THE WORKERS' COMPENSATION LAWS OF CALIFORNIA

Compiled from
THE LABOR CODE, INSURANCE CODE,
UNEMPLOYMENT INSURANCE CODE, AND
OTHER SOURCES

2009 Edition

LexisNexis

QUESTIONS ABOUT THIS PUBLICATION?

For questions about the **Editorial Content** appearing in these volumes or reprint permission, please call:

Robin Kobayashi at .... 1-800-424-0651 EXT. 3352
Email: .... robin.e.kobayashi@lexisnexis.com
Katie Solomon at .... 1-800-424-0651 EXT. 3251
Email: .... katie.k.solomon@lexisnexis.com
or e-mail at .... CalCodes@lexisnexis.com

For assistance with replacement pages, shipments, billing or other customer service matters, please call:

Customer Services Department at .... (800) 833-9844

Outside the United States and Canada, please call .... (518) 487-3000

Fax number .... (518) 487-3584

Customer Service Website .... http://www.lexisnexis.com/custserv/

For information on other Matthew Bender publications, please call:

Your account manager .... (800) 2273-1940

Outside the United States and Canada, please call .... (518) 487-3000

ISBN 978-1-4224-2743-9

Editorial Offices
744 Broad Street, Newark, NJ 07102 (973) 820-2000
201 Mission St., San Francisco, CA 94105-1831 (415) 908-3200
www.lexis.com

Publisher's Editorial Staff

Robert D. Bae, J.D.

Director, Editorial Content & Development

Karen Mawyer, J.D.

Manager, Statutory Editorial Operations

Katie K. Solomon

Senior Legal Analyst

Kathy Hoover

Senior Editor

Michael Dougherty
Timothy Maness

Coordinating Editors

Stephen Sofinski, J.D.

Index Manager

Mark Dempsey, J.D.

Index Analyst

Cheryl Kirby

Index Editor

BOARD OF EDITORIAL CONSULTANTS

PREFACE

California Statutes

This publication contains selected provisions relating to workers' compensation law from the Insurance, Labor, and Unemployment Insurance Codes. Following these provisions are miscellaneous related statutes from the California Constitution and the following Codes: Business & Professions, Civil, Code of Civil Procedure, Education, Evidence, Government, Harbors & Navigation, Health & Safety, Military & Veterans, Penal, Vehicle, and Welfare & Institutions. Legislative histories ("Leg.H.") beginning with 1991 are given for each statute.

This 2009 Edition of the Workers' Compensation Laws of California incorporates all changes required by legislative enactments up to and including the second year of the 2007–2008 Regular Session. Amendments made in 2008 are highlighted by printing in **boldface** type all matter added to a section and indicating by a figure within brackets, such as [1], each point of deletion. The deleted matter is then shown by bracketed footnotes keyed to the corresponding figures. Where changes are extensive, the former section may be reprinted in full. Some sections contain bracketed notes indicating material is not reproduced; this indicates that portions of the section having no workers' compensation applications have not been reproduced.

The following reproduction of Section 3710.2 of the Labor Code clearly illustrates the "stressed amendment" feature:

> **§3710.2. Penalties for failure to observe stop order.**
> Failure of an employer, officer, or anyone having direction, management, or control of any place of employment or of employees to observe a stop order issued and served upon him or her pursuant to Section 3710.1 is a misdemeanor punishable by imprisonment in the county jail not exceeding 60 days or by a fine not exceeding [1] **ten** thousand dollars [2] **($10,000)**, or both. Fines shall be paid into the State Treasury to the credit of the Uninsured Employers Fund. The director may also obtain injunctive and other relief from the courts to carry out the purposes of Section 3710.1. The failure to obtain a policy of workers' compensation insurance or a certificate of consent to self-insure as required by Section 3700 is a misdemeanor in accordance with Section 3700.5. **Leg.H.** 1991 ch. 600.
> **§3710.2. 1991 Deletes. [1]** one **[2]** ($1,000)

To read Section 3710.2 as amended, you read the section as printed, omitting the bracketed figures "[1]" and "[2]":

> Failure of an employer, officer, or anyone having direction, management, or control of any place of employment or of employees to observe a stop order issued and served upon him or her pursuant to Section 3710.1 is a misdemeanor punishable by imprisonment in the county jail not exceeding 60 days or by a fine not exceeding **ten** thousand dollars **($10,000)**, or both. Fines shall be paid into the State Treasury to the credit of the Uninsured Employers Fund. The director may also obtain injunctive and other relief from the courts to carry out the purposes of Section 3710.1. The failure to obtain a policy of workers' compensation insurance or a certificate of consent to self-insure as required by Section 3700 is a misdemeanor in accordance with Section 3700.5.

To reconstruct the section as it read before being amended, you read the section as printed, omitting the words in boldface type and inserting the words appearing in the footnote under Section 3710.2 and referred to by the [1] and [2] in the section:

> Failure of an employer, officer, or anyone having direction, management, or control of any place of employment or of employees to observe a stop order issued and served upon him or her pursuant to Section 3710.1 is a misdemeanor punishable by imprisonment in the county jail not exceeding 60 days or by a fine not exceeding one thousand dollars ($1,000), or both. Fines shall be paid into the State Treasury to the credit of the Uninsured Employers Fund. The director may also obtain injunctive and other relief from the courts to carry out the purposes of Section 3710.1. The failure to obtain a policy of workers' compensation insurance or a certificate of consent to self-insure as required by Section 3700 is a misdemeanor in accordance with Section 3700.5.

California Code of Regulations

This publication contains selected Title 2, Title 8 and Title 10 regulations relating to workers' compensation. This 2009 Edition of the Workers' Compensation Laws of California incorporates all changes made to the regulations through Register 2008, Number 44 (October 31, 2008).

United States Code

This publication contains selected provisions relating to workers' compensation law from Titles 5, 26, 28, 33, 40, 42, 43, 45, and 46 of the United States Code. These code provisions are current through Public Law 110-448 (October 22, 2008).

Cross-References

Where applicable, statutes and regulations in this publication are followed by cross-reference lines ("Ref.") containing citations to related sections of the following:

"CACI" — Judicial Council of California Civil Jury Instructions (Matthew Bender, Official Publisher);

"CALCRIM" — Judicial Council of California Criminal Jury Instructions (Matthew Bender, Official Publisher);

"C.C.R." — California Code of Regulations;

"Hanna" — *California Law of Employee Injuries and Workers' Compensation*, a three-volume treatise (Matthew Bender);

"Herlick Handbook" — *California Workers' Compensation Handbook* (Matthew Bender);

"Lawyer's Guide to AMA *Guides* and Calif. Workers' Comp." — *The Lawyer's Guide to the AMA* Guides *and California Workers' Compensation* (Matthew Bender);

"MB Prac. Guide: Cal. Civ. Disc." — Matthew Bender® Practice Guide: California Civil Discovery;

"MB Prac. Guide: Cal. Contract Lit." — Matthew Bender® Practice Guide: California Contract Litigation;

"MB Prac. Guide: Cal. Debt Collection & Enforcement of Judgments" — Matthew Bender® California Debt Collection and Enforcement of Judgments;

"MB Prac. Guide: Fed. Pretrial Proc. in Cal." — Matthew Bender® Practice Guide: Federal Pretrial Civil Procedure in California;

"MB Prac. Guide: Landlord-Tenant" — Matthew Bender® Practice Guide: California Landlord-Tenant Litigation;

"MB Prac. Guide: Cal. Pretrial Proc." — Matthew Bender® Practice Guide: California Pretrial Civil Procedure;

"MB Prac. Guide: Cal. Trial & Post-Trial Civ. Proc." — Matthew Bender® Practice Guide: California Trial and Post-Trial Civil Procedure;

"W. Cal. Ev." — Witkin's California Evidence, 4th Ed.; and

"W. Cal. Sum." — Witkin's Summary of California Law, 10th Ed.

To order the Matthew Bender products listed above, please contact our Customer Service Department at 1-800-833-9844.

In presenting this Edition of the Workers' Compensation Laws of California, we wish to acknowledge with gratitude the many helpful suggestions received from users, and to express the hope that this Edition will serve effectively the needs of the workers' compensation community.

THE PUBLISHER

TABLE OF CONTENTS

REFERENCE DIRECTORY

FOR ASSISTANCE ON HOW TO READ AND USE THIS EDITION:

See the Preface on pages vii-ix

Contact Robin Kobayashi, J.D., Practice Area Editor at Matthew Bender, 800-424-0651 ext. 3352, robin.e.kobayashi@lexisnexis.com with questions about:

- Location of statutes and regulations covered in this and prior editions
- Coverage of recent workers' comp legislation
- Index entries

Contact Katie Solomon, Senior Legal Analyst at Matthew Bender, 800-424-0651 ext. 3251, katie.k.solomon@lexisnexis.com with questions about:

- Tables and schedules
- Permission to reprint parts of this edition

FOR QUESTIONS REGARDING INTERPRETATION OF THE LAW AND WORKERS' COMP PROCEDURE, CONTACT:

Workers' Compensation Appeals Board Information and Assistance (I&A) at the field office near you:

Toll Free:	800-736-7401
Anaheim:	714-738-4000
Bakersfield:	661-395-2723
Eureka:	707-445-6518
Fresno:	559-445-5051
Goleta:	805-968-0258
Grover Beach:	805-481-4912
Long Beach:	562-590-5001
Los Angeles:	213-576-7335
Marina Del Rey:	310-482-3820
Oakland:	510-622-2866
Oxnard:	805-485-2533
Pomona:	909-623-4301
Redding:	530-225-2845
Riverside:	951-782-4269
Sacramento:	916-263-2735
Salinas:	831-443-3060
San Bernardino:	909-383-4341
San Diego:	619-767-2083
San Francisco:	415-703-5011
San Jose:	408-277-1246
Santa Ana:	714-558-4121
Santa Rosa:	707-576-2391

Stockton:	209-948-7759
Van Nuys:	818-901-5367

OTHER RESOURCES:

LexisNexis: Print and Electronic Products toll-free ordering (800-223-1940) *www.lexis.com*

- *California Compensation Cases* (monthly advance sheets and yearly hardbound volumes covering workers' comp cases)
- *LexisNexis Automated California Workers' Compensation Forms* (forms software)
- Hanna, *California Law of Employee Injuries and Workers' Compensation* (3-volume treatise)
- Herlick, *California Workers' Compensation Law* (2-volume treatise)
- Herlick, *California Workers' Compensation Handbook* (softbound volume)
- *The Lawyer's Guide to the AMA* Guides *and California Workers' Compensation (softbound volume)*
- *Judicial Council of California Civil Jury Instructions (Matthew Bender, Official Publisher)*
- *Larson's Workers' Compensation Law* (12-volume treatise)
- *Larson's Workers' Compensation, Desk Edition* (3-volume treatise)
- *Matthew Bender® Practice Guide: California Civil Discovery*
- *Matthew Bender® Practice Guide: California Contract Litigation*
- *Matthew Bender® Practice Guide: California Debt Collection and Enforcement of Judgments*
- *Matthew Bender® Practice Guide: Federal Pretrial Civil Procedure in California*
- *Matthew Bender® Practice Guide: California Landlord-Tenant Litigation*
- *Matthew Bender® Practice Guide: California Pretrial Civil Procedure*
- *Matthew Bender® Practice Guide: California Trial and Post-Trial Civil Procedure*
- NOSSCR, *Social Security Practice Guide* (5-volume treatise)
- *Attorneys' Textbook of Medicine* (23-volume treatise)
- *Attorneys' Dictionary of Medicine*
- *Proving Medical Diagnosis and Prognosis* (14-volume treatise)
- *Common Diagnostic Procedures* (1-volume treatise)
- *Occupational Injuries and Illnesses* (3-volume treatise)

Other Publications

- *California Workers' Comp: How to Take Charge When You're Injured on the Job* (Nolo Press, 800-728-3555 *www.nolo.com*)
- *Official Medical Fee Schedule (OMFS),* (see 8 CCR §9791.1 for information on ordering a copy of the fee schedule or obtain an order form at *http://www.dir.ca.gov/DWC/OMFS9904.htm*)

- *Work Comp Index,* 7th Ed., May, 2008 (James T. Stewart, 559-291-9081, fax 559-485-3804, *stewshe@comcast.net*) Alphabetical subject index to workers' compensation in California
- *Rehab Index,* 10th Ed., May, 2005 (James T. Stewart, 559-291-9081, fax 559-485-3804, *stewshe@comcast.net*) Alphabetical subject index to vocational rehabilitation in California

Websites on the Internet

- Dept. of Industrial Relations: *http://www.dir.ca.gov*
- LexisNexis Workers' Compensation Law Center: *http://law.lexisnexis.com/practiceareas/Workers-Compensation*
- State Compensation Insurance Fund: *http://www.scif.com*
- California Applicants' Attorneys Association: *http://www.caaa.org*
- California Manufacturers & Technology Association: *http://www.cmta.net*
- California Self-Insurers Association: *http://www.caself-insurers.com*
- California Society of Industrial Medicine and Surgery: *http://www.csims.net*
- California Workers' Comp. Defense Attorneys' Assoc.: *http://www.cwcdaa.org*
- California Workers' Compensation Institute: *http://www.cwci.org*
- Council on Education in Management: *http://www.counciloned.com*
- Insurance Educational Association: *http://www.ieatraining.com*
- Combined Claims Conference: *http://www.combinedclaims.com*
- San Francisco Industrial Claims Association: *http://sfica.tripod.com*
- Valley Industrial Claims Association: *http://www.valleyica.org*
- Diablo Valley Industrial Claims Association: *http://www.dvica.org*
- South Bay Industrial Claims Association: *http://southbayica.tripod.com/southbayindustrialclaimsassociation/id3.html*
- Mid Valley Claims Association: *http://www.midvalleyclaims.org*
- Sacramento Claims Association: *http://www.sacramentoclaims.org*
- Professionals in Workers' Comp: *http://thepiwc.tripod.com*

Sponsors of Educational Programs

- WCAB information and assistance injured worker workshops (call your local WCAB office)
- California Applicants' Attorneys Association (916-444-5155, 800-648-3132)
- California Manufacturers & Technology Association (916-441-5420)
- California Self-Insurers Association (925-648-2002)
- California Society of Industrial Medicine and Surgery (916-446-4199, 800-692-4199)
- California Workers' Compensation Defense Attorneys' Association (619-694-4630)
- California Workers' Compensation Institute (510-251-9470)
- Combined Claims Conference (888-811-6930)
- Council on Education in Management (800-942-4494)

- Insurance Educational Association (800-655-4432)
- San Francisco Industrial Claims Association (510-862-3700)

2008 LEGISLATIVE ACTION

Effective January 1, 2009, unless otherwise noted at end of section.

CIVIL CODE

Section	Effect	Chap.
56.10	Amended	179
56.103	Amended	699, 700

CODE OF CIVIL PROCEDURE

Section	Effect	Chap.
2034.430	Amended	303

GOVERNMENT CODE

Section	Effect	Chap.
21156	Amended	370
21537	Amended	74

INSURANCE CODE

Section	Effect	Chap.
1063.1	Amended	80, 179
1063.2	Amended	80
1063.17	Added	407
1063.75	Amended	80
1877.1	Amended	369
1877.35	Added	369
11770	Amended	322
11770.5	Repealed	344
11785	Amended	344
11873	Amended	344

LABOR CODE

Section	Effect	Chap.
62.5	Amended	751
62.9	Amended	751
77.7	Amended	179
139.48	Amended	751
2699.5	Amended	169
3212.1	Amended	747
3212.8	Amended	684
4600.6	Amended	682
4604.5	Amended	179
4658.5	Amended	179
5307.2	Amended	193
6409.1	Amended	740
6410	Amended	740

UNITED STATES CODE

Section	Effect	P.L.
Title 42		
1655	Added	110-417
Title 46		
30104	Amended	110-181
30104 Note	Added	110-181

2008 REGULATORY ACTION

Effective on the dates shown below.

Title 8

Reg.	Effect	Eff. Date
Art. 1.6 Hdg (comm w/§9720.1)	Amended	9-24-08
9720.1	Amended	9-24-08
9720.2	Amended	9-24-08
9721.1	Amended	9-24-08
9721.2	Amended	9-24-08
9721.11	Added	9-24-08
9721.12	Added	9-24-08
9721.13	Added	9-24-08
9721.14	Added	9-24-08
9721.21	Added	9-24-08
9721.31	Amended	9-24-08
9721.32	Amended	9-24-08
9721.33	Added	9-24-08
9722	Amended	9-24-08
9722.1	Amended	9-24-08
9722.2	Amended	9-24-08
9723	Amended	9-24-08
9767.1	Amended	4-9-08
9767.16	Added	4-9-08
Art. 8 Hdg (comm w/§9810)	Repealed & Added	4-9-08
9810	Amended	4-9-08
9811	Amended	4-9-08
9812	Amended	4-9-08
9813	Amended	4-9-08
9813.1	Added	4-9-08
9813.2	Added	4-9-08
Art. 5.5 Hdg (comm w/§10112.1)	Renumbered from Art. 1 (comm w/§10225)	4-7-08
10112.1	Renumbered from §10225	4-7-08
10112.2	Renumbered from §10225.1	4-7-08
10112.3	Amended & Renumbered from §10225.2	4-7-08
Art. 6 Hdg (comm w/§10116)	Renumbered to Art. 9 (comm w/§10136)	4-7-08
10116	Amended & Renumbered to §10136	4-7-08
10116.1	Renumbered to §10137	4-7-08
10117.1	Amended & Renumbered to §10138	4-7-08
10118.1	Renumbered to §10139	4-7-08
10119	Renumbered to §10140	4-7-08

10120	Renumbered to §10141	4-7-08
10121	Renumbered to §10142	4-7-08
Art. 9 Hdg (comm w/§10136)	Repealed / Renumbered from Art. 6 (comm w/§10116)	4-7-08
10136	Amended & Renumbered to §10252 / Amended & Renumbered from §10116	4-7-08
10137	Renumbered to §10252.1 / Renumbered from §10116.1	4-7-08
10138	Amended & Renumbered from §10117.1	4-7-08
10139	Renumbered from §10118.1	4-7-08
10140	Renumbered from §10119	4-7-08
10141	Renumbered from §10120	4-7-08
10142	Renumbered from §10121	4-7-08
Art. 1 Hdg (comm w/§10225)	Renumbered to Art. 5.5 (comm w/§10112.1)	4-7-08
10225	Renumbered to §10112.1	4-7-08
10225.1	Renumbered to §10112.2	4-7-08
10225.2	Amended & Renumbered to §10112.3	4-7-08
10252	Amended & Renumbered from §10136	4-7-08
10252.1	Renumbered from §10137	4-7-08

INSURANCE CODE
[Selected Provisions]

SYNOPSIS

GENERAL PROVISIONS
[Selected Provisions]

DIVISION 1
GENERAL RULES GOVERNING INSURANCE

PART 1
The Contract

CHAPTER 1
CLASSES OF INSURANCE
[Selected Provisions]

CHAPTER 11
CANCELLATION AND FAILURE TO RENEW CERTAIN PROPERTY INSURANCE
[Selected Provisions]

PART 2
The Business of Insurance

CHAPTER 1
GENERAL REGULATIONS

ARTICLE 3
Certificate of Authority
[Selected Provisions]

ARTICLE 4
Examination by Commissioner
[Selected Provisions]

ARTICLE 5.1
Unlawful Practices
[Selected Provisions]

ARTICLE 10
Financial Statements of Insurers
[Selected Provisions]

ARTICLE 14.2
California Insurance Guarantee Association
[Selected Provisions]

ARTICLE 14.26
Workers' Compensation Bond Fund

CHAPTER 12
THE INSURANCE FRAUDS PREVENTION ACT

ARTICLE 1
False and Fraudulent Claims
[Selected Provisions]

ARTICLE 2
Bureau of Fraudulent Claims
[Selected Provisions]

ARTICLE 4
Motor Vehicle Theft and Motor Vehicle Insurance Fraud Reporting

ARTICLE 7
Workers' Compensation Insurance Fraud Reporting

DIVISION 2
CLASSES OF INSURANCE

PART 3
Liability, Workers' Compensation, and Common Carrier Liability Insurance

CHAPTER 1
GENERAL REGULATIONS

ARTICLE 2
Actions on Policies Containing Liability Provisions
[Selected Provisions]

ARTICLE 2.5
Personal Liability Insurance Providing Workers' Compensation Coverage for Household Employees

CHAPTER 2
WORKERS' COMPENSATION POLICIES

ARTICLE 1
Definitions

ARTICLE 2
Policy Provisions
[Selected Provisions]

CHAPTER 3
REGULATION OF BUSINESS OF WORKERS' COMPENSATION INSURANCE

ARTICLE 1
Deposits by Workers' Compensation Insurers

ARTICLE 2
State Rate Supervision

ARTICLE 3
Rating and Other Organizations

ARTICLE 4
Penalties for Misrepresentation

ARTICLE 5
Standards Applicable to Claims Adjusters

CHAPTER 4
THE STATE COMPENSATION INSURANCE FUND

ARTICLE 1
Organization and Powers

ARTICLE 2
Rates

ARTICLE 3
Policies

ARTICLE 4
Reports and Statements

ARTICLE 5
Coverage of Public Employers

ARTICLE 6
Penalties

SELECTED PROVISIONS Of The INSURANCE CODE

GENERAL PROVISIONS [Selected Provisions]

§20.5. Terms referring to Division of Industrial Accidents.

Whenever in this code the terms "State Industrial Accident Commission" or "Industrial Accident Commission" or "commission," relating to the said "State Industrial Accident Commission" or the said "Industrial Accident Commission," appear, said terms shall mean "Division of Industrial Accidents," including "administrative director" of said division or "appeals board," or both, as the context may require.

§42. Use of "group" in designating insurance coverage; application of section.

The designation of insurance coverage as "group" in any code or law of this State other than this code does not authorize its representation as a group coverage or as a group policy, certificate or contract by any person licensed or certificated by the commissioner unless the policy providing the coverage is defined as group insurance by a specific provision of this code or of the laws of the state in which the policy, certificate or contract is issued. This section shall apply only to life, disability and workmen's compensation insurance.

§46. "Workmen's compensation" to become "workers' compensation."

The Legislature hereby declares its intent that the term "workmen's compensation" shall hereafter also be known as "workers' compensation." In furtherance of this policy it is the desire of the Legislature that references to the term "workmen's compensation" in this code be changed to "workers' compensation" when such code sections are being amended for any purpose. This act is declaratory and not amendatory of existing law.

DIVISION 1
GENERAL RULES GOVERNING INSURANCE

PART 1
The Contract

CHAPTER 1
CLASSES OF INSURANCE
[Selected Provisions]

§100. Classes of insurance.

Insurance in this state is divided into the following classes:

(1) Life
(2) Fire
(3) Marine
(4) Title
(5) Surety
(6) Disability
(7) Plate glass
(8) Liability
(9) Workers' compensation
(10) Common carrier liability
(11) Boiler and machinery
(12) Burglary
(13) Credit
(14) Sprinkler
(15) Team and vehicle
(16) Automobile
(17) Mortgage
(18) Aircraft
(19) Mortgage guaranty
(19.5) Insolvency
(19.6) Legal insurance
(20) Miscellaneous

Ref.: Hanna § 1.22; W. Cal. Sum., 2 "Insurance" §§3, 133.

§108. Liability insurance.

Liability insurance includes:

(a) Insurance against loss resulting from liability for injury, fatal or nonfatal, suffered by any natural person, or resulting from liability for damage to property, or property interests of others but does not include workers' compensation, common carrier liability, boiler and machinery, or team and vehicle insurance.

[Subsections (b)–(e) Not Reproduced]

Ref.: W. Cal. Sum., 2 "Insurance" §§3, 135, 155, 161, 180.

§108.1. Liability insurers as workers' compensation insurers.

Insurers admitted to transact liability insurance are also deemed to be admitted to transact workers' compensation insurance for the purpose of covering those persons defined as employees by subdivision (d) of Section 3351 of the Labor Code.

§109. "Workers' compensation insurance."

Workers' compensation insurance includes insurance against loss from liability imposed by law upon employers to compensate employees and their dependents for injury sustained by the employees arising out of and in the course of the employment, irrespective of negligence or of the fault of either party.

Ref.: Hanna §§ 1.22, 2.10[2]; W. Cal. Sum., 2 "Insurance" §3.

§110. "Common carrier liability insurance."

Common carrier liability insurance includes insurance against loss resulting from liability of a common carrier for accident or injury, fatal or nonfatal, to any person but does not include liability or workers' compensation insurance.

Ref.: W. Cal. Sum., 2 "Insurance" §3.

CHAPTER 11 CANCELLATION AND FAILURE TO RENEW CERTAIN PROPERTY INSURANCE [Selected Provisions]

§676. Grounds for cancellation.

After a policy specified in Section 675 has been in effect for 60 days, or, if the policy is a renewal, effective immediately, no notice of cancellation shall be effective unless it is based on the occurrence, after the effective date of the policy, of one or more of the following:

(a) Nonpayment of premium, including nonpayment of any additional premiums, calculated in accordance with the current rating manual of the insurer, justified by a physical change in the insured property or a change in its occupancy or use.

(b) Conviction of the named insured of a crime having as one of its necessary elements an act increasing any hazard insured against.

(c) Discovery of fraud or material misrepresentation by either of the following:

(1) The insured or his or her representative in obtaining the insurance.

(2) The named insured or his or her representative in pursuing a claim under the policy.

(d) Discovery of grossly negligent acts or omissions by the insured or his or her representative substantially increasing any of the hazards insured against.

(e) Physical changes in the insured property which result in the property becoming uninsurable. **Leg.H.** 1970 ch. 313 §1, 1986 ch. 1321 §2.

Ref.: W. Cal. Sum., 2 "Insurance" §219.

§676.1. Arbitrary cancellation or refusal to renew homeowners' policy due to operation of family day care business; coverage to be by separate endorsement.

(a) The arbitrary cancellation of a policy of homeowners' insurance solely on the basis that the policyholder has a license to operate a family day care home at the insured location shall subject the insurer to administrative sanctions authorized by this code unless, there has been a material misrepresentation of fact, the risk has changed substantially since the policy was issued, there has been a nonpayment of premium, or the insurer no longer writes homeowners policies.

(b) The arbitrary refusal to renew a policy of homeowners' insurance solely on the basis that the policyholder has a license to operate a family day care home at the insured location shall subject the insurer to administrative sanctions authorized by this code unless, there has been a material misrepresentation of fact, the risk has changed substantially since the policy was issued, there has been a nonpayment of premium, or the insurer no longer writes homeowners' policies. For purposes of this subdivision, an insured's purchase of a policy of homeowner's insurance to cover a new, primary residence from the same insurer which insured his or her previous primary residence, provided that the insurer then underwrites homeowners' insurance in the geographic area containing the new residence, shall be deemed a renewal of the policy on the previous, primary residence.

(c) It shall be against public policy for a residential property insurance policy to provide coverage for liability for losses arising out of, or in connection with, the operation of a family day care home. This coverage shall only be provided by a separate endorsement or insurance policy for which premiums have been assessed and collected. **Leg.H.** 1985 ch. 1362 §2, effective October 1, 1985, 1991 ch. 784 (AB 676) §1.

Ref.: W. Cal. Sum., 2 "Insurance" §§150, 219.

§676.2. Grounds for cancellation of commercial insurance policies.

(a) This section applies only to policies of commercial insurance that are subject to Section 675.5.

(b) After a policy has been in effect for more than 60 days, or if the policy is a renewal, effective immediately, no notice of cancellation shall be effective unless it complies with Section 677.2 and it is based on the occurrence, after the effective date of the policy, of one or more of the following:

(1) Nonpayment of premium, including payment due on a prior policy issued by the insurer and due during the current policy term covering the same risks.

(2) A judgment by a court or an administrative tribunal that the named insured has violated any law of this state or of the United States having as one of its necessary elements an act

that materially increases any of the risks insured against.

(3) Discovery of fraud or material misrepresentation by either of the following:

(A) The insured or his or her representative in obtaining the insurance.

(B) The named insured or his or her representative in pursuing a claim under the policy.

(4) Discovery of willful or grossly negligent acts or omissions, or of any violations of state laws or regulations establishing safety standards, by the named insured or his or her representative, which materially increase any of the risks insured against.

(5) Failure by the named insured or his or her representative to implement reasonable loss control requirements that were agreed to by the insured as a condition of policy issuance or that were conditions precedent to the use by the insurer of a particular rate or rating plan, if the failure materially increases any of the risks insured against.

(6) A determination by the commissioner that the loss of, or changes in, an insurer's reinsurance covering all or part of the risk would threaten the financial integrity or solvency of the insurer. A certification made under penalty of perjury to the commissioner by an officer of the insurer of the loss of, or change in, reinsurance and that the loss or change will threaten the financial integrity or solvency of the insurer if the cancellation of the policy is not permitted shall constitute this determination unless disapproved by the commissioner within 30 days of the filing. There shall be no extensions to this 30-day period.

(7) A determination by the commissioner that a continuation of the policy coverage would place the insurer in violation of the laws of this state or the state of its domicile or that the continuation of coverage would threaten the solvency of the insurer.

(8) A change by the named insured or his or her representative in the activities or property of the commercial or industrial enterprise that results in a material added risk, a materially increased risk, or a materially changed risk, unless the added, increased, or changed risk is included in the policy.

(c)(1) After a policy has been in effect for more than 60 days, or if the policy is a renewal, effective immediately upon renewal, no increase in the rate upon which the premium is based, reduction in limits, or change in the conditions of coverage shall be effective during the policy period unless a written notice is mailed or delivered to the named insured and the producer of record at the mailing address shown on the policy, at least 30 days prior to the effective date of the increase, reduction, or change. Subdivision (a) of Section 1013 of the Code of Civil Procedure is applicable if the notice is mailed. The notice shall state the effective date of, and the reasons for, the increase, reduction, or change.

(2) The increase, reduction, or change shall not be effective unless it is based upon one of the following reasons:

(A) Discovery of willful or grossly negligent acts or omissions, or of any violations of state laws or regulations establishing safety standards by the named insured that materially increase any of the risks or hazards insured against.

(B) Failure by the named insured to implement reasonable loss control requirements that were agreed to by the insured as a condition of policy issuance or that were conditions precedent to the use by the insurer of a particular rate or rating plan, if the failure materially increases any of the risks insured against.

(C) A determination by the commissioner that loss of or changes in an insurer's reinsurance covering all or part of the risk covered by the policy would threaten the financial integrity or solvency of the insurer unless the change in the terms or conditions or rate upon which the premium is based is permitted.

(D) A change by the named insured in the activities or property of the commercial or industrial enterprise that results in a materially added risk, a materially increased risk, or a materially changed risk, unless the added, increased, or changed risk is included in the policy.

(E) With respect to a change in the rate of a policy of professional liability insurance for a health care provider, the insurer's offer of renewal notifies the policyholder that the insurer has an application filed pursuant to Section 1861.05 pending with the commissioner for approval of a change in the rate upon which the premium is based, and the commissioner subsequently approves the rate change, or some different amount for the policy period. The change shall not be retroactive.

(d) The Administrative Procedure Act (Chapter 3.5 (commencing with Section 11340), Chapter 4 (commencing with Section 11370), and

Chapter 5 (commencing with Section 11500) of Title 2 of Division 3 of the Government Code) shall not apply to a determination pursuant to paragraph (6) or (7) of subdivision (b) or subparagraph (C) of paragraph (2) of subdivision (c). The commissioner shall charge an insurer who requests a determination pursuant to paragraph (6) or (7) of subdivision (b) a fee sufficient to recover the costs of making the determination. If the commissioner does not act upon a request by an insurer to cancel or change a policy pursuant to those provisions within 30 days, the request shall be deemed to be approved.

(e) This section shall not prohibit an insurer from increasing a premium during the policy period if the increase is calculated in accordance with the current rating manual of the insurer and is justified by a physical change in the insured property or by a change in the activities of the commercial or industrial enterprise that materially increases any of the risks insured against.

(f) This section shall not apply to a transfer of a policy without a change in its terms or conditions or the rate upon which the premium is based between insurers that are members of the same insurance group. **Leg.H.** 1986 ch. 1321 §3, 1990 ch. 216 (SB 2510) §84, 1993 ch. 1198 (SB 581) §1, 2006 ch. 538 (SB 1852) §451.

Ref.: W. Cal. Sum., 2 "Insurance" §219.

§676.3. Remedial underwriting on medical malpractice insurance for dentists, physicians and surgeons.

Nothing in Section 676.2 shall preclude the imposition of remedial underwriting action upon coverage insuring dentists or physicians and surgeons against legal liability arising from the rendering of professional services by an insured licensed pursuant to Chapter 4 (commencing with Section 1600) or Chapter 5 (commencing with Section 2000) of Division 2 of the Business and Professions Code, respectively, if remedial underwriting action is imposed pursuant to the recommendation of an underwriting committee advising the insurer; provided that a majority of the members of that committee are licensed pursuant to the chapter of Division 2 of the Business and Professions Code that is applicable to that particular insured, and written notification of the proposed remedial underwriting action is first given to the insured, and the insured is afforded not less than 30 days to present opposition or argument to the underwriting committee as to why the remedial underwriting action should be modified or withheld, prior to any imposition thereof. Remedial underwriting action includes all actions described in subdivision (c) of Section 676.2. Remedial underwriting action imposed pursuant to this section shall not be subject to Article 7 (commencing with Section 1858) of Chapter 9 of Part 2, but nothing in this section shall deny the right of the commissioner to investigate, pursue enforcement action, and seek other remedies as authorized by Article 1 (commencing with Section 12919) of Chapter 2 of Division 3.

It is the intent of the Legislature to encourage peer review by insurers providing coverage to persons engaged in the provision of health services and the adoption of conditions of coverage which are intended to protect the public. **Leg.H.** 1988 ch. 1618 §1, 1995 ch. 600 (AB 852) §1.

§676.4. Changes in rate on which premium based or conditions of coverage of policies insuring health care facilities.

Nothing in Section 676.2 shall preclude, while the policies are in force, changes in the rate upon which the premium is based or the conditions of coverage, or both, of policies insuring health care facilities licensed pursuant to Chapter 2 (commencing with Section 1250) of Division 2 of the Health and Safety Code, if the change is imposed pursuant to the recommendation of a health care facility professional liability advisory committee advising the insurer; provided that a majority of the members of the committee are duly authorized representatives of health care facilities licensed pursuant to that Chapter 2 (commencing with Section 1250) of Division 2 of the Health and Safety Code, and written notification of the change is given to all affected insureds at least 30 days prior to any such change. **Leg.H.** 1988 ch. 1618 §2.

§676.5. Length of term for commercial insurance policies.

(a) This section applies only to policies of commercial insurance which are subject to Section 675.5.

(b) Except as provided in subdivision (c), for purposes of this chapter only, a policy with no fixed expiration, or with a term of less than one year, shall be considered to be a policy for a term of one year, and a policy written for a term of more than one year shall be considered as if written for successive terms of one year.

(c) For purposes of this chapter, a policy shall be considered to be for a term of less than one year if the policy is issued for a specific risk which does not continue beyond the period of the policy, or if the insured requests a policy for a term of less than one year. **Leg.H.** 1986 ch. 1321 §4.

§676.6. Commercial umbrella liability, commercial excess liability, and commercial excess property insurance policies; notice of cancellation or nonrenewal.

(a) This section applies to commercial umbrella liability insurance policies, commercial excess liability insurance policies, and commercial excess property insurance policies.

(b) As used in this section:

(1) "Umbrella liability insurance policy" means an insurance policy providing liability coverage per person or per occurrence or per claim, when written over one or more underlying liability policies or over a specified amount of self-insured retention.

(2) "Excess liability insurance policy" means an insurance policy providing liability covrage per person or per occurrence or per claim when written over one or more underlying liability policies. Excess liability policies shall include policies written over umbrella liability policies.

(3) "Excess property insurance policy" means a policy providing property coverage per occurrence or per location when written over one or more underlying property insurance policies or a specified amount of self-insured retention.

(c) After a policy defined in subdivision (b) of this section has been in effect for more than 60 days, or if the policy is a renewal, effective immediately, no notice of cancellation shall be effective unless it complies with Section 677.2, is based on one or more of the grounds set forth in subdivision (b) of Section 676.2, or is based on one or more of the following:

(1) A material change in limits, type or scope of coverage, or exclusions in one or more of the underlying policies.

(2) Cancellation or nonrenewal of one or more of the underlying policies where such policies are not replaced without lapse.

(3) A reduction in financial rating or grade of one or more insurers, insuring one or more underlying policies based on an evaluation obtained from a recognized financial rating organization.

(d) A notice of nonrenewal shall not be required in any of the following situations:

(1) The transfer of, or renewal of, a policy without a change in its terms or conditions or the rate on which the premium is based between insurers which are members of the same insurance group.

(2) The policy has been extended for 90 days or less, if the notice required in subdivision (c) has been given prior to the extension.

(3) The named insured has obtained replacement coverage or has agreed, in writing, within 60 days of the termination of the policy, to obtain that coverage.

(4) The policy is for a period of no more than 60 days and the insured is notified at the time of issuance that it may not be renewed.

(5) The named insured requests a change in the terms or conditions or risks covered by the policy within 60 days prior to the end of the policy period.

(6) The insurer has made a written offer to the insured, within the time period specified in subdivision (c), to renew the policy under changed terms or conditions or at a changed premium rate. As used herein, "terms or conditions" includes, but is not limited to, a reduction in limits, elimination of coverages, or an increase in deductibles. **Leg.H.** 1988 ch. 1618 §3.

Ref.: W. Cal. Sum., 2 "Insurance" §222.

§676.7. Applicant or policyholder engaged in foster home activities.

(a) No admitted insurer, licensed to issue and issuing homeowner's or tenant's policies, as described in Section 122, shall (1) fail or refuse to accept an application for that insurance or to issue that insurance to an applicant or (2) cancel that insurance, solely on the basis that the applicant or policyholder is engaged in foster home activities in a licensed foster family home or licensed small family home, as defined in Section 1502 of the Health and Safety Code.

(b) Coverage under policies described in subdivision (a) with respect to a foster child shall be the same as that provided for a natural child. However, unless specifically provided in the policy, there shall be no coverage expressly provided in the policy for any bodily injury arising out of the operation or use of any motor vehicle, aircraft, or watercraft owned or operated by, or rented or loaned to, any foster parent.

(c) It is against public policy for a policy of homeowner's or tenant's insurance subject to this section to provide liability coverage for any of the following losses:

(1) Claims of a foster child, or a parent, guardian, or guardian ad litem thereof, of a type payable by the Foster Family Home and Small Family Home Insurance Fund established by Section 1527.1 of the Health and Safety Code, regardless of whether the claim is within the limits of coverage specified in Section 1527.4 of the Health and Safety Code.

(2) An insurer shall not be liable, under a policy of insurance subject to this section, to any governmental agency for damage arising from occurrences peculiar to the foster-care relationship and the provision of foster-care services.

(3) Alienation of affection of a foster child.

(4) Any loss arising out of licentious, immoral, or sexual behavior on the part of a foster parent intended to lead to, or culminating in, any sexual act.

(5) Any loss arising out of a dishonest, fraudulent, criminal, or intentional act.

(d) There shall be no penalty for violations of this section prior to January 1, 1987.

(e) Insurers may provide a special endorsement to a homeowners' or tenants' policy covering claims related to foster care that are not excluded by subdivision (c).

(f) Insurers may provide by a separate policy for some or all of the claims related to foster care that are excluded by subdivision (c). **Leg.H.** 1986 ch. 1330 §4, effective September 29, 1986, as §676.2, 1988 ch. 195 §3, effective June 16, 1988, 1990 ch. 216 §85 (renumbered).

§676.8. Workers' compensation insurance policies.

(a) This section applies only to policies of workers' compensation insurance.

(b) After a policy is in effect, no notice of cancellation shall be effective unless it complies with the notice requirements of this section and is based upon the occurrence, after the effective date of the policy, of one or more of the following:

(1) The policyholder's failure to make any workers' compensation insurance premium payment when due.

(2) The policyholder's failure to report payroll, to permit the insurer to audit payroll as required by the terms of the policy or of a previous policy issued by the insurer, or to pay any additional premium as a result of a audit of payroll as required by the terms of the policy or of a previous policy.

(3) The policyholder's material failure to comply with federal or state safety orders or written recommendations of the insurer's designated loss control representative.

(4) A material change in ownership or any change in the policyholder's business or operations that materially increases the hazard for frequency or severity of loss, requires additional or different classifications for premium calculations, or contemplates an activity excluded by the insurer's reinsurance treaties.

(5) Material misrepresentation by the policyholder or its agent.

(6) Failure to cooperate with the insurer in the insurer's investigation of a claim.

(c) A policy shall not be canceled for the conditions specified in paragraph (1), (2), (5), or (6) of subdivision (b) except upon 10 days' written notice to the policyholder by the insurer. A policy shall not be canceled for the conditions specified in paragraph (3) or (4) of subdivision (b) except upon 30 days' written notice to the policyholder by the insurer, provided that no notice is required if an insured and insurer consent to the cancellation and reissuance of a policy effective upon a material change in ownership or operations of the insured. If the policyholder remedies the condition to the insurer's satisfaction within the specified time period, the policy shall not be canceled by the insurer.

(d) Nothing in this section shall preclude, while policies are in force, changes in the premium rate required or authorized by law, regulation, or order of the commissioner, or otherwise agreed to between the policyholder and insurer.

(e) Any policy written for a term longer than one year, or any policy with no fixed expiration date, shall be considered as if written for successive policy periods of one year. **Leg.H.** 1993 ch. 121 (AB 110) §2, effective July 16, 1993, 1993 ch. 1242 (SB 223) §1.

Ref.: Hanna § 2.61[2]; Herlick Handbook § 3.15.

§676.9. Discrimination against domestic violence victims; nature and use of information about domestic violence victims.

(a) This section applies to policies covered by Sections 675 and 675.5.

(b) No insurer issuing policies subject to this section shall deny or refuse to accept an application, refuse to insure, refuse to renew, cancel, restrict, or otherwise terminate, or charge a different rate for the same coverage, on the basis that the applicant or insured person is, has been, or may be, a victim of domestic violence.

(c) Nothing in this section shall prevent an insurer subject to this section from taking any of the actions set forth in subdivision (b) on the basis of criteria not otherwise made invalid by this section or any other act, regulation, or rule of law. If discrimination by an insurer is not in violation of this section but is based on any other criteria that are allowable by law, the fact that the applicant or insured is, has been, or may be the subject of domestic violence shall be irrelevant.

(d) For purposes of this section, information that indicates that a person is, has been, or may be a victim of domestic violence is personal information within the meaning of Article 6.6 (commencing with Section 791) of Chapter 1 of Part 2.

(e) No insurer that issues policies subject to this section, and no person employed by or under contract with an insurer that issues policies subject to this section, shall request any information the insurer or person knows or reasonably should know relates to acts of domestic violence or an applicant's or insured's status as a victim of domestic violence, or make use of this information however obtained, except for the limited purpose of complying with legal obligations, verifying a person's claim to be a subject of domestic violence, or cooperating with a victim of domestic violence in seeking protection from domestic violence or facilitating the treatment of a domestic violence-related medical condition. This subdivision does not prohibit an insurer from asking an applicant or insured about a property and casualty claim, even if the claim is related to domestic violence, or from using information thereby obtained in evaluating and carrying out its rights and duties under the policy, to the extent otherwise permitted by this section and other applicable law.

(f) As used in this section, "domestic violence" means domestic violence as defined in Section 6211 of the Family Code. **Leg.H.** 1997 ch. 845 (AB 588) §1.

Ref.: W. Cal. Sum., 8 "Constitutional Law" §891, 11 "Husband and Wife" §371.

§676.10. Applicability of section; cancellation or nonrenewal due to hate crime or anti-reproductive-rights crime losses; "hate crime" and "anti-reproductive-rights crime"; reporting procedures; violation.

(a) This section applies to policies covered by Section 675, 675.5, or 676.5 if the insured is a religious organization described in clause (i) of subparagraph (A) of paragraph (1) of subsection (b) of Section 170 of Title 26 of the United States Code, an educational organization described in clause (ii) of subparagraph (A) of paragraph (1) of subsection (b) of Section 170 of Title 26 of the United States Code, or other nonprofit organization described in clause (vi) of subparagraph (A) of paragraph (1) of subsection (b) of Section 170 of Title 26 of the United States Code that is organized and operated for religious, charitable, or educational purposes, or a reproductive health services facility, as defined in subdivision (h) of Section 423.1 of the Penal Code, or its administrative offices.

(b) No insurer issuing policies subject to this section shall cancel or refuse to renew the policy, nor shall any premium be excessive or unfairly discriminatory solely on the basis that one or more claims has been made against the policy during the preceding 60 months for a loss that is the result of a hate crime committed against the person or property of the insured, or an anti-reproductive-rights crime.

(c) As it relates to this section, if determined by a law enforcement agency, a "hate crime" may include any of the following:

(1) By force or threat of force, willfully injure, intimidate, interfere with, oppress, or threaten any other person in the free exercise or enjoyment of any right or privilege secured to him or her by the Constitution or laws of this state or by the Constitution or laws of the United States because of the other person's race, color, religion, ancestry, national origin, disability, gender, or sexual orientation, or because he or she

perceives that the other person has one or more of those characteristics. However, the foregoing offense does not include speech alone, except upon a showing that the speech itself threatened violence against a specific person or group of persons and that the defendant had the apparent ability to carry out the threat.

(2) Knowingly deface, damage, or destroy the real or personal property of any other person for the purpose of intimidating or interfering with the free exercise or enjoyment of any right or privilege secured to the other person by the Constitution or laws of this state or by the Constitution or laws of the United States, because of the other person's race, color, religion, ancestry, national origin, disability, gender, or sexual orientation, or because he or she perceives that the other person has one or more of those characteristics.

(d) As it relates to this section, if determined by a law enforcement agency, "anti-reproductive-rights crime" shall have the meaning set forth in subdivision (a) of Section 13776 of the Penal Code, and shall also include a violation of subdivision (e) of Section 423.2 of the Penal Code, if the crime results in a covered loss under a policy subject to this section.

(e) Upon cancellation of or refusal to renew a policy subject to this section after an insured has submitted a claim to the insurer that is the result of a hate crime committed against the person or property of the insured, or an anti-reproductive-rights crime, the insurer shall report the cancellation or nonrenewal to the commissioner.

(f) A violation of this section shall be an unfair practice subject to Article 6.5 (commencing with Section 790) of Chapter 1 of Division 2.

(g) Nothing in this section shall prevent an insurer subject to this section from taking any of the actions set forth in subdivision (b) on the basis of criteria not otherwise made invalid by this section or any other act, regulation, or law. **Leg.H.** 2001 ch. 253 (AB 1193) §1, 2003 ch. 647 (AB 996).

Ref.: W. Cal. Sum., 2 "Insurance" §§219, 223.

§677. Notice of cancellation.

(a) All notices of cancellation shall be in writing, mailed to the named insured at the address shown in the policy, or to his or her last known address, and shall state, with respect to policies in effect after the time limits specified in Section 676, (1) which of the grounds set forth in Section 676 is relied upon, and, in accordance with the requirements of subdivisions (a) and (e) of Section 791.10, and (2) the specific information supporting the cancellation, the specific items of personal and privileged information that support those reasons, if applicable, and corresponding summary of rights.

(b) For purposes of this section, a lienholder's copy of those notices shall be deemed mailed if, with the lienholder's consent, it is delivered by electronic transmittal, facsimile, or personal delivery. **Leg.H.** 1970 ch. 313 §1, 1972 ch. 237 §1, 1987 ch. 800 §2, 2004 chs. 939 (AB 1979), 940 (AB 2693), 2006 ch. 740 (AB 2125) §3.

Ref.: W. Cal. Sum., 2 "Insurance" §222.

§677.2. Notice of cancellation for commercial insurance policies.

(a) This section applies only to policies covered by Section 675.5.

(b) A notice of cancellation shall be in writing and shall be delivered or mailed to the producer of record, provided that the producer of record is not an employee of the insurer, and to the named insured at the mailing address shown on the policy. Subdivision (a) of Section 1013 of the Code of Civil Procedure is applicable if the notice is mailed.

The notice of cancellation shall include the effective date of the cancellation and the reasons for the cancellation.

(c) The notice of cancellation shall be given at least 30 days prior to the effective date of the cancellation, except that in the case of cancellation for nonpayment of premiums or for fraud the notice shall be given no less than 10 days prior to the effective date of the cancellation. Notice of a proposed cancellation pursuant to subdivision (d) of Section 676.2 given prior to a finding of the commissioner shall satisfy the requirements of this section if it is given no less than 30 days prior to the effective date of the cancellation and if it states that cancellation will be effective only upon the approval of the commissioner.

(d) This section applies only to cancellations pursuant to Section 676.2. **Leg.H.** 1986 ch. 1321 §5.

Ref.: W. Cal. Sum., 2 "Insurance" §§20, 222.

§677.4. Notice of cancellation for certain property insurance policies.

A notice of cancellation with respect to a policy covered under Section 675 shall be delivered at least 20 calendar days prior to the effective date of the cancellation, except that in the case of a cancellation for nonpayment of premiums, or for fraud, the notice shall be given at least 10 calendar days prior to the effective date of the cancellation. Subdivision (a) of Section 1013 of the Code of Civil Procedure is applicable if the notice is mailed. **Leg.H.** 2003 ch. 148 (AB 1727).

§678. Notice of nonrenewal.

(a) At least 45 days prior to policy expiration, an insurer shall deliver to the named insured or mail to the named insured at the address shown in the policy, either of the following:

(1) An offer of renewal of the policy contingent upon payment of premium as stated in the offer, stating each of the following:

(A) Any reduction of limits or elimination of coverage.

(B) The telephone number of the insurer's representatives who handle consumer inquiries or complaints. The telephone number shall be displayed prominently in a font size consistent with the other text of the renewal offer.

(2) A notice of nonrenewal of the policy. That notice shall contain each of the following:

(A) The reason or reasons for the nonrenewal.

(B) The telephone number of the insurer's representatives who handle consumer inquiries or complaints. The telephone number shall be displayed prominently in a font size consistent with the other text of the notice of nonrenewal.

(C) A brief statement indicating that if the consumer has contacted the insurer to discuss the nonrenewal and remains unsatisfied, he or she may have the matter reviewed by the department. The statement shall include the telephone number of the unit within the department that responds to consumer inquiries and complaints.

(b) In the event an insurer fails to give the named insured either an offer of renewal or notice of nonrenewal as required by this section, the existing policy, with no change in its terms and conditions, shall remain in effect for 45 days from the date that either the offer to renew or the notice of nonrenewal is delivered or mailed to the named insured. A notice to this effect shall be provided by the insurer to the named insured with the policy or the notice of renewal or nonrenewal.

(c) Any policy written for a term of less than one year shall be considered as if written for a term of one year. Any policy written for a term longer than one year, or any policy with no fixed expiration date, shall be considered as if written for successive policy periods or terms of one year.

(d) This section applies only to policies of insurance specified in Section 675. **Leg.H.** 1970 ch. 313 §1, 1986 chs. 1321, 1322 §2, operative July 1, 1987, 1995 ch. 791 (SB 306) §2, 2003 ch. 571 (AB 1191), operative March 1, 2004.

Ref.: W. Cal. Sum., 2 "Insurance" §223.

PART 2
The Business of Insurance

CHAPTER 1
GENERAL REGULATIONS

ARTICLE 3
Certificate of Authority
[Selected Provisions]

§703.5. Advertising of qualifications to advise employers—Penalty.

Any person, including, but not limited to, persons licensed or certificated under this code or exempted from regulation under this code, who as a part of any business advertises as, or holds himself or herself out as, qualified to advise the public concerning insurance or qualified to administer workers' compensation for employers and who in connection with or as part of that business also, with or without consideration, (a) suggests or recommends to an employer, or advises an employer, that the employer purchase aggregate excess or aggregate stop-loss workers' compensation insurance, or (b) names or suggests to an employer, or advises an employer of, a nonadmitted insurer from whom aggregate excess or aggregate stop-loss workers' compensation insurance might be purchased, is guilty of a misdemeanor. This section does not apply if the employer is a self-insured public entity, including any agency, board, or commission provided for by a joint exercise of powers agreement, or those who have been issued a certificate by the Director of the Department of Industrial Relations to self-insure. **Leg.H.** 1992 ch. 378.

Ref.: Herlick Handbook §§ 3.16, 3.22.

ARTICLE 4
Examination by Commissioner
[Selected Provisions]

§738. Authority of commissioner to examine State Compensation Insurance Fund.

The commissioner shall have the same powers and authority to examine the State Compensation Insurance Fund as are conferred upon him by law relative to the examination of other insurers except where the fund is specifically exempted by reference. **Leg.H.** 2006 ch. 740 (AB 2125) §3.3.

ARTICLE 5.1
Unlawful Practices
[Selected Provisions]

§756. Misrepresentation of payroll; penalty.

When the premium on a policy insuring an employer is based upon the amount or segregation of the employer's payroll, and the employer, personally or knowingly through his or her employee, procures a lower premium by willfully misrepresenting the amount or segregation, that misrepresentation is an unlawful act as to the employer.

In addition to any penalty provided by law, the employer in that case is liable to the state in an amount 10 times the difference between the lower premium paid and the premium properly payable. The commissioner shall collect the amount so payable and may bring a civil action in his or her name as commissioner to enforce collection unless the misrepresentation is made to, and the lower premium procured from the State Compensation Insurance Fund. In the latter case the liability to the state under this section shall be enforced in a civil action in the name of the State Compensation Insurance Fund and any amount so collected shall become a part of that fund.

Ref.: Herlick Handbook §§ 3.2, 3.15.

§757. Insurer's acceptance of false payroll information.

When a statement of the amount or segregation of a payroll is materially false, and an insurer, through a person employed by it in a managerial capacity, accepts the statement as the basis for the premium on a policy, the acceptance is an unlawful act if the accepting employee knows of the falsity.

ARTICLE 10
Financial Statements of Insurers
[Selected Provisions]

§923.5. Required reserves.

Each insurer transacting business in this state shall at all times maintain reserves in an amount estimated in the aggregate to provide for the payment of all losses and claims for which the insurer may be liable, and to provide for the expense of adjustment or settlement of losses and claims.

The reserves shall be computed in accordance with regulations made from time to time by the commissioner. The promulgation of the regulations by the commissioner, or any changes thereto or amendments thereof, shall be in accordance with the procedure provided in Chapter 3.5 (commencing with Section 11340) of Part 1 of Division 3 of Title 2 of the Government Code. The commissioner shall make the regulations upon reasonable consideration of the ascertained experience and the character of such kinds of business for the purpose of adequately protecting the insured and securing the solvency of the insurer.

With respect to liability and common carrier liability, the regulations shall be consistent with Section 11558.

The commissioner may prescribe the manner and form of reporting pertinent information concerning the reserves provided for in this section.

This section shall not apply to life insurance, title insurance, disability insurance, mortgage insurance, or mortgage guaranty insurance. **Leg.H.** 2007 ch. 431 (SB 316) §1.

Ref.: Herlick Handbook §§ 3.2, 3.12, 12.13; W. Cal. Sum., 2 "Insurance" §6.

ARTICLE 14.2
California Insurance Guarantee Association
[Selected Provisions]

§1063. California Insurance Guarantee Association.

(a) Within 60 days after the original effective date of this article, all insurers, including reciprocal insurers, admitted to transact insurance in this state of any or all of the following classes only in accordance with the provisions of Chapter 1 (commencing with Section 100) of Part 1 of this division: fire (see Section 102), marine (see Section 103), plate glass (see Section 107), liability (see Section 108), workers' compensation (see Section 109), common carrier liability (see Section 110), boiler and machinery (see Section 111), burglary (see Section 112), sprinkler (see Section 114), team and vehicle (see Section 115), automobile (see Section 116), aircraft (see Section 118), and miscellaneous (see Section 120), shall establish the California Insurance Guarantee Association (the association); provided, however, this article shall not apply to the following classes or kinds of insurance: life and annuity (see Section 101), title (see Section 104), fidelity or surety including fidelity or surety bonds, or any other bonding obligations (see Section 105), disability or health (see Section 106), credit (see Section 113), mortgage (see Section 117), mortgage guaranty, insolvency or legal (see Section 119), financial guaranty or other forms of insurance offering protection against investment risks (see Section 124), the ocean marine portion of any marine insurance or ocean marine coverage under any insurance policy including the following: the Jones Act (46 U.S.C. Sec. 688), the Longshore and Harbor Workers' Compensation Act (33 U.S.C. Sec. 901 et seq.), or any other similar federal statutory enactment, or any endorsement or policy affording protection and indemnity coverage, or reinsurance as defined in Section 620, or fraternal fire insurance written by associations organized and operating under Sections 9080 to 9103, inclusive. Any insurer admitted to transact only those classes or kinds of insurance excluded from this article shall not be a member insurer of the association. Each insurer admitted to transact a class of insurance included in this article, including the State Compensation Insurance Fund, as a condition of its authority to transact insurance in this state, shall participate in the association whether established voluntarily or by order of the commissioner after the elapse of 60 days following the original effective date of this article in accordance with rules to be established as provided in this article. It shall be the purpose of the association to provide for each member insurer insolvency insurance as defined in Section 119.5.

[Subsections (b)–(j) Not Reproduced]

Leg.H. 1994 ch. 6, effective February 10, 1994, 1996 ch. 252, 2001 ch. 296, effective September 12, 2001, 2002 ch. 431 (AB 2007), 2003 ch. 635 (AB 227).

Ref.: Hanna § 2.84; Herlick Handbook §§ 3.13, 8.23; W. Cal. Sum., 2 "Insurance" §§12, 13.

§1063.1. Definitions.

As used in this article:

(a) "Member insurer" means an insurer required to be a member of the association in accordance with subdivision (a) of Section 1063, except and to the extent that the insurer is participating in an insolvency program adopted by the United States government.

(b) "Insolvent insurer" means an insurer that was a member insurer of the association, consistent with paragraph (11) of subdivision (c), either at the time the policy was issued or when the insured event occurred, and against which an order of liquidation or receivership with a finding of insolvency has been entered by a court of competent jurisdiction, or, in the case of the State Compensation Insurance Fund, if a finding of insolvency is made by a duly enacted legislative measure.

(c)(1) "Covered claims" means the obligations of an insolvent insurer, including the obligation for unearned premiums, (A) imposed by law and within the coverage of an insurance policy of the insolvent insurer; (B) which were unpaid by the insolvent insurer; (C) which are presented as a claim to the liquidator in this state or to the association on or before the last date fixed for the filing of claims in the domiciliary liquidating proceedings; (D) which were incurred prior to the date coverage under the policy terminated and prior to, on, or within 30 days after the date the liquidator was appointed; (E) for which the assets of the insolvent insurer are insufficient to discharge in full; (F) in the case of a policy of workers' compensation insurance, to provide workers' compensation benefits under the workers' compensation law of this state; and (G) in the case of other classes of insurance if the claimant or insured is a resident of this state at the time of the insured occurrence, or the property from which the claim arises is permanently located in this state.

(2) "Covered claims" also include the obligations assumed by an assuming insurer from a ceding insurer where the assuming insurer subsequently becomes an insolvent insurer if, at the time of the insolvency of the assuming insurer, the ceding insurer is no longer admitted to transact business in this state. Both the assuming insurer and the ceding insurer shall have been member insurers at the time the assumption was made. "Covered claims" under this paragraph shall be required to satisfy the requirements of subparagraphs (A) to (G), inclusive, of paragraph (1), except for the requirement that the claims be against policies of the insolvent insurer. The association shall have a right to recover any deposit, bond, or other assets that may have been required to be posted by the ceding company to the extent of covered claim payments and shall be subrogated to any rights the policyholders may have against the ceding insurer.

(3) "Covered claims" does not include obligations arising from the following:

(A) Life, annuity, health, or disability insurance.

(B) Mortgage guaranty, financial guaranty, or other forms of insurance offering protection against investment risks.

(C) Fidelity or surety insurance including fidelity or surety bonds, or any other bonding obligations.

(D) Credit insurance.

(E) Title insurance.

(F) Ocean marine insurance or ocean marine coverage under any insurance policy including claims arising from the following: the Jones Act (46 U.S.C. Sec. 688), the Longshore and Harbor Workers' Compensation Act (33 U.S.C. Sec. 901 et seq.), or any other similar federal statutory enactment, or any endorsement or policy affording protection and indemnity coverage.

(G) Any claims servicing agreement or insurance policy providing retroactive insurance of a known loss or losses, except a special excess workers' compensation policy issued pursuant to subdivision (c) of Section 3702.8 of the Labor Code that covers all or any part of workers' compensation liabilities of an employer that is issued, or was previously issued, a certificate of consent to self-insure pursuant to subdivision (b) of Section 3700 of the Labor Code.

(4) "Covered claims" does not include any obligations of the insolvent insurer arising out of any reinsurance contracts, nor any obligations incurred after the expiration date of the insurance policy or after the insurance policy has been replaced by the insured or canceled at the insured's request, [1] or after the insurance policy has been canceled by the liquidator, nor any obligations to any state or to the federal government.

(5) "Covered claims" does not include any obligations to insurers, insurance pools, or underwriting associations, nor their claims for contribution, indemnity, or subrogation, equita-

ble or otherwise, except as otherwise provided in this chapter.

An insurer, insurance pool, or underwriting association may not maintain, in its own name or in the name of its insured, any claim or legal action against the insured of the insolvent insurer for contribution, indemnity or by way of subrogation, except insofar as, and to the extent only, that the claim exceeds the policy limits of the insolvent insurer's policy. In those claims or legal actions, the insured of the insolvent insurer is entitled to a credit or setoff in the amount of the policy limits of the insolvent insurer's policy, or in the amount of the limits remaining, where those limits have been diminished by the payment of other claims.

(6) "Covered claims," except in cases involving a claim for workers' compensation benefits or for unearned premiums, does not include any claim in an amount of one hundred dollars ($100) or less, nor that portion of any claim that is in excess of any applicable limits provided in the insurance policy issued by the insolvent insurer.

(7) "Covered claims" does not include that portion of any claim, other than a claim for workers' compensation benefits, that is in excess of five hundred thousand dollars ($500,000).

(8) "Covered claims" does not include any amount awarded as punitive or exemplary damages, nor any amount awarded by the Workers' Compensation Appeals Board pursuant to Section 5814 or 5814.5 because payment of compensation was unreasonably delayed or refused by the insolvent insurer.

(9) "Covered claims" does not include (A) any claim to the extent it is covered by any other insurance of a class covered by this article available to the claimant or insured nor (B) any claim by any person other than the original claimant under the insurance policy in his or her own name, his or her assignee as the person entitled thereto under a premium finance agreement as defined in Section 673 and entered into prior to insolvency, his or her executor, administrator, guardian or other personal representative or trustee in bankruptcy and does not include any claim asserted by an assignee or one claiming by right of subrogation, except as otherwise provided in this chapter.

(10) "Covered claims" does not include any obligations arising out of the issuance of an insurance policy written by the separate division of the State Compensation Insurance Fund pursuant to Sections 11802 and 11803.

(11) "Covered claims" does not include any obligations of the insolvent insurer arising from any policy or contract of insurance issued or renewed prior to the insolvent insurer's admission to transact insurance in the State of California.

(12) "Covered claims" does not include surplus deposits of subscribers as defined in Section 1374.1.

(13) "Covered claims" shall also include obligations arising under an insurance policy written to indemnify a permissibly self-insured employer pursuant to subdivision (b) or (c) of Section 3700 of the Labor Code for its liability to pay workers' compensation benefits in excess of a specific or aggregate retention, provided, however, that for purposes of this article, those claims shall not be considered workers' compensation claims and therefore are subject to the per claim limit in paragraph (7) and any payments and expenses related thereto shall be allocated to category (c) for claims other than workers' compensation, homeowners, and automobile, as provided in Section 1063.5.

These provisions shall apply to obligations arising under any policy as described herein issued to a permissibly self-insured employer or group of self-insured employers pursuant to Section 3700 of the Labor Code and notwithstanding any other provision of the Insurance Code, those obligations shall be governed by this provision in the event that the Self-Insurers' Security Fund is ordered to assume the liabilities of a permissibly self-insured employer or group of self-insured employers pursuant to Section 3701.5 of the Labor Code. The provisions of this paragraph apply only to insurance policies written to indemnify a permissibly self-insured employer or group of self-insured employers under subdivision (b) or (c) of Section 3700, for its liability to pay workers' compensation benefits in excess of a specific or aggregate retention, and this paragraph does not apply to special excess workers' compensation insurance policies unless issued pursuant to authority granted in subdivision (c) of Section 3702.8 of the Labor Code, and as provided for in subparagraph (G) of paragraph (3) of subdivision (c). In addition, this paragraph does not apply to any claims servicing agreement or insurance policy providing retroactive insurance of a known loss or losses as are excluded in subparagraph (G) of paragraph (3) of subdivision (c).

Each permissibility self-insured employer or group of self-insured employers, or the Self-Insurers' Security Fund, shall, to the extent required by the Labor Code, be responsible for paying, adjusting, and defending each claim arising under policies of insurance covered under this section, unless the benefits paid on a claim exceed the specific or aggregate retention, in which case [2]:

(A) If the benefits paid on the claim exceed the specific or aggregate retention, and the policy requires the insurer to defend and adjust the claim, the California Insurance Guarantee Association (CIGA) shall be solely responsible for adjusting and defending the claim, and shall make all payments due under the claim, subject to the limitations and exclusions of this article with regards to covered claims. As to each claim subject to this paragraph, notwithstanding any other provisions of the Insurance Code or the Labor Code, and regardless of whether the amount paid by CIGA is adequate to discharge a claim obligation, neither the self-insured employer, group of employers, nor the Self-Insurers' Security Fund, shall have any obligation to pay benefits over and above the specific or aggregate retention, except as provided in subdivision (c).

(B) If the benefits paid on the claim exceed the specific or aggregate retention, and the policy does not require the insurer to defend and adjust the claim, the permissibility self-insured employer or group of self-insured employers, or the Self-Insurers' Security Fund, shall not have any further payment obligations with respect to the claim, but shall continue defending and adjusting the claim, and shall have the right, but not the obligation, in any proceeding to assert all applicable statutory limitations and exclusions as contained in this article with regard to the covered claim. CIGA shall have the right, but not the obligation, to intervene in any proceeding where the self-insured employer, group of self-insured employers, or the Self-Insurers' Security Fund is defending any such claim and shall be permitted to raise the appropriate statutory limitations and exclusions as contained in this article with respect to covered claims. Regardless of whether the self-insured employer or group of employers, or the Self-Insurers' Security Fund, asserts the applicable statutory limitations and exclusions, or whether CIGA intervenes in any such proceeding, CIGA shall be solely responsible for paying all benefits due on the claim, subject to the exclusions and limitations of this article with respect to covered claims. As to each claim subject to this paragraph, notwithstanding any other provision of the Insurance Code or the Labor Code and regardless of whether the amount paid by CIGA is adequate to discharge a claim obligation, neither the self-insured employer, group of employers, nor the Self-Insurers' Security Fund, shall have any obligation to pay benefits over and above the specific or aggregate retention, except as provided in this subdivision.

[3] **(C)** In the event that the benefits paid on the covered claim exceed the per claim limit in paragraph (7) of subdivision (c), the responsibility for paying, adjusting, and defending the claim shall be returned to the permissibly self-insured employer or group of employers, or the Self-Insurers' Security Fund.

These provisions shall apply to all pending and future insolvencies. For purposes of this paragraph, a pending insolvency is one involving a company that is currently receiving benefits from the guaranty association.

[4] **(d)** "Admitted to transact insurance in this state" means an insurer possessing a valid certificate of authority issued by the department.

[5] **(e)** "Affiliate" means a person who directly or indirectly, through one or more intermediaries, controls, is controlled by, or is under common control with an insolvent insurer on December 31 of the year next preceding the date the insurer becomes an insolvent insurer.

[6] **(f)** "Control" means the possession, direct or indirect, of the power to direct or cause the direction of the management and policies of a person, whether through the ownership of voting securities, by contract other than a commercial contract for goods or nonmanagement services, or otherwise, unless the power is the result of an official position with or corporate office held by the person. Control is presumed to exist if any person, directly or indirectly, owns, controls, holds with the power to vote, or holds proxies representing, 10 percent or more of the voting securities of any other person. This presumption may be rebutted by showing that control does not in fact exist.

[7] **(g)** "Claimant" means any insured making a first party claim or any person instituting a liability claim; provided that no person who is

an affiliate of the insolvent insurer may be a claimant.

[8] **(h)** "Ocean marine insurance" includes marine insurance as defined in Section 103, except for inland marine insurance, as well as any other form of insurance, regardless of the name, label, or marketing designation of the insurance policy, that insures against maritime perils or risks and other related perils or risks, which are usually insured against by traditional marine insurance such as hull and machinery, marine builders' risks, and marine protection and indemnity. Those perils and risks insured against include, without limitation, loss, damage, or expense or legal liability of the insured arising out of or incident to ownership, operation, chartering, maintenance, use, repair, or construction of any vessel, craft or instrumentality in use in ocean or inland waterways, including liability of the insured for personal injury, illness, or death for loss or damage to the property of the insured or another person.

[9] **(i)** "Unearned premium" means that portion of a premium as calculated by the liquidator that had not been earned because of the cancellation of the insolvent insurer's policy and is that premium remaining for the unexpired term of the insolvent insurer's policy. "Unearned premium" does not include any amount sought as return of a premium under any policy providing retroactive insurance of a known loss or return of a premium under any retrospectively rated policy or a policy subject to a contingent surcharge or any policy in which the final determination of the premium cost is computed after expiration of the policy and is calculated on the basis of actual loss experience during the policy period. **Leg.H.** 1991 ch. 537, 1992 ch. 227, 1994 ch. 6, effective February 10, 1994, 1997 ch. 372 §1, ch. 497 §2.5, 1999 ch. 721, 2003 ch. 635 (AB 227), 2005 ch. 395 (AB 817) §1, 2006 ch. 740 (AB 2125) §4, 2007 ch. 100 (SB 1038) §2, 2008 chs. 80 (AB 3055) §1, 179 (SB 1498) §166 (ch. 80 prevails; ch. 179 not effective).

§1063.1. 2008 Deletes. **[1]** or after the insurance policy has been canceled by the association as provided in this chapter, **[2]** . **[3]** (d) **[4]** (e) **[5]** (f) **[6]** (g) **[7]** (h) **[8]** (i) **[9]** (j)

Ref.: Hanna § 2.84; Herlick Handbook § 3.13; W. Cal. Sum., 2 "Insurance" §§12, 13.

§1063.2. Association's duties; authority; exceptions to "covered claims."

(a) The association shall pay and discharge covered claims and in connection therewith pay for or furnish loss adjustment services and defenses of claimants when required by policy provisions. It may do so either directly by itself or through a servicing facility or through a contract for reinsurance and assumption of liabilities by one or more member insurers or through a contract with the liquidator, upon terms satisfactory to the association and to the liquidator, under which payments on covered claims would be made by the liquidator using funds provided by the association.

(b) The association shall be a party in interest in all proceedings involving a covered claim, and shall have the same rights as the insolvent insurer would have had if not in liquidation, including, but not limited to, the right to: (1) appear, defend, and appeal a claim in a court of competent jurisdiction; (2) receive notice of, investigate, adjust, compromise, settle, and pay a covered claim; and (3) investigate, handle, and deny a noncovered claim. The association shall have no cause of action against the insureds of the insolvent insurer for any sums it has paid out, except as provided by this article.

(c)(1) If damages against uninsured motorists are recoverable by the claimant from his or her own insurer, the applicable limits of the uninsured motorists coverage shall be a credit against a covered claim payable under this article. Any person having a claim that may be recovered under more than one insurance guaranty association or its equivalent shall seek recovery first from the association of the place of residence of the insured, except that if it is a first-party claim for damage to property with a permanent location, he or she shall seek recovery first from the association of the permanent location of the property, and if it is a workers' compensation claim, he or she shall seek recovery first from the association of the residence of the claimant. Any recovery under this article shall be reduced by the amount of recovery from any other insurance guaranty association or its equivalent. A member insurer may recover in subrogation from the association only one-half of any amount paid by such insurer under uninsured motorist coverage for bodily injury or wrongful death (and nothing for a payment for anything else), in those cases where the injured person insured by such an insurer has proceeded under his or her uninsured motorist coverage on the ground that the [1] **tort-feasor** is uninsured as a result of the insolvency of his or her liability insurer (an insolvent insurer as defined in this article), provided that such member insurer shall waive all rights of subrogation against such [2] **tort-feasor**. Any amount paid a claimant in excess of the amount authorized by this section may be recovered by action**, or other proceeding,** brought by the association.

(2) Any claimant having collision coverage on a loss which is covered by the insolvent company's liability policy shall first proceed against his or her collision carrier. Neither that claimant nor the collision carrier, if it is a member of the association, shall have the right to sue or continue a suit against the insured of the insolvent insurance company for such collision damage.

(d) The association shall have the right to recover from any person who is an affiliate of the insolvent insurer and whose liability obligations to other persons are satisfied in whole or in part by payments made under this article the amount of any covered claim and allocated claims expense paid on behalf of that person pursuant to this article.

(e) Any person having a claim or legal right of recovery under any governmental insurance or guaranty program which is also a covered claim, shall be required to first exhaust his or her right under the program. Any amount payable on a covered claim shall be reduced by the amount of any recovery under the program.

(f) "Covered claims" for unearned premium by lenders under insurance premium finance agreements as defined in Section 673 shall be computed as of the earliest cancellation date of the policy pursuant to Section 673 or subdivision (g) of this section.

(g) "Covered claims" shall not include any judgments against or obligations or liabilities of the insolvent insurer or the commissioner, as liquidator, or otherwise resulting from alleged or proven torts, nor shall any default judgment or stipulated judgment against the insolvent insurer, or against the insured of the insolvent insurer, be binding against the association.

(h) "Covered claims" shall not include any loss adjustment expenses, including adjustment fees and expenses, attorney fees and expenses, court costs, interest, and bond premiums, incurred prior to the appointment of a liquidator. **Leg.H.** 1991 ch. 537, 1992 chs. 227, 427 (ch. 227 prevails; ch. 427 not effective), 1994 ch. 6, effective February 10, 1994, 2008 ch. 80 (AB 3055) §2.

§1063.2. 2008 Deletes. [1] tort feasor **[2]** tort feasor

Ref.: Hanna § 2.84; Herlick Handbook § 3.13; W. Cal. Sum., 2 "Insurance" §12.

§1063.3. Reports and recommendations pertaining to regulation for solvency.

To aid in the detection and prevention of member insurer insolvencies:

(a) The board may, upon majority vote, make recommendations to the commissioner on matters pertaining to regulation for solvency.

(b) The board may prepare a report on the history and causes of any member insurer insolvency in which the association was obligated to pay covered claims, based on the information available to the association, and submit that report along with any recommendations resulting therefrom to the commissioner.

(c) The board may request the Self-Insurers' Security Fund to prepare, and the Self-Insurers' Security Fund may provide to the board, a report identifying the aggregate amount of liability, including the estimated exposure for every insurance carrier admitted to transact workers' compensation insurance in this state, under all specific excess workers' compensation policies in existence for a given period in this state as reported by the private self-insured employers to the Director of Industrial Relations in the annual reports submitted pursuant to Section 3702.2 of the Labor Code. **Leg.H.** 1994 ch. 6 (AB 1667) §5, effective February 10, 1994, 2005 ch. 395 (AB 817) §2.

§1063.5. Premiums.

Each time an insurer becomes insolvent then, to the extent necessary to secure funds for the association for payment of covered claims of that insolvent insurer and also for payment of reasonable costs of adjusting the claims, the association shall collect premium payments from its member insurers sufficient to discharge its obligations. The association shall allocate its claim payments and costs, incurred or estimated to be incurred, to one or more of the following categories: (a) workers' compensation claims; (b) homeowners' claims, and automobile claims, which shall include: automobile material damage, automobile liability (both personal injury and death and property damage), medical payments and uninsured motorist claims; and (c) claims other than workers' compensation, homeowners', and automobile, as above defined. Separate premium payments shall be required for each category. The premium payments for each category shall be used to pay the claims and costs allocated to that category. The rate of premium charged shall be a uniform percentage of net direct written premium in the preceding calendar year applicable to that category. The rate of premium charges to each member in the appropriate categories shall initially be based on the written premium of each insurer as shown in the latest year's annual financial statement on file with the commissioner. The initial premium shall be adjusted by applying the same rate of premium charge as initially used to each insurer's written premium as shown on the annual statement for the second year following the year in which the initial premium charge is made. The difference between the initial premium charge and the adjusted premium charge shall be charged or credited to each member insurer by the association as soon as practical after the filing of the annual statements of the member insurers with the commissioner for the year on which the adjusted premium is based. Any credit due in a specific category to a member insurer as a result of the adjusted premium calculation may be refunded to the member insurer at the discretion of the association if the member insurer has agreed with the commissioner to no longer write insurance in that category but has not withdrawn from the state and surrendered its certificate of authority. However, in the case of an insurer that was a member insurer when the initial premium charge was made and that paid the initial assessment but is no longer a member insurer at the time of the adjusted premium charge by reason of its insolvency or its withdrawal from the state and surrender of its certificate of authority to transact insurance in this state, any credit accruing to that insurer shall be refunded to it by the association. "Net direct written premiums" shall mean the amount of gross premiums, less return premiums, received in that calendar year upon business done in this state, other than premiums received for reinsurance. In cases of a dispute as to the amount of the net direct written premium between the association and one of its members the written decision of the commissioner shall be final. The premium charged to any member insurer for any of the three categories or a category established by the association shall not be more than 2 percent of the net direct premium written in that category in this state by that member per year, starting on January 1, 2003, until December 31, 2007, and thereafter shall be 1 percent per year. The association may exempt or defer, in whole or in part, the premium charge of any member insurer, if the premium charge would cause the member insurer's financial statement to reflect an amount of capital or surplus less than the minimum amounts required for a certificate of authority by any jurisdiction in which the member insurer is authorized to transact insurance. However, during the period of deferment, no dividends shall be paid to shareholders or policyholders by the company whose premium charge was deferred. Deferred premium charges shall be paid when the payment will not reduce capital or surplus below required minimums. These payments shall be credited against future premium charges to those companies receiving larger premium charges by virtue of the deferment. After all covered claims of the insolvent insurer and expenses of administration have been paid, any unused premiums and any reimbursements or claims dividends from the liquidator remaining in any category shall be retained by the association and applied to reduce future premium charges in the appropriate category. However, an insurer which ceases to be a member of the association, other than an insurer that has become insolvent or has withdrawn from the state and has surrendered its certificate of authority following an initial assessment that is entitled to a refund based upon an adjusted assessment as provided above in this section, shall have no right to a refund of any premium previously remitted to the association. The commissioner may suspend or revoke the certificate of authority to transact business in this state of a member insurer which fails to pay a premium when due and after demand has been made.

Interest at a rate equal to the current federal reserve discount rate plus 2½ percent per annum shall be added to the premium of any member insurer which fails to submit the premium requested by the association within 30 days after the mailing request. However, in no event shall the interest rate exceed the legal maximum. **Leg.H.** 1992 ch. 227, 1994 ch. 6, effective February 10, 1994, 2001 ch. 296, effective

September 12, 2001, 2002 ch. 431 (AB 2007), 2006 ch. 740 (AB 2125) §4.1.

Ref.: Herlick Handbook § 3.13.

§1063.14. Surcharges on premiums.

(a) The plan of operation adopted pursuant to subdivision (c) of Section 1063 shall contain provisions whereby each member insurer is required to recoup over a reasonable length of time a sum reasonably calculated to recoup the assessments paid by the member insurer under this article by way of a surcharge on premiums charged for insurance policies to which this article applies. Amounts recouped shall not be considered premiums for any other purpose, including the computation of gross premium tax or agents' commission.

(b) The amount of any surcharge shall be separately stated on either a billing or policy declaration sent to an insured. The association shall determine the rate of the surcharge and the collection period for each category and these shall be mandatory for all member insurers of the association who write business in those categories. Member insurers who collect surcharges in excess of premiums paid pursuant to Section 1063.5 for an insolvent insurer shall remit the excess to the association as an additional premium within 30 days after the association has determined the amount of the excess recoupment and given notice to the member of that amount. The excess shall be applied to reduce future premium charges in the appropriate category.

(c) The plan of operation may permit a member insurer to omit collection of the surcharge from its insureds when the expense of collecting the surcharge would exceed the amount of the surcharge. However, nothing in this section shall relieve the member insurer of its obligation to recoup the amount of surcharge otherwise collectible. **Leg.H.** 1992 ch. 227.

Ref.: Herlick Handbook § 3.13; W. Cal. Sum., 2 "Insurance" §12.

§1063.15. Association's time limits.

In any workers' compensation matter the association shall have the same period of time within which to act or to exercise a right as is accorded to the insurer by the Labor Code, and those time periods shall be tolled against the association until 45 days after the appointment of a domiciliary or receiver. **Leg.H.** 1991 ch. 537.

Ref.: Hanna § 2.84; Herlick Handbook § 3.13.

§1063.17. Public meeting; scope; notice; certain closed meeting or session permitted; requirements.

(a) All meetings of the board of governors of the association and its investment and audit committees shall be open and public, and all persons shall be permitted to attend any meeting of the association except as otherwise provided in subdivision (g). This shall apply to meetings conducted in person and via teleconference. Attendance at telephonically conducted meetings by members of the public shall be made available by the publication by the association in its meeting notices as set forth below of a call-in number and passcode that members of the public may use to participate in the meeting.

(b) As used in this section, "meeting" includes any congregation of a majority of the members of the board of governors or the investment and audit committee, as applicable, at the same time to hear, discuss, or deliberate upon any item that is within the responsibility of the association as set forth in this article or in the association's plan of operations. Notwithstanding the foregoing, a meeting shall not include any of the following:

(1) Individual contacts or conversations between a member of the board of governors and any other person, including, but not limited to, any employee or official of the association, that do not violate subdivision (c).

(2) The attendance of a majority of the members of the board of governors or a committee at an industry conference or other gathering organized by a person or organization other than the association, provided that a majority of the members do not discuss among themselves any item that is within the responsibility of the association as set forth in this article or in the association's plan of operations.

(3) The attendance of a majority of the members, the board of governors, or a committee at a purely social or ceremonial occasion, provided that a majority of the members do not discuss among themselves any item that is within the responsibility of the association as set forth in this article or in the association's plan of operations.

(c)(1) A majority of the members of the board of governors shall not, outside a meeting authorized by this article, use a series of communications of any kind, directly or through intermediaries, to discuss, deliberate, or take action on any item of business that is within the responsibility of the association as set forth in this article or in the association's plan of operations.

(2) Paragraph (1) shall not be construed as preventing any employee or officer of the association from engaging in separate conversations or communications outside of a meeting authorized by this article with members of the board of governors in order to answer questions or provide information regarding matters within the responsibility of the association, if that person does not communicate to members of the board of governors the comments or position of any other member or members of the board.

(d) All meetings of the association authorized under this article shall comply with the protections and prohibitions contained in Section 202 of the Americans with Disabilities Act of 1990 (42 U.S.C. Sec. 12132), and the federal rules and regulations adopted in implementation of that act.

(e) The association shall provide notice of its meetings that are open and public pursuant to subdivision (a). This notice and an agenda of items to be discussed shall be provided at least 10 days in advance of the meeting via the association's Internet Web site, and the notice shall be published in a newspaper of general circulation in the State of California. In addition, members of the public may request notice by regular mail or by e-mail by making a written request to the association for notice of meetings that are open and public pursuant to subdivision (a). Notice may be waived, or the 10-day period modified with respect to any particular meeting by the board of governors of the association upon request submitted to the commissioner stating the need for a modified notice and exigent circumstances requiring waiver of the notice requirement at least 24 hours in advance of the meeting time set. The approval of the commissioner shall be deemed granted if a written denial of the request for waiver or modification of the notice period is not received at least four hours prior to the commencement of the meeting to be conducted under the modified notice. Notice of a meeting that does not meet the 10-day notice requirement under this subdivision shall be posted on the association's Internet Web site and provided by e-mail to members of the public who have made a written request for e-mail notice to the association of meetings that are open and public pursuant to subdivision (a). A summary agenda shall be included in each such notice, but members of the board of governors may bring additional items of business to any such meeting.

(f) At any meeting where notice is required pursuant to this section, the association shall reserve time for public comment on the issues addressed at the meeting.

(g) Nothing in this section shall be construed to prohibit the board of governors of the association or its investment and audit committees from holding a closed meeting or a closed session of an open and public meeting to discuss any of the following subjects:

(1) Bond issuances or other matters relating to borrowings of the association.

(2) Matters regarding the detection and prevention of insolvency of members of the association as contemplated by this article.

(3) Nonpublic information received from liquidators, receivers, and regulators regarding members of the association.

(4) Nonpublic information received from the California Liquidation Office.

(5) Proprietary information regarding third-party administrators, vendors that provide products and services in connection with claims administration, or investments made by the association. Proprietary information also includes information which the association and its corresponding out-of-state associations only have access to pursuant to binding contractual confidentiality provisions.

(6) Nonpublic financial information regarding members of the association, including information in support of requests for assessment deferrals.

(7) Statutory interpretations and other advice received from legal counsel to the association, whether in connection with litigation or otherwise.

(8) Appointment, employment, evaluation of performance, or dismissal of any employee or vendor that provides products and services in connection with claims administration of the association.

(9) Deliberations concerning the purchase, sale, exchange, or lease of real or personal property, including investment property.

(10) Matters posing a threat of criminal or terrorist activity against the association, its personnel, or its property.

(11) Covered claims and purported covered claims against the association.

(12) Disputes and purported disputes with or involving members of the association.

(13) Any other matters as permitted by the commissioner under the association's approved plan, provided such matters may be heard in a closed meeting or a closed session consistent with Section 11126 of the Government Code.

(h) With respect to any closed meeting or session held as permitted by subdivision (g), the association shall do both of the following:

(1) Disclose, prior to the closed meeting or the closed session, the general nature of the item or items to be discussed in the closed session. The disclosure may take the form of a reference to the item or items as they are listed by number or letter on the agenda. In the closed session, the board of governors may consider only those matters covered in its disclosure. After any closed session, the board of governors shall reconvene in open session prior to adjournment and shall make any reports, provide any documentation, or make any other disclosures that may be required consistent with this article. The announcements required to be made in open session pursuant to this subdivision may be made at the location announced in the agenda for the closed session, as long as the public is allowed to be present at that location for the purpose of hearing the announcement.

(2) Provide periodic reports to the commissioner identifying the matters covered in each such closed meeting or session and the provision of subdivision (g) pursuant to which the subject was discussed.

(i) Nothing in this section shall require or authorize the disclosure of names or other information that would constitute an invasion of privacy or otherwise unnecessarily divulge the particular facts concerning the closed session or the disclosure of which is prohibited by state or federal law.

(j) The commissioner or his or her designated representative shall be permitted to attend all meetings of the board of governors and its investment and audit committees, specifically including closed meetings and sessions. Any information discussed in closed meetings or sessions shall be treated by the commissioner and his or her designated representatives as confidential pursuant to the provisions of Section 12919. **Leg.H.** 2008 ch. 407 (SB 1467) §1.

ARTICLE 14.26
Workers' Compensation Bond Fund

§1063.70. Issuance of bonds for payment of covered claims against insolvent insurers.

The California Insurance Guarantee Association is authorized to pay and discharge certain claims of insolvent insurers as defined in Section 1063.1 through the collection of premiums from its members, which amounts are limited by law and take time to assess and collect. This article provides for the ability of CIGA to request the issuance of bonds by the California Infrastructure and Economic Development Bank pursuant to Article 8 (commencing with Section 63049.6) of Chapter 2 of Division 1 of Title 6.7 of the Government Code to more expeditiously and effectively provide for the payment of covered claims that arise as a result of the insolvencies of insurance companies providing workers' compensation insurance. The bonds are to be paid from the special bond assessments assessed by CIGA for those purposes and the other funds provided pursuant to Section 1063.74. Special bond assessments to repay bonds issued for payment of workers compensation benefits shall be assessed, to the extent necessary, for the claims category. It is a public purpose and in the best interest of the public health, safety, and general welfare of the residents of this state to provide for the issuance of bonds to pay claimants and policyholders having covered claims against insolvent insurers operating in this state. **Leg.H.** 2003 ch. 635 (AB 227).

Ref.: Herlick Handbook § 3.13.

§1063.71. Definitions.

(a) The terms "member insurer," "insolvent insurer," and "covered claims" have the meanings assigned those terms in Section 1063.1.

(b) The terms "CIGA," "commissioner," "board," and "department" have the meanings assigned those terms in Section 1063.51.

(c) "Bank" means the California Infrastructure and Economic Development Bank created pursuant to Article 1 (commencing with Section 63020) of Chapter 2, Division 1 of Title 6.7 of the Government Code.

(d) "Bonds" means bonds issued by the Bank pursuant to Article 8 (commencing with Section 63049.6) of Chapter 2 of Division 1 of

Title 6.7 of the Government Code to provide funds for the payment of the covered claims and the adjusting and defense expenses relating to those claims that are issued at the request of the board pursuant to Section 1063.73.

(e) "Collateral" means the special bond assessments, the right of CIGA to be paid the special bond assessments, all revenues therefrom, the separate account of the Workers' Comp Bond Fund into which special bond assessments are deposited, and the proceeds thereof.

(f) "Special bond assessment" means the premiums collected by CIGA pursuant to Section 1063.74.

(g) "Workers' Comp Bond Fund" means the fund created pursuant to Section 1063.72. **Leg.H.** 2003 ch. 635 (AB 227).

Ref.: Herlick Handbook § 3.13.

§1063.72. Workers' Comp Bond Fund.

The Workers' Comp Bond Fund is hereby created. Proceeds from the sale of bonds shall be deposited in a separate account in the Workers' Comp Bond Fund. Only CIGA, and with respect to payment of the bonds, the trustee for the bonds, shall have the ability to authorize disbursements from the separate account. Special bond assessments shall be deposited in a separate account in the Workers' Comp Bond Fund and shall not be commingled with any other moneys. Only the trustee for the bonds shall have the ability to authorize disbursements from this separate account, and CIGA shall have no right or authority to authorize disbursements from this separate account. The Workers' Comp Bond Fund shall be maintained with the trustee for the bonds. Following payment or provision for payment of the bonds, amounts in the Workers' Comp Bond Fund shall be transferred to the fund that is designated in the indenture. All money in the Workers' Comp Bond Fund and all special bond assessments shall be used by CIGA for the exclusive purpose of carrying out the purposes of this part, and, notwithstanding any other provisions of law, the Workers' Comp Bond Fund shall not be a state fund, shall not be subject to the rules or procedures of any fund in the State Treasury, and application of the fund shall not be subject to the supervision or budgetary approval of any officer or division of state government. CIGA and the trustee for the bonds may as necessary or convenient to the accomplishment of any other purpose under this article, divide the fund into separate accounts. **Leg.H.** 2003 ch. 635 (AB 227).

Ref.: Herlick Handbook § 3.13.

§1063.73. CIGA's request for issuance of bonds—Copy to commissioner; commissioner may modify, cancel, or delay requested issuance.

In the event CIGA determines that the insolvency of one or more member insurers providing workers' compensation insurance will result in covered claim obligations for workers' compensation claims in excess of CIGA's capacity to pay from current funds, the board, in its sole discretion, may by resolution request the Bank to issue bonds pursuant to Article 8 (commencing with Section 63049.6) of Chapter 2 of Division 1 of Title 6.7 of the Government Code to provide funds for the payment of the covered claims and the adjusting and defense expenses relating to those claims. Notwithstanding any other provision of law, CIGA is hereby authorized to borrow proceeds of the bonds to provide for those purposes. CIGA may request the Bank to issue bonds pursuant to Article 8 (commencing with Section 63049.6) of Chapter 2 of Division 1 of Title 6.7 of the Government Code. CIGA shall provide the commissioner with a copy of the request and the commissioner may, within 30 days of receipt of the request, modify, cancel, or require a delay in the requested issuance. The proceeds of bonds issued for workers' compensation benefits may be used by CIGA to reimburse funds advanced or temporarily loaned from other categories to fund workers' compensation claims. **Leg.H.** 2003 ch. 635 (AB 227).

Ref.: Herlick Handbook § 3.13.

§1063.74. Funding workers' compensation claims—Special bond assessments, current funds, premium assessments, and advances or dividends.

(a) Notwithstanding any other limits on assessments, CIGA shall have the authority to levy upon member insurers special bond assessments in the amount necessary to pay the principal of and interest on the bonds, and to meet other requirements established by agreements relating to the bonds. The assessments shall be collected only from the member insurers providing workers' compensation insurance, in the same manner as separate premium payments are used to pay the claims and costs allocated to that category pursuant to Section 1063.5. Special bond assessments made pursuant to this section shall also be subject to the surcharge provisions in Sections 1063.14 and 1063.145.

(b) In addition to the special bond assessments provided for in this section, the board in its discretion and subject to other obligations of the association, may utilize current funds of CIGA, premium assessments made under Section 1063.5, and advances or dividends received from the liquidators of insolvent insurers to pay the principal and interest on any bonds issued at the board's request and shall utilize, to the extent feasible, the recoveries from the liquidators of the estates of insolvent workers' compensation carriers to pay bonds issued at the board's request to fund workers' compensation claims. **Leg.H.** 2003 ch. 635 (AB 227).

Ref.: Herlick Handbook § 3.13.

§1063.75. Terms and conditions of bonds.

Any bonds issued to provide funds for covered claim obligations for workers' compensation claims shall be issued prior to January 1, [1] **2011**, in an aggregate principal amount outstanding at any one time not to exceed $1.5 billion, and any bonds issued or issued to refund bonds shall not have a final maturity exceeding 20 years from the date of issuance. The bonds shall be issued at the request of CIGA, shall be in the form, shall bear the date or dates, and shall mature at the time or times as the indenture authorized by the request may provide. The bonds may be issued in one or more series, as serial bonds or as term bonds, or as a combination thereof, and, notwithstanding any other provision of law, the amount of principal of, or interest on, bonds maturing at each date of maturity need not be equal. The bonds shall bear interest at the rate or rates, variable or fixed or a combination thereof, be in the denominations, be in the form, either coupon or registered, carry the registration privileges, be executed in the manner, be payable in the medium of payment at the place or places within or without the state, be subject to the terms of redemption, contain the terms and conditions, and be secured by the covenants as the indenture may provide. The indenture may provide for the proceeds of the bonds and funds securing the bonds to be invested in any securities and investments, including investment agreements, as specified therein. CIGA may enter into or authorize any ancillary obligations or derivative agreements as it determines necessary or desirable to manage interest rate risk or security features related to the bonds. The bonds shall be sold at public or private sale by the Treasurer at, above, or below the principal amount thereof, on the terms and conditions and for the consideration in the medium of payment that the Treasurer shall determine prior to the sale. **Leg.H.** 2003 ch. 635 (AB 227), 2006 ch. 112 (AB 3072) §1, 2008 ch. 80 (AB 3055) §3.

§1063.75. 2008 Deletes. [1] 2009

Ref.: Herlick Handbook § 3.13.

§1063.76. Collateral—Permitted use; subject to first priority statutory lien; exempt from specified claims.

(a) The collateral shall be used solely for the purpose of paying the principal and redemption price of, and interest on, the bonds and any amounts owing by CIGA under contracts entered into pursuant to Section 1063.77, and shall not be used for any other purpose. Member insurers shall pay the special bond assessments directly to the trustee for the bonds. Any collateral in the possession of CIGA shall be held by CIGA in trust for the benefit of the trustee for the bonds.

(b) Upon the issuance of the first bond, the collateral shall be subject to a first priority statutory lien in favor of the trustee for the bonds, for the benefit of the holders of the bonds and the parties to the contracts entered into pursuant to Section 1063.77, to secure the payment of the principal and redemption price of, and interest on, the bonds and any amounts owing by CIGA under contracts entered into pursuant to Section 1063.77. This lien shall arise by operation of law automatically without any action on the part of CIGA, the bank, or any other person. This lien is a continuous lien on all collateral effective from the time the first bond is issued, whether or not a particular item of collateral exists at the time of the issuance. From the time the first bond is issued, this lien shall be valid, effective, prior, perfected, binding, and enforceable against CIGA, its successors, purchasers of the collateral, creditors, and all others asserting rights in the collateral, irrespective of whether those parties have notice of the lien and without the need for any physical delivery, recordation, filing, or further act. Upon default in the payment of the principal or redemption price of, or interest on, the bonds, or any amounts owing by CIGA under contracts entered into pursuant to Section 1063.77, the trustee for the bonds shall be entitled to foreclose or otherwise enforce this lien on the collateral.

(c) No person acting under any provision of law or principle of equity shall be permitted in any way to impede or in any manner interfere with (1) the full and timely payment of the principal and redemption price of, and interest on, the bonds and any amounts owing by CIGA under contracts entered into pursuant to Section 1063.77, or (2) the statutory lien created by this section and the full and timely application of the collateral to the payment of the principal and redemption price of, and interest on, the bonds and any amounts owing by CIGA under contracts entered into pursuant to Section 1063.77.

(d) None of the collateral shall be subject to garnishment, levy, execution, attachment, or other process, writ (including writ of mandate), or remedy in connection with the assertion or enforcement of any debt, claim, settlement, or judgment against the state, the department, the commissioner, the bank, CIGA, or the board, nor shall any of the collateral be subject to the claims of any creditor of the state, the department, the commissioner, the bank, CIGA, or the board. This paragraph shall not limit the rights or remedies of the trustee for the bonds, the holders of the bonds, or the parties to contracts entered into pursuant to Section 1063.77.

(e) As long as any bond is outstanding, CIGA shall not be subject to Article 14 (commencing with Section 1010) or Article 14.3 (commencing with Section 1064.1) of Chapter 1 of Part 2 of Division 1 of the Insurance Code. **Leg.H.** 2003 ch. 635 (AB 227).

Ref.: Herlick Handbook § 3.13.

§1063.77. Contracts or agreements with banks, insurers, or other financial institutions or parties; optional terms in contracts or agreements.

CIGA is authorized to enter into those contracts or agreements with those banks, insurers, or other financial institutions or parties that it determines are necessary or desirable to improve the security and marketability of, or to manage interest rates or other risks associated with, the bonds issued pursuant to Article 8 (commencing with Section 63049.6) of Chapter 2 of Division 1 of Title 6.7 of the Government Code. Those contracts or agreements may contain an obligation to reimburse, with interest, any of those banks, insurers, or other financial institutions or partics for advances used to pay the purchase price of, or principal or interest on, the bonds or other obligations. **Leg.H.** 2003 ch. 635 (AB 227).

Ref.: Herlick Handbook § 3.13.

CHAPTER 12 THE INSURANCE FRAUDS PREVENTION ACT

ARTICLE 1 False and Fraudulent Claims [Selected Provisions]

§1871. Insurance fraud—Generally.

The Legislature finds and declares as follows:

(a) The business of insurance involves many transactions that have the potential for abuse and illegal activities. There are numerous law enforcement agencies on the state and local levels charged with the responsibility for investigating and prosecuting fraudulent activity. This chapter is intended to permit the full utilization of the expertise of the commissioner and the department so that they may more effectively investigate and discover insurance frauds, halt fraudulent activities, and assist and receive assistance from federal, state, local, and administrative law enforcement agencies in the prosecution of persons who are parties in insurance frauds.

(b) Insurance fraud is a particular problem for automobile policyholders; fraudulent activities account for 15 to 20 percent of all auto insurance payments. Automobile insurance fraud is the biggest and fastest growing segment of insurance fraud and contributes substantially to the high cost of automobile insurance with particular significance in urban areas.

(c) Prevention of automobile insurance fraud will significantly reduce the incidence of severity and automobile insurance claim payments and will therefore produce a commensurate reduction in automobile insurance premiums.

(d) Workers' compensation fraud harms employers by contributing to the increasingly high cost of workers' compensation insurance and self-insurance and harms employees by undermining the perceived legitimacy of all workers' compensation claims.

(e) Prevention of workers' compensation insurance fraud may reduce the number of workers' compensation claims and claim payments thereby producing a commensurate reduction in workers' compensation costs. Prevention of workers' compensation insurance fraud will assist in restoring confidence and faith in the workers' compensation system, and will facilitate expedient and full compensation for employees injured at the workplace.

(f) The actions of employers who fraudulently underreport payroll or fail to report payroll for all employees to their insurance company in order to pay a lower workers' compensation premium result in significant additional premium costs and an unfair burden to honest employers and their employees.

(g) The actions of employers who fraudulently fail to secure the payment of workers' compensation as required by Section 3700 of the Labor Code harm employees, cause unfair competition for honest employers, and increase costs to taxpayers.

(h) Health insurance fraud is a particular problem for health insurance policyholders. Although there are no precise figures, it is believed that fraudulent activities account for billions of dollars annually in added health care costs nationally. Health care fraud causes losses in premium dollars and increases health care costs unnecessarily. **Leg.H.** 1991 chs. 116, 1008, 1995 ch. 885, 2001 ch. 159, 2002 ch. 6 (AB 749).

Ref.: Hanna § 2.03[1]; Herlick Handbook § 9.18.

§1871.1. Access to records required to be open for inspection in fraud claims.

Insurers and their agents, while they are investigating suspected fraud claims, shall have access to all relevant public records that are required to be open for inspection under Chapter 3.5 (commencing with Section 6250) of Division 7 of Title 1 of the Government Code, and any regulations thereunder. This section restates existing law, and the Legislature does not intend to grant insurers or their agents access to public records other than to those public records available to them under existing law. **Leg.H.** 1993 ch. 323.

Ref.: 8 C.C.R. §2695.7; Hanna §§ 2.03[2], 2.03[5]; Herlick Handbook § 9.18; W. Cal. Ev., "Witnesses" §284.

§1871.2. Notice of penalties on claim forms; exception.

(a) Any insurer who, in connection with any insurance contract or provision of contract described in Section 108, prints, reproduces, or furnishes a form to any person upon which that person gives notice to the insurer or makes claim against it by reason of accident, injury, death, or other noticed or claimed loss, or on a rider attached thereto, shall cause to be printed or displayed in comparative prominence with other content the statement: "Any person who knowingly presents false or fraudulent claim for the payment of a loss is guilty of a crime and may be subject to fines and confinement in state prison." This statement shall be preceded by the words: "For your protection California law requires the following to appear on this form" or other explanatory words of similar meaning.

(b) This section is not applicable to a contract of reinsurance as defined in Section 620. **Leg.H.** 1989 ch. 1119, 2000 ch. 470.

Ref.: Hanna § 25.20[2]; Herlick Handbook § 9.18.

§1871.4. Penalties for making false or fraudulent written or oral statements.

(a) It is unlawful to do any of the following:

(1) Make or cause to be made a knowingly false or fraudulent material statement or material representation for the purpose of obtaining or denying any compensation, as defined in Section 3207 of the Labor Code.

(2) Present or cause to be presented a knowingly false or fraudulent written or oral material statement in support of, or in opposition to, a claim for compensation for the purpose of obtaining or denying any compensation, as defined in Section 3207 of the Labor Code.

(3) Knowingly assist, abet, conspire with, or solicit a person in an unlawful act under this section.

(4) Make or cause to be made a knowingly false or fraudulent statement with regard to entitlement to benefits with the intent to discourage an injured worker from claiming benefits or pursuing a claim.

For the purposes of this subdivision, "statement" includes, but is not limited to, a notice, proof of injury, bill for services, payment for services, hospital or doctor records, X-ray, test results, medical-legal expense as defined in Section 4620 of the Labor Code, other evidence of loss, injury, or expense, or payment.

(5) Make or cause to be made a knowingly false or fraudulent material statement or material representation for the purpose of obtaining or denying any of the benefits or reimbursement provided in the Return-to-Work Program established under Section 139.48 of the Labor Code.

(6) Make or cause to be made a knowingly false or fraudulent material statement or material representation for the purpose of discouraging an employer from claiming any of the benefits or reimbursement provided in the Return-to-Work Program established under Section 139.48 of the Labor Code.

(b) Every person who violates subdivision (a) shall be punished by imprisonment in the county jail for one year, or in the state prison, for two, three, or five years, or by a fine not exceeding one hundred fifty thousand dollars ($150,000) or double the value of the fraud, whichever is greater, or by both that imprisonment and fine. Restitution shall be ordered, including restitution for any medical evaluation or treatment services obtained or provided. The court shall determine the amount of restitution and the person or persons to whom the restitution shall be paid. A person convicted under this section may be charged the costs of investigation at the discretion of the court.

(c) A person who violates subdivision (a) and who has a prior felony conviction of that subdivision, of former Section 556, of former Section 1871.1, or of Section 548 or 550 of the Penal Code, shall receive a two-year enhancement for each prior conviction in addition to the sentence provided in subdivision (b).

The existence of any fact that would subject a person to a penalty enhancement shall be alleged in the information or indictment and either admitted by the defendant in open court, or found to be true by the jury trying the issue of guilt or by the court where guilt is established by plea of guilty or nolo contendere or by trial by the court sitting without a jury.

(d) This section may not be construed to preclude the applicability of any other provision of criminal law that applies or may apply to a transaction. **Leg.H.** 1991 chs. 116, 934, 1992 chs. 675, 1352 §2, effective September 30, 1992, §2.5, operative January 1, 1993, 1993 ch. 120, effective July 16, 1993, 1995 ch. 574, 2002 ch. 6 (AB 749), 2003 ch. 635 (AB 227), 2004 ch. 2 (SB 2 Fourth Extra. Sess.), effective March 6, 2005.

Ref.: Hanna §§ 2.03[1]–[3], [5], 5.06, 20.07, 22.16, 28.02; Herlick Handbook §§ 9.18, 14.18; W. Cal. Sum., 2 "Workers' Compensation" §§23, 427.

§1871.5. Ineligibility to receive or retain compensation.

Any person convicted of workers' compensation fraud pursuant to Section 1871.4 or Section 550 of the Penal Code shall be ineligible to receive or retain any compensation, as defined in Section 3207 of the Labor Code, where that compensation was owed or received as a result of a violation of Section 1871.4 or Section 550 of the Penal Code for which the recipient of the compensation was convicted. **Leg.H.** 1993 ch. 120, effective July 16, 1993.

Ref.: Hanna § 2.03[2]; Herlick Handbook §§ 9.18, 14.18; W. Cal. Sum., 2 "Workers' Compensation" §§23, 427.

§1871.6. Provisions of Penal Code §781 applicable to prosecutions for violations of §1871.4.

The provisions of Section 781 of the Penal Code are applicable to any prosecutions for violations of Section 1871.4. This section is declaratory of existing law and shall not be interpreted to limit the applicability of Section 781 of the Penal Code to any other criminal provisions. **Leg.H.** 1993 ch. 120, effective July 16, 1993.

Ref.: Herlick Handbook § 9.18.

§1871.7. Employing persons to procure clients or patients to perform or obtain benefits unlawful; penalties; bringing action.

(a) It is unlawful to knowingly employ runners, cappers, steerers, or other persons to procure clients or patients to perform or obtain services or benefits pursuant to Division 4 (commencing with Section 3200) of the Labor Code or to procure clients or patients to perform or obtain services or benefits under a contract of insurance or that will be the basis for a claim against an insured individual or his or her insurer.

(b) Every person who violates any provision of this section or Section 549, 550, or 551 of the Penal Code shall be subject, in addition to any other penalties that may be prescribed by law, to a civil penalty of not less than five thousand dollars ($5,000) nor more than ten thousand dollars ($10,000), plus an assessment of not more than three times the amount of each claim for compensation, as defined in Section 3207 of the Labor Code or pursuant to a contract of insurance. The court shall have the power to grant other equitable relief, including temporary injunctive relief, as is necessary to prevent the transfer, concealment, or dissipation of illegal proceeds, or to protect the public. The penalty prescribed in this paragraph shall be assessed for each fraudulent claim presented to an insurance company by a defendant and not for each violation.

(c) The penalties set forth in subdivision (b) are intended to be remedial rather than punitive, and shall not preclude, nor be precluded by, a criminal prosecution for the same conduct. If the court finds, after considering the goals of disgorging unlawful profit, restitution, compensating the state for the costs of investigation and prosecution, and alleviating the social costs of increased insurance rates due to fraud, that such a penalty would be punitive and would preclude, or be precluded by, a criminal prosecution, the court shall reduce that penalty appropriately.

(d) The district attorney or commissioner may bring a civil action under this section. Before the commissioner may bring that action, the commissioner shall be required to present the evidence obtained to the appropriate local district attorney for possible criminal or civil filing. If the district attorney elects not to pursue the matter due to insufficient resources, then the commissioner may proceed with the action.

(e)(1) Any interested persons, including an insurer, may bring a civil action for a violation of this section for the person and for the State of California. The action shall be brought in the name of the state. The action may be dismissed only if the court and the district attorney or the commissioner, whichever is participating, give written consent to the dismissal and their reasons for consenting.

(2) A copy of the complaint and written disclosure of substantially all material evidence and information the person possesses shall be served on the district attorney and commissioner. The complaint shall be filed in camera, shall remain under seal for at least 60 days, and shall not be served on the defendant until the court so orders. The local district attorney or commissioner may elect to intervene and proceed with the action within 60 days after he or she receives both the complaint and the material evidence and information. If more than one governmental entity elects to intervene, the district attorney shall have precedence.

(3) The district attorney or commissioner may, for good cause shown, move the court for extensions of the time during which the complaint remains under seal under paragraph (2). The motions may be supported by affidavits or other submissions in camera. The defendant shall not be required to respond to any complaint filed under this section until 20 days after the complaint is unsealed and served upon the defendant.

(4) Before the expiration of the 60-day period or any extensions obtained under paragraph (3), the district attorney or commissioner shall either:

(A) Proceed with the action, in which case the action shall be conducted by the district attorney or commissioner.

(B) Notify the court that it declines to take over the action, in which case the person bringing the action shall have the right to conduct the action.

(5) When a person or governmental agency brings an action under this section, no person other than the district attorney or commissioner may intervene or bring a related action based on the facts underlying the pending action unless that action is authorized by another statute or common law.

(f)(1) If the district attorney or commissioner proceeds with the action, he or she shall have the primary responsibility for prosecuting the action, and shall not be bound by an act of the person bringing the action. That person shall have the right to continue as a party to the action, subject to the limitations set forth in paragraph (2).

(2)(A) The district attorney or commissioner may dismiss the action notwithstanding the objections of the person initiating the action if the person has been notified by the district attorney or commissioner of the filing of the motion, and the court has provided the person with an opportunity for a hearing on the motion.

(B) The district attorney or commissioner may settle the action with the defendant notwithstanding the objections of the person initiating the action if the court determines, after a hearing, that the proposed settlement is fair, adequate, and reasonable under all the circumstances. Upon a showing of good cause, the hearing may be held in camera.

(C) Upon a showing by the district attorney or commissioner that unrestricted participation during the course of the litigation by the person initiating the action would interfere with or unduly delay the district attorney's or commissioner's prosecution of the case, or would be repetitious, irrelevant, or for purposes of harassment, the court may, in its discretion, impose limitations on the person's participation, including, but not limited to, the following:

(i) Limiting the number of witnesses the person may call.

(ii) Limiting the length of the testimony of those witnesses.

(iii) Limiting the person's cross-examination of witnesses.

(iv) Otherwise limiting the participation by the person in the litigation.

(D) Upon a showing by the defendant that unrestricted participation during the course of the litigation by the person initiating the action would be for purposes of harassment or would cause the defendant undue burden or unnecessary expense, the court may limit the participation by the person in the litigation.

(3) If the district attorney or commissioner elects not to proceed with the action, the person who initiated the action shall have the right to conduct the action. If the district attorney or commissioner so requests, he or she shall be served with copies of all pleadings filed in the action and shall be supplied with copies of all deposition transcripts, at the district attorney's or commissioner's expense. When a person proceeds with the action, the court, without limiting the status and rights of the person initiating the action, may nevertheless permit the district attorney or commissioner to intervene at a later date upon a showing of good cause.

(4) If at any time both a civil action for penalties and equitable relief pursuant to this section and a criminal action are pending against a defendant for substantially the same conduct, whether brought by the government or a private party, the civil action shall be stayed until the criminal action has been concluded at the trial court level. The stay shall not preclude the court from granting or enforcing temporary equitable relief during the pendency of the actions. Whether or not the district attorney or commissioner proceeds with the action, upon a showing by the district attorney or commissioner that certain actions of discovery by the person initiating the action would interfere with a law enforcement or governmental agency investigation or prosecution of a criminal or civil matter arising out of the same facts, the court may stay discovery for a period of not more than 180 days. A hearing on a request for the stay shall be conducted in camera. The court may extend the 180-day period upon a further showing in camera that the agency has pursued the criminal or civil investigation or proceedings with reasonable diligence and any proposed discovery in the civil action will interfere with the ongoing criminal or civil investigation or proceedings.

(5) Notwithstanding subdivision (e), the district attorney or commissioner may elect to pursue its claim through any alternate remedy available to the district attorney or commissioner.

(g)(1)(A)(i) If the district attorney proceeds with an action brought by a person under subdivision (e), that person shall, subject to subparagraph (B), receive at least 30 percent but not more than 40 percent of the proceeds of the action or settlement of the claim, depending upon the extent to which the person substantially contributed to the prosecution of the action.

(ii) If the commissioner has brought an action or has proceeded with an action brought by another person under this section on or after January 1, 2006, and prior to January 1, 2011, the commissioner shall be entitled to attorney's fees and costs in addition to any judgment, regardless of the date that judgment is entered. The court shall determine and award the commissioner the amount of reasonable attorney's fees, including, but not limited to, reasonable fees for time expended by attorneys employed by the department and for costs incurred. Any attorney's fees or costs awarded to the commissioner and collected shall be deposited in the Insurance Fund. In cases in which the commissioner has intervened, the commissioner and the person bringing the claim may stipulate to an allocation. The court may allocate the funds pursuant to the stipulation if, after the court's ruling on objection by the district attorney, if any, the court finds it is in the interests of justice to follow the stipulation.

(iii) If the commissioner has proceeded with an action, if there is no stipulation regarding allocation, and if a judgment has been obtained or a settlement has been reached with the defendants, the court shall determine the allocation, upon motion of the commissioner or the person bringing the action, according to the following priority:

(I) The person bringing the action, regardless of whether that person paid money to the defendants as part of the acts alleged in the complaint, shall first receive the amount the court determines is reasonable for attorney's fees, costs, and expenses that the court determines to have been necessarily incurred.

(II) The commissioner shall receive the amount the court determines for reasonable attorney's fees and costs.

(III) If the person bringing the suit has paid moneys to the defendants as part of the acts alleged in the complaint, that person shall receive the amount paid to the defendants.

(IV) At least 30 percent, but not more than 40 percent, of the remaining assets or moneys, shall be allocated to the person bringing the action, depending upon the extent to which the person substantially contributed to the prosecution of the action.

(iv) Those portions of a judgment or settlement not distributed pursuant to this subdivision shall be paid to the General Fund of the state and, upon appropriation by the Legislature, shall be apportioned between the Department of Justice and the Department of Insurance for enhanced fraud investigation and prevention efforts.

(B) Where the action is one that the court finds to be based primarily on disclosures of specific information, other than information provided by the person bringing the action, relating to allegations or transactions in a criminal, civil, or administrative hearing, in a legislative or administrative report, hearing, audit, or investigation, or from the news media, the court may award those sums that it considers appropriate, but in no case more than 10 percent of the proceeds, taking into account the significance of the information and the role of the person bringing the action in advancing the case to litigation.

(C) Any payment to a person under subparagraph (A) or under subparagraph (B) shall be made from the proceeds. The person shall also receive an amount for reasonable expenses that the court finds to have been necessarily incurred, plus reasonable attorney's fees and costs. All of those expenses, fees, and costs shall be awarded against the defendant.

(2)(A) If the district attorney or commissioner does not proceed with an action under this section, the person bringing the action or settling the claim shall receive an amount that the court decides is reasonable for collecting the civil penalty and damages. Except as provided in subparagraph (B), the amount shall not be less than 40 percent and not more than 50 percent of the proceeds of the action or settlement and shall be paid out of the proceeds. That person shall also receive an amount for reasonable expenses that the court finds to have been necessarily incurred, plus reasonable attorney's fees and costs. All of those attorney's fees and costs shall be imposed against the defendant. The parties shall serve the commissioner and the local district attorney with complete copies of any and all settlement agreements, and terms and conditions, for actions brought under this article at least 10 days prior to filing any motion for allocation with the court under this paragraph. The court may allocate the funds pursuant to the settlement agreement if, after the court's ruling on objection by the commissioner or the local district attorney, if any, the court finds it is in the interests of justice to follow the settlement agreement.

(B) If the person bringing the action, as a result of a violation of this section has paid money to the defendant or to an attorney acting on behalf of the defendant in the underlying claim, then he or she shall be entitled to up to double the amount paid to the defendant or the attorney if that amount is greater than 50 percent of the proceeds. That person shall also receive an amount for reasonable expenses that the court finds to have been necessarily incurred, plus reasonable attorney's fees and costs. All of those expenses, fees, and costs shall be awarded against the defendant.

(3) If a local district attorney has proceeded with an action under this section, one-half of the penalties not awarded to a private party, as well as any costs awarded shall go to the treasurer of the appropriate county. Those funds shall be used to investigate and prosecute fraud, augmenting existing budgets rather than replacing them. All remaining funds shall go to the state and be deposited in the General Fund and, when appropriated by the Legislature, shall be apportioned between the Department of Justice and the Department of Insurance for enhanced fraud investigation and prevention efforts.

(4) Whether or not the district attorney or commissioner proceeds with the action, if the court finds that the action was brought by a person who planned and initiated the violation of this section, that person shall be dismissed

from the civil action and shall not receive any share of the proceeds of the action. The dismissal shall not prejudice the right of the district attorney or commissioner to continue the action on behalf of the state.

(5) If the district attorney or commissioner does not proceed with the action, and the person bringing the action conducts the action, the court may award to the defendant its reasonable attorney's fees and expenses if the defendant prevails in the action and the court finds that the claim of the person bringing the action was clearly frivolous, clearly vexatious, or brought primarily for purposes of harassment.

(h)(1) In no event may a person bring an action under subdivision (e) that is based upon allegations or transactions that are the subject of a civil suit or an administrative civil money penalty proceeding in which the Attorney General, district attorney, or commissioner is already a party.

(2)(A) No court shall have jurisdiction over an action under this section based upon the public disclosure of allegations or transactions in a criminal, civil, or administrative hearing in a legislative or administrative report, hearing, audit, or investigation, or from the news media, unless the action is brought by the Attorney General or the person bringing the action is an original source of the information.

(B) For purposes of this paragraph, "original source" means an individual who has direct and independent knowledge of the information on which the allegations are based and has voluntarily provided the information to the district attorney or commissioner before filing an action under this section which is based on the information.

(i) Except as provided in subdivision (j), the district attorney or commissioner is not liable for expenses that a person incurs in bringing an action under this section.

(j) In civil actions brought under this section in which the commissioner or a district attorney is a party, the court shall retain discretion to impose sanctions otherwise allowed by law, including the ability to order a party to pay expenses as provided in Sections 128.5 and 1028.5 of the Code of Civil Procedure.

(k) Any employee who is discharged, demoted, suspended, threatened, harassed, or in any other manner discriminated against in the terms and conditions of employment by his or her employer because of lawful acts done by the employee on behalf of the employee or others in furtherance of an action under this section, including investigation for, initiation of, testimony for, or assistance in an action filed or to be filed under this section, shall be entitled to all relief necessary to make the employee whole. That relief shall include reinstatement with the same seniority status the employee would have had but for the discrimination, two times the amount of backpay, interest on the backpay, and compensation for any special damages sustained as a result of the discrimination, including litigation costs and reasonable attorney's fees. An employee may bring an action in the appropriate superior court for the relief provided in this subdivision. The remedies under this section are in addition to any other remedies provided by existing law.

(*l*)(1) An action pursuant to this section may not be filed more than three years after the discovery of the facts constituting the grounds for commencing the action.

(2) Notwithstanding paragraph (1) no action may be filed pursuant to this section more than eight years after the commission of the act constituting a violation of this section or a violation of Section 549, 550, or 551 of the Penal Code. **Leg.H.** 1993 ch. 120, effective July 16, 1993, 1994 ch. 1247, 1995 ch. 574, 1999 ch. 885, 2005 ch. 380 (SB 706) §1.

Ref.: Hanna §§ 20.01[1][e], 22.15; Herlick Handbook § 9.18; W. Cal. Sum., 2 "Insurance" §311, 2 "Workers' Compensation" §23.

§1871.8. Notice to injured worker regarding penalties and prosecution for fraudulent receipt of temporary disability benefits.

An insurer or self-insured employer shall provide the following notice, in both English and Spanish, to an injured worker on or with a check for temporary disability benefits:

WARNING: You are required to report to your employer or the insurance company any money that you earned for work during the time covered by this check, and before cashing this check. If you do not follow these rules, you may be in violation of the law and the penalty may be jail or prison, a fine, and loss of benefits.

ADVERTENCIA: Es necesario que usted le avise a su patrón o a su compañía de seguro todo dinero que usted ha ganado por trabajar, durante el tiempo cubierto por éste cheque, y antes de cambiar éste cheque. Si usted no sigue estos reglamentos, Usted puede estar en violación de la ley y el castigo podría ser cárcel o prisión, una multa, y pérdida de beneficios.

Leg.H. 1996 ch. 1005, 2004 ch. 2 (SB 2 Fourth Extra. Sess.), effective March 6, 2005, operative January 1, 2005.

2004 Note: The changes to Section 1871.8 of the Insurance Code made by Section 2 of this act shall become operative on January 1, 2005. Stats. 2004 ch. 2 (SB 2 (Fourth Extra. Sess.)) §9.

Ref.: Hanna § 7.03[1]; Herlick Handbook § 9.18; W. Cal. Sum., 2 "Workers' Compensation" §23.

§1871.9. Posting information on Web site of person convicted of violation of article.

The department shall post all of the following information on its Internet Web site for each person, as defined in Section 19, convicted of a violation of this article, Section 11760 or 11880, Section 3700.5 of the Labor Code, or Section 487 or 550 of the Penal Code, if the violation involved workers' compensation insurance, services, or benefits:

(a) The name, case number, county or court, and other identifying information with respect to the case.

(b) The full name of the defendant.

(c) The city and county of the defendant's last known residence or business address.

(d) The date of conviction.

(e) A description of the offense.

(f) The amount of money alleged to have been defrauded.

(g) A description of the punishment imposed, including the length of any sentence of imprisonment and the amount of any fine imposed.

The information required to be posted under this section shall be maintained on the department's Web site for a period of five years from the date of conviction or until the department is notified in writing by the person that the conviction has been reversed or expunged. **Leg.H.** 2004 ch. 281 (AB 2866).

Ref.: Hanna § 2.03[3]; Herlick Handbook § 9.18; W. Cal. Sum., 2 "Workers' Compensation" §146.

ARTICLE 2
Bureau of Fraudulent Claims
[Selected Provisions]

§1872.84. Information to be forwarded to appropriate disciplinary body.

The commissioner shall ensure that the Fraud Division forwards to the appropriate disciplinary body, in addition to the names and supporting evidence of individuals described in subdivision (a) of Section 1872.83, the names, along with all supporting evidence, of any individuals licensed under the Chiropractic Initiative Act who are suspected of actively engaging in fraudulent activity. **Leg.H.** 2005 ch. 415 (AB 1760) §2.

§1872.95. Medical and chiropractic boards and State Bar; investigation of workers' compensation, motor vehicle, or disability insurance fraud by licensees.

(a) Within existing resources, the Medical Board of California, the Board of Chiropractic Examiners, and the State Bar shall each designate employees to investigate and report on possible fraudulent activities relating to workers' compensation, motor vehicle insurance, or disability insurance by licensees of the board or the bar. Those employees shall actively cooperate with the Fraud Division in the investigation of those activities.

(b) The Medical Board of California, the Board of Chiropractic Examiners, and the State Bar shall each report annually, on or before March 1, to the committees of the Senate and Assembly having jurisdiction over insurance on their activities established pursuant to subdivision (a) for the previous year. That report shall specify, at a minimum, the number of cases investigated, the number of cases forwarded to the Fraud Division or other law enforcement agencies, the outcome of all cases listed in the report, and any other relevant information concerning those cases or general activities conducted under subdivision (a) for the previous year. The report shall include information regarding activities conducted in connection with cases of suspected automobile insurance fraud. **Leg.H.** 1995 ch. 167, 1999 ch. 885, 2005 ch. 717 (AB 1183) §11.

Ref.: Hanna § 2.03[3].

ARTICLE 4
Motor Vehicle Theft and Motor Vehicle Insurance Fraud Reporting

§1874.1. Definitions.

The following definitions govern the construction of this article, unless the context requires otherwise:

(a) "Authorized governmental agency" means the Department of the California Highway Patrol, the Department of Insurance, the Department of Justice, the Department of Motor Vehicles, the police department of a city, or a city and county, the sheriff's office or department of a county, a law enforcement agency of the federal government, the district attorney of any county, or city and county, and any licensing agency governed by the Business and Professions Code or the Chiropractic Initiative Act.

(b) "Relevant" means having a tendency to make the existence of any fact that is of consequence to the investigation or determination of an issue more probable or less probable than it would be without the information.

(c) Information shall be deemed important if, within the sole discretion of the authorized governmental agency, that information is requested by that authorized governmental agency.

(d) "Insurer" means the automobile assigned risk plan established pursuant to Section 11620 of the Insurance Code, as well as any insurer writing insurance for motor vehicles or otherwise liable for any loss due to motor vehicle theft or motor vehicle insurance fraud.

(e) "Motor vehicle" means motor vehicle as defined in Section 415 of the Vehicle Code. **Leg.H.** 1989 ch. 1119, 2005 ch. 415 (AB 1760) §3.

ARTICLE 7
Workers' Compensation Insurance Fraud Reporting

§1877. Title.

This article shall be known and may be cited as the Workers' Compensation Insurance Fraud Reporting Act. **Leg.H.** 1991 ch. 116.

Ref.: Hanna § 2.03[3]; Herlick Handbook § 9.18.

§1877.1. Definitions.

The following definitions govern the construction of this article, unless the context requires otherwise:

(a) "Authorized governmental agency" means the district attorney of any county, any city attorney whose duties include criminal prosecutions, any law enforcement agency investigating workers' compensation fraud, the office of the Attorney General, the Department of Insurance, the Department of Industrial Relations, the Employment Development Department, the Department of Corrections **and Rehabilitation, the Public Employees' Retirement System**, and any licensing agency governed by the Business and Professions Code.

(b) "Relevant" means having a tendency to make the existence of any fact that is of consequence to the investigation or determination of an issue more probable or less probable than it would be without the information.

(c) "Insurer" means an insurer admitted to transact workers' compensation insurance in this state, the State Compensation Insurance Fund, an employer that has secured a certificate of consent to self-insure pursuant to subdivision (b) or (c) of Section 3700 of the Labor Code, or a third-party administrator that has secured a certificate pursuant to Section 3702.1 of the Labor Code.

(d) "Licensed rating organization" means a rating organization licensed by the Insurance Commissioner pursuant to Section 11750.1.

(e) Information shall be deemed important if, within the sole discretion of the authorized governmental agency, that information is requested by that authorized governmental agency. **Leg.H.** 1991 chs. 116, 934, 2003 ch. 636 (AB 1099), 2004 chs. 490 (SB 1344), 1 (AB 13 Fourth Extra. Sess.), effective March 6, 2005 (ch. 490 prevails; ch. 1 (Fourth Extra. Sess.) not effective), 2008 ch. 369 (AB 1844) §6.

Ref.: Hanna §§ 2.03[2], 2.03[3]; Herlick Handbook § 9.18.

§1877.2. Authorized governmental agency.

For the purposes of this article, "authorized governmental agency" includes, in addition to the entities listed in subdivision (a) of Section

1877.1, any licensing agency governed by the Chiropractic Initiative Act. **Leg.H.** 2005 ch. 415 (AB 1760) §4.

§1877.3. Insurer's or licensed rating organization's release of requested information to governmental agency; requirement to notify when fraud committed.

(a) Upon written request to an insurer or a licensed rating organization by an authorized governmental agency, an insurer, an agent authorized by that insurer, or a licensed rating organization to act on behalf of the insurer, shall release to the requesting authorized governmental agency any or all relevant information deemed important to the authorized governmental agency that the insurer or licensed rating organization may possess relating to any specific workers' compensation insurance fraud investigation.

(b)(1) When an insurer or licensed rating organization knows or reasonably believes it knows the identity of a person or entity whom it has reason to believe committed a fraudulent act relating to a workers' compensation insurance claim or a workers' compensation insurance policy, including any policy application, or has knowledge of such a fraudulent act that is reasonably believed not to have been reported to an authorized governmental agency, then, for the purpose of notification and investigation, the insurer, or agent authorized by an insurer to act on its behalf, or licensed rating organization shall notify the local district attorney's office and the Fraud Division of the Department of Insurance, and may notify any other authorized governmental agency of that suspected fraud and provide any additional information in accordance with subdivision (a). The insurer or licensed rating organization shall state in its notice the basis of the suspected fraud.

(2) Insurers shall use a form prescribed by the department for the purposes of reporting suspected fraudulent workers' compensation acts pursuant to this subdivision.

(3) Nothing in this subdivision shall abrogate or impair the rights or powers created under subdivision (a).

(c) The authorized governmental agency provided with information pursuant to subdivision (a), (b), or (e) may release or provide that information in a confidential manner to any other authorized governmental agency for purposes of investigation, prosecution, or prevention of insurance fraud or workers' compensation fraud.

(d) An insurer or licensed rating organization providing information to an authorized governmental agency pursuant to this section shall provide the information within a reasonable time, but not exceeding 60 days from the day on which the duty arose.

(e) Upon written request by an authorized governmental agency, as specified in subdivision (o) of Section 1095 of the Unemployment Insurance Code, the Employment Development Department shall release to the requesting agency any or all relevant information that the Employment Development Department may possess relating to any specific workers' compensation insurance fraud investigation. Relevant information may include, but is not limited to, all of the following:

(1) Copies of unemployment and disability insurance application and claim forms and copies of any supporting medical records, documentation, and records pertaining thereto.

(2) Copies of returns filed by an employer pursuant to Section 1088 of the Unemployment Insurance Code and copies of supporting documentation.

(3) Copies of benefit payment checks issued to claimants.

(4) Copies of any documentation that specifically identifies the claimant by social security number, residence address, or telephone number. **Leg.H.** 1991 chs. 116, 934, 1992 ch. 1352, effective September 30, 1992, 1995 ch. 885, 2003 ch. 636 (AB 1099), 2005 ch. 717 (AB 1183) §16.

Ref.: Hanna § 2.03[3]; Herlick Handbook § 9.18.

§1877.35. Public Employees' Retirement System—Request for information from insurer relating to investigation of eligibility, unlawful application, or receipt of benefits.

(a) The Public Employees' Retirement System may request information from an insurer for any specific investigation of eligibility for, and unlawful application or receipt of, benefits provided under Part 3 (commencing with Section 20000) of Division 5 of Title 2 of the Government Code.

(b) Information received by the Public Employees' Retirement System pursuant to this article may be used for purposes of determining eligibility for, and unlawful application or receipt of, benefits provided under Part 3 (commencing with Section 20000) of Division 5 of Title 2 of the Government Code. **Leg.H.** 2008 ch. 369 (AB 1844) §7.

§1877.4. Confidentiality of information acquired; exception to privilege.

(a) Any information acquired pursuant to this article shall not be a part of the public record. Except as otherwise provided by law, any authorized governmental agency, an insurer, or an agent authorized to act on its behalf, which receives any information furnished pursuant to this article shall not release that information to any person not authorized to receive the information under this article. Any person who violates the prohibition of this subdivision is guilty of a misdemeanor.

(b) The evidence or information described in this section shall be privileged and shall not be subject to subpoena or subpoena duces tecum in a civil or criminal proceeding, unless, after reasonable notice to any insurer, an agent authorized by an insurer to act on its behalf, licensed rating organization, or authorized governmental agency which has an interest in the information, and a hearing, the court determines that the public interest and any ongoing investigation by the authorized governmental agency, insurer, or an agent authorized by the insurer to act on its behalf, or licensed rating organization will not be jeopardized by its disclosure, or by the issuance of and compliance with a subpoena or subpoena duces tecum. **Leg.H.** 1991 ch. 116, 2003 ch. 636 (AB 1099).

Ref.: Hanna §§ 2.03[3], 2.35; Herlick Handbook § 9.18.

§1877.5. Immunity from civil liability when acting in good faith.

No insurer, agent authorized by an insurer to act on its behalf, or licensed rating organization who furnishes information, written or oral, pursuant to this article, and no authorized governmental agency or its employees who (a) furnishes or receives information, written or oral, pursuant to this article, or (b) assists in any investigation of a suspected violation of Section 1871.1, 1871.4, 11760, or 11880, or of Section 549 of the Penal Code, or of Section 3215 or 3219 of the Labor Code conducted by an authorized governmental agency, shall be subject to any civil liability in a cause or action of any kind where the insurer, authorized agent, licensed rating organization, or authorized governmental agency acts in good faith, without malice, and reasonably believes that the action taken was warranted by the then known facts, obtained by reasonable efforts. Nothing in this chapter is intended to, nor does in any way or manner, abrogate or lessen the existing common law or statutory privileges and immunities of an insurer, agent authorized by that insurer to act on its behalf, licensed rating organization, or any authorized governmental agency or its employees. **Leg.H.** 1991 chs. 116, 934, 1993 ch. 120, effective July 16, 1993, 2003 ch. 636 (AB 1099).

Ref.: Hanna § 2.03[3]; Herlick Handbook §§ 9.18, 12.13.

DIVISION 2
CLASSES OF INSURANCE

PART 3
Liability, Workers' Compensation, and Common Carrier Liability Insurance

CHAPTER 1
GENERAL REGULATIONS

ARTICLE 2
Actions on Policies Containing Liability Provisions
[Selected Provisions]

§11580.1. Required provisions for automobile liability insurance.

(a) No policy of automobile liability insurance described in Section 16054 of the Vehicle Code covering liability arising out of the ownership, maintenance, or use of any motor vehicle shall be issued or delivered in this state on or after the effective date of this section unless it contains the provisions set forth in subdivision (b). However, none of the requirements of subdivision (b) shall apply to the insurance afforded under the policy (1) to the extent that the insurance exceeds the limits specified in subdivision (a) of Section 16056 of the Vehicle Code, or (2) if the policy contains an underlying insurance requirement, or provides for a retained limit of self-insurance, equal to or greater than the limits specified in subdivision (a) of Section 16056 of the Vehicle Code.

(b) Every policy of automobile liability insurance to which subdivision (a) applies shall contain all of the following provisions:

[Subsections (b)(1)–(3) Not Reproduced]

(4) Provision affording insurance to the named insured with respect to any owned or leased motor vehicle covered by the policy, and to the same extent that insurance is afforded to the named insured, to any other person using the motor vehicle, provided the use is by the named insured or with his or her permission, express or implied, and within the scope of that permission, except that: (A) … (B) the insurance afforded to any person other than the named insured need not apply to: (i) any employee with respect to bodily injury sustained by a fellow employee injured in the scope and course of his or her employment, or (ii) ….

(c) In addition to any exclusion provided in paragraph (3) of subdivision (b), the insurance afforded by any policy of automobile liability insurance to which subdivision (a) applies, including the insurer's obligation to defend, may, by appropriate policy provision, be made inapplicable to any or all of the following:

[Subsections (c)(1) and (2) Not Reproduced]

(3) Liability imposed upon or assumed by the insured under any workers' compensation law.

(4) Liability for bodily injury to any employee of the insured arising out of and in the course of his or her employment.

[Subsections (c)(5)–(h) Not Reproduced]

Leg.H. 1993 ch. 408, 1999 ch. 313, 2006 ch. 538 (SB 1852) §471.

Ref.: Hanna § 7.04[9][b]; Herlick Handbook § 12.15; W. Cal. Sum., 2 "Insurance" §§152, 163–168, 170–177, 196.

§11580.2. Uninsured vehicle coverage; limitations.

[Subsections (a) and (b) Not Reproduced]

(c) The insurance coverage provided for in this section does not apply either as primary or as excess coverage:

[Subsections (c)(1)–(3) Not Reproduced]

(4) In any instance where it would inure directly or indirectly to the benefit of any

workers' compensation carrier or to any person qualified as a self-insurer under any workers' compensation law, or directly to the benefit of the United States, or any state or any political subdivision thereof.

[Subsections (c)(5)–(e) Not Reproduced]

(f) The policy or an endorsement added thereto shall provide that the determination as to whether the insured shall be legally entitled to recover damages, and if so entitled, the amount thereof, shall be made by agreement between the insured and the insurer or, in the event of disagreement, by arbitration. The arbitration shall be conducted by a single neutral arbitrator. An award or a judgment confirming an award shall not be conclusive on any party in any action or proceeding between (i) the insured, his or her insurer, his or her legal representative, or his or her heirs and (ii) the uninsured motorist to recover damages arising out of the accident upon which the award is based. If the insured has or may have rights to benefits, other than nonoccupational disability benefits, under any workers' compensation law, the arbitrator shall not proceed with the arbitration until the insured's physical condition is stationary and ratable. In those cases in which the insured claims a permanent disability, the claims shall, unless good cause be shown, be adjudicated by award or settled by compromise and release before the arbitration may proceed. Any demand or petition for arbitration shall contain a declaration, under penalty of perjury, stating whether (i) the insured has a workers' compensation claim; (ii) the claim has proceeded to findings and award or settlement on all issues reasonably contemplated to be determined in that claim; and (iii) if not, what reasons amounting to good cause are grounds for the arbitration to proceed immediately. The arbitration shall be deemed to be a proceeding and the hearing before the arbitrator shall be deemed to be the trial of an issue therein for purposes of issuance of a subpoena by an attorney of a party to the arbitration under Section 1985 of the Code of Civil Procedure. Title 4 (commencing with Section 2016.010) of Part 4 of the Code of Civil Procedure shall be applicable to these determinations, and all rights, remedies, obligations, liabilities and procedures set forth in Title 4 (commencing with Section 2016.010) of Part 4 of the Code of Civil Procedure shall be available to both the insured and the insurer at any time after the accident, both before and after the commencement of arbitration, if any, with the following limitations:

[Subsections (f)(1)–(g) Not Reproduced]

(h) An insured entitled to recovery under the uninsured motorist endorsement or coverage shall be reimbursed within the conditions stated herein without being required to sign any release or waiver of rights to which he or she may be entitled under any other insurance coverage applicable; nor shall payment under this section to the insured be delayed or made contingent upon the decisions as to liability or distribution of loss costs under other bodily injury liability insurance or any bond applicable to the accident. Any loss payable under the terms of the uninsured motorist endorsement or coverage to or for any person may be reduced:

(1) By the amount paid and the present value of all amounts payable to him or her, his or her executor, administrator, heirs, or legal representative under any workers' compensation law, exclusive of nonoccupational disability benefits.

[Subsections (h)(2)–(q) Not Reproduced]

Leg.H. 1995 ch. 738, 2001 ch. 95, 2003 ch. 56 (SB 333), 2005 ch. 294 (AB 333) §23.

Ref.: Hanna § 2.85; Herlick Handbook § 12.15; MB Prac. Guide: Cal. Contract Lit., §5.20[6][d]; MB Prac. Guide: Cal. Trial & Post-Trial Civ. Proc., §24.07[1]; W. Cal. Sum., 2 "Insurance" §§4, 162, 172, 174, 177, 180–187, 189–200, 202, 205–215, 13 "Equity" §119.

ARTICLE 2.5
Personal Liability Insurance Providing Workers' Compensation Coverage for Household Employees

§11590. Personal liability insurance policies to contain coverage for workers' compensation; inapplicability.

Except as provided in Section 11591, no policy providing comprehensive personal liability insurance may be issued or renewed in this state on or after January 1, 1977, unless it contains a provision for coverage against liability for the payment of compensation, as defined in Section 3207 of the Labor Code, to any person defined as an employee by subdivision (d) of Section 3351 of the Labor Code. Any such policy in effect on or after January 1, 1977, whether or not actually containing such provisions, shall be construed as if such provisions were embodied therein. However, such coverage shall not apply if any other existing, valid and collectible, workers' compensation insurance for such liability is applicable to the injury or death of such employee.

Ref.: Hanna §§ 2.82, 3.80; Herlick Handbook §§ 2.4, 2.5, 3.17; W. Cal. Sum., 2 "Workers' Compensation" §187.

§11591. Exception to §11590.

The requirements of Section 11590 shall be inapplicable to any such policy of insurance or endorsement where the services of such employee are in connection with the trade, business, profession, or occupation, as such terms are defined in Sections 3355 and 3356 of the Labor Code, of the insured.

Ref.: Hanna § 2.82; Herlick Handbook §§ 2.5, 3.17.

§11592. Law governing rates, rating systems, and classifications for workers' compensation insurance.

Notwithstanding the provisions of subdivision (f) of Section 1851, the rates, classifications, and rating systems for the workers' compensation insurance covering those persons defined as employees by subdivision (d) of Section 3351 of the Labor Code, and the insurers issuing such insurance coverage, shall be subject to the provisions of Chapter 9 (commencing with Section 1850) of Part 2 of Division 1.

Ref.: Herlick Handbook § 3.17.

§11593. Premium charge for workers' compensation insurance not to be separately stated.

The premium charge for the coverage required by Section 11590 shall not be separately stated from that charged for other coverage under the policy in the insured's copy of the following: premium notice, policy, endorsement or memorandum of insurance.

Ref.: Herlick Handbook § 3.17.

CHAPTER 2 WORKERS' COMPENSATION POLICIES

ARTICLE 1 Definitions

§11630. "Compensation."

As used in this chapter, the term "compensation" means the benefits insured by workers' compensation insurance.

§11631. "Insurer."

As used in this chapter, the term "insurer" includes the State Compensation Insurance Fund.

ARTICLE 2 Policy Provisions [Selected Provisions]

§11650. Conclusive presumption of compliance with this article.

Every contract insuring against liability for compensation and every compensation policy is conclusively presumed to contain all of the provisions required by this article.

Ref.: Hanna §§ 2.50[1][a], [b], 26.06[9][b]; Herlick Handbook § 3.1; W. Cal. Ev., "Burden of Proof and Presumptions" §163.

§11651. Contract/policy statement of insurer's liability.

Every such contract or policy shall contain a clause to the effect that the insurer will be directly and primarily liable to any proper claimant for payment of any compensation for which the employer is liable, subject to the provisions, conditions and limitations of the policy.

Ref.: 8 C.C.R. §9811; Hanna §§ 2.50[1][a], [b], 5.04[4]; Herlick Handbook § 3.1.

§11652. Employer knowledge of injury as imputed to insurer.

Every such contract or policy shall contain a clause to the effect that, as between the employee and the insurer, notice to or knowledge of the occurrence of the injury on the part of the employer will be deemed notice or knowledge, as the case may be, on the part of the insurer.

Ref.: 8 C.C.R. §9811; Hanna §§ 2.50[1][a], [b], 5.04[4]; Herlick Handbook § 3.1.

§11653. Employer's and insurer's jurisdiction.

Every such contract or policy shall contain a clause to the effect that jurisdiction of the employer will, for the purpose of the law imposing liability for compensation, be jurisdiction of the insurer.

Ref.: Hanna §§ 2.50[1][a], [b], 5.04[4], 21.03[5]; Herlick Handbook § 3.1.

§11654. Insurer bound by findings against employer; insurance contract to govern liability.

Every such contract or policy shall contain a clause to the effect that the insurer will in all things be bound by and subject to the orders, findings, decisions or awards rendered against the employer under the provisions of the law imposing liability for compensation, subject to the provisions, conditions and limitations of the policy. The insurance contract shall govern as between the employer and insurer as to payments by either in discharge of the employer's liability for compensation.

Ref.: Hanna §§ 2.50[1][a], [b], 5.04[4].

§11655. Effect of employer's insolvency or bankruptcy on insurer's liability.

Such policy shall not contain any provisions relieving the insurer from payment when the employer becomes insolvent or is discharged in bankruptcy, or otherwise, during the period that the policy is in operation or the compensation remains owing.

Ref.: Hanna §§ 2.50[1][a], [b], 5.04[4], 27.04.

§11656. Employee's lien.

Such policy shall also provide that the employee has a first lien upon any amount which becomes owing to the employer from the insurer on account of the policy, and that in case of the legal incapacity or inability of the employer to receive the money and pay it to the claimant, the insurer will pay it directly to the claimant. To the extent of such payment, the obligations of the employer to the claimant are thereby discharged.

Ref.: Hanna §§ 2.50[1][a], [b], 5.04[4].

§11661. Insurance for employer's serious and willful misconduct.

An insurer shall not insure against the liability of the employer for the additional compensation recoverable for serious and willful misconduct of the employer or his agent. An insurer may, however, provide insurance against the expense of defending any suit for serious and willful misconduct against an employer or his agent.

Ref.: Hanna §§ 2.50[4][b], 2.62[2][b], 10.01[2], 25.10[7]; Herlick Handbook §§ 3.8, 9.6; W. Cal. Sum., 2 "Workers' Compensation" §157.

§11661.5. Injuries to illegally employed minors.

An insurer shall not insure an employer against his liability for additional compensation arising out of injuries to illegally employed persons under 16 years of age, as provided for by Part 4 (commencing with Section 1171) of Division 2 of the Labor Code.

Note: See Labor Code §4557.

Ref.: Hanna §§ 2.50[3], [4][b], 2.62[2][c], 2.63[3][c], 10.10; Herlick Handbook § 3.8; W. Cal. Sum., 2 "Workers' Compensation" §§157, 174.

§11661.6. Insuring compensation for increased indemnity prohibited.

(a) An insurer shall not insure an employer against his or her obligation to reimburse the insurer for the amount of increase in indemnity payment as provided for by subdivision (e) of Section 4650 of the Labor Code. Every contract insuring against liability for compensation and every compensation policy shall provide that the insured employer is obligated to reimburse the insurer for the amount of increase in indemnity payment required by Section 4650 of the Labor Code, if the late indemnity payment which gives rise to the increase in the amount of payment is due less than seven days after the insurer receives the completed claim form from the employer.

(b) An insurer shall not report the amount of any increase in indemnity required by Section 4650 of the Labor Code as incurred indemnity to the Insurance Commissioner's designated statistical agent.

Ref.: Hanna §§ 2.62[2][f], 2.72[2]; Herlick Handbook §§ 5.15, 9.5.

§11662. Insurer's subrogation to employer's rights.

Whenever any employer is insured against liability for compensation with any insurer, such insurer is subrogated to the rights of the employer to recover losses arising out of any of the following acts by the insurer:

(a) Assuming the liability of the employer for compensation in the manner provided by the law relating thereto.

(b) Payment of any compensation for which the employer is liable.

Such insurer may enforce any such subrogated rights in its own name.

Ref.: Hanna §§ 2.71, 5.05[4], [11], 11.40[1], 11.41; Herlick Handbook §§ 3.7, 12.2; W. Cal. Sum., 2 "Workers' Compensation" §149.

§11663. Liability of general and special employers.

As between insurers of general and special employers, one which insures the liability of the general employer is liable for the entire cost of compensation payable on account of injury occurring in the course of and arising out of general and special employments unless the special employer had the employee on his or her payroll at the time of injury, in which case the insurer of the special employer is solely liable. For the purposes of this section, a self-insured or lawfully uninsured employer is deemed and treated as an insurer of his or her workers' compensation liability.

Ref.: Hanna §§ 2.60[3], 3.142[5]; Herlick Handbook § 3.9; W. Cal. Sum., 2 "Workers' Compensation" §167.

§11663.5. Insurer provides premium and loss history report.

(a) Upon receiving a written request from an insured or the agent or broker of record where authorized by the insured, an insurer shall provide a premium and loss history report to the requesting party for the account's tenure or the three-year period ending with the inception of the current policy period, whichever is shorter, plus loss experience during the current policy period that is in force if any of the following occur.

(1) The policy is canceled or nonrenewed.

(2) The policyholder requests the information within 60 days prior to the renewal date of an existing policy.

(3) The policyholder's current insurer's rating is downrated by a nationally recognized insurance rating service to a financial rating below secure or good or to a rating that would negatively impact the ability of the policyholder to conduct its business operations.

(4) The policyholder's current insurer is conserved by the department under Section 1011, or is ordered to cease writing business under Sections 1065.1 and 1065.2.

The premium and loss history report, and the loss experience information for the current policy period, shall be provided within 10 business days of receiving the request.

(b) This section applies only to workers' compensation insurance.

(c) This section shall not apply to a policyholder who, through automated or other means, is provided direct, ongoing access to claims information by the insurer.

(d) For purposes of this section, a loss history report includes, but is not limited to, a list of individual claims detailed by date of claim and total incurred and paid losses. **Leg.H.** 2001 ch. 102.

§11664. Notice of nonrenewal.

(a) This section applies only to policies of workers' compensation insurance.

(b) A notice of nonrenewal shall be in writing and shall be delivered or mailed to the producer of record and to the named insured at the mailing address shown on the policy. Subdivision (a) of Section 1013 of the Code of Civil Procedure shall be applicable if the notice is mailed.

(c) An insurer, at least 30 days, but not more than 120 days, in advance of the end of the policy period, shall give notice of nonrenewal, and the reasons for the nonrenewal, if the insurer intends not to renew the policy.

(d) If an insurer fails to give timely notice required by subdivision (c), the policy of insurance shall be continued, with no change in its premium rate, for a period of 60 days after the insurer gives the notice.

(e) A notice of nonrenewal shall not be required in any of the following situations.

(1) The transfer of, or renewal of, a policy without a change in its terms or conditions or the

rate on which the premium is based between insurers that are members of the same insurance group.

(2) The policy has been extended for 90 days or less, if the notice required in subdivision (c) has been given prior to the extension.

(3) The named insured has obtained replacement coverage or has agreed, in writing, within 60 days of the termination of the policy, to obtain that coverage.

(4) The policy is for a period of no more than 60 days and the insured is notified at the time of issuance that it may not be renewed.

(5) The named insured requests a change in the terms or conditions or risks covered by the policy within 60 days prior to the end of the policy period.

(6) The insurer has made a written offer to the insured to renew the policy at a premium rate increase of less than 25 percent.

(A) If the premium rate in the governing classification for the insured is to be increased 25 percent or greater and the insurer intends to renew the policy, the insurer shall provide a written notice of a renewal offer not less than 30 days prior to the policy renewal date. The governing classification shall be determined by the rules and regulations established in accordance with subdivision (c) of Section 11750.3.

(B) For purposes of this section, "premium rate" means the cost of insurance per unit of exposure prior to the application of individual risk variations based on loss or expense considerations such as scheduled rating and experience rating. **Leg.H.** 1994 ch. 398, effective September 1, 1994, operative November 30, 1994, 1995 ch. 375, 1997 ch. 385, 2000 ch. 884, effective September 29, 2000, 2001 ch. 102.

Ref.: Herlick Handbook §§ 3.2, 3.15.

§11665. [Repealed January 1, 2011] Payroll audits for roofing contractors; annual report.

(a) An insurer who issues a workers' compensation insurance policy to a roofing contractor holding a C-39 license from the Contractors State License Board shall perform an annual payroll audit for the contractor. The insurer may impose a surcharge on each policyholder audited under this subdivision in an amount necessary to recoup the reasonable costs of conducting the annual payroll audits.

(b) The commissioner shall direct the rating organization designated as his or her statistical agent to compile pertinent statistical data on those holding C-39 licenses, as reported by the appropriate state entity, on an annual basis and provide a report to him or her each year. The data shall track the total annual payroll and loss data reported on those holding C-39 licenses in accordance with the standard workers' compensation insurance classifications applicable to roofing operations. The first report shall be filed no later than March 1, 2008, and shall cover the data compiled for the 2005 calendar year.

(c) This section shall become operative on January 1, 2007, and shall remain in effect only until January 1, 2011, and as of that date is repealed, unless a later enacted statute, that is enacted before January 1, 2011, deletes or extends that date. **Leg.H.** 2006 ch. 38 (AB 881) §3.

Ref.: Hanna § 3.134; Herlick Handbook § 3.23.

CHAPTER 3 REGULATION OF BUSINESS OF WORKERS' COMPENSATION INSURANCE

ARTICLE 1 Deposits by Workers' Compensation Insurers

§11690. Definitions.

For purposes of this article:

(a) "Compensable workers' compensation claim" means a claim where the claimant is entitled to benefits under the workers' compensation law of the state.

(b) "Delinquency proceeding" means any proceeding commenced against an insurer for the purpose of liquidating, rehabilitating, reorganizing, or conserving that insurer, where there has not been a court order finding the insurer insolvent.

(c) "Receiver" means liquidator, rehabilitator, or conservator, as appropriate. **Leg.H.** 2002 ch. 899 (SB 2093) §2.

Ref.: Hanna § 2.30[2]–[5]; Herlick Handbook §§ 3.12, 3.13, 3.15.

§11691. Deposit required by insurer desiring admission to transact workers' compensation insurance, or reinsurance, or desiring to reinsure the injury, disablement, or death portions of policies; notice to commissioner; trust agreement; fee.

(a) In order to provide protection to the workers of this state in the event that the insurers issuing workers' compensation insurance to employers fail to pay compensable workers' compensation claims when due, except in the case of the State Compensation Insurance Fund, every insurer desiring admission to transact workers' compensation insurance, or workers' compensation reinsurance business, or desiring to reinsure the injury, disablement, or death portions of policies of workers' compensation insurance under the class of disability insurance shall, as a prerequisite to admission, or ability to reinsure the injury, disablement, or death portion of policies of workers' compensation insurance under the class of disability insurance, deposit cash instruments or approved interest-bearing securities or approved stocks readily convertible into cash, investment certificates, or share accounts issued by a savings and loan association doing business in this state and insured by the Federal Deposit Insurance Corporation, certificates of deposit or savings deposits in a bank licensed to do business in this state, or approved letters of credit that perform in material respects as any other security allowable as a form of deposit for purposes of a workers' compensation deposit and that meet the standard set forth in Section 922.5, or approved securities registered with a qualified depository located in a reciprocal state as defined in Section 1104.9, with that deposit to be in an amount and subject to any exceptions as set forth in this article. The deposit shall be made from time to time as demanded by the commissioner and may be made with the Treasurer, or a bank or savings and loan association authorized to engage in the trust business pursuant to Division 1 (commencing with Section 99) or Division 2 (commencing with Section 5000) of the Financial Code, or a trust company. A deposit of securities registered with a qualified depository located in a reciprocal state as defined in Section 1104.9 may only be made in a bank or savings and loan association authorized to engage in the trust business pursuant to Division 1 (commencing with Section 99) or Division 2 (commencing with Section 5000) of the Financial Code, or a trust company, licensed to do business and located in this state that is a qualified custodian as defined in paragraph (1) of subdivision (a) of Section 1104.9 and that maintains deposits of at least seven hundred fifty million dollars ($750,000,000). The deposit shall be made subject to the approval of the commissioner under those rules and regulations that he or she shall promulgate. The deposit shall be maintained at a deposit value specified by the commissioner, but in any event no less than one hundred thousand dollars ($100,000), nor less than the reserves required of the insurer to be maintained under any of the provisions of Article 1 (commencing with Section 11550) of Chapter 1 of Part 3 of Division 2, relating to loss reserves on workers' compensation business of the insurer in this state, nor less than the sum of the amounts specified in subdivision (a) of Section 11693, whichever is greater. The deposit shall be for the purpose of paying compensable workers' compensation claims under policies issued by the insurer or reinsured by the admitted reinsurer and expenses as provided in Section 11698.02, in the event the insurer or reinsurer fails to pay those claims when they come due. If the insurer providing the deposit is domiciled in a state where a state statute, regulation, or court decision provides that, with respect to covered claims within the deductible amount that are paid by a guarantee association after the entry of an order of liquidation under large deductible workers' compensation policies, any part of the reimbursement proceeds, other than the reasonable expenses of the receiver related to treatment of deductible policy arrangements of insurance companies in liquidation, owed by insureds on those deductible amounts, whether paid directly or through a draw of collateral, are general assets of the estate, then the amount of the insurer's deposit pursuant to this article shall be calculated based on the gross amount of that insurer's liabilities for loss and loss adjustment expenses under those policies without regard to the deductible, and those reserves shall not be reduced by any collateral or reimbursement obligations insureds were required to provide under those policies.

Nothing in this section shall require that the deposit be calculated based on gross amounts of liabilities described above if the domiciliary state does not have an existing statute, regulation, or court decision providing that the reimbursement proceeds described above are general assets of the estate.

(b) Each insurer or reinsurer desiring to have the ability to reinsure the injury, disablement, or death portions of policies of workers' compensation under the class of disability insurance shall provide prior notice to the commissioner, in the manner and form prescribed by the commissioner of its intent to reinsure that insurance. In the event of late notice, a late filing fee shall be imposed on the reinsurer pursuant to Section 924 for failure to notify the commissioner of its intent to reinsure workers' compensation insurance.

(c) If the deposit required by this section is not made with the Treasurer, then the depositor shall execute a trust agreement in a form approved by the commissioner between the insurer, the institution in which the deposit is made or, where applicable, the qualified custodian of the deposit, and the commissioner, that grants to the commissioner the authority to withdraw the deposit as set forth in Sections 11691.2, 11696, 11698, and 11698.3. The insurer shall also execute and deliver in duplicate to the commissioner a power of attorney in favor of the commissioner for the purposes specified herein, supported by a resolution of the depositor's board of directors. The power of attorney and director's resolution shall be on forms approved by the commissioner, shall provide that the power of attorney cannot be revoked or withdrawn without the consent of the commissioner, and shall be acknowledged as required by law.

(d)(1) The commissioner shall require payment in advance of fees for the initial filing of a trust agreement with a bank, savings and loan association, or trust company on deposits made pursuant to subdivision (a); for each amendment, supplement, or other change to the deposit agreement; for receiving and processing deposit schedules pursuant to this section; and for each withdrawal, substitution, or any other change in the deposit. The fees shall be set forth in the department's Schedule of Fees and Charges.

(2) The commissioner shall require payment in advance of a fee for the initial filing of each letter of credit utilized pursuant to subdivision (a). In addition, the commissioner shall require payment in advance of a fee for each amendment of a letter of credit. The fees shall be set forth in the department's Schedule of Fees and Charges.

(e) Any workers' compensation insurer that deposits cash or cash equivalents pursuant to this section shall be entitled to a prompt refund of those deposits in excess of the amount determined by the commissioner pursuant to subdivision (a). The commissioner shall cause to be refunded any deposits determined by the commissioner to be in excess of the amount required by subdivision (a) within 30 days of that determination. In the alternative, an insurer may use any excess deposit funds to offset a demand by the commissioner to increase its deposit due to the failure of a reinsurer to make a deposit pursuant to this section.

(f)(1) As of January 1, 2003, an admitted insurer reinsuring business covered in this article (hereafter referred to as reinsurer) shall identify to the commissioner, in a form prescribed by the commissioner, amounts deposited for credit in the name of each ceding insurer.

(2) Beginning January 1, 2005, all reinsurance agreements covering claims and obligations under business covered by this article, and allowable for purposes of granting a ceding carrier a deposit credit, shall include a provision granting the commissioner, in the event of a delinquency proceeding, receivership, or insolvency of a ceding insurer, any sums from a reinsurer's deposit that are necessary for the commissioner to pay those reinsured claims and obligations, or to ensure their payment by the California Insurance Guarantee Association, deemed by the commissioner due under the reinsurance agreement, upon failure of the reinsurer for any reason to make payments under the policy of reinsurance. The commissioner shall give 30 days' notice prior to drawing upon these funds of an intent to do so. Notwithstanding the commissioner's right to draw on these funds, the reinsurer shall otherwise retain its right to determine the validity of those claims and obligations and to contest their payment under the reinsurance agreement. Prior to a reinsurer's deposit being drawn upon, in whole or in part, by the department, the department shall provide a reinsurer with an explanation of procedures that a reinsurer may use to explain to the department why the use of the reinsurer's deposit may not be appropriate under the reinsurance agreement.

(3) No reinsurer entering into a contract identified in paragraph (2), beginning on or after January 1, 2005, may cede claims or obligations assumed from a ceding insurer unless the de-

posit securing the ceded claims or obligations is governed by paragraph (2) or, upon approval of the commissioner, would secure the ceded claims or obligations in all material respects and in the same manner as a deposit identified in paragraph (2) above.

(4) All sums received from the reinsurer by the commissioner for those claims paid by the California Insurance Guarantee Association shall be held separate and apart from and not included in the general assets of the insolvent insurer, and shall be transferred to the California Insurance Guarantee Association upon receipt by the commissioner. In the event of a final judgment or settlement adverse to the drawing of funds by the commissioner pursuant to paragraph (2) or (3), the California Insurance Guarantee Association shall repay funds it obtained to pay covered claims and shall, if necessary, either levy a surcharge as needed or seek legislative approval to levy the surcharge if the California Insurance Guarantee Association is already levying the maximum surcharge permissible under law.

(g) If a reinsurer has not maintained deposits as required by subdivision (a) in amounts equal to the amounts of deposit credits claimed by its ceding insurers, the commissioner, after notifying the reinsurer and its ceding insurers of the deposit shortfall and allowing 15 days from the date of the notice for the deposit shortfall to be corrected, may disallow all or a portion of the reserve credits claimed by the ceding insurers. A ceding insurer disallowed a reserve credit pursuant to this provision shall immediately make the deposit required by this section.

(h) For interest-bearing securities that are debt securities and include principal payment features prior to maturity that are utilized pursuant to subdivision (a), all principal payments received must be retained as part of the deposit.

(i) Withdrawal of any amount of the deposit required under subdivision (a) that results in a reduction of the required amount of the deposit may only occur with the prior written consent of the commissioner. **Leg.H.** 2002 ch. 899 (SB 2093) §2, 2005 ch. 415 (AB 1760) §6, 2007 ch. 117 (AB 1364) §1.

Ref.: Hanna § 2.30[2]–[5]; Herlick Handbook §§ 3.12, 3.13, 3.15.

§11691.1. Fee for filing schedule of securities.

The fees for filing a schedule of securities with the Treasurer, and making a deposit of the same, and for each withdrawal, substitution, or any other change in the securities comprising this deposit with the Treasurer, shall be paid to the commissioner for the costs of review and approval of deposits, and shall be the same as are prescribed by Article 11 (commencing with Section 939) of Chapter 1 of Part 2 of Division 1.

All other reasonable charges made by the Treasurer for servicing securities deposited with him or her shall be paid to the Treasurer by the insurer that has deposited the security, and shall not be charged to the commissioner. **Leg.H.** 2002 ch. 899 (SB 2093) §2.

Ref.: Hanna § 2.30[2]–[5]; Herlick Handbook §§ 3.12, 3.13, 3.15.

§11691.2. Deposit as security for payment of obligations on workers' compensation insurance transacted in state.

The deposit required pursuant to Section 11691 shall be security for the payment of the insurer's obligations on worker's compensation insurance transacted in this state. The deposit shall not be withdrawn except upon the written order of the commissioner to use the proceeds thereof in payment of compensable worker's compensation claims and expenses as provided in Section 11698.02, or as otherwise provided in this article, but shall be forthwith payable to the commissioner or at the direction of the commissioner by the Treasurer or the bank, savings and loan association, or trust company approved by the commissioner upon that order. No deposit so placed with a bank, savings and loan association, or trust company shall be subject to any lien or claim asserted by it or be subject to any disposition obligation, demand, liability, cause of action, judgment, or other claim, or cost or expense attendant thereon, other than as is permitted by the commissioner. Notwithstanding any other provisions of this code, the deposit shall be retained by the Treasurer or the bank, savings and loan association, or trust company approved by the commissioner and only released in accordance with the provisions of this article or pursuant to regulations or a written order of the commissioner. **Leg.H.** 2002 ch. 899 (SB 2093) §2.

Ref.: Hanna § 2.30[2]–[5]; Herlick Handbook §§ 3.12, 3.13, 3.15.

§11691.3. List of authorized insurers and reinsurers.

The commissioner shall establish a list of all insurers or reinsurers authorized to reinsure the injury, disablement, or death portions of policies of workers' compensation insurance under the class of disability insurance. An insurer or reinsurer shall be authorized to reinsure the injury, disablement, or death portions of policies of workers' compensation insurance under the class of disability insurance if it has complied with Section 11691. The commissioner shall publish a master list of those insurers or reinsurers at least semiannually. Any insurer or reinsurer providing the notification and deposit required by Section 11691, shall be added by addendum to the list at the time of approval, and shall be incorporated into the master list at the next date of publication. The list and addenda required by this section shall be published so that they are readily accessible to insurers and producers. The list and addenda required by this section shall also contain a notice that if an insurer enters into a contract of reinsurance with an insurer or reinsurer reinsuring the injury, disablement, or death portions of policies of workers' compensation insurance under the class of disability insurance that is not authorized pursuant to this section, the ceding insurer may not be able to claim that reinsurance for reserve credit. **Leg.H.** 2002 ch. 899 (SB 2093) §2.

Ref.: Hanna § 2.30[2]–[5]; Herlick Handbook §§ 3.12, 3.13, 3.15.

§11692. Issuance of certificate of authority.

A certificate of authority to transact workers' compensation insurance in this state shall not be issued nor renewed to any insurer until the deposit required pursuant to Section 11691 is approved by the commissioner. **Leg.H.** 2002 ch. 899 (SB 2093) §2, 2005 ch. 415 (AB 1760) §7.

Ref.: Hanna § 2.30[2]–[5]; Herlick Handbook §§ 3.12, 3.13, 3.15.

§11692.5. Late filing fee.

On and after the effective date of this article, the commissioner shall collect a late filing fee from any admitted insurer or reinsurer that fails to deposit the securities when required by this code in the following amount:

(a) If the deposit shortfall is outstanding for less than 31 days, 0.5 percent of the deposit shortfall, but in no event not less than six hundred dollars ($600).

(b) If the deposit shortfall is outstanding for more than 30 days but less than 61 days, an additional late filing fee in the amount of 1 percent of the deposit shortfall, but in no event not less than one thousand two hundred dollars ($1,200) shall be due.

(c) If the deposit shortfall is outstanding for 61 days or greater, an additional late filing fee of 1.5 percent of the deposit shortfall for every 30-day period thereafter, or fraction thereof, but in no event shall this portion of the late filing fee for each additional 30-day period or fraction thereof be less than three thousand dollars ($3,000). The late filing fees provided herein are in addition to all other rights and remedies granted the commissioner by this article. **Leg.H.** 2002 ch. 899 (SB 2093) §2, 2005 ch. 415 (AB 1760) §8.

Ref.: Hanna § 2.30[2]–[5]; Herlick Handbook §§ 3.12, 3.13, 3.15.

§11693. Annual adjustment of deposit.

The deposit required pursuant to Section 11691 shall be adjusted on or prior to March 31 of each year in an amount as follows:

(a) Not less than the sum of the following amounts computed, less credits and deductions allowable with respect to reinsurance in admitted insurers, as provided under Section 11691, as of the close of the last preceding December 31 or as of any calendar quarter end as directed by the commissioner pursuant to Section 11694 in respect to workers' compensation insurance written subject to the workers' compensation laws of this state:

(1) The aggregate of the present values at 6 percent interest, or at the rate of the company's investment yield as determined by the NAIC Insurance Regulatory Information System Ratio Number 5 for Property and Casualty Companies, whichever is lower, of the determined and estimated future payments upon compensation claims not included in paragraph (2), including in those claims both benefits and loss expenses.

(2) The aggregate of the amounts computed as follows:

For each of the preceding three years, 65 percent of the earned compensation premiums for that year less all loss and loss expense payments made upon claims incurred in the corresponding year from that 65 percent; except that the amount for each year shall not be less than the present value at 6 percent interest of the determined and the estimated unpaid claims incurred in that year, including both benefits and loss expenses.

(b) Not less than one hundred thousand dollars ($100,000).

(c) If the aggregate amount computed under subdivision (a) exceeds fifty thousand dollars ($50,000), not more than double the aggregate amount.

(d) The commissioner may utilize securities valuation software programs or services to validate the value of securities held in workers' compensation deposits of insurers authorized to transact workers' compensation insurance in California as direct writers or reinsurers, or reinsurers of workers' compensation under the class of disability. **Leg.H.** 2002 ch. 899 (SB 2093) §2, 2005 ch. 415 (AB 1760) §9.

Ref.: Hanna § 2.30[2]–[5]; Herlick Handbook §§ 3.12, 3.13, 3.15.

§11694. Computation of deposit from figures in annual report.

After the first annual statement to the commissioner covering business of the insurer for a full year in this state, the deposit required pursuant to Section 11691 shall be computed from the figures shown in the last preceding report of business as of December 31, filed with the commissioner, and shall be reported to the commissioner on or before March 1 of each year in a form and manner prescribed by the commissioner. Notwithstanding anything to the contrary in this article, should the commissioner determine that there has been a material change in the insurer's ultimate liability for future payments upon compensable workers' compensation claims in this state, at the commissioner's discretion, the amount of the deposit shall then be fixed by the commissioner at the amount that he or she deems sufficient to secure the payment of the insurer's ultimate obligations on its workers' compensation insurance transacted in this state, and upon notification from the commissioner the insurer shall immediately, but in no event less than 30 days after notification, increase the deposit as directed. **Leg.H.** 2002 ch. 899 (SB 2093) §2, 2005 ch. 415 (AB 1760) §10.

Ref.: Hanna § 2.30[2]–[5]; Herlick Handbook §§ 3.12, 3.13, 3.15.

§11694.5. Deposit reports.

On or before March 1 and May 15 of each year, the insurers or reinsurers subject to Section 11694 shall file a report in the form and manner prescribed by the commissioner that valuates and details the deposit as of December 31 of the preceding year and March 31 of the current year. The commissioner may require additional reporting by any insurer or reinsurer when it is deemed necessary. **Leg.H.** 2005 ch. 415 (AB 1760) §11.

§11695. Fixing deposit for insurer who voluntarily ceases to do business in state.

Where an admitted insurer has voluntarily ceased to do in this state the business for which a deposit is required pursuant to Section 11691, the deposit shall be fixed by the commissioner at the amount that he or she deems sufficient for the protection of the beneficiaries of the policies of that insurer. **Leg.H.** 2002 ch. 899 (SB 2093) §2.

Ref.: Hanna § 2.30[2]–[5]; Herlick Handbook §§ 3.12, 3.13, 3.15.

§11696. Use of deposit when insurer fails to pay compensation claim.

In the event an insurer not in a delinquency proceeding fails to pay any compensable workers' compensation claim against it, or fails to pay, to the extent of its liability as a reinsurer, any compensable workers' compensation claim covered by a policy wholly or partly reinsured by it, the commissioner shall use the proceeds of the deposit required pursuant to Section 11691 to pay all those compensable workers' compensation claims and related expenses as described in Section 11698.02. **Leg.H.** 2002 ch. 899 (SB 2093) §2.

Ref.: Hanna § 2.30[2]–[5]; Herlick Handbook §§ 3.12, 3.13, 3.15.

§11697. Payment of claim by commissioner as satisfaction of claim.

The payment of a workers' compensation claim by the commissioner shall constitute a satisfaction of the claim to the extent of the payment made. In the event any judgment is entered on the claim, the commissioner shall file a proportionate satisfaction thereof in the office of the clerk of the court wherein the judgment is entered. **Leg.H.** 2002 ch. 899 (SB 2093) §2.

Ref.: Hanna § 2.30[2]–[5]; Herlick Handbook §§ 3.12, 3.13, 3.15.

§11698. Circumstances authorizing commissioner to take control or possession of deposit.

(a) In the event any one of the eventualities described in paragraph (1), (2), (3), or (4), transpires, the commissioner shall immediately take control or possession of the deposit required pursuant to Section 11691 and may use the deposit to pay or procure the payment of those compensable workers' compensation claims against the insurer, and those expenses described in Section 11698.02. The proceeds of the deposit shall in that event inure to the commissioner as a trust to be held separate and apart from all other assets of the insurer held by the commissioner. They shall be used only for the purposes set forth and in accordance with the procedures established in this article. Once it is determined that there are no remaining undischarged liabilities for compensable workers' compensation claims or it is actuarially demonstrated that the deposit exceeds those liabilities, the commissioner shall transfer the remaining amount of the deposit to the general assets of the estate.

(1) If the commissioner is named conservator of that insurer pursuant to Article 14 (commencing with Section 1011) of Chapter 1 of Part 2 of Division 1.

(2) The proper court has appointed the commissioner ancillary receiver of the insurer or reinsurer.

(3) A delinquency proceeding has been instituted by the proper court against the insurer or reinsurer.

(4) If it appears to the commissioner that any of the conditions set forth in Section 1011 exist or that irreparable loss and injury to the property and business of the insurer or reinsurer has occurred or may occur unless the commissioner acts immediately without notice and before applying to the court for any order.

(b) If the commissioner has proceeded under subdivision (a) or Section 11696 or 11698.3 and a deposit of securities registered with a qualified depository located in a reciprocal state and in the custody of a qualified custodian pursuant to Section 1104.9 cannot be released to the commissioner according to the terms of the agreement entered into pursuant to Section 11691 or the requirements of Section 11691.2 because of a delinquency proceeding initiated in the reciprocal state in which the qualified depository is located, or, if the deposit of securities registered with a qualified depository has been executed upon at any time by any creditor of an insurer and that execution has been affirmed by a written opinion of a court of competent federal appellate jurisdiction, the commissioner may, after a public hearing and upon a finding that deposits of securities registered with that depository do not allow the commissioner to discharge his or her responsibilities as set forth in this chapter, require workers' compensation insurers authorized to transact insurance in this state to cease and desist making any further deposits authorized by Section 11691 in approved securities registered with that depository. For the purposes of this subdivision, the term "delinquency proceeding" shall have the same meaning as contained in subdivision (b) of Section 1064.1. **Leg.H.** 2002 ch. 899 (SB 2093) §2.

Ref.: Hanna § 2.30[2]–[5]; Herlick Handbook §§ 3.12, 3.13, 3.15.

§11698.01. Options of commissioner upon taking control or possession of deposit.

When the commissioner is authorized to proceed under Section 11698 he or she may do either of the following:

(a) Subject to Sections 11698.2, 11698.21, and 11698.22, enter into reinsurance and assumption agreements with one or more admitted solvent workers' compensation insurers by the terms of which liability for all those obligations is reinsured and assumed by such insurer.

(b) Use the deposit required pursuant to Section 11691 to pay or procure payment of the insurer's compensable workers' compensation claims and those expenses authorized in Section 11698.02. **Leg.H.** 2002 ch. 899 (SB 2093) §2.

Ref.: Hanna § 2.30[2]–[5]; Herlick Handbook §§ 3.12, 3.13, 3.15.

§11698.02. Use of proceeds from deposit.

The proceeds of the deposit required pursuant to Section 11691 shall be used solely to pay compensable workers' compensation claims under the insured or reinsured policies, allocated claims expense necessary to pay those claims, and the expenses connected with all proceedings statistical plan or classification system developed by the rating organization.

(d) The designated rating organization shall also develop and file with the commissioner a weekly premium per employee for each classification used or proposed for use by that organization. The weekly premium shall be developed by applying the proposed rate for each classification to the state average weekly wage. For the purpose of this section, "state average weekly wage" means the average weekly wage paid by employers to employees covered by unemployment insurance as reported by the United States Department of Labor for California for the 12 months ending March 31 of the calendar year preceding the year in which the injury occurred. **Leg.H.** 1993 ch. 228 §2, operative January 1, 1995, ch. 1242, 2002 ch. 6 (AB 749).

Ref.: Hanna §§ 2.01, 2.02[2], 2.40[1]; Herlick Handbook § 3.2.

§11735. Filing of rates and supplementary rate information; filings open to public inspection; using rates in excess of those stated in filing; disallowance of rating systems violating Unruh Act; filing requirements for plans with deductibles; reporting losses subject to deductibles.

(a) Every insurer shall file with the commissioner all rates and supplementary rate information that are to be used in this state. The rates and supplementary rate information shall be filed not later than 30 days prior to the effective date. Upon application by the filer, the commissioner may authorize an earlier effective date. To the extent possible, rates and supplementary rate information shall be based upon supporting information derived from the experience or data of the insurer, rating organization, advisory organization, or other insurers. For the purposes of this subdivision, "rating organization" shall have the same meaning as set forth in subdivision (b) of Section 11750.1, and "advisory organization" shall have the same meaning as set forth in subdivision (e) of that section.

(b) Rates filed pursuant to this section shall be filed in the form and manner prescribed by the commissioner. All rates, supplementary rate information, and any supporting information for rates filed under this article, as soon as filed, shall be open to public inspection at any reasonable time. Copies may be obtained by any person upon request and the payment of a reasonable charge.

(c) Upon the written application of the insurer and insured, stating its reasons therefor, filed with the commissioner, a rate in excess of that provided by a filing otherwise applicable may be used on any specific risk.

(d) Notwithstanding Section 679.70, no rating organization may issue, nor may any insurer use, any classification system or rate, as applied or used, that violates Section 679.71 or 679.72 or that violates the Unruh Civil Rights Act.

(e) Notwithstanding Sections 11657 to 11660, inclusive, supplementary rate information filed with the commissioner for purposes of offering deductibles to policyholders for all or part of benefits payable under the policy shall be deemed complete if the filing contains all of the following:

(1) A copy of the deductible endorsement that is to be attached to the policy to effectuate deductible coverage.

(2) Endorsement language that protects the rights of injured workers and ensures that benefits are paid by the insurer without regard to any deductible. The endorsement shall specify that the nonpayment of deductible amounts by the policyholder shall not relieve the insurer from the payment of compensation for injuries sustained by the employee during the period of time the endorsed policy was in effect. The endorsement shall provide that deductible policies for workers' compensation insurance coverage shall not be terminated retroactively for the nonpayment of deductible amounts.

(3) The endorsement shall provide that notwithstanding the deductible, the insurer shall pay all of the obligations of the employer for workers' compensation benefits for injuries occurring during the policy period. Payment by the insurer of any amounts within the deductible shall be treated as an advancement of funds by the insurer to the employer and shall create a legal obligation for reimbursements, and may be secured by appropriate security.

(4) The endorsement shall specify whether loss adjustment expenses are to be treated as advancements within the deductible to be reimbursed by the employer.

(5) An explanation of premium reductions reflecting the type and level of the deductible shall be clearly set forth for the policyholder.

(6) The filing shall provide that premium reductions for deductibles are determined before application of any experience modification, premium surcharge, or premium discount, and the premium reductions reflect the type and level of deductible consistent with accepted actuarial standards.

(7) The filing shall provide that the nonpayment of deductible amounts by the insured employer to its insurer, or the failure to comply with any security-related terms of the policy, shall be treated under the policy in the same manner as the payment or nonpayment of the premium pursuant to paragraph (1) of subdivision (b) of Section 676.8.

(f) The insurer shall report and record losses subject to the deductible as losses for purposes of ratemaking and application of an experience rating plan on the same basis as losses under policies providing first dollar coverage. **Leg.H.** 1993 ch. 228 §2, operative January 1, 1995, 1994 chs. 732, 1097, 1131 §1.5, 1997 ch. 748, 2002 ch. 873 (AB 1985).

Ref.: Hanna § 2.40[1]; Herlick Handbook §§ 3.2, 3.14.

§11736. Requirements of experience rating plan.

An experience rating plan shall contain reasonable eligibility standards, provide adequate incentives for loss prevention, and shall provide for sufficient premium differentials so as to encourage safety. **Leg.H.** 1993 ch. 228 §2, operative January 1, 1995, 1997 ch. 748.

Ref.: Hanna § 2.40[1]; Herlick Handbook § 3.2.

§11736.5. Collateral or security for deductible amount on policy; reserves and recognition of receivables.

(a) The commissioner shall establish, by regulation, those forms of collateral or security that an insurer may designate to secure the deductible amount of any policy of workers' compensation insurance and the establishment of reserves and recognition of receivables for insurers writing workers' compensation deductible policies.

The commissioner, by order, exempt from the requirements of the Administrative Procedure Act, shall establish those forms of security or collateral that the insurer may designate to secure the deductible amount of any policy of workers' compensation insurance that provides for a deductible and the establishment of reserves and recognition of receivables for insurers writing workers' compensation deductible policies. This authority shall expire if regulations required by subdivision (a) are not drafted and filed with the Office of Administrative Law by December 31, 1995; if the regulations are filed with the Office of Administrative Law by December 31, 1995, this authority shall expire December 31, 1996, or upon filing of the regulations with the Secretary of State, whichever is earlier. **Leg.H.** 1994 ch. 1131.

1994 Note: The Legislature inadvertently added a subsection (a) designation without any additional subsection designations.

Ref.: Herlick Handbook § 3.2.

§11737. Disapproval of rate by commissioner; notice of disapproval; request for review of rating system of insurer or rating organization by aggrieved party; appeal to commissioner after request; hearing; issuance of order by commissioner upon disapproval; specification of interim rates; rate increase for policies with inception dates before January 1, 2003.

(a) The commissioner may disapprove a rate if the insurer fails to comply with the filing requirements under Section 11735.

(b) The commissioner may disapprove rates if the commissioner determines that premiums charged, in the aggregate, resulting from the use of the rates or the rates as modified by any supplementary rate information, would be inadequate to cover an insurer's losses and expenses, unfairly discriminatory, or tend to create a monopoly in the market pursuant to Section 11732, 11732.5, or 11733.

(c) The commissioner shall disapprove rates if the commissioner determines that premiums charged, in the aggregate, resulting from the use of the rates or the rates as modified by any supplementary rate information would, if continued in use, tend to impair or threaten the solvency of an insurer. In determining whether the premium charged in the aggregate would, if continued in use, tend to impair or threaten the solvency of the insurer, the commissioner shall consider the insurer's experience in other states.

(d) If the commissioner intends to disapprove rates pursuant to subdivision (a) or (b), the commissioner shall serve notice on the insurer of the intent to disapprove and shall schedule a hearing to commence within 60 days of the date of the notice.

(e) If the commissioner disapproves rates pursuant to subdivision (c), the commissioner shall immediately serve notice on the insurer of the disapproval. An insurer whose rates have been disapproved pursuant to that subdivision may, within 20 days of the date of the notice of disapproval, request a hearing, and the commissioner shall hold a hearing within 60 days of the date of the notice of disapproval.

(f) Every insurer or rating organization shall provide within this state reasonable means whereby any person aggrieved by the application of its filings may be heard by the insurer or rating organization on written request to review the manner in which the rating system has been applied in connection with the insurance afforded or offered. If the insurer or rating organization fails to grant or reject the request within 30 days, the applicant may proceed in the same manner as if the application had been rejected. Any party affected by the action of the insurer or rating organization on the request may appeal, within 30 days after written notice of the action, to the commissioner who, after a hearing held within 60 days from the date on which the party requests the appeal, or longer upon agreement of the parties and not less than 10 days' written notice to the appellant and to the insurer or rating organization, may affirm, modify, or reverse that action. If the commissioner has information on the subject from which the appeal is taken and believes that a reasonable basis for the appeal does not exist or that the appeal is not made in good faith, the commissioner may deny the appeal without a hearing. The denial shall be in writing, set forth the basis for the denial, and be served on all parties.

(g) If the commissioner disapproves a rate, the commissioner shall issue an order specifying in what respects the rate fails to meet the requirements of this article and stating when, within a reasonable period thereafter, that rate shall be discontinued for any policy issued or renewed after a date specified in the order. The order shall be issued within 20 days after the notice prescribed in subdivision (e) is served. If a hearing is held pursuant to subdivision (d) or (e), the order shall be issued, instead, within 30 days after the close of the hearing. The order may include a provision for premium adjustment for the period after the effective date of the order for policies in effect on that date.

(h) Whenever an insurer has no legally effective rates as a result of the commissioner's disapproval of rates or other act, the commissioner shall specify interim rates for the insurer that protect the interests of all parties and may order that a specified portion of the premiums be placed in an escrow account approved by the commissioner. When new rates become legally effective, the commissioner shall order the escrowed funds or any overcharge in the interim rates to be distributed appropriately, except that refunds of less than ten dollars ($10) per policyholder shall not be required. However, if the commissioner has disapproved rates pursuant to subdivision (c), the commissioner shall order the insurer in the interim to use, at a minimum, the approved advisory pure premium rates pursuant to subdivision (b) of Section 11750, as modified by the uniform experience rating plan established pursuant to subdivision (c) of Section 11734, without any deviations on account of any supplementary rate information and reflecting the actual expenses of the insurer, until the time that a final determination of rates is adjudicated and ordered through a hearing.

(i) Notwithstanding any other provision of law, an insurer may increase rates on policies with inception dates prior to January 1, 2003, in an amount no greater than the pure premium rate increase approved by the commissioner reflecting the cost of the change in benefit levels authorized by the act adding this subdivision. **Leg.H.** 1993 ch. 228 §2, operative January 1, 1995, ch. 1242, 1994 ch. 1097, 1997 ch. 517, 2002 chs. 6 (AB 749), 873 (AB 1985).

Ref.: Hanna § 2.40[1]; Herlick Handbook § 3.2.

§11738. Factors not considered in classification.

A classification shall take no account of any physical impairment of employees or the extent to which employees may have persons dependent upon them for support. **Leg.H.** 1993 ch. 228 §2, operative January 1, 1995.

Ref.: Hanna § 2.40[1]; Herlick Handbook § 3.2.

§11739. Dividend payments to policyholders—Restrictions and filing requirement.

(a) An insurer shall not use any plan for the payment of dividends to policyholders by reason of a participating provision in a workers' compensation insurance policy which is unfairly discriminatory.

(b) Every insurer issuing workers' compensation insurance policies under the laws of this state shall file annually with the rating organization designated by the commissioner information relating to dividend payments made to its policyholders. Information filed shall be in sufficient detail to permit the rating organization to prepare for the commissioner's review and approval, a report showing in the aggregate for all companies premiums earned, losses incurred, and dividends paid the preceding calendar year under policies containing a participating provision, separately by premium size and loss ratio categories, as may reasonably be prescribed by the commissioner.

(c) Information submitted by individual companies pursuant to this section shall be confidential and not subject to public disclosure under any law of this state. **Leg.H.** 1993 ch. 228 §2, operative January 1, 1995.

Ref.: Herlick Handbook § 3.2.

§11740. Effective dates for rates and supplementary rate information pursuant to this article.

Rates and supplementary rate information filed for use in this state pursuant to this article and Article 3 (commencing with Section 11750), as added and amended by Chapter 228 of the Statutes of 1993, shall not be effective prior to the first normal anniversary rating date of a policy on or after January 1, 1995. Rates, any rating plan or plans, and policy forms issued or approved prior to January 1, 1995, shall remain in effect only until the first normal anniversary rating date on or after January 1, 1995, as determined by a licensed rating organization pursuant to rules issued or approved by the commissioner in effect on July 16, 1993. Prior to January 1, 1995, no policy may be issued or renewed for a term of less than one year for the purpose of changing the normal anniversary date of the policy or the preceding policy. No policy may be canceled, amended, or rewritten for the purpose of avoiding this section.

Notwithstanding Section 7 of Chapter 228 of the Statutes of 1993, this section shall become operative January 1, 1994. **Leg.H.** 1993 ch. 1242.

Ref.: Hanna § 2.40[1].

§11742. Workers' compensation insurance online rate comparison guide.

(a) The Legislature finds and declares that the insolvencies of more than a dozen workers' compensation insurance carriers have seriously constricted the market and led to a dangerous increase in business at the State Compensation Insurance Fund. Yet more than 200 insurance companies are still licensed to offer workers' compensation insurance in California. Unfortunately, many employers do not know which carriers are offering coverage, and it is both difficult and time consuming to try to get information on rates and coverages from competing insurance companies. A central information source would help employers find the required coverage at the best competitive rate.

(b) On or before July 1, 2004, the commissioner shall establish and maintain, on the Internet Web site maintained by the department, an online rate comparison guide showing workers' compensation insurance rates for the 50 insurance companies writing the highest volume of business in this line during the two preceding years.

(c) The online comparison shall display rates for each class set forth in the classification system adopted by the commissioner pursuant to Section 11734, shall include the effective date of each rate, and shall list the rates for each class from the lowest to the highest rate.

(d) The rating organization designated by the commissioner as his or her statistical agent pursuant to Section 11751.5 shall determine the cost savings achieved in the 2003 workers' compensation reform legislation. Each insurer shall certify, in the form and manner determined by the commissioner, that its rates reflect those cost savings. The certifications shall be made available to the public on the Internet Web site maintained by the department. **Leg.H.** 2003 ch. 635 (AB 227).

Ref.: Hanna § 2.40[1]; Herlick Handbook §§ 3.2, 3.10.

ARTICLE 3
Rating and Other Organizations

§11750. Purpose of this article.

(a) The purpose of this article is to promote the public welfare by regulating concert of action between insurers in collecting and tabulating rating information and other data that may be helpful in the making of adequate pure premium rates for workers' compensation insurance and for employers liability insurance incidental thereto and written in connection therewith for all admitted insurers and in submitting them to the commissioner for approval; to authorize and regulate the existence and cooperation of qualified rating organizations to one of which each workers' compensation insurer shall belong; to authorize and regulate cooperation between insurers, rating organizations and advisory organizations in ratemaking and other related matters to the end that the purposes of this chapter may be complied with and carried into effect.

(b) Notwithstanding any other provision of law, within 60 days of receiving an advisory pure premium rate filing made pursuant to subdivision (b) of Section 11750.3, the Insurance Commissioner shall hold a public hearing, and within 30 days of the conclusion of the hearing, approve, disapprove, or modify the proposed rate. **Leg.H.** 1993 ch. 1242, 2000 ch. 884, effective September 29, 2000.

Ref.: Hanna §§ 2.01, 2.02[2], 2.16, 2.40[1], 2.50[1][a], 2.70[2]; Herlick Handbook § 3.10.

§11750.1. Definitions.

As used in this article, unless a different meaning is manifest, the term:

(a) "Insurer" means every insurer authorized to transact workers' compensation insurance and employer's liability insurance incidental thereto and written in connection therewith in this state, including the State Compensation Insurance Fund;

(b) "Rating organization" means any organization which has as its primary object or purpose the collecting of loss and expense statistics and other statistical information and data, the making of pure premium rates and those rating plans authorized by Section 11734 for workers' compensation insurance and employer's liability insurance incidental thereto and written in connection therewith and presenting them to the commissioner for approval;

(c) "Insurance" means workers' compensation insurance and employer's liability insurance incidental thereto and written in connection therewith;

(d) "Willful" or "willfully" in relation to an act or omission which constitutes a violation of this article means with actual knowledge or belief that such act or omission constitutes such violation and with specific intent to commit such violation.

(e) "Advisory organization" means every person, group or organization, other than an insurer, whether located within or without this state, which prepares policy forms or underwriting rules incidental to or in connection with workers' compensation insurance and employer's liability insurance incidental thereto and written in connection therewith or which collects and furnishes to admitted insurers or rating organizations loss statistics or other statistical information and data relating to workers' compensation insurance and employer's liability insurance incidental thereto and written in connection therewith and acts in an advisory capacity to such insurers or rating organizations as distinguished from a ratemaking capacity. No duly authorized attorney at law acting in the usual course of his profession shall be deemed to be an advisory organization.

(f) "Employer's liability insurance incidental thereto and written in connection therewith" means insurance of any liability of employers for injuries to, or death of, employees arising out of, and in the course of, employment when this insurance is incidental to, and written in connection with, the workers' compensation insurance issued to the same employer and covering the same employer interests. **Leg.H.** 1993 chs. 228, 1242.

Ref.: Hanna §§ 2.02[2], 2.16, 2.63[1]; Herlick Handbook § 3.10.

§11750.2. Scope of article.

The provisions of this article shall apply to all workers' compensation insurance and employer's liability insurance incidental thereto and written in connection therewith in this state, except reinsurance.

Ref.: Herlick Handbook § 3.10.

§11750.3. Permissible purposes of rating organization.

A rating organization may be organized pursuant to this article and maintained in this state for the following purposes:

(a) To provide reliable statistics and rating information with respect to workers' compensation insurance and employer's liability insurance incidental thereto and written in connection therewith.

(b) To collect and tabulate information and statistics for the purpose of developing pure premium rates to be submitted to the commissioner for issuance or approval.

(c) To formulate rules and regulations in connection with pure premium rates and the administration of classifications and rating systems.

(d) To inspect risks for classification or rate purposes and to furnish to the insurer and upon request of the employer and after notice to the insurer, to furnish to the employer full information concerning the rates applicable to the employer's insurance.

(e) To examine policies, daily reports, endorsements or other evidences of insurance for the purpose of ascertaining whether they comply with the provisions of law and to make reasonable rules governing their submission. A rating organization may develop loss data on behalf of its members to assist members in developing plans pursuant to subdivision (e) of Section 11735 and other loss sensitive plans.

(f) Within one year after expiration of any workers' compensation insurance policy, to initiate test audits of insured employer's payrolls and insurer's audits of those payrolls to check the accuracy and reliability thereof, and to examine all records relative thereto and premises of insured employers.

(g) To exchange information and experience data with rating organizations, advisory organizations, and insurers in this and other states, with respect to ratemaking.

(h) To become a member or subscriber of any lawfully authorized ratemaking or advisory organization whenever membership in the organization is necessary or helpful to the rating organization.

(i) To perform all acts necessary, incidental, or convenient to carry out the foregoing purposes or the provisions of this chapter relating to rating organizations. **Leg.H.** 1993 ch. 228, operative January 1, 1995, 1994 ch. 1131.

Ref.: Hanna §§ 2.02[2], 2.16, 2.50[1][a]; Herlick Handbook §§ 3.2, 3.10, 12.13.

§11751. License; fee; required information.

On and after January 1, 1952, no rating organization shall conduct its operations in this state without first having filed with the commissioner a written application for and securing a license to act as a rating organization. Any rating organization may make application for and obtain a license as a rating organization if it shall meet the requirements for license set forth in this article. The fee for filing an application for a license as a rating organization is one hundred fifty dollars ($150) payable in advance to the commissioner. Every such rating organization shall file with its application:

(a) A copy of its constitution, its articles of incorporation, agreement of association, and of its bylaws, rules and regulations governing the conduct of its business, all certified by the custodian of the originals thereof.

(b) A list of its members who shall not number less than five insurers authorized to write and writing workers' compensation insurance in this state and whose combined experience shall be determined by the commissioner to be reasonably adequate for ratemaking purposes.

(c) The name and address of a resident of this state upon whom notices of the commissioner or process affecting such rating organization may be served.

(d) A statement of its qualifications as a rating organization.

Ref.: Herlick Handbook § 3.10.

§11751.1. License requirements.

To obtain and retain a license, a rating organization shall provide satisfactory evidence to the commissioner that it shall do all of the following:

(a) Permit any insurer to become a member at a reasonable cost and without discrimination, or to withdraw therefrom.

(b) Neither have nor adopt any rule or exact any agreement, the effect of which would be to require any member as a condition of membership to adhere to any rates.

(c) Neither adopt any rule nor exact any agreement, the effect of which would be to prohibit or regulate the payment of dividends, savings, or unabsorbed premium deposits allowed or returned by insurers to their policyholders or members.

(d) Neither practice nor sanction any plan or act of boycott, coercion, or intimidation.

(e) Neither enter into nor sanction any contract or act by which any person is restrained from lawfully engaging in the insurance business.

(f) Notify the commissioner promptly of every change in its constitution or articles of incorporation, agreement of association, or in its bylaws, rules and regulations governing the conduct of its business; its list of members; and the name and address of the resident of this state designated by it upon whom notices or orders of the commissioner or process affecting the organization may be served.

(g) Agree that the commissioner or his or her representative may attend all meetings of the organization or any of its committees.

(h) Agree to permit four members of the public, two representing organized labor and two representing insured employers, to serve on the managing or governing committee of the organization as specified in Section 11751.35.

(i) Maintain reasonable records of the experience of its members and of the data, statistics or information collected or used in connection with the pure premium rates, classifications, manual rules, and policy and endorsement forms used by its members so that these records will be available at all reasonable times to enable the commissioner to determine whether the rating organization and its members comply with the provisions of this chapter applicable to them. These records shall be maintained in an office within this state. The commissioner may prescribe a uniform system for the keeping of the records which shall be reasonably adapted to the rating organization and its members' method of operation and which shall be applicable to all rating organizations licensed under this article and their members. **Leg.H.** 1993 ch. 228, operative January 1, 1995.

1989 Note: This section is applicable only to injuries occurring on or after January 1, 1990. Stats. 1989 ch. 893 §6.

Ref.: Herlick Handbook § 3.10.

§11751.2. Investigation of rating organizations; findings of commissioner; denial of application; duration of license.

The commissioner shall examine each application for license to act as a rating organization and the documents filed therewith and may make any further investigation of the applicant, its affairs and its proposed plan of business, as he deems desirable.

The commissioner shall issue the license applied for within 60 days of its filing with him if from such examination and investigation he is satisfied that:

(a) The business reputation of the applicant and its officers is good.

(b) The facilities of the applicant are adequate to enable it to furnish the services it proposes to furnish.

(c) The applicant and its proposed plan of operation conform to the requirements of this chapter.

Otherwise, but only after hearing upon notice, the commissioner shall in writing deny the application and notify the applicant of his decision and his reasons therefor.

Licenses issued pursuant to this section shall remain in effect until suspended or revoked.

Ref.: Herlick Handbook § 3.10.

§11751.25. License fee due annually.

Notwithstanding the provisions of Section 11751, each rating organization possessing a license of indefinite term pursuant to this article shall owe and pay to the commissioner an annual fee of one hundred dollars ($100) in advance on account of such license until its final termination. Such fee shall be for periods commencing on July 1, 1969, and on each July 1st thereafter, and ending on June 30, 1970, and each June 30th thereafter, and shall be due and payable on March 1, 1969, and on each March 1st thereafter, and shall be delinquent on April 1, 1969, and each April 1st thereafter.

Ref.: Herlick Handbook § 3.10.

§11751.3. Rules of rating organizations; State Fund's committee membership.

(a) Subject to the approval of the commissioner, a rating organization licensed under this article may adopt any reasonable constitution, articles of incorporation, or agreement of association, and may make reasonable rules for the regulation of its members and the conduct of its business by bylaws or otherwise. In a rating organization of which the State Compensation Insurance Fund is a member, it shall be entitled without election to membership on the managing or governing committee and on the classification and rating committee thereof.

(b) In addition, after consultation with the California Labor Federation, AFL-CIO, other statewide organized labor organizations, and statewide associations representing business, the commissioner shall appoint two public members representing insured employers and two public members representing organized labor to serve on the managing or governing committee of a rating organization. The bylaws of a rating organization shall permit a public member from time to time to designate in his or her stead a representative from the same employer organization or an affiliated employee union, as the case may be, to attend and participate in any meeting of the governing committee of a rating organization.

1989 Note: This section is applicable only to injuries occurring on or after January 1, 1990. Stats. 1989 ch. 893 §6.

Ref.: Herlick Handbook § 3.10.

§11751.35. Public members of managing committee.

(a) Four members of the public, two representing organized labor and two representing insured employers, appointed pursuant to subdivision (b) of Section 11751.3, shall be entitled to serve on the managing or governing committee of a rating organization licensed under this article. A public member shall be entitled to vote on all issues involving pure premium rates, classifications, rating plans, rating systems, manual rules and policy, and endorsement forms which are properly brought before the committee. A public member shall be removed by the commissioner only for cause.

(b) In the event a public member is unable or unwilling to complete his or her term, after consultation with the California Labor Federation, AFL-CIO, other statewide organized labor organizations, and statewide organizations representing business, as the case may be, the commissioner shall appoint a successor from organized labor or an insured employer to complete the unexpired term.

(c) The public members who serve on the governing committee of a rating organization licensed under this article together may, by a majority vote, retain experts who shall include a fellow of the Casualty Actuarial Society, to advise them on any matter specified in subdivision (a). The actuary hired may participate in all proceedings of the actuarial committee of the rating organization. The reasonable expense of retaining these experts shall not exceed one hundred thousand dollars ($100,000) per year and shall be paid from the budget of the department. The commissioner shall increase this amount annually to reflect any needed cost-of-living adjustments. The public members may submit information obtained from these experts, as well as any other information they deem appropriate, to the commissioner for his or her consideration in approving a change of any matter specified in subdivision (a).

(d) In addition to the expenses authorized pursuant to subdivision (c), the public members who serve on the governing committee of a rating organization licensed under this article may expend up to an additional one hundred thousand dollars ($100,000) per year, which shall be paid by insurer members of the rating organization. Those funds shall be used to retain staff, who shall be hired by a majority vote of the public members. **Leg.H.** 1993 ch. 121, effective July 16, 1993, ch. 1242, 1995 ch. 375.

1989 Note: This section is applicable only to injuries occurring on or after January 1, 1990. Stats. 1989 ch. 893 §6.

Ref.: Herlick Handbook § 3.10.

§11751.4. Insurer as rating organization member.

From and after the taking effect of this act, it shall be the duty of every insurer to be a member of a rating organization. No insurer may at the same time belong to more than one rating organization licensed under this article.

Ref.: Hanna §§ 2.50[1][a], 2.16; Herlick Handbook § 3.10.

§11751.5. Provision of statistics to commissioner.

The commissioner, after notice and hearing, may promulgate reasonable rules and statistical plans, which may be modified from time to time and which shall be used thereafter in the recording and reporting by insurers of their loss and expense experience in order that the experiences of all insurers may be made available in such form and detail as may be necessary to aid the commissioner in administering the provisions of Article 2 (commencing with Section 11730). The commissioner shall designate a rating organization licensed under this article as his or her statistical agent to gather and compile such experience statistics and all licensed rating organizations shall report the experience of their members to such designated rating organization. Subject to reasonable rules approved by the commissioner, such designated rating organization shall make such experience statistics, when compiled, available to all licensed rating organizations and may make a reasonable charge to other rating organizations for the expense incurred by it in combining, tabulating and compiling the experience of all workers' compensation insurers. **Leg.H.** 1993 ch. 1242.

Ref.: Herlick Handbook § 3.10.

§11751.55. Filing fee if public hearing is required.

If an insurer, the State Compensation Insurance Fund, a rating organization, or an advisory organization requests an official action by the commissioner under Chapters 2 (commencing with Section 11630), 3 (commencing with Section 11690), or 4 (commencing with Section 11770) of this part which he can lawfully consummate only after a noticed public hearing required by law, the commissioner shall require the request to be in writing and require the payment of five hundred ninety dollars ($590), in advance, as a fee for filing such request. Such fee shall be earned even if the request is denied or is granted in an altered form.

Ref.: Herlick Handbook § 3.10.

§11751.7. Statistical agent information request.

(a) The rating organization designated the statistical agent pursuant to Section 11751.5 shall provide to the Director of Industrial Relations, upon request, any information in the possession of, or reasonably attainable by the rating organization, that would assist the Director of Industrial Relations to identify employers who fail to secure adequate insurance in violation of Section 3700 of the Labor Code. The information requested pursuant to this section shall be provided by the rating organization in a form and manner prescribed by the Director of Industrial Relations.

(b) The rating organization designated the statistical agent pursuant to Section 11751.5 shall provide to the Registrar of Contractors of the Contractor's State License Board, upon request, any information in the possession of, or reasonably attainable by, the rating organization that would assist in identifying licensed contractors who fail to secure adequate insurance in violation of Section 3700 of the Labor Code. The information requested pursuant to this section shall be provided by the rating organization in a form and manner prescribed by the Registrar of Contractors. **Leg.H.** 1992 ch. 1276, 2005 ch. 428 (AB 1027) §1.

Ref.: Herlick Handbook § 3.10.

§11751.8. Reporting loss corrections or revisions to rating organization; when insurer must report.

An insurer shall report to its rating organization as corrections or revisions of losses, pursuant to the unit statistical plan and uniform experience rating plans approved by the commissioner, if any of the following is applicable:

(a) A loss record detail was incorrectly reported through mistake other than error of judgment.

(b) One or more claims are declared noncompensable. A claim is declared noncompensable if any of the following applies:

(1) There is an official ruling specifically holding that a claimant is not entitled to benefits under the workers' compensation laws of the state, even though the claimant may have been awarded reimbursement for expenses incurred by the claimant in presenting the case.

(2) No claim was filed during the period of limitation provided by the workers' compensation laws for the filing of the claim, and the carrier, therefore, closes the claim.

(3) Where the carrier contends, prior to the valuation date, that a claimant is not entitled to benefits under the workers' compensation laws and the claim is officially closed because of the claimant's failure to prosecute the claim.

(c) The carrier has recovered in an action against a third party.

(d) A death claim has been compromised over the sole issue of the applicability of the workers' compensation laws of the state.

(e) The exposure has been reassigned to another classification through the revision of an audit, in which case the insurer shall file with the revision of exposure a revision of losses that will reassign all claims to the appropriate classification.

(f) A clerical error in either the classification assignment or the type of injury assignment of a given claim, or a group of claims, has been discovered by the insurer.

(g) A clerical error in either the classification assignment or the type of injury assignment of a given claim has been discovered by the rating organization. The insurer shall, when notified by the rating organization, file a revision of losses or make satisfactory explanation.

(h) A correction is made in a classification assignment of a given claim, or a group of claims, as a result of the organization test audit of an insured for which the experience has been submitted.

(i) The claim has been determined to be a joint coverage claim in accordance with the unit statistical plan approved by the commissioner. **Leg.H.** 1994 ch. 776, 1995 ch. 161, 1997 ch. 748.

Ref.: Hanna § 2.36; Herlick Handbook § 3.10.

§11751.82. Reporting workers' compensation losses and payroll information by insurer under wrap-up insurance policy.

(a) An insurer under a wrap-up insurance policy shall report workers' compensation losses and payroll information for each contractor and subcontractor to its rating organization on a timely basis and in accordance with the uniform statistical plan. Within 10 days, upon request, the insurer shall provide to each contractor and subcontractor copies of the report covering workers' compensation losses and payroll information for that contractor or subcontractor.

(b) For the purposes of this section, a "wrap-up insurance policy" is an insurance policy, or series of policies, written to cover risks associated with a work of improvement, as defined in Section 3106 of the Civil Code, and covering two or more of the contractors or subcontractors that work on that work of improvement. **Leg.H.** 2004 ch. 777 (AB 2147).

§11751.9. Revision of experience rating upon closure and reporting of claims.

Whenever a claim or claims used in an experience rating are closed and reported pursuant to the unit statistical plan approved by the commissioner and are valued, in the aggregate, at an amount that is less than 60 percent of the highest reported aggregate value of all of these claims, then the experience rating shall be revised pursuant to the uniform experience rating plan approved by the commissioner based on the most current reported values for all claims used in the experience rating. **Leg.H.** 1997 ch. 748.

Ref.: Hanna § 2.36; Herlick Handbook § 3.10.

§11752. Examination of rating organizations; acceptable substitutes.

The commissioner may, as often as reasonable and necessary, make or cause to be made an examination of each rating or advisory organization to ascertain whether such organizations comply with the legal requirements applicable to it under this article.

In lieu of any such examination the commissioner may accept the report of an examination made by the insurance supervisory official of another state or the report of a representative designated by the National Association of Insurance Commissioners.

Ref.: Herlick Handbook § 3.10.

§11752.1. Examination of personnel and records.

The officers, managers, agents and employees of any such organization may be examined by the commissioner at any time under oath and shall exhibit all books, records, accounts, documents or agreements governing its method of operation together with all data, statistics and information of every kind and character collected or considered by such organization in the conduct of the operations to which the examination relates.

Ref.: Herlick Handbook § 3.10.

§11752.2. Cost of commissioner's examination.

The reasonable cost of any examination authorized by this article of any rating or advisory organization shall be paid by the organization examined.

Ref.: Herlick Handbook § 3.10.

§11752.5. Release of policy information to governmental agencies.

(a) Subject to subdivision (b), a licensed rating organization shall make available any policy information contained in its records to the following:

(1) The Department of Industrial Relations.

(2) Any other governmental agency if the Insurance Commissioner, after consultation with the licensed rating organization, approves the release of the policy information requested to the agency.

(b) The Department of Industrial Relations and any other governmental agency shall specify to the licensed rating organization, in writing, the information requested, that the information requested is to be used to facilitate the agency's performance of its constitutional or statutory duties, and that the information received will not be released to others, except in the discharge of a specific statutory or constitutional duty, or published without the prior written consent of the licensed rating organization. In addition, if the Insurance Commissioner's approval is required for the release of the policy information requested, a written copy of the approval shall be submitted to the licensed rating organization.

(c) As used in this section, "policy information" means information which is contained in a workers' compensation policy, including, but not limited to, the identity and address of the employer, the identity of the insurer, the policy number, and the policy period.

(d) Information obtained by a governmental agency pursuant to this section shall be confidential and not subject to public disclosure under any other law of this state.

(e) No licensed rating organization or member thereof, or member of a committee of a licensed rating organization when acting in its capacity as a member of the committee, or officer or employee of a licensed rating organization, when acting within the scope of his or her employment, shall be liable to any person for injury, personal or otherwise, or damages caused or alleged to have been caused, either directly or indirectly, by the disclosure of information to a governmental agency pursuant to this section, or for the accuracy or completeness of the information so disclosed.

(f) This section shall not be construed as implying the existence of liability in circumstances not defined in this section, nor as implying a legislative recognition that, except for enactment of this section, a liability has existed or would exist in the circumstances stated in this section.

(g) This section shall not be construed as limiting any authority of a licensed rating organization to disclose information contained in its records to others. **Leg.H.** 1984 ch. 909 §1, 2006 ch. 452 (SB 1452) §5.

Ref.: Herlick Handbook § 3.10.

§11752.6. Release of policy information to employer.

(a) A licensed rating organization shall make available, in writing, to an employer insured under a workers' compensation policy, all policyholder information contained in its records upon request of the employer and after notice to the employer's insurer.

(b) As used in this section, "policyholder information" means all information relating to the employer's loss experience, claims, classification assignments, and policy contracts. Policyholder information also includes information relating to rating plans, rating systems, manual rules, and any other information that impacts the policyholder's pure premium rates.

(c) If a licensed rating organization rejects an employer's request for policyholder information, the rating organization shall notify the employer in writing of the reasons for the rejection. An employer whose request has been rejected in whole or in part may appeal to the commissioner in accordance with Section 11753.1. If the commissioner finds that the reasons for the rejection are not justified, he or she may order the rating organization to furnish that information to the employer.

(d) No licensed rating organization or member of the organization, or member of a committee of a licensed rating organization when acting in its capacity as a member of the committee, or officer or employee of a licensed rating organization, when acting within the scope of his or her employment, is liable to any person for injury, personal or otherwise, or damages caused or alleged to have been caused, either directly or indirectly, by the disclosure of information to an employer under this section or for the accuracy or completeness of the information disclosed.

(e) This section does not imply the existence of liability in circumstances not defined in this section, nor does it imply a legislative recognition that, except for enactment of this section, a liability has existed or would exist in the circumstances stated in this section.

(f) This section does not limit any authority of a licensed rating organization to disclose information contained in its records to others.

(g) There shall be established in all licensed rating organizations a policyholder ombudsman. The policyholder ombudsman shall be a person with sufficient knowledge of the workers' compensation ratemaking process to provide information and assistance to policyholders in obtaining and evaluating the information provided in Article 2 (commencing with Section 11730) and this article, and in Sections 3761 and 3762 of the Labor Code. Every rating organization licensed in this state shall provide compensation for the ombudsman and necessary staff and other necessary resources to allow the ombudsman to provide prompt and complete service to workers' compensation policyholders of this state. The policyholder ombudsman may advise the policyholder in any dispute with insurers or the rating organization that the ombudsman serves, or on appeal to the commissioner as provided in Section 11737.

(h) For all policies of insurance issued or renewed on or after January 1, 1994, the insurer shall advise the policyholder in writing of the following:

(1) The policyholder's right to request a written report containing the information set forth in this section from the licensed rating organization of which the insurer is a member, and the policyholder's right to contact the policyholder ombudsman to assist in obtaining and evaluating information relating to rates, together with the telephone number and address of the ombudsman, as well as the policyholder's right to contact the department to resolve a dispute with an insurer, as provided in this section and Section 11737.

(2) If a participating policy, that upon payment or nonpayment of a dividend the policyholder shall be provided a written explanation, in clear and understandable language, setting forth the basis of the calculation and expressing any dividend in both dollar amount and as a percentage of earned premium under the policy.

(3) The date when the insurer is required to file the first unit statistical report with the licensed rating organization designated by the commissioner. **Leg.H.** 1993 ch. 121, effective July 16, 1993, 1995 ch. 582.

Ref.: Herlick Handbook § 3.10.

§11752.7. Availability of experience rating information.

(a) A licensed rating organization may make available experience rating information contained in its records to any insurer admitted to transact workers' compensation insurance in this state or to any insurance agent or broker that is licensed to transact workers' compensation insurance in this state, if the insurer, agent, or broker submits a written request to the licensed rating organization stating all of the following:

(1) The requesting insurer is admitted to transact workers' compensation insurance in this state or that the requesting agent or broker is licensed to transact workers' compensation insurance in this state.

(2) The information requested.

(3) The information requested will be used to facilitate the transaction of workers' compensation insurance by the insurer, agent, or broker.

(4) The information received will not be released by the agent or broker to others, except to facilitate the transaction of workers' compensation insurance by the requesting agent or broker.

(b) The licensed rating organization may, but shall not be required to, verify that an insurer requesting information under this section is admitted to transact workers' compensation insurance in this state or that an insurance agent or broker requesting information under this section is licensed to transact workers' compensation insurance in this state.

(c) For purposes of this section:

(1) "Experience rating information" means information released on microfiche, at an Internet Web site or other electronic format, or in other forms or media by a licensed rating organization that identifies all experience-rated employers, and the experience ratings and classifications or experience modifications that apply or applied to those employers.

(2) "Transaction," as applied to workers' compensation insurance, includes any of the following:

(A) Solicitation.

(B) Negotiations preliminary to execution of a contract of insurance.

(C) Execution of a contract of insurance.

(D) Resolution of matters arising out of the contract and subsequent to its execution.

(d) Experience rating information made available pursuant to this section shall be confidential and shall not be used for any purpose other than to facilitate the transaction of workers' compensation insurance by the insurer, agent, or broker receiving the information pursuant to this section.

(e) Notwithstanding any other provision of law, including this section, a licensed rating organization may not enter into a contract or other agreement, including its constitution, articles of incorporation, or bylaws that prohibits information services companies in the business of publishing or providing experience rating information immediately prior to September 15, 1989, from continuing on or after September 15, 1989, to receive and provide to others experience rating information from whatever sources and in whatever forms or media.

(f) No licensed rating organization, member of a licensed rating organization, member of a committee of a licensed rating organization when acting in its capacity as a member of the committee, or officer or employee of a licensed rating organization when acting within the scope of his or her employment, shall be liable to any person for injury, personal or otherwise, or damages caused or alleged to have been caused, either directly or indirectly, by the disclosure of information pursuant to this section, or to the members of those organizations, or for the accuracy or completeness of the information disclosed.

(g) This section shall not be construed as implying the existence of liability in circumstances not defined in this section, nor as implying a legislative recognition that, except for the enactment of this section, a liability has existed or would exist in the circumstances stated in this section.

(h) This section shall not be construed as limiting any authority of a licensed rating organization to disclose information contained in its records to others. **Leg.H.** 1998 ch. 176, 2002 ch. 879 (AB 2192).

Ref.: Herlick Handbook § 3.10.

§11752.8. Notice of workers' compensation rating laws to be provided to policyholder.

(a) For all policies of insurance issued, or renewed for the first time on or after January 1, 1995, the insurer shall provide a notice, approved by the commissioner, to the policyholder, explaining in easily understandable language the workers' compensation rating laws. For policies issued or renewed between January 1, 1994, and January 1, 1995, inclusive, the insurer shall include a notice to the policyholder, in easily understandable language, containing a summary of the changes in the rating laws enacted during the 1993-94 Regular Session of the Legislature.

(b) The notice required by this section may be combined with the notice required by subdivision (h) of Section 11752.6. **Leg.H.** 1993 ch. 121, effective July 16, 1993, ch. 1242 §12.

Ref.: Hanna § 2.33; Herlick Handbook § 3.10.

§11752.9. Written notification of change in classification assignment to be provided to policyholder.

Notwithstanding subdivision (d) of Section 11750.3, a rating organization shall provide a policyholder with written notification if it imposes a change in the classification assignment of the policyholder. The written notification shall be provided to the policyholder at the same time that it is provided to the insurer. A rating organization may satisfy this requirement by furnishing the policyholder with a copy of the notice that it provides to the insurer regarding the change in classification assignment. **Leg.H.** 2003 ch. 121 (SB 176).

Ref.: Hanna § 2.02[2].

§11753. Information required of advisory organizations; notification of all changes; prohibition on unfair practices.

No advisory organization shall conduct its operations in this State unless and until it has filed with the commissioner:

(a) A copy of its constitution, articles of incorporation, agreement of association, and of its by-laws, rules and regulations governing its activities, all duly certified by the custodian of the originals thereof.

(b) A list of its members and subscribers.

(c) The name and address of a resident of this State upon whom notices or orders of the commissioner or process may be served.

Every such advisory organization shall notify the commissioner promptly of every change in its constitution, its articles of incorporation, agreement of association, and of its by-laws, rules and regulations governing the conduct of its business; its list of members and subscribers; and the name and address of the resident of this State designated by it upon whom notices or orders of the commissioner or process affecting such organizations may be served.

No such advisory organization shall engage in any unfair or unreasonable practice with respect to its activities.

Ref.: Herlick Handbook § 3.10.

§11753.1. Appeal of decision, action, or omission of rating organization by aggrieved party; hearing by commissioner; notice to employer of change in classification assignment; request for reconsideration by employer.

(a) Any person aggrieved by any decision, action, or omission to act of a rating organization may request that the rating organization reconsider the decision, action, or omission. If the request for reconsideration is rejected or is not acted upon within 30 days by the rating organization, the person requesting reconsideration may, within a reasonable time, appeal from the decision, action, or omission of the rating organization. The appeal shall be made to the commissioner by filing a written complaint and request for a hearing specifying the grounds relied upon. If the commissioner has information on the subject appealed from and believes that probable cause for the appeal does not exist or that the appeal is not made in good faith, the commissioner may deny the appeal without a hearing. The commissioner shall otherwise hold a hearing to consider and determine the matter presented by the appeal.

(b) Any insurer adopting a change in the classification assignment of an employer that results in an increased premium shall notify the employer in writing, or if the insurance was transacted through an insurance agent or broker, the insurer shall notify the agent or broker who shall notify the employer in writing of the change and the reasons for the change. Any employer receiving this notice shall have the right to request reconsideration and appeal the reclassification pursuant to this section. The notice required by this section shall inform the employer of his or her rights pursuant to this section. No notification shall be required when the change is a result of a regulation adopted by the Department of Insurance or other action by or under the authority of the commissioner.

An insurer shall provide written notification of the revised classification assignment to an employer within 30 days after adoption. **Leg.H.** 1994 ch. 501, 1995 ch. 91, 1997 ch. 517, 2002 ch. 873 (AB 1985).

Ref.: Hanna §§ 2.02[1][c], 2.02[2], 2.16; Herlick Handbook § 3.10.

§11753.2. Effective date of classification change resulting in a decreased premium.

(a) If a change in a classification assignment on a workers' compensation insurance policy is due to an erroneous classification and results in a decreased premium, the classification change shall become effective as of the inception date of a policy in effect on the date the revised classification assignment is published by an insurer or, if the classification is assigned by the designated rating organization, when the insurer and insured are notified in writing by the designated rating organization that the erroneous classification assignment is under review. The revised classification assignment shall be applied as of the inception date of a policy that expired no more than 12 months prior to the date the revised classification assignment was published or the insurer and insured were notified in writing by the designated rating organization that assigned the classification that the erroneous classification assignment was under review, provided that the erroneous classification assignment was applicable to that policy.

(b) If a change in a classification assignment on a workers' compensation insurance policy is due to an erroneous classification and results in an increased premium, the classification change shall become effective on the effective date of the erroneous classification assignment provided any of the following conditions occur:

(1) The revised classification assignment is published within three months of the effective date or publication date of the erroneous assignment.

(2) The insurer or, where applicable, the designated rating organization, was notified in writing within three months of the effective date or publication date of the erroneous classification assignment of a possible error.

(3) The designated rating organization notified the insurer in writing within three months of the effective date or publication date of the erroneous classification assignment that the erroneous classification assignment was under review.

If one or more of the conditions set forth in paragraphs (1), (2), and (3) do not occur, the revised classification assignment shall become effective as of the date it is published unless the publication date is less than three months prior to the expiration date of the outstanding policy, in which case the revised classification assignment shall become effective as of the inception date of the policy that replaced the outstanding policy.

(c) If a change in a classification assignment on a workers' compensation policy is due to an insured's change of operations, any resulting increase or decrease in premium shall become effective on the date of the change of operations.

(d) Any insurer that violates this section shall be subject to civil penalties in an amount of up to five thousand dollars ($5,000) per violation. **Leg.H.** 1994 ch. 501, 1995 ch. 375.

Ref.: Hanna §§ 2.02[1][c], 2.16; Herlick Handbook § 3.10.

§11753.3. Workers' compensation insurance rating organization's exemption and authority.

Notwithstanding Section 1851.1, a workers' compensation insurance rating organization licensed pursuant to the provisions of this article which does not make rates, rating plans or rating systems for insurance covering employers against their liability for compensation or damages under the United States Longshoremen's and Harbor Workers' Compensation Act (33 U.S.C. 901, et seq.) shall not be required to be licensed as a rating organization or registered as an advisory organization pursuant to the provisions of Chapter 9 (commencing with Section 1850) of Part 2 of Division 1, and shall have authority under its license as a workers' compensation insurance rating organization issued pursuant to this article to:

(a) Collect and tabulate loss and expense experience statistics and other information and data relating to insurance covering employers against their liability for compensation under the United States Longshoremen's and Harbor Workers' Compensation Act.

(b) Furnish or exchange such information and experience data to or with rating organizations, advisory organizations and insurers in this and other states.

(c) Adopt and enforce compliance by its insurer members with reasonable rules and statistical plans to be used in the recording and reporting by insurer members of their California longshoremen and harbor workers' insurance loss and expense experience in order that such experience of all of its insurer members shall be available in such form and detail as will be of aid to the commissioner in the enforcement of and to its insurer members in complying with the provisions of Chapter 9 (commencing with Section 1850) of Part 2 of Division 1.

(d) Engage in the same activities and carry out the same functions with respect to insurance covering the liability of employers for compensation or damages under the United States Longshoremen's and Harbor Workers' Compensation Act that it is authorized to engage in or carry out with respect to California workers' compensation insurance generally under the provisions of this article other than the making of rates, rating plans and rating systems.

Ref.: Herlick Handbook § 3.10.

§11754. Noncompliance.

If the commissioner has good cause to believe that a rating or advisory organization or an insurer does not comply with the requirements of this article applicable to it, he shall, unless he has good cause to believe that such noncompliance is wilful, give notice in writing to such organization or insurer, stating therein in what manner and to what extent such noncompliance is alleged to exist and specifying therein a reasonable time, not less than 10 days thereafter, in which such noncompliance may be corrected. Notices under this section shall be confidential as between the commissioner and the organization or insurer unless a hearing is held under Section 11754.1.

Ref.: Herlick Handbook § 3.10.

§11754.1. Wilful or uncorrected noncompliance.

If the commissioner has good cause to believe such noncompliance to be wilful, or if within the period prescribed by the commissioner in the notice required by Section 11754 the organization or insurer does not make such change as may be necessary to correct the noncompliance specified by the commissioner or establish to the satisfaction of the commissioner that such noncompliance does not exist, then the commissioner may hold a public hearing in connection therewith, provided that within a reasonable period of time, which shall not be less than 10 days before the date of such hearing, he shall mail written notice specifying the matters to be considered at such hearing to such organization or insurer. Such notice shall conform to the requirements for an accusation as prescribed by Section 11503 of the Government Code. If no notice has been given as provided in Section

11754 such notice shall state therein in what manner and to what extent noncompliance is alleged to exist. The hearing shall not include any additional subjects not specified in the notices required by Section 11754 or this section.

Ref.: Herlick Handbook § 3.10.

§11754.2. Ordering compliance; suspension or revocation of license.

If, after a hearing pursuant to Section 11754.1, the commissioner finds:

(a) That any rating or advisory organization or other organization authorized by this article or any insurer has violated the provisions of this article applicable to it, he may issue an order to such organization or insurer which has been the subject of the hearing, specifying in what respect such violation exists and stating when, within a reasonable period of time, the violation shall cease.

(b) That any conditions prerequisite to the granting of a license to a rating organization no longer exists, he may issue an order to such organization which has been the subject of the hearing specifying the condition which has ceased to exist and stating when within a reasonable time the condition shall be complied with. If the condition is not complied with within the time specified the commissioner may suspend or revoke the license of such organization, in addition to any other penalty provided in this article.

(c) That any rating organization has wilfully engaged in any fraudulent, dishonest act or practice, he may suspend or revoke the license of such organization, in addition to any other penalty provided for in this article.

Ref.: Herlick Handbook § 3.10.

§11754.3. Suspension or revocation for noncompliance within time limits.

In addition to other penalties provided in this code the commissioner may suspend or revoke the license of any rating organization or insurer which fails to comply within the time limited by such order or extension thereof which the commissioner may grant, with an order of the commissioner lawfully made by him pursuant to Section 11754.1 and effective pursuant to Section 11754.5.

Ref.: Herlick Handbook § 3.10.

§11754.4. Procedures for denial, suspension, or revocation of license.

Except as otherwise provided in this article, all proceedings in connection with the denial, suspension or revocation of a license of a rating organization or insurer under this article shall be conducted in accordance with the provisions of Chapter 5 of Part 1 of Division 3 of Title 2 of the Government Code and the commissioner shall have all the powers granted to him therein.

Ref.: Herlick Handbook § 3.10.

§11754.5. Court review of commissioner's rulings.

Any finding, determination, rule, ruling, or order made by the commissioner under this article or Article 2 (commencing with Section 11730) shall be subject to review by the courts of the state pursuant to Section 1094.5 of the Code of Civil Procedure. **Leg.H.** 1995 ch. 582.

Ref.: Hanna § 2.02[2]; Herlick Handbook § 3.10.

§11755. False or misleading information; refusal to allow examination.

No person, insurer, rating or advisory organization shall willfully withhold information from, or knowingly give false or misleading information to, the commissioner or to any rating organization, which will affect the rates, rating systems or premiums for workers' compensation insurance and employer's liability insurance incidental thereto and written in connection therewith.

In the event of the refusal by any insured employer to permit an audit or an examination provided for in subdivision (f) of Section 11750.3, the commissioner shall, upon the verified petition of the rating organization concerned, take such action as the commissioner may be authorized to take pursuant to and subject to the provisions of this code and of the Government Code.

Ref.: Hanna § 2.02[2]; Herlick Handbook § 3.10.

§11756. Penalties for noncompliance with final order.

(a) Any person, insurer, or organization, who fails to comply with a final order of the commissioner under this article shall be liable to the State in an amount not exceeding fifty dollars ($50), but if the failure is wilful, he, she, or it shall be liable to the state in an amount not exceeding five thousand dollars ($5,000) for the failure. The commissioner shall collect the amount so payable and may bring an action in the name of the people of the state of California to enforce collection. These penalties may be in addition to any other penalties provided by law.

(b) A willful violation of the provisions of this article by any person is a misdemeanor.

Ref.: Herlick Handbook § 3.10.

§11757. Dividends, savings, or unabsorbed premium deposits.

Nothing in this article shall be construed to prohibit or regulate the payment of dividends, savings or unabsorbed premium deposits allowed or returned by insurers to their policyholders, members or subscribers. A plan for the payment of dividends, savings or unabsorbed premium deposits allowed or returned by insurers to their policyholders, members or subscribers shall not be deemed a rating plan or system.

Ref.: Hanna § 2.43; Herlick Handbook § 3.10.

§11758. Violation of other state laws.

No act done, action taken or agreement made pursuant to the authority conferred by this article shall constitute a violation of or grounds for prosecution or civil proceedings under any other law of this State heretofore or hereafter enacted which does not specifically refer to insurance.

Ref.: Hanna § 2.70[2]; Herlick Handbook §§ 3.10, 12.13; W. Cal. Sum., 5 "Torts" §222.

§11758.1. Exemption for household employees.

The provisions of this article shall not apply to the workers' compensation insurance covering those persons defined as employees by subdivision (d) of Section 3351 of the Labor Code.

Ref.: Herlick Handbook § 3.10.

§11759. Rating organizations' and personnel's exemption from liability.

The Legislature hereby finds and declares as follows: The Legislature pursuant to its plenary power over workers' compensation granted by Section 4 of Article XIV of the California Constitution has authorized classification of risks and premium rates and systems of merit rating for workers' compensation insurance. The selective and discretionary inspection of locations, plants and operations of employers for classification and rating purposes, the gathering and compiling of experience statistics and other data by rating organizations licensed by the Insurance Commissioner, and the application of standards predicated upon the reliability of such classifications and merit rating data are essential to the proper functioning of the classifications of risks and premium rates and systems of merit rating which are regulated by the Insurance Commissioner as authorized by the Legislature.

In order to implement and facilitate the proper and adequate administration of such classifications of risks and rates and systems of rating by such licensed rating organizations and the Insurance Commissioner, it is important and in the public interest that licensed rating organizations and their officers and employees shall not be liable for injury or death or other damage caused or alleged to have been caused by their failure to inspect, or negligent or incomplete inspection of, an employer's location, plant or operation for classification or rating purposes.

No licensed rating organization or member thereof in its character as a member, or officer or employee of such licensed rating organization when acting within the scope of his employment, shall be liable for injury or death or other damage proximately caused by a failure to inspect, or the manner or extent of inspection of, an employer's locations, plants or operations for classification or rating purposes, or by such person's comment, or failure to comment, on the subject matter or object of such inspection.

This section shall not be construed as implying the existence of liability in circumstances not defined in this section; nor as implying a legislative recognition that, except for the enactment of this section, a liability has existed or would exist in circumstances stated in this section.

Ref.: Herlick Handbook §§ 3.10, 12.13.

§11759.1. Rating organizations must make available report of prior year's losses and expenses.

A rating organization shall, no later than June 1 of each year, notify the Governor and the Legislature that a report containing an analysis of all losses and expenses for the prior year by all insurers who are members of the organization is available on request. The first report shall be due June 1, 1996. The report shall include, but not be limited to, the following:

(a) An analysis of all medical costs identifying separately the amounts paid for medical treatment to hospitals and physicians, and the amounts paid for medical-legal expenses. The amounts paid for medical treatment to physicians shall also identify the amounts paid for each specialty authorized to provide medical services pursuant to Sections 3209.3, 3209.5, and 3209.8 of the Labor Code. The amounts paid for medical-legal evaluations shall also be subcategorized by specialty and shall identify average costs paid per claim.

(b) An analysis of indemnity benefits paid for temporary disability, permanent total disability, permanent partial disability, life pensions, death benefits, and funeral expenses. The permanent partial disability benefits also shall be reported according to the degree of impairment in the following categories: .25 to 24.75 percent, 25 to 69.75 percent, and 70 to 99.75 percent.

(c) An analysis of amounts paid for vocational rehabilitation subcategorized by amounts paid for maintenance allowance, evaluation, education and training.

(d) An analysis of expenses of insurers categorized by loss adjustment, acquisition, general expenses, profit, and taxes. Amounts spent for defense attorneys' expense shall be separately identified.

(e) An analysis of attorney's fees paid to applicant attorneys.

(f) An analysis of workers' compensation costs by the type of injury or illness generally following the injury classification in the Annual Redesigned Occupational Safety and Health Statistical Program used by the Department of Industrial Relations in its annual report on California work injuries and illnesses. **Leg.H.** 1993 ch. 121, effective July 16, 1993, ch. 1242, 1995 ch. 556.

Ref.: Herlick Handbook § 3.10.

§11759.2. Report on underreported workers' compensation exposure in taxicab industry.

(a) A licensed rating organization designated as the Insurance Commissioner's statistical agent shall prepare a report to be submitted to the Insurance Commissioner by April 1, 2003, on the potential underreporting of workers' compensation exposure in the taxicab industry. The report shall include an analysis of workers' compensation exposure, loss, and premium in the taxicab industry. The licensed rating organization shall submit a report to the Governor, the Legislature, and the commissioner by May 1, 2003, that describes its findings.

(b) A licensed rating organization designated as the insurance commissioner's statistical agent may confer with state agencies, including, but not limited to, the Employment Development Department, in the preparation of the study. The state agencies shall provide all necessary statistical or other information requested by the licensed rating organization designated as the Insurance Commissioner's statistical agent. **Leg.H.** 2002 ch. 893 (SB 1407).

ARTICLE 4
Penalties for Misrepresentation

§11760. Penalties for misrepresentation to obtain reduced rate.

(a) It is unlawful to make or cause to be made any knowingly false or fraudulent statement, whether made orally or in writing, of any fact material to the determination of the premium, rate, or cost of any policy of workers' compensation insurance, for the purpose of reducing the premium, rate, or cost of the insurance. Any person convicted of violating this subdivision shall be punished by imprisonment in the county jail for one year, or in the state prison for two, three, or five years, or by a fine not exceeding fifty thousand dollars ($50,000), or double the value of the fraud, whichever is greater, or by both imprisonment and fine.

(b) Any person who violates subdivision (a) and who has a prior felony conviction of the offense set forth in that subdivision shall receive a two-year enhancement for each prior conviction in addition to the sentence provided in subdivision (a). The existence of any fact that would subject a person to a penalty enhancement shall be alleged in the information or indictment and either admitted by the defendant in open court, or found to be true by the jury trying the issue of guilt or by the court where guilt is established by plea of guilty or nolo contendere or by trial by the court sitting without a jury. **Leg.H.** 1991 chs. 116, 934, 1995 ch. 885.

Ref.: Hanna § 2.03[3], [4]; Herlick Handbook § 9.18.

§11760.1. Audit of employer; failure to provide access to records; costs.

(a) If an employer fails to provide for access by the insurer or its authorized representative to its records, to enable the insurer to perform an audit to determine the remuneration earned by the employer's employees and by any of its uninsured subcontractors and the employees of any of its uninsured subcontractors during the policy period, the employer shall be liable to pay to the insurer a total premium for the policy equal to three times the insurer's then-current estimate of the annual premium on the expiration date of the policy. The employer shall also be liable, in addition to the premium, for costs incurred by the insurer in its attempts to perform an audit, after the insured has failed upon the insurer's third request during at least a 90-day period to provide access, and the insured has provided no compelling business reason for the failure. This section shall only apply if the insurer elects to comply with the conditions set forth in subdivision (d).

(b) "Access" shall mean access at any time during regular business hours during the policy period and within three years after the policy period ends. "Access" may also include any other time mutually agreed upon by the employer and insurer.

(c) The insurer shall have and follow regular and reasonable rules and procedures to notify employers of their duty to provide for access to records, and to contact employers to make appointments during regular business hours for that purpose.

(d) Upon the employer's failure to provide access after the insurer's third request during at least a 90-day period, the insurer may notify the employer through its mailing of a certified, return-receipt, document of the increased premium and the total amount of the costs incurred by the insurer for its attempts to perform an audit as described under subdivision (a). Upon the expiration of 30 days after the delivery of the notice, collection by the insurer of the amount of premium and costs described under subdivision (a), less all premiums previously paid by the employer for the policy, shall be fully enforceable and executable.

(e) If the employer provides for access to its records after having received the notice described in subdivision (d), and if the insurer then succeeds in performing the audit to its satisfaction, the insurer shall revise the total premium and costs payable for the policy by the employer to reflect the results of its audit. **Leg.H.** 2007 ch. 615 (AB 812) §1.

ARTICLE 5
Standards Applicable to Claims Adjusters

§11761. Workers' compensation claims adjusters—Minimum standards of training, experience, and skill; certification to commissioner by specified entities that employees meet minimum standards.

(a) The commissioner shall adopt regulations setting forth the minimum standards of training, experience, and skill that workers' compensation claims adjusters must possess to perform their duties with regard to workers' compensation claims. The regulations adopted pursuant to this section shall, to the greatest extent possible, encourage the use of existing private and public education, training, and certification programs.

(b) Every insurer shall certify to the commissioner that the personnel employed by the insurer to adjust workers' compensation claims, or employed for that purpose by any medical billing entity with which the insurer contracts, meet the minimum standards adopted by the commissioner pursuant to subdivision (a).

(c) For the purposes of this section, "medical billing entity" means a third party that reviews or adjusts workers' compensation medical bills for insurers.

(d) For the purposes of this section, "insurer" means an insurer admitted to transact workers' compensation insurance in this state, the State Compensation Insurance Fund, an employer that has secured a certificate of consent to self-insure pursuant to subdivision (b) or (c) of Section 3700 of the Labor Code, or a third-party administrator that has secured a certificate of consent pursuant to Section 3702.1 of the Labor Code. **Leg.H.** 2003 ch. 637 (AB 1262).

Ref.: Hanna § 2.70[2]; Herlick Handbook § 3.15.

CHAPTER 4
THE STATE COMPENSATION INSURANCE FUND

ARTICLE 1
Organization and Powers

§11770. State Compensation Insurance Fund; board of directors.

(a) The State Compensation Insurance Fund is continued in existence, to be administered by its board of directors for the purpose of transacting workers' compensation insurance, and insurance against the expense of defending any suit for serious and willful misconduct, against an employer or his or her agent, and insurance to employees and other persons of the compensation fixed by the workers' compensation laws for employees and their dependents. Any appropriation made therefrom or thereto before the effective date of this code shall continue to be available for the purposes for which it was made.

(b)(1) The [1] **Board of Directors** of the State Compensation Insurance Fund is composed of [2] **11 members, nine** of whom shall be [3] appointed by the Governor. The Governor shall appoint the chairperson [4]**. One of the members appointed by the Governor shall be from organized labor. The members appointed by the Governor, other than the labor member, shall have substantial experience in positions involving workers' compensation, legal, investment, financial, corporate governance and management, accounting, or auditing responsibilities with entities of sufficient size as to make their qualifications relevant to an enterprise of the financial and operational size of the State Compensation Insurance Fund. At all times the board shall have a member with auditing background for the purposes of fulfilling the responsibility of the chair of the audit committee. A quorum is a majority of those appointed, provided that at no time shall a quorum be established with less than five members.**

(2) The Speaker of the Assembly shall appoint one member who shall represent organized labor, and the Senate Committee on Rules shall appoint one member who shall have been a policyholder of the State Compensation Insurance Fund, or an officer or employee of a policyholder, for one year immediately preceding the appointment, and must continue in this status during the period of his or her membership.

(3) The Director of Industrial Relations [5] shall be **an** ex officio, nonvoting [6] **member** of the board, and shall not be counted as members of the board for quorum purposes or any other purpose.

(4) Notwithstanding subdivision (c), the initial term of the members of the board added in the 2008 portion of the 2007–2008 Regular Session shall be as follows:

(A) One of the members appointed by the Governor shall serve an initial term of two years, one shall serve an initial term of four years, and two shall serve an initial term of five years.

(B) The member appointed by the Senate Committee on Rules shall serve an initial term of four years.

(C) The member appointed by the Speaker of the Assembly shall serve an initial term of three years.

(c) The term of office of the members of the board, other than that of the director, [7] shall be five years and they shall hold office until the appointment and qualification of their successors. [8]

(d)(1) Each member **of the board** shall receive his or her actual and necessary traveling expenses incurred in the performance of his or her [9] **duties** as a member and, with the exception of the ex officio members, one hundred dollars ($100) for each day of his or her actual attendance at meetings of the board. [10]

(2)(A) Each member of the board appointed pursuant to paragraphs (1) and (2) of subdivision (b) shall receive the compensation fixed pursuant to subparagraph (B).

(B) Each board member described in subparagraph (A) shall be paid an annual compensation of fifty thousand dollars ($50,000), to be automatically adjusted beginning January 1, 2010, by multiplying the compensation in effect the prior June 30 by the percentage of inflation that occurred during the previous year, adding this amount to the annual compensation from the previous year, and rounding off the result to the nearest dollar. "Percentage of inflation" means the percentage of inflation specified in the Consumer Price Index for All Urban Consumers, as published by the Department of Industrial

Relations, Division of Labor Statistics and Research, or its successor index.

(e) Each member of the board of directors shall attend training approved by the board of directors that covers topics, including, but not limited to, the duties and obligations of members of a board of directors, corporate governance, ethics, board of director legal issues, insurance, finance and investment, and information technology. The training shall be conducted by persons or entities not affiliated with the State Compensation Insurance Fund.

(f) No person who has had a direct or indirect interest in any transaction with the State Compensation Insurance Fund since the beginning of the last fiscal year of the fund, or who has a direct or indirect material interest in any proposed transaction with the fund, where the amount involved in the transaction exceeds one hundred twenty thousand dollars ($120,000) shall be eligible for appointment as a member of the board of directors of the fund. Once appointed, no member of the board of directors shall have a financial conflict of interest, as defined in Chapter 7 of Title 9 (commencing with Section 87100) of the Government Code. Every member shall be subject to Article 4 (commencing with Section 1090) of Chapter 1 of Division 4 of Title 1 of the Government Code, provided that the existence of a contract of insurance between the State Compensation Insurance Fund and the policyholder member appointed by the Senate Committee on Rules shall not constitute a conflict pursuant to this subdivision.

(g) The appointing authority of a member of the board may remove the member and make an appointment replacing the member for the duration of the term if the member ceases to discharge the duties of his or her office for the period of three consecutive board meetings.

(h) The board of the State Compensation Insurance Fund shall create, at a minimum, an audit committee, an investment committee, a corporate governance committee, and other committees as the board determines are necessary. **Leg.H.** 2002 ch. 6 (AB 749), 2008 ch. 322 (AB 1874) §3.

§11770. 2008 Deletes. **[1]** board of directors **[2]** five members, one **[3]** from organized labor, **[4]** who shall serve at the pleasure of the Governor **[5]** , the Speaker of the Assembly, and the President pro Tempore of the Senate, or their designees, **[6]** members **[7]** the Speaker of the Assembly, and the President pro Tempore of the Senate, **[8]** The term of office of the first additional member appointed pursuant to amendment of this section effective January 1, 1990, shall expire on January 15, 1995. Commencing January 15, 1991, the terms of office of other members shall be extended to five years as each four-year term expires, so that one member's term of office expires January 15 of each year. **[9]** duty **[10]** In order to qualify for membership on the board, each member other than the ex officio members shall have been a policyholder or the employee or member of a policyholder in the State Compensation Insurance Fund for one year immediately preceding the appointment, and must continue in this status during the period of his or her membership

Ref.: W. Cal. Sum., 2 "Workers' Compensation" §147, 3 "Agency and Employment" §314.

§11770.5. Enacted 1967. Repealed 2008 ch. 344 (SB 1145) §4, effective September 26, 2008.

§11771. State's limited liability.

The State shall not be liable beyond the assets of the State Compensation Insurance Fund for any obligations in connection therewith.

Ref.: Hanna § 1.20[4].

§11771.5. Advertising disclaimer.

Any advertising of the State Compensation Insurance Fund shall include the following disclaimer: "The State Compensation Insurance Fund is not a branch of the State of California." **Leg.H.** 2002 ch. 6 (AB 749).

§11772. Directors' and personnel's limited liability.

There shall not be any liability in a private capacity on the part of the board of directors or any member thereof, or any officer or employee of the fund for or on account of any act performed or obligation entered into in an official capacity, when done in good faith, without intent to defraud and in connection with the administration, management or conduct of the fund or affairs relating thereto.

Ref.: Hanna § 1.20[4].

§11773. Organization as public enterprise fund.

The fund shall be organized as a public enterprise fund.

Ref.: Hanna § 1.20[1].

§11774. Use of fund assets.

The assets of the fund shall be applicable to the payment of losses sustained on account of insurance and to the payment of the salaries and other expenses charged against it in accordance with the provisions of this chapter.

Ref.: Hanna §§ 1.20[1], 2.30[1].

§11775. Competitiveness with other insurers.

The fund shall, after a reasonable time during which it may establish a business, be fairly competitive with other insurers, and it is the intent of the Legislature that the fund shall ultimately become neither more nor less than self-supporting. For that purpose loss experience and expense shall be ascertained and dividends or credits may be made as provided in this article.

Ref.: Hanna §§ 1.20[1], 2.30[1].

§11776. Annual accountings; possible dividends and credits.

The actual loss experience and expense of the fund shall be ascertained on or about the first of January in each year for the year preceding. If it is then shown that there exists an excess of assets over liabilities, necessary reserves, and a reasonable surplus for the catastrophe hazard, then a cash dividend may be declared to, or a credit allowed on the renewal premium of each employer who has been insured with the fund.

Ref.: Hanna §§ 1.20[5], 2.30[1]; Herlick Handbook § 3.2.

§11777. Amount of dividends or credits.

Such cash dividend or credit is to be an amount which the board of directors in its discretion considers to be the employer's proportion of divisible surplus.

Ref.: Hanna §§ 1.20[5], 2.30[1]; Herlick Handbook § 3.2.

§11778. Ability to transact workers' compensation insurance.

The fund may transact workers' compensation insurance required or authorized by law of this state to the same extent as any other insurer. The fund shall be subject to the powers and authority of the commissioner to the same extent as any other insurer transacting workers' compensation insurance, except where specifically exempted by reference. For purposes of Section 700, the fund shall be deemed admitted to transact this class of insurance. **Leg.H.** 1981 ch. 714 §305, 2006 ch. 740 (AB 2125) §13.1.

Ref.: Hanna §§ 1.20[1], [2], 2.30[1].

§11779. Ability to insure under federal or maritime laws.

The fund may insure California employers against their liability for compensation or damages for injury or death under the United States Longshoremen's and Harbor Workers' Compensation Act, or other federal or maritime laws, as fully as any private insurer.

Ref.: Hanna §§ 1.20[2], 2.30[1]; Herlick Handbook § 13.2.

§11780. Ability to insure under state law.

The fund may also insure an employer against his or her liability for damages under the laws of the State of California arising out of bodily injury to or death of the employer's employees occurring within the State of California if the fund also issues workers' compensation insurance to the employer as to his or her employees.

Ref.: Hanna §§ 1.20[2], 2.30[1].

§11780.5. Ability to insure employees temporarily out of California.

The fund may also insure a California employer against his liability for workers' compensation benefits, under the law of any other state, for California employees temporarily working outside of California on a specific assignment if the fund insures the employer's other employees who work within California.

Ref.: Hanna §§ 1.20[2], 2.30[1]; Herlick Handbook § 13.2; W. Cal. Sum., 2 "Workers' Compensation" §147.

§11781. Board of directors' powers.

The board of directors is hereby vested with full power, authority and jurisdiction over the State Compensation Insurance Fund. The board of directors may perform all acts necessary or convenient in the exercise of any power, authority or jurisdiction over the fund, either in the administration thereof or in connection with the insurance business to be carried on by it under the provisions of this chapter, as fully and completely as the governing body of a private insurance carrier. The principal office for the transaction of the business of the State Compensation Insurance Fund is located in the City and County of San Francisco.

Ref.: Hanna §§ 1.20[1], [3], 2.30[1].

§11781.5. Authority to acquire property in Los Angeles.

The State Compensation Insurance Fund may acquire and own real property for a branch office in the City of Los Angeles when so determined by the board of directors, and may, if necessary, construct suitable buildings thereon in accordance with law.

Ref.: Hanna § 2.30[1].

§11782. Business name.

All business and affairs of the fund shall be conducted in the name of the State Compensation Insurance Fund, and in that name, without any other name or title, the board of directors may perform the acts authorized by this chapter.

Ref.: Hanna § 2.30[1].

§11783. Powers of fund.

The State Compensation Insurance Fund may:

(a) Sue and be sued in all actions arising out of any act or omission in connection with its business or affairs.

(b) Enter into any contracts or obligations relating to the State Compensation Insurance Fund which are authorized or permitted by law.

(c) Invest and reinvest the moneys belonging to the fund as provided by this chapter.

(d) Conduct all business and affairs and perform all acts relating to the fund whether or not specifically designated in this chapter.

(e) Commission an independent study, with the assistance of an investment banking firm, to determine the feasibility of the State Compensation Insurance Fund issuing bonds or securities. The study may include, among other things, the purpose for issuing bonds and any potential adverse consequences that may arise from that issuance. **Leg.H.** 2002 ch. 6 (AB 749).

§11784. Powers of fund president.

In conducting the business and affairs of the fund, the president of the fund may do any of the following:

(a) Enter into contracts of workers' compensation insurance.

(b) Sell annuities covering compensation benefits.

(c) Decline to insure any risk in which the minimum requirements of the industrial accident prevention authorities with regard to construction, equipment, and operation are not complied with, or which is beyond the safe carrying of the fund. Otherwise, he or she shall not refuse to insure any workers' compensation risk under state law, tendered with the premium therefor.

(d) Reinsure any risk or any part thereof.

(e) Cause to be inspected and audited the payrolls of employers applying to the fund for insurance.

(f) Make rules for the settlement of claims against the fund and determine to whom and through whom the payments of compensation are to be made.

(g) Contract with physicians and surgeons, and hospitals, for medical and surgical treatment and the care and nursing of injured persons entitled to benefits from the fund. **Leg.H.** 2001 ch. 159, 2002 ch. 6 (AB 749).

§11785. Appointment of officers to fund; applicability of Government Code and Public Contract Code provisions.

(a) The board of directors shall appoint a president [1], **a chief financial officer, a chief operating officer, a chief information technology officer, a chief investment officer, a chief risk officer, and a general counsel. The board of directors shall set the salary for each position. These positions shall not be subject to otherwise applicable provisions of the Government Code and the Public Contract Code, and for those purposes the fund shall not be considered a state agency or other public entity**. The president shall manage and conduct the business and affairs of the fund under the general direction and subject to the approval of the board of directors, and shall perform other duties as the board of directors prescribes.

(b) Section 87406 of the Government Code, the Milton Marks Postgovernment Employment Restrictions Act of 1990, shall apply to the fund. Members of the board, the president, the chief financial officer, the chief operating officer, the general counsel, and any other person designated by the fund shall

be deemed to be designated employees for the purpose of that act.

(c) Both the Bagley-Keene Open Meeting Act (Article 9 (commencing with Section 11120) of Chapter 1 of Part 1 of Division 3 of Title 2 of the Government Code) and the California Public Records Act (Chapter 3.5 (commencing with Section 6250) of Division 7 of Title 1 of the Government Code) shall apply to the fund. **Leg.H.** 2002 ch. 6 (AB 749), 2008 ch. 344 (SB 1145) §5, effective September 26, 2008.

§11785. 2008 Deletes. [1] of the fund and fix his or her salary

§11786. President's bond and oath.

Before entering on the duties of his or her office, the president shall qualify by giving an official bond approved by the board of directors in the sum of fifty thousand dollars ($50,000) and by taking and subscribing to an official oath. The approval of the board shall be by written endorsement on the bond. The bond shall be filed in the office of the Secretary of State. **Leg.H.** 2001 ch. 159, 2002 ch. 6 (AB 749).

§11787. Board's delegation of authority to president.

The board of directors may delegate to the president of the fund, under those rules and regulations and subject to those conditions as it from time to time prescribes, any power, function, or duty conferred by law on the board of directors in connection with the fund or in connection with the administration, management, and conduct of the business and affairs of the fund. The president may exercise those powers and functions and perform those duties with the same force and effect as the board of directors, but subject to its approval. **Leg.H.** 2001 ch. 159, 2002 ch. 6 (AB 749).

§11788. State Treasurer as custodian of fund's securities.

The State Treasurer shall be custodian of all securities belonging to the State Compensation Insurance Fund, except as otherwise provided in this chapter. He shall be liable on his official bond for the safekeeping thereof.

§11790. Delivery of securities to State Treasurer.

All securities belonging to the fund shall be delivered to the State Treasurer and held by him until otherwise disposed of as provided in this chapter. Upon delivery of such securities into the custody of the State Treasurer, such securities shall be credited by the State Treasurer to the fund.

§11793. Exemption for fund's expenditures.

Expenditures made by the State Compensation Insurance Fund are exempted from the provisions of Part 3 (commencing with Section 900) of Division 3.6 of Title I of the Government Code.

§11797. Investment of excess moneys.

The board of directors shall cause all moneys in the State Compensation Insurance Fund which are in excess of current requirements to be invested and reinvested, from time to time, in the same manner as provided for private insurance carriers pursuant to Article 3 (commencing with Section 1170) of Chapter 2 of Part 2 of Division 1.

§11800. Deposit of excess moneys.

All moneys in the State Compensation Insurance Fund, in excess of current requirements and not otherwise invested, may be deposited by the board of directors from time to time in financial institutions authorized by law to receive deposits of public moneys.

§11800.1. Fund account in State Treasury.

The board of directors may, with the approval of the State Treasurer, authorize the establishment of an account or fund in the State Treasury in the name of the State Compensation Insurance Fund, but such moneys deposited with the State Treasurer are not state moneys within the intent of Section 16305.2 of the Government Code.

§11800.2. Special ledger account by State Controller.

The State Controller shall keep a special ledger account pertaining to the State Compensation Insurance Fund. In the State Controller's general ledger this account may appear as a cash account, like other accounts of funds in the State Treasury, and only the actual cash credited or deposited to the credit of the State Compensation Insurance Fund shall be entered in the account.

§11801. Prohibition on use of certain assets to satisfy federal claims.

The assets, premiums, reserves, investment income, and any and all property of whatsoever kind derived or acquired by the fund from its transaction of its workers' compensation insurance business shall not be used, attached or levied upon in any manner whatsoever by any person to satisfy claims or any other obligations or liability incurred, arising out of, or related to, the fund's transaction of insurance pursuant to the United States Longshoremen's and Harbor Workers' Compensation Act.

Ref.: Hanna § 1.20[2].

§11802. Separate accounts for funds acquired for federal claims.

All premiums, reserves, investment income, and all property of whatsoever kind derived or acquired by the fund from its transaction of insurance pursuant to the United States Longshoremen's and Harbor Workers' Compensation Act shall be maintained and identified in separate accounts and records.

Ref.: Hanna § 1.20[2].

§11803. Federal claims and costs to be paid from separate account.

All claims, costs of doing business, liabilities, expenses, and obligations arising out of or related to the fund's transaction of insurance pursuant to the United States Longshoremen's and Harbor Workers' Compensation Act shall be paid and charged to the income of whatsoever nature derived from its United States Longshoremen's and Harbor Workers' Compensation Act insurance business only.

Ref.: Hanna § 1.20[2].

§11804. Charges for insurance classes' use of facilities, supplies, or equipment.

Joint or shared use of office building space, whether owned, leased or rented, and the joint use of all furniture, automobiles, office equipment, supplies and services shall be charged to each class of insurance business on an equitable and proportional basis.

§11805. Annual report to Legislature.

The State Compensation Insurance Fund shall report annually to the Legislature as soon after the close of the calendar year as is feasible, with respect to its experience handling United States longshoremen's and harbor workers' insurance pursuant to this chapter, including, but not limited to, a statement of resources and liabilities at the close of each annual period commencing December 31, 1979.

Ref.: Hanna § 1.20[2].

ARTICLE 2
Rates

§11820. Rates.

Subject to the provisions of Article 2 (commencing with Section 11730) of Chapter 3, the board of directors shall establish the rates to be charged by the State Compensation Insurance Fund for insurance issued by it. These rates shall be fixed with due regard to the physical hazards of each industry, occupation, or employment. **Leg.H.** 2002 ch. 6 (AB 749).

§11821. Factors considered in setting rates.

Within each class of business insured such rates shall be fixed, so far as practicable, in accordance with the following elements:

(a) Bodily risk or safety, or other hazard of the plant, premises or work of each insured employer.

(b) The manner in which the work is conducted.

(c) A reasonable regard for the accident experience and history of each such insured.

(d) A reasonable regard for the insured's means and methods of caring for injured persons.

Such rates shall take no account of the extent to which the employees in any particular establishment have or have not persons dependent upon them for support.

§11822. Percentage basis of rates.

The rates fixed by the board of directors shall be that percentage of the payroll of any employer which, in the long run and on the average, will produce a sufficient sum, when invested in a way as to realize the maximum return consistent with safe and prudent management practices:

(a) To carry all claims to maturity. The rates shall be based upon the "reserve" and not upon the "assessment" plan.

(b) To meet the reasonable expenses of conducting the business of the fund.

(c) To produce a reasonable surplus to cover the catastrophe hazard. **Leg.H.** 2002 ch. 6 (AB 749).

ARTICLE 3
Policies

§11840. Insurance contracts and policies.

The insurance contracts or policies of the State Compensation Insurance Fund may be either limited or unlimited. The insurance contracts or policies may be issued for like periods as are allowed by law to other workers' compensation insurers or, in the form of stamps or tickets or otherwise, for one month, for any number of months less than one year, for one day, for any number of days less than one month or during the performance of any particular work, job or contract. The rates charged shall be proportionately greater for a shorter than for a longer period and a minimum premium charge shall be fixed in accordance with a reasonable rate for insuring one person for one day.

§11841. Chapter's limitations on temporary coverage and policy surrender.

Nothing in this chapter shall prevent:

(a) Any applicant for insurance from being covered temporarily until the application is finally acted upon.

(b) An insured from surrendering any policy at any time and having returned to him the difference between the premium paid and the premium at the customary short term for the shorter period which such policy has already run.

§11843. Policies for employers and families.

The State Compensation Insurance Fund may issue policies including, with their employees, employers who perform labor incidental to their occupations, and including also members of the families of such employers engaged in the same occupation.

Ref.: Hanna § 1.20[2]; Herlick Handbook § 3.2.

§11844. Same compensation and rates for employers and employees.

Such policies covering employers shall insure to such employers and working members of their families the same compensations provided for their employees, and at the same rates.

Ref.: Hanna § 1.20[2]; Herlick Handbook § 3.2.

§11845. Estimates of employers' wage values.

The estimations of the wage values, respectively, of such insured employers and members of their families shall be reasonable and shall be separately stated in and added to the valuation of the pay rolls upon which their premium is computed.

Ref.: Herlick Handbook § 3.2.

§11846. Policies for self-employed persons and casual employees.

The policies may likewise be sold to self-employing persons and to casual employees. The insureds, for the purpose of the insurance, shall be deemed to be employees within the meaning of the workers' compensation laws.

Ref.: Hanna §§ 1.20[2], 2.10[4], 3.144; Herlick Handbook § 3.2.

ARTICLE 4
Reports and Statements

§11860. Quarterly report to Governor; annual audit publication; reports to commissioner.

Each quarter the president of the State Compensation Insurance Fund shall make a report to the Governor of the business done by the State Compensation Insurance Fund during the previous quarter and a statement of the fund's resources and liabilities at the close of that previous quarter. The State Compensation Insurance Fund shall, at its own expense, hire a recognized firm of certified public accountants to audit annually the books and records of the State Compensation Insurance Fund and cause an abstract summary thereof to be published one or more times in at least two newspapers of general circulation in the state. The president of the fund shall additionally provide the commissioner with all reports required by law to be made to him or her by other insurers. **Leg.H.** 2002 ch. 6 (AB 749).

ARTICLE 5
Coverage of Public Employers

§11870. Potential insurers; premiums.

The state, any agency, department, division, commission, board, bureau, officer or other authority thereof, and each county, city and county, city, school district, irrigation district, any other district established by law, or other public corporation or quasi public corporation within the state, including any public utility operated by a private corporation may insure against its liability for compensation with the State Compensation Insurance Fund. Where the state or any agency, department, division, commission, board, bureau, officer or authority thereof is the insured, the premium for that insurance shall be a proper charge against any moneys appropriated for the support of or expenditure by the insured, except that in the case of an insured supported by or authorized to expend moneys appropriated out of more than one fund, the insured, with the approval of the Director of Finance, may determine the proportion of the premium to be paid out of each fund. In that case the insured, with the approval of the Director of Finance, may pay the entire premium out of any of those funds and thereafter the funds used for payment shall be reimbursed in proper proportion out of the other funds. In case a county, city and county, city, school district, irrigation district, or other district established by law, or other public corporation or quasi public corporation within the state is the insured, the premium therefor shall be a proper charge against the general fund of the insured. **Leg.H.** 1994 ch. 373.

Ref.: Hanna §§ 2.10[4], 3.111; Herlick Handbook § 3.21.

§11871. Master agreement with Department of Personnel Administration.

The State Compensation Insurance Fund may enter into a master agreement with the Department of Personnel Administration to render services in the adjustment and disposition of claims for workers' compensation to any state agencies, including any officer, department, division, bureau, commission, board or authority, not insured with the fund.

The master agreement shall provide for rendition of services at a uniform rate to all agencies, except that the rate for the California Highway Patrol may be fixed independently of the uniform rate.

The fund may, in accordance with the agreement, adjust and dispose of claims for workers' compensation made by an officer or employee of any state agency not insured with the fund.

The fund may make all expenditures, including payment to claimants for medical care or for adjustment or settlement of claims, necessary to the adjustment and final disposition of claims. The agreement shall provide that the state agency whose officer or employee is a claimant shall reimburse the fund for the expenditures and for the actual cost of services rendered.

The fund may in its own name, or in the name of the state agency for which the services are performed, do any and all things necessary to recover on behalf of the state agency for which it renders service any and all amounts which an employer might recover from third persons under Chapter 5 (commencing with Section 3850) of Part 1 of Division 4 of the Labor Code, or which an insurer might recover pursuant to Section 11662 including the right to commence and prosecute actions, to file, pursuant to Chapter 5 (commencing with Section 3850) of Part 1 of Division 4 of the Labor Code, liens for whatever sums would be recoverable by suit against a third person, to intervene in other court proceedings, and to compromise claims and actions before or after commencement of suit or after entry of judgment when in the opinion of the fund full collection cannot be enforced.

Ref.: Hanna § 11.41; Herlick Handbook § 3.21.

§11872. Annual agreements with state agencies.

The fund may annually enter into agreements with state agencies for service to be rendered to the fund. These state agencies include, but shall not be limited to: the Department of Finance, Department of General Services, State Personnel Board, and the Public Employees' Retirement System. If these agencies and the fund cannot agree upon the cost of services provided by the agreements, the California Victim Compensation and Government Claims Board shall be requested to arrive at an equitable settlement.

Leg.H. 1979 ch. 738 §14, 2006 ch. 538 (SB 1852) §472.

Ref.: Herlick Handbook § 3.21.

§11873. Laws applicable to fund.

(a) Except as provided by subdivision (b), the fund shall not be subject to the provisions of the Government Code made applicable to state agencies generally or collectively, unless the section specifically names the fund as an agency to which the provision applies.

(b) The fund shall be subject to the provisions of Chapter 10.3 (commencing with Section 3512) of Division 4 of Title 1 of, [1] **Chapter 3.5 (commencing with Section 6250) of Division 7 of Title 1 of,** Chapter 6.5 (commencing with Section 8543) of Division 1 of Title 2 of, **Article 9 (commencing with Section 11120) of Chapter 1 of Part 1 of Division 3 of Title 2 of,** the Government Code, and Division 5 (commencing with Section 18000) of Title 2 of the Government Code, with the exception of all of the following provisions of that division:

(1) Article 1 (commencing with Section 19820) and Article 2 (commencing with Section 19823) of Chapter 2 of Part 2.6 of Division 5.

(2) Sections 19849.2, 19849.3, 19849.4, and 19849.5.

(3) Chapter 4.5 (commencing with Section 19993.1) of Part 2.6 of Division 5.

(c) Notwithstanding any provision of the Government Code or any other provision of law, the positions funded by the State Compensation Insurance Fund are exempt from any hiring freezes and staff cutbacks otherwise required by law. This subdivision is declaratory of existing law. **Leg.H.** 2003 ch. 635 (AB 227), 2006 ch. 452 (SB 1452) §6, 2008 ch. 344 (SB 1145) §6, effective September 26, 2008.

§11873. 2008 Deletes. [1] and

Ref.: Hanna § 1.20[1], [4]; W. Cal. Sum., 2 "Workers' Compensation" §147, 5 "Torts" §222.

§11874. Treasurer's payment of warrant.

On the effective date of this act the Controller shall draw his warrant in favor of the State Compensation Insurance Fund for the total amount of the funds in the custody of the Treasurer belonging to the State Compensation Insurance Fund and the Treasurer shall pay such warrant.

ARTICLE 6
Penalties

§11880. Willful misrepresentation to obtain reduced rate—Punishment; enhancement for prior conviction.

(a) It is unlawful to make or cause to be made any knowingly false or fraudulent statement, whether made orally or in writing, of any fact material to the determination of the premium, rate, or cost of any policy of workers' compensation insurance issued or administered by the State Compensation Insurance Fund for the purpose of reducing the premium, rate, or cost of the insurance. Any person convicted of violating this subdivision shall be punished by imprisonment in the county jail for one year, or in the state prison for two, three, or five years, or by a fine not exceeding fifty thousand dollars ($50,000), or double the value of the fraud, whichever is greater, or by both imprisonment and fine.

(b) Any person who violates subdivision (a) and who has a prior felony conviction of the offense set forth in that subdivision shall receive a two-year enhancement for each prior conviction in addition to the sentence provided in subdivision (a). The existence of any fact that would subject a person to a penalty enhancement shall be alleged in the information or indictment and either admitted by the defendant in open court, or found to be true by the jury trying the issue of guilt or by the court where guilt is established by plea of guilty or nolo contendere or by trial by the court sitting without a jury. **Leg.H.** 1991 chs. 116, 934, 1995 ch. 885.

Ref.: Hanna §§ 2.03[3], 2.03[4]; Herlick Handbook § 9.18.

§11881. Other names for Board of Directors.

Whenever in Chapter 4, Part 3, Division 2 of the Insurance Code the term "State Industrial Accident Commission" or "Industrial Accident Commission" or "commission" or "director" or similar designation occurs, it means the Board of Directors of the State Compensation Insurance Fund except when such meaning is inconsistent with the intent and context of said chapter.

LABOR CODE
[Selected Provisions]

SYNOPSIS

GENERAL PROVISIONS
[Selected Provisions]

DIVISION 1
DEPARTMENT OF INDUSTRIAL RELATIONS

CHAPTER 1
GENERAL POWERS AND DUTIES
[Selected Provisions]

CHAPTER 3
COMMISSION ON HEALTH AND SAFETY AND WORKERS' COMPENSATION

CHAPTER 4
DIVISION OF LABOR STANDARDS ENFORCEMENT
[Selected Provisions]

CHAPTER 5
DIVISION OF WORKERS' COMPENSATION

CHAPTER 6
OCCUPATIONAL SAFETY AND HEALTH STANDARDS BOARD

CHAPTER 6.5
OCCUPATIONAL SAFETY AND HEALTH APPEALS BOARD

Labor

DIVISION 2
EMPLOYMENT REGULATION AND SUPERVISION

PART 4
Employees

CHAPTER 1
WAGES, HOURS AND WORKING CONDITIONS

PART 7
Public Works and Public Agencies

CHAPTER 1
PUBLIC WORKS

ARTICLE 5
Securing Workers' Compensation

PART 9
Health

CHAPTER 1
SANITARY CONDITIONS

ARTICLE 5
General Health Provisions

PART 13
The Labor Code Private Attorneys General Act of 2004

DIVISION 3
EMPLOYMENT RELATIONS

CHAPTER 1
SCOPE OF DIVISION

CHAPTER 2
EMPLOYER AND EMPLOYEE

ARTICLE 1
The Contract of Employment
[Selected Provisions]

ARTICLE 2
Obligations of Employer
[Selected Provisions]

DIVISION 4 WORKERS' COMPENSATION AND INSURANCE

PART 1 Scope and Operation

CHAPTER 1 GENERAL PROVISIONS

Labor

CHAPTER 2
EMPLOYERS, EMPLOYEES, AND DEPENDENTS

ARTICLE 1
Employers

ARTICLE 2
Employees

community classroom, or student apprenticeship program by school, school district, or county superintendent; school, school district, or county superintendent as "employer"; exceptions; "registered student apprentice"; regional and joint supervision of program.

§3369. Effect of coverage by this division.

§3370. State penal or correctional institution inmates.

§3371. Attorney referral for inmates.

ARTICLE 3
Dependents

§3501. Presumption; minor's or incapacitated adult's dependence on deceased parent.

§3502. Factual determination of dependency.

§3503. Qualifications for dependency.

ARTICLE 4
Employee Notice

§3550. Posting of notice; failure to post; applicability; form and content of notice.

§3551. Written notice to new employee; contents.

§3553. Employee who is victim of workplace crime; provision of written notice to employee concerning workers' compensation eligibility; when employer must provide notice.

CHAPTER 3
CONDITIONS OF COMPENSATION LIABILITY

§3600. Conditions of compensation for employer liability.

§3600.1. State firefighters not acting under employer's immediate direction.

§3600.2. Peace officers not acting under employer's immediate direction.

§3600.3. Scope of employment; off-duty peace officers.

§3600.4. Local firefighters not acting under employer's immediate direction.

§3600.5. Out-of-state injury of resident; exemption; certificate of insurance for out-of-state employer.

§3600.6. Disaster service workers.

§3600.8. Participation in alternative commute program not acting within course of employment—Definitions; exceptions.

§3601. Employee's liability to another employee.

§3602. Employer's personal liability.

§3603. Discharge of claims.

§3604. Unavailable defense for public employers.

§3605. Injured minors; compensation.

CHAPTER 4
COMPENSATION INSURANCE AND SECURITY

ARTICLE 1
Insurance and Security

§3700. Employer's possible means of securing payment.

§3700.1. Definitions.

§3700.5. Penalty for failure to secure payment; enhancement for subsequent conviction; recovery of investigative costs.

§3701. Private self-insuring employer; surety.

§3701.3. Return of overpayments to self-insured employers.

§3701.5. Private self-insured employer; payment of obligations.

§3701.7. Special conditions to be met after period of unlawful uninsurance.

§3701.8. Alternative security system for securing aggregate liabilities of private, self-insured employers through the Self-Insurers' Security Fund.

§3702. Certificate of consent to self-insure; revocation.

§3702.1. Third-party administrators; certificate of consent.

§3702.2. Self-insurer's annual report; director's annual aggregated summary.

§3702.3. Failure to submit reports or information; fines; handling of funds.

§3702.5. Costs of administration of self-insured programs; fines for late filing; handling of funds.

§3702.6. Audit cycle for private self-insured employers; special audit of public self-insured employers.

§3702.7. Revocation of certificate of consent; fine in lieu of.

§3702.8. Obligations of former self-insured employers.

§3702.9. Director's order for compliance, restitution, and civil penalty.

ARTICLE 2
Uninsured Employers Fund

ARTICLE 2.5
Self-Insurers' Security Fund

ARTICLE 3
Insurance Rights and Privileges

ARTICLE 4
Construction Permit

ARTICLE 5
Workers' Compensation Misrepresentations

CHAPTER 5
SUBROGATION OF EMPLOYER

CHAPTER 7
MEDICAL EXAMINATIONS

ARTICLE 1
[In General]

ARTICLE 2
Determination of Medical Issues

CHAPTER 8
ELECTION TO BE SUBJECT TO COMPENSATION LIABILITY

CHAPTER 9
ECONOMIC OPPORTUNITY PROGRAMS

ARTICLE 1
General Provisions

ARTICLE 2
Benefits

ARTICLE 3
Adjustment of Claims

CHAPTER 10
DISASTER SERVICE WORKERS

CHAPTER 11
ASBESTOS WORKERS' ACCOUNT

ARTICLE 1
General Provisions

ARTICLE 2
Benefits

ARTICLE 3
Collections

PART 2
Computation of Compensation

CHAPTER 1
AVERAGE EARNINGS

CHAPTER 2
COMPENSATION SCHEDULES

ARTICLE 1
General Provisions

ARTICLE 2
Medical and Hospital Treatment

Labor

seeking to reimburse health care providers.

§4600.4. Availability during normal business day.

§4600.5. Application for certification as health care organization; application fee; certification requirements for health care service plan, disability insurer, workers' compensation insurer, third-party administrator, workers' compensation health care provider and other entities; claimant's medical treatment records; health care service plan charges; limitations and allowances of act; grounds for refusal, revocation or suspension of certification; provision and regulation of chiropractic care, acupuncture treatment; individual patient information.

§4600.6. Rules and procedures for certification as health care organization; application requirements; disclosure requirements; contracts with prospective purchasers; restrictions on advertisements; name of organization; licensing requirements for facilities, personnel, and equipment; scope of workers' compensation health care; grievance system; cause of action against organization; delegation of responsibility to subcommittees; periodic on-site medical survey by Administrative Director.

§4600.7. Workers' Compensation Managed Care Fund.

§4601. Employee request to change physician.

§4602. Employee request for certification of competency of consulting physicians.

§4603. Employer request for change of physician.

§4603.2. Notice to employer of selected physician; reports to employer; payment by employer; penalties and liabilities for late payment; review of itemization.

§4603.4. Regulatory authority for payment processing and confidentiality of medical information.

§4603.5. Adoption of rules; notice to employees of rights.

§4604. Jurisdiction of appeals board to settle disputes.

§4604.5. Medical treatment utilization schedule—Guidelines; rebuttable presumption on issue of extent and scope of medical treatment; limitations on chiropractic, occupational therapy, and physical therapy visits.

§4605. Consulting or attending physicians provided at employee's expense.

§4606. Public self-insured employer; 90-day limitation inapplicable.

§4607. Denial of petition to terminate benefits; attorney's fees.

§4608. Pharmacy benefits; form requirements.

§4609. Disclosure relating to health care provider's participation in network; disclosures by contracting agent conveying its list of contracted health care providers and reimbursement rates; election by provider to be excluded from list; demonstration by payor of entitlement to pay contracted rate.

§4610. Utilization review process to be established; administrative penalties for failure to meet certain requirements.

§4610.1. Increase in compensation under §5814—Inapplicable for unreasonable delay in medical treatment for periods of time necessary to complete utilization review process; exception.

§4611. Rights and obligations of health care provider contract governed by underlying contract between provider and contracting agent upon contracting agent's sale, lease, or transfer of contract to payor.

§4614. Payment for services.

§4614.1. Certified health care service plan permitted to accept payment from self-insured employers.

ARTICLE 2.3
Medical Provider Networks

§4616. Establishment of medical provider network; goal; requirements; regulations.

§4616.1. Economic profiling; filing of policies and procedures; disclosure to public.

§4616.2. Continuity of care policy; filing and approval; revisions; notice; completion of treatment by terminated provider; terms and conditions.

ARTICLE 2.5
Medical-Legal Expenses

ARTICLE 3
Disability Payments

ARTICLE 4
Death Benefits

ARTICLE 4.5
Public Official Death Benefits

ARTICLE 5
Subsequent Injuries Payments

ARTICLE 6
Special Payments to Certain Persons

law enforcement officers of University of California Police Department.

§4807. Appeals board to determine relationship of disability to duty.

§4808. Medical, surgical, and hospital benefits for University of California police officers.

§4809. University of California police officer's disability continuing beyond one year.

§4810. Prohibition on temporary disability payments concurrent with salary payments for University of California police officers.

§4816. California State University Police Department collective bargaining agreement for enhanced industrial disability leave.

§4817. Appeals board to determine relationship of disability to duty.

§4819. California State University police officer's disability continuing beyond one year.

§4820. Prohibition on temporary disability payments concurrent with salary payments for California State University police officers.

ARTICLE 7
City Police and Firemen, Sheriffs, and Others

§4850. Paid leave of absence for specified public employees.

§4850.3. Advanced disability pension payments—Local safety officer.

§4850.4. Advanced disability pension payments.

§4850.5. Benefits for firefighters, sheriff's and probation office employees, and other specified employees of San Luis Obispo County.

§4850.7. Firefighters' entitlement to benefits.

§4851. Request to make disability determinations.

§4852. Article's effect on medical, surgical, and hospital benefits.

§4853. Disability continuing beyond one year.

§4854. Prohibition on temporary disability payments concurrent with salary payments.

§4855. Non-applicability to reserve public safety employees.

§4856. Continued provision of health benefits to surviving spouse and dependents of deceased firefighter or peace officer; limitations.

PART 3
Compensation Claims

CHAPTER 1
PAYMENT AND ASSIGNMENT

§4900. Claim for compensation; assignment.

§4901. Effect of debts on claims.

§4902. Payment of claim directly to attorney or agent.

§4903. Determination of liens against compensation payable.

§4903.1. Determination of reimbursement for benefits paid or services provided.

§4903.2. Attorney's fee allowed from lien claimant's recovery.

§4903.3. Compensation provided from fund.

§4903.4. Disputes over liens for expenses.

§4903.5. Limitations period for filing lien claim.

§4903.6. Lien claim or application for adjudication; requirements for filing; exemptions.

§4904. Adjustment and disallowance of liens; liens on unemployment compensation benefits.

§4904.1. Lien does not affect payment of balance of award.

§4905. Determination when lien not duly requested.

§4906. Only reasonable legal and medical services claims valid.

§4907. Removal of privilege to represent party.

§4908. Compensation claim's equal preference over other debts.

§4909. Effect of employer's payment of benefits before settlement.

§4909.1. State fund may administer benefits.

CHAPTER 2
COMPROMISE AND RELEASE

§5000. Limitations of this division.

§5001. "Compensation"; validity of compromise and release.

§5002. Appeals board's power to enter award once copy of compromise and release filed.

§5003. Required information for compromise and release.

§5004. Additional required information

CHAPTER 3
LUMP SUM PAYMENTS

PART 3.5
Arbitration

PART 4
Compensation Proceedings

CHAPTER 1
JURISDICTION

CHAPTER 2
LIMITATIONS OF PROCEEDINGS

CHAPTER 2.3
WORKERS' COMPENSATION—TRUTH IN ADVERTISING

CHAPTER 2.5
ADMINISTRATIVE ASSISTANCE

CHAPTER 3
APPLICATIONS AND ANSWERS

CHAPTER 4
ATTACHMENTS

CHAPTER 5
HEARINGS

CHAPTER 6
FINDINGS AND AWARDS

CHAPTER 7
RECONSIDERATION AND JUDICIAL REVIEW

ARTICLE 1
Reconsideration

ARTICLE 2
Judicial Review

Labor

CHAPTER 2
EDUCATION AND RESEARCH
[Selected Provisions]

CHAPTER 2.5
HAZARDOUS SUBSTANCES INFORMATION AND TRAINING

ARTICLE 3
Hazardous Substances
[Selected Provisions]

ARTICLE 4
Duties

CHAPTER 3
RESPONSIBILITIES AND DUTIES OF EMPLOYERS AND EMPLOYEES

CHAPTER 4
PENALTIES

CHAPTER 5
TEMPORARY VARIANCES

CHAPTER 6
PERMIT REQUIREMENTS

CHAPTER 7
APPEAL PROCEEDINGS

CHAPTER 8
ENFORCEMENT OF CIVIL PENALTIES

§6652. Notice to Contractors' State License Board of civil penalty.

CHAPTER 9
MISCELLANEOUS SAFETY PROVISIONS

§6700. Gas pipelines; conclusive presumptions.
§6701. Internal combustion engines used within structures.
§6702. Exhaust purifier devices.
§6703. Exceptions to rules for internal combustion engines used within structures.
§6704. Boomstops for crawler and wheel cranes.
§6705. Restrictions on contracts involving trench excavations.
§6705.5. Application of shoring, bracing, and sloping regulations to swimming pool excavations found unsafe.
§6706. One permit per project; exceptions.
§6707. Bids for local government projects involving trenches or open excavations.
§6708. Adequate emergency first aid treatment; requirement.
§6710. Explosives.
§6711. Examination of persons using explosives for snow avalanche blasting.
§6712. Occupational safety and health standard for field sanitation.
§6716. "Lead-related construction work."
§6717. Standard that protects employees engaged in lead-related construction.
§6718. Restrictions on test procedures for vapor emission from vehicles transporting gasoline.
§6719. Concern over repetitive motion injuries.

PART 3
Safety on Buildings

CHAPTER 1
BUILDINGS UNDER CONSTRUCTION OR REPAIR

ARTICLE 1
Floors and Walls

§7100. "Building."
§7101. Protective flooring.
§7102. Protective flooring in concrete buildings.
§7103. Protective wooden flooring.
§7104. Supportive intermediate beams.
§7105. Replanking.
§7106. Building sections as "buildings."
§7107. Planked floors.
§7108. Safety belts and nets.
§7109. Working without required planking or nets.
§7110. Enforcement by Division.

ARTICLE 2
Scaffolding

§7150. "Scaffolding."
§7151. Suspended scaffolding.
§7152. Employers using scaffolding.
§7153. Scaffolding platforms or floors.
§7154.1. Prohibition of lean-to scaffolds.
§7155. Penalty for scaffolding requirement violations.
§7156. Employer violations and penalty.
§7157. Division's power regarding safety orders.
§7158. Enforcement by division.

ARTICLE 3
Construction Elevators

§7200. "Construction elevator" and "building."
§7201. Signals for construction elevators.
§7202. Employee to give signals.
§7203. Board's regulation of signals.
§7204. Inspection of construction elevators.
§7205. Penalties for violation.

ARTICLE 4
Structural Steel Framed Buildings

§7250. "Building."
§7251. Buildings affected.
§7252. Decking of derricks or working floors.
§7253. Temporary floor and safety belt protection.
§7254. Temporary floors.
§7255. Protection against temporary floor displacement.
§7256. Plank extension.
§7257. Covering openings by columns.
§7258. Metal decking instead of wood planking.
§7259. Replacement of floor planks.
§7260. Employee instruction before planking removed.
§7261. Removing temporary planking.
§7262. Protection while removing temporary planking.
§7263. Constantly maintaining structural frame's stability.

CHAPTER 2
ELEVATORS, ESCALATORS, PLATFORM AND STAIRWAY CHAIR LIFTS, DUMBWAITERS, MOVING WALKS, AUTOMATED PEOPLE MOVERS, AND OTHER CONVEYANCES

CHAPTER 3
SAFETY DEVICES UPON BUILDINGS TO SAFEGUARD WINDOW CLEANERS

CHAPTER 4
AERIAL PASSENGER TRAMWAYS

§7349. Inspectors; temporary permits.
§7350. Fees.
§7351. Payment of fees; temporary permit exception.
§7352. Disposition of fees.
§7353. Certification of construction and repair plans.
§7354. Certification.
§7354.5. Ski lift inspections.
§7355. Division's authority.
§7356. Report of tramway injury.
§7357. Qualification of tramway operators.

CHAPTER 5
CRANES

ARTICLE 1
Permits for Tower Cranes

§7370. Legislative declaration; priority of tower crane safety inspections.
§7371. Definitions.
§7372. Employment of safety inspectors; establishment of safety inspection program.
§7373. Issuance and validity of permits.
§7374. Suspension or revocation of permit.

ARTICLE 2
Certification
[Selected Provisions]

§7376. Suspension or revocation of license to certify crane safety.
§7377. Appeal of revocation of license.
§7378. Penalties for fraudulent certification.
§7379. Penalties for certifying without license.
§7380. Collection of fees.
§7381. Penalties for violation of safety standards if serious injury or death results; penalties for serious violations.
§7382. Presence of safety representative required while installing, dismantling, or "jumping" crane.

PART 6
Tanks and Boilers

CHAPTER 6
MISMANAGEMENT OF STEAM BOILERS

§7770. Penalty for undue quantity of steam endangering human life.
§7771. Imprisonment for causing death.

PART 7
Volatile Flammable Liquids
[Selected Provisions]

§7800. "Volatile flammable liquids."
§7803. Means of flame extinguishment.

PART 7.5
Refinery and Chemical Plants

CHAPTER 1
GENERAL

§7850. Title of part.
§7851. Legislative declaration.
§7852. Legislative intent.
§7853. "Process safety management" defined.

CHAPTER 2
PROCESS SAFETY MANAGEMENT STANDARDS

§7855. Purpose of chapter.
§7856. Process safety management standards—Adoption of federal standards; facilities not covered under federal rules.
§7857. Standards to include prescribed items.
§7858. Written safety information; employee participation; content and availability.
§7859. Hazard analysis; availability of risk management prevention program information.
§7860. Written operating procedures; availability; review.
§7861. Safety and health hazard training; refresher courses; employer duty to train; training certification and testing.
§7862. Contractor's employees working near potential hazard.
§7863. Prestartup safety review for new and modified facilities.
§7864. Inspection and testing procedures.
§7865. Permits for "hot work."
§7866. Procedure for managing changes.
§7867. Procedure for investigating incidents and potential incidents.
§7868. Emergency action plan.
§7870. Collection of fees.

PART 9
Tunnel and Mine Safety

CHAPTER 1
TUNNELS AND MINES

§7950. Citation of part.

CHAPTER 2
GASSY AND EXTRAHAZARDOUS TUNNELS

CHAPTER 3
LICENSING AND PENALTIES
[Selected Provisions]

SELECTED PROVISIONS Of The LABOR CODE

GENERAL PROVISIONS [Selected Provisions]

Labor

§1. Title.

This Act shall be known as the Labor Code.

§2. Construction of Labor Code.

The provisions of this code, in so far as they are substantially the same as existing provisions relating to the same subject matter, shall be construed as restatements and continuations thereof and not as new enactments.

Ref.: W. Cal. Sum., 2 "Workers' Compensation" §4.

§5. General provisions govern construction.

Unless the context otherwise requires, the general provisions hereinafter set forth shall govern the construction of this code.

§6. Headings not to affect meaning or intent.

Division, part, chapter, article and section headings contained herein shall not be deemed to govern, limit, modify or in any manner affect the scope, meaning, or intent of the provisions of any division, part, chapter, article, or section hereof.

§7. Administrative powers.

Whenever, by the provisions of this code, an administrative power is granted to a public officer or duty imposed upon such an officer, the power may be exercised or the duty performed by a deputy of the officer or by a person authorized pursuant to law.

Ref.: 8 C.C.R. §§9820, 9821, 9822, 9823, 9824, 9825, 9826, 9827, 9828, 9829, 9830, 9831, 9832, 9833, 9834, 9835, 9836, 9837, 10100, 10100.1, 10100.2, 10106, 10106.1, 10113, 10114, 10114.1, 10114.2, 10114.3, 10114.4, 10115.2.

§8. "Writing"; mailings by certified mail.

Writing includes any form of recorded message capable of comprehension by ordinary visual means. Whenever any notice, report, statement or record is required by this code, it shall be made in writing.

Wherever any notice or other communication is required by this code to be mailed by registered mail by or to any person or corporation, the mailing of such notice or other communication by certified mail shall be deemed to be a sufficient compliance with the requirements of law.

§9. References to code include amendments and additions.

Whenever any reference is made to any portion of this code or of any other law of this State, such reference shall apply to all amendments and additions thereto now or hereafter made.

§10. "Section."

"Section" means a section of this code unless some other statute is specifically mentioned.

§11. Tenses.

The present tense includes the past and future tenses; and the future, the present.

§12. Gender.

The masculine gender includes the feminine and neuter.

§12.1. References to "man" to be changed to "person."

The Legislature hereby declares its intent that the terms "man" or "men" where appropriate shall be deemed "person" or "persons" and any references to the terms "man" or "men" in sections of this code be changed to "person" or "persons" when such code sections are being amended for any purpose. This section is declaratory and not amendatory of existing law.

§13. Singulars and plurals.

The singular number includes the plural, and the plural the singular.

§14. "County."

"County" includes "city and county."

§15. "Shall"; "may."

"Shall" is mandatory and "may" is permissive.

§16. "Oath."

"Oath" includes affirmation.

§17. "Signature" or "subscription" includes mark; acknowledgement of mark.

"Signature" or "subscription" includes mark when the signer or subscriber can not write, such signer's or subscriber's name being written near the mark by a witness who writes his own name near the signer's or subscriber's name; but a signature or subscription by mark can be acknowledged or can serve as a signature or subscription to a sworn statement only when two witnesses so sign their own names thereto.

§18. "Person."

"Person" means any person, association, organization, partnership, business trust, limited liability company, or corporation. **Leg.H.** 1994 ch. 1010.

§18.5. "Agency."

"Agency" means the Labor and Workforce Development Agency. **Leg.H.** 2002 ch. 859 (SB 1236).

§19. "Department."

"Department" means Department of Industrial Relations.

Ref.: W. Cal. Sum., 3 "Agency and Employment" §314.

§19.5. "Secretary."

"Secretary" means the Secretary of Labor and Workforce Development. **Leg.H.** 2002 ch. 859 (SB 1236).

§20. "Director."

"Director" means Director of Industrial Relations.

Ref.: W. Cal. Sum., 3 "Agency and Employment" §314.

§21. "Labor Commissioner."

"Labor Commissioner" means Chief of the Division of Labor Standards Enforcement.

Ref.: W. Cal. Sum., 3 "Agency and Employment" §315.

§22. "Violation."

"Violation" includes a failure to comply with any requirement of the code.

§23. Punishment for offenses.

Except in cases where a different punishment is prescribed, every offense declared by this code to be a misdemeanor is punishable by imprisonment in a county jail, not exceeding six months, or by a fine not exceeding one thousand dollars ($1,000), or both.

Ref.: Hanna §§ 10.26, 10.52.

§24. Invalid provisions.

If any provision of this code, or the application thereof to any person or circumstances, is held invalid the remainder of the code, and the application of its provisions to other persons or circumstances, shall not be affected thereby.

§25. "Sheriff."

"Sheriff" includes "marshal." **Leg.H.** 1996 ch. 872.

§26. Rehabilitated criminals.

Notwithstanding any other provision of this code, no person who has not previously obtained a license regulated by this code shall be denied a license solely on the basis that he has been convicted of a crime if he has obtained a certificate of rehabilitation under Section 4852.01 and following of the Penal Code, and if his probation has been terminated and the information or accusation has been dismissed pursuant to Section 1203.4 of the Penal Code.

§27. Use of term "workers' compensation judge" or "workers' compensation referee" means "workers' compensation administrative law judge."

Whenever the term "workers' compensation judge" or "workers' compensation referee" is used in this code in connection with the workers' compensation law, the term shall mean "workers' compensation administrative law judge." **Leg.H.** 1993 ch. 121, effective July 16, 1993, 1998 ch. 448.

Ref.: Hanna § 1.11[3]; W. Cal. Sum., 2 "Workers' Compensation" §395.

§28. "Independent medical examiner" means "qualified medical evaluator."

For injuries occurring on and after January 1, 1991, whenever the term "independent medical examiner" is used in this code, the term shall mean "qualified medical evaluator."

Ref.: Hanna § 27.07[3].

§29. Definition of "medical director."

"Medical director" means the physician appointed by the administrative director pursuant to Section 122. **Leg.H.** 2003 ch. 639 (SB 228).

DIVISION 1
DEPARTMENT OF INDUSTRIAL RELATIONS

CHAPTER 1
GENERAL POWERS AND DUTIES
[Selected Provisions]

§50. Department of Industrial Relations.

There is in the Labor and Workforce Development Agency the Department of Industrial Relations. **Leg.H.** 2002 ch. 859 (SB 1236).

Ref.: Hanna § 1.10; W. Cal. Sum., 3 "Agency and Employment" §§314, 324, 4 "Secured Transactions in Personal Property" §24.

§50.5. Functions of department.

One of the functions of the Department of Industrial Relations is to foster, promote, and develop the welfare of the wage earners of California, to improve their working conditions, and to advance their opportunities for profitable employment.

Ref.: W. Cal. Sum., 3 "Agency and Employment" §314.

§50.6. Enforcement of Fair Labor Standards Act of 1938.

The Department of Industrial Relations may assist and cooperate with the Wage and Hour Division, and the Children's Bureau, United States Department of Labor, in the enforcement within this State of the Fair Labor Standards Act of 1938, and, subject to the regulations of the Administrator of the Wage and Hour Division, or the Chief of the Children's Bureau, and subject to the laws of the State applicable to the receipt and expenditures of money, may be reimbursed by the division or the bureau for the reasonable cost of such assistance and cooperation.

Ref.: W. Cal. Sum., 3 "Agency and Employment" §314.

§50.7. Administration and enforcement of OSHA standards.

(a) The Department of Industrial Relations is the state agency designated to be responsible for administering the state plan for the development and enforcement of occupational safety and health standards relating to issues covered by corresponding standards promulgated under the federal Occupational Safety and Health Act of 1970 (Public Law 91-596). The state plan shall be consistent with the provisions of state law governing occupational safety and health, including, but not limited to, Chapter 6 (commencing with Section 140) and Chapter 6.5 (commencing with Section 148) of Division 1, and Division 5 (commencing with Section 6300), of this code.

(b) The budget and budget bill submitted pursuant to Article IV, Section 12 of the California Constitution shall include in the item for the support of the Department of Industrial Relations amounts sufficient to fully carry out the purposes and provisions of the state plan and this code in a manner which assures that the risk of industrial injury, exposure to toxic substances, illness and death to employees will be minimized.

(c) Because Federal grants are available, maximum Federal funding shall be sought and, to the extent possible, the cost of administering the state plan shall be paid by funds obtained from federal grants.

(d) The Governor and the Department of Industrial Relations shall take all steps necessary to prevent withdrawal of approval for the state plan by the Federal government. If Federal approval of the state plan has been withdrawn before passage of this initiative, or if it is withdrawn at any time after passage of this initiative, the Governor shall submit a new state plan immediately so that California shall be approved and shall continue to have access to Federal funds. **Leg.H.** Amended November 8, 1988, by initiative Proposition 95.

Note: Sec. 4 of Prop. 95 provides for direct amendment by the Legislature.

§50.8. Occupational health and medicine programs; occupational health centers; reports.

The department shall develop a long range program for upgrading and expanding the resources of the State of California in the area of occupational health and medicine. The program shall include a contractual agreement with the University of California for the creation of occupational health centers affiliated with regional schools of medicine and public health. One such occupational health center shall be situated in the northern part of the state and one in the southern part. The primary function of these occupational health centers shall be the training of occupational physicians and nurses, toxicologists, epidemiologists, and industrial hygienists. In addition, the centers shall serve as referral centers for occupational illnesses and shall engage in research on the causes, diagnosis, and prevention of occupational illnesses.

The centers shall also inform the Division of Occupational Safety and Health Administration of the Department of Industrial Relations, State Department of Health Services, and the Department of Food and Agriculture of their clinical and research findings.

Ref.: W. Cal. Sum., 3 "Agency and Employment" §378.

§50.9. Director's comments.

In furtherance of the provisions of Section 50.5, the director, or the Director of Employment Development, may comment on the impact of actions or projects proposed by public agencies on opportunities for profitable employment, and such agencies shall consider such comments in their decisions.

§51. Appointment of director.

The department shall be conducted under the control of an executive officer known as Director of Industrial Relations. The Director of Industrial Relations shall be appointed by the Governor with the advice and consent of the Senate and hold office at the pleasure of the Governor and shall receive an annual salary provided for by Chapter 6 (commencing with Section 11550) of Part 1 of Division 3 of Title 2 of the Government Code.

Ref.: 8 C.C.R. §15600; W. Cal. Sum., 3 "Agency and Employment" §314.

§52. Application of Government Code to state departments.

Except as otherwise prescribed in this code, the provisions of the Government Code relating to departments of the State shall govern and apply to the conduct of the department.

§53. Head of department.

Whenever in Section 1001 or in Part 1 (commencing with Section 11000) of Division 3 of Title 2 of the Government Code "head of the department" or similar designation occurs, the same shall, for the purposes of this code, mean the director, except that in respect to matters which by the express provisions of this code are committed to or retained under the jurisdiction of the Division of Workers' Compensation, the State Compensation Insurance Fund, the Occupational Safety and Health Standards Board, the Occupational Safety and Health Appeals Board, or the Industrial Welfare Commission the designation shall mean the Division of Workers' Compensation, the Administrative Director of the Division of Workers' Compensation, the Workers' Compensation Appeals Board, the State Compensation Insurance Fund, the Occupational Safety and Health Standards Board, the Occupational Safety and Health Appeals Board, or the Industrial Welfare Commission, as the case may be. **Leg.H.** 1994 chs. 146, 1097.

Ref.: 8 C.C.R. §§10106, 10106.1; Hanna § 1.10.

§54. Duties of director.

The director shall perform all duties, exercise all powers and jurisdiction, assume and discharge all responsibilities, and carry out and effect all purposes vested by law in the department, except as otherwise expressly provided by this code.

Ref.: 8 C.C.R. §§15202, 15250.1, 15300, 15301, 15302, 15303, 15354, 15420, 15422, 15424, 15425, 15426, 15427, 15428.

§54.5. Legal services.

The director may appoint an attorney and assistants licensed to practice law in this state. In the absence of an appointment, the attorney for the Division of Workers' Compensation shall also perform legal services for the department as the Director of Industrial Relations may direct. **Leg.H.** 1994 chs. 146, 1097.

§55. Administrative organization.

For the purpose of administration the director shall organize the department subject to the approval of the Governor, in the manner he deems necessary properly to segregate and conduct the work of the department. Notwithstanding any provision in this code to the contrary, the director may require any division in the department to assist in the enforcement of any or all laws within the jurisdiction of the department. Except as provided in Section 18930 of the Health and Safety Code, the director may, in accordance with the provisions of Chapter 4.5 (commencing with Section 11371), Part 1, Division 3, Title 2 of the Government Code, make rules and regulations that are reasonably necessary to carry out the provisions of this chapter and to effectuate its purposes. The provisions of this section, however, shall not apply to the Division of Workers' Compensation or the State Compensation Insurance Fund, except as to any power or jurisdiction within those divisions as may have been specifically conferred upon the director by law. **Leg.H.** 1994 chs. 146, 1097.

Ref.: 8 C.C.R. §§15202, 15300, 15301, 15302, 15303, 15354, 15420, 15422, 15424, 15425, 15426, 15427, 15428.

§56. Departmental divisions.

The work of the department shall be divided into at least six divisions known as the Division of Workers' Compensation, the Division of Occupational Safety and Health, the Division of Labor Standards Enforcement, the Division of Labor Statistics and Research, the Division of Apprenticeship Standards, and the State Compensation Insurance Fund. **Leg.H.** 1994 chs. 146, 1097.

Ref.: Hanna §§ 1.10, 1.16[1], 1.17; W. Cal. Sum., 3 "Agency and Employment" §314.

§57. Division chiefs.

Each division shall be in charge of a chief who shall be appointed by the Governor and shall receive a salary fixed in accordance with law, and shall serve at the pleasure of the director.

Ref.: W. Cal. Sum., 3 "Agency and Employment" §314.

§57.1. Chief's salary; appointments; salaries.

(a) The Chief of the Division of Occupational Safety and Health shall receive an annual salary as provided by Chapter 6 (commencing with Section 11550) of Part 1 of Division 3 of Title 2 of the Government Code.

(b) All officers or employees of the Division of Occupational Safety and Health employed after the operative date of this section shall be appointed by the director in accordance with the provisions of the State Civil Service Act. Notwithstanding the foregoing, two deputy chiefs of the Division of Occupational Safety and Health shall be appointed by the Governor, with the advice of the Director of Industrial Relations, to serve at the pleasure of the Director of Industrial Relations. The two deputy chiefs shall be exempt from civil service. The annual salaries of the two exempted deputy chiefs shall be fixed by the Director of Industrial Relations, subject to the approval of the Director of Finance.

§57.5. Board of Directors of State Compensation Insurance Fund.

All duties, powers, and jurisdiction relating to the administration of the State Compensation Insurance Fund shall be vested in the Board of Directors of the State Compensation Insurance Fund.

Ref.: Hanna § 1.20[3].

§58. Title to departmental property.

The department shall have possession and control of all records, books, papers, offices, equipment, supplies, moneys, funds, appropriations, land, and other property, real and personal, held for the benefit or use of all commissions, divisions, and offices of the department and the title to all such property held for the use and benefit of the State is hereby transferred to the State.

§59. Departmental law enforcement.

The department through its appropriate officers shall administer and enforce all laws imposing any duty, power, or function upon the offices or officers of the department.

Ref.: 8 C.C.R. §§10106.5, 15201, 15202, 15203.1, 15203.2, 15203.3, 15203.4, 15203.5, 15203.6, 15203.7, 15203.8, 15203.9, 15203.10, 15204, 15205, 15210, 15210.1, 15210.2, 15210.3, 15211.2, 15211.3, 15212, 15213, 15214, 15215, 15216, 15230, 15231, 15232, 15233, 15234, 15251, 15300, 15301, 15302, 15303, 15353, 15354, 15400, 15400.1, 15400.2, 15402, 15402.1, 15402.2, 15402.3, 15402.4, 15403, 15403.1, 15404, 15404.1, 15404.2, 15405, 15420, 15422, 15424, 15425, 15426, 15427, 15428, 15430, 15431, 15431.1, 15431.2, 15432, 15433, 15434, 15435, 15436, 15437, 15438, 15450, 15452, 15454, 15458, 15459, 15463, 15470.

§60. Administration and enforcement of code.

Except as otherwise provided, the provisions of Divisions 4 and 4.5 of this code shall be administered and enforced by the Division of Workers' Compensation. **Leg.H.** 1994 ch. 146.

Ref.: 8 C.C.R. §10106.5; Hanna § 1.10.

§60.5. Division of Occupational Safety and Health: duties and powers.

(a) The provisions of Part 1 of Division 5 of this code shall be administered and enforced by the department through the Division of Occupational Safety and Health, subject to the direction of the director pursuant to Section 50.7.

(b) The Division of Occupational Safety and Health succeeds to, and is vested with, all of the powers, duties, purposes, responsibilities, and jurisdiction of the Division of Industrial Safety, which is hereby abolished, and any other jurisdiction conferred by law.

(c) All powers, duties, and responsibilities of the Chief of the Division of Industrial Safety are hereby transferred to the Chief of the Division of Occupational Safety and Health.

(d) Any regulation or other action made, prescribed, issued, granted, or performed by the abolished Division of Industrial Safety in the administration of a function transferred pursuant to subdivision (b) shall remain in effect and shall be deemed to be a regulation or action of the Division of Occupational Safety and Health unless and until repealed, modified, or rescinded by such division.

(e) Whenever any reference is made in any law to the abolished Division of Industrial Safety, it shall be deemed to be a reference to, and to mean, the Division of Occupational Safety and Health.

Ref.: Hanna § 1.16[1].

§61. Enforcement of chapter.

The provisions of Chapter 1 (commencing with Section 1171) of Part 4 of Division 2 shall be administered and enforced by the department through the Division of Labor Standards Enforcement.

§62. Expenditures.

The department may expend money appropriated for the administration of the provisions of the laws, the enforcement of which is committed to the department. The department may expend such money for the use, support, or maintenance of any commission or office of the department. Such expenditures by the department shall be made in accordance with law in carrying on the work for which such appropriations were made.

§62.5. Workers' Compensation Administration Revolving Fund; Uninsured Employers Benefits Trust Fund; Subsequent Injuries Benefits Trust Fund; Occupational Safety and Health Fund.

(a)**(1)** The Workers' Compensation Administration Revolving Fund is hereby created as a special account in the State Treasury. Money in the fund may be expended by the department, upon appropriation by the Legislature, for all of the following purposes, and may not be used or borrowed for any other purpose:

[1] **(A)** For the administration of the workers' compensation program set forth in this division and Division 4 (commencing with Section 3200), other than the activities financed pursuant to Section 3702.5.

[2] **(B)** For the Return-to-Work Program set forth in Section 139.48.

[3] **(C)** For the enforcement of the insurance coverage program established and maintained by the Labor Commissioner pursuant to Section 90.3.

[4] **(2)** The fund shall consist of surcharges made pursuant to subdivision (e).

[5] **(b)**(1) The Uninsured Employers Benefits Trust Fund is hereby created as a special trust fund account in the State Treasury, of which the director is trustee, and its sources of funds are as provided in subdivision (e). Notwithstanding Section 13340 of the Government Code, the fund is continuously appropriated for the payment of nonadministrative expenses of the workers' compensation program for workers injured while employed by uninsured employers in accordance with Article 2 (commencing with Section 3710) of Chapter 4 of Part 1 of Division 4, and shall not be used for any other purpose. All moneys collected shall be retained in the trust fund until paid as benefits to workers injured while employed by uninsured employers. Nonadministrative expenses include audits and reports of services prepared pursuant to subdivision (b) of Section 3716.1. The surcharge amount for this fund shall be stated separately.

Labor

(2) Notwithstanding any other provision of law, all references to the Uninsured Employers Fund shall mean the Uninsured Employers Benefits Trust Fund.

(3) Notwithstanding paragraph (1), in the event that budgetary restrictions or impasse prevent the timely payment of administrative expenses from the Workers' Compensation Administration Revolving Fund, those expenses shall be advanced from the Uninsured Employers Benefits Trust Fund. Expense advances made pursuant to this paragraph shall be reimbursed in full to the Uninsured Employers Benefits Trust Fund upon enactment of the annual Budget Act.

(4) Any moneys from penalties collected pursuant to Section 3722 as a result of the insurance coverage program established under Section 90.3 shall be deposited in the State Treasury to the credit of the Workers' Compensation Administration Revolving Fund created under Section 62.5, to cover expenses incurred by the director under the insurance coverage program. The amount of any penalties in excess of payment of administrative expenses incurred by the director for the insurance coverage program established under Section 90.3 shall be deposited in the State Treasury to the credit of the Uninsured Employers Benefits Trust Fund for nonadministrative expenses, as prescribed in paragraph (1), and notwithstanding paragraph (1), shall only be available upon appropriation by the Legislature.

[6] **(c)**(1) The Subsequent Injuries Benefits Trust Fund is hereby created as a special trust fund account in the State Treasury, of which the director is trustee, and its sources of funds are as provided in subdivision (e). Notwithstanding Section 13340 of the Government Code, the fund is continuously appropriated for the nonadministrative expenses of the workers' compensation program for workers who have suffered serious injury and who are suffering from previous and serious permanent disabilities or physical impairments, in accordance with Article 5 (commencing with Section 4751) of Chapter 2 of Part 2 of Division 4, and Section 4 of Article XIV of the California Constitution, and shall not be used for any other purpose. All moneys collected shall be retained in the trust fund until paid as benefits to workers who have suffered serious injury and who are suffering from previous and serious permanent disabilities or physical impairments. Nonadministrative expenses include audits and reports of services pursuant to subdivision (c) of Section 4755. The surcharge amount for this fund shall be stated separately.

(2) Notwithstanding any other provision of law, all references to the Subsequent Injuries Fund shall mean the Subsequent Injuries Benefits Trust Fund.

(3) Notwithstanding paragraph (1), in the event that budgetary restrictions or impasse prevent the timely payment of administrative expenses from the Workers' Compensation Administration Revolving Fund, those expenses shall be advanced from the Subsequent Injuries Benefits Trust Fund. Expense advances made pursuant to this paragraph shall be reimbursed in full to the Subsequent Injuries Benefits Trust Fund upon enactment of the annual Budget Act.

(d) The Occupational Safety and Health Fund is hereby created as a special account in the State Treasury. Moneys in the account may be expended by the department, upon appropriation by the Legislature, for support of the Division of Occupational Safety and Health, the Occupational Safety and Health Standards Board, and the Occupational Safety and Health Appeals Board, and the activities these entities perform as set forth in this division, and Division 5 (commencing with Section 6300).

(e)(1) Separate surcharges shall be levied by the director upon all employers, as defined in Section 3300, for purposes of deposit in the Workers' Compensation Administration Revolving Fund, the Uninsured Employers Benefits Trust Fund, [7] the Subsequent Injuries Benefits Trust Fund**, and the Occupational Safety and Health Fund**. The total amount of the surcharges shall be allocated between self-insured employers and insured employers in proportion to payroll respectively paid in the most recent year for which payroll information is available. The director shall adopt reasonable regulations governing the manner of collection of the surcharges. The regulations shall require the surcharges to be paid by self-insurers to be expressed as a percentage of indemnity paid during the most recent year for which information is available, and the surcharges to be paid by insured employers to be expressed as a percentage of premium. In no event shall the surcharges paid by insured employers be considered a premium for computation of a gross premium tax or agents' commission. In no event shall the total amount of the surcharges paid by insured and self-insured employers exceed the amounts reasonably necessary to carry out the purposes of this section.

(2) The regulations adopted pursuant to paragraph (1) shall be exempt from the rulemaking provisions of the Administrative Procedure Act (Chapter 3.5 (commencing with Section 11340) of Part 1 of Division 3 of Title 2 of the Government Code). **Leg.H.** 1999 ch. 746, 2002 ch. 1124 (AB 3000), effective September 30, 2002, 2003 chs. 228 (AB 1756), effective August 11, 2003, 635 (AB 227), 757 (AB 296), 2004 ch. 34 (SB 899), effective April 19, 2004, 2007 ch. 662 (SB 869) §1, 2008 ch. 751 (AB 1389) §59, effective September 30, 2008.

§62.5. 2008 Deletes. **[1]** (1) **[2]** (2) **[3]** (3) **[4]** (b) **[5]** (c) **[6]** (d) **[7]** and

2004 Note: The amendment to §62.5 made by this act shall apply prospectively from the date of enactment of this act, regardless of the date of injury, unless otherwise specified, but shall not constitute good cause to reopen or rescind, alter, or amend any existing order, decision, or award of the Workers' Compensation Appeals Board. Stats. 2004 ch. 34 (SB 899) §47.

Ref.: 8 C.C.R. §§15232, 15600, 15601, 15602, 15603, 15604, 15605, 15606, 15607, 15608, 15609, 15611; Hanna § 1.12[2]; Herlick Handbook § 1.2; W. Cal. Sum., 2 "Workers' Compensation" §297.

§62.6. Assessments.

(a) The director shall levy and collect assessments from employers in accordance with subdivision (b), as necessary, to collect the aggregate amount determined by the Fraud Assessment Commission pursuant to Section 1872.83 of the Insurance Code. Revenues derived from the assessments shall be deposited in the Workers' Compensation Fraud Account in the Insurance Fund and shall only be expended, upon appropriation by the Legislature, for the investigation and prosecution of workers' compensation fraud and the willful failure to secure payment of workers' compensation, as prescribed by Section 1872.83 of the Insurance Code.

(b) Assessments shall be levied by the director upon all employers as defined in Section 3300. The total amount of the assessment shall be allocated between self-insured employers and insured employers in proportion to payroll respectively paid in the most recent year for which payroll information is available. The director shall promulgate reasonable rules and regulations governing the manner of collection of the assessment. The rules and regulations shall require the assessment to be paid by self-insurers to be expressed as a percentage of indemnity paid during the most recent year for which information is available, and the assessment to be paid by insured employers to be expressed as a percentage of premium. In no event shall the assessment paid by insured employers be considered a premium for computation of a gross premium tax or agents' commission. **Leg.H.** 1991 chs. 116, 934, 2002 ch. 6 (AB 749).

Ref.: 8 C.C.R. §§15600, 15601.5, 15602, 15603, 15605, 15606, 15607, 15608, 15609.

§62.7. Cal-OSHA Targeted Inspection and Consultation Fund.

(a) The Cal-OSHA Targeted Inspection and Consultation Fund is hereby created as a special account in the State Treasury. Proceeds of the fund may be expended by the department, upon appropriation by the Legislature, for the costs of the Cal-OSHA targeted inspection program provided by Section 6314.1 and the costs of the Cal-OSHA targeted consultation program provided by subdivision (a) of Section 6354, and for costs related to assessments levied and collected pursuant to Section 62.9.

(b) The fund shall consist of the assessments made pursuant to Section 62.9 and other moneys transferred to the fund. **Leg.H.** 1993 ch. 121, effective July 16, 1993, chs. 1241, 1242, 1995 ch. 33, effective June 30, 1995, ch. 556.

Ref.: 8 C.C.R. §§15234, 15601.7, 15601.8.

§62.9. Levy and collection of assessments on employers having workers' compensation insurance and on private self-insured employers.

(a)(1) The director shall levy and collect assessments from employers in accordance with this section. The total amount of the assessment collected shall be the amount determined by the director to be necessary to produce the revenue sufficient to fund the programs specified by Section 62.7, except that the amount assessed in any year for those purposes shall not exceed 50 percent of the amounts appropriated from the General Fund for the support of the occupational safety and health program for the 1993–94 fiscal year, adjusted for inflation. The director also shall include in the total assessment amount the department's costs for administering the assessment, including the collections process and the cost of reimbursing the Franchise Tax Board for its cost of collection activities pursuant to subdivision (c).

(2) The insured employers and private sector self-insured employers that, pursuant to subdivision (b), are subject to assessment shall be assessed, respectively, on the basis of their annual payroll subject to premium charges or their annual payroll that would be subject to premium charges if the employer were insured, as follows:

(A) An employer with a payroll of less than two hundred fifty thousand dollars ($250,000) shall be assessed one hundred dollars ($100).

(B) An employer with a payroll of two hundred fifty thousand dollars ($250,000) or more, but not more than five hundred thousand dollars ($500,000), shall be assessed two hundred dollars ($200).

(C) An employer with a payroll of more than five hundred thousand dollars ($500,000), but not more than seven hundred fifty thousand dollars ($750,000), shall be assessed four hundred dollars ($400).

(D) An employer with a payroll of more than seven hundred fifty thousand dollars ($750,000), but not more than one million dollars ($1,000,000), shall be assessed six hundred dollars ($600).

(E) An employer with a payroll of more than one million dollars ($1,000,000), but not more than one million five hundred thousand dollars ($1,500,000), shall be assessed eight hundred dollars ($800).

(F) An employer with a payroll of more than one million five hundred thousand dollars ($1,500,000), but not more than two million dollars ($2,000,000), shall be assessed one thousand dollars ($1,000).

(G) An employer with a payroll of more than two million dollars ($2,000,000), but not more than two million five hundred thousand dollars ($2,500,000), shall be assessed one thousand five hundred dollars ($1,500).

(H) An employer with a payroll of more than two million five hundred thousand dollars ($2,500,000), but not more than three million five hundred thousand dollars ($3,500,000), shall be assessed two thousand dollars ($2,000).

(I) An employer with a payroll of more than three million five hundred thousand dollars ($3,500,000)**, but not more than four million five hundred thousand dollars ($4,500,000),** shall be assessed two thousand five hundred dollars ($2,500).

(J) An employer with a payroll of more than four million five hundred thousand dollars ($4,500,000), but not more than five million five hundred thousand dollars ($5,500,000), shall be assessed three thousand dollars ($3,000).

(K) An employer with a payroll of more than five million five hundred thousand dollars ($5,500,000), but not more than seven million dollars ($7,000,000), shall be assessed three thousand five hundred dollars ($3,500).

(L) An employer with a payroll of more than seven million dollars ($7,000,000), but not more than twenty million dollars ($20,000,000), shall be assessed six thousand seven hundred dollars ($6,700).

(M) An employer with a payroll of more than twenty million dollars ($20,000,000) shall be assessed ten thousand dollars ($10,000).

(b)(1) In the manner as specified by this section, the director shall identify those insured employers having a workers' compensation experience modification rating of 1.25 or more, and private sector self-insured employers having an equivalent experience modification rating of 1.25 or more as determined pursuant to subdivision (e).

(2) The assessment required by this section shall be levied annually, on a calendar year basis, on those insured employers and private sector self-insured employers, as identified pursuant to paragraph (1), having the highest workers' compensation experience modification ratings or equivalent experience modification ratings, that the director determines to be required numerically to produce the total amount of the assessment to be collected pursuant to subdivision (a).

(c) The director shall collect the assessment from insured employers as follows:

(1) Upon the request of the director, the Department of Insurance shall direct the licensed rating organization designated as the department's statistical agent to provide to the director, for purposes of subdivision (b), a list of all insured employers having a workers' compensation experience rating modification of 1.25 or more, according to the organization's records at the time the list is requested, for policies commencing the year preceding the year in which the assessment is to be collected.

(2) The director shall determine the annual payroll of each insured employer subject to assessment from the payroll that was reported to the licensed rating organization identified in paragraph (1) for the most recent period for which one full year of payroll information is available for all insured employers.

(3) On or before September 1 of each year, the director shall determine each of the current insured employers subject to assessment, and the amount of the total assessment for which each insured employer is liable. The director immediately shall notify each insured employer, in a format chosen by the insurer, of the insured's obligation to submit payment of the assessment to the director within 30 days after the date the billing was mailed, and warn the insured of the penalties for failure to make timely and full payment as provided by this subdivision.

(4) The director shall identify any insured employers that, within 30 days after the mailing of the billing notice, fail to pay, or object to, their assessments. The director shall mail to each of these employers a notice of delinquency and a notice of the intention to assess penalties, advising that, if the assessment is not paid in full within 15 days after the mailing of the notices, the director will levy against the employer a penalty equal to 25 percent of the employer's assessment, and will refer the assessment and penalty to the Franchise Tax Board **or another agency** for collection. The notices required by this paragraph shall be sent by United States first-class mail.

(5) If an assessment is not paid by an insured employer within 15 days after the mailing of the notices required by paragraph (4), the director shall refer the delinquent assessment and the penalty to the Franchise Tax Board**, or another agency, as deemed appropriate by the director,** for collection pursuant to Section 19290.1 of the Revenue and Taxation Code.

(d) The director shall collect the assessment directly from private sector self-insured employers. The failure of any private sector self-insured employer to pay the assessment as billed constitutes grounds for the suspension or termination of the employer's certificate to self-insure.

(e) The director shall adopt regulations implementing this section that include provision for a method of determining experience modification ratings for private sector self-insured employers that is generally equivalent to the modification ratings that apply to insured employers and is weighted by both severity and frequency.

(f) The director shall determine whether the amount collected pursuant to any assessment exceeds expenditures, as described in subdivision (a), for the current year and shall credit the amount of any excess to any deficiency in the prior year's assessment or, if there is no deficiency, against the assessment for the subsequent year. **Leg.H.** 1995 ch. 33, effective June 30, 1995, 1998 ch. 814, 1999 ch. 469, 2008 ch. 751 (AB 1389) §60, effective September 30, 2008.

Ref.: 8 C.C.R. §§15234, 15601.7.

CHAPTER 3 COMMISSION ON HEALTH AND SAFETY AND WORKERS' COMPENSATION

§75. Composition of Commission; selection of chair; terms; meetings.

(a) There is in the department the Commission on Health and Safety and Workers' Compensation. The commission shall be composed of eight voting members. Four voting members shall represent organized labor, and four voting members shall represent employers. Not more than one employer member shall represent public agencies. Two of the employer and two of the labor members shall be appointed by the Governor. The Senate Committee on Rules and the Speaker of the Assembly shall each appoint one employer and one labor representative. The public employer representative shall be appointed by the Governor. No action of the commission shall be valid unless agreed to by a majority of the membership and by not less than two members representing organized labor and two members representing employers.

(b) The commission shall select one of the members representing organized labor to chair the commission during the 1994 calendar year, and thereafter the commission shall alternatively select an employer and organized labor representative to chair the commission for one-year terms.

(c) The initial terms of the members of the commission shall be four years, and they shall hold office until the appointment of a successor. However, the initial terms of one employer and one labor member appointed by the Governor shall expire on December 31, 1995; the initial terms of the members appointed by the Senate Committee on Rules shall expire December 31, 1996; the initial terms of the members appointed by the Speaker of the Assembly shall expire on December 31, 1997; and the initial term of one employer and one labor member appointed by the Governor shall expire on December 31, 1998. Any vacancy shall be filled by appointment to the unexpired term.

(d) The commission shall meet every other month and upon the call of the chair. Meetings shall be open to the public. Members of the commission shall receive one hundred dollars ($100) for each day of their actual attendance at meetings of the commission and other official business of the commission and shall also receive their actual and necessary traveling expenses incurred in the performance of their duty as a member. Payment of per diem and traveling expenses shall be made from the Workers' Compensation Administration Revolving Fund, when appropriated by the Legislature. **Leg.H.** 1993 ch. 227, 2002 ch. 6 (AB 749).

Ref.: Hanna §§ 1.10, 1.18; Herlick Handbook § 1.10.

§76. Commission personnel.

The commission may employ officers, assistants, experts, and other employees it deems necessary. All personnel of the commission shall be under the supervision of the chair or an executive officer to whom he or she delegates this responsibility. All personnel shall be appointed pursuant to the State Civil Service Act (Part 2 (commencing with Section 18500) of Division 5 of Title 2 of the Government Code), except for the one exemption allowed by subdivision (e) of Section 4 of Article VII of the California Constitution. **Leg.H.** 1993 ch. 227.

Ref.: Herlick Handbook § 1.10.

§77. Commission duties and powers.

(a) The commission shall conduct a continuing examination of the workers' compensation system, as defined in Section 4 of Article XIV of the California Constitution, and of the state's activities to prevent industrial injuries and occupational diseases. The commission may conduct or contract for studies it deems necessary to carry out its responsibilities. In carrying out its duties, the commission shall examine other states' workers' compensation programs and activities to prevent industrial injuries and occupational diseases. All state departments and agencies, and any rating organization licensed by the Insurance Commissioner pursuant to Article 3 (commencing with Section 11750) of Chapter 3 of Part 3 of Division 2 of the Insurance Code, shall cooperate with the commission and upon reasonable request provide information and data in their possession that the commission deems necessary for the purpose of carrying out its responsibilities. The commission shall issue an annual report on the state of the workers' compensation system, including recommendations for administrative or legislative modifications which would improve the operation of the system. The report shall be made available to the Governor, the Legislature, and the public on request.

(b) On or before July 1, 2003, and periodically thereafter as it deems necessary, the commission shall issue a report and recommendations on the improvement and simplification of the notices required to be provided by insurers and self-insured employers.

(c) The commission succeeds to, and is vested with, all of the powers, duties, purposes, responsibilities, and jurisdiction of the Health and Safety Commission which is hereby abolished, including the administration of grants to assist in establishing effective occupational injury and illness prevention programs. **Leg.H.** 1993 ch. 227, 2002 ch. 6 (AB 749).

Ref.: Hanna § 1.18; Herlick Handbook § 1.10.

§77.5. Medical treatment utilization standards—Survey and evaluation of standards of care; report to administrative director.

(a) On or before July 1, 2004, the commission shall conduct a survey and evaluation of evidence-based, peer-reviewed, nationally recognized standards of care, including existing medical treatment utilization standards, including independent medical review, as used in other states, at the national level, and in other medical benefit systems. The survey shall be updated periodically.

(b) On or before October 1, 2004, the commission shall issue a report of its findings and recommendations to the administrative director for purposes of the adoption of a medical treatment utilization schedule. **Leg.H.** 2003 ch. 639 (SB 228).

Ref.: Hanna § 1.18.

§77.7. Study of causes of insolvencies among workers' compensation insurers; contents; costs; disclosure of data.

(a) A study shall be undertaken to examine the causes of the number of insolvencies among workers' compensation insurers within the past 10 years. The study shall be conducted by an independent research organization under the direction of the commission. Not later than July 1, 2009, the commission and the department shall publish the report of the study on [1] **its** Internet Web site and shall inform the Legislature and the Governor of the availability of the report.

(b) The study shall include an analysis of the following: the access to capital for workers' compensation insurance from all sources between 1993 and 2003; the availability, source, and risk assumed of reinsurers during this period; the use of deductible policies and their effect on solvency regulation; market activities by insurers and producers that affected market concentration; activities, including financial oversight of insurers, by insurance regulators and the National Association of Insurance Commissioners during this period; the quality of data reporting to the commissioner's designated statistical agent and the accuracy of recommendations provided by the commissioner's designated statistical agent during this period of time; and underwriting, claims adjusting, and reserving practices of insolvent insurers. The study shall also include a survey of reports of other state agencies analyzing the insurance market response to rising system costs within the applicable time period.

(c) Data reasonably required for the study shall be made available by the California Insurance Guarantee Association, Workers' Compensation Insurance Rating Bureau, third-party administrators for the insolvent insurers, whether prior to or after the insolvency, the State Compensation Insurance Fund, and the Department of Insurance. The commission shall also include a survey of reports by the commission and other state agencies analyzing the insurance market response to rising system costs within the applicable period of time.

(d) The cost of the study is not to exceed one million dollars ($1,000,000). Confidential information identifiable to [2] **a** natural person or insurance company held by [3] **an agency, organization,** association, or other person or entity shall be released to researchers upon satisfactory agreement to maintain confidentiality. Information or material that is not subject to subpoena from the agency [4]**, organization,** association, or other person or entity shall not be subject to subpoena from the commission or the contracted research organization.

(e) The costs of the study shall be borne one-half by the commission from funds derived from the Workers' Compensation Administration Revolving Fund and one-half by insurers from assessments allocated to each insurer based on the insurer's proportionate share of the market as shown by the Market Share Report for Calendar Year 2006 published by the Department of Insurance.

(f) In order to protect individual company trade secrets, this study shall not lead to the disclosure of, either directly or indirectly, the business practices of [5] **a** company that provides data pursuant to this section. This prohibition shall not apply to insurance companies that have been ordered by a court of competent jurisdiction to be placed in liquidation under the supervision of a liquidator or other authority. **Leg.H.** 2007 ch. 431 (SB 316) §3, 2008 ch. 179 (SB 1498) §174.

§77.7. 2008 Deletes. [1] it's **[2]** any **[3]** any agency or organization or **[4]** or organization or **[5]** any

§78. Review of grant applications.

(a) The commission shall review and approve applications from employers and employee organizations, as well as applications submitted jointly by an employer organization and an employee organization, for grants to assist in establishing effective occupational injury and illness prevention programs. The commission shall establish policies for the evaluation of these applications and shall give priority to applications proposing to target high-risk industries and occupations, including those with high injury or illness rates, and those in which employees are exposed to one or more hazardous substances or conditions or where there is a demonstrated need for research to determine effective strategies for the prevention of occupational illnesses or injuries.

(b) Civil and administrative penalties assessed and collected pursuant to Sections 129.5 and 4628 shall be deposited in the Workers'

Compensation Administration Revolving Fund. Moneys in the fund, when appropriated by the Legislature to fund the grants under subdivision (a) and other activities and expenses of the commission set forth in this code, shall be expended by the department, upon approval by the commission. **Leg.H.** 1993 ch. 227, 2002 chs. 6 (AB 749), 866 (AB 486).

Ref.: Hanna § 1.18; Herlick Handbook § 1.10.

CHAPTER 4 DIVISION OF LABOR STANDARDS ENFORCEMENT [Selected Provisions]

§90.3. Enforcement of payment for workers' compensation coverage; targeted program; contact and inspection; annual report.

(a) It is the policy of this state to vigorously enforce the laws requiring employers to secure the payment of compensation as required by Section 3700 and to protect employers who comply with the law from those who attempt to gain a competitive advantage at the expense of their workers by failing to secure the payment of compensation.

(b) In order to ensure that the laws requiring employers to secure the payment of compensation are adequately enforced, the Labor Commissioner shall establish and maintain a program that systematically identifies unlawfully uninsured employers. The Labor Commissioner, in consultation with the Administrative Director of the Division of Workers' Compensation and the director, may prioritize targets for the program in consideration of available resources. The employers shall be identified from data from the Uninsured Employers' Fund, the Employment Development Department, the rating organizations licensed by the Insurance Commissioner pursuant to Article 3 (commencing with Section 11750) of Chapter 3 of Part 3 of Division 2 of the Insurance Code, and any other sources deemed likely to lead to the identification of unlawfully uninsured employers. All state departments and agencies and any rating organization licensed by the Insurance Commissioner pursuant to Article 3 (commencing with Section 11750) of Chapter 3 of Part 3 of Division 2 of the Insurance Code shall cooperate with the Labor Commissioner and on reasonable request provide information and data in their possession reasonably necessary to carry out the program.

(c) As part of the program, the Labor Commissioner shall establish procedures for ensuring that employers with payroll but with no record of workers' compensation coverage are contacted and, if no valid reason for the lack of record of coverage is shown, inspected on a priority basis.

(d) The Labor Commissioner shall annually, not later than March 1, prepare a report concerning the effectiveness of the program, publish it on the Labor Commissioner's Web site, as well as notify the Legislature, the Governor, the Insurance Commissioner, and the Administrative Director of the Division of Workers' Compensation of the report's availability. The report shall include, but not be limited to, all of the following:

(1) The number of employers identified from records of the Employment Development Department who were screened for matching records of insurance coverage or self-insurance.

(2) The number of employers identified from records of the Employment Development Department that were matched to records of insurance coverage or self-insurance.

(3) The number of employers identified from records of the Employment Development Department that were notified that there was no record of their insurance coverage.

(4) The number of employers responding to the notices, and the nature of the responses, including the number of employers who failed to provide satisfactory proof of workers' compensation coverage and including information about the reasons that employers who provided satisfactory proof of coverage were not appropriately recognized in the comparison performed under subdivision (b). The report may include recommendations to improve the accuracy and efficiency of the program in screening for unlawfully uninsured employers.

(5) The number of employers identified as unlawfully uninsured from records of the Uninsured Employers' Benefits Trust Fund or from records of the Division of Workers' Compensation, and the number of those employers that are also identifiable from the records of the Employment Development Department. These statistics shall be reported in a manner to permit analysis and estimation of the percentage of unlawfully

uninsured employers that do not report wages to the Employment Development Department.

(6) The number of employers inspected.

(7) The number and amount of penalties assessed pursuant to Section 3722 as a result of the program.

(8) The number and amount of penalties collected pursuant to Section 3722 as a result of the program.

(e) The allocation of funds from the Workers' Compensation Administration Revolving Fund pursuant to subdivision (a) of Section 62.5 shall not increase the total amount of surcharges pursuant to subdivision (e) of Section 62.5. Startup costs for this program shall be allocated from the fiscal year 2007–08 surcharges collected. The total amount allocated for this program under subdivision (a) of Section 62.5 in subsequent years shall not exceed the amount of penalties collected pursuant to Section 3722 as a result of the program. **Leg.H.** 2002 ch. 6 (AB 749), 2007 ch. 662 (SB 869) §2.

§90.5. Enforcement of minimum labor standards; establishment of field units; adoption of plan; report to Legislature.

(a) It is the policy of this state to vigorously enforce minimum labor standards in order to ensure employees are not required or permitted to work under substandard unlawful conditions or for employers that have not secured the payment of compensation, and to protect employers who comply with the law from those who attempt to gain a competitive advantage at the expense of their workers by failing to comply with minimum labor standards.

(b) In order to ensure that minimum labor standards are adequately enforced, the Labor Commissioner shall establish and maintain a field enforcement unit, which shall be administratively and physically separate from offices of the division that accept and determine individual employee complaints. The unit shall have offices in Los Angeles, San Francisco, San Jose, San Diego, Sacramento, and any other locations that the Labor Commissioner deems appropriate. The unit shall have primary responsibility for administering and enforcing those statutes and regulations most effectively enforced through field investigations, including Sections 226, 1021, 1021.5, 1193.5, 1193.6, 1194.5, 1197, 1198, 1771, 1776, 1777.5, 2651, 2673, 2675, and 3700, in accordance with the plan adopted by the Labor Commissioner pursuant to subdivision (c). Nothing in this section shall be construed to limit the authority of this unit in enforcing any statute or regulation in the course of its investigations.

(c) The Labor Commissioner shall adopt an enforcement plan for the field enforcement unit. The plan shall identify priorities for investigations to be undertaken by the unit that ensure the available resources will be concentrated in industries, occupations, and areas in which employees are relatively low paid and unskilled, and those in which there has been a history of violations of the statutes cited in subdivision (b), and those with high rates of noncompliance with Section 3700.

(d) The Labor Commissioner shall annually report to the Legislature, not later than March 1, concerning the effectiveness of the field enforcement unit. The report shall include, but not be limited to, all of the following:

(1) The enforcement plan adopted by the Labor Commissioner pursuant to subdivision (c), and the rationale for the priorities identified in the plan.

(2) The number of establishments investigated by the unit, and the number of types of violations found.

(3) The amount of wages found to be unlawfully withheld from workers, and the amount of unpaid wages recovered for workers.

(4) The amount of penalties and unpaid wages transferred to the General Fund as a result of the efforts of the unit. **Leg.H.** 2002 ch. 6 (AB 749).

§96. Assignment of claims.

The Labor Commissioner and his or her deputies and representatives authorized by him or her in writing shall, upon the filing of a claim therefor by an employee, or an employee representative authorized in writing by an employee, with the Labor Commissioner, take assignments of:

(a) Wage claims and incidental expense accounts and advances.

(b) Mechanics' and other liens of employees.

(c) Claims based on "stop orders" for wages and on bonds for labor.

(d) Claims for damages for misrepresentations of conditions of employment.

(e) Claims for unreturned bond money of employees.

(f) Claims for penalties for nonpayment of wages.

(g) Claims for the return of workers' tools in the illegal possession of another person.

(h) Claims for vacation pay, severance pay, or other compensation supplemental to a wage agreement.

(i) Awards for workers' compensation benefits in which the Workers' Compensation Appeals Board has found that the employer has failed to secure payment of compensation and where the award remains unpaid more than 10 days after having become final.

(j) Claims for loss of wages as the result of discharge from employment for the garnishment of wages.

(k) Claims for loss of wages as the result of demotion, suspension, or discharge from employment for lawful conduct occurring during nonworking hours away from the employer's premises. **Leg.H.** 1999 ch. 692.

Ref.: Hanna §§ 27.05, 30.01; W. Cal. Sum., 2 "Workers' Compensation" §152, 3 "Agency and Employment" §§248, 262, 316.

§96.3. Employees represented by collective bargaining agreements.

In cases where employees are covered by a collective bargaining agreement, the collective bargaining representative by virtue of such agreement may be the assignee of all such covered employees for purposes of filing claims for wages with the Labor Commissioner, subject to the option of the employee to reject such representation and to represent himself or herself.

§96.5. Certification of claims.

The Labor Commissioner shall conduct such hearings as may be necessary for the purpose of Section 7071.11 of the Business and Professions Code. In any action to recover upon a cash deposit after a determination made under Section 7071.11, the Labor Commissioner shall certify in writing to the appropriate court that he has heard and determined the validity of claims and demands and that the sum specified therein is the amount found due and payable. The certificate of the commissioner shall be considered by the court but shall not, by itself, be sufficient evidence to support a judgment.

§96.6. Industrial Relations Unpaid Wage Fund.

The Industrial Relations Unpaid Wage Fund is hereby created as a special fund in the State Treasury, which is continuously appropriated for the purposes of subdivision (c) of Section 96.7.

Ref.: W. Cal. Sum., 3 "Agency and Employment" §255.

§96.7. Collection and disbursement of unpaid wages and benefits.

The Labor Commissioner, after investigation and upon determination that wages or monetary benefits are due and unpaid to any worker in the State of California, may collect such wages or benefits on behalf of the worker without assignment of such wages or benefits to the commissioner.

(a) The Labor Commissioner shall act as trustee of all such collected unpaid wages or benefits, and shall deposit such collected moneys in the Industrial Relations Unpaid Wage Fund.

(b) The Labor Commissioner shall make a diligent search to locate any worker for whom the Labor Commissioner has collected unpaid wages or benefits.

(c) All wages or benefits collected under this section shall be remitted to the worker, his lawful representative, or to any trust or custodial fund established under a plan to provide health and welfare, pension, vacation, retirement, or similar benefits from the Industrial Relations Unpaid Wage Fund.

(d) Any unpaid wages or benefits collected by the Labor Commissioner pursuant to this section shall be retained in the Industrial Relations Unpaid Wage Fund until remitted pursuant to subdivision (c), or until deposited in the General Fund.

(e) The Controller shall, at the end of each fiscal year, transfer to the General Fund the unencumbered balance, less six months of expenditures as determined by the Director of Finance, in the Industrial Relations Unpaid Wage Fund.

(f) All wages or benefits collected under this section which cannot be remitted from the Industrial Relations Unpaid Wage Fund pursuant to subdivision (c) because money has been transmitted to the General Fund shall be paid out of the General Fund from funds appropriated for that purpose. **Leg.H.** 1975 ch. 714, 1981 ch.

562, effective September 19, 1981, 2005 ch. 74 (AB 139) §54, effective July 19, 2005.

Ref.: W. Cal. Sum., 3 "Agency and Employment" §317.

CHAPTER 5 DIVISION OF WORKERS' COMPENSATION

§110. Definitions.

As used in this chapter:

(a) "Appeals board" means the Workers' Compensation Appeals Board. The title of a member of the board is "commissioner."

(b) "Administrative director" means the Administrative Director of the Division of Workers' Compensation.

(c) "Division" means the Division of Workers' Compensation.

(d) "Medical director" means the physician appointed by the administrative director pursuant to Section 122.

(e) "Qualified medical evaluator" means physicians appointed by the administrative director pursuant to Section 139.2.

(f) "Court administrator" means the administrator of the workers' compensation adjudicatory process at the trial level. **Leg.H.** 1965 ch. 1513 §5, operative January 15, 1966, 1967 ch. 1462 §1, 1981 ch. 21 §2, effective April 18, 1981, 1989 ch. 892 §10, 1990 ch. 1550 (AB 2910) §8, 1993 ch. 121, effective July 16, 1993, 2002 ch. 6 (AB 749), 2003 ch. 639 (SB 228).

1989 Note: This section is applicable only to injuries occurring on or after January 1, 1990. Stats. 1989 ch. 893 §6.

Ref.: Hanna §§ 1.10, 1.12[2A]; Herlick Handbook § 1.2; W. Cal. Sum., 2 "Workers' Compensation" §§10–13, 400, 3 "Agency and Employment" §314.

§111. Powers of appeals board and administrative director.

(a) The Workers' Compensation Appeals Board, consisting of seven members, shall exercise all judicial powers vested in it under this code. In all other respects, the Division of Workers' Compensation is under the control of the administrative director and, except as to those duties, powers, jurisdiction, responsibilities, and purposes as are specifically vested in the appeals board, the administrative director shall exercise the powers of the head of a department within the meaning of Article 1 (commencing with Section 11150) of Chapter 2 of Part 1 of Division 3 of Title 2 of the Government Code with respect to the Division of Workers' Compensation which shall include supervision of, and responsibility for, personnel, and the coordination of the work of the division, except personnel of the appeals board.

(b) The administrative director shall prepare and submit, on March 1 of each year, a report to the Governor and the Legislature covering the activities of the division during the prior year. The report shall include recommendations for improvement and the need, if any, for legislation to enhance the delivery of compensation to injured workers. The report shall include data on penalties imposed on employers or insurers due to delays in compensation or notices, or both, by category of penalty imposed.

1989 Note: This section is applicable only to injuries occurring on or after January 1, 1990. Stats. 1989 ch. 893 §6.

Ref.: 8 C.C.R. §§9720.1, 9720.2, 9721.1, 9721.2, 9721.31, 9721.32, 9722, 9722.1, 9722.2, 9723, 10106, 10106.1, 10106.5, 10107, 10107.1, 10563, 10582, 10622, 10753; Hanna §§ 1.10, 1.11[1], [6], 1.12[2], 21.02[1]; Herlick Handbook § 1.2; W. Cal. Sum., 2 "Workers' Compensation" §§10, 11, 13, 14.

§112. Appointment and composition of appeals board.

The members of the appeals board shall be appointed by the Governor with the advice and consent of the Senate. The term of office of the members appointed prior to January 1, 1990, shall be four years, and the term of office of members appointed on or after January 1, 1990, shall be six years and they shall hold office until the appointment and qualification of their successors.

Five of the members of the appeals board shall be experienced attorneys at law admitted to practice in the State of California. The other two members need not be attorneys at law. All members shall be selected with due consideration of their judicial temperament and abilities. Each member shall receive the salary provided for by Chapter 6 (commencing with Section 11550) of Part 1 of Division 3 of Title 2 of the Government Code.

1990 Note: The amendments made by this act to Section 112 of the Labor Code are declaratory of existing law. Stats. 1990 ch. 1550 §66.

1989 Note: This section is applicable only to injuries occurring on or after January 1, 1990. Stats. 1989 ch. 893 §6.

Ref.: Hanna § 1.11[1]; Herlick Handbook § 1.2; W. Cal. Sum., 2 "Workers' Compensation" §13.

§113. Appointment of chairperson.

The Governor shall designate the chairman of the appeals board from the membership of the appeals board. The person so designated shall hold the office of chairman at the pleasure of the Governor.

The chairman may designate in writing one of the other members of the appeals board to act as chairman during such time as he may be absent from the state on official business, on vacation, or absent due to illness.

Ref.: Hanna § 1.11[2]; Herlick Handbook § 1.2; W. Cal. Sum., 2 "Workers' Compensation" §13.

§115. Appeals board decisions; reconsideration.

Actions of the appeals board shall be taken by decision of a majority of the appeals board except as otherwise expressly provided.

The chairman shall assign pending cases in which reconsideration is sought to any three members thereof for hearing, consideration and decision. Assignments by the chairman of members to such cases shall be rotated on a case-by-case basis with the composition of the members so assigned being varied and changed to assure that there shall never be a fixed and continued composition of members. Any such case assigned to any three members in which the finding, order, decision or award is made and filed by any two or more of such members shall be the action of the appeals board unless reconsideration is had in accordance with the provisions of Article 1 (commencing with Section 5900), Chapter 7, Part 4, Division 4 of this code. Any case assigned to three members shall be heard and decided only by them, unless the matter has been reassigned by the chairman on a majority vote of the appeals board to the appeals board as a whole in order to achieve uniformity of decision, or in cases presenting novel issues.

Ref.: 8 C.C.R. §§10340, 10341, 10342; Hanna §§ 1.11[2], 28.35[1]; Herlick Handbook § 1.2; W. Cal. Sum., 2 "Workers' Compensation" §13.

§116. Appeals board seal.

The seal of the appeals board bearing the inscription "Workers' Compensation Appeals Board, Seal" shall be affixed to all writs and authentications of copies of records and to such other instruments as the appeals board directs.

Ref.: Herlick Handbook § 1.2.

§117. Appointment of attorney.

The administrative director may appoint an attorney licensed to practice law in the state as counsel to the division.

1989 Note: This section is applicable only to injuries occurring on or after January 1, 1990. Stats. 1989 ch. 893 §6.

Ref.: Hanna § 1.12[4]; Herlick Handbook § 1.2; W. Cal. Sum., 2 "Workers' Compensation" §11.

§119. Duties of attorney.

The attorney shall:

(a) Represent and appear for the state and the Division of Workers' Compensation and the appeals board in all actions and proceedings arising under any provision of this code administered by the division or under any order or act of the division or the appeals board and, if directed so to do, intervene, if possible, in any action or proceeding in which any such question is involved.

(b) Commence, prosecute, and expedite the final determination of all actions or proceedings, directed or authorized by the administrative director or the appeals board.

(c) Advise the administrative director and the appeals board and each member thereof, upon request, in regard to the jurisdiction, powers or duties of the administrative director, the appeals board and each member thereof.

(d) Generally perform the duties and services as attorney to the Division of Workers' Compensation and the appeals board which are required of him or her. **Leg.H.** 1994 chs. 146, 1097.

Ref.: Herlick Handbook § 1.2.

§120. Appointment of secretaries.

The administrative director and the chairman of the appeals board may each respectively appoint a secretary and assistant secretaries to perform such services as shall be prescribed.

Ref.: Herlick Handbook § 1.2; W. Cal. Sum., 2 "Workers' Compensation" §§11, 13.

§121. Acts by deputies; validity.

The chairman of the appeals board may authorize its secretary and any two assistant secretaries to act as deputy appeals board members and may delegate authority and duties to these deputies. Not more than three deputies may act as appeals board members at any one time. No act of any deputy shall be valid unless it is concurred in by at least one member of the appeals board.

Ref.: 8 C.C.R. §§10348, 10349, 10350, 10351, 10352; Herlick Handbook § 1.2; W. Cal. Sum., 2 "Workers' Compensation" §13.

§122. Medical director and assistants; appointment; qualifications; salaries.

The administrative director shall appoint a medical director who shall possess a physician's and surgeon's certificate granted under Chapter 5 (commencing with Section 2000) of Division 2 of the Business and Professions Code. The medical director shall employ medical assistants who shall also possess physicians' and surgeons' certificates and other staff necessary to the performance of his or her duties. The salaries for the medical director and his or her assistants shall be fixed by the Department of Personnel Administration, commensurate with the salaries paid by private industry to medical directors and assistant medical directors. **Leg.H.** 2003 ch. 639 (SB 228).

1989 Note: This section is applicable only to injuries occurring on or after January 1, 1990. Stats. 1989 ch. 893 §6.

Ref.: Herlick Handbook §§ 1.2, 1.8; W. Cal. Sum., 2 "Workers' Compensation" §11.

§123. Administrative personnel; salaries of workers' compensation administrative law judges.

The administrative director may employ necessary assistants, officers, experts, statisticians, actuaries, accountants, workers' compensation administrative law judges, stenographic shorthand reporters, legal secretaries, disability evaluation raters, program technicians, and other employees to implement new, efficient court management systems. The salaries of the workers' compensation administrative law judges shall be fixed by the Department of Personnel Administration for a class of positions which perform judicial functions. **Leg.H.** 2002 ch. 6 (AB 749).

Ref.: Herlick Handbook § 1.2; W. Cal. Sum., 2 "Workers' Compensation" §§11, 14.

§123.3. Official reporters.

Any official reporter employed by the administrative director shall render stenographic or clerical assistance as directed by the presiding workers' compensation administrative law judge of the office to which the reporter is assigned, when the presiding workers' compensation administrative law judge determines that the reporter is not engaged in the performance of any other duty imposed by law. **Leg.H.** 2002 ch. 6 (AB 749).

Ref.: Herlick Handbook § 1.2.

§123.5. Workers' compensation administrative law judges.

(a) Workers' compensation administrative law judges employed by the administrative director and supervised by the court administrator pursuant to this chapter shall be taken from an eligible list of attorneys licensed to practice law in this state, who have the qualifications prescribed by the State Personnel Board. In establishing eligible lists for this purpose, state civil service examinations shall be conducted in accordance with the State Civil Service Act (Part 2 (commencing with Section 18500) of Division 5 of Title 2 of the Government Code). Every workers' compensation judge shall maintain membership in the State Bar of California during his or her tenure.

A workers' compensation administrative law judge may not receive his or her salary as a workers' compensation administrative law judge while any cause before the workers' compensation administrative law judge remains pending and undetermined for 90 days after it has been submitted for decision.

(b) All workers' compensation administrative law judges appointed on or after January 1, 2003, shall be attorneys licensed to practice law in California for five or more years prior to their appointment and shall have experience in workers' compensation law. **Leg.H.** 2002 chs. 6 (AB 749), 866 (AB 486).

1989 Note: This section is applicable only to injuries occurring on or after January 1, 1990. Stats. 1989 ch. 893 §6.

Ref.: 8 C.C.R. §§9710, 9711, 9712, 9713, 9714, 9714.5, 9715, 10302; Hanna §§ 1.11[3], 24.11[1]; Herlick Handbook § 1.2; W. Cal. Sum., 2 "Workers' Compensation" §14.

§123.6. Workers' compensation administrative law judges to adhere to Code of Judicial Ethics; prior approval by court administrator for honoraria or travel payments.

(a) All workers' compensation administrative law judges employed by the administrative director and supervised by the court administrator shall subscribe to the Code of Judicial Ethics adopted by the Supreme Court pursuant to subdivision (m) of Section 18 of Article VI of the California Constitution for the conduct of judges and shall not otherwise, directly or indirectly, engage in conduct contrary to that code or to the commentary to the Code of Judicial Ethics.

In consultation with both the court administrator and the Commission on Judicial Performance, the administrative director shall adopt regulations to enforce this section. Existing regulations shall remain in effect until new regulations based on the recommendations of the court administrator and the Commission on Judicial Performance have become effective. To the extent possible, the rules shall be consistent with the procedures established by the Commission on Judicial Performance for regulating the activities of state judges, and, to the extent possible, with the gift, honoraria, and travel restrictions on legislators contained in the Political Reform Act of 1974 (Title 9 (commencing with Section 81000) of the Government Code). The court administrator shall have the authority to enforce the rules adopted by the administrative director.

(b) Honoraria or travel allowed by the court administrator, and not otherwise prohibited by this section in connection with any public or private conference, convention, meeting, social event, or like gathering, the cost of which is significantly paid for by attorneys who practice before the board, may not be accepted unless the court administrator has provided prior approval in writing to the workers' compensation administrative law judge allowing him or her to accept those payments. **Leg.H.** 1993 ch. 483, effective September 27, 1993, 1998 chs. 95, 448, 2002 chs. 6 (AB 749), 866 (AB 486), 2005 ch. 706 (AB 1742) §35.

Ref.: 8 C.C.R. §§9720.1, 9720.2, 9721.1, 9721.2, 9721.31, 9721.32, 9722, 9722.1, 9722.2, 9723, 10166; Hanna § 1.11[3][a]; Herlick Handbook § 1.2; W. Cal. Sum., 2 "Workers' Compensation" §§14, 395.

§123.7. Certified workers' compensation specialists; pro tempore judges.

The appeals board may, by rule or regulation, establish procedures whereby attorneys who are either certified specialists in workers' compensation by the California State Bar, or are eligible for this certification, may be appointed by the presiding workers' compensation judge of each board office to serve as a pro tempore workers' compensation judge in a particular case, upon the stipulation of the employee or his or her representative, and the employer or the insurance carrier. Service in this capacity by an attorney shall be voluntary and without pay. It is the intent of the Legislature that the use of pro tempore workers' compensation judges pursuant to this section shall not result in a reduction of the number of permanent civil service employees or the number of authorized full-time equivalent positions.

Ref.: 8 C.C.R. §§10166, 10349, 10350, 10351, 10352; Hanna § 1.11[1]; Herlick Handbook § 1.2.

§124. Administration and enforcement of benefits.

(a) In administering and enforcing this division and Division 4 (commencing with Section 3200), the division shall protect the interests of injured workers who are entitled to the timely provision of compensation.

(b) Forms and notices required to be given to employees by the division shall be in English and Spanish. **Leg.H.** 1993 ch. 1241, 2002 ch. 6 (AB 749), 2003 ch. 639 (SB 228).

1989 Note: This section is applicable only to injuries occurring on or after January 1, 1990. Stats. 1989 ch. 893 §6.

Ref.: 8 C.C.R. §§10100, 10100.1, 10100.2, 10101, 10101.1, 10102, 10103, 10103.1, 10103.2, 10106, 10106.1, 10106.5, 10107, 10108, 10109, 10111, 10111.1, 10111.2, 10113, 10114, 10114.1, 10114.2, 10114.3, 10114.4, 10122, 10133.50, 10150, 10151, 10152, 10156, 10158, 10160, 10160.1, 10160.5, 10161, 10162, 10163, 10164, 10165, 10165.5, 10166, 10168; Hanna § 1.12[15]; Herlick Handbook §§ 1.2, 1.5.

§125. Blank forms.

The administrative director shall cause to be printed and furnished free of charge to any person blank forms that may facilitate or promote the efficient performance of the duties of the Division of Workers' Compensation. **Leg.H.** 1994 ch. 146.

Ref.: Hanna §§ 1.12[2], 23.12[1]; Herlick Handbook § 1.2; W. Cal. Sum., 2 "Workers' Compensation" §11.

§126. Records.

The Division of Workers' Compensation, including the administrative director and the appeals board, shall keep minutes of all their proceedings and other books or records requisite for proper and efficient administration. All records shall be kept in their respective offices. **Leg.H.** 1994 ch. 146.

Ref.: 8 C.C.R. §§10306, 10308, 10360, 10390, 10392, 10395, 10396, 10400, 10412, 10450, 10630, 10750, 10751, 10753, 10842; Hanna §§ 1.11[5], 1.12[5]; Herlick Handbook § 1.2.

§127. Administrative director and court administrator—Authority.

The administrative director and court administrator may:

(a) Charge and collect fees for copies of papers and records, for certified copies of official documents and orders or of the evidence taken or proceedings had, for transcripts of testimony, and for inspection of case files not stored in the place where the inspection is requested. The administrative director shall fix those fees in an amount sufficient to recover the actual costs of furnishing the services. No fees for inspection of case files shall be charged to an injured employee or his or her representative.

(b) Publish and distribute from time to time, in addition to the reports to the Governor, further reports and pamphlets covering the operations, proceedings, and matters relative to the work of the division.

(c) Prepare, publish, and distribute an office manual, for which a reasonable fee may be charged, and to which additions, deletions, amendments, and other changes from time to time may be adopted, published, and distributed, for which a reasonable fee may be charged for the revision, or for which a reasonable fee may be fixed on an annual subscription basis.

(d) Fix and collect reasonable charges for publications issued. **Leg.H.** 2002 ch. 6 (AB 749).

Ref.: 8 C.C.R. §§9990, 9992, 9994, 10322, 10740; Hanna §§ 1.12[2], [5], 23.13[1]; Herlick Handbook § 1.2; W. Cal. Sum., 2 "Workers' Compensation" §12.

§127.5. Court administrator; additional duties.

In the exercise of his or her functions, the court administrator shall further the interests of uniformity and expedition of proceedings before workers' compensation administrative law judges, assure that all workers' compensation administrative law judges are qualified and adhere to deadlines mandated by law or regulations, and manage district office procedural matters at the trial level. **Leg.H.** 2002 ch. 6 (AB 749).

Ref.: Hanna § 1.12[3]; Herlick Handbook § 1.2; W. Cal. Sum., 2 "Workers' Compensation" §12.

§127.6. Administrative director; additional duties.

(a) The administrative director shall, in consultation with the Commission on Health and Safety and Workers' Compensation, other state agencies, and researchers and research institutions with expertise in health care delivery and occupational health care service, conduct a study of medical treatment provided to workers who have sustained industrial injuries and illnesses. The study shall focus on, but not be limited to, all of the following:

(1) Factors contributing to the rising costs and utilization of medical treatment and case management in the workers' compensation system.

(2) An evaluation of case management procedures that contribute to or achieve early and sustained return to work within the employee's temporary and permanent work restrictions.

(3) Performance measures for medical services that reflect patient outcomes.

(4) Physician utilization, quality of care, and outcome measurement data.

(5) Patient satisfaction.

(b) The administrative director shall begin the study on or before July 1, 2003, and shall report and make recommendations to the Legislature based on the results of the study on or before July 1, 2004.

(c) In implementing this section, the administrative director shall ensure the confidentiality and protection of patient-specific data. **Leg.H.** 2002 ch. 6 (AB 749), 2003 ch. 639 (SB 228).

Ref.: Hanna § 1.12[2].

§128. Enforcement of Longshoremen's and Harbor Workers' Compensation Act.

The appeals board may accept appointment as deputy commissioner under, or any delegation of authority to enforce, the United States Longshoremen's and Harbor Worker's Compensation Act. The appeals board may enter into arrangements with the United States, subject to the approval of the Department of Finance, for the payment of any expenses incurred in the performance of services under said act. In the performance of any duties under said act, appointment, or authority, the appeals board may, subject to the provisions thereof, exercise any authority conferred upon the appeals board by the laws of this state.

Ref.: Hanna § 21.01[5]; Herlick Handbook §§ 1.2, 1.4; W. Cal. Sum., 2 "Workers' Compensation" §14.

§129. Audits.

(a) To make certain that injured workers, and their dependents in the event of their death, receive promptly and accurately the full measure of compensation to which they are entitled, the administrative director shall audit insurers, self-insured employers, and third-party administrators to determine if they have met their obligations under this code. Each audit subject shall be audited at least once every five years. The audit subjects shall be selected and the audits conducted pursuant to subdivision (b). The results of audits of insurers shall be provided to the Insurance Commissioner, and the results of audits of self-insurers and third-party administrators shall be provided to the Director of Industrial Relations. Nothing in this section shall restrict the authority of the Director of Industrial Relations or the Insurance Commissioner to audit their licensees.

(b) The administrative director shall schedule and conduct audits as follows:

(1) A profile audit review of every audit subject shall be conducted once every five years and on additional occasions indicated by target audit criteria. The administrative director shall annually establish a profile audit review performance standard that will identify the poorest performing audit subjects.

(2) A full compliance audit shall be conducted of each profile audited subject failing to meet or exceed the profile audit review performance standard. The full compliance audit shall be a comprehensive and detailed evaluation of the audit subject's performance. The administrative director shall annually establish a full compliance audit performance standard that will identify the audit subjects that are performing satisfactorily. Any full compliance audit subject that fails to meet or exceed the full compliance audit performance standard shall be audited again within two years.

(3) A targeted profile audit review or a full compliance audit may be conducted at any time in accordance with target audit criteria adopted by the administrative director. The target audit criteria shall be based on information obtained from benefit notices, from information and assistance officers, and from other reliable sources providing factual information that indicates an insurer, self-insured employer, or third-party administrator is failing to meet its obligations under this division or Division 4 (commencing with Section 3200) or the regulations of the administrative director.

(c) If, as a result of a profile audit review or a full compliance audit, the administrative director determines that any compensation, interest, or penalty is due and unpaid to an employee or dependent, the administrative director shall issue and cause to be served upon the insurer, self-insured employer, or third-party administrator a notice of assessment detailing the amounts due and unpaid in each case, and shall order the amounts paid to the person entitled thereto. The notice of assessment shall be served personally or by registered mail in accordance with subdivision (c) of Section 11505 of the Government Code. A copy of the notice of assessment shall also be sent to the affected employee or dependent.

If the amounts are not paid within 30 days after service of the notice of assessment, the employer shall also be liable for reasonable attorney's fees necessarily incurred by the employee or dependent to obtain amounts due. The administrative director shall advise each employee or dependent still owed compensation after this 30-day period of his or her rights with respect to the commencement of proceedings to collect the compensation owed. Amounts unpaid because the person entitled thereto cannot be located shall be paid to the Workers' Compensation Administration Revolving Fund. The Director of Industrial Relations shall promulgate rules and regulations establishing standards and procedures for the payment of compensation from moneys deposited in the Workers' Compensation Administration Revolving Fund whenever the person entitled thereto applies for compensation.

(d) A determination by the administrative director that an amount is or is not due to an employee or dependent shall not in any manner limit the jurisdiction or authority of the appeals board to determine the issue.

(e) Annually, commencing on April 1, 1991, the administrative director shall publish a report detailing the results of audits conducted pursuant to this section during the preceding calendar year. The report shall include the name of each insurer, self-insured employer, and third-party administrator audited during that period. For each insurer, self-insured employer, and third-party administrator audited, the report shall specify the total number of files audited, the number of violations found by type and amount of compensation, interest and penalties payable, and the amount collected for each violation. The administrative director shall also publish and make available to the public on request a list ranking all insurers, self-insured employers, and third-party administrators audited during the period according to their performance measured by the profile audit review and full compliance audit performance standards.

These reports shall not identify the particular claim file that resulted in a particular violation or penalty. Except as required by this subdivision or other provisions of law, the contents of individual claim files and auditor's working papers shall be confidential. Disclosure of claim information to the administrative director pursuant to an audit shall not waive the provisions of the Evidence Code relating to privilege.

(f) A profile audit review of the adjustment of claims against the Uninsured Employers Fund by the claims and collections unit of the Division of Workers' Compensation shall be conducted at least every five years. The results of this profile audit review shall be included in the report required by subdivision (e). **Leg.H.** 1993 ch. 1241, 2001 ch. 159, 2002 ch. 6 (AB 749).

1989 Note: This section is applicable only to injuries occurring on or after January 1, 1990. Stats. 1989 ch. 893 §6.

Ref.: 8 C.C.R. §§9703, 10100, 10100.1, 10100.2, 10101, 10101.1, 10102, 10103, 10103.1, 10103.2, 10104, 10105, 10106, 10106.1. 10106.5, 10107, 10107.1, 10108, 10109, 10110, 10111, 10111.1, 10111.2, 10112, 10113, 10113.1, 10113.2, 10113.3, 10113.4, 10113.5, 10113.6, 10115, 10115.1, 10115.2, 10952, 15201, 15210.2, 15210.3, 15211, 15211.2, 15212, 15216, 15251, 15300, 15301, 15302, 15303, 15360, 15362, 15400, 15400.1, 15400.2, 15402, 15402.1, 15402.2, 15402.4, 15403, 15403.1, 15403.2, 15404, 15404.1, 15404.2, 15405, 15420, 15422, 15423, 15424, 15425, 15426, 15427, 15428, 15458, 15459; Hanna §§ 1.12[8]–[9], 2.02[1]; Herlick Handbook §§ 1.2, 1.5; W. Cal. Sum., 2 "Workers' Compensation" §11.

§129.5. Administrative and civil penalties; schedule of violations.

(a) The administrative director may assess an administrative penalty against an insurer, self-insured employer, or third-party administrator for any of the following:

(1) Failure to comply with the notice of assessment issued pursuant to subdivision (c) of Section 129 within 15 days of receipt.

(2) Failure to pay when due the undisputed portion of an indemnity payment, the reasonable cost of medical treatment of an injured worker, or a charge or cost implementing an approved vocational rehabilitation plan.

(3) Failure to comply with any rule or regulation of the administrative director.

(b) The administrative director shall promulgate regulations establishing a schedule of violations and the amount of the administrative penalty to be imposed for each type of violation. The schedule shall provide for imposition of a penalty of up to one hundred dollars ($100) for each violation of the less serious type and for imposition of penalties in progressively higher amounts for the most serious types of violations to be set at up to five thousand dollars ($5,000) per violation. The administrative director is authorized to impose penalties pursuant to rules and regulations which give due consideration to the appropriateness of the penalty with respect to the following factors:

(1) The gravity of the violation.

(2) The good faith of the insurer, self-insured employer, or third-party administrator.

(3) The history of previous violations, if any.

(4) The frequency of the violations.

(5) Whether the audit subject has met or exceeded the profile audit review performance standard.

(6) Whether a full compliance audit subject has met or exceeded the full compliance audit performance standard.

(7) The size of the audit subject location.

(c) The administrative director shall assess penalties as follows:

Labor

(1) If, after a profile audit review, the administrative director determines that the profile audit subject met or exceeded the profile audit review performance standard, no penalties shall be assessed under this section, but the audit subject shall be required to pay any compensation due and penalties due under subdivision (d) of Section 4650 as provided in subdivision (c) of Section 129.

(2) If, after a full compliance audit, the administrative director determines that the audit subject met or exceeded the full compliance audit performance standards, penalties for unpaid or late paid compensation, but no other penalties under this section, shall be assessed. The audit subject shall be required to pay any compensation due and penalties due under subdivision (d) of Section 4650 as provided in subdivision (c) of Section 129.

(3) If, after a full compliance audit, the administrative director determines that the audit subject failed to meet the full compliance audit performance standards, penalties shall be assessed as provided in a full compliance audit failure penalty schedule to be adopted by the administrative director. The full compliance audit failure penalty schedule shall adjust penalty levels relative to the size of the audit location to mitigate inequality between total penalties assessed against small and large audit subjects. The penalty amounts provided in the full compliance audit failure penalty schedule for the most serious type of violations shall not be limited by subdivision (b), but in no event shall the penalty for a single violation exceed forty thousand dollars ($40,000).

(d) The notice of penalty assessment shall be served personally or by registered mail in accordance with subdivision (c) of Section 11505 of the Government Code. The notice shall be in writing and shall describe the nature of the violation, including reference to the statutory provision or rule or regulation alleged to have been violated. The notice shall become final and the assessment shall be paid unless contested within 15 days of receipt by the insurer, self-insured employer, or third-party administrator.

(e) In addition to the penalty assessments permitted by subdivisions (a), (b), and (c), the administrative director may assess a civil penalty, not to exceed one hundred thousand dollars ($100,000), upon finding, after hearing, that an employer, insurer, or third-party administrator for an employer has knowingly committed or performed with sufficient frequency so as to indicate a general business practice any of the following:

(1) Induced employees to accept less than compensation due, or made it necessary for employees to resort to proceedings against the employer to secure compensation.

(2) Refused to comply with known and legally indisputable compensation obligations.

(3) Discharged or administered compensation obligations in a dishonest manner.

(4) Discharged or administered compensation obligations in a manner as to cause injury to the public or those dealing with the employer or insurer.

Any employer, insurer, or third-party administrator that fails to meet the full compliance audit performance standards in two consecutive full compliance audits shall be rebuttably presumed to have engaged in a general business practice of discharging and administering its compensation obligations in a manner causing injury to those dealing with it.

Upon a second or subsequent finding, the administrative director shall refer the matter to the Insurance Commissioner or the Director of Industrial Relations and request that a hearing be conducted to determine whether the certificate of authority, certificate of consent to self-insure, or certificate of consent to administer claims of self-insured employers, as the case may be, shall be revoked.

(f) An insurer, self-insured employer, or third-party administrator may file a written request for a conference with the administrative director within seven days after receipt of a notice of penalty assessment issued pursuant to subdivision (a) or (c). Within 15 days of the conference, the administrative director shall issue a notice of findings and serve it upon the contesting party by registered or certified mail. Any amount found due by the administrative director shall become due and payable 30 days after receipt of the notice of findings. The 30-day period shall be tolled during any appeal. A writ of mandate may be taken from the findings to the appropriate superior court upon the execution by the contesting party of a bond to the state in the principal sum that is double the amount found due and ordered by the administrative director, on the condition that the contesting party shall pay any judgment and costs rendered against it for the amount.

(g) An insurer, self-insured employer, or third-party administrator may file a written request for a hearing before the Workers' Compensation Appeals Board within seven days after receipt of a notice of penalty assessment issued pursuant to subdivision (e). Within 30 days of the hearing, the appeals board shall issue findings and orders and serve them upon the contesting party in the manner provided in its rules. Any amount found due by the appeals board shall become due and payable 45 days after receipt of the notice of findings. Judicial review of the findings and order shall be had in the manner provided by Article 2 (commencing with Section 5950) of Chapter 7 of Part 4 of Division 4. The 45-day period shall be tolled during appellate proceedings upon execution by the contesting party of a bond to the state in a principal sum that is double the amount found due and ordered by the appeals board on the condition that the contesting party shall pay the amount ultimately determined to be due and any costs awarded by an appellate court.

(h) Nothing in this section shall create nor eliminate a civil cause of action for the employee and his or her dependents.

(i) All moneys collected under this section shall be deposited in the State Treasury and credited to the Workers' Compensation Administration Revolving Fund. **Leg.H.** 1993 ch. 1241, 2002 ch. 6 (AB 749).

1989 Note: This section is applicable only to injuries occurring on or after January 1, 1990. Stats. 1989 ch. 893 §6.

Ref.: 8 C.C.R. §§10100, 10100.1, 10100.2, 10101, 10101.1, 10102, 10103, 10103.1, 10103.2, 10104, 10105, 10106, 10106.1, 10106.5, 10107, 10107.1, 10108, 10111, 10111.1, 10111.2, 10112, 10113, 10113.1, 10113.2, 10113.3, 10113.4, 10113.5, 10113.6, 10114, 10114.1, 10114.2, 10114.3, 10114.4, 10115, 10115.1, 10115.2, 10953; Hanna § 10.51[2][a]; Herlick Handbook §§ 1.2, 1.5, 9.5; W. Cal. Sum., 2 "Workers' Compensation" §§11, 150.

§130. Authority to administer oaths and issue subpoenas.

The appeals board and each of its members, its secretary, assistant secretaries, and workers' compensation judges, may administer oaths, certify to all official acts, and issue subpoenas for the attendance of witnesses and the production of papers, books, accounts, documents and testimony in any inquiry, investigation, hearing or proceeding in any part of the state.

Ref.: 8 C.C.R. §§10530, 10534, 10536, 10563, 10820, 10825, 10828; Hanna §§ 1.11[3], [6], 21.03[8], 25.29[3], 25.43; Herlick Handbook §§ 1.2, 1.4; W. Cal. Ev., "Introduction" §73.

§131. Fees and mileage for witnesses.

Each witness who appears by order of the appeals board or any of its members, or a workers' compensation judge, shall receive, if demanded, for his or her attendance the same fees and mileage allowed by law to a witness in civil cases, paid by the party at whose request the witness is subpoenaed, unless otherwise ordered by the appeals board. When any witness who has not been required to attend at the request of any party is subpoenaed by the appeals board, his or her fees and mileage may be paid from the funds appropriated for the use of the appeals board in the same manner as other expenses of the appeals board are paid. Any witness subpoenaed, except one whose fees and mileage are paid from the funds of the appeals board, may, at the time of service, demand the fee to which he or she is entitled for travel to and from the place at which he or she is required to appear, and one day's attendance. If a witness demands his or her fees at the time of service, and they are not at that time paid or tendered, he or she shall not be required to attend as directed in the subpoena. All fees and mileage to which any witness is entitled under this section may be collected by action therefor instituted by the person to whom the fees are payable.

Ref.: 8 C.C.R. §10536; Hanna §§ 21.03[8], 23.10[2], 23.13[2], 25.10[2]; Herlick Handbook § 1.2; W. Cal. Ev., "Introduction" §73.

§132. Refusal to obey subpoena; contempt.

The superior court in and for the county in which any proceeding is held by the appeals board or a workers' compensation judge may compel the attendance of witnesses, the giving of testimony and the production of papers, including books, accounts, and documents, as required by any subpoena regularly issued hereunder. In case of the refusal of any witness to obey the subpoena the appeals board or the workers' compensation judge, before whom the testimony is to be given or produced, may report to the superior court in and for the county in which the proceeding is pending, by petition, setting forth that due notice has been given of the time and place of attendance of the witness, or the production of the papers, that the witness has been subpoenaed in the prescribed manner, and that the witness has failed and refused to obey the subpoena, or has refused to answer questions propounded to him or her in the course of the proceeding, and ask an order of the court, compelling the witness to attend and testify or produce the papers before the appeals board. The court shall thereupon enter an order directing the witness to appear before the court at a time and place fixed in the order, the time to be not more than 10 days from the date of the order, and then and there show cause why he or she had not attended and testified or produced the papers before the appeals board or the workers' compensation judge. A copy of the order shall be served upon the witness. If it appears to the court that the subpoena was regularly issued hereunder and that the witness was legally bound to comply therewith, the court shall thereupon enter an order that the witness appear before the appeals board or the workers' compensation judge at a time and place fixed in the order, and testify or produce the required papers, and upon failure to obey the order, the witness shall be dealt with as for contempt of court. The remedy provided in this section is cumulative, and shall not impair or interfere with the power of the appeals board or a member thereof to enforce the attendance of witnesses and the production of papers, and to punish for contempt in the same manner and to the same extent as courts of record.

Ref.: 8 C.C.R. §§10532, 10534, 10536, 10537; Hanna §§ 20.01[2], 21.09[1]–[3], 25.43; Herlick Handbook § 1.2; W. Cal. Ev., "Introduction" §73.

§132a. Nondiscrimination policy.

It is the declared policy of this state that there should not be discrimination against workers who are injured in the course and scope of their employment.

(1) Any employer who discharges, or threatens to discharge, or in any manner discriminates against any employee because he or she has filed or made known his or her intention to file a claim for compensation with his or her employer or an application for adjudication, or because the employee has received a rating, award, or settlement, is guilty of a misdemeanor and the employee's compensation shall be increased by one-half, but in no event more than ten thousand dollars ($10,000), together with costs and expenses not in excess of two hundred fifty dollars ($250). Any such employee shall also be entitled to reinstatement and reimbursement for lost wages and work benefits caused by the acts of the employer.

(2) Any insurer that advises, directs, or threatens an insured under penalty of cancellation or a raise in premium or for any other reason, to discharge an employee because he or she has filed or made known his or her intention to file a claim for compensation with his or her employer or an application for adjudication, or because the employee has received a rating, award, or settlement, is guilty of a misdemeanor and subject to the increased compensation and costs provided by paragraph (1).

(3) Any employer who discharges, or threatens to discharge, or in any manner discriminates against any employee because the employee testified or made known his or her intentions to testify in another employee's case before the appeals board, is guilty of a misdemeanor, and the employee shall be entitled to reinstatement and reimbursement for lost wages and work benefits caused by the acts of the employer.

(4) Any insurer that advises, directs, or threatens an insured employer under penalty of cancellation or a raise in premium or for any other reason, to discharge or in any manner discriminate against an employee because the employee testified or made known his or her intention to testify in another employee's case before the appeals board, is guilty of a misdemeanor.

Proceedings for increased compensation as provided in paragraph (1), or for reinstatement and reimbursement for lost wages and work benefits, are to be instituted by filing an appropriate petition with the appeals board, but these proceedings may not be commenced more than one year from the discriminatory act or date of termination of the employee. The appeals board is vested with full power, authority, and jurisdiction to try and determine finally all matters specified in this section subject only to judicial review, except that the appeals board shall have no jurisdiction to try and determine a misdemeanor charge. The appeals board may refer and any worker may complain of suspected violations of the criminal misdemeanor provisions of this section to the Division of Labor Standards Enforcement, or directly to the office of the public prosecutor.

1989 Note: This section is applicable only to injuries occurring on or after January 1, 1990. Stats. 1989 ch. 893 §6.

Ref.: 8 C.C.R. §10447; Hanna §§ 10.11[1]–[4], 21.03[2][d], 21.07[7], 35.103[2], 35.104[2]; Herlick Handbook §§ 1.2, 9.12; W. Cal. Sum., 1 "Contracts" §888, 2 "Workers' Compensation" §§17–22, 107, 276, 3 "Agency and Employment" §350, 8 "Constitutional Law" §936.

§133. Division of Workers' Compensation—Power and jurisdiction.

The Division of Workers' Compensation, including the administrative director, the court administrator, and the appeals board, shall have power and jurisdiction to do all things necessary or convenient in the exercise of any power or jurisdiction conferred upon it under this code. **Leg.H.** 1994 chs. 146, 1097, 2002 ch. 6 (AB 749).

Ref.: 8 C.C.R. §§151, 9900, 10109, 10122.1, 10304, 10450, 10946; Herlick Handbook § 1.2; W. Cal. Sum., 2 "Workers' Compensation" §§11–13.

§134. Contempt proceedings; process service.

The appeals board or any member thereof may issue writs or summons, warrants of attachment, warrants of commitment and all necessary process in proceedings for contempt, in like manner and to the same extent as courts of record. The process issued by the appeals board or any member thereof shall extend to all parts of the state and may be served by any person authorized to serve process of courts of record or by any person designated for that purpose by the appeals board or any member thereof. The person executing process shall receive compensation allowed by the appeals board, not to exceed the fees prescribed by law for similar services. Such fees shall be paid in the same manner as provided herein for the fees of witnesses.

Ref.: 8 C.C.R. §§10348, 10414, 10416, 10536, 10820, 10825, 10828; Hanna § 21.09[1]; Herlick Handbook § 1.2; W. Cal. Sum., 2 "Workers' Compensation" §§14, 353, 388, 397.

§135. Destruction of files.

In accordance with rules of practice and procedure that it may adopt, the appeals board may, with the approval of the Department of Finance, destroy or otherwise dispose of any file kept by it in connection with any proceeding under Division 4 (commencing with Section 3200) or Division 4.5 (commencing with Section 6100). **Leg.H.** 1995 ch. 556.

Ref.: 8 C.C.R. §§10168, 10755, 10758; Herlick Handbook § 1.2.

§138. Appointment of deputy in director's or court administrator's absence.

The administrative director and the court administrator may each appoint a deputy to act during that time as he or she may be absent from the state due to official business, vacation, or illness. **Leg.H.** 2002 ch. 6 (AB 749).

Ref.: Hanna § 1.12[1]; Herlick Handbook § 1.2; W. Cal. Sum., 2 "Workers' Compensation" §§11, 12.

§138.1. Administrative director, court administrator; appointment; salary.

(a) The administrative director shall be appointed by the Governor with the advice and consent of the Senate and shall hold office at the pleasure of the Governor. He or she shall receive the salary provided for by Chapter 6 (commencing with Section 11550) of Part 1 of Division 3 of Title 2 of the Government Code.

(b) The court administrator shall be appointed by the Governor with the advice and consent of the Senate. The court administrator shall hold office for a term of five years. The court administrator shall receive the salary provided for by Chapter 6 (commencing with Section 11550) of Part 1 of Division 3 of Title 2 of the Government Code. **Leg.H.** 2002 ch. 6 (AB 749), 2003 ch. 639 (SB 228).

Ref.: Hanna § 1.12[1]; Herlick Handbook § 1.2; W. Cal. Sum., 2 "Workers' Compensation" §§11, 12.

§138.2. Division of Workers' Compensation headquarters; administrative offices; notice of public meetings.

(a) The headquarters of the Division of Workers' Compensation shall be based at and operated from a centrally located city.

The administrative director and the court administrator shall have an office in that city with suitable rooms, necessary office furniture, stationery, and supplies, and may rent quarters in other places for the purpose of establishing branch or service offices, and for that purpose may provide those offices with necessary furniture, stationery and supplies.

(b) The administrative director shall provide suitable rooms, with necessary office furniture, stationery and supplies, for the appeals board at the centrally located city in which the board shall be based and from which it shall operate, and may rent quarters in other places for the purpose of establishing branch or service offices for the appeals board, and for that purpose may provide those offices with necessary furniture, stationery, and supplies.

(c) All meetings held by the administrative director shall be open and public. Notice thereof shall be published in papers of general circulation not more than 30 days and not less than 10 days prior to each meeting in Sacramento, San Francisco, Fresno, Los Angeles and San Diego. Written notice of all meetings shall be given to all persons who request in writing directed to the administrative director that they be given notice. **Leg.H.** 1994 chs. 146, 1097, 2002 ch. 6 (AB 749).

Ref.: 8 C.C.R. §9900; Hanna §§ 1.11[1], 1.12[1], [5]; Herlick Handbook § 1.2.

§138.3. Notice to injured employee of right to benefits.

The administrative director shall, with respect to all injuries, prescribe, pursuant to Section 5402, reasonable rules and regulations requiring the employer to serve notice on the injured employee that he may be entitled to benefits under this division.

Ref.: 8 C.C.R. §§9900, 10101, 10101.1, 10102; Herlick Handbook §§ 1.2, 16.3; W. Cal. Sum., 2 "Workers' Compensation" §381.

§138.4. Injuries involving lost time; claims administrator's duties and responsibilities; claim form and notice of potential eligibility of benefits; regulatory authority of administrative director.

(a) For the purpose of this section, "claims administrator" means a self-administered workers' compensation insurer; or a self-administered self-insured employer; or a self-administered legally uninsured employer; or a self-administered joint powers authority; or a third-party claims administrator for an insurer, a self-insured employer, a legally uninsured employer, or a joint powers authority.

(b) With respect to injuries resulting in lost time beyond the employee's work shift at the time of injury or medical treatment beyond first aid:

(1) If the claims administrator obtains knowledge that the employer has not provided a claim form or a notice of potential eligibility for benefits to the employee, it shall provide the form and notice to the employee within three working days of its knowledge that the form or notice was not provided.

(2) If the claims administrator cannot determine if the employer has provided a claim form and notice of potential eligibility for benefits to the employee, the claims administrator shall provide the form and notice to the employee within 30 days of the administrator's date of knowledge of the claim.

(c) The administrative director shall prescribe reasonable rules and regulations for serving on the employee (or employee's dependents, in the case of death), notices dealing with the payment, nonpayment, or delay in payment of temporary disability, permanent disability, and death benefits and the provision of vocational rehabilitation services, notices of any change in the amount or type of benefits being provided, the termination of benefits, the rejection of any liability for compensation, and an accounting of benefits paid. **Leg.H.** 1999 ch. 83, 2002 ch. 6 (AB 749).

Ref.: 8 C.C.R. §§9702, 9703, 9810, 9811, 9812, 9813, 9815, 10101, 10101.1, 10103, 10103.1, 10103.2; Hanna § 24.01[2]; Herlick Handbook §§ 14.2, 16.3; W. Cal. Sum., 2 "Workers' Compensation" §§386, 413.

§138.5. Enforcement of child support obligations; Workers' Compensation Notification Project.

The Division of Workers' Compensation shall cooperate in the enforcement of child support obligations. At the request of the Department of Child Support Services, the administrative director shall assist in providing to the State Department of Child Support Services information concerning persons who are receiving permanent disability benefits or who have filed an application for adjudication of a claim which the Department of Child Support Services determines is necessary to carry out its responsibilities pursuant to Section 17510 of the Family Code.

The process of sharing information with regard to applicants for and recipients of permanent disability benefits required by this section shall be known as the Workers' Compensation Notification Project. **Leg.H.** 1994 chs. 146, 1097, 2000 ch. 808, effective September 28, 2000.

Ref.: W. Cal. Sum., 11 "Husband and Wife" §314.

§138.6. Development of workers' compensation information system.

(a) The administrative director, in consultation with the Insurance Commissioner and the Workers' Compensation Insurance Rating Bureau, shall develop a cost-efficient workers' compensation information system, which shall be administered by the division. The administrative director shall adopt regulations specifying the data elements to be collected by electronic data interchange.

(b) The information system shall do the following:

(1) Assist the department to manage the workers' compensation system in an effective and efficient manner.

(2) Facilitate the evaluation of the efficiency and effectiveness of the benefit delivery system.

(3) Assist in measuring how adequately the system indemnifies injured workers and their dependents.

(4) Provide statistical data for research into specific aspects of the workers' compensation program.

(c) The data collected electronically shall be compatible with the Electronic Data Interchange System of the International Association of Industrial Accident Boards and Commissions. The administrative director may adopt regulations authorizing the use of other nationally recognized data transmission formats in addition to those set forth in the Electronic Data Interchange System for the transmission of data required pursuant to this section. The administrative director shall accept data transmissions in any authorized format. If the administrative director determines that any authorized data transmission format is not in general use by claims administrators, conflicts with the requirements of state or federal law, or is obsolete, the administrative director may adopt regulations eliminating that data transmission format from those authorized pursuant to this subdivision. **Leg.H.** 1993 ch. 121, effective July 16, 1993, ch. 1242, 1997 ch. 729, 2000 ch. 318.

Ref.: 8 C.C.R. §§9700, 9701, 9702, 9703, 9704; Hanna § 1.12[2]; Herlick Handbook § 1.2; W. Cal. Sum., 2 "Workers' Compensation" §11.

§138.65. Study on 2003 and 2004 legislative reforms on workers' compensation insurance rates; data from insurers; study and recommendations; allocation of costs.

(a) The administrative director, after consultation with the Insurance Commissioner, shall contract with a qualified organization to study the effects of the 2003 and 2004 legislative reforms on workers' compensation insurance rates. The study shall do, but not be limited to, all of the following:

(1) Identify and quantify the savings generated by the reforms.

(2) Review workers' compensation insurance rates to determine the extent to which the reform savings were reflected in rates. When reviewing the rates, consideration shall be given to an insurer's premium revenue, claim costs, and surplus levels.

(3) Assess the effect of the reform savings on replenishing surpluses for workers' compensation insurance coverage.

(4) Review the effects of the reforms on the workers' compensation insurance rates, marketplace, and competition.

(5) Review the adequacy and accuracy of the pure premium rate as recommended by the Workers' Compensation Insurance Bureau and the pure premium rate adopted by the Insurance Commissioner.

(b) Insurers shall submit to the contracting organization premium revenue, claims costs, and surplus levels in different timing aggregates as established by the contracting organization, but at least quarterly and annually. The contracting organization may also request additional materials when appropriate. The contracting organization and the commission shall maintain strict confidentiality of the data. An insurer that fails to comply with the reporting requirements of this subdivision is subject to Section 11754 of the Insurance Code.

(c) The administrative director shall submit to the Governor, the Insurance Commissioner, and the President pro Tempore of the Senate, the Speaker of the Assembly, and the chairs of the appropriate policy committees of the Legislature, a progress report on the study on January 1, 2005, and July 1, 2005, and the final study on or before January 1, 2006. The Governor and the Insurance Commissioner shall review the results of the study and make recommendations as to the appropriateness of regulating insurance rates. If, after reviewing the study, the Governor and the Insurance Commissioner determine that the rates do not appropriately reflect the savings and the timing of the savings associated with the 2003 and 2004 reforms, the Governor and the Insurance Commissioner may submit proposals to the Legislature. The proposals shall take into consideration how rates should be regulated, and by whom. In no event shall the proposals unfairly penalize insurers that have properly reflected the 2003 and 2004 reforms in their rates, or can verify that they have not received any cost savings as a result of the reforms.

(d) The cost of the study shall be borne by the insurers up to one million dollars ($1,000,000). The cost of the study shall be allocated to an insurer based on the insurer's proportionate share of the market. **Leg.H.** 2004 ch. 34 (SB 899), effective April 19, 2004.

2004 Note: The addition of §138.65 made by this act shall apply prospectively from the date of enactment of this act, regardless of the date of injury, unless otherwise specified, but shall not constitute good cause to reopen or rescind, alter, or amend any existing order, decision, or award of the Workers' Compensation Appeals Board. Stats. 2004 ch. 34 (SB 899) §47.

Ref.: Hanna § 1.12[2]; Herlick Handbook § 1.2.

§138.7. "Individually identifiable information"; restricted access.

(a) Except as expressly permitted in subdivision (b), a person or public or private entity not a party to a claim for workers' compensation benefits may not obtain individually identifiable information obtained or maintained by the division on that claim. For purposes of this section, "individually identifiable information" means any data concerning an injury or claim that is linked to a uniquely identifiable employee, employer, claims administrator, or any other person or entity.

(b)(1) The administrative director, or a statistical agent designated by the administrative director, may use individually identifiable information for purposes of creating and maintaining the workers' compensation information system as specified in Section 138.6.

(2) The State Department of Health Services may use individually identifiable information for purposes of establishing and maintaining a program on occupational health and occupational disease prevention as specified in Section 105175 of the Health and Safety Code.

(3)(A) Individually identifiable information may be used by the Division of Workers' Compensation, the Division of Occupational Safety and Health, and the Division of Labor Statistics and Research as necessary to carry out their duties. The administrative director shall adopt regulations governing the access to the information described in this subdivision by these divisions. Any regulations adopted pursuant to this subdivision shall set forth the specific uses for which this information may be obtained.

(B) Individually identifiable information maintained in the workers' compensation information system and the Division of Workers' Compensation may be used by researchers employed by or under contract to the Commission on Health and Safety and Workers' Compensation as necessary to carry out the commission's research. The administrative director shall adopt regulations governing the access to the information described in this subdivision by commission researchers. These regulations shall set forth the specific uses for which this information may be obtained and include provisions guaranteeing the confidentiality of individually identifiable information. Individually identifiable information obtained under this subdivision shall not be disclosed to commission members. No individually identifiable information obtained by researchers under contract to the commission pursuant to this subparagraph may be disclosed to any other person or entity, public or private, for a use other than that research project for which the information was obtained. Within a reasonable period of time after the research for which the information was obtained has been completed, the data collected shall be modified in a manner so that the subjects cannot be identified, directly or through identifiers linked to the subjects.

(4) The administrative director shall adopt regulations allowing reasonable access to individually identifiable information by other persons or public or private entities for the purpose of bona fide statistical research. This research shall not divulge individually identifiable information concerning a particular employee, employer, claims administrator, or any other person or entity. The regulations adopted pursuant to this paragraph shall include provisions guaran-

teeing the confidentiality of individually identifiable information. Within a reasonable period of time after the research for which the information was obtained has been completed, the data collected shall be modified in a manner so that the subjects cannot be identified, directly or through identifiers linked to the subjects.

(5) This section shall not operate to exempt from disclosure any information that is considered to be a public record pursuant to the California Public Records Act (Chapter 3.5 (commencing with Section 6250) of Division 7 of Title 1 of the Government Code) contained in an individual's file once an application for adjudication has been filed pursuant to Section 5501.5.

However, individually identifiable information shall not be provided to any person or public or private entity who is not a party to the claim unless that person identifies himself or herself or that public or private entity identifies itself and states the reason for making the request. The administrative director may require the person or public or private entity making the request to produce information to verify that the name and address of the requester is valid and correct. If the purpose of the request is related to preemployment screening, the administrative director shall notify the person about whom the information is requested that the information was provided and shall include the following in 12-point type:

"IT MAY BE A VIOLATION OF FEDERAL AND STATE LAW TO DISCRIMINATE AGAINST A JOB APPLICANT BECAUSE THE APPLICANT HAS FILED A CLAIM FOR WORKERS' COMPENSATION BENEFITS."

Any residence address is confidential and shall not be disclosed to any person or public or private entity except to a party to the claim, a law enforcement agency, an office of a district attorney, any person for a journalistic purpose, or other governmental agency.

Nothing in this paragraph shall be construed to prohibit the use of individually identifiable information for purposes of identifying bona fide lien claimants.

(c) Except as provided in subdivision (b), individually identifiable information obtained by the division is privileged and is not subject to subpoena in a civil proceeding unless, after reasonable notice to the division and a hearing, a court determines that the public interest and the intent of this section will not be jeopardized by disclosure of the information. This section shall not operate to restrict access to information by any law enforcement agency or district attorney's office or to limit admissibility of that information in a criminal proceeding.

(d) It shall be unlawful for any person who has received individually identifiable information from the division pursuant to this section to provide that information to any person who is not entitled to it under this section. **Leg.H.** 1997 ch. 674, 1998 ch. 624, 2001 ch. 792.

Ref.: 8 C.C.R. §§9700, 9701, 9702, 9703, 9704, 9990; Hanna § 1.12[2]; Herlick Handbook § 1.2; W. Cal. Sum., 2 "Workers' Compensation" §11.

§139.2. Appointment, qualification, suspension, termination of QMEs; timeframes, guidelines, procedures, and admissibility of medical evaluations.

(a) The administrative director shall appoint qualified medical evaluators in each of the respective specialties as required for the evaluation of medical-legal issues. The appointments shall be for two-year terms.

(b) The administrative director shall appoint or reappoint as a qualified medical evaluator a physician, as defined in Section 3209.3, who is licensed to practice in this state and who demonstrates that he or she meets the requirements in paragraphs (1), (2), (6), and (7), and, if the physician is a medical doctor, doctor of osteopathy, doctor of chiropractic, or a psychologist, that he or she also meets the applicable requirements in paragraph (3), (4), or (5).

(1) Prior to his or her appointment as a qualified medical evaluator, passes an examination written and administered by the administrative director for the purpose of demonstrating competence in evaluating medical-legal issues in the workers' compensation system. Physicians shall not be required to pass an additional examination as a condition of reappointment. A physician seeking appointment as a qualified medical evaluator on or after January 1, 2001, shall also complete prior to appointment, a course on disability evaluation report writing approved by the administrative director. The administrative director shall specify the curriculum to be covered by disability evaluation report writing courses, which shall include, but is not limited to, 12 or more hours of instruction.

(2) Devotes at least one-third of total practice time to providing direct medical treatment, or has served as an agreed medical evaluator on

eight or more occasions in the 12 months prior to applying to be appointed as a qualified medical evaluator.

(3) Is a medical doctor or doctor of osteopathy and meets one of the following requirements:

(A) Is board certified in a specialty by a board recognized by the administrative director and either the Medical Board of California or the Osteopathic Medical Board of California.

(B) Has successfully completed a residency training program accredited by the American College of Graduate Medical Education or the osteopathic equivalent.

(C) Was an active qualified medical evaluator on June 30, 2000.

(D) Has qualifications that the administrative director and either the Medical Board of California or the Osteopathic Medical Board of California, as appropriate, both deem to be equivalent to board certification in a specialty.

(4) Is a doctor of chiropractic and meets either of the following requirements:

(A) Has completed a chiropractic postgraduate specialty program of a minimum of 300 hours taught by a school or college recognized by the administrative director, the Board of Chiropractic Examiners and the Council on Chiropractic Education.

(B) Has been certified in California workers' compensation evaluation by a provider recognized by the administrative director. The certification program shall include instruction on disability evaluation report writing that meets the standards set forth in paragraph (1).

(5) Is a psychologist and meets one of the following requirements:

(A) Is board certified in clinical psychology by a board recognized by the administrative director.

(B) Holds a doctoral degree in psychology, or a doctoral degree deemed equivalent for licensure by the Board of Psychology pursuant to Section 2914 of the Business and Professions Code, from a university or professional school recognized by the administrative director and has not less than five years' postdoctoral experience in the diagnosis and treatment of emotional and mental disorders.

(C) Has not less than five years' postdoctoral experience in the diagnosis and treatment of emotional and mental disorders, and has served as an agreed medical evaluator on eight or more occasions prior to January 1, 1990.

(6) Does not have a conflict of interest as determined under the regulations adopted by the administrative director pursuant to subdivision (o).

(7) Meets any additional medical or professional standards adopted pursuant to paragraph (6) of subdivision (j).

(c) The administrative director shall adopt standards for appointment of physicians who are retired or who hold teaching positions who are exceptionally well qualified to serve as a qualified medical evaluator even though they do not otherwise qualify under paragraph (2) of subdivision (b). In no event shall a physician whose full-time practice is limited to the forensic evaluation of disability be appointed as a qualified medical evaluator under this subdivision.

(d) The qualified medical evaluator, upon request, shall be reappointed if he or she meets the qualifications of subdivision (b) and meets all of the following criteria:

(1) Is in compliance with all applicable regulations and evaluation guidelines adopted by the administrative director.

(2) Has not had more than five of his or her evaluations that were considered by a workers' compensation administrative law judge at a contested hearing rejected by the workers' compensation administrative law judge or the appeals board pursuant to this section during the most recent two-year period during which the physician served as a qualified medical evaluator. If the workers' compensation administrative law judge or the appeals board rejects the qualified medical evaluator's report on the basis that it fails to meet the minimum standards for those reports established by the administrative director or the appeals board, the workers' compensation administrative law judge or the appeals board, as the case may be, shall make a specific finding to that effect, and shall give notice to the medical evaluator and to the administrative director. Any rejection shall not be counted as one of the five qualifying rejections until the specific finding has become final and time for appeal has expired.

(3) Has completed within the previous 24 months at least 12 hours of continuing education in impairment evaluation or workers' compensation-related medical dispute evaluation approved by the administrative director.

(4) Has not been terminated, suspended, placed on probation, or otherwise disciplined by the administrative director during his or her

most recent term as a qualified medical evaluator.

If the evaluator does not meet any one of these criteria, the administrative director may in his or her discretion reappoint or deny reappointment according to regulations adopted by the administrative director. In no event may a physician who does not currently meet the requirements for initial appointment or who has been terminated under subdivision (e) because his or her license has been revoked or terminated by the licensing authority be reappointed.

(e) The administrative director may, in his or her discretion, suspend or terminate a qualified medical evaluator during his or her term of appointment without a hearing as provided under subdivision (k) or (*l*) whenever either of the following conditions occurs:

(1) The evaluator's license to practice in California has been suspended by the relevant licensing authority so as to preclude practice, or has been revoked or terminated by the licensing authority.

(2) The evaluator has failed to timely pay the fee required by the administrative director pursuant to subdivision (n).

(f) The administrative director shall furnish a physician, upon request, with a written statement of its reasons for termination of, or for denying appointment or reappointment as, a qualified medical evaluator. Upon receipt of a specific response to the statement of reasons, the administrative director shall review his or her decision not to appoint or reappoint the physician or to terminate the physician and shall notify the physician of its final decision within 60 days after receipt of the physician's response.

(g) The administrative director shall establish agreements with qualified medical evaluators to assure the expeditious evaluation of cases assigned to them for comprehensive medical evaluations.

(h)(1) When requested by an employee or employer pursuant to Section 4062.1, the medical director appointed pursuant to Section 122 shall assign three-member panels of qualified medical evaluators within five working days after receiving a request for a panel. If a panel is not assigned within 15 working days, the employee shall have the right to obtain a medical evaluation from any qualified medical evaluator of his or her choice. The medical director shall use a random selection method for assigning panels of qualified medical evaluators. The medical director shall select evaluators who are specialists of the type requested by the employee. The medical director shall advise the employee that he or she should consult with his or her treating physician prior to deciding which type of specialist to request.

(2) The administrative director shall promulgate a form that shall notify the employee of the physicians selected for his or her panel after a request has been made pursuant to Section 4062.1 or 4062.2. The form shall include, for each physician on the panel, the physician's name, address, telephone number, specialty, number of years in practice, and a brief description of his or her education and training, and shall advise the employee that he or she is entitled to receive transportation expenses and temporary disability for each day necessary for the examination. The form shall also state in a clear and conspicuous location and type: "You have the right to consult with an information and assistance officer at no cost to you prior to selecting the doctor to prepare your evaluation, or you may consult with an attorney. If your claim eventually goes to court, the workers' compensation administrative law judge will consider the evaluation prepared by the doctor you select to decide your claim."

(3) When compiling the list of evaluators from which to select randomly, the medical director shall include all qualified medical evaluators who meet all of the following criteria:

(A) He or she does not have a conflict of interest in the case, as defined by regulations adopted pursuant to subdivision (o).

(B) He or she is certified by the administrative director to evaluate in an appropriate specialty and at locations within the general geographic area of the employee's residence.

(C) He or she has not been suspended or terminated as a qualified medical evaluator for failure to pay the fee required by the administrative director pursuant to subdivision (n) or for any other reason.

(4) When the medical director determines that an employee has requested an evaluation by a type of specialist that is appropriate for the employee's injury, but there are not enough qualified medical evaluators of that type within the general geographic area of the employee's residence to establish a three-member panel, the medical director shall include sufficient qualified medical evaluators from other geographic areas and the employer shall pay all necessary

travel costs incurred in the event the employee selects an evaluator from another geographic area.

(i) The medical director appointed pursuant to Section 122 shall continuously review the quality of comprehensive medical evaluations and reports prepared by agreed and qualified medical evaluators and the timeliness with which evaluation reports are prepared and submitted. The review shall include, but not be limited to, a review of a random sample of reports submitted to the division, and a review of all reports alleged to be inaccurate or incomplete by a party to a case for which the evaluation was prepared. The medical director shall submit to the administrative director an annual report summarizing the results of the continuous review of medical evaluations and reports prepared by agreed and qualified medical evaluators and make recommendations for the improvement of the system of medical evaluations and determinations.

(j) After public hearing pursuant to Section 5307.3, the administrative director shall adopt regulations concerning the following issues:

(1)(A) Standards governing the timeframes within which medical evaluations shall be prepared and submitted by agreed and qualified medical evaluators. Except as provided in this subdivision, the timeframe for initial medical evaluations to be prepared and submitted shall be no more than 30 days after the evaluator has seen the employee or otherwise commenced the medical evaluation procedure. The administrative director shall develop regulations governing the provision of extensions of the 30-day period in both of the following cases:

(i) When the evaluator has not received test results or consulting physician's evaluations in time to meet the 30-day deadline.

(ii) To extend the 30-day period by not more than 15 days when the failure to meet the 30-day deadline was for good cause.

(B) For purposes of subparagraph (A), "good cause" means any of the following:

(i) Medical emergencies of the evaluator or evaluator's family.

(ii) Death in the evaluator's family.

(iii) Natural disasters or other community catastrophes that interrupt the operation of the evaluator's business.

(C) The administrative director shall develop timeframes governing availability of qualified medical evaluators for unrepresented employees under Sections 4061 and 4062. These timeframes shall give the employee the right to the addition of a new evaluator to his or her panel, selected at random, for each evaluator not available to see the employee within a specified period of time, but shall also permit the employee to waive this right for a specified period of time thereafter.

(2) Procedures to be followed by all physicians in evaluating the existence and extent of permanent impairment and limitations resulting from an injury in a manner consistent with Section 4660.

(3) Procedures governing the determination of any disputed medical treatment issues in a manner consistent with Section 5307.27.

(4) Procedures to be used in determining the compensability of psychiatric injury. The procedures shall be in accordance with Section 3208.3 and shall require that the diagnosis of a mental disorder be expressed using the terminology and criteria of the American Psychiatric Association's Diagnostic and Statistical Manual of Mental Disorders, Third Edition-Revised, or the terminology and diagnostic criteria of other psychiatric diagnostic manuals generally approved and accepted nationally by practitioners in the field of psychiatric medicine.

(5) Guidelines for the range of time normally required to perform the following:

(A) A medical-legal evaluation that has not been defined and valued pursuant to Section 5307.6. The guidelines shall establish minimum times for patient contact in the conduct of the evaluations, and shall be consistent with regulations adopted pursuant to Section 5307.6.

(B) Any treatment procedures that have not been defined and valued pursuant to Section 5307.1.

(C) Any other evaluation procedure requested by the Insurance Commissioner, or deemed appropriate by the administrative director.

(6) Any additional medical or professional standards that a medical evaluator shall meet as a condition of appointment, reappointment, or maintenance in the status of a medical evaluator.

(k) Except as provided in this subdivision, the administrative director may, in his or her discretion, suspend or terminate the privilege of a physician to serve as a qualified medical evaluator if the administrative director, after hearing pursuant to subdivision (*l*), determines, based on substantial evidence, that a qualified medical evaluator:

(1) Has violated any material statutory or administrative duty.

(2) Has failed to follow the medical procedures or qualifications established pursuant to paragraph (2), (3), (4), or (5) of subdivision (j).

(3) Has failed to comply with the timeframe standards established pursuant to subdivision (j).

(4) Has failed to meet the requirements of subdivision (b) or (c).

(5) Has prepared medical-legal evaluations that fail to meet the minimum standards for those reports established by the administrative director or the appeals board.

(6) Has made material misrepresentations or false statements in an application for appointment or reappointment as a qualified medical evaluator.

No hearing shall be required prior to the suspension or termination of a physician's privilege to serve as a qualified medical evaluator when the physician has done either of the following:

(A) Failed to timely pay the fee required pursuant to subdivision (n).

(B) Had his or her license to practice in California suspended by the relevant licensing authority so as to preclude practice, or had the license revoked or terminated by the licensing authority.

(*l*) The administrative director shall cite the qualified medical evaluator for a violation listed in subdivision (k) and shall set a hearing on the alleged violation within 30 days of service of the citation on the qualified medical evaluator. In addition to the authority to terminate or suspend the qualified medical evaluator upon finding a violation listed in subdivision (k), the administrative director may, in his or her discretion, place a qualified medical evaluator on probation subject to appropriate conditions, including ordering continuing education or training. The administrative director shall report to the appropriate licensing board the name of any qualified medical evaluator who is disciplined pursuant to this subdivision.

(m) The administrative director shall terminate from the list of medical evaluators any physician where licensure has been terminated by the relevant licensing board, or who has been convicted of a misdemeanor or felony related to the conduct of his or her medical practice, or of a crime of moral turpitude. The administrative director shall suspend or terminate as a medical evaluator any physician who has been suspended or placed on probation by the relevant licensing board. If a physician is suspended or terminated as a qualified medical evaluator under this subdivision, a report prepared by the physician that is not complete, signed, and furnished to one or more of the parties prior to the date of conviction or action of the licensing board, whichever is earlier, shall not be admissible in any proceeding before the appeals board nor shall there be any liability for payment for the report and any expense incurred by the physician in connection with the report.

(n) Each qualified medical evaluator shall pay a fee, as determined by the administrative director, for appointment or reappointment. These fees shall be based on a sliding scale as established by the administrative director. All revenues from fees paid under this subdivision shall be deposited into the Workers' Compensation Administration Revolving Fund and are available for expenditure upon appropriation by the Legislature, and shall not be used by any other department or agency or for any purpose other than administration of the programs the Division of Workers' Compensation related to the provision of medical treatment to injured employees.

(o) An evaluator may not request or accept any compensation or other thing of value from any source that does or could create a conflict with his or her duties as an evaluator under this code. The administrative director, after consultation with the Commission on Health and Safety and Workers' Compensation, shall adopt regulations to implement this subdivision. **Leg.H.** 1992 ch. 1352, effective September 30, 1992, 1993 ch. 4, effective April 3, 1993, ch. 121, effective July 16, 1993, ch. 1242, 1994 ch. 301, effective July 21, 1994, ch. 1118, 1995 ch. 319, 2000 ch. 54, 2003 chs. 228 (AB 1756), effective August 11, 2003, 639 (SB 228), 2004 ch. 34 (SB 899), effective April 19, 2004.

2004 Note: The amendment to §139.2 made by this act shall apply prospectively from the date of enactment of this act, regardless of the date of injury, unless otherwise specified, but shall not constitute good cause to reopen or rescind, alter, or amend any existing order, decision, or award of the Workers' Compensation Appeals Board. Stats. 2004 ch. 34 (SB 899) §47.

2003 Note: The regulations adopted by the Industrial Medical Council contained in Chapter 1 (commencing with Section 1) of Division 1 of Title 8 of the California Code of Regulations, except for those regulations repealed in Section 50 of this act, shall remain in effect and shall be deemed to be regulations adopted by the Administrative Director of the Division of Workers' Compensation. The terms of all qualified medical examiners appointed by the Industrial Medical Council shall be unaffected by the changes made by this act. All qualified medical examiners appointed by the Industrial Medical Council shall be deemed to be appointments made by the Administrative Director of the Division of Workers' Compensation. Any pending disciplinary actions against qualified medical examiners shall not be affected by the changes made by this act. Stats. 2003 ch. 639 (SB 228) §52.

1993 Note: Section 139.2, as amended by ch. 121, applies only to injuries occurring on or after January 1, 1994. Stats. 1993 ch. 121 §77.

Ref.: 8 C.C.R. §§1, 10, 10.2, 10.5, 11, 11.5, 12, 13, 14, 15, 16, 17, 18, 19, 30, 30.5, 31, 31.5, 32, 33, 35, 38, 39, 39.5, 40, 41, 43, 44, 45, 46, 47, 48, 49, 49.2, 49.4, 49.6, 49.8, 49.9, 50, 51, 52, 53, 54, 55, 56, 57, 60, 61, 62, 65, 74, 107, 108, 109, 110, 111, 112, 113, 114, 115, 116, 117, 150, 153, 154, 9795, 10631; Hanna §§ 22.11, 22.13; Herlick Handbook §§ 1.2, 1.8, 4.21, 9.18, 14.4, 14.21; W. Cal. Sum., 2 "Workers' Compensation" §§11, 23, 245.

§139.3. Referral to person with whom physician has financial interest unlawful.

(a) Notwithstanding any other provision of law, to the extent those services are paid pursuant to Division 4 (commencing with Section 3200), it is unlawful for a physician to refer a person for clinical laboratory, diagnostic nuclear medicine, radiation oncology, physical therapy, physical rehabilitation, psychometric testing, home infusion therapy, outpatient surgery, or diagnostic imaging goods or services whether for treatment or medical-legal purposes if the physician or his or her immediate family, has a financial interest with the person or in the entity that receives the referral.

(b) For purposes of this section and Section 139.31, the following shall apply:

(1) "Diagnostic imaging" includes, but is not limited to, all X-ray, computed axial tomography magnetic resonance imaging, nuclear medicine, positron emission tomography, mammography, and ultrasound goods and services.

(2) "Immediate family" includes the spouse and children of the physician, the parents of the physician, and the spouses of the children of the physician.

(3) "Physician" means a physician as defined in Section 3209.3.

(4) A "financial interest" includes, but is not limited to, any type of ownership, interest, debt, loan, lease, compensation, remuneration, discount, rebate, refund, dividend, distribution, subsidy, or other form of direct or indirect payment, whether in money or otherwise, between a licensee and a person or entity to whom the physician refers a person for a good or service specified in subdivision (a). A financial interest also exists if there is an indirect relationship between a physician and the referral recipient, including, but not limited to, an arrangement whereby a physician has an ownership interest in any entity that leases property to the referral recipient. Any financial interest transferred by a physician to, or otherwise established in, any person or entity for the purpose of avoiding the prohibition of this section shall be deemed a financial interest of the physician.

(5) A "physician's office" is either of the following:

(A) An office of a physician in solo practice.

(B) An office in which the services or goods are personally provided by the physician or by employees in that office, or personally by independent contractors in that office, in accordance with other provisions of law. Employees and independent contractors shall be licensed or certified when that licensure or certification is required by law.

(6) The "office of a group practice" is an office or offices in which two or more physicians are legally organized as a partnership, professional corporation, or not-for-profit corporation licensed according to subdivision (a) of Section 1204 of the Health and Safety Code for which all of the following are applicable:

(A) Each physician who is a member of the group provides substantially the full range of services that the physician routinely provides, including medical care, consultation, diagnosis, or treatment, through the joint use of shared office space, facilities, equipment, and personnel.

(B) Substantially all of the services of the physicians who are members of the group are provided through the group and are billed in the name of the group and amounts so received are treated as receipts of the group, and except that in the case of multispecialty clinics, as defined in subdivision (*l*) of Section 1206 of the Health and Safety Code, physician services are billed in the name of the multispecialty clinic and amounts so received are treated as receipts of the multispecialty clinic.

(C) The overhead expenses of, and the income from, the practice are distributed in accordance with methods previously determined by members of the group.

(7) Outpatient surgery includes both of the following:

(A) Any procedure performed on an outpatient basis in the operating rooms, ambulatory surgery rooms, endoscopy units, cardiac catheterization laboratories, or other sections of a freestanding ambulatory surgery clinic, whether or not licensed under paragraph (1) of subdivision (b) of Section 1204 of the Health and Safety Code.

(B) The ambulatory surgery itself.

(c)(1) It is unlawful for a licensee to enter into an arrangement or scheme, such as a cross-referral arrangement, that the licensee knows, or should know, has a principal purpose of ensuring referrals by the licensee to a particular entity that, if the licensee directly made referrals to that entity, would be in violation of this section.

(2) It shall be unlawful for a physician to offer, deliver, receive, or accept any rebate, refund, commission, preference, patronage dividend, discount, or other consideration, whether in the form of money or otherwise, as compensation or inducement for a referred evaluation or consultation.

(d) No claim for payment shall be presented by an entity to any individual, third-party payor, or other entity for any goods or services furnished pursuant to a referral prohibited under this section.

(e) A physician who refers to or seeks consultation from an organization in which the physician has a financial interest shall disclose this interest to the patient or if the patient is a minor, to the patient's parents or legal guardian in writing at the time of the referral.

(f) No insurer, self-insurer, or other payor shall pay a charge or lien for any goods or services resulting from a referral in violation of this section.

(g) A violation of subdivision (a) shall be a misdemeanor. The appropriate licensing board shall review the facts and circumstances of any conviction pursuant to subdivision (a) and take appropriate disciplinary action if the licensee has committed unprofessional conduct. Violations of this section may also be subject to civil penalties of up to five thousand dollars ($5,000) for each offense, which may be enforced by the Insurance Commissioner, Attorney General, or a district attorney. A violation of subdivision (c), (d), (e), or (f) is a public offense and is punishable upon conviction by a fine not exceeding fifteen thousand dollars ($15,000) for each violation and appropriate disciplinary action, including revocation of professional licensure, by the Medical Board of California or other appropriate governmental agency. **Leg.H.** 1993 ch. 121 §20, effective July 16, 1993, ch. 1242, 2003 ch. 639 (SB 228).

1993 Note: Section 139.3, as added by ch. 121, applies only to injuries occurring on or after January 1, 1994. Stats. 1993 ch. 121 §77.

Ref.: 8 C.C.R. §9768.12; Hanna §§ 22.14, 25.06[3]; Herlick Handbook §§ 1.2, 1.5, 1.8, 9.18; W. Cal. Sum., 2 "Workers' Compensation" §§261, 387, 389, 399.

§139.31. Exceptions to §139.3.

The prohibition of Section 139.3 shall not apply to or restrict any of the following:

(a) A physician may refer a patient for a good or service otherwise prohibited by subdivision (a) of Section 139.3 if the physician's regular practice is where there is no alternative provider of the service within either 25 miles or 40 minutes traveling time, via the shortest route on a paved road. A physician who refers to, or seeks consultation from, an organization in which the physician has a financial interest under this subdivision shall disclose this interest to the patient or the patient's parents or legal guardian in writing at the time of referral.

(b) A physician who has one or more of the following arrangements with another physician, a person, or an entity, is not prohibited from referring a patient to the physician, person, or entity because of the arrangement:

(1) A loan between a physician and the recipient of the referral, if the loan has commercially reasonable terms, bears interest at the prime rate or a higher rate that does not constitute usury, is adequately secured, and the loan terms are not affected by either party's referral of any person or the volume of services provided by either party.

(2) A lease of space or equipment between a physician and the recipient of the referral, if the lease is written, has commercially reasonable terms, has a fixed periodic rent payment, has a term of one year or more, and the lease payments are not affected by either party's referral of any person or the volume of services provided by either party.

(3) A physician's ownership of corporate investment securities, including shares, bonds, or other debt instruments that were purchased on terms that are available to the general public through a licensed securities exchange or NASDAQ, do not base profit distributions or other transfers of value on the physician's referral of persons to the corporation, do not have a separate class or accounting for any persons or for any physicians who may refer persons to the corporation, and are in a corporation that had, at the end of the corporation's most recent fiscal year, total gross assets exceeding one hundred million dollars ($100,000,000).

(4) A personal services arrangement between a physician or an immediate family member of the physician and the recipient of the referral if the arrangement meets all of the following requirements:

(A) It is set out in writing and is signed by the parties.

(B) It specifies all of the services to be provided by the physician or an immediate family member of the physician.

(C) The aggregate services contracted for do not exceed those that are reasonable and necessary for the legitimate business purposes of the arrangement.

(D) A written notice disclosing the existence of the personal services arrangement and including information on where a person may go to file a complaint against the licensee or the immediate family member of the licensee, is provided to the following persons at the time any services pursuant to the arrangement are first provided:

(i) An injured worker who is referred by a licensee or an immediate family member of the licensee.

(ii) The injured worker's employer, if self-insured.

(iii) The injured worker's employer's insurer, if insured.

(iv) If the injured worker is known by the licensee or the recipient of the referral to be represented, the injured worker's attorney.

(E) The term of the arrangement is for at least one year.

(F) The compensation to be paid over the term of the arrangement is set in advance, does not exceed fair market value, and is not determined in a manner that takes into account the volume or value of any referrals or other business generated between the parties, except that if the services provided pursuant to the arrangement include medical services provided under Division 4, compensation paid for the services shall be subject to the official medical fee schedule promulgated pursuant to Section 5307.1 or subject to any contract authorized by Section 5307.11.

(G) The services to be performed under the arrangement do not involve the counseling or promotion of a business arrangement or other activity that violates any state or federal law.

(c)(1) A physician may refer a person to a health facility as defined in Section 1250 of the Health and Safety Code, to any facility owned or leased by a health facility, or to an outpatient surgical center, if the recipient of the referral does not compensate the physician for the patient referral, and any equipment lease arrangement between the physician and the referral recipient complies with the requirements of paragraph (2) of subdivision (b).

(2) Nothing shall preclude this subdivision from applying to a physician solely because the physician has an ownership or leasehold interest in an entire health facility or an entity that owns or leases an entire health facility.

(3) A physician may refer a person to a health facility for any service classified as an emergency under subdivision (a) or (b) of Section 1317.1 of the Health and Safety Code. For nonemergency outpatient diagnostic imaging services performed with equipment for which, when new, has a commercial retail price of four hundred thousand dollars ($400,000) or more, the referring physician shall obtain a service preauthorization from the insurer, or self-insured employer. Any oral authorization shall be memorialized in writing within five business days.

(d) A physician compensated or employed by a university may refer a person to any facility owned or operated by the university, or for a physician service, to another physician employed by the university, provided that the facility or university does not compensate the referring physician for the patient referral. For nonemergency diagnostic imaging services performed with equipment that, when new, has a commercial retail price of four hundred thousand dollars ($400,000) or more, the referring physician shall obtain a service preauthorization from the insurer or self-insured employer. An oral authorization shall be memorialized in writing within five business days. In the case of a facility which is totally or partially owned by an entity other than the university, but which is staffed by university physicians, those physicians may not refer patients to the facility if the facility compensates the referring physician for those referrals.

(e) The prohibition of Section 139.3 shall not apply to any service for a specific patient that is performed within, or goods that are supplied by, a physician's office, or the office of a group practice. Further, the provisions of Section 139.3 shall not alter, limit, or expand a physician's ability to deliver, or to direct or supervise the delivery of, in-office goods or services according to the laws, rules, and regulations governing his or her scope of practice. With respect to diagnostic imaging services performed with equipment that, when new, had a commercial retail price of four hundred thousand dollars ($400,000) or more, or for physical therapy services, or for psychometric testing that exceeds the routine screening battery protocols, with a time limit of two to five hours, established by the administrative director, the referring physician obtains a service preauthorization from the insurer or self-insured employer. Any oral authorization shall be memorialized in writing within five business days.

(f) The prohibition of Section 139.3 shall not apply where the physician is in a group practice as defined in Section 139.3 and refers a person for services specified in Section 139.3 to a multispecialty clinic, as defined in subdivision (*l*) of Section 1206 of the Health and Safety Code. For diagnostic imaging services performed with equipment that, when new, had a commercial retail price of four hundred thousand dollars ($400,000) or more, or physical therapy services, or psychometric testing that exceeds the routine screening battery protocols, with a time limit of two to five hours, established by the administrative director, performed at the multispecialty facility, the referring physician shall obtain a service preauthorization from the insurer or self-insured employer. Any oral authorization shall be memorialized in writing within five business days.

(g) The requirement for preauthorization in Sections (c), (e), and (f) shall not apply to a patient for whom the physician or group accepts payment on a capitated risk basis.

(h) The prohibition of Section 139.3 shall not apply to any facility when used to provide health care services to an enrollee of a health care service plan licensed pursuant to the Knox-Keene Health Care Service Plan Act of 1975 (Chapter 2.2 (commencing with Section 1340) of Division 2 of the Health and Safety Code).

(i) The prohibition of Section 139.3 shall not apply to an outpatient surgical center, as defined in paragraph (7) of subdivision (b) of Section 139.3, where the referring physician obtains a service preauthorization from the insurer or self-insured employer after disclosure of the financial relationship. **Leg.H.** 1993 ch. 121, effective July 16, 1993, ch. 1242, 2002 ch. 309 (SB 1907), 2003 ch. 639 (SB 228).

1993 Note: Section 139.31, as added by ch. 121, applies only to injuries occurring on or after January 1, 1994. Stats. 1993 ch. 121 §77.

Ref.: Hanna § 22.14; Herlick Handbook §§ 1.8, 9.18; W. Cal. Sum., 2 "Workers' Compensation" §261.

Labor

§139.4. Council review of advertising; disciplinary actions and proceedings; adoption of advertising regulations and report to Legislature.

(a) The administrative director may review advertising copy to ensure compliance with Section 651 of the Business and Professions Code and may require qualified medical evaluators to maintain a file of all advertising copy for a period of 90 days from the date of its use. Any file so required to be maintained shall be available to the administrative director upon the administrative director's request for review.

(b) No advertising copy shall be used after its use has been disapproved by the administrative director and the qualified medical evaluator has been notified in writing of the disapproval.

(c) A qualified medical evaluator who is found by the administrative director to have violated any provision of this section may be terminated, suspended, or placed on probation.

(d) Proceedings to determine whether a violation of this section has occurred shall be conducted pursuant to Chapter 4 (commencing with Section 11370) of Part 1 of Division 3 of Title 2 of the Government Code.

(e) The administrative director shall adopt regulations governing advertising by physicians with respect to industrial injuries or illnesses.

(f) Subdivision (a) shall not be construed to alter the application of Section 651 of the Business and Professions Code. **Leg.H.** 1991 ch. 116, 2003 ch. 639 (SB 228).

Ref.: 8 C.C.R. §§150, 151, 152, 153, 154, 155, 156, 157, 158, 159; Hanna § 1.12[2A].

§139.43. False or misleading advertising prohibited; adoption of regulations by administrative director; physicians and attorneys exempted.

(a) No person or entity shall advertise, print, display, publish, distribute, or broadcast, or cause or permit to be advertised, printed, displayed, published, distributed, or broadcast in any manner, any statement concerning services or benefits to be provided to an injured worker, that is paid for directly or indirectly by that person or entity and is false, misleading, or deceptive, or that omits material information necessary to make the statement therein not false, misleading, or deceptive.

(b) As soon as reasonably possible, but not later than January 1, 1994, the administrative director shall adopt regulations governing advertising by persons or entities other than physicians and attorneys with respect to services or benefits for injured workers. In promulgating regulations pursuant to this subdivision, the administrative director shall review existing regulations, including those adopted by the State Bar, to identify those regulatory approaches that may serve as a model for regulations required by this subdivision.

(c) A violation of subdivision (a) is a misdemeanor, punishable by incarceration in the county jail for not more than one year, or by a fine not exceeding ten thousand dollars ($10,000), or both.

(d) This section shall not apply to physicians or attorneys. It is the intent of the Legislature to exempt physicians and attorneys from this section because the conduct regulated by this section, with respect to physicians and attorneys, is governed by other provisions of law. **Leg.H.** 1991 ch. 116, 1992 ch. 1352, effective September 30, 1992, 2004 ch. 193 (SB 111).

Ref.: 8 C.C.R. §§9820, 9821, 9822, 9823, 9824, 9825, 9826, 9827, 9828, 9829, 9830, 9831, 9832, 9833, 9834, 9835, 9836, 9837; Hanna § 1.23.

§139.45. Care required in promulgating advertising regulations; description of false or misleading advertisements.

(a) In promulgating regulations pursuant to Sections 139.4 and 139.43, the administrative director shall take particular care to preclude any advertisements with respect to industrial injuries or illnesses that are false or mislead the public with respect to workers' compensation. In promulgating rules with respect to advertising, the State Bar and physician licensing boards shall also take particular care to achieve the same goal.

(b) For purposes of subdivision (a), false or misleading advertisements shall include advertisements that do any of the following:

(1) Contain an untrue statement.

(2) Contain any matter, or present or arrange any matter in a manner or format that is false, deceptive, or that tends to confuse, deceive, or mislead.

(3) Omit any fact necessary to make the statement made, in the light of the circumstances under which the statement is made, not misleading.

(4) Are transmitted in any manner that involves coercion, duress, compulsion, intimidation, threats, or vexatious or harassing conduct.

(5) Entice a person to respond by the offering of any consideration, including a good or service but excluding free medical evaluations or treatment, that would be provided either at no charge or for less than market value. No free medical evaluation or treatment shall be offered for the purpose of defrauding any entity. **Leg.H.** 1991 ch. 116, 1992 ch. 1352, effective September 30, 1992, 2003 ch. 639 (SB 228).

Ref.: 8 C.C.R. §§150, 151, 152, 153, 154, 155, 156, 157, 158, 159, 9820, 9821, 9822, 9823, 9824, 9825, 9826, 9827, 9828, 9829, 9830, 9831, 9832, 9833, 9834, 9835, 9836, 9837; Hanna §§ 1.12[2A], 1.23; Herlick Handbook §§ 1.2, 9.18.

§139.47. Program established to educate employers about early and sustained return to work after employee's occupational injury or illness.

The Director of Industrial Relations shall establish and maintain a program to encourage, facilitate, and educate employers to provide early and sustained return to work after occupational injury or illness. The program shall do both of the following:

(a) Develop educational materials and guides, in easily understandable language in both print and electronic form, for employers, health care providers, employees, and labor unions. These materials shall address issues including, but not limited to, early return to work, assessment of functional abilities and limitations, development of appropriate work restrictions, job analysis, worksite modifications, assistive equipment and devices, and available resources.

(b) Conduct training for employee and employer organizations and health care providers concerning the accommodation of injured employees and the prevention of reinjury. **Leg.H.** 2002 ch. 6 (AB 749).

Ref.: Hanna §§ 7.02[3][d][i], [ii], 35.03[3A]; Herlick Handbook § 5.20; W. Cal. Sum., 2 "Workers' Compensation" §11.

§139.48. [Repealed January 1, 2010] Return-to-Work Program; reimbursement; restrictions on return to work of injured employee; regulatory authority; fund.

(a)(1) The administrative director shall establish the Return-to-Work Program in order to promote the early and sustained return to work of the employee following a work-related injury or illness.

(2) This section shall be implemented to the extent funds are available.

(b) Upon submission by eligible employers of documentation in accordance with regulations adopted pursuant to subdivision (h), the administrative director shall pay the workplace modification expense reimbursement allowed under this section.

(c) The administrative director shall reimburse an eligible employer for expenses incurred to make workplace modifications to accommodate the employee's return to modified or alternative work, as follows:

(1) The maximum reimbursement to an eligible employer for expenses to accommodate each temporarily disabled injured worker is one thousand two hundred fifty dollars ($1,250).

(2) The maximum reimbursement to an eligible employer for expenses to accommodate each permanently disabled worker who is a qualified injured worker is two thousand five hundred dollars ($2,500). If the employer received reimbursement under paragraph (1), the amount of the reimbursement under paragraph (1) and this paragraph shall not exceed two thousand five hundred dollars ($2,500).

(3) The modification expenses shall be incurred in order to allow a temporarily disabled worker to perform modified or alternative work within physician-imposed temporary work restrictions, or to allow a permanently disabled worker who is an injured worker to return to sustained modified or alternative employment with the employer within physician-imposed permanent work restrictions.

(4) Allowable expenses may include physical modifications to the worksite, equipment, devices, furniture, tools, or other necessary costs for accommodation of the employee's restrictions.

(d) This section shall not create a preference in employment for injured employees over noninjured employees. It shall be unlawful for an employer to discriminatorily terminate, lay off, demote, or otherwise displace an employee in order to return an industrially injured employee to employment for the purpose of obtaining the reimbursement set forth in subdivision (c).

(e) For purposes of this section, the following definitions apply:

(1) "Eligible employer" means any employer, except the state or an employer eligible to secure the payment of compensation pursuant to subdivision (c) of Section 3700, who employs 50 or fewer full-time employees on the date of injury.

(2) "Employee" means a worker who has suffered a work-related injury or illness on or after July 1, 2004.

(f) The administrative director shall adopt regulations to carry out this section. Regulations allocating budget funds that are insufficient to implement the workplace modification expense reimbursement provided for in this section shall include a prioritization schema.

(g) The Workers' Compensation Return-to-Work Fund is hereby created as a special fund in the State Treasury. The fund shall consist of all penalties collected pursuant to Section 5814.6 and transfers made by the administrative director from the Workers' Compensation Administration Revolving Fund established pursuant to Section 62.5. The fund shall be administered by the administrative director. Moneys in the fund may be expended by the administrative director, upon appropriation by the Legislature, only for purposes of implementing this section.

(h) This section shall be operative on July 1, 2004.

(i) This section shall remain in effect only until January 1, [1] **2010**, and as of that date is repealed, unless a later enacted statute, that is enacted before January 1, [2] **2010**, deletes or extends that date. **Leg.H.** 2002 ch. 6 (AB 749), 2004 ch. 34 (SB 899), effective April 19, 2004, 2008 ch. 751 (AB 1389) §61, effective September 30, 2008.

§139.48. 2008 Deletes. [1] 2009 **[2]** 2009

2004 Note: The amendment to §139.48 made by this actshall apply prospectively from the date of enactment of this act, regardless of the date of injury, unless otherwise specified, but shall not constitute good cause to reopen or rescind, alter, or amend any existing order, decision, or award of the Workers' Compensation Appeals Board. Stats. 2004 ch. 34 (SB 899) §47.

Ref.: Hanna §§7.02[3][d][i], [iii], [iv], 35.03[3A]; Hanna §§ 23.02, 23.03[1], [2]; Herlick Handbook §§ 5.20, 9.18.

§139.49. Enacted 2002. Repealed operative January 1, 2009, by its own provisions. 2002 ch. 6 (AB 749).

§139.5. Enacted 2004. Repealed operative January 1, 2009, by its own provisions. 2004 ch. 34 (SB 899) §5, effective April 19, 2004.

§139.6. Program to provide workers' compensation information.

(a) The administrative director shall establish and effect within the Division of Workers' Compensation a continuing program to provide information and assistance concerning the rights, benefits, and obligations of the workers' compensation law to employees and employers subject thereto. The program shall include, but not be limited to, the following:

(1) The preparation, publishing, and as necessary, updating, of guides to the California workers' compensation system for employees and employers. The guides shall detail, in easily understandable language, the rights and obligations of employees and employers, the procedures for obtaining benefits, and the means provided for resolving disputes. Separate guides may be prepared for employees and employers. The appropriate guide shall be provided to all labor and employer organizations known to the administrative director, and to any other person upon request.

(2) The preparation, publishing, and as necessary, updating, of a pamphlet advising injured workers of their basic rights under workers' compensation law, and informing them of rights under the Americans with Disabilities Act, and the provisions of the Fair Employment and Housing Act relating to individuals with a disability. The pamphlet shall be written in easily understandable language. The pamphlet shall be available in both English and Spanish, and shall include basic information concerning the circumstances under which injured employees are entitled to the various types of workers' compensation benefits, the protections against discrimination because of an injury, the procedures for resolving any disputes which arise, and the right to seek information and advice from an information and assistance officer or an attorney.

(b) In each district office of the division, the administrative director shall appoint an information and assistance officer, and any other deputy information and assistance officers as the work of the district office may require. The administrative director shall provide office facilities and clerical support appropriate to the functions of these information and assistance officers.

(c) Each information and assistance officer shall be responsible for the performance of the following duties:

(1) Providing continuing information concerning rights, benefits, and obligations under workers' compensation laws to injured workers, employers, lien claimants, and other interested parties.

(2) Upon request by the injured worker, assisting in the prompt resolution of misunderstanding, disputes, and controversies arising out of claims for compensation, without formal proceedings, in order that full and timely compensation benefits shall be furnished. In performing this duty, information and assistance officers shall not be responsible for reviewing applications for adjudication or declarations of readiness to proceed. This function shall be performed by workers' compensation judges. This function may also be performed by settlement conference referees upon delegation by the appeals board.

(3) Distributing any information pamphlets in English and Spanish as are prepared and approved by the administrative director to all inquiring injured workers and any other parties that may request copies of these pamphlets.

(4) Establishing and maintaining liaison with the persons located in the geographic area served by the district office, with other affected state agencies, and with organizations representing employees, employers, insurers, and the medical

community. **Leg.H.** 1993 ch. 121, effective July 16, 1993.

Ref.: 8 C.C.R. §§9880, 9883, 9885, 9900, 9928.1; Hanna §§ 23.02, 23.03[1], [2]; Herlick Handbook §§ 1.2, 1.9, 14.11, 16.3.

CHAPTER 6 OCCUPATIONAL SAFETY AND HEALTH STANDARDS BOARD

§140. Occupational Safety and Health Standards Board.

(a) There is in the Department of Industrial Relations, the Occupational Safety and Health Standards Board which consists of seven members who shall be appointed by the Governor. Two members shall be from the field of management, two members shall be from the field of labor, one member shall be from the field of occupational health, one member shall be from the field of occupational safety and one member shall be from the general public. Members representing occupational safety and health fields and the public member shall be selected from other than the fields of management or labor.

(b) Terms of office for members of the Industrial Safety Board shall expire 60 days after the effective date of the amendment of this section enacted at the 1973–74 Regular Session. Newly appointed members of the Occupational Safety and Health Standards Board shall assume their duties upon that date.

(c) The Governor shall designate the chairman of the board from the membership of the board. The person so designated shall hold the office of chairman at the pleasure of the Governor. The chairman shall designate a member of the board to act as chairman in his absence.

(d) As used in this chapter, "board" means the Occupational Safety and Health Standards Board.

(e) All references in this or any other code to the Industrial Safety Board shall be deemed to mean the Occupational Safety and Health Standards Board.

Ref.: Herlick Handbook § 9.10; W. Cal. Sum., 3 "Agency and Employment" §§314, 365.

§141. Term of office; compensation.

(a) The terms of office of the members of the board shall be four years and they shall hold office until the appointment and qualification of a successor. The terms of the members of the board first appointed shall expire as follows: three members, one representative from management, one representative from labor, and one representative from occupational health, on June 1, 1974; three members, one representative from management, one representative from labor, and one representative from occupational safety, on June 1, 1975; one member June 1, 1976. The terms shall thereafter expire in the same relative order. Vacancies occurring shall be filled by appointment to the unexpired term.

(b) Each member of the board shall receive one hundred dollars ($100) for each day of his or her actual attendance at meetings of the board, and other official business of the board, and his or her actual and necessary traveling expenses incurred in the performance of his or her duty as a member. **Leg.H.** 2004 ch. 183 (AB 3082).

Ref.: Herlick Handbook § 9.10.

§142. Enforcement of occupational safety and health standards.

The Division of Occupational Safety and Health shall enforce all occupational safety and health standards adopted pursuant to this chapter, and those heretofore adopted by the Industrial Accident Commission or the Industrial Safety Board. General safety orders heretofore adopted by the Industrial Accident Commission or the Industrial Safety Board shall continue to remain in effect, but they may be amended or repealed pursuant to this chapter. **Leg.H.** 2002 ch. 1124 (AB 3000), effective September 30, 2002.

Ref.: Hanna §§ 1.16[1], 25.10[7]; Herlick Handbook § 9.10; W. Cal. Sum., 3 "Agency and Employment" §366.

§142.1. Public meetings; notice.

The board shall meet at least monthly. The meetings shall be rotated throughout the state at locations designated by the chairman. All meetings held by the board shall be open and public. Written notice of all meetings and a proposed agenda shall be given to all persons who make request for the notice in writing to the board.

Ref.: Hanna § 1.16[2]; Herlick Handbook § 9.10; W. Cal. Sum., 3 "Agency and Employment" §365.

§142.2. Proposals at meetings.

At each of its meetings, the board shall make time available to interested persons to propose new or revised orders or standards appropriate for adoption pursuant to this chapter or other items concerning occupational safety and health. The board shall consider such proposed orders or standards and report its decision no later than six months following receipt of such proposals.

Ref.: Herlick Handbook § 9.10.

§142.3. Standards: vote required; state building standards; warnings of hazards to employees; medical examinations provided by employer.

(a)(1) The board, by an affirmative vote of at least four members, may adopt, amend or repeal occupational safety and health standards and orders. The board shall be the only agency in the state authorized to adopt occupational safety and health standards.

(2) The board shall adopt standards at least as effective as the federal standards for all issues for which federal standards have been promulgated under Section 6 of the Occupational Safety and Health Act of 1970 (P.L. 91-596) within six months of the promulgation date of the federal standards and which, when applicable to products which are distributed or used in interstate commerce, are required by compelling local conditions and do not unduly burden interstate commerce.

(3) No standard or amendment to any standard adopted by the board that is substantially the same as a federal standard shall be subject to Article 5 (commencing with Section 11346) and Article 6 (commencing with Section 11349) of Chapter 3.5 of Part 1 of Division 3 of Title 2 of the Government Code. For purposes of this subdivision, "substantially the same" means identical to the federal standard with the exception of editorial and format differences needed to conform to other state laws and standards.

(4) If a federal standard is promulgated and no state standard that is at least as effective as the federal standard is adopted by the board within six months of the date of promulgation of the federal standard, the following provisions shall apply unless adoption of the state standard is imminent:

(A) If there is no existing state standard covering the same issues, the federal standard shall be deemed to be a standard adopted by the board and enforceable by the division pursuant to Section 6317. This standard shall not be subject to Article 5 (commencing with Section 11346) and Article 6 (commencing with Section 11349) of Chapter 3.5 of Part 1 of Division 3 of Title 2 of the Government Code.

(B) If a state standard is in effect at the time a federal standard is promulgated covering the same issue or issues, the board may adopt the federal standard, or a portion thereof, as a standard enforceable by the division pursuant to Section 6317; provided, however, if a federal standard or portion thereof is adopted which replaces an existing state standard or portion thereof, the federal standard shall be as effective as the state standard or portion thereof. No adoption of or amendment to any federal standard, or portion thereof shall be subject to Article 5 (commencing with Section 11346) and Article 6 (commencing with Section 11349) of Chapter 3.5 of Part 1 of Division 3 of Title 2 of the Government Code.

(C) Any state standard adopted pursuant to subparagraph (A) or (B) shall become effective at the time the standard is filed with the Secretary of State, unless otherwise provided, but shall not take effect before the effective date of the equivalent federal standard and shall remain in effect for six months unless readopted by the board for an additional six months or superseded by a standard adopted by the board pursuant to paragraph (2) of subdivision (a).

(D) Any standard adopted pursuant to subparagraph (A), (B), or (C), shall be published in Title 8 of the California Code of Regulations in a manner similar to any other standards adopted pursuant to paragraphs (1) and (2) of subdivision (a) of this section.

(b) The State Building Standards Commission shall codify and publish in a semiannual supplement to the California Building Standards Code, or in a more frequent supplement if required by federal law, all occupational safety and health standards that would otherwise meet the definition of a building standard described in Section 18909 of the Health and Safety Code adopted by the board in the State Building Standards Code without reimbursement from the board. These occupational safety and health standards may also be published by the Occupational Safety and Health Standards Board in other provisions in Title 8 of the California Code of Regulations prior to publication in the California Building Standards Code if that other publication includes an appropriate identification of occupational safety and health standards contained in the other publication.

(c) Any occupational safety or health standard or order promulgated under this section shall prescribe the use of labels or other appropriate forms of warning as are necessary to ensure that employees are apprised of all hazards to which they are exposed, relevant symptoms and appropriate emergency treatment, and proper conditions and precautions for safe use or exposure. Where appropriate, these standards or orders shall also prescribe suitable protective equipment and control or technological procedures to be used in connection with these hazards and shall provide for monitoring or measuring employee exposure at such locations and intervals and in a manner as may be necessary for the protection of employees. In addition, where appropriate, the occupational safety or health standard or order shall prescribe the type and frequency of medical examinations or other tests which shall be made available, by the employer or at his or her cost, to employees exposed to such hazards in order to most effectively determine whether the health of such employee is adversely affected by this exposure.

(d) The results of these examinations or tests shall be furnished only to the Division of Occupational Safety and Health, the State Department of Health Services, any other authorized state agency, the employer, the employee, and, at the request of the employee, to his or her physician. **Leg.H.** 1992 ch. 1214, 2002 ch. 1124 (AB 3000), effective September 30, 2002.

Ref.: Herlick Handbook § 9.10; W. Cal. Sum., 3 "Agency and Employment" §365.

§142.4. Adoption of standards; emergency regulations.

(a) Occupational safety and health standards and orders shall be adopted, amended, or repealed as provided in Chapter 3.5 (commencing with Section 11340) of Part 1 of Division 3 of Title 2 of the Government Code, except as modified by this chapter.

(b) If an emergency regulation is based upon an emergency temporary standard published in the Federal Register by the Secretary of Labor pursuant to Section 6(c)(1) of the Federal Occupational Safety and Health Act of 1970 (P.L. 91–596; 29 U.S.C. Sec. 655(c)(1)), the 120-day period specified in Section 11346.1 of the Government Code shall be deemed not to expire until 120 days after a permanent standard is promulgated by the Secretary of Labor pursuant to Section 6(c)(3) of the Federal Occupational Safety and Health Act of 1970 (29 U.S.C. Sec. 655(c)(3)). **Leg.H.** 1973 ch. 993 §17, effective October 1, 1973, 1982 ch. 454 §129, 2006 ch. 538 (SB 1852) §478.

Ref.: Herlick Handbook § 9.10.

§142.7. Standards for hazardous substance removal work.

(a) On or before October 1, 1987, the board shall adopt an occupational safety and health standard concerning hazardous substance removal work, so as to protect most effectively the health and safety of employees. The standard shall include, but not be limited to, requirements for all of the following:

(1) Specific work practices.

(2) Certification of all employees engaged in hazardous substance removal-related work, except that no certification shall be required for an employee whose only activity is the transportation of hazardous substances which are subject to the requirement for a certificate under Section 12804.1 of the Vehicle Code.

(3) Certification of supervisors with sufficient experience and authority to be responsible for hazardous substance removal work.

(4) Designation of a qualified person who shall be responsible for scheduling any air sampling, laboratory calibration of sampling equipment, evaluation of soil or other contaminated materials sampling results, and for conducting any equipment testing and evaluating the results of the tests.

(5) Requiring that a safety and health conference be held for all hazardous substance removal jobs before the start of actual work. The conference shall include representatives of the owner or contracting agency, the contractor, the employer, employees, and employee representatives, and shall include a discussion of the employer's safety and health program and the means, methods, devices, processes, practices, conditions, or operations which the employer intends to use in providing a safe and healthy place of employment.

(b) For purposes of this section, "hazardous substance removal work" means cleanup work at any of the following:

(1) A site where removal or remedial action is taken pursuant to either of the following:

(A) Chapter 6.8 (commencing with Section 25300) of Division 20 of the Health and Safety Code, regardless of whether the site is listed pursuant to Section 25356 of the Health and Safety Code.

(B) The federal Comprehensive Environmental Response, Compensation, and Liability Act of 1980 (42 U.S.C. Sec. 9601 et seq.).

(2) A site where corrective action is taken pursuant to Section 25187 or 25200.10 of the Health and Safety Code or the federal Resource Conservation and Recovery Act of 1976 (42 U.S.C. Sec. 6901 et seq.).

(3) A site where cleanup of a discharge of a hazardous substance is required pursuant to Division 7 (commencing with Section 13000) of the Water Code.

(4) A site where removal or remedial action is taken because a hazardous substance has been discharged or released in an amount that is reportable pursuant to Section 13271 of the Water Code or the federal Comprehensive Environmental Response, Compensation, and Liability Act of 1980 (42 U.S.C. Sec. 9601 et seq.). "Hazardous substance removal work" does not include work related to a hazardous substance spill on a highway.

(c) Until the occupational safety and health standard required by subdivision (a) is adopted by the board and becomes effective, the occupational safety and health standard concerning hazardous substance removal work shall be the standard adopted by the federal government and codified in Section 1910.120 of Title 29 of the Code of Federal Regulations. In addition, before actual work is started on a hazardous substance removal job, a safety and health conference shall be held that shall include the participants and involve a discussion of the subjects described in paragraph (5) of subdivision (a).

Ref.: Herlick Handbook § 9.10.

§143. Permanent variances.

(a) Any employer may apply to the board for a permanent variance from an occupational safety and health standard, order, special order, or portion thereof, upon a showing of an alternate program, method, practice, means, device, or process which will provide equal or superior safety for employees.

(b) The board shall issue such variance if it determines on the record, after opportunity for an investigation where appropriate and a hearing, that the proponent of the variance has demonstrated by a preponderance of the evidence that the conditions, practices, means, methods, operations, or processes used or proposed to be used by an employer will provide employment and places or employment to his employees which are as safe and healthful as those which would prevail if he complied with the standard. The variance so issued shall prescribe the conditions the employer must maintain, and the practices, means, methods, operations, and processes which he must adopt and utilize to the extent they differ from the standard in question.

(c) The board is authorized to grant a variance from any standard or portion thereof whenever it determines such variance is necessary to permit an employer to participate in an experiment approved by the director designed to demonstrate or validate new and improved techniques to safeguard the health or safety of workers.

(d) A permanent variance may be modified or revoked upon application by an employer, employees, or the division, or by the board on its own motion, in the manner prescribed for its issuance under this section at any time.

Ref.: Herlick Handbook § 9.10; W. Cal. Sum., 3 "Agency and Employment" §365.

§143.1. Variance requests; hearings.

The board shall conduct hearings on such requests for a permanent variance after employees or employee representatives are properly notified and given an opportunity to appear. All board decisions on permanent variance requests shall be final except for any rehearing or judicial review provided for by law.

Ref.: Herlick Handbook § 9.10; W. Cal. Sum., 3 "Agency and Employment" §369.

§143.2. Procedural rules for hearings.

The board, acting as a whole, may adopt, amend, or repeal rules of practice and procedure pertaining to hearings on applications for permanent variances, variance appeals, and other matters within its jurisdiction. All rules of practice and procedure amendments thereto, or repeal thereof, shall be made in accordance with the provisions of Chapter 3.5 (commencing with Section 11340) of Part 1 of Division 3 of Title 2 of the Government Code. **Leg.H.** 2004 ch. 183 (AB 3082).

Ref.: Herlick Handbook § 9.10; W. Cal. Sum., 3 "Agency and Employment" §368.

§144. Enforcement of occupational safety and health standards; assistance of other agencies.

(a) The authority of any agency, department, division, bureau or any other political subdivision other than the Division of Occupational Safety and Health to assist in the administration or enforcement of any occupational safety or health standard, order, or rule adopted pursuant to this chapter shall be contained in a written agreement with the Department of Industrial Relations or an agency authorized by the department to enter into such agreement.

(b) No such agreement shall deprive the Division of Occupational Safety and Health or other state agency to which authority has been delegated of any power or authority of the state agency.

(c) Such an agreement may provide for the right of access of an authorized representative of the designated agency to enter any place of employment which is under the jurisdiction of the Division of Occupational Safety and Health.

(d) If any representative of an agency operating under such an agreement becomes aware of an imminent hazard, he shall notify the employer and affected employees of the hazard and immediately notify the Division of Occupational Safety and Health.

(e) Nothing in this section shall affect or limit the authority of any state or local agency as to any matter other than the enforcement of occupational safety and health standards adopted by the board; however, nothing herein shall limit or reduce the authority of local agencies to adopt and enforce higher standards relating to occupational safety and health for their own employees.

Ref.: Herlick Handbook § 9.10.

§144.5. Division of Occupational Safety and Health; duties.

(a) The Division of Occupational Safety and Health in connection with the enforcement of occupational safety and health standards adopted pursuant to this chapter shall do all of the following:

(1) Conduct inspections or investigations related to specific workplaces for the evaluation of occupational health problems or environmental conditions which may be harmful to the health of employees.

(2) Upon request of any employer or employee, or on its own initiative, conduct special investigations or studies of occupational health problems which are unrelated to a specific enforcement action to the extent the circumstances indicate and priorities permit.

(3) Provide a continuing program of training for safety engineers of the Division of Occupational Safety and Health in the recognition of health hazards, in dealing with such hazards that do not require specialized competence or equipment and in acquainting them with the skills available from the State Department of Health Services and local health agencies.

(b) (1) When requested by a local health department, the Division of Occupational Safety and Health shall enter into a written agreement with such local health department to conduct inspections and evaluations of occupational health problems, including environmental and sanitary conditions, in places of employment.

(2) Any such agreement shall be subject to the provisions of Section 144. It shall be entered into only after a finding that the local health department can meet the necessary standards of performance for inspections and evaluations to be conducted pursuant to the agreement.

(3) Such agreement shall not be binding upon either party unless and until it has been fully approved by the United States Department of Labor.

(4) Such agreements shall be completed by the Division of Occupational Safety and Health and submitted for approval to the United States Department of Labor not later than six months from the date of request by the local health department.

(5) Inspection services performed under the agreement shall be conducted pursuant to the occupational safety and health standards adopted pursuant to this chapter.

Ref.: Hanna § 1.16[1]; Herlick Handbook § 9.10.

§144.6. Toxic materials; standards.

In promulgating standards dealing with toxic materials or harmful physical agents, the board shall adopt that standard which most adequately assures, to the extent feasible, that no employee will suffer material impairment of health or functional capacity even if such employee has regular exposure to a hazard regulated by such standard for the period of his working life. Development of standards under this section shall be based upon research, demonstrations, experiments, and such other information as may be appropriate. In addition to the attainment of the highest degree of health and safety protection for the employee, other considerations shall be the latest available scientific data in the field, the reasonableness of the standards, and experience gained under this and other health and safety laws. Whenever practicable, the standard promulgated shall be expressed in terms of objective criteria and of the performance desired.

Ref.: Herlick Handbook § 9.10.

§144.7. Needle safety standards.

(a) The board shall, no later than January 15, 1999, adopt an emergency regulation revising the bloodborne pathogen standard currently set forth in Section 5193 of Title 8 of the California Code of Regulations in accordance with subdivision (b). Following adoption of the emergency regulation, the board shall complete the regulation adoption process and shall formally adopt a regulation embodying a bloodborne pathogen standard meeting the requirements of subdivision (b), which regulation shall become operative no later than August 1, 1999. Notwithstanding Section 11346.1 of the Government Code, the emergency regulation adopted pursuant to this subdivision shall remain in effect until the nonemergency regulation becomes operative or until August 1, 1999, whichever first occurs.

(b) The board shall adopt a standard, as described in subdivision (a), to be developed by the Division of Occupational Safety and Health. The standard shall include, but not be limited to, the following:

(1) A revised definition of "engineering controls" that includes sharps injury prevention technology including, but not limited to, needleless systems and needles with engineered sharps injury protection, which shall be defined in the standard.

(2) A requirement that sharps injury prevention technology specified in paragraph (1) be included as engineering or work practice controls, except in cases where the employer or other appropriate party can demonstrate circumstances in which the technology does not promote employee or patient safety or interferes with a medical procedure. Those circumstances shall be specified in the standard, and shall include, but not be limited to, circumstances where the technology is medically contraindicated or not more effective than alternative measures used by the employer to prevent exposure incidents.

(3) A requirement that written exposure control plans include an effective procedure for identifying and selecting existing sharps injury prevention technology of the type specified in paragraph (1).

(4) A requirement that written exposure control plans be updated when necessary to reflect progress in implementing the sharps injury prevention technology specified in paragraph (1).

(5) A requirement that information concerning exposure incidents be recorded in a sharps injury log, including, but not limited to, the type and brand of device involved in the incident.

(c) The Division of Occupational Safety and Health may consider and propose for adoption by the board additional revisions to the bloodborne pathogen standards to prevent sharps injuries or exposure incidents including, but not limited to, training requirements and measures to increase vaccinations.

(d) The Division of Occupational Safety and Health and the State Department of Health Services shall jointly compile and maintain a list of existing needleless systems and needles with engineered sharps injury protection, which shall be available to assist employers in complying with the requirements of the bloodborne pathogen standard adopted pursuant to this section. The list may be developed from existing sources of information, including, but not limited to, the federal Food and Drug Administration, the federal Centers for Disease Control, the National Institute of Occupational Safety and Health, and the United States Department of Veterans Affairs. **Leg.H.** 1998 ch. 999, 2001 ch. 370.

Ref.: Herlick Handbook § 9.10; W. Cal. Sum., 3 "Agency and Employment" §378.

§145. Employment of personnel.

The board may employ necessary assistants, officers, experts, and such other employees as it deems necessary. All such personnel of the board shall be under the supervision of the chairman of the board or an executive officer to whom he delegates such responsibility. All such personnel shall be appointed pursuant to the State Civil Service Act (Part 1 (commencing with Section 18000) of Division 5 of Title 2 of the Government Code), except for the one exempt deputy or employee allowed by subdivision (e) of Section 4 of Article XXIV of the California Constitution.

Ref.: Herlick Handbook § 9.10.

§145.1. Powers of board.

The board and its duly authorized representatives in the performance of its duties shall have the powers of a head of a department as set forth in Article 2 (commencing with Section 11180) of Chapter 2 of Part 1 of Division 3 of Title 2 of the Government Code.

Ref.: Herlick Handbook § 9.10.

§146. Permanent variances; hearings.

In the conduct of hearings related to permanent variances, the board and its representatives are not bound by common law or statutory rules of evidence or by technical or formal rules of procedure but shall conduct the hearings in accordance with Article 8 (commencing with Section 11435.05) of Chapter 4.5 of Part 1 of Division 3 of Title 2 of, and Section 11513 of, the Government Code. A full and complete record shall be kept of all proceedings. **Leg.H.** 1995 ch. 938, operative July 1, 1997.

Ref.: Herlick Handbook § 9.10; W. Cal. Sum., 3 "Agency and Employment" §365.

§147. Evaluation of standards and variances from other sources.

The board shall refer to the Division of Occupational Safety and Health for evaluation any proposed occupational safety or health standard or variance from adopted standards received by the board from sources other than the division. The division shall submit a report on the proposed standard or variance within 60 days of receipt thereof.

Ref.: Herlick Handbook § 9.10.

§147.1. Division of Occupational Safety and Health; duties; federal standards; proposed standards.

In connection with the development and promulgation of occupational health standards the Division of Occupational Safety and Health shall perform all of the following functions:

(a) Analyze proposed and new federal occupational health standards, evaluate their impact on California, determine any necessity for their modification, and present proposed standards to the board in sufficient time for the board to conduct hearings and adopt standards within the time required.

(b) Maintain liaison with the National Institute of Occupational Safety and Health and the federal Occupational Safety and Health Administration in the development of recommended federal standards and when appropriate provide representation on federal advisory committees dealing with the development of occupational health standards.

(c) On occupational health issues not covered by federal standards maintain surveillance, determine the necessity for standards, develop and present proposed standards to the board.

(d) Evaluate any proposed occupational health standard or application for a variance of an occupational health standard received by the board, and submit a report to the board on the proposed standard or variance within 60 days of receipt thereof.

(e) Appear and testify at board hearings and other public proceedings involving occupational health matters.

Ref.: Herlick Handbook § 9.10.

§147.2. Information repository on toxic materials.

In accordance with Chapter 2 (commencing with Section 6350) of Part 1 of Division 5 of this code and Section 105175 of the Health and Safety Code, the Department of Industrial Relations shall, by interagency agreement with the State Department of Health Services, establish a repository of current data on toxic materials and harmful physical agents in use or potentially in use in places of employment in the state.

The repository shall fulfill all of the following functions:

(1) Provide reliable information of practical use to employers, employees, representatives of employees, and other governmental agencies on the possible hazards to employees of exposure to toxic materials or harmful physical agents.

(2) Collect and evaluate toxicological and epidemiological data and any other information that may be pertinent to establishing harmful effects on health of exposure to toxic materials or harmful physical agents. Nothing in this subdivision shall be construed as authorizing the repository to require employers to report any information not otherwise required by law.

(3) Recommend to the Chief of the Division of Occupational Safety and Health Administration that an occupational safety and health standard be developed whenever it has been

determined that a substance in use or potentially in use in places of employment is potentially toxic at the concentrations or under the conditions used.

(4) Notify the Director of Food and Agriculture of any information developed by the repository that is relevant to carrying out his or her responsibilities under Chapters 2 (commencing with Section 12751) and 3 (commencing with Section 14001) of Division 7 of the Food and Agricultural Code.

The Director of Industrial Relations shall appoint an Advisory Committee to the repository. The Advisory Committee shall consist of four representatives from labor, four representatives from management, four active practitioners in the occupational health field, and three persons knowledgeable in biomedical statistics or information storage and retrieval systems. The Advisory Committee shall meet on a regular basis at the request of the director. The committee shall be consulted by, and shall advise the director at each phase of the structuring and functioning of the repository and alert system with regard to, the procedures, methodology, validity, and practical utility of collecting, evaluating, and disseminating information concerning hazardous substances, consistent with the primary goals and objectives of the repository.

Nothing in this section shall be construed to limit the ability of the State Department of Health Services to propose occupational safety and health standards to the Occupational Safety and Health Standards Board.

Policies and procedures shall be developed to assure, to the extent possible, that the repository uses and does not duplicate the resources of the federal government and other states.

On or before December 31 of each year, the Department of Industrial Relations shall submit a report to the Legislature detailing the implementation and operation of the repository including, but not limited to, the amount and source of funds allocated and spent on repository activities, the toxic materials and harmful physical agents investigated during the past year and recommendations made concerning them, actions taken to inform interested persons of the possible hazards of exposure to toxic materials and harmful physical agents, and any recommendations for legislative changes relating to the functions of the repository. **Leg.H.** 1996 ch. 1023, effective September 29, 1996.

Ref.: Herlick Handbook § 9.10; W. Cal. Sum., 3 "Agency and Employment" §378.

CHAPTER 6.5 OCCUPATIONAL SAFETY AND HEALTH APPEALS BOARD

§148. Occupational Safety and Health Appeals Board; designation of chairperson.

(a) There is in the Department of Industrial Relations the Occupational Safety and Health Appeals Board, consisting of three members appointed by the Governor, subject to the approval of the Senate. One member shall be from the field of management, one shall be from the field of labor and one member shall be from the general public. The public member shall be chosen from other than the fields of management and labor. Each member of the appeals board shall devote his full time to the performance of his duties.

(b) The chairman and each member of the appeals board shall receive the annual salary provided for by Chapter 6 (commencing with Section 11550) of Part 1 of Division 3 of Title 2 of the Government Code.

(c) The Governor shall designate the chairman of the appeals board from the membership of the appeals board. The person so designated shall hold the office of chairman at the pleasure of the Governor. The chairman shall designate a member of the appeals board to act as chairman in his absence.

Ref.: Hanna § 1.16[3]; Herlick Handbook § 9.10; W. Cal. Sum., 3 "Agency and Employment" §368.

§148.1. Term of office.

Each member of the appeals board shall serve for a term of four years and until his successor is appointed and qualifies. The terms of the first three members appointed to the appeals board shall expire on the second, third, and fourth January 15th following the date of the appointment of the first appointed member. A vacancy shall be filled by the Governor, subject to the approval of the Senate by appointment for the unexpired term.

Ref.: Herlick Handbook § 9.10.

§148.2. Employment of appeals board personnel; salaries of hearing officers.

The appeals board may employ necessary assistants, officers, experts, hearing officers, and such other employees as it deems necessary. All such personnel of the appeals board shall be under the supervision of the chairman of the appeals board or an executive officer to whom the chairman delegates such responsibility. All such personnel shall be appointed pursuant to the State Civil Service Act (Part 2 (commencing with Section 18500) of Division 5 of Title 2 of the Government Code), except for the one exempt deputy or employee allowed by subdivision (e) of Section 4 of Article XXIV of the California Constitution. The salaries of the hearing officers shall be fixed by the State Personnel Board at a rate comparable to that of other referees or hearing officers in state service whose duties and responsibilities are comparable, without regard to whether such other positions have membership in the State Bar of California as a prerequisite to appointment.

Ref.: Herlick Handbook § 9.10.

§148.4. Orders and decisions to be in writing.

All decisions and orders of the appeals board shall be in writing.

Ref.: Herlick Handbook § 9.10.

§148.5. Finality of decisions.

A decision of the appeals board is final, except for any rehearing or judicial review as permitted by Chapter 4 (commencing with Section 6600) of Part 1 of Division 5.

Ref.: Herlick Handbook § 9.10.

§148.6. Director's right to seek judicial review.

A decision of the appeals board is binding on the director and the Division of Occupational Safety and Health with respect to the parties involved in the particular appeal. The director shall have the right to seek judicial review of an appeals board decision irrespective of whether or not he or she appeared or participated in the appeal to the appeals board or its hearing officer.

Ref.: Herlick Handbook § 9.10.

§148.7. Procedural rules for hearings; adoption.

The appeals board, acting as a whole, may adopt, amend, or repeal rules of practice and procedure pertaining to hearing appeals and other matters falling within its jurisdiction. All such rules, amendments thereto, or repeals thereof shall be made in accordance with the provisions of Chapter 3.5 (commencing with Section 11340) of Part 1 of Division 3 of Title 2 of the Government Code.

Ref.: Herlick Handbook § 9.10.

§148.8. Powers of appeals board.

The appeals board and its duly authorized representatives in the performance of its duties shall have the powers of a head of a department as set forth in Article 2 (commencing with Section 11180) of Chapter 2 of Part 1 of Division 3 of Title 2 of the Government Code, except for Section 11185 of the Government Code.

Ref.: Herlick Handbook § 9.10.

§148.9. Decisions by majority of board.

Decisions of the appeals board shall be made by a majority of the appeals board, except as otherwise expressly provided.

Ref.: Herlick Handbook § 9.10.

§149. Executive officer as acting deputy.

The chairman of the appeals board may authorize its executive officer to act as deputy appeals board member, and may delegate authority and duties to the executive officer in the event of the absence of a member of the appeals board.

Ref.: Herlick Handbook § 9.10.

§149.5. Costs and attorney's fees.

The appeals board may award reasonable costs, including attorney's fees, consultant's fees, and witness' fees, not to exceed five thousand dollars ($5,000) in the aggregate, to any employer who appeals a citation resulting from an inspection or investigation conducted on or after January 1, 1980, issued for violation of an occupational safety and health standard, rule, order, or regulation established pursuant to Chapter 6 (commencing with Section 140) of

Division 1, if (1) either the employer prevails in the appeal, or the citation is withdrawn, and (2) the appeals board finds that the issuance of the citation was the result of arbitrary or capricious action or conduct by the division.

The appeals board shall adopt rules of practice and procedure to implement this section.

The payment of costs pursuant to this section shall be from funds in the regular operating budget of the division. The division shall show in its proposed budget for each fiscal year the following information with respect to the prior fiscal year:

(a) The total costs paid.

(b) The number of cases in which costs were paid.

Ref.: Herlick Handbook § 9.10.

DIVISION 2
EMPLOYMENT REGULATION AND SUPERVISION

PART 4
Employees

CHAPTER 1
WAGES, HOURS AND WORKING CONDITIONS

§1171.5. Legislative findings and declarations regarding employment protections available regardless of immigration status.

The Legislature finds and declares the following:

(a) All protections, rights, and remedies available under state law, except any reinstatement remedy prohibited by federal law, are available to all individuals regardless of immigration status who have applied for employment, or who are or who have been employed, in this state.

(b) For purposes of enforcing state labor and employment laws, a person's immigration status is irrelevant to the issue of liability, and in proceedings or discovery undertaken to enforce those state laws no inquiry shall be permitted into a person's immigration status except where the person seeking to make this inquiry has shown by clear and convincing evidence that the inquiry is necessary in order to comply with federal immigration law.

(c) The provisions of this section are declaratory of existing law.

(d) The provisions of this section are severable. If any provision of this section or its application is held invalid, that invalidity shall not affect other provisions or applications that can be given effect without the invalid provision or application. **Leg.H.** 2002 ch. 1071 (SB 1818).

Ref.: Hanna §§ 3.31, 35.30[4]; Herlick Handbook § 2.3; W. Cal. Sum., 8 "Constitutional Law" §§897, 914, 951.

PART 7
Public Works and Public Agencies

CHAPTER 1
PUBLIC WORKS

ARTICLE 5
Securing Workers' Compensation

§1860. Public works contracts; compensation clause required.

The awarding body shall cause to be inserted in every public works contract a clause providing that, in accordance with the provisions of Section 3700 of the Labor Code, every contractor will be required to secure the payment of compensation to his employees.

§1861. Public works contracts; certificate of insurance.

Each contractor to whom a public works contract is awarded shall sign and file with the awarding body the following certification prior to performing the work of the contract: "I am aware of the provisions of Section 3700 of the Labor Code which require every employer to be insured against liability for workers' compensation or to undertake self-insurance in accordance with the provisions of that code, and I will comply with such provisions before commencing the performance of the work of this contract."

PART 9
Health

CHAPTER 1
SANITARY CONDITIONS

ARTICLE 5
General Health Provisions

§2440. Employers' compliance with medical services and first aid standards.

All employers shall comply with standards relating to the ready availability of medical services and first aid adopted by the Occupational Safety and Health Standards Board, pursuant to Chapter 6 (commencing with Section 140) of Division 1. **Leg.H.** 1994 ch. 486 §9.

Ref.: Hanna § 5.02[4]; Herlick Handbook § 4.8; W. Cal. Sum., 3 "Agency and Employment" §371.

§2441. Provision of drinking water.

(a) Every employer of labor in this state shall, without making a charge therefor, provide fresh and pure drinking water to his or her employees during working hours. Access to the drinking water shall be permitted at reasonable and convenient times and places. Any violation of this section is punishable for each offense by a fine of not less than fifty dollars ($50), nor more than two hundred dollars ($200), or by imprisonment for not more than 30 days, or by both the fine and imprisonment.

(b) The State Department of Health Services and all health officers of counties, cities, and health districts shall enforce the provisions of this section pursuant to subdivision (b) of Section 118390 of the Health and Safety Code. The enforcement shall not be construed to abridge or limit in any manner the jurisdiction of the Division of Industrial Safety of the Department of Industrial Relations pursuant to Division 5 (commencing with Section 6300). **Leg.H.** 1996 ch. 1023, effective September 29, 1996.

Ref.: Herlick Handbook § 4.8; W. Cal. Sum., 3 "Agency and Employment" §371.

Labor

PART 13
The Labor Code Private Attorneys General Act of 2004

§2698. Citation of part.

This part shall be known and may be cited as the Labor Code Private Attorneys General Act of 2004. **Leg.H.** 2003 ch. 906 (SB 796).

Ref.: W. Cal. Sum., 3 "Agency and Employment" §324.

§2699. Recovery of civil penalty for violation of Labor Code through civil action brought by aggrieved employee; amount of penalty; attorney's fees and costs; distribution of penalty proceeds; applicability of section.

(a) Notwithstanding any other provision of law, any provision of this code that provides for a civil penalty to be assessed and collected by the Labor and Workforce Development Agency or any of its departments, divisions, commissions, boards, agencies, or employees, for a violation of this code, may, as an alternative, be recovered through a civil action brought by an aggrieved employee on behalf of himself or herself and other current or former employees pursuant to the procedures specified in Section 2699.3.

(b) For purposes of this part, "person" has the same meaning as defined in Section 18.

(c) For purposes of this part, "aggrieved employee" means any person who was employed by the alleged violator and against whom one or more of the alleged violations was committed.

(d) For purposes of this part, "cure" means that the employer abates each violation alleged by any aggrieved employee, the employer is in compliance with the underlying statutes as specified in the notice required by this part, and any aggrieved employee is made whole.

(e)(1) For purposes of this part, whenever the Labor and Workforce Development Agency, or any of its departments, divisions, commissions, boards, agencies, or employees, has discretion to assess a civil penalty, a court is authorized to exercise the same discretion, subject to the same limitations and conditions, to assess a civil penalty.

(2) In any action by an aggrieved employee seeking recovery of a civil penalty available under subdivision (a) or (f), a court may award a lesser amount than the maximum civil penalty amount specified by this part if, based on the facts and circumstances of the particular case, to do otherwise would result in an award that is unjust, arbitrary and oppressive, or confiscatory.

(f) For all provisions of this code except those for which a civil penalty is specifically provided, there is established a civil penalty for a violation of these provisions, as follows:

(1) If, at the time of the alleged violation, the person does not employ one or more employees, the civil penalty is five hundred dollars ($500).

(2) If, at the time of the alleged violation, the person employs one or more employees, the civil penalty is one hundred dollars ($100) for each aggrieved employee per pay period for the initial violation and two hundred dollars ($200) for each aggrieved employee per pay period for each subsequent violation.

(3) If the alleged violation is a failure to act by the Labor and Workplace Development Agency, or any of its departments, divisions, commissions, boards, agencies, or employees, there shall be no civil penalty.

(g)(1) Except as provided in paragraph (2), an aggrieved employee may recover the civil penalty described in subdivision (f) in a civil action pursuant to the procedures specified in Section 2699.3 filed on behalf of himself or herself and other current or former employees against whom one or more of the alleged violations was committed. Any employee who prevails in any action shall be entitled to an award of reasonable attorney's fees and costs. Nothing in this part shall operate to limit an employee's right to pursue or recover other remedies available under state or federal law, either separately or concurrently with an action taken under this part.

(2) No action shall be brought under this part for any violation of a posting, notice, agency reporting, or filing requirement of this code, except where the filing or reporting requirement involves mandatory payroll or workplace injury reporting.

(h) No action may be brought under this section by an aggrieved employee if the agency or any of its departments, divisions, commissions, boards, agencies, or employees, on the same facts and theories, cites a person within the timeframes set forth in Section 2699.3 for a violation of the same section or sections of the Labor Code under which the aggrieved employee is attempting to recover a civil penalty on behalf of himself or herself or others or initiates a proceeding pursuant to Section 98.3.

(i) Except as provided in subdivision (j), civil penalties recovered by aggrieved employees shall be distributed as follows: 75 percent to the Labor and Workforce Development Agency for enforcement of labor laws and education of employers and employees about their rights and responsibilities under this code, to be continuously appropriated to supplement and not supplant the funding to the agency for those purposes; and 25 percent to the aggrieved employees.

(j) Civil penalties recovered under paragraph (1) of subdivision (f) shall be distributed to the Labor and Workforce Development Agency for enforcement of labor laws and education of employers and employees about their rights and responsibilities under this code, to be continuously appropriated to supplement and not supplant the funding to the agency for those purposes.

(k) Nothing contained in this part is intended to alter or otherwise affect the exclusive remedy provided by the workers' compensation provisions of this code for liability against an employer for the compensation for any injury to or death of an employee arising out of and in the course of employment.

(*l*) The superior court shall review and approve any penalties sought as part of a proposed settlement agreement pursuant to this part.

(m) This section shall not apply to the recovery of administrative and civil penalties in connection with the workers' compensation law as contained in Division 1 (commencing with Section 50) and Division 4 (commencing with Section 3200), including, but not limited to, Sections 129.5 and 132a.

(n) The agency or any of its departments, divisions, commissions, boards, or agencies may promulgate regulations to implement the provisions of this part. **Leg.H.** 2003 ch. 906 (SB 796), 2004 chs. 34 (SB 899), effective April 19, 2004, 221 (SB 1809), effective August 11, 2004.

2004 Notes: The amendment, addition, or repeal of, any provision of law made by this act shall apply prospectively from the date of enactment of this act, regardless of the date of injury, unless otherwise specified, but shall not constitute good cause to reopen or rescind, alter, or amend any existing order, decision, or award of the Workers' Compensation Appeals Board. Stats. 2004 ch. 34 (SB 899) §34.

(a) The Legislature finds and declares that, as enunciated in long-standing judicial precedent, its inherent authority to create causes of action or remedies necessarily includes the authority to abolish them. Therefore, a plaintiff seeking recovery upon a legislatively created cause of action runs the risk that the Legislature may repeal or alter that cause during the pendency of the claim. Thus, the Legislature further finds and declares that the alteration of the right to recover civil penalties for violations of the Labor Code made by this act may be applied retroactively to any applicable pending proceeding without depriving any person of a substantive right without due process of law.

(b) (1) The provisions of paragraph (2) of subdivision (g) of Section 2699 of the Labor Code shall apply retroactively to January 1, 2004, the effective date of Chapter 906 of the Statutes of 2003, and shall affect all applicable pending proceedings.

(2) The provisions of subdivision (*l*) of Section 2699 of the Labor Code shall apply retroactively to January 1, 2004, the effective date of Chapter 906 of the Statutes of 2003, and shall affect all applicable pending proceedings. Stats. 2004 ch. 221 (SB 1809) §6.

Ref.: Hanna § 11.01[9]; Herlick Handbook § 9.1; W. Cal. Sum., 3 "Agency and Employment" §§255, 324.

§2699.3. Requirements for commencement of civil actions under Labor Code §2699 alleging specified violations; time limits.

(a) A civil action by an aggrieved employee pursuant to subdivision (a) or (f) of Section 2699 alleging a violation of any provision listed in Section 2699.5 shall commence only after the following requirements have been met:

(1) The aggrieved employee or representative shall give written notice by certified mail to the Labor and Workforce Development Agency and the employer of the specific provisions of this code alleged to have been violated, including the facts and theories to support the alleged violation.

(2)(A) The agency shall notify the employer and the aggrieved employee or representative by certified mail that it does not intend to investigate the alleged violation within 30 calendar days of the postmark date of the notice received pursuant to paragraph (1). Upon receipt of that notice or if no notice is provided within 33 calendar days of the postmark date of the notice given pursuant to paragraph (1), the aggrieved employee may commence a civil action pursuant to Section 2699.

(B) If the agency intends to investigate the alleged violation, it shall notify the employer and the aggrieved employee or representative by certified mail of its decision within 33 calendar days of the postmark date of the notice received pursuant to paragraph (1). Within 120 calendar days of that decision, the agency may investigate the alleged violation and issue any appropriate citation. If the agency determines that no citation will be issued, it shall notify the employer and aggrieved employee of that decision within five business days thereof by certified mail. Upon receipt of that notice or if no citation is issued by the agency within the 158-day period prescribed by subparagraph (A) and this subparagraph or if the agency fails to provide timely or any notification, the aggrieved employee may commence a civil action pursuant to Section 2699.

(C) Notwithstanding any other provision of law, a plaintiff may as a matter of right amend an existing complaint to add a cause of action arising under this part at any time within 60 days of the time periods specified in this part.

(b) A civil action by an aggrieved employee pursuant to subdivision (a) or (f) of Section 2699 alleging a violation of any provision of Division 5 (commencing with Section 6300) other than those listed in Section 2699.5 shall commence only after the following requirements have been met:

(1) The aggrieved employee or representative shall give notice by certified mail to the Division of Occupational Safety and Health and the employer, with a copy to the Labor and Workforce Development Agency, of the specific provisions of Division 5 (commencing with Section 6300) alleged to have been violated, including the facts and theories to support the alleged violation.

(2)(A) The division shall inspect or investigate the alleged violation pursuant to the procedures specified in Division 5 (commencing with Section 6300).

(i) If the division issues a citation, the employee may not commence an action pursuant to Section 2699. The division shall notify the aggrieved employee and employer in writing within 14 calendar days of certifying that the employer has corrected the violation.

(ii) If by the end of the period for inspection or investigation provided for in Section 6317, the division fails to issue a citation and the aggrieved employee disputes that decision, the employee may challenge that decision in the superior court. In such an action, the superior court shall follow precedents of the Occupational Safety and Health Appeals Board. If the court finds that the division should have issued a citation and orders the division to issue a citation, then the aggrieved employee may not commence a civil action pursuant to Section 2699.

(iii) A complaint in superior court alleging a violation of Division 5 (commencing with Section 6300) other than those listed in Section 2699.5 shall include therewith a copy of the notice of violation provided to the division and employer pursuant to paragraph (1).

(iv) The superior court shall not dismiss the action for nonmaterial differences in facts or theories between those contained in the notice of violation provided to the division and employer pursuant to paragraph (1) and the complaint filed with the court.

(B) If the division fails to inspect or investigate the alleged violation as provided by Section 6309, the provisions of subdivision (c) shall apply to the determination of the alleged violation.

(3)(A) Nothing in this subdivision shall be construed to alter the authority of the division to permit long-term abatement periods or to enter into memoranda of understanding or joint agreements with employers in the case of long-term abatement issues.

(B) Nothing in this subdivision shall be construed to authorize an employee to file a notice or to commence a civil action pursuant to Section 2699 during the period that an employer has voluntarily entered into consultation with the division to ameliorate a condition in that particular worksite.

(C) An employer who has been provided notice pursuant to this section may not then enter into consultation with the division in order to avoid an action under this section.

(4) The superior court shall review and approve any proposed settlement of alleged violations of the provisions of Division 5 (com-

mencing with Section 6300) to ensure that the settlement provisions are at least as effective as the protections or remedies provided by state and federal law or regulation for the alleged violation. The provisions of the settlement relating to health and safety laws shall be submitted to the division at the same time that they are submitted to the court. This requirement shall be construed to authorize and permit the division to comment on those settlement provisions, and the court shall grant the division's commentary the appropriate weight.

(c) A civil action by an aggrieved employee pursuant to subdivision (a) or (f) of Section 2699 alleging a violation of any provision other than those listed in Section 2699.5 or Division 5 (commencing with Section 6300) shall commence only after the following requirements have been met:

(1) The aggrieved employee or representative shall give written notice by certified mail to the Labor and Workforce Development Agency and the employer of the specific provisions of this code alleged to have been violated, including the facts and theories to support the alleged violation.

(2)(A) The employer may cure the alleged violation within 33 calendar days of the postmark date of the notice. The employer shall give written notice by certified mail within that period of time to the aggrieved employee or representative and the agency if the alleged violation is cured, including a description of actions taken, and no civil action pursuant to Section 2699 may commence. If the alleged violation is not cured within the 33-day period, the employee may commence a civil action pursuant to Section 2699.

(B) No employer may avail himself or herself of the notice and cure provisions of this subdivision more than three times in a 12-month period for the same violation or violations contained in the notice, regardless of the location of the worksite.

(3) If the aggrieved employee disputes that the alleged violation has been cured, the aggrieved employee or representative shall provide written notice by certified mail, including specified grounds to support that dispute, to the employer and the agency. Within 17 calendar days of the postmark date of that notice, the agency shall review the actions taken by the employer to cure the alleged violation, and provide written notice of its decision by certified mail to the aggrieved employee and the employer. The agency may grant the employer three additional business days to cure the alleged violation. If the agency determines that the alleged violation has not been cured or if the agency fails to provide timely or any notification, the employee may proceed with the civil action pursuant to Section 2699. If the agency determines that the alleged violation has been cured, but the employee still disagrees, the employee may appeal that determination to the superior court.

(d) The periods specified in this section are not counted as part of the time limited for the commencement of the civil action to recover penalties under this part. **Leg.H.** 2004 ch. 221 (SB 1809), effective August 11, 2004.

Ref.: Hanna § 11.01[9]; W. Cal. Sum., 3 "Agency and Employment" §324.

§2699.5. Applicability of Labor Code §2699.3.

The provisions of subdivision (a) of Section 2699.3 [1] apply to any alleged violation of the following provisions: subdivision (k) of Section 96, [2] **Sections** 98.6, 201, **201.3,** 201.5, 201.7, 202, 203, 203.1, 203.5, 204, 204a, 204b, 204.1, 204.2, 205, 205.5, 206, 206.5, 208, 209, [3] **and** 212, subdivision (d) of Section 213, [4] **Sections** 221, 222, 222.5, 223, [5] **and** 224, subdivision (a) of Section 226, [6] **Sections** 226.7, 227, 227.3, 230, 230.1, 230.2, 230.3, 230.4, 230.7, 230.8, [7] **and** 231, subdivision (c) of Section 232, subdivision (c) of Section 232.5, [8] **Sections** 233, 234, 351, 353, [9] **and** 403, subdivision (b) of Section 404, [10] **Sections** 432.2, 432.5, 432.7, 435, 450, 510, 511, 512, 513, 551, 552, 601, 602, 603, 604, 750, 751.8, 800, 850, 851, 851.5, 852, 921, 922, 923, 970, 973, 976, 1021, 1021.5, 1025, 1026, 1101, 1102, 1102.5, [11] **and 1153, subdivisions (c) and** (d) of Section 1174, [12] **Sections** 1194, 1197, 1197.1, 1197.5, [13] **and** 1198, subdivision (b) of Section 1198.3, [14] **Sections** 1199, 1199.5, 1290, 1292, 1293, 1293.1, 1294, 1294.1, 1294.5, 1296, 1297, 1298, 1301, 1308, 1308.1, 1308.7, 1309, 1309.5, 1391, 1391.1, 1391.2, 1392, 1683, [15] **and** 1695, subdivision (a) of Section 1695.5, [16] **Sections** 1695.55, 1695.6, 1695.7, 1695.8, 1695.9, 1696, 1696.5, 1696.6, 1697.1, 1700.25, 1700.26, 1700.31, 1700.32, 1700.40, [17] **and 1700.47, paragraphs** (1), (2), [18] **and** (3) of subdivision (a) of [19] **and** subdivision (e) of Section 1701.4, subdivision (a) of Section 1701.5,

[20] **Sections** 1701.8, 1701.10, 1701.12, 1735, 1771, 1774, 1776, 1777.5, 1811, 1815, 2651, [21] **and** 2673, subdivision (a) of Section 2673.1, [22] **Sections** 2695.2, 2800, 2801, 2802, 2806, [23] **and** 2810, subdivision (b) of Section 2929, [24] **and Sections** 3095, 6310, 6311, [25] **and** 6399.7. **Leg.H.** 2004 ch. 221 (SB 1809), effective August 11, 2004, 2005 ch. 22 (SB 1108) §141, 2008 ch. 169 (SB 940) §8.

§2699.5. 2008 Deletes. **[1]** shall **[2]** Section **[3]** or **[4]** Section **[5]** or **[6]** Section **[7]** or **[8]** Section **[9]** or **[10]** Section **[11]** or 1153, subdivision (c) or **[12]** Section **[13]** or **[14]** Section **[15]** or **[16]** Section **[17]** or 1700.47, paragraph **[18]** or **[19]** or **[20]** Section **[21]** or **[22]** Section **[23]** or **[24]** or Section **[25]** or

2004 Note: Notwithstanding any other provision of law, the provisions of Section 2699.5 relating to the duties and functions of the Division of Occupational Safety and Health shall be subject to review by the Joint Committee on Boards, Commissions, and Consumer Protection pursuant to Chapter 2 (commencing with Section 474) of Division 1.2 of the Business and Professions Code in consultation with the Senate Committee on Labor and Industrial Relations and the Assembly Committee on Labor and Employment. The first review shall be completed no later than three years from the effective date of this act. Stats 2004 ch. 221 (SB 1809) §8.

Ref.: Hanna § 11.01[9].

DIVISION 3
EMPLOYMENT RELATIONS

CHAPTER 1
SCOPE OF DIVISION

§2700. Scope.

The provisions of this division shall not limit, change, or in any way qualify the provisions of Division 4 of this code, but shall be fully operative and effective in all cases where the provisions of Division 4 are not applicable.

Ref.: Hanna § 3.100[1]; W. Cal. Sum., 2 "Workers' Compensation" §190, 3 "Agency and Employment" §33.

CHAPTER 2
EMPLOYER AND EMPLOYEE

ARTICLE 1
The Contract of Employment
[Selected Provisions]

§2750. "Employment contract."

The contract of employment is a contract by which one, who is called the employer, engages another, who is called the employee, to do something for the benefit of the employer or a third person.

Ref.: Hanna § 3.21[1]; Herlick Handbook § 2.8; CACI No. 2400 (Matthew Bender); W. Cal. Sum., 3 "Agency and Employment" §3.

§2750.5. Rebuttable presumption that worker is employee; proof of independent contractor status.

There is a rebuttable presumption affecting the burden of proof that a worker performing services for which a license is required pursuant to Chapter 9 (commencing with Section 7000) of Division 3 of the Business and Professions Code, or who is performing such services for a person who is required to obtain such a license is an employee rather than an independent contractor. Proof of independent contractor status includes satisfactory proof of these factors:

(a) That the individual has the right to control and discretion as to the manner of performance of the contract for services in that the result of the work and not the means by which it is accomplished is the primary factor bargained for.

(b) That the individual is customarily engaged in an independently established business.

(c) That the individual's independent contractor status is bona fide and not a subterfuge to avoid employee status. A bona fide independent contractor status is further evidenced by the presence of cumulative factors such as substantial investment other than personal services in the business, holding out to be in business for oneself, bargaining for a contract to complete a specific project for compensation by project rather than by time, control over the time and place the work is performed, supplying the tools or instrumentalities used in the work other than tools and instrumentalities normally and customarily provided by employees, hiring employees, performing work that is not ordinarily in the course of the principal's work, performing work that requires a particular skill, holding a license pursuant to the Business and Professions Code, the intent by the parties that the work relationship is of an independent contractor status, or that the relationship is not severable or terminable at will by the principal but gives rise to an action for breach of contract.

In addition to the factors contained in subdivisions (a), (b), and (c), any person performing any function or activity for which a license is required pursuant to Chapter 9 (commencing with Section 7000) of Division 3 of the Business and Professions Code shall hold a valid contractors' license as a condition of having independent contractor status.

For purposes of workers' compensation law, this presumption is a supplement to the existing statutory definitions of employee and independent contractor, and is not intended to lessen the coverage of employees under Division 4 and Division 5.

Ref.: Hanna §§ 3.49[1]–[5], 10.24[5]; Herlick Handbook §§ 2.8, 12.11; W. Cal. Sum., 1 "Contracts" §496, 2 "Workers' Compensation" §§52, 190, 3 "Agency and Employment" §§21, 23, 32, 33.

§2750.6. Physician contracting with primary care clinic as independent contractor; rebuttable presumption.

There is a rebuttable presumption affecting the burden of proof that a physician and sur-

Labor

geon, licensed pursuant to Division 2 (commencing with Section 500) of the Business and Professions Code, who enters into a contract for the performance of health services on behalf of a licensed primary care clinic, as defined in paragraph (1) of subdivision (a) of Section 1204 of the Health and Safety Code, is an independent contractor rather than an employee. Nothing in this section shall authorize the employment of a physician and surgeon to provide professional services when the employment would violate any other provision of law.

Ref.: Herlick Handbook § 2.8; W. Cal. Sum., 3 "Agency and Employment" §39.

ARTICLE 2
Obligations of Employer [Selected Provisions]

§2800. Indemnification of employee; employer's want of care.

An employer shall in all cases indemnify his employee for losses caused by the employer's want of ordinary care.

Ref.: Hanna § 11.02[4][m]; W. Cal. Sum., 3 "Agency and Employment" §§122, 123.

§2800.1. Safeguard of musical instruments.

An employer shall in all cases take reasonable and necessary precautions to safeguard musical instruments and equipment, belonging to an employed musician, located on premises under the employer's control. In the event such equipment is damaged or stolen as a result of the employer's failure or refusal to take such reasonable and necessary precautions, the employer shall be liable to the owner for repair or replacement thereof if the employed musician has taken reasonable and necessary precautions to safeguard the musical instruments and equipment.

For the purposes of this section: (a) "employer" includes a purchaser of services and the owner of premises upon which an employed musician is working; and (b) "employee" is any employed musician working on premises which are under an employer's control.

Ref.: W. Cal. Sum., 3 "Agency and Employment" §§122, 123.

§2800.2. Employer provided medical coverage; notice of conversion coverage; continuation coverage under COBRA and notification of conversion coverage.

(a) Any employer, employee association, or other entity otherwise providing hospital, surgical, or major medical benefits to its employees or members is solely responsible for notification of its employees or members of the conversion coverage made available pursuant to Part 6.1 (commencing with Section 12670) of Division 2 of the Insurance Code or Section 1373.6 of the Health and Safety Code.

(b) Any employer, employee association, or other entity, whether private or public, that provides hospital, medical, or surgical expense coverage that a former employee may continue under Section 4980B of Title 26 of the United States Code, Section 1161 et seq. of Title 29 of the United States Code, or Section 300bb of Title 42 of the United States Code, as added by the Consolidated Omnibus Budget Reconciliation Act of 1985 (Public Law 99-272), and as may be later amended (hereafter "COBRA"), shall, in conjunction with the notification required by COBRA that COBRA continuation coverage will cease and conversion coverage is available, and as a part of the notification required by subdivision (a), also notify the former employee, spouse, or former spouse of the availability of the continuation coverage under Section 1373.621 of the Health and Safety Code, and Sections 10116.5 and 11512.03 of the Insurance Code.

(c) On or after July 1, 2006, notification provided to employees, members, former employees, spouses, or former spouses under subdivisions (a) and (b) shall also include the following notification:

"Please examine your options carefully before declining this coverage. You should be aware that companies selling individual health insurance typically require a review of your medical history that could result in a higher premium or you could be denied coverage entirely." **Leg.H.** 1995 ch. 489, 1996 ch. 1118, effective September 30, 1996, operative January 1, 1997, 2005 ch. 526 (AB 356) §8.

Ref.: W. Cal. Sum., 3 "Agency and Employment" §404.

§2800.3. Availability of coverage conversion.

Any employer, other than a self-insurer, employee association or other entity otherwise providing hospital, surgical or major medical benefits to its employees or members shall also make available conversion coverage which complies with the provisions of Part 6.1 (commencing with Section 12670) of Division 2 of the Insurance Code and Section 1373.6 of the Health and Safety Code.

§2801. Contributory negligence no bar to recovery; employer defenses limited.

In any action to recover damages for a personal injury sustained within this State by an employee while engaged in the line of his duty or the course of his employment as such, or for death resulting from personal injury so sustained, in which recovery is sought upon the ground of want of ordinary or reasonable care of the employer, or of any officer, agent or servant of the employer, the fact that such employee has been guilty of contributory negligence shall not bar a recovery therein where his contributory negligence was slight and that of the employer was gross, in comparison, but the damages may be diminished by the jury in proportion to the amount of negligence attributable to such employee.

It shall be conclusively presumed that such employee was not guilty of contributory negligence in any case where the violation of any law enacted for the safety of employees contributed to such employee's injury.

It shall not be a defense that:

(a) The employee either expressly or impliedly assumed the risk of the hazard complained of.

(b) The injury or death was caused in whole or in part by the want of ordinary or reasonable care of a fellow servant.

No contract, or regulation, shall exempt the employer from any provisions of this section.

Ref.: Hanna §§ 1.01[3], 11.03[2]; Herlick Handbook § 12.11.

§2802. Employee indemnification; loss sustained in performance of duties.

(a) An employer shall indemnify his or her employee for all necessary expenditures or losses incurred by the employee in direct consequence of the discharge of his or her duties, or of his or her obedience to the directions of the employer, even though unlawful, unless the employee, at the time of obeying the directions, believed them to be unlawful.

(b) All awards made by a court or by the Division of Labor Standards Enforcement for reimbursement of necessary expenditures under this section shall carry interest at the same rate as judgments in civil actions. Interest shall accrue from the date on which the employee incurred the necessary expenditure or loss.

(c) For purposes of this section, the term "necessary expenditures or losses" shall include all reasonable costs, including, but not limited to, attorney's fees incurred by the employee enforcing the rights granted by this section. **Leg.H.** 1937 ch. 90, 2000 ch. 990.

2000 Note: Nothing in this act is intended to establish the right of the Division of Labor Standards Enforcement to be awarded costs and attorney's fees. Stats. 2000 ch. 990 §2.

Ref.: Hanna § 4.01[2]; W. Cal. Sum., 2 "Workers' Compensation" §42, 3 "Agency and Employment" §§122–124, 5 "Torts" §373.

§2803. Death of employee; survivor's rights.

When death, whether instantaneously or otherwise, results from an injury to an employee caused by the want of ordinary or reasonable care of an employer or of any officer, agent, a servant of the employer, the personal representative of such employee shall have a right of action therefor against such employer, and may recover damages in respect thereof, for and on behalf of the surviving spouse, children, dependent parents, and dependent brothers and sisters, in order of precedence as stated, but no more than one action shall be brought for such recovery.

Ref.: W. Cal. Sum., 14 "Wills and Probate" §521.

§2803.4. Health benefits under ERISA; no reduction of benefits for Medi-Cal or medicaid coverage.

(a) Any employer providing health benefits under the Employee Retirement Income Security Act of 1974 (29 U.S.C. Sec. 1001, et seq.) shall not provide an exception for other coverage where the other coverage is entitlement to Medi-Cal benefits under Chapter 7 (commencing with Section 14000) or Chapter 8 (commencing with Section 14200) of Part 3 of Division 9

Labor

of the Welfare and Institutions Code, or medicaid benefits under Subchapter 19 (commencing with Section 1396) of Chapter 7 of Title 42 of the United States Code. Any employer providing health benefits under the Employee Retirement Income Security Act of 1974 shall not provide an exception for the Medi-Cal or medicaid benefits.

(b) Any employer providing health benefits under the Employee Retirement Income Security Act of 1974 shall not provide that the benefits payable are subject to reduction if the individual insured has entitlement to Medi-Cal or medicaid benefits.

(c) Any employer providing health benefits under the Employee Retirement Income Security Act of 1974 shall not provide an exception for enrollment for benefits because of an applicant's entitlement to Medi-Cal benefits under Chapter 7 (commencing with Section 14000) or Chapter 8 (commencing with Section 14200) of Part 3 of Division 9 of the Welfare and Institutions Code, or medicaid benefits under Subchapter 19 (commencing with Section 1396) of Chapter 7 of Title 42 of the United States Code.

(d) The State Department of Health Services shall consider health benefits available under the Employee Retirement Income Security Act of 1974 in determining legal liability of any third party for medical expenses incurred by a Medi-Cal or medicaid recipient under Section 14124.90 of the Welfare and Institutions Code and Subchapter 19 (commencing with Section 1396) of Chapter 7 of Title 42 of the United States Code. **Leg.H.** 1994 ch. 147, effective July 11, 1994.

Ref.: W. Cal. Sum., 3 "Agency and Employment" §404.

§2803.5. Compliance with provisions on health care coverage of children.

Any employer who offers health care coverage, including employers and insurers, shall comply with the standards set forth in Chapter 7 (commencing with Section 3750) of Part 1 of Division 9 of the Family Code and Section 14124.94 of the Welfare and Institutions Code. **Leg.H.** 1994 ch. 147, effective July 11, 1994, 1996 ch. 1062.

Ref.: W. Cal. Sum., 3 "Agency and Employment" §404.

§2804. Waiver of benefits as null and void.

Any contract or agreement, express or implied, made by any employee to waive the benefits of this article or any part thereof, is null and void and this article shall not deprive any employee or his personal representative of any right or remedy to which he is entitled under the laws of this State.

Ref.: MB Prac. Guide: Cal. Contract Lit., §18.06[1][d]; W. Cal. Sum., 1 "Contracts" §682.

§2806. Employer discontinuing coverage; notice.

(a) No employer, whether private or public, shall discontinue coverage for medical, surgical, or hospital benefits for employees unless the employer has notified and advised all covered employees in writing of any discontinuation of coverage, inclusive of nonrenewal and cancellation, but not inclusive of employment termination or cases in which substitute coverage has been provided, at least 15 days in advance of such discontinuation.

(b) If coverage is provided by a third party, failure of the employer to give the necessary notice shall not require the third party to continue the coverage beyond the date it would otherwise terminate.

(c) This section shall not apply to any employee welfare benefit plan that is subject to the Employee Retirement Income Security Act of 1974. **Leg.H.** 1992 ch. 722, effective September 15, 1992.

Ref.: W. Cal. Sum., 3 "Agency and Employment" §404.

§2807. Notification to former employees of availability of continued medical coverage.

(a) All employers, whether private or public, shall provide notification to former employees, along with the notification required by federal law pursuant to the Consolidated Omnibus Budget Reconciliation Act of 1985 (Public Law 99-272), of the availability of continued coverage for medical, surgical, or hospital benefits, a standardized written description of the Health Insurance Premium Program established by the State Department of Health Services pursuant to Section 120835 of the Health and Safety Code and Section 14124.91 of the Welfare and Institutions Code. The employer shall utilize the standardized written description prepared by the State Department of Health Services pursuant to subdivision (b).

(b) The State Department of Health Services shall prepare and make available, on request, a standardized written description of the Health Insurance Premium Program, at cost. **Leg.H.** 1992 ch. 722, effective September 15, 1992, 1996 ch. 1023, effective September 29, 1996.

Ref.: W. Cal. Sum., 3 "Agency and Employment" §404.

§2809. Employer-managed deferred compensation plans—Risks; summary of financial condition.

(a) Any employer, whether private or public, that offers its employees an employer-managed deferred compensation plan shall provide to each employee, prior to the employee's enrollment in the plan, written notice of the reasonably foreseeable financial risks accompanying participation in the plan, historical information to date as to the performance of the investments or funds available under the plan, and an annual balance sheet, annual audit, or similar document that describes the employer's financial condition as of a date no earlier than the immediately preceding year.

(b) Within 30 days after the end of each quarter of the calendar year, the employer, who directly manages the investments of a deferred compensation plan, shall provide, to each employee enrolled in a deferred compensation plan offered by the employer, a written report summarizing the current financial condition of the employer, summarizing the financial performance during the preceding quarter of each investment or fund available under the plan, and describing the actual performance of the employee's funds that are invested in each investment or fund in the plan.

(c) The obligations described in subdivisions (a) and (b) may be performed by a plan manager designated by the employer, who may contract with an investment manager for that purpose.

(d) If an employee is enrolled in a deferred compensation plan that is self-directed through a financial institution, the requirements set forth in this section shall be deemed to have been met. **Leg.H.** 1996 ch. 1160.

Ref.: W. Cal. Sum., 3 "Agency and Employment" §404.

§2810. Persons contracting for specified labor or services without providing sufficient funds for compliance with applicable laws or regulations subject to liability and civil penalties; rebuttable presumption; exceptions.

(a) A person or entity may not enter into a contract or agreement for labor or services with a construction, farm labor, garment, janitorial, or security guard contractor, where the person or entity knows or should know that the contract or agreement does not include funds sufficient to allow the contractor to comply with all applicable local, state, and federal laws or regulations governing the labor or services to be provided.

(b) There is a rebuttable presumption affecting the burden of proof that there has been no violation of subdivision (a) where the contract or agreement with a construction, farm labor, garment, janitorial, or security guard contractor meets all of the requirements in subdivision (d).

(c) Subdivision (a) does not apply to a person or entity who executes a collective bargaining agreement covering the workers employed under the contract or agreement, or to a person who enters into a contract or agreement for labor or services to be performed on his or her home residences, provided that a family member resides in the residence or residences for which the labor or services are to be performed for at least a part of the year.

(d) To meet the requirements of subdivision (b), a contract or agreement with a construction, farm labor, garment, janitorial, or security guard contractor for labor or services must be in writing, in a single document, and contain all of the following provisions, in addition to any other provisions that may be required by regulations adopted by the Labor Commissioner from time to time:

(1) The name, address, and telephone number of the person or entity and the construction, farm labor, garment, janitorial, or security guard contractor through whom the labor or services are to be provided.

(2) A description of the labor or services to be provided and a statement of when those services are to be commenced and completed.

(3) The employer identification number for state tax purposes of the construction, farm labor, garment, janitorial, or security guard contractor.

(4) The workers' compensation insurance policy number and the name, address, and telephone number of the insurance carrier of the construction, farm labor, garment, janitorial, or security guard contractor.

(5) The vehicle identification number of any vehicle that is owned by the construction, farm labor, garment, janitorial, or security guard contractor and used for transportation in connection with any service provided pursuant to the contract or agreement, the number of the vehicle liability insurance policy that covers the vehicle, and the name, address, and telephone number of the insurance carrier.

(6) The address of any real property to be used to house workers in connection with the contract or agreement.

(7) The total number of workers to be employed under the contract or agreement, the total amount of all wages to be paid, and the date or dates when those wages are to be paid.

(8) The amount of the commission or other payment made to the construction, farm labor, garment, janitorial, or security guard contractor for services under the contract or agreement.

(9) The total number of persons who will be utilized under the contract or agreement as independent contractors, along with a list of the current local, state, and federal contractor license identification numbers that the independent contractors are required to have under local, state, or federal laws or regulations.

(10) The signatures of all parties, and the date the contract or agreement was signed.

(e)(1) To qualify for the rebuttable presumption set forth in subdivision (b), a material change to the terms and conditions of a contract or agreement between a person or entity and a construction, farm labor, garment, janitorial, or security guard contractor must be in writing, in a single document, and contain all of the provisions listed in subdivision (d) that are affected by the change.

(2) If a provision required to be contained in a contract or agreement pursuant to paragraph (7) or (9) of subdivision (d) is unknown at the time the contract or agreement is executed, the best estimate available at that time is sufficient to satisfy the requirements of subdivision (d). If an estimate is used in place of actual figures in accordance with this paragraph, the parties to the contract or agreement have a continuing duty to ascertain the information required pursuant to paragraph (7) or (9) of subdivision (d) and to reduce that information to writing in accordance with the requirements of paragraph (1) once that information becomes known.

(f) A person or entity who enters into a contract or agreement referred to in subdivisions (d) or (e) shall keep a copy of the written contract or agreement for a period of not less than four years following the termination of the contract or agreement.

(g)(1) An employee aggrieved by a violation of subdivision (a) may file an action for damages to recover the greater of all of his or her actual damages or two hundred fifty dollars ($250) per employee per violation for an initial violation and one thousand dollars ($1,000) per employee for each subsequent violation, and, upon prevailing in an action brought pursuant to this section, may recover costs and reasonable attorney's fees. An action under this section may not be maintained unless it is pleaded and proved that an employee was injured as a result of a violation of a labor law or regulation in connection with the performance of the contract or agreement.

(2) An employee aggrieved by a violation of subdivision (a) may also bring an action for injunctive relief and, upon prevailing, may recover costs and reasonable attorney's fees.

(h) The phrase "construction, farm labor, garment, janitorial, or security guard contractor" includes any person, as defined in this code, whether or not licensed, who is acting in the capacity of a construction, farm labor, garment, janitorial, or security guard contractor.

(i)(1) The term "knows" includes the knowledge, arising from familiarity with the normal facts and circumstances of the business activity engaged in, that the contract or agreement does not include funds sufficient to allow the contractor to comply with applicable laws.

(2) The phrase "should know" includes the knowledge of any additional facts or information that would make a reasonably prudent person undertake to inquire whether, taken together, the contract or agreement contains sufficient funds to allow the contractor to comply with applicable laws.

(3) A failure by a person or entity to request or obtain any information from the contractor that is required by any applicable statute or by the contract or agreement between them, constitutes knowledge of that information for purposes of this section. **Leg.H.** 2003 ch. 908 (SB 179).

Ref.: W. Cal. Sum., 3 "Agency and Employment" §451.

Labor

DIVISION 4
WORKERS' COMPENSATION AND INSURANCE

PART 1
Scope and Operation

CHAPTER 1
GENERAL PROVISIONS

§3200. "Workmen's compensation" to become "workers' compensation."

The Legislature hereby declares its intent that the term "workmen's compensation" shall hereafter also be known as "workers' compensation." and that the "Workmen's Compensation Appeals Board" shall hereafter be known as the "Workers' Compensation Appeals Board." In furtherance of this policy it is the desire of the Legislature that references to the terms "workmen's compensation" and "Workmen's Compensation Appeals Board" in this code or elsewhere be changed to "workers' compensation" and "Workers' Compensation Appeals Board" when such laws are being amended for any purpose. This act is declaratory and not amendatory of existing law.

Ref.: Hanna § 4.06[1]; W. Cal. Ev., "Discovery" §§230, 236; W. Cal. Sum., 2 "Workers' Compensation" §4, 3 "Agency and Employment" §324, 4 "Secured Transactions in Personal Property" §24.

§3201. Purposes of Divisions 4 and 5 of Labor Code.

This division and Division 5 (commencing with Section 6300) are an expression of the police power and are intended to make effective and apply to a complete system of workers' compensation the provisions of Section 4 of Article XIV of the California Constitution.

Ref.: Hanna § 1.10; Herlick Handbook § 3.4; W. Cal. Ev., "Discovery" §§230, 236; W. Cal. Sum., 2 "Workers' Compensation" §§4, 77.

§3201.5. Validity of collective bargaining agreements—Prohibitions; applicability; premium rate; filing with Director; reports to Department, Legislature; confidentiality.

(a) Except as provided in subdivisions (b) and (c), the Department of Industrial Relations and the courts of this state shall recognize as valid and binding any provision in a collective bargaining agreement between a private employer or groups of employers engaged in construction, construction maintenance, or activities limited to rock, sand, gravel, cement and asphalt operations, heavy-duty mechanics, surveying, and construction inspection and a union that is the recognized or certified exclusive bargaining representative that establishes any of the following:

(1) An alternative dispute resolution system governing disputes between employees and employers or their insurers that supplements or replaces all or part of those dispute resolution processes contained in this division, including, but not limited to, mediation and arbitration. Any system of arbitration shall provide that the decision of the arbiter or board of arbitration is subject to review by the appeals board in the same manner as provided for reconsideration of a final order, decision, or award made and filed by a workers' compensation administrative law judge pursuant to the procedures set forth in Article 1 (commencing with Section 5900) of Chapter 7 of Part 4 of Division 4, and the court of appeals pursuant to the procedures set forth in Article 2 (commencing with Section 5950) of Chapter 7 of Part 4 of Division 4, governing orders, decisions, or awards of the appeals board. The findings of fact, award, order, or decision of the arbitrator shall have the same force and effect as an award, order, or decision of a workers' compensation administrative law judge. Any provision for arbitration established pursuant to this section shall not be subject to Sections 5270, 5270.5, 5271, 5272, 5273, 5275, and 5277.

(2) The use of an agreed list of providers of medical treatment that may be the exclusive source of all medical treatment provided under this division.

(3) The use of an agreed, limited list of qualified medical evaluators and agreed medical evaluators that may be the exclusive source of qualified medical evaluators and agreed medical evaluators under this division.

(4) Joint labor management safety committees.

(5) A light-duty, modified job or return-to-work program.

(6) A vocational rehabilitation or retraining program utilizing an agreed list of providers of rehabilitation services that may be the exclusive source of providers of rehabilitation services under this division.

(b)(1) Nothing in this section shall allow a collective bargaining agreement that diminishes the entitlement of an employee to compensation payments for total or partial disability, temporary disability, vocational rehabilitation, or medical treatment fully paid by the employer as otherwise provided in this division. The portion of any agreement that violates this paragraph shall be declared null and void.

(2) The parties may negotiate any aspect of the delivery of medical benefits and the delivery of disability compensation to employees of the employer or group of employers that are eligible for group health benefits and nonoccupational disability benefits through their employer.

(c) Subdivision (a) shall apply only to the following:

(1) An employer developing or projecting an annual workers' compensation insurance premium, in California, of two hundred fifty thousand dollars ($250,000) or more, or any employer that paid an annual workers' compensation insurance premium, in California, of two hundred fifty thousand dollars ($250,000) in at least one of the previous three years.

(2) Groups of employers engaged in a workers' compensation safety group complying with Sections 11656.6 and 11656.7 of the Insurance Code, and established pursuant to a joint labor management safety committee or committees, that develops or projects annual workers' compensation insurance premiums of two million dollars ($2,000,000) or more.

(3) Employers or groups of employers that are self-insured in compliance with Section 3700 that would have projected annual workers' compensation costs that meet the requirements of, and that meet the other requirements of, paragraph (1) in the case of employers, or paragraph (2) in the case of groups of employers.

(4) Employers covered by an owner or general contractor provided wrap-up insurance policy applicable to a single construction site that develops workers' compensation insurance premiums of two million dollars ($2,000,000) or more with respect to those employees covered by that wrap-up insurance policy.

(d) Employers and labor representatives who meet the eligibility requirements of this section shall be issued a letter by the administrative director advising each employer and labor representative that, based upon the review of all documents and materials submitted as required by the administrative director, each has met the eligibility requirements of this section.

(e) The premium rate for a policy of insurance issued pursuant to this section shall not be subject to the requirements of Section 11732 or 11732.5 of the Insurance Code.

(f) No employer may establish or continue a program established under this section until it has provided the administrative director with all of the following:

(1) Upon its original application and whenever it is renegotiated thereafter, a copy of the collective bargaining agreement and the approximate number of employees who will be covered thereby.

(2) Upon its original application and annually thereafter, a valid and active license where that license is required by law as a condition of doing business in the state within the industries set forth in subdivision (a) of Section 3201.5.

(3) Upon its original application and annually thereafter, a statement signed under penalty of perjury, that no action has been taken by any administrative agency or court of the United States to invalidate the collective bargaining agreement.

(4) The name, address, and telephone number of the contact person of the employer.

(5) Any other information that the administrative director deems necessary to further the purposes of this section.

(g) No collective bargaining representative may establish or continue to participate in a program established under this section unless all of the following requirements are met:

(1) Upon its original application and annually thereafter, it has provided to the administrative director a copy of its most recent LM-2 or LM-3 filing with the United States Depart-

ment of Labor, along with a statement, signed under penalty of perjury, that the document is a true and correct copy.

(2) It has provided to the administrative director the name, address, and telephone number of the contact person or persons of the collective bargaining representative or representatives.

(h) Commencing July 1, 1995, and annually thereafter, the Division of Workers' Compensation shall report to the Director of the Department of Industrial Relations the number of collective bargaining agreements received and the number of employees covered by these agreements.

(i) By June 30, 1996, and annually thereafter, the Administrative Director of the Division of Workers' Compensation shall prepare and notify Members of the Legislature that a report authorized by this section is available upon request. The report based upon aggregate data shall include the following:

(1) Person hours and payroll covered by agreements filed.

(2) The number of claims filed.

(3) The average cost per claim shall be reported by cost components whenever practicable.

(4) The number of litigated claims, including the number of claims submitted to mediation, the appeals board, or the court of appeal.

(5) The number of contested claims resolved prior to arbitration.

(6) The projected incurred costs and actual costs of claims.

(7) Safety history.

(8) The number of workers participating in vocational rehabilitation.

(9) The number of workers participating in light-duty programs.

The division shall have the authority to require those employers and groups of employers listed in subdivision (c) to provide the data listed above.

(j) The data obtained by the administrative director pursuant to this section shall be confidential and not subject to public disclosure under any law of this state. However, the Division of Workers' Compensation shall create derivative works pursuant to subdivisions (h) and (i) based on the collective bargaining agreements and data. Those derivative works shall not be confidential, but shall be public. On a monthly basis the administrative director shall make available an updated list of employers and unions entering into collective bargaining agreements containing provisions authorized by this section. **Leg.H.** 1993 ch. 117, effective July 16, 1993, 1994 ch. 963, effective September 28, 1994, 1995 ch. 886, 2002 ch. 866 (AB 486), 2004 ch. 34 (SB 899), effective April 19, 2004.

2004 Note: The amendment to §3201.5 made by this act shall apply prospectively from the date of enactment of this act, regardless of the date of injury, unless otherwise specified, but shall not constitute good cause to reopen or rescind, alter, or amend any existing order, decision, or award of the Workers' Compensation Appeals Board. Stats. 2004 ch. 34 (SB 899) §47.

Ref.: 8 C.C.R. §§10200, 10201, 10202, 10203, 10203.1, 10203.2, 10204, 10865; Hanna §§ 1.04[1], 1.04[2], 1.04[4], 1.04A[2], 28.27; Herlick Handbook §§ 3.4, 14.4, 14.32; W. Cal. Ev., "Discovery" §§230, 236; W. Cal. Sum., 2 "Workers' Compensation" §§4, 261, 393.

§3201.7. Labor-management agreements—Criteria; applicability; requirements.

(a) Except as provided in subdivision (b), the Department of Industrial Relations and the courts of this state shall recognize as valid and binding any labor-management agreement that meets all of the following requirements:

(1) The labor-management agreement has been negotiated separate and apart from any collective bargaining agreement covering affected employees.

(2) The labor-management agreement is restricted to the establishment of the terms and conditions necessary to implement this section.

(3) The labor-management agreement has been negotiated in accordance with the authorization of the administrative director pursuant to subdivision (d), between an employer or groups of employers and a union that is the recognized or certified exclusive bargaining representative that establishes any of the following:

(A) An alternative dispute resolution system governing disputes between employees and employers or their insurers that supplements or replaces all or part of those dispute resolution processes contained in this division, including, but not limited to, mediation and arbitration. Any system of arbitration shall provide that the decision of the arbiter or board of arbitration is subject to review by the appeals board in the same manner as provided for reconsideration of a final order, decision, or award made and filed by a workers' compensation administrative law judge pursuant to the procedures set forth in Article 1 (commencing with Section 5900) of Chapter 7 of Part 4 of Division 4, and the court of appeals pursuant to the procedures set forth in Article 2 (commencing with Section 5950) of Chapter 7 of Part 4 of Division 4, governing orders, decisions, or awards of the appeals board. The findings of fact, award, order, or decision of the arbitrator shall have the same force and effect as an award, order, or decision of a workers' compensation administrative law judge. Any provision for arbitration established pursuant to this section shall not be subject to Sections 5270, 5270.5, 5271, 5272, 5273, 5275, and 5277.

(B) The use of an agreed list of providers of medical treatment that may be the exclusive source of all medical treatment provided under this division.

(C) The use of an agreed, limited list of qualified medical evaluators and agreed medical evaluators that may be the exclusive source of qualified medical evaluators and agreed medical evaluators under this division.

(D) Joint labor management safety committees.

(E) A light-duty, modified job, or return-to-work program.

(F) A vocational rehabilitation or retraining program utilizing an agreed list of providers of rehabilitation services that may be the exclusive source of providers of rehabilitation services under this division.

(b)(1) Nothing in this section shall allow a labor-management agreement that diminishes the entitlement of an employee to compensation payments for total or partial disability, temporary disability, vocational rehabilitation, or medical treatment fully paid by the employer as otherwise provided in this division; nor shall any agreement authorized by this section deny to any employee the right to representation by counsel at all stages during the alternative dispute resolution process. The portion of any agreement that violates this paragraph shall be declared null and void.

(2) The parties may negotiate any aspect of the delivery of medical benefits and the delivery of disability compensation to employees of the employer or group of employers that are eligible for group health benefits and nonoccupational disability benefits through their employer.

(c) Subdivision (a) shall apply only to the following:

(1) An employer developing or projecting an annual workers' compensation insurance premium, in California, of fifty thousand dollars ($50,000) or more, and employing at least 50 employees, or any employer that paid an annual workers' compensation insurance premium, in California, of fifty thousand dollars ($50,000), and employing at least 50 employees in at least one of the previous three years.

(2) Groups of employers engaged in a workers' compensation safety group complying with Sections 11656.6 and 11656.7 of the Insurance Code, and established pursuant to a joint labor management safety committee or committees, that develops or projects annual workers' compensation insurance premiums of five hundred thousand dollars ($500,000) or more.

(3) Employers or groups of employers, including cities and counties, that are self-insured in compliance with Section 3700 that would have projected annual workers' compensation costs that meet the requirements of, and that meet the other requirements of, paragraph (1) in the case of employers, or paragraph (2) in the case of groups of employers.

(d) Any recognized or certified exclusive bargaining representative in an industry not covered by Section 3201.5, may file a petition with the administrative director seeking permission to negotiate with an employer or group of employers to enter into a labor-management agreement pursuant to this section. The petition shall specify the bargaining unit or units to be included, the names of the employers or groups of employers, and shall be accompanied by proof of the labor union's status as the exclusive bargaining representative. The current collective bargaining agreement or agreements shall be attached to the petition. The petition shall be in the form designated by the administrative director. Upon receipt of the petition, the administrative director shall promptly verify the petitioner's status as the exclusive bargaining representative. If the petition satisfies the requirements set forth in this subdivision, the administrative director shall issue a letter advising each employer and labor representative of their eligibility to enter into negotiations, for a period not to exceed one year, for the purpose of reaching agreement on a labor-management agreement pursuant to this section. The parties may jointly request, and shall be granted, by the administrative-tive director, an additional one-year period to negotiate an agreement.

(e) No employer may establish or continue a program established under this section until it has provided the administrative director with all of the following:

(1) Upon its original application and whenever it is renegotiated thereafter, a copy of the labor-management agreement and the approximate number of employees who will be covered thereby.

(2) Upon its original application and annually thereafter, a statement signed under penalty of perjury, that no action has been taken by any administrative agency or court of the United States to invalidate the labor-management agreement.

(3) The name, address, and telephone number of the contact person of the employer.

(4) Any other information that the administrative director deems necessary to further the purposes of this section.

(f) No collective bargaining representative may establish or continue to participate in a program established under this section unless all of the following requirements are met:

(1) Upon its original application and annually thereafter, it has provided to the administrative director a copy of its most recent LM-2 or LM-3 filing with the United States Department of Labor, where such filing is required by law, along with a statement, signed under penalty of perjury, that the document is a true and correct copy.

(2) It has provided to the administrative director the name, address, and telephone number of the contact person or persons of the collective bargaining representative or representatives.

(g) Commencing July 1, 2005, and annually thereafter, the Division of Workers' Compensation shall report to the Director of Industrial Relations the number of labor-management agreements received and the number of employees covered by these agreements.

(h) By June 30, 2006, and annually thereafter, the administrative director shall prepare and notify Members of the Legislature that a report authorized by this section is available upon request. The report based upon aggregate data shall include the following:

(1) Person hours and payroll covered by agreements filed.

(2) The number of claims filed.

(3) The average cost per claim shall be reported by cost components whenever practicable.

(4) The number of litigated claims, including the number of claims submitted to mediation, the appeals board, or the court of appeal.

(5) The number of contested claims resolved prior to arbitration.

(6) The projected incurred costs and actual costs of claims.

(7) Safety history.

(8) The number of workers participating in vocational rehabilitation.

(9) The number of workers participating in light-duty programs.

(10) Overall worker satisfaction.

The division shall have the authority to require employers and groups of employers participating in labor-management agreements pursuant to this section to provide the data listed above.

(i) The data obtained by the administrative director pursuant to this section shall be confidential and not subject to public disclosure under any law of this state. However, the Division of Workers' Compensation shall create derivative works pursuant to subdivisions (f) and (g) based on the labor-management agreements and data. Those derivative works shall not be confidential, but shall be public. On a monthly basis, the administrative director shall make available an updated list of employers and unions entering into labor-management agreements authorized by this section. **Leg.H.** 2003 ch. 639 (SB 228) §14.7, 2004 ch. 34 (SB 899), effective April 19, 2004.

2004 Note: The amendment to §3201.7 made by this act shall apply prospectively from the date of enactment of this act, regardless of the date of injury, unless otherwise specified, but shall not constitute good cause to reopen or rescind, alter, or amend any existing order, decision, or award of the Workers' Compensation Appeals Board. Stats. 2004 ch. 34 (SB 899) §47.

Ref.: 8 C.C.R. §§10200, 10202, 10203, 10203.1, 10203.2, 10204, 10865; Hanna §§ 1.04[1], 1.04A; Herlick Handbook §§ 3.4, 14.4; W. Cal. Ev., "Discovery" §§230, 236; W. Cal. Sum., 2 "Workers' Compensation" §§4, 261, 393.

§3201.81. Collective bargaining agreements for licensed jockeys.

In the horse racing industry, the organization certified by the California Horse Racing Board to represent the majority of licensed jockeys pursuant to subdivision (b) of Section 19612.9 of the Business and Professions Code is the labor organization authorized to negotiate the collective bargaining agreement establishing an alternative dispute resolution system for licensed jockeys pursuant to Section 3201.7. **Leg.H.** 2003 ch. 884 (AB 1719), 2007 ch. 130 (AB 299) §184.

Ref.: W. Cal. Ev., "Discovery" §§230, 236.

§3201.9. Reports under collective bargaining agreements; required provisions.

(a) On or before June 30, 2004, and biannually thereafter, the report required in subdivision (i) of Section 3201.5 and subdivision (h) of Section 3201.7 shall include updated loss experience for all employers and groups of employers participating in a program established under those sections. The report shall include updated data on each item set forth in subdivision (i) of Section 3201.5 and subdivision (h) of Section 3201.7 for the previous year for injuries in 2003 and beyond. Updates for each program shall be done for the original program year and for subsequent years. The insurers, the Department of Insurance, and the rating organization designated by the Insurance Commissioner pursuant to Article 3 (commencing with Section 11750) of Chapter 3 of Part 3 of Division 2 of the Insurance Code, shall provide the administrative director with any information that the administrative director determines is reasonably necessary to conduct the study.

(b) Commencing on and after June 30, 2004, the Insurance Commissioner, or the commissioner's designee, shall prepare for inclusion in the report required in subdivision (i) of Section 3201.5 and subdivision (h) of Section 3201.7 a review of both of the following:

(1) The adequacy of rates charged for these programs, including the impact of scheduled credits and debits.

(2) The comparative results for these programs with other programs not subject to Section 3201.5 or Section 3201.7.

(c) Upon completion of the report, the administrative director shall report the findings to the Legislature, the Department of Insurance, the designated rating organization, and the programs and insurers participating in the study.

(d) The data obtained by the administrative director pursuant to this section shall be confidential and not subject to public disclosure under any law of this state. **Leg.H.** 2002 ch. 6 (AB 749), 2004 ch. 34 (SB 899), effective April 19, 2004.

2004 Note: The amendment to §3201.9 made by this act shall apply prospectively from the date of enactment of this act, regardless of the date of injury, unless otherwise specified, but shall not constitute good cause to reopen or rescind, alter, or amend any existing order, decision, or award of the Workers' Compensation Appeals Board. Stats. 2004 ch. 34 (SB 899) §47.

Ref.: 8 C.C.R. §§10203, 10203.1, 10203.2, 10204; W. Cal. Ev., "Discovery" §§230, 236.

§3202. Liberal construction of Divisions 4 and 5.

This division and Division 5 (commencing with Section 6300) shall be liberally construed by the courts with the purpose of extending their benefits for the protection of persons injured in the course of their employment.

Ref.: Hanna §§ 3.23, 4.05[1], 28.36[2][d]; Herlick Handbook § 14.6; W. Cal. Ev., "Discovery" §§230, 236; W. Cal. Sum., 2 "Workers' Compensation" §§6, 19, 113, 143, 187, 351, 391.

§3202.5. Preponderance of evidence standard.

All parties and lien claimants shall meet the evidentiary burden of proof on all issues by a preponderance of the evidence in order that all parties are considered equal before the law. "Preponderance of the evidence" means that evidence that, when weighed with that opposed to it, has more convincing force and the greater probability of truth. When weighing the evidence, the test is not the relative number of witnesses, but the relative convincing force of the evidence. **Leg.H.** 1993 ch. 4, effective April 3, 1993, 2004 ch. 34 (SB 899), effective April 19, 2004.

2004 Note: The amendment to §3202.5 made by this act shall apply prospectively from the date of enactment of this act, regardless of the date of injury, unless otherwise specified, but shall not constitute good cause to reopen or rescind, alter, or amend any existing order, decision, or award of the Workers' Compensation Appeals Board. Stats. 2004 ch. 34 (SB 899) §47.

Ref.: Hanna §§ 3.05, 4.05[1], 4.05[2][a], 26.06[6]; Herlick Handbook §§ 10.1, 14.6; W. Cal. Ev., "Discovery" §§230, 236; W. Cal. Sum., 2 "Workers' Compensation" §§6, 231, 351.

§3203. Inapplicability of Divisions 4 and 5 to interstate commerce.

This division and Division 5 (commencing with Section 6300) do not apply to employers or employments which, according to law, are so engaged in interstate commerce as not to be subject to the legislative power of the state, nor to employees injured while they are so engaged, except in so far as these divisions are permitted to apply under the Constitution or laws of the United States.

Ref.: Hanna § 21.01[1], [3]; Herlick Handbook § 13.2; W. Cal. Ev., "Discovery" §§230, 236; W. Cal. Sum., 2 "Workers' Compensation" §118.

§3204. Chapter's definitions to govern construction.

Unless the context otherwise requires, the definitions hereinafter set forth in this chapter shall govern the construction and meaning of the terms and phrases used in this division.

Ref.: W. Cal. Ev., "Discovery" §§230, 236.

§3205. "Division."

"Division" means the Division of Workers' Compensation. **Leg.H.** 1994 chs. 146, 1097.

Ref.: W. Cal. Ev., "Discovery" §§230, 236.

§3205.5. "Appeals board."

"Appeals board" means the Workers' Compensation Appeals Board of the Division of Workers' Compensation. **Leg.H.** 1994 chs. 146, 1097.

Ref.: W. Cal. Ev., "Discovery" §§230, 236; W. Cal. Sum., 2 "Workers' Compensation" §13.

§3206. "Administrative director."

"Administrative director" means the Director of the Division of Workers' Compensation. **Leg.H.** 1994 chs. 146, 1097.

Ref.: W. Cal. Ev., "Discovery" §§230, 236.

§3207. "Compensation."

"Compensation" means compensation under this division and includes every benefit or payment conferred by this division upon an injured employee, or in the event of his or her death, upon his or her dependents, without regard to negligence. **Leg.H.** 2004 ch. 34 (SB 899), effective April 19, 2004.

2004 Note: The amendment to §3207 made by this act shall apply prospectively from the date of enactment of this act, regardless of the date of injury, unless otherwise specified, but shall not constitute good cause to reopen or rescind, alter, or amend any existing order, decision, or award of the Workers' Compensation Appeals Board. Stats. 2004 ch. 34 (SB 899) §47.

Ref.: 8 C.C.R. §§10110, 10115; Hanna §§ 2.70[1], 10.01[1][b], 20.01[1][d], 22.02[6], 22.08[3][b], 35.03[1]; W. Cal. Ev., "Discovery" §§230, 236; W. Cal. Sum., 2 "Insurance" §281, 2 "Workers' Compensation" §§18, 23, 151, 317.

§3208. "Injury."

"Injury" includes any injury or disease arising out of the employment, including injuries to artificial members, dentures, hearing aids, eyeglasses and medical braces of all types; provided, however, that eyeglasses and hearing aids will not be replaced, repaired, or otherwise compensated for, unless injury to them is incident to an injury causing disability.

Ref.: 8 C.C.R. §§9767.1, 9811; Hanna § 4.01[2][a]; Herlick Handbook §§ 4.13, 8.19; W. Cal. Sum., 2 "Workers' Compensation" §§55, 236, 265.

§3208.05. Injury to health care worker from preventative care.

(a) "Injury" includes a reaction to or a side effect arising from health care provided by an employer to a health care worker, which health care is intended to prevent the development or manifestation of any bloodborne disease, illness, syndrome, or condition recognized as occupationally incurred by Cal-OSHA, the Federal Centers for Disease Control, or other appropriate governmental entities. This section shall apply only to preventive health care that the employer provided to a health care worker under the following circumstances: (1) prior to an exposure because of risk of occupational exposure to such a disease, illness, syndrome, or condition, or (2) where the preventive care is provided as a consequence of a documented exposure to blood or bodily fluid containing blood that arose out of and in the course of employment. Such a disease, illness, syndrome, or condition includes, but is not limited to, hepatitis, and the human immunodeficiency virus. Such preventive health care, and any disability indemnity or other benefits required as a result of the preventive health care provided by the employer, shall be compensable under the workers' compensation system. The employer may require the health care worker to document that the employer provided the preventive health care and that the reaction or side effects arising from the preventive health care resulted in lost work time, health care costs, or other costs normally compensable under workers' compensation.

(b) The benefits of this section shall not be provided to a health care worker for a reaction to or side effect from health care intended to prevent the development of the human immunodeficiency virus if the worker claims a work-related exposure and if the worker tests positive within 48 hours of that exposure to a test to determine the presence of the human immunodeficiency virus.

(c) For purposes of this section, "health care worker" includes any person who is an employee of a provider of health care as defined in subdivision (d) of Section 56.05 of the Civil Code, and who is exposed to human blood or other bodily fluids contaminated with blood in the course of employment, including, but not limited to, a registered nurse, a licensed vocational nurse, a certified nurse aide, clinical laboratory technologist, dental hygienist, physician, janitor, and housekeeping worker. "Health care worker" does not include an employee who provides employee health services for an employer primarily engaged in a business other than providing health care. **Leg.H.** 1992 ch. 1085.

Ref.: Hanna § 4.71; Herlick Handbook §§ 8.19, 8.22; W. Cal. Sum., 2 "Workers' Compensation" §236.

§3208.1. Specific and cumulative injuries.

An injury may be either: (a) "specific," occurring as the result of one incident or exposure which causes disability or need for medical treatment; or (b) "cumulative," occurring as repetitive mentally or physically traumatic activities extending over a period of time, the combined effect of which causes any disability or need for medical treatment. The date of a cumulative injury shall be the date determined under Section 5412.

Ref.: Hanna § 4.01[2][a]; Herlick Handbook § 8.23; W. Cal. Ev., "Discovery" §§230, 236; W. Cal. Sum., 2 "Workers' Compensation" §§292, 368, 371.

§3208.2. Combined injuries; separate determinations.

When disability, need for medical treatment, or death results from the combined effects of two or more injuries, either specific, cumulative, or both, all questions of fact and law shall be separately determined with respect to each such injury, including, but not limited to, the apportionment between such injuries of liability for disability benefits, the cost of medical treatment, and any death benefit.

Ref.: 8 C.C.R. §10401; Hanna §§ 8.02[3], 26.10[2]; Herlick Handbook § 8.23; W. Cal. Ev., "Discovery" §§230, 236; W. Cal. Sum., 2 "Workers' Compensation" §§279, 292, 371.

§3208.3. Threshold of compensability for psychiatric injury.

(a) A psychiatric injury shall be compensable if it is a mental disorder which causes disability or need for medical treatment, and it is diagnosed pursuant to procedures promulgated under paragraph (4) of subdivision (j) of Section 139.2 or, until these procedures are promulgated, it is diagnosed using the terminology and criteria of the American Psychiatric Association's Diagnostic and Statistical Manual of Mental Disorders, Third Edition-Revised, or the terminology and diagnostic criteria of other psychiatric diagnostic manuals generally approved and accepted nationally by practitioners in the field of psychiatric medicine.

(b)(1) In order to establish that a psychiatric injury is compensable, an employee shall demonstrate by a preponderance of the evidence that actual events of employment were predominant as to all causes combined of the psychiatric injury.

(2) Notwithstanding paragraph (1), in the case of employees whose injuries resulted from being a victim of a violent act or from direct exposure to a significant violent act, the employee shall be required to demonstrate by a preponderance of the evidence that actual events of employment were a substantial cause of the injury.

(3) For the purposes of this section, "substantial cause" means at least 35 to 40 percent of the causation from all sources combined.

(c) It is the intent of the Legislature in enacting this section to establish a new and higher threshold of compensability for psychiatric injury under this division.

(d) Notwithstanding any other provision of this division, no compensation shall be paid pursuant to this division for a psychiatric injury related to a claim against an employer unless the employee has been employed by that employer for at least six months. The six months of employment need not be continuous. This subdivision shall not apply if the psychiatric injury is caused by a sudden and extraordinary employment condition. Nothing in this subdivision shall be construed to authorize an employee, or his or her dependents, to bring an action at law or equity for damages against the employer for a psychiatric injury, where those rights would not exist pursuant to the exclusive remedy doctrine set forth in Section 3602 in the absence of the amendment of this section by the act adding this subdivision.

(e) Where the claim for compensation is filed after notice of termination of employment or layoff, including voluntary layoff, and the claim is for an injury occurring prior to the time of notice of termination or layoff, no compensation shall be paid unless the employee demonstrates by a preponderance of the evidence that actual events of employment were predominant as to all causes combined of the psychiatric injury and one or more of the following conditions exist:

(1) Sudden and extraordinary events of employment were the cause of the injury.

(2) The employer has notice of the psychiatric injury under Chapter 2 (commencing with Section 5400) prior to the notice of termination or layoff.

(3) The employee's medical records existing prior to notice of termination or layoff contain evidence of treatment of the psychiatric injury.

(4) Upon a finding of sexual or racial harassment by any trier of fact, whether contractual, administrative, regulatory, or judicial.

(5) Evidence that the date of injury, as specified in Section 5411 or 5412, is subsequent to the date of the notice of termination or layoff, but prior to the effective date of the termination or layoff.

(f) For purposes of this section, an employee provided notice pursuant to Sections 44948.5, 44949, 44951, 44955, 44955.6, 72411, 87740, and 87743 of the Education Code shall be considered to have been provided a notice of termination or layoff only upon a district's final decision not to reemploy that person.

(g) A notice of termination or layoff that is not followed within 60 days by that termination or layoff shall not be subject to the provisions of this subdivision, and this subdivision shall not apply until receipt of a later notice of termination or layoff. The issuance of frequent notices of termination or layoff to an employee shall be considered a bad faith personnel action and shall make this subdivision inapplicable to the employee.

(h) No compensation under this division shall be paid by an employer for a psychiatric injury if the injury was substantially caused by a lawful, nondiscriminatory, good faith personnel action. The burden of proof shall rest with the party asserting the issue.

(i) When a psychiatric injury claim is filed against an employer, and an application for adjudication of claim is filed by an employer or employee, the division shall provide the employer with information concerning psychiatric injury prevention programs.

(j) An employee who is an inmate, as defined in subdivision (e) of Section 3351, or his or her family on behalf of an inmate, shall not be entitled to compensation for a psychiatric injury except as provided in subdivision (d) of Section 3370. **Leg.H.** 1991 ch. 115, effective July 16, 1991, 1993 ch. 118, effective July 16, 1993, ch. 1242, 1994 ch. 497.

1989 Note: This section is applicable only to injuries occurring on or after January 1, 1990. 1989 ch. 893 §6.

Ref.: Hanna §§ 4.02[3][b]–[f], 4.65[1], 4.69[3][d]; Herlick Handbook §§ 8.19, 8.21; Lawyer's Guide to AMA *Guides* and Calif. Workers' Comp. §§ 2.06, 13.14; W. Cal. Ev., "Discovery" §§230, 236; W. Cal. Sum., 2 "Workers' Compensation" §§180, 193, 244–247, 381.

§3208.4. Discovery requirements in proceedings involving injury arising from sexual conduct; nonadmissible evidence.

In any proceeding under this division involving an injury arising out of alleged conduct that constitutes sexual harassment, sexual assault, or sexual battery, any party seeking discovery concerning sexual conduct of the applicant with any person other than the defendant, whether consensual or nonconsensual or prior or subsequent to the alleged act complained of, shall establish specific facts showing good cause for that discovery on a noticed motion to the appeals board. The motion shall not be made or considered at an ex parte hearing.

The procedures set forth in Section 783 of the Evidence Code shall be followed if evidence of sexual conduct of the applicant is offered to attack his or her credibility. Opinion evidence,

evidence of reputation, and evidence of specific instances of sexual conduct of the applicant with any person other than the defendant, or any of such evidence, is not admissible by the defendant to prove consent by or the absence of injury to the applicant, unless the injury alleged by the applicant is in the nature of loss of consortium. **Leg.H.** 1993 ch. 121, effective July 16, 1993.

1993 Note: Section 3208.4, as added by 1993 ch. 121, applies only to injuries occurring on or after January 1, 1994. Stats. 1993 ch. 121 §77.

Ref.: Herlick Handbook § 8.8; W. Cal. Sum., 2 "Workers' Compensation" §402.

§3209. "Damages."

"Damages" means the recovery allowed in an action at law as contrasted with compensation.

Ref.: Hanna § 2.70[1]; W. Cal. Sum., 2 "Insurance" §281.

§3209.3. "Physician"; "psychologist"; "acupuncturist"; request for medical collaboration; acupuncturist unauthorized to determine disability.

(a) "Physician" includes physicians and surgeons holding an M.D. or D.O. degree, psychologists, acupuncturists, optometrists, dentists, podiatrists, and chiropractic practitioners licensed by California state law and within the scope of their practice as defined by California state law.

(b) "Psychologist" means a licensed psychologist with a doctoral degree in psychology, or a doctoral degree deemed equivalent for licensure by the Board of Psychology pursuant to Section 2914 of the Business and Professions Code, and who either has at least two years of clinical experience in a recognized health setting or has met the standards of the National Register of the Health Service Providers in Psychology.

(c) When treatment or evaluation for an injury is provided by a psychologist, provision shall be made for appropriate medical collaboration when requested by the employer or the insurer.

(d) "Acupuncturist" means a person who holds an acupuncturist's certificate issued pursuant to Chapter 12 (commencing with Section 4925) of Division 2 of the Business and Professions Code.

(e) Nothing in this section shall be construed to authorize acupuncturists to determine disability for the purposes of Article 3 (commencing with Section 4650) of Chapter 2 of Part 2, or under Section 2708 of the Unemployment Insurance Code. **Leg.H.** 1992 ch. 824 §1, 1994 ch. 1118 §3, 1996 ch. 26 §1, 1997 ch. 98 §1.

Ref.: 8 C.C.R. §§9767.1, 9767.3, 9773, 9773.1, 9792.6; Hanna §§ 22.05[2], 22.09[5], 26.06[12]; Herlick Handbook §§ 4.18, 10.3; W. Cal. Ev., "Discovery" §§230, 236; W. Cal. Sum., 2 "Workers' Compensation" §§261, 399.

§3209.4. Optometrists not physicians.

The inclusion of optometrists in Section 3209.3 does not imply any right or entitle any optometrist to represent, advertise, or hold himself out as a physician.

Ref.: W. Cal. Ev., "Discovery" §§230, 236.

§3209.5. Osteopathic and chiropractic practitioners.

Medical, surgical, and hospital treatment, including nursing, medicines, medical and surgical supplies, crutches, and apparatus, includes but is not limited to services and supplies by physical therapists, chiropractic practitioners, and acupuncturists, as licensed by California state law and within the scope of their practice as defined by law. **Leg.H.** 1998 ch. 440.

Ref.: 8 C.C.R. §9767.1; W. Cal. Ev., "Discovery" §§230, 236; W. Cal. Sum., 2 "Workers' Compensation" §266.

§3209.6. Chiropractors not physicians.

The inclusion of chiropractors in Sections 3209.3 and 3209.5 does not imply any right or entitle any chiropractor to represent, advertise, or hold himself out as a physician.

Ref.: W. Cal. Ev., "Discovery" §§230, 236.

§3209.7. Agreements on other healing practices.

Treatment of injuries at the expense of the employer may also include, either in addition to or in place of medical, surgical, and hospital services, as specified in Section 3209.5, any other form of therapy, treatment, or healing practice agreed upon voluntarily in writing, between the employee and his employer. Such agreement may be entered into at any time after employment and shall be in a form approved by the Department of Industrial Relations, and shall include at least the following items:

(a) A description of the form of healing practice intended to be relied upon and designation of individuals and facilities qualified to administer it.

(b) The employee shall not by entering into such an agreement or by selecting such therapy, treatment or healing practice, waive any rights conferred upon him by law, or forfeit any benefits to which he might otherwise be entitled.

(c) The employer and the employee shall each reserve the right to terminate such agreement upon seven days written notice to the other party.

No liability shall be incurred by the employer under the provisions of this section, except as provided for in Chapter 3 (commencing with Section 3600), of this part.

Ref.: W. Cal. Ev., "Discovery" §§230, 236; W. Cal. Sum., 2 "Workers' Compensation" §266.

§3209.8. Treatment by marriage and family therapists and clinical social workers.

Treatment reasonably required to cure or relieve from the effects of an injury shall include the services of marriage and family therapists and clinical social workers licensed by California state law and within the scope of their practice as defined by California state law if the injured person is referred to the marriage and family therapist or the clinical social worker by a licensed physician and surgeon, with the approval of the employer, for treatment of a condition arising out of the injury. Nothing in this section shall be construed to authorize marriage and family therapists or clinical social workers to determine disability for the purposes of Article 3 (commencing with Section 4650) of Chapter 2 of Part 2. The requirement of this section that the employer approve the referral by a licensed physician or surgeon shall not be construed to preclude reimbursement for self-procured treatment, found by the appeals board to be otherwise compensable pursuant to this division, where the employer has refused to authorize any treatment for the condition arising from the injury treated by the marriage and family therapist or clinical social worker. **Leg.H.** 1991 ch. 234, 2002 ch. 1013 (SB 2026).

Ref.: Herlick Handbook § 4.18; W. Cal. Sum., 2 "Workers' Compensation" §266.

§3209.9. Acupuncturists not physicians or surgeons.

The inclusion of acupuncturists in Section 3209.3 does not imply any right or entitle any acupuncturist to represent, advertise, or hold himself or herself out as a physician or surgeon holding an M.D. or D.O. degree. **Leg.H.** 1997 ch. 98.

Ref.: Herlick Handbook § 4.18; W. Cal. Ev., "Discovery" §§230, 236.

§3209.10. Physician assistant or nurse practitioner may provide treatment for work-related injury under supervision; supervising physician deemed treating physician.

(a) Medical treatment of a work-related injury required to cure or relieve the effects of the injury may be provided by a state licensed physician assistant or nurse practitioner, acting under the review or supervision of a physician and surgeon pursuant to standardized procedures or protocols within their lawfully authorized scope of practice. The reviewing or supervising physician and surgeon of the physician assistant or nurse practitioner shall be deemed to be the treating physician. For the purposes of this section, "medical treatment" includes the authority of the nurse practitioner or physician assistant to authorize the patient to receive time off from work for a period not to exceed three calendar days if that authority is included in a standardized procedure or protocol approved by the supervising physician. The nurse practitioner or physician assistant may cosign the Doctor's First Report of Occupational Injury or Illness. The treating physician shall make any determination of temporary disability and shall sign the report.

(b) The provision of subdivision (a) that requires the cosignature of the treating physician applies to this section only and it is not the intent of the Legislature that the requirement apply to any other section of law or to any other statute or regulation. Nothing in this section implies that a nurse practitioner or physician assistant is a physician as defined in Section 3209.3. **Leg.H.** 2001 ch. 229, 2004 ch. 100 (AB 2919).

2001 Notes: The addition of Section 3209.10 to the Labor Code made by this act does not constitute a change in, but is declaratory of, existing law and neither expands nor limits the scope of practice of nurse practitioners or physician assistants with regard to the delivery of care pursuant to Division 4 of the Labor Code. Stats. 2001 ch. 229 §2.

In enacting this act, the Legislature intends to abrogate the opinions expressed by the Administrative Director or the Division of Workers' Compensation as set forth in *Minnie Martin* v. *Los Angeles Unified School District,* AD No. 9786-4895, July 6, 1999, to the extent that it precluded a physician assistant from practicing within the scope of the protocol approved by the supervising physician and their lawful scope of practice. Stats. 2001 ch. 229 §3.

Ref.: Hanna § 5.02[2][a]; Herlick Handbook §§ 4.18, 4.19; W. Cal. Ev., "Discovery" §§230, 236; W. Cal. Sum., 2 "Workers' Compensation" §261.

§3210. "Persons."

"Persons" includes an individual, firm, voluntary association, or a public, or quasi public, or private corporation.

Ref.: W. Cal. Ev., "Discovery" §§230, 236.

§3211. "Insurer."

"Insurer" includes the State Compensation Insurance Fund and any private company, corporation, mutual association, reciprocal or interinsurance exchange authorized under the laws of this State to insure employers against liability for compensation and any employer to whom a certificate of consent to self-insure has been issued.

Ref.: W. Cal. Ev., "Discovery" §§230, 236; W. Cal. Sum., 2 "Workers' Compensation" §105.

§3211.5. "Firefighter," "firefighting member," or "member of a fire department."

For purposes of this division, whenever the term "firefighter," "firefighting member," and "member of a fire department" is used, the term shall include, but shall not be limited to, unless the context expressly provides otherwise, a person engaged in providing firefighting services who is an apprentice, volunteer, or employee on a partly paid or fully paid basis. **Leg.H.** 2002 ch. 870 (AB 1847).

Ref.: Herlick Handbook § 2.5; W. Cal. Ev., "Discovery" §§230, 236; W. Cal. Sum., 2 "Workers' Compensation" §239.

§3211.9. "Disaster council."

"Disaster council" means a public agency established by ordinance which is empowered to register and direct the activities of disaster service workers within the area of the county, city, city and county, or any part thereof, and is thus, because of such registration and direction, acting as an instrumentality of the state in aid of the carrying out of the general governmental functions and policy of the state.

Ref.: W. Cal. Ev., "Discovery" §§230, 236.

§3211.91. "Accredited disaster council."

"Accredited disaster council" means a disaster council that is certified by the Office of Emergency Services as conforming with the rules and regulations established by the office pursuant to Article 10 (commencing with Section 8610) of Chapter 7 of Division 1 of Title 2 of the Government Code. A disaster council remains accredited only while the certification of the Office of Emergency Services is in effect and is not revoked. **Leg.H.** 1971 ch. 438 §139, 2006 ch. 502 (AB 1889) §9.

Ref.: W. Cal. Ev., "Discovery" §§230, 236.

§3211.92. "Disaster service worker."

(a) "Disaster service worker" means any natural person who is registered with an accredited disaster council or a state agency for the purpose of engaging in disaster service pursuant to the California Emergency Services Act without pay or other consideration.

(b) "Disaster service worker" includes public employees performing disaster work that is outside the course and scope of their regular employment without pay and also includes any unregistered person impressed into service during a state of war emergency, a state of emergency, or a local emergency by a person having authority to command the aid of citizens in the execution of his or her duties.

(c) Persons registered with a disaster council at the time that council becomes accredited need not reregister in order to be entitled to the benefits provided by Chapter 10 (commencing with Section 4351).

(d) "Disaster service worker" does not include any member registered as an active firefighting member of any regularly organized volunteer fire department, having official recognition, and full or partial support of the county, city, or district in which the fire department is located. **Leg.H.** 2000 ch. 506.

Ref.: Hanna §§ 3.117[1], 21.07[4]; W. Cal. Ev., "Discovery" §§230, 236.

§3211.93. "Disaster service."

"Disaster service" means all activities authorized by and carried on pursuant to the California Emergency Services Act, including training necessary or proper to engage in such activities.

Ref.: W. Cal. Ev., "Discovery" §§230, 236.

§3211.93a. Exception to "disaster service."

"Disaster service" does not include any activities or functions performed by a person if the accredited disaster council with which that person is registered receives a fee or other compensation for the performance of those activities or functions by that person. **Leg.H.** 2000 ch. 506.

Ref.: W. Cal. Ev., "Discovery" §§230, 236.

§3212. Hernia; heart trouble; pneumonia.

In the case of members of a sheriff's office or the California Highway Patrol, district attorney's staff of inspectors and investigators or of police or fire departments of cities, counties, cities and counties, districts or other public or municipal corporations or political subdivisions, whether those members are volunteer, partly paid, or fully paid, and in the case of active firefighting members of the Department of Forestry and Fire Protection whose duties require firefighting or of any county forestry or firefighting department or unit, whether voluntary, fully paid, or partly paid, and in the case of members of the warden service of the Wildlife Protection Branch of the Department of Fish and Game whose principal duties consist of active law enforcement service, excepting those whose principal duties are clerical or otherwise do not clearly fall within the scope of active law enforcement service such as stenographers, telephone operators, and other officeworkers, the term "injury" as used in this act includes hernia when any part of the hernia develops or manifests itself during a period while the member is in the service in the office, staff, division, department, or unit, and in the case of members of fire departments, except those whose principal duties are clerical, such as stenographers, telephone operators, and other officeworkers, and in the case of county forestry or firefighting departments, except those whose principal duties are clerical, such as stenographers, telephone operators, and other officeworkers, and in the case of active firefighting members of the Department of Forestry and Fire Protection whose duties require firefighting, and in the case of members of the warden service of the Wildlife Protection Branch of the Department of Fish and Game whose principal duties consist of active law enforcement service, excepting those whose principal duties are clerical or otherwise do not clearly fall within the scope of active law enforcement service such as stenographers, telephone operators, and other officeworkers, the term "injury" includes pneumonia and heart trouble that develops or manifests itself during a period while the member is in the service of the office, staff, department, or unit. In the case of regular salaried county or city and county peace officers, the term "injury" also includes any hernia that manifests itself or develops during a period while the officer is in the service. The compensation that is awarded for the hernia, heart trouble, or pneumonia shall include full hospital, surgical, medical treatment, disability indemnity, and death benefits, as provided by the workers' compensation laws of this state.

The hernia, heart trouble, or pneumonia so developing or manifesting itself in those cases shall be presumed to arise out of and in the course of the employment. This presumption is disputable and may be controverted by other evidence, but unless so controverted, the appeals board is bound to find in accordance with it. The presumption shall be extended to a member following termination of service for a period of three calendar months for each full year of the requisite service, but not to exceed 60 months in any circumstance, commencing with the last date actually worked in the specified capacity.

The hernia, heart trouble, or pneumonia so developing or manifesting itself in those cases shall in no case be attributed to any disease existing prior to that development or manifestation. **Leg.H.** 1992 ch. 427, 2001 ch. 833, 2002 ch. 664 (AB 3034).

Ref.: Hanna § 3.113[4]; Herlick Handbook §§ 5.3, 8.27; W. Cal. Ev., "Discovery" §§230, 236; W. Cal. Sum., 2 "Workers' Compensation" §§235, 239–242.

§3212.1. Cancer presumption; active firefighters and peace officers.

(a) This section applies to **all of the following:**

(1) Active firefighting members, whether volunteers, partly paid, or fully paid, of all of the following fire departments:

[1] **(A)** A fire department of a city, county, city and county, district, or other public or municipal corporation or political subdivision [2].

(B) A fire department of the University of California and the California State University [3].

(C) The Department of Forestry and Fire Protection [4].

(D) A county forestry or firefighting department or unit. [5]

(2) Active firefighting members of a fire department that serves a United States Department of Defense installation and who are certified by the Department of Defense as meeting its standards for firefighters.

(3) Peace officers, as defined in Section 830.1, subdivision (a) of Section 830.2, and subdivisions (a) and (b) of Section 830.37, of the Penal Code, who are primarily engaged in active law enforcement activities.

(4)(A) Fire and rescue services coordinators who work for the Office of Emergency Services.

(B) For purposes of this paragraph, "fire and rescue services coordinator" means a coordinator with any of the following job classifications: coordinator, senior coordinator, or chief coordinator.

(b) The term "injury," as used in this division, includes cancer, including leukemia, that develops or manifests itself during a period in which any member described in subdivision (a) is in the service of the department or unit, if the member demonstrates that he or she was exposed, while in the service of the department or unit, to a known carcinogen as defined by the International Agency for Research on Cancer, or as defined by the director.

(c) The compensation that is awarded for cancer shall include full hospital, surgical, medical treatment, disability indemnity, and death benefits, as provided by this division.

(d) The cancer so developing or manifesting itself in these cases shall be presumed to arise out of and in the course of the employment. This presumption is disputable and may be controverted by evidence that the primary site of the cancer has been established and that the carcinogen to which the member has demonstrated exposure is not reasonably linked to the disabling cancer. Unless so controverted, the appeals board is bound to find in accordance with the presumption. This presumption shall be extended to a member following termination of service for a period of three calendar months for each full year of the requisite service, but not to exceed 60 months in any circumstance, commencing with the last date actually worked in the specified capacity.

(e) The amendments to this section enacted during the 1999 portion of the 1999–2000 Regular Session shall be applied to claims for benefits filed or pending on or after January 1, 1997, including, but not limited to, claims for benefits filed on or after that date that have previously been denied, or that are being appealed following denial. **Leg.H.** 1999 ch. 595, 2000 ch. 887, 2008 ch. 747 (SB 1271) §1.

§3212.1. 2008 Deletes. [1] (1) **[2]** , (2) **[3]** , (3) **[4]** , and (4) **[5]** This section also applies to

Ref.: Hanna § 3.113[4][b]; Herlick Handbook § 8.28; W. Cal. Ev., "Discovery" §§230, 236; W. Cal. Sum., 2 "Workers' Compensation" §§239, 240.

§3212.2. Employees of Department of Corrections, Department of Youth Authority, Atascadero State Hospital—Heart trouble.

In the case of officers and employees in the Department of Corrections having custodial duties, each officer and employee in the Department of Youth Authority having group supervisory duties, and each security officer employed at the Atascadero State Hospital, the term "injury" includes heart trouble which develops or manifests itself during a period while such officer or employee is in the service of such department or hospital.

The compensation which is awarded for such heart trouble shall include full hospital, surgical, medical treatment, disability indemnity, and death benefits, as provided by the workers' compensation laws of this state.

Such heart trouble so developing or manifesting itself in such cases shall be presumed to arise out of and in the course of the employment. This presumption is disputable and may be controverted by other evidence, but unless so controverted, the appeals board is bound to find in accordance with it. This presumption shall be extended to a member following termination of service for a period of three calendar months for each full year of the requisite service, but not to exceed 60 months in any circumstance, commencing with the last date actually worked in the specified capacity.

Ref.: Herlick Handbook § 8.27; W. Cal. Ev., "Discovery" §§230, 236; W. Cal. Sum., 2 "Workers' Compensation" §239.

§3212.3. California Highway Patrol—Heart trouble; pneumonia.

In the case of a peace officer who is designated under subdivision (a) of Section 2250.1 of the Vehicle Code and who has graduated from an academy certified by the Commission on Peace Officer Standards and Training, when that officer is employed upon a regular, full-time salary, the term "injury," as used in this division, includes heart trouble and pneumonia which develops or manifests itself during a period while that officer is in the service of the Department of the California Highway Patrol. The compensation which is awarded for the heart trouble or pneumonia shall include full hospital, surgical, medical treatment, disability indemnity, and death benefits as provided by this division.

The heart trouble or pneumonia so developing or manifesting itself shall be presumed to arise out of and in the course of the employment. However, a peace officer of the Department of the California Highway Patrol, as designated under subdivision (a) of Section 2250.1 of the Vehicle Code, shall have served five years or more in that capacity or as a peace officer with the former California State Police Division, or in both capacities, before the presumption shall arise as to the compensability of heart trouble so developing or manifesting itself. This presumption is disputable and may be controverted by other evidence, but unless so controverted, the appeals board is bound to find in accordance with it. This presumption shall be extended to a member following termination of service for a period of three calendar months for each full year of the requisite service, but not to exceed 60 months in any circumstance, commencing with the last date actually worked in the specified capacity.

The heart trouble or pneumonia so developing or manifesting itself in these cases shall in no case be attributed to any disease existing prior to that development or manifestation.

The term "peace officers" as used herein shall be limited to those employees of the Department of the California Highway Patrol who are designated as peace officers under subdivision (a) of Section 2250.1 of the Vehicle Code. **Leg.H.** 1995 Gov. Reorg. Plan 1, effective May 12, 1995, 1996 ch. 305 (codification of the 1995 Gov. Reorg. Plan).

Ref.: W. Cal. Ev., "Discovery" §§230, 236; W. Cal. Sum., 2 "Workers' Compensation" §§239, 240.

§3212.4. University of California fire department—Heart trouble; hernia; pneumonia.

In the case of a member of a University of California fire department located at a campus or other facility administered by the Regents of University of California, when any such member is employed by such a department upon a regular, full-time salary, on a nonprobationary basis, the term "injury" as used in this division includes heart trouble, hernia, or pneumonia which develops or manifests itself during a period while such member is in the service of such a University of California fire department. The compensation which is awarded for such heart trouble, hernia, or pneumonia shall include full hospital, surgical, medical treatment disability indemnity, and death benefits as provided by the provisions of this division.

Such heart trouble, hernia, or pneumonia so developing or manifesting itself shall be presumed to arise out of and in the course of the employment. This presumption is disputable and may be controverted by other evidence, but unless so controverted, the appeals board is bound to find in accordance with it. This presumption shall be extended to a member following termination of service for a period of three calendar months for each full year of the requisite service, but not to exceed 60 months in any circumstance, commencing with the last date actually worked in the specified capacity.

Such heart trouble, hernia, or pneumonia so developing or manifesting itself in such cases shall in no case be attributed to any disease existing prior to such development or manifestation.

The term "member" as used herein shall exclude those employees of a University of California fire department whose principal duties are those of a telephone operator, clerk, stenographer, machinist, mechanic, or otherwise, and whose functions do not clearly fall within the scope of active firefighting and prevention service.

Ref.: W. Cal. Ev., "Discovery" §§230, 236; W. Cal. Sum., 2 "Workers' Compensation" §239.

§3212.5. Peace officers—Heart trouble; pneumonia.

In the case of a member of a police department of a city or municipality, or a member of the State Highway Patrol, when any such member is employed upon a regular, full-time salary, and in the case of a sheriff or deputy sheriff, or an inspector or investigator in a district attorney's office of any county, employed upon a regular, full-time salary, the term "injury" as used in this division includes heart trouble and pneumonia which develops or manifests itself during a period while such member, sheriff, or deputy sheriff, inspector or investigator is in the service of the police department, the State Highway Patrol, the sheriff's office or the district attorney's office, as the case may be. The compensation which is awarded for such heart trouble or pneumonia shall include full hospital, surgical, medical treatment, disability indemnity, and death benefits as provided by the provisions of this division.

Such heart trouble or pneumonia so developing or manifesting itself shall be presumed to arise out of and in the course of the employment; provided, however, that the member of the police department, State Highway Patrol, the sheriff or deputy sheriff, or an inspector or investigator in a district attorney's office of any county shall have served five years or more in such capacity before the presumption shall arise as to the compensability of heart trouble so developing or manifesting itself. This presumption is disputable and may be controverted by other evidence, but unless so controverted, the appeals board is bound to find in accordance with it. This presumption shall be extended to a member following termination of service for a period of three calendar months for each full year of the requisite service, but not to exceed 60 months in any circumstance, commencing with the last date actually worked in the specified capacity.

Such heart trouble or pneumonia so developing or manifesting itself in such cases shall in no case be attributed to any disease existing prior to such development or manifestation.

The term "members" as used herein shall be limited to those employees of police departments, the California Highway Patrol and sheriffs' departments and inspectors and investigators of a district attorney's office who are defined as peace officers in Section 830.1, 830.2, or 830.3 of the Penal Code.

Ref.: Hanna § 10.40[3][c], 33.02[4][d][i]; W. Cal. Ev., "Discovery" §§230, 236; "Burden" §110; W. Cal. Sum., 2 "Workers' Compensation" §§3, 239, 240–242, 368.

§3212.6. Peace officers, prison guards, correctional officers, and firefighters—Tuberculosis; tuberculosis test for firefighter applicants.

In the case of a member of a police department of a city or county, or a member of the sheriff's office of a county, or a member of the California Highway Patrol, or an inspector or investigator in a district attorney's office of any county whose principal duties consist of active law enforcement service, or a prison or jail guard or correctional officer who is employed by a public agency, when that person is employed upon a regular, full-time salary, or in the case of members of fire departments of any city, county, or district, or other public or municipal corporations or political subdivisions, when those members are employed on a regular fully paid basis, and in the case of active firefighting members of the Department of Forestry and Fire Protection whose duties require firefighting and first-aid response services, or of any county forestry or firefighting department or unit, where those members are employed on a regular fully paid basis, excepting those whose principal duties are clerical or otherwise do not clearly fall within the scope of active law enforcement, firefighting, or emergency first-aid response service such as stenographers, telephone operators, and other officeworkers, the term "injury" includes tuberculosis that develops or manifests itself during a period while that member is in the service of that department or office. The compensation that is awarded for the tuberculosis shall include full hospital, surgical, medical treatment, disability indemnity, and death benefits as provided by the provisions of this division.

The tuberculosis so developing or manifesting itself shall be presumed to arise out of and in the course of the employment. This presumption is disputable and may be controverted by other evidence, but unless so controverted, the appeals board is bound to find in accordance with it. This presumption shall be extended to a member following termination of service for a period of three calendar months for each full year of the requisite service, but not to exceed 60 months in any circumstance, commencing with the last date actually worked in the specified capacity.

A public entity may require applicants for employment in firefighting positions who would be entitled to the benefits granted by this section to be tested for infection for tuberculosis. **Leg.H.** 1995 ch. 683, 1996 ch. 802, 2001 ch. 833.

Ref.: Herlick Handbook § 8.27; W. Cal. Ev., "Discovery" §§230, 236; W. Cal. Sum., 2 "Workers' Compensation" §239.

§3212.7. Department of Justice—Heart trouble; hernia; pneumonia; tuberculosis.

In the case of an employee in the Department of Justice falling within the "state safety" class, when any such individual is employed under civil service upon a regular, full-time salary, the term "injury", as used in this division, includes heart trouble or hernia or pneumonia or tuberculosis which develops or manifests itself during the period while such individual is in the service of the Department of Justice. The compensation which is awarded for any such injury shall include full hospital, surgical, medical treatment, disability indemnity, and death benefits as provided by the provisions of this division.

Such heart trouble, hernia, pneumonia, or tuberculosis so developing or manifesting itself shall be presumed to arise out of and in the course of the employment. This presumption is disputable and may be controverted by other evidence but unless so controverted, the appeals board is bound to find in accordance with it. This presumption shall be extended to a member following termination of service for a period of three calendar months for each full year of the requisite service, but not to exceed 60 months in any circumstance, commencing with the last date actually worked in the specified capacity.

Such heart trouble, hernia, peneumonia, or tuberculosis developing or manifesting itself in such cases shall in no case be attributed to any disease existing prior to such development or manifestation.

Ref.: Herlick Handbook §§ 5.3, 8.27; W. Cal. Ev., "Discovery" §§230, 236; W. Cal. Sum., 2 "Workers' Compensation" §239.

§3212.8. "Injury" includes blood-borne infectious disease or methicillin-resistant Staphylococcus aureus skin infection.

(a) In the case of members of a sheriff's office, of police or fire departments of cities, counties, cities and counties, districts, or other public or municipal corporations or political subdivisions, or individuals described in Chapter 4.5 (commencing with Section 830) of Title 3 of Part 2 of the Penal Code, whether those persons are volunteer, partly paid, or fully paid, and in the case of active firefighting members of the Department of Forestry and Fire Protection, or of any county forestry or firefighting department or unit, whether voluntary, fully paid, or partly paid, excepting those whose principal duties are clerical or otherwise do not clearly fall within the scope of active law enforcement service or active firefighting services, such as stenographers, telephone operators, and other office workers, the term "injury" as used in this division, includes a blood-borne infectious disease **or methicillin-resistant Staphylococcus aureus skin infection** when any part of the blood-borne infectious disease **or methicillin-resistant Staphylococcus aureus skin infection** develops or manifests itself during a period while that person is in the service of that office, staff, division, department, or unit. The compensation that is awarded for a blood-borne infectious disease **or methicillin-resistant Staphylococcus aureus skin infection** shall include, but not be limited to, full hospital, surgical, medical treatment, disability indemnity, and death benefits, as provided by the workers' compensation laws of this state.

(b)**(1)** The blood-borne infectious disease **or methicillin-resistant Staphylococcus aureus skin infection** so developing or manifesting itself in those cases shall be presumed to arise out of and in the course of the employment or service. This presumption is disputable and may be controverted by other evidence, but unless so controverted, the appeals board is bound to find in accordance with it.

[1] **(2) The blood-borne infectious disease** presumption shall be extended to a person covered by subdivision (a) following termination of service for a period of three calendar months for each full year of service, but not to exceed 60 months in any circumstance, commencing with the last date actually worked in the specified capacity.

(3) Notwithstanding paragraph (2), the methicillin-resistant Staphylococcus aureus skin infection presumption shall be extended to a person covered by subdivision (a) following termination of service for a period of 90 days, commencing with the last day actually worked in the specified capacity.

(c) The blood-borne infectious disease **or methicillin-resistant Staphylococcus aureus skin infection** so developing or manifesting itself in those cases shall in no case be attributed to any disease **or skin infection** existing prior to that development or manifestation.

(d) For the purposes of this section, "blood-borne infectious disease" means a disease caused by exposure to pathogenic microorganisms that are present in human blood that can cause disease in humans, including those pathogenic microorganisms defined as blood-borne pathogens by the Department of Industrial Relations. **Leg.H.** 2000 ch. 490, 2001 ch. 833, 2008 ch. 684 (AB 2754) §2.

§3212.8. 2008 Deletes. [1] That

Ref.: Herlick Handbook § 8.27; W. Cal. Sum., 2 "Workers' Compensation" §239.

§3212.85. "Injury" includes death or illness from exposure to biochemical substances.

(a) This section applies to peace officers described in Sections 830.1 to 830.5, inclusive, of the Penal Code, and members of a fire department.

(b) The term "injury," as used in this division, includes illness or resulting death due to exposure to a biochemical substance that develops or occurs during a period in which any member described in subdivision (a) is in the service of the department or unit.

(c) The compensation that is awarded for injury pursuant to this section shall include full hospital, surgical, medical treatment, disability indemnity, and death benefits, as provided by this division.

(d) The injury that develops or manifests itself in these cases shall be presumed to arise out of, and in the course of, the employment. This presumption is disputable and may be controverted by other evidence. Unless controverted, the appeals board is bound to find in accordance with the presumption. This presumption shall be extended to a member following termination of service for a period of three calendar months for each full year of the requisite service, but not to exceed 60 months in any circumstance, commencing with the last date actually worked in the specified capacity.

(e) For purposes of this section, the following definitions apply:

(1) "Biochemical substance" means any biological or chemical agent that may be used as a weapon of mass destruction, including, but not limited to, any chemical warfare agent, weaponized biological agent, or nuclear or radiological agent, as these terms are defined in Section 11417 of the Penal Code.

(2) "Members of a fire department" includes, but is not limited to, an apprentice, volunteer, partly paid, or fully paid member of any of the following:

(A) A fire department of a city, county, city and county, district, or other public or municipal corporation or political subdivision.

(B) A fire department of the University of California and the California State University.

(C) The Department of Forestry and Fire Protection.

(D) A county forestry or firefighting department or unit. **Leg.H.** 2002 ch. 870 (AB 1847).

Ref.: Herlick Handbook § 8.27; W. Cal. Ev., "Discovery" §§230, 236; W. Cal. Sum., 2 "Workers' Compensation" §239.

§3212.9. Peace officers, probation officers, district attorney investigators, and firefighters—Meningitis.

In the case of a member of a police department of a city, county, or city and county, or a member of the sheriff's office of a county, or a member of the California Highway Patrol, or a county probation officer, or an inspector or investigator in a district attorney's office of any county whose principal duties consist of active law enforcement service, when that person is employed on a regular, full-time salary, or in the case of a member of a fire department of any city, county, or district, or other public or municipal corporation or political subdivision, or any county forestry or firefighting department or unit, when those members are employed on a regular full-time salary, excepting those whose principal duties are clerical or otherwise do not clearly fall within the scope of active law enforcement or firefighting, such as stenographers, telephone operators, and other officeworkers, the term "injury" includes meningitis that develops or manifests itself during a period while that person is in the service of that department, office, or unit. The compensation that is awarded for the meningitis shall include full hospital, surgical, medical treatment, disability indemnity, and death benefits as provided by the provisions of this division.

The meningitis so developing or manifesting itself shall be presumed to arise out of and in the course of the employment. This presumption is disputable and may be controverted by other evidence, but unless so controverted, the appeals board is bound to find in accordance with it. This presumption shall be extended to a person following termination of service for a period of three calendar months for each full year of the requisite service, but not to exceed 60 months in any circumstance, commencing with the last date actually worked in the specified capacity. **Leg.H.** 2000 ch. 883, 2001 ch. 833.

Ref.: W. Cal. Ev., "Discovery" §§230, 236; W. Cal. Sum., 2 "Workers' Compensation" §239.

§3212.10. Heart trouble, pneumonia, tuberculosis, and meningitis as compensable for certain peace officers.

In the case of a peace officer of the Department of Corrections who has custodial or supervisory duties of inmates or parolees, or a peace officer of the Department of the Youth Authority who has custodial or supervisory duties of wards or parolees, or a peace officer as defined in Section 830.5 of the Penal Code and employed by a local agency, the term "injury" as used in this division includes heart trouble, pneumonia, tuberculosis, and meningitis that develops or manifests itself during a period in which any peace officer covered under this section is in the service of the department or unit. The compensation that is awarded for that injury shall include full hospital, surgical, medical treatment, disability indemnity, and death benefits as provided by the provisions of this division.

The heart trouble, pneumonia, tuberculosis, and meningitis so developing or manifesting itself shall be presumed to arise out of and in the course of employment. This presumption is disputable and may be controverted by other evidence, but unless so controverted, the appeals board is bound to find in accordance with it. This presumption shall be extended to a member following termination of service for a period of three calendar months for each full year of requisite service, but not to exceed 60 months in any circumstance, commencing with the last date actually worked in the specified capacity. **Leg.H.** 2001 ch. 835, 2002 ch. 664 (AB 3034).

Ref.: Herlick Handbook §§ 3.113[4][m], 8.27; W. Cal. Ev., "Discovery" §§230, 236; W. Cal. Sum., 2 "Workers' Compensation" §239.

§3212.11. Skin cancer as "injury" for lifeguards arising out of and in course of employment.

This section applies to both of the following: (a) active lifeguards employed by a city, county, city and county, district, or other public or municipal corporation or political subdivision, and (b) active state lifeguards employed by the Department of Parks and Recreation. The term "injury," as used in this division, includes skin cancer that develops or manifests itself during the period of the lifeguard's employment. The compensation awarded for that injury shall include full hospital, surgical, and medical treatment, disability indemnity, and death benefits, as provided by the provisions of this division.

Skin cancer so developing or manifesting itself shall be presumed to arise out of and in the course of the employment. This presumption is disputable and may be controverted by other evidence, but unless so controverted, the appeals board shall find in accordance with it. This presumption shall be extended to a lifeguard following termination of service for a period of three calendar months for each full year of the requisite service, but not to exceed 60 months in any circumstance, commencing with the last date actually worked in the specified capacity.

Skin cancer so developing or manifesting itself in these cases shall not be attributed to any disease existing prior to that development or manifestation.

This section shall only apply to lifeguards employed for more than three consecutive months in a calendar year. **Leg.H.** 2001 ch. 846.

Ref.: Herlick Handbook §§ 3.113[4][n], 8.27; W. Cal. Ev., "Discovery" §§230, 236; W. Cal. Sum., 2 "Workers' Compensation" §§236, 239.

§3212.12. Lyme disease as injury for specified peace officers and corpsmembers.

(a) This section applies to peace officers, as defined in subdivision (b) of Section 830.1 of the Penal Code, subdivisions (e), (f), and (g) of Section 830.2 of the Penal Code, and corpsmembers, as defined by Section 14302 of the Public Resources Code, and other employees at the California Conservation Corps classified as any of the following:

Title	Class
Backcounty Trails Camp Supervisor,	

Title	Class
California Conservation Corps	1030
Conservationist I, California Conservation Corps	1029
Conservationist II, California Conservation Corps	1003
Conservationist II, Nursery California Conservation Corps	7370

(b) The term "injury," as used in this division, includes Lyme disease that develops or manifests itself during a period in which any person described in subdivision (a) is in the service of the department.

(c) The compensation that is awarded for Lyme disease shall include full hospital, surgical, medical treatment, disability indemnity, and death benefits, as provided by this division.

(d) Lyme disease so developing or manifesting itself in these cases shall be presumed to arise out of and in the course of the employment. This presumption is disputable and may be controverted by evidence that the Lyme disease is not reasonably linked to the work performance. Unless so controverted, the appeals board shall find in accordance with the presumption. This presumption shall be extended to a person described in subdivision (a) following termination of service for a period of three calendar months for each full year of the requisite service, but not to exceed 60 months in any circumstance, commencing with the last date actually worked in the specified capacity. **Leg.H.** 2002 ch. 876 (AB 2125).

Ref.: Hanna § 3.113[4][o]; Herlick Handbook § 8.27; W. Cal. Ev., "Discovery" §§230, 236; W. Cal. Sum., 2 "Workers' Compensation" §239.

§3213. University of California police—Heart trouble; pneumonia.

In the case of a member of the University of California Police Department who has graduated from an academy certified by the Commission on Peace Officer Standards and Training, when he and all members of the campus department of which he is a member have graduated from such an academy, and when any such member is employed upon a regular, full-time salary, the term "injury" as used in this division includes heart trouble and pneumonia which develops or manifests itself during a period while such member is in the service of such campus department of the University of California Police Department. The compensation which is awarded for such heart trouble or pneumonia shall include full hospital, surgical, medical treatment, disability indemnity, and death benefits as provided by the provisions of this division.

Such heart trouble or pneumonia so developing or manifesting itself shall be presumed to arise out of and in the course of the employment; provided, however, that the member of the University of California Police Department shall have served five years or more in such capacity before the presumption shall arise as to the compensability of heart trouble so developing or manifesting itself. This presumption is disputable and may be controverted by other evidence, but unless so controverted, the appeals board is bound to find in accordance with it. This presumption shall be extended to a member following termination of service for a period of three calendar months for each full year of the requisite service, but not to exceed 60 months in any circumstance, commencing with the last date actually worked in the specified capacity.

Such heart trouble or pneumonia so developing or manifesting itself in such cases shall in no case be attributed to any disease existing prior to such development or manifestation.

As used in this section:

(a) "Members" shall be limited to those employees of the University of California Police Department who are defined as peace officers in Section 830.2 of the Penal Code.

(b) "Campus" shall include any campus or other installation maintained under the jurisdiction of the Regents of the University of California.

(c) "Campus department" means all members of the University of California Police Department who are assigned and serve on a particular campus.

Ref.: Herlick Handbook § 8.27; W. Cal. Ev., "Discovery" §§230, 236; W. Cal. Sum., 2 "Workers' Compensation" §§239, 241.

§3213.2. "Injury" includes lower back impairment for certain law enforcement officers; "duty belt" defined.

(a) In the case of a member of a police department of a city, county, or city and county, or a member of the sheriff's office of a county, or a peace officer employed by the Department of the California Highway Patrol, or a peace officer employed by the University of California, who has been employed for at least five years as a peace officer on a regular, full-time salary and has been required to wear a duty belt as a condition of employment, the term "injury," as used in this division, includes lower back impairments. The compensation that is awarded for lower back impairments shall include full hospital, surgical, medical treatment, disability indemnity, and death benefits as provided by the provisions of this division.

(b) The lower back impairment so developing or manifesting itself in the peace officer shall be presumed to arise out of and in the course of the employment. This presumption is disputable and may be controverted by other evidence, but unless so controverted, the appeals board is bound to find in accordance with it. This presumption shall be extended to a person following termination of service for a period of three calendar months for each full year of the requisite service, but not to exceed 60 months in any circumstance, commencing with the last date actually worked in the specified capacity.

(c) For purposes of this section, "duty belt" means a belt used for the purpose of holding a gun, handcuffs, baton, and other items related to law enforcement. **Leg.H.** 2001 ch. 834.

Ref.: Hanna §3.113[4][*l*]; Herlick Handbook § 8.27; W. Cal. Ev., "Discovery" §§230, 236; W. Cal. Sum., 2 "Workers' Compensation" §239.

§3214. Early intervention program.

(a) The Department of Corrections and the Department of the Youth Authority shall, in conjunction with all recognized employee representative associations, develop policy and implement the workers' compensation early intervention program by December 31, 1989, for all department employees who sustain an injury. The program shall include, but not be limited to, counseling by an authorized independent early intervention counselor and the services of an agreed medical panel to assist in timely decisions regarding compensability. Costs of services through early intervention shall be borne by the departments.

(b) It is the intent of the Legislature to reduce all costs associated with the delivery of workers' compensation benefits, in balance with the need to ensure timely and adequate benefits to the injured worker. Toward this goal the workers' compensation early intervention program was established in the Department of Corrections and the Department of the Youth Authority. The fundamental concept of the program is to settle disputes rather than to litigate them. This is a worthwhile concept in terms of cost control for the employer and timely receipt of benefits for the worker. To ascertain the effectiveness of the program is crucial in helping guide policy in this arena. **Leg.H.** 1994 ch. 1034, effective September 29, 1994, 2001 ch. 745, effective October 12, 2001.

Ref.: Herlick Handbook § 2.5; W. Cal. Ev., "Discovery" §§230, 236.

§3215. Crime to offer or receive compensation for referring clients or patients.

Except as otherwise permitted by law, any person acting individually or through his or her employees or agents, who offers, delivers, receives, or accepts any rebate, refund, commission, preference, patronage, dividend, discount or other consideration, whether in the form of money or otherwise, as compensation or inducement for referring clients or patients to perform or obtain services or benefits pursuant to this division, is guilty of a crime. **Leg.H.** 1991 ch. 116.

Ref.: Hanna §§ 20.01[1][d], 22.14; Herlick Handbook § 9.18; W. Cal. Ev., "Discovery" §§230, 236; W. Cal. Sum., 2 "Workers' Compensation" §23.

§3217. Exceptions to prohibitions of §3215.

(a) Section 3215 shall not be construed to prevent the recommendation of professional employment where that recommendation is not prohibited by the Rules of Professional Conduct of the State Bar.

(b) Section 3215 shall not be construed to prohibit a public defender or assigned counsel from making known his or her availability as a criminal defense attorney to persons unable to afford legal counsel, whether or not those persons are in custody.

(c) Any person who commits an act that violates both Section 3215 and either Section 650 of the Business and Professions Code or Section 750 of the Insurance Code shall, upon conviction, have judgment and sentence imposed for only one violation for any act.

(d) Section 3215 shall not be construed to prohibit the payment or receipt of consideration or services that is lawful pursuant to Section 650 of the Business and Professions Code.

(e) Notwithstanding Sections 3215 and 3219, and Section 750 of the Insurance Code, nothing shall prevent an attorney at law or a law firm from providing any person or entity with legal advice, information, or legal services, including the providing of printed, copied, or written documents, either without charge or for an otherwise lawfully agreed upon attorney fee.

(f) Section 3215 shall not be construed to prohibit a workers' compensation insurer from offering, and an employer from accepting, a workers' compensation insurance policy with rates that reflect premium discounts based upon the employer securing coverage for occupational or nonoccupational illnesses or injuries from a health care service plan or disability insurer that is owned by, affiliated with, or has a contractual relationship with, the workers' compensation insurer. **Leg.H.** 1991 ch. 116, 1993 ch. 120, effective July 16, 1993, ch. 1242, 1995 ch. 886.

Ref.: Herlick Handbook §§ 3.2, 9.18; W. Cal. Ev., "Discovery" §§230, 236.

§3218. Penalties for violating §3215.

A violation of Section 3215 is a public offense punishable upon a first conviction by incarceration in the county jail for not more than one year, or by incarceration in the state prison, or by a fine not exceeding ten thousand dollars ($10,000), or by both incarceration and fine. A second or subsequent conviction is punishable by incarceration in state prison. **Leg.H.** 1991 ch. 116.

Ref.: Herlick Handbook § 9.18; W. Cal. Ev., "Discovery" §§230, 236.

§3219. Felony to offer compensation to claims adjuster; felony for adjuster to accept compensation; contract for services obtained through false statements is void; allocation of recoverable fees.

(a)(1) Except as otherwise permitted by law, any person acting individually or through his or her employees or agents, who offers or delivers any rebate, refund, commission, preference, patronage, dividend, discount, or other consideration to any adjuster of claims for compensation, as defined in Section 3207, as compensation, inducement, or reward for the referral or settlement of any claim, is guilty of a felony.

(2) Except as otherwise permitted by law, any adjuster of claims for compensation, as defined in Section 3207, who accepts or receives any rebate, refund, commission, preference, patronage, dividend, discount, or other consideration, as compensation, inducement, or reward for the referral or settlement of any claim, is guilty of a felony.

(b) Any contract for professional services secured by any medical clinic, laboratory, physician or other health care provider in this state in violation of Section 550 of the Penal Code, Section 1871.4 of the Insurance Code, Section 650 or 651 of the Business and Professions Code, or Section 3215 or subdivision (a) of Section 3219 of this code is void. In any action against any medical clinic, laboratory, physician, or other health care provider, or the owners or operators thereof, under Chapter 4 (commencing with Section 17000) or Chapter 5 (commencing with Section 17200) of Division 7 of the Business and Professions Code, any judgment shall include an order divesting the medical clinic, laboratory, physician, or other health care provider, and the owners and operators thereof, of any fees and other compensation received pursuant to any such void contract. Those fees and compensation shall be recoverable as additional civil penalties under Chapter 4 (commencing with Section 17000) or Chapter 5 (commencing with Section 17200) of Division 7 of the Business and Professions Code. The judgment may also include an order prohibiting the person from further participating in any manner in the entity in which that person directly or indirectly owned or operated for a time period that the court deems appropriate. For the purpose of this section, "operated" means participated in the management, direction, or control of the entity.

(c) Notwithstanding Section 17206 or any other provision of law, any fees recovered pursuant to subdivision (b) in an action involving professional services related to the provision of workers' compensation shall be allocated as follows: if the action is brought by the Attorney General, one-half of the penalty collected shall be paid to the State General Fund, and one-half of the penalty collected shall be paid to the Workers' Compensation Fraud Account in the Insurance Fund; if the action is brought by a district attorney, one-half of the penalty collected shall be paid to the treasurer of the county

Labor

in which the judgment was entered, and one-half of the penalty collected shall be paid to the Workers' Compensation Fraud Account in the Insurance Fund; if the action is brought by a city attorney or city prosecutor, one-half of the penalty collected shall be paid to the treasurer of the city in which the judgment was entered, and one-half of the penalty collected shall be paid to the Workers' Compensation Fraud Account in the Insurance Fund. Moneys deposited into the Workers' Compensation Fraud Account pursuant to this subdivision shall be used in the investigation and prosecution of workers' compensation fraud, as appropriated by the Legislature. **Leg.H.** 1993 ch. 120, effective July 16, 1993.

Ref.: Herlick Handbook § 9.18; W. Cal. Sum., 2 "Workers' Compensation" §23.

CHAPTER 2 EMPLOYERS, EMPLOYEES, AND DEPENDENTS

ARTICLE 1 Employers

§3300. "Employer."

As used in this division, "employer" means:

(a) The State and every State agency.

(b) Each county, city, district, and all public and quasi public corporations and public agencies therein.

(c) Every person including any public service corporation, which has any natural person in service.

(d) The legal representative of any deceased employer.

Ref.: 8 C.C.R. §§9770, 9811, 15430.1; Herlick Handbook § 2.1; W. Cal. Sum., 2 "Workers' Compensation" §§159, 162, 6 "Torts" §1236.

§3301. Specified sponsors not "employers."

As used in this division, "employer" excludes the following:

(a) Any person while acting solely as the sponsor of a bowling team.

(b) Any private, nonprofit organization while acting solely as the sponsor of a person who, as a condition of sentencing by a superior or municipal court, is performing services for the organization.

The exclusions of this section do not exclude any person or organization from the application of this division which is otherwise an employer for the purposes of this division.

Ref.: Herlick Handbook §§ 2.1, 2.2, 2.4, 8.7; W. Cal. Sum., 2 "Workers' Compensation" §159.

§3302. Payment of workers' compensation premiums by temporary employment agency, employment referral service, labor contractor, or similar entity.

(a)(1) When a licensed contractor enters an agreement with a temporary employment agency, employment referral service, labor contractor, or other similar entity for the entity to supply the contractor with an individual to perform acts or contracts for which the contractor's license is required under Chapter 9 (commencing with Section 7000) of Division 3 of the Business and Professions Code and the licensed contractor is responsible for supervising the employee's work, the temporary employment agency, employment referral service, labor contractor, or other similar entity shall pay workers' compensation premiums based on the contractor's experience modification rating.

(2) The temporary employment agency, employment referral service, labor contractor, or other similar entity described in paragraph (1) shall report to the insurer both of the following:

(A) Its payroll on a monthly basis in sufficient detail to allow the insurer to determine the number of workers provided and the wages paid to these workers during the period the workers were supplied to the licensed contractor.

(B) The licensed contractor's name, address, and experience modification factor as reported by the licensed contractor.

(C) The workers' compensation classifications associated with the payroll reported pursuant to subparagraph (A). Classifications shall be assigned in accordance with the rules set forth in the California Workers' Compensation Uniform Statistical Reporting Plan published by the Workers' Compensation Insurance Rating Bureau.

(b) The temporary employment agency, employment referral service, labor contractor, or other similar entity supplying the individual under the conditions specified in subdivision (a) shall be solely responsible for the individual's workers' compensation, as specified in subdivision (a).

(c) Nothing in this section is intended to change existing law in effect on December 31, 2002, as it relates to the sole remedy provisions of this division and the special employer provisions of Section 11663 of the Insurance Code.

(d) A licensed contractor that is using a temporary worker supplied pursuant to subdivision (a) shall notify the temporary employment agency, employment referral service, labor contractor, or other similar entity that supplied that temporary worker when either of the following occurs:

(1) The temporary worker is being used on a public works project.

(2) The contractor reassigns a temporary worker to a position other than the classification to which the worker was originally assigned.

(e) A temporary employment agency, employment referral service, labor contractor, or other similar entity may pass through to a licensed contractor any additional costs incurred as a result of this section. **Leg.H.** 2002 ch. 1098 (AB 2816).

Ref.: Hanna § 3.134; W. Cal. Sum., 2 "Workers' Compensation" §166.

ARTICLE 2
Employees

§3350. Division's definitions to govern construction.

Unless the context otherwise requires, the definitions set forth in this article shall govern the construction and meaning of the terms and phrases used in this division.

§3351. "Employee."

"Employee" means every person in the service of an employer under any appointment or contract of hire or apprenticeship, express or implied, oral or written, whether lawfully or unlawfully employed, and includes:

(a) Aliens and minors.

(b) All elected and appointed paid public officers.

(c) All officers and members of boards of directors of quasi-public or private corporations while rendering actual service for the corporations for pay; provided that, where the officers and directors of the private corporation are the sole shareholders thereof, the corporation and the officers and directors shall come under the compensation provisions of this division only by election as provided in subdivision (a) of Section 4151.

(d) Except as provided in subdivision (h) of Section 3352, any person employed by the owner or occupant of a residential dwelling whose duties are incidental to the ownership, maintenance, or use of the dwelling, including the care and supervision of children, or whose duties are personal and not in the course of the trade, business, profession, or occupation of the owner or occupant.

(e) All persons incarcerated in a state penal or correctional institution while engaged in assigned work or employment as defined in paragraph (1) of subdivision (a) of Section 10021 of Title 8 of the California Code of Regulations, or engaged in work performed under contract.

(f) All working members of a partnership or limited liability company receiving wages irrespective of profits from the partnership or limited liability company; provided that where the working members of the partnership or limited liability company are general partners or managers, the partnership or limited liability company and the partners or managers shall come under the compensation provisions of this division only by election as provided in subdivision (a) of Section 4151. If a private corporation is a general partner or manager, "working members of a partnership or limited liability company" shall include the corporation and the officers and directors of the corporation, provided that the officers and directors are the sole shareholders of the corporation. If a limited liability company is a partner or member, "working members of the partnership or limited liability company" shall include the managers of the limited liability company.

(g) For the purposes of subdivisions (c) and (f), the persons holding the power to revoke a trust as to shares of a private corporation or as to general partnership or limited liability company interests held in the trust, shall be deemed to be the shareholders of the private corporation, or the general partners of the partnership, or the managers of the limited liability company. **Leg.H.** 1994 ch. 497, 1996 ch. 57, effective June 6, 1996.

Ref.: 8 C.C.R. §§9811, 10133.4; Hanna §§ 2.50[4][f], 2.63[3][c], 2.82, 3.30, 3.34, 3.36[3]; Herlick Handbook §§ 2.3, 2.4, 8.21; CACI Nos. 2800, 2810 (Matthew Bender); W. Cal. Sum., 2 "Insurance" §64, 2 "Workers' Compensation" §§52, 66, 170, 172–174, 176, 181, 184, 187, 191.

§3351.5. Employees included.

"Employee" includes:

(a) Any person whose employment training is arranged by the State Department of Rehabilitation with any employer. Such person shall be deemed an employee of such employer for workers' compensation purposes; provided that, the department shall bear the full amount of any additional workers' compensation insurance premium expense incurred by the employer due to the provisions of this section.

(b) Any person defined in subdivision (d) of Section 3351 who performs domestic service comprising in-home supportive services under Article 7 (commencing with Section 12300), Chapter 3, Part 3, Division 9 of the Welfare and Institutions Code. For purposes of Section 3352, such person shall be deemed an employee of the recipient of such services for workers' compensation purposes if the state or county makes or provides for direct payment to such person or to the recipient of in-home supportive services for the purchase of services, subject to the provisions of Section 12302.2 of the Welfare and Institutions Code.

(c) Any person while engaged by contract for the creation of a specially ordered or commissioned work of authorship in which the parties expressly agree in a written instrument signed by them that the work shall be considered a work made for hire, as defined in Section 101 of Title 17 of the United States Code, and the ordering or commissioning party obtains ownership of all the rights comprised in the copyright in the work.

Ref.: 8 C.C.R. §9811; Herlick Handbook § 2.5; W. Cal. Sum., 2 "Workers' Compensation" §§172, 187, 188.

§3352. Employees excluded.

"Employee" excludes the following:

(a) Any person defined in subdivision (d) of Section 3351 who is employed by his or her parent, spouse, or child.

(b) Any person performing services in return for aid or sustenance only, received from any religious, charitable, or relief organization.

(c) Any person holding an appointment as deputy clerk or deputy sheriff appointed for his or her own convenience, and who receives no compensation from the county or municipal corporation or from the citizens thereof for his or her services as the deputy. This exclusion is operative only as to employment by the county or municipal corporation and does not deprive any person so deputized from recourse against a private person employing him or her for injury occurring in the course of and arising out of the employment.

(d) Any person performing voluntary services at or for a recreational camp, hut, or lodge operated by a nonprofit organization, exempt from federal income tax under Section 101(6) of the Internal Revenue Code, of which he or she or a member of his or her family is a member and who receives no compensation for those services other than meals, lodging, or transportation.

(e) Any person performing voluntary service as a ski patrolman who receives no compensation for those services other than meals or lodging or the use of ski tow or ski lift facilities.

(f) Any person employed by a ski lift operator to work at a snow ski area who is relieved of and not performing any prescribed duties, while participating in recreational activities on his or her own initiative.

(g) Any person, other than a regular employee, participating in sports or athletics who receives no compensation for the participation other than the use of athletic equipment, uniforms, transportation, travel, meals, lodgings, or other expenses incidental thereto.

(h) Any person defined in subdivision (d) of Section 3351 who was employed by the employer to be held liable for less than 52 hours during the 90 calendar days immediately preceding the date of the injury for injuries, as defined in Section 5411, or during the 90 calendar days immediately preceding the date of the last employment in an occupation exposing the employee to the hazards of the disease or injury for injuries, as defined in Section 5412, or who earned less than one hundred dollars ($100) in wages from the employer during the 90 calendar days immediately preceding the date of the injury for injuries, as defined in Section 5411, or during the 90 calendar days immediately preceding the date of the last employment in an occupation exposing the employee to the hazards of the disease or injury for injuries, as defined in Section 5412.

(i) Any person performing voluntary service for a public agency or a private, nonprofit organization who receives no remuneration for the services other than meals, transportation, lodging, or reimbursement for incidental expenses.

(j) Any person, other than a regular employee, performing officiating services relating to amateur sporting events sponsored by any public agency or private, nonprofit organization, who receives no remuneration for these services other than a stipend for each day of service no greater than the amount established by the Department of Personnel Administration as a per diem expense for employees or officers of the state. The stipend shall be presumed to cover incidental expenses involved in officiating, including, but not limited to, meals, transportation, lodging, rule books and courses, uniforms, and appropriate equipment.

(k) Any student participating as an athlete in amateur sporting events sponsored by any public agency, public or private nonprofit college, university or school, who receives no remuneration for the participation other than the use of athletic equipment, uniforms, transportation, travel, meals, lodgings, scholarships, grants-in-aid, or other expenses incidental thereto.

(*l*) Any law enforcement officer who is regularly employed by a local or state law enforcement agency in an adjoining state and who is deputized to work under the supervision of a California peace officer pursuant to paragraph (4) of subdivision (a) of Section 832.6 of the Penal Code.

(m) Any law enforcement officer who is regularly employed by the Oregon State Police, the Nevada Department of Motor Vehicles and Public Safety, or the Arizona Department of Public Safety and who is acting as a peace officer in this state pursuant to subdivision (a) of Section 830.32 of the Penal Code.

(n) Any person, other than a regular employee, performing services as a sports official for an entity sponsoring an intercollegiate or interscholastic sports event, or any person performing services as a sports official for a public agency, public entity, or a private nonprofit organization, which public agency, public entity, or private nonprofit organization sponsors an amateur sports event. For purposes of this subdivision, "sports official" includes an umpire, referee, judge, scorekeeper, timekeeper, or other person who is a neutral participant in a sports event.

(o) Any person who is an owner-builder, as defined in subdivision (a) of Section 50692 of the Health and Safety Code, who is participating in a mutual self-help housing program, as defined in Section 50087 of the Health and Safety Code, sponsored by a nonprofit corporation. **Leg.H.** 1995 ch. 725, 1996 chs. 320, 872 (ch. 320 prevails; ch. 872 not effective), 1998 ch. 931, effective September 28, 1998, 2004 ch. 83 (AB 2649).

Ref.: Hanna §§ 3.36[1], 3.36[2][a]–[b], 3.36[3], 3.40, 3.80, 21.04[1][a]; Herlick Handbook §§ 2.1, 2.4, 2.5; CACI No. 2800 (Matthew Bender); W. Cal. Sum., 2 "Workers' Compensation" §§170, 172, 183, 187, 190, 191, 5 "Torts" §238, 7 "Constitutional Law" §625.

§3352.94. Exclusions for disaster service workers as "employees."

"Employee" excludes a disaster service worker while performing services as a disaster service worker except as provided in Chapter 10 of this part. "Employee" excludes any unregistered person performing like services as a disaster service worker without pay or other consideration, except as provided by Section 3211.92 of this code.

Ref.: Herlick Handbook § 2.4.

§3353. "Independent contractor."

"Independent contractor" means any person who renders service for a specified recompense for a specified result, under the control of his principal as to the result of his work only and not as to the means by which such result is accomplished.

Ref.: Herlick Handbook §§ 2.7, 2.8; W. Cal. Sum., 2 "Workers' Compensation" §189, 3 "Agency and Employment" §21.

§3354. Employers of household workers.

Employers of employees defined by subdivision (d) of Section 3351 shall not be subject to the provisions of Sections 3710, 3710.1, 3710.2, 3711, 3712, and 3722, or any other penalty provided by law, for failure to secure the payment of compensation for such employees.

This section shall not apply to employers of employees specified in subdivision (b) of Section 3715, with respect to such employees.

Ref.: Hanna § 10.27; Herlick Handbook § 2.4.

§3355. "Course of trade, business, profession, or occupation."

As used in subdivision (d) of Section 3351, the term "course of trade, business, profession, or occupation" includes all services tending toward the preservation, maintenance, or operation of the business, business premises, or business property of the employer.

Ref.: Herlick Handbook § 2.5; W. Cal. Sum., 2 "Workers' Compensation" §187.

§3356. "Trade, business, profession, or occupation."

As used in subdivision (d) of Section 3351 and in Section 3355, the term "trade, business, profession, or occupation" includes any undertaking actually engaged in by the employer with some degree of regularity, irrespective of the trade name, articles of incorporation, or principal business of the employer.

Ref.: Herlick Handbook §§ 2.4, 2.5; W. Cal. Sum., 2 "Workers' Compensation" §187.

§3357. Presumption that one rendering service is employee.

Any person rendering service for another, other than as an independent contractor, or unless expressly excluded herein, is presumed to be an employee.

Ref.: Herlick Handbook §§ 2.3, 2.7, 2.8; CACI Nos. 2800, 2810 (Matthew Bender); W. Cal. Sum., 2 "Workers' Compensation" §§172, 173, 189.

§3358. Watchmen.

Watchmen for nonindustrial establishments, paid by subscription by several persons, are not employees under this division. In other cases where watchmen, paid by subscription by several persons, have at the time of the injury sustained by them taken out and maintained in force insurance upon themselves as self-employing persons, conferring benefits equal to those conferred by this division, the employer is not liable under this division.

Ref.: Herlick Handbook § 2.4; W. Cal. Sum., 2 "Workers' Compensation" §191.

§3360. Partners for particular piece of work.

Workers associating themselves under a partnership agreement, the principal purpose of which is the performance of the labor on a particular piece of work are employees of the person having such work executed. In respect to injuries which occur while such workers maintain in force insurance in an insurer, insuring to themselves and all persons employed by them benefits identical with those conferred by this division the person for whom such work is to be done is not liable as an employer under this division.

Ref.: Herlick Handbook § 2.4; W. Cal. Sum., 2 "Workers' Compensation" §184.

§3361. Volunteer firefighters.

Each member registered as an active firefighting member of any regularly organized volunteer fire department, having official recognition, and full or partial support of the government of the county, city, town, or district in which the volunteer fire department is located, is an employee of that county, city, town, or district for the purposes of this division, and is entitled to receive compensation from the county, city, town, or district in accordance with the provisions thereof.

Ref.: Herlick Handbook § 2.5; W. Cal. Sum., 2 "Workers' Compensation" §177.

§3361.5. Authorized volunteers of recreation and park districts.

Notwithstanding Section 3351, a volunteer, unsalaried person authorized by the governing board of a recreation and park district to perform volunteer services for the district shall, upon the adoption of a resolution of the governing board of the district so declaring, be deemed an employee of the district for the purposes of this division and shall be entitled to the workers' compensation benefits provided by this division for any injury sustained by him or her while engaged in the performance of any service under the direction and control of the governing board of the recreation and park district.

Ref.: W. Cal. Sum., 2 "Workers' Compensation" §179.

§3362. Active police officers.

Each male or female member registered as an active policeman or policewoman of any regularly organized police department having official recognition and full or partial support of the government of the county, city, town, or district in which such police department is located, shall, upon the adoption of a resolution by the governing body of the county, city, town or district so declaring, be deemed an employee of such county, city, town or district for the purpose of this division and shall be entitled to receive compensation from such county, city, town or district in accordance with the provisions thereof.

Ref.: Hanna § 33.02[3][a]; Herlick Handbook § 2.5; W. Cal. Sum., 2 "Workers' Compensation" §178.

§3362.5. Reserve and auxiliary peace officers.

Whenever any qualified person is deputized or appointed by the proper authority as a reserve or auxiliary sheriff or city police officer, a deputy sheriff, or a reserve police officer of a regional park district or a transit district, and is assigned specific police functions by that authority, the person is an employee of the county, city, city and county, town, or district for the purposes of this division while performing duties as a peace officer if the person is not performing services as a disaster service worker for purposes of Chapter 10 (commencing with Section 4351).

1989 Note: This section is applicable only to injuries occurring on or after January 1, 1990. Stats. 1989 ch. 893 §6.

Ref.: W. Cal. Sum., 2 "Workers' Compensation" §178.

§3363. Registered members of reserve fish and game warden program.

Each member registered with the Department of Fish and Game as an active member of the reserve fish and game warden program of the department is an employee of the department for the purposes of this division and is entitled to receive compensation from the department in accordance with the provisions thereof.

Ref.: Herlick Handbook § 2.5; W. Cal. Sum., 2 "Workers' Compensation" §179.

§3363.5. Public agency volunteers.

(a) Notwithstanding Sections 3351, 3352, and 3357, a person who performs voluntary service without pay for a public agency, as designated and authorized by the governing body of the agency or its designee, shall, upon adoption of a resolution by the governing body of the agency so declaring, be deemed to be an employee of the agency for purposes of this division while performing such service.

(b) For purposes of this section, "voluntary service without pay" shall include services performed by any person, who receives no remuneration other than meals, transportation, lodging, or reimbursement for incidental expenses.

Ref.: Herlick Handbook § 2.5; W. Cal. Sum., 2 "Workers' Compensation" §179.

§3363.6. Volunteers for private, nonprofit organizations.

(a) Notwithstanding Sections 3351, 3352, and 3357, a person who performs voluntary service without pay for a private, nonprofit organization, as designated and authorized by the board of directors of the organization, shall, when the board of directors of the organization, in its sole discretion, so declares in writing and prior to the injury, be deemed an employee of the organization for purposes of this division while performing such service.

(b) For purposes of this section, "voluntary service without pay" shall include the performance of service by a parent, without remuneration in cash, when rendered to a cooperative parent participation nursery school if such service is required as a condition of participation in the organization.

(c) For purposes of this section, "voluntary service without pay" shall include the performance of services by a person who receives no remuneration other than meals, transportation, lodging, or reimbursement for incidental expenses.

Ref.: Herlick Handbook § 2.5; W. Cal. Sum., 2 "Workers' Compensation" §§172, 191.

§3364. Sheriff's reserve volunteers.

Notwithstanding subdivision (c) of Section 3352, a volunteer, unsalaried member of a sheriff's reserve in any county who is not deemed an employee of the county under Section 3362.5, shall, upon the adoption of a resolution of the board of supervisors declaring that the member is deemed an employee of the county for the purposes of this division, be entitled to the workers' compensation benefits provided by this division for any injury sustained by him or her while engaged in the performance of any active law enforcement service under the direction and control of the sheriff. **Leg.H.** 1961 ch. 901 §1, 1989 ch. 892 §26, 2006 ch. 538 (SB 1852) §488.

1989 Note: This section is applicable only to injuries occurring on or after January 1, 1990. Stats. 1989 ch. 893 §6.

Ref.: Herlick Handbook §§ 2.4, 2.5; W. Cal. Sum., 2 "Workers' Compensation" §178.

§3364.5. Volunteers for school districts and county superintendents of schools.

Notwithstanding Section 3351 of the Labor Code, a volunteer, unsalaried person authorized by the governing board of a school district or the county superintendent of schools to perform volunteer services for the school district or the county superintendent shall, upon the adoption of a resolution of the governing board of the school district or the county board of education so declaring, be deemed an employee of the district or the county superintendent for the purposes of this division and shall be entitled to the workers' compensation benefits provided by this division for any injury sustained by him while engaged in the performance of any service under the direction and control of the governing board of the school district or the county superintendent.

Ref.: Herlick Handbook § 2.5; W. Cal. Sum., 2 "Workers' Compensation" §179.

§3364.55. Juvenile court wards doing rehabilitative work.

A ward of the juvenile court engaged in rehabilitative work without pay, under an assignment by order of the juvenile court to a work project on public property within the jurisdiction of any governmental entity, including the federal government, shall, upon the adoption of a resolution of the board of supervisors declaring that such ward is deemed an employee of the county for purposes of this division, be entitled to the workers' compensation benefits provided by this division for injury sustained while in the performance of such assigned work project, provided:

(a) That such ward shall not be entitled to any temporary disability indemnity benefits.

(b) That in determining permanent disability benefits, average weekly earnings shall be taken at the minimum provided therefor in Section 4453.

Ref.: Herlick Handbook § 2.5; W. Cal. Sum., 2 "Workers' Compensation" §§179, 182.

§3364.6. Juvenile traffic offenders doing rehabilitative work.

Notwithstanding Sections 3351 and 3352, juvenile traffic offenders pursuant to Section 564 of the Welfare and Institutions Code, or juvenile probationers pursuant to subdivision (a) of Section 725 of the Welfare and Institutions Code, engaged in rehabilitative work without pay, under an assignment by order of the juvenile court to a work project on public property within the jurisdiction of any governmental entity, including the federal government, shall, upon the adoption of a resolution of the board of supervisors declaring that such traffic offenders or probationers, or both such groups, shall be deemed employees of the county for purposes of this division, be entitled to the workers' compensation benefits provided by this division for injury sustained while in the performance of such assigned work project, provided:

(a) That such traffic offender or probationer shall not be entitled to any temporary disability indemnity benefits.

(b) That in determining permanent disability benefits, average weekly earnings shall be taken at the minimum provided therefor in Section 4453.

Ref.: Herlick Handbook §2.5; W. Cal. Sum., 2 "Workers' Compensation" §179.

§3364.7. Juvenile court wards committed to regional youth educational facility.

Notwithstanding Sections 3351 and 3352, a ward of the juvenile court committed to a regional youth educational facility pursuant to Article 24.5 (commencing with Section 894), engaged in rehabilitative work without pay on public property within the jurisdiction of any governmental entity, including the federal government, shall, upon the adoption of a resolution of the board of supervisors declaring that such wards shall be deemed employees of the county for purposes of this division, be entitled to the workers' compensation benefits provided by this division for injury sustained while in the performance of such public work project, provided:

(a) That the ward shall not be entitled to any disability indemnity benefits.

(b) That in determining permanent disability benefits, average weekly earnings shall be taken at the minimum provided therefor in Section 4453.

§3365. Persons engaged in suppressing fires.

For the purposes of this division:

(a) Except as provided in subdivisions (b) and (c), each person engaged in suppressing a fire pursuant to Section 4153 or 4436 of the

Public Resources Code, and each person (other than an independent contractor or an employee of an independent contractor) engaged in suppressing a fire at the request of a public officer or employee charged with the duty of preventing or suppressing fires, is deemed, except when the entity is the United States or an agency thereof, to be an employee of the public entity that he is serving or assisting in the suppression of the fire, and is entitled to receive compensation from such public entity in accordance with the provisions of this division. When the entity being served is the United States or an agency thereof, the State Department of Corrections shall be deemed the employer and the cost of workers' compensation may be considered in fixing the reimbursement paid by the United States for the service of prisoners. A person is engaged in suppressing a fire only during the period he (1) is actually fighting the fire, (2) is being transported to or from the fire, or (3) is engaged in training exercises for fire suppression.

(b) A member of the armed forces of the United States while serving under military command in suppressing a fire is not an employee of a public entity.

(c) Neither a person who contracts to furnish aircraft with pilots to a public entity for fire prevention or suppression service, nor his employees, shall be deemed to be employees of the public entity; but a person who contracts to furnish aircraft to a public entity for fire prevention or suppression service and to pilot the aircraft himself shall be deemed to be an employee of the public entity.

Ref.: Hanna § 6.05[2]; Herlick Handbook § 2.5; W. Cal. Sum., 2 "Workers' Compensation" §177.

§3366. Persons assisting in active law enforcement.

(a) For the purposes of this division, each person engaged in the performance of active law enforcement service as part of the posse comitatus or power of the county, and each person (other than an independent contractor or an employee of an independent contractor) engaged in assisting any peace officer in active law enforcement service at the request of such peace officer, is deemed to be an employee of the public entity that he or she is serving or assisting in the enforcement of the law, and is entitled to receive compensation from the public entity in accordance with the provisions of this division.

(b) Nothing in this section shall be construed to provide workers' compensation benefits to a person who is any of the following:

(1) A law enforcement officer who is regularly employed by a local or state law enforcement agency in an adjoining state and who is deputized to work under the supervision of a California peace officer pursuant to paragraph (4) of subdivision (a) of Section 832.6 of the Penal Code.

(2) A law enforcement officer who is regularly employed by the Oregon State Police, the Nevada Department of Motor Vehicles and Public Safety, or the Arizona Department of Public Safety and who is acting as a peace officer in this state pursuant to subdivision (a) of Section 830.32 of the Penal Code.

Ref.: Herlick Handbook §§ 2.4, 2.5; W. Cal. Sum., 2 "Workers' Compensation" §§178, 191.

§3367. Technical assistants to fire or law enforcement officers.

(a) For purposes of this division any person voluntarily rendering technical assistance to a public entity to prevent a fire, explosion, or other hazardous occurrence, at the request of a duly authorized fire or law enforcement officer of that public entity is deemed an employee of the public entity to whom the technical assistance was rendered, and is entitled to receive compensation benefits in accordance with the provisions of this division. Rendering technical assistance shall include the time that person is traveling to, or returning from, the location of the potentially hazardous condition for which he or she has been requested to volunteer his or her assistance.

(b) Nothing in this section shall be construed to provide workers' compensation benefits to a person who is any of the following:

(1) A law enforcement officer who is regularly employed by a local or state law enforcement agency in an adjoining state and who is deputized to work under the supervision of a California peace officer pursuant to paragraph (4) of subdivision (a) of Section 832.6 of the Penal Code.

(2) A law enforcement officer who is regularly employed by the Oregon State Police, the Nevada Department of Motor Vehicles and Public Safety, or the Arizona Department of Public Safety and who is acting as a peace officer in this state pursuant to subdivision (a) of Section 830.32 of the Penal Code.

Ref.: Herlick Handbook §§ 2.4, 2.5; W. Cal. Sum., 2 "Workers' Compensation" §§177, 191.

§3368. Supervision of work experience education, cooperative vocational education, community classroom, or student apprenticeship program by school, school district, or county superintendent; school, school district, or county superintendent as "employer"; exceptions; "registered student apprentice"; regional and joint supervision of program.

Notwithstanding any provision of this code or the Education Code to the contrary, the school district, county superintendent of schools, or any school administered by the State Department of Education under whose supervision work experience education, cooperative vocational education, or community classrooms, as defined by regulations adopted by the Superintendent of Public Instruction, or student apprenticeship programs registered by the Division of Apprenticeship Standards for registered student apprentices, are provided, shall be considered the employer under Division 4 (commencing with Section 3200) of persons receiving this training unless the persons during the training are being paid a cash wage or salary by a private employer. However, in the case of students being paid a cash wage or salary by a private employer in supervised work experience education or cooperative vocational education, or in the case of registered student apprentices, the school district, county superintendent of schools, or any school administered by the State Department of Education may elect to provide workers' compensation coverage, unless the person or firm under whom the persons are receiving work experience or occupational training elects to provide workers' compensation coverage. If the school district or other educational agency elects to provide workers' compensation coverage for students being paid a cash wage or salary by a private employer in supervised work experience education or cooperative vocational education, it may only be for a transitional period not to exceed three months. A registered student apprentice is a registered apprentice who is (1) at least 16 years of age, (2) a full-time high school student in the 10th, 11th, or 12th grade, and (3) in an apprenticeship program for registered student apprentices registered with the Division of Apprenticeship Standards. An apprentice, while attending related and supplemental instruction classes, shall be considered to be in the employ of the apprentice's employer and not subject to this section, unless the apprentice is unemployed. Whenever this work experience education, cooperative vocational education, community classroom education, or student apprenticeship program registered by the Division of Apprenticeship Standards for registered student apprentices, is under the supervision of a regional occupational center or program operated by two or more school districts pursuant to Section 52301 of the Education Code, the district of residence of the persons receiving the training shall be deemed the employer for the purposes of this section. **Leg.H.** 1997 ch. 345, 1998 ch. 541.

Ref.: Herlick Handbook § 2.5.

§3369. Effect of coverage by this division.

The inclusion of any person or groups of persons within the coverage of this division shall not cause any such person or group of persons to be within the coverage of any other statute unless any other such statute expressly so provides.

Ref.: Herlick Handbook § 2.1.

§3370. State penal or correctional institution inmates.

(a) Each inmate of a state penal or correctional institution shall be entitled to the workers' compensation benefits provided by this division for injury arising out of and in the course of assigned employment and for the death of the inmate if the injury proximately causes death, subject to all of the following conditions:

(1) The inmate was not injured as the result of an assault in which the inmate was the initial aggressor, or as the result of the intentional act of the inmate injuring himself or herself.

(2) The inmate shall not be entitled to any temporary disability indemnity benefits while incarcerated in a state prison.

(3) No benefits shall be paid to an inmate while he or she is incarcerated. The period of benefit payment shall instead commence upon release from incarceration. If an inmate who has been released from incarceration, and has been receiving benefits under this section, is reincarcerated in a city or county jail, or state penal or correctional institution, the benefits

shall cease immediately upon the inmate's reincarceration and shall not be paid for the duration of the reincarceration.

(4) This section shall not be construed to provide for the payment to an inmate, upon release from incarceration, of temporary disability benefits which were not paid due to the prohibition of paragraph (2).

(5) In determining temporary and permanent disability indemnity benefits for the inmate, the average weekly earnings shall be taken at not more than the minimum amount set forth in Section 4453.

(6) Where a dispute exists respecting an inmate's rights to the workers' compensation benefits provided herein, the inmate may file an application with the appeals board to resolve the dispute. The application may be filed at any time during the inmate's incarceration.

(7) After release or discharge from a correctional institution, the former inmate shall have one year in which to file an original application with the appeals board, unless the time of injury is such that it would allow more time under Section 5804 of the Labor Code.

(8) The percentage of disability to total disability shall be determined as for the occupation of a laborer of like age by applying the schedule for the determination of the percentages of permanent disabilities prepared and adopted by the administrative director.

(9) This division shall be the exclusive remedy against the state for injuries occurring while engaged in assigned work or work under contract. Nothing in this division shall affect any right or remedy of an injured inmate for injuries not compensated by this division.

(b) The Department of Corrections shall present to each inmate of a state penal or correctional institution, prior to his or her first assignment to work at the institution, a printed statement of his or her rights under this division, and a description of procedures to be followed in filing for benefits under this section. The statement shall be approved by the administrative director and be posted in a conspicuous place at each place where an inmate works.

(c) Not withstanding any other provision of this division, the Department of Corrections shall have medical control over treatment provided an injured inmate while incarcerated in a state prison, except, that in serious cases, the inmate is entitled, upon request, to the services of a consulting physician.

(d) Paragraphs (2), (3), and (4) of subdivision (a) shall also be applicable to an inmate of a state penal or correctional institution who would otherwise be entitled to receive workers' compensation benefits based on an injury sustained prior to his or her incarceration. However, temporary and permanent disability benefits which, except for this subdivision, would otherwise be payable to an inmate during incarceration based on an injury sustained prior to incarceration shall be paid to the dependents of the inmate. If the inmate has no dependents, the temporary disability benefits which, except for this subdivision, would otherwise be payable during the inmate's incarceration shall be paid to the State Treasury to the credit of the Uninsured Employers Fund, and the permanent disability benefits which would otherwise be payable during the inmate's incarceration shall be held in trust for the inmate by the Department of Corrections during the period of incarceration.

For purposes of this subdivision, "dependents" means the inmate's spouse or children, including an inmate's former spouse due to divorce and the inmate's children from that marriage.

(e) Notwithstanding any other provision of this division, an employee who is an inmate, as defined in subdivision (e) of Section 3351 who is eligible for vocational rehabilitation services as defined in Section 4635 shall only be eligible for direct placement services. **Leg.H.** 1994 ch. 497.

Ref.: 8 C.C.R. §10133.4; Hanna §§ 3.100[1], 3.100[2][b], 6.05[3]; Herlick Handbook § 2.4; W. Cal. Sum., 2 "Workers' Compensation" §§180, 244, 250, 261, 305, 326.

§3371. Attorney referral for inmates.

If the issues are complex or if the inmate applicant requests, the Department of Corrections shall furnish a list of qualified workers' compensation attorneys to permit the inmate applicant to choose an attorney to represent him or her before the appeals board. **Leg.H.** 1994 ch. 497 §5.

Ref.: W. Cal. Sum., 2 "Workers' Compensation" §354.

ARTICLE 3
Dependents

§3501. Presumption; minor's or incapacitated adult's dependence on deceased parent.

(a) A child under the age of 18 years, or a child of any age found by any trier of fact, whether contractual, administrative, regulatory, or judicial, to be physically or mentally incapacitated from earning, shall be conclusively presumed to be wholly dependent for support upon a deceased employee-parent with whom that child is living at the time of injury resulting in death of the parent or for whose maintenance the parent was legally liable at the time of injury resulting in death of the parent, there being no surviving totally dependent parent.

(b) A spouse to whom a deceased employee is married at the time of death shall be conclusively presumed to be wholly dependent for support upon the deceased employee if the surviving spouse earned thirty thousand dollars ($30,000) or less in the twelve months immediately preceding the death. **Leg.H.** 2002 chs. 6 (AB 749), 866 (AB 486).

1989 Note: This section is applicable only to injuries occurring on or after January 1, 1990. Stats. 1989 ch. 893 §6.

Ref.: Hanna §§ 9.05[3][a]–[d], [4][a], [b]; Herlick Handbook §§ 7.1, 7.2, 7.6, 7.9, 7.10, 14.38; W. Cal. Ev., "Burden" §163; W. Cal. Sum., 2 "Workers' Compensation" §§280, 312, 313, 8 "Constitutional Law" §773, 10 "Parent and Child" §420.

§3502. Factual determination of dependency.

In all other cases, questions of entire or partial dependency and questions as to who are dependents and the extent of their dependency shall be determined in accordance with the facts as they exist at the time of the injury of the employee.

Ref.: Hanna §§ 9.05[2], [3][b]–[c], [4][a], [b], 25.10[6]; Herlick Handbook §§ 7.2, 7.9; W. Cal. Sum., 2 "Workers' Compensation" §313, 8 "Constitutional Law" §773.

§3503. Qualifications for dependency.

No person is a dependent of any deceased employee unless in good faith a member of the family or household of the employee, or unless the person bears to the employee the relation of husband or wife, child, posthumous child, adopted child or stepchild, grandchild, father or mother, father-in-law or mother-in-law, grandfather or grandmother, brother or sister, uncle or aunt, brother-in-law or sister-in-law, nephew or niece.

Ref.: Hanna § 9.05[2]; Herlick Handbook §§ 7.1, 7.9, 7.12, 14.38; W. Cal. Sum., 2 "Workers' Compensation" §313.

ARTICLE 4
Employee Notice

§3550. Posting of notice; failure to post; applicability; form and content of notice.

(a) Every employer subject to the compensation provisions of this division shall post and keep posted in a conspicuous location frequented by employees, and where the notice may be easily read by employees during the hours of the workday, a notice that states the name of the current compensation insurance carrier of the employer, or when such is the fact, that the employer is self-insured, and who is responsible for claims adjustment.

(b) Failure to keep any notice required by this section conspicuously posted shall constitute a misdemeanor, and shall be prima facie evidence of noninsurance.

(c) This section shall not apply with respect to the employment of employees as defined in subdivision (d) of Section 3351.

(d) The form and content of the notice required by this section shall be prescribed by the administrative director, after consultation with the Commission on Health and Safety and Workers' Compensation, and shall advise employees that all injuries should be reported to their employer. The notice shall be easily understandable. It shall be posted in both English and Spanish where there are Spanish-speaking employees. The notice shall include the following information:

(1) How to get emergency medical treatment, if needed.

(2) The kinds of events, injuries, and illnesses covered by workers' compensation.

(3) The injured employee's right to receive medical care.

(4) The rights of the employee to select and change the treating physician pursuant to the provisions of Section 4600.

(5) The rights of the employee to receive temporary disability indemnity, permanent disability indemnity, vocational rehabilitation services, and death benefits, as appropriate.

(6) To whom injuries should be reported.

(7) The existence of time limits for the employer to be notified of an occupational injury.

(8) The protections against discrimination provided pursuant to Section 132a.

(9) The location and telephone number of the nearest information and assistance officer.

(e) Failure of an employer to provide the notice required by this section shall automatically permit the employee to be treated by his or her personal physician with respect to an injury occurring during that failure.

(f) The form and content of the notice required to be posted by this section shall be made available to self-insured employers and insurers by the administrative director. Insurers shall provide this notice to each of their policyholders, with advice concerning the requirements of this section and the penalties for a failure to post this notice. **Leg.H.** 2002 ch. 6 (AB 749).

Ref.: 8 C.C.R. §§9880, 9881, 9883, 15203.1, 15203.7; Hanna §§ 2.10[1], 10.20, 10.26, 10.27, 22.01[2]–[3]; Herlick Handbook §§ 9.3, 14.3; W. Cal. Sum., 2 "Workers' Compensation" §146.

§3551. Written notice to new employee; contents.

(a) Every employer subject to the compensation provisions of this code, except employers of employees defined in subdivision (d) of Section 3351, shall give every new employee, either at the time the employee is hired or by the end of the first pay period, written notice of the information contained in Section 3550. The content of the notice required by this section shall be prescribed by the administrative director after consultation with the Commission on Health and Safety and Workers' Compensation.

(b) The notice required by this section shall be easily understandable and available in both English and Spanish. In addition to the information contained in Section 3550, the content of the notice required by this section shall include:

(1) Generally, how to obtain appropriate medical care for a job injury.

(2) The role and function of the primary treating physician.

(3) A form that the employee may use as an optional method for notifying the employer of the name of the employee's "personal physician," as defined by Section 4600, or "personal chiropractor," as defined by Section 4601.

(c) The content of the notice required by this section shall be made available to employers and insurers by the administrative director. Insurers shall provide this notice to each of their policyholders, with advice concerning the requirements of this section and the penalties for a failure to provide this notice to all employees. **Leg.H.** 2002 ch. 6 (AB 749).

Ref.: 8 C.C.R. §§9880, 9883; Herlick Handbook §§ 4.1, 9.3, 14.3, 16.3; W. Cal. Sum., 2 "Workers' Compensation" §146.

§3553. Employee who is victim of workplace crime; provision of written notice to employee concerning workers' compensation eligibility; when employer must provide notice.

Every employer subject to the compensation provisions of this code shall give any employee who is a victim of a crime that occurred at the employee's place of employment written notice that the employee is eligible for workers' compensation for injuries, including psychiatric injuries, that may have resulted from the place of employment crime. The employer shall provide this notice, either personally or by first-class mail, within one working day of the place of employment crime, or within one working day of the date the employer reasonably should have known of the crime. **Leg.H.** 1997 ch. 527.

Ref.: Herlick Handbook §§ 3.23, 8.9, 8.15, 14.3.

CHAPTER 3
CONDITIONS OF COMPENSATION LIABILITY

§3600. Conditions of compensation for employer liability.

(a) Liability for the compensation provided by this division, in lieu of any other liability whatsoever to any person except as otherwise specifically provided in Sections 3602, 3706, and 4558, shall, without regard to negligence, exist against an employer for any injury sustained by his or her employees arising out of and in the course of the employment and for the death of any employee if the injury proximately causes death, in those cases where the following conditions of compensation concur:

(1) Where, at the time of the injury, both the employer and the employee are subject to the compensation provisions of this division.

(2) Where, at the time of the injury, the employee is performing service growing out of and incidental to his or her employment and is acting within the course of his or her employment.

(3) Where the injury is proximately caused by the employment, either with or without negligence.

(4) Where the injury is not caused by the intoxication, by alcohol or the unlawful use of a controlled substance, of the injured employee. As used in this paragraph, "controlled substance" shall have the same meaning as prescribed in Section 11007 of the Health and Safety Code.

(5) Where the injury is not intentionally self-inflicted.

(6) Where the employee has not willfully and deliberately caused his or her own death.

(7) Where the injury does not arise out of an altercation in which the injured employee is the initial physical aggressor.

(8) Where the injury is not caused by the commission of a felony, or a crime which is punishable as specified in subdivision (b) of Section 17 of the Penal Code, by the injured employee, for which he or she has been convicted.

(9) Where the injury does not arise out of voluntary participation in any off-duty recreational, social, or athletic activity not constituting part of the employee's work-related duties, except where these activities are a reasonable expectancy of, or are expressly or impliedly required by, the employment. The administrative director shall promulgate reasonable rules and regulations requiring employers to post and keep posted in a conspicuous place or places a notice advising employees of the provisions of this subdivision. Failure of the employer to post the notice shall not constitute an expression of intent to waive the provisions of this subdivision.

(10) Except for psychiatric injuries governed by subdivision (e) of Section 3208.3, where the claim for compensation is filed after notice of termination or layoff, including voluntary layoff, and the claim is for an injury occurring prior to the time of notice of termination or layoff, no compensation shall be paid unless the employee demonstrates by a preponderance of the evidence that one or more of the following conditions apply:

(A) The employer has notice of the injury, as provided under Chapter 2 (commencing with Section 5400), prior to the notice of termination or layoff.

(B) The employee's medical records, existing prior to the notice of termination or layoff, contain evidence of the injury.

(C) The date of injury, as specified in Section 5411, is subsequent to the date of the notice of termination or layoff, but prior to the effective date of the termination or layoff.

(D) The date of injury, as specified in Section 5412, is subsequent to the date of the notice of termination or layoff.

For purposes of this paragraph, an employee provided notice pursuant to Sections 44948.5, 44949, 44951, 44955, 44955.6, 72411, 87740, and 87743 of the Education Code shall be considered to have been provided a notice of termination or layoff only upon a district's final decision not to reemploy that person.

A notice of termination or layoff that is not followed within 60 days by that termination or layoff shall not be subject to the provisions of this paragraph, and this paragraph shall not apply until receipt of a later notice of termination or layoff. The issuance of frequent notices of termination or layoff to an employee shall be considered a bad faith personnel action and shall make this paragraph inapplicable to the employee.

(b) Where an employee, or his or her dependents, receives the compensation provided by this division and secures a judgment for, or settlement of, civil damages pursuant to those specific exemptions to the employee's exclusive remedy set forth in subdivision (b) of Section 3602 and Section 4558, the compensation paid under this division shall be credited against the judgment or settlement, and the employer shall be relieved from the obligation to pay further compensation to, or on behalf of, the employee or his or her dependents up to the net amount of the judgment or settlement received by the employee or his or her heirs, or that portion of the judgment as has been satisfied. **Leg.H.** 1993 ch. 118, effective July 16, 1993, ch. 1242.

Ref.: 8 C.C.R. §§9880, 9881; Hanna §§ 11.01[1], [4][b], 11.02[3][a], 11.04[2], 21.03[1][b]; Herlick Handbook §§ 8.1–8.7, 8.17; CACI Nos. 2800–2803, 2810–2812, 3726 (Matthew Bender); W. Cal. Sum., 2 "Workers' Compensation" §§5, 20, 24–26, 28, 30, 49, 54, 55, 65, 105, 183, 193, 194, 197, 225, 226, 230, 247, 250–253, 256, 325–327, 3 "Agency and Employment" §176.

§3600.1. State firefighters not acting under employer's immediate direction.

(a) Whenever any firefighter of the state, as defined in Section 19886 of the Government Code, is injured, dies, or is disabled from performing his or her duties as a firefighter by reason of his or her proceeding to or engaging in a fire-suppression or rescue operation, or the protection or preservation of life or property, anywhere in this state, including the jurisdiction in which he or she is employed, but is not at the time acting under the immediate direction of his or her employer, he or she or his or her dependents, as the case may be, shall be accorded by his or her employer all of the same benefits of this division that he, she, or they would have received had that firefighter been acting under the immediate direction of his or her employer. Any injury, disability, or death incurred under the circumstances described in this section shall be deemed to have arisen out of, and been sustained in, the course of employment for purposes of workers' compensation and all other benefits.

(b) Nothing in this section shall be deemed to do either of the following:

(1) Require the extension of any benefits to a firefighter who, at the time of his or her injury, death, or disability, is acting for compensation from one other than the state.

(2) Require the extension of any benefits to a firefighter employed by the state where by departmental regulation, whether now in force or hereafter enacted or promulgated, the activity giving rise to the injury, disability, or death is expressly prohibited.

(c) If the provisions of this section are in conflict with the provisions of a memorandum of understanding reached pursuant to Section 3517.5 of the Government Code, the memorandum of understanding shall be controlling without further legislative action, except that if the provisions of a memorandum of understanding require the expenditure of funds, the provisions shall not become effective unless approved by the Legislature in the annual Budget Act. **Leg.H.** 2004 ch. 183 (AB 3082), 2005 ch. 22 (SB 1108) §143.

Ref.: W. Cal. Sum., 2 "Workers' Compensation" §§177, 193.

§3600.2. Peace officers not acting under employer's immediate direction.

(a) Whenever any peace officer, as defined in Section 50920 of the Government Code, is injured, dies or is disabled from performing his duties as a peace officer by reason of engaging in the apprehension or attempted apprehension of law violators or suspected law violators, or protection or preservation of life or property, or the preservation of the peace anywhere in this state, including the local jurisdiction in which he is employed, but is not at the time acting under the immediate direction of his employer, he or his dependants, as the case may be, shall be accorded by his employer all of the same benefits, including the benefits of this division, which he or they would have received had that peace officer been acting under the immediate direction of his employer. Any injury, disability, or death incurred under the circumstances described in this section shall be deemed to have arisen out of and been sustained in the course of employment for purposes of workers' compensation and all other benefits.

(b) Nothing in this section shall be deemed to:

(1) Require the extension of any benefits to a peace officer who at the time of his injury, death, or disability is acting for compensation from one other than the city, county, city and county, judicial district, or town of his primary employment.

(2) Require the extension of any benefits to a peace officer employed by a city, county, city and county, judicial district, or town which by charter, ordinance, or departmental regulation, whether now in force or hereafter enacted or promulgated, expressly prohibits the activity giving rise to the injury, disability, or death.

(3) Enlarge or extend the authority of any peace officer to make an arrest; provided, however, that illegality of the arrest shall not affect the extension of benefits by reason of this act if the peace officer reasonably believed that the arrest was not illegal.

Ref.: W. Cal. Sum., 2 "Workers' Compensation" §178.

§3600.3. Scope of employment; off-duty peace officers.

(a) For the purposes of Section 3600, an off-duty peace officer, as defined in subdivision (b), who is performing, within the jurisdiction of his or her employing agency, a service he or she would, in the course of his or her employment, have been required to perform if he or she were on duty, is performing a service growing out of and incidental to his or her employment and is acting within the course of his or her employment if, as a condition of his or her employment, he or she is required to be on call within the jurisdiction during off-duty hours.

Labor

(b) As used in subdivision (a), "peace officer" means those employees of the Department of Forestry and Fire Protection named as peace officers for purposes of subdivision (b) of Section 830.37 of the Penal Code.

(c) This section does not apply to any off-duty peace officer while he or she is engaged, either as an employee or as an independent contractor, in any capacity other than as a peace officer. **Leg.H.** 1992 ch. 427.

Ref.: Hanna § 4.130[2]; W. Cal. Sum., 2 "Workers' Compensation" §178.

§3600.4. Local firefighters not acting under employer's immediate direction.

(a) Whenever any firefighter of a city, county, city and county, district, or other public or municipal corporation or political subdivision, or any firefighter employed by a private entity, is injured, dies, or is disabled from performing his or her duties as a firefighter by reason of his or her proceeding to or engaging in a fire suppression or rescue operation, or the protection or preservation of life or property, anywhere in this state, including the local jurisdiction in which he or she is employed, but is not at the time acting under the immediate direction of his or her employer, he or she or his or her dependents, as the case may be, shall be accorded by his or her employer all of the same benefits of this division which he or she or they would have received had that firefighter been acting under the immediate direction of his or her employer. Any injury, disability, or death incurred under the circumstances described in this section shall be deemed to have arisen out of and been sustained in the course of employment for purposes of workers' compensation and all other benefits.

(b) Nothing in this section shall be deemed to:

(1) Require the extension of any benefits to a firefighter who at the time of his or her injury, death, or disability is acting for compensation from one other than the city, county, city and county, district, or other public or municipal corporation or political subdivision, or private entity, of his or her primary employment or enrollment.

(2) Require the extension of any benefits to a firefighter employed by a city, county, city and county, district, or other public or municipal corporation or political subdivision, or private entity, which by charter, ordinance, departmental regulation, or private employer policy, whether now in force or hereafter enacted or promulgated, expressly prohibits the activity giving rise to the injury, disability, or death. However, this paragraph shall not apply to relieve the employer from liability for benefits for any injury, disability, or death of a firefighter when the firefighter is acting pursuant to Section 1799.107 of the Health and Safety Code. **Leg.H.** 1998 ch. 617.

Ref.: W. Cal. Sum., 2 "Workers' Compensation" §177.

§3600.5. Out-of-state injury of resident; exemption; certificate of insurance for out-of-state employer.

(a) If an employee who has been hired or is regularly employed in this state receives personal injury by accident arising out of and in the course of such employment outside of this state, he, or his dependents, in the case of his death, shall be entitled to compensation according to the law of this state.

(b) Any employee who has been hired outside of this state and his employer shall be exempted from the provisions of this division while such employee is temporarily within this state doing work for his employer if such employer has furnished workers' compensation insurance coverage under the workers' compensation insurance or similar laws of a state other than California, so as to cover such employee's employment while in this state; provided, the extraterritorial provisions of this division are recognized in such other state and provided employers and employees who are covered in this state are likewise exempted from the application of the workers' compensation insurance or similar laws of such other state. The benefits under the Workers' Compensation Insurance Act or similar laws of such other state, or other remedies under such act or such laws, shall be the exclusive remedy against such employer for any injury, whether resulting in death or not, received by such employee while working for such employer in this state.

A certificate from the duly authorized officer of the appeals board or similar department of another state certifying that the employer of such other state is insured therein and has provided extraterritorial coverage insuring his employees while working within this state shall be prima facie evidence that such employer carries such workers' compensation insurance.

Ref.: Hanna §§ 21.06, 21.07[5]; W. Cal. Sum., 2 "Workers' Compensation" §§111, 113, 116, 193.

§3600.6. Disaster service workers.

Disaster service workers registered by a disaster council while performing services under the general direction of the disaster council shall be entitled to all of the same benefits of this division as any other injured employee, except as provided by Chapter 10 (commencing with Section 4351) of Part 1. For purposes of this section, an unregistered person impressed into performing service as a disaster service worker during a state of war emergency, a state of emergency, or a local emergency by a person having authority to command the aid of citizens in the execution of his or her duties shall also be deemed a disaster service worker and shall be entitled to the same benefits of this division as any other disaster service worker.

Ref.: W. Cal. Sum., 2 "Workers' Compensation" §177.

§3600.8. Participation in alternative commute program not acting within course of employment—Definitions; exceptions.

(a) No employee who voluntarily participates in an alternative commute program that is sponsored or mandated by a governmental entity shall be considered to be acting within the course of his or her employment while utilizing that program to travel to or from his or her place of employment, unless he or she is paid a regular wage or salary in compensation for those periods of travel. An employee who is injured while acting outside the course of his or her employment, or his or her dependents in the event of the employee's death, shall not be barred from bringing an action at law for damages against his or her employer as a result of this section.

(b) Any alternative commute program provided, sponsored, or subsidized by an employee's employer in order to comply with any trip reduction mandates of an air quality management district or local government shall be considered a program mandated by a governmental entity. An employer's reimbursement of employee expenses or subsidization of costs related to an alternative commute program shall not be considered payment of a wage or salary in compensation for the period of travel. If an employer's salary is not based on the hours the employee works, payment of his or her salary shall not be considered to be in compensation for the period of travel unless there is a specific written agreement between the employer and the employee to that effect. If an employer elects to provide workers' compensation coverage for those employees who are passengers in a vehicle owned and operated by the employer or an agent thereof, those employees shall be considered to be within the course of their employment, provided the employer notifies employees in writing prior to participation of the employee or coverage becoming effective.

(c) As used in this section, "governmental entity" means a regional air district, air quality management district, congestion management agency, or other local jurisdiction having authority to enact air pollution or congestion management controls or impose them upon entities within its jurisdiction.

(d) Notwithstanding any other provision of law, vanpool programs may continue to provide workers' compensation benefits to employees who participate in an alternative commute program by riding in a vanpool, in the case in which the vanpool vehicle is owned or registered to the employer.

(e) Employees of the state who participate in an alternative commute program, while riding in a vanpool vehicle that is registered to or owned by the state, shall be deemed to be within the course and scope of employment for workers' compensation purposes only. **Leg.H.** 1994 ch. 622.

1994 Note: It is the intent of the Legislature in enacting this section only to declare existing law and to clarify, and not to expand, limit, or otherwise alter the ability under existing law of any employee, or his or her dependents, to bring an action at law for damages. Stats. 1994 ch. 622 §5.

Ref.: Hanna § 4.151[3]; W. Cal. Sum., 2 "Workers' Compensation" §§201, 214.

§3601. Employee's liability to another employee.

(a) Where the conditions of compensation set forth in Section 3600 concur, the right to recover such compensation, pursuant to the provisions of this division is, except as specifically provided in this section, the exclusive remedy for injury or death of an employee against any other employee of the employer acting within the scope of his or her employment, except that an employee, or his or her dependents in the event of his or her death, shall,

Labor

in addition to the right to compensation against the employer, have a right to bring an action at law for damages against the other employee, as if this division did not apply, in either of the following cases:

(1) When the injury or death is proximately caused by the willful and unprovoked physical act of aggression of the other employee.

(2) When the injury or death is proximately caused by the intoxication of the other employee.

(b) In no event, either by legal action or by agreement whether entered into by the other employee or on his or her behalf, shall the employer be held liable, directly or indirectly, for damages awarded against, or for a liability incurred by the other employee under paragraph (1) or (2) of subdivision (a).

(c) No employee shall be held liable, directly or indirectly, to his or her employer, for injury or death of a coemployee except where the injured employee or his or her dependents obtain a recovery under subdivision (a).

Ref.: Hanna §§ 2.10[2], 3.142[2][a], 4.51[1], 11.21[2][a]; Herlick Handbook §§ 12.10, 12.11; CACI Nos. 2801, 2810–2812, VF-2804, VF-2805 (Matthew Bender); W. Cal. Sum., 2 "Workers' Compensation" §§24, 25, 30, 42, 52, 59, 63, 67, 68, 105, 128, 160, 251, 6 "Torts" §1260.

§3602. Employer's personal liability.

(a) Where the conditions of compensation set forth in Section 3600 concur, the right to recover such compensation is, except as specifically provided in this section and Sections 3706 and 4558, the sole and exclusive remedy of the employee or his or her dependents against the employer, and the fact that either the employee or the employer also occupied another or dual capacity prior to, or at the time of, the employee's industrial injury shall not permit the employee or his or her dependents to bring an action at law for damages against the employer.

(b) An employee, or his or her dependents in the event of his or her death, may bring an action at law for damages against the employer, as if this division did not apply, in the following instances:

(1) Where the employee's injury or death is proximately caused by a willful physical assault by the employer.

(2) Where the employee's injury is aggravated by the employer's fraudulent concealment of the existence of the injury and its connection with the employment, in which case the employer's liability shall be limited to those damages proximately caused by the aggravation. The burden of proof respecting apportionment of damages between the injury and any subsequent aggravation thereof is upon the employer.

(3) Where the employee's injury or death is proximately caused by a defective product manufactured by the employer and sold, leased, or otherwise transferred for valuable consideration to an independent third person, and that product is thereafter provided for the employee's use by a third person.

(c) In all cases where the conditions of compensation set forth in Section 3600 do not concur, the liability of the employer shall be the same as if this division had not been enacted.

(d) For the purposes of this division, including Sections 3700 and 3706, an employer may secure the payment of compensation on employees provided to it by agreement by another employer by entering into a valid and enforceable agreement with that other employer under which the other employer agrees to obtain, and has, in fact, obtained workers' compensation coverage for those employees. In those cases, both employers shall be considered to have secured the payment of compensation within the meaning of this section and Sections 3700 and 3706 if there is a valid and enforceable agreement between the employers to obtain that coverage, and that coverage, as specified in subdivision (a) or (b) of Section 3700, has been in fact obtained, and the coverage remains in effect for the duration of the employment providing legally sufficient coverage to the employee or employees who form the subject matter of the coverage. That agreement shall not be made for the purpose of avoiding an employer's appropriate experience rating as defined in subdivision (c) of Section 11730 of the Insurance Code.

Employers who have complied with this subdivision shall not be subject to civil, criminal, or other penalties for failure to provide workers' compensation coverage or tort liability in the event of employee injury, but may, in the absence of compliance, be subject to all three. **Leg.H.** 1995 ch. 800.

Ref.: Hanna §§ 11.02[1], [6][a], [c], [7][a]–[c], [8]; Herlick Handbook §§ 12.10, 12.11; CACI Nos. 2800–2803, VF-2800–VF-2802 (Matthew Bender); W. Cal. Sum., 2 "Insurance" §306, 2 "Workers' Compensation" §§20, 24, 25, 38, 42–45, 48, 54, 58, 62, 63, 65, 146, 183, 253, 6 "Torts" §1597.

§3603. Discharge of claims.

Payment of compensation in accordance with the order and direction of the appeals board shall discharge the employer from all claims therefor.

§3604. Unavailable defense for public employers.

It is not a defense to the State, any county, city, district or institution thereof, or any public or quasi-public corporation, that a person injured while rendering service for it was not lawfully employed by reason of the violation of any civil service or other law or regulation respecting the hiring of employees.

Ref.: Hanna § 3.111; W. Cal. Sum., 2 "Workers' Compensation" §174.

§3605. Injured minors; compensation.

The compensation due an injured minor may be paid to him until his parent or guardian gives the employer or the latter's compensation insurance carrier written notice that he claims such compensation.

Compensation paid to such injured minor prior to receipt of such written notice is in full release of the employer and insurance carrier for the amount so paid. The minor cannot disaffirm such payment upon appointment of a guardian or coming of age.

CHAPTER 4 COMPENSATION INSURANCE AND SECURITY

ARTICLE 1 Insurance and Security

§3700. Employer's possible means of securing payment.

Every employer except the state shall secure the payment of compensation in one or more of the following ways:

(a) By being insured against liability to pay compensation by one or more insurers duly authorized to write compensation insurance in this state.

(b) By securing from the Director of Industrial Relations a certificate of consent to self-insure either as an individual employer, or as one employer in a group of employers, which may be given upon furnishing proof satisfactory to the Director of Industrial Relations of ability to self-insure and to pay any compensation that may become due to his or her employees.

(c) For any county, city, city and county, municipal corporation, public district, public agency, or any political subdivision of the state, including each member of a pooling arrangement under a joint exercise of powers agreement (but not the state itself), by securing from the Director of Industrial Relations a certificate of consent to self-insure against workers' compensation claims, which certificate may be given upon furnishing proof satisfactory to the director of ability to administer workers' compensation claims properly, and to pay workers' compensation claims that may become due to its employees. On or before March 31, 1979, a political subdivision of the state which, on December 31, 1978, was uninsured for its liability to pay compensation, shall file a properly completed and executed application for a certificate of consent to self-insure against workers' compensation claims. The certificate shall be issued and be subject to the provisions of Section 3702.

For purposes of this section, "state" shall include the superior courts of California. **Leg.H.** 1993 ch. 121, effective July 16, 1993, 2002 ch. 905 (SB 2011).

Ref.: 8 C.C.R. §§9767.1, 9767.4, 9767.8, 9811, 10100, 10100.1, 10100.2, 10181, 14000, 15201, 15203, 15203.1, 15203.2, 15203.3, 15203.4, 15203.6, 15203.7, 15203.8, 15203.10, 15204, 15205, 15210, 15210.1, 15210.2, 15210.3, 15211, 15211.2, 15212, 15213, 15214, 15215, 15230, 15231, 15232, 15233, 15234, 15251, 15300, 15301, 15302, 15303, 15353, 15354, 15360, 15400, 15400.1, 15400.2, 15402, 15402.1, 15402.2, 15402.3, 15402.4, 15403, 15405, 15420, 15422, 15423, 15424, 15425, 15426, 15427, 15428, 15430, 15430.1, 15431, 15431.1, 15431.2, 15432, 15433, 15434, 15435, 15436, 15437, 15438, 15450.1, 15458, 15459, 15470, 15471, 15472, 15473, 15474, 15475, 15476, 15477, 15478, 15479, 15480, 15481, 15550, 15551, 15552, 15553, 15554, 15555, 15556, 15557, 15558, 15559, 15560, 15561, 15562, 15563, 15564, 15565, 15566, 15567, 15568, 15569, 15570, 15571, 15571.5, 15572, 15573, 15574, 15575, 15576, 15578, 15579, 15580, 15581, 15582, 15583, 15584, 15585, 15586, 15587, 15588, 15589, 15590, 15591, 15592, 15593, 15594, 15595, 15596, 15600; Hanna §§ 1.03, 2.12, 21.05[1]; Herlick Handbook §§ 3.1, 3.14, 3.19, 3.21; W. Cal. Sum., 2 "Workers' Compensation" §§53, 146, 148, 170.

§3700.1. Definitions.

As used in this article:

(a) "Director" means the Director of Industrial Relations.

(b) "Private self-insurer" means a private employer which has secured the payment of compensation pursuant to Section 3701.

(c) "Insolvent self-insurer" means a private self-insurer who has failed to pay compensation and whose security deposit has been called by the director pursuant to Section 3701.5.

(d) "Fund" means the Self-Insurers' Security Fund established pursuant to Section 3742.

(e) "Trustees" means the Board of Trustees of the Self-Insurers' Security Fund.

(f) "Member" means a private self-insurer which participates in the Self-Insurers' Security Fund.

(g) "Incurred liabilities for the payment of compensation" means the sum of an estimate of future compensation, as compensation is defined by Section 3207, plus an estimate of the amount necessary to provide for the administration of claims, including legal costs.

Ref.: 8 C.C.R. §15475.

§3700.5. Penalty for failure to secure payment; enhancement for subsequent conviction; recovery of investigative costs.

(a) The failure to secure the payment of compensation as required by this article by one who knew, or because of his or her knowledge or experience should be reasonably expected to have known, of the obligation to secure the payment of compensation, is a misdemeanor punishable by imprisonment in the county jail for up to one year, or by a fine of up to double the amount of premium, as determined by the court, that would otherwise have been due to secure the payment of compensation during the time compensation was not secured, but not less than ten thousand dollars ($10,000), or by both that imprisonment and fine.

(b) A second or subsequent conviction shall be punished by imprisonment in the county jail for a period not to exceed one year, by a fine of triple the amount of premium, or by both that imprisonment and fine, as determined by the court, that would otherwise have been due to secure the payment of compensation during the time payment was not secured, but not less than fifty thousand dollars ($50,000).

(c) Upon a first conviction of a person under this section, the person may be charged the costs of investigation at the discretion of the court. Upon a subsequent conviction, the person shall be charged the costs of investigation in addition to any other penalties pursuant to subdivision (b). The costs of investigation shall be paid only after the payment of any benefits that may be owed to injured workers, any reimbursement that may be owed to the director for benefits provided to the injured worker pursuant to Section 3717, and any other penalty assessments that may be owed. **Leg.H.** 1999 ch. 553, 2004 ch. 2 (SB 2 Fourth Extra. Session), effective March 6, 2005.

Ref.: Hanna §§ 2.11[5], 2.17; Herlick Handbook § 3.19; W. Cal. Sum., 2 "Workers' Compensation" §146.

§3701. Private self-insuring employer; surety.

(a) Each year every private self-insuring employer shall secure incurred liabilities for the payment of compensation and the performance of the obligations of employers imposed under this chapter by renewing the prior year's security deposit or by making a new deposit of security. If a new deposit is made, it shall be posted within 60 days of the filing of the self-insured employer's annual report with the director, but in no event later than May 1.

(b) The minimum deposit shall be 125 percent of the private self-insurer's estimated future liability for compensation to secure payment of compensation plus 10 percent of the private self-insurer's estimated future liability for compensation to secure payment of all administrative and legal costs relating to or arising from the employer's self-insuring. In no event shall the security deposit for the incurred liabilities for compensation be less than two hundred twenty thousand dollars ($220,000).

(c) In determining the amount of the deposit required to secure incurred liabilities for the payment of compensation and the performance of obligations of a self-insured employer imposed under this chapter, the director shall offset estimated future liabilities for the same claims covered by a self-insured plan under the Longshore and Harbor Workers' Compensation Act (33 U.S.C. Sec. 901 et seq.), but in no event shall the offset exceed the estimated future liabilities for the claims under this chapter.

(d) The director may only accept as security, and the employer shall deposit as security, cash, securities, surety bonds, or irrevocable letters of credit in any combination the director, in his or her discretion, deems adequate security. The current deposit shall include any amounts covered by terminated surety bonds or excess insurance policies, as shall be set forth in regulations adopted by the director pursuant to Section 3702.10.

(e) Surety bonds, irrevocable letters of credit, and documents showing issuance of any irrevocable letter of credit shall be deposited with, and be in a form approved by, the director, shall be exonerated only according to its terms and, in no event, by the posting of additional security.

(f) The director may accept as security a joint security deposit that secures an employer's obligation under this chapter and that also secures that employer's obligations under the federal Longshore and Harbor Workers' Compensation Act.

(g) The liability of the Self-Insurers' Security Fund, with respect to any claims brought under both this chapter and under the federal Longshore and Harbor Workers' Compensation Act, to pay for shortfalls in a security deposit shall be limited to the amount of claim liability owing the employee under this chapter offset by the amount of any claim liability owing under the Longshore and Harbor Workers' Compensation Act, but in no event shall the liability of the fund exceed the claim liability under this chapter. The employee shall be entitled to pursue recovery under either or both the state and federal programs.

(h) Securities shall be deposited on behalf of the director by the self-insured employer with the Treasurer. Securities shall be accepted by the Treasurer for deposit and shall be withdrawn only upon written order of the director.

(i) Cash shall be deposited in a financial institution approved by the director, and in the account assigned to the director. Cash shall be withdrawn only upon written order of the director.

(j) Upon the sending by the director of a request to renew, request to post, or request to increase or decrease a security deposit, a perfected security interest is created in the private self-insured's assets in favor of the director to the extent of any then unsecured portion of the self-insured's incurred liabilities. That perfected security interest is transferred to any cash or securities thereafter posted by the private self-insured with the director and is released only upon either of the following:

(1) The acceptance by the director of a surety bond or irrevocable letter of credit for the full amount of the incurred liabilities for the payment of compensation.

(2) The return of cash or securities by the director.

The private self-insured employer loses all right, title, and interest in, and any right to control, all assets or obligations posted or left on deposit as security. The director may liquidate the deposit as provided in Section 3701.5 and apply it to the self-insured employer's incurred liabilities either directly or through the Self-Insurers' Security Fund. **Leg.H.** 1993 chs. 917, 1242, 1994 ch. 56.

Ref.: 8 C.C.R. §§15201, 15203, 15203.1, 15203.2, 15203.3, 15203.5, 15203.7, 15203.8, 15203.9, 15203.10, 15210, 15210.1, 15210.2, 15210.3, 15211, 15211.1, 15211.2, 15211.3, 15212, 15213, 15214, 15215, 15216, 15220, 15220.4, 15302, 15303, 15360, 15400, 15420, 15422, 15423, 15424, 15425, 15426, 15427, 15428, 15430, 15430.1, 15431, 15431.1, 15431.2, 15432, 15433, 15434, 15435, 15436, 15437, 15438, 15450.1, 15458, 15459, 15470, 15471, 15472, 15475, 15476, 15477, 15478, 15479, 15480, 15481, 15600; Hanna § 27.10[1]; Herlick Handbook § 3.20; W. Cal. Sum., 2 "Workers' Compensation" §148.

§3701.3. Return of overpayments to self-insured employers.

The director shall return to a private self-insured employer all amounts determined, in the director's discretion, to be in excess of that needed to assure the administration of the employer's self-insuring, including legal fees, and the payment of any future claims.

§3701.5. Private self-insured employer; payment of obligations.

(a) If the director determines that a private self-insured employer has failed to pay workers' compensation as required by this division, the security deposit shall be utilized to administer and pay the employer's compensation obligations.

(b) If the director determines the security deposit has not been immediately made available for the payment of compensation, the director shall determine the method of payment and claims administration as appropriate, which may include, but is not limited to, payment by a surety that issued the bond, or payment by an issuer of an irrevocable letter of credit, and administration by a surety or by an adjusting agency, or through the Self-Insurers' Security Fund, or any combination thereof.

(c) If the director determines the payment of benefits and claims administration shall be made through the Self-Insurers' Security Fund, the fund shall commence payment of the private self-insured employer's obligations for which it is liable under Section 3743 within 30 days of notification. Payments shall be made to claimants whose entitlement to benefits can be ascertained by the fund, with or without proceedings before the appeals board. Upon the assumption of obligations by the fund pursuant to the director's determination, the fund shall have a right to immediate possession of any posted security and the custodian, surety, or issuer of any irrevocable letter of credit shall turn over the security to the fund together with the interest that has accrued since the date of the self-insured employer's default or insolvency.

(d) The director shall promptly audit an employer upon making a determination under subdivision (a) or (b). The employer, any excess insurer, and any adjusting agency shall provide any relevant information in their possession. If the audit results in a preliminary estimate that liabilities exceed the amount of the security deposit, the director shall direct the custodian of the security deposit to liquidate it and provide all proceeds to the Self-Insurers' Security Fund. If the preliminary estimate is that liabilities are less than the security deposit, the director shall ensure the administration and payment of compensation pursuant to subdivision (b).

(e) The payment of benefits by the Self-Insurers' Security Fund from security deposit proceeds shall release and discharge any custodian of the security deposit, surety, any issuer of a letter of credit, and the self-insured employer, from liability to fulfill obligations to provide those same benefits as compensation, but does not release any person from any liability to the fund for full reimbursement. Payment by a surety constitutes a full release of the surety's liability under the bond to the extent of that payment, and entitles the surety to full reimbursement by the principal or his or her estate. Full reimbursement includes necessary attorney fees and other costs and expenses, without prior claim or proceedings on the part of the injured employee or other beneficiaries. Any decision or determination made, or any settlement approved, by the director or by the appeals board under subdivision (g) shall conclusively be presumed valid and binding as to any and all known claims arising out of the underlying dispute, unless an appeal is made within the time limit specified in Section 5950.

(f) The director shall advisc the Self-Insurers' Security Fund promptly after receipt of information indicating that a private self-insured employer may be unable to meet its compensation obligations. The director shall also advise the Self-Insurers' Security Fund of all determinations and directives made or issued pursuant to this section.

(g) Disputes concerning the posting, renewal, termination, exoneration, or return of all or any portion of the security deposit, or any liability arising out of the posting or failure to post security, or adequacy of the security or reasonableness of administrative costs, including legal fees, and arising between or among a surety, the issuer of an agreement of assumption and guarantee of workers' compensation liabilities, the issuer of a letter of credit, any custodian of the security deposit, a self-insured employer, or the Self-Insurers' Security Fund shall be resolved by the director. An appeal from the director's decision or determination may be taken to the appropriate superior court by petition for writ of mandate. Payment of claims from the security deposit or by the Self-Insurers' Security Fund shall not be stayed pending the resolution of the disputes unless and until the superior court issues a determination staying a payment of claims decision or determination of the director.

Ref.: 8 C.C.R. §§15201, 15203.1, 15203.5, 15203.8, 15203.9, 15210, 15210.1, 15210.2, 15210.3, 15211.2, 15211.3, 15212, 15213, 15214, 15215, 15216, 15251, 15301, 15302, 15303, 15420, 15422, 15424, 15425, 15426, 15427, 15428, 15430, 15430.1, 15431, 15431.1, 15431.2, 15432, 15433, 15434, 15435, 15436, 15437, 15438, 15450.1, 15470, 15472, 15475, 15477, 15478, 15479, 15480, 15481; Hanna §§ 2.11[1], 2.11[5]; W. Cal. Sum., 2 "Workers' Compensation" §148.

§3701.7. Special conditions to be met after period of unlawful uninsurance.

Where any employer requesting coverage under a new or existing certificate of consent to self-insure has had a period of unlawful uninsurance, either for an applicant in its entirety or for a subsidiary or member of a joint powers authority legally responsible for its own workers' compensation obligations, the following special conditions shall apply before the requesting employer can operate under a certificate of consent to self-insure:

(a) The director may require a deposit of not less than 200 percent of the outstanding liabilities remaining unpaid at the time of application, which had been incurred during the uninsurance period.

(b) At the discretion of the director, where a public or private employer has been previously totally uninsured for workers' compensation pursuant to Section 3700, the director may require an additional deposit not to exceed 100 percent of the total outstanding liabilities for the uninsured period, or the sum of two hundred fifty thousand dollars ($250,000), whichever is greater.

(c) In addition to the deposits required by subdivisions (a) and (b), a penalty shall be paid to the Uninsured Employers Fund of 10 percent per year of the remaining unpaid liabilities, for every year liabilities remain outstanding. In addition, an additional application fee, not to exceed one thousand dollars ($1,000), plus assessments, pursuant to Section 3702.5 and subdivision (b) of Section 3745, may be imposed by the director and the Self-Insurers' Security Fund, respectively, against private self-insured employers.

(d) An employer may retrospectively insure the outstanding liabilities arising out of the uninsured period, either before or after an application for self-insurance has been approved. Upon proof of insurance acceptable to the director, no deposit shall be required for the period of uninsurance.

The penalties to be paid to the Uninsured Employers Fund shall consist of a one-time payment of 20 percent of the outstanding liabilities for the period of uninsurance remaining unpaid at the time of application, in lieu of any other penalty for being unlawfully uninsured pursuant to this code.

(e) In the case of a subsidiary which meets all of the following conditions, a certificate shall issue without penalty:

(1) The subsidiary has never had a certificate revoked for reasons set forth in Section 3702.

(2) Employee injuries were reported to the Office of Self-Insurance Plans in annual reports.

(3) The security deposit of the certificate holder was calculated to include the entity's compensation liabilities.

(4) Application for a separate certificate or corrected certificate is made within 90 days and completed within 180 days of notice from the Office of Self-Insurance Plans. If the requirements of this subdivision are not met, all penalties pursuant to subdivision (b) of Section 3702.9 shall apply.

(f) The director may approve an application on the date the application is substantially completed, subject to completion requirements, and may make the certificate effective on an earlier date, covering a period of uninsurance, if the employer complies with the requirements of this section.

(g) Any decision by the director may be contested by an entity in the manner provided in Section 3701.5.

(h) Nothing in this section shall abrogate the right of an employee to bring an action against an uninsured employer pursuant to Section 3706.

(i) Nothing in this statute shall abrogate the right of a self-insured employer to insure against known or unknown claims arising out of the self-insurance period.

Ref.: 8 C.C.R. §15210.1; Hanna § 2.11[1]; W. Cal. Sum., 2 "Workers' Compensation" §148.

§3701.8. Alternative security system for securing aggregate liabilities of private, self-insured employers through the Self-Insurers' Security Fund.

(a) As an alternative to each private self-insuring employer securing its own incurred liabilities as provided in Section 3701, the director may provide by regulation for an alternative security system whereby all private self-insureds designated for full participation by the director shall collectively secure their aggregate incurred liabilities through the Self-Insurers' Security Fund. The regulations shall provide for the director to set a total security requirement for these participating self-insured employers based on a review of their annual reports and any other self-insurer information as may be specified by the director. The Self-Insurers' Security Fund shall propose to the director a combination of cash and securities, surety bonds, irrevocable letters of credit, insurance, or other financial instruments or guarantees satisfactory to the director sufficient to meet the security requirement set by the director. Upon approval by the director and posting by the Self-Insurers' Security Fund on or before the date set by the director, that combination shall be the composite deposit. The noncash elements of the composite deposit may be one-year or multiple-year instruments. If the Self-Insurers' Security Fund fails to post the required composite deposit by the date set by the director, then within 30 days after that date, each private self-insuring employer shall secure its incurred liabilities in the manner required by Section 3701. Self-insured employers not designated for full participation by the director shall meet all requirements as may be set by the director pursuant to subdivision (g).

(b) In order to provide for the composite deposit approved by the director, the Self-Insurers' Security Fund shall assess, in a manner approved by the director, each fully participating private self-insuring employer a deposit assessment payable within 30 days of assessment. The amount of the deposit assessment charged each fully participating self-insured employer shall be set by the Self-Insurers' Security Fund, based on its reasonable consideration of all the following factors:

(1) The total amount needed to provide the composite deposit.

(2) The self-insuring employer's paid or incurred liabilities as reflected in its annual report.

(3) The financial strength and creditworthiness of the self-insured.

(4) Any other reasonable factors as may be authorized by regulation.

(5) In order to make a composite deposit proposal to the director and set the deposit assessment to be charged each fully participating self-insured, the Self-Insurers' Security Fund shall have access to the annual reports and other information submitted by all self-insuring employers to the director, under terms and conditions as may be set by the director, to preserve the confidentiality of the self-insured's financial information.

(c) Upon payment of the deposit assessment and except as provided herein, the self-insuring employer loses all right, title, and interest in the deposit assessment. To the extent that in any one year the deposit assessment paid by self-insurers is not exhausted in the purchase of securities, surety bonds, irrevocable letters of credit, insurance, or other financial instruments to post with the director as part of the composite deposit, the surplus shall remain posted with the director, and the principal and interest earned on that surplus shall remain as part of the composite deposit in subsequent years. In the event that in any one year the Self-Insurers' Security Fund fails to post the required composite deposit by the date set the by the director, and the director requires each private self-insuring employer to secure its incurred liabilities in the manner required by Section 3701, then any deposit assessment paid in that year shall be refunded to the self-insuring employer that paid the deposit assessment.

(d) If any private self-insuring employer objects to the calculation, posting, or any other aspect of its deposit assessment, upon payment of the assessment in the time provided, the employer shall have the right to appeal the assessment to the director, who shall have exclusive jurisdiction over this dispute. If any private self-insuring employer fails to pay the deposit assessment in the time provided, the director shall order the self-insuring employer to pay a penalty of not less than 10 percent of its deposit assessment, and to post a separate security deposit in the manner provided by Section 3701. The penalty shall be added to the composite deposit held by the director. The director may also revoke the certificate of consent to self-insure of any self-insuring employer who fails to pay the deposit assessment in the time provided.

(e) Upon the posting by the Self-Insurers' Security Fund of the composite deposit with the director, the deposit shall be held until the director determines that a private self-insured employer has failed to pay workers' compensation as required by this division, and the director orders the Self-Insurers' Security Fund to commence payment. Upon ordering the Self-Insurers' Security Fund to commence payment, the director shall make available to the fund that portion of the composite deposit necessary to pay the workers' compensation benefits of the defaulting self-insuring employer. In the event additional funds are needed in subsequent years to pay the workers' compensation benefits of any self-insuring employer who defaulted in earlier years, the director shall make available to the Self-Insurers' Security Fund any portions of the composite deposit as may be needed to pay those benefits. In making the deposit available to the Self-Insurers' Security Fund, the director shall also allow any amounts as may be reasonably necessary to pay for the administrative and other activities of the fund.

(f) The cash portion of the composite deposit shall be segregated from all other funds held by the director, and shall be invested by the director for the sole benefit of the Self-Insurers' Security Fund and the injured workers of private self-insured employers, and may not be used for any other purpose by the state. Alternatively, the director, in his discretion, may allow the Self-Insurers' Security Fund to hold, invest, and draw upon the cash portion of the composite deposit as prescribed by regulation.

(g) Notwithstanding any other provision of this section, the director shall, by regulation, set minimum credit, financial, or other conditions that a private self-insured must meet in order to be a fully participating self-insurer in the alternative security system. In the event any private self-insuring employer is unable to meet the conditions set by the director, or upon application of the Self-Insurers' Security Fund to exclude an employer for credit or financial reasons, the director shall exclude the self-insuring employer from full participation in the alternative security system. In the event a self-insuring employer is excluded from full participation, the nonfully participating private self-insuring employer shall post a separate security deposit in the manner provided by Section 3701 and pay a deposit assessment set by the director. Alternatively, the director may order that the nonfully participating private self-insuring employer post a separate security deposit to secure a portion of its incurred liabilities and pay a deposit assessment set by the director.

(h) An employer who self-insures through group self-insurance and an employer whose certificate to self-insure has been revoked may fully participate in the alternative security system if both the director and the Self-Insurers' Security Fund approve the participation of the self-insurer. If not approved for full participation, or if an employer is issued a certificate to self-insure after the composite deposit is posted, the employer shall satisfy the requirements of subdivision (g) for nonfully participating private self-insurers.

(i) At all times, a self-insured employer shall have secured its incurred workers' compensation liabilities either in the manner required by Section 3701 or through the alternative security system, and there shall not be any lapse in the security. **Leg.H.** 2002 ch. 866 (AB 486).

Ref.: 8 C.C.R. §§15201, 15210, 15210.1, 15210.2, 15216, 15220, 15220.1, 15220.2, 15220.3, 15220.4, 15220.5, 15220.6, 15220.7, 15220.8, 15430; Hanna § 2.11[5]; Herlick Handbook § 3.20.

§3702. Certificate of consent to self-insure; revocation.

(a) A certificate of consent to self-insure may be revoked by the director at any time for good cause after a hearing. Good cause includes, among other things, the impairment of the solvency of the employer to the extent that there is a marked reduction of the employer's financial strength, failure to maintain a security deposit as required by Section 3701, failure to pay assessments of the Self-Insurers' Security Fund, frequent or flagrant violations of state safety and health orders, the failure or inability of the employer to fulfill his or her obligations, or any of the following practices by the employer or his or her agent in charge of the administration of obligations under this division:

(1) Habitually and as a matter of practice and custom inducing claimants for compensation to accept less than the compensation due or making it necessary for them to resort to proceedings against the employer to secure compensation due.

(2) Where liability for temporary disability indemnity is not in dispute, intentionally failing to pay temporary disability indemnity without good cause in order to influence the amount of permanent disability benefits due.

(3) Intentionally refusing to comply with known and legally indisputable compensation obligations.

(4) Discharging or administering his or her compensation obligations in a dishonest manner.

(5) Discharging or administering his or her compensation obligations in such a manner as to cause injury to the public or those dealing with the employer.

(b) Where revocation is in part based upon the director's finding of a marked reduction of the employer's financial strength or the failure or inability of the employer to fulfill his or her obligations, or a practice of discharging obligations in a dishonest manner, it is a condition precedent to the employer's challenge or appeal of the revocation that the employer have in effect insurance against liability to pay compensation.

(c) The director may hold a hearing to determine whether good cause exists to revoke an employer's certificate of consent to self-insure if the employer is cited for a willful, or repeat serious violation of the standard adopted pursuant to Section 6401.7 and the citation has become final.

Ref.: 8 C.C.R. §§9767.1, 15201, 15203, 15203.1, 15203.2, 15203.3, 15203.4, 15203.7, 15203.8, 15203.10, 15210, 15210.1, 15210.2, 15210.3, 15211, 15211.2, 15211.3, 15212, 15213, 15214, 15215, 15216, 15302, 15353, 15354, 15360, 15400, 15402.2, 15420, 15422, 15423, 15424, 15425, 15426, 15427, 15428, 15430, 15431, 15431.1, 15431.2, 15432, 15433, 15434, 15435, 15436, 15437, 15438, 15450, 15450.1, 15452, 15470, 15472, 15479, 15480; Hanna § 2.11[3]; Herlick Handbook § 3.20; W. Cal. Sum., 2 "Workers' Compensation" §148.

§3702.1. Third-party administrators; certificate of consent.

(a) No person, firm, or corporation, other than an insurer admitted to transact workers' compensation insurance in this state, shall contract to administer claims of self-insured employers as a third-party administrator unless in possession of a certificate of consent to administer self-insured employers workers' compensation claims.

(b) As a condition of receiving a certificate of consent, all persons given discretion by a third-party administrator to deny, accept, or negotiate a workers' compensation claim shall demonstrate their competency to the director by written examination, or other methods approved by the director.

(c) A separate certificate shall be required for each adjusting location operated by a third-party administrator. A third-party administrator holding a certificate of consent shall be subject to regulation only under this division with respect to the adjustment, administration, and management of workers' compensation claims for any self-insured employer.

(d) A third-party administrator retained by a self-insured employer to administer the employer's workers' compensation claims shall estimate the total accrued liability of the employer for the payment of compensation for the employer's annual report to the director and shall make the estimate both in good faith and with the exercise of a reasonable degree of care. The use of a third-party administrator shall not, however, discharge or alter the employer's responsibilities with respect to the report.

Ref.: 8 C.C.R. §§10100, 10100.1, 10100.2, 15400, 15400.1, 15400.2, 15402, 15402.1, 15402.2, 15402.4, 15430, 15430.1, 15431, 15431.1, 15431.2, 15432, 15433, 15434, 15435, 15436, 15437, 15438, 15450, 15450.1, 15452, 15454, 15458, 15459, 15463, 15471, 15474, 15475, 15479; Hanna §§ 2.11[2], 2,11[4], 20.01[1][d], 22.14; Herlick Handbook § 3.22; W. Cal. Sum., 2 "Workers' Compensation" §148.

§3702.2. Self-insurer's annual report; director's annual aggregated summary.

(a) All self-insured employers shall file a self-insurer's annual report in a form prescribed by the director.

(b) To enable the director to determine the amount of the security deposit required by subdivision (c) of Section 3701, the annual report of a self-insured employer who has self-insured both state and federal workers' compensation liability shall also set forth (1) the amount of all compensation liability incurred, paid-to-date, and estimated future liability under both this chapter and under the federal Longshore and Harbor Workers' Compensation Act (33 U.S.C. Sec. 901 et seq.), and (2) the identity and the amount of the security deposit securing the employer's liability under state and federal self-insured programs.

(c) The director shall annually prepare an aggregated summary of all self-insured employer liability to pay compensation reported on the self-insurers' employers annual reports, including a separate summary for public and private employer self-insurers. The summaries shall be in the same format as the individual self-insured employers are required to report that liability on the employer self-insurer's annual report forms prescribed by the director. The aggregated summaries shall be made available to the public on the self-insurance section of the department's Internet Web site. Nothing in this subdivision shall authorize the director to release or make available information that is aggregated by industry or business type, that identifies individual self-insured filers, or that includes any individually identifiable claimant information.

(d) The director may release a copy, or make available an electronic version, of the data contained in any public sector employer self-insurer's annual reports received from an individual public entity self-insurer or from a joint powers authority employer and its membership. However, the release of any annual report information by the director shall not include any portion of any listing of open indemnity claims that contains individually identifiable claimant information, or any portion of excess insurance coverage information that contains any individually identifiable claimant information. **Leg.H.** 1993 ch. 917, 2006 ch. 115 (AB 2087) §1.

Ref.: 8 C.C.R. §§15251, 15402.1, 15402.2, 15450.1, 15470, 15472, 15474, 15475, 15479; Hanna §§ 1.19, 2.11[2].

§3702.3. Failure to submit reports or information; fines; handling of funds.

Failure to submit reports or information as deemed necessary by the director to implement the purposes of Section 3701, 3702, or 3702.2 may result in the assessment of a civil penalty as set forth in subdivision (a) of Section 3702.9. Moneys collected shall be used for the administration of self-insurance plans. **Leg.H.** 1992 ch. 532.

Ref.: 8 C.C.R. §§15201, 15203.8, 15210, 15210.1, 15210.2, 15215, 15216, 15251, 15300, 15301, 15302, 15303, 15420, 15422, 15424, 15425, 15426, 15427, 15428, 15450.1, 15479; Hanna § 2.11[2]; W. Cal. Sum., 2 "Workers' Compensation" §148.

§3702.5. Costs of administration of self-insured programs; fines for late filing; handling of funds.

(a) The cost of administration of the public self-insured program by the Director of Industrial Relations shall be a General Fund item. The cost of administration of the private self-insured program by the Director of Industrial Relations shall be borne by the private self-insurers through payment of certificate fees which shall be established by the director in broad ranges based on the comparative numbers of employees insured by the private self-insurers and the number of adjusting locations. The director may assess other fees as necessary to cover the costs of special audits or services rendered to private self-insured employers. The director may assess a civil penalty for late filing as set forth in subdivision (a) of Section 3702.9.

(b) All revenues from fees and penalties paid by private self-insured employers shall be deposited into the Self-Insurance Plans Fund, which is hereby created for the administration of the private self-insurance program. Any unencumbered balance in subdivision (a) of Item 8350-001-001 of the Budget Act of 1983 shall be transferred to the Self-Insurance Plans Fund. The director shall annually eliminate any unused surplus in the Self-Insurance Plans Fund by reducing certificate fee assessments by an appropriate amount in the subsequent year. Moneys paid into the Self-Insurance Plans Fund for administration of the private self-insured program shall not be used by any other department or agency or for any purpose other than administration of the private self-insurance program. Detailed accountability shall be maintained by the director for any security deposit or other funds held in trust for the Self-Insurer's Security Fund in the Self-Insurance Plans Funds.

Moneys held by the director shall be invested in the Surplus Money Investment Fund. Interest shall be paid on all moneys transferred to the General Fund in accordance with Section 16310 of the Government Code. The Treasurer's and Controller's administrative costs may be charged to the interest earnings upon approval of the director. **Leg.H.** 1992 ch. 532.

Ref.: 8 C.C.R. §§15201, 15203, 15204, 15205, 15211, 15211.2, 15212, 15230, 15231, 15233, 15234, 15360, 15400, 15402.3, 15420, 15422, 15423, 15430, 15432, 15433, 15434, 15435, 15436, 15437, 15438, 15454, 15470, 15479; W. Cal. Sum., 2 "Workers' Compensation" §148.

Labor

§3702.6. Audit cycle for private self-insured employers; special audit of public self-insured employers.

(a) The director shall establish an audit program addressing the adequacy of estimates of future liability of claims for all private self-insured employers, and shall ensure that all private self-insured employers are audited within a three-year cycle by the Office of Self Insurance Plans.

(b) Each public self-insurer shall advise its governing board within 90 days after submission of the self-insurer's annual report of the total liabilities reported and whether current funding of those workers' compensation liabilities is in compliance with the requirements of Government Accounting Standards Board Publication No. 10.

(c) The director shall, upon a showing of good cause, order a special audit of any public self-insured employer to determine the adequacy of estimates of future liability of claims.

(d) For purposes of this section, "good cause" means that there exists circumstances sufficient to raise concerns regarding the adequacy of estimates of future liability of claims to justify a special audit. **Leg.H.** 1992 ch. 532.

1989 Note: This section is applicable only to injuries occurring on or after January 1, 1990. Stats. 1989 ch. 893 §6.

Ref.: 8 C.C.R. §§15201, 15210, 15210.1, 15210.2, 15211, 15211.2, 15211.3, 15212, 15213, 15214, 15215, 15216, 15300, 15301, 15302, 15303, 15360, 15400, 15403, 15403.1, 15404, 15404.1, 15404.2, 15405, 15420, 15422, 15423, 15424, 15425, 15426, 15427, 15428, 15430, 15432, 15433, 15434, 15435, 15436, 15437, 15438; Hanna § 2.11[2]; Herlick Handbook § 3.20; W. Cal. Sum., 2 "Workers' Compensation" §11.

§3702.7. Revocation of certificate of consent; fine in lieu of.

A certificate of consent to administer claims of self-insured employers may be revoked by the director at any time for good cause after a hearing. Good cause includes, but is not limited to, the violation of subsection (1), (2), (3), (4), or (5) of subdivision (a) of Section 3702. In lieu of revocation of a certificate of consent, the director may impose a fine of not less than fifty dollars ($50) nor more than five hundred dollars ($500) for each violation.

Ref.: 8 C.C.R. §§15402.2, 15430, 15430.1, 15431, 15431.1, 15431.2, 15432, 15433, 15434, 15435, 15436, 15437, 15438, 15463, 15479; Hanna § 2.11[4]; Herlick Handbook § 3.22; W. Cal. Sum., 2 "Workers' Compensation" §148.

§3702.8. Obligations of former self-insured employers.

(a) Employers who have ceased to be self-insured employers shall discharge their continuing obligations to secure the payment of workers' compensation that accrued during the period of self-insurance, for purposes of Sections 3700, 3700.5, 3706, and 3715, and shall comply with all of the following obligations of current certificate holders:

(1) Filing annual reports as deemed necessary by the director to carry out the requirements of this chapter.

(2) In the case of a private employer, depositing and maintaining a security deposit for accrued liability for the payment of any workers' compensation that may become due, pursuant to subdivision (b) of Section 3700 and Section 3701, except as provided in subdivision (c).

(3) Paying within 30 days all assessments of which notice is sent, pursuant to subdivision (b) of Section 3745, within 36 months from the last day the employer's certificate of self-insurance was in effect. Assessments shall be based on the benefits paid by the employer during the last full calendar year of self-insurance on claims incurred during that year.

(b) In addition to proceedings to establish liabilities and penalties otherwise provided, a failure to comply may be the subject of a proceeding before the director. An appeal from the director's determination shall be taken to the appropriate superior court by petition for writ of mandate.

(c) Notwithstanding subdivision (a), any employer who is currently self-insured or who has ceased to be self-insured may purchase a special excess workers' compensation policy to discharge any or all of the employer's continuing obligations as a self-insurer to pay compensation or to secure the payment of compensation.

(1) The special excess workers' compensation insurance policy shall be issued by an insurer authorized to transact workers' compensation insurance in this state.

(2) Each carrier's special excess workers' compensation policy shall be approved as to form and substance by the Insurance Commissioner, and rates for special excess workers' compensation insurance shall be subject to the filing requirements set forth in Section 11735 of the Insurance Code.

(3) Each special excess workers' compensation insurance policy shall be submitted by the employer to the director. The director shall adopt and publish minimum insurer financial rating standards for companies issuing special excess workers' compensation policies.

(4) Upon acceptance by the director, a special excess workers' compensation policy shall provide coverage for all or any portion of the purchasing employer's claims for compensation arising out of injuries occurring during the period the employer was self-insured in accordance with Sections 3755, 3756, and 3757 of the Labor Code and Sections 11651 and 11654 of the Insurance Code. The director's acceptance shall discharge the Self-Insurer's Security Fund, without recourse or liability to the Self-Insurer's Security Fund, of any continuing liability for the claims covered by the special excess workers' compensation insurance policy.

(5) For public employers, no security deposit or financial guarantee bond or other security shall be required. The director shall set minimum financial rating standards for insurers issuing special excess workers' compensation policies for public employers.

(d)(1) In order for the special excess workers' compensation insurance policy to discharge the full obligations of a private employer to maintain a security deposit with the director for the payment of self-insured claims, applicable to the period to be covered by the policy, the special excess policy shall provide coverage for all claims for compensation arising out of that liability. The employer shall maintain the required deposit for the period covered by the policy with the director for a period of three years after the issuance date of the special excess policy.

(2) If the special workers' compensation insurance policy does not provide coverage for all of the continuing obligations for which the private self-insured employer is liable, to the extent the employer's obligations are not covered by the policy a private employer shall maintain the required deposit with the director. In addition, the employer shall maintain with the director the required deposit for the period covered by the policy for a period of three years after the issuance date of the special excess policy.

(e) The director shall adopt regulations pursuant to Section 3702.10 that are reasonably necessary to implement this section in order to reasonably protect injured workers, employers, the Self-Insurers' Security Fund, and the California Insurance Guarantee Association.

(f) The posting of a special excess workers' compensation insurance policy with the director shall discharge the obligation of the Self-Insurer's Security Fund pursuant to Section 3744 to pay claims in the event of an insolvency of a private employer to the extent of coverage of compensation liabilities under the special excess workers' compensation insurance policy. The California Insurance Guarantee Association shall be advised by the director whenever a special excess workers' compensation insurance policy is posted.

Ref.: 8 C.C.R. §§10103, 10103.1, 10103.2, 15210.2, 15360, 15437; Hanna § 1.19; Herlick Handbook § 3.20.

§3702.9. Director's order for compliance, restitution, and civil penalty.

(a) In addition to remedies and penalties otherwise provided for a failure to secure the payment of compensation, the director may, after a determination that an obligation created in this article has been violated, also enter an order against any self-insured employer, including employers who are no longer self-insured, but who are required to comply with Section 3702.8, directing compliance, restitution for any losses, and a civil penalty in an amount not to exceed the following:

(1) For a failure to file a complete or timely annual report, an amount up to 5 percent of the incurred liabilities in the last report or one thousand five hundred dollars ($1,500), whichever is less, for each 30 days or portion thereof during which there is a failure.

(2) For failure to deposit and maintain a security deposit, an amount up to 10 percent of the increase not timely filed or five thousand dollars ($5,000), whichever is less, for each 30 days or portion thereof during which there is a failure.

(3) For a failure to timely or completely pay an assessment, an amount up to the assessment or two thousand five hundred dollars ($2,500), whichever is less, for each 30 days or portion thereof during which there is a failure.

(4) Where the failure was by an employer which knew or reasonably should have know of the obligation, the director shall, in addition, award reimbursement for all expenditures and costs by the fund or any intervening party, including a reasonable attorney fee.

(5) Where the failure was malicious, fraudulent, in bad faith, or a repeated violation, the director may award, as an additional civil penalty, liquidated damages of up to double the amounts assessed under paragraphs (1) to (4), inclusive, for deposit in the General Fund.

(b) An employer may deposit and maintain a security deposit or pay an assessment, reserving its right to challenge the amount or liability therefor at a hearing. If the director or the appeals board or a court, upon appeal, concludes that the employer is not liable or the amounts are excessive, then the director may waive, release, compromise, refund, or otherwise remit amounts which had been paid or deposited by an employer. The director may condition the waiver, release, compromise, refund, or remittance upon the present and continued future compliance with the obligations of subdivision (a) of Section 3702.8 for a period up to two years.

(c) Notwithstanding subdivision (b), where a violation has occurred, the director may waive, release, compromise, or otherwise reduce any civil penalty otherwise due upon a showing that

Labor

a violation occurred through the employer's mistake, inadvertence, surprise, or excusable neglect. Neglect is not excusable within the meaning of this subdivision where the employer knew, or reasonably should have known, of the obligations.

Ref.: 8 C.C.R. §§15232, 15251, 15430, 15431.1, 15431.2, 15432, 15433, 15434, 15435, 15436, 15437, 15438; Hanna § 2.11[1].

§3702.10. Authorization to adopt, amend, and repeal regulations.

The director, in accordance with Chapter 3.5 (commencing with Section 11340) of Part 1 of Division 3 of Title 2 of the Government Code, may adopt, amend, and repeal rules and regulations reasonably necessary to carry out the purposes of Section 129 and Article 1 (commencing with Section 3700), Article 2 (commencing with Section 3710), and Article 2.5 (commencing with Section 3740). This authorization includes, but is not limited to, the adoption of regulations to do all of the following:

(a) Specifying what constitutes ability to self-insure and to pay any compensation which may become due under Section 3700.

(b) Specifying what constitutes a marked reduction of an employer's financial strength.

(c) Specifying what constitutes a failure or inability to fulfill the employer's obligations under Section 3702.

(d) Interpreting and defining the terms used.

(e) Establishing procedures and standards for hearing and determinations, and providing for those determinations to be appealed to the appeals board.

(f) Specifying the standards, form, and content of agreements, forms, and reports between parties who have obligations pursuant to this chapter.

(g) Providing for the combinations and relative liabilities of security deposits, assumptions, and guarantees used pursuant to this chapter.

(h) Disclosing otherwise confidential financial information concerning self-insureds to courts or the Self-Insurers' Security Fund and specifying appropriate safeguards for that information.

(i) Requiring an amount to be added to each security deposit to secure the cost of administration of claims and to pay all legal costs.

(j) Authorizing and encouraging group self-insurance. **Leg.H.** 1993 ch. 121, effective July 16, 1993.

Ref.: 8 C.C.R. §§15201, 15202, 15203.1, 15203.2, 15203.3, 15203.4, 15203.5, 15203.6, 15203.7, 15203.8, 15203.9, 15203.10, 15204, 15205, 15210, 15210.1, 15211.2, 15211.3, 15212, 15213, 15214, 15215, 15220.1, 15220.2, 15220.4, 15230, 15231, 15232, 15233, 15234, 15250, 15250.1, 15251, 15300, 15301, 15302, 15353, 15354, 15400.1, 15400.2, 15402, 15402.1, 15402.2, 15402.3, 15402.4, 15403, 15403.1, 15404, 15404.1, 15404.2, 15405, 15420, 15424, 15425, 15426, 15427, 15428, 15431.1, 15431.2, 15432, 15433, 15434, 15435, 15436, 15437, 15438, 15452, 15454, 15458, 15459, 15461, 15463, 15470, 15472, 15473, 15474, 15475, 15476, 15477, 15478, 15479, 15480, 15481; Hanna § 2.10[5]; Herlick Handbook § 3.20.

§3703. Self-insurer's independent administration.

So long as the certificate has not been revoked, and the self-insurer maintains on deposit the requisite bond or securities, the self-insurer shall not be required or obliged to pay into the State Compensation Insurance Fund any sums covering liability for compensation excepting life pensions; and the self-insurer may fully administer any compensation benefits assessed against the self-insurer.

Ref.: 8 C.C.R. §§15201, 15203.8, 15211, 15211.2, 15211.3, 15212, 15213, 15214, 15216, 15300, 15303, 15360, 15400, 15420, 15422, 15423, 15424, 15425, 15426, 15427, 15428; Hanna § 2.11[1].

§3705. Surety's equal preference over other debts.

The Self-Insurers' Security Fund or the surety making payment of compensation hereunder shall have the same preference over the other debts of the principal or his or her estate as is given by law to the person directly entitled to the compensation.

Ref.: 8 C.C.R. §§15201, 15203.1, 15211, 15211.2, 15211.3, 15212, 15213, 15214, 15216, 15360, 15400, 15420, 15422, 15423, 15424, 15425, 15426, 15427, 15428, 15430, 15432, 15433, 15434, 15435, 15436, 15437, 15438.

§3706. Employer's failure to secure payment.

If any employer fails to secure the payment of compensation, any injured employee or his dependents may bring an action at law against such employer for damages, as if this division did not apply.

Ref.: Hanna §§ 10.25, 11.02[4], 11.03[2], 21.05[1], 27.12[1][c]; Herlick Handbook §§ 9.2, 12.11; CACI No. 2800 (Matthew Bender); W. Cal. Sum., 2 "Workers' Compensation" §§24, 25, 32, 52, 146, 150, 151.

§3706.5. Exceptions to penalty for failure to secure payment.

The provisions of this article and Sections 4553, 4554, and 4555, and any other penalty provided by law for failure to secure the payment of compensation for employees, shall not apply to individual members of a board or governing body of a public agency or to members of a private, nonprofit organization, if the agency or organization performs officiating services relating to amateur sporting events and such members are excluded from the definition of "employee" pursuant to subdivision (j) of Section 3352.

Ref.: Hanna § 21.05[1].

§3707. Attachment of employer's property.

The injured employee or his dependents may in such action attach the property of the employer, at any time upon or after the institution of such action, in an amount fixed by the court, to secure the payment of any judgment which is ultimately obtained. The provisions of the Code of Civil Procedure, not inconsistent with this division, shall govern the issuance of, and proceedings upon such attachment.

Ref.: W. Cal. Sum., 2 "Workers' Compensation" §53.

§3708. Employer's negligence; presumption; defenses unavailable.

In such action it is presumed that the injury to the employee was a direct result and grew out of the negligence of the employer, and the burden of proof is upon the employer, to rebut the presumption of negligence. It is not a defense to the employer that the employee was guilty of contributory negligence, or assumed the risk of the hazard complained of, or that the injury was caused by the negligence of a fellow servant. No contract or regulation shall restore to the employer any of the foregoing defenses.

This section shall not apply to any employer of an employee, as defined in subdivision (d) of Section 3351, with respect to such employee, but shall apply to employers of employees described in subdivision (b) of Section 3715, with respect to such employees.

Ref.: Hanna §§ 2.17, 11.02[4][e]–[f], 11.03[2]; Herlick Handbook § 2.5; W. Cal. Sum., 2 "Workers' Compensation" §53.

§3708.5. Employee's complaint; service; consolidation of actions.

If an employee brings such an action for damages, the employee shall forthwith give a copy of the complaint to the Uninsured Employers Fund of the action by personal service or certified mail. Proof of such service shall be filed in such action. If a civil action has been initiated against the employer pursuant to Section 3717, the actions shall be consolidated.

Ref.: W. Cal. Sum., 2 "Workers' Compensation" §53.

§3709. Judgments.

If, as a result of such action for damages, a judgment is obtained against the employer, any compensation awarded, paid, or secured by the employer shall be credited against the judgment. The court shall allow as a first lien against such judgment the amount of compensation paid by the director from the Uninsured Employers Fund pursuant to Section 3716.

Such judgment shall include a reasonable attorney's fee fixed by the court. The director, as administrator of the Uninsured Employers Fund, shall have a first lien against any proceeds of settlement in such action, before or after judgment, in the amount of compensation paid by the director from the Uninsured Employers Fund pursuant to section 3716.

No satisfaction of a judgment in such action, in whole or in part, shall be valid as against the director without giving the director notice and a reasonable opportunity to perfect and satisfy his lien.

Ref.: Herlick Handbook § 12.11; W. Cal. Sum., 2 "Workers' Compensation" §§52, 53.

§3709.5. Employer's and Uninsured Employers Fund's relief from obligation to pay more.

After the payment of attorney's fees fixed by the court, the employer shall be relieved from the obligation to pay further compensation to or on behalf of the employee under this division up to the entire amount of the balance of the judgment, if satisfied, or such portion as has been satisfied.

After the satisfaction by the employer of the attorney's fees fixed by the court, the Uninsured Employers Fund shall be relieved from the obligation to pay further compensation to or on behalf of the employee pursuant to Section 3716, up to the entire amount of thc balance of the judgment, if satisfied, or such portion as has been satisfied.

The appeals board shall allow as a credit to the employer and to the Uninsured Employers Fund, to be applied against the liability for compensation, the amount recovered by the employee in such action, either by settlement or after the judgment, as has not been applied to the expense of attorney's fees and costs.

Ref.: W. Cal. Sum., 2 "Workers' Compensation" §52.

ARTICLE 2
Uninsured Employers Fund

§3710. Director of Industrial Relations; powers; "director."

(a) The Director of Industrial Relations shall enforce the provisions of this article. He may employ necessary investigators, clerks, and other employees, and make use of the services of any employee of the department whom he may assign to assist him in the enforcement of this article. Prosecutions for criminal violations of this division may be conducted by the appropriate public official of the county in which the offense is committed, by the Attorney General, or by any attorney in the civil service of the Department of Industrial Relations designated by the director for such purpose.

(b) The director, in accordance with the provisions of Chapter 4 (commencing at Section 11370) of Part 1 of Division 3 of Title 2 of the Government Code, may adopt, amend and repeal such rules and regulations as are reasonably necessary for the purpose of enforcing and administering this article and as are not inconsistent with law.

(c) As used in this article, "director" means the Director of Industrial Relations or the director's designated agents.

Ref.: 8 C.C.R. §§15550, 15551, 15552, 15553, 15554, 15555, 15556, 15557, 15558, 15559, 15560, 15561, 15562, 15563, 15564, 15565, 15566, 15567, 15568, 15569, 15570, 15571, 15571.5, 15572, 15573, 15574, 15575, 15576, 15578, 15579, 15580, 15581, 15582, 15583, 15584, 15585, 15586, 15587, 15588, 15589, 15590, 15591, 15592, 15593, 15594, 15595, 15596; Herlick Handbook §§ 3.14, 3.19, 3.23; W. Cal. Sum., 2 "Workers' Compensation" §150.

§3710.1. Stop orders.

Where an employer has failed to secure the payment of compensation as required by Section 3700, the director shall issue and serve on such employer a stop order prohibiting the use of employee labor by such employer until the employer's compliance with the provisions of Section 3700. Such stop order shall become effective immediately upon service. Any employee so affected by such work stoppage shall be paid by the employer for such time lost, not exceeding 10 days, pending compliance by the employer. Such employer may protest the stop order by making and filing with the director a written request for a hearing within 20 days after service of such stop order. Such hearing shall be held within 5 days from the date of filing such request. The director shall notify the employer of the time and place of the hearing by mail. At the conclusion of the hearing, the stop order shall be immediately affirmed or dismissed, and within 24 hours thereafter the director shall issue and serve on all parties to the hearing by registered or certified mail a written notice of findings and findings. A writ of mandate may be taken from the findings to the appropriate superior court. Such writ must be taken within 45 days after the mailing of the notice of findings and findings.

Ref.: 8 C.C.R. §§15550, 15551, 15552, 15553, 15554, 15555, 15556, 15557, 15558, 15559, 15560, 15561, 15562, 15563, 15564, 15565, 15566, 15567, 15568, 15569, 15570, 15571, 15571.5, 15572, 15573, 15574, 15575, 15576, 15578, 15579, 15580, 15581, 15582, 15583, 15584, 15585, 15586, 15587, 15588, 15589, 15590, 15591, 15592, 15593, 15594, 15595, 15596; W. Cal. Sum., 2 "Workers' Compensation" §150.

§3710.2. Penalties for failure to observe stop order.

Failure of an employer, officer, or anyone having direction, management, or control of any place of employment or of employees to observe a stop order issued and served upon him or her pursuant to Section 3710.1 is a misdemeanor punishable by imprisonment in the county jail not exceeding 60 days or by a fine not exceeding ten thousand dollars ($10,000), or both. Fines shall be paid into the State Treasury to the credit of the Uninsured Employers Fund. The director may also obtain injunctive and other relief from the courts to carry out the purposes of Section 3710.1. The failure to obtain a policy of workers' compensation insurance or a certificate of consent to self-insure as required by Section 3700 is a misdemeanor in accordance with Section 3700.5. **Leg.H.** 1991 ch. 600.

Ref.: 8 C.C.R. §§15550, 15551, 15552, 15553, 15554, 15555, 15556, 15557, 15558, 15559, 15560, 15561, 15562, 15563, 15564, 15565, 15566, 15567, 15568, 15569, 15570, 15571, 15571.5, 15572, 15573, 15574, 15575, 15576, 15578, 15579, 15580, 15581, 15582, 15583, 15584, 15585, 15586, 15587, 15588, 15589, 15590, 15591, 15592, 15593, 15594, 15595, 15596; W. Cal. Sum., 2 "Workers' Compensation" §§146, 150.

§3710.3. Transmittal of stop orders issued to certain carriers.

Whenever a stop order has been issued pursuant to Section 3710.1 to a motor carrier of property subject to the jurisdiction and control of the Department of Motor Vehicles or to a household goods carrier, passenger stage corporation, or charter-party carrier of passengers subject to the jurisdiction and control of the Public Utilities Commission, the director shall transmit the stop order to the Public Utilities Commission or the Department of Motor Vehicles, whichever has jurisdiction over the affected carrier, within 30 days. **Leg.H.** 1991 ch. 1071, 1996 ch. 1042, effective September 29, 1996, 1998 ch. 485.

Ref.: Herlick Handbook § 3.23.

§3711. Proof of insurance.

The director, an investigator for the Department of Insurance Fraud Bureau or its successor, or a district attorney investigator assigned to investigate workers' compensation fraud may, at any time, require an employer to furnish a written statement showing the name of his or her insurer or the manner in which the employer has complied with Section 3700. Failure of the employer for a period of 10 days to furnish the written statement is prima facie evidence that he or she has failed or neglected in respect to the matters so required. The 10-day period may not be construed to allow an uninsured employer, so found by the director, any extension of time from the application of the provisions of Section 3710.1. An insured employer who fails to respond to an inquiry respecting his or her status as to his or her workers' compensation security shall be assessed and required to pay a penalty of five hundred dollars ($500) to the director for deposit in the State Treasury to the credit of the Uninsured Employers Fund. In any prosecution under this article, the burden of proof is upon the defendant to show that he or she has secured the payment of compensation in one of the two ways set forth in Section 3700. **Leg.H.** 1991 ch. 600, 1992 ch. 1276, 1993 ch. 60, effective June 30, 1993, 2004 ch. 2 (SB 2 Fourth Extra. Sess.), effective March 6, 2005.

Ref.: 8 C.C.R. §§15550, 15551, 15552, 15553, 15554, 15555, 15556, 15557, 15558, 15559, 15560, 15561, 15562, 15563, 15564, 15565, 15566, 15567, 15568, 15569, 15570, 15571, 15571.5, 15572, 15573, 15574, 15575, 15576, 15578, 15579, 15580, 15581, 15582, 15583, 15584, 15585, 15586, 15587, 15588, 15589, 15590, 15591, 15592, 15593, 15594, 15595, 15596; Hanna §§ 2.14, 10.20; Herlick Handbook § 3.23.

§3712. Purpose for compensation laws; court procedure.

(a) The securing of the payment of compensation in a way provided in this division is essential to the functioning of the expressly declared social public policy of this state in the matter of workers' compensation. The conduct or operation of any business or undertaking without full compensation security, in continuing violation of social policy, shall be subject to imposition of business strictures and monetary penalties by the director, including, but not limited to, resort to the superior court of any county in which all or some part of the business is being thus unlawfully conducted or operated, for carrying out the intent of this article.

(b) In a proceeding before the superior court in matters concerned with this article, no filing fee shall be charged to the plaintiff; nor may any charge or cost be imposed for any act or service required of or done by any state or county officer or employee in connection with the proceeding. If the court or the judge before whom the order to show cause in the proceeding is made returnable, finds that the defendant is conducting or operating a business or undertaking without the full compensation security required, the court or judge shall forthwith, and without continuance, issue an order restraining the future or further conduct and operation of the business or undertaking so long as the violation of social public policy continues. The action shall be prosecuted by the Attorney General of California, the district attorney of the county in which suit is brought, the city attorney of any city in which such a business or undertaking is being operated or conducted without full compensation security, or any attorney possessing civil service status who is an employee of the Department of Industrial Relations who may be designated by the director for that purpose. No finding made in the course of any such action is binding on the appeals board in any subsequent proceeding before it for benefits under this division.

Ref.: 8 C.C.R. §§15550, 15551, 15552, 15553, 15554, 15555, 15556, 15557, 15558, 15559, 15560, 15561, 15562, 15563, 15564, 15565, 15566, 15567, 15568, 15569, 15570, 15571, 15571.5, 15572, 15573, 15574, 15575, 15576, 15578, 15579, 15580, 15581, 15582, 15583, 15584, 15585, 15586, 15587, 15588, 15589, 15590, 15591, 15592, 15593, 15594, 15595, 15596; W. Cal. Sum., 2 "Workers' Compensation" §150.

§3714. [See Subsection (d) for Inoperative and Repeal Information] Case hearing and filing procedures.

(a) All cases involving the Uninsured Employers Fund or the Subsequent Injuries Fund as a party or involving death without dependents shall only be heard for conference, mandatory settlement conference pursuant to subdivision (d) of Section 5502, standby conference, or rating calendar at the district Workers' Compensation Appeals Board located in San Francisco, Los Angeles, Van Nuys, Anaheim, Sacramento, or San Diego, except for good cause shown and with the consent of the director. This subdivision shall not apply to trials or hearings pursuant to Section 5309 or to expedited hearings pursuant to subdivision (b) of Section 5502.

(b) For the cases specified in subdivision (a), the presiding judge of the Workers' Compensation Appeals Board located in San Francisco, Los Angeles, Van Nuys, Anaheim, Sacramento, or San Diego shall have the authority, either by standing order or on a case-by-case basis, to order a conference, mandatory settlement conference pursuant to subdivision (d) of Section 5502, standby conference, or rating calendar in which no testimony will be taken to be conducted by telephone conference call among the parties and their attorneys of record who do not reside in the county in which that appeals board is located. The cost of the scheduling of the conference call shall be charged against the appropriate fund of the department.

(c) Any filings of documents necessary for the proceedings specified in subdivisions (a) and (b) may be served on the appeals board and the parties by facsimile machine, but if so served, within five workings days service shall be made on the appeals board and the parties as required by regulation.

(d) This section shall remain in effect for two years commencing on the date that the administrative director certifies and publishes that the rearrangement of judicial resources required by this section, and conference call facilities required for this section are in place. The certification shall be published in the California Notice Register, but shall be required to have been posted in the office of each appeals board at least 30 days prior to that publication. Notwithstanding this section, with the permission of the presiding judge and under standards set by the administrative director, parties may be permitted to conclude existing cases where they were filed. This section shall cease to be operative at the end of that two-year period, and shall be repealed on January 1 following that date. **Leg.H.** 1992 ch. 611.

Ref.: 8 C.C.R. §§15550, 15551, 15552, 15553, 15554, 15555, 15556, 15557, 15558, 15559, 15560, 15561, 15562, 15563, 15564, 15565, 15566, 15567, 15568, 15569, 15570, 15571, 15571.5, 15572, 15573, 15574, 15575, 15576, 15578, 15579, 15580, 15581, 15582, 15583, 15584, 15585, 15586, 15587, 15588, 15589, 15590, 15591, 15592, 15593, 15594, 15595, 15596; Herlick Handbook § 14.15.

§3715. Employee's remedies.

(a) Any employee, except an employee as defined in subdivision (d) of Section 3351, whose employer has failed to secure the payment of compensation as required by this division, or his or her dependents in case death has ensued, may, in addition to proceeding against his or her employer by civil action in the courts as provided in Section 3706, file his or her application with the appeals board for compensation and the appeals board shall hear and determine the application for compensation in like manner as in other claims and shall make the award to the claimant as he or she would be entitled to receive if the employer had secured the payment of compensation as required, and the employer shall pay the award in the manner and amount fixed thereby or shall furnish to the appeals board a bond, in any amount and with any sureties as the appeals board requires, to pay the employee the award in the manner and amount fixed thereby.

(b) Notwithstanding this section or any other provision of this chapter except Section 3708, any person described in subdivision (d) of Section 3351 who is (1) engaged in household domestic service who is employed by one employer for over 52 hours per week, (2) engaged as a part-time gardener in connection with a private dwelling, if the number of hours devoted to the gardening work for any individual regularly exceeds 44 hours per month, or (3) engaged in casual employment where the work contemplated is to be completed in not less than 10 working days, without regard to the number of persons employed, and where the total labor cost of the work is not less than one hundred dollars ($100) (which amount shall not include charges other than for personal services), shall be entitled, in addition to proceeding against his or her employer by civil action in the courts as provided in Section 3706, to file his or her application with the appeals board for compensation. The appeals board shall hear and determine the application for compensation in like manner as in other claims, and shall make the award to the claimant as he or she would be entitled to receive if the person's employer had secured the payment of compensation as required, and the employer shall pay the award in the manner and amount fixed thereby, or shall furnish to the appeals board a bond, in any amount and with any sureties as the appeals board requires, to pay the employee the award in the manner and amount fixed thereby.

It is the intent of the Legislature that the amendments to this section by Chapter 17 of the Statutes of 1977, make no change in the law as it applied to those types of employees covered by this subdivision prior to the effective date of Chapter 1263 of the 1975 Regular Session.

(c) In any claim in which it is alleged that the employer has failed to secure the payment of compensation, the director, only for purposes of this section and Section 3720, shall determine, on the basis of the evidence available to him or her, whether the employer was prima facie illegally uninsured. A finding that the employer was prima facie illegally uninsured shall be made when the director determines that there is sufficient evidence to constitute a prima facie case that the employer employed an employee on the date of the alleged injury and had failed to secure the payment of compensation, and that the employee was injured arising out of, and occurring in the course of, the employment.

Failure of the employer to furnish within 10 days the written statement in response to a written demand for a written statement prescribed in Section 3711, addressed to the employer at its address as shown on the official address record of the appeals board, shall constitute in itself sufficient evidence for a prima facie case that the employer failed to secure the payment of compensation.

A written denial by the insurer named in the statement furnished by the employer as prescribed in Section 3711, that the employer was so insured as claimed, or the nonexistence of a valid certificate of consent to self-insure for the time of the claimed injury, if the statement furnished by the employer claims the employer was self-insured, shall constitute in itself sufficient evidence for a prima facie case that the employer had failed to secure the payment of compensation.

The nonexistence of a record of the employer's insurance with the Workers' Compensation Insurance Rating Bureau shall constitute in itself sufficient evidence for a prima facie case that the employer failed to secure the payment of compensation.

The unrebutted written declaration under penalty of perjury by the injured employee, or applicant other than the employee, that the employee was employed by the employer at the time of the injury, and that he or she was injured in the course of his or her employment, shall constitute, in itself, sufficient evidence for a prima facie case that the employer employed the employee at the time of the injury, and that the employee was injured arising out of, and occurring in the course of, the employment.

(d) When the director determines that an employer was prima facie illegally uninsured, the director shall mail a written notice of the determination to the employer at his or her address as shown on the official address record of the appeals board, and to any other more recent address the director may possess. The notice shall advise the employer of its right to appeal the finding, and that a lien may be placed against the employer's and any parent corporation's property, or the property of substantial shareholders of a corporate employer as defined by Section 3717.

Any employer aggrieved by a finding of the director that it was prima facie illegally uninsured may appeal the finding by filing a petition before the appeals board. The petition shall be filed within 20 days after the finding is issued. The appeals board shall hold a hearing on the petition within 20 days after the petition is filed with the appeals board. The appeals board shall have exclusive jurisdiction to determine appeals of the findings by the director, and no court of this state has jurisdiction to review, annul, or suspend the findings or the liens created thereunder, except as provided by Article 2 (commencing with Section 5950) of Chapter 7 of Part 4 of Division 4.

(e) Any claim brought against an employer under this section may be resolved by the director by compromise and release or stipulated findings and award as long as the appeals board has acquired jurisdiction over the employer and the employer has been given notice and an opportunity to object.

Notice may be given by service on the employer of an appeals board notice of intention to approve the compromise and release or stipulated findings and award. The employer shall have 20 days after service of the notice of intention to file an objection with the appeals board and show good cause therefor.

If the employer objects, the appeals board shall determine if there is good cause for the objection.

If the appeals board finds good cause for the objection, the director may proceed with the compromise and release or stipulated findings and award if doing so best serves the interest of the Uninsured Employers Fund, but shall have no cause of action against the employer under Section 3717 unless the appeals board case is tried to its conclusion and the employer is found liable.

If the appeals board does not find good cause for the objection, and the compromise and release or stipulated findings and award is approved, the Uninsured Employers Fund shall have a cause of action against the employer pursuant to Section 3717.

(f) The director may adopt regulations to implement and interpret the procedures provided for in this section.

Ref.: 8 C.C.R. §§15710, 15720, 15721, 15722, 15723, 15730, 15731; Hanna §§ 10.24[3]–[4], 11.02[4][c]; Herlick Handbook §§ 2.5, 3.2; W. Cal. Sum., 2 "Workers' Compensation" §§52, 150, 153, 154, 187, 5 "Torts" §248.

§3716. Uninsured Employers Benefits Trust Fund.

(a) If the employer fails to pay the compensation required by Section 3715 to the person entitled thereto, or fails to furnish the bond required by Section 3715 within a period of 10 days after notification of the award, the award, upon application by the person entitled thereto, shall be paid by the director from the Uninsured Employers Benefits Trust Fund. The expenses of the director in administering these provisions, directly or by contract pursuant to Section 3716.1, shall be paid from the Workers' Compensation Administration Revolving Fund. Refunds may be paid from the Uninsured Employers Benefits Trust Fund for amounts remitted erroneously to the fund, or the director may authorize offsetting subsequent remittances to the fund.

(b) It is the intent of the Legislature that the Uninsured Employers Benefits Trust Fund is created to ensure that workers who happen to be employed by illegally uninsured employers are not deprived of workers' compensation benefits, and is not created as a source of contribution to insurance carriers, or self-insured, or legally insured employers. The Uninsured Employers Benefits Trust Fund has no liability for claims of occupational disease or cumulative injury unless no employer during the period of the occupational disease or cumulative injury during which liability is imposed under Section 5500.5 was insured for workers' compensation, was permissibly self-insured, or was legally uninsured. No employer has a right of contribution against the Uninsured Employers Benefits Trust Fund for the liability of an illegally uninsured employer under an award of benefits for occupational disease or cumulative injury, nor may an employee in a claim of occupational disease or cumulative injury elect to proceed against an illegally uninsured employer.

(c) The Uninsured Employers Benefits Trust Fund has no liability to pay for medical, surgical, chiropractic, hospital, or other treatment, the liability for which treatment is imposed upon the employer pursuant to Section 4600, and which treatment has been provided or paid for by the State Department of Health Services pursuant to the California Medical Assistance Program.

(d) The Uninsured Employers Benefits Trust Fund shall have no liability to pay compensation, nor shall it be joined in any appeals board proceeding, unless the employer alleged to be illegally uninsured shall first either have made a general appearance or have been served with the application specified in Section 3715 and with a special notice of lawsuit issued by the appeals board. The special notice of lawsuit shall be in a form to be prescribed by the appeals board, and it shall contain at least the information and warnings required by the Code of Civil Procedure to be contained in the summons issued in a civil action. The special notice of lawsuit shall also contain a notice that if the appeals board makes an award against the defendant that his or her house or other dwelling and other property may be taken to satisfy the award in a nonjudicial sale, with no exemptions from execution. The special notice of lawsuit shall, in addition, contain a notice that a lien may be imposed upon the defendant's property without further hearing and before the issuance of an award. The applicant shall identify a legal person or entity as the employer named in the special notice of lawsuit. The reasonable expense of serving the application and special notice of lawsuit, when incurred by the employee, shall be awarded as a cost. Proof of service of the special notice of lawsuit and application shall be filed with the appeals board.

(1) The application and special notice of lawsuit may be served, within or without this state, in the manner provided for service of summons in the Code of Civil Procedure. Thereafter, an employer, alleged to be illegally uninsured, shall notify the appeals board of the address at which it may be served with official notices and papers, and shall notify the appeals board of any changes in the address. No findings, order, decision, award, or other notice or paper need be served in this manner on an employer, alleged to be illegally uninsured, who has been served as provided in this section, and who has not filed an answer, otherwise made a general appearance, or furnished the appeals board with its address. The findings, orders, decisions, awards, or other notice or paper may be mailed to the employer as the board, by regulation, may provide.

(2) Notwithstanding paragraph (1), if the employer alleged to be illegally uninsured has not filed an answer, otherwise made a general appearance, or furnished the appeals board with its address, the appeals board shall serve any findings, order, decision, award, or other notice or paper on the employer by mail at the address the appeals board has for the employer. The failure of delivery at that address or the lack of personal service on an employer who has been served as provided in this section, of these findings, order, decision, award, or other notice or paper, shall not constitute grounds for reopening or invalidating any appeals board action pursuant to Section 5506, or for contesting the validity of any judgment obtained under Section 3716 or 5806, a lien under Section 3720, or a settlement under subdivision (e) of Section 3715.

(3) The board, by regulation, may provide for service procedures in cases where a request for new and further benefits is made after the issuance of any findings and award and a substantial period of time has passed since the first service or attempted service.

(4) The director, on behalf of the Uninsured Employers Benefits Trust Fund, shall furnish information as to the identities, legal capacities, and addresses of uninsured employers known to the director upon request of the board or upon a showing of good cause by the employee or the employee's representative. Good cause shall include a declaration by the employee's representative, filed under penalty of perjury, that the information is necessary to represent the employee in proceedings under this division. **Leg.H.** 1993 ch. 1241, 2003 ch. 228 (AB 1756), effective August 11, 2003.

Ref.: 8 C.C.R. §§15740, 15741; Herlick Handbook §§ 2.5, 3.19, 14.11; W. Cal. Sum., 2 "Workers' Compensation" §§52, 153–155.

Labor

§3716.1. Representation and investigation.

(a) In any hearing, investigation, or proceeding, the Attorney General, or attorneys of the Department of Industrial Relations, shall represent the director and the state. Expenses incident to representation of the director and the state, before the appeals board and in civil court, by the Attorney General or Department of Industrial Relations attorneys, shall be reimbursed from the Workers' Compensation Administration Revolving Fund. Expenses incident to representation by the Attorney General or attorneys of the Department of Industrial Relations incurred in attempts to recover moneys pursuant to Section 3717 of the Labor Code shall not exceed the total amounts recovered by the director on behalf of the Uninsured Employers Benefits Trust Fund pursuant to this chapter.

(b) The director shall assign investigative and claims' adjustment services respecting matters concerning uninsured employers injury cases. The director or his or her representative may make these service assignments within the department, or he or she may contract for these services with the State Compensation Insurance Fund, except insofar as these matters might conflict with the interests of the State Compensation Insurance Fund. The administrative costs associated with these services shall be reimbursed from the Workers' Compensation Administration Revolving Fund and the nonadministrative costs from the Uninsured Employers Benefits Trust Fund, except when a budget impasse requires advances as described in subdivision (c) of Section 62.5. To the extent permitted by state law, the director may contract for audits or reports of services under this section.

(c) Commencing November 1, 2004, the State Compensation Insurance Fund and the director shall report annually to the fiscal committees of both houses of the Legislature and the Director of Finance, regarding any of the following:

(1) The number of uninsured employers claims paid in the previous fiscal year, the total cost of those claims, and levels of reserves for incurred claims.

(2) The administrative costs associated with claims payment activities.

(3) Annual revenues to the Uninsured Employers Benefits Trust Fund from all of the following:

(A) Assessments collected pursuant to subdivision (c) of Section 62.5.

(B) Fines and penalties collected by the department.

(C) Revenues collected pursuant to Section 3717.

(4) Projected annual program and claims costs for the current and upcoming fiscal years. **Leg.H.** 2003 ch. 228 (AB 1756), effective August 11, 2003.

Ref.: 8 C.C.R. §§15740, 15741.

§3716.2. Extent of payments from Uninsured Employers Fund.

Notwithstanding the precise elements of an award of compensation benefits, and notwithstanding the claim and demand for payment being made therefor to the director, the director, as administrator of the Uninsured Employers Fund, shall pay the claimant only such benefits allowed, recognizing proper liens thereon, that would have accrued against an employer properly insured for workers' compensation liability. The Uninsured Employers Fund shall not be liable for any penalties or for the payment of interest on any awards. However, in civil suits by the director to enforce payment of an award, including procedures pursuant to Section 3717, the total amount of the award, including interest, other penalties, and attorney's fees granted by the award, shall be sought. Recovery by the director, in a civil suit or by other means, of awarded benefits in excess of amounts paid to the claimant by the Uninsured Employers Fund shall be paid over to the injured employee or his representative, as the case may be. **Leg.H.** 1999 ch. 83.

Ref.: 8 C.C.R. §§15740, 15741; Hanna §§ 1.21, 2.13, 10.24[7], 27.10[6]; W. Cal. Sum., 2 "Workers' Compensation" §153.

§3716.3. Enforcement of judgment by nonjudicial foreclosure.

(a) Notwithstanding any other provision of law to the contrary, when the director obtains a judgment against an uninsured employer, the director may, in addition to any other remedies provided by law, enforce the judgment by nonjudicial foreclosure. This enforcement shall not be subject to Chapter 4 (commencing with Section 703.010) of Division 2 of Title 9 of Part 2 of the Code of Civil Procedure relating to claiming exemptions after levy.

(b) To enforce the judgment by nonjudicial foreclosure, the director shall record with the county recorder of any county in which real property of the parties against whom the judgment is taken is located, a certified copy of the judgment together with the director's notice of intent to foreclose. The notice of intent to foreclose shall set forth all of the following:

(1) The name, address, and telephone number of the trustee authorized by the director to enforce the lien by sale.

(2) The legal description of the real property to be foreclosed upon.

(3) Proof of service by registered or certified mail on the following:

(A) The parties against whom the foreclosure is sought at their last known address as shown on the official records of the appeals board and as shown on the latest recorded deed, deed of trust, or mortgage affecting the real property which is the subject of the foreclosure.

(B) All of the owners of the real property which is subject to the foreclosure at their last address as shown on the latest equalized assessment roll.

(c) Upon the expiration of 20 days following recording of the judgment and notice of intent to foreclose, the trustee may proceed to sell the real property. Any sale by the trustee shall be conducted in accordance with Article 1 (commencing with Section 2920) of Chapter 2 of Title 14 of Part 4 of Division 3 of the Civil Code applicable to the exercise of powers of sale of property under powers created by mortgages and deeds of trust.

(d) The director may authorize any person, including an attorney, corporation, or other business entity, to act as trustee pursuant to subdivision (b).

(e) Except as provided in subdivision (f), this section shall apply to all judgments which the director has obtained or may obtain pursuant to Section 3717, 3726, or 5806.

(f) This section shall not apply to the principal residence of an employer if the appeals board finds that the employer, on the date of injury, employed 10 or fewer employees. An employer seeking this exemption shall provide proof of payment of tax withholding required pursuant to Division 6 (commencing with Section 13000) of the Unemployment Insurance Code, to assist in determining the number of employees on the date of injury.

1990 Note: Section 3716.3 shall be retroactive in effect and shall apply to all obligations of illegally uninsured employers to the director, regardless of the date of injury to the employee. Stats. 1990 ch. 770 §4.

Ref.: W. Cal. Sum., 2 "Workers' Compensation" §155.

§3716.4. Copy of judgment against carrier may be transmitted to Public Utilities Commission.

Whenever a final judgment has been entered against a motor carrier of property subject to the jurisdiction and control of the Department of Motor Vehicles or a passenger stage corporation, charter-party carrier of passengers, or a household goods carrier subject to the jurisdiction and control of the Public Utilities Commission as a result of an award having been made pursuant to Section 3716.2, the director may transmit to the Public Utilities Commission or the Department of Motor Vehicles, whichever has jurisdiction over the affected carrier, a copy of the judgment along with the name and address of the regulated entity and any other persons, corporations, or entities named in the judgment which are jointly and severally liable for the debt to the State Treasury with a complaint requesting that the Public Utilities Commission or the Department of Motor Vehicles immediately revoke the carrier's Public Utilities Commission certificate of public convenience and necessity or Department of Motor Vehicles motor carrier permit. **Leg.H.** 1991 ch. 1071, 1996 ch. 1042, effective September 29, 1996.

§3716.5. Director's responsibility to designate job classifications of payees.

In the payment of workers' compensation benefits from the Uninsured Employers Fund, the director shall do the following:

(a) Designate the job classifications of employees who are paid compensation from the fund.

(b) Compile data on the job classifications of employees paid compensation from the fund and report this data to the Legislature by November 1, 1990, and annually thereafter.

§3717. Employer's liability to Uninsured Employers Fund; corporation's liability; definitions.

(a) A findings and award that is the subject of a demand on the Uninsured Employers Fund or an approved compromise and release or stipulated findings and award entered into by the director pursuant to subdivision (e) of Section 3715, or a decision and order of the rehabilitation unit of the Division of Workers' Compensation, that has become final, shall constitute a liquidated claim for damages against an employer in the amount so ascertained and fixed by the appeals board, and the appeals board shall certify the same to the director who may institute a civil action against the employer in the name of the director, as administrator of the Uninsured Employers Fund, for the collection of the award, or may obtain a judgment against the employer pursuant to Section 5806. In the event that the appeals board finds that a corporation is the employer of an injured employee, and that the corporation has not secured the payment of compensation as required by this chapter, the following persons shall be jointly and severally liable with the corporation to the director in the action:

(1) All persons who are a parent, as defined in Section 175 of the Corporations Code, of the corporation.

(2) All persons who are substantial shareholders, as defined in subdivision (b), of the corporation or its parent. In the action it shall be

sufficient for plaintiff to set forth a copy of the findings and award of the appeals board relative to the claims as certified by the appeals board to the director and to state that there is due to plaintiff on account of the finding and award of the appeals board a specified sum which plaintiff claims with interest. The director shall be further entitled to costs and reasonable attorney fees, and to his or her investigation and litigation expenses for the appeals board proceedings, and a reasonable attorney fee for litigating the appeals board proceedings. A certified copy of the findings and award in the claim shall be attached to the complaint. The contents of the findings and award shall be deemed proved. The answer or demurrer to the complaint shall be filed within 10 days, the reply or demurrer to the answer within 20 days, and the demurrer to the reply within 30 days after the return day of the summons or service by publication. All motions and demurrers shall be submitted to the court within 10 days after they are filed. At the time the civil action filed pursuant to this section is at issue, it shall be placed at the head of the trial docket and shall be first in order for trial.

Nothing in this chapter shall be construed to preclude informal adjustment by the director of a claim for compensation benefits before the issuance of findings and award wherever it appears to the director that the employer is uninsured and that informal adjustment will facilitate the expeditious delivery of compensation benefits to the injured employee.

(b) As used in this section, "substantial shareholder" means a shareholder who owns at least 15 percent of the total value of all classes of stock, or, if no stock has been issued, who owns at least 15 percent of the beneficial interests in the corporation.

(c) For purposes of this section, in determining the ownership of stock or beneficial interest in the corporation, in the determination of whether a person is a substantial shareholder of the corporation, the rules of attribution of ownership of Section 17384 of the Revenue and Taxation Code shall be applied.

(d) For purposes of this section, "corporation" shall not include:

(1) Any corporation which is the issuer of any security which is exempted by Section 25101 of the Corporations Code from Section 25130 of the Corporations Code.

(2) Any corporation which is the issuer of any security exempted by subdivision (c), (d), or (i) of Section 25100 of the Corporations Code from Sections 25110, 25120, and 25130 of the Corporations Code.

(3) Any corporation which is the issuer of any security which has qualified either by coordination, as provided by Section 25111 of the Corporations Code, or by notification, as provided by Section 25112 of the Corporations Code. **Leg.H.** 1994 ch. 146.

Ref.: Hanna §§ 10.24[4], 10.24[7]; Herlick Handbook § 3.19; W. Cal. Sum., 2 "Workers' Compensation" §§155, 410.

§3717.1. Substantial shareholders and parents joined in action against uninsured employer.

In any claim in which an alleged uninsured employer is a corporation, the director may cause substantial shareholders and parents, as defined by Section 3717, to be joined as parties. Substantial shareholders may be served as provided in this division for service on adverse parties, or if they cannot be found with reasonable diligence, by serving the corporation. The corporation, upon this service, shall notify the shareholder of the service, and mail the served document to him or her at the shareholder's last address known to the corporation.

Ref.: Hanna § 10.24[7]; W. Cal. Sum., 2 "Workers' Compensation" §155.

§3717.2. Board of appeals determination as to shareholder or parent status.

Upon request of the director, the appeals board shall make findings of whether persons are substantial shareholders or parents, as defined in Section 3717. The director may in his or her discretion proceed against substantial shareholders and parents pursuant to Section 3717 without those findings of the appeals board.

Ref.: 8 C.C.R. §§15710, 15720, 15721, 15722, 15723, 15730, 15731; W. Cal. Sum., 2 "Workers' Compensation" §155.

§3718. Joinder of actions against employers; recovered amount paid into State Treasury.

The cause of action provided in Section 3717 and any cause of action arising out of Section 3722 may be joined in one action against an employer. The amount recovered in such action from such employer shall be paid into the State

Treasury to the credit of the Uninsured Employers Fund.

Ref.: 8 C.C.R. §§15550, 15551, 15552, 15553, 15554, 15555, 15556, 15557, 15558, 15559, 15560, 15561, 15562, 15563, 15564, 15565, 15566, 15567, 15568, 15569, 15570, 15571, 15571.5, 15572, 15573, 15574, 15575, 15576, 15578, 15579, 15580, 15581, 15582, 15583, 15584, 15585, 15586, 15587, 15588, 15589, 15590, 15591, 15592, 15593, 15594, 15595, 15596.

§3719. Suit against uninsured employers.

Any suit, action, proceeding, or award brought or made against any employer under Section 3717 may be compromised by the director, or such suit, action, or proceeding may be prosecuted to final judgment as in the discretion of the director may best subserve the interests of the Uninsured Employers Fund.

§3720. Certificate that employer is uninsured; effect; service.

(a) When the appeals board or the director determines under Section 3715 or 3716 that an employer has not secured the payment of compensation as required by this division or when the director has determined that the employer is prima facie illegally uninsured, the director may file for record in the office of the county recorder in the counties where the employer's property is possibly located, a certificate of lien showing the date that the employer was determined to be illegally uninsured or the date that the director has determined that the employer was prima facie illegally uninsured. The certificate shall show the name and address of the employer against whom it was filed, and the fact that the employer has not secured the payment of compensation as required by this division. Upon the recordation, the certificate shall constitute a valid lien in favor of the director, and shall have the same force, effect and priority as a judgment lien and shall continue for 10 years from the time of the recording of the certificate unless sooner released or otherwise discharged. A copy of the certificate shall be served upon the employer by mail, by the director. A facsimile signature of the director accompanied by the seal imprint of the department shall be sufficient for recording purposes of liens and releases or cancellations thereof considered herein. Certificates of liens may be filed in any or all counties of the state, depending upon the information the director obtains concerning the employer's assets.

(b) For purposes of this section, in the event the employer is a corporation, those persons whom either the appeals board finds are the parent or the substantial shareholders of the corporation or its parent, or whom the director finds pursuant to Section 3720.1 to be prima facie the parent or the substantial shareholders of the corporation or its parent, as defined in Section 3717, shall be deemed to be the employer, and the director may file the certificates against those persons.

(c) A person who claims to be aggrieved by the filing of a lien against the property of an uninsured employer because he or she has the same or a similar name, may apply to the director to have filed an amended certificate of lien which shows that the aggrieved applicant is not the uninsured employer which is the subject of the lien. If the director finds that the aggrieved applicant is not the same as the uninsured employer, the director shall file an amended certificate of lien with the county recorder of the county in which the aggrieved applicant has property, which shall show, by reasonably identifying information furnished by the aggrieved applicant, that the uninsured employer and the aggrieved applicant are not the same. If the director does not file the amended certificate of lien within 60 days of application therefor, the applicant may appeal the director's failure to so find by filing a petition with the appeals board, which shall make a finding as to whether the applicant and the uninsured employer are the same.

(d) Liens filed under this section have continued existence independent of, and may be foreclosed upon independently of, any right of action arising out of Section 3717 or 5806. **Leg.H.** 1992 ch. 1226.

Ref.: 8 C.C.R. §§15710, 15720, 15721, 15722, 15723, 15730, 15731; Hanna § 27.10[6][c][i]; Herlick Handbook § 3.19; W. Cal. Sum., 2 "Workers' Compensation" §§154, 155.

§3720.1. Determination of person as prima facie parent or shareholder; appeal of determination.

(a) In any claim in which the alleged uninsured employer is a corporation, for purposes of filing certificates of lien pursuant to Section 3720, the director may determine, according to the evidence available to him or her, whether a

Labor

person is prima facie a parent or substantial shareholder, as defined in Section 3717. A finding that a person was prima facie a parent or substantial shareholder shall be made when the director determines that there is sufficient evidence to constitute a prima facie case that the person was a parent or substantial shareholder.

(b) Any person aggrieved by a finding of the director that he or she was prima facie a parent or substantial shareholder may request a hearing on the finding by filing a written request for hearing with the director. The director shall hold a hearing on the matter within 20 days of the receipt of the request for hearing, and shall mail a notice of time and place of hearing to the person requesting hearing at least 10 days prior to the hearing. The hearing officer shall hear and receive evidence, and within 10 days of the hearing, file his or her findings on whether there is sufficient evidence to constitute a prima facie case that the person was a substantial shareholder or parent. The hearing officer shall serve with his or her findings a summary of evidence received and relied upon, and the reasons for the findings. A party may at his or her own expense require that the hearing proceedings be recorded and transcribed.

(c) A party aggrieved by the findings of the hearing officer may within 20 days apply for a writ of mandate to the superior court. Venue shall lie in the county in which is located the office of the director which issued the findings after the hearing.

Ref.: 8 C.C.R. §§15710, 15720, 15721, 15722, 15723, 15730, 15731; Hanna § 10.24[8][a]–[b]; W. Cal. Sum., 2 "Workers' Compensation" §155.

§3721. Certificate of cancellation of lien.

The director shall provide the employer with a certificate of cancellation of lien after the employer has paid to the claimant or to the Uninsured Employers Fund the amount of the compensation or benefits which has been ordered paid to the claimant, or when the application has finally been denied after the claimant has exhausted the remedies provided by law in those cases, or when the employer has filed a bond in the amount and with such surety as the appeals board approves conditioned on the payment of all sums ordered paid to the claimant, or when, after a finding that the employer was prima facie illegally uninsured, it is finally determined that the finding was in error. The recorder shall make no charge for filing the certificates of lien, for filing amended certificates of lien, or for cancellation when liens are filed in error. Cancellation of lien certificates provided to the employer may be filed for recordation by the employer at his or her expense.

Ref.: 8 C.C.R. §§15710, 15720, 15721, 15722, 15723, 15730, 15731; Hanna § 10.24[8][d].

§3722. Penalty assessments.

(a) At the time the stop order is issued and served pursuant to Section 3710.1, the director shall also issue and serve a penalty assessment order requiring the uninsured employer to pay to the director, for deposit in the State Treasury to the credit of the Uninsured Employers Fund, the sum of one thousand dollars ($1,000) per employee employed at the time the order is issued and served, as an additional penalty for being uninsured at that time.

(b) At any time that the director determines that an employer has been uninsured for a period in excess of one week during the calendar year preceding the determination, the director may issue and serve a penalty assessment order requiring the uninsured employer to pay to the director, for deposit in the State Treasury to the credit of the Uninsured Employers Fund, the greater of (1) twice the amount the employer would have paid in workers' compensation premiums during the period the employer was uninsured, determined according to subdivision (c), or (2) the sum of one thousand dollars ($1,000) per employee employed during the period the employer was uninsured. A penalty assessment issued and served by the director pursuant to this subdivision shall be in lieu of, and not in addition to, any other penalty issued and served by the director pursuant to subdivision (a).

(c) If the employer is currently insured, or becomes insured during the period during which the penalty under subdivision (b) is being determined, the amount an employer would have paid in workers' compensation premiums shall be calculated by prorating the current premium for the number of weeks the employer was uninsured. If the employer is uninsured at the time the penalty under subdivision (b) is being determined, the amount an employer would have paid in workers' compensation premiums shall be calculated by applying the weekly premium per employee calculated according to subdivision (d) of Section 11734 of the Insurance Code to the number of weeks the employer was uninsured. Each employee of the uninsured employer shall be assumed to be assigned to the governing classification for that employer as determined by the director after consultation with the Insurance Commissioner. If the employer contends that the assignment of the governing classification is incorrect, or that any employee should be assigned to a different classification, the employer has the burden to prove that the different classification should be utilized.

(d) If upon the filing of a claim for compensation under this division the Workers' Compensation Appeals Board finds that any employer has not secured the payment of compensation as required by this division and finds the claim either noncompensable or compensable, the appeals board shall mail a copy of their findings to the uninsured employer and the director, together with a direction to the uninsured employer to file a verified statement pursuant to subdivision (e).

After the time for any appeal has expired and the adjudication of the claim has become final, the uninsured employer shall be assessed and pay as a penalty either of the following:

(1) In noncompensable cases, two thousand dollars ($2,000) per each employee employed at the time of the claimed injury.

(2) In compensable cases, ten thousand dollars ($10,000) per each employee employed on the date of the injury.

(e) In order to establish the number of employees the uninsured employer had on the date of the claimed injury in noncompensable cases and on the date of injury in compensable cases, the employer shall submit to the director within 10 days after service of findings, awards, and orders of the Workers' Compensation Appeals Board a verified statement of the number of employees in his or her employ on the date of injury. If the employer fails to submit to the director this verified statement or if the director disputes the accuracy of the number of employees reported by the employer, the director shall use any information regarding the number of employees as the director may have or otherwise obtains.

(f) Except for penalties assessed under subdivision (b), the maximum amount of penalties which may be assessed pursuant to this section is one hundred thousand dollars ($100,000). Payment shall be transmitted to the director for deposit in the State Treasury to the credit of the Uninsured Employers Fund.

(g)(1) The Workers' Compensation Appeals Board may provide for a summary hearing on the sole issue of compensation coverage to effect the provisions of this section.

(2) In the event a claim is settled by the director pursuant to subdivision (e) of Section 3715 by means of a compromise and release or stipulations with request for award, the appeals board may also provide for a summary hearing on the issue of compensability. **Leg.H.** 1991 ch. 600, 2002 ch. 6 (AB 749).

Ref.: 8 C.C.R. §§15550, 15551, 15552, 15553, 15554, 15555, 15556, 15557, 15558, 15559, 15560, 15561, 15562, 15563, 15564, 15565, 15566, 15567, 15568, 15569, 15570, 15571, 15571.5, 15572, 15573, 15574, 15575, 15576, 15578, 15579, 15580, 15581, 15582, 15583, 15584, 15585, 15586, 15587, 15588, 15589, 15590, 15591, 15592, 15593, 15594, 15595, 15596; Hanna § 10.22[2]; Herlick Handbook § 3.19; W. Cal. Sum., 2 "Workers' Compensation" §§150, 153, 7 "Constitutional Law" §146.

§3725. Penalty assessment order; contest procedure.

If an employer desires to contest a penalty assessment order, the employer shall file with the director a written request for a hearing within 15 days after service of the order. Upon receipt of the request, the director shall set the matter for a hearing within 30 days thereafter and shall notify the employer of the time and place of the hearing by mail at least 10 days prior to the date of the hearing. The decision of the director shall consist of a notice of findings and findings which shall be served on all parties to the hearing by registered or certified mail within 15 days after the hearing. Any amount found due by the director as a result of a hearing shall become due and payable 45 days after notice of the findings and written findings have been mailed by registered or certified mail to the party assessed. A writ of mandate may be taken from these findings to the appropriate superior court upon the execution by the party assessed of a bond to the state in double the amount found due and ordered paid by the director, as long as the party agrees to pay any judgment and costs rendered against the party for the assessment. The writ shall be taken within 45 days after mailing the notice of findings and findings.

Ref.: 8 C.C.R. §§15550, 15551, 15552, 15553, 15554, 15555, 15556, 15557, 15558, 15559, 15560,

15561, 15562, 15563, 15564, 15565, 15566, 15567, 15568, 15569, 15570, 15571, 15571.5, 15572, 15573, 15574, 15575, 15576, 15578, 15579, 15580, 15581, 15582, 15583, 15584, 15585, 15586, 15587, 15588, 15589, 15590, 15591, 15592, 15593, 15594, 15595, 15596; Hanna §§ 10.22[4], 22.08[2]; Herlick Handbook §§ 3.19, 14.2.

§3726. Penalty assessment order; uncontested procedure.

(a) When no petition objecting to a penalty assessment order is filed, a certified copy of the order may be filed by the director in the office of the clerk of the superior court in any country in which the employer has property or in which the employer has or had a place of business. The clerk, immediately upon such filing, shall enter judgment for the state against the employer in the amount shown on the penalty assessment order.

(b) When findings are made affirming or modifying a penalty assessment order after hearing, a certified copy of such order and a certified copy of such findings may be filed by the director in the office of the clerk of the superior court in any county in which the employer has property or in which the employer has or had a place of business. The clerk, immediately upon such filing, shall enter judgment for the state against the employer in the amount shown on the penalty assessment order or in the amount shown in the findings if the order has been modified.

(c) A judgment entered pursuant to the provisions of this section may be filed by the clerk in a looseleaf book entitled "Special Judgments for State Uninsured Employers Fund." Such judgment shall bear the same rate of interest and shall have the same effect as other judgments and be given the same preference allowed by law on other judgments rendered for claims for taxes. The clerk shall make no charge for the service provided by this section to be performed by him.

Ref.: 8 C.C.R. §§15550, 15551, 15552, 15553, 15554, 15555, 15556, 15557, 15558, 15559, 15560, 15561, 15562, 15563, 15564, 15565, 15566, 15567, 15568, 15569, 15570, 15571, 15571.5, 15572, 15573, 15574, 15575, 15576, 15578, 15579, 15580, 15581, 15582, 15583, 15584, 15585, 15586, 15587, 15588, 15589, 15590, 15591, 15592, 15593, 15594, 15595, 15596; Hanna § 10.22[5]; W. Cal. Sum., 2 "Workers' Compensation" §155.

§3727. Certificate of penalty assessment; filing; recording certificate of cancellation.

If the director determines pursuant to Section 3722 that an employer has failed to secure the payment of compensation as required by this division, the director may file with the county recorder of any counties in which such employer's property may be located his certificate of the amount of penalty due from such employer and such amount shall be a lien in favor of the director from the date of such filing against the real property and personal property of the employer within the county in which such certificate is filed. The recorder shall accept and file such certificate and record the same as a mortgage on real estate and shall file the same as a security interest and he shall index the same as mortgage on real estate and as a security interest. Certificates of liens may be filed in any and all counties of the state, depending upon the information the director obtains concerning the employer's assets. The recorder shall make no charge for the services provided by this section to be performed by him. Upon payment of the penalty assessment, the director shall issue a certificate of cancellation of penalty assessment, which may be recorded by the employer at his expense.

Ref.: 8 C.C.R. §§15550, 15551, 15552, 15553, 15554, 15555, 15556, 15557, 15558, 15559, 15560, 15561, 15562, 15563, 15564, 15565, 15566, 15567, 15568, 15569, 15570, 15571, 15571.5, 15572, 15573, 15574, 15575, 15576, 15578, 15579, 15580, 15581, 15582, 15583, 15584, 15585, 15586, 15587, 15588, 15589, 15590, 15591, 15592, 15593, 15594, 15595, 15596; Hanna § 10.22[7].

§3727.1. Withdrawal of stop order or penalty assessment order.

The director may withdraw a stop order or a penalty assessment order where investigation reveals the employer had secured the payment of compensation as required by Section 3700 on the date and at the time of service of such order. The director also may withdraw a penalty assessment order where investigation discloses that the employer was insured on the date and at the time of an injury or claimed injury, or where an insured employer responded in writing to a request to furnish the status of his workers' compensation coverage within the time prescribed.

Ref.: Hanna §§ 10.21[4], 10.22[6]; W. Cal. Sum., 2 "Workers' Compensation" §150.

§3728. Cash revolving fund.

(a) The director may draw from the State Treasury out of the Uninsured Employers Benefits Trust Fund for the purposes of Sections 3716 and 3716.1, without at the time presenting vouchers and itemized statements, a sum not to exceed in the aggregate the level provided for pursuant to Section 16400 of the Government Code, to be used as a cash revolving fund. The revolving fund shall be deposited in any banks and under any conditions as the Department of General Services determines. The Controller shall draw his or her warrants in favor of the Director of Industrial Relations for the amounts so withdrawn and the Treasurer shall pay these warrants.

(b) Expenditures made from the revolving fund in payment of claims for compensation due from the Uninsured Employers Benefits Trust Fund and from the Workers' Compensation Administration Revolving Fund for administrative and adjusting services rendered are exempted from the operation of Section 925.6 of the Government Code. Reimbursement of the revolving fund from the Uninsured Employers Benefits Trust Fund or the Workers' Compensation Administration Revolving Fund for expenditures shall be made upon presentation to the Controller of an abstract or statement of the expenditures. The abstract or statement shall be in any form as the Controller requires. **Leg.H.** 1992 ch. 100, effective June 26, 1992, 2003 ch. 228 (AB 1756), effective August 11, 2003.

§3730. Effect of weekend or holiday on last day for filing.

When the last day for filing any instrument or other document pursuant to this chapter falls upon a Saturday, Sunday, or other holiday, such act may be performed upon the next business day with the same effect as if it had been performed upon the day appointed.

§3731. Personal service of stop orders or penalty assessment orders.

Any stop order or penalty assessment order may be personally served upon the employer either by (1) manual delivery of the order to the employer personally or by (2) leaving signed copies of the order during usual office hours with the person who is apparently in charge of the office and by thereafter mailing copies of the order by first class mail, postage prepaid to the employer at the place where signed copies of the order were left.

Ref.: Hanna § 10.22[3].

§3732. Payment from Uninsured Employers Fund: third party liability.

(a) If compensation is paid or becomes payable from the Uninsured Employers Fund, whether as a result of a findings and award, award based upon stipulations, compromise and release executed on behalf of the director, or payments voluntarily furnished by the director pursuant to Section 4903.3, the director may recover damages from any person or entity, other than the employer, whose tortious act or omission proximately caused the injury or death of the employee. The damages shall include any compensation, including additional compensation by way of interest or penalty, paid or payable by the director, plus the expense incurred by the director in investigating and litigating the workers' compensation claim and a reasonable attorney fee for litigating the workers' compensation claim. The director may compromise, or settle and release any claim, and may waive any claim, including the lien allowed by this section, in whole or in part, for the convenience of the director.

(b) Except as otherwise provided in this section, Chapter 5 (commencing with Section 3850) of Part 1 of Division 4 shall be applicable to these actions, the director being treated as an employer within the meaning of Chapter 5 to the extent not inconsistent with this section.

(c) Actions brought under this section shall be commenced within one year after the later of either the time the director pays or the time the director becomes obligated to pay any compensation from the Uninsured Employers Fund.

(d) In the trial of these actions, any negligence attributable to the employer shall not be imputed to the director or to the Uninsured Employers Fund, and the damages recoverable by the director shall not be reduced by any percentage of fault or negligence attributable to the employer or to the employee.

(e) In determining the credit to the Uninsured Employers Fund provided by Section 3861, the appeals board shall not take into consideration any negligence of the employer, but shall allow a credit for the entire amount of the employee's recovery either by settlement or after judgment, as has not theretofore been applied to the payment of expenses or attorney's fees.

(f) When an action or claim is brought by an employee, his or her guardian, conservator, personal representative, estate, survivors, or heirs against a third party who may be liable for causing the injury or death of the employee, any settlement or judgment obtained is subject to the director's claim for damages recoverable by the director pursuant to subdivision (a), and the director shall have a lien against any settlement in the amount of the damages.

(g) No judgment or settlement in any action or claim by an employee, his or her guardian, conservator, personal representative, survivors, or heirs to recover damages for injuries, where the director has an interest, shall be satisfied without first giving the director notice and a reasonable opportunity to perfect and satisfy his or her lien. The director shall be mailed a copy of the complaint in the third-party action as soon as reasonable after it is filed with the court.

(h) When the director has perfected a lien upon a judgment or settlement in favor of an employee, his or her guardian, conservator, personal representative, survivors or heirs against any third party, the director shall be entitled to a writ of execution as a lien claimant to enforce payment of the lien against the third party with interest and other accruing costs as in the case of other executions. In the event the amount of the judgment or settlement so recovered has been paid to the employee, his or her guardian, conservator, personal representative, survivors, or heirs, the director shall be entitled to a writ of execution against the employee, his or her guardian, conservator, personal representative, survivors, or heirs to the extent of the director's lien, with interest and other accruing costs as in the cost of other executions.

(i) Except as otherwise provided in this section, notwithstanding any other provision of law, the entire amount of any settlement of the action or claim of the employee, his or her guardian, conservator, personal representative, survivors, or heirs, with or without suit, is subject to the director's lien claim for the damages recoverable by the director pursuant to subdivision (a).

(j) Where the action or claim is brought by the employee, his or her guardian, conservator, personal representative, estate, survivors, or heirs, and the director has not joined in the action, and the employee, his or her guardian, conservator, personal representative, estate, survivors, or heirs incur a personal liability to pay attorney's fees and costs of litigation, the director's claim for damages shall be limited to the amount of the director's claim for damages less that portion of the costs of litigation expenses determined by multiplying the total cost of litigation expenses by the ratio of the full amount of the director's claim for damages to the full amount of the judgment, award, or settlement, and less 25 percent of the balance after subtracting the director's share of litigation expenses, which represents the director's reasonable share of attorney's fees incurred.

(k) In the trial of the director's action for damages, and in the allowance of his or her lien in an action by the employee, guardian, executor, personal representative, survivors, or heirs, the compensation paid from the Uninsured Employers Fund pursuant to an award as provided in Section 3716 is conclusively presumed to be reasonable in amount and to be proximately caused by the event or events which caused the employee's injury or death.

(*l*) In the action for damages the director shall be entitled to recover, if he or she prevails, the entire amount of the damages recoverable by the director pursuant to subdivision (a), regardless of whether the damages recoverable by the employee, guardian, conservator, personal representative, survivors, or heirs are of lesser amount.

Ref.: Hanna §§ 11.42[3][b], 11.44[3], 27.10[6][c][ii]; W. Cal. Sum., 2 "Workers' Compensation" §156.

ARTICLE 2.5
Self-Insurers' Security Fund

§3740. Intent of Legislature.

It is the intent of the Legislature in enacting this article and Article 1 (commencing with Section 3700) to provide for the continuation of workers' compensation benefits delayed due to the failure of a private self-insured employer to meet its compensation obligations when the employers' security deposit is either inadequate or not immediately accessible for the payment of benefits. With respect to the continued liability of a surety for claims that arose under a bond after termination of that bond and to a surety's liability for the cost of administration of claims, it is the intent of the Legislature to clarity existing law. The Legislature finds and declares that the establishment of the Self-Insurers' Security Fund is a necessary component of a complete system of workers' compensation, required by Section 4 of Article XIV of the California Constitution, to have adequate provisions for the comfort, health and safety, and general welfare of any and all workers and their dependents to the extent of relieving the consequences of any industrial injury or death, and full provision for securing the payment of compensation.

Ref.: 8 C.C.R. §§15201, 15210, 15210.1, 15210.2, 15210.3, 15211, 15211.2, 15211.3, 15212, 15213, 15214, 15215, 15216, 15300, 15301, 15302, 15303, 15360, 15420, 15422, 15424, 15425, 15426, 15427, 15428, 15430, 15430.1, 15431, 15431.1, 15431.2, 15432, 15433, 15434, 15435, 15436, 15437, 15438, 15478; Hanna § 2.11[5]; Herlick Handbook § 3.20; W. Cal. Sum., 2 "Workers' Compensation" §148.

§3741. Definitions.

As used in this article:

(a) "Director" means the Director of Industrial Relations.

(b) "Private self-insurer" means a private employer which has secured the payment of compensation pursuant to subdivision (b) of Section 3700.

(c) "Insolvent self-insurer" means a private self-insurer who has failed to pay compensation and whose security deposit has been called by the director pursuant to Section 3701.5.

(d) "Fund" means the Self-Insurers' Security Fund established pursuant to Section 3742.

(e) "Trustees" means the Board of Trustees of the Self-Insurers' Security Fund.

(f) "Member" means a private self-insurer which participates in the Self-Insurers' Security Fund.

Ref.: 8 C.C.R. §§15201, 15210, 15210.1, 15210.2, 15211, 15211.2, 15211.3, 15212, 15213, 15214, 15215, 15216, 15300, 15301, 15302, 15303, 15360, 15420, 15422, 15424, 15425, 15426, 15427, 15428, 15430, 15430.1, 15431, 15431.1, 15431.2, 15432, 15433, 15434, 15435, 15436, 15437, 15438, 15478.

§3742. Establishment of fund; governing board; bylaws; obligations; requirement of fund members.

(a) The Self-Insurers' Security Fund shall be established as a Nonprofit Mutual Benefit Corporation pursuant to Part 3 (commencing with Section 7110) of Division 2 of Title 1 of the Corporations Code and this article. If any provision of the Nonprofit Mutual Benefit Corporation Law conflicts with any provision of this article, the provisions of this article shall apply. Each private self-insurer shall participate as a member in the fund as a condition of maintaining its certificate of consent to self-insure.

(b) The fund shall be governed by a seven member board of trustees. The director shall hold ex officio status, with full powers equal to those of a trustee, except that the director shall not have a vote. The director, or a delegate authorized in writing to act as the director's representative on the board of trustees, shall carry out exclusively the responsibilities set forth in Division 1 (commencing with Section 50) through Division 4 (commencing with Section 3200) and shall not have the obligations of a trustee under the Nonprofit Mutual Benefit Corporation Law. The fund shall adopt bylaws to segregate the director from all matters that may involve fund litigation against the department or fund participation in legal proceedings before the director. Although not voting, the director or a delegate authorized in writing to represent the director, shall be counted toward a quorum of trustees. The remaining six trustees shall be representatives of private self-insurers. The self-insurer trustees shall be elected by the members of the fund, each member having one vote. Three of the trustees initially elected by the members shall serve two-year terms, and three shall serve four-year terms. Thereafter, trustees shall be elected to four-year terms, and shall serve until their successors are elected and assume office pursuant to the bylaws of the fund.

(c) The fund shall establish bylaws as are necessary to effectuate the purposes of this article and to carry out the responsibilities of the fund, including, but not limited to, any obligations imposed by the director pursuant to Section 3701.8. The fund may carry out its responsibilities directly or by contract, and may purchase services and insurance and borrow funds as it deems necessary for the protection of the members and their employees. The fund may receive confidential information concerning the financial condition of self-insured employers whose liabilities to pay compensation may devolve upon it and shall adopt bylaws to prevent dissemination of that information.

(d) The director may also require fund members to subscribe to financial instruments or guarantees to be posted with the director in

Labor

order to satisfy the security requirements set by the director pursuant to Section 3701.8. **Leg.H.** 2002 ch. 866 (AB 486).

Ref.: 8 C.C.R. §§15201, 15210, 15210.1, 15210.2, 15211, 15211.2, 15211.3, 15212, 15213, 15214, 15215, 15216, 15300, 15301, 15302, 15303, 15360, 15420, 15422, 15424, 15425, 15426, 15427, 15428, 15430, 15430.1, 15431, 15431.1, 15431.2, 15432, 15433, 15434, 15435, 15436, 15437, 15438, 15478; W. Cal. Sum., 2 "Workers' Compensation" §148.

§3743. Assumption of workers' compensation obligations.

(a) Upon order of the director pursuant to Section 3701.5, the fund shall assume the workers' compensation obligations of an insolvent self-insurer.

(b) Notwithstanding subdivision (a), the fund shall not be liable for the payment of any penalties assessed for any act or omission on the part of any person other than the fund, including, but not limited to, the penalties provided in Section 132a, 3706, 4553, 4554, 4556, 4557, 4558, 4601.5, 5814, or 5814.1.

(c) The fund shall be a party in interest in all proceedings involving compensation claims against an insolvent self-insurer whose compensation obligations have been paid or assumed by the fund. The fund shall have the same rights and defenses as the insolvent self-insurer, including, but not limited to, all of the following:

(1) To appear, defend, and appeal claims.

(2) To receive notice of, investigate, adjust, compromise, settle, and pay claims.

(3) To investigate, handle, and deny claims.

Ref.: 8 C.C.R. §§9767.1, 9767.4, 9767.8, 15201, 15210, 15210.2, 15210.3, 15211, 15211.2, 15211.3, 15212, 15213, 15214, 15216, 15300, 15301, 15302, 15303, 15360, 15420, 15422, 15424, 15425, 15426, 15427, 15428, 15430, 15430.1, 15431, 15431.1, 15431.2, 15432, 15433, 15434, 15435, 15436, 15437, 15438, 15478; Hanna §§ 2.11[5], 11.41; W. Cal. Sum., 2 "Workers' Compensation" §148.

§3744. Rights and obligations of fund.

(a) The fund shall have the right and obligation to obtain reimbursement from an insolvent self-insurer up to the amount of the self-insurer's workers' compensation obligations paid and assumed by the fund, including reasonable administrative and legal costs. This right includes, but is not limited to, a right to claim for wages and other necessities of life advanced to claimants as subrogee of the claimants in any action to collect against the self-insured as debtor.

(b) The fund shall have the right and obligation to obtain from the security deposit of an insolvent self-insurer the amount of the self-insurer's compensation obligations, including reasonable administrative and legal costs, paid or assumed by the fund. Reimbursement of administrative costs, including legal costs, shall be subject to approval by a majority vote of the fund's trustees. The fund shall be a party in interest in any action to obtain the security deposit for the payment of compensation obligations of an insolvent self-insurer.

(c) The fund shall have the right to bring an action against any person to recover compensation paid and liability assumed by the fund, including, but not limited to, any excess insurance carrier of the self-insured employer, and any person whose negligence or breach of any obligation contributed to any underestimation of the self-insured employer's total accrued liability as reported to the director.

(d) The fund may be a party in interest in any action brought by any other person seeking damages resulting from the failure of an insolvent self-insurer to pay workers' compensation required pursuant to this division.

Ref.: 8 C.C.R. §§15201, 15210, 15210.2, 15210.3, 15211, 15211.2, 15211.3, 15212, 15213, 15214, 15216, 15300, 15301, 15302, 15303, 15360, 15420, 15422, 15424, 15425, 15426, 15427, 15428, 15430, 15430.1, 15431, 15431.1, 15431.2, 15432, 15433, 15434, 15435, 15436, 15437, 15438, 15478; W. Cal. Sum., 2 "Workers' Compensation" §148.

§3745. Maintenance of assets; assessment of members.

(a) The fund shall maintain cash, readily marketable securities, or other assets, or a line of credit, approved by the director, sufficient to immediately continue the payment of the compensation obligations of an insolvent self-insurer pending assessment of the members. The director may establish the minimum amount to be maintained by, or immediately available to, the fund for this purpose.

(b) The fund may assess each of its members a pro rata share of the funding necessary to carry out the purposes of this article. However, no member shall be assessed at one time in excess of 1.5 percent of the benefits paid by the member for claims incurred during the previous calendar year as a self-insurer, and total annual assessments in any calendar year shall not exceed 2 percent of the benefits paid for claims incurred during the previous calendar year. Funds obtained by assessments pursuant to this subdivision may only be used for the purposes of this article.

(c) The trustees shall certify to the director the collection and receipt of all moneys from assessments, noting any delinquencies. The trustees shall take any action deemed appropriate to collect any delinquent assessments.

Ref.: 8 C.C.R. §§15201, 15210, 15210.2, 15211, 15211.3, 15213, 15214, 15216, 15220.4, 15300, 15301, 15302, 15303, 15360, 15420, 15422, 15424, 15425, 15426, 15427, 15428, 15430, 15430.1, 15431, 15431.1, 15431.2, 15432, 15433, 15434, 15435, 15436, 15437, 15438, 15478.

§3746. Annual contract for audit; annual report.

The trustees shall annually contract for an independent certified audit of the financial activities of the fund. An annual report on the financial status of the fund as of June 30 shall be submitted to the director and to each member.

Ref.: 8 C.C.R. §§15201, 15430, 15430.1, 15431, 15431.1, 15431.2, 15432, 15433, 15434, 15435, 15436, 15437, 15438, 15478.

§3747. How to refer to article.

This article shall be known and may be referred to as the "Young-La Follette Self-Insurers' Security Act."

Ref.: 8 C.C.R. §§15201, 15430, 15430.1, 15431, 15431.1, 15431.2, 15432, 15433, 15434, 15435, 15436, 15437, 15438, 15478.

ARTICLE 3
Insurance Rights and Privileges

§3750. Limitations on division.

Nothing in this division shall affect:

(a) The organization of any mutual or other insurer.

(b) Any existing contract for insurance.

(c) The right of the employer to insure in mutual or other insurers, in whole or in part, against liability for the compensation provided by this division.

(d) The right to provide by mutual or other insurance, or by arrangement with his employees, or otherwise, for the payment to such employees, their families, dependents or representatives, of sick, accident, or death benefits, in addition to the compensation provided for by this division.

(e) The right of the employer to waive the waiting period provided for herein by insurance coverage.

§3751. Cost of compensation; no employee contribution; violation; no employee payments to medical provider while claim pending.

(a) No employer shall exact or receive from any employee any contribution, or make or take any deduction from the earnings of any employee, either directly or indirectly, to cover the whole or any part of the cost of compensation under this division. Violation of this subdivision is a misdemeanor.

(b) If an employee has filed a claim form pursuant to Section 5401, a provider of medical services shall not, with actual knowledge that a claim is pending, collect money directly from the employee for services to cure or relieve the effects of the injury for which the claim form was filed, unless the medical provider has received written notice that liability for the injury has been rejected by the employer and the medical provider has provided a copy of this notice to the employee. Any medical provider who violates this subdivision shall be liable for three times the amount unlawfully collected, plus reasonable attorney's fees and costs.

Ref.: 8 C.C.R. §§10107, 10107.1; Hanna §§ 2.10[2], 11.02[4][b][i]; Herlick Handbook §§ 3.2, 4.19, 4.21, 9.5; W. Cal. Sum., 2 "Workers' Compensation" §§77, 192, 337, 338, 343, 376, 386.

§3752. Effect of insurance or other benefits.

Liability for compensation shall not be reduced or affected by any insurance, contribution or other benefit whatsoever due to or received by the person entitled to such compensation, except as otherwise provided by this division.

Ref.: 8 C.C.R. §§10107, 10107.1; Hanna §§ 2.10[2], 7.04[9][b]; Herlick Handbook § 12.15; W. Cal. Sum., 2 "Workers' Compensation" §343.

§3753. Effect of insurance.

The person entitled to compensation may, irrespective of any insurance or other contract, except as otherwise provided in this division, recover such compensation directly from the employer. In addition thereto, he may enforce in his own name, in the manner provided by this division the liability of any insurer either by making the insurer a party to the original application or by filing a separate application for any portion of such compensation.

Ref.: 8 C.C.R. §9811; Hanna § 2.71; W. Cal. Sum., 2 "Workers' Compensation" §349.

§3754. Effect of amount paid on recovery.

Payment in whole or in part of compensation by either the employer or the insurer shall, to the extent thereof, be a bar to recovery against each of them of the amount so paid.

§3755. Substitution of insurer.

If the employer is insured against liability for compensation, and if after the suffering of any injury the insurer causes to be served upon any compensation claimant a notice that it has assumed and agreed to pay any compensation to the claimant for which the employer is liable, such employer shall be relieved from liability for compensation to such claimant upon the filing of a copy of such notice with the appeals board. The insurer shall, without further notice, be substituted in place of the employer in any proceeding theretofore or thereafter instituted by such claimant to recover such compensation, and the employer shall be dismissed therefrom.

Such proceedings shall not abate on account of such substitution but shall be continued against such insurer.

Ref.: Hanna § 25.28; Herlick Handbook §§ 14.7, 14.43; W. Cal. Sum., 2 "Workers' Compensation" §§149, 349.

§3756. Notice of insurer liability.

If at the time of the suffering of a compensable injury, the employer is insured against liability for the full amount of compensation payable, he may cause to be served upon the compensation claimant and upon the insurer a notice that the insurer has agreed to pay any compensation for which the employer is liable. The employer may also file a copy of such notice with the appeals board.

Ref.: Hanna § 25.28.

§3757. Substitution of insurer; employer's relief from liability.

If it thereafter appears to the satisfaction of the appeals board that the insurer has assumed the liability for compensation, the employer shall thereupon be relieved from liability for compensation to the claimant. The insurer shall, after notice, be substituted in place of the employer in any proceeding instituted by the claimant to recover compensation, and the employer shall be dismissed therefrom.

Ref.: Hanna § 25.28; W. Cal. Sum., 2 "Workers' Compensation" §149.

§3758. Substitution of insurer; no abatement of proceeding.

A proceeding to obtain compensation shall not abate on account of substitution of the insurer in place of the employer and on account of the dismissal of the employer, but shall be continued against such insurer.

Ref.: Hanna § 25.28.

§3759. Joinder of insurer; employer's relief from liability.

The appeals board may enter its order relieving the employer from liability where it appears from the pleadings, stipulations, or proof that an insurer joined as party to the proceeding is liable for the full compensation for which the employer in such proceeding is liable.

Ref.: Herlick Handbook §§ 3.6, 14.43; W. Cal. Sum., 2 "Workers' Compensation" §149.

§3760. Employer notice to insurer.

Every employer who is insured against any liability imposed by this division shall file with the insurer a complete report of every injury to each employee as specified in Section 6409.1. If not so filed, the insurer may petition the appeals board for an order, or the appeals board may of its own motion issue an order, directing the employer to submit a report of the injury within five days after service of the order. Failure of the employer to comply with the appeals board's order may be punished by the appeals board as a contempt..

Ref.: Hanna § 25.20[3]; Herlick Handbook § 14.2.

§3761. Insurer must notify employer of indemnity claims; employer's notification of insurer regarding facts to disprove claim, report of reserve amount.

(a) An insurer securing an employer's liability under this division shall notify the employer, within 15 days, of each claim for indemnity filed against the employer directly with the insurer if the employer has not timely provided to the insurer a report of occupational injury or occupational illness pursuant to Section 6409.1. The insurer shall furnish an employer who has not filed this report with an opportunity to provide to the insurer, prior to the expiration of the 90-day period specified in Section 5402, all relevant information available to the employer concerning the claim.

(b) An employer shall promptly notify its insurer in writing at any time during the pendency of a claim when the employer has actual knowledge of any facts which would tend to disprove any aspect of the employee's claim. When an employer notifies its insurer in writing that, in the employer's opinion, no compensation is payable to an employee, at the employer's written request, to the appeals board, the appeals board may approve a compromise and release agreement, or stipulation, that provides compensation to the employee only where there is proof of service upon the employer by the insurer, to the employer's last known address, not less than 15 days prior to the appeals board action, of notice of the time and place of the hearing at which the compromise and release agreement or stipulation is to be approved. The insurer shall file proof of this service with the appeals board.

Failure by the insurer to provide the required notice shall not prohibit the board from approving a compromise and release agreement, or stipulation; however, the board shall order the insurer to pay reasonable expenses as provided in Section 5813.

(c) In establishing a reserve pursuant to a claim that affects premiums against an employer, an insurer shall provide the employer, upon request, a written report of the reserve amount established. The written report shall include, at a minimum, the following:

(1) Estimated medical-legal costs.

(2) Estimated vocational rehabilitation costs, if any.

(3) Itemization of all other estimated expenses to be paid from the reserve.

(d) When an employer properly provides notification to its insurer pursuant to subdivision (b), and the appeals board thereafter determines that no compensation is payable under this division, the insurer shall reimburse the employer for any premium paid solely due to the inclusion of the successfully challenged payments in the calculation of the employer's experience modification. The employee shall not be required to refund the challenged payment. **Leg.H.** 1991 ch. 116, 1993 ch. 121, effective July 16, 1993, 1994 ch. 1118.

1993 Note: Section 3761, as amended by ch. 121, applies only to injuries occurring on or after January 1, 1994. Stats. 1993 ch. 121 §77.

Ref.: 8 C.C.R. §10875; Hanna §§ 2.34, 2.70[1], 29.04[7]; Herlick Handbook §§ 3.2, 11.1, 14.2, 14.32; W. Cal. Sum., 2 "Workers' Compensation" §361.

Labor

§3762. Employer's right to information and documents affecting premium—Exceptions; disclosure of employee's medical information prohibited—Exceptions.

(a) Except as provided in subdivisions (b) and (c), the insurer shall discuss all elements of the claim file that affect the employer's premium with the employer, and shall supply copies of the documents that affect the premium at the employer's expense during reasonable business hours.

(b) The right provided by this section shall not extend to any document that the insurer is prohibited from disclosing to the employer under the attorney-client privilege, any other applicable privilege, or statutory prohibition upon disclosure, or under Section 1877.4 of the Insurance Code.

(c) An insurer, third-party administrator retained by a self-insured employer pursuant to Section 3702.1 to administer the employer's workers' compensation claims, and those employees and agents specified by a self-insured employer to administer the employer's workers' compensation claims, are prohibited from disclosing or causing to be disclosed to an employer, any medical information, as defined in subdivision (b) of Section 56.05 of the Civil Code, about an employee who has filed a workers' compensation claim, except as follows:

(1) Medical information limited to the diagnosis of the mental or physical condition for which workers' compensation is claimed and the treatment provided for this condition.

(2) Medical information regarding the injury for which workers' compensation is claimed that is necessary for the employer to have in order for the employer to modify the employee's work duties. **Leg.H.** 1993 ch. 121, effective July

16, 1993, ch. 1242, 1999 ch. 766, 2000 ch. 135, 2002 ch. 6 (AB 749).

1993 Note: Section 3762, as added by ch. 121, applies only to injuries occurring on or after January 1, 1994. Stats. 1993 ch. 121 §77.

Ref.: Herlick Handbook §§ 3.2, 4.24; W. Cal. Sum., 2 "Workers' Compensation" §158.

ARTICLE 4
Construction Permit

§3800. Construction permits; verification of workers' compensation coverage.

(a) Every county or city which requires the issuance of a permit as a condition precedent to the construction, alteration, improvement, demolition, or repair of any building or structure shall require that each applicant for the permit sign a declaration under penalty of perjury verifying workers' compensation coverage or exemption from coverage, as required by Section 19825 of the Health and Safety Code.

(b) At the time of permit issuance, contractors shall show their valid workers' compensation insurance certificate, or the city or county may verify the workers' compensation coverage by electronic means. **Leg.H.** 1994 ch. 178, 1999 ch. 982.

Ref.: Hanna § 2.10[1]; Herlick Handbook § 3.23; W. Cal. Sum., 5 "Torts" §248.

ARTICLE 5
Workers' Compensation Misrepresentations

§3820. Workers' compensation fraud—Civil penalties; additional penalties for prior felony conviction; Worker's Compensation Fraud Account.

(a) In enacting this section, the Legislature declares that there exists a compelling interest in eliminating fraud in the workers' compensation system. The Legislature recognizes that the conduct prohibited by this section is, for the most part, already subject to criminal penalties pursuant to other provisions of law. However, the Legislature finds and declares that the addition of civil money penalties will provide necessary enforcement flexibility. The Legislature, in exercising its plenary authority related to workers' compensation, declares that these sections are both necessary and carefully tailored to combat the fraud and abuse that is rampant in the workers' compensation system.

(b) It is unlawful to do any of the following:

(1) Willfully misrepresent any fact in order to obtain workers' compensation insurance at less than the proper rate.

(2) Present or cause to be presented any knowingly false or fraudulent written or oral material statement in support of, or in opposition to, any claim for compensation for the purpose of obtaining or denying any compensation, as defined in Section 3207.

(3) Knowingly solicit, receive, offer, pay, or accept any rebate, refund, commission, preference, patronage, dividend, discount, or other consideration, whether in the form of money or otherwise, as compensation or inducement for soliciting or referring clients or patients to obtain services or benefits pursuant to Division 4 (commencing with Section 3200) unless the payment or receipt of consideration for services other than the referral of clients or patients is lawful pursuant to Section 650 of the Business and Professions Code or expressly permitted by the Rules of Professional Conduct of the State Bar.

(4) Knowingly operate or participate in a service that, for profit, refers or recommends clients or patients to obtain medical or medical-legal services or benefits pursuant to Division 4 (commencing with Section 3200).

(5) Knowingly assist, abet, solicit, or conspire with any person who engages in an unlawful act under this section.

(c) For the purposes of this section, "statement" includes, but is not limited to, any notice, proof of injury, bill for services, payment for services, hospital or doctor records, X-ray, test results, medical-legal expenses as defined in Section 4620, or other evidence of loss, expense, or payment.

(d) Any person who violates any provision of this section shall be subject, in addition to any other penalties that may be prescribed by law, to a civil penalty of not less than four thousand dollars ($4,000) nor more than ten thousand dollars ($10,000), plus an assessment of not more than three times the amount of the medical treatment expenses paid pursuant to Article 2 (commencing with Section 4600) and medical-legal expenses paid pursuant to Article 2.5 (commencing with Section 4620) for each claim for compensation submitted in violation of this section.

(e) Any person who violates subdivision (b) and who has a prior felony conviction of an offense set forth in Section 1871.1 or 1871.4 of the Insurance Code, or in Section 549 of the Penal Code, shall be subject, in addition to the penalties set forth in subdivision (d), to a civil penalty of four thousand dollars ($4,000) for each item or service with respect to which a violation of subdivision (b) occurred.

(f) The penalties provided for in subdivisions (d) and (e) shall be assessed and recovered in a civil action brought in the name of the people of the State of California by any district attorney.

(g) In assessing the amount of the civil penalty the court shall consider any one or more of the relevant circumstances presented by any of the parties to the case, including, but not limited to, the following: the nature and seriousness of the misconduct, the number of violations, the persistence of the misconduct, the length of time over which the misconduct occurred, the willfulness of the defendant's misconduct, and the defendant's assets, liabilities, and net worth.

(h) All penalties collected pursuant to this section shall be paid to the Workers' Compensation Fraud Account in the Insurance Fund pursuant to Section 1872.83 of the Insurance Code. All costs incurred by district attorneys in carrying out this article shall be funded from the Workers' Compensation Fraud Account. It is the intent of the Legislature that the program instituted by this article be supported entirely from funds produced by moneys deposited into the Workers' Compensation Fraud Account from the imposition of civil money penalties for workers' compensation fraud collected pursuant to this section. All moneys claimed by district attorneys as costs of carrying out this article shall be paid pursuant to a determination by the Fraud Assessment Commission established by Section 1872.83 of the Insurance Code and on appropriation by the Legislature. **Leg.H.** 1993 ch. 120, effective July 16, 1993, ch. 1242, 2002 ch. 6 (AB 749).

Ref.: Hanna § 2.03[5]; Herlick Handbook § 9.18; W. Cal. Sum., 2 "Workers' Compensation" §23.

§3822. Annual fraud warning notices.

The administrative director shall, on an annual basis, provide to every employer, claims adjuster, third party administrator, physician, and attorney who participates in the workers' compensation system, a notice that warns the recipient against committing workers' compensation fraud. The notice shall specify the penalties that are applied for committing workers' compensation fraud. The Fraud Assessment Commission, established by Section 1872.83 of the Insurance Code, shall provide the administrative director with all funds necessary to carry out this section. **Leg.H.** 2002 ch. 6 (AB 749).

§3823. Medical billing and provider fraud—Protocols for reporting apparent fraudulent claims; immunity from civil liability for reporting apparent fraud.

(a) The administrative director shall, in coordination with the Bureau of Fraudulent Claims of the Department of Insurance, the Medi-Cal Fraud Task Force, and the Bureau of Medi-Cal Fraud and Elder Abuse of the Department of Justice, or their successor entities, adopt protocols, to the extent that these protocols are applicable to achieve the purpose of subdivision (b), similar to those adopted by the Department of Insurance concerning medical billing and provider fraud.

(b) Any insurer, self-insured employer, third-party administrator, workers' compensation administrative law judge, audit unit, attorney, or other person that believes that a fraudulent claim has been made by any person or entity providing medical care, as described in Section 4600, shall report the apparent fraudulent claim in the manner prescribed by subdivision (a).

(c) No insurer, self-insured employer, third-party administrator, workers' compensation administrative law judge, audit unit, attorney, or other person that reports any apparent fraudulent claim under this section shall be subject to any civil liability in a cause of action of any kind when the insurer, self-insured employer, third-party administrator, workers' compensation administrative law judge, audit unit, attorney, or other person acts in good faith, without malice, and reasonably believes that the action taken was warranted by the known facts, obtained by reasonable efforts. Nothing in this section is intended to, nor does in any manner, abrogate or lessen the existing common law or statutory privileges and immunities of any insurer, self-insured employer, third-party administrator, workers' compensation administrative law judge, audit unit, attorney, or other person. **Leg.H.** 2003 ch. 639 (SB 228), 2004 ch. 34 (SB 899), effective April 19, 2004.

2004 Note: The amendment to §3823 made by this act shall apply prospectively from the date of enactment of this act, regardless of the date of injury, unless otherwise specified, but shall not constitute good cause to reopen or rescind, alter, or amend any existing order, decision, or award of the Workers' Compensation Appeals Board. Stats. 2004 ch. 34 (SB 899) §47.

Ref.: Hanna § 2.03[3]; Herlick Handbook § 9.18.

CHAPTER 5 SUBROGATION OF EMPLOYER

§3850. "Employee"; "employer."

As used in this chapter:

(a) "Employee" includes the person injured and any other person to whom a claim accrues by reason of the injury or death of the former.

(b) "Employer" includes insurer as defined in this division.

(c) "Employer" also includes the Self-Insurers' Security Fund, where the employer's compensation obligations have been assumed pursuant to Section 3743.

Ref.: 8 C.C.R. §15201; Hanna §§ 11.06[1], 11.21[1], 11.40[1], 21.03[5]; Herlick Handbook § 12.2; W. Cal. Sum., 2 "Workers' Compensation" §§31, 35, 38, 156, 159, 170, 6 "Torts" §1637.

§3851. Death of employee; effect.

The death of the employee or of any other person, does not abate any right of action established by this chapter.

Ref.: W. Cal. Sum., 2 "Workers' Compensation" §69.

§3852. Claim for compensation; effect on third party action.

The claim of an employee, including, but not limited to, any peace officer or firefighter, for compensation does not affect his or her claim or right of action for all damages proximately resulting from the injury or death against any person other than the employer. Any employer who pays, or becomes obligated to pay compensation, or who pays, or becomes obligated to pay salary in lieu of compensation, or who pays or becomes obligated to pay an amount to the Department of Industrial Relations pursuant to Section 4706.5, may likewise make a claim or bring an action against the third person. In the latter event the employer may recover in the same suit, in addition to the total amount of compensation, damages for which he or she was liable including all salary, wage, pension, or other emolument paid to the employee or to his or her dependents. The respective rights against the third person of the heirs of an employee claiming under Section 377.60 of the Code of Civil Procedure, and an employer claiming pursuant to this section, shall be determined by the court. **Leg.H.** 1993 ch. 589.

Ref.: Hanna §§ 11.04[1], 11.06[2], 11.20[2], 11.24[1][a], 11.25[2]; Herlick Handbook §§ 12.2, 12.5, 12.6, 12.7, 12.10; W. Cal. Sum., 2 "Workers' Compensation" §§35, 38, 62, 68–72, 74, 82–84, 91, 104, 339, 13 "Equity" §185, 14 "Wills and Probate" §620.

§3853. Service of complaint on employer or employee; consolidation of actions.

If either the employee or the employer brings an action against such third person, he shall forthwith give to the other a copy of the complaint by personal service or certified mail. Proof of such service shall be filed in such action. If the action is brought by either the employer or employee, the other may, at any time before trial on the facts, join as party plaintiff or shall consolidate his action, if brought independently.

Ref.: Hanna §§ 11.22[3]–[4], 11.42[3][b]; Herlick Handbook §§ 12.2, 12.3, 12.7; W. Cal. Sum., 2 "Workers' Compensation" §§69, 83, 85, 86.

§3854. Action by employer alone; evidence of amounts paid.

If the action is prosecuted by the employer alone, evidence of any amount which the employer has paid or become obligated to pay by reason of the injury or death of the employee is admissible, and such expenditures or liability shall be considered as proximately resulting from such injury or death in addition to any other items of damage proximately resulting therefrom.

Ref.: Hanna §§ 11.42[2], [3][e], 11.43; Herlick Handbook §§ 12.6, 12.7; W. Cal. Sum., 2 "Workers' Compensation" §§82, 91.

§3855. Joint action; evidence of damages.

If the employee joins in or prosecutes such action, either the evidence of the amount of disability indemnity or death benefit paid or to be paid by the employer or the evidence of loss of earning capacity by the employee shall be admissible, but not both. Proof of all other items of damage to either the employer or employee proximately resulting from such injury or death is admissible and is part of the damages.

Ref.: Hanna §§ 11.22[6], 11.24[1][a]; Herlick Handbook §§ 12.3, 12.7.

§3856. Suit against third party; costs and attorney's fees.

In the event of suit against such third party:

(a) If the action is prosecuted by the employer alone, the court shall first order paid from any judgment for damages recovered the reasonable litigation expenses incurred in preparation and prosecution of such action, together with a reasonable attorney's fee which shall be based solely upon the services rendered by the employer's attorney in effecting recovery both for the benefit of the employer and the employee. After the payment of such expenses and attorney's fees, the court shall apply out of the amount of such judgment an amount sufficient to reimburse the employer for the amount of his expenditure for compensation together with any amounts to which he may be entitled as special damages under Section 3852 and shall order any excess paid to the injured employee or other person entitled thereto.

(b) If the action is prosecuted by the employee alone, the court shall first order paid from any judgment for damages recovered the reasonable litigation expenses incurred in preparation and prosecution of such action, together with a reasonable attorney's fee which shall be based solely upon the services rendered by the employee's attorney in effecting recovery both for the benefit of the employee and the employer. After the payment of such expenses and attorney's fee the court shall, on application of the employer, allow as a first lien against the amount of such judgment for damages, the amount of the employer's expenditure for compensation together with any amounts to which he may be entitled as special damages under Section 3852.

(c) If the action is prosecuted both by the employee and the employer, in a single action or in consolidated actions, and they are represented by the same agreed attorney or by separate attorneys, the court shall first order paid from any judgment for damages recovered, the reasonable litigation expenses incurred in preparation and prosecution of such action or actions, together with reasonable attorneys' fees based solely on the services rendered for the benefit of both parties where they are represented by the same attorney, and where they are represented by separate attorneys, based solely upon the service rendered in each instance by the attorney in effecting recovery for the benefit of the party represented. After the payment of such expenses and attorneys' fees the court shall apply out of the amount of such judgment for damages an amount sufficient to reimburse the employer for the amount of his expenditures for compensation together with any other amounts to which he may be entitled as special damages under Section 3852.

(d) The amount of reasonable litigation expenses and the amount of attorneys' fees under subdivisions (a), (b), and (c) of this section shall be fixed by the court. Where the employer and employee are represented by separate attorneys they may propose to the court, for its consideration and determination, the amount and division of such expenses and fees.

Ref.: Hanna §§ 11.24[2], 11.42[2][f], [3][a], 11.46, 11.47; Herlick Handbook §§ 12.4, 12.7; W. Cal. Sum., 2 "Workers' Compensation" §§72, 76, 77, 79, 80, 83, 84, 87–89.

§3857. Subsequent compensation paid by employer; application for further lien.

The court shall, upon further application at any time before the judgment is satisfied, allow as a further lien the amount of any expenditures of the employer for compensation subsequent to the original order.

Ref.: Herlick Handbook §§ 12.3, 12.7; W. Cal. Sum., 2 "Insurance" §13, 2 "Workers' Compensation" §72.

§3858. Employer's release from further compensation.

After payment of litigation expenses and attorneys' fees fixed by the court pursuant to Section 3856 and payment of the employer's lien, the employer shall be relieved from the obligation to pay further compensation to or on behalf of the employee under this division up to the entire amount of the balance of the judg-

Labor

ment, if satisfied, without any deduction. No satisfaction of such judgment in whole or in part, shall be valid without giving the employer notice and a reasonable opportunity to perfect and satisfy his lien.

Ref.: Herlick Handbook §§ 9.12, 10.16, 12.3, 12.6, 12.7; W. Cal. Sum., 2 "Insurance" §13, 2 "Workers' Compensation" §§75, 99, 339.

§3859. Release or settlement; written agreement; claims against third parties.

(a) No release or settlement of any claim under this chapter as to either the employee or the employer is valid without the written consent of both. Proof of service filed with the court is sufficient in any action or proceeding where such approval is required by law.

(b) Notwithstanding anything to the contrary contained in this chapter, an employee may settle and release any claim he may have against a third party without the consent of the employer. Such settlement or release shall be subject to the employer's right to proceed to recover compensation he has paid in accordance with Section 3852.

Ref.: Hanna §§ 11.25[2], 11.42[4][a]; Herlick Handbook §§ 12.4, 12.5, 12.6; W. Cal. Sum., 2 "Workers' Compensation" §§69–71, 83.

§3860. Release or settlement; notice; employer's claim for reimbursement; settlement expenses.

(a) No release or settlement under this chapter, with or without suit, is valid or binding as to any party thereto without notice to both the employer and the employee, with opportunity to the employer to recover the amount of compensation he has paid or become obligated to pay and any special damages to which he may be entitled under Section 3852, and opportunity to the employee to recover all damages he has suffered and with provision for determination of expenses and attorney's fees as herein provided.

(b) Except as provided in Section 3859, the entire amount of such settlement, with or without suit, is subject to the employer's full claim for reimbursement for compensation he has paid or become obligated to pay and any special damages to which he may be entitled under Section 3852, together with expenses and attorney fees, if any, subject to the limitations in this section set forth.

(c) Where settlement is effected, with or without suit, solely through the efforts of the employee's attorney, then prior to the reimbursement of the employer, as provided in subdivision (b) hereof, there shall be deducted from the amount of the settlement the reasonable expenses incurred in effecting such settlement, including costs of suit, if any, together with a reasonable attorney's fee to be paid to the employee's attorney, for his services in securing and effecting settlement for the benefit of both the employer and the employee.

(d) Where settlement is effected, with or without suit, solely through the efforts of the employer's attorney, then, prior to the reimbursement of the employer as provided in subdivision (b) hereof, there shall be deducted from the amount of the settlement the reasonable expenses incurred in effecting such settlement, including costs of suit, if any, together with a reasonable attorney's fee to be paid to the employer's attorney, for his services in securing and effecting settlement for the benefit of both the employer and the employee.

(e) Where both the employer and the employee are represented by the same agreed attorney or by separate attorneys in effecting a settlement, with or without suit, prior to reimbursement of the employer, as provided in subdivision (b) hereof, there shall be deducted from the amount of the settlement the reasonable expenses incurred by both the employer and the employee or on behalf of either, including costs of suit, if any, together with reasonable attorneys' fees to be paid to the respective attorneys for the employer and the employee, based upon the respective services rendered in securing and effecting settlement for the benefit of the party represented. In the event both parties are represented by the same attorney, by agreement, the attorney's fee shall be based on the services rendered for the benefit of both.

(f) The amount of expenses and attorneys' fees referred to in this section shall, on settlement of suit, or on any settlement requiring court approval, be set by the court. In all other cases these amounts shall be set by the appeals board. Where the employer and the employee are represented by separate attorneys they may propose to the court or the appeals board, for consideration and determination, the amount and division of such expenses and fees.

Ref.: Hanna §§ 11.25[2]–[3], 20.02[2][m]; Herlick Handbook §§ 12.3, 12.4, 12.6, 12.7; W. Cal. Sum., 2 "Workers' Compensation" §§7, 69–71, 76, 77, 79, 81, 83, 84, 88–90.

§3861. Employee recovery credited to employer's liability.

The appeals board is empowered to and shall allow, as a credit to the employer to be applied against his liability for compensation, such amount of any recovery by the employee for his injury, either by settlement or after judgment, as has not theretofore been applied to the payment of expenses or attorneys' fees, pursuant to the provisions of Sections 3856, 3858, and 3860 of this code, or has not been applied to reimburse the employer.

Ref.: Hanna §§ 11.42[5][a]–[d], 31.14[2]; W. Cal. Sum., 2 "Workers' Compensation" §§73–75, 93, 99, 156.

§3862. Enforcement of judgment lien by employer against third party.

Any employer entitled to and who has been allowed and has perfected a lien upon the judgment or award in favor of an employee against any third party for damages occasioned to the same employer by payment of compensation, expenses of medical treatment, and any other charges under this act, may enforce payment of the lien against the third party, or, in case the damages recovered by the employee have been paid to the employee, against the employee to the extent of the lien, in the manner provided for enforcement of money judgments generally.

Ref.: Hanna § 11.42[2][f]; W. Cal. Sum., 2 "Workers' Compensation" §72.

§3864. Action against third party; prior written agreement of employer to reimburse.

If an action as provided in this chapter prosecuted by the employee, the employer, or both jointly against the third person results in judgment against such third person, or settlement by such third person, the employer shall have no liability to reimburse or hold such third person harmless on such judgment or settlement in absence of a written agreement so to do executed prior to the injury.

Ref.: Hanna §§ 2.63[3][a], 11.48; Herlick Handbook §§ 12.8, 12.12; W. Cal. Sum., 2 "Workers' Compensation" §§40, 102, 105, 107, 6 "Torts" §§1260, 1357, 1369.

§3865. Duplication of payment under this chapter.

Any judgment or settlement of an action as provided for in this chapter is, upon notice to the court, subject to the same lien claims of the Employment Development Department as are provided for in Chapter 1 (commencing with Section 4900) of Part 3, and shall be allowed by the court as it determines necessary to avoid a duplication of payment as compensation to the employee for lost earnings.

CHAPTER 7
MEDICAL EXAMINATIONS

ARTICLE 1
[In General]

§4050. Medical examinations; written request of employer; order of Appeals Board.

Whenever the right to compensation under this division exists in favor of an employee, he shall, upon the written request of his employer, submit at reasonable intervals to examination by a practicing physician, provided and paid for by the employer, and shall likewise submit to examination at reasonable intervals by any physician selected by the administrative director or appeals board or referee thereof.

Ref.: Hanna §§ 5.02[10][[b], 22.07[2][a], 31.11[3]; Herlick Handbook §§ 4.4, 4.20, 14.21, 14.22; W. Cal. Sum., 2 "Workers' Compensation" §328.

§4051. Time and place of examination.

The request or order for the medical examination shall fix a time and place therefor, due consideration being given to the convenience of the employee and his physical condition and ability to attend at the time and place fixed.

Ref.: Hanna § 22.07[2][a]; W. Cal. Sum., 2 "Workers' Compensation" §328.

§4052. Presence of employee's physician.

The employee may employ at his own expense a physician, to be present at any examination required by his employer.

§4053. Failure or refusal to submit to examination at employer's request.

So long as the employee, after written request of the employer, fails or refuses to submit to such examination or in any way obstructs it, his right to begin or maintain any proceeding for the collection of compensation shall be suspended.

Ref.: 8 C.C.R. §10890; Hanna §§ 5.02[10][b], 22.07[2][b], 25.40[2], 31.11[3]; Herlick Handbook § 4.20; W. Cal. Sum., 2 "Workers' Compensation" §328.

§4054. Failure or refusal to submit to examination on order of Appeals Board.

If the employee fails or refuses to submit to examination after direction by the appeals board, or a referee thereof, or in any way obstructs the examination, his right to the disability payments which accrue during the period of such failure, refusal or obstruction, shall be barred.

Ref.: 8 C.C.R. §10890; Hanna §§ 5.02[10][b], 22.07[2][b]; Herlick Handbook §§ 4.20, 14.43; W. Cal. Sum., 2 "Workers' Compensation" §328.

§4055. Physician's report.

Any physician who makes or is present at any such examination may be required to report or testify as to the results thereof.

Ref.: Hanna § 22.08[3][c].

§4055.2. Subpoena of records; copies.

Any party who subpoenas records in any proceeding under this division shall concurrent with service of the subpoena upon the person who has possession of the records, send a copy of the subpoena to all parties of record in the proceeding. **Leg.H.** 1999 ch. 444.

Ref.: Hanna §§ 22.08[4][c], 25.29[3][a], 25.43; Herlick Handbook § 14.21; W. Cal. Ev., "Discovery" §221.

§4056. Disability caused or aggravated by refusal to submit to medical treatment.

No compensation is payable in case of the death or disability of an employee when his death is caused, or when and so far as his disability is caused, continued, or aggravated, by an unreasonable refusal to submit to medical treatment, or to any surgical treatment, if the risk of the treatment is, in the opinion of the appeals board, based upon expert medical or surgical advice, inconsiderable in view of the seriousness of the injury.

Ref.: Hanna §§ 5.05[9][a]–[c], 5.05[10][e], 22.02[6]; Herlick Handbook § 14.22; W. Cal. Sum., 2 "Workers' Compensation" §§329, 330.

ARTICLE 2
Determination of Medical Issues

§4060. Comprehensive medical-legal evaluation.

(a) This section shall apply to disputes over the compensability of any injury. This section shall not apply where injury to any part or parts of the body is accepted as compensable by the employer.

(b) Neither the employer nor the employee shall be liable for any comprehensive medical-legal evaluation performed by other than the treating physician, except as provided in this section. However, reports of treating physicians shall be admissible.

(c) If a medical evaluation is required to determine compensability at any time after the filing of the claim form, and the employee is represented by an attorney, a medical evaluation to determine compensability shall be obtained only by the procedure provided in Section 4062.2.

(d) If a medical evaluation is required to determine compensability at any time after the claim form is filed, and the employee is not represented by an attorney, the employer shall provide the employee with notice either that the employer requests a comprehensive medical evaluation to determine compensability or that the employer has not accepted liability and the employee may request a comprehensive medical evaluation to determine compensability. Either party may request a comprehensive medical evaluation to determine compensability. The evaluation shall be obtained only by the procedure provided in Section 4062.1.

(e)(1) Each notice required by subdivision (d) shall describe the administrative procedures available to the injured employee and advise the employee of his or her right to consult an information and assistance officer or an attorney. It shall contain the following language:

"Should you decide to be represented by an attorney, you may or may not receive a larger award, but, unless you are determined to be ineligible for an award, the attorney's fee will be deducted from any award you might receive for disability benefits. The decision to be represented by an attorney is yours to make, but it is voluntary and may not be necessary for you to receive your benefits."

(2) The notice required by subdivision (d) shall be accompanied by the form prescribed by the administrative director for requesting the assignment of a panel of qualified medical evaluators. **Leg.H.** 1993 ch. 121, effective July 16, 1993, ch. 1242, 2004 ch. 34 (SB 899), effective April 19, 2004.

2004 Note: The amendment to §4060 made by this act shall apply prospectively from the date of enactment of this act, regardless of the date of injury, unless otherwise specified, but shall not constitute good cause to reopen or rescind, alter, or amend any existing order, decision, or award of the Workers' Compensation Appeals Board. Stats. 2004 ch. 34 (SB 899) §47.

1993 Note: Section 4060, as added by ch. 121, applies only to injuries occurring on or after January 1, 1994. Stats. 1993 ch. 121 §77.

Ref.: 8 C.C.R. §§1, 10, 10.2, 11.5, 12, 13, 14, 15, 20, 30, 30.1, 35, 35.5, 36, 39, 39.5, 40, 41, 44, 45, 46, 46.1, 47, 50, 53, 55, 62, 112, 113, 114, 115, 116; Hanna § 22.06[8]; Herlick Handbook §§ 8.25, 14.1, 14.4, 14.11, 14.21; W. Cal. Sum., 2 "Workers' Compensation" §§4, 274, 386.

§4061. Notice of permanent disability indemnity; formal medical evaluation.

(a) Together with the last payment of temporary disability indemnity, the employer shall, in a form prescribed by the administrative director pursuant to Section 138.4, provide the employee one of the following:

(1) Notice either that no permanent disability indemnity will be paid because the employer alleges the employee has no permanent impairment or limitations resulting from the injury or notice of the amount of permanent disability indemnity determined by the employer to be payable. The notice shall include information concerning how the employee may obtain a formal medical evaluation pursuant to subdivision (c) or (d) if he or she disagrees with the position taken by the employer. The notice shall be accompanied by the form prescribed by the administrative director for requesting assignment of a panel of qualified medical evaluators, unless the employee is represented by an attorney. If the employer determines permanent disability indemnity is payable, the employer shall advise the employee of the amount determined payable and the basis on which the determination was made and whether there is need for continuing medical care.

(2) Notice that permanent disability indemnity may be or is payable, but that the amount cannot be determined because the employee's medical condition is not yet permanent and stationary. The notice shall advise the employee that his or her medical condition will be monitored until it is permanent and stationary, at which time the necessary evaluation will be performed to determine the existence and extent of permanent impairment and limitations for the purpose of rating permanent disability and to determine the need for continuing medical care, or at which time the employer will advise the employee of the amount of permanent disability indemnity the employer has determined to be payable. If an employee is provided notice pursuant to this paragraph and the employer later takes the position that the employee has no permanent impairment or limitations resulting from the injury, or later determines permanent disability indemnity is payable, the employer shall in either event, within 14 days of the determination to take either position, provide the employee with the notice specified in paragraph (1).

(b) Each notice required by subdivision (a) shall describe the administrative procedures available to the injured employee and advise the employee of his or her right to consult an information and assistance officer or an attorney. It shall contain the following language:

"Should you decide to be represented by an attorney, you may or may not receive a larger award, but, unless you are determined to be ineligible for an award, the attorney's fee will be deducted from any award you might receive for disability benefits. The decision to be represented by an attorney is yours to make, but it is voluntary and may not be necessary for you to receive your benefits."

(c) If the parties do not agree to a permanent disability rating based on the treating physician's evaluation, and the employee is represented by an attorney, a medical evaluation to determine permanent disability shall be obtained as provided in Section 4062.2.

(d) If the parties do not agree to a permanent disability rating based on the treating physician's evaluation, and if the employee is not represented by an attorney, the employer shall immediately provide the employee with a form prescribed by the medical director with which to

Labor

request assignment of a panel of three qualified medical evaluators. Either party may request a comprehensive medical evaluation to determine permanent disability, and the evaluation shall be obtained only by the procedure provided in Section 4062.1.

(c) The qualified medical evaluator who has evaluated an unrepresented employee shall serve the comprehensive medical evaluation and the summary form on the employee, employer, and the administrative director. The unrepresented employee or the employer may submit the treating physician's evaluation for the calculation of a permanent disability rating. Within 20 days of receipt of the comprehensive medical evaluation, the administrative director shall calculate the permanent disability rating according to Section 4660 and serve the rating on the employee and employer.

(f) Any comprehensive medical evaluation concerning an unrepresented employee which indicates that part or all of an employee's permanent impairment or limitations may be subject to apportionment pursuant to Sections 4663 and 4664 shall first be submitted by the administrative director to a workers' compensation judge who may refer the report back to the qualified medical evaluator for correction or clarification if the judge determines the proposed apportionment is inconsistent with the law.

(g) Within 30 days of receipt of the rating, if the employee is unrepresented, the employee or employer may request that the administrative director reconsider the recommended rating or obtain additional information from the treating physician or medical evaluator to address issues not addressed or not completely addressed in the original comprehensive medical evaluation or not prepared in accord with the procedures promulgated under paragraph (2) or (3) of subdivision (j) of Section 139.2. This request shall be in writing, shall specify the reasons the rating should be reconsidered, and shall be served on the other party. If the administrative director finds the comprehensive medical evaluation is not complete or not in compliance with the required procedures, the administrative director shall return the report to the treating physician or qualified medical evaluator for appropriate action as the administrative director instructs. Upon receipt of the treating physician's or qualified medical evaluator's final comprehensive medical evaluation and summary form, the administrative director shall recalculate the permanent disability rating according to Section 4660 and serve the rating, the comprehensive medical evaluation, and the summary form on the employee and employer.

(h)(1) If a comprehensive medical evaluation from the treating physician or an agreed medical evaluator or a qualified medical evaluator selected from a three-member panel resolves any issue so as to require an employer to provide compensation, the employer shall commence the payment of compensation or promptly commence proceedings before the appeals board to resolve the dispute.

(2) If the employee and employer agree to a stipulated findings and award as provided under Section 5702 or to compromise and release the claim under Chapter 2 (commencing with Section 5000) of Part 3, or if the employee wishes to commute the award under Chapter 3 (commencing with Section 5100) of Part 3, the appeals board shall first determine whether the agreement or commutation is in the best interests of the employee and whether the proper procedures have been followed in determining the permanent disability rating. The administrative director shall promulgate a form to notify the employee, at the time of service of any rating under this section, of the options specified in this subdivision, the potential advantages and disadvantages of each option, and the procedure for disputing the rating.

(i) No issue relating to the existence or extent of permanent impairment and limitations resulting from the injury may be the subject of a declaration of readiness to proceed unless there has first been a medical evaluation by a treating physician or an agreed or qualified medical evaluator. With the exception of an evaluation or evaluations prepared by the treating physician or physicians, no evaluation of permanent impairment and limitations resulting from the injury shall be obtained, except in accordance with Section 4062.1 or 4062.2. Evaluations obtained in violation of this prohibition shall not be admissible in any proceeding before the appeals board. **Leg.H.** 1993 ch. 121, effective July 16, 1993, chs. 1241, 1242, 2002 ch. 6 (AB 749), 2003 ch. 639 (SB 228), 2004 ch. 34 (SB 899), effective April 19, 2004.

2004 Note: The amendment to §4061 made by this act shall apply prospectively from the date of enactment of this act, regardless of the date of injury, unless otherwise specified, but shall not constitute good cause to reopen or rescind, alter, or amend any existing order, decision, or award of the Workers' Compensation Appeals Board. Stats. 2004 ch. 34 (SB 899) §47.

1993 Note: Section 4061, as amended by ch. 121, applies only to injuries occurring on or after January 1, 1994. Stats. 1993 ch. 121 §77.

Ref.: 8 C.C.R. §§1, 10, 10.2, 11.5, 12, 13, 14, 15, 20, 30, 30.5, 31, 31.5, 32, 32.5, 33, 34, 35, 36, 37, 38, 39, 39.5, 40, 41, 44, 45, 46, 46.1, 47, 50, 53, 55, 62, 108, 109, 110, 111, 112, 113, 114, 115, 116, 9785, 9793, 9795, 9810, 9812, 9813, 9815, 10101, 10101.1, 10102, 10109, 10111, 10111.1, 10111.2, 10150, 10152, 10156, 10158, 10160, 10160.1, 10160.5, 10161, 10162, 10163, 10164, 10165, 10165.5, 10168; Hanna §§ 22.06[1][a], [b], [e], [f], [g], 32.06[2][a], [b], [f], [g], [h]; Herlick Handbook §§ 4.20, 4.21, 6.19, 14.4; Lawyer's Guide to AMA *Guides* and Calif. Workers' Comp. §§ 2.02, 2.05, 2.06[2]; W. Cal. Sum., 2 "Workers' Compensation" §§274, 291, 386.

§4061.5. Treating physician to render opinions on medical issues needed to determine eligibility for compensation.

The treating physician primarily responsible for managing the care of the injured worker or the physician designated by that treating physician shall, in accordance with rules promulgated by the administrative director, render opinions on all medical issues necessary to determine eligibility for compensation. In the event that there is more than one treating physician, a single report shall be prepared by the physician primarily responsible for managing the injured worker's care that incorporates the findings of the various treating physicians. **Leg.H.** 1993 ch. 121, effective July 16, 1993.

1993 Note: Section 4061.5, as added by ch. 121, applies only to injuries occurring on or after January 1, 1994. Stats. 1993 ch. 121 §77.

Ref.: 8 C.C.R. §§1, 11.5, 31.5, 32.7, 37, 46.1, 50, 62, 108, 113, 9770, 9785, 9785.2, 9785.3, 9785.4, 9785.5, 9793, 9795, 10160.1; Hanna § 22.08[3][b]; Herlick Handbook § 14.4.

§4062. Objections to medical determination; procedures when employer objects to treating physician's recommendations.

(a) If either the employee or employer objects to a medical determination made by the treating physician concerning any medical issues not covered by Section 4060 or 4061 and not subject to Section 4610, the objecting party shall notify the other party in writing of the objection within 20 days of receipt of the report if the employee is represented by an attorney or within 30 days of receipt of the report if the employee is not represented by an attorney. Employer objections to the treating physician's recommendation for spinal surgery shall be subject to subdivision (b), and after denial of the physician's recommendation, in accordance with Section 4610. If the employee objects to a decision made pursuant to Section 4610 to modify, delay, or deny a treatment recommendation, the employee shall notify the employer of the objection in writing within 20 days of receipt of that decision. These time limits may be extended for good cause or by mutual agreement. If the employee is represented by an attorney, a medical evaluation to determine the disputed medical issue shall be obtained as provided in Section 4062.2, and no other medical evaluation shall be obtained. If the employee is not represented by an attorney, the employer shall immediately provide the employee with a form prescribed by the medical director with which to request assignment of a panel of three qualified medical evaluators, the evaluation shall be obtained as provided in Section 4062.1, and no other medical evaluation shall be obtained.

(b) The employer may object to a report of the treating physician recommending that spinal surgery be performed within 10 days of the receipt of the report. If the employee is represented by an attorney, the parties shall seek agreement with the other party on a California licensed board-certified or board-eligible orthopedic surgeon or neurosurgeon to prepare a second opinion report resolving the disputed surgical recommendation. If no agreement is reached within 10 days, or if the employee is not represented by an attorney, an orthopedic surgeon or neurosurgeon shall be randomly selected by the administrative director to prepare a second opinion report resolving the disputed surgical recommendation. Examinations shall be scheduled on an expedited basis. The second opinion report shall be served on the parties within 45 days of receipt of the treating physician's report. If the second opinion report recommends surgery, the employer shall authorize the surgery. If the second opinion report does not recommend surgery, the employer shall file a declaration of readiness to proceed. The employer shall not be liable for medical treatment costs for the disputed surgical procedure, whether through a lien filed with the appeals board or as a self-procured medical expense, or for periods of temporary disability resulting from the surgery, if the disputed surgical procedure is performed prior to the completion of the second opinion process required by this subdivision.

(c) The second opinion physician shall not have any material professional, familial, or financial affiliation, as determined by the administrative director, with any of the following:

(1) The employer, his or her workers' compensation insurer, third-party claims administrator, or other entity contracted to provide utilization review services pursuant to Section 4610.

(2) Any officer, director, or employee of the employer's health care provider, workers' compensation insurer, or third-party claims administrator.

(3) A physician, the physician's medical group, or the independent practice association involved in the health care service in dispute.

(4) The facility or institution at which either the proposed health care service, or the alternative service, if any, recommended by the employer's health care provider, workers' compensation insurer, or third-party claims administrator, would be provided.

(5) The development or manufacture of the principal drug, device, procedure, or other therapy proposed by the employee or his or her treating physician whose treatment is under review, or the alternative therapy, if any, recommended by the employer or other entity.

(6) The employee or the employee's immediate family. **Leg.H.** 2003 ch. 639 (SB 228) §17, 2004 ch. 34 (SB 899), effective April 19, 2004.

2004 Note: The amendment to §4062 made by this act shall apply prospectively from the date of enactment of this act, regardless of the date of injury, unless otherwise specified, but shall not constitute good cause to reopen or rescind, alter, or amend any existing order, decision, or award of the Workers' Compensation Appeals Board. Stats. 2004 ch. 34 (SB 899) §47.

2003 Note: The Commission on Health and Safety and Workers' Compensation shall conduct a study of the spinal surgery second opinion procedure established in subdivision (b) of Section 4062 of the Labor Code. The study shall be completed by June 30, 2006. The commission shall issue a report concerning the findings of the study and recommendations for further legislation. Stats. 2003 ch. 639 (SB 228) §48.

Ref.: 8 C.C.R. §§1, 10, 10.2, 11.5, 12, 13, 14, 15, 20, 30, 30.5, 31, 31.5, 32, 32.5, 33, 34, 35, 35.5, 36, 38, 39, 39.5, 40, 41, 44, 45, 46, 46.1, 47, 50, 62, 108, 109, 110, 112, 113, 114, 115, 116, 9785, 9788.01, 9788.1, 9788.11, 9788.2, 9788.3, 9788.31, 9788.32, 9788.4, 9788.45, 9788.5, 9788.6, 9788.7, 9788.8, 9788.9, 9788.91, 9792.6, 9792.7, 9792.8, 9792.9, 9792.10, 9793, 10152, 10160, 10160.1, 10160.5, 10163, 10165.5; Hanna §§ 22.05[6][c], 22.06[2], 32.06[3]; Herlick Handbook §§ 4.19, 14.4; W. Cal. Sum., 2 "Workers' Compensation" §§263, 274, 291, 386.

§4062.1. Unrepresented employee—Medical evaluation.

(a) If an employee is not represented by an attorney, the employer shall not seek agreement with the employee on an agreed medical evaluator, nor shall an agreed medical evaluator prepare the formal medical evaluation on any issues in dispute.

(b) If either party requests a medical evaluation pursuant to Section 4060, 4061, or 4062, either party may submit the form prescribed by the administrative director requesting the medical director to assign a panel of three qualified medical evaluators in accordance with Section 139.2. However, the employer may not submit the form unless the employee has not submitted the form within 10 days after the employer has furnished the form to the employee and requested the employee to submit the form. The party submitting the request form shall designate the specialty of the physicians that will be assigned to the panel.

(c) Within 10 days of the issuance of a panel of qualified medical evaluators, the employee shall select a physician from the panel to prepare a medical evaluation, the employee shall schedule the appointment, and the employee shall inform the employer of the selection and the appointment. If the employee does not inform the employer of the selection within 10 days of the assignment of a panel of qualified medical evaluators, then the employer may select the physician from the panel to prepare a medical evaluation. If the employee informs the employer of the selection within 10 days of the assignment of the panel but has not made the appointment, or if the employer selects the physician pursuant to this subdivision, then the employer shall arrange the appointment. Upon receipt of written notice of the appointment arrangements from the employee, or upon giving the employee notice of an appointment arranged by the employer, the employer shall furnish payment of estimated travel expense.

(d) The evaluator shall give the employee, at the appointment, a brief opportunity to ask questions concerning the evaluation process and the evaluator's background. The unrepresented employee shall then participate in the evaluation as requested by the evaluator unless the employee has good cause to discontinue the evaluation. For purposes of this subdivision, "good cause" shall include evidence that the evaluator is biased against the employee because of his or her race, sex, national origin, religion, or sexual preference or evidence that the evaluator has requested the employee to submit to an unnecessary medical examination or procedure. If the unrepresented employee declines to proceed with the evaluation, he or she shall have the right to a new panel of three qualified medical evaluators from which to select one to prepare a comprehensive medical evaluation. If the appeals board subsequently determines that the employee did not have good cause to not proceed with the evaluation, the cost of the evaluation shall be deducted from any award the employee obtains.

(e) If an employee has received a comprehensive medical-legal evaluation under this section, and he or she later becomes represented by an attorney, he or she shall not be entitled to an additional evaluation. **Leg.H.** 2004 ch. 34 (SB 899), effective April 19, 2004.

2004 Note: The amendment to §4062.1 made by this act shall apply prospectively from the date of enactment of this act, regardless of the date of injury, unless otherwise specified, but shall not constitute good cause to reopen or rescind, alter, or amend any existing order, decision, or award of the Workers' Compensation Appeals Board. Stats. 2004 ch. 34 (SB 899) §47.

Ref.: 8 C.C.R. §§10152, 10160, 10160.1, 10160.5, 10161, 10163, 10165.5; Hanna §§ 22.06[1][b], 32.06[2][b]; Herlick Handbook § 14.4; W. Cal. Sum., 2 "Workers' Compensation" §§274, 291.

§4062.2. Comprehensive medical evaluation to resolve dispute over injuries on or after January 1, 2005, when employee is represented by attorney.

(a) Whenever a comprehensive medical evaluation is required to resolve any dispute arising out of an injury or a claimed injury occurring on or after January 1, 2005, and the employee is represented by an attorney, the evaluation shall be obtained only as provided in this section.

(b) If either party requests a medical evaluation pursuant to Section 4060, 4061, or 4062, either party may commence the selection process for an agreed medical evaluator by making a written request naming at least one proposed physician to be the evaluator. The parties shall seek agreement with the other party on the physician, who need not be a qualified medical evaluator, to prepare a report resolving the disputed issue. If no agreement is reached within 10 days of the first written proposal that names a proposed agreed medical evaluator, or any additional time not to exceed 20 days agreed to by the parties, either party may request the assignment of a three-member panel of qualified medical evaluators to conduct a comprehensive medical evaluation. The party submitting the request shall designate the specialty of the medical evaluator, the specialty of the medical evaluator requested by the other party if it has been made known to the party submitting the request, and the specialty of the treating physician. The party submitting the request form shall serve a copy of the request form on the other party.

(c) Within 10 days of assignment of the panel by the administrative director, the parties shall confer and attempt to agree upon an agreed medical evaluator selected from the panel. If the parties have not agreed on a medical evaluator from the panel by the 10th day after assignment of the panel, each party may then strike one name from the panel. The remaining qualified medical evaluator shall serve as the medical evaluator. If a party fails to exercise the right to strike a name from the panel within three working days of gaining the right to do so, the other party may select any physician who remains on the panel to serve as the medical evaluator. The administrative director may prescribe the form, the manner, or both, by which the parties shall conduct the selection process.

(d) The represented employee shall be responsible for arranging the appointment for the examination, but upon his or her failure to inform the employer of the appointment within 10 days after the medical evaluator has been selected, the employer may arrange the appointment and notify the employee of the arrangements.

(e) If an employee has received a comprehensive medical-legal evaluation under this section, and he or she later ceases to be represented, he or she shall not be entitled to an additional evaluation. **Leg.H.** 2004 ch. 34 (SB 899) §18, effective April 19, 2004.

2004 Note: The addition of §4062.2 made by this act shall apply prospectively from the date of enactment of this act, regardless of the date of injury, unless otherwise specified, but shall not constitute good cause to reopen or rescind, alter, or amend any existing order, decision, or award of the Workers' Compensation Appeals Board. Stats. 2004 ch. 34 (SB 899) §47.

Ref.: 8 C.C.R. §§41, 10160, 10160.1, 10160.5, 10161, 10163, 10165.5; Hanna §§ 22.06[1][a], 32.06[2][a]; Herlick Handbook § 14.4; W. Cal. Sum., 2 "Workers' Compensation" §§274, 291.

§4062.3. Information provided to qualified medical evaluator; service on opposing party; discovery; ex parte communications; contempt; evaluation and summary form; new medical issues.

(a) Any party may provide to the qualified medical evaluator selected from a panel any of the following information:

(1) Records prepared or maintained by the employee's treating physician or physicians.

(2) Medical and nonmedical records relevant to determination of the medical issue.

(b) Information that a party proposes to provide to the qualified medical evaluator selected from a panel shall be served on the opposing party 20 days before the information is provided to the evaluator. If the opposing party objects to consideration of nonmedical records within 10 days thereafter, the records shall not be provided to the evaluator. Either party may use discovery to establish the accuracy or authenticity of nonmedical records prior to the evaluation.

(c) If an agreed medical evaluator is selected, as part of their agreement on an evaluator, the parties shall agree on what information is to be provided to the agreed medical evaluator.

(d) In any formal medical evaluation, the agreed or qualified medical evaluator shall identify the following:

(1) All information received from the parties.

(2) All information reviewed in preparation of the report.

(3) All information relied upon in the formulation of his or her opinion.

(e) All communications with an agreed medical evaluator or a qualified medical evaluator selected from a panel before a medical evaluation shall be in writing and shall be served on the opposing party 20 days in advance of the evaluation. Any subsequent communication with the medical evaluator shall be in writing and shall be served on the opposing party when sent to the medical evaluator.

(f) Ex parte communication with an agreed medical evaluator or a qualified medical evaluator selected from a panel is prohibited. If a party communicates with the agreed medical evaluator or the qualified medical evaluator in violation of subdivision (e), the aggrieved party may elect to terminate the medical evaluation and seek a new evaluation from another qualified medical evaluator to be selected according to Section 4062.1 or 4062.2, as applicable, or proceed with the initial evaluation.

(g) The party making the communication prohibited by this section shall be subject to being charged with contempt before the appeals board and shall be liable for the costs incurred by the aggrieved party as a result of the prohibited communication, including the cost of the medical evaluation, additional discovery costs, and attorney's fees for related discovery.

(h) Subdivisions (e) and (f) shall not apply to oral or written communications by the employee or, if the employee is deceased, the employee's dependent, in the course of the examination or at the request of the evaluator in connection with the examination.

(i) Upon completing a determination of the disputed medical issue, the medical evaluator shall summarize the medical findings on a form prescribed by the administrative director and shall serve the formal medical evaluation and the summary form on the employee and the employer. The medical evaluation shall address all contested medical issues arising from all injuries reported on one or more claim forms prior to the date of the employee's initial appointment with the medical evaluator.

(j) If, after a medical evaluation is prepared, the employer or the employee subsequently objects to any new medical issue, the parties, to the extent possible, shall utilize the same medical evaluator who prepared the previous evaluation to resolve the medical dispute.

(k) No disputed medical issue specified in subdivision (a) may be the subject of declaration of readiness to proceed unless there has first been an evaluation by the treating physician or an agreed or qualified medical evaluator. **Leg.H.** 2004 ch. 34 (SB 899), effective April 19, 2004.

2004 Note: The addition of §4062.3 made by this act shall apply prospectively from the date of enactment of this act, regardless of the date of injury, unless otherwise specified, but shall not constitute good cause to reopen or rescind, alter, or amend any existing order, decision, or award of the Workers' Compensation Appeals Board. Stats. 2004 ch. 34 (SB 899) §47.

Ref.: Hanna §§ 22.06[1][d], [e], [4], 32.06[2][c], [f]; Herlick Handbook § 14.4; W. Cal. Sum., 2 "Workers' Compensation" §§274, 291.

§4062.5. Failure of QME to complete timely evaluation.

If a qualified medical evaluator selected from a panel fails to complete the formal medical evaluation within the timeframes established by the administrative director pursuant to paragraph (1) of subdivision (j) of Section 139.2, a new evaluation may be obtained upon the request of either party, as provided in Sections 4062.1 or 4062.2. Neither the employee nor the employer shall have any liability for payment for the formal medical evaluation which was not completed within the required timeframes unless the employee or employer, on forms prescribed by the administrative director, each waive the right to a new evaluation and elects to accept the original evaluation even though it was not completed within the required timeframes. **Leg.H.** 2003 ch. 639 (SB 228), 2004 ch. 34 (SB 899), effective April 19, 2004.

2004 Note: The amendment to §4062.5 made by this act shall apply prospectively from the date of enactment of this act, regardless of the date of injury, unless otherwise specified, but shall not constitute good cause to reopen or rescind, alter, or amend any existing order, decision, or award of the Workers' Compensation Appeals Board. Stats. 2004 ch. 34 (SB 899) §47.

Ref.: 8 C.C.R. §§112, 113, 114, 115, 116, 10160, 10160.1, 10160.5, 10161, 10163, 10165.5; Hanna § 22.06[5]; Herlick Handbook § 14.4; W. Cal. Sum., 2 "Workers' Compensation" §291.

§4062.8. Educational materials for treating physicians and other providers.

The administrative director shall develop, not later than January 1, 2004, and periodically revise as necessary thereafter, educational materials to be used to provide treating physicians, as described in Section 3209.3, or other providers, as described in Section 3209.5, with information and training in basic concepts of workers' compensation, the role of the treating physician, the conduct of permanent and stationary evaluations, and report writing, as appropriate. **Leg.H.** 2004 ch. 34 (SB 899), effective April 19, 2004.

2004 Note: The addition of §4062.8 made by this act shall apply prospectively from the date of enactment of this act, regardless of the date of injury, unless otherwise specified, but shall not constitute good cause to reopen or rescind, alter, or amend any existing order, decision, or award of the Workers' Compensation Appeals Board. Stats. 2004 ch. 34 (SB 899) §47.

Ref.: Hanna § 1.12[2]; Herlick Handbook § 1.8.

§4063. Commencement of payment; adjudication of claim.

If a formal medical evaluation from an agreed medical evaluator or a qualified medical evaluator selected from a three member panel resolves any issue so as to require an employer to provide compensation, the employer shall commence the payment of compensation or file an application for adjudication of claim.

Ref.: Herlick Handbook § 14.4.

§4064. Employer liability for costs and attorney's fees.

(a) The employer shall be liable for the cost of each reasonable and necessary comprehensive medical-legal evaluation obtained by the employee pursuant to Sections 4060, 4061, and 4062. Each comprehensive medical-legal evaluation shall address all contested medical issues arising from all injuries reported on one or more claim forms.

(b) For injuries occurring on or after January 1, 2003, if an unrepresented employee obtains an attorney after the evaluation pursuant to subdivision (d) of Section 4061 or subdivision (b) of Section 4062 has been completed, the employee shall be entitled to the same reports at employer expense as an employee who has been represented from the time the dispute arose and those reports shall be admissible in any proceeding before the appeals board.

(c) Subject to Section 4906, if an employer files an application for adjudication and the employee is unrepresented at the time the application is filed, the employer shall be liable for any attorney's fees incurred by the employee in connection with the application for adjudication.

(d) The employer shall not be liable for the cost of any comprehensive medical evaluations obtained by the employee other than those authorized pursuant to Sections 4060, 4061, and 4062. However, no party is prohibited from

Labor

obtaining any medical evaluation or consultation at the party's own expense. In no event shall an employer or employee be liable for an evaluation obtained in violation of subdivision (b) of Section 4060. All comprehensive medical evaluations obtained by any party shall be admissible in any proceeding before the appeals board except as provided in subdivisions (d) and (m) of Section 4061 and subdivisions (b) and (e) of Section 4062. **Leg.H.** 1993 ch. 121, effective July 16, 1993, ch. 1242 §30, 1998 ch. 485, 2002 ch. 6 (AB 749).

1993 Notes: The elimination of subdivision (d) of Section 4064 of the Labor Code made by this act shall not affect the applicability of Section 4064 of the Labor Code, as it existed prior to changes made during the 1993-94 Regular Session, to injuries arising prior to those changes. Stats. 1993 ch. 1242 §44.

Section 4064, as amended by ch. 121, applies only to injuries occurring on or after January 1, 1994. Stats. 1993 ch. 121 §77.

Ref.: 8 C.C.R. §§10160, 10160.1, 10160.5, 10161, 10163, 10165.5; Hanna §§ 22.06[1][b], 22.06[6], 22.06[7], 22.06[9]; Herlick Handbook §§ 14.4, 14.21; W. Cal. Sum., 2 "Workers' Compensation" §§273, 274, 354.

§4066. Costs incurred by adjudication of claim.

When the employer files an application for adjudication of claim contesting the formal medical evaluation prepared by an agreed medical evaluator under this article, regardless of outcome, the workers' compensation judge or the appeals board shall assess the employee's attorney's fees against the employer, subject to Section 4906.

Ref.: Herlick Handbook § 14.4.

§4067. Subsequent formal evaluations.

If the jurisdiction of the appeals board is invoked pursuant to Section 5803 upon the grounds that the effects of the injury have recurred, increased, diminished, or terminated, a formal medical evaluation shall be obtained pursuant to this article.

When an agreed medical evaluator or a qualified medical evaluator selected by an unrepresented employee from a three-member panel has previously made a formal medical evaluation of the same or similar issues, the subsequent or additional formal medical evaluation shall be conducted by the same agreed medical evaluator or qualified medical evaluator, unless the workers' compensation judge has made a finding that he or she did not rely on the prior evaluator's formal medical evaluation, any party contested the original medical evaluation by filing an application for adjudication, the unrepresented employee hired an attorney and selected a qualified medical evaluator to conduct another evaluation pursuant to subdivision (b) of Section 4064, or the prior evaluator is no longer qualified or readily available to prepare a formal medical evaluation, in which case Sections 4061 or 4062, as the case may be, shall apply as if there had been no prior formal medical evaluation. **Leg.H.** 2002 ch. 6 (AB 749).

Ref.: 8 C.C.R. §§10160, 10160.1, 10160.5, 10161, 10163, 10165.5; Herlick Handbook §§ 4.20, 14.4, 14.9, 14.21, 14.22.

§4067.5. Operative date.

This article shall become operative for injuries occurring on and after January 1, 1991.

Ref.: 8 C.C.R. §38; Hanna §§ 20.02[2][b], 32.04[1][a], 32.06[1]; Herlick Handbook §§ 4.20, 4.21.

§4068. Determination that treating physician's reports are biased and unsupported; notification to appropriate licensing body.

(a) Upon determining that a treating physician's report contains opinions that are the result of conjecture, are not supported by adequate evidence, or that indicate bias, the appeals board shall so notify the administrative director in writing in a manner he or she has specified.

(b) If the administrative director believes that any treating physician's reports show a pattern of unsupported opinions, he or she shall notify in writing the physician's applicable licensing body of his or her findings. **Leg.H.** 1993 ch. 121, effective July 16, 1993, 2003 ch. 639 (SB 228).

1993 Note: Section 4068, as added by ch. 121, applies only to injuries occurring on or after January 1, 1994. Stats. 1993 ch. 121 §77.

Ref.: Herlick Handbook §§ 4.20, 14.4.

CHAPTER 8
ELECTION TO BE SUBJECT TO COMPENSATION LIABILITY

§4150. Person not "employee"; joint election of employer and employee.

When an employer has in his employment any person not included within the term "employee" as defined by Article 2 of Chapter 2 of Part 1 of this division or a person not entitled to compensation under this division, such employer and such person employed by him may, by their joint election, come under the compensation provisions of this division in the manner hereinafter provided.

Ref.: Hanna § 21.04[2][a]; Herlick Handbook §§ 2.5, 2.9; W. Cal. Sum., 2 "Workers' Compensation" §192.

§4151. Methods of employer election.

Election on the part of the employer shall be made in one of the following ways:

(a) By insuring against liability for compensation, in which case he is deemed, as to all persons employed by him and covered by insurance, to have so elected during the period such insurance remains in force.

(b) By filing with the administrative director a statement to the effect that he accepts the compensation provisions of this division.

Ref.: Hanna §§ 3.33, 3.34, 3.88, 11.03[1], 21.04[2][a]; Herlick Handbook §§ 2.3, 2.4, 2.5; W. Cal. Sum., 2 "Workers' Compensation" §§172, 184, 187, 192.

§4152. Effect statement of acceptance.

The statement, when filed, shall operate, within the meaning of Chapter 3 (commencing with Section 3600), to subject him or her to the compensation provisions thereof for the term of one year from the date of filing. Thereafter, without further act on his or her part, he or she shall be so subject for successive terms of one year each, unless at least 60 days prior to the expiration of such first or succeeding year, he or she files with the administrative director a notice that he or she withdraws his or her election.

Ref.: W. Cal. Sum., 2 "Workers' Compensation" §192.

§4153. Persons included in statement of acceptance.

Such statement of acceptance includes persons whose employment is both casual and not in the course of the trade, business, profession, or occupation of the employer, unless expressly excluded therefrom.

§4154. Employer election.

Where any employer has made an election in either of the modes above prescribed, any person in his service is deemed to have accepted the compensation provisions of this division if, at the time of the injury for which liability is claimed:

(a) Such employer is subject to the compensation provisions of this division and;

(b) Such person in his service has not, either upon entering into the employment, or within five days after the filing of an election by the employer, given to such employer notice in writing that he elects not to be subject to the compensation provisions of this division.

In case of such acceptance, the person employed becomes subject to the compensation provisions at the time of the filing of the election or entry in the employment.

Ref.: Hanna § 3.88; W. Cal. Sum., 2 "Workers' Compensation" §§187, 192.

§4155. Coverage of state institutions; presumption.

The State and each county, city, district, and public agency thereof and all State institutions are conclusively presumed to have elected to come within the provisions of this division as to all employments otherwise excluded from this division.

Ref.: W. Cal. Ev., "Burden" §163; W. Cal. Sum., 2 "Workers' Compensation" §192.

§4156. Liability for compensation; effective date of division.

No liability for compensation shall attach to any employer of a person excluded by subdivision (h) of Section 3352 from the definition of "employee" for an injury to or the death of a person so excluded which occurs on or after the effective date of this section if such employer elected to come under the compensation provisions of this division pursuant to subdivision (a) of Section 4151 prior to the effective date of this section by purchasing or renewing a policy providing comprehensive personal liability insurance containing a provision for coverage against liability for the payment of compensation, as defined in Section 3207 of the Labor Code, to any person defined as an employee by subdivision (d) of Section 3351 of the Labor Code; provided, however, nothing in this section shall prohibit an employer from providing compensation pursuant to the provisions of this chapter.

Ref.: Herlick Handbook §§ 2.5, 2.9.

§4157. Application of chapter to independent contractor vending periodicals.

Where any employer has made an election pursuant to this chapter to include under the compensation provisions of this division an independent contractor engaged in vending, selling, offering for sale, or delivering directly to the public any newspaper, magazine, or periodical, the status of such person as an independent contractor for all other purposes shall not be affected by such election.

Ref.: Herlick Handbook §§ 2.5, 2.8; W. Cal. Sum., 2 "Workers' Compensation" §192.

CHAPTER 9
ECONOMIC OPPORTUNITY PROGRAMS

ARTICLE 1
General Provisions

§4201. Legislative intent; application of chapter.

It is the intent of this chapter to apply to all enrollees in economic opportunity programs, including, but not limited to, work training or work study authorized by or financed in whole or in part through provisions of Public Law 88–452 (Economic Opportunity Act of 1964).

Ref.: W. Cal. Sum., 3 "Agency and Employment" §326.

§4202. "Economic Opportunity Program."

"Economic Opportunity Program" means any program adopted pursuant to Public Law 88–452, including, but not limited to, work training and work study.

§4203. "Enrollee."

"Enrollee" means any person enrolled in an economic opportunity program.

§4204. "Sponsoring agency."

"Sponsoring agency" means any agency, entity, or institution, public or private, receiving grants or financial assistance, either directly or as a subcontractor, pursuant to Public Law 88–452.

§4205. "Participating agency."

"Participating agency" means any agency, entity or institution, public or private, taking part in an economic opportunity program, other than a sponsoring agency.

§4206. Enrollee's right to compensation.

Except as provided in this chapter, an enrollee within a given economic opportunity program shall have no right to receive compensation from sponsoring or participating agencies, entities, and institutions, public or private.

Ref.: Herlick Handbook § 2.5.

§4207. Conditions for compensation.

Compensation shall be furnished an enrollee for injury or to dependents if injury causes death, suffered within or without the state occurring in the course of his duties for a sponsoring agency within an economic opportunity program if the following conditions occur:

(a) Where, at the time of injury, the enrollee is performing services and is acting within the scope of his duties as a recipient of aid within an economic opportunity program.

(b) Where injury is proximately caused by his service as an enrollee within an economic opportunity program either with or without negligence.

(c) Where injury is not caused by the intoxication of the injured enrollee.

(d) Where the injury is not intentionally self-inflicted.

Ref.: W. Cal. Sum., 2 "Workers' Compensation" §250.

§4208. Compensation under chapter; exclusive remedy.

Where the conditions of compensation exist, the right to recover such compensation pursuant to the provisions of this chapter is the exclusive remedy for injury or death of an enrollee against the sponsoring agency, or the participating agency.

§4209. Application of Division to enrollees.

Insofar as not inconsistent with the provisions of this chapter, all of the provisions of this division shall pertain to enrollees and their dependents and the furnishing of compensation benefits thereto.

ARTICLE 2
Benefits

§4211. Limitations on compensation.

Where liability for compensation exists, such compensation shall be provided as limited by this chapter.

§4212. Injury or death of enrollee.

If an enrollee suffers injury or death in the performance of his duties under an economic opportunity program, then, irrespective of his remuneration from this or other employment, his average weekly earnings for the purpose of determining temporary and permanent disability indemnity shall be determined in accordance with Section 4453, provided that for the purpose of this chapter only, there shall be no statutory minimum average weekly earnings for temporary disability indemnity. If the injury sustained by an enrollee causes death, death benefits shall be determined in accordance with Sections 4701 and 4702 of this code.

§4213. Injury causing permanent disability; percentage of disability.

If the injury sustained by an enrollee causes permanent disability, the percentage of disability to total disability shall be determined for the occupation of a laborer of like age by applying the schedule for the determination of the percentage of permanent disabilities prepared and adopted by the appeals board.

§4214. Fatal injury; enrollee's burial expenses.

In addition to death benefit in the event of fatal injury, the reasonable expenses of the enrollee's burial shall be paid not to exceed six hundred dollars ($600).

ARTICLE 3
Adjustment of Claims

§4226. Effect of benefits provided under federal statute.

Should the United States government or any agent thereof, pursuant to federal statute, rule or regulations furnish benefits to enrollees or dependents of enrollees under an economic opportunity program, then the amount of indemnity which an enrollee or his dependents are entitled to receive under this chapter shall be reduced by the amount of monetary benefits the enrollee or his dependents have and will receive from the above source as a result of injury.

§4227. Effect of medical treatment provided by federal government.

If the United States government or any agent thereof furnishes medical treatment to an injured enrollee, the enrollee will have no right to receive the same or similar treatment under this chapter.

§4228. Effect of medical treatment provided by federal government; reimbursement.

If the furnishing of medical treatment by the United States government or its agent takes the form of reimbursement of the enrollee, he shall have no right to receive the same or similar treatment under this chapter.

§4229. Right to recover benefits under federal statute supersedes rights under chapter.

If the furnishing of compensation benefits to an enrollee or his dependents under this chapter prevents such enrollee or his dependents from receiving benefits under the provisions of federal statute, rule or regulations, then the enrollee or his dependents shall have not right and shall not receive compensation benefits under this chapter.

Ref.: Herlick Handbook § 2.5.

CHAPTER 10
DISASTER SERVICE WORKERS

§4350. Office of Emergency Services to administer benefits for volunteer disaster service workers.

The Office of Emergency Services shall administer this chapter as it relates to volunteer disaster service workers. **Leg.H.** 2003 ch. 228 (AB 1756), effective August 11, 2003.

Ref.: Hanna § 3.117[1], [4].

§4351. Exclusive remedy.

Compensation provided by this division is the exclusive remedy of a disaster service worker, or his or her dependents, for injury or death arising out of, and in the course of, his or her activities as a disaster service worker as against the state, the disaster council with which he or she is registered, and the county or city which has empowered the disaster council to register and direct his or her activities. Liability for compensation provided by this division is in lieu of any other liability whatsoever to a disaster service worker or his or her dependents or any other person on his or her behalf against the state, the disaster council with which the disaster service worker is registered, and the county or city which has empowered the disaster council to register and direct his or her activities, for any injury or death arising out of, and in the course of, his or her activities as a disaster service worker.

Ref.: Hanna § 3.117[1]; W. Cal. Sum., 2 "Workers' Compensation" §177.

§4352. Liability for compensation limited to appropriated money; reserve fund.

No compensation shall be paid or furnished to disaster service workers or their dependents pursuant to this division except from money appropriated for the purpose of furnishing compensation to disaster service workers and their dependents. Liability for the payment or furnishing of compensation is dependent upon and limited to the availability of money so appropriated.

After all money so appropriated is expended or set aside in bookkeeping reserves for the payment or furnishing of compensation and reimbursing the State Compensation Insurance Fund for its services, the payment or furnishing of compensation for an injury to a disaster service worker or his or her dependents is dependent upon there having been a reserve set up for the payment or furnishing of compensation to that disaster service worker or his or her dependents and for that injury, and liability is limited to the amount of the reserve. The excess in a reserve for the payment or furnishing of compensation or for reimbursing the State Compensation Insurance Fund for its services may be transferred to reserves of other disaster service workers for the payment or furnishing of compensation and reimbursing the State Compensation Insurance Fund, or may be used to set up reserves for other disaster service workers.

§4353. Maximum benefits.

If a disaster service worker suffers injury or death while in the performance of duties as a disaster service worker, then, irrespective of his or her remuneration from this or other employment or from both, the average weekly earnings for the purposes of determining temporary and permanent disability indemnity shall be taken at the maximum fixed for each, respectively, in Section 4453.

Ref.: Hanna § 3.117[3]; W. Cal. Sum., 2 "Workers' Compensation" §250.

§4354. Determination of permanent disability percentage.

If the injury sustained by a disaster service worker causes permanent disability, the percentage of disability to total disability shall be determined as for the occupation of a laborer of like age by applying the schedule for the determination of the percentages of permanent disabilities prepared and adopted by the administrative director. The amount of the weekly payment for permanent disability shall be the same as the weekly benefit which would be paid for temporary total disability pursuant to Section 4353.

Ref.: Hanna § 3.117[3]; Herlick Handbook § 2.4.

§4355. State benefits reduced by amount of federal benefits received.

(a) Should the United States Government or any agent thereof, in accordance with any federal statute, rule, or regulation, furnish monetary assistance, benefits, or other temporary or permanent relief to disaster service workers or to disaster service workers and their dependents for injuries arising out of and occurring in the course of their activities as disaster service workers, the amount of compensation that any disaster service worker or his or her dependents are otherwise entitled to receive from the State of California under this division for any injury shall be reduced by the amount of monetary assistance, benefits, or other temporary or permanent relief the disaster service worker or his or her dependents have received and will receive from the United States or any agent thereof as a result of the injury.

(b) If, in addition to monetary assistance, benefits, or other temporary or permanent relief, the United States Government or any agent thereof furnishes medical, surgical, or hospital treatment, or any combination thereof, to an injured disaster service worker, the disaster service worker has no right to receive similar medical, surgical, or hospital treatment under this division.

(c) If, in addition to monetary assistance, benefits, or other temporary or permanent relief, the United States Government or any agent thereof will reimburse a disaster service worker or his or her dependents for medical, surgical, or hospital treatment, or any combination thereof, furnished to the injured disaster service worker, the disaster service worker has no right to receive similar medical, surgical, or hospital treatment under this division.

(d) If the furnishing of compensation under this division to a disaster service worker or his or her dependents prevents the disaster service worker or his or her dependents from receiving assistance, benefits, or other temporary or permanent relief under a federal statute, rule, regulation, the disaster service worker and his or her dependents shall have no right to, and may not receive, any compensation from the State of California under this division for any injury for which the United States Government or any agent thereof will furnish assistance, benefits, or other temporary or permanent relief in the absence of the furnishing of compensation by the State of California. **Leg.H.** 2003 ch. 228 (AB 1756), effective August 11, 2003.

CHAPTER 11 ASBESTOS WORKERS' ACCOUNT

ARTICLE 1 General Provisions

§4401. Asbestosis; state policy.

It is the declared policy of the state that qualified injured workers with asbestosis which arises out of and occurs in the course of employment shall receive workers' compensation asbestos workers' benefits promptly and not be subjected to delays of litigation to determine the responsible employer.

Ref.: Herlick Handbook § 3.19; MB Prac. Guide: Cal. Debt Collection & Enforcement of Judgments, §§12.36, 17.06; W. Cal. Sum., 2 "Workers' Compensation" §406.

§4402. Definitions.

(a) "Asbestosis" means any pathology, whether or not combined with preexisting pathology, which results in disability or need for medical treatment from inhalation of asbestos fibers.

(b) "Asbestos worker" means any person whose occupation subjected him or her to an exposure to asbestos fibers.

(c) "Asbestos workers' benefits" means temporary total disability benefits, permanent total disability benefits, death benefits, and medical benefits.

(d) "Dependents" means, and is limited to, a surviving spouse who at the time of injury was dependent on the deceased asbestos worker for half or more of his or her support, and minor children of the deceased asbestos worker.

§4403. Asbestos Workers' Account.

The Asbestos Workers' Account is hereby created in the Uninsured Employers Fund in the State Treasury, and shall be administered by the Director of Industrial Relations. The money in the Asbestos Workers' Account is hereby continuously appropriated for the purposes of this chapter, and to pay the expenses of the director in administering these provisions.

§4404. Scope.

Insofar as not inconsistent with the provisions of this chapter, all of the provisions of this division shall pertain to asbestos workers and their dependents for purposes of furnishing workers' compensation asbestos workers' benefits thereto.

§4405. Asbestos workers' benefits; temporary remedy.

Where the conditions of compensation exist under this division the right to recover workers' compensation asbestos workers' benefits pursuant to the provisions of this chapter is a temporary remedy for injury to an asbestos worker against the Asbestos Workers' Account, and such asbestos worker or his or her dependents shall make all reasonable effort to establish the identity of the employer responsible for securing the payment of compensation.

§4406. Conditions for receiving asbestos workers' benefits.

(a) Payments as advances on workers' compensation asbestos workers' benefits shall be furnished an asbestos worker for injury resulting in asbestosis, or the dependents of the asbestos worker in the case of his or her death due to asbestosis, subject to the provisions of this division, if all of the following conditions occur:

(1) The asbestos worker demonstrates to the account that at the time of exposure, the asbestos worker was performing services and was acting within the scope of his or her duties in an occupation that subjected the asbestos worker to the exposure to asbestos.

(2) The asbestos worker demonstrates to the account that he or she is suffering from asbestosis.

(3) The asbestos worker demonstrates to the account that he or she developed asbestosis from the employment.

(4) The asbestos worker is entitled to compensation for asbestosis as otherwise provided for in this division.

(b) The findings of the account with regard to the conditions in subdivision (a) shall not be evidence in any other proceeding.

(c) The account shall require the asbestos worker to submit to an independent medical examination unless the information and assistance officer, in consultation with the medical director or his or her designee, determines that there exists adequate medical evidence that the worker developed asbestosis from the employment.

ARTICLE 2
Benefits

§4407. Payments as advances.

When the account determines that the conditions in Section 4406 have occurred, payments as advances on workers' compensation asbestos workers' benefits shall be provided in accordance with this chapter, notwithstanding the right of the asbestos worker to secure compensation as otherwise provided for in this division.

§4407.3. Death benefit.

For purposes of this chapter, the death benefit shall be paid in installments in the same manner and amounts as temporary disability indemnity.

§4407.5. No lump-sum payment.

Benefits provided by this chapter shall not be commuted into a lump-sum payment.

§4408. Compensation procedures.

Prior to seeking compensation benefits under this chapter, the asbestos worker shall first make claim on the employer or its workers' compensation insurance carrier for payment of compensation under this division. If the asbestos worker is unable to locate the responsible employer or insurance carrier, or if the employer or insurance carrier fails to pay or denies liability for the compensation required by this division to the person entitled thereto, within a period of 30 days after the assertion of such a claim, the asbestos worker may seek payment of workers' compensation asbestos workers' benefits required by this division from the Asbestos Workers' Account.

§4409. Investigations and claims adjustment.

The Director of Industrial Relations, or his or her representative, shall assign investigative and claims adjustment services respecting matters concerning Asbestos Workers' Account cases. Those assignments may be made within the department, including the Division of Workers' Compensation, and excluding the State Compensation Insurance Fund. **Leg.H.** 1994 chs. 146, 1097.

§4409.5. Workers' compensation judges and support staff; appointment.

The administrative director shall appoint workers' compensation judges and support staff who shall give priority to the processing of the claims of asbestos workers.

Ref.: Hanna § 26.02[2].

§4410. Information and assistance officers; duties.

The administrative director shall appoint at least two information and assistance officers who shall give priority to assisting asbestos workers pursuant to the provisions of this chapter. The information and assistance officer shall assist to the fullest extent possible any asbestos worker seeking benefits under this chapter. In assisting the asbestos worker, the information and assistance officer shall conduct necessary investigation and procure those records, reports, and information which are necessary to the identification of responsible employers and insurance carriers, and to facilitate in the expediting of payments of benefits that may be due under this division.

Ref.: 8 C.C.R. §9928.1.

§4411. Claims against Account; responsible employer; Account as party; termination of benefits.

(a) When a claim is made against the Asbestos Workers' Account, the account shall secure appropriate information, adjust the claim, and pay benefits provided by this chapter in accordance with the provisions of this division.

(b) The asbestos worker shall, prior to the first payment of benefits by the Asbestos Workers' Account, file an application before the Workers' Compensation Appeals Board to determine the responsible employer for payment of compensation under this division.

(c) In every case before the Workers' Compensation Appeals Board in which a claim of injury from exposure to asbestos is alleged, the appeals board shall join the Asbestos Workers' Account as a party to the proceeding and serve the fund with copies of all decisions and orders including findings and awards, and order approving compromise and release.

(d) Once a decision establishing the responsible employer or insurance carrier is agreed upon between the parties, or is issued by the Workers' Compensation Appeals Board, and becomes final, the Asbestos Workers' Account shall terminate payment of compensation benefits, notify all interested parties accordingly, and seek collection as provided for under this chapter. Responsibility for payment of all future compensation benefits shall be in accordance with such agreement, order, or decision.

(e) The account shall terminate the payment of benefits to any employee who fails to cooperate fully in determining the responsible employer or insurance carrier.

(f) The Asbestos Workers' Account may, at any time, commence or join in proceedings before the Workers' Compensation Appeals Board by filing an application on its own behalf. In any case in which the Asbestos Workers' Account has been joined as a party or has filed an application on its own behalf, the Asbestos Workers' Account shall have all of the rights and privileges of a party applicant.

Ref.: Hanna § 30.10.

ARTICLE 3
Collections

§4412. Benefits paid and costs incurred; recovery.

The Asbestos Workers' Account shall take all reasonable and appropriate action to insure that recovery is made by the account for all moneys paid as compensation benefits and as costs.

In the event that the responsible employer is uninsured, the account shall not be entitled to reimbursement from the Uninsured Employers Fund.

§4413. Statutes of limitation under division inapplicable against account.

No limitation of time provided by this division shall run against the Asbestos Workers' Account to initiate proceedings before the Workers' Compensation Appeals Board when the account has made any payment of moneys, incurred any costs for services, or encumbered any liability of the account.

§4414. Liens filed by account.

Immediately following the receipt of knowledge of initiation of proceedings before the Workers' Compensation Appeals Board, or any other jurisdiction providing benefits for the same injury, the Asbestos Workers' Account shall file a lien and may invoke such other remedies as are available to recover moneys expended for compensation benefits.

Ref.: Herlick Handbook § 10.17.

§4415. Legal representation for Director of Industrial Relations.

In any hearing or proceeding, the Director of Industrial Relations may use attorneys from within the department, or the Attorney General, to represent the director and the state.

§4416. Responsible employer; notice of amount to satisfy lien; priority of lien.

Once an agreement as to the responsible employer is reached, or a decision is issued by the Workers' Compensation Appeals Board and becomes final, the Asbestos Workers' Account shall notify the responsible employer or insurance carrier of the amount of payment necessary to satisfy the lien in full. Full payment of the lien shall be made by the responsible employer or insurance carrier within 30 days of the issue of such notification. The account may grant a reasonable extension of time for payment of the lien beyond 30 days. This payment shall be for all moneys expended for compensation benefits, and for all recoverable costs including the cost of independent medical examination and all costs reasonably incidental thereto, including, but not limited to, costs of transportation, hospitalization, consultative evaluation, X-rays, laboratory tests, and other diagnostic procedures. The payment shall bear interest, as provided in Section 5800, from the date of the agreement or decision through the date of payment.

The lien of the Asbestos Workers' Account shall be allowed as a first lien against compensation, and shall have priority over all other liens. The lien of the Asbestos Workers' Account may not be reduced by the Workers' Compensation Appeals Board or by the parties unless express written consent to the proposed reduction of the lien is given by the Asbestos Workers' Account and is filed in the record of proceedings before the Workers' Compensation Appeals Board.

Ref.: Hanna § 30.10.

§4417. Suit against third party.

Nothing in this chapter shall be construed to preclude the filing by an asbestos worker of a claim or suit for damages or indemnity against any person other than his or her employer. The Asbestos Workers' Account shall be entitled to recover from, and shall have a first lien against, any amount which is recoverable by the injured employee pursuant to civil judgment or settlement in relation to a claim for damages or indemnity for the effect of exposure to asbestos, for all compensation benefits paid to the injured employee by the Asbestos Workers' Account which have not previously been recovered from the responsible employer or employers by the Asbestos Workers' Account. Recovery by the Asbestos Workers' Account pursuant to the provisions of this section shall not have the effect of extinguishing or diminishing the liability of the responsible employer or employers to the injured employee for compensation payable under the provisions of this division.

Ref.: Herlick Handbook § 12.2.

§4418. Termination date of chapter; benefits under chapter.

The provisions of this chapter providing for the payment of workers' compensation asbestos workers' benefits from the Asbestos Workers' Account shall be operative only until January 1, 1989, and as of that date all payments from the fund shall be terminated, and the state shall have no further obligation to pay asbestos workers' benefits, unless a later enacted statute which is chaptered before January 1, 1989, deletes or extends that date. However, if no statute is enacted to delete or extend that date prior to January 1, 1989, the authority of the Asbestos Workers' Account under this chapter to recover the benefits and costs paid to asbestos workers prior to that date shall continue until the benefits and costs have been recovered.

Ref.: Hanna § 7.06; Herlick Handbook § 3.19; W. Cal. Sum., 2 "Workers' Compensation" §406.

PART 2
Computation of Compensation

CHAPTER 1
AVERAGE EARNINGS

§4451. "Average annual earnings."

Average annual earnings shall be taken as fifty-two times the average weekly earnings referred to in this chapter.

§4452. Minimum and maximum limits.

Four times the average annual earnings shall be taken at not less than four thousand eight hundred dollars and sixty-four cents ($4,800.64) nor more than fifteen thousand two hundred dollars and sixty-four cents ($15,200.64) in disability cases, and in death cases shall be taken at not less than the minimum nor more than the maximum limits as provided in section 4702 of this code.

§4452.5. "Permanent total disability"; "permanent partial disability."

As used in this division:

(a) "Permanent total disability" means a permanent disability with a rating of 100 percent permanent disability only.

(b) "Permanent partial disability" means a permanent disability with a rating of less than 100 percent permanent disability.

Ref.: Hanna § 6.01[2]; W. Cal. Sum., 2 "Workers' Compensation" §287.

§4453. Computing average weekly earnings.

(a) In computing average annual earnings for the purposes of temporary disability indemnity and permanent total disability indemnity only, the average weekly earnings shall be taken at:

(1) Not less than one hundred twenty-six dollars ($126) nor more than two hundred ninety-four dollars ($294), for injuries occurring on or after January 1, 1983.

(2) Not less than one hundred sixty-eight dollars ($168) nor more than three hundred thirty-six dollars ($336), for injuries occurring on or after January 1, 1984.

(3) Not less than one hundred sixty-eight dollars ($168) for permanent total disability, and, for temporary disability, not less than the lesser of one hundred sixty-eight dollars ($168) or 1.5 times the employee's average weekly earnings from all employers, but in no event less than one hundred forty-seven dollars ($147), nor more than three hundred ninety-nine dollars ($399), for injuries occurring on or after January 1, 1990.

(4) Not less than one hundred sixty-eight dollars ($168) for permanent total disability, and for temporary disability, not less than the lesser of one hundred eighty-nine dollars ($189) or 1.5 times the employee's average weekly earnings from all employers, nor more than five hundred four dollars ($504), for injuries occurring on or after January 1, 1991.

(5) Not less than one hundred sixty-eight dollars ($168) for permanent total disability, and for temporary disability, not less than the lesser of one hundred eighty-nine dollars ($189) or 1.5 times the employee's average weekly earnings from all employers, nor more than six hundred nine dollars ($609), for injuries occurring on or after July 1, 1994.

(6) Not less than one hundred sixty-eight dollars ($168) for permanent total disability, and for temporary disability, not less than the lesser of one hundred eighty-nine dollars ($189) or 1.5 times the employee's average weekly earnings from all employers, nor more than six hundred seventy-two dollars ($672), for injuries occurring on or after July 1, 1995.

(7) Not less than one hundred sixty-eight dollars ($168) for permanent total disability, and for temporary disability, not less than the lesser of one hundred eighty-nine dollars ($189) or 1.5 times the employee's average weekly earnings from all employers, nor more than seven hundred thirty-five dollars ($735), for injuries occurring on or after July 1, 1996.

(8) Not less than one hundred eighty-nine dollars ($189), nor more than nine hundred three dollars ($903), for injuries occurring on or after January 1, 2003.

(9) Not less than one hundred eighty-nine dollars ($189), nor more than one thousand ninety-two dollars ($1,092), for injuries occurring on or after January 1, 2004.

(10) Not less than one hundred eighty-nine dollars ($189), nor more than one thousand two hundred sixty dollars ($1,260), for injuries occurring on or after January 1, 2005. For injuries occurring on or after January 1, 2006, average weekly earnings shall be taken at not less than one hundred eighty-nine dollars ($189), nor more than one thousand two hundred sixty dollars ($1,260) or 1.5 times the state average weekly wage, whichever is greater. Commencing on January 1, 2007, and each January 1 thereafter, the limits specified in this paragraph shall be increased by an amount equal to the percentage increase in the state average weekly wage as compared to the prior year. For purposes of this paragraph, "state average weekly wage" means the average weekly wage paid by employers to employees covered by unemployment insurance as reported by the United States Department of Labor for California for the 12 months ending March 31 of the calendar year preceding the year in which the injury occurred.

(b) In computing average annual earnings for purposes of permanent partial disability indemnity, except as provided in Section 4659, the average weekly earnings shall be taken at:

(1) Not less than seventy-five dollars ($75), nor more than one hundred ninety-five dollars ($195), for injuries occurring on or after January 1, 1983.

(2) Not less than one hundred five dollars ($105), nor more than two hundred ten dollars ($210), for injuries occurring on or after January 1, 1984.

(3) When the final adjusted permanent disability rating of the injured employee is 15 percent or greater, but not more than 24.75 percent: (A) not less than one hundred five dollars ($105), nor more than two hundred twenty-two dollars ($222), for injuries occurring on or after July 1, 1994; (B) not less than one hundred five dollars ($105), nor more than two hundred thirty-one dollars ($231), for injuries occurring on or after July 1, 1995; (C) not less than one hundred five dollars ($105), nor more than two hundred forty dollars ($240), for injuries occurring on or after July 1, 1996.

(4) When the final adjusted permanent disability rating of the injured employee is 25 percent or greater, not less than one hundred five dollars ($105), nor more than two hundred twenty-two dollars ($222), for injuries occurring on or after January 1, 1991.

(5) When the final adjusted permanent disability rating of the injured employee is 25 percent or greater but not more than 69.75 percent: (A) not less than one hundred five dollars ($105), nor more than two hundred thirty-seven dollars ($237), for injuries occurring on or after July 1, 1994; (B) not less than one hundred five dollars ($105), nor more than two hundred forty-six dollars ($246), for injuries occurring on or after July 1, 1995; and (C) not less than one hundred five dollars ($105), nor more than two hundred fifty-five dollars ($255), for injuries occurring on or after July 1, 1996.

(6) When the final adjusted permanent disability rating of the injured employee is less than 70 percent: (A) not less than one hundred fifty dollars ($150), nor more than two hundred seventy-seven dollars and fifty cents ($277.50), for injuries occurring on or after January 1, 2003; (B) not less than one hundred fifty-seven dollars and fifty cents ($157.50), nor more than three hundred dollars ($300), for injuries occurring on or after January 1, 2004; (C) not less than one hundred fifty-seven dollars and fifty cents ($157.50), nor more than three hundred thirty dollars ($330), for injuries occurring on or after January 1, 2005; and (D) not less than one hundred ninety-five dollars ($195), nor more than three hundred forty-five dollars ($345), for injuries occurring on or after January 1, 2006.

(7) When the final adjusted permanent disability rating of the injured employee is 70 percent or greater, but less than 100 percent: (A) not less than one hundred five dollars ($105), nor more than two hundred fifty-two dollars ($252), for injuries occurring on or after July 1, 1994; (B) not less than one hundred five dollars ($105), nor more than two hundred ninety-seven dollars ($297), for injuries occurring on or after July 1, 1995; (C) not less than one hundred five dollars ($105), nor more than three hundred forty-five dollars ($345), for injuries occurring on or after July 1, 1996; (D) not less than one hundred fifty dollars ($150), nor more than three hundred forty-five dollars ($345), for injuries occurring on or after January 1, 2003; (E) not less than one hundred fifty-seven dollars and fifty cents ($157.50), nor more than three hundred seventy-five dollars ($375), for injuries occurring on or after January 1, 2004; (F) not less than one hundred fifty-seven dollars and fifty cents ($157.50), nor more than four hundred five dollars ($405), for injuries occurring on or after January 1, 2005; and (G) not less than one hundred ninety-five dollars ($195), nor

more than four hundred five dollars ($405), for injuries occurring on or after January 1, 2006.

(c) Between the limits specified in subdivisions (a) and (b), the average weekly earnings, except as provided in Sections 4456 to 4459, shall be arrived at as follows:

(1) Where the employment is for 30 or more hours a week and for five or more working days a week, the average weekly earnings shall be the number of working days a week times the daily earnings at the time of the injury.

(2) Where the employee is working for two or more employers at or about the time of the injury, the average weekly earnings shall be taken as the aggregate of these earnings from all employments computed in terms of one week; but the earnings from employments other than the employment in which the injury occurred shall not be taken at a higher rate than the hourly rate paid at the time of the injury.

(3) If the earnings are at an irregular rate, such as piecework, or on a commission basis, or are specified to be by week, month, or other period, then the average weekly earnings mentioned in subdivision (a) shall be taken as the actual weekly earnings averaged for this period of time, not exceeding one year, as may conveniently be taken to determine an average weekly rate of pay.

(4) Where the employment is for less than 30 hours per week, or where for any reason the foregoing methods of arriving at the average weekly earnings cannot reasonably and fairly be applied, the average weekly earnings shall be taken at 100 percent of the sum which reasonably represents the average weekly earning capacity of the injured employee at the time of his or her injury, due consideration being given to his or her actual earnings from all sources and employments.

(d) Every computation made pursuant to this section beginning January 1, 1990, shall be made only with reference to temporary disability or the permanent disability resulting from an original injury sustained after January 1, 1990. However, all rights existing under this section on January 1, 1990, shall be continued in force. Except as provided in Section 4661.5, disability indemnity benefits shall be calculated according to the limits in this section in effect on the date of injury and shall remain in effect for the duration of any disability resulting from the injury. **Leg.H.** 1993 ch. 121, effective July 16, 1993, 2002 chs. 6 (AB 749), 866 (AB 486).

1993 Note: Section 4453, as amended by ch. 121, applies only to injuries occurring on or after January 1, 1994. Stats. 1993 ch. 121 §77.

Ref.: 8 C.C.R. §§10101, 10101.1, 10102, 10110, 10111, 10111.1, 10111.2; Hanna §§ 6.02[1]–[2], 6.05[2], 7.04[1][a]–[b], 8.08[4]; Herlick Handbook §§ 5.1–5.3, 5.5–5.8, 5.11, 6.4, 14.37; W. Cal. Sum., 2 "Workers' Compensation" §§180, 303–308.

§4453.5. Subsequent statutory changes in allowable indemnity.

Benefits payable on account of an injury shall not be affected by a subsequent statutory change in amounts of indemnity payable under this division, and shall be continued as authorized, and in the amounts provided for, by the law in effect at the time the injury giving rise to the right to such benefits occurred.

Ref.: Hanna § 32.04[1][b]; Herlick Handbook §§ 5.2, 5.8; W. Cal. Sum., 2 "Workers' Compensation" §9.

§4454. Overtime and value of board and lodging; determination of average weekly earnings.

In determining average weekly earnings within the limits fixed in Section 4453, there shall be included overtime and the market value of board, lodging, fuel, and other advantages received by the injured employee as part of his remuneration, which can be estimated in money, but such average weekly earnings shall not include any sum which the employer pays to or for the injured employee to cover any special expenses entailed on the employee by the nature of his employment, nor shall there be included either the cost or the market value of any savings, wage continuation, wage replacement, or stock acquisition program or of any employee benefit programs for which the employer pays or contributes to persons other than the employee or his family.

Ref.: 8 C.C.R. §§10101, 10101.1, 10102, 10111, 10111.1, 10111.2; Hanna § 6.04[4]; Herlick Handbook § 5.3; W. Cal. Sum., 2 "Workers' Compensation" §303.

§4455. Injured employee under 18 years old; average weekly earnings.

If the injured employee is under 18 years of age, and his or her incapacity is permanent, his or her average weekly earnings shall be deemed, within the limits fixed in Section 4453, to be the weekly sum that under ordinary circumstances he or she would probably be able to earn at the age of 18 years, in the occupation in which he or she was employed at the time of the injury or in any occupation to which he or she would reasonably have been promoted if he or she had not been injured. If the probable earnings at the age of 18 years cannot reasonably be determined, his or her average weekly earnings shall be taken at the maximum limit established in Section 4453. **Leg.H.** 2001 ch. 159, 2002 ch. 6 (AB 749).

Ref.: Herlick Handbook § 5.7; W. Cal. Sum., 2 "Workers' Compensation" §305.

§4456. Injured employee engaged in unemployment work relief program conducted by state.

Where any employee is injured while engaged on any unemployment work relief program conducted by the State, or a political subdivision, or any State or governmental agency, the disability payments due under this division shall be determined solely on the monthly earnings or anticipated earnings of such person from such program, such payments to be within the minimum and maximum limits set forth in section 4453.

Ref.: W. Cal. Sum., 2 "Workers' Compensation" §305.

§4457. Workers under partnership agreement; average weekly earnings.

In the event the average weekly earnings of workers associating themselves under a partnership agreement, the principal purpose of which is the performance of labor on a particular piece of work, are not otherwise ascertainable, they shall be deemed to be forty dollars ($40).

Ref.: Hanna § 6.05[6]; Herlick Handbook § 5.3; W. Cal. Sum., 2 "Workers' Compensation" §305.

§4458. Active firefighter; average weekly earnings.

If a member registered as an active firefighting member of any regularly organized volunteer fire department as described in Section 3361 suffers injury or death while in the performance of his duty as a fireman, or if a person engaged in fire suppression as described in Section 3365 suffers injury or death while so engaged, then, irrespective of his remuneration from this or other employment or from both, his average weekly earnings for the purposes of determining temporary disability indemnity and permanent disability indemnity shall be taken at the maximum fixed for each, respectively, in Section 4453. Four times his average annual earnings in disability cases and in death cases shall be taken at the maximum limits provided in Sections 4452 and 4702 respectively.

Ref.: Herlick Handbook § 5.3; W. Cal. Sum., 2 "Workers' Compensation" §305.

§4458.2. Active police officer; average weekly earnings.

If an active peace officer of any department as described in Section 3362 suffers injury or death while in the performance of his or her duties as a peace officer, or if a person engaged in the performance of active law enforcement service as described in Section 3366 suffers injury or death while in the performance of that active law enforcement service, or if a person registered as a reserve peace officer of any regularly organized police or sheriff's department as described in Section 3362.5 suffers injury or death while in the performance of his or her duties as a peace officer, then, irrespective of his or her remuneration from this or other employment or from both, his or her average weekly earnings for the purposes of determining temporary disability indemnity and permanent disability indemnity shall be taken at the maximum fixed for each, respectively, in Section 4453. Four times his or her average annual earnings in disability cases and in death cases shall be taken at the maximum limits provided in Sections 4452 and 4702 respectively.

1989 Note: This section is applicable only to injuries occurring on or after January 1, 1990. Stats. 1989 ch. 893 §6.

§4458.5. Injury after termination of active service; average weekly earnings.

If a member suffers "an injury" following termination of active service, and within the time prescribed in Section 3212, 3212.2, 3212.3, 3212.4, 3212.5, 3212.6, 3212.7, or 3213, then, irrespective of his remuneration from any postactive service employment, his average weekly earnings for the purposes of determining temporary disability indemnity, permanent total disability indemnity, and permanent partial disability indemnity, shall be taken at the maximum fixed for each such disability, respectively, in Section 4453.

§4459. Previous disability and compensation; determination of average weekly earnings.

The fact that an employee has suffered a previous disability, or received compensation therefor, does not preclude him from compensation for a later injury, or his dependents from compensation for death resulting therefrom, but in determining compensation for the later injury, or death resulting therefrom, his average weekly earnings shall be fixed at the sum which reasonably represents his earning capacity at the time of the later injury.

Ref.: W. Cal. Sum., 2 "Workers' Compensation" §311.

CHAPTER 2 COMPENSATION SCHEDULES

ARTICLE 1 General Provisions

§4550. Payment of compensation by employer.

Where liability for compensation exists under this division, such compensation shall be furnished or paid by the employer and shall be as provided in this chapter.

Ref.: 8 C.C.R. §§10109, 10110, 10111, 10111.1, 10111.2, 10115, 10440, 10445.

§4551. Willful misconduct of injured employee.

Where the injury is caused by the serious and willful misconduct of the injured employee, the compensation otherwise recoverable therefor shall be reduced one-half, except:

(a) Where the injury results in death.

(b) Where the injury results in a permanent disability of 70 percent or over.

(c) Where the injury is caused by the failure of the employer to comply with any provision of law, or any safety order of the Division of Occupational Safety and Health, with reference to the safety of places of employment.

(d) Where the injured employee is under 16 years of age at the time of injury.

Ref.: 8 C.C.R. §§10440, 10445; Hanna §§ 10.02[2], 24.03[6][b]; Herlick Handbook §§ 9.6, 14.36; W. Cal. Sum., 2 "Workers' Compensation" §331.

§4552. Reduction of compensation; determination by Appeals Board.

The reduction of compensation because of the serious and willful misconduct of an employee is not enforceable, valid, or binding in any respect until the appeals board has so determined by its findings and award as provided in Chapter 6 of Part 4 of this division.

Ref.: 8 C.C.R. §§10440, 10445; Hanna § 31.20[3]; Herlick Handbook § 9.6.

§4553. Willful misconduct of employer.

The amount of compensation otherwise recoverable shall be increased one-half, together with costs and expenses not to exceed two hundred fifty dollars ($250), where the employee is injured by reason of the serious and willful misconduct of any of the following:

(a) The employer, or his managing representative.

(b) If the employer is a partnership, on the part of one of the partners or a managing representative or general superintendent thereof.

(c) If the employer is a corporation, on the part of an executive, managing officer, or general superintendent thereof.

Ref.: 8 C.C.R. §§10440, 10445; Hanna §§ 10.01[1][a]–[b], 10.01[1][d]–[e], 10.01[3], 10.01[4][b], 24.03[6][a]; Herlick Handbook §§ 9.6, 9.7, 12.10, 14.42; CACI No. 2800 (Matthew Bender); W. Cal. Sum., 2 "Workers' Compensation" §§39, 56, 305, 316, 317, 321, 323, 5 "Torts" §230.

§4553.1. Serious and willful misconduct; appeals board findings.

In order to support a holding of serious and willfull misconduct by an employer based upon violation of a safety order, the appeals board must specifically find all of the following:

(1) The specific manner in which the order was violated.

(2) That the violation of the safety order did proximately cause the injury or death, and the specific manner in which the violation constituted the proximate cause.

(3) That the safety order, and the conditions making the safety order applicable, were known to, and violated by, a particular named person, either the employer, or a representative designated by Section 4553, or that the condition making the safety order applicable was obvious, created a probability of serious injury, and that

Labor

the failure of the employer, or a representative designated by Section 4553, to correct the condition constituted a reckless disregard for the probable consequences.

Ref.: 8 C.C.R. §§10440, 10445; Hanna §§ 10.03, 25.05[4], 25.10[7]; Herlick Handbook §§ 9.7, 14.36; W. Cal. Sum., 2 "Workers' Compensation" §321.

§4554. Employer's willful failure to secure payment of compensation.

In case of the willful failure by an employer to secure the payment of compensation, the amount of compensation otherwise recoverable for injury or death as provided in this division shall be increased 10 percent. Failure of the employer to secure the payment of compensation as provided in Article 1 (commencing at Section 3700) of Chapter 4 of Part 1 of this division is prima facie evidence of willfulness on his part.

Ref.: Hanna §§ 2.17, 10.24[5], 10.25, 11.02[4][a]; W. Cal. Sum., 2 "Workers' Compensation" §§52, 53, 151.

§4555. Employer's failure to secure payment of compensation; attorney's fees.

In case of failure by an employer to secure the payment of compensation, the appeals board may award a reasonable attorney's fee in addition to the amount of compensation recoverable. When a fee is awarded under this section no further fee shall be allowed under Section 4903 but the provisions of Section 4903 shall be applicable to secure the payment of any fee awarded under this section.

Ref.: Hanna §§ 10.24[6], 20.02[2][f]; Herlick Handbook §§ 9.2, 10.2, 14.42; W. Cal. Sum., 2 "Workers' Compensation" §§150, 358.

§4555.5. Denial of petition to reduce award.

Whenever a petition to reduce an award, based upon a permanent disability rating which has become final, is denied, the appeals board may order the petitioner to pay to the injured employee all costs incident to the furnishing of X-rays, laboratory services, medical reports, and medical testimony incurred by such employee in connection with the proceeding on such petition.

Ref.: Herlick Handbook § 9.13.

§4556. Increases unaffected by maximums for computation of average earnings.

The increases provided for by this article shall not be limited by the provisions of Chapter 1 of this part relating to maximum amounts in the computation of average earnings.

§4557. Injury to illegally employed person under 16.

Where the injury is to an employee under 16 years of age and illegally employed at the time of injury, the entire compensation otherwise recoverable shall be increased fifty percent (50%), and such additional sum shall be paid by the employer at the same time and in the same manner as the normal compensation benefits.

An employer shall not be held liable for the additional compensation provided by this section if such an employee is hired pursuant to a birth certificate, automobile driver's license, or other reasonable evidence of the fact that the employee is over the age of 15 years, even though such evidence of the age were falsely obtained by the employee. The additional compensation provided by this section shall not exceed the maximum sum specified by Section 4553 for additional compensation payable for serious and willful misconduct on the part of an employer. This section shall not apply to the State or any of its political subdivisions or districts.

Note: See Insurance Code §11661.5.

Ref.: W. Cal. Sum., 2 "Workers' Compensation" §174.

§4558. Definitions; employee's action against employer; injury from absence of power press guard.

(a) As used in this section:

(1) "Employer" means a named identifiable person who is, prior to the time of the employee's injury or death, an owner or supervisor having managerial authority to direct and control the acts of employees.

(2) "Failure to install" means omitting to attach a point of operation guard either provided or required by the manufacturer, when the attachment is required by the manufacturer and made known by him or her to the employer at the time of acquisition, installation, or manufacturer-required modification of the power press.

(3) "Manufacturer" means the designer, fabricator, or assembler of a power press.

(4) "Power press" means any material-forming machine that utilizes a die which is designed for use in the manufacture of other products.

(5) "Removal" means physical removal of a point of operation guard which is either installed by the manufacturer or installed by the employer pursuant to the requirements or instructions of the manufacturer.

(6) "Specifically authorized" means an affirmative instruction issued by the employer prior to the time of the employee's physical injury or death, but shall not mean any subsequent acquiescence in, or ratification of, removal of a point of operation safety guard.

(b) An employee, or his or her dependents in the event of the employee's death, may bring an action at law for damages against the employer where the employee's injury or death is proximately caused by the employer's knowing removal of, or knowing failure to install, a point of operation guard on a power press, and this removal or failure to install is specifically authorized by the employer under conditions known by the employer to create a probability of serious injury or death.

(c) No liability shall arise under this section absent proof that the manufacturer designed, installed, required, or otherwise provided by specification for the attachment of the guards and conveyed knowledge of the same to the employer. Proof of conveyance of this information to the employer by the manufacturer may come from any source.

(d) No right of action for contribution or indemnity by any defendant shall exist against the employer; however, a defendant may seek contribution after the employee secures a judgment against the employer pursuant to the provisions of this section if the employer fails to discharge his or her comparative share of the judgment.

Ref.: Hanna §§ 11.02[5][a]–[c], 11.02[5][e]–[f], 21.05[3][d]; Herlick Handbook §§ 12.8, 12.11, 13.3; CACI Nos. 2800, 2804, 3800, VF-2803 (Matthew Bender); W. Cal. Sum., 2 "Workers' Compensation" §§24, 25, 49–51, 144.

ARTICLE 2
Medical and Hospital Treatment

§4600. Medical treatment provided by employer; expenses included.

(a) Medical, surgical, chiropractic, acupuncture, and hospital treatment, including nursing, medicines, medical and surgical supplies, crutches, and apparatuses, including orthotic and prosthetic devices and services, that is reasonably required to cure or relieve the injured worker from the effects of his or her injury shall be provided by the employer. In the case of his or her neglect or refusal reasonably to do so, the employer is liable for the reasonable expense incurred by or on behalf of the employee in providing treatment.

(b) As used in this division and notwithstanding any other provision of law, medical treatment that is reasonably required to cure or relieve the injured worker from the effects of his or her injury means treatment that is based upon the guidelines adopted by the administrative director pursuant to Section 5307.27 or, prior to the adoption of those guidelines, the updated American College of Occupational and Environmental Medicine's Occupational Medicine Practice Guidelines.

(c) Unless the employer or the employer's insurer has established a medical provider network as provided for in Section 4616, after 30 days from the date the injury is reported, the employee may be treated by a physician of his or her own choice or at a facility of his or her own choice within a reasonable geographic area.

(d)(1) If an employee has notified his or her employer in writing prior to the date of injury that he or she has a personal physician, the employee shall have the right to be treated by that physician from the date of injury if either of the following conditions exist:

(A) The employer provides nonoccupational group health coverage in a health care service plan, licensed pursuant to Chapter 2.2 (commencing with Section 1340) of Division 2 of the Health and Safety Code.

(B) The employer provides nonoccupational health coverage in a group health plan or a group health insurance policy as described in Section 4616.7.

(2) For purposes of paragraph (1), a personal physician shall meet all of the following conditions:

(A) The physician is the employee's regular physician and surgeon, licensed pursuant to Chapter 5 (commencing with Section 2000) of Division 2 of the Business and Professions Code.

(B) The physician is the employee's primary care physician and has previously directed the medical treatment of the employee, and who

Labor

retains the employee's medical records, including his or her medical history. "Personal physician" includes a medical group, if the medical group is a single corporation or partnership composed of licensed doctors of medicine or osteopathy, which operates an integrated multispecialty medical group providing comprehensive medical services predominantly for nonoccupational illnesses and injuries.

(C) The physician agrees to be predesignated.

(3) If the employer provides nonoccupational health care pursuant to Chapter 2.2 (commencing with Section 1340) of Division 2 of the Health and Safety Code, and the employer is notified pursuant to paragraph (1), all medical treatment, utilization review of medical treatment, access to medical treatment, and other medical treatment issues shall be governed by Chapter 2.2 (commencing with Section 1340) of Division 2 of the Health and Safety Code. Disputes regarding the provision of medical treatment shall be resolved pursuant to Article 5.55 (commencing with Section 1374.30) of Chapter 2.2 of Division 2 of the Health and Safety Code.

(4) If the employer provides nonoccupational health care, as described in Section 4616.7, all medical treatment, utilization review of medical treatment, access to medical treatment, and other medical treatment issues shall be governed by the applicable provisions of the Insurance Code.

(5) The insurer may require prior authorization of any nonemergency treatment or diagnostic service and may conduct reasonably necessary utilization review pursuant to Section 4610.

(6) An employee shall be entitled to all medically appropriate referrals by the personal physician to other physicians or medical providers within the nonoccupational health care plan. An employee shall be entitled to treatment by physicians or other medical providers outside of the nonoccupational health care plan pursuant to standards established in Article 5 (commencing with Section 1367) of Chapter 2.2 of Division 2 of the Health and Safety Code.

(7) The division shall conduct an evaluation of this program and present its findings to the Governor and the Legislature on or before December 31, 2008.

(8) This subdivision shall remain in effect only until December 31, 2009, and as of that date is repealed, unless a later enacted statute that is enacted before December 31, 2009, deletes or extends that date.

(e)(1) When at the request of the employer, the employer's insurer, the administrative director, the appeals board, or a workers' compensation administrative law judge, the employee submits to examination by a physician, he or she shall be entitled to receive, in addition to all other benefits herein provided, all reasonable expenses of transportation, meals, and lodging incident to reporting for the examination, together with one day of temporary disability indemnity for each day of wages lost in submitting to the examination.

(2) Regardless of the date of injury, "reasonable expenses of transportation" includes mileage fees from the employee's home to the place of the examination and back at the rate of twenty-one cents ($0.21) a mile or the mileage rate adopted by the Director of the Department of Personnel Administration pursuant to Section 19820 of the Government Code, whichever is higher, plus any bridge tolls. The mileage and tolls shall be paid to the employee at the time he or she is given notification of the time and place of the examination.

(f) When at the request of the employer, the employer's insurer, the administrative director, the appeals board, or a workers' compensation administrative law judge, an employee submits to examination by a physician and the employee does not proficiently speak or understand the English language, he or she shall be entitled to the services of a qualified interpreter in accordance with conditions and a fee schedule prescribed by the administrative director. These services shall be provided by the employer. For purposes of this section, "qualified interpreter" means a language interpreter certified, or deemed certified, pursuant to Article 8 (commencing with Section 11435.05) of Chapter 4.5 of Part 1 of Division 3 of Title 2 of, or Section 68566 of, the Government Code. **Leg.H.** 1993 ch. 121, effective July 16, 1993, 1994 ch. 477, 1995 ch. 938, operative July 1, 1997, 1998 ch. 440 §2, 2004 ch. 34 (SB 899), effective April 19, 2004, 2006 ch. 819 (AB 2068) §2.

2004 Note: The amendment to §4600 made by this act shall apply prospectively from the date of enactment of this act, regardless of the date of injury, unless otherwise specified, but shall not constitute good cause to reopen or rescind, alter, or amend any existing order, decision, or award of the Workers' Compensation Appeals Board. Stats. 2004 ch. 34 (SB 899) §47.

1993 Note: Section 4600, as amended by ch. 121, applies only to injuries occurring on or after January 1, 1994. Stats. 1993 ch. 121 §77.

1989 Note: This section is applicable only to injuries occurring on or after January 1, 1990. Stats. 1989 ch. 893 §6.

Ref.: 8 C.C.R. §§9771, 9773, 9773.1, 9774, 9775, 9777, 9778, 9779, 9779.1, 9779.2, 9779.3, 9779.4, 9779.45, 9779.5, 9779.8, 9779.9, 9785, 9785.2, 9785.3, 9785.4, 9786, 9786.1, 9787, 9788.01, 9788.1, 9788.11, 9788.2, 9788.3, 9788.31, 9788.32, 9788.4, 9788.45, 9788.5, 9788.6, 9788.7, 9788.8, 9788.9, 9788.91, 9789.10, 9789.11, 9789.20, 9789.21, 9789.22, 9789.24, 9789.30, 9789.31, 9789.32, 9789.33, 9789.34, 9789.35, 9789.36, 9789.37, 9789.38, 9789.40, 9789.50, 9789.60, 9789.70, 9789.110, 9789.111, 9790, 9790.1, 9791, 9791.1, 9792, 9792.1, 9792.6, 9792.7, 9792.8, 9792.9, 9792.10, 9795.1, 9795.2, 9795.3, 9795.4, 9880, 9881, 10101, 10101.1, 10102, 10108, 10109, 10110, 10111, 10111.1, 10111.2, 10115, 10118.1, 10564, 10606, 10608, 10616, 10618, 10626, 10727, 10950; Hanna §§ 5.02[1], 5.02[3], 5.03[4], 5.05[1], 5.05[6][b], 5.05[7][a], 22.02[1]; Herlick Handbook §§ 4.1, 4.4, 4.15, 14.22, 14.26, 14.33, 15.6; W. Cal. Sum., 2 "Workers' Compensation" §§4, 23, 261–265, 268, 269, 271–273, 276, 301, 350, 376.

§4600.1. Dispensing generic drug equivalent.

(a) Subject to subdivision (b), any person or entity that dispenses medicines and medical supplies, as required by Section 4600, shall dispense the generic drug equivalent.

(b) A person or entity shall not be required to dispense a generic drug equivalent under either of the following circumstances:

(1) When a generic drug equivalent is unavailable.

(2) When the prescribing physician specifically provides in writing that a nongeneric drug must be dispensed.

(c) For purposes of this section, "dispense" has the same meaning as the definition contained in Section 4024 of the Business and Professions Code.

(d) Nothing in this section shall be construed to preclude a prescribing physician, who is also the dispensing physician, from dispensing a generic drug equivalent. **Leg.H.** 2003 ch. 639 (SB 228) §24.

Ref.: Hanna § 5.02[8]; W. Cal. Sum., 2 "Workers' Compensation" §261.

§4600.2. Continuing availability of medicines and medical supplies to injured employees.

(a) Notwithstanding Section 4600, when a self-insured employer, group of self-insured employers, insurer of an employer, or group of insurers contracts with a pharmacy, group of pharmacies, or pharmacy benefit network to provide medicines and medical supplies required by this article to be provided to injured employees, those injured employees that are subject to the contract shall be provided medicines and medical supplies in the manner prescribed in the contract for as long as medicines or medical supplies are reasonably required to cure or relieve the injured employee from the effects of the injury.

(b) Nothing in this section shall affect the ability of employee-selected physicians to continue to prescribe and have the employer provide medicines and medical supplies that the physicians deem reasonably required to cure or relieve the injured employee from the effects of the injury.

(c) Each contract described in subdivision (a) shall comply with standards adopted by the administrative director. In adopting those standards, the administrative director shall seek to reduce pharmaceutical costs and may consult any relevant studies or practices in other states. The standards shall provide for access to a pharmacy within a reasonable geographic distance from an injured employee's residence. **Leg.H.** 2002 ch. 6 (AB 749).

Ref.: Hanna § 5.02[8]; Herlick Handbook § 4.15; W. Cal. Sum., 2 "Workers' Compensation" §261.

§4600.3. Employee to choose health care provider; health care organization contract—Standards; payment for services; option to switch health care provider.

(a)(1) Notwithstanding Section 4600, when a self-insured employer, group of self-insured employers, or the insurer of an employer contracts with a health care organization certified pursuant to Section 4600.5 for health care services required by this article to be provided to injured employees, those employees who are subject to the contract shall receive medical services in the manner prescribed in the contract, providing that the employee may choose to be treated by a personal physician, personal

Labor

chiropractor, or personal acupuncturist that he or she has designated prior to the injury, in which case the employee shall not be treated by the health care organization. Every employee shall be given an affirmative choice at the time of employment and at least annually thereafter to designate or change the designation of a health care organization or a personal physician, personal chiropractor, or personal acupuncturist. The choice shall be memorialized in writing and maintained in the employee's personnel records. The employee who has designated a personal physician, personal chiropractor, or personal acupuncturist may change their designated caregiver at any time prior to the injury. Any employee who fails to designate a personal physician, personal chiropractor, or personal acupuncturist shall be treated by the health care organization selected by the employer. If the health care organization offered by the employer is the workers' compensation insurer that covers the employee or is an entity that controls or is controlled by that insurer, as defined by Section 1215 of the Insurance Code, this information shall be included in the notice of contract with a health care organization.

(2) Each contract described in paragraph (1) shall comply with the certification standards provided in Section 4600.5, and shall provide all medical, surgical, chiropractic, acupuncture, and hospital treatment, including nursing, medicines, medical and surgical supplies, crutches, and apparatus, including artificial members, that is reasonably required to cure or relieve the effects of the injury, as required by this division, without any payment by the employee of deductibles, copayments, or any share of the premium. However, an employee may receive immediate emergency medical treatment that is compensable from a medical service or health care provider who is not a member of the health care organization.

(3) Insured employers, a group of self-insured employers, or self-insured employers who contract with a health care organization for medical services shall give notice to employees of eligible medical service providers and any other information regarding the contract and manner of receiving medical services as the administrative director may prescribe. Employees shall be duly notified that if they choose to receive care from the health care organization they must receive treatment for all occupational injuries and illnesses as prescribed by this section.

(b) Notwithstanding subdivision (a), no employer which is required to bargain with an exclusive or certified bargaining agent which represents employees of the employer in accordance with state or federal employer-employee relations law shall contract with a health care organization for purposes of Section 4600.5 with regard to employees whom the bargaining agent is recognized or certified to represent for collective bargaining purposes pursuant to state or federal employer-employee relations law unless authorized to do so by mutual agreement between the bargaining agent and the employer. If the collective bargaining agreement is subject to the National Labor Relations Act, the employer may contract with a health care organization for purposes of Section 4600.5 at any time when the employer and bargaining agent have bargained to impasse to the extent required by federal law.

(c)(1) When an employee is not receiving or is not eligible to receive health care coverage for nonoccupational injuries or illnesses provided by the employer, if 90 days from the date the injury is reported the employee who has been receiving treatment from a health care organization or his or her physician, chiropractor, acupuncturist, or other agent notifies his or her employer in writing that he or she desires to stop treatment by the health care organization, he or she shall have the right to be treated by a physician, chiropractor, or acupuncturist or at a facility of his or her own choosing within a reasonable geographic area.

(2) When an employee is receiving or is eligible to receive health care coverage for nonoccupational injuries or illnesses provided by the employer, and has agreed to receive care for occupational injuries and illnesses from a health care organization provided by the employer, the employee may be treated for occupational injuries and diseases by a physician, chiropractor, or acupuncturist of his or her own choice or at a facility of his or her own choice within a reasonable geographic area if the employee or his or her physician, chiropractor, acupuncturist, or other agent notifies his or her employer in writing only after 180 days from the date the injury was reported, or upon the date of contract renewal or open enrollment of the health care organization, whichever occurs first, but in no case until 90 days from the date the injury was reported.

(3) For purposes of this subdivision, an employer shall be deemed to provide health care

coverage for nonoccupational injuries and illnesses if the employer pays more than one-half the costs of the coverage, or if the plan is established pursuant to collective bargaining.

(d) An employee and employer may agree to other forms of therapy pursuant to Section 3209.7.

(e) An employee enrolled in a health care organization shall have the right to no less than one change of physician on request, and shall be given a choice of physicians affiliated with the health care organization. The health care organization shall provide the employee a choice of participating physicians within five days of receiving a request. In addition, the employee shall have the right to a second opinion from a participating physician on a matter pertaining to diagnosis or treatment from a participating physician.

(f) Nothing in this section or Section 4600.5 shall be construed to prohibit a self-insured employer, a group of self-insured employers, or insurer from engaging in any activities permitted by Section 4600.

(g) Notwithstanding subdivision (c), in the event that the employer, group of employers, or the employer's workers' compensation insurer no longer contracts with the health care organization that has been treating an injured employee, the employee may continue treatment provided or arranged by the health care organization. If the employee does not choose to continue treatment by the health care organization, the employer may control the employee's treatment for 30 days from the date the injury was reported. After that period, the employee may be treated by a physician of his or her own choice or at a facility of his or her own choice within a reasonable geographic area. **Leg.H.** 1993 ch. 121, effective July 16, 1993, ch. 1242, 1998 chs. 440, 485 (ch. 440 prevails; ch. 485 not effective), 2002 ch. 6 (AB 749).

1993 Note: Section 4600.3, as added by ch. 121, applies only to injuries occurring on or after January 1, 1994. Stats. 1993 ch. 121 §77.

Ref.: 8 C.C.R. §§9771.1, 9771.2, 9771.6, 9771.60, 9771.61, 9771.62, 9771.63, 9771.64, 9771.65, 9771.66, 9771.67, 9771.68, 9771.69, 9771.70, 9771.71, 9771.72, 9771.73, 9771.74, 9771.75, 9771.76, 9771.77, 9771.78, 9771.79, 9771.80, 9771.81, 9771.82, 9771.83, 9779.3, 9779.45, 9785; Hanna § 22.01[6]; Herlick Handbook §§ 4.1, 4.18; W. Cal. Sum., 2 "Workers' Compensation" §§261, 269, 270.

§4600.35. Licensing requirements for entities seeking to reimburse health care providers.

Any entity seeking to reimburse health care providers for health care services rendered to injured workers on a capitated, or per person per month basis, shall be licensed pursuant to the Knox-Keene Health Care Service Plan Act of 1975 (Chapter 2.2 (commencing with Section 1340) of Division 2 of the Health and Safety Code). **Leg.H.** 2002 ch. 6 (AB 749).

§4600.4. Availability during normal business day.

(a) A workers' compensation insurer, third-party administrator, or other entity that requires, or pursuant to regulation requires, a treating physician to obtain either utilization review or prior authorization in order to diagnose or treat injuries or diseases compensable under this article, shall ensure the availability of those services from 9 a.m. to 5:30 p.m. Pacific coast time of each normal business day.

(b) For purposes of this section "normal business day" means a business day as defined in Section 9 of the Civil Code. **Leg.H.** 1999 ch. 124.

Ref.: 8 C.C.R. §§9792.6, 9792.7, 9792.8, 9792.9, 9792.10; Hanna § 22.05[6][c][iii].

§4600.5. Application for certification as health care organization; application fee; certification requirements for health care service plan, disability insurer, workers' compensation insurer, third-party administrator, workers' compensation health care provider and other entities; claimant's medical treatment records; health care service plan charges; limitations and allowances of act; grounds for refusal, revocation or suspension of certification; provision and regulation of chiropractic care, acupuncture treatment; individual patient information.

(a) Any health care service plan licensed pursuant to the Knox-Keene Health Care Service Plan Act, a disability insurer licensed by the Department of Insurance, or any entity, including, but not limited to, workers' compensation insurers and third-party administrators authorized by the administrative director under subdivision (e), may make written application to the administrative director to become certified as a health care organization to provide health care to injured employees for injuries and diseases compensable under this article.

(b) Each application for certification shall be accompanied by a reasonable fee prescribed by the administrative director, sufficient to cover the actual cost of processing the application. A certificate is valid for the period that the director may prescribe unless sooner revoked or suspended.

(c) If the health care organization is a health care service plan licensed pursuant to the Knox-Keene Health Care Service Plan Act, and has provided the Managed Care Unit of the Division of Workers' Compensation with the necessary documentation to comply with this subdivision, that organization shall be deemed to be a health care organization able to provide health care pursuant to Section 4600.3, without further application duplicating the documentation already filed with the Department of Managed Health Care. These plans shall be required to remain in good standing with the Department of Managed Health Care, and shall meet the following additional requirements:

(1) Proposes to provide all medical and health care services that may be required by this article.

(2) Provides a program involving cooperative efforts by the employees, the employer, and the health plan to promote workplace health and safety, consultative and other services, and early return to work for injured employees.

(3) Proposes a timely and accurate method to meet the requirements set forth by the administrative director for all carriers of workers' compensation coverage to report necessary information regarding medical and health care service cost and utilization, rates of return to work, average time in medical treatment, and other measures as determined by the administrative director to enable the director to determine the effectiveness of the plan.

(4) Agrees to provide the administrative director with information, reports, and records prepared and submitted to the Department of Managed Health Care in compliance with the Knox-Keene Health Care Service Plan Act, relating to financial solvency, provider accessibility, peer review, utilization review, and quality assurance, upon request, if the administrative director determines the information is necessary to verify that the plan is providing medical treatment to injured employees in compliance with the requirements of this code.

Disclosure of peer review proceedings and records to the administrative director shall not alter the status of the proceedings or records as privileged and confidential communications pursuant to Sections 1370 and 1370.1 of the Health and Safety Code.

(5) Demonstrates the capability to provide occupational medicine and related disciplines.

(6) Complies with any other requirement the administrative director determines is necessary to provide medical services to injured employees consistent with the intent of this article, including, but not limited to, a written patient grievance policy.

(d) If the health care organization is a disability insurer licensed by the Department of Insurance, and is in compliance with subdivision (d) of Sections 10133 and 10133.5 of the Insurance Code, the administrative director shall certify the organization to provide health care pursuant to Section 4600.3 if the director finds that the plan is in good standing with the Department of Insurance and meets the following additional requirements:

(1) Proposes to provide all medical and health care services that may be required by this article.

(2) Provides a program involving cooperative efforts by the employees, the employer, and the health plan to promote workplace health and safety, consultative and other services, and early return to work for injured employees.

(3) Proposes a timely and accurate method to meet the requirements set forth by the administrative director for all carriers of workers' compensation coverage to report necessary information regarding medical and health care service cost and utilization, rates of return to work, average time in medical treatment, and other measures as determined by the administrative director to enable the director to determine the effectiveness of the plan.

(4) Agrees to provide the administrative director with information, reports, and records prepared and submitted to the Department of Insurance in compliance with the Insurance Code relating to financial solvency, provider accessibility, peer review, utilization review, and quality assurance, upon request, if the administrative director determines the information is

necessary to verify that the plan is providing medical treatment to injured employees consistent with the intent of this article.

Disclosure of peer review proceedings and records to the administrative director shall not alter the status of the proceedings or records as privileged and confidential communications pursuant to subdivision (d) of Section 10133 of the Insurance Code.

(5) Demonstrates the capability to provide occupational medicine and related disciplines.

(6) Complies with any other requirement the administrative director determines is necessary to provide medical services to injured employees consistent with the intent of this article, including, but not limited to, a written patient grievance policy.

(e) If the health care organization is a workers' compensation insurer, third-party administrator, or any other entity that the administrative director determines meets the requirements of Section 4600.6, the administrative director shall certify the organization to provide health care pursuant to Section 4600.3 if the director finds that it meets the following additional requirements:

(1) Proposes to provide all medical and health care services that may be required by this article.

(2) Provides a program involving cooperative efforts by the employees, the employer, and the health plan to promote workplace health and safety, consultative and other services, and early return to work for injured employees.

(3) Proposes a timely and accurate method to meet the requirements set forth by the administrative director for all carriers of workers' compensation coverage to report necessary information regarding medical and health care service cost and utilization, rates of return to work, average time in medical treatment, and other measures as determined by the administrative director to enable the director to determine the effectiveness of the plan.

(4) Agrees to provide the administrative director with information, reports, and records relating to provider accessibility, peer review, utilization review, quality assurance, advertising, disclosure, medical and financial audits, and grievance systems, upon request, if the administrative director determines the information is necessary to verify that the plan is providing medical treatment to injured employees consistent with the intent of this article.

Disclosure of peer review proceedings and records to the administrative director shall not alter the status of the proceedings or records as privileged and confidential communications pursuant to subdivision (d) of Section 10133 of the Insurance Code.

(5) Demonstrates the capability to provide occupational medicine and related disciplines.

(6) Complies with any other requirement the administrative director determines is necessary to provide medical services to injured employees consistent with the intent of this article, including, but not limited to, a written patient grievance policy.

(7) Complies with the following requirements:

(A) An organization certified by the administrative director under this subdivision may not provide or undertake to arrange for the provision of health care to employees, or to pay for or to reimburse any part of the cost of that health care in return for a prepaid or periodic charge paid by or on behalf of those employees.

(B) Every organization certified under this subdivision shall operate on a fee-for-service basis. As used in this section, fee for service refers to the situation where the amount of reimbursement paid by the employer to the organization or providers of health care is determined by the amount and type of health care rendered by the organization or provider of health care.

(C) An organization certified under this subdivision is prohibited from assuming risk.

(f)(1) A workers' compensation health care provider organization authorized by the Department of Corporations on December 31, 1997, shall be eligible for certification as a health care organization under subdivision (e).

(2) An entity that had, on December 31, 1997, submitted an application with the Commissioner of Corporations under Part 3.2 (commencing with Section 5150) shall be considered an applicant for certification under subdivision (e) and shall be entitled to priority in consideration of its application. The Commissioner of Corporations shall provide complete files for all pending applications to the administrative director on or before January 31, 1998.

(g) The provisions of this section shall not affect the confidentiality or admission in evidence of a claimant's medical treatment records.

(h) Charges for services arranged for or provided by health care service plans certified by this section and that are paid on a per-enrollee-periodic-charge basis shall not be subject to the schedules adopted by the administrative director pursuant to Section 5307.1.

(i) Nothing in this section shall be construed to expand or constrict any requirements imposed by law on a health care service plan or insurer when operating as other than a health care organization pursuant to this section.

(j) In consultation with interested parties, including the Department of Corporations and the Department of Insurance, the administrative director shall adopt rules necessary to carry out this section.

(k) The administrative director shall refuse to certify or may revoke or suspend the certification of any health care organization under this section if the director finds that:

(1) The plan for providing medical treatment fails to meet the requirements of this section.

(2) A health care service plan licensed by the Department of Managed Health Care, a workers' compensation health care provider organization authorized by the Department of Corporations, or a carrier licensed by the Department of Insurance is not in good standing with its licensing agency.

(3) Services under the plan are not being provided in accordance with the terms of a certified plan.

(*l*)(1) When an injured employee requests chiropractic treatment for work-related injuries, the health care organization shall provide the injured worker with access to the services of a chiropractor pursuant to guidelines for chiropractic care established by paragraph (2). Within five working days of the employee's request to see a chiropractor, the health care organization and any person or entity who directs the kind or manner of health care services for the plan shall refer an injured employee to an affiliated chiropractor for work-related injuries that are within the guidelines for chiropractic care established by paragraph (2). Chiropractic care rendered in accordance with guidelines for chiropractic care established pursuant to paragraph (2) shall be provided by duly licensed chiropractors affiliated with the plan.

(2) The health care organization shall establish guidelines for chiropractic care in consultation with affiliated chiropractors who are participants in the health care organization's utilization review process for chiropractic care, which may include qualified medical evaluators knowledgeable in the treatment of chiropractic conditions. The guidelines for chiropractic care shall, at a minimum, explicitly require the referral of any injured employee who so requests to an affiliated chiropractor for the evaluation or treatment, or both, of neuromusculoskeletal conditions.

(3) Whenever a dispute concerning the appropriateness or necessity of chiropractic care for work-related injuries arises, the dispute shall be resolved by the health care organization's utilization review process for chiropractic care in accordance with the health care organization's guidelines for chiropractic care established by paragraph (2).

Chiropractic utilization review for work-related injuries shall be conducted in accordance with the health care organization's approved quality assurance standards and utilization review process for chiropractic care. Chiropractors affiliated with the plan shall have access to the health care organization's provider appeals process and, in the case of chiropractic care for work-related injuries, the review shall include review by a chiropractor affiliated with the health care organization, as determined by the health care organization.

(4) The health care organization shall inform employees of the procedures for processing and resolving grievances, including those related to chiropractic care, including the location and telephone number where grievances may be submitted.

(5) All guidelines for chiropractic care and utilization review shall be consistent with the standards of this code that require care to cure or relieve the effects of the industrial injury.

(m) Individually identifiable medical information on patients submitted to the division shall not be subject to the California Public Records Act (Chapter 3.5 (commencing with Section 6250) of Division 7 of Title 1 of the Government Code).

(n)(1) When an injured employee requests acupuncture treatment for work-related injuries, the health care organization shall provide the injured worker with access to the services of an acupuncturist pursuant to guidelines for acupuncture care established by paragraph (2). Within five working days of the employee's request to see an acupuncturist, the health care organization and any person or entity who directs the kind or manner of health care services for the plan shall refer an injured employee to an affiliated acupuncturist for work-related injuries that are within the guidelines for acupuncture care established by paragraph (2). Acupuncture care rendered in accordance with guidelines for acupuncture care established pursuant to paragraph (2) shall be provided by duly licensed acupuncturists affiliated with the plan.

(2) The health care organization shall establish guidelines for acupuncture care in consultation with affiliated acupuncturists who are participants in the health care organization's utilization review process for acupuncture care, which may include qualified medical evaluators. The guidelines for acupuncture care shall, at a minimum, explicitly require the referral of any injured employee who so requests to an affiliated acupuncturist for the evaluation or treatment, or both, of neuromusculoskeletal conditions.

(3) Whenever a dispute concerning the appropriateness or necessity of acupuncture care for work-related injuries arises, the dispute shall be resolved by the health care organization's utilization review process for acupuncture care in accordance with the health care organization's guidelines for acupuncture care established by paragraph (2).

Acupuncture utilization review for work-related injuries shall be conducted in accordance with the health care organization's approved quality assurance standards and utilization review process for acupuncture care. Acupuncturists affiliated with the plan shall have access to the health care organization's provider appeals process and, in the case of acupuncture care for work-related injuries, the review shall include review by an acupuncturist affiliated with the health care organization, as determined by the health care organization.

(4) The health care organization shall inform employees of the procedures for processing and resolving grievances, including those related to acupuncture care, including the location and telephone number where grievances may be submitted.

(5) All guidelines for acupuncture care and utilization review shall be consistent with the standards of this code that require care to cure or relieve the effects of the industrial injury. **Leg.H.** 1993 ch. 121, effective July 16, 1993, ch. 1242, 1994 chs. 285, 1118, 1997 ch. 346, 1998 ch. 440, 1999 ch. 525, operative July 1, 2000, 2000 ch. 857, 2002 chs. 6, 866 (AB 486).

1993 Note: Section 4600.5, as added by ch. 121, applies only to injuries occurring on or after January 1, 1994. Stats. 1993 ch. 121 §77.

Ref.: 8 C.C.R. §§9770, 9771, 9771.1, 9771.2, 9771.6, 9771.60, 9771.61, 9771.62, 9771.63, 9771.64, 9771.65, 9771.66, 9771.67, 9771.68, 9771.69, 9771.70, 9771.71, 9771.72, 9771.73, 9771.74, 9771.75, 9771.76, 9771.77, 9771.78, 9771.79, 9771.80, 9771.81, 9771.82, 9771.83, 9772, 9773, 9773.1, 9774, 9775, 9777, 9778, 9779, 9779.1, 9779.2, 9779.3, 9779.4, 9779.45, 9779.5, 9779.8, 9779.9; Hanna § 1.24; Herlick Handbook §§ 4.1, 4.19, 16.20; W. Cal. Sum, 2 "Workers' Compensation" §§261, 266.

§4600.6. Rules and procedures for certification as health care organization; application requirements; disclosure requirements; contracts with prospective purchasers; restrictions on advertisements; name of organization; licensing requirements for facilities, personnel, and equipment; scope of workers' compensation health care; grievance system; cause of action against organization; delegation of responsibility to subcommittees; periodic on-site medical survey by Administrative Director.

Any workers' compensation insurer, third-party administrator, or other entity seeking certification as a health care organization under subdivision (e) of Section 4600.5 shall be subject to the following rules and procedures:

(a) Each application for authorization as an organization under subdivision (e) of Section 4600.5 shall be verified by an authorized representative of the applicant and shall be in a form prescribed by the administrative director. The application shall be accompanied by the prescribed fee and shall set forth or be accompanied by each and all of the following:

(1) The basic organizational documents of the applicant, such as the articles of incorporation, articles of association, partnership agreement, trust agreement, or other applicable documents and all amendments thereto.

(2) A copy of the bylaws, rules, and regulations, or similar documents regulating the conduct of the internal affairs of the applicant.

(3) A list of the names, addresses, and official positions of the persons who are to be responsible for the conduct of the affairs of the applicant, which shall include, among others, all members of the board of directors, board of

trustees, executive committee, or other governing board or committee, the principal officers, each shareholder with over 5 percent interest in the case of a corporation, and all partners or members in the case of a partnership or association, and each person who has loaned funds to the applicant for the operation of its business.

(4) A copy of any contract made, or to be made, between the applicant and any provider of health care, or persons listed in paragraph (3), or any other person or organization agreeing to perform an administrative function or service for the plan. The administrative director by rule may identify contracts excluded from this requirement and make provision for the submission of form contracts. The payment rendered or to be rendered to the provider of health care services shall be deemed confidential information that shall not be divulged by the administrative director, except that the payment may be disclosed and become a public record in any legislative, administrative, or judicial proceeding or inquiry. The organization shall also submit the name and address of each provider employed by, or contracting with, the organization, together with his or her license number.

(5) A statement describing the organization, its method of providing for health services, and its physical facilities. If applicable, this statement shall include the health care delivery capabilities of the organization, including the number of full-time and part-time physicians under Section 3209.3, the numbers and types of licensed or state-certified health care support staff, the number of hospital beds contracted for, and the arrangements and the methods by which health care will be provided, as defined by the administrative director under Sections 4600.3 and 4600.5.

(6) A copy of the disclosure forms or materials that are to be issued to employees.

(7) A copy of the form of the contract that is to be issued to any employer, insurer of an employer, or a group of self-insured employers.

(8) Financial statements accompanied by a report, certificate, or opinion of an independent certified public accountant. However, the financial statements from public entities or political subdivisions of the state need not include a report, certificate, or opinion by an independent certified public accountant if the financial statement complies with any requirements that may be established by regulation of the administrative director.

(9) A description of the proposed method of marketing the organization and a copy of any contract made with any person to solicit on behalf of the organization or a copy of the form of agreement used and a list of the contracting parties.

(10) A statement describing the service area or areas to be served, including the service location for each provider rendering professional services on behalf of the organization and the location of any other organization facilities where required by the administrative director.

(11) A description of organization grievance procedures to be utilized as required by this part, and a copy of the form specified by paragraph (3) of subdivision (j).

(12) A description of the procedures and programs for internal review of the quality of health care pursuant to the requirements set forth in this part.

(13) Evidence of adequate insurance coverage or self-insurance to respond to claims for damages arising out of the furnishing of workers' compensation health care.

(14) Evidence of adequate insurance coverage or self-insurance to protect against losses of facilities where required by the administrative director.

(15) Evidence of adequate workers' compensation coverage to protect against claims arising out of work-related injuries that might be brought by the employees and staff of an organization against the organization.

(16) Evidence of fidelity bonds in such amount as the administrative director prescribes by regulation.

(17) Other information that the administrative director may reasonably require.

(b)(1) An organization, solicitor, solicitor firm, or representative may not use or permit the use of any advertising or solicitation that is untrue or misleading, or any form of disclosure that is deceptive. For purposes of this chapter:

(A) A written or printed statement or item of information shall be deemed untrue if it does not conform to fact in any respect that is or may be significant to an employer or employee, or potential employer or employee.

(B) A written or printed statement or item of information shall be deemed misleading whether or not it may be literally true, if, in the total context in which the statement is made or the item of information is communicated, the statement or item of information may be understood by a person not possessing special knowledge regarding health care coverage, as indicating any benefit or advantage, or the absence of any exclusion, limitation, or disadvantage of possible significance to an employer or employee, or potential employer or employee.

(C) A disclosure form shall be deemed to be deceptive if the disclosure form taken as a whole and with consideration given to typography and format, as well as language, shall be such as to cause a reasonable person, not possessing special knowledge of workers' compensation health care, and the disclosure form therefor, to expect benefits, service charges, or other advantages that the disclosure form does not provide or that the organization issuing that disclosure form does not regularly make available to employees.

(2) An organization, solicitor, or representative may not use or permit the use of any verbal statement that is untrue, misleading, or deceptive or make any representations about health care offered by the organization or its cost that does not conform to fact. All verbal statements are to be held to the same standards as those for printed matter provided in paragraph (1).

(c) It is unlawful for any person, including an organization, subject to this part, to represent or imply in any manner that the person or organization has been sponsored, recommended, or approved, or that the person's or organization's abilities or qualifications have in any respect been passed upon, by the administrative director.

(d)(1) An organization may not publish or distribute, or allow to be published or distributed on its behalf, any advertisement unless (A) a true copy thereof has first been filed with the administrative director, at least 30 days prior to any such use, or any shorter period as the administrative director by rule or order may allow, and (B) the administrative director by notice has not found the advertisement, wholly or in part, to be untrue, misleading, deceptive, or otherwise not in compliance with this part or the rules thereunder, and specified the deficiencies, within the 30 days or any shorter time as the administrative director by rule or order may allow.

(2) If the administrative director finds that any advertisement of an organization has materially failed to comply with this part or the rules thereunder, the administrative director may, by order, require the organization to publish in the same or similar medium, an approved correction or retraction of any untrue, misleading, or deceptive statement contained in the advertising.

(3) The administrative director by rule or order may classify organizations and advertisements and exempt certain classes, wholly or in part, either unconditionally or upon specified terms and conditions or for specified periods, from the application of subdivision (a).

(e)(1) The administrative director shall require the use by each organization of disclosure forms or materials containing any information regarding the health care and terms of the workers' compensation health care contract that the administrative director may require, so as to afford the public, employers, and employees with a full and fair disclosure of the provisions of the contract in readily understood language and in a clearly organized manner. The administrative director may require that the materials be presented in a reasonably uniform manner so as to facilitate comparisons between contracts of the same or other types of organizations. The disclosure form shall describe the health care that is required by the administrative director under Sections 4600.3 and 4600.5, and shall provide that all information be in concise and specific terms, relative to the contract, together with any additional information as may be required by the administrative director, in connection with the organization or contract.

(2) All organizations, solicitors, and representatives of a workers' compensation health care provider organization shall, when presenting any contract for examination or sale to a prospective employee, provide the employee with a properly completed disclosure form, as prescribed by the administrative director pursuant to this section for each contract so examined or sold.

(3) In addition to the other disclosures required by this section, every organization and any agent or employee of the organization shall, when representing an organization for examination or sale to any individual purchaser or the representative of a group consisting of 25 or fewer individuals, disclose in writing the ratio of premium cost to health care paid for contracts with individuals and with groups of the same or similar size for the organization's preceding fiscal year. An organization may report that information by geographic area, provided the organization identifies the geographic area and

reports information applicable to that geographic area.

(4) Where the administrative director finds it necessary in the interest of full and fair disclosure, all advertising and other consumer information disseminated by an organization for the purpose of influencing persons to become members of an organization shall contain any supplemental disclosure information that the administrative director may require.

(f) When the administrative director finds it necessary in the interest of full and fair disclosure, all advertising and other consumer information disseminated by an organization for the purpose of influencing persons to become members of an organization shall contain any supplemental disclosure information that the administrative director may require.

(g)(1) An organization may not refuse to enter into any contract, or may not cancel or decline to renew or reinstate any contract, because of the [1] age **or any characteristic listed or defined in subdivision (b) or (e) of Section 51 of the Civil Code** of any contracting party, prospective contracting party, or person reasonably expected to benefit from that contract as an employee or otherwise.

(2) The terms of any contract shall not be modified, and the benefits or coverage of any contract shall not be subject to any limitations, exceptions, exclusions, reductions, copayments, coinsurance, deductibles, reservations, or premium, price, or charge differentials, or other modifications because of the [2] age **or any characteristic listed or defined in subdivision (b) or (e) of Section 51 of the Civil Code** of any contracting party, potential contracting party, or person reasonably expected to benefit from that contract as an employee or otherwise; except that premium, price, or charge differentials because of the sex or age of any individual when based on objective, valid, and up-to-date statistical and actuarial data are not prohibited. Nothing in this section shall be construed to permit an organization to charge different rates to individual employees within the same group solely on the basis of the employee's sex.

(3) It shall be deemed a violation of subdivision (a) for any organization to utilize marital status, living arrangements, occupation, gender, beneficiary designation, ZIP Codes or other territorial classification, or any combination thereof for the purpose of establishing sexual orientation. Nothing in this section shall be construed to alter in any manner the existing law prohibiting organizations from conducting tests for the presence of human immunodeficiency virus or evidence thereof.

(4) This section shall not be construed to limit the authority of the administrative director to adopt or enforce regulations prohibiting discrimination because of sex, marital status, or sexual orientation.

(h)(1) An organization may not use in its name any of the words "insurance," "casualty," "health care service plan," "health plan," "surety," "mutual," or any other words descriptive of the health plan, insurance, casualty, or surety business or use any name similar to the name or description of any health care service plan, insurance, or surety corporation doing business in this state unless that organization controls or is controlled by an entity licensed as a health care service plan or insurer pursuant to the Health and Safety Code or the Insurance Code and the organization employs a name related to that of the controlled or controlling entity.

(2) Section 2415 of the Business and Professions Code, pertaining to fictitious names, does not apply to organizations certified under this section.

(3) An organization or solicitor firm may not adopt a name style that is deceptive, or one that could cause the public to believe the organization is affiliated with or recommended by any governmental or private entity unless this affiliation or endorsement exists.

(i) Each organization shall meet the following requirements:

(1) All facilities located in this state, including, but not limited to, clinics, hospitals, and skilled nursing facilities, to be utilized by the organization shall be licensed by the State Department of Health Services, if that licensure is required by law. Facilities not located in this state shall conform to all licensing and other requirements of the jurisdiction in which they are located.

(2) All personnel employed by or under contract to the organization shall be licensed or certified by their respective board or agency, where that licensure or certification is required by law.

(3) All equipment required to be licensed or registered by law shall be so licensed or registered and the operating personnel for that equipment shall be licensed or certified as required by law.

(4) The organization shall furnish services in a manner providing continuity of care and ready referral of patients to other providers at any time as may be appropriate and consistent with good professional practice.

(5) All health care shall be readily available at reasonable times to all employees. To the extent feasible, the organization shall make all health care readily accessible to all employees.

(6) The organization shall employ and utilize allied health manpower for the furnishing of health care to the extent permitted by law and consistent with good health care practice.

(7) The organization shall have the organizational and administrative capacity to provide services to employees. The organization shall be able to demonstrate to the department that health care decisions are rendered by qualified providers, unhindered by fiscal and administrative management.

(8) All contracts with employers, insurers of employers, and self-insured employers and all contracts with providers, and other persons furnishing services, equipment, or facilities to or in connection with the workers' compensation health care organization, shall be fair, reasonable, and consistent with the objectives of this part.

(9) Each organization shall provide to employees all workers' compensation health care required by this code. The administrative director shall not determine the scope of workers' compensation health care to be offered by an organization.

(j)(1) Every organization shall establish and maintain a grievance system approved by the administrative director under which employees may submit their grievances to the organization. Each system shall provide reasonable procedures in accordance with regulations adopted by the administrative director that shall ensure adequate consideration of employee grievances and rectification when appropriate.

(2) Every organization shall inform employees upon enrollment and annually thereafter of the procedures for processing and resolving grievances. The information shall include the location and telephone number where grievances may be submitted.

(3) Every organization shall provide forms for complaints to be given to employees who wish to register written complaints. The forms used by organizations shall be approved by the administrative director in advance as to format.

(4) The organization shall keep in its files all copies of complaints, and the responses thereto, for a period of five years.

(k) Every organization shall establish procedures in accordance with regulations of the administrative director for continuously reviewing the quality of care, performance of medical personnel, utilization of services and facilities, and costs. Notwithstanding any other provision of law, there shall be no monetary liability on the part of, and no cause of action for damages shall arise against, any person who participates in quality of care or utilization reviews by peer review committees that are composed chiefly of physicians, as defined by Section 3209.3, for any act performed during the reviews if the person acts without malice, has made a reasonable effort to obtain the facts of the matter, and believes that the action taken is warranted by the facts, and neither the proceedings nor the records of the reviews shall be subject to discovery, nor shall any person in attendance at the reviews be required to testify as to what transpired thereat. Disclosure of the proceedings or records to the governing body of an organization or to any person or entity designated by the organization to review activities of the committees shall not alter the status of the records or of the proceedings as privileged communications.

The above prohibition relating to discovery or testimony does not apply to the statements made by any person in attendance at a review who is a party to an action or proceeding the subject matter of which was reviewed, or to any person requesting hospital staff privileges, or in any action against an insurance carrier alleging bad faith by the carrier in refusing to accept a settlement offer within the policy limits, or to the administrative director in conducting surveys pursuant to subdivision (o).

This section shall not be construed to confer immunity from liability on any workers' compensation health care organization. In any case in which, but for the enactment of the preceding provisions of this section, a cause of action would arise against an organization, the cause of action shall exist notwithstanding the provisions of this section.

(*l*) Nothing in this chapter shall be construed to prevent an organization from utilizing subcommittees to participate in peer review activities, nor to prevent an organization from delegating the responsibilities required by subdivision (i) as it determines to be appropriate, to

Labor

subcommittees including subcommittees composed of a majority of nonphysician health care providers licensed pursuant to the Business and Professions Code, as long as the organization controls the scope of authority delegated and may revoke all or part of this authority at any time. Persons who participate in the subcommittees shall be entitled to the same immunity from monetary liability and actions for civil damages as persons who participate in organization or provider peer review committees pursuant to subdivision (i).

(m) Every organization shall have and shall demonstrate to the administrative director that it has all of the following:

(1) Adequate provision for continuity of care.

(2) A procedure for prompt payment and denial of provider claims.

(n) Every contract between an organization and an employer or insurer of an employer, and every contract between any organization and a provider of health care, shall be in writing.

(o)(1) The administrative director shall conduct periodically an onsite medical survey of the health care delivery system of each organization. The survey shall include a review of the procedures for obtaining health care, the procedures for regulating utilization, peer review mechanisms, internal procedures for assuring quality of care, and the overall performance of the organization in providing health care and meeting the health needs of employees.

(2) The survey shall be conducted by a panel of qualified health professionals experienced in evaluating the delivery of workers' compensation health care. The administrative director shall be authorized to contract with professional organizations or outside personnel to conduct medical surveys. These organizations or personnel shall have demonstrated the ability to objectively evaluate the delivery of this health care.

(3) Surveys performed pursuant to this section shall be conducted as often as deemed necessary by the administrative director to assure the protection of employees, but not less frequently than once every three years. Nothing in this section shall be construed to require the survey team to visit each clinic, hospital, office, or facility of the organization.

(4) Nothing in this section shall be construed to require the medical survey team to review peer review proceedings and records conducted and compiled under this section or in medical records. However, the administrative director shall be authorized to require onsite review of these peer review proceedings and records or medical records where necessary to determine that quality health care is being delivered to employees. Where medical record review is authorized, the survey team shall ensure that the confidentiality of the physician-patient relationship is safeguarded in accordance with existing law and neither the survey team nor the administrative director or the administrative director's staff may be compelled to disclose this information except in accordance with the physician-patient relationship. The administrative director shall ensure that the confidentiality of the peer review proceedings and records is maintained. The disclosure of the peer review proceedings and records to the administrative director or the medical survey team shall not alter the status of the proceedings or records as privileged and confidential communications.

(5) The procedures and standards utilized by the survey team shall be made available to the organizations prior to the conducting of medical surveys.

(6) During the survey, the members of the survey team shall offer such advice and assistance to the organization as deemed appropriate.

(7) The administrative director shall notify the organization of deficiencies found by the survey team. The administrative director shall give the organization a reasonable time to correct the deficiencies, and failure on the part of the organization to comply to the administrative director's satisfaction shall constitute cause for disciplinary action against the organization.

(8) Reports of all surveys, deficiencies, and correction plans shall be open to public inspection, except that no surveys, deficiencies or correction plans shall be made public unless the organization has had an opportunity to review the survey and file a statement of response within 30 days, to be attached to the report.

(p)(1) All records, books, and papers of an organization, management company, solicitor, solicitor firm, and any provider or subcontractor providing medical or other services to an organization, management company, solicitor, or solicitor firm shall be open to inspection during normal business hours by the administrative director.

(2) To the extent feasible, all the records, books, and papers described in paragraph (1)

shall be located in this state. In examining those records outside this state, the administrative director shall consider the cost to the organization, consistent with the effectiveness of the administrative director's examination, and may upon reasonable notice require that these records, books, and papers, or a specified portion thereof, be made available for examination in this state, or that a true and accurate copy of these records, books, and papers, or a specified portion thereof, be furnished to the administrative director.

(q)(1) The administrative director shall conduct an examination of the administrative affairs of any organization, and each person with whom the organization has made arrangements for administrative, or management services, as often as deemed necessary to protect the interest of employees, but not less frequently than once every five years.

(2) The expense of conducting any additional or nonroutine examinations pursuant to this section, and the expense of conducting any additional or nonroutine medical surveys pursuant to subdivision (o) shall be charged against the organization being examined or surveyed. The amount shall include the actual salaries or compensation paid to the persons making the examination or survey, the expenses incurred in the course thereof, and overhead costs in connection therewith as fixed by the administrative director. In determining the cost of examinations or surveys, the administrative director may use the estimated average hourly cost for all persons performing examinations or surveys of workers' compensation health care organizations for the fiscal year. The amount charged shall be remitted by the organization to the administrative director.

(3) Reports of all examinations shall be open to public inspection, except that no examination shall be made public, unless the organization has had an opportunity to review the examination report and file a statement or response within 30 days, to be attached to the report. **Leg.H.** 1997 ch. 346, 2008 ch. 682 (AB 2654) §9.

§4600.6. 2008 Deletes. [1] race, color, national origin, ancestry, religion, sex, marital status, sexual orientation, or **[2]** race, color, national origin, ancestry, religion, sex, marital status, sexual orientation, or

Ref.: 8 C.C.R. §§9771.6, 9771.60, 9771.61, 9771.62, 9771.63, 9771.64, 9771.65, 9771.66, 9771.67, 9771.68, 9771.69, 9771.70, 9771.71, 9771.72, 9771.73, 9771.74, 9771.75, 9771.76, 9771.77, 9771.78, 9771.79, 9771.80, 9771.81, 9771.82, 9771.83; Herlick Handbook § 4.1; W. Cal. Sum., 2 "Workers' Compensation" §261.

§4600.7. Workers' Compensation Managed Care Fund.

(a) The Workers' Compensation Managed Care Fund is hereby created in the State Treasury for the administration of Sections 4600.3 and 4600.5 by the Division of Workers' Compensation. The administrative director shall establish a schedule of fees and revenues to be charged to certified health care organizations and applicants for certification to fully fund the administration of these provisions and to repay amounts received as a loan from the General Fund. All fees and revenues shall be deposited in the Workers' Compensation Managed Care Fund and shall be used when appropriated by the Legislature solely for the purpose of carrying out the responsibilities of the Division of Workers' Compensation under Section 4600.3 or 4600.5.

(b) On and after July 1, 1998, no funds received as a loan from the General Fund shall be used to support the administration of Sections 4600.3 and 4600.5. The loan amount shall be repaid to the General Fund by assessing a surcharge on the enrollment fee for each of the next five fiscal years. In the event the surcharge does not produce sufficient revenue over this period, the surcharge shall be adjusted to fully repay the loan over the following three fiscal years, with the final assessment calculated by dividing the balance of the loan by the enrollees at the end of the final fiscal year. **Leg.H.** 1994 ch. 152, effective July 11, 1994, 1998 ch. 282.

Ref.: 8 C.C.R. §§9779, 9779.1; W. Cal. Sum., 2 "Workers' Compensation" §261.

§4601. Employee request to change physician.

(a) If the employee so requests, the employer shall tender the employee one change of physician. The employee at any time may request that the employer tender this one-time change of physician. Upon request of the employee for a change of physician, the maximum amount of time permitted by law for the employer or insurance carrier to provide the employee an alternative physician or, if requested by the employee, a chiropractor, or an acupuncturist shall be five working days from the date of the request. Notwithstanding the 30-day time period specified in Section 4600, a request for a

Labor

change of physician pursuant to this section may be made at any time. The employee is entitled, in any serious case, upon request, to the services of a consulting physician, chiropractor, or acupuncturist of his or her choice at the expense of the employer. The treatment shall be at the expense of the employer.

(b) If an employee requesting a change of physician pursuant to subdivision (a) has notified his or her employer in writing prior to the date of injury that he or she has a personal chiropractor, the alternative physician tendered by the employer to the employee, if the employee so requests, shall be the employee's personal chiropractor. For the purpose of this article, "personal chiropractor" means the employee's regular chiropractor licensed pursuant to Chapter 2 (commencing with Section 1000) of Division 2 of the Business and Professions Code, who has previously directed treatment of the employee, and who retains the employee's chiropractic treatment records, including his or her chiropractic history.

(c) If an employee requesting a change of physician pursuant to subdivision (a) has notified his or her employer in writing prior to the date of injury that he or she has a personal acupuncturist, the alternative physician tendered by the employer to the employee, if the employee so requests, shall be the employee's personal acupuncturist. For the purpose of this article, "personal acupuncturist" means the employee's regular acupuncturist licensed pursuant to Chapter 12 (commencing with Section 4935) of Division 2 of the Business and Professions Code, who has previously directed treatment of the employee, and who retains the employee's acupuncture treatment records, including his or her acupuncture history. **Leg.H.** 1998 ch. 440.

Ref.: 8 C.C.R. §§9880, 9881; Hanna § 5.05[7][a]; Herlick Handbook §§ 4.1, 4.2[a], 4.21; W. Cal. Sum., 2 "Workers' Compensation" §§270, 271.

§4602. Employee request for certification of competency of consulting physicians.

If the employee so requests, the employer shall procure certification by either the administrative director or the appeals board as the case may be of the competency, for the particular case, of the consulting or additional physicians.

Ref.: Hanna § 22.04.

§4603. Employer request for change of physician.

If the employer desires a change of physicians or chiropractor, he may petition the administrative director who, upon a showing of good cause by the employer, may order the employer to provide a panel of five physicians, or if requested by the employee, four physicians and one chiropractor competent to treat the particular case, from which the employee must select one.

Ref.: 8 C.C.R. §§9786, 9786.1, 9787, 9880, 9881, 10950; Hanna §§ 5.05[7][b], 23.03[2]; Herlick Handbook § 4.1; W. Cal. Sum., 2 "Workers' Compensation" §270.

§4603.2. Notice to employer of selected physician; reports to employer; payment by employer; penalties and liabilities for late payment; review of itemization.

(a) Upon selecting a physician pursuant to Section 4600, the employee or physician shall forthwith notify the employer of the name and address of the physician. The physician shall submit a report to the employer within five working days from the date of the initial examination and shall submit periodic reports at intervals that may be prescribed by rules and regulations adopted by the administrative director.

(b)(1) Except as provided in subdivision (d) of Section 4603.4, or under contracts authorized under Section 5307.11, payment for medical treatment provided or authorized by the treating physician selected by the employee or designated by the employer shall be made at reasonable maximum amounts in the official medical fee schedule, pursuant to Section 5307.1, in effect on the date of service. Payments shall be made by the employer within 45 working days after receipt of each separate, itemization of medical services provided, together with any required reports and any written authorization for services that may have been received by the physician. If the itemization or a portion thereof is contested, denied, or considered incomplete, the physician shall be notified, in writing, that the itemization is contested, denied, or considered incomplete, within 30 working days after receipt of the itemization by the employer. A notice that an itemization is incomplete shall state all additional information required to make a decision. Any properly documented list of services provided not paid at the rates then in effect under Section 5307.1 within the 45-working-day period shall be increased by 15 percent, together with interest at the same rate as judgments in civil actions retroactive to the date of receipt of the itemization, unless the employer does both of the following:

(A) Pays the provider at the rates in effect within the 45-working-day period.

(B) Advises, in the manner prescribed by the administrative director, the physician, or another provider of the items being contested, the reasons for contesting these items, and the remedies available to the physician or the other provider if he or she disagrees. In the case of an itemization that includes services provided by a hospital, outpatient surgery center, or independent diagnostic facility, advice that a request has been made for an audit of the itemization shall satisfy the requirements of this paragraph.

An employer's liability to a physician or another provider under this section for delayed payments shall not affect its liability to an employee under Section 5814 or any other provision of this division.

(2) Notwithstanding paragraph (1), if the employer is a governmental entity, payment for medical treatment provided or authorized by the treating physician selected by the employee or designated by the employer shall be made within 60 working days after receipt of each separate itemization, together with any required reports and any written authorization for services that may have been received by the physician.

(c) Any interest or increase in compensation paid by an insurer pursuant to this section shall be treated in the same manner as an increase in compensation under subdivision (d) of Section 4650 for the purposes of any classification of risks and premium rates, and any system of merit rating approved or issued pursuant to Article 2 (commencing with Section 11730) of Chapter 3 of Part 3 of Division 2 of the Insurance Code.

(d)(1) Whenever an employer or insurer employs an individual or contracts with an entity to conduct a review of an itemization submitted by a physician or medical provider, the employer or insurer shall make available to that individual or entity all documentation submitted together with that itemization by the physician or medical provider. When an individual or entity conducting a itemization review determines that additional information or documentation is necessary to review the itemization, the individual or entity shall contact the claims administrator or insurer to obtain the necessary information or documentation that was submitted by the physician or medical provider pursuant to subdivision (b).

(2) An individual or entity reviewing an itemization of service submitted by a physician or medical provider shall not alter the procedure codes listed or recommend reduction of the amount of the payment unless the documentation submitted by the physician or medical provider with the itemization of service has been reviewed by that individual or entity. If the reviewer does not recommend payment for services as itemized by the physician or medical provider, the explanation of review shall provide the physician or medical provider with a specific explanation as to why the reviewer altered the procedure code or changed other parts of the itemization and the specific deficiency in the itemization or documentation that caused the reviewer to conclude that the altered procedure code or amount recommended for payment more accurately represents the service performed.

(3) The appeals board shall have jurisdiction over disputes arising out of this subdivision pursuant to Section 5304. **Leg.H.** 1999 ch. 124, 2000 ch. 1069, 2001 ch. 240, 2003 ch. 639 (SB 228), 2004 ch. 34 (SB 899), effective April 19, 2004, 2006 ch. 69 (AB 1806) §24, effective July 12, 2006.

2004 Note: The amendment to §4603.2 made by this act shall apply prospectively from the date of enactment of this act, regardless of the date of injury, unless otherwise specified, but shall not constitute good cause to reopen or rescind, alter, or amend any existing order, decision, or award of the Workers' Compensation Appeals Board. Stats. 2004 ch. 34 (SB 899) §47.

Ref.: 8 C.C.R. §§9785, 9785.2, 9785.3, 9785.4, 9786, 9786.1, 9787, 9789.10, 9789.11, 9789.20, 9789.21, 9789.22, 9789.24, 9789.30, 9789.31, 9789.32, 9789.33, 9789.34, 9789.35, 9789.36, 9789.37, 9789.38, 9789.40, 9789.50, 9789.60, 9789.70, 9789.110, 9789.111, 9790, 9790.1, 9791, 9791.1, 9792, 9792.1, 9792.5, 9900, 10101, 10101.1, 10102, 10111, 10111.1, 10111.2, 10606, 10950; Hanna §§ 5.05[6][b], [10][b], 10.40[3][b], 22.02[2], [3], 22.05[1], [3]; Herlick Handbook §§ 4.19, 9.5, 10.3; W. Cal. Sum., 2 "Workers' Compensation" §§268, 408.

§4603.4. Regulatory authority for payment processing and confidentiality of medical information.

(a) The administrative director shall adopt rules and regulations to do all of the following:

Labor

(1) Ensure that all health care providers and facilities submit medical bills for payment on standardized forms.

(2) Require acceptance by employers of electronic claims for payment of medical services.

(3) Ensure confidentiality of medical information submitted on electronic claims for payment of medical services.

(b) To the extent feasible, standards adopted pursuant to subdivision (a) shall be consistent with existing standards under the federal Health Insurance Portability and Accountability Act of 1996.

(c) The rules and regulations requiring employers to accept electronic claims for payment of medical services shall be adopted on or before January 1, 2005, and shall require all employers to accept electronic claims for payment of medical services on or before July 1, 2006.

(d) Payment for medical treatment provided or authorized by the treating physician selected by the employee or designated by the employer shall be made by the employer within 15 working days after electronic receipt of an itemized electronic billing for services at or below the maximum fees provided in the official medical fee schedule adopted pursuant to Section 5307.1. If the billing is contested, denied, or incomplete, payment shall be made in accordance with Section 4603.2. **Leg.H.** 2002 ch. 6 (AB 749), 2003 ch. 639 (SB 228).

Ref.: Hanna §§ 1.12[6], 5.05[6][b], 22.02[3], 22.05[1].

§4603.5. Adoption of rules; notice to employees of rights.

The administrative director shall adopt rules pertaining to the format and content of notices required by this article; define reasonable geographic areas for the purposes of Section 4600; specify time limits for all such notices, and responses thereto; and adopt any other rules necessary to make effective the requirements of this article.

Employers shall notify all employees of their rights under this section.

Ref.: 8 C.C.R. §§9900, 10950; Herlick Handbook § 4.1.

§4604. Jurisdiction of appeals board to settle disputes.

Controversies between employer and employee arising under this chapter shall be determined by the appeals board, upon the request of either party.

Ref.: 8 C.C.R. §10950; Hanna §§ 5.05[10][d], 21.02[1], 22.10; Herlick Handbook §§ 4.2[a], 4.3; W. Cal. Sum., 2 "Workers' Compensation" §268.

§4604.5. Medical treatment utilization schedule—Guidelines; rebuttable presumption on issue of extent and scope of medical treatment; limitations on chiropractic, occupational therapy, and physical therapy visits.

(a) Upon adoption by the administrative director of a medical treatment utilization schedule pursuant to Section 5307.27, the recommended guidelines set forth in the schedule shall be presumptively correct on the issue of extent and scope of medical treatment. The presumption is rebuttable and may be controverted by a preponderance of the scientific medical evidence establishing that a variance from the guidelines [1] reasonably **is** required to cure or relieve the injured worker from the effects of his or her injury. The presumption created is one affecting the burden of proof.

(b) The recommended guidelines set forth in the schedule adopted pursuant to subdivision (a) shall reflect practices that are evidence and scientifically based, nationally recognized, and peer reviewed. The guidelines shall be designed to assist providers by offering an analytical framework for the evaluation and treatment of injured workers, and shall constitute care in accordance with Section 4600 for all injured workers diagnosed with industrial conditions.

(c) Three months after the publication date of the updated American College of Occupational and Environmental Medicine's Occupational Medicine Practice Guidelines, and continuing until the effective date of a medical treatment utilization schedule, pursuant to Section 5307.27, the recommended guidelines set forth in the American College of Occupational and Environmental Medicine's Occupational Medicine Practice Guidelines shall be presumptively correct on the issue of extent and scope of medical treatment, regardless of date of injury.

The presumption is rebuttable and may be controverted by a preponderance of the evidence establishing that a variance from the guidelines [2] reasonably **is** required to cure and relieve the employee from the effects of his or her injury, in accordance with Section 4600. The presumption created is one affecting the burden of proof.

(d)(1) Notwithstanding the medical treatment utilization schedule or the guidelines set forth in the American College of Occupational and Environmental Medicine's Occupational Medicine Practice Guidelines, for injuries occurring on and after January 1, 2004, an employee shall be entitled to no more than 24 chiropractic, 24 occupational therapy, and 24 physical therapy visits per industrial injury.

(2) Paragraph (1) shall not apply when an employer authorizes, in writing, additional visits to a health care practitioner for physical medicine services.

(3) Paragraph (1) shall not apply to visits for postsurgical physical medicine and postsurgical rehabilitation services provided in compliance with a postsurgical treatment utilization schedule established by the administrative director pursuant to Section 5307.27.

(e) For all injuries not covered by the American College of Occupational and Environmental Medicine's Occupational Medicine Practice Guidelines or **the** official utilization schedule after adoption pursuant to Section 5307.27, authorized treatment shall be in accordance with other [3] **evidence-based** medical treatment guidelines [4] **that are** recognized **generally** by the national medical community and [5] scientifically based. **Leg.H.** 2003 ch. 639 (SB 228), 2004 ch. 34 (SB 899), effective April 19, 2004, 2007 ch. 621 (AB 1073) §1, 2008 ch. 179 (SB 1498) §175.

§4604.5. 2008 Deletes. [1] is **[2]** is **[3]** evidence based **[4]** generally **[5]** that are

2004 Note: The amendment to §4604.5 made by this act shall apply prospectively from the date of enactment of this act, regardless of the date of injury, unless otherwise specified, but shall not constitute good cause to reopen or rescind, alter, or amend any existing order, decision, or award of the Workers' Compensation Appeals Board. Stats. 2004 ch. 34 (SB 899) §47.

Ref.: 8 C.C.R. §§9767.6, 9792.6, 9792.7, 9792.8, 9792.9, 9792.10, 9881, 10118.1, 10950; Hanna §§ 5.02[3A], 22.05[6][b]; Herlick Handbook § 4.19; W. Cal. Sum., 2 "Workers' Compensation" §§4, 266.

§4605. Consulting or attending physicians provided at employee's expense.

Nothing contained in this chapter shall limit the right of the employee to provide, at his own expense, a consulting physician or any attending physicians whom he desires.

Ref.: Herlick Handbook § 4.3; W. Cal. Sum., 2 "Workers' Compensation" §§107, 268, 350.

§4606. Public self-insured employer; 90-day limitation inapplicable.

Any county, city and county, city, school district, or other public corporation within the state which was a self-insured employer under the "Workmen's Compensation, Insurance and Safety Act," enacted by Chapter 176 of the Statutes of 1913, may provide such medical, and hospital treatment, including nursing, medicines, medical and surgical supplies, crutches, and apparatus, including artificial members which is reasonably required to cure or relieve from the effects of an injury to a former employee who was covered under such act, without regard to the 90-day limitation of subdivision (a) of Section 15 of such act for medical treatment. The provisions of this section shall not be operative in any such county, city and county, city, school district, or other public corporation unless adopted by a resolution of the governing body of such public entity.

§4607. Denial of petition to terminate benefits; attorney's fees.

Where a party to a proceeding institutes proceedings to terminate an award made by the appeals board to an applicant for continuing medical treatment and is unsuccessful in such proceedings, the appeals board may determine the amount of attorney's fees reasonably incurred by the applicant in resisting the proceeding to terminate the medical treatment, and may assess such reasonable attorney's fees as a cost upon the party instituting the proceedings to terminate the award of the appeals board.

Ref.: Hanna § 20.02[2][h]; Herlick Handbook §§ 9.13, 10.2, 14.42; W. Cal. Sum., 2 "Workers' Compensation" §357.

§4608. Pharmacy benefits; form requirements.

No workers' compensation insurer, self-insured employer, or agent of an insurer or self-insured employer, shall refuse to pay pharmacy benefits solely because the claim form utilized is reproduced by the person providing the pharmacy benefits, provided the reproduced form is an exact copy of that used by the insurer, self-insured employer, or agent.

Ref.: Herlick Handbook § 4.19.

§4609. Disclosure relating to health care provider's participation in network; disclosures by contracting agent conveying its list of contracted health care providers and reimbursement rates; election by provider to be excluded from list; demonstration by payor of entitlement to pay contracted rate.

(a) In order to prevent the improper selling, leasing, or transferring of a health care provider's contract, it is the intent of the Legislature that every arrangement that results in any payor paying a health care provider a reduced rate for health care services based on the health care provider's participation in a network or panel shall be disclosed by the contracting agent to the provider in advance and shall actively encourage employees to use the network, unless the health care provider agrees to provide discounts without that active encouragement.

(b) Beginning July 1, 2000, every contracting agent that sells, leases, assigns, transfers, or conveys its list of contracted health care providers and their contracted reimbursement rates to a payor, as defined in subparagraph (A) of paragraph (3) of subdivision (d), or another contracting agent shall, upon entering or renewing a provider contract, do all of the following:

(1) Disclose whether the list of contracted providers may be sold, leased, transferred, or conveyed to other payors or other contracting agents, and specify whether those payors or contracting agents include workers' compensation insurers or automobile insurers.

(2) Disclose what specific practices, if any, payors utilize to actively encourage employees to use the list of contracted providers when obtaining medical care that entitles a payor to claim a contracted rate. For purposes of this paragraph, a payor is deemed to have actively encouraged employees to use the list of contracted providers if the employer provides information directly to employees during the period the employer has medical control advising them of the existence of the list of contracted providers through the use of a variety of advertising or marketing approaches that supply the names, addresses, and telephone numbers of contracted providers to employees; or in advance of a workplace injury, or upon notice of an injury or claim by an employee, the approaches may include, but are not limited to, the use of provider directories, the use of a list of all contracted providers in an area geographically accessible to the posting site, the use of wall cards that direct employees to a readily accessible listing of those providers at the same location as the wall cards, the use of wall cards that direct employees to a toll-free telephone number or Internet Web site address, or the use of toll-free telephone numbers or Internet Web site addresses supplied directly during the period the employer has medical control. However, Internet Web site addresses alone shall not be deemed to satisfy the requirements of this paragraph. Nothing in this paragraph shall prevent contracting agents or payors from providing only listings of providers located within a reasonable geographic range of an employee. A payor who otherwise meets the requirements of this paragraph is deemed to have met the requirements of this paragraph regardless of the employer's ability to control medical treatment pursuant to Sections 4600 and 4600.3.

(3) Disclose whether payors to which the list of contracted providers may be sold, leased, transferred, or conveyed may be permitted to pay a provider's contracted rate without actively encouraging the employees to use the list of contracted providers when obtaining medical care. Nothing in this subdivision shall be construed to require a payor to actively encourage the employees to use the list of contracted providers when obtaining medical care in the case of an emergency.

(4) Disclose, upon the initial signing of a contract, and within 15 business days of receipt of a written request from a provider or provider panel, a payor summary of all payors currently eligible to claim a provider's contracted rate due to the provider's and payor's respective written agreements with any contracting agent.

(5) Allow providers, upon the initial signing, renewal, or amendment of a provider contract, to decline to be included in any list of contracted providers that is sold, leased, transferred, or conveyed to payors that do not actively encourage the employees to use the list of

contracted providers when obtaining medical care as described in paragraph (2). Each provider's election under this paragraph shall be binding on the contracting agent with which the provider has the contract and any other contracting agent that buys, leases, or otherwise obtains the list of contracted providers.

A provider shall not be excluded from any list of contracted providers that is sold, leased, transferred, or conveyed to payors that actively encourage the employees to use the list of contracted providers when obtaining medical care, based upon the provider's refusal to be included on any list of contracted providers that is sold, leased, transferred, or conveyed to payors that do not actively encourage the employees to use the list of contracted providers when obtaining medical care.

(6) If the payor's explanation of benefits or explanation of review does not identify the name of the network that has a written agreement signed by the provider whereby the payor is entitled, directly or indirectly, to pay a preferred rate for the services rendered, the contracting agent shall do the following:

(A) Maintain a Web site that is accessible to all contracted providers and updated at least quarterly and maintain a toll-free telephone number accessible to all contracted providers whereby providers may access payor summary information.

(B) Disclose through the use of an Internet Web site, a toll-free telephone number, or through a delivery or mail service to its contracted providers, within 30 days, any sale, lease assignment, transfer or conveyance of the contracted reimbursement rates to another contracting agent or payor.

(7) Nothing in this subdivision shall be construed to impose requirements or regulations upon payors, as defined in subparagraph (A) of paragraph (3) of subdivision (d).

(c) Beginning July 1, 2000, a payor, as defined in subparagraph (B) of paragraph (3) of subdivision(d), shall do all of the following:

(1) Provide an explanation of benefits or explanation of review that identifies the name of the network with which the payor has an agreement that entitles them to pay a preferred rate for the services rendered.

(2) Demonstrate that it is entitled to pay a contracted rate within 30 business days of receipt of a written request from a provider who has received a claim payment from the payor. The provider shall include in the request a statement explaining why the payment is not at the correct contracted rate for the services provided. The failure of the provider to include a statement shall relieve the payor from the responsibility of demonstrating that it is entitled to pay the disputed contracted rate. The failure of a payor to make the demonstration to a properly documented request of the provider within 30 business days shall render the payor responsible for the lesser of the provider's actual fee or, as applicable, any fee schedule pursuant to this division, which amount shall be due and payable within 10 days of receipt of written notice from the provider, and shall bar the payor from taking any future discounts from that provider without the provider's express written consent until the payor can demonstrate to the provider that it is entitled to pay a contracted rate as provided in this subdivision. A payor shall be deemed to have demonstrated that it is entitled to pay a contracted rate if it complies with either of the following:

(A) Describes the specific practices the payor utilizes to comply with paragraph (2) of subdivision (b), and demonstrates compliance with paragraph (1).

(B) Identifies the contracting agent with whom the payor has a written agreement whereby the payor is not required to actively encourage employees to use the list of contracted providers pursuant to paragraph (5) of subdivision (b).

(d) For the purposes of this section, the following terms have the following meanings:

(1) "Contracting agent" means an insurer licensed under the Insurance Code to provide workers' compensation insurance, a health care service plan, including a specialized health care service plan, a preferred provider organization, or a self-insured employer, while engaged, for monetary or other consideration, in the act of selling, leasing, transferring, assigning, or conveying a provider or provider panel to provide health care services to employees for work-related injuries.

(2) "Employee" means a person entitled to seek health care services for a work-related injury.

(3)(A) For the purposes of subdivision (b), "payor" means a health care service plan, including a specialized health care service plan, an insurer licensed under the Insurance Code to provide disability insurance that covers hospital, medical, or surgical benefits, automobile insurance, or workers' compensation insurance, or a self-insured employer that is responsible to pay for health care services provided to beneficiaries.

(B) For the purposes of subdivision (c), "payor" means an insurer licensed under the Insurance Code to provide workers' compensation insurance, a self-insured employer, a third-party administrator or trust, or any other third party that is responsible to pay health care services provided to employees for work-related injuries, or an agent of an entity included in this definition.

(4) "Payor summary" means a written summary that includes the payor's name and the type of plan, including, but not limited to, a group health plan, an automobile insurance plan, and a workers' compensation insurance plan.

(5) "Provider" means any of the following:

(A) Any person licensed or certified pursuant to Division 2 (commencing with Section 500) of the Business and Professions Code.

(B) Any person licensed pursuant to the Chiropractic Initiative Act or the Osteopathic Initiative Act.

(C) Any person licensed pursuant to Chapter 2.5 (commencing with Section 1440) of Division 2 of the Health and Safety Code.

(D) A clinic, health dispensary, or health facility licensed pursuant to Division 2 (commencing with Section 1200) of the Health and Safety Code.

(E) Any entity exempt from licensure pursuant to Section 1206 of the Health and Safety Code.

(e) This section shall become operative on July 1, 2000. **Leg.H.** 1999 ch. 545, 2000 ch. 1069, 2001 ch. 159.

2000 Note: The amendments made by this act to Section 4609 of the Labor Code do not apply retroactively, and shall become operative on January 1, 2001. Stats. 2000 ch. 1069 §6.

Ref.: 8 C.C.R. §§9767.3, 9767.15.

§4610. Utilization review process to be established; administrative penalties for failure to meet certain requirements.

(a) For purposes of this section, "utilization review" means utilization review or utilization management functions that prospectively, retrospectively, or concurrently review and approve, modify, delay, or deny, based in whole or in part on medical necessity to cure and relieve, treatment recommendations by physicians, as defined in Section 3209.3, prior to, retrospectively, or concurrent with the provision of medical treatment services pursuant to Section 4600.

(b) Every employer shall establish a utilization review process in compliance with this section, either directly or through its insurer or an entity with which an employer or insurer contracts for these services.

(c) Each utilization review process shall be governed by written policies and procedures. These policies and procedures shall ensure that decisions based on the medical necessity to cure and relieve of proposed medical treatment services are consistent with the schedule for medical treatment utilization adopted pursuant to Section 5307.27. Prior to adoption of the schedule, these policies and procedures shall be consistent with the recommended standards set forth in the American College of Occupational and Environmental Medicine Occupational Medical Practice Guidelines. These policies and procedures, and a description of the utilization process, shall be filed with the administrative director and shall be disclosed by the employer to employees, physicians, and the public upon request.

(d) If an employer, insurer, or other entity subject to this section requests medical information from a physician in order to determine whether to approve, modify, delay, or deny requests for authorization, the employer shall request only the information reasonably necessary to make the determination. The employer, insurer, or other entity shall employ or designate a medical director who holds an unrestricted license to practice medicine in this state issued pursuant to Section 2050 or Section 2450 of the Business and Professions Code. The medical director shall ensure that the process by which the employer or other entity reviews and approves, modifies, delays, or denies requests by physicians prior to, retrospectively, or concurrent with the provision of medical treatment services, complies with the requirements of this section. Nothing in this section shall be construed as restricting the existing authority of the Medical Board of California.

(e) No person other than a licensed physician who is competent to evaluate the specific clinical issues involved in the medical treatment services, and where these services are within the scope of the physician's practice, requested by the physician may modify, delay, or deny requests for authorization of medical treatment for reasons of medical necessity to cure and relieve.

(f) The criteria or guidelines used in the utilization review process to determine whether to approve, modify, delay, or deny medical treatment services shall be all of the following:

(1) Developed with involvement from actively practicing physicians.

(2) Consistent with the schedule for medical treatment utilization adopted pursuant to Section 5307.27. Prior to adoption of the schedule, these policies and procedures shall be consistent with the recommended standards set forth in the American College of Occupational and Environmental Medicine Occupational Medical Practice Guidelines.

(3) Evaluated at least annually, and updated if necessary.

(4) Disclosed to the physician and the employee, if used as the basis of a decision to modify, delay, or deny services in a specified case under review.

(5) Available to the public upon request. An employer shall only be required to disclose the criteria or guidelines for the specific procedures or conditions requested. An employer may charge members of the public reasonable copying and postage expenses related to disclosing criteria or guidelines pursuant to this paragraph. Criteria or guidelines may also be made available through electronic means. No charge shall be required for an employee whose physician's request for medical treatment services is under review.

(g) In determining whether to approve, modify, delay, or deny requests by physicians prior to, retrospectively, or concurrent with the provisions of medical treatment services to employees all of the following requirements must be met:

(1) Prospective or concurrent decisions shall be made in a timely fashion that is appropriate for the nature of the employee's condition, not to exceed five working days from the receipt of the information reasonably necessary to make the determination, but in no event more than 14 days from the date of the medical treatment recommendation by the physician. In cases where the review is retrospective, the decision shall be communicated to the individual who received services, or to the individual's designee, within 30 days of receipt of information that is reasonably necessary to make this determination.

(2) When the employee's condition is such that the employee faces an imminent and serious threat to his or her health, including, but not limited to, the potential loss of life, limb, or other major bodily function, or the normal timeframe for the decisionmaking process, as described in paragraph (1), would be detrimental to the employee's life or health or could jeopardize the employee's ability to regain maximum function, decisions to approve, modify, delay, or deny requests by physicians prior to, or concurrent with, the provision of medical treatment services to employees shall be made in a timely fashion that is appropriate for the nature of the employee's condition, but not to exceed 72 hours after the receipt of the information reasonably necessary to make the determination.

(3)(A) Decisions to approve, modify, delay, or deny requests by physicians for authorization prior to, or concurrent with, the provision of medical treatment services to employees shall be communicated to the requesting physician within 24 hours of the decision. Decisions resulting in modification, delay, or denial of all or part of the requested health care service shall be communicated to physicians initially by telephone or facsimile, and to the physician and employee in writing within 24 hours for concurrent review, or within two business days of the decision for prospective review, as prescribed by the administrative director. If the request is not approved in full, disputes shall be resolved in accordance with Section 4062. If a request to perform spinal surgery is denied, disputes shall be resolved in accordance with subdivision (b) of Section 4062.

(B) In the case of concurrent review, medical care shall not be discontinued until the employee's physician has been notified of the decision and a care plan has been agreed upon by the physician that is appropriate for the medical needs of the employee. Medical care provided during a concurrent review shall be care that is medically necessary to cure and relieve, and an insurer or self-insured employer shall only be liable for those services determined medically necessary to cure and relieve. If the insurer or self-insured employer disputes whether or not one or more services offered concurrently with a utilization review were medically necessary to cure and relieve, the dispute shall be resolved pursuant to Section 4062, except in cases involving recommendations for the performance of spinal surgery, which shall be governed by the provisions of subdivision (b) of Section 4062. Any compromise between the parties that an insurer or self-insured employer believes may result in payment for services that were not medically necessary to cure and relieve shall be reported by the insurer or the self-insured employer to the licensing board of the provider or providers who received the payments, in a manner set forth by the respective board and in such a way as to minimize reporting costs both to the board and to the insurer or self-insured employer, for evaluation as to possible violations of the statutes governing appropriate professional practices. No fees shall be levied upon insurers or self-insured employers making reports required by this section.

(4) Communications regarding decisions to approve requests by physicians shall specify the specific medical treatment service approved. Responses regarding decisions to modify, delay, or deny medical treatment services requested by physicians shall include a clear and concise explanation of the reasons for the employer's decision, a description of the criteria or guidelines used, and the clinical reasons for the decisions regarding medical necessity.

(5) If the employer, insurer, or other entity cannot make a decision within the timeframes specified in paragraph (1) or (2) because the employer or other entity is not in receipt of all of the information reasonably necessary and requested, because the employer requires consultation by an expert reviewer, or because the employer has asked that an additional examination or test be performed upon the employee that is reasonable and consistent with good medical practice, the employer shall immediately notify the physician and the employee, in writing, that the employer cannot make a decision within the required timeframe, and specify the information requested but not received, the expert reviewer to be consulted, or the additional examinations or tests required. The employer shall also notify the physician and employee of the anticipated date on which a decision may be rendered. Upon receipt of all information reasonably necessary and requested by the employer, the employer shall approve, modify, or deny the request for authorization within the timeframes specified in paragraph (1) or (2).

(h) Every employer, insurer, or other entity subject to this section shall maintain telephone access for physicians to request authorization for health care services.

(i) If the administrative director determines that the employer, insurer, or other entity subject to this section has failed to meet any of the timeframes in this section, or has failed to meet any other requirement of this section, the administrative director may assess, by order, administrative penalties for each failure. A proceeding for the issuance of an order assessing administrative penalties shall be subject to appropriate notice to, and an opportunity for a hearing with regard to, the person affected. The administrative penalties shall not be deemed to be an exclusive remedy for the administrative director. These penalties shall be deposited in the Workers' Compensation Administration Revolving Fund. **Leg.H.** 2003 ch. 639 (SB 228).

Ref.: 8 C.C.R. §§9785.2, 9792.6, 9792.7, 9792.8, 9792.9, 9792.10; Hanna § 22.05[6][c]; Herlick Handbook § 4.19; W. Cal. Sum., 2 "Workers' Compensation" §§263, 291.

§4610.1. Increase in compensation under §5814—Inapplicable for unreasonable delay in medical treatment for periods of time necessary to complete utilization review process; exception.

An employee shall not be entitled to an increase in compensation under Section 5814 for unreasonable delay in the provision of medical treatment for periods of time necessary to complete the utilization review process in compliance with Section 4610. A determination by the appeals board that medical treatment is appropriate shall not be conclusive evidence that medical treatment was unreasonably delayed or denied for purposes of penalties under Section 5814. In no case shall this section preclude an employee from entitlement to an increase in compensation under Section 5814 when an employer has unreasonably delayed or denied medical treatment due to an unreasonable delay in completion of the utilization review process set forth in Section 4610. **Leg.H.** 2003 ch. 638 (AB 1557).

Ref.: Hanna § 22.05[6][c][v]; Herlick Handbook § 4.19.

§4611. Rights and obligations of health care provider contract governed by underlying contract between provider and contracting agent upon contracting agent's sale, lease, or transfer of contract to payor.

(a) When a contracting agent sells, leases, or transfers a health provider's contract to a payor, the rights and obligations of the provider shall be governed by the underlying contract between the health care provider and the contracting agent.

(b) For purposes of this section, the following terms have the following meanings:

(1) "Contracting agent" has the meaning set forth in paragraph (2) of subdivision (d) of Section 4609.

(2) "Payor" has the meaning set forth in paragraph (3) of subdivision (d) of Section 4609. **Leg.H.** 2003 ch. 203 (AB 175), 2004 ch. 183 (AB 3082) (amended & renumbered from §4610).

§4614. Payment for services.

(a)(1) Notwithstanding Section 5307.1, where the employee's individual or organizational provider of health care services rendered under this division and paid on a fee-for-service basis is also the provider of health care services under contract with the employee's health benefit program, and the service or treatment provided is included within the range of benefits of the employee's health benefit program, and paid on a fee-for-service basis, the amount of payment for services provided under this division, for a work-related occurrence or illness, shall be no more than the amount that would have been paid for the same services under the health benefit plan, for a non-work-related occurrence or illness.

(2) A health care service plan that arranges for health care services to be rendered to an employee under this division under a contract, and which is also the employee's organizational provider for nonoccupational injuries and illnesses, with the exception of a nonprofit health care service plan that exclusively contracts with a medical group to provide or arrange for medical services to its enrollees in a designated geographic area, shall be paid by the employer for services rendered under this division only on a capitated basis.

(b)(1) Where the employee's individual or organizational provider of health care services rendered under this division who is not providing services under a contract is not the provider of health care services under contract with the employee's health benefit program or where the services rendered under this division are not within the benefits provided under the employer-sponsored health benefit program, the provider shall receive payment that is no more than the average of the payment that would have been paid by five of the largest preferred provider organizations by geographic region. Physicians, as defined in Section 3209.3, shall be reimbursed at the same averaged rates, regardless of licensure, for the delivery of services under the same procedure code. This subdivision shall not apply to a health care service plan that provides its services on a capitated basis.

(2) The administrative director shall identify the regions and the five largest carriers in each region. The carriers shall provide the necessary information to the administrative director in the form and manner requested by the administrative director. The administrative director shall make this information available to the affected providers on an annual basis.

(c) Nothing in this section shall prohibit an individual or organizational health care provider from being paid fees different from those set forth in the official medical fee schedule by an employer, insurance carrier, third-party administrator on behalf of employers, or preferred provider organization representing an employer or insurance carrier provided that the administrative director has determined that the alternative negotiated rates between the organizational or individual provider and a payer, a third-party administrator on behalf of employers, or a preferred provider organization will produce greater savings in the aggregate than if each item on billings were to be charged at the scheduled rate.

(d) For the purposes of this section, "organizational provider" means an entity that arranges for health care services to be rendered directly by individual caregivers. An organizational provider may be a health care service plan, disability insurer, health care organization, preferred provider organization, or workers' compensation insurer arranging for care through a managed care network or on a fee-for-service basis. An individual provider is either an individual or institution that provides care directly to the injured worker. **Leg.H.** 1993 ch. 121, effective July 16, 1993, ch. 1242, 2002 ch. 866 (AB 486).

1993 Note: Section 4614, as added by ch. 121, applies only to injuries occurring on or after January 1, 1994. Stats. 1993 ch. 121 §77.

Ref.: Herlick Handbook § 4.19.

Labor

§4614.1. Certified health care service plan permitted to accept payment from self-insured employers.

Notwithstanding subdivision (f) of Section 1345 of the Health and Safety Code, a health care service plan licensed pursuant to the Knox-Keene Health Care Service Plan Act and certified by the administrative director pursuant to Section 4600.5 to provide health care pursuant to Section 4600.3 shall be permitted to accept payment from a self-insured employer, a group of self-insured employers, or the insurer of an employer on a fee-for-service basis for the provision of such health care as long as the health care service plan is not both the health care organization in which the employee is enrolled and the plan through which the employee receives regular health benefits. **Leg.H.** 1993 ch. 121, effective July 16, 1993, ch. 1242.

1993 Note: Section 4614.1, as added by ch. 121, applies only to injuries occurring on or after January 1, 1994. Stats. 1993 ch. 121 §77.

Ref.: Herlick Handbook § 4.19.

ARTICLE 2.3
Medical Provider Networks

§4616. Establishment of medical provider network; goal; requirements; regulations.

(a)(1) On or after January 1, 2005, an insurer or employer may establish or modify a medical provider network for the provision of medical treatment to injured employees. The network shall include physicians primarily engaged in the treatment of occupational injuries and physicians primarily engaged in the treatment of nonoccupational injuries. The goal shall be at least 25 percent of physicians primarily engaged in the treatment of nonoccupational injuries. The administrative director shall encourage the integration of occupational and nonoccupational providers. The number of physicians in the medical provider network shall be sufficient to enable treatment for injuries or conditions to be provided in a timely manner. The provider network shall include an adequate number and type of physicians, as described in Section 3209.3, or other providers, as described in Section 3209.5, to treat common injuries experienced by injured employees based on the type of occupation or industry in which the employee is engaged, and the geographic area where the employees are employed.

(2) Medical treatment for injuries shall be readily available at reasonable times to all employees. To the extent feasible, all medical treatment for injuries shall be readily accessible to all employees. With respect to availability and accessibility of treatment, the administrative director shall consider the needs of rural areas, specifically those in which health facilities are located at least 30 miles apart.

(b) The employer or insurer shall submit a plan for the medical provider network to the administrative director for approval. The administrative director shall approve the plan if he or she determines that the plan meets the requirements of this section. If the administrative director does not act on the plan within 60 days of submitting the plan, it shall be deemed approved.

(c) Physician compensation may not be structured in order to achieve the goal of reducing, delaying, or denying medical treatment or restricting access to medical treatment.

(d) If the employer or insurer meets the requirements of this section, the administrative director may not withhold approval or disapprove an employer's or insurer's medical provider network based solely on the selection of providers. In developing a medical provider network, an employer or insurer shall have the exclusive right to determine the members of their network.

(e) All treatment provided shall be provided in accordance with the medical treatment utilization schedule established pursuant to Section 5307.27 or the American College of Occupational Medicine's Occupational Medicine Practice Guidelines, as appropriate.

(f) No person other than a licensed physician who is competent to evaluate the specific clinical issues involved in the medical treatment services, when these services are within the scope of the physician's practice, may modify, delay, or deny requests for authorization of medical treatment.

(g) On or before November 1, 2004, the administrative director, in consultation with the Department of Managed Health Care, shall adopt regulations implementing this article. The administrative director shall develop regulations that establish procedures for purposes of making medical provider network modifications. **Leg.H.** 2004 ch. 34 (SB 899), effective April 19, 2004.

2004 Note: The addition of §4616 made by this act shall apply prospectively from the date of enactment of this act, regardless of the date of injury, unless otherwise specified, but shall not constitute good cause to reopen or rescind, alter, or amend any existing order, decision, or award of the Workers' Compensation Appeals Board. Stats. 2004 ch. 34 (SB 899) §47.

Ref.: 8 C.C.R. §§9767.1, 9767.2, 9767.3, 9767.4, 9767.5, 9767.6, 9767.7, 9767.8, 9767.9, 9767.12, 9767.13, 9767.14, 9767.15, 9881, 10118.1; Hanna § 5.05[13][a]; Herlick Handbook § 4.19A; W. Cal. Sum., 2 "Workers' Compensation" §§4, 261, 262, 268.

§4616.1. Economic profiling; filing of policies and procedures; disclosure to public.

(a) An insurer or employer that offers a medical provider network under this division and that uses economic profiling shall file with the administrative director a description of any policies and procedures related to economic profiling utilized by the insurer or employer. The filing shall describe how these policies and procedures are used in utilization review, peer review, incentive and penalty programs, and in provider retention and termination decisions. The insurer or employer shall provide a copy of the filing to an individual physician, provider, medical group, or individual practice association.

(b) The administrative director shall make each insurer's or employer's filing available to the public upon request. The administrative director may not publicly disclose any information submitted pursuant to this section that is determined by the administrative director to be confidential pursuant to state or federal law.

(c) For the purposes of this article, "economic profiling" shall mean any evaluation of a particular physician, provider, medical group, or individual practice association based in whole or in part on the economic costs or utilization of services associated with medical care provided or authorized by the physician, provider, medical group, or individual practice association. **Leg.H.** 2004 ch. 34 (SB 899), effective April 19, 2004.

2004 Note: The addition of §4616.1 made by this act shall apply prospectively from the date of enactment of this act, regardless of the date of injury, unless otherwise specified, but shall not constitute good cause to reopen or rescind, alter, or amend any existing order, decision, or award of the Workers' Compensation Appeals Board. Stats. 2004 ch. 34 (SB 899) §47.

Ref.: 8 C.C.R. §§9767.1, 9767.3, 9767.11; Hanna § 5.05[13][b]; Herlick Handbook § 4.19A; W. Cal. Sum., 2 "Workers' Compensation" §262.

§4616.2. Continuity of care policy; filing and approval; revisions; notice; completion of treatment by terminated provider; terms and conditions.

(a) An insurer or employer that arranges for care for injured employees through a medical provider network shall file a written continuity of care policy with the administrative director.

(b) If approved by the administrative director, the provisions of the written continuity of care policy shall replace all prior continuity of care policies. The insurer or employer shall file a revision of the continuity of care policy with the administrative director if it makes a material change to the policy.

(c) The insurer or employer shall provide to all employees entering the workers' compensation system notice of its written continuity of care policy and information regarding the process for an employee to request a review under the policy and shall provide, upon request, a copy of the written policy to an employee.

(d)(1) An insurer or employer that offers a medical provider network shall, at the request of an injured employee, provide the completion of treatment as set forth in this section by a terminated provider.

(2) The completion of treatment shall be provided by a terminated provider to an injured employee who, at the time of the contract's termination, was receiving services from that provider for one of the conditions described in paragraph (3).

(3) The insurer or employer shall provide for the completion of treatment for the following conditions subject to coverage through the workers' compensation system:

(A) An acute condition. An acute condition is a medical condition that involves a sudden onset of symptoms due to an illness, injury, or other medical problem that requires prompt medical attention and that has a limited duration. Completion of treatment shall be provided for the duration of the acute condition.

(B) A serious chronic condition. A serious chronic condition is a medical condition due to a disease, illness, or other medical problem or medical disorder that is serious in nature and

Labor

that persists without full cure or worsens over an extended period of time or requires ongoing treatment to maintain remission or prevent deterioration. Completion of treatment shall be provided for a period of time necessary to complete a course of treatment and to arrange for a safe transfer to another provider, as determined by the insurer or employer in consultation with the injured employee and the terminated provider and consistent with good professional practice. Completion of treatment under this paragraph shall not exceed 12 months from the contract termination date.

(C) A terminal illness. A terminal illness is an incurable or irreversible condition that has a high probability of causing death within one year or less. Completion of treatment shall be provided for the duration of a terminal illness.

(D) Performance of a surgery or other procedure that is authorized by the insurer or employer as part of a documented course of treatment and has been recommended and documented by the provider to occur within 180 days of the contract's termination date.

(4)(A) The insurer or employer may require the terminated provider whose services are continued beyond the contract termination date pursuant to this section to agree in writing to be subject to the same contractual terms and conditions that were imposed upon the provider prior to termination. If the terminated provider does not agree to comply or does not comply with these contractual terms and conditions, the insurer or employer is not required to continue the provider's services beyond the contract termination date.

(B) Unless otherwise agreed by the terminated provider and the insurer or employer, the services rendered pursuant to this section shall be compensated at rates and methods of payment similar to those used by the insurer or employer for currently contracting providers providing similar services who are practicing in the same or a similar geographic area as the terminated provider. The insurer or provider is not required to continue the services of a terminated provider if the provider does not accept the payment rates provided for in this paragraph.

(5) An insurer or employer shall ensure that the requirements of this section are met.

(6) This section shall not require an insurer or employer to provide for completion of treatment by a provider whose contract with the insurer or employer has been terminated or not renewed for reasons relating to a medical disciplinary cause or reason, as defined in paragraph (6) of subdivision (a) of Section 805 of the Business and Profession Code, or fraud or other criminal activity.

(7) Nothing in this section shall preclude an insurer or employer from providing continuity of care beyond the requirements of this section.

(e) The insurer or employer may require the terminated provider whose services are continued beyond the contract termination date pursuant to this section to agree in writing to be subject to the same contractual terms and conditions that were imposed upon the provider prior to termination. If the terminated provider does not agree to comply or does not comply with these contractual terms and conditions, the insurer or employer is not required to continue the provider's services beyond the contract termination date. **Leg.H.** 2004 ch. 34 (SB 899), effective April 19, 2004.

2004 Note: The addition of §4616.2 made by this act shall apply prospectively from the date of enactment of this act, regardless of the date of injury, unless otherwise specified, but shall not constitute good cause to reopen or rescind, alter, or amend any existing order, decision, or award of the Workers' Compensation Appeals Board. Stats. 2004 ch. 34 (SB 899) §47.

Ref.: 8 C.C.R. §§9767.3, 9767.7, 9767.8, 9767.9, 9767.10, 9767.12, 9767.15; Hanna § 5.05[13][c]; Herlick Handbook § 4.19A; W. Cal. Sum., 2 "Workers' Compensation" §262.

§4616.3. Initial medical evaluation; notice of right to be treated by physician of employee's choice; second and third opinions; specialists.

(a) When the injured employee notifies the employer of the injury or files a claim for workers' compensation with the employer, the employer shall arrange an initial medical evaluation and begin treatment as required by Section 4600.

(b) The employer shall notify the employee of his or her right to be treated by a physician of his or her choice after the first visit from the medical provider network established pursuant to this article, and the method by which the list of participating providers may be accessed by the employee.

(c) If an injured employee disputes either the diagnosis or the treatment prescribed by the treating physician, the employee may seek the opinion of another physician in the medical provider network. If the injured employee disputes the diagnosis or treatment prescribed by the second physician, the employee may seek the opinion of a third physician in the medical provider network.

(d)(1) Selection by the injured employee of a treating physician and any subsequent physicians shall be based on the physician's specialty or recognized expertise in treating the particular injury or condition in question.

(2) Treatment by a specialist who is not a member of the medical provider network may be permitted on a case-by-case basis if the medical provider network does not contain a physician who can provide the approved treatment and the treatment is approved by the employer or the insurer. **Leg.H.** 2004 ch. 34 (SB 899), effective April 19, 2004.

2004 Note: The addition of §4616.3 made by this act shall apply prospectively from the date of enactment of this act, regardless of the date of injury, unless otherwise specified, but shall not constitute good cause to reopen or rescind, alter, or amend any existing order, decision, or award of the Workers' Compensation Appeals Board. Stats. 2004 ch. 34 (SB 899) §47.

Ref.: 8 C.C.R. §§9767.1, 9767.3, 9767.5, 9767.6, 9767.15, 9768.9, 9768.10; Hanna § 5.05[13][d]; Herlick Handbook § 4.19A; W. Cal. Sum., 2 "Workers' Compensation" §§262, 268, 269.

§4616.4. Contract for independent medical reviews; duties; requirements; when employee may request independent medical review; standard; applications; examination, determination, and report; deadlines; treatment.

(a)(1) The administrative director shall contract with individual physicians, as described in paragraph (2), or an independent medical review organization to perform independent medical reviews pursuant to this section.

(2) Only physicians licensed pursuant to Chapter 5 (commencing with Section 2000) of the Business and Professions Code may be independent medical reviewers.

(3) The administrative director shall ensure that the independent medical reviewers or those within the review organization shall do all of the following:

(A) Be appropriately credentialed and privileged.

(B) Ensure that the reviews provided by the medical professionals are timely, clear, and credible, and that reviews are monitored for quality on an ongoing basis.

(C) Ensure that the method of selecting medical professionals for individual cases achieves a fair and impartial panel of medical professionals who are qualified to render recommendations regarding the clinical conditions consistent with the medical utilization schedule established pursuant to Section 5307.27, or the American College of Occupational and Environmental Medicine's Occupational Medicine Practice Guidelines.

(D) Ensure that confidentiality of medical records and the review materials, consistent with the requirements of this section and applicable state and federal law.

(E) Ensure the independence of the medical professionals retained to perform the reviews through conflict-of-interest policies and prohibitions, and ensure adequate screening for conflicts of interest.

(4) Medical professionals selected by the administrative director or the independent medical review organizations to review medical treatment decisions shall be physicians, as specified in paragraph (2) of subdivision (a), who meet the following minimum requirements:

(A) The medical professional shall be a clinician knowledgeable in the treatment of the employee's medical condition, knowledgeable about the proposed treatment, and familiar with guidelines and protocols in the area of treatment under review.

(B) Notwithstanding any other provision of law, the medical professional shall hold a nonrestricted license in any state of the United States, and for physicians, a current certification by a recognized American medical specialty board in the area or areas appropriate to the condition or treatment under review.

(C) The medical professional shall have no history of disciplinary action or sanctions, including, but not limited to, loss of staff privileges or participation restrictions taken or pending by any hospital, government, or regulatory body.

(b) If, after the third physician's opinion, the treatment or diagnostic service remains disputed, the injured employee may request independent medical review regarding the disputed treatment or diagnostic service still in dispute after the third physician's opinion in accordance

Labor

with Section 4616.3. The standard to be utilized for independent medical review is identical to that contained in the medical treatment utilization schedule established in Section 5307.27, or the American College of Occupational and Environmental Medicine's Occupational Medicine Practice Guidelines, as appropriate.

(c) Applications for independent medical review shall be submitted to the administrative director on a one-page form provided by the administrative director entitled "Independent Medical Review Application." The form shall contain a signed release from the injured employee, or a person authorized pursuant to law to act on behalf of the injured employee, authorizing the release of medical and treatment information. The injured employee may provide any relevant material or documentation with the application. The administrative director or the independent medical review organization shall assign the independent medical reviewer.

(d) Following receipt of the application for independent medical review, the employer or insurer shall provide the independent medical reviewer, assigned pursuant to subdivision (c), with all information that was considered in relation to the disputed treatment or diagnostic service, including both of the following:

(1) A copy of all correspondence from, and received by, any treating physician who provided a treatment or diagnostic service to the injured employee in connection with the injury.

(2) A complete and legible copy of all medical records and other information used by the physicians in making a decision regarding the disputed treatment or diagnostic service.

(e) Upon receipt of information and documents related to the application for independent medical review, the independent medical reviewer shall conduct a physical examination of the injured employee at the employee's discretion. The reviewer may order any diagnostic tests necessary to make his or her determination regarding medical treatment. Utilizing the medical treatment utilization schedule established pursuant to Section 5307.27, or the American College of Occupational and Environmental Medicine's Occupational Medicine Practice Guidelines, as appropriate, and taking into account any reports and information provided, the reviewer shall determine whether the disputed health care service was consistent with Section 5307.27 or the American College of Occupational and Environmental Medicine's Occupational Medicine Practice Guidelines based on the specific medical needs of the injured employee.

(f) The independent medical reviewer shall issue a report to the administrative director, in writing, and in layperson's terms to the maximum extent practicable, containing his or her analysis and determination whether the disputed health care service was consistent with the medical treatment utilization schedule established pursuant to Section 5307.27, or the American College of Occupational and Environmental Medicine's Occupational Medicine Practice Guidelines, as appropriate, within 30 days of the examination of the injured employee, or within less time as prescribed by the administrative director. If the disputed health care service has not been provided and the independent medical reviewer certifies in writing that an imminent and serious threat to the health of the injured employee may exist, including, but not limited to, serious pain, the potential loss of life, limb, or major bodily function, or the immediate and serious deterioration of the injured employee, the report shall be expedited and rendered within three days of the examination by the independent medical reviewer. Subject to the approval of the administrative director, the deadlines for analyses and determinations involving both regular and expedited reviews may be extended by the administrative director for up to three days in extraordinary circumstances or for good cause.

(g) The independent medical reviewer's analysis shall cite the injured employee's medical condition, the relevant documents in the record, and the relevant findings associated with the documents or any other information submitted to the reviewer in order to support the determination.

(h) The administrative director shall immediately adopt the determination of the independent medical reviewer, and shall promptly issue a written decision to the parties.

(i) If the determination of the independent medical reviewer finds that the disputed treatment or diagnostic service is consistent with Section 5307.27 or the American College of Occupational and Environmental Medicine's Occupational Medicine Practice Guidelines, the injured employee may seek the disputed treatment or diagnostic service from a physician of his or her choice from within or outside the medical provider network. Treatment outside the medical provider network shall be provided consistent with Section 5307.27 or the American College of Occupational and Environmental Medicine's Occupational Practice Guidelines. The employer shall be liable for the cost of any approved medical treatment in accordance with Section 5307.1 or 5307.11. **Leg.H.** 2004 ch. 34 (SB 899), effective April 19, 2004.

2004 Note: The addition of §4616.4 made by this act shall apply prospectively from the date of enactment of this act, regardless of the date of injury, unless otherwise specified, but shall not constitute good cause to reopen or rescind, alter, or amend any existing order, decision, or award of the Workers' Compensation Appeals Board. Stats. 2004 ch. 34 (SB 899) §47.

Ref.: 8 C.C.R. §§9768.1, 9768.2, 9768.3, 9768.4, 9768.5, 9768.6, 9768.7, 9768.8, 9768.9, 9768.10, 9768.11, 9768.12, 9768.13, 9768.14, 9768.15, 9768.17; Hanna § 5.05[13][e]; Herlick Handbook § 4.19A; W. Cal. Sum., 2 "Workers' Compensation" §§262, 269.

§4616.5. "Employer" defined.

For purposes of this article, "employer" means a self-insured employer, joint powers authority, or the state. **Leg.H.** 2004 ch. 34 (SB 899), effective April 19, 2004.

2004 Note: The addition of §4616.5 made by this act shall apply prospectively from the date of enactment of this act, regardless of the date of injury, unless otherwise specified, but shall not constitute good cause to reopen or rescind, alter, or amend any existing order, decision, or award of the Workers' Compensation Appeals Board. Stats. 2004 ch. 34 (SB 899) §47.

Ref.: 8 C.C.R. §§9767.1, 9767.3, 9767.4, 9767.8; Hanna § 5.05[13][a]; W. Cal. Sum., 2 "Workers' Compensation" §262.

§4616.6. Additional examinations and reports precluded.

No additional examinations shall be ordered by the appeals board and no other reports shall be admissable to resolve any controversy arising out of this article. **Leg.H.** 2004 ch. 34 (SB 899), effective April 19, 2004.

2004 Note: The addition of §4616.6 made by this act shall apply prospectively from the date of enactment of this act, regardless of the date of injury, unless otherwise specified, but shall not constitute good cause to reopen or rescind, alter, or amend any existing order, decision, or award of the Workers' Compensation Appeals Board. Stats. 2004 ch. 34 (SB 899) §47.

Ref.: Hanna § 5.05[13][e]; Herlick Handbook § 4.19A; W. Cal. Sum., 2 "Workers' Compensation" §262.

§4616.7. Requirements for approval; health care organization; health care service plan; group disability insurance policy; Taft-Hartley Health and Welfare Fund.

(a) A health care organization certified pursuant to Section 4600.5 shall be deemed approved pursuant to this article if it meets the percentage required for physicians primarily engaged in nonoccupational medicine specified in subdivision (a) of Section 4616 and all the other requirements of this article are met, as determined by the administrative director.

(b) A health care service plan, licensed pursuant to Chapter 2.2 (commencing with Section 1340) of Division 2 of the Health and Safety Code, shall be deemed approved for purposes of this article if it has a reasonable number of physicians with competency in occupational medicine, as determined by the administrative director.

(c) A group disability insurance policy, as defined in subdivision (b) of Section 106 of the Insurance Code, that covers hospital, surgical, and medical care expenses shall be deemed approved for purposes of this article if it has a reasonable number of physicians with competency in occupational medicine, as determined by the administrative director. For the purposes of this section, a group disability insurance policy shall not include Medicare supplement, vision-only, dental-only, and Champus-supplement insurance. For purposes of this section, a group disability insurance policy shall not include hospital indemnity, accident-only, and specified disease insurance that pays benefits on a fixed benefit, cash-payment-only basis.

(d) Any Taft-Hartley health and welfare fund shall be deemed approved for purposes of this article if it has a reasonable number of physicians with competency in occupational medicine, as determined by the administrative director. **Leg.H.** 2004 ch. 34 (SB 899), effective April 19, 2004.

2004 Note: The addition of §4616.7 made by this act shall apply prospectively from the date of enactment of this act, regardless of the date of injury, unless otherwise specified, but shall not constitute good cause to reopen or rescind, alter, or amend any existing order, decision, or award of the Workers' Compensation Appeals Board. Stats. 2004 ch. 34 (SB 899) §47.

Ref.: 8 C.C.R. §§9767.1, 9767.3, 9767.4; Hanna §§ 5.05[1], 22.02[1]; Herlick Handbook § 4.19A; W. Cal. Sum., 2 "Workers' Compensation" §§262, 269.

ARTICLE 2.5
Medical-Legal Expenses

§4620. Definitions.

(a) For purposes of this article, a medical-legal expense means any costs and expenses incurred by or on behalf of any party, the administrative director, the board, or a referee for X-rays, laboratory fees, other diagnostic tests, medical reports, medical records, medical testimony, and, as needed, interpreter's fees, for the purpose of proving or disproving a contested claim.

(b) A contested claim exists when the employer knows or reasonably should know that the employee is claiming entitlement to any benefit arising out of a claimed industrial injury and one of the following conditions exists:

(1) The employer rejects liability for a claimed benefit.

(2) The employer fails to accept liability for benefits after the expiration of a reasonable period of time within which to decide if it will contest the claim.

(3) The employer fails to respond to a demand for payment of benefits after the expiration of any time period fixed by statute for the payment of indemnity.

(c) Costs of medical evaluations, diagnostic tests, and interpreters incidental to the production of a medical report do not constitute medical-legal expenses unless the medical report is capable of proving or disproving a disputed medical fact, the determination of which is essential to an adjudication of the employee's claim for benefits. In determining whether a report meets the requirements of this subdivision, a judge shall give full consideration to the substance as well as the form of the report, as required by applicable statutes and regulations. **Leg.H.** 1993 ch. 4, effective April 3, 1993.

Ref.: 8 C.C.R. §§9793, 9794, 9795, 9795.1, 9795.2, 9795.3, 9795.4, 10564, 10771; Hanna §§ 5.04[2][a], 5.04[2][c], 22.09[1], 22.09[3], 23.13[3]; Herlick Handbook §§ 4.20, 4.21, 10.1, 10.3; W. Cal. Sum., 2 "Workers' Compensation" §§23, 273, 274.

§4621. Reimbursement of medical-legal expenses.

(a) In accordance with the rules of practice and procedure of the appeals board, the employee, or the dependents of a deceased employee, shall be reimbursed for his or her medical-legal expenses and reasonably, actually, and necessarily incurred, except as provided in Section 4064. The reasonableness of, and necessity for, incurring these expenses shall be determined with respect to the time when the expenses were actually incurred. Costs for medical evaluations, diagnostic tests, and interpreters' services incidental to the production of a medical report shall not be incurred earlier than the date of receipt by the employer, the employer's insurance carrier, or, if represented, the attorney of record, of all reports and documents required by the administrative director incidental to the services. This subdivision is not applicable unless there has been compliance with Section 4620.

(b) Except as provided in subdivision (c) and Sections 4061 and 4062, no comprehensive medical-legal evaluations, except those at the request of an employer, shall be performed during the first 60 days after the notice of claim has been filed pursuant to Section 5401, and neither the employer nor the employee shall be liable for any expenses incurred for comprehensive medical-legal evaluations performed within the first 60 days after the notice of claim has been filed pursuant to Section 5401.

(c) Comprehensive medical-legal evaluations may be performed at any time after the claim form has been filed pursuant to Section 5401 if the employer has rejected the claim.

(d) Where, at the request of the employer, the employer's insurance carrier, the administrative director, the appeals board, or a referee, the employee submits to examination by a physician, he or she shall be entitled to receive, in addition to all other benefits herein provided, all reasonable expenses of transportation, meals, and lodging incident to reporting for the examination to the same extent and manner as provided for in Section 4600. **Leg.H.** 1993 ch. 4, effective April 3, 1993, ch. 121, effective July 16, 1993.

1993 Note: Section 4621, as amended by ch. 121, applies only to injuries occurring on or after January 1, 1994. Stats. 1993 ch. 121 §77.

Ref.: 8 C.C.R. §§9793, 9794, 9795, 9795.1, 9795.2, 9795.3, 9795.4, 10101, 10101.1, 10102, 10108, 10110,

10111, 10111.1, 10111.2, 10115, 10536, 10564, 10608, 10771; Herlick Handbook §§ 4.20, 4.21, 4.23, 14.33; MB Prac. Guide: Cal. Debt Collection & Enforcement of Judgments, §§12.36, 17.06; W. Cal. Sum., 2 "Workers' Compensation" §§273, 274.

§4622. Employer's liability for expenses; penalty.

All medical-legal expenses for which the employer is liable shall, upon receipt by the employer of all reports and documents required by the administrative director incident to the services, be paid to whom the funds and expenses are due, as follows:

(a) Except as provided in subdivision (b), within 60 days after receipt by the employer of each separate, written billing and report, and where payment is not made within this period, that portion of the billed sum then unreasonably unpaid shall be increased by 10 percent, together with interest thereon at the rate of 7 percent per annum retroactive to the date of receipt of the bill and report by the employer. Where the employer, within the 60-day period, contests the reasonableness and necessity for incurring the fees, services, and expenses, payment shall be made within 20 days of the filing of an order of the appeals board directing payment.

The penalty provided for in this subdivision shall not apply if (1) the employer pays the provider that portion of his or her charges which do not exceed the amount deemed reasonable pursuant to subdivision (c) of Section 4624 within 60 days of receipt of the report and itemized billing, and, (2) the appeals board sustains the employer's position in contesting the reasonableness or necessity for incurring the expenses. If the employer prevails before the appeals board, the referee shall order the physician to reimburse the employer for the amount of the paid charges found to be unreasonable.

(b) Where requested by the employee, or the dependents of a deceased employee, within 20 days from the filing of an order of the appeals board directing payment, and where payment is not made within that period, that portion of the billed sum then unpaid shall be increased by 10 percent, together with interest thereon at the rate of 7 percent per annum retroactive to the date of the filing of the order of the board directing payment.

(c) The employer shall notify, in writing, the provider of the services, the employee, or if represented, his or her attorney, if the employer contests the reasonableness or necessity of incurring these expenses, and shall indicate the reasons therefor.

The appeals board shall promulgate all necessary and reasonable rules and regulations to insure compliance with this section, and shall take such further steps as may be necessary to guarantee that the rules and regulations are enforced.

The provisions of Sections 5800 and 5814 shall not apply to this section.

(d) Nothing contained in this section shall be construed to create a rebuttable presumption of entitlement to payment of an expense upon receipt by the employer of the required reports and documents. This section is not applicable unless there has been compliance with Sections 4620 and 4621. **Leg.H.** 1993 ch. 4, effective April 3, 1993.

Ref.: 8 C.C.R. §§9793, 9794, 9795, 10101, 10101.1, 10102, 10111, 10111.1, 10111.2, 10771; Hanna §§ 5.04[2][c], 10.43, 22.09[2]–[3], 27.01[8][b][iv], 27.12[3]; Herlick Handbook §§ 4.21, 9.5, 10.1, 10.3, 14.33; W. Cal. Sum., 2 "Workers' Compensation" §§273, 408.

§4625. Prompt payment of all reasonable charges for reports.

(a) Notwithstanding subdivision (d) of Section 4628, all charges for medical-legal expenses for which the employer is liable that are not in excess of those set forth in the official medical-legal fee schedule adopted pursuant to Section 5307.6 shall be paid promptly pursuant to Section 4622.

(b) If the employer contests the reasonableness of the charges it has paid, the employer may file a petition with the appeals board to obtain reimbursement of the charges from the physician that are considered to be unreasonable. **Leg.H.** 1993 ch. 4, effective April 3, 1993.

Ref.: 8 C.C.R. §§9793, 9794, 9795, 10111, 10111.1, 10111.2, 10771; Herlick Handbook §§ 4.19, 4.21, 10.1, 10.3; W. Cal. Sum., 2 "Workers' Compensation" §273.

§4626. Billing of diagnostic tests in accordance with official medical fee schedule.

All charges for X-rays, laboratory services, and other diagnostic tests provided in connection with an industrial medical-legal evaluation shall be billed in accordance with the official medical fee schedule adopted by the administra-

Labor

tive director pursuant to Section 5307.1 and shall be itemized separately in accordance with rules promulgated by the administrative director.

Ref.: 8 C.C.R. §§9794, 9795; Herlick Handbook § 4.21.

§4627. Appeals board and administrative director may promulgate rules and regulations.

The board and the administrative director may promulgate such reasonable rules and regulations as may be necessary to interpret this article and compel compliance with its provisions.

Ref.: Herlick Handbook §§ 4.21, 10.3, 14.26, 14.42.

§4628. Responsibilities of physician signing medical-legal report; information required in report; billable amounts; admissibility of report; civil penalty; contempt; declaration by physician; provision of physician's curriculum vitae.

(a) Except as provided in subdivision (c), no person, other than the physician who signs the medical-legal report, except a nurse performing those functions routinely performed by a nurse, such as taking blood pressure, shall examine the injured employee or participate in the nonclerical preparation of the report, including all of the following:

(1) Taking a complete history.

(2) Reviewing and summarizing prior medical records.

(3) Composing and drafting the conclusions of the report.

(b) The report shall disclose the date when and location where the evaluation was performed; that the physician or physicians signing the report actually performed the evaluation; whether the evaluation performed and the time spent performing the evaluation was in compliance with the guidelines established by the administrative director pursuant to paragraph (5) of subdivision (j) of Section 139.2 or Section 5307.6 and shall disclose the name and qualifications of each person who performed any services in connection with the report, including diagnostic studies, other than its clerical preparation. If the report discloses that the evaluation performed or the time spent performing the evaluation was not in compliance with the guidelines established by the administrative director, the report shall explain, in detail, any variance and the reason or reasons therefor.

(c) If the initial outline of a patient's history or excerpting of prior medical records is not done by the physician, the physician shall review the excerpts and the entire outline and shall make additional inquiries and examinations as are necessary and appropriate to identify and determine the relevant medical issues.

(d) No amount may be charged in excess of the direct charges for the physician's professional services and the reasonable costs of laboratory examinations, diagnostic studies, and other medical tests, and reasonable costs of clerical expense necessary to producing the report. Direct charges for the physician's professional services shall include reasonable overhead expense.

(e) Failure to comply with the requirements of this section shall make the report inadmissible as evidence and shall eliminate any liability for payment of any medical-legal expense incurred in connection with the report.

(f) Knowing failure to comply with the requirements of this section shall subject the physician to a civil penalty of up to one thousand dollars ($1,000) for each violation to be assessed by a workers' compensation judge or the appeals board. All civil penalties collected under this section shall be deposited in the Workers' Compensation Administration Revolving Fund.

(g) A physician who is assessed a civil penalty under this section may be terminated, suspended, or placed on probation as a qualified medical evaluator pursuant to subdivisions (k) and (*l*) of Section 139.2.

(h) Knowing failure to comply with the requirements of this section shall subject the physician to contempt pursuant to the judicial powers vested in the appeals board.

(i) Any person billing for medical-legal evaluations, diagnostic procedures, or diagnostic services performed by persons other than those employed by the reporting physician or physicians, or a medical corporation owned by the reporting physician or physicians shall specify the amount paid or to be paid to those persons for the evaluations, procedures, or services. This subdivision shall not apply to any procedure or service defined or valued pursuant to Section 5307.1.

(j) The report shall contain a declaration by the physician signing the report, under penalty of perjury, stating:

"I declare under penalty of perjury that the information contained in this report and its attachments, if any, is true and correct to the best of my knowledge and belief, except as to information that I have indicated I received from others. As to that information, I declare under penalty of perjury that the information accurately describes the information provided to me and, except as noted herein, that I believe it to be true."

The foregoing declaration shall be dated and signed by the reporting physician and shall indicate the county wherein it was signed.

(k) The physician shall provide a curriculum vitae upon request by a party and include a statement concerning the percent of the physician's total practice time that is annually devoted to medical treatment. **Leg.H.** 1992 ch. 1352, effective September 30, 1992, 1993 ch. 120, effective July 16, 1993, 2002 ch. 6 (AB 749), 2003 ch. 639 (SB 228).

1989 Note: This section is applicable only to injuries occurring on or after January 1, 1990. Stats. 1989 ch. 893 §6.

Ref.: 8 C.C.R. §§43, 49, 49.2, 49.4, 49.6, 49.8, 49.9, 9774, 9793, 9794, 9795, 10606, 10634; Hanna §§ 22.09[5], 26.06[12]; Herlick Handbook §§ 4.20, 4.21, 10.1, 10.3, 14.20, 14.23; Lawyer's Guide to AMA *Guides* and Calif. Workers' Comp. § 3.03; W. Cal. Sum., 2 "Workers' Compensation" §§274, 399.

ARTICLE 3
Disability Payments

§4650. Timing of payments; when employer obligated to reimburse insurer.

(a) If an injury causes temporary disability, the first payment of temporary disability indemnity shall be made not later than 14 days after knowledge of the injury and disability, on which date all indemnity then due shall be paid, unless liability for the injury is earlier denied.

(b) If the injury causes permanent disability, the first payment shall be made within 14 days after the date of last payment of temporary disability indemnity. When the last payment of temporary disability indemnity has been made pursuant to subdivision (c) of Section 4656, and regardless of whether the extent of permanent disability can be determined at that date, the employer nevertheless shall commence the timely payment required by this subdivision and shall continue to make these payments until the employer's reasonable estimate of permanent disability indemnity due has been paid, and if the amount of permanent disability indemnity due has been determined, until that amount has been paid.

(c) Payment of temporary or permanent disability indemnity subsequent to the first payment shall be made as due every two weeks on the day designated with the first payment.

(d) If any indemnity payment is not made timely as required by this section, the amount of the late payment shall be increased 10 percent and shall be paid, without application, to the employee, unless the employer continues the employee's wages under a salary continuation plan, as defined in subdivision (g). No increase shall apply to any payment due prior to or within 14 days after the date the claim form was submitted to the employer under Section 5401. No increase shall apply when, within the 14-day period specified under subdivision (a), the employer is unable to determine whether temporary disability indemnity payments are owed and advises the employee, in the manner prescribed in rules and regulations adopted pursuant to Section 138.4, why payments cannot be made within the 14-day period, what additional information is required to make the decision whether temporary disability indemnity payments are owed, and when the employer expects to have the information required to make the decision.

(e) If the employer is insured for its obligation to provide compensation, the employer shall be obligated to reimburse the insurer for the amount of increase in indemnity payments, made pursuant to subdivision (d), if the late payment which gives rise to the increase in indemnity payments, is due less than seven days after the insurer receives the completed claim form from the employer. Except as specified in this subdivision, an employer shall not be obligated to reimburse an insurer nor shall an insurer be permitted to seek reimbursement, directly or indirectly, for the amount of increase in indemnity payments specified in this section.

(f) If an employer is obligated under subdivision (e) to reimburse the insurer for the amount of increase in indemnity payments, the insurer shall notify the employer in writing, within 30 days of the payment, that the employer is obligated to reimburse the insurer and shall bill and collect the amount of the payment no later than at final audit. However, the insurer shall not be obligated to collect, and the employer shall not be obligated to reimburse, amounts paid pursuant to subdivision (d) unless the aggregate total paid in a policy year exceeds one hundred dollars ($100). The employer shall have 60 days, following notice of the obligation to reimburse, to appeal the decision of the insurer to the Department of Insurance. The notice of the obligation to reimburse shall specify that the employer has the right to appeal the decision of the insurer as provided in this subdivision.

(g) For purposes of this section, "salary continuation plan" means a plan that meets both of the following requirements:

(1) The plan is paid for by the employer pursuant to statute, collective bargaining agreement, memorandum of understanding, or established employer policy.

(2) The plan provides the employee on his or her regular payday with salary not less than the employee is entitled to receive pursuant to statute, collective bargaining agreement, memorandum of understanding, or established employer policy and not less than the employee would otherwise receive in indemnity payments.

Leg.H. Enacted 1937, amended 1947 ch. 1033 §5, 1949 chs. 408 §1, 705 §1, 1959 ch. 1189 §11, 1971 ch. 1750 §4, operative April 1, 1972, 1973 ch. 1021 §1, operative April 1, 1974, 1989 ch. 892 §34, 1990 ch. 1550 (AB 2910) §41, 2004 ch. 34 (SB 899), effective April 19, 2004.

2004 Note: The amendment to §4650 made by this act shall apply prospectively from the date of enactment of this act, regardless of the date of injury, unless otherwise specified, but shall not constitute good cause to reopen or rescind, alter, or amend any existing order, decision, or award of the Workers' Compensation Appeals Board. Stats. 2004 ch. 34 (SB 899) §47.

1989 Note: This section is applicable only to injuries occurring on or after January 1, 1990. Stats. 1989 ch. 893 §6.

Ref.: 8 C.C.R. §§9793, 9810, 9811, 9812, 9813, 9814, 9815, 9880, 10100, 10100.1, 10100.2, 10101, 10101.1, 10102, 10109, 10111, 10111.1, 10111.2, 10462, 10464, 10466; Hanna §§ 2.62[2][f], 2.72[2], 8.08[1], 8.08[4], 10.40[3][b], 32.04[1][a]; Herlick Handbook §§ 4.19, 5.9, 6.6, 7.15, 9.5; W. Cal. Sum., 2 "Workers' Compensation" §§260, 275, 277, 386, 413.

§4650.5. Time of first payment; civil service employees; employees of Regents of University of California; Board of Trustees of California State University.

Notwithstanding Section 4650, in the case of state civil service employees, employees of the Regents of the University of California, and employees of the Board of Trustees of the California State University, the disability payment shall be made from the first day the injured employee leaves work as a result of the injury, if the injury is the result of a criminal act of violence against the employee.

Ref.: Hanna § 7.03[2]; Herlick Handbook § 5.9; W. Cal. Sum., 2 "Workers' Compensation" §277.

§4651. Acceptable methods of payment; delay in negotiation of written instrument caused by state or federal banking laws; report on providing injured workers better access to funds in light of state and federal banking law requirements.

(a) No disability indemnity payment shall be made by any written instrument unless it is immediately negotiable and payable in cash, on demand, without discount at some established place of business in the state.

Nothing in this section shall prohibit an employer from depositing the disability indemnity payment in an account in any bank, savings and loan association or credit union of the employee's choice in this state, provided the employee has voluntarily authorized the deposit, nor shall it prohibit an employer from electronically depositing the disability indemnity payment in an account in any bank, savings and loan association, or credit union, that the employee has previously authorized to receive electronic deposits of payroll, unless the employee has requested, in writing, that disability indemnity benefits not be electronically deposited in the account.

(b) It is not a violation of this section if a delay in the negotiation of a written instrument is caused solely by the application of state or federal banking laws or regulations.

(c) On or before July 1, 2004, the administrative director shall present to the Governor recommendations on how to provide better access to funds paid to injured workers in light of the requirements of federal and state laws and regulations governing the negotiability of disability indemnity payments. The administrative director shall make specific recommendations regarding payments to migratory and seasonal farmworkers. The Commission on Health and Safety and Workers' Compensation and the Employment Development Department shall assist the administrative director in the completion of this report. **Leg.H.** 2002 ch. 6 (AB 749).

1989 Note: This section is applicable only to injuries occurring on or after January 1, 1990. Stats. 1989 ch. 893 §6.

Ref.: 8 C.C.R. §§9880, 10111, 10111.1, 10111.2; Hanna § 10.40[3][b]; Herlick Handbook §§ 5.15, 10.1; W. Cal. Sum., 2 "Workers' Compensation" §260.

§4651.1. Petition alleging disability has decreased or terminated.

Where a petition is filed with the appeals board concerning a continuing award of such appeals board, in which it is alleged that the disability has decreased or terminated, there shall be a rebuttable presumption that such temporary disability continues for at least one week following the filing of such petition. In such case, payment for such week shall be made in accordance with the provisions of Sections 4650 and 4651 of this code.

Where the employee has returned to work at or prior to the date of such filing, however, no such presumption shall apply.

Service of a copy of such petition on the employee shall be made as provided by Section 5316 of this code.

Ref.: 8 C.C.R. §§10462, 10464, 10466; Hanna §§ 20.02[2][i], 23.14[2][i], 35.11[1].

§4651.2. Limitations on filing petition alleging disability has decreased or terminated.

No petitions filed under Section 4651.1 shall be granted while the injured worker is pursuing a rehabilitation plan under Section 139.5 of this code.

§4651.3. Denial of petition alleging disability has decreased or terminated; attorney's fees.

Where a petition is filed with the appeals board pursuant to the provisions of Section 4651.1, and is subsequently denied wholly by the appeals board, the board may determine the amount of attorney's fees reasonably incurred by the applicant in resisting the petition and may assess such reasonable attorney's fees as a cost upon the party filing the petition to decrease or terminate the award of the appeals board.

Ref.: Hanna §§ 20.02[2][i], 31.10[1][c]; W. Cal. Sum., 2 "Workers' Compensation" §357.

§4652. Disability suffered after employee leaves work because of injury.

Except as otherwise provided by Section 4650.5, no temporary disability indemnity is recoverable for the disability suffered during the first three days after the employee leaves work as a result of the injury unless temporary disability continues for more than 14 days or the employee is hospitalized as an inpatient for treatment required by the injury, in either of which cases temporary disability indemnity shall be payable from the date of disability. For purposes of calculating the waiting period, the day of the injury shall be included unless the employee was paid full wages for that day.

1989 Note: This section is applicable only to injuries occurring on or after January 1, 1990. Stats. 1989 ch. 893 §6.

Ref.: Herlick Handbook § 5.9; W. Cal. Sum., 2 "Workers' Compensation" §§275, 277.

§4653. Temporary total disability; amount.

If the injury causes temporary total disability, the disability payment is two-thirds of the average weekly earnings during the period of such disability, consideration being given to the ability of the injured employee to compete in an open labor market.

Ref.: 8 C.C.R. §§9811, 10110; Hanna § 7.04[4]; Herlick Handbook § 5.10; W. Cal. Sum., 2 "Workers' Compensation" §§275, 285.

§4654. Temporary partial disability; amount.

If the injury causes temporary partial disability, the disability payment is two-thirds of the weekly loss in wages during the period of such disability. However, such disability payment shall be reduced by the sum of unemployment compensation benefits and extended duration benefits received by the employee during the period of temporary partial disability.

Ref.: 8 C.C.R. §9811; Herlick Handbook §§ 5.10, 5.12; W. Cal. Sum., 2 "Workers' Compensation" §§275, 341.

§4655. Temporary disability, both total and partial; amount.

If the injury causes temporary disability which is at times total and at times partial, the weekly disability payment during the period of each total or partial disability is in accordance with sections 4653 and 4654 respectively.

Ref.: Herlick Handbook § 5.10.

§4656. Maximum period for temporary disability payments.

(a) Aggregate disability payments for a single injury occurring prior to January 1, 1979, causing temporary disability shall not extend for more than 240 compensable weeks within a period of five years from the date of the injury.

(b) Aggregate disability payments for a single injury occurring on or after January 1, 1979, and prior to April 19, 2004, causing temporary partial disability shall not extend for more than 240 compensable weeks within a period of five years from the date of the injury.

(c)(1) Aggregate disability payments for a single injury occurring on or after April 19, 2004, causing temporary disability shall not extend for more than 104 compensable weeks within a period of two years from the date of commencement of temporary disability payment.

(2) Aggregate disability payments for a single injury occurring on or after January 1, 2008, causing temporary disability shall not extend for more than 104 compensable weeks within a period of five years from the date of injury.

(3) Notwithstanding paragraphs (1) and (2), for an employee who suffers from the following injuries or conditions, aggregate disability payments for a single injury occurring on or after April 19, 2004, causing temporary disability shall not extend for more than 240 compensable weeks within a period of five years from the date of the injury:

(A) Acute and chronic hepatitis B.

(B) Acute and chronic hepatitis C.

(C) Amputations.

(D) Severe burns.

(E) Human immunodeficiency virus (HIV).

(F) High-velocity eye injuries.

(G) Chemical burns to the eyes.

(H) Pulmonary fibrosis.

(I) Chronic lung disease. **Leg.H.** 2004 ch. 34 (SB 899), effective April 19, 2004, 2007 ch. 595 (AB 338) §1.

2004 Note: The amendment to §4656 made by this act shall apply prospectively from the date of enactment of this act, regardless of the date of injury, unless otherwise specified, but shall not constitute good cause to reopen or rescind, alter, or amend any existing order, decision, or award of the Workers' Compensation Appeals Board. Stats. 2004 ch. 34 (SB 899) §47.

Ref.: Hanna §§ 7.02[1], 7.03[5], 7.04[2], 24.03[3][b]; Herlick Handbook §§ 5.10, 14.9, 16.5; W. Cal. Sum., 2 "Workers' Compensation" §§4, 275, 430.

§4657. Temporary partial disability; lost wages.

In case of temporary partial disability the weekly loss in wages shall consist of the difference between the average weekly earnings of the injured employee and the weekly amount which the injured employee will probably be able to earn during the disability, to be determined in view of the nature and extent of the injury. In computing such probable earnings, due regard shall be given to the ability of the injured employee to compete in an open labor market. If evidence of exact loss of earnings is lacking, such weekly loss in wages may be computed from the proportionate loss of physical ability or earning power caused by the injury.

Ref.: Hanna §§ 7.02[3][c], 7.04[2]; Herlick Handbook §§ 5.10, 5.12, 16.1; W. Cal. Sum., 2 "Workers' Compensation" §§275, 286.

§4658. Permanent disability; computation.

(a) For injuries occurring prior to January 1, 1992, if the injury causes permanent disability, the percentage of disability to total disability shall be determined, and the disability payment computed and allowed, according to paragraph (1). However, in no event shall the disability payment allowed be less than the disability payment computed according to paragraph (2).

(1)

Column 1—Range of percentage of permanent disability incurred:	Column 2—Number of weeks for which two-thirds of average weekly earnings allowed for each 1 percent of permanent disability within percentage range:
Under 10	3
10–19.75	4
20–29.75	5
30–49.75	6
50–69.75	7
70–99.75	8

The number of weeks for which payments shall be allowed set forth in column 2 above based upon the percentage of permanent disability set forth in column 1 above shall be cumulative, and the number of benefit weeks shall increase with the severity of the disability. The following schedule is illustrative of the computation of the number of benefit weeks:

Column 1—Percentage of permanent disability incurred:	Column 2—Cumulative number of benefit weeks:
5	15.00
10	30.25
15	50.25
20	70.50
25	95.50
30	120.75
35	150.75
40	180.75
45	210.75
50	241.00
55	276.00
60	311.00
65	346.00
70	381.25
75	421.25
80	461.25
85	501.25
90	541.25
95	581.25
100	for life

(2) Two-thirds of the average weekly earnings for four weeks for each 1 percent of disability, where, for the purposes of this subdivision, the average weekly earnings shall be taken at not more than seventy-eight dollars and seventy-five cents ($78.75).

(b) This subdivision shall apply to injuries occurring on or after January 1, 1992. If the injury causes permanent disability, the percentage of disability to total disability shall be determined, and the disability payment computed and allowed, according to paragraph (1). However, in no event shall the disability payment allowed be less than the disability payment computed according to paragraph (2).

(1)

Column 1—Range of percentage of permanent disability incurred:	Column 2—Number of weeks for which two-thirds of average weekly earnings allowed for each 1 percent of permanent disability within percentage range:
Under 10	3
10–19.75	4
20–24.75	5
25–29.75	6
30–49.75	7
50–69.75	8
70–99.75	9

The numbers set forth in column 2 above are based upon the percentage of permanent disability set forth in column 1 above and shall be cumulative, and shall increase with the severity of the disability in the manner illustrated in subdivision (a).

(2) Two-thirds of the average weekly earnings for four weeks for each 1 percent of disability, where, for the purposes of this subdivision, the average weekly earnings shall be taken at not more than seventy-eight dollars and seventy-five cents ($78.75).

(c) This subdivision shall apply to injuries occurring on or after January 1, 2004. If the injury causes permanent disability, the percentage of disability to total disability shall be determined, and the disability payment computed and allowed as follows:

Column 1—Range of percentage of permanent disability incurred:	Column 2—Number of weeks for which two-thirds of average weekly earnings allowed for each 1 percent of permanent disability within percentage range:
Under 10	4
10–19.75	5
20–24.75	5
25–29.75	6
30–49.75	7
50–69.75	8
70–99.75	9

The numbers set forth in column 2 above are based upon the percentage of permanent disability set forth in column 1 above and shall be cumulative, and shall increase with the severity of the disability in the manner illustrated in subdivision (a).

(d)(1) This subdivision shall apply to injuries occurring on or after the effective date of the revised permanent disability schedule adopted by the administrative director pursuant to Section 4660. If the injury causes permanent disability, the percentage of disability to total disability shall be determined, and the basic disability payment computed as follows:

Column 1—Range of percentage of permanent disability incurred:	Column 2—Number of weeks for which two-thirds of average weekly earnings allowed for each 1 percent of permanent disability within percentage range:
0.25–9.75	3
10–14.75	4
15–24.75	5
25–29.75	6
30–49.75	7
50–69.75	8
70–99.75	16

The numbers set forth in column 2 above are based upon the percentage of permanent disability set forth in column 1 above and shall be cumulative, and shall increase with the severity of the disability in the manner illustrated in subdivision (a).

(2) If, within 60 days of a disability becoming permanent and stationary, an employer does not offer the injured employee regular work, modified work, or alternative work, in the form and manner prescribed by the administrative director, for a period of at least 12 months, each disability payment remaining to be paid to the injured employee from the date of the end of the 60-day period shall be paid in accordance with paragraph (1) and increased by 15 percent. This paragraph shall not apply to an employer that employs fewer than 50 employees.

(3)(A) If, within 60 days of a disability becoming permanent and stationary, an employer offers the injured employee regular work, modified work, or alternative work, in the form and manner prescribed by the administrative director, for a period of at least 12 months, and regardless of whether the injured employee accepts or rejects the offer, each disability payment remaining to be paid to the injured employee from the date the offer was made shall be paid in accordance with paragraph (1) and decreased by 15 percent.

(B) If the regular work, modified work, or alternative work is terminated by the employer before the end of the period for which disability payments are due the injured employee, the amount of each of the remaining disability payments shall be paid in accordance with paragraph (1) and increased by 15 percent. An employee who voluntarily terminates employment shall not be eligible for payment under this subparagraph. This paragraph shall not apply to an employer that employs fewer than 50 employees.

(4) For compensable claims arising before April 30, 2004, the schedule provided in this subdivision shall not apply to the determination of permanent disabilities when there has been either a comprehensive medical-legal report or a report by a treating physician, indicating the existence of permanent disability, or when the employer is required to provide the notice required by Section 4061 to the injured worker. **Leg.H.** 2002 ch. 6 (AB 749), 2004 ch. 34 (SB 899), effective April 19, 2004.

2004 Note: The amendment to §4658 made by this act shall apply prospectively from the date of enactment of this act, regardless of the date of injury, unless otherwise specified, but shall not constitute good cause to reopen or rescind, alter, or amend any existing order, decision, or award of the Workers' Compensation Appeals Board. Stats. 2004 ch. 34 (SB 899) §47.

Ref.: 8 C.C.R. §§10110, 10133.53; Hanna §§ 8.02[2], 8.08[1], 32.04[3][a]; Herlick Handbook §§ 5.8, 6.1–6.5; W. Cal. Sum., 2 "Workers' Compensation" §§4, 275, 278, 287, 293.

§4658.1. Meaning of "regular work," "modified work," and "alternative work"; equivalent wages and compensation; location.

As used in this article, the following definitions apply:

(a) "Regular work" means the employee's usual occupation or the position in which the employee was engaged at the time of injury and that offers wages and compensation equivalent to those paid to the employee at the time of injury, and located within a reasonable commuting distance of the employee's residence at the time of injury.

(b) "Modified work" means regular work modified so that the employee has the ability to perform all the functions of the job and that offers wages and compensation that are at least

85 percent of those paid to the employee at the time of injury, and located within a reasonable commuting distance of the employee's residence at the time of injury.

(c) "Alternative work" means work that the employee has the ability to perform, that offers wages and compensation that are at least 85 percent of those paid to the employee at the time of injury, and that is located within reasonable commuting distance of the employee's residence at the time of injury.

(d) For the purpose of determining whether wages and compensation are equivalent to those paid at the time of injury, the wages and compensation for any increase in working hours over the average hours worked at the time of injury shall not be considered.

(e) For the purpose of determining whether wages and compensation are equivalent to those paid at the time of injury, actual wages and compensation shall be determined without regard to the minimums and maximums set forth in Chapter 1 (commencing with Section 4451).

(f) The condition that regular work, modified work, or alternative work be located within a reasonable distance of the employee's residence at the time of injury may be waived by the employee. The condition shall be deemed to be waived if the employee accepts the regular work, modified work, or alternative work and does not object to the location within 20 days of being informed of the right to object. The condition shall be conclusively deemed to be satisfied if the offered work is at the same location and the same shift as the employment at the time of injury. **Leg.H.** 2004 ch. 34 (SB 899), effective April 19, 2004.

2004 Note: The addition of §4658.1 made by this act shall apply prospectively from the date of enactment of this act, regardless of the date of injury, unless otherwise specified, but shall not constitute good cause to reopen or rescind, alter, or amend any existing order, decision, or award of the Workers' Compensation Appeals Board. Stats. 2004 ch. 34 (SB 899) §47.

Ref.: 8 C.C.R. §§10133.50, 10133.53, 10133.60; Hanna § 32.04[3][a]; Herlick Handbook § 6.3; W. Cal. Sum., 2 "Workers' Compensation" §278.

§4658.5. Supplemental job displacement benefits—Eligibility; voucher; notice of employee's rights; applicability.

(a) Except as provided in Section 4658.6, if the injury causes permanent partial disability and the injured employee does not return to work for the employer within 60 days of the termination of temporary disability, the injured employee shall be eligible for a supplemental job displacement benefit in the form of a nontransferable voucher for education-related retraining or skill enhancement, or both, at state-approved or accredited schools, as follows:

(1) Up to four thousand dollars ($4,000) for permanent partial disability awards of less than 15 percent.

(2) Up to six thousand dollars ($6,000) for permanent partial disability awards between 15 and 25 percent.

(3) Up to eight thousand dollars ($8,000) for permanent partial disability awards between 26 and 49 percent.

(4) Up to ten thousand dollars ($10,000) for permanent partial disability awards between 50 and 99 percent.

(b) The voucher may be used for payment of tuition, fees, books, and other expenses required by the school for retraining or skill enhancement. No more than 10 percent of the voucher moneys may be used for vocational or [1] **return-to-work** counseling. The administrative director shall adopt regulations governing the form of payment, direct reimbursement to the injured employee upon presentation to the employer of appropriate documentation and receipts, and [2] other matters necessary to the proper administration of the supplemental job displacement benefit.

(c) Within 10 days of the last payment of temporary disability, the employer shall provide to the employee, in the form and manner prescribed by the administrative director, information that provides notice of rights under this section. This notice shall be sent by certified mail.

(d) This section shall apply to injuries occurring on or after January 1, 2004. **Leg.H.** 2003 ch. 635 (AB 227), 2005 ch. 22 (SB 1108) §144, 2008 ch. 179 (SB 1498) §176.

§4658.5. 2008 Deletes. [1] return to work **[2]** any

Ref.: 8 C.C.R. §§9880, 9881, 10118.1, 10133.50, 10133.51, 10133.52, 10133.53, 10133.54, 10133.55, 10133.56, 10133.57, 10133.58, 10133.59, 10133.60; Hanna Ch. 35; Herlick Handbook Ch. 16; W. Cal. Sum., 2 "Workers' Compensation" §283.

§4658.6. When employer not liable for supplemental job displacement benefit.

The employer shall not be liable for the supplemental job displacement benefit if the employer meets either of the following conditions:

(a) Within 30 days of the termination of temporary disability indemnity payments, the employer offers, and the employee rejects, or fails to accept, in the form and manner prescribed by the administrative director, modified work, accommodating the employee's work restrictions, lasting at least 12 months.

(b) Within 30 days of the termination of temporary disability indemnity payments, the employer offers, and the employee rejects, or fails to accept, in the form and manner prescribed by the administrative director, alternative work meeting all of the following conditions:

(1) The employee has the ability to perform the essential functions of the job provided.

(2) The job provided is in a regular position lasting at least 12 months.

(3) The job provided offers wages and compensation that are within 15 percent of those paid to the employee at the time of injury.

(4) The job is located within reasonable commuting distance of the employee's residence at the time of injury. **Leg.H.** 2003 ch. 635 (AB 227).

Ref.: 8 C.C.R. §§9880, 9881, 10118.1, 10133.50, 10133.53, 10133.54, 10133.56, 10133.60; Hanna Ch. 35; Herlick Handbook Ch. 16; W. Cal. Sum., 2 "Workers' Compensation" §283.

§4659. Permanent disability; average weekly earnings; life pensions or total permanent disability.

(a) If the permanent disability is at least 70 percent, but less than 100 percent, 1.5 percent of the average weekly earnings for each 1 percent of disability in excess of 60 percent is to be paid during the remainder of life, after payment for the maximum number of weeks specified in Section 4658 has been made. For the purposes of this subdivision only, average weekly earnings shall be taken at not more than one hundred seven dollars and sixty-nine cents ($107.69). For injuries occurring on or after July 1, 1994, average weekly wages shall not be taken at more than one hundred fifty-seven dollars and sixty-nine cents ($157.69). For injuries occurring on or after July 1, 1995, average weekly wages shall not be taken at more than two hundred seven dollars and sixty-nine cents ($207.69). For injuries occurring on or after July 1, 1996, average weekly wages shall not be taken at more than two hundred fifty-seven dollars and sixty-nine cents ($257.69). For injuries occurring on or after January 1, 2006, average weekly wages shall not be taken at more than five hundred fifteen dollars and thirty-eight cents ($515.38).

(b) If the permanent disability is total, the indemnity based upon the average weekly earnings determined under Section 4453 shall be paid during the remainder of life.

(c) For injuries occurring on or after January 1, 2003, an employee who becomes entitled to receive a life pension or total permanent disability indemnity as set forth in subdivisions (a) and (b) shall have that payment increased annually commencing on January 1, 2004, and each January 1 thereafter, by an amount equal to the percentage increase in the "state average weekly wage" as compared to the prior year. For purposes of this subdivision, "state average weekly wage" means the average weekly wage paid by employers to employees covered by unemployment insurance as reported by the United States Department of Labor for California for the 12 months ending March 31 of the calendar year preceding the year in which the injury occurred. **Leg.H.** 1993 ch. 121, effective July 16, 1993, 2002 ch. 6 (AB 749).

1993 Note: Section 4659, as amended by ch. 121, applies only to injuries occurring on or after January 1, 1994. Stats. 1993 ch. 121 §77.

Ref.: 8 C.C.R. §10110; Hanna §§ 8.08[2], 32.04[3][a]; Herlick Handbook §§ 6.2, 6.4; W. Cal. Sum., 2 "Workers' Compensation" §304.

§4660. Percentage of permanent disability; schedule.

(a) In determining the percentages of permanent disability, account shall be taken of the nature of the physical injury or disfigurement, the occupation of the injured employee, and his or her age at the time of the injury, consideration being given to an employee's diminished future earning capacity.

(b)(1) For purposes of this section, the "nature of the physical injury or disfigurement" shall incorporate the descriptions and measurements of physical impairments and the corresponding percentages of impairments published in the American Medical Association (AMA)

Guides to the Evaluation of Permanent Impairment (5th Edition).

(2) For purposes of this section, an employee's diminished future earning capacity shall be a numeric formula based on empirical data and findings that aggregate the average percentage of long-term loss of income resulting from each type of injury for similarly situated employees. The administrative director shall formulate the adjusted rating schedule based on empirical data and findings from the Evaluation of California's Permanent Disability Rating Schedule, Interim Report (December 2003), prepared by the RAND Institute for Civil Justice, and upon data from additional empirical studies.

(c) The administrative director shall amend the schedule for the determination of the percentage of permanent disability in accordance with this section at least once every five years. This schedule shall be available for public inspection and, without formal introduction in evidence, shall be prima facie evidence of the percentage of permanent disability to be attributed to each injury covered by the schedule.

(d) The schedule shall promote consistency, uniformity, and objectivity. The schedule and any amendment thereto or revision thereof shall apply prospectively and shall apply to and govern only those permanent disabilities that result from compensable injuries received or occurring on and after the effective date of the adoption of the schedule, amendment or revision, as the fact may be. For compensable claims arising before January 1, 2005, the schedule as revised pursuant to changes made in legislation enacted during the 2003-04 Regular and Extraordinary Sessions shall apply to the determination of permanent disabilities when there has been either no comprehensive medical-legal report or no report by a treating physician indicating the existence of permanent disability, or when the employer is not required to provide the notice required by Section 4061 to the injured worker.

(e) On or before January 1, 2005, the administrative director shall adopt regulations to implement the changes made to this section by the act that added this subdivision. **Leg.H.** 1993 ch. 121, effective July 16, 1993, 2004 ch. 34 (SB 899), effective April 19, 2004.

2004 Note: The amendment to §4660 made by this act shall apply prospectively from the date of enactment of this act, regardless of the date of injury, unless otherwise specified, but shall not constitute good cause to reopen or rescind, alter, or amend any existing order, decision, or award of the Workers' Compensation Appeals Board. Stats. 2004 ch. 34 (SB 899) §47.

1993 Note: Section 4660, as amended by ch. 121, applies only to injuries occurring on or after January 1, 1994. Stats. 1993 ch. 121 §77.

Ref.: 8 C.C.R. §§9725, 9726, 9727, 9785, 9785.2, 9785.3, 9785.4, 9805, 9805.1, 10110, 10150, 10152, 10156, 10158, 10160, 10163, 10165.5, 10602; Hanna §§ 8.01, 8.02[3], 8.02[4][a], 8.06[5][a], 8.08[1], 32.01[3][a][i], 32.02[2][a], 32.02[4], 32.04[3][a]; Herlick Handbook §§ 6.1, 6.3, 6.8, 14.20, 16.1; Lawyer's Guide to AMA *Guides* and Calif. Workers' Comp. §§ 2.02, 3.02, 3.03, 5.03; W. Cal. Sum., 2 "Workers' Compensation" §§4, 288.

§4661. Compensation for causing both temporary and permanent disability.

Where an injury causes both temporary and permanent disability, the injured employee is entitled to compensation for any permanent disability sustained by him in addition to any payment received by such injured employee for temporary disability.

Every computation made pursuant to this section shall be made only with reference to disability resulting from an original injury sustained after this section as amended during the 1949 Regular Session of the Legislature becomes effective; provided, however, that all rights presently existing under this section shall be continued in force.

Ref.: Hanna §§ 8.01, 21.01[5][b], 32.04[1][a]; Herlick Handbook § 6.6; W. Cal. Sum., 2 "Workers' Compensation" §§9, 143, 275, 287.

§4661.5. Temporary total disability; payment made two years after injury.

Notwithstanding any other provision of this division, when any temporary total disability indemnity payment is made two years or more from the date of injury, the amount of this payment shall be computed in accordance with the temporary disability indemnity average weekly earnings amount specified in Section 4453 in effect on the date each temporary total disability payment is made unless computing the payment on this basis produces a lower payment because of a reduction in the minimum average weekly earnings applicable under Section 4453.

1989 Note: This section is applicable only to injuries occurring on or after January 1, 1990. Stats. 1989 ch. 893 §6.

Ref.: 8 C.C.R. §§9812, 9813, 9815, 10110: Hanna §§ 7.04[1][b], 35.11[2], 35.11[3]; Herlick Handbook §§ 5.2, 5.11, 7.15, 10.4, 16.1, 16.5; W. Cal. Sum., 2 "Workers' Compensation" §§304, 344.

§4662. Permanent disability; presumption of total disability.

Any of the following permanent disabilities shall be conclusively presumed to be total in character:

(a) Loss of both eyes or the sight thereof.

(b) Loss of both hands or the use thereof.

(c) An injury resulting in a practically total paralysis.

(d) An injury to the brain resulting in incurable mental incapacity or insanity.

In all other cases, permanent total disability shall be determined in accordance with the fact. **Leg.H.** 2007 ch. 31 (AB 1640) §2.

2007 Note: It is the intent of the Legislature, in enacting this act, not to adversely affect decisional case law that has previously interpreted, or used, the terms "idiot," "imbecility," or "lunatic," or any variation thereof. Stats. 2007 ch. 31 (AB 1640) §5.

Ref.: 8 C.C.R. §§9725, 9726, 9727, 9785, 9785.2, 9785.3, 9785.4, 9805, 9805.1, 10150, 10152, 10156, 10158, 10160, 10161, 10163, 10165.5; Hanna §§ 8.02[2], 8.06[5][d], 8.07[2][a], 8.07[2][c], 32.03[1]; Herlick Handbook §§ 6.2, 6.8; W. Cal. Ev., "Burden" §163; W. Cal. Sum., 2 "Workers' Compensation" §§287, 296.

§4663. Apportionment of permanent disability; causation as basis; physician's report; apportionment determination; disclosure by employee.

(a) Apportionment of permanent disability shall be based on causation.

(b) Any physician who prepares a report addressing the issue of permanent disability due to a claimed industrial injury shall in that report address the issue of causation of the permanent disability.

(c) In order for a physician's report to be considered complete on the issue of permanent disability, the report must include an apportionment determination. A physician shall make an apportionment determination by finding what approximate percentage of the permanent disability was caused by the direct result of injury arising out of and occurring in the course of employment and what approximate percentage of the permanent disability was caused by other factors both before and subsequent to the industrial injury, including prior industrial injuries. If the physician is unable to include an apportionment determination in his or her report, the physician shall state the specific reasons why the physician could not make a determination of the effect of that prior condition on the permanent disability arising from the injury. The physician shall then consult with other physicians or refer the employee to another physician from whom the employee is authorized to seek treatment or evaluation in accordance with this division in order to make the final determination.

(d) An employee who claims an industrial injury shall, upon request, disclose all previous permanent disabilities or physical impairments.

(e) Subdivisions (a), (b), and (c) shall not apply to injuries or illnesses covered under Sections 3212, 3212.1, 3212.2, 3212.3, 3212.4, 3212.5, 3212.6, 3212.7, 3212.8, 3212.85, 3212.9, 3212.10, 3212.11, 3212.12, 3213, and 3213.2. **Leg.H.** 2004 ch. 34 (SB 899) §34, effective April 19, 2004, 2006 ch. 836 (AB 1368) §1.

2006 Note: It is the intent of the Legislature that this act be construed as declaratory of existing law. Stats. 2006 ch. 836 (AB 1368) §2.

2004 Note: The addition of §4663 made by this act shall apply prospectively from the date of enactment of this act, regardless of the date of injury, unless otherwise specified, but shall not constitute good cause to reopen or rescind, alter, or amend any existing order, decision, or award of the Workers' Compensation Appeals Board. Stats. 2004 ch. 34 (SB 899) §47.

Ref.: 8 C.C.R. §§9725, 9726, 9727, 9785, 9785.2, 9785.3, 9785.4, 9805, 9805.1, 10150, 10152, 10156, 10158, 10160, 10161, 10163, 10165.5; Hanna §§ 8.01, 8.05[1]–[3], 8.06[1], [3], [4], [5][a]; Herlick Handbook § 6.16; Lawyer's Guide to AMA *Guides* and Calif. Workers' Comp. §§ 2.06[3], 5.02, 6.01; W. Cal. Sum., 2 "Workers' Compensation" §§4, 293, 294, 296.

§4664. Liability of employer for percentage of permanent disability directly caused by injury; conclusive presumption from prior award of permanent disability; accumulation of permanent disability awards.

(a) The employer shall only be liable for the percentage of permanent disability directly caused by the injury arising out of and occurring in the course of employment.

(b) If the applicant has received a prior award of permanent disability, it shall be conclusively presumed that the prior permanent disability exists at the time of any subsequent industrial injury. This presumption is a presumption affecting the burden of proof.

(c)(1) The accumulation of all permanent disability awards issued with respect to any one region of the body in favor of one individual employee shall not exceed 100 percent over the employee's lifetime unless the employee's injury or illness is conclusively presumed to be total in character pursuant to Section 4662. As used in this section, the regions of the body are the following:

(A) Hearing.

(B) Vision.

(C) Mental and behavioral disorders.

(D) The spine.

(E) The upper extremities, including the shoulders.

(F) The lower extremities, including the hip joints.

(G) The head, face, cardiovascular system, respiratory system, and all other systems or regions of the body not listed in subparagraphs (A) to (F), inclusive.

(2) Nothing in this section shall be construed to permit the permanent disability rating for each individual injury sustained by an employee arising from the same industrial accident, when added together, from exceeding 100 percent. **Leg.H.** 2004 ch. 34 (SB 899), effective April 19, 2004.

2004 Note: The addition of §4664 made by this act shall apply prospectively from the date of enactment of this act, regardless of the date of injury, unless otherwise specified, but shall not constitute good cause to reopen or rescind, alter, or amend any existing order, decision, or award of the Workers' Compensation Appeals Board. Stats. 2004 ch. 34 (SB 899) §47.

Ref.: 8 C.C.R. §§9725, 9726, 9727, 9785, 9785.2, 9785.3, 9785.4, 9805, 9805.1, 10150, 10152, 10156, 10158, 10160, 10161, 10163, 10165.5; Hanna §§ 8.01, 8.05[1]–[3], 8.06[1], [3], [4], [5][a]; Herlick Handbook § 6.16; Lawyer's Guide to AMA *Guides* and Calif. Workers' Comp. § 5.02; W. Cal. Sum., 2 "Workers' Compensation" §§293, 296.

ARTICLE 4
Death Benefits

§4700. Death of employee; employer's liability.

The death of an injured employee does not affect the liability of the employer under Articles 2 (commencing with Section 4600) and 3 (commencing with Section 4650). Neither temporary nor permanent disability payments shall be made for any period of time subsequent to the death of the employee. Any accrued and unpaid compensation shall be paid to the dependents, or, if there are no dependents, to the personal representative of the deceased employee or heirs or other persons entitled thereto, without administration.

Ref.: 8 C.C.R. §§9811, 9812, 9813, 9815, 9880; Hanna §§ 9.01[2], 24.03[5], 27.03[2]; Herlick Handbook §§ 7.1, 7.3, 7.4, 10.2, 14.38; W. Cal. Sum., 2 "Workers' Compensation" §§275, 358, 14 "Wills and Probate" §834.

§4701. Fatal injury; burial expenses; death benefits.

When an injury causes death, either with or without disability, the employer shall be liable, in addition to any other benefits provided by this division, for all of the following:

(a) Reasonable expenses of the employee's burial, not exceeding two thousand dollars ($2,000) and for injuries occurring on and after January 1, 1991, not exceeding five thousand dollars ($5,000).

(b) A death benefit, to be allowed to the dependents when the employee leaves any person dependent upon him or her for support.

1989 Note: This section is applicable only to injuries occurring on or after January 1, 1990. Stats. 1989 ch. 893 §6.

Ref.: 8 C.C.R. §§9811, 9812, 9813, 9815, 10101, 10101.1, 10102, 10109, 10110, 10111, 10111.1, 10111.2, 10115; Hanna § 9.01[3][a]–[b]; Herlick Handbook § 10.5; W. Cal. Sum., 2 "Workers' Compensation" §§279, 280, 314.

§4702. Death benefits; computation; payable in installments; no deduction for disability indemnity.

(a) Except as otherwise provided in this section and Sections 4553, 4554, 4557, and 4558, and notwithstanding any amount of compensation paid or otherwise owing to the surviving dependent, personal representative, heir, or other person entitled to a deceased employee's accrued and unpaid compensation, the death benefit in cases of total dependency shall be as follows:

(1) In the case of two total dependents and regardless of the number of partial dependents, for injuries occurring before January 1, 1991, ninety-five thousand dollars ($95,000), for injuries occurring on or after January 1, 1991, one

hundred fifteen thousand dollars ($115,000), for injuries occurring on or after July 1, 1994, one hundred thirty-five thousand dollars ($135,000), for injuries occurring on or after July 1, 1996, one hundred forty-five thousand dollars ($145,000), and for injuries occurring on or after January 1, 2006, two hundred ninety thousand dollars ($290,000).

(2) In the case of one total dependent and one or more partial dependents, for injuries occurring before January 1, 1991, seventy thousand dollars ($70,000), for injuries occurring on or after January 1, 1991, ninety-five thousand dollars ($95,000), for injuries occurring on or after July 1, 1994, one hundred fifteen thousand dollars ($115,000), for injuries occurring on or after July 1, 1996, one hundred twenty-five thousand dollars ($125,000), and for injuries occurring on or after January 1, 2006, two hundred fifty thousand dollars ($250,000), plus four times the amount annually devoted to the support of the partial dependents, but not more than the following: for injuries occurring before January 1, 1991, a total of ninety-five thousand dollars ($95,000), for injuries occurring on or after January 1, 1991, one hundred fifteen thousand dollars ($115,000), for injuries occurring on or after July 1, 1994, one hundred twenty-five thousand dollars ($125,000), for injuries occurring on or after July 1, 1996, one hundred forty-five thousand dollars ($145,000), and for injuries occurring on or after January 1, 2006, two hundred ninety thousand dollars ($290,000).

(3) In the case of one total dependent and no partial dependents, for injuries occurring before January 1, 1991, seventy thousand dollars ($70,000), for injuries occurring on or after January 1, 1991, ninety-five thousand dollars ($95,000), for injuries occurring on or after July 1, 1994, one hundred fifteen thousand dollars ($115,000), for injuries occurring on or after July 1, 1996, one hundred twenty-five thousand dollars ($125,000), and for injuries occurring on or after January 1, 2006, two hundred fifty thousand dollars ($250,000).

(4)(A) In the case of no total dependents and one or more partial dependents, for injuries occurring before January 1, 1991, four times the amount annually devoted to the support of the partial dependents, but not more than seventy thousand dollars ($70,000), for injuries occurring on or after January 1, 1991, a total of ninety-five thousand dollars ($95,000), for injuries occurring on or after July 1, 1994, one hundred fifteen thousand dollars ($115,000), and for injuries occurring on or after July 1, 1996, but before January 1, 2006, one hundred twenty-five thousand dollars ($125,000).

(B) In the case of no total dependents and one or more partial dependents, eight times the amount annually devoted to the support of the partial dependents, for injuries occurring on or after January 1, 2006, but not more than two hundred fifty thousand dollars ($250,000).

(5) In the case of three or more total dependents and regardless of the number of partial dependents, one hundred fifty thousand dollars ($150,000), for injuries occurring on or after July 1, 1994, one hundred sixty thousand dollars ($160,000), for injuries occurring on or after July 1, 1996, and three hundred twenty thousand dollars ($320,000), for injuries occurring on or after January 1, 2006.

(6)(A) In the case of a police officer who has no total dependents and no partial dependents, for injuries occurring on or after January 1, 2003, and prior to January 1, 2004, two hundred fifty thousand dollars ($250,000) to the estate of the deceased police officer.

(B) For injuries occurring on or after January 1, 2004, in the case of no total dependents and no partial dependents, two hundred fifty thousand dollars ($250,000) to the estate of the deceased employee.

(b) A death benefit in all cases shall be paid in installments in the same manner and amounts as temporary total disability indemnity would have to be made to the employee, unless the appeals board otherwise orders. However, no payment shall be made at a weekly rate of less than two hundred twenty-four dollars ($224).

(c) Disability indemnity shall not be deducted from the death benefit and shall be paid in addition to the death benefit when the injury resulting in death occurs after September 30, 1949.

(d) All rights under this section existing prior to January 1, 1990, shall be continued in force. **Leg.H.** 1993 ch. 121, effective July 16, 1993, 1994 ch. 1097, 2002 chs. 6 (AB 749), 866 (AB 486), 2004 ch. 92 (AB 1840), 2006 ch. 119 (AB 2292) §2.

2006 Note: It is the intent of the Legislature to clarify existing statutory requirements governing the payment of death benefits to the survivors of deceased employees under the workers' compensation system when the employee suffered a fatal injury. Stats. 2006 ch. 119 (AB 2292) §1.

2004 Note: It is the intent of the Legislature that the amendment to Section 4702 of the Labor Code made by ch. 92 shall have retroactive effect. Stats. 2004 ch. 92 §2.

1993 Note: Section 4702, as amended by ch. 121, applies only to injuries occurring on or after January 1, 1994. Stats. 1993 ch. 121 §77.

1990 Note: The amendments made by this act to subdivision (c) of Section 139.5 of the Labor Code, pertaining to the payment of additional living expenses, and subdivisions (a) and (c) of Section 4702, of the Labor Code, with respect to the crediting of accrued disability indemnity against the amount of the death benefit, and subdivision (a) of Section 4906 of the Labor Code, with respect to legal services, are not intended by the Legislature to make a change in the law as it existed with respect to these provisions prior to January 1, 1990. Stats. 1990 ch. 1550 §67.

1989 Note: This section is applicable only to injuries occurring on or after January 1, 1990. Stats. 1989 ch. 893 §6.

Ref.: 8 C.C.R. §§9812, 9813, 9815, 9880, 10101, 10101.1, 10102, 10109, 10110, 10111, 10111.1, 10111.2, 10115; Hanna §§ 9.02[3], 9.02[4][d.2], 9.02[5], 9.03[1], 9.03[3], 27.03[2]; Herlick Handbook §§ 5.11, 7.5, 7.6, 7.8, 7.9, 7.10, 7.15; W. Cal. Sum., 2 "Workers' Compensation" §§260, 275, 279–281, 298, 314.

§4703. Dependent's right to death benefits.

Subject to the provisions of section 4704, this section shall determine the right to a death benefit.

If there is any person wholly dependent for support upon a deceased employee, that person shall receive a full death benefit as set forth in Section 4702 for one total dependent, and any additional partial dependents shall receive a death benefit as set forth in subdivision (b) of Section 4702 to a maximum aggregate amount of twenty-five thousand dollars ($25,000).

If there are two or more persons wholly dependent for support upon a deceased employee, those persons shall receive the death benefit set forth in subdivision (a) of Section 4702, and any person partially dependent shall receive no part thereof.

If there is more than one person wholly dependent for support upon a deceased employee, the death benefit shall be divided equally among them.

If there is more than one person partially dependent for support upon a deceased employee, and no person wholly dependent for support, the amount allowed as a death benefit shall be divided among the persons so partially dependent in proportion to the relative extent of their dependency.

Ref.: 8 C.C.R. §§9812, 9813, 9815, 9880, 10101, 10101.1, 10102, 10109, 10110, 10111, 10111.1, 10111.2, 10115; Hanna § 9.03[1]–[2]; Herlick Handbook §§ 7.6, 7.9, 7.13; W. Cal. Sum., 2 "Workers' Compensation" §§280, 314.

§4703.5. Payment of death benefits to dependent children.

In the case of one or more totally dependent minor children, as defined in Section 3501, after payment of the amount specified in Section 4702, and notwithstanding the maximum limitations specified in Sections 4702 and 4703, payment of death benefits shall continue until the youngest child attains age 18, or until the death of a child physically or mentally incapacitated from earning, in the same manner and amount as temporary total disability indemnity would have been paid to the employee, except that no payment shall be made at a weekly rate of less than two hundred twenty-four dollars ($224). **Leg.H.** 2002 ch. 6 (AB 749).

1989 Note: This section is applicable only to injuries occurring on or after January 1, 1990. Stats. 1989 ch. 893 §6.

Ref.: 8 C.C.R. §§9812, 9813, 9815, 10101, 10101.1, 10102, 10109, 10110, 10111, 10111.1, 10111.2, 10115; Hanna §§ 9.02[5], 9.03[3]; Herlick Handbook §§ 5.11, 7.7, 7.9, 7.15; W. Cal. Sum., 2 "Workers' Compensation" §280.

§4703.6. Application of death benefit payments to totally dependent minor child of certain local safety members.

The provisions of Section 4703.5 shall also apply to a totally dependent minor child of a local safety member as defined in Article 4 (commencing with Section 20420) of Chapter 4 of Part 3 of Division 5 of Title 2 of the Government Code, or a safety member as defined in Section 31469.3 of the Government Code, other than a member performing duties related to juvenile hall group counseling and group supervision, or a safety member subject to any public retirement system, or a patrol member as defined in Section 20390 of the Government Code, if that member was killed in the line of duty prior to January 1, 1990, and the totally dependent minor child is otherwise entitled to benefits under Section 4703.5. **Leg.H.** 2001 ch.

589, 2002 ch. 296 (AB 2008), effective August 28, 2002.

2002 Note: The provisions of this act shall apply retroactively to January 1, 2002. Stats. 2002 ch. 296 (AB 2008) §2.

Ref.: Hanna § 9.02[5]; Herlick Handbook § 7.6; W. Cal. Sum., 2 "Workers' Compensation" §280.

§4704. Control assignment of death benefits.

The appeals board may set apart or reassign the death benefit to any one or more of the dependents in accordance with their respective needs and in a just and equitable manner, and may order payment to a dependent subsequent in right, or not otherwise entitled thereto, upon good cause being shown therefor. The death benefit shall be paid to such one or more of the dependents of the deceased or to a trustee appointed by the appeals board for the benefit of the person entitled thereto, as determined by the appeals board.

Ref.: Hanna §§ 3.115[1], 33.02[5][c]; Herlick Handbook §§ 7.9, 7.13; W. Cal. Sum., 2 "Workers' Compensation" §314.

§4705. Trustee to application of death benefits to beneficiaries.

The person to whom the death benefit is paid for the use of the several beneficiaries shall apply it in compliance with the findings and directions of the appeals board.

§4706. Death of dependent beneficiary.

(a) If a dependent beneficiary of any deceased employee dies and there is no surviving dependent, the payments of the death benefit accrued and payable at the time of the death of the sole remaining dependent shall be paid upon the order of the appeals board to the heirs of the dependent or, if none, to the heirs of the deceased employee, without administration.

(b) In the event there is no surviving dependent and no surviving heir, the appeals board may order the burial expense of the deceased employee, not to exceed the amount specified in Section 4701, paid to the proper person, without administration.

Ref.: 8 C.C.R. §§10111, 10111.1, 10111.2; Hanna § 9.03[5]; Herlick Handbook § 14.38; W. Cal. Sum., 2 "Workers' Compensation" §§279, 406.

§4706.5. Payment of death benefits where no surviving dependent.

(a) Whenever any fatal injury is suffered by an employee under circumstances that would entitle the employee to compensation benefits, but for his or her death, and the employee does not leave surviving any person entitled to a dependency death benefit, the employer shall pay a sum to the Department of Industrial Relations equal to the total dependency death benefit that would be payable to a surviving spouse with no dependent minor children.

(b) When the deceased employee leaves no surviving dependent, personal representative, heir, or other person entitled to the accrued and unpaid compensation referred to in Section 4700, the accrued and unpaid compensation shall be paid by the employer to the Department of Industrial Relations.

(c) The payments to be made to the Department of Industrial Relations, as required by subdivisions (a) and (b), shall be deposited in the General Fund and shall be credited, as a reimbursement, to any appropriation to the Department of Industrial Relations for payment of the additional compensation for subsequent injury provided in Article 5 (commencing with Section 4751), in the fiscal year in which the Controller's receipt is issued.

(d) The payments to be made to the Department of Industrial Relations, as required by subdivision (a), shall be paid to the department in a lump sum in the manner provided in subdivision (b) of Section 5101.

(e) The Department of Industrial Relations shall keep a record of all payments due the state under this section, and shall take any steps as may be necessary to collect those amounts.

(f) Each employer, or the employer's insurance carrier, shall notify the administrative director, in any form as the administrative director may prescribe, of each employee death, except when the employer has actual knowledge or notice that the deceased employee left a surviving dependent.

(g) When, after a reasonable search, the employer concludes that the deceased employee left no one surviving who is entitled to a dependency death benefit, and concludes that the death was under circumstances that would entitle the employee to compensation benefits, the employer may voluntarily make the payment referred to in subdivision (a). Payments so made shall be construed as payments made pursuant to an appeals board findings and award. Thereafter, if the appeals board finds that the deceased employee did in fact leave a person surviving who is entitled to a dependency death benefit, upon that finding, all payments referred to in subdivision (a) that have been made shall be forthwith returned to the employer, or if insured, to the employer's workers' compensation carrier that indemnified the employer for the loss.

(h) This section does not apply where there is no surviving person entitled to a dependency death benefit or accrued and unpaid compensation if a death benefit is paid to any person under paragraph (6) of subdivision (a) of Section 4702. **Leg.H.** 2004 ch. 34 (SB 899), effective April 19, 2004, 2006 ch. 119 (AB 2292) §3.

2006 Note: It is the intent of the Legislature to clarify existing statutory requirements governing the payment of death benefits to the survivors of deceased employees under the workers' compensation system when the employee suffered a fatal injury. Stats. 2006 ch. 119 (AB 2292) §1.

2004 Note: The amendment to §4706.5 made by this act shall apply prospectively from the date of enactment of this act, regardless of the date of injury, unless otherwise specified, but shall not constitute good cause to reopen or rescind, alter, or amend any existing order, decision, or award of the Workers' Compensation Appeals Board. Stats. 2004 ch. 34 (SB 899) §47.

Ref.: 8 C.C.R. §§10111, 10111.1, 10111.2, 10501; Hanna §§ 9.03[5], 27.03[2], 28.01[1]; Herlick Handbook §§ 6.26, 7.18, 12.2; W. Cal. Sum., 2 "Workers' Compensation" §§69, 275, 279, 298, 314.

§4707. Limitation on benefits for member of Public Employees' Retirement System.

(a) Except as provided in subdivision (b), no benefits, except reasonable expenses of burial not exceeding one thousand dollars ($1,000), shall be awarded under this division on account of the death of an employee who is an active member of the Public Employees' Retirement System unless it is determined that a special death benefit, as defined in the Public Employees' Retirement Law, or the benefit provided in lieu of the special death benefit in Sections 21547 and 21548 of the Government Code, will not be paid by the Public Employees' Retirement System to the surviving spouse or children under 18 years of age, of the deceased, on account of the death, but if the total death allowance paid to the surviving spouse and children is less than the benefit otherwise payable under this division the surviving spouse and children are entitled, under this division, to the difference.

The amendments to this section during the 1977–78 Regular Session shall be applied retroactively to July 1, 1976.

(b) The limitation prescribed by subdivision (a) shall not apply to local safety members, or patrol members, as defined in Section 20390 of the Government Code, of the Public Employees' Retirement System. This subdivision shall be applied retroactively. **Leg.H.** 1998 ch. 770, 1999 ch. 83, 2001 ch. 589.

Ref.: Hanna §§ 3.115[1], 9.04[1], 33.02[5][c]; Herlick Handbook §§ 3.21, 7.20, 14.17; W. Cal. Sum., 2 "Workers' Compensation" §§314, 333.

§4708. Joinder of Public Employees' Retirement System.

Upon application of any party in interest for a death benefit provided by this division on the death of an employee member of the Public Employees' Retirement System, the latter shall be joined as a defendant, and the appeals board shall determine whether the death resulted from injury or illness arising out of and in the course of his employment, for the purpose of enabling the appeals board to apply the provision of this division and the board of administration to apply the provisions of the Public Employees' Retirement Law.

Ref.: Hanna §§ 9.04[1], 32.02[5][b]–[c].

§4709. Scholarships for dependents of specified employees; "dependent."

(a) Notwithstanding any other provisions of law, a dependent of a peace officer, as defined in Section 830.1, 830.2, 830.3, 830.31, 830.32, 830.33, 830.34, 830.35, 830.36, 830.37, 830.38, 830.39, 830.4, 830.5, or 830.6 of the Penal Code, who is killed in the performance of duty or who dies or is totally disabled as a result of an accident or an injury caused by external violence or physical force, incurred in the performance of duty, when the death, accident, or injury is compensable under this division or Division 4.5 (commencing with Section 6100) shall be entitled to a scholarship at any institution described in subdivision (*l*) of Section 69535 of the Education Code. The scholarship shall be in an amount equal to the amount provided a student who has been awarded a Cal Grant scholarship as specified in Article 3 (com-

Labor

mencing with Section 69530) of Chapter 2 of Part 42 of the Education Code.

(b) A dependent of an officer or employee of the Department of Corrections or the Department of the Youth Authority described in Section 20017.77 of the Government Code who is killed in the performance of duty, or who dies or is totally disabled as a result of an accident or an injury incurred in the performance of duty, when the death, accident, or injury is caused by the direct action of an inmate, and is compensable under this division or Division 4.5 (commencing with Section 6100), shall also be entitled to a scholarship specified in this section.

(c) Notwithstanding any other provisions of law, a dependent of a firefighter employed by a county, city, city and county, district, or other political subdivision of the state, who is killed in the performance of duty or who dies or is totally disabled as a result of an accident or injury incurred in the performance of duty, when the death, accident, or injury is compensable under this division or Division 4.5 (commencing with Section 6100), shall also be entitled to a scholarship specified in this section.

(d) Nothing in this section shall be interpreted to allow the admittance of the dependent into a college or university unless the dependent is otherwise qualified to gain admittance to the college or university.

(e) The scholarship provided for by this section shall be paid out of funds annually appropriated in the Budget Act to the Student Aid Commission established by Article 2 (commencing with Section 69510) of Chapter 2 of Part 42 of the Education Code.

(f) The receipt of a scholarship provided for by this section shall not preclude a dependent from receiving a Cal Grant award pursuant to Article 3 (commencing with Section 69530) of Chapter 2 of Part 42 of the Education Code, any other grant, or any fee waivers that may be provided by an institution of higher education. The receipt of a Cal Grant award pursuant to Article 3 (commencing with Section 69530) of Chapter 2 of Part 42 of the Education Code, any other grant, or any fee waivers that may be provided by an institution of higher education shall not preclude a dependent from receiving a scholarship provided for by this section.

(g) The amendments made to this section during the 1995 portion of the 1995–96 Regular Session shall apply to a student receiving a scholarship on the effective date of the amendments unless that application would result in the student receiving a scholarship on less favorable terms or in a lesser amount, in which case the student shall continue to receive the scholarship on the same terms and conditions in effect prior to the effective date of the amendments.

(h) As used in this section, "dependent" means the children (natural or adopted) or spouse, at the time of the death or injury, of the peace officer, law enforcement officer, or firefighter.

(i) Eligibility for a scholarship under this section shall be limited to a person who demonstrates financial need as determined by the Student Aid Commission pursuant to Article 1.5 (commencing with Section 69503) of Chapter 2 of Part 42 of the Education Code. For purposes of determining financial need, the proceeds of death benefits received by the dependent, including, but not limited to, a continuation of income received from the Public Employees' Retirement System, the proceeds from the federal Public Safety Officers' Benefits Act, life insurance policies, proceeds from Sections 4702 and 4703.5, any private scholarship where receipt is predicated upon the recipient being the survivor of a deceased public safety officer, the scholarship awarded pursuant to Section 68120 of the Education Code, and any interest received from these benefits, shall not be considered. **Leg.H.** 1995 ch. 646, 2001 ch. 806.

Ref.: Hanna §§ 3.115[2], 9.04[2].

ARTICLE 4.5
Public Official Death Benefits

§4720. "Elected public official"; "assassination."

As used in this article:

(a) "Elected public official" means any person other than the President or Vice President of the United States who holds any federal, state, local, or special district elective office as a result of winning election in California to such office or being appointed to fill a vacancy in such office.

(b) "Assassination" means the killing of an elected public official as a direct result of an intentional act perpetrated by an individual or individuals acting to prevent, or retaliate for, the performance of official duties, acting because of the public position held by the official, or acting because of pathological reasons.

Ref.: Hanna §§ 9.04[3], 33.02[5][c]; Herlick Handbook § 7.22; W. Cal. Sum., 2 "Workers' Compensation" §279.

§4721. Special death benefits upon assassination of elected public official.

The surviving spouse or dependent minor children of an elected public official who is killed by assassination shall be entitled to a special death benefit which shall be in addition to any other benefits provided for by this division or Division 4.5 (commencing with Section 6100).

§4722. Persons entitled to special death benefits.

If the deceased elected public official is survived by a spouse with or without dependent minor children, such special death benefit shall be payable to the surviving spouse. If the deceased elected public official leaves no surviving spouse but one or more dependent minor children, benefits shall be paid to a guardian ad litem and trustee for such child or children appointed by the Workers' Compensation Appeals Board. In the absence of a surviving spouse and dependent minor children, the benefit shall be payable to any legally recognized dependent parent of the deceased elected public official.

§4723. Types of special death benefits; election.

The person or persons to whom the special death benefit is payable pursuant to Section 4722 shall, within one year of the date of death of the elected public official, choose either of the following benefits:

(a) An annual benefit equal to one-half of the average annual salary paid to the elected public official in his or her elected capacity, less credit for any other death benefit provided for under existing law or by public funds, except benefits payable pursuant to this division or Division 4.5 (commencing with Section 6100). Payments shall be paid not less frequently than monthly, and shall be paid from the date of death until the spouse dies or remarries, or until the youngest minor dependent child reaches the age of 18 years, whichever occurs last. If payments are being made to a dependent parent or parents they shall continue during dependency.

(b) A lump-sum benefit of one hundred fifty thousand dollars ($150,000), less any other death benefit provided for under existing law or by public funds, except benefits payable pursuant to this division or Division 4.5 (commencing with Section 6100).

§4724. Filing claim for special death benefits.

The person or persons to whom the special death benefit is payable pursuant to Section 4722 shall file a claim therefor with the State Board of Control, which shall be processed pursuant to the provisions of Chapter 3 (commencing with Section 900) of Part 2 of Division 3.6 of Title 1 of the Government Code.

§4725. State Compensation Insurance Fund as disbursing agent.

The State Compensation Insurance Fund shall be the disbursing agent for payments made pursuant to this article and shall receive a fee for its services to be negotiated by the State Board of Control. Unless otherwise provided herein, payments shall be made in accordance with the provisions of this division.

§4726. Joint adoption of rules to carry out article's provisions.

The State Board of Control and the Administrative Director of the Division of Workers' Compensation shall jointly adopt rules and regulations as may be necessary to carry out the provisions of this article. **Leg.H.** 1994 ch. 146.

§4727. Assassin's ineligibility for benefits.

Any person who is convicted of any crime in connection with the assassination of an elected public official shall not be eligible for any benefits pursuant to this article.

§4728. Scholarships for dependents of elected public officials intentionally killed in retaliation for or to prevent their performance of official duties.

(a) A dependent of an elected public official, who was intentionally killed while holding office, in retaliation for, or to prevent the performance of, an official duty, shall be entitled to a scholarship at any institution described in subdivision (k) of Section 69535 of the Education Code. The scholarship shall be in an amount equal to the amount provided a student who has been awarded a Cal Grant scholarship as specified in Article 3 (commencing with Section 69530) of Chapter 2 of Part 42 of the Education Code. Eligibility for a scholarship under this section shall be limited to a person who demonstrates financial need as determined by the Student Aid Commission pursuant to Article 1.5 (commencing with Section 69503) of Chapter 2 of Part 42 of the Education Code.

(b) The scholarship provided for by this section shall be paid out of funds annually appropriated in the Budget Act to the Student Aid Commission established by Article 2 (commencing with Section 69510) of Chapter 2 of Part 42 of the Education Code.

(c) The receipt of a scholarship provided for by this section shall not preclude a dependent from receiving a Cal Grant award pursuant to Article 3 (commencing with Section 69530) of Chapter 2 of Part 42 of the Education Code, any other grant, or any fee waivers that may be provided by an institution of higher education. The receipt of a Cal Grant award pursuant to Article 3 (commencing with Section 69530) of Chapter 2 of Part 42 of the Education Code, any other grant, or any fee waivers that may be provided by an institution of higher education shall not preclude a dependent from receiving a scholarship provided for by this section.

(d) This section shall apply to a student receiving a scholarship on the effective date of the section unless that application would result in the student receiving a scholarship on less favorable terms or in a lesser amount, in which case the student shall continue to receive the scholarship on the same terms and conditions in effect prior to the effective date of this section.

(e) As used in this section, "dependent" means the children (natural or adopted) or spouse, at the time of the death or injury, of the elected public official. **Leg.H.** 1995 ch. 646.

Ref.: Hanna § 3.115[2]; Herlick Handbook § 7.22.

ARTICLE 5
Subsequent Injuries Payments

§4751. Compensation for specified additions to permanent partial disabilities.

If an employee who is permanently partially disabled receives a subsequent compensable injury resulting in additional permanent partial disability so that the degree of disability caused by the combination of both disabilities is greater than that which would have resulted from the subsequent injury alone, and the combined effect of the last injury and the previous disability or impairment is a permanent disability equal to 70 percent or more of total, he shall be paid in addition to the compensation due under this code for the permanent partial disability caused by the last injury compensation for the remainder of the combined permanent disability existing after the last injury as provided in this article; provided, that either (a) the previous disability or impairment affected a hand, an arm, a foot, a leg, or an eye, and the permanent disability resulting from the subsequent injury affects the opposite and corresponding member, and such latter permanent disability, when considered alone and without regard to, or adjustment for, the occupation or age of the employee, is equal to 5 percent or more of total, or (b) the permanent disability resulting from the subsequent injury, when considered alone and without regard to or adjustment for the occupation or the age of the employee, is equal to 35 percent or more of total.

Ref.: 8 C.C.R. §§10940, 10942, 15740, 15741; Hanna § 8.09[2]; Herlick Handbook §§ 6.21, 14.17; W. Cal. Sum., 2 "Workers' Compensation" §§260, 297, 299.

§4753. Reduction of additional compensation.

Such additional compensation is not in addition to but shall be reduced to the extent of any monetary payments received by the employee, from any source whatsoever, for or on account of such preexisting disability or impairment, except as to payments being made to the employee or to which he is entitled as a pension or other compensation for disability incurred in service in the armed forces of the United States, and except as to payments being made to him or to which he is entitled as assistance under the provisions of Chapter 2 (commencing with Section 11200), Chapter 3 (commencing with Section 12000), Chapter 4 (commencing with Section 12500), Chapter 5 (commencing with Section 13000), or Chapter 6 (commencing with Section 13500) of Part 3, or Part 5 (commencing with Section 17000), of Division 9 of the Welfare and Institutions Code, and excluding from such monetary payments received by the employee for or on account of such preexisting disability or impairment a sum equal to all sums reasonably and necessarily expended by the employee for or on account of attorney's fees, costs and expenses incidental to the recovery of such monetary payments.

All cases under this section and under Section 4751 shall be governed by the terms of this section and Section 4751 as in effect on the date of the particular subsequent injury.

Ref.: 8 C.C.R. §§10940, 10942, 15740, 15741; W. Cal. Sum., 2 "Workers' Compensation" §300.

§4753.5. Legal representation of state.

In any hearing, investigation, or proceeding, the state shall be represented by the Attorney General, or the attorneys of the Department of Industrial Relations, as appointed by the director. Expenses incident to representation, including costs for investigation, medical examinations, other expert reports, fees for witnesses, and other necessary and proper expenses, but excluding the salary of any of the Attorney General's deputies, shall be reimbursed from the Workers' Compensation Administration Revolving Fund. No witness fees or fees for medical services shall exceed those fees prescribed by the appeals board for the same services in those cases where the appeals board, by rule, has prescribed fees. Reimbursement pursuant to this section shall be in addition to, and in augmentation of, any other appropriations made or funds available for the use or support of the legal representation. **Leg.H.** 1994 ch. 146, 2003 ch. 228 (AB 1756), effective August 11, 2003, 2006 ch. 538 (SB 1852) §489.

Ref.: 8 C.C.R. §§10940, 10942; Hanna § 31.20[4][e]; Herlick Handbook § 6.21; W. Cal. Sum., 2 "Workers' Compensation" §301.

§4754. Special additional compensation; awards, payment; reimbursement.

The appeals board shall fix and award the amounts of special additional compensation to be paid under this article, and shall direct the State Compensation Insurance Fund to pay the additional compensation so awarded. Such additional compensation may be paid only from funds appropriated for such purpose. Out of any such appropriation the fund may reimburse itself for the cost of service rendered in payment of compensation awards pursuant to this article and maintenance of accounts and records pertaining thereto, which cost shall not exceed 5 percent of the amount of award paid.

Ref.: 8 C.C.R. §§15740, 15741; W. Cal. Sum., 2 "Workers' Compensation" §301.

§4754.5. Compromises and release agreements.

Nothing in this article shall impair the right of the Attorney General or the Department of Industrial Relations to release by compromise any claims brought under the provisions of this article. No such compromise and release agreement is valid unless it is approved by the appeals board; however, the provisions of Sections 5000 to 5004, inclusive, of this code, shall not apply to such compromise and release agreements.

Ref.: 8 C.C.R. §§10940, 10942, 15740, 15741; W. Cal. Sum., 2 "Workers' Compensation" §301.

§4755. Cash revolving funds.

(a) The State Compensation Insurance Fund may draw from the State Treasury out of the Subsequent Injuries Benefits Trust Fund for the purposes specified in Section 4751, without at the time presenting vouchers and itemized statements, a sum not to exceed in the aggregate fifty thousand dollars ($50,000), to be used as a cash revolving fund. The revolving fund shall be deposited in any banks and under any conditions as the Department of Finance determines. The Controller shall draw his or her warrants in favor of the State Compensation Insurance Fund for the amounts so withdrawn and the Treasurer shall pay these warrants.

(b) Expenditures made from the revolving fund in payments on claims for any additional compensation and for adjusting services are exempted from the operation of Section 16003 of the Government Code. Reimbursement of the revolving fund for these expenditures shall be made upon presentation to the Controller of an abstract or statement of the expenditures. The abstract or statement shall be in any form as the Controller requires.

(c) The director shall assign claims adjustment services and legal representation services respecting matters concerning subsequent injuries. The director or his or her representative may make these service assignments within the department, or he or she may contract for these services with the State Compensation Insurance Fund, for a fee in addition to that authorized by Section 4754, except insofar as these matters might conflict with the interests of the State Compensation Insurance Fund. The administrative costs associated with these services shall be reimbursed from the Workers' Compensation Administration Revolving Fund, except when a budget impasse requires advances as provided in subdivision (d) of Section 62.5. To the extent permitted by state law, the director may contract for audits or reports of services under this section.

(d) Commencing November 1, 2004, the State Compensation Insurance Fund and the director shall report annually to the fiscal committees of both houses of the Legislature and the Director of Finance, regarding all of the following:

(1) The number of subsequent injuries claims paid in the previous fiscal year, the total costs of those claims, and the levels of reserves on incurred claims.

(2) The administrative costs associated with claims payment activities.

(3) Annual revenues to the Subsequent Injuries Benefits Trust Fund from both of the following:

(A) Assessments collected pursuant to subdivision (d) of Section 62.5.

(B) Other revenues collected by the department.

(4) Projected annual program and claims costs for the current and upcoming fiscal years. **Leg.H.** 2003 ch. 228 (AB 1756), effective August 11, 2003.

Ref.: 8 C.C.R. §§15740, 15741; W. Cal. Sum., 2 "Workers' Compensation" §301.

ARTICLE 6
Special Payments to Certain Persons

§4800. Paid leave of absence for specified employees of Department of Justice and San Francisco Port Commission.

Whenever any member of the Department of Justice falling within the "state peace officer/firefighter" class is disabled by injury arising out of and in the course of his or her duties, he or she shall become entitled, regardless of his or her period of service with the Department of Justice to leave of absence while so disabled without loss of salary, in lieu of disability payments under this chapter, for a period of not exceeding one year. This section shall apply only to members of the Department of Justice whose principal duties consist of active law enforcement and shall not apply to persons employed in the Department of Justice whose principal duties are those of telephone operator, clerk, stenographer, machinist, mechanic or otherwise clearly not falling within the scope of active law enforcement service, even though this person is subject to occasional call or is occasionally called upon to perform duties within the scope of active law enforcement service.

This section shall apply to harbor policemen employed by the San Francisco Port Commission who are described in Section 20017.76 of the Government Code.

This section shall not apply to periods of disability which occur subsequent to termination of employment by resignation, retirement or dismissal. When this section does not apply, the employee shall be eligible for those benefits which would apply if this section had not been enacted. **Leg.H.** 1994 ch. 762, effective September 23, 1994.

Ref.: 8 C.C.R. §9814; Hanna §§ 3.114[2]–[3], 33.02[3][a], 34.03[2]; Herlick Handbook §§ 5.17, 14.17, 16.5; W. Cal. Sum., 2 "Workers' Compensation" §334.

§4800.5. Paid leave of absence for specified employees of Department of the California Highway Patrol—Limitations; appeals board jurisdiction in determining disability; eligibility of other peace officers.

(a) Whenever any sworn member of the Department of the California Highway Patrol is disabled by a single injury, excluding disabilities that are the result of cumulative trauma or cumulative injuries, arising out of and in the course of his or her duties, he or she shall become entitled, regardless of his or her period of service with the patrol, to leave of absence while so disabled without loss of salary, in lieu of disability payments under this chapter, for a period of not exceeding one year. This section shall apply only to members of the Department of the California Highway Patrol whose principal duties consist of active law enforcement and shall not apply to persons employed in the Department of the California Highway Patrol whose principal duties are those of telephone operator, clerk, stenographer, machinist, mechanic, or otherwise clearly not falling within the scope of active law enforcement service, even though this person is subject to occasional call or is occasionally called upon to perform the duties of active law enforcement service.

(b) Benefits payable for eligible sworn members of the Department of the California Highway Patrol whose disability is solely the result of cumulative trauma or injury shall be limited to the actual period of temporary disability or entitlement to maintenance allowance, or for one year, whichever is less.

(c) This section shall not apply to periods of disability that occur subsequent to termination of employment by resignation, retirement, or dismissal. When this section does not apply, the employee shall be eligible for those benefits that would apply had this section not been enacted.

(d) The appeals board may determine, upon request of any party, whether or not the disability referred to in this section arose out of and in the course of duty. In any action in which a dispute exists regarding the nature of the injury or the period of temporary disability or entitlement to maintenance allowance, or both, and upon the request of any party thereto, the appeals board shall determine when the disability commenced and ceased, and the amount of benefits provided by this division to which the employee is entitled during the period of this disability. The appeals board shall have the jurisdiction to award and enforce payment of these benefits, subject to subdivision (a) or (b), pursuant to Part 4 (commencing with Section 5300). A decision issued by the appeals board under this section is final and binding upon the parties subject to the rights of appeal contained in Chapter 7 (commencing with Section 5900) of Part 4.

(e) Except as provided in subdivision (g), this section shall apply for periods of disability commencing on or after January 1, 1995.

(f) This section does not apply to peace officers designated under subdivision (a) of Section 2250.1 of the Vehicle Code.

(g) Peace officers of the California State Police Division who become sworn members of the Department of the California Highway Patrol as a result of the Governor's Reorganization Plan No. 1 of 1995, other than those officers described in subdivision (f), shall be eligible for injury benefits accruing to sworn members of the Department of the California Highway Patrol under this division only for injuries occurring on or after July 12, 1995. **Leg.H.** 1994 ch. 762, effective September 23, 1994, 1995 Gov. Reorg. Plan 1, effective May 12, 1995, ch. 91, 1996 ch. 305.

Ref.: 8 C.C.R. §10405; Hanna § 3.114[2]–[3]; Herlick Handbook § 5.17; W. Cal. Sum., 2 "Workers' Compensation" §334.

§4801. Disability occurring in course of duty.

It shall be the duty of the appeals board to determine in the case of members of the California Highway Patrol, upon request of the Department of the California Highway Patrol or Department of Justice, and, in the case of the harbor policemen, upon the request of the San Francisco Port Commission, whether or not the disability referred to in Section 4800 arose out of and in the course of duty. The appeals board shall, also, in any disputed case, determine when such disability ceases.

Ref.: 8 C.C.R. §10405; Hanna § 21.07[6].

§4802. Medical, surgical, and hospital benefits.

Any such member of the California Highway Patrol or Department of Justice, or any such harbor policeman, so disabled is entitled from the date of injury and regardless of retirement under the Public Employees' Retirement System, to the medical, surgical and hospital benefits prescribed by this division as part of the compensation for persons injured in the course of and arising out of their employment, at the expense of the Department of the California Highway Patrol, the Department of Justice, or the San Francisco Port Commission, as the case may be, and such expense shall be charged upon the fund out of which the compensation of the member is paid.

Ref.: Hanna § 22.01[5].

§4803. Disability continuing beyond one year.

Whenever such disability of such member of the California Highway Patrol, or Department of Justice, or of such harbor policeman, continues for a period beyond one year, such member or harbor policeman shall thereafter be subject, as to disability indemnity, to the provisions of this division other than Section 4800, which refers to temporary disability only, during the remainder of the disability, except that such compensation shall be paid out of funds available for the support of the Department of the California

Labor

Highway Patrol, the Department of Justice, or the San Francisco Port Commission, as the case may be, and the leave of absence shall continue.

§4804. Prohibition on temporary disability payments concurrent with salary payments.

No disability indemnity shall be paid to said member of the California Highway Patrol or harbor policeman as temporary disability concurrently with wages or salary payments.

§4804.1. Paid leave of absence for specified University of California fire department employees.

Whenever any member of a University of California fire department specified in Section 3212.4 falling within the active "firefighting and prevention service" class is disabled by injury arising out of and in the course of his duties, he shall become entitled, regardless of his period of service with a University of California fire department, to leave of absence while so disabled without loss of salary, in lieu of disability payments under this chapter, for a period of not exceeding one year. This section shall apply only to members of a University of California fire department whose principal duties consists of active firefighting and prevention service and shall not apply to persons employed in a University of California fire department whose principal duties are those of telephone operator, clerk, stenographer, machinist, mechanic, or otherwise clearly not falling within the scope of active firefighting and prevention service, even though such person is subject to occasional call or is occasionally called upon to perform duties within the scope of active firefighting and prevention service.

Ref.: 8 C.C.R. §9814.

§4804.2. University of California firefighter's disability occurring in course of duty; determination.

It shall be the duty of the appeals board to determine in the case of members of a University of California fire department specified in Section 4804.1, upon request of the Regents of the University of California, whether or not the disability referred to in Section 4804.1 arose out of and in the course of duty. The appeals board shall, also in any disputed case, determine when such disability ceases.

Ref.: 8 C.C.R. §10405.

§4804.3. Medical, surgical, and hospital benefits for University of California firefighters.

Any such member of a University of California fire department specified in Section 4804.1, so disabled is entitled from the date of injury and regardless of retirement under the Public Employees' Retirement System, or other retirement system, to the medical, surgical, and hospital benefits prescribed by this division as part of the compensation for persons injured in the course of and arising out of their employment, at the expense of the Regents of the University of California, and such expense shall be charged upon the fund out of which the compensation of the member is paid.

§4804.4. University of California firefighter's disability continuing beyond one year.

Whenever such disability of such member of a University of California fire department, specified in Section 4804.1, continues for a period beyond one year, such member shall thereafter be subject, as to disability indemnity, to the provisions of this division other than Section 4804.1, which refers to temporary disability only, during the remainder of the disability, except that such compensation shall be paid out of funds available for the support of the Regents of the University of California, and the leave of absence shall continue.

§4804.5. Prohibition on temporary disability payments concurrent with salary payments for University of California firefighters.

No disability indemnity shall be paid to said member of a University of California fire department, specified in Section 4804.1, as temporary disability concurrently with wages or salary payments.

§4806. Paid leave of absence for active law enforcement officers of University of California Police Department.

Whenever any member of the University of California Police Department falling within the "law enforcement" class is disabled by injury arising out of and in the course of his duties, he shall become entitled, regardless of his period of service with the police department, to leave of absence while so disabled without loss of salary, in lieu of disability payments under this chapter, for a period of not exceeding one year. This section shall apply only to members of the University of California Police Department whose principal duties consist of active law enforcement, and shall not apply to persons employed in the University of California Police Department whose principal duties are those of telephone operator, clerk, stenographer, machinist, mechanic or otherwise clearly not falling within the scope of active law enforcement service, even though such person is subject to occasional call or is occasionally called upon to perform duties within the scope of active law enforcement service.

This section shall apply only to those members of the University of California Police Department specified in Section 3213.

Ref.: 8 C.C.R. §9814; W. Cal. Sum., 2 "Workers' Compensation" §334.

§4807. Appeals board to determine relationship of disability to duty.

It shall be the duty of the appeals board to determine, in the case of members of the University of California Police Department, upon the request of the Regents of the University of California, whether or not the disability referred to in Section 4806 arose out of and in the course of duty. The appeals board shall, also in any disputed case, determine when such disability ceases.

Ref.: 8 C.C.R. §10405; Hanna § 3.114[3]; Herlick Handbook § 14.17.

§4808. Medical, surgical, and hospital benefits for University of California police officers.

Any such member of the University of California Police Department so disabled is entitled from the date of injury, and regardless of retirement under either the University of California Retirement System or Public Employees' Retirement System, to the medical, surgical, and hospital benefits prescribed by this division as part of the compensation for persons injured in the course of and arising out of their employment, at the expense of the Regents of the University of California, and such expense shall be charged upon the fund out of which the compensation of the member is paid.

§4809. University of California police officer's disability continuing beyond one year.

Whenever such disability of such member of the University of California Police Department continues for a period beyond one year, such member shall thereafter be subject, as to disability indemnity, to the provisions of this division other than Section 4806, which refers to temporary disability only, during the remainder of the disability, except that such compensation shall be paid out of funds available for the support of the Regents of the University of California and the leave of absence shall continue.

§4810. Prohibition on temporary disability payments concurrent with salary payments for University of California police officers.

No disability indemnity shall be paid to such member of the University of California Police Department as temporary disability concurrently with wages or salary payments.

§4816. California State University Police Department collective bargaining agreement for enhanced industrial disability leave.

Pursuant to a collective bargaining agreement applicable to members of the California State University Police Department, whenever any member of that police department falling within the "law enforcement" class is disabled by injury or illness arising out of and in the course of his or her duties, he or she shall become entitled, regardless of his or her period of service with the police department, to enhanced industrial disability leave equivalent to the injured employee's net take home salary on the date of occurrence of the injury. For the purposes of this section, "net take home salary" means the amount of salary received after federal income tax, state income tax, and the employee's retirement contribution has been deducted from the employee's gross salary, in lieu of disability payments under this chapter, for a period of not exceeding one year. No benefits shall be paid under this section for any psychiatric disability or any physical disability arising from a psychiatric injury.

This section shall apply only to members of the California State University Police Department whose principal duties consist of active

Labor

law enforcement, and shall not apply to persons employed in the California State University Police Department whose principal duties are those of telephone operator, clerk, stenographer, machinist, mechanic, or otherwise clearly not falling within the scope of active law enforcement service, even though the person is subject to occasional call or is occasionally called upon to perform duties within the scope of active law enforcement service. **Leg.H.** 1994 ch. 50.

Ref.: Herlick Handbook § 8.21.

§4817. Appeals board to determine relationship of disability to duty.

It shall be the duty of the appeals board to determine, in the case of members of the California State University Police Department, upon the request of the Board of Trustees of the California State University, whether or not the disability referred to in Section 4816 arose out of and in the course of duty. The appeals board shall, also in any disputed case, determine when such disability ceases. **Leg.H.** 1994 ch. 50.

§4819. California State University police officer's disability continuing beyond one year.

Whenever the disability of a member of the California State University Police Department continues for a period beyond one year, that member shall thereafter be subject, as to disability indemnity, to the provisions of this division other than Section 4816, which refers to temporary disability only, during the remainder of the disability. **Leg.H.** 1994 ch. 50.

§4820. Prohibition on temporary disability payments concurrent with salary payments for California State University police officers.

No disability indemnity shall be paid to a member of the California State University Police Department as temporary disability concurrently with wages or salary payments. **Leg.H.** 1994 ch. 50.

ARTICLE 7
City Police and Firemen, Sheriffs, and Others

§4850. Paid leave of absence for specified public employees.

(a) Whenever any person listed in subdivision (b) who is a member of the Public Employees' Retirement System or the Los Angeles City Employees' Retirement System or subject to the County Employees Retirement Law of 1937 (Chapter 3 (commencing with Section 31450) of Part 3 of Division 4 of Title 3 of the Government Code), is disabled, whether temporarily or permanently, by injury or illness arising out of and in the course of his or her duties, he or she shall become entitled, regardless of his or her period of service with the city, county, or district, to a leave of absence while so disabled without loss of salary in lieu of temporary disability payments or maintenance allowance payments under Section 139.5, if any, which would be payable under this chapter, for the period of the disability, but not exceeding one year, or until that earlier date as he or she is retired on permanent disability pension, and is actually receiving disability pension payments, or advanced disability pension payments pursuant to Section 4850.3.

(b) The persons eligible under subdivision (a) include all of the following:

(1) City police officers.

(2) City, county, or district firefighters.

(3) Sheriffs.

(4) Officers or employees of any sheriff's offices.

(5) Inspectors, investigators, detectives, or personnel with comparable titles in any district attorney's office.

(6) County probation officers, group counselors, or juvenile services officers.

(7) Officers or employees of a probation office.

(8) Peace officers under Section 830.31 of the Penal Code employed on a regular, full-time basis by a county of the first class.

(9) Lifeguards employed year round on a regular, full-time basis by a county of the first class.

(10) Airport law enforcement officers under subdivision (d) of Section 830.33 of the Penal Code.

(11) Harbor or port police officers, wardens, or special officers of a harbor or port district or city or county harbor department under subdivision (a) of Section 830.1 or subdivision (b) of Section 830.33 of the Penal Code.

(12) Police officers of the Los Angeles Unified School District.

(c) This section shall apply only to persons listed in subdivision (b) who meet the requirements of subdivision (a) and does not include any of the following:

(1) Employees of a police department whose principal duties are those of a telephone operator, clerk, stenographer, machinist, mechanic, or otherwise, and whose functions do not clearly fall within the scope of active law enforcement service.

(2) Employees of a county sheriff's office whose principal duties are those of a telephone operator, clerk, stenographer, machinist, mechanic, or otherwise, and whose functions do not clearly come within the scope of active law enforcement service.

(3) Employees of a county probation office whose principal duties are those of a telephone operator, clerk, stenographer, machinist, mechanic, or otherwise, and whose functions do not clearly come within the scope of active law enforcement service.

(4) Employees of a city fire department, county fire department, or fire district whose principal duties are those of a telephone operator, clerk, stenographer, machinist, mechanic, or otherwise, and whose functions do not clearly fall within the scope of active firefighting and prevention service.

(d) If the employer is insured, the payments which, except for this section, the insurer would be obligated to make as disability indemnity to the injured, the insurer may pay to the insured.

(e) No leave of absence taken pursuant to this section by a peace officer, as defined by Chapter 4.5 (commencing with Section 830) of Title 3 of Part 2 of the Penal Code, or by a city, county, or district firefighter, shall be deemed to constitute family care and medical leave, as defined in Section 12945.2 of the Government Code, or to reduce the time authorized for family care and medical leave by Section 12945.2 of the Government Code. **Leg.H.** 1995 ch. 474, 1999 chs. 270, 970 §1.5, 2000 chs. 920, 929 §3, 2001 ch. 791.

Ref.: 8 C.C.R. §9814; Hanna §§ 3.114, 7.04[9][a], 21.07[6], 21.08[1], 33.02[3]; Herlick Handbook §§ 5.17, 13.4, 14.17, 16.5; W. Cal. Sum., 2 "Workers' Compensation" §§282, 334.

§4850.3. Advanced disability pension payments—Local safety officer.

A city, county, special district, or harbor district that is a member of the Public Employees' Retirement System, is subject to the County Employees Retirement Law of 1937, or is subject to the Los Angeles City Employees' Retirement System, may make advanced disability pension payments to any local safety officer who has qualified for benefits under Section 4850 and is approved for a disability allowance. The payments shall be no less than 50 percent of the estimated highest average annual compensation earnable by the local safety officer during the three consecutive years of employment immediately preceding the effective date of his or her disability retirement, unless the local safety officer chooses an optional settlement in the permanent disability retirement application process which would reduce the pension allowance below 50 percent. In the case where the local safety officer's choice lowers the disability pension allowance below 50 percent of average annual compensation as calculated, the advanced pension payments shall be set at an amount equal to the disability pension allowance. If a local agency has an adopted policy of paying for any accumulated sick leave after the safety officer is eligible for a disability allowance, the advanced disability pension payments under this section may only be made when the local safety officer has exhausted all sick leave payments. Advanced disability pension payments shall not be considered a salary under this or any other provision of law. All advanced disability pension payments made by a local agency with membership in the Public Employees' Retirement System shall be reimbursed by the Public Employees' Retirement System pursuant to Section 21293.1 of the Government Code. **Leg.H.** 1989 ch. 1464, 2000 ch. 920.

Ref.: 8 C.C.R. §9814; Hanna § 3.114[2]; Herlick Handbook § 5.17.

§4850.4. Advanced disability pension payments.

(a) A city, county, special district, or harbor district that is a member of the Public Employees' Retirement System, is subject to the County Employees Retirement Law of 1937, or is subject to the Los Angeles City Employees' Retirement Systems, shall make advanced disability pension payments in accordance with Section 4850.3 unless any of the following is applicable:

(1) After an examination of the employee by a physician, the physician determines that there is no discernable injury to, or illness of, the employee.

Labor

(2) The employee was incontrovertibly outside the course of his or her employment duties when the injury occurred.

(3) There is proof of fraud associated with the filing of the employee's claim.

(b) Any employer described in subdivision (a) who is required to make advanced disability pension payments, shall make the payments commencing no later than 30 days from the date of issuance of the last disbursed of the following:

(1) The employee's last regular payment of wages or salary.

(2) The employee's last payment of benefits under Section 4850.

(3) The employee's last payment for sick leave.

(c) The advanced disability payments shall continue until the claimant is approved or disapproved for a disability allowance pursuant to final adjudication as provided by law.

(d) An employer described in subdivision (a) shall be required to make advanced disability pension payments only if the employee does all of the following:

(1) Files an application for disability retirement at least 60 days prior to the payment of benefits pursuant to subdivision (a).

(2) Fully cooperates in providing the employer with medical information and in attending all statutorily required medical examinations and evaluations set by the employer.

(3) Fully cooperates with the evaluation process established by the retirement plan.

(e) The 30-day period for the commencement of payments pursuant to subdivision (b) shall be tolled by whatever period of time is directly related to the employee's failure to comply with the provisions of subdivision (d).

(f) After final adjudication, if an employee's disability application is denied, the local agency and the employee shall arrange for the employee to repay any advanced disability pension payments received by the employee pursuant to this subdivision. The repayment plan shall take into account the employee's ability to repay the advanced disability payments received. Absent an agreement on repayment, the matter shall be submitted for a local agency administrative appeals remedy that includes an independent level of resolution to determine a reasonable repayment plan. If repayment is not made according to the repayment plan, the local agency may take reasonable steps, including litigation, to recover the payments advanced. **Leg.H.** 2002 chs. 189 (AB 1982), 877 (AB 2131).

Ref.: See Govt. Code §21419; 8 C.C.R. §9814; Hanna § 3.114[2]; Herlick Handbook § 5.17.

§4850.5. Benefits for firefighters, sheriff's and probation office employees, and other specified employees of San Luis Obispo County.

Any firefighter employed by the County of San Luis Obispo, and the sheriff or any officer or employee of the sheriff's office of the County of San Luis Obispo, and any county probation officer, group counselor, or juvenile services officer, or any officer or employee of a probation office, employed by the County of San Luis Obispo, shall, upon the adoption of a resolution of the board of supervisors so declaring, be entitled to the benefits of this article, if otherwise entitled to these benefits, even though the employee is not a member of the Public Employees' Retirement System or subject to the County Employees Retirement Law of 1937 (Chapter 3 (commencing with Section 31450) of Part 3 of Division 4 of Title 3 of the Government Code). **Leg.H.** 1999 ch. 970.

Ref.: 8 C.C.R. §9814; Hanna §§ 3.114[1], 33.02[2][a]; Herlick Handbook § 5.17.

§4850.7. Firefighters' entitlement to benefits.

(a) Any firefighter employed by a dependent or independent fire district may be entitled to the benefits of this article, if otherwise entitled to these benefits, even though the employee is not a member of the Public Employees' Retirement System or subject to the County Employees Retirement Law of 1937 (Chapter 3 (commencing with Section 31450) of Part 3 of Division 4 of Title 3 of the Government Code).

(b) The issue of whether the firefighters employed by a fire district are entitled to the benefits of this article is subject to Article 10 (commencing with Section 3500) of Chapter 3 of Division 4 of Title 1 of the Government Code.

(c) If the governing body of the district agrees that the benefits shall apply, it shall adopt a resolution to that effect.

Ref.: 8 C.C.R. §9814.

§4851. Request to make disability determinations.

The governing body of any city, county, or city and county, in addition to anyone else properly entitled, including the Public Employees' Retirement System, may request the appeals board to determine in any case, and the appeals board shall determine, whether or not the disability referred to in Section 4850 arose out of and in the course of duty. The appeals board shall also, in any disputed case, determine when the disability commenced and ceased, and the amount of benefits provided by this division to which the employee is entitled during the period of the disability. The appeals board shall have jurisdiction to award and enforce payment of these benefits pursuant to Part 4 (commencing with Section 5300).

Ref.: 8 C.C.R. §10405; Hanna §§ 3.114[3], 33.02[3][b]; Herlick Handbook §§ 13.4, 14.17; W. Cal. Sum., 2 "Workers' Compensation" §334.

§4852. Article's effect on medical, surgical, and hospital benefits.

The provisions of this article do not diminish or affect the right of any such officer or employee to the medical, surgical, and hospital benefits prescribed by this division.

Ref.: Hanna §§ 3.114[2], 22.01[5].

§4853. Disability continuing beyond one year.

Whenever such disability of any such officer or employee continues for a period beyond one year, such member shall thereafter be subject as to disability indemnity to the provisions of this division other than Section 4850 during the remainder of the period of said disability or until the effective date of his retirement under the Public Employees' Retirement Act, and the leave of absence shall continue.

Ref.: Hanna §§ 3.114[2], 35.19; Herlick Handbook § 16.5; W. Cal. Sum., 2 "Workers' Compensation" §334.

§4854. Prohibition on temporary disability payments concurrent with salary payments.

No disability indemnity shall be paid to any such officer or employee concurrently with wages or salary.

§4855. Non-applicability to reserve public safety employees.

This article shall not be applicable to individuals who are appointed as reserve public safety employees and are deemed to be employees of a county, city, town or district for workers' compensation purposes pursuant to Section 3362.

Ref.: Hanna § 33.02[3][a].

§4856. Continued provision of health benefits to surviving spouse and dependents of deceased firefighter or peace officer; limitations.

(a) Whenever any local employee who is a firefighter, or peace officer as described in Chapter 4.5 (commencing with Section 830) of Title 3 of Part 2 of the Penal Code, is killed in the performance of his or her duty or dies as a result of an accident or injury caused by external violence or physical force incurred in the performance of his or her duty, the employer shall continue providing health benefits to the deceased employee's spouse under the same terms and conditions provided prior to the death, or prior to the accident or injury that caused the death, of the employee unless the surviving spouse elects to receive a lump-sum survivors benefit in lieu of monthly benefits. Minor dependents shall continue to receive benefits under the coverage provided the surviving spouse or, if there is no surviving spouse, until the age of 21 years. However, pursuant to Section 22822 of the Government Code, the surviving spouse may not add the new spouse or stepchildren as family members under the continued health benefits coverage of the surviving spouse.

(b) Subdivision (a) also applies to the employer of any local employee who is a firefighter, or peace officer as described in Chapter 4.5 (commencing with Section 830) of Title 3 of Part 2 of the Penal Code, who was killed in the performance of his or her duty or who died as a result of an accident or injury caused by external violence or physical force incurred in the performance of his or her duty prior to September 30, 1996. **Leg.H.** 1996 ch. 1120, effective September 30, 1996, 1997 ch. 193, 2004 ch. 69 (SB 626), effective June 24, 2004.

Ref.: Hanna § 3.115[3]; Herlick Handbook § 7.23; W. Cal. Sum., 2 "Workers' Compensation" §336.

Labor

PART 3
Compensation Claims

CHAPTER 1
PAYMENT AND ASSIGNMENT

§4900. Claim for compensation; assignment.

No claim for compensation, except as provided in Section 96, is assignable before payment, but this provision does not affect the survival thereof.

Ref.: 8 C.C.R. §§10110, 10115; Hanna §§ 7.03[3], 27.05, 30.01; Herlick Handbook § 10.1; MB Prac. Guide: Cal. Debt Collection & Enforcement of Judgments, §§16.38, 17.06; W. Cal. Sum., 1 "Contracts" §721.

§4901. Effect of debts on claims.

No claim for compensation nor compensation awarded, adjudged, or paid, is subject to be taken for the debts of the party entitled to such compensation except as hereinafter provided.

Ref.: Hanna §§ 27.05, 30.01; Herlick Handbook § 10.1.

§4902. Payment of claim directly to attorney or agent.

No compensation, whether awarded or voluntarily paid, shall be paid to any attorney at law or in fact or other agent, but shall be paid directly to the claimant entitled thereto unless otherwise ordered by the appeals board. No payment made to an attorney at law or in fact or other agent in violation of this section shall be credited to the employer.

Ref.: 8 C.C.R. §§10110, 10115; Hanna § 30.03[1].

§4903. Determination of liens against compensation payable.

The appeals board may determine, and allow as liens against any sum to be paid as compensation, any amount determined as hereinafter set forth in subdivisions (a) through (i). If more than one lien is allowed, the appeals board may determine the priorities, if any, between the liens allowed. The liens that may be allowed hereunder are as follows:

(a) A reasonable attorney's fee for legal services pertaining to any claim for compensation either before the appeals board or before any of the appellate courts, and the reasonable disbursements in connection therewith. No fee for legal services shall be awarded to any representative who is not an attorney, except with respect to those claims for compensation for which an application, pursuant to Section 5501, has been filed with the appeals board on or before December 31, 1991, or for which a disclosure form, pursuant to Section 4906, has been sent to the employer, or insurer or third-party administrator, if either is known, on or before December 31, 1991.

(b) The reasonable expense incurred by or on behalf of the injured employee, as provided by Article 2 (commencing with Section 4600) and, to the extent the employee is entitled to reimbursement under Section 4621, medical-legal expenses as provided by Article 2.5 (commencing with Section 4620) of Chapter 2 of Part 2.

(c) The reasonable value of the living expenses of an injured employee or of his or her dependents, subsequent to the injury.

(d) The reasonable burial expenses of the deceased employee, not to exceed the amount provided for by Section 4701.

(e) The reasonable living expenses of the spouse or minor children of the injured employee, or both, subsequent to the date of the injury, where the employee has deserted or is neglecting his or her family. These expenses shall be allowed in the proportion that the appeals board deems proper, under application of the spouse, guardian of the minor children, or the assignee, pursuant to subdivision (a) of Section 11477 of the Welfare and Institutions Code, of the spouse, a former spouse, or minor children. A collection received as a result of a lien against a workers' compensation award imposed pursuant to this subdivision for payment of child support ordered by a court shall be credited as provided in Section 695.221 of the Code of Civil Procedure.

(f) The amount of unemployment compensation disability benefits that have been paid under or pursuant to the Unemployment Insurance Code in those cases where, pending a determination under this division there was uncertainty whether the benefits were payable under the Unemployment Insurance Code or payable hereunder; provided, however, that any lien under this subdivision shall be allowed and paid as provided in Section 4904.

(g) The amount of unemployment compensation benefits and extended duration benefits paid to the injured employee for the same day or days for which he or she receives, or is entitled to receive, temporary total disability indemnity payments under this division; provided, however, that any lien under this subdivision shall be allowed and paid as provided in Section 4904.

(h) The amount of family temporary disability insurance benefits that have been paid to the injured employee pursuant to the Unemployment Insurance Code for the same day or days for which that employee receives, or is entitled to receive, temporary total disability indemnity payments under this division, provided, however, that any lien under this subdivision shall be allowed and paid as provided in Section 4904.

(i) The amount of indemnification granted by the California Victims of Crime Program pursuant to Article 1 (commencing with Section 13959) of Chapter 5 of Part 4 of Division 3 of Title 2 of the Government Code.

(j) The amount of compensation, including expenses of medical treatment, and recoverable costs that have been paid by the Asbestos Workers' Account pursuant to the provisions of Chapter 11 (commencing with Section 4401) of Part 1. **Leg.H.** 1991 chs. 116, 934, 1993 ch. 876, effective October 6, 1993, 1994 ch. 75, effective May 20, 1994, 1996 ch. 1077, 2003 ch. 797 (SB 727).

Ref.: 8 C.C.R. §§9812, 9813, 9815, 10770, 10771, 10772, 10774, 10775, 10776, 10778, 10886, 10888; Hanna §§ 30.01–30.10, 30.24[3], 30.25[3], 30.27; MB Prac. Guide: Cal. Debt Collection & Enforcement of Judgments, §§12.35, 12.36, 17.06; W. Cal. Sum., 2 "Insurance" §212, 2 "Workers' Compensation" §§42, 150, 341, 342, 358, 359, 405–409.

§4903.1. Determination of reimbursement for benefits paid or services provided.

(a) The appeals board, arbitrator, or settlement conference referee, before issuing an award or approval of any compromise of claim, shall determine, on the basis of liens filed with it pursuant to subdivision (b) or (c), whether any benefits have been paid or services provided by a health care provider, a health care service plan, a group disability policy, including a loss of income policy, a self-insured employee welfare benefit plan, or a hospital service contract, and its award or approval shall provide for reimbursement for benefits paid or services provided under these plans as follows:

(1) When the referee issues an award finding that an injury or illness arises out of and in the course of employment, but denies the applicant reimbursement for self-procured medical costs solely because of lack of notice to the applicant's employer of his need for hospital, surgical, or medical care, the appeals board shall nevertheless award a lien against the employee's recovery, to the extent of benefits paid or services provided, for the effects of the industrial injury or illness, by a health care provider, a health care service plan, a group disability policy, a self-insured employee welfare benefit plan, or a hospital service contract.

(2) When the referee issues an award finding that an injury or illness arises out of and in the course of employment, and makes an award for reimbursement for self-procured medical costs, the appeals board shall allow a lien, to the extent of benefits paid or services provided, for the effects of the industrial injury or illness, by a health care provider, a health care service plan, a group disability policy, a self-insured employee welfare benefit plan, or a hospital service contract.

(3) When the referee issues an award finding that an injury or illness arises out of and in the course of employment and makes an award for temporary disability indemnity, the appeals board shall allow a lien as living expense under Section 4903, for benefits paid by a group disability policy providing loss of time benefits. Such lien shall be allowed to the extent that benefits have been paid for the same day or days for which temporary disability indemnity is awarded and shall not exceed the award for temporary disability indemnity. No lien shall be allowed hereunder unless the group disability policy provides for reduction, exclusion, or coordination of loss of time benefits on account of workers' compensation benefits.

(4) When the parties propose that the case be disposed of by way of a compromise and release agreement, in the event the lien claimant, other than a health care provider, does not agree to the amount allocated to it, then the referee shall determine the potential recovery and reduce the amount of the lien in the ratio of the applicant's recovery to the potential recovery in full satisfaction of its lien claim.

Labor

(b) When a compromise of claim or an award is submitted to the appeals board, arbitrator, or settlement conference referee for approval, the parties shall file with the appeals board, arbitrator, or settlement conference referee any liens served on the parties.

(c) Any lien claimant under Section 4903 or this section shall file its lien with the appeals board in writing upon a form approved by the appeals board. The lien shall be accompanied by a full statement or itemized voucher supporting the lien and justifying the right to reimbursement and proof of service upon the injured worker, or if deceased, upon the worker's dependents, the employer, the insurer, and the respective attorneys or other agents of record.

(d) The appeals board shall file liens required by subdivision (c) immediately upon receipt. Numbers shall be assigned pursuant to subdivision (c) of Section 5500.

Ref.: 8 C.C.R. §§10609, 10770, 10771, 10886, 10888; Hanna §§ 23.14[2][l], 29.04[3][c], 30.24[2][b], 30.27; Herlick Handbook §§ 10.1, 10.3, 10.4; W. Cal. Sum., 2 "Workers' Compensation" §§344, 361, 406–409.

§4903.2. Attorney's fee allowed from lien claimant's recovery.

Where a lien claimant is reimbursed pursuant to subdivision (f) or (g) of Section 4903 or Section 4903.1, for benefits paid or services provided, the appeals board may award an attorney's fee out of the lien claimant's recovery if the appeals board determines that all of the following occurred:

(a) The lien claimant received notice of all hearings following the filing of the lien and received notice of intent to award the applicant's attorney a fee.

(b) An attorney or other representative of the lien claimant did not participate in the proceedings before the appeals board with respect to the lien claim.

(c) There were bona fide issues respecting compensability, or respecting allowability of the lien, such that the services of an attorney were reasonably required to effectuate recovery on the claim of lien and were instrumental in effecting the recovery.

(d) The case was not disposed of by compromise and release.

The amount of the attorney's fee out of the lien claimant's recovery shall be based on the extent of applicant's attorney's efforts on behalf of the lien claimant. The ratio of the amount of the attorney's fee awarded against the lien claimant's recovery to that recovery shall not exceed the ratio of the amount of the attorney's fee awarded against the applicant's award to that award.

Ref.: Hanna § 30.27; Herlick Handbook §§ 10.2, 10.6, 10.8; W. Cal. Sum., 2 "Workers' Compensation" §§351, 407.

§4903.3. Compensation provided from fund.

The director, as administrator of the Uninsured Employers Fund, may, in his discretion, provide compensation, including medical treatment, from the Uninsured Employers Fund in cases to which the director is a party before the issuance of any award, if such compensation is not being provided to the applicant.

The appeals board shall determine and allow as a first lien against any sum to be paid as compensation the amount of compensation, including the cost of medical treatment, provided by the director pursuant to this section.

Ref.: Herlick Handbook § 10.17; W. Cal. Sum., 2 "Workers' Compensation" §156.

§4903.4. Disputes over liens for expenses.

When a dispute arises concerning a lien for expenses incurred by or on behalf of the injured employee as provided by Article 2 (commencing with Section 4600) of Chapter 2 of Part 2, the appeals board may resolve the dispute in a separate proceeding, which may include binding arbitration upon agreement of the employer, lien claimant, and the employee, if the employee remains a party to the dispute, according to the rules of practice and procedure.

1989 Note: This section is applicable only to injuries occurring on or after January 1, 1990. Stats. 1989 ch. 893 §6.

Ref.: 8 C.C.R. §§10773, 10886; Hanna §§ 22.05[5], 30.26; W. Cal. Sum., 2 "Workers' Compensation" §408.

§4903.5. Limitations period for filing lien claim.

(a) No lien claim for expenses as provided in subdivision (b) of Section 4903 may be filed after six months from the date on which the appeals board or a workers' compensation administrative law judge issues a final decision, findings, order, including an order approving compromise and release, or award, on the merits of the claim, after five years from the date of the injury for which the services were provided, or after one year from the date the services were provided, whichever is later.

(b) Notwithstanding subdivision (a), any health care provider, health care service plan, group disability insurer, employee benefit plan, or other entity providing medical benefits on a nonindustrial basis, may file a lien claim for expenses as provided in subdivision (b) of Section 4903 within six months after the person or entity first has knowledge that an industrial injury is being claimed.

(c) The injured worker shall not be liable for any underlying obligation if a lien claim has not been filed and served within the allowable period. Except when the lien claimant is the applicant as provided in Section 5501, a lien claimant shall not file a declaration of readiness to proceed in any case until the case-in-chief has been resolved.

(d) This section shall not apply to civil actions brought under the Cartwright Act (Chapter 2 (commencing with Section 16700) of Part 2 of Division 7 of the Business and Professions Code), the Unfair Practices Act (Chapter 4 (commencing with Section 17000) of Part 2 of Division 7 of the Business and Professions Code), or the federal Racketeer Influenced and Corrupt Organization Act (Chapter 96 (commencing with Section 1961) of Title 18 of the United States Code) based on concerted action with other insurers that are not parties to the case in which the lien or claim is filed. **Leg.H.** 2002 ch. 6 (AB 749).

Ref.: Hanna § 30.21[1]; Herlick Handbook § 10.1; W. Cal. Sum., 2 "Workers' Compensation" §408.

§4903.6. Lien claim or application for adjudication; requirements for filing; exemptions.

(a) Except as necessary to meet the requirements of Section 4903.5, no lien claim or application for adjudication shall be filed under subdivision (b) of Section 4903 until the expiration of one of the following:

(1) Sixty days after the date of acceptance or rejection of liability for the claim, or expiration of the time provided for investigation of liability pursuant to subdivision (b) of Section 5402, whichever date is earlier.

(2) The time provided for payment of medical treatment bills pursuant to Section 4603.2.

(3) The time provided for payment of medical-legal expenses pursuant to Section 4622.

(b) No declaration of readiness to proceed shall be filed for a lien under subdivision (b) of Section 4903 until the underlying case has been resolved or where the applicant chooses not to proceed with his or her case.

(c) The appeals board shall adopt reasonable regulations to ensure compliance with this section, and shall take any further steps as may be necessary to enforce the regulations, including, but not limited to, impositions of sanctions pursuant to Section 5813.

(d) The prohibitions of this section shall not apply to lien claims, applications for adjudication, or declarations of readiness to proceed filed by or on behalf of the employee, or to the filings by or on behalf of the employer. **Leg.H.** 2006 ch. 69 (AB 1806) §26, effective July 12, 2006.

Ref.: Hanna §§ 30.04, 30.05; Herlick Handbook § 10.3; W. Cal. Sum., 2 "Workers' Compensation" §408.

§4904. Adjustment and disallowance of liens; liens on unemployment compensation benefits.

(a) If notice is given in writing to the insurer, or to the employer if uninsured, setting forth the nature and extent of any claim that is allowable as a lien, the claim is a lien against any amount thereafter payable as compensation, subject to the determination of the amount and approval of the lien by the appeals board. When the Employment Development Department has served an insurer or employer with a lien claim, the insurer or employer shall notify the Employment Development Department, in writing, as soon as possible, but in no event later than 15 working days after commencing disability indemnity payments. When a lien has been served on an insurer or an employer by the Employment Development Department, the insurer or employer shall notify the Employment Development Department, in writing, within 10 working days of filing an application for adjudication, a stipulated award, or a compromise and release with the appeals board.

(b)(1) In determining the amount of lien to be allowed for unemployment compensation disability benefits under subdivision (f) of Section 4903, the appeals board shall allow the lien in the amount of benefits which it finds were

Labor

paid for the same day or days of disability for which an award of compensation for any permanent disability indemnity resulting solely from the same injury or illness or temporary disability indemnity, or both, is made and for which the employer has not reimbursed the Employment Development Department pursuant to Section 2629.1 of the Unemployment Insurance Code.

(2) In determining the amount of lien to be allowed for unemployment compensation benefits and extended duration benefits under subdivision (g) of Section 4903, the appeals board shall allow the lien in the amount of benefits which it finds were paid for the same day or days for which an award of compensation for temporary total disability is made.

(3) In determining the amount of lien to be allowed for family temporary disability insurance benefits under subdivision (h) of Section 4903, the appeals board shall allow the lien in the amount of benefits that it finds were paid for the same day or days for which an award of compensation for temporary total disability is made and for which the employer has not reimbursed the Employment Development Department pursuant to Section 2629.1 of the Unemployment Insurance Code.

(c) In the case of agreements for the compromise and release of a disputed claim for compensation, the applicant and defendant may propose to the appeals board, as part of the compromise and release agreement, an amount out of the settlement to be paid to any lien claimant claiming under subdivision (f), (g), or (h) of Section 4903. If the lien claimant objects to the amount proposed for payment of its lien under a compromise and release settlement or stipulation, the appeals board shall determine the extent of the lien claimant's entitlement to reimbursement on its lien and make and file findings on all facts involved in the controversy over this issue in accordance with Section 5313. The appeals board may approve a compromise and release agreement or stipulation which proposes the disallowance of a lien, in whole or in part, only where there is proof of service upon the lien claimant by the defendant, not less than 15 days prior to the appeals board action, of all medical and rehabilitation documents and a copy of the proposed compromise and release agreement or stipulation. The determination of the appeals board, subject to petition for reconsideration and to the right of judicial review, as to the amount of lien allowed under subdivision (f), (g), or (h) of Section 4903, whether in connection with an award of compensation or the approval of a compromise and release agreement, shall be binding on the lien claimant, the applicant, and the defendant, insofar as the right to benefits paid under the Unemployment Insurance Code for which the lien was claimed. The appeals board may order the amount of any lien claim, as determined and allowed by it, to be paid directly to the person entitled, either in a lump sum or in installments.

(d) Where unemployment compensation disability benefits, including family temporary disability insurance benefits, have been paid pursuant to the Unemployment Insurance Code while reconsideration of an order, decision, or award is pending, or has been granted, the appeals board shall determine and allow a final amount on the lien as of the date the board is ready to issue its decision denying a petition for reconsideration or affirming, rescinding, altering or amending the original findings, order, decision, or award.

(e) The appeals board may not be prohibited from approving a compromise and release agreement on all other issues and deferring to subsequent proceedings the determination of a lien claimant's entitlement to reimbursement if the defendant in any of these proceedings agrees to pay the amount subsequently determined to be due under the lien claim. **Leg.H.** 1993 ch. 748, 2003 ch. 797 (SB 727).

Ref.: 8 C.C.R. §§10772, 10886, 10888; Hanna §§ 30.08, 30.24[1], 30.24[3]; Herlick Handbook §§ 10.1, 10.6, 10.8, 10.9, 10.11; MB Prac. Guide: Cal. Debt Collection & Enforcement of Judgments, §§12.36, 17.06; W. Cal. Sum., 2 "Workers' Compensation" §§342, 406, 408, 409.

§4904.1. Lien does not affect payment of balance of award.

The payment of liens as provided in Section 4904, shall in no way affect the commencement of immediate payments on any balance of the award to the injured claimant where an installment payment for his disability has been determined.

Ref.: 8 C.C.R. §10886; W. Cal. Sum., 2 "Workers' Compensation" §408.

§4905. Determination when lien not duly requested.

Where it appears in any proceeding pending before the appeals board that a lien should be allowed if it had been duly requested by the party entitled thereto, the appeals board may, without any request for such lien having been made, order the payment of the claim to be made directly to the person entitled, in the same manner and with the same effect as though the lien had been regularly requested, and the award to such person shall constitute a lien against unpaid compensation due at the time of service of the award.

Ref.: 8 C.C.R. §10886; Hanna §§ 20.04[3], 30.23; Herlick Handbook §§ 5.17, 10.14.

§4906. Only reasonable legal and medical services claims valid.

(a) No charge, claim, or agreement for the legal services or disbursements mentioned in subdivision (a) of Section 4903, or for the expense mentioned in subdivision (b) of Section 4903, is enforceable, valid, or binding in excess of a reasonable amount. The appeals board may determine what constitutes a reasonable amount.

(b) No attorney or agent shall demand or accept any fee from an employee or dependent of an employee for the purpose of representing the employee or dependent of an employee in any proceeding of the division, appeals board, or any appellate procedure related thereto until the amount of the fee has been approved or set by the appeals board.

(c) Any fee agreement shall be submitted to the appeals board for approval within 10 days after the agreement is made.

(d) In establishing a reasonable attorney's fee, consideration shall be given to the responsibility assumed by the attorney, the care exercised in representing the applicant, the time involved, and the results obtained.

(e) At the initial consultation, an attorney shall furnish the employee a written disclosure form promulgated by the administrative director which shall clearly and prominently describe the procedures available to the injured employee or his or her dependents. The disclosure form shall describe this section, the range of attorney's fees customarily approved by the appeals board, and the attorney's fees provisions of Section 4064 and the extent to which an employee may receive compensation without incurring attorney's fees. The disclosure form shall include the telephone number of the administrative director together with the statement that the employee may receive answers at that number to questions concerning entitlement to compensation or the procedures to follow to receive compensation. A copy of the disclosure form shall be signed by the employee and the attorney and sent to the employer, or insurer or third-party administrator, if either is known, by the attorney within 15 days of the employee's and attorney's execution thereof.

(f) The disclosure form set forth in subdivision (e) shall contain, prominently stated, the following statement:

"Any person who makes or causes to be made any knowingly false or fraudulent material statement or representation for the purpose of obtaining or denying worker's compensation benefits or payments is guilty of a felony."

(g) The employee, the insurer, the employer, and the attorneys for each party shall sign and file with the board a statement, with the application or answer, under penalty of perjury that they have not violated Section 139.3 and that they have not offered, delivered, received, or accepted any rebate, refund, commission, preference, patronage dividend, discount, or other consideration, whether in the form of money or otherwise, as compensation or inducement for any referred examination or evaluation. **Leg.H.** 1991 ch. 934, 1993 ch. 120, effective July 16, 1993, ch. 1241.

1990 Note: The amendments made by this act to subdivision (c) of Section 139.5 of the Labor Code, pertaining to the payment of additional living expenses, and subdivisions (a) and (c) of Section 4702, of the Labor Code, with respect to the crediting of accrued disability indemnity against the amount of the death benefit, and subdivision (a) of Section 4906 of the Labor Code, with respect to legal services, are not intended by the Legislature to make a change in the law as it existed with respect to these provisions prior to January 1, 1990. Stats. 1990 ch. 1550 §67.

1989 Note: This section is applicable only to injuries occurring on or after January 1, 1990. Stats. 1989 ch. 893 §6.

Ref.: 8 C.C.R. §§10134, 10135, 10135.1, 10404, 10774, 10775, 10776, 10778, 10886; Hanna §§ 20.02[1][b], 22.06[6][b], 25.01[4], 30.03[2]; Herlick Handbook §§ 9.18, 10.2, 14.11, 14.13, 16.16; W. Cal. Sum., 2 "Workers' Compensation" §§350, 354, 387, 389, 406.

§4907. Removal of privilege to represent party.

The privilege of any person, including attorneys admitted to practice in the Supreme Court of the state to appear in any proceeding as a representative of any party before the appeals board, or any of its referees, may, after a hearing, be removed, denied, or suspended by the appeals board for a violation of this chapter or for other good cause.

Ref.: 8 C.C.R. §§10773, 10779; Hanna §§ 20.01[2], 21.09[5]; Herlick Handbook § 10.2; W. Cal. Sum., 2 "Workers' Compensation" §353.

§4908. Compensation claim's equal preference over other debts.

A claim for compensation for the injury or death of any employee, or any award or judgment entered thereon, has the same preference over the other debts of the employer, or his estate and of the insurer which is given by the law to claims for wages. Such preference is for the entire amount of the compensation to be paid. This section shall not impair the lien of any previous award.

Ref.: MB Prac. Guide: Cal. Debt Collection & Enforcement of Judgments, §§12.37, 17.06; W. Cal. Sum., 2 "Workers' Compensation" §410.

§4909. Effect of employer's payment of benefits before settlement.

Any payment, allowance, or benefit received by the injured employee during the period of his incapacity, or by his dependents in the event of his death, which by the terms of this division was not then due and payable or when there is any dispute or question concerning the right to compensation, shall not, in the absence of any agreement, be an admission of liability for compensation on the part of the employer, but any such payment, allowance, or benefit may be taken into account by the appeals board in fixing the amount of the compensation to be paid. The acceptance of any such payment, allowance, or benefit shall not operate as a waiver of any right or claim which the employee or his dependents has against the employer.

Ref.: Hanna §§ 7.04[6], 7.04[8], 7.04[9][b]; Herlick Handbook § 11.1; W. Cal. Sum., 2 "Workers' Compensation" §§332, 391.

§4909.1. State fund may administer benefits.

Authorized representatives of the Department of Corrections, and the Department of the Youth Authority may request the State Compensation Insurance Fund to provide any payment, allowance, or benefit as described in Section 4909. When requested by an authorized representative, the State Compensation Insurance Fund shall administer the benefits in a timely fashion.

CHAPTER 2
COMPROMISE AND RELEASE

§5000. Limitations of this division.

No contract, rule, or regulation shall exempt the employer from liability for the compensation fixed by this division, but nothing in this division shall:

(a) Impair the right of the parties interested to compromise, subject to the provisions herein contained, any liability which is claimed to exist under this division on account of injury or death.

(b) Confer upon the dependents of any injured employee any interest which the employee may not release by compromise or for which he, or his estate is in the event of such compromise by him accountable to dependents.

Ref.: 8 C.C.R. §§10878, 10882; Hanna §§ 29.01[1], 29.04[4]; Herlick Handbook §§ 7.19, 11.1, 11.8; W. Cal. Sum., 2 "Workers' Compensation" §§104, 113, 361, 364.

§5001. "Compensation"; validity of compromise and release.

Compensation is the measure of the responsibility which the employer has assumed for injuries or deaths which occur to employees in his employment when subject to this division. No release of liability or compromise agreement is valid unless it is approved by the appeals board or referee.

Ref.: 8 C.C.R. §§10608, 10870, 10874, 10878, 10882, 10888, 10890; Hanna §§ 29.01[2], 29.04[1], 29.05[1]; Herlick Handbook §§ 11.1, 14.5; W. Cal. Sum., 2 "Workers' Compensation" §§361, 362, 14 "Wills and Probate" §1014.

§5002. Appeals board's power to enter award once copy of compromise and release filed.

A copy of the release or compromise agreement signed by both parties shall forthwith be filed with the appeals board. Upon filing with and approval by the appeals board, it may, without notice, of its own motion or on the application of either party, enter its award based upon the release or compromise agreement.

Ref.: 8 C.C.R. §§10870, 10874, 10878, 10882, 10888, 10890; W. Cal. Sum., 2 "Workers' Compensation" §363.

§5003. Required information for compromise and release.

Every release or compromise agreement shall be in writing and duly executed, and the signature of the employee or other beneficiary shall be attested by two disinterested witnesses or acknowledged before a notary public. The document shall specify:

(a) The date of the accident.

(b) The average weekly wages of the employee, determined according to Chapter 1 of Part 2 of this division.

(c) The nature of the disability, whether total or partial, permanent or temporary.

(d) The amount paid, or due and unpaid, to the employee up to the date of the release or agreement or death, and the amount of the payment or benefits then or thereafter to be made.

(e) The length of time such payment or benefit is to continue.

(f) In the event a claim of lien under subdivision (f) or (g) of Section 4903 has been filed, the number of days and the amount of temporary disability indemnity which should be allowed to the lien claimant.

Ref.: 8 C.C.R. §§10874, 10878, 10882; Hanna §§ 29.03[1], 29.03[6]; Herlick Handbook §§ 10.1, 11.2; W. Cal. Sum., 2 "Workers' Compensation" §363.

§5004. Additional required information for compromise and release agreements in case of death.

In case of death there shall also be stated in the release or compromise agreement:

(a) The date of death.

(b) The name of the widow.

(c) The names and ages of all children.

(d) The names of all other dependents.

(e) Whether the dependents are total or partial.

(f) The amount paid or to be paid as a death benefit and to whom payment is to be made.

Ref.: 8 C.C.R. §§10874, 10878, 10882; Hanna § 29.03[1]; Herlick Handbook § 11.2; W. Cal. Sum., 2 "Workers' Compensation" §363.

§5005. Compromises and release agreements; occupational disease or cumulative injury.

In any case involving a claim of occupational disease or cumulative injury, as set forth in Section 5500.5, the employee and any employer, or any insurance carrier for any employer, may enter into a compromise and release agreement settling either all or any part of the employee's claim, including a part of his claim against any employer. Such compromise and release agreement, upon approval by the appeals board or a referee, shall be a total release as to such employer or insurance carrier for the portion or portions of the claim released, but shall not constitute a bar to a recovery from any one or all of the remaining employers or insurance carriers for the periods of exposure not so released.

In any case where a compromise and release agreement of a portion of a claim has been made and approved, the employee may elect to proceed as provided in Section 5500.5 against any one or more of the remaining employers, or against an employer for that portion of his exposure not so released; in any such proceeding after election following compromise and release, that portion of liability attributable to the portion or portions of the exposure so released shall be assessed and deducted from the liability of the remaining defendant or defendants, but any such defendant shall receive no credit for any moneys paid by way of compromise and release in excess of the liability actually assessed against the released employments and the employee shall not receive any further benefits from the released employments for any liability assessed to them above what was paid by way of compromise and release.

In approving a compromise and release agreement under this section, the appeals board or referee shall determine the adequacy of the compromise and release agreement as it shall then reflect the potential liability of the released exposure after apportionment, but need not make a final actual determination of the potential liability of the employer or employers for that portion of the exposure being released.

Ref.: 8 C.C.R. §§10878, 10882; Hanna § 29.06; Herlick Handbook §§ 8.23, 11.8, 14.35; W. Cal. Sum., 2 "Workers' Compensation" §361.

§5006. Board's findings as having no collateral estoppel effect on subsequent criminal proceedings.

A determination of facts by the appeals board under this chapter has no collateral estoppel effect on a subsequent criminal prosecution and does not preclude litigation of those same facts

Labor

in the criminal proceeding. **Leg.H.** 1995 ch. 158.

CHAPTER 3
LUMP SUM PAYMENTS

§5100. Lump sum payments; commutation.

At the time of making its award, or at any time thereafter, the appeals board, on its own motion either upon notice, or upon application of either party with due notice to the other, may commute the compensation payable under this division to a lump sum and order it to be paid forthwith or at some future time if any of the following conditions appear:

(a) That such commutation is necessary for the protection of the person entitled thereto, or for the best interest of the applicant. In determining what is in the best interest of the applicant, the appeals board shall consider the general financial condition of the applicant, including but not limited to, the applicant's ability to live without periodic indemnity payments and to discharge debts incurred prior to the date of injury.

(b) That commutation will avoid inequity and will not cause undue expense or hardship to the applicant.

(c) That the employer has sold or otherwise disposed of the greater part of his assets or is about to do so.

(d) That the employer is not a resident of this state.

Ref.: 8 C.C.R. §§10169, 10169.1; Hanna §§ 9.03[4], 27.02[1]–[5][a], 27.10[2][b]; Herlick Handbook §§ 6.7, 7.17; W. Cal. Sum., 2 "Workers' Compenation" §§260, 426.

§5100.5. When commutation not possible.

Notwithstanding the provisions of Section 5100, the appeals board shall not commute the compensation payable under this division to a lump sum when such compensation is payable under Section 4751 of the Labor Code.

Ref.: 8 C.C.R. §10169.1; Hanna § 27.02[2]; W. Cal. Sum., 2 "Workers' Compensation" §260.

§5100.6. No commutation or settlement of rehabilitation benefits.

Notwithstanding the provisions of Section 5100, the appeals board shall not permit the commutation or settlement of prospective compensation or indemnity payments or other benefits to which the employee is entitled under vocational rehabilitation. **Leg.H.** 1998 ch. 524.

1998 Note: The amendments made by this act do not constitute a change in, but are declaratory of, existing law. Stats. 1998 ch. 524 §3.

Ref.: 8 C.C.R. §§10169.1, 10870; Hanna §§ 29.03[3], 35.03[1], 35.54; Herlick Handbook §§ 11.5, 16.5, 16.15; W. Cal. Sum., 2 "Workers' Compensation" §260.

§5101. Determination of lump sum amount.

The amount of the lump sum shall be determined as follows:

(a) If the injury causes temporary disability, the appeals board shall estimate the probable duration thereof and the probable amount of the temporary disability payments therefor, in accordance with Chapter 2 of Part 2 of this division, and shall fix the lump sum at the amount so determined.

(b) If the injury causes permanent disability or death, the appeals board shall fix the total amount of the permanent disability payment or death benefit payable therefor in accordance with Chapter 2 of Part 2 of this division, and shall estimate the present value thereof, assuming interest at the rate of 3 percent per annum and disregarding the probability of the beneficiary's death in all cases except where the percentage of permanent disability is such as to entitle the beneficiary to a life pension, and then taking into consideration the probability of the beneficiary's death only in estimating the present value of such life pension.

Ref.: 8 C.C.R. §§10169, 10169.1; Hanna §§ 27.02[2], 27.02[6].

§5102. Method of payment of lump sums.

The appeals board may order the lump sum paid directly to the injured employee or his dependents, or deposited with any savings bank or trust company authorized to transact business in this state, which agrees to accept the same as a deposit bearing interest; or the appeals board may order the lump sum deposited with the State Compensation Insurance Fund. Any lump sum so deposited, together with all interest derived therefrom, shall thereafter be held in trust for the injured employee, or in the event of his death, for his dependents. In the event of the employee's death, his dependents shall have no further recourse against the employer under this chapter.

§5103. Trustee's payments from deposited lump sum.

Payments from the lump sum so deposited shall be made by the trustee only in the amounts and at the time fixed by order of the appeals board and until the lump sum and interest thereon are exhausted.

§5104. Preference in trustee appointment.

In the appointment of the trustee, preference may be given to the choice of the injured employee or his dependents.

§5105. Receipt and certificate for lump sum payment.

Upon the payment of a lump sum, the employer shall present to the appeals board a proper receipt evidencing the same, executed either by the injured employee or his dependents, or by the trustee. The appeals board shall thereupon issue its certificate in proper form evidencing such payment. Such certificate, upon filing with the clerk of the superior court in which any judgment upon an award has been entered, operates as a satisfaction of the award and fully discharges the employer from any further liability on account thereof.

Ref.: 8 C.C.R. §§10820, 10825, 10828.

§5106. Present worth of uninsured employer's future payments.

The appeals board shall, upon the request of the Director of Industrial Relations, where the employer is uninsured and the installments of compensation awarded are to be paid in the future, determine the present worth of the future payments, discounted at the rate of 3 percent per annum, and order the present worth paid into the Uninsured Employers Fund, which fund shall thereafter pay to the beneficiaries of the award the future payments as they become due.

PART 3.5
Arbitration

§5270. Representation.

This part shall not apply in cases where an injured employee or dependent is involved unless the employee or dependent is represented by an attorney.

1989 Note: This section is applicable only to injuries occurring on or after January 1, 1990. Stats. 1989 ch. 893 §6.

Ref.: 8 C.C.R. §§10995, 10996, 10997; Hanna § 33.01[6]; Herlick Handbook §§ 14.4, 14.32, 15.1, 16.1; W. Cal. Sum., 2 "Workers' Compensation" §§392, 393.

§5270.5. List of eligible arbitrators.

(a) The presiding workers' compensation judge at each district office shall prepare a list of all eligible attorneys who apply to be placed on the list of eligible arbitrators. Attorneys are eligible to become arbitrators if they are active members of the California State Bar Association and are one of the following:

(1) A certified specialist in workers' compensation, or eligible to become certified.

(2) A retired workers' compensation judge.

(3) A retired appeals board member.

(4) An attorney who has been certified to serve as a judge pro tempore.

(b) No attorney shall be included in a panel of arbitrators, if he or she has served as a judge in any proceeding involving the same case, or has represented, or whose firm has represented, any party in the same case.

1989 Note: This section is applicable only to injuries occurring on or after January 1, 1990. Stats. 1989 ch. 893 §6.

Ref.: 8 C.C.R. §§10995, 10996, 10997; Herlick Handbook § 14.32; W. Cal. Sum., 2 "Workers' Compensation" §§392, 393, 396.

§5271. Selection of arbitrator.

(a) The parties to a dispute submitted for arbitration may select any eligible attorney from the list prepared by the presiding workers' compensation judge to serve as arbitrator. However, when the disputed issue involves insurance coverage, the parties may select any attorney as arbitrator upon agreement of the parties.

(b) If the parties cannot select an arbitrator by agreement, either party may request the presiding workers' compensation judge to assign a panel of five arbitrators selected at random from the list of eligible attorneys. No more than three arbitrators on a five-member panel may be defense attorneys, no more than three may be applicant's attorneys, and no more than two may be retired workers' compensation judges or appeals board commissioners.

(c) For each party in excess of one party in the capacity of employer and one party in the capacity of injured employee or lien claimant, the presiding judge shall randomly select two additional arbitrators to add to the panel. For each additional party in the capacity of employer, the presiding judge shall assign a retired workers' compensation judge or retired appeals board commissioner and an applicant's attorney. For each additional party in the capacity of injured employee or lien claimant, the presiding judge shall assign a retired workers' compensation judge or retired appeals board commissioner and a defense attorney. For each additional other party, the presiding judge shall assign two arbitrators to the panel, in order of rotation from case to case, as follows: a retired workers' compensation judge or retired appeals board commissioner, an applicant's attorney, a defense attorney.

(d) A party may petition the presiding workers' compensation judge to remove a member from the panel pursuant to Section 170.1 of the Code of Civil Procedure. The presiding workers' compensation judge shall assign another eligible attorney to replace any member removed under this subdivision.

(e) Each party or lien claimant shall strike two members from the panel, and the remaining attorney shall serve as arbitrator.

1989 Note: This section is applicable only to injuries occurring on or after January 1, 1990. Stats. 1989 ch. 893 §6.

Ref.: 8 C.C.R. §§10995, 10996, 10997, 10998; W. Cal. Sum., 2 "Workers' Compensation" §§392, 393.

§5272. Arbitrators' duties and limits of power.

Arbitrators shall have all of the statutory and regulatory duties and responsibilities of a workers' compensation judge, as set forth in Chapter

1 (commencing with Section 5300) of Part 4, except for the following:

(a) Arbitrators shall have no power to order the injured worker to be examined by a qualified medical evaluator pursuant to Sections 5701 and 5703.5.

(b) Arbitrators shall not have power of contempt.

1989 Note: This section is applicable only to injuries occurring on or after January 1, 1990. Stats. 1989 ch. 893 §6.

Ref.: 8 C.C.R. §§10995, 10996, 10997; W. Cal. Sum., 2 "Workers' Compensation" §393.

§5273. Payment of costs of proceedings.

(a) In disputes between an employee and an employer, the employer shall pay all costs related to the arbitration proceeding, including use of facilities, hearing reporter per diems and transcript costs.

(b) In all other disputes, the costs of the arbitration proceedings, including the arbitrator's compensation, shall be paid as follows:

(1) By the parties equally in any dispute between an employer and an insurer, or an employer and a lien claimant.

(2) By the parties equally in proceedings subject to Section 5500.5.

(3) By the dependents in accordance with their proportionate share of death benefits, where there is no dispute as to the injury causing death.

(c) Disputes regarding the costs or fees for arbitration shall be within the exclusive jurisdiction of the appeals board, and shall be determined initially by the presiding judge of the district office.

1989 Note: This section is applicable only to injuries occurring on or after January 1, 1990. Stats. 1989 ch. 893 §6.

Ref.: 8 C.C.R. §§10995, 10996, 10997, 10999; W. Cal. Sum., 2 "Workers' Compensation" §§392, 393.

§5275. Types of disputes submitted.

(a) Disputes involving the following issues shall be submitted for arbitration:

(1) Insurance coverage.

(2) Right of contribution in accordance with Section 5500.5.

(b) By agreement of the parties, any issue arising under Division 1 (commencing with Section 50) or Division 4 (commencing with Section 3200) may be submitted for arbitration, regardless of the date of injury. **Leg.H.** 1993 ch. 121, effective July 16, 1993, 1994 ch. 470, 2002 ch. 6 (AB 749).

1993 Note: Section 5275, as amended by ch. 121, applies only to injuries occurring on or after January 1, 1994. Stats. 1993 ch. 121 §77.

1989 Note: This section is applicable only to injuries occurring on or after January 1, 1990. Stats. 1989 ch. 893 §6.

Ref.: 8 C.C.R. §§10166, 10866, 10867, 10995, 10996, 10997, 10999; Hanna §§ 33.01[1][a.1], 33.01[6]; Herlick Handbook §§ 8.23, 14.32, 15.2, 16.1, 16.8; W. Cal. Sum., 2 "Workers' Compensation" §§392, 393.

§5276. Date, time, and place of proceedings.

(a) Arbitration proceedings may commence at any place and time agreed upon by all parties.

(b) If the parties cannot agree on a time or place to commence arbitration proceedings, the arbitrator shall order the date, time and place for commencement of the proceeding. Unless all parties agree otherwise, arbitration proceedings shall commence not less than 30 days nor more than 60 days from the date an arbitrator is selected.

(c) Ten days before the arbitration, each party shall submit to the arbitrator and serve on the opposing party reports, records and other documentary evidence on which that party intends to rely. If a party intends to rely upon excerpts of records or depositions, only copies of the excerpts shall be submitted to the arbitrator.

1989 Note: This section is applicable only to injuries occurring on or after January 1, 1990. Stats. 1989 ch. 893 §6.

Ref.: 8 C.C.R. §§10995, 10996, 10997; W. Cal. Sum., 2 "Workers' Compensation" §392.

§5277. Findings and award.

(a) The arbitrator's findings and award shall be served on all parties within 30 days of submission of the case for decision.

(b) The arbitrator's award shall comply with Section 5313 and shall be filed with the appeals board office pursuant to venue rules published by the appeals board.

(c) The findings of fact, award, order, or decision of the arbitrator shall have the same force and effect as an award, order, or decision of a workers' compensation judge.

(d) Use of an arbitrator for any part of a proceeding or any issue shall not bind the parties to the use of the same arbitrator for any subsequent issues or proceedings.

(e) Unless all parties agree to a longer period of time, the failure of the arbitrator to submit the decision within 30 days shall result in forfeiture of the arbitrator's fee and shall vacate the submission order and all stipulations.

(f) The presiding workers' compensation judge may submit supplemental proceedings to arbitration pursuant to this part. **Leg.H.** 1989 ch. 892 §44, 2006 ch. 538 (SB 1852) §490.

1989 Note: This section is applicable only to injuries occurring on or after January 1, 1990. Stats. 1989 ch. 893 §6.

Ref.: 8 C.C.R. §§10866, 10867, 10995, 10996, 10997; Hanna § 33.01[4]; Herlick Handbook §§ 14.4, 14.32, 15.1; W. Cal. Sum., 2 "Workers' Compensation" §§392, 393.

§5278. Disclosure of settlement to arbitrator prior to award prohibited.

(a) No disclosure of any offers of settlement made by any party shall be made to the arbitrator prior to the filing of the award.

(b) Article 7 (commencing with Section 11430.10) of Chapter 4.5 of Part 1 of Division 3 of Title 2 of the Government Code applies to a communication to the arbitrator or a potential arbitrator. **Leg.H.** 1995 ch. 938, operative July 1, 1997.

Ref.: Hanna § 33.01[4]; Herlick Handbook § 14.32.

PART 4
Compensation Proceedings

CHAPTER 1
JURISDICTION

§5300. Proceedings to be handled by appeals board.

All the following proceedings shall be instituted before the appeals board and not elsewhere, except as otherwise provided in Division 4:

(a) For the recovery of compensation, or concerning any right or liability arising out of or incidental thereto.

(b) For the enforcement against the employer or an insurer of any liability for compensation imposed upon the employer by this division in favor of the injured employee, his or her dependents, or any third person.

(c) For the determination of any question as to the distribution of compensation among dependents or other persons.

(d) For the determination of any question as to who are dependents of any deceased employee, or what persons are entitled to any benefit under the compensation provisions of this division.

(e) For obtaining any order which by Division 4 the appeals board is authorized to make.

(f) For the determination of any other matter, jurisdiction over which is vested by Division 4 in the Division of Workers' Compensation, including the administrative director and the appeals board. **Leg.H.** 1994 ch. 146.

Ref.: 8 C.C.R. §§9768.6, 9768.16, 10181, 10364, 10952; Hanna §§ 2.02[3], 11.01[5], 34.01; Herlick Handbook §§ 3.11, 16.13; W. Cal. Sum., 2 "Insurance" §281, 2 "Workers' Compensation" §§14, 15, 38.

§5301. Appeals board power and jurisdiction.

The appeals board is vested with full power, authority and jurisdiction to try and determine finally all the matters specified in Section 5300 subject only to the review by the courts as specified in this division.

Ref.: 8 C.C.R. §10952; Hanna § 34.01; W. Cal. Sum., 2 "Workers' Compensation" §15.

§5302. Presumptions regarding all appeals board decisions.

All orders, rules, findings, decisions, and awards of the appeals board shall be prima facie lawful and conclusively presumed to be reasonable and lawful, until and unless they are modified or set aside by the appeals board or upon a review by the courts within the time and in the manner specified in this division.

Ref.: 8 C.C.R. §10950; Hanna § 27.10[2][a].

§5303. Separate cause of action; joined claims.

There is but one cause of action for each injury coming within the provisions of the division. All claims brought for medical expense, disability payments, death benefits, burial expense, liens, or any other matter arising out of such injury may, in the discretion of the appeals board, be joined in the same proceeding at any time; provided, however, that no injury, whether specific or cumulative, shall, for any purpose whatsoever, merge into or form a part of another injury; nor shall any award based on a cumulative injury include disability caused by any specific injury or by any other cumulative injury causing or contributing to the existing disability, need for medical treatment or death.

Ref.: 8 C.C.R. §§10364, 10589, 10590, 10591, 10592; Hanna §§ 7.05[2], 8.02[3], 26.10[2], 31.01; Herlick Handbook § 8.23; W. Cal. Sum., 2 "Workers' Compensation" §§292, 348, 371.

§5304. Appeals board jurisdiction over medical, surgical, and hospital treatment.

The appeals board has jurisdiction over any controversy relating to or arising out of Sections 4600 to 4605 inclusive, unless an express agreement fixing the amounts to be paid for medical, surgical or hospital treatment as such treatment is described in those sections has been made between the persons or institutions rendering such treatment and the employer or insurer.

Ref.: Hanna §§ 5.05[10][d], 30.04; Herlick Handbook §§ 4.3, 13.4; W. Cal. Sum., 2 "Workers' Compensation" §350.

§5305. Jurisdiction of resident's out-of-state injuries.

The Division of Workers' Compensation, including the administrative director, and the appeals board have jurisdiction over all controversies arising out of injuries suffered outside the territorial limits of this state in those cases where the injured employee is a resident of this state at the time of the injury and the contract of hire was made in this state. Any employee described by this section, or his or her dependents, shall be entitled to the compensation or death benefits provided by this division. **Leg.H.** 1994 ch. 146, 2002 ch. 6 (AB 749).

Ref.: Hanna §§ 3.22[2], 21.06, 21.07[5]; Herlick Handbook § 13.2; W. Cal. Sum., 2 "Workers' Compensation" §§111–113.

§5306. Employee's rights against employer's estate.

The death of an employer subsequent to the sustaining of an injury by an employee shall not impair the right of the employee to proceed before the appeals board against the estate of the employer, and the failure of the employee or his dependents to cause the claim to be presented to the executor or administrator of the estate shall not in any way bar or suspend such right.

Ref.: W. Cal. Sum., 2 "Workers' Compensation" §5.

§5307. Appeals board powers; procedure for adopting, amending or rescinding regulations; uniform rules for trial level proceedings.

(a) Except for those rules and regulations within the authority of the court administrator regarding trial level proceedings as defined in subdivision (c), the appeals board may by an order signed by four members:

(1) Adopt reasonable and proper rules of practice and procedure.

(2) Regulate and provide the manner in which, and by whom, minors and incompetent persons are to appear and be represented before it.

(3) Regulate and prescribe the kind and character of notices, where not specifically prescribed by this division, and the service thereof.

(4) Regulate and prescribe the nature and extent of the proofs and evidence.

(b) No rule or regulation of the appeals board pursuant to this section shall be adopted, amended, or rescinded without public hearings. Any written request filed with the appeals board seeking a change in its rules or regulations shall be deemed to be denied if not set by the appeals board for public hearing to be held within six months of the date on which the request is received by the appeals board.

(c) The court administrator shall adopt reasonable, proper, and uniform rules for district office procedure regarding trial level proceedings of the workers' compensation appeals board. These rules shall include, but not be limited to, all of the following:

(1) Rules regarding conferences, hearings, continuances, and other matters deemed reasonable and necessary to expeditiously resolve disputes.

(2) The kind and character of forms to be used at all trial level proceedings.

All rules and regulations adopted by the court administrator pursuant to this subdivision shall be subject to the requirements of the rulemaking provisions of the Administrative Procedure Act (Chapter 3.5 (commencing with Section 11340) of Part 1 of Division 3 of Title 2 of the Government Code). **Leg.H.** 2002 ch. 6 (AB 749).

Ref.: 8 C.C.R. §§10250, 10301, 10304, 10450, 10602, 10869, 10946; Hanna § 1.11[6][a]; W. Cal. Sum., 2 "Workers' Compensation" §§12, 13, 345.

§5307.1. Official medical fee schedule.

(a) The administrative director, after public hearings, shall adopt and revise periodically an official medical fee schedule that shall establish reasonable maximum fees paid for medical services other than physician services, drugs and pharmacy services, health care facility fees, home health care, and all other treatment, care, services, and goods described in Section 4600 and provided pursuant to this section. Except for physician services, all fees shall be in accordance with the fee-related structure and rules of the relevant Medicare and Medi-Cal payment systems, provided that employer liability for medical treatment, including issues of reasonableness, necessity, frequency, and duration, shall be determined in accordance with Section 4600. Commencing January 1, 2004, and continuing until the time the administrative director has adopted an official medical fee schedule in accordance with the fee-related structure and rules of the relevant Medicare payment systems, except for the components listed in subdivision (j), maximum reasonable fees shall be 120 percent of the estimated aggregate fees prescribed in the relevant Medicare payment system for the same class of services before application of the inflation factors provided in subdivision (g), except that for pharmacy services and drugs that are not otherwise covered by a Medicare fee schedule payment for facility services, the maximum reasonable fees shall be 100 percent of fees prescribed in the relevant Medi-Cal payment system. Upon adoption by the administrative director of an official medical fee schedule pursuant to this section, the maximum reasonable fees paid shall not exceed 120 percent of estimated aggregate fees prescribed in the Medicare payment system for the same class of services before application of the inflation factors provided in subdivision (g). Pharmacy services and drugs shall be subject to the requirements of this section, whether furnished through a pharmacy or dispensed directly by the practitioner pursuant to subdivision (b) of Section 4024 of the Business and Professions Code.

(b) In order to comply with the standards specified in subdivision (f), the administrative director may adopt different conversion factors, diagnostic related group weights, and other factors affecting payment amounts from those used in the Medicare payment system, provided estimated aggregate fees do not exceed 120 percent of the estimated aggregate fees paid for the same class of services in the relevant Medicare payment system.

(c) Notwithstanding subdivisions (a) and (d), the maximum facility fee for services performed in an ambulatory surgical center, or in a hospital outpatient department, may not exceed 120 percent of the fee paid by Medicare for the same services performed in a hospital outpatient department.

(d) If the administrative director determines that a medical treatment, facility use, product, or service is not covered by a Medicare payment system, the administrative director shall establish maximum fees for that item, provided that the maximum fee paid shall not exceed 120 percent of the fees paid by Medicare for services that require comparable resources. If the administrative director determines that a pharmacy service or drug is not covered by a Medi-Cal payment system, the administrative director shall establish maximum fees for that item. However, the maximum fee paid shall not exceed 100 percent of the fees paid by Medi-Cal for pharmacy services or drugs that require comparable resources.

(e) Prior to the adoption by the administrative director of a medical fee schedule pursuant to this section, for any treatment, facility use, product, or service not covered by a Medicare payment system, including acupuncture services, or, with regard to pharmacy services and drugs, for a pharmacy service or drug that is not covered by a Medi-Cal payment system, the maximum reasonable fee paid shall not exceed the fee specified in the official medical fee schedule in effect on December 31, 2003.

(f) Within the limits provided by this section, the rates or fees established shall be adequate to ensure a reasonable standard of services and care for injured employees.

(g)(1)(A) Notwithstanding any other provision of law, the official medical fee schedule shall be adjusted to conform to any relevant changes in the Medicare and Medi-Cal payment systems no later than 60 days after the effective date of those changes, provided that both of the following conditions are met:

(i) The annual inflation adjustment for facility fees for inpatient hospital services provided by acute care hospitals and for hospital outpatient services shall be determined solely by the estimated increase in the hospital market basket for the 12 months beginning October 1 of the preceding calendar year.

(ii) The annual update in the operating standardized amount and capital standard rate for inpatient hospital services provided by hospitals excluded from the Medicare prospective payment system for acute care hospitals and the conversion factor for hospital outpatient services shall be determined solely by the estimated increase in the hospital market basket for excluded hospitals for the 12 months beginning October 1 of the preceding calendar year.

(B) The update factors contained in clauses (i) and (ii) of subparagraph (A) shall be applied beginning with the first update in the Medicare fee schedule payment amounts after December 31, 2003.

(2) The administrative director shall determine the effective date of the changes, and shall issue an order, exempt from Sections 5307.3 and 5307.4 and the rulemaking provisions of the Administrative Procedure Act (Chapter 3.5 (commencing with Section 11340) of Part 1 of Division 3 of Title 2 of the Government Code), informing the public of the changes and their

effective date. All orders issued pursuant to this paragraph shall be published on the Internet Web site of the Division of Workers' Compensation.

(3) For the purposes of this subdivision, the following definitions apply:

(A) "Medicare Economic Index" means the input price index used by the federal Centers for Medicare and Medicaid Services to measure changes in the costs of a providing physician and other services paid under the resource-based relative value scale.

(B) "Hospital market basket" means the input price index used by the federal Centers for Medicare and Medicaid Services to measure changes in the costs of providing inpatient hospital services provided by acute care hospitals that are included in the Medicare prospective payment system.

(C) "Hospital market basket for excluded hospitals" means the input price index used by the federal Centers for Medicare and Medicaid Services to measure changes in the costs of providing inpatient services by hospitals that are excluded from the Medicare prospective payment system.

(h) Nothing in this section shall prohibit an employer or insurer from contracting with a medical provider for reimbursement rates different from those prescribed in the official medical fee schedule.

(i) Except as provided in Section 4626, the official medical fee schedule shall not apply to medical-legal expenses, as that term is defined by Section 4620.

(j) The following Medicare payment system components may not become part of the official medical fee schedule until January 1, 2005:

(1) Inpatient skilled nursing facility care.

(2) Home health agency services.

(3) Inpatient services furnished by hospitals that are exempt from the prospective payment system for general acute care hospitals.

(4) Outpatient renal dialysis services.

(k) Notwithstanding subdivision (a), for the calendar years 2004 and 2005, the existing official medical fee schedule rates for physician services shall remain in effect, but these rates shall be reduced by 5 percent. The administrative director may reduce fees of individual procedures by different amounts, but in no event shall the administrative director reduce the fee for a procedure that is currently reimbursed at a rate at or below the Medicare rate for the same procedure.

(*l*) Notwithstanding subdivision (a), the administrative director, commencing January 1, 2006, shall have the authority, after public hearings, to adopt and revise, no less frequently than biennially, an official medical fee schedule for physician services. If the administrative director fails to adopt an official medical fee schedule for physician services by January 1, 2006, the existing official medical fee schedule rates for physician services shall remain in effect until a new schedule is adopted or the existing schedule is revised.

(m)(1) Notwithstanding subdivisions (a), (b), (f), and (g), commencing January 1, 2008, the administrative director, after public hearings, may adopt and revise, no less frequently than biennially, an official medical fee schedule for inpatient facility fees for burn cases in accordance with this subdivision. Until the date that the administrative director adopts a fee schedule pursuant to this subdivision, the inpatient fee schedule adopted and revised in accordance with subdivisions (a) and (g) shall continue to apply to inpatient facility fees for burn cases.

(2) In order to establish inpatient facility fees for burn cases that are adequate to ensure a reasonable standard of services and care, the administrative director may do any of the following:

(A) Adopt a fee schedule in accordance with the Medicare payment system, or adopt different conversion factors, diagnostic related group weights, and other factors affecting payment amounts from those used in the Medicare payment system.

(B) Adopt a fee schedule utilizing payment methodologies other than those utilized by the Medicare payment system.

(C) Adopt a fee schedule that utilizes both Medicare and non-Medicare methodologies.

(3) Inpatient facility fees for burn cases may exceed 120 percent, but in no case shall exceed 180 percent, of the fees paid by Medicare. Inpatient facility fees for burn cases shall be excluded from the calculation of estimated aggregate fees for purposes of other subdivisions of this section.

(4) The changes to this section made by this subdivision shall remain in effect only until January 1, 2011. **Leg.H.** 2003 ch. 639 (SB 228) §35, 2006 ch. 538 (SB 1852) §491, 2007 ch. 697 (AB 1269) §1.

Ref.: 8 C.C.R. §§9768.17, 9789.10, 9789.11, 9789.20, 9789.21, 9789.22, 9789.24, 9789.30, 9789.31, 9789.32, 9789.33, 9789.34, 9789.35, 9789.36, 9789.37, 9789.38, 9789.40, 9789.50, 9789.60, 9789.70, 9789.110, 9789.111, 9790, 9790.1, 9791, 9791.1, 9792, 9792.1, 9792.5, 9900, 10100, 10100.1, 10100.2; Hanna §§ 5.05[6][b], 22.05[2]; Herlick Handbook § 4.19.

§5307.11. Permissible contracts for reimbursement rates outside official fee schedule.

A health care provider or health facility licensed pursuant to Section 1250 of the Health and Safety Code, and a contracting agent, employer, or carrier may contract for reimbursement rates different from those in the fee schedule adopted and revised pursuant to Section 5307.1. When a health care provider or health facility licensed pursuant to Section 1250 of the Health and Safety Code, and a contracting agent, employer, or carrier contract for reimbursement rates different from those in the fee schedule, the medical fee schedule for that health care provider or health facility licensed pursuant to Section 1250 of the Health and Safety Code shall not apply to the contracted reimbursement rates. Except as provided in subdivision (b) of Section 5307.1, the official medical fee schedule shall establish maximum reimbursement rates for all medical services for injuries subject to this division provided by a health care provider or health care facility licensed pursuant to Section 1250 of the Health and Safety Code other than those specified in contracts subject to this section. **Leg.H.** 2001 ch. 252.

Ref.: Hanna §§ 5.05[10][d], 22.05[2].

§5307.2. Study of access to medical treatment, quality health care or products, including prescription drugs and pharmacy services, for injured workers; authority of administrative director to adjust medical and facilities' fees.

The administrative director shall contract with an independent consulting firm, to the extent permitted by state law, to perform an annual study of access to medical treatment for injured workers. The study shall analyze whether there is adequate access to quality health care and products, **including prescription drugs and pharmacy services,** for injured workers and make recommendations to ensure continued access. If the administrative director determines, based on this study, that there is insufficient access to quality health care or products for injured workers, **including access to prescription drugs and pharmacy services,** the administrative director may make appropriate adjustments to medical**, prescription drugs and pharmacy services,** and facilities' fees. When there has been a determination that substantial access problems exist, the administrative director may, in accordance with the notification and hearing requirements of Section 5307.1, adopt fees in excess of 120 percent of the applicable Medicare payment system fee**, or in excess of 100 percent of the fees prescribed in the relevant Medi-Cal payment system,** for the applicable services or products. **Leg.H.** 2003 ch. 639 (SB 228) §37, 2008 ch. 193 (AB 2091) §1.

Ref.: Hanna § 22.05[2]; Herlick Handbook § 4.19.

§5307.27. Adoption of medical treatment utilization schedule.

On or before December 1, 2004, the administrative director, in consultation with the Commission on Health and Safety and Workers' Compensation, shall adopt, after public hearings, a medical treatment utilization schedule, that shall incorporate the evidence-based, peer-reviewed, nationally recognized standards of care recommended by the commission pursuant to Section 77.5, and that shall address, at a minimum, the frequency, duration, intensity, and appropriateness of all treatment procedures and modalities commonly performed in workers' compensation cases. **Leg.H.** 2003 ch. 639 (SB 228).

Ref.: 8 C.C.R. §§9767.6, 9768.11, 9768.12; Hanna § 22.05[6][b]; Herlick Handbook § 4.19; W. Cal. Sum., 2 "Workers' Compensation" §§261, 262, 266, 269.

§5307.3. Administrative director's powers; changing regulations.

The administrative director may adopt, amend, or repeal any rules and regulations that are reasonably necessary to enforce this division, except where this power is specifically reserved to the appeals board or the court administrator.

No rule or regulation of the administrative director pursuant to this section shall be adopted, amended, or rescinded without public hearings. Any written request filed with the administrative director seeking a change in its rules or regulations shall be deemed to be denied if not set by the administrative director for public hearing to be held within six months of the date on which the request is received by the administrative director. **Leg.H.** 2003 ch. 639 (SB 228).

1989 Note: This section is applicable only to injuries occurring on or after January 1, 1990. Stats. 1989 ch. 893 §6.

Ref.: 8 C.C.R. §§10.5, 9900; W. Cal. Sum., 2 "Workers' Compensation" §11.

§5307.4. Public hearings.

(a) Public hearings required under Section 5307 and 5307.3 shall be subject to the provisions of this section except to the extent that there is involved a matter relating to the management, or to personnel, or to public property, loans, grants, benefits, or to contracts, of the appeals board or the administrative director.

(b) Notice of the rule of regulation proposed to be adopted, amended, or rescinded, shall be given to such business and labor organizations and firms or individuals who have requested notice thereof. The notice shall include all the following:

(1) A statement of the time, place, and nature of the public hearings.

(2) Reference to the legal authority under which the rule is proposed.

(3) Either the terms or substance of the proposed rule, or a description of the subjects and the issues involved.

(c) Except where the proposed rule or regulation has a significant impact on the public, this section shall not apply to interpretive rules, general statements of policy, or rules of agency organization.

(d) After notice required by this section, the appeals board or the administrative director shall give interested persons the opportunity to participate in the rulemaking through submission of written data, views, or arguments, with opportunity for oral presentation. If, after consideration of the relevant matter presented, the appeals board or the administrative director adopts a rule, it or he shall publish a concise, general statement of reasons for the adoption of the rule. The rule and statement of reasons shall be given to the same individuals and organizations who have requested notice of hearings.

(e) The notice required under this section shall be made not less than 30 days prior to the public hearing date.

Ref.: 8 C.C.R. §§10.5, 10300; Hanna §§ 1.11[4], 1.12[6], 23.10[3]; W. Cal. Sum., 2 "Workers' Compensation" §345.

§5307.5. Appeals board or workers' compensation judge's powers.

The appeals board or a workers' compensation judge may:

(a) Appoint a trustee or guardian ad litem to appear for and represent any minor or incompetent upon the terms and conditions which it deems proper. The guardian or trustee shall, if required by the appeals board, give a bond in the form and of the character required by law from a guardian appointed by a superior court and in the amount which the appeals board determines. The bond shall be approved by the appeals board, and the guardian or trustee shall not be discharged from the liability until he or she files an account with the appeals board or with the superior court and the account is approved. The trustee or guardian shall receive the compensation for his or her services fixed and allowed by the appeals board or by the superior court.

(b) Provide for the joinder in the same proceeding of all persons interested therein, whether as employer, insurer, employee, dependent, creditor, or otherwise.

Ref.: 8 C.C.R. §§10360, 10364, 10380, 10402, 10570, 10718; Hanna § 1.11[4]; Herlick Handbook § 14.11.

§5307.6. Director to adopt fee schedule for medical-legal expenses.

(a) The administrative director shall adopt and revise a fee schedule for medical-legal expenses as defined by Section 4620, which shall be prima facie evidence of the reasonableness of fees charged for medical-legal expenses at the same time he or she adopts and revises the medical fee schedule pursuant to Section 5307.1.

The schedule shall consist of a series of procedure codes, relative values, and a conversion factor producing fees which provide remuneration to physicians performing medical-legal evaluations at a level equivalent to that provided to physicians for reasonably comparable work, and which additionally recognizes the relative complexity of various types of evaluations, the amount of time spent by the physician in direct contact with the patient, and the need to prepare a written report.

(b) A provider shall not be paid fees in excess of those set forth in the fee schedule established under this section unless the provider provides an itemization and explanation of the fee that shows that it is both a reasonable fee and that extraordinary circumstances relating to the medical condition being evaluated justify a higher fee; provided, however, that in no event shall a provider charge in excess of his or her usual fee. The employer and employee shall have standing to contest fees in excess of those set forth in the fee schedule.

(c) In the event of a dispute between the provider and the employer, employee, or carrier concerning the fees charged, the provider may be allowed a reasonable fee for testimony if the provider testified pursuant to the employer's or carrier's subpoena and the judge or referee determines that the fee charged was reasonable and justified by extraordinary circumstances.

(d)(1) No provider may request nor accept any compensation, including, but not limited to, any kind of remuneration, discount, rebate, refund, dividend, distribution, subsidy, or other form of direct or indirect payment, whether in money or otherwise, from any source for medical-legal expenses if such compensation is in addition to the fees authorized by this section. In addition to being subject to discipline pursuant to the provisions of subdivision (k) of Section 139.2, any provider violating this subdivision is subject to disciplinary action by the appropriate licensing board.

(2) This subdivision does not apply to medical-legal expenses for which the administrative director has not adopted a fee schedule. **Leg.H.** 1993 ch. 4, effective April 3, 1993, ch. 121, effective July 16, 1993, ch. 1242.

1993 Note: Section 5307.6, as amended by ch. 121, applies only to injuries occurring on or after January 1, 1994. Stats. 1993 ch. 121 §77.

Ref.: 8 C.C.R. §§9793, 9794, 9795; Hanna § 5.04[2][b]–[c]; Herlick Handbook § 4.21; W. Cal. Sum., 2 "Workers' Compensation" §§23, 273.

§5308. Appeals board jurisdiction over insurance controversies involving self-employed persons.

The appeals board has jurisdiction to determine controversies arising out of insurance policies issued to self-employing persons, conferring benefits identical with those prescribed by this division.

The appeals board may try and determine matters referred to it by the parties under the provisions of Title 9 (commencing with Section 1280) of Part 3 of the Code of Civil Procedure, with respect to controversies arising out of insurance issued to self-employing persons under the provisions of this division. Such controversies may be submitted to it by the signed agreement of the parties, or by the application of one party and the submission of the other to its jurisdiction, with or without an express request for arbitration.

The State Compensation Insurance Fund, when the consent of the other party is obtained, shall submit to the appeals board all controversies susceptible of being arbitrated under this section.

In acting as arbitrator under this section, the appeals board has all the powers which it may lawfully exercise in compensation cases, and its findings and award upon such arbitration have the same conclusiveness and are subject to the same mode or reopening, review, and enforcement as in compensation cases. No fee or cost shall be charged by the appeals board for arbitrating the issues presented under this section.

Ref.: Hanna § 21.07[2]; W. Cal. Sum., 2 "Workers' Compensation" §168.

§5309. Appeals board power over workers' compensation judge.

The appeals board may, in accordance with rules of practice and procedure which it shall adopt and upon the agreement of the parties, on the application of either, or of its own motion, and with or without notice, direct and order a workers' compensation judge:

(a) To try the issues in any proceeding before it, whether of fact or of law, and make and file a finding, order, decision, or award based thereon.

(b) To hold hearings and ascertain facts necessary to enable the appeals board to determine any proceeding or to make any order, decision, or award that the appeals board is authorized to make under Divisions 4 or 5, or necessary for the information of the appeals board.

(c) To issue writs or summons, warrants of attachment, warrants of commitment, and all necessary process in proceedings for direct and hybrid contempt in a like manner and to the same extent as courts of record. For the purposes of this section, "hybrid contempt" means a charge of contempt which arises from events occurring in the immediate presence of the workers' compensation judge for reasons which occur outside the presence of the workers' compensation judge.

Ref.: 8 C.C.R. §§10302, 10346, 10347, 10348, 10349, 10350, 10351, 10352, 10858, 10862; Herlick Handbook §§ 1.2, 14.5; W. Cal. Sum., 2 "Workers' Compensation" §§395, 397, 3 "Agency and Employment" §368.

§5310. Workers' compensation administrative law judges appointed by appeals board or administrative director.

The appeals board may appoint one or more workers' compensation administrative law judges in any proceeding, as it may deem necessary or advisable, and may refer, remove to itself, or transfer to a workers' compensation administrative law judge the proceedings on any claim. The administrative director, after consideration of the recommendation of the court administrator, may appoint workers' compensation administrative law judges. Any workers' compensation administrative law judge appointed by the administrative director has the powers, jurisdiction, and authority granted by law, by the order of appointment, and by the rules of the appeals board. **Leg.H.** 2002 ch. 6 (AB 749).

Ref.: 8 C.C.R. §§10302, 10346, 10347, 10348, 10349, 10350, 10351, 10352, 10417, 10420, 10452, 10453, 10454, 10591, 10843, 10850; Herlick Handbook §§ 14.32, 15.3, 15.5; W. Cal. Sum., 2 "Workers' Compensation" §§14, 395.

§5311. Objections to particular workers' compensation judges.

Any party to the proceeding may object to the reference of the proceeding to a particular workers' compensation judge upon any one or more of the grounds specified in Section 641 of the Code of Civil Procedure and the objection shall be heard and disposed of by the appeals board. Affidavits may be read and witnesses examined as to the objections.

Ref.: 8 C.C.R. §§10340, 10347, 10417, 10452, 10453, 10850; Herlick Handbook § 14.19; W. Cal. Sum., 2 "Workers' Compensation" §395.

§5311.5. Requirement that workers' compensation administrative law judges participate in continuing education.

The administrative director or the court administrator shall require all workers' compensation administrative law judges to participate in continuing education to further their abilities as workers' compensation administrative law judges, including courses in ethics and conflict of interest. The director may coordinate the requirements with those imposed upon attorneys by the State Bar in order that the requirements may be consistent. **Leg.H.** 1993 ch. 483, effective September 27, 1993, 2002 ch. 6 (AB 749).

Ref.: W. Cal. Sum., 2 "Workers' Compensation" §395.

§5312. Swearing in of workers' compensation judge.

Before entering upon his or her duties, the workers' compensation judge shall be sworn, before an officer authorized to administer oaths, faithfully and fairly to hear and determine the matters and issues referred to him or her, to make just findings and to report according to his or her understanding.

Ref.: 8 C.C.R. §10302.

§5313. Decisions of appeals board or workers' compensation judge.

The appeals board or the workers' compensation judge shall, within 30 days after the case is submitted, make and file findings upon all facts involved in the controversy and an award, order, or decision stating the determination as to the rights of the parties. Together with the findings, decision, order or award there shall be served upon all the parties to the proceedings a summary of the evidence received and relied upon and the reasons or grounds upon which the determination was made.

Ref.: 8 C.C.R. §§9710, 9711, 9712, 9713, 9714, 9714.5, 9715, 10566, 10862; Hanna §§ 22.06[9], 24.11[2], 26.08, 27.01[1][b], 31.14[4]; Herlick Handbook §§ 10.2, 14.5, 14.28; W. Cal. Sum., 2 "Workers' Compensation" §§392, 403, 404, 448.

§5315. Time limits for appeals board to act on decision of workers' compensation judge.

Within 60 days after the filing of the findings, decision, order or award, the appeals board may confirm, adopt, modify or set aside the findings, order, decision, or award of a workers' compensation judge and may, with or without further proceedings, and with or without notice, enter its order, findings, decision, or award based upon the record in the case.

Ref.: Herlick Handbook § 15.5.

§5316. Method of service.

Any notice, order, or decision required by this division to be served upon any person either before, during, or after the institution of any proceeding before the appeals board, may be served in the manner provided by Chapter 5, Title 14 of Part 2 of the Code of Civil Procedure, unless otherwise directed by the appeals board. In the latter event the document shall be served in accordance with the order or direction of the appeals board. The appeals board may, in the cases mentioned in the Code of Civil Procedure, order service to be made by publication of notice of time and place of hearing. Where service is ordered to be made by publication the date of the hearing may be fixed at more than 30 days from the date of filing the application.

Ref.: 8 C.C.R. §§10380, 10400, 10417, 10500, 10505, 10506, 10507, 10510, 10514, 10520, 10590, 10591, 10592; W. Cal. Sum., 2 "Workers' Compensation" §388.

§5317. Service of public official.

Any such notice, order or decision affecting the State or any county, city, school district, or public corporation therein, shall be served upon the person upon whom the service of similar notices, orders, or decisions is authorized by law.

§5318. Separate reimbursement for medical devices, hardware, and instrumentation for specified DRGs.

(a) Implantable medical devices, hardware, and instrumentation for Diagnostic Related Groups (DRGs) 004, 496, 497, 498, 519, and 520 shall be separately reimbursed at the provider's documented paid cost, plus an additional 10 percent of the provider's documented paid cost, not to exceed a maximum of two hundred fifty dollars ($250), plus any sales tax and shipping and handling charges actually paid.

(b) This section shall be operative only until the administrative director adopts a regulation specifying separate reimbursement, if any, for implantable medical hardware or instrumentation for complex spinal surgeries. **Leg.H.** 2003 ch. 639 (SB 228) §44.

Ref.: 8 C.C.R. §§9789.20, 9789.21, 9789.22, 9789.24, 9792.3.

CHAPTER 2 LIMITATIONS OF PROCEEDINGS

§5400. Time limits for notice of injury.

Except as provided by sections 5402 and 5403, no claim to recover compensation under this division shall be maintained unless within thirty days after the occurrence of the injury which is claimed to have caused the disability or death, there is served upon the employer notice in writing, signed by the person injured or someone in his behalf, or in case of the death of the person injured, by a dependent or someone in the dependent's behalf.

Ref.: 8 C.C.R. §9770; Hanna §§ 24.01[1], 24.04[6], 25.03[1]; Herlick Handbook §§ 4.5, 8.17, 8.21, 9.4, 14.2; W. Cal. Sum., 2 "Workers' Compensation" §§247, 366, 381, 385, 386.

§5401. Claim form and notice of potential eligibility for benefits; form and content; when and where to file claim form.

(a) Within one working day of receiving notice or knowledge of injury under Section 5400 or 5402, which injury results in lost time beyond the employee's work shift at the time of injury or which results in medical treatment beyond first aid, the employer shall provide, personally or by first-class mail, a claim form and a notice of potential eligibility for benefits under this division to the injured employee, or in the case of death, to his or her dependents. As used in this subdivision, "first aid" means any one-time treatment, and any followup visit for the purpose of observation of minor scratches, cuts, burns, splinters, or other minor industrial injury, which do not ordinarily require medical care. This one-time treatment, and followup visit for the purpose of observation, is considered first aid even though provided by a physician or registered professional personnel. "Minor industrial injury" shall not include serious exposure to a hazardous substance as defined in subdivision (i) of Section 6302. The claim form shall request the injured employee's name and address, social security number, the time and address where the injury occurred, and the nature of and part of the body affected by the injury. Claim forms shall be available at district offices of the Employment Development Depart-

Labor

ment and the division. Claim forms may be made available to the employee from any other source.

(b) Insofar as practicable, the notice of potential eligibility for benefits required by this section and the claim form shall be a single document and shall instruct the injured employee to fully read the notice of potential eligibility. The form and content of the notice and claim form shall be prescribed by the administrative director after consultation with the Commission on Health and Safety and Workers' Compensation. The notice shall be easily understandable and available in both English and Spanish. The content shall include, but not be limited to, the following:

(1) The procedure to be used to commence proceedings for the collection of compensation for the purposes of this chapter.

(2) A description of the different types of workers' compensation benefits.

(3) What happens to the claim form after it is filed.

(4) From whom the employee can obtain medical care for the injury.

(5) The role and function of the primary treating physician.

(6) The rights of an employee to select and change the treating physician pursuant to subdivision (e) of Section 3550 and Section 4600.

(7) How to get medical care while the claim is pending.

(8) The protections against discrimination provided pursuant to Section 132a.

(9) The following written statements:

(A) You have a right to disagree with decisions affecting your claim.

(B) You can obtain free information from an information and assistance officer of the state Division of Workers' Compensation, or you can hear recorded information and a list of local offices by calling [applicable information and assistance telephone number(s)].

(C) You can consult an attorney. Most attorneys offer one free consultation. If you decide to hire an attorney, his or her fee will be taken out of some of your benefits. For names of workers' compensation attorneys, call the State Bar of California at [telephone number of the State Bar of California's legal specialization program, or its equivalent].

(c) The completed claim form shall be filed with the employer by the injured employee, or, in the case of death, by a dependent of the injured employee, or by an agent of the employee or dependent. Except as provided in subdivision (d), a claim form is deemed filed when it is personally delivered to the employer or received by the employer by first-class or certified mail. A dated copy of the completed form shall be provided by the employer to the employer's insurer and to the employee, dependent, or agent who filed the claim form.

(d) The claim form shall be filed with the employer prior to the injured employee's entitlement to late payment supplements under subdivision (d) of Section 4650, or prior to the injured employee's request for a medical evaluation under Section 4060, 4061, or 4062. Filing of the claim form with the employer shall toll, for injuries occurring on or after January 1, 1994, the time limitations set forth in Sections 5405 and 5406 until the claim is denied by the employer or the injury becomes presumptively compensable pursuant to Section 5402. For purposes of this subdivision, a claim form is deemed filed when it is personally delivered to the employer or mailed to the employer by first-class or certified mail. **Leg.H.** 1993 ch. 121, effective July 16, 1993, ch. 1242, 1994 ch. 1118, 2002 ch. 6 (AB 749).

1993 Note: Section 5401, as amended by ch. 121, applies only to injuries occurring on or after January 1, 1994. Stats. 1993 ch. 121 §77.

1989 Note: This section is applicable only to injuries occurring on or after January 1, 1990. Stats. 1989 ch. 893 §6.

Ref.: 8 C.C.R. §§9767.6, 9770, 10101, 10101.1, 10102, 10103, 10103.1, 10103.2, 10111, 10111.1, 10111.2, 10116, 10116.1, 10117.1, 10118.1, 10119, 10120, 10121, 10430, 10530, 14001, 14005; Hanna §§ 22.05[4], 24.01[1], 25.20[2]; Herlick Handbook §§ 4.20, 7.3, 8.26, 14.2; W. Cal. Sum., 2 "Workers' Compensation" §§274, 381, 386, 387, 413.

§5401.7. Statement required on claim form; optional statements.

The claim form shall contain, prominently stated, the following statement:

"Any person who makes or causes to be made any knowingly false or fraudulent material statement or material representation for the purpose of obtaining or denying workers' compensation benefits or payments is guilty of a felony."

The statements required to be printed or displayed pursuant to Sections 1871.2 and 1879.2 of the Insurance Code may, but are not required to, appear on the claim form. **Leg.H.** 1991 chs. 116, 934, 1993 ch. 121, effective July 16, 1993, 1997 ch. 346.

1993 Note: Section 5401.7, as amended by ch. 121, applies only to injuries occurring on or after January 1, 1994. Stats. 1993 ch. 121 §77.

Ref.: 8 C.C.R. §§10116, 10117.1, 10118.1, 10120, 10121, 14005, 14006, 14007; Herlick Handbook §§ 9.18, 14.2; W. Cal. Sum., 2 "Workers' Compensation" §386.

§5402. Employer's knowledge equivalent to notice; employer's notice to employee or employee's dependents.

(a) Knowledge of an injury, obtained from any source, on the part of an employer, his or her managing agent, superintendent, foreman, or other person in authority, or knowledge of the assertion of a claim of injury sufficient to afford opportunity to the employer to make an investigation into the facts, is equivalent to service under Section 5400.

(b) If liability is not rejected within 90 days after the date the claim form is filed under Section 5401, the injury shall be presumed compensable under this division. The presumption of this subdivision is rebuttable only by evidence discovered subsequent to the 90-day period.

(c) Within one working day after an employee files a claim form under Section 5401, the employer shall authorize the provision of all treatment, consistent with Section 5307.27 or the American College of Occupational and Environmental Medicine's Occupational Medicine Practice Guidelines, for the alleged injury and shall continue to provide the treatment until the date that liability for the claim is accepted or rejected. Until the date the claim is accepted or rejected, liability for medical treatment shall be limited to ten thousand dollars ($10,000).

(d) Treatment provided under subdivision (c) shall not give rise to a presumption of liability on the part of the employer. **Leg.H.** 1990 ch. 1550, 2000 ch. 883, 2004 ch. 34 (SB 899), effective April 19, 2004.

2004 Note: The amendment to §5402 made by this act shall apply prospectively from the date of enactment of this act, regardless of the date of injury, unless otherwise specified, but shall not constitute good cause to reopen or rescind, alter, or amend any existing order, decision, or award of the Workers' Compensation Appeals Board. Stats. 2004 ch. 34 (SB 899) §47.

1989 Note: This section is applicable only to injuries occurring on or after January 1, 1990. Stats. 1989 ch. 893 §6.

Ref.: 8 C.C.R. §§9770, 9793, 9812, 9813, 9815, 9884, 10100, 10100.1, 10100.2, 10109, 10111, 10111.1, 10111.2, 10116, 10117.1, 10118.1, 10119, 10120; Hanna §§ 4.02[3][d], 5.05[3][a], 24.01[1], 24.01[4], 25.03[2], 25.20[2], 25.20[4]; Herlick Handbook §§ 8.26, 14.2, 14.3, 14.7, 14.20, 14.34, 14.40; W. Cal. Ev., "Burden" §110; W. Cal. Sum., 2 "Workers' Compensation" §§246, 381, 382, 385, 386.

§5403. Effect of failure to give notice or of defective notice.

The failure to give notice under section 5400, or any defect or inaccuracy in a notice is not a bar to recovery under this division if it is found as a fact in the proceedings for the collection of the claim that the employer was not in fact misled or prejudiced by such failure.

Ref.: Herlick Handbook §§ 4.5, 9.4; W. Cal. Sum., 2 "Workers' Compensation" §385.

§5404. Barring of untimely claims; further claims barred by timely filing.

Unless compensation is paid within the time limited in this chapter for the institution of proceedings for its collection, the right to institute such proceedings is barred. The timely filing of an application with the appeals board by any party in interest for any part of the compensation defined by Section 3207 renders this chapter inoperative as to all further claims by such party against the defendants therein named for compensation arising from that injury, and the right to present such further claims is governed by Sections 5803 to 5805, inclusive.

Ref.: Hanna §§ 24.02[2], 35.50[2]; Herlick Handbook §§ 14.7–14.9; W. Cal. Sum., 2 "Workers' Compensation" §§366, 378, 382.

§5404.5. Dismissal of claims with no activity for 180 days.

(a) Where a claim form has been filed prior to January 1, 1994, and where the claim is denied by the employer, the claim may be dismissed if there has been no activity for the previous 180 days and if the claims adjuster has served notice pursuant to Article 3 (commencing with Section 415.10) of Chapter 4 of Title 5 of the Code of Civil Procedure. The notice shall specify that the claim will be dismissed by operation of law unless an application for adjudication of the claim is filed within 180 days of service of the notice.

(b) Where a claim form has been filed prior to January 1, 1994, and where benefits have been furnished by the employer, the claim may be dismissed if there has been no activity for the previous 180 days and if the claims adjuster has served notice pursuant to Article 3 (commencing with Section 415.10) of Chapter 4 of Title 5 of the Code of Civil Procedure. The notice shall specify that the claim will be dismissed by operation of law unless an application for adjudication of the claim is filed within five years of the date of injury or within one year of the last furnishing of benefits, whichever is later.

(c) The administrative director may adopt rules of practice and procedure consistent with this section.

(d) The provisions of subdivisions (a) and (b) do not limit the jurisdiction of the appeals board.

(e) This section is applicable to injuries occurring before January 1, 1994. **Leg.H.** 1993 ch. 121, effective July 16, 1993, ch. 1242.

Ref.: 8 C.C.R. §§10116, 10120, 10562, 10583; Hanna § 25.20[2]; Herlick Handbook § 14.2.

§5405. Time limits for benefits collection proceedings.

The period within which proceedings may be commenced for the collection of the benefits provided by Article 2 (commencing with Section 4600) or Article 3 (commencing with Section 4650), or both, of Chapter 2 of Part 2 is one year from any of the following:

(a) The date of injury.

(b) The expiration of any period covered by payment under Article 3 (commencing with Section 4650) of Chapter 2 of Part 2.

(c) The last date on which any benefits provided for in Article 2 (commencing with Section 4600) of Chapter 2 of Part 2 were furnished. **Leg.H.** 2002 ch. 6 (AB 749).

Ref.: 8 C.C.R. §§10102, 10852; Hanna §§ 24.03[1], [3][c], 24.04[2]–[3], 31.03[3], 31.05[3]; Herlick Handbook §§ 14.2, 14.7; W. Cal. Sum., 2 "Workers' Compensation" §§302, 367, 372, 375, 376, 378, 379, 382, 384, 386.

§5406. Time limits for commencement of benefits collection proceedings; generally.

Except as provided in Section 5406.5 or 5406.6, the period within which may be commenced proceedings for the collection of the benefits provided by Article 4 (commencing with Section 4700) of Chapter 2 of Part 2 is one year from:

(a) The date of death where death occurs within one year from date of injury; or

(b) The date of last furnishing of any benefits under Chapter 2 (commencing with Section 4550) of Part 2, where death occurs more than one year from the date of injury; or

(c) The date of death, where death occurs more than one year after the date of injury and compensation benefits have been furnished.

No such proceedings may be commenced more than one year after the date of death, nor more than 240 weeks from the date of injury. **Leg.H.** 1999 ch. 358.

Ref.: 8 C.C.R. §10852; Hanna §§ 9.01[4], 24.03[5]; Herlick Handbook §§ 7.14, 14.2, 14.7; W. Cal. Sum., 2 "Workers' Compensation" §§372, 373, 386.

§5406.5. Time limits for commencement of benefits collection proceedings; asbestosis.

In the case of the death of an asbestos worker or firefighter from asbestosis, the period within which proceedings may be commenced for the collection of the benefits provided by Article 4 (commencing with Section 4700) of Chapter 2 of Part 2 is one year from the date of death. **Leg.H.** 2003 ch. 831 (AB 149).

Ref.: Hanna § 24.03[5]; Herlick Handbook § 7.4; W. Cal. Sum., 2 "Workers' Compensation" §372.

§5406.6. Limitations period for claim for workers' compensation benefits for death from HIV-related disease.

(a) In the case of the death of a health care worker, a worker described in Section 3212, or a worker described in Section 830.5 of the Penal Code from an HIV-related disease, the period within which proceedings may be commenced for the collection of benefits provided by Article 4 (commencing with Section 4700) of Chapter 2 of Part 2 is one year from the date of death, providing that one or more of the following events has occurred:

(1) A report of the injury or exposure was made to the employer or to a governmental agency authorized to administer industrial injury claims, within one year of the date of the injury.

(2) The worker has complied with the notice provisions of this chapter and the claim has

not been finally determined to be noncompensable.

(3) The employer provided, or was ordered to provide, workers' compensation benefits for the injury prior to the date of death.

(b) For the purposes of this section, "health care worker" means an employee who has direct contact, in the course of his or her employment, with blood or other bodily fluids contaminated with blood, or with other bodily fluids identified by the Division of Occupational Safety and Health as capable of transmitting HIV, who is either (1) any person who is an employee of a provider of health care, as defined in subdivision (d) of Section 56.05 of the Civil Code, including, but not limited to, a registered nurse, licensed vocational nurse, certified nurse aide, clinical laboratory technologist, dental hygienist, physician, janitor, or housekeeping worker, or (2) an employee who provides direct patient care. **Leg.H.** 1999 ch. 358.

Ref.: Hanna §§ 9.01[4], 24.03[5]; W. Cal. Sum., 2 "Workers' Compensation" §372.

§5407. Time limits for commencement of compensation collection proceedings in case of misconduct.

The period within which may be commenced proceedings for the collection of compensation on the ground of serious and willful misconduct of the employer, under provision of Section 4553, is as follows:

Twelve months from the date of injury. This period shall not be extended by payment of compensation, agreement therefor, or the filing of application for compensation benefits under other provisions of this division.

Ref.: Herlick Handbook § 14.7; W. Cal. Sum., 2 "Workers' Compensation" §367.

§5407.5. Time limits for commencement of compensation reduction proceedings in case of employee misconduct.

The period within which may be commenced proceedings for the reduction of compensation on the ground of serious and willful misconduct of the employee, under provisions of Section 4551, is as follows:

Twelve months from the date of injury. However, this limitation shall not apply in any case where the employee has commenced proceedings for the increase of compensation on the ground of serious and willful misconduct of the employer.

Ref.: Herlick Handbook § 14.7; W. Cal. Sum., 2 "Workers' Compensation" §367.

§5408. Guardian/conservator to exercise minor's or incompetent's rights.

If an injured employee or, in the case of the employee's death, any of the employee's dependents, is under 18 years of age or incompetent at any time when any right or privilege accrues to such employee or dependent under this division, a guardian or conservator of the estate, appointed by the court, or a guardian ad litem or trustee appointed by the appeals board may, on behalf of the employee or dependent, claim and exercise any right or privilege with the same force and effect as if no disability existed.

No limitation of time provided by this division shall run against any person under 18 years of age or any incompetent unless and until a guardian or conservator of the estate or trustee is appointed. The appeals board may determine the fact of the minority or incompetency of any injured employee and may appoint a trustee to receive and disburse compensation payments for the benefit of such minor or incompetent and his family.

Ref.: Hanna §§ 9.01[4], 24.03[5], 24.05[1], 31.03[3], 31.21[1]; Herlick Handbook § 14.7; W. Cal. Sum., 2 "Workers' Compensation" §374.

§5409. Statute of limitations is affirmative defense.

The running of the period of limitations prescribed by this chapter is an affirmative defense and operates to bar the remedy and not to extinguish the right of the employee. Such defense may be waived. Failure to present such defense prior to the submission of the cause for decision is a sufficient waiver.

Ref.: Herlick Handbook §§ 14.7, 14.9, 14.18; W. Cal. Sum., 2 "Workers' Compensation" §§366, 375.

§5410. Time limits; proceedings for aggravated disabilities.

Nothing in this chapter shall bar the right of any injured worker to institute proceedings for the collection of compensation, including vocational rehabilitation services, within five years after the date of the injury upon the ground that the original injury has caused new and further

Labor

disability or that the provision of vocational rehabilitation services has become feasible because the employee's medical condition has improved or because of other factors not capable of determination at the time the employer's liability for vocational rehabilitation services otherwise terminated. The jurisdiction of the appeals board in these cases shall be a continuing jurisdiction within this period. This section does not extend the limitation provided in Section 5407.

1989 Note: This section is applicable only to injuries occurring on or after January 1, 1990. Stats. 1989 ch. 893 §6.

Ref.: 8 C.C.R. §10133.60; Hanna §§ 8.07[2][d][ii], 24.03[2], 24.03[3][c], 24.04[2][a], 31.05[1]–[5]; Herlick Handbook §§ 14.7, 14.8, 14.9; W. Cal. Sum., 2 "Workers' Compensation" §§290, 302, 369, 375, 378, 379, 383, 384, 426, 430, 432.

§5410.1. Attorney's fee for defendant in action to reduce permanent disability benefits.

Should any party to a proceeding institute proceedings to reduce the amount of permanent disability awarded to an applicant by the appeals board and be unsuccessful in such proceeding, the board may make a finding as to the amount of a reasonable attorney's fee incurred by the applicant in resisting such proceeding to reduce permanent disability benefits previously awarded by the appeals board and assess the same as costs upon the party instituting the proceeding for the reduction of permanent disability benefits.

Ref.: Herlick Handbook § 14.19; W. Cal. Sum., 2 "Workers' Compensation" §357.

§5411. Date of injury.

The date of injury, except in cases of occupational disease or cumulative injury, is that date during the employment on which occurred the alleged incident or exposure, for the consequences of which compensation is claimed.

Ref.: Herlick Handbook §§ 5.2, 8.17, 14.7; W. Cal. Sum., 2 "Workers' Compensation" §§193, 247, 367.

§5412. Date of injury for occupational diseases or cumulative injuries.

The date of injury in cases of occupational diseases or cumulative injuries is that date upon which the employee first suffered disability therefrom and either knew, or in the exercise of reasonable diligence should have known, that such disability was caused by his present or prior employment.

Ref.: Hanna §§ 24.03[4], 24.03[7][a], 31.04[3]; Herlick Handbook §§ 14.7, 14.35; W. Cal. Sum., 2 "Workers' Compensation" §§170, 193, 236, 247, 280, 292, 306, 313, 368, 369, 371, 373, 379, 426, 430.

§5413. Board's findings as having no collateral estoppel effect on subsequent criminal proceedings.

A determination of facts by the appeals board under this chapter has no collateral estoppel effect on a subsequent criminal prosecution and does not preclude litigation of those same facts in the criminal proceeding. **Leg.H.** 1995 ch. 158.

Ref.: Herlick Handbook § 9.18.

CHAPTER 2.3 WORKERS' COMPENSATION—TRUTH IN ADVERTISING

§5430. Title.

This chapter shall be known and may be cited as the Workers' Compensation Truth in Advertising Act of 1992. **Leg.H.** 1992 ch. 904.

Ref.: 8 C.C.R. §§9820, 9821, 9822, 9823, 9824, 9825, 9826, 9827, 9828, 9829, 9830, 9831, 9832, 9833, 9834, 9835, 9836, 9837; Herlick Handbook § 9.18; W. Cal. Sum., 2 "Workers' Compensation" §360.

§5431. Purpose.

The purpose of this chapter is to assure truthful and adequate disclosure of all material and relevant information in the advertising which solicits persons to file workers' compensation claims or to engage or consult counsel or a medical care provider or clinic to consider a workers' compensation claim. **Leg.H.** 1992 ch. 904.

Ref.: 8 C.C.R. §§9820, 9821, 9822, 9823, 9824, 9825, 9826, 9827, 9828, 9829, 9830, 9831, 9832, 9833, 9834, 9835, 9836, 9837; Hanna § 20.07; W. Cal. Sum., 2 "Workers' Compensation" §360.

§5432. Notice requirements.

(a) Any advertisement which solicits persons to file workers' compensation claims or to engage or consult counsel or a medical care provider or clinic to consider a workers' compensation claim in any newspaper, magazine, circular, form letter, or open publication, published, distributed, or circulated in this state, or on any billboard, card, label, transit advertisement or other written advertising medium shall state at the top or bottom on the front side or surface of the document in at least 12-point roman boldface type font, except for any billboard which shall be in type whose letters are 12 inches in height or any transit advertisement which shall be in type whose letters are seven inches in height and for any television announcement which shall be in 12-point roman boldface type font and appear in a dark background and remain on the screen for a minimum of five seconds and for any radio announcement which shall be read at an understandable pace with no loud music or sound effects, or both, to compete for the listener's attention, the following:

NOTICE

Making a false or fraudulent workers' compensation claim is a felony subject to up to 5 years in prison or a fine of up to $50,000 or double the value of the fraud, whichever is greater, or by both imprisonment and fine.

(b) Any television or radio announcement published or disseminated in this state which solicits persons to file workers' compensation claims or to engage or consult counsel to consider a workers' compensation claim under this code shall include the following spoken statement by the announcer of the advertisement:

"Making a false or fraudulent workers' compensation claim is a felony subject to up to 5 years in prison or a fine of up to $50,000 or double the value of the fraud, whichever is greater, or by both imprisonment and fine."

(c) This chapter does not supersede or repeal any regulation which governs advertising under this code and those regulations shall continue to be in force in addition to this chapter.

(d) For purposes of subdivisions (a) and (b), the notice or statement shall be written or spoken in English. In those cases where the preponderance of the listening or reading public receives information other than in the English language, the written notice or spoken statement shall be in those other languages. **Leg.H.** 1992 ch. 904.

Ref.: 8 C.C.R. §§9820, 9821, 9822, 9823, 9824, 9825, 9826, 9827, 9828, 9829, 9830, 9831, 9832, 9833, 9834, 9835, 9836, 9837; W. Cal. Sum., 2 "Workers' Compensation" §360.

§5433. Disclosure requirements.

(a) Any advertisement or other device designed to produce leads based on a response from a person to file a workers' compensation claim or to engage or consult counsel or a medical care provider or clinic shall disclose that an agent may contact the individual if that is the fact. In addition, an individual who makes contact with a person as a result of acquiring that individual's name from a lead generating device shall disclose that fact in the initial contact with that person.

(b) No person shall solicit persons to file a workers' compensation claim or to engage or consult counsel or a medical care provider or clinic to consider a workers' compensation claim through the use of a true or fictitious name which is deceptive or misleading with regard to the status, character, or proprietary or representative capacity of the entity or person, or to the true purpose of the advertisement.

(c) For purposes of this section, an advertisement includes a solicitation in any newspaper, magazine, circular, form letter, or open publication, published, distributed, or circulated in this state, or on any billboard, card, label, transit advertisement, or other written advertising medium, and includes envelopes, stationery, business cards, or other material designed to encourage the filing of a workers' compensation claim.

(d) Advertisements shall not employ words, initials, letters, symbols, or other devices which are so similar to those used by governmental agencies, a nonprofit or charitable institution, or other entity that they could have the capacity or tendency to mislead the public. Examples of misleading materials include, but are not limited to, those that imply any of the following:

(1) The advertisement is in some way provided by or is endorsed by a governmental agency or charitable institution.

(2) The advertiser is the same as, is connected with, or is endorsed by a governmental agency or charitable institution.

(e) Advertisements may not use the name of a state or political subdivision thereof in an advertising solicitation.

(f) Advertisements may not use any name, service mark, slogan, symbol, or any device in any manner which implies that the advertiser, or any person or entity associated with the advertiser, or that any agency who may call upon the person in response to the advertisement, is connected with a governmental agency.

(g) Advertisements may not imply that the reader, listener, or viewer may lose a right or privilege or benefits under federal, state, or local law if he or she fails to respond to the advertisement. **Leg.H.** 1992 ch. 904, 1998 ch. 485, 1999 ch. 83.

Ref.: 8 C.C.R. §§9820, 9821, 9822, 9823, 9824, 9825, 9826, 9827, 9828, 9829, 9830, 9831, 9832, 9833, 9834, 9835, 9836, 9837; Hanna § 20.07; W. Cal. Sum., 2 "Workers' Compensation" §360.

§5434. Penalty for violation; "advertiser" defined.

(a) Any advertiser who violates Section 5431 or 5432 is guilty of a misdemeanor.

(b) For the purposes of this chapter, "advertiser" means any person who provides workers' compensation claims services which are described in the written or broadcast advertisements, any person to whom persons solicited by the advertisements are directed to for inquiries or the provision of workers' compensation claims related services, or any person paying for the preparation, broadcast, printing, dissemination, or placement of the advertisements. **Leg.H.** 1992 ch. 904.

Ref.: 8 C.C.R. §§9820, 9821, 9822, 9823, 9824, 9825, 9826, 9827, 9828, 9829, 9830, 9831, 9832, 9833, 9834, 9835, 9836, 9837; Herlick Handbook § 9.18; W. Cal. Sum., 2 "Workers' Compensation" §360.

CHAPTER 2.5 ADMINISTRATIVE ASSISTANCE

§5450. Assistance from Division of Workers' Compensation.

The Division of Workers' Compensation shall make available to employees, employers and other interested parties information, assistance, and advice to assure the proper and timely furnishing of benefits and to assist in the resolution of disputes on an informal basis. **Leg.H.** 1994 chs. 146, 1097.

Ref.: 8 C.C.R. §§9900, 9922, 9923, 9924, 9925, 9926, 9927, 9928; Herlick Handbook § 1.9.

§5451. Duties of information and assistance officer.

Any party may consult with, or seek the advice of, an information and assistance officer within the Division of Workers' Compensation as designated by the administrative director. If no application is filed, if the employee is not represented, or upon agreement of the parties, the information and assistance officer shall consider the contentions of the parties and may refer the matter to the appropriate bureau or unit within the Division of Workers' Compensation for review and recommendations. The information and assistance officer shall advise the employer and the employee of their rights, benefits, and obligations under this division. Upon making a referral, the information and assistance officer shall arrange for a copy of any pertinent material submitted to be served upon the parties or their representatives, if any. The procedures to be followed by the information and assistance officer shall be governed by the rules and regulations of the administrative director adopted after public hearings. **Leg.H.** 1994 chs. 146, 1097.

Ref.: 8 C.C.R. §§9900, 9922, 9923, 9924, 9925, 9926, 9927, 9928, 9928.1, 10166.

§5453. Recommendation of information and assistance officer.

After consideration of the information submitted, including the reports of any bureau or unit within the Division of Workers' Compensation which have been received, the information and assistance officer shall make a recommendation which shall be served on the parties or their representatives, if any. **Leg.H.** 1994 chs. 146, 1097.

Ref.: 8 C.C.R. §§9900, 9922, 9923, 9924, 9925, 9926, 9927, 9928.

§5454. Statute of limitations tolled by submission to information and assistance officer.

Submission of any matter to an information and assistance officer of the Division of Workers' Compensation shall toll any applicable statute of limitations for the period that the matter is under consideration by the information and assistance officer, and for 60 days following the issuance of his or her recommendation. **Leg.H.** 1994 chs. 146, 1097.

Ref.: 8 C.C.R. §§9900, 9922, 9923, 9924, 9925, 9926, 9927, 9928; Hanna § 23.03[2][f].

§5455. Application for benefits; admissible evidence.

Nothing in this chapter shall prohibit any party from filing an application for benefits under this division. In any proceeding pursuant to such application, the admissibility of written evidence or reports submitted by any party pursuant to this chapter, or Section 5502, shall be governed by Chapter 5 (commencing with Section 5700).

Ref.: 8 C.C.R. §§9900, 9922, 9923, 9924, 9925, 9926, 9927, 9928; Herlick Handbook § 1.9.

CHAPTER 3 APPLICATIONS AND ANSWERS

§5500. Required pleadings.

No pleadings other than the application and answer shall be required. Both shall be in writing and shall conform to forms prescribed by the appeals board in its rules of practice and procedure, simply but clearly and completely delineating all relevant matters of agreement and all issues of disagreement within the jurisdiction of the appeals board, and providing for the furnishing of any additional information as the appeals board may properly determine necessary to expedite its hearing and determination of the claim.

The amendment of this section made during the 1993 portion of the 1993-94 Regular Session shall apply to all applications filed on or after January 1, 1994.

Notwithstanding Section 5401, except where a claim form has been filed for an injury occurring on or after January 1, 1990, and before January 1, 1994, the filing of an application for adjudication and not the filing of a claim form shall establish the jurisdiction of the appeals board and shall commence proceedings before the appeals board for the collection of benefits. **Leg.H.** 1993 ch. 121, effective July 16, 1993, 1994 ch. 1118.

1993 Note: Section 5500, as amended by ch. 121, applies only to injuries occurring on or after January 1, 1994. Stats. 1993 ch. 121 §77.

1989 Note: This section is applicable only to injuries occurring on or after January 1, 1990. Stats. 1989 ch. 893 §6.

Ref.: 8 C.C.R. §§10353, 10364, 10400, 10401, 10402, 10408, 10480, 10484, 10490, 10878, 10955; Hanna §§ 25.05[1], 25.22[1]; Herlick Handbook §§ 14.2, 14.11; W. Cal. Sum., 2 "Workers' Compensation" §§347, 387.

§5500.3. Uniformity among offices.

(a) The court administrator shall establish uniform district office procedures, uniform forms, and uniform time of court settings for all district offices of the appeals board. No district office of the appeals board or workers' compensation administration law judge shall require forms or procedures other than as established by the court administrator. The court administrator shall take reasonable steps to ensure enforcement of this section. A workers' compensation administrative law judge who violates this section may be subject to disciplinary proceedings.

(b) The appeals board shall establish uniform court procedures and uniform forms for all other proceedings of the appeals board. No district office of the appeals board or workers' compensation administrative law judge shall require forms or procedures other than as established by the appeals board. **Leg.H.** 2002 ch. 6 (AB 749).

Ref.: Herlick Handbook § 14.5; W. Cal. Sum., 2 "Workers' Compensation" §§12, 345.

§5500.5. Employers liable for occupational disease or cumulative injury.

(a) Except as otherwise provided in Section 5500.6, liability for occupational disease or cumulative injury claims filed or asserted on or after January 1, 1978, shall be limited to those employers who employed the employee during a period of four years immediately preceding either the date of injury, as determined pursuant to Section 5412, or the last date on which the employee was employed in an occupation exposing him or her to the hazards of the occupational disease or cumulative injury, whichever occurs first. Commencing January 1, 1979, and thereafter on the first day of January for each of the next two years, the liability period for occupational disease or cumulative injury shall be decreased by one year so that liability is limited in the following manner:

For claims filed or asserted on or after:	The period shall be:
January 1, 1979	three years
January 1, 1980	two years

Labor

January 1, 1981 and
thereafter . . . . one year

In the event that none of the employers during the above referenced periods of occupational disease or cumulative injury are insured for workers' compensation coverage or an approved alternative thereof, liability shall be imposed upon the last year of employment exposing the employee to the hazards of the occupational disease or cumulative injury for which an employer is insured for workers' compensation coverage or an approved alternative thereof.

Any employer held liable for workers' compensation benefits as a result of another employer's failure to secure the payment of compensation as required by this division shall be entitled to reimbursement from the employers who were unlawfully uninsured during the last year of the employee's employment, and shall be subrogated to the rights granted to the employee against the unlawfully uninsured employers under the provisions of Article 1 (commencing with Section 3700) of Chapter 4 of Part 1 of Division 4.

If, based upon all the evidence presented, the appeals board or workers' compensation judge finds the existence of cumulative injury or occupational disease, liability for the cumulative injury or ocupational disease shall not be apportioned to prior or subsequent years; however, in determining the liability, evidence of disability due to specific injury, disability due to nonindustrial causes, or disability previously compensated for by way of a findings and award or order approving compromise and release, or a voluntary payment of disability, may be admissible for purposes of apportionment.

(b) Where a claim for compensation benefits is made on account of an occupational disease or cumulative injury which may have arisen out of more than one employment, the application shall state the names and addresses of all employers liable under subdivision (a), the places of employment, and the approximate periods of employment where the employee was exposed to the hazards of the occupational disease or cumulative injury. If the application is not so prepared or omits necessary and proper employers, any interested party, at or prior to the first hearing, may request the appeals board to join as defendant any necessary or proper party. If the request is made prior to the first hearing on the application, the appeals board shall forthwith join the employer as a party defendant and cause a copy of the application together with a notice of the time and place of hearing to be served upon the omitted employer; provided, the notice can be given within the time specified in this division. If the notice cannot be timely given or if the motion for joinder is made at the time of the first hearing, then the appeals board or the workers' compensation judge before whom the hearing is held, if it is found that the omitted employer named is a necessary or proper party, may order a joinder of the party and continue the hearing so that proper notice may be given to the party or parties so joined. Only one continuance shall be allowed for the purpose of joining additional parties. Subsequent to the first hearing the appeals board shall join as a party defendant any additional employer when it appears that the employer is a proper party, but the liability of the employer shall not be determined until supplemental proceedings are instituted.

(c) In any case involving a claim of occupational disease or cumulative injury occurring as a result of more than one employment within the appropriate time period set forth in subdivision (a), the employee making the claim, or his or her dependents, may elect to proceed against any one or more of the employers. Where such an election is made, the employee must successfully prove his or her claim against any one of the employers named, and any award which the appeals board shall issue awarding compensation benefits shall be a joint and several award as against any two or more employers who may be held liable for compensation benefits. If, during the pendency of any claim wherein the employee or his or her dependents has made an election to proceed against one or more employers, it should appear that there is another proper party not yet joined, the additional party shall be joined as a defendant by the appeals board on the motion of any party in interest, but the liability of the employer shall not be determined until supplemental proceedings are instituted. Any employer joined as a defendant subsequent to the first hearing or subsequent to the election provided herein shall not be entitled to participate in any of the proceedings prior to the appeal board's final decision, nor to any continuance or further proceedings, but may be permitted to ascertain from the employee or his or her dependents such information as will enable the employer to determine the time, place, and duration of the alleged employment. On supplemental proceedings, however, the right of the employer to full and complete examination or cross-examination shall not be restricted.

(d)(1) In the event a self-insured employer which owns and operates a work location in the State of California, sells or has sold the ownership and operation of the work location pursuant to a sale of a business or all or part of the assets of a business to another self-insured person or entity after January 1, 1974, but before January 1, 1978, and all the requirements of subparagraphs (A) to (D), inclusive, exist, then the liability of the employer-seller and employer-buyer, respectively, for cumulative injuries suffered by employees employed at the work location immediately before the sale shall, until January 1, 1986, be governed by the provisions of this section which were in effect on the date of that sale.

(A) The sale constitutes a material change in ownership of such work location.

(B) The person or entity making the purchase continues the operation of the work location.

(C) The person or entity becomes the employer of substantially all of the employees of the employer-seller.

(D) The agreement of sale makes no special provision for the allocation of liabilities for workers' compensation between the buyer and the seller.

(2) For purposes of this subdivision:

(A) "Work location" shall mean any fixed place of business, office, or plant where employees regularly work in the trade or business of the employer.

(B) A "material change in ownership" shall mean a change in ownership whereby the employer-seller does not retain, directly or indirectly, through one or more corporate entities, associations, trusts, partnerships, joint ventures, or family members, a controlling interest in the work location.

(3) This subdivision shall have no force or effect on or after January 1, 1986, unless otherwise extended by the Legislature prior to that date, and it shall not have any force or effect as respects an employee who, subsequent to the sale described in paragraph (1) and prior to the date of his or her application for compensation benefits has been filed, is transferred to a different work location by the employer-buyer.

(4) If any provision of this subdivision or the application thereof to any person or circumstances is held invalid, that invalidity shall not affect other provisions or applications of this subdivision which can be given effect without the invalid provision or application, and to this end the provisions of this subdivision are severable.

(e) At any time within one year after the appeals board has made an award for compensation benefits in connection with an occupational disease or cumulative injury, any employer held liable under the award may institute proceedings before the appeals board for the purpose of determining an apportionment of liability or right of contribution. The proceeding shall not diminish, restrict, or alter in any way the recovery previously allowed the employee or his or her dependents, but shall be limited to a determination of the respective contribution rights, interest or liabilities of all the employers joined in the proceeding, either initially or supplementally; provided, however, if the appeals board finds on supplemental proceedings for the purpose of determining an apportionment of liability or of a right of contribution that an employer previously held liable in fact has no liability, it may dismiss the employer and amend its original award in such manner as may be required.

(f) In any proceeding before the appeals board for the purpose of determining an apportionment of liability or of a right of contribution where any employee incurred a disability or death resulting from silicosis in underground metal mining operations, the determination of the respective rights and interests of all of the employers joined in the proceedings either initially or supplementally shall be as follows:

(1) All employers whose underground metal mining operations resulted in a silicotic exposure during the period of the employee's employment in those operations shall be jointly and severally liable for the payment of compensation and of medical, surgical, legal and hospital expense which may be awarded to the employee or his or her estate or dependents as the result of disability or death resulting from or aggravated by the exposure.

(2) In making its determination in the supplemental proceeding for the purpose of determining an apportionment of liability or of a right of contribution of percentage liabilities of the various employers engaged in underground metal mining operations the appeals board shall consider as a rebuttable presumption that employment in underground work in any mine for a

Labor

continuous period of more than three calendar months will result in a silicotic exposure for the employee so employed during the period of employment if the underground metal mine was driven or sunk in rock having a composition which will result in dissemination of silica or silicotic dust particles when drilled, blasted, or transported.

(g) Any employer shall be entitled to rebut the presumption by showing to the satisfaction of the appeals board, or the workers' compensation judge, that the mining methods used by the employer in the employee's place of employment did not result during his or her employment in the creation of silica dust in sufficient amount or concentration to constitute a silicotic hazard. Dust counts, competently made, at intervals and in locations as meet the requirements of the Division of Occupational Safety and Health for safe working conditions may be received as evidence of the amount and concentration of silica dust in the workings where the counts have been made at the time when they were made. The appeals board may from time to time, as its experience may indicate proper, promulgate orders as to the frequency with which dust counts shall be taken in different types of workings in order to justify their acceptance as evidence of the existence or nonexistence of a silicotic hazard in the property where they have been taken.

(h) The amendments to this section adopted at the 1959 Regular Session of the Legislature shall operate retroactively, and shall apply retrospectively to any cases pending before the appeals board or courts. From and after the date this section becomes effective no payment shall be made out of the fund used for payment of the additional compensation provided for in Section 4751, or out of any other state funds, in satisfaction of any liability heretofore incurred or hereafter incurred, except awards which have become final without regard to the continuing jurisdiction of the appeals board on that effective date, and the state and its funds shall be without liability therefor. This subdivision shall not in any way effect a reduction in any benefit conferred or which may be conferred upon any injured employee or his dependents.

(i) The amendments to this section adopted at the 1977 Regular Session of the Legislature shall apply to any claims for benefits under this division which are filed or asserted on or after January 1, 1978, unless otherwise specified in this section.

Ref.: Hanna §§ 8.06[2], 25.05[6], 26.01[2][c], 31.13[2][a]–[d]; Herlick Handbook §§ 6.22, 8.22, 8.23, 8.27, 11.8, 14.35; W. Cal. Sum., 2 "Workers' Compensation" §§169–171, 392.

§5500.6. Employers liable for occupational disease or cumulative injury; household employee.

Liability for occupational disease or cumulative injury which results from exposure solely during employment as an employee, as defined in subdivision (d) of Section 3351, shall be limited to those employers in whose employment the employee was exposed to the hazards of the occupational disease or cumulative injury during the last day on which the employee was employed in an occupation exposing the employee to the hazards of the disease or injury. In the event that none of the employers of the last day of hazardous employment is insured for workers' compensation liability, that liability, shall be imposed upon the last employer exposing the employee to the hazards of the occupational disease or cumulative injury who has secured workers' compensation insurance coverage or an approved alternative thereto. If, based upon all the evidence presented, the appeals board or the workers' compensation judge finds the existence of cumulative injury or occupational disease, liability for the cumulative injury or occupational disease shall not be apportioned to prior employers. However, in determining liability, evidence of disability due to specific injury, disability due to non-work-related causes, or disability previously compensated for by way of a findings and award or order approving compromise and release, or a voluntary payment of disability, may be admissible for purposes of apportionment.

Ref.: W. Cal. Sum., 2 "Workers' Compensation" §170.

§5501. Filing of application; subsequent procedure.

The application may be filed with the appeals board by any party in interest, his attorney, or other representative authorized in writing. A representative who is not an attorney licensed by the State Bar of this state shall notify the appeals board in writing that he or she is not an attorney licensed by the State Bar of this state. Upon the filing of the application, the appeals board shall, where the applicant is represented by an attorney or other representative, serve a conformed copy of the application showing the date of filing and the case number upon applicant's attorney or representative. The applicant's attorney or representative shall, upon receipt of the conformed copy, forthwith serve a copy of the conformed application upon all other parties to the claim. If the applicant is unrepresented, a copy thereof shall forthwith be served upon all adverse parties by the appeals board. **Leg.H.** 1991 ch. 934.

Ref.: Hanna §§ 23.14[1][b], 23.14[2][b]; Herlick Handbook §§ 10.1, 10.2, 14.11, 14.12; W. Cal. Sum., 2 "Workers' Compensation" §§349, 353, 382, 388.

§5501.5. Where application for adjudication of claim may be filed.

(a) The application for adjudication of claim shall be filed in any of the following locations:

(1) In the county where the injured employee or dependent of a deceased employee resides on the date of filing.

(2) In the county where the injury allegedly occurred, or, in cumulative trauma and industrial disease claims, where the last alleged injurious exposure occurred.

(3) In the county where the employee's attorney maintains his or her principal place of business, if the employee is represented by an attorney.

(b) If the county selected for filing has more than one office of the appeals board, the application shall be filed at any location of the appeals board within that county that meets the criteria specified in subdivision (a). The written consent of the employee, or dependent of a deceased employee, to the selected venue site shall be filed with application.

(c) If the venue site where the application is to be filed is the county where the employee's attorney maintains his or her principal place of business, the attorney for the employee shall indicate that venue site when forwarding the information request form required by Section 5401.5. The employer shall have 30 days from receipt of the information request form to object to the selected venue site. Where there is an employer objection to a venue site under paragraph (3) of subdivision (a), then the application shall be filed pursuant to either paragraph (1) or (2) of subdivision (a).

(d) If there is no appeals board office in the county where venue is permitted under subdivision (a), the application shall be filed at the appeals board office nearest the residence on the date of filing of the injured employee or dependent of a deceased employee, or the nearest place where the injury allegedly occurred, or, in cumulative trauma and industrial disease claims, where the last injurious exposure occurred, or nearest the location where the attorney of the employee maintains his or her principal place of business, unless the employer objects under subdivision (c).

Ref.: 8 C.C.R. §§10408, 10410, 15740; Herlick Handbook § 14.15; W. Cal. Sum., 2 "Workers' Compensation" §346.

§5501.6. Petition for change of venue.

(a) An applicant or defendant may petition the appeals board for a change of venue and a change of venue shall be granted for good cause. The reasons for the change of venue shall be specifically set forth in the request for change of venue.

(b) If a change of venue is requested for the convenience of witnesses, the names and addresses of these witnesses and the substance of their testimony shall be specifically set forth in the request for change of venue.

Ref.: 8 C.C.R. §§10411, 10412; Hanna §25.27; W. Cal. Sum., 2 "Workers' Compensation" §346.

§5502. Time for hearing; priority calendar; reports; mandatory settlement conference.

(a) Except as provided in subdivisions (b) and (d), the hearing shall be held not less than 10 days, and not more than 60 days, after the date a declaration of readiness to proceed, on a form prescribed by the court administrator, is filed. If a claim form has been filed for an injury occurring on or after January 1, 1990, and before January 1, 1994, an application for adjudication shall accompany the declaration of readiness to proceed.

(b) The court administrator shall establish a priority calendar for issues requiring an expedited hearing and decision. A hearing shall be held and a determination as to the rights of the parties shall be made and filed within 30 days after the declaration of readiness to proceed is filed if the issues in dispute are any of the following:

(1) The employee's entitlement to medical treatment pursuant to Section 4600.

(2) The employee's entitlement to, or the amount of, temporary disability indemnity payments.

(3) The employee's entitlement to vocational rehabilitation services, or the termination of an employer's liability to provide these services to an employee.

(4) The employee's entitlement to compensation from one or more responsible employers when two or more employers dispute liability as among themselves.

(5) Any other issues requiring an expedited hearing and determination as prescribed in rules and regulations of the administrative director.

(c) The court administrator shall establish a priority conference calendar for cases in which the employee is represented by an attorney and the issues in dispute are employment or injury arising out of employment or in the course of employment. The conference shall be conducted by a workers' compensation administrative law judge within 30 days after the declaration of readiness to proceed. If the dispute cannot be resolved at the conference, a trial shall be set as expeditiously as possible, unless good cause is shown why discovery is not complete, in which case status conferences shall be held at regular intervals. The case shall be set for trial when discovery is complete, or when the workers' compensation administrative law judge determines that the parties have had sufficient time in which to complete reasonable discovery. A determination as to the rights of the parties shall be made and filed within 30 days after the trial.

(d) The court administrator shall report quarterly to the Governor and to the Legislature concerning the frequency and types of issues which are not heard and decided within the period prescribed in this section and the reasons therefor.

(e)(1) In all cases, a mandatory settlement conference shall be conducted not less than 10 days, and not more than 30 days, after the filing of a declaration of readiness to proceed. If the dispute is not resolved, the regular hearing shall be held within 75 days after the declaration of readiness to proceed is filed.

(2) The settlement conference shall be conducted by a workers' compensation administrative law judge or by a referee who is eligible to be a workers' compensation administrative law judge or eligible to be an arbitrator under Section 5270.5. At the mandatory settlement conference, the referee or workers' compensation administrative law judge shall have the authority to resolve the dispute, including the authority to approve a compromise and release or issue a stipulated finding and award, and if the dispute cannot be resolved, to frame the issues and stipulations for trial. The appeals board shall adopt any regulations needed to implement this subdivision. The presiding workers' compensation administrative law judge shall supervise settlement conference referees in the performance of their judicial functions under this subdivision.

(3) If the claim is not resolved at the mandatory settlement conference, the parties shall file a pretrial conference statement noting the specific issues in dispute, each party's proposed permanent disability rating, and listing the exhibits, and disclosing witnesses. Discovery shall close on the date of the mandatory settlement conference. Evidence not disclosed or obtained thereafter shall not be admissible unless the proponent of the evidence can demonstrate that it was not available or could not have been discovered by the exercise of due diligence prior to the settlement conference.

(f) In cases involving the Director of the Department of Industrial Relations in his or her capacity as administrator of the Uninsured Employers Fund, this section shall not apply unless proof of service, as specified in paragraph (1) of subdivision (d) of Section 3716 has been filed with the appeals board and provided to the Director of Industrial Relations, valid jurisdiction has been established over the employer, and the fund has been joined.

(g) Except as provided in subdivision (a) and in Section 4065, the provisions of this section shall apply irrespective of the date of injury. **Leg.H.** 1992 ch. 1226, 1993 ch. 121, effective July 16, 1993, 1994 ch. 1118, 2002 chs. 6 (AB 749), 866 (AB 486).

1993 Note: Section 5502, as amended by ch. 121, applies only to injuries occurring on or after January 1, 1994. Stats. 1993 ch. 121 §77.

1989 Note: This section is applicable only to injuries occurring on or after January 1, 1990. Stats. 1989 ch. 893 §6.

Ref.: 8 C.C.R. §§10136, 10137, 10166, 10353, 10414, 10415, 10417, 10555, 10562, 10563, 10590, 10591, 10601, 10607, 10608; Hanna § 26.04[2]; Herlick Handbook §§ 14.8, 14.11, 14.18, 14.20, 14.30, 14.40; W. Cal. Sum., 2 "Workers' Compensation" §§12, 396, 400.

§5502.5. Hearing continuance—Good cause required.

A continuance of any conference or hearing required by Section 5502 shall not be favored, but may be granted by a workers' compensation judge upon any terms as are just upon a showing of good cause. When determining a request for continuance, the workers' compensation judge shall take into consideration the complexity of the issues, the diligence of the parties, and the prejudice incurred on the part of any party by reasons of granting or denying a continuance.

Ref.: 8 C.C.R. §§10353, 10548; W. Cal. Sum., 2 "Workers' Compensation" §396.

§5503. "Applicant"; "defendant."

The person so applying shall be known as the applicant and the adverse party shall be known as the defendant.

Ref.: 8 C.C.R. §§10360, 10364.

§5504. Service of notice of hearing.

A notice of the time and place of hearing shall be served upon the applicant and all adverse parties and may be served either in the manner of service of a summons in a civil action or in the same manner as any notice that is authorized or required to be served under the provisions of this division.

Ref.: 8 C.C.R. §§10500, 10544; W. Cal. Sum., 2 "Workers' Compensation" §§388, 396.

§5505. Defendant's answer.

If any defendant desires to disclaim any interest in the subject matter of the claim in controversy, or considers that the application is in any respect inaccurate or incomplete, or desires to bring any fact, paper, or document to the attention of the appeals board as a defense to the claim or otherwise, he may, within 10 days after the service of the application upon him, file with or mail to the appeals board his answer in such form as the appeals board may prescribe, setting forth the particulars in which the application is inaccurate or incomplete, and the facts upon which he intends to rely. A copy of the answer shall be forthwith served upon all adverse parties. Evidence upon matters not pleaded by answer shall be allowed only upon the terms and conditions imposed by the appeals board or referee holding the hearing.

Ref.: 8 C.C.R. §§10484, 10544; Herlick Handbook § 14.18; W. Cal. Sum., 2 "Workers' Compensation" §389.

§5506. Defendant's failure to appear or answer.

If the defendant fails to appear or answer, no default shall be taken against him, but the appeals board shall proceed to the hearing of the matter upon the terms and conditions which it deems proper. A defendant failing to appear or answer, or subsequently contending that no service was made upon him, or claiming to be aggrieved in any other manner by want of notice of the pendency of the proceedings, may apply to the appeals board for relief substantially in accordance with the provisions of Section 473 of the Code of Civil Procedure. The appeals board may afford such relief. No right to relief, including the claim that the findings and award of the appeals board or judgment entered thereon are void upon their face, shall accrue to such defendant in any court unless prior application is made to the appeals board in accordance with this section. In no event shall any petition to any court be allowed except as prescribed in Sections 5950 and 5951.

Ref.: Herlick Handbook § 14.43; W. Cal. Sum., 2 "Workers' Compensation" §§154, 388, 389, 408.

§5507. Dismissal of application without hearing.

If an application shows upon its face that the applicant is not entitled to compensation, the appeals board may, after opportunity to the applicant to be heard orally or to submit his claim or argument in writing dismiss the application without any hearing thereon. Such dismissal may be upon the motion of the appeals board or upon motion of the adverse party. The pendency of such motion or notice of intended dismissal shall not, unless otherwise ordered by the appeals board, delay the hearing on the application upon its merits.

Ref.: 8 C.C.R. §10780; Herlick Handbook § 14.43; W. Cal. Sum., 2 "Workers' Compensation" §§389, 390.

CHAPTER 4
ATTACHMENTS

§5600. Appeals board authority to order writs of attachment.

The appeals board may, upon the filing of an application by or on behalf of an injured em-

Labor

ployee, the employee's dependents, or any other party in interest, direct the clerk of the superior court of any county to issue writs of attachment authorizing the sheriff to attach the property of the defendant as security for the payment of any compensation which may be awarded in any of the following cases:

(a) In any case mentioned in Section 415.50 of the Code of Civil Procedure.

(b) Where the employer has failed to secure the payment of compensation as required by Article 1 (commencing with Section 3700) of Chapter 4 of Part 1.

The attachment shall be in an amount fixed by the appeals board, not exceeding the greatest probable award against the defendant in the matter. **Leg.H.** 2002 ch. 784 (SB 1316).

Ref.: W. Cal. Sum., 2 "Workers' Compensation" §150.

§5601. Procedure for attachment proceedings.

The provisions of Title 6.5 (commencing with Section 481.010) of Part 2 of the Code of Civil Procedure, as far as applicable, shall govern the proceedings upon attachment, the appeals board being substituted therein for the proper court.

§5602. Issuance and discharge of attachment.

No writ of attachment shall be issued except upon the order of the appeals board. Such order shall not be made where it appears from the application or affidavit in support thereof that the employer was, at the time of the injury to the employee, insured against liability imposed by this division by any insurer. If, at any time after the levying of an attachment, it appears that such employer was so insured, and the requisites for dismissing the employer from the proceeding and substituting the insurer as defendant under any method prescribed by this division are established, the appeals board shall forthwith discharge the attachment.

§5603. Preference when attachments levied.

In levying attachments preference shall be given to the real property of the employer.

CHAPTER 5
HEARINGS

§5700. Adjournment of hearing; parties permitted at hearing.

The hearing on the application may be adjourned from time to time and from place to place in the discretion of the appeals board or the workers' compensation judge holding the hearing. Any hearing adjourned by the workers' compensation judge shall be continued to be heard by and shall be concluded and the decision made by the workers' compensation judge who previously heard it. Either party may be present at any hearing, in person, by attorney, or by any other agent, and may present testimony pertinent under the pleadings.

Ref.: Herlick Handbook § 14.5; W. Cal. Ev., "Witnesses" §103; W. Cal. Sum., 2 "Workers' Compensation" §353.

§5701. Appeals board authority to take testimony or direct examination.

The appeals board may, with or without notice to either party, cause testimony to be taken, or inspection of the premises where the injury occurred to be made, or the timebooks and payroll of the employer to be examined by any member of the board or a workers' compensation judge appointed by the appeals board. The appeals board may also from time to time direct any employee claiming compensation to be examined by a regular physician. The testimony so taken and the results of any inspection or examination shall be reported to the appeals board for its consideration.

Ref.: 8 C.C.R. §§10156, 10166, 10718; Herlick Handbook §§ 14.22, 14.40; W. Cal. Sum., 2 "Workers' Compensation" §§396, 400.

§5702. Stipulations.

The parties to a controversy may stipulate the facts relative thereto in writing and file such stipulation with the appeals board. The appeals board may thereupon make its findings and award based upon such stipulation, or may set the matter down for hearing and take further testimony or make the further investigation necessary to enable it to determine the matter in controversy.

Ref.: 8 C.C.R. §§10492, 10496, 10497, 10578, 10878, 10882, 10888, 10890; Hanna §§ 23.11[3], 26.06[2]; Herlick Handbook § 14.44; W. Cal. Sum., 2 "Workers' Compensation" §391.

§5703. Specified additional evidence allowed.

The appeals board may receive as evidence either at or subsequent to a hearing, and use as proof of any fact in dispute, the following matters, in addition to sworn testimony presented in open hearing:

(a) Reports of attending or examining physicians.

(1) Statements concerning any bill for services are admissible only if made under penalty of perjury that they are true and correct to the best knowledge of the physician.

(2) In addition, reports are admissible under this subdivision only if the physician has further stated in the body of the report that there has not been a violation of Section 139.3 and that the contents of the report are true and correct to the best knowledge of the physician. The statement shall be made under penalty of perjury.

(b) Reports of special investigators appointed by the appeals board or a workers' compensation judge to investigate and report upon any scientific or medical question.

(c) Reports of employers, containing copies of timesheets, book accounts, reports, and other records properly authenticated.

(d) Properly authenticated copies of hospital records of the case of the injured employee.

(e) All publications of the Division of Workers' Compensation.

(f) All official publications of the State of California and United States governments.

(g) Excerpts from expert testimony received by the appeals board upon similar issues of scientific fact in other cases and the prior decisions of the appeals board upon similar issues.

(h) Relevant portions of medical treatment protocols published by medical specialty societies. To be admissible, the party offering such a protocol or portion of a protocol shall concurrently enter into evidence information regarding how the protocol was developed, and to what extent the protocol is evidence-based, peer-reviewed, and nationally recognized. If a party offers into evidence a portion of a treatment protocol, any other party may offer into evidence additional portions of the protocol. The party offering a protocol, or portion thereof, into evidence shall either make a printed copy of the full protocol available for review and copying, or shall provide an Internet address at which the entire protocol may be accessed without charge.

(i) The medical treatment utilization schedule in effect pursuant to Section 5307.27 or the guidelines in effect pursuant to Section 4604.5.

Leg.H. 1993 ch. 120, effective July 16, 1993, 1994 ch. 146, 2003 ch. 639 (SB 228), 2004 ch. 34 (SB 899), effective April 19, 2004.

2004 Note: The amendment to §5703 made by this act shall apply prospectively from the date of enactment of this act, regardless of the date of injury, unless otherwise specified, but shall not constitute good cause to reopen or rescind, alter, or amend any existing order, decision, or award of the Workers' Compensation Appeals Board. Stats. 2004 ch. 34 (SB 899) §47.

Ref.: 8 C.C.R. §§10430, 10600, 10601, 10604, 10606, 10608, 10616; Hanna § 26.06[12]; Herlick Handbook § 14.40; W. Cal. Ev., "Introduction" §§67, 71; W. Cal. Sum., 2 "Workers' Compensation" §§399, 447.

§5703.5. Examination of injured employee by QME.

(a) The appeals board, at any time after an application is filed and prior to the expiration of its jurisdiction may, upon the agreement of a party to pay the cost, direct an unrepresented employee to be examined by a qualified medical evaluator selected by the appeals board, within the scope of the qualified medical evaluator's professional training, upon any clinical question then at issue before the appeals board.

(b) The administrative director or his or her designees, upon the submission of a matter to an information and assistance officer, may, upon the agreement of a party to pay the cost, and with the consent of an unrepresented employee direct the injured employee to be examined by a qualified medical evaluator selected by the medical director, within the scope of the qualified medical evaluator's professional training, upon any clinical question, other than those issues specified in Section 4061, then pertinent to the investigation of the information and assistance officer.

(c) The 1989 and 1990 amendments to this section shall become operative for injuries occurring on and after January 1, 1991.

Ref.: 8 C.C.R. §§10166, 10700, 10718; Hanna §§ 22.07[4], 23.03[2][c]; Herlick Handbook §§ 1.9, 4.20, 14.22; W. Cal. Sum., 2 "Workers' Compensation" §400.

§5704. Transcripts of testimony.

Transcripts of all testimony taken without notice and copies of all reports and other matters added to the record, otherwise than during the course of an open hearing, shall be served upon the parties to the proceeding, and an opportunity shall be given to produce evidence in explanation or rebuttal thereof before decision is rendered.

Labor

Ref.: 8 C.C.R. §10580; Herlick Handbook §14.40; W. Cal. Ev., "Introduction" §§71, 85; W. Cal. Sum., 2 "Workers' Compensation" §§399, 447.

§5705. Burden of proof; affirmative defenses.

The burden of proof rests upon the party or lien claimant holding the affirmative of the issue. The following are affirmative defenses, and the burden of proof rests upon the employer to establish them:

(a) That an injured person claiming to be an employee was an independent contractor or otherwise excluded from the protection of this division where there is proof that the injured person was at the time of his or her injury actually performing service for the alleged employer.

(b) Intoxication of an employee causing his or her injury.

(c) Willful misconduct of an employee causing his or her injury.

(d) Aggravation of disability by unreasonable conduct of the employee.

(e) Prejudice to the employer by failure of the employee to give notice, as required by Sections 5400 and 5401. **Leg.H.** 1993 ch. 4, effective April 3, 1993.

Ref.: 8 C.C.R. §10541; Hanna §§ 3.03, 3.05, 3.61, 5.05[9][b], 21.03[4][c]; Herlick Handbook §§ 14.6, 14.18; W. Cal. Ev., "Introduction" §61; W. Cal. Sum., 2 "Workers' Compensation" §§172, 325.

§5706. Appeals board authority to order autopsy.

Where it is represented to the appeals board, either before or after the filing of an application, that an employee has died as a result of injuries sustained in the course of his employment, the appeals board may require an autopsy. The report of the physician performing the autopsy may be received in evidence in any proceedings theretofore or thereafter brought. If at the time the autopsy is requested, the body of the employee is in the custody of the coroner, the coroner shall, upon the request of the appeals board or of any party interested, afford reasonable opportunity for the attendance of any physicians named by the appeals board at any autopsy ordered by him. If the coroner does not require, or has already performed the autopsy, he shall permit an autopsy or reexamination to be performed by physicians named by the appeals board. No fee shall be charged by the coroner for any service, arrangement, or permission given by him.

Ref.: 8 C.C.R. §10342; Hanna § 22.07[5]; Herlick Handbook §§ 9.15, 14.20, 14.38.

§5707. Appeals board limited authority to order autopsy when body not in coroner's custody.

If the body of a deceased employee is not in the custody of the coroner, the appeals board may authorize the performance of such autopsy and, if necessary, the exhumation of the body therefor. If the dependents, or a majority thereof, of any such deceased employee, having the custody of the body refuse to allow the autopsy, it shall not be performed. In such case, upon the hearing of any application for compensation it is a disputable presumption that the injury or death was not due to causes entitling the claimants to benefits under this division.

Ref.: 8 C.C.R. §10342; Hanna § 31.12[1]; Herlick Handbook §§ 9.15, 14.38.

§5708. Appeals board authority to conduct hearings by own rules.

All hearings and investigations before the appeals board or a workers' compensation judge are governed by this division and by the rules of practice and procedures adopted by the appeals board. In the conduct thereof they shall not be bound by the common law or statutory rules of evidence and procedure, but may make inquiry in the manner, through oral testimony and records, which is best calculated to ascertain the substantial rights of the parties and carry out justly the spirit and provisions of this division. All oral testimony, objections, and rulings shall be taken down in shorthand by a competent phonographic reporter.

Ref.: 8 C.C.R. §§10324, 10490, 10541, 10560, 10562, 10563, 10589, 10591, 10600, 10601, 10602, 10604, 10605, 10606, 10607, 10608, 10609, 10610, 10616, 10618, 10622, 10727, 10740, 10750, 10754, 10762, 10957, 10958; Hanna §§ 23.10[1], 25.41[2], 26.06[4]; Herlick Handbook § 14.5; W. Cal. Ev., "Introduction" §55; W. Cal. Sum., 2 "Workers' Compensation" §§345, 398.

§5709. Informality in proceedings; no effect on validity.

No informality in any proceeding or in the manner of taking testimony shall invalidate any order, decision, award, or rule made and filed as specified in this division. No order, decision, award, or rule shall be invalidated because of the admission into the record, and use as proof of any fact in dispute, of any evidence not admissible under the common law or statutory rules of evidence and procedure.

Ref.: 8 C.C.R. §§10541, 10600, 10601, 10604, 10606, 10608, 10609, 10616, 10618, 10619, 10620, 10622, 10957, 10958; Hanna § 26.06[1]; W. Cal. Ev., "Introduction" §67; W. Cal. Sum., 2 "Workers' Compensation" §394.

§5710. Deposition of witnesses.

(a) The appeals board, a workers' compensation judge, or any party to the action or proceeding, may, in any investigation or hearing before the appeals board, cause the deposition of witnesses residing within or without the state to be taken in the manner prescribed by law for like depositions in civil actions in the superior courts of this state under Title 4 (commencing with Section 2016.010) of Part 4 of the Code of Civil Procedure. To that end the attendance of witnesses and the production of records may be required. Depositions may be taken outside the state before any officer authorized to administer oaths. The appeals board or a workers' compensation judge in any proceeding before the appeals board may cause evidence to be taken in other jurisdictions before the agency authorized to hear workers' compensation matters in those other jurisdictions.

(b) Where the employer or insurance carrier requests a deposition to be taken of an injured employee, or any person claiming benefits as a dependent of an injured employee, the deponent is entitled to receive in addition to all other benefits:

(1) All reasonable expenses of transportation, meals, and lodging incident to the deposition.

(2) Reimbursement for any loss of wages incurred during attendance at the deposition.

(3) A copy of the transcript of the deposition, without cost.

(4) A reasonable allowance for attorney's fees for the deponent, if represented by an attorney licensed by the State Bar of this state. The fee shall be discretionary with, and, if allowed, shall be set by, the appeals board, but shall be paid by the employer or his or her insurer.

(5) A reasonable allowance for interpreter's fees for the deponent, if interpretation services are needed and provided by a language interpreter certified or deemed certified pursuant to Article 8 (commencing with Section 11435.05) of Chapter 4.5 of Part 1 of Division 3 of Title 2 of, or Section 68566 of, the Government Code. The fee shall be in accordance with the fee schedule set by the administrative director and paid by the employer or his or her insurer. Payment for interpreter's services shall be allowed for deposition of a non-English-speaking injured worker, and for any other deposition-related events as permitted by the administrative director. **Leg.H.** 1991 ch. 116, 1993 ch. 121, effective July 16, 1993, 1995 ch. 938, operative July 1, 1997, 1998 ch. 931, effective September 28, 1998, 2004 ch. 182 (AB 3081), operative July 1, 2005.

1993 Note: Section 5710, as amended by ch. 121, applies only to injuries occurring on or after January 1, 1994. Stats. 1993 ch. 121 §77.

Ref.: 8 C.C.R. §§9795.1, 9795.2, 9795.3, 9795.4, 10536, 10564, 10890; Hanna § 25.41[2]; Herlick Handbook §§ 10.2, 14.20, 14.33, 14.40, 14.43; W. Cal. Ev., "Introduction" §81; W. Cal. Sum., 2 "Workers' Compensation" §§359, 396, 406.

CHAPTER 6
FINDINGS AND AWARDS

§5800. Interest on compensation or death benefit payments.

All awards of the appeals board either for the payment of compensation or for the payment of death benefits, shall carry interest at the same rate as judgments in civil actions on all due and unpaid payments from the date of the making and filing of said award. Such interest shall run from the date of making and filing of an award, as to amounts which by the terms of the award are payable forthwith. As to amounts which under the terms of the award subsequently become due in installments or otherwise, such interest shall run from the date when each such amount becomes due and payable.

Ref.: 8 C.C.R. §§10111, 10111.1, 10111.2; Hanna § 27.01[7]; Herlick Handbook §§ 9.12, 14.41; W. Cal. Sum., 2 "Workers' Compensation" §§18, 403, 404, 411.

§5800.5. Clarification of §5313.

The 30-day period specified in Section 5313, shall run from the date of the submission of the application for decision and the provisions requiring the decision within such 30-day period shall be deemed mandatory and not merely directive.

Ref.: W. Cal. Sum., 2 "Workers' Compensation" §403.

§5801. Appeals board determination of payment matters; attorney's fees.

The appeals board in its award may fix and determine the total amount of compensation to be paid and specify the manner of payment, or may fix and determine the weekly disability payment to be made and order payment thereof during the continuance of disability.

In the event the injured employee or the dependent of a deceased employee prevails in any petition by the employer for a writ of review from an award of the appeals board and the reviewing court finds that there is no reasonable basis for the petition, it shall remand the cause to the appeals board for the purpose of making a supplemental award awarding to the injured employee or his attorney, or the dependent of a deceased employee or his attorney a reasonable attorney's fee for services rendered in connection with the petition for writ of review. Any such fee shall be in addition to the amount of compensation otherwise recoverable and shall be paid as part of the award by the party liable to pay such award.

Ref.: Hanna §§ 20.02[2][l], 34.24; Herlick Handbook §§ 14.42, 15.6; W. Cal. Sum., 2 "Workers' Compensation" §§357, 358, 439.

§5802. Nominal disability indemnity.

If, in any proceeding under this division, it is proved that an injury has been suffered for which the employer would be liable to pay compensation if disability had resulted therefrom, but it is not proved that any disability has resulted, the appeals board may, instead of dismissing the application, award a nominal disability indemnity, if it appears that disability is likely to result at a future time.

§5803. Appeals board continuing jurisdiction.

The appeals board has continuing jurisdiction over all its orders, decisions, and awards made and entered under the provisions of this division, and the decisions and orders of the rehabilitation unit established under Section 139.5. At any time, upon notice and after an opportunity to be heard is given to the parties in interest, the appeals board may rescind, alter, or amend any order, decision, or award, good cause appearing therefor.

This power includes the right to review, grant or regrant, diminish, increase, or terminate, within the limits prescribed by this division, any compensation awarded, upon the grounds that the disability of the person in whose favor the award was made has either recurred, increased, diminished, or terminated.

Ref.: 8 C.C.R. §§10454, 10455, 10458; Hanna §§ 21.08[1], 26.01[3], 29.05[3], 31.04[2][a]; Herlick Handbook §§ 14.7, 14.9; W. Cal. Sum., 2 "Workers' Compensation" §§296, 415, 426, 427, 429, 430, 432.

§5803.5. Grounds for reconsideration of order, decision, or award.

Any conviction pursuant to Section 1871.4 of the Insurance Code that materially affects the basis of any order, decision, or award of the appeals board shall be sufficient grounds for a reconsideration of that order, decision, or award. **Leg.H.** 1991 ch. 116.

Ref.: Hanna § 28.02; Herlick Handbook §§ 9.18, 14.18, 15.4.

§5804. Altering award after five years.

No award of compensation shall be rescinded, altered, or amended after five years from the date of the injury except upon a petition by a party in interest filed within such five years and any counterpetition seeking other relief filed by the adverse party within 30 days of the original petition raising issues in addition to those raised by such original petition. Provided, however, that after an award has been made finding that there was employment and the time to petition for a rehearing or reconsideration or review has expired or such petition if made has been determined, the appeals board upon a petition to reopen shall not have the power to find that there was no employment.

Ref.: 8 C.C.R. §10102; Hanna §§ 24.03[4], 24.13[2], 31.04[1][a], 31.04[1][c], 31.04[3]; Herlick Handbook §§ 14.34, 15.3, 15.4, 16.14; W. Cal. Sum., 2 "Workers' Compensation" §§180, 290, 296, 378, 383, 415, 421, 426, 430, 432.

§5805. Effect of altered decision.

Any order, decision, or award rescinding, altering or amending a prior order, decision, or award shall have the effect herein provided for original orders, decisions, and awards.

Ref.: Herlick Handbook §§ 14.9, 14.44, 1614.

§5806. Certified copy of decision; filing.

Any party affected thereby may file a certified copy of the findings and order, decision, or award of the appeals board with the clerk of the superior court of any county. Judgment shall be entered immediately by the clerk in conformity therewith. The words "any party affected thereby" include the Uninsured Employers Fund. In any case in which the findings and order, decision, or award of the appeals board is against an employer that has failed to secure the payment of compensation, the State of California on behalf of the Uninsured Employers Fund shall be entitled to have judgment entered not only against the employer, but also against any person found to be parents or substantial shareholders under Section 3717. **Leg.H.** 1992 ch. 1226.

Ref.: 8 C.C.R. §§10820, 10825, 10828; Hanna § 27.11[2][a]; MB Prac. Guide: Cal. Debt Collection & Enforcement of Judgments, §§17.06, 24.05[5]; W. Cal. Sum., 2 "Workers' Compensation" §§152, 154, 155, 410, 411.

§5807. Certified copy as judgment roll.

The certified copy of the findings and order, decision, or award of the appeals board and a copy of the judgment constitute the judgment-roll. The pleadings, all orders of the appeals board, its original findings and order, decision, or award, and all other papers and documents filed in the cause shall remain on file in the office of the appeals board.

Ref.: 8 C.C.R. §§10820, 10825, 10828.

§5808. Stay of execution of appeals board decision.

The appeals board or a member thereof may stay the execution of any judgment entered upon an order, decision, or award of the appeals board, upon good cause appearing therefor and may impose the terms and conditions of the stay of execution. A certified copy of such order shall be filed with the clerk entering judgment. Where it is desirable to stay the enforcement of an order, decision, or award and a certified copy thereof and of the findings has not been issued, the appeals board or a member thereof may order the certified copy to be withheld with the same force and under the same conditions as it might issue a stay of execution if the certified copy had been issued and judgment entered thereon.

Ref.: 8 C.C.R. §§10820, 10825, 10828; Hanna §§ 27.10[3][b], 27.11[3][a]–[b].

§5809. Satisfaction of judgment in fact.

When a judgment is satisfied in fact, otherwise than upon an execution, the appeals board may, upon motion of either party or of its own motion, order the entry of satisfaction of the judgment. The clerk shall enter satisfaction of judgment only upon the filing of a certified copy of such order.

Ref.: 8 C.C.R. §§10820, 10825, 10828; Hanna § 27.11[4][a]; MB Prac. Guide: Cal. Debt Collection & Enforcement of Judgments, §§17.06, 24.05[5].

§5810. Court review.

The orders, findings, decisions, or awards of the appeals board made and entered under this division may be reviewed by the courts specified in Sections 5950 and 5956 within the time and in the manner therein specified and not otherwise.

Ref.: Hanna § 34.03[1]; Herlick Handbook § 14.41.

§5811. Limited fees; appeals board allowance of costs; interpreter fees.

(a) No fees shall be charged by the clerk of any court for the performance of any official service required by this division, except for the docketing of awards as judgments and for certified copies of transcripts thereof. In all proceedings under this division before the appeals board, costs as between the parties may be allowed by the appeals board.

(b) It shall be the responsibility of any party producing a witness requiring an interpreter to arrange for the presence of a qualified interpreter. A qualified interpreter is a language interpreter who is certified, or deemed certified, pursuant to Article 8 (commencing with Section 11435.05) of Chapter 4.5 of Part 1 of Division 3 of Title 2 of, or Section 68566 of, the Government Code.

Interpreter fees which are reasonably, actually, and necessarily incurred shall be allowed as cost under this section, provided they are in accordance with the fee schedule set by the administrative director.

A qualified interpreter may render services during the following:

(1) A deposition.

(2) An appeals board hearing.

(3) During those settings which the administrative director determines are reasonably necessary to ascertain the validity or extent of injury to an employee who cannot communicate in English. **Leg.H.** 1993 ch. 121, effective July 16, 1993, 1995 ch. 938, operative July 1, 1997.

1993 Note: Section 5811, as amended by ch. 121, applies only to injuries occurring on or after January 1, 1994. Stats. 1993 ch. 121 §77.

Ref.: 8 C.C.R. §§9795.1, 9795.2, 9795.3, 9795.4, 10322, 10564; Hanna §§ 23.13[3], 23.13[4], 27.01[8][a], 34.23; Herlick Handbook §§ 14.33, 14.42; W. Cal. Sum., 2 "Workers' Compensation" §§396, 439.

§5813. Sanctions for bad-faith actions or tactics.

(a) The workers' compensation referee or appeals board may order a party, the party's attorney, or both, to pay any reasonable expenses, including attorney's fees and costs, incurred by another party as a result of bad-faith actions or tactics that are frivolous or solely intended to cause unnecessary delay. In addition, a workers' compensation referee or the appeals board, in its sole discretion, may order additional sanctions not to exceed two thousand five hundred dollars ($2,500) to be transmitted to the General Fund.

(b) The determination of sanctions shall be made after written application by the party seeking sanctions or upon the appeal board's own motion.

(c) This section shall apply to all applications for adjudication that are filed on or after January 1, 1994. **Leg.H.** 1993 ch. 121, effective July 16, 1993, ch. 1242.

Ref.: 8 C.C.R. §§10414, 10416, 10561, 10592; Hanna § 23.15; Herlick Handbook §§ 3.2, 10.2, 11.1, 14.42; W. Cal. Sum., 2 "Workers' Compensation" §§361, 414.

§5814. Unreasonable delay or refusal of payment of compensation; increase; self-imposed penalty; conclusive presumption on approval of compromise and release, etc.; actions; applicability.

(a) When payment of compensation has been unreasonably delayed or refused, either prior to or subsequent to the issuance of an award, the amount of the payment unreasonably delayed or refused shall be increased up to 25 percent or up to ten thousand dollars ($10,000), whichever is less. In any proceeding under this section, the appeals board shall use its discretion to accomplish a fair balance and substantial justice between the parties.

(b) If a potential violation of this section is discovered by the employer prior to an employee claiming a penalty under this section, the employer, within 90 days of the date of the discovery, may pay a self-imposed penalty in the amount of 10 percent of the amount of the payment unreasonably delayed or refused, along with the amount of the payment delayed or refused. This self-imposed penalty shall be in lieu of the penalty in subdivision (a).

(c) Upon the approval of a compromise and release, findings and awards, or stipulations and orders by the appeals board, it shall be conclusively presumed that any accrued claims for penalty have been resolved, regardless of whether a petition for penalty has been filed, unless the claim for penalty is expressly excluded by the terms of the order or award. Upon the submission of any issue for determination at a regular trial hearing, it shall be conclusively presumed that any accrued claim for penalty in connection with the benefit at issue has been resolved, regardless of whether a petition for penalty has been filed, unless the issue of penalty is also submitted or is expressly excluded in the statement of issues being submitted.

(d) The payment of any increased award pursuant to subdivision (a) shall be reduced by any amount paid under subdivision (d) of Section 4650 on the same unreasonably delayed or refused benefit payment.

(e) No unreasonable delay in the provision of medical treatment shall be found when the treatment has been authorized by the employer in a timely manner and the only dispute concerns payment of a billing submitted by a physician or medical provider as provided in Section 4603.2.

(f) Nothing in this section shall be construed to create a civil cause of action.

(g) Notwithstanding any other provision of law, no action may be brought to recover penalties that may be awarded under this section more than two years from the date the payment of compensation was due.

(h) This section shall apply to all injuries, without regard to whether the injury occurs before, on, or after the operative date of this section.

(i) This section shall become operative on June 1, 2004. **Leg.H.** 2004 ch. 34 (SB 899) §43, effective April 19, 2004.

2004 Note: The addition of §5814 made by this act shall apply prospectively from the date of enactment of this act, regardless of the date of injury, unless otherwise specified, but shall not constitute good cause to reopen or rescind, alter, or amend any existing order, decision, or award of the Workers' Compensation Appeals Board. Stats. 2004 ch. 34 (SB 899) §47.

Ref.: 8 C.C.R. §§10109, 10111, 10111.1, 10111.2; Hanna §§ 10.40[1], [3]–[6], 27.12[2][a], [c]–[d]; Herlick Handbook § 9.5; W. Cal. Sum., 2 "Workers' Compensation" §§4, 18, 31, 38, 282, 412, 413.

§5814.1. Employer's penalty paid to director.

When the payment of compensation has been unreasonably delayed or refused prior to the issuance of an award, and the director has provided discretionary compensation pursuant to Section 4903.3, the appeals board shall award to the director a penalty to be paid by the employer in the amount of 10 percent of the compensation so provided by the director, such penalty to be in addition to the penalty imposed by Section 5814. The question of delay and the reasonableness of the cause therefor shall be determined by the appeals board in accordance with the facts.

Ref.: Herlick Handbook § 3.19.

§5814.5. Reasonable attorneys' fees awarded when payment of compensation delayed or refused.

When the payment of compensation has been unreasonably delayed or refused subsequent to the issuance of an award by an employer that has secured the payment of compensation pursuant to Section 3700, the appeals board shall, in addition to increasing the order, decision, or award pursuant to Section 5814, award reasonable attorneys' fees incurred in enforcing the payment of compensation awarded. **Leg.H.** 2002 ch. 6 (AB 749).

Ref.: Hanna §§ 10.42, 27.12[5]; Herlick Handbook § 10.2.

§5814.6. Administrative penalties for knowing violation of §5814.

(a) Any employer or insurer that knowingly violates Section 5814 with a frequency that indicates a general business practice is liable for administrative penalties of not to exceed four hundred thousand dollars ($400,000). Penalty payments shall be imposed by the administrative director and deposited into the Return-to-Work Fund established pursuant to Section 139.48.

(b) The administrative director may impose a penalty under either this section or subdivision (e) of Section 129.5.

(c) This section shall become operative on June 1, 2004. **Leg.H.** 2004 ch. 34 (SB 899), effective April 19, 2004.

2004 Note: The addition of §5814.6 made by this act shall apply prospectively from the date of enactment of this act, regardless of the date of injury, unless otherwise specified, but shall not constitute good cause to reopen or rescind, alter, or amend any existing order, decision, or award of the Workers' Compensation Appeals Board. Stats. 2004 ch. 34 (SB 899) §47.

Ref.: Hanna §§ 10.40[1], 27.12[2][b]; Herlick Handbook § 9.5; W. Cal. Sum., 2 "Workers' Compensation" §413.

§5815. Statement of determination of issues raised.

Every order, decision or award, other than an order merely appointing a trustee or guardian, shall contain a determination of all issues presented for determination by the appeals board prior thereto and not theretofore determined. Any issue not so determined will be deemed decided adversely as to the party in whose interest such issue was raised.

Ref.: W. Cal. Sum., 2 "Workers' Compensation" §404.

§5816. No collateral estoppel effect on subsequent criminal proceedings.

A determination of facts by the appeals board under this chapter has no collateral estoppel effect on a subsequent criminal prosecution and does not preclude litigation of those same facts in the criminal proceeding. **Leg.H.** 1995 ch. 158.

Ref.: Herlick Handbook § 9.18; W. Cal. Sum., 2 "Workers' Compensation" §§404, 417.

CHAPTER 7 RECONSIDERATION AND JUDICIAL REVIEW

ARTICLE 1 Reconsideration

§5900. Reconsideration; petition.

(a) Any person aggrieved directly or indirectly by any final order, decision, or award made and filed by the appeals board or a workers' compensation judge under any provision contained in this division, may petition the appeals board for reconsideration in respect to any matters determined or covered by the final order, decision, or award, and specified in the petition for reconsideration. The petition shall be made only within the time and in the manner specified in this chapter.

(b) At any time within 60 days after the filing of an order, decision, or award made by a workers' compensation judge and the accompanying report, the appeals board may, on its own motion, grant reconsideration.

Ref.: 8 C.C.R. §§10352, 10840, 10842, 10848, 10860, 10864, 10866, 10867; Hanna §§ 28.01[1]–[3], 28.05, 28.20, 34.10; Herlick Handbook §§ 15.1, 15.3, 15.5; MB Prac. Guide: Cal. Debt Collection & Enforcement of Judgments, §17.06; W. Cal. Sum., 2 "Workers' Compensation" §§13, 14, 351, 418, 425, 426.

§5901. Accrual of cause of action in court.

No cause of action arising out of any final order, decision or award made and filed by the appeals board or a workers' compensation judge shall accrue in any court to any person until and unless the appeals board on its own motion sets aside the final order, decision, or award and removes the proceeding to itself or if the person files a petition for reconsideration, and the reconsideration is granted or denied. Nothing herein contained shall prevent the enforcement of any final order, decision, or award, in the manner provided in this division.

Ref.: 8 C.C.R. §§10352, 10866, 10867; MB Prac. Guide: Cal. Debt Collection & Enforcement of Judgments, §17.06; W. Cal. Sum., 2 "Workers' Compensation" §418.

§5902. Requirements of petition for reconsideration.

The petition for reconsideration shall set forth specifically and in full detail the grounds upon which the petitioner considers the final order, decision or award made and filed by the appeals board or a workers' compensation judge to be unjust or unlawful, and every issue to be considered by the appeals board. The petition shall be verified upon oath in the manner required for verified pleadings in courts of record and shall contain a general statement of any evidence or other matters upon which the applicant relies in support thereof.

Ref.: 8 C.C.R. §§10352, 10842, 10846, 10850, 10852, 10856, 10866, 10867; Herlick Handbook § 15.4; MB Prac. Guide: Cal. Debt Collection & Enforcement of Judgments, §17.06; W. Cal. Sum., 2 "Workers' Compensation" §419.

§5903. Grounds for reconsideration.

At any time within 20 days after the service of any final order, decision, or award made and filed by the appeals board or a workers' compensation judge granting or denying compensation, or arising out of or incidental thereto, any person aggrieved thereby may petition for reconsideration upon one or more of the following grounds and no other:

(a) That by the order, decision, or award made and filed by the appeals board or a the workers' compensation judge, the appeals board acted without or in excess of its powers.

(b) That the order, decision, or award was procured by fraud.

(c) That the evidence does not justify the findings of fact.

(d) That the petitioner has discovered new evidence material to him or her, which he or she could not, with reasonable diligence, have discovered and produced at the hearing.

(e) That the findings of fact do not support the order, decision, or award.

Nothing contained in this section shall limit the grant of continuing jurisdiction contained in Sections 5803 to 5805, inclusive.

Ref.: 8 C.C.R. §§10352, 10850, 10852, 10856, 10866, 10867; Hanna §§ 28.02, 28.22[1], 28.22[2], 28.25; Herlick Handbook §§ 14.34, 15.4; MB Prac. Guide: Cal. Debt Collection & Enforcement of Judgments, §17.06; W. Cal. Sum., 2 "Workers' Compensation" §§418–420.

§5904. Waiver of irregularities.

The petitioner for reconsideration shall be deemed to have finally waived all objections, irregularities, and illegalities concerning the matter upon which the reconsideration is sought other than those set forth in the petition for reconsideration.

Ref.: 8 C.C.R. §§10352, 10866, 10867; Hanna §§ 28.06, 34.20; Herlick Handbook § 15.4; MB Prac. Guide: Cal. Debt Collection & Enforcement of Judgments, §17.06; W. Cal. Sum., 2 "Workers' Compensation" §419.

§5905. Petition for reconsideration; service; answer.

A copy of the petition for reconsideration shall be served forthwith upon all adverse parties by the person petitioning for reconsideration. Any adverse party may file an answer thereto within 10 days thereafter. Such answer shall likewise be verified. The appeals board may require the petition for reconsideration to be served on other persons designated by it.

Ref.: 8 C.C.R. §§10352, 10840, 10866, 10867; Hanna §§ 28.23, 28.24; Herlick Handbook § 15.3; MB Prac. Guide: Cal. Debt Collection & Enforcement of Judgments, §17.06; W. Cal. Sum., 2 "Workers' Compensation" §420.

§5906. Petition for reconsideration; notice of hearings on reconsideration.

Upon the filing of a petition for reconsideration, or having granted reconsideration upon its own motion, the appeals board may, with or without further proceedings and with or without notice affirm, rescind, alter, or amend the order, decision, or award made and filed by the appeals board or the workers' compensation judge on the basis of the evidence previously submitted in the case, or may grant reconsideration and direct the taking of additional evidence. Notice of the time and place of any hearing on reconsideration shall be given to the petitioner and adverse parties and to other persons as the appeals board orders.

Ref.: 8 C.C.R. §§10352, 10859, 10860, 10866, 10867; Herlick Handbook §§ 4.20, 15.3, 15.4; MB Prac. Guide: Cal. Debt Collection & Enforcement of Judgments, §17.06; W. Cal. Sum., 2 "Workers' Compensation" §§400, 422.

§5907. Decision without hearing.

If, at the time of granting reconsideration, it appears to the satisfaction of the appeals board that no sufficient reason exists for taking further testimony, the appeals board may affirm, rescind, alter, or amend the order, decision, or award made and filed by the appeals board or the workers' compensation judge and may, without further proceedings, without notice, and without setting a time and place for further hearing, enter its findings, order, decision, or award based upon the record in the case. **Leg.H.** 1937 ch. 90, 1951 ch. 778 §21, 1965 ch. 1513 §177, operative January 15, 1966, 1985 ch. 326 §32, 2006 ch. 538 (SB 1852) §492.

Ref.: 8 C.C.R. §§10352, 10859, 10866, 10867; Hanna §§ 28.33[2], 28.36[2][b]; MB Prac. Guide: Cal. Debt Collection & Enforcement of Judgments, §17.06; W. Cal. Sum., 2 "Workers' Compensation" §422.

§5908. Effect of order on reconsideration.

(a) After the taking of additional evidence and a consideration of all of the facts the appeals board may affirm, rescind, alter, or amend the original order, decision, or award. An order, decision, or award made following reconsideration which affirms, rescinds, alters, or amends the original order, decision, or award shall be made by the appeals board but shall not affect any right or the enforcement of any right arising from or by virtue of the original order, decision, or award, unless so ordered by the appeals board.

(b) In any case where the appeals board rescinds or reduces an order, decision, or award on the grounds specified in paragraph (b) of Section 5903, the appeals board shall refer the case to the Bureau of Fraudulent Claims pursuant to Article 4 (commencing with Section 12990) of Chapter 2 of Division 3 of the Insurance Code, if the employer is insured, or to the district attorney of the county in which the fraud occurred if the employer is self-insured.

1989 Note: This section is applicable only to injuries occurring on or after January 1, 1990. Stats. 1989 ch. 893 §6.

Ref.: 8 C.C.R. §§10352, 10866, 10867; Herlick Handbook §§ 9.18, 15.3; MB Prac. Guide: Cal. Debt Collection & Enforcement of Judgments, §17.06; W. Cal. Sum., 2 "Workers' Compensation" §422.

§5908.5. Decision on reconsideration.

Any decision of the appeals board granting or denying a petition for reconsideration or affirming, rescinding, altering, or amending the original findings, order, decision, or award following reconsideration shall be made by the appeals board and not by a workers' compensation judge and shall be in writing, signed by a majority of the appeals board members assigned thereto, and shall state the evidence relied upon and specify in detail the reasons for the decision.

The requirements of this section shall in no way be construed so as to broaden the scope of judicial review as provided for in Article 2 (commencing with Section 5950) of this chapter.

Ref.: 8 C.C.R. §§10352, 10859, 10866, 10867; Hanna §§ 28.36[2][c], 34.17[1]; Herlick Handbook §§ 10.2, 15.3; MB Prac. Guide: Cal. Debt Collection & Enforcement of Judgments, §17.06; W. Cal. Sum., 2 "Workers' Compensation" §§421–424.

§5909. Denial of reconsideration.

A petition for reconsideration is deemed to have been denied by the appeals board unless it is acted upon within 60 days from the date of filing. **Leg.H.** 1992 ch. 1226.

Ref.: 8 C.C.R. §§10352, 10866, 10867; Hanna § 28.32; Herlick Handbook § 15.4; MB Prac. Guide: Cal. Debt Collection & Enforcement of Judgments, §17.06; W. Cal. Sum., 2 "Workers' Compensation" §423.

§5910. Filing petition for reconsideration.

The filing of a petition for reconsideration shall suspend for a period of 10 days the order, decision, or award affected, in so far as it applies to the parties to the petition, unless otherwise ordered by the appeals board. The appeals board upon the terms and conditions which it by order directs, may stay, suspend, or postpone the order, decision, or award during the pendency of the reconsideration.

Ref.: 8 C.C.R. §§10352, 10864, 10866, 10867; Hanna § 27.10[2][d]; MB Prac. Guide: Cal. Debt Collection & Enforcement of Judgments, §17.06; W. Cal. Sum., 2 "Workers' Compensation" §420.

§5911. Limitations on article.

Nothing contained in this article shall be construed to prevent the appeals board, on petition of an aggrieved party or on its own motion, from granting reconsideration of an original order, decision, or award made and filed by the appeals board within the same time specified for reconsideration of an original order, decision, or award.

Ref.: 8 C.C.R. §§10352, 10864, 10866, 10867; Hanna § 24.12[2]; Herlick Handbook § 15.3; MB Prac. Guide: Cal. Debt Collection & Enforcement of Judgments, §17.06.

ARTICLE 2
Judicial Review

§5950. Writ of review; time limit for filing.

Any person affected by an order, decision, or award of the appeals board may, within the time limit specified in this section, apply to the Supreme Court or to the court of appeal for the appellate district in which he resides, for a writ of review, for the purpose of inquiring into and determining the lawfulness of the original order, decision, or award or of the order, decision, or award following reconsideration. The application for writ of review must be made within 45 days after a petition for reconsideration is denied, or, if a petition is granted or reconsideration is had on the appeals board's own motion, within 45 days after the filing of the order, decision, or award following reconsideration.

Ref.: Hanna §§ 28.32, 34.10[3], 34.11[1], 34.12[1]; Herlick Handbook § 15.6; MB Prac. Guide: Cal. Debt Collection & Enforcement of Judgments, §17.06; W. Cal. Sum., 2 "Workers' Compensation" §§434, 436–438.

§5951. Writ of review; based on record of appeals board.

The writ of review shall be made returnable at a time and place then or thereafter specified by court order and shall direct the appeals board to certify its record in the case to the court within the time therein specified. No new or additional evidence shall be introduced in such court, but the cause shall be heard on the record of the appeals board, as certified to by it.

Ref.: Herlick Handbook § 15.6; MB Prac. Guide: Cal. Debt Collection & Enforcement of Judgments, §17.06; W. Cal. Sum., 2 "Workers' Compensation" §439.

§5952. Extent of review.

The review by the court shall not be extended further than to determine, based upon the entire record which shall be certified by the appeals board, whether:

(a) The appeals board acted without or in excess of its powers.

(b) The order, decision, or award was procured by fraud.

(c) The order, decision, or award was unreasonable.

(d) The order, decision, or award was not supported by substantial evidence.

(e) If findings of fact are made, such findings of fact support the order, decision, or award under review.

Nothing in this section shall permit the court to hold a trial de novo, or take evidence, or to exercise its independent judgment on the evidence.

Ref.: Hanna §§ 27.01[1][c], 34.16[1]–[2], 34.18[1]–[2]; Herlick Handbook § 15.6; MB Prac. Guide: Cal. Debt Collection & Enforcement of Judgments, §17.06; W. Cal. Sum., 2 "Workers' Compensation" §§439, 441–443.

§5953. Appeals board's findings of fact are final; right to appear at hearing.

The findings and conclusions of the appeals board on questions of fact are conclusive and final and are not subject to review. Such questions of fact shall include ultimate facts and the findings and conclusions of the appeals board. The appeals board and each party to the action or proceeding before the appeals board shall have the right to appear in the review proceeding. Upon the hearing, the court shall enter judgment either affirming or annulling the order, decision, or award, or the court may remand the case for further proceedings before the appeals board.

Ref.: Herlick Handbook § 15.6; MB Prac. Guide: Cal. Debt Collection & Enforcement of Judgments, §17.06; W. Cal. Sum., 2 "Workers' Compensation" §§439, 443.

§5954. Code of Civil Procedure governs proceedings; service of pleadings.

The provisions of the Code of Civil Procedure relating to writs of review shall, so far as applicable, apply to proceedings in the courts under the provisions of this article. A copy of every pleading filed pursuant to the terms of this article shall be served on the appeals board and upon every party who entered an appearance in the action before the appeals board and whose interest therein is adverse to the party filing such pleading.

Ref.: MB Prac. Guide: Cal. Debt Collection & Enforcement of Judgments, §17.06; W. Cal. Sum., 2 "Workers' Compensation" §438.

§5955. Exclusive jurisdiction of Supreme Court or appellate courts.

No court of this state, except the Supreme Court and the courts of appeal to the extent herein specified, has jurisdiction to review, reverse, correct, or annul any order, rule, decision, or award of the appeals board, or to suspend or delay the operation or execution thereof, or to restrain, enjoin, or interfere with the appeals board in the performance of its duties but a writ of mandate shall lie from the Supreme Court or a court of appeal in all proper cases.

Ref.: Hanna §§ 34.02, 34.03[2]–[3]; MB Prac. Guide: Cal. Debt Collection & Enforcement of Judgments, §17.06; W. Cal. Sum., 2 "Workers' Compensation" §§434, 435.

§5956. Stay of appeals board decision not automatic.

The filing of a petition for, or the pendency of, a writ of review shall not of itself stay or suspend the operation of any order, rule, decision, or award of the appeals board, but the court before which the petition is filed may stay or suspend, in whole or in part, the operation of the order, decision, or award of the appeals board subject to review, upon the terms and conditions which it by order directs, except as provided in Article 3 of this chapter.

Ref.: 8 C.C.R. §10828; MB Prac. Guide: Cal. Debt Collection & Enforcement of Judgments, §17.06; W. Cal. Sum., 2 "Workers' Compensation" §438.

ARTICLE 3
Undertaking on Stay Order

§6000. Limitations on authority of reviewing court to issue stay order.

The operation of any order, decision, or award of the appeals board under the provisions of this division or any judgment entered thereon, shall not at any time be stayed by the court to which petition is made for a writ of review, unless an undertaking is executed on the part of the petitioner.

Ref.: 8 C.C.R. §§10342, 10344, 10820, 10825, 10828; MB Prac. Guide: Cal. Debt Collection & Enforcement of Judgments, §17.06; W. Cal. Sum., 2 "Workers' Compensation" §438.

§6001. Undertaking.

The undertaking shall provide that:

(a) The petitioner and sureties are bound in double the amount named in such order, decision, or award.

(b) If the order, decision, or award appealed from, or any part thereof, is affirmed, or the proceeding upon review is dismissed, the petitioner will pay the amount directed to be paid by the order, decision, or award or the part of such amount as to which the order, decision, or award is affirmed, and all damages and costs which are awarded against the petitioner.

(c) If the petitioner does not make such payment within 30 days after the filing with the appeals board of the remittitur from the reviewing court, judgment in favor of the adverse party may be entered on motion of the adverse party, and the undertaking shall apply to any judgment entered thereon. Such judgment may be entered in any superior court in which a certified copy of the order, decision, or award is filed, against the sureties for such amount, together with interest that is due thereon, and the damages and costs which are awarded against the petitioner. The provisions of the Code of Civil Procedure, except insofar as they are inconsistent with this division, are applicable to the undertaking.

Ref.: 8 C.C.R. §§10342, 10344, 10820, 10825, 10828; MB Prac. Guide: Cal. Debt Collection & Enforcement of Judgments, §17.06.

§6002. Filing of undertaking with appeals board.

The undertaking shall be filed with the appeals board. The certificate of the appeals board or any proper officer thereof, of the filing and approval of such undertaking, is sufficient evidence of the compliance of the petitioner with the provisions of this article.

Ref.: 8 C.C.R. §§10342, 10344, 10346, 10820, 10825, 10828; MB Prac. Guide: Cal. Debt Collection & Enforcement of Judgments, §17.06.

DIVISION 4.5 WORKERS' COMPENSATION AND INSURANCE: STATE EMPLOYEES NOT OTHERWISE COVERED

CHAPTER 1 GENERAL PROVISIONS

§6100. Purpose of division.

The purpose of this division is to effect economy, efficiency and continuity in the public service by providing means for increasing the willingness of competent persons to assume the risk of injuries or death in State employment and for restoring experienced employees to productive work at the earliest possible moment following injury in the course of and arising out of State employment, irrespective of fault, in circumstances which make the injury or resulting death non-compensable under the provisions of Division 4 of this code.

Ref.: W. Cal. Ev., "Discovery" §§230, 236.

§6101. Definitions.

Unless the context otherwise requires, as used in this division:

(a) "State agency" means any agency, department, division, commission, board, bureau, officer, or other authority of the State of California.

(b) "Fund" means State Compensation Insurance Fund.

(c) "Appeals board" means the Workers' Compensation Appeals Board.

Ref.: W. Cal. Ev., "Discovery" §§230, 236.

CHAPTER 2 DIRECT PAYMENTS

§6110. Voluntary offering of benefits.

Any State agency may, by appropriate action, undertake to provide hospitalization, medical treatment and indemnity, including death benefits, to its employees and to their dependents for injury or death suffered from accident, irrespective of fault, occurring in the course of and arising out of the employment with such State agency, where the injury or death is not compensable under the provisions of Division 4 of this code.

Ref.: W. Cal. Ev., "Discovery" §§230, 236; W. Cal. Sum., 2 "Workers' Compensation" §192.

§6111. State Compensation Insurance Fund; master agreement to dispose of claims.

The State Compensation Insurance Fund may enter into a master agreement with the State Department of Finance to render services in accordance with the agreement in the adjustment and disposition of claims against any State agency arising under this chapter.

Ref.: W. Cal. Ev., "Discovery" §§230, 236.

§6112. Master agreement; uniform rates for state agencies.

The master agreement shall provide for the rendition of services at a uniform rate to all State agencies.

Ref.: W. Cal. Ev., "Discovery" §§230, 236.

§6113. Authorization for fund to make expenditures.

The fund may make all expenditures, including payments to claimants for medical care or for adjustment or settlement of claims.

Ref.: W. Cal. Ev., "Discovery" §§230, 236.

§6114. Reimbursement of expenditures by claimant's agency.

The agreement shall provide that the State agency whose officer or employee is a claimant shall reimburse the fund for the expenditures and for the actual cost of services rendered.

Ref.: W. Cal. Ev., "Discovery" §§230, 236.

§6115. Right of fund to recover from third parties.

The fund may in its own name, or in the name of the State agency for which services are performed, do any and all things necessary to recover on behalf of the State agency any and all amounts which an employer might recover from third persons under Chapter 5 of Part 1 of Division 4 of this code, or which an insurer might recover pursuant to Section 11662 of the Insurance Code, including the rights to commence and prosecute actions or to intervene in other court proceedings, or to compromise claims before or after commencement of suit.

Ref.: W. Cal. Ev., "Discovery" §§230, 236.

CHAPTER 3
INSURANCE

§6130. Insurance from other insurer.

In lieu of direct payments pursuant to Chapter 2 of this division, any State agency may obtain by insurance from the State Compensation Insurance Fund, if the fund accepts the risk when the application for insurance is made, otherwise from any other insurer, hospitalization, medical treatment, and indemnity, including death benefits, on behalf of its employees and of their dependents for injury or death suffered from accident, irrespective of fault, occurring in the course of and arising out of the employment with such State agency, where the injury or death is not compensable under the provisions of Division 4 of this Code.

Ref.: W. Cal. Ev., "Discovery" §§230, 236.

§6131. Payment of premium.

The premium for such insurance shall be a proper charge against any moneys appropriated for the support of or expenditure by such State agency. In case such State agency is supported by or authorized to expend moneys appropriated out of more than one fund, it may, with the approval of the Director of Finance, determine the proportion of such premium to be paid out of each such fund.

Ref.: W. Cal. Ev., "Discovery" §§230, 236.

CHAPTER 4
BENEFITS AND PROCEDURE

§6140. Benefits employees entitled to.

The hospitalization, medical treatment, and indemnity, including death benefits, provided pursuant to this division shall be the same as provided by Division 4 of this code for employees entitled to the benefits of that division.

Ref.: W. Cal. Ev., "Discovery" §§230, 236.

§6141. Applicable procedure and limitations.

Except as otherwise provided in this chapter, the provisions of Division 4 of this code, relating to benefits, procedure, and limitations, and all other provisions of that division, so far as they are consistent with the intent and purpose of this division, are made a part hereof the same as if set forth herein verbatim.

Ref.: W. Cal. Ev., "Discovery" §§230, 236.

§6142. Exceptions.

The provisions of Sections 3212, 3212.5, 3361, 4458, 4800 to 4855, inclusive, of this code, as well as of other sections of Division 4 of this code, which are restrictive to particular persons or occupations, are excepted from this division and its operation.

Ref.: W. Cal. Ev., "Discovery" §§230, 236.

§6143. Powers of appeals board.

The appeals board is vested with all power not inconsistent with Article VI of the Constitution of the State of California to hear and determine any dispute or matter arising out of an obligation under this division to provide directly, or through the medium of insurance, benefits identical with those prescribed by Division 4 of this code, with such limitations as are authorized, in the case of insurance, by Section 11657 of the Insurance Code.

Ref.: W. Cal. Ev., "Discovery" §§230, 236.

§6144. Trial and determination of controversies.

The appeals board may try and determine controversies under this division referred to it by the parties under the provisions of Part 3, Title 10, of the Code of Civil Procedure, when such controversies are submitted to it by the signed agreement of the parties, or by the application of one party and the submission of the other to its jurisdiction, with or without an express request for arbitration.

Ref.: W. Cal. Ev., "Discovery" §§230, 236.

§6145. Submission of controversies for arbitration.

The state, acting by or through any state agency or when the consent of the opposing party is obtained, shall submit to the appeals board all controversies under this division susceptible of being arbitrated.

Ref.: W. Cal. Ev., "Discovery" §§230, 236.

§6146. Powers of appeals board as arbitrator.

In acting as arbitrator, the appeals board has all the powers which it has in compensation cases, and its findings and award upon an arbitration have the same conclusiveness and are subject to the same mode of reopening, review, and enforcement as in compensation cases.

No fee or cost shall be charged by the appeals board for acting as arbitrator.

Ref.: W. Cal. Ev., "Discovery" §§230, 236.

§6147. Benefits received by state agency.

No state agency, either directly or through its adjusting agency, the State Compensation Insurance Fund, shall pay or provide any benefit authorized by this division unless and until the claimant makes and delivers to such state agency or to the fund an agreement in writing that if he, or his dependents in the event of his death, elects or elect to bring suit against the state with respect to the injury or death, except an action before the appeals board pursuant to the provisions of this division, or an action against the state for damages resulting from the negligence of an employee of another state agency, he or they will allow, and take all proper measures to effect, a credit to the reasonable value of all benefits which he or they have received under the provisions of this division, deductible from any verdict or judgment obtained in such suit, and from the date of commencement of suit will forego further benefits under this division.

Ref.: W. Cal. Ev., "Discovery" §§230, 236.

§6148. Payment of benefits by insurer.

The insurer, when insurance exists, shall not pay or provide any benefit authorized by this division unless and until the claimant makes and delivers to the insurer an agreement in writing that if he, or his dependents in the event of his death, elects or elect to bring suit against the state or the insurer with respect to the injury or death, except an action before the appeals board pursuant to the provisions of this division, or an action against the state for damages resulting from the negligence of an employee of another state agency, he or they will allow, and take all proper measures to effect, a credit to the reasonable value of all benefits which he or they have received under the provisions of this division, deductible from any verdict or judgment obtained in such suit, and from the date of commencement of suit will forego further benefits under such insurance.

Ref.: W. Cal. Ev., "Discovery" §§230, 236.

§6149. Negotiation of agreement.

Nothing shall preclude an employee from negotiating the agreement mentioned in Sections 6147 and 6148 prior to the occurrence of injury.

Ref.: W. Cal. Ev., "Discovery" §§230, 236.

DIVISION 4.7
RETRAINING AND REHABILITATION

§6200. Rehabilitation procedures; purpose of division.

Every public agency, its insurance carrier, and the State Department of Rehabilitation shall jointly formulate procedures for the selection and orderly referral of injured full-time public employees who may be benefited by rehabilitation services and retrained for other positions in public service. The State Department of Rehabilitation shall cooperate in both designing and monitoring results of rehabilitation programs for the disabled employees. The primary purpose of this division is to encourage public agencies to reemploy their injured employees in suitable and gainful employment.

Ref.: Hanna § 35.19; Herlick Handbook § 16.2; W. Cal. Ev., "Discovery" §§230, 236.

§6201. Availability of rehabilitation services; notice to employee.

The employer or insurance carrier shall notify the injured employee of the availability of rehabilitation services in those cases where there is continuing disability of 28 days and beyond. Notification shall be made at the time the employee is paid retroactively for first day of disability (in cases of 28 days of continuing disability or hospitalization) which has previously been uncompensated. A copy of said notification shall be forwarded to the State Department of Rehabilitation.

Ref.: Herlick Handbook § 16.2; W. Cal. Ev., "Discovery" §§230, 236.

§6202. Initiation of rehabilitation plan.

The initiation of a rehabilitation plan shall be the joint responsibility of the injured employee, and the employer or the insurance carrier.

Ref.: Herlick Handbook § 16.2; W. Cal. Ev., "Discovery" §§230, 236.

§6203. Subsistence allowance.

If a rehabilitation plan requires an injured employee to attend an educational or medical facility away from his home, the injured employee shall be paid a reasonable and necessary subsistence allowance in addition to temporary disability indemnity. The subsistence allowance shall be regarded neither as indemnity nor as replacement for lost earnings, but rather as an amount reasonable and necessary to sustain the employee. The determination of need in a particular case shall be established as part of the rehabilitation plan.

Ref.: Herlick Handbook § 16.2; W. Cal. Ev., "Discovery" §§230, 236.

§6204. Rehabilitation plan; employee cooperation.

An injured employee agreeing to a rehabilitation plan shall cooperate in carrying it out. On his unreasonable refusal to comply with the provisions of the rehabilitation plan, the injured employee's rights to further subsistence shall be suspended until compliance is obtained, except that the payment of temporary or permanent disability indemnity, which would be payable regardless of the rehabilitation plan, shall not be suspended.

Ref.: Herlick Handbook § 16.2; W. Cal. Ev., "Discovery" §§230, 236.

§6205. Rehabilitation plan without state approval.

The injured employee may agree with his employer or insurance carrier upon a rehabilitation plan without submission of such plan for approval to the State Department of Rehabilitation. Provision of service under such plans shall be at no cost to the State General Fund.

Ref.: Herlick Handbook § 16.2; W. Cal. Ev., "Discovery" §§230, 236.

§6206. Rehabilitative services; extent.

The injured employee shall receive such medical and vocational rehabilitative services as may be reasonably necessary to restore him to suitable employment.

Ref.: Herlick Handbook § 16.2; W. Cal. Ev., "Discovery" §§230, 236.

§6207. Rehabilitative benefits; nature.

The injured employee's rehabilitation benefit is an additional benefit and shall not be converted to or replace any workers' compensation benefit available to him.

Ref.: Herlick Handbook § 16.2; W. Cal. Ev., "Discovery" §§230, 236.

§6208. Initiation and acceptance of rehabilitation program.

The initiation and acceptance of a rehabilitation program shall be voluntary and not compulsory upon the employer, the insurance carrier, or the injured employee.

Ref.: Hanna § 35.19; Herlick Handbook § 16.2; W. Cal. Ev., "Discovery" §§230, 236.

Labor

DIVISION 5
SAFETY IN EMPLOYMENT

PART 1
Occupational Safety and Health

CHAPTER 1
JURISDICTION AND DUTIES

§6300. Purpose.

The California Occupational Safety and Health Act of 1973 is hereby enacted for the purpose of assuring safe and healthful working conditions for all California working men and women by authorizing the enforcement of effective standards, assisting and encouraging employers to maintain safe and healthful working conditions, and by providing for research, information, education, training, and enforcement in the field of occupational safety and health.

Ref.: Herlick Handbook §§ 2.5, 9.10, 12.11; W. Cal. Ev., "Hearsay" §116; W. Cal. Sum., 3 "Agency and Employment" §§275, 314, 363, 364.

§6301. Construction and interpretation.

The definitions set forth in this chapter shall govern the construction and interpretation of this part.

Ref.: Herlick Handbook § 12.11; W. Cal. Ev., "Hearsay" §116.

§6302. Definitions.

As used in this division:

(a) "Director" means the Director of Industrial Relations.

(b) "Department" means the Department of Industrial Relations.

(c) "Insurer" includes the State Compensation Insurance Fund and any private company, corporation, mutual association, and reciprocal or interinsurance exchange, authorized under the laws of this state to insure employers against liability for compensation under this part and under Division 4 (commencing with Section 3201), and any employer to whom a certificate of consent to self-insure has been issued.

(d) "Division" means the Division of Occupational Safety and Health.

(e) "Standards board" means the Occupational Safety and Health Standards Board, within the department.

(f) "Appeals board" means the Occupational Safety and Health Appeals Board, within the department.

(g) "Aquaculture" means a form of agriculture as defined in Section 17 of the Fish and Game Code.

(h) "Serious injury or illness" means any injury or illness occurring in a place of employment or in connection with any employment which requires inpatient hospitalization for a period in excess of 24 hours for other than medical observation or in which an employee suffers a loss of any member of the body or suffers any serious degree of permanent disfigurement, but does not include any injury or illness or death caused by the commission of a Penal Code violation, except the violation of Section 385 of the Penal Code, or an accident on a public street or highway.

(i) "Serious exposure" means any exposure of an employee to a hazardous substance when the exposure occurs as a result of an incident, accident, emergency, or exposure over time and is in a degree or amount sufficient to create a substantial probability that death or serious physical harm in the future could result from the exposure.

Ref.: Herlick Handbook § 12.11; W. Cal. Ev., "Hearsay" §116.

§6303. "Place of employment" and "employment."

(a) "Place of employment" means any place, and the premises appurtenant thereto, where employment is carried on, except a place where the health and safety jurisdiction is vested by law in, and actively exercised by, any state or federal agency other than the division.

(b) "Employment" includes the carrying on of any trade, enterprise, project, industry, business, occupation, or work, including all excavation, demolition, and construction work, or any process or operation in any way related thereto, in which any person is engaged or permitted to work for hire, except household domestic service.

(c) "Employment," for purposes of this division only, also includes volunteer firefighting when covered by Division 4 (commencing with Section 3200) pursuant to Section 3361.

(d) Subdivision (c) shall become operative on January 1, 2004. **Leg.H.** 2001 ch. 807, 2002 ch. 368 (AB 2118), effective September 5, 2002.

Ref.: Herlick Handbook § 12.11; W. Cal. Ev., "Hearsay" §116; W. Cal. Sum., 3 "Agency and Employment" §367.

§6303.5. Unlimited jurisdiction of state where federal law authorizes concurrent jurisdiction.

Nothing in this division shall be construed to limit the jurisdiction of the state over any employment or place of employment by reason of the exercise of occupational safety and health jurisdiction by any federal agency if federal jurisdiction is being exercised under a federal law which expressly authorizes concurrent state jurisdiction over occupational safety or health issues.

Ref.: W. Cal. Ev., "Hearsay" §116.

§6304. "Employer."

"Employer" shall have the same meaning as in Section 3300.

Ref.: Herlick Handbook §§ 12.7, 12.12; W. Cal. Ev., "Hearsay" §116; W. Cal. Sum., 6 "Torts" §1236.

§6304.1. "Employee."

(a) "Employee" means every person who is required or directed by any employer to engage in any employment or to go to work or be at any time in any place of employment.

(b) "Employee" also includes volunteer firefighters covered by Division 4 (commencing with Section 3200) pursuant to Section 3361.

(c) Subdivision (b) shall become operative on January 1, 2004.

(d) This act does not affect claims that arose pursuant to Division 5 of this code between January 1, 2002, and the effective date of this act. **Leg.H.** 2001 ch. 807, 2002 ch. 368 (AB 2118), effective September 5, 2002.

Ref.: W. Cal. Ev., "Hearsay" §116.

§6304.2. State prisoners as employees; Department of Corrections as employer.

Notwithstanding Section 6413, and except as provided in Sections 6304.3 and 6304.4, any state prisoner engaged in correctional industry, as defined by the Department of Corrections, shall be deemed to be an "employee," and the Department of Corrections shall be deemed to be an "employer," with regard to such prisoners for the purposes of this part.

Ref.: W. Cal. Ev., "Hearsay" §116.

§6304.3. Correctional Industry Safety Committee; establishment and duties.

(a) A Correctional Industry Safety Committee shall be established in accordance with Department of Corrections administrative procedures at each facility maintaining a correctional industry, as defined by the Department of Corrections. The Division of Occupational Safety and Health shall promulgate, and the Department of Corrections shall implement, regulations concerning the duties and functions which shall govern the operation of each such committee.

(b) All complaints alleging unsafe or unhealthy working conditions in a correctional industry shall initially be directed to the Correctional Industry Safety Committee of the facility prison. The committee shall attempt to resolve all complaints.

If a complaint is not resolved by the committee within 15 calendar days, the complaint shall be referred by the committee to the division where it shall be reviewed. When the division receives a complaint which, in its determination, constitutes a bona fide allegation of a safety or health violation, the division shall summarily investigate the same as soon as possible, but not later than three working days after receipt of a complaint charging a serious violation, as defined in Section 6309, and not later than 14 calendar days after receipt of a complaint charging a nonserious violation.

(c) Except as provided in subdivision (b) and in Section 6313, the inspection or investigation of a facility maintaining a correctional industry, as defined by the Department of Corrections, shall be discretionary with the division.

(d) Notwithstanding Section 6321, the division may give advance notice of an inspection or investigation and may postpone the same if such action is necessary for the maintenance of security at the facility where the inspection or investigation is to be held, or for insuring the safety and health of the division's representative who will be conducting such inspection or investigation.

Ref.: W. Cal. Ev., "Hearsay" §116.

§6304.4. When prisoners are not "employees."

A prisoner engaged in correctional industry, as defined by the Department of Corrections, shall not be considered an employee for purposes of the provisions relating to appeal proceedings set forth in Chapter 7 (commencing with Section 6600).

Ref.: W. Cal. Ev., "Hearsay" §116.

§6304.5. Applicability.

It is the intent of the Legislature that the provisions of this division, and the occupational safety and health standards and orders promulgated under this code, are applicable to proceedings against employers for the exclusive purpose of maintaining and enforcing employee safety.

Neither the issuance of, or failure to issue, a citation by the division shall have any application to, nor be considered in, nor be admissible into, evidence in any personal injury or wrongful death action, except as between an employee and his or her own employer. Sections 452 and 669 of the Evidence Code shall apply to this division and to occupational safety and health standards adopted under this division in the same manner as any other statute, ordinance, or regulation. The testimony of employees of the division shall not be admissible as expert opinion or with respect to the application of occupational safety and health standards. It is the intent of the Legislature that the amendments to this section enacted in the 1999–2000 Regular Session shall not abrogate the holding in *Brock v. State of California* (1978) 81 Cal.App.3d 752. **Leg.H.** 1999 ch. 615.

Ref.: Hanna § 11.22[5]; Herlick Handbook § 12.12; CACI No. 418 (Matthew Bender); W. Cal. Ev., "Hearsay" §116, "Judicial Notice" §18, "Opinion Evidence" §32; W. Cal. Sum., 3 "Agency and Employment" §364, 6 "Torts" §908.

§6305. Definitions.

(a) "Occupational safety and health standards and orders" means standards and orders adopted by the standards board pursuant to Chapter 6 (commencing with Section 140) of Division 1 and general orders heretofore adopted by the Industrial Safety Board or the Industrial Accident Commission.

(b) "Special order" means any order written by the chief or the chief's authorized representative to correct an unsafe condition, device, or place of employment which poses a threat to the health or safety of an employee and which cannot be made safe under existing standards or orders of the standards board. These orders shall have the same effect as any other standard or order of the standards board, but shall apply only to the employment or place of employment described in the written order of the chief's authorized representative.

§6306. Definitions.

(a) "Safe," "safety," and "health" as applied to an employment or a place of employment mean such freedom from danger to the life, safety, or health of employees as the nature of the employment reasonably permits.

(b) "Safety device" and "safeguard" shall be given a broad interpretation so as to include any practicable method of mitigating or preventing a specific danger, including the danger of exposure to potentially injurious levels of ionizing radiation or potentially injurious quantities of radioactive materials.

Ref.: Herlick Handbook § 12.7; W. Cal. Ev., "Hearsay" §116; W. Cal. Sum., 3 "Agency and Employment" §365.

§6307. Scope of power and jurisdiction.

The division has the power, jurisdiction, and supervision over every employment and place of employment in this state, which is necessary to adequately enforce and administer all laws and lawful standards and orders, or special orders requiring such employment and place of employment to be safe, and requiring the protection of the life, safety, and health of every employee in such employment or place of employment.

Ref.: W. Cal. Ev., "Hearsay" §116; W. Cal. Sum., 3 "Agency and Employment" §§366, 367.

§6307.1. Role of State Department of Health Services.

The State Department of Health Services shall assist the division in the enforcement of

Section 25910 of the Health and Safety Code in the manner prescribed by a written agreement between the State Department of Health Services and the Department of Industrial Relations, pursuant to Section 144.

Ref.: W. Cal. Ev., "Hearsay" §116.

§6308. Enforcement powers.

The division, in enforcing occupational safety and health standards and orders and special orders may do any of the following:

(a) Declare and prescribe what safety devices, safeguards, or other means or methods of protection are well adapted to render the employees of every employment and place of employment safe as required by law or lawful order.

(b) Enforce Section 25910 of the Health and Safety Code and standards and orders adopted by the standards board pursuant to Chapter 6 (commencing with Section 140) of Division 1 of the Labor Code, for the installation, use, maintenance, and operation of reasonable uniform safety devices, safeguards, and other means or methods of protection, which are necessary to carry out all laws and lawful standards or special orders relative to the protection of the life and safety of employees in employments and places of employment.

(c) Require the performance of any other act which the protection of the life and safety of the employees in employments and places of employment reasonably demands.

An employer may request a hearing on a special order or action ordered pursuant to this section, at which the employer, owner, or any other person may appear. The appeals board shall conduct the hearing at the earliest possible time.

All orders, rules, regulations, findings, and decisions of the division made or entered under this part, except special orders and action orders, may be reviewed by the Supreme Court and the courts of appeal as may be provided by law.

Ref.: W. Cal. Ev., "Hearsay" §116; W. Cal. Sum., 3 "Agency and Employment" §§366, 369, 6 "Torts" §1236.

§6308.5. Hearings.

Hearings conducted by the division pursuant to this part shall give any affected employer or other affected person the opportunity to submit facts or arguments, but may be conducted informally, either orally or in writing.

Ref.: W. Cal. Ev., "Hearsay" §116.

§6309. Investigation procedures.

If the division learns or has reason to believe that an employment or place of employment is not safe or is injurious to the welfare of an employee, it may, on its own motion, or upon complaint, summarily investigate the same with or without notice or hearings. However, if the division receives a complaint from an employee, an employee's representative, including, but not limited to, an attorney, health or safety professional, union representative, or government agency representative, or an employer of an employee directly involved in an unsafe place of employment, that his or her employment or place of employment is not safe, it shall, with or without notice or hearing, summarily investigate the complaint as soon as possible, but not later than three working days after receipt of a complaint charging a serious violation, and not later than 14 calendar days after receipt of a complaint charging a nonserious violation. The division shall attempt to determine the period of time in the future that the complainant believes the unsafe condition may continue to exist, and shall allocate inspection resources so as to respond first to those situations in which time is of the essence. For purposes of this section, a complaint is deemed to allege a serious violation if the division determines that the complaint charges that there is a substantial probability that death or serious physical harm could result from a condition which exists, or from one or more practices, means, methods, operations, or processes which have been adopted or are in use in a place of employment. When a complaint charging a serious violation is received from a state or local prosecutor, or a local law enforcement agency, the division shall summarily investigate the employment or place of employment within 24 hours of receipt of the complaint. All other complaints are deemed to allege nonserious violations. The division may enter and serve any necessary order relative thereto. The division is not required to respond to a complaint within this period where, from the facts stated in the complaint, it determines that the complaint is intended to willfully harass an employer or is without any reasonable basis.

The division shall keep complete and accurate records of all complaints, whether verbal or written, and shall inform the complainant, whenever his or her identity is known, of any action taken by the division in regard to the subject matter of the complaint, and the reasons for the action, within 14 calendar days of taking any action. The records of the division shall include the dates on which any action was taken on the complaint, or the reasons for not taking any action on the complaint. The division shall, pursuant to authorized regulations, conduct an informal review of any refusal by a representative of the division to issue a citation with respect to an alleged violation. The division shall furnish the employee or the representative of employees requesting the review a written statement of the reasons for the division's final disposition of the case.

The name of a person who submits to the division a complaint regarding the unsafe condition of an employment or place of employment shall be kept confidential by the division, unless that person requests otherwise.

The division shall annually compile and release on its Web site data pertaining to complaints received and citations issued.

The requirements of this section do not relieve the division of its requirement to inspect and assure that all places of employment are safe and healthful for employees. The division shall maintain the capability to receive and act upon complaints at all times. **Leg.H.** 1999 ch. 615, 2002 ch. 885 (AB 2837), 2003 ch. 884 (AB 1719).

Ref.: W. Cal. Ev., "Hearsay" §116; W. Cal. Sum., 3 "Agency and Employment" §366.

§6310. Employer action against employees filing complaints.

(a) No person shall discharge or in any manner discriminate against any employee because the employee has done any of the following:

(1) Made any oral or written complaint to the division, other governmental agencies having statutory responsibility for or assisting the division with reference to employee safety or health, his or her employer, or his or her representative.

(2) Instituted or caused to be instituted any proceeding under or relating to his or her rights or has testified or is about to testify in the proceeding or because of the exercise by the employee on behalf of himself, herself, or others of any rights afforded him or her.

(3) Participated in an occupational health and safety committee established pursuant to Section 6401.7.

(b) Any employee who is discharged, threatened with discharge, demoted, suspended, or in any other manner discriminated against in the terms and conditions of employment by his or her employer because the employee has made a bona fide oral or written complaint to the division, other governmental agencies having statutory responsibility for or assisting the division with reference to employee safety or health, his or her employer, or his or her representative, of unsafe working conditions, or work practices, in his or her employment or place of employment or has participated in an employer-employee occupational health and safety committee, shall be entitled to reinstatement and reimbursement for lost wages and work benefits caused by the acts of the employer. Any employer who willfully refuses to rehire, promote, or otherwise restore an employee or former employee who has been determined to be eligible for rehiring or promotion by a grievance procedure, arbitration, or hearing authorized by law, is guilty of a misdemeanor.

Ref.: 8 C.C.R. §14300.36; W. Cal. Ev., "Hearsay" §116; W. Cal. Sum., 3 "Agency and Employment" §§212, 370, 7 "Constitutional Law" §28.

§6311. Employee's refusal to work when health or safety threatened.

No employee shall be laid off or discharged for refusing to perform work in the performance of which this code, including Section 6400, any occupational safety or health standard or any safety order of the division or standards board will be violated, where the violation would create a real and apparent hazard to the employee or his or her fellow employees. Any employee who is laid off or discharged in violation of this section or is otherwise not paid because he or she refused to perform work in the performance of which this code, any occupational safety or health standard or any safety order of the division or standards board will be violated and where the violation would create a real and apparent hazard to the employee or his or her fellow employees shall have a right of action for wages for the time the employee is without work as a result of the layoff or discharge.

Ref.: 8 C.C.R. §14300.36; W. Cal. Ev., "Hearsay" §116; W. Cal. Sum., 3 "Agency and Employment" §§212, 370.

§6312. Employee's recourse for violation of §6310 or §6311.

Any employee who believes that he or she has been discharged or otherwise discriminated against by any person in violation of Section 6310 or 6311 may file a complaint with the Labor Commissioner pursuant to Section 98.7.

Ref.: W. Cal. Ev., "Hearsay" §116; W. Cal. Sum., 3 "Agency and Employment" §212.

§6313. Cases for investigation.

(a) The division shall investigate the causes of any employment accident that is fatal to one or more employees or that results in a serious injury or illness, or a serious exposure, unless it determines that an investigation is unnecessary. If the division determines that an investigation of an accident is unnecessary, it shall summarize the facts indicating that the accident need not be investigated and the means by which the facts were determined. The division shall establish guidelines for determining the circumstances under which an investigation of these accidents and exposures is unnecessary.

(b) The division may investigate the causes of any other industrial accident or occupational illness which occurs within the state in any employment or place of employment, or which directly or indirectly arises from or is connected with the maintenance or operation of the employment or place of employment, and shall issue any orders necessary to eliminate the causes and to prevent reoccurrence. The orders may not be admitted as evidence in any action for damages, or any proceeding to recover compensation, based on or arising out of injury or death caused by the accident or illness. **Leg.H.** 2002 ch. 885 (AB 2837).

Ref.: W. Cal. Ev., "Hearsay" §116; W. Cal. Sum., 3 "Agency and Employment" §366, 7 "Constitutional Law" §659.

§6313.5. Transmittal of investigative reports.

The division shall transmit to the Registrar of Contractors copies of any reports made in any investigation conducted pursuant to subdivision (a) of Section 6313, and may, upon its own motion or at the request of the Registrar of Contractors, transmit copies of any other reports made in any investigation conducted pursuant to subdivision (b) of Section 6313 involving a contractor licensed pursuant to the Contractors License Law (Chapter 9 (commencing with Section 7000) of Division 3 of the Business and Professions Code).

Ref.: W. Cal. Ev., "Hearsay" §116.

§6314. Access to place of employment for investigative purposes.

(a) To make an investigation or inspection, the chief of the division and all qualified divisional inspectors and investigators authorized by him or her shall, upon presenting appropriate credentials to the employer, have free access to any place of employment to investigate and inspect during regular working hours, and at other reasonable times when necessary for the protection of safety and health, and within reasonable limits and in a reasonable manner. The chief or his or her authorized representative may, during the course of any investigation or inspection, obtain any statistics, information, or any physical materials in the possession of the employer that are directly related to the purpose of the investigation or inspection, conduct any tests necessary to the investigation or inspection, and take photographs. Photographs taken by the division during the course of any investigation or inspection shall be considered to be confidential information pursuant to the provisions of Section 6322, and shall not be deemed to be public records for purposes of the California Public Records Act.

(b) If permission to investigate or inspect the place of employment is refused, or the facts or circumstances reasonably justify the failure to seek permission, the chief or his or her authorized representative may obtain an inspection warrant pursuant to the provisions of Title 13 (commencing with Section 1822.50) of the Code of Civil Procedure. Cause for the issuance of a warrant shall be deemed to exist if there has been an industrial accident, injury, or illness reported, if any complaint that violations of occupational safety and health standards exist at the place of employment has been received by the division, or if the place of employment to be inspected has been chosen on the basis of specific neutral criteria contained in a general administrative plan for the enforcement of this division.

(c) The chief and his or her authorized representatives may issue subpoenas to compel the attendance of witnesses and the production of books, papers, records, and physical materials, administer oaths, examine witnesses under oath, take verification or proof of written materials, and take depositions and affidavits for the purpose of carrying out the duties of the division.

(d) In the course of any investigation or inspection of an employer or place of employment by an authorized representative of the division, a representative of the employer and a representative authorized by his or her employees shall have an opportunity to accompany him or her on the tour of inspection. Any employee or employer, or their authorized representatives, shall have the right to discuss safety and health violations or safety and health problems with the inspector privately during the course of an investigation or inspection. Where there is no authorized employee representative, the chief or his or her authorized representatives shall consult with a reasonable number of employees concerning matters of health and safety of the place of employment.

(e) During any investigation of an industrial accident or occupational illness conducted by the division pursuant to the provisions of Section 6313, the chief or his or her authorized representative may issue an order to preserve physical materials or the accident site as they were at the time the accident or illness occurred if, in the opinion of the division, it is necessary to do so in order to determine the cause or causes of the accident or illness, and the evidence is in potential danger of being removed, altered, or tampered with. Under these circumstances, the division shall issue that order in a manner that will avoid, to the extent possible, any interference with normal business operations.

A conspicuous notice that an order has been issued shall be prepared by the division and shall be posted by the employer in the area or on the article to be preserved. The order shall be limited to the immediate area and the machines, devices, apparatus, or equipment directly associated with the accident or illness.

Any person who knowingly violates an order issued by the division pursuant to this subdivision shall, upon conviction, be punished by a fine of not more than five thousand dollars ($5,000). **Leg.H.** 1993 ch. 998.

Ref.: W. Cal. Ev., "Hearsay" §116.

§6314.1. High hazardous industries.

(a) The division shall establish a program for targeting employers in high hazardous industries with the highest incidence of preventable occupational injuries and illnesses and workers' compensation losses. The employers shall be identified from any or all of the following data sources: the California Work Injury and Illness program, the Occupational Injuries and Illness Survey, the federal hazardous employers' list, experience modification and other relevant data maintained and furnished by all rating organizations as defined in Section 11750.1 of the Insurance Code, histories of violations of Occupational Safety and Health Act standards, and any other source deemed to be appropriate that identifies injury and illness rates.

(b) The division shall establish procedures for ensuring that the highest hazardous employers in the most hazardous industries are inspected on a priority basis. The division may send a letter to the high hazard employers who are identified pursuant to this section informing them of their status and directing them to submit a plan, including the establishment of joint labor-management health and safety committees, within a time determined by the division for reducing their occupational injury and illness rates. Employers who submit plans that meet the requirements of the division may be placed on a secondary inspection schedule. Employers on that schedule shall be inspected on a random basis as determined by the division. Employers who do not submit plans meeting the requirements of the division within the time specified by the division shall be placed on the primary inspection list. Every employer on the primary inspection list shall be subject to an inspection. The division shall employ sufficient personnel to meet minimum federal targeted inspection standards.

(c) The division shall establish and maintain regional plans for allocating the division's resources for the targeted inspection program in addition to the inspections required or authorized in Section 6309, 6313, and 6320. Each regional plan shall focus on industries selected from the targeted inspection program as well as any other scheduled inspections that the division determines to be appropriate to the region, including the cleanup of hazardous waste sites. All targeted inspections shall be conducted on a priority basis, targeting the worst employers first.

(d) In order to maximize the impact of the regional plans, the division shall coordinate its education, training, and consulting services with the priorities established in the regional plans.

Leg.H. 1993 ch. 121 §68, effective July 16, 1993.

Ref.: W. Cal. Ev., "Hearsay" §116.

§6314.5. Scope of inspection.

(a) Every inspection conducted by the division shall include an evaluation of the employer's injury prevention program established pursuant to Section 6401.7. The division shall evaluate injury prevention programs using the criteria for substantial compliance determined by the standards board. The evaluation shall include interviews with a sample of employees and the members of any employer-employee occupational safety and health committee. In any inspection which includes work for which a permit is required pursuant to Section 6500 and for which a permit has been issued pursuant to Section 6502, the evaluation of the employer's injury prevention program shall be limited to the implementation of the plan approved by the division in the issuance of the permit. Before any inspection is concluded, the division shall notify the employer of the services available from the department to assist the employer to establish, maintain, improve, and evaluate the employer's injury prevention program.

(b) Inspections also shall include an evaluation of the following:

(1) The condition or conditions alleged in the complaint if the inspection is conducted pursuant to Section 6309.

(2) The condition or conditions involved in the accident if the inspection is conducted pursuant to Section 6313.

(3) The condition or conditions involving work for which a permit is required pursuant to Section 6500, for which notification of asbestos related work is required pursuant to Section 6501.5, or for which a report of use of a carcinogen is required pursuant to Section 9030.

(4) The condition or conditions related to significant safety or health hazards in the industries identified in the regional plans developed pursuant to Section 6314.1.

(5) The condition or conditions involved in abatement of previous violations, special orders, or action orders if the inspection is conducted pursuant to Section 6320.

(c) The scope of any inspection may be expanded beyond the evaluations specified in subdivisions (a) and (b) whenever, in the opinion of the division, a more complete inspection is warranted.

Ref.: 8 C.C.R. §§15353, 15354; W. Cal. Ev., "Hearsay" §116.

§6315. Bureau of Investigations.

(a) There is within the division a Bureau of Investigations. The bureau is responsible for directing accident investigations involving violations of standards, orders, special orders, or Section 25910 of the Health and Safety Code, in which there is a serious injury to five or more employees, death, or request for prosecution by a division representative. The bureau shall review inspection reports involving a serious violation where there have been serious injuries to one to four employees or a serious exposure, and may investigate those cases in which the bureau finds criminal violations may have occurred. The bureau is responsible for preparing cases for the purpose of prosecution, including evidence and findings.

(b) The division shall provide the bureau with all of the following:

(1) All initial accident reports.

(2) The division's inspection report for any inspection involving a serious violation where there is a fatality, and the reports necessary for the bureau's review required pursuant to subdivision (a).

(3) Any other documents in the possession of the division requested by the bureau for its review or investigation of any case or which the division determines will be helpful to the bureau in its investigation of the case.

(c) The supervisor of the bureau is the administrative chief of the bureau, and shall be an attorney.

(d) The bureau shall be staffed by as many attorneys and investigators as are necessary to carry out the purposes of this chapter. To the extent possible, the attorneys and investigators shall be experienced in criminal law.

(e) The supervisor of the bureau and bureau representatives designated by the supervisor have a right of access to all places of employment necessary to the investigation, may collect any evidence or samples they deem necessary to an investigation, and have all of the powers enumerated in Section 6314.

(f) The supervisor of the bureau and bureau representatives designated by the supervisor may serve all processes and notices throughout the state.

(g) In any case where the bureau is required to conduct an investigation, and in which there is a serious injury or death, the results of the investigation shall be referred in a timely manner by the bureau to the appropriate prosecuting authority having jurisdiction for appropriate action, unless the bureau determines that there is legally insufficient evidence of a violation of the law. If the bureau determines that there is legally insufficient evidence of a violation of the law, the bureau shall notify the appropriate prosecuting authority, if the prosecuting authority requests notice.

(h) The bureau may communicate with the appropriate prosecuting authority at any time the bureau deems appropriate.

(i) Upon the request of a county district attorney, the department may develop a protocol for the referral of cases that may involve criminal conduct to the appropriate prosecuting authority in lieu of or in cooperation with an investigation by the bureau. The protocol shall provide for the voluntary acceptance of referrals after a review of the case by the prosecuting authority. In cases accepted for investigation by the prosecuting authority, the protocol shall provide for cooperation between the prosecuting authority, the division, and the bureau. Where a referral is declined by the prosecuting authority, the bureau shall comply with subdivisions (a) to (h), inclusive. **Leg.H.** 2002 ch. 885 (AB 2837), 2003 ch. 884 (AB 1719).

Ref.: W. Cal. Ev., "Hearsay" §116; W. Cal. Sum., 3 "Agency and Employment" §366, 7 "Constitutional Law" §659.

§6315.3. Submission of report of bureau activities.

The bureau shall, not later than February 15, annually submit to the division for submission to the director a report on the activities of the bureau, including, but not limited to, the following:

(a) Totals of each type of report provided the bureau under each category in subdivision (b) of Section 6315.

(b) Totals of each type of case reflecting the number of investigations and court cases in progress at the start of the calendar year being reported, investigations completed in the calendar year, cases referred to appropriate prosecuting authorities in the calendar year, and investigations and court cases in progress at the end of the calendar year. The types of cases shall include the following:

(1) Those that the bureau is required to investigate, divided into fatalities, serious injuries to five or more employees, and requests for prosecution from a division representative.

(2) Those that were initiated by the bureau following the review required in subdivision (a) of Section 6315, divided into serious injuries to fewer than five employees and serious exposures.

(c) A summary of the dispositions in the calendar year of cases referred by the bureau to appropriate prosecuting authorities. The summary shall be divided into the types of cases, as described in subdivision (b), and shall show at least the violation, the statute for which the case was referred for prosecution, and the dates of referral to the bureau for investigation, referral from the bureau for prosecution, and the final court action if the case was prosecuted.

(d) A summary of investigations completed in the calendar year that did not result in a referral for prosecution, divided into the types of cases as described in subdivision (b), showing the violation and the reasons for nonreferral.

(e) A summary of the use of the bureau's resources in accomplishing the bureau's mission. **Leg.H.** 1984 ch. 1317 §6, 2006 ch. 538 (SB 1852) §493.

Ref.: W. Cal. Ev., "Hearsay" §116.

§6315.5. Admissibility as evidence of division's standards, findings, etc.

All occupational safety and health standards and orders, rules, regulations, findings, and decisions of the division made and entered pursuant to this part are admissible as evidence in any prosecution for the violation of any provision of this part, and shall, in every such prosecution, be presumed to be reasonable and lawful and to fix a reasonable and proper standard and requirement of safety unless, prior to the institution of the prosecution for such violation, proceedings for a hearing on a special order are instituted, or a petition is filed under Section 11426 of the Government Code.

Ref.: W. Cal. Ev., "Hearsay" §116.

§6316. Limitations on powers of other governing bodies.

Except as limited by Chapter 6 (commencing with Section 140) of Division 1, nothing in this part shall deprive the governing body of any county, city, or public corporation, board, or department, of any power or jurisdiction over or relative to any place of employment.

Ref.: W. Cal. Ev., "Hearsay" §116.

§6317. Steps taken against employers violating regulations.

If, upon inspection or investigation, the division believes that an employer has violated Section 25910 of the Health and Safety Code or any standard, rule, order, or regulation established pursuant to Chapter 6 (commencing with Section 140) of Division 1 of the Labor Code, or any standard, rule, order, or regulation established pursuant to this part, it shall with reasonable promptness issue a citation to the employer. Each citation shall be in writing and shall describe with particularity the nature of the violation, including a reference to the provision of the code, standard, rule, regulation, or order alleged to have been violated. In addition, the citation shall fix a reasonable time for the abatement of the alleged violation. The period specified for abatement shall not commence running until the date the citation or notice is received by certified mail and the certified mail receipt is signed, or if not signed, the date the return is made to the post office. If the division officially and directly delivers the citation or notice to the employer, the period specified for abatement shall commence running on the date of the delivery.

A "notice" in lieu of citation may be issued with respect to violations found in an inspection or investigation which meet either of the following requirements:

(1) The violations do not have a direct relationship upon the health or safety of an employee.

(2) The violations do not have an immediate relationship to the health or safety of an employee, and are of a general or regulatory nature. A notice in lieu of a citation may be issued only if the employer agrees to correct the violations within a reasonable time, as specified by the division, and agrees not to appeal the finding of the division that the violations exist. A notice issued pursuant to this paragraph shall have the same effect as a citation for purposes of establishing repeat violations or a failure to abate. Every notice shall clearly state the abatement period specified by the division, that the notice may not be appealed, and that the notice has the same effect as a citation for purposes of establishing a repeated violation or a failure to abate. The employer shall indicate agreement to the provisions and conditions of the notice by his or her signature on the notice.

Under no circumstances shall a notice be issued in lieu of a citation if the violations are serious, repeated, willful, or arise from a failure to abate.

The director shall prescribe guidelines for the issuance of these notices.

The division may impose a civil penalty against an employer as specified in Chapter 4 (commencing with Section 6423) of this part. A notice in lieu of a citation may not be issued if the number of first instance violations found in the inspection (other than serious, willful, or repeated violations) is 10 or more violations.

No citation or notice shall be issued by the division for a given violation or violations after six months have elapsed since occurrence of the violation.

The director shall prescribe procedures for the issuance of a citation or notice.

The division shall prepare and maintain records capable of supplying an inspector with previous citations and notices issued to an employer. **Leg.H.** 1991 ch. 599, effective October 5, 1991.

Ref.: W. Cal. Ev., "Hearsay" §116; W. Cal. Sum., 3 "Agency and Employment" §§366, 368.

§6317.5. Employer's falsification of materials posted or distributed in workplace—Notice of violation; posting of citation.

(a) If, upon inspection or investigation, the division finds that an employer has falsified any materials posted in the workplace or distributed to employees related to the California Occupational Safety and Health Act, the division shall issue a citation to the employer.

(b) Each citation issued pursuant to this section, or a copy or copies thereof, shall be prominently posted, as prescribed in regulations issued by the director.

(c) Any employer served with a citation pursuant to subdivision (a) may appeal to the appeals board pursuant to the provisions of Chapter 7 (commencing with Section 6600). The appeal shall be subject to the timeframes and procedures set forth in that chapter.

(d) The provisions of this section are in addition to, and not in lieu of, all other criminal penalties and civil remedies that may be applicable to any act leading to issuance of a citation pursuant to this section. **Leg.H.** 1993 ch. 580.

Ref.: W. Cal. Ev., "Hearsay" §116.

§6317.7. Notice of no violations.

If, upon inspection or investigation, the division finds no violations pursuant to this chapter, the division with reasonable promptness shall issue a written notice to the employer specifying the areas inspected and stating that no violations were found.

The director shall prescribe procedures for the issuance of this notice. **Leg.H.** 1993 ch. 580.

Ref.: W. Cal. Ev., "Hearsay" §116; W. Cal. Sum., 3 "Agency and Employment" §366.

§6318. Posting of citations.

(a) Each citation issued under Section 6317, and each special order or action ordered pursuant to Section 6308, or a copy or copies thereof, shall be prominently posted, as prescribed in regulations issued by the director, at or near each place a violation referred to in the citation or order occurred. All postings shall be maintained for three working days, or until the unsafe condition is abated, whichever is longer. Following each investigation of an industrial accident or occupational illness, if no violations are found, the employer shall post a notice prepared by the division so indicating for three working days.

(b) When the division verifies abatement of a serious violation or an order at the time of inspection or upon reinspection, the employer shall post a notice prepared by the division so indicating for three working days. In all other cases of abatement of serious violations, the employer shall post the signed statement confirming abatement prepared pursuant to Section 6320.

Ref.: W. Cal. Ev., "Hearsay" §116.

§6319. Procedures for citation or order issuance; appeal; setting of penalties.

(a) If, after an inspection or investigation, the division issues a citation pursuant to Section 6317 or an order pursuant to Section 6308, it shall, within a reasonable time after the termination of the inspection or investigation, notify the employer by certified mail of the citation or order, and that the employer has 15 working days from receipt of the notice within which to notify the appeals board that he or she wishes to contest the citation or order for any reason set forth in Section 6600 or 6600.5.

(b) Any employer served by certified mail with a notice of civil penalty may appeal to the appeals board within 15 working days from receipt of that notice for any reason set forth in Section 6600. If the citation is issued for a violation involving the condition or operation of any machine, device, apparatus, or equipment, and a person other than the employer is obligated to the employer to repair the machine, device, apparatus, or equipment and to pay any penalties assessed against the employer, the other person may appeal to the appeals board within 15 working days of the receipt of the citation by the employer for any reasons set forth in Section 6600.

(c) The director shall promulgate regulations covering the assessment of civil penalties under this chapter which give due consideration to the appropriateness of the penalty with respect to the following factors:

(1) The size of the business of the employer being charged.

(2) The gravity of the violation.

(3) The good faith of the employer, including timely abatement.

(4) The history of previous violations.

(d) Notwithstanding subdivision (c), if serious injury, illness, exposure, or death is caused by any serious, willful, or repeated violation, or by any failure to correct a serious violation within the time permitted for its correction, the penalty shall not be reduced for any reason other than the size of the business of the employer being charged. Whenever the division issues a citation for a violation covered by this subdivision, it shall notify the employer of its determination that serious injury, illness, exposure or death was caused by the violation and shall, upon request, provide the employer with a copy of the inspection report.

(e) The employer shall not be liable for a civil penalty under this part for any citation issued by a division representative providing consulting services pursuant to Sections 6354 and 6355.

(f) Whenever a citation of a self-insured employer for a willful, or repeat serious violation of the standard adopted pursuant to Section 6401.7 becomes final, the division shall notify the director so that a hearing may be held to determine whether good cause exists to revoke the employer's certificate of consent to self-insure as provided in Section 3702.

(g) Based upon the evidence, the division may propose appropriate modifications concerning the characterization of violations and corresponding modifications to civil penalties as a result thereof.

Ref.: 8 C.C.R. §§15210.1, 15353, 15354; W. Cal. Ev., "Hearsay" §116; W. Cal. Sum., 3 "Agency and Employment" §§366, 368.

§6319.3. Civil penalty assessed against new employer.

(a) Except as provided in subdivision (b) of this section and subdivision (j) of Section 6401.7, no civil penalty shall be assessed against any new employer in the state for a violation of any standard developed pursuant to subdivision (a) of Section 6401.7 for a period of one year after the date the new employer establishes a business in the state.

(b) Subdivision (a) shall only apply to an employer who has made a good faith effort to comply with any standard developed pursuant to subdivision (a) of Section 6401.7, but shall not apply if the employer is found to have committed a serious, willful, or repeated violation of that standard, or fails to abate the violation and is assessed a penalty pursuant to Section 6430. **Leg.H.** 1993 ch. 928.

Ref.: W. Cal. Ev., "Hearsay" §116.

§6319.5. Employer's showing of good-faith compliance effort.

Upon a showing by an employer of a good-faith effort to comply with the abatement requirement of a citation, and that abatement has not been completed because of factors beyond his reasonable control, the division, after an opportunity for a hearing, shall issue an order affirming or modifying the abatement requirements in such citation.

Ref.: W. Cal. Ev., "Hearsay" §116.

§6320. Reinspection.

(a) If, after inspection or investigation, the division issues a special order, order to take special action, or a citation for a serious violation, and if at the time of inspection the order is not complied with or the violation is not abated, the division shall conduct a reinspection in the following cases:

(1) All inspections or investigations involving a serious violation of a standard adopted pursuant to Section 6401.7, a special order or order to take special action, serious violations of those orders, and serious violations characterized as repeat or willful or with abatement periods of less than six days. These reinspections shall be conducted at the end of the period fixed for compliance with the order or abatement of the violation or within 30 days thereafter.

(2) At least 20 percent of the inspections or investigations involving a serious violation not otherwise scheduled for reinspection. These inspections shall be randomly selected and shall be conducted at the end of the period fixed for abatement of the violation or within a reasonable time thereafter.

(b) Whenever a serious violation is not abated at the time of the initial or subsequent inspection, the division shall require the employer to submit a signed statement under penalty of perjury that he or she has complied with the abatement terms within the period fixed for abatement of the violation. If the statement is not received by the division within 10 working days after the end of the period fixed for abatement, the division shall revoke any adjustments to the civil penalty based on abatement of the violation. The division shall include on the initial notice of civil penalty a clear warning of reinspection and automatic revocation of any civil penalty adjustments based on abatement for failure to submit the required statement in the time allotted, and of an additional, potentially substantial monetary penalty for failure to abate the violation. If the division fails to receive evidence of abatement or the statement within 10 working days after the end of the abatement period, the division shall notify the employer that the additional civil penalty for failure to abate, as provided in Section 6430, will be assessed retroactive to the end of the abatement period unless the employer can provide sufficient evidence that the violation was abated prior to that date. The division shall conduct a reinspection of serious violations within 45 days following the end of the abatement period whenever it still has no evidence of abatement.

Ref.: W. Cal. Ev., "Hearsay" §116.

§6321. Limitation on advance warning; penalties for violation.

No person or employer shall be given advance warning of an inspection or investigation by any authorized representative of the division unless authorized under provisions of this part.

Only the chief or, in the case of his absence, his authorized representatives shall have the authority to permit advance notice of an inspection or investigation. The director shall, as soon as practicable, set down limitations under which an employer may be granted advance notice by the chief. In no case, except an imminent danger to the health or safety of an employee or employees, is advance notice to be authorized when the investigation or inspection is to be made as a result of an employee complaint.

Any person who gives advance notice of any inspection to be conducted, without authority from the chief or his designees, is guilty of a misdemeanor and shall, upon conviction, be punished by a fine of not more than one thousand dollars ($1,000) or by imprisonment for not more than six months, or by both.

Ref.: W. Cal. Ev., "Hearsay" §116.

§6322. Confidentiality of information obtained.

All information reported to or otherwise obtained by the chief or his representatives in connection with any inspection or proceeding of the division which contains or which might reveal a trade secret referred to in Section 1905 of Title 18 of the United States Code, or other information that is confidential pursuant to Chapter 3.5 (commencing with Section 6250) of Division 7 of Title 1 of the Government Code, shall be considered confidential, except that such information may be disclosed to other officers or employees of the division concerned with carrying out the purposes of the division or when relevant in any proceeding of the division. The appeals board, standards board, the courts, or the director shall in any such proceeding issue such orders as may be appropriate to protect the confidentiality of trade secrets. Violation of this section is a misdemeanor.

Ref.: W. Cal. Ev., "Hearsay" §116, "Witnesses" §300.

§6323. Injunctions.

If the condition of any employment or place of employment or the operation of any machine, device, apparatus, or equipment constitutes a serious menace to the lives or safety of persons about it, the division may apply to the superior court of the county in which such place of employment, machine, device, apparatus, or equipment is situated, for an injunction restraining the use or operation thereof until such condition is corrected.

Ref.: W. Cal. Ev., "Hearsay" §116; W. Cal. Sum., 3 "Agency and Employment" §366.

§6324. Temporary restraining orders.

The application to the superior court accompanied by affidavit showing that such place of employment, machine, device, apparatus, or equipment is being operated in violation of a safety order or standard, or in violation of Section 25910 of the Health and Safety Code, and that such use or operation constitutes a menace to the life or safety of any person employed thereabout and accompanied by a copy of the order or standard applicable thereto is a sufficient prima facie showing to warrant, in the discretion of the court, the immediate granting of a temporary restraining order. No bond shall be required from the division as a prerequisite to the granting of any restraining order.

Ref.: W. Cal. Ev., "Hearsay" §116.

§6325. Prohibition of workplace entry or use of equipment.

When, in the opinion of the division, a place of employment, machine, device, apparatus, or equipment or any part thereof is in a dangerous condition, is not properly guarded or is dangerously placed so as to constitute an imminent hazard to employees, entry therein, or the use thereof, as the case may be, shall be prohibited by the division, and a conspicuous notice to that effect shall be attached thereto. Such prohibition of use shall be limited to the immediate area in which the imminent hazard exists, and the division shall not prohibit any entry in or use of a place of employment, machine, device, apparatus, or equipment, or any part thereof, which is outside such area of imminent hazard. Such notice shall not be removed except by an authorized representative of the division, nor until the place of employment, machine, device, apparatus, or equipment is made safe and the required safeguards or safety appliances or devices are provided. This section shall not prevent the entry or use with the division's knowledge and permission for the sole purpose of eliminating the dangerous conditions.

Ref.: W. Cal. Ev., "Hearsay" §116; W. Cal. Sum., 3 "Agency and Employment" §366.

§6325.5. Order prohibiting use of workplace containing friable asbestos.

If the division has reasonable cause to believe that any workplace contains friable asbestos, and if there appears to be inadequate protection for employees at that workplace to the hazards from airborne asbestos fibers, the division may issue an order prohibiting use.

Ref.: W. Cal. Ev., "Hearsay" §116.

§6326. Penalties for violation of no-entry or no-use orders.

Every person who, after such notice is attached as provided in Section 6325, enters any such place of employment, or uses or operates any such place of employment, machine, device, apparatus, or equipment before it is made safe and the required safeguards or safety appliances or devices are provided, or who defaces, destroys or removes any such notice without the authority of the division, is guilty of a misdemeanor punishable by a fine of up to one thousand dollars ($1,000), or up to one year in the county jail, or both.

Ref.: W. Cal. Ev., "Hearsay" §116.

§6327. Contesting prohibition of use or entry.

Once an authorized representative of the division has prohibited entry in or use of a place of employment, machine device, apparatus, or equipment, as specified in Section 6325, the employer may contest the order and shall be granted, upon request, a hearing by the division to review the validity of the representative's order. The hearing shall be held within 24 hours following the employer's request.

Ref.: W. Cal. Ev., "Hearsay" §116.

§6327.5. Employee action if division fails to act.

If the division arbitrarily or capriciously fails to take action to prevent or prohibit any conditions or practices in any employment or place of employment which are such that danger exists which could reasonably be expected to cause death or serious physical harm immediately or before the imminence of such danger can be eliminated through other available means, any employee who may be injured by reason of such failure, or the representatives of such employees, may bring an action against the chief of the division in any appropriate court for a writ of mandate to compel the division to prevent or prohibit the condition. Nothing contained in this section shall be deemed to prevent the bringing of a writ of mandate against any appropriate person or entity as may be provided by law.

Ref.: W. Cal. Ev., "Hearsay" §116; W. Cal. Sum., 3 "Agency and Employment" §366.

§6328. Informational notices.

The division shall prepare a notice containing pertinent information regarding safety rules and regulations. The notice shall contain the address and telephone number of the nearest division office; a clear explanation of an employee's right to report any unsafe working conditions; the right to request a safety inspection by the division for unsafe conditions; the right to refuse to work under conditions which endanger his life or health; the right to receive information under the Hazardous Substances Information and Training Act (Ch. 2.5 (commencing with Section 6360)); posting and notice requirements of employers and the division; and any other information the division deems necessary. It shall be supplied to employers as soon as practical. The division shall promulgate regulations on the content and the required location and number of notices which must be posted by employers. Sufficient posters in both English and Spanish shall be printed to supply employers in this state.

Ref.: W. Cal. Ev., "Hearsay" §116.

§6329. Payment of money collected from employers.

All money collected for violation of standards, orders, or special orders of, or for fees paid pursuant to this division shall be paid into the state treasury to the credit of the General Fund.

The Department of Industrial Relations shall account to the Department of Finance and the State Controller for all moneys so received and furnish proper vouchers therefor.

Ref.: W. Cal. Ev., "Hearsay" §116.

§6330. Annual report to Legislature.

The director shall prepare and submit to the Legislature, not later than March 1, an annual report on the division activities. The report shall include, but need not be limited to, the following information for the previous calendar year:

(a) The amount of funds allocated and spent in enforcement, education and research, and administration by the division.

(b) Total inspections made, and citations issued by the division.

(c) The number of civil penalties assessed, total amount of fines collected and the number of appeals heard.

(d) The number of contractors referred to the Contractor's State License Board for hearing, pursuant to Section 7109.5 of the Business and Professions Code, and the total number of these cases resulting in suspension or revocation of a license.

(e) The report from the division prepared by the Bureau of Investigations for submission to the director pursuant to Section 6315.3.

(f) Recommendations for legislation which improves the ability of the division to provide safety in places of employment.

The report shall be made to the Speaker of the Assembly and the Chairman of the Rules Committee of the Senate, for assignment to the appropriate committee or committees for evaluation.

Ref.: W. Cal. Ev., "Hearsay" §116.

§6331. Testing of self-contained breathing apparatus.

The division shall enter into a contract for the development and execution of tests to define safety standards for the use of positive pressure, closed circuit, breathing apparatus in interior structural fires. The testing shall define numerically what constitutes positive pressure in breathing apparatus. The testing shall also address the issues of the heat of the oxygen coming into the mask, the condensation inside the mask, the possibility of, and effect of, moisture condensation in the lungs of the wearer of the mask, and the risks associated with a dislodgement of the mask in an interior structural fire situation. The development of these tests shall utilize the resources of recognized specialists in fire research to design, conduct, and execute the tests and develop the standards. The standards board shall adopt or revise safety standards based on the results of these tests.

The test parameters, the location where the testing will take place, and the level of expertise required shall be determined by the Cal-OSHA Self Contained Breathing Apparatus Advisory Committee.

Ref.: W. Cal. Ev., "Hearsay" §116.

§6332. Employers to keep record of violence committed against community health care worker.

(a) For purposes of this section, the following terms have the following meanings:

(1) "Community health care worker" means an individual who provides health care or health care-related services to clients in home settings.

(2) "Employer" means a person or entity that employs a community health care worker. "Employer" does not include an individual who is a recipient of home-based services and who is responsible for hiring his or her own community health care worker.

(3) "Violence" means a physical assault or a threat of a physical assault.

(b) Every employer shall keep a record of any violence committed against a community health care worker and shall file a copy of that record with the Division of Labor Statistics and Research in the form and detail and within the time limits prescribed by the Division of Labor Statistics and Research. **Leg.H.** 2000 ch. 493.

Ref.: W. Cal. Ev., "Hearsay" §116.

CHAPTER 2
EDUCATION AND RESEARCH
[Selected Provisions]

§6350. Educational and research program.

The division shall maintain an education and research program for the purpose of providing in-service training of division personnel, safety education for employees and employers, research and consulting safety services.

Ref.: W. Cal. Ev., "Hearsay" §116.

§6351. Preparation and distribution of health and safety information.

The division shall be responsible for preparation and distribution of information concerning occupational safety and health programs, methods, techniques or devices. Such information may include but is not limited to safety publications, films and audiovisual material, speeches and conferences on safety.

Ref.: W. Cal. Ev., "Hearsay" §116.

§6352. Safety training programs; priority of program development.

The division shall provide safety training programs, upon request, for employees and employers. Priority for the development of safety training programs shall be in those occupations which pose the greatest hazard to the safety and health of employees.

Ref.: W. Cal. Ev., "Hearsay" §116.

§6353. Continuing research.

The division shall conduct continuing research into methods, means, operations, techniques, processes and practices necessary for improvement of occupational safety and health of employees.

Ref.: W. Cal. Ev., "Hearsay" §116.

§6354. Consulting services.

The division shall, upon request, provide a full range of occupational safety and health consulting services to any employer or employee group. These consulting services shall include:

(a) A program for identifying categories of occupational safety and health hazards causing the greatest number and most serious preventable injuries and illnesses and workers' compensation losses and the places of employment where they are occurring. The hazards, industries, and places of employment shall be identified from the data system that is used in the targeted inspection program pursuant to Section 6314.1. The division shall develop procedures for offering consultation services to high hazard employers who are identified pursuant to this section. The services may include the development of educational material and procedures for reducing or eliminating safety and health hazards, conducting workplace surveys to identify health and safety problems, and development of plans to improve employer health and safety loss records.

The program shall include a component for reducing the number of work-related, repetitive motion injuries, including, but not limited to, back injuries. The division may formulate recommendations for reducing repetitive motion injuries after conducting a survey of the workplace of the employer who accepts services of the division. The recommendations shall include, wherever appropriate, the application of generally accepted ergonomic and engineering principles to eliminate repetitive motions that are generally expected to result in injuries to workers. The recommendations shall also include, wherever appropriate, training programs to instruct workers in methods for performing job-related movements, such as lifting heavy objects, in a manner that minimizes strain and provides safeguards against injury.

The division shall establish model injury and illness prevention training programs to prevent repetitive motion injuries, including recommendations for the minimum qualifications of instructors. The model programs shall be made available to employers, employer associations, workers' compensation insurers, and employee organizations on request.

(b) A program for providing assistance in the development of injury prevention programs for employees and employers. The highest priority for the division's consulting services shall be given to development of these programs for businesses with fewer than 250 employees in industries identified in the regional plans developed pursuant to subdivision (b) of Section 6314.1.

(c) A program for providing employers or employees with information, advice, and recommendations on maintaining safe employment or place of employment, and on applicable occupational safety and health standards, techniques, devices, methods, practices, or programs. **Leg.H.** 1993 ch. 121, effective July 16, 1993, 1995 ch. 903.

Ref.: W. Cal. Ev., "Hearsay" §116.

§6354.5. Insurer's provision of occupational safety and health loss control consultation services; standards; insurance loss control services coordinator.

(a) Any insurer desiring to write workers' compensation insurance shall maintain or provide occupational safety and health loss control consultation services. The insurer may employ qualified personnel to provide these services or provide the services through another entity.

(b) The program of an insurer for furnishing loss control consultation services shall be adequate to meet minimum standards prescribed by this section. Required loss control consultation services shall be adequate to identify the hazards exposing the insured to, or causing the insured, significant workers' compensation losses, and to advise the insured of steps needed to mitigate the identified workers' compensation losses or exposures. The program of an insurer for furnishing loss control consultation services shall provide all of the following:

(1) A workplace survey, including discussions with management and, where appropriate, nonmanagement personnel with permission of the employer.

(2) A review of injury records with appropriate personnel.

(3) The development of a plan to improve the employer's health and safety loss control experience, which shall include, where appropriate, modifications to the employer's injury and illness prevention program established pursuant to Section 6401.7. At the time that an insurance policy is issued and annually thereafter, and again when notified by Cal-OSHA that an insured employer has been identified as a targeted employer pursuant to Section 6314.1, the insurer shall provide each insured employer with a written description of the consultation services together with a notice that the services are available at no additional charge to the employer. These notices to the employer shall appear in at least 10-point bold type.

(c) The insurer shall not charge any fee in addition to the insurance premium for safety and health loss control consultation services.

(d) Nothing in this section shall be construed to require insurers to provide loss control services to places of employment that do not pose significant preventable hazards to workers.

(e) The director shall establish an insurance loss control services coordinator position in the Department of Industrial Relations. The coordinator shall provide information to employers about the availability of loss control consultation services and respond to employers' questions and complaints about loss control consultation services provided by their insurer. The coordinator shall notify the insurer of every complaint concerning loss control consultation services. If the employer and the insurer are unable to agree on a mutually satisfactory solution to the complaint, the coordinator shall investigate the complaint. Whenever the coordinator determines that the loss control consultation services provided by the insurer are inadequate or inappropriate, he or she shall recommend to the employer and the insurer the actions required to bring the loss control program into compliance. If the employer and the insurer are unable to agree on a mutually satisfactory solution to the complaint, the coordinator shall forward his or her recommendations to the director. The cost of providing the coordinator services shall be paid out of the Workers' Occupational Safety and Health Education Fund created by subdivision (a) of Section 6354.7. However, no more than 20 percent of that fund may be expended for this purpose each year. **Leg.H.** 1995 ch. 556, 2002 ch. 6 (AB 749).

Ref.: Herlick Handbook § 3.15; W. Cal. Ev., "Hearsay" §116; W. Cal. Sum., 2 "Workers' Compensation" §147.

§6354.7. [First Enacted Section] Workers' Occupational Safety and Health Education Fund; development of worker safety and health training and education program.

(a) The Workers' Occupational Safety and Health Education Fund is hereby created as a special account in the State Treasury. Proceeds of the fund may be expended, upon appropriation by the Legislature, by the Commission on Health and Safety and Workers' Compensation for the purpose of establishing and maintaining a worker occupational safety and health training and education program and insurance loss control services coordinator. The director shall levy and collect fees to fund these purposes from insurers subject to Section 6354.5. However, the fee assessed against any insurer shall not exceed the greater of one hundred dollars ($100) or 0.0286 percent of paid workers' compensation indemnity claims as reported for the previous calendar year to the designated rating organization for the analysis required under subdivision (b) of Section 11759.1 of the Insurance Code. All fees shall be deposited in the fund.

(b) The commission shall establish and maintain a worker safety and health training and education program. The purpose of the worker occupational safety and health training and education program shall be to promote awareness of the need for prevention education programs, to develop and provide injury and illness prevention education programs for employees and their representatives, and to deliver those awareness and training programs through a network of providers throughout the state. The commission may conduct the program directly or by means of contracts or interagency agreements.

(c) The commission shall establish an employer and worker advisory board for the program. The advisory board shall guide the development of curricula, teaching methods, and specific course material about occupational safety and health, and shall assist in providing links to the target audience and broadening the partnerships with worker-based organizations, labor studies programs, and others that are able to reach the target audience.

(d) The program shall include the development and provision of a needed core curriculum addressing competencies for effective participation in workplace injury and illness prevention programs and on joint labor-management health and safety committees. The core curriculum shall include an overview of the requirements related to injury and illness prevention programs and hazard communication.

(e) The program shall include the development and provision of additional training programs for any or all of the following categories:

(1) Industries on the high hazard list.

(2) Hazards that result in significant worker injuries, illnesses, or compensation costs.

(3) Industries or trades where workers are experiencing numerous or significant injuries or illnesses.

(4) Occupational groups with special needs, such as those who do not speak English as their first language, workers with limited literacy, young workers, and other traditionally underserved industries or groups of workers. Priority shall be given to training workers who are able to train other workers and workers who have significant health and safety responsibilities, such as those workers serving on a health and safety committee or serving as designated safety representatives.

(f) The program shall operate one or more libraries and distribution systems of occupational safety and health training material, which shall include, but not be limited to, all material developed by the program pursuant to this section.

(g) The advisory board shall annually prepare a written report evaluating the use and impact of programs developed.

(h) The payment of administrative costs incurred by the commission in conducting the program shall be made from the Workers' Occupational Safety and Health Education Fund. **Leg.H.** 2002 ch. 6 (AB 749).

2002 Note: The Legislature inadvertently enacted another §6354.7, which follows.

Ref.: Hanna § 1.18; Herlick Handbook § 3.15.

§6354.7. [Second Enacted Section] Workers' Occupational Safety and Health Education Fund; development of worker safety and health training and education program.

(a) The Workers' Occupational Safety and Health Education Fund is hereby created as a special account in the State Treasury. Proceeds of the fund may be expended, upon appropriation by the Legislature, by the Commission on Health and Safety and Workers' Compensation for the purpose of establishing and maintaining a worker occupational safety and health training and education program and an insurance loss control services coordinator. The director shall levy and collect fees to fund these purposes from insurers subject to Section 6354.5. However, the fee assessed against any insurer shall not exceed the greater of one hundred dollars ($100) or 0.0286 percent of paid workers' compensation indemnity amounts for claims as reported for the previous calendar year to the designated rating organization for the analysis required under subdivisions (b) and (c) of Section 11759.1 of the Insurance Code. All fees shall be deposited in the fund.

(b) The commission shall establish and maintain a worker safety and health training and education program. The purpose of the worker occupational safety and health training and education program shall be to promote awareness of the need for prevention education programs, to develop and provide injury and illness prevention education programs for employees and their representatives, and to deliver those awareness and training programs through a network of providers throughout the state. The commission may conduct the program directly or by means of contracts or interagency agreements.

(c) The commission shall establish an employer and worker advisory board for the program. The advisory board shall guide the development of curricula, teaching methods, and specific course material about occupational safety and health, and shall assist in providing links to the target audience and broadening the partnerships with worker-based organizations, labor studies programs, and others that are able to reach the target audience.

(d) The program shall include the development and provision of a needed core curriculum addressing competencies for effective participation in workplace injury and illness prevention programs and on joint labor-management health and safety committees. The core curriculum shall include an overview of the requirements related to injury and illness prevention programs and hazard communication.

(e) The program shall include the development and provision of additional training programs for any or all of the following categories:

(1) Industries on the high hazard list.

(2) Hazards that result in significant worker injuries, illnesses, or compensation costs.

(3) Industries or trades in which workers are experiencing numerous or significant injuries or illnesses.

(4) Occupational groups with special needs, such as those who do not speak English as their first language, workers with limited literacy, young workers, and other traditionally underserved industries or groups of workers. Priority shall be given to training workers who are able to train other workers and workers who have significant health and safety responsibilities, such as those workers serving on a health and safety committee or serving as designated safety representatives.

(f) The program shall operate one or more libraries and distribution systems of occupational safety and health training material, which shall include, but not be limited to, all material developed by the program pursuant to this section.

(g) The advisory board shall annually prepare a written report evaluating the use and impact of programs developed.

(h) The payment of administrative costs incurred by the commission in conducting the program shall be made from the Workers' Occupational Safety and Health Education Fund. **Leg.H.** 2002 ch. 866 (AB 486).

Ref.: Hanna § 1.18; Herlick Handbook § 3.15; W. Cal. Ev., "Hearsay" §116.

§6355. Employer's immunity from prosecution or penalties.

If the employer requests or accepts consulting services offered pursuant to Section 6354, the division in providing such services at the employer's employment or place of employment shall neither institute any prosecution under Section 6423 nor issue any citations for a violation of any standard or order adopted pursuant to Chapter 6 (commencing with Section 140) of Division 1. In any instance in which the division representative providing the consulting service finds that the conditions of employment, place of employment, any work procedure, or the operation of any machine, device, apparatus, or equipment constitutes an imminent hazard or danger, within the meaning of Section 6325, to the lives, safety, or health of employees, entry therein, or the use thereof, as the case may be, shall be prohibited by the division pursuant to Section 6325. The employer shall not, however, be liable to prosecution under Section 6423, nor shall the division issue any citations or assess any civil penalties, except in any case where the employer fails to comply with the division's prohibition of entry or use, or in any case where the provisions of Section 6326 apply. **Leg.H.** 1993 ch. 121, effective July 16, 1993.

Ref.: W. Cal. Ev., "Hearsay" §116.

§6356. Worker Safety Bilingual Investigative Support, Enforcement, and Training Account.

(a) There is hereby created, in the General Fund, the Worker Safety Bilingual Investigative Support, Enforcement, and Training Account. The moneys in the account may be expended by the department, upon appropriation by the Legislature, for the purposes of this part.

(b) The department may receive and accept a contribution of funds from an individual or private organization, including the proceeds from a judgment in a state or federal court, if the contribution is made to carry out the purposes of this part. The department shall immediately deposit the contribution in the account established by subdivision (a).

(c) The department may not receive or accept a contribution of funds under this section made from the proceeds of a judgment in a criminal action filed pursuant to Section 6423 or 6425 of the Labor Code. **Leg.H.** 2002 ch. 885 (AB 2837).

Ref.: W. Cal. Ev., "Hearsay" §116.

§6357. Adoption of standards for ergonomics in the workplace.

On or before January 1, 1995, the Occupational Safety and Health Standards Board shall adopt standards for ergonomics in the workplace designed to minimize the instances of injury from repetitive motion. **Leg.H.** 1993 ch. 121, effective July 16, 1993.

Ref.: W. Cal. Ev., "Hearsay" §116; W. Cal. Sum., 3 "Agency and Employment" §378.

CHAPTER 2.5 HAZARDOUS SUBSTANCES INFORMATION AND TRAINING

ARTICLE 3 Hazardous Substances [Selected Provisions]

§6380. List of hazardous substances.

For the purposes of this chapter, the director, pursuant to Section 6382, shall establish a list of hazardous substances and shall make the list available to manufacturers, employers, and the public. Substances on the list shall be designated by their chemical and common name or names. The director shall adopt, amend, and repeal regulations for the establishment of the list of hazardous substances pursuant to the provisions of Chapter 3.5 (commencing with Section 11340) of Part 1 of Division 3 of Title 2 of the Government Code. **Leg.H.** 1980 ch. 874 § 1.

Ref.: W. Cal. Ev., "Hearsay" §116.

ARTICLE 4 Duties

§6390. Preparation and provision of MSDS.

The manufacturer of any hazardous substance listed pursuant to the provisions of Section 6380 shall prepare and provide its direct purchasers of the hazardous substance with an MSDS containing the information specified in Section 6391 which, to the best of the manufacturer's knowledge, is current, accurate, and complete, based on information then reasonably available to the manufacturer. For purposes of this section, a substance, mixture, or product shall not be considered a hazardous substance if present in a physical state, volume, or concentration for which there is no valid and substantial evidence that any adverse acute or chronic risk to human health may occur from exposure. The manufacturer shall revise an MSDS on a timely basis as appropriate to the importance of any new information which would affect the contents of the existing MSDS, and in any event within one year of such information becoming available to the manufacturer. If the new information indicates significantly increased risks to, or measures necessary to protect, employee health, as compared to those stated on the MSDS previously provided, the manufacturer shall provide such new information to persons who have purchased the product directly from the manufacturer within the last year. **Leg.H.** 1980 ch. 874.

Ref.: W. Cal. Ev., "Hearsay" §116.

§6390.5. Labeling.

The manufacturer, importer, and distributor of any hazardous substance, and the employer, shall label each container of a hazardous substance in a manner consistent with the federal Hazard Communication Standard (29 C.F.R. Sec. 1910.1200) and as set forth in applicable occupational safety and health standards adopted by the standards board. **Leg.H.** 1985 ch. 1000 §4.

Ref.: W. Cal. Ev., "Hearsay" §116.

§6391. Information manufacturers must provide purchasers.

The information which manufacturers shall provide to their purchasers pursuant to the provisions of Section 6390 shall include the following, if pertinent:

(a) The chemical name, any common names, and the CAS number of the hazardous substance.

(b) The hazards or other risks in the use of the hazardous substance, including all of the following:

(1) The potential for fire, explosion, and reactivity.

(2) The acute and chronic health effects or risks from exposure.

(3) The potential routes of exposure and symptoms of overexposure.

(c) The hazards or other risks of exposure to the combustion products of the hazardous substance.

(d) The proper precautions, handling practices, necessary personal protective equipment, and other safety precautions in the use of or exposure to the hazardous substance, and its combustion products.

(e) The emergency procedures for spills, fire, disposal, and first aid.

(f) A description in lay terms, if not otherwise provided, on either a separate sheet or with the body of the information specified in this section, of the specific potential health risks posed by the hazardous substance and its combustion products intended to alert any person reading the information.

(g) The month and year that the information was compiled and, for an MSDS issued after January 1, 1981, the name and address of the manufacturer responsible for preparing the information. **Leg.H.** 1988 ch. 423 §1.

Ref.: W. Cal. Ev., "Hearsay" §116.

§6392. Proof of compliance—Federal MSDS.

Provision of a federal Material Safety Data Sheet or equivalent shall constitute prima facie proof of compliance with Section 6390. **Leg.H.** 1980 ch. 874, 1992 ch. 1214.

Ref.: W. Cal. Ev., "Hearsay" §116.

§6393. Relief of obligation to provide MSDS.

The manufacturer shall be relieved of the obligation to provide a specific purchaser of a hazardous substance with an MSDS pursuant to Section 6390 if the manufacturer has a record of having provided the specific purchaser with the most current version of the MSDS, or if the product is one sold at retail and is incidentally sold to an employer or the employer's employees, in the same form, approximate amount, concentration, and manner as it is sold to consumers, and, to the seller's knowledge, employee exposure to the product is not significantly greater than the consumer exposure occurring during the principal consumer use of the product. Except for products so labeled, this section does not relieve the manufacturer of the requirement to provide direct purchasers with new, revised, or later information or an MSDS pursuant to Section 6390. **Leg.H.** 1991 ch. 274 §3, 1992 ch. 427.

Ref.: W. Cal. Ev., "Hearsay" §116.

§6394. Transmission of copy of MSDS to department.

The preparer of an MSDS shall provide the department with a copy of the MSDS on each hazardous substance it manufactures. The preparer may transmit the MSDS to the department in either paper or electronic form. In the electronic filing of an MSDS, it is the responsibility of the preparer to protect any trade secret information contained in the MSDS during transmission to the department. Upon receipt by the department of the MSDS, it is the responsibility of the department to protect any trade secret information. **Leg.H.** 1980 ch. 874, 1999 ch. 366.

Ref.: W. Cal. Ev., "Hearsay" §116.

§6395. MSDS for entire product mixture.

(a) The manufacturer may provide the information required by Section 6390 on an entire product mixture, instead of on each hazardous substance in it, when all of the following conditions exist:

(1) Hazard test information exists on the mixture itself, or adequate information exists to form a valid judgment of the hazardous properties of the mixture itself and the MSDS indicates that the information presented and the conclusions drawn are from some source other than direct test data on the mixture itself, and that an MSDS on each constituent hazardous substance identified on the MSDS is available upon request.

(2) Provision of information on the mixture will be as effective in protecting employee health as information on the ingredients.

(3) The hazardous substances in the mixture are identified on the MSDS unless it is either unfeasible to describe all the ingredients in the mixture or the identity of the ingredients is itself a valid trade secret, in either case the reason why the hazardous substances in the mixture are not identified shall be stated on the MSDS.

(b) A single mixture MSDS may be provided for more than one formulation of a product mixture if the information provided pursuant to Section 6390 does not vary for the formulation. **Leg.H.** 1980 ch. 874.

Ref.: W. Cal. Ev., "Hearsay" §116.

§6396. Protection from disclosure of trade secrets.

(a) The Director of Industrial Relations shall protect from disclosure any and all trade secrets coming into his or her possession, as defined in subdivision (d) of Section 6254.7 of the Government Code, when requested in writing or by appropriate stamping or marking of documents by the manufacturer or producer of a mixture.

(b) Any information reported to or otherwise obtained by the Director of Industrial Relations, or any of his or her representatives or employees, which is exempt from disclosure under subdivision (a), shall not be disclosed to anyone except an officer or employee of the state or of the United States of America, in connection with the official duties of that officer or employee under any law for the protection of health, or to contractors with the state and their employees if in the opinion of the director the disclosure is necessary and required for the satisfactory performance of a contract for performance of work in connection with this act.

(c) Any officer or employee of the state, or former officer or employee, who by virtue of that employment or official position has obtained possession of or has access to material the disclosure of which is prohibited by this section, and who, knowing that disclosure of the material is prohibited, knowingly and willfully discloses the material in any manner to any person not entitled to receive it, is guilty of a misdemeanor. Any contractor with the state and any employee of that contractor, who has been furnished information as authorized by this section, shall be considered to be an employee of the state for purposes of this section.

(d) Information certified to by appropriate officials of the United States, as necessarily kept secret for national defense purposes, shall be accorded the full protections against disclosure as specified by that official or in accordance with the laws of the United States.

(e)(1) The director, upon his or her own initiative, or upon receipt of a request pursuant to the California Public Records Act, (Chapter 3.5 (commencing with Section 6250) of Division 7 of Title 1 of the Government Code) for the release of data submitted and designated as a trade secret by an employer, manufacturer, or producer of a mixture, shall determine whether any or all of the data so submitted are a properly designated trade secret.

(2) If the director determines that the data is not a trade secret, the director shall notify the employer, manufacturer, or producer of a mixture by certified mail.

(3) The employer, manufacturer, or producer of a mixture shall have 15 days after receipt of notification to provide the director with a complete justification and statement of the grounds on which the trade secret privilege is claimed. This justification and statement shall be submitted by certified mail.

(4) The director shall determine whether the data are protected as a trade secret within 15 days after receipt of the justification and statement, or if no justification and statement is filed, within 30 days of the original notice, and shall notify the employer or manufacturer and any party who has requested the data pursuant to the California Public Records Act of that determination by certified mail. If the director determines that the data are not protected as a trade secret, the final notice shall also specify a date, not sooner than 15 days after the date of mailing of the final notice, when the data shall be available to the public.

(5) Prior to the date specified in the final notice, an employer, manufacturer, or producer of a mixture may institute an action in an appropriate superior court for a declaratory judgment as to whether the data are subjected to protection under subdivision (a).

(f) This section does not authorize a manufacturer to refuse to disclose information required pursuant to this chapter to the director. **Leg.H.** 1983 ch. 142 §112, 1995 ch. 91.

Ref.: W. Cal. Ev., "Hearsay" §116.

§6397. Provision of MSDS to direct purchaser at time of sale.

(a) Any person other than a manufacturer who sells a mixture or any hazardous substance shall provide its direct purchasers of the mixture or hazardous substance at the time of sale with a copy of the most recent MSDS or equivalent information prepared and supplied to the person pursuant to either Section 6390 or subdivision (b) whenever it is foreseeable that the provisions of this chapter may apply to the purchaser.

(b) Any person who produces a mixture may, for the purposes of this section, prepare and use a mixture MSDS, subject to the provisions of Section 6395.

(c) Any person subject to the provisions of subdivision (a) shall be relieved of the obligation to provide a specific purchaser of a hazardous substance with an MSDS if he or she has a record of having provided the specific purchaser with the most recent version of the MSDS, or if the product is one sold at retail and is incidentally sold to an employer or the employer's employees, in the same form, approximate amount, concentration, and manner as it is sold to consumers, and, to the seller's knowledge, employee exposure to the product is not significantly greater than the consumer exposure oc-

Labor

curring during the principal consumer use of the product. **Leg.H.** 1991 ch. 274 §4.

Ref.: W. Cal. Ev., "Hearsay" §116.

§6398. Employer's duties toward employees.

The Occupational Safety and Health Standards Board shall adopt a standard setting forth an employer's duties toward its employees under this chapter, on or before July 1, 1981, consistent with the following guidelines:

(a) An MSDS shall be available to an employee, collective bargaining representative, or the employee's physician, on a timely and reasonable basis, on substances in the workplace.

(b) Employers shall furnish employees who may be exposed to a hazardous substance with information on the contents of the MSDS for the hazardous substances or equivalent information, either in written form or through training programs, which may be generic to the extent appropriate and related to the job.

(c) Provision shall be made for employees to be informed of their rights under this chapter and under the standard to be adopted. **Leg.H.** 1980 ch. 874.

Ref.: W. Cal. Ev., "Hearsay" §116.

§6399. Availability of MSDS to employees.

Upon request, the manufacturer of a hazardous substance or the producer of a mixture who has produced a mixture MSDS pursuant to the provisions of subdivision (b) of Section 6397 shall make available to any employer, whose employees may be exposed to its product in the workplace, an MSDS on its product. If the employer does not already have an MSDS and has not already made written inquiry within 12 months as to whether a substance or product is subject to the requirements of this chapter or if the employer has not already made written inquiry within 6 months as to whether any new, revised, or later information has been issued for a hazardous substance, the employer shall do so within seven working days of a request to do so by an employee or employee's collective bargaining representative or physician. The employer may adopt reasonable procedures for acting upon such employee requests to avoid interruption of normal work operations. The manufacturer or the producer of a mixture MSDS pursuant to the provisions of Section 6397 shall answer such inquiries within 15 working days of their receipt, stating that the substance or product is subject to the requirements of this chapter and furnishing the most current MSDS or a statement that the MSDS is under development and the estimated completion date, or stating that it is not subject to the requirements of this chapter, with a brief explanation of why the chapter is not applicable. If an employer has not received a response from a manufacturer within 25 working days of the date the request was made, the employer shall send a copy of the request made of the manufacturer to the director with the notation that no response has been received. **Leg.H.** 1980 ch. 874.

Ref.: W. Cal. Ev., "Hearsay" §116.

§6399.1. Compliance with Food and Agricultural Code §12981.

Compliance with regulations of the Director of Pesticide Regulation issued pursuant to Section 12981 of the Food and Agricultural Code shall be deemed compliance with the obligations of an employer toward his or her employees under this chapter. **Leg.H.** 1980 ch. 874, 1991 Gov. Reorg. Plan 1, effective July 17, 1991.

Ref.: W. Cal. Ev., "Hearsay" §116.

§6399.2. Operative date of article.

This article shall become operative 180 days after adoption of the initial list of hazardous substances pursuant to Article 3 (commencing with Section 6380). **Leg.H.** 1980 ch. 874.

1982 Note: Section 339 of Title 8 of the California Code of Regulations, as filed August 25, 1982, contains a hazardous substances list.

Ref.: W. Cal. Ev., "Hearsay" §116.

CHAPTER 3
RESPONSIBILITIES AND DUTIES OF EMPLOYERS AND EMPLOYEES

§6400. Employer to furnish safe and healthy workplace; employer categories that may be issued citations when employee exposed to hazard on multiemployer worksites.

(a) Every employer shall furnish employment and a place of employment that is safe and healthful for the employees therein.

(b) On multiemployer worksites, both construction and nonconstruction, citations may be issued only to the following categories of employers when the division has evidence that an employee was exposed to a hazard in violation of any requirement enforceable by the division:

(1) The employer whose employees were exposed to the hazard (the exposing employer).

(2) The employer who actually created the hazard (the creating employer).

(3) The employer who was responsible, by contract or through actual practice, for safety and health conditions on the worksite, which is the employer who had the authority for ensuring that the hazardous condition is corrected (the controlling employer).

(4) The employer who had the responsibility for actually correcting the hazard (the correcting employer).

The employers listed in paragraphs (2) to (4), inclusive, of this subdivision may be cited regardless of whether their own employees were exposed to the hazard.

(c) It is the intent of the Legislature, in adding subdivision (b) to this section, to codify existing regulations with respect to the responsibility of employers at multiemployer worksites. Subdivision (b) of this section is declaratory of existing law and shall not be construed or interpreted as creating a new law or as modifying or changing an existing law. **Leg.H.** 1999 ch. 615.

Ref.: Herlick Handbook §§ 9.6, 9.10, 12.7, 12.12; W. Cal. Ev., "Hearsay" §116; W. Cal. Sum., 3 "Agency and Employment" §§275, 364, 370, 6 "Torts" §§1236, 1247.

§6401. Safe and healthy equipment and practices requirement.

Every employer shall furnish and use safety devices and safeguards, and shall adopt and use practices, means, methods, operations, and processes which are reasonably adequate to render such employment and place of employment safe and healthful. Every employer shall do every other thing reasonably necessary to protect the life, safety, and health of employees.

Ref.: Herlick Handbook § 9.10; W. Cal. Ev., "Hearsay" §116; W. Cal. Sum., 6 "Torts" §1236.

§6401.5. Prohibition against salvaging materials during demolition.

No salvage of materials shall be permitted while demolition is in progress on any building, structure, falsework, or scaffold more than three stories high or the equivalent height for which a permit is required under subdivision (c) of Section 6500.

For this purpose salvage does not include removal of material from premises solely for the purpose of clearing the area to facilitate the continuation of the demolition.

Ref.: Herlick Handbook § 12.7; W. Cal. Ev., "Hearsay" §116.

§6401.7. Injury prevention programs.

(a) Every employer shall establish, implement, and maintain an effective injury prevention program. The program shall be written, except as provided in subdivision (e), and shall include, but not be limited to, the following elements:

(1) Identification of the person or persons responsible for implementing the program.

(2) The employer's system for identifying and evaluating workplace hazards, including scheduled periodic inspections to identify unsafe conditions and work practices.

(3) The employer's methods and procedures for correcting unsafe or unhealthy conditions and work practices in a timely manner.

(4) An occupational health and safety training program designed to instruct employees in general safe and healthy work practices and to provide specific instruction with respect to hazards specific to each employee's job assignment.

(5) The employer's system for communicating with employees on occupational health and safety matters, including provisions designed to encourage employees to inform the employer of hazards at the worksite without fear of reprisal.

(6) The employer's system for ensuring that employees comply with safe and healthy work practices, which may include disciplinary action.

(b) The employer shall correct unsafe and unhealthy conditions and work practices in a timely manner based on the severity of the hazard.

(c) The employer shall train all employees when the training program is first established, all new employees, and all employees given a new job assignment, and shall train employees whenever new substances, processes, procedures, or equipment are introduced to the workplace and represent a new hazard, and whenever the employer receives notification of a new or previously unrecognized hazard. Beginning January 1, 1994, an employer in the construction industry who is required to be licensed under Chapter 9 (commencing with Section 7000) of Division 3 of the Business and Professions Code may use employee training provided to the employer's employees under a construction industry occupational safety and health training program approved by the division to comply with the requirements of subdivision (a) relating to employee training, and shall only be required to provide training on hazards specific to an employee's job duties.

(d) The employer shall keep appropriate records of steps taken to implement and maintain the program. Beginning January 1, 1994, an employer in the construction industry who is required to be licensed under Chapter 9 (commencing with Section 7000) of Division 3 of the Business and Professions Code may use records relating to employee training provided to the employer in connection with an occupational safety and health training program approved by the division to comply with the requirements of this subdivision, and shall only be required to keep records of those steps taken to implement and maintain the program with respect to hazards specific to an employee's job duties.

(e)(1) The standards board shall adopt a standard setting forth the employer's duties under this section, on or before January 1, 1991, consistent with the requirements specified in subdivisions (a), (b), (c), and (d). The standards board, in adopting the standard, shall include substantial compliance criteria for use in evaluating an employer's injury prevention program. The board may adopt less stringent criteria for employers with few employees and for employers in industries with insignificant occupational safety or health hazards.

(2) Notwithstanding subdivision (a), for employers with fewer than 20 employees who are in industries that are not on a designated list of high hazard industries and who have a workers' compensation experience modification rate of 1.1 or less, and for any employers with fewer than 20 employees who are in industries that are on a designated list of low hazard industries, the board shall adopt a standard setting forth the employer's duties under this section consistent with the requirements specified in subdivisions (a), (b), and (c), except that the standard shall only require written documentation to the extent of documenting the person or persons responsible for implementing the program pursuant to paragraph (1) of subdivision (a), keeping a record of periodic inspections pursuant to paragraph (2) of subdivision (a), and keeping a record of employee training pursuant to paragraph (4) of subdivision (a). To any extent beyond the specifications of this subdivision, the standard shall not require the employer to keep the records specified in subdivision (d).

(3) The division shall establish a list of high hazard industries using the methods prescribed in Section 6314.1 for identifying and targeting employers in high hazard industries. For purposes of this subdivision, the "designated list of high hazard industries" shall be the list established pursuant to this paragraph.

For the purpose of implementing this subdivision, the Department of Industrial Relations shall periodically review, and as necessary revise, the list.

(4) For the purpose of implementing this subdivision, the Department of Industrial Relations shall also establish a list of low hazard industries, and shall periodically review, and as necessary revise, that list.

(f) The standard adopted pursuant to subdivision (e) shall specifically permit employer and employee occupational safety and health committees to be included in the employer's injury prevention program. The board shall establish criteria for use in evaluating employer and employee occupational safety and health committees. The criteria shall include minimum duties, including the following:

(1) Review of the employer's (A) periodic, scheduled worksite inspections, (B) investigation of causes of incidents resulting in injury, illness, or exposure to hazardous substances, and (C) investigation of any alleged hazardous condition brought to the attention of any committee member. When determined necessary by the committee, the committee may conduct its own inspections and investigations.

(2) Upon request from the division, verification of abatement action taken by the employer as specified in division citations.

If an employer's occupational safety and health committee meets the criteria established by the board, it shall be presumed to be in substantial compliance with paragraph (5) of subdivision (a).

(g) The division shall adopt regulations specifying the procedures for selecting employee representatives for employer-employee occupational health and safety committees when these procedures are not specified in an applicable collective bargaining agreement. No employee or employee organization shall be held liable for any act or omission in connection with a health and safety committee.

(h) The employer's injury prevention program, as required by this section, shall cover all of the employer's employees and all other workers who the employer controls or directs and directly supervises on the job to the extent these workers are exposed to worksite and job assignment specific hazards. Nothing in this subdivision shall affect the obligations of a contractor or other employer that controls or directs and directly supervises its own employees on the job.

(i) When a contractor supplies its employee to a state agency employer on a temporary basis, the state agency employer may assess a fee upon the contractor to reimburse the state agency for the additional costs, if any, of including the contract employee within the state agency's injury prevention program.

(j)(1) The division shall prepare a Model Injury and Illness Prevention Program for Non-High-Hazard Employment, and shall make copies of the model program prepared pursuant to this subdivision available to employers, upon request, for posting in the workplace. An employer who adopts and implements the model program prepared by the division pursuant to this paragraph in good faith shall not be assessed a civil penalty for the first citation for a violation of this section issued after the employer's adoption and implementation of the model program.

(2) For purposes of this subdivision, the division shall establish a list of non-high-hazard industries in California. These industries, identified by their Standard Industrial Classification Codes, as published by the United States Office of Management and Budget in the Manual of Standard Industrial Classification Codes, 1987 Edition, are apparel and accessory stores (Code 56), eating and drinking places (Code 58), miscellaneous retail (Code 59), finance, insurance, and real estate (Codes 60–67), personal services (Code 72), business services (Code 73), motion pictures (Code 78) except motion picture production and allied services (Code 781), legal services (Code 81), educational services (Code 82), social services (Code 83), museums, art galleries, and botanical and zoological gardens (Code 84), membership organizations (Code 86), engineering, accounting, research, management, and related services (Code 87), private households (Code 88), and miscellaneous services (Code 89). To further identify industries that may be included on the list, the division shall also consider data from a rating organization, as defined in Section 11750.1 of the Insurance Code, the Division of Labor Statistics and Research, and all other appropriate information. The list shall be established by June 30, 1994, and shall be reviewed, and as necessary revised, biennially.

(3) The division shall prepare a Model Injury and Illness Prevention Program for Employers in Industries with Intermittent Employment, and shall determine which industries have historically utilized seasonal or intermittent employees. An employer in an industry determined by the division to have historically utilized seasonal or intermittent employees shall be deemed to have complied with the requirements of subdivision (a) with respect to a written injury prevention program if the employer adopts the model program prepared by the division pursuant to this paragraph and complies with any instructions relating thereto.

(k) With respect to any county, city, city and county, or district, or any public or quasi-public corporation or public agency therein, including any public entity, other than a state agency, that is a member of, or created by, a joint powers agreement, subdivision (d) shall not apply.

(*l*) Every workers' compensation insurer shall conduct a review, including a written report as specified below, of the injury and illness prevention program (IIPP) of each of its insureds with an experience modification of 2.0 or greater within six months of the commencement of the initial insurance policy term. The review shall determine whether the insured has implemented all of the required components of the IIPP, and evaluate their effectiveness. The training component of the IIPP shall be evaluated to determine whether training is provided to line employees, supervisors, and upper level management, and effectively imparts the information and skills each of these groups needs to ensure that all of the insured's specific health and safety issues are fully addressed by the insured. The reviewer shall prepare a detailed written report specifying the findings of the review and all recommended changes deemed necessary to make the IIPP effective. The reviewer shall be or work under the direction of a

Labor

licensed California professional engineer, certified safety professional, or a certified industrial hygienist. **Leg.H.** 1991 ch. 964, 1993 chs. 927, 928, 929 §4, 2003 ch. 639 (SB 228), 2004 ch. 34 (SB 899), effective April 19, 2004.

2004 Note: The amendment to §6401.7 made by this act shall apply prospectively from the date of enactment of this act, regardless of the date of injury, unless otherwise specified, but shall not constitute good cause to reopen or rescind, alter, or amend any existing order, decision, or award of the Workers' Compensation Appeals Board. Stats. 2004 ch. 34 (SB 899) §47.

Ref.: 8 C.C.R. §§15203, 15210.1, 15353, 15354; Herlick Handbook §§ 3.20, 9.10, 12.7; W. Cal. Ev., "Hearsay" §116.

§6402. Allowing employee to work in unsafe conditions prohibited.

No employer shall require, or permit any employee to go or be in any employment or place of employment which is not safe and healthful.

Ref.: Herlick Handbook § 12.7; W. Cal. Ev., "Hearsay" §116.

§6403. Requirements of employer.

No employer shall fail or neglect to do any of the following:

(a) To provide and use safety devices and safeguards reasonably adequate to render the employment and place of employment safe.

(b) To adopt and use methods and processes reasonably adequate to render the employment and place of employment safe.

(c) To do every other thing reasonably necessary to protect the life, safety, and health of employees.

Ref.: Herlick Handbook § 12.7; W. Cal. Ev., "Hearsay" §116.

§6404. Prohibition against unsafe or unhealthy work sites.

No employer shall occupy or maintain any place of employment that is not safe and healthful.

Ref.: Herlick Handbook § 12.7; W. Cal. Ev., "Hearsay" §116.

§6404.5. Prohibition against smoking in the workplace.

(a) The Legislature finds and declares that regulation of smoking in the workplace is a matter of statewide interest and concern. It is the intent of the Legislature in enacting this section to prohibit the smoking of tobacco products in all (100 percent of) enclosed places of employment in this state, as covered by this section, thereby eliminating the need of local governments to enact workplace smoking restrictions within their respective jurisdictions. It is further the intent of the Legislature to create a uniform statewide standard to restrict and prohibit the smoking of tobacco products in enclosed places of employment, as specified in this section, in order to reduce employee exposure to environmental tobacco smoke to a level that will prevent anything other than insignificantly harmful effects to exposed employees, and also to eliminate the confusion and hardship that can result from enactment or enforcement of disparate local workplace smoking restrictions. Notwithstanding any other provision of this section, it is the intent of the Legislature that any area not defined as a "place of employment" pursuant to subdivision (d) or in which the smoking of tobacco products is not regulated pursuant to subdivision (e) shall be subject to local regulation of smoking of tobacco products.

(b) No employer shall knowingly or intentionally permit, and no person shall engage in, the smoking of tobacco products in an enclosed space at a place of employment. "Enclosed space" includes lobbies, lounges, waiting areas, elevators, stairwells, and restrooms that are a structural part of the building and not specifically defined in subdivision (d).

(c) For purposes of this section, an employer who permits any nonemployee access to his or her place of employment on a regular basis has not acted knowingly or intentionally in violation of this section if he or she has taken the following reasonable steps to prevent smoking by a nonemployee:

(1) Posted clear and prominent signs, as follows:

(A) Where smoking is prohibited throughout the building or structure, a sign stating "No smoking" shall be posted at each entrance to the building or structure.

(B) Where smoking is permitted in designated areas of the building or structure, a sign stating "Smoking is prohibited except in designated areas" shall be posted at each entrance to the building or structure.

(2) Has requested, when appropriate, that a nonemployee who is smoking refrain from smoking in the enclosed workplace.

For purposes of this subdivision, "reasonable steps" does not include (A) the physical ejection of a nonemployee from the place of employment or (B) any requirement for making a request to a nonemployee to refrain from smoking, under circumstances involving a risk of physical harm to the employer or any employee.

(d) For purposes of this section, "place of employment" does not include any of the following:

(1) Sixty-five percent of the guestroom accommodations in a hotel, motel, or similar transient lodging establishment.

(2) Areas of the lobby in a hotel, motel, or other similar transient lodging establishment designated for smoking by the establishment. An establishment may permit smoking in a designated lobby area that does not exceed 25 percent of the total floor area of the lobby or, if the total area of the lobby is 2,000 square feet or less, that does not exceed 50 percent of the total floor area of the lobby. For purposes of this paragraph, "lobby" means the common public area of an establishment in which registration and other similar or related transactions, or both, are conducted and in which the establishment's guests and members of the public typically congregate.

(3) Meeting and banquet rooms in a hotel, motel, other transient lodging establishment similar to a hotel or motel, restaurant, or public convention center, except while food or beverage functions are taking place, including setup, service, and cleanup activities, or when the room is being used for exhibit purposes. At times when smoking is not permitted in a meeting or banquet room pursuant to this paragraph, the establishment may permit smoking in corridors and prefunction areas adjacent to and serving the meeting or banquet room if no employee is stationed in that corridor or area on other than a passing basis.

(4) Retail or wholesale tobacco shops and private smokers' lounges. For purposes of this paragraph:

(A) "Private smokers' lounge" means any enclosed area in or attached to a retail or wholesale tobacco shop that is dedicated to the use of tobacco products, including, but not limited to, cigars and pipes.

(B) "Retail or wholesale tobacco shop" means any business establishment the main purpose of which is the sale of tobacco products, including, but not limited to, cigars, pipe tobacco, and smoking accessories.

(5) Cabs of motortrucks, as defined in Section 410 of the Vehicle Code, or truck tractors, as defined in Section 655 of the Vehicle Code, if no nonsmoking employees are present.

(6) Warehouse facilities. For purposes of this paragraph, "warehouse facility" means a warehouse facility with more than 100,000 square feet of total floorspace, and 20 or fewer full-time employees working at the facility, but does not include any area within a facility that is utilized as office space.

(7) Gaming clubs, in which smoking is permitted by subdivision (f). For purposes of this paragraph, "gaming club" means any gaming club, as defined in Section 19802 of the Business and Professions Code, or bingo facility, as defined in Section 326.5 of the Penal Code, that restricts access to minors under 18 years of age.

(8) Bars and taverns, in which smoking is permitted by subdivision (f). For purposes of this paragraph, "bar" or "tavern" means a facility primarily devoted to the serving of alcoholic beverages for consumption by guests on the premises, in which the serving of food is incidental. "Bar or tavern" includes those facilities located within a hotel, motel, or other similar transient occupancy establishment. However, when located within a building in conjunction with another use, including a restaurant, "bar" or "tavern" includes only those areas used primarily for the sale and service of alcoholic beverages. "Bar" or "tavern" does not include the dining areas of a restaurant, regardless of whether alcoholic beverages are served therein.

(9) Theatrical production sites, if smoking is an integral part of the story in the theatrical production.

(10) Medical research or treatment sites, if smoking is integral to the research and treatment being conducted.

(11) Private residences, except for private residences licensed as family day care homes, during the hours of operation as family day care homes and in those areas where children are present.

(12) Patient smoking areas in long-term health care facilities, as defined in Section 1418 of the Health and Safety Code.

(13) Breakrooms designated by employers for smoking, provided that all of the following conditions are met:

(A) Air from the smoking room shall be exhausted directly to the outside by an exhaust fan. Air from the smoking room shall not be recirculated to other parts of the building.

(B) The employer shall comply with any ventilation standard or other standard utilizing appropriate technology, including, but not limited to, mechanical, electronic, and biotechnical systems, adopted by the Occupational Safety and Health Standards Board or the federal Environmental Protection Agency. If both adopt inconsistent standards, the ventilation standards of the Occupational Safety and Health Standards Board shall be no less stringent than the standards adopted by the federal Environmental Protection Agency.

(C) The smoking room shall be located in a nonwork area where no one, as part of his or her work responsibilities, is required to enter. For purposes of this subparagraph, "work responsibilities" does not include any custodial or maintenance work carried out in the breakroom when it is unoccupied.

(D) There are sufficient nonsmoking breakrooms to accommodate nonsmokers.

(14) Employers with a total of five or fewer employees, either full time or part time, may permit smoking where all of the following conditions are met:

(A) The smoking area is not accessible to minors.

(B) All employees who enter the smoking area consent to permit smoking. No one, as part of his or her work responsibilities, shall be required to work in an area where smoking is permitted. An employer who is determined by the division to have used coercion to obtain consent or who has required an employee to work in the smoking area shall be subject to the penalty provisions of Section 6427.

(C) Air from the smoking area shall be exhausted directly to the outside by an exhaust fan. Air from the smoking area shall not be recirculated to other parts of the building.

(D) The employer shall comply with any ventilation standard or other standard utilizing appropriate technology, including, but not limited to, mechanical, electronic, and biotechnical systems, adopted by the Occupational Safety and Health Standards Board or the federal Environmental Protection Agency. If both adopt inconsistent standards, the ventilation standards of the Occupational Safety and Health Standards Board shall be no less stringent than the standards adopted by the federal Environmental Protection Agency.

This paragraph shall not be construed to (i) supersede or render inapplicable any condition or limitation on smoking areas made applicable to specific types of business establishments by any other paragraph of this subdivision or (ii) apply in lieu of any otherwise applicable paragraph of this subdivision that has become inoperative.

(e) Paragraphs (13) and (14) of subdivision (d) shall not be construed to require employers to provide reasonable accommodation to smokers, or to provide breakrooms for smokers or nonsmokers.

(f)(1) Except as otherwise provided in this subdivision, smoking may be permitted in gaming clubs, as defined in paragraph (7) of subdivision (d), and in bars and taverns, as defined in paragraph (8) of subdivision (d), until the earlier of the following:

(A) January 1, 1998.

(B) The date of adoption of a regulation (i) by the Occupational Safety and Health Standards Board reducing the permissible employee exposure level to environmental tobacco smoke to a level that will prevent anything other than insignificantly harmful effects to exposed employees or (ii) by the federal Environmental Protection Agency establishing a standard for reduction of permissible exposure to environmental tobacco smoke to an exposure level that will prevent anything other than insignificantly harmful effects to exposed persons.

(2) If a regulation specified in subparagraph (B) of paragraph (1) is adopted on or before January 1, 1998, smoking may thereafter be permitted in gaming clubs and in bars and taverns, subject to full compliance with, or conformity to, the standard in the regulation within two years following the date of adoption of the regulation. An employer failing to achieve compliance with, or conformity to, the regulation within this two-year period shall prohibit smoking in the gaming club, bar, or tavern until compliance or conformity is achieved. If the Occupational Safety and Health Standards Board and the federal Environmental Protection Agency both adopt regulations specified in subparagraph (B) of paragraph (1) that are inconsistent, the regulations of the Occupational Safety and Health

Standards Board shall be no less stringent than the regulations of the federal Environmental Protection Agency.

(3) If a regulation specified in subparagraph (B) of paragraph (1) is not adopted on or before January 1, 1998, the exemptions specified in paragraphs (7) and (8) of subdivision (d) shall become inoperative on and after January 1, 1998, until a regulation is adopted. Upon adoption of such a regulation on or after January 1, 1998, smoking may thereafter be permitted in gaming clubs and in bars and taverns, subject to full compliance with, or conformity to, the standard in the regulation within two years following the date of adoption of the regulation. An employer failing to achieve compliance with, or conformity to, the regulation within this two-year period shall prohibit smoking in the gaming club, bar, or tavern until compliance or conformity is achieved. If the Occupational Safety and Health Standards Board and the federal Environmental Protection Agency both adopt regulations specified in subparagraph (B) of paragraph (1) that are inconsistent, the regulations of the Occupational Safety and Health Standards Board shall be no less stringent than the regulations of the federal Environmental Protection Agency.

(4) From January 1, 1997, to December 31, 1997, inclusive, smoking may be permitted in gaming clubs, as defined in paragraph (7) of subdivision (d), and in bars and taverns, as defined in paragraph (8) of subdivision (d), subject to both of the following conditions:

(A) If practicable, the gaming club or bar or tavern shall establish a designated nonsmoking area.

(B) If feasible, no employee shall be required, in the performance of ordinary work responsibilities, to enter any area in which smoking is permitted.

(g) The smoking prohibition set forth in this section shall constitute a uniform statewide standard for regulating the smoking of tobacco products in enclosed places of employment and shall supersede and render unnecessary the local enactment or enforcement of local ordinances regulating the smoking of tobacco products in enclosed places of employment. Insofar as the smoking prohibition set forth in this section is applicable to all (100-percent) places of employment within this state and, therefore, provides the maximum degree of coverage, the practical effect of this section is to eliminate the need of local governments to enact enclosed workplace smoking restrictions within their respective jurisdictions.

(h) Nothing in this section shall prohibit an employer from prohibiting smoking in an enclosed place of employment for any reason.

(i) The enactment of local regulation of smoking of tobacco products in enclosed places of employment by local governments shall be suspended only for as long as, and to the extent that, the (100-percent) smoking prohibition provided for in this section remains in effect. In the event this section is repealed or modified by subsequent legislative or judicial action so that the (100-percent) smoking prohibition is no longer applicable to all enclosed places of employment in California, local governments shall have the full right and authority to enforce previously enacted, and to enact and enforce new, restrictions on the smoking of tobacco products in enclosed places of employment within their jurisdictions, including a complete prohibition of smoking. Notwithstanding any other provision of this section, any area not defined as a "place of employment" or in which smoking is not regulated pursuant to subdivision (d) or (e), shall be subject to local regulation of smoking of tobacco products.

(j) Any violation of the prohibition set forth in subdivision (b) is an infraction, punishable by a fine not to exceed one hundred dollars ($100) for a first violation, two hundred dollars ($200) for a second violation within one year, and five hundred dollars ($500) for a third and for each subsequent violation within one year. This subdivision shall be enforced by local law enforcement agencies, including, but not limited to, local health departments, as determined by the local governing body.

(k) Notwithstanding Section 6309, the division shall not be required to respond to any complaint regarding the smoking of tobacco products in an enclosed space at a place of employment, unless the employer has been found guilty pursuant to subdivision (j) of a third violation of subdivision (b) within the previous year.

(*l*) If any provision of this act or the application thereof to any person or circumstances is held invalid, that invalidity shall not affect other provisions or applications of the act that can be given effect without the invalid provision or application, and to this end the provisions of this act are severable. **Leg.H.** 1994 ch. 310, 1995 ch.

91, 1996 ch. 989, 1998 ch. 606, 2006 ch. 736 (AB 2067) §2.

Ref.: W. Cal. Ev., "Hearsay" §116; W. Cal. Sum., 3 "Agency and Employment" §377, 8 "Constitutional Law" §§992, 1074, 12 "Real Property" §902.

§6405. Prohibition against construction of unhealthy or unsafe work sites.

No employer, owner, or lessee of any real property shall construct or cause to be constructed any place of employment that is not safe and healthful.

Ref.: W. Cal. Ev., "Hearsay" §116.

§6406. Prohibition against interfering with or neglecting to provide safe or healthful equipment or practices.

No person shall do any of the following:

(a) Remove, displace, damage, destroy or carry off any safety device, safeguard, notice, or warning, furnished for use in any employment or place of employment.

(b) Interfere in any way with the use thereof by any other person.

(c) Interfere with the use of any method or process adopted for the protection of any employee, including himself, in such employment, or place of employment.

(d) Fail or neglect to do every other thing reasonably necessary to protect the life, safety, and health of employees.

Ref.: Herlick Handbook § 9.6; W. Cal. Ev., "Hearsay" §116.

§6407. Employer's and employee's obligation to comply with regulations.

Every employer and every employee shall comply with occupational safety and health standards, with Section 25910 of the Health and Safety Code, and with all rules, regulations, and orders pursuant to this division which are applicable to his own actions and conduct.

Ref.: W. Cal. Ev., "Hearsay" §116.

§6408. Obligation to provide specified information to employees.

All employers shall provide information to employees in the following ways, as prescribed by authorized regulations:

(a) Posting of information regarding protections and obligations of employees under occupational safety and health laws.

(b) Posting prominently each citation issued under Section 6317, or a copy or copies thereof, at or near each place a violation referred to in the notice of violation occurred.

(c) The opportunity for employees or their representatives to observe monitoring or measuring of employee exposure to hazards conducted pursuant to standards promulgated under Section 142.3.

(d) Allow access by employees or their representatives to accurate records of employee exposures to potentially toxic materials or harmful physical agents.

(e) Notification of any employee who has been or is being exposed to toxic materials or harmful physical agents in concentrations or at levels exceeding those prescribed by an applicable standard, order, or special order, and informing any employee so exposed of corrective action being taken.

Ref.: W. Cal. Ev., "Hearsay" §116.

§6409. Requirements of physicians treating injured employees; "occupational illness."

(a) Every physician as defined in Section 3209.3 who attends any injured employee shall file a complete report of every occupational injury or occupational illness to the employee with the employer, or if insured, with the employer's insurer, on forms prescribed for that purpose by the Division of Labor Statistics and Research. A portion of the form shall be completed by the injured employee, if he or she is able to do so, describing how the injury or illness occurred. The form shall be filed within five days of the initial examination. Inability or failure of an injured employee to complete his or her portion of the form shall not affect the employee's rights under this code, and shall not excuse any delay in filing the form. The employer or insurer, as the case may be, shall file the physician's report with the Department of Industrial Relations, through its Division of Labor Statistics and Research, within five days of receipt. Each report of occupational injury or occupational illness shall indicate the social security number of the injured employee. If the treatment is for pesticide poisoning or a condition suspected to be pesticide poisoning, the physician shall also file a complete report, which need not include the affidavit required pursuant to this section, with the Division of Labor Statistics and Research, and within 24 hours of the initial examination shall file a complete report with the local health officer by facsimile transmission or other means. If the treatment is for pesticide poisoning or a condition suspected to be pesticide poisoning, the physician shall not be compensated for the initial diagnosis and treatment unless the report is filed with the employer, or if insured, with the employer's insurer, and includes or is accompanied by a signed affidavit which certifies that a copy of the report was filed with the local health officer pursuant to the requirements of this section.

(b) As used in this section, "occupational illness" means any abnormal condition or disorder caused by exposure to environmental factors associated with employment, including acute and chronic illnesses or diseases which may be caused by inhalation, absorption, ingestion, or direct contact. **Leg.H.** 1994 ch. 667.

Ref.: 8 C.C.R. §§10101, 10101.1, 10181, 14000, 14001, 14002, 14003; Hanna § 22.08[2]; Herlick Handbook §§ 3.6, 9.18, 14.2; W. Cal. Ev., "Hearsay" §116; W. Cal. Sum., 2 "Workers' Compensation" §399.

§6409.1. [Effective Until Conditions in 2008 Ch. 740 §3 Met] Requirements of employers when employee is occupationally injured/ill; subsequent death of employee.

(a) Every employer shall file a complete report of every occupational injury or occupational illness, as defined in subdivision (b) of Section 6409, to each employee which results in lost time beyond the date of the injury or illness, or which requires medical treatment beyond first aid, with the Department of Industrial Relations, through its Division of Labor Statistics and Research or, if an insured employer, with the insurer, on a form prescribed for that purpose by the Division of Labor Statistics and Research. A report shall be filed concerning each injury and illness which has, or is alleged to have, arisen out of and in the course of employment, within five days after the employer obtains knowledge of the injury or illness. Each report of occupational injury or occupational illness shall indicate the social security number of the injured employee.In the case of an insured employer, the insurer shall file with the division immediately upon receipt, a copy of the employer's report, which has been received from the insured employer. In the event an employer has filed a report of injury or illness pursuant to this subdivision and the employee subsequently dies as a result of the reported injury or illness, the employer shall file an amended report indicating the death with the Department of Industrial Relations, through its Division of Labor Statistics and Research or, if an insured employer, with the insurer, within five days after the employer is notified or learns of the death. A copy of any amended reports received by the insurer shall be filed with the division immediately upon receipt.

(b) In every case involving a serious injury or illness, or death, in addition to the report required by subdivision (a), a report shall be made immediately by the employer to the Division of Occupational Safety and Health by telephone or telegraph. An employer who violates this subdivision may be assessed a civil penalty of not less than five thousand dollars ($5,000). Nothing in this subdivision shall be construed to increase the maximum civil penalty, pursuant to Sections 6427 to 6430, inclusive, that may be imposed for a violation of this section. **Leg.H.** 1992 ch. 386, 2002 ch. 885 (AB 2837).

Ref.: 8 C.C.R. §§10101, 10101.1, 10181, 14001, 14002, 14004, 14005; Hanna § 25.20[3]; Herlick Handbook § 14.2; W. Cal. Ev., "Hearsay" §116; W. Cal. Sum., 2 "Workers' Compensation" §399.

§6409.1. [Effective Upon Conditions in 2008 Ch. 740 §3 Being Met; See Note Below] Requirements of employers when employee is occupationally injured/ill; subsequent death of employee.

(a) Every employer shall file a complete report of every occupational injury or occupational illness, as defined in subdivision (b) of Section 6409, to each employee which results in lost time beyond the date of the injury or illness, or which requires medical treatment beyond first aid [1]. An insured employer [2] **shall file the report** with the insurer [3] on a form prescribed [4] **by the Administrative Director of the Division of Workers' Compensation for that purpose within five days after the employer obtains knowledge of the injury or illness that** has, or is alleged to have, arisen out of and in the course of employment [5]. **A self-insured employer, the state, or the insurer of an insured**

Labor

employer shall file the report in the electronic form prescribed for that purpose by the administrative director pursuant to Section 138.6 within the time prescribed by the administrative director. The administrative director shall ensure that the report required by this subdivision contains necessary information to continue to be acceptable as substitute documentation for purposes of recordkeeping required under the federal Occupational Safety and Health Act of 1970 (29 U.S.C. Sec. 651 et seq.). Each report of occupational injury or occupational illness shall indicate the social security number of the injured employee. [6] In the event an employer has filed a report of injury or illness pursuant to this subdivision and the employee subsequently dies as a result of the reported injury or illness, the employer shall file an amended report indicating the death with the Department of Industrial Relations, through its Division of [7] **Workers' Compensation** or, if an insured employer, with the insurer, within five days after the employer is notified or learns of the death. A copy of any amended reports received by the insurer shall be filed with the [8] **Division of Workers' Compensation in electronic form as prescribed by the administrative director**.

(b) In every case involving a serious injury or illness, or death, in addition to the report required by subdivision (a), a report shall be made immediately by the employer to the Division of Occupational Safety and Health by telephone or telegraph. An employer who violates this subdivision may be assessed a civil penalty of not less than five thousand dollars ($5,000). Nothing in this subdivision shall be construed to increase the maximum civil penalty, pursuant to Sections 6427 to 6430, inclusive, that may be imposed for a violation of this section. **Leg.H.** 1992 ch. 386, 2002 ch. 885 (AB 2837), 2008 ch. 740 (AB 2181) §1.

§6409.1. 2008 Deletes. [1] , with the Department of Industrial Relations, through its Division of Labor Statistics and Research or, if **[2]** , **[3]** , **[4]** for that purpose by the Division of Labor Statistics and Research. A report shall be filed concerning each injury and illness which **[5]** , within five days after the employer obtains knowledge of the injury or illness **[6]** In the case of an insured employer, the insurer shall file with the division immediately upon receipt, a copy of the employer's report, which has been received from the insured employer. **[7]** Labor Statistics and Research **[8]** division immediately upon receipt

2008 Note: The changes to subdivision (a) of Section 6409.1 and Section 6410 of the Labor Code made by Stats. 2008 ch. 740 shall become effective upon the effective date of regulations adopted by the administrative director to implement the changes made to subdivision (a) of Section 6409.1 of the Labor Code by this act, provided that the regulations specify a transition period of no less than 180 days and no more than 545 days in which the employer or insurer may continue to comply with Section 6409.1 as it was last amended by Chapter 885 of the Statutes of 2002. Stats. 2008 ch. 740 §3.

Ref.: 8 C.C.R. §§10101, 10101.1, 10181, 14001, 14002, 14004, 14005; Hanna § 25.20[3]; Herlick Handbook § 14.2; W. Cal. Ev., "Hearsay" §116; W. Cal. Sum., 2 "Workers' Compensation" §399.

§6409.2. Notification when fire or police are called to serious or fatal accident.

Whenever a state, county, or local fire or police agency is called to an accident involving an employee covered by this part in which a serious injury or illness, or death occurs, the responding agency shall immediately notify the nearest office of the Division of Occupational Safety and Health by telephone. Thereafter, the division shall immediately notify the appropriate prosecuting authority of the accident. **Leg.H.** 2002 ch. 885 (AB 2837).

Ref.: W. Cal. Ev., "Hearsay" §116.

§6409.3. Pesticide poisoning treatment.

In no case shall the treatment administered for pesticide poisoning or a condition suspected as pesticide poisoning be deemed to be first aid treatment.

Ref.: 8 C.C.R. §14003; W. Cal. Ev., "Hearsay" §116.

§6409.5. Notification of Division of Occupational Safety and Health and Division of Labor Standards Enforcement regarding garment manufacturing hazards—Investigation by local public fire agency.

(a) Whenever any local public fire agency has knowledge that a place of employment where garment manufacturing operations take place contains fire or safety hazards for which fire and injury prevention measures have not been taken in accordance with local fire and life safety ordinances, the agency may notify the

Division of Occupational Safety and Health. This referral shall be made only after the garment manufacturing employer has been given a reasonable amount of time to correct violations.

(b) Whenever the Division of Occupational Safety and Health has knowledge or reasonable suspicion that a place of employment where garment manufacturing operations take place contains fire or safety hazards for which fire and injury prevention measures have not been taken in accordance with local fire and life safety ordinances, the division shall notify the appropriate local public fire agency.

(c) Whenever the Division of Occupational Safety and Health receives a referral by a local public fire agency pursuant to subdivision (a) which informs the division that a place of employment where garment manufacturing operations take place is not safe or is injurious to the welfare of any employee, it shall constitute a complaint for purposes of Section 6309 and shall be investigated.

(d) Whenever a local public fire agency receives a referral by the Division of Occupational Safety and Health pursuant to subdivision (b) which informs the local public fire agency that a place of employment where garment manufacturing operations take place is not safe or is injurious to the welfare of any employee, the local public fire agency may investigate the referral at its discretion.

(e)(1) If the Division of Occupational Safety and Health acquires knowledge that the garment manufacturing employer is not currently registered, it shall notify the Division of Labor Standards Enforcement.

(2) Local public fire agencies may make referrals of individuals not registered as garment manufacturers to the Division of Labor Standards Enforcement.

(3) Whenever the Division of Labor Standards Enforcement is informed by the Division of Occupational Safety and Health or by a local public fire agency that a garment manufacturing employer is unregistered, the Division of Labor Standards Enforcement shall take measures it deems appropriate to obtain compliance. **Leg.H.** 1991 ch. 7, effective December 13, 1990, operative January 1, 1991.

§6410. [Effective Until Conditions in 2008 Ch. 740 §3 Met] Requirements for reports and records.

The reports required by subdivision (a) of Section 6409, subdivision (a) of Section 6409.1, and Section 6413 shall be made in the form and detail and within the time limits prescribed by reasonable rules and regulations adopted by the Division of Labor Statistics and Research in accordance with Chapter 3.5 (commencing with Section 11340) of Part 1 of Division 3 of Title 2 of the Government Code.

Nothing in this chapter requiring recordkeeping and reporting by employers shall relieve the employer of maintaining records and making reports to the assistant secretary, United States Department of Labor, as required under the Federal Occupational Safety and Health Act of 1970 (P.L. 91–596). The Division of Labor Statistics and Research shall prescribe and provide the forms necessary for maintenance of the required records, and the Division of Occupational Safety and Health shall enforce by citation and penalty assessment any violation of the recordkeeping requirements of this chapter.

All state and local government employers shall maintain records and make reports in the same manner and to the same extent as required of other employers by this section.

Ref.: 8 C.C.R. §§14300, 14300.1, 14300.2, 14300.3, 14300.4, 14300.5, 14300.6, 14300.7, 14300.8, 14300.9, 14300.10, 14300.11, 14300.12, 14300.29, 14300.30, 14300.31, 14300.32, 14300.33, 14300.34, 14300.35, 14300.36, 14300.38, 14300.40, 14300.41, 14300.42, 14300.43, 14300.44, 14300.46, 14300.47, 14300.48; Herlick Handbook §§ 8.28, 9.10; W. Cal. Ev., "Hearsay" §116.

§6410. [Effective Upon Conditions in 2008 Ch. 740 §3 Being Met; See Note Below] Requirements for reports and records.

The reports required by subdivision (a) of Section 6409 [1] and Section 6413 shall be made in the form and detail and within the time limits prescribed by reasonable rules and regulations adopted by the Division of Labor Statistics and Research in accordance with Chapter 3.5 (commencing with Section 11340) of Part 1 of Division 3 of Title 2 of the Government Code.

Nothing in this chapter requiring recordkeeping and reporting by employers shall relieve the employer of maintaining records and making reports to the assistant secretary, United States Department of Labor, as required under the Federal Occupational Safety and Health Act of 1970 (P.L. 91–596). The Division of Labor Statistics and Research shall prescribe and provide the forms necessary for maintenance of the required records, and the Division of Occupational Safety and Health shall enforce by citation and penalty assessment any violation of the recordkeeping requirements of this chapter.

All state and local government employers shall maintain records and make reports in the same manner and to the same extent as required of other employers by this section. **Leg.H.** 2008 ch. 740 (AB 2181) §2.

§6410. 2008 Deletes. [1] , subdivision (a) of Section 6409.1,

2008 Note: The changes to subdivision (a) of Section 6409.1 and Section 6410 of the Labor Code made by Stats. 2008 ch. 740 shall become effective upon the effective date of regulations adopted by the administrative director to implement the changes made to subdivision (a) of Section 6409.1 of the Labor Code by this act, provided that the regulations specify a transition period of no less than 180 days and no more than 545 days in which the employer or insurer may continue to comply with Section 6409.1 as it was last amended by Chapter 885 of the Statutes of 2002. Stats. 2008 ch. 740 §3.

Ref.: 8 C.C.R. §§14300, 14300.1, 14300.2, 14300.3, 14300.4, 14300.5, 14300.6, 14300.7, 14300.8, 14300.9, 14300.10, 14300.11, 14300.12, 14300.29, 14300.30, 14300.31, 14300.32, 14300.33, 14300.34, 14300.35, 14300.36, 14300.38, 14300.40, 14300.41, 14300.42, 14300.43, 14300.44, 14300.46, 14300.47, 14300.48; Herlick Handbook §§ 8.28, 9.10; W. Cal. Ev., "Hearsay" §116.

§6410.5. Statement must accompany reports.

The reports required by subdivision (a) of Section 6409, subdivision (a) of Section 6409.1, and Section 6413 shall contain, prominently stated, the statement set forth in Section 5401.7. **Leg.H.** 1991 ch. 116.

Ref.: Herlick Handbook §§ 9.18, 14.2; W. Cal. Ev., "Hearsay" §116.

§6411. Requirement to fully and accurately complete forms.

Every employer or insurer receiving forms with directions from the Division of Labor Statistics and Research to complete them shall cause them to be properly filled out so as to answer fully and correctly each question propounded therein. In case of inability to answer any such questions, a good and sufficient reason shall be given for such failure.

Ref.: W. Cal. Ev., "Hearsay" §116.

§6412. Report's confidentiality and admissibility as evidence.

No report of injury or illness required by subdivision (a) of Section 6409.1 shall be open to public inspection or made public, nor shall those reports be admissible as evidence in any adversary proceeding before the Workers' Compensation Appeals Board. However, the reports required of physicians by subdivision (a) of Section 6409 shall be admissible as evidence in the proceeding, except that no physician's report shall be admissible as evidence to bar proceedings for the collection of compensation, and the portion of any physician's report completed by an employee shall not be admissible as evidence in any proceeding before the Workers' Compensation Appeals Board.

Ref.: Herlick Handbook §§ 3.6, 4.21, 14.2; W. Cal. Ev., "Hearsay" §116; W. Cal. Sum., 2 "Workers' Compensation" §399.

§6413. Requirements when state prisoner is injured.

(a) The Department of Corrections, and every physician or surgeon who attends any injured state prisoner, shall file with the Division of Labor Statistics and Research a complete report, on forms prescribed under Sections 6409 and 6409.1, of every injury to each state prisoner, resulting from any labor performed by the prisoner unless disability resulting from such injury does not last through the day or does not require medical service other than ordinary first aid treatment.

(b) Where the injury results in death a report, in addition to the report required by subdivision (a), shall forthwith be made by the Department of Corrections to the Division of Labor Statistics and Research by telephone or telegraph.

(c) Except as provided in Section 6304.2, nothing in this section or in this code shall be deemed to make a prisoner an employee, for any purpose, of the Department of Corrections.

(d) Notwithstanding subdivision (a), no physician or surgeon who attends any injured state prisoner outside of a Department of Corrections institution shall be required to file the report required by subdivision (a), but the Department of Corrections shall file the report. **Leg.H.** 1992 ch. 386.

Ref.: Herlick Handbook § 9.18; W. Cal. Ev., "Hearsay" §116.

§6413.2. Division's powers regarding Department of Corrections.

(a) The Division of Labor Statistics and Research shall, within five working days of their receipt, transmit to the Division of Occupational Safety and Health copies of all reports received by the Division of Labor Statistics and Research pursuant to Section 6413.

(b) With regard to any report required by Section 6413, the Division of Occupational Safety and Health may make recommendations to the Department of Corrections of ways in which the department might improve the safety of the working conditions and work areas of state prisoners, and other safety matters. The Department of Corrections shall not be required to comply with these recommendations.

(c) With regard to any report required by Section 6413, the Division of Occupational Safety and Health may, in any case in which the Department of Corrections has not complied with recommendations made by the division pursuant to subdivision (b), or in any other case in which the division deems the safety of any state prisoner shall require it, conduct hearings and, after these hearings, adopt special orders, rules, or regulations or otherwise proceed as authorized in Chapter 1 (commencing with Section 6300) of this part as it deems necessary. The Department of Corrections shall comply with any order, rule or regulation so adopted by the Division of Occupational Safety and Health.

Ref.: W. Cal. Ev., "Hearsay" §116.

§6413.5. Penalties for violation of reporting requirements.

Any employer or physician who fails to comply with any provision of subdivision (a) of Section 6409, or Section 6409.1, 6409.2, 6409.3, or 6410 may be assessed a civil penalty of not less than fifty dollars ($50) nor more than two hundred dollars ($200) by the director or his or her designee if he or she finds a pattern or practice of violations, or a willful violation of any of these provisions. Penalty assessments may be contested in the manner provided in Section 3725. Penalties assessed pursuant to this section shall be deposited in the General Fund.

Ref.: Herlick Handbook § 14.2; W. Cal. Ev., "Hearsay" §116.

CHAPTER 4
PENALTIES

§6423. Violations as misdemeanors; penalties.

(a) Except where another penalty is specifically provided, every employer and every officer, management official, or supervisor having direction, management, control, or custody of any employment, place of employment, or of any other employee, who does any of the following is guilty of a misdemeanor:

(1) Knowingly or negligently violates any standard, order, or special order, or any provision of this division, or of any part thereof in, or authorized by, this part the violation of which is deemed to be a serious violation pursuant to Section 6432.

(2) Repeatedly violates any standard, order, or special order, or provision of this division, or any part thereof in, or authorized by, this part, which repeated violation creates a real and apparent hazard to employees.

(3) Knowingly fails to report to the division a death, as required by subdivision (b) of Section 6409.1.

(4) Fails or refuses to comply, after notification and expiration of any abatement period, with any such standard, order, special order, or provision of this division, or any part thereof, which failure or refusal creates a real and apparent hazard to employees.

(5) Directly or indirectly, knowingly induces another to commit any of the acts in paragraph (1), (2), (3), or (4) of subdivision (a).

(b) Any violation of paragraph (1) of subdivision (a) is punishable by imprisonment in the county jail for a period not to exceed six months, or by a fine not to exceed five thousand dollars ($5,000), or by both that imprisonment and fine.

(c) Any violation of paragraph (3) of subdivision (a) is punishable by imprisonment in county jail for up to one year, or by a fine not to exceed fifteen thousand dollars ($15,000), or by both that imprisonment and fine. If the violator is a corporation or a limited liability company, the fine prescribed by this subdivision may not exceed one hundred fifty thousand dollars ($150,000).

(d) Any violation of paragraph (2), (4), or (5) of subdivision (a) is punishable by imprisonment in a county jail for a term not exceeding one year, or by a fine not exceeding fifteen thousand dollars ($15,000), or by both that imprisonment and fine. If the defendant is a corporation or a limited liability company, the fine may not exceed one hundred fifty thousand dollars ($150,000).

(e) In determining the amount of fine to impose under this section, the court shall consider all relevant circumstances, including, but not limited to, the nature, circumstance, extent, and gravity of the violation, any prior history of violations by the defendant, the ability of the defendant to pay, and any other matters the court determines the interests of justice require. **Leg.H.** 1999 ch. 615, 2002 ch. 885 (AB 2837).

Ref.: Herlick Handbook § 9.6; W. Cal. Ev., "Hearsay" §116; W. Cal. Sum., 3 "Agency and Employment" §366.

§6425. Penalties for willful violations causing death or serious bodily impairment; violations within 7 years of first conviction.

(a) Any employer and any employee having direction, management, control, or custody of any employment, place of employment, or of any other employee, who willfully violates any occupational safety or health standard, order, or special order, or Section 25910 of the Health and Safety Code, and that violation caused death to any employee, or caused permanent or prolonged impairment of the body of any employee, is guilty of a public offense punishable by imprisonment in a county jail for a term not exceeding one year, or by a fine not exceeding one hundred thousand dollars ($100,000), or by both that imprisonment and fine; or by imprisonment in the state prison for 16 months, or two or three years, or by a fine of not more than two hundred fifty thousand dollars ($250,000), or by both that imprisonment and fine; and in either case, if the defendant is a corporation or a limited liability company, the fine may not exceed one million five hundred thousand dollars ($1,500,000).

(b) If the conviction is for a violation committed within seven years after a conviction under subdivision (b), (c), or (d) of Section 6423 or subdivision (c) of Section 6430, punishment shall be by imprisonment in state prison for a term of 16 months, two, or three years, or by a fine not exceeding two hundred fifty thousand dollars ($250,000), or by both that fine and imprisonment, but if the defendant is a corporation or limited liability company, the fine may not be less than five hundred thousand dollars ($500,000) or more than two million five hundred thousand dollars ($2,500,000).

(c) If the conviction is for a violation committed within seven years after a first conviction of the defendent for any crime involving a violation of subdivision (a), punishment shall be by imprisonment in the state prison for two, three, or four years, or by a fine not exceeding two hundred fifty thousand dollars ($250,000), or by both that fine and imprisonment, but if the defendant is a corporation or a limited liability company, the fine shall not be less than one million dollars ($1,000,000) but may not exceed three million five hundred thousand dollars ($3,500,000).

(d) In determining the amount of fine to be imposed under this section, the court shall consider all relevant circumstances, including, but not limited to, the nature, circumstance, extent, and gravity of the violation, any prior history of violations by the defendant, the ability of the defendant to pay, and any other matters the court determines the interests of justice require.

(e) As used in this section, "willfully" has the same definition as it has in Section 7 of the Penal Code. This subdivision is intended to be a codification of existing law.

(f) This section does not prohibit a prosecution under Section 192 of the Penal Code. **Leg.H.** 1991 ch. 599, effective October 5, 1991, 1999 ch. 615.

Ref.: W. Cal. Ev., "Hearsay" §116.

§6426. Penalties for knowingly falsifying reports or records.

Whoever knowingly makes any false statement, representation, or certification in any application, record, report, plan, or other document filed or required to be maintained pursuant to this division shall, upon conviction, be punished by a fine of not more than seventy thousand dollars ($70,000), or by imprisonment for not more than six months, or by both. **Leg.H.** 1991 ch. 599, effective October 5, 1991.

Ref.: W. Cal. Ev., "Hearsay" §116.

§6427. Civil penalty for non-serious violations.

Any employer who violates any occupational safety or health standard, order, or special order, or Section 25910 of the Health and Safety Code, and the violation is specifically determined not to be of a serious nature, may be assessed a civil penalty of up to seven thousand dollars ($7,000) for each violation. **Leg.H.** 1991 ch. 599, effective October 5, 1991, 1993 ch. 928.

Ref.: W. Cal. Ev., "Hearsay" §116.

§6428. Civil penalty for serious violations.

Any employer who violates any occupational safety or health standard, order, or special order, or Section 25910 of the Health and Safety Code, if that violation is a serious violation, shall be assessed a civil penalty of up to twenty-five thousand dollars ($25,000) for each violation. Employers who do not have an operative injury prevention program shall receive no adjustment for good faith of the employer or history of previous violations as provided in paragraphs (3) and (4) of subdivision (c) of Section 6319. **Leg.H.** 1991 ch. 599, effective October 5, 1991, 1999 ch. 615.

Ref.: W. Cal. Ev., "Hearsay" §116.

§6428.5. Criteria for "operative" injury prevention program.

An employer's injury prevention program shall be deemed to be operative for the purposes of Sections 6427 and 6428 if it meets the criteria for substantial compliance established by the standards board pursuant to Section 6401.7.

§6429. Civil penalties for willful or repetitious violations.

(a) Any employer who willfully or repeatedly violates any occupational safety or health standard, order, or special order, or Section 25910 of the Health and Safety Code, may be assessed a civil penalty of not more than seventy thousand dollars ($70,000) for each violation, but in no case less than five thousand dollars ($5,000) for each willful violation.

(b) Any employer who repeatedly violates any occupational safety or health standard, order, or special order, or Section 25910 of the Health and Safety Code, shall not receive any adjustment of a penalty assessed pursuant to this section on the basis of the regulations promulgated pursuant to subdivision (c) of Section 6319 pertaining to the good faith of the employer or the history of previous violations of the employer.

(c) The division shall preserve and maintain records of its investigations and inspections and citations for a period of not less than seven years. **Leg.H.** 1991 ch. 599, effective October 5, 1991, 1999 ch. 615, 2000 ch. 135.

Ref.: W. Cal. Ev., "Hearsay" §116.

§6430. Civil penalties for failure to correct violations.

(a) Any employer who fails to correct a violation of any occupational safety or health standard, order, or special order, or Section 25910 of the Health and Safety Code, within the period permitted for its correction shall be assessed a civil penalty of not more than fifteen thousand dollars ($15,000) for each day during which the failure or violation continues.

(b) Notwithstanding subdivision (a), for any employer who submits a signed statement affirming compliance with the abatement terms pursuant to Section 6320, and is found upon a reinspection not to have abated the violation, any adjustment to the civil penalty based on abatement shall be rescinded and the additional civil penalty assessed for failure to abate shall not be adjusted for good faith of the employer or history of previous violations as provided in paragraphs (3) and (4) of subdivision (c) of Section 6319.

(c) Notwithstanding subdivision (a), any employer who submits a signed statement affirming compliance with the abatement terms pursuant to subdivision (b) of Section 6320, and is found not to have abated the violation, is guilty of a public offense punishable by imprisonment in a county jail for a term not exceeding one year, or by a fine not exceeding thirty thousand dollars ($30,000), or by both that fine and imprisonment; but if the defendant is a corporation or a limited liability company the fine shall not exceed three hundred thousand dollars ($300,000). In determining the amount of the fine to be imposed under this section, the court shall consider all relevant circumstances, including, but not limited to, the nature, circumstance, extent, and gravity of the violation, any prior history of violations by the defendant, the ability of the defendant to pay, and any other matters the court determines the interests of justice require. Nothing in this section shall be construed to prevent prosecution under any law that may apply. **Leg.H.** 1991 ch. 599, effective October 5, 1991, 1999 ch. 615.

Ref.: W. Cal. Ev., "Hearsay" §116.

§6431. Civil penalty for violation of posting or recordkeeping requirements.

Any employer who violates any of the posting or recordkeeping requirements as prescribed by regulations adopted pursuant to Sections 6408 and 6410, or who fails to post any notice required by Section 3550, shall be assessed a civil penalty of up to seven thousand dollars ($7,000) for each violation. **Leg.H.** 1991 ch. 599, effective October 5, 1991.

Ref.: Herlick Handbook § 14.3; W. Cal. Ev., "Hearsay" §116.

§6432. "Serious violation" and "substantial probability" defined.

(a) As used in this part, a "serious violation" shall be deemed to exist in a place of employment if there is a substantial probability that death or serious physical harm could result from a violation, including, but not limited to, circumstances where there is a substantial probability that either of the following could result in death or great bodily injury:

(1) A serious exposure exceeding an established permissible exposure limit.

(2) The existence of one or more practices, means, methods, operations, or processes which have been adopted or are in use, in the place of employment.

(b) Notwithstanding subdivision (a), a serious violation shall not be deemed to exist if the employer can demonstrate that it did not, and could not with the exercise of reasonable diligence, know of the presence of the violation.

(c) As used in this section, "substantial probability" refers not to the probability that an accident or exposure will occur as a result of the violation, but rather to the probability that death or serious physical harm will result assuming an accident or exposure occurs as a result of the violation. **Leg.H.** 1999 ch. 615.

Ref.: W. Cal. Ev., "Hearsay" §116.

§6433. Civil penalties distinguished.

The civil penalties set forth in Sections 6427 to 6431, inclusive, shall not be considered as other penalties specifically provided within the meaning of Section 6423.

Ref.: W. Cal. Ev., "Hearsay" §116.

§6434. Civil or administrative penalties assessed against educational entities to be deposited with fund; application for refund upon abatement—Time limit.

(a) Any civil or administrative penalty assessed pursuant to this chapter against a school district, county board of education, county superintendent of schools, charter school, community college district, California State University, University of California, or joint powers agency performing education functions shall be deposited with the Workplace Health and Safety Revolving Fund established pursuant to Section 78.

(b) Any school district, county board of education, county superintendent of schools, charter school, community college district, California State University, University of California, or joint powers agency performing education functions may apply for a refund of their civil penalty, with interest, if all conditions previously cited have been abated, they have abated any other outstanding citation, and if they have not been cited by the division for a serious violation at the same school within two years of the date of the original violation. Funds not applied for within two years and six months of the time of the original violation shall be expended as provided for in Section 78 to assist schools in establishing effective occupational injury and illness prevention programs. **Leg.H.** 1991 ch. 599, effective October 5, 1991, 1999 ch. 615, 2000 ch. 135.

Ref.: W. Cal. Ev., "Hearsay" §116.

§6434.5. Refund plan for civil and administrative penalties.

(a) Any civil or administrative penalty assessed pursuant to this chapter against a public police or city, county, or special district fire department or the California Department of Forestry and Fire Protection shall be deposited into the Workers' Compensation Administration Revolving Fund established pursuant to Section 62.5.

(b) Any public police or city, county, or special district fire department or the California Department of Forestry and Fire Protection may apply for a refund of any civil or administrative penalty assessed pursuant to this chapter, with interest, if all conditions previously cited have been abated, the department has abated any other outstanding citation, and the department has not been cited by the division for a serious violation within two years of the date of the original violation. Funds received as a result of a penalty, for which a refund is not applied for within two years and six months of the time of the original violation, shall be expended in accordance with Section 78 as follows:

(1) Funds received as a result of a civil or administrative penalty imposed on a city, county, or special district fire department or the California Department of Forestry and Fire Protection shall be allocated to the California Firefighter Joint Apprenticeship Program for the purpose of establishing and maintaining effective occupational injury and illness prevention programs.

(2) Funds received as a result of a civil or administrative penalty imposed on a police department shall be allocated to the Office of Criminal Justice Planning, or any succeeding agency, for the purpose of establishing and maintaining effective occupational injury and illness prevention programs.

(c) This section does not apply to that portion of any civil or administrative penalty that is distributed directly to an aggrieved employee or employees pursuant to the provisions of Section 2699. **Leg.H.** 2005 ch. 141 (AB 186) §1.

Ref.: W. Cal. Ev., "Hearsay" §116.

§6435. Civil penalty for violation of permit requirements.

(a) Any employer who violates any of the requirements of Chapter 6 (commencing with Section 6500) of this part shall be assessed a civil penalty under the appropriate provisions of Sections 6427 to 6430, inclusive.

(b) This section shall become inoperative on January 1, 1987, and shall remain inoperative until January 1, 1991, at which time it shall become operative, unless a later enacted statute, which becomes effective on or before January 1, 1991, deletes or extends that date.

Ref.: W. Cal. Ev., "Hearsay" §116.

§6436. Jurisdiction of actions involving asbestos-related complaints.

The criminal complaint regarding a violation of Section 6505.5 may be brought by the Attorney General or by the district attorney or prosecuting attorney of any city, in the superior court of any county in the state with jurisdiction over the contractor or employer, by reason of the contractor's or employer's act or failure to act within that county. Any penalty assessed by the court shall be paid to the office of the prosecutor bringing the complaint, but if the case was referred to the prosecutor by the division, or some other governmental unit, one-half of the civil or criminal penalty assessed shall be paid to that governmental unit. **Leg.H.** 2003 ch. 449 (AB 1712).

Ref.: W. Cal. Ev., "Hearsay" §116.

CHAPTER 5
TEMPORARY VARIANCES

§6450. Temporary order for variance from health and safety standards.

(a) Any employer may apply to the division for a temporary order granting a variance from an occupational safety or health standard. Such temporary order shall be granted only if the employer files an application which meets the requirements of Section 6451, and establishes that (1) he is unable to comply with a standard by its effective date because of unavailability of professional or technical personnel or of materials and equipment needed to come into compliance with the standard or because necessary construction or alteration of facilities cannot be completed by the effective date, (2) he is taking all available steps to safeguard his employees against the hazards covered by the standard, and (3) he has an effective program for coming into compliance with the standard as quickly as practicable.

(b) Any temporary order issued under this section shall prescribe the practices, means, methods, operations, and processes which the employer must adopt and use while the order is in effect and state in detail his program for coming into compliance with the standard. Such a temporary order may be granted only after notice to employees and an opportunity for a hearing. However, the division may issue one interim order for a temporary variance upon submission of an application showing that the employment or place of employment will be safe for employees pending a hearing on the application for a temporary variance. No temporary order may be in effect for longer than the period needed by the employer to achieve compliance with the standard or one year, whichever is shorter, except that such an order may be renewed not more than twice provided that the requirements of this section are met and an application for renewal is filed prior to the expiration date of the order. No single renewal of an order may remain in effect for longer than 180 days.

Ref.: W. Cal. Ev., "Hearsay" §116; W. Cal. Sum., 3 "Agency and Employment" §365.

§6451. Information needed for temporary variance application.

An application for a temporary order under Section 6450 shall contain all of the following:

(a) A specification of the standard or portion thereof from which the employer seeks a variance.

(b) A representation by the employer, supported by representations from qualified persons having firsthand knowledge of the facts represented, that he is unable to comply with the standard or portion thereof and a detailed statement of the reasons therefor.

(c) A statement of the steps he has taken and will take, with specific dates, to protect employees against the hazard covered by the standard.

(d) A statement of when he expects to be able to comply with the standard and what steps he has taken and what steps he will take, with dates specified, to come into compliance with the standard.

(e) A certification that he has informed his employees of the application by giving a copy thereof to their authorized representative, posting a statement giving a summary of the application and specifying where a copy may be examined at the place or places where notices to employees are normally posted, and by other appropriate means. A description of how employees have been informed shall be contained in the certification. The information to employees shall also inform them of their right to petition the division for a hearing.

Ref.: W. Cal. Ev., "Hearsay" §116.

§6452. Temporary variance to test new techniques.

The division is authorized to grant a temporary variance from any standard or portion thereof whenever it determines such variance is necessary to permit an employer to participate in an experiment approved by the director designed to demonstrate or validate new and improved techniques to safeguard the health or safety of workers.

Ref.: W. Cal. Ev., "Hearsay" §116.

§6454. Rules for temporary variances.

The division may, in accordance with Chapter 3.5 (commencing with Section 11340) of Part 1 of Division 3 of Title 2 of the Government Code, make such rules and regulations as are reasonably necessary to carry out the provisions of this chapter and to establish rules and regulations relating to the granting or denial of temporary variances.

Ref.: W. Cal. Ev., "Hearsay" §116.

§6455. Time limits to appeal temporary variance.

Any employer or other person adversely affected by the granting or denial of a temporary variance may appeal to the standards board within 15 working days from receipt of the notice granting or denying the variance. The 15-day period may be extended by the standards board for good cause.

Ref.: W. Cal. Ev., "Hearsay" §116; W. Cal. Sum., 3 "Agency and Employment" §368.

§6456. Temporary variance decisions binding on parties.

A decision of the standards board on a variance appeal is binding on the director and the division with respect to the parties involved in the particular appeal. The director shall have the right to seek judicial review of a standards board decision irrespective of whether he appeared or participated in the appeal to the standards board.

Ref.: W. Cal. Ev., "Hearsay" §116; W. Cal. Sum., 3 "Agency and Employment" §369.

§6457. Standards board decisions.

The standards board shall conduct hearings and render decisions on appeals of decisions of the division relating to allowance or denial of temporary variances. All board decisions on such variance appeals shall be in writing and shall be final except for any rehearing or judicial review.

Ref.: W. Cal. Ev., "Hearsay" §116; W. Cal. Sum., 3 "Agency and Employment" §369.

CHAPTER 6
PERMIT REQUIREMENTS

§6500. Permit requirement for dangerous employment or place of employment; application to certain construction, demolition, and underground activities and motion picture, television, and theater stages or sets on and after January 1, 2000.

(a) For those employments or places of employment that by their nature involve a substantial risk of injury, the division shall require the issuance of a permit prior to the initiation of any practices, work, method, operation, or process of employment. The permit requirement of this section is limited to employment or places of employment that are any of the following:

(1) Construction of trenches or excavations that are five feet or deeper and into which a person is required to descend.

(2) The construction of any building, structure, falsework, or scaffolding more than three stories high or the equivalent height.

(3) The demolition of any building, structure, falsework, or scaffold more than three stories high or the equivalent height.

(4) The underground use of diesel engines in work in mines and tunnels.

This subdivision does not apply to motion picture, television, or theater stages or sets, including, but not limited to, scenery, props, backdrops, flats, greenbeds, and grids.

(b) On or after January 1, 2000, this subdivision shall apply to motion picture, television, or theater stages or sets, if there has occurred within any one prior calendar year in any combination at separate locations three serious injuries, fatalities, or serious violations related to the construction or demolition of sets more than 36 feet in height for the motion picture, television, and theatrical production industry.

An annual permit shall be required for employers who construct or dismantle motion picture, television, or theater stages or sets that are more than three stories or the equivalent height. A single permit shall be required under this subdivision for each employer, regardless of the number of locations where the stages or sets are located. An employer with a currently valid annual permit issued under this subdivision shall not be required to provide notice to the division prior to commencement of any work activity authorized by the permit. The division may adopt procedures to permit employers to renew by mail the permits issued under this subdivision. For purposes of this subdivision, "motion picture, television, or theater stages or sets" include, but are not limited to, scenery, props, backdrops, flats, greenbeds, and grids. **Leg.H.** 1996 ch. 664, 1997 ch. 17.

Ref.: W. Cal. Ev., "Hearsay" §116; W. Cal. Sum., 3 "Agency and Employment" §366.

§6501. Permit information required of employer.

Any employer subject to Section 6500 shall apply to the division for a permit pursuant to Section 6500. Such application for a permit shall contain such information as the division may deem necessary to evaluate the safety of the proposed employment or place of employment.

An application by an employer shall include a provision that the applicant has knowledge of applicable occupational safety and health standards and will comply with such standards and any other lawful order of the division.

Ref.: W. Cal. Ev., "Hearsay" §116.

§6501.5. Employer registration of asbestos-related work.

Effective January 1, 1987, any employer or contractor who engages in asbestos-related work, as defined in Section 6501.8, and which involves 100 square feet or more of surface area of asbestos-containing material, shall register with the division.

The division may grant registration based on a determination that the employer has demonstrated evidence that the conditions, practices, means, methods, operations, or processes used, or proposed to be used, will provide a safe and healthful place of employment. This section is not intended to supersede existing laws and regulations under Title 8, California Administrative Code, Section 5208.

An application for registration shall contain such information and attachments, given under penalty of perjury, as the division may deem necessary to evaluate the safety and health of the proposed employment or place of employment. It shall include, but not be limited to, all of the following:

(a) Every employer shall meet each of the following criteria:

(1) If the employer is a contractor, the contractor shall be certified pursuant to Section 7058.5 of the Business and Professions Code.

(2) Provide health insurance coverage to cover the entire cost of medical examinations and monitoring required by the law and be insured for workers' compensation, or provide a five hundred dollar ($500) trust account for each employee engaged in asbestos-related work. The health insurance coverage may be provided through a union, association, or employer.

(3) Train and certify all employees in accordance with all training required by law and Title 8 of the California Administrative Code.

(4) Be proficient and have the necessary equipment to safely do asbestos-related work.

(b) Provide written notice to the division of each separate job or phase of work, where the work process used is different or the work is performed at noncontiguous locations, noting all of the following:

(1) The address of the job.

(2) The exact physical location of the job at that address.

(3) The start and projected completion date.

(4) The name of a certified supervisor with sufficient experience and authority who shall be responsible for the asbestos-related work at that job.

(5) The name of a qualified person, who shall be responsible for scheduling any air sampling, laboratory calibration of air sampling equipment, evaluation of sampling results, and conducting respirator fit testing and evaluating the results of those tests.

(6) The type of work to be performed, the work practices that will be utilized, and the potential for exposure.

Should any change be necessary, the employer or contractor shall so inform the division at or before the time of the change. Any oral notification shall be confirmed in writing.

(c) Post the location where any asbestos-related work occurs so as to be readable at 20 feet stating, "Danger—Asbestos. Cancer and Lung Hazard. Keep Out."

(d) A copy of the registration shall be provided before the start of the job to the prime contractor or other employers on the site and shall be posted on the jobsite beside the Cal-OSHA poster.

(e) The division shall obtain the services of three industrial hygienists and one clerical employee to implement and to enforce the requirements of this section unless the director makes a finding that these services are not necessary or that the services are not obtainable due to a lack of qualified hygienists applying for available positions. Funding may, at the director's discretion, be appropriated from the Asbestos Abatement Fund.

(f) Not later than January 1, 1987, the Division of Occupational Safety and Health shall propose to the Occupational Safety and Health Standards Board for review and adoption a regulation concerning asbestos-related work, as defined in Section 6501.8, which involves 100 square feet or more of surface area of asbestos-containing material. The regulation shall protect most effectively the health and safety of employees and shall include specific requirements for certification of employees, supervisors with sufficient experience and authority to be responsible for asbestos-related work, and a qualified person who shall be responsible for scheduling any air sampling, for arranging for calibration of the air sampling equipment and for analysis of the air samples by a NIOSH approved method, for conducting respirator fit testing, and for evaluating the results of the air sampling.

The Division of Occupational Safety and Health shall also propose a regulation to the Occupational Safety and Health Standards Board for review and adoption specifying sampling methodology for use in taking air samples.

Ref.: W. Cal. Ev., "Hearsay" §116; W. Cal. Sum., 3 "Agency and Employment" §373.

§6501.7. Definition of "asbestos."

"Asbestos" means fibrous forms of various hydrated minerals, including chrysotile (fibrous serpentine), crocidolite (fibrous riebecktite), amosite (fibrous cummingtonite—grunerite), fibrous tremolite, fibrous actinolite, and fibrous anthophyllite.

Ref.: W. Cal. Ev., "Hearsay" §116.

§6501.8. "Asbestos-related work" and "asbestos containing construction material."

(a) For purposes of this chapter, "asbestos-related work" means any activity which by disturbing asbestos-containing construction materials may release asbestos fibers into the air and which is not related to its manufacture, the mining or excavation of asbestos-bearing ore or materials, or the installation or repair of automotive materials containing asbestos.

(b) For purposes of this chapter, "asbestos containing construction material" means any manufactured construction material that contains more than one-tenth of 1 percent asbestos by weight.

(c) For purposes of this chapter, "asbestos-related work" does not include the installation, repair, maintenance, or nondestructive removal of asbestos cement pipe used outside of buildings, if the installation, repair, maintenance, or nondestructive removal of asbestos cement pipe does not result in asbestos exposures to employees in excess of the action level determined in accordance with Sections 1529 and 5208 of Title 8 of the California Code of Regulations, and if the employees and supervisors involved in the operation have received training through a task-specific training program, approved pursuant to Section 9021.9, with written certification of completion of that training by the training entity responsible for the training. **Leg.H.** 1993 ch. 1075.

Ref.: W. Cal. Ev., "Hearsay" §116.

§6501.9. Employer or contractor shall determine if asbestos is present.

The owner of a commercial or industrial building or structure, employer, or contractor who engages in, or contracts for, asbestos-related work shall make a good faith effort to determine if asbestos is present before the work is begun. The contractor or employer shall first inquire of the owner if asbestos is present in any building or structure built prior to 1978.

Ref.: W. Cal. Ev., "Hearsay" §116.

§6502. Division's issuance of permits.

The division may issue a permit based on a determination the employer has demonstrated evidence that the conditions, practices, means, methods, operations or processes used or proposed to be used will provide a safe and healthful place of employment. The division may issue a single permit for two or more projects to be performed by a single employer if similar conditions exist on each project and the chief or his representative is satisfied an adequate safety program has been developed for all the projects. The division may, upon its motion, conduct any investigation or hearing it deems necessary for the purpose of this section, and may require a safety conference prior to the start of actual work.

Ref.: W. Cal. Ev., "Hearsay" §116.

§6503. Safety conferences.

A safety conference shall include representatives of the owner or contracting agency, the contractor, the employer, employees and employee representatives. The safety conference shall include a discussion of the employer's safety program and such means, methods, devices, processes, practices, conditions or operations as he intends to use in providing safe employment and a safe place of employment.

Ref.: W. Cal. Ev., "Hearsay" §116.

§6503.5. Safety conference for all asbestos handling jobs.

A safety conference shall be held for all asbestos handling jobs prior to the start of actual work. It shall include representatives of the owner or contracting agency, the contractor, the employer, employees, and employee representatives. It shall include a discussion of the employer's safety program and such means, methods, devices, processes, practices, conditions, or operations as the employer intends to use in providing a safe place of employment.

Ref.: W. Cal. Ev., "Hearsay" §116.

§6504. Employers to post copies of permits.

Any employer issued a permit pursuant to this chapter shall post a copy or copies of the permit pursuant to subdivision (a) of Section 6408.

Ref.: W. Cal. Ev., "Hearsay" §116.

§6505. Revocation of permits.

The division may at any time, upon good cause being shown therefor, and after notice and an opportunity to be heard revoke any permit issued pursuant to this chapter.

Ref.: W. Cal. Ev., "Hearsay" §116.

§6505.5. Penalties for failure to determine if asbestos is present.

(a) The division may, upon good cause shown, and after notice to the employer or contractor by the division and an opportunity to be heard, revoke or suspend any registration issued to the employer or contractor to do

Labor

asbestos-related work until certain specified written conditions are met.

(b) Any person who owns a commercial or industrial building or structure, any employer who engages in or contracts for asbestos-related work, any contractor, public agency, or any employee acting for any of the foregoing, who, contracts for, or who begins, asbestos-related work in any commercial or industrial building or structure built prior to 1978 without first determining if asbestos-containing material is present, and thereby fails to comply with the applicable laws and regulations, is subject to one of the following penalties:

(1) For a knowing or negligent violation, a fine of not more than five thousand dollars ($5,000) or imprisonment in the county jail for not more than six months, or both the fine and imprisonment.

(2) For a willful violation which results in death, serious injury or illness, or serious exposure, a fine of not more than ten thousand dollars ($10,000) or imprisonment in the county jail for not more than one year, or both the fine and imprisonment. A second or subsequent conviction under this paragraph may be punishable by a fine of not more than twenty thousand dollars ($20,000) or by imprisonment in the county jail for not more than one year, or by both the fine and imprisonment.

(3) A civil penalty of not more than two thousand dollars ($2,000) for each violation, to be imposed pursuant to the procedures set forth in Sections 6317, 6318, and 6319.

(4) For a willful or repeat violation, a civil penalty of not more than twenty thousand dollars ($20,000) for each violation.

(c) It is a defense to an action for violation of this section if the owner, contractor, employer, public agency, or agent thereof, proves, by a preponderance of the evidence, that he or she made a reasonable effort to determine whether asbestos was present.

Ref.: W. Cal. Ev., "Hearsay" §116.

§6506. Appeal of permit denial or revocation.

(a) Any employer denied a permit upon application, or whose permit is revoked, may appeal such denial or revocation to the director.

(b) The filing of an appeal to the director from a permit revocation by the division shall not stay the revocation. Upon application by the employer with proper notice to the division, and after an opportunity for the division to respond to the application, the director may issue an order staying the revocation while the appeal is pending.

Ref.: W. Cal. Ev., "Hearsay" §116; W. Cal. Sum., 3 "Agency and Employment" §368.

§6507. Permit fees.

The division shall set a fee to be charged for such permits in an amount reasonably necessary to cover the costs involved in investigating and issuing such permits.

Ref.: W. Cal. Ev., "Hearsay" §116.

§6508. Entities exempt from permit requirements.

No permit shall be required of the State of California, a city, city and county, county, district, or public utility subject to the jurisdiction of the Public Utilities Commission.

Ref.: W. Cal. Ev., "Hearsay" §116.

§6508.5. No exemption from registration.

No entity shall be exempt from registration. The State of California, a city, city and county, county, district, or public utility subject to the jurisdiction of the Public Utilities Commission, shall be required to apply for a registration through the designated chief executive officer of that body. No registration fees shall be required of any public agencies.

Ref.: W. Cal. Ev., "Hearsay" §116.

§6509. Penalty for permit violations.

Any person, or agent or officer thereof, who violates this chapter is guilty of a misdemeanor.

Ref.: W. Cal. Ev., "Hearsay" §116.

§6509.5. Asbestos consultant may not require contract for corrective work as condition to performing inspection.

(a) If an asbestos consultant has made an inspection for the purpose of determining the presence of asbestos or the need for related remedial action with knowledge that the report has been required by a person as a condition of making a loan of money secured by the property, or is required by a public entity as a condition of issuing a permit concerning the property, the asbestos consultant or any employee, subsidiary, or any company with common ownership, shall not require, as a condition of performing the inspection, that the consultant also perform any corrective work on the property that was recommended in the report.

(b) This section does not prohibit an asbestos consultant that has contracted to perform corrective work after the report of another company has indicated the presence of asbestos or the need for related remedial action from making its own inspection prior to performing that corrective work or from making an inspection to determine whether the corrective measures were successful and, if not, thereafter performing additional corrective work.

(c) A violation of this section is grounds for disciplinary action against any asbestos consultant who engages in that work pursuant to any license from a state agency.

(d) A violation of this section is a misdemeanor punishable by a fine of not less than three thousand dollars ($3,000) and not more than five thousand dollars ($5,000), or by imprisonment in the county jail for not more than one year, or both.

(e) For the purpose of this section:

(1) "Asbestos consultant" means any person who, for compensation, inspects property to identify asbestos containing materials, determining the risks, or the need for related remedial action.

(2) "Asbestos" has the meaning set forth in Section 6501.7.

Ref.: W. Cal. Ev., "Hearsay" §116.

§6510. Temporary restraining order for permit violation.

(a) If, after inspection or investigation, the division finds that an employer, without a valid permit, is engaging in activity for which a permit is required, it may, through its attorneys, apply to the superior court of the county in which such activity is taking place for an injunction restraining such activity.

(b) The application to the superior court, accompanied by an affidavit showing that the employer, without a valid permit, is engaging in activity for which a permit is required, is a sufficient prima facie showing to warrant, in the discretion of the court, the immediate granting of a temporary restraining order. No bond shall be required of the division as a prerequisite to the granting of any restraining order.

Ref.: W. Cal. Ev., "Hearsay" §116; W. Cal. Sum., 3 "Agency and Employment" §366.

CHAPTER 7
APPEAL PROCEEDINGS

§6600. Time limit for appeal of citation or penalty.

Any employer served with a citation or notice pursuant to Section 6317, or a notice of proposed penalty under this part, or any other person obligated to the employer as specified in subdivision (b) of Section 6319, may appeal to the appeals board within 15 working days from the receipt of such citation or such notice with respect to violations alleged by the division, abatement periods, amount of proposed penalties, and the reasonableness of the changes required by the division to abate the condition.

Ref.: W. Cal. Ev., "Hearsay" §116; W. Cal. Sum., 3 "Agency and Employment" §368.

§6600.5. Time limit for appeal of special order or action order.

Any employer served with a special order or any action order by the division pursuant to Section 6308, or any other person obligated to the employer as specified in subdivision (b) of Section 6319, may appeal to the appeals board within 15 working days from the receipt of the order with respect to the action ordered by the division, abatement periods, the reasonableness of the changes required by the division to abate the condition.

Ref.: W. Cal. Ev., "Hearsay" §116.

§6601. Failure to act within time limit for appeal of citation or penalty.

If within 15 working days from receipt of the citation or notice of civil penalty issued by the division, the employer fails to notify the appeals board that he intends to contest the citation or notice of proposed penalty, and no notice contesting the abatement period is filed by any employee or representative of the employee within such time, the citation or notice of proposed penalty shall be deemed a final order of the appeals board and not subject to review by any court or agency. The 15-day period may be extended by the appeals board for good cause.

Ref.: W. Cal. Ev., "Hearsay" §116.

§6601.5. Failure to act within time limit for appeal of special order or action order.

If, within 15 working days from receipt of a special order, or action order by the division, the employer fails to notify the appeals board that he or she intends to contest the order, and no notice contesting the abatement period is filed by any employee or representative of the employee within that time, the order shall be deemed a final order of the appeals board and not subject to review by any court or agency. The 15-day period may be extended by the appeals board for good cause.

Ref.: W. Cal. Ev., "Hearsay" §116.

§6602. Appeal procedures.

If an employer notifies the appeals board that he or she intends to contest a citation issued under Section 6317, or notice of proposed penalty issued under Section 6319, or order issued under Section 6308, or if, within 15 working days of the issuance of a citation or order any employee or representative of an employee files a notice with the division or appeals board alleging that the period of time fixed in the citation or order for the abatement of the violation is unreasonable, the appeals board shall afford an opportunity for a hearing. The appeals board shall thereafter issue a decision, based on findings of fact, affirming, modifying or vacating the division's citation, order, or proposed penalty, or directing other appropriate relief.

Ref.: W. Cal. Ev., "Hearsay" §116.

§6603. Appeals board rules of practice and procedure.

(a) The rules of practice and procedure adopted by the appeals board shall be consistent with Article 8 (commencing with Section 11435.05) of Chapter 4.5 of Part 1 of Division 3 of Title 2 of, and Sections 11507, 11507.6, 11507.7, 11513, 11514, 11515, and 11516 of, the Government Code, and shall provide affected employees or representatives of affected employees an opportunity to participate as parties to a hearing under Section 6602.

(b) The superior courts shall have jurisdiction over contempt proceedings, as provided in Article 12 (commencing with Section 11455.10) of Chapter 4.5 of Part 1 of Division 3 of Title 2 of the Government Code. **Leg.H.** 1995 ch. 938, operative July 1, 1997;

Ref.: W. Cal. Ev., "Hearsay" §116; W. Cal. Sum., 3 "Agency and Employment" §368.

§6604. Duties of hearing officer.

The appeals board may, in accordance with rules of practice and procedure which it shall adopt, direct and order a hearing officer:

(a) To try the issues in any proceeding before it, whether of fact or of law, and make and file a finding, order or decision based thereon.

(b) To hold hearings and ascertain facts necessary to enable the appeals board to determine any proceeding or to make any order or decision that the appeals board is authorized to make, or necessary for the information of the appeals board.

Ref.: W. Cal. Ev., "Hearsay" §116; W. Cal. Sum., 3 "Agency and Employment" §368.

§6605. Powers of hearing officer.

The appeals board may appoint one or more hearing officers in any proceeding, as it may deem necessary or advisable, and may defer, remove to itself, or transfer to a hearing officer the proceedings on any appeal. Any hearing officer appointed by the appeals board has the powers, jurisdiction, and authority granted by law, by the order of appointment, and by the rules of the appeals board.

Ref.: W. Cal. Ev., "Hearsay" §116.

§6606. Objection to hearing officer.

Any party to the proceeding may object to the reference of the proceeding to a particular hearing officer upon any one or more of the grounds specified in Section 641 of the Code of Civil Procedure and such objection shall be heard and disposed of by the appeals board. Affidavits may be read and witnesses examined as to such objections.

Ref.: W. Cal. Ev., "Hearsay" §116.

§6607. Hearing officer must be sworn.

Before entering upon his duties, the hearing officer shall be sworn, before an officer authorized to administer oaths, faithfully and fairly to hear and determine the matters and issues referred to him, to make just findings and to report according to his understanding. In any proceedings under this chapter, the hearing officer shall have the power to administer oaths and affirmations and to certify official acts.

Ref.: W. Cal. Ev., "Hearsay" §116.

§6608. Findings; decision.

The appeals board or a hearing officer shall, within 30 days after the case is submitted, make and file findings upon all facts involved in the appeal and file an order or decision. Together with the findings or the decision, there shall be served upon all the parties to the proceedings a summary of the evidence received and relied upon and the reasons or grounds upon which the decision was made.

Ref.: W. Cal. Ev., "Hearsay" §116.

§6609. Appeals board's action on decision.

Within 30 days after the filing of the findings, decision, or order, the appeals board may confirm, adopt, modify or set aside the findings, order, or decision of a hearing officer and may, with or without further proceedings, and with or without notice, enter its order, findings, or decision based upon the record in the case.

Ref.: W. Cal. Ev., "Hearsay" §116.

§6610. Service of notice, order, decision.

Any notice, order, or decision required by this part to be served upon any person either before, during, or after the institution of any proceeding before the appeals board, shall be served in the manner provided by Chapter 5 (commencing with Section 1010) of Title 14 of Part 2 of the Code of Civil Procedure, unless otherwise directed by the appeals board. In the latter event the document shall be served in accordance with the order or direction of the appeals board. The appeals board may, in the cases mentioned in the Code of Civil Procedure, order service to be made by publication of notice of time and place of hearing. Where service is ordered to be made by publication the date of the hearing shall be fixed at more than 30 days from the date of filing the application.

Ref.: W. Cal. Ev., "Hearsay" §116.

§6611. Employer's failure to appear at appeal.

(a) If the employer fails to appear, the appeals board may dismiss the appeal or may take action upon the employer's express admissions or upon other evidence, and affidavits may be used without any notice to the employer. Where the burden of proof is upon the employer to establish the appeals board action sought, the appeals board may act without taking evidence. Nothing in this section shall be construed to deprive the employer of the right to make any showing by way of mitigation.

(b) The appeal may be reinstated by the appeals board upon a showing of good cause by the employer for his failure to appear.

Ref.: W. Cal. Ev., "Hearsay" §116.

§6612. Informality of proceedings does not affect decision.

No informality in any proceeding or in the manner of taking testimony shall invalidate any order, decision, or finding made and filed as specified in this division. No order, decision, or finding shall be invalidated because of the admission into the record, and use as proof of any fact in dispute of any evidence not admissible under the common law or statutory rules of evidence and procedure.

Ref.: W. Cal. Ev., "Hearsay" §116.

§6613. Use of depositions on appeal.

The appeals board, a hearing officer, or any party to the action or proceeding, may, in any investigation or hearing before the appeals board, cause the deposition of witnesses residing within or without the state to be taken in the manner prescribed by law for like depositions in civil actions in the superior courts of this state under Title 4 (commencing with Section 2016.010) of Part 4 of the Code of Civil Procedure. To that end the attendance of witnesses and the production of records may be required. Depositions may be taken outside the state before any officer authorized to administer oaths. The appeals board or a hearing officer in any proceeding before the appeals board may cause evidence to be taken in other jurisdictions before the agency authorized to hear similar matters in such other jurisdictions. **Leg.H.** 1998 ch. 931, effective September 28, 1998, 2004 ch. 182 (AB 3081), operative July 1, 2005.

Ref.: W. Cal. Ev., "Hearsay" §116.

§6614. Time for reconsideration.

(a) At any time within 30 days after the service of any final order or decision made and filed by the appeals board or a hearing officer, any party aggrieved directly or indirectly by any final order or decision, made and filed by the

Labor

appeals board or a hearing officer under any provision contained in this division, may petition the appeals board for reconsideration in respect to any matters determined or covered by the final order or decision and specified in the petition for reconsideration. Such petition shall be made only within the time and in the manner specified in this chapter.

(b) At any time within 30 days after the filing of an order or decision made by a hearing officer and the accompanying report, the appeals board may, on its own motion, grant reconsideration.

Ref.: W. Cal. Ev., "Hearsay" §116.

§6615. Accrual of cause of action; role of appeals board.

No cause of action arising out of any final order or decision made and filed by the appeals board or a hearing officer shall accrue in any court to any person until and unless the appeals board on its own motion sets aside such final order or decision and removes such proceeding to itself or such person files a petition for reconsideration, and such reconsideration is granted or denied. Nothing herein contained shall prevent the enforcement of any such final order or decision, in the manner provided in this division.

Ref.: W. Cal. Ev., "Hearsay" §116.

§6616. Information required in petition for reconsideration.

The petition for reconsideration shall set forth specifically and in full detail the grounds upon which the petitioner considers the final order or decision made and filed by the appeals board or a hearing officer to be unjust or unlawful, and every issue to be considered by the appeals board. The petition shall be verified upon oath in the manner required for verified pleadings in courts of record and shall contain a general statement of any evidence or other matters upon which the applicant relies in support thereof.

Ref.: W. Cal. Ev., "Hearsay" §116.

§6617. Grounds for reconsideration.

The petition for reconsideration may be based upon one or more of the following grounds and no other:

(a) That by such order or decision made and filed by the appeals board or hearing officer, the appeals board acted without or in excess of its powers.

(b) That the order or decision was procured by fraud.

(c) That the evidence does not justify the findings of fact.

(d) That the petitioner has discovered new evidence material to him, which he could not, with reasonable diligence, have discovered and produced at the hearing.

(e) That the findings of fact do not support the order or decision.

Ref.: W. Cal. Ev., "Hearsay" §116.

§6618. Waiver of objections not set forth in petition for reconsideration.

The petitioner for reconsideration shall be deemed to have finally waived all objections, irregularities, and illegalities concerning the matter upon which the reconsideration is sought other than those set forth in the petition for reconsideration.

Ref.: W. Cal. Ev., "Hearsay" §116.

§6619. Service petition for reconsideration; answer.

A copy of the petition for reconsideration shall be served forthwith upon all parties by the person petitioning for reconsideration. Any party may file an answer thereto within 30 days thereafter. Such answer shall likewise be verified. The appeals board may require the petition for reconsideration to be served on other persons designated by it.

Ref.: W. Cal. Ev., "Hearsay" §116.

§6620. Appeals board's power to reconsider; notice of hearing.

Upon the filing of a petition for reconsideration, or having granted reconsideration upon its own motion, the appeals board may, with or without further proceedings and with or without notice affirm, rescind, alter, or amend the order or decision made and filed by the appeals board or hearing officer on the basis of the evidence previously submitted in the case, or may grant reconsideration and direct the taking of additional evidence. Notice of the time and place of any hearing on reconsideration shall be given to the petitioner and adverse parties and to such other persons as the appeals board orders.

Ref.: W. Cal. Ev., "Hearsay" §116.

§6621. Decision based on record without further hearing.

If at the time of granting reconsideration, it appears to the satisfaction of the appeals board that no sufficient reason exists for taking further testimony, the appeals board may affirm, rescind, alter or amend the order or decision made and filed by the appeals board or hearing officer and may, without further proceedings, without notice, and without setting a time and place for further hearing, enter its findings, order or decision based upon the record in the case.

Ref.: W. Cal. Ev., "Hearsay" §116.

§6622. Effect of appeals board's alteration of decision.

After the taking of additional evidence and a consideration of all of the facts the appeals board may affirm, rescind, alter, or amend the original order or decision. An order or decision made following reconsideration which affirms, rescinds, alters, or amends the original order or decision shall be made by the appeals board but shall not affect any right or the enforcement of any right arising from or by virtue of the original order or decision unless so ordered by the appeals board.

Ref.: W. Cal. Ev., "Hearsay" §116.

§6623. Procedure for decisions.

Any decision of the appeals board granting or denying a petition for reconsideration or affirming, rescinding, altering, or amending the original findings, order, or decision following reconsideration shall be made by the appeals board and not by a hearing officer and shall be in writing, signed by a majority of the appeals board members assigned thereto, and shall state the evidence relied upon and specify in detail the reasons for the decision.

Ref.: W. Cal. Ev., "Hearsay" §116.

§6624. Denial of reconsideration; presumption.

A petition for reconsideration is deemed to have been denied by the appeals board unless it is acted upon within 45 days from the date of filing. The appeals board may, upon good cause being shown therefor, extend the time within which it may act upon that petition for not exceeding 15 days. **Leg.H.** 1991 ch. 734.

Ref.: W. Cal. Ev., "Hearsay" §116.

§6625. Filing for reconsideration; effect on original decision.

The filing of a petition for reconsideration shall suspend for a period of 10 days the order or decision affected, insofar as it applies to the parties to the petition, unless otherwise ordered by the appeals board. The appeals board upon the terms and conditions which it by order directs, may stay, suspend, or postpone the order or decision during the pendency of the reconsideration.

Ref.: W. Cal. Ev., "Hearsay" §116.

§6626. Time for reconsideration of appeals board order.

Nothing contained in this chapter shall be construed to prevent the appeals board, on petition of an aggrieved party or on its own motion, from granting reconsideration of an original order or decision made and filed by the appeals board within the same time specified for reconsideration of an original order or decision.

Ref.: W. Cal. Ev., "Hearsay" §116.

§6627. Writ of mandate in superior court.

Any person affected by an order or decision of the appeals board may, within the time limit specified in this section, apply to the superior court of the county in which he resides, for a writ of mandate, for the purpose of inquiring into and determining the lawfulness of the original order or decision or of the order or decision following reconsideration. The application for writ of mandate must be made within 30 days after a petition for reconsideration is denied, or, if a petition is granted or reconsideration is had on the appeals board's own motion, within 30 days after the filing of the order or decision following reconsideration.

Ref.: W. Cal. Ev., "Hearsay" §116; W. Cal. Sum., 3 "Agency and Employment" §369.

§6628. Procedure for superior court's consideration.

The writ of mandate shall be made returnable at a time and place then or thereafter specified by court order and shall direct the appeals board to certify its record in the case to the court within the time therein specified. No new or additional evidence shall be introduced in such court, but the cause shall be heard on the record of the appeals board, as certified to by it.

Ref.: W. Cal. Ev., "Hearsay" §116; W. Cal. Sum., 3 "Agency and Employment" §369.

§6629. Scope of superior court review.

The review by the court shall not be extended further than to determine, based upon the entire record which shall be certified by the appeals board, whether:

(a) The appeals board acted without or in excess of its powers.

(b) The order or decision was procured by fraud.

(c) The order or decision was unreasonable.

(d) The order or decision was not supported by substantial evidence.

(e) If findings of fact are made, such findings of fact support the order or decision under review.

Nothing in this section shall permit the court to hold a trial de novo, to take evidence, or to exercise its independent judgment on the evidence.

Ref.: W. Cal. Ev., "Hearsay" §116; W. Cal. Sum., 3 "Agency and Employment" §369.

§6630. Appeals board's factual findings and conclusions as controlling.

The findings and conclusions of the appeals board on questions of fact are conclusive and final and are not subject to review. Such questions of fact shall include ultimate facts and the findings and conclusions of the appeals board. The appeals board and each party to the action or proceeding before the appeals board shall have the right to appear in the mandate proceeding. Upon the hearing, the court shall enter judgment either affirming or annulling the order or decision, or the court may remand the case for further proceedings before the appeals board.

Ref.: W. Cal. Ev., "Hearsay" §116.

§6631. Procedure for writ of mandate.

The provisions of the Code of Civil Procedure relating to writs of mandate shall, so far as applicable, apply to proceedings in the courts under the provisions of this part. A copy of every pleading filed pursuant to the terms of this part shall be served on the appeals board and upon every party who entered an appearance in the action before the appeals board and whose interest therein is adverse to the party filing such pleading.

Ref.: W. Cal. Ev., "Hearsay" §116; W. Cal. Sum., 3 "Agency and Employment" §369.

§6632. Courts having jurisdiction over appeals board decisions.

No court of this state, except the Supreme Court, the courts of appeal, and the superior court to the extent herein specified, has jurisdiction to review, reverse, correct, or annul any order or rule, or decision of the appeals board, or to suspend or delay the operation or execution thereof, or to restrain, enjoin, or interfere with the appeals board in the performance of its duties.

Ref.: W. Cal. Ev., "Hearsay" §116.

§6633. Court's power to postpone operation of appeals board decision.

The filing of a petition for, or the pendency of, a writ of mandate shall not of itself stay or suspend the operation of any order, rule or decision of the appeals board, but the court before which the petition is filed may stay or suspend, in whole or in part, the operation of the order or decision of the appeals board subject to review, upon the terms and conditions which it by order directs.

Ref.: W. Cal. Ev., "Hearsay" §116.

CHAPTER 8
ENFORCEMENT OF CIVIL PENALTIES

§6650. Procedures for unpaid civil penalty.

(a) After the expiration of the period during which a penalty may be appealed, no appeal having been filed, the department may file with the clerk of the superior court in any county a certified copy of the citation and notice of civil penalty, the certification by the department that the penalty remains unpaid, and the division's proof of service on the employer of the items filed with the clerk of the court.

(b) After the exhaustion of the review procedures provided for in Chapter 7 (commencing with Section 6600), an appeal having been filed, the department may file with the clerk of the superior court in any county a certified copy of the citation and notice of civil penalty, a certified copy of the order, findings or decision of the appeals board, the certification of the department that the penalty remains unpaid, and proof of service on the employer at the employer's address as shown on the official address record by the appeals board.

(c) The clerk, immediately upon the filing of a notice of civil penalty by the department pursuant to subdivision (a) or (b), shall enter judgment for the state against the person assessed the civil penalty in the amount of the penalty, plus interest due for each day from the date of issuance of the notice of civil penalty that the penalty remains unpaid.

(d) The department shall serve the notice of entry of judgment provided by Section 664.5 of the Code of Civil Procedure on the employer.

(e) A judgment entered pursuant to this section shall bear the same rate of interest, have the same effect as other judgments, and be given the same preference allowed by law on other judgments rendered for claims for taxes pursuant to Section 7170 of the Government Code.

(f) No fees shall be charged by the clerk of any court for the performance of any official service required by this chapter. **Leg.H.** 1991 ch. 1210, 2000 ch. 135.

Ref.: W. Cal. Ev., "Hearsay" §116; W. Cal. Sum., 3 "Agency and Employment" §366.

§6651. Deadline to commence action to collect civil penalty.

(a) Notwithstanding Section 340 of the Code of Civil Procedure, an action to collect any civil penalty, fee, or penalty fee under this division shall be commenced within three years from the date the penalty or fee became final.

(b) The amendments made to this section by the act adding this subdivision shall only apply to penalty assessments or fees for which the three-year period prescribed in this section for the commencement of an action to collect a civil penalty or fee has not expired on the effective date of the act adding this subdivision. **Leg.H.** 1991 ch. 1210 §3, 1993 ch. 998.

Ref.: W. Cal. Ev., "Hearsay" §116.

§6652. Notice to Contractors' State License Board of civil penalty.

The division shall provide the Contractors' State License Board with a certified copy of every notice of civil penalty deemed to be a final order pursuant to Section 6601 or after the exhaustion of all other review procedures pursuant to Chapter 7 (commencing with Section 6600) when both of the following have occurred:

(a) The employer served with the notice of civil penalty is, or is thought to be, a licensee licensed by the Contractors' State License Board.

(b) The employer referred to in subdivision (a) has failed to pay the civil penalty after a period of 60 days following that employer's receipt of the notice of civil penalty.

(c) When the employer has paid the civil penalty referenced in the certified copy of notice of civil penalty that was provided to the Contractors' State License Board, including all interest owed thereon, then the division shall provide to the employer who was the subject of the certified copy of notice a written confirmation or receipt stating that the employer has paid the amount owed that was the subject of the certified notice provided to the board. **Leg.H.** 1991 ch. 1210.

Ref.: W. Cal. Ev., "Hearsay" §116.

CHAPTER 9 MISCELLANEOUS SAFETY PROVISIONS

§6700. Gas pipelines; conclusive presumptions.

(a) Any employer who causes or allows the use of any flammable or combustible material for the installation acceptance pressure test of any gas houseline or piping shall be conclusively presumed to be maintaining an unsafe place of employment.

(b) Any employer who causes or allows gas pipelines to be tested with gas at pressures in excess of that permitted by applicable sections of the American Society of Mechanical Engineers Code for Pressure Piping shall be conclusively presumed to be maintaining an unsafe place of employment.

Ref.: W. Cal. Ev., "Hearsay" §116.

§6701. Internal combustion engines used within structures.

It shall be the duty of the standards board to determine by the maximum allowable standards of emissions of contaminants from portable and from mobile internal combustion engines used inside factories, manufacturing plants, warehouses, buildings and other enclosed structures, which standards are compatible with the safety and health of employees.

Ref.: W. Cal. Ev., "Hearsay" §116.

§6702. Exhaust purifier devices.

All portable and all mobile internal combustion engines that are used inside factories, manufacturing plants, warehouses, buildings and other enclosed structures shall be equipped with a certified exhaust purifier device after the certification of the device by the State Air Resources Board.

The Division of Occupational Safety and Health shall be responsible for the enforcement of the provisions of this section.

Ref.: W. Cal. Ev., "Hearsay" §116.

§6703. Exceptions to rules for internal combustion engines used within structures.

Sections 6701 and 6702 shall apply to all portable and all mobile internal combustion engines used inside factories, manufacturing plants, warehouses, buildings and other enclosed structures unless the operation of such an engine used inside a particular factory, plant, warehouse, building or enclosed structure does not result in harmful exposure to concentrations of dangerous gases or fumes in excess of maximum acceptable concentrations as determined by the standards board.

Ref.: W. Cal. Ev., "Hearsay" §116.

§6704. Boomstops for crawler and wheel cranes.

All crawler and wheel cranes with cable-controlled booms and with rated lifting capacity of more than 10 tons sold or operated in this state shall be equipped with boomstops that meet standards that shall be established therefor by the standards board.

Ref.: W. Cal. Ev., "Hearsay" §116.

§6705. Restrictions on contracts involving trench excavations.

No contract for public works involving an estimated expenditure in excess of twenty-five thousand dollars ($25,000), for the excavation of any trench or trenches five feet or more in depth, shall be awarded unless it contains a clause requiring submission by the contractor and acceptance by the awarding body or by a registered civil or structural engineer, employed by the awarding body, to whom authority to accept has been delegated, in advance of excavation, of a detailed plan showing the design of shoring, bracing, sloping, or other provisions to be made for worker protection from the hazard of caving ground during the excavation of such trench or trenches. If such plan varies from the shoring system standards, the plan shall be prepared by a registered civil or structural engineer.

Nothing in this section shall be deemed to allow the use of a shoring, sloping, or protective system less effective than that required by the Construction Safety Orders.

Nothing in this section shall be construed to impose tort liability on the awarding body or any of its employees.

The terms "public works" and "awarding body", as used in this section, shall have the same meaning as in Sections 1720 and 1722, respectively, of the Labor Code.

Ref.: W. Cal. Ev., "Hearsay" §116.

§6705.5. Application of shoring, bracing, and sloping regulations to swimming pool excavations found unsafe.

Regulations of the department requiring the shoring, bracing, or sloping of excavations, or which contain similar requirements for excavations, shall only apply to the excavation of swimming pools where a reasonable examination by a qualified person reveals recognizable conditions which would expose employees to injury from possible moving ground. If these conditions are found to exist with respect to a swimming pool excavation, employees shall not be permitted to enter the excavation until the condition is abated or otherwise no longer exists.

Ref.: W. Cal. Ev., "Hearsay" §116.

§6706. One permit per project; exceptions.

For the purposes of subdivision (a) of Section 6500, only one permit shall be required for a project involving several trenches or excavations. The provisions of Section 6500 shall not apply to the construction of trenches or excavations for the purpose of performing emergency repair work to underground facilities, or the construction of swimming pools, or the construction of "graves" as defined in Section 7014 of the Health and Safety Code or to the construction or final use of excavations or trenches where the construction or final use does not require a person to descend into the excavations or trenches.

Ref.: W. Cal. Ev., "Hearsay" §116.

§6707. Bids for local government projects involving trenches or open excavations.

Whenever the state, a county, city and county, or city issues a call for bids for the construction of a pipeline, sewer, sewage disposal system, boring and jacking pits, or similar trenches or open excavations, which are five feet or deeper, such call shall specify that each bid submitted in response thereto shall contain, as a bid item, adequate sheeting, shoring, and bracing, or equipment method, for the protection of life or limb, which shall conform to applicable safety orders. Nothing in this section shall be construed to impose tort liability on the body awarding the contract or any of its employees. This section shall not apply to contracts awarded pursuant to the provisions of Chapter 3 (commencing with Section 14250) of Part 5 of Division 3 of Title 2 of the Government Code.

Ref.: W. Cal. Ev., "Hearsay" §116.

§6708. Adequate emergency first aid treatment; requirement.

Every contractor on a construction project, including, but not limited to any public works, shall maintain adequate emergency first aid treatment for his employees. As used in this section, "adequate" shall be construed to mean sufficient to comply with the Federal Occupational Safety and Health Act of 1970 (P.L. 91–596).

Ref.: Herlick Handbook § 9.10; W. Cal. Ev., "Hearsay" §116.

§6710. Explosives.

(a) At every place of employment where explosives are used in the course of employment, there shall be a person licensed pursuant to the provisions of Chapter 3 (commencing with Section 7990) of Part 9 of Division 5, to supervise and visually direct the blasting operation.

(b) For the purposes of this section, "explosives" shall include, but not be limited to, class A and B explosives, blasting caps, detonating cord, and charges or projectiles used in the control of avalanches. For the purposes of this section, "explosives" shall not include small arms ammunition or class C explosives such as explosive powerpacks in the form of explosive cartridges or explosive-charged construction devices, explosive rivets, bolts, and charges for driving pins and studs, and cartridges for explosive-actuated power devices.

This section shall not apply to persons, firms, or corporations licensed pursuant to Part 2 (commencing with Section 12500) of Division 11 of the Health and Safety Code.

Ref.: W. Cal. Ev., "Hearsay" §116.

§6711. Examination of persons using explosives for snow avalanche blasting.

(a) The division shall develop and administer an oral and written examination for persons using explosives, as defined in Section 6710, while engaged in snow avalanche blasting. Any person engaged in snow avalanche blasting shall pass this examination prior to being licensed by the division.

(b) The division shall select an advisory committee to assist the division in preparing the data and information for the written and oral qualifying examination. The advisory committee shall consist of not less than seven members, nor more than nine members, with at least one representative from explosive manufacturers, snow avalanche blasting consultants, the recreational snow ski industry, a public recreation area, the California Department of Transportation, and the division.

Ref.: W. Cal. Ev., "Hearsay" §116.

§6712. Occupational safety and health standard for field sanitation.

(a) The standards board shall, no later than December 1, 1991, adopt an occupational safety and health standard for field sanitation. The standard shall comply with all of the following:

(1) The standard shall be at least as effective as the federal field sanitation standard contained in Section 1928.110 of Title 29 of the Code of Federal Regulations.

(2) The standard shall be at least as effective as California field sanitation requirements in effect as of July 1, 1990, pursuant to Article 4 (commencing with Section 113310) of Chapter 11 of Part 6 of Division 104 of the Health and

Labor

Safety Code, Article 1 (commencing with Section 118375) of Chapter 1 of Part 15 of Division 104 of the Health and Safety Code, and Section 2441 of this code.

(3) The standard shall apply to all agricultural places of employment.

(4) The standard shall require that toilets are serviced and maintained in a clean, sanitary condition and kept in good repair at all times, including written records of that service and maintenance.

(b) Consistent with its mandatory investigation and reinspection duties under Sections 6309, 6313, and 6320, the division shall develop and implement a special emphasis program for enforcement of the standard for at least two years following its adoption. Not later than March 15, 1995, the division shall also develop a written plan to coordinate its enforcement program with other state and local agencies. The division shall be the lead enforcement agency. Other state and local agencies shall cooperate with the division in the development and implementation of the plan. The division shall report to the Legislature, not later than January 1, 1994, on its enforcement program. The plan shall provide for coordination between the division and local officials in counties where the field sanitation facilities required by the standard adopted pursuant to subdivision (a) are registered by the county health officer or other appropriate official of the county where the facilities are located. The division shall establish guidelines to assist counties that choose to register sanitation facilities pursuant to this section, for developing service charges, fees, or assessments to defray the costs of registering the facilities, taking into consideration the differences between small and large employers.

(c)(1) Past violations by a fixed-site or nonfixed-site employer, occurring anywhere in the state within the previous five years, of one or more field sanitation regulations established pursuant to this section, or of Section 1928.110 of Title 29 of the Code of Federal Regulations, shall be considered for purposes of establishing whether a current violation is a repeat violation under Section 6429.

(2) Past violations by a fixed-site or nonfixed-site employer, occurring anywhere in the state within the previous five years, of one or more field sanitation regulations established pursuant to this section, Article 4 (commencing with Section 113310) of Chapter 11 of Part 6 of Division 104 of the Health and Safety Code, Article 1 (commencing with Section 118375) of Part 15 of Division 104 of the Health and Safety Code, or Section 2441 of this code, or of Section 1928.110 of Title 29 of the Code of Federal Regulations, shall constitute evidence of willfulness for purposes of Section 6429.

(d)(1) Notwithstanding Sections 6317 and 6434, any employer who fails to provide the facilities required by the field sanitation standard shall be assessed a civil penalty under the appropriate provisions of Sections 6427 to 6430, inclusive, except that in no case shall the penalty be less than seven hundred fifty dollars ($750) for each violation.

(2) Abatement periods fixed by the division pursuant to Section 6317 for violations shall be limited to one working day. However, the division may, pursuant to Section 6319.5, modify the period in cases where a good faith effort to comply with the abatement requirement is shown. The filing of an appeal with the appeals board pursuant to Sections 6319 and 6600 shall not stay the abatement period.

(3) An employer cited pursuant to paragraph (1) of this subdivision shall be required to annually complete a field sanitation compliance form which shall list the estimated peak number of employees, the toilets, washing, and drinking water facilities to be provided by the employer, any rental and maintenance agreements, and any other information considered relevant by the division for a period of five years following the citation. The employer shall be required to annually submit the completed form, subscribed under penalty of perjury, to the division, or to an agency designated by the division.

(e) The division shall notify the State Department of Health Services and the appropriate local health officers whenever a violation of the standard adopted pursuant to this section may result in the adulteration of food with harmful bacteria or other deleterious substances within the meaning of Article 5 (commencing with Section 110545) of Chapter 5 of Part 5 of Division 104 of the Health and Safety Code.

(f) Pending final adoption and approval of the standard required by subdivision (a), the division may enforce the field sanitation standards prescribed by Section 1928.110 of Title 29 of the Code of Federal Regulations, except subdivision (a) of Section 1928.110, in the same manner as other standards contained in this division. **Leg.H.** 1994 ch. 1203, 1996 ch. 1023, effective September 29, 1996.

Ref.: W. Cal. Ev., "Hearsay" §116.

§6716. "Lead-related construction work."

For the purposes of this division, "lead-related construction work" means any of the following:

(a) Any construction, alteration, painting, demolition, salvage, renovation, repair, or maintenance of any building or structure, including preparation and cleanup, that, by using or disturbing lead-containing material or soil, may result in significant exposure of employees to lead as determined by the standard adopted pursuant to Section 6717.

(b) The transportation, disposal, storage, or containment of materials containing lead on site or at a location at which construction activities are performed. "Lead-related construction work" does not include any activity related to the manufacture or mining of lead or the installation or repair of automotive materials containing lead. **Leg.H.** 1993 ch. 1122.

Ref.: W. Cal. Ev., "Hearsay" §116.

§6717. Standard that protects employees engaged in lead-related construction.

(a) On or before February 1, 1994, the division shall propose to the standards board for its review and adoption, a standard that protects the health and safety of employees who engage in lead-related construction work and meets all requirements imposed by the federal Occupational Safety and Health Administration. The standards board shall adopt the standard on or before December 31, 1994. The standard shall at least prescribe protective measures appropriate to the work activity and the lead content of materials to be disturbed by the activity, and shall include requirements and specifications pertaining to the following:

(1) Sampling and analysis of surface coatings and other materials that may contain significant amounts of lead.

(2) Concentrations and amounts of lead in surface coatings and other materials that may constitute a health hazard to employees engaged in lead-related construction work.

(3) Engineering controls, work practices, and personal protective equipment, including respiratory protection, fit-testing requirements, and protective clothing and equipment.

(4) Washing and showering facilities.

(5) Medical surveillance and medical removal protection.

(6) Establishment of regulated areas and appropriate posting and warning requirements.

(7) Recordkeeping.

(8) Training of employees engaged in lead-related construction work and their supervisors, that shall consist of current certification as required by regulations adopted under subdivision (c) of Section 105250 of the Health and Safety Code and include training with respect to at least the following:

(A) Health effects of lead exposure, including symptoms of overexposure.

(B) The construction activities, methods, processes, and materials that can result in lead exposure.

(C) The requirements of the lead standard promulgated pursuant to this section.

(D) Appropriate engineering controls, work practices, and personal protection for lead-related work.

(E) The necessity for fit-testing for respirator use and how fit-testing is conducted. **Leg.H.** 1993 ch. 1122, 1996 ch. 1023, effective September 29, 1996.

1993 Note: Section 6717 has no subsection (b).

Ref.: W. Cal. Ev., "Hearsay" §116.

§6718. Restrictions on test procedures for vapor emission from vehicles transporting gasoline.

Notwithstanding any other provision of law, any test procedures adopted by a state agency to determine compliance with vapor emission standards, by vapor recovery systems of cargo tanks on tank vehicles used to transport gasoline, shall not require any person to climb upon the cargo tank during loading operations. **Leg.H.** 1997 ch. 84.

Ref.: W. Cal. Ev., "Hearsay" §116.

§6719. Concern over repetitive motion injuries.

The Legislature reaffirms its concern over the prevalence of repetitive motion injuries in the workplace and reaffirms the Occupational Safety and Health Standards Board's continuing duty to carry out Section 6357. **Leg.H.** 1999 ch. 615.

Ref.: W. Cal. Ev., "Hearsay" §116.

PART 3
Safety on Buildings

CHAPTER 1
BUILDINGS UNDER CONSTRUCTION OR REPAIR

ARTICLE 1
Floors and Walls

§7100. "Building."

As used in this article, "building" means any multifloor building, other than structural steel framed building, more than two stories high in the course of construction.

Ref.: W. Cal. Sum., 3 "Agency and Employment" §371.

§7101. Protective flooring.

Every building shall have the joists, beams, or girders of floors below the floor or level where any work is being done, or about to be done, covered with flooring laid close together, or with other suitable material to protect workers engaged in such building from falling through joists or girders, and from falling substances, whereby life or safety is endangered.

§7102. Protective flooring in concrete buildings.

Every building which is of reinforced concrete construction, with reinforced concrete floors, shall have the floor filled in, either with forms or concrete, on each floor before the commencement of work upon the walls of the second floor above or the commencement of work upon the floor of the next floor above.

§7103. Protective wooden flooring.

Every building having wooden floors other than a steel frame building shall have the underflooring, if double flooring is to be used, laid on each floor within the time prescribed above for reinforced concrete floors. Where single wooden floors are to be used, each floor shall be planked over within the time prescribed above for reinforced concrete floors.

§7104. Supportive intermediate beams.

If a span of a floor on a building exceeds 13 feet, an intermediate beam shall be used to support the temporary flooring, but spans not to exceed 16 feet may be covered by three-inch planks without an intermediate beam. The intermediate beam shall be of a sufficient strength to sustain a live load of 50 pounds per square foot of the area supported.

§7105. Replanking.

If building operations are suspended and the temporary flooring required by this article is removed, the building shall be replanked upon the resumption of work so that every man at work has a covered floor not more than two stories below.

§7106. Building sections as "buildings."

Where a building is being constructed in sections each section constitutes a building for the purpose of this article.

§7107. Planked floors.

Planked floors on buildings shall be tightly laid together of proper thickness, grade and span to carry the working load; such working load to be assumed as at least 25 pounds per square foot.

§7108. Safety belts and nets.

Safety belts and nets shall be required in accordance with Article 24 (commencing with Section 1669) of subchapter 4 of Chapter 4 of Part 1 of Title 8 of the California Administrative Code, Construction Safety Orders of the Division of Occupational Safety and Health.

§7109. Working without required planking or nets.

No person shall proceed with any work assigned to or undertaken by him, or require or permit any other person to proceed with work assigned to or undertaken by either, unless the planking or nets required by this article are in place. Violation of this section is a misdemeanor.

§7110. Enforcement by Division.

The Division of Occupational Safety and Health shall enforce this article.

ARTICLE 2
Scaffolding

§7150. "Scaffolding."

As used in this article, "scaffolding" includes scaffolding and staging.

§7151. Suspended scaffolding.

If the working platform of any scaffolding swung or suspended from an overhead support is more than 10 feet above the ground, floor or area to which an employee on the scaffolding might fall, it shall have a safety rail of wood or other equally rigid material of adequate strength. The rail shall comply with the applicable orders of the Division of Occupational Safety and Health.

Suspended scaffolding shall be fastened so as to prevent the scaffolding from swaying from the building, or structure, or other object being worked on from the scaffolding. All parts of the scaffolding shall be of sufficient strength to support, bear, or withstand with safety any weight of persons, tools, appliances, or materials which might reasonably be placed on it or which are to be supported by it.

§7152. Employers using scaffolding.

In addition to the duties imposed by any law regulating or relating to scaffolding, an employer who uses or permits the use of scaffolding described in Section 7151 in connection with construction, alteration, repairing, painting, cleaning or doing of any work upon any building or structure, shall:

(a) Furnish safety lines to tie all hooks and hangers back on the roof of such building or structure.

(b) Provide safety lines hanging from the roof, securely tied thereto, for all swinging scaffolds which rely upon stirrups of the single point suspension type to support the working platform. One such line shall be provided for each workman with a minimum of one line between each pair of hangers or falls.

The standards board may adopt occupational safety and health standards different from the requirements of this section or grant variances from these requirements if the standards or variances provide equivalent or superior safety for employees.

§7153. Scaffolding platforms or floors.

Platforms or floors of such scaffolding shall be not less than 14 inches in width and shall be free from knots or fractures impairing their strength.

§7154.1. Prohibition of lean-to scaffolds.

The use of lean-to scaffolds, sometimes known as jack scaffolds, as support for scaffolds is hereby prohibited.

§7155. Penalty for scaffolding requirement violations.

Violation of any provision of sections 7151 to 7154 inclusive is a misdemeanor.

§7156. Employer violations and penalty.

Any person employing or directing another to do or perform any labor in the construction, alteration, repairing, painting, or cleaning of any house, building, or structure within this state is guilty of a misdemeanor who does any of the following:

(a) Knowingly or negligently furnishes or erects, or causes to be furnished or erected for the performance of that labor, unsafe or improper scaffolding, slings, hammers, blocks, pulleys, stays, braces, ladders, irons, ropes, or other mechanical contrivances.

(b) Hinders or obstructs any officer or inspector of the Division of Occupational Safety and Health attempting to inspect such equipment under the provisions of this article or any law or safety order of this state.

(c) Destroys or defaces, or removes any notice posted thereon by any division officer or inspector, or permits the use thereof, after the equipment has been declared unsafe by the officer or inspector.

§7157. Division's power regarding safety orders.

The division may make and enforce safety orders in the manner prescribed by law, to supplement and carry into effect the purposes and provisions of this article.

§7158. Enforcement by division.

The division shall enforce the provisions of this article.

ARTICLE 3
Construction Elevators

§7200. "Construction elevator" and "building."

As used in this article:

(a) "Construction elevator" includes any means used to hoist persons or material of any kind on a building under course of construction, when operated by any power other than muscular power.

(b) "Building" includes structures of all kinds during the course of construction, regardless of the purposes for which they are intended and whether such construction be below or above the level of the ground.

§7201. Signals for construction elevators.

Every construction elevator used in buildings shall have a system of signals for the purpose of signaling the person operating or controlling the machinery which operates or controls the construction elevator.

§7202. Employee to give signals.

The person in charge of a building shall appoint one or more persons to give such signals. Such person shall be selected from those most familiar with the work for which the construction elevator is being used. The signaling devices provided shall be protected against unauthorized or accidental operation.

§7203. Board's regulation of signals.

The board shall make, and may from time to time amend, general safety orders in the manner prescribed by law. Such orders shall specify and fix the nature and methods of signals and signaling devices and uniform signals to be used in this State under this article.

§7204. Inspection of construction elevators.

The division shall inspect all construction elevators. If any part of the construction or system of signals used on a construction elevator is defective or endangers the lives of the persons working in the immediate vicinity of the construction elevator, the division shall direct the person in charge thereof to remedy such defect. Such construction elevator shall not be used again until the order of the division is complied with.

§7205. Penalties for violation.

Any person, or the agent or officer thereof, who violates any provision of this article is guilty of a misdemeanor, punishable by a fine of not less than one hundred dollars ($100) and not more than one thousand dollars ($1,000), or imprisonment in the county jail for not less than thirty days and not more than six months, or both.

ARTICLE 4
Structural Steel Framed Buildings

§7250. "Building."

As used in this article "building" means any multifloor structural steel framed building more than two stories high in the course of construction.

§7251. Buildings affected.

As defined above, these provisions shall apply to buildings erected in tiers or stories and shall not apply to steel framed buildings having large open spans or areas such as, mill buildings, gymnasiums, auditoriums, hangars, arenas, or stadiums.

§7252. Decking of derricks or working floors.

The derrick or working floor of every building shall be solidly decked over its entire surface except for access openings.

§7253. Temporary floor and safety belt protection.

There shall be a tight and substantial temporary floor within two floors below and directly under that portion of each tier of beams on which erection, riveting, bolting, welding or painting is being done. For operations of short duration of exposure to falling, safety belts shall be required as set forth in Section 7265.

§7254. Temporary floors.

Temporary floors shall be wood planking of proper thickness, grade and span to carry the working load, but shall not be less than two inches thick, full size undressed.

§7255. Protection against temporary floor displacement.

Provision shall be made to secure temporary flooring against displacement by strong winds or other forces.

§7256. Plank extension.

Planks shall extend a minimum of 12 inches beyond centerline of their supports at each end.

§7257. Covering openings by columns.

Wire mesh or plywood (exterior grade) shall be used to cover openings adjacent to columns where planks do not fit tightly.

§7258. Metal decking instead of wood planking.

Metal decking where used in lieu of wood planking shall be of equivalent strength and shall be laid tightly and secured to prevent movement.

§7259. Replacement of floor planks.

Floor planks that are temporarily removed for any reason whatsoever shall be replaced as soon as work requiring their removal is completed or the open area shall be properly guarded.

§7260. Employee instruction before planking removed.

Prior to removal of temporary floor plank, employees shall be instructed by assigned supervision the steps to be taken to perform the work safely and in proper sequence.

§7261. Removing temporary planking.

When gathering and stacking temporary floor plank on a lower floor, in preparation for transferring such plank for use on an upper working floor, the steel erector's personnel shall remove such plank successively, working toward the last panel of such floor, so that the work is always being done from the planked floor.

§7262. Protection while removing temporary planking.

When gathering and stacking temporary floor planks from the last panel, the steel erector's personnel assigned to such work shall be protected by safety belts with life lines attached to a catenary line or other substantial anchorage.

§7263. Constantly maintaining structural frame's stability.

The sequence of erection, bolting, temporary guying, riveting and welding shall be such as to maintain the stability of the structural frame at all times during construction. This applies to the dead weight of the structure, plus weight and working reactions of all construction equipment placed thereon plus any external forces that may be applied.

§7264. Section as "building."

Where a building is being constructed in sections, each section constitutes a building as defined in Section 7250.

§7265. Safety belts and nets.

Safety belts and nets shall be required in accordance with Article 24 (commencing with Section 1669) of subchapter 4 of Chapter 4 of Part 1 of Title 8 of the California Administrative Code, Construction Safety Orders of the Division of Occupational Safety and Health.

§7266. Penalty for violation.

No person shall proceed with any work assigned to or undertaken by him, or require or permit any other person to proceed with work assigned to or undertaken by either, unless the planking or nets required by this article are in place. Violation of this section is a misdemeanor.

§7267. Enforcement by Division.

The Division of Occupational Safety and Health shall enforce this article.

CHAPTER 2 ELEVATORS, ESCALATORS, PLATFORM AND STAIRWAY CHAIR LIFTS, DUMBWAITERS, MOVING WALKS, AUTOMATED PEOPLE MOVERS, AND OTHER CONVEYANCES

§7300. Standards to promote public safety awareness.

The Legislature finds and declares all of the following:

(a) It is the purpose of this chapter to promote public safety awareness and to assure, to the extent feasible, the safety of the public and of workers with respect to conveyances covered by this chapter.

(b) The use of unsafe or defective conveyances imposes a substantial probability of serious and preventable injury to employees and the public. The prevention of these injuries and protection of employees and the public from unsafe conditions is in the best interest of the people of this state. Therefore, this chapter also establishes minimum standards for persons operating or maintaining conveyances covered by this chapter. These standards include familiarity with the operation and safety functions of the components and equipment, and documented training or experience or both, which shall include, but not be limited to, recognizing the safety hazards and performing the procedures to which they are assigned in conformance with all legal requirements.

(c) This chapter is not intended to prevent the division from implementing regulations, nor to prevent the use of systems, methods, or devices of equivalent or superior quality, strength, fire resistance, code effectiveness, durability, and safety to those required by the law, provided that there is technical documentation to demonstrate that the equivalency of the system, method, or device, is at least as effective as that prescribed in ASME A17.1, ASME A17.3, ASME A18.1, or ASCE 21. **Leg.H.** 2002 ch. 1149 (SB 1886) §3.

§7300.1. Definitions.

As used in this chapter:

(a) "ASCE 21" means the Automated People Mover Standards, as adopted by the American Society of Civil Engineers.

(b) "ASME A17.1" means the Safety Code for Elevators and Escalators, an American National Standard, as adopted by the American Society of Mechanical Engineers.

(c) "ASME A17.3" means the Safety Code for Existing Elevators and Escalators, an American National Standard, as adopted by the American Society of Mechanical Engineers.

(d) "ASME A18.1" means the Safety Standard for Platform Lifts and Stairway Chairlifts, an American National Standard, as adopted by the American Society of Mechanical Engineers.

(e) "Automated people mover" has the same meaning as defined in ASCE 21.

(f) "Board" or "standards board" means the Occupational Safety and Health Standards Board.

(g) "Certified qualified conveyance company" means any person, firm, or corporation that (1) possesses a valid contractor's license if required by Chapter 9 (commencing with Section 7000) of Division 3 of the Business and Professions Code and (2) is certified as a qualified conveyance company by the division in accordance with this chapter.

(h) "Certified competent conveyance mechanic" means any person who has been determined by the division to have the qualifications and ability of a competent journey-level conveyance mechanic and is so certified by the division in accordance with this chapter.

(i) "Conveyance" means any elevator, dumbwaiter, escalator, moving platform lift, stairway chairlift, material lift or dumbwaiter with automatic transfer device, automated people mover, or other equipment subject to this chapter.

(j) "Division" means the Division of Occupational Safety and Health.

(k) "Dormant elevator, dumbwaiter, or escalator" means an installation placed out of service as specified in ASME A17.1 and ASME A18.1.

(*l*) "Elevator" means an installation defined as an "elevator" in ASME A17.1.

(m) "Conveyance inspector" means any conveyance safety inspector of the division or other conveyance inspector determined by the division to be qualified pursuant to this chapter.

(n) "Escalator" means an installation defined as an "escalator" in ASME A17.1.

(o) "Existing installation" means an installation defined as an "installation, existing" in ASME A17.1.

(p) "Full maintenance service contract" means an agreement by a certified competent conveyance company and the person owning or having the custody, management, or control of the operation of the conveyance, if the agreement provides that the certified competent conveyance company is responsible for effecting repairs necessary to the safe operation of the equipment and will provide services as frequently as is necessary, but no less often than monthly.

(q) "Material alteration" means an alteration as defined in ASME A17.1 or A18.1.

(r) "Moving walk" or "moving sidewalk" means an installation defined as a "moving walk" in ASME A17.1.

(s) "Permit" means a document issued by the division that indicates that the conveyance has had the required safety inspection and tests and fees have been paid as set forth in this chapter.

(t) "Temporary permit" means a document issued by the division which permits the use of a noncompliant conveyance by the general public for a limited time while minor repairs are being completed or until permit fees are paid.

(u) "Repair" has the same meaning as defined in ASME A17.1 or A18.1. A "repair" does not require a permit.

(v) "Temporarily dormant elevator, dumbwaiter, or escalator" means a conveyance, the power supply of which has been disconnected by removing fuses and placing a padlock on the mainline disconnect switch in the "off" position. In the case of an elevator or dumbwaiter, the car shall be parked and the hoistway doors shall be in the closed and latched position. A wire seal shall be installed on the mainline disconnect switch by a conveyance inspector of the division. The wire seal and padlock shall not be removed for any purpose without permission from a conveyance inspector of the division. A temporarily dormant elevator, dumbwaiter, or escalator shall not be used again until it has been put in safe running order and is in condition for use. Annual inspections by a conveyance inspector shall continue for the duration of the temporarily dormant status. Temporarily dormant status may be renewed annually, but shall not exceed five years. After each inspection, the conveyance inspector shall file a report with the chief of the division describing the current condition of the conveyance.

(w) The meanings of building transportation terms not otherwise defined in this section shall be as defined in the latest editions of ASME A17.1 and ASME A18.1. **Leg.H.** 2002 ch. 1149 (SB 1886), 2004 ch. 503 (AB 2350).

§7300.2. Equipment covered.

Except as provided in Section 7300.3, this chapter covers the design, erection, construction, installation, material alteration, inspection, testing, maintenance, repair, service, and operation of the following conveyances and their associated parts and hoistways:

(a) Hoisting and lowering mechanisms equipped with a car or platform which move between two or more landings. This equipment includes, but is not limited to, the following:

(1) Elevators.

(2) Platform lifts and stairway chair lifts.

(b) Power-driven stairways and walkways for carrying persons between landings. This equipment includes, but is not limited to, the following:

(1) Escalators.

(2) Moving walks.

(c) Hoisting and lowering mechanisms equipped with a car which serve two or more landings and are restricted to the carrying of material by limited size or limited access to the car. This equipment includes, but is not limited to, the following:

(1) Dumbwaiters.

(2) Material lifts and dumbwaiters with automatic transfer devices.

(d) Automatic guided transit vehicles on guideways with an exclusive right-of-way. This equipment includes, but is not limited to, automated people movers. **Leg.H.** 2002 ch. 1149 (SB 1886).

§7300.3. Equipment not covered.

Equipment not covered by this chapter includes the following:

(a) Material hoists within the scope of standard A10.5 as adopted by the American National Standards Institute.

(b) Mobile scaffolds, towers, and platforms within the scope of standard A92 as adopted by the American National Standards Institute.

(c) Powered platforms and equipment for exterior and interior maintenance within the scope of standard 120.1 as adopted by the American National Standards Institute.

(d) Cranes, derricks, hoists, hooks, jacks, and slings within the scope of standard B30 as adopted by the American Society of Mechanical Engineers.

(e) Industrial trucks within the scope of standard B56 as adopted by the American Society of Mechanical Engineers.

(f) Portable equipment, except for portable escalators that are covered by standard A17.1 as adopted by the American National Standards Institute.

(g) Tiering or piling machines used to move materials to and from storage located and operating entirely within one story.

(h) Equipment for feeding or positioning materials, including that equipment used with machine tools or printing presses.

(i) Skip or furnace hoists.

(j) Wharf ramps.

(k) Railroad car lifts or dumpers.

(*l*) Line jacks, false cars, shafters, moving platforms, and similar equipment used for installing a conveyance by a contractor licensed in this state. **Leg.H.** 2002 ch. 1149 (SB 1886), 2004 ch. 503 (AB 2350).

§7300.4. Work exemptions.

This chapter does not apply to work that is not related to standards for conveyances that are (a) incorporated in codes promulgated by the American National Standards Institute or the American Society of Mechanical Engineers or (b) included in regulations of the division, in effect immediately prior to January 1, 2003, prescribing conveyance safety orders. Work exempted pursuant to this section includes, but is not limited to, routine nonmechanical maintenance, such as cleaning panels and changing light fixtures. **Leg.H.** 2002 ch. 1149 (SB 1886), 2004 ch. 503 (AB 2350).

§7301. Permit required for conveyance operation.

No conveyance shall be operated in this state unless a permit for its operation is issued by or in behalf of the division, and unless the permit remains in effect and is kept posted conspicuously on the conveyance. Operation of a conveyance without a permit or failure to post the permit conspicuously shall constitute cause for the division to prohibit use of the conveyance, unless it can be shown that a request for issuance or renewal of a permit has been made and the request has not been acted upon by the division. **Leg.H.** 1991 ch. 258, 2002 ch. 1149 (SB 1886).

§7301.1. Requirements for permit.

(a) On and after June 30, 2003, no conveyance may be erected, constructed, installed, or materially altered, as defined by regulation of the division, unless a permit has been obtained from the division before the work is commenced. A copy of the permit shall be kept at the construction site at all times while the work is in progress and shall be made available for inspection upon request. This section shall not apply to platform lifts and stairway chairlifts installed in a private residence as provided in paragraph (2) or (3) of subdivision (a) of Section 7317.

(b) Before March 1, 2003, the division shall establish an application procedure and all requirements for a permit under this section, which shall include the following:

(1) At a minimum, the applicant for a permit under this section shall meet all of the following requirements:

(A) The applicant shall hold a current elevator contractor's license issued pursuant to Chapter 9 (commencing with Section 7000) of Division 3 of the Business and Professions Code.

(B) The applicant shall be a certified qualified conveyance company.

(C) The applicant shall submit proof of the following types of insurance coverage, in the form of certified copies of policies or certificates of insurance:

(i) Liability insurance to provide general liability coverage of not less than one million dollars ($1,000,000) for the injury or death of any one person or persons in any one occurrence, with coverage of not less than five hundred thousand dollars ($500,000) for property damage in any one occurrence.

(ii) Workers' compensation insurance coverage.

(D) In the event of any material alteration, nonrenewal, or cancellation of any insurance required by this subparagraph, the applicant or permitholder shall submit written notice thereof to the division within five working days.

(2) At a minimum, each application for a permit under this section shall include all of the following:

(A) Copies of specifications and accurately scaled and fully dimensioned plans showing the

Labor

location of the installation in relation to the plans and elevation of the building; the location of the machinery room and the equipment to be installed, relocated, or altered; and all structural supporting members thereof, including foundations. The plans and specifications shall identify all materials to be employed and all loads to be supported or conveyed. The plans and specifications shall be sufficiently complete to illustrate all details of construction and design.

(B) The name, residence, and business address of the applicant and each partner, or for a corporation, the principal officers and anyone who is authorized to accept service of process or official notices; the number of years the applicant has engaged in the business of constructing, erecting, installing, or altering conveyances; and the approximate number of persons to be employed on the permitted job.

(C) The permit fee.

(3) The division shall establish, and may from time to time amend, a fee for a permit under this section in an amount sufficient to defray the division's actual costs in administering the permit process, including the costs of investigation, revocation, or other associated costs. Permit fees collected by the division are nonrefundable.

(c)(1) The permit shall expire when the work authorized by that permit is not commenced within six months after the date of issuance, or within a shorter period as the division may specify at the time the permit is issued.

(2) The permit shall expire following commencement of work, if the permitholder suspends or abandons the work for a period of 60 days, or for a shorter period of time as the division may specify at the time the permit is issued.

(3) Upon application and for good cause shown, the division may extend a permit that would otherwise expire under this subdivision.

(d) The division may revoke any permit at any time, upon good cause, and after notice and an opportunity to be heard. **Leg.H.** 2002 ch. 1149 (SB 1886), 2004 ch. 503 (AB 2350).

§7301.5. Adoption of fire and emergency regulations for conveyance operation; emergency certification.

(a) The standards board shall adopt regulations pertaining to conveyances, including, but not limited to, conveyance emergency and signal devices, and the operation of conveyances under fire and other emergency conditions.

(b) Before January 1, 2003, the division shall establish an application procedure and all requirements for certification under this subdivision as an emergency certified competent conveyance mechanic. To ensure the safety of the public when a disaster or other emergency exists within the state and the number of certified competent conveyance mechanics in the state is insufficient to cope with the emergency, any certified qualified conveyance company may, within five business days after commencing work requiring certified competent conveyance mechanics, apply to the division, on behalf of all persons performing the work who are not certified competent conveyance mechanics, for certification as emergency certified competent conveyance mechanics. Any person for whom emergency certification is sought under this subdivision shall be certified by a certified qualified conveyance company to have an acceptable combination of documented experience and education to perform work covered by this chapter without direct and immediate supervision. The certified qualified conveyance company shall furnish proof of competency as the division may require. The division shall issue an emergency certified competent conveyance mechanic certificate upon receipt of acceptable documentation and payment of the required fee. Each certificate issued pursuant to this subdivision shall recite that it is valid for a period of 30 days from the date of issuance and for those particular conveyances and geographical areas as the division may designate, and otherwise shall entitle the person being certified to the rights and privileges of a certified competent conveyance mechanic as set forth in this chapter. The division shall renew an emergency certified competent conveyance mechanic certificate during the existence of the emergency.

(c) Before January 1, 2004, the division shall establish an application procedure and all requirements for certification under this subdivision as a temporary certified competent conveyance mechanic. If there are no certified qualified conveyance mechanics available to perform elevator work, a certified qualified conveyance company may apply to the division for certification of one or more temporary certified competent conveyance mechanics. Any person seeking to work as a temporary certified competent conveyance mechanic shall, before beginning work, be approved by the division as having an acceptable combination of documented experience and education to perform work covered by this chapter without direct and immediate supervision. The certified qualified conveyance company shall furnish proof of competency as the division may require. The division may issue a temporary certified competent conveyance mechanic certificate upon acceptable documentation and payment of the required fee. Each certificate issued pursuant to this subdivision shall recite that it is valid for a period of 30 days from the date of issuance and while the certificate holder is employed by the certified qualified conveyance company that certified the individual as competent. The certificate shall be renewable as long as the shortage of certified competent conveyance mechanics continues. **Leg.H.** 2002 ch. 1149 (SB 1886), 2004 ch. 503 (AB 2350).

§7302. Conveyance operation without permit.

The operation of a conveyance without a permit by any person owning or having the custody, management, or control of the operation of the conveyance, is a misdemeanor, punishable by a fine of not more than one thousand dollars ($1,000), imprisonment in the county jail for not more than 10 days, or by both that fine and imprisonment. Each day of operation for each conveyance without a permit is a separate offense. Any person who has requested the issuance or renewal of a permit if the request has not been acted upon by the division may not be prosecuted for a violation of this section. **Leg.H.** 2002 ch. 1149 (SB 1886) §12.

§7302.1. Conveyance authorization without permit.

(a) Any person who contracts for or authorizes the erection, construction, installation, or material alteration of a conveyance without a permit in violation of Section 7301.1 is guilty of a misdemeanor punishable by a fine of not more than seventy thousand dollars ($70,000), imprisonment in the county jail for not more than one year, or by both that fine and imprisonment.

(b) Any employer or contractor who contracts for or engages in the erection, construction, installation, or material alteration of a conveyance without a permit in violation of Section 7301.1 is guilty of a misdemeanor punishable by a fine of not more than seventy thousand dollars ($70,000), imprisonment in the county jail for not more than one year, or by both that fine and imprisonment. **Leg.H.** 2002 ch. 1149 (SB 1886).

§7302.2. Assessment of penalty.

The division may assess a civil penalty of not more than seventy thousand dollars ($70,000) against any person, and against any employer or contractor, who contracts for or authorizes the erection, construction, installation, or material alteration of a conveyance without a permit issued pursuant to Section 7301.1. **Leg.H.** 2002 ch. 1149 (SB 1886).

§7303. Remedies for dangerous operation without permit.

(a) Whenever any conveyance is operated without a current valid permit issued pursuant to Section 7304, and is in a condition that its use is dangerous to the life or safety of any person, the division or any affected person may apply to the superior court of the county in which the conveyance is located for an injunction restraining the operation of the conveyance until the condition is corrected. Proof by certification of the division that a permit has not been issued, has expired, or has been revoked, together with the affidavit of any safety inspector of the division or other expert that the operation of the conveyance is dangerous to the life or safety of any person, is sufficient ground, in the discretion of the court, for the immediate granting of a temporary restraining order.

(b) No bond shall be required from the division as a prerequisite for the division to seek or obtain any restraining order under subdivision (a).

(c) Any person who intentionally violates any injunction prohibiting the operation of the conveyance issued pursuant to subdivision (a) shall be liable for a civil penalty, to be assessed by the division, not to exceed seven thousand dollars ($7,000) for each violation. Each day of operation for each conveyance is a separate violation. **Leg.H.** 2002 ch. 1149 (SB 1886).

§7304. Conveyance inspection and permit issuance.

(a) Except as provided in subdivision (b), the division shall cause all conveyances to be inspected at least once each year. If a conveyance is found upon inspection to be in a safe condition for operation, a permit for operation

Labor

for not longer than one year shall be issued by the division.

(b) If a conveyance is subject to a full maintenance service contract, the division may, after investigation and inspection, issue a permit for operation for not longer than two years. **Leg.H.** 2002 ch. 1149 (SB 1886), 2004 ch. 183 (AB 3082).

§7305. Division's power over unsafe conveyances.

If inspection shows that a conveyance is in an unsafe condition, the division may issue a preliminary order requiring repairs or alterations to be made to the conveyance that are necessary to render it safe, and may prohibit its operation or use until the repairs or alterations are made or the unsafe conditions are removed. **Leg.H.** 2002 ch. 1149 (SB 1886).

§7306. Challenging division orders.

Unless the preliminary order is complied with, a hearing before the division shall be allowed, upon request, at which the owner, operator, or other person in charge of the conveyance may appear and show cause why he or she should not comply with the order. **Leg.H.** 2002 ch. 1149 (SB 1886).

§7307. Procedural choices of division; later review.

(a) If it thereafter appears to the division that the conveyance is unsafe and that the requirements contained in the preliminary order should be complied with, or that other things should be done to make the conveyance safe, the division may order or confirm the withholding of the permit and may impose requirements as it deems proper for the repair or alteration of the conveyance or for the correction of the unsafe condition. The order may thereafter be reheard by the division or reviewed by the courts in the manner specified for safety orders by Part 1 (commencing with Section 6300) of this division, and not otherwise.

(b) The operation of a conveyance by any person owning or having the custody, management, or control of the operation thereof, while an order to repair is outstanding pursuant to subdivision (a), is a misdemeanor punishable by a fine of not more than seven thousand dollars ($7,000), by imprisonment in the county jail for not more than 30 days, or by both that fine and imprisonment. Each day of operation for each conveyance without a permit is a separate offense. **Leg.H.** 2002 ch. 1149 (SB 1886).

§7308. Temporary permits.

If the operation of a conveyance during the making of repairs or alterations is not immediately dangerous to the safety of persons, the division may issue a temporary permit for its operation for a period not to exceed 30 days during the making of repairs or alterations. **Leg.H.** 2002 ch. 1149 (SB 1886).

§7309. Inspectors.

The division may cause the inspection herein provided for to be made either by its safety inspectors or by any qualified elevator inspector employed by an insurance company.

§7309.1. Requirements for certification of inspectors.

(a) On and after June 30, 2003, no conveyance subject to this chapter shall be reinspected by any person unless the person is a conveyance inspector employed by the division or certified as qualified by the division.

(b) Before March 1, 2003, the division shall establish an application procedure and all requirements for the certification of conveyance inspectors. Each application for certification shall include information as the division may require and the applicable fee. At a minimum, the applicant shall present proof of certification as a qualified conveyance inspector by the American Society of Mechanical Engineers or proof of education and experience equivalent to what is required to obtain that certification from the American Society of Mechanical Engineers. **Leg.H.** 2002 ch. 1149 (SB 1886), 2004 ch. 503 (AB 2350).

§7310. Division's acceptance of other inspections.

The division may also issue its permit or a permit may be issued on its behalf based upon a certificate of inspection issued by a conveyance inspector of any municipality, upon proof to the satisfaction of the division that the safety requirements of the municipality are equal to the minimum safety requirements for conveyances adopted by the board. **Leg.H.** 1991 ch. 258, 2002 ch. 1149 (SB 1886), 2004 ch. 503 (AB 2350).

§7311. Requirements for inspectors.

All persons inspecting conveyances shall first secure from the division a certificate of competency to make those inspections. The division may determine the competency of any applicant for the certificate, either by examination or by other satisfactory proof of qualifications. The division may rescind at any time, upon good cause being shown therefor, and after hearing, if requested, any certificate of competency issued by it to a conveyance inspector. **Leg.H.** 2002 ch. 1149 (SB 1886), 2004 ch. 503 (AB 2350).

§7311.1. Certified qualified conveyance company—Application and certification.

(a) On and after June 30, 2003, no conveyance subject to this chapter shall be erected, constructed, installed, materially altered, tested, maintained, repaired, or serviced by any person, firm, or corporation unless the person, firm, or corporation is certified by the division as a certified qualified conveyance company. A copy of the certificate shall be kept at the site of the conveyance at all times while any work is in progress, and shall be made available for inspection upon request. However, certification under this section is not required for removing or dismantling conveyances that are destroyed as a result of the complete demolition of a secured building or structure or where the hoistway or wellway is demolished back to the basic support structure and no access is permitted that would endanger the safety of any person. This section does not apply to platform lifts and stairway chairlifts installed in a private residence as provided in paragraph (2) or (3) of subdivision (a) of Section 7317.

(b) Before March 1, 2003, the division shall establish an application procedure and all requirements for certification under this section as a certified qualified conveyance company, consistent with this section. At a minimum, the individual qualifying on behalf of a corporation, the owner on behalf of a sole ownership, or the partners on behalf of a partnership, shall meet either of the following requirements:

(1) Five years' work experience at a journey person level in the conveyance industry in construction, installation, alteration, testing, maintenance, and service and repair of conveyances covered by this chapter. This experience shall be verified by current and previously licensed elevator contractors or by current and previously certified qualified conveyance companies.

(2) Satisfactory completion of a written examination administered by the division on the most recent applicable codes and standards.

(c) At a minimum, each application for certification as a certified qualified conveyance company shall include:

(1) The name, residence and business address, and telephone numbers and other means to contact the sole owner or each partner, or for a corporation of the principal officers and the individual qualifying for the corporation; the number of years the applicant business has engaged in the business of constructing, maintaining, and service and repair of conveyances; and other information as the division may require.

(2) The fee required by this chapter.

(d) Before bidding for or engaging in any work covered by this chapter, a certified qualified conveyance company shall submit proof to the division by certified copies of policies or certificates of insurance, of all of the following:

(1) Liability insurance providing general liability coverage of not less than one million dollars ($1,000,000) for injury or death of any one person or persons in any one occurrence, with coverage of not less than five hundred thousand dollars ($500,000) for property damage of any one person or persons in any one occurrence.

(2) Workers' compensation insurance coverage.

(3) In the event of any material alteration or cancellation of any policy specified in paragraph (1) or (2), the certified qualified conveyance company shall provide written notice thereof to the division within five working days. **Leg.H.** 2002 ch. 1149 (SB 1886), 2004 ch. 503 (AB 2350).

§7311.2. Certified competent conveyance mechanic.

(a) On and after June 30, 2003, except as provided in subdivisions (b) and (c) of Section 7301.5, any person who, without supervision, erects, constructs, installs, alters, tests, maintains, services or repairs, removes, or dismantles any conveyance covered by this chapter, shall be certified as a certified competent conveyance mechanic by the division. This section does not apply to platform lifts and stairway chairlifts installed in a private residence as provided in paragraph (2) or (3) of subdivision (a) of Section 7317.

(b) Before March 1, 2003, the division shall establish an application procedure and all requirements for certification under this section as a certified competent conveyance mechanic, consistent with all of the following:

(1) At a minimum, a certified competent conveyance mechanic applicant shall meet both of the following requirements:

(A) Three years' work experience in the conveyance industry in construction, maintenance, and service and repair of conveyances covered by this chapter. This experience shall be verified by current and previously licensed elevator contractors or by current and previously certified qualified conveyance companies, as required by the division.

(B) One of the following:

(i) Satisfactory completion of a written examination administered by the division on the most recent applicable codes and standards.

(ii) A certificate of completion and successfully passing the mechanic examination of a nationally recognized training program for the conveyance industry, such as the National Elevator Industry Educational Program or its equivalent.

(iii) A certificate of completion of an apprenticeship program for elevator mechanic, having standards substantially equal to those of this chapter, and which program shall be registered with the Bureau of Apprenticeship and Training of the United States Department of Labor or a state apprenticeship council.

(iv) A certificate or license from another state having standards substantially equal to or more comprehensive than those of this chapter.

(v) The applicant applies on or before December 31, 2003, and within the three years immediately prior to January 1, 2003, has documented at least three years of actual work experience in the conveyance industry in construction, maintenance, and service and repair of conveyances covered by this chapter. This experience shall be as a journey-level mechanic working without direct and immediate supervision, and shall be verified by currently and previously licensed conveyance contractors or by current and previously certified qualified conveyance companies, as required by the division.

(2) At a minimum, each application for certification as a certified competent conveyance mechanic shall include the information required by the division and the fee required by this chapter. **Leg.H.** 2002 ch. 1149 (SB 1886), 2004 ch. 503 (AB 2350).

§7311.3. Certificate—2-year term; renewal—Continuing education of certificate holders.

(a) A certificate issued by the division to the certified qualified conveyance inspector, certified qualified conveyance company, or certified competent conveyance mechanic as set forth in Sections 7309.1, 7311.1, and 7311.2, shall have a term of two years. The fee for biennial renewal shall be established by the division in an amount sufficient to defray the division's costs of administering this chapter.

(b) The renewal of all certificates issued under this chapter shall be conditioned upon the submission of a certificate of completion of a course designed to ensure the continuing education of certificate holders on new and existing provisions of the regulations of the board. This continuing education course shall consist of not less than eight hours of instruction that shall be attended and completed within one year immediately preceding any certificate renewal.

(c) The courses shall be taught by instructors through continuing education providers that may include, but not be limited to, division programs, association seminars, and joint labor-management apprenticeship and journeyman upgrade training programs. The division shall approve the continuing education providers and curriculum. All instructors shall be approved by the division and shall be exempt from the requirements of subdivision (b), provided that the applicant is qualified as an instructor at any time during the one-year period immediately preceding the scheduled date for renewal.

(d) A certificate holder who is unable to complete the continuing education course required under this section prior to the expiration of his or her certificate due to a temporary disability may apply for a waiver from the division. Waiver applications shall be submitted to the division on a form provided by the division. Waiver applications shall be signed and accompanied by a declaration signed by a competent physician attesting to the applicant's temporary disability. Upon the termination of the temporary disability, the certificate holder shall submit to the division a declaration from the same physician, if practicable, attesting to the termination of the temporary disability, and a waiver sticker, valid for 90 days, shall be issued to the certificate holder and affixed to his or her certificate.

(e) Continuing education providers approved by the division shall keep uniform records, for a period of 10 years, of attendance of certificate holders, following a format approved by the division. These records shall be available for inspection by the division at its request. Approved continuing education providers shall keep secure all attendance records and certificates of completion. Falsifying or knowingly allowing another to falsify attendance records or certificates of completion of continuing education provided pursuant to this section shall constitute grounds for suspension or revocation of the approval required under this section. **Leg.H.** 2002 ch. 1149 (SB 1886), 2004 ch. 503 (AB 2350).

§7311.4. Certification fees.

(a) The division shall establish fees for initial and renewal applications for certification under this chapter as a certified qualified conveyance inspector, certified qualified conveyance company, or certified competent conveyance mechanic based upon the actual costs involved with the certification process, including the cost of developing and administering any tests as well as any costs related to continuing education, investigation, revocation, or other associated costs.

(b) Fees collected pursuant to this chapter are nonrefundable. **Leg.H.** 2002 ch. 1149 (SB 1886), 2004 ch. 503 (AB 2350).

§7311.5. Persons maintaining certain personnel elevators on marine terminal cranes; experiential requirements; proscriptions.

(a) A person, firm, or corporation that maintains and repairs solely special purpose personnel elevators on cranes that utilize a rack and pinion system in marine terminals as part of crane maintenance activities qualifies as a certified qualified conveyance company under Section 7311.1 if the individual qualifying individually or on behalf of the firm or corporation has five years' work experience at a journeyperson level in the crane maintenance industry, including experience in the maintenance and repair of crane elevators. This experience shall be verified by a person, firm, or corporation in the business of maintaining and repairing cranes in marine terminals.

(b) A person qualifies as a certified competent conveyance mechanic under Section 7311.2 if the person has three years' work experience in the crane maintenance industry, including experience in the maintenance and repair of crane elevators, as a journey-level mechanic without direct and immediate supervision. This experience shall be verified by a crane maintenance company approved as a certified qualified conveyance company pursuant to subdivision (a).

(c) The certifications obtained pursuant to this section may only be used for the limited purposes of maintaining and repairing special purpose personnel elevators on cranes that utilize a rack and pinion system in marine terminals.

(d) A person, firm, or corporation that qualifies for certification as a certified qualified conveyance company or certified competent conveyance mechanic is not authorized to perform any of the following procedures:

(1) Any work on a conveyance other than a special purpose personnel elevator on cranes that utilize a rack and pinion system in marine terminals.

(2) Any work related to new elevator installations.

(3) Any modifications or alterations of existing elevator systems.

(4) Testing or replacing of emergency brakes, centrifugal brakes, emergency safety devices, or electrical systems.

(5) Annual certifications of any type of conveyance or elevator.

(e) The certifications authorized by this section require experience but do not require an examination because the general examination given pursuant to this chapter is inapplicable to the work described in this section. The division is not required to set up specialty examinations to certify persons pursuant to this chapter.

(f) For purposes of this section, the following terms shall have the following meanings:

(1) "Special purpose personnel elevators" shall have the same meaning as defined in Section 3085 of Title 8 of the California Code of Regulations.

(2) "Marine terminal" shall have the same meaning as used in Section 3460 of Title 8 of the California Code of Regulations.

(g) Nothing in this section exempts a person, firm, or corporation applying for certification as a certified qualified conveyance company or a certified competent conveyance mechanic under this section from paying the administration fees required under this chapter. **Leg.H.** 2006 ch. 448 (SB 727) §1.

§7312. Revocation of conveyance operation permit.

The division may at any time, upon good cause being shown therefor, and after notice and an opportunity to be heard, revoke any permit to operate a conveyance. **Leg.H.** 2002 ch. 1149 (SB 1886).

§7313. Requirements for inspection reports.

Each conveyance inspector shall, within 21 days after he or she makes an inspection, forward to the division on forms provided by it, a report of the inspection. Failure to comply with this section shall be grounds for the division to cancel his or her certificate. **Leg.H.** 2002 ch. 1149 (SB 1886), 2004 ch. 503 (AB 2350).

§7314. Inspection fees.

(a) The division may fix and collect fees for the inspection of conveyances as it deems necessary to cover the actual costs of having the inspection performed by a division safety engineer, including administrative costs, and the costs related to regulatory development as required by Section 7323. An additional fee may, in the discretion of the division, be charged for necessary subsequent inspections to determine if applicable safety orders have been complied with. The division may fix and collect fees for field consultations regarding conveyances as it deems necessary to cover the actual costs of the time spent in the consultation by a division safety engineer, including administrative and travel expenses.

(b) Notwithstanding Section 6103 of the Government Code, the division may collect the fees authorized by subdivision (a) from the state or any county, city, district, or other political subdivision.

(c) Whenever a person owning or having the custody, management, or operation of a conveyance fails to pay the fees required under this chapter within 60 days after the date of notification, he or she shall pay, in addition to the fees required under this chapter, a penalty fee equal to 100 percent of the fee. Failure to pay fees within 60 days after the date of notification constitutes cause for the division to prohibit use of the conveyance.

(d) Any fees required pursuant to this section shall be set forth in regulations that shall be adopted as emergency regulations. These emergency regulations shall not be subject to the review and approval of the Office of Administrative Law pursuant to the provisions of the Administrative Procedure Act provided for in Chapter 3.5 (commencing with Section 11340) of Part 1 of Division 3 of Title 2 of the Government Code. These regulations shall become effective immediately upon filing with the Secretary of State.

(e) For purposes of this section, the date of the invoice assessing a fee pursuant to this section shall be considered the date of notification. **Leg.H.** 1993 ch. 998, 2002 ch. 1149 (SB 1886), 2007 ch. 179 (SB 86) §30, effective August 24, 2007.

§7315. Payment of inspection fees; temporary permit issuance; fees—Exceptions.

Fees shall be paid before the issuance of any permit to operate a conveyance, but a temporary permit may be issued pending receipt of fee payment. No fee may be charged by the division where an inspection has been made by an inspector of an insurance company or municipality if that inspector holds a certificate as a conveyance inspector and an inspection report is filed with the division within 21 days after inspection is made. **Leg.H.** 2002 ch. 1149 (SB 1886), 2004 ch. 503 (AB 2350).

§7316. Disposition and reporting requirements for inspection fee funds.

All fees collected by the division under this chapter shall be paid into the Elevator Safety Account which is hereby created for the administration of the division's conveyance safety program. The division shall establish criteria upon which fee charges are based and prepare an annual report concerning revenues obtained and expenditures appropriated for the conveyance safety program. The division shall file the report with the Legislative Analyst, the Joint Legislative Audit Committee, and the Department of Finance. **Leg.H.** 2002 ch. 1149 (SB 1886), 2004 ch. 503 (AB 2350).

§7317. Exempted conveyances.

(a) Except as provided in subdivision (b), the following conveyances are exempt from this chapter:

(1) Conveyances under the jurisdiction of the United States government.

(2) Conveyances located in a single-unit private home and not accessible to the public.

(3) Conveyances located in a multiunit residential building serving no more than two dwelling units and not accessible to the public.

(b) Conveyances otherwise exempted pursuant to paragraph (3) of subdivision (a) shall be inspected by the division upon completion of installation prior to being placed in service or after major alterations. The inspection shall be for safety and compliance with orders or regulations applicable to the type of conveyance installed. **Leg.H.** 2002 ch. 1149 (SB 1886).

§7318. Division's authority over safety orders.

Nothing in this chapter limits the authority of the division to prescribe or enforce general or special safety orders. **Leg.H.** 2002 ch. 1149 (SB 1886).

§7319. Seat for elevator operator; penalty for violation.

All elevators used for the carriage of passengers shall be provided with a suitable seat for the operator in charge. Failure to comply with this section is a misdemeanor punishable by a fine not exceeding fifty dollars ($50) for each offense.

§7320. Penalty for failure to display permit.

The division may assess a civil penalty not to exceed one thousand dollars ($1,000) against any person owning or having custody, management, or control of the operation of a conveyance, who operates the conveyance without a permit or who fails to conspicuously post the permit in the conveyance. No penalty shall be assessed against any person who has requested the issuance or renewal of a permit and the request has not been acted upon by the division. **Leg.H.** 2002 ch. 1149 (SB 1886).

§7321. Penalty for operation of unsafe conveyance.

(a) The division may assess a civil penalty not to exceed seventy thousand dollars ($70,000) against any person owning or having custody, management, or control of the operation of a conveyance, who operates or permits the operation of the conveyance in a condition that is dangerous to the life or safety of any person, or who operates or permits the operation of the conveyance in violation of an order prohibiting use issued pursuant to Section 7301, 7305, or 7314.

(b) The division shall issue an order prohibiting use and may assess a civil penalty not to exceed seventy thousand dollars ($70,000) against any person who constructs, installs, or materially alters a conveyance without a permit issued pursuant to Section 7301.1 that is dangerous to the life or safety of any person. **Leg.H.** 2002 ch. 1149 (SB 1886).

Labor

§7321.5. Enforcement of penalties; appeals.

The division shall enforce Sections 7320 and 7321 by issuance of a citation and notice of civil penalty in a manner consistent with Sections 6317 and 6319. Any person owning or having custody, management, or control of the operation of a conveyance who receives a citation and notice of civil penalty may appeal to the Occupational Safety and Health Appeals Board in a manner consistent with Section 6319. **Leg.H.** 2002 ch. 1149 (SB 1886).

§7322. Hearing on order prohibiting use of conveyance.

(a) Once an authorized representative of the division has issued an order prohibiting the use of a conveyance as specified in Sections 7301, 7305, 7314, or subdivision (b) of Section 7321, the person owning or having custody, management, or operation of the conveyance may contest the order and shall be granted, upon request, a hearing to review the validity of the order. The hearing shall be held no later than 10 working days following receipt of the request for hearing.

(b) After a notice is attached as provided in Section 7305 or subdivision (b) of Section 7321, every person who enters or uses, or directs or causes another to enter or use, any conveyance before it is made safe, or who defaces, destroys, or removes the notice without the authority of the division, is guilty of a misdemeanor punishable by a fine of not more than seventy thousand dollars ($70,000), by imprisonment in the county jail for not more than one year, or by both that fine and imprisonment.

(c) After a notice is attached for failure to comply with the requirements of Section 7301 or 7314, every person who enters or uses, or directs or causes another to enter or use, any conveyance before it is made safe, or who defaces, destroys, or removes the notice without the authority of the division, is guilty of a misdemeanor punishable by a fine of not more than seven thousand dollars ($7,000), imprisonment in the county jail for not more than six months, or by both that fine and imprisonment. **Leg.H.** 2002 ch. 1149 (SB 1886).

§7323. Regulations for equipment.

The division shall propose to the standards board for review, and the standards board shall adopt, regulations for the equipment covered by this chapter. Not later than December 31, 2003, the division shall propose final rulemaking proposals to the standards board for review and adoption, which shall include provisions at least as effective as ASME A17.1, ASME A17.3, ASME A18.1, and ASCE 21, as in effect prior to September 30, 2002. Not later than nine months after the effective date of any revision or any substantive revision to any addendum to these codes, the division shall propose additional final rulemaking proposals to the standards board for review and adoption at least as effective as those in the revised code or addendum. The standards board shall notice the division's final rulemaking proposals for public hearing within three months of their receipt and shall adopt the proposed regulations promptly and in accordance with subdivision (b) of Section 11346.4 of the Government Code. **Leg.H.** 2002 ch. 1149 (SB 1886).

§7324. Compliance with State Fire Prevention and Building Code.

Individuals, firms, or companies certified as described in this chapter shall ensure that installation, service, and maintenance of conveyances are performed in compliance with the provisions contained in the State Fire Prevention and Building Code and with generally accepted standards referenced in that code. **Leg.H.** 2002 ch. 1149 (SB 1886), 2004 ch. 503 (AB 2350).

§7324.1. Responsibility and liability of persons, firms or corporations.

This chapter shall not be construed to relieve or lessen the responsibility or liability of any person, firm, or corporation owning, operating, controlling, maintaining, erecting, constructing, installing, altering, testing, or repairing any conveyance or other related mechanisms covered by this chapter for damages to any person or property caused by any defect therein. **Leg.H.** 2002 ch. 1149 (SB 1886).

§7324.2. Requirements not retroactive.

The provisions of this chapter added or amended by the act enacting this section shall not be applied retroactively. Equipment subject to this chapter shall be required to comply with the applicable standards in effect on the date of its installation or within the period determined by the board for compliance with ASME A17.3, whichever is more stringent. **Leg.H.** 2002 ch. 1149 (SB 1886).

CHAPTER 3
SAFETY DEVICES UPON BUILDINGS TO SAFEGUARD WINDOW CLEANERS

§7325. "Building."

"Building," as used in this chapter, means any building three stories or more in height, and whether heretofore constructed or hereafter to be constructed, including commercial buildings of all types, office buildings, apartment houses, hotels and buildings used for manufacturing purposes, but excluding dwelling houses occupied by not more than three families, and excluding all buildings constructed with windows that may be, and are, entirely washed and cleaned from the inside of the building or from a sitting position on the window sill in the manner provided by safety orders issued, or which may be issued from time to time, by the division.

§7326. Window sill or frame fixtures.

There shall be securely attached to the outside window sills or frames of the window of any building, rings, bolts, lugs, fittings, or other devices to which may be fastened safety belts or other devices to be used, or which may hereafter be used by persons engaged in cleaning windows. The division shall, prior to the installation of any such bolts, lugs, rings, fittings, or other devices, approve such bolts, lugs, rings, fittings, or other devices as to their design, durability, and safety. Except as provided in Section 18930 of the Health and Safety Code, the division shall by appropriate rules and orders designate the manner in which said safety devices are to be attached, installed, and used.

§7327. Approval of alternative fixtures.

In lieu of the safety devices enumerated in Section 7326, the division may approve the installation or use of any other devices or means which will effectively safeguard persons engaged in cleaning windows.

§7328. Penalty for employer violation.

Any person employing, directing or permitting another to do or perform any labor upon any windows which have not the safety devices as provided for in Sections 7326 and 7327 shall be guilty of a misdemeanor.

§7329. Obligation to install and maintain safety fixtures; penalty for violation.

Every person owning or entitled to possession, under any lease, sublease, or agreement for a longer period than one year, or under any renewal lease, sublease, or agreement for a period of less than one year, of any building heretofore constructed shall, within six months following the effective date of this chapter, install and provide the safety devices as provided for in this chapter, and thereafter maintain such safety devices in good condition. Any person failing to install or provide and maintain said safety devices as provided for in this chapter shall be guilty of a misdemeanor.

§7330. Penalty for failure to provide safety devices.

Every person who fails to provide the safety devices as set forth in this chapter upon any building hereafter to be constructed, and who thereafter fails to maintain such devices in good condition, shall be guilty of a misdemeanor.

§7331. Division's powers.

The division may make and enforce such safety orders and rules as it considers necessary and proper to carry into effect the purposes and provisions of this chapter.

The division shall give notice to the owner or person entitled to possession of any building that is existing in violation of this chapter or of any rules issued under this chapter. Failure of the person so notified to comply with this chapter and rules issued under it, within 15 days, shall be authority for the division to proceed against such person as authorized in this chapter.

§7332. Enforcement by division.

The division shall enforce the provisions of this chapter.

CHAPTER 4
AERIAL PASSENGER TRAMWAYS

§7340. "Aerial passenger tramway" and "permit."

As used in this chapter:

(a) "Aerial passenger tramway" includes any method or device used primarily for the purpose of transporting persons by means of cables or ropes suspended between two or more points or structures.

(b) "Permit" means a permit issued by the division to operate an aerial passenger tramway in any place.

§7341. Permit requirement.

No aerial passenger tramway shall be operated in any place in this state unless a permit for the operation thereof is issued by the division, and unless such permit remains in effect and is kept posted conspicuously in the main operating terminal of the tramway.

§7342. Violation by operation without permit.

The operation of an aerial passenger tramway by any person owning or having the custody, management, or operation thereof without a permit is a misdemeanor, and each day of operation without a permit is a separate offense. No prosecution shall be maintained where the issuance or renewal of a permit has been requested and remains unacted upon.

§7343. Remedies for dangerous operation.

Whenever an aerial passenger tramway in any place is being operated without the permit herein required, and is in such condition that its use is dangerous to the life or safety of any person, the division, or any person affected thereby, may apply to the superior court of the county in which the aerial passenger tramway is located for an injunction restraining the operation of the aerial passenger tramway until the condition is corrected. Proof by certification of the division that a permit has not been issued, together with the affidavit of any safety engineer of the division that the operation of the aerial passenger tramway is dangerous to the life or safety of any person, is sufficient ground, in the discretion of the court, for the immediate granting of a temporary restraining order.

§7344. Inspection and permit issuance.

(a) The division shall cause all aerial passenger tramways to be inspected at least two times each year.

(b) At least one of the inspections required by subdivision (a) shall take place between November 15 of each year and March 15 of the succeeding year.

(c) If an aerial passenger tramway is found upon inspection to be in a safe condition for operation, a permit for operation for not longer than one year shall be issued by the division.

§7345. Division's powers when tramways are unsafe.

If inspection shows an aerial passenger tramway to be in an unsafe condition, the division may issue a preliminary order requiring repairs or alterations to be made to the aerial passenger tramway which are necessary to render it safe, and may order the operation or use thereof discontinued until the repairs or alterations are made or the unsafe conditions are removed.

§7346. Procedure to challenge division orders.

Unless the preliminary order is complied with, a hearing before the division shall be allowed, upon request, at which the owner, operator, or other person in charge of the aerial passenger tramway may appear and show cause why he should not comply with the order.

§7347. Procedural choices of division; later review.

If it thereafter appears to the division that the aerial passenger tramway is unsafe and that the requirements contained in the preliminary order should be complied with, or that other things should be done to make such aerial passenger tramway safe, the division may order or confirm the withholding of the permit and may make such requirements as it deems proper for its repair or alteration or for the correction of such unsafe condition. Such order may thereafter be reheard by the division or reviewed by the courts in the manner specified for safety orders by Part 1 of this division and not otherwise.

§7348. Temporary permits.

If the operation of an aerial passenger tramway during the making of repairs or alterations is not immediately dangerous to the safety of employees or others, the division may issue a temporary permit for the operation thereof for not to exceed 30 days during the making of repairs or alterations.

§7349. Inspectors; temporary permits.

The inspection herein provided for shall be made by a division safety engineer or, on ski lifts, by a certified tramway inspector qualified under Section 7354.5 and employed by a licensed insurance company. A temporary permit for operation may be issued by a division engineer or by the qualified insurance inspector, on a form furnished by the division, under conditions of Sections 7348 and 7351.

§7350. Fees.

(a) The division may fix and collect fees for the inspection of aerial passenger tramways as it deems necessary to cover the actual cost of having the inspection performed by a division safety engineer. The division may not charge for inspections performed by certified insurance inspectors, but may charge a fee of not more than ten dollars ($10) to cover the cost of processing the permit when issued by the division as a result of the inspection. Notwithstanding Section 6103 of the Government Code, the division may collect the fees authorized by this section from the state or any county, city, district, or other political subdivision.

(b) Whenever a person owning or having custody, management, or operation of an aerial passenger tramway fails to pay any fee required under this chapter within 60 days after the date of notification by the division, the division shall assess a penalty fee equal to 100 percent of the initial fee. For purposes of this section, the date of the invoice fixing the fee shall be considered the date of notification. **Leg.H.** 1993 ch. 998, 2007 ch. 179 (SB 86) §31, effective August 24, 2007.

§7351. Payment of fees; temporary permit exception.

Fees shall be paid before issuance of a permit to operate an aerial passenger tramway, except that the division, at its own discretion, may issue a temporary operating permit not to exceed 30 days, pending receipt of payment of fees.

§7352. Disposition of fees.

All fees collected by the division under this chapter shall be deposited into the Elevator Safety Account to support the division's aerial passenger tramway inspection program. **Leg.H.** 2007 ch. 179 (SB 86) §32, effective August 24, 2007.

§7353. Certification of construction and repair plans.

No aerial passenger tramway shall be constructed or altered until the plans and design information have been properly certified to the division by an engineer qualified under the Civil and Professional Engineers Act (Chapter 7, commencing with Section 6700, of Division 3 of the Business and Professions Code).

Any person who owns, has custody of, manages, or operates an aerial passenger tramway shall notify the division prior to any major repair of such tramway.

§7354. Certification.

The division shall not issue an operating permit to operate an aerial passenger tramway until it receives certification in writing by an engineer qualified under the Civil and Professional Engineers Act (Chapter 7, commencing with Section 6700, of Division 3 of the Business and Professions Code) that the erection work on such tramway has been completed in accordance with the design and erection plans for such tramway.

§7354.5. Ski lift inspections.

Notwithstanding any other provision of this chapter, in any case in which an insurer admitted to transact insurance in this state has inspected or caused to be inspected, by a qualified, licensed professional engineer who is registered in California pursuant to Chapter 7 (commencing with Section 6700) of Division 3 of the Business and Professions Code, any aerial passenger tramway used as a ski lift, the division may, if it finds such inspections were made according to the provisions of subdivisions (a) and (b) of Section 7344, accept such inspections in lieu of any other inspections for that year, except that the initial inspection of a new ski lift or of a major alteration to an existing ski lift shall be performed by a division safety engineer. Such private inspector shall, before commencing his duties therein, secure from the division a certificate of competency to make such inspections. The division may determine the competency of any applicant for such certificate, either by examination or by other satisfactory proof of qualification.

The division may rescind at any time, upon good cause being shown therefor, and after hearing, if requested, any certificate of competency issued by it to a ski lift inspector. The inspection reports made to the division shall be in such form and content as the division may find necessary for acceptance as a proper inspection made by such private inspector.

§7355. Division's authority.

Nothing in the foregoing sections of this chapter shall limit the authority of the division to prescribe or enforce general or special safety orders.

§7356. Report of tramway injury.

The division shall, under the authority of Section 7355, promulgate and cause to be published safety orders directing each owner or operator of an aerial passenger tramway to report to the division each known incident where the maintenance, operation, or use of such tramway results in injury to any person, unless such injury does not require medical service other than ordinary first aid treatment.

§7357. Qualification of tramway operators.

The division shall establish standards for the qualification of persons engaged in the operation of aerial passenger tramways, whether as employees or otherwise. The standards shall be consistent with the general objective of this chapter in providing for the safety of members of the public who use aerial passenger tramways and those engaged in their operation.

CHAPTER 5
CRANES

ARTICLE 1
Permits for Tower Cranes

§7370. Legislative declaration; priority of tower crane safety inspections.

(a) The Legislature finds and declares that recent statewide spot inspections of cranes have uncovered a pattern of numerous safety violations so serious and pervasive that safety inspections shall be a continuing priority with regard to all tower cranes in the state.

1990 Note: It appears the Legislature inadvertently enacted a subsection (a) designation without enacting subsection (b).

§7371. Definitions.

As used in this chapter, the following definitions shall apply:

(a) "Crane" means a machine for lifting or lowering a load and moving it horizontally, in which the hoisting mechanism is an integral part of the machine. It may be driven manually or by power and may be a fixed or a mobile machine, but does not include stackers, lift trucks, power shovels, backhoes, excavators, concrete pumping equipment, or straddle type mobile boat hoists.

(b) "Straddle type mobile boat hoist" means a straddle type carrier supported by four wheels with pneumatic tires capable of straddling and carrying boats with high masts and superstructure.

(c) "Tower crane" means a crane in which a boom, swinging jib, or other structural member is mounted on a vertical mast or tower.

(d) "Mobile tower crane" means a tower crane which is mounted on a crawler, truck, or similar carrier for travel or transit.

(e) "Crane employer" means an employer who is responsible for the maintenance and operation of a tower crane.

(f) "Certificating agency" shall have the same definition as in Section 4885 of Title 8 of the California Code of Regulations. **Leg.H.** 1992 ch. 254.

§7372. Employment of safety inspectors; establishment of safety inspection program.

(a) The division shall employ safety engineers trained to inspect tower cranes.

(b) The division shall establish a safety inspection program for all tower cranes operated in the state. This safety program shall include:

(1) Safety inspection of tower cranes twice a year.

(2) Increased penalties for the violation of tower crane safety orders and standards.

(3) Permit fees as described in Section 7373.

§7373. Issuance and validity of permits.

(a) No tower crane shall be operated at any worksite unless an employer obtains a permit from the division. The division shall conduct an investigation for purposes of issuing a permit in an expeditious manner. If the division does not issue a permit within 10 days after being requested to do so by a crane employer, the crane employer may operate the crane without a permit.

(b) The division shall set a fee to be charged for these permits in an amount sufficient to cover the cost of funding the issuance of the permits and the safety engineers as provided by subdivision (a) of section 7372.

(c) The permit for a fixed tower crane shall be valid for the period of time that the tower crane is fixed to the site.

(d) The permit for a mobile tower crane shall be valid for one calendar year.

§7374. Suspension or revocation of permit.

(a) The division may suspend or revoke the permit of a crane where the employer engages in gross negligence, gross incompetence, or willful or repeated disregard of any occupational safety standard or order involving the crane.

(b) The permit of the crane shall be suspended or revoked for a six-month period for first-time suspensions or revocations, and for a one-year period for each subsequent suspension or revocation. The division shall establish a suspension and revocation hearing procedure and appeal process.

ARTICLE 2
Certification
[Selected Provisions]

§7376. Suspension or revocation of license to certify crane safety.

(a) The division shall suspend or revoke a license to certify for the following reasons:

(1) Gross negligence, gross incompetency, a pattern of incompetence, or fraud in the certification of a crane.

(2) Willful or deliberate disregard of any occupational safety standard while certifying a crane.

(3) Misrepresentation of a material fact in applying for, or obtaining, a license to certify under this chapter.

(4) Upon a showing of good cause.

(b) The period of suspension or revocation shall be for six months for a first suspension or revocation, and one year for each subsequent suspension or revocation. The certificating agency shall obtain a new license from the division following a suspension or revocation. The division shall establish a hearing procedure and an appeal process for license suspensions and revocations.

§7377. Appeal of revocation of license.

Revocation of a license to certify may be appealed to the Director of Industrial Relations.

§7378. Penalties for fraudulent certification.

A licensed certifier who fraudulently certifies that a crane is in compliance with the criteria established by the division under subdivision (a) of Section 7375 is guily of a misdemeanor punishable by imprisonment in the county jail for a period not to exceed six months, or by a fine not to exceed one thousand dollars ($1,000), or both.

§7379. Penalties for certifying without license.

It shall be a misdemeanor for an individual to engage in the certification of a crane as specified in this chapter if that individual is not licensed pursuant to this chapter. Any violation of this section shall be punishable by imprisonment in the county jail for a period not to exceed six months, or by a fine not to exceed one thousand dollars ($1,000), or both.

§7380. Collection of fees.

The division may collect fees for the examination and licensing of crane certifiers as necessary to cover the actual costs, including administrative costs. All fees collected by the division under this chapter shall be paid into the General Fund.

§7381. Penalties for violation of safety standards if serious injury or death results; penalties for serious violations.

(a) Nothwithstanding Sections 6319 and 6425, if serious injury or death is caused by any serious or willful repeated violation of a crane standard, order, or special order, or by any failure to correct a serious violation of a crane standard, order, or special order within the time specified for its correction, the employer shall be assessed a civil penalty in an amount equal to double the maximum penalty allowable for each violation contributing to the injury or death.

(b) Notwithstanding any provision of this division, any employer who violates any tower crane standard, order, or special order, if that violation is a serious violation, shall be assessed a civil penalty of not less than one thousand dollars ($1,000) nor more than two thousand dollars ($2,000) for each serious violation. The penalty shall not be reduced for any of the reasons listed in Section 6319.

§7382. Presence of safety representative required while installing, dismantling, or "jumping" crane.

No person shall install or dismantle a tower crane, or increase the height of a crane, known in the construction trade as "jumping or climbing a crane," without a safety representative of the crane manufacturer, distributor, or a representative of a licensed crane certifier being present on site for consultation during the procedure. The standards board shall adopt a regulation making failure to provide the designated safety representative a serious violation of a safety order. Local governmental entities may restrict the hours during which these procedures may be performed.

PART 6
Tanks and Boilers

CHAPTER 6
MISMANAGEMENT OF STEAM BOILERS

§7770. Penalty for undue quantity of steam endangering human life.

Every engineer or other person having charge of any steam-boiler, steam-engine, or other apparatus for generating or employing steam, used in any manufactory, railway, or other mechanical works, who wilfully, or from ignorance or from gross neglect, creates, or allows to be created, such an undue quantity of steam as to burst or break the boiler, engine or apparatus, or to cause any other accident whereby human life is endangered, is guilty of a felony.

§7771. Imprisonment for causing death.

Every person having charge of any steam boiler, steam engine, or other apparatus for generating or employing steam, used in any manufactory, railroad, vessel, or other mechanical works, who willfully, or from ignorance or neglect, creates, or allows to be created, such an undue quantity of steam as to burst or break the boiler, engine, or apparatus, or to cause any other accident whereby the death of a human being is caused, is punishable by imprisonment in the state prison for two, three, or four years.

PART 7
Volatile Flammable Liquids
[Selected Provisions]

§7800. "Volatile flammable liquids."

"Volatile flammable liquids" as used in this part means any petroleum or liquid product of petroleum or natural gas having a flash point below 100 degrees Fahrenheit, and includes any petroleum or liquid product of petroleum or natural gas while at a temperature above its flash point. Flash points shall be as determined by means of the Tag Closed Tester, Designation D56–36 American Society for Testing Materials, or the Pensky-Martens Closed Tester, Designation D93–42 American Society for Testing Materials.

Ref.: W. Cal. Sum., 3 "Agency and Employment" §371.

§7803. Means of flame extinguishment.

Every employer who engages in any business requiring any employee to handle or use any volatile flammable liquid or to work in the close proximity of any such liquid in sufficient quantity and under conditions affording opportunity for the person or clothing becoming ignited shall provide adequate means of extinguishment whereby such employee may extinguish flames on his person or clothing.

PART 7.5
Refinery and Chemical Plants

CHAPTER 1
GENERAL

§7850. Title of part.

This part shall be known and cited as the California Refinery and Chemical Plant Worker Safety Act of 1990.

Ref.: W. Cal. Sum., 3 "Agency and Employment" §371.

§7851. Legislative declaration.

The Legislature finds and declares that because of the potentially hazardous nature of handling large quantities of chemicals and recent disasters involving chemical handling in other states, a greater state effort is required to assure worker safety. The Legislature also recognizes that a key element for assuring workplace safety is adequate employee training. The potential consequences of explosions, fires, and releases of dangerous chemicals may be catastrophic; thus immediate and comprehensive government action must be taken to ensure that workers in petroleum refineries, chemical plants, and other related facilities are thoroughly trained and that adequate process safety management practices are implemented.

§7852. Legislative intent.

(a) It is the intent of the Legislature, in enacting this part, that the Occupational Safety and Health Standards Board and the Division of Occupational Health and Safety (OSHA) promote worker safety through implementation of training and process safety management practices in petroleum refineries and chemical plants and other facilities deemed appropriate.

(b) To the maximum extent practicable, the board and the division shall minimize duplications with other state statutory programs and business reporting requirements when developing standards pursuant to Chapter 2 (commencing with Section 7855).

(c) It is further the intent of the Legislature, in enacting this part, that in the interest of promoting worker safety, standards be adopted at the earliest reasonably possible date, but in no case later than July 1, 1992.

§7853. "Process safety management" defined.

For the purposes of this part, "process safety management" means the application of management programs, which are not limited to engineering guidelines, when dealing with the risks associated with handling or working near hazardous chemicals. Process safety management is intended to prevent or minimize the consequences of catastrophic releases of acutely hazardous, flammable, or explosive chemicals.

CHAPTER 2
PROCESS SAFETY MANAGEMENT STANDARDS

§7855. Purpose of chapter.

The purpose of this chapter is to prevent or minimize the consequences of catastrophic releases of toxic, flammable, or explosive chemicals. The establishment of process safety management standards are intended to eliminate, to a substantial degree, the risks to which workers are exposed in petroleum refineries, chemical plants, and other related manufacturing facilities.

§7856. Process safety management standards—Adoption of federal standards; facilities not covered under federal rules.

No later than July 1, 1992, the board shall adopt process safety management standards for refineries, chemical plants, and other manufacturing facilities, as specified in Codes 28 (Chemical and Allied Products) and 29 (Petroleum Refining and Related Industries) of the Manual of Standard Industrial Classification Codes, published by the United States Office of Management and Budget, 1987 Edition, that handle acutely hazardous material as defined in subdivision (a) of Section 25532 and subdivision (a) of Section 25536 of the Health and Safety Code and pose a significant likelihood of accident risk, as determined by the board. Alternately, upon making a finding that there is a significant likelihood of risk to employees at a facility not included in Codes 28 and 29 resulting from the presence of acutely hazardous materials or explosives as identified in Part 172 (commencing with Section 172.1) of Title 49 of the Code of Federal Regulations, the board may require that these facilities by subject to the jurisdiction of the standards provided for in this section. When adopting these standards, the board shall give priority to facilities and areas of facilities where the potential is greatest for preventing severe or catastrophic accidents because of the size or nature of the process or business. The standards adopted pursuant to this section shall require that injury prevention programs of employers subject to this part and implemented pursuant to Section 6401.7 include the requirements of this part.

§7857. Standards to include prescribed items.

The process safety management standards shall include provisions dealing with the items prescribed by Sections 7858 to 7868, inclusive, of this chapter.

§7858. Written safety information; employee participation; content and availability.

The employer shall develop and maintain a compilation of written safety information to enable the employer and the employees operating the process to identify and understand the hazards posed by processes involving acutely hazardous and flammable material. The employer shall provide for employee participation in this process. This safety information shall be communicated to employees involved in the processes, and shall include information pertaining to hazards of acutely hazardous and flammable materials used in the process, information pertaining to the technology of the process, and information pertaining to the equipment in the process. A copy of this information and communication shall be accessible to all workers who perform any duties in or near the process area.

§7859. Hazard analysis; availability of risk management prevention program information.

The employer shall perform a hazard analysis for identifying, evaluating, and controlling hazards involved in the process. The employer shall provide for the participation of knowledgeable operating employees in these analyses. The final report containing the results of the hazardous analysis for each process shall be available, in the respective work area, for review by any person working in that area. Upon request of any worker or any labor union representative of any worker in the area, the employer shall provide or make available a copy of any risk management prevention program prepared for that facility pursuant to Article 2 (commencing with Section 25531) of Chapter 6.95 of Division 20 of the Health and Safety Code. The board, when adopting a standard or standards pertaining to this section, may authorize employers to submit risk management prevention programs prepared pursuant to Article 2 (commencing with Section 25531) of Chapter 6.95 of Division 20 of the Health and Safety Code to satisfy related requirements in whole or in part.

§7860. Written operating procedures; availability; review.

(a) The employer shall develop and implement written operating procedures that provide clear instructions for safely conducting activities involved in each process consistent with the process safety information.

(b) A copy of the operating procedures shall be readily accessible to employees or to any other person who works in or near the process area.

(c) The operating procedures shall be reviewed as often as necessary to assure that they reflect current operating practice, including changes that result from changes in process chemicals, technology, and equipment, and changes to facilities.

§7861. Safety and health hazard training; refresher courses; employer duty to train; training certification and testing.

(a) Each employee whose primary duties include the operating or maintenance of a process, and each employee prior to assuming operations and maintenance duties in a newly assigned process, shall be trained in an overview of the process and in the operating procedures as specified in Section 7860. The training shall include emphasis on the specific safety and health hazards, procedures, and safe practices applicable to the employee's job tasks.

(b) Refresher and supplemental training shall be provided to each operating or maintenance employee, or both, and other worker necessary to ensure safe operation of the facility and on a recurring regular schedule as determined adequate by the board.

(c) The employer shall ensure that each worker necessary to ensure safe operation of the facility has received and successfully completed training as specified by this section. The employer, after the initial or refresher training shall prepare a certification record which contains the identity of the employee, the date of training, and the signature of the person conducting the training. Testing procedures shall be established by each employer to ensure competency in job skill levels and safe and healthy work practices.

§7862. Contractor's employees working near potential hazard.

(a) The employer shall inform contractors performing work on, or near, a process of the known potential fire, explosion, or toxic release hazards related to the contractor's work and the process, and require that contractors have trained their employees to a level adequate to safely perform their job. The employer shall also inform contractors of any applicable safety rules of the facility, and assure that the contractors have so informed their employees.

(b) The employer shall explain to contractors the applicable provisions of the emergency action plan required by Section 7868.

(c) Contractors shall assure that their employees have received training to safely perform their jobs and that these employees will adhere to all applicable work practices and safety rules of the facility.

§7863. Prestartup safety review for new and modified facilities.

The employer shall perform a prestartup safety review for new facilities and for modified facilities for which the modification necessitates a change in the process safety information. These reviews shall include knowledgeable operating employees.

§7864. Inspection and testing procedures.

The employer shall establish and implement written procedures and inspection and testing programs to maintain the ongoing integrity of process equipment. These programs shall include a process for allowing employees to identify and report potentially faulty or unsafe equipment, and to record their observations and suggestions in writing. The employer shall respond regarding the disposition of the employee's concerns contained in the reports in a timely manner.

§7865. Permits for "hot work."

The employer shall develop and implement a written procedure governing the issuance of "hot work" permits. "Hot work" includes electric or gas welding, cutting, brazing, or similar flame- or spark-producing operations.

§7866. Procedure for managing changes.

The employer shall establish and implement written procedures to manage changes, except for replacements in kind, to process chemicals, technology, and equipment, and to make changes to facilities.

§7867. Procedure for investigating incidents and potential incidents.

The employer shall establish a written procedure for investigating every incident which results in, or, as determined by board criteria, could reasonably have resulted in, a major accident in the workplace. The procedure shall, at a minimum, require that a written report be prepared and be provided to all employees whose work assignments are within the facility where the incident occurred at the time the incident occurred and shall also include establishing a method for dealing with findings and recommendations.

§7868. Emergency action plan.

The employer shall establish and implement an emergency action plan. The employer may use the business plan for emergency response submitted pursuant to subdivision (a) of Section 25503.5 and subdivision (b) of Section 25505 of the Health and Safety Code if it meets the standards adopted by the board.

§7870. Collection of fees.

Notwithstanding the availability of federal funds to carry out the purposes of this part, the division may fix and collect reasonable fees for consultation, inspection, adoption of standards, and other duties conducted pursuant to this part. The expenditure of these funds shall be subject to appropriation by the Legislature in the annual Budget Act.

PART 9
Tunnel and Mine Safety

CHAPTER 1
TUNNELS AND MINES

§7950. Citation of part.

This part shall be known and may be cited as "The Tom Carrell Memorial Tunnel and Mine Safety Act of 1972."

Ref.: W. Cal. Sum., 3 "Agency and Employment" §371.

§7951. Definitions.

As used in this part:

(a) Tunnel shall include excavation, construction, alteration, repairing, renovating, or demolishing of any tunnel except tunnel work covered under the compressed air safety orders adopted by the Occupational Safety and Health Standards Board and manhole construction.

(b) "Tunnel" means an underground passageway, excavated by men and equipment working below the earth's surface, that provides a subterranean route along which men, equipment, or substances can move.

(c) "Mine" means any excavation or opening above or below ground used for removal of ore, minerals, gravel, sand, rock, or other materials intended for manufacturing or sale. It shall include quarries and open pit operations, other than a gravel pit or other pit where material is removed by a contractor or other person for his own use and not for sale to others. The term "mine" shall not include a mine that is operated exclusively by persons having a proprietary interest in such mine or by persons who are paid only a share of the profits from the mine, nor shall it include during any calendar year, any mine that produced less than five thousand dollars ($5,000) in ore, minerals, sand, rock, or other material during the preceding calendar year.

(d) "Access shaft" means a vertical shaft used as a regular means of worker access to underground mines and tunnels under construction, renovation, or demolition.

(e) "Lower explosive limit" means the lowest concentration at which a gas or vapor can be ignited or will explode.

(f) "Face" means the head of the tunnel where soil is being removed, or that area in a mine where digging is underway.

(g) "Muck" means excavated dirt, rock, or other material.

(h) "Permissible equipment" means equipment tested and approved by the U.S. Bureau of Mines or acceptable to other authorities recognized by the division, and acceptable by the division, which is safe for use in gassy or extrahazardous tunnels or underground mines.

(i) "Division" means the Division of Occupational Safety and Health.

(j) "Board" means the Occupational Safety and Health Standards Board.

(k) "Underground mine" means a mine that consists of a subterranean excavation.

§7952. Safety engineers unit.

There shall be within the division a separate unit of safety engineers trained to inspect all tunnel construction and mine operations.

§7953. Inspection of mines and tunnels.

Sufficient manpower shall be maintained to provide for four annual inspections of underground mines, one inspection of surface mines or quarries annually, and six inspections of tunnels under construction annually.

§7954. Availability of additional personnel, facilities, and services.

To assist the unit of safety engineers in determining the safety of tunnel construction and mine operation, the division shall make available at least one industrial hygiene engineer and one chemist. A laboratory for analysis of dust, gas, vapors, soil, or other materials shall be available to members of this unit. Contracts to provide for geological and other services may be signed by the division whenever it is necessary to assure safety for employees engaged in mining or tunnel work.

§7955. Notification before operation or construction; prejob safety conferences; classification of tunnels and underground mines; reclassification.

The division and the owner of a mine, if he is not the operator of the mine, shall be notified before any initial mining operation or construction may be started at any mines or tunnels. A prejob safety conference shall be held with an authorized representative of the division for all underground operations. Representatives of the tunnel or mine owner, the employer, and employees shall be included in the prejob safety conference.

The division shall classify all tunnels or underground mines operating on the effective date of this section, or which commence operation thereafter, as one of the classifications set forth in subdivisions (a) to (d), inclusive. Such classification shall be made prior to the request for bids on all public works projects, whenever possible. This shall not, however, prevent the division from reclassifying such mines or tunnels when conditions warrant it.

(a) Nongassy, which classification shall be applied to tunnels or underground mines where there is little likelihood of encountering gas during the construction of the tunnel or operation of an underground mine. Such tunnels shall be constructed or underground mines operated under regulations, rules, and orders developed by the division and board and approved by the board. This subdivision shall not prohibit the division chief or his representatives from establishing any special orders that they feel are necessary for safety.

(b) Potentially gassy, which classification shall be applied to tunnels or underground mines where there exists a possibility gas will be encountered.

(c) Gassy, which classification shall be applied to tunnels or underground mines where it is likely gas will be encountered. Special safety measures, including those set forth in Sections 7965 to 7976, inclusive, those established by the division and board and adopted by the board, or special orders written by the chief or his representatives shall be observed in construction of gassy tunnels in addition to regular rules, orders, special orders, or regulations.

(d) Extrahazardous, which classification may, when the division finds that there is a serious danger to the safety of the employees, be applied to tunnels or underground mines where gas or vapors have caused an explosion or fire, where the likelihood of encountering pertroleum vapors exists, or where tests show, with normal ventilation, a concentration of hydrocarbon petroleum vapors in excess of 20 percent of the lower explosive limit within three inches of the roof, face, floor, or walls of any open workings. Construction in extrahazardous tunnels or operation in extrahazardous underground mines shall conform to safety measures set forth in Sections 7977 to 7985, inclusive, any rules, regulations, orders, or special orders of the division, or any special rules, orders, or regulations adopted by the board.

The division shall not be required to reclassify any tunnel or underground mine that is shut down seasonally, when such tunnel or underground mine is put back into operation in not less than six months after date of the shutdown.

§7956. Posting of classification and special regulations.

All personnel, including both employees working above ground and those in the tunnel or underground mine, shall be informed of the classification designated by the division for that job. A notice of the classification and any special orders, rules, or regulations to be used in construction, remodeling, demolition, or operation of the tunnel or underground mine shall be prominently posted at the site.

§7957. Emergency rescue plans.

An emergency rescue plan shall be developed by the employer for every tunnel or underground mine. Such plan, including a current map of the tunnel or underground mine, shall be provided to local fire and rescue units, to the division, and to every employee at the place of employment.

§7958. Trained rescue crews.

A trained rescue crew of at least five men shall be provided at underground mines with more than 25 men or tunnels with 10 or more men underground at any one time. Smaller mines shall have one man for each 10 men underground who receives annual training in the use of breathing apparatus. Two trained crews shall be provided at mines with more than 50 men underground and at tunnels with more than 25 men underground.

§7959. Rescue crews: equipment familiarity, regular practices, placement.

Rescue crews shall be familiar with all emergency equipment necessary to effect a rescue or search for missing employees in case of an accident or explosion. Such rescue crews shall hold practices with equipment and using emergency rescue plan procedures at least once monthly during construction or operation of the tunnel or underground mines. At least one rescue crew shall be maintained above ground at all times and within 30 minutes travel of the tunnel or underground mine site classified as gassy or extrahazardous.

§7960. Tests in potentially gassy tunnels and mines.

In any tunnel or underground mine classified as potentially gassy, tests for gas or vapors shall be made prior to start of work at each shift. If any concentration of gas at or above 10 percent of the lower explosive limit is recorded, the division shall be notified immediately.

§7961. Investigation of specified gas readings.

The division shall investigate immediately any notification of a gas reading 10 percent of the lower explosive limit or higher by an employer in a tunnel or underground mine classified as potentially gassy. If the inspection determines the likelihood of encountering more gas or vapor, the division may halt operations until the tunnel or mine can be reclassified.

§7962. Safety representatives.

A safety representative qualified to recognize hazardous conditions and certified by the division shall be designated by the employer in any tunnel or underground mine. He shall have the authority to correct unsafe conditions and unsafe practices, and shall be responsible for directing the required safety programs.

§7963. Communication systems.

All underground mines and tunnels with more than five men underground at one time shall have telephone or other communication systems to the surface in operation at any time there are persons underground. Such systems shall be installed in such a manner that destruction or removal of one phone or communication device does not make other phones or communication devices inoperative.

§7964. Fireproof access shafts.

Whenever an access shaft is used as the normal means of entrance or exit to an underground mine or tunnel, it shall be constructed of fireproof material or fireproofed by chemical or other means.

§7964.5. Division's authority.

Nothing contained in this part shall restrict the division in contracting with the Secretary of the Interior for an approved state plan for mines under P.L. 89–577 (30 U.S.C. 721 et seq.).

CHAPTER 2 GASSY AND EXTRAHAZARDOUS TUNNELS

§7965. Operational procedures for gassy tunnels and mines.

Any tunnel or underground mine classified by the division as gassy shall operate under special procedures adopted by the board, as well as rules, regulations, special orders, or general orders for nongassy underground mines and tunnels.

§7966. Gas tests and probe holes.

In any tunnel classified as gassy by the division, there shall be tests for gas or vapors taken prior to each shift and at least hourly during actual operation. If a mechanical excavator is used, gas tests shall be made prior to removal of muck or material and before any cutting or drilling in tunnels or underground mines where explosives are used. A log shall be maintained for inspection by the division showing results of each test. Whenever a tunnel excavation or underground mine operation approaches a geologic formation in which there is a likelihood of encountering gas or water, a probe hole at least 20 feet ahead of the tunnel face or area where material is being mined shall be maintained.

§7967. Division notification of specified gas levels.

Whenever gas levels in excess of 10 percent of the lower explosive limit are encountered initially in a tunnel or underground mine classified as gassy, the division shall be notified immediately by telephone or telegraph. The chief of the division or his authorized representative may waive subsequent notification for gas readings less than 20 percent of the lower explosive limits upon a finding that adequate ventilation and other safety measures are provided to assure employee safety.

§7968. Shutdown orders for gas or vapor testing.

In any gassy tunnel or underground mine, the division may order work halted until adequate testing can be completed to determine the level of hazard from gases or vapors. A notice of such shutdown shall be filed by the division inspector with his superiors as soon as practicable. Any overruling of such order must be made by the chief or his designated representative and must be in writing. An onsite inspection must be made by the person overruling an inspector's order prior to resumption of work.

§7969. Review of electric plans for gassy tunnels and mines.

In any gassy tunnel or underground mine the division shall review plans for electrical lighting and power for equipment. When it is necessary for safety, the inspector may require changes in the amount and type of lighting, and may require permissive-type wiring, switches, tools, and equipment.

§7970. Smoking and ignition sources prohibited in gassy mines; employer's responsibility.

In any tunnel or underground mine classified gassy, smoking shall be prohibited and the employer shall be responsible for collecting all personal sources of ignition such as lighters and matches from employees entering the the tunnel.

§7971. Procedures when gas or vapor ignites.

Whenever there is any ignition of gas or vapor in a tunnel or underground mine, all work shall cease, employees shall be removed, and reentry except for rescue purposes shall be prohibited until the division has conducted an inspection and authorized reentry for maintenance or production in writing.

§7972. Removal of workers at specified gas levels.

If the level of gas in any tunnel or underground mine reaches 20 percent of its lower explosive limit at any time all men shall be removed, the division notified immediately by telephone or telegram, and no one shall reenter the tunnel or underground mine until approval is given by the division.

§7973. Employee notification and posting of special orders following inspection.

In any tunnel or underground mine classified as gassy, all employees shall be informed of any special orders made by the division following an inspection. Such notice shall be given before entering the tunnel or underground mine. A copy of any orders subsequently written by the division shall be posted and all employees shall be notified at a safety meeting called by the safety representative before they are permitted to start work.

§7974. Ventilation in gassy tunnels.

In any tunnel classified as gassy by the division, ventilation shall include continuous exhausting of fumes and air, unless an alternative ventilation plan which is as effective or better is approved by the division. Fans for this purpose shall be located at the surface, and shall be reversible from a single switch at the portal or shaft. These requirements shall not preclude the use of auxiliary fans to supply more air or greater exhaust to a tunnel or underground mine.

§7975. "Kill" buttons for electrical equipment; procedures.

A "kill" button capable of cutting off all electrical equipment shall be maintained in any gassy tunnel or underground mine. The safety representative or his designated representative shall cut off power at any time gas or vapor levels reach 20 percent of the lower explosive limit or more. Before work is restarted every employee underground shall be informed of the level of gas or vapor recorded, and a permanent record shall be called to the surface and retained in a special log.

§7976. Fire extinguishers in gassy tunnels and mines.

In any tunnel or underground mine classified as gassy, the division shall determine the number of fire extinguishers necessary and their locations.

§7977. Extrahazardous tunnels and mines.

Any tunnel or underground mine classified as extrahazardous by the division shall comply with the provisions for gassy tunnels in this chapter, as well as regulations, rules, special orders, and general orders of the division or board.

§7978. Smoking or open flame in extrahazardous tunnel or mine; welding or cutting.

In any extrahazardous tunnel or underground mine smoking by employees or open flame shall be prohibited. Welding or cutting with arc or flame underground in other than fresh air shall be done under the direct supervision of qualified persons who shall test for gas and vapors before welding or cutting starts and continuously during such an operation. No cutting or welding shall be permitted in atmospheres where any concentration of gas or vapor reaches 20 percent of the lower explosive limit or more while a probe hole is being drilled or when the tunnel face or material from a mine is being excavated.

§7979. Air composition of extrahazardous tunnels and mines.

In tunnels or underground mines classified extrahazardous, sufficient air shall be supplied to maintain an atmosphere of all of the following conditions:

(a) Not less than 19 percent oxygen.

(b) Not more than 0.5 percent carbon dioxide.

(c) Not more than 5 parts per million nitrogen dioxide.

(d) No petroleum vapors or toxic gases in concentrations exceeding the threshold limit values established annually by the American Conference of Governmental Industrial Hygienists.

§7980. Equipment in extrahazardous tunnels and mines.

All electrical equipment and machines, including diesel engines, used in tunnels or underground mines classified extrahazardous shall be permissible equipment. The division may, however, permit the use of nonpermissive equipment in a tunnel or underground mine in areas where it finds there is no longer danger from gas or other hazards.

§7981. Escape chambers and routes; rescue equipment.

An escape chamber or alternate escape route shall be maintained within 5,000 feet of the tunnel face or areas being used to excavate material in an underground mine classifed as gassy or extrahazardous. Workers shall be provided with emergency rescue equipment and trained in its use.

§7982. Employer's obligation to record air flow and air samples.

Records of air flow and air sample tests to assure compliance with required standards shall be maintained by the employer at the site of any tunnel or underground mine classified extrahazardous. Such records shall be made available to any division representative upon request.

§7983. Main fan lines.

The main fan line used for ventilation in any tunnel or underground mine classified extrahazardous shall contain a cutoff switch capable of halting all machinery underground automatically should the fan fail or its performance fall below minimum power needed to maintain a safe atmosphere.

§7984. Testing for gases or vapors using mechanical excavation.

In any tunnel or underground mine classified extrahazardous a device or devices which automatically and continuously test the atmosphere for gases or vapors shall be maintained. Such device or devices shall be placed as near the face or area of operation as practical, but never more than 50 feet from such point. The division shall determine if additional monitors are necessary and where they should be located. This requirement shall apply only to tunnels or underground mines where excavation of material is by mechanical means.

§7985. Testing device requirements; permissible levels.

All such testing device or devices shall be U.S. Bureau of Mines approved or acceptable to other authorities recognized by the division and shall automatically sound an alarm and activate flashing red signals visible to employees underground whenever the concentration of gases or vapors reaches or exceeds permissible levels. Permissible levels may be established lower than the limits set in division rules, regulations, or general orders whenever a division inspector considers such action necessary to make the operation safe for employees.

CHAPTER 3
LICENSING AND PENALTIES
[Selected Provisions]

§7990. Limitation on explosive use.

In any tunnel or mine under jurisdiction of the division, the use of explosives shall be limited to persons licensed by the division.

§7991. License to use explosives.

To obtain a license under Section 7990, and to renew such a license, a person shall pass an oral and written examination given by the division. The division shall offer such examination in Spanish, or any other language, when requested by the applicant. The division shall administer such examination orally when requested by an applicant who cannot write. Application for such license shall cost fifteen dollars ($15), which is nonreturnable. Licenses shall be renewable every five years at a fee of fifteen dollars ($15).

§7996. Acceptable safety equipment.

All safety equipment required to provide safe employment in tunnels or underground mines shall be U.S. Bureau of Mines approved, or acceptable to other authorities recognized by the division, and acceptable by the division.

§7997. General orders; review; update; suggested changes.

The board shall review and update general orders for tunnels and mines at least every two years. Representatives of the unit inspecting tunnels and mines shall be consulted during each review and shall be permitted to submit suggested changes to the general orders at any time.

UNEMPLOYMENT INSURANCE CODE
[Selected Provisions]

SYNOPSIS

CHAPTER 6
VOLUNTARY PLANS

§3251.	Voluntary plans.
§3252.	Worker contributions.
§3253.	Simultaneous voluntary plan and Disability Fund benefits.
§3254.	Requirements for voluntary plan approval.
§3254.5.	Acquisition by other employing unit; effect.
§3255.	Voluntary plans; several employers.
§3256.	Deductions under §3255.
§3257.	Establishment and coverage of voluntary plans.
§3258.	Employer's surety required.
§3259.	Substituted liability of insurer.
§3260.	Deductions from employee wages.
§3260.5.	Remittance of excess wage deductions to Disability Fund; assessments for noncompliance; increase in amount deducted.
§3261.	Employee contributions treated as voluntary plan trust fund.
§3262.	Termination of voluntary plan by director; remittance of moneys for deposit into Disability Fund; assessments for noncompliance; appeal.
§3263.	Cessation of coverage; availability of benefits from Fund.
§3264.	Appeal procedure when benefits under approved plan are denied.
§3265.	Director's intercession on failure to pay.
§3266.	Determination of credits and refunds.
§3267.	Availability of information.
§3268.	Director's obligation to furnish information.
§3269.	Director's obligation to determine administrative costs.
§3270.	Operative date for selection of risks.
§3271.	Amendment of voluntary plans.
§3272.	Applicability of specified article.

CHAPTER 7
PAID FAMILY LEAVE

§3300.	Legislative findings and declarations.
§3301.	Family temporary disability insurance program.
§3302.	Definitions.
§3302.1.	Disability benefit period.
§3303.	Individual eligibility.
§3303.1.	Eligibility restrictions.
§3304.	Receiving benefits under this division.
§3305.	Penalty for false certification of medical condition.
§3306.	Director may request additional evidence; care recipient to submit to examinations to determine care provider's participation.

SELECTED PROVISIONS Of The UNEMPLOYMENT INSURANCE CODE

DIVISION 1 UNEMPLOYMENT AND DISABILITY COMPENSATION

PART 1 Unemployment Compensation

CHAPTER 1 GENERAL PROVISIONS

ARTICLE 2 General Definitions [Selected Provisions]

§128. "Benefits."

"Benefits" means the money payments payable to an individual, pursuant to this division, with respect to his unemployment and includes unemployment compensation benefits, federal-state extended benefits, or extended duration benefits, or disability benefits, or all of them.

§140.5. "Unemployment compensation disability benefits."

"Unemployment compensation disability benefits" or "disability benefits" refers to money payments payable under Part 2 (commencing with Section 2601) to either of the following:

(a) An eligible unemployed individual with respect to his or her wage losses due to unemployment as a result of illness or other disability, resulting in that individual being unavailable or unable to work.

(b) An eligible individual with respect to his or her wage losses who is unable to work due to caring for a seriously ill or injured family member or bonding with a minor child within one year of the birth or placement of the child in connection with foster care or adoption. **Leg.H.** 2003 ch. 797 (SB 727).

2003 Note: This act shall become operative on January 1, 2004, except that benefits shall be payable for family temporary disability insurance claims commencing on or after July 1, 2004. Stats. 2003 ch. 797 (SB 727) §28.

§144. Contributions to Disability Fund.

"Worker contributions," "contributions by workers," "employee contributions," or "contributions by employees" mean contributions to the Disability Fund.

CHAPTER 4 CONTRIBUTIONS AND REPORTS

ARTICLE 3 Contribution Rates [Selected Provisions]

§984. Worker's contribution percentage.

(a)(1) Each worker shall pay worker contributions at the rate determined by the director pursuant to this section with respect to wages, as defined by Sections 926, 927, and 985. On or before October 31 of each calendar year, the director shall prepare a statement, which shall be a public record, declaring the rate of worker contributions for the calendar year and shall notify promptly all employers of employees covered for disability insurance of the rate.

(2)(A) Except as provided in paragraph (3), the rate of worker contributions for calendar year 1987 and for each subsequent calendar year shall be 1.45 times the amount disbursed from the Disability Fund during the 12-month period ending September 30 and immediately preceding the calendar year for which the rate is to be effective, less the amount in the Disability Fund on that September 30, with the resulting figure divided by total wages paid pursuant to Sections 926, 927, and 985 during the same 12-month period, and then rounded to the nearest one-tenth of 1 percent.

(B) The director shall increase the rate of worker contributions by .08 percent for the 2004 and 2005 calendar years to cover the initial cost of family temporary disability insurance benefits provided in Chapter 7 (commencing with Section 3300) of Part 2.

(3) The rate of worker contributions shall not exceed 1.5 percent or be less than 0.1 percent. The rate of worker contributions shall not decrease from the rate in the previous year by more than two-tenths of 1 percent.

(b) Worker contributions required under Sections 708 and 708.5 shall be at a rate determined by the director to reimburse the Disability Fund for unemployment compensation disability benefits paid and estimated to be paid to all employers and self-employed individuals covered by those sections. On or before November 30th of each calendar year, the director shall prepare a statement, which shall be a public record, declaring the rate of contributions for the succeeding calendar year for all employers and self-employed individuals covered under Sections 708 and 708.5 and shall notify promptly the employers and self-employed individuals of the rate. The rate shall be determined by dividing the estimated benefits and administrative costs paid in the prior year by the product of the annual remuneration deemed to have been received under Sections 708 and 708.5 and the estimated number of persons who were covered at any time in the prior year. The resulting rate shall be rounded to the next higher one-hundredth percentage point. The rate may also be reduced or increased by a factor estimated to maintain as nearly as practicable a cumulative zero balance in the funds contributed pursuant to Sections 708 and 708.5. Estimates made pursuant to this subdivision may be made on the basis of statistical sampling, or another method determined by the director.

(c) The director's action in determining a rate under this section shall not constitute an authorized regulation.

(d)(1) Notwithstanding subdivision (a), and except as provided in paragraph (2), the director may, at his or her discretion, increase or decrease, by not to exceed 0.1 percent, the rate of worker contributions determined pursuant to subdivision (a), up to a maximum worker contribution rate of 1.5 percent, if he or she determines the adjustment is necessary to reimburse the Disability Fund for disability benefits paid or estimated to be paid to individuals covered by this section or to prevent the accumulation of funds in excess of those needed to maintain an adequate fund balance.

(2) Notwithstanding paragraph (1), for the 2004, 2005, and 2006 calendar years, the director may not decrease the rate of worker contributions, regardless of whether the director determines that a decrease is necessary to prevent the accumulation of funds in excess of those needed to maintain the adequacy of the Disability Fund during program implementation. **Leg.H.** 1991 ch. 793 §1, 1993 chs. 747, 748, 2002 ch. 901 (SB 1661), operative January 1, 2004, 2003 ch. 797 (SB 727).

2003 Note: This act shall become operative on January 1, 2004, except that benefits shall be payable for family temporary disability insurance claims commencing on or after July 1, 2004. Stats. 2003 ch. 797 (SB 727) §28.

2002 Note: This act shall become operative on January 1, 2004, except that benefits shall be payable for periods of family temporary disability leave commencing on or after July 1, 2004. Stats. 2002 ch. 901 §7.

CHAPTER 5 UNEMPLOYMENT COMPENSATION BENEFITS

ARTICLE 1 Eligibility and Disqualifications [Selected Provisions]

§1255.5. Ineligibility when interim cash payments made.

(a) An individual is not eligible for unemployment compensation benefits or extended duration benefits for the same day or days of unemployment for which he is allowed by the Workmen's Compensation Appeals Board, or for which he receives, benefits in the form of cash payments for temporary total disability indemnity, under a workmen's compensation law, or employer's liability law of this state, or of any other state, or of the federal government, except that if such cash payments are less than the amount he would otherwise receive as unemployment compensation benefits or extended duration benefits under this division, he shall be entitled to receive for such day or days, if otherwise eligible, unemployment compensation benefits or extended duration benefits reduced by the amount of such cash payments.

(b) Notwithstanding any other provision of this division, an individual who is ineligible to receive unemployment compensation benefits or extended duration benefits under subdivision (a) of this section for one or more days of a week of unemployment and who is eligible to receive unemployment compensation benefits or extended duration benefits for the other days of that week is, with respect to that week, entitled to an amount of unemployment compensation benefits or extended duration benefits computed by reducing his weekly benefit amount by the amount of temporary total disability indemnity received for that week.

(c) The amount determined under subdivision (a) or (b), if not a multiple of one dollar ($1), shall be computed to the next higher multiple of one dollar ($1).

Ref.: W. Cal. Sum., 2 "Workers' Compensation" §341.

ARTICLE 4 Overpayments [Selected Provisions]

§1375.3. Liability for overpayment of benefits.

No determination of overpayment shall be based upon the disallowance by the Workmen's Compensation Appeals Board of a claim of lien filed under subdivision (g) of Section 4903 of the Labor Code, or the allowance of such lien for less than the amount claimed as a lien, or upon the approval by the said appeals board of a compromise and release agreement providing for the allowance of such lien in an amount less than the amount claimed as a lien.

PART 2
Disability Compensation

CHAPTER 2
DISABILITY BENEFITS

ARTICLE 1
Eligibility
[Selected Provisions]

§2626. "Disability" or "disabled."

(a) An individual shall be deemed disabled on any day in which, because of his or her physical or mental condition, he or she is unable to perform his or her regular or customary work.

(b) For purposes of this section, "disability" or "disabled" includes:

(1) Illness or injury, whether physical or mental, including any illness or injury resulting from pregnancy, childbirth, or related medical condition.

(2) Inability to work because of a written order from a state or local health officer to an individual infected with, or suspected of being infected with, a communicable disease.

(3) Acute alcoholism being medically treated or, to the extent specified in Section 2626.1, resident status in an alcoholic recovery home.

(4) Acute drug-induced illness being medically treated or, to the extent specified in Section 2626.2, resident status in a drug-free residential facility.

(c) For purposes of this section, if an individual participates in a vocational rehabilitation plan under Article 2.6 (commencing with Section 4635) of Chapter 2 of Part 2 of Division 4 of the Labor Code, regular or customary work shall, upon completion of the plan, mean only that employment for which the individual has been retrained under the vocational rehabilitation plan. **Leg.H.** 1993 ch. 748.

Ref.: W. Cal. Sum., 3 "Agency and Employment" §465.

§2629. Eligibility while receiving specified "other benefits."

(a) Except as provided in this section, an individual is not eligible for disability benefits under this part for any day of unemployment and disability for which he or she has received, or is entitled to receive, "other benefits" in the form of cash payments.

(b) "Other benefits," as used in this section and Section 2629.1, means any of the following:

(1) Temporary disability indemnity under a workers' compensation law of this state or of any other state or of the federal government including, for purposes of this code and Sections 4903 and 4904 of the Labor Code, a maintenance allowance paid pursuant to Section 139.5 of the Labor Code.

(2) Temporary disability benefits under any employer's liability law of this state or of any other state or of the federal government.

(3) Permanent disability benefits for the same injury or illness under the workers' compensation law of this state, any other state, or the federal government.

(c) Except for a maintenance allowance paid pursuant to Section 139.5 of the Labor Code, if these "other benefits" are less than the amount an individual would otherwise receive as disability benefits under this part, he or she shall be entitled to receive, for that day, if otherwise eligible, disability benefits under this part reduced by the amount of these "other benefits."

(d) An individual shall be entitled to receive, for any day, if otherwise eligible, disability benefits under this part reduced by the amount of the maintenance allowance and permanent disability indemnity if both of the following conditions are met:

(1) The individual elects to receive the maximum permanent disability indemnity pursuant to paragraph (2) of subdivision (d) of Section 139.5 of the Labor Code.

(2) The sum of the maintenance allowance and permanent disability indemnity is less than the amount an individual would otherwise receive as disability benefits under this part. **Leg.H.** 1953, 1957 ch. 1977 §6 p. 3526, 1972 ch. 833 §11, 1973 ch. 86 §2, effective June 12, 1973, 1980 ch. 1040 §2, 1989 ch. 1280 §3, 1990 ch. 1550 §64 (AB 2910), 1993 ch. 748 §8 (SB 4).

§2629.1. Determination of entitlement to workers' compensation benefits; notice; assessment of employer for liability; penalty.

(a) Nothing in Section 2629 shall be construed to authorize the delay of payment of unemployment compensation disability benefits except where the claimant is currently in receipt of other benefits or where the department has received notice that the claimant's employer or insurer has agreed to commence the payment of other benefits.

(b) Notwithstanding Section 2701.5, payments shall commence within 14 days after notice to the employer or insurer under this section unless the employer or insurer has either paid or has agreed to commence the payment of other benefits.

(c) Upon the filing of a claim for unemployment compensation disability benefits, the department shall make an initial determination as to the claimant's entitlement to other benefits for purposes of Section 2629.

(1) The department shall notify the claimant and the claimant's employer if it determines that the claimant is entitled to other benefits.

(2) The notice to the claimant shall inform the claimant that disability benefits will be paid pending receipt of other benefits if the employer fails to agree to pay these other benefits within 14 days of notification of industrial injury and shall advise the claimant of the provisions of Section 2629.

(3) The department shall also include with the claimant's notice a pamphlet to be provided by the Department of Industrial Relations which meets the criteria specified in subdivision (b) of Section 139.6 of the Labor Code.

(4) The notice to the employer shall constitute a claim for compensation and knowledge of an injury for purposes of Section 5402 of the Labor Code, and shall inform the employer of its potential liability for interest and penalties under this section.

(d) If the employer or the insurance carrier disputes liability for the payment of other benefits, or the extent thereof, the department's right to reimbursement shall be subject to the jurisdiction of the Workers' Compensation Appeals Board in accordance with Part 4 (commencing with Section 5300) of Division 4 of the Labor Code.

(e) An employer or insurance carrier who subsequently assumes liability or is determined to be liable for reimbursement to the department for unemployment compensation disability benefits which the department has paid in lieu of other benefits shall be assessed for this liability by the department. In addition, the employer shall pay the department interest on the disability benefits at the annual rate provided in Section 19521 of the Revenue and Taxation Code. The employer shall also pay a penalty of 10 percent of the amount reimbursed to the department if the Workers' Compensation Appeals Board finds that the failure of the employer to pay other benefits upon notice by the department under this section was unreasonable and a penalty has not been awarded for the delay under Section 5814 of the Labor Code. All funds received by the department pursuant to this section shall be deposited in the Disability Fund.

(f) The employer shall reimburse the department in accordance with subdivision (e) within 60 days of either voluntarily accepting liability for other benefits or after a final award, order, or decision of the Workers' Compensation Appeals Board. **Leg.H.** 1989 ch. 1280 §5, 1993 ch. 877 §95 (SB 673), effective October 6, 1993, operative January 1, 1994.

ARTICLE 5
Overpayments
[Selected Provisions]

§2741. Satisfaction by payment of lien claim.

Any claim of lien filed with the Workers' Compensation Appeals Board under the provisions of Section 4903 of the Labor Code shall be fully discharged and satisfied by payment of the amount of such lien allowed by the said appeals board under the provisions of Section 4904 of said code or the amount specified in any compromise and release agreement filed and approved by the said appeals board pursuant to Sections 5000 through 5004 of said code.

ARTICLE 7
Rights of Industrially Disabled Persons

§2775. Industrially disabled persons; rights.

Notwithstanding any inconsistent provisions of this part, the benefit rights of industrially disabled persons shall be determined in accordance with the provisions of this article for the period and with respect to the matters specified in this article. Except as otherwise provided in this article, all of the provisions of this part shall continue to be applicable in connection with such benefits.

Ref.: W. Cal. Sum., 3 "Agency and Employment" §464.

§2776. "Industrially disabled person"; "industrial disability."

As used in this article:

(a) "Industrially disabled person" means an individual who has received or is entitled to receive benefits under Division 4 (commencing with Section 3201) of the Labor Code, and who is unable to perform his regular or customary work for 60 consecutive days or more, but not to exceed two calendar years from the date of commencement of his industrial disability.

(b) "Industrial disability" means a disability compensable under Division 4 (commencing with Section 3201) of the Labor Code.

§2777. Determining quarters of base period.

Except as provided in subdivision (b) of Section 2611, in determining the benefit rights of any industrially disabled person the disability base period shall exclude those quarters during which such person was industrially disabled for 60 days or more. For all quarters so excluded there shall be substituted an equal number of quarters immediately preceding the commencement of his or her industrial disability. In the event the base period so determined includes wages in calendar quarters for which the records have been destroyed under proper approval, a claimant may establish the amount of wages by affidavit in accordance with authorized regulations. The quarter of commencement of an industrial disability shall be counted as a completed quarter if the director finds that the inclusion thereof would be more equitable to the industrially disabled person.

§2778. Actions before disability; effect.

No disqualification shall be applied to any industrially disabled person after the termination of his industrial disability, by reason of any act or course of action on his part prior to the date on which his industrial disability commenced.

CHAPTER 2.4 NONINDUSTRIAL DISABILITY INSURANCE FOR STATE EMPLOYEES

§2781. State employees; eligibility for benefits.

Except as provided in this chapter and Chapter 2.5 (commencing with Section 19878) of Part 2.6 of Division 5 of Title 2 of the Government Code, a state employee shall be eligible for nonindustrial disability benefits on the same terms and conditions as are specified by this part. Except as inconsistent with the provisions of this chapter and Chapter 2.6 (commencing with Section 19878) of Part 2.6 of Division 5 of Title 2 of the Government Code, the provisions of this division and authorized regulations shall apply to any matter arising pursuant to this chapter. **Leg.H.** 1976 ch. 341 §14, effective July 7, 1976, operative July 1, 1976, 2005 ch. 152 (AB 1577) §26.

Ref.: W. Cal. Sum., 3 "Agency and Employment" §464.

§2782. Limitations on this chapter.

(a) The provisions of Chapter 4 (commencing with Section 2901), Chapter 5 (commencing with Section 3001), and Chapter 6 (commencing with Section 3251) of Part 2 do not apply to this chapter.

(b) The provisions of Article 2 (commencing with Section 2652), Article 6 (commencing with Section 2765) and Article 7 (commencing with Section 2775) of Chapter 2 of Part 2 do not apply to this chapter.

(c) Sections 2609, 2610, 2611, 2625, 2712, and 2712.5 do not apply to this chapter.

§2783. Payment; publishing information; records.

(a) Nonindustrial disability benefits are payable by the Controller upon authorization by the Employment Development Department to individuals who are eligible to receive such benefit payments under this chapter.

(b) In lieu of the contributions required of employees, the State of California shall pay into the Disability Fund in the State Treasury at the times and in the manner provided in subdivision (c), an amount equal to the additional cost to the Disability Fund for added administrative work arising out of nonindustrial disability insurance for state employees.

(c) In making the payments prescribed by subdivision (b), there shall be paid or credited to the Disability Fund, either in advance or by way of reimbursement, as may be determined by the director, such sums as he estimates the Disability Fund will be entitled to receive from the State of California under this section for each fiscal year, reduced or increased by any sum by which he finds that his estimates for any prior fiscal year were greater or less than the amounts which should have been paid to the fund. Such estimates may be made upon the basis of statistical sampling, or other method as may be determined by the director.

Upon making such determination, the director shall certify to the Controller the amount determined with respect to the State of California. The Controller shall pay to the Disability Fund the contributions due from the State of California.

(d) The director may require from each state agency such employment, wage, financial, statistical, or other information and reports, properly verified, as may be deemed necessary by the director to carry out his duties under this chapter, which shall be filed with the director at the time and in the manner prescribed by him.

(e) The director may tabulate and publish information obtained pursuant to this chapter in statistical form and may divulge the name of the employing unit.

(f) Each state agency shall keep such work records as may be prescribed by the director for the proper administration of this chapter.

CHAPTER 6
VOLUNTARY PLANS

§3251. Voluntary plans.

An employer, a majority of the employees employed in this state of an employer, or both, may apply to the Director of Employment Development for approval of a voluntary plan for the payment of disability benefits to the employees so electing. The benefits payable as indemnification for loss of wages under any voluntary plan shall be separately stated and designated in the plan "unemployment compensation disability benefits" separate and distinct from other benefits, if any.

Ref.: W. Cal. Sum., 3 "Agency and Employment" §464.

§3252. Worker contributions.

(a) Except as provided by subdivision (b) of this section, neither an employee nor his or her employer shall be liable for the worker contributions required under this division with respect to wages paid by the employer while the employee is covered by an approved voluntary plan.

(b) Each voluntary plan shall pay to the department for the Disability Fund 14 percent of the product obtained by multiplying the rate of worker contributions, as determined in Section 984, by the amount of the taxable wages paid to employees covered by the voluntary plan for disability benefit coverage for each calendar year. Such payments shall not constitute a part of the voluntary plan premium for purposes of any tax under any provision of law. Payments under this section shall be deposited in the Disability Fund.

(c) The payments made under subdivision (b) of this section in excess of the credit to the unemployed disabled account made pursuant to Section 3012 shall reimburse the Disability Fund for the amounts paid for administrative costs arising out of voluntary plans as determined pursuant to Section 3269, and the aggregate amount paid as refunds and credits made to employees applicable to voluntary plans pursuant to Section 1176 as determined pursuant to Section 3266.

(d) Each voluntary plan shall file with the director within the time required for payments under subdivision (e) of this section, a return containing the employer's business name, address, and account number, and such other information as the director shall prescribe. The director shall prescribe the form for the return.

(e) Payments required under this section are due and payable on the first day of the calendar month following the close of each calendar quarter and shall become delinquent if not paid on or before the last day of such month.

(f) The provisions of Article 8 (commencing with Section 1126) of Chapter 4 of Part 1 of this division with respect to the assessment of contributions and the provisions of Chapter 7 (commencing with Section 1701) of Part 1 of this division with respect to the collection of contributions shall apply to payments required by this section.

(g) Whenever the director believes that a change in the percentage rate of payment specified in subdivision (b) may be necessary, he or she shall inform the Governor and the Legislature thereof and make recommendations accordingly.

§3253. Simultaneous voluntary plan and Disability Fund benefits.

Except as provided in this part, an employee covered by an approved voluntary plan at the commencement of a disability benefit period shall not be entitled to benefits from the Disability Fund. Benefits payable to that employee shall be the liability of the approved voluntary plan under which the employee was covered at the commencement of the disability benefit period, regardless of any subsequent disabling condition which may occur during that disability benefit period. The Director of Employment Development shall prescribe authorized regulations to allow benefits to individuals simultaneously covered by one or more approved voluntary plans and the Disability Fund. **Leg.H.** 2003 ch. 797 (SB 727).

2003 Note: This act shall become operative on January 1, 2004, except that benefits shall be payable for family temporary disability insurance claims commencing on or after July 1, 2004. Stats. 2003 ch. 797 (SB 727) §28.

§3254. Requirements for voluntary plan approval.

The Director of Employment Development shall approve any voluntary plan, except one filed pursuant to Section 3255, as to which he or she finds that there is at least one employee in employment and all of the following exist:

(a) The rights afforded to the covered employees are greater than those provided for in Chapter 2 (commencing with Section 2625), including those provided for in Chapter 7 (commencing with Section 3300).

(b) The plan has been made available to all of the employees of the employer employed in this state or to all employees at any one distinct, separate establishment maintained by the employer in this state. "Employees" as used in this subdivision includes those individuals in partial or other forms of short-time employment and employees not in employment as the Director of Employment Development shall prescribe by authorized regulations.

(c) A majority of the employees of the employer employed in this state or a majority of the employees employed at any one distinct, separate establishment maintained by the employer in this state have consented to the plan.

(d) If the plan provides for insurance the form of the insurance policies to be issued have been approved by the Insurance Commissioner and are to be issued by an admitted disability insurer.

(e) The employer has consented to the plan and has agreed to make the payroll deductions required, if any, and transmit the proceeds to the plan insurer, if any.

(f) The plan provides for the inclusion of future employees.

(g) The plan will be in effect for a period of not less than one year and, thereafter, continuously unless the Director of Employment Development finds that the employer or a majority of its employees employed in this state covered by the plan have given notice of withdrawal from the plan. The notice shall be filed in writing with the Director of Employment Development and shall be effective only on the anniversary of the effective date of the plan next following the filing of the notice, but in any event not less than 30 days from the time of the filing of the notice; except that the plan may be withdrawn on the operative date of any law increasing the benefit amounts provided by Sections 2653 and 2655 or the operative date of any change in the rate of worker contributions as determined by Section 984, if notice of the withdrawal from the plan is transmitted to the Director of Employment Development not less than 30 days prior to the operative date of that law or change. If the plan is not withdrawn on the 30 days' notice because of the enactment of a law increasing benefits or because of a change in the rate of worker contributions as determined by Section 984, the plan shall be amended to conform to that increase or change on the operative date of the increase or change.

(h) The amount of deductions from the wages of an employee in effect for any plan shall not be increased on other than an anniversary of the effective date of the plan except to the extent that any increase in the deductions from the wages of an employee allowed by Section 3260 permits that amount to exceed the amount of deductions in effect.

(i) The approval of the plan or plans will not result in a substantial selection of risks adverse to the Disability Fund. **Leg.H.** 2002 chs. 52 (SB 467), 901 (SB 1661), operative January 1, 2004, 2003 ch. 797 (SB 727).

2003 Note: This act shall become operative on January 1, 2004, except that benefits shall be payable for family temporary disability insurance claims commencing on or after July 1, 2004. Stats. 2003 ch. 797 (SB 727) §28.

2002 Note: This act shall become operative on January 1, 2004, except that benefits shall be payable for periods of family temporary disability leave commencing on or after July 1, 2004. Stats. 2002 ch. 901 §7.

§3254.5. Acquisition by other employing unit; effect.

A voluntary plan in force and effect at the time a successor employing unit acquires the organization, trade, or business, or substantially all the assets thereof, or a distinct and severable portion of the organization, trade, or business, and continues its operation without substantial reduction of personnel resulting from the acquisition, shall not withdraw without specific request for withdrawal thereof. The successor employing unit and the insurer shall be deemed to have consented to the provisions of the plan unless written request for withdrawal, effective as of the date of acquisition, is transmitted to the Director of Employment Development, by the employer or the insurer, within 30 days after the acquisition date, or within 30 days after notification from the Director of Employment Development that the plan is to continue, whichever is later. Unless the plan is withdrawn as of the date of acquisition by the successor employer or the insurer, a written request for withdrawal shall be effective only on the anniversary of the effective date of the plan next occurring on or after the date of acquisition, except that the plan may be withdrawn on the operative date of any law increasing the benefit amounts provided by Sections 2653 and 2655 or the operative date of any change in the rate of worker contributions as determined by Section 984, if notice of the withdrawal of the plan is transmitted to the Director of Employment Development not less than 30 days prior to the operative date of law or change. If the plan is not withdrawn on 30 days' notice because of the enactment of a law increasing benefits or because of a change in the rate of worker contributions as determined by Section 984, the plan shall be amended to conform to the increase or change on the operative date of the increase or change. Promptly, upon notice of change in ownership, any insurer of a plan shall prepare and issue policy forms and amendments as required, unless the plan is withdrawn. Nothing contained in this section shall prevent future withdrawal of any plans on an anniversary of the effective date of the plan upon 30 days' notice, except that the plan may be withdrawn on the operative date of any law increasing the benefit amounts provided by Sections 2653 and 2655 or the operative date of any change in the rate of worker contributions as determined by Section 984, if notice of the withdrawal of the plan is transmitted to the Director of Employment Development not less than 30 days prior to the operative date of the law or change. If the plan is not withdrawn on 30 days' notice because of the enactment of a law increasing benefits or because of a change in the rate of worker contributions as determined by Section 984, the plan shall be amended to conform to the increase or change on the operative date of the increase or change. **Leg.H.** 1957 ch. 2107 §9, operative January 1, 1958, 1961 ch. 1905 §2, operative January 1, 1962, 1963 ch. 1864 §1.5, 1973 ch. 1212 §275, operative July 1, 1974, 1977 ch. 1143 §12, 1980 ch. 1308 §5, 2005 ch. 152 (AB 1577) §27, 2006 ch. 538 (SB 1852) §647.

§3255. Voluntary plans; several employers.

When workers are engaged in an employment that normally involves working for several employers in the same industry interchangeably, and several employers or some of them cooperate to establish a plan for the payment of wages at a central place or places, and have appointed an agent under Section 1096, that agent, or a majority of workers regularly paid through a central place or places, or both, may apply to the Director of Employment Development for approval of a voluntary plan for the payment of disability benefits applicable to all employees whose wages are paid at one or more central place or places. The Director of Employment Development shall approve any voluntary plan under this section as to which he or she finds that all of the following exist:

(a) The rights afforded to the covered employees are greater than those provided for in Chapter 2 (commencing with Section 2625) of this part, and are separately stated and designated "unemployment compensation disability benefits" separate and distinct from other benefits, if any.

(b) The plan applies to all employees whose wages are paid at a central place or places with respect to all employment for which wages are paid at central place or places.

(c) Seventy-five percent of the workers regularly paid at the central place or places have consented to the plan prior to the filing of the initial application for approval.

(d) If the plan provides for insurance the form of the insurance policies to be issued have been approved by the Insurance Commissioner and are to be issued by an admitted disability insurer.

(e) All employers paying wages through the central place or places have agreed to participate in the plan and the agent appointed under Section 1096 has agreed to make the payroll deductions required, if any, and transmit the proceeds to the plan insurer, if any.

(f) The plan provides for the inclusion of all future employees paid at the central place or places.

(g) The plan is to be in effect for a period of not less than one year and, thereafter, continuously unless the Director of Employment Development finds that the agent or a majority of the employees regularly paid at the central place or places has given written notice of withdrawal from the plan. The notice shall be filed in writing with the Director of Employment Development at least 30 days before it is to become effective and, upon the filing, will be effective only as to wages paid after the beginning of the calendar quarter next occurring on or after the anniversary of the effective date of the plan; except that the plan may be withdrawn on the operative date of any law increasing the benefit amounts provided by Sections 2653 and 2655 or the operative date of any change in the rate of worker contributions as determined by Section 984, if notice of the withdrawal from the plan is transmitted to the Director of Employment Development not less than 30 days prior to the operative date of that law or change. If the plan is not withdrawn on 30 days' notice because of the enactment of a law increasing benefits or because of a change in the rate of worker contributions as determined by Section 984, the plan shall be amended to conform to that increase or change on the operative date of the increase or change.

(h) The amount of deductions from the wages of an employee in effect for any plan shall not be increased on other than an anniversary of the effective date of the plan except to the extent that any increase in the deductions from the wages of an employee allowed by Section 3260 permits that amount to exceed the amount of deductions in effect.

(i) The approval of the plan or plans will not result in a substantial selection of risks adverse to the Disability Fund. **Leg.H.** 2002 ch. 52 (SB 467).

§3256. Deductions under §3255.

During the effective period of a plan approved under Section 3255 the employer, or his agent appointed under Section 1096, may make the pay roll deductions provided for by the plan, with respect to all employment covered by the plan.

§3257. Establishment and coverage of voluntary plans.

Whenever eighty-five percent (85%) of the employees to whom a plan is available have consented to the plan, the employer, or seventy-five percent (75%) of the employees who have consented to the plan, or both, may elect to make the plan applicable to all employees to whom it is available, except those who reject the plan. In such case, there shall be filed with the Director of Employment Development a notice stating that the requisite percentage of employees has consented to the plan and fixing the date upon which the plan will become applicable to all employees to whom it is available. At least 10 days before the date fixed in the notice, a notice shall be posted and circulated in a manner reasonably calculated to bring it to the attention of all employees to whom the plan is available but who have not consented thereto. The notice to such employees shall set forth the date the plan is to become applicable and the manner in which an employee may reject it.

From the time fixed in the notice filed with the Director of Employment Development all employees to whom the plan is available shall be deemed to have elected to be covered by the plan, except those who advise the employer in writing of their rejection within the time fixed.

Every person employed after the date the plan becomes applicable and to whom the plan is available, shall be deemed to have elected to be covered by the plan from the time of employment unless he rejects the plan prior to or at the time of employment. Each employee at the time of employment shall be given a written notice specifying his right to consent to or to reject such plan and a written statement setting forth the essential features of the plan.

Any employee covered by a plan may withdraw from the plan as of the beginning of any calendar quarter upon giving reasonable notice in writing directed to the employer.

The form of the statement and the forms of the notices required under this Section shall be approved by the Director of Employment Development.

§3258. Employer's surety required.

If a voluntary plan does not provide for the assumption by an admitted disability insurer of the liability of the employer to pay the benefits afforded by the plan, the director shall not approve it unless the employer files with the director the bond of an admitted surety insurer conditioned on the payment by the employer of its obligations under the plan, deposits with the director securities approved by the director to secure the payment of the obligations, or deposits with the director an irrevocable letter of credit. The penal sum of the bond or the amount of the deposit of securities or letter of credit shall be determined by the director and shall be not less than the product obtained by multiplying the rate of worker contributions in the ensuing year, as determined in Section 984, by 0.5 of the estimated taxable wages prescribed by Section 985 to be paid to the employees for the ensuing year. Upon approval, the bond, money, or securities shall upon the director's written order be deposited with the Treasurer for the purpose specified in this section. The Treasurer shall give a receipt for the deposits and the state shall be responsible for the custody and safe return of any securities so deposited. **Leg.H.** 1994 ch. 960, operative May 31, 1995.

§3259. Substituted liability of insurer.

Whenever an approved voluntary plan is insured by an admitted disability insurer, the insurer shall be substituted for the employer with respect to any assessments under this part which relate to the portion of the voluntary plan insured by such insurer.

§3260. Deductions from employee wages.

An employer may, but need not, assume all or part of the cost of the plan, and may deduct from the wages of an employee covered by the plan, for the purpose of providing the disability benefits specified in this part, an amount not in excess of that which would be required by Sections 984 and 985 if the employee were not covered by the plan. **Leg.H.** 2002 ch. 52 (SB 467).

§3260.5. Remittance of excess wage deductions to Disability Fund; assessments for noncompliance; increase in amount deducted.

(a) All deductions from the wages of an employee remaining in the possession of the employer upon its voluntary withdrawal of the plan as a result of plan contributions being in excess of plan costs, that are not disposed of in conformity with authorized regulations of the Director of Employment Development, shall be remitted to the department and deposited in the Disability Fund. If an employer fails to remit any deductions to the Disability Fund, the Director of Employment Development shall assess the amount thereof against the employer.

(b) The provisions of Article 8 (commencing with Section 1126) of Chapter 4 of Part 1, with respect to the assessment of contributions, and the provisions of Chapter 7 (commencing with Section 1701) of Part 1, with respect to the collection of contributions, shall apply to assessments provided by this section, except that interest may not accrue until 30 days after issuance of the notice of assessment.

(c) With respect to individuals covered by a voluntary plan on January 1 of any calendar year for which the limitation on wages under Section 985 is increased or the tax rate under Section 984 is increased, the amount of the deduction on or after that date may be increased to apply to not more than the maximum limitation on taxable wages or to not more than the maximum tax rate, as applicable, without any further consent of the individual or approval of the Director of Employment Development, but only if such increase in the amount of the deductions is made effective as of January 1 of the affected calendar year. **Leg.H.** 2002 ch. 52 (SB 467).

§3261. Employee contributions treated as voluntary plan trust fund.

All employee contributions and income arising therefrom received or retained by an employer under an approved voluntary plan are trust funds that are not considered to be part of an employer's assets. An employer shall either maintain a separate, specifically identifiable account for voluntary plan trust funds in a financial institution, or an employer may transmit voluntary plan trust funds, including any earned interest or income, directly to the admitted disability insurer. If an employer, with prior approval from the Director of Employment Development, invests voluntary plan trust funds in securities purchased through a commercial bank under Article 4 of Chapter 10 of Division 1 of the Financial Code, the securities account shall be separately identifiable from any other securities accounts maintained by the employer. In the event of commingling of voluntary plan trust funds, or the bankruptcy or insolvency of the employer, or the appointment of a receiver for the business of the employer, those voluntary plan trust funds are entitled to the same preference as are the claims of the state under Sections 1701 and 1702. **Leg.H.** 2002 ch. 52 (SB 467).

§3262. Termination of voluntary plan by director; remittance of moneys for deposit into Disability Fund; assessments for noncompliance; appeal.

(a) The Director of Employment Development may terminate any voluntary plan if the director finds that there is danger that the benefits accrued or to accrue will not be paid, that the security for the payment is insufficient, or for other good cause shown. The Director of Employment Development shall give notice of his or her intention to terminate a plan to the employer, employee group, and insurer. The notice shall state the effective date and the reason for the withdrawal. The Director of Employment Development may change or stay the effective date of the termination.

(b) Notwithstanding Section 3260.5, on the effective date of the termination of a plan by the Director of Employment Development, all moneys in the plan, including moneys paid by the employer, moneys paid by the employee, moneys owed to the voluntary plan by the employer but not yet paid to the plan, and any interest accrued on all these moneys, shall be remitted to the department and deposited into the Disability Fund.

(c) If an employer fails to remit all moneys owed to the Disability Fund after termination of the plan, the Director of Employment Development shall make an assessment against the employer equal to the amount of the moneys owed. The Director of Employment Development shall also make an assessment against the employer for all benefits paid from the Disability Fund after the termination of the plan, less any moneys received from the employer after the termination of the plan.

(d) The provisions of Article 8 (commencing with Section 1126) of Chapter 4 of Part 1, with respect to the assessment of moneys, and the provisions of Chapter 7 (commencing with Section 1701) of Part 1, with respect to the collection of moneys owed, shall apply to assessments authorized under this section, except that interest may not accrue until 30 days after issuance of the notice of assessment.

(e) The employer, employee group or insurer may, within 10 days from mailing or personal service of the notice, appeal to the Appeals Board. The 10-day period may be extended for good cause. The Appeals Board may prescribe by regulation the time, manner, method and procedure through which it may determine appeals under this section.

(f) The payment of benefits from the Disability Fund and the transfer of moneys in the voluntary plan may not be delayed during an employer's appeal of the termination of a voluntary plan. **Leg.H.** 2002 ch. 52 (SB 467).

§3263. Cessation of coverage; availability of benefits from Fund.

(a) An employee is no longer covered by an approved voluntary plan if a disability arose after the employment relationship with the voluntary plan employer ends, or if the Director of Employment Development terminates a voluntary plan in accordance with Section 3262.

(b) An employee who has ceased to be covered by an approved voluntary plan shall, if otherwise eligible, thereupon immediately become entitled to benefits from the Disability Fund to the same extent as though there had been no exemption from contributions as provided in this chapter. **Leg.H.** 2002 ch. 52 (SB 467).

§3264. Appeal procedure when benefits under approved plan are denied.

If any employer or insurer wholly or partially denies liability upon the claim of an employee for disability benefits under an approved plan, the employee may appeal the denial in the manner provided by law and authorized regulations for an appeal on a claim for benefits payable out of the Disability Fund. All decisions of the Appeals Board denying benefits under this section shall be subject to review by the courts of this State by the exclusive remedy of filing a petition for writ of mandate. No such petition may be filed, however, until the employee exhausts the administrative remedies provided for in this division, nor may any other action be commenced by an employee upon a denial of his claim by his employer or insurer, as the case may be, other than that prescribed herein.

§3265. Director's intercession on failure to pay.

(a) If, on appeal, it is decided that an employee is entitled to receive disability benefits under an approved voluntary plan and the employer or insurer fails to pay the same within 15 days after notice of a decision by an administrative law judge or the appeals board, the director shall pay such benefits and shall assess the amount thereof against the employer or the insurer, and the provisions of Article 8 (commencing with Section 1126) of Chapter 4 of Part 1 of this division with respect to the assessment of contributions and the provisions of Chapter 7 (commencing with Section 1701) of Part 1 of this division with respect to the collection of contributions shall apply to the recovery of such benefit payments. Amounts so collected shall be deposited in the Disability Fund.

(b) If an approved voluntary plan is not terminated because of the enactment of any law increasing the benefit amounts provided by Sections 2653 and 2655, and the employer or insurer fails to pay such increase under the plan, the director shall pay such benefits to an employee, if otherwise eligible, and shall assess the amount thereof against the employer or the insurer and the provisions of Article 8 (commencing with Section 1126) of Chapter 4 of Part 1 of this division with respect to the assessment of contributions and the provisions of Chapter 7 (commencing with Section 1701) of Part 1 of this division with respect to the collection of contributions shall apply to the recovery of such benefit payments. Amounts so collected shall be deposited in the Disability Fund.

§3266. Determination of credits and refunds.

The director shall in accordance with his or her authorized regulations determine the portion of the aggregate amount of refunds and credits to employees made under Section 1176 during any calendar year which is applicable to voluntary plans for which deductions were made under Section 3260, such determination to be based upon the relation during the preceding calendar year of the amount of wages subject to contributions to the Disability Fund to the amount of wages exempt from contributions to the Disability Fund under Section 3252.

§3267. Availability of information.

Employers whose employees are participating in an approved voluntary plan and any insurer of an approved plan shall furnish such reports and information and make available to the department such records as the director may by authorized regulations require for the proper administration of this part.

§3268. Director's obligation to furnish information.

The Director of Employment Development shall, in accordance with his authorized regulations, promptly furnish to employers, employees, or insurers, such information as may be required for the proper administration of an approved voluntary plan.

§3269. Director's obligation to determine administrative costs.

The director shall in accordance with his or her authorized regulations, determine each fiscal year the total amount expended for added administrative work arising out of voluntary plans.

§3270. Operative date for selection of risks.

The provisions of subdivision (i) of Section 3254 and subdivision (i) of Section 3255, dealing with substantial selection of risks adverse to the Disability Fund, shall be operative as of January 1, 1962.

§3271. Amendment of voluntary plans.

(a) The director shall approve any amendment to a voluntary plan adjusting the provisions thereof as to periods after the effective date of the amendment as to which he or she finds that the plan, as amended, will conform to the standards set forth in Section 3254, and that any of the following exist:

(1) A majority of the employees covered by the plan have consented in writing to the amendment.

(2) All of the employees covered by the plan who are adversely affected by the amendment have consented in writing to the amendment.

(3) The insurer of such plan, if any, has certified to the director that notice of the amendment either separately or as a part of a new certificate or statement of coverage, has, at least 10 days prior to the effective date of the proposed amendment, been delivered to the employer for distribution to his or her employees within 10 days thereafter and has further certified that such notice specifically included notification to the employees covered by the plan of their right to withdraw from the plan.

(b) Nothing contained in this section is intended to deny or limit the right of the director to make regulations supplementary thereto, nor on the general subject of requirements for amendments of voluntary plans.

§3272. Applicability of specified article.

The provisions of Article 9 (commencing with Section 1176) of Chapter 4 of Part 1 of this division shall apply to amounts collected under Sections 3252, 3260, and 3265, to amounts remitted to the Disability Fund under Section 3260, and to amounts paid to an employee by an employer or insurer after a final decision on appeal under Section 3264 to an administrative judge or the appeals board that the employee is entitled to disability benefits.

CHAPTER 7
PAID FAMILY LEAVE

§3300. Legislative findings and declarations.

The Legislature finds and declares all of the following:

(a) It is in the public benefit to provide family temporary disability insurance benefits to workers to care for their family members. The need for family temporary disability insurance benefits has intensified as the participation of both parents in the workforce has increased, and the number of single parents in the workforce has grown. The need for partial wage replacement for workers taking family care leave will be exacerbated as the population of those needing care, both children and parents of workers, increases in relation to the number of working age adults.

(b) Family Temporary Disability Insurance shall be known as Paid Family Leave.

(c) Developing systems that help families adapt to the competing interests of work and home not only benefits workers, but also benefits employers by increasing worker productivity and reducing employee turnover.

(d) The federal Family and Medical Leave Act (FMLA) and California's Family Rights Act (CFRA) entitle eligible employees working for covered employers to take unpaid, job-protected leave for up to 12 workweeks in a 12-month period. Under the FMLA and the CFRA, unpaid leave may be taken for the birth, adoption, or foster placement of a new child; to care for a seriously ill child, parent, or spouse; or for the employee's own serious health condition.

(e) State disability insurance benefits currently provide wage replacement for workers who need time off due to their own non-work-related injuries, illnesses, or conditions, including pregnancy, that prevent them from working, but do not cover leave to care for a sick or injured child, spouse, parent, domestic partner, or leave to bond with a new child.

(f) The majority of workers in this state are unable to take family care leave because they are unable to afford leave without pay. When workers do not receive some form of wage replacement during family care leave, families suffer from the worker's loss of income, increasing the demand on the state unemployment insurance system and dependence on the state's welfare system.

(g) It is the intent of the Legislature to create a family temporary disability insurance program to help reconcile the demands of work and family. The family temporary disability insurance program shall be a component of the state's unemployment compensation disability insurance program, shall be funded through employee contributions, and shall be administered in accordance with the policies of the state disability insurance program created pursuant to this part. Initial and ongoing administrative costs associated with the family temporary disability insurance program shall be payable from the Disability Fund. **Leg.H.** 2002 ch. 901 (SB 1661), operative January 1, 2004, 2003 ch. 797 (SB 727).

2003 Note: This act shall become operative on January 1, 2004, except that benefits shall be payable for family temporary disability insurance claims commencing on or after July 1, 2004. Stats. 2003 ch. 797 (SB 727) §28.

Ref.: W. Cal. Sum., 3 "Agency and Employment" §§421, 466, 524.

§3301. Family temporary disability insurance program.

(a)(1) The purpose of this chapter is to establish, within the state disability insurance program, a family temporary disability insurance program. Family temporary disability insurance shall provide up to six weeks of wage replacement benefits to workers who take time off work to care for a seriously ill child, spouse, parent, domestic partner, or to bond with a minor child within one year of the birth or placement of the child in connection with foster care or adoption.

(2) Nothing in this chapter shall be construed to abridge the rights and responsibilities conveyed under the CFRA or pregnancy disability leave.

(b) An individual's "weekly benefit amount" shall be the amount provided in Section 2655. An individual is eligible to receive family temporary disability insurance benefits equal to one-seventh of his or her weekly benefit amount for each full day during which he or she is unable to work due to caring for a seriously ill or injured family member or bonding with a minor child within one year of the birth or placement of the child in connection with foster care or adoption.

(c) The maximum amount payable to an individual during any disability benefit period for family temporary disability insurance shall be six times his or her "weekly benefit amount," but in no case shall the total amount of benefits payable be more than the total wages paid to the individual during his or her disability base period. If the benefit is not a multiple of one dollar ($1), it shall be computed to the next higher multiple of one dollar ($1).

(d) No more than six weeks of family temporary disability insurance benefits shall be paid within any 12-month period.

(e) An individual shall file a claim for family temporary disability insurance benefits not later than the 41st consecutive day following the first compensable day with respect to which the claim is made for benefits, which time shall be extended by the department upon a showing of good cause. If a first claim is not complete, the claim form shall be returned to the claimant for completion and it shall be completed and returned not later than the 10th consecutive day after the date it was mailed by the department to the claimant, except that such time shall be extended by the department upon a showing of good cause. **Leg.H.** 2002 ch. 901 (SB 1661), operative January 1, 2004, 2003 ch. 797 (SB 727).

2003 Note: This act shall become operative on January 1, 2004, except that benefits shall be payable for family temporary disability insurance claims commencing on or after July 1, 2004. Stats. 2003 ch. 797 (SB 727) §28.

Ref.: W. Cal. Sum., 3 "Agency and Employment" §421.

§3302. Definitions.

For purposes of this part:

(a) "Care recipient" means the family member who is receiving care for a serious health condition or the new child with whom the care provider is bonding.

(b) "Care provider" means the family member who is providing the required care for a serious health condition or the family member who is bonding with the new child.

(c) "Child" means a biological, adopted, or foster son or daughter, a stepson or stepdaughter, a legal ward, a son or daughter of a domestic partner, or the person to whom the employee stands in loco parentis.

(d) "Domestic partner" has the same meaning as defined in Section 297 of the Family Code.

(e) "Family care leave" means any of the following:

(1) Leave to bond with a minor child within the first year of the child's birth or placement in connection with foster care or adoption.

(2) Leave to care for a child, parent, spouse, or domestic partner who has a serious health condition.

(f) "Family member" means child, parent, spouse, or domestic partner as defined in this section.

(g) "Parent" means a biological, foster, or adoptive parent, a stepparent, a legal guardian, or other person who stood in loco parentis to the employee when the employee was a child.

(h) "Serious health condition" means an illness, injury, impairment, or physical or mental condition that involves inpatient care in a hospital, hospice, or residential health care facility, or continuing treatment or continuing supervision by a health care provider, as defined in Section 12945.2 of the Government Code.

(i) "Spouse" means a partner to a lawful marriage.

(j) "Valid claim" means any claim for family temporary disability insurance benefits made in accordance with the provisions of this code, and any rules and regulations adopted thereunder, if the individual claiming benefits is unemployed and has been paid the necessary wages in employment for employers to qualify for benefits under Section 2652 and is caring for a seriously ill family member, or bonding with a minor child during the first year after the birth or placement of the child in connection with foster care or adoption.

(k) "Twelve-month period," with respect to any individual, means the 365 consecutive days that begin with the first day the individual first establishes a valid claim for family temporary disability benefits. **Leg.H.** 2002 ch. 901 (SB 1661), operative January 1, 2004, 2003 ch. 797 (SB 727).

2003 Note: This act shall become operative on January 1, 2004, except that benefits shall be payable for family temporary disability insurance claims commencing on or after July 1, 2004. Stats. 2003 ch. 797 (SB 727) §28.

2002 Note: This act shall become operative on January 1, 2004, except that benefits shall be payable for periods of family temporary disability leave commencing on or after July 1, 2004. Stats. 2002 ch. 901 §7.

Ref.: W. Cal. Sum., 3 "Agency and Employment" §421.

§3302.1. Disability benefit period.

For purposes of this chapter:

(a) "Disability benefit period" with respect to any individual, means the period of unemployment beginning with the first day an individual establishes a valid claim for family temporary disability insurance benefits to care for a seriously ill family member, or to bond with a minor child during the first year after the birth or placement of the child in connection with foster care or adoption.

(b) Periods of family care leave for the same care recipient within a 12-month period shall be considered one disability benefit period.

(c) Periods of disability for pregnancy, as defined in Section 2608, and periods of family care leave for bonding associated with the birth of that child shall be considered one disability benefit period. **Leg.H.** 2003 ch. 797 (SB 727).

2003 Note: This act shall become operative on January 1, 2004, except that benefits shall be payable for family temporary disability insurance claims commencing on or after July 1, 2004. Stats. 2003 ch. 797 (SB 727) §28.

§3303. Individual eligibility.

An individual shall be deemed eligible for family temporary disability insurance benefits equal to one-seventh of his or her weekly benefit amount on any day in which he or she is unable to perform his or her regular or customary work because he or she is bonding with a minor child during the first year after the birth or placement of the child in connection with foster care or adoption or caring for a seriously ill child, parent, spouse, or domestic partner, only if the director finds all of the following:

(a) The individual has made a claim for temporary disability benefits as required by authorized regulations.

(b) The individual has been unable to perform his or her regular or customary work for a seven-day waiting period during each disability benefit period, with respect to which waiting period no family temporary disability insurance benefits are payable.

(c) The individual has filed a certificate, as required by Sections 2708 and 2709. **Leg.H.** 2002 ch. 901 (SB 1661), operative January 1, 2004, 2003 ch. 797 (SB 727).

2003 Note: This act shall become operative on January 1, 2004, except that benefits shall be payable for family temporary disability insurance claims commencing on or after July 1, 2004. Stats. 2003 ch. 797 (SB 727) §28.

Ref.: W. Cal. Sum., 3 "Agency and Employment" §421.

§3303.1. Eligibility restrictions.

(a) An individual is not eligible for family temporary disability insurance benefits with respect to any day that any of the following apply:

(1) The individual has received, or is entitled to receive, unemployment compensation benefits under Part 1 (commencing with Section 100) or under an unemployment compensation act of any other state or of the federal government.

(2) The individual has received, or is entitled to receive, "other benefits" in the form of cash benefits as defined in Section 2629.

(3) The individual has received, or is entitled to receive, state disability insurance benefits under Part 2 (commencing with Section 2601) or under a disability insurance act of any other state.

(4) Another family member, as defined in Section 3302, is ready, willing, and able and available for the same period of time in a day that the individual is providing the required care.

(b) An individual who is entitled to leave under the FMLA and the CFRA must take Family Temporary Disability Insurance (FTDI) leave concurrent with leave taken under the FMLA and the CFRA.

(c) As a condition of an employee's initial receipt of family temporary disability insurance benefits during any 12-month period in which an employee is eligible for these benefits, an employer may require an employee to take up to two weeks of earned but unused vacation leave prior to the employee's initial receipt of these benefits. If an employer so requires an employee to take vacation leave, that portion of the vacation leave that does not exceed one week shall be applied to the waiting period required under subdivision (b) of Section 3303. This subdivision may not be construed in a manner that relieves an employer of any duty of collective bargaining the employer may have with respect to the subject matter of this subdivision. **Leg.H.** 2003 ch. 797 (SB 727).

2003 Note: This act shall become operative on January 1, 2004, except that benefits shall be payable for family temporary disability insurance claims commencing on or after July 1, 2004. Stats. 2003 ch. 797 (SB 727) §28.

Ref.: W. Cal. Sum., 3 "Agency and Employment" §421.

§3304. Receiving benefits under this division.

Eligible workers shall receive benefits in accordance with provisions established under this division. **Leg.H.** 2002 ch. 901 (SB 1661), operative January 1, 2004.

2002 Note: This act shall become operative on January 1, 2004, except that benefits shall be payable for periods of family temporary disability leave commencing on or after July 1, 2004. Stats. 2002 ch. 901 §7.

Ref.: W. Cal. Sum., 3 "Agency and Employment" §421.

§3305. Penalty for false certification of medical condition.

If the director finds that any individual falsely certifies the medical condition of any person in order to obtain family temporary disability insurance benefits, with the intent to defraud, whether for the maker or for any other person, the director shall assess a penalty against the individual in the amount of 25 percent of the benefits paid as a result of the false certification. The provisions of Article 8 (commencing with Section 1126) of Chapter 4 of Part 1, with respect to assessments, the provisions of Article 9 (commencing with Section 1176) of Chapter 4 of Part 1, with respect to refunds, and the provisions of Chapter 7 (commencing with Section 1701) of Part 1, with respect to collections, shall apply to the assessments provided by this section. Penalties collected under this section shall be deposited in the contingent fund. **Leg.H.** 2002 ch. 901 (SB 1661), operative January 1, 2004, 2003 ch. 797 (SB 727), 2004 ch. 183 (AB 3082).

2003 Note: This act shall become operative on January 1, 2004, except that benefits shall be payable for family temporary disability insurance claims commencing on or after July 1, 2004. Stats. 2003 ch. 797 (SB 727) §28.

2002 Note: This act shall become operative on January 1, 2004, except that benefits shall be payable for periods of family temporary disability leave commencing on or after July 1, 2004. Stats. 2002 ch. 901 §7.

Ref.: W. Cal. Sum., 3 "Agency and Employment" §421.

§3306. Director may request additional evidence; care recipient to submit to examinations to determine care provider's participation.

(a) The director may request additional medical evidence to supplement the first or any continued claim if the additional evidence can be procured without additional cost to the care recipient. The director may require that the additional evidence include any or all of the following information:

(1) Identification of diagnoses.

(2) Identification of symptoms.

(3) A statement setting forth the facts of the care recipient's serious health condition that warrants the participation of the employee. The statement shall be completed by any of the following people:

(A) The physician or practitioner treating the care recipient.

(B) The registrar, authorized medical officer, or other duly authorized official of the hospital or health facility treating the care recipient.

(C) An examining physician or other representative of the department.

(b) Except as provided in Section 2709, the director may require the care recipient to submit to reasonable examinations for the purpose of determining all of the following:

(1) Whether a serious health condition exists.

(2) Whether a care provider's participation is warranted.

(3) The period of time that the care provider's participation is warranted. **Leg.H.** 2003 ch. 797 (SB 727).

2003 Note: This act shall become operative on January 1, 2004, except that benefits shall be payable for family temporary disability insurance claims commencing on or after July 1, 2004. Stats. 2003 ch. 797 (SB 727) §28.

MISCELLANEOUS PROVISIONS

SYNOPSIS

Misc. Provisions

CHAPTER 2.5
DISCLOSURE OF GENETIC TEST RESULTS BY A HEALTH CARE SERVICE PLAN

CHAPTER 3
USE AND DISCLOSURE OF MEDICAL INFORMATION BY EMPLOYERS
[Selected Provisions]

CHAPTER 6
RELATIONSHIP TO EXISTING LAW
[Selected Provisions]

DIVISION 3
OBLIGATIONS

PART 3
Obligations Imposed by Law
[Selected Provisions]

DIVISION 4
GENERAL PROVISIONS

PART 1
Relief

TITLE 2
COMPENSATORY RELIEF

CHAPTER 2
MEASURE OF DAMAGES

ARTICLE 2
Damages for Wrongs
[Selected Provisions]

CODE OF CIVIL PROCEDURE

PART 2
OF CIVIL ACTIONS

TITLE 9
Enforcement of Judgments

DIVISION 2
ENFORCEMENT OF MONEY JUDGMENTS

CHAPTER 2
LIENS

ARTICLE 2
Judgment Lien on Real Property
[Selected Provisions]

lien based on workers' compensation award.

CHAPTER 4
EXEMPTIONS

ARTICLE 3
Exempt Property
[Selected Provisions]

§704.160. Workers' compensation claim, award, or payment—Application to support judgment.

TITLE 14
Miscellaneous Provisions

CHAPTER 5
NOTICES, AND FILING AND SERVICE OF PAPERS
[Selected Provisions]

§1013. Service by mail, Express Mail, overnight delivery, or facsimile transmission—Method of service.

PART 4
Miscellaneous Provisions

TITLE 4
CIVIL DISCOVERY ACT

CHAPTER 1
GENERAL PROVISIONS

§2016.010. Short title.
§2016.020. Definitions.
§2016.030. Modification by written stipulation.
§2016.040. What meet and confer declaration in support of motion to show.
§2016.050. Applicability of CCP §1013.
§2016.060. Specified date falling on Saturday, Sunday or holiday; extension of time limit.
§2016.070. Applicability of title to enforcement of money judgment.

CHAPTER 2
SCOPE OF DISCOVERY
[Selected Provisions]

ARTICLE 1
General Provisions

§2017.010. What matters may be subject to discovery.
§2017.020. When court may limit scope of discovery; motion for protective order; monetary sanction.

ARTICLE 2
Scope of Discovery in Specific Contexts

§2017.210. Information concerning insurance.
§2017.220. Discovery regarding plaintiff's sexual conduct in certain actions; showing of good cause; monetary sanction.

CHAPTER 3
USE OF TECHNOLOGY IN CONDUCTING DISCOVERY IN A COMPLEX CASE

§2017.710. Meaning of "technology" as used in chapter.
§2017.720. Effect of chapter on rights, duties and responsibilities of parties; use of stenographic court reporter.
§2017.730. Order authorizing use of technology in conducting discovery; when permitted; criteria; promulgation of rules and standards.
§2017.740. Service provider; selection and appointment; removal; periodic review.

CHAPTER 4
ATTORNEY WORK PRODUCT

§2018.010. Meaning of "client" for purposes of chapter.
§2018.020. Policy of state.
§2018.030. Certain writings not discoverable; when other work product may be subject to discovery.
§2018.040. Restatement of existing law.
§2018.050. Work product enabling commission of crime not protected in official investigations.
§2018.060. Right to request in camera hearing.
§2018.070. Discovery for purposes of State Bar disciplinary proceedings; protective order; client approval.
§2018.080. No privilege when work product relevant to issue of breach of attorney-client relationship.

CHAPTER 5
METHODS AND SEQUENCE OF DISCOVERY

ARTICLE 1
General Provisions

§2019.010. Methods of discovery.
§2019.020. Sequence and timing of discovery.

ARTICLE 2
Methods and Sequence of Discovery in Specific Contexts

CHAPTER 6
NONPARTY DISCOVERY

ARTICLE 1
General Provisions

ARTICLE 2
Procedures Applicable to All Types of Deposition Subpoenas

ARTICLE 3
Subpoena Commanding Only Attendance and Testimony of the Deponent

ARTICLE 4
Subpoena Commanding Only Production of Business Records for Copying

ARTICLE 5
Subpoena Commanding Both Production of Business Records and Attendance and Testimony of the Deponent

CHAPTER 7
SANCTIONS

CHAPTER 14
INSPECTION AND PRODUCTION OF DOCUMENTS, TANGIBLE THINGS, LAND, AND OTHER PROPERTY
[Selected Provisions]

ARTICLE 1
Inspection Demand

ARTICLE 2
Response to Inspection Demand

ARTICLE 3
Deposition of Expert Witness

EDUCATION CODE

TITLE 1
GENERAL EDUCATION CODE PROVISIONS

DIVISION 1
General Education Code Provisions

PART 2
COUNTY EDUCATIONAL AGENCIES

CHAPTER 2
COUNTY SUPERINTENDENT OF SCHOOLS

ARTICLE 2
Duties, Responsibilities, and General Powers
[Selected Provisions]

ARTICLE 3
Staff
[Selected Provisions]

PART 13
STATE TEACHERS' RETIREMENT SYSTEM

CHAPTER 30
SUBROGATION

PART 19
MISCELLANEOUS

CHAPTER 3
MISCELLANEOUS

ARTICLE 6
District Liability on Loaned Equipment

DIVISION 3
Local Administration

PART 25
EMPLOYEES

CHAPTER 1
EMPLOYEES

ARTICLE 1
General Provisions
[Selected Provisions]

ARTICLE 2
Rights and Duties
[Selected Provisions]

CHAPTER 4
EMPLOYMENT—CERTIFICATED EMPLOYEE

ARTICLE 3
Resignations, Dismissals, and Leaves of Absence [Selected Provisions]

CHAPTER 5
CLASSIFIED EMPLOYEES

ARTICLE 4
Resignation and Leaves of Absence [Selected Provisions]

TITLE 3
POSTSECONDARY EDUCATION

DIVISION 8
California State University

PART 55
CALIFORNIA STATE UNIVERSITY

CHAPTER 5
PERSONNEL

ARTICLE 1.1
Industrial Disability Leave

EVIDENCE CODE

DIVISION 2
WORDS AND PHRASES DEFINED
[Selected Provisions]

DIVISION 4
JUDICIAL NOTICE
[Selected Provisions]

DIVISION 6
WITNESSES

CHAPTER 5
METHOD AND SCOPE OF EXAMINATION

ARTICLE 2
Examination of Witnesses [Selected Provisions]

DIVISION 8
PRIVILEGES

CHAPTER 1
DEFINITIONS

CHAPTER 2
APPLICABILITY OF DIVISION

CHAPTER 3
GENERAL PROVISIONS RELATING TO PRIVILEGES

§911. General provision.
§912. Waiver by disclosure—Joint holders of privilege.
§913. Comment on exercise of privilege prohibited—No presumption or inference.
§914. Determination of claim of privilege—Contempt for failure to disclose information.
§915. Disclosure of information to determine claim—Official information—Identity of informer—Trade secrets.
§916. Exclusion of information where holder of privilege not a party.
§917. Presumption of confidential nature of communication; electronic communication retains privileged character.
§918. Error in disallowing claim.
§919. Inadmissibility of privileged information erroneously disclosed.
§920. Construction against repeal by implication.

CHAPTER 4
PARTICULAR PRIVILEGES

ARTICLE 3
Lawyer-Client Privilege
[Selected Provisions]

§953. "Holder of privilege" defined.

ARTICLE 4
Privilege Not to Testify Against Spouse
[Selected Provisions]

§971. Spouse of party called as witness by adverse party.
§972. Exceptions to privilege.
§973. Waiver—Proceeding brought or defended for benefit of spouse.

ARTICLE 5
Privilege for Confidential Marital Communications
[Selected Provisions]

§980. General provision.

ARTICLE 6
Physician-Patient Privilege
[Selected Provisions]

§996. Condition of patient in issue.

ARTICLE 7
Psychotherapist-Patient Privilege
[Selected Provisions]

§1010. "Psychotherapist" defined.
§1010.5. Application of privilege to educational psychologist.
§1011. "Patient" defined.
§1012. "Confidential communication between patient and psychotherapist" defined.
§1013. "Holder of privilege" defined.
§1014. Who may claim privilege.
§1015. When psychotherapist must claim privilege.
§1016. Condition of patient in issue.

ARTICLE 9
Official Information and Identity of Informer
[Selected Provisions]

§1043. Investigation of citizens' complaints—Discovery or disclosure of peace or custodial officer personnel records.

DIVISION 10
HEARSAY EVIDENCE

CHAPTER 2
EXCEPTIONS TO THE HEARSAY RULE

ARTICLE 7
Business Records

§1270. "Business" defined.
§1271. Record as evidence.
§1272. Absence of record as evidence.

DIVISION 11
WRITINGS

CHAPTER 2
SECONDARY EVIDENCE OF WRITINGS

ARTICLE 3
Photographic Copies and Printed Representations of Writings

§1550. Business records.
§1550.1. Admissibility of reproductions of files, records, writings, photographs, fingerprints or other instruments.
§1551. Lost or destroyed writings.
§1552. Printed representations of computer information.
§1553. Printed representation of images

ARTICLE 4
Production of Business Records

GOVERNMENT CODE

GENERAL PROVISIONS
[Selected Provisions]

TITLE 1
GENERAL

DIVISION 7
Miscellaneous

CHAPTER 5
JOINT EXERCISE OF POWERS

ARTICLE 1
Joint Powers Agreements
[Selected Provisions]

TITLE 2
GOVERNMENT OF THE STATE OF CALIFORNIA

DIVISION 1
General

CHAPTER 7
CALIFORNIA EMERGENCY SERVICES ACT

ARTICLE 3.5
Oil Spills
[Selected Provisions]

ARTICLE 5
Office of Emergency Services
[Selected Provisions]

ARTICLE 9.8
Disaster Preparedness
[Selected Provisions]

ARTICLE 10
Local Disaster Councils
[Selected Provisions]

ARTICLE 17
Privileges and Immunities
[Selected Provisions]

DIVISION 3
Executive Department

PART 2.8
DEPARTMENT OF FAIR EMPLOYMENT AND HOUSING

CHAPTER 4
DEFINITIONS
[Selected Provisions]

CHAPTER 6
DISCRIMINATION PROHIBITED

ARTICLE 1
Unlawful Practices, Generally
[Selected Provisions]

DIVISION 5
Personnel

PART 2.6
PERSONNEL ADMINISTRATION

CHAPTER 2
ADMINISTRATION OF SALARIES

ARTICLE 1
Claims for Reimbursement
[Selected Provisions]

PART 3
PUBLIC EMPLOYEES' RETIREMENT SYSTEM

CHAPTER 1
GENERAL PROVISIONS AND DEFINITIONS

ARTICLE 2
Definitions
[Selected Provisions]

CHAPTER 2
ADMINISTRATION OF SYSTEM

ARTICLE 2
Powers and Duties of the Board
[Selected Provisions]

ARTICLE 8
Subrogation

CHAPTER 12
RETIREMENT FROM EMPLOYMENT

ARTICLE 6
Disability Retirement
[Selected Provisions]

ARTICLE 7
Reinstatement from Retirement

CHAPTER 13
RETIREMENT BENEFITS

ARTICLE 1
General Provisions
[Selected Provisions]

ARTICLE 5
Disability Retirement Benefits
[Selected Provisions]

CHAPTER 14
DEATH BENEFITS

ARTICLE 2
Preretirement Death Benefits
[Selected Provisions]

TITLE 3
GOVERNMENT OF COUNTIES

DIVISION 2
Officers

PART 2
BOARD OF SUPERVISORS

CHAPTER 3
FINANCIAL POWERS
[Selected Provisions]

DIVISION 4
Employees

PART 1
GENERAL
[Selected Provisions]

PART 3
RETIREMENT SYSTEMS

CHAPTER 3
COUNTY EMPLOYEES RETIREMENT LAW OF 1937

ARTICLE 3
Retirement Board
[Selected Provisions]

ARTICLE 14
Subrogation
[Selected Provisions]

CHAPTER 5
COUNTY FIRE SERVICE RETIREMENT LAW

ARTICLE 5
Contributions
[Selected Provisions]

TITLE 5
LOCAL AGENCIES

DIVISION 1
Cities and Counties

PART 1
POWERS AND DUTIES COMMON TO CITIES AND COUNTIES

CHAPTER 4
POLICE OFFICERS' PENSION FUND AND FIREMEN'S PENSION FUND

ARTICLE 5
Extraterritorial Activities of County and City Peace Officers
[Selected Provisions]

ARTICLE 6
Extraterritorial Activities of Firemen
[Selected Provisions]

DIVISION 2
Cities, Counties, and Other Agencies

PART 1
POWERS AND DUTIES COMMON TO CITIES, COUNTIES, AND OTHER AGENCIES

CHAPTER 1
GENERAL

ARTICLE 2
Emergency Powers
[Selected Provisions]

CHAPTER 6
REVENUE BOND LAW OF 1941

ARTICLE 5
Additional Powers to Secure Bonds
[Selected Provisions]

TITLE 8
THE ORGANIZATION AND GOVERNMENT OF COURTS

CHAPTER 2
THE JUDICIAL COUNCIL

ARTICLE 4
Court Interpreter Services
[Selected Provisions]

§68562. Certification of court interpreters—Procedures, standards, and guidelines.

HARBORS AND NAVIGATION CODE

DIVISION 8
HARBOR AND PORT DISTRICTS

PART 4
PORT DISTRICTS

CHAPTER 2
BOARD OF PORT COMMISSIONERS

ARTICLE 2
Jurisdiction and Powers of the Board
[Selected Provisions]

§6276. Stevedore employee workers' compensation benefits.

PART 6
RIVER PORT DISTRICTS

CHAPTER 2
PORT COMMISSION

ARTICLE 2
Jurisdiction and Powers of the Board
[Selected Provisions]

§6869. Federal benefits in lieu of state benefits.

HEALTH AND SAFETY CODE

DIVISION 13
HOUSING

PART 1.5
Regulation of Buildings Used for Human Habitation

CHAPTER 2
RULES AND REGULATIONS
[Selected Provisions]

§17922.5. Building permits from state or local agencies.

MILITARY AND VETERANS CODE

DIVISION 2
THE MILITARY FORCES OF THE STATE

PART 1
The State Militia

CHAPTER 5
COMPENSATION, ALLOWANCE, AND INSURANCE

ARTICLE 3
Casualty Insurance

§340. Members of National Guard, organized or unorganized militia injured in line of duty.

§340.1. Disability for those wounded in service of state.

§340.2. Disability for those transferred under mutual aid or interagency agreements.

§341. Member of militia; determination of average yearly earnings; "injury suffered in line of duty."

§342. Jurisdiction of Appeals Board.

ARTICLE 4
State Militia Disability Equality Act

§345. Citation of article.

§346. Disability benefits.

PART 2
California Cadet Corps and Voluntary Organizations

CHAPTER 1
CALIFORNIA CADET CORPS
[Selected Provisions]

§520. Supervisors of cadet instruction; right to compensation; determination of average yearly earnings; "injury suffered in line of duty."

CHAPTER 3
STATE MILITARY RESERVE ACT
[Selected Provisions]

§562. Members of State Military Reserve; right to compensation; determination of average yearly earnings; "injury suffered in line of duty."

PENAL CODE

PART 1
Of Crimes and Punishments

TITLE 10
OF CRIMES AGAINST THE PUBLIC HEALTH AND SAFETY
[Selected Provisions]

§385. "High voltage"; "overhead conductor"; penalty for activity within specified distance of high voltage overhead conductor and for failure to post warning sign; exceptions.

TITLE 13
OF CRIMES AGAINST PROPERTY

CHAPTER 10
CRIMES AGAINST INSURED PROPERTY AND INSURERS
[Selected Provisions]

§549. Solicitation or referral for purposes of insurance fraud.

§550. Making false or fraudulent claims—Punishment.

PART 2
Of Criminal Procedure

TITLE 3
ADDITIONAL PROVISIONS REGARDING CRIMINAL PROCEDURE

CHAPTER 2
TIME OF COMMENCING CRIMINAL ACTIONS
[Selected Provisions]

§803. Limitation not tolled or extended—Does not commence until discovery of offense.

TITLE 12
OF SPECIAL PROCEEDINGS OF A CRIMINAL NATURE

CHAPTER 3
OF SEARCH WARRANTS
[Selected Provisions]

§1524. Grounds for issuance.

PART 3
Of Imprisonment and the Death Penalty

TITLE 4
COUNTY JAILS, FARMS AND CAMPS

CHAPTER 1
COUNTY JAILS
[Selected Provisions]

§4017. Prisoner labor for firefighting; benefits for injuries; "labor on the public works."

§4017.5. Work required of persons imprisoned for contempt.

CHAPTER 2
COUNTY INDUSTRIAL FARMS AND ROAD CAMPS

ARTICLE 1
County Industrial Farms
[Selected Provisions]

§4125.1. Credit for fire suppression work.

TITLE 7
ADMINISTRATION OF THE STATE CORRECTIONAL SYSTEM

CHAPTER 2
THE SECRETARY OF THE DEPARTMENT OF CORRECTIONS AND REHABILITATION
[Selected Provisions]

§5069. Rehabilitation for injured inmates; notice to inmate.

VEHICLE CODE

DIVISION 13
TOWING AND LOADING EQUIPMENT

CHAPTER 5
TRANSPORTING OTHER LOADS

ARTICLE 2
Vehicles Transporting Workmen
[Selected Provisions]

§31402. Operation of farm labor vehicle after notice that vehicle is in unsafe condition.

§31403. Transportation of passengers in unsafe farm labor vehicles.

WELFARE AND INSTITUTIONS CODE

DIVISION 2 CHILDREN

PART 1 Delinquents and Wards of the Juvenile Court

CHAPTER 2 JUVENILE COURT LAW

ARTICLE 1 General Provisions [Selected Provisions]

§219. Ward of juvenile court engaged in rehabilitative work; right to benefits.

ARTICLE 24 Wards and Dependent Children—Juvenile Homes, Ranches and Camps [Selected Provisions]

§883. Wards of juvenile homes, ranches, or camps; right to benefits.

DIVISION 9 PUBLIC SOCIAL SERVICES

PART 3 Aid and Medical Assistance

CHAPTER 3 STATE SUPPLEMENTARY PROGRAM FOR AGED, BLIND AND DISABLED

ARTICLE 7 In-Home Supportive Services [Selected Provisions]

§12302.2. Performance of statutory compensation and benefit obligations when direct payment made to provider or recipient; payment of administrative costs.

§12302.21. Workers' compensation coverage for employees of nonprofit and proprietary agencies who contract with counties to provide in-home supportive services.

§12302.5. Establishment of agents for employers in order to comply with federal and state laws.

CHAPTER 7 BASIC HEALTH CARE

ARTICLE 1 General Provisions [Selected Provisions]

§14011. Verification of income required to obtain benefits.

ARTICLE 3 Administration [Selected Provisions]

§14101.7. Reimbursement from Appeals Board.

DIVISION 10 STATE DEPARTMENT OF REHABILITATION

PART 1 General Provisions

CHAPTER 1 POWERS AND DUTIES [Selected Provisions]

§19005.5. Federal targeted jobs tax credit eligibility.

SELECTED PROVISIONS Of The CALIFORNIA CONSTITUTION

ARTICLE XIV LABOR RELATIONS [Selected Provisions]

§1. Minimum wages; general welfare of employees.

The Legislature may provide for minimum wages and for the general welfare of employees and for those purposes may confer on a commission legislative, executive, and judicial powers. **Leg.H.** Adopted June 8, 1976.

§4. Workers' compensation system.

The Legislature is hereby expressly vested with plenary power, unlimited by any provision of this Constitution, to create, and enforce a complete system of workers' compensation, by appropriate legislation, and in that behalf to create and enforce a liability on the part of any or all persons to compensate any or all of their workers for injury or disability, and their dependents for death incurred or sustained by the said workers in the course of their employment, irrespective of the fault of any party. A complete system of workers' compensation includes adequate provisions for the comfort, health and safety and general welfare of any and all workers and those dependent upon them for support to the extent of relieving from the consequences of any injury or death incurred or sustained by workers in the course of their employment, irrespective of the fault of any party; also full provision for securing safety in places of employment; full provision for such medical, surgical hospital and other remedical treatment as is requisite to cure and relieve from the effects of such injury; full provision for adequate insurance coverage against liability to pay or furnish compensation; full provision for regulating such insurance coverage in all its aspects, including the establishment and management of a State compensation insurance fund; full provision for otherwise securing the payment of compensation; and full provision for vesting power, authority and jurisdiction in an administrative body with all the requisite governmental functions to determine any dispute or matter arising under such legislation, to the end that the administration of such legislation shall accomplish substantial justice in all cases expeditiously, inexpensively, and without incumbrance of any character; all of which matters are expressly declared to be the social public policy of this State, binding upon all departments of the State government.

The Legislature is vested with plenary powers, to provide for the settlement of any disputes arising under such legislation by arbitration, or by an industrial accident commission, by the courts, or by either, any, or all of these agencies, either separately or in combination, and may fix and control the method and manner of trial of any such dispute, the rules of evidence and the manner of review of decisions rendered by the tribunal or tribunals designated by it; provided, that all decisions of any such tribunal shall be subject to review by the appellate court of this State. The Legislature may combine in one statute all the provisions for a complete system of workers' compensation, as herein defined.

The Legislature shall have power to provide for the payment of an award to the state in the case of the death, arising out of and in the course of the employment, of an employee without dependents, and such awards may be used for the payment of extra compensation for subsequent injuries beyond the liability of a single employer for awards to employees of the employer.

Nothing contained herein shall be taken or construed to impair or render ineffectual in any measure the creation and existence of the industrial accident commission of this State or the State compensation insurance fund, the creation and existence of which, with all the functions vested in them, are hereby ratified and confirmed. **Leg.H.** Adopted June 8, 1976.

Ref.: 8 C.C.R. §§10109, 10548, 10560, 10562, 10727; W. Cal. Sum., 2 "Workers' Compensation" §§2, 3, 5, 14, 74, 99, 241, 353, 394, 434, 439, 7 "Constitutional Law" §217, 9 "Taxation" §121.

§5. Convicts' labor; state benefit.

(a) The Director of Corrections or any county Sheriff or other local government official charged with jail operations, may enter into contracts with public entities, nonprofit or for profit organizations, entities, or businesses for the purpose of conducting programs which use inmate labor. Such programs shall be operated and implemented pursuant to statutes enacted by or in accordance with the provisions of the Prison Inmate Labor Initiative of 1990, and by rules and regulations prescribed by the Director of Corrections and, for county jail programs, by local ordinances.

(b) No contract shall be executed with an employer that will initiate employment by inmates in the same job classification as non-inmate employees of the same employer who are on strike, as defined in Section 1132.6 of the Labor Code, as it reads on January 1, 1990, or who are subject to lockout, as defined in Section 1132.8 of the Labor Code, as it reads on January 1, 1990. Total daily hours worked by inmates employed in the same job classification as non-inmate employees of the same employer who are on strike, as defined in Section 1132.6 of the Labor Code, as it reads on January 1, 1990, or who are subject to lockout, as defined in Section 1132.8 of the Labor Code, as it reads on January 1, 1990, shall not exceed, for the duration of the strike, the average daily hours worked for the preceding six months, or if the program has been in operation for less than six months, the average for the period of operation.

(c) Nothing in this section shall be interpreted as creating a right of inmates to work. **Leg.H.** Former section repealed operative November 7, 1990; new section adopted operative November 7, 1990.

SELECTED PROVISIONS Of The BUSINESS AND PROFESSIONS CODE

DIVISION 3 PROFESSIONS AND VOCATIONS GENERALLY

CHAPTER 2.7 ADVERTISING FOR WORKERS' COMPENSATION LEGAL SERVICES

§5499.30. Name of attorney required in advertisement for workers' compensation legal services.

(a) Any individual, firm, corporation, partnership, organization, or association which prints, displays, publishes, distributes, or broadcasts or causes or permits to be advertised, printed, displayed, published, distributed, or broadcast any advertising which purports to provide legal services for obtaining workers' compensation benefits shall include the name of at least one attorney associated with the individual, firm, corporation, partnership, organization, or association in all such advertising.

(b) As used in this section, the term "legal services" includes any service which refers potential clients to any attorney.

(c) A violation of this section is a misdemeanor, punishable by imprisonment in the county jail for not more than one year, or by a fine not exceeding ten thousand dollars ($10,000), or both. **Leg.H.** 1993 ch. 120, effective July 16, 1993.

CHAPTER 9 CONTRACTORS

ARTICLE 7 Disciplinary Proceedings [Selected Provisions]

§7110. Grounds for disciplinary action.

Willful or deliberate disregard and violation of the building laws of the state, or of any political subdivision thereof, or of Section 8505 or 8556 of this code, or of Sections 1689.5 to 1689.8, inclusive, or Sections 1689.10 to 1689.13, inclusive, of the Civil Code, or of the safety laws or labor laws or compensation insurance laws or Unemployment Insurance Code of the state, or violation by any licensee of any provision of the Health and Safety Code or Water Code, relating to the digging, boring, or drilling of water wells, or Article 2 (commencing with Section 4216) of Chapter 3.1 of Division 5 of Title 1 of the Government Code, constitutes a

Misc. Provisions

cause for disciplinary action. **Leg.H.** 1994 ch. 362, 2002 ch. 1013 (SB 2026).

ARTICLE 7.5
Workers' Compensation Insurance Reports

§7125. [Repealed January 1, 2011] Certificate of Worker's Compensation Insurance or Certification of Self-Insurance required for licensure; exceptions; report to registrar.

(a) Except as provided in subdivision (b), the board shall require as a condition precedent to the issuance, reinstatement, reactivation, renewal, or continued maintenance of a license, that the applicant or licensee have on file at all times a current and valid Certificate of Workers' Compensation Insurance or Certification of Self-Insurance. A Certificate of Workers' Compensation Insurance shall be issued and filed, electronically or otherwise, by one or more insurers duly licensed to write workers' compensation insurance in this state. A Certification of Self-Insurance shall be issued and filed by the Director of Industrial Relations. If reciprocity conditions exist, as defined in Section 3600.5 of the Labor Code, the registrar shall require the information deemed necessary to assure compliance with this section.

(b) This section does not apply to an applicant or licensee who meets both of the following conditions:

(1) Has no employees provided that he or she files a statement with the board on a form prescribed by the registrar prior to the issuance, reinstatement, reactivation, or continued maintenance of a license, certifying that he or she does not employ any person in any manner so as to become subject to the workers' compensation laws of California or is not otherwise required to provide for workers' compensation insurance coverage under California law.

(2) Does not hold a C-39 license, as defined in Section 832.39 of Title 16 of the California Code of Regulations.

(c) No Certificate of Workers' Compensation Insurance, Certification of Self-Insurance, or exemption-certificate is required of a holder of a license that has been inactivated on the official records of the board during the period the license is inactive.

(d) The insurer, including the State Compensation Insurance Fund, shall report to the registrar the following information for any policy required under this section: name, license number, policy number, dates that coverage is scheduled to commence and lapse, and cancellation date if applicable.

(e) For any license that, on January 1, 2007, is active and includes a C-39 classification in addition to any other classification, the registrar shall, in lieu of the automatic license suspension otherwise required under this article, remove the C-39 classification from the license unless a valid Certificate of Workers' Compensation Insurance or Certification of Self-Insurance is received by the registrar prior to the operative date of this section.

(f) This section shall remain in effect only until January 1, 2011, and as of that date is repealed, unless a later enacted statute, that is enacted before January 1, 2011, deletes or extends that date. **Leg.H.** 1991 ch. 1160, 1995 ch. 467, 1996 ch. 331, 2002 ch. 311 (AB 264), 2006 ch. 38 (AB 881) §1.

Ref.: Hanna § 3.134; Herlick Handbook § 3.23; W. Cal. Sum., 2 "Workers' Compensation" §§146, 150, 190.

§7125. [Operative January 1, 2011] Certificate of Worker's Compensation Insurance or Certification of Self-Insurance required for licensure; exceptions; report to registrar.

(a) The board shall require as a condition precedent to the issuance, reinstatement, reactivation, renewal, or continued maintenance of a license, that the applicant or licensee have on file at all times a current and valid Certificate of Workers' Compensation Insurance or Certification of Self-Insurance. A Certificate of Workers' Compensation Insurance shall be issued and filed, electronically or otherwise, by one or more insurers duly licensed to write workers' compensation insurance in this state. A Certification of Self-Insurance shall be issued and filed by the Director of Industrial Relations. If reciprocity conditions exist, as defined in Section 3600.5 of the Labor Code, the registrar shall require the information deemed necessary to assure compliance with this section.

(b) This section does not apply to an applicant or licensee who has no employees provided that he or she files a statement with the board on a form prescribed by the registrar prior to the issuance, reinstatement, reactivation, or continued maintenance of a license, certifying that he or she does not employ any person in any manner so as to become subject to the workers' compensation laws of California or is not otherwise required to provide for workers' compensation insurance coverage under California law.

(c) No Certificate of Workers' Compensation Insurance, Certification of Self-Insurance, or exemption-certificate is required of a holder of a license that has been inactivated on the official records of the board during the period the license is inactive.

(d) The insurer, including the State Compensation Insurance Fund, shall report to the registrar the following information for any policy required under this section: name, license number, policy number, dates that coverage is scheduled to commence and lapse, and cancellation date, if applicable.

(e) This section shall become operative on January 1, 2011. **Leg.H.** 2006 ch. 38 (AB 881) §2.

Ref.: Hanna § 3.134; Herlick Handbook § 3.23; W. Cal. Sum., 2 "Workers' Compensation" §§146, 150, 190.

§7125.1. License reinstatement retroactive to effective date of certificate if submitted within 90 days; exception.

(a) The registrar shall accept a certificate required by Section 7125 as of the effective date shown on the certificate, if the certificate is received by the registrar within 90 days after that date, and shall reinstate the license to which the certificate pertains, if otherwise eligible, retroactive to the effective date of the certificate.

(b) Notwithstanding subdivision (a), the registrar shall accept the certificate as of the effective date shown on the certificate, even if the certificate is not received by the registrar within 90 days after that date, upon a showing by the licensee, on a form acceptable to the registrar, that the failure to have a certificate on file was due to circumstances beyond the control of the licensee. The registrar shall reinstate the license to which the certificate pertains, if otherwise eligible, retroactive to the effective date of the certificate. **Leg.H.** 1995 ch. 467 §18.

§7125.2. Failure to obtain or maintain insurance—Automatic license suspension; registrar notice and citation; reinstatement.

The failure of a licensee to obtain or maintain workers' compensation insurance coverage, if required under this chapter, shall result in the automatic suspension of the license by operation of law in accordance with the provisions of this section, but this suspension shall not affect, alter, or limit the status of the licensee as an employer for purposes of Section 3716 of the Labor Code.

(a) The license suspension imposed by this section is effective upon the earlier of either of the following:

(1) On the date that the relevant workers' compensation insurance coverage lapses.

(2) On the date that workers' compensation coverage is required to be obtained.

(b) A licensee who is subject to suspension under paragraph (1) of subdivision (a) shall be provided a notice by the registrar that includes all of the following:

(1) The reason for the license suspension and the effective date.

(2) A statement informing the licensee that a pending suspension will be posted to the license record for not more than 45 days prior to the posting of any license suspension periods required under this article.

(3) The procedures required to reinstate the license.

(c) Reinstatement may be made at any time following the suspension by showing proof of compliance as specified in Sections 7125 and 7125.1.

(d) In addition, with respect to an unlicensed individual acting in the capacity of a contractor who is not otherwise exempted from the provisions of this chapter, a citation may be issued by the registrar under Section 7028.7 for failure to comply with this article and to maintain workers' compensation insurance. An opportunity for a hearing as specified in Section 7028.10 will be granted if requested within 15 working days after service of the citation. **Leg.H.** 1995 ch. 467 §20, 2002 ch. 311 (AB 264).

Ref.: W. Cal. Sum., 2 "Workers' Compensation" §§150, 190.

§7125.3. Periods of licensure.

A contractor shall be considered duly licensed during all periods in which the registrar is required to accept the certificate prescribed by Section 7125, provided the licensee has otherwise complied with the provisions of this chapter. **Leg.H.** 2002 ch. 311 (AB 264).

§7125.4. Causes for disciplinary action.

(a) The filing of the exemption certificate prescribed by this article that is false, or the employment of a person subject to coverage under the workers' compensation laws after the filing of an exemption certificate without first filing a Certificate of Workers' Compensation Insurance or Certification of Self-Insurance in accordance with the provisions of this article, or the employment of a person subject to coverage under the workers' compensation laws without maintaining coverage for that person, constitutes cause for disciplinary action.

(b) Any qualifier for a license who, under Section 7068.1 is responsible for assuring that a licensee complies with the provisions of this chapter, is also guilty of a misdemeanor for committing or failing to prevent the commission of any of the acts that are cause for disciplinary action under this section. **Leg.H.** 2002 ch. 311 (AB 264), 2005 ch. 205 (SB 488) §2.

§7126. Penalty for violation.

Any licensee or agent or officer thereof, who violates, or omits to comply with, any of the provisions of this article is guilty of a misdemeanor.

CHAPTER 14
STRUCTURAL PEST CONTROL OPERATORS

ARTICLE 7
Disciplinary Proceedings [Selected Provisions]

§8636. Grounds for disciplinary action.

Disregard and violation of the buildings laws of the state, or of any of its political subdivisions, or of the safety laws, labor laws, health laws, or compensation insurance laws of the state relating to the practice of structural pest control is a ground for disciplinary action.

DIVISION 7
GENERAL BUSINESS REGULATIONS

PART 1
Licensing for Revenue and Regulation

CHAPTER 6
NOTICE TO LICENSEES

§16545. Business license application form.

Every state agency which licenses any kind of business transacted or carried on within their respective jurisdictions shall require applications filed to designate the name of the applicant's workers' compensation insurance carrier, if any. This section does not apply to licensing under the Outdoor Advertising Act. The license application form shall contain a statement substantially as follows: "I am aware of the provisions of Section 3700 of the Labor Code which requires every employer to be insured against liability for workers' compensation."

SELECTED PROVISIONS Of The CIVIL CODE

DIVISION 1 PERSONS

PART 2.6 Confidentiality of Medical Information

CHAPTER 1 DEFINITIONS [Selected Provisions]

§56.05. Definitions.

For purposes of this part:

(a) "Authorization" means permission granted in accordance with Section 56.11 or 56.21 for the disclosure of medical information.

(b) "Authorized recipient" means any person who is authorized to receive medical information pursuant to Section 56.10 or 56.20.

(c) "Contractor" means any person or entity that is a medical group, independent practice association, pharmaceutical benefits manager, or a medical service organization and is not a health care service plan or provider of health care. "Contractor" does not include insurance institutions as defined in subdivision (k) of Section 791.02 of the Insurance Code or pharmaceutical benefits managers licensed pursuant to the Knox-Keene Health Care Service Plan Act of 1975 (Chapter 2.2 (commencing with Section 1340) of Division 2 of the Health and Safety Code).

(d) "Health care service plan" means any entity regulated pursuant to the Knox-Keene Health Care Service Plan Act of 1975 (Chapter 2.2 (commencing with Section 1340) of Division 2 of the Health and Safety Code).

(e) "Licensed health care professional" means any person licensed or certified pursuant to Division 2 (commencing with Section 500) of the Business and Professions Code, the Osteopathic Initiative Act or the Chiropractic Initiative Act, or Division 2.5 (commencing with Section 1797) of the Health and Safety Code.

(f) "Marketing" means to make a communication about a product or service that encourages recipients of the communication to purchase or use the product or service.

"Marketing" does not include any of the following:

(1) Communications made orally or in writing for which the communicator does not receive direct or indirect remuneration, including, but not limited to, gifts, fees, payments, subsidies, or other economic benefits, from a third party for making the communication.

(2) Communications made to current enrollees solely for the purpose of describing a provider's participation in an existing health care provider network or health plan network of a Knox-Keene licensed health plan to which the enrollees already subscribe; communications made to current enrollees solely for the purpose of describing if, and the extent to which, a product or service, or payment for a product or service, is provided by a provider, contractor, or plan or included in a plan of benefits of a Knox-Keene licensed health plan to which the enrollees already subscribe; or communications

made to plan enrollees describing the availability of more cost-effective pharmaceuticals.

(3) Communications that are tailored to the circumstances of a particular individual to educate or advise the individual about treatment options, and otherwise maintain the individual's adherence to a prescribed course of medical treatment, as provided in Section 1399.901 of the Health and Safety Code, for a chronic and seriously debilitating or life-threatening condition as defined in subdivisions (d) and (e) of Section 1367.21 of the Health and Safety Code, if the health care provider, contractor, or health plan receives direct or indirect remuneration, including, but not limited to, gifts, fees, payments, subsidies, or other economic benefits, from a third party for making the communication, if all of the following apply:

(A) The individual receiving the communication is notified in the communication in typeface no smaller than 14-point type of the fact that the provider, contractor, or health plan has been remunerated and the source of the remuneration.

(B) The individual is provided the opportunity to opt out of receiving future remunerated communications.

(C) The communication contains instructions in typeface no smaller than 14-point type describing how the individual can opt out of receiving further communications by calling a toll-free number of the health care provider, contractor, or health plan making the remunerated communications. No further communication may be made to an individual who has opted out after 30 calendar days from the date the individual makes the opt out request.

(g) "Medical information" means any individually identifiable information, in electronic or physical form, in possession of or derived from a provider of health care, health care service plan, pharmaceutical company, or contractor regarding a patient's medical history, mental or physical condition, or treatment. "Individually identifiable" means that the medical information includes or contains any element of personal identifying information sufficient to allow identification of the individual, such as the patient's name, address, electronic mail address, telephone number, or social security number, or other information that, alone or in combination with other publicly available information, reveals the individual's identity.

(h) "Patient" means any natural person, whether or not still living, who received health care services from a provider of health care and to whom medical information pertains.

(i) "Pharmaceutical company" means any company or business, or an agent or representative thereof, that manufactures, sells, or distributes pharmaceuticals, medications, or prescription drugs. "Pharmaceutical company" does not include a pharmaceutical benefits manager, as included in subdivision (c), or a provider of health care.

(j) "Provider of health care" means any person licensed or certified pursuant to Division 2 (commencing with Section 500) of the Business and Professions Code; any person licensed pursuant to the Osteopathic Initiative Act or the Chiropractic Initiative Act; any person certified pursuant to Division 2.5 (commencing with Section 1797) of the Health and Safety Code; any clinic, health dispensary, or health facility licensed pursuant to Division 2 (commencing with Section 1200) of the Health and Safety Code. "Provider of health care" does not include insurance institutions as defined in subdivision (k) of Section 791.02 of the Insurance Code. **Leg.H.** 1981 ch. 782, 1984 ch. 1391, 1999 ch. 526, 2000 ch. 1067, 2002 ch. 853 (AB 2191), 2003 ch. 562 (AB 715).

Ref.: Hanna § 22.02[6]; Herlick Handbook § 4.24; W. Cal. Ev., "Witnesses" §§200, 202, 230, 518–520; W. Cal. Sum., 2 "Workers' Compensation" §158, 10 "Parent and Child" §150.

CHAPTER 2
DISCLOSURE OF MEDICAL INFORMATION BY PROVIDERS

§56.10. When medical information may be disclosed.

(a) No provider of health care, health care service plan, or contractor shall disclose medical information regarding a patient of the provider of health care or an enrollee or subscriber of a health care service plan without first obtaining an authorization, except as provided in subdivision (b) or (c).

(b) A provider of health care, a health care service plan, or a contractor shall disclose medical information if the disclosure is compelled by any of the following:

(1) By a court pursuant to an order of that court.

(2) By a board, commission, or administrative agency for purposes of adjudication pursuant to its lawful authority.

(3) By a party to a proceeding before a court or administrative agency pursuant to a subpoena, subpoena duces tecum, notice to appear served pursuant to Section 1987 of the Code of Civil Procedure, or any provision authorizing discovery in a proceeding before a court or administrative agency.

(4) By a board, commission, or administrative agency pursuant to an investigative subpoena issued under Article 2 (commencing with Section 11180) of Chapter 2 of Part 1 of Division 3 of Title 2 of the Government Code.

(5) By an arbitrator or arbitration panel, when arbitration is lawfully requested by either party, pursuant to a subpoena duces tecum issued under Section 1282.6 of the Code of Civil Procedure, or [1] **another** provision authorizing discovery in a proceeding before an arbitrator or arbitration panel.

(6) By a search warrant lawfully issued to a governmental law enforcement agency.

(7) By the patient or the patient's representative pursuant to Chapter 1 (commencing with Section 123100) of Part 1 of Division 106 of the Health and Safety Code.

(8) By a coroner, when requested in the course of an investigation by the coroner's office for the purpose of identifying the decedent or locating next of kin, or when investigating deaths that may involve public health concerns, organ or tissue donation, child abuse, elder abuse, suicides, poisonings, accidents, sudden infant deaths, suspicious deaths, unknown deaths, or criminal deaths, or when otherwise authorized by the decedent's representative. Medical information requested by the coroner under this paragraph shall be limited to information regarding the patient who is the decedent and who is the subject of the investigation and shall be disclosed to the coroner without delay upon request.

(9) When otherwise specifically required by law.

(c) A provider of health care or a health care service plan may disclose medical information as follows:

(1) The information may be disclosed to providers of health care, health care service plans, contractors, or other health care professionals or facilities for purposes of diagnosis or treatment of the patient. This includes, in an emergency situation, the communication of patient information by radio transmission or other means between emergency medical personnel at the scene of an emergency, or in an emergency medical transport vehicle, and emergency medical personnel at a health facility licensed pursuant to Chapter 2 (commencing with Section 1250) of Division 2 of the Health and Safety Code.

(2) The information may be disclosed to an insurer, employer, health care service plan, hospital service plan, employee benefit plan, governmental authority, contractor, or any other person or entity responsible for paying for health care services rendered to the patient, to the extent necessary to allow responsibility for payment to be determined and payment to be made. If (A) the patient is, by reason of a comatose or other disabling medical condition, unable to consent to the disclosure of medical information and (B) no other arrangements have been made to pay for the health care services being rendered to the patient, the information may be disclosed to a governmental authority to the extent necessary to determine the patient's eligibility for, and to obtain, payment under a governmental program for health care services provided to the patient. The information may also be disclosed to another provider of health care or health care service plan as necessary to assist the other provider or health care service plan in obtaining payment for health care services rendered by that provider of health care or health care service plan to the patient.

(3) The information may be disclosed to a person or entity that provides billing, claims management, medical data processing, or other administrative services for providers of health care or health care service plans or for any of the persons or entities specified in paragraph (2). However, [2] information so disclosed shall **not** be further disclosed by the recipient in [3] **a** way that would violate this part.

(4) The information may be disclosed to organized committees and agents of professional societies or of medical staffs of licensed hospitals, licensed health care service plans, professional standards review organizations, independent medical review organizations and their selected reviewers, utilization and quality control peer review organizations as established by Congress in Public Law 97-248 in 1982, contractors, or persons or organizations insuring, responsible for, or defending professional

liability that a provider may incur, if the committees, agents, health care service plans, organizations, reviewers, contractors, or persons are engaged in reviewing the competence or qualifications of health care professionals or in reviewing health care services with respect to medical necessity, level of care, quality of care, or justification of charges.

(5) The information in the possession of a provider of health care or health care service plan may be reviewed by a private or public body responsible for licensing or accrediting the provider of health care or health care service plan. However, no patient-identifying medical information may be removed from the premises except as expressly permitted or required elsewhere by law, nor shall that information be further disclosed by the recipient in [4] **a** way that would violate this part.

(6) The information may be disclosed to the county coroner in the course of an investigation by the coroner's office when requested for all purposes not included in paragraph (8) of subdivision (b).

(7) The information may be disclosed to public agencies, clinical investigators, including investigators conducting epidemiologic studies, health care research organizations, and accredited public or private nonprofit educational or health care institutions for bona fide research purposes. However, no information so disclosed shall be further disclosed by the recipient in [5] **a** way that would disclose the identity of a patient or violate this part.

(8) A provider of health care or health care service plan that has created medical information as a result of employment-related health care services to an employee conducted at the specific prior written request and expense of the employer may disclose to the employee's employer that part of the information that:

(A) Is relevant in a lawsuit, arbitration, grievance, or other claim or challenge to which the employer and the employee are parties and in which the patient has placed in issue his or her medical history, mental or physical condition, or treatment, provided that information may only be used or disclosed in connection with that proceeding.

(B) Describes functional limitations of the patient that may entitle the patient to leave from work for medical reasons or limit the patient's fitness to perform his or her present employment, provided that no statement of medical cause is included in the information disclosed.

(9) Unless the provider of health care or health care service plan is notified in writing of an agreement by the sponsor, insurer, or administrator to the contrary, the information may be disclosed to a sponsor, insurer, or administrator of a group or individual insured or uninsured plan or policy that the patient seeks coverage by or benefits from, if the information was created by the provider of health care or health care service plan as the result of services conducted at the specific prior written request and expense of the sponsor, insurer, or administrator for the purpose of evaluating the application for coverage or benefits.

(10) The information may be disclosed to a health care service plan by providers of health care that contract with the health care service plan and may be transferred among providers of health care that contract with the health care service plan, for the purpose of administering the health care service plan. Medical information [6] **shall** not otherwise be disclosed by a health care service plan except in accordance with [7] this part.

(11) [8] This part [9] **does not** prevent the disclosure by a provider of health care or a health care service plan to an insurance institution, agent, or support organization, subject to Article 6.6 (commencing with Section 791) **of Chapter 1** of Part 2 of Division 1 of the Insurance Code, of medical information if the insurance institution, agent, or support organization has complied with all **of the** requirements for obtaining the information pursuant to Article 6.6 (commencing with Section 791) **of Chapter 1** of Part 2 of Division 1 of the Insurance Code.

(12) The information relevant to the patient's condition [10]**,** care**,** and treatment provided may be disclosed to a probate court investigator in the course of [11] **an** investigation required or authorized in a conservatorship proceeding under the Guardianship-Conservatorship Law as defined in Section 1400 of the Probate Code, or to a probate court investigator, probation officer, or domestic relations investigator engaged in determining the need for an initial guardianship or continuation of an [12] **existing** guardianship.

(13) The information may be disclosed to an organ procurement organization or a tissue bank processing the tissue of a decedent for transplantation into the body of another person,

but only with respect to the donating decedent, for the purpose of aiding the transplant. For the purpose of this paragraph, [13] "tissue bank" and "tissue" have the same [14] **meanings** as defined in Section 1635 of the Health and Safety Code.

(14) The information may be disclosed when the disclosure is otherwise specifically authorized by law, including, but not limited to, the voluntary reporting, either directly or indirectly, to the federal Food and Drug Administration of adverse events related to drug products or medical device problems.

(15) Basic information, including the patient's name, city of residence, age, sex, and general condition, may be disclosed to a [15] **state-recognized** or federally recognized disaster relief organization for the purpose of responding to disaster welfare inquiries.

(16) The information may be disclosed to a third party for purposes of encoding, encrypting, or otherwise anonymizing data. However, no information so disclosed shall be further disclosed by the recipient in [16] **a** way that would violate this part, including the unauthorized manipulation of coded or encrypted medical information that reveals individually identifiable medical information.

(17) For purposes of disease management programs and services as defined in Section 1399.901 of the Health and Safety Code, information may be disclosed as follows: (A) to an entity contracting with a health care service plan or the health care service plan's contractors to monitor or administer care of enrollees for a covered benefit, if the disease management services and care are authorized by a treating physician, or (B) to a disease management organization, as defined in Section 1399.900 of the Health and Safety Code, that complies fully with the physician authorization requirements of Section 1399.902 of the Health and Safety Code, if the health care service plan or its contractor provides or has provided a description of the disease management services to a treating physician or to the health care service plan's or contractor's network of physicians. [17] This paragraph [18] **does not** require physician authorization for the care or treatment of the adherents of a well-recognized church or religious denomination who depend solely upon prayer or spiritual means for healing in the practice of the religion of that church or denomination.

(18) The information may be disclosed, as permitted by state and federal law or regulation, to a local health department for the purpose of preventing or controlling disease, injury, or disability, including, but not limited to, the reporting of disease, injury, vital events, including, but not limited to, birth or death, and the conduct of public health surveillance, public health investigations, and public health interventions, as authorized or required by state or federal law or regulation.

(19) The information may be disclosed, consistent with applicable law and standards of ethical conduct, by a psychotherapist, as defined in Section 1010 of the Evidence Code, if the psychotherapist, in good faith, believes the disclosure is necessary to prevent or lessen a serious and imminent threat to the health or safety of a reasonably foreseeable victim or victims, and the disclosure is made to a person or persons reasonably able to prevent or lessen the threat, including the target of the threat.

(20) The information may be disclosed as described in Section 56.103.

(d) Except to the extent expressly authorized by [19] **a** patient or enrollee or subscriber or as provided by subdivisions (b) and (c), [20] **a** provider of health care, health care service plan, contractor, or corporation and its subsidiaries and affiliates shall **not** intentionally share, sell, use for marketing, or otherwise use [21] medical information for [22] **a** purpose not necessary to provide health care services to the patient.

(e) Except to the extent expressly authorized by [23] **a** patient or enrollee or subscriber or as provided by subdivisions (b) and (c), [24] **a** contractor or corporation and its subsidiaries and affiliates shall **not** further disclose medical information regarding a patient of the provider of health care or an enrollee or subscriber of a health care service plan or insurer or self-insured employer received under this section to [25] **a** person or entity that is not engaged in providing direct health care services to the patient or his or her provider of health care or health care service plan or insurer or self-insured employer. **Leg.H.** 2000 ch. 1068 §1.16, 2002 ch. 123 (AB 1958), 2003 ch. 562 (AB 715), 2006 ch. 874 (SB 1430) §2, 2007 chs. 506 (AB 1178) §1, 552 (AB 1687) §2, 553 (AB 1727) §1.9, 2008 ch. 179 (SB 1498) §27.

§56.10. 2008 Deletes. [1] any other **[2]** no **[3]** any **[4]** any **[5]** any **[6]** may **[7]** the provisions of **[8]**

Nothing in **[9]** shall **[10]** and **[11]** any **[12]** existent **[13]** the terms **[14]** meaning **[15]** state **[16]** any **[17]** Nothing in **[18]** shall be construed to **[19]** the **[20]** no **[21]** any **[22]** any **[23]** the **[24]** no **[25]** any

2006 Note: This act shall be known, and may be cited as the Local Pandemic and Emergency Health Preparedness Act of 2006. Stats. 2006 ch. 874 (SB 1430) §1.

Ref.: Hanna § 22.02[5]; Herlick Handbook § 4.24; W. Cal. Ev., "Witnesses" §§518–520; W. Cal. Sum., 7 "Constitutional Law" §580.

§56.101. Preservation of confidentiality of records.

Every provider of health care, health care service plan, pharmaceutical company, or contractor who creates, maintains, preserves, stores, abandons, destroys, or disposes of medical records shall do so in a manner that preserves the confidentiality of the information contained therein. Any provider of health care, health care service plan, pharmaceutical company, or contractor who negligently creates, maintains, preserves, stores, abandons, destroys, or disposes of medical records shall be subject to the remedies and penalties provided under subdivisions (b) and (c) of Section 56.36. **Leg.H.** 1999 ch. 526, 2000 ch. 1067, 2002 ch. 853 (AB 2191).

Ref.: W. Cal. Ev., "Witnesses" §518.

§56.102. Pharmaceutical company cannot require patient to sign form permitting disclosure of medical information as condition of receiving pharmaceuticals; exceptions.

(a) A pharmaceutical company may not require a patient, as a condition of receiving pharmaceuticals, medications, or prescription drugs, to sign an authorization, release, consent, or waiver that would permit the disclosure of medical information that otherwise may not be disclosed under Section 56.10 or any other provision of law, unless the disclosure is for one of the following purposes:

(1) Enrollment of the patient in a patient assistance program or prescription drug discount program.

(2) Enrollment of the patient in a clinical research project.

(3) Prioritization of distribution to the patient of a prescription medicine in limited supply in the United States.

(4) Response to an inquiry from the patient communicated in writing, by telephone, or by electronic mail.

(b) Except as provided in subdivision (a) or Section 56.10, a pharmaceutical company may not disclose medical information provided to it without first obtaining a valid authorization from the patient. **Leg.H.** 2002 ch. 853 (AB 2191).

Ref.: W. Cal. Ev., "Witnesses" §518.

§56.103. Disclosure of minor's medical information for purpose of coordinating health care services and medical treatment.

(a) A provider of health care may disclose medical information to a county social worker, a probation officer, or any other person who is legally authorized to have custody or care of a minor for the purpose of coordinating health care services and medical treatment provided to the minor.

(b) For purposes of this section, health care services and medical treatment includes one or more providers of health care providing, coordinating, or managing health care and related services, including, but not limited to, a provider of health care coordinating health care with a third party, consultation between providers of health care and medical treatment relating to a minor, or a provider of health care referring a minor for health care services to another provider of health care.

(c) For purposes of this section, a county social worker, a probation officer, or any other person who is legally authorized to have custody or care of a minor shall be considered a third party who may receive any of the following:

(1) Medical information described in Sections 56.05 and 56.10.

(2) Protected health information described in Section 160.103 of Title 45 of the Code of Federal Regulations.

(d) Medical information disclosed to a county social worker, probation officer, or any other person who is legally authorized to have custody or care of a minor shall not be further disclosed by the recipient unless the disclosure is for the purpose of coordinating health care services and medical treatment of the minor and the disclosure is authorized by law. Medical information disclosed pursuant to this section may not be admitted into evidence in any criminal or delinquency proceeding against the minor. Nothing in this subdivision shall prohibit identical evidence from being admissible in a criminal proceeding if that evidence is derived solely from lawful means other than this section and is permitted by law.

(e)(1) Notwithstanding Section 56.104, if a provider of health care determines that the disclosure of medical information concerning the diagnosis and treatment of a mental health condition of a minor is reasonably necessary for the purpose of assisting in coordinating the treatment and care of the minor, that information may be disclosed to a county social worker, probation officer, or any other person who is legally authorized to have custody or care of the minor. The information shall not be further disclosed by the recipient unless the disclosure is for the purpose of coordinating mental health services and treatment of the minor and the disclosure is authorized by law.

(2) As used in this subdivision, "medical information" does not include psychotherapy notes as defined in Section 164.501 of Title 45 of the Code of Federal Regulations.

(f) The disclosure of information pursuant to this section is not intended to limit the disclosure of information when that disclosure is otherwise required by law.

(g) For purposes of this section, "minor" means a minor taken into temporary custody or as to who a petition has been filed with the court, or who has been adjudged to be a dependent child or ward of the juvenile court pursuant to Section 300 or [1] **601** of the Welfare and Institutions Code.

(h)(1) Except as described in paragraph (1) of subdivision (e), nothing in this section shall be construed to limit or otherwise affect existing privacy protections provided for in state or federal law.

(2) Nothing in this section shall be construed to expand the authority of a social worker, probation officer, or custodial caregiver beyond the authority provided under existing law to a parent or a patient representative regarding access to medical information. **Leg.H.** 2007 ch. 552 (AB 1687) §3, 2008 chs. 699 (SB 1241) §1, 700 (AB 2352) §1.

§56.103. 2008 Deletes. [1] 600

§56.104. Release of information on psychotherapy.

(a) Notwithstanding subdivision (c) of Section 56.10, except as authorized in paragraph (1) of subdivision (c) of Section 56.10, no provider of health care, health care service plan, or contractor may release medical information to persons or entities authorized by law to receive that information pursuant to subdivision (c) of Section 56.10, if the requested information specifically relates to the patient's participation in outpatient treatment with a psychotherapist, unless the person or entity requesting that information submits to the patient pursuant to subdivision (b) and to the provider of health care, health care service plan, or contractor a written request, signed by the person requesting the information or an authorized agent of the entity requesting the information, that includes all of the following:

(1) The specific information relating to a patient's participation in outpatient treatment with a psychotherapist being requested and its specific intended use or uses.

(2) The length of time during which the information will be kept before being destroyed or disposed of. A person or entity may extend that timeframe, provided that the person or entity notifies the provider, plan, or contractor of the extension. Any notification of an extension shall include the specific reason for the extension, the intended use or uses of the information during the extended time, and the expected date of the destruction of the information.

(3) A statement that the information will not be used for any purpose other than its intended use.

(4) A statement that the person or entity requesting the information will destroy the information and all copies in the person's or entity's possession or control, will cause it to be destroyed, or will return the information and all copies of it before or immediately after the length of time specified in paragraph (2) has expired.

(b) The person or entity requesting the information shall submit a copy of the written request required by this section to the patient within 30 days of receipt of the information requested, unless the patient has signed a written waiver in the form of a letter signed and submitted by the patient to the provider of health care or health care service plan waiving notification.

(c) For purposes of this section, "psychotherapist" means a person who is both a "psychotherapist" as defined in Section 1010 of the Evidence Code and a "provider of health care" as defined in subdivision (i) of Section 56.05.

(d) This section does not apply to the disclosure or use of medical information by a law enforcement agency or a regulatory agency when required for an investigation of unlawful activity or for licensing, certification, or regulatory purposes, unless the disclosure is otherwise prohibited by law.

(e) Nothing in this section shall be construed to grant any additional authority to a provider of health care, health care service plan, or contractor to disclose information to a person or entity without the patient's consent. **Leg.H.** 1999 ch. 527, 2004 ch. 463 (SB 598).

Ref.: W. Cal. Ev., "Witnesses" §518.

§56.105. Authorization to disclose medical information in connection with settlement or compromise of medical malpractice case.

Whenever, prior to the service of a complaint upon a defendant in any action arising out of the professional negligence of a person holding a valid physician's and surgeon's certificate issued pursuant to Chapter 5 (commencing with Section 2000) of Division 2 of the Business and Professions Code, a demand for settlement or offer to compromise is made on a patient's behalf, the demand or offer shall be accompanied by an authorization to disclose medical information to persons or organizations insuring, responsible for, or defending professional liability that the certificate holder may incur. The authorization shall be in accordance with Section 56.11 and shall authorize disclosure of that information that is necessary to investigate issues of liability and extent of potential damages in evaluating the merits of the demand for settlement or offer to compromise.

Notice of any request for medical information made pursuant to an authorization as provided by this section shall be given to the patient or the patient's legal representative. The notice shall describe the inclusive subject matter and dates of the materials requested and shall also authorize the patient or the patient's legal representative to receive, upon request, copies of the information at his or her expense.

Nothing in this section shall be construed to waive or limit any applicable privileges set forth in the Evidence Code except for the disclosure of medical information subject to the patient's authorization. Nothing in this section shall be construed as authorizing a representative of any person from whom settlement has been demanded to communicate in violation of the physician-patient privilege with a treating physician except for the medical information request.

The requirements of this section are independent of the requirements of Section 364 of the Code of Civil Procedure. **Leg.H.** 1985 ch. 484, 1991 ch. 591.

Ref.: W. Cal. Ev., "Witnesses" §518.

§56.1007. Disclosure to family member, partner, or friend; disclosure for notification purposes; disaster relief efforts.

(a) A provider of health care, health care service plan, or contractor may, in accordance with subdivision (c) or (d), disclose to a family member, other relative, domestic partner, or a close personal friend of the patient, or any other person identified by the patient, the medical information directly relevant to that person's involvement with the patient's care or payment related to the patient's health care.

(b) A provider of health care, health care service plan, or contractor may use or disclose medical information to notify, or assist in the notification of, including identifying or locating, a family member, a personal representative of the patient, a domestic partner, or another person responsible for the care of the patient of the patient's location, general condition, or death. Any use or disclosure of medical information for those notification purposes shall be in accordance with the provisions of subdivision (c), (d), or (e), as applicable.

(c)(1) Except as provided in paragraph (2), if the patient is present for, or otherwise available prior to, a use or disclosure permitted by subdivision (a) or (b) and has the capacity to make health care decisions, the provider of health care, health care service plan, or contractor may use or disclose the medical information if it does any of the following:

(A) Obtains the patient's agreement.

(B) Provides the patient with the opportunity to object to the disclosure, and the patient does not express an objection.

(C) Reasonably infers from the circumstances, based on the exercise of professional judgment, that the patient does not object to the disclosure.

(2) A provider of health care who is a psychotherapist, as defined in Section 1010 of the Evidence Code, may use or disclose medical information pursuant to this subdivision only if the psychotherapist complies with subparagraph (A) or (B) of paragraph (1).

(d) If the patient is not present, or the opportunity to agree or object to the use or disclosure cannot practicably be provided because of the patient's incapacity or an emergency circumstance, the provider of health care, health care service plan, or contractor may, in the exercise of professional judgment, determine whether the disclosure is in the best interests of the patient and, if so, disclose only the medical information that is directly relevant to the person's involvement with the patient's health care. A provider of health care, health care service plan, or contractor may use professional judgment and its experience with common practice to make reasonable inferences of the patient's best interest in allowing a person to act on behalf of the patient to pick up filled prescriptions, medical supplies, X-rays, or other similar forms of medical information.

(e) A provider of health care, health care service plan, or contractor may use or disclose medical information to a public or private entity authorized by law or by its charter to assist in disaster relief efforts, for the purpose of coordinating with those entities the uses or disclosures permitted by subdivision (b). The requirements in subdivisions (c) and (d) apply to those uses and disclosures to the extent that the provider of health care, health care service plan, or contractor, in the exercise of professional judgment, determines that the requirements do not interfere with the ability to respond to the emergency circumstances.

(f) Nothing in this section shall be construed to interfere with or limit the access authority of Protection and Advocacy, Inc., the Office of Patients' Rights, or any county patients' rights advocates to access medical information pursuant to any state or federal law. **Leg.H.** 2006 ch. 833 (AB 3013) §1.

§56.11. Requirements for authorizing release of medical information.

Any person or entity that wishes to obtain medical information pursuant to subdivision (a) of Section 56.10, other than a person or entity authorized to receive medical information pursuant to subdivision (b) or (c) of Section 56.10, shall obtain a valid authorization for the release of this information.

An authorization for the release of medical information by a provider of health care, health care service plan, pharmaceutical company, or contractor shall be valid if it:

(a) Is handwritten by the person who signs it or is in a typeface no smaller than 14-point type.

(b) Is clearly separate from any other language present on the same page and is executed by a signature which serves no other purpose than to execute the authorization.

(c) Is signed and dated by one of the following:

(1) The patient. A patient who is a minor may only sign an authorization for the release of medical information obtained by a provider of health care, health care service plan, pharmaceutical company, or contractor in the course of furnishing services to which the minor could lawfully have consented under Part 1 (commencing with Section 25) or Part 2.7 (commencing with Section 60).

(2) The legal representative of the patient, if the patient is a minor or an incompetent. However, authorization may not be given under this subdivision for the disclosure of medical information obtained by the provider of health care, health care service plan, pharmaceutical company, or contractor in the course of furnishing services to which a minor patient could lawfully have consented under Part 1 (commencing with Section 25) or Part 2.7 (commencing with Section 60).

(3) The spouse of the patient or the person financially responsible for the patient, where the medical information is being sought for the sole purpose of processing an application for health insurance or for enrollment in a nonprofit hospital plan, a health care service plan, or an employee benefit plan, and where the patient is to be an enrolled spouse or dependent under the policy or plan.

(4) The beneficiary or personal representative of a deceased patient.

(d) States the specific uses and limitations on the types of medical information to be disclosed.

(e) States the name or functions of the provider of health care, health care service plan, pharmaceutical company, or contractor that may disclose the medical information.

(f) States the name or functions of the persons or entities authorized to receive the medical information.

(g) States the specific uses and limitations on the use of the medical information by the persons or entities authorized to receive the medical information.

(h) States a specific date after which the provider of health care, health care service plan, pharmaceutical company, or contractor is no longer authorized to disclose the medical information.

(i) Advises the person signing the authorization of the right to receive a copy of the authorization. **Leg.H.** 1981 ch. 782, 1999 ch. 526, 2000 ch. 1066, 2002 ch. 853 (AB 2191), 2003 ch. 562 (AB 715).

Ref.: W. Cal. Ev., "Witnesses" §518.

§56.12. Furnishing copy of authorization to patient.

Upon demand by the patient or the person who signed an authorization, a provider of health care, health care service plan, pharmaceutical company, or contractor possessing the authorization shall furnish a true copy thereof. **Leg.H.** 1981 ch. 782, 1999 ch. 526, 2002 ch. 853 (AB 2191).

Ref.: W. Cal. Ev., "Witnesses" §518.

§56.13. Confidentiality of released medical information.

A recipient of medical information pursuant to an authorization as provided by this chapter or pursuant to the provisions of subdivision (c) of Section 56.10 may not further disclose that medical information except in accordance with a new authorization that meets the requirements of Section 56.11, or as specifically required or permitted by other provisions of this chapter or by law. **Leg.H.** 1981 ch. 782.

Ref.: W. Cal. Ev., "Witnesses" §518.

§56.14. Provider non-liability for unauthorized use of medical information.

A provider of health care, health care service plan, or contractor that discloses medical information pursuant to the authorizations required by this chapter shall communicate to the person or entity to which it discloses the medical information any limitations in the authorization regarding the use of the medical information. No provider of health care, health care service plan, or contractor that has attempted in good faith to comply with this provision shall be liable for any unauthorized use of the medical information by the person or entity to which the provider, plan, or contractor disclosed the medical information. **Leg.H.** 1981 ch. 782, 1999 ch. 526.

Ref.: W. Cal. Ev., "Witnesses" §518.

§56.15. Cancellation or modification of authorization.

Nothing in this part shall be construed to prevent a person who could sign the authorization pursuant to subdivision (c) of Section 56.11 from cancelling or modifying an authorization. However, the cancellation or modification shall be effective only after the provider of health care actually receives written notice of the cancellation or modification. **Leg.H.** 1981 ch. 782.

Ref.: W. Cal. Ev., "Witnesses" §518.

§56.16. Disclosure of nonmedical information permitted.

For disclosures not addressed by Section 56.1007, unless there is a specific written request by the patient to the contrary, nothing in this part shall be construed to prevent a general acute care hospital, as defined in subdivision (a) of Section 1250 of the Health and Safety Code, upon an inquiry concerning a specific patient, from releasing at its discretion any of the following information: the patient's name, address, age, and sex; a general description of the reason for treatment (whether an injury, a burn, poisoning, or some unrelated condition); the general nature of the injury, burn, poisoning, or other condition; the general condition of the patient; and any information that is not medical information as defined in subdivision (c) of Section 56.05. **Leg.H.** 1981 ch. 782, 2006 ch. 833 (AB 3013) §2.

Ref.: Hanna § 22.02[5].

CHAPTER 2.5 DISCLOSURE OF GENETIC TEST RESULTS BY A HEALTH CARE SERVICE PLAN

§56.17. Insurers prohibited from offering or providing different terms, conditions, or benefits based on genetic characteristics; penalties; disclosure of test results for genetic characteristic—Civil and criminal liability.

(a) This section shall apply to the disclosure of genetic test results contained in an applicant's or enrollee's medical records by a health care service plan.

(b) Any person who negligently discloses results of a test for a genetic characteristic to any third party in a manner that identifies or provides identifying characteristics of the person to whom the test results apply, except pursuant to a written authorization as described in subdivision (g), shall be assessed a civil penalty in an amount not to exceed one thousand dollars ($1,000) plus court costs, as determined by the court, which penalty and costs shall be paid to the subject of the test.

(c) Any person who willfully discloses the results of a test for a genetic characteristic to any third party in a manner that identifies or provides identifying characteristics of the person to whom the test results apply, except pursuant to a written authorization as described in subdivision (g), shall be assessed a civil penalty in an amount not less than one thousand dollars ($1,000) and no more than five thousand dollars ($5,000) plus court costs, as determined by the court, which penalty and costs shall be paid to the subject of the test.

(d) Any person who willfully or negligently discloses the results of a test for a genetic characteristic to a third party in a manner that identifies or provides identifying characteristics of the person to whom the test results apply, except pursuant to a written authorization as described in subdivision (g), that results in economic, bodily, or emotional harm to the subject of the test, is guilty of a misdemeanor punishable by a fine not to exceed ten thousand dollars ($10,000).

(e) In addition to the penalties listed in subdivisions (b) and (c), any person who commits any act described in subdivision (b) or (c) shall be liable to the subject for all actual damages, including damages for economic, bodily, or emotional harm which is proximately caused by the act.

(f) Each disclosure made in violation of this section is a separate and actionable offense.

(g) The applicant's "written authorization," as used in this section, shall satisfy the following requirements:

(1) Is written in plain language and is in a typeface no smaller than 14-point type.

(2) Is dated and signed by the individual or a person authorized to act on behalf of the individual.

(3) Specifies the types of persons authorized to disclose information about the individual.

(4) Specifies the nature of the information authorized to be disclosed.

(5) States the name or functions of the persons or entities authorized to receive the information.

(6) Specifies the purposes for which the information is collected.

(7) Specifies the length of time the authorization shall remain valid.

(8) Advises the person signing the authorization of the right to receive a copy of the authorization. Written authorization is required for each separate disclosure of the test results.

(h) This section shall not apply to disclosures required by the Department of Health Services necessary to monitor compliance with Chapter 1 (commencing with Section 124975) of Part 5 of Division 106 of the Health and Safety Code, nor to disclosures required by the Department of Managed Care necessary to administer and enforce compliance with Section 1374.7 of the Health and Safety Code.

(i) For purposes of this section, "genetic characteristic" has the same meaning as that set forth in subdivision (d) of Section 1374.7 of the Health and Safety Code. **Leg.H.** 1995 ch. 695, 1996 ch. 1023, effective September 29, 1996, ch. 532, operative January 1, 1997 (ch. 532 prevails), 1999 chs. 311, 525, operative July 1, 2000, 2000 chs. 857, 941, 2003 ch. 562 (AB 715).

Ref.: W. Cal. Ev., "Witnesses" §518; W. Cal. Sum., 7 "Constitutional Law" §605.

CHAPTER 3 USE AND DISCLOSURE OF MEDICAL INFORMATION BY EMPLOYERS [Selected Provisions]

§56.20. Employer's duty to ensure confidentiality of medical information; employee's right to refuse release of such information.

(a) Each employer who receives medical information shall establish appropriate procedures to ensure the confidentiality and protection from unauthorized use and disclosure of that information. These procedures may include, but are not limited to instruction regarding confidentiality of employees and agents handling files containing medical information, and security systems restricting access to files containing medical information.

(b) No employee shall be discriminated against in terms or conditions of employment due to that employee's refusal to sign an authorization under this part. However, nothing in this section shall prohibit an employer from taking such action as is necessary in the absence of medical information due to an employee's refusal to sign an authorization under this part.

(c) No employer shall use, disclose, or knowingly permit its employees or agents to use or disclose medical information which the employer possesses pertaining to its employees without the patient having first signed an authorization under Section 56.11 or Section 56.21 permitting such use or disclosure, except as follows:

(1) The information may be disclosed if the disclosure is compelled by judicial or administrative process or by any other specific provision of law.

(2) That part of the information which is relevant in a lawsuit, arbitration, grievance, or other claim or challenge to which the employer and employee are parties and in which the patient has placed in issue his or her medical history, mental or physical condition, or treatment may be used or disclosed in connection with that proceeding.

(3) The information may be used only for the purpose of administering and maintaining employee benefit plans, including health care plans and plans providing short-term and long-term disability income, workers' compensation and for determining eligibility for paid and unpaid leave from work for medical reasons.

(4) The information may be disclosed to a provider of health care or other health care professional or facility to aid the diagnosis or treatment of the patient, where the patient or other person specified in subdivision (c) of Section 56.21 is unable to authorize the disclosure.

(d) If an employer agrees in writing with one or more of its employees or maintains a written policy which provides that particular types of medical information shall not be used or disclosed by the employer in particular ways, the employer shall obtain an authorization for such uses or disclosures even if an authorization would not otherwise be required by subdivision (c). **Leg.H.** 1981 ch. 782.

Ref.: W. Cal. Ev., "Witnesses" §§518, 519.

§56.21. Requirements for authorized release of medical information.

An authorization for an employer to disclose medical information shall be valid if it complies with all of the following:

(a) Is handwritten by the person who signs it or is in a typeface no smaller than 14-point type.

(b) Is clearly separate from any other language present on the same page and is executed by a signature that serves no purpose other than to execute the authorization.

(c) Is signed and dated by one of the following:

(1) The patient, except that a patient who is a minor may only sign an authorization for the disclosure of medical information obtained by a provider of health care in the course of furnishing services to which the minor could lawfully have consented under Part 1 (commencing with Section 25) or Part 2.7 (commencing with Section 60) of Division 1.

(2) The legal representative of the patient, if the patient is a minor or incompetent. However, authorization may not be given under this subdivision for the disclosure of medical information that pertains to a competent minor and that was created by a provider of health care in the course of furnishing services to which a minor patient could lawfully have consented under

Part 1 (commencing with Section 25) or Part 2.7 (commencing with Section 60) of Division 1.

(3) The beneficiary or personal representative of a deceased patient.

(d) States the limitations, if any, on the types of medical information to be disclosed.

(e) States the name or functions of the employer or person authorized to disclose the medical information.

(f) States the names or functions of the persons or entities authorized to receive the medical information.

(g) States the limitations, if any, on the use of the medical information by the persons or entities authorized to receive the medical information.

(h) States a specific date after which the employer is no longer authorized to disclose the medical information.

(i) Advises the person who signed the authorization of the right to receive a copy of the authorization. **Leg.H.** 1981 ch. 782, 2003 ch. 562 (AB 715), 2006 ch. 538 (SB 1852) §39.

Ref.: W. Cal. Ev., "Witnesses" §518.

CHAPTER 6
RELATIONSHIP TO EXISTING LAW
[Selected Provisions]

§56.30. Disclosure of medical information not subject to limitations of Part 2.6.

The disclosure and use of the following medical information shall not be subject to the limitations of this part:

(a) (Mental health and developmental disabilities) Information and records obtained in the course of providing services under Division 4 (commencing with Section 4000), Division 4.1 (commencing with Section 4400), Division 4.5 (commencing with Section 4500), Division 5 (commencing with Section 5000), Division 6 (commencing with Section 6000), or Division 7 (commencing with Section 7100) of the Welfare and Institutions Code.

(b) (Public social services) Information and records that are subject to Sections 10850, 14124.1, and 14124.2 of the Welfare and Institutions Code.

(c) (State health services, communicable diseases, developmental disabilities) Information and records maintained pursuant to former Chapter 2 (commencing with Section 200) of Part 1 of Division 1 of the Health and Safety Code and pursuant to the Communicable Disease Prevention and Control Act (subdivision (a) of Section 27 of the Health and Safety Code).

(d) (Licensing and statistics) Information and records maintained pursuant to Division 2 (commencing with Section 1200) and Part 1 (commencing with Section 102100) of Division 102 of the Health and Safety Code; pursuant to Chapter 3 (commencing with Section 1200) of Division 2 of the Business and Professions Code; and pursuant to Section 8608, 8817, or 8909 of the Family Code.

(e) (Medical survey, workers' safety) Information and records acquired and maintained or disclosed pursuant to Sections 1380 and 1382 of the Health and Safety Code and pursuant to Division 5 (commencing with Section 6300) of the Labor Code.

(f) (Industrial accidents) Information and records acquired, maintained, or disclosed pursuant to Division 1 (commencing with Section 50), Division 4 (commencing with Section 3200), Division 4.5 (commencing with Section 6100), and Division 4.7 (commencing with Section 6200) of the Labor Code.

(g) (Law enforcement) Information and records maintained by a health facility which are sought by a law enforcement agency under Chapter 3.5 (commencing with Section 1543) of Title 12 of Part 2 of the Penal Code.

(h) (Investigations of employment accident or illness) Information and records sought as part of an investigation of an on-the-job accident or illness pursuant to Division 5 (commencing with Section 6300) of the Labor Code or pursuant to Section 105200 of the Health and Safety Code.

(i) (Alcohol or drug abuse) Information and records subject to the federal alcohol and drug abuse regulations (Part 2 (commencing with Section 2.1) of subchapter A of Chapter 1 of Title 42 of the Code of Federal Regulations) or to Section 11977 of the Health and Safety Code dealing with narcotic and drug abuse.

(j) (Patient discharge data) Nothing in this part shall be construed to limit, expand, or otherwise affect the authority of the California Health Facilities Commission to collect patient discharge information from health facilities.

(k) Medical information and records disclosed to, and their use by, the Insurance Commissioner, the Director of the Department of

Managed Health Care, the Division of Industrial Accidents, the Workers' Compensation Appeals Board, the Department of Insurance, or the Department of Managed Health Care. **Leg.H.** 1981 ch. 782, 1990 ch. 1363, operative July 1, 1991, 1992 ch. 163, operative January 1, 1994, 1993 ch. 1004, 1996 ch. 1023, effective September 29, 1996, 1999 ch. 526, 2000 ch. 1067.

Ref.: Herlick Handbook § 4.24; W. Cal. Ev., "Witnesses" §518.

§56.31. Disclosure of human immunodeficiency virus.

Notwithstanding any other provision of law, nothing in subdivision (f) of Section 56.30 shall permit the disclosure or use of medical information regarding whether a patient is infected with or exposed to the human immunodeficiency virus without the prior authorization from the patient unless the patient is an injured worker claiming to be infected with or exposed to the human immunodeficiency virus through an exposure incident arising out of and in the course of employment. **Leg.H.** 1999 ch. 766.

1999 Note: The addition of Section 56.31 to the Civil Code by Chapter 766 is not intended either to abrogate the holdings in *Allison v. Workers' Comp. Appeals Bd.* (1999) 72 Cal.App.4th 654, or to prohibit a redaction decision by a workers' compensation judge from being appealed to the Workers' Compensation Appeals Board. Stats. 1999 ch. 766 §3.

Ref.: Herlick Handbook § 4.24; W. Cal. Ev., "Witnesses" §518.

DIVISION 3
OBLIGATIONS

PART 3
Obligations Imposed by Law
[Selected Provisions]

§1708.8. Invasion of privacy—Visual images or sound recordings.

(a) A person is liable for physical invasion of privacy when the defendant knowingly enters onto the land of another person without permission or otherwise committed a trespass in order to physically invade the privacy of the plaintiff with the intent to capture any type of visual image, sound recording, or other physical impression of the plaintiff engaging in a personal or familial activity and the physical invasion occurs in a manner that is offensive to a reasonable person.

(b) A person is liable for constructive invasion of privacy when the defendant attempts to capture, in a manner that is offensive to a reasonable person, any type of visual image, sound recording, or other physical impression of the plaintiff engaging in a personal or familial activity under circumstances in which the plaintiff had a reasonable expectation of privacy, through the use of a visual or auditory enhancing device, regardless of whether there is a physical trespass, if this image, sound recording, or other physical impression could not have been achieved without a trespass unless the visual or auditory enhancing device was used.

(c) An assault committed with the intent to capture any type of visual image, sound recording, or other physical impression of the plaintiff is subject to subdivisions (d), (e), and (h).

(d) A person who commits any act described in subdivision (a), (b), or (c) is liable for up to three times the amount of any general and special damages that are proximately caused by the violation of this section. This person may also be liable for punitive damages, subject to proof according to Section 3294. If the plaintiff proves that the invasion of privacy was committed for a commercial purpose, the defendant shall also be subject to disgorgement to the plaintiff of any proceeds or other consideration obtained as a result of the violation of this section.

(e) A person who directs, solicits, actually induces, or actually causes another person, regardless of whether there is an employer-employee relationship, to violate any provision of subdivision (a), (b), or (c) is liable for any general, special, and consequential damages resulting from each said violation. In addition, the person that directs, solicits, instigates, induces, or otherwise causes another person, regardless of whether there is an employer-employee relationship, to violate this section shall be liable for punitive damages to the extent that an employer would be subject to punitive damages pursuant to subdivision (b) of Section 3294.

(f) Sale, transmission, publication, broadcast, or use of any image or recording of the type, or under the circumstances, described in this section shall not itself constitute a violation of this section, nor shall this section be construed to limit all other rights or remedies of plaintiff in law or equity, including, but not limited to, the publication of private facts.

(g) This section shall not be construed to impair or limit any otherwise lawful activities of law enforcement personnel or employees of governmental agencies or other entities, either public or private who, in the course and scope of their employment, and supported by an articulable suspicion, attempt to capture any type of visual image, sound recording, or other physical impression of a person during an investigation, surveillance, or monitoring of any conduct to obtain evidence of suspected illegal activity, the suspected violation of any administrative rule or regulation, a suspected fraudulent insurance claim, or any other suspected fraudulent conduct or activity involving a violation of law or pattern of business practices adversely affecting the public health or safety.

(h) In any action pursuant to this section, the court may grant equitable relief, including, but not limited to, an injunction and restraining order against further violations of subdivision (a) or (b).

(i) The rights and remedies provided in this section are cumulative and in addition to any other rights and remedies provided by law.

(j) It is not a defense to a violation of this section that no image, recording, or physical impression was captured or sold.

(k) For the purposes of this section, "for a commercial purpose" means any act done with the expectation of a sale, financial gain, or other consideration. A visual image, sound recording, or other physical impression shall not be found to have been, or intended to have been captured for a commercial purpose unless it is intended to be, or was in fact, sold, published, or transmitted.

(*l*) For the purposes of this section, "personal and familial activity" includes, but is not limited to, intimate details of the plaintiff's personal life, interactions with the plaintiff's family or significant others, or other aspects of plaintiff's private affairs or concerns. Personal and familial activity does not include illegal or otherwise criminal activity as delineated in subdivision (f). However, "personal and familial activity" shall include the activities of victims of crime in circumstances where either subdivision (a) or (b), or both, would apply.

(m) The provisions of this section are severable. If any provision of this section or its application is held invalid, that invalidity shall not affect other provisions or applications that can be given effect without the invalid provision or application. **Leg.H.** 1998 ch. 1000, 2005 ch. 424 (AB 381) §1.

Ref.: CACI No. 1800 (Matthew Bender); W. Cal. Sum., 5 "Torts" §663.

DIVISION 4
GENERAL PROVISIONS

PART 1
Relief

TITLE 2
COMPENSATORY RELIEF

CHAPTER 2
MEASURE OF DAMAGES

ARTICLE 2
Damages for Wrongs
[Selected Provisions]

§3333.1. Introduction of evidence of amount payable as benefit in action for personal injury—Health care provider defined—Professional negligence defined.

(a) In the event the defendant so elects, in an action for personal injury against a health care provider based upon professional negligence, he may introduce evidence of any amount payable as a benefit to the plaintiff as a result of the personal injury pursuant to the United States Social Security Act, any state or federal income disability or worker's compensation act, any health, sickness or income-disability insurance, accident insurance that provides health benefits or income-disability coverage, and any contract or agreement of any group, organization, partnership, or corporation to provide, pay for, or reimburse the cost of medical, hospital, dental, or other health care services. Where the defendant elects to introduce such evidence, the plaintiff may introduce evidence of any amount which the plaintiff has paid or contributed to secure his right to any insurance benefits concerning which the defendant has introduced evidence.

(b) No source of collateral benefits introduced pursuant to subdivision (a) shall recover any amount against the plaintiff nor shall it be subrogated to the rights of the plaintiff against a defendant.

(c) For the purposes of this section:

(1) "Health care provider" means any person licensed or certified pursuant to Division 2 (commencing with Section 500) of the Business and Professions Code, or licensed pursuant to the Osteopathic Initiative Act, or the Chiropractic Initiative Act, or licensed pursuant to Chapter 2.5 (commencing with Section 1440) of Division 2 of the Health and Safety Code; and any clinic, health dispensary, or health facility, licensed pursuant to Division 2 (commencing with Section 1200) of the Health and Safety Code. "Health care provider" includes the legal representatives of a health care provider;

(2) "Professional negligence" means a negligent act or omission to act by a health care provider in the rendering of professional services, which act or omission is the proximate cause of a personal injury or wrongful death, provided that such services are within the scope of services for which the provider is licensed and which are not within any restriction imposed by the licensing agency or licensed hospital.

Ref.: CACI No. 500 (Matthew Bender); W. Cal. Ev., "Circumstantial Evidence" §160; W. Cal. Sum., 2 "Workers' Compensation" §74, 6 "Torts" §§956, 957, 1631, 1637.

SELECTED PROVISIONS Of The CODE OF CIVIL PROCEDURE

PART 2 OF CIVIL ACTIONS

TITLE 9 Enforcement of Judgments

DIVISION 2 ENFORCEMENT OF MONEY JUDGMENTS

CHAPTER 2 LIENS

ARTICLE 2 Judgment Lien on Real Property [Selected Provisions]

§697.330. Creation and duration of judgment lien based on workers' compensation award.

(a) In the case of a money judgment entered on an order, decision, or award made under Division 4 (commencing with Section 3200) of the Labor Code (workers' compensation):

(1) If the judgment is for a lump sum, a judgment lien on real property is created by recording an abstract of the judgment as provided in Section 697.310 and, except as otherwise provided in Division 4 (commencing with Section 3200) of the Labor Code, the judgment lien is governed by the provisions applicable to a judgment lien created under Section 697.310.

(2) If the judgment is for the payment of money in installments, a judgment lien on real property is created by recording a certified copy of the judgment as provided in Section 697.320 and, except as otherwise provided in Division 4 (commencing with Section 3200) of the Labor Code, the lien is governed by the provisions applicable to a judgment lien created under Section 697.320.

(b) Nothing in this section limits or affects any provision of Division 4 (commencing with Section 3200) of the Labor Code.

Ref.: MB Prac. Guide: Cal. Debt Collection & Enforcement of Judgments, §§11.02, 11.03, 11.08[1], [2], 17.04, 17.06.

CHAPTER 4 EXEMPTIONS

ARTICLE 3 Exempt Property [Selected Provisions]

§704.160. Workers' compensation claim, award, or payment—Application to support judgment.

(a) Except as provided by Chapter 1 (commencing with Section 4900) of Part 3 of Division 4 of the Labor Code, before payment, a claim for workers' compensation or workers' compensation awarded or adjudged is exempt without making a claim. Except as specified in

Misc. Provisions

subdivision (b), after payment, the award is exempt.

(b) Notwithstanding any other provision of law, during the payment of workers' compensation temporary disability benefits described in subdivision (a) to a support judgment debtor, the support judgment creditor may, through the appropriate local child support agency, seek to apply the workers' compensation temporary disability benefit payment to satisfy the support judgment as provided by Section 17404 of the Family Code.

(c) Notwithstanding any other provision of law, during the payment of workers' compensation temporary disability benefits described in subdivision (a) to a support judgment debtor under a support judgment, including a judgment for reimbursement of public assistance, the judgment creditor may, directly or through the appropriate local child support agency, seek to apply the temporary disability benefit payments to satisfy the support judgment by an earnings assignment order for support, as defined in Section 5208 of the Family Code, or any other applicable enforcement procedure. The amount to be withheld pursuant to the earnings assignment order for support or other enforcement procedure shall be 25 percent of the amount of each periodic payment or any lower amount specified in writing by the judgment creditor or court order, rounded down to the nearest dollar. Otherwise, the amount to be withheld shall be the amount the court determines under subdivision (c) of Section 703.070. The paying entity may deduct from each payment made pursuant to an order assigning earnings under this subdivision an amount reflecting the actual cost of administration of this assignment, up to two dollars ($2) for each payment.

(d) Unless the provision or context otherwise requires, the following definitions govern the construction of this section.

(1) "Judgment debtor" or "support judgment debtor" means a person who is owing a duty of support.

(2) "Judgment creditor" or "support judgment creditor" means the person to whom support has been ordered to be paid.

(3) "Support" refers to an obligation owing on behalf of a child, spouse, or family; or an amount owing pursuant to Section 17402 of the Family Code. It also includes past due support or arrearage when it exists. **Leg.H.** 1982 ch. 1364, operative July 1, 1983, 1992 ch. 848, effective September 22, 1992, 1993 ch. 219, 2000 ch. 808, effective September 28, 2000.

Ref.: MB Prac. Guide: Cal. Debt Collection & Enforcement of Judgments, §§1.40, 10.03, 10.07[1], 16.02, 16.03[1], 16.05, 16.06[3], 16.17, 16.18, 16.38, 16.45, 16.53; MB Prac. Guide: Fed. Pretrial Proc. in Cal., §19.48[1].

TITLE 14
Miscellaneous Provisions

CHAPTER 5
NOTICES, AND FILING AND SERVICE OF PAPERS
[Selected Provisions]

§1013. Service by mail, Express Mail, overnight delivery, or facsimile transmission—Method of service.

(a) In case of service by mail, the notice or other paper shall be deposited in a post office, mailbox, subpost office, substation, or mail chute, or other like facility regularly maintained by the United States Postal Service, in a sealed envelope, with postage paid, addressed to the person on whom it is to be served, at the office address as last given by that person on any document filed in the cause and served on the party making service by mail; otherwise at that party's place of residence. The service is complete at the time of the deposit, but any period of notice and any right or duty to do any act or make any response within any period or on a date certain after the service of the document, which time period or date is prescribed by statute or rule of court, shall be extended five calendar days, upon service by mail, if the place of address and the place of mailing is within the State of California, 10 calendar days if either the place of mailing or the place of address is outside the State of California but within the United States, and 20 calendar days if either the place of mailing or the place of address is outside the United States, but the extension shall not apply to extend the time for filing notice of intention to move for new trial, notice of intention to move to vacate judgment pursuant to Section 663a, or notice of appeal. This extension applies in the absence of a specific exception provided for by this section or other statute or rule of court.

(b) The copy of the notice or other paper served by mail pursuant to this chapter shall bear a notation of the date and place of mailing or be accompanied by an unsigned copy of the affidavit or certificate of mailing.

(c) In case of service by Express Mail, the notice or other paper must be deposited in a post office, mailbox, subpost office, substation, or mail chute, or other like facility regularly maintained by the United States Postal Service for receipt of Express Mail, in a sealed envelope, with Express Mail postage paid, addressed to the person on whom it is to be served, at the office address as last given by that person on any document filed in the cause and served on the party making service by Express Mail; otherwise at that party's place of residence. In case of service by another method of delivery providing for overnight delivery, the notice or other paper must be deposited in a box or other facility regularly maintained by the express service carrier, or delivered to an authorized courier or driver authorized by the express service carrier to receive documents, in an envelope or package designated by the express service carrier with delivery fees paid or provided for, addressed to the person on whom it is to be served, at the office address as last given by that person on any document filed in the cause and served on the party making service; otherwise at that party's place of residence. The service is complete at the time of the deposit, but any period of notice and any right or duty to do any act or make any response within any period or on a date certain after the service of the document served by Express Mail or other method of delivery providing for overnight delivery shall be extended by two court days, but the extension shall not apply to extend the time for filing notice of intention to move for new trial, notice of intention to move to vacate judgment pursuant to Section 663a, or notice of appeal. This extension applies in the absence of a specific exception provided for by this section or other statute or rule of court.

(d) The copy of the notice or other paper served by Express Mail or another means of delivery providing for overnight delivery pursuant to this chapter shall bear a notation of the date and place of deposit or be accompanied by an unsigned copy of the affidavit or certificate of deposit.

(e) Service by facsimile transmission shall be permitted only where the parties agree and a written confirmation of that agreement is made. The Judicial Council may adopt rules implementing the service of documents by facsimile transmission and may provide a form for the confirmation of the agreement required by this subdivision. In case of service by facsimile transmission, the notice or other paper must be transmitted to a facsimile machine maintained by the person on whom it is served at the facsimile machine telephone number as last given by that person on any document which he or she has filed in the cause and served on the party making the service. The service is complete at the time of transmission, but any period of notice and any right or duty to do any act or make any response within any period or on a date certain after the service of the document, which time period or date is prescribed by statute or rule of court, shall be extended, after service by facsimile transmission, by two court days, but the extension shall not apply to extend the time for filing notice of intention to move for new trial, notice of intention to move to vacate judgment pursuant to Section 663a, or notice of appeal. This extension applies in the absence of a specific exception provided for by this section or other statute or rule of court.

(f) The copy of the notice or other paper served by facsimile transmission pursuant to this chapter shall bear a notation of the date and place of transmission and the facsimile telephone number to which transmitted or be accompanied by an unsigned copy of the affidavit or certificate of transmission which shall contain the facsimile telephone number to which the notice or other paper was transmitted.

(g) Subdivisions (b), (d), and (f) are directory. **Leg.H.** 1872, 1874 p. 343, 1907 p. 602, 1929 p. 845, 1931 ch. 739, 1949 ch. 456, 1967 ch. 169, 1968 ch. 166, 1974 ch. 281, 282 §2, 1980 ch. 196, 1992 ch. 339, 1995 ch. 576, 2001 ch. 812.

Ref.: MB Prac. Guide: Cal. Contract Lit., §§5.15, 5.20[4], [5][d], 5.25[1]; MB Prac. Guide: Cal. Debt Collection & Enforcement of Judgments, §§9.35[1][d], [2][c], 16.51[5][d]; MB Prac. Guide: Cal. Pretrial Proc., Ch. 27; MB Prac. Guide: Cal. Trial & Post-Trial Civ. Proc., §§3.09[3], 7.18, 20.25, 21.25, 22.14, 24.35[3][b], [c], 24.36, 24.41[3], 24.46, 27.03, 27.06[2], 29.15[5], 29.32[1][c]; CACI Nos. 4303, 4305, 4307, 4320 (Matthew Bender); W. Cal. Ev., "Discovery" §§7, 24, 97, 175, 232, 237; W. Cal. Sum., 2 "Workers' Compensation" §§388, 438, 3 "Agency and Employment" §§319, 672, 10 "Parent and Child" §416, 11 "Husband and Wife" §§107, 251, 270, 272, 313, 12 "Real Property" §§521, 526, 680, 727, 737.

PART 4
Miscellaneous Provisions

TITLE 4
CIVIL DISCOVERY ACT

CHAPTER 1
GENERAL PROVISIONS

§2016.010. Short title.

This title may be cited as the "Civil Discovery Act." **Leg.H.** 2004 ch. 182 (AB 3081), operative July 1, 2005.

Ref.: Herlick Handbook § 14.20; MB Prac. Guide: Cal. Debt Collection & Enforcement of Judgments, §8.43; W. Cal. Sum., 2 "Insurance" §210, 11 "Husband and Wife" §291.

§2016.020. Definitions.

As used in this title:

(a) "Action" includes a civil action and a special proceeding of a civil nature.

(b) "Court" means the trial court in which the action is pending, unless otherwise specified.

(c) "Document" and "writing" mean a writing, as defined in Section 250 of the Evidence Code. **Leg.H.** 2004 ch. 182 (AB 3081), operative July 1, 2005.

Ref.: Herlick Handbook § 14.20.

§2016.030. Modification by written stipulation.

Unless the court orders otherwise, the parties may by written stipulation modify the procedures provided by this title for any method of discovery permitted under Section 2019.010. **Leg.H.** 2004 ch. 182 (AB 3081), operative July 1, 2005.

Ref.: Herlick Handbook § 14.20.

§2016.040. What meet and confer declaration in support of motion to show.

A meet and confer declaration in support of a motion shall state facts showing a reasonable and good faith attempt at an informal resolution of each issue presented by the motion. **Leg.H.** 2004 ch. 182 (AB 3081), operative July 1, 2005.

Ref.: Herlick Handbook § 14.20.

§2016.050. Applicability of CCP §1013.

Section 1013 applies to any method of discovery or service of a motion provided for in this title. **Leg.H.** 2004 ch. 182 (AB 3081), operative July 1, 2005.

Ref.: Herlick Handbook § 14.20.

§2016.060. Specified date falling on Saturday, Sunday or holiday; extension of time limit.

When the last day to perform or complete any act provided for in this title falls on a Saturday, Sunday, or holiday as specified in Section 10, the time limit is extended until the next court day closer to the trial date. **Leg.H.** 2004 ch. 182 (AB 3081) §23.5, operative July 1, 2005.

Ref.: Herlick Handbook § 14.20.

§2016.070. Applicability of title to enforcement of money judgment.

This title applies to discovery in aid of enforcement of a money judgment only to the extent provided in Article 1 (commencing with Section 708.010) of Chapter 6 of Title 9 of Part 2. **Leg.H.** 2004 ch. 182 (AB 3081), operative July 1, 2005.

Ref.: Herlick Handbook § 14.20.

CHAPTER 2
SCOPE OF DISCOVERY
[Selected Provisions]

ARTICLE 1
General Provisions

§2017.010. What matters may be subject to discovery.

Unless otherwise limited by order of the court in accordance with this title, any party may obtain discovery regarding any matter, not privileged, that is relevant to the subject matter involved in the pending action or to the determination of any motion made in that action, if the matter either is itself admissible in evidence or appears reasonably calculated to lead to the discovery of admissible evidence. Discovery may relate to the claim or defense of the party seeking discovery or of any other party to the action. Discovery may be obtained of the identity and location of persons having knowledge of any discoverable matter, as well as of the existence, description, nature, custody, condition, and location of any document, tangible thing, or land or other property. **Leg.H.** 2004 ch. 182 (AB 3081), operative July 1, 2005.

Ref.: MB Prac. Guide: Cal. Debt Collection & Enforcement of Judgments, §9.39[2][d]; MB Prac. Guide: Fed. Pretrial Proc. in Cal., §24.06; MB Prac. Guide: Cal. Trial & Post-Trial Civ. Proc., §7.15[4]; W. Cal. Sum., 7 "Constitutional Law" §581.

§2017.020. When court may limit scope of discovery; motion for protective order; monetary sanction.

(a) The court shall limit the scope of discovery if it determines that the burden, expense, or intrusiveness of that discovery clearly outweighs the likelihood that the information sought will lead to the discovery of admissible evidence. The court may make this determination pursuant to a motion for protective order by a party or other affected person. This motion shall be accompanied by a meet and confer declaration under Section 2016.040.

(b) The court shall impose a monetary sanction under Chapter 7 (commencing with Section 2023.010) against any party, person, or attorney who unsuccessfully makes or opposes a motion for a protective order, unless it finds that the one subject to the sanction acted with substantial justification or that other circumstances make the imposition of the sanction unjust. **Leg.H.** 2004 ch. 182 (AB 3081), operative July 1, 2005.

ARTICLE 2
Scope of Discovery in Specific Contexts

§2017.210. Information concerning insurance.

A party may obtain discovery of the existence and contents of any agreement under which any insurance carrier may be liable to satisfy in whole or in part a judgment that may be entered in the action or to indemnify or reimburse for payments made to satisfy the judgment. This discovery may include the identity of the carrier and the nature and limits of the coverage. A party may also obtain discovery as to whether that insurance carrier is disputing the agreement's coverage of the claim involved in the action, but not as to the nature and substance of that dispute. Information concerning the insurance agreement is not by reason of disclosure admissible in evidence at trial. **Leg.H.** 2004 ch. 182 (AB 3081), operative July 1, 2005.

Ref.: W. Cal. Sum., 2 "Insurance" §260.

§2017.220. Discovery regarding plaintiff's sexual conduct in certain actions; showing of good cause; monetary sanction.

(a) In any civil action alleging conduct that constitutes sexual harassment, sexual assault, or sexual battery, any party seeking discovery concerning the plaintiff's sexual conduct with individuals other than the alleged perpetrator shall establish specific facts showing that there is good cause for that discovery, and that the matter sought to be discovered is relevant to the subject matter of the action and reasonably calculated to lead to the discovery of admissible evidence. This showing shall be made by a noticed motion, accompanied by a meet and confer declaration under Section 2016.040, and shall not be made or considered by the court at an ex parte hearing.

(b) The court shall impose a monetary sanction under Chapter 7 (commencing with Section 2023.010) against any party, person, or attorney who unsuccessfully makes or opposes a motion for discovery under subdivision (a), unless it finds that the one subject to the sanction acted with substantial justification or that other circumstances make the imposition of the sanction unjust. **Leg.H.** 2004 ch. 182 (AB 3081), operative July 1, 2005.

CHAPTER 3
USE OF TECHNOLOGY IN CONDUCTING DISCOVERY IN A COMPLEX CASE

§2017.710. Meaning of "technology" as used in chapter.

Subject to the findings required by Section 2017.730 and the purpose of permitting and encouraging cost-effective and efficient discovery, "technology," as used in this chapter, includes, but is not limited to, telephone, e-mail, CD-ROM, Internet Web sites, electronic documents, electronic document depositories, Internet depositions and storage, videoconferencing, and other electronic technology that may be used to improve communication and the discovery process. **Leg.H.** 2004 ch. 182 (AB 3081), operative July 1, 2005.

§2017.720. Effect of chapter on rights, duties and responsibilities of parties; use of stenographic court reporter.

(a) Nothing in this chapter diminishes the rights and duties of the parties regarding discovery, privileges, procedural rights, or substantive law.

(b) Nothing in this chapter modifies the requirement for use of a stenographic court reporter as provided in Section 2025.330. The rules, standards, and guidelines adopted pursuant to this chapter shall be consistent with the requirement of Section 2025.330 that deposition testimony be taken stenographically unless the parties agree or the court orders otherwise.

(c) Nothing in this chapter modifies or affects in any way the process used for the selection of a stenographic court reporter. **Leg.H.** 2004 ch. 182 (AB 3081), operative July 1, 2005.

§2017.730. Order authorizing use of technology in conducting discovery; when permitted; criteria; promulgation of rules and standards.

(a) Pursuant to a noticed motion, a court may enter an order authorizing the use of technology in conducting discovery in any of the following:

(1) A case designated as complex under Section 19 of the Judicial Administration Standards.

(2) A case ordered to be coordinated under Chapter 3 (commencing with Section 404) of Title 4 of Part 2.

(3) An exceptional case exempt from case disposition time goals under Article 5 (commencing with Section 68600) of Chapter 2 of Title 8 of the Government Code.

(4) A case assigned to Plan 3 under paragraph (3) of subdivision (b) of Section 2105 of the California Rules of Court.

(b) In a case other than one listed in subdivision (a), the parties may stipulate to the entry of an order authorizing the use of technology in conducting discovery.

(c) An order authorizing the use of technology in conducting discovery may be made only upon the express findings of the court or stipulation of the parties that the procedures adopted in the order meet all of the following criteria:

(1) They promote cost-effective and efficient discovery or motions relating thereto.

(2) They do not impose or require an undue expenditure of time or money.

(3) They do not create an undue economic burden or hardship on any person.

(4) They promote open competition among vendors and providers of services in order to facilitate the highest quality service at the lowest reasonable cost to the litigants.

(5) They do not require the parties or counsel to purchase exceptional or unnecessary services, hardware, or software.

(d) Pursuant to an order authorizing the use of technology in conducting discovery, discovery may be conducted and maintained in electronic media and by electronic communication. The court may enter orders prescribing procedures relating to the use of electronic technology in conducting discovery, including orders for service of discovery requests and responses, service and presentation of motions, conduct of discovery in electronic media, and production, storage, and access to information in electronic form.

(e) The Judicial Council may promulgate rules, standards, and guidelines relating to electronic discovery and the use of electronic discovery data and documents in court proceedings. **Leg.H.** 2004 ch. 182 (AB 3081), operative July 1, 2005.

§2017.740. Service provider; selection and appointment; removal; periodic review.

(a) If a service provider is to be used and compensated by the parties in discovery under this chapter, the court shall appoint the person or organization agreed on by the parties and approve the contract agreed on by the parties and the service provider. If the parties do not agree on selection of a service provider, each party shall submit to the court up to three nominees for appointment, together with a contract acceptable to the nominee. The court shall appoint a service provider from among the nominees. The court may condition this appointment on the acceptance of modifications in the terms of the contract. If no nominations are received from any of the parties, the court shall appoint one or more service providers.

(b) Pursuant to a noticed motion at any time and on a showing of good cause, the court may order the removal of the service provider or vacate any agreement between the parties and the service provider, or both, effective as of the date of the order. The continued service of the service provider shall be subject to review periodically, as agreed by the parties and the service provider, or annually if they do not agree. Any disputes involving the contract or the duties, rights, and obligations of the parties or the service provider may be determined on a noticed motion in the action. **Leg.H.** 2004 ch. 182 (AB 3081), operative July 1, 2005.

CHAPTER 4
ATTORNEY WORK PRODUCT

§2018.010. Meaning of "client" for purposes of chapter.

For purposes of this chapter, "client" means a "client" as defined in Section 951 of the Evidence Code. **Leg.H.** 2004 ch. 182 (AB 3081), operative July 1, 2005.

§2018.020. Policy of state.

It is the policy of the state to do both of the following:

(a) Preserve the rights of attorneys to prepare cases for trial with that degree of privacy necessary to encourage them to prepare their cases thoroughly and to investigate not only the favorable but the unfavorable aspects of those cases.

(b) Prevent attorneys from taking undue advantage of their adversary's industry and efforts. **Leg.H.** 2004 ch. 182 (AB 3081), operative July 1, 2005.

§2018.030. Certain writings not discoverable; when other work product may be subject to discovery.

(a) A writing that reflects an attorney's impressions, conclusions, opinions, or legal research or theories is not discoverable under any circumstances.

(b) The work product of an attorney, other than a writing described in subdivision (a), is not discoverable unless the court determines that denial of discovery will unfairly prejudice the party seeking discovery in preparing that party's claim or defense or will result in an injustice. **Leg.H.** 2004 ch. 182 (AB 3081), operative July 1, 2005.

§2018.040. Restatement of existing law.

This chapter is intended to be a restatement of existing law relating to protection of work product. It is not intended to expand or reduce the extent to which work product is discoverable under existing law in any action. **Leg.H.** 2004 ch. 182 (AB 3081), operative July 1, 2005.

§2018.050. Work product enabling commission of crime not protected in official investigations.

Notwithstanding Section 2018.040, when a lawyer is suspected of knowingly participating in a crime or fraud, there is no protection of work product under this chapter in any official investigation by a law enforcement agency or proceeding or action brought by a public prosecutor in the name of the people of the State of California if the services of the lawyer were sought or obtained to enable or aid anyone to commit or plan to commit a crime or fraud. **Leg.H.** 2004 ch. 182 (AB 3081), operative July 1, 2005.

§2018.060. Right to request in camera hearing.

Nothing in this chapter is intended to limit an attorney's ability to request an in camera hearing as provided for in People v. Superior Court (Laff) (2001) 25 Cal.4th 703. **Leg.H.** 2004 ch. 182 (AB 3081), operative July 1, 2005.

§2018.070. Discovery for purposes of State Bar disciplinary proceedings; protective order; client approval.

(a) The State Bar may discover the work product of an attorney against whom disciplinary charges are pending when it is relevant to issues of breach of duty by the lawyer and requisite client approval has been granted.

(b) Where requested and for good cause, discovery under this section shall be subject to a protective order to ensure the confidentiality of the work product except for its use by the State Bar in disciplinary investigations and its consideration under seal in State Bar Court proceedings.

(c) For purposes of this chapter, whenever a client has initiated a complaint against an attorney, the requisite client approval shall be deemed to have been granted. **Leg.H.** 2004 ch. 182 (AB 3081), operative July 1, 2005.

§2018.080. No privilege when work product relevant to issue of breach of attorney-client relationship.

In an action between an attorney and a client or a former client of the attorney, no work product privilege under this chapter exists if the work product is relevant to an issue of breach by the attorney of a duty to the client arising out of the attorney-client relationship. **Leg.H.** 2004 ch. 182 (AB 3081), operative July 1, 2005.

CHAPTER 5
METHODS AND SEQUENCE OF DISCOVERY

ARTICLE 1
General Provisions

§2019.010. Methods of discovery.

Any party may obtain discovery by one or more of the following methods:

(a) Oral and written depositions.

(b) Interrogatories to a party.

(c) Inspections of documents, things, and places.

(d) Physical and mental examinations.

(e) Requests for admissions.

(f) Simultaneous exchanges of expert trial witness information. **Leg.H.** 2004 ch. 182 (AB 3081), operative July 1, 2005.

§2019.020. Sequence and timing of discovery.

(a) Except as otherwise provided by a rule of the Judicial Council, a local court rule, or a local uniform written policy, the methods of discovery may be used in any sequence, and the fact that a party is conducting discovery, whether by deposition or another method, shall not operate to delay the discovery of any other party.

(b) Notwithstanding subdivision (a), on motion and for good cause shown, the court may establish the sequence and timing of discovery for the convenience of parties and witnesses and in the interests of justice. **Leg.H.** 2004 ch. 182 (AB 3081), operative July 1, 2005.

§2019.030. When frequency or extent of discovery may be restricted; motion for protective order; monetary sanction.

(a) The court shall restrict the frequency or extent of use of a discovery method provided in Section 2019.010 if it determines either of the following:

(1) The discovery sought is unreasonably cumulative or duplicative, or is obtainable from some other source that is more convenient, less burdensome, or less expensive.

(2) The selected method of discovery is unduly burdensome or expensive, taking into account the needs of the case, the amount in controversy, and the importance of the issues at stake in the litigation.

(b) The court may make these determinations pursuant to a motion for a protective order by a party or other affected person. This motion shall be accompanied by a meet and confer declaration under Section 2016.040.

(c) The court shall impose a monetary sanction under Chapter 7 (commencing with Section 2023.010) against any party, person, or attorney who unsuccessfully makes or opposes a motion for a protective order, unless it finds that the one subject to the sanction acted with substantial justification or that other circumstances make the imposition of the sanction unjust. **Leg.H.** 2004 ch. 182 (AB 3081), operative July 1, 2005.

Ref.: MB Prac. Guide: Cal. Trial & Post-Trial Civ. Proc., §7.15[6].

ARTICLE 2
Methods and Sequence of Discovery in Specific Contexts

§2019.210. Misappropriation of trade secret.

In any action alleging the misappropriation of a trade secret under the Uniform Trade Secrets Act (Title 5 (commencing with Section 3426) of Part 1 of Division 4 of the Civil Code), before commencing discovery relating to the trade secret, the party alleging the misappropriation shall identify the trade secret with reasonable particularity subject to any orders that may be appropriate under Section 3426.5 of the Civil Code. **Leg.H.** 2004 ch. 182 (AB 3081), operative July 1, 2005.

Ref.: MB Prac. Guide: Cal. Contract Lit., §§25.02, 25.22[4]; MB Prac. Guide: Fed. Pretrial Proc. in Cal., §24.93; W. Cal. Sum., 13 "Equity" §92.

CHAPTER 6 NONPARTY DISCOVERY

ARTICLE 1 General Provisions

§2020.010. Methods for discovery within state from nonparty.

(a) Any of the following methods may be used to obtain discovery within the state from a person who is not a party to the action in which the discovery is sought:

(1) An oral deposition under Chapter 9 (commencing with Section 2025.010).

(2) A written deposition under Chapter 11 (commencing with Section 2028.010).

(3) A deposition for production of business records and things under Article 4 (commencing with Section 2020.410) or Article 5 (commencing with Section 2020.510).

(b) Except as provided in subdivision (a) of Section 2025.280, the process by which a nonparty is required to provide discovery is a deposition subpoena. **Leg.H.** 2004 ch. 182 (AB 3081), operative July 1, 2005.

Ref.: W. Cal. Sum., 14 "Wills and Probate" §597.

§2020.020. What deposition subpoena may command.

A deposition subpoena may command any of the following:

(a) Only the attendance and the testimony of the deponent, under Article 3 (commencing with Section 2020.310).

(b) Only the production of business records for copying, under Article 4 (commencing with Section 2020.410).

(c) The attendance and the testimony of the deponent, as well as the production of business records, other documents, and tangible things, under Article 5 (commencing with Section 2020.510). **Leg.H.** 2004 ch. 182 (AB 3081), operative July 1, 2005.

§2020.030. Provisions applicable to deposition subpoena.

Except as modified in this chapter, the provisions of Chapter 2 (commencing with Section 1985) of Title 3 of Part 4 of this code, and of Article 4 (commencing with Section 1560) of Chapter 2 of Division 11 of the Evidence Code, apply to a deposition subpoena. **Leg.H.** 2004 ch. 182 (AB 3081), operative July 1, 2005.

ARTICLE 2 Procedures Applicable to All Types of Deposition Subpoenas

§2020.210. Issuance of deposition subpoena by clerk of court or attorney of record.

(a) The clerk of the court in which the action is pending shall issue a deposition subpoena signed and sealed, but otherwise in blank, to a party requesting it, who shall fill it in before service.

(b) Instead of a court-issued deposition subpoena, an attorney of record for any party may sign and issue a deposition subpoena. A deposition subpoena issued under this subdivision need not be sealed. A copy may be served on the nonparty, and the attorney may retain the original. **Leg.H.** 2004 ch. 182 (AB 3081), operative July 1, 2005.

Ref.: MB Prac. Guide: Cal. Trial & Post-Trial Civ. Proc., §7.15[2], [3].

§2020.220. Service of deposition subpoena.

(a) Subject to subdivision (c) of Section 2020.410, service of a deposition subpoena shall be effected a sufficient time in advance of the deposition to provide the deponent a reasonable opportunity to locate and produce any designated business records, documents, and tangible things, as described in Article 4 (commencing with Section 2020.410), and, where personal attendance is commanded, a reasonable time to travel to the place of deposition.

(b) Any person may serve the subpoena by personal delivery of a copy of it as follows:

(1) If the deponent is a natural person, to that person.

(2) If the deponent is an organization, to any officer, director, custodian of records, or to any

agent or employee authorized by the organization to accept service of a subpoena.

(c) Personal service of any deposition subpoena is effective to require all of the following of any deponent who is a resident of California at the time of service:

(1) Personal attendance and testimony, if the subpoena so specifies.

(2) Any specified production, inspection, testing, and sampling.

(3) The deponent's attendance at a court session to consider any issue arising out of the deponent's refusal to be sworn, or to answer any question, or to produce specified items, or to permit inspection or photocopying, if the subpoena so specifies, or specified testing and sampling of the items produced. **Leg.H.** 2004 ch. 182 (AB 3081), operative July 1, 2005.

§2020.230. Witness fee and mileage.

(a) If a deposition subpoena requires the personal attendance of the deponent, under Article 3 (commencing with Section 2020.310) or Article 5 (commencing with Section 2020.510), the party noticing the deposition shall pay to the deponent in cash or by check the same witness fee and mileage required by Chapter 1 (commencing with Section 68070) of Title 8 of the Government Code for attendance and testimony before the court in which the action is pending. This payment, whether or not demanded by the deponent, shall be made, at the option of the party noticing the deposition, either at the time of service of the deposition subpoena, or at the time the deponent attends for the taking of testimony.

(b) Service of a deposition subpoena that does not require the personal attendance of a custodian of records or other qualified person, under Article 4 (commencing with Section 2020.410), shall be accompanied, whether or not demanded by the deponent, by a payment in cash or by check of the witness fee required by paragraph (6) of subdivision (b) of Section 1563 of the Evidence Code. **Leg.H.** 2004 ch. 182 (AB 3081), operative July 1, 2005.

§2020.240. Punishment for disobeying deposition subpoena; contempt; forfeiture and damages.

A deponent who disobeys a deposition subpoena in any manner described in subdivision (c) of Section 2020.220 may be punished for contempt under Chapter 7 (commencing with Section 2023.010) without the necessity of a prior order of court directing compliance by the witness. The deponent is also subject to the forfeiture and the payment of damages set forth in Section 1992. **Leg.H.** 2004 ch. 182 (AB 3081), operative July 1, 2005.

ARTICLE 3
Subpoena Commanding Only Attendance and Testimony of the Deponent

§2020.310. Rules applicable to deposition subpoena commanding only attendance and testimony.

The following rules apply to a deposition subpoena that commands only the attendance and the testimony of the deponent:

(a) The subpoena shall specify the time when and the place where the deponent is commanded to attend the deposition.

(b) The subpoena shall set forth a summary of all of the following:

(1) The nature of a deposition.

(2) The rights and duties of the deponent.

(3) The penalties for disobedience of a deposition subpoena, as described in Section 2020.240.

(c) If the deposition will be recorded using audio or video technology by, or at the direction of, the noticing party under Section 2025.340, the subpoena shall state that it will be recorded in that manner.

(d) If the deposition testimony will be conducted using instant visual display, the subpoena shall state that it will be conducted in that manner.

(e) If the deponent is an organization, the subpoena shall describe with reasonable particularity the matters on which examination is requested. The subpoena shall also advise the organization of its duty to make the designation of employees or agents who will attend the deposition, as described in Section 2025.230. **Leg.H.** 2004 ch. 182 (AB 3081), operative July 1, 2005.

ARTICLE 4
Subpoena Commanding Only Production of Business Records for Copying

§2020.410. What deposition subpoena commanding only production of business records to contain; description of records; records pertaining to consumer.

(a) A deposition subpoena that commands only the production of business records for copying shall designate the business records to be produced either by specifically describing each individual item or by reasonably particularizing each category of item.

(b) Notwithstanding subdivision (a), specific information identifiable only to the deponent's records system, like a policy number or the date when a consumer interacted with the witness, is not required.

(c) A deposition subpoena that commands only the production of business records for copying need not be accompanied by an affidavit or declaration showing good cause for the production of the business records designated in it. It shall be directed to the custodian of those records or another person qualified to certify the records. It shall command compliance in accordance with Section 2020.430 on a date that is no earlier than 20 days after the issuance, or 15 days after the service, of the deposition subpoena, whichever date is later.

(d) If, under Section 1985.3 or 1985.6, the one to whom the deposition subpoena is directed is a witness, and the business records described in the deposition subpoena are personal records pertaining to a consumer, the service of the deposition subpoena shall be accompanied either by a copy of the proof of service of the notice to the consumer described in subdivision (e) of Section 1985.3, or subdivision (b) of Section 1985.6, as applicable, or by the consumer's written authorization to release personal records described in paragraph (2) of subdivision (c) of Section 1985.3, or paragraph (2) of subdivision (c) of Section 1985.6, as applicable. **Leg.H.** 2004 ch. 182 (AB 3081), operative July 1, 2005.

§2020.420. Deposition officer.

The officer for a deposition seeking discovery only of business records for copying under this article shall be a professional photocopier registered under Chapter 20 (commencing with Section 22450) of Division 8 of the Business and Professions Code, or a person exempted from the registration requirements of that chapter under Section 22451 of the Business and Professions Code. This deposition officer shall not be financially interested in the action, or a relative or employee of any attorney of the parties. Any objection to the qualifications of the deposition officer is waived unless made before the date of production or as soon thereafter as the ground for that objection becomes known or could be discovered by reasonable diligence. **Leg.H.** 2004 ch. 182 (AB 3081), operative July 1, 2005.

§2020.430. Delivery to deposition officer; copy of records and affidavit; duties of custodian; date for delivery; applicability of specified provisions.

(a) Except as provided in subdivision (e), if a deposition subpoena commands only the production of business records for copying, the custodian of the records or other qualified person shall, in person, by messenger, or by mail, deliver both of the following only to the deposition officer specified in the subpoena:

(1) A true, legible, and durable copy of the records.

(2) An affidavit in compliance with Section 1561 of the Evidence Code.

(b) If the delivery required by subdivision (a) is made to the office of the deposition officer, the records shall be enclosed, sealed, and directed as described in subdivision (c) of Section 1560 of the Evidence Code.

(c) If the delivery required by subdivision (a) is made at the office of the business whose records are the subject of the deposition subpoena, the custodian of those records or other qualified person shall do one of the following:

(1) Permit the deposition officer specified in the deposition subpoena to make a copy of the originals of the designated business records during normal business hours, as defined in subdivision (e) of Section 1560 of the Evidence Code.

(2) Deliver to the deposition officer a true, legible, and durable copy of the records on receipt of payment in cash or by check, by or on behalf of the party serving the deposition subpoena, of the reasonable costs of preparing that copy, together with an itemized statement of the

cost of preparation, as determined under subdivision (b) of Section 1563 of the Evidence Code. This copy need not be delivered in a sealed envelope.

(d) Unless the parties, and if the records are those of a consumer as defined in Section 1985.3 or 1985.6, the consumer, stipulate to an earlier date, the custodian of the records shall not deliver to the deposition officer the records that are the subject of the deposition subpoena prior to the date and time specified in the deposition subpoena. The following legend shall appear in boldface type on the deposition subpoena immediately following the date and time specified for production: "Do not release the requested records to the deposition officer prior to the date and time stated above."

(e) This section does not apply if the subpoena directs the deponent to make the records available for inspection or copying by the subpoenaing party's attorney or a representative of that attorney at the witness' business address under subdivision (e) of Section 1560 of the Evidence Code.

(f) The provisions of Section 1562 of the Evidence Code concerning the admissibility of the affidavit of the custodian or other qualified person apply to a deposition subpoena served under this article. **Leg.H.** 2004 ch. 182 (AB 3081), operative July 1, 2005.

§2020.440. Deposition officer to provide copies to specified parties.

Promptly on or after the deposition date and after the receipt or the making of a copy of business records under this article, the deposition officer shall provide that copy to the party at whose instance the deposition subpoena was served, and a copy of those records to any other party to the action who then or subsequently, within a period of six months following the settlement of the case, notifies the deposition officer that the party desires to purchase a copy of those records. **Leg.H.** 2004 ch. 182 (AB 3081), operative July 1, 2005.

ARTICLE 5
Subpoena Commanding Both Production of Business Records and Attendance and Testimony of the Deponent

§2020.510. Requirements for deposition subpoena that commands attendance, testimony and production of business records, etc.; records pertaining to consumer or employee.

(a) A deposition subpoena that commands the attendance and the testimony of the deponent, as well as the production of business records, documents, and tangible things, shall:

(1) Comply with the requirements of Section 2020.310.

(2) Designate the business records, documents, and tangible things to be produced either by specifically describing each individual item or by reasonably particularizing each category of item.

(3) Specify any testing or sampling that is being sought.

(b) A deposition subpoena under subdivision (a) need not be accompanied by an affidavit or declaration showing good cause for the production of the documents and things designated.

(c) If, as described in Section 1985.3, the person to whom the deposition subpoena is directed is a witness, and the business records described in the deposition subpoena are personal records pertaining to a consumer, the service of the deposition subpoena shall be accompanied either by a copy of the proof of service of the notice to the consumer described in subdivision (e) of Section 1985.3, or by the consumer's written authorization to release personal records described in paragraph (2) of subdivision (c) of Section 1985.3.

(d) If, as described in Section 1985.6, the person to whom the deposition subpoena is directed is a witness and the business records described in the deposition subpoena are employment records pertaining to an employee, the service of the deposition subpoena shall be accompanied either by a copy of the proof of service of the notice to the employee described in subdivision (e) of Section 1985.6, or by the employee's written authorization to release personal records described in paragraph (2) of subdivision (c) of Section 1985.6. **Leg.H.** 2004 ch. 182 (AB 3081), operative July 1, 2005, 2007 ch. 113 (AB 1126) §4.

CHAPTER 7
SANCTIONS

§2023.010. Misuses of discovery process.

Misuses of the discovery process include, but are not limited to, the following:

(a) Persisting, over objection and without substantial justification, in an attempt to obtain information or materials that are outside the scope of permissible discovery.

(b) Using a discovery method in a manner that does not comply with its specified procedures.

(c) Employing a discovery method in a manner or to an extent that causes unwarranted annoyance, embarrassment, or oppression, or undue burden and expense.

(d) Failing to respond or to submit to an authorized method of discovery.

(e) Making, without substantial justification, an unmeritorious objection to discovery.

(f) Making an evasive response to discovery.

(g) Disobeying a court order to provide discovery.

(h) Making or opposing, unsuccessfully and without substantial justification, a motion to compel or to limit discovery.

(i) Failing to confer in person, by telephone, or by letter with an opposing party or attorney in a reasonable and good faith attempt to resolve informally any dispute concerning discovery, if the section governing a particular discovery motion requires the filing of a declaration stating facts showing that an attempt at informal resolution has been made. **Leg.H.** 2004 ch. 182 (AB 3081), operative July 1, 2005.

Ref.: MB Prac. Guide: Cal. Trial & Post-Trial Civ. Proc., §23.07[2][a].

§2023.020. Monetary sanction for failure to confer.

Notwithstanding the outcome of the particular discovery motion, the court shall impose a monetary sanction ordering that any party or attorney who fails to confer as required pay the reasonable expenses, including attorney's fees, incurred by anyone as a result of that conduct. **Leg.H.** 2004 ch. 182 (AB 3081), operative July 1, 2005.

§2023.030. Sanctions which may be imposed for misuse of discovery process.

To the extent authorized by the chapter governing any particular discovery method or any other provision of this title, the court, after notice to any affected party, person, or attorney, and after opportunity for hearing, may impose the following sanctions against anyone engaging in conduct that is a misuse of the discovery process:

(a) The court may impose a monetary sanction ordering that one engaging in the misuse of the discovery process, or any attorney advising that conduct, or both pay the reasonable expenses, including attorney's fees, incurred by anyone as a result of that conduct. The court may also impose this sanction on one unsuccessfully asserting that another has engaged in the misuse of the discovery process, or on any attorney who advised that assertion, or on both. If a monetary sanction is authorized by any provision of this title, the court shall impose that sanction unless it finds that the one subject to the sanction acted with substantial justification or that other circumstances make the imposition of the sanction unjust.

(b) The court may impose an issue sanction ordering that designated facts shall be taken as established in the action in accordance with the claim of the party adversely affected by the misuse of the discovery process. The court may also impose an issue sanction by an order prohibiting any party engaging in the misuse of the discovery process from supporting or opposing designated claims or defenses.

(c) The court may impose an evidence sanction by an order prohibiting any party engaging in the misuse of the discovery process from introducing designated matters in evidence.

(d) The court may impose a terminating sanction by one of the following orders:

(1) An order striking out the pleadings or parts of the pleadings of any party engaging in the misuse of the discovery process.

(2) An order staying further proceedings by that party until an order for discovery is obeyed.

(3) An order dismissing the action, or any part of the action, of that party.

(4) An order rendering a judgment by default against that party.

(e) The court may impose a contempt sanction by an order treating the misuse of the discovery process as a contempt of court. **Leg.H.** 2004 ch. 182 (AB 3081), operative July 1, 2005.

Ref.: MB Prac. Guide: Cal. Trial & Post-Trial Civ. Proc., §§1.23, 23.07[2][a].

§2023.040. Request for sanction and notice of motion; what to be included therein.

A request for a sanction shall, in the notice of motion, identify every person, party, and attorney against whom the sanction is sought, and specify the type of sanction sought. The notice of motion shall be supported by a memorandum of points and authorities, and accompanied by a declaration setting forth facts supporting the amount of any monetary sanction sought. **Leg.H.** 2004 ch. 182 (AB 3081), operative July 1, 2005.

CHAPTER 14
INSPECTION AND PRODUCTION OF DOCUMENTS, TANGIBLE THINGS, LAND, AND OTHER PROPERTY
[Selected Provisions]

ARTICLE 1
Inspection Demand

§2031.010. Right to discovery by inspection of documents, tangible things, and land or other property.

(a) Any party may obtain discovery within the scope delimited by Chapters 2 (commencing with Section 2017.010) and 3 (commencing with Section 2017.710), and subject to the restrictions set forth in Chapter 5 (commencing with Section 2019.010), by inspecting documents, tangible things, and land or other property that are in the possession, custody, or control of any other party to the action.

(b) A party may demand that any other party produce and permit the party making the demand, or someone acting on that party's behalf, to inspect and to copy a document that is in the possession, custody, or control of the party on whom the demand is made.

(c) A party may demand that any other party produce and permit the party making the demand, or someone acting on that party's behalf, to inspect and to photograph, test, or sample any tangible things that are in the possession, custody, or control of the party on whom the demand is made.

(d) A party may demand that any other party allow the party making the demand, or someone acting on that party's behalf, to enter on any land or other property that is in the possession, custody, or control of the party on whom the demand is made, and to inspect and to measure, survey, photograph, test, or sample the land or other property, or any designated object or operation on it. **Leg.H.** 2004 ch. 182 (AB 3081), operative July 1, 2005.

Ref.: MB Prac. Guide: Cal. Debt Collection & Enforcement of Judgments, §§10.23, 10.28; W. Cal. Sum., 5 "Torts" §563.

§2031.020. Demand for inspection by defendant authorized at any time; when plaintiff may make demand for inspection.

(a) A defendant may make a demand for inspection without leave of court at any time.

(b) A plaintiff may make a demand for inspection without leave of court at any time that is 10 days after the service of the summons on, or appearance by, the party to whom the demand is directed, whichever occurs first.

(c) Notwithstanding subdivision (b), in an unlawful detainer action or other proceeding under Chapter 4 (commencing with Section 1159) of Title 3 of Part 3, a plaintiff may make a demand for inspection without leave of court at any time that is five days after service of the summons on, or appearance by, the party to whom the demand is directed, whichever occurs first.

(d) Notwithstanding subdivisions (b) and (c), on motion with or without notice, the court, for good cause shown, may grant leave to a plaintiff to make an inspection demand at an earlier time. **Leg.H.** 2004 ch. 182 (AB 3081), operative July 1, 2005, 2007 ch. 113 (AB 1126) §9.

§2031.030. Format and requirements for demands for inspection.

(a) A party demanding an inspection shall number each set of demands consecutively.

(b) In the first paragraph immediately below the title of the case, there shall appear the identity of the demanding party, the set number, and the identity of the responding party.

(c) Each demand in a set shall be separately set forth, identified by number or letter, and shall do all of the following:

(1) Designate the documents, tangible things, or land or other property to be inspected either by specifically describing each individual item or by reasonably particularizing each category of item.

(2) Specify a reasonable time for the inspection that is at least 30 days after service of the demand, unless the court for good cause shown has granted leave to specify an earlier date. In an unlawful detainer action or other proceeding

under Chapter 4 (commencing with Section 1159) of Title 3 of Part 3, the demand shall specify a reasonable time for the inspection that is at least five days after service of the demand, unless the court, for good cause shown, has granted leave to specify an earlier date.

(3) Specify a reasonable place for making the inspection, copying, and performing any related activity.

(4) Specify any related activity that is being demanded in addition to an inspection and copying, as well as the manner in which that related activity will be performed, and whether that activity will permanently alter or destroy the item involved. **Leg.H.** 2004 ch. 182 (AB 3081), operative July 1, 2005, 2007 ch. 113 (AB 1126) §10.

Ref.: W. Cal. Sum., 12 "Real Property" §736.

§2031.040. Service of inspection demand.

The party demanding an inspection shall serve a copy of the inspection demand on the party to whom it is directed and on all other parties who have appeared in the action. **Leg.H.** 2004 ch. 182 (AB 3081), operative July 1, 2005.

§2031.050. When supplemental demand may be propounded.

(a) In addition to the inspection demands permitted by this chapter, a party may propound a supplemental demand to inspect any later acquired or discovered documents, tangible things, or land or other property that are in the possession, custody, or control of the party on whom the demand is made.

(b) A party may propound a supplemental inspection demand twice before the initial setting of a trial date, and, subject to the time limits on discovery proceedings and motions provided in Chapter 8 (commencing with Section 2024.010), once after the initial setting of a trial date.

(c) Notwithstanding subdivisions (a) and (b), on motion, for good cause shown, the court may grant leave to a party to propound an additional number of supplemental demands for inspection. **Leg.H.** 2004 ch. 182 (AB 3081), operative July 1, 2005.

§2031.060. Motion for protective order; what protective order may provide; denial of protective order; monetary sanction.

(a) When an inspection of documents, tangible things or places has been demanded, the party to whom the demand has been directed, and any other party or affected person or organization, may promptly move for a protective order. This motion shall be accompanied by a meet and confer declaration under Section 2016.040.

(b) The court, for good cause shown, may make any order that justice requires to protect any party or other natural person or organization from unwarranted annoyance, embarrassment, or oppression, or undue burden and expense. This protective order may include, but is not limited to, one or more of the following directions:

(1) That all or some of the items or categories of items in the inspection demand need not be produced or made available at all.

(2) That the time specified in Section 2030.260 to respond to the set of inspection demands, or to a particular item or category in the set, be extended.

(3) That the place of production be other than that specified in the inspection demand.

(4) That the inspection be made only on specified terms and conditions.

(5) That a trade secret or other confidential research, development, or commercial information not be disclosed, or be disclosed only to specified persons or only in a specified way.

(6) That the items produced be sealed and thereafter opened only on order of the court.

(c) If the motion for a protective order is denied in whole or in part, the court may order that the party to whom the demand was directed provide or permit the discovery against which protection was sought on terms and conditions that are just.

(d) The court shall impose a monetary sanction under Chapter 7 (commencing with Section 2023.010) against any party, person, or attorney who unsuccessfully makes or opposes a motion for a protective order, unless it finds that the one subject to the sanction acted with substantial justification or that other circumstances make the imposition of the sanction unjust. **Leg.H.** 2004 ch. 182 (AB 3081), operative July 1, 2005.

ARTICLE 2
Response to Inspection Demand

§2031.210. Nature and format of response to inspection demand.

(a) The party to whom an inspection demand has been directed shall respond separately to each item or category of item by any of the following:

(1) A statement that the party will comply with the particular demand for inspection by the date set for inspection pursuant to paragraph (2) of subdivision (c) of Section 2031.030 and any related activities.

(2) A representation that the party lacks the ability to comply with the demand for inspection of a particular item or category of item.

(3) An objection to the particular demand.

(b) In the first paragraph of the response immediately below the title of the case, there shall appear the identity of the responding party, the set number, and the identity of the demanding party.

(c) Each statement of compliance, each representation, and each objection in the response shall bear the same number and be in the same sequence as the corresponding item or category in the demand, but the text of that item or category need not be repeated. **Leg.H.** 2004 ch. 182 (AB 3081), operative July 1, 2005, 2007 ch. 738 (AB 1248) §7.

Ref.: MB Prac. Guide: Cal. Debt Collection & Enforcement of Judgments, §§10.20, 10.24; MB Prac. Guide: Cal. Trial & Post-Trial Civ. Proc., §§29.12[4], 29.18[3][d].

§2031.220. Statement regarding compliance in whole or in part.

A statement that the party to whom an inspection demand has been directed will comply with the particular demand shall state that the production, inspection, and related activity demanded will be allowed either in whole or in part, and that all documents or things in the demanded category that are in the possession, custody, or control of that party and to which no objection is being made will be included in the production. **Leg.H.** 2004 ch. 182 (AB 3081), operative July 1, 2005.

§2031.230. Representation of inability to comply.

A representation of inability to comply with the particular demand for inspection shall affirm that a diligent search and a reasonable inquiry has been made in an effort to comply with that demand. This statement shall also specify whether the inability to comply is because the particular item or category has never existed, has been destroyed, has been lost, misplaced, or stolen, or has never been, or is no longer, in the possession, custody, or control of the responding party. The statement shall set forth the name and address of any natural person or organization known or believed by that party to have possession, custody, or control of that item or category of item. **Leg.H.** 2004 ch. 182 (AB 3081), operative July 1, 2005.

§2031.240. Statements regarding demand that is objectionable in whole or in part.

(a) If only part of an item or category of item in an inspection demand is objectionable, the response shall contain a statement of compliance, or a representation of inability to comply with respect to the remainder of that item or category.

(b) If the responding party objects to the demand for inspection of an item or category of item, the response shall do both of the following:

(1) Identify with particularity any document, tangible thing, or land falling within any category of item in the demand to which an objection is being made.

(2) Set forth clearly the extent of, and the specific ground for, the objection. If an objection is based on a claim of privilege, the particular privilege invoked shall be stated. If an objection is based on a claim that the information sought is protected work product under Chapter 4 (commencing with Section 2018.010), that claim shall be expressly asserted. **Leg.H.** 2004 ch. 182 (AB 3081), operative July 1, 2005.

§2031.250. Signing of response to demand.

(a) The party to whom the demand for inspection is directed shall sign the response under oath unless the response contains only objections.

(b) If that party is a public or private corporation or a partnership or association or governmental agency, one of its officers or agents shall sign the response under oath on behalf of that party. If the officer or agent signing the response on behalf of that party is an attorney acting in that capacity for a party, that party waives any lawyer-client privilege and any protection for work product under Chapter 4 (commencing with Section 2018.010) during any subsequent discovery from that attorney concerning the identity of the sources of the information contained in the response.

(c) The attorney for the responding party shall sign any responses that contain an objection. **Leg.H.** 2004 ch. 182 (AB 3081), operative July 1, 2005.

Ref.: MB Prac. Guide: Cal. Debt Collection & Enforcement of Judgments, §10.24.

§2031.260. Time for service of response; unlawful detainer action.

(a) Within 30 days after service of an inspection demand, the party to whom the demand is directed shall serve the original of the response to it on the party making the demand, and a copy of the response on all other parties who have appeared in the action, unless on motion of the party making the demand, the court has shortened the time for response, or unless on motion of the party to whom the demand has been directed, the court has extended the time for response.

(b) Notwithstanding subdivision (a), in an unlawful detainer action or other proceeding under Chapter 4 (commencing with Section 1159) of Title 3 of Part 3, the party to whom an inspection demand is directed shall have at least five days from the date of service of the demand to respond, unless on motion of the party making the demand, the court has shortened the time for the response, or unless on motion of the party to whom the demand has been directed, the court has extended the time for response. **Leg.H.** 2004 ch. 182 (AB 3081), operative July 1, 2005, 2007 ch. 113 (AB 1126) §11.

Ref.: W. Cal. Sum., 12 "Real Property" §736.

§2031.270. Extension of time for inspection or service of response; written confirmation of agreement.

(a) The party demanding an inspection and the responding party may agree to extend the date for inspection or the time for service of a response to a set of inspection demands, or to particular items or categories of items in a set, to a date or dates beyond those provided in Sections 2031.030, 2031.210, 2031.260, and 2031.280.

(b) This agreement may be informal, but it shall be confirmed in a writing that specifies the extended date for inspection or service of a response.

(c) Unless this agreement expressly states otherwise, it is effective to preserve to the responding party the right to respond to any item or category of item in the demand to which the agreement applies in any manner specified in Sections 2031.210, 2031.220, 2031.230, 2031.240, and 2031.280. **Leg.H.** 2004 ch. 182 (AB 3081), operative July 1, 2005, 2007 ch. 738 (AB 1248) §8.

§2031.280. Production of documents—Form; date of inspection; translation; expense.

(a) Any documents produced in response to an inspection demand shall either be produced as they are kept in the usual course of business, or be organized and labeled to correspond with the categories in the demand.

(b) The documents shall be produced on the date specified in the inspection demand pursuant to paragraph (2) of subdivision (c) of Section 2031.030, unless an objection has been made to that date. If the date for inspection has been extended pursuant to Section 2031.270, the documents shall be produced on the date agreed to pursuant to that section.

(c) If necessary, the responding party at the reasonable expense of the demanding party shall, through detection devices, translate any data compilations included in the demand into reasonably usable form. **Leg.H.** 2004 ch. 182 (AB 3081), operative July 1, 2005, 2007 ch. 738 (AB 1248) §9.

§2031.290. Retention of inspection demand, proof of service, and response by demanding party.

(a) The inspection demand and the response to it shall not be filed with the court.

(b) The party demanding an inspection shall retain both the original of the inspection demand, with the original proof of service affixed to it, and the original of the sworn response until six months after final disposition of the action. At that time, both originals may be destroyed, unless the court, on motion of any party and for good cause shown, orders that the originals be preserved for a longer period. **Leg.H.** 2004 ch. 182 (AB 3081), operative July 1, 2005.

§2031.300. Effect of failure to serve timely response to inspection demand; motion for order; monetary and other sanctions.

If a party to whom an inspection demand is directed fails to serve a timely response to it, the following rules apply:

(a) The party to whom the inspection demand is directed waives any objection to the demand, including one based on privilege or on the protection for work product under Chapter 4 (commencing with Section 2018.010). The court, on motion, may relieve that party from this waiver on its determination that both of the following conditions are satisfied:

(1) The party has subsequently served a response that is in substantial compliance with Sections 2031.210, 2031.220, 2031.230, 2031.240, and 2031.280.

(2) The party's failure to serve a timely response was the result of mistake, inadvertence, or excusable neglect.

(b) The party making the demand may move for an order compelling response to the inspection demand.

(c) The court shall impose a monetary sanction under Chapter 7 (commencing with Section 2023.010) against any party, person, or attorney who unsuccessfully makes or opposes a motion to compel a response to an inspection demand, unless it finds that the one subject to the sanction acted with substantial justification or that other circumstances make the imposition of the sanction unjust. If a party then fails to obey the order compelling a response, the court may make those orders that are just, including the imposition of an issue sanction, an evidence sanction, or a terminating sanction under Chapter 7 (commencing with Section 2023.010). In lieu of or in addition to this sanction, the court may impose a monetary sanction under Chapter 7 (commencing with Section 2023.010). **Leg.H.** 2004 ch. 182 (AB 3081), operative July 1, 2005, 2005 ch. 22 (SB 1108) §23.

Ref.: MB Prac. Guide: Cal. Debt Collection & Enforcement of Judgments, §10.24; MB Prac. Guide: Cal. Trial & Post-Trial Civ. Proc., §§29.04[1], 29.11[1][b], 29.12[4], 29.18[3][d].

§2031.310. Motion for order compelling further response; grounds; notice; waiver; monetary and other sanctions.

(a) On receipt of a response to an inspection demand, the party demanding an inspection may move for an order compelling further response to the demand if the demanding party deems that any of the following apply:

(1) A statement of compliance with the demand is incomplete.

(2) A representation of inability to comply is inadequate, incomplete, or evasive.

(3) An objection in the response is without merit or too general.

(b) A motion under subdivision (a) shall comply with both of the following:

(1) The motion shall set forth specific facts showing good cause justifying the discovery sought by the inspection demand.

(2) The motion shall be accompanied by a meet and confer declaration under Section 2016.040.

(c) Unless notice of this motion is given within 45 days of the service of the response, or any supplemental response, or on or before any specific later date to which the demanding party and the responding party have agreed in writing, the demanding party waives any right to compel a further response to the inspection demand.

(d) The court shall impose a monetary sanction under Chapter 7 (commencing with Section 2023.010) against any party, person, or attorney who unsuccessfully makes or opposes a motion to compel further response to an inspection demand, unless it finds that the one subject to the sanction acted with substantial justification or that other circumstances make the imposition of the sanction unjust.

(e) If a party fails to obey an order compelling further response, the court may make those orders that are just, including the imposition of an issue sanction, an evidence sanction, or a terminating sanction under Chapter 7 (commencing with Section 2023.010). In lieu of or in addition to that sanction, the court may impose a monetary sanction under Chapter 7 (commencing with Section 2023.010). **Leg.H.** 2004 ch. 182 (AB 3081), operative July 1, 2005.

§2031.320. Motion for order compelling compliance on failure to permit inspection in accordance with response; monetary and other sanctions.

(a) If a party filing a response to a demand for inspection under Section 2031.210, 2031.220, 2031.230, 2031.240, and 2031.280 thereafter fails to permit the inspection in accordance with that party's statement of compliance, the party demanding the inspection may move for an order compelling compliance.

(b) The court shall impose a monetary sanction under Chapter 7 (commencing with Section 2023.010) against any party, person, or attorney who unsuccessfully makes or opposes a motion to compel compliance with an inspection demand, unless it finds that the one subject to the sanction acted with substantial justification or that other circumstances make the imposition of the sanction unjust.

(c) If a party then fails to obey an order compelling inspection, the court may make those orders that are just, including the imposition of an issue sanction, an evidence sanction, or a terminating sanction under Chapter 7 (commencing with Section 2023.010). In lieu of or in addition to that sanction, the court may impose a monetary sanction under Chapter 7 (commencing with Section 2023.010). **Leg.H.** 2004 ch. 182 (AB 3081), operative July 1, 2005.

ARTICLE 3
Deposition of Expert Witness

§2034.430. Payment of certain experts' reasonable and customary hourly or daily fees for time spent at deposition; tardy counsel; workers' compensation cases.

(a) Except as provided in subdivision (f), this section applies to an expert witness, other than a party or an employee of a party, who is any of the following:

(1) An expert described in subdivision (b) of Section [1] **2034.210**.

(2) A treating physician and surgeon or other treating health care practitioner who is to be asked during the deposition to express opinion testimony, including opinion or factual testimony regarding the past or present diagnosis or prognosis made by the practitioner or the reasons for a particular treatment decision made by the practitioner, but not including testimony requiring only the reading of words and symbols contained in the relevant medical record or, if those words and symbols are not legible to the deponent, the approximation by the deponent of what those words or symbols are.

(3) An architect, professional engineer, or licensed land surveyor who was involved with the original project design or survey for which that person is asked to express an opinion within the person's expertise and relevant to the action or proceeding.

(b) A party desiring to depose an expert witness described in subdivision (a) shall pay the expert's reasonable and customary hourly or daily fee for any time spent at the deposition from the time noticed in the deposition subpoena, or from the time of the arrival of the expert witness should that time be later than the time noticed in the deposition subpoena, until the time the expert witness is dismissed from the deposition, regardless of whether the expert is actually deposed by any party attending the deposition.

(c) If any counsel representing the expert or a nonnoticing party is late to the deposition, the expert's reasonable and customary hourly or daily fee for the time period determined from the time noticed in the deposition subpoena until the counsel's late arrival, shall be paid by that tardy counsel.

(d) Notwithstanding subdivision (c), the hourly or daily fee charged to the tardy counsel shall not exceed the fee charged to the party who retained the expert, except where the expert donated services to a charitable or other non-profit organization.

(e) A daily fee shall only be charged for a full day of attendance at a deposition or where the expert was required by the deposing party to be available for a full day and the expert necessarily had to [2] **forgo** all business that the expert would otherwise have conducted that day but for the request that the expert be available all day for the scheduled deposition.

(f) In a worker's compensation case arising under Division 4 (commencing with Section 3201) or Division 4.5 (commencing with Section 6100) of the Labor Code, a party desiring to depose any expert on another party's expert witness list shall pay the fee under this section. **Leg.H.** 2004 ch. 182 (AB 3081), operative July 1, 2005, 2008 ch. 303 (AB 2619) §2.

§2034.430. 2008 Deletes. [1] 2034.260 **[2]** forego

Ref.: MB Prac. Guide: Fed. Pretrial Proc. in Cal., §16.07[2][b]; MB Prac. Guide: Cal. Trial & Post-Trial Civ. Proc., §24.11[2].

SELECTED PROVISIONS Of The EDUCATION CODE

TITLE 1 GENERAL EDUCATION CODE PROVISIONS

DIVISION 1 General Education Code Provisions

PART 2 COUNTY EDUCATIONAL AGENCIES

CHAPTER 2 COUNTY SUPERINTENDENT OF SCHOOLS

ARTICLE 2 Duties, Responsibilities, and General Powers [Selected Provisions]

§1252. Workers' compensation insurance for schools.

The county superintendent of schools of any county may, with the approval of the State Compensation Insurance Fund, insure the liability for compensation of any school districts and community college districts in the territory under his or her jurisdiction, the governing boards of which consent thereto, with the State Compensation Insurance Fund under one policy or contract of insurance and pay the premium for the insurance from the county school service fund. Immediately following the payment of the final premium the county superintendent of schools shall transfer from the funds of each insured district to the county school service fund an amount which bears the same ratio to the premium as the payroll of each district bears to the total payroll of all the insured districts.

Any dividends earned on the premiums paid under this section shall be credited to the individual districts in proportion to the amount of the premium charged to each district.

The expenses of the county superintendent of schools incurred under this section shall be charged to and paid from the county school service fund, which fund shall be reimbursed for those expenses from the general funds of the school districts and community college districts on whose behalf the expenditures are incurred.

ARTICLE 3 Staff [Selected Provisions]

§1297. Extent of coverage; payment of costs.

For the purpose of insurance under the workers' compensation laws of this state, any person employed by a county superintendent of schools to supervise instruction or to give instruction in the school districts or community college districts located in the territory under the jurisdic-

Misc. Provisions

tion of the county superintendent of schools shall be deemed an employee of the county. The cost of insuring any person employed to supervise instruction shall be paid by the county superintendent of schools from the county school service fund. The cost of insuring any person employed by the county superintendent of schools to give instruction shall be paid by the county superintendent of schools from the county school service fund.

PART 13
STATE TEACHERS' RETIREMENT SYSTEM

CHAPTER 30
SUBROGATION

§24500. Board's right of subrogation.

Notwithstanding Sections 11042 and 11043 of the Government Code, if a disability retirement allowance, disability allowance, family allowance, or survivor benefit allowance is payable under this part due to the injury to or death of a member and the injury or death is the proximate consequence of the act of a third person or entity, other than the member's employer, the board may, upon adoption of a resolution, recover from that person or entity on behalf of the plan, an amount equal to the actuarial equivalent of benefits paid under the plan because of the injury to or death of the member less any amounts the system may be obligated to pay under the plan without regard to the actions of the third party. This chapter shall be deemed to create a right of subrogation only to amounts paid as disability retirement allowances, disability allowances, family allowances, or survivor benefit allowances. **Leg.H.** 1993 ch. 893, 1996 ch. 634.

§24501. Board may contract with SCIF or AG to act as agent.

The board may act on its own or contract with the State Compensation Insurance Fund or Attorney General for recovery on behalf of the plan of any amounts recoverable from third persons under this chapter, Chapter 5 (commencing with Section 3850) of Part 1 of Division 4 of the Labor Code, Section 11662 of the Insurance Code, or otherwise. **Leg.H.** 1993 ch. 893, 1996 ch. 634.

§24502. Actions board may take to enforce subrogation right.

In the exercise of its rights under this part, the board or the agent under contract may commence or prosecute actions, file liens, intervene in court proceedings, join parties to the action and consolidate actions all in the same manner and to the same extent provided in Chapter 5 (commencing with Section 3850) of Part 1 of Division 4 of the Labor Code except that recovery shall not be made from benefits payable under this part because of the injury or death. **Leg.H.** 1993 ch. 893.

§24503. SCIF or AG may compromise claims.

The State Compensation Insurance Fund or Attorney General as agent for the board may compromise claims before or after commencement of suit or entry of judgment for an amount as may be approved by a person duly authorized by the board for that purpose. **Leg.H.** 1993 ch. 893.

§24504. Application of recovery.

Any amount recovered by way of subrogation by the board on behalf of the member, shall be applied first to the amount which the plan paid or is obligated to pay including court costs, attorney fees, and expenses. **Leg.H.** 1993 ch. 893, 1996 ch. 634.

§24505. Three-year limitation period.

Actions brought by the board or its agent under contract pursuant to this chapter shall be commenced within three years after the liability of the system to pay benefits under the plan is fixed. Liability of the plan is fixed at the time the board approves the payment of benefits under this plan. **Leg.H.** 1993 ch. 893, 1996 ch. 634, 1998 ch. 965.

PART 19
MISCELLANEOUS

CHAPTER 3
MISCELLANEOUS

ARTICLE 6
District Liability on Loaned Equipment

§32350. Liability for loaned equipment or services; "public entity."

Any person, corporation, firm, or public entity, or employee thereof, who gratuitously loans equipment of any description or the services of an employee to a school district or community college district shall not be liable, and the school district or community college district shall be liable, for damages because of personal injuries to, or the death of any person or damage to property resulting from the operation of such equipment or an act or omission of such employee occurring while such equipment or employee is under the supervision and control of the district.

This section does not apply to any person, corporation, firm, or public entity who gratuitously loans mechanically defective equipment of any description or who gratuitously loans the services of an employee who is not fully qualified to perform such service, and such defect or lack of qualification is the cause of any damage or injury.

An employee whose services are loaned to a school district or community college district pursuant to this section remains an employee of his employer for all purposes, including the application of the provisions of the Labor Code relating to workers' compensation.

For the purposes of this section, "public entity" includes the state, the Regents of the University of California, a county, city, city and county, district, public authority, public agency, or any other political subdivision or public corporation in this state.

Ref.: W. Cal. Sum., 2 "Workers' Compensation" §161.

Misc. Provisions

DIVISION 3
LOCAL ADMINISTRATION

PART 25
EMPLOYEES

CHAPTER 1
EMPLOYEES

ARTICLE 1
General Provisions
[Selected Provisions]

§44017. Possible payment to surviving spouse.

Notwithstanding any provision of law to the contrary, a school district may, from funds under its jurisdiction, pay the surviving spouse of any employee who is murdered while in the course of his employment the amount that the deceased would have received if he had lived to complete the time remaining in his contract with the district.

This section shall be applicable to the surviving spouse of any such employee who was murdered during or after the 1973–74 school year.

ARTICLE 2
Rights and Duties
[Selected Provisions]

§44043. Restrictions on salary and paid leave when temporary disability benefits received.

Any school employee of a school district who is absent because of injury or illness which arose out of and in the course of the person's employment, and for which the person is receiving temporary disability benefits under the workers' compensation laws of this state, shall not be entitled to receive wages or salary from the district which, when added to the temporary disability benefits, will exceed a full day's wages or salary.

During such periods of temporary disability so long as the employee has available for the employee's use sick leave, vacation, compensating time off or other paid leave of absence, the district shall require that temporary disability checks be endorsed payable to the district. The district shall then cause the employee to receive the person's normal wage or salary less appropriate deductions including but not limited to employee retirement contributions.

When sick leave, vacation, compensating time off or other available paid leave is used in conjunction with temporary disability benefits derived from workers' compensation, as provided in this section, it shall be reduced only in that amount necessary to provide a full day's wage or salary when added to the temporary disability benefits.

CHAPTER 4
EMPLOYMENT—CERTIFICATED EMPLOYEE

ARTICLE 3
Resignations, Dismissals, and Leaves of Absence
[Selected Provisions]

§44977. Salaries for those on extended leave and substitutes.

(a) During each school year, when a person employed in a position requiring certification qualifications has exhausted all available sick leave, including all accumulated sick leave, and continues to be absent from his or her duties on account of illness or accident for an additional period of five school months, whether or not the absence arises out of or in the course of the employment of the employee, the amount deducted from the salary due him or her for any of the additional five months in which the absence occurs shall not exceed the sum that is actually paid a substitute employee employed to fill his or her position during his or her absence or, if no substitute employee was employed, the amount that would have been paid to the substitute had he or she been employed. The school district shall make every reasonable effort to secure the services of a substitute employee.

(b) For purposes of subdivision (a):

(1) The sick leave, including accumulated sick leave, and the five-month period shall run consecutively.

(2) An employee shall not be provided more than one five-month period per illness or accident. However, if a school year terminates before the five-month period is exhausted, the employee may take the balance of the five-month period in a subsequent school year.

(c) The governing board of every school district shall adopt a salary schedule for substitute employees. The salary schedule shall indicate a salary for a substitute for all categories or classes of certificated employees of the district.

(d) Excepting in a district the governing board of which has adopted a salary schedule for substitute employees of the district, the amount paid the substitute employee during any month shall be less than the salary due the employee absent from his or her duties.

(e) When a person employed in a position requiring certification qualifications is absent from his or her duties on account of illness for a period of more than five school months, or when a person is absent from his or her duties for a cause other than illness, the amount deducted from the salary due him or her for the month in which the absence occurs shall be determined according to the rules and regulations established by the governing board of the district. The rules and regulations shall not conflict with rules and regulations of the State Board of Education.

(f) Nothing in this section shall be construed so as to deprive any district, city, or city and county of the right to make any reasonable rule for the regulation of accident or sick leave or cumulative accident or sick leave without loss of salary for persons acquiring certification qualifications.

(g) This section shall be applicable whether or not the absence from duty is by reason of a leave of absence granted by the governing board of the employing district. **Leg.H.** 1998 ch. 30.

§44983. Salary deductions for those on extended leave.

Section 44977 shall not apply to any school district which adopts and maintains in effect a rule which provides that when a person employed in a position requiring certification qualifications is absent from his duties on account of illness or accident for a period of five school months or less whether or not the absence arises out of or in the course of the employment of the employee, he shall receive 50 percent or more of his regular salary during the period of such absence and nothing in Section 44977 shall be construed as preventing the governing board of any district from adopting any such rule.

Notwithstanding the foregoing, when a person employed in a position requiring certification qualifications is absent from his duties on account of illness for a period of more than five school months, or when a person is absent from his duties for a cause other than illness, the amount deducted from the salary due him for the month in which the absence occurs shall be determined according to the rules and regulations established by the governing board of the district. Such rules and regulations shall not conflict with rules and regulations of the State Board of Education.

Nothing in this section shall be construed so as to deprive any district, city, or city and county of the right to make any reasonable rule for the regulation of accident or sick leave or cumulative accident or sick leave without loss of salary for persons requiring certification qualifications.

This section shall be applicable whether or not the absence from duty is by reason of a leave of absence granted by the governing board of the employing district.

§44984. Rules for industrial accident or illness leave.

Governing boards of school districts shall provide by rules and regulations for industrial accident and illness leaves of absence for all certificated employees. The governing board of any district which is created or whose boundaries or status is changed by an action to organize or reorganize districts completed after the effective date of this section shall provide by rules and regulations for such leaves of absence on or before the date on which the organization or reorganization of the district becomes effective for all purposes as provided in Section 4064.

Such rules or regulations shall include the following provisions:

a. Allowable leave shall be for not less than 60 days during which the schools of the district are required to be in session or when the employee would otherwise have been performing work for the district in any one fiscal year for the same accident;

b. Allowable leave shall not be accumulated from year to year;

c. Industrial accident or illness leave shall commence on the first day of absence;

d. When a certificated employee is absent from his duties on account of an industrial accident or illness, he shall be paid such portion of the salary due him for any month in which the absence occurs as, when added to his temporary disability indemnity under Division 4 or Division 4.5 of the Labor Code, will result in a payment to him of not more than his full salary;

The phrase "full salary" as utilized in this subdivision shall be computed so that it shall not be less than the employee's "average weekly earnings" as that phrase is utilized in Section 4453 of the Labor Code. For purposes of this section, however, the maximum and minimum average weekly earnings set forth in Section 4453 of the Labor Code shall otherwise not be deemed applicable.

e. Industrial accident or illness leave shall be reduced by one day for each day of authorized absence regardless of a temporary disability indemnity award;

f. When an industrial accident or illness leave overlaps into the next fiscal year, the employee shall be entitled to only the amount of unused leave due him for the same illness or injury.

Upon termination of the industrial accident or illness leave, the employee shall be entitled to the benefits provided in Sections 44977, 44978 and 44983, and for the purposes of each of these sections, his absence shall be deemed to have commenced on the date of termination of the industrial accident or illness leave, provided that if the employee continues to receive temporary disability indemnity, he may elect to take as much of his accumulated sick leave which, when added to his temporary disability indemnity, will result in a payment to him of not more than his full salary.

The governing board may, by rule or regulation, provide for such additional leave of absence for industrial accident or illness as it deems appropriate.

During any paid leave of absence, the employee may endorse to the district the temporary disability indemnity checks received on account of his industrial accident or illness. The district, in turn, shall issue the employee appropriate salary warrants for payment of the employee's salary and shall deduct normal retirement, other authorized contributions, and the temporary disability indemnity, if any, actually paid to and retained by the employee for periods covered by such salary warrants.

Any employee receiving benefits as a result of this section shall, during periods of injury or illness, remain within the State of California unless the governing board authorizes travel outside the state.

In the absence of rules and regulations adopted by the governing board pursuant to this section an employee shall be entitled to industrial accident or illness leave as provided in this section but without limitation as to the number of days of such leave.

CHAPTER 5
CLASSIFIED EMPLOYEES

ARTICLE 4
Resignation and Leaves of Absence [Selected Provisions]

§45192. Rules for industrial accident or illness leave of classified service employees.

Governing boards of school districts shall provide by rules and regulations for industrial accident or illness leaves of absence for employees who are a part of the classified service. The governing board of any district which is created or whose boundaries or status is changed by an action to organize or reorganize districts completed after the effective date of this section shall provide by rules and regulations for these leaves of absence on or before the date on which the organization or reorganization of the district becomes effective for all purposes as provided in Section 4064.

The rules and regulations shall include the following provisions:

(a) Allowable leave shall not be for less than 60 working days in any one fiscal year for the same accident.

(b) Allowable leave shall not be accumulative from year to year.

(c) Industrial accident or illness leave will commence on the first day of absence.

(d) Payment for wages lost on any day shall not, when added to an award granted the employee under the workers' compensation laws of this state, exceed the normal wage for the day.

(e) Industrial accident leave will be reduced by one day for each day of authorized absence regardless of a compensation award made under workers' compensation.

(f) When an industrial accident or illness occurs at a time when the full 60 days will overlap into the next fiscal year, the employee shall be entitled to only that amount remaining at the end of the fiscal year in which the injury or illness occurred, for the same illness or injury.

The industrial accident or illness leave of absence is to be used in lieu of entitlement acquired under Section 45191. When entitlement to industrial accident or illness leave has been exhausted, entitlement or other sick leave will then be used; but if an employee is receiving workers' compensation the person shall be entitled to use only so much of the person's accumulated or available sick leave, accumulated compensating time, vacation or other available leave which, when added to the workers' compensation award, provide for a full day's wage or salary.

The governing board may, by rule or regulation, provide for as much additional leave of absence, paid or unpaid, as it deems appropriate and during this leave the employee may return to the person's position without suffering any loss of status or benefits. The employee shall be notified, in writing, that available paid leave has been exhausted, and shall be offered an opportunity to request additional leave.

Periods of leave of absence, paid or unpaid, shall not be considered to be a break in service of the employee.

During all paid leaves of absence, whether industrial accident leave as provided in this section, sick leave, vacation, compensated time off or other available leave provided by law or the action of a governing board, the employee shall endorse to the district wage loss benefit checks received under the workers' compensation laws of this state. The district, in turn, shall issue the employee appropriate warrants for payment of wages or salary and shall deduct normal retirement and other authorized contributions. Reduction of entitlement to leave shall be made only in accordance with this section.

When all available leaves of absence, paid or unpaid, have been exhausted and if the employee is not medically able to assume the duties of the person's position, the person shall, if not placed in another position, be placed on a reemployment list for a period of 39 months. When available, during the 39-month period, the person shall be employed in a vacant position in the class of the person's previous assignment over all other available candidates except for a reemployment list established because of lack of work or lack of funds, in which case the person shall be listed in accordance with appropriate seniority regulations.

The governing board may require that an employee serve or have served continuously a specified period of time with the district before the benefits provided by this section are made available to the person provided that this period shall not exceed three years and that all service of an employee prior to the effective date of this section shall be credited in determining compliance with the requirement.

Any employee receiving benefits as a result of this section shall, during periods of injury or illness, remain within the State of California unless the governing board authorizes travel outside the state.

In the absence of rules and regulations adopted by the governing board, pursuant to this section, an employee shall be entitled to industrial and accident or illness leave as provided in this section but without limitation as to the number of days of this leave and without any requirement of a specified period of service.

An employee who has been placed on a reemployment list, as provided herein, who has been medically released for return to duty and who fails to accept an appropriate assignment shall be dismissed.

This section shall apply to districts that have adopted the merit system in the same manner and effect as if it were a part of Article 6 (commencing with Section 45240) of this chapter.

TITLE 3
POSTSECONDARY EDUCATION

DIVISION 8
California State University

PART 55
CALIFORNIA STATE UNIVERSITY

CHAPTER 5
PERSONNEL

ARTICLE 1.1
Industrial Disability Leave

§89529. Application of article.

(a) This article applies to employees of the trustees who are members of the Public Employees' Retirement System or the State Teachers' Retirement System in compensated employment on and after July 1, 1974.

(b) This article also applies to a participant in the optional retirement program pursuant to Chapter 5.5 (commencing with Section 89600), provided that he or she would otherwise be eligible to participate in the Public Employees' Retirement System except for the election to participate in the optional retirement program.

(c) This article does not apply to employees of the trustees who are included in the provisions of Article 6 (commencing with Section 4800) of Chapter 2 of Part 2 of Division 4 of the Labor Code. **Leg.H.** 1996 ch. 385.

§89529.01. Resolution of conflicts with memorandum of understanding.

If the provisions of this article are in conflict with the provisions of a memorandum of understanding reached pursuant to Chapter 12 (commencing with Section 3560) of Division 4 of Title 1 of the Government Code, the memorandum of understanding shall be controlling without further legislative action, except that if the provisions of a memorandum of understanding require the expenditure of funds, the provisions shall not become effective unless approved by the Legislature in the annual Budget Act.

§89529.02. Definitions.

As used in this article:

(a) "Industrial disability leave" means temporary disability as defined in Division 4 (commencing with Section 3200) and 4.5 (commencing with Section 6100) of the Labor Code and includes any period in which the disability is permanent and stationary and the disabled employee is undergoing vocational rehabilitation.

(b) "Full pay" means the gross base pay earnable by the employee and subject to retirement contribution if he or she had not vacated his or her position.

§89529.03. Industrial disability leave: entitlement; amount; frequency; deductions.

If an employee is temporarily disabled by illness or injury arising out of and in the course of state employment, he or she shall become entitled, regardless of his or her period of service, to receive industrial disability leave and payments, in lieu of workers' compensation temporary disability payments and payment under Section 89527, for a period not exceeding 52 weeks within two years from the first day of disability. The payments shall be in the amount of the employee's full pay less withholding based on his or her exemptions in effect on the date of his or her disability for federal income taxes, state income taxes, and social security taxes not to exceed 22 working days of disability subject to Section 89529.08. Thereafter, the payment shall be two-thirds of full pay. Payments shall be additionally adjusted to offset disability benefits, excluding those disability benefits payable from the State Teachers' Retirement System, the employee may receive from other employer-subsidized programs, except that no adjustment will be made for benefits to which the employee's family is entitled up to a maximum of three-quarters of full pay. Contributions to the Public Employees' Retirement System or the State Teachers' Retirement System shall be deducted in the amount based on full pay. Discretionary deductions of the employee including those for coverage under a state health benefits plan in which the employee is enrolled shall continue to be deducted unless canceled by the employee. State employer contributions to the Public Employees' Retirement System and state employer normal retirement contributions to the State Teachers' Retirement System shall be made on the basis of full pay and state contributions pursuant to Sections 22871 and 22885 of the Government Code because of the employee's enrollment in a health benefits plan shall continue. **Leg.H.** 2004 ch. 69 (SB 626), effective June 24, 2004.

§89529.04. Continuation of other employee benefits.

An employee who is receiving industrial disability leave benefits shall continue to receive all employee benefits which he or she would have received had he or she not incurred disability.

§89529.05. Coordination of industrial disability leave and temporary disability indemnity.

The disabled employee shall not receive temporary disability indemnity or sick leave or annual leave with pay for any period for which he or she receives industrial disability leave; however, he or she may elect to waive the provisions of this article and to receive disability indemnity pursuant to Divisions 4 (commencing with Section 3200) and 4.5 (commencing with Section 6100) of the Labor Code and to receive payments under Section 89527 in lieu of the benefits provided in this article. If the amount of the employee's benefits payable under this article is less than the amount he or she would receive under Divisions 4 (commencing with Section 3200) and 4.5 (commencing with Section 6100) of the Labor Code, the employee shall be deemed to have rejected the benefits of this article and shall be paid benefits pursuant to Divisions 4 (commencing with Section 3200) and 4.5 (commencing with Section 6100) of the Labor Code.

§89529.06. Inapplicability of article.

Division 4.7 (commencing with Section 6200) of the Labor Code shall not apply to employees to which this article applies.

§89529.07. Continuation of disability after expiration of industrial disability leave.

If an employee continues to be temporarily disabled after termination of benefits under this article, he or she shall be entitled to the benefits provided by Division 4 (commencing with Section 3200) and 4.5 (commencing with Section 6100) of the Labor Code and to payments under Section 89527.

§89529.08. Commencement of industrial disability leave.

(a) If an illness or injury causes temporary disability, the employee shall be placed on industrial disability leave on the fourth calendar day after the injured employee leaves work as the result of the illness or injury, except that in case the injury causes disability of more than 14 days or necessitates hospitalization, the employee shall be placed on industrial disability leave from the first day he or she leaves work or is hospitalized as a result of the injury.

(b) Notwithstanding subdivision (a), the disability payment shall be made from the first day the injured employee leaves work as a result of the injury, if the injury is the result of a criminal act of violence against the employee.

§89529.09. Contingencies that must be satisfied to receive payments.

Payments shall be contingent on the complete medical certification of the illness or injury including diagnosis and any prognosis of recovery. Further, payments shall be contingent on the employee's agreement to cooperate and participate in a reasonable and appropriate vocational rehabilitation plan when furnished by the state subject to appropriate medical approval as determined by the trustees.

§89529.10. Rules and regulations.

The trustees or its designee shall adopt any rules and regulations necessary for the administration of this article for its employees.

§89529.11. Effective date.

(a) This article shall be effective upon the adoption of applicable rules and regulations, but not later than January 1, 1975.

(b) The reenactment of this article at the 1987–88 Regular Session of the Legislature does not constitute a change in, but is declaratory of, the existing law.

SELECTED PROVISIONS Of The EVIDENCE CODE

DIVISION 2 WORDS AND PHRASES DEFINED [Selected Provisions]

§110. Burden of producing evidence defined.

"Burden of producing evidence" means the obligation of a party to introduce evidence sufficient to avoid a ruling against him on the issue. **Leg.H.** 1965 ch. 299, operative January 1, 1967.

Ref.: Cal. Courtroom Ev., §§2.03, 2.04[3][d] (Matthew Bender); MB Prac. Guide: Cal. Trial & Post-Trial Civ. Proc., §§9.05[1], 9.10, 9.11[1], 11.83[4].

§115. Burden of proof defined.

"Burden of proof" means the obligation of a party to establish by evidence a requisite degree of belief concerning a fact in the mind of the trier of fact or the court. The burden of proof may require a party to raise a reasonable doubt concerning the existence or nonexistence of a fact or that he establish the existence or nonexistence of a fact by a preponderance of the evidence, by clear and convincing proof, or by proof beyond a reasonable doubt.

Except as otherwise provided by law, the burden of proof requires proof by a preponderance of the evidence. **Leg.H.** 1965 ch. 299, operative January 1, 1967.

Ref.: Hanna § 26.06[6]; Cal. Courtroom Ev., §§2.03[2], [3][b], 2.04, 13.01[2] (Matthew Bender); MB Prac. Guide: Cal. Trial & Post-Trial Civ. Proc., §§9.04, 9.05[1], [4], 9.09, 9.16, 9.17, 9.18[1], 11.83[4], 14.03, 14.07[1], 15.12; CACI Nos. 200, 201 (Matthew Bender); W. Cal. Sum., 5 "Torts" §769, 9 "Partnership" §10, 10 "Parent and Child" §§345, 679, 741, 11 "Community Property" §11, 14 "Wills and Probate" §996.

§140. Evidence defined.

"Evidence" means testimony, writings, material objects, or other things presented to the senses that are offered to prove the existence or nonexistence of a fact. **Leg.H.** 1965 ch. 299, operative January 1, 1967.

Ref.: Cal. Courtroom Ev., §2.09 (Matthew Bender); CACI Nos. 106, 5002 (Matthew Bender).

§240. Unavailable as a witness defined.

(a) Except as otherwise provided in subdivision (b), "unavailable as a witness" means that the declarant is any of the following:

(1) Exempted or precluded on the ground of privilege from testifying concerning the matter to which his or her statement is relevant.

(2) Disqualified from testifying to the matter.

(3) Dead or unable to attend or to testify at the hearing because of then existing physical or mental illness or infirmity.

(4) Absent from the hearing and the court is unable to compel his or her attendance by its process.

(5) Absent from the hearing and the proponent of his or her statement has exercised reasonable diligence but has been unable to procure his or her attendance by the court's process.

(b) A declarant is not unavailable as a witness if the exemption, preclusion, disqualification, death, inability, or absence of the declarant was brought about by the procurement or wrongdoing of the proponent of his or her statement for the purpose of preventing the declarant from attending or testifying.

(c) Expert testimony which establishes that physical or mental trauma resulting from an alleged crime has caused harm to a witness of sufficient severity that the witness is physically unable to testify or is unable to testify without suffering substantial trauma may constitute a sufficient showing of unavailability pursuant to paragraph (3) of subdivision (a). As used in this section, the term "expert" means a physician and surgeon, including a psychiatrist, or any person described by subdivision (b), (c), or (e) of Section 1010.

The introduction of evidence to establish the unavailability of a witness under this subdivision shall not be deemed procurement of unavailability, in absence of proof to the contrary. **Leg.H.** 1965 ch. 299, operative January 1, 1967, 1984 ch. 401, 1988 ch. 485.

Ref.: Cal. Courtroom Ev., §§2.28, 21.46[2], 21.49[2] (Matthew Bender); CACI No. 208 (Matthew Bender); W. Cal. Sum., 10 "Parent and Child" §578, 14 "Wills and Probate" §545.

§250. Writing defined.

"Writing" means handwriting, typewriting, printing, photostating, photographing, photocopying, transmitting by electronic mail or facsimile, and every other means of recording upon any tangible thing, any form of communication or representation, including letters, words, pictures, sounds, or symbols, or combinations thereof, and any record thereby created, regardless of the manner in which the record has been stored. **Leg.H.** 1965 ch. 299, operative January 1, 1967, 2002 ch. 945 (AB 1962).

Ref.: Cal. Courtroom Ev., §2.29 (Matthew Bender); W. Cal. Sum., 5 "Torts" §563.

DIVISION 4
JUDICIAL NOTICE
[Selected Provisions]

§450. General provision.

Judicial notice may not be taken of any matter unless authorized or required by law. **Leg.H.** 1965 ch. 299, operative January 1, 1967.

Ref.: Hanna § 26.06[8]; Cal. Courtroom Ev., §§12.00[2], 12.01 (Matthew Bender); MB Prac. Guide: Cal. Pretrial Proc., §§26.17, 26.50.

§451. Mandatory judicial notice.

Judicial notice shall be taken of the following:

(a) The decisional, constitutional, and public statutory law of this state and of the United States and the provisions of any charter described in Section 3, 4, or 5 of Article XI of the California Constitution.

(b) Any matter made a subject of judicial notice by Section 11343.6, 11344.6, or 18576 of the Government Code or by Section 1507 of Title 44 of the United States Code.

(c) Rules of professional conduct for members of the bar adopted pursuant to Section 6076 of the Business and Professions Code and rules of practice and procedure for the courts of this state adopted by the Judicial Council.

(d) Rules of pleading, practice, and procedure prescribed by the United States Supreme Court, such as the Rules of the United States Supreme Court, the Federal Rules of Civil Procedure, the Federal Rules of Criminal Procedure, the Admiralty Rules, the Rules of the Court of Claims, the Rules of the Customs Court, and the General Orders and Forms in Bankruptcy.

(e) The true signification of all English words and phrases and of all legal expressions.

(f) Facts and propositions of generalized knowledge that are so universally known that they cannot reasonably be the subject of dispute. **Leg.H.** 1965 ch. 299, operative January 1, 1967, 1971 ch. 438, 1972 ch. 764, 1982 ch. 454, 1985 ch. 106, 1986 ch. 248.

Ref.: Hanna § 26.06[8]; Cal. Courtroom Ev., §§12.01[2], 12.02, 12.03[2], 12.07[2], 12.11[2] (Matthew Bender); MB Prac. Guide: Cal. Contract Lit., §11.20; MB Prac. Guide: Cal. Debt Collection & Enforcement of Judgments, §§7.03, 7.09; MB Prac. Guide: Cal. Pretrial Proc., §§26.17, 26.50, 26.74; MB Prac. Guide: Cal. Trial & Post-Trial Civ. Proc., §§4.16[1], 11.113, 11.116.

§452. Permissive judicial notice.

Judicial notice may be taken of the following matters to the extent that they are not embraced within Section 451:

(a) The decisional, constitutional, and statutory law of any state of the United States and the resolutions and private acts of the Congress of the United States and of the Legislature of this state.

(b) Regulations and legislative enactments issued by or under the authority of the United States or any public entity in the United States.

(c) Official acts of the legislative, executive, and judicial departments of the United States and of any state of the United States.

(d) Records of (1) any court of this state or (2) any court of record of the United States or of any state of the United States.

(e) Rules of court of (1) any court of this state or (2) any court of record of the United States or of any state of the United States.

(f) The law of an organization of nations and of foreign nations and public entities in foreign nations.

(g) Facts and propositions that are of such common knowledge within the territorial jurisdiction of the court that they cannot reasonably be the subject of dispute.

(h) Facts and propositions that are not reasonably subject to dispute and are capable of immediate and accurate determination by resort to sources of reasonably indisputable accuracy. **Leg.H.** 1965 ch. 299, operative January 1, 1967.

Ref.: Hanna § 26.06[8]; Cal. Courtroom Ev., §§12.01[2], 12.02[2], 12.03, 12.05[2], 12.07[2], 12.11[2] (Matthew Bender); MB Prac. Guide: Cal. Contract Lit., §11.20; MB Prac. Guide: Cal. Debt Collection & Enforcement of Judgments, §§7.03, 7.09; MB Prac. Guide: Cal. Pretrial Proc., §§26.17, 26.43, 26.50, 26.66, 26.71–26.74; MB Prac. Guide: Cal. Trial & Post-Trial Civ. Proc., §§4.16[1], 11.113, 11.116, 29.32[1][b], 29.76.

DIVISION 6
WITNESSES

CHAPTER 5
METHOD AND SCOPE OF EXAMINATION

ARTICLE 2
Examination of Witnesses
[Selected Provisions]

§776. Adverse witnesses.

(a) A party to the record of any civil action, or a person identified with such a party, may be called and examined as if under cross-examination by any adverse party at any time during the presentation of evidence by the party calling the witness.

(b) A witness examined by a party under this section may be cross-examined by all other parties to the action in such order as the court directs; but, subject to subdivision (e), the witness may be examined only as if under redirect examination by:

(1) In the case of a witness who is a party, his own counsel and counsel for a party who is not adverse to the witness.

(2) In the case of a witness who is not a party, counsel for the party with whom the witness is identified and counsel for a party who is not adverse to the party with whom the witness is identified.

(c) For the purpose of this section, parties represented by the same counsel are deemed to be a single party.

(d) For the purpose of this section, a person is identified with a party if he is:

(1) A person for whose immediate benefit the action is prosecuted or defended by the party.

(2) A director, officer, superintendent, member, agent, employee, or managing agent of the party or of a person specified in paragraph (1), or any public employee of a public entity when such public entity is the party.

(3) A person who was in any of the relationships specified in paragraph (2) at the time of the act or omission giving rise to the cause of action.

(4) A person who was in any of the relationships specified in paragraph (2) at the time he obtained knowledge of the matter concerning which he is sought to be examined under this section.

(e) Paragraph (2) of subdivision (b) does not require counsel for the party with whom the witness is identified and counsel for a party who is not adverse to the party with whom the witness is identified to examine the witness as if under redirect examination if the party who called the witness for examination under this section:

(1) Is also a person identified with the same party with whom the witness is identified.

(2) Is the personal representative, heir, successor, or assignee of a person identified with the same party with whom the witness is identified.

Ref.: Cal. Courtroom Ev., §§16.38[2], 16.42, 18.36[3] (Matthew Bender); MB Prac. Guide: Cal. Debt Collection & Enforcement of Judgments, §7.32; MB Prac. Guide: Cal. Trial & Post-Trial Civ. Proc., §§11.99, 11.103[8].

§777. Exclusion of witnesses from courtroom.

(a) Subject to subdivisions (b) and (c), the court may exclude from the courtroom any witness not at the time under examination so that such witness cannot hear the testimony of other witnesses.

(b) A party to the action cannot be excluded under this section.

(c) If a person other than a natural person is a party to the action, an officer or employee designated by its attorney is entitled to be present.

Ref.: Cal. Courtroom Ev., §16.43 (Matthew Bender); MB Prac. Guide: Cal. Trial & Post-Trial Civ. Proc., §§4.17[5], 11.03, 11.05–11.07, 11.118; W. Cal. Sum., 10 "Parent and Child" §809.

DIVISION 8
PRIVILEGES

CHAPTER 1
DEFINITIONS

§900. Applicability.

Unless the provision or context otherwise requires, the definitions in this chapter govern the construction of this division. They do not govern the construction of any other division. **Leg.H.** 1965 ch. 299, operative January 1, 1967.

Ref.: Herlick Handbook § 14.40; Cal. Courtroom Ev., §18.01 (Matthew Bender).

§901. Proceeding defined.

"Proceeding" means any action, hearing, investigation, inquest, or inquiry (whether conducted by a court, administrative agency, hearing officer, arbitrator, legislative body, or any other person authorized by law) in which, pursuant to law, testimony can be compelled to be given. **Leg.H.** 1965 ch. 299, operative January 1, 1967.

Ref.: Herlick Handbook § 14.40; Cal. Courtroom Ev., §18.02 (Matthew Bender); MB Prac. Guide: Fed. Pretrial Proc. in Cal., §§22.03[1], 22.12[9].

§902. Civil proceeding defined.

"Civil proceeding" means any proceeding except a criminal proceeding. **Leg.H.** 1965 ch. 299, operative January 1, 1967.

Ref.: Herlick Handbook § 14.40; Cal. Courtroom Ev., §18.03 (Matthew Bender).

§903. Criminal proceeding defined.

"Criminal proceeding" means:

(a) A criminal action; and

(b) A proceeding pursuant to Article 3 (commencing with Section 3060) of Chapter 7 of Division 4 of Title 1 of the Government Code to determine whether a public officer should be removed from office for willful or corrupt misconduct in office. **Leg.H.** 1965 ch. 299, operative January 1, 1967.

Ref.: Herlick Handbook § 14.40; Cal. Courtroom Ev., §18.04 (Matthew Bender).

§905. Presiding officer defined.

"Presiding officer" means the person authorized to rule on a claim of privilege in the proceeding in which the claim is made. **Leg.H.** 1965 ch. 299, operative January 1, 1967.

Ref.: Herlick Handbook § 14.40; Cal. Courtroom Ev., §18.05 (Matthew Bender).

CHAPTER 2
APPLICABILITY OF DIVISION

§910. Applicability of division.

Except as otherwise provided by statute, the provisions of this division apply in all proceedings. The provisions of any statute making rules of evidence inapplicable in particular proceedings, or limiting the applicability of rules of evidence in particular proceedings, do not make this division inapplicable to such proceedings. **Leg.H.** 1965 ch. 299, operative January 1, 1967.

Ref.: Herlick Handbook § 14.40; Cal. Courtroom Ev., §18.06 (Matthew Bender).

CHAPTER 3 GENERAL PROVISIONS RELATING TO PRIVILEGES

§911. General provision.

Except as otherwise provided by statute:

(a) No person has a privilege to refuse to be a witness.

(b) No person has a privilege to refuse to disclose any matter or to refuse to produce any writing, object, or other thing.

(c) No person has a privilege that another shall not be a witness or shall not disclose any matter or shall not produce any writing, object, or other thing. **Leg.H.** 1965 ch. 299, operative January 1, 1967.

Ref.: Herlick Handbook § 14.40; Cal. Courtroom Ev., §§18.07, 18.65[2] (Matthew Bender); MB Prac. Guide: Cal. Trial & Post-Trial Civ. Proc., §§11.80, 11.85[1].

§912. Waiver by disclosure—Joint holders of privilege.

(a) Except as otherwise provided in this section, the right of any person to claim a privilege provided by Section 954 (lawyer-client privilege), 980 (privilege for confidential marital communications), 994 (physician-patient privilege), 1014 (psychotherapist-patient privilege), 1033 (privilege of penitent), 1034 (privilege of clergyman), 1035.8 (sexual assault counselor-victim privilege), or 1037.5 (domestic violence counselor-victim privilege) is waived with respect to a communication protected by the privilege if any holder of the privilege, without coercion, has disclosed a significant part of the communication or has consented to disclosure made by anyone. Consent to disclosure is manifested by any statement or other conduct of the holder of the privilege indicating consent to the disclosure, including failure to claim the privilege in any proceeding in which the holder has the legal standing and opportunity to claim the privilege.

(b) Where two or more persons are joint holders of a privilege provided by Section 954 (lawyer-client privilege), 994 (physician-patient privilege), 1014 (psychotherapist-patient privilege), 1035.8 (sexual assault counselor-victim privilege), or 1037.5 (domestic violence counselor-victim privilege), a waiver of the right of a particular joint holder of the privilege to claim the privilege does not affect the right of another joint holder to claim the privilege. In the case of the privilege provided by Section 980 (privilege for confidential marital communications), a waiver of the right of one spouse to claim the privilege does not affect the right of the other spouse to claim the privilege.

(c) A disclosure that is itself privileged is not a waiver of any privilege.

(d) A disclosure in confidence of a communication that is protected by a privilege provided by Section 954 (lawyer-client privilege), 994 (physician-patient privilege), 1014 (psychotherapist-patient privilege), 1035.8 (sexual assault counselor-victim privilege), or 1037.5 (domestic violence counselor-victim privilege), when disclosure is reasonably necessary for the accomplishment of the purpose for which the lawyer, physician, psychotherapist, sexual assault counselor, or domestic violence counselor was consulted, is not a waiver of the privilege. **Leg.H.** 1965 ch. 299, operative January 1, 1967, 1980 ch. 917, 2002 ch. 72 (SB 2061), 2004 ch. 405 (SB 1796).

Ref.: Herlick Handbook § 14.40; Cal. Courtroom Ev., §§18.00[3], 18.08, 18.21[3] (Matthew Bender); MB Prac. Guide: Cal. Trial & Post-Trial Civ. Proc., §§11.80, 11.85[2][g], [3].

§913. Comment on exercise of privilege prohibited—No presumption or inference.

(a) If in the instant proceeding or on a prior occasion a privilege is or was exercised not to testify with respect to any matter, or to refuse to disclose or to prevent another from disclosing any matter, neither the presiding officer nor counsel may comment thereon, no presumption shall arise because of the exercise of the privilege, and the trier of fact may not draw any inference therefrom as to the credibility of the witness or as to any matter at issue in the proceeding.

(b) The court, at the request of a party who may be adversely affected because an unfavorable inference may be drawn by the jury because a privilege has been exercised, shall instruct the jury that no presumption arises because of the exercise of the privilege and that the jury may not draw any inference therefrom as to the credibility of the witness or as to any matter at issue in the proceeding. **Leg.H.** 1965 ch. 299, operative January 1, 1967.

Ref.: Herlick Handbook § 14.40; Cal. Courtroom Ev., §§11.03[2], 18.00[4], 18.09 (Matthew Bender); MB Prac. Guide: Cal. Trial & Post-Trial Civ. Proc., §§11.80, 11.85[4]; CACI Nos. 215, 216 (Matthew Bender).

§914. Determination of claim of privilege—Contempt for failure to disclose information.

(a) The presiding officer shall determine a claim of privilege in any proceeding in the same manner as a court determines such a claim under Article 2 (commencing with Section 400) of Chapter 4 of Division 3.

(b) No person may be held in contempt for failure to disclose information claimed to be privileged unless he has failed to comply with an order of a court that he disclose such information. This subdivision does not apply to any governmental agency that has constitutional contempt power, nor does it apply to hearings and investigations of the Industrial Accident Commission, nor does it impliedly repeal Chapter 4 (commencing with Section 9400) of Part 1 of Division 2 of Title 2 of the Government Code. If no other statutory procedure is applicable, the procedure prescribed by Section 1991 of the Code of Civil Procedure shall be followed in seeking an order of a court that the person disclose the information claimed to be privileged. **Leg.H.** 1965 ch. 299, operative January 1, 1967.

Ref.: Herlick Handbook § 14.40; Cal. Courtroom Ev., §18.10 (Matthew Bender).

§915. Disclosure of information to determine claim—Official information—Identity of informer—Trade secrets.

(a) Subject to subdivision (b), the presiding officer may not require disclosure of information claimed to be privileged under this division or attorney work product under subdivision (a) of Section 2018.030 of the Code of Civil Procedure in order to rule on the claim of privilege; provided, however, that in any hearing conducted pursuant to subdivision (c) of Section 1524 of the Penal Code in which a claim of privilege is made and the court determines that there is no other feasible means to rule on the validity of the claim other than to require disclosure, the court shall proceed in accordance with subdivision (b).

(b) When a court is ruling on a claim of privilege under Article 9 (commencing with Section 1040) of Chapter 4 (official information and identity of informer) or under Section 1060 (trade secret) or under subdivision (b) of Section 2018.030 of the Code of Civil Procedure (attorney work product) and is unable to do so without requiring disclosure of the information claimed to be privileged, the court may require the person from whom disclosure is sought or the person authorized to claim the privilege, or both, to disclose the information in chambers out of the presence and hearing of all persons except the person authorized to claim the privilege and any other persons as the person authorized to claim the privilege is willing to have present. If the judge determines that the information is privileged, neither the judge nor any other person may ever disclose, without the consent of a person authorized to permit disclosure, what was disclosed in the course of the proceedings in chambers. **Leg.H.** 1965 ch. 299, operative January 1, 1967, 1979 ch. 1034, 2001 ch. 812, 2004 ch. 182 (AB 3081), operative July 1, 2005.

Ref.: Herlick Handbook § 14.40; Cal. Courtroom Ev., §18.11 (Matthew Bender).

§916. Exclusion of information where holder of privilege not a party.

(a) The presiding officer, on his own motion or on the motion of any party, shall exclude information that is subject to a claim of privilege under this division if:

(1) The person from whom the information is sought is not a person authorized to claim the privilege; and

(2) There is no party to the proceeding who is a person authorized to claim the privilege.

(b) The presiding officer may not exclude information under this section if:

(1) He is otherwise instructed by a person authorized to permit disclosure; or

(2) The proponent of the evidence establishes that there is no person authorized to claim the privilege in existence. **Leg.H.** 1965 ch. 299, operative January 1, 1967.

Ref.: Herlick Handbook § 14.40.

§917. Presumption of confidential nature of communication; electronic communication retains privileged character.

(a) If a privilege is claimed on the ground that the matter sought to be disclosed is a communication made in confidence in the course of the lawyer-client, physician-patient, psychotherapist-patient, clergy-penitent, husband-wife, sexual assault counselor-victim, or domestic violence counselor-victim relationship, the communication is presumed to have been made in confidence and the opponent of the claim of privilege has the burden of proof to establish that the communication was not confidential.

(b) A communication between persons in a relationship listed in subdivision (a) does not lose its privileged character for the sole reason that it is communicated by electronic means or because persons involved in the delivery, facilitation, or storage of electronic communication may have access to the content of the communication.

(c) For purposes of this section, "electronic" has the same meaning provided in Section 1633.2 of the Civil Code. **Leg.H.** 1965 ch. 299, operative January 1, 1967, 2002 ch. 72 (SB 2061), 2003 ch. 468 (SB 851), 2004 ch. 183 (AB 3082), 2006 ch. 689 (SB 1743) §2.

Ref.: Herlick Handbook § 14.40; Cal. Courtroom Ev., §18.13 (Matthew Bender); MB Prac. Guide: Cal. Trial & Post-Trial Civ. Proc., §§11.80, 11.85[5].

§918. Error in disallowing claim.

A party may predicate error on a ruling disallowing a claim of privilege only if he is the holder of the privilege, except that a party may predicate error on a ruling disallowing a claim of privilege by his spouse under Section 970 or 971. **Leg.H.** 1965 ch. 299, operative January 1, 1967.

Ref.: Herlick Handbook § 14.40.

§919. Inadmissibility of privileged information erroneously disclosed.

(a) Evidence of a statement or other disclosure of privileged information is inadmissible against a holder of the privilege if:

(1) A person authorized to claim the privilege claimed it but nevertheless disclosure erroneously was required to be made; or

(2) The presiding officer did not exclude the privileged information as required by Section 916.

(b) If a person authorized to claim the privilege claimed it, whether in the same or a prior proceeding, but nevertheless disclosure erroneously was required by the presiding officer to be made, neither the failure to refuse to disclose nor the failure to seek review of the order of the presiding officer requiring disclosure indicates consent to the disclosure or constitutes a waiver and, under these circumstances, the disclosure is one made under coercion. **Leg.H.** 1965 ch. 299, operative January 1, 1967, 1974 ch. 227.

Ref.: Herlick Handbook § 14.40; Cal. Courtroom Ev., §18.15 (Matthew Bender).

§920. Construction against repeal by implication.

Nothing in this division shall be construed to repeal by implication any other statute relating to privileges. **Leg.H.** 1965 ch. 299, operative January 1, 1967.

Ref.: Herlick Handbook § 14.40; Cal. Courtroom Ev., §§2.26[3], 18.16 (Matthew Bender).

CHAPTER 4
PARTICULAR PRIVILEGES

ARTICLE 3
Lawyer-Client Privilege
[Selected Provisions]

§953. "Holder of privilege" defined.

As used in this article, "holder of the privilege" means:

(a) The client when he has no guardian or conservator.

(b) A guardian or conservator of the client when the client has a guardian or conservator.

(c) The personal representative of the client if the client is dead.

(d) A successor, assign, trustee in dissolution, or any similar representative of a firm, association, organization, partnership, business trust, corporation, or public entity that is no longer in existence. **Leg.H.** 1965 ch. 299, operative January 1, 1967.

Ref.: Herlick Handbook § 14.40; Cal. Courtroom Ev., §18.22 (Matthew Bender); MB Prac. Guide: Fed. Pretrial Proc. in Cal., §§24.31, 24.32[2][c]; MB Prac. Guide: Cal. Trial & Post-Trial Civ. Proc., §§11.80, 11.85[2][b].

ARTICLE 4
Privilege Not to Testify Against Spouse
[Selected Provisions]

§971. Spouse of party called as witness by adverse party.

Except as otherwise provided by statute, a married person whose spouse is a party to a proceeding has a privilege not to be called as a witness by an adverse party to that proceeding without the prior express consent of the spouse having the privilege under this section unless the party calling the spouse does so in good faith without knowledge of the marital relationship. **Leg.H.** 1965 ch. 299, operative January 1, 1967.

Ref.: Herlick Handbook § 14.40; Cal. Courtroom Ev., §18.34 (Matthew Bender); MB Prac. Guide: Fed. Pretrial Proc. in Cal., §24.59[4].

§972. Exceptions to privilege.

A married person does not have a privilege under this article in:

(a) A proceeding brought by or on behalf of one spouse against the other spouse.

(b) A proceeding to commit or otherwise place his or her spouse or his or her spouse's property, or both, under the control of another because of the spouse's alleged mental or physical condition.

(c) A proceeding brought by or on behalf of a spouse to establish his or her competence.

(d) A proceeding under the Juvenile Court Law, Chapter 2 (commencing with Section 200) of Part 1 of Division 2 of the Welfare and Institutions Code.

(e) A criminal proceeding in which one spouse is charged with:

(1) A crime against the person or property of the other spouse or of a child, parent, relative, or cohabitant of either, whether committed before or during marriage.

(2) A crime against the person or property of a third person committed in the course of committing a crime against the person or property of the other spouse, whether committed before or during marriage.

(3) Bigamy.

(4) A crime defined by Section 270 or 270a of the Penal Code.

(f) A proceeding resulting from a criminal act which occurred prior to legal marriage of the spouses to each other regarding knowledge acquired prior to that marriage if prior to the legal marriage the witness spouse was aware that his or her spouse had been arrested for or had been formally charged with the crime or crimes about which the spouse is called to testify.

(g) A proceeding brought against the spouse by a former spouse so long as the property and debts of the marriage have not been adjudicated, or in order to establish, modify, or enforce a child, family or spousal support obligation arising from the marriage to the former spouse; in a proceeding brought against a spouse by the other parent in order to establish, modify, or enforce a child support obligation for a child of a nonmarital relationship of the spouse; or in a proceeding brought against a spouse by the guardian of a child of that spouse in order to establish, modify, or enforce a child support obligation of the spouse. The married person does not have a privilege under this subdivision to refuse to provide information relating to the issues of income, expenses, assets, debts, and employment of either spouse, but may assert the privilege as otherwise provided in this article if other information is requested by the former spouse, guardian, or other parent of the child.

Any person demanding the otherwise privileged information made available by this subdivision, who also has an obligation to support the child for whom an order to establish, modify, or enforce child support is sought, waives his or her marital privilege to the same extent as the spouse as provided in this subdivision. **Leg.H.** 1965 ch. 299, 1975 ch. 71, 1982 ch. 256, 1983 ch. 244, 1986 ch. 769, 1989 ch. 1359.

Ref.: Herlick Handbook § 14.40; Cal. Courtroom Ev., §18.35 (Matthew Bender); MB Prac. Guide: Fed. Pretrial Proc. in Cal., §24.59[4]; MB Prac. Guide: Cal. Trial & Post-Trial Civ. Proc., §§11.80, 11.85[2][c]; W. Cal. Sum., 10 "Parent and Child" §§620, 873.

§973. Waiver—Proceeding brought or defended for benefit of spouse.

(a) Unless erroneously compelled to do so, a married person who testifies in a proceeding to which his spouse is a party, or who testifies against his spouse in any proceeding, does not have a privilege under this article in the proceeding in which such testimony is given.

(b) There is no privilege under this article in a civil proceeding brought or defended by a married person for the immediate benefit of his spouse or of himself and his spouse. **Leg.H.** 1965 ch. 299, operative January 1, 1967.

Ref.: Herlick Handbook § 14.40; Cal. Courtroom Ev., §18.36 (Matthew Bender); MB Prac. Guide: Fed. Pretrial Proc. in Cal., §24.59[4].

ARTICLE 5
Privilege for Confidential Marital Communications [Selected Provisions]

§980. General provision.

Subject to Section 912 and except as otherwise provided in this article, a spouse (or his guardian or conservator when he has a guardian or conservator), whether or not a party, has a privilege during the marital relationship and afterwards to refuse to disclose, and to prevent another from disclosing, a communication if he claims the privilege and the communication was made in confidence between him and the other spouse while they were husband and wife. **Leg.H.** 1965 ch. 299, operative January 1, 1967.

Ref.: Herlick Handbook § 14.40; Cal. Courtroom Ev., §18.37 (Matthew Bender); MB Prac. Guide: Fed. Pretrial Proc. in Cal., §24.58[6]; MB Prac. Guide: Cal. Trial & Post-Trial Civ. Proc., §§11.80, 11.85[2][d]; W. Cal. Sum., 11 "Husband and Wife" §151.

ARTICLE 6
Physician-Patient Privilege [Selected Provisions]

§996. Condition of patient in issue.

There is no privilege under this article as to a communication relevant to an issue concerning the condition of the patient if such issue has been tendered by:

(a) The patient;

(b) Any party claiming through or under the patient;

(c) Any party claiming as a beneficiary of the patient through a contract to which the patient is or was a party; or

(d) The plaintiff in an action brought under Section 376 or 377 of the Code of Civil Procedure for damages for the injury or death of the patient.

Ref.: Cal. Courtroom Ev., §18.51 (Matthew Bender); MB Prac. Guide: Fed. Pretrial Proc. in Cal., §§24.41, 24.43[6]; MB Prac. Guide: Cal. Trial & Post-Trial Civ. Proc., §§11.80, 11.85[2][e].

ARTICLE 7
Psychotherapist-Patient Privilege [Selected Provisions]

§1010. "Psychotherapist" defined.

As used in this article, "psychotherapist" means a person who is, or is reasonably believed by the patient to be:

(a) A person authorized to practice medicine in any state or nation who devotes, or is reasonably believed by the patient to devote, a substantial portion of his or her time to the practice of psychiatry.

(b) A person licensed as a psychologist under Chapter 6.6 (commencing with Section 2900) of Division 2 of the Business and Professions Code.

(c) A person licensed as a clinical social worker under Article 4 (commencing with Section 4996) of Chapter 14 of Division 2 of the Business and Professions Code, when he or she is engaged in applied psychotherapy of a nonmedical nature.

(d) A person who is serving as a school psychologist and holds a credential authorizing that service issued by the state.

(e) A person licensed as a marriage and family therapist under Chapter 13 (commencing with Section 4980) of Division 2 of the Business and Professions Code.

(f) A person registered as a psychological assistant who is under the supervision of a licensed psychologist or board certified psychiatrist as required by Section 2913 of the Business and Professions Code, or a person registered as a marriage and family therapist intern who is under the supervision of a licensed marriage and family therapist, a licensed clinical social worker, a licensed psychologist, or a licensed physician certified in psychiatry, as specified in Section 4980.44 of the Business and Professions Code.

(g) A person registered as an associate clinical social worker who is under the supervision of a licensed clinical social worker, a licensed psychologist or a board certified psychiatrist as required by Section 4996.20 or 4996.21 of the Business and Professions Code.

(h) A person exempt from the Psychology Licensing Law pursuant to subdivision (d) of Section 2909 of the Business and Professions Code who is under the supervision of a licensed psychologist or board certified psychiatrist.

(i) A psychological intern as defined in Section 2911 of the Business and Professions Code who is under the supervision of a licensed psychologist or board certified psychiatrist.

(j) A trainee, as defined in subdivision (c) of Section 4980.03 of the Business and Professions Code, who is fulfilling his or her supervised practicum required by subdivision (b) of Section 4980.40 of the Business and Professions Code and is supervised by a licensed psychologist, board certified psychiatrist, a licensed clinical social worker, or a licensed marriage and family therapist.

(k) A person licensed as a registered nurse pursuant to Chapter 6 (commencing with Section 2700) of Division 2 of the Business and Professions Code, who possesses a master's degree in psychiatric-mental health nursing and is listed as a psychiatric-mental health nurse by the Board of Registered Nursing.

(*l*) An advanced practice registered nurse who is certified as a clinical nurse specialist pursuant to Article 9 (commencing with Section 2838) of Chapter 6 of Division 2 of the Business and Professions Code and who participates in expert clinical practice in the specialty of psychiatric-mental health nursing.

(m) A person rendering mental health treatment or counseling services as authorized pursuant to Section 6924 of the Family Code. **Leg.H.** 1965 ch. 299, operative January 1, 1967, 1967 ch. 1677, 1970 chs. 1396, 1397 §1.5, 1972 ch. 888, 1974 ch. 546, 1983 ch. 928, 1987 ch. 724, 1988 ch. 488, 1989 ch. 1104, 1990 ch. 662, 1992 ch. 308, 1994 ch. 1270, 2001 chs. 142, 420, effective October 2, 2001, §1, operative until January 1, 2002, §1.5, operative January 1, 2002.

Ref.: Herlick Handbook § 14.40; Cal. Courtroom Ev., §18.63 (Matthew Bender); MB Prac. Guide: Fed. Pretrial Proc. in Cal., §24.50; CACI No. 503A (Matthew Bender); W. Cal. Sum., 1 "Contracts" §45.

§1010.5. Application of privilege to educational psychologist.

A communication between a patient and an educational psychologist, licensed under Article 5 (commencing with Section 4986) of Chapter 13 of Division 2 of the Business and Professions Code, shall be privileged to the same extent, and subject to the same limitations, as a communication between a patient and a psychotherapist described in subdivisions (c), (d), and (e) of Section 1010. **Leg.H.** 1985 ch. 545.

Ref.: Herlick Handbook § 14.40; MB Prac. Guide: Fed. Pretrial Proc. in Cal., §24.50.

§1011. "Patient" defined.

As used in this article, "patient" means a person who consults a psychotherapist or submits to an examination by a psychotherapist for the purpose of securing a diagnosis or preventive, palliative, or curative treatment of his mental or emotional condition or who submits to an examination of his mental or emotional condition for the purpose of scientific research on mental or emotional problems. **Leg.H.** 1965 ch. 299, operative January 1, 1967.

Ref.: Herlick Handbook § 14.40; Cal. Courtroom Ev., §18.65 (Matthew Bender); MB Prac. Guide: Fed. Pretrial Proc. in Cal., §24.50.

§1012. "Confidential communication between patient and psychotherapist" defined.

As used in this article, "confidential communication between patient and psychotherapist" means information, including information obtained by an examination of the patient, transmitted between a patient and his psychotherapist in the course of that relationship and in confidence by a means which, so far as the patient is aware, discloses the information to no third persons other than those who are present to further the interest of the patient in the consultation, or those to whom disclosure is reasonably necessary for the transmission of the information or the accomplishment of the purpose for which the psychotherapist is consulted, and includes a diagnosis made and the advice given by the psychotherapist in the course of that relationship. **Leg.H.** 1965 ch. 299, operative January 1, 1967, 1967 ch. 650, 1970 chs. 1396, 1397.

Ref.: Herlick Handbook § 14.40; Cal. Courtroom Ev., §18.66 (Matthew Bender); MB Prac. Guide: Fed. Pretrial Proc. in Cal., §24.50; W. Cal. Sum., 10 "Parent and Child" §§620, 873.

§1013. "Holder of privilege" defined.

As used in this article, "holder of the privilege" means:

(a) The patient when he has no guardian or conservator.

(b) A guardian or conservator of the patient when the patient has a guardian or conservator.

(c) The personal representative of the patient if the patient is dead. **Leg.H.** 1965 ch. 299, operative January 1, 1967.

Ref.: Herlick Handbook § 14.40; Cal. Courtroom Ev., §18.67 (Matthew Bender); MB Prac. Guide: Fed. Pretrial Proc. in Cal., §24.50; MB Prac. Guide: Cal. Trial & Post-Trial Civ. Proc., §§11.80, 11.85[2][f].

§1014. Who may claim privilege.

Subject to Section 912 and except as otherwise provided in this article, the patient, whether or not a party, has a privilege to refuse to disclose, and to prevent another from disclosing, a confidential communication between patient and psychotherapist if the privilege is claimed by:

(a) The holder of the privilege.

(b) A person who is authorized to claim the privilege by the holder of the privilege.

(c) The person who was the psychotherapist at the time of the confidential communication, but the person may not claim the privilege if there is no holder of the privilege in existence or if he or she is otherwise instructed by a person authorized to permit disclosure.

The relationship of a psychotherapist and patient shall exist between a psychological corporation as defined in Article 9 (commencing with Section 2995) of Chapter 6.6 of Division 2 of the Business and Professions Code, a marriage and family therapy corporation as defined in Article 6 (commencing with Section 4987.5) of Chapter 13 of Division 2 of the Business and Professions Code, or a licensed clinical social workers corporation as defined in Article 5 (commencing with Section 4998) of Chapter 14 of Division 2 of the Business and Professions Code, and the patient to whom it renders professional services, as well as between those patients and psychotherapists employed by those corporations to render services to those patients. The word "persons" as used in this subdivision includes partnerships, corporations, limited liability companies, associations and other groups and entities. **Leg.H.** 1965 ch. 299, operative January 1, 1967, 1969 ch. 1436, 1972 ch. 1286, 1989 ch. 1104, 1990 ch. 605, 1994 ch. 1010, 2002 ch. 1013 (SB 2026).

Ref.: Herlick Handbook § 14.40; Cal. Courtroom Ev., §18.68 (Matthew Bender); MB Prac. Guide: Fed. Pretrial Proc. in Cal., §24.50; MB Prac. Guide: Cal. Trial & Post-Trial Civ. Proc., §§11.80, 11.85[2][f]; W. Cal. Sum., 10 "Parent and Child" §§284, 873.

§1015. When psychotherapist must claim privilege.

The psychotherapist who received or made a communication subject to the privilege under this article shall claim the privilege whenever he is present when the communication is sought to be disclosed and is authorized to claim the privilege under subdivision (c) of Section 1014. **Leg.H.** 1965 ch. 299, operative January 1, 1967.

Ref.: Herlick Handbook § 14.40; Cal. Courtroom Ev., §18.70 (Matthew Bender); MB Prac. Guide: Fed. Pretrial Proc. in Cal., §24.50.

§1016. Condition of patient in issue.

There is no privilege under this article as to a communication relevant to an issue concerning the mental or emotional condition of the patient if such issue has been tendered by:

(a) The patient;

(b) Any party claiming through or under the patient;

(c) Any party claiming as a beneficiary of the patient through a contract to which the patient is or was a party; or

(d) The plaintiff in an action brought under Section 376 or 377 of the Code of Civil Procedure for damages for the injury or death of the patient. **Leg.H.** 1965 ch. 299, operative January 1, 1967.

Ref.: Herlick Handbook § 14.40; Cal. Courtroom Ev., §§18.71, 18.72[2], 18.78[2] (Matthew Bender); MB Prac. Guide: Fed. Pretrial Proc. in Cal., §24.50; MB Prac. Guide: Cal. Trial & Post-Trial Civ. Proc., §§11.80, 11.85[2][f]; W. Cal. Sum., 10 "Parent and Child" §620.

ARTICLE 9
Official Information and Identity of Informer [Selected Provisions]

§1043. Investigation of citizens' complaints—Discovery or disclosure of peace or custodial officer personnel records.

(a) In any case in which discovery or disclosure is sought of peace or custodial officer personnel records or records maintained pursuant to Section 832.5 of the Penal Code or information from those records, the party seeking the discovery or disclosure shall file a written motion with the appropriate court or administrative body upon written notice to the governmental agency which has custody and control of the records. The written notice shall be given at the times prescribed by subdivision (b) of Section 1005 of the Code of Civil Procedure. Upon receipt of the notice the governmental agency served shall immediately notify the individual whose records are sought.

(b) The motion shall include all of the following:

(1) Identification of the proceeding in which discovery or disclosure is sought, the party seeking discovery or disclosure, the peace or custodial officer whose records are sought, the governmental agency which has custody and control of the records, and the time and place at which the motion for discovery or disclosure shall be heard.

(2) A description of the type of records or information sought.

(3) Affidavits showing good cause for the discovery or disclosure sought, setting forth the materiality thereof to the subject matter involved in the pending litigation and stating upon reasonable belief that the governmental agency identified has the records or information from the records.

(c) No hearing upon a motion for discovery or disclosure shall be held without full compliance with the notice provisions of this section except upon a showing by the moving party of good cause for noncompliance, or upon a waiver of the hearing by the governmental agency identified as having the records. **Leg.H.** 1978 ch. 630, 1989 ch. 693, 2002 ch. 391 (AB 2040).

Ref.: Herlick Handbook § 14.40; Cal. Courtroom Ev., §18.111 (Matthew Bender).

DIVISION 10
HEARSAY EVIDENCE

CHAPTER 2
EXCEPTIONS TO THE HEARSAY RULE

ARTICLE 7
Business Records

§1270. "Business" defined.

As used in this article, "a business" includes every kind of business, governmental activity, profession, occupation, calling, or operation of institutions, whether carried on for profit or not. **Leg.H.** 1965 ch. 299, operative January 1, 1967.

Ref.: Cal. Courtroom Ev., §21.37 (Matthew Bender); MB Prac. Guide: Cal. Trial & Post-Trial Civ. Proc., §§11.101, 11.104[25], [49].

§1271. Record as evidence.

Evidence of a writing made as a record of an act, condition, or event is not made inadmissible by the hearsay rule when offered to prove the act, condition, or event if:

(a) The writing was made in the regular course of a business;

(b) The writing was made at or near the time of the act, condition, or event;

(c) The custodian or other qualified witness testifies to its identity and the mode of its preparation; and

(d) The sources of information and method and time of preparation were such as to indicate its trustworthiness. **Leg.H.** 1965 ch. 299, operative January 1, 1967.

Ref.: Cal. Courtroom Ev., §§21.38, 21.40[3] (Matthew Bender); MB Prac. Guide: Cal. Debt Collection & Enforcement of Judgments, §§7.03, 7.07[1]; MB Prac. Guide: Cal. Trial & Post-Trial Civ. Proc., §§11.101, 11.104[25], [40].

§1272. Absence of record as evidence.

Evidence of the absence from the records of a business of a record of an asserted act, condition, or event is not made inadmissible by the hearsay rule when offered to prove the nonoccurrence of the act or event, or the nonexistence of the condition, if:

(a) It was the regular course of that business to make records of all such acts, conditions, or events at or near the time of the act, condition, or event and to preserve them; and

(b) The sources of information and method and time of preparation of the records of that business were such that the absence of a record of an act, condition, or event is a trustworthy indication that the act or event did not occur or the condition did not exist. **Leg.H.** 1965 ch. 299, operative January 1, 1967.

Ref.: Cal. Courtroom Ev., §21.39 (Matthew Bender); MB Prac. Guide: Cal. Debt Collection & Enforcement of Judgments, §§7.03, 7.07[2]; MB Prac. Guide: Cal. Trial & Post-Trial Civ. Proc., §§11.101, 11.104[25].

DIVISION 11
WRITINGS

CHAPTER 2
SECONDARY EVIDENCE OF WRITINGS

ARTICLE 3
Photographic Copies and Printed Representations of Writings

§1550. [Operative Until Amendment by Stats. 2002 Ch. 124 Becomes Operative] Business records.

A nonerasable optical image reproduction provided that additions, deletions, or changes to the original document are not permitted by the technology, a photostatic, microfilm, microcard, miniature photographic, or other photographic copy or reproduction, or an enlargement thereof, of a writing is as admissible as the writing itself if the copy or reproduction was made and preserved as a part of the records of a business (as defined by Section 1270) in the regular course of that business. The introduction of the copy, reproduction, or enlargement does not preclude admission of the original writing if it is still in existence. A court may require the introduction of a hard copy printout of the document. **Leg.H.** 1965 ch. 299, operative January 1, 1967, 1992 ch. 876.

Ref.: Cal. Courtroom Ev., §23.08 (Matthew Bender).

§1550. [See Note for Operative Information] Business records.

(a) If made and preserved as a part of the records of a business, as defined in Section 1270, in the regular course of that business, the following types of evidence of a writing are as admissible as the writing itself:

(1) A nonerasable optical image reproduction or any other reproduction of a public record by a trusted system, as defined in Section 12168.7 of the Government Code, if additions, deletions, or changes to the original document are not permitted by the technology.

(2) A photostatic copy or reproduction.

(3) A microfilm, microcard, or miniature photographic copy, reprint, or enlargement.

(4) Any other photographic copy or reproduction, or an enlargement thereof.

(b) The introduction of evidence of a writing pursuant to subdivision (a) does not preclude admission of the original writing if it is still in existence. A court may require the introduction of a hard copy printout of the document. **Leg.H.** 1965 ch. 299, operative January 1, 1967, 1992 ch. 876, 2002 ch. 124 (AB 2033).

2002 Note: This act shall become operative on the date the Secretary of State adopts uniform standards for storing and recording permanent and nonpermanent documents in electronic media, as required by Section 12168.7 of the Government Code. Stats. 2002 ch. 124 (AB 2033) §2.

Ref.: Cal. Courtroom Ev., §23.08 (Matthew Bender).

§1550.1. Admissibility of reproductions of files, records, writings, photographs, fingerprints or other instruments.

Reproductions of files, records, writings, photographs, fingerprints or other instruments in the official custody of a criminal justice agency that were microphotographed or otherwise reproduced in a manner that conforms with the provisions of Section 11106.1, 11106.2, or 11106.3 of the Penal Code shall be admissible to the same extent and under the same circumstances as the original file, record, writing or other instrument would be admissible. **Leg.H.** 2004 ch. 65 (AB 883).

2004 Note: The addition of §1550.1 is declarative of existing law. Stats. 2004 ch. 65 (AB 883) §3.

Ref.: MB Prac. Guide: Cal. Trial & Post-Trial Civ. Proc., §§9.10, 11.108.

§1551. Lost or destroyed writings.

A print, whether enlarged or not, from a photographic film (including a photographic plate, microphotographic film, photostatic negative, or similar reproduction) of an original writing destroyed or lost after such film was taken is as admissible as the original writing itself if, at the time of the taking of such film, the person under whose direction and control it was taken attached thereto, or to the sealed container in which it was placed and has been kept, or incorporated in the film, a certification complying with the provisions of Section 1531 and stating the date on which, and the fact that, it was so taken under his direction and control.

Ref.: Cal. Courtroom Ev., §23.10 (Matthew Bender).

§1552. Printed representations of computer information.

(a) A printed representation of computer information or a computer program is presumed to be an accurate representation of the computer information or computer program that it purports to represent. This presumption is a presumption affecting the burden of producing evidence. If a party to an action introduces evidence that a printed representation of computer information or computer program is inaccurate or unreliable, the party introducing the printed representation into evidence has the burden of proving, by a preponderance of evidence, that the printed representation is an accurate representation of the existence and content of the computer information or computer program that it purports to represent.

(b) Subdivision (a) shall not apply to computer-generated official records certified in accordance with Section 452.5 or 1530. **Leg.H.** 1998 ch. 100.

1998 Note: Stats. 1998 ch. 100 applies in an action or proceeding commenced before, on, or after January 1, 1999. Stats. 1998 ch. 100 §9(b).

Ref.: Cal. Courtroom Ev., §23.11 (Matthew Bender); MB Prac. Guide: Cal. Trial & Post-Trial Civ. Proc., §§9.10, 9.11[3].

§1553. Printed representation of images stored on video or digital medium.

A printed representation of images stored on a video or digital medium is presumed to be an accurate representation of the images it purports to represent. This presumption is a presumption affecting the burden of producing evidence. If a party to an action introduces evidence that a printed representation of images stored on a video or digital medium is inaccurate or unreliable, the party introducing the printed representation into evidence has the burden of proving, by a preponderance of evidence, that the printed representation is an accurate representation of the existence and content of the images that it purports to represent. **Leg.H.** 1998 ch. 100.

1998 Note: Stats. 1998 ch. 100 applies in an action or proceeding commenced before, on, or after January 1, 1999. Stats. 1998 ch. 100 §9(b).

Ref.: Cal. Courtroom Ev., §23.12 (Matthew Bender).

ARTICLE 4
Production of Business Records

§1560. Copies—Transmittal.

(a) As used in this article:

(1) "Business" includes every kind of business described in Section 1270.

(2) "Record" includes every kind of record maintained by a business.

(b) Except as provided in Section 1564, when a subpoena duces tecum is served upon the custodian of records or other qualified witness of a business in an action in which the business is neither a party nor the place where any cause of action is alleged to have arisen, and the subpoena requires the production of all or any part of the records of the business, it is sufficient compliance therewith if the custodian or other qualified witness delivers by mail or otherwise a true, legible, and durable copy of all of the records described in the subpoena to the clerk of the court or to another person described in subdivision (d) of Section 2026.010 of the Code of Civil Procedure, together with the affidavit described in Section 1561, within one of the following time periods:

(1) In any criminal action, five days after the receipt of the subpoena.

(2) In any civil action, within 15 days after the receipt of the subpoena.

(3) Within the time agreed upon by the party who served the subpoena and the custodian or other qualified witness.

(c) The copy of the records shall be separately enclosed in an inner envelope or wrapper, sealed, with the title and number of the action, name of witness, and date of subpoena clearly inscribed thereon; the sealed envelope or wrapper shall then be enclosed in an outer envelope or wrapper, sealed, and directed as follows:

(1) If the subpoena directs attendance in court, to the clerk of the court.

(2) If the subpoena directs attendance at a deposition, to the officer before whom the deposition is to be taken, at the place designated in the subpoena for the taking of the deposition or at the officer's place of business.

(3) In other cases, to the officer, body, or tribunal conducting the hearing, at a like address.

(d) Unless the parties to the proceeding otherwise agree, or unless the sealed envelope or wrapper is returned to a witness who is to appear personally, the copy of the records shall remain sealed and shall be opened only at the time of trial, deposition, or other hearing, upon the direction of the judge, officer, body, or tribunal conducting the proceeding, in the presence of all parties who have appeared in person or by counsel at the trial, deposition, or hearing. Records that are original documents and that are not introduced in evidence or required as part of the record shall be returned to the person or entity from whom received. Records that are copies may be destroyed.

(e) As an alternative to the procedures described in subdivisions (b), (c), and (d), the subpoenaing party in a civil action may direct the witness to make the records available for inspection or copying by the party's attorney, the attorney's representative, or deposition officer as described in Section 2020.420 of the Code of Civil Procedure, at the witness' business address under reasonable conditions during normal business hours. Normal business hours, as used in this subdivision, means those hours that the business of the witness is normally open for business to the public. When provided with at least five business days' advance notice by the party's attorney, attorney's representative, or deposition officer, the witness shall designate a time period of not less than six continuous hours on a date certain for copying of records subject to the subpoena by the party's attorney, attorney's representative, or deposition officer. It shall be the responsibility of the attorney's representative to deliver any copy of the records as directed in the subpoena. Disobedience to the deposition subpoena issued pursuant to this subdivision is punishable as provided in Section 2020.240 of the Code of Civil Procedure. **Leg.H.** 1965 ch. 299, operative January 1, 1967, 1969 ch. 199, 1982 ch. 452, 1984 ch. 481, 1986 ch. 603, 1991 ch. 1090, 1997 ch. 442, 1999 ch. 444, 2000 ch. 287, 2004 chs. 162 (AB 1249), 182 (AB 3081), operative July 1, 2005 (ch. 162 prevails; ch. 182 not effective), 2005 ch. 294 (AB 333) §18, 2006 ch. 538 (SB 1852) §155.

Ref.: Cal. Courtroom Ev., §23.13 (Matthew Bender); MB Prac. Guide: Cal. Trial & Post-Trial Civ. Proc., §7.15[1].

§1561. Affidavit accompanying record.

(a) The records shall be accompanied by the affidavit of the custodian or other qualified witness, stating in substance each of the following:

(1) The affiant is the duly authorized custodian of the records or other qualified witness and has authority to certify the records.

(2) The copy is a true copy of all the records described in the subpoena duces tecum, or pursuant to subdivision (e) of Section 1560 the records were delivered to the attorney, the attorney's representative, or deposition officer for copying at the custodian's or witness' place of business, as the case may be.

(3) The records were prepared by the personnel of the business in the ordinary course of business at or near the time of the act, condition, or event.

(4) The identity of the records.

(5) A description of the mode of preparation of the records.

(b) If the business has none of the records described, or only part thereof, the custodian or other qualified witness shall so state in the affidavit, and deliver the affidavit and those records that are available in one of the manners provided in Section 1560.

(c) Where the records described in the subpoena were delivered to the attorney or his or her representative or deposition officer for copying at the custodian's or witness' place of business, in addition to the affidavit required by subdivision (a), the records shall be accompanied by an affidavit by the attorney or his or her representative or deposition officer stating that the copy is a true copy of all the records delivered to the attorney or his or her representative or deposition officer for copying. **Leg.H.** 1965 ch. 299, operative January 1, 1967, 1969 ch. 199, 1986 ch. 603, 1987 ch. 19, effective May 12, 1987, 1996 ch. 146, 1999 ch. 444.

Ref.: Cal. Courtroom Ev., §§23.14, 23.15[2] (Matthew Bender); MB Prac. Guide: Cal. Trial & Post-Trial Civ. Proc., §7.15[1]; W. Cal. Sum., 11 "Husband and Wife" §291.

§1562. Admissibility of copies and affidavits.

If the original records would be admissible in evidence if the custodian or other qualified witness had been present and testified to the matters stated in the affidavit, and if the requirements of Section 1271 have been met, the copy of the records is admissible in evidence. The affidavit is admissible as evidence of the matters stated therein pursuant to Section 1561 and the matters so stated are presumed true. When more than one person has knowledge of the facts, more than one affidavit may be made. The presumption established by this section is a presumption affecting the burden of producing evidence. **Leg.H.** 1965 ch. 299, operative January 1, 1967, 1989 ch. 1416, 1996 ch. 146.

Ref.: Cal. Courtroom Ev., §23.15 (Matthew Bender); MB Prac. Guide: Cal. Trial & Post-Trial Civ. Proc., §7.15[1]; W. Cal. Sum., 11 "Husband and Wife" §291.

§1563. Witness fees.

(a) This article shall not be interpreted to require tender or payment of more than one witness fee and one mileage fee or other charge, to a witness or witness' business, unless there is an agreement to the contrary between the witness and the requesting party.

(b) All reasonable costs incurred in a civil proceeding by any witness which is not a party with respect to the production of all or any part of business records the production of which is requested pursuant to a subpoena duces tecum may be charged against the party serving the subpoena duces tecum.

(1) "Reasonable cost," as used in this section, shall include, but not be limited to, the following specific costs: ten cents ($0.10) per page for standard reproduction of documents of a size 8½ by 14 inches or less; twenty cents ($0.20) per page for copying of documents from microfilm; actual costs for the reproduction of oversize documents or the reproduction of documents requiring special processing which are made in response to a subpoena; reasonable clerical costs incurred in locating and making the records available to be billed at the maximum rate of twenty-four dollars ($24) per hour per person, computed on the basis of six dollars ($6) per quarter hour or fraction thereof; actual postage charges; and the actual cost, if any, charged to the witness by a third person for the retrieval and return of records held offsite by that third person.

(2) The requesting party, or the requesting party's deposition officer, shall not be required to pay those costs or any estimate thereof prior to the time the records are available for delivery pursuant to the subpoena, but the witness may demand payment of costs pursuant to this section simultaneous with actual delivery of the subpoenaed records, and until payment is made, is under no obligation to deliver the records.

(3) The witness shall submit an itemized statement for the costs to the requesting party, or the requesting party's deposition officer, setting forth the reproduction and clerical costs incurred by the witness. Should the costs exceed those authorized in paragraph (1), or the witness refuses to produce an itemized statement of costs as required by paragraph (3), upon demand by the requesting party, or the requesting party's deposition officer, the witness shall furnish a statement setting forth the actions taken by the witness in justification of the costs.

(4) The requesting party may petition the court in which the action is pending to recover from the witness all or a part of the costs paid to the witness, or to reduce all or a part of the costs charged by the witness, pursuant to this subdivision, on the grounds that those costs were excessive. Upon the filing of the petition the court shall issue an order to show cause and from the time the order is served on the witness the court has jurisdiction over the witness. The court may hear testimony on the order to show cause and if it finds that the costs demanded and collected, or charged but not collected, exceed the amount authorized by this subdivision, it shall order the witness to remit to the requesting party, or reduce its charge to the requesting party by an amount equal to, the amount of the excess. In the event that the court finds the costs excessive and charged in bad faith by the witness, the court shall order the witness to remit the full amount of the costs demanded and collected, or excuse the requesting party from any payment of costs charged but not collected, and the court shall also order the witness to pay the requesting party the amount of the reasonable expenses incurred in obtaining the order including attorney's fees. If the court finds the costs were not excessive, the court shall order the requesting party to pay the witness the amount of the reasonable expenses incurred in defending the petition, including attorney's fees.

(5) If a subpoena is served to compel the production of business records and is subse-

quently withdrawn, or is quashed, modified or limited on a motion made other than by the witness, the witness shall be entitled to reimbursement pursuant to paragraph (1) for all costs incurred in compliance with the subpoena to the time that the requesting party has notified the witness that the subpoena has been withdrawn or quashed, modified or limited. In the event the subpoena is withdrawn or quashed, if those costs are not paid within 30 days after demand therefor, the witness may file a motion in the court in which the action is pending for an order requiring payment, and the court shall award the payment of expenses and attorney's fees in the manner set forth in paragraph (4).

(6) Where the records are delivered to the attorney, the attorney's representative, or the deposition officer for inspection or photocopying at the witness' place of business, the only fee for complying with the subpoena shall not exceed fifteen dollars ($15), plus the actual cost, if any, charged to the witness by a third person for retrieval and return of records held offsite by that third person. If the records are retrieved from microfilm, the reasonable cost, as defined in paragraph (1), shall also apply.

(c) When the personal attendance of the custodian of a record or other qualified witness is required pursuant to Section 1564, in a civil proceeding, he or she shall be entitled to the same witness fees and mileage permitted in a case where the subpoena requires the witness to attend and testify before a court in which the action or proceeding is pending and to any additional costs incurred as provided by subdivision (b). **Leg.H.** 1965 ch. 299, operative January 1, 1967, 1972 ch. 396, 1981 ch. 1014, 1982 ch. 452, 1986 ch. 603, 1987 ch. 19, effective May 12, 1987, 1997 ch. 442, 1999 ch. 444.

Ref.: Cal. Courtroom Ev., §23.16 (Matthew Bender); MB Prac. Guide: Cal. Trial & Post-Trial Civ. Proc., §7.15[1].

§1564. Personal attendance of custodian or witness.

The personal attendance of the custodian or other qualified witness and the production of the original records is not required unless, at the discretion of the requesting party, the subpoena duces tecum contains a clause which reads:

"The personal attendance of the custodian or other qualified witness and the production of the original records are required by this subpoena. The procedure authorized pursuant to subdivision (b) of Section 1560, and Sections 1561 and 1562, of the Evidence Code will not be deemed sufficient compliance with this subpoena."

Ref.: MB Prac. Guide: Cal. Trial & Post-Trial Civ. Proc., §7.15[1].

§1565. Custodian as witness of party serving first subpoena.

If more than one subpoena duces tecum is served upon the custodian of records or other qualified witness and the personal attendance of the custodian or other qualified witness is required pursuant to Section 1564, the witness shall be deemed to be the witness of the party serving the first such subpoena duces tecum.

Ref.: MB Prac. Guide: Cal. Trial & Post-Trial Civ. Proc., §7.15[1].

§1566. Applicable proceedings.

This article applies in any proceeding in which testimony can be compelled.

Ref.: Cal. Courtroom Ev., §23.19 (Matthew Bender); MB Prac. Guide: Cal. Trial & Post-Trial Civ. Proc., §7.15[1].

§1567. Admissibility of certain income and benefit information provided by employer in proceeding to modify or terminate order for child, family, or spousal support.

A completed form described in Section 3664 of the Family Code for income and benefit information provided by the employer may be admissible in a proceeding for modification or termination of an order for child, family, or spousal support if both of the following requirements are met:

(a) The completed form complies with Sections 1561 and 1562.

(b) A copy of the completed form and notice was served on the employee named therein pursuant to Section 3664 of the Family Code. **Leg.H.** 1995 ch. 506.

Ref.: W. Cal. Sum., 11 "Husband and Wife" §291.

SELECTED PROVISIONS
Of The
GOVERNMENT CODE

GENERAL PROVISIONS
[Selected Provisions]

§24. "Workmen's compensation" changed to "workers' compensation."

The Legislature hereby declares its intent that the term "workmen's compensation" shall hereafter also be known as "workers' compensation." In furtherance of this policy it is the desire of the Legislature that references to the term "workmen's compensation" in this code be changed to "workers' compensation" when such code sections are being amended for any purpose. This act is declaratory and not amendatory of existing law.

TITLE 1
GENERAL

DIVISION 7
Miscellaneous

CHAPTER 5
JOINT EXERCISE OF POWERS

ARTICLE 1
Joint Powers Agreements
[Selected Provisions]

§6516. Public agencies' joint powers agreement for insurance and risk pooling; reserve fund.

Public agencies conducting agricultural, livestock, industrial, cultural, or other types of fairs or exhibitions may enter into a joint powers agreement to form an insurance pooling arrangement for the payment of workers' compensation, unemployment compensation, tort liability, public liability, or other losses incurred by those agencies. An insurance and risk pooling arrangement formed in accordance with a joint powers agreement pursuant to this section is not subject to Section 11007.7 of the Government Code. The Department of Food and Agriculture may enter into such a joint powers agreement for the California Exposition and State Fair, district agricultural associations, or citrus fruit fairs, and the department shall have authority to contract with the California Exposition and State Fair, district agricultural associations, or citrus fruit fairs with respect to such a joint powers agreement entered into on behalf of the California Exposition and State Fair, district agricultural association, or citrus fruit fair. Any county contracting with a nonprofit corporation to conduct a fair pursuant to Sections 25905 and 25906 of the Government Code may enter into such a joint powers agreement for a fair conducted by the nonprofit corporation, and shall have authority to contract with a nonprofit corporation with respect to such a joint powers agreement entered into on behalf of the fair of the nonprofit corporation.

Any county contracting with a nonprofit corporation to conduct a fair shall assume all workers' compensation and liability obligations accrued prior to the dissolution or nonrenewal of the nonprofit corporation's contract with the county.

Any public entity entering into a joint powers agreement under this section shall establish or maintain a reserve fund to be used to pay losses incurred under the agreement. The reserve fund shall contain sufficient moneys to maintain the fund on an actuarially sound basis. **Leg.H.** 1996 ch. 373.

TITLE 2
GOVERNMENT OF THE STATE OF CALIFORNIA

DIVISION 1
General

CHAPTER 7
CALIFORNIA EMERGENCY SERVICES ACT

ARTICLE 3.5
Oil Spills
[Selected Provisions]

§8574.3. Volunteers of state agencies; entitlement to benefits.

State agencies granted authority to implement a plan adopted under this article may use volunteer workers. The volunteers shall be deemed employees of the state for the purpose of workers' compensation under Article 2 (commencing with Section 3350) of Chapter 2 of Part 1 of Division 4 of the Labor Code. Any payments for workers' compensation under this section shall be made from the account specified in Section 8574.4.

ARTICLE 5
Office of Emergency Services
[Selected Provisions]

§8585.5. Office of Emergency Services; classes of disaster workers; procedures for payment of benefits.

The Office of Emergency Services shall establish by rule and regulation various classes of disaster service workers and the scope of the duties of each class. The Office of Emergency Services shall also adopt rules and regulations prescribing the manner in which disaster service workers of each class are to be registered. All of the rules and regulations shall be designed to facilitate the payment of workers' compensation. **Leg.H.** 1970 ch. 1454 §2, 1981 ch. 714 §171, 2006 ch. 502 (AB 1889) §4 (amended & renumbered from §8580).

ARTICLE 9.8
Disaster Preparedness
[Selected Provisions]

§8609. Volunteer workers.

State agencies granted authority by the Governor, the Business Continuity Task Force, the Emergency Preparedness Task Force, or the Executive Committee established by Executive Order D-3-99 to implement any type of disaster, contingency, or business continuity plan may use volunteer workers. The volunteers shall be deemed disaster service workers for the purpose of workers' compensation under Chapter 3 (commencing with Section 3600) of Part 1 of Division 4 of the Labor Code. **Leg.H.** 1999 ch. 784, effective October 10, 1999.

ARTICLE 10
Local Disaster Councils
[Selected Provisions]

§8610. Authority to create local disaster councils.

Counties, cities and counties, and cities may create disaster councils by ordinance. A disaster council shall develop plans for meeting any condition constituting a local emergency or state of emergency, including, but not limited to, earthquakes, natural or manmade disasters specific to that jurisdiction, or state of war emergency; those plans shall provide for the effective mobilization of all of the resources within the political subdivision, both public and private. The disaster council shall supply a copy of any plans developed pursuant to this section to the Office of Emergency Services. The governing body of a county, city and county, or city may, in the ordinance or by resolution adopted pursuant to the ordinance, provide for the organization, powers and duties, divisions, services, and staff of the emergency organization. The governing body of a county, city and county, or city may, by ordinance or resolution, authorize public officers, employees, and registered volunteers to command the aid of citizens when necessary in the execution of their duties during a state of war emergency, a state of emergency, or a local emergency.

Counties, cities and counties, and cities may enact ordinances and resolutions and either establish rules and regulations or authorize disaster councils to recommend to the director of the local emergency organization rules and regulations for dealing with local emergencies that can be adequately dealt with locally; and further may act to carry out mutual aid on a voluntary basis and, to this end, may enter into agreements. **Leg.H.** 2007 ch. 130 (AB 299) §110.

§8612. Certification of accredited disaster councils.

Any disaster council that both agrees to follow the rules and regulations established by the Office of Emergency Services pursuant to Section 8585.5 and substantially complies with those rules and regulations shall be certified by the office. Upon that certification, and not before, the disaster council becomes an accredited disaster council. **Leg.H.** 1970 ch. 1454 §2, 2006 ch. 502 (AB 1889) §7.

ARTICLE 17
Privileges and Immunities [Selected Provisions]

§8656. Public employees; privileges applying in territory apply outside territory.

All of the privileges and immunities from liability; exemptions from laws, ordinances, and rules; all pension, relief, disability, workers' compensation, and other benefits which apply to the activity of officers, agents, or employees of any political subdivision when performing their respective functions within the territorial limits of their respective political subdivisions, shall apply to them to the same degree and extent while engaged in the performance of any of their functions and duties extraterritorially under this chapter.

Ref.: W. Cal. Sum., 5 "Torts" §341.

§8657. Liability for damages suffered by volunteer engaged in emergency preparedness training or relief activity; responsibilities and immunities of California Earthquake Prediction Evaluation Council.

(a) Volunteers duly enrolled or registered with the Office of Emergency Services or any disaster council of any political subdivision, or unregistered persons duly impressed into service during a state of war emergency, a state of emergency, or a local emergency, in carrying out, complying with, or attempting to comply with, any order or regulation issued or promulgated pursuant to the provisions of this chapter or any local ordinance, or performing any of their authorized functions or duties or training for the performance of their authorized functions or duties, shall have the same degree of responsibility for their actions and enjoy the same immunities as officers and employees of the state and its political subdivisions performing similar work for their respective entities.

(b) No political subdivision or other public agency under any circumstances, nor the officers, employees, agents, or duly enrolled or registered volunteers thereof, or unregistered persons duly impressed into service during a state of war emergency, a state of emergency, or a local emergency, acting within the scope of their official duties under this chapter or any local ordinance shall be liable for personal injury or property damage sustained by any duly enrolled or registered volunteer engaged in or training for emergency preparedness or relief activity, or by any unregistered person duly impressed into service during a state of war emergency, a state of emergency, or a local emergency and engaged in such service. The foregoing shall not affect the right of any such person to receive benefits or compensation which may be specifically provided by the provisions of any federal or state statute nor shall it affect the right of any person to recover under the terms of any policy of insurance.

(c) The California Earthquake Prediction Evaluation Council, an advisory committee established pursuant to Section 8590 of this chapter, may advise the Governor of the existence of an earthquake or volcanic prediction having scientific validity. In its review, hearings, deliberations, or other validation procedures, members of the council, jointly and severally, shall have the same degree of responsibility for their actions and enjoy the same immunities as officers and employees of the state and its political subdivisions engaged in similar work in their respective entities. Any person making a presentation to the council as part of the council's validation process, including presentation of a prediction for validation, shall be deemed a member of the council until the council has found the prediction to have or not have scientific validity.

Ref.: W. Cal. Sum., 5 "Torts" §§341, 342.

§8659. State of emergency; limitations of physician's liability.

Any physician or surgeon (whether licensed in this state or any other state), hospital, pharmacist, nurse, or dentist who renders services during any state of war emergency, a state of emergency, or a local emergency at the express or implied request of any responsible state or local official or agency shall have no liability for any injury sustained by any person by reason of such services, regardless of how or under what circumstances or by what cause such injuries are sustained; provided, however, that the immunity herein granted shall not apply in the event of a willful act or omission.

Ref.: W. Cal. Sum., 5 "Torts" §341.

§8660. Limitations on liability; other state rendering aid in emergency.

No other state or its officers or employees rendering aid in this state pursuant to any interstate arrangement, agreement, or compact shall be liable on account of any act or omission in good faith on the part of such state or its officers or employees while so engaged, or on account of the maintenance or use of any equipment or supplies in connection with an emergency.

Ref.: W. Cal. Sum., 5 "Torts" §341.

DIVISION 3
Executive Department

PART 2.8
DEPARTMENT OF FAIR EMPLOYMENT AND HOUSING

CHAPTER 4
DEFINITIONS
[Selected Provisions]

§12925. Definitions.

As used in this part, unless a different meaning clearly appears from the context:

(a) "Commission" means the Fair Employment and Housing Commission and "commissioner" means a member of the commission.

(b) "Department" means the Department of Fair Employment and Housing.

(c) "Director" means the Director of Fair Employment and Housing.

(d) "Person" includes one or more individuals, partnerships, associations, corporations, limited liability companies, legal representatives, trustees, trustees in bankruptcy, and receivers or other fiduciaries. **Leg.H.** 1980 ch. 992 §4, 1994 ch. 1010 (SB 2053) §142.

Ref.: CACI Nos. 2505, 2520, 2521A–2521C (Matthew Bender).

§12926. Definitions regarding unlawful practices.

As used in this part in connection with unlawful practices, unless a different meaning clearly appears from the context:

(a) "Affirmative relief" or "prospective relief" includes the authority to order reinstatement of an employee, awards of backpay, reimbursement of out-of-pocket expenses, hiring, transfers, reassignments, grants of tenure, promotions, cease and desist orders, posting of notices, training of personnel, testing, expunging of records, reporting of records, and any other similar relief that is intended to correct unlawful practices under this part.

(b) "Age" refers to the chronological age of any individual who has reached his or her 40th birthday.

(c) "Employee" does not include any individual employed by his or her parents, spouse, or child, or any individual employed under a special license in a nonprofit sheltered workshop or rehabilitation facility.

(d) "Employer" includes any person regularly employing five or more persons, or any person acting as an agent of an employer, directly or indirectly, the state or any political or civil subdivision of the state, and cities, except as follows:

"Employer" does not include a religious association or corporation not organized for private profit.

(e) "Employment agency" includes any person undertaking for compensation to procure employees or opportunities to work.

(f) "Essential functions" means the fundamental job duties of the employment position the individual with a disability holds or desires. "Essential functions" does not include the marginal functions of the position.

(1) A job function may be considered essential for any of several reasons, including, but not limited to, any one or more of the following:

(A) The function may be essential because the reason the position exists is to perform that function.

(B) The function may be essential because of the limited number of employees available among whom the performance of that job function can be distributed.

(C) The function may be highly specialized, so that the incumbent in the position is hired for his or her expertise or ability to perform the particular function.

(2) Evidence of whether a particular function is essential includes, but is not limited to, the following:

(A) The employer's judgment as to which functions are essential.

(B) Written job descriptions prepared before advertising or interviewing applicants for the job.

(C) The amount of time spent on the job performing the function.

(D) The consequences of not requiring the incumbent to perform the function.

(E) The terms of a collective bargaining agreement.

(F) The work experiences of past incumbents in the job.

(G) The current work experience of incumbents in similar jobs.

(g) "Labor organization" includes any organization that exists and is constituted for the purpose, in whole or in part, of collective bargaining or of dealing with employers concerning grievances, terms or conditions of employment, or of other mutual aid or protection.

(h) "Medical condition" means either of the following:

(1) Any health impairment related to or associated with a diagnosis of cancer or a record or history of cancer.

(2) Genetic characteristics. For purposes of this section, "genetic characteristics" means either of the following:

(A) Any scientifically or medically identifiable gene or chromosome, or combination or alteration thereof, that is known to be a cause of a disease or disorder in a person or his or her offspring, or that is determined to be associated with a statistically increased risk of development of a disease or disorder, and that is presently not associated with any symptoms of any disease or disorder.

(B) Inherited characteristics that may derive from the individual or family member, that are known to be a cause of a disease or disorder in a person or his or her offspring, or that are determined to be associated with a statistically increased risk of development of a disease or disorder, and that are presently not associated with any symptoms of any disease or disorder.

(i) "Mental disability" includes, but is not limited to, all of the following:

(1) Having any mental or psychological disorder or condition, such as mental retardation, organic brain syndrome, emotional or mental illness, or specific learning disabilities, that limits a major life activity. For purposes of this section:

(A) "Limits" shall be determined without regard to mitigating measures, such as medications, assistive devices, or reasonable accommodations, unless the mitigating measure itself limits a major life activity.

(B) A mental or psychological disorder or condition limits a major life activity if it makes the achievement of the major life activity difficult.

(C) "Major life activities" shall be broadly construed and shall include physical, mental, and social activities and working.

(2) Any other mental or psychological disorder or condition not described in paragraph (1) that requires special education or related services.

(3) Having a record or history of a mental or psychological disorder or condition described in paragraph (1) or (2), which is known to the employer or other entity covered by this part.

(4) Being regarded or treated by the employer or other entity covered by this part as having, or having had, any mental condition that makes achievement of a major life activity difficult.

(5) Being regarded or treated by the employer or other entity covered by this part as having, or having had, a mental or psychological disorder or condition that has no present disabling effect, but that may become a mental disability as described in paragraph (1) or (2).

"Mental disability" does not include sexual behavior disorders, compulsive gambling, kleptomania, pyromania, or psychoactive substance use disorders resulting from the current unlawful use of controlled substances or other drugs.

(j) "On the bases enumerated in this part" means or refers to discrimination on the basis of one or more of the following: race, religious creed, color, national origin, ancestry, physical disability, mental disability, medical condition, marital status, sex, age, or sexual orientation.

(k) "Physical disability" includes, but is not limited to, all of the following:

(1) Having any physiological disease, disorder, condition, cosmetic disfigurement, or anatomical loss that does both of the following:

(A) Affects one or more of the following body systems: neurological, immunological, musculoskeletal, special sense organs, respiratory, including speech organs, cardiovascular, reproductive, digestive, genitourinary, hemic and lymphatic, skin, and endocrine.

(B) Limits a major life activity. For purposes of this section:

(i) "Limits" shall be determined without regard to mitigating measures such as medications, assistive devices, prosthetics, or reasonable accommodations, unless the mitigating measure itself limits a major life activity.

(ii) A physiological disease, disorder, condition, cosmetic disfigurement, or anatomical loss limits a major life activity if it makes the achievement of the major life activity difficult.

(iii) "Major life activities" shall be broadly construed and includes physical, mental, and social activities and working.

(2) Any other health impairment not described in paragraph (1) that requires special education or related services.

(3) Having a record or history of a disease, disorder, condition, cosmetic disfigurement, anatomical loss, or health impairment described in paragraph (1) or (2), which is known to the employer or other entity covered by this part.

(4) Being regarded or treated by the employer or other entity covered by this part as having, or having had, any physical condition that makes achievement of a major life activity difficult.

(5) Being regarded or treated by the employer or other entity covered by this part as having, or having had, a disease, disorder, condition, cosmetic disfigurement, anatomical loss, or health impairment that has no present disabling effect but may become a physical disability as described in paragraph (1) or (2).

(6) "Physical disability" does not include sexual behavior disorders, compulsive gambling, kleptomania, pyromania, or psychoactive substance use disorders resulting from the current unlawful use of controlled substances or other drugs.

(*l*) Notwithstanding subdivisions (i) and (k), if the definition of "disability" used in the Americans with Disabilities Act of 1990 (Public Law 101-336) would result in broader protection of the civil rights of individuals with a mental disability or physical disability, as defined in subdivision (i) or (k), or would include any medical condition not included within those definitions, then that broader protection or coverage shall be deemed incorporated by reference into, and shall prevail over conflicting provisions of, the definitions in subdivisions (i) and (k).

(m) "Race, religious creed, color, national origin, ancestry, physical disability, mental disability, medical condition, marital status, sex, age, or sexual orientation" includes a perception that the person has any of those characteristics or that the person is associated with a person who has, or is perceived to have, any of those characteristics.

(n) "Reasonable accommodation" may include either of the following:

(1) Making existing facilities used by employees readily accessible to, and usable by, individuals with disabilities.

(2) Job restructuring, part-time or modified work schedules, reassignment to a vacant position, acquisition or modification of equipment or devices, adjustment or modifications of examinations, training materials or policies, the provision of qualified readers or interpreters, and other similar accommodations for individuals with disabilities.

(o) "Religious creed," "religion," "religious observance," "religious belief," and "creed" include all aspects of religious belief, observance, and practice.

(p) "Sex" includes, but is not limited to, pregnancy, childbirth, or medical conditions related to pregnancy or childbirth. "Sex" also includes, but is not limited to, a person's gender, as defined in Section 422.56 of the Penal Code.

(q) "Sexual orientation" means heterosexuality, homosexuality, and bisexuality.

(r) "Supervisor" means any individual having the authority, in the interest of the employer, to hire, transfer, suspend, lay off, recall, promote, discharge, assign, reward, or discipline other employees, or the responsibility to direct them, or to adjust their grievances, or effectively to recommend that action, if, in connection with the foregoing, the exercise of that authority is not of a merely routine or clerical nature, but requires the use of independent judgment.

(s) "Undue hardship" means an action requiring significant difficulty or expense, when considered in light of the following factors:

(1) The nature and cost of the accommodation needed.

(2) The overall financial resources of the facilities involved in the provision of the reasonable accommodations, the number of persons employed at the facility, and the effect on expenses and resources or the impact otherwise of these accommodations upon the operation of the facility.

(3) The overall financial resources of the covered entity, the overall size of the business of a covered entity with respect to the number of employees, and the number, type, and location of its facilities.

(4) The type of operations, including the composition, structure, and functions of the workforce of the entity.

(5) The geographic separateness, administrative, or fiscal relationship of the facility or facilities. **Leg.H.** 1980 ch. 992 §4, 1985 ch. 1151 §1, 1990 ch. 15 (SB 1027) §1, 1992 ch. 911 (AB 311) §3, ch. 912 (AB 1286) §3, ch. 913 (AB 1077) §21.3, 1993 ch. 1214 (AB 551) §5, 1998 ch. 99 (SB 654) §1, 1999 ch. 311 (SB

1185) §2, ch. 591 (AB 1670) §5.1, ch. 592 (AB 1001) §3.7, 2000 ch. 1049 (AB 2222) §5, 2003 ch. 164 (AB 196), 2004 ch. 700 (SB 1234).

Ref.: Hanna § 10.60[4]; CACI Nos. 2500, 2520, 2521A–2521C, 2522A–2522C, 2525, 2540–2543, 2545, 2560, 3020, 3021 (Matthew Bender); CALCRIM No. 523 (Matthew Bender); W. Cal. Sum., 3 "Agency and Employment" §§248, 332, 339, 340, 345, 422, 8 "Constitutional Law" §§892, 916–919, 925, 926, 931, 932, 936–938, 941.

§12926.1. Physical and mental disabilities.

The Legislature finds and declares as follows:

(a) The law of this state in the area of disabilities provides protections independent from those in the federal Americans with Disabilities Act of 1990 (Public Law 101-336). Although the federal act provides a floor of protection, this state's law has always, even prior to passage of the federal act, afforded additional protections.

(b) The law of this state contains broad definitions of physical disability, mental disability, and medical condition. It is the intent of the Legislature that the definitions of physical disability and mental disability be construed so that applicants and employees are protected from discrimination due to an actual or perceived physical or mental impairment that is disabling, potentially disabling, or perceived as disabling or potentially disabling.

(c) Physical and mental disabilities include, but are not limited to, chronic or episodic conditions such as HIV/AIDS, hepatitis, epilepsy, seizure disorder, diabetes, clinical depression, bipolar disorder, multiple sclerosis, and heart disease. In addition, the Legislature has determined that the definitions of "physical disability" and "mental disability" under the law of this state require a "limitation" upon a major life activity, but do not require, as does the Americans with Disabilities Act of 1990, a "substantial limitation." This distinction is intended to result in broader coverage under the law of this state than under that federal act. Under the law of this state, whether a condition limits a major life activity shall be determined without respect to any mitigating measures, unless the mitigating measure itself limits a major life activity, regardless of federal law under the Americans with Disabilities Act of 1990. Further, under the law of this state, "working" is a major life activity, regardless of whether the actual or perceived working limitation implicates a particular employment or a class or broad range of employments.

(d) Notwithstanding any interpretation of law in Cassista v. Community Foods (1993) 5 Cal.4th 1050, the Legislature intends (1) for state law to be independent of the Americans with Disabilities Act of 1990, (2) to require a "limitation" rather than a "substantial limitation" of a major life activity, and (3) by enacting paragraph (4) of subdivision (i) and paragraph (4) of subdivision (k) of Section 12926, to provide protection when an individual is erroneously or mistakenly believed to have any physical or mental condition that limits a major life activity.

(e) The Legislature affirms the importance of the interactive process between the applicant or employee and the employer in determining a reasonable accommodation, as this requirement has been articulated by the Equal Employment Opportunity Commission in its interpretive guidance of the Americans with Disabilities Act of 1990. **Leg.H.** 2000 ch. 1049 (AB 2222) §6.

Ref.: CACI Nos. 2540–2542, 2546 (Matthew Bender); W. Cal. Sum., 8 "Constitutional Law" §§936–938.

§12926.2. Definitions.

As used in this part in connection with unlawful practices, unless a different meaning clearly appears from the context:

(a) "Religious corporation" means any corporation formed under, or otherwise subject to, Part 4 (commencing with Section 9110) or Part 6 (commencing with Section 10000) of Division 2 of Title 1 of the Corporations Code, and also includes a corporation that is formed primarily or exclusively for religious purposes under the laws of any other state to administer the affairs of an organized religious group and that is not organized for private profit.

(b) "Religious duties" means duties of employment connected with carrying on the religious activities of a religious corporation or association.

(c) Notwithstanding subdivision (d) of Section 12926 and except as otherwise provided in subdivision (d) of this section, "employer" includes a religious corporation or association with respect to persons employed by the religious association or corporation to perform duties, other than religious duties, at a health care facility operated by the religious association or corporation for the provision of health care that is not restricted to adherents of the religion that established the association or corporation.

(d) "Employer" does not include a religious corporation with respect to either the employment, including promotion, of an individual of a particular religion, or the application of the employer's religious doctrines, tenets, or teachings, in any work connected with the provision of health care.

(e) Notwithstanding subdivision (d) of Section 12926, "employer" does not include a nonprofit public benefit corporation incorporated to provide health care on behalf of a religious organization under Part 2 (commencing with Section 5110) of Division 2 of Title 1 of the Corporations Code, with respect to employment, including promotion, of an individual of a particular religion in an executive or pastoral-care position connected with the provision of health care.

(f)(1) Notwithstanding any other provision of law, a nonprofit public benefit corporation formed by, or affiliated with, a particular religion and that operates an educational institution as its sole or primary activity, may restrict employment, including promotion, in any or all employment categories to individuals of a particular religion.

(2) Notwithstanding paragraph (1) or any other provision of law, employers that are nonprofit public benefit corporations specified in paragraph (1) shall be subject to the provisions of this part in all other respects, including, but not limited to, the prohibitions against discrimination made unlawful employment practices by this part. **Leg.H.** 1999 ch. 913 (AB 1541) §2, 2001 ch. 910 (SB 504) §1.

Ref.: W. Cal. Sum., 3 "Agency and Employment" §335, 8 "Constitutional Law" §918.

CHAPTER 6
DISCRIMINATION PROHIBITED

ARTICLE 1
Unlawful Practices, Generally [Selected Provisions]

§12940. Unlawful employment practices.

It shall be an unlawful employment practice, unless based upon a bona fide occupational qualification, or, except where based upon applicable security regulations established by the United States or the State of California:

(a) For an employer, because of the race, religious creed, color, national origin, ancestry, physical disability, mental disability, medical condition, marital status, sex, age, or sexual orientation of any person, to refuse to hire or employ the person or to refuse to select the person for a training program leading to employment, or to bar or to discharge the person from employment or from a training program leading to employment, or to discriminate against the person in compensation or in terms, conditions, or privileges of employment.

(1) This part does not prohibit an employer from refusing to hire or discharging an employee with a physical or mental disability, or subject an employer to any legal liability resulting from the refusal to employ or the discharge of an employee with a physical or mental disability, where the employee, because of his or her physical or mental disability, is unable to perform his or her essential duties even with reasonable accommodations, or cannot perform those duties in a manner that would not endanger his or her health or safety or the health or safety of others even with reasonable accommodations.

(2) This part does not prohibit an employer from refusing to hire or discharging an employee who, because of the employee's medical condition, is unable to perform his or her essential duties even with reasonable accommodations, or cannot perform those duties in a manner that would not endanger the employee's health or safety or the health or safety of others even with reasonable accommodations. Nothing in this part shall subject an employer to any legal liability resulting from the refusal to employ or the discharge of an employee who, because of the employee's medical condition, is unable to perform his or her essential duties, or cannot perform those duties in a manner that would not endanger the employee's health or safety or the health or safety of others even with reasonable accommodations.

(3) Nothing in this part relating to discrimination on account of marital status shall do either of the following:

(A) Affect the right of an employer to reasonably regulate, for reasons of supervision, safety, security, or morale, the working of spouses in the same department, division, or facility, consistent with the rules and regulations adopted by the commission.

(B) Prohibit bona fide health plans from providing additional or greater benefits to employees with dependents than to those employees without or with fewer dependents.

(4) Nothing in this part relating to discrimination on account of sex shall affect the right of an employer to use veteran status as a factor in employee selection or to give special consideration to Vietnam era veterans.

(5) Nothing in this part prohibits an employer from refusing to employ an individual because of his or her age if the law compels or provides for that refusal. Promotions within the existing staff, hiring or promotion on the basis of experience and training, rehiring on the basis of seniority and prior service with the employer, or hiring under an established recruiting program from high schools, colleges, universities, or trade schools do not, in and of themselves, constitute unlawful employment practices.

(b) For a labor organization, because of the race, religious creed, color, national origin, ancestry, physical disability, mental disability, medical condition, marital status, sex, age, or sexual orientation of any person, to exclude, expel or restrict from its membership the person, or to provide only second-class or segregated membership or to discriminate against any person because of the race, religious creed, color, national origin, ancestry, physical disability, mental disability, medical condition, marital status, sex, age, or sexual orientation of the person in the election of officers of the labor organization or in the selection of the labor organization's staff or to discriminate in any way against any of its members or against any employer or against any person employed by an employer.

(c) For any person to discriminate against any person in the selection or training of that person in any apprenticeship training program or any other training program leading to employment because of the race, religious creed, color, national origin, ancestry, physical disability, mental disability, medical condition, marital status, sex, age, or sexual orientation of the person discriminated against.

(d) For any employer or employment agency to print or circulate or cause to be printed or circulated any publication, or to make any non-job-related inquiry of an employee or applicant, either verbal or through use of an application form, that expresses, directly or indirectly, any limitation, specification, or discrimination as to race, religious creed, color, national origin, ancestry, physical disability, mental disability, medical condition, marital status, sex, age, or sexual orientation, or any intent to make any such limitation, specification or discrimination. Nothing in this part prohibits an employer or employment agency from inquiring into the age of an applicant, or from specifying age limitations, where the law compels or provides for that action.

(e)(1) Except as provided in paragraph (2) or (3), for any employer or employment agency to require any medical or psychological examination of an applicant, to make any medical or psychological inquiry of an applicant, to make any inquiry whether an applicant has a mental disability or physical disability or medical condition, or to make any inquiry regarding the nature or severity of a physical disability, mental disability, or medical condition.

(2) Notwithstanding paragraph (1), an employer or employment agency may inquire into the ability of an applicant to perform job-related functions and may respond to an applicant's request for reasonable accommodation.

(3) Notwithstanding paragraph (1), an employer or employment agency may require a medical or psychological examination or make a medical or psychological inquiry of a job applicant after an employment offer has been made but prior to the commencement of employment duties, provided that the examination or inquiry is job-related and consistent with business necessity and that all entering employees in the same job classification are subject to the same examination or inquiry.

(f)(1) Except as provided in paragraph (2), for any employer or employment agency to require any medical or psychological examination of an employee, to make any medical or psychological inquiry of an employee, to make any inquiry whether an employee has a mental disability, physical disability, or medical condition, or to make any inquiry regarding the nature or severity of a physical disability, mental disability, or medical condition.

(2) Notwithstanding paragraph (1), an employer or employment agency may require any examinations or inquiries that it can show to be job-related and consistent with business necessity. An employer or employment agency may conduct voluntary medical examinations, including voluntary medical histories, which are part

of an employee health program available to employees at that worksite.

(g) For any employer, labor organization, or employment agency to harass, discharge, expel, or otherwise discriminate against any person because the person has made a report pursuant to Section 11161.8 of the Penal Code that prohibits retaliation against hospital employees who report suspected patient abuse by health facilities or community care facilities.

(h) For any employer, labor organization, employment agency, or person to discharge, expel, or otherwise discriminate against any person because the person has opposed any practices forbidden under this part or because the person has filed a complaint, testified, or assisted in any proceeding under this part.

(i) For any person to aid, abet, incite, compel, or coerce the doing of any of the acts forbidden under this part, or to attempt to do so.

(j)(1) For an employer, labor organization, employment agency, apprenticeship training program or any training program leading to employment, or any other person, because of race, religious creed, color, national origin, ancestry, physical disability, mental disability, medical condition, marital status, sex, age, or sexual orientation, to harass an employee, an applicant, or a person providing services pursuant to a contract. Harassment of an employee, an applicant, or a person providing services pursuant to a contract by an employee, other than an agent or supervisor, shall be unlawful if the entity, or its agents or supervisors, knows or should have known of this conduct and fails to take immediate and appropriate corrective action. An employer may also be responsible for the acts of nonemployees, with respect to sexual harassment of employees, applicants, or persons providing services pursuant to a contract in the workplace, where the employer, or its agents or supervisors, knows or should have known of the conduct and fails to take immediate and appropriate corrective action. In reviewing cases involving the acts of nonemployees, the extent of the employer's control and any other legal responsibility which the employer may have with respect to the conduct of those nonemployees shall be considered. An entity shall take all reasonable steps to prevent harassment from occurring. Loss of tangible job benefits shall not be necessary in order to establish harassment.

(2) The provisions of this subdivision are declaratory of existing law, except for the new duties imposed on employers with regard to harassment.

(3) An employee of an entity subject to this subdivision is personally liable for any harassment prohibited by this section that is perpetrated by the employee, regardless of whether the employer or covered entity knows or should have known of the conduct and fails to take immediate and appropriate corrective action.

(4)(A) For purposes of this subdivision only, "employer" means any person regularly employing one or more persons or regularly receiving the services of one or more persons providing services pursuant to a contract, or any person acting as an agent of an employer, directly or indirectly, the state, or any political or civil subdivision of the state, and cities. The definition of "employer" in subdivision (d) of Section 12926 applies to all provisions of this section other than this subdivision.

(B) Notwithstanding subparagraph (A), for purposes of this subdivision, "employer" does not include a religious association or corporation not organized for private profit, except as provided in Section 12926.2.

(C) For purposes of this subdivision, "harassment" because of sex includes sexual harassment, gender harassment, and harassment based on pregnancy, childbirth, or related medical conditions.

(5) For purposes of this subdivision, "a person providing services pursuant to a contract" means a person who meets all of the following criteria:

(A) The person has the right to control the performance of the contract for services and discretion as to the manner of performance.

(B) The person is customarily engaged in an independently established business.

(C) The person has control over the time and place the work is performed, supplies the tools and instruments used in the work, and performs work that requires a particular skill not ordinarily used in the course of the employer's work.

(k) For an employer, labor organization, employment agency, apprenticeship training program, or any training program leading to employment, to fail to take all reasonable steps necessary to prevent discrimination and harassment from occurring.

(*l*) For an employer or other entity covered by this part to refuse to hire or employ a person or to refuse to select a person for a training program leading to employment or to bar or to discharge a person from employment or from a training program leading to employment, or to discriminate against a person in compensation or in terms, conditions, or privileges of employment because of a conflict between the person's religious belief or observance and any employment requirement, unless the employer or other entity covered by this part demonstrates that it has explored any available reasonable alternative means of accommodating the religious belief or observance, including the possibilities of excusing the person from those duties that conflict with his or her religious belief or observance or permitting those duties to be performed at another time or by another person, but is unable to reasonably accommodate the religious belief or observance without undue hardship on the conduct of the business of the employer or other entity covered by this part. Religious belief or observance, as used in this section, includes, but is not limited to, observance of a Sabbath or other religious holy day or days, and reasonable time necessary for travel prior and subsequent to a religious observance.

(m) For an employer or other entity covered by this part to fail to make reasonable accommodation for the known physical or mental disability of an applicant or employee. Nothing in this subdivision or in paragraph (1) or (2) of subdivision (a) shall be construed to require an accommodation that is demonstrated by the employer or other covered entity to produce undue hardship to its operation.

(n) For an employer or other entity covered by this part to fail to engage in a timely, good faith, interactive process with the employee or applicant to determine effective reasonable accommodations, if any, in response to a request for reasonable accommodation by an employee or applicant with a known physical or mental disability or known medical condition.

(o) For an employer or other entity covered by this part, to subject, directly or indirectly, any employee, applicant, or other person to a test for the presence of a genetic characteristic. **Leg.H.** 1980 ch. 992 §4, 1981 ch. 11 §1, ch. 270 §1, 1982 ch. 1184 §1, ch. 1193 §2, 1984 ch. 1754 §2, 1985 ch. 1151 §2, 1987 ch. 605 §1, 1989 ch. 1309 §3, 1992 ch. 912 (AB 1286) §5, ch. 913 (AB 1077) §23.1, 1993 ch. 711 (AB 675) §2, 1998 ch. 485 (AB 2803) §85, 1999 chs. 591 (AB 1670) §8, 592 (AB 1001) §7.5, 2000 chs. 1047 (AB 1856) §1, 1049 (AB 2222) §7.5, 2001 ch. 909 (AB 1475) §1, 2002 chs. 525 (AB 1599), 664 (AB 3034) (ch. 525 prevails; ch. 664 not effective), 2003 ch. 671 (AB 76).

2003 Note: It is the intent of the Legislature in enacting this act to construe and clarify the meaning and effect of existing law and to reject the interpretation given to the law in *Salazar v. Diversified Paratransit, Inc.* (2002) 103 Cal.App.4th 131. Stats. 2003 ch. 671 (AB 76) §2.

2002 Note: It is the intent of the Legislature in enacting this act to construe and clarify the meaning and effect of existing law and to reject the interpretation given to the law in *Esberg v. Union Oil Company of California*, 87 Cal.App.4th 378 (2001). Stats. 2002 ch. 525 (AB 1599) §4.

Ref.: Hanna §§ 10.60[4], 11.05[4], 21.03[2][d], 21.07[7]; Herlick Handbook §§ 3.15, 9.12, 12.11, 12.13; CACI Nos. 2500–2502, 2505, 2507, 2520, 2521A–2521C, 2522A–2522C, 2523, 2525, 2527, 2540–2546, 2560, 2561, 2620, VF-2500–VF-2504, VF-2506A–VF-2506C, VF-2507A–VF-2507C, VF-2509–VF-2512 (Matthew Bender); W. Cal. Ev., "Introduction" §68; W. Cal. Sum., 2 "Insurance" §§103, 279, 282, 2 "Workers' Compensation" §20, 3 "Agency and Employment" §§200, 243, 244, 261, 332, 334, 335, 337, 340, 342, 345, 346, 499, 658, 5 "Torts" §240, 6 "Torts" §§1582, 1596, 7 "Constitutional Law" §§292, 624, 8 "Constitutional Law" §§897, 916, 918, 919, 921–932, 934, 936–938, 940, 941.

DIVISION 5
Personnel

PART 2.6
PERSONNEL ADMINISTRATION

CHAPTER 2
Administration of Salaries

ARTICLE 1
Claims for Reimbursement
[Selected Provisions]

§19820. Adoption of general rules and regulations by the director.

The director shall adopt general rules and regulations doing all of the following:

(a) Limiting the amount, time, and place of expenses and allowances to be paid to officers, employees, experts, and agents of the state while traveling on official state business. The rules and regulations shall provide for reasonable reimbursement to an officer, employee, expert, or agent of the state for expenses incurred by him or her to repair a privately owned vehicle which was damaged through no fault of the officer, employee, expert, or agent, if the damage occurred while the vehicle was used on official state business with the permission or authorization of an employing agency.

As used in this subdivision, "officers and employees of the state" means all officers and employees of the state other than elected state officers, officers and employees of the state provided for in Article VI of the California Constitution, and officers and employees of the California State University. "Officers and employees of the state" is not limited by subdivision (d) of Section 19815.

(b) Governing such matters as are specifically committed to the jurisdiction of the department.

(c) Governing the computation of pay in the case of any employee on a monthly basis salary who is entitled to less than a full month's pay.

If this section is in conflict with a memorandum of understanding reached pursuant to Section 3517.5, the memorandum of understanding shall be controlling without further legislative action, except that if any conflicting provision of a memorandum of understanding requires the expenditure of funds, that provision shall not become effective unless approved by the Legislature in the annual Budget Act. **Leg.H.** 1981 ch. 230 §55, 1982 ch. 1095 §14, 1987 ch. 351 §1.

Ref.: Herlick Handbook § 4.12; W. Cal. Sum., 2 "Workers' Compensation" §264.

PART 3
PUBLIC EMPLOYEES' RETIREMENT SYSTEM

CHAPTER 1
GENERAL PROVISIONS AND DEFINITIONS

ARTICLE 2
Definitions
[Selected Provisions]

§20046. "Industrial"; death or disability of members.

"Industrial," in reference to the death or disability of any member of this system who is in a membership category under which special benefits are provided by this part because the death or disability is industrial, means disability or death as a result of injury or disease arising out of and in the course of his or her employment as such a member. **Leg.H.** 1995 ch. 379 §2 (former §20038).

Ref.: W. Cal. Sum., 2 "Workers' Compensation" §245.

CHAPTER 2
ADMINISTRATION OF SYSTEM

ARTICLE 2
Powers and Duties of the Board
[Selected Provisions]

§20130. Representation of retirement system before Appeals Board; determination of disability.

The board may enter into an agreement with the State Compensation Insurance Fund under which the latter shall represent this system, as its agent, or the Attorney General under which the latter shall represent this system, in proceedings instituted or to be instituted before the Workers' Compensation Appeals Board as may be referred to it by the board to determine whether the death or disability of a member is industrial. The agreed cost of this service and the expenses incidental thereto shall be paid from the retirement fund, except that there shall be no charge to this system by the Attorney General in cases involving members of this system who are employees of the General Fund state agencies. **Leg.H.** 1995 ch. 379 §2 (former §20126).

ARTICLE 8
Subrogation

§20250. Right of subrogation—Limitation.

The provisions of this article shall be deemed to create a right of subrogation only to amounts paid as disability retirement allowances and special death benefits. **Leg.H.** 1995 ch. 379 §2 (former §21456).

§20251. "State fund."

As used in this article, "state fund" means the State Compensation Insurance Fund. **Leg.H.** 1995 ch. 379 §2 (former §21450).

§20252. Amounts recoverable from third person.

If benefits are payable under this part because of an injury to or the death of a member and the injury or death is the proximate consequence of the act of a person other than his or her employer (the state or the employing contracting agency), the board may on behalf of this system recover from that person an amount that is the lesser of the following:

(1) An amount that is equal to one-half of the actuarial equivalent of the benefits for which this system is liable because of such injury or death.

(2) An amount that is equal to one-half of the remaining balance of the amount recovered after allowance of that amount that the employer or its insurance carrier have paid or become obligated to pay. **Leg.H.** 1995 ch. 379 §2 (former §21451).

Ref.: W. Cal. Sum., 2 "Workers' Compensation" §103.

§20253. Contracts with state fund or Attorney General for third-party recovery.

The board may contract with the state fund or the Attorney General for the recovery on behalf of this system of any amounts that the board might recover from third persons under this article or Chapter 5 (commencing with Section 3850) of Part 1 of Division 4 of the Labor Code, or that an insurer might recover under Section 11662 of the Insurance Code, or otherwise.

Under the contract, the state fund, in its own name or in the name of the board, or the Attorney General for the board, may, to recover the amounts regardless of whether the injury or death is industrial, commence and prosecute actions, file liens, or intervene in court proceedings all in the same manner and to the same extent, provided in Chapter 5 (commencing with Section 3850) of Part 1 of Division 4 of the Labor Code, for the state fund or employer, except that the recovery shall not be made from benefits payable under this part because of the injury or death. The state fund or the Attorney General, as the case may be, may compromise claims before or after commencement of suit or entry of judgment for the amount as may be approved by a person duly authorized by the board for that purpose. The agreed cost of the service and the expense incidental thereto is a proper charge against the retirement fund. **Leg.H.** 1995 ch. 379 §2 (former §21452).

§20254. Application of amounts recovered by subrogation.

Any amount recovered by way of subrogation by the employer, workers' compensation insurer or this system shall be applied first to the amounts that the employer or its insurer has paid or become obligated to pay. The balance of the amount recovered as specified in Section 20252 shall be paid to, or retained by, this system. **Leg.H.** 1995 ch. 379 §2 (former §21454).

§20255. Statute of limitations.

Actions brought by the board under this article shall be commenced within three years after the liability of this system to pay benefits is fixed. Liability of this system is fixed at the time the board approves the payment of benefits under this part. **Leg.H.** 1995 ch. 379 §2 (former §21455).

CHAPTER 12
RETIREMENT FROM EMPLOYMENT

ARTICLE 6
Disability Retirement
[Selected Provisions]

§21150. Retirement of incapacitated member.

(a) A member incapacitated for the performance of duty shall be retired for disability pursuant to this chapter if he or she is credited with five years of state service, regardless of age, unless the person has elected to become subject to Section 21076 or 21077.

(b) A member subject to Section 21076 or 21077 who becomes incapacitated for the performance of duty shall be retired for disability pursuant to this chapter if he or she is credited with 10 years of state service, regardless of age, except that a member may retire for disability if he or she had five years of state service prior to January 1, 1985.

(c) For purposes of this section, "state service" includes service to the state for which the member, pursuant to Section 20281.5, did not receive credit. **Leg.H.** 1995 ch. 379 (SB 541) §2, 2006 ch. 118 (AB 2244) §9, 2007 ch. 130 (AB 299) §124.

§21151. Members subject to mandatory retirement for incapacity resulting from industrial disability.

(a) Any patrol, state safety, state industrial, state peace officer/firefighter, or local safety member incapacitated for the performance of duty as the result of an industrial disability shall be retired for disability, pursuant to this chapter, regardless of age or amount of service.

(b) This section also applies to local miscellaneous members if the contracting agency employing those members elects to be subject to this section by amendment to its contract.

(c) This section also applies to all of the following:

(1) State miscellaneous members employed by the Department of Justice who perform the duties now performed in positions with the class title of Criminalist (Class Code 8466), or Senior Criminalist (Class Code 8478), or Criminalist Supervisor (Class Code 8477), or Criminalist Manager (Class Code 8467), Latent Print Analyst I (Class Code 8460), Latent Print Analyst II (Class Code 8472), or Latent Print Supervisor (Class Code 8473).

(2) State miscellaneous members employed by the Department of the California Highway Patrol who perform the duties now performed in positions with the class title of Communications Operator I, California Highway Patrol (Class Code 1663), Communications Operator II, California Highway Patrol (Class Code 1664), Communications Supervisor I, California Highway Patrol (Class Code 1662), or Communications Supervisor II, California Highway Patrol (Class Code 1665).

(3) State miscellaneous members whose disability resulted under the conditions specified in Sections 20046.5 and 20047.

(4) State miscellaneous members in State Bargaining Unit 12 employed by the Department of Transportation, if a memorandum of understanding has been agreed to by the state employer and the recognized employee organization making this paragraph applicable to those members.

(d) This section does not apply to local safety members described in Section 20423.6, unless this section has been made applicable to local miscellaneous members pursuant to subdivision (b).

(e) This section does not apply to state safety members described in Section 20401.5. **Leg.H.** 1995 ch. 379 (SB 541) §2, 1996 chs. 906 (SB 1859) §137, 907 (SB 2039) §7, 1997 ch. 951 (AB 1595) §5, 2002 chs. 1152 (AB 2023), 1153 (SB 1984) §1.5, 2005 ch. 328 (AB 1166) §7.

Ref.: Hanna §§ 3.116[1], 33.02[4][a].

§21153. Required application by employer.

Notwithstanding any other provision of law, an employer may not separate because of disability a member otherwise eligible to retire for disability but shall apply for disability retirement of any member believed to be disabled, unless the member waives the right to retire for disability and elects to withdraw contributions or to permit contributions to remain in the fund with rights to service retirement as provided in Section 20731. **Leg.H.** 1995 ch. 379 (SB 541) §2.

§21154. Application for retirement for disability.

The application shall be made only (a) while the member is in state service, or (b) while the member for whom contributions will be made under Section 20997, is absent on military service, or (c) within four months after the discontinuance of the state service of the member, or while on an approved leave of absence, or (d) while the member is physically or mentally incapacitated to perform duties from the date of discontinuance of state service to the time of application or motion. On receipt of an application for disability retirement of a member, other than a local safety member with the exception of a school safety member, the board shall, or of its own motion it may, order a medical examination of a member who is otherwise eligible to retire for disability to determine whether the member is incapacitated for the performance of duty. On receipt of the application with respect to a local safety member other than a school safety member, the board shall request the governing body of the contracting agency employing the member to make the determination. **Leg.H.** 1995 ch. 379 §2 (former §21024).

§21155. Medical examination; reimbursement for expenses.

If the board requests a person to submit to a medical examination, he or she shall be entitled to reimbursement for expenses of transportation, and meals and lodging incident to the examination if he or she is required to travel more than 50 miles one way. Standard per diem rates in effect for state employees as authorized by current law shall be used for the reimbursement; provided, that higher costs of lodging may be paid if supported by receipt and determined necessary by the board. "Expenses of transportation" with respect to the use of private transportation includes mileage fees from the person's home to the place of examination and back to a maximum of 300 miles round trip or within the state at the appropriate current rate per mile authorized to state employees for use of private vehicles in accordance with current law plus bridge tolls. The per diem and mileage may be paid to the person by this system at the time he or she is given notification of the time and place of examination. **Leg.H.** 1995 ch. 379 §2 (former §21024.1), 1996 chs. 320, 907.

§21156. When board to retire member for disability; retirement for service in lieu of retirement for disability; competent medical evidence; appeal.

(a)(1) If the medical examination and other available information show to the satisfaction of the board, or in case of a local safety member, other than a school safety member, the governing body of the contracting agency employing the member, that the member in the state service is incapacitated physically or mentally for the performance of his or her duties and is eligible to retire for disability, the board shall immediately retire him or her for disability, unless the member is qualified to be retired for service and applies therefor prior to the effective date of his or her retirement for disability or within 30 days after the member is notified of his or her eligibility for retirement on account of disability, in which event the board shall retire the member for service.

(2) In determining whether a member is eligible to retire for disability, the board or governing body of the contracting agency shall make a determination on the basis of competent medical opinion and shall not use disability retirement as a substitute for the disciplinary process.

(b)(1) The governing body of a contracting agency upon receipt of the request of the board pursuant to Section 21154 shall certify to the board its determination under this section that the member is or is not incapacitated.

(2) The local safety member may appeal the determination of the governing body. Appeal hearings shall be conducted by an administrative law judge of the Office of Administrative Hearings pursuant to Chapter 5 (commencing with Section 11500) of Part 1 of Division 3 of this title. **Leg.H.** 1995 ch. 379 (SB 541), 2006 ch. 118 (AB 2244) §10, 2008 ch. 370 (AB 2023) §3.

Ref.: Hanna § 3.114[2].

§21157. Time limit for contracting agency to make determination as to local safety member.

The governing body of a contracting agency shall make its determination within six months of the date of the receipt by the contracting agency of the request by the board pursuant to Section 21154 for a determination with respect to a local safety member.

A local safety member may waive the requirements of this section. **Leg.H.** 1995 ch. 379 (SB 541) §2.

§21158. Time allowed for determination relating to state peace officer/firefighter, state patrol member, or state safety member.

Upon the receipt by the board of an application for disability retirement with respect to a state peace officer/firefighter member, state patrol member, or a state safety member, the board shall inform both the employer and the member of all information required for the board to make its determination. The board shall make its determination within three months of the receipt by the board of all information required to make a determination for disability retirement on an application submitted by a state peace officer/firefighter member, state patrol member, or a state safety member for disability retirement pursuant to this article. **Leg.H.** 1995 ch. 379 (SB 541) §2.

§21163. Retirement of member granted or entitled to sick leave or entitled to compensating time off for overtime.

Notwithstanding any other provision of this article, the retirement of a member who has been granted or is entitled to sick leave or who is entitled to compensating time off for overtime, shall not become effective until the expiration of the sick leave with compensation and the expiration of the compensating time off with compensation, unless the member applies for or consents to his or her retirement as of an earlier date, or unless, with respect to sick leave, the provisions of a local ordinance or resolution or the rules or regulations of the employer provide to the contrary. This section shall also be applicable to a state member who participates in the annual leave program and who has been granted annual leave for the reasons applicable to sick leave. **Leg.H.** 1995 ch. 379 (SB 541) §2.

§21164. Disability retirement of local safety member.

Notwithstanding any other provision of this article, the retirement for disability of a local safety member, other than a school safety member, shall not be effective without the member's consent earlier than the date upon which leave of absence without loss of salary under Section 4850 of the Labor Code because of the disability terminates, or the earlier date during the leave as of which the disability is permanent and stationary as found by the Workers' Compensation Appeals Board. **Leg.H.** 1995 ch. 379 §2 (former §21025.4).

§21166. Determination of industrial disability; limitation on Appeals Board jurisdiction.

If a member is entitled to a different disability retirement allowance according to whether the disability is industrial or nonindustrial and the member claims that the disability as found by the board, or in the case of a local safety member by the governing body of his or her employer, is industrial and the claim is disputed by the board, or in case of a local safety member by the governing body, the Workers' Compensation Appeals Board, using the same procedure as in workers' compensation hearings, shall determine whether the disability is industrial.

The jurisdiction of the Workers' Compensation Appeals Board shall be limited solely to the issue of industrial causation, and this section shall not be construed to authorize the Workers' Compensation Appeals Board to award costs against this system pursuant to Section 4600, 5811, or any other provision of the Labor Code. **Leg.H.** 1995 ch. 379 §2 (former §21026).

Ref.: W. Cal. Sum., 2 "Workers' Compensation" §245.

§21167. Petition for rehearing; grounds.

At any time within 20 days after the service of any findings of fact by the Workers' Compensation Appeals Board under this part, any party aggrieved thereby, or the board, may petition for a rehearing upon one or more of the following grounds, and no other:

(a) That the Workers' Compensation Appeals Board acted without or in excess of its powers.

(b) That the findings of fact were procured by fraud.

(c) That the evidence does not justify the findings of fact.

(d) That the petitioner has discovered new evidence material to him or her, that he or she could not, with reasonable diligence, have discovered and produced at the hearing. **Leg.H.** 1995 ch. 379 §2 (former §21026.1).

§21168. Petition for rehearing denied or granted; application for writ of review.

Within 30 days after the petition for rehearing is denied, or, if the petition is granted, within 30 days after the rendition of amended findings of fact on rehearing, any person affected thereby, including this system, may apply to the Supreme Court or to the court of appeal of the appellate district in which he or she resides, for a writ of review, for the purpose of inquiring into and determining the lawfulness of the findings of the Workers' Compensation Appeals Board. **Leg.H.** 1995 ch. 379 §2 (former §21026.2).

§21169. Evidence on writ of review; Appeals Board record.

The writ of review shall be made returnable not later than 30 days after the date of issuance thereof, and shall direct the Workers' Compensation Appeals Board to certify its record in the case to the court. On the return day the cause shall be heard in the court unless continued for good cause. No new or additional evidence shall be introduced in the court, but the cause shall be heard on the record of the appeals board, as certified to by it. **Leg.H.** 1995 ch. 379 §2 (former §21026.3).

§21170. Scope of review.

The review by the court shall not be extended further than to determine whether the Workers' Compensation Appeals Board acted without or in excess of its powers, or unreasonably, or whether its act was procured by fraud. **Leg.H.** 1995 ch. 379 §2 (former §21026.4).

§21171. Appeals Board continuing jurisdiction.

The Workers' Compensation Appeals Board shall have continuing jurisdiction over its determinations made under Section 21166 and may at any time within five years of the date of injury, upon notice and after an opportunity to be heard is given to the parties in interest, rescind, alter, or amend the determination, good cause appearing therefor. **Leg.H.** 1995 ch. 379 §2 (former §21026.5).

§21173. Delegation of authority.

The governing body of a contracting agency may delegate any authority or duty conferred or imposed under this article to a subordinate officer subject to conditions it may impose. **Leg.H.** 1995 ch. 379 (SB 541) §2.

§21174. Subsequent determination that disability is industrial.

If it is not claimed that the disability is industrial or if the claim is made and the member so requests, the board shall proceed with retirement and with the payment of the benefits as are payable when disability is not industrial. If the Workers' Compensation Appeals Board subsequently determines that disability is industrial, an amount equal to the benefits paid shall be deducted from the benefits payable under this system because of the determination. No additional benefits shall be payable, however, because disability is determined to be industrial unless the application for that determination is filed with the Workers' Compensation Appeals Board or in the office of this system in Sacramento, for transmission to the Workers' Compensation Appeals Board within two years after the effective date of the member's retirement. **Leg.H.** 1995 ch. 379 §2 (former §21027).

§21175. Refusal to submit to medical examination.

If any recipient of a disability retirement allowance under the minimum age for voluntary retirement for service applicable to members of his or her class refuses to submit to medical examination the pension portions of his or her allowance may be discontinued until his or her withdrawal of the refusal. If the refusal continues for one year his or her disability retirement allowance may be canceled. **Leg.H.** 1995 ch. 379 (SB 541) §2.

ARTICLE 7
Reinstatement from Retirement

§21190. Reinstatement and employment of retiree.

A person who has been retired under this system for service may be reinstated from retirement by the board as provided in this article, and thereafter may be employed by the state or by a contracting agency in accordance with the laws governing that service, in the same manner as a person who has not been so retired. **Leg.H.** 1995 ch. 379 (SB 541) §2.

§21191. Reinstatement of person retired for disability.

Subject to Sections 21197 and 21201, notwithstanding any other provision of law to the contrary, a person who has been retired under this system for industrial disability shall be reinstated from retirement pursuant to this article, upon his or her application to the board, if, upon reinstatement, he or she will be employed by the state or any contracting agency as a state or local miscellaneous member. **Leg.H.** 1995 ch. 379 (SB 541) §2.

§21192. Disability retirement recipient under minimum age for voluntary retirement; medical examination; application for reinstatement.

The board, or in case of a local safety member, other than a school safety member, the governing body of the employer from whose employment the person was retired, may require any recipient of a disability retirement allowance under the minimum age for voluntary retirement for service applicable to members of his or her class to undergo medical examination, and upon his or her application for reinstatement, shall cause a medical examination to be made of the recipient who is at least six months less than the age of compulsory retirement for service applicable to members of the class or category in which it is proposed to employ him or her. The board, or in case of a local safety member, other than a school safety member, the governing body of the employer from whose employment the person was retired, shall also cause the examination to be made upon application for reinstatement to the position held at retirement or any position in the same class, of a person who was incapacitated for performance of duty in the position at the time of a prior reinstatement to another position. The examination shall be made by a physician or surgeon, appointed by the board or the governing body of the employer, at the place of residence of the recipient or other place mutually agreed upon. Upon the basis of the examination, the board or the governing body shall determine whether he or she is still incapacitated, physically or mentally, for duty in the state agency, the university, or contracting agency, where he or she was employed and in the position held by him or her when retired for disability, or in a position in the same classification, and for the duties of the position with regard to which he or she has applied for reinstatement from retirement. **Leg.H.** 1995 ch. 379 (SB 541) §2.

§21193. Cancellation of allowance and reinstatement to position, on determination that recipient not incapacitated.

If the determination pursuant to Section 21192 is that the recipient is not so incapacitated for duty in the position held when retired for disability or in a position in the same classification or in the position with regard to which he or she has applied for reinstatement and his or her employer offers to reinstate that employee, his or her disability retirement allowance shall be canceled immediately, and he or she shall become a member of this system.

If the recipient was an employee of the state or of the university and is so determined to be not incapacitated for duty in the position held when retired for disability or in a position in the same class, he or she shall be reinstated, at his or her option, to that position. However, in that case, acceptance of any other position shall immediately terminate any right to reinstatement. A recipient who is found to continue to be incapacitated for duty in his or her former position and class, but not incapacitated for duty in another position for which he or she has applied for reinstatement and who accepts employment in the other position, shall upon subsequent discontinuance of incapacity for service in his or her former position or a position in the same class, as determined by the board under Section 21192, be reinstated at his or her option to that position.

If the recipient was an employee of a contracting agency other than a local safety member, with the exception of a school safety member, the board shall notify it that his or her disability has terminated and that he or she is eligible for reinstatement to duty. The fact that he or she was retired for disability does not prejudice any right to reinstatement to duty which he or she may claim. **Leg.H.** 1995 ch. 379 (SB 541) §2.

Ref.: Hanna § 3.116[3].

§21194. Reinstatement from partial retirement.

A person who has been partially retired under this system pursuant to Article 1.7 (commencing with Section 19996.30) of Chapter 7 of Part 2.6 or pursuant to Sections 21110 through 21115 may be reinstated from partial retirement by the board as provided in this article, and thereafter may continue to be employed on a full-time basis by the state, in the same manner as a person who has not been so retired. **Leg.H.** 1995 ch. 379 (SB 541) §2.

§21195. Reinstatement requirements.

(a) Notwithstanding any other section in Article 6 (commencing with Section 21150) or in this article, the Department of Personnel Administration may reinstate a person who has retired for industrial disability pursuant to Section 21410, within 12 months after the effective date of retirement, if it has identified an available position with duties that the employee is able to perform. Upon reinstatement, the person shall become entitled to benefits under the partial disability retirement program pursuant to Section 21160.

(b) This section shall not apply to any job-related or job-incurred illness or injury that occurs on or after January 1, 2000. **Leg.H.** 1995 ch. 379 (SB 541) §2, 2000 ch. 402 (AB 649) §18, effective September 11, 2000.

§21196. Reinstatement procedure.

The board may reinstate a person from retirement upon (a) his or her application to the board for reinstatement and (b) the determination of the board that his or her age at the date of application for reinstatement is at least six months less than the age of compulsory retirement for service applicable to members of the class or category in which it is proposed to employ him or her. The provisions of clause (b) of this section shall apply only to patrol, state peace officer/firefighters, and safety members. The effective date of reinstatement for purposes of this article shall be the first day of compensated employment following approval of reinstatement. **Leg.H.** 1995 chs. 379 (SB 541), 850 (SB 860), 1996 ch. 906 (SB 1859) §135 (former §21101).

§21197. Reinstatement procedure for person retired for disability.

The board may reinstate a person from industrial disability retirement to a miscellaneous member position upon all of the following:

(a) His or her application to the board for reinstatement.

(b) The determination of the board, based upon medical examination, that he or she is not incapacitated for the duties to be assigned to him or her.

(c) The determination of the board that the employer from whose employment the person was retired for industrial disability has been furnished a notice of intent to reinstate that person, that contains information that he or she may be entitled to resume an industrial disability retirement allowance using the salaries earnable under the miscellaneous member position upon termination of the miscellaneous member employment. **Leg.H.** 1995 ch. 379 (SB 541) §2.

§21198. Reinstatement after involuntary termination of employment.

A person who has been retired under this system for service following an involuntary termination of his or her employment, and who is subsequently reinstated to that employment pursuant to an administrative or judicial proceeding, shall be reinstated from retirement. The requirements of Section 21196 shall not apply to that reinstatement. Reinstatement shall be effective as of the date from which salary is awarded in the administrative or judicial proceedings, and his or her rights and obligations shall be as specified in this article. However, amounts paid to the person during retirement for any period after the date from which salary is awarded, shall be repaid by him or her to this system, and contributions shall be made for any period for which salary is awarded in the administrative or judicial proceedings in the amount that he or she would have contributed had his or her employment not been terminated, and he or she shall receive credit as state service for the period for which salary is awarded. **Leg.H.** 1995 ch. 379 (SB 541) §2, 1996 ch. 906 (SB 1859) §142.

§21199. Reinstatement if person will be appointed to position by Governor.

A person who has been retired under this system for service may be reinstated from retirement pursuant to this article, without regard to the requirements of Section 21196, upon his or her application to the board, if, upon reinstatement, he or she will be appointed by the Governor to any state office or employment. **Leg.H.** 1995 ch. 379 (SB 541) §2.

§21200. Cancellation of retirement allowance; crediting account; future rate of contribution and allowance.

When any person is reinstated from retirement under this article, his or her retirement allowance shall be canceled immediately, and he or she shall become a member of this system as of the date of reinstatement. His or her individual account shall be credited with an amount that is the actuarial equivalent of his or her annuity at the date of reinstatement, not to exceed the amount of his or her accumulated contributions as it was at the date of retirement. His or her future rate of contributions and his or her retirement allowance upon subsequent retirement shall be determined in accordance with Chapter 8 (commencing with Section 20670) and Chapter 13 (commencing with Section 21250), respectively.

The actuarial equivalent under this section shall be adjusted by the board every 10 years, or more frequently, to agree with the interest rate and mortality tables in effect at the commencement of each such 10-year or succeeding interval. **Leg.H.** 1995 ch. 379 (SB 541) §2, 1996 ch. 906 (SB 1859) §143.

§21201. Cancellation of allowance for person reinstated from disability retirement.

When any person is reinstated from industrial disability retirement under Sections 21191 and 21197, his or her retirement allowance shall be canceled immediately, and he or she shall become a member of this system as of the date of reinstatement. His or her individual account shall be credited with an amount that is the actuarial equivalent of his or her annuity at the date of reinstatement, not to exceed the amount of his or her accumulated contributions as it was at the date of retirement. Upon subsequent retirement, the board shall resume the payment of his or her previous industrial disability retirement allowance using the highest compensation earnable during any period of membership, notwithstanding Section 20036, to recalculate the industrial disability retirement allowance. The member shall receive, in addition to the disability retirement allowance from the employment in which he or she was granted the industrial disability retirement, an annuity purchased with his or her accumulated normal contributions made in respect to other employment covered by this system. If the member is qualified for service retirement, he or she shall receive his or her service retirement allowance, in lieu of the industrial retirement allowance, if the service retirement allowance is greater. **Leg.H.** 1995 ch. 379 (SB 541) §2, 1999 ch. 785 (AB 813) §7.

§21202. Reinstatement of unlawfully employed retiree.

A person employed in violation of Section 21220 shall be reinstated to membership in the category in which, and on the date on which, the unlawful employment occurred. **Leg.H.** 1995 ch. 379 (SB 541) §2.

§21203. Reinstatement of employee with special qualifications.

A person who has been retired under this system for service may be reinstated from retirement pursuant to this article, without regard to the requirements of Section 21196, upon his or her application to the board if both of the following conditions occur:

(a) Upon reinstatement, he or she will be appointed by a state board or commission to the position to which the board or commission is entitled to appoint an employee exempt from civil service under the provisions of Article VII of the California Constitution.

(b) In the judgment of the board or commission he or she has special knowledge, experience and qualifications respecting the activities of the board or commission. **Leg.H.** 1995 ch. 379 (SB 541) §2.

CHAPTER 13
RETIREMENT BENEFITS

ARTICLE 1
General Provisions
[Selected Provisions]

§21257. No modification due to workers' compensation benefits received.

The benefits payable after August 4, 1943 under this system shall not be modified on account of any amounts paid to a retired member or beneficiary under Division 4 (commencing with Section 3200) of the Labor Code. **Leg.H.** 1995 ch. 379 §2 (former §21202).

ARTICLE 5
Disability Retirement Benefits
[Selected Provisions]

§21413. Local safety member retired for industrial disability.

Upon retirement of a local safety member for industrial disability he or she shall receive a disability retirement allowance of 50 percent of his or her final compensation plus an annuity purchased with his or her accumulated additional contributions, if any, or, if qualified for service retirement, he or she shall receive his or her service retirement allowance if the allowance, after deducting the annuity, is greater. **Leg.H.** 1995 ch. 379 (SB 541) §2.

§21416. Disability allowance for state safety member; retroactive payments.

Notwithstanding any provision of this part, a state safety member employed by the Department of Corrections or the Department of the Youth Authority with 25 years or more of service credit as such, shall, upon retirement on or after January 1, 1982, for industrial disability, receive the disability allowance provided for in Section 21411 or a disability allowance equal to 1/50th of final compensation multiplied by the number of years of state safety member service in the Department of Corrections or the Department of the Youth Authority with which the member is credited at retirement.

This section shall not become operative for any eligible member, until it is first agreed to in a memorandum of understanding reached between the state and the exclusive representatives of the employees in State Bargaining Unit No. 6 pursuant to Chapter 10.3 (commencing with Section 3512) of Division 4 of Title 1, and approved by the Legislature pursuant to law.

Payment of benefits pursuant to this section for any eligible member shall be retroactive to the effective date of the retirement of the member. **Leg.H.** 1995 ch. 379 §2 (former §21292.51).

§21419. Deduction of advanced disability payments from retroactive disability allowance.

This system shall deduct the amount of advanced disability pension payments made to a local safety member pursuant to Section 4850.3 or 4850.4 of the Labor Code from the member's retroactive disability allowance, and reimburse the local agency that has made the advanced disability pension payments. If the retroactive disability allowance is not sufficient to reimburse the total advanced disability pension payments, an amount no greater than 10 percent of the member's monthly disability allowance shall be deducted and reimbursed to the local agency until the total advanced disability pension payments have been repaid. The local safety member and this system may agree to any other arrangement or schedule for the member to repay the advanced disability pension payments. **Leg.H.** 1995 ch. 379 (SB 541), 2002 ch. 877 (AB 2131).

Ref.: See Labor Code § 4850.4; Hanna § 3.114[2].

§21430. Increased industrial disability allowance of local members based on percentage disability determined by Workers' Compensation Appeals Board subject to employer election.

Upon retirement of a local safety member for industrial disability, the member shall receive in lieu of the allowance otherwise provided by this article a disability retirement allowance in the amount of the percentage of final compensation equal to the percentage of permanent disability determined by the Workers' Compensation Appeals Board for the purposes of permanent disability payments pursuant to Article 3 (commencing with Section 4650) of Chapter 2 of Part 2 of the Labor Code with respect solely to the injury resulting in the disability retirement and giving effect to Section 4750 of the Labor Code, but not less than 50 percent nor in excess of 90 percent of the member's final compensation.

This section shall not apply to any contracting agency nor to the employees of any contracting agency unless and until the agency elects to be subject to the provisions of this section by amendment to its contract made in the manner prescribed for approval of contracts, or in the case of contracts made after June 14, 1975, by express provision in such contract making the contracting agency subject to the provisions of this section.

This section shall only apply to members who retire for disability on and after the date the agency elects to be subject to this section. **Leg.H.** 1995 ch. 379 (SB 541) §2.

Ref.: Hanna § 33.02[4][a].

CHAPTER 14
DEATH BENEFITS

ARTICLE 2
Preretirement Death Benefits
[Selected Provisions]

§21537. Special death benefit; industrial death; determination by Appeals Board; limitations on jurisdiction; applicability.

(a) The special death benefit is payable if the deceased was a patrol, state peace officer/firefighter, state safety, state industrial, or local safety member, if his or her death was industrial and if there is a survivor who qualifies under subdivision (b) of Section 21541. The Workers' Compensation Appeals Board, using the same procedures as in workers' compensation hearings, shall in disputed cases determine whether the death of a member was industrial.

(b) The jurisdiction of the Workers' Compensation Appeals Board shall be limited solely to the issue of industrial causation, and this section shall not be construed to authorize the Workers' Compensation Appeals Board to award costs against this system pursuant to Section 4600, 5811, or any other provision of the Labor Code.

(c) This section does not apply to state safety members described in Section 20401.5 or local safety members described in Section 20423.6.

(d)(1) For purposes of this section, the special death benefit is payable as of the effective date of the industrial disability retirement of the member if the death of the member occurred from a single event injury arising out of and in the course of his or her official duties which, based on competent medical opinion, rendered the member into a persistent vegetative state devoid of cognitive function at the time of injury until the time of death.

(2) This subdivision applies only to a member who retired and then died on or after July 3, 2006. Leg.H. 1995 ch. 379 §2 (former §21363), 2002 ch. 1152 (AB 2023), 2008 ch. 74 (AB 2156) §1.

Ref.: W. Cal. Sum., 2 "Workers' Compensation" §314.

§21537.5. [See Subsection (c) for Operative Information] Special death benefit for state miscellaneous member in State Bargaining Unit 12.

(a) The special death benefit is payable if the deceased was a state miscellaneous member in State Bargaining Unit 12 employed by the Department of Transportation, if his or her death occurred as a direct result of injury arising out of and in the course of his or her official duties with the department working on the California highway system performing highway maintenance, and if there is a survivor who qualifies under subdivision (b) of Section 21541. The Workers' Compensation Appeals Board, using the same procedures as in workers' compensation hearings, shall in disputed cases determine whether the death of the member occurred as a result of that injury.

(b) The jurisdiction of the Workers' Compensation Appeals Board shall be limited solely to the issue of industrial causation, and this section may not be construed to authorize the Workers' Compensation Appeals Board to award costs against this system pursuant to Section 4600, 5811, or any other provision of the Labor Code.

(c) This section shall not become operative unless and until a memorandum of understanding has been agreed to by the state employer and the recognized employee organization making this section applicable to those members described in subdivision (a). **Leg.H.** 2002 ch. 1153 (SB 1984), 2006 ch. 210 (SB 357) §6, effective September 6, 2006.

§21538. Special death benefit for appointed state member.

The special death benefit is also payable if the deceased was a state member appointed by the Governor, the Director of Corrections, or the Board of Prison Terms, if his or her death occurred as a result of injury or disease arising out of and in the course of his or her official duties within a state prison or facility of the

Department of Corrections, and if there is a survivor who qualifies under subdivision (b) of Section 21541. The Workers' Compensation Appeals Board, using the same procedure as in workers' compensation hearings, shall in disputed cases determine whether the death of the member occurred as a result of the injury or disease.

The jurisdiction of the Workers' Compensation Appeals Board shall be limited solely to the issue of industrial causation, and this section shall not be construed to authorize the Workers' Compensation Appeals Board to award costs against this system pursuant to Section 4600 or 5811 or any other provision of the Labor Code. **Leg.H.** 1995 ch. 379 §2 (former §21363.3).

§21540. Special death benefit for appointed state member—Death resulting from conduct of correctional institution inmate.

The special death benefit is also payable if the deceased was the Secretary of the Youth and Adult Corrections Agency, or was a state member appointed by the Secretary of the Youth and Adult Corrections Agency, the Department of the Youth Authority, the Superintendent of the California Institution for Women, or the Women's Board of Terms and Paroles, the Board of Corrections, or was a member of the Board of Corrections or the Department of the Youth Authority not already classified as a prison member, provided that his or her death occurred as a result of misconduct of an inmate of a state prison, correctional school, or facility of the Department of Corrections or the Department of the Youth Authority, or a parolee therefrom.

The special death benefit provided by this section is not payable unless the death of the member arose out of and was in the course of his or her official duties and unless there is a survivor who qualifies under subdivision (b) of Section 21541. The Workers' Compensation Appeals Board, using the same procedure as in workers' compensation hearings, shall, in disputed cases, determine whether the member's death arose out of and in the course of his or her official duties.

A natural parent of surviving children eligible to receive an allowance payable under this section shall not be required to become the guardian of surviving unmarried children under 18 years of age in order to be paid the benefits prescribed for those children.

The jurisdiction of the Workers' Compensation Appeals Board shall be limited solely to the issue of industrial causation, and this section shall not be construed to authorize the Workers' Compensation Appeals Board to award costs against this system pursuant to Section 4600 or 5811 or any other provision of the Labor Code. **Leg.H.** 1995 ch. 379 §2 (former §21363.6).

§21540.5. Special death benefit for state, school, or local miscellaneous member or local or state safety member; conditions; jurisdiction and determination of Workers' Compensation Appeals Board; inapplicability of section.

(a) The special death benefit is also payable if the deceased was a state, school, or local miscellaneous member, a local safety member described in Section 20423.6, or a state safety member described in Section 20401.5, if the death of the member was a direct consequence of a violent act perpetrated on his or her person that arose out of and was in the course of his or her official duties and there is a survivor who qualifies under paragraph (2) of subdivision (a) of Section 21541. The Workers' Compensation Appeals Board, using the same procedure as in workers' compensation hearings, shall, in disputed cases determine whether the member's death was a direct consequence of a violent act perpetrated on his or her person that arose out of and in the course of his or her official duties.

(b) A natural parent of surviving children eligible to receive an allowance payable under this section is not required to become the guardian of surviving unmarried children under 18 years of age in order to be paid the benefits prescribed for those children.

(c) The jurisdiction of the Workers' Compensation Appeals Board shall be limited solely to the issue of industrial causation, and this section may not be construed to authorize the Workers' Compensation Appeals Board to award costs against this system pursuant to Section 4600 or 5811 or any other provision of the Labor Code.

(d) This section does not apply to a contracting agency nor its employees unless and until the agency elects to be subject to it by amendment to its contract made in the manner prescribed for approval of contracts, or in the case of a new contract, by express provision of the contract. **Leg.H.** 1995 ch. 379 §2 (former

§21363.7), 1997 ch. 386, 2002 ch. 1152 (AB 2023), 2005 ch. 328 (AB 1166) §16.

1997 Note: The amendments to Section 21540.5 of the Government Code during the 1997–98 Regular Session shall not be construed to affect the liability of the Public Employees' Retirement System for any acts respecting state or local miscellaneous members that occurred prior to July 1, 1993, nor any acts respecting school members that occurred prior to January 1, 1998. Stats. 1997 ch. 386 §5.

§21541. Special death benefit.

(a) The special death benefit consists of the following:

(1) An amount equal to and derived from the same source as the basic death benefit exclusive of the contributions from which the annuity provided under paragraph (4) is paid.

(2) An amount sufficient, when added to the amount provided under paragraph (1), to provide, when applied according to tables adopted by the board, a monthly death allowance equal to one-half of his or her final compensation in the membership category applicable to him or her at the time of the injury, or the onset of the disease, causing death, as adjusted pursuant to subdivision (b), which amount shall be payable to the surviving spouse to whom he or she was married either continuously for at least one year prior to death, or prior to sustaining the injury or disease resulting in death, as long as the surviving spouse lives; or, if there is no surviving spouse or if the spouse dies before all children of the deceased member attain the age of 22 years, to his or her children under the age of 22 years collectively until every child shall have died, married, or attained the age of 22 years. However, no child shall receive any part of the allowance after marrying or attaining the age of 22 years. The increases described in this section shall only apply to spouses of deceased members who would have been less than 50 years of age, if still living on January 1, 2001.

(3) During the lifetime of the surviving spouse, an additional percentage of the death benefit allowed by this section, exclusive of the annuity under paragraph (4), shall be paid to the spouse of a member who is killed in the performance of his or her duty or who dies as a result of an accident or an injury caused by external violence or physical force, incurred in the performance of his or her duty, for each of his or her children during the lifetime of the child, or until the child marries or reaches the age of 22 years, as follows: for one child, 25 percent; for two children, 40 percent; and for three or more children, 50 percent.

(4) An annuity that is the actuarial equivalent, assuming monthly payments for life to the surviving spouse, of the deceased's accumulated additional contributions at the date of his or her death, plus his or her accumulated contributions at that date based on compensation earned in any membership category other than the category applicable to him or her at the time of the injury or the onset of the disease causing death.

(b) For purposes of this section only, the deceased member's final compensation shall be deemed to increase, and the death benefit under paragraph (2) of subdivision (a) shall be increased correspondingly, at any time and to the extent the compensation is increased for then-active members employed in the job classification and membership category that was applicable to the deceased member at the time of the injury, or the onset of the disease, causing death. The deceased member's final compensation shall be deemed to be subject to further increases hereunder only until the earlier of (1) the death of the surviving spouse or (2) the date that the deceased member would have attained the age of 50 years.

(c) Monthly allowances shall be adjusted annually for time commencing on the first day of September and effective with the monthly allowance regularly payable on the first day of the October beginning with October 1, 2001. The employer of the deceased member shall be responsible for reporting and certifying top range salary rates by the first day of July, beginning with July 1, 2001.

(d) If the surviving spouse does not have custody of the member's children, the additional amount payable pursuant to this section shall be payable to the person having custody of the children for each child during the lifetime of the child, or until the child marries or reaches the age of 22 years.

(e) The computation for time prior to entering the membership category applicable to the deceased at the time of the injury, or the onset of the disease, causing death shall be based on the compensation earnable by him or her in the position first held by him or her in that category.

(f) For purposes of this section:

(1) "Child" means a natural or adopted child of the deceased member, or a stepchild living or domiciled with the deceased member at the time of his or her death.

(2) "Spouse" means a wife or husband.

(g) This section shall apply to all contracting agencies and to the employees of all contracting agencies.

(h) For purposes of Section 21313, the base allowance shall be the allowance as increased under this section. The base year for annual adjustments of allowances increased by this section shall be the calendar year preceding the year of the adjustment.

(i) The amount of the death benefit payable pursuant to this section on and after January 1, 2001, with respect to any member who died prior to that date, shall be recalculated on and after that date pursuant to subdivision (b). **Leg.H.** 1945 ch. 123 §1, as Gov C §21364, 1949 ch. 298 §41, 1953 ch. 1186 §30, effective October 1, 1953, 1955 ch. 1766 §1, 1961 ch. 2197 §1, 1965 ch. 977 §5, operative October 1, 1965, ch. 1772 §1, ch. 1773 §1, operative October 1, 1965, 1967 ch. 1699 §2, 1974 ch. 92 §1, 1976 ch. 1436 §16, 1980 ch. 1102 §22, 1981 ch. 609 §27, ch. 963 §7, 1982 ch. 432 §10, 1995 chs. 379 (SB 541) §1, 850 (SB 860) §11, 1996 ch. 906 (SB 1859) §166 (amended & renumbered from §21364), 1999 ch. 800 (AB 232) §1.6, 2000 ch. 1031 (AB 2621) §1, 2003 ch. 840 (AB 933).

2003 Note: This act shall apply retroactively to the survivors of a deceased person who dies or is killed in the line of duty on or after January 1, 2001. Stats. 2003 ch. 840 (AB 933) §4.

Ref.: Hanna §§ 3.115[1], 9.04[1].

§21541.5. Benefits terminated upon adoption.

Any child whose benefits under Section 21541 were terminated upon his or her adoption, pursuant to that section as it read prior to January 1, 2001, shall have those benefits restored as follows:

(a) The child shall receive a lump-sum payment in the amount that would have paid, if he or she had not been adopted, from the date of adoption to the earlier of (1) the date his or her eligibility for benefits under Section 21541 would have otherwise terminated had he or she not been adopted or (2) January 1, 2001.

(b) If on January 1, 2001, the child is eligible for benefits under Section 21541, he or she shall receive benefits from and after that date pursuant to Section 21541. **Leg.H.** 2000 ch. 1031 (AB 2621) §2.

§21542. Special death benefit—Accrual; election to receive death benefit in lieu of special death benefit.

The special death benefit shall begin to accrue on the day next following the date of the member's death, and shall be paid in monthly installments to the surviving spouse and children as prescribed in Section 21541. The surviving spouse or the guardian of the minor child or children entitled to the special death benefit may elect, before the first payment, to receive the basic death benefit in lieu of the special death benefit. The election precludes a claim to benefits under Section 4707 of the Labor Code as the special death benefit is deemed payable by this system and is irrevocable. **Leg.H.** 1995 ch. 379 §2.

§21543. Special death benefit payment—Conditions for lump sum payment; accumulated additional contributions.

If payment of the special death benefit is stopped because of death of the surviving spouse or death, marriage, or attainment of the age of 22 years by a child before the sum of the monthly payment made, exclusive of the annuity derived from the accumulated additional contribution of the deceased, equals the basic death benefit, a lump sum equal to the difference shall be paid to the surviving children of the deceased member, share and share alike, or if there are no children, to the estate of the person last entitled to the allowance. In that event, the accumulated additional contributions of the deceased, as they were at his or her death, less the annuity paid as derived from those contributions, and plus interest credited to the accumulated additional contributions, shall be paid in the manner provided in this article for the payments of amounts due in the absence of a designated beneficiary. **Leg.H.** 1995 ch. 379 (SB 541) §2, 2004 ch. 231 (SB 1603).

§21544. Special death benefit—Determination of death as industrial in nature.

Upon notice of a death as a result of which the special death benefit may be payable, and when there is a survivor who would qualify under subdivision (b) of Section 21541, the board, or in disputed cases, the Workers' Compensation

Appeals Board, shall determine whether the death was industrial, and pending final determination of the issue, the board shall temporarily pay special death benefits. The temporary payments shall be deducted from any other death benefits otherwise payable if the death is determined not to be industrial. **Leg.H.** 1995 ch. 379 §2 (former §21367).

§21546. Death of qualified member while in state service and before retirement; beneficiaries; monthly allowance; application.

(a) Upon the death of a member who has attained the minimum age for voluntary service retirement applicable to the member in his or her last employment preceding death, and who is eligible to retire and in circumstances in which the basic death benefit is payable other than solely that of membership in a county retirement system, or a retirement system maintained by the university, a monthly allowance shall be payable as follows:

(1) To the member's surviving spouse as long as the spouse lives.

(2) To the children under the age of 18 years collectively if there is no surviving spouse or if the surviving spouse dies before all children of the deceased member attain the age of 18 years, until every child dies or attains the age of 18 years. No child shall receive any allowance after marrying or attaining the age of 18 years.

(b) The monthly allowance under this section shall be equal to one-half of, and derived from the same source as, the unmodified retirement allowance the member would have been entitled to receive if he or she had retired for service on the date of death. If, however, the member made a specific beneficiary designation under Section 21490, the monthly allowance shall be equal to one-half of that portion of the member's unmodified retirement allowance that would have been derived from the nonmember spouse's community property interest in the member's contributions and service credit.

(c) If a member does not have a surviving spouse nor any children under the age of 18 years at the time of death, no allowance shall be payable under this section.

(d) No allowance shall be payable under this section if a special death benefit is payable.

(e)(1) The allowance provided by this section shall be paid in lieu of the basic death benefit but a surviving spouse qualifying for the allowance may elect, before the first payment on account of it, to receive the basic death benefit in lieu of the allowance.

(2) The allowance provided by this section shall be paid in lieu of the basic death benefit but the guardian of the minor child or children qualifying for the allowance may elect, before the first payment on account of it, to receive the basic death benefit in lieu of the allowance. If an election of the basic death benefit is made, the basic death benefit shall be paid to all the member's surviving children, regardless of age or marital status, in equal shares.

(f) If the total of the payments made pursuant to this section are less than the basic death benefit that was otherwise payable on account of the member's death, the amount of the basic death benefit less any payments made pursuant to this section shall be paid in a lump sum to the surviving children of the member, share and share alike, or if there are no children, to the estate of the person last entitled to the allowance.

(g) The board shall compute the amount by which benefits paid pursuant to this section exceed the benefits that would otherwise be payable and shall charge any excess against the contributions of the state so that there shall be no increase in contributions of members by reason of benefits paid pursuant to this section.

(h) As used in this section, "a surviving spouse" means a spouse who was either married to the member for at least one year prior to the member's death, or was married to the member prior to the occurrence of the injury or the onset of the illness that resulted in death, and "child" includes a posthumously born child of the member.

(i) On and after April 1, 1972, this section shall apply to all contracting agencies and to the employees of those agencies with respect to deaths occurring after April 1, 1972, whether or not the agencies have previously elected to be subject to this section. **Leg.H.** 1995 ch. 379 (SB 541) §2, 1999 ch. 800 (AB 232) §2, 2000 ch. 1002 (SB 1998) §8.

§21547. Monthly allowance in lieu of basic death benefit for members in state bargaining units subject to memoranda of understanding.

(a) Notwithstanding any other provision of this article requiring attainment of the minimum age for voluntary service retirement to the member in his or her last employment preceding death, upon the death of a state member on or after January 1, 1993, who is credited with 20 years or more of state service, the surviving spouse, or eligible children if there is no surviving spouse, may receive a monthly allowance in lieu of the basic death benefit. The board shall notify the eligible survivor, as defined in Section 21546, of this alternate death benefit. The board shall calculate the monthly allowance that shall be payable as follows:

(1) To the member's surviving spouse, an amount equal to the amount the member would have received if the member had retired for service at minimum retirement age on the date of death and had elected optional settlement 2 and Section 21459.

(2) If the member made a specific beneficiary designation under Section 21490, the monthly allowance shall be based only on that portion of the amount the member would have received described in paragraph (1) that would have been derived from the nonmember spouse's community property interest in the member's contributions and service credit.

(3) If there is no surviving spouse or the spouse dies before all of the children of the deceased member attain the age of 18 years, to the surviving children, under the age of 18 years, collectively, an amount equal to one-half of, and derived from the same source as, the unmodified allowance the member would have received if he or she had retired for service at minimum retirement age on the date of death. No child shall receive any allowance after marrying or attaining the age of 18 years. As used in this paragraph, "surviving children" includes a posthumously born child or children of the member.

(b) This section shall only apply to members employed in state bargaining units for which a memorandum of understanding has been agreed to by the state employer and the recognized employee organization to become subject to this section, members who are excluded from the definition of state employees in subdivision (c) of Section 3513, and members employed by the executive branch of government who are not members of the civil service.

(c) For purposes of this section, "state service" means service rendered as a state employee, as defined in Section 19815. This section shall not apply to any contracting agency nor to the employees of any contracting agency.

(d) For purposes of this section, "state service" includes service to the state for which the member, pursuant to Section 20281.5, did not receive credit. **Leg.H.** 1995 ch. 379 (SB 541) §2, 1999 ch. 457 (SB 401) §14, effective September 21, 1999, 2000 ch. 1002 (SB 1998) §9, 2004 ch. 214 (SB 1105), effective August 11, 2004.

Ref.: Herlick Handbook § 7.20; W. Cal. Sum., 2 "Workers' Compensation" §333.

§21547.5. Adjustment of monthly allowance that began prior to specified date.

For any survivor receiving a monthly allowance pursuant to Section 21547 prior to January 1, 2000, that allowance shall be adjusted as of January 1, 2000, to equal the amount that the survivor would have been entitled to receive if the member's death had occurred on or after January 1, 2000. The adjusted allowance shall be payable only on and after January 1, 2000. **Leg.H.** 1999 ch. 457 (SB 401) §15, effective September 21, 1999.

§21547.7. Monthly allowance in lieu of basic death benefit.

(a) Notwithstanding any other provision of this article requiring attainment of the minimum age for voluntary service retirement applicable to him or her in his or her last employment preceding death, upon the death of a local firefighter member while in the employ of an agency subject to this section on or after January 1, 2001, who is credited with 20 years or more of state service, the surviving spouse, or eligible children, if there is no eligible spouse, may receive a monthly allowance in lieu of the basic death benefit. The board shall notify the eligible survivor, as defined in Section 21546, of this alternate death benefit. The board shall calculate the monthly allowance that shall be payable as follows:

(1) To the member's surviving spouse, an amount equal to the amount the member would have received if he or she had retired for service at the minimum retirement age on the date of death and had elected optional settlement 2 and Section 21459. The retirement allowance shall be calculated using all service earned by the member in this system.

(2) If there is no surviving spouse or the spouse dies before all of the children of the deceased member attain the age of 18 years, to

the surviving children, under the age of 18 years, collectively, an amount equal to one-half of, and derived from the same source as, the unmodified allowance the member would have received if he or she had retired for service at the minimum retirement age on the date of death. No child shall receive any allowance after marrying or attaining the age of 18 years. As used in this paragraph, "surviving children" includes a posthumously born child or children of the member. The retirement allowance shall be calculated using all service earned by the member in this system.

(3) The cost of the allowance paid pursuant to this subdivision shall be paid from the assets of the employer at the member's date of death. All member contributions made by the member to this system shall be transferred to the plan assets of the employer liable for the funding of this benefit.

(b)(1) Upon the death of a local firefighter member while in the employ of an agency subject to this section on or after January 1, 2001, who is credited with 20 years or more of state service and who has attained the minimum age for voluntary service retirement applicable to him or her in his or her last employment preceding death, the surviving spouse, or eligible children, if there is no eligible spouse, may elect to receive a monthly allowance that is equal to the amount that member would have received if the member had been retired from service on the date of death and had elected optional settlement 2 and Section 21459 in lieu of the basic death benefit. The retirement allowance will be calculated using all service earned by the member in this system.

(2) If there is no surviving spouse or the spouse dies before all of the children of the deceased member attain the age of 18 years, the allowance shall continue to the surviving children, under the age of 18 years, collectively, in an amount equal to one-half of, and derived from the same source as, the unmodified allowance the member would have received if he or she had been retired from service on the date of death. No child shall receive any allowance after marrying or attaining the age of 18 years. As used in this paragraph, "surviving children" includes a posthumously born child or children of the member. The retirement allowance will be calculated using all service earned by the member in this system.

(3) The cost of the increase in service allowance paid pursuant to this subdivision shall be paid from the assets of the employer at the member's date of death.

(c) This section shall not apply to any contracting agency, nor to the employees of any contracting agency, unless and until the agency elects to be subject to this section by amendment to its contract made in the manner prescribed for approval of contracts, except that an election among the employees is not required. **Leg.H.** 2000 ch. 855 (SB 1695) §1, 2001 chs. 159 (SB 662) §114, 793 (AB 1683) §31.

§21548. Allowance to surviving spouse of member eligible pursuant to specified provision; application.

(a) The surviving spouse of a member who has attained the minimum age for voluntary service retirement applicable to the member in his or her last employment preceding death, and who is eligible to receive an allowance pursuant to Section 21546, shall instead receive an allowance that is equal to the amount that the member would have received if the member had been retired from service on the date of death and had elected optional settlement 2 and Section 21459.

(b) The surviving spouse of a member who has attained the minimum age for voluntary service retirement applicable to the member in his or her last employment preceding death, and who is eligible to receive a special death benefit in lieu of an allowance under Section 21546, may elect to instead receive an allowance that is equal to the amount that the member would have received if the member had been retired from service on the date of death and had elected optional settlement 2 and Section 21459.

(c) If the member made a specific beneficiary designation under Section 21490, the allowance under this section shall be based only on that portion of the amount the member would have received described in subdivision (a) or (b) that would have been derived from the nonmember spouse's community property interest in the member's contributions and service credit.

(d) The allowance provided by this section shall be payable as long as the surviving spouse lives. Upon the death of the surviving spouse, the benefit shall be continued to minor children, as defined in Section 6500 of the Family Code, or a lump sum shall be paid as provided under circumstances specified in Section 21546 or in Sections 21541 and 21543, as the case may be.

(e) The allowance provided by this section shall be paid in lieu of the basic death benefit, but the surviving spouse qualifying for the allowance may elect before the first payment on account of it to receive the basic death benefit in lieu of the allowance.

(f) This section shall apply with respect to state members whose death occurs on and after July 1, 1976.

(g) All references in this code to Section 21546 shall be deemed to include this section in the alternative.

(h) This section shall not apply to any contracting agency nor to the employees of any contracting agency unless and until the agency elects to be subject to this section by amendment to its contract made in the manner prescribed for approval of contracts, except that an election among the employees is not required, or, in the case of contracts made after January 1, 1985, by express provision in the contract making the contracting agency subject to this section. **Leg.H.** 1995 ch. 379 (SB 541) §2, 1999 ch. 800 (AB 232) §3, 2000 ch. 1002 (SB 1998) §10.

Ref.: Herlick Handbook § 7.20; W. Cal. Sum., 2 "Workers' Compensation" §333.

§21551. Surviving spouse benefits.

Notwithstanding any other provision of this part, the benefits payable to a surviving spouse pursuant to Sections 21541, 21546, 21547, 21548, and Article 3 (commencing with Section 21570), do not cease upon remarriage if the remarriage occurs on or after September 19, 1989, for surviving spouses of deceased state members, January 1, 1991, for surviving spouses of deceased school members, upon the date a contracting agency elected to be subject to this section for deceased local members, or January 1, 2000, for spouses of deceased local members if the contracting agency has not elected to be subject to this section. Any surviving spouse who elected the reduction specified in Section 21500 as it read prior to January 1, 2000, shall be restored to the lifetime allowance to which he or she was originally entitled effective September 19, 1989, for state members, January 1, 1991, for school members, upon the date a contracting agency elected to be subject to this section, or January 1, 2000, if the contracting agency has not elected to be subject to this section.

Pursuant to Section 22822, the surviving spouse who remarries may not enroll his or her new spouse or stepchildren as family members under the continued health benefits coverage of the surviving spouse.

Any surviving spouse whose allowance has been discontinued as a result of remarriage prior to the effective date of this section shall have that allowance restored and resumed on January 1, 2000, or the first of the month, following receipt by the board of a written application from the spouse for resumption of the allowance, whichever is later. The amount of the benefits due shall be calculated as though the allowance had never been reduced or discontinued because of remarriage, and is not payable for the period between the date of discontinuance because of remarriage and January 1, 2000. The board has no duty to identify, locate, or notify a spouse who previously had his or her allowance discontinued because of remarriage. **Leg.H.** 1989 ch. 497 §4, effective September 19, 1989, as Gov C §21373, 1990 ch. 862 §2, 1995 chs. 379 (SB 541) §1, 850 (SB 860) §12, 1996 chs. 906 (SB 1859) §168, 1120 (AB 3478) §1, effective September 30, 1996 (amended & renumbered from §21373), 1999 ch. 800 (AB 232) §5, 2004 ch. 69 (SB 626), effective June 24, 2004.

§21552. Effect of remarriage by surviving spouse of firefighter or peace officer.

Notwithstanding any other provision of this part, on and after the effective date of this section, the remarriage of any surviving spouse of any deceased local safety member who was a firefighter, or peace officer as described in Chapter 4.5 (commencing with Section 830) of Title 3 of Part 2 of the Penal Code, who died in the line of duty, shall not result in the reduction or cessation of any monthly allowance the spouse was receiving pursuant to Section 21541 and Article 3 (commencing with Section 21570). **Leg.H.** 1996 ch. 1120 (AB 3478) §2, effective September 30, 1996.

§21553. Restoration of allowance to remarried surviving spouse of firefighter or peace officer.

(a) The monthly allowance pursuant to Section 21541 and Article 3 (commencing with Section 21570), paid to the surviving spouse of any deceased local safety member who was a firefighter, or peace officer as described in Chapter 4.5 (commencing with Section 830) of Title

3 of Part 2 of the Penal Code, who died in the line of duty, shall be restored if that allowance has been reduced or discontinued upon the spouse's remarriage. The allowance shall be resumed on the effective date of this section, or the first of the month, following receipt by the board of a written application from the spouse for resumption of the allowance, whichever is later.

(b) The amount of the benefits due shall be calculated as though the allowance had never been reduced or discontinued because of remarriage, and shall not be payable for the period between the date of reduction or discontinuance and the effective date of resumption.

(c) The board has no duty to identify, locate, or notify a spouse who previously had his or her allowance reduced or discontinued because of remarriage.

(d) Any surviving spouse shall be entitled to restoration of terminated or diminished benefits upon application to the system if he or she previously qualified for special death benefits because his or her spouse died in the line of duty. **Leg.H.** 1996 ch. 1120 (AB 3478) §3, effective September 30, 1996.

TITLE 3
GOVERNMENT OF COUNTIES

DIVISION 2
Officers

PART 2
BOARD OF SUPERVISORS

CHAPTER 3
FINANCIAL POWERS
[Selected Provisions]

§25263. County workers' compensation reserve account.

Notwithstanding any other law to the contrary, the board of supervisors of a county may, by resolution, establish and maintain a reserve account to insure against its liability or the liability of its employees for injuries, for liability under the workers' compensation laws, for casualty losses incurred by the county, and for providing health and welfare benefits for its employees. In such event, a county may elect to be wholly or partially self-insured, and if such reserves are established, the board of supervisors shall prescribe procedures whereby the reserves may be used to pay for settlement of claims; payment of property losses; payment of attorney and investigator fees; and payment of insurance and broker fees if the county elects to be partially insured. If such reserves are established, appropriations shall be made to such reserves, and payments may be made from such reserves for the above purposes without specific appropriation. All interest earned by the reserve shall be credited to the reserve.

The board of supervisors may authorize any district for which the board is the governing body to establish and maintain the reserves authorized by this section.

Ref.: W. Cal. Sum., 3 "Agency and Employment" §403.

Misc. Provisions

DIVISION 4
Employees

PART 1
GENERAL
[Selected Provisions]

§31000.8. Self-insured county; definitions.

Notwithstanding any other law to the contrary, the board of supervisors of a county which is wholly or partially self-insured under the workers' compensation laws, which is wholly or partially self-insured against public liability, or which is wholly or partially self-insured for employee health and welfare benefits, may contract with a qualified firm for the purpose of having such firm render investigative, administrative, and claims adjustment services relating to workers' compensation and public liability and employee health and welfare benefit claims against the county. The contract may provide that the contracting firm may reject, settle, compromise and approve workers' compensation, and public liability and employee health and welfare benefit claims against the county, its officers or employees, within such limits and for such amounts as the board of supervisors may specify, and may provide that the contracting firm may execute and issue checks in payment of such claims, which checks shall be payable only from a trust fund which may be established by the board of supervisors. Funds in the trust fund established by the board pursuant to the provisions of this section shall not exceed a sum sufficient to provide for the settlement of claims for a 30–day period as determined by the board of supervisors or the sum of twenty thousand dollars ($20,000), whichever is larger, at any one time. The rejection or settlement and approval of a claim by the contracting firm in accordance with the terms of the contract shall have the same effect as would the rejection or settlement and approval of such a claim by the board of supervisors and the county auditor. The contract may also provide that the contracting firm may employ legal counsel, subject to such terms and limitations as the board may prescribe, to advise such contracting firm concerning the legality and advisability of rejecting, settling, compromising and paying claims referred to said contracting firm by the county for investigation and adjustment, or to represent the county in litigation concerning such claims. The compensation and expenses of such attorney for services rendered to the county shall be county charges.

The contract provided for in this section may contain such other terms and conditions as the board of supervisors may consider necessary or desirable to effectuate the county's self-insured programs.

In lieu of, or in addition to, contracting for the services described in this section, the board of supervisors may authorize a county employee to perform any or all of the services and functions which the board may contract for under the provisions of this section.

As used in this section:

(a) "Firm" includes a person, corporation, or other legal entity.

(b) "Board of supervisors" includes governing boards of districts and other public agencies for which the board of supervisors acts as the governing board.

(c) "County" includes such districts and other public agencies for which the board of supervisors acts as the governing board.

PART 3
RETIREMENT SYSTEMS

CHAPTER 3
COUNTY EMPLOYEES RETIREMENT LAW OF 1937

ARTICLE 3
Retirement Board
[Selected Provisions]

§31520.4. Benefits for retirement board member injured or killed.

In any county with a board of retirement composed of nine members pursuant to Section 31520.1, if the second, third, seventh, or alternate member of the board is injured or killed while performing his or her duties as a member of the board, that member shall be deemed to have been acting in the course and scope of his or her duties as an employee of the county or district employing the member, for the limited purpose of determining eligibility for workers' compensation benefits or disability or death benefits from the retirement system.

This section shall not be operative in any county until the board of supervisors, by resolution adopted by a majority vote, makes this section operative in that county.

ARTICLE 14
Subrogation
[Selected Provisions]

§31820. Recovery of value of benefits from third party.

If benefits are payable under this chapter because of any injury to, or the death of, a member of the retirement association, and such injury or death is the proximate consequence of the act of any person other than his employer, the board on behalf of the retirement association may recover from such person an amount which is the lesser of the following:

(1) An amount which is equal to one-half of the actuarial equivalent of the benefits for which the association is liable because of such injury or death; or

(2) An amount which is equal to one-half of the remaining balance of the amount recovered after allowance of that amount which the employer or its insurance carrier have paid or become obligated to pay. The right shall be determined under the subrogation provisions of any workmen's compensation law.

CHAPTER 5
COUNTY FIRE SERVICE RETIREMENT LAW

ARTICLE 5
Contributions
[Selected Provisions]

§32338. Contributions by member absent from employment due to incapacity.

If any member is compelled to be absent from his employment because temporarily incapacitated for the performance of duty as the result of injury or disease occurring in and arising out of his employment, because of which he becomes entitled to workmen's compensation, within 90 days after his return to active employment, or within 90 days after the effective date of this section, whichever first occurs, or within such further time as may be granted by the board, he may pay into the fund an amount equal to that which would have been deducted had he remained in active employment. Upon the making of such payment, such time, whether before or after the effective date of this section, shall be considered as time served as a county forester, firewarden, or fireman.

TITLE 5
LOCAL AGENCIES

DIVISION 1
Cities and Counties

PART 1
POWERS AND DUTIES COMMON TO CITIES AND COUNTIES

CHAPTER 4
POLICE OFFICERS' PENSION FUND AND FIREMEN'S PENSION FUND

ARTICLE 5
Extraterritorial Activities of County and City Peace Officers
[Selected Provisions]

§50920. "Peace officer."

As used in this article, the term "peace officer" means a sheriff, undersheriff, deputy sheriff, marshal, or deputy marshal of a county or city and county, or a marshal or police officer of a city or town, employed and compensated as such, whether the members are volunteer, partly paid, or fully paid, except those whose principal duties are clerical, such as stenographers, telephone operators, and other workers not engaged in law enforcement operations, or the protection or preservation of life or property, and not under suspension or otherwise lacking in good standing. **Leg.H.** 1998 ch. 931, effective September 28, 1998, 2002 ch. 784 (SB 1316).

1989 Note: This section is applicable only to injuries occurring on or after January 1, 1990. Stats. 1989 ch. 893 §6.

§50921. Peace officer performing duty, not under direction of employer.

Whenever any peace officer of a city, county, or city and county of this state is injured, dies or is disabled from performing his or her duties as a peace officer by reason of engaging in the apprehension or attempted apprehension of law violators or suspected law violators or protection or preservation of life or property, or the preservation of the peace anywhere in this state, including the local jurisdiction in which he or she is employed, but is not at the time acting under the immediate direction of his or her employer, he, she, or his or her dependents, as the case may be, shall be accorded by his or her employer all of the same benefits including the benefits of the Workers' Compensation Law, which he, she, or they would have received had that peace officer been acting under the immediate direction of his or her employer. Any injury, disability or death incurred under the circumstances described in this section shall be deemed to have arisen out of and been sustained in the course of employment for purposes of workers' compensation and all other benefits.

ARTICLE 6
Extraterritorial Activities of Firemen
[Selected Provisions]

§50926. Public firefighter performing duty, not under direction of employer.

Whenever any fireman of a city, county, city and county, district, or other public or municipal corporation or political subdivision is injured, dies or is disabled from performing his duties as a fireman by reason of his proceeding to or engaging in a fire suppression or rescue operation, or the protection or preservation of life or property, anywhere in this state, including the local jurisdiction in which he is employed, but is not at the time acting under the immediate direction of his employer, he or his dependents, as the case may be, shall be accorded by his employer all of the same benefits of the Workers' Compensation Law, which he or they would have received had that fireman been acting under the immediate direction of his employer. Any injury, disability or death incurred under the circumstances described in this section shall be deemed to have arisen out of and been sustained in the course of employment for purposes of workers' compensation and all other benefits.

Ref.: W. Cal. Sum., 3 "Workers' Compensation" §177.

DIVISION 2
Cities, Counties, and Other Agencies

PART 1
POWERS AND DUTIES COMMON TO CITIES, COUNTIES, AND OTHER AGENCIES

CHAPTER 1
GENERAL

ARTICLE 2
Emergency Powers
[Selected Provisions]

§53023. Privileges and immunities of local agent apply extraterritorially.

Notwithstanding any other provisions of law or any local ordinance all the privileges and immunities from liability, exemptions from laws and rules, all pension, relief, disability, workmen's compensation, and other benefits, which apply to officers, agents, or employees of the local agency when performing functions within the local agency's limits apply to them to the same extent while performing functions extraterritorially pursuant to this article.

CHAPTER 6
REVENUE BOND LAW OF 1941

ARTICLE 5
Additional Powers to Secure Bonds
[Selected Provisions]

§54462. Provision for amount and kind of insurance.

The legislative body may provide for the amount and kind of insurance on the enterprise including insurance against:

(a) Accident to or destruction of any enterprise from any or all risks.

(b) Loss of revenues from an enterprise.

(c) Public liability or property damage and workmen's compensation.

TITLE 8
THE ORGANIZATION AND GOVERNMENT OF COURTS

CHAPTER 2
THE JUDICIAL COUNCIL

ARTICLE 4
Court Interpreter Services
[Selected Provisions]

§68562. Certification of court interpreters—Procedures, standards, and guidelines.

(a) The Judicial Council shall designate the languages for which certification programs shall be established under subdivision (b). The language designations shall be based on (1) the courts' needs as determined by the language and interpreter use and need studies under Section 68563, (2) the language needs of non-English-speaking persons in the courts, and (3) other information the Judicial Council deems relevant.

(b) By July 1, 1996, the Judicial Council shall approve one or more entities to certify Spanish language interpreters and interpreters for as many other languages designated under subdivision (a) as practicable by that date. The Judicial Council may give provisional approval to an entity to examine interpreters and establish a list of recommended court interpreters pending final approval of one or more certification entities. Certification entities may include educational institutions, testing organizations, joint powers agencies, or public agencies.

The Judicial Council shall adopt and publish guidelines, standards, and procedures to determine which certification entities will be approved to test and certify interpreters.

(c) The Judicial Council shall develop and implement procedures to administer the list of recommended court interpreters previously established by the State Personnel Board and the list established by an entity provisionally approved under subdivision (b).

The Judicial Council shall develop procedures and standards for certifying without reexamination interpreters on the list of recommended court interpreters (1) previously established by the State Personnel Board, or (2) established by an entity provisionally approved under subdivision (b). Certification of these interpreters shall be based on criteria determined by the Judicial Council, such as recent interpreting experience, performance in court or at administrative hearings, training, and continuing education.

(d) The Judicial Council shall adopt standards and requirements for interpreter proficiency, continuing education, certification renewal, and discipline. The Judicial Council shall adopt standards of professional conduct for court interpreters.

(e) The Judicial Council shall adopt programs for interpreter recruiting, training, and continuing education and evaluation to ensure that an adequate number of interpreters is available and that they interpret competently.

(f) The Judicial Council shall establish guidelines for fees or shall set and charge fees for applications to take the court interpreter examinations, for renewal of certifications, for certification of interpreters on the list of recommended court interpreters, for maintaining interpreters on the recommended list until January 1, 1996, and for other functions and services provided under this article. All fees and other revenues received by the Judicial Council under this article shall be transferred promptly to the Controller, and shall be placed in the Court Interpreters' Fund, which is hereby created, the moneys in which shall be available to carry out the purposes of this article upon appropriation by the Legislature.

(g) Each superior court may adopt local rules to impose additional requirements, standards, examinations, and programs as necessary for equity or to recognize local conditions. **Leg.H.** 1992 ch. 770, 1995 ch. 143, effective July 18, 1995, 2002 ch. 784 (SB 1316).

Ref.: 8 C.C.R. §9795.4; MB Prac. Guide: Cal. Trial & Post-Trial Civ. Proc., §§8.10, 8.15[3], 8.19[3][a]; W. Cal. Ev., "Presentation at Trial" §26.

SELECTED PROVISIONS Of The HARBORS AND NAVIGATION CODE

DIVISION 8 HARBOR AND PORT DISTRICTS

PART 4 PORT DISTRICTS

CHAPTER 2 BOARD OF PORT COMMISSIONERS

ARTICLE 2 Jurisdiction and Powers of the Board [Selected Provisions]

§6276. Stevedore employee workers' compensation benefits.

(a) In lieu of the benefits afforded pursuant to Division 4 (commencing with Section 3200) and Division 4.7 (commencing with Section 6200) of the Labor Code, the district may agree to provide workers' compensation benefits to its stevedore employees in amounts, and under such conditions, as would be payable to stevedore employees of private employers pursuant to the Longshoremen's and Harbor Workers' Compensation Act (33 U.S.C. 901, et seq.).

(b) Such an agreement shall be binding upon the parties only if it is in writing and signed by the employee and by a representative of the district. It shall acknowledge, in writing, that the benefits agreed upon are authorized by this section and are expressly in lieu of any benefits available under Division 4 (commencing with Section 3200) and Division 4.7 (commencing with Section 6200) of the Labor Code.

(c) All claims for benefits against the district which are authorized by this section shall be determined pursuant to law and the rules and regulations of the Workers' Compensation Appeals Board. To the fullest extent possible, the Workers' Compensation Appeals Board shall attempt to apply the Longshoremen's and Harbor Workers' Compensation Act to employees covered by this section in the same manner as applicable to private employees.

(d) Notwithstanding the provisions of Sections 11779 and 11870 of the Insurance Code or any other provision of law, the State Compensation Insurance Fund or any private insurer may provide insurance coverage for the benefits authorized by this section.

PART 6
RIVER PORT DISTRICTS

CHAPTER 2
PORT COMMISSION

ARTICLE 2
Jurisdiction and Powers of the Board
[Selected Provisions]

§6869. Federal benefits in lieu of state benefits.

(a) In lieu of the benefits afforded pursuant to Division 4 (commencing with Section 3200) and Division 4.7 (commencing with Section 6200) of the Labor Code, the district may agree to provide workers' compensation benefits to its stevedore employees in amounts, and under such conditions, as would be payable to stevedore employees of private employers pursuant to the Longshoremen's and Harbor Workers' Compensation Act (33 U.S.C. 901, et seq.).

(b) Such an agreement shall be binding upon the parties only if it is in writing and signed by the employee and by a representative of the district. It shall acknowledge, in writing, that the benefits agreed upon are authorized by this section and are expressly in lieu of any benefits available under Division 4 (commencing with Section 3200) and Division 4.7 (commencing with Section 6200) of the Labor Code.

(c) All claims for benefits against the district which are authorized by this section shall be determined pursuant to law and the rules and regulations of the Workers' Compensation Appeals Board. To the fullest extent possible, the Workers' Compensation Appeals Board shall attempt to apply the Longshoremen's and Harbor Workers' Compensation Act to employees covered by this section in the same manner as applicable to private employees.

(d) Notwithstanding the provisions of Section 11779 of the Insurance Code or any other provision of law, the State Compensation Insurance Fund may provide insurance coverage for the benefits authorized by this section.

SELECTED PROVISIONS Of The HEALTH AND SAFETY CODE

DIVISION 13 HOUSING

PART 1.5 Regulation of Buildings Used for Human Habitation

CHAPTER 2 RULES AND REGULATIONS [Selected Provisions]

§17922.5. Building permits from state or local agencies.

Any state or local agency which issues building permits shall require, as a condition of issuing any building permit where the working conditions of the construction would require an employer to obtain a permit from the Division of Occupational Safety and Health pursuant to Chapter 6 (commencing with Section 6500) of Part 1 of Division 5 of the Labor Code, that proof be submitted showing that the employer has received such a permit from the Division of Occupational Safety and Health.

An employer may apply for a building permit prior to receiving the permit from the Division of Occupational Safety and Health.

SELECTED PROVISIONS Of The MILITARY AND VETERANS CODE

DIVISION 2
THE MILITARY FORCES OF THE STATE

PART 1
The State Militia

CHAPTER 5
COMPENSATION, ALLOWANCE, AND INSURANCE

ARTICLE 3
Casualty Insurance

§340. Members of National Guard, organized or unorganized militia injured in line of duty.

(a) Subject to Section 340.1, whenever any officer, warrant officer, or enlisted member of the California National Guard, the organized militia, or the unorganized militia, when called into the active service of the state, pursuant to Section 142, 143, or 146, is wounded, injured, disabled, or killed in the active service of the state in the line of duty, the member or the member's dependents shall receive compensation under Division 4 (commencing with Section 3201) of the Labor Code. For these purposes, the member is deemed to be an employee of the state. The compensation shall be based on the member's average income from all sources during the year immediately preceding the date of wounding, injury, death, or the commencement of disability and shall not exceed the maximum prescribed in Division 4 (commencing with Section 3200) of the Labor Code.

(b) For the purposes of this article, any officer, warrant officer, or enlisted member performing military duty of any nature pursuant to Title 32 or Title 10 of the United States Code shall not be entitled to benefits described in subdivision (a) or in Section 340.1.

(c) Notwithstanding subdivision (a), any officer, warrant officer, or enlisted member on full-time active duty with the Office of the Adjutant General who suffers disability or death in the line of duty from either injury or disease is entitled to receive, from the state, benefits or compensation for that disability or death comparable to that provided to members of the United States armed forces on active duty. **Leg.H.** 1993 ch. 287, 2006 ch. 538 (SB 1852) §496.

§340.1. Disability for those wounded in service of state.

(a) Any officer, warrant officer, or enlisted member of the California National Guard, the organized militia, or the unorganized militia, when called into the active service of the state, pursuant to Sections 142, 143, or 146, except an officer, warrant officer, or enlisted member on

Misc. Provisions

full-time duty with the Office of the Adjutant General, who is wounded, injured, or disabled in the active service of the state in the line of duty shall be retained on active duty and shall receive regular military pay and allowances for not to exceed 52 weeks from the date of wounding, injury, or disability, regardless of the date of expiration of the period of state active duty, unless any of the following occurs:

(1) The member becomes entitled to disability compensation through any private or other public employer.

(2) The member is able to return to his or her regular civilian employment, as determined by proper authority.

(3) The member requests an earlier release from active duty.

(b) A member who has received benefits under subdivision (a) and who is unable to return to his or her regular civilian employment following 52 weeks after the date of wounding, injury, or disability is entitled to compensation under Division 4 (commencing with Section 3201) of the Labor Code, pursuant to Section 340. **Leg.H.** 1993 ch. 287.

§340.2. Disability for those transferred under mutual aid or interagency agreements.

Any officer, warrant officer, or enlisted member of the California National Guard, the organized militia, or the unorganized militia, when called into the active service of the state, pursuant to Sections 142, 143, or 146, who, while in that active service, is transferred by the California National Guard or other military authority to any other state or local agency for purposes of fulfilling active service requirements pursuant to either a mutual aid agreement or an interagency agreement and is wounded, injured, or disabled in the line of duty, is entitled to the benefits provided under Section 340.1. **Leg.H.** 1993 ch. 287.

§341. Member of militia; determination of average yearly earnings; "injury suffered in line of duty."

In the determination of the benefits to be awarded any member of the militia or his dependents under the provisions of Section 340, it shall be conclusively presumed that the average yearly earning of such injured or deceased member is not less than two thousand five hundred dollars ($2,500). Any injury, death, or disability shall be deemed to have been suffered in line of duty unless the same resulted from misconduct or disobedience of lawful orders by the injured or deceased member.

§342. Jurisdiction of Appeals Board.

The appeals board is empowered to hear and determine all issues concerning any obligation of the State of California to provide to any officer, warrant officer, or enlisted man or woman on active duty with the Office of the Adjutant General any rights or benefits provided in Section 3, Public Law 108, Chapter 225, 81st Congress, First Session, and any and all issues arising under or in connection with that law. In doing so, the appeals board shall follow the same procedures in all respects as are provided in Division 4 (commencing with Section 3200) of the Labor Code for the determination of workers' compensation claims. The orders, decisions, and awards of the appeals board issued in exercising this jurisdiction are subject to review and rehearing in the manner provided in Sections 5900 to 5956, inclusive, of the Labor Code. **Leg.H.** 1994 ch. 114.

Note: Section 3 of this law (63 Stats. 201, approved June 20, 1949) reads as follows:

All officers, warrant officers, and enlisted men of the National Guard of the United States, both ground and air, the federal recognized National Guard of the several States, Territories, and the District of Columbia—

(1) if engaged for periods in excess of thirty days in any type of training or active duty under sections 5, 81, 92, 94, 97 or 99 of the National Defense Act, as amended, suffer disability or death in line of duty from disease while so engaged; or

(2) if engaged for any period of time in any type of training or inactive duty under such sections of the National Defense Act as amended, suffer disability or death in line of duty from injury while so employed.

shall be in all respects entitled to receive the same pensions, compensation, death gratuity, retirement pay, hospital benefits, and pay and allowances as are now or may hereafter be provided by law or regulation for officers and enlisted men of corresponding grades and length of service of the Regular Army.

ARTICLE 4
State Militia Disability Equality Act

§345. Citation of article.

This article shall be known and may be cited as the State Militia Disability Equality Act. **Leg.H.** 2005 ch. 319 (AB 980) §2.

2005 Note: It is the intent of the Legislature to ensure that all California National Guard reservists and military personnel, when called into federal active status, receive the same military combat disability compensation that is provided to regular active military service personnel that are injured in combat. Stats. 2005 ch. 319 (AB 980) §1.

§346. Disability benefits.

(a) When any officer, warrant officer, or enlisted member of the California National Guard or the organized militia who is not in active service in this state is wounded, injured, or disabled in the line of duty when performing military duty of any nature under Title 10 or Title 32 of the United States Code, the Military Department shall determine both of the following amounts:

(1) The amount of disability benefits to which a member of the United States Armed Forces of the same or equivalent rank would be entitled from the federal government as a result of a comparable wound, injury, or disability.

(2) The amount of disability benefits to which the officer, warrant officer, or enlisted member is entitled from the federal government as a result of the wound, injury, or disability.

(b) If the Military Department determines that the amount described in paragraph (1) of subdivision (a) is greater than the amount described in paragraph (2) of subdivision (a), that department shall, upon an appropriation of funds to the department by the Legislature for this purpose, provide to the officer, warrant officer, or enlisted member an amount equal to the difference between those two amounts. **Leg.H.** 2005 ch. 319 (AB 980) §2.

2005 Note: It is the intent of the Legislature to ensure that all California National Guard reservists and military personnel, when called into federal active status, receive the same military combat disability compensation that is provided to regular active military service personnel that are injured in combat. Stats. 2005 ch. 319 (AB 980) §1.

Misc. Provisions

PART 2
California Cadet Corps and Voluntary Organizations

CHAPTER 1
CALIFORNIA CADET CORPS
[Selected Provisions]

§520. Supervisors of cadet instruction; right to compensation; determination of average yearly earnings; "injury suffered in line of duty."

In all cases in which any executive officer, assistant executive officer, regional or other supervisor of cadet instruction, and officers appointed or detailed, pursuant to Sections 502, 502.1, 512, 513, 515, or 516.1, when in the performance of duty ordered by the Adjutant General, is wounded, injured, disabled or killed in the performance of ordered duty and in line of duty, such executive officer, assistant executive officer, regional, or other supervisor of cadet instruction, or officers appointed or detailed, pursuant to Sections 505, 502.1, 512, 513, 515, or 516.1, shall be entitled to receive compensation from the State in accordance with the provisions of Division 4 of the Labor Code. In all such cases, such officers and those so appointed or detailed shall be held and deemed to be employees of the State. The compensation to be awarded to any such officer and those so appointed or detailed shall be ascertained, determined and fixed upon the basis of his average income from all sources during the year immediately preceding the date of such injury or death, or the commencement of such disability, but such compensation shall in no case exceed the maximum prescribed in Division 4 of the Labor Code.

In the determination of benefits to be awarded any such officer and those so appointed or detailed, under the provisions of this section, it shall be conclusively presumed that the average yearly earning of such injured or deceased officer is not less than two thousand five hundred dollars ($2,500). Any injury, death or disability shall be deemed to have been suffered in line of duty unless the same resulted from misconduct or disobedience of lawful orders by the injured or deceased officer.

CHAPTER 3
STATE MILITARY RESERVE ACT
[Selected Provisions]

§562. Members of State Military Reserve; right to compensation; determination of average yearly earnings; "injury suffered in line of duty."

In all cases in which any officer, warrant officer or enlisted man or woman of the State Military Reserve, when organized or authorized as a cadre or otherwise, when in the performance of ordered duty, or when ordered into the active service of the state, is wounded, injured, disabled, or killed in active service, or in the performance of ordered duty and in line of duty, the officer or warrant officer or enlisted man or woman or the dependents of that officer or warrant officer or enlisted man or woman shall be entitled to receive compensation from the state in accordance with the provisions of Division 4 (commencing with Section 3201) of the Labor Code. In all such cases, such an officer, warrant officer, enlisted man or woman shall be held and deemed to be an employee of the state. The compensation to be awarded to any such officer, warrant officer, enlisted man or woman shall be ascertained, determined, and fixed upon the basis of his or her average income from all sources during the year immediately preceding the date of the injury or death or the commencement of the disability, but the compensation shall in no case exceed the maximum prescribed in Division 4 (commencing with Section 3201) of the Labor Code.

In the determination of the benefits to be awarded any member of the State Military Reserve or his or her dependents under the provisions of this section it shall be conclusively presumed that the average yearly earning of the injured or deceased member is not less than two thousand five hundred dollars ($2,500). Any injury, death, or disability shall be deemed to have been suffered in line of duty unless the same resulted from misconduct or disobedience of lawful orders by the injured or deceased member.

SELECTED PROVISIONS Of The PENAL CODE

PART 1
Of Crimes and Punishments

TITLE 10
OF CRIMES AGAINST THE PUBLIC HEALTH AND SAFETY
[Selected Provisions]

§385. "High voltage"; "overhead conductor"; penalty for activity within specified distance of high voltage overhead conductor and for failure to post warning sign; exceptions.

(a) The term "high voltage" as used in this section means, a voltage in excess of 750 volts, measured between conductors or measured between the conductor and the ground.

The term "overhead conductor" as used in this section means any electrical conductor (either bare or insulated) installed above the ground except such conductors as are enclosed in iron pipe or other metal covering of equal strength.

(b) Any person who either personally or through an employee or agent, or as an employee or agent of another operates, places, erects or moves any tools, machinery, equipment, material, building or structure within six feet of a high voltage overhead conductor is guilty of a misdemeanor.

(c) It shall be a misdemeanor to own, operate or to employ any person to operate, any crane, derrick, power shovel, drilling rig, hay loader, hay stacker, piledriver, or similar apparatus, any part of which is capable of vertical, lateral, or swinging motion, unless there is posted and maintained in plain view of the operator thereof, a durable warning sign legible at 12 feet, reading: "Unlawful to operate this equipment within six feet of high voltage lines."

Each day's failure to post or maintain such sign shall constitute a separate violation.

(d) The provisions of this section shall not apply to (1) the construction, reconstruction, operation or maintenance of any high voltage overhead conductor, or its supporting structures or appurtenances by persons authorized by the owner, or (2) the operation of standard rail equipment which is normally used in the transportation of freight or passengers, or the operation of relief trains or other emergency railroad equipment by persons authorized by the owner, or (3) any construction, reconstruction, operation or maintenance of any overhead structures covered by the rules for overhead line construction prescribed by the Public Utilities Commission of the State of California.

TITLE 13
OF CRIMES AGAINST PROPERTY

CHAPTER 10
CRIMES AGAINST INSURED PROPERTY AND INSURERS
[Selected Provisions]

§549. Solicitation or referral for purposes of insurance fraud.

Any firm, corporation, partnership, or association, or any person acting in his or her individual capacity, or in his or her capacity as a public or private employee, who solicits, accepts, or refers any business to or from any individual or entity with the knowledge that, or with reckless disregard for whether, the individual or entity for or from whom the solicitation or referral is made, or the individual or entity who is solicited or referred, intends to violate Section 550 of this code or Section 1871.4 of the Insurance Code is guilty of a crime, punishable upon a first conviction by imprisonment in the county jail for not more than one year or by imprisonment in the state prison for 16 months, two years, or three years, or by a fine not exceeding fifty thousand dollars ($50,000) or double the amount of the fraud, whichever is greater, or by both that imprisonment and fine. A second or subsequent conviction is punishable by imprisonment in the state prison or by imprisonment in the state prison and a fine of fifty thousand dollars ($50,000). Restitution shall be ordered, including restitution for any medical evaluation or treatment services obtained or provided. The court shall determine the amount of restitution and the person or persons to whom the restitution shall be paid. **Leg.H.** 1991 chs. 116, 934, 1992 ch. 1352, effective September 30, 1992, 1993 ch. 589, 1994 chs. 841, 1031, 2000 ch. 843, 2004 ch. 2 (SB 2 Fourth Extra. Sess.), effective March 6, 2005.

Ref.: W. Cal. Sum., 2 "Workers' Compensation" §23.

§550. Making false or fraudulent claims—Punishment.

(a) It is unlawful to do any of the following, or to aid, abet, solicit, or conspire with any person to do any of the following:

(1) Knowingly present or cause to be presented any false or fraudulent claim for the payment of a loss or injury, including payment of a loss or injury under a contract of insurance.

(2) Knowingly present multiple claims for the same loss or injury, including presentation of multiple claims to more than one insurer, with an intent to defraud.

(3) Knowingly cause or participate in a vehicular collision, or any other vehicular accident, for the purpose of presenting any false or fraudulent claim.

(4) Knowingly present a false or fraudulent claim for the payments of a loss for theft, destruction, damage, or conversion of a motor vehicle, a motor vehicle part, or contents of a motor vehicle.

(5) Knowingly prepare, make, or subscribe any writing, with the intent to present or use it, or to allow it to be presented, in support of any false or fraudulent claim.

(6) Knowingly make or cause to be made any false or fraudulent claim for payment of a health care benefit.

(7) Knowingly submit a claim for a health care benefit that was not used by, or on behalf of, the claimant.

(8) Knowingly present multiple claims for payment of the same health care benefit with an intent to defraud.

(9) Knowingly present for payment any undercharges for health care benefits on behalf of a specific claimant unless any known overcharges for health care benefits for that claimant are presented for reconciliation at that same time.

(10) For purposes of paragraphs (6) to (9), inclusive, a claim or a claim for payment of a health care benefit also means a claim or claim for payment submitted by or on the behalf of a provider of any workers' compensation health benefits under the Labor Code.

(b) It is unlawful to do, or to knowingly assist or conspire with any person to do, any of the following:

(1) Present or cause to be presented any written or oral statement as part of, or in support of or opposition to, a claim for payment or other benefit pursuant to an insurance policy, knowing

that the statement contains any false or misleading information concerning any material fact.

(2) Prepare or make any written or oral statement that is intended to be presented to any insurer or any insurance claimant in connection with, or in support of or opposition to, any claim or payment or other benefit pursuant to an insurance policy, knowing that the statement contains any false or misleading information concerning any material fact.

(3) Conceal, or knowingly fail to disclose the occurrence of, an event that affects any person's initial or continued right or entitlement to any insurance benefit or payment, or the amount of any benefit or payment to which the person is entitled.

(4) Prepare or make any written or oral statement, intended to be presented to any insurer or producer for the purpose of obtaining a motor vehicle insurance policy, that the person to be the insured resides or is domiciled in this state when, in fact, that person resides or is domiciled in a state other than this state.

(c)(1) Every person who violates paragraph (1), (2), (3), (4), or (5) of subdivision (a) is guilty of a felony punishable by imprisonment in the state prison for two, three, or five years, and by a fine not exceeding fifty thousand dollars ($50,000), or double the amount of the fraud, whichever is greater.

(2) Every person who violates paragraph (6), (7), (8), or (9) of subdivision (a) is guilty of a public offense.

(A) When the claim or amount at issue exceeds four hundred dollars ($400), the offense is punishable by imprisonment in the state prison for two, three, or five years, or by a fine not exceeding fifty thousand dollars ($50,000) or double the amount of the fraud, whichever is greater, or by both that imprisonment and fine, or by imprisonment in a county jail not to exceed one year, by a fine of not more than ten thousand dollars ($10,000), or by both that imprisonment and fine.

(B) When the claim or amount at issue is four hundred dollars ($400) or less, the offense is punishable by imprisonment in a county jail not to exceed six months, or by a fine of not more than one thousand dollars ($1,000), or by both that imprisonment and fine, unless the aggregate amount of the claims or amount at issue exceeds four hundred dollars ($400) in any 12-consecutive-month period, in which case the claims or amounts may be charged as in subparagraph (A).

(3) Every person who violates paragraph (1), (2), (3), or (4) of subdivision (b) shall be punished by imprisonment in the state prison for two, three, or five years, or by a fine not exceeding fifty thousand dollars ($50,000) or double the amount of the fraud, whichever is greater, or by both that imprisonment and fine, or by imprisonment in a county jail not to exceed one year, or by a fine of not more than ten thousand dollars ($10,000), or by both that imprisonment and fine.

(4) Restitution shall be ordered for a person convicted of violating this section, including restitution for any medical evaluation or treatment services obtained or provided. The court shall determine the amount of restitution and the person or persons to whom the restitution shall be paid.

(d) Notwithstanding any other provision of law, probation shall not be granted to, nor shall the execution or imposition of a sentence be suspended for, any adult person convicted of felony violations of this section who previously has been convicted of felony violations of this section or Section 548, or of Section 1871.4 of the Insurance Code, or former Section 556 of the Insurance Code, or former Section 1871.1 of the Insurance Code as an adult under charges separately brought and tried two or more times. The existence of any fact that would make a person ineligible for probation under this subdivision shall be alleged in the information or indictment, and either admitted by the defendant in an open court, or found to be true by the jury trying the issue of guilt or by the court where guilt is established by plea of guilty or nolo contendere or by trial by the court sitting without a jury.

Except when the existence of the fact was not admitted or found to be true or the court finds that a prior felony conviction was invalid, the court shall not strike or dismiss any prior felony convictions alleged in the information or indictment.

This subdivision does not prohibit the adjournment of criminal proceedings pursuant to Division 3 (commencing with Section 3000) or Division 6 (commencing with Section 6000) of the Welfare and Institutions Code.

(e) Except as otherwise provided in subdivision (f), any person who violates subdivision (a) or (b) and who has a prior felony conviction of an offense set forth in either subdivision (a) or (b), in Section 548, in Section 1871.4 of the Insurance Code, in former Section 556 of the Insurance Code, or in former Section 1871.1 of the Insurance Code shall receive a two-year enhancement for each prior felony conviction in addition to the sentence provided in subdivision (c). The existence of any fact that would subject a person to a penalty enhancement shall be alleged in the information or indictment and either admitted by the defendant in open court, or found to be true by the jury trying the issue of guilt or by the court where guilt is established by plea of guilty or nolo contendere or by trial by the court sitting without a jury. Any person who violates this section shall be subject to appropriate orders of restitution pursuant to Section 13967 of the Government Code.

(f) Any person who violates paragraph (3) of subdivision (a) and who has two prior felony convictions for a violation of paragraph (3) of subdivision (a) shall receive a five-year enhancement in addition to the sentence provided in subdivision (c). The existence of any fact that would subject a person to a penalty enhancement shall be alleged in the information or indictment and either admitted by the defendant in open court, or found to be true by the jury trying the issue of guilt or by the court where guilt is established by plea of guilty or nolo contendere or by trial by the court sitting without a jury.

(g) Except as otherwise provided in Section 12022.7, any person who violates paragraph (3) of subdivision (a) shall receive a two-year enhancement for each person other than an accomplice who suffers serious bodily injury resulting from the vehicular collision or accident in a violation of paragraph (3) of subdivision (a).

(h) This section shall not be construed to preclude the applicability of any other provision of criminal law or equitable remedy that applies or may apply to any act committed or alleged to have been committed by a person.

(i) Any fine imposed pursuant to this section shall be doubled if the offense was committed in connection with any claim pursuant to any automobile insurance policy in an auto insurance fraud crisis area designated by the Insurance Commissioner pursuant to Article 4.6 (commencing with Section 1874.90) of Chapter 12 of Part 2 of Division 1 of the Insurance Code. **Leg.H.** 1992 ch. 675, 1993 ch. 120, effective July 16, 1993, ch. 605, 1994 chs. 841, 1008 §3.1, 1995 ch. 573 §2, effective October 4, 1995, ch. 574 §4, 1998 ch. 189, 1999 ch. 83, 2000 ch. 867, 2004 ch. 2 (SB 2 Fourth Extra. Sess.), effective March 6, 2005.

Ref.: Hanna § 2.03[2]; W. Cal. Sum., 2 "Workers' Compensation" §23, 5 "Torts" §14, 13 "Equity" §119.

PART 2
Of Criminal Procedure

TITLE 3
ADDITIONAL PROVISIONS REGARDING CRIMINAL PROCEDURE

CHAPTER 2
TIME OF COMMENCING CRIMINAL ACTIONS
[Selected Provisions]

§803. Limitation not tolled or extended—Does not commence until discovery of offense.

(a) Except as provided in this section, a limitation of time prescribed in this chapter is not tolled or extended for any reason.

(b) No time during which prosecution of the same person for the same conduct is pending in a court of this state is a part of a limitation of time prescribed in this chapter.

(c) A limitation of time prescribed in this chapter does not commence to run until the discovery of an offense described in this subdivision. This subdivision applies to an offense punishable by imprisonment in the state prison, a material element of which is fraud or breach of a fiduciary obligation, the commission of the crimes of theft or embezzlement upon an elder or dependent adult, or the basis of which is misconduct in office by a public officer, employee, or appointee, including, but not limited to, the following offenses:

(1) Grand theft of any type, forgery, falsification of public records, or acceptance of a bribe by a public official or a public employee.

(2) A violation of Section 72, 118, 118a, 132, 134, or 186.10.

(3) A violation of Section 25540, of any type, or Section 25541 of the Corporations Code.

(4) A violation of Section 1090 or 27443 of the Government Code.

(5) Felony welfare fraud or Medi-Cal fraud in violation of Section 11483 or 14107 of the Welfare and Institutions Code.

(6) Felony insurance fraud in violation of Section 548 or 550 of this code or former Section 1871.1, or Section 1871.4, of the Insurance Code.

(7) A violation of Section 580, 581, 582, 583, or 584 of the Business and Professions Code.

(8) A violation of Section 22430 of the Business and Professions Code.

(9) A violation of Section 10690 of the Health and Safety Code.

(10) A violation of Section 529a.

(11) A violation of subdivision (d) or (e) of Section 368.

(d) If the defendant is out of the state when or after the offense is committed, the prosecution may be commenced as provided in Section 804 within the limitations of time prescribed by this chapter, and no time up to a maximum of three years during which the defendant is not within the state shall be a part of those limitations.

(e) A limitation of time prescribed in this chapter does not commence to run until the offense has been discovered, or could have reasonably been discovered, with regard to offenses under Division 7 (commencing with Section 13000) of the Water Code, under Chapter 6.5 (commencing with Section 25100) of, Chapter 6.7 (commencing with Section 25280) of, or Chapter 6.8 (commencing with Section 25300) of, Division 20 of, or Part 4 (commencing with Section 41500) of Division 26 of, the Health and Safety Code, or under Section 386, or offenses under Chapter 5 (commencing with Section 2000) of Division 2 of, Chapter 9 (commencing with Section 4000) of Division 2 of, Section 6126 of, Chapter 10 (commencing with Section 7301) of Division 3 of, or Chapter 19.5 (commencing with Section 22440) of Division 8 of, the Business and Professions Code.

(f)(1) Notwithstanding any other limitation of time described in this chapter, a criminal complaint may be filed within one year of the date of a report to a California law enforcement agency by a person of any age alleging that he or she, while under the age of 18 years, was the victim of a crime described in Section 261, 286, 288, 288a, 288.5, or 289, or Section 289.5, as enacted by Chapter 293 of the Statutes of 1991 relating to penetration by an unknown object.

(2) This subdivision applies only if all of the following occur:

(A) The limitation period specified in Section 800, 801, or 801.1, whichever is later, has expired.

(B) The crime involved substantial sexual conduct, as described in subdivision (b) of Section 1203.066, excluding masturbation that is not mutual.

(C) There is independent evidence that corroborates the victim's allegation. If the victim was 21 years of age or older at the time of the report, the independent evidence shall clearly and convincingly corroborate the victim's allegation.

(3) No evidence may be used to corroborate the victim's allegation that otherwise would be inadmissible during trial. Independent evidence does not include the opinions of mental health professionals.

(4)(A) In a criminal investigation involving any of the crimes listed in paragraph (1) committed against a child, when the applicable limitations period has not expired, that period shall be tolled from the time a party initiates litigation challenging a grand jury subpoena until the end of the litigation, including any associated writ or appellate proceeding, or until the final disclosure of evidence to the investigating or prosecuting agency, if that disclosure is ordered pursuant to the subpoena after the litigation.

(B) Nothing in this subdivision affects the definition or applicability of any evidentiary privilege.

(C) This subdivision shall not apply where a court finds that the grand jury subpoena was issued or caused to be issued in bad faith.

(g)(1) Notwithstanding any other limitation of time described in this chapter, a criminal complaint may be filed within one year of the date on which the identity of the suspect is conclusively established by DNA testing, if both of the following conditions are met:

(A) The crime is one that is described in subdivision (c) of Section 290.

(B) The offense was committed prior to January 1, 2001, and biological evidence collected in connection with the offense is analyzed for DNA type no later than January 1, 2004, or the offense was committed on or after January 1, 2001, and biological evidence collected in connection with the offense is analyzed for DNA type no later than two years from the date of the offense.

(2) For purposes of this section, "DNA" means deoxyribonucleic acid.

(h) For any crime, the proof of which depends substantially upon evidence that was seized under a warrant, but which is unavailable to the prosecuting authority under the procedures described in People v. Superior Court (Laff) (2001) 25 Cal.4th 703, People v. Superior Court (Bauman & Rose) (1995) 37 Cal.App.4th 1757, or subdivision (c) of Section 1524, relating to claims of evidentiary privilege or attorney work product, the limitation of time prescribed in this chapter shall be tolled from the time of the seizure until final disclosure of the evidence to the prosecuting authority. Nothing in this section otherwise affects the definition or applicability of any evidentiary privilege or attorney work product. **Leg.H.** 2005 chs. 2 (SB 16) §3, effective February 28, 2005, 479 (SB 111) §3, 2007 ch. 579 (SB 172) §41, effective October 13, 2007.

2005 Note: This act shall be known, and may be cited, as the Child Sexual Abuse Prevention Act. Stats. 2005 ch. 479 (SB 111) §1.

Ref.: W. Cal. Sum., 7 "Constitutional Law" §144.

TITLE 12
OF SPECIAL PROCEEDINGS OF A CRIMINAL NATURE

CHAPTER 3
OF SEARCH WARRANTS
[Selected Provisions]

§1524. Grounds for issuance.

(a) A search warrant may be issued upon any of the following grounds:

(1) When the property was stolen or embezzled.

(2) When the property or things were used as the means of committing a felony.

(3) When the property or things are in the possession of any person with the intent to use them as a means of committing a public offense, or in the possession of another to whom he or she may have delivered them for the purpose of concealing them or preventing them from being discovered.

(4) When the property or things to be seized consist of any item or constitute any evidence that tends to show a felony has been committed, or tends to show that a particular person has committed a felony.

(5) When the property or things to be seized consist of evidence that tends to show that sexual exploitation of a child, in violation of Section 311.3, or possession of matter depicting sexual conduct of a person under the age of 18 years, in violation of Section 311.11, has occurred or is occurring.

(6) When there is a warrant to arrest a person.

(7) When a provider of electronic communication service or remote computing service has records or evidence, as specified in Section 1524.3, showing that property was stolen or embezzled constituting a misdemeanor, or that property or things are in the possession of any person with the intent to use them as a means of committing a misdemeanor public offense, or in the possession of another to whom he or she may have delivered them for the purpose of concealing them or preventing their discovery.

(8) When the property or things to be seized include an item or any evidence that tends to show a violation of Section 3700.5 of the Labor Code, or tends to show that a particular person has violated Section 3700.5 of the Labor Code.

(b) The property, things, person, or persons described in subdivision (a) may be taken on the warrant from any place, or from any person in whose possession the property or things may be.

(c) Notwithstanding subdivision (a) or (b), no search warrant shall issue for any documentary evidence in the possession or under the control of any person who is a lawyer as defined in Section 950 of the Evidence Code, a physician as defined in Section 990 of the Evidence Code, a psychotherapist as defined in Section 1010 of the Evidence Code, or a member of the clergy as defined in Section 1030 of the Evidence Code, and who is not reasonably suspected of engaging or having engaged in criminal activity related to the documentary evidence for which a warrant is requested unless the following procedure has been complied with:

(1) At the time of the issuance of the warrant, the court shall appoint a special master in accordance with subdivision (d) to accompany the person who will serve the warrant. Upon service of the warrant, the special master shall inform the party served of the specific items being sought and that the party shall have the opportunity to provide the items requested. If the party, in the judgment of the special master, fails to provide the items requested, the special master shall conduct a search for the items in the areas indicated in the search warrant.

(2)(A) If the party who has been served states that an item or items should not be disclosed, they shall be sealed by the special master and taken to court for a hearing.

(B) At the hearing, the party searched shall be entitled to raise any issues that may be raised pursuant to Section 1538.5 as well as a claim that the item or items are privileged, as provided by law. The hearing shall be held in the superior court. The court shall provide sufficient time for the parties to obtain counsel and make any motions or present any evidence. The hearing shall be held within three days of the service of the warrant unless the court makes a finding that the expedited hearing is impracticable. In that case the matter shall be heard at the earliest possible time.

(C) If an item or items are taken to court for a hearing, any limitations of time prescribed in Chapter 2 (commencing with Section 799) of Title 3 of Part 2 shall be tolled from the time of the seizure until the final conclusion of the hearing, including any associated writ or appellate proceedings.

(3) The warrant shall, whenever practicable, be served during normal business hours. In addition, the warrant shall be served upon a party who appears to have possession or control of the items sought. If, after reasonable efforts, the party serving the warrant is unable to locate the person, the special master shall seal and return to the court, for determination by the court, any item that appears to be privileged as provided by law.

(d)(1) As used in this section, a "special master" is an attorney who is a member in good standing of the California State Bar and who has been selected from a list of qualified attorneys that is maintained by the State Bar particularly for the purposes of conducting the searches described in this section. These attorneys shall serve without compensation. A special master shall be considered a public employee, and the governmental entity that caused the search warrant to be issued shall be considered the employer of the special master and the applicable public entity, for purposes of Division 3.6 (commencing with Section 810) of Title 1 of the Government Code, relating to claims and actions against public entities and public employees. In selecting the special master, the court shall make every reasonable effort to ensure that the person selected has no relationship with any of the parties involved in the pending matter. Any information obtained by the special master shall be confidential and may not be divulged except in direct response to inquiry by the court.

(2) In any case in which the magistrate determines that, after reasonable efforts have been made to obtain a special master, a special master is not available and would not be available within a reasonable period of time, the magistrate may direct the party seeking the order to conduct the search in the manner described in this section in lieu of the special master.

(e) Any search conducted pursuant to this section by a special master may be conducted in a manner that permits the party serving the warrant or his or her designee to accompany the special master as he or she conducts his or her search. However, that party or his or her designee may not participate in the search nor shall he or she examine any of the items being searched by the special master except upon agreement of the party upon whom the warrant has been served.

(f) As used in this section, "documentary evidence" includes, but is not limited to, writings, documents, blueprints, drawings, photographs, computer printouts, microfilms, X-rays, files, diagrams, ledgers, books, tapes, audio and video recordings, films, and papers of any type or description.

(g) No warrant shall issue for any item or items described in Section 1070 of the Evidence Code.

(h) Notwithstanding any other law, no claim of attorney work product as described in Chapter 4 (commencing with Section 2018.010) of Title 4 of Part 4 of the Code of Civil Procedure shall be sustained where there is probable cause to believe that the lawyer is engaging or has engaged in criminal activity related to the documentary evidence for which a warrant is requested unless it is established at the hearing with respect to the documentary evidence seized under the warrant that the services of the lawyer were not sought or obtained to enable or aid anyone to commit or plan to commit a crime or a fraud.

(i) Nothing in this section is intended to limit an attorney's ability to request an in camera hearing pursuant to the holding of the Supreme Court of California in People v. Superior Court (Laff) (2001) 25 Cal.4th 703.

(j) In addition to any other circumstance permitting a magistrate to issue a warrant for a person or property in another county, when the property or things to be seized consist of any item or constitute any evidence that tends to show a violation of Section 530.5, the magistrate may issue a warrant to search a person or property located in another county if the person whose identifying information was taken or used resides in the same county as the issuing court. **Leg.H.** 1872, 1899 p. 87, 1957 ch. 1884, 1978 ch. 1054, 1979 ch. 1034, 1980 ch. 441, 1982 ch. 438, 1996 chs. 1078, 1079 §11, 2002 chs. 864 (SB 1980), 1059 (AB 2055), effective September 29, 2002, §3 operative until January 1, 2003, §3.2, operative January 1, 2003, 2003 ch. 137 (AB 1773), 2004 ch. 182 (AB 3081), operative July 1, 2005, ch. 2 (SB 2 Fourth Extra. Sess.), effective March 6, 2005, 2005 chs. 279 (SB 1107) §12, 294 (AB 333) §24, 2006 ch. 538 (SB 1852) §507.

PART 3
Of Imprisonment and the Death Penalty

TITLE 4
COUNTY JAILS, FARMS AND CAMPS

CHAPTER 1
COUNTY JAILS
[Selected Provisions]

§4017. Prisoner labor for firefighting; benefits for injuries; "labor on the public works."

All persons confined in the county jail, industrial farm, road camp, or city jail under a final judgment of imprisonment rendered in a criminal action or proceeding and all persons confined in the county jail, industrial farm, road camp, or city jail as a condition of probation after suspension of imposition of a sentence or suspension of execution of sentence may be required by an order of the board of supervisors or city council to perform labor on the public works or ways in the county or city, respectively, and to engage in the prevention and suppression of forest, brush and grass fires upon lands within the county or city, respectively, or upon lands in adjacent counties where the suppression of fires would afford fire protection to lands within the county.

Whenever any such person so in custody shall suffer injuries or death while working in the prevention or suppression of forest, brush or grass fires he shall be considered to be an employee of the county or city, respectively, for the purposes of compensation under the provisions of the Labor Code regarding workers' compensation and such work shall be performed under the direct supervision of a local, state or federal employee whose duties include fire prevention and suppression work. A regularly employed member of an organized fire department shall not be required to directly supervise more than 20 such persons so in custody.

As used in this section, "labor on the public works" includes clerical and menial labor in the county jail, industrial farm, camps maintained for the labor of such persons upon the ways in the county, or city jail.

Ref.: W. Cal. Sum., 2 "Workers' Compensation" §177.

§4017.5. Work required of persons imprisoned for contempt.

In any case in which a person is confined to a city or county jail for a definite period of time for contempt pursuant to an action or proceeding other than a criminal action or proceeding, all of the provisions of law authorizing, requiring, or otherwise relating to, the performance of labor or work by persons sentenced to such facilities for like periods of time under a judgment of imprisonment, or a fine and imprisonment until the fine is paid or as a condition of probation after suspension of imposition of a sentence or suspension of execution of sentence, in a criminal action or proceeding, shall apply.

Nothing in this section shall be construed to authorize the confinement of any prisoner contrary to the provisions of Section 4001.

CHAPTER 2
COUNTY INDUSTRIAL FARMS AND ROAD CAMPS

ARTICLE 1
County Industrial Farms
[Selected Provisions]

§4125.1. Credit for fire suppression work.

The board of supervisors may contract with the United States or the State of California, or any department or agency thereof, for the performance of work and labor by any person in custody on any county industrial farm or industrial road camp or confined in the county jail or branch thereof under a final judgment of imprisonment rendered in a criminal action or proceeding or as a condition of probation in the suppression of fires within and upon the national forests, state parks, or other lands of the United

States or the State of California, or within and upon such other lands, of whatever ownership, contiguous to, or adjacent to said state or federal lands, the suppression of fires upon which other lands affords fire protection to said state or federal lands. Such payments as may be so contracted for and to be paid by the United States or by the State of California for the work and labor so performed by any person so in custody may, by order of the board of supervisors, be credited in full or in part, and upon such terms and conditions as the board shall determine, to any such person so in custody and performing such work and labor, and all in addition to those credits hereinbefore provided in Section 4125 of this code.

Whenever any such person so in custody shall perform the services herein specified he shall be subject to workmen's compensation benefits to the same extent as a county employee, and the board of supervisors shall provide and cover any such person so in custody, while performing such services, with accident, death and compensation insurance as is otherwise regularly provided for employees of the county.

The term "suppression of fires" as herein used shall include the construction of fire-breaks and other works of improvement for the prevention and suppression of fire whether or not constructed in the actual course of suppression of existing fires.

TITLE 7
ADMINISTRATION OF THE STATE CORRECTIONAL SYSTEM

CHAPTER 2
THE SECRETARY OF THE DEPARTMENT OF CORRECTIONS AND REHABILITATION
[Selected Provisions]

§5069. Rehabilitation for injured inmates; notice to inmate.

(a) The administrative director of the Division of Industrial Accidents shall formulate procedures for the selection and orderly referral of injured inmates of state penal or correctional institutions who may be benefited by rehabilitation services and retrained for other positions upon release from incarceration. The State Department of Rehabilitation shall cooperate in both designing and monitoring results of rehabilitation programs for the disabled inmates. The primary purpose of this section is to rehabilitate injured inmates in order that they might engage in suitable and gainful employment upon their release.

(b) The director shall notify the injured inmate of the availability of rehabilitation services in those cases where there is continuing disability of 28 days and beyond. A copy of such notification shall be forwarded to the State Department of Rehabilitation.

(c) The initiation of a rehabilitation plan shall be the responsibility of the director.

(d) Upon establishment of a rehabilitation plan, the injured inmate shall cooperate in carrying it out.

(e) The injured inmate shall receive such medical and vocational rehabilitative services as may be reasonably necessary to restore him to suitable employment.

(f) The injured inmates rehabilitation benefit is an additional benefit and shall not be converted to or replace any workers' compensation benefit available to him.

SELECTED PROVISIONS Of The VEHICLE CODE

DIVISION 13 TOWING AND LOADING EQUIPMENT

CHAPTER 5 TRANSPORTING OTHER LOADS

ARTICLE 2 Vehicles Transporting Workmen [Selected Provisions]

§31402. Operation of farm labor vehicle after notice that vehicle is in unsafe condition.

(a) No person may operate any farm labor vehicle except as may be necessary to return the unladen vehicle or combination of vehicles to the residence or place of business of the owner or driver, or to a garage, after notice by the department to the owner that the vehicle is in an unsafe condition or is not equipped as required by this code, or any regulations adopted thereunder, until the vehicle and its equipment have been made to conform with the requirements of this code, or any regulations adopted thereunder, and approved by the department.

(b)(1) A person who operates a farm labor vehicle in violation of this section while the vehicle is in a condition that presents an immediate safety hazard is guilty of a misdemeanor punishable by a fine of not less than one thousand dollars ($1,000) and not more than five thousand dollars ($5,000), or both that fine and a sentence of confinement for not more than six months in the county jail. No part of any fine imposed under this subdivision may be suspended.

(2) As used in this subdivision, an "immediate safety hazard" is any equipment violation described in subdivision (a) of Section 31401 or Section 31405, including any violation of a regulation adopted pursuant to that provision or those provisions.

(c) Any member of the Department of the California Highway Patrol may impound a farm labor vehicle operated in violation of this section pursuant to Section 34506.4. A farm labor vehicle shall not be impounded unless a member of that department determines that a person has failed to comply with subdivision (a) or a person fails to comply with a lawful out-of-service order, as described in subdivision (b) of Section 2800. **Leg.H.** 1974 ch. 1447, effective September 26, 1974, 1980 ch. 676, 2000 ch. 873.

§31403. Transportation of passengers in unsafe farm labor vehicles.

A farm labor vehicle known to an owner, farm labor contractor, or driver, to be unsafe, or not equipped as required by this code, or any regulations adopted thereunder, shall not be used for transporting any passengers until it is examined and repaired or equipped as required by this code, or any regulations adopted thereunder, and certified by a competent mechanic to be safe and lawfully equipped.

SELECTED PROVISIONS Of The WELFARE AND INSTITUTIONS CODE

DIVISION 2 CHILDREN

PART 1 Delinquents and Wards of the Juvenile Court

CHAPTER 2 JUVENILE COURT LAW

ARTICLE 1 General Provisions [Selected Provisions]

§219. Ward of juvenile court engaged in rehabilitative work; right to benefits.

The board of supervisors of a county may provide a ward of the juvenile court engaged in rehabilitative work without pay, under an assignment by order of the juvenile court to a work project in a county department, with workers' compensation benefits for injuries sustained while performing such rehabilitative work, in accordance with Section 3364.55 of the Labor Code.

Ref.: W. Cal. Sum., 10 "Parent and Child" §942.

ARTICLE 24 Wards and Dependent Children—Juvenile Homes, Ranches and Camps [Selected Provisions]

§883. Wards of juvenile homes, ranches, or camps; right to benefits.

The wards committed to ranches, camps, or forestry camps may be required to labor on the buildings and grounds thereof, on the making of forest roads for fire prevention or firefighting, on forestation or reforestation of public lands, or on the making of firetrails or firebreaks, or to perform any other work or engage in any studies or activities on or off of the grounds of those ranches, camps, or forestry camps prescribed by the probation department, subject to such approval as the county board of supervisors by ordinance requires.

Wards may not be required to labor in fire suppression when under the age of 16 years.

Wards between the ages of 16 years and 18 years may be required to labor in fire suppression if all of the following conditions are met:

(a) The parent or guardian of the ward has given permission for that labor by the ward.

(b) The ward has completed 80 hours of training in forest firefighting and fire safety, including, but not limited to, the handling of equipment and chemicals, survival techniques, and first aid.

Whenever any ward committed to a camp is engaged in fire prevention work or the suppression of existing fires, he or she shall be subject to worker's compensation benefits to the same extent as a county employee, and the board of supervisors shall provide and cover any ward committed to a camp while performing that service, with accident, death and compensation insurance as is otherwise regularly provided for employees of the county. **Leg.H.** 1998 ch. 694.

Ref.: W. Cal. Sum., 2 "Workers' Compensation" §§177, 305, 10 "Parent and Child" §747.

DIVISION 9
PUBLIC SOCIAL SERVICES

PART 3
Aid and Medical Assistance

CHAPTER 3
STATE SUPPLEMENTARY PROGRAM FOR AGED, BLIND AND DISABLED

ARTICLE 7
In-Home Supportive Services
[Selected Provisions]

§12302.2. Performance of statutory compensation and benefit obligations when direct payment made to provider or recipient; payment of administrative costs.

(a)(1) If the state or a county makes or provides for direct payment to a provider chosen by a recipient or to the recipient for the purchase of in-home supportive services, the department shall perform or assure the performance of all rights, duties and obligations of the recipient relating to those services as required for purposes of unemployment compensation, unemployment compensation disability benefits, workers' compensation, federal and state income tax, and federal old-age survivors and disability insurance benefits. Those rights, duties, and obligations include, but are not limited to, registration and obtaining employer account numbers, providing information, notices, and reports, making applications and returns, and withholding in trust from the payments made to or on behalf of a recipient amounts to be withheld from the wages of the provider by the recipient as an employer and transmitting those amounts along with amounts required for all contributions, premiums, and taxes payable by the recipient as the employer to the appropriate person or state or federal agency. The department may assure the performance of any or all of these rights, duties, and obligations by contract with any person, or any public or private agency.

(2) Contributions, premiums, and taxes shall be paid or transmitted on the recipient's behalf as the employer for any period commencing on or after January 1, 1978, except that contributions, premiums, and taxes for federal and state income taxes and federal old-age, survivors and disability insurance contributions shall be paid or transmitted pursuant to this section commencing with the first full month that begins 90 days after the effective date of this section.

(3) Contributions, premiums, and taxes paid or transmitted on the recipient's behalf for unemployment compensation, workers' compensation, and the employer's share of federal old-age survivors and disability insurance benefits shall be payable in addition to the maximum monthly amount established pursuant to Section 12303.5 or subdivision (a) of Section 12304 or other amount payable to or on behalf of a recipient. Contributions, premiums, or taxes resulting from liability incurred by the recipient as employer for unemployment compensation, workers' compensation, and federal old-age, survivors and disability insurance benefits with respect to any period commencing on or after January 1, 1978, and ending on or before the effective date of this section shall also be payable in addition to the maximum monthly amount established pursuant to Section 12303.5 or subdivision (a) of Section 12304 or other amount payable to or on behalf of the recipient. Nothing in this section shall be construed to permit any interference with the recipient's right to select the provider of services or to authorize a charge for administrative costs against any amount payable to or on behalf of a recipient.

(b) If the state makes or provides for direct payment to a provider chosen by a recipient, the Controller shall make any deductions from the wages of in-home supportive services personnel that are authorized by Sections 1152 and 1153 of the Government Code, as limited by Section 3515.6 of the Government Code.

(c) Funding for the costs of administering this section and for contributions, premiums, and taxes paid or transmitted on the recipient's behalf as an employer pursuant to this section shall qualify, where possible, for the maximum federal reimbursement. To the extent that federal funds are inadequate, notwithstanding Section 12306, the state shall provide funding for the purposes of this section. **Leg.H.** 1978 ch. 463, effective July 18, 1978, 2002 ch. 1135 (AB 2235).

§12302.21. Workers' compensation coverage for employees of nonprofit and proprietary agencies who contract with counties to provide in-home supportive services.

(a) For purposes of providing cost-efficient workers' compensation coverage for in-home supportive services providers under this article, the department shall assume responsibility for providing workers' compensation coverage for employees of nonprofit agencies and proprietary agencies who provide in-home supportive services pursuant to contracts with counties. The workers' compensation coverage provided for these employees shall be provided on the same terms as provided to providers under Section 12302.2 and 12302.5.

(b) A county that has existing contracts with nonprofit agencies or proprietary agencies whose employees will be provided workers' compensation coverage by the department pursuant to subdivision (a), shall reduce the contract hourly rate by fifty cents ($0.50) per hour, effective on the date that the department implements this section. **Leg.H.** 2003 ch. 209 (AB 632), effective August 11, 2003.

Ref.: Hanna § 3.36[3].

§12302.5. Establishment of agents for employers in order to comply with federal and state laws.

(a) Counties may establish entities or agents to act on behalf of the employers for those recipients who are designated as the employer of the in-home supportive services worker and who elect not to, or who are unable to, ensure compliance with all applicable federal, state, and county wage, hour, and workplace laws.

(b) Any entity or agent established pursuant to this section shall not restrict or interfere with the right of a recipient to select, replace, and terminate the employment of his or her own provider of in-home supportive services and to set his or her own service schedule. **Leg.H.** 1994 ch. 1006 (SB 1484).

CHAPTER 7
BASIC HEALTH CARE

ARTICLE 1
General Provisions
[Selected Provisions]

§14011. Verification of income required to obtain benefits.

(a) Each applicant who is not a recipient of aid under the provisions of Chapter 2 (commencing with Section 11200) or Chapter 3 (commencing with Section 12000) shall be required to file an affirmation setting forth such facts about his annual income and other resources and qualifications for eligibility as may be required by the department. Such statements shall be on forms prescribed by the department.

(b) To the extent permitted by federal law, eligibility for medical assistance for such applicants shall not be granted until the applicant or designated representative provides independent documentation verifying statements of gross income by type and source; income amounts withheld for taxes, health care benefits available through employment, retirement, military service, work related injuries or settlements from prior injuries, employee retirement contributions, and other employee benefit contributions, deductible expenses for maintenance or improvement of income-producing property and status and value of property owned, other than property exempt under Section 14006. The director may prescribe those items of exempt property which the director deems should be verified as to status and value in order to reasonably assure a correct designation of those items as exempt.

(c) The verification requirements of subdivision (b) apply to income, income deductions and property both of applicants for medical assistance (other than applicants for public assistance) and to persons whose income, income deductions, expenses or property holdings must be considered in determining the applicant's eligibility and share of cost.

(d) A determination of eligibility and share of cost may be extended beyond otherwise prescribed time frames if, in the county department's judgment, and subject to standards of the director, the applicant or designated representative has good cause for failure to provide the required verification and continues to make a good faith effort to provide such verification.

(e) To the extent permitted by federal law, in addition to the other verification requirements of this section, a county department may require verification of any other applicant statements, or conduct a full and complete investigation of the statements, whenever a verification or investigation is warranted in the judgment of the county department.

(f) If documentation is unavailable, as defined in regulations promulgated by the department, the applicant's signed statement as to the value or amount shall be deemed to constitute verification.

ARTICLE 3
Administration
[Selected Provisions]

§14101.7. Reimbursement from Appeals Board.

The Workers' Compensation Appeals Board and the department shall exchange information and cooperate to assure that health services provided by Medi-Cal which are reimbursable by Workers' Compensation are identified, and that Workers' Compensation reimburses the department for those services.

DIVISION 10
STATE DEPARTMENT OF REHABILITATION

PART 1
General Provisions

CHAPTER 1
POWERS AND DUTIES
[Selected Provisions]

§19005.5. Federal targeted jobs tax credit eligibility.

(a) The Department of Rehabilitation shall establish a program authorizing rehabilitation professionals serving industrially injured workers under the provisions of Labor Code Section 139.5 to refer clients to the Department of Rehabilitation for federal targeted jobs tax credit eligibility determination. The Department shall set forth the specific requirements, procedures, and eligibility criteria. The Department shall not be required to certify, for purposes of the federal targeted jobs tax credit, industrially injured workers who do not meet the eligibility requirements set forth in the federal Rehabilitation Act.

(b) The Department shall be authorized to collect a fee from the insurer or self-insured employer in the amount necessary to determine eligibility and to certify the industrially injured worker for this program.

CALIFORNIA CODE OF REGULATIONS

SYNOPSIS

TITLE 2
ADMINISTRATION

DIVISION 1
Administrative Personnel

CHAPTER 3
DEPARTMENT OF PERSONNEL ADMINISTRATION

SUBCHAPTER 1
GENERAL CIVIL SERVICE RULES

ARTICLE 2
Traveling Expenses

TITLE 8
INDUSTRIAL RELATIONS

DIVISION 1
Department of Industrial Relations

CHAPTER 1
INDUSTRIAL MEDICAL COUNCIL

ARTICLE 1
General

ARTICLE 2
QME Eligibility

ARTICLE 2.5
Time Periods for Processing Applications for QME Status

ARTICLE 3
Assignment of Qualified Medical Evaluators, Evaluation Procedure

ARTICLE 4
Evaluation Procedures

ARTICLE 4.5
Minimum Time Guidelines

ARTICLE 5
QME Reappointment

ARTICLE 6
QME Discipline

ARTICLE 7
Practice Parameters for the Treatment of Common Industrial Injuries

ARTICLE 10
QME Application Forms

ARTICLE 10.5
QME Process Forms

§113. The Time Extension Approval Form.
§114. The Denial of Time Extension Form.
§115. The Notice of Late Qualified Medical Evaluator Report Form.
§116. The Notice of Late Qualified Medical Evaluator Report Form—Extension Not Requested Form.
§117. Qualified Medical Evaluator Continuing Education Response Form.
§118. Application for Accreditation or Re-Accreditation As Education Provider.
§119. Faculty Disclosure of Commercial Interest.

ARTICLE 15
Fraudulent or Misleading Advertising

§150. Definitions.
§151. Filing of Documents.
§152. Statement of Intent.
§153. False or Misleading Advertising Copy Prohibited.
§154. Permissible Advertising Content.
§155. Filing of Complaints.
§156. Council Requests to Review Advertising Copy.
§157. Determinations.
§158. Penalties.
§159. Severability.

CHAPTER 4.5 DIVISION OF WORKERS' COMPENSATION

SUBCHAPTER 1 ADMINISTRATIVE DIRECTOR—ADMINISTRATIVE RULES

ARTICLE 1.1
Workers' Compensation Information System

§9700. Authority.
§9701. Definitions.
§9702. Electronic Data Reporting.
§9703. Access to Individually Identifiable Information.
§9704. WCIS Advisory Committee.

ARTICLE 1.5
Receipt of Salary by Workers' Compensation Administrative Law Judge

§9710. Authority.
§9711. Operative Date.
§9712. Definitions.
§9713. Receipt of Salary.
§9714. Procedures for Compliance With Labor Code Section 123.5(a).
§9714.5. Affidavit.
§9715. Procedures for Submitting a Cause for Decision.

ARTICLE 1.6
Ethical Standards of Workers' Compensation Administrative Law Judges; Enforcement of Standards

§9720.1. Authority.
§9720.2. Definitions.
§9721.1. Code of Judicial Ethics.
§9721.2. Gifts, Honoraria and Travel.
§9721.11. Requirement for Disclosure.
§9721.12. Disqualification.
§9721.13. What Are Not Grounds for Disqualification.
§9721.14. Manner of Disclosure.
§9721.21. Restriction on Investments.
§9721.31. Financial Interests in Educational Programs.
§9721.32. Duty to Report Ethics Violations.
§9721.33. Previously Earned Compensation.
§9722. The Workers' Compensation Ethics Advisory Committee.
§9722.1. Commencing an Investigation.
§9722.2. Investigation and Action by the Administrative Director or Court Administrator.
§9723. Miscellaneous Provisions.

ARTICLE 2
Disabilities, Description of

§9725. Method of Measurement.
§9726. Method of Measurement (Psychiatric).
§9727. Subjective Disability.

ARTICLE 3.5
Medical Provider Network

§9767.1. Medical Provider Networks—Definitions.
§9767.2. Review of Medical Provider Network Application.
§9767.3. Application for a Medical Provider Network Plan.
§9767.4. Cover Page for Medical Provider Network Application.
§9767.5. Access Standards.
§9767.6. Treatment and Change of Physicians Within MPN.
§9767.7. Second and Third Opinions.
§9767.8. Modification of Medical Provider Network Plan.
§9767.9. Transfer of Ongoing Care into the MPN.
§9767.10. Continuity of Care Policy.
§9767.11. Economic Profiling Policy.

ARTICLE 3.6
Independent Medical Review

ARTICLE 4
Certification Standards for Health Care Organizations

ARTICLE 5

Predesignation of Personal Physician; Request for Change of Physician; Reporting Duties of the Primary Treating Physician; Petition for Change of Primary Treating Physician

ARTICLE 5.1

Spinal Surgery Second Opinion Procedure

ARTICLE 5.3

Official Medical Fee Schedule

§9789.37. DWC Form 15 Election for High Cost Outlier.
§9789.38. Appendix X.
§9789.40. Pharmacy.
§9789.50. Pathology and Laboratory.
§9789.60. Durable Medical Equipment, Prosthetics, Orthotics, Supplies.
§9789.70. Ambulance Services.
§9789.80. Skilled Nursing Facility. [Reserved]
§9789.90. Home Health Care. [Reserved]
§9789.100. Outpatient Renal Dialysis. [Reserved]
§9789.110. Update of Rules to Reflect Changes in the Medicare Payment System.
§9789.111. Effective Date of Fee Schedule Provisions.

ARTICLE 5.5
Application of the Official Medical Fee Schedule (Treatment)

§9790. Authority.
§9790.1. Definitions.
§9791. Services Covered.
§9791.1. Medical Fee Schedule.
§9792. Determination of the Fee.
§9792.1. Payment of Inpatient Services of Health Facilities.
§9792.5. Payment for Medical Treatment.

ARTICLE 5.5.1
Utilization Review Standards

§9792.6. Utilization Review Standards—Definitions.
§9792.7. Utilization Review Standards—Applicability.
§9792.8. Utilization Review Standards—Medically-Based Criteria.
§9792.9. Utilization Review Standards—Timeframe, Procedures and Notice Content.
§9792.10. Utilization Review Standards—Dispute Resolution.
§9792.11. Investigation Procedures: Labor Code §4610 Utilization Review Violations.
§9792.12. Administrative Penalty Schedule for Labor Code §4610 Utilization Review Violations.
§9792.13. Assessment of Administrative Penalties — Penalty Adjustment Factors.
§9792.14. Liability for Penalty Assessments.
§9792.15. Administrative Penalties Pursuant to Labor Code §4610 — Order to Show Cause, Notice of Hearing, Determination and Order, and Review Procedure.

ARTICLE 5.5.2
Medical Treatment Utilization Schedule

§9792.20. Medical Treatment Utilization Schedule — Definitions.
§9792.21. Medical Treatment Utilization Schedule.
§9792.22. Presumption of Correctness, Burden of Proof and Strength of Evidence.
§9792.23. Medical Evidence Evaluation Advisory Committee.

ARTICLE 5.6
Medical-Legal Expenses and Comprehensive Medical-Legal Evaluations

§9793. Definitions.
§9794. Reimbursement of Medical-Legal Expenses.
§9795. Reasonable Level of Fees for Medical-Legal Expenses, Follow-up, Supplemental and Comprehensive Medical-Legal Evaluations, and Medical-Legal Testimony.

ARTICLE 5.7
Fees for Interpreter Services

§9795.1. Definitions.
§9795.2. Notice of Right to Interpreter.
§9795.3. Fees for Interpreter Services.
§9795.4. Time for Payment; Effective Date.

ARTICLE 6
Consulting Physician, Certification of

§9796. Certification of Consulting Physician, How Initiated.
§9799. Criterion for Certifying Competence.
§9802. Notification by Administrative Director.

ARTICLE 7
Schedule for Rating Permanent Disabilities

§9805. Schedule for Rating Permanent Disabilities, Adoption, Amendment.
§9805.1. Data Collection, Evaluation, and Revision of Schedule.

ARTICLE 8
Benefit Notices; Claims Administrator's Duties and Responsibilities; Claim Form and Notice of Potential Eligibility for Benefits; Regulatory Authority of the Administrative Director

§9810. General Provisions.
§9811. Definitions.
§9812. Benefit Payment and Notice.

ARTICLE 8.1
Workers' Compensation Advertising by Non-Attorneys and Non-Physicians; Prohibition of False or Misleading Advertising

ARTICLE 8.5
Employee Information

ARTICLE 10
Employee Death, Notice of

ARTICLE 10.5
Operation of the Information and Assistance Program of the Division of Workers' Compensation

ARTICLE 11
Document Copy and Electronic Transaction Fees

ARTICLE 12
Return to Work

SUBCHAPTER 1.5
INJURIES ON OR AFTER JANUARY 1, 1990

ARTICLE 1
Audit, General Definitions

ARTICLE 7.5
Supplemental Job Displacement Benefit

§10133.58. State Approved or Accredited Schools.
§10133.59. The Administrative Director's List of Vocational Return to Work Counselors.
§10133.60. Termination of Claims Administrator's Liability for the Supplemental Job Displacement Benefit.

ARTICLE 8
Attorney Fee Disclosure Statement

§10134. Attorney Fee Disclosure Statement Form.
§10135. Required Use of Form.
§10135.1. Service of Form.

ARTICLE 9
Claim Form: Availability, Filing, Acknowledgement of Receipt, Dismissal

§10136. General: Definitions.
§10137. General: Employer Obligation.
§10138. Claim Form and Notice of Potential Eligibility for Benefits.
§10139. Workers' Compensation Claim Form (DWC 1) and Notice of Potential Eligibility.
§10140. Employer's Responsibility to Process Claim Form, Claims Administrator's Duty to Provide Claim Form.
§10141. Dismissal of Inactive Claim by Operation of Law After Notice.
§10142. Date of Denial for Purposes of End of Tolling of Limitations Period.

SUBCHAPTER 1.6
PERMANENT DISABILITY RATING DETERMINATION

§10150. Disability Evaluation Unit.
§10152. Disability, When Considered Permanent.
§10156. Formal Rating Determinations.
§10158. Formal Rating Determinations As Evidence.
§10160. Summary Rating Determinations, Comprehensive Medical Evaluation of Unrepresented Employee.
§10160.1. Summary Rating Determinations, Report of Primary Treating Physician for Unrepresented Employee.
§10160.5. Summary Rating Determinations, Represented Employees.
§10161. Forms.
§10161.1. Reproduction of Forms.
§10162. Summary Rating Determination, Apportionment.
§10163. Apportionment Referral.
§10164. Summary Rating Determinations, Reconsideration If Employee Is Unrepresented.
§10165. Service of Summary Rating Determination and Notice of Options Following Permanent Disability Rating.
§10165.5. Notice of Options Following Disability Rating (DEU Form 110).
§10166. Consultative Rating Determinations.
§10167. Informal Ratings.
§10168. Records, Destruction of.
§10169. Commutation Tables and Instructions.
§10169.1. Commutation of Life Pension and Permanent Disability Benefits.

SUBCHAPTER 1.7

§10175. Definitions.
§10176. Eligible Employers and Employees.
§10177. Eligible Applicants.
§10178. Pilot Project Proposal Requirements.
§10179. Selection of Proposals; Priorities; Pilot Termination.
§10180. Employee Choice of Plans.
§10181. Records, Claims Administration, Auditing, and Termination.

SUBCHAPTER 1.8
ADMINISTRATIVE DIRECTOR – ADMINISTRATIVE RULES COLLECTIVE BARGAINING AGREEMENTS UNDER LABOR CODE SECTIONS 3201.5 AND 3201.7

§10200. Definitions.
§10201. Procedure for Determining Eligibility Under Labor Code Section 3201.5.
§10202. Procedure for Recognizing Labor-Management Agreements Under Labor Code Section 3201.7.
§10202.1. Petition for Permission to Negotiate a Section 3201.7 Labor-Management Agreement (DWC Form RGS-1).
§10203. Reporting Data.
§10203.1. Aggregate Employer Annual Report (DWC Form GV-1).
§10203.2. Individual Employer Annual Report (DWC Form GV-2).
§10204. Annual Reports.

SUBCHAPTER 1.9 RULES OF THE COURT ADMINISTRATOR

SUBCHAPTER 2 WORKERS' COMPENSATION APPEALS BOARD—RULES OF PRACTICE AND PROCEDURE

ARTICLE 1
General

ARTICLE 2
Powers, Duties and Responsibilities

ARTICLE 3
Parties and Joinder

ARTICLE 4
Filing of Documents

ARTICLE 5
Pleadings

ARTICLE 6
Service

ARTICLE 7
Subpoenas

ARTICLE 8
Hearings

ARTICLE 9
Evidence and Reports

ARTICLE 10
Medical Examiners

ARTICLE 11
Transcript of Testimony

ARTICLE 12
Record of Proceedings

ARTICLE 13
Liens

§10772. Unemployment Compensation Disability Liens.
§10773. Law Firm Employees.

ARTICLE 14
Attorneys and Representatives

§10774. Substitution or Dismissal of Attorneys.
§10775. Reasonable Attorney's Fee.
§10776. Approval of Attorney's Fee.
§10778. Request for Increase of Attorney's Fee.
§10779. Disbarred and Suspended Attorneys.

ARTICLE 15
Findings, Awards and Orders

§10780. Dismissal Orders.

ARTICLE 16
Executions and Certified Copies

§10820. When Certified Copies Will Issue.
§10825. Withholding Certified Copies.
§10828. Necessity for Bond.

ARTICLE 17
Reconsideration

§10840. Filing Petitions for Reconsideration and Answers.
§10842. Contents of Petition for Reconsideration and Answer.
§10843. Petitions to Remove.
§10846. Skeletal Petitions.
§10848. Supplemental Petitions.
§10850. Proof of Service.
§10852. Insufficiency of Evidence.
§10856. Allegations of Newly Discovered Evidence and Fraud.
§10858. Correction of Errors.
§10859. Orders After Filing of Petition for Reconsideration.
§10860. Report of Workers' Compensation Judge.
§10862. Hearing After Reconsideration Granted.
§10864. Authority of Workers' Compensation Judge After Decision After Reconsideration.
§10865. Reconsideration—Labor Code Sections 3201.5 and 3201.7.
§10866. Reconsideration of Arbitrator's Decisions or Awards.
§10867. Report of Arbitrator.

ARTICLE 18
Settlements

§10870. Approval of Compromise and Release.
§10874. Form.
§10875. Procedures—Labor Code Section 3761.
§10878. Settlement Document as an Application.
§10882. Action on Settlement Agreement.
§10886. Service on Lien Claimants.
§10888. Resolution of Liens.
§10890. Walk-Through Documents.

ARTICLE 19
Subsequent Injuries Fund

§10940. Application.
§10942. Service.
§10946. Medical Reports.

ARTICLE 20
Review of Administrative Orders

§10950. Appeal from Order Granting or Denying Petition for Order Requiring Employee to Select Employer-Designated Physician.
§10952. Appeal of Notice of Compensation Due.
§10953. Petition Appealing Audit Penalty Assessment—Labor Code Section 129.5(g).
§10955. Rehabilitation Appeals.
§10957. Deposition of Rehabilitation Consultants.
§10958. Hearing and Burden of Proof.

ARTICLE 22
Arbitration

§10995. Mandatory Arbitration.
§10996. Voluntary Arbitration.
§10997. Request for Arbitration.
§10998. Disqualification of Arbitrator.
§10999. Arbitrator Fee and Cost Disputes.

CHAPTER 7
DIVISION OF LABOR STATISTICS AND RESEARCH

SUBCHAPTER 1
OCCUPATIONAL INJURY OR ILLNESS REPORTS AND RECORDS

ARTICLE 1
Reporting of Occupational Injury or Illness

§14000. Definitions.
§14001. Employer.
§14002. Insurer.
§14003. Physician.
§14004. Employer's Report of Occupational Injury or Illness, Form 5020, Rev. 7.

ARTICLE 2
Employer Records of Occupational Injury or Illness

SUBCHAPTER 2
REPORTS OF INJURY TO BE FILED BY THE CALIFORNIA DEPARTMENT OF CORRECTIONS

ARTICLE 1
Prison Labor

ARTICLE 2
Reports to Be Filed by the Department of Corrections

CHAPTER 8
OFFICE OF THE DIRECTOR

SUBCHAPTER 2
ADMINISTRATION OF SELF-INSURANCE PLANS

ARTICLE 1
Definitions

ARTICLE 2
Certificate to Self Insure

ARTICLE 3
Security Deposit Requirements

ARTICLE 3.1
Alternative Composite Deposits

ARTICLE 4
Assessments

ARTICLE 5
Self Insurer's Annual Report

ARTICLE 6
Estimating Work Injury Claims and Medical Reports

ARTICLE 7
Injury and Illness Prevention Program

ARTICLE 8
Transfer of Liabilities

ARTICLE 9
Recordkeeping and Audits

§15403.1. Notice of Special Audit.
§15404. Expense of Out-of-State Audit.
§15404.1. Expense of Revoked Certificate Audit.
§15404.2. Expense of Special Audit.
§15405. Confidentiality.

ARTICLE 10
Revocation of a Certificate to Self Insure or Certificate to Administer and Continuing Jurisdiction

§15420. Compliance With Statutes and Regulatory Requirements.
§15422. Voluntary Revocation.
§15423. Revocation.
§15424. Revoked Certificate Report.
§15425. Revoked Certificate Audit.
§15426. Release of Security Deposit.
§15427. Continuing Jurisdiction.
§15428. Administration of Claims After Revocation.

ARTICLE 11
Hearing and Appeal Procedures

§15430. Hearing.
§15430.1. Definitions.
§15431. Delegation of Authority.
§15431.1. Appeals and/or Requests for Hearings.
§15431.2. Complaints.
§15432. Hearings; Special Requirements: Failure to Appear.
§15433. Hearing Officer: Appointment and Delegation of Authority.
§15434. Hearing Procedures.
§15435. Decision.
§15436. Reconsideration.
§15437. Appellate Review.
§15438. Severability.

ARTICLE 12
Claims Administration

§15450. Certificate to Administer.
§15450.1. Third Party Claims Administration for New Private Self Insurers.
§15452. Administrator Competence.
§15454. Certificate to Administer: Fees.
§15458. Claims Administration and Recordkeeping.
§15459. Notification of Willful Failure to Pay Benefits.
§15463. Revocation of Certificate.

ARTICLE 13
Group Self Insurance

§15470. General.
§15471. Initial Feasibility Study.
§15472. Minimum Net Worth of a Group Self Insurer.
§15473. Homogeneity of Group Members.
§15474. Reporting Periods.
§15475. Board of Trustees.
§15476. Advance Premium Discounts.
§15477. Surplus or Insufficient Funding.
§15478. Excess Insurance.
§15479. Indemnity Agreement and Power of Attorney.
§15480. Termination of Membership in a Group.
§15481. Actuarial Certification of Losses.

SUBCHAPTER 2.05
ENFORCEMENT OF WORKERS' COMPENSATION COVERAGE, PENALTY ASSESSMENT ORDERS, STOP ORDERS AND POSTING AND NOTICE REQUIREMENTS

ARTICLE 1
Delegation of Enforcement Authority

§15550. Delegation of Enforcement Authority.

ARTICLE 2
Definitions

§15551. Direction to File Verified Statement.
§15552. Director.
§15553. Division.
§15554. Findings.
§15555. Issue.
§15556. Notice of Findings on Penalty Assessment Order or Stop Order.
§15557. Penalty Assessment Order.
§15558. Special Judgment.
§15559. Stop Order.
§15560. Uninsured Employer.
§15561. Verified Statement.
§15562. Verified Petition.

ARTICLE 3
Investigation of Employer's Workers' Compensation Status

§15563. Access to Places of Labor.
§15564. Inquiry Into Workers' Compensation Status.
§15565. Posting Notice of Workers' Compensation Carrier.

ARTICLE 4
Penalties

§15566. Assessment of Penalty.
§15567. Penalty Assessment Orders.
§15568. Types of Penalty Assessment Orders.

ARTICLE 5
Stop Order

ARTICLE 6
Contents of Orders, of Direction to File Verified Statement and of Verified Statement

ARTICLE 7
Service of Stop Order and Penalty Assessment Order

ARTICLE 8
Review of Proceedings and Withdrawal Proceedings

ARTICLE 9
Appeal Procedures

ARTICLE 10
Hearing

ARTICLE 11
Writ of Review

ARTICLE 12
Special Judgment Procedure as to Penalty Assessment Orders

ARTICLE 14
Penalty Liens

ARTICLE 15
Notice of Right to Benefits

SUBCHAPTER 2.06
WORKERS' COMPENSATION—ADMINISTRATION REVOLVING FUND ASSESSMENT, UNINSURED EMPLOYERS BENEFITS TRUST FUND ASSESSMENT, SUBSEQUENT INJURIES BENEFITS TRUST FUND ASSESSMENTS, FRAUD SURCHARGE AND CAL–OSHA TARGETED INSPECTION ASSESSMENT

ARTICLE 1
Definitions

ARTICLE 2
Determination of Assessments and/or Surcharge

ARTICLE 3
Collection of Assessments and/or Surcharges

SUBCHAPTER 2.1
ILLEGALLY UNINSURED EMPLOYERS. DETERMINATIONS BY THE DIRECTOR: PRIMA FACIE ILLEGALLY UNINSURED, CORPORATE PARENT AND SUBSTANTIAL SHAREHOLDER; NOTICE; HEARINGS; APPEALS

ARTICLE 1
General

ARTICLE 2
Determinations by Director

ARTICLE 3
Hearings Under Code Section 3720.1

SUBCHAPTER 2.1.1
UNINSURED EMPLOYERS FUND AND SUBSEQUENT INJURIES FUND BENEFITS TO ALIENS

ARTICLE 1
Limitations on Benefits

TITLE 10
INVESTMENTS

CHAPTER 5
INSURANCE COMMISSIONER

SUBCHAPTER 3
INSURERS

ARTICLE 20
Standards Applicable to Workers' Compensation Claims Adjusters and Medical Billing Entities and Certification of Those Standards by Insurers

§2592.14. Post-Designation Training Form.

SELECTED PROVISIONS Of The CALIFORNIA CODE OF REGULATIONS

TITLE 2 ADMINISTRATION

DIVISION 1 Administrative Personnel

CHAPTER 3 DEPARTMENT OF PERSONNEL ADMINISTRATION

SUBCHAPTER 1 GENERAL CIVIL SERVICE RULES

ARTICLE 2 Traveling Expenses

§599.631. Transportation by Privately Owned Automobile—Excluded Employees.

(a) Where the employee is authorized to use a privately owned automobile on official state business the reimbursement rate shall be 34 cents per mile. Claims for reimbursement for private vehicle expenses must include the vehicle license number and the name of each state officer, employee or board, commission or authority member transported on the trip. No reimbursement of transportation expense shall be allowed any passenger in any vehicle operated by another state officer, employee or member.

(1) Expenses arising from travel between home and headquarters or garage shall not be allowed, except as provided in 599.626(d)(2) or 599.626.1(c), regardless of the employee's normal mode of transportation.

(2) When a trip is commenced or terminated at a claimant's home on a regularly scheduled work day, the distance traveled shall be computed from either his/her residence or headquarters, whichever shall result in the lesser distance except as provided in 599.626.1(c).

(3) However, if the employee commences or terminates travel on a regularly scheduled day off, mileage may be computed from his/her residence.

(b) Where the employee's use of a privately owned automobile is authorized for travel to or from a common carrier terminal, and the automobile is not parked at the terminal during the period of travel, the employee may claim double the number of miles between the terminal and the employee's headquarters or residence, whichever is less, at a rate as defined in Section 599.631(a), while the employee occupies the automobile for the distance between the terminal and his/her residence or headquarters. If the employee commences or terminates travel one hour before or after his/her regularly scheduled work day, or on a regularly scheduled day off, mileage may be computed from his/her residence.

(c) All ferry, bridge, or toll road charges will be allowed with any required receipts.

(d) All necessary parking charges while on state business will be allowed, with any required receipts, for:

(1) Day parking on trips away from the headquarters office and excluded employee's primary residence.

(2) Overnight public parking on trips away from the headquarters and excluded employee's primary residence, except that parking shall not be claimed if expense-free overnight parking is available.

(3) Day parking adjacent to either a headquarters office, a temporary job site or training site, but only if the excluded employee had other reimbursable private or state automobile expenses for the same day. An employee may not prorate weekly or monthly parking fees.

(e) Gasoline, maintenance and automobile repair expenses will not be allowed.

(f) The mileage reimbursement rates include the cost of maintaining liability insurance at the minimum amount prescribed by a law and collision insurance sufficient to cover the reasonable value of the automobile, less a deductible. When a privately owned automobile operated by state officer, agent or excluded employee is damaged by collision or is otherwise accidentally damaged, reimbursement for repair or the deductible to a maximum of $500.00 will be allowed if:

(1) The damage occurred while the automobile was used on official state business by permission or authorization of the employing agency; and

(2) The automobile was damaged through no fault of the state officer, agent or excluded employee; and

(3) The amount claimed is an actual loss to the state officer, agent or excluded employee, and is not recoverable directly from or through the insurance coverage of any party involved in the accident; and

(4) The loss claimed does not result from a decision of a state officer, agent or excluded employee not to maintain collision coverage; and

(5) The claim is processed in accordance with the procedures prescribed by the Department of Personnel Administration.

(g) Specialized Vehicles. An employee with a physical disability who must operate a motor vehicle on official state business and who can operate only specially equipped or modified vehicles may claim a rate of 34 cents per mile without certification and up to 37 cents per mile with certification. Where travel is authorized to and from a common carrier terminal, as specified in Section 599.631(b) the employee may compute the mileage as defined in Section 599.631(b). Supervisors approving these claims must determine the employee's need for the use of such vehicles.

Note: Authority cited: Sections 3539.5, 19815.4(d), 19816 and 19820, Government Code. Reference: Section 11030, Government Code.

History: 1. Amendment of subsections (a)-(c) and (h) filed by the Department of Personnel Administration with the Secretary of State on 8-20-84; effective upon filing. Submitted to OAL for printing only pursuant to Government Code section 11343.8 (Register 85, No. 18).

2. Amendment filed by the Department of Personnel Administration with the Secretary of State on 7-8-87; operative 7-8-87. Submitted to OAL for printing only pursuant to Government Code section 11343.8 (Register 87, No. 32).

3. Amendment filed by the Department of Personnel Administration with the Secretary of State on 6-27-88 pursuant to Government Code section 3539.5. Submitted to OAL for printing only pursuant to Government Code section 11343.8 (Register 88, No. 31).

4. Amendment filed by the Department of Personnel Administration with the Secretary of State on 6-30-89; operative 6-30-89. Submitted to OAL for printing only pursuant to Government Code section 11343.8 (Register 89, No. 33).

5. Amendment filed 12-31-91 with Secretary of State by Department of Personnel Administration; operative 12-31-91. Submitted to OAL for printing only pursuant to Government Code section 3539.5 (Register 92, No. 12).

6. Amendment of section heading and section filed 12-27-95; operative 1-1-96. Submitted to OAL for printing only pursuant to Government Code section 3539.5 (Register 95, No. 52).

7. Amendment of subsection (a)(1) filed 1-10-96; operative 1-10-96. Submitted to OAL for printing only pursuant to Government Code section 3539.5 (Register 96, No. 38).

8. Editorial correction of subsection (g) (Register 96, No. 38).

9. Amendment of subsection (a) filed 7-1-97; operative 7-1-97 pursuant to Government Code section 11343.4(d). Submitted to OAL for printing only pursuant to Government Code section 3539.5 (Register 97, No. 27).

10. Amendment of subsections (a), (a)(2) and (g) filed 10-28-99; operative 11-2-99. Submitted to OAL for printing only (Register 99, No. 51). At the request of DPA pursuant to Government Code section 3539.5, OAL is directing the printing of this regulation in the CCR. Title 1, CCR, section 6(b)(2)(F)1 defines "print only" regulations as "regulations *adopted pursuant to the requirements of the APA*, but which are expressly exempted by statute from OAL review ..." (Emphasis added.) In complying with DPA's request, OAL makes no determination concerning whether or not DPA has met the statutory requirements for adoption of regulations set forth in Government Code sections 11346-11347.3, including but not limited to public notice and comment. See 1998 OAL Determination No. 40 (Department of Personnel Administration, 96-008, December 9, 1998), California Regulatory Notice Register 99, No. 3-Z, January 15, 1999, p. 139, at p. 145; typewritten version, p. 18.

11. Amendment of subsections (a) and (g) filed 10-1-2001; operative 10-1-2001. Submitted to OAL for printing only pursuant to Government Code section 3539.5 (Register 2001, No. 46).

Ref.: Hanna §§ 5.04[1], 22.07[2][a]; Herlick Handbook § 4.12.

TITLE 8
INDUSTRIAL RELATIONS

DIVISION 1
Department of Industrial Relations

CHAPTER 1
INDUSTRIAL MEDICAL COUNCIL

ARTICLE 1
General

§1. [See Note Following §159 Regarding Elimination of the IMC] Definitions.

As used in these regulations:

(a) "Accreditation" means the conferring of recognized status as a provider of physician education by the Industrial Medical Council.

(b) "Administrative Director" means the administrative director of the Division of Workers' Compensation of the State of California Department of Industrial Relations.

(c) "AME" means Agreed Medical Examiner or Agreed Medical Evaluator, a physician selected by agreement between the employer and the employees to resolve disputed medical issues referred by the parties in a workers' compensation proceeding.

(d) "Appeals Board" means the Workers' Compensation Appeals Board within the State of California Department of Industrial Relations.

(e) "Audit" means a formal evaluation of a continuing education program, disability evaluation report writing course, or an accredited provider which is conducted at the request of the Medical Director.

(f) "Comprehensive Medical-Legal Evaluation" means a medical evaluation performed pursuant to Labor Code Sections 4060, 4061, or 4062 and meeting the requirements of Section 9793 of this Title.

(g) "Claims Administrator" means a self-administered insurer providing security for the payment of compensation required by Divisions 4 and 4.5 of the Labor Code, a self-administered self-insured employer, a group self-insurer, or a third-party claims administrator for a self-insured employer, insurer, legally uninsured employer, group self-insurer, or joint powers authority.

(h) "Continuing Education Program" means a systematic learning experience (such as a course, seminar, or audiovisual or computer learning program) which serves to develop, maintain, or increase the knowledge, skills and professional performance of physicians who serve as Qualified Medical Evaluators in the California workers' compensation system.

(i) "Council" means the Industrial Medical Council as defined in Labor Code Section 139.

(j) "Course" means the 12 hours of instruction in disability evaluation report writing which is required of a Qualified Medical Evaluator prior to appointment. A course must be approved by the Council.

(k) "Credit Hour" means a sixty minute hour. A credit hour may include time for questions and answers related to the presentation.

(*l*) "Direct medical treatment" means that special phase of the health care provider-patient relationship which—(1) attempts to clinically diagnose and alter or modify the expression of a non-industrial illness, injury or pathological condition; or (2) attempts to cure or relieve the effects of an industrial injury.

(m) "Distance Learning" means an education program in which the instructor and student are in different locations, as in programs based on audio or video tapes, computer programs, or printed educational material.

(n) "DEU" is the Disability Evaluation Unit

under the Administrative Director responsible for issuing summary disability ratings.

(o) "Employer" means an uninsured employer and the Uninsured Employers Fund pursuant to Labor Code Section 3716. The UEF shall only be subject to these regulations after proper service has been made on the uninsured employer and the Appeals Board has obtained jurisdiction over the UEF by joinder as a party.

(p) "Evaluator" means "Qualified Medical Evaluator" or "Agreed Medical Evaluator."

(q) "Medical Director" means the Executive Medical Director appointed by the Industrial Medical Council pursuant to Labor Code Section 122, who is Executive Secretary of the Council.

(r) "Provider" means the individual or organization which has been accredited by the Council to offer physician education programs. There are two categories of providers: (1) the Council and (2) individuals, partnerships, or corporations; hospitals; clinics or other patient care facilities; educational institutions; medical or health-related organizations whose membership includes L.C. 3209.3 physicians; organizations of non-medical participants in the California workers' compensation system; and governmental agencies. In the case of a national organization seeking accreditation, the California Chapter or organization affiliated with the national organization shall be accredited by the Council in lieu of the national organization.

(s) "Qualified Injured Worker" means a employee defined pursuant to subdivision (c) of Section 10003 of this Title.

(t) "Qualified Medical Evaluator" (QME) means a physician licensed by the appropriate licensing body for the state of California and appointed by the Council pursuant to Labor Code Section 139.2, provided however, that acupuncturist QMEs shall not perform comprehensive medical-legal evaluations to determine disability.

(u) "QME competency examination" means an examination administered by the Industrial Medical Council for the purpose of demonstrating competence in evaluating medical-legal issues in the workers' compensation system. This examination shall be given at least as often as twice annually.

(v) "Physician's office" means a bona fide office facility which is identified by a street address and any other more specific designation such as a suite or room number and which contains the usual and customary equipment for the evaluation and treatment appropriate to the physician's medical specialty or practice.

(w) "Rebuttal examination" means a comprehensive medical-legal evaluation performed at the request of a party concerning a disputed medical finding or conclusion by a QME concerning an unrepresented employee.

(x) "Significant Financial Interest or Affiliation" means grant or research support; status as a consultant, member of a speakers' bureau, or major stock shareholder; or other financial or material interest for the program faculty member or his or her family.

(y) "Treating physician" means a physician who has provided direct medical treatment to an employee which is reasonably required to cure or relieve the effects of an industrial injury pursuant to section 4600 of the Labor Code.

(z) "Treatment Guideline" means the advisory guideline issued by the Industrial Medical Council which sets out a systematic statement intended to assist health care providers in the California workers' compensation community in making decisions about appropriate medical treatment for specific industrial injuries.

(aa) "Unrepresented employee" means an employee not represented by an attorney.

Note: Authority cited: Sections 139, 139.2, 4060, 4061 and 4062, Labor Code. Reference: Sections 139, 139.2, 4060, 4061, 4061.5 and 4062, Labor Code.

History: 1. Repealer and new section filed 8-1-94; operative 8-31-94 (Register 94, No. 31). For prior history, see Register 93, No. 38.

2. Change without regulatory effect amending subsections (c), (g), (h), (k) and (p) filed 9-19-94 pursuant to section 100, title 1, California Code of Regulations (Register 94, No. 38).

3. Amendment of subsections (d) and (f), repealer and new subsection (m), amendment of subsections (n) and (o), new subsections (p) and (q) and subsection relettering, and amendment of newly designated subsection (r) filed 8-23-96; operative 9-22-96 (Register 96, No. 34).

4. New subsection (s) and subsection relettering filed 6-3-97; operative 7-3-97 (Register 97, No. 23).

5. Amendment of subsections (f) and (r) filed 4-14-2000; operative 5-14-2000 (Register 2000, No. 15).

6. New subsections (a) and (e), repealer of former subsection (f), new subsections (h), (j), (k), (m), (r) and (x) and subsection relettering filed 10-16-2000 as an emergency; operative 1-1-2001 (Register 2000, No. 42). A Certificate of Compliance must be transmitted to OAL by 5-1-2001 or emergency language will be repealed by operation of law on the following day.

7. New subsections (a) and (e), repealer of former subsection (f), new subsections (h), (j), (k), (r) and (x) and subsection relettering refiled 5-2-2001 as an emergency; operative 5-2-2001 (Register 2001, No. 18). A Certificate of Compliance must be transmitted to OAL by 8-30-2001 or emergency language will be repealed by operation of law on the following day.

8. Certificate of Compliance as to 5-2-2001 order, including further amendment of section, transmitted to OAL 7-12-2001 and filed 8-23-2001 (Register 2001, No. 34).

Ref.: W. Cal. Sum., 3 "Agency and Employment" §314.

ARTICLE 2
QME Eligibility

§10. [See Note Following §159 Regarding Elimination of the IMC] Appointment of QMEs.

Applications for appointment as a QME shall be submitted on the form in Section 100. The completed application form, and any supporting documentation as required by the application, shall be filed at the Council's headquarters office. Upon its approval of each application form and supporting documentation, the Council shall certify as eligible to sit for the QME competency examination those applicants who meet all of the statutory and regulatory eligibility requirements. Any application for appointment may be rejected if it is incompletely filled out, contains false information or does not contain the required supporting documentation listed in Section 11.

Note: Authority cited: Sections 133, 139 and 139.2, Labor Code. Reference: Sections 139.2, 4060, 4061 and 4062, Labor Code.

History: 1. Relocation of article 2 heading and new section filed 8-1-94; operative 8-31-94 (Register 94, No. 31).

2. Amendment of section filed 8-23-96; operative 9-22-96 (Register 96, No. 34).

3. Amendment filed 4-14-2000; operative 5-14-2000 (Register 2000, No. 15).

Ref.: Herlick Handbook § 1.8.

§10.1. The Application for Appointment as Qualified Medical Evaluator Form.

Note: Authority cited: Sections 133, 139 and 139.2, Labor Code. Reference: Sections 139.2, 4060, 4061 and 4062, Labor Code.

History: 1. New section filed 8-1-94; operative 8-31-94 (Register 94, No. 31).

2. Change without regulatory effect updating QME Application Form filed 6-27-95 pursuant to section 100, title 1, California Code of Regulations (Register 95, No. 26).

3. Change without regulatory effect amending specialty codes filed 10-11-95 pursuant to section 100, title 1, California Code of Regulations (Register 95, No. 41).

4. Change without regulatory effect amending QME Application form and adding MAP specialty code filed 12-27-95 pursuant to section 100, title 1, California Code of Regulations (Register 95, No. 52).

5. Change without regulatory effect amending MD/DO specialty codes filed 6-19-97 pursuant to section 100, title 1, California Code of Regulations (Register 97, No. 25).

6. Change without regulatory effect amending MD/DO specialty codes and updating form revision date filed 4-15-98 pursuant to section 100, title 1, California Code of Regulations (Register 98, No. 16).

7. Change without regulatory effect amending QME appointment application form filed 8-19-98 pursuant to section 100, title 1, California Code of Regulations (Register 98, No. 34).

8. Change without regulatory effect amending MD/DO specialty codes and updating form revision date filed 7-12-99 pursuant to section 100, title 1, California Code of Regulations (Register 99, No. 29).

9. Repealer filed 4-14-2000; operative 5-14-2000 (Register 2000, No. 15).

§10.1A. Reappointment Application as Qualified Medical Evaluator Form.

History: 1. Change without regulatory effect adding new section filed 6-20-96 pursuant to section 100, title 1, California Code of Regulations (Register 96, No. 25).

2. Change without regulatory effect repealing section and adding new section filed 4-16-98 pursuant to section 100, title 1, California Code of Regulations (Register 98, No. 16).

3. Change without regulatory effect amending block 2, item 3 and verification statement in block 5 filed 8-12-98 pursuant to section 100, title 1, California Code of Regulations (Register 98, No. 33).

4. Change without regulatory effect amending block 5 filed 10-30-98 pursuant to section 100, title 1, California Code of Regulations (Register 98, No. 44).

5. Repealer filed 4-14-2000; operative 5-14-2000 (Register 2000, No. 15).

§10.2. [See Note Following §159 Regarding Elimination of the IMC] The QME Fee Assessment Notice Form.

[Form Not Reproduced]

Editor's Note: To acquire a copy of IMC Form 5 (Rev. 4/99), please contact the local I&A office. *See* Reference Directory, p. xiii, for phone numbers.

Note: Authority cited: Sections 133, 139 and 139.2, Labor Code. Reference: Sections 139.2, 4060, 4061 and 4062, Labor Code.

History: 1. New section filed 8-1-94; operative 8-31-94 (Register 94, No. 31).

2. Repealer and new section filed 6-7-99 as an emergency; operative 6-7-99 (Register 99, No. 24). A Certificate of Compliance must be transmitted to OAL by 10-5-99 or emergency language will be repealed by operation of law on the following day.

3. Repealed by operation of Government Code section 11346.1(g) (Register 2000, No. 3).

4. New section filed 1-19-2000; operative 1-19-2000 pursuant to Government Code section 11343.4(d) (Register 2000, No. 3).

Ref.: Herlick Handbook § 1.8.

§10.5. [See Note Following §159 Regarding Elimination of the IMC] Limitations on Certification as Qualified Medical Evaluators.

(a) All eligibility requirements contained herein shall be applied without regard to the race, creed, color, gender, religion, or national origin of the individual applying for the public benefit.

(b) Pursuant to Section 411 of the Personal Responsibility and Work Opportunity Reconciliation Act of 1996, (Pub. L. No. 104-193 (PRWORA)), (8 U.S.C. § 1621), and notwithstanding any other provision of this division, aliens who are not qualified aliens, nonimmigrant aliens under the Immigration and Nationality Act (INA) (8 U.S.C. § 1101 et seq.), or aliens paroled into the United States under Section 212(d)(5) of the INA (8 U.S.C. § 1182(d)(5)), for less than one year, are not eligible to receive QME certification as set forth in Labor Code Section 139.2.

(c) A qualified alien is an alien who, at the time he or she applies for, receives, or attempts to receive QME certification is, under Section 431(b) of the PRWORA (8 U.S.C. § 1641(b)), any of the following:

(1) An alien who is lawfully admitted for permanent residence under the INA (8 U.S.C. § 1101 et seq.).

(2) An alien who is granted asylum under Section 208 of the INA (8 U.S.C. § 1158).

(3) A refugee who is admitted to the United States under Section 207 of the INA (8 U.S.C. § 1157).

(4) An alien who is paroled into the United States under Section 212(d)(5) of the INA (8 U.S.C. § 1182(d)(5)) for a period of at least one year.

(5) An alien whose deportation is being withheld under Section 243(h) of the INA (8 U.S.C. § 1253(h)) (as in effect immediately before the effective date of Section 307 of division C of Public Law 104-208) or Section 241(b)(3) of such Act (8 U.S.C. § 1251(b)(3)) (as amended by Section 305(a) of division C of Public Law 104-208).

(6) An alien who is granted conditional entry pursuant to Section 203(a)(7) of the INA as in effect prior to April 1, 1980. (8 U.S.C. § 1153(a)(7)) (See editorial note under 8 U.S.C. § 1101, "Effective Date of 1980 Amendment").

(7) An alien who is a Cuban or Haitian entrant (as defined in Section 501(e) of the Refugee Education Assistance Act of 1980 (8 U.S.C. § 1522 note)).

(8) An alien who meets all of the conditions of subparagraphs (A), (B), (C), and (D) below:

(A) The alien has been battered or subjected to extreme cruelty in the United States by a spouse or parent, or by a member of the spouse's or parent's family residing in the same household as the alien, and the spouse or parent of the alien consented to, or acquiesced in, such battery or cruelty. For purpose of this subsection, the term "battered or subjected to extreme cruelty" includes, but is not limited to being the victim of any act or threatened act of violence including any forceful detention, which results or threatens to result in physical or mental injury. Rape, molestation, incest (if the victim is a minor), or forced prostitution shall be considered as acts of violence.

(B) There is a substantial connection between such battery or cruelty and the need for QME certification in the opinion of the IMC. For purposes of this subsection, the following circumstances demonstrate a substantial connection between the battery or cruelty and the need for QME certification:

(1) QME certification is needed to enable the alien to become self-sufficient following separation from the abuser.

(2) QME certification is needed to enable the alien to escape the abuser and/or the community in which the abuser lives, or to ensure the safety of the alien from the abuser.

(3) QME certification is needed due to a loss of financial support resulting from the alien's separation from the abuser.

(4) QME certification is needed because the battery or cruelty, separation from the abuser, or work absences or lower job performance resulting from the battery or extreme cruelty or from legal proceedings relating thereto (including resulting child support, child custody, and divorce actions) cause the alien to lose his or her job or to earn less or to require the alien to leave his or her job for safety reasons.

(5) QME certification is needed because the alien requires medical attention, health counseling, or has become disabled, as a result of the battery or extreme cruelty.

(6) QME certification is needed because the loss of a dwelling or source of income or fear of the abuser following separation from the abuser jeopardizes the alien's ability to care for his or her children (e.g., inability to house, feed, or clothe children or to put children into daycare for fear of being found by the abuser).

(7) QME certification is needed to alleviate nutritional risk or need resulting from the abuse or following separation from the abuser.

(8) QME certification is needed to provide medical care during a pregnancy resulting from the abuser's sexual assault or abuse of, or relationship with, the alien and/or to care for any resulting children.

(9) Where medical coverage and/or health care services are needed to replace medical coverage or health care services the alien had when living with the abuser.

(C) The alien has a petition that has been approved or has a petition pending which sets forth a prima facie case for:

(1) status as a spouse or child of a United States citizen or legal permanent resident pursuant to clause (ii), (iii), or (iv) of Section 204(a)(1)(A) of the INA (8 U.S.C. § 1154(a)(1)(A)(ii), (iii) or (iv) and (B)(i)),

(2) classification pursuant to (ii) or (iii) of Section 204(a)(1)(B) of the INA (8 U.S.C. § 1154(a)(1)(B)(ii) or (iii)),

(3) suspension of deportation and adjustment of status pursuant to Section 244(a)(3) of the INA (8 U.S.C. § 1254) as in effect prior to April 1, 1997 [Pub.L. 104-208, § 501 (effective September 30, 1996, pursuant to § 591); Pub.L. 104-208, § 304 (effective April 1, 1997, pursuant to § 309; Pub.L. 105-33, § 5581 (effective pursuant to § 5582)] (incorrectly codified as "cancellation of removal under Section 240A of such Act [8 U.S.C. § 1229b] (as in effect prior to April 1, 1997)."

(4) status as a spouse or child of a United States citizen pursuant to clause (i) or Section 204(a)(1)(A) of the INA (8 U.S.C. § 1157(a)(1)(A)(i)) or classification pursuant to clause (i) of Section 204(a)(1)(B) of the INA (8 U.S.C. § 1154(a)(1)(B)(i)), or

(5) cancellation of removal pursuant to section 240(b)(2) of the INA (8 U.S.C. § 1229b(b)(2)).

(D) For the period for which QME certification is sought, the individual responsible for the battery or cruelty does not reside in the same household or family eligibility unit as the individual subjected to the battery or cruelty.

(9) An alien who, under Section 431(c)(2) of the PRWORA (8 U.S.C. § 1641(c)(2)), meets all of the conditions of subparagraphs (A), (B), (C), (D), and (E) below:

(A) The alien has a child who has been battered or subjected to extreme cruelty in the United States by a spouse or a parent of the alien (without the active participation of the alien in the battery or cruelty), or by a member of the spouse's or parent's family residing in the same household as the alien, and the spouse or parent consented or acquiesced to such battery or cruelty. For purposes of this subsection, the term "battered or subjected to extreme cruelty" includes but is not limited to being the victim of any act or threatened act of violence including any forceful detention, which results or threatens to result in physical or mental injury. Rape, molestation, incest (if the victim is a minor), or forced prostitution shall be considered as acts of violence.

(B) The alien did not actively participate in such battery or cruelty.

(C) There is a substantial connection between such battery or cruelty and the need for QME certification to be provided in the opinion

IMC. For purposes of this subsection, the following circumstances demonstrate a substantial connection between the battery or cruelty and the need for the benefits to be provided:

(1) QME certification is needed to enable the alien's child to become self-sufficient following separation from the abuser.

(2) QME certification is needed to enable the alien's child to escape the abuser and/or the community in which the abuser lives, or to ensure the safety of the alien's child from the abuser.

(3) QME certification is needed due to a loss of financial support resulting from the alien's child's separation from the abuser.

(4) QME certification is needed because the battery or cruelty, separation from the abuser, or work absences are lower job performance resulting from the battery or extreme cruelty or from legal proceedings relating thereto (including resulting child support, child support, child custody, and divorce actions) cause the alien's child to lose his or her job or to earn less or to require the alien's child to leave his or her job for safety reasons.

(5) QME certification is needed because the alien's child requires medical attention or mental health counseling, or has become disabled, as a result of the battery or extreme cruelty.

(6) QME certification is needed because the loss of a dwelling or source of income or fear of the abuser following separation from the abuser jeopardizes the alien's child's ability to care for his or her children (e.g., inability to house, feed, or clothe children or to put children into day care for fear of being found by the abuser).

(7) QME certification is needed to alleviate nutritional risk or need resulting from the abuse or following separation from the abuser.

(8) QME certification is needed to provide medical care during a pregnancy resulting from the abuser's sexual assault or abuse of, or relationship with, the alien's child and/or care for any resulting children.

(9) Where medical coverage and/or health care services are needed to replace medical coverage or health care services the alien's child had when living with the abuser.

(D) The alien meets the requirements of subsection (c)(8)(C) above.

(E) For the period for which benefits are sought, thc individual responsible for the battery or cruelty does not reside in the same household or family eligibility unit as the individual subjected to the battery or cruelty.

(10) An alien child who meets all of the conditions of subparagraphs (A), (B), and (C) below:

(A) The alien child resides in the same household as a parent who has been battered or subjected to extreme cruelty in the United States by that parent's spouse or by a member of the spouse's family residing in the same household as the parent and the spouse consented or acquiesced to such battery or cruelty. For purposes of this subsection, the term "battered or subjected to extreme cruelty" includes but is not limited to being the victim of any act or threatened act of violence including any forceful detention, which results or threatens to result in physical or mental injury. Rape, molestation, incest (if the victim is a minor), or forced prostitution shall be considered as acts of violence.

(B) There is a substantial connection between such battery or cruelty and the need for QME certification in the opinion of IMC. For purposes of this subsection, the following circumstances demonstrate a substantial connection between the battery or cruelty and the need for the benefits to be provided:

(1) QME certification is needed to enable the alien child's parent to become self-sufficient following separation from the abuser.

(2) QME certification is needed to enable the alien child's parent to escape the abuser and/or the community in which the abuser lives, or to ensure the safety of the alien child's parent from the abuser.

(3) QME certification is needed due to a loss of financial support resulting from the alien child's parent's separation from the abuser.

(4) QME certification is needed because the battery or cruelty, separation from the abuser, or work absences or lower job performance resulting from the battery or extreme cruelty or from legal proceedings relating thereto (including resulting child support, child custody, and divorce actions) cause the alien child's parent to lose his or her job or to earn less or to require the alien child's parent to leave his her job for safety reasons.

(5) QME certification is needed because the alien child's parent requires medical attention or mental health counseling, or has become disabled, as a result of the battery or extreme cruelty.

(6) QME certification is needed because the loss of a dwelling or source of income or fear of the abuser following separation from the abuser jeopardizes the alien child's parent's ability to care for his or her children (e.g., inability to house, feed, or clothe children or to put children into day care for fear of being found by the abuser).

(7) QME certification is needed to alleviate nutritional risk or need resulting from the abuse or following separation from the abuser.

(8) QME certification is needed to provide medical care during a pregnancy resulting from the abuser's sexual assault or abuse of, or relationship with, the alien child's parent and/or to care for any resulting children.

(9) Where medical coverage and/or health care services are needed to replace medical coverage or health care services the alien child's parent had when living with the abuser.

(C) The alien child meets the requirements of subsection (c)(8)(C) above.

(d) For purposes of this section, "nonimmigrant" is defined the same as in Section 101(a)(15) of the INA (8 U.S.C. § 1101(a)(15)).

(e) For purposes of establishing eligibility for certification as a QME pursuant to Labor Code Section 139.2, all of the following must be met:

(1) The applicant must declare himself or herself to be a citizen of the United States or a qualified alien under subsection (c), a nonimmigrant alien under subsection (d), or an alien paroled into the United States for less than one year under Section 212(d)(5) of the INA (8 U.S.C. § 1182(d)(5)). The applicant shall declare that status through use of the "Statement of Citizenship, Alienage, and Immigration Status for QME Certification," Form 101.

(2) The applicant must present documents of a type acceptable to the Immigration and Naturalization Service (INS) which serve as reasonable evidence of the applicant's declared status. A fee receipt from the INS for replacement of a lost, stolen, or unreadable INS document is reasonable evidence of the alien's declared status.

(3) The applicant must complete and sign Form 101 and submit the from to the IMC with any other required information under Article 2 and Article 5 of this division.

(4) Where the documents presented do not on their face appear to be genuine or to relate to the individual presenting them, the government entity that originally issued the documents shall be contacted for verification. With regard to naturalized citizens and derivative citizens presenting certificates of citizenship and aliens, the INS is the appropriate government entity to contact for verification. The IMC shall request verification from the INS by filing INS Form G-845 with copies of the pertinent documents provided by the applicant with the local INS office. If the applicant has lost his or her original documents or presents expired documents or is unable to present any documentation evidencing his or her immigration status, the applicant shall be referred to the local INS office to obtain documentation.

(5) The type of documentation referred to the INS for verification pursuant to INS Form G-845 shall include the following:

(A) The document presented indicates immigration status but does not include an alien registration or alien admission number.

(B) The document is suspected to be counterfeit or to have been altered.

(C) The document includes an alien registration number in the A60 000 000 (not yet issued) or A80 000 000 (illegal border crossing) series.

(D) The document is one of the following: an INS Form, I-181b notification letter issued in connection with an INS Form I-181 Memorandum of Creation of Records of Permanent Residence, and Arrival-Departure Record (INS Form I-94) or an foreign passport stamped "PROCESSED FOR I-551, TEMPORARY EVIDENCE OF LAWFUL PERMANENT RESIDENCE" that INS issued more than one year before the date of application for QME certification.

(6) If the INS advises that the applicant has citizenship status or immigration status which makes him or her a qualified alien, a nonimmigrant or alien paroled for less than one year under Section 212(d)(5) of the INA, the INS verification shall be accepted. If the INS advises that it cannot verify that the applicant has citizenship status or an immigration status that makes him or her a qualified alien, a nonimmigrant or an alien paroled for less than one year under Section 212(d)(5) of the INA, QME certification shall be denied and the applicant notified pursuant to the Administrative Procedure Act (Gov't Code § 11370 et seq. of his or her right to appeal the denial of his or her certification.

(f) Pursuant to Section 434 of PRWORA (8 U.S.C. § 1644), where the Industrial Medical Council reasonably believes that an alien is unlawfully in the State based on the failure of the alien to provide reasonable evidence of the alien's declared status, after an opportunity to do so, said alien shall be reported to the Immigration and Naturalization Service.

(g) Eligibility for QME certification is established where subsections (e)(1)-(3) are satisfied. Any alien who provides documentation specified under subsection (e)(5) shall be eligible for QME certification until and unless the Industrial Medical Council receives written confirmation from the Immigration and Naturalization Service that the alien is not eligible for QME certification.

(h) Nothing in this section shall be construed to withdraw eligibility for QME certification if any of the conditions in U.S.C. § 1621(b) are present.

(i) Any applicant who was made eligible for QME certification whose services are terminated, suspended, or reduced pursuant to subsections (b) and (e), is entitled to a hearing under Section 61 of these regulations.

Note: Authority cited: Sections 139 and 139.2. Reference: 8 U.S.C. Sections 1621, 1641 and 1642; Sections 139.2, 5307.3 and 5307.4, Labor Code; and Section 11507 et seq., Government Code.

History: 1. New section filed 11-5-98; operative 12-5-98 (Register 98, No. 45).

2. Change without regulatory effect repealing and adding new Form 10.5, Rev. 5/99 (incorporated by reference) filed 7-12-99 pursuant to section 100, title 1, California Code of Regulations (Register 99, No. 29).

3. Amendment of subsections (e)(1), (e)(3) and (i) and repealer of subsections (i)(1)-(6) filed 4-14-2000; operative 5-14-2000 (Register 2000, No. 15).

Ref.: Hanna § 1.12[2A].

§11. [See Note Following §159 Regarding Elimination of the IMC] Eligibility Requirements for Initial Appointment as a QME.

The Council shall appoint as QMEs all applicants who meet the requirements set forth in Labor Code Section 139.2(b) and all applicants:

(a) Shall submit the required supporting documentation:

(1) Copy of current license to practice in California;

(2) For Medical Doctors, or Doctors of Osteopathy:

(A) A copy of the applicant's certificate of completion of postgraduate specialty training at an institution recognized by the Accreditation Council for Graduate Medical Education or the osteopathic equivalent as defined pursuant to Section 12, or;

(B) A copy of the applicant's Board certification by a specialty board recognized by the Council or as defined pursuant to Section 12, or;

(C) A declaration under penalty of perjury accompanied by supporting documentation that the physician has qualifications that the Council and the Medical Board of California or the Osteopathic Medical Board of California both deem to be equivalent to board certification in a specialty.

(3) If a psychologist, (i) a copy of a doctoral degree in psychology or a doctoral degree deemed equivalent for licensure by the Board of Psychology pursuant to Section 2914 of the Business and Professions Code, and has not had less than five years postdoctoral experience in the treatment of emotional and mental disorders or (ii) served as an AME on eight or more occasions prior to January 1, 1990 and has not less than five years postdoctoral experience in the diagnosis and treatment of emotional and mental disorders.

(4) For Doctors of Chiropractic, the physician shall provide (1) a copy of a current or otherwise valid certificate in California Workers Compensation Evaluation by either a California professional chiropractic association or an accredited California college recognized by the Council (i.e. Workers' Compensation Evaluation Certificate with a minimum 44 hours completed or; (2) a certificate of completion of a chiropractic postgraduate specialty program of at least 300 hours taught by a school or college recognized by the Council, the Board of Chiropractic Examiners and the Council on Chiropractic Education.

(5) Or, for other physicians, a copy of the physician's professional diploma.

(b) Prior to appointment as a QME, each applicant shall complete a course of at least 12 hours in disability evaluation report writing pursuant to Section 11.5 of this Article. Doctors of Chiropractic who submit documentation showing compliance with section 11(a)(4) are exempt from this requirement.

(c)(1) Shall provide supplemental information and/or documentation to the Council after an application form is submitted if requested to verify an applicant's eligibility for appointment.

(2) Shall declare that he or she has not performed a QME Evaluation without QME Certification. The Council, after hearing pursuant to Section 61 may deny appointment to any applicant who has performed a QME Evaluation without QME Certification prior to appointment.

(d) Shall agree that during a QME exam he or she will not treat or offer or solicit to provide medical treatment for that injury for which he or she has done a QME evaluation for an injured worker unless a medical emergency arises as defined under subdivision (a) or (b) of Section 1317.1 of the Health and Safety Code. A QME may also provide treatment if requested by the employee pursuant to section 4600 of the Labor Code, but he or she shall not offer or solicit to provide it. A QME who solicits an injured employee to receive direct medical treatment or to become the primary treating physician of that employee shall be subject to disciplinary action pursuant to Section 60.

(e) Shall declare under penalty of perjury on the QME application he or she:

(1) has an unrestricted license or is currently on probation from the state licensing board and;

(2) devotes at least one-third of their total practice time to providing direct medical treatment during each year of the applicant's term of appointment. This requirement shall not apply if the applicant has served as an AME on 8 or more occasions in the year prior to application and each year of the applicant's term; or if the applicant meets the requirements of section 15.

(f) Shall pass the QME Competency Examination.

(1) In order to take this examination, a physician who is not currently appointed as a QME and not exempt pursuant to Labor Code §139(b)(1), shall be considered to have applied to take the QME competency examination upon submitting the properly-completed Application for Appointment Form in Section 100, and the Registration Form for the QME Competency Examination in Section 102 and the appropriate fee as specified in Section 11(f)(2).

(2) The fee for applying to take or retake the QME competency examination is $125.00 and may be waived by the Council at its discretion for first time applicants.

(3) The Medical Director shall give appropriate public notice of the date, time and location of the examination no fewer than 60 calendar days before a competency examination is to be given.

(4) An applicant must submit the properly completed forms as required in Section 11(f)(1) to the Medical Director at least 30 calendar days prior to the date of the next scheduled competency examination unless the Medical Director finds good cause to grant an extension to the physician(s).

(5) The Medical Director shall inform the applicant in writing whether he or she shall be allowed to take the examination within 15 calendar days from the date the Council receives the properly-completed forms and appropriate fee.

(6) The Medical Director shall inform the applicant in writing whether or not he or she passed the examination within 60 calendar days from the date the applicant takes the competency examination.

(7) An applicant who passes the QME competency examination shall file the QME Fee Assessment Form in Section 103 including the appropriate fee within 30 days of the date of the notice. The physician shall not be appointed to the official QME list until the appropriate fee is paid and has completed a disability evaluation report writing course pursuant to Section 11.5. Appointments shall be for two-year terms beginning with the date of appointment by the Council.

(8) Any applicant who fails to follow test instructions and/or proctor instructions either before or during or at the conclusion of an examination shall be disqualified from the examination procedure and the applicant's exam shall be nullified.

(9) If an applicant fails the competency examination or fails to appear for a noticed QME examination for which the applicant has submitted a QME Exam Registration Form 102, the applicant may apply to take any subsequent examinations, upon submission of a new test application form and a fee of $125. An applicant who fails the exam three times shall show proof of having completed six (6) hours continuing education from a course approved by the Council prior to taking the examination again.

(10) Any applicant who receives a failing grade on a competency exam may appeal the failing grade to the Council. Appeals shall be

considered on a case by case basis. Appeals will be accepted immediately after a candidate has completed the examination and until 10 days after the date of the examination results letter. The appeal shall state specific facts as to why the failing grade should be overturned. Pursuant to Section 6254(g) of the Government Code, the Council will consider appeals of test questions in closed session with counsel and will base its decision solely on the written appeal including any supporting documentation submitted by the physician. Appeals will only be accepted for the current examination period. Grounds for appeal are:

(A) Significant procedural error in the examination process;

(B) Unfair Discrimination;

(C) Bias or fraud.

(g) Each applicant shall pay the annual fee required by section 17 of this Article prior to appointment.

Note: Authority cited: Section 139.2, Labor Code. Reference: Section 139.2, Labor Code; and Section 6254, Government Code.

History: 1. New section filed 8-1-94; operative 8-31-94 (Register 94, No. 31).

2. New subsections (a)-(c) and subsection relettering, amendment of newly designated subsections (d)-(f)(6), new subsections (f)(7) and (f)(8) and subsection renumbering, amendment of newly designated subsections (f)(9) and (f)(10), and new subsection (g) filed 8-23-96; operative 9-22-96 (Register 96, No. 34).

3. Change without regulatory effect amending section (f)(5) filed 6-20-97 pursuant to section 100, title 1, California Code of Regulations (Register 97, No. 25).

4. Amendment filed 4-14-2000; operative 5-14-2000 (Register 2000, No. 15).

5. Amendment of section heading and section filed 8-23-2001; operative 8-23-2001 pursuant to Government Code section 11343.4 (Register 2001, No. 34).

Ref.: Herlick Handbook § 1.8.

§11.1. Application for QME Competency Examination Form.

Note: Authority cited: Section 139.2, Labor Code. Reference: Section 139.2, Labor Code.

History: 1. New section filed 8-1-94; operative 8-31-94 (Register 94, No. 31).

2. Change without regulatory effect amending form filed 3-11-96 pursuant to section 100, title 1, California Code of Regulations (Register 96, No. 11).

3. Change without regulatory effect amending form filed 7-23-96 pursuant to section 100, title 1, California Code of Regulations (Register 96, No. 30).

4. Amendment of form filed 3-15-99; operative 4-14-99 (Register 99, No. 12).

5. Repealer filed 4-14-2000; operative 5-14-2000 (Register 2000, No. 15).

§11.5. [See Note Following §159 Regarding Elimination of the IMC] Disability Evaluation Report Writing Course.

Prior to appointment as a QME, a physician shall complete a course of at least twelve hours of instruction in disability evaluation report writing. The course curriculum shall be specified by the Council.

(a) To apply to the Council for accreditation, a provider shall submit:

(1) a completed IMC Form 118 which contains

(A) the applicant's name; address; director of education with contact information; type of organization; length of time in business; nature of business; and past experience providing continuing education courses (including a list of other accrediting agencies that have approved such courses);

(B) a description of the proposed education program or course which includes the title; type (continuing education program or disability evaluation report writing course); location(s); date(s); length of training in clock hours; educational objectives; a complete description of the program or course content; faculty; and the names of other accrediting agencies that have approved the program.

(2) A curriculum vitae for each proposed instructor. A proposed instructor shall have education and/or training and recent work experience relevant to the subject of his/her presentation.

(3) To apply to the Council for accreditation, an applicant shall submit the application to the Council, at least 60 calendar days before any public advertisement of the applicant's course.

(b) The Council shall accredit an applicant that meets the definition of provider in Section 1(r); submits a completed, signed and dated application which demonstrates past experience in providing continuing education programs; and proposes a program which meets the requirements of 55(c) or a course which meets the requirements of 11.5(a) and (i). The applicant must demonstrate that adequate time is allocated to the curriculum set forth in section 11(5)(i) for the course to be approved by the Council.

Proposed content for continuing education program credit must relate directly to disability evaluation or California workers' compensation-related medical dispute evaluation. No credit shall be recognized by the IMC for material primarily discussing the business aspects of workers' compensation medical practice, including but not limited to billing, coding and marketing.

(c) The Council shall notify the applicant within 20 calendar days following the next scheduled Council meeting after receipt of the application containing all the information listed in Section 11.5(a) whether that provider has been accredited for a two year period and the proposed course has been approved. Incomplete applications will be returned to the provider.

(d) A provider that has been accredited by the Council will be given a number which must be displayed on course promotional material.

(e) On or before the date the course is first presented, the provider shall submit the program syllabus (all program handouts) to the Council.

(f) An approved course may be offered for two (2) years. A provider shall notify the Council in writing of any change to the faculty in an approved course. The provider shall send the Council the program outline, promotional material and faculty for each offering of the program at least 45 days prior to the date of the presentation of the program. The Council may require submission of the program syllabi. The Council may require changes in the program based on its review of the program outline, program syllabi, promotional material or faculty if the IMC finds that any aspect of the program is not in compliance with these regulations.

(g) To apply for re-accreditation, a provider must submit a completed IMC Form 118, using the application process in 11.5(a). The provider may complete section 2 of the form using a new program or course or one which was given by the provider during the recent accreditation period. The Council shall give the provider 90 days' notice of the need to seek re-accreditation.

(h) Promotional materials for a course must state the provider's educational objectives; the professional qualifications of course faculty (at the least, all relevant professional degrees); the content of course activities; and the intended audience.

(i) The minimum of 12 hours of instruction in disability evaluation report writing shall include:

(1) The Qualified Medical Evaluator's Role in the Disability Evaluation Process (minimum recommended 1 hour)

How disability evaluation reports are used

The reasons why reports must be clear, complete and timely

The QME's role as an expert witness

Impact of the QME's report on the injured worker

QME ethics and the Confidentiality of Medical Information Act

(2) Elements of the Medical-Legal Report (minimum recommended 1 hour)

The Labor Code and regulatory requirements for medical-legal reports.

(3) The Language of Reports (minimum recommended 4 hours)

Evaluation of disability in California (impairment and disability)

The occupational history

The physician examination and the role of testing

Labor Code requirements to use Packard Thurber's Evaluation of Industrial Disability

Factors of disability

Subjective

Objective

Work restrictions

Loss of pre-injury capacity

Causation

Determination of permanent and stationary status

Vocational rehabilitation

Apportionment

Future medical treatment

Review of records

Providing sufficient support for conclusions

(4) The Council's Disability Evaluation Protocols (minimum recommended 1 hour)

An overview of the protocols and an in-depth discussion of one or more of the Neuromusculoskeletal, Pulmonary, Cardiac, Immunologic, or Psychiatric protocols.

(5) The Third Party Perspective (minimum recommended 1 hour)

The report from the perspective of those who read it:

Judge(s), attorney(ies), insurer(s), rater(s), employer(s), qualified rehabilitation representative(s).

(6) Anatomy of a Good Report (small group or other interactive sessions — minimum recommended 3 hours)

Discussion of examples of good reports and identification of weaknesses in reports

Opportunities for the practitioner to critique and/or correct reports.

If feasible, physician should have the opportunity to write a sample report.

Review of results of IMC annual report review and identification of common problems with reports

(7) Mechanics of Report Writing (minimum recommended 1 hour)

The QME Process

Face to face time

Timelines for submission of report

Completion of required forms

Service of reports

Final questions and answers

(j) No more than four hours of the required twelve hours of instruction may be taken by distance learning. All audio or video tapes, computer programs and printed educational material used in the course must be submitted to the Council on or before the date the course is first given. All distance learning materials shall bear a date of release and shall be updated yearly. The provider shall notify the Council in writing of the revision.

(k) No one shall recruit members or promote commercial products or services in the instruction room immediately before, during, or immediately after the presentation of a course. Providers or vendors may display/sell educational materials related to workers' compensation or applications for membership in an area adjoining a course. A course provider or faculty member shall disclose on IMC form 119 any significant financial interest in or affiliation with any commercial product or service which is discussed in a course and that interest or affiliation must be disclosed to all attendees. A provider shall file every form 119 in its possession with the Council.

(*l*) The provider shall maintain attendance records for each disability evaluation report writing course for a period of no less than three years after the course is given. A physician attending the course must be identified by signature. The provider must submit a copy of the signature list to the Council within 60 days of completion of the course.

(m) The provider is required to give the IMC's Evaluation Form 117) to course attendees and request they submit the form to the IMC. This information shall not be used in lieu of a certification of completion given by the provider, as specified pursuant to section (n). Destruction by a provider or its employee of a QME's Evaluation Form or failure by such provider or its employee to distribute Form 117 as part of its course shall constitute grounds for revocation of a provider's accredited status. The Council shall tabulate the responses and return a summary to the provider within 90 days of completion of the course.

(n) The provider shall issue a certificate of completion to the physician which states the name of the provider, the provider's number, the date(s) and location and title of the course. To be eligible for appointment as a QME, a physician must complete no less than 12 hours of the curriculum specified in Section 11.5(i) and must submit a copy of that certificate to the Council.

(o) Joint sponsorship of courses (as between an accredited and an unaccredited provider) must be approved by the Council prior to presentation of the course.

(p) The Council may audit a provider's course(s) at the request of the medical director to determine if the provider meets the criteria for accreditation. The Council may audit courses given by providers randomly, when a complaint is received, or on the basis of responses on IMC Form 117. An auditor shall not receive QME credit for auditing a course. The Council shall make written results of the audit available to the provider no more than 30 days after the audit is completed.

(q) Accredited providers that cease to offer disability evaluation report writing courses shall notify the Council in writing no later than 60 days prior to the discontinuing an approved course.

(r) The Council may withdraw accreditation of a provider or deny such a provider's application for accreditation on the following grounds (in addition to failure to meet the relevant requirements of subsections 11.5(a):

(1) Conviction of a felony or any offense substantially related to the activities of the provider.

(2) Any material misrepresentation of fact made by the provider.

(3) Failure to comply with Council regulations

(4) False or misleading advertising

(5) Failure to comply with Council recommendations following an audit

(6) Failure to distribute Council form 117 cards to course attendees.

Note: Authority cited: Sections 139, 139.2, 4060, 4061 and 4062, Labor Code. Reference: Sections 139, 139.2, 4060, 4061, 4061.5 and 4062, Labor Code.

History: 1. New section filed 10-16-2000 as an emergency; operative 1-1-2001 (Register 2000, No. 42). A Certificate of Compliance must be transmitted to OAL by 5-1-2001 or emergency language will be repealed by operation of law on the following day.

2. New section refiled 5-2-2001 as an emergency; operative 5-2-2001 (Register 2001, No. 18). A Certificate of Compliance must be transmitted to OAL by 8-30-2001 or emergency language will be repealed by operation of law on the following day.

3. Certificate of Compliance as to 5-2-2001 order, including further amendment of section, transmitted to OAL 7-12-2001 and filed 8-23-2001 (Register 2001, No. 34).

§12. [See Note Following §159 Regarding Elimination of the IMC] Recognition of Specialty Boards.

The Council shall recognize all specialty boards accredited by the American Board of Medical Specialties (ABMS), the American Osteopathic Association, the American Board of Professional Psychology, Inc. and those boards either accredited or considered equivalent to ABMS recognized boards by the Medical Board, the Osteopathic Medical Board and the Board of Psychology of State of California. The Council shall recognize chiropractic diplomate boards whose programs are taught by the Council on Chiropractic Education accredited colleges.

Note: Authority cited: Sections 139 and 139.2, Labor Code. Reference: Sections 139.2(b)(2)(A), 4060, 4061 and 4062, Labor Code.

History: 1. New section filed 8-1-94; operative 8-31-94 (Register 94, No. 31).

2. Amendment of section filed 8-23-96; operative 9-22-96 (Register 96, No. 34).

Ref.: Herlick Handbook § 1.8.

§13. [See Note Following §159 Regarding Elimination of the IMC] Physician's Specialty.

A physician's specialty(ies) is one for which the physician is board certified or, has completed a postgraduate specialty training as defined in Section 11(a)(2)(A), or held an appointment as a QME in that specialty on June 30, 2000, pursuant to Labor Code Section 139.2, having provided to the Council documentation from the relevant board of certification or qualification or has provided documentation which meets the requirements of Section 11.

Note: Authority cited: Sections 139 and 139.2, Labor Code. Reference: Sections 139.2(b)(2)(A), 4060, 4061 and 4062, Labor Code.

History: 1. New section filed 8-1-94; operative 8-31-94 (Register 94, No. 31).

2. Amendment of section filed 8-23-96; operative 9-22-96 (Register 96, No. 34).

3. Amendment filed 4-14-2000; operative 5-14-2000 (Register 2000, No. 15).

4. Amendment filed 8-23-2001; operative 8-23-2001 pursuant to Government Code section 11343.4 (Register 2001, No. 34).

Ref.: Herlick Handbook § 1.8.

§13.5. Chiropractic Certification in Workers' Compensation Evaluation.

Note: Authority cited: Sections 139, 139.2 and 139.3, Labor Code. Reference: Sections 139.2, 4060, 4061 and 4062, Labor Code.

History: 1. New section filed 8-1-94; operative 8-31-94 (Register 94, No. 31).

2. Change without regulatory effect amending subsection (a) filed 12-2-96 pursuant to section 100, title 1, California Code of Regulations (Register 96, No. 49).

3. Amendment filed 3-15-99; operative 4-14-99 (Register 99, No. 12).

4. Renumbering of former section 13.5 to section 14 filed 4-14-2000; operative 5-14-2000 (Register 2000, No. 15).

§13.7. Appointment of Retired or Teaching Physicians.

Note: Authority cited: Sections 139 and 139.2, Labor Code. Reference: Sections 139.2, 4060, 4061 and 4062, Labor Code.

History: 1. New section filed 8-1-94; operative 8-31-94 (Register 94, No. 31).

2. Amendment of opening paragraph and subsections (c)(2) and (c)(3) and new subsection (e) filed 8-23-96; operative 9-22-96 (Register 96, No. 34).

3. Renumbering of former section 13.7 to section 15 filed 4-14-2000; operative 5-14-2000 (Register 2000, No. 15).

§14. [See Note Following §159 Regarding Elimination of the IMC] Doctors of Chiropractic: Certification in Workers' Compensation Evaluation.

(a) All doctors of chiropractic, in lieu of board certification, shall be certified in workers' compensation evaluation by either a California professional chiropractic association, or an accredited California college recognized by the Council. The certification program shall include instruction in disability evaluation report writing that meets the standards set forth in Section 11.5.

(b) California professional chiropractic associations or accredited California colleges applying to be recognized by the Council for the purpose of providing these required courses to chiropractors in California workers' compensation evaluation, shall meet the following criteria:

(1) The provider's courses shall be administered and taught by a California professional chiropractic association or a California chiropractic college accredited by the Council on Chiropractic Education. Instructors shall be licensed or certified in their profession or if a member of a non-regulated profession have at least two years experience in their area of instruction regarding workers' compensation issues.

(2) The provider's method of instruction and testing shall include all of the following:

(A) lecture, didactic sessions and group discussion including an initial 8 hours of overview of the workers' compensation system and 36 additional hours in medical-legal issues for total minimum class time of 44 hours. Up to 4 hours of the instruction covering the regulations affecting QMEs and/or writing ratable reports may be satisfied by distance learning. The initial 8 hours of overview are transferable to any other approved program provider for credit;

(B) passing a written test at the completion of the program to determine proficiency and application of course material;

(C) writing a narrative conclusion to medical-legal issues in response to facts presented or a narrative report, in appropriate format, which would meet the standards of a ratable report;

(3) The initial 8 hours of the course material shall cover the following information:

(A) overview of California Labor Code, DWC (Division of Workers' Compensation of the California Department of Industrial Relations) and Council regulations governing medical-legal reports and evaluations;

(B) obligations of the treating and evaluating physicians;

(C) review of appropriate workers' compensation terminology;

(4) The remaining 36 hours shall include but not be limited to the following:

(A) history and examination procedure requirements, including all relevant IMC guidelines;

(B) work capacity guidelines and disability ratings;

(C) apportionment;

(D) vocational rehabilitation;

(E) continued or future medical care.

(5) The provider's course material and tests shall be submitted to the Council for annual review and the Council shall monitor a provider's course as necessary to determine if the provider meets the criteria for recognition.

(6) The provider's course advertising shall clearly state whether or not the course is recognized to satisfy the requirement for chiropractic California workers' compensation evaluation by the Council.

(c) Course Material shall also cover at a minimum, the material within the text of the "Physicians Guide to Medical Practice in the California Workers' Compensation system (Current Edition)."

Note: The "Physicians Guide" does not appear as a part of this regulation. Copies are available through the Executive Medical Director of the Industrial Medical Council; P. O. Box 8888, San Francisco, CA 94128-8888.

Note: Authority cited: Sections 139, 139.2 and 139.3, Labor Code. Reference: Sections 139.2, 4060, 4061 and 4062, Labor Code.

History: 1. New section filed 4-9-93 as an emergency; operative 4-9-93 (Register 93, No. 15). A Certificate of Compliance must be transmitted to OAL 8-9-93 or emergency language will be repealed by operation of law on the following day.

2. Editorial correction amending subsections (a)(1) and (b) and Note (Register 93, No. 17).

3. New section refiled 9-16-93 with amendment of subsections (a)(1)-(b) as an emergency; operative 9-16-93 (Register 93, No. 38). A Certificate of Compliance must be transmitted to OAL by 1-14-94 or emergency language will be repealed by operation of law on the following day.

4. Certificate of Compliance as to 9-16-93 order including amendment of subsections (b) and (c) transmitted to OAL 10-28-93 and filed 12-14-93 (Register 93, No. 51).

5. Relocation of article 2 filed 8-1-94; operative 8-31-94 (Register 94, No. 31).

6. Amendment of subsections (a)(1) and (a)(2), repealer of subsections (b)-(b)(2) and subsection relet-

tering, and amendment of newly designated subsections (b) and (c) filed 8-23-96; operative 9-22-96 (Register 96, No. 34).

7. Amendment filed 6-7-99 as an emergency; operative 6-7-99 (Register 99, No. 24). A Certificate of Compliance must be transmitted to OAL by 10-5-99 or emergency language will be repealed by operation of law on the following day.

8. Reinstatement of section as it existed prior to 6-7-99 emergency amendment by operation of Government Code section 11346.1(f) (Register 2000, No. 3).

9. Amendment filed 1-19-2000; operative 1-19-2000 pursuant to Government Code section 11343.4(d) (Register 2000, No. 3).

10. Renumbering of former section 14 to section 16 filed 4-14-2000 pursuant to section 100, title 1, California Code of Regulations (Register 2000, No. 15).

11. Renumbering and amendment of former section 13.5 to section 14 filed 4-14-2000; operative 5-14-2000 (Register 2000, No. 15).

12. Amendment of subsections (a), (b), (b)(4) and (b)(6) and redesignation and amendment of former subsection (b)(7) as new subsection (c) filed 8-23-2001; operative 8-23-2001 pursuant to Government Code section 11343.4 (Register 2001, No. 34).

Ref.: Herlick Handbook § 1.8.

§15. [See Note Following §159 Regarding Elimination of the IMC] Appointment of Retired or Teaching Physicians.

In order to be considered for appointment as a QME pursuant to Labor Code Section 139.2(c), a physician shall submit written documentation to the Council that he or she meets either (a), (b) or (c) of this section. A physician applying for appointment pursuant to this section shall also pass the QME competency examination.

The physician shall:

(a) Be a current salaried faculty member at an accredited university or college, have a current license to practice as a physician and have been engaged in teaching, lecturing, published writing or medical research at that university or college in the area of his or her specialty for not less than one-third of his or her professional time. The physician's practice in the three consecutive years immediately preceding the time of application shall not have been devoted solely to the forensic evaluation of disability.

(b) Be retired from full-time practice, retaining a current license to practice as a physician with his or her licensing board; and

(1) Has a minimum of 25 years' experience in his or her practice as a physician; and

(2) Has had a minimum of 10 years' experience in workers' compensation medical issues; and

(3) Is currently practicing fewer than 10 hours per week on direct medical treatment as a physician, and;

(4) Whose practice in the three consecutive years immediately preceding the time of application was not devoted solely to the forensic evaluation of disability.

(c) Be retired from active practice due to a documented medical or physical disability as defined pursuant to Gov't Code § 12926 and currently practicing in his or her specialty fewer than 10 hours per week. The physician shall have 10 years experience in workers' compensation medical issues as a physician. The physician's practice in the three consecutive years immediately preceding the time of application shall not have been devoted solely to the forensic evaluation of disability.

(d) A physician appointed under Section 11 or this section shall, notify the Council of changes in his or her status and shall complete the requirements for continuing education pursuant to section 55 prior to reappointment.

Note: Authority cited: Sections 139 and 139.2, Labor Code. Reference: Sections 139.2, 4060, 4061 and 4062, Labor Code.

History: 1. New section filed 4-9-93 as an emergency; operative 4-9-93 (Register 93, No. 15). A Certificate of Compliance must be transmitted to OAL 8-9-93 or emergency language will be repealed by operation of law on the following day.

2. Editorial correction amending subsection (b) and Note (Register 93, No. 17).

3. New section refiled 9-16-93 with amendment of subsections (a)(1)-(b) as an emergency; operative 9-16-93 (Register 93, No. 38). A Certificate of Compliance must be transmitted to OAL by 1-14-94 or emergency language will be repealed by operation of law on the following day.

4. Certificate of Compliance as to 9-16-93 order including amendment of subsection (b) transmitted to OAL 10-28-93 and filed 12-14-93 (Register 93, No. 51).

5. Amendment filed 6-7-99 as an emergency; operative 6-7-99 (Register 99, No. 24). A Certificate of Compliance must be transmitted to OAL by 10-5-99

or emergency language will be repealed by operation of law on the following day.

6. Reinstatement of section as it existed prior to 6-7-99 emergency amendment by operation of Government Code section 11346.1(f) (Register 2000, No. 3).

7. Amendment filed 1-19-2000; operative 1-19-2000 pursuant to Government Code section 11343.4(d) (Register 2000, No. 3).

8. Renumbering of former section 15 to section 17 filed 4-14-2000 pursuant to section 100, title 1, California Code of Regulations (Register 2000, No. 15).

9. Renumbering and amendment former section 13.7 to section 15 filed 4-14-2000; operative 5-14-2000 (Register 2000, No. 15).

Ref.: Herlick Handbook § 1.8.

§16. [See Note Following §159 Regarding Elimination of the IMC] Determination of Fees for QME Eligibility.

(a) For purposes of establishing the annual fee for any qualified medical evaluator pursuant to Article 2, physicians (as defined under Section 3209.3 of the Labor Code) shall be classified into one of three categories:

(1) QMEs who meet all applicable requirements under Article 2 and 5 and who have conducted 0-10 comprehensive medical-legal evaluations in the twelve months prior to the assessment of the fee. Comprehensive medical-legal evaluations are evaluations as defined under Section (1)(d) of this Chapter performed by a physician.

(2) QMEs who meet all applicable requirements under Article 2 and 5 and who have conducted 11-24 comprehensive medical-legal evaluations in the twelve months prior to assessment of the fee. Comprehensive medical-legal evaluations are evaluations as defined under Section (1)(d) of this Chapter performed by a physician.

(3) QMEs who meet all applicable requirements under Article 2 and 5 and who have conducted 25 or more comprehensive medical-legal evaluations in the twelve months prior to assessment of the fee. Comprehensive medical-legal evaluations are evaluations as defined under Section (1)(d) of this Chapter performed by a physician.

(b) The evaluations shall be conducted in compliance with all applicable statutes and regulations.

(c) Verification of the number of examinations shall be made by the Council using The Findings Summary Form in Section 36.1. Misrepresentation of the number of evaluations performed for purposes of establishing a physician's QME fee shall constitute grounds for disciplinary proceedings under Section 60 of this chapter.

Note: Authority cited: Section 139.2, Labor Code. Reference: Sections 139, 139.1 and 139.2, Labor Code.

History: 1. New section filed 4-9-93 as an emergency; operative 4-9-93 (Register 93, No. 15). A Certificate of Compliance must be transmitted to OAL 8-9-93 or emergency language will be repealed by operation of law on the following day.

2. Editorial correction amending Note (Register 93, No. 17).

3. New section refiled 9-16-93 with amendment of subsection (a) as an emergency; operative 9-16-93 (Register 93, No. 38). A Certificate of Compliance must be transmitted to OAL by 1-14-94 or emergency language will be repealed by operation of law on the following day.

4. Certificate of Compliance as to 9-16-93 order including amendments transmitted to OAL 10-28-93 and filed 12-14-93 (Register 93, No. 51).

5. Amendment of section filed 8-23-96; operative 9-22-96 (Register 96, No. 34).

6. Amendment filed 6-7-99 as an emergency; operative 6-7-99 (Register 99, No. 24). A Certificate of Compliance must be transmitted to OAL by 10-5-99 or emergency language will be repealed by operation of law on the following day.

7. Reinstatement of section as it existed prior to 6-7-99 emergency amendment by operation of Government Code section 11346.1(f) (Register 2000, No. 3).

8. Amendment filed 1-19-2000; operative 1-19-2000 pursuant to Government Code section 11343.4(d) (Register 2000, No. 3).

9. Renumbering of former section 16 to section 18 and renumbering of former section 14 to section 16 filed 4-14-2000 pursuant to section 100, title 1, California Code of Regulations (Register 2000, No. 15).

Ref.: Herlick Handbook § 1.8.

§17. [See Note Following §159 Regarding Elimination of the IMC] Fee Schedule for QME.

(a) All physicians seeking QME status shall be required to pay to the Industrial Medicine Fund within the Industrial Medical Council, the following fee:

(1) QMEs performing 0-10 comprehensive medical-legal evaluations, $110 during each of the years or any part of a year the physician retains his or her eligibility on the approved QME list.

(2) QMEs performing 11-24 comprehensive medical-legal evaluations, $125 during each of the years or part of a year the physician retains his or her eligibility on the approved QME list.

(3) QMEs performing 25 or more comprehensive medical-legal evaluations, $250 during each of the years or any part of a year the physician retains his or her eligibility on the approved QME list.

(b) Individual QMEs who perform comprehensive medical-legal evaluations at more than one medical office location within the state which is identified by a street address and any other more specific designation such as a suite or room number and which contains the usual and customary equipment for the evaluations and treatment appropriate to the medical specialty or practice shall be required to pay an additional $100 annually per additional office location. This requirement applies to all QMEs regardless of whether the QME is a sole practitioner, or corporation, or partnership pursuant to Corporations Code Chapter 1 (sections 15001-15045) Chapter 2 (sections 15501-15533) and/or Chapter 3 (sections 15611-15723).

(c) The IMC may waive or return the statutory fee in the amount of $110 for the completion of a survey of QMEs to validate the QME competency examination. The term "completion of the survey" means the return of the survey to the testing agency designated by the IMC on or before the date for the return of the survey.

Note: Authority cited: Section 139.2, Labor Code. Reference: Sections 139, 139.1 and 139.2, Labor Code.

History: 1. New section filed 4-9-93 as an emergency; operative 4-9-93 (Register 93, No. 15). A Certificate of Compliance must be transmitted to OAL 8-9-93 or emergency language will be repealed by operation of law on the following day.

2. Editorial correction amending Note (Register 93, No. 17).

3. New section refiled 9-16-93 with amendments as an emergency; operative 9-16-93 (Register 93, No. 38). A Certificate of Compliance must be transmitted to OAL by 1-14-94 or emergency language will be repealed by operation of law on the following day.

4. Certificate of Compliance as to 9-16-93 order including amendments transmitted to OAL 10-28-93 and filed 12-14-93 (Register 93, No. 51).

5. Renumbering former section 17 to new section 19 filed 4-14-2000; operative 5-14-2000 (Register 2000, No. 15).

6. Renumbering of former section 15 to section 17 filed 4-14-2000 pursuant to section 100, title 1, California Code of Regulations (Register 2000, No. 15).

7. New subsection (c) and amendment of Note filed 2-14-2002 as an emergency; operative 2-14-2002 (Register 2002, No. 7). A Certificate of Compliance must be transmitted to OAL by 6-14-2002 or emergency language will be repealed by operation of law on the following day.

Ref.: Herlick Handbook § 1.8.

§18. [See Note Following §159 Regarding Elimination of the IMC] QME Fee Due Dates.

(a) All physicians, regardless of the number of comprehensive medical-legal evaluations performed under Section 17 shall pay the required QME fees at yearly intervals within 30 days of receipt of notice from the Council that the QME fee for the next 12 months is due and payable. No physician who has passed the competency examination shall be placed on the active QME roster until the appropriate fee under section 15 has been paid.

(b) Any QME who fails to pay the required statutory fee within 30 days of receipt of a final notice that the fee is due shall be notified that he or she shall be terminated from the official QME roster of physicians within 30 days and shall not perform any panel QME or represented QME comprehensive medical-legal evaluation until the fee is paid. If the fee is not paid within two years from the due date in the QMEs final notice from the Council that the fee is due, then the physician shall resubmit a new application pursuant to Sections 10 and 11, pass the QME competency examination and pay the appropriate fee prior to regaining QME eligibility.

Note: Authority cited: Section 139.2, Labor Code. Reference: Sections 139 and 139.2, Labor Code.

History: 1. New section filed 4-9-93 as an emergency; operative 4-9-93 (Register 93, No. 15). A Certificate of Compliance must be transmitted to OAL 8-9-93 or emergency language will be repealed by operation of law on the following day.

2. Editorial correction amending subsections (b) and (b)(1) and Note (Register 93, No. 17).

3. New section refiled 9-16-93 with amendment of section heading and text as an emergency; operative 9-16-93 (Register 93, No. 38). A Certificate of Compliance must be transmitted to OAL by 1-14-94 or

emergency language will be repealed by operation of law on the following day.

4. Certificate of Compliance as to 9-16-93 order including amendments transmitted to OAL 10-28-93 and filed 12-14-93 (Register 93, No. 51).

5. Repealer filed 8-23-96; operative 9-22-96 (Register 96, No. 34).

6. Renumbering of former section 16 to section 18 filed 4-14-2000 pursuant to section 100, title 1, California Code of Regulations (Register 2000, No. 15).

§19. [See Note Following §159 Regarding Elimination of the IMC] Certificate of QME Status.

(a) Upon receipt of the QME fees and review by the council to ensure current compliance with section 139.2 of Labor Code and any other applicable regulations promulgated by the council concerning QME eligibility, the council shall within 45 days send to the physician a certificate of approved status as Qualified Medical Evaluator. The certificate of QME status shall be displayed in a conspicuous manner at the QME's office location at all times during the period the QME is approved by the council to conduct evaluations under council appointment.

(b) It shall be unlawful for any physician who has been terminated or suspended from the QME list or who has failed to pay the required QME fee pursuant to sections 17 and 18 to display a certificate of approved status as a Qualified Medical Evaluator.

Note: Authority cited: Section 139.2, Labor Code. Reference: Sections 139 and 139.2, Labor Code.

History: 1. Renumbering and amendment of former section 17 to new section 19 filed 4-14-2000; operative 5-14-2000 (Register 2000, No. 15).

Ref.: Herlick Handbook § 1.8.

ARTICLE 2.5
Time Periods for Processing Applications for QME Status

§20. [See Note Following §159 Regarding Elimination of the IMC] Time Periods.

(a) Within 45 days of receipt of an application for QME status, the Council shall either inform the applicant, in writing, that the application is complete and accepted for filing, or that the application is deficient and what specific information is required.

(b) Within 45 days of receipt of a completed application, the Council shall inform the applicant, in writing, of its decision to allow or not to allow the applicant to proceed to take the required QME competency examination as per Section 11(c) of these regulations.

(c) Within 45 days of receipt of a completed application, the Council must inform the applicant, in writing, of its decision to grant or deny the application.

(d) Based upon the two years immediately preceding October 1, 1993, the Council's minimum time for processing an application for QME status is 14 days. The median time is 60 days. The maximum time is 2 years.

Note: Authority cited: Sections 139 and 139.2, Labor Code; and Section 15376, Government Code. Reference: Sections 4060, 4061 and 4062, Labor Code; and Section 15376, Government Code.

History: 1. New article 2.5 and section filed 8-1-94; operative 8-31-94 (Register 94, No. 31).

Ref.: Herlick Handbook § 1.8.

ARTICLE 3
Assignment of Qualified Medical Evaluators, Evaluation Procedure

§30. [See Note Following §159 Regarding Elimination of the IMC] QME Panel Requests.

(a) Requests for a QME panel made by an unrepresented employee pursuant to Labor Code Sections 4061 and 4062 shall be submitted on the form in Section 106.

(b) In the event a request form is incomplete, or improperly completed so that a QME panel selection cannot properly be made, the request form shall be returned to the employee with an explanation why the selection could not be made.

(c) The Request for Qualified Medical Evaluator Form along with the instruction form in Section 105 entitled "How to Request a Qualified Medical Evaluator" shall be provided by the claims administrator (or, if there is no claims administrator, the employer) to the unrepresented employee by personal delivery to the employee or by first class or certified mailing.

(d)(1) For admitted injuries between January 1, 1991 and December 31, 1993, a panel request form and notice in a form prescribed by the Administrative Director pursuant to Article 8 of Chapter 4.5 of this Title shall be provided to an unrepresented employee where the employee, the claims administrator or, if none, the employer alleges a medical conclusion that the employee is no longer entitled to temporary disability indemnity and permanent disability cannot be determined or is or is not payable. The QME shall address all medical issues raised by the parties, including but not limited to the employee's permanent and stationary status, the extent and scope of medical treatment, the employee's status as a Qualified Injured Worker or the existence of new and further disability in order to produce a complete comprehensive medical-legal evaluation.

(2) For admitted injuries occurring on or after January 1, 1994 a panel request form and the Administrative Director's notice pursuant to Article 8 of Chapter 4.5 of this Title shall be provided to an unrepresented employee where a party disputes a medical conclusion by the primary treating physician. If the issues are other than the level of permanent impairment and limitations or the need for medical care, the objecting party shall, absent good cause as determined by the Appeals Board, notify the other party of the nature of the objection within 30 days of receipt of the report from the primary treating physician. The objecting party shall submit a written copy of the objection to the QME along with any medical records submitted pursuant to the requirements of Section 35. After the QME evaluation is complete, either the employee or the employer may object to any new or unresolved issue. The parties shall utilize the same QME to the extent possible. Where the issue is outside the QME's scope of practice pursuant to the QMEs licensing authority, the parties may select another QME pursuant to subdivision (a) of Section 4064 of the Labor Code.

(e) If the request form is submitted by an unrepresented employee who no longer resides within the state of California, the geographic area of the QME panel selection within the state shall be determined by agreement between the claims administrator or, if none, the employer, and the employee. If no agreement can be reached, the geographic area of the QME panel selection shall be determined by the employee's former residence within the state.

Note: Authority cited: Sections 139, 139.2, 4061 and 4062, Labor Code. Reference: Sections 139.2, 4061 and 4062, Labor Code.

History: 1. New article 3 and section filed 8-1-94; operative 8-31-94 (Register 94, No. 31).

2. Amendment of subsection (b) and new subsections (d)-(e) filed 8-23-96; operative 9-22-96 (Register 96, No. 34).

3. Amendment of subsections (a), (c) and (d)(1) filed 4-14-2000; operative 5-14-2000 (Register 2000, No. 15).

Ref.: See Labor Code §4060; Herlick Handbook § 1.8.

§30.1. The Request for Qualified Medical Evaluator Form.

Note: Authority cited: Sections 133, 139 and 139.2, Labor Code. Reference: Sections 139.2, 4060, 4061 and 4062, Labor Code.

History: 1. New section filed 8-1-94; operative 8-31-94 (Register 94, No. 31).

2. Change without regulatory effect amending specialty codes filed 6-27-95 pursuant to section 100, title 1, California Code of Regulations (Register 95, No. 26).

3. Editorial correction adding History 3 and including previously filed amendments (Register 95, No. 41).

4. Change without regulatory effect amending specialty code MPT, repealing specialty codes DDS and DMD and adding specialty code DEN filed 10-11-95 pursuant to section 100, title 1, California Code of Regulations (Register 95, No. 41).

5. Change without regulatory effect adding MAP specialty code filed 12-27-95 pursuant to section 100, title 1, California Code of Regulations (Register 95, No. 52).

6. Change without regulatory effect amending form filed 6-20-96 pursuant to section 100, title 1, California Code of Regulations (Register 96, No. 25).

7. Change without regulatory effect amending form filed 2-25-97 pursuant to section 100, title 1, California Code of Regulations (Register 97, No. 9).

8. Change without regulatory effect amending MD/DO specialty codes filed 6-19-97 pursuant to section 100, title 1, California Code of Regulations (Register 97, No. 25).

9. Change without regulatory effect amending MD/DO specialty codes and updating form revision date filed 4-15-98 pursuant to section 100, title 1, California Code of Regulations (Register 98, No. 16).

10. Change without regulatory effect amending MD/DO specialty codes and updating form revision date filed 7-12-99 pursuant to section 100, title 1, California Code of Regulations (Register 99, No. 29).

11. Repealer filed 4-14-2000; operative 5-14-2000 (Register 2000, No. 15).

§30.2. The Request for Qualified Medical Evaluator Instruction Form.

Note: Authority cited: Sections 4061 and 4062, Labor Code. Reference: Sections 4061 and 4062, Labor Code.

History: 1. New section filed 8-1-94; operative 8-31-94 (Register 94, No. 31).

2. Change without regulatory effect amending third paragraph filed 2-25-97 pursuant to section 100, title 1, California Code of Regulations (Register 97, No. 9).

3. Repealer filed 4-14-2000; operative 5-14-2000 (Register 2000, No. 15).

§30.5. [See Note Following §159 Regarding Elimination of the IMC] Specialist Designation.

The Medical Director shall utilize in the selection process the specialist(s) indicated on the Request for Qualified Medical Evaluator Form 105.

Note: Authority cited: Sections 139, 139.2, 4061 and 4062, Labor Code. Reference: Sections 139.2, 4061 and 4062, Labor Code.

History: 1. Renumbering and amendment of former section 32 to new section 30.5 filed 4-14-2000; operative 5-14-2000 (Register 2000, No. 15).

Ref.: Herlick Handbook § 1.8.

§31. [See Note Following §159 Regarding Elimination of the IMC] QME Panel Selection.

(a) The panels shall be selected randomly from the appropriate specialty requested by the employee, with consideration given to the proximity of the QME's medical office to the employee's residence.

(b) The unrepresented employee shall make an appointment request with a QME listed on the panel and may consult with his or her primary treating physician as to an appropriate QME specialist. Neither the claims representative nor a representative of the employer nor a QME may discuss or make the selection of a panel QME for an unrepresented worker at any time.

(c) The Medical Director shall exclude from the panel selection process any QME who has informed the Medical Director that he or she is unavailable pursuant to Section 33.

(d) Any physician who has served as a primary treating physician or secondary physician and who has provided treatment in accordance with Section 9785.5 of this Title for this injury for an unrepresented employee shall not perform a QME evaluation on that employee. If that QME appears on a panel, he or she shall disqualify him or herself, and the employee may request a replacement QME pursuant to Section 31.5.

Note: Authority cited: Sections 4061 and 4062, Labor Code. Reference: Sections 139.2, 4061 and 4062, Labor Code.

History: 1. New section filed 8-1-94; operative 8-31-94 (Register 94, No. 31).

2. Repealer of subsection (d) and subsection relettering, and amendment of newly designated subsection (d) filed 8-23-96; operative 9-22-96 (Register 96, No. 34).

3. Amendment of subsections (b) and (d) filed 4-14-2000; operative 5-14-2000 (Register 2000, No. 15).

Ref.: Herlick Handbook § 1.8.

§31.1. The Qualified Medical Evaluator Panel Selection Form.

Note: Authority cited: Sections 139.2, 4061 and 4062, Labor Code. Reference: Section 139.2, Labor Code.

History: 1. New section filed 8-1-94; operative 8-31-94 (Register 94, No. 31).

2. Amendment of section heading and form filed 8-23-96; operative 9-22-96 (Register 96, No. 34).

3. Repealer filed 4-14-2000; operative 5-14-2000 (Register 2000, No. 15).

§31.2. The Qualified Medical Evaluator Panel Selection Instruction Form.

Note: Authority cited: Sections 133, 139, 139.2, 4061 and 4062, Labor Code. Reference: Sections 139.2, 4061, 4061.5 and 4062, Labor Code.

History: 1. New section filed 8-1-94; operative 8-31-94 (Register 94, No. 31).

2. Amendment of section heading and form filed 8-23-96; operative 9-22-96 (Register 96, No. 34).

3. Change without regulatory effect amending paragraph 1) filed 2-25-97 pursuant to section 100, title 1, California Code of Regulations (Register 97, No. 9).

4. Repealer filed 4-14-2000; operative 5-14-2000 (Register 2000, No. 15).

§31.5. [See Note Following §159 Regarding Elimination of the IMC] QME Replacement Requests.

(a) A replacement QME to a panel shall be provided to an unrepresented worker upon the employee's request if any of the following occurs:

(1) A QME on the panel issued does not practice in the specialty requested by the employee.

(2) A QME on the panel issued cannot schedule an examination for the employee within 60 days of the employee's request.

(3) The employee has changed his or her residence address since the QME panel was issued.

(4) A physician on the QME panel is a member of the same group practice as defined by Labor Code section 139.3 as another QME on the panel.

(5) The QME is unavailable pursuant to section 33.

(b) Any party may request a replacement QME if any of the following occurs:

(1) The employee's primary treating physician in accordance with Section 9785 of this Title is on the panel.

(2) The claims administrator or, if none, the employer and the unrepresented employee agree that a new panel may be issued in the geographic area of the employee's work place.

(3) The Medical Director, upon written request, finds good cause that a replacement QME is appropriate for reasons related to the medical nature of the injury. For purposes of this subsection, "good cause" is defined as a documented medical or psychological impairment.

(4) The Medical Director, upon written request, determines after a review of all appropriate records that the specialty chosen by the injured worker is medically or otherwise inappropriate for the injury to be evaluated.

(5) Any violation of Section 34.

(c) The Medical Director shall select replacement QME(s) at random.

Note: Authority cited: Sections 139, 139.2, 4061 and 4062, Labor Code. Reference: Sections 139.2, 4061 and 4062, Labor Code.

History: 1. New section filed 8-23-96; operative 9-22-96 (Register 96, No. 34).

2. Amendment of subsections (b), (b)(1) and (b)(3) and new subsections (b)(4)-(5) filed 4-14-2000; operative 5-14-2000 (Register 2000, No. 15).

Ref.: Herlick Handbook § 1.8.

§32. [See Note Following §159 Regarding Elimination of the IMC] Consultations.

(a) For injuries occurring between January 1, 1991 and December 31, 1993, a party may request the Medical Director to direct the QME to consult with a physician in an appropriate specialty to address issues outside the QME's specialty if the party believes such a consultation is necessary to provide a complete and accurate examination pursuant to section 4061 of the Labor Code. The party requesting the consultation shall specify in writing the reasons for the consultation. Valid reasons for providing the QME consultation shall include, but not be limited to, the expertise of the QME, the accuracy of the QME comprehensive medical-legal evaluation in question and the complexity of the medical issue involved.

(b) The Medical Director shall appoint a separate list of physicians for requests pursuant to subsection (a), and shall, in his or her discretion, grant or deny the request within 30 days.

(c) For injuries occurring on or after January 1, 1994 a QME may obtain a consultation from any physician who has treated the unrepresented employee for the injury listed on the panel request form or by any physician as reasonable and necessary pursuant to Labor Code section 4064 or upon agreement by a party to pay the cost.

(d) In any case where an acupuncturist has been selected by the injured worker from a three-member panel and an issue of disability is in dispute, the acupuncturist shall request a consult from a QME defined under § 1(n) to evaluate the disability issue(s). The acupuncturist shall evaluate all other issues as required for a complete evaluation.

Note: Authority cited: Sections 139.2, 4061, 4062 and 4064, Labor Code. Reference: Sections 4061 and 4062, Labor Code.

History: 1. New section filed 8-1-94; operative 8-31-94 (Register 94, No. 31).

2. Renumbering of former section 32 to new section 30.5 and renumbering and amendment of former section 32.5 to section 32 filed 4-14-2000; operative 5-14-2000 (Register 2000, No. 15).

Ref.: Herlick Handbook § 1.8.

§32.5. [See Note Following §159 Regarding Elimination of the IMC] Rebuttal QME Examinations.

(a) For injuries occurring between January 1, 1991 and December 31, 1993, an unrepresented employee shall have the right to a QME panel for one comprehensive medical-legal evaluation to rebut the findings of a panel QME, provided however, that the rebuttal evaluation is reasonable and necessary to resolve a disputed medical fact as defined in section 9793(e) of this Title. The employee shall notify in writing the claims administrator, or if none, the employer, the justification for the rebuttal evaluation. A copy of this notice shall be submitted to the Medical Director with this request. Reasonable and necessary justification shall include but not be limited to a discrepancy between the treating physician's conclusions and the QME's conclusions as to the level of permanent impairment, the need for medical treatment or the employee's status as a Qualified Injured Worker.

(b) For injuries occurring on or after January 1, 1994, and upon request by the Appeals Board, the Medical Director shall assign a QME to address disputed issues provided, however, that the claims administrator or if none, the employer, agrees to pay for the cost of this rebuttal examination.

Note: Authority cited: Sections 139.2, 4061, 4062 and 4064, Labor Code. Reference: Sections 4061 and 4062, Labor Code.

History: 1. New section filed 8-23-96; operative 9-22-96 (Register 96, No. 34).

2. Renumbering of former section 32.5 to section 32 and renumbering and amendment of former section 32.7 to section 32.5 filed 4-14-2000; operative 5-14-2000 (Register 2000, No. 15).

Ref.: Herlick Handbook § 1.8.

§32.7. Rebuttal QME Examinations.

Note: Authority cited: Sections 139.2, 4061 and 4062, Labor Code. Reference: Sections 4061 and 4064, Labor Code.

History: 1. New section filed 8-23-96; operative 9-22-96 (Register 96, No. 34).

2. Renumbering of former section 32.7 to section 32.5 filed 4-14-2000; operative 5-14-2000 (Register 2000, No. 15).

§33. [See Note Following §159 Regarding Elimination of the IMC] Unavailability of QME.

(a) A QME who will be unavailable to accept appointments to a QME panel for a period of 14 days or more for any reason, including a change of address, absent good cause including but not limited to medical or family emergency, shall notify the Medical Director by submitting the form in Section 109. The form shall be filed with the Medical Director 30 days prior to the period of unavailability. The Medical Director may, in his or her discretion, grant a notice of unavailability within the 30 day period in cases of injury or illness to the QME or his or her immediate family.

(b) It shall not be an acceptable reason for unavailability that a QME does not intend to perform comprehensive medical-legal evaluations for unrepresented workers. A QME who has filed notification for unavailability for more than 90 days during the QME fee period without good cause may be denied reappointment subject to Section 52. Good cause includes, but is not limited to sabbaticals or death of immediate family member.

(c) If an unrepresented employee is unable to obtain an appointment for an evaluation with a selected QME within 60 days after an appointment request, the employee may report the unavailability of the QME to the Medical Director. The Medical Director shall provide a replacement QME at random to be added to the employee's panel in accordance with Section 31(d). The employee may choose to waive his or her right to replacement QME and accept a later appointment with the originally selected QME or select one of the two remaining QME's on the panel.

(d) If a QME fails to notify the Medical Director, by submitting the form in Section 109, of his or her unavailability at a medical office due to a change in address for that office within 30 days of the change, the Medical Director may designate the QME to be unavailable at that location for 30 days from the date the Medical Director learns of the change in address. At that time, a certified letter will be sent to the QME by the IMC regarding his/her unavailability. If the IMC does not receive a response within 30 days of the date of certification of the letter, then the QME will be made inactive at that location.

Note: Authority cited: Sections 139 and 139.2, Labor Code. Reference: Sections 139.2, 4061 and 4062, Labor Code.

History: 1. New section filed 8-1-94; operative 8-31-94 (Register 94, No. 31).

2. Amendment filed 4-14-2000; operative 5-14-2000 (Register 2000, No. 15).

Ref.: Herlick Handbook § 1.8.

§33.1. The Notice of QME Unavailability Form.

Note: Authority cited: Sections 139 and 139.2, Labor Code. Reference: Sections 139.2, 4061 and 4062, Labor Code.

History: 1. New section filed 8-1-94; operative 8-31-94 (Register 94, No. 31).

2. Amendment of section heading, repealer and new section filed 8-23-96; operative 9-22-96 (Register 96, No. 34).

3. Repealer filed 4-14-2000; operative 5-14-2000 (Register 2000, No. 15).

§34. [See Note Following §159 Regarding Elimination of the IMC] Appointment Notification.

(a) When an unrepresented employee makes an appointment with a QME, the QME shall complete an appointment notification form by submitting the form in Section 110. This completed form shall be postmarked or sent by facsimile to the employee and the claims administrator or, if none, the employer within 5 working days of the date the appointment was made. Failure to comply with this requirement shall constitute grounds for denial of reappointment under Section 51.

(b) The QME shall schedule an appointment for a comprehensive medical-legal examination which shall be conducted only at the medical office listed on the panel selection form.

(c) The QME shall include within the notification whether a Certified Interpreter, as defined by Labor Code Section 5811 and subject to the provisions of section 9795.3 of this Title, is required and specify the language. The interpreter shall be arranged by the party who is to pay the cost as provided for in Section 5811 of the Labor Code.

Note: Authority cited: Sections 139 and 139.2, Labor Code. Reference: Sections 4061 and 4062, Labor Code.

History: 1. New section filed 8-1-94; operative 8-31-94 (Register 94, No. 31).

2. Amendment of subsections (a) and (c) filed 4-14-2000; operative 5-14-2000 (Register 2000, No. 15).

Ref.: Herlick Handbook § 1.8.

§34.1. The Appointment Notification Form.

Note: Authority cited: Sections 139 and 139.2, Labor Code. Reference: Sections 139.2, 4061 and 4062, Labor Code.

History: 1. New section filed 8-1-94; operative 8-31-94 (Register 94, No. 31).

2. Repealer filed 4-14-2000; operative 5-14-2000 (Register 2000, No. 15).

§35. [See Note Following §159 Regarding Elimination of the IMC] Exchange of Information.

(a) Where an employee is unrepresented, the claims administrator or, if none, the employer shall, and the employee may, provide to the QME:

(1) All records prepared or maintained by the employee's treating physician or physicians;

(2) Other medical records in their possession, including any previous treatment records, and/or non-medical records or information which are relevant to the evaluation of the employee's injury;

(3) A letter outlining the issues which the QME is requested to address in the evaluation, which shall be served on the opposing party no less than 20 days in advance of the evaluation;

(b) In no fewer than 20 days before the information is to be provided to the QME, the party providing such information shall serve on the opposing party the following:

(1) A copy of all medical records and medical reports to be sent.

(2) A copy of all non-medical documents or other non-medical information, including films or videotapes, to be sent. The claims administrator or employer shall include a cover letter or other document when providing such information to the employee which shall clearly and conspicuously include the following language: "Please look carefully at the enclosed information. It may be used by the doctor who is evaluating your medical condition as it relates to your workers' compensation claim. If you do not want the doctor to see this information, you must let me know within 10 days."

(3) Copies of all records being sent to the QME shall be sent to all parties except as otherwise provided in section (c). Failure to do so shall constitute ex parte communication by the party transmitting the information under section (f).

(c) In the event that the unrepresented employee schedules an appointment within 20 days of receipt of the panel, the employer or if none, the claims administrator shall not be required to comply with the 20 day time frame for sending medical information in subsection (b)(1) provided, however, that the unrepresented employee is served all non-medical information in subsection (b)(2) 20 days prior to the information being served on the QME so the employee has an opportunity to object to any non-medical information.

(d) In the event that a party fails to provide to the QME any relevant medical record which the QME deems necessary to perform a comprehensive medical-legal evaluation, the QME may contact the treating physicians or other health care provider, to obtain such record(s). If the party fails to provide relevant medical records under section (a) within 10 days after the date of the evaluation, and the QME is unable to obtain the records, the QME shall complete and serve the report to comply with the statutory time frames under Section 38. The QME shall note in the report that the records were not received within the required time period. Upon request by the party, or the Appeals Board, the QME shall complete a supplemental evaluation when the relevant medical records are received. For a supplemental report the QME need not conduct an additional physical examination of the employee if the QME believes a review of the additional records is sufficient.

(e) The QME and the employee's treating physician(s) may consult as necessary to produce a complete and accurate report. The QME shall note within the report new or additional information received from the treating physician.

(f) If an employer or claims administrator communicates with a QME in violation of Labor Code section 4062.2, the Medical Director shall provide the unrepresented employee with a new panel in which to select a new QME or the employee may elect to proceed with the original QME. If an employee communicates with a QME either before or after the evaluation, in violation of Labor Code section 4062.2, the claims administrator or employer may request the Medical Director to issue a new panel to the unrepresented employee. The Appeals Board shall retain jurisdiction to determine whether ex parte contact has occurred in all cases.

Note: Authority cited: Sections 139 and 139.2, Labor Code. Reference: Sections 139.2, 4060, 4061, 4062, 4062.2, Labor Code.

History: 1. New section filed 8-1-94; operative 8-31-94 (Register 94, No. 31).

2. New subsection (c) and subsection relettering, amendment of newly designated subsections (d) and (e) and new subsection (f) filed 8-23-96; operative 9-22-96 (Register 96, No. 34).

3. New subsection (b)(3) and amendment of subsection (e) filed 4-14-2000; operative 5-14-2000 (Register 2000, No. 15).

Ref.: Herlick Handbook § 1.8.

§35.5. [See Note Following §159 Regarding Elimination of the IMC] Compliance by QMEs with IMC Guidelines.

Any evaluation pursuant to Labor Code 4060, 4061 and 4062 shall be performed in compliance with all appropriate evaluation procedures pursuant to Article 4 of this Chapter.

History: 1. New section filed 4-14-2000; operative 5-14-2000 (Register 2000, No. 15).

§36. [See Note Following §159 Regarding Elimination of the IMC] Summary Form for Comprehensive Medical-Legal Evaluation Performed Pursuant to Labor Code Section 4061 by QMEs or AMEs; Service of Form and Evaluation.

(a) Upon completion of either a comprehensive medical-legal evaluation or follow-up medical legal evaluation as defined under Section 9793(f) of this Title, of an unrepresented employee, the evaluator shall complete the QME/AME Findings Summary Form in Section 111. The Form shall not be required for a supplemental medical legal evaluation under 9793(k) of this Title. The evaluator shall serve the comprehensive medical-legal evaluation, the summary form, and DEU forms 100 and 101 on the employee, and the claims administrator, or if none, the employer, as well as the appropriate local DEU office within the time frames specified in Section 38.

(b) If an evaluation is completed under subsection (a) for an unrepresented employee, in which the QME determines that the employees condition has not become permanent and stationary as of the date of the evaluation, the parties shall request any further evaluation from the same QME if the QME is currently an active QME and available at the time of the request for the additional evaluation. If the QME is unavailable, a new panel may be issued to resolve any disputed issue(s). If the evaluator is no longer a QME, he/she may issue a supplemental report as long as a face-to-face evaluation (as defined in section 49(b) of these regulations) with the injured worker is not required. In no event shall a physician who is not a QME or no longer a QME perform a follow up evaluation on an injured worker.

Note: Authority cited: Section 139, Labor Code. Reference: Sections 4060, 4061 and 4062, Labor Code; and 8 CCR 10161.

History: 1. New section filed 8-1-94; operative 8-31-94 (Register 94, No. 31).

2. Amendment of section heading, section and Note filed 4-14-2000; operative 5-14-2000 (Register 2000, No. 15).

Ref.: Herlick Handbook § 1.8.

§36.1. The Qualified or Agreed Medical Evaluator's Findings Summary Form.

Note: Authority cited: Sections 139, 139.2, 4061 and 4062, Labor Code. Reference: Sections 139.2, 4061 and 4062, Labor Code.

History: 1. New section filed 8-1-94; operative 8-31-94 (Register 94, No. 31).

2. Change without regulatory effect amending section filed 11-9-94 pursuant to section 100, title 1, California Code of Regulations (Register 94, No. 45).

3. Amendment of section filed 8-23-96; operative 9-22-96 (Register 96, No. 34).

4. Repealer filed 4-14-2000; operative 5-14-2000 (Register 2000, No. 15).

§37. [See Note Following §159 Regarding Elimination of the IMC] Treating Physician's Determination of Medical Issues Form.

Pursuant to Labor Code Sections 4061.5 and 139(e)(9), this form may be used by the treating physician primarily responsible for managing the care of the injured worker, or the physician designated by that physician, when rendering opinions on all medical issues necessary to determine eligibility for compensation. The Treating Physician's Determination of Medical Issues Form (Treating Physician's Form) is as follows:

[Form Not Reproduced]

Editor's Note: To acquire a copy of IMC Form 81556 (4/95), please contact the local I&A office. *See* Reference Directory, p. xiii, for phone numbers.

Note: Authority cited: Sections 139, 4061 and 4061.5, Labor Code. Reference: Sections 139(e)(9), 4061 and 4061.5, Labor Code.

History: 1. New section and forms filed 5-17-95; operative 5-24-95 pursuant to Government Code section 11343.4(d) (Register 95, No. 20).

Ref.: Herlick Handbook § 1.8.

§38. [See Note Following §159 Regarding Elimination of the IMC] Medical Evaluation Time Frames; Extensions for QMEs and AMEs.

(a) For a late report, regardless of the date of injury, if any of the following occur, the unrepresented injured worker shall be entitled to a new three-member QME panel:

(1) the QME fails to request an extension

(2) the timeframe extension is denied

(3) the QME does not issue the report by the approved extension date.

The injured worker shall have 15 days from the date of notice by the Medical Director to complete, sign and return IMC Forms 113, 115, 116 as applicable. If the employee requests a new panel, the claims administrator or, if none, the employer shall have no liability for the late report. If the employee is represented by an attorney and the extension is denied to an AME, either party may withdraw from the AME and no party shall be liable for payment to the AME.

(b) For injuries between January 1, 1991 and December 31, 1993, the time frame for comprehensive medical-legal evaluations to be prepared and submitted shall not exceed 45 days after the QME or AME has seen the employee or otherwise commenced the comprehensive medical-legal evaluation procedure. Extension of the 45-day limit shall be approved when the evaluator has good cause or has not received test results or consulting physicians' evaluations necessary to address all disputed medical issues in time to meet the initial 45-day deadline. If the evaluation is not completed on the scheduled date through no fault of the QME, the QME may request an extension not to exceed an additional 45 days from the Medical Director. The evaluator shall notify the employee and the claims administrator or, if none, the employer not later than 5 days before the initial 45-day period expires that an extension is warranted. A copy of the notice shall be sent to the Medical Director. The notice shall be on the form in Section 112. If the extension of time requires additional days greater than 90 days from the date of the evaluation for the submission of the report, approval or denial shall be granted within 10 days by the Medical Director.

(c) For injuries on or after January 1, 1994, the time frame for comprehensive medical-legal evaluations to be prepared and submitted shall not exceed 30 days after the QME or AME has seen the employee or otherwise commenced the comprehensive medical-legal evaluation procedure. Extension of the 30-day limit shall be approved when the evaluator has good cause or not received test results or consulting physicians' evaluations necessary to address all disputed medical issues in time to meet the initial 30-day deadline. If the evaluation is not completed on the scheduled date through no fault of the QME, the QME may request an extension not to exceed an additional 30 days from the Medical Director. The evaluator shall notify the employee and the claims administrator, or if none, the employer not later than 5 days before the initial 30-day period expires that an extension is warranted. A copy of the notice shall be sent to the Medical Director. The notice shall be on the form in Section 112. If the extension of time requires additional days greater than 60 days from the date of the evaluation for the submission of the report, approval or denial shall be granted within 10 days by the Medical Director.

(d) Extensions for good cause shall not exceed an additional 15 days from the date the report is to be served. Good cause means:

(1) medical emergencies of the evaluator or the evaluator's family;

(2) death in the evaluator's family;

(3) natural disasters or other community catastrophies that interrupt the operation of the evaluator's office operations;

(e) Extensions shall not be granted because relevant medical information/records (including Disability Evaluation Form 101 8 CCR § 10161(b)) have not been received. The evaluator shall complete the report based on the information available and state that the opinions and/or conclusions may or may not change after review of the relevant medical information/records.

(f) The time frame for supplemental reports in unrepresented cases shall be no more than 60 days from the date of a written or electronically transmitted request to the physician by a party. The request for a supplemental report shall be accompanied by any new medical records unavailable to the QME at the time of the original QME evaluation in compliance with section 10160(f) of this Title. An extension of the 60 days may be agreed to by the parties.

(g) Evaluators giving notice of time extensions will be monitored and advised by the Medical Director when such notices appear unreasonable or excessive. Failure to comply with this section may constitute grounds for denial of the QME's request for reappointment pursuant to Section 51.

Note: Authority cited: Sections 139.2, 4061 and 4062, Labor Code. Reference: Sections 139.2, 4061, 4062 and 4067.5, Labor Code.

History: 1. New section filed 8-1-94; operative 8-31-94 (Register 94, No. 31).

2. Amendment of subsections (a) and (b), new subsections (c)-(c)(3) and subsection relettering, and amendment of newly designated subsection (d) filed 8-23-96; operative 9-22-96 (Register 96, No. 34).

3. Amendment filed 4-14-2000; operative 5-14-2000 (Register 2000, No. 15).

Ref.: Herlick Handbook § 1.8.

§38.1. The QME and AME Time Frame Extension Request Form.

Note: Authority cited: Sections 139 and 139.2, Labor Code. Reference: Sections 139.2, 4060, 4061, 4062 and 4062.5, Labor Code.

History: 1. New section filed 8-1-94; operative 8-31-94 (Register 94, No. 31).

2. Change without regulatory effect amending form filed 4-2-96 pursuant to section 100, title 1, California Code of Regulations (Register 96, No. 14).

3. Repealer filed 4-14-2000; operative 5-14-2000 (Register 2000, No. 15).

§38.2. "The Time Extension Approval" Form.

Note: Authority cited: Sections 139 and 139.2, Labor Code. Reference: Sections 139.2, 4060, 4061, 4062 and 4062.5, Labor Code.

History: 1. New section filed 8-1-94; operative 8-31-94 (Register 94, No. 31).

2. Change without regulatory effect amending section filed 3-28-96 pursuant to section 100, title 1, California Code of Regulations (Register 96, No. 13).

3. Repealer filed 4-14-2000; operative 5-14-2000 (Register 2000, No. 15).

§38.3. The "Denial of Time Extension" Form.

Note: Authority cited: Sections 139 and 139.2, Labor Code. Reference: Sections 139.2, 4060, 4061, 4062 and 4062.5, Labor Code.

History: 1. New section filed 8-1-94; operative 8-31-94 (Register 94, No. 31).

2. Amendment of section heading and repealer and new section filed 8-23-96; operative 9-22-96 (Register 96, No. 34).

3. Repealer filed 4-14-2000; operative 5-14-2000 (Register 2000, No. 15).

§38.4. The "Notice of Late QME Report" Form.

Note: Authority cited: Sections 139 and 139.2, Labor Code. Reference: Sections 139.2, 4060, 4061, 4062 and 4062.5, Labor Code.

History: 1. New section filed 8-1-94; operative 8-31-94 (Register 94, No. 31).

2. Repealer filed 4-14-2000; operative 5-14-2000 (Register 2000, No. 15).

§39. [See Note Following §159 Regarding Elimination of the IMC] Records, Destruction of.

The Medical Director may destroy any forms included in these regulations five years after the date of receipt, provided that the completed "Application for Appointment as Qualified Medical Evaluator" form shall be preserved for each QME during the period(s) of his or her appointment as a QME. The "Request for Qualified Medical Evaluator" forms may be destroyed by the Medical Director two years after the date of receipt.

Note: Authority cited: Sections 139 and 139.2, Labor Code. Reference: Sections 139.2, 4060, 4061 and 4062, Labor Code; and Section 14755, Government Code.

History: 1. New section filed 8-1-94; operative 8-31-94 (Register 94, No. 31).

Ref.: Herlick Handbook § 1.8.

§39.5. [See Note Following §159 Regarding Elimination of the IMC] Records, Retention by QMEs.

(a) All QMEs shall retain all comprehensive medical-legal reports completed by the QME for a period of five years from the date of the employee's evaluation. Upon written request, a QME is required to return original radiological and imaging studies and or original medical records.

(b) An evaluator shall submit all comprehensive medical/legal reports performed as a QME under this article to the Medical Director upon request for a review by the Medical Director. Failure to submit evaluations upon request by the Medical Director may constitute grounds for disciplinary action pursuant to Section 60.

Note: Authority cited: Sections 139 and 139.2, Labor Code. Reference: Sections 139.2, 4060, 4061 and 4062, Labor Code; and Section 14755, Government Code.

History: 1. New section filed 8-23-96; operative 9-22-96 (Register 96, No. 34).

2. Amendment filed 4-14-2000; operative 5-14-2000 (Register 2000, No. 15).

Ref.: Herlick Handbook § 1.8.

ARTICLE 4
Evaluation Procedures

§40. [See Note Following §159 Regarding Elimination of the IMC] Disclosure Requirements: Unrepresented Workers.

(a) A QME shall advise an unrepresented injured worker prior to or at the time of the actual evaluation of the following:

(1) That he or she is entitled to ask the QME and the QME shall promptly answer questions about any matter concerning the evaluation process in which the QME and the injured worker are involved;

(2) That subject to Section 41(e), the injured worker may discontinue the evaluation based on good cause. Good cause includes discriminatory conduct by the evaluator towards the worker based on race, sex, national origin, religion, or sexual preference, and instances where the evaluator requests the worker to submit to an unnecessary exam or procedure.

(b) When required as a condition of probation by the Council or his/her licensing authority, the QME shall disclose his/her probationary status. The QME shall be entitled to explain any circumstances surrounding the probation. If at that time, the injured worker declines to proceed with the evaluation, such termination shall be considered by the Council to have occurred for good cause.

(c) If the injured worker declines to ask any questions relating to the evaluation procedure as set forth in Section 40(a), and does not otherwise object on the grounds of good cause to the exam proceedings under Section 41(a) during the exam itself, the injured worker shall have no right to object to the QME comprehensive medical-legal evaluation based on a violation of this section.

Note: Authority cited: Sections 139.2 and 5307.3, Labor Code. Reference: Sections 139, 139.2, 4060, 4061 and 4062, Labor Code.

History: 1. New article 4 heading and section filed 4-11-95; operative 5-11-95 (Register 95, No. 15).

Ref.: Herlick Handbook § 1.8.

§41. [See Note Following §159 Regarding Elimination of the IMC] Ethical Requirements.

(a) All QMEs, regardless of whether the injured worker is represented by an attorney, shall:

(1) Maintain a clean, professional medical office (as defined in Section 1(m)) at all times including functioning evaluating medical instruments and equipment appropriate to conducting the evaluation within the physician's scope of practice.

(2) Schedule all appointments for comprehensive medical-legal evaluations without regard to whether a worker is unrepresented or represented by an attorney. A QME shall not refuse to schedule an appointment with an injured worker solely because the worker is not represented by an attorney or because a promise to reimburse or reimbursement is not made prior to the evaluation.

(3) Not request the employee to submit to an unnecessary exam or procedure.

(b) QMEs selected by an unrepresented injured worker from a three-member panel provided by the Council shall not engage in ex parte communication in violation of Labor Code Section 4062.2.

(c) All QMEs, regardless of whether the injured worker is represented by an attorney, shall with respect to his or her comprehensive medical-legal evaluation:

(1) Refuse any compensation from any source contingent upon writing an opinion that in any way could be construed as unfavorable to a party to the case.

(2) Review all available relevant medical and non-medical records and/or facts necessary for an accurate and objective assessment of the injured workers' case before generating a written report.

(3) Render expert opinions or conclusions without regard to an injured workers' race, sex, national origin, religion or sexual preference.

(4) Render expert opinions or conclusions only on issues with regard to which the QME has adequate qualifications, education, and training. All conclusions shall be based on the facts and on the QME's training and specialty-based knowledge and shall be without bias either for or against the injured worker or the employer.

(5) Present a report that addresses all relevant issues, is ratable by the DEU, if applicable, and complies with all relevant guidelines of the Industrial Medical Council.

(d) All aspects of all physical and/or psychological comprehensive medical-legal evaluations, including history taking, shall be directly related to medical issues as presented by any party or addressed in the reports of treating physician(s).

(e) No physician certified by the IMC as a QME, or his or her agent, shall contact a QME for the purpose of influencing that QME's opinions or conclusions in any QME evaluation.

(f) No QME shall schedule appointments to the extent that any injured worker will be required to wait for more than one hour at a QME's office prior to being seen for the previously agreed upon appointment time for an evaluation. If the injured worker is unrepresented and is not seen by the QME within one hour, he or she may terminate the exam and request a replacement evaluator from the Council. No party shall be liable for the terminated exam. The QME may explain any reasons for the delay to the injured worker and, provided both parties agree, the evaluation may proceed or be rescheduled at a later date. If the evaluation is rescheduled, the QME shall provide notice to the claims administrator or, if none, the employer within 5 working days after rescheduling the appointment.

(g) If the injured worker terminates the examination process based on an alleged violation of either Section 40 or Section 41(a) and the Appeals Board later determines that good cause did not exist for the termination, the cost of the evaluation shall be deducted from the injured worker's award. A violation of Section 40 or of any part of section 41(a) shall constitute good cause for purposes of an Appeals Board determination. No party shall be liable for any cost for medical reports or medical services delivered as a result of an exam terminated for good cause.

(h) Nothing in this section shall require a QME to undertake or continue a comprehensive medical-legal evaluation where the injured worker or his/her representative uses abusive language towards the QME or the QME's staff or deliberately attempts to disrupt the operation of the QME's office in any way. The QME shall state under penalty of perjury, the facts supporting the termination of the evaluation process. Upon request, the Medical Director shall investigate the facts and make a final determination of the issue(s).

(i) Nothing in this section shall require a QME to undertake or continue a comprehensive medical-legal evaluation where the injured worker is intoxicated or under the influence of any medication which impairs the injured worker's ability to participate in the evaluation process. The QME shall state under penalty of perjury, the facts supporting the termination of the evaluation process. Upon request, the Medical Director shall investigate the facts and make a final determination of the issue(s).

Note: Authority cited: Sections 139.2, 5307.3 and 5307.6, Labor Code. Reference: Sections 139, 139.2, 4060, 4061, 4062 and 4062.2, Labor Code.

History: 1. New section filed 4-11-95; operative 5-11-95 (Register 95, No. 15).

2. New subsection (b), subsection relettering, and amendment of redesignated subsection (b)(1) filed 7-18-95 as an emergency; operative 7-18-95 (Register 95, No. 29). A Certificate of Compliance must be transmitted to OAL by 11-15-95 or emergency language will be repealed by operation of law on the following day.

3. Certificate of Compliance as to 7-18-95 order including amendment of subsection (b), deletion of subsection (b)(1) designator, and amendment of Note transmitted to OAL 11-14-95 and filed 12-21-95 (Register 95, No. 51).

4. Amendment filed 4-14-2000; operative 5-14-2000 (Register 2000, No. 15).

Ref.: Herlick Handbook § 1.8.

§42. Disciplinary Proceedings.

Note: Authority cited: Sections 139.2 and 5307.3, Labor Code; Section 11370 et seq., Government Code; and Section 11500 et seq., Government Code. Reference: Sections 139, 139.2, 4060, 4061 and 4062, Labor Code.

History: 1. New section filed 4-11-95; operative 5-11-95 (Register 95, No. 15).

2. Repealer filed 4-14-2000; operative 5-14-2000 (Register 2000, No. 15).

§43. [See Note Following §159 Regarding Elimination of the IMC] Method of Measurement of Psychiatric Disability.

The Method of measuring the psychiatric elements of a disability shall be as set forth below in the "Psychiatric Protocols" as adopted by the Industrial Medical Council on July 16, 1992, and amended on March 18 and October 25, 1993.

[Psychiatric Protocols Not Reproduced]

Editor's Note: Copies are available through the local I&A office. *See* Reference Directory, p. xiii, for phone numbers.

Note: Authority cited: Section 139.2(j)(4), Labor Code. Reference: Sections 139.2(j)(4) and 4628, Labor Code.

History: 1. New section filed 12-7-93; operative 1-6-94 (Register 93, No. 50).

2. Change without regulatory effect amending section filed 3-15-94 pursuant to title 1, section 100, California Code of Regulations (Register 94, No. 11).

3. Change without regulatory effect amending section filed 9-7-95 pursuant to section 100, title 1, California Code of Regulations (Register 95, No. 36).

4. Change without regulatory effect amending section filed 7-12-2001 pursuant to section 100, title 1, California Code of Regulations (Register 2001, No. 28). Pursuant to this filing, material adopted pursuant to the Administrative Procedure Act that had previously been incorporated by reference in the California Code of Regulations was instead printed in full in the California Code of Regulations.

Ref.: Herlick Handbook §§ 1.8, 6.14, 14.23.

§44. [See Note Following §159 Regarding Elimination of the IMC] Method of Evaluation of Pulmonary Disability.

The method of measuring the pulmonary elements of disability shall be as set forth below in the "Guidelines for Evaluation of Pulmonary Disability" as adopted by the Industrial Medical Council on December 4, 1997.

[Guidelines for Evaluation of Pulmonary Disability Not Reproduced]

Editor's Note: Copies are available through the local I&A office. *See* Reference Directory, p. xiii, for phone numbers.

Note: Authority cited: Section 139.2(j)(2), Labor Code. Reference: Sections 139.2(j)(2), 4060, 4061 and 4062, Labor Code.

History: 1. New section filed 5-23-94; operative 6-22-94 (Register 94, No. 21).

2. Amendment of section and Note filed 6-19-98; operative 7-19-98 (Register 98, No. 25).

3. Change without regulatory effect amending section filed 7-12-2001 pursuant to section 100, title 1, California Code of Regulations (Register 2001, No. 28). Pursuant to this filing, material adopted pursuant to the Administrative Procedure Act that had previously been incorporated by reference in the California Code of Regulations was instead printed in full in the California Code of Regulations.

Ref.: Herlick Handbook §§ 1.8, 14.23.

§45. [See Note Following §159 Regarding Elimination of the IMC] Method of Evaluation of Cardiac Disability.

The method of measuring the cardiac elements of disability shall be set forth below in the "Guidelines for Evaluation of Cardiac Disability" as adopted by the Industrial Medical Council on December 4, 1997.

[Guidelines for Evaluation of Cardiac Disability Not Reproduced]

Editor's Note: Copies are available through the local I&A office. *See* Reference Directory, p. xiii, for phone numbers.

Note: Authority cited: Section 139.2(j)(2), Labor Code. Reference: Sections 139.2(j)(2), 4060, 4061 and 4062, Labor Code.

History: 1. New section filed 5-23-94; operative 6-22-94 (Register 94, No. 21).

2. Amendment of section and Note filed 6-19-98; operative 7-19-98 (Register 98, No. 25).

3. Change without regulatory effect amending section filed 7-12-2001 pursuant to section 100, title 1, California Code of Regulations (Register 2001, No. 28). Pursuant to this filing, material adopted pursuant to the Administrative Procedure Act that had previously been incorporated by reference in the California Code of Regulations was instead printed in full in the California Code of Regulations.

Ref.: Herlick Handbook §§ 1.8, 14.23.

§46. [See Note Following §159 Regarding Elimination of the IMC] Method of Evaluation of Neuromusculoskeletal Disability.

The method of measuring the neuromusculoskeletal elements of disability shall be as set forth below in the "Guidelines for Evaluation of Neuromusculoskeletal Disability" as adopted by the Industrial Medical Council on October 20, 1994.

[Guidelines for Evaluation of Neuromusculoskeletal Disability Not Reproduced]

Editor's Note: Copies are available through the local I&A office. *See* Reference Directory, p. xiii, for phone numbers.

Note: Authority cited: Section 139.2(j)(2), Labor Code. Reference: Sections 139, 139.2, 4060, 4061 and 4062, Labor Code.

History: 1. New section filed 4-18-96; operative 4-18-96 pursuant to Government Code section 11343.4(d) (Register 96, No. 16).

2. Change without regulatory effect amending "Guidelines for Evaluation of Neuromusculoskeletal Disability, 2nd Ed." (incorporated by reference) filed 6-6-96 pursuant to section 100, title 1, California Code of Regulations (Register 96, No. 23).

3. Change without regulatory effect amending Note filed 8-1-96 pursuant to section 100, title 1, California Code of Regulations (Register 96, No. 31).

4. Amendment of section and Note filed 4-14-2000; operative 5-14-2000 (Register 2000, No. 15).

5. Change without regulatory effect amending section filed 7-12-2001 pursuant to section 100, title 1, California Code of Regulations (Register 2001, No. 28). Pursuant to this filing, material adopted pursuant to the Administrative Procedure Act that had previously been incorporated by reference in the California Code of Regulations was instead printed in full in the California Code of Regulations.

Ref.: Herlick Handbook §§ 1.8, 14.23.

§46.1. [See Note Following §159 Regarding Elimination of the IMC] Guidelines for the Evaluation of Foot and Ankle Disability.

[Guidelines for Evaluation of Foot and Ankle Disability Not Reproduced]

Appendix A to Section 46.1
[Muscle Grading Chart]

Appendix B to Section 46.1
[Description of Subjective Disability]

Appendix C to Section 46.1
[Description of Activities]

Editor's Note: Copies are available through the local I&A office. *See* Reference Directory, p. xiii, for phone numbers.

Note: Authority cited: Sections 139, 139.2, 4060, 4061 and 4062, Labor Code. Reference: Sections 139, 139.2, 4060, 4061, 4061.5 and 4062, Labor Code.

History: 1. New section and appendices A-C filed 1-8-2003; operative 2-7-2003 (Register 2003, No. 2).

§47. [See Note Following §159 Regarding Elimination of the IMC] Method of Evaluation of Immunologic Disability.

The method of measuring immunologic elements of disability shall be as set forth below in the "Guidelines for Immunologic Testing" as adopted by the Industrial Medical Council on March 17, 1994.

[Guidelines for Immunologic Testing Not Reproduced]

Editor's Note: Copies are available through the local I&A office. *See* Reference Directory, p. xiii, for phone numbers.

Note: Authority cited: Section 139.2(j)(2), Labor Code. Reference: Sections 139.2(j)(2), 4060, 4061 and 4062, Labor Code.

History: 1. New section filed 5-23-94; operative 6-22-94 (Register 94, No. 21).

2. Amendment of Note filed 4-14-2000; operative 5-14-2000 (Register 2000, No. 15).

3. Change without regulatory effect amending section filed 7-12-2001 pursuant to section 100, title 1, California Code of Regulations (Register 2001, No. 28). Pursuant to this filing, material adopted pursuant to the Administrative Procedure Act that had previously been incorporated by reference in the California Code of Regulations was instead printed in full in the California Code of Regulations.

Ref.: Herlick Handbook §§ 1.8, 14.23.

§48. Repealed.

Note: Authority cited: Sections 139.2(j)(2) and (3) and 5307.3, Labor Code. Reference: Sections 139.2(j)(2) and (3), 4060, 4061 and 4062, Labor Code.

History: 1. New section filed 5-23-94; operative 6-22-94 (Register 94, No. 21).

2. Repealer filed 4-11-95; operative 5-11-95 (Register 95, No. 15).

ARTICLE 4.5
Minimum Time Guidelines

§49. [See Note Following §159 Regarding Elimination of the IMC] Definitions.

The following definitions apply to this Article:

(a) Cardiovascular evaluation. "Cardiovascular evaluation" means the determination of disability due to pathological changes of the heart and/or the central circulatory system.

(b) Face to Face time. "Face to face time" means only that time the evaluator is present with an injured worker. This includes the time in which the evaluator performs such tasks as taking a history, performing a physical examination or discussing the worker's medical condition with the worker. Face to face time excludes time spent on research, records review and report writing. Any time spent with clinical or clerical staff in performing diagnostic or laboratory tests (such as blood tests or x-rays) or time spent by the injured worker in a waiting room or other area outside the evaluation room is not included in face to face time.

(c) Medical evaluation. "Medical evaluation" means a comprehensive medical-legal evaluation as defined under section 9793 of Article 5.6, Subchapter 1, Chapter 4.5 of this Title.

(d) Neuromusculoskeletal evaluation. "Neuromusculoskeletal evaluation" means the determination of disability due to injury to the central nervous systems, the spine and extremities, and the various muscle groups of the body.

(e) Psychiatric evaluation. "Psychiatric evaluation" means the determination, by either a psychiatrist or psychologist following the IMC guidelines on psychiatric protocols, of disability due to psychopathology.

(f) Pulmonary evaluation. "Pulmonary evaluation" means the determination of disability due to pathological changes of the lungs and/or other components of the respiratory system.

(g) QME. "QME" means Qualified Medical Evaluator appointed by the Council pursuant to Labor Code section 139.2.

(h) Uncomplicated evaluation. "Uncomplicated evaluation" means a face to face evaluation in which all of the following are recorded in the medical report: Minimal or no review of records, minimal or no diagnostic studies or laboratory testing, minimal or no research, and minimal or no medical history taking.

Note: Authority cited: Section 139, Labor Code. Reference: Sections 139, 139.2 and 4628, Labor Code.

History: 1. Change without regulatory effect relocating article 4.5 heading and renumbering former section 149 to new section 49 filed 8-31-94 pursuant to section 100, title 1, California Code of Regulations (Register 94, No. 35).

2. Change without regulatory effect amending article

heading filed 9-28-94 pursuant to section 100, title 1, California Code of Regulations (Register 94, No. 39).

3. Amendment of subsection (b) filed 4-14-2000; operative 5-14-2000 (Register 2000, No. 15).

Ref.: Herlick Handbook § 1.8.

§49.2. [See Note Following §159 Regarding Elimination of the IMC] Neuromusculoskeletal Evaluation.

A medical evaluation concerning a claim for neuromusculoskeletal injury (whether specific or cumulative in nature) shall not be completed by a QME in fewer than 20 minutes of face to face time. Twenty minutes is the minimum allowable face to face time for an uncomplicated evaluation. The evaluator shall state in the evaluation report that he or she has complied with these guidelines and explain in detail any variance.

Note: Authority cited: Sections 139 and 139.2(j), Labor Code. Reference: Sections 139, 139.2 and 4628, Labor Code.

History: 1. Change without regulatory effect renumbering former section 149.2 to new section 49.2 filed 8-31-94 pursuant to section 100, title 1, California Code of Regulations (Register 94, No. 35).

Ref.: Herlick Handbook § 1.8.

§49.4. [See Note Following §159 Regarding Elimination of the IMC] Cardiovascular Evaluation.

A medical evaluation concerning a claim for cardiovascular injury (whether specific or cumulative in nature) shall not be completed by a QME in fewer than 30 minutes of face to face time. Thirty minutes is the minimum allowable face to face time for an uncomplicated evaluation. The evaluator shall state in the evaluation report that he or she has complied with these guidelines and explain in detail any variance.

Note: Authority cited: Sections 139 and 139.2(j), Labor Code. Reference: Sections 139, 139.2 and 4628, Labor Code.

History: 1. Change without regulatory effect renumbering former section 149.4 to new section 49.4 filed 8-31-94 pursuant to section 100, title 1, California Code of Regulations (Register 94, No. 35).

Ref.: Herlick Handbook § 1.8.

§49.6. [See Note Following §159 Regarding Elimination of the IMC] Pulmonary Evaluation.

A medical evaluation concerning a claim for pulmonary injury (whether specific or cumulative in nature) shall not be completed by a QME in fewer than 30 minutes of face to face time. Thirty minutes is the minimum allowable face to face time for an uncomplicated evaluation. The evaluator shall state in the evaluation report that he or she has complied with these guidelines and explain in detail any variance.

Note: Authority cited: Sections 139 and 139.2(j), Labor Code. Reference: Sections 139, 139.2 and 4628, Labor Code.

History: 1. Change without regulatory effect renumbering former section 149.6 to new section 49.6 filed 8-31-94 pursuant to section 100, title 1, California Code of Regulations (Register 94, No. 35).

Ref.: Herlick Handbook § 1.8.

§49.8. [See Note Following §159 Regarding Elimination of the IMC] Psychiatric Evaluation.

A medical evaluation concerning a claim for psychiatric injury (whether specific or cumulative in nature) shall not be completed by a QME in less than one hour of face to face time. One hour is considered the minimum allowable face to face time for an uncomplicated evaluation. The evaluator shall state in the evaluation report that he or she has complied with these guidelines and explain in detail any variance.

Note: Authority cited: Sections 139 and 139.2(j), Labor Code. Reference: Sections 139, 139.2 and 4628, Labor Code.

History: 1. Change without regulatory effect renumbering former section 149.8 to new section 49.8 filed 8-31-94 pursuant to section 100, title 1, California Code of Regulations (Register 94, No. 35).

Ref.: Herlick Handbook § 1.8.

§49.9. [See Note Following §159 Regarding Elimination of the IMC] Other Evaluation.

A medical evaluation concerning a claim for any injury (whether specific or cumulative in nature) not specifically included in this article shall not be completed by a QME in fewer than 30 minutes of face to face time. Thirty minutes is the minimum allowable face to face time for an uncomplicated evaluation. The evaluator shall state in the evaluation report that he or she has complied with these guidelines and explain in detail any variance.

Note: Authority cited: Sections 139 and 139.2(j), Labor Code. Reference: Sections 139, 139.2 and 4628, Labor Code.

History: 1. Change without regulatory effect renumbering former section 149.9 to new section 49.9 filed 8-31-94 pursuant to section 100, title 1, California Code of Regulations (Register 94, No. 35).

Ref.: Herlick Handbook § 1.8.

ARTICLE 5
QME Reappointment

§50. [See Note Following §159 Regarding Elimination of the IMC] Reappointment: Requirements and Application Form.

(a) In addition to the eligibility requirements set forth in section 11, a physician may seek reappointment on the basis that he or she was an active QME on June 30, 2000. For all physicians, applications for reappointment shall include a Reappointment Application Form in Section 10.1A, a statement of citizenship form 101 if not previously submitted, and the appropriate fee under Section 17 and shall be filed at the Council's headquarters office.

(b) Any Reappointment Application Form may be rejected if it is incompletely filled out or does not contain the required supporting documentation listed in Section 11. Upon its approval of the Reappointment Application Form, the Council shall verify that the QME has complied with all requirements under this Article.

(c) When a QME applies for reappointment, he or she shall submit a statement signed under penalty of perjury (1) that he or she has completed the education requirement and (2) that lists the dates, locations, and titles of continuing education programs and the names of the providers of those programs which he or she has taken to meet the requirement of Labor Code Section 139.2(d)(3), as well as the number of hours of attendance at each program. The Council may randomly audit QMEs for documentation of program attendance, which supports compliance with this requirement.

Note: Authority cited: Sections 139, 139.2, 4060, 4061 and 4062, Labor Code. Reference: Sections 139, 139.2, 4060, 4061, 4061.5 and 4062, Labor Code.

History: 1. New article 5 and repealer and new section filed 8-1-94; operative 8-31-94 (Register 94, No. 31). For prior history, see Register 91, No. 26.

2. Change without regulatory effect amending first paragraph and subsection (i) filed 4-19-95 pursuant to section 100, title 1, California Code of Regulations (Register 95, No. 16).

3. Amendment of article 5 heading and renumbering of former section 50 to new section 53 and new section filed 8-23-96; operative 9-22-96 (Register 96, No. 34).

4. Amendment filed 4-14-2000; operative 5-14-2000 (Register 2000, No. 15).

5. Amendment of section heading and section and new Note filed 9-6-2001; operative 10-6-2001 (Register 2001, No. 36).

Ref.: Herlick Handbook § 1.8.

§50.1. Reappointment: Failure to Comply with Time Frames.

Note: Authority cited: Section 139.2, Labor Code. Reference: Section 139.2(d)(1), Labor Code.

History: 1. New section filed 8-1-94; operative 8-31-94 (Register 94, No. 31).

2. Change without regulatory effect amending section filed 12-2-96 pursuant to section 100, title 1, California Code of Regulations (Register 96, No. 49).

3. Renumbering of former section 50.1 to section 51 filed 4-14-2000; operative 5-14-2000 (Register 2000, No. 15).

§50.2. Reappointment: Unavailability Notification.

Note: Authority cited: Section 139.2, Labor Code. Reference: Sections 139.2(d) and 139.2(j)(6), Labor Code.

History: 1. New section filed 8-1-94; operative 8-31-94 (Register 94, No. 31).

2. Change without regulatory effect amending section filed 12-2-96 pursuant to section 100, title 1, California Code of Regulations (Register 96, No. 49).

3. Renumbering of former section 50.2 to section 52 filed 4-14-2000; operative 5-14-2000 (Register 2000, No. 15).

§50.3. Renumbered.

Note: Authority cited: Section 139.2, Labor Code. Reference: Sections 139.2(d) and 139.2(j)(6), Labor Code.

History: 1. New section filed 8-1-94; operative 8-31-94 (Register 94, No. 31).

2. Renumbering of former section 50.3 to new section 52 filed 8-23-96; operative 9-22-96 (Register 96, No. 34).

Ref.: Herlick Handbook § 1.8.

§51. [See Note Following §159 Regarding Elimination of the IMC] Reappointment: Failure to Comply with Time Frames.

All QMEs shall comply with the time frames in Sections 34 and 38 as a condition for reappointment. The Council, after hearing pursuant to Section 61, may deny reappointment to any QME who has failed to comply with the evaluation time frames in Section 34 and 38 on at least three occasions during the calendar year.

Note: Authority cited: Section 139.2, Labor Code. Reference: Sections 139.2(d)(1), Labor Code.

History: 1. Repealer and new section filed 8-1-94; operative 8-31-94 (Register 94, No. 31). For prior history, see Register 91, No. 26.

2. Renumbering of former section 51 to new section 60 and new section filed 8-23-96; operative 9-22-96 (Register 96, No. 34).

3. Renumbering of former section 51 to section 53 and renumbering of former section 50.1 to section 51 filed 4-14-2000; operative 5-14-2000 (Register 2000, No. 15).

Ref.: Herlick Handbook § 1.8.

§52. [See Note Following §159 Regarding Elimination of the IMC] Reappointment: Unavailability Notification.

All QMEs shall comply with the unavailability notification requirements in Section 33 as a condition for reappointment. The Council, after hearing pursuant to Section 61, may deny reappointment of any QME who has filed notification for unavailability under Section 33 for more than 90 calendar days during the calendar year, or who has on any single occasion refused without good cause to perform a medical-legal evaluation for an unrepresented employee.

Note: Authority cited: Section 139.2, Labor Code. Reference: Sections 139.2(d) and 139.2(j)(6), Labor Code.

History: 1. Repealer and new section filed 8-1-94; operative 8-31-94 (Register 94, No. 31). For prior history, see Register 91, No. 26.

2. Renumbering of former section 52 to new section 61, renumbering of former section 50.3 to new section 52 and amendment of section filed 8-23-96; operative 9-22-96 (Register 96, No. 34).

3. Renumbering of former section 52 to section 54 and renumbering of former section 50.2 to section 52 filed 4-14-2000; operative 5-14-2000 (Register 2000, No. 15).

Ref.: Herlick Handbook § 1.8.

§53. [See Note Following §159 Regarding Elimination of the IMC] Reappointment: Failure of Board Certification Examination.

For Medical Doctors or Doctors of Osteopathy, in order to be reappointed, a QME shall submit a declaration under penalty of perjury that, if not board certified at the time for reappointment, he or she has not failed a board certification exam after 1985. This section shall not apply to any physician who meets the requirement of Labor Code § 139.2(b)(3)(C), (D) or (G).

History: 1. Repealer and new section filed 8-1-94; operative 8-31-94 (Register 94, No. 31). For prior history, see Register 91, No. 26.

2. Renumbering of former section 53 to new section 62, renumbering of former section 50 to new section 53 and amendment of section filed 8-23-96; operative 9-22-96 (Register 96, No. 34).

3. Amendment filed 3-15-99; operative 4-14-99 (Register 99, No. 12).

4. Renumbering of former section 53 to section 55 and renumbering of former section 51 to section 53 filed 4-14-2000; operative 5-14-2000 (Register 2000, No. 15).

Ref.: See Labor Code §§4060, 4061; Herlick Handbook § 1.8.

§53.1. QME Continuing Education Response Form.

Note: Authority cited: Section 139.2, Labor Code. Reference: Section 139.2, Labor Code.

History: 1. New section filed 3-15-99; operative 4-14-99 (Register 99, No. 12).

2. Repealer filed 4-14-2000; operative 5-14-2000 (Register 2000, No. 15).

§54. [See Note Following §159 Regarding Elimination of the IMC] Reappointment: Evaluations Rejected by Appeals Board.

The Council, after hearing pursuant to Section 61, may deny reappointment to any QME who has had more than five evaluations rejected by a Workers' Compensation Judge or the Appeals Board originally submitted at a contested hearing. The rejection shall be based on the failure of the QME's evaluation to prove or disprove a contested issue or failure to comply with guidelines promulgated by the Council pursuant to Labor Code Section 139.2(j)(2), (3), (4) or (5). A specific finding must become final and the time for appeal must have expired before any rejected evaluation shall be counted as one of the five rejections.

Note: Authority cited: Section 139.2, Labor Code. Reference: Sections 139.2(d) and 139.2(j)(6), Labor Code.

History: 1. New section filed 5-9-91; operative 5-9-91 (Register 91, No. 26). New section is exempt from review by OAL pursuant to Government Code section 11351(a).

2. Repealer filed 8-1-94; operative 8-31-94 (Register 94, No. 31).

3. Renumbering of former section 52 to section 54 filed 4-14-2000; operative 5-14-2000 (Register 2000, No. 15).

§55. [See Note Following §159 Regarding Elimination of the IMC] Reappointment: Continuing Education Programs.

A QME shall complete within the previous 24 months of his or her term of appointment 12 hours of continuing education in disability evaluation or workers' compensation related medical dispute evaluation given by a provider accredited by the Council.

(a) There are two types of continuing education programs:

(1) On-site programs, in which the instructor and QME are in the same location; and

(2) Distance learning programs.

(A) Providers of distance learning programs shall give either a pre-or post-course self-examination based on the program material. The provider shall grade the QME's test. Credit for the course can be given only for a passing rate of no lower than 70 percent correct responses. The Council may audit physicians' examinations and scores.

(B) Credit for distance learning courses shall be granted for the actual time spent viewing, listening to or participating in the program and for the reasonable and necessary time to take the examinations for up to six hours per program. Credit for the same distance learning program may be taken only once.

(C) All distance learning materials shall bear a date of release and shall be updated every three years. The provider shall notify the Council in writing of the revision.

(b) In addition to granting credit for attending a course or program which it gives, the Council may grant credit for:

(1) Participating in a panel on the development or review of the QME competency examination. A physician may receive one hour credit for each hour of participation on a panel. The QME shall obtain documentation of participation from the test administrator for submission to the Council.

(2) Instructing in a program given for QME credit by a provider accredited by the Council. The instructor may receive two hours of credit for each hour of instruction in an accredited provider's program or one hour of credit for each hour of participation on a panel. Credit for the same presentation may be taken only once during each calendar year. The QME shall submit documentation of participation from the program provider to the Council.

(3) Attending a program which is accepted by the QME's licensing board for renewal of his or her professional license, provided the subject matter is directly related to California impairment evaluation or workers' compensation medical dispute evaluation.

To request credit for this type of course, the QME must submit:

(A) proof of attendance;

(B) written material which describes the program content and program faculty; and

(C) documentation that the program is for continuing education credit by the physician's licensing board.

(4) Passing the QME competency examination. A QME may be granted six hours of continuing education credit for passing this examination for the purpose of receiving an initial appointment as a QME.

(c) To apply to the Council for accreditation, a provider shall submit to the Council, at least 60 calendar days before any public advertisement of the applicant's program or course is made:

(1) a completed form 118, in section 118 of these regulations.

(2) A curriculum vitae for each proposed instructor or author (for paper-based programs). A proposed instructor or author shall have education and/or training and recent work experience relevant to the subject of his/her presentation.

(3) The proposed promotional material for the program.

(d) The Council shall accredit an applicant who meets the definition of a provider in Section 1(r); submits a completed, signed and dated application which demonstrates past experience in providing continuing education programs; and proposes a program which meets the requirements of section 55(c) or a course which meets the requirements of section 11.5(a) and (i). Proposed content for continuing education program credit must relate directly to disability evaluation or California workers' compensation-related medical dispute evaluation. No credit shall be recognized by the IMC for material solely discussing the business aspects of workers' compensation medical practice such as billing, coding and marketing.

(e) The Council shall notify the applicant within 30 calendar days following the next scheduled council meeting after receipt of the application containing all the information listed in Section 55(c) whether that provider has been accredited for a two year period. Incomplete applications will be returned to the applicant.

(f) A provider that has been accredited by the Council will be given a number which must be displayed on any public advertisements of QME continuing education programs for that provider with the statement "Accredited by the California Industrial Medical Council for Qualified Medical Evaluator continuing education. Physicians may report up to _____ hours of credit for QME reappointment."

(g) On or before the date the program is first presented or distributed, the provider shall submit the program syllabus (all program handouts) to the Council. Each distance learning program shall also submit one copy of the examinations and one copy of the audio/video tapes, computer program or each issue of the journal or newsletter for which credit is to be granted.

(h) A provider may offer different QME continuing education programs during the two-year accreditation period provided the subject matter is in disability evaluation or workers' compensation related medical dispute resolution. The provider shall send the Council the program outlined and faculty for each new program at least 45 days prior to the date of presentation of the new program. The Council may require submission of program syllabi. The Council may require changes in the program based on its review of the program outline, program syllabi, promotional material or faculty if the IMC finds that any aspect of the program is not in compliance with these regulations.

(i) Promotional materials for a program must state the provider's educational objectives; the professional qualifications of program faculty (at least all relevant professional degrees); the content of program activities; the maximum number of credit hours to be granted; and the intended audience.

(j) Joint sponsorship of education programs (as between an accredited and an unaccredited provider) must be approved by the Council prior to presentation of the program.

(k) Accredited providers that cease to offer education programs shall notify the Council in writing.

(*l*) Instructors shall not recruit members or promote commercial products or services immediately before, during or after a course. Providers or vendors may display/sell educational materials related to workers' compensation or applications for membership in an area adjoining a course. A course provider or faculty member shall disclose on IMC form 119, located in section 119, any significant financial interest in or affiliation with any commercial product or service discussed in a course and that interest or affiliation must be disclosed to all attendees. A provider shall file every form 119 in its possession or in its control with the Council.

(m) The provider shall issue a certificate of completion to each QME who successfully completes a continuing education program. The certificate must list the provider; provider number; date(s); location and title of the continuing education program; and the number of hours in attendance for which credit is to be granted. Credit shall be granted only for the actual time of attendance at or participation in a program. Each accredited provider may in its sole discretion limit the amount of credit hours that a course will be granted to less than the amount of time actually spent in attendance in the course.

(n) To apply for re-accreditation, a provider must submit a completed IMC Form 118. The provider may complete section 2 of the form using a new program or course or one which was given by the provider during the recent accreditation period. The Council shall give the provider 90 days' notice of the need to seek re-accreditation.

(o) The provider shall maintain attendance records for each continuing education program for a period of no less than three years after the program is given. A physician attending the program must be identified by signature. The provider must submit a copy of the signature list to the Council within 60 days of completion of the program.

(p) The provider is required to give the IMC's Evaluation Form 117 to program attendees and request they submit the form to the IMC. This information shall not be used in lieu of a certification of completion given by the provider, as specified pursuant to section (m).

Destruction by a provider or its employee of a QME's Evaluation Form or failure by such provider or its employee to distribute Form 117 as part of its program shall constitute grounds for revocation of a provider's accredited status. The Council shall tabulate the responses and return a summary to the provider within 90 days of completion of the program.

(q) The Council may audit a provider's program(s) at the request of the medical director to determine if the provider meets the criteria for accreditation. The Council may audit programs randomly, when a complaint is received, or on the basis of responses on IMC Form 117. An auditor shall not receive QME credit for an audited program. The Council shall make written results of the audit available to the provider no more than 30 days after the audit is completed.

(r) The Council may withdraw accreditation of a provider or deny such a provider's application for accreditation on the following grounds (in addition to failure to meet the relevant requirements of subsection 11.5(a) or 55(c)):

(1) Conviction of a felony or any offense substantially related to the activities of the provider.

(2) Any material misrepresentation of fact made by the provider.

(3) Failure to comply with Council regulations.

(4) False or misleading advertising.

(5) Failure to comply with Council recommendations following an audit.

(6) Failure to distribute Council Form 117 cards to program attendees.

Note: Authority cited: Sections 139 and 139.2, Labor Code. Reference: Sections 139.2, 4060, 4061 and 4062, Labor Code.

History: 1. New section filed 5-9-91; operative 5-9-91 (Register 91, No. 26). New section is exempt from review by OAL pursuant to Government Code section 11351(a).

2. Repealer filed 8-1-94; operative 8-31-94 (Register 94, No. 31).

3. Renumbering of former section 53 to section 55 filed 4-14-2000; operative 5-14-2000 (Register 2000, No. 15).

4. Amendment of section heading and section filed 9-6-2001; operative 10-6-2001 (Register 2001, No. 36).

§56. [See Note Following §159 Regarding Elimination of the IMC] Reappointment: Failure to Comply with WCAB Order or Ruling.

The Council, after hearing pursuant to Section 61, may deny reappointment to any QME who has been found in violation of any order or ruling by a Workers' Compensation Judge or the Appeals Board.

Note: Authority cited: Section 139.2, Labor Code. Reference: Sections 139.2(d) and 139.2(j)(6), Labor Code.

History: 1. New section filed 4-14-2000; operative 5-14-2000 (Register 2000, No. 15). For prior history see Register 94, No. 31.

§57. [See Note Following §159 Regarding Elimination of the IMC] Reappointment: Professional Standard—Violation of Business and Professions Code Section 730.

The Council, after hearing pursuant to Section 61, may deny reappointment to any QME who has performed a QME Evaluation without QME Certification.

Note: Authority cited: Section 139.2, Labor Code; and Section 730, Business and Professions Code. Reference: Sections 139.2(d) and 139.2(j)(6), Labor Code; and Section 730, Business and Professions Code.

History: 1. New section filed 4-14-2000; operative 5-14-2000 (Register 2000, No. 15).

ARTICLE 6
QME Discipline

§60. [See Note Following §159 Regarding Elimination of the IMC] Discipline.

(a) The Council may, in its discretion, suspend or terminate any physician from the QME list without hearing:

(1) whose license has been revoked;

(2) whose license has been suspended or terminated by the relevant licensing board so as to preclude practice;

(3) who has been convicted of a misdemeanor or felony related to the conduct of his or her practice or who has been suspended or placed on probation by his or her licensing board;

(4) based on a stipulation or a decision by the physician's licensing board that the physician has been placed on probation;

(5) who has failed to pay timely the appropriate fee as required under section 17.

(b) The council may, based on a complaint by the Medical Director, and following a hearing pursuant to Section 61, suspend, terminate or place on probation a QME found in violation of a statutory or administrative duty as described in the IMC Sanction Guidelines under Section 65 of these regulations. Such violations include, but are not limited to:

(1) one violation of Labor Code Section 139.3 or 4628;

(2) failure to follow the medical procedures established by the Council pursuant to Labor Code Section 139.2(j)(1)(2)(3)(4)(5) or (6);

(3) failure to comply with the requirements of Labor Code Section 139.2(b) or (c) and/or Section 10, 10.5, 11 or 12 of these regulations;

(4) failure to comply with the unavailability notification requirements pursuant to Section 33.

(5) failure to comply with the disclosure and ethical requirements pursuant to Sections 40 and 41;

(6) failure to complete accurate and complete reports pursuant to Labor Code Section 139.2(i) or to comply with section 39.5 of these regulations.

(7) A finding by the Appeals Board of ex parte contact by the QME prohibited by Labor Code Section 4062.2.

(8) A finding by the Council that the QME solicited an injured worker to take over that worker's treatment for his or her workers compensation claim.

(c) The Medical Director may file a complaint with the Council against a QME on any of the grounds listed in subsection (b) based on a complaint from a member of the public and/or the Medical Director's own initiative. The Medical Director may assign legal counsel and investigators to conduct all matters related to this Article.

(d) A report prepared by a QME which has not been completed and served on one or more parties prior to the date of the final decision taken by the licensing board or the date of the conviction, whichever is earlier, shall be inadmissible before the Appeals Board and no party shall have liability for payment for the report.

Note: Authority cited: Sections 139 and 139.2, Labor Code. Reference: Section 139.2, Labor Code.

History: 1. New article 6 (sections 60-62), renumbering of former section 51 to new section 60, repealer and new subsection (a), amendment of subsection (b), new subsection (b)(6) and subsection renumbering, and new subsections (b)(8) and (d) filed 8-23-96; operative 9-22-96 (Register 96, No. 34).

2. Amendment filed 4-14-2000; operative 5-14-2000 (Register 2000, No. 15).

§61. [See Note Following §159 Regarding Elimination of the IMC] Hearing Procedure.

(a) Where the Medical Director determines that there is a prima facie evidence of any violation of Section 60, he or she shall make and submit a prima facie case of the violation to a committee within the Council assigned to review disciplinary matters.

(b) If the Committee sustains the Medical Director's prima facie case, the QME shall be notified in writing of the determination and shall also be notified of his or her right to a hearing in accordance with Chapter 4 (commencing with Section 11370) and Chapter 5 (commencing with Section 11500) and Part 1 of Division 3 of the Government Code.

(1) The committee may, notwithstanding Government Code Section 11502, assign the hearing to a hearing officer designated by the Medical Director who shall act as an Administrative Law Judge for the purposes of Government Code Sections 11370 et. seq. and 11500 et. seq., or may delegate in whole or in part to an Administrative Law Judge the authority to conduct the hearing and decide the case. In the event of a hearing, the hearing officer or Administrative Law Judge shall fix the time and place of the hearing and notify interested parties in writing no fewer than 10 days in advance of the hearing and in accordance with Code or Civil Procedure Sections 1013(a) and 2015.5 specifying the time and place of the hearing.

(2) If an Administrative Law Judge conducts a hearing, the Administrative Law Judge selected to preside over the hearing shall hear the case alone, and exercise all powers related to the conduct of the hearing.

(3) Upon a decision being made regarding the prima facie case, the Administrative Law Judge or hearing officer shall file a written statement of findings and decisions with the full Council. The decision made pursuant to this

action shall include specific findings in accordance with Section 60(b), and under Section 65 of these Regulations shall recommend, but defer to the Council the final decision, with respect to sanctions. The Council shall, at the next scheduled Council meeting, accept, alter, or not adopt the proposed decision.

(4) The Council's decision on which sanction(s) to impose on a QME, pursuant to Labor Code Section 139.2(k) or any other statute giving the Council disciplinary authority, shall be in accordance with the IMC Sanction Guidelines under Section 65 of this Title.

(5) In accordance with Government Code Section 11517(c), if the proposed decision is not adopted by the Council, the Council shall determine in accordance with Labor Code Section 139(g) whether or not to decide the case as a body, based on the record and transcript, and/or whether or not to take additional evidence or to refer the case back to the Administrative Law Judge to take additional evidence on any issue or issues requested by the Council.

(6) Within 30 days of the date the written decision is served upon the QME, the QME may file a petition for reconsideration with the Council. The petition shall be governed by Government Code Section 11521 and shall set forth any legal or factual basis as to why the decision should not be confirmed. The Council Chairperson(s) shall appoint a three member panel, (excluding members of the committee) to review the physician's petition.

(c) Judicial Review of the Council's decision may be had by the filing of a petition for writ of mandate pursuant to Government Code Section 11523 no later than 30 days after the last day on which the Council can order reconsideration in accordance with (b)(6) of this Section.

Note: Authority cited: Sections 133, 139, 139.2, 5307.3 and 5307.4, Labor Code; and Sections 11370 et seq. and 11500 et seq., Government Code. Reference: Section 139.2, Labor Code; and Sections 11502 et seq., Government Code.

History: 1. Renumbering of former section 52 to new section 61, and amendment of subsections (c) and (d) filed 8-23-96; operative 9-22-96 (Register 96, No. 34).

2. Repealer and new section and amendment of Note filed 4-14-2000; operative 5-14-2000 (Register 2000, No. 15).

§62. [See Note Following §159 Regarding Elimination of the IMC] Probation.

(a) A physician on probationary status from his or her licensing authority may be placed on probationary status by the Council in its discretion in accordance with IMC Sanction Guidelines under Section 65 of this Title.

(b) A QME on probationary status from the Council may be required to report periodically to the Medical Director to ensure compliance with any conditions of probation that have been imposed by the Council. These conditions may include the completion of specific courses and training.

(c) A QME shall be deemed to have passed probation and be eligible for reappointment if he or she has complied with the conditions imposed by the Council during the probation period, and meets the requirements for reappointment in accordance with Article 5.

(d) A QME shall be deemed to have failed probation if upon completion of the probation period it is determined that he or she has not complied with the conditions imposed by the Council during the probation period, and/or has failed to meet the requirements for reappointment in accordance with Article 5.

(e) The Council shall terminate probation, which shall be equivalent to a failure to pass probation, before completion of the probation period if during the probation period it is determined that a QME has not complied with the conditions of probation.

Note: Authority cited: Sections 139 and 139.2, Labor Code. Reference: Sections 139.2, 4060, 4061 and 4062, Labor Code.

History: 1. Renumbering of former section 53 to new section 62, new subsection (a) and subsection relettering, and amendment of subsections (c) and (d) filed 8-23-96; operative 9-22-96 (Register 96, No. 34).

2. Amendment of subsections (a), (c) and (d) filed 4-14-2000; operative 5-14-2000 (Register 2000, No. 15).

§65. [See Note Following §159 Regarding Elimination of the IMC] Sanction Guidelines.

The guidelines for determining appropriate sanctions for physicians licensed as Qualified Medical Evaluators shall be set forth in the Sanction Guidelines as adopted by the Industrial Medical Council on October 21, 1999.

[IMC Sanction Guidelines Not Reproduced]

Editor's Note: Copies are available through the local I&A office. *See* Reference Directory, p. xiii, for phone numbers.

Note: Authority cited: Sections 133, 139 and 139.2, Labor Code. Reference: Section 139.2, Labor Code.

History: 1. New section filed 4-14-2000; operative 5-14-2000 (Register 2000, No. 15).

2. Change without regulatory effect amending section filed 10-29-2001 pursuant to section 100, title 1, California Code of Regulations (Register 2001, No. 44). Pursuant to this filing, material adopted pursuant to the Administrative Procedure Act that had previously been incorporated by reference in the California Code of Regulations was instead printed in full in the California Code of Regulations.

ARTICLE 7
Practice Parameters for the Treatment of Common Industrial Injuries

§70. [See Note Following §77 Regarding Legislative Repeal by 2003 Ch. 639 §50] Treatment Guideline for Low Back Problems.

The Industrial Medical Council recommends treatment of industrial injury to the low back, consistent with the "Treatment Guideline for Low Back Problems," as adopted by the Industrial Medical Council on April 17, 1997 as set forth below.

[Treatment Guidelines Not Reproduced]

Editor's Note: Copies are available through the local I&A office. *See* Reference Directory, p. xiii, for phone numbers.

Note: Authority cited: Section 139(e)(8), Labor Code. Reference: Section 139(e)(8) Labor Code.

History: 1. Editorial correction changing placement of article 7 heading (Register 97, No. 23).

2. New section filed 6-3-97; operative 7-3-97 (Register 97, No. 23).

3. Amendment filed 4-14-2000; operative 5-14-2000 (Register 2000, No. 15).

4. Change without regulatory effect amending section filed 7-12-2001 pursuant to section 100, title 1, California Code of Regulations (Register 2001, No. 28). Pursuant to this filing, material adopted pursuant to the Administrative Procedure Act that had previously been incorporated by reference in the California Code of Regulations was instead printed in full in the California Code of Regulations.

Ref.: Herlick Handbook § 4.1.

§71. [See Note Following §77 Regarding Legislative Repeal by 2003 Ch. 639 §50] Treatment Guideline for Industrial Neck Injuries.

The method of treating industrial injury to the neck shall be as set forth below in the "Treatment Guideline for Industrial Neck Injuries" as adopted by the Industrial Medical Council on May 15, 1997.

[Treatment Guidelines for Industrial Neck Injury Not Reproduced]

Editor's Note: Copies are available through the local I&A office. *See* Reference Directory, p. xiii, for phone numbers.

Note: Authority cited: Section 139(e)(8), Labor Code. Reference: Section 139(e)(8), Labor Code.

History: 1. New section filed 7-18-97; operative 8-17-97 (Register 97, No. 29).

2. Amendment filed 4-14-2000; operative 5-14-2000 (Register 2000, No. 15).

3. Change without regulatory effect amending section filed 7-12-2001 pursuant to section 100, title 1, California Code of Regulations (Register 2001, No. 28). Pursuant to this filing, material adopted pursuant to the Administrative Procedure Act that had previously been incorporated by reference in the California Code of Regulations was instead printed in full in the California Code of Regulations.

Ref.: Herlick Handbook § 4.1.

§72. [See Note Following §77 Regarding Legislative Repeal by 2003 Ch. 639 §50] Treatment Guideline for Occupational Asthma.

The method of treating occupational asthma shall be as set forth below in the "Treatment Guideline for Occupational Asthma" as adopted by the Industrial Medical Council on July 20, 1995.

[Treatment Guidelines for Occupational Asthma Not Reproduced]

Editor's Note: Copies are available through the local I&A office. *See* Reference Directory, p. xiii, for phone numbers.

Note: Authority cited: Section 139(e)(8), Labor Code. Reference: Section 139(e)(8), Labor Code.

History: 1. New section filed 9-18-95; operative 10-18-95 (Register 95, No. 38).

2. Change without regulatory effect amending section heading and section filed 9-25-95 pursuant to section 100, title 1, California Code of Regulations (Register 95, No. 39).

3. Amendment filed 4-14-2000; operative 5-14-2000 (Register 2000, No. 15).

4. Change without regulatory effect amending section filed 7-12-2001 pursuant to section 100, title 1, California Code of Regulations (Register 2001, No. 28). Pursuant to this filing, material adopted pursuant to the Administrative Procedure Act that had previously been incorporated by reference in the California Code of Regulations was instead printed in full in the California Code of Regulations.

§73. [See Note Following §77 Regarding Legislative Repeal by 2003 Ch. 639 §50] Treatment Guideline for Contact Dermatitis.

The method of treating contact dermatitis shall be as set forth below in the "Treatment Guideline for Contact Dermatitis" as adopted by the Industrial Medical Council on July 20, 1995.

[Treatment Guideline for Contact Dermatitis Not Reproduced]

Editor's Note: Copies are available through the local I&A office. *See* Reference Directory, p. xiii, for phone numbers.

Note: Authority cited: Section 139(e)(8), Labor Code. Reference: Section 139(e)(8), Labor Code.

History: 1. New section filed 9-18-95; operative 10-18-95 (Register 95, No. 38).

2. Change without regulatory effect amending section heading and section filed 9-25-95 pursuant to section 100, title 1, California Code of Regulations (Register 95, No. 39).

3. Amendment filed 4-14-2000; operative 5-14-2000 (Register 2000, No. 15).

4. Change without regulatory effect amending section filed 7-12-2001 pursuant to section 100, title 1, California Code of Regulations (Register 2001, No. 28). Pursuant to this filing, material adopted pursuant to the Administrative Procedure Act that had previously been incorporated by reference in the California Code of Regulations was instead printed in full in the California Code of Regulations.

§74. [See Note Following §77 Regarding Legislative Repeal by 2003 Ch. 639 §50] Treatment Guideline for Post-Traumatic Stress Disorder.

The method for treating post-traumatic stress disorder shall be as set forth below in the "Treatment Guideline for Post-Traumatic Stress Disorder" as adopted by the Industrial Medical Council on December 17, 1996.

[Treatment Guideline for Post-Traumatic Stress Disorder Not Reproduced]

Editor's Note: Copies are available through the local I&A office. *See* Reference Directory, p. xiii, for phone numbers.

Note: Authority cited: Section 139(e)(8), Labor Code. Reference: Section 139 and 139.2, Labor Code.

History: 1. New section filed 1-24-97; operative 2-23-97 (Register 97, No. 4).

2. Change without regulatory effect amending section filed 7-12-2001 pursuant to section 100, title 1, California Code of Regulations (Register 2001, No. 28). Pursuant to this filing, material adopted pursuant to the Administrative Procedure Act that had previously been incorporated by reference in the California Code of Regulations was instead printed in full in the California Code of Regulations.

§75. [See Note Following §77 Regarding Legislative Repeal by 2003 Ch. 639 §50] Treatment Guidelines for Shoulder Problems.

The method of treating industrial injury to the shoulder shall be as set forth below in the "Treatment Guideline for Shoulder Problems" as adopted by the Industrial Medical Council on May 15, 1997.

[Shoulder Problems Not Reproduced]

Editor's Note: Copies are available through the local I&A office. *See* Reference Directory, p. xiii, for phone numbers.

Note: Authority cited: Section 139(e)(8), Labor Code. Reference: Section 139(e)(8), Labor Code.

History: 1. New section filed 7-16-97; operative 8-15-97 (Register 97, No. 29).

2. Amendment filed 4-14-2000; operative 5-14-2000 (Register 2000, No. 15).

3. Change without regulatory effect amending section filed 7-12-2001 pursuant to section 100, title 1, California Code of Regulations (Register 2001, No. 28). Pursuant to this filing, material adopted pursuant to the

Administrative Procedure Act that had previously been incorporated by reference in the California Code of Regulations was instead printed in full in the California Code of Regulations.

§76. [See Note Following §77 Regarding Legislative Repeal by 2003 Ch. 639 §50] Treatment Guideline for Knee Problems.

The method of treating industrial injury to the knee shall be as set forth below in the "Treatment Guideline for Knee Problems" as adopted by the Industrial Medical Council on March 20, 1997.

[Knee Problems Not Reproduced]

Editor's Note: Copies are available through the local I&A office. *See* Reference Directory, p. xiii, for phone numbers.

Note: Authority cited: Section 139(e)(8), Labor Code. Reference: Section 139(e)(8), Labor Code.

History: 1. New article 7 (section 76) and section filed 5-13-97; operative 6-12-97 (Register 97, No. 20).

2. Amendment filed 4-14-2000; operative 5-14-2000 (Register 2000, No. 15).

3. Change without regulatory effect amending section filed 7-12-2001 pursuant to section 100, title 1, California Code of Regulations (Register 2001, No. 28). Pursuant to this filing, material adopted pursuant to the Administrative Procedure Act that had previously been incorporated by reference in the California Code of Regulations was instead printed in full in the California Code of Regulations.

§76.5. [See Note Following §77 Regarding Legislative Repeal by 2003 Ch. 639 §50] Treatment Guideline for Elbow Problems.

The method of treating industrial injury to the elbow shall be as set forth below in the "Treatment Guideline for Elbow Problems" as adopted by the Industrial Medical Council on May 15, 1997.

[Elbow Problems Not Reproduced]

Editor's Note: Copies are available through the local I&A office. *See* Reference Directory, p. xiii, for phone numbers.

Note: Authority cited: Section 139(e)(8), Labor Code. Reference: Section 139(e)(8), Labor Code.

History: 1. New section filed 7-17-97; operative 8-16-97 (Register 97, No. 29).

2. Amendment filed 4-14-2000; operative 5-14-2000 (Register 2000, No. 15).

3. Change without regulatory effect amending section filed 7-12-2001 pursuant to section 100, title 1, California Code of Regulations (Register 2001, No. 28). Pursuant to this filing, material adopted pursuant to the Administrative Procedure Act that had previously been incorporated by reference in the California Code of Regulations was instead printed in full in the California Code of Regulations.

§77. [See Note, Below, Regarding Legislative Repeal by 2003 Ch. 639 §50] Treatment Guideline for Problems of the Hand and Wrist.

The method of treating industrial injury to the hand and wrist shall be set forth below in the "Treatment Guideline for Problems of the Hand & Wrist" as adopted by the Industrial Medical Council on May 15, 1997.

[Problems of the Hand and Wrist Not Reproduced]

Editor's Note: Copies are available through the local I&A office. *See* Reference Directory, p. xiii, for phone numbers.

Note: Authority cited: Section 139(e)(8), Labor Code. Reference: Section 139(e)(8), Labor Code.

History: 1. New section filed 7-18-97; operative 8-17-97 (Register 97, No. 29).

2. Change without regulatory effect amending section filed 7-12-2001 pursuant to section 100, title 1, California Code of Regulations (Register 2001, No. 28). Pursuant to this filing, material adopted pursuant to the Administrative Procedure Act that had previously been incorporated by reference in the California Code of Regulations was instead printed in full in the California Code of Regulations.

2003 Note: Article 7 (commencing with Section 70) of Chapter 1 of Division 1 of the California Code of Regulations is repealed effective January 1, 2004, by 2003 ch. 639 (SB 228) §50. The publisher, however, has not received a CCR register confirming this change and has elected to leave the text of the repealed regulations in the volume.

ARTICLE 10
QME Application Forms

§100. [See Note Following §159 Regarding Elimination of the IMC] The Application for Appointment as Qualified Medical Evaluator Form.

[Form Not Reproduced]

Editor's Note: To acquire a copy of QME Form 100 (Rev. 1/2006), please contact the local

I&A office. *See* Reference Directory, p. xiii, 2006 Edition, for phone numbers.

History: 1. Renumbering of former article 10 to new article 15, new article 10 (sections 100-104) and new section filed 4-14-2000; operative 5-14-2000 (Register 2000, No. 15). For prior history see Register 94, No. 31.

2. Amendment filed 8-23-2001; operative 8-23-2001 pursuant to Government Code section 11343.4 (Register 2001, No. 34).

3. Change without regulatory effect amending section filed 5-2-2002 pursuant to section 100, title 1, California Code of Regulations (Register 2002, No. 18).

4. Change without regulatory effect amending section filed 1-27-2006 pursuant to section 100, title 1, California Code of Regulations (Register 2006, No. 4).

§101. [See Note Following §159 Regarding Elimination of the IMC] The Alien Application Form.

[Form Not Reproduced]

Editor's Note: To acquire a copy of IMC Form 101 (Rev. 3/01/00), please contact the local I&A office. *See* Reference Directory, p. xiii, for phone numbers.

History: 1. New section filed 4-14-2000; operative 5-14-2000 (Register 2000, No. 15). For prior history see Register 94, No. 31.

§102. [See Note Following §159 Regarding Elimination of the IMC] The Application for QME Competency Examination Form.

[Form Not Reproduced]

Editor's Note: To acquire a copy of QME Form 102 (Rev. 1/2006), please contact the local I&A office. *See* Reference Directory, p. xiii, 2006 Edition, for phone numbers.

History: 1. New section filed 4-14-2000; operative 5-14-2000 (Register 2000, No. 15). For prior history see Register 94, No. 31.

2. Change without regulatory effect amending section filed 1-27-2006 pursuant to section 100, title 1, California Code of Regulations (Register 2006, No. 4).

§103. [See Note Following §159 Regarding Elimination of the IMC] The QME Fee Assessment Form.

[Form Not Reproduced]

Editor's Note: To acquire a copy of IMC Form 103 (Rev. 5/05/00), please contact the local I&A office. *See* Reference Directory, p. xiii, for phone numbers.

History: 1. New section filed 4-14-2000; operative 5-14-2000 (Register 2000, No. 15). For prior history see Register 94, No. 31.

2. Change without regulatory effect amending section filed 6-27-2000 pursuant to section 100, title 1, California Code of Regulations (Register 2000, No. 26).

§104. [See Note Following §159 Regarding Elimination of the IMC] The Reappointment Application as Qualified Medical Evaluator Form.

[Form Not Reproduced]

Editor's Note: To acquire a copy of IMC Form 104 (Rev. 8/30/01), please contact the local I&A office. *See* Reference Directory, p. xiii, for phone numbers.

History: 1. New section filed 4-14-2000; operative 5-14-2000 (Register 2000, No. 15). For prior history see Register 94, No. 31.

2. Amendment filed 9-6-2001; operative 10-6-2001 (Register 2001, No. 36).

ARTICLE 10.5
QME Process Forms

§105. [See Note Following §159 Regarding Elimination of the IMC] The Request for Qualified Medical Evaluator Instruction Form.

[Form Not Reproduced]

Editor's Note: To acquire a copy of IMC Form 105 (Rev. 3/01/00), please contact the local I&A office. *See* Reference Directory, p. xiii, for phone numbers.

History: 1. New article 10.5 (sections 105–117) and new section filed 4-14-2000; operative 5-14-2000 (Register 2000, No. 15). For prior history see Register 94, No. 31.

§106. [See Note Following §159 Regarding Elimination of the IMC] The Request for Qualified Medical Evaluator Form.

[Form Not Reproduced]

Editor's Note: To acquire a copy of IMC Form 106 (Rev. 4/14/00(A)), please contact the local I&A office. *See* Reference Directory, p. xiii, for phone numbers.

History: 1. New section filed 4-14-2000; operative 5-14-2000 (Register 2000, No. 15). For prior history see Register 94, No. 31.

2. Change without regulatory effect amending section filed 5-2-2002 pursuant to section 100, title 1, California Code of Regulations (Register 2002, No. 18).

§107. [See Note Following §159 Regarding Elimination of the IMC] The Qualified Medical Evaluator Panel Selection Form.

[Form Not Reproduced]

Editor's Note: To acquire a copy of IMC Form 107 (Rev. 3/01/00), please contact the local I&A office. *See* Reference Directory, p. xiii, for phone numbers.

Note: Authority cited: Sections 139.2, 4061 and 4062, Labor Code. Reference: Section 139.2, Labor Code.

History: 1. New section filed 4-14-2000; operative 5-14-2000 (Register 2000, No. 15). For prior history see Register 94, No. 31.

§108. [See Note Following §159 Regarding Elimination of the IMC] The Request for Qualified Medical Evaluator Panel Selection Instruction Form.

[Form Not Reproduced]

Editor's Note: To acquire a copy of IMC Form 108 (Rev. 3/01/00), please contact the local I&A office. *See* Reference Directory, p. xiii, for phone numbers.

Note: Authority cited: Sections 133, 139, 139.2, 4061 and 4062, Labor Code. Reference: Sections 139.2, 4061, 4061.5 and 4062, Labor Code.

History: 1. New section filed 4-14-2000; operative 5-14-2000 (Register 2000, No. 15). For prior history see Register 94, No. 31.

§109. [See Note Following §159 Regarding Elimination of the IMC] The Notice of Qualified Medical Evaluator Unavailability Form.

[Form Not Reproduced]

Editor's Note: To acquire a copy of IMC Form 109 (Rev. 3/01/00), please contact the local I&A office. *See* Reference Directory, p. xiii, for phone numbers.

Note: Authority cited: Sections 139 and 139.2, Labor Code. Reference: Sections 139.2, 4061 and 4062, Labor Code.

History: 1. New section filed 4-14-2000; operative 5-14-2000 (Register 2000, No. 15). For prior history see Register 94, No. 31.

§110. [See Note Following §159 Regarding Elimination of the IMC] The Appointment Notification Form.

[Form Not Reproduced]

Editor's Note: To acquire a copy of IMC Form 110 (Rev. 3/01/00), please contact the local I&A office. *See* Reference Directory, p. xiii, for phone numbers.

Note: Authority cited: Sections 139 and 139.2, Labor Code. Reference: Sections 139.2, 4061 and 4062, Labor Code.

History: 1. New section filed 4-14-2000; operative 5-14-2000 (Register 2000, No. 15). For prior history see Register 94, No. 31.

§111. [See Note Following §159 Regarding Elimination of the IMC] The Qualified or Agreed Medical Evaluator Findings Summary Form.

[Form Not Reproduced]

Editor's Note: To acquire a copy of IMC Form 111 (Rev. 3/01/00), please contact the local I&A office. *See* Reference Directory, p. xiii, for phone numbers.

Note: Authority cited: Sections 139, 139.2 and 4061, Labor Code. Reference: Sections 139.2 and 4061, Labor Code.

History: 1. New section filed 4-14-2000; operative 5-14-2000 (Register 2000, No. 15).

§112. [See Note Following §159 Regarding Elimination of the IMC] The Qualified or Agreed Medical Evaluator Extension Request Form.

[Form Not Reproduced]

Editor's Note: To acquire a copy of IMC Form 112 (Rev. 3/01/00), please contact the local I&A office. *See* Reference Directory, p. xiii, for phone numbers.

Note: Authority cited: Sections 139 and 139.2, Labor Code. Reference: Sections 139.2, 4060, 4061, 4062 and 4062.5, Labor Code.

History: 1. New section filed 4-14-2000; operative 5-14-2000 (Register 2000, No. 15).

§113. [See Note Following §159 Regarding Elimination of the IMC] The Time Extension Approval Form.

[Form Not Reproduced]

Editor's Note: To acquire a copy of IMC Form 113 (Rev. 3/01/00), please contact the local I&A office. *See* Reference Directory, p. xiii, for phone numbers.

Note: Authority cited: Sections 139 and 139.2, Labor Code. Reference: Sections 139.2, 4060, 4061, 4062 and 4062.5, Labor Code.

History: 1. New section filed 4-14-2000; operative 5-14-2000 (Register 2000, No. 15).

§114. [See Note Following §159 Regarding Elimination of the IMC] The Denial of Time Extension Form.

[Form Not Reproduced]

Editor's Note: To acquire a copy of IMC Form 114 (Rev. 3/01/00), please contact the local I&A office. *See* Reference Directory, p. xiii, for phone numbers.

Note: Authority cited: Sections 139 and 139.2, Labor Code. Reference: Sections 139.2, 4060, 4061, 4062 and 4062.5, Labor Code.

History: 1. New section filed 4-14-2000; operative 5-14-2000 (Register 2000, No. 15).

§115. [See Note Following §159 Regarding Elimination of the IMC] The Notice of Late Qualified Medical Evaluator Report Form.

[Form Not Reproduced]

Editor's Note: To acquire a copy of IMC Form 115 (Rev. 3/01/00), please contact the local I&A office. *See* Reference Directory, p. xiii, for phone numbers.

Note: Authority cited: Sections 139 and 139.2, Labor Code. Reference: Sections 139.2, 4060, 4061, 4062 and 4062.5, Labor Code.

History: 1. New section filed 4-14-2000; operative 5-14-2000 (Register 2000, No. 15).

§116. [See Note Following §159 Regarding Elimination of the IMC] The Notice of Late Qualified Medical Evaluator Report Form—Extension Not Requested Form.

[Form Not Reproduced]

Editor's Note: To acquire a copy of IMC Form 116 (Rev. 3/01/00), please contact the local I&A office. *See* Reference Directory, p. xiii, for phone numbers.

Note: Authority cited: Sections 139 and 139.2, Labor Code. Reference: Sections 139.2, 4060, 4061, 4062 and 4062.5, Labor Code.

History: 1. New section filed 4-14-2000; operative 5-14-2000 (Register 2000, No. 15).

§117. [See Note Following §159 Regarding Elimination of the IMC] Qualified Medical Evaluator Continuing Education Response Form.

[Form Not Reproduced]

Editor's Note: To acquire a copy of IMC Form 117 (Rev. 3/01/00(A)), please contact the local I&A office. *See* Reference Directory, p. xiii, for phone numbers.

Note: Authority cited: Section 139.2, Labor Code. Reference: Section 139.2, Labor Code.

History: 1. New section filed 4-14-2000; operative 5-14-2000 (Register 2000, No. 15).

2. Change without regulatory effect amending section filed 5-2-2002 pursuant to section 100, title 1, California Code of Regulations (Register 2002, No. 18).

§118. [See Note Following §159 Regarding Elimination of the IMC] Application for Accreditation or Re-Accreditation As Education Provider.

[Form Not Reproduced]

Editor's Note: To acquire a copy of IMC Form 118 (Rev. 5/01), please contact the local

I&A office. *See* Reference Directory, p. xiii, for phone numbers.

History: 1. New section filed 10-16-2000 as an emergency; operative 1-1-2001 (Register 2000, No. 42). A Certificate of Compliance must be transmitted to OAL by 5-1-2001 or emergency language will be repealed by operation of law on the following day.

2. New section refiled 5-2-2001 as an emergency; operative 5-2-2001 (Register 2001, No. 18). A Certificate of Compliance must be transmitted to OAL by 8-30-2001 or emergency language will be repealed by operation of law on the following day.

3. Certificate of Compliance as to 5-2-2001 order, including further amendment of section, transmitted to OAL 7-12-2001 and filed 8-23-2001 (Register 2001, No. 34).

§119. [See Note Following §159 Regarding Elimination of the IMC] Faculty Disclosure of Commercial Interest.

[Form Not Reproduced]

Editor's Note: To acquire a copy of IMC Form 119 (Rev. 5/01), please contact the local I&A office. *See* Reference Directory, p. xiii, for phone numbers.

History: 1. New section filed 10-16-2000 as an emergency; operative 1-1-2001 (Register 2000, No. 42). A Certificate of Compliance must be transmitted to OAL by 5-1-2001 or emergency language will be repealed by operation of law on the following day.

2. New section refiled 5-2-2001 as an emergency; operative 5-2-2001 (Register 2001, No. 18). A Certificate of Compliance must be transmitted to OAL by 8-30-2001 or emergency language will be repealed by operation of law on the following day.

3. Certificate of Compliance as to 5-2-2001 order, including further amendment of section, transmitted to OAL 7-12-2001 and filed 8-23-2001 (Register 2001, No. 34).

ARTICLE 15
Fraudulent or Misleading Advertising

§150. [See Note Following §159 Regarding Elimination of the IMC] Definitions.

As used in this Article:

(a) Advertising copy — includes any "public communication" as defined in Business and Professions Code Section 651, or any other communication of any message in any form or medium regarding the availability for professional employment of any physician, which is made by or on behalf of any physician to the general public or any substantial portion thereof.

Advertising concerning medical services regarding industrial injuries or illnesses which benefits any physician, and which is placed by any medical clinic, medical service organization or other non-physician third party shall be deemed advertising copy subject to these regulations.

(b) Council — means the Industrial Medical Council as defined in Labor Code Section 139.

(c) Medical Board — means the Medical Board of California as established in Business and Professions Code Section 2001.

(d) Medical Director — means the physician appointed pursuant to Labor Code Section 122 or such person as he or she may designate.

(e) Physician — has the meaning defined in Labor Code Section 3209.3.

(f) QME — means a Qualified Medical Evaluator as defined in Labor Code Section 139.2.

Note: Authority cited: Sections 139, 139.4 and 139.45, Labor Code. Reference: Sections 139, 139.2, 139.4 and 139.45, Labor Code.

History: 1. New article 10 and section filed 3-31-93; operative 4-30-93 (Register 93, No. 14).

Ref.: Herlick Handbook § 1.8.

§151. [See Note Following §159 Regarding Elimination of the IMC] Filing of Documents.

Any document filed under these regulations shall be deemed filed on the date when it is received by the Council.

Note: Authority cited: Sections 139, 139.4 and 139.45, Labor Code. Reference: Sections 133, 139, 139.4 and 139.45, Labor Code.

History: 1. New section filed 3-31-93; operative 4-30-93 (Register 93, No. 14.)

Ref.: Herlick Handbook § 1.8.

§152. [See Note Following §159 Regarding Elimination of the IMC] Statement of Intent.

Nothing in these regulations is intended to alter the interpretation or application of Business and Professions Code Section 651. These regulations are promulgated under the authority of Labor Code Sections 139.4 and 139.45 and are intended to reflect the Industrial Medical

Council's understanding of the Legislature's intent that the Council apply a higher and independent standard, pursuant to those Sections, to physician advertising which relates to industrial injuries or illnesses.

Note: Authority cited: Sections 139, 139.4 and 139.45, Labor Code. Reference: Sections 139, 139.4 and 139.45, Labor Code.

History: 1. New section filed 3-31-93; operative 4-30-93 (Register 93, No. 14.)

Ref.: Herlick Handbook § 1.8.

§153. [See Note Following §159 Regarding Elimination of the IMC] False or Misleading Advertising Copy Prohibited.

No physician subject to these regulations, or any person acting on his or her behalf or for his or her benefit, shall use, cause to be used, or allow to be used:

(a) Any advertising copy which, through endorsements, testimonials or other representations, makes or implies any guarantee, warranty, or prediction that is intended, or is likely, to create a false or unjustified expectation of favorable results concerning the outcome of the employment of the physician.

(b) Any advertising copy which by use of a firm name, trade name, fictitious business name, or other professional designation states or implies a relationship between any physician in private practice and any governmental agency or entity, with the exception that, as provided in section 154 below, a physician designated by the Council as a Qualified Medical Evaluator may state this fact in advertising copy.

(c) Any advertising copy which states or implies that a medical-legal report written by any physician, or group or association of physicians enjoys any special degree of credibility by any workers' compensation judge or judges.

(d) Any advertising copy which advises or recommends the securing of any medical-legal examination, or which suggests that a tactical advantage may be secured by obtaining any medical-legal evaluation.

(e) Any advertising copy which contains the phrase "Qualified Medical Evaluator" or the designation "QME" unless such phrase is used to identify individual physicians who have been formally designated as QMEs by the Industrial Medical Council in accordance with Labor Code Section 139.2.

(f) Any advertising copy which contains a firm name, trade name, or fictitious business name which contains the phrases "Qualified Medical Evaluator," "Independent Medical Examiner" or the designations "QME" or "IME."

(g) Any advertising copy which states or implies that any physician has an ongoing appointment, title or professional status as an "Agreed Medical Examiner," "Independent Medical Examiner," "AME," or "IME."

Note: Authority cited: Sections 139, 139.4 and 139.45, Labor Code. Reference: Sections 139, 139.2, 139.4 and 139.45, Labor Code.

History: 1. New section filed 3-31-93; operative 4-30-93 (Register 93, No. 14.)

Ref.: Herlick Handbook § 1.8.

§154. [See Note Following §159 Regarding Elimination of the IMC] Permissible Advertising Content.

(a) A physician subject to these regulations, or any person acting on his or her behalf, may use, disseminate, or cause to be disseminated to the public, or any portion of the public, advertising copy which relates to any industrial injury or illness which accurately states:

(1) The name of each physician affiliated with or participating in the physician's practice.

(2) The address, telephone number and business hours of the office or offices.

(3) The areas of practice each physician engages in.

(4) An individual physician's appointment as a QME.

(5) A statement that the physician is Board Certified or limits his or her practice to specific fields as authorized by Business and Professions Code Section 651. Any statement of Board Certification shall include the name of the certifying board.

(6) Any languages spoken fluently by the physician or his or her staff.

(7) A description of any diagnostic or therapeutic facilities available.

(8) The availability of surgery or hospitalization on a lien basis.

(9) The usual time frame for scheduling appointments or producing medical reports.

(10) That all billings are made in compliance with the Official Medical Fee Schedule promulgated by the Administrative Director of the Division of Workers' Compensation.

(11) Biographic information concerning the physician's educational background, internships

and residencies, hospital affiliations, professional affiliations and professional publications.

(b) Any physician who wishes to use, disseminate, or cause to be disseminated to the public, or any portion of the public, any advertising copy which relates to any industrial injury or illness which contains any material not specified in subsection (a) above, shall apply in writing to the Council for approval before using such material. The Council shall approve all requests which do not contain material which is false or likely to mislead the public with respect to workers' compensation. No advertising copy submitted to the Council pursuant to this subsection shall be used until the Council has given its written approval.

Note: Authority cited: Sections 139, 139.4 and 139.45, Labor Code. Reference: Sections 139, 139.2, 139.4 and 139.45, Labor Code.

History: 1. New section filed 3-31-93; operative 4-30-93 (Register 93, No. 14.)

Ref.: Herlick Handbook § 1.8.

§155. [See Note Following §159 Regarding Elimination of the IMC] Filing of Complaints.

(a) Any person may file a complaint with the Medical Director, alleging that any physician is using advertising copy which violates the provisions of Business and Professions Code Section 651, or the provisions of these regulations.

(b) Complaints filed with the Medical Director shall be in writing and contain the following:

(1) The full name and address of the party filing the complaint.

(2) The full name and address of the physician against whom the complaint is made, or if the complainant is unable to identify the physician using the advertising, as much information as the complainant can provide to assist the Council in identifying the physician who used the advertisement.

(3) A copy, if available to the complaining party, of the advertising copy against which the complaint is made, or a description of the medium in which the advertising copy appeared. Such description should contain sufficient details regarding the manner and form in which the advertising copy was published to allow a copy of the advertising copy to be obtained by the council.

(4) A detailed statement of the grounds on which the advertising copy is alleged to violate Business and Professions Code Section 651 or these regulations.

(5) All complaints filed under this section shall be filed the Executive Medical Director, at either 395 Oyster Point Blvd., South San Francisco, CA 94080, or P.O. Box 8888, San Francisco, CA 94128-8888.

(6) Nothing in these regulations shall prevent the Council or Medical Director from acting independently, and without receipt of a complaint, to initiate an investigation and issue a complaint on the Council's own motion whenever the Council or Medical Director has reason to believe that there has been a violation of Business and Professions Code Section 651 or these regulations.

Note: Authority cited: Sections 139, 139.4 and 139.45, Labor Code. Reference: Sections 139, 139.4 and 139.45, Labor Code.

History: 1. New section filed 3-31-93; operative 4-30-93 (Register 93, No. 14.)

Ref.: Herlick Handbook § 1.8.

§156. [See Note Following §159 Regarding Elimination of the IMC] Council Requests to Review Advertising Copy.

(a) Upon receipt of a complaint under Section 155 of these regulations, the Council shall serve a written notice of complaint on the physician against whom the complaint was filed. Such notice shall direct the physician to file a copy of his or her advertising with the Medical Director within 15 working days of the date on which the notice was served.

(b) The Medical Director may take such steps as he or she deems necessary to determine whether the complaint has merit.

(1) The Medical Director shall respond to the complaint within 15 working days of the Council's receipt of the physician's response and notify the complainant that the Council:

(A) will investigate the complaint; or

(B) will require additional time to ascertain whether the complaint has merit; or

(C) will refer a copy of the complaint to another agency which also has jurisdiction over the subject matter of the complaint; or

(D) will take no further action on the complaint because the council lacks jurisdiction over the person or conduct complained of; or

CHAPTER 4.5 DIVISION OF WORKERS' COMPENSATION

SUBCHAPTER 1 ADMINISTRATIVE DIRECTOR—ADMINISTRATIVE RULES

ARTICLE 1.1 Workers' Compensation Information System

§9700. Authority.

This article is adopted to implement the Workers' Compensation Information System mandated by Sections 138.6 and 138.7 of the Labor Code.

Note: Authority cited: Sections 133, 138.6 and 138.7, Labor Code. Reference: Sections 138.6 and 138.7, Labor Code.

History: 1. New article 1.1 (sections 9700-9704) and section filed 10-6-99; operative 11-5-99 (Register 99, No. 41).

Ref.: W. Cal. Sum., 2 "Workers' Compensation" §10.

§9701. Definitions.

(a) The following definitions apply in this article:

Bona Fide Statistical Research. The analysis of existing workers' compensation data for the purpose of developing or contributing to basic knowledge regarding the California workers' compensation system.

California EDI Implementation Guide for First and Subsequent Reports of Injury. California EDI Implementation Guide, Version 2.1, dated February 2006, contains California specific reporting requirements and information excerpted from the IAIABC EDI Implementation Guide for First, Subsequent, Acknowledgment Detail, Header & Trailer Records, Release 1, issued February 15, 2002, by the International Association of Industrial Accident Boards and Commissions. The California EDI Implementation Guide for First and Subsequent Reports of Injury, Version 2.1, dated February 2006, is posted on the Division's Web site at http://www.dir.ca.gov/dwc/WCIS.htm, will be made available by the Division of Workers' Compensation upon request, and is incorporated by reference.

California EDI Implementation Guide for Medical Bill Payment Records. California EDI Implementation Guide for Medical Bill Payment Records, Version 1.0, dated December 2005, contains the California-specific protocols and excerpts from the IAIABC EDI Implementation Guide for Medical Bill Payment Records, explains the technical design and functionality of the WCIS system, testing options for the trading partners, instructions regarding the data elements for medical billing, and copies of the required medical billing electronic forms. The California EDI Implementation Guide for Medical Bill Payment Records, Version 1.0, dated December 2005, is posted on the Division's Web site at http://www.dir.ca.gov/dwc/WCIS.htm, will be made available by the Division of Workers' Compensation upon request, and is incorporated by reference.

Claim. An injury as defined in Division 4 of the Labor Code, occurring on or after March 1, 2000, that has resulted in the receipt of one or more of the following by a claims administrator:

(1) Employer's Report of Occupational Injury or Illness, as required by Title 8, California Code of Regulations §§ 14004-14005.

(2) Doctor's First Report of Occupational Injury or Illness, as required by Title 8, California Code of Regulations §§ 14006-14007.

(3) Application for Adjudication filed with the Workers' Compensation Appeals Board under Labor Code § 5500 and Title 8, California Code of Regulations § 10408.

(4) Any information indicating that the injury requires medical treatment by a physician as defined in Labor Code § 3209.3.

(b) Claims Administrator. A self-administered insurer providing security for the payment of compensation required by Divisions 4 and 4.5 of the Labor Code, a self-administered self-insured employer, California Insurance Guarantee Association (CIGA), or a third-party claims administrator for a self-insured employer, insurer, legally uninsured employer, or joint powers authority.

Claims Administrator's Agents. Any entity contracted by the claims administrator to assist in adjusting the claim(s) including third party administrators, bill reviewers, utilization review vendors, and electronic data interchange vendors.

Closed Claim. A claim in which future payment of indemnity benefits and/or provision of medical benefits cannot be reasonably expected to be due.

Data Elements. Information identified by data number (DN) and defined in the dictionary of the IAIABC EDI Implementation Guide, Release 1. Data elements set forth in Section 9702 must be transmitted on all claims, where applicable, as indicated in Section 9702. The data elements set forth in the IAIABC EDI Implementation Guide, Release 1 that are not enumerated in Section 9702 are optional and may, but need not be, submitted on any or all claims.

Electronic Data Interchange. ("EDI"). A computer to computer exchange of data or information in a standardized format acceptable to the Administrative Director.

Health Care Organization ("HCO"). Any entity certified as a health care organization by the Administrative Director pursuant to Labor Code Sections 4600.5 and 4600.6.

IAIABC EDI Implementation Guide, Release 1. EDI Implementation Guide for First, Subsequent, Acknowledgment Detail, Header & Trailer Records, Release 1, issued February 15, 2002, by the International Association of Industrial Accident Boards and Commissions. Sections 4, 5, 6, and the Appendix of EDI Implementation Guide, Release 1, are linked to the Division's Web site at http://www.dir.ca.gov/dwc/WCIS.htm, and are hereby incorporated by reference.

IAIABC EDI Implementation Guide for Medical Bill Payment Records. IAIABC EDI Implementation Guide for Medical Bill Payment Records, Release 1, approved July 4, 2002, by the International Association of Industrial Accident Boards and Commissions. Sections 1 through 3, and 5 through 11 of the IAIABC EDI Implementation Guide for Medical Bill Payment Records, Release 1, are linked to the Division's Web site at http://www.dir.ca.gov/dwc/WCIS.htm, and are incorporated by reference.

Indemnity Benefits. Payments conferred, including those made by settlement, for any of the following: temporary disability indemnity, permanent disability indemnity, death benefits, vocational rehabilitation maintenance allowance, and employer-paid salary in lieu of compensation.

Individually Identifiable Information. Any data concerning an injury or claim that is linked to a uniquely identifiable employee, employer, claims administrator, or any other person or entity.

International Association of Industrial Accident Boards and Commissions ("IAIABC"). A professional association of workers' compensation specialists, located at 5610 Medical Circle, Suite 14, Madison, Wisconsin 53711, which is, in addition to other activities, engaged in the production and publication of EDI standards for filing workers' compensation information. Note: IAIABC asserts ownership of such EDI standards which are published in various ways and include Implementation Guides with instructions on their use, technical and business specifications and coding information to permit the transfer of data between regulatory bodies and regulated entities in a uniform and consistent manner.

WCIS. The Workers' Compensation Information System established pursuant to sections 138.6 and 138.7 of the Labor Code.

Note; Authority cited: Sections 133, 138.6 and 138.7, Labor Code. Reference: Sections 138.6 and 138.7, Labor Code.

History: 1. New section filed 10-6-99; operative 11-5-99 (Register 99, No. 41).

2. Amendment filed 3-22-2006; operative 4-21-2006 (Register 2006, No. 12).

§9702. Electronic Data Reporting.

(a) Each claims administrator shall transmit data elements, by electronic data interchange in the manner set forth in the California EDI Implementation Guide for First and Subsequent Reports of Injury and the California EDI Implementation Guide for Medical Bill Payment Records, to the WCIS by the dates specified in this section. Each claims administrator shall, at a minimum, provide complete, valid, accurate data for the data elements set forth in this section. The data elements required in subdivisions (b), (c), (d) and (e) are taken from California EDI Implementation Guide for First and Subsequent Reports of Injury and the California EDI Implementation Guide for Medical Bill Payment Records. Claims administrators shall only transmit the data elements that are set forth in the California EDI Implementation Guide for First and Subsequent Reports of Injury and the California EDI Implementation Guide for Medical Bill Payment Records. Each transmission of data elements shall include appropriate header and trailer records as set forth in the California EDI Implementation Guide for First and Subsequent Reports of Injury and the California EDI

Implementation Guide for Medical Bill Payment Records.

(1) The Administrative Director, upon written request, may grant a claims administrator either a partial or total variance in reporting all or part of the data elements required pursuant to subdivision (e) of this section. Any variance granted by the Administrative Director under this subdivision shall be set forth in writing.

(A) A partial variance requested on the basis that the claims administrator is unable to transmit some of the required data elements to the WCIS shall be granted for a six month period only if all of the following are shown:

1. a documented showing that compliance with the reporting deadlines set forth in subdivision (e) would cause undue hardship to the claims administrator;

2. a documented showing that any medical data elements currently being transmitted by the claims administrator or the claims administrator's agent to public or private research or statistical entities shall be reported by the claims administrator to the WCIS; and

3. submission of a plan, prior to the applicable deadline set forth in subdivision (e), documenting the means by which the claims administrator will ensure full compliance with the data reporting within six months from the request.

(B) A partial variance requested on the basis that the claims administrator is unable to report some of the required data elements to the WCIS because the data elements are not available to the claims administrator or the claims administrator's agent shall be granted for a six month period only if all of the following are shown:

1. a documented showing that compliance with the reporting deadlines set forth in subdivision (e) would cause undue hardship to the claims administrator;

2. a documented showing that any medical data elements currently being transmitted by the claims administrator or the claims administrator's agent to public or private research or statistical entities shall be reported by the claims administrator to the WCIS;

3. a documented showing that the claims administrator will submit to the WCIS the medical data elements available to the claims administrator or the claims administrator's agents; and

4. submission of a plan, prior to the applicable deadline set forth in subdivision (e), documenting the means by which the claims administrator will ensure full compliance with the data reporting within six months from the request.

(C) A total variance shall be granted for a twelve month period if all of the following are shown:

1. a documented showing that compliance with the reporting deadlines set forth in subdivision (e) would cause undue hardship to the claims administrator;

2. a documented showing that the claims administrator has not contracted with a bill review company to review medical bills submitted by providers in its workers' compensation claims;

3. a documented showing that the claims administrator is unable to transmit medical data to public or private research or statistical entities; and

4. submission of a plan, prior to the applicable deadline set forth in subdivision (e), documenting the means by which the claims administrator will ensure full compliance with the data reporting within twelve months from the request.

(2) "Undue hardship" shall be determined based upon a review of the documentation submitted by the claims administrator. The documentation shall include: the claims administrator's total required expenses; the reporting cost per claim if transmitted in house; and the total cost per claim if reported by a vendor. The costs and expenses shall be itemized to reflect costs and expenses related to reporting the data elements listed in subdivision (e) only.

(3) The variance period for reporting data elements under subdivisions (a)(1)(A) and (B) shall not be extended. The variance period for reporting data elements under subdivision (a)(1)(C) may be extended for additional twelve month periods if the claims administrator resubmits a written request for a variance. A claims administrator granted a variance shall submit to the WCIS all data elements that were required to be submitted under subdivision (e) during the variance period except for data elements that were not known to the claims administrator, the claims administrator's agents, or not captured on the claims administrator's electronic data systems. The data shall be submitted in an electronic format acceptable to the Division.

(b) Each claims administrator shall submit to the WCIS on each claim, within five (5) business days of knowledge of the claim, each of the following data elements known to the claims administrator:

Data Element Name	*DN*
ACCIDENT DESCRIPTION/CAUSE	38
CAUSE OF INJURY CODE	37
CLAIM ADMINISTRATOR ADDRESS LINE 2	11
CLAIM ADMINISTRATOR ADDRESS LINE 1	10
CLAIM ADMINISTRATOR CITY	12
CLAIM ADMINISTRATOR CLAIM NUMBER	15
CLAIM ADMINISTRATOR POSTAL CODE	14
CLAIM ADMINISTRATOR STATE	13
CLASS CODE(3)	59
DATE DISABILITY BEGAN	56
DATE LAST DAY WORKED	65
DATE OF HIRE(1)	61
DATE OF INJURY	31
DATE OF RETURN TO WORK	68
DATE REPORTED TO CLAIM ADMINISTRATOR	41
DATE REPORTED TO EMPLOYER	40
EMPLOYEE ADDRESS LINE 1(1)	46
EMPLOYEE ADDRESS LINE 2(1)	47
EMPLOYEE CITY(1)	48
EMPLOYEE DATE OF BIRTH	52
EMPLOYEE DATE OF DEATH	57
EMPLOYEE FIRST NAME	44
EMPLOYEE LAST NAME	43
EMPLOYEE MIDDLE INITIAL(1)	45
EMPLOYEE PHONE(1)	51
EMPLOYEE POSTAL CODE(1)	50
EMPLOYEE STATE(1)	49
EMPLOYER ADDRESS LINE 1	19
EMPLOYER ADDRESS LINE 2	20
EMPLOYER CITY	21
EMPLOYER FEIN	16
EMPLOYER NAME	18
EMPLOYER POSTAL CODE	23
EMPLOYER STATE	22
EMPLOYMENT STATUS CODE(1)	58
GENDER CODE	53
INDUSTRY CODE	25
INSURER FEIN	6
INSURER NAME	7
JURISDICTION	4
MAINTENANCE TYPE CODE	2
MAINTENANCE TYPE CODE DATE	3
MARITAL STATUS CODE(2)	54
NATURE OF INJURY CODE	35
NUMBER OF DEPENDENTS(2)	55
OCCUPATION DESCRIPTION	60
PART OF BODY INJURED CODE	36
POSTAL CODE OF INJURY SITE	33
SALARY CONTINUED INDICATOR	67
SELF INSURED INDICATOR	24
SOCIAL SECURITY NUMBER(1)	42
THIRD PARTY ADMINISTRATOR FEIN	8
THIRD PARTY ADMINISTRATOR NAME	9
WAGE(1)	62
WAGE PERIOD(1)	63

(1) Required only when provided to the claims administrator.

(2) Death Cases Only.

(3) Required for insured claims only; optional for self-insured claims.

Data elements omitted under this subsection because they were not known by the claims administrator shall be submitted within sixty (60) days from the date of the first report under this subsection.

(c) Each transmission of data elements listed under (b), (d), (e), (f), or (g) of this section shall also include the following elements for data linkage:

Data Element Name	*DN*
CLAIM ADMINISTRATOR CLAIM NUMBER(2) (3) (4)	15
DATE OF INJURY(2)	31
INSURER FEIN(4)	6
JURISDICTION CLAIM NUMBER NUMBER(2) (3) (4)	5
MAINTENANCE TYPE CODE(1)	2
MAINTENANCE TYPE CODE DATE(1)	3
SOCIAL SECURITY NUMBER NUMBER(2) (3)	42
THIRD PARTY ADMINISTRATOR FEIN(4)	8

(1) Maintenance Type Code (DN 2) and Maintenance Type Code Date (DN 3) are required for transmissions under Subsections (b), (d), (f), and (g).

(2) This number will be provided by WCIS upon receipt of the first report. The Jurisdiction Claim Number (DN 5) is required when changing a Claim Administrator Claim Number (DN 15); it is optional for other transmissions under this subsection.

(3) The Date of Injury (DN 31), Employee SSN (DN 42), and Claim Administrator Claim Number (DN 15) need not be submitted if the Jurisdiction Claim Number (DN 5) accompanies the transmission, except for transmissions required under Subsection (f).

(4) If the Jurisdiction Claim Number (DN 5) is not provided, trading partners must provide the Claim Administrator Claim Number (DN 15) and the Third Party Administrator FEIN (DN 8), or, if there is no third party administrator, the Insurer FEIN (DN 6).

(d) Each claims administrator shall submit to the WCIS within fifteen (15) business days the following data elements, whenever indemnity benefits of a particular type and amount are started, changed, suspended, restarted, stopped, delayed, or denied, or when a claim is closed or reopened, or when the claims administrator is notified of a change in employee representation. Submissions under this subsection are required only for claims with a date of injury on or after July 1, 2000, and shall not include data on routine payments made during the course of an uninterrupted period of indemnity benefits.

Data Element Name	*DN*
CLAIM STATUS	73
DATE DISABILITY BEGAN	56
DATE OF MAXIMUM MEDICAL IMPROVEMENT	70
DATE OF REPRESENTATION	76
DATE OF RETURN TO WORK	68
DATE OF RETURN TO WORK/RELEASE TO WORK	72
EMPLOYMENT STATUS CODE	58
LATE REASON CODE	77
PAID TO DATE/REDUCED EARNINGS/RECOVERIES AMOUNT	96
PAID TO DATE/REDUCED EARNINGS/RECOVERIES CODE	95
PAYMENT/ADJUSTMENT CODE	85
PAYMENT/ADJUSTMENT DAYS PAID	91
PAYMENT/ADJUSTMENT END DATE	89
PAYMENT/ADJUSTMENT PAID TO DATE	86
PAYMENT/ADJUSTMENT START DATE	88
PAYMENT/ADJUSTMENT WEEKLY AMOUNT	87
PAYMENT/ADJUSTMENT WEEKS PAID	90
PERMANENT IMPAIRMENT BODY PART CODE[(1) (2)]	83
PERMANENT IMPAIRMENT PERCENTAGE[(2)]	84
WAGE	62
WAGE PERIOD	63

[(1)] May use Code 90 (Multiple Body Parts) to reflect combined rating for any/all impairments.

[(2)] Use actual permanent disability rating at the time of initial payment of permanent disability benefits. For compromise and release cases and stipulated settlements, use permanent disability estimate as reported to the appropriate rating organization established under Insurance Code § 11750, et seq.

(e) On and after September 22, 2006, claims administrators handling one hundred and fifty (150) or more total claims per year shall submit to the WCIS on each claim with a date of service on or after September 22, 2006, the following data elements for all medical services for which the claims administrator has received a billing or other report of provided medical services. The California EDI Implementation Guide for Medical Bill Payment Records sets forth the specific California reporting requirements. The data elements required in this subdivision are taken from California EDI Implementation Guide for Medical Bill Payment Records and the IAIABC EDI Implementation Guide for Medical Bill Payment Records. The claims administrator shall submit the data within ninety (90) calendar days of the medical bill payment. Each claims administrator shall transmit the data elements by electronic data interchange in the manner set forth in the California EDI Implementation Guide for Medical Bill Payment Records.

Data Element Name	*DN*
ACKNOWLEDGMENT TRANSACTION SET ID	110
ADMISSION DATE	513
ADMITTING DIAGNOSIS CODE	535
APPLICATION ACKNOWLEDGMENT CODE	111
BASIS OF COST DETERMINATION CODE	564
BATCH CONTROL NUMBER	532
BILL ADJUSTMENT AMOUNT	545
BILL ADJUSTMENT GROUP CODE[(5)]	543
BILL ADJUSTMENT REASON CODE	544
BILL ADJUSTMENT UNITS	546
BILL SUBMISSION REASON CODE	508
BILLING FORMAT CODE	503
BILLING PROVIDER FEIN	629
BILLING PROVIDER LAST/GROUP NAME	528
BILLING PROVIDER POSTAL CODE	542
BILLING PROVIDER PRIMARY SPECIALTY CODE[(4)]	537
BILLING PROVIDER STATE LICENSE NUMBER[(4)]	630
BILLING PROVIDER UNIQUE BILL IDENTIFICATION NUMBER	523
BILLING TYPE CODE	502
CLAIM ADMINISTRATOR CLAIM NUMBER	15
CLAIM ADMINISTRATOR FEIN	187
CLAIM ADMINISTRATOR NAME	188
CONTRACT TYPE CODE	515
DATE INSURER PAID BILL	512
DATE INSURER RECEIVED BILL	511
DATE OF BILL	510
DATE OF INJURY	31
DATE PROCESSED	108

Data Element Name	*DN*
DATE TRANSMISSION SENT	100
DAYS/UNITS BILLED	554
DAYS/UNITS CODE	553
DIAGNOSIS POINTER	557
DISCHARGE DATE	514
DISPENSE AS WRITTEN CODE	562
DME BILLING FREQUENCY CODE	567
DRG CODE	518
DRUG NAME	563
DRUGS/SUPPLIES BILLED AMOUNT	572
DRUGS/SUPPLIES DISPENSING FEE	579
DRUGS/SUPPLIES NUMBER OF DAYS	571
DRUGS/SUPPLIES QUANTITY DISPENSED	570
ELEMENT ERROR NUMBER	116
ELEMENT NUMBER	115
EMPLOYEE FIRST NAME	44
EMPLOYEE LAST NAME	43
EMPLOYEE MIDDLE NAME/INITIAL	45
EMPLOYEE EMPLOYMENT VISA	152
EMPLOYEE GREEN CARD	153
EMPLOYEE PASSPORT NUMBER	156
EMPLOYEE SOCIAL SECURITY NUMBER	42
FACILITY CODE	504
FACILITY FEIN	679
FACILITY MEDICARE NUMBER	681
FACILITY NAME	678
FACILITY POSTAL CODE	688
FACILITY STATE LICENSE NUMBER	680
HCPCS BILL PROCEDURE CODE	737
HCPCS LINE PROCEDURE BILLED CODE	714
HCPCS LINE PROCEDURE PAID CODE	726
HCPCS MODIFIER BILLED CODE	717
HCPCS MODIFIER PAID CODE	727
HCPCS PRINCIPLE PROCEDURE BILLED CODE	626
ICD-9 CM DIAGNOSIS CODE	522
ICD-9 CM PRINCIPAL PROCEDURE CODE	525
ICD-9 CM PROCEDURE CODE	736
INSURER FEIN	6
INSURER NAME	7
INTERCHANGE VERSION ID	105
JURISDICTION CLAIM NUMBER	5
JURISDICTION MODIFIER BILLED CODE[(8)] [(10)]	718
JURISDICTION MODIFIER PAID CODE[(8)]	730
JURISDICTION PROCEDURE BILLED CODE[(8)]	715
JURISDICTION PROCEDURE PAID CODE[(8)] [(9)]	729
LINE NUMBER	547
MANAGED CARE ORGANIZATION FEIN[(1)]	704
MANAGED CARE ORGANIZATION IDENTIFICATION NUMBER	208
MANAGED CARE ORGANIZATION NAME	209
MANAGED CARE ORGANIZATION POSTAL CODE	712
NDC BILLED CODE	721
NDC PAID CODE	728
ORIGINAL TRANSMISSION DATE	102
ORIGINAL TRANSMISSION TIME	103
PLACE OF SERVICE BILL CODE	555
PLACE OF SERVICE LINE CODE	600
PRESCRIPTION BILL DATE	527
PRESCRIPTION LINE DATE	604
PRESCRIPTION LINE NUMBER	561
PRINCIPLE DIAGNOSIS CODE	521
PRINCIPLE PROCEDURE DATE	550
PROCEDURE DATE	524
PROVIDER AGREEMENT CODE[(3)]	507
RECEIVER ID	99
RELEASE OF INFORMATION CODE	526
RENDERING BILL PROVIDER FEIN	642
RENDERING BILL PROVIDER LAST/GROUP NAME	638
RENDERING BILL PROVIDER POSTAL CODE	656
RENDERING BILL PROVIDER PRIMARY SPECIALTY CODE	651
RENDERING BILL PROVIDER SPECIALTY LICENSE NUMBER	649
RENDERING BILL PROVIDER STATE LICENSE NUMBER	643
RENDERING LINE PROVIDER NATIONAL ID[(7)]	592
RENDERING LINE PROVIDER FEIN	586
RENDERING LINE PROVIDER LAST/GROUP NAME[(6)]	589
RENDERING LINE PROVIDER POSTAL CODE	593
RENDERING LINE PROVIDER PRIMARY SPECIALTY CODE[(6)]	595
RENDERING LINE PROVIDER STATE LICENSE NUMBER[(6)]	599
REPORTING PERIOD	615
REVENUE BILLED CODE	559
REVENUE PAID CODE	576
SENDER ID	98
SERVICE ADJUSTMENT AMOUNT	733
SERVICE ADJUSTMENT GROUP CODE[(5)]	731
SERVICE ADJUSTMENT REASON CODE[(5)]	732
SERVICE BILL DATE(S) RANGE	509
SERVICE LINE DATE(S) RANGE	605
TEST/PRODUCTION INDICATOR	104
TIME PROCESSED	109
TIME TRANSMISSION SENT	101
TOTAL AMOUNT PAID PER BILL[(2)]	516
TOTAL AMOUNT PAID PER LINE[(2)]	574
TOTAL CHARGE PER BILL	501

Data Element Name	*DN*
TOTAL CHARGE PER LINE — PURCHASE	566
TOTAL CHARGE PER LINE — RENTAL	565
TOTAL CHARGE PER LINE	552
TRANSACTION TRACKING NUMBER	266
UNIQUE BILL ID NUMBER	500

(1) For HCO claims use the FEIN of the sponsoring organization in DN 704.

(2) Not required on non-denied bills if amount paid equals amount charged.

(3) For MPN claims use code P "Participation Agreement"

(4) Does not apply if billing provider is an organization.

(5) Required if charged and paid amounts differ.

(6) Optional if rendering provider equals billing provider.

(7) To be provided following the assignment of a National Provider Identifier by the United States Department of Health and Human Services, Centers for Medicare & Medicaid Services ("CMS").

(8) The codes for this data element are the codes that are set forth in the California Official Medical Fee Schedule, a publication of the State of California, Department of Industrial Relations (adopted pursuant to Labor Code § 5307.1 and Title 8, California Code of Regulations § 9790 et seq.).

(9) Optional if procedure billed equals procedure paid.

(10) Use when a modifier has been provided.

(f) Notwithstanding the requirement in Subsection (b) to submit data elements omitted from the first report within 60 days from the date of transmission of the first report, when a claims administrator becomes aware of an error or need to update data elements previously transmitted, or learns of information that was previously omitted, the claims administrator shall transmit the corrected, updated or omitted data to WCIS no later than the next submission of data for the affected claim.

(g) No later than January 31 of every year, commencing in 2001, claims administrators shall, for each claim with a date of injury on or after July 1, 2000 and with any payment in any benefit category in the previous calendar year, report the total paid in each payment category through the previous calendar year by submitting the following data elements:

Data Element Name	*DN*
PAID TO DATE/REDUCED EARNINGS/RECOVERIES AMOUNT	96
PAID TO DATE/REDUCED EARNINGS/RECOVERIES CODE	95
PAYMENT/ADJUSTMENT CODE	85
PAYMENT/ADJUSTMENT END DATE	89
PAYMENT/ADJUSTMENT PAID TO DATE	86
PAYMENT/ADJUSTMENT START DATE	88

(h) Final reports (MTC = FN) are required only for claims where indemnity benefits are paid. For medical-only claims, the final report may be reported under this section or on the annual report (MTC = AN) with claim status = "closed."

(i)(1) A claims administrator's obligation to submit copies of benefit notices to the Administrative Director pursuant to Labor Code Section 138.4 is satisfied upon written determination by the Administrative Director that the claims administrator has demonstrated the capability to submit complete, valid, and accurate data as required under Subsection (d) and continued compliance with that subsection.

(2) Reserved.

(3) On and after September 22, 2006, a claims administrator's obligation to submit an Annual Report of Inventory pursuant to Title 8, California Code of Regulations, section 10104 is satisfied upon determination by the Administrative Director that the claims administrator has demonstrated the capability to submit complete, valid, and accurate data as required under subdivisions (b), (d), (e), and (g), and continued compliance with those subsections.

(j) The data submitted pursuant to this section shall not have any application to, nor be considered in, nor be admissible into, evidence in any personal injury or wrongful death action, except as between an employee and the employee's employer. Nothing in this subdivision shall be construed to expand access to information held in the WCIS beyond that authorized in section 9703 and Labor Code section 138.7.

(k) Each claims administrator required to submit data under this section shall submit to the Administrative Director an EDI Trading Partner Profile at least thirty days prior to its first transmission of EDI data. Each claims administrator shall advise the Administrative Director of any subsequent changes and/or corrections made to the information provided in the EDI Trading

Partner Profile by filing a corrected copy of the EDI Trading Partner Profile with the Administrative Director.

Note: Authority cited: Sections 133, 138.4, 138.6 and 138.7, Labor Code. Reference: Sections 138.4, 138.6 and 138.7, Labor Code.

History: 1. New section filed 10-6-99; operative 11-5-99 (Register 99, No. 41).

2. Amendment filed 3-22-2006; operative 4-21-2006 (Register 2006, No. 12).

§9703. Access to Individually Identifiable Information.

(a) No person shall have access to individually identifiable data held in the WCIS except as provided in this section and subdivision (c) of section 138.7 of the Labor Code.

(b) The Division of Workers' Compensation may obtain and use individually identifiable information for the following purposes:

(1) To create and maintain the WCIS, including the selection of claims to survey in order to obtain information not available from the data elements provided by claims administrators.

(2) To help select claims administrators for audits under section 129 of the Labor Code.

(3) To report the promptness with which claims administrators make payments.

(4) To electronically import names, addresses, and other information into Division of Workers' Compensation case files which would otherwise have to be key entered by agency staff.

(5) To conduct research related to the workers' compensation system for the purpose of carrying out the duties of the Division of Workers' Compensation or the Administrative Director.

(c) The following agencies may obtain individually identifiable information from the WCIS, in the manner set forth in a memorandum of understanding between the Administrative Director and the agency, for the purposes specified:

(1) The Division of Occupational Safety and Health may use individually identifiable information to help select employers for health and safety consultations and inspections.

(2) The Division of Labor Statistics and Research may use individually identifiable information to carry out its research and reporting responsibilities under Labor Code sections 150 and 156.

(3) The Department of Health Services may use individually identifiable information to carry out its occupational health and occupational disease prevention responsibilities under section 105175 of the Health and Safety Code.

(d) Upon written request to the Administrative Director, researchers employed by or under contract to the Commission on Health and Safety and Workers' Compensation (CHSWC) may obtain individually identifiable information from the WCIS, in the manner set forth in a memorandum of understanding between the Administrative Director, the commission, and the person or entity conducting research, for the purpose of bona fide statistical research.

(1) Any request from the CHSWC for individually identifiable information under this subdivision shall include the identity of the person or entity conducting the research, the purpose of the research, the research protocol, the need for individually identifiable WCIS data, and an anticipated completion date for the research.

(2) Researchers under contract to the CHSWC seeking individually identifiable WCIS data under this subdivision shall also submit to the Administrative Director written approval of the research protocol by an Institutional Review Board in the same manner as required under subdivision (e). If the researcher under contract to the CHSWC is the University of California or a non profit educational institution, the researcher shall comply with the provisions of Civil Code section 1789.24 subdivision (t).

(3) Individually identifiable information obtained under this subdivision shall not be disclosed to the members of the CHSWC.

(4) No individually identifiable information obtained by researchers under this subdivision may be disclosed to any other person or entity, public or private, for a use other than that research project for which the information was obtained.

(5) Researchers obtaining individually identifiable information under this subdivision shall notify the Administrative Director when the research has been completed. Except as required by researchers subject to subdivision (f), within 30 days thereafter, the CHSWC shall present evidence to the Administrative Director that the data collected has been modified in a manner so that the subjects cannot be identified, directly or through identifiers linked to the subjects.

(e) Individually identifiable information may be provided to other persons or public or private entities for the purpose of bona fide statistical research which does not divulge individually identifiable information concerning any employee, employer, claims administrator, or any other person or entity. Any request for individually identifiable information for this purpose shall include the identity of the requester, the purpose of the research, the methods of research, and the need for individually identifiable WCIS data. The requester shall also submit written approval of the research protocol by an Institutional Review Board, under Title 45, Code of Federal Regulations, Part 46, Subpart A. "Approval" means a determination by the Institutional Review Board that the research protocol was reviewed and provides sufficient safeguards to ensure the confidentiality of individually identifiable information. Any agreement to permit use of the data shall be in writing between the requester and the Administrative Director. Note: The Division shall make available upon request a list of Institutional Review Boards known to the Division that have the authority to grant the required approval and that expressed willingness to review research proposals under this section.

(f) The University of California or any non profit educational institution conducting scientific research must comply with the provisions of Civil Code section 1798.24 subdivision (t).

(g) Each agreement or memorandum of understanding entered concerning the use of individually identifiable information by any agency, entity, or person shall specify the methods to be used to protect the information from unlawful disclosure, and shall include a warning to the receiving party that it is unlawful for any person who has received individually identifiable information from the Division of Workers' Compensation under this section to provide the information to any person who is not entitled to it under this section and Labor Code § 138.7.

(h) Nothing in this section shall be construed to exempt from disclosure any public record contained in an individual's file once an Application for Adjudication has been filed with the Workers' Compensation Appeals Board. This includes any data from an individual's file that are converted to or stored in an electronic format for the purpose of case processing and tracking.

(i) Nothing in this section shall be construed to exempt from disclosure WCIS data in a format that does not contain individually identifiable information.

Note: Authority cited: Sections 127, 133, 138.4, 138.6 and 138.7, Labor Code. Reference: Sections 129, 138.4, 138.6 and 138.7, Labor Code; and Section 1798.24, Civil Code.

History: 1. New section filed 10-6-99; operative 11-5-99 (Register 99, No. 41).

2. Amendment filed 3-22-2006; operative 4-21-2006 (Register 2006, No. 12).

§9704. WCIS Advisory Committee.

(a) The Administrative Director shall maintain a Workers' Compensation Information System Advisory Committee, which shall include, but not be limited to, representatives of claims administrators (including self-insured employers, insurers, and third party administrators), insured employers, organized labor, attorneys, physicians as defined in Labor Code § 3209.3, vocational rehabilitation counselors, academic researchers, the Department of Insurance statistical agent, and appropriate legislative committees and state agencies with jurisdiction over workers' compensation, occupational health, and related areas, including the Commission on Health and Safety and Workers' Compensation and the Employment Development Department.

(b) The advisory committee shall meet at least annually on the call of the Administrative Director, and may provide advice on all aspects of WCIS. The Administrative Director, or his or her designee, shall present to the advisory committee any plan to collect survey data, including any expanded collection of the data elements specified in subdivision (d) of section 9702.

Note: Authority cited: Sections 133 and 138.6, Labor Code. Reference: Sections 138.6 and 138.7, Labor Code.

History: 1. New section filed 10-6-99; operative 11-5-99 (Register 99, No. 41).

ARTICLE 1.5
Receipt of Salary by Workers' Compensation Administrative Law Judge

§9710. Authority.

The rules and regulations contained in Article 1.5 are adopted pursuant to the authority contained in Sections 123, 123.5(a) and 133 of the California Labor Code.

Note: Authority cited: Sections 123, 123.5(a) and 133, Labor Code. Reference: Sections 123.5(a) and 5313, Labor Code.

History: 1. New Article 1.5 (Sections 9710-9715) filed 1-16-81; effective thirtieth day thereafter (Register 81, No. 3).

2. Amendment of article heading, section and Note filed 1-12-99; operative 2-11-99 (Register 99, No. 3).

Ref.: Herlick Handbook § 1.6.

§9711. Operative Date.

The provisions of this Article shall first apply to cases submitted after January 1, 1981, and the affidavit shall first be required for the April 1981 pay period. For the purposes of this Article, all cases submitted prior to January 1, 1981 shall be deemed to have been submitted on January 2, 1981.

Note: Authority cited: Sections 123, 123.5(a) and 133, Labor Code. Reference: Sections 123.5(a) and 5313, Labor Code.

History: 1. New Note filed 1-12-99; operative 2-11-99 (Register 99, No. 3).

Ref.: Herlick Handbook § 1.6.

§9712. Definitions.

For the purposes of this Article and Section 123.5(a) of the Labor Code, the following definitions shall apply:

(a) "Salary" shall include ordinary pay, but shall not include sick leave pay, industrial disability leave or non-industrial disability insurance substantiated by a physician's report.

(b) "Cause" shall mean a cause of action arising out of the substantive rights, liabilities and duties provided for in Sections 132(a) and 139.5, and in Divisions 4 and 4.5 of the Labor Code which is pending before a Workers' Compensation Administrative Law Judge for decision. "Cause" shall not include Compromise and Release agreements, Stipulations with Request for Award, or petitions and motions which have been filed ex parte and are not part of a submission ordered by a Workers' Compensation Administrative Law Judge.

(c) "Pending and Undetermined" means that the Workers' Compensation Administrative Law Judge's decision has not been filed in the record.

(d) "Submitted" means the closing of the record for the receipt of further evidence or argument.

Note: Authority cited: Sections 123, 123.5(a) and 133, Labor Code. Reference: Sections 123.5(a) and 5313, Labor Code.

History: 1. Amendment of section and new Note filed 1-12-99; operative 2-11-99 (Register 99, No. 3).

Ref.: Herlick Handbook § 1.6.

§9713. Receipt of Salary.

A Workers' Compensation Administrative Law Judge may not receive his or her salary while any cause before the Workers' Compensation Administrative Law Judge remains pending and undetermined for ninety (90) days after it has been submitted for decision.

Note: Authority cited: Sections 123, 123.5(a) and 133, Labor Code. Reference: Sections 123.5(a) and 5313, Labor Code.

History: 1. Amendment of section and new Note filed 1-12-99; operative 2-11-99 (Register 99, No. 3).

Ref.: Herlick Handbook § 1.6.

§9714. Procedures for Compliance With Labor Code Section 123.5(a).

(a) In order to receive his or her salary for each pay period, at some time before 5:00 p.m. on the last working day of each State payroll period, the Workers' Compensation Administrative Law Judge shall submit to the Division of Workers' Compensation an affidavit based upon information and belief in the form prescribed by Section 9714.5, and executed under penalty of perjury, declaring that no cause submitted before him or her remains pending and undetermined for a period of ninety (90) days or more.

(b) When a Workers' Compensation Administrative Law Judge who receives salary by automatic direct deposit does not timely submit the affidavit required by subsection (a), he or she shall, before 5:00 p.m. on the next working day following the direct deposit of salary into his or her account, deliver to the Presiding Workers' Compensation Administrative Law Judge of the district office to which the judge is assigned a money order or cashier's check for the amount of salary automatically deposited.

Note: Authority cited: Section 133, Labor Code. Reference: Sections 123.5(a) and 5313, Labor Code.

History: 1. Amendment of section heading and section and new Note filed 1-12-99; operative 2-11-99 (Register 99, No. 3).

2. Amendment of subsection (a) and Note filed 5-23-2001; operative 6-22-2001 (Register 2001, No. 21).

Ref.: Herlick Handbook § 1.6.

§9714.5. Affidavit.

Department of Industrial Relations
Division of Workers' Compensation
Workers' Compensation Appeals Board

AFFIDAVIT
(Labor Code Section 123.5(a))

I, ___________, (Name) Workers' Compensation Administrative Law Judge in the ___________ (City) office of the Division of Workers' Compensation/Workers' Compensation Appeals Board, Department of Industrial Relations, State of California, declare that I have made a reasonable and diligent inquiry concerning those matters submitted to me, and based on information and belief, state that no cause remains pending and undetermined that has been submitted to me for the period of ninety (90) days prior to the first day of ___________, 20_____. (Date) (Year)

Executed on ___________ (Date) at ___________ (City), California. I declare under penalty of perjury that the foregoing is true and correct.

____

(Signature)
Workers' Compensation Administrative Law Judge

Note: Authority cited: Section 133, Labor Code. Reference: Sections 123.5(a) and 5313, Labor Code.

History: 1. Amendment filed 1-12-99; operative 2-11-99 (Register 99, No. 3).

2. Amendment of section and new Note filed 5-23-2001; operative 6-22-2001 (Register 2001, No. 21).

Ref.: Herlick Handbook § 1.6.

§9715. Procedures for Submitting a Cause for Decision.

Minutes of Hearing must be prepared at the conclusion of each hearing and filed in the record. Workers' Compensation Administrative Law Judges are to follow the provisions of Rules of Practice and Procedure Section 10566. Each set of minutes must include a disposition which includes the time and action, if any, required for submissions.

Thereafter, any change in or modification of the disposition must be served on all parties forthwith, together with the statement of the reasons for the change of disposition.

A hearing has not been concluded if the disposition includes an order taking off calendar or an order of continuance for further hearing with or without notice. Continuances and further hearings are governed by Rules of Practice and Procedure Sections 10548 and 10560.

Note: Authority cited: Sections 123, 123.5(a) and 133, Labor Code. Reference: Sections 123.5(a) and 5313, Labor Code.

History: 1. Amendment of first paragraph and new Note filed 1-12-99; operative 2-11-99 (Register 99, No. 3).

Ref.: Herlick Handbook § 1.6.

ARTICLE 1.6
Ethical Standards of Workers' Compensation Administrative Law Judges; Enforcement of Standards

§9720.1. Authority.

The rules and regulations contained in Article 1.6 are adopted pursuant to the authority contained in Sections 123.6, 133, and 5307.3 of the Labor Code. This article is designed to enforce the highest ethical standards among workers' compensation administrative law judges and to provide all parties with an independent, impartial investigation into allegations of ethics violations by workers' compensation administrative law judges.

Note: Authority cited: Sections 123.6, 133 and 5307.3, Labor Code. Reference: Sections 111 and 123.6, Labor Code.

History: 1. New article 1.6 and section filed 11-30-95; operative 12-1-95. Submitted to OAL for printing only pursuant to Government Code section 11351 (Register 95, No. 48).

2. Amendment of article heading and section filed 8-25-2008; operative 9-24-2008 (Register 2008, No. 35).

Ref.: Herlick Handbook §§ 1.2, 1.6.

§9720.2. Definitions.

For purposes of this Article and Section 123.6 of the Labor Code, the following definitions shall apply:

(a) "Code of Judicial Ethics" shall mean the Code of Judicial Ethics adopted by the Supreme Court pursuant to subdivision (m) of Section 18 of Article VI of the California Constitution and any subsequent revision thereof.

(b) "Committee" shall mean the Workers' Compensation Ethics Advisory Committee specified in Section 9722 of these regulations.

(c) "Complaint" shall mean a statement alleging facts that, if true, might constitute an ethics violation.

(d) "Ethics violation" shall mean any conduct of a workers' compensation administrative law judge that is contrary to the Code of Judicial Ethics or to the other rules of conduct that apply to workers' compensation administrative law judges.

(e) "Financial interest" shall mean a legal or equitable interest of either more than one per cent (1%) or a fair market value in excess of two thousand dollars ($2,000). Ownership in a mutual fund or other common investment fund that holds securities is not a "financial interest" in those securities unless the judge participates in the management of the fund.

(f) "Gift" means any payment or furnishing of value to the extent that consideration of equal or greater value is not given and includes a rebate or discount in the price of anything of value unless the rebate or discount is made in the regular course of business to members of the public without regard to official status. Any person who claims that a payment is not a gift by reason of the giving of consideration has the burden of proving that the consideration received is of equal or greater value. The term "gift" does not include:

(1) Informational material such as books, reports, pamphlets, calendars, periodicals, cassettes and discs, or free or reduced-price admission, tuition, or registration, for informational conferences or seminars. No payment for travel or reimbursement for any expenses shall be deemed "informational material."

(2) Gifts which are not used and which, within 30 days after receipt, are returned to the donor or delivered to a charitable organization without being claimed as a charitable contribution for tax purposes.

(3) Gifts from a judge's spouse, fiancée, child, parent, grandparent, grandchild, brother, sister, parent-in-law, brother-in-law, sister-in-law, nephew, niece, aunt, uncle, or first cousin or the spouse of any such person; provided that a gift from any such person shall be considered a gift if the donor is acting as an agent or intermediary for any person not covered by this paragraph.

(4) Campaign contributions required to be reported under Chapter 4 (commencing with Section 84100) of Title 9 of the Government Code.

(5) Gifts of comestible items of nominal value that are not directed to a particular judge, such as holiday baskets of candy or fruit delivered to a District office of the Division, and placed in public areas for consumption by members of the public.

(6) Any devise, inheritance, or other transfer to the judge occurring as a result of death or distribution from an irrevocable trust.

(7) Personalized plaques and trophies with an individual value of less than the amount specified from time to time in Government Code § 82028 (which at the time of this amendment is two hundred fifty dollars ($ 250).

(8) Admission to events and refreshments and similar non-cash nominal benefits provided to a judge during the entire event at which the judge gives a speech, participates in a panel or seminar, or provides a similar service, and payments, advances, or reimbursements for actual transportation and any reasonably necessary lodging and subsistence provided directly in connection with the speech, panel, seminar, or service, provided that the lodging and subsistence expenses are limited to the day immediately preceding, the day of, and the day immediately following the speech, panel participation or seminar, and the travel is within the United States.

(9) Complimentary admission to events and refreshments and similar non-cash nominal benefits, at legal educational events at which the judge is not a speaker or participant in a panel, if:

A. the educational event is open to the public who wish to purchase admission;

B. continuing legal education credits are available for attorneys who attend; and

C. the free admission is offered to all workers' compensation administrative law judges;

"Complimentary admission to events" does not include admission to non-educational functions, such as golf tournaments, excursions, picnics, and dances. "Refreshments" does not include meals other than meals served contemporaneously with an educational presentation, and is limited to those refreshments offered to all who pay admission to the event.

(g) "Honorarium" shall mean any payment made in consideration for any speech given, article published, or attendance at any public or private conference, convention, meeting, social event, meal, or like gathering.

(1) "Honorarium" does not include earned income for personal services which are customarily provided in connection with the practice of a bona fide business, trade, or profession, such as teaching or writing for a publisher.

(2) For purposes of this article, "teaching" includes presentations to impart educational information to students in bona fide educational institutions, to associations or groups of judges, and to presentations of the State Bar of California or a section of the State Bar of California. An individual is presumed to be engaged in the bona fide profession of teaching in any of the following circumstances:

(A) The individual receives payment for teaching students at a bona fide educational institution.

(B) The individual receives payment for teaching students enrolled in an examination preparation program, such as a bar examination review course.

(C) The individual receives payment for teaching or making a presentation or participating in a panel presentation at an educational program offered by an association or group of judges, or at an educational program of the State Bar of California or of a section of the State Bar of California.

(h) "Judge" shall mean a worker's compensation administrative law judge and presiding workers' compensation administrative law judge employed by the Administrative Director and supervised by the Court Administrator pursuant to Section 123.5 of the Labor Code. The term shall also include Vocational Rehabilitation Consultants, Regional Managers (Associate Chief Judges) the Chief Judge, the Court Administrator, the Administrative Director, pro tem administrative law judges, and the Administrative Director's designees, but only while they are exercising judicial or quasi-judicial powers. The term does not include Information and Assistance Officers, Workers' Compensation Compliance Officers (Auditors), nor Disability Evaluation Specialists.

(i) "Previously earned compensation" shall mean legal fees and other compensation to which a workers' compensation administrative law judge may be entitled arising out of the practice of law, engaged in before the judge was appointed to be a judge. Previously earned compensation includes compensation to which the judge was contingently entitled as of the time of appointment, but which became fixed in amount after appointment.

(j) "Spouse" shall include "domestic partner".

(k) "Third degree of relationship" shall mean the following persons: great-grandparent, grandparent, parent, uncle, aunt, brother, sister, child, grandchild, great-grandchild, nephew, and niece.

Note: Authority cited: Sections 123.6, 133 and 5307.3, Labor Code. Reference: Sections 111 and 123.6, Labor Code.

History: 1. New section filed 11-30-95; operative 12-1-95. Submitted to OAL for printing only pursuant to Government Code section 11351 (Register 95, No. 48).

2. Amendment filed 8-25-2008; operative 9-24-2008 (Register 2008, No. 35).

Ref.: Herlick Handbook §§ 1.2, 1.6.

§9721.1. Code of Judicial Ethics.

Every workers' compensation administrative law judge shall abide by the Code of Judicial Ethics.

Note: Authority cited: Sections 123.6, 133 and 5307.3, Labor Code. Reference: Sections 111 and 123.6, Labor Code.

History: 1. New section filed 11-30-95; operative 12-1-95. Submitted to OAL for printing only pursuant to Government Code section 11351 (Register 95, No. 48).

2. Amendment of section heading and section filed 8-25-2008; operative 9-24-2008 (Register 2008, No. 35).

Ref.: Herlick Handbook §§ 1.2, 1.6.

§9721.2. Gifts, Honoraria and Travel.

(a) No workers' compensation administrative law judge shall accept any gift or favor, the acceptance of which is prohibited by the Code of Judicial Ethics, or the transmission of which is prohibited by the Rules of Professional Conduct of the State Bar of California.

(b) No workers' compensation administrative law judge shall accept gifts from any single source in any calendar year with a total value of more than the greater of three hundred ninety dollars ($390) and the amount specified for that year in regulations of the Fair Political Practices Commission interpreting Government Code § 89503 (currently Title 2, Regulation § 18940.2). This section shall not be construed to authorize the receipt of gifts that would otherwise be prohibited by the Code of Judicial Ethics, Government Code section 19990, the Political Reform Act of 1974 and any amendment thereto, the Rules of Professional Conduct of the State Bar of California, or any other provision of law.

(c) The limitation of subdivision (b) shall not apply to or limit the following:

(1) Payments, advances, or reimbursements for travel and related lodging and subsistence described in subdivision (d).

(2) Wedding gifts and gifts exchanged between individuals on birthdays, holidays and other similar occasions, provided that the gifts exchanged are not substantially disproportionate in value.

(3) A gift from any person whose preexisting relationship with a judge would disqualify the judge under the Code of Judicial Ethics from hearing a case involving that person.

(d) Payments, advances, or reimbursements, for travel, including actual transportation and related lodging and subsistence which is reasonably related to a judicial or governmental purpose, or to an issue of state, national, or international public policy, are excluded from the limits prescribed by subdivision (b) if any of the following apply:

(1) The travel is provided by a government, a governmental agency or authority, a foreign government, a bona fide public or private educational institution, as defined in Section 203 of the Revenue and Taxation Code, a nonprofit organization which is exempt from taxation under Section 501(c)(3) of the Internal Revenue Code, or by a person domiciled outside the United States who substantially satisfies the requirements for tax exempt status under Section 501(c)(3) of the Internal Revenue Code.

(2) The travel is provided by the California State Bar or a section of the California State Bar, a state bar association, or professional association of judges in connection with testimony before a governmental body or attendance at any professional function hosted by the bar, bar association or professional association of judges, and the lodging and subsistence expenses are limited to the day immediately preceding, the day of, and the day immediately following the professional function.

(e) Payments, advances, and reimbursements for travel not described in either subdivision (c) of this Section or subdivision (f)(8) of Section 9720.2 are subject to the limit in subdivision (b).

(f) No workers' compensation administrative law judge shall accept any honorarium unless allowed in writing by the Court Administrator, if either:

(1) the cost of the honorarium is significantly paid for by attorneys who practice before the Workers' Compensation Appeals Board; or

(2) the judge would be required to report the receipt of income or gifts from the source of payment for the honorarium on the judge's statement of economic interests

(g) This section does not apply to any honorarium that is not used and within 30 days after receipt, is either returned to the donor or delivered to the Controller for deposit in the General Fund without being claimed as a deduction from income for tax purposes.

(h) The Court Administrator shall enforce the prohibitions of this section.

(i) Judges may not accept honoraria or travel allowed by the Court Administrator, and not otherwise prohibited by this section in connection with any public or private conference, convention, meeting, social event, or like gathering, the cost of which is significantly paid for by attorneys who practice before the board, unless the Court Administrator, or his or her designee, has provided prior approval in writing to the workers' compensation administrative law judge allowing him or her to accept the payments. This section shall not be construed to authorize the acceptance of an honorarium, as defined by Government Code section 89501, the acceptance of which is prohibited by Government Code section 89502.

(j) Honoraria to give a speech, participate in a panel or seminar, or provide a similar service, are allowed within the meaning of Labor Code section 123.6 where the event is sponsored by one of the following:

A professional association of judges, the State Bar of California, a section of the State Bar of California, a government, a governmental agency or authority, a foreign government, a state, national or local bar association not comprised primarily of either defense or applicant workers' compensation attorneys, a foreign bar association, an international service organization, a bona fide public or private educational institution as defined in Section 203 of the Revenue and Taxation Code, a nonprofit organization which is exempt from taxation under Section 501(c)(3) of the Internal Revenue Code, or by a person domiciled outside the United States who substantially satisfies the requirements for tax exempt status under Section 501(c)(3) of the Internal Revenue Code.

(k) Upon request to the Court Administrator by a judge, the Court Administrator may approve honoraria and travel reimbursement to give a speech, participate in a panel or seminar, or provide a similar service, where the event is sponsored by a person or entity not listed in subdivision (j) of this section.

(*l*) Payment, provision, or reimbursement for travel in connection with a judge's speech, participation in a panel or seminar, or provision of a similar service, if the event is sponsored by a professional association of judges, the State Bar of California, or a section of the State Bar of California, a government, a governmental agency or authority, a foreign government, a foreign bar association, a bona fide public or private educational institution as defined in Section 203 of the Revenue and Taxation Code, a nonprofit organization which is exempt from taxation under Section 501(c)(3) of the Internal Revenue Code, or by a person domiciled outside the United States who substantially satisfies the requirements for tax exempt status under Section 501(c)(3) of the Internal Revenue Code, is allowed within the meaning of Labor Code section 123.6 for actual transportation and any reasonably necessary lodging and subsistence provided directly in connection with the speech, panel, seminar, or service, provided that the lodging and subsistence expenses are limited to the day immediately preceding, the day of, and the day immediately following the speech, panel participation or seminar, and the travel is within the United States.

(m) Payment, provision, or reimbursement for a judge's travel, including actual transportation and related lodging and subsistence, that is reasonably related to a legislative or governmental purpose, or to an issue of state, national, or international public policy, that is provided by a government, a governmental agency or authority, a foreign government, a bona fide public or private educational institution as defined in Section 203 of the Revenue and Taxation Code, a nonprofit organization which is exempt from taxation under Section 501(c)(3) of the Internal Revenue Code, or by a person domiciled outside the United States who substantially satisfies the requirements for tax exempt status under Section 501(c)(3) of the Internal Revenue Code, is allowed within the meaning of Labor Code section 123.6, and may also be accepted when prior approval of the Court Administrator is not required.

(n) Upon approval by the Court Administrator, payment, provision, or reimbursement for a judge's travel in connection with a speech, participation in a panel or seminar, or provision of a similar service, if the event is sponsored by, or if the payment or reimbursement is to be made by, an association or group of attorneys who practice before the appeals board, will be allowed for the following:

Refreshments and similar non-cash nominal benefits provided to a judge during the entire event at which the judge gives a speech, participates in a panel or seminar, or provides a similar service, actual transportation and any reasonably necessary lodging and subsistence provided directly in connection with the speech, panel, seminar, or service. Reasonably necessary subsistence is limited to meals and beverages served contemporaneously with a breakfast, dinner, or luncheon speech, panel participation or seminar, and to meals consumed while traveling to or from the activity, limited to the days of necessary travel.

(o) When prior approval of the Court Administrator is not required, payment or reimbursement for travel in connection with a speech, participation in a panel or seminar, or provision of a similar service, if the event is sponsored by a professional association of judges, the State Bar of California, or a section of the State Bar of California, a government, a governmental agency or authority, a foreign government, a foreign bar association, an international service organization, a bona fide public or private educational institution as defined in Section 203 of the Revenue and Taxation Code, a nonprofit organization which is exempt from taxation under Section 501(c)(3) of the Internal Revenue Code, or by a person domiciled outside the United States who substantially satisfies the requirements for tax exempt status under Section 501(c)(3) of the Internal Revenue Code, may be accepted for actual transportation and any reasonably necessary lodging and subsistence provided directly in connection with the speech, panel, seminar, or service, provided that the lodging and subsistence expenses are limited to the day immediately preceding, the day of, and the day immediately following the speech, panel participation or seminar, and the travel is within the United States.

Note: Authority cited: Sections 123.6, 133 and 5307.3, Labor Code. Reference: Sections 111 and 123.6, Labor Code.

History: 1. New section filed 11-30-95; operative 12-1-95. Submitted to OAL for printing only pursuant to Government Code section 11351 (Register 95, No. 48).

2. Amendment filed 8-25-2008; operative 9-24-2008 (Register 2008, No. 35).

Ref.: Hanna § 1.11[3][a]; Herlick Handbook §§ 1.2, 1.6.

§9721.11. Requirement for Disclosure.

A judge shall disclose to all parties or attorneys in a case, at the time the judge first becomes aware of the existence of the facts, any and all of the following:

(a) That the judge served as a lawyer for a party at any time within the three years before being assigned to the case. "Serving as a lawyer" includes having interviewed a prospective client and learned confidential information, although the judge did not become a lawyer for the prospective client. A judge shall use the resources reasonably available to the judge to ascertain the identity of the judge's former clients.

(b) That the judge provided legal advice on the specific issue presently at bar to a party involved in the instant action or proceeding.

(c) That within the past two years, a party, officer, director, or trustee of a party was a client of the judge or of a lawyer with whom the judge was associated in private practice, as an employee or on a contract basis.

(d) That a lawyer, associate of the lawyer in private practice, or spouse of a lawyer in the proceeding is a spouse, former spouse, child, sibling, or parent of the judge or of the judge's spouse.

(e) That the judge has, as a lawyer or public official, participated in the drafting of enacted laws or actively participated in the effort to pass or defeat laws, the meaning, effect, or application of which is in issue in the proceeding. "Actively participated" means the judge has engaged in lobbying, or made other substantial efforts to change law. Mere membership in an organization which advocates or has advocated change in law does not constitute active participation.

(f) Any information that the workers' compensation administrative law judge believes would be relevant to the issue of disqualification, such that a person aware of the facts might reasonably entertain a doubt as to the workers' compensation administrative law judge's ability to be impartial.

(g) Any situation known to the judge, disclosure of which is required by the Code of Judicial Ethics.

(h) That the judge has a disputed workers' compensation claim against a party.

Note: Authority cited: Sections 123.6, 133 and 5307.3, Labor Code. Reference: Sections 111 and 123.6, Labor Code.

History: 1. New section filed 8-25-2008; operative 9-24-2008 (Register 2008, No. 35).

§9721.12. Disqualification.

(a) A judge is disqualified in a workers' compensation case if any of the following is true:

(1) The judge has personal knowledge of disputed evidentiary facts.

(2) The judge served as lawyer for a party in the past two years.

(3) The judge has actual bias in favor of or against any party and the judge has substantial doubt as to his or her capacity to be impartial.

(4) Because of physical impairment, the judge is unable to perceive evidence or properly conduct proceedings.

(5) Within the past two years, the judge served as a lawyer for an officer, director, trustee of a party.

(6) Within the past two years, the judge was associated in private practice, as an employee or on a contract basis, with a lawyer in the proceedings.

(7) The judge, the judge's spouse, or minor child of the judge, personally or as a fiduciary, has a financial interest in the subject matter in a proceeding or in a party to the proceeding, or has a relationship of director, advisor, or active participant to a party to the proceeding.

(8) The judge, the judge's spouse, a relative of either within the third degree of relationship, or spouse of such relative, is likely to be a material witness.

(9) A party to the action before the judge, or the party's spouse, is related within the third degree of relationship to either the judge or to the judge's spouse.

(10) The judge believes that recusal would further the interests of justice or believes there is a substantial doubt as to his or her capacity to be impartial.

(11) The judge has actual bias against or in favor of an attorney for a party and the judge has a substantial doubt as to his or her capacity to be impartial. A judge is not disqualified as to other members or associates in a law firm, or as to the law firm itself, solely because of actual bias

against or in favor of individual attorneys in or associated with the firm. Actual bias in favor of or against an attorney does not in itself create the appearance of bias as to a law firm of which the attorney is a member or associate. A doubt of a person aware of the facts that a judge could be impartial towards a law firm or other members or associates of a law firm, based only on knowledge of a judge's bias in favor of or against an individual attorney or attorneys, is not a doubt which is reasonably entertained. If the workers' compensation appeals board, on a petition for disqualification alleging bias against or in favor of an attorney, determines that a judge is disqualified because of the appearance of bias or because a person aware of the facts might reasonably entertain a doubt that the judge could be impartial, it shall not be presumed, as to a law firm of which the attorney is a member or associate, or as to other members or associates of the law firm:

A. that there is the appearance of bias; or

B. that a person aware of the facts might reasonably entertain a doubt that the judge could be impartial.

(b) The parties may waive the disqualification of a judge after written disclosure of the facts constituting a ground of disqualification. A judge who believes he or she is disqualified shall recuse or shall state in writing the basis of disqualification. All waivers shall be in writing and shall be made part of the file, or shall be made on the record. The judge may ask the parties and their attorneys whether they wish to waive the disqualification. The judge may not request the parties or attorneys to waive the disqualification The parties and any attorney for the employee shall execute any waiver. An attorney for a party other than the employee may execute the waiver on behalf of the attorney's clients. Such a waiver shall state that the attorney has advised the client of the disqualification information, and that the client has agreed to waive the disqualification.

(c) Disqualification for the following circumstances cannot be waived:

(1) The judge, the judge's spouse, a relative of either within the third degree of relationship, or spouse of such relative, is likely to be a material witness

(2) The judge served as a lawyer in the case.

Note: Authority cited: Sections 123.6, 133 and 5307.3, Labor Code. Reference: Sections 111 and 123.6, Labor Code.

History: 1. New section filed 8-25-2008; operative 9-24-2008 (Register 2008, No. 35).

§9721.13. What Are Not Grounds for Disqualification.

The following factors do not in themselves disqualify a judge:

(a) That the judge is or is not a member of a racial, ethnic, religious, gender, or sexual orientation classification, and the proceedings involve the rights of a person of the same classification.

(b) That the judge has, in any capacity, expressed a view on a legal or factual issue presented in the proceeding, except if the judge has formed or expressed an unqualified opinion or belief as to the merits of the particular action before the judge.

(c) That the judge has a policy of insurance with an insurance company that is a party or is a carrier of a party in the proceeding, unless the judge also has a pending claim or dispute with the insurance company.

(d) That the judge has a currently disputed or recently finalized workers' compensation claim against a party.

Note: Authority cited: Sections 123.6, 133 and 5307.3, Labor Code. Reference: Sections 111 and 123.6, Labor Code.

History: 1. New section filed 8-25-2008; operative 9-24-2008 (Register 2008, No. 35).

§9721.14. Manner of Disclosure.

(a) Facts or circumstances which are required to be disclosed pursuant to §9721.11 or §9721.12, except for those which must be disclosed pursuant to subdivision (a) of §9721.11, shall be disclosed on the record.

(b) Facts or circumstances which are required to be disclosed pursuant to subdivision (a) of §9721.11 may be disclosed by the judge by providing a list of former clients. The posting in the courtroom of a list of the judge's former clients will satisfy this requirement as to former clients who were not employee workers' compensation claimants. A judge shall not post a list of former clients who were employee workers' compensation claimants, but shall make a list available to the parties in a case, and shall disclose the availability of the list.

Note: Authority cited: Sections 123.6, 133 and 5307.3, Labor Code. Reference: Sections 111 and 123.6, Labor Code.

History: 1. New section filed 8-25-2008; operative 9-24-2008 (Register 2008, No. 35).

§9721.21. Restriction on Investments.

(a) A workers' compensation administrative law judge may not have an ownership interest in, either in his individual capacity or as a fiduciary, and may not purchase an interest in, an insurance carrier which either writes policies of workers' compensation insurance to employers in the state of California or is authorized to write policies of workers' compensation insurance to employers in the state of California.

(b) A workers' compensation administrative law judge who, as of the date this regulation becomes effective, has an interest in an insurance company described in subdivision (a), shall dispose of the interest or terminate the fiduciary relationship within one year of the date this regulation becomes effective.

(c) A workers' compensation administrative law judge who acquires an interest in an insurance company described in subdivision (a) through gift, inheritance or devise, or by becoming a fiduciary for a person, estate, or trust which has an interest in such an insurance company, shall dispose of the acquired interest or terminate the fiduciary relationship within one year.

(d) Upon application by a workers' compensation administrative law judge who acquired an interest in an insurance company described in subdivision (a) through gift, inheritance or devise, or by becoming a fiduciary for a person, estate, or trust which has an interest in such an insurance company, and upon the showing of hardship to the judge or to the person, trust, or estate for whom the judge is serving as fiduciary, the Administrative Director may grant an extension of time to dispose of the acquired interest or to terminate the fiduciary relationship or may grant an exemption if the value of the interest is de minimus.

(e) The obligation of a workers' compensation administrative law judge under the California Code of Judicial Ethics to "manage personal investments and financial activities so as to minimize the necessity for disqualification" includes the obligation not to acquire or hold investments in self-insured employers who are reasonably likely to be defendant employers in cases at the district office where the judge is usually employed.

(f) An ownership interest in a corporation which owns, wholly or in part, an insurance carrier which either writes policies of workers' compensation insurance to employers in the state of California or is authorized to write policies of workers' compensation insurance to employers in the state of California, is not an ownership interest in that insurance carrier. This subdivision shall not affect a judge's disqualification or obligation to disclose.

Note: Authority cited: Sections 123.6, 133 and 5307.3, Labor Code. Reference: Sections 111 and 123.6, Labor Code.

History: 1. New section filed 8-25-2008; operative 9-24-2008 (Register 2008, No. 35).

§9721.31. Financial Interests in Educational Programs.

(a) A workers' compensation administrative law judge may not have an ownership interest in, nor may the workers' compensation administrative law judge receive a percentage of revenue or any other contingent economic interest relating to, educational programs servicing the workers' compensation community.

(b) As used in this section, "percentage of revenues or any other contingent financial interest" does not include:

(1) Usual and customary royalties or residuals paid by commercial publishers in the normal course of business, provided that the publisher does not appear before the workers' compensation administrative law judge in question.

(2) Usual and customary royalties or residuals earned by a workers' compensation administrative law judge who self-publishes or owns the company that publishes his or her work, provided that the book is not available for purchase or delivery at any office of the Division of Workers' Compensation and is not sold or distributed by any Division of Workers' Compensation employee on behalf of the workers' administrative law judge. Any workers' compensation administrative law judge who self-publishes or owns the company that publishes his or her work has the responsibility to submit to the Court Administrator, or his or her designee, for approval a proposed plan that complies with this subdivision. If there is no Court Administrator, then the workers' compensation administrative law judge shall submit the proposed plan to the Administrative Director.

Note: Authority cited: Sections 123.6, 133 and 5307.3, Labor Code. Reference: Sections 111 and 123.6, Labor Code.

History: 1. New section filed 11-30-95; operative 12-1-95. Submitted to OAL for printing only pursuant to Government Code section 11351 (Register 95, No. 48).

2. Amendment filed 8-25-2008; operative 9-24-2008 (Register 2008, No. 35).

Ref.: Hanna § 1.11[3][a]; Herlick Handbook §§ 1.2, 1.6.

§9721.32. Duty to Report Ethics Violations.

When circumstances warrant, a workers' compensation administrative law judge shall take or initiate appropriate corrective action, which may include reporting to the appropriate authority, in respect to a workers' compensation administrative law judge, lawyer, party, or other person who engages in unprofessional, fraudulent or other improper conduct of which the workers' compensation administrative law judge becomes aware through personal knowledge or based upon information the judge reasonably believes to be competent and reliable.

Note: Authority cited: Sections 123.6, 133 and 5307.3, Labor Code. Reference: Sections 111 and 123.6, Labor Code.

History: 1. New section filed 11-30-95; operative 12-1-95. Submitted to OAL for printing only pursuant to Government Code section 11351 (Register 95, No. 48).

2. Amendment of section heading and section filed 8-25-2008; operative 9-24-2008 (Register 2008, No. 35).

Ref.: Hanna § 1.11[3][a]; Herlick Handbook §§ 1.2, 1.6.

§9721.33. Previously Earned Compensation.

A Workers' Compensation Administrative Law Judge may receive previously earned compensation.

Note: Authority cited: Sections 123.6, 133 and 5307.3, Labor Code. Reference: Sections 111 and 123.6, Labor Code.

History: 1. New section filed 8-25-2008; operative 9-24-2008 (Register 2008, No. 35).

§9722. The Workers' Compensation Ethics Advisory Committee.

(a) There shall be a Workers' Compensation Ethics Advisory Committee consisting of nine members appointed by the Administrative Director or by his/her designee:

(1) a member of the public representing organized labor,

(2) a member of the public representing insurers,

(3) a member of the public representing self-insured employers,

(4) an attorney who formerly practiced before the Workers' Compensation Appeals Board and who usually represented insurers or employers,

(5) an attorney who formerly practiced before the Workers' Compensation Appeals Board and who usually represented applicants,

(6) a presiding workers' compensation administrative law judge,

(7) a workers' compensation administrative law judge or retired workers' compensation administrative law judge,

(8) and (9) two members of the public outside the workers' compensation community.

Members shall serve for a term of four years. However, to create staggered terms, the first term of members in odd-numbered categories above shall be two years. The Administrative Director shall designate a chairperson.

(b) The Committee shall meet as necessary to carry out its responsibilities under this article. State employees shall meet on state time and at state expense.

(c) The Committee may do the following:

(1) Receive complaints made against workers' compensation administrative law judges,

(2) Forward those complaints to the Administrative Director or Court Administrator with a recommendation to investigate or not to investigate,

(3) Monitor the outcome of complaints, and

(4) Make reports and recommendations to the Administrative Director, the Court Administrator, the legislature and the public concerning the integrity of the workers' compensation adjudicatory process. The Committee shall make a public report on or before April 15 or each year, summarizing the activities of the Committee in the previous calendar year. The report shall not contain personally identifiable information concerning complainants or workers' compensation administrative law judges, unless the information is already public.

(d) The Administrative Director shall make staff available to the Committee to assist it in carrying out its functions.

(e) The Committee may receive information that is not available to the public. The Committee shall hold such information strictly confidential from public disclosure. However, this rule of confidentiality shall not prevent the Administrative Director or Court Administrator from disclosing information to the workers' compensation administrative law judge, if the workers' compensation administrative law judge is otherwise entitled to the information.

Note: Authority cited: Sections 123.6, 133 and 5307.3, Labor Code. Reference: Sections 111 and 123.6, Labor Code.

History: 1. New section filed 11-30-95; operative 12-1-95. Submitted to OAL for printing only pursuant to Government Code section 11351 (Register 95, No. 48).

2. Amendment filed 8-25-2008; operative 9-24-2008 (Register 2008, No. 35).

Ref.: Hanna § 1.11[3][a]; Herlick Handbook §§ 1.2, 1.6.

§9722.1. Commencing an Investigation.

(a) Any person may file a complaint concerning an ethics violation by a workers' compensation administrative law judge with the Committee. The Committee or the Administrative Director may require complaints to be filed in a particular form. Nothing in these regulations prohibits any person from complaining directly to a presiding workers' compensation administrative law judge, the Chief Judge, the Court Administrator or to the Administrative Director. The presiding workers' compensation administrative law judge, the Chief Judge, and Court Administrator or the Administrative Director may, but is not required to, refer such complaints to the Committee.

(b) The Committee shall review the complaint. The Committee may make inquiries to obtain information needed to clarify the complaint and/or to obtain additional information necessary to determine if the complaint might have merit.

(c) If the Committee determines that the complaint does not allege facts that might constitute an ethics violation, or if the complaint is merely conjectural or conclusory, specious, obviously unfounded, or stale, or alleges only legal error by the workers' compensation administrative law judge, the Committee shall forward the complaint to the Administrative Director or Court Administrator with a recommendation not to proceed with the complaint.

(d) If the Committee determines that the complaint might have merit, the Committee shall refer the complaint to the Administrative Director or Court Administrator. Complaints against the Administrative Director or Court Administrator shall be referred to the Director of Industrial Relations.

(e) Except as otherwise provided in subdivision (c) of section 9722.2, reports and recommendations of the Committee regarding individual complaints shall remain confidential.

Note: Authority cited: Sections 123.6, 133 and 5307.3, Labor Code. Reference: Sections 111 and 123.6, Labor Code.

History: 1. New section filed 11-30-95; operative 12-1-95. Submitted to OAL for printing only pursuant to Government Code section 11351 (Register 95, No. 48).

2. Amendment filed 8-25-2008; operative 9-24-2008 (Register 2008, No. 35).

Ref.: Hanna § 1.11[3][a]; Herlick Handbook §§ 1.2, 1.6.

§9722.2. Investigation and Action by the Administrative Director or Court Administrator.

(a) Upon receiving a complaint from the Committee, the Administrative Director or Court Administrator shall investigate whether a workers' compensation administrative law judge has committed an ethics violation.

(b) If the Administrative Director or Court Administrator determines after investigation that misconduct has occurred, he or she shall take appropriate disciplinary or other action against the workers' compensation administrative law judge. The Administrative Director's or Court Administrator's action shall be in the form required by Government Code section 19574 or section 19590(b), or other applicable laws governing the ethics violation.

(c) The Administrative Director or Court Administrator shall provide the Committee with a copy of his or her decision and shall inform the complaining party whether an ethical violation occurred, and whether corrective action was taken.

Note: Authority cited: Sections 123.6, 133 and 5307.3, Labor Code. Reference: Sections 111 and 123.6, Labor Code.

History: 1. New section filed 11-30-95; operative 12-1-95. Submitted to OAL for printing only pursuant to Government Code section 11351 (Register 95, No. 48).

2. Amendment of section heading and section filed 8-25-2008; operative 9-24-2008 (Register 2008, No. 35).

Ref.: Hanna § 1.11[3][a]; Herlick Handbook §§ 1.2, 1.6.

§9723. Miscellaneous Provisions.

(a) This article does not replace or diminish the procedural rights of a workers' compensation administrative law judge under the State Civil Service Act. Documentation of unfounded or unsubstantiated complaints shall not be retained in the employee's personnel file.

(b) This article does not replace or diminish the authority of the Administrative Director or Court Administrator to investigate allegations of ethics violations, to impose appropriate discipline, or to take any other action authorized by law.

(c) Nothing in this article shall affect the rights and obligations of the Administrative Director or Court Administrator and workers' compensation administrative law judges concerning the probationary period under Government Code sections 19170 through 19180.

(d) Pursuant to Government Code section 19574.5, the Administrative Director or Court Administrator may place a workers' compensation administrative law judge on leave of absence pending investigation of the accusations listed in that section.

(e) A workers' compensation administrative law judge or other interested person may request the Administrative Director or Court Administrator to issue an advisory opinion on the application of the Code or other rules to a particular situation. The Administrative Director or Court Administrator may, in his or her sole discretion, issue an advisory opinion. The Administrative Director or Court Administrator may issue an advisory opinion on his or her own initiative.

Note: Authority cited: Sections 123.6, 133 and 5307.3, Labor Code. Reference: Sections 111 and 123.6, Labor Code.

History: 1. New section filed 11-30-95; operative 12-1-95. Submitted to OAL for printing only pursuant to Government Code section 11351 (Register 95, No. 48).

2. Amendment filed 8-25-2008; operative 9-24-2008 (Register 2008, No. 35).

Ref.: Herlick Handbook §§ 1.2, 1.6.

ARTICLE 2
Disabilities, Description of

§9725. Method of Measurement.

The method of measuring physical elements of a disability should follow the Report of the Joint Committee of the California Medical Association and Industrial Accident Commission, as contained in "*Evaluation of Industrial Disability*" edited by Packard Thurber, Second Edition, Oxford University Press, New York, 1960. This section shall not apply to any permanent disability evaluations performed pursuant to the permanent disability rating schedule adopted on or after January 1, 2005.

Note: Authority cited: Sections 133 and 5307.3, Labor Code. Reference: Sections 4660, 4662, 4663 and 4664, Labor Code.

History: 1. New Subchapter (§§9725, 9727, 9732, 9735, 9738, 9739, 9742-9744, 9750, 9753, 9756-9760, 9770, 9773, 9775, 9778, 9784, 9787, 9790, 9796, 9799, 9802 and 9805) filed 4-18-66; effective thirtieth day thereafter (Register 65, No. 10).

2. Amendment of section and Note filed 12-31-2004 as an emergency; operative 1-1-2005 (Register 2004, No. 53). A Certificate of Compliance must be transmitted to OAL by 5-2-2005 or emergency language will be repealed by operation of law on the following day.

3. Certificate of Compliance as to 12-31-2004 order transmitted to OAL 4-29-2005 and filed 6-10-2005 (Register 2005, No. 23).

Editor's Note: "*Evaluation of Industrial Disability*" is available in major law libraries in California.

Ref.: Hanna §§ 22.08[5][b], 32.02[2][b]; Herlick Handbook §§ 1.6, 14.23.

§9726. Method of Measurement (Psychiatric).

The method of measuring the psychiatric elements of a disability shall follow the Report of the Subcommittee on Permanent Psychiatric Disability to the Medical Advisory Committee of the California Division of Industrial Accidents, entitled "The Evaluation of Permanent Psychiatric Disability," (hereinafter referred to as the "Psychiatric Protocols") as adopted, forwarded for adoption on July 10, 1987, and subsequent amendments and/or revisions thereto adopted after a public hearing. This section shall not apply to any permanent disability evaluations performed pursuant to the permanent disability rating schedule adopted on or after January 1, 2005.

Note: The Report (which contains these Protocols) of the Subcommittee on Permanent Psychiatric Disability, as adopted, does not appear as a printed part of the Administrative Director's Regulations (8 California Code of Regulations, Section 9726); copies will be available through the Medical Director of the Division of Industrial Accidents.

Note: Authority cited: Sections 133 and 5307.3, Labor Code. Reference: Sections 4660, 4662, 4663 and 4664, Labor Code.

History: 1. New section filed 8-24-87; operative 8-24-87 (Register 87, No. 36). This regulation was filed pursuant to Government Code Section 11351 and thus this filing is exempted from compliance with Article 5 (commencing with Section 11346), (except subdivision (e) of Section 11346.4), Article 6 (commencing with Section 11349), and Article 7 (commencing with Section 11350) of Chapter 3.5 of the Government Code. The provisions of Government Code Section 11343.6 are not applicable to this filing.

2. Amendment filed 6-30-88; operative 7-1-88 (Register 88, No. 28). The amendment was filed pursuant to Government Code Section 11351.

3. Amendment of section and Note filed 12-31-2004 as an emergency; operative 1-1-2005 (Register 2004, No. 53). A Certificate of Compliance must be transmitted to OAL by 5-2-2005 or emergency language will be repealed by operation of law on the following day.

4. Certificate of Compliance as to 12-31-2004 order transmitted to OAL 4-29-2005 and filed 6-10-2005 (Register 2005, No. 23).

Ref.: Hanna §§ 4.69[3][a], 4.69[3][c], 8.02[4][c][i], 22.08[5][c], 32.02[5][b][i]–[ii]; Herlick Handbook §§ 1.6, 6.14, 14.23; Lawyer's Guide to AMA *Guides* and Calif. Workers' Comp. §§ 2.06, 13.14.

§9727. Subjective Disability.

Subjective Disability should be identified by:

1. A description of the activity which produces the disability.

2. The duration of the disability.

3. The activities which are precluded and those which can be performed with the disability.

4. The means necessary for relief. The terms shown below are presumed to mean the following:

1. A *severe* pain would preclude the activity precipitating the pain.

2. A *moderate* pain could be tolerated, but would cause marked handicap in the performance of the activity precipitating the pain.

3. A *slight* pain could be tolerated, but would cause some handicap in the performance of the activity precipitating the pain.

4. A *minimal* (mild) pain would constitute an annoyance, but causing no handicap in the performance of the particular activity, would be considered as nonratable permanent disability.

This section shall not apply to any permanent disability evaluations performed pursuant to the permanent disability rating schedule adopted on or after January 1, 2005.

Note: Authority cited: Sections 133 and 5307.3, Labor Code. Reference: Sections 4660, 4662, 4663 and 4664, Labor Code.

History: 1. New last paragraph and new Note filed 12-31-2004 as an emergency; operative 1-1-2005 (Register 2004, No. 53). A Certificate of Compliance must be transmitted to OAL by 5-2-2005 or emergency language will be repealed by operation of law on the following day.

2. Certificate of Compliance as to 12-31-2004 order transmitted to OAL 4-29-2005 and filed 6-10-2005 (Register 2005, No. 23).

Ref.: Hanna §§ 8.02[4][b], 22.08[5][b], 32.02[2][c][i]–[ii]; Herlick Handbook §§ 1.6, 6.11, 6.13.

ARTICLE 3
Permanent Disability Ratings and Evaluations

§9732. Repealed.

Note: Authority cited: Sections 124, 127, 133, 138.2, 138.3, 138.4, 139, 139.5, 139.6, 4600, 4601, 4602, 4603, 4603.2, 4603.5, 5307.3, 5450, 5451, 5452, 5453, 5454, and 5455, Labor Code. Reference: Chapters 442, 709, and 1172, Statutes of 1977; Chapter 1017, Statutes of 1976.

History: 1. Amendment filed 11-7-78; effective thirtieth day thereafter (Register 78, No. 45).

2. Repealer of article 3 (sections 9732-9766, nonconsecutive) and section filed 12-27-96; operative 12-27-96. Submitted to OAL for printing only pursuant to Government Code section 11351 (Register 96, No. 52).

§9735. Repealed.

History: 1. Repealer of section filed 12-27-96; operative 12-27-96. Submitted to OAL for printing only pursuant to Government Code section 11351 (Register 96, No. 52).

§9738. Repealed.

History: 1. Amendment filed 11-7-78; effective thirtieth day thereafter (Register 78, No. 45).

2. Amendment filed 10-16-81; effective thirtieth day thereafter (Register 81, No. 42).

3. Repealer of section filed 12-27-96; operative 12-27-96. Submitted to OAL for printing only pursuant to Government Code section 11351 (Register 96, No. 52).

§9739. Repealed.

Note: Authority cited: Sections 124, 133 and 5307.3, Labor Code. Reference: Section 124, Labor Code.

History: 1. Change without regulatory effect filed 7-11-86; effective upon filing (Register 86, No. 28).

2. Repealer of section filed 12-27-96; operative 12-27-96. Submitted to OAL for printing only pursuant to Government Code section 11351 (Register 96, No. 52).

§9742. Repealed.

Note: Authority cited: Sections 124, 5307.3 and 5451, Labor Code. Reference: Sections 124, 5451 and 5453, Labor Code.

History: 1. Amendment filed 12-8-69; designated effective 1-1-70 (Register 69, No. 50).

2. Amendment filed 11-7-78; effective thirtieth day thereafter (Register 78, No. 45).

3. Amendment filed 10-16-81; effective thirtieth day thereafter (Register 81, No. 42).

4. Amendment filed 7-15-83; effective thirtieth day thereafter (Register 83, No. 30).

5. Editorial correction of 7-15-83 order redesignating effective date to 8-1-83 pursuant to Government Code Section 11346.2(d) filed 7-19-83 (Register 83, No. 30).

6. Amendment filed 8-29-84; effective thirtieth day thereafter (Register 84, No. 35).

7. Repealer of section filed 12-27-96; operative 12-27-96. Submitted to OAL for printing only pursuant to Government Code section 11351 (Register 96, No. 52).

§9750. Repealed.

Note: Authority cited: Sections 124, 133 and 5307.3, Labor Code. Reference: Section 124, Labor Code.

History: 1. Change without regulatory effect filed 7-11-86; effective upon filing (Register 86, No. 28).

2. Repealer of section filed 12-27-96; operative 12-27-96. Submitted to OAL for printing only pursuant to Government Code section 11351 (Register 96, No. 52).

§9753. Repealed.

History: 1. Repealer of section filed 12-27-96; operative 12-27-96. Submitted to OAL for printing only pursuant to Government Code section 11351 (Register 96, No. 52).

§9757. Repealed.

Note: Authority cited: Sections 124 and 5307.3, Labor Code. Reference: Section 124, Labor Code.

History: 1. Amendment filed 10-16-81; effective thirtieth day thereafter (Register 81, No. 42.)

2. Change without regulatory effect filed 7-11-86; effective upon filing (Register 86, No. 28).

3. Repealer of section filed 12-27-96; operative 12-27-96. Submitted to OAL for printing only pursuant to Government Code section 11351 (Register 96, No. 52).

§9758. Repealed.

Note: Authority cited: Sections 124, 5307.3 and 5451, Labor Code. Reference: Sections 123.7, 124 and 5453, Labor Code.

History: 1. Amendment filed 12-14-72; designated effective 1-1-73 (Register 72, No. 51).

2. Amendment filed 11-7-78; effective thirtieth day thereafter (Register 78, No. 45).

3. Amendment filed 10-16-81; effective thirtieth day thereafter (Register 81, No. 42).

4. Amendment filed 7-15-83; effective thirtieth day thereafter (Register 83, No. 30).

5. Editorial correction of 7-15-83 order redesignating effective date to 8-1-83 pursuant to Government Code Section 11346.2(d) filed 7-19-83 (Register 83, No. 30).

6. Repealer of section filed 12-27-96; operative 12-27-96. Submitted to OAL for printing only pursuant to Government Code section 11351 (Register 96, No. 52).

§9759. Repealed.

Note: Authority cited: Sections 124, 133, 5307.3 and 5451, Labor Code. Reference: Sections 123.7, 124 and 5453, Labor Code.

History: 1. Amendment filed 7-15-83; effective thirtieth day thereafter (Register 83, No. 30).

2. Editorial correction of 7-15-83 order redesignating effective date to 8-1-83 pursuant to Government Code Section 11346.2(d) filed 7-19-83 (Register 83, No. 30).

3. Change without regulatory effect filed 7-11-86; effective upon filing (Register 86, No. 28).

4. Repealer of section filed 12-27-96; operative 12-27-96. Submitted to OAL for printing only pursuant to

Government Code section 11351 (Register 96, No. 52).

§9766. Repealed.

Note: Authority cited: Sections 124, 127, 133, 138.2, 138.3, 138.4, 139, 139.5, 139.6, 4600, 4601, 4602, 4603, 4603.2, 4603.5, 5307.3, 5450, 5451, 5452, 5453, 5454 and 5455, Labor Code. Reference: Section 124, Labor Code; and Section 14755, Government Code.

History: 1. New section filed 6-27-66; effective thirtieth day thereafter (Register 66, No. 20).

2. Amendment of subsection (a) filed 11-7-7; effective thirtieth day thereafter (Register 78, No. 45).

3. Amendment filed 7-15-83; effective thirtieth day thereafter (Register 83, No. 30).

4. Editorial correction of 7-15-83 order redesignating effective date to 8-1-83 pursuant to Government Code Section 11346.2(d) filed 7-19-83 (Register 83, No. 30).

5. Change without regulatory effect of subsections (a) and (b) filed 7-11-86; effective upon filing (Register 86, No. 28).

6. Repealer of section filed 12-27-96; operative 12-27-96. Submitted to OAL for printing only pursuant to Government Code section 11351 (Register 96, No. 52).

ARTICLE 3.5
Medical Provider Network

§9767.1. Medical Provider Networks—Definitions.

(a) As used in this article:

(1) "Ancillary services" means any provision of medical services or goods as allowed in Labor Code section 4600 by a non-physician.

(2) "Cessation of use" means the discontinued use of an implemented MPN that continues to do business.

(3) "Covered employee" means an employee or former employee whose employer has ongoing workers' compensation obligations and whose employer or employer's insurer has established a Medical Provider Network for the provision of medical treatment to injured employees unless:

(A) the injured employee has properly designated a personal physician pursuant to Labor Code section 4600(d) by notice to the employer prior to the date of injury, or;

(B) the injured employee's employment with the employer is covered by an agreement providing medical treatment for the injured employee and the agreement is validly established under Labor Code section 3201.5, 3201.7 and/or 3201.81.

(4) "Division" means the Division of Workers' Compensation.

(5) "Economic profiling" means any evaluation of a particular physician, provider, medical group, or individual practice association based in whole or in part on the economic costs or utilization of services associated with medical care provided or authorized by the physician, provider, medical group, or individual practice association.

(6) "Emergency health care services" means health care services for a medical condition manifesting itself by acute symptoms of sufficient severity such that the absence of immediate medical attention could reasonably be expected to place the patient's health in serious jeopardy.

(7) "Employer" means a self-insured employer, the Self-Insurer's Security Fund, a group of self-insured employers pursuant to Labor Code section 3700(b) and as defined by Title 8, California Code of Regulations, section 15201(s), a joint powers authority, or the state.

(8) "Group Disability Insurance Policy" means an entity designated pursuant to Labor Code section 4616.7(c).

(9) "Health Care Organization" means an entity designated pursuant to Labor Code section 4616.7(a).

(10) "Health Care Service Plan" means an entity designated pursuant to Labor Code section 4616.7(b).

(11) "Insurer" means an insurer admitted to transact workers' compensation insurance in the state of California, California Insurance Guarantee Association, or the State Compensation Insurance Fund.

(12) "Medical Provider Network" ("MPN") means any entity or group of providers approved as a Medical Provider Network by the Administrative Director pursuant to Labor Code sections 4616 to 4616.7 and this article.

(13) "Medical Provider Network Plan" means an employer's or insurer's detailed description for a medical provider network contained in an application submitted to the Administrative Director by a MPN applicant.

(14) "MPN Applicant" means an insurer or employer as defined in subdivisions (7) and (11) of this section.

(15) "MPN Contact" means an individual(s) designated by the MPN Applicant in the employee notification who is responsible for answering employees' questions about the Medical Provider Network and is responsible for assisting the employee in arranging for an independent medical review.

(16) "Nonoccupational Medicine" means the diagnosis or treatment of any injury or disease not arising out of and in the course of employment.

(17) "Occupational Medicine" means the diagnosis or treatment of any injury or disease arising out of and in the course of employment.

(18) "Physician primarily engaged in treatment of nonoccupational injuries" means a provider who spends more than 50 percent of his/her practice time providing non-occupational medical services.

(19) "Primary treating physician" means a primary treating physician within the medical provider network and as defined by section 9785(a)(1).

(20) "Provider" means a physician as described in Labor Code section 3209.3 or other provider as described in Labor Code section 3209.5.

(21) "Regional area listing" means either:

(A) a listing of all MPN providers within a 15-mile radius of an employee's worksite and/or residence; or

(B) a listing of all MPN providers in the county where the employee resides and/or works if

1. the employer or insurer cannot produce a provider listing based on a mile radius

2. or by choice of the employer or insurer, or upon request of the employee.

(C) If the listing described in either (A) or (B) does not provide a minimum of three physicians of each specialty, then the listing shall be expanded by adjacent counties or by 5-mile increments until the minimum number of physicians per specialty are met.

(22) "Residence" means the covered employee's primary residence.

(23) "Second Opinion" means an opinion rendered by a medical provider network physician after an in person examination to address an employee's dispute over either the diagnosis or the treatment prescribed by the treating physician.

(24) "Taft-Hartley health and welfare fund" means an entity designated pursuant to Labor Code section 4616.7(d).

(25) "Termination" means the discontinued use of an implemented MPN that ceases to do business.

(26) "Third Opinion" means an opinion rendered by a medical provider network physician after an in person examination to address an employee's dispute over either the diagnosis or the treatment prescribed by either the treating physician or physician rendering the second opinion.

(27) "Treating physician" means any physician within the MPN applicant's medical provider network other than the primary treating physician who examines or provides treatment to the employee, but is not primarily responsible for continuing management of the care of the employee.

(28) "Workplace" means the geographic location where the covered employee is regularly employed.

Note: Authority cited: Sections 133 and 4616(g), Labor Code. Reference: Sections 1063.1, 3208, 3209.3, 3209.5, 3700, 3702, 3743, 4616, 4616.1, 4616.3, 4616.5 and 4616.7, Labor Code; and *California Insurance Guarantee Association v. Division of Workers' Compensation* (April 26, 2005) WCAB No. Misc. #249.

History: 1. New article 3.5 (sections 9767.1–9767.14) and section filed 11-1-2004 as an emergency; operative 11-1-2004 (Register 2004, No. 45). A Certificate of Compliance must be transmitted to OAL by 3-1-2005 or emergency language will be repealed by operation of law on the following day.

2. New article 3.5 (sections 9767.1–9767.14) and section refiled 2-28-2005 as an emergency; operative 3-1-2005 (Register 2005, No. 9). A Certificate of Compliance must be transmitted to OAL by 6-29-2005 or emergency language will be repealed by operation of law on the following day.

3. New article 3.5 (sections 9767.1–9767.14) and section refiled 6-20-2005 as an emergency; operative 6-29-2005 (Register 2005, No. 25). A Certificate of Compliance must be transmitted to OAL by 10-27-2005 or emergency language will be repealed by operation of law on the following day.

4. Certificate of Compliance as to 6-20-2005 order, including amendment of section and Note, transmitted to OAL 7-29-2005 and filed 9-9-2005 (Register 2005, No. 36).

5. New subsections (a)(2) and (a)(25), subsection renumbering and amendment of newly designated

subsection (a)(14) filed 12-11-2007; operative 4-9-2008 (Register 2007, No. 50).

Ref.: Hanna § 5.05[13]; Herlick Handbook § 4.19A.

§9767.2. Review of Medical Provider Network Application.

(a) Within 60 days of the Administrative Director's receipt of a complete application, the Administrative Director shall approve or disapprove an application based on the requirements of Labor Code section 4616 et seq. and this article. An application shall be considered complete if it includes information responsive to each applicable subdivision of section 9767.3. Pursuant to Labor Code section 4616(b), if the Administrative Director has not acted on a plan within 60 days of submittal of a complete plan, it shall be deemed approved.

(b) The Administrative Director shall provide notification(s) to the MPN applicant: (1) setting forth the date the MPN application was received by the Division; and (2) informing the MPN applicant if the MPN application is not complete and the item(s) necessary to complete the application.

(c) No additional materials shall be submitted by the MPN applicant or considered by the Administrative Director until the MPN applicant receives the notification described in (b).

(d) The Administrative Director's decision to approve or disapprove an application shall be limited to his/her review of the information provided in the application.

(e) Upon approval of the Medical Provider Network Plan, the MPN applicant shall be assigned a MPN approval number.

Note: Authority cited: Sections 133 and 4616(g), Labor Code. Reference: Section 4616, Labor Code.

History: 1. New section filed 11-1-2004 as an emergency; operative 11-1-2004 (Register 2004, No. 45). A Certificate of Compliance must be transmitted to OAL by 3-1-2005 or emergency language will be repealed by operation of law on the following day.

2. New section refiled 2-28-2005 as an emergency; operative 3-1-2005 (Register 2005, No. 9). A Certificate of Compliance must be transmitted to OAL by 6-29-2005 or emergency language will be repealed by operation of law on the following day.

3. New section refiled 6-20-2005 as an emergency; operative 6-29-2005 (Register 2005, No. 25). A Certificate of Compliance must be transmitted to OAL by 10-27-2005 or emergency language will be repealed by operation of law on the following day.

4. Certificate of Compliance as to 6-20-2005 order, including new subsection (c) and subsection relettering, transmitted to OAL 7-29-2005 and filed 9-9-2005 (Register 2005, No. 36).

Ref.: Hanna § 5.05[13][a]; Herlick Handbook § 4.19A.

§9767.3. Application for a Medical Provider Network Plan.

(a) As long as the application for a medical provider network plan meets the requirements of Labor Code section 4616 et seq. and this article, nothing in this section precludes an employer or insurer from submitting for approval one or more medical provider network plans in its application.

(b) Nothing in this section precludes an insurer and an insured employer from agreeing to submit for approval a medical provider network plan which meets the specific needs of an insured employer considering the experience of the insured employer, the common injuries experienced by the insured employer, the type of occupation and industry in which the insured employer is engaged and the geographic area where the employees are employed.

(c) All MPN applicants shall submit an original Cover Page for Medical Provider Network Application with original signature, an original application, and a copy of the Cover Page for Medical Provider Network and application to the Division.

(1) A MPN applicant may submit the provider information and/or ancillary service provider information required in section 9767.3(a)(8)(C) and (D) on a computer disk(s) or CD ROM(s). The information shall be submitted as a Microsoft Excel spread sheet or as a Microsoft Access File unless an alternative format is approved by the Administrative Director.

(2) If the network provider information is submitted on a disk(s) or CD ROM(s), the provider file must have at a minimum five columns. These columns shall be: (1) physician name (2) license number (3) the taxpayer identification number (4) specialty and (5) location of each physician.

(3) If the ancillary service provider information is submitted on a disk(s) or CD ROM(s), the file must have at a minimum five columns. The columns shall be (1) the name of the each ancillary provider (2) license number (3) the taxpayer identification number (4) specialty or

type of service and (5) location of each ancillary service provider.

(d) If the network is not a Health Care Organization, Health Care Service Plan, Group Disability Insurance Policy, or Taft-Hartley Health and Welfare Fund, a Medical Provider Network application shall include all of the following information:

(1) Type of MPN Applicant: Insurer or Employer.

(2) Name of MPN Applicant.

(3) MPN Applicant's Taxpayer Identification Number.

(4) Name of Medical Provider Network, if applicable.

(5) Division Liaison: Provide the name, title, address, e-mail address, and telephone number of the person designated as the liaison for the Division, who is responsible for receiving compliance and informational communications from the Division and for disseminating the same within the MPN.

(6) The application must be verified by an officer or employee of the MPN applicant authorized to sign on behalf of the MPN applicant. The verification shall state: "I, the undersigned officer or employee of the MPN applicant, have read and signed this application and know the contents thereof, and verify that, to the best of my knowledge and belief, the information included in this application is true and correct."

(7) Nothing in this section precludes a network, entity, administrator, or other third-party, upon agreement with an MPN applicant, from preparing an MPN application on behalf of an insurer or employer.

(8) Description of Medical Provider Network Plan:

(A) State the number of employees expected to be covered by the MPN plan;

(B) Describe the geographic service area or areas within the State of California to be served;

(C) The name, license number, taxpayer identification number, specialty, and location of each physician as described in Labor Code Section 3209.3, or other providers as described in Labor Code Section 3209.5, who will be providing occupational medicine services under the plan. Alternatively, if the physicians are also part of a medical group practice, the name and taxpayer identification number of the medical group practice shall be identified in the application. By submission of the application, the MPN applicant is confirming that a contractual agreement exists with the physicians, providers or medical group practice in the MPN to provide treatment for injured workers in the workers' compensation system and that the contractual agreement is in compliance with Labor Code section 4609, if applicable.

(D) The name, license number (if required by the State of California), taxpayer identification number, specialty or type of service and location of each ancillary service, other than a physician or provider covered under subdivision (d)(8)(C), who will be providing medical services within the medical provider network. By submission of the application, the MPN applicant is confirming that a contractual agreement exists between the MPN and these ancillary services in the MPN or the MPN applicant and these ancillary services in the MPN;

(E) Describe how the MPN complies with the second and third opinion process set forth in section 9767.7;

(F) Describe how the MPN complies with the goal of at least 25% of physicians (not including pediatricians, OB/GYNs, or other specialties not likely to routinely provide care for common injuries and illnesses expected to be encountered in the MPN) primarily engaged in the treatment of nonoccupational injuries;

(G) Describe how the MPN arranges for providing ancillary services to its covered employees. Set forth which ancillary services, if any, will be within the MPN. For ancillary services not within the MPN, affirm that referrals will be made to services outside the MPN;

(H) Describe how the MPN complies with the access standards set forth in section 9767.5 for all covered employees;

(I) Describe the employee notification process, and attach an English and Spanish sample of the employee notification material described in sections 9767.12(a) and (b);

(J) Attach a copy of the written continuity of care policy as described in Labor Code section 4616.2;

(K) Attach a copy of the written transfer of care policy that complies with section 9767.9;

(L) Attach any policy or procedure that is used by the MPN applicant to conduct "economic profiling of MPN providers" pursuant to Labor Code section 4616.1 and affirm that a copy of the policy or procedure has been provided to the MPN providers or attach a statement that the MPN applicant does not conduct economic profiling of MPN providers;

(M) Provide an affirmation that the physician compensation is not structured in order to achieve the goal of reducing, delaying, or denying medical treatment or restricting access to medical treatment; and

(N) Describe how the MPN applicant will ensure that no person other than a licensed physician who is competent to evaluate the specific clinical issues involved in the medical treatment services, when these services are within the scope of the physician's practice, will modify, delay, or deny requests for authorization of medical treatment.

(e) If the entity is a Health Care Organization, a Medical Provider Network application shall set forth the following:

(1) Type of MPN Applicant: Insurer or Employer

(2) Name of MPN Applicant

(3) MPN Applicant's Taxpayer Identification Number

(4) Name of Medical Provider Network, if applicable.

(5) Division Liaison: Provide the name, title, address, e-mail address, and telephone number of the person designated as the liaison for the Division, who is responsible for receiving compliance and informational communications from the Division and for disseminating the same within the MPN.

(6) The application must be verified by an officer or employee of the MPN applicant authorized to sign on behalf of the MPN applicant. The verification shall state: "I, the undersigned officer or employee of the MPN applicant, have read and signed this application and know the contents thereof, and verify that, to the best of my knowledge and belief, the information included in this application is true and correct."

(7) Nothing in this section precludes a network, entity, administrator, or other third-party, upon agreement with an MPN applicant, from preparing an MPN application on behalf of an insurer or employer.

(8) Describe how the MPN complies with the second and third opinion process set forth in section 9767.7;

(9) Confirm that the application shall set forth that at least 25% of the network physicians are primarily engaged in nonoccupational medicine;

(10) Describe the geographic service area or areas within the State of California to be served and affirm that this access plan complies with the access standards set forth in section 9767.5;

(11) Describe the employee notification process, and attach an English and Spanish sample of the employee notification material described in sections 9767.12(a) and (b);

(12) Attach a copy of the written continuity of care policy as described in Labor Code section 4616.2;

(13) Attach a copy of the written transfer of care policy that complies with section 9767.9 with regard to the transfer of on-going cases from the HCO to the MPN;

(14) Attach a copy of the policy or procedure that is used by the MPN applicant to conduct "economic profiling of MPN providers" pursuant to Labor Code section 4616.1 and affirm that a copy of the policy or procedure has been provided to the MPN providers or attach a statement that the MPN applicant does not conduct economic profiling of MPN providers; and

(15) Describe the number of employees expected to be covered by the MPN plan and confirm that the number of employees is within the approved capacity of the HCO.

(16) By submission of the application, the MPN applicant is confirming that a contractual agreement exists with the physicians, providers or medical group practice in the MPN to provide treatment for injured workers in the workers' compensation system and that the contractual agreement with the providers is in compliance with Labor Code section 4609, if applicable.

(f) If the entity is a Health Care Service Plan, Group Disability Insurance Policy, or Taft-Hartley Health and Welfare Fund, in addition to the requirements set forth in subdivision (e) [excluding (e)(9) and (e)(15)], a Medical Provider Network application shall include the following information:

(1) The application shall set forth that the entity has a reasonable number of providers with competency in occupational medicine.

(A) The MPN applicant may show that a physician has competency by confirming that the physician either is Board Certified or was residency trained in that specialty.

(B) If (A) is not applicable, describe any other relevant procedure or process that assures that providers of medical treatment are competent to provide treatment for occupational injuries and illnesses.

(g) If the MPN applicant is providing for ancillary services within the MPN that are in addition to the services provided by the Health Care Organization, Health Care Service Plan, Group Disability Insurance Policy, or Taft-Hartley Health and Welfare Fund, it shall set forth the ancillary services in the application.

(h) If a Health Care Organization, Health Care Service Plan, Group Disability Insurance Policy, or Taft-Hartley Health and Welfare Fund has been approved as a MPN, and the entity does not maintain its certification or licensure or regulated status, then the entity must file a new Medical Provider Network Application pursuant to section 9767.3(d).

(i) If a Health Care Organization, Health Care Service Plan, Group Disability Insurance Policy, or Taft-Hartley Health and Welfare Fund has been modified from its certification or licensure or regulated status, the application shall comply with subdivision (d).

Note: Authority cited: Sections 133 and 4616(g), Labor Code. Reference: Sections 3209.3, 4609, 4616, 4616.1, 4616.2, 4616.3, 4616.5 and 4616.7, Labor Code.

History: 1. New section filed 11-1-2004 as an emergency; operative 11-1-2004 (Register 2004, No. 45). A Certificate of Compliance must be transmitted to OAL by 3-1-2005 or emergency language will be repealed by operation of law on the following day.

2. New section refiled 2-28-2005 as an emergency; operative 3-1-2005 (Register 2005, No. 9). A Certificate of Compliance must be transmitted to OAL by 6-29-2005 or emergency language will be repealed by operation of law on the following day.

3. New section refiled 6-20-2005 as an emergency; operative 6-29-2005 (Register 2005, No. 25). A Certificate of Compliance must be transmitted to OAL by 10-27-2005 or emergency language will be repealed by operation of law on the following day.

4. Certificate of Compliance as to 6-20-2005 order, including amendment of section and Note, transmitted to OAL 7-29-2005 and filed 9-9-2005 (Register 2005, No. 36).

Ref.: Hanna § 5.05[13][a]; Herlick Handbook § 4.19A.

§9767.4. Cover Page for Medical Provider Network Application.

For DWC only: MPN Approval Number Date Application Received: / /

Cover Page for Medical Provider Network Application

1. Name of MPN Applicant ____________________

2. Address ____________________ 3. Tax Identification Number __ __–__ __ __ __ __ __ __

____

4. Type of MPN Applicant

☐ Self–Insured Employer ☐ Group of Self–Insured Employers

☐ Self–Insurer Security Fund ☐ Joint Powers Authority ☐ State ☐ Insurer

5. Name of Medical Provider Network(s), if applicable: ____________________

6. If the medical provider network is one of the following deemed entities, check the appropriate box:

☐ Health Care Organization (HCO)
☐ Health Care Service Plan
☐ Group Disability Insurer
☐ Taft–Hartley Health and Welfare Trust Fund

7. Name of entity, administrator or other third–party who prepared MPN Application on behalf of MPN applicant (if applicable): ____________________

8. Signature of authorized individual: "I, the undersigned officer or employee of the MPN applicant, have read and signed this application and know the contents thereof, and verify that, to the best of my knowledge and ability, the information included in this application is true and correct."

____
Name of Authorized Individual Title Phone/Email

____
Signature of Authorized Individual Date Signed

9. Authorized Liaison to DWC:

____
Name Title Organization Phone/Email

____
Address Fax number

Submit an original Cover Page for Medical Provider Network Application with original signature, an original Application with the information required by Title 8, California Code of Regulations, section 9767.3 and a copy of the Cover Page and Application to the Division of Workers' Compensation. Mailing address: DWC, MPN Application, P.O. Box 71010, Oakland, CA 94612.

[DWC Mandatory Form — Section 9767.4 — May 2007]

Note: Authority cited: Sections 133 and 4616(g), Labor Code. Reference: Sections 3700, 3743, 4616, 4616.5 and 4616.7, Labor Code.

History: 1. New section filed 11-1-2004 as an emergency; operative 11-1-2004 (Register 2004, No. 45). A Certificate of Compliance must be transmitted to OAL by 3-1-2005 or emergency language will be repealed by operation of law on the following day.

2. New section refiled 2-28-2005 as an emergency; operative 3-1-2005 (Register 2005, No. 9). A Certificate of Compliance must be transmitted to OAL by 6-29-2005 or emergency language will be repealed by operation of law on the following day.

3. New section refiled 6-20-2005 as an emergency; operative 6-29-2005 (Register 2005, No. 25). A Certificate of Compliance must be transmitted to OAL by 10-27-2005 or emergency language will be repealed by operation of law on the following day.

4. Certificate of Compliance as to 6-20-2005 order, including amendment of section and Note, transmitted to OAL 7-29-2005 and filed 9-9-2005 (Register 2005, No. 36).

5. Change without regulatory effect amending section filed 5-23-2007 pursuant to section 100, title 1, California Code of Regulations (Register 2007, No. 21).

Ref.: Hanna § 5.05[13][a]; Herlick Handbook § 4.19A.

§9767.5. Access Standards.

(a) A MPN must have at least three physicians of each specialty expected to treat common injuries experienced by injured employees based on the type of occupation or industry in which the employee is engaged and within the access standards set forth in (b) and (c).

(b) A MPN must have a primary treating physician and a hospital for emergency health care services, or if separate from such hospital, a provider of all emergency health care services, within 30 minutes or 15 miles of each covered employee's residence or workplace.

(c) A MPN must have providers of occupational health services and specialists within 60 minutes or 30 miles of a covered employee's residence or workplace.

(d) If a MPN applicant believes that, given the facts and circumstances with regard to a portion of its service area, specifically rural areas including those in which health facilities are located at least 30 miles apart, the accessibility standards set forth in subdivisions (b) and/or (c) are unreasonably restrictive, the MPN applicant may propose alternative standards of accessibility for that portion of its service area. The MPN applicant shall do so by including the proposed alternative standards in writing in its plan approval application or in a notice of MPN plan modification. The alternative standards shall provide that all services shall be available and accessible at reasonable times to all covered employees.

(e)(1) The MPN applicant shall have a written policy for arranging or approving non-emergency medical care for: (A) a covered employee authorized by the employer to temporarily work or travel for work outside the MPN geographic service area when the need for medical care arises; (B) a former employee whose employer has ongoing workers' compensation obligations and who permanently resides outside the MPN geographic service area; and (C) an injured employee who decides to temporarily reside outside the MPN geographic service area during recovery.

(2) The written policy shall provide the employees described in subdivision (e)(1) above with the choice of at least three physicians outside the MPN geographic service area who either have been referred by the employee's primary treating physician within the MPN or have been selected by the MPN applicant. In addition to physicians within the MPN, the employee may change physicians among the referred physicians and may obtain a second and third opinion from the referred physicians.

(3) The referred physicians shall be located within the access standards described in paragraphs (c) and (d) of this section.

(4) Nothing in this section precludes a MPN applicant from having a written policy that allows a covered employee outside the MPN geographic service area to choose his or her own provider for non-emergency medical care.

(f) For non-emergency services, the MPN applicant shall ensure that an appointment for initial treatment is available within 3 business days of the MPN applicant's receipt of a request for treatment within the MPN.

(g) For non-emergency specialist services to treat common injuries experienced by the covered employees based on the type of occupation or industry in which the employee is engaged, the MPN applicant shall ensure that an appointment is available within 20 business days of the MPN applicant's receipt of a referral to a specialist within the MPN.

(h) If the primary treating physician refers the covered employee to a type of specialist not included in the MPN, the covered employee may select a specialist from outside the MPN.

(i) The MPN applicant shall have a written policy to allow an injured employee to receive emergency health care services from a medical service or hospital provider who is not a member of the MPN.

Note: Authority cited: Sections 133 and 4616(g), Labor Code. Reference: Sections 4616 and 4616.3, Labor Code.

History: 1. New section filed 11-1-2004 as an emergency; operative 11-1-2004 (Register 2004, No. 45). A Certificate of Compliance must be transmitted to OAL by 3-1-2005 or emergency language will be repealed by operation of law on the following day.

2. New section refiled 2-28-2005 as an emergency; operative 3-1-2005 (Register 2005, No. 9). A Certificate of Compliance must be transmitted to OAL by 6-29-2005 or emergency language will be repealed by operation of law on the following day.

3. New section refiled 6-20-2005 as an emergency; operative 6-29-2005 (Register 2005, No. 25). A Certificate of Compliance must be transmitted to OAL by 10-27-2005 or emergency language will be repealed by operation of law on the following day.

4. Certificate of Compliance as to 6-20-2005 order, including amendment of section, transmitted to OAL 7-29-2005 and filed 9-9-2005 (Register 2005, No. 36).

Ref.: Hanna § 5.05[13][a]; Herlick Handbook § 4.19A.

§9767.6. Treatment and Change of Physicians Within MPN.

(a) When the injured covered employee notifies the employer or insured employer of the injury or files a claim for workers' compensation with the employer or insured employer, the employer or insurer shall arrange an initial medical evaluation with a MPN physician in compliance with the access standards set forth in section 9767.5.

(b) Within one working day after an employee files a claim form under Labor Code section 5401, the employer or insurer shall provide for all treatment, consistent with guidelines adopted by the Administrative Director pursuant to Labor Code section 5307.27 or, prior to the adoption of these guidelines, the American College of Occupational and Environmental Medicine's Occupational Medicine Practice Guidelines (ACOEM), and for all injuries not covered by the ACOEM guidelines or guidelines adopted by the Administrative Director, authorized treatment shall be in accordance with other evidence based medical treatment guidelines generally recognized by the national medical community and that are scientifically based. The Administrative Director incorporates by reference the American College of Occupational and Environmental Medicine's Occupational Medicine Practice Guidelines (ACOEM), 2nd Edition (2004), published by OEM Press. A copy may be obtained from OEM Press, 8 West Street, Beverly Farms, Massachusetts 01915 (www.oempress.com).

(c) The employer or insurer shall provide for the treatment with MPN providers for the alleged injury and shall continue to provide the treatment until the date that liability for the claim is rejected. Until the date the claim is rejected, liability for the claim shall be limited to ten thousand dollars ($10,000).

(d) The insurer or employer shall notify the employee of his or her right to be treated by a physician of his or her choice within the MPN after the first visit with the MPN physician and the method by which the list of participating providers may be accessed by the employee.

(e) At any point in time after the initial medical evaluation with a MPN physician, the covered employee may select a physician of his or her choice from within the MPN. Selection by the covered employee of a treating physician and any subsequent physicians shall be based on the physician's specialty or recognized expertise in treating the particular injury or condition in question.

(f) The employer or insurer shall not be entitled to file a Petition for Change of Treating Physician, as set forth at section 9786, if a covered employee is treating with a physician within the MPN.

Note: Authority cited: Sections 133 and 4616(g), Labor Code. Reference: Sections 4604.5, 4616, 4616.3, 5307.27 and 5401, Labor Code.

History: 1. New section filed 11-1-2004 as an emergency; operative 11-1-2004 (Register 2004, No. 45). A Certificate of Compliance must be transmitted to OAL by 3-1-2005 or emergency language will be repealed by operation of law on the following day.

2. New section refiled 2-28-2005 as an emergency; operative 3-1-2005 (Register 2005, No. 9). A Certificate of Compliance must be transmitted to OAL by 6-29-2005 or emergency language will be repealed by operation of law on the following day.

3. New section refiled 6-20-2005 as an emergency; operative 6-29-2005 (Register 2005, No. 25). A Certificate of Compliance must be transmitted to OAL by 10-27-2005 or emergency language will be repealed by operation of law on the following day.

4. Certificate of Compliance as to 6-20-2005 order, including amendment of section, transmitted to OAL 7-29-2005 and filed 9-9-2005 (Register 2005, No. 36).

Ref.: Hanna § 5.05[13][d]; Herlick Handbook § 4.19A.

§9767.7. Second and Third Opinions.

(a) If the covered employee disputes either the diagnosis or the treatment prescribed by the primary treating physician or the treating physician, the employee may obtain a second and third opinion from physicians within the MPN. During this process, the employee is required to continue his or her treatment with the treating physician or a physician of his or her choice within the MPN.

(b) If the covered employee disputes either the diagnosis or the treatment prescribed by primary treating physician or the treating physician, it is the employee's responsibility to: (1) inform the person designated by the employer or insurer that he or she disputes the treating physician's opinion and requests a second opinion (the employee may notify the person designated by the employer or insurer either in writing or orally); (2) select a physician or specialist from a list of available MPN providers; (3) make an appointment with the second opinion physician within 60 days; and (4) inform the person designated by the employer or insurer of the appointment date. It is the employer's or insurer's responsibility to (1) provide a regional area listing of MPN providers and/or specialists to the employee for his/her selection based on the specialty or recognized expertise in treating the particular injury or condition in question and inform the employee of his or her right to request a copy of the medical records that will be sent to the second opinion physician; (2) contact the treating physician, provide a copy of the medical records or send the necessary medical records to the second opinion physician prior to the appointment date, and provide a copy of the records to the covered employee upon request; and (3) notify the second opinion physician in writing that he or she has been selected to provide a second opinion and the nature of the dispute with a copy to the employee. If the appointment is not made within 60 days of receipt of the list of the available MPN providers, then the employee shall be deemed to have waived the second opinion process with regard to this disputed diagnosis or treatment of this treating physician.

(c) If, after reviewing the covered employee's medical records, the second opinion physician determines that the employee's injury is outside the scope of his or her practice, the physician shall notify the person designated by the employer or insurer and employee so the employer or insurer can provide a new list of MPN providers and/or specialists to the employee for his/her selection based on the specialty or recognized expertise in treating the particular injury or condition in question.

(d) If the covered employee disagrees with either the diagnosis or treatment prescribed by the second opinion physician, the injured employee may seek the opinion of a third physician within the MPN. It is the employee's responsibility to: (1) inform the person designated by the employer or insurer that he or she disputes the treating physician's opinion and requests a third opinion (the employee may notify the person designated by the employer or insurer either in writing or orally); (2) select a physician or specialist from a list of available MPN providers; and (3) make an appointment with the third opinion physician within 60 days; and (4) inform the person designated by the employer or insurer of the appointment date. It is the employer's or insurer's responsibility to (1) provide a regional area listing of MPN providers and/or specialists to the employee for his/her selection based on the specialty or recognized expertise in treating the particular injury or condition in question and inform the employee of his or her right to request a copy of the medical records that will be sent to the third opinion physician; and (2) contact the treating physician, provide a copy of the medical records or send the necessary medical records to the third opinion physician prior to the appointment date, and provide a copy of the records to the covered employee upon request; and (3) notify the third opinion physician in writing that he or she has been selected to provide a third opinion and the nature of the dispute with a copy to the employee. If the appointment is not made within 60 days of receipt of the list of the available MPN providers, then the employee shall be deemed to have waived the third opinion process with regard to this disputed diagnosis or treatment of this treating physician.

(e) If, after reviewing the covered employee's medical records, the third opinion physician determines that the employee's injury is outside the scope of his or her practice, the physician shall notify the person designated by the employer or insurer and employee so the MPN can provide a new list of MPN providers and/or specialists to the employee for his/her selection based on the specialty or recognized expertise in treating the particular injury or condition in question.

(f) The second and third opinion physicians shall each render his or her opinion of the disputed diagnosis or treatment in writing and offer alternative diagnosis or treatment recommendations, if applicable. Any recommended treatment shall be in accordance with Labor Code section 4616(e). The second and third opinion physicians may order diagnostic testing if medically necessary. A copy of the written report shall be served on the employee, the person designated by the employer or insurer, and the treating physician within 20 days of the date of the appointment or receipt of the results of the diagnostic tests, whichever is later.

(g) The employer or insurer shall permit the employee to obtain the recommended treatment within the MPN. The covered employee may obtain the recommended treatment by changing physicians to the second opinion physician, third opinion physician, or other MPN physician.

(h) If the injured covered employee disagrees with the diagnosis or treatment of the third opinion physician, the injured employee may file with the Administrative Director a request for an Independent Medical Review.

Note: Authority cited: Sections 133 and 4616(g), Labor Code. Reference: Sections 4616(a) and 4616.3, Labor Code.

History: 1. New section filed 11-1-2004 as an emergency; operative 11-1-2004 (Register 2004, No. 45). A Certificate of Compliance must be transmitted to OAL by 3-1-2005 or emergency language will be repealed by operation of law on the following day.

2. New section refiled 2-28-2005 as an emergency; operative 3-1-2005 (Register 2005, No. 9). A Certificate of Compliance must be transmitted to OAL by 6-29-2005 or emergency language will be repealed by operation of law on the following day.

3. New section refiled 6-20-2005 as an emergency; operative 6-29-2005 (Register 2005, No. 25). A Certificate of Compliance must be transmitted to OAL by 10-27-2005 or emergency language will be repealed by operation of law on the following day.

4. Certificate of Compliance as to 6-20-2005 order, including amendment of section, transmitted to OAL 7-29-2005 and filed 9-9-2005 (Register 2005, No. 36).

Ref.: Hanna § 5.05[13][d]–[e]; Herlick Handbook § 4.19A.

§9767.8. Modification of Medical Provider Network Plan.

(a) The MPN applicant shall serve the Administrative Director with an original Notice of MPN Plan Modification with original signature, any necessary documentation, and a copy of the Notice and any necessary documentation before any of the following changes occur:

(1) A change of 10% or more in the number or specialty of providers participating in the network since the approval date of the previous MPN Plan application or modification.

(2) A change of 25% or more in the number of covered employees since the approval date of the previous MPN Plan application or modification.

(3) A material change in the continuity of care policy.

(4) A material change in the transfer of care policy.

(5) Change in policy or procedure that is used by the MPN to conduct "economic profiling of MPN providers" pursuant to Labor Code section 4616.1.

(6) Change in the name of the MPN.

(7) Change in geographic service area within the State of California.

(8) Change in how the MPN complies with the access standards.

(9) A material change in any of the employee notification materials required by section 9767.12.

(b) The MPN applicant shall serve the Administrative Director with a Notice of MPN Plan Modification within 5 business days of a change of the DWC liaison.

(c) The modification must be verified by an officer or employee of the MPN authorized to sign on behalf of the MPN applicant. The verification shall state: "I, the undersigned officer or employee of the MPN applicant, have read and signed this notice and know the contents thereof, and verify that, to the best of my knowledge and belief, the information included in this notice is true and correct."

(d) Within 60 days of the Administrative Director's receipt of a Notice of MPN Plan Modification, the Administrative Director shall approve or disapprove the plan modification based on information provided in the Notice of MPN Plan Modification. The Administrative Director shall approve or disapprove a plan modification based on the requirements of Labor

Code section 4616 et seq. and this article. If the Administrative Director has not acted on a plan within 60 days of submittal of a Notice of MPN Plan Modification, it shall be deemed approved. Except for (a)(6) and (b), modifications shall not be made until the Administrative Director has approved the plan or until 60 days have passed, which ever occurs first. If the Administrative Director disapproves of the MPN plan modification, he or she shall serve the MPN applicant with a Notice of Disapproval within 60 days of the submittal of a Notice of MPN Plan Modification.

(e) A MPN applicant denied approval of a MPN plan modification may either:

(1) Submit a new request addressing the deficiencies; or

(2) Request a re-evaluation by the Administrative Director.

(f) Any MPN applicant may request a re-evaluation of the denial by submitting with the Division, within 20 days of the issuance of the Notice of Disapproval, a written request for a re-evaluation with a detailed statement explaining the basis upon which a re-evaluation is requested. The request for re-evaluation shall be accompanied by supportive documentary material relevant to the specific allegations raised and shall be verified under penalty of perjury. The MPN application and modification at issue shall not be refiled; they shall be made part of the administrative record by incorporation by reference.

(g) The Administrative Director shall, within 45 days of the receipt of the request for a re-evaluation, either:

(1) Issue a Decision and Order affirming or modifying the Notice of Disapproval based on a failure to meet the procedural requirements of this section or based on a failure to meet the requirements of Labor Code section 4616 et seq. and this article; or

(2) Issue a Decision and Order revoking the Notice of Disapproval and issue an approval of the modification;

(h) The Administrative Director may extend the time specified in subdivision (h) within which to act upon the request for a re-evaluation for a period of 30 days and may order a party to submit additional documents or information.

(i) A MPN applicant may appeal the Administrative Director's decision and order regarding the MPN by filing, within twenty (20) days of the issuance of the decision and order, a petition at the district office of the Workers' Compensation Appeals Board closest to the MPN applicant's principal place of business, together with a Declaration of Readiness to Proceed. The petition shall set forth the specific factual and/or legal reason(s) for the appeal. A copy of the petition and of the Declaration of Readiness to Proceed shall be concurrently served on the Administrative Director.

(j) The MPN applicant shall use the following Notice of MPN Plan Modification form:

For DWC only: MPN Approval Number Date Notice Received: / /

Notice of Medical Provider Network Plan Modification §9767.8

1. Name of MPN Applicant____________________

2. Address ____________________ ____________________

3. Tax Identification Number __ __ – __ __ __ __ __ __ __

4. Type of MPN Applicant

☐ Self–Insured Employer ☐ Group of Self–Insured Employers

☐ Self–Insurer Security Fund ☐ Joint Powers Authority ☐ State ☐ Insurer

5. Name of MPN, if applicable: ____________________

6. Date of initial application approval and MPN approval number: ____________________

7. Dates of prior plan modifications approvals: ____________________

8. If the medical provider network is one of the following deemed entities, check the appropriate box:

☐ Health Care Organization (HCO)
☐ Health Care Service Plan
☐ Group Disability Insurer
☐ Taft–Hartley Health and Welfare Trust Fund

9. Name of entity, administrator or other third–party who prepared MPN Modification on behalf of MPN applicant (if applicable):____________________

10. Signature of authorized individual: "I, the undersigned officer or employee of the MPN applicant, have read and signed this notice and know the contents thereof, and verify that, to the best of my knowledge and ability, the information included in this application is true and correct."

____
Name of Authorized Individual Title Phone/Email

____
Signature of Authorized Individual Date Signed

11. Authorized Liaison to DWC:

____
Name Title Organization Phone/Email

____
Address Fax number

Please give a short summary of the proposed modifications in the space provided below and place a check mark against the box that reflects the proposed modification. Please explain whether the modification will adversely affect the ability of the MPN to meet the regulatory and statutory MPN requirements.

____
____
____

☐ Change in Service Area: Provide documentation in compliance with section 9767.5.

☐ Change of MPN name: Provide new MPN name.

☐ Change of Division Liaison: Provide the name and contact information.

☐ Change of 10% or more in the number or specialty of Network Providers since the approval date of the previous MPN Plan application or modification: Provide the name, license number, and location of each physician by specialty type or name of provider, if other than physician.

☐ Change of 25% or more in the number of covered employees since the approval date of the previous MPN Plan application or modification.

☐ Change in continuity of care policy: Provide a copy of the revised written continuity of care policy.

☐ Change in transfer of care policy: Provide a copy of the revised written transfer of care policy.

☐ Change in Economic Profiling: Provide a copy of the revised policy or procedure.

☐ Change in how the MPN complies with the access standards: Explain what change has been made and describe how the MPN still complies with the access standards.

☐ Change of employee notification materials: Provide a copy of the revised notification materials.

☐ Other (please describe): Attach documentation.

Submit an original Notice of MPN Plan Modification with original signature, any necessary documentation, and a copy of the Notice and documents to the Division of Workers' Compensation. Mailing address: DWC, MPN Application, P.O. Box 71010, Oakland, CA 94612.

[DWC Mandatory Form — Section 9767.8 — May 2007]

Note: Authority cited: Sections 133, 4616(g) and 5300(f), Labor Code. Reference: Sections 3700, 3743, 4616, 4616.2 and 4616.5, Labor Code.

History: 1. New section filed 11-1-2004 as an emergency; operative 11-1-2004 (Register 2004, No. 45). A Certificate of Compliance must be transmitted to OAL by 3-1-2005 or emergency language will be repealed by operation of law on the following day.

2. New section refiled 2-28-2005 as an emergency; operative 3-1-2005 (Register 2005, No. 9). A Certificate of Compliance must be transmitted to OAL by 6-29-2005 or emergency language will be repealed by operation of law on the following day.

3. New section refiled 6-20-2005 as an emergency; operative 6-29-2005 (Register 2005, No. 25). A Certificate of Compliance must be transmitted to OAL by 10-27-2005 or emergency language will be repealed by operation of law on the following day.

4. Certificate of Compliance as to 6-20-2005 order, including amendment of section and Note, transmitted to OAL 7-29-2005 and filed 9-9-2005 (Register 2005, No. 36).

5. Change without regulatory effect amending form filed 5-23-2007 pursuant to section 100, title 1, California Code of Regulations (Register 2007, No. 21).

Ref.: Herlick Handbook § 4.19A.

§9767.9. Transfer of Ongoing Care into the MPN.

(a) If the injured covered employee's injury or illness does not meet the conditions set forth in (e)(1) through (e)(4), the injured covered employee may be transferred into the MPN for medical treatment.

(b) Until the injured covered employee is transferred into the MPN, the employee's physician may make referrals to providers within or outside the MPN.

(c) Nothing in this section shall preclude an insurer or employer from agreeing to provide medical care with providers outside of the MPN.

(d) If an injured covered employee is being treated for an occupational injury or illness by a physician or provider prior to coverage of a medical provider network, and the injured covered employee's physician or provider becomes a provider within the MPN that applies to the injured covered employee, then the employer or insurer shall inform the injured covered employee and his or her physician or provider if his/her treatment is being provided by his/her physician or provider under the provisions of the MPN.

(e) The employer or insurer shall authorize the completion of treatment for injured covered employees who are being treated outside of the MPN for an occupational injury or illness that occurred prior to the coverage of the MPN and whose treating physician is not a provider within the MPN, including injured covered employees who pre-designated a physician and do not fall within the Labor Code section 4600(d), for the following conditions:

(1) An acute condition. For purposes of this subdivision, an acute condition is a medical condition that involves a sudden onset of symptoms due to an illness, injury, or other medical problem that requires prompt medical attention and that has a duration of less than 90 days. Completion of treatment shall be provided for the duration of the acute condition.

(2) A serious chronic condition. For purposes of this subdivision, a serious chronic condition is a medical condition due to a disease, illness, catastrophic injury, or other medical problem or medical disorder that is serious in nature and that persists without full cure or worsens over 90 days and requires ongoing treatment to maintain remission or prevent de-

terioration. Completion of treatment shall be authorized for a period of time necessary, up to one year: (A) to complete a course of treatment approved by the employer or insurer; and (B) to arrange for transfer to another provider within the MPN, as determined by the insurer or employer. The one year period for completion of treatment starts from the date of the injured covered employee's receipt of the notification, as required by subdivision (f), of the determination that the employee has a serious chronic condition.

(3) A terminal illness. For purposes of this subdivision, a terminal illness is an incurable or irreversible condition that has a high probability of causing death within one year or less. Completion of treatment shall be provided for the duration of a terminal illness.

(4) Performance of a surgery or other procedure that is authorized by the insurer or employer as part of a documented course of treatment and has been recommended and documented by the provider to occur within 180 days from the MPN coverage effective date.

(f) If the employer or insurer decides to transfer the covered employee's medical care to the medical provider network, the employer or insurer shall notify the covered employee of the determination regarding the completion of treatment and the decision to transfer medical care into the medical provider network. The notification shall be sent to the covered employee's residence and a copy of the letter shall be sent to the covered employee's primary treating physician. The notification shall be written in English and Spanish and use layperson's terms to the maximum extent possible.

(g) If the injured covered employee disputes the medical determination under this section, the injured covered employee shall request a report from the covered employee's primary treating physician that addresses whether the covered employee falls within any of the conditions set forth in subdivisions (e)(1-4). The treating physician shall provide the report to the covered employee within twenty calendar days of the request. If the treating physician fails to issue the report, then the determination made by the employer or insurer referred to in (f) shall apply.

(h) If the employer or insurer or injured covered employee objects to the medical determination by the treating physician, the dispute regarding the medical determination made by the treating physician concerning the transfer of care shall be resolved pursuant to Labor Code section 4062.

(i) If the treating physician agrees with the employer's or insurer's determination that the injured covered employee's medical condition does not meet the conditions set forth in subdivisions (e)(1) through (e)(4), the transfer of care shall go forward during the dispute resolution process.

(j) If the treating physician does not agree with the employer's or insurer's determination that the injured covered employee's medical condition does not meet the conditions set forth in subdivisions (e)(1) through (e)(4), the transfer of care shall not go forward until the dispute is resolved.

Note: Authority cited: Sections 133, 4616(g), and 4062, Labor Code. Reference: Sections 4616 and 4616.2, Labor Code.

History: 1. New section filed 11-1-2004 as an emergency; operative 11-1-2004 (Register 2004, No. 45). A Certificate of Compliance must be transmitted to OAL by 3-1-2005 or emergency language will be repealed by operation of law on the following day.

2. New section refiled 2-28-2005 as an emergency; operative 3-1-2005 (Register 2005, No. 9). A Certificate of Compliance must be transmitted to OAL by 6-29-2005 or emergency language will be repealed by operation of law on the following day.

3. New section refiled 6-20-2005 as an emergency; operative 6-29-2005 (Register 2005, No. 25). A Certificate of Compliance must be transmitted to OAL by 10-27-2005 or emergency language will be repealed by operation of law on the following day.

4. Certificate of Compliance as to 6-20-2005 order, including amendment of section, transmitted to OAL 7-29-2005 and filed 9-9-2005 (Register 2005, No. 36).

Ref.: Hanna § 5.05[13][c]; Herlick Handbook § 4.19A.

§9767.10. Continuity of Care Policy.

(a) At the request of a covered employee, an insurer or employer that offers a medical provider network shall complete the treatment by a terminated provider as set forth in Labor Code sections 4616.2(d) and (e).

(b) An "acute condition," as referred to in Labor Code section 4616.2(d)(3)(A), shall have a duration of less than ninety days.

(c) "An extended period of time," as referred to in Labor Code section 4616.2(d)(3)(B) with regard to a serious and chronic condition, means a duration of at least ninety days.

(d) The MPN applicant's continuity of care policy shall include a dispute resolution procedure that contains the following requirements:

(1) Following the employer's or insurer's determination of the injured covered employee's medical condition, the employer or insurer shall notify the covered employee of the determination regarding the completion of treatment and whether or not the employee will be required to select a new provider from within the MPN. The notification shall be sent to the covered employee's residence and a copy of the letter shall be sent to the covered employee's primary treating physician. The notification shall be written in English and Spanish and use layperson's terms to the maximum extent possible.

(2) If the terminated provider agrees to continue treating the injured covered employee in accordance with Labor Code section 4616.2 and if the injured covered employee disputes the medical determination, the injured covered employee shall request a report from the covered employee's primary treating physician that addresses whether the covered employee falls within any of the conditions set forth in Labor Code section 4616.2(d)(3); an acute condition; a serious chronic condition; a terminal illness; or a performance of a surgery or other procedure that is authorized by the insurer or employer as part of a documented course of treatment and has been recommended and documented by the provider to occur within 180 days of the contract's termination date. The treating physician shall provide the report to the covered employee within twenty calendar days of the request. If the treating physician fails to issue the report, then the determination made by the employer or insurer referred to in (d)(1) shall apply.

(3) If the employer or insurer or injured covered employee objects to the medical determination by the treating physician, the dispute regarding the medical determination made by the treating physician concerning the continuity of care shall be resolved pursuant to Labor Code section 4062.

(4) If the treating physician agrees with the employer's or insurer's determination that the injured covered employee's medical condition does not meet the conditions set forth in Labor Code section 4616.2(d)(3), the employee shall choose a new provider from within the MPN during the dispute resolution process.

(5) If the treating physician does not agree with the employer's or insurer's determination that the injured covered employee's medical condition does not meet the conditions set forth in Labor Code section 4616.2(d)(3), the injured covered employee shall continue to treat with the terminated provider until the dispute is resolved.

Note: Authority cited: Sections 133 and 4616(g), Labor Code. Reference: Section 4616.2, Labor Code.

History: 1. New section filed 11-1-2004 as an emergency; operative 11-1-2004 (Register 2004, No. 45). A Certificate of Compliance must be transmitted to OAL by 3-1-2005 or emergency language will be repealed by operation of law on the following day.

2. New section refiled 2-28-2005 as an emergency; operative 3-1-2005 (Register 2005, No. 9). A Certificate of Compliance must be transmitted to OAL by 6-29-2005 or emergency language will be repealed by operation of law on the following day.

3. New section refiled 6-20-2005 as an emergency; operative 6-29-2005 (Register 2005, No. 25). A Certificate of Compliance must be transmitted to OAL by 10-27-2005 or emergency language will be repealed by operation of law on the following day.

4. Certificate of Compliance as to 6-20-2005 order, including amendment of section, transmitted to OAL 7-29-2005 and filed 9-9-2005 (Register 2005, No. 36).

Ref.: Hanna § 5.05[13][c]; Herlick Handbook § 4.19A.

§9767.11. Economic Profiling Policy.

(a) An insurer's or employer's filing of its economic profiling policies and procedures shall include:

(1) An overall description of the profiling methodology, data used to create the profile and risk adjustment;

(2) A description of how economic profiling is used in utilization review;

(3) A description of how economic profiling is used in peer review; and

(4) A description of any incentives and penalties used in the program and in provider retention and termination decisions.

Note: Authority cited: Sections 133 and 4616(g), Labor Code. Reference: Section 4616.1, Labor Code.

History: 1. New section filed 11-1-2004 as an emergency; operative 11-1-2004 (Register 2004, No. 45). A Certificate of Compliance must be transmitted to OAL by 3-1-2005 or emergency language will be repealed by operation of law on the following day.

2. New section refiled 2-28-2005 as an emergency; operative 3-1-2005 (Register 2005, No. 9). A Certificate of Compliance must be transmitted to OAL by 6-29-2005 or emergency language will be repealed by operation of law on the following day.

3. New section refiled 6-20-2005 as an emergency; operative 6-29-2005 (Register 2005, No. 25). A Certificate of Compliance must be transmitted to OAL by 10-27-2005 or emergency language will be repealed by operation of law on the following day.

4. Certificate of Compliance as to 6-20-2005 order transmitted to OAL 7-29-2005 and filed 9-9-2005 (Register 2005, No. 36).

Ref.: Hanna § 5.05[13][b]; Herlick Handbook § 4.19A.

§9767.12. Employee Notification.

(a) An employer or insurer that offers a Medical Provider Network Plan under this article shall notify each covered employee in writing about the use of the Medical Provider Network 30 days prior to the implementation of an approved MPN, at the time of hire, or when an existing employee transfers into the MPN, whichever is appropriate to ensure that the employee has received the initial notification. The notification shall also be sent to a covered employee at the time of injury. The notification(s) shall be written in English and Spanish. The initial written notification shall include the following information:

(1) How to contact the person designated by the employer or insurer to be the MPN contact for covered employees. The employer or insurer shall provide a toll free telephone number of the MPN geographical service area includes more than one area code;

(2) A description of MPN services;

(3) How to review, receive or access the MPN provider directory. Nothing precludes an employer or insurer from initially providing covered employees with a regional area listing of MPN providers in addition to maintaining and making available its complete provider listing in writing. If the provider directory is also accessible on a website, the URL address shall be listed;

(4) How to access initial care and subsequent care, and what the access standards are under section 9767.5;

(5) How to access treatment if (A) the employee is authorized by the employer to temporarily work or travel for work outside the MPN's geographical service area; (B) a former employee whose employer has ongoing workers' compensation obligations permanently resides outside the MPN geographical service area; and (C) an injured employee decides to temporarily reside outside the MPN geographical service area during recovery;

(6) How to choose a physician within the MPN;

(7) What to do if a covered employee has trouble getting an appointment with a provider within the MPN;

(8) How to change a physician within the MPN;

(9) How to obtain a referral to a specialist within the MPN or outside the MPN, if needed;

(10) How to use the second and third opinion process;

(11) How to request and receive an independent medical review;

(12) A description of the standards for transfer of ongoing care into the MPN and a notification that a copy of the policy shall be provided to an employee upon request; and

(13) A description of the continuity of care policy and a notification that a copy of the policy shall be provided to an employee upon request.

(b) At the time of the selection of the physician for a third opinion, the covered employee shall be notified about the Independent Medical Review process. The notification shall be written in English and Spanish.

(c) Covered employees shall be notified 30 days prior to a change of the medical provider network. If the MPN applicant is an insurer, then a copy of the notification shall be served on the insured employer. The notification shall be written in English and Spanish.

Note: Authority cited: Sections 133 and 4616, Labor Code. Reference: Sections 4616, 4616.2 and 4616.3, Labor Code.

History: 1. New section filed 11-1-2004 as an emergency; operative 11-1-2004 (Register 2004, No. 45). A Certificate of Compliance must be transmitted to OAL by 3-1-2005 or emergency language will be repealed by operation of law on the following day.

2. New section refiled 2-28-2005 as an emergency; operative 3-1-2005 (Register 2005, No. 9). A Certificate of Compliance must be transmitted to OAL by 6-29-2005 or emergency language will be repealed by operation of law on the following day.

3. New section refiled 6-20-2005 as an emergency; operative 6-29-2005 (Register 2005, No. 25). A Certificate of Compliance must be transmitted to OAL by 10-27-2005 or emergency language will be repealed by operation of law on the following day.

4. Certificate of Compliance as to 6-20-2005 order, including amendment of section, transmitted to OAL 7-29-2005 and filed 9-9-2005 (Register 2005, No. 36).

Ref.: Hanna § 5.05[13][c]; Herlick Handbook § 4.19A.

§9767.13. Denial of Approval of Application and Re-Evaluation.

(a) The Administrative Director shall deny approval of a plan if the MPN applicant does not satisfy the requirements of this article and Labor Code section 4616 et seq. and shall state the reasons for disapproval in writing in a Notice of Disapproval, and shall transmit the Notice to the MPN applicant by U.S. Mail.

(b) An MPN applicant denied approval may either:

(1) Submit a new application addressing the deficiencies; or

(2) Request a re-evaluation by the Administrative Director.

(c) Any MPN applicant may request a re-evaluation by submitting with the Division, within 20 days of the issuance of the Notice of Disapproval, a written request for re-evaluation with a detailed statement explaining the basis upon which a re-evaluation is requested. The request for a re-evaluation shall be accompanied by supportive documentary material relevant to the specific allegations raised and shall be verified under penalty of perjury. The MPN application at issue shall not be re-filed; it shall be made part of the administrative record by incorporation by reference.

(d) The Administrative Director shall, within 45 days of the receipt of the request for a re-evaluation, either:

(1) Issue a Decision and Order affirming or modifying the Notice of Disapproval based on a failure to meet the procedural requirements of this section or based on a failure to meet the requirements of Labor Code section 4616 et seq. and this article; or

(2) Issue a Decision and Order revoking the Notice of Disapproval and issue an approval of the MPN.

(e) The Administrative Director may extend the time specified in subdivision (d) within which to act upon the request for a re-evaluation for a period of 30 days and may order a party to submit additional documents or information.

(f) A MPN applicant may appeal the Administrative Director's decision and order regarding the MPN by filing, within twenty (20) days of the issuance of the decision and order, a petition at the district office of the Workers' Compensation Appeals Board closest to the MPN applicant's principal place of business, together with a Declaration of Readiness to Proceed. The petition shall set forth the specific factual and/or legal reason(s) for the appeal. A copy of the petition and of the Declaration of Readiness to Proceed shall be concurrently served on the Administrative Director.

Note: Authority cited: Sections 133, 4616(g) and 5300(f), Labor Code. Reference: Section 4616, Labor Code.

History: 1. New section filed 11-1-2004 as an emergency; operative 11-1-2004 (Register 2004, No. 45). A Certificate of Compliance must be transmitted to OAL by 3-1-2005 or emergency language will be repealed by operation of law on the following day.

2. New section refiled 2-28-2005 as an emergency; operative 3-1-2005 (Register 2005, No. 9). A Certificate of Compliance must be transmitted to OAL by 6-29-2005 or emergency language will be repealed by operation of law on the following day.

3. New section refiled 6-20-2005 as an emergency; operative 6-29-2005 (Register 2005, No. 25). A Certificate of Compliance must be transmitted to OAL by 10-27-2005 or emergency language will be repealed by operation of law on the following day.

4. Certificate of Compliance as to 6-20-2005 order, including amendment of section heading, section and Note, transmitted to OAL 7-29-2005 and filed 9-9-2005 (Register 2005, No. 36).

Ref.: Hanna § 5.05[13][a]; Herlick Handbook § 4.19A.

§9767.14. Suspension or Revocation of Medical Provider Network Plan; Hearing.

(a) The Administrative Director may suspend or revoke approval of a MPN Plan if:

(1) Service under the MPN is not being provided according to the terms of the approved MPN plan.

(2) The MPN fails to meet the requirements of Labor Code section 4616 et seq. and this article.

(3) False or misleading information is knowingly or repeatedly submitted by the MPN or a participating provider or the MPN knowingly or repeatedly fails to report information required by this article.

(4) The MPN knowingly continues to use the services of a provider or medical reviewer whose license, registration, or certification has

been suspended or revoked or who is otherwise ineligible to provide treatment to an injured worker under California law.

(b) If one of the circumstances in subdivision (a) exists, the Administrative Director shall notify the MPN applicant in writing of the specific deficiencies alleged. The Administrative Director shall allow the MPN applicant an opportunity to correct the deficiency and/or to respond within ten days. If the Administrative Director determines that the deficiencies have not been cured, he or she shall issue a Notice of Action to the MPN applicant that specifies the time period in which the suspension or revocation will take effect and shall transmit the Notice of Action to the MPN applicant by U.S. Mail.

(c) A MPN applicant may request a re-evaluation of the suspension or revocation by submitting to the Administrative Director, within 20 days of the issuance of the Notice of Action, a written notice of the request for a re-evaluation with a detailed statement explaining the basis upon which a re-evaluation is requested. The request for a re-evaluation shall be accompanied by supportive documentary material relevant to the specific allegations raised and shall be verified under penalty of perjury. The MPN application at issue shall not be re-filed; it shall be made part of the administrative record and incorporated by reference.

(d) The Administrative Director shall, within 45 days of the receipt of the request for a re-evaluation, either:

(1) Issue a Decision and Order affirming or modifying the Notice of Action based on a failure to meet the procedural requirements of this section or based on a failure to meet the requirements of Labor Code section 4616 et seq. and this article;

(2) Issue a Decision and Order revoking the Notice of Action;

(e) The Administrative Director may extend the time specified in subdivision (d) within which to act upon the request for a re-evaluation for a period of 30 days and may order a party to submit additional documents or information.

(f) A MPN applicant may appeal the Administrative Director's decision and order regarding the MPN by filing, within twenty (20) days of the issuance of the decision and order, a petition at the district office of the Workers' Compensation Appeals Board closest to the MPN applicant's principal place of business, together with a Declaration of Readiness to Proceed. The petition shall set forth the specific factual and/or legal reason(s) for the appeal. A copy of the petition and of the Declaration of Readiness to Proceed shall be concurrently served on the Administrative Director.

Note: Authority cited: Sections 133, 4616(g) and 5300(f), Labor Code. Reference: Section 4616, Labor Code.

History: 1. New section filed 11-1-2004 as an emergency; operative 11-1-2004 (Register 2004, No. 45). A Certificate of Compliance must be transmitted to OAL by 3-1-2005 or emergency language will be repealed by operation of law on the following day.

2. New section refiled 2-28-2005 as an emergency; operative 3-1-2005 (Register 2005, No. 9). A Certificate of Compliance must be transmitted to OAL by 6-29-2005 or emergency language will be repealed by operation of law on the following day.

3. New section refiled 6-20-2005 as an emergency; operative 6-29-2005 (Register 2005, No. 25). A Certificate of Compliance must be transmitted to OAL by 10-27-2005 or emergency language will be repealed by operation of law on the following day.

4. Certificate of Compliance as to 6-20-2005 order, including amendment of section, transmitted to OAL 7-29-2005 and filed 9-9-2005 (Register 2005, No. 36).

Ref.: Herlick Handbook § 4.19A.

§9767.15. Compliance with Permanent MPN Regulations.

a. This section applies to MPNs that were approved by the Administrative Director pursuant to the emergency Medical Provider Network regulations effective November 1, 2004

b. Employers or insurers whose MPNs were approved pursuant to the emergency Medical Provider Network regulations are not required to submit a Notice of MPN Plan Modification to comply with the new or revised sections of the permanent regulations, including:

1. Section 9767.3(d)(8)(C) or Section 9767.3(d)(16) regarding the contractual agreements contained in the Application for a Medical Provider Network Plan provisions.

2. Sections 9767.5(e)(1), (e)(2), (e)(3), (e)(4), 9767.5(h) and 9767.5(i) of the Access Standards provisions.

3. Section 9767.9(g) provision providing a timeline for the treating physician's report and what happens if the treating physician fails to issue a timely report contained in the Transfer of Ongoing Care into the MPN provisions.

4. Section 9767.10(b)(c) and (d) of the Continuity of Care provisions.

5. Section 9767.12(a), (a)(1), (a)(2), (a)(3), (a)(4) and (a)(5) of the Employee Notification provisions.

c. At the time an employer or insurer with an approved MPN pursuant to the emergency Medical Provider Network regulations submits a Notice of MPN Plan Modification, the employer or insurer shall be required to verify compliance with the sections of the MPN permanent regulations listed in subdivision (b) above.

Note: Authority cited: Sections 133, 4616(g) and 5300(f), Labor Code. Reference: Sections 4609, 4616, 4616.2 and 4616.3, Labor Code.

History: 1. New section filed 9-9-2005; operative 9-9-2005 (Register 2005, No. 36).

Ref.: Herlick Handbook § 4.19A.

§9767.16. Notice of Employee Rights upon Termination or Cessation of Use of Medical Provider Network.

(a) The Medical Provider Network ("MPN") Applicant is responsible for ensuring that each covered employee is informed in writing of the MPN policies under which he or she is covered and when the employee is no longer covered by an MPN. The MPN Applicant shall ensure each covered employee is given written notice of the date of termination or cessation of use of its MPN. The written notice shall be provided to covered employees prior to the effective date of termination or cessation of use of an MPN. The notices required by this section shall be made available in English and Spanish.

(1) The MPN Applicant shall advise every covered employee of the following information in all notices of termination or cessation of use of an MPN by an MPN Applicant or insured employer:

(A) The effective date of termination or cessation of use of the MPN.

(B) The insurer's or employer's liability for continuing care for ongoing claims, and the potential penalties that may be imposed by the WCAB for unreasonable delay or interruption of that care.

(C) The name, address and telephone number of the person to contact with questions concerning the termination or cessation of use, including any questions about continuity of care or transfer of care.

(D) If there will be a period of no MPN coverage due to a termination, cessation of use, or before a change to a different MPN is effective, then notice shall be given of an employee's rights to a choice of physician under Labor Code section 4600. Specifically, an employee who has an existing industrial illness or injury that is being treated under the MPN shall have the right under Labor Code section 4600 to be treated by a physician of his or her own choice or at a facility of his or her own choice within a reasonable geographic area after 30 days have elapsed from the date the employee notified the employer of his or her injury.

(E) Any pending Independent Medical Review under that MPN shall also be terminated.

(2) If an MPN Applicant or insured employer is also changing MPN coverage to a different MPN, the MPN Applicant is responsible for ensuring that every covered employee is given notice of the following information in addition to the information required for an MPN termination or cessation of use:

(A) Notice that any injured worker receiving treatment from a provider not in the subsequent MPN, may be entitled to transfer of care to continue treatment with his or her current provider. Transfer of care applies when an employee has an acute, serious chronic or terminal illness or has a prior scheduled medical procedure with the non-MPN provider, pursuant to section 9767.9 of these regulations. The notice shall also advise that an employee may be required to treat within the new MPN after the transfer of care period.

(B) Notice that is required by sections 9767.12(a) and (c) for new MPN coverage and for a change of MPNs.

(b) Notice of termination or cessation of use of an MPN may be combined with the notice of the change to new MPN coverage if the combined notice meets all the MPN regulatory requirements.

(c) Notice of a change of MPNs shall be transmitted by the MPN Applicant providing the new MPN coverage to the Division, not less than 45 calendar days prior to the effective date of the termination or cessation of use of the MPN. A written letter signed by the MPN Applicant's authorized individual shall be submitted to DWC stating the effective date of the termination or cessation of use of the prior MPN, the planned effective date of the new MPN coverage, and shall attach a copy of the employee notice(s) to be sent to the covered employees pursuant to this section. The notices of a change of MPNs shall not be distributed without approval from DWC. If a notice is timely filed and DWC does not act by the date the notice should be distributed, then the notice shall be deemed approved.

(1) If a change in MPN coverage results in modifications to an MPN's plan application or results in the filing of a new MPN application, the MPN modification or new application filing shall be submitted to DWC pursuant to section 9767.8 or 9767.3, whichever is applicable. Distribution to covered employees of the 30-day notice of a change of MPNs shall occur after DWC's approval of an MPN modification or new MPN.

Note: Authority cited: Sections 59, 124, 133, 138.3, 138.4, 4616 and 5307.3, Labor Code. Reference: Section 4616.2, Labor Code.

History: 1. New section filed 12-11-2007; operative 4-9-2008 (Register 2007, No. 50).

Ref.: Hanna § 5.05[13][f].

ARTICLE 3.6
Independent Medical Review

§9768.1. Definitions.

(a) As used in this article, the following definitions apply:

(1) "American College of Occupational and Environmental Medicine's Occupational Medicine Practice Guidelines" ("ACOEM") means the American College of Occupational and Environmental Medicine's Occupational Medicine Practice Guidelines, 2nd Edition (2004), published by OEM Press. The Administrative Director incorporates ACOEM by reference. A copy may be obtained from OEM Press, 8 West Street, Beverly Farms, Massachusetts 01915 (www.oempress.com).

(2) "Appropriate specialty" means a medical specialty in an area or areas appropriate to the condition or treatment under review.

(3) "Independent Medical Reviewer" ("IMR") means the physician who is randomly selected pursuant to subdivision (b) of Labor Code section 4616.4.

(4) "In-person examination" means an examination of an injured employee by a physician which involves more than a review of records, and may include a physical examination, discussing the employee's medical condition with the employee, taking a history and performing an examination.

(5) "Material familial affiliation" means a relationship in which one of the persons or entities listed in section 9768.2 is the parent, child, grandparent, grandchild, sibling, uncle, aunt, nephew, niece, spouse, or cohabitant of the Independent Medical Reviewer.

(6) "Material financial affiliation" means a financial interest (owns a legal or equitable interest of more than 1% interest in the party, or a fair market value in excess of $2000, or relationship of director, advisor, or active participant) in any person or entity listed in section 9768.2. It also means any gift or income of more than $300 in the preceding year except for income for services as a second opinion physician, third opinion physician, treating physician, Agreed Medical Evaluator, Qualified Medical Evaluator, or Independent Medical Reviewer.

(7) "Material professional affiliation" means any relationship in which the Independent Medical Reviewer shares office space with, or works in the same office of, any person or entity listed in section 9768.2.

(8) "Medical emergency" means a medical condition manifesting itself by acute symptoms of sufficient severity such that the absence of immediate medical attention could reasonably be expected to place the patient's health in serious jeopardy.

(9) "Medical Provider Network Contact" ("MPN Contact") means the individual(s) designated by the MPN Applicant in the employee notification who is responsible for answering employees' questions about the Medical Provider Network and is responsible for assisting the employee in arranging for an Independent Medical Review.

(10) "Panel" means the contracted providers in a specific specialty.

(11) "Relevant medical records" means all information that was considered in relation to the disputed treatment or diagnostic service, including: (A) a copy of all correspondence from, and received by, any treating physician who provided a treatment or diagnostic service to the injured employee in connection with the injury; (B) a complete and legible copy of all medical records and other information used by the physicians in making a decision regarding the disputed treatment or diagnostic service; (C) the treating physician's report with the disputed treatment or diagnosis; and (D) the second and third opinion physicians' reports.

(12) "Residence" means the covered employee's primary residence.

Note: Authority cited: Sections 133 and 4616, Labor Code. Reference: Section 4616.4, Labor Code.

History: 1. New article 3.6 (sections 9768.1-9768.17) and section filed 12-31-2004 as an emergency; operative 1-1-2005 (Register 2004, No. 53). A Certificate of Compliance must be transmitted to OAL by 5-2-2005 or emergency language will be repealed by operation of law on the following day.

2. Certificate of Compliance as to 12-31-2004 order, including amendment of section, transmitted to OAL 4-29-2005 and filed 6-10-2005 (Register 2005, No. 23).

Ref.: Hanna § 5.05[13][e]; Herlick Handbook § 4.19A.

§9768.2. Conflicts of Interest.

(a) The IMR shall not have any material, professional, familial, or financial affiliation with any of the following:

(1) The injured employee's employer or employer's workers' compensation insurer;

(2) Any officer, director, management employee, or attorney of the injured employee's medical provider network, employer or employer's workers' compensation insurer;

(3) Any treating health care provider proposing the service or treatment;

(4) The institution at which the service or treatment would be provided, if known;

(5) The development or manufacture of the principal drug, device, procedure, or other therapy proposed for the injured employee whose treatment is under review; or

(6) The injured employee, the injured employee's immediate family, or the injured employee's attorney.

(b) The IMR shall not have a contractual agreement to provide physician services for the injured employee's MPN if the IMR is within a 35 mile radius of the treating physician.

(c) The IMR shall not have previously treated or examined the injured employee.

Note: Authority cited: Sections 133 and 4616, Labor Code. Reference: Section 4616.4, Labor Code.

History: 1. New section filed 12-31-2004 as an emergency; operative 1-1-2005 (Register 2004, No. 53). A Certificate of Compliance must be transmitted to OAL by 5-2-2005 or emergency language will be repealed by operation of law on the following day.

2. Certificate of Compliance as to 12-31-2004 order transmitted to OAL 4-29-2005 and filed 6-10-2005 (Register 2005, No. 23).

Ref.: Hanna § 5.05[13][e]; Herlick Handbook § 4.19A.

§9768.3. Qualifications of Independent Medical Reviewers.

(a) To qualify to be on the Administrative Director's list of Independent Medical Reviewers, a physician shall file a Physician Contract Application pursuant to section 9768.5 that demonstrates to the satisfaction of the Administrative Director that the physician:

(1) Is board certified. For physicians, the Administrative Director shall recognize only specialty boards recognized by the appropriate California licensing board.

(2) Has an unrestricted license as a physician in California under the appropriate licensing Board;

(3) Is not currently under accusation by any governmental licensing agency for a quality of care violation, fraud related to medical practice, or felony conviction or conviction of a crime related to the conduct of his or her practice of medicine;

(4) Has not been terminated or had discipline imposed by the Industrial Medical Council or Administrative Director in relation to the physician's role as a Qualified Medical Evaluator; is not currently under accusation by the Industrial Medical Council or Administrative Director; has not been denied renewal of Qualified Medical Evaluator status, except for non-completion of continuing education or for non-payment of fees; has neither resigned nor failed to renew Qualified Medical Evaluator status while under accusation or probation by the Industrial Medical Council or Administrative Director or after notification that reappointment as a Qualified Medical Evaluator may or would be denied for reasons other than non-completion of continuing education or non-payment of fees; and has not filed any applications or forms with the Industrial Medical Council or Administrative Director which contained any untrue material statements;

(5) Has not been convicted of a felony crime or a crime related to the conduct of his or her practice of medicine; and

(6) Has no history of disciplinary action or sanction, including but not limited to, loss of staff privileges or participation restrictions taken or pending by any hospital, government or regulatory body.

Note: Authority cited: Sections 133 and 4616, Labor Code. Reference: Section 4616.4, Labor Code.

History: 1. New section filed 12-31-2004 as an emergency; operative 1-1-2005 (Register 2004, No.

53). A Certificate of Compliance must be transmitted to OAL by 5-2-2005 or emergency language will be repealed by operation of law on the following day.

2. Certificate of Compliance as to 12-31-2004 order, including amendment of subsections (a) and (a)(3), transmitted to OAL 4-29-2005 and filed 6-10-2005 (Register 2005, No. 23).

Ref.: Hanna § 5.05[13][e]; Herlick Handbook § 4.19A.

§9768.4. IMR Contract Application Procedures.

(a) A physician seeking to serve as an Independent Medical Reviewer shall:

(1) Apply to the Administrative Director on the Physician Contract Application set forth in section 9768.5.

(2) Furnish a certified copy of his or her board certification, a copy of his or her current license to practice medicine, and submit other documentation of his or her qualifications as the Administrative Director may require.

(3) Designate specialties based on each of his or her board certifications.

(4) Designate the address(es) of the physician's office with necessary medical equipment where in-person examinations will be held.

(5) Agree to see any injured worker assigned to him or her within 30 days unless there is a conflict of interest as defined in section 9768.2.

(6) During the application process and after being notified by the Administrative Director that the contract application has been accepted, the physician shall keep the Administrative Director informed of any change of address, telephone, email address or fax number, and of any disciplinary action taken by a licensing board.

(b) The contract application, completed by the physician, and any supporting documentation included with the contract application, shall be filed at the Administrative Director's office listed on the form. The contract application submitted by the physician may be rejected if it is incomplete, contains false information or does not contain the required supporting documentation listed in this section.

(c) The Administrative Director shall maintain a list of physicians who have applied, and whom the Administrative Director has contracted with to conduct Independent Medical Reviews under Labor Code section 4616.4.

(d) The IMR contract term is two years. A physician may apply to serve for subsequent two year terms by following the procedure set forth in subdivision (a).

Note: Authority cited: Sections 133 and 4616, Labor Code. Reference: Section 4616.4, Labor Code.

History: 1. New section filed 12-31-2004 as an emergency; operative 1-1-2005 (Register 2004, No. 53). A Certificate of Compliance must be transmitted to OAL by 5-2-2005 or emergency language will be repealed by operation of law on the following day.

2. Certificate of Compliance as to 12-31-2004 order, including amendment of subsections (a) and (c), transmitted to OAL 4-29-2005 and filed 6-10-2005 (Register 2005, No. 23).

Ref.: Hanna § 5.05[13][e]; Herlick Handbook § 4.19A.

§9768.5. Physician Contract Application Form.

PHYSICIAN CONTRACT APPLICATION
(INDEPENDENT MEDICAL REVIEWER)
For the Department of Industrial Relations
Division of Workers' Compensation
P.O. Box 71010
Oakland, CA 94612

FOR OFFICE USE ONLY
NO.:
INPUT DATE:
INPUT BY:

BLOCK 1

PLEASE TYPE OR PRINT LEGIBLY

Please list your primary location. DO NOT USE P.O. BOX. You may provide additional office addresses at which you may schedule appointments, on a separate sheet.

LAST NAME	FIRST NAME	MI	JR/SR

BUSINESS ADDRESS	CITY	ZIP+4

MAILING ADDRESS, if different from above	CITY	ZIP+4

E-MAIL ADDRESS

(AREA CODE) PHONE NO.	(AREA CODE) FAX NO.	CAL. PROFESSIONAL LICENSE NUMBER	EXPIRATION (MM/YY)

BLOCK 2

MEDICAL/GRADUATE SCHOOL

CITY	STATE	DEGREE	DATE OF DEGREE

ALL PHYSICIANS are to furnish their board certification and current hospital privileges, if applicable.
PLEASE LIST:

Hospital/Facility	Location (City/State)	Type	From	To

Hospital/Facility	Location (City/State)	Type	From	To

DWC Form 9768.5
May 2007

BLOCK 3 PHYSICIANS MUST MEET THE FOLLOWING REQUIREMENTS **Yes No**

1) I am board certified in a specialty recognized by the appropriate California licensing Board. ☐ ☐
List name(s) of board: ____________________

2) Date of expiration of board certification, if applicable ____________________

3) List the requested specialty codes using the three digit specialty codes listed on page 5 __________

BLOCK 4

Physicians are prohibited from serving as an IMR in cases in which they have a material professional, familial, or financial affiliation with any of the parties or companies involved. YOU are responsible for determining whether you have one of these affiliations in any particular case, and for recusing yourself, although the Administrative Director will attempt to screen out any cases in which a conflict of interest is apparent from the names of all companies with which you have a material professional, familial or financial affiliation, as defined in the Regulations. **Please list entities with which you have an affiliation, and respond "not applicable" if appropriate.**

Workers' Compensation Insurance Companies

1.	3.
2.	4.

Workers' Compensation Third Party Administrators

1.	3.
2.	4.

Utilization Review Companies

1.	3.
2.	4.

Medical Provider Networks (Name or MPN number)

1.	3.
2.	4.

Hospitals or Ambulatory Surgery Centers (Please include the address(es) of the facility)

1.	3.
2.	4.

Drugs, Devices, Procedures or Therapies

1.	3.
2.	4.

** PROVIDE ADDITIONAL SHEETS WHEN NECESSARY**

BLOCK 5 PLEASE CHECK:

1) That the physician sections of this contract are fully completed, dated and signed with an original signature. We will not accept faxed applications.
2) That all necessary documentation is attached:
   - ❖ A Copy of your current California Professional License.
   - ❖ A Copy of your board certification(s).
   - ❖ Certification of your current hospital privileges, if applicable.

IMPORTANT: Your contract application to be an Independent Medical Review Physician shall be returned if it is incomplete, and it must be submitted prior to obtaining your appointment.

DWC Form 9768.5
May 2007

BLOCK 6 **Yes** **No**

License Status

1) Have you ever been formally disciplined by any State Medical Licensing Board? ☐ ☐
*If the answer is "Yes", please furnish full particulars on a separate sheet.

2) Is any accusation by any State medical licensing board for a quality of care violation, fraud related to medical practice, or felony conviction or conviction of a crime related to the conduct of your practice of medicine currently pending against you? ☐ ☐
*If the answer is "Yes", please furnish full particulars on a separate sheet.

3) Have you ever lost hospital staff privileges? ☐ ☐
*If the answer is "Yes", please furnish full particulars on a separate sheet.

4) My license to practice medicine is active and is neither restricted nor encumbered by suspension, interim suspension or probation. ☐ ☐
*If the answer is "No", please furnish full particulars on a separate sheet.

5) I agree to notify the Administrative Director if my license to practice medicine is placed on suspension, interim suspension, probation or is restricted by my licensing agency, if my Board Certification is revoked, if my hospital staff privileges are revoked, or if I am convicted of a felony crime or a crime related to the conduct of my practice of medicine. ☐ ☐

Verification

I understand that by submitting this contract application, I am offering to be an Independent Medical Reviewer. I have used reasonable diligence in preparing and completing this contract application. I have reviewed this completed contract application and to the best of my knowledge the information contained herein and in the attached supporting documentation is true, correct and complete. I understand that if this contract application is accepted that I will be placed on the list of eligible Independent Medical Reviewers. I understand that the Title 8, California Code of Regulations, sections 9768.1 et seq. set forth requirements that I must comply with and I agree to comply with those requirements. I understand that I must maintain the confidentiality of medical records and the rview materials consistent wit the applicable state and federal law. I confirm that I am familiar with the *American College of Occupational and Environmental Medicine's Occupational Medicine Practice Guidelines*, 2nd Edition (2004), published by OEM Press. If the Administrative Director adopts a medical treatment utilization schedule pursuant to Labor Code section 5307.27 during the two-year term of this contract, I agree to become familiar with that schedule no later than its effective date. I understand that this contract application is not accepted by the Administrative Director of the Division of Workers' Compensation until is it signed by the Administrative Director. I declare under penalty of perjury under the laws of the State of California that the foregoing is true and correct.

Executed on ______________ at ______________, CA ______________
(MM/DD/YY) County Applicant's Signature

DWC Form 9768.5
May 2007

A PUBLIC DOCUMENT

PRIVACY NOTICE – The Information Practices Act of 1977 and the Federal Privacy Act Require the Administrative Director to provide the following notice to individuals who are asked by a governmental entity to supply information for appointment as an Independent Medical Reviewer physician.

The California Labor Code provides for physicians and surgeons to participate in the workers' compensation Independent Medical Reviewer program. The Division of Workers' Compensation has adopted regulations which require applicants under this program to provide: name; business address, professional education, training, license number, board certifications, fellowships, conflicts of interest, and documents deemed necessary by the Administrative Director of the Division of Workers' Compensation. It is mandatory to furnish all the appropriate information requested by the Administrative Director. This contract may not be accepted if all the requested information is not provided.

The principal purpose for requesting information from physicians and surgeons is to administer the Independent Medical Review program within the California workers' compensation system. Additional information may be requested.

As authorized by law, information furnished on this form may be given to: you, upon request; the public, pursuant to the Public Records Act; a governmental entity, when required by state of federal law; to any person, pursuant to a subpoena or court order or pursuant to any other exception in Civil Code § 1798.24.

An individual has a right of access to records containing his/her personal information that are maintained by the Administrative Director. An individual may also amend, correct, or dispute information in such personal records. (Civil Code § 1798.34-1798.37.)
Requests should be sent to:

Division of Workers' Compensation – Medical Unit
P.O. Box 71010
Oakland, CA 94612

Copies of all records are ten cents ($0.10) per page, payable in advance. (Civil Code § 1798.33.)

ACCEPTANCE OF CONTRACT APPLICATION BY ADMINISTRATIVE DIRECTOR

The Administrative Director of the Division of Workers' Compensation accepts this contract application and agrees to add this physician's name to the list of eligible Independent Medical Reviewers for a two year term beginning with the date this contract is executed.

Executed on ________________ at ________________, CA ________________________
(MM/DD/YY) County Administrative Director

DWC Form 9768.5
May 2007

(Note to physicians: please use three letter specialty code when completing block 3 of application form)

SPECIALTY CODES

MAI	Allergy and Immunology
MAA	Anesthesiology
MRS	Colon & Rectal Surgery
MDE	Dermatology
MEM	Emergency Medicine
MFP	Family Practice
MPM	General Preventive Medicine
MOSU	Hand – Orthopaedic Surgery, Plastic Surgery, General Surgery
MMM	Internal Medicine
MMV	Internal Medicine – Cardiovascular Disease
MME	Internal Medicine – Endocrinology Diabetes and Metabolism
MMG	Internal Medicine – Gastroenterology
MMH	Internal Medicine – Hematology
MMI	Internal Medicine – Infectious Disease
MMO	Internal Medicine – Medical Oncology
MMN	Internal Medicine - Nephrology
MMP	Internal Medicine – Pulmonary Disease
MMR	Internal Medicine – Rheumatology
MPN	Neurology
MNS	Neurological Surgery
MNM	Nuclear Medicine
MOG	Obstetrics and Gynecology
MPO	Occupational Medicine
MOP	Opthalmology
MOSG	Orthopaedic Surgery (General)
MOSS	Orthopaedic –Shoulder
MOSK	Orthopaedic –Knee
MOSB	Orthopaedic –Spine
MOSF	Orthopaedic –Foot and ankle
MTO	Otolaryngology
MAP	Pain Management –Psychiatry and Neurology, Physical Medicine and Rehabilitation, Anesthesiology
MHA	Pathology
MEP	Pediatrics
MPR	Physical Medicine & Rehabilitation
MPS	Plastic Surgery
MPD	Psychiatry
MSY	Surgery
MSG	Surgery – General Vascular
MTS	Thoracic Surgery
MTO	Toxicology – Preventive Medicine, Pediatrics, Emergency
MUU	Urology
MRD	Radiology
POD	Podiatry

DWC Form 9768.5
May 2007

Note: Authority cited: Sections 133 and 4616, Labor Code. Reference: Section 4616.4, Labor Code.

History: 1. New section filed 12-31-2004 as an emergency; operative 1-1-2005 (Register 2004, No.

53). A Certificate of Compliance must be transmitted to OAL by 5-2-2005 or emergency language will be repealed by operation of law on the following day.

2. Certificate of Compliance as to 12-31-2004 order, including amendment of section, transmitted to OAL 4-29-2005 and filed 6-10-2005 (Register 2005, No. 23).

3. Change without regulatory effect amending form filed 10-18-2006 pursuant to section 100, title 1, California Code of Regulations (Register 2006, No. 42).

4. Change without regulatory effect amending form filed 5-21-2007 pursuant to section 100, title 1, California Code of Regulations (Register 2007, No. 21).

Ref.: Hanna § 5.05[13][e]; Herlick Handbook § 4.19A.

§9768.6. Administrative Director's Action on Contract Application Submitted by Physician.

(a) After reviewing a completed contract application submitted by a physician, if the Administrative Director finds that the physician meets the qualifications, he/she shall accept the contract application made by the physician to be an Independent Medical Reviewer by executing the IMR contract, notify the physician by mail, and add the physician's name to the list of Independent Medical Reviewers. The contract term shall be for a two-year term beginning with the date of acceptance by the Administrative Director.

(b) If the Administrative Director determines that a physician does not meet the qualifications, he/she shall notify the physician by mail that the physician's contract application is not accepted and the reason for the rejection.

(c) A physician whose contract application has not been accepted may reapply.

(d) If the Administrative Director denies a physician's contract application following at least two subsequent submissions, the physician may seek further review of the Administrative Director's decision by filing an appeal with the Workers' Compensation Appeals Board, and serving a copy on the Administrative Director, within twenty days after receipt of the denial.

Note: Authority cited: Sections 133 and 4616, Labor Code. Reference: Sections 4616.4 and 5300(f), Labor Code.

History: 1. New section filed 12-31-2004 as an emergency; operative 1-1-2005 (Register 2004, No. 53). A Certificate of Compliance must be transmitted to OAL by 5-2-2005 or emergency language will be repealed by operation of law on the following day.

2. Certificate of Compliance as to 12-31-2004 order, including amendment of subsection (a), transmitted to OAL 4-29-2005 and filed 6-10-2005 (Register 2005, No. 23).

Ref.: Hanna § 5.05[13][e]; Herlick Handbook § 4.19A.

§9768.7. IMR Request to Be Placed on Voluntary Inactive Status.

A physician may request to be placed on the inactive list during the IMR contract term. The physician shall submit the request to the Administrative Director and specify the time period that he or she is requesting to be on voluntary inactive status. The two-year contract term is not extended due to a physician's request to be placed on voluntary inactive status.

Note: Authority cited: Sections 133 and 4616, Labor Code. Reference: Section 4616.4, Labor Code.

History: 1. New section filed 12-31-2004 as an emergency; operative 1-1-2005 (Register 2004, No. 53). A Certificate of Compliance must be transmitted to OAL by 5-2-2005 or emergency language will be repealed by operation of law on the following day.

2. Certificate of Compliance as to 12-31-2004 order transmitted to OAL 4-29-2005 and filed 6-10-2005 (Register 2005, No. 23).

§9768.8. Removal of Physicians from Independent Medical Reviewer List.

(a) The Administrative Director may cancel the IMR contract and remove a physician from the Independent Medical Reviewer list if the Administrative Director determines based upon the Administrative Director's monitoring of reports:

(1) That the physician, having been notified by the Administrative Director of the physician's selection to render an Independent Medical Review, has not issued the Independent Medical Review report in a case within the time limits prescribed in these regulations on more than one occasion; or

(2) That the physician has not met the reporting requirements on more than one occasion; or

(3) That the physician has at any time failed to disclose to the Administrative Director that the physician had a conflict of interest pursuant to section 9768.2; or

(4) That the physician has failed to schedule appointments within the time frame required by these regulations on more than one occasion; or

(5) That the physician has failed to maintain the confidentiality of medical records and the review materials consistent with the applicable state and federal law.

(b) The Administrative Director shall cancel the IMR contract and remove a physician from the Independent Medical Reviewer list if the Administrative Director determines:

(1) That the physician no longer meets the qualifications to be on the list; or

(2) That the physician's contract application to be on the list contained material statements which were not true.

(c) The Administrative Director shall place a physician on an inactive list for up to the end of the two year contract term whenever the Administrative Director determines that the appropriate licensing Board from whom the physician is licensed has filed an accusation for a quality of care violation, fraud related to medical practice, or conviction of a felony crime or a crime related to the conduct of his or her practice of medicine against the physician or taken other action restricting the physician's medical license. If the accusation or action is later withdrawn, dismissed or determined to be without merit during the two year contract term, the physician shall advise the Administrative Director who will then remove the physician's name from the inactive list. If the accusation or action is withdrawn, dismissed or determined to be without merit after the expiration of the two year contract term, the physician may reapply to serve as an Independent Medical Reviewer pursuant to section 9768.4.

(d) Upon removal of a physician from the Independent Medical Reviewer list or placement on the inactive list, the Administrative Director shall advise the physician by mail of the removal or placement on the inactive list, the Administrative Director's reasons for such action, and the right to request a hearing on the removal from the IMR list or placement on the inactive list.

(e) A physician who has been mailed a notice of removal from the list or placement on the inactive list, may, within 30 calendar days of the mailing of the notice, request a hearing by filing a written request for hearing with the Administrative Director. If a written request for hearing is not received by the Administrative Director within 30 calendar days of the mailing of the notice, the physician shall be deemed to have waived any appeal or request for hearing.

(f) Upon receipt of a written request for hearing, the Administrative Director shall prepare an accusation and serve the applicant physician with the accusation, as provided in Government Code section 11503.

(g) Hearings shall be held by the Administrative Director or his or her designee under the procedures of Chapter 5 of Part 1 of Division 3 of Title 2 of the Government Code (commencing with section 11500) and the regulations of the Office of Administrative Hearings (Title 1, California Code of Regulations, section 1000 et seq.).

(h) Failure to timely file a notice of defense or failure to appear at a noticed hearing or conference shall constitute a waiver of a right to a hearing.

(i) A physician who has been removed from the list may petition for reinstatement after one year has elapsed since the effective date of the Administrative Director's decision on the physician's removal. The provisions of Government Code section 11522 shall apply to such petition.

Note: Authority cited: Sections 133 and 4616, Labor Code; and Section 11400.20, Government Code. Reference: Section 4616.4, Labor Code; and Sections 11415.10, 11503 and 11522, Government Code.

History: 1. New section filed 12-31-2004 as an emergency; operative 1-1-2005 (Register 2004, No. 53). A Certificate of Compliance must be transmitted to OAL by 5-2-2005 or emergency language will be repealed by operation of law on the following day.

2. Certificate of Compliance as to 12-31-2004 order, including amendment of section, transmitted to OAL 4-29-2005 and filed 6-10-2005 (Register 2005, No. 23).

Ref.: Hanna § 5.05[13][e]; Herlick Handbook § 4.19A.

§9768.9. Procedure for Requesting an Independent Medical Review.

(a) If a covered employee disputes the diagnostic service, diagnosis, or medical treatment prescribed by the second opinion physician, the injured employee may seek the opinion of a third physician in the MPN. The covered employee and the employer or insurer shall comply with the requirements of section 9767.7(d). Additionally, at the time of the selection of the physician for a third opinion, the MPN Contact shall notify the covered employee about the

Independent Medical Review process and provide the covered employee with an "Independent Medical Review Application" form set forth in section 9768.10. The MPN Contact shall fill out the "MPN Contact Section" of the form and list the specialty of the treating physician and an alternative specialty, if any, that is different from the specialty of the treating physician.

(b) If a covered employee disputes either the diagnostic service, diagnosis or medical treatment prescribed by the third opinion physician, the covered employee may request an Independent Medical Review by filing the completed Independent Medical Review Application form with the Administrative Director. The covered employee shall complete the "employee section" of the form, indicate on the form whether he or she requests an in-person examination or record review, and may list an alternative specialty, if any, that is different from the specialty of the treating physician.

(c) The Administrative Director shall select an IMR with an appropriate specialty within ten business days of receiving the Independent Medical Review Application form. The Administrative Director's selection of the IMR shall be based on the specialty of the treating physician, the alternative specialties listed by the covered employee and the MPN Contact, and the information submitted with the Independent Medical Review Application.

(d) If the covered employee requests an in-person examination, the Administrative Director shall randomly select a physician from the panel of available Independent Medical Reviewers, with an appropriate specialty, who has an office located within thirty miles of the employee's residence address, to be the Independent Medical Reviewer. If there is only one physician with an appropriate specialty within thirty miles of the employee's residence address, that physician shall be selected to be the Independent Medical Reviewer. If there are no physicians with an appropriate specialty who have offices located within thirty miles of the employee's residence address, the Administrative Director shall search in increasing five mile increments, until one physician is located. If there are no available physicians with this appropriate specialty, the Administrative Director may choose another specialty based on the information submitted.

(e) If the covered employee requests a record review, then the Administrative Director shall randomly select a physician with an appropriate specialty from the panel of available Independent Medical Reviewers to be the IMR. If there are no physicians with an appropriate specialty, the Administrative Director may choose another specialty based on the information submitted.

(f) The Administrative Director shall send written notification of the name and contact information of the IMR to the covered employee, the employee's attorney, if any, the MPN Contact and the IMR. The Administrative Director shall send a copy of the completed Independent Medical Review Application to the IMR.

(g) The covered employee, MPN Contact, or the selected IMR can object within 10 calendar days of receipt of the name of the IMR to the selection if there is a conflict of interest as defined by section 9768.2. If the IMR determines that he or she does not practice the appropriate specialty, the IMR shall withdraw within 10 calendar days of receipt of the notification of selection. If this conflict is verified or the IMR withdraws, the Administrative Director shall select another IMR from the same specialty. If there are no available physicians with the same specialty, the Administrative Director may select an IMR with another specialty based on the information submitted and in accordance with the procedure set forth in subdivision (d) for an in-person examination and subdivision (e) for a record review.

(h) If the covered employee requests an in-person exam, within 60 calendar days of receiving the name of the IMR, the covered employee shall contact the IMR to arrange an appointment. If the covered employee fails to contact the IMR for an appointment within 60 calendar days of receiving the name of the IMR, then the employee shall be deemed to have waived the IMR process with regard to this disputed diagnosis or treatment of this treating physician. The IMR shall schedule an appointment with the covered employee within 30 calendar days of the request for an appointment, unless all parties agree to a later date. The IMR shall notify the MPN Contact of the appointment date.

(i) The covered employee shall provide written notice to the Administrative Director and the MPN Contact if the covered employee decides to withdraw the request for an Independent Medical Reviewer.

(j) During this process, the employee shall remain within the MPN for treatment pursuant to section 9767.6.

Note: Authority cited: Sections 133 and 4616, Labor Code. Reference: Sections 4616.3 and 4616.4, Labor Code.

History: 1. New section filed 12-31-2004 as an emergency; operative 1-1-2005 (Register 2004, No. 53). A Certificate of Compliance must be transmitted to OAL by 5-2-2005 or emergency language will be repealed by operation of law on the following day.

2. Certificate of Compliance as to 12-31-2004 order, including amendment of section, transmitted to OAL 4-29-2005 and filed 6-10-2005 (Register 2005, No. 23).

Ref.: Hanna § 5.05[13][e]; Herlick Handbook § 4.19A.

§9768.10. Independent Medical Review Application (Form).

Independent Medical Review Application
(Division of Workers' Compensation – 8 CCR §9768.10 Mandatory Form)

Employee Section: The Employee shall complete this section and send the completed form to the Administrative Director. Mailing address: Dept. of Industrial Relations, Division of Workers' Compensation, P.O. Box 71010, Oakland, CA 94612.

Employee Name ______ Employee Phone Number / Fax ______ Employee's Address ______

Employee's Attorney's Name, if applicable ______ Attorney's Phone Number / Fax ______ Attorney's Address ______

Pursuant to Labor Code section 4616.4, I request that the Administrative Director set an Independent Medical Review within 30 days from receipt of this Application.

Check one: ☐ Request for In-Person Examination ☐ Request for Record Review (no In-Person Examination)

Is interpreter needed for exam? ______ If yes, language: ______

Describe diagnosis and part of body affected: ______

Reason for request for Independent Medical Review. Please explain if the dispute involves the diagnosis, treatment or a test (attach additional page or additional materials, such as medical records, if necessary):

______

Select an alternative specialty, other than specialty of treating physician, if any, from the list on the instructions for this form:

______

Release: I, ______ (injured employee or person authorized pursuant to law to act on behalf of the injured employee), authorize the release of relevant medical records to the Independent Medical Reviewer.

Signature of injured employee or authorized person ______ Date ______

Medical Provider Network Contact Section: The MPN Contact shall complete this section and send the form to the employee.

Employee ______ Employer ______

Insurer ______ Claim Number ______

Medical Provider Network ______ Date of Injury ______

Treating Physician ______ Specialty ______ Address ______

2nd Opinion Physician and specialty ______ 3rd Opinion Physician and specialty ______

Select an alternative specialty other than specialty of treating physician, if any, from the list on the back of this form:

______

I declare under penalty of perjury that I mailed a copy of the Application for IMR to the above named Employee on

Date ______ Signature ______ Phone number, fax, and email of MPN Contact ______

Name of MPN Contact ______ Address ______

DWC Form 9768.10
May 2007

Instructions for Independent Medical Review Application Form

Instructions for MPN Contact: At the time of the selection of the physician for a third opinion, you are required to notify the covered employee about the Independent Medical Review process and provide the covered employee with this "Independent Medical Review Application" form. You are required to fill out the "MPN Contact section" of the form. You must then send the form to the employee, who will fill out the top section of the form and send it to the Division of Workers' Compensation. The DWC will send you written notification of the name and contact information of the Independent Medical Reviewer. You must then send the employee's relevant medical records as defined by section 9768.1(a)(11) to the Independent Medical Reviewer. A copy of the medical reports must also be sent to the employee.

Instructions for Injured Employee: This application is being sent to you because you have requested a third opinion to address your dispute with your treating doctor's diagnosis, suggested test, or suggested medical treatment. **Please wait until you read the report from the third opinion doctor before you fill out this form.** If the report resolves your dispute, then you do not need to fill out this form. If you still have a dispute with your treating doctor, then you may request an Independent Medical Review by completing this form and sending it to:

Dept. of Industrial Relations
Division of Workers' Compensation
P.O. Box 71010
Oakland, CA 94612.

An Independent Medical Review is done by a physician who does not work directly with your doctor. You can visit that doctor and be examined or you can choose to have the doctor review your records. Indicate on the form whether you want to be examined (in-person examination) or if you only want to have your records reviewed.

The specialty of the doctor will be the same as the specialty of your treating physician, if possible. Not all types of doctors can be an Independent Medical Reviewer. You may select another type of doctor in case your doctor's specialty is not available. To do this, look at the list of specialists below and chose one type. Indicate this choice on the application. You will receive the name and contact information of the Independent Medical Reviewer from the Division of Workers' Compensation. When you receive the name of the Independent Medical Reviewer, you must make an appointment within 60 days. The Independent Medical Reviewer is required to schedule an appointment with you within 30 days. If you fail to make the appointment with the Independent Medical Reviewer within 60 days, you will not be allowed to have an Independent Medical Review on this dispute. **Written notice must be made to the Administrative Director and MPN Contact if you wish to withdraw the request for an Independent Medical Review after this form has been submitted.**

SPECIALTY CODES

MAI Allergy and Immunology	**MAA** Anesthesiology
MRS Colon & Rectal Surgery	**MDE** Dermatology
MEM Emergency Medicine	**MFP** Family Practice
MPM General Preventive Medicine	**MHD** Hand – Orthopaedic Surgery, Plastic Surgery, General Surgery
MMM Internal Medicine	**MMV** Internal Medicine – Cardiovascular Disease
MME Internal Medicine – Endocrinology Diabetes and Metabolism	**MMG** Internal Medicine - Gastroenterology
MMH Internal Medicine – Hematology	**MMI** Internal Medicine – Infectious Disease
MMO Internal Medicine – Medical Oncology	**MMN** Internal Medicine - Nephrology
MMP Internal Medicine – Pulmonary Disease	**MMR** Internal Medicine – Rheumatology
MPN Neurology	**MNS** Neurological Surgery
MNM Nuclear Medicine	**MOG** Obstetrics and Gynecology
MPO Occupational Medicine	**MOP** Ophthalmology
MOS Orthopaedic Surgery	**MTO** Otolaryngology
MAP Pain Management –Psychiatry and Neurology, Physical Medicine and Rehabilitation, Anesthesiology	**MHA** Pathology
MEP Pediatrics	**MPR** Physical Medicine & Rehabilitation
MPS Plastic Surgery	**MPD** Psychiatry
MRD Radiology	**MSY** Surgery
MSG Surgery – General Vascular	**MTS** Thoracic Surgery
MTX Toxicology – Preventive Medicine, Pediatrics, Emergency	**MUU** Urology
POD Podiatry	

DWC Form 9768.10
May 2007

Note: Authority cited: Sections 133 and 4616, Labor Code. Reference: Sections 4616.3 and 4616.4, Labor Code.

History: 1. New section filed 12-31-2004 as an emergency; operative 1-1-2005 (Register 2004, No. 53). A Certificate of Compliance must be transmitted to OAL by 5-2-2005 or emergency language will be repealed by operation of law on the following day.

2. Certificate of Compliance as to 12-31-2004 order, including amendment of section heading and section, transmitted to OAL 4-29-2005 and filed 6-10-2005 (Register 2005, No. 23).

3. Change without regulatory effect amending form filed 10-18-2006 pursuant to section 100, title 1, California Code of Regulations (Register 2006, No. 42).

4. Change without regulatory effect amending section filed 5-23-2007 pursuant to section 100, title 1, California Code of Regulations (Register 2007, No. 21).

Ref.: Hanna § 5.05[13][e]; Herlick Handbook § 4.19A.

§9768.11. In-Person Examination or Record Review IMR Procedure.

(a) The MPN Contact shall send all relevant medical records to the IMR. The MPN Contact shall also send a copy of the documents to the covered employee. The employee may furnish any relevant medical records or additional materials to the Independent Medical Reviewer, with a copy to the MPN Contact. If an in-person examination is requested and if a special form of transportation is required because of the employee's medical condition, it is the obligation of the MPN Contact to arrange for it. The MPN Contact shall furnish transportation and arrange for an interpreter, if necessary, in advance of the in-person examination. All reasonable expenses of transportation shall be incurred by the insurer or employer pursuant to Labor Code section 4600. Except for the in-person examination itself, the Independent Medical Reviewer shall have no ex parte contact with any party. Except for matters dealing with scheduling appointments, scheduling medical tests and obtaining medical records, all communications between the Independent Medical Reviewer and any party shall be in writing, with copies served on all parties.

(b) If the IMR requires further tests, the IMR shall notify the MPN Contact within one working day of the appointment. All tests shall be consistent with the medical treatment utilization schedule adopted pursuant to Labor Code section 5307.27 or, prior to the adoption of this schedule, the ACOEM guidelines, and for all injuries not covered by the medical treatment utilization schedule or the ACOEM guidelines, in accordance with other evidence based medical treatment guidelines generally recognized by the national medical community and that are scientifically based.

(c) The IMR may order any diagnostic tests necessary to make his or her determination regarding medical treatment or diagnostic services for the injury or illness but shall not request the employee to submit to an unnecessary exam or procedure. If a test duplicates a test already given, the IMR shall provide justification for the duplicative test in his or her report.

(d) If the employee fails to attend an examination with the IMR and fails to reschedule the appointment within five business days of the missed appointment, the IMR shall perform a review of the record and make a determination based on those records.

(e) The IMR shall serve the report on the Administrative Director, the MPN Contact, the employee and the employee's attorney, if any, within 20 days after the in-person examination or completion of the record review.

(f) If the disputed health care service has not been provided and the IMR certifies in writing that an imminent and serious threat to the health of the injured employee exists, including, but not limited to, the potential loss of life, limb, or bodily function, or the immediate and serious deterioration of the injured employee, the report shall be expedited and rendered within three business days of the in-person examination by the IMR.

(g) Subject to approval by the Administrative Director, reviews not covered under subdivision (f) may be extended for up to three business days in extraordinary circumstances or for good cause.

(h) Extensions for good cause shall be granted for:

(1) Medical emergencies of the IMR or the IMR's family;

(2) Death in the IMR's family; or

(3) Natural disasters or other community catastrophes that interrupt the operation of the IMR's office operations.

(i) Utilizing the medical treatment utilization schedule established pursuant to Labor Code section 5307.27 or, prior to the adoption of this schedule, the ACOEM guidelines, and taking into account any reports and information provided, the IMR shall determine whether the disputed health care service is consistent with the recommended standards. For injuries not covered by the medical treatment utilization schedule or by the ACOEM guidelines, the treatment rendered shall be in accordance with other evidence-based medical treatment guidelines which are generally recognized by the national medical community and scientifically based.

(j) The IMR shall not treat or offer to provide medical treatment for that injury or illness for which he or she has done an Independent Medical Review evaluation for the employee unless a medical emergency arises during the in-person examination.

(k) Neither the employee nor the employer nor the insurer shall have any liability for payment for the Independent Medical Review which was not completed within the required timeframes unless the employee and the employer each waive the right to a new Independent Medical Review and elect to accept the original evaluation.

Note: Authority cited: Sections 133 and 4616, Labor Code. Reference: Sections 4616.4 and 5307.27, Labor Code.

History: 1. New section filed 12-31-2004 as an emergency; operative 1-1-2005 (Register 2004, No. 53). A Certificate of Compliance must be transmitted to OAL by 5-2-2005 or emergency language will be repealed by operation of law on the following day.

2. Certificate of Compliance as to 12-31-2004 order, including amendment of subsections (a), (e), (j) and (k), transmitted to OAL 4-29-2005 and filed 6-10-2005 (Register 2005, No. 23).

Ref.: Hanna § 5.05[13][e]; Herlick Handbook § 4.19A.

§9768.12. Contents of Independent Medical Review Reports.

(a) Reports of Independent Medical Reviewers shall include:

(1) The date of the in-person examination or record review;

(2) The patient's complaint(s);

(3) A listing of all information received from the parties reviewed in preparation of the report or relied upon for the formulation of the physician's opinion;

(4) The patient's medical history relevant to the diagnostic services, diagnosis or medical treatment;

(5) Findings on record review or in-person examination;

(6) The IMR's diagnosis;

(7) The physician's opinion whether or not the proposed treatment or diagnostic services are appropriate and indicated. If the proposed treatment or diagnostic services are not appropriate or indicated, any alternative diagnosis or treatment recommendation consistent with the medical treatment utilization schedule shall be included;

(8) An analysis and determination whether the disputed health care service is consistent with the medical treatment utilization schedule established pursuant to Labor Code section 5307.27 or, prior to the adoption of this schedule, the ACOEM guidelines. For injuries not covered by the medical treatment utilization schedule or by the ACOEM guidelines, an analysis and determination whether the treatment rendered is in accordance with other evidence-based medical treatment guidelines which are generally recognized by the national medical community and scientifically based; and

(9) The signature of the physician.

(b) The report shall be in writing and use layperson's terms to the maximum extent possible.

(c) An Independent Medical Reviewer shall serve with each report the following executed declaration made under penalty of perjury:

"I declare under penalty of perjury that this report is true and correct to the best of my knowledge and that I have not violated Labor Code section 139.3.

________________ ________________"

Date Signature

Note: Authority cited: Sections 133 and 4616, Labor Code. Reference: Sections 139.3, 4616.4 and 5307.27, Labor Code.

History: 1. New section filed 12-31-2004 as an emergency; operative 1-1-2005 (Register 2004, No. 53). A Certificate of Compliance must be transmitted to OAL by 5-2-2005 or emergency language will be repealed by operation of law on the following day.

2. Certificate of Compliance as to 12-31-2004 order, including amendment of subsections (a) and (c), transmitted to OAL 4-29-2005 and filed 6-10-2005 (Register 2005, No. 23).

Ref.: Hanna § 5.05[13][e]; Herlick Handbook § 4.19A.

§9768.13. Destruction of Records by the Administrative Director.

The Administrative Director may destroy any forms or documents submitted to the Administrative Director as part of the IMR process two years after the date of receipt.

Note: Authority cited: Sections 133 and 4616, Labor Code. Reference: Section 4616.4, Labor Code.

History: 1. New section filed 12-31-2004 as an emergency; operative 1-1-2005 (Register 2004, No. 53). A Certificate of Compliance must be transmitted to OAL by 5-2-2005 or emergency language will be repealed by operation of law on the following day.

2. Certificate of Compliance as to 12-31-2004 order transmitted to OAL 4-29-2005 and filed 6-10-2005 (Register 2005, No. 23).

§9768.14. Retention of Records by Independent Medical Reviewer.

Each Independent Medical Reviewer shall retain all comprehensive medical reports completed by the Independent Medical Reviewer for a period of five years from the date of the IMR report.

Note: Authority cited: Sections 133 and 4616, Labor Code. Reference: Section 4616.4, Labor Code.

History: 1. New section filed 12-31-2004 as an emergency; operative 1-1-2005 (Register 2004, No. 53). A Certificate of Compliance must be transmitted to OAL by 5-2-2005 or emergency language will be repealed by operation of law on the following day.

2. Certificate of Compliance as to 12-31-2004 order, including amendment of section, transmitted to OAL 4-29-2005 and filed 6-10-2005 (Register 2005, No. 23).

§9768.15. Charges for Independent Medical Reviewers.

(a) Payment for the services of the Independent Medical Reviewers shall be made by the employer or insurer.

(b) The fee shall be based on the Official Medical Fee Schedule using confirmatory consultation codes (99271 through 99275 for in-person examinations or 99271 through 99273 for evaluations not requiring an in-person examination), 99080 for reports, and 99358 for record reviews, and any other appropriate codes or modifiers.

(c) An IMR shall not accept any additional compensation from any source for his or her services as an IMR except for services provided to treat a medical emergency that arose during an in-person examination pursuant to section 9768.11(j).

Note: Authority cited: Sections 133 and 4616, Labor Code. Reference: Section 4616.4, Labor Code.

History: 1. New section filed 12-31-2004 as an emergency; operative 1-1-2005 (Register 2004, No. 53). A Certificate of Compliance must be transmitted to OAL by 5-2-2005 or emergency language will be repealed by operation of law on the following day.

2. Certificate of Compliance as to 12-31-2004 order, including amendment of subsections (a) and (b), transmitted to OAL 4-29-2005 and filed 6-10-2005 (Register 2005, No. 23).

Ref.: Hanna § 5.05[13][e]; Herlick Handbook § 4.19A.

§9768.16. Adoption of Decision.

(a) The Administrative Director shall immediately adopt the determination of the Independent Medical Reviewer and issue a written decision within 5 business days of receipt of the report.

(b) The parties may appeal the Administrative Director's written decision by filing a petition with the Workers' Compensation Appeals Board and serving a copy on the Administrative Director, within twenty days after receipt of the decision.

Note: Authority cited: Sections 133 and 4616, Labor Code. Reference: Sections 4616.4 and 5300(f), Labor Code.

History: 1. New section filed 12-31-2004 as an emergency; operative 1-1-2005 (Register 2004, No. 53). A Certificate of Compliance must be transmitted to OAL by 5-2-2005 or emergency language will be repealed by operation of law on the following day.

2. Certificate of Compliance as to 12-31-2004 order, including amendment of subsection (a), transmitted to OAL 4-29-2005 and filed 6-10-2005 (Register 2005, No. 23).

Ref.: Hanna § 5.05[13][e]; Herlick Handbook § 4.19A.

§9768.17. Treatment Outside the Medical Provider Network.

(a) If the IMR agrees with the diagnosis, diagnostic service or medical treatment prescribed by the treating physician, the covered employee shall continue to receive medical treatment from physicians within the MPN.

(b) If the IMR does not agree with the disputed diagnosis, diagnostic service or medical treatment prescribed by the treating physician, the covered employee shall seek medical treatment with a physician of his or her choice either within or outside the MPN. If the employee chooses to receive medical treatment with a physician outside the MPN, the treatment is limited to the treatment recommended by the IMR or the diagnostic service recommended by the IMR.

(c) The medical treatment shall be consistent with the medical treatment utilization schedule established pursuant to Labor Code section 5307.27 or, prior to the adoption of this schedule, the ACOEM guidelines. For injuries not covered by the medical treatment utilization schedule or by the ACOEM guidelines, the treatment rendered shall be in accordance with other evidence-based medical treatment guidelines which are generally recognized by the national medical community and scientifically based.

(d) The employer or insurer shall be liable for the cost of any approved medical treatment in accordance with Labor Code section 5307.1 or 5307.11.

Note: Authority cited: Sections 133 and 4616, Labor Code. Reference: Sections 4616.4, 5307.1, 5307.11 and 5307.27, Labor Code.

History: 1. New section filed 12-31-2004 as an emergency; operative 1-1-2005 (Register 2004, No. 53). A Certificate of Compliance must be transmitted to OAL by 5-2-2005 or emergency language will be repealed by operation of law on the following day.

2. Certificate of Compliance as to 12-31-2004 order, including amendment of Note, transmitted to OAL 4-29-2005 and filed 6-10-2005 (Register 2005, No. 23).

Ref.: Hanna § 5.05[13][e]; Herlick Handbook § 4.19A.

ARTICLE 4
Certification Standards for Health Care Organizations

§9770. Definitions.

(a) "Administrative Director" means the administrative director of the Division of Workers' Compensation.

(b) "Claims Administrator" means a self-administered insurer providing security for the payment of compensation required by Divisions 4 and 4.5 of the Labor Code, a self-administered self-insured employer, or a third-party claims administrator for a self-insured employer, insurer, legally uninsured employer, or joint powers authority.

(c) "Division" means the Division of Workers' Compensation.

(d) "Employer" means an employer as defined in Section 3300 of the Labor Code.

(e) "HCO Enrollee" means a person who is eligible to receive services from an HCO.

(f) "Health care organization" ("HCO") means any entity certified as a health care organization by the administrative director pursuant to Section 4600.5 of the Labor Code and this article.

(g) "International Classification of Diseases—9th Revision (ICD-9) code" means the 4 or 5 digit number which identifies the illness, injury, disease, cause of death, or other morbid state of an enrollee that corresponds to the numeric classifications and descriptions listed in *International Classification of Diseases. Clinical Modification. 9th Revision (ICD-9CM)* US Department of Health and Human Services, Health Care Financing Administration. Washington DC: Superintendent of Documents, and updated successor revised manuals.

(h) "Material": A factor is "material" with respect to a matter if it is one to which a reasonable person would attach importance in determining the action to be taken upon the matter.

(i) "Participating provider" means a provider who is employed by or under contract with an HCO for purposes of providing occupational medical or health services or services required by this article.

(j) "Patient" means an HCO enrollee who is currently obtaining treatment or services for a work-related injury or illness.

(k) "Primary treating physician" means the treating physician primarily responsible for managing the care of the injured worker in accordance with Section 9785.5.

(*l*) "Professionally recognized standards of care" means health care practice encompassing the learning, skill and clinical judgment ordinarily possessed and and used by a provider of good standing in similar circumstances.

(m) "Provider" means any professional person, organization, health facility, or other person or institution licensed by the state to deliver or furnish health care services.

(n) "Revocation" means the termination of a health care organization's certification to provide services pursuant to Section 4600.5 of the Labor Code and this article.

(o) "Standard Industrial Classification code" means the 4 digit number which identifies the primary type of economic activity which the employer is engaged in that corresponds to the numeric classifications and descriptions listed in The Standard Industrial Classification Manual 1987, Office of Management and Budget, Washington DC: Superintendent of Documents, US Government Printing Office, 1989, and updated successor revised manuals.

(p) "Suspension" means the health care organization's authority to enter into new, renewed, or amended contracts with claims administrators has been suspended by the administrative director for a specific period of time.

(q) "Utilization review" or "Utilization Management" is the system used to manage, assess, improve, or review patient care and decision-making through case by case assessments of the medical reasonableness or medical necessity of the frequency, duration, level and appropriateness of medical care and services, based upon professionally recognized standards of care. Utilization review may include, but is not limited to, prospective, concurrent, and retrospective review of a request for authorization of medical treatment.

Note: Authority cited: Sections 133, 4600.5, 4603.5 and 5307.3, Labor Code. Reference: Sections 3300, 4061.5, 4600.5, 5400, 5401 and 5402, Labor Code.

History: 1. New article 4 and section filed 12-31-93; operative 1-1-94. Submitted to OAL for printing only pursuant to Government Code section 11351 (Register 93, No. 53). For prior history, see Register 84, No. 35.

2. New subsection (h) and subsection relettering filed 2-14-96; operative 2-14-96. Submitted to OAL for printing only pursuant to Government Code section 11351 (Register 96, No. 7).

Ref.: Herlick Handbook § 1.6.

§9771. Applications for Certification.

(a) Any of the following entities may apply for certification as a health care organization:

(1) A disability insurer licensed by the Department of Insurance to transact health insurance or disability income insurance pursuant to Part 2 of Division 2 of the Insurance Code.

(2) Any workers compensation health care provider organization.

(b) An applicant must meet all of the requirements set forth in this article in order to be certified as a health care organization by the administrative director. Applicants must initially submit to the administrative director, as part of the application, a plan which will provide a clear and concise description of how occupational medical and health care services are to be provided and how each of the requirements in this article are met, and, where specified, in the manner required under each section. HCOs must include all documentation necessary to demonstrate that they meet the requirements for certification.

(c) Health care service plans must provide written certification that at the time of application the applicant is not in violation of any provision of law or rules or orders of the Director of the Department of Managed Health Care, and that there are no outstanding orders, undertakings, or deficiency letters which involve the applicant. Disability insurers must provide written certification that at the time of application they are in good standing with the Department of Insurance. The requirement of this subdivision may be satisfied by verified statement under penalty of perjury by the president or managing officer of an applicant that the applicant meets the requirements of this subdivision, subject to verification by the administrative director.

(d) An applicant who is in compliance with requirements for certification by the Department of Insurance may submit copies of any relevant exhibits, sections or other documents submitted as part of the primary certification application to meet any of the requirements of this article, provided that the applicant (1) verifies that the Department of Insurance has fully reviewed and approved the submitted information, (2) provides a concise narrative identifying any manner in which HCO services will be provided differently from those provided under the primary certification, and (3) provides a concise description for each requirement of this article, specifying how occupational medical and health care services or other services specifically and exclusively required by this article will be met.

(e) Applications must be in writing in the form and manner prescribed by the administrative director, and must be submitted on or after January 1, 1994. The original plus one copy of the application shall be submitted together with a fee as specified in subdivision (c). Each application shall provide, in addition to the plan specified in subdivision (b), the following information:

(1) The names of all directors and officers of the health care organization;

(2) The title and name of the person designated to be the day-to-day administrator of the health care organization.

(3) The title and name of the person designated to be the administrator of the financial affairs of the health care organization.

(4) The name, medical specialty, if any, board certification, if any, and any unrestricted licenses (including states where licensed), of the medical director.

(5) The name, address, and telephone number of a person designated to serve as a liaison for the Division, who is responsible for receiving compliance and informational communications from the Division and for disseminating the same within the HCO organization.

(6) A sample of each type of contract with participating providers, claims administrators, and insurers, and any entities specifically providing services required by this article; and a list of contractors for each type of contract. Copies of contracts shall be made available to the administrative director upon request. The Division will maintain as confidential information pertaining to provider rates and other financial information in accordance with Government Code Section 6254(d)(1).

(7) An organizational chart demonstrating the structural relationships between the medical director, fiscal or financial administrator, and executive officers and administrators.

(8) The identity of any worker's compensation insurer that controls or is controlled by the applicant, as defined by Section 1215 of the Insurance Code.

(f) Each application for certification must be accompanied by a non refundable fee of $20,000.

(g) In lieu of an application for certification, an entity licensed as a full service health care service plan under Section 1353 of the Health and Safety Code (a Knox-Keene Health Care Service Plan Act) and deemed to be an HCO pursuant to Labor Code Section 4600.5(c) shall submit to the administrative director:

(1) a concise description of how the health plan will satisfy the requirements of Labor Code Section 4600.5(c)(1–5) and Sections 9772 through 9778, inclusive, of these regulations. At the time the materials required by this subsection are submitted to the administrative director for review, the health plan shall pay a nonrefundable documentation processing and review fee of $10,000; and,

(2) written certification that the health plan is not in violation of any provisions of law or rules or orders of the Director of the Department of Managed Health Care, and that there are no outstanding orders, undertakings, or deficiency letters which involve the health plan. The requirements of this subdivision may be satisfied by verified statement under penalty of perjury by the president or managing officer of the health plan that the plan meets the requirements of this subdivision, subject to verification by the administrative director.

Note: Authority cited: Sections 133, 4600.5, 4600.7, 4603.5 and 5307.3, Labor Code. Reference: Sections 4600 and 4600.5, Labor Code.

History: 1. New section filed 12-31-93; operative 1-1-94. Submitted to OAL for printing only pursuant to Government Code section 11351 (Register 93, No. 53).

2. Amendment of subsection (d), new subsection (e)(8) and amendment of subsection (f) filed 2-14-96; operative 2-14-96. Submitted to OAL for printing only pursuant to Government Code section 11351 (Register 96, No. 7).

3. Repealer of subsection (a)(1), subsection renumbering, amendment of newly designated subsection (a)(2) and subsections (c), (d) and (f), new subsections (g)-(g)(2) and amendment of Note filed 1-9-2003; operative 1-9-2003 pursuant to Government Code section 11343.4 (Register 2003, No. 2).

Ref.: Hanna § 22.01[6]; Herlick Handbook § 1.6.

§9771.1. Updating Applications.

(a) Every application submitted under Section 9771(e) shall be kept current to reflect accurately the actual operation of the HCO. An applicant or a certified HCO shall file an amendment to its application to show any change in any information contained in the application. Amendments include changes, deletions, additions and variations to the original application and its exhibits, including sample contracts. Amendments shall be filed as set forth in this section. However, the administrative director may approve an alternative form of submitting an amendment if it substantially accomplishes the purposes of this section.

(b) An original and one copy of an amendment shall be submitted to the administrative director as follows:

(1) Submit an Execution Page of the application, indicating it is an "Amendment to Pend-

ing Application" or "Amendment to Application of a Certified Organization";

(2) Furnish only those pages of the application and/or those exhibits which are changed by the amendment.

(3) If a page of the application is amended, complete all items on that page and "redline" or otherwise clearly designated the changed item. At the lower left-hand corner of each page, type "Rev. [date]", giving the effective date of the amendment.

(4) If an exhibit is being amended:

(A) Furnish the complete exhibit as amended, bearing the same number as the original exhibit, with the changed portions of the exhibit "redlined" or otherwise clearly designated, or

(B) Furnish the pages of the exhibit which are amended, each page to be marked with the exhibit number and the page number of the exhibit, and with the changed portions "redlined" or otherwise clearly designated. At the lower left-hand corner of each page, type "Rev. [date]", giving the effective date of the amendment. If this method of amendment is employed, the applicant shall refile the entire exhibit as amended whenever more than 10 percent if its pages have been amended.

(2) In the event that it is impossible to submit a proposed material change in the application 30 days before the change is implemented, the applicant shall submit the change as soon as the applicant becomes aware that a change is required. If, in the opinion of the administrative director, the change or proposed changed raises a question as to the ability of a certified HCO to meet the requirements of this article, the administrative director may, within 30 days of receiving notice of the change inform the HCO of the question. When the administrative director informs the HCO that a question exists, the HCO may not implement the proposed change, or shall cease implementing the change. The HCO may submit whatever materials it deems appropriate to justify the amendment and may meet with the administrative director or staff to discuss the question. Within 30 days after informing the HCO of the question, the administrative director shall inform the HCO whether the amendment is approved or disapproved.

(d) Amendments making non-material changes shall be filed quarterly on dates specified by the administrative director. However, a list of providers need be amended only when 10 percent or more of the names contained in the list for a service area have been changed or when the sole or principal provider for a particular health care service in a service area is added or deleted. When amended, the complete list (or the list for the service area) shall be furnished following the instructions for the particular item, with each added "redlined" or otherwise clearly designated and the names of persons deleted from the list shown at the end under the heading "deletions."

(e) Review of amendments submitted under section 9771.1, except quarterly updates under section 9771.1(e)(2), will be charged based on the actual cost for performing the review. The amount shall include the actual salaries or compensation paid to the persons reviewing amendment; the expenses incurred in the course thereof, and overhead costs in connection therewith as fixed by the Administrative Director. Overhead costs shall be based on the total expenditure for operating expenses and equipment, except travel, of the managed care unit of the Division of Workers' Compensation for the previous fiscal year. The invoice will be sent upon the completion of the review and shall be paid within 30 calendar days.

Note: Authority: Sections 133, 4600.5, 4600.7, 5307.3, Labor Code. Reference: Sections 4600.3, 4600.5, Labor Code.

History: 1. New section filed 2-14-96; operative 2-14-96. Submitted to OAL for printing only pursuant to Government Code section 11351 (Register 96, No. 7).

1996 Note: It appears that the subsection preceding subsection (d) should be designated as subsection (c).

Ref.: Herlick Handbook § 1.6.

§9771.2. Information to Be Furnished as it Becomes Available.

(a) If an HCO, or any person listed in section 9771(e)(8), is named as a defendant in a lawsuit that is materially related to the provision of medical treatment under Labor Code section 4600, the HCO shall inform the administrative director within 5 days of the day it becomes aware the suit is filed and shall provide a copy of the complaint.

(b)(1) If a certified HCO is a health care services plan and if the Director of the Department of Managed Health Care begins proceedings against the plan under Articles 7 or 8 of the Knox-Keene Health Care Service Plan Act of 1975, the certified HCO shall inform the administrative director within 5 days of the day it becomes aware of the proceedings. The requirements of this subdivision shall also apply to an HMO deemed an HCO pursuant to Labor Code Section 4600.5(c) while the administrative director is reviewing the documentation required by Section 9771 subdivisions (g)(1) and (2) prior to issuing the HMO its certification.

(2) If an applicant or a certified HCO is a disability insurer and if the Commissioner of Insurance begins proceedings against the insurer under Insurance Code section 704 or an examination under section 730, the applicant or certified HCO shall inform the administrative director within 5 days of the day it becomes aware of the proceedings or examination.

(c) A change in the information required by Section 9771(e)(1), (2), (3), (4), (5), and (8) shall be submitted within 5 days of the change.

(d) If an applicant or an affiliate of an applicant enters a contract whereby the applicant is to be purchased by or otherwise come under the control of another entity, the applicant shall notify the administrative director within 5 days of entry into the contract.

Note: Authority: Sections 133, 4600.5, 5307.3, Labor Code. Reference: Sections 4600.3, 4600.5, Labor Code.

History: 1. New section filed 2-14-96; operative 2-14-96. Submitted to OAL for printing only pursuant to Government Code section 11351 (Register 96, No. 7).

2. Amendment of subsection (b)(2) and repealer of subsection (b)(3) filed 1-9-2003; operative 1-9-2003 pursuant to Government Code section 11343.4 (Register 2003, No. 2).

Ref.: Herlick Handbook § 1.6.

§9771.6. Application of Regulations Concerning Workers' Compensation Health Care Provider Organizations.

Sections 9771.6 through 9771.83 apply only to workers' compensation health care organizations as defined by Section 9771.60(m).

Note: Authority cited: Stats. 1997, Ch. 346, Section 5. Reference: Sections 4600.3, 4500.5 and 4600.6, Labor Code.

History: 1. New section filed 4-15-98; operative 4-15-98. Submitted to OAL for printing only pursuant to Stats. 1997, Ch. 346, Section 5 (Register 98, No. 16).

Ref.: See Labor Code §4600.5; Herlick Handbook § 1.6.

§9771.60. Further Definitions.

The following definitions apply to the interpretation of these rules and the Act:

(a) "Act" means Sections 4600.3, 4600.5 and 4600.6 of the Code.

(b) "Advertisement" includes the disclosure form required pursuant to Section 4600.6(e) of the Code.

(c)(1) An "affiliate" of a person is a person controlled by, under common control with, or controlling such person.

(2) A person's relationship with another person is that of an "affiliated person" if such person is, as to such other person, a director, trustee or a member of its executive committee or other governing board or committee, or that of an officer or general partner, or holds any other position involving responsibility and authority similar to that of a principal officer or general partner; or who is the holder of 5 percent or more of its outstanding equity securities; or who has any such relationship with an affiliate of such person. An affiliate is also an affiliated person.

(d) The term "control" (including the terms "controlling," "controlled by" and "under common control with") means the possession, direct or indirect, of the power to direct or cause the direction of the management and policies of a person, whether through the ownership of voting shares, debt, by contract, or otherwise.

(e) The term "certified" or "audited," when used in regard to financial statements, means examined and reported upon with an opinion expressed by an independent public or certified public accountant.

(f) "Code" means the California Labor Code.

(g) "Administrative Director" means the Administrative Director of the Division of Workers' Compensation.

(h) "Facility" means (1) any premises owned, leased, used or operated directly or indirectly by or for the benefit of an organization or any affiliate thereof, and (2) any premises maintained by a provider to provide services on behalf of an organization.

(i) "Material": A factor is "material" with respect to a matter if it is one to which a reasonable person would attach importance in determining the action to be taken upon the matter.

(j) "Principal creditor" means (1) a person who has loaned funds to another for the operation of such other person's business, and (2) a person who has, directly or indirectly, 20 percent or more of the outstanding debts of a person.

(k) "Principal officer" means a president, vice-president, secretary, treasurer or chairman of the board of a corporation, a sole proprietor, the managing general partner of a partnership, or a person having similar responsibilities or functions.

(*l*) The term "generally accepted accounting principles," when used in regard to financial statements, assets, liabilities and other accounting items, means generally accepted accounting principles as used by business enterprises organized for profit. Accordingly, Financial Accounting Standards Board statements, Accounting Principles Board opinions, accounting research bulletins and other authoritative pronouncements of the accounting profession should be applied in determining generally accepted accounting principles unless such statements, opinions, bulletins and pronouncements are inapplicable. Section 510.05 of the AICPA Professional Standards, in and of itself, shall not be sufficient reason for determining inapplicability of statements, opinions, bulletins and pronouncements.

(m) "Workers' compensation health care provider organization" or "organization" means an entity authorized by the Administrative Director to be a health care organization pursuant to Section 4600.5(e) and 4600.6, or an entity applying for such authorization.

Note: Authority cited: Stats. 1997, Ch. 346, Section 5. Reference: Sections 4600.3, 4500.5 and 4600.6, Labor Code.

History: 1. New section filed 4-15-98; operative 4-15-98. Submitted to OAL for printing only pursuant to Stats. 1997, Ch. 346, Section 5 (Register 98, No. 16).

Ref.: See Labor Code §4600.5; Herlick Handbook § 1.6.

§9771.61. Prohibition of Bonuses or Gratuities in Solicitations.

No person subject to the provisions of the Act shall offer or otherwise distribute any bonus or gratuity to a potential self-insured employer, group of self-insured employers, or insurer of an employer for the purpose of inducing enrollment or to an existing self-insured employer, group of self-insured employers, or insurer of an employer for the purpose of inducing the continuation of enrollment.

Note: Authority cited: Stats. 1997, Ch. 346, Section 5. Reference: Sections 4600.3, 4500.5 and 4600.6, Labor Code.

History: 1. New section filed 4-15-98; operative 4-15-98. Submitted to OAL for printing only pursuant to Stats. 1997, Ch. 346, Section 5 (Register 98, No. 16).

Ref.: See Labor Code §4600.5; Herlick Handbook § 1.6.

§9771.62. Application for Authorization as a Workers' Compensation Health Care Provider Organization.

(a) An application for authorization as a workers' compensation health care provider organization shall be filed in the form specified in subsection (c) and contain the information specified in this section.

(b) Applications will be processed in the order in which they are filed; provided however, that applications under Section 4600.5(f)(2) shall have priority.

(c) Application Form (WHWCPO-1).

DIVISION OF WORKERS' COMPENSATION SUPPLEMENTARY APPLICATION UNDER LABOR CODE SECTION 4600.6.

Date of Application:

WORKERS' COMPENSATION HEALTH CARE PROVIDER ORGANIZATION AUTHORIZATION APPLICATION LABOR CODE SECTION 4600.6 (EXECUTION PAGE)

Identification of Organization.

Name of Applicant.

a. Legal name: ____________________

b. Please list all fictitious names you intend to use

A. Type of Filing: Indicate the type of filing by checking and completing the appropriate items:

1. ( ) Original application for organization authorization.

2. ( ) Amendment #__ to a pending application dated ________ for organization authorization. (Complete Item A-5 below.)

3. ( ) Notice of a proposed material modification (Complete Item A-5 below.)

4. ( ) Amendment filed by an organization because of a change in the information contained in the original application. (Complete Item A-5 below.)

5. Item numbers being amended

Exhibit numbers being amended

B. Other Agencies.

1. If applicant has made or intends to make any filing relating to its plan of operation to any other state or federal agency, check here _____, and attach Exhibit B-1 identifying each such agency, and the nature, purpose and (projected) date of each such filing.

Additional Exhibits: An original application for organization authorization must include the completed form specified in this subsection and the exhibits required.

C. Summary of Information in Application.

1. Summary Description of Organization and Operation. Provide as Exhibit C-1 a summary description of the organization and operation of applicant's business as a workers' compensation health care provider organization, covering the highlights and essential features of the information provided in response to the other portions of this application which is essential or desirable to an effective overview of the applicant's workers' compensation health care business, including a summary of the applicant's experience in the provision of workers' compensation health care.

2. Summary Description of Start-up. Provide as Exhibit C-2 a concise description of applicant's start-up program and its assumptions, including such program's operating, capitalization and financial assumptions. Indicate applicant's projected date for the beginning of operations, and discuss the factors which require such date.

D. Organization and Affiliated Persons.

1. Type of Organization.

a. Corporation. If applicant is a corporation, attach as Exhibits D-1-a-I, D-1-a-ii, D-1-a-iii and D-1-a-iv respectively, the Articles of Incorporation, Bylaws, the Corporation Information Form (Form WCHCPO 1-A) and any other organizational documents or agreements relating to the internal affairs of the applicant.

b. Partnership. If applicant is a partnership, attach as Exhibits D-1-b-I, D-1-b-ii and D-1-b-iii respectively, the Partnership Agreement, the Partnership Information Form (Form WCHCPO 1-B) and any other organizational documents or agreements relating to the internal affairs of the applicant.

c. Sole Proprietor. If applicant is a sole proprietorship, attach as Exhibit D-1-c the Sole Proprietorship Information Form. (Form WCHCPO 1-C)

d. Other Organization. If applicant is any other type of organization, attach as Exhibit D-1-d Articles of Association, trust agreement, or any other applicable documents, and any other organizational documents or agreements relating to the conduct of the internal affairs of the applicant, and attach as Exhibit D-1-d-ii the Information Form for other than Corporations, Partnerships, and Sole Proprietorships. (Form WCHCPO 1-D)

e. Individual Information Sheet. Attach as Exhibit D-1-e, an Individual Information Sheet (Form WCHCPO 2) for each natural person named in any exhibit in Item D-1.

2. Contracts with Affiliated Persons, Principal Creditors and Providers of Administrative Services.

a. Persons to Be Identified. Attach as Exhibit D-2-a, a list identifying each individual or entity who is a party to a contract with applicant, if such contract is one for the provision of administrative services to the applicant or any such party is an Affiliated Person or Principal Creditor (Rule 9771.60(c) and (j)) of the applicant. As to each such person, show the following information in columnar form:

(i) The names in alphabetical order.

(ii) The exhibit and page number of the contract (including loans and other obligations).

(iii) The type of contract or loan.

(iv) Each relationship which such individual or entity bears to the applicant (officer, director, partner, trustee, member, Principal Creditor, employee, administrative services provider, health care services provider, or shareholder).

3. Other Controlling Persons. Does any individual or entity not named as a contracting party in Item D-2 or any exhibit thereto have any power, directly or indirectly, to manage, influence, or administer the operation, or to control the operations or decisions, of applicant?

If the appropriate response to this item is "yes," attach as Exhibit D-3 a statement identifying each such person or entity and explaining fully such person's power or control, and summarizing every contract or other arrangement or understanding (if any) with each such person.

(Each such contract should be submitted pursuant to Subsection D-2.)

4. Criminal, Civil and Administrative Proceedings. Within the preceding 10 years, has the applicant, its management company, or any Affiliate of the applicant (Rule 9771.60(c)), or any controlling person, officer, director or other person occupying a principal management or supervisory position in such organization, management company or Affiliate, or any person intended to hold such a relationship or position, been convicted of or pleaded nolo contendere to a crime, or been held to have committed any act involving dishonesty, fraud or deceit in a judicial or administrative proceeding to which such person was a party?

If "yes," attach a separate exhibit as to each such person designated Exhibit D-4, identifying such person and fully explaining the crime or act committed. Also, attach a copy of the exhibit to any Individual Information Sheet required by Item D-1-e for such individual.

5. Employment of Barred Persons. Has the organization engaged or does the organization intend to engage, as an officer, director, employee, associate, or provider, any person named in (i) any order of the Commissioner pursuant to Section 1386(c) or Section 1388(d) of the Knox-Keene Health Care Service Plan Act of 1975, (ii) any similar order of the Insurance Commissioner under the Insurance Code barring or otherwise prohibiting such person from being employed or otherwise engaged as an officer, director, employee, associate or provider of any entity subject to the jurisdiction of the Insurance Commissioner, or (iii) any administrative orders issued by a professional licensing board or by the Department of Industrial Relations? If the appropriate response to this item is "yes," attach as Exhibit D-5 a statement identifying each such person and explaining fully the scope of, and the circumstances giving rise to, such order.

E. Contracts with Providers.

1. Compliance with Requirements. Attach as Exhibit E a statement in tabular form for each provider contract, and for each standard form contract and its variations, if any, specifying the provisions of such contract which comply with the following provisions of the Act and rules:

Section 4600.6(g)
4600.6(I)(8)
4600.6(n)

Rules 9771.69
9771.70
9772 through 9778

2. The provisions describing the mechanism by which payments are to be rendered to the provider clearly identified by the name of the provider.

F. Workers' Compensation Health Care Contracts.

Compliance with Requirements. Attach as Exhibit F a schedule in tabular form for each workers' compensation health care contract and each standard form workers' compensation contract, identifying the particular provision of such contract which complies with the sections listed below, covering also any variations made in standard form contracts. As to any provision which varies from the applicable provision of the Act or rules, identify such provision in Exhibit F.

Section 4600.5(e)(7)(B)
4600.6(e)

Rules 9771.67
9771.69
9772 – 9778

G. Advertising.

Attach as Exhibit G a copy of any advertising which is subject to Section 4600.6 of the Code and which applicant proposes to use. With respect to each proposed advertisement indicate the contract(s) by name and by exhibit number(s) to which such advertisement relates and identify the employer segment to which the advertisement is directed.

H. Marketing of Workers' Compensation Health Care Contracts.

Attach as Exhibit H a statement describing the methods by which applicant proposes to market workers' compensation health care contracts, including the use of employees, or contracting solicitors or solicitor firms, their method or form of compensation, and the methods by which applicant will obtain compliance with Rules 9771.64, 9771.65, and 9771.83.

I. Supervision of Marketing.

Attach as Exhibit I a statement setting forth applicant's internal arrangements to supervise the marketing of its workers' compensation health care contracts, including the name and title of each person who has primary management responsibility for the employment and qualification of solicitors, advertising, contracts with solicitors and solicitor firms and for monitoring and supervising compliance with contractual and regulatory provisions.

J. Solicitation Contracts.

1. Attach as Exhibit J-1 a list of all persons (other than any employee of the organization whose only compensation is by salary) soliciting or agreeing to solicit the sale of workers' compensation health care contracts on behalf of the applicant. For each such person, identify by exhibit number that person's contract furnished pursuant to Item K-2 and, if such contract does not show the rate of compensation to be paid, specify the person's rate of compensation.

2. Attach as Exhibit J-2, a copy of each contract or proposed contract between applicant and the persons named in Exhibit J-1 for soliciting the sale of or selling workers' compensation health care contracts on behalf of applicant. If a standard form contract is used, furnish a specimen of the form, identify the provision and terms of the form which may be varied and include a copy of each variation.

K. Workers' Compensation Health Care Contract Enrollment Projections.

NOTE: All projections are to cover the period commencing from the applicant's commencement of operations as an authorized and certified workers' compensation health care provider organization for two years.

1. Projections. Attach as Exhibit K-1 projections of applicant's enrollments under workers' compensation health care provider contracts with self-insured employers, groups of self-insured employers, or insurers of employers (individually, "Employer"; collectively, "Employers") for the periods specified in the above note. Exhibit K-1 is to contain the following information with respect to each anticipated workers' compensation health care contract:

a. The name of the Employer.

b. The number of potential employees eligible to receive workers' compensation health care from the organization who are employed by the Employer.

c. The locations within and around applicant's service area in which the potential employees live and work.

d. The estimated date (or period after authorization by the Administrative Director and certification by the Workers' Compensation Division of the Department of Industrial Relations) for entry into the workers' compensation health care contract.

e. Identification of the workers' compensation health care contract anticipated with the Employer, by reference to Exhibit F. If more than one type of workers' compensation health care contract is expected with an Employer, each contract must be covered separately.

f. The projected number of employees on a monthly basis for the initial period specified in the Note, above, and quarterly for the following year.

2. Substantiation of Projections. Attach as Exhibit K-2 for each workers' compensation health care contract specified in Exhibit K-1 a description of the facts and assumptions used in connection with the information specified in that exhibit and include documentation of the source and validity of such facts and assumptions.

3. Letters of Interest. Attach as Exhibit K-3 letters of interest or intent from each Employer listed in Exhibit K-1, on the letterhead of the Employer and signed by its representative.

L. (Reserved for future use.)

M. Current Viability.

1. Financial Statements.

a. Attach as Exhibit M-1-a the most recent audited financial statements of applicant, accompanied by a report, certificate, or opinion of an independent certified public accountant, together with all footnotes to such financial statements.

b. If the financial statements attached as Exhibit M-1-a are for a period ended more than 60 days before the date of filing of this application, also attach as Exhibit M-1-b financial statements prepared as of date no later than 60 days prior to the filing of this application consisting of at least a balance sheet, a statement of income and expenses, and any accompanying footnotes; these more recent financial statements need not be audited, so long as they are prepared in accordance with generally accepted accounting principles.

2. Provision for Extraordinary Losses. The following requirements require an initial applicant to submit legible copies of the actual policies of insurance (including any riders or endorsements) or specimen copies of the policies of insurance which show all of the terms and conditions of coverage, or with respect to those items expressly allowing for self-insurance, allow applicant to provide evidence of self-insurance at least as adequate as insurance coverage.

a. Attach as Exhibit M-2-a evidence of adequate insurance coverage or self- insurance to respond to claims for damages arising out of furnishing workers' compensation health care (malpractice insurance).

b. Attach as Exhibit M-2-b evidence of adequate insurance coverage or self-insurance (e.g., appropriate reserve set aside to fund likely liabilities associated with uninsured costs) to respond to claims for tort claims, other than with respect to claims for damages arising out of furnishing health care services.

c. Attach as Exhibit M-2-c evidence of adequate insurance coverage or self-insurance to protect applicant against losses of facilities upon which it has the risk of loss due to fire or other causes. Identify facilities covered by individual policies and indicate the basis upon which applicant believes that the insurance thereon is adequate.

d. Attach as Exhibit M-2-d, evidence of fidelity bond coverage for at least the amounts specified in Rule 9771.74, in the form of a primary commercial blanket bond or a blanket position bond written by an insurer licensed by the California Insurance Commissioner, providing 30 days' notice to the Administrative Director prior to cancellation, and covering each officer, director, trustee, partner and employee of the organization, whether or not compensated.

e. Attach as Exhibit M-2-e evidence of adequate workers' compensation insurance coverage against claims which may arise against applicant.

N. Fiscal Arrangements.

1. Maintenance of Financial Viability. Attach as Exhibit N-1 a statement describing applicant's arrangements to comply with Section 4600.6(m) of the Code and Rule 9771/73.

2. Provider Claims. Attach as Exhibit N-2 a statement describing applicant's system for processing claims from providers for payment, including the rules defining applicant's obligation to reimburse, the standards and procedures for applicant's claims processing system (including receipt, identification, handling, screening, and payment of claims), the timetable for processing claims, and procedures for monitoring the claims processing system.

3. Other Business. If the applicant is or will engage in any business other than as a workers' compensation health care provider organization, attach as Exhibit N-3 a statement describing such other business, its relationship to applicant's business as an organization, and the anticipated financial risks and liabilities of such other business. If the financial statements and projections in Exhibits M-1-a, do not include such other business, explain.

(d) Information Forms Required by Item D-1:

(1) Corporation Information Form (WCHCPO 1-A).

STATE OF CALIFORNIA
DIVISION OF WORKERS' COMPENSATION

D-1-a-iii CORPORATION INFORMATION FORM

To be used in response to Item D-1-a of Form WCHCPO 1.

---

1. Name of Applicant (as in Item 1-a) _____
2. State of Incorporation. _______________
3. Date of Incorporation. _______________
4. Is applicant a nonprofit corporation?
( ) Yes ( ) No

5. Is applicant exempted from taxation as a nonprofit corporation? ( ) Yes ( ) No

6. Names of principal officers, directors and shareholders: List (a) each person who is a director or principal officer or who performs similar functions or duties and (b) each person who holds of record or beneficially 5 percent or more of the voting securities of applicant or 5 percent or more of applicant's equity securities. If this is an amended exhibit, place an asterisk (*) before the names for whom a change in title, status or stock ownership is being reported and a double asterisk (**) before the names of persons which are added to those furnished in the most recent previous filing.

Full Name Last First Middle	Relationship Beginning Date Mo. Year	Class of Equity Title or Security Status	Percent of Class

7. If this is an amended exhibit, list below the names reported in the most recent filing of this exhibit which are deleted by this amendment:

____
____

(2) Partnership Information Form (WCHCPO 1-B)

STATE OF CALIFORNIA
DIVISION OF WORKERS'
COMPENSATION

EXHIBIT D-1-ii PARTNERSHIP
INFORMATION FORM.

To be used in response to Item D-1-b of Form WCHCPO 1.

1. Name of Applicant (as in Item 1-a). ______
2. State of organization. ______
3. Date of organization. ______
4. Names of Partners and Principal Management: List all general, limited and special partners and all persons who perform principal management functions. If this is an amended exhibit, place an asterisk (*) before the names of persons for whom a change in title, status or partnership interest is being reported and place a double asterisk (**) before the names of persons which are added to those furnished in the most recent previous filing.

Full Name Last First Middle	Beginning Date Mo. Year	Type of Partner	Capital Contribution (percentage)	Title or Duties

5. If this is an amended exhibit, list below the names reported in the most recent filing of this exhibit which are deleted by this amendment:

______
______
______

(3) Sole Proprietor Information Form (WCHCPO 1-C).

STATE OF CALIFORNIA
DIVISION OF WORKERS'
COMPENSATION

EXHIBIT D-1-c SOLE PROPRIETORSHIP
INFORMATION FORM

To be used in response to Item D-1-c of Form WCHCPO 1.

1. Name of Applicant (as in Item 1-a). ______
2. Residence Address. ______
3. Names of persons performing principal management functions: List each person who occupies a principal management position or who performs principal management functions for the applicant. If this is an amended exhibit, place an asterisk (*) before the names of persons for whom a change in title or duties is being reported and place a double asterisk (**) before the names of persons which are being added to those furnished in the most recent previous filing of this exhibit.

Full Name Last First Middle	Beginning Date Mo. Year	Title and Duties

4. If this is an amended exhibit, list below the names reported in the most recent filing of this exhibit which are deleted by this amendment:

______
______
______

(4) Information Form for Miscellaneous Types of Entities (WCHCPO 1-D).

STATE OF CALIFORNIA
DIVISION OF WORKERS'
COMPENSATION

EXHIBIT D-1-d INFORMATION FORM
FOR MISCELLANEOUS TYPES OF
ENTITIES.

To be used in response to Item D-1-d of Form WCHCPO 1.

1. Name of Applicant (as in Item 1-a)

______

2. State of Organization ______
3. Date of Organization ______
4. Form of Organization (describe briefly)

______

5. Names of Principal Officers and Beneficial Owners: List below the names of (a) each person who is a principal officer or trustee of the applicant or who performs principal management functions, and (b) each person who owns of record or beneficially over 5 percent of any class of equity security of the applicant. If this is an amended exhibit, place an asterisk (*) before the name of each person for whom a change in title, status or interest is reported, and a double asterisk (**) before the name of persons which are added to those reported in the most recent previous filing.

Full Name Last First	Beginning Date Mo. Year	Class of Equity Security	Percent of Class	Title and Duties

6. If this is an amended exhibit, list below the names reported in the most recent filing of this exhibit which are deleted by this amendment:

____

____

____

Note: Authority cited: Stats. 1997, Ch. 346, Section 5. Reference: Sections 4600.3, 4500.5 and 4600.6, Labor Code.

History: 1. New section filed 4-15-98; operative 4-15-98. Submitted to OAL for printing only pursuant to Stats. 1997, Ch. 346, Section 5 (Register 98, No. 16).

Ref.: See Labor Code §4600.5; Herlick Handbook § 1.6.

§9771.63. Individual Information Sheet (WCHCPO 2).

An individual information sheet required pursuant to these rules shall be in the following form:

CONFIDENTIAL
DIVISION OF WORKERS' COMPENSATION
State of California
INDIVIDUAL INFORMATION SHEET
under Labor Code Section 4600.6

1. Name of Applicant: ____________ File No. ____________

2. Exact full name of person completing this statement:

____

First Middle Last

3. Have you ever had a certificate, license, permit registration or exemption issued pursuant to the Business and Professions Code, Health and Safety Code, Insurance Code, or Labor Code denied, revoked or suspended or been otherwise subject to disciplinary action, while you were in the employ of the applicant, or while you had a contract with the applicant as a provider or otherwise? [ ] Yes [ ] No

If "yes" state the date of the action and the administrative body taking such action.

____

____

____

4. Have you ever been convicted or pled nolo contendere to a misdemeanor involving moral turpitude or any felony, other than traffic violations? [ ] Yes [ ] No

If the answer is "yes" give details:

____

____

____

5. Have you ever changed your name or ever been known by any name other than that herein listed? (Including a married person's prior surname, if any.) [ ] Yes [ ] No

If so, explain. Change in name through marriage or court order should also be listed. EXACT DATE OF EACH NAME CHANGE MUST BE LISTED.

____

____

____

6. Have you ever engaged in business under a fictitious firm name either as an individual or in the partnership or corporate form?
[ ] Yes [ ] No

If the answer is "yes" set forth particulars:

____

____

____

VERIFICATION

I, the undersigned, state that I am the person named in the foregoing Individual Information Sheet, that I have read and signed said Individual Information Sheet and know the contents thereof, including all exhibits attached thereto; and that the statements made therein, including any exhibits attached thereto, are true and correct.

I certify (or declare) under penalty of perjury under the laws of the State of California that I have read this Individual Information Sheet and the exhibits thereto and know the contents thereto, and that the statements therein are true and correct.

Executed at ____________ (Place) on ____________ (Date)

____
(Signature of Declarant)

NOTE: If this form is signed outside California complete the verification before a notary public in the space provided below.

State of ______________________________

County of ____________________________

Dated, _______________________________

at ___________________________________

____

(Signature of Affiant)

Subscribed and sworn to before me,

____

Notary Public in and for said
County and State

Note: Authority cited: Stats. 1997, Ch. 346, Section 5. Reference: Sections 4600.3, 4500.5 and 4600.6, Labor Code.

History: 1. New section filed 4-15-98; operative 4-15-98. Submitted to OAL for printing only pursuant to Stats. 1997, Ch. 346, Section 5 (Register 98, No. 16).

Ref.: See Labor Code §4600.5; Herlick Handbook § 1.6.

§9771.64. Organization Assurances Prior to Solicitation.

Prior to allowing any person to engage in acts of solicitation on its behalf, each organization shall reasonably assure itself that such person has sufficient knowledge of its organization, procedures, workers' compensation health care contracts, and the provisions of the Act and these rules to do so lawfully.

Note: Authority cited: Stats. 1997, Ch. 346, Section 5. Reference: Sections 4600.3, 4500.5 and 4600.6, Labor Code.

History: 1. New section filed 4-15-98; operative 4-15-98. Submitted to OAL for printing only pursuant to Stats. 1997, Ch. 346, Section 5 (Register 98, No. 16).

Ref.: See Labor Code §4600.5; Herlick Handbook § 1.6.

§9771.65. Filing of Advertising and Disclosure Forms.

(a) Two copies of a proposed advertisement shall be filed. To minimize the expense of changes in advertising copy, it may be submitted in draft form for preliminary review subject to the later filing of a proof or final copy, and the later filing of a proof or final copy may be waived when the draft copy is presented in a manner reasonably representing the final appearance of the advertisement. The text of audio or audio/visual advertising should indicate any directions for presentation, including voice qualities and the juxtaposition of the visual materials with the text.

(b) The Administrative Director will not issue letters of nondisapproval of advertising. If the person submitting the advertisement requests an order shortening the 30-day waiting period under Section 4600.6(d) of the Code, such order will be issued when an appropriate showing of the need therefor is made.

Note: Authority cited: Stats. 1997, Ch. 346, Section 5. Reference: Sections 4600.3, 4500.5 and 4600.6, Labor Code.

History: 1. New section filed 4-15-98; operative 4-15-98. Submitted to OAL for printing only pursuant to Stats. 1997, Ch. 346, Section 5 (Register 98, No. 16).

Ref.: See Labor Code §4600.5; Herlick Handbook § 1.6.

§9771.66. Deceptive Advertising.

Without limitation upon the meaning of Section 4600.6 of the Code, an advertisement or other consumer information is untrue, misleading or deceptive if:

(a) It represents that payment is provided in full for the charge for workers' compensation health care other than in accordance with what is required under the Labor Code.

(b) It represents that payment is provided for the customary charges for workers' compensation health care other than in accordance with what is required under the Labor Code.

(c) It represents that the organization, firm or solicitor or any provider or other person associated therewith is licensed or regulated by the Department of Managed Health Care or Administrative Director or other governmental agency, unless such statement is required by law or regulation or unless such statement is accompanied by a satisfactory statement which counters any inference that such licensing or regulation is an assurance of financial soundness or the quality or extent of workers' compensation health care.

Note: Authority cited: Stats. 1997, Ch. 346, Section 5. Reference: Sections 4600.3, 4500.5 and 4600.6, Labor Code.

History: 1. New section filed 4-15-98; operative 4-15-98. Submitted to OAL for printing only pursuant to Stats. 1997, Ch. 346, Section 5 (Register 98, No. 16).

2. Amendment of subsection (c) filed 1-9-2003; operative 1-9-2003 pursuant to Government Code section 11343.4 (Register 2003, No. 2).

Ref.: See Labor Code §4600.5; Herlick Handbook § 1.6.

§9771.67. Disclosure Form.

(a) The disclosure form required under subdivision (a) of Section 4600.6(e) of the Code and made available to employers and employees shall conform to the requirements established by the Administrative Director of the Division of Workers' Compensation of the Department of Industrial Relations (Cal. Code Regs., Tit. 8, Sec. 9770 et seq.).

Note: Authority cited: Stats. 1997, Ch. 346, Section 5. Reference: Sections 4600.3, 4500.5 and 4600.6, Labor Code.

History: 1. New section filed 4-15-98; operative 4-15-98. Submitted to OAL for printing only pursuant to Stats. 1997, Ch. 346, Section 5 (Register 98, No. 16).

Ref.: See Labor Code §4600.5; Herlick Handbook § 1.6.

§9771.68. Deceptive Workers' Compensation Health Care Provider Organization Names.

(a) A change of organization name is a "material modification".

(b) An organization name will be considered deceptive if it suggests the quality of care furnished by the organization or if it suggests that the cost of workers' compensation health care provided to employees is lower than the cost of similar health care purchased elsewhere, and in any such case the express or implied representation contained in the organization name is demonstrably untrue or is not supported by substantial evidence at all times while such name is used by the organization. Nothing in this subsection limits or restricts the Administrative Director from a determination that an organization or solicitor firm name is deceptive for reasons other than those stated herein.

Note: Authority cited: Stats. 1997, Ch. 346, Section 5. Reference: Sections 4600.3, 4500.5 and 4600.6, Labor Code.

History: 1. New section filed 4-15-98; operative 4-15-98. Submitted to OAL for printing only pursuant to Stats. 1997, Ch. 346, Section 5 (Register 98, No. 16).

Ref.: See Labor Code §4600.5; Herlick Handbook § 1.6.

§9771.69. Workers' Compensation Health Care Contracts.

(a) All workers' compensation health care contracts and endorsements and amendments shall be printed legibly and shall include at least the following:

(1) The information required to be included on disclosure forms by Section 4600.6(e) of the Code and the information required to be included on disclosure forms by Rule 9771.67.

(2) Definitions of all terms contained in the contract which:

(A) Are defined by the Act, relevant Labor Code provisions, and the Regulations of the Administrative Director.

(B) Require definition in order to be understood by a reasonable person not possessing special knowledge of law, medicine, or organizations;

(C) Specifically describes the eligibility of employees.

(3) Appropriate captions, in boldface type, regarding the provision of workers' compensation health care, consistent with the requirements of the certification standards for health care organizations promulgated by the Administrative Director of the Division of Workers' Compensation of the Department of Industrial Relations (Cal. Code Regs., Tit. 8, Sec. 9770, et seq.).

(A) A benefit afforded by the contract shall not be subject to any limitation, exclusion, exception, reduction, deductible, or copayment, if any, which renders the benefit illusory.

(4) Provisions relating to cancellation under appropriate caption, in boldface type, which provisions shall include a statement of the time when a notice of cancellation becomes effective.

(5) A provision requiring the organization to provide written notice within a reasonable time to the other party of any termination or breach of contract by, or inability to perform of, any contracting provider if the other party may be materially and adversely affected thereby.

(6) A provision requiring a self-insured employer, group of self-insured employers, or insurer of an employer to mail promptly to each employee a legible, true copy of any notice of cancellation of the organization contract which may be received from the organization and to provide promptly to the organization proof of such mailing and the date thereof.

(7) A provision that (i) the organization is subject to the requirements of the Labor Code, the Regulations of the Administrative Director, and (ii) any provision required to be in the contract by the above shall bind the organization whether or not provided in the contract.

(b) For the purposes of this section:

(1) "Other party" means (A) in the case of a group of self-insured employers, the group representative designated in the contract, and (B) in

the case of a self-insured employer or issuer of an employer, the self-insured employer or insurer of an employer and the insured employer.

(2) Any express or implied requirement of notice to the other party, in the context of a contract with a group of self-insured employers, requires notice to the group representative designated in the contract and, with respect to material matters, to the employers and employees under the contract. An organization may fulfill any obligation imposed by this section to notify employers and employees under such contract if the organization provider notice to the group representative designated in the contract, and the contract requires the group representative to disseminate such notice to employers and employees by the next regular communication to the group, but in no event later than 30 days after the receipt thereof.

Note: Authority cited: Stats. 1997, Ch. 346, Section 5. Reference: Sections 4600.3, 4500.5 and 4600.6, Labor Code.

History: 1. New section filed 4-15-98; operative 4-15-98. Submitted to OAL for printing only pursuant to Stats. 1997, Ch. 346, Section 5 (Register 98, No. 16).

Ref.: See Labor Code §4600.5; Herlick Handbook § 1.6.

§9771.70. Contracts with Providers.

Written contracts must be executed between the organization and each provider of workers' compensation health care which regularly furnishes health care under the organization. All contracts with providers shall be subject to the following requirements:

(a) A written contract shall be prepared or arranged in a manner which permits confidential treatment by the Administrative Director of payment rendered or to be rendered to the provider without concealment or misunderstanding of other terms and provisions of the contract.

(b) The contract shall require that the provider submit claims for workers' compensation health care services to the organization within a reasonable period of time following the delivery of health care services to an employee.

Contracts which contain the following language shall be deemed to meet the timing requirements of this subsection (b), and there shall be no other agreements or other language in the contract which negates or diminishes the effect of the following language:

"[Name of Provider] shall submit claims for the cost of workers' compensation health care services to [Organization] according to the compensation provisions of [Section and paragraph] of this agreement, within 60 days after [Name of Provider] has rendered the workers' compensation health care services to the employee. However, failure to submit claims within 60 days does not alter the obligation of the organization to pay claims of contracting providers for which the organization has received payment."

(c) The contract shall provide that the organization shall forward claims from providers to the self-insured employer, group of self-insured employers or insurers of employers within 30 days after receipt of the claim from the provider, and that the organization shall pay the provider's claim no later than 30 days after receiving payment from the self-insured employer, group of self-insured employers or insurer of employers.

(d) The contract shall require that the provider maintain such records and provide such information to the organization or to the Administrative Director as may be necessary for compliance by the organization with the provisions of the Code and the rules thereunder, that such records will be retained by the provider for at least five years, and that such obligation is not terminated upon a termination of the agreement, whether by rescission or otherwise. (See Rule 9771.83) Contracts which contain the following language shall be deemed to meet the requirements of this subsection (d), and there shall be no other agreements or other language in the contract which negates or diminishes the effect of the following language:

"[Name of Provider] shall maintain all books, records of account, medical records, reports and papers as may be necessary for compliance by the organization with the provisions of Labor Code Section 4600.6 and the rules thereunder. All such books, records and reports shall be available to the organization or to the Administrative Director, as necessary or required, under the Act and Rules.

All such books, records, reports and papers must be maintained for at least five years after the initial date of delivery of health care services under this Agreement. The obligation of [Name of Provider] to maintain books, records, reports and papers and to make them available shall not terminate upon the termination of [this Agreement]."

(e) The contract shall require that the organization shall have access at reasonable times upon demand to the books, records and papers of the provider relating to the workers' compensation health care provided to employees, to the cost thereof, to payments received by the provider from the organization, self-insured employer, group of self-insured employers, an insurer of an employer, employee, or from others on the behalf of the foregoing.

Contracts which contain the following language shall be deemed to meet the requirements of this subsection (e), and there shall be no other agreements or other language in the contract which negates or diminishes the effect of the following language:

"The [Organization] shall have access during regular business hours to all administrative, financial and medical books, records reports and papers relating to the delivery of workers' compensation health care to employees, and to the cost of such delivery, payments received by [the Provider] from [the Organization] and/or any self-insured employer, group of self-insured employers, or insurer of an employer, an employee, or others."

(f) The contract shall prohibit surcharges or other payments in violation of the Labor Code for workers' compensation health care services and shall provide that whenever the organization receives notice of any such surcharge it shall take appropriate action.

(g) The contract shall disclose whether there are any other agreements between the organization and the provider, and shall incorporate by reference all such other agreements. Contracts which contain the following language shall be deemed to meet the requirements of this subsection (g):

"This [Agreement], including all addenda, supersedes any and all other agreements between [the Organization] and [the Provider] which are not attached hereto and incorporated herein and which are related to the delivery of, or to the compensation for, workers' compensation health care services. No future statements or promises relating to the delivery of workers' compensation health care services shall be valid or binding unless written and incorporated herein as addenda, subject to the approval of the Administrative Director".

(h) The contract shall contain provisions complying with Section 4600.6(n) of the Code and shall comply with the provisions of subsection (a)(7) of Rule 9771.69.

(i) The contract shall require that the provider cooperate with the organization's quality assurance and utilization review system established pursuant to Section 4600.6(k) of the Code, and cooperate with the Administrative Director in accordance with the provisions of Section 4600.6(o) of the Code and Sections 9771.76 and 9771.77 of the Rules.

Note: Authority cited: Stats. 1997, Ch. 346, Section 5. Reference: Sections 4600.3, 4500.5 and 4600.6, Labor Code.

History: 1. New section filed 4-15-98; operative 4-15-98. Submitted to OAL for printing only pursuant to Stats. 1997, Ch. 346, Section 5 (Register 98, No. 16).

Ref.: See Labor Code §4600.5; Herlick Handbook § 1.6.

§9771.71. Disclosure of Conflicts of Interest.

(a) An organization shall not enter into any transaction with a person currently named in Item D of its application under Rule 9771.62 unless, prior thereto, each of the following conditions is met:

(1) The material facts concerning the transaction and the person's interest therein are disclosed to the governing body of the organization.

(2) The transaction is approved by a disinterested majority of the governing body.

(3) Such facts and such approval are made a part of the minutes of such governing body or, if no minutes are required of such governing body, otherwise retained as a record of the organization.

(b) An organization shall promptly give written notice to the Administrative Director if a transaction with a person currently named in Item D of its application under Rule 9771.62 is entered into otherwise than in conformity with the terms of this section.

(c) For the purposes of this section, "governing body" means the board of directors, all general partners, the sole proprietor, the board of trustees, and any other persons occupying a similar position or performing similar functions.

Note: Authority cited: Stats. 1997, Ch. 346, Section 5. Reference: Sections 4600.3, 4500.5 and 4600.6, Labor Code.

History: 1. New section filed 4-15-98; operative 4-15-98. Submitted to OAL for printing only pursuant to Stats. 1997, Ch. 346, Section 5 (Register 98, No. 16).

Ref.: See Labor Code §4600.5; Herlick Handbook § 1.6.

§9771.72. Contracts with Solicitor Firms.

An organization shall not permit a solicitor firm to solicit self-insured employers, groups of self-insured employers, or insurers of an employer on its behalf except pursuant to a written contract which meets all of the following minimum requirements:

(a) The solicitor firm shall comply, and shall cause its principal persons and employees to comply, with all applicable provisions of the Act and the rules thereunder.

(b) The solicitor firm shall promptly notify the organization of the institution of any disciplinary proceedings against it or against any of its principal persons or employees relating to any license issued to any such person by the California Insurance Commissioner.

Note: Authority cited: Stats. 1997, Ch. 346, Section 5. Reference: Sections 4600.3, 4500.5 and 4600.6, Labor Code.

History: 1. New section filed 4-15-98; operative 4-15-98. Submitted to OAL for printing only pursuant to Stats. 1997, Ch. 346, Section 5 (Register 98, No. 16).

Ref.: See Labor Code §4600.5; Herlick Handbook § 1.6.

§9771.73. Fiscal Soundness, Insurance, and Other Arrangements.

(a) An organization shall demonstrate fiscal soundness as follows:

Demonstrate an approach to the risk of insolvency which allows for the continuation of health care services for the duration of the contract period, the continuation of health care services to employees who are under treatment or confined on the date of insolvency in an in-patient facility until their discharge, and payments to unaffiliated providers for health care services rendered.

(b) In passing upon an organization's showing pursuant to this section, the Administrative Director will consider all relevant factors, including but not limited to:

(1) The method of compensating providers and the terms of provider contracts, especially as to the obligations of providers to employees in the event of the organization's insolvency.

(2) The methods by which the organization controls and monitors the utilization of health care services.

Note: Authority cited: Stats. 1997, Ch. 346, Section 5. Reference: Sections 4600.3, 4500.5 and 4600.6, Labor Code.

History: 1. New section filed 4-15-98; operative 4-15-98. Submitted to OAL for printing only pursuant to Stats. 1997, Ch. 346, Section 5 (Register 98, No. 16).

Ref.: See Labor Code §4600.5; Herlick Handbook § 1.6.

§9771.74. Fidelity Bond.

(a) Each organization shall at all times maintain a fidelity bond covering each officer, director, trustee, partner and employee of the organization, whether or not they are compensated. The fidelity bond may be either a primary commercial blanket bond or a blanket position bond written by an insurer licensed by the California Insurance Commissioner, and it shall provide for 30 days' notice to the Administrative Director prior to cancellation. The fidelity bond shall provide at least the minimum coverage for the organization determined by the following schedule:

Annual Gross Income	*Minimum Coverage*
Up to $ 100,000	$ 10,000
100,000 to 300,000	20,000
300,000 to 500,000	30,000
500,000 to 750,000	50,000
750,000 to 1,000,000	75,000
1,000,000 to 2,000,000	100,000
2,000,000 to 4,000,000	200,000
4,000,000 to 6,000,000	400,000
6,000,000 to 10,000,000	600,000
10,000,000 to 20,000,000	1,000,000
20,000,000 and over	2,000,000

(b) The fidelity bond required pursuant to subsection (a) may contain a provision for a deductible amount from any loss which, except for such deductible provision, would be recoverable from the insurer. A deductible provision shall not be in excess of 10 percent of the required minimum bond coverage, but in no event shall the deductible amount be in excess of $100,000.

Note: Authority cited: Stats. 1997, Ch. 346, Section 5. Reference: Sections 4600.3, 4500.5 and 4600.6, Labor Code.

History: 1. New section filed 4-15-98; operative 4-15-98. Submitted to OAL for printing only pursuant to Stats. 1997, Ch. 346, Section 5 (Register 98, No. 16).

Ref.: See Labor Code §4600.5; Herlick Handbook § 1.6.

§9771.75. Reimbursements on a Fee-for-Services Basis: Determination of Status of Claims.

Every organization shall institute procedures whereby all claim forms received by the organization from providers of workers' compensation health care for reimbursement on a fee-for-service basis are maintained and accounted for in a manner which permits the determination of the date of receipt of any claim, the status of any claim, the dollar amount of unpaid claims at any time, and rapid retrieval of any claim. Although any categories for status-determination held unobjectionable by the Administrative Director may be used, for the purposes of this section, the following status-determination categories, as a group, shall be presumptively reasonable:

(1) to be processed,

(2) processed, waiting for payment,

(3) pending, waiting for approval for payment or denial,

(4) pending, waiting for additional information,

(5) denied,

(6) paid, and, if appropriate,

(7) other.

These procedures shall involve the use of either a claims log, claims numbering system, electronic data processing records, and/or any other method held unobjectionable by the Administrative Director.

Note: Authority cited: Stats. 1997, Ch. 346, Section 5. Reference: Sections 4600.3, 4500.5 and 4600.6, Labor Code.

History: 1. New section filed 4-15-98; operative 4-15-98. Submitted to OAL for printing only pursuant to Stats. 1997, Ch. 346, Section 5 (Register 98, No. 16).

Ref.: See Labor Code §4600.5; Herlick Handbook § 1.6.

§9771.76. Medical Survey Procedure.

(a) Unless the Administrative Director in his discretion determines that advance notice will render the survey less useful, an organization will be notified approximately four weeks in advance of the date for commencement of an onsite medical survey. The Administrative Director may, without prior notice, conduct inspections of organization facilities or other elements of a medical survey, either in conjunction with the medical survey or as part of an unannounced inspection program.

(b) The onsite medical survey of an organization shall include, but not be limited to, the following procedures to the extent considered necessary based upon prior experience with the organization and in accordance with the procedures and standards developed by the Administrative Director.

(1) Review of the procedures for obtaining workers' compensation health care including, but not limited to, the scope of health care.

(A) The availability and adequacy of facilities for telephone communication with health personnel, emergency health care facilities, out-of-the-area coverage, referral procedures, and medical encounters.

(B) The means of advising employees of the procedures to obtain health care, including the hours of operation, location and nature of facilities, types of health care, telephone and other arrangements for appointment setting.

(C) The availability of qualified personnel at each facility referred to in Section 4600.6(j) of the Code to receive and handle inquiries concerning health care and grievances.

(2) Review of the design and implementation of procedures for reviewing and regulating utilization of health care and facilities.

(3) Review of the design and implementation of procedures to review and control costs.

(4) Review of the design, implementation and effectiveness of the internal quality of care review systems, including review of medical records and medical records systems. A review of medical records and medical records systems may include, but is not limited to, determining whether:

(A) The entries establish the diagnosis stated, including an appropriate history and physical findings;

(B) The therapies noted reflect an awareness of current therapies;

(C) The important diagnoses are summarized or highlighted; (Important are those conditions that have a bearing on future clinical management.)

(D) Drug allergies and idiosyncratic medical problems are conspicuously noted;

(E) Pathology, laboratory and other reports are recorded;

(F) The health professional responsible for each entry is identifiable;

(G) Any necessary consultation and progress notes are evidenced as indicated;

(H) The maintenance of an appropriate system for coordination and availability of the medical records of the employee, including out-patient, in-patient and referral services and significant telephone consultations.

(5) Review of the overall performance of the organization in providing workers' compensation health care, by consideration of the following:

(A) The numbers and qualifications of health professional and other personnel;

(B) The provision of, incentives for, and participation in, continuing education for health personnel and the provision for access to current medical literature;

(C) The adequacy of all physical facilities, including lighting, cleanliness, maintenance, equipment, furnishings, and convenience to employees, organization personnel and visitors;

(D) The practice of health professionals and allied personnel in a functionally integrated manner, including the extent of shared responsibility for patient care and coordinated use of equipment, medical records and other facilities and services;

(E) The appropriate functioning of health professionals and other health personnel, including specialists, consultants and referrals;

(F) Nursing practices, including reasonable supervision;

(G) Written nondiscriminatory personnel practices which attract and retain qualified health professionals and other personnel;

(H) The adequacy and utilization of pathology and other laboratory facilities, including the quality, efficiency and appropriateness of laboratory procedures and records and quality control procedures;

(I) X-ray and radiological services, including staffing, utilization, equipment, and the promptness of interpretation of X-ray films by a qualified provider;

(J) The handling and adequacy of medical record systems, including filing procedures, provisions for maintenance of confidentiality, the efficiency of procedures for retrieval and transmittal, and the utilization of sampling techniques for medical records audits and quality of care review;

(K) The adequacy, including convenience and readiness of availability to employees, of all provided health care;

(L) How the organization is organized and its mechanisms for furnishing workers' compensation health care, including the supervision of health professionals and other personnel;

(M) The extent to which individual medical decisions by qualified medical personnel are unduly constrained by fiscal or administrative personnel, policies or considerations;

(N) The adequacy of staffing, including medical specialties.

(6) Review of the overall performance of the organization in meeting the health needs of employees.

(A) Accessibility of facilities and workers' compensation health care, based upon location of facilities, hours of operation, waiting periods for health care and appointments, the availability of parking and transportation;

(B) Continuity of health care, including the ability of employees to select a primary treating physician, staffing in medical specialties or arrangements therefor; the referral system (including instructions, monitoring and follow-up); the maintenance and ready availability of medical records; and the availability of health care education to employees;

(C) The grievance procedure required by Section 4600.6(j) of the Code, including the availability to employees of grievance procedure information, the time required for and the adequacy of the response to grievances and the utilization of grievance information by the organization's management.

(7) In considering the above and in pursuit of the survey objectives, the survey team may perform any or all of the following procedures:

(A) Private interviews and group conferences with employees, physicians and other health care professionals and providers, and members of its administrative staff including, but not limited to, persons in principal management positions.

(B) Examination of any records, books, reports and papers of the organization and of any management company, provider or subcontractor providing workers' compensation health care or other services to the organization including, but not limited to, the minutes of medical staff meetings, peer review, and quality of care review records, duty rosters of medical personnel, surgical logs, appointment records, the written procedures for the internal operation of the organization, and contracts and correspondence with employees and with providers of workers' compensation health care and of other services to the organization, and such additional documentation the Administrative Director may specifically direct the surveyors to examine.

(C) Physical examination of facilities, including equipment.

(D) Investigation of grievances or complaints from employees, or from the general public.

Note: Authority cited: Stats. 1997, Ch. 346, Section 5. Reference: Sections 4600.3, 4500.5 and 4600.6, Labor Code.

History: 1. New section filed 4-15-98; operative 4-15-98. Submitted to OAL for printing only pursuant to Stats. 1997, Ch. 346, Section 5 (Register 98, No. 16).

Ref.: See Labor Code §4600.5; Herlick Handbook § 1.6.

§9771.77. Medical Survey: Report of Correction of Deficiencies.

Prior to or immediately upon the expiration of the 30-day period following notice to an organization of a deficiency as provided in subdivision (8) of Section 4600.6(o) of the Code, the organization shall file a written statement with the Administrative Director identifying the deficiency and describing the action taken to correct the deficiency and the results of such action. The report shall be signed by a principal officer of the organization.

Where such deficiencies reasonably may be adjudged to require long-term corrective action or to be of a nature which reasonably may be expected to require a period longer than 30 days to remedy, evidence that the organization has initiated remedial action and is on the way to achieving acceptable levels of compliance may be submitted for review by the Administrative Director.

Note: Authority cited: Stats. 1997, Ch. 346, Section 5. Reference: Sections 4600.3, 4500.5 and 4600.6, Labor Code.

History: 1. New section filed 4-15-98; operative 4-15-98. Submitted to OAL for printing only pursuant to Stats. 1997, Ch. 346, Section 5 (Register 98, No. 16).

Ref.: See Labor Code §4600.5; Herlick Handbook § 1.6.

§9771.78. Removal of Books and Records from State.

The books and records of an organization, management company, solicitor firm, and any provider or subcontractor providing workers' compensation health care or other services to an organization, management company, or solicitor firm shall not be removed from this state without the prior written consent of the Administrative Director.

Note: Authority cited: Stats. 1997, Ch. 346, Section 5. Reference: Sections 4600.3, 4500.5 and 4600.6, Labor Code.

History: 1. New section filed 4-15-98; operative 4-15-98. Submitted to OAL for printing only pursuant to Stats. 1997, Ch. 346, Section 5 (Register 98, No. 16).

Ref.: See Labor Code §4600.5; Herlick Handbook § 1.6.

§9771.79. Examination Procedure.

Regular and additional or nonroutine examinations conducted by the Administrative Director pursuant to Section 4600.6(q) of the Code will ordinarily be commenced on an unannounced basis. To the extent feasible, deficiencies noted will be called to the attention of the responsible officers of the company under examination during the course of the examination, and in that event the company should take the corrective action indicated. When deemed appropriate, the company will be advised by letter of the deficiencies noted upon the examination. If the deficiency letter requires a report from the organization, such report must be furnished within 15 days or such additional time as may be allowed.

Note: Authority cited: Stats. 1997, Ch. 346, Section 5. Reference: Sections 4600.3, 4500.5 and 4600.6, Labor Code.

History: 1. New section filed 4-15-98; operative 4-15-98. Submitted to OAL for printing only pursuant to Stats. 1997, Ch. 346, Section 5 (Register 98, No. 16).

Ref.: See Labor Code §4600.5; Herlick Handbook § 1.6.

§9771.80. Additional or Nonroutine Examinations and Surveys.

(a) An examination or survey is additional or nonroutine for good cause for the purposes of Section 4600.6(q) of the Code when the reason for such examination or survey is any of the following:

(1) The organization's noncompliance with written instructions from the Administrative Director;

(2) The organization has violated, or the Administrative Director has reason to believe that the organization has violated, any of the provisions of Sections 4600.3, 4600.5, or 4600.6 of the Code or regulations referring to those sections.

(3) The organization has committed, or the Administrative Director has reason to believe that the organization has committed, any of the acts or omissions enumerated in Section 4600.5(k) of the Code.

(4) The Administrative Director deems such additional or nonroutine examination or survey necessary to verify representations made to the Administrative Director by an organization in response to a deficiency letter.

(b) Each situation giving rise to an additional or nonroutine examination or survey shall be evaluated on a case-by-case basis as to the seriousness of the violation, or lack of timely or adequate response by the organization to the Administrative Director's request to correct the violation. The organization shall be notified in writing of the provisions of the Act or regulations which have been, or may have been, violated and which therefore caused such additional or nonroutine examination or survey to be performed. The expense of such examinations and surveys shall be charged to the organization being examined or surveyed in accordance with Section 4600.6(q) of the Code.

Note: Authority cited: Stats. 1997, Ch. 346, Section 5. Reference: Sections 4600.3, 4500.5 and 4600.6, Labor Code.

History: 1. New section filed 4-15-98; operative 4-15-98. Submitted to OAL for printing only pursuant to Stats. 1997, Ch. 346, Section 5 (Register 98, No. 16).

Ref.: See Labor Code §4600.5; Herlick Handbook § 1.6.

§9771.81. Financial Statements.

(a) Whenever pursuant to these rules or pursuant to an order or request of the Administrative Director under the Code a financial statement or other report is required to be audited or be accompanied by the opinion of a certified public accountant, such accountant shall be independent of the licensee, determined in accordance with Section 602.02 of Financial Reporting Release No. 1 issued by the Securities and Exchange Commission (Securities Act Release 6395, April 15, 1982).

(b) The financial statements shall be audited by an independent accountant in accordance with Rule 9771.60(e).

(c) Except as provided in subsection (d), financial statements of an organization required pursuant to these rules must be on a combining basis with an affiliate, if the organization or such affiliate is substantially dependent upon the other for the provision of workers' compensation health care, management or other services. An affiliate will normally be required to be combined, regardless of its form of organization, if the following conditions exist:

(1) The affiliate controls, is controlled by, or is under common control with, the organization, either directly or indirectly (see subsections (c) and (d) of Rule 9771.60), and

(2) The organization or the affiliate is substantially dependent, either directly or indirectly, upon the other for services or revenue.

(d) Upon written request of an organization, the Administrative Director may waive the requirement that an affiliate be combined in financial statements required pursuant to these rules. Normally, a waiver will be granted only when

(1) the affiliate is not directly engaged in the delivery of workers' compensation health care or

(2) the affiliate is operating under an authority granted by a governmental agency pursuant to which the affiliate is required to submit periodic financial reports in a form prescribed by such governmental agency that cannot practicably be reformatted into the form prescribed by these rules (such as an insurance company).

(e) When combined financial statements are required by this section, the independent accountant's report or opinion must cover all the entities included in the combined financial statements. If the accountant's report or opinion makes reference to the fact that a part of the examination was performed by another auditor, the organization shall also file the individual financial statements and report or opinion issued by the other auditor.

(f) Organizations which have subsidiaries that are required to be consolidated under generally accepted accounting principles must present either

(1) consolidating financial statements, or

(2) consolidating schedules for the balance sheet and statement of operations, which in

either case must show the organization separate from the other entities included in the consolidated balances.

(g) This section shall not apply to an organization which is a public entity or political subdivision.

(h) All filings of financial statements required pursuant to these rules must include an original and one copy.

Note: Authority cited: Stats. 1997, Ch. 346, Section 5. Reference: Sections 4600.3, 4500.5 and 4600.6, Labor Code.

History: 1. New section filed 4-15-98; operative 4-15-98. Submitted to OAL for printing only pursuant to Stats. 1997, Ch. 346, Section 5 (Register 98, No. 16).

Ref.: See Labor Code §4600.5; Herlick Handbook § 1.6.

§9771.82. Books and Records.

(a) Each organization, solicitor firm, and solicitor shall keep and maintain their books of account and other records on a current basis.

(b) Each organization shall make or cause to be made and retain books and records which accurately reflect:

(1) The names and last known addresses of all employees eligible to receive workers' compensation health care, and all contracting self-insured employers, groups of self-insured employers and insurers of employers.

(2) All contracts required to be submitted to the Administrative Director and all other contracts entered into by the organization.

(3) All requests made to the organization for payment of moneys for workers' compensation health care, the date of such requests, and the dispositions thereof.

(4) A current list of the names and addresses of all individuals employed by the organization as solicitors.

(5) A current list of the names and addresses of all solicitor firms with which the organization contracts.

(6) A current list of the names and addresses of all of the organization's officers, directors, principal shareholders, general managers, and other principals.

(7) The amount of any commissions paid to persons who obtain self-insured employers, groups of self-insured employers, and insurers of employers for workers' compensation health care provider organizations, and the manner in which said commissions are determined.

(c) Each solicitor firm shall make and retain books and records which include a current list of the names and addresses of its partners, if any, and all of its employees who make act as solicitors.

Note: Authority cited: Stats. 1997, Ch. 346, Section 5. Reference: Sections 4600.3, 4500.5 and 4600.6, Labor Code.

History: 1. New section filed 4-15-98; operative 4-15-98. Submitted to OAL for printing only pursuant to Stats. 1997, Ch. 346, Section 5 (Register 98, No. 16).

Ref.: See Labor Code §4600.5; Herlick Handbook § 1.6.

§9771.83. Retention of Books and Records.

Every organization and solicitor firm shall preserve for a period of not less than five years, the last two years of which shall be in an easily accessible place at the offices of the organization or solicitor firm, the books of account and other records required under the provisions, and for the purposes, of the Act. After such books and records have been preserved for two years, they may be warehoused or stored, or microfilmed, subject to their availability to the Administrative Director within not more than 5 days after request therefore.

Note: Authority cited: Stats. 1997, Ch. 346, Section 5. Reference: Sections 4600.3, 4500.5 and 4600.6, Labor Code.

History: 1. New section filed 4-15-98; operative 4-15-98. Submitted to OAL for printing only pursuant to Stats. 1997, Ch. 346, Section 5 (Register 98, No. 16).

Ref.: See Labor Code §4600.5; Herlick Handbook § 1.6.

§9772. General Standards.

(a) HCOs must demonstrate that they meet the following requirements:

(1) All facilities located in this state including, but not limited to, clinics, hospitals, laboratories, and skilled nursing facilities to be utilized by the HCO for the delivery of occupational medical and health care services or other services specifically required by this article shall be licensed by the State Department of Health Services, if such licensure is required by law, and shall meet any other relevant certification requirements. Facilities not located in this state

shall conform to all licensing and other requirements of the jurisdiction in which they are located.

(2) All personnel employed by or under contract to the HCO shall be licensed or certified by their respective board or agency, where such licensure or certification is required by law.

(3) All equipment required to be licensed or registered by law shall be so licensed or registered and the operating personnel for such equipment shall be licensed or certified as required by law.

(4) The HCO shall provide continuity of care and timely referral of patients to other providers in a manner consistent with professionally recognized standards of care.

(5) All services shall be available and accessible at reasonable times to all HCO enrollees.

(6) The HCO may employ and utilize allied health personnel for the furnishing of occupational health services to the extent permitted by law and provided such use is consistent with professionally recognized standards of care; however, any course of treatment beyond first aid, as defined in subdivision (c) of Section 14311, shall provide for at least one face to face visit with a primary treating physician.

(7) The HCO shall have the organizational, financial, and administrative capacity to provide services to employers, claims administrators, and HCO enrollees. The HCO shall be able to demonstrate to the Division that medical decisions are rendered by qualified providers unhindered by fiscal and administrative management, and that such decisions adhere to professionally recognized standards of care.

Any applicant that is owned in whole or in part or controlled by a workers' compensation insurer or self-insured employer shall, in addition to the requirements set forth above, further demonstrate that the organization's claims function shall have no influence or control over medical decision-making. The applicant shall further demonstrate that the clear authority of its Medical Director over all medical decisions is reflected both in its organizational chart and any internal procedure manual or other internal description of HCO operations.

(8) All contracts with claims administrators, employers, providers and other persons or entities furnishing services specifically required by this article shall be consistent with the requirements of this article and Division 4 of the Labor Code.

Note: Authority cited: Sections 133, 4600.5, 4603.5 and 5307.3, Labor Code. Reference: Section 4600.5, Labor Code.

History: 1. New section filed 12-31-93; operative 1-1-94. Submitted to OAL for printing only pursuant to Government Code section 11351 (Register 93, No. 53).

2. Amendment of subsection (b)(7) filed 1-9-2003; operative 1-9-2003 pursuant to Government Code section 11343.4 (Register 2003, No. 2).

Ref.: Hanna § 22.01[6]; Herlick Handbook § 1.6.

§9773. Treatment Standards.

(a) HCOs shall provide all HCO enrollees with access to all medical, surgical, chiropractic, and hospital treatment which is reasonably required to cure or relieve the effects of an injury in accordance with Section 4600 of the Labor Code. This treatment must be provided without payment of any co-payment, deductible, or premium share by an HCO enrollee. HCOs must provide a description of the method for providing treatment required under the code, including a list of its physical facilities. The description must include the occupational health care delivery capabilities of the HCO, including the number of primary treating physicians and specialists, the number and types of licensed or state-certified health care support staff, the number of hospital beds, and the arrangements and the methods by which occupational health care services will be provided, which shall include the following:

(1) Provider services, including consultation and referral. HCOs must identify the total number of full time equivalent physicians and providers of each different specialty type available to provide treatment for work injuries or illnesses on a regular basis.

(2) Inpatient hospital services, which shall include acute hospital services, general nursing care, use of operating room and related facilities, intensive care unit and services, diagnostic laboratory and x-ray services, special duty nursing as medically necessary, physical therapy, respiratory therapy, administration of blood and blood products, and other diagnostic, therapeutic and rehabilitative services as medically reasonable or medically necessary, and coordinated discharge planning including planning of such continuing care as may be necessary, both med-

ically and as a means of preventing possible rehospitalization.

(3) Ambulatory care services, (including outpatient hospital services) which shall include diagnostic and treatment services, physical therapy, speech therapy, occupational therapy services as appropriate, and those hospital services which can reasonably be provided on an ambulatory basis.

(4) Emergency services, including ambulance services and out-of-area coverage for emergency care.

(5) Diagnostic laboratory services, diagnostic and therapeutic radiological services, and other diagnostic services.

(6) Home health service, which shall include, where medically appropriate, health services provided at the home of an HCO enrollee as provided or prescribed by a physician or osteopath licensed to practice in California. Such home health services shall be provided in the home, including nursing care, performed by a registered nurse, public health nurse, licensed vocational nurse or licensed home health aide.

(b) HCOs shall provide a description of the times, places and manner of providing services under the HCO, including a description of the geographical service area. The geographical service area shall be designated by a list of the postal zip codes in the service area, and a map indicating the type and number of facilities within the service area. The following requirements must be met unless the HCO shows that a lack of a type of provider exists in an area and that the minimum number is not available:

(1) At least one full-time equivalent primary treating physician shall be available within the geographical proximity specified in paragraph (2) for every 1,200 expected injuries or illnesses. The HCO shall provide information on expected case-load and the methodology, data and assumptions used in the calculations.

(2) HCO enrollees must have a residence or workplace within 30 minutes or 15 miles of (i) a primary treating physician or (ii) a contracting or HCO-operating hospital, or if separate from such hospital, a contracting or HCO-operated provider of all emergency health care services. Enrollees must have a residence or workplace within 60 minutes or 30 miles of all other occupational health services listed in subdivision (a).

(3) The HCO must provide a description of how access to any of the basic health services listed in subdivision (a) will be provided to HCO enrollees who reside outside the HCO's geographical service area such that the requirements of this subdivision are met.

(4) Initial treatment for non-emergency services must be made available by an HCO within 24 hours of the HCO's receipt of a request for treatment.

(5) The HCO must describe how treatment is initiated and how an HCO enrollee is assigned a primary treating physician.

(6) Enrollees shall be entitled to at least one change of physician for an injury. The HCO shall provide the employee, within five days of a request by an HCO enrollee, with a choice of any other available participating provider in the appropriate specialty.

(7) HCO enrollees shall be provided with a second opinion, upon request, from a participating provider.

(8) The HCO must describe how it will make available interpreter's services, as required, for the treatment or evaluation of patients.

(9) The HCO must describe how the HCO will treat an injury or illness pending a claims administrator's decision concerning liability for treatment.

(10) HCOs must maintain and make available or insure that their contracted medical providers maintain and make available medical records to treating or evaluating physicians in a timely manner.

(c) The HCO shall describe its process for coordinating all aspects of medical treatment, including the coordination and monitoring of referrals to consultants, therapeutic or diagnostic facilities, reporting of treatment, being responsive to the HCO patient's request for change of physician or physician referrals as may be required by this article, and for ensuring timeliness of referrals and timely response to the primary treating physician.

(d) The HCO must include at least one full-time equivalent board-certified occupational medicine employed or contracting physician to provide expertise on workplace health and safety issues and prevention and treatment of occupational injuries and illnesses. The HCO shall describe its ongoing educational program to ensure that all primary treating physicians receive education, training or experience in occupational medicine and workers compensation, including but not limited to, the following:

(1) The regulatory requirements for primary treating physicians in workers' compensation;

(2) Familiarity with workplace hazards, causes of workplace injury, work restrictions, and vocational rehabilitation;

(3) The requirements of medical-legal reports in workers compensation.

Note: Authority cited: Sections 133, 4600.5, 4603.5 and 5307.3, Labor Code. Reference: Sections 3209.3, 4600 and 4600.5, Labor Code.

History: 1. New section filed 12-31-93; operative 1-1-94. Submitted to OAL for printing only pursuant to Government Code section 11351 (Register 93, No. 53).

Ref.: Herlick Handbook § 1.6.

§9773.1. Referrals to Chiropractors.

HCOs shall maintain guidelines for chiropractor care in accordance with paragraph (2) of subdivision (1) of Section 4600.5 of the Labor Code. The HCO must include a description of the HCO's guidelines and utilization review process for chiropractic care, including the HCO's definition of "neuromusculoskeletal condition", and the procedure whereby enrollees may be referred to chiropractors in accordance with the HCO's guidelines.

Note: Authority cited: Sections 133, 4600.5, 4603.5 and 5307.3, Labor Code. Reference: Section 3209.3, 4600 and 4600.5, Labor Code.

History: 1. New section filed 12-31-93; operative 1-1-94. Submitted to OAL for printing only pursuant to Government Code section 11351 (Register 93, No. 53).

Ref.: Herlick Handbook § 1.6.

§9774. Quality of Care.

(a) An HCO must include a written program designed to ensure a level of care for occupational injuries and illnesses which meets professionally recognized standards of care. The program must be designed and directed by providers to document that the quality of care provided is reviewed, that problems are identified, that effective action is taken to improve care where deficiencies are identified, that follow-up measures are planned where indicated, and that all of the requirements of this division are met. The plans must describe the goals and objectives of the program and organizational arrangements, including staffing, the methodology for ongoing monitoring and evaluation of health services, the scope of the program, and required levels of activity. Quality of care problems must be identified and corrected. The program must demonstrate that the HCO's utilization review activities are designed to improve the quality of care provided.

The HCO shall describe and implement a program, including the following:

(1) A description of the process whereby the medical reasonableness or medical necessity of requests for authorization are reviewed and decisions on such requests are made by the HCO. The description shall include the specific criteria utilized in the review and throughout the decision-making process, including treatment protocols or standards in any software, database, or other resource used in the process. Treatment protocols must be consistent with any guidelines adopted pursuant to paragraph (8) of subdivision (e) of Section 139 of the Labor Code.

(2) A description of the qualifications of the personnel involved in reviewing and making decisions concerning requests for authorization, including the professional qualifications of the personnel, and the manner in which such personnel are involved in the review process. Medical decisions must be rendered by physicians with licenses unrestricted by their licensing board.

(3) A description of manual and automated data storage and retrieval systems for medical and utilization review; and the types of data analyses, reports, and manner in which results are communicated to providers.

(b) The HCO's quality assurance committee shall meet on at least a quarterly basis or more frequently if problems have been identified, to oversee its quality assurance program responsibilities. Reports to the HCO's governing body shall be sufficiently detailed to include findings and actions taken as a result of the quality assurance program and to identify those internal or contracting provider components which the quality assurance program had identified as presenting significant or chronic quality of care issues.

(c) The HCO is responsible for establishing a quality assurance program to monitor and evaluate the care provided by each contracting provider group or facility. Medical groups or other provider entities may have active quality assurance programs which the HCO may use. However, the HCO must retain responsibility for reviewing the overall quality of care delivered to HCO enrollees. To the extent that the HCO's quality assurance responsibilities are delegated within the HCO or to a contracting provider or facility, the HCO shall provide evidence of an oversight mechanism for ensuring that delegated quality assurance functions are adequately performed.

(d) Physicians must be an integral part of the quality assurance program. Design and implementation of the quality assurance program shall be supervised by designated physicians. Physician participation in quality assurance activity must be adequate to monitor the full scope of clinical services rendered, resolve problems and ensure that corrective action is taken when indicated. Specialist providers must also be involved in peer review of like specialties.

(e) The HCO may delegate inpatient quality assurance functions to hospitals, however in such case a HCO must fully describe and monitor that hospital's quality assurance program.

(f) The HCO must insure that all comprehensive medical-legal reports are prepared in an objective, fair, and unbiased manner, and that such reports are prepared in accordance with Section 4628 of the Labor Code, any applicable procedures promulgated under Section 139.2 of the Labor Code, and the requirements of Section 10606. The HCO or physician shall retain, for no less than three years, copies of all comprehensive medical evaluation reports which are prepared by any of its physicians to determine an employee's eligibility for compensation. These reports shall be made available to the administrative director upon request. The administrative director may review such reports as he or she deems necessary to insure compliance with this subdivision, and the results of this review may be used to deny recertification if it is determined that a significant number of an HCO's reports show bias or are legally inadequate.

(g) The HCO must describe how it will assess its activities as required by Sections 9776 and 9776.1 and the HCO's system for assuring data quality.

Note: Authority cited: Sections 133, 4600.5, 4603.5 and 5307.3, Labor Code. Reference: Sections 4600, 4600.5 and 4628, Labor Code.

History: 1. New section filed 12-31-93; operative 1-1-94. Submitted to OAL for printing only pursuant to Government Code section 11351 (Register 93, No. 53).

Ref.: Herlick Handbook § 1.6.

§9775. Grievance and Dispute Resolution Procedure.

(a) HCOs must maintain a grievance procedure under which HCO enrollees or participating providers may submit grievances to the HCO. Each HCO must include a system for resolving disputes which shall include HCO enrollee disputes with a provider and a provider's dispute with the HCO. The HCO must provide that either an HCO enrollee or a provider shall be able to initiate a grievance. Each HCO must provide reasonable procedures which insure adequate consideration of enrollee and provider grievances or disputes and which provide prompt rectification when appropriate.

(b) Compliant forms and a copy of the grievance procedure shall be readily available through each provider facility and through the claims administrator, and shall be furnished promptly upon receipt of a verbal or written request.

(c) If a grievance or dispute concerns the medical reasonableness or medical necessity of treatment recommended by a provider, the HCO must provide for an expedited procedure for review of the grievance or dispute by physicians or qualified professional providers not previously involved in the grievance or dispute and who possess the specialty which is appropriate to the medical nature of the disputed treatment. Under no circumstance may the appeal decision be made by a registered nurse. The HCO must issue a written decision as to the grievance or dispute within 30 days unless the HCO enrollee's medical condition requires a more expedited decision.

(d) Each HCO shall inform providers and HCO enrollees, or their representatives, that they may file a written complaint to the administrative director

(e) The HCO shall annually provide to the administrative director a summary of written grievances received concerning the provision of occupational health services, including the number of total grievances received and processed. Records of all written grievances concerning the provision of occupational health services, including the name of the grievant, the nature of the complaint or grievance, and the manner in which the grievance was resolved or referred for further action, shall be kept by the HCO for a period of not less than 3 years and shall be made available by the HCO to the administrative director as he or she deems necessary.

Note: Authority cited: Sections 133, 4600.5, 4603.5 and 5307.3, Labor Code. Reference: Sections 4600 and 4600.5, Labor Code.

History: 1. New section filed 12-31-93; operative 1-1-94. Submitted to OAL for printing only pursuant to Government Code section 11351 (Register 93, No. 53).

Ref.: Herlick Handbook § 1.6.

§9776. Workplace Safety and Health.

(a) The HCO must maintain the capability to work cooperatively and in conjunction with claims administrators, employers, and employees to promote workplace health and safety and to detect workplace exposures and hazards, including:

(1) education of employees and employers on health and medical aspects of workplace health and safety issues;

(2) consultation on employee medical screening for early detection of occupational disease, and assessment of workplace risk factors.

(b) An HCO shall include in contracts with claims administrators a provision which enables the HCO to obtain upon request information to allow appropriate provider decision-making regarding diagnoses, patient medical restrictions, early disease detection, or return-to-work, which may include:

(1) the employer's written Injury and Illness Prevention Plan, including the name and title of individual responsible for implementing the plan.

(2) information concerning exposure levels for specified materials, and information, including Material Safety Data Sheets, concerning health, safety, and ergonomic risk factors in the workplace.

(3) the name and title of the individual responsible for loss control services for each employer.

(c) The HCO shall have in place a program for prompt reporting, to the employer or insurer loss control program and to the employer's designee responsible for the Injury and Illness Prevention Plan, of the following occupational injuries and illnesses: occupational asthma; cumulative trauma disorders of the upper extremities; lead poisoning; amputations (excluding amputations of the distal phalanges); noise-induced hearing loss; pesticide illness; electrocutions; asphyxiation; and burns and falls from heights requiring hospitalization.

(d) The HCO shall annually report to the insurer loss control program or to the employer's designee responsible for the Injury and Illness Prevention Plan as designated in the contract between the HCO and the claims administrator, aggregate data on injuries and illnesses.

History: 1. New section filed 12-31-93; operative 1-1-94. Submitted to OAL for printing only pursuant to Government Code section 11351 (Register 93, No. 53).

Ref.: Herlick Handbook § 1.6.

§9776.1. Return to Work Coordination.

An HCO shall maintain a return to work program in conjunction with the employer and claims administrator to facilitate and coordinate returning injured workers to the workplace, to assess the feasibility and availability of modified work or modified duty, and to minimize risk of employee exposure after return to work to risk factors which may aggravate or cause recurrence of injury. The duties of the HCO shall be specified in the contract between the HCO and the claims administrator.

History: 1. New section filed 12-31-93; operative 1-1-94. Submitted to OAL for printing only pursuant to Government Code section 11351 (Register 93, No. 53).

Ref.: Herlick Handbook § 1.6.

§9777. Patient Assistance and Notification.

(a) The HCO shall inform HCO enrollees upon enrollment in the plan and annually thereafter of the details of their coverage, and their rights and options under the HCO including: (1) how HCO enrollees are informed of the procedure for processing and resolving grievances, including the location(s) and telephone number where grievances may be submitted; and (2) how HCO enrollees are informed of their right to file a complaint with the administrative director in accordance with subdivision (d) of Section 9775.

(b) The HCO shall provide patient education specifically designed for injured workers with work-related injuries or illnesses.

(c) HCO enrollees must be able to receive information on a 24-hour basis regarding the availability of necessary medical services available within the HCO. The information may be provided through recorded telephone message after normal working hours. It must include information on how the enrollee can obtain emergency services or other urgently needed care and how the employee can access an evaluation within 24 hours of the injury as required under paragraph 4 of subdivision (b) of section 9773.

(d) Informational materials must be in a form understandable to all enrollees and available in Spanish. HCOs must provide in their application a description of how the information specified in subdivisions (a) through (c) will be provided to HCO enrollees. A copy of the informational material provided to HCO enrollees, including the text of phone messages, shall be made available to the administrative director upon request.

(e) The HCO shall provide for periodic evaluation of the HCO by enrollees. The HCO must provide a survey to HCO enrollees and patients, which shall be in the form and manner prescribed by the administrative director. The HCO must describe its method for incorporating the results of the survey in its quality assurance program. The completed forms and any data extracted from such forms shall be made available to the administrative director upon request.

Note: Authority cited: Sections 133, 4600.5, 4603.5 and 5307.3, Labor Code. Reference: Sections 4600 and 4600.5, Labor Code.

History: 1. New section filed 12-31-93; operative 1-1-94. Submitted to OAL for printing only pursuant to Government Code section 11351 (Register 93, No. 53).

Ref.: Herlick Handbook § 1.6.

§9778. Evaluation.

(a) The HCO must include a timely and accurate method to report to the administrative director the following information, in a standardized format to be prescribed by the administrative director:

(1) Cost of services under the plan, specific to particular industries and occupations, diagnoses, and procedures.

(2) Aggregated information on the number of HCO enrollees and their age, sex, geographical distribution, occupation, and SIC, by federal employer identification number.

(b) The HCO shall provide the following information on each injured enrollee.

i. For HCO enrollee claims opened in the calendar year:

(1) Patient's Employer's Federal Identification Number and SIC code.

(2) Injured enrollee name, date of birth, gender, social security number, and occupation.

(3) Date of injury.

(4) Diagnosis (ICD-9).

ii. For HCO enrollee claims closed during a calendar year, the following information linked with enrollee name, date of birth, and social security number:

(5) Medical Treatment, including dates of surgery and hospitalization.

(6) Date injured HCO enrollee released to return to work by the primary treating physician.

(7) Date injured HCO enrollee actually returned to work (not "released to work").

(8) HCO enrollee's job status at time of return to work (full or modified duty, or job different from pre-injury job), and employee's job status, including no longer employed, at time of close of claim.

(9) Permanent Disability rating.

(10) Whether injured HCO enrollee was represented by an attorney at any time through the claims process.

(c) Effective March 1, 2000, data elements required pursuant to paragraph (b) may instead be provided to the administrative director directly by the claims administrator in the format specified in Article 1.1 (commencing with section 9700), provided that:

(1) The claims administrator provides the data for all injured HCO enrollees for whom it contracts for medical care; and

(2) The HCO provides to the administrative director all information required by this section which is not provided by the claims administrator.

Information on claims opened and closed in the previous calendar year shall be made available by the HCO to the administrative director, in a form and manner to be prescribed by the administrative director, annually, on March 1, commencing with March 1, 1995.

Note: Authority cited: Sections 133, 4600.5, 4603.5 and 5307.3, Labor Code. Reference: Sections 4600 and 4600.5, Labor Code.

History: 1. New section filed 12-31-93; operative 1-1-94. Submitted to OAL for printing only pursuant to Government Code section 11351 (Register 93, No. 53).

2. New subsections (c)-(c)(2) filed 10-7-99; operative 3-1-2000 (Register 99, No. 41).

Ref.: Herlick Handbook § 1.6.

§9779. Certification.

(a) Once an applicant has completed an application and submitted a fee in accordance with Section 9771 and has demonstrated to the administrative director that its organization has met all of the criteria for certification, the administrative director will certify the organization as an HCO for a period of three years, unless earlier revoked or suspended.

(b) Once the Administrative Director has determined that an entity licensed as a full service health care service plan under Section 1353 of the Health and Safety Code (a Knox-Keene Health Care Service Plan Act) and deemed to be an HCO pursuant to Labor Code Section 4600.5(c) has complied with the requirements of Section 9771 subsections (g)(1) and (2) the administrative director shall certify the organization as an HCO, pursuant to Section 4600.5(c), for a period of three years unless earlier revoked or suspended.

(c) A certification shall state that a particular entity is certified as a health care organization to provide health care to injured employees for injuries and diseases and other services in accordance with the terms of the entity's application. The certification shall also state: (1) the geographic service area in which the health care organization is permitted to provide health care, (2) the maximum number of enrollees, (3) the name or names under which the health care organization is permitted to provide health care, (4) the date of expiration of the certification, and (5) any other conditions or limitations.

(d) The HCO will be recertified at the expiration of each subsequent three year period, provided it continues to meet the requirements of this article and timely pays a recertification fee of $10,000.

Note: Authority cited: Sections 133, 4600.5, 4600.7, 4603.5 and 5307.3, Labor Code. Reference: Sections 4600, 4600.5 and 4600.7, Labor Code.

History: 1. New section filed 12-31-93; operative 1-1-94. Submitted to OAL for printing only pursuant to Government Code section 11351 (Register 93, No. 53).

2. Amendment of subsection (a), repealer and new subsection (b), amendment of subsection (c), repealer and new subsection (d), repealer of subsection (e), and amendment of Note filed 2-14-96; operative 2-14-96. Submitted to OAL for printing only pursuant to Government Code section 11351 (Register 96, No. 7).

3. New subsection (b), repealer of subsection (d) and subsection relettering filed 1-9-2003; operative 1-9-2003 pursuant to Government Code section 11343.4 (Register 2003, No. 2).

Ref.: Herlick Handbook § 1.6.

§9779.1. On-Site Surveys.

(a) The HCO must ensure that it will be available for and cooperate with on-site surveys as the administrative director deems necessary to insure compliance with this article, including during the initial certification process. The administrative director will coordinate on-site surveys with the Department of Managed Health Care to the extent feasible.

(b) The administrative director will notify the HCO of deficiencies found by the survey team. The administrative director will provide the HCO a reasonable time to correct the deficiencies. Failure on the part of the HCO to timely correct noted deficiencies may result in suspension or revocation of an HCO's certification in accordance with Section 9779.2.

(c) Reports of all surveys shall be open to public inspection, except that no survey shall be made public unless the HCO has had an opportunity to review the survey and file a statement in response within 30 days, to be attached to the report. Deficiencies shall not be made public if they are corrected within 30 days of the date that the HCO was notified.

(d) Non-routine audits will be charged based on the actual cost for performing the audit. The amount shall include the actual salaries or compensation paid to the persons making the audit, the expenses incurred in the course thereof, and overhead costs in connection therewith as fixed by the Administrative Director. Overhead costs shall be based on the total expenditure for operating expenses and equipment, except travel, of the managed care unit of the Division of Workers' Compensation for the previous fiscal year. The invoice will be sent upon the completion of the audit and shall be paid within 30 calendar days.

Note: Authority cited: Sections 133, 4600.5, 4600.7, 4603.5 and 5307.3, Labor Code. Reference: Sections 4600, 4600.5 and 4600.7, Labor Code.

History: 1. New section filed 12-31-93; operative 1-1-94. Submitted to OAL for printing only pursuant to Government Code section 11351 (Register 93, No. 53).

2. Editorial correction of section heading (Register 96, No. 7).

3. New subsection (d) and amendment of Note filed 2-14-96; operative 2-14-96. Submitted to OAL for

printing only pursuant to Government Code section 11351 (Register 96, No. 7).

4. Amendment of subsection (a) filed 1-9-2003; operative 1-9-2003 pursuant to Government Code section 11343.4 (Register 2003, No. 2).

Ref.: Herlick Handbook § 1.6.

§9779.2. Suspension; Revocation; Hearing.

(a) Complaints pertaining to an HCO's violations of this article may be directed in writing to the administrative director. Upon receipt of a complaint, or in the course of monitoring the HCO's operations, the administrative director may investigate an alleged violation. The investigation may include, but not be limited to, a request for and review of pertinent HCO records, interviewing medical and administrative personnel, or an on-site medical survey. If the investigation reveals reasonable cause to belive that the HCO has violated a requirement of this article, the administrative director may initiate proceedings to suspend or revoke an HCO's certification.

(b) Certification of an HCO may be suspended or revoked if:

(1) Service under the HCO is not being provided according to the terms of the certified HCO.

(2) The HCO fails to meet the requirements of this article, the Labor Code, or other applicable law.

(3) False or misleading information is knowingly or repeatedly submitted by the HCO or a participating provider or the HCO knowingly or repeatedly fails to report information required by this article.

(4) The HCO knowingly continues to use the services of a provider or medical reviewer whose license, registration, or certification has been suspended or revoked or who is otherwise ineligible to provide treatment to an inured worker under California law.

(c) In the event an HCO or organization is formally notified of the administrative director's intention to revoke or suspend the HCO's certification, or to refuse certification or recertification as an HCO, the HCO or organization shall be entitled to a hearing before the administrative director or an administrative law judge which shall be shall be held in accordance with the Administrative Procedure Act (Chapter 5 (commencing with Section 11500), of Part 1 of Division 3 of Title 2 of the Government Code), and the administrative director shall have all of the powers granted under that act.

Note: Authority cited: Sections 133, 4600.5, 4603.5 and 5307.3, Labor Code. Reference: Sections 4600 and 4600.5, Labor Code.

History: 1. New section filed 12-31-93; operative 1-1-94. Submitted to OAL for printing only pursuant to Government Code section 11351 (Register 93, No. 53).

Ref.: Herlick Handbook § 1.6.

§9779.3. Obligations of Employer Covered by a Contract with a Health Care Organization.

(a) When an insurer or employers, a group of self-insured employers, or self-insured employers have contracted with a health care organization certified pursuant to Section 4600.5 of the Labor Code the employer shall provide information to all employees who are eligible to be enrolled in the health care organization as follows:

(1) a new employee shall be provided with the choice of enrolling in an HCO or designating the employee's own personal physician or personal chiropractor no later than 30 days following the employee's date of hire.

(2) a current employee shall be provided with the choice of enrolling in an HCO or designating the employee's own personal physician or personal chiropractor no later than 30 days before the initial enrollment period ends;

(3) an employer must provide information concerning the HCO it is offering to its employees no later than 30 days prior to the final date for enrollment. Information shall be provided in written form, in no less than twelve (12) point typeface, and in a language understandable to employees. The information provided must include, at a minimum, the following:

(i) the name of the HCO offered;

(ii) the corporate or business name of all entities which own or control the HCO offered; and indication of relationship, if any, of the HCO to workers' compensation carrier or self-insured employer;

(iii) the services offered by the HCO;

(iv) a complete listing of all primary treating physicians, specialist physicians, and clinics participating in the HCO who would be reasonably accessible to the employee for the provision of occupational health services. Primary treating physicians who are not accepting new patients must be clearly identified;

(v) If the HCO is also the provider of group health coverage for non-occupational health services, the HCO policy regarding enrollees' ability to use their personal physician (for non-occupational health services) for treatment of work injuries.

(vi) any provider risk-sharing arrangements related to utilization of services.

(4) Within fifteen days following enrollment, the HCO must provide to each enrollee complete information regarding HCO services and processes, including but not limited to:

(i) the services offered, including interpreters services, how such services are obtained, hours of services;

(ii) the definition of emergency care, how to obtain out-of-service treatment, how to obtain after-hours services;

(iii) case management and medical management processes, selection of the primary treating physician, and method for obtaining second opinions, change of physician, or referrals to chiropractors, physical therapists, or specialists;

(iv) the grievance and dispute resolution procedures;

(v) additional services offered, including return to work, health and safety, patient assistance, and patient education.

(b) Employees shall designate their enrollment option on form DWC 1194. This form must be maintained in the employee's personnel file for a minimum of three (3) years, and be made available to the employee or employee's representative on request.

Employees who designate on form DWC 1194 that they do not wish to enroll in an HCO and wish to pre-designate their own personal physician or personal chiropractor or personal acupuncturist shall pre-designate that personal physician or personal chiropractor or personal acupuncturist on the form 1194. At least once each year the employer shall provide the employee with a notice informing the employee of his or her right to continue as an enrollee of the HCO, change to another HCO if another HCO is offered by the employer, or designate the employee's own personal physician, personal chiropractor or personal acupuncturist instead of the HCO. If another HCO is offered by the employer and the employee chooses to change to another HCO, or if the employee chooses to designate a personal physician, personal chiropractor or personal acupuncturist, the employee shall designate such choice on a form DWC 1194, which shall be provided by the employer.

Note: Authority cited: Sections 133, 4600.3, 4600.5, 4603.5 and 5307.3, Labor Code. Reference: Sections 4600, 4600.3 and 4600.5, Labor Code.

History: 1. New section filed 3-27-95; operative 3-27-95. Submitted to OAL for printing only pursuant to Government Code section 11351 (Register 95, No. 13).

2. Amendment filed 5-17-99; operative 5-17-99 pursuant to Government Code section 11343.4(d) (Register 99, No. 21).

3. Amendment of section heading and section filed 1-9-2003; operative 1-9-2003 pursuant to Government Code section 11343.4 (Register 2003, No. 2).

Ref.: Hanna § 22.01[6]; Herlick Handbook §§ 1.6, 4.1.

§9779.4. DWC Form 1194.

CHOOSING MEDICAL CARE FOR WORK-RELATED INJURIES and ILLNESSES

California law requires your employer to provide and pay for medical treatment if you are injured at work. Your employer has chosen to provide this medical care by using a health plan called a Workers' Compensation Health Care Organization, or HCO. This form gives you information about the HCO program, and describes your rights in choosing medical care for work-related injuries and illnesses.

What is an HCO?

A Workers' Compensation Health Care Organization is an organization which has been certified by the State of California Division of Workers' Compensation to provide health care to injured workers. HCOs must meet the quality and service standards set by the Division of Workers' Compensation. They must have health care providers who understand the workers' compensation system and occupational health care. The HCO must be able to work with employers and workers to improve worksite health and safety. If you choose an HCO, the HCO will coordinate all aspects of the care for your work injury, including working with your employer to help you get back to work in a job that will not make the injury worse. The HCO must provide information on the services they provide to injured workers and must answer your questions and complaints. By choosing an HCO, you may help your employer save money. There is no cost to you in choosing an HCO.

Choosing an HCO

Your employer has offered you enrollment in an HCO. If your employer's workers' compensation insurance company owns or controls this HCO, your employer must tell you this during the enrollment process. Your employer must give you information about the HCO before you make a choice.

If you choose to enroll in the HCO, you must use the HCO for any medical treatment you need as a result of a work injury for at least 90 days after the injury. If you choose an HCO and your employer pays for at least one-half of your health insurance (for non-work injuries), then you must use the HCO for at least 180 days after a work injury. In some HCOs, your own personal physician, personal chiropractor or personal acupuncturist for your regular health care is available to treat you for work injuries/illnesses.

Choosing Your Own Doctor—Not in an HCO

If you do not want to be treated by the HCO after a work injury, you can "designate" your own personal physician, personal chiropractor or personal acupuncturist who has treated you before and who has your medical records. If you choose your own personal physician, personal chiropractor or personal acupuncturist, you may go to him or her any time for treatment of a work injury.

DWC Form 1194: front (rev. 1/03)

MAKING YOUR CHOICE
For Workers' Compensation Health Care

Use this form to choose how you want to get medical care if you have a work-related injury or illness. You may choose the Workers' Compensation Health Care Organization offered by your employer, or you may designate your own personal physician, personal chiropractor or personal acupuncturist. If you choose to designate your own personal physician, personal chiropractor or personal acupuncturist, you should do so in the space provided below. If you do not make one of these choices, your employer will enroll you in the HCO in order for you to receive treatment for a work injury or illness.

If you have questions about HCOs or medical treatment after a work injury, you may call an Information and Assistance officer. Find the telephone number in the phone book listed under State of California, Department of Industrial Relations, Division of Workers Compensation. If you have concerns, complaints or questions regarding a specific HCO or the enrollment process you can call 1-800-277-1767.

THIS IS AN IMPORTANT LEGAL DOCUMENT THAT AFFECTS YOUR RIGHTS IF YOU HAVE A WORK INJURY.

☐ I want to enroll in an HCO for my medical care for any work-related injury or illness. I have received information about the Health Care Organization offered by my employer and want to enroll in that HCO.

____

☐ I do not want to enroll in an HCO. I want my personal physician, personal chiropractor or personal acupuncturist to treat me for any work-related injury or illness. My personal physician, personal chiropractor or personal acupuncturist is:

____

(Write in the name, and address and telephone number of your personal physician, personal chiropractor or personal acupuncturist.)

☐ I do not want to enroll in an HCO or designate a personal physician, personal chiropractor or personal acupuncturist to treat me for any work-related injury or illness. I understand that my employer will enroll me in the HCO for treatment of any work-related injury or illness.

______________________________ ______________________________
(Print) Name of Employee Signature

____
Date Signed DWC Form 1194: back (rev. 1/03)

Note: Authority cited: Sections 133, 4600.5, 4603.5 and 5307.3, Labor Code. Reference: Sections 4600 and 4600.5, Labor Code.

History: 1. New section filed 3-27-95; operative 3-27-95. Submitted to OAL for printing only pursuant to Government Code section 11351 (Register 95, No. 13).

2. Amendment filed 1-9-2003; operative 1-9-2003 pursuant to Government Code section 11343.4 (Register 2003, No. 2).

Ref.: Hanna § 22.01[6]; Herlick Handbook §§ 1.6, 4.1.

§9779.45. Minimum Periods of Enrollment.

Pursuant to Labor Code Section 4600.3:

(a) An employee whose employer does not offer non-occupational health coverage under a plan established pursuant to collective bargaining, and does not offer to pay more than one-half the cost of non-occupational health coverage for that employee under another plan, may be treated for occupational injuries and illnesses by a physician of the employee's choosing after 90 days from the date the injury was reported.

(b) An employee whose employer offers non-occupational health coverage under a plan established pursuant to collective bargaining, or offers to pay more than one-half the cost of non-occupational health coverage for that employee under another plan, may be treated for occupational injuries and illnesses by a physician of the employee's choosing after 180 days from the date the injury was reported or upon the date of contract renewal or open enrollment of the health care organization, whichever occurs first, but in no case until 90 days from the date the injury was reported.

Note: Authority cited: Sections 133, 4600.3, 4600.5, 4603.5 and 5307.3, Labor Code. Reference: Sections 4600, 4600.3 and 4600.5, Labor Code.

History: 1. New section filed 5-17-99; operative 5-17-99 pursuant to Government Code section 11343.4(d) (Register 99, No. 21).

2. Repealer of subsection (c) filed 1-9-2003; operative 1-9-2003 pursuant to Government Code section 11343.4 (Register 2003, No. 2).

§9779.5. Reimbursement of Costs to the Administrative Director; Obligation to Pay Share of Administrative Expense.

(a) Each organization certified under this article shall pay to the administrative director an amount as estimated by the administrative director for the ensuing fiscal year, as a reimbursement of a share of all costs and expenses, including routine on-site surveys, data collection and dissemination and overhead, reasonably incurred in the administration of this article and not otherwise recovered by the administrative director under this article or from the Worker's Compensation Managed Care Fund. The amount shall be assessed annually on or before April 15 and may be paid to the Workers' Compensation Managed Care Fund in two equal installments. The first installment shall be paid on or before July 1 of each year and the second installment shall be paid on or before December 15 of each year.

(1) Annual Assessment: The assessment shall be calculated on the basis of the number of enrollees in each individual HCO. Each HCO will be assessed a sum equivalent to $1.00 per enrollee, based on the number of enrollees enrolled in the HCO on December 31 of the prior calendar year.

(2) Loan Repayment Surcharge: Each HCO will be assessed an annual surcharge of fifty cents per enrollee, based on the number of enrollees in the HCO on December 31 of the prior claendar year, until the loan is fully repaid. This surcharge will be used solely to reimburse the general fund for the loan made to the Workers' Compensation Managed Care Fund. The surcharge shall be assessed at this level for up to five years, commencing with the 1999 assessment. If the general fund loan has not been fully repaid after five years, the annual surcharge for each HCO shall be adjusted the following three years to fully repay the loan as follows:

2004: (One-third of outstanding loan balance) divided by (total number of enrollees in all certified HCOs) times (number of enrollees in HCO)

2005: (One-half of outstanding loan balance) divided by (total number of enrollees in all certified HCOs) times (number of enrollees in HCO)

2006: (Total outstanding loan balance) divided by (total number of enrollees in all certified HCOs) times (number of enrollees in HCO)

(b) Non-routine audits conducted in response to complaints will be charged based on the actual cost for performing the audit. The invoice will be sent within sixty days of the completion of the audit and shall be paid within 30 calendar days after the billing date.

(c) In no case shall the reimbursement, payment, or other fee authorized by this section exceed the cost, including overhead, reasonably incurred in the administration of this article.

Note: Authority cited: Sections 133, 4600.5, 4600.7, 4603.5 and 5307.3, Labor Code. Reference: Sections 4600 and 4600.5, Labor Code.

History: 1. New section filed 2-14-96; operative 2-14-96. Submitted to OAL for printing only pursuant to Government Code section 11351 (Register 96, No. 7).

2. Amendment of subsection (a)(1) and repealer and new subsection (a)(2) filed 5-17-99; operative 5-17-99 pursuant to Government Code section 11343.4(d) (Register 99, No. 21).

Ref.: Herlick Handbook § 1.6.

§9779.8. Copies of Documents.

Fees for copies of documents will be charged as set forth in Section 9990. Any request for copies of documents must include payment of fees by check or money order made payable to the Workers' Compensation Managed Care Fund.

Note: Authority: Sections 133, 4600.5, 4600.7, 4603.5, 5307.3, Labor Code. Reference: Sections 4600, 4600.5, Labor Code.

History: 1. New section filed 2-14-96; operative 2-14-96. Submitted to OAL for printing only pursuant to Government Code section 11351 (Register 96, No. 7).

Ref.: Herlick Handbook § 1.6.

§9779.9. Late Payment.

Failure to pay fees and assessments within sixty days after the date due pursuant to this section shall allow the administrative director to charge a late payment fee for any outstanding amount at a rate of ten percent after sixty days or one hundred dollars, whichever is greater. In addition, after sixty days a late fee of ten percent per year shall be assessed on any outstanding amount. In addition, the administrative director may suspend or revoke certifications of HCOs which fail to pay fees and assessment in a timely manner.

Note: Authority: Sections 133, 4600.5, 4600.7, 4603.5, 5307.3, Labor Code. Reference: Sections 4600, 4600.5, Labor Code.

History: 1. New section filed 2-14-96; operative 2-14-96. Submitted to OAL for printing only pursuant to Government Code section 11351 (Register 96, No. 7).

Ref.: Herlick Handbook § 1.6.

ARTICLE 5
Predesignation of Personal Physician; Request for Change of Physician; Reporting Duties of the Primary Treating Physician; Petition for Change of Primary Treating Physician

§9780. Definitions.

As used in this Article:

(a) "Claims Administrator" means a self-administered insurer providing security for the payment of compensation required by Divisions 4 and 4.5 of the Labor Code, a self-administered self-insured employer, a self-administered joint powers authority, a self-administered legally uninsured, or a third-party claims administrator for a self-insured employer, insurer, legally uninsured employer, or joint powers authority.

(b) "Emergency health care services" means health care services for a medical condition manifesting itself by acute symptoms of sufficient severity such that the absence of immediate medical attention could reasonably be expected to place the patient's health in serious jeopardy.

(c) "Facility" means a hospital, clinic or other institution capable of providing the medical, surgical, chiropractic or hospital treatment which is reasonably required to cure or relieve the employee from the effects of the injury.

(d) "First aid" is any one-time treatment, and a follow-up visit for the purpose of observation of minor scratches, cuts, burns, splinters, etc., which do not ordinarily require medical care. Such one-time treatment, and follow-up visit for the purpose of observation, is considered first aid, even though provided by a physician or registered professional personnel.

(e) "Nonoccupational group health coverage" means coverage for nonoccupational health care that the employer makes available to the employee, including, but not limited to, a Taft Hartley or Employee Retirement Income Security Act (ERISA) trust, or a health plan negotiated between a union or employee's association and the employer or employer's association.

(f) "Personal Physician" means (1) the employee's regular physician and surgeon, licensed pursuant to Chapter 5 (commencing with section

2000) of Division 2 of the Business and Professions Code, (2) who has been the employee's primary care physician, and has previously directed the medical treatment of the employee, and (3) who retains the employee's medical records, including the employee's medical history. "Personal physician" includes a medical group, if the medical group is a single corporation or partnership composed of licensed doctors of medicine or osteopathy, which operates an integrated multispecialty medical group providing comprehensive medical services predominantly for nonoccupational illnesses and injuries.

(g) "Primary Care Physician" means a physician who has the responsibility for providing initial and primary care to patients, for maintaining the continuity of patient care, and for initiating referral for specialist care. A primary care physician shall be either a physician who has limited his or her practice of medicine to general practice or who is a board-certified or board-eligible internist, pediatrician, obstetrician-gynecologist, or family practitioner.

(h) "Reasonable geographic area" within the context of Labor Code section 4600 shall be determined by giving consideration to:

(1) The employee's place of residence, place of employment and place where the injury occurred; and

(2) The availability of physicians in the fields of practice, and facilities offering treatment reasonably required to cure or relieve the employee from the effects of the injury;

(3) The employee's medical history;

(4) The employee's primary language.

Note: Authority cited: Sections 59, 133 and 4603.5, Labor Code. Reference: Section 4600, Labor Code.

History: 1. Repealer of Article 5 (Sections 9783-9785, 9787 and 9788) and new Article 5 (Sections 9780-9787) filed 1-28-76 as an emergency; effective upon filing (Register 76, No. 5). For prior history, see Register 70, No. 49, and Register 72, No. 51.

2. Certificate of Compliance filed 1-29-76 (Register 76, No. 5).

3. New subsections (f)-(i) filed 11-7-78; effective thirtieth day thereafter (Register 78, No. 45).

4. Repealer and new article 5 heading and amendment of section and Note filed 3-14-2006; operative 3-14-2006 pursuant to Government Code section 11343.4 (Register 2006, No. 11).

5. Editorial correction of subsection (f) (Register 2007, No. 7).

6. Change without regulatory effect amending subsection (f) filed 2-21-2007 pursuant to section 100, title 1, California Code of Regulations (Register 2007, No. 8).

Ref.: Hanna §§ 5.02[1], 5.02[4], 5.05[6][a], 22.01[4], 22.02[1]–[2], 22.03[2]; Herlick Handbook §§ 1.6, 4.1, 4.2(a), 4.8.

§9780.1. Employee's Predesignation of Personal Physician.

(a) An employee may be treated for an industrial injury in accordance with section 4600 of the Labor Code by a personal physician that the employee predesignates prior to the industrial injury if the following three conditions are met:

(1) Notice of the predesignation of a personal physician is in writing, and is provided to the employer prior to the industrial injury for which treatment by the personal physician is sought. The notice shall include the personal physician's name and business address. The employee may use the optional predesignation form (DWC Form 9783) in section 9783 for this purpose.

(2) The employer provides: (i) nonoccupational group health coverage in a health care service plan, licensed pursuant to Chapter 2.2 (commencing with section 1340) of Division 2 of the Health and Safety Code, or (ii) nonoccupational health coverage in a group health plan or a group health insurance policy as described in section 4616.7 of the Labor Code. The employer's provision of health coverage as defined herein is sufficient to meet this requirement, regardless of whether the employee accepts or participates in this health coverage.

(3) The employee's personal physician agrees to be predesignated prior to the injury. The personal physician may sign the optional predesignation form (DWC Form 9783) in section 9783 as documentation of such agreement. The physician may authorize a designated employee of the physician to sign the optional predesignation form on his or her behalf. If the personal physician or the designated employee of the physician does not sign a predesignation form, there must be other documentation that the physician agrees to be predesignated prior to the injury in order to satisfy this requirement.

(b) If an employee has predesignated a personal physician prior to the effective date of these regulations, such predesignation shall be considered valid if the conditions in subdivision (a) have been met.

(c) Where an employer or an employer's insurer has a Medical Provider Network pursuant to section 4616 of the Labor Code, an employee's predesignation which has been made in accordance with this section shall be valid and the employee shall not be subject to the Medical Provider Network.

(d) Where an employee has made a valid predesignation pursuant to this section, and where the employer or employer's insurer has a Medical Provider Network, any referral to another physician for other treatment need not be within the Medical Provider Network.

(e) An employer who qualifies under (a)(2) of this section shall notify its employees of all of the requirements of this section and provide its employees with an optional form for predesignating a personal physician, in accordance with section 9880. The employer may use the predesignation form (DWC Form 9783) in section 9783 for this purpose.

(f) Unless the employee agrees, neither the employer nor the claims administrator shall contact the predesignated personal physician to confirm predesignation status or contact the personal physician regarding the employee's medical information or medical history prior to the personal physician's commencement of treatment for an industrial injury.

(g) Where the employer has been notified of an employee's predesignation of a personal physician in accordance with this section and where the employer becomes liable for an employee's medical treatment, the claims administrator shall:

(1) authorize the predesignated physician to provide all medical treatment reasonably required to cure or relieve the injured employee from the effects of his or her injury;

(2) furnish the name and address of the person to whom billing for treatment should be sent;

(3) where there has been treatment of an injury prior to commencement of treatment by the predesignated physician, arrange for the delivery to the predesignated physician of all medical information relating to the claim, all X-rays, the results of all laboratory studies done in relation to the injured employee's treatment; and

(4) provide the physician with (1) the fax number, if available, to be used to request authorization of treatment plans; (2) the complete requirements of section 9785; and (3) the forms set forth in sections 9785.2 and 9785.4. In lieu of providing the materials required in (2) and (3) immediately above, the claims administrator may refer the physician to the Division of Workers' Compensation's website where the applicable information and forms can be found at http://www.dir.ca.gov/DWC/dwc_home_page.htm.

(h) Notwithstanding subdivision (g), the employer shall provide first aid and appropriate emergency health care services reasonably required by the nature of the injury or illness. Thereafter, if further medical treatment is reasonably required to cure or relieve the injured employee from the effects of his or her injury, the claims administrator shall authorize treatment with the employee's predesignated personal physician in accordance with subdivision (g).

(i) If documentation of a physician's agreement to be predesignated has not been provided to the employer as of the time of injury, treatment shall be provided in accordance with Labor Code section 4600, or Labor Code section 4616, if the employer or insurer has established a Medical Provider Network, as though no predesignation had occurred. Upon provision of the documented agreement that was made prior to injury that meets the conditions of Labor Code section 4600(d), the employer or claims administrator shall authorize treatment with the employee's predesignated physician as set forth in subdivision (g).

Note: Authority cited: Sections 59, 133 and 4603.5, Labor Code. Reference: Sections 3551, 4600 and 4616, Labor Code.

History: 1. New section filed 11-7-78; effective thirtieth day thereafter (Register 78, No. 45).

2. Amendment of section heading, repealer and new section and amendment of Note filed 3-14-2006; operative 3-14-2006 pursuant to Government Code section 11343.4 (Register 2006, No. 11).

Ref.: Hanna § 5.05[1]; Herlick Handbook §§ 1.6, 4.1, 4.2(a).

§9780.2. Employer's Duty to Provide First Aid and Emergency Treatment. [Repealed]

Note: Authority cited: Sections 124, 127, 133, 138.2, 138.3, 138.4, 139, 139.5, 139.6, 4600, 4601, 4602, 4603, 4603.2, 4603.5, 5307.3, 5450, 5451, 5452, 5453, 5454, and 5455, Labor Code. Reference:

Chapters 442, 709, and 1172, Statutes of 1977; Chapter 1017, Statutes of 1976.

History: 1. New section filed 11-7-78; effective thirtieth day thereafter (Register 78, No. 45).

2. Repealer filed 3-14-2006; operative 3-14-2006 pursuant to Government Code section 11343.4 (Register 2006, No. 11).

Ref.: Hanna §§ 5.02[4], 22.01[4]; Herlick Handbook §§ 1.6, 4.1, 4.2(a), 4.8.

§9781. Employee's Request for Change of Physician.

(a) This section shall not apply to self-insured and insured employers who offer a Medical Provider Network pursuant to section 4616 of the Labor Code.

(b) Pursuant to section 4601 of the Labor Code, and notwithstanding the 30 day time period specified in subdivision (c), the employee may request a one time change of physician at any time.

(1) An employee's request for change of physician pursuant to this subdivision need not be in writing. The claims administrator shall respond to the employee in the manner best calculated to inform the employee, and in no event later than 5 working days from receipt of said request, the claims administrator shall provide the employee an alternative physician, or if the employee so requests, a chiropractor or acupuncturist.

(2) Notwithstanding subdivision (a) of section 9780.1, if an employee requesting a change of physician pursuant to this subdivision has notified his or her employer in writing prior to the date of injury that he or she has either a personal chiropractor or a personal acupuncturist, and where the employee so requests, the alternative physician tendered by the claims administrator to the employee shall be the employee's personal chiropractor or personal acupuncturist as defined in subdivisions (b) and (c), respectively, of Labor Code section 4601. The notification to the employer must include the name and business address of the chiropractor or acupuncturist. The employer shall notify its employees of the requirements of this subdivision and provide its employees with an optional form for notification of a personal chiropractor or acupuncturist, in accordance with section 9880. DWC Form 9783.1 in section 9783.1 may be used for this purpose.

(3) Except where the employee is permitted to select a personal chiropractor or acupuncturist as defined in subdivisions (b) and (c), respectively, of Labor Code section 4601, the claims administrator shall advise the employee of the name and address of the alternative physician, or chiropractor or acupuncturist if requested, the date and time of an initial scheduled appointment, and any other pertinent information.

(c) Pursuant to section 4600, after 30 days from the date the injury is reported, the employee shall have the right to be treated by a physician or at a facility of his or her own choice within a reasonable geographic area.

(1) The employee shall notify the claims administrator of the name and address of the physician or facility selected pursuant to this subdivision. However, this notice requirement will be deemed to be satisfied if the selected physician or facility gives notice to the claims administrator of the commencement of treatment or if the claims administrator receives this information promptly from any source.

(2) If so requested by the selected physician or facility, the employee shall sign a release permitting the selected physician or facility to report to the claims administrator as required by section 9785.

(d) When the claims administrator is notified of the name and address of an employee-selected physician or facility pursuant to subdivision (c), or of a personal chiropractor or acupuncturist pursuant to paragraph (2) of subdivision (b), the claims administrator shall:

(1) authorize such physician or facility or personal chiropractor or acupuncturist to provide all medical treatment reasonably required pursuant to section 4600 of the Labor Code;

(2) furnish the name and address of the person to whom billing for treatment should be sent;

(3) arrange for the delivery to the selected physician or facility of all medical information relating to the claim, all X-rays and the results of all laboratory studies done in relation to the injured employee's treatment; and

(4) provide the physician or facility with (1) the fax number, if available, to be used to request authorization of treatment plans; (2) the complete requirements of section 9785; and (3) the forms set forth in sections 9785.2 and 9785.4. In lieu of providing the materials required in (2) and (3) immediately above, the claims administrator may refer the physician or facility to the Division of Workers' Compensation's website where the applicable information

and forms can be found at http://www.dir.ca.gov/DWC/dwc_home_page.htm.

Note: Authority cited: Sections 133 and 4603.5, Labor Code. Reference: Sections 3551, 4600 and 4601, Labor Code.

History: 1. Repealer and new section filed 11-9-77; effective thirtieth day thereafter (Register 77, No. 46).

2. Repealer and new section and amendment of Note filed 3-14-2006; operative 3-14-2006 pursuant to Government Code section 11343.4 (Register 2006, No. 11).

Ref.: Hanna §§ 5.05[7][a], 22.03[1]; Herlick Handbook §§ 1.6, 4.1, 4.2(a); W. Cal. Sum., 2 "Workers' Compensation" §270.

§9782. Notice to Employee of Right to Choose Physician.

(a) Except for an employer who has established a Medical Provider Network, or an employer whose insurer has established a Medical Provider Network, every employer shall advise its employees in writing of an employee's right (1) to request a change of treating physician if the original treating physician is selected initially by the employer pursuant to Labor Code section 4601, and (2) to be treated by a physician of his or her own choice 30 days after reporting an injury pursuant to subdivision (c) of Labor Code 4600.

(b) Every employer shall advise its employees in writing of an employee's right to predesignate a personal physician pursuant to subdivision (d) of Labor Code section 4600, and section 9780.1.

(c) The notices required by this section shall be provided in accordance with section 9880 and posted in accordance with section 9881.

Note: Authority cited: Sections 133 and 4603.5, Labor Code. Reference: Sections 3550, 3551, 4600, 4601 and 4616, Labor Code.

History: 1. Repealer and new section filed 11-9-77; effective thirtieth day thereafter (Register 77, No. 46).

2. Repealer and new section filed 11-7-78; effective thirtieth day thereafter (Register 78, No. 45).

3. Amendment of section and Note filed 3-14-2006; operative 3-14-2006 pursuant to Government Code section 11343.4 (Register 2006, No. 11).

Ref.: Hanna § 5.05[2]; Herlick Handbook §§ 1.6, 4.1, 4.2(a).

§9783. DWC Form 9783 Predesignation of Personal Physician.

PREDESIGNATION OF PERSONAL PHYSICIAN

In the event you sustain an injury or illness related to your employment, you may be treated for such injury or illness by your personal medical doctor (M.D.), doctor of osteopathic medicine (D.O.) or medical group if:

- your employer offers group health coverage;
- the doctor is your regular physician, who shall be either a physician who has limited his or her practice of medicine to general practice or who is a board-certified or board-eligible internist, pediatrician, obstetrician-gynecologist, or family practitioner, and has previously directed your medical treatment, and retains your medical records;
- your "personal physician" may be a medical group if it is a single corporation or partnership composed of licensed doctors of medicine or osteopathy, which operates an integrated multispecialty medical group providing comprehensive medical services predominantly for nonoccupational illnesses and injuries;
- prior to the injury your doctor agrees to treat you for work injuries or illnesses;
- prior to the injury you provided your employer the following in writing: (1) notice that you want your personal doctor to treat you for a work-related injury or illness, and (2) your personal doctor's name and business address.

You may use this form to notify your employer if you wish to have your personal medical doctor or a doctor of osteopathic medicine treat you for a work-related injury or illness and the above requirements are met.

NOTICE OF PREDESIGNATION OF PERSONAL PHYSICIAN

Employee: Complete this section.

To: ____________ (name of employer)

If I have a work-related injury or illness, I choose to be treated by:

____

(name of doctor) (M.D., D.O., or medical group)

____

(street address, city, state, ZIP)

____

(telephone number)

Employee Name (please print):

____

Employee's Address:

____

Employee's Signature ______________

Date: ______________________

Physician: I agree to this Predesignation:

Signature: ______________________

Date: ______________________

(Physician or Designated Employee of the Physician or Medical Group)

The physician is not required to sign this form, however, if the physician or designated employee of the physician or medical group does not sign, other documentation of the physician's agreement to be predesignated will be required pursuant to Title 8, California Code of Regulations, section 9780.1(a)(3).

Title 8, California Code of Regulations, section 9783.

(Optional DWC Form 9783–March 1, 2007)

Note: Authority cited: Sections 133, 4603.5 and 5307.3, Labor Code. Reference: Section 4600, Labor Code.

History: 1. Amendment filed 11-11-78; effective thirtieth day thereafter (Register 78, No. 45).

2. Repealer and new section heading, section and Note filed 3-14-2006; operative 3-14-2006 pursuant to Government Code section 11343.4 (Register 2006, No. 11).

3. Change without regulatory effect amending section filed 2-21-2007 pursuant to section 100, title 1, California Code of Regulations (Register 2007, No. 8).

Ref.: Hanna §§ 5.05[6][b], 22.02[2], 25.10[4]; Herlick Handbook §§ 1.6, 4.1, 4.2(a).

§9783.1. DWC Form 9783.1 Notice of Personal Chiropractor or Personal Acupuncturist.

NOTICE OF PERSONAL CHIROPRACTOR OR PERSONAL ACUPUNCTURIST

If your employer or your employer's insurer does not have a Medical Provider Network, you may be able to change your treating physician to your personal chiropractor or acupuncturist following a work-related injury or illness. In order to be eligible to make this change, you must give your employer the name and business address of a personal chiropractor or acupuncturist in writing prior to the injury or illness. Your claims administrator generally has the right to select your treating physician within the first 30 days after your employer knows of your injury or illness. After your claims administrator has initiated your treatment with another doctor during this period, you may then, upon request, have your treatment transferred to your personal chiropractor or acupuncturist.

You may use this form to notify your employer of your personal chiropractor or acupuncturist.

Your Chiropractor or Acupuncturist's Information:

____

(name of chiropractor or acupuncturist)

____

(street address, city, state, zip code)

____

(telephone number)

____

Employee Name (please print):

____

Employee's Address:

____

Employee's Signature ________ Date: ______

Title 8, California Code of Regulations, section 9783.1.

(DWC Form 9783.1-Effective date March 2006)

Note: Authority cited: Sections 133, 4603.5 and 5307.3, Labor Code. Reference: Sections 4600 and 4601, Labor Code.

History: 1. New section filed 3-14-2006; operative 3-14-2006 pursuant to Government Code section 11343.4 (Register 2006, No. 11).

§9784. Duties of the Employer. [Repealed]

Note: Authority cited: Sections 124, 127, 133, 138.2, 138.3, 138.4, 139, 139.5, 139.6, 4600, 4601, 4602, 4603, 4603.2, 4603.5, 5307.3, 5450, 5451, 5452, 5453, 5454, and 5455, Labor Code. Reference: Chapters 442, 709, and 1172, Statutes of 1977; Chapter 1017, Statutes of 1976.

History: 1. Repealer and new section filed 11-9-77; effective thirtieth day thereafter (Register 77, No. 46).

2. Amendment filed 11-11-78; effective thirtieth day thereafter (Register 78, No. 45).

3. Repealer filed 3-14-2006; operative 3-14-2006 pursuant to Government Code section 11343.4 (Register 2006, No. 11).

Ref.: Hanna §§ 5.05[6][b], 22.02[3]–[4]; Herlick Handbook §§ 1.6, 4.1, 4.2(a), 4.19.

§9785. Reporting Duties of the Primary Treating Physician.

(a) For the purposes of this section, the following definitions apply:

(1) The "primary treating physician" is the physician who is primarily responsible for managing the care of an employee, and who has examined the employee at least once for the purpose of rendering or prescribing treatment and has monitored the effect of the treatment thereafter. The primary treating physician is the physician selected by the employer, the employee pursuant to Article 2 (commencing with section 4600) of Chapter 2 of Part 2 of Division 4 of the Labor Code, or under the contract or procedures applicable to a Health Care Organization certified under section 4600.5 of the Labor Code, or in accordance with the physician selection procedures contained in the medical provider network pursuant to Labor Code section 4616.

(2) A "secondary physician" is any physician other than the primary treating physician who examines or provides treatment to the employee, but is not primarily responsible for continuing management of the care of the employee.

(3) "Claims administrator" is a self-administered insurer providing security for the payment of compensation required by Divisions 4 and 4.5 of the Labor Code, a self-administered self-insured employer, or a third-party administrator for a self-insured employer, insurer, legally uninsured employer, or joint powers authority.

(4) "Medical determination" means, for the purpose of this section, a decision made by the primary treating physician regarding any and all medical issues necessary to determine the employee's eligibility for compensation. Such issues include but are not limited to the scope and extent of an employee's continuing medical treatment, the decision whether to release the employee from care, the point in time at which the employee has reached permanent and stationary status, and the necessity for future medical treatment.

(5) "Released from care" means a determination by the primary treating physician that the employee's condition has reached a permanent and stationary status with no need for continuing or future medical treatment.

(6) "Continuing medical treatment" is occurring or presently planned treatment that is reasonably required to cure or relieve the employee from the effects of the injury.

(7) "Future medical treatment" is treatment which is anticipated at some time in the future and is reasonably required to cure or relieve the employee from the effects of the injury.

(8) "Permanent and stationary status" is the point when the employee has reached maximal medical improvement, meaning his or her condition is well stabilized, and unlikely to change substantially in the next year with or without medical treatment.

(b)(1) An employee shall have no more than one primary treating physician at a time.

(2) An employee may designate a new primary treating physician of his or her choice pursuant to Labor Code §§4600 or 4600.3 provided the primary treating physician has determined that there is a need for:

(A) continuing medical treatment; or

(B) future medical treatment. The employee may designate a new primary treating physician to render future medical treatment either prior to or at the time such treatment becomes necessary.

(3) If the employee disputes a medical determination made by the primary treating physician, including a determination that the employee should be released from care, or if the employee objects to a decision made pursuant to Labor Code section 4610 to modify, delay, or deny a treatment recommendation, the dispute shall be resolved under the applicable procedures set forth at Labor Code sections 4061 and 4062. No other primary treating physician shall be designated by the employee unless and until the dispute is resolved.

(4) If the claims administrator disputes a medical determination made by the primary treating physician, the dispute shall be resolved under the applicable procedures set forth at Labor Code sections 4610, 4061 and 4062.

(c) The primary treating physician, or a physician designated by the primary treating physician, shall make reports to the claims administrator as required in this section. A primary treating physician has fulfilled his or her reporting duties under this section by sending one copy of a required report to the claims administrator. A claims administrator may designate any person or entity to be the recipient of its copy of the required report.

(d) The primary treating physician shall render opinions on all medical issues necessary to determine the employee's eligibility for compensation in the manner prescribed in subdivisions (e), (f) and (g) of this section. The primary treating physician may transmit reports to the claims administrator by mail or FAX or by any other means satisfactory to the claims administrator, including electronic transmission.

(e)(1) Within 5 working days following initial examination, a primary treating physician shall submit a written report to the claims administrator on the form entitled "Doctor's First Report of Occupational Injury or Illness," Form DLSR 5021. Emergency and urgent care physicians shall also submit a Form DLSR 5021 to the claims administrator following the initial visit to the treatment facility. On line 24 of the Doctor's First Report, or on the reverse side of the form, the physician shall (A) list methods, frequency, and duration of planned treatment(s), (B) specify planned consultations or referrals, surgery or hospitalization and (C) specify the type, frequency and duration of planned physical medicine services (e.g., physical therapy, manipulation, acupuncture).

(2) Each new primary treating physician shall submit a Form DLSR 5021 following the initial examination in accordance with subdivision (e)(1).

(3) Secondary physicians, physical therapists, and other health care providers to whom the employee is referred shall report to the primary treating physician in the manner required by the primary treating physician.

(4) The primary treating physician shall be responsible for obtaining all of the reports of secondary physicians and shall, unless good cause is shown, within 20 days of receipt of each report incorporate, or comment upon, the findings and opinions of the other physicians in the primary treating physician's report and submit all of the reports to the claims administrator.

(f) A primary treating physician shall, unless good cause is shown, within 20 days report to the claims administrator when any one or more of the following occurs:

(1) The employee's condition undergoes a previously unexpected significant change;

(2) There is any significant change in the treatment plan reported, including, but not limited to, (A) an extension of duration or frequency of treatment, (B) a new need for hospitalization or surgery, (C) a new need for referral to or consultation by another physician, (D) a change in methods of treatment or in required physical medicine services, or (E) a need for rental or purchase of durable medical equipment or orthotic devices;

(3) The employee's condition permits return to modified or regular work;

(4) The employee's condition requires him or her to leave work, or requires changes in work restrictions or modifications;

(5) The employee is released from care;

(6) The primary treating physician concludes that the employee's permanent disability precludes, or is likely to preclude, the employee from engaging in the employee's usual occupation or the occupation in which the employee was engaged at the time of the injury, as required pursuant to Labor Code Section 4636(b);

(7) The claims administrator reasonably requests appropriate additional information that is necessary to administer the claim. "Necessary" information is that which directly affects the provision of compensation benefits as defined in Labor Code Section 3207.

(8) When continuing medical treatment is provided, a progress report shall be made no later than forty-five days from the last report of any type under this section even if no event described in paragraphs (1) to (7) has occurred. If an examination has occurred, the report shall be signed and transmitted within 20 days of the examination.

Except for a response to a request for information made pursuant to subdivision (f)(7), reports required under this subdivision shall be submitted on the "Primary Treating Physician's Progress Report" form (Form PR-2) contained in Section 9785.2, or in the form of a narrative report. If a narrative report is used, it must be entitled "Primary Treating Physician's Progress Report" in bold-faced type, must indicate clearly the reason the report is being submitted, and must contain the same information using the same subject headings in the same order as Form PR-2. A response to a request for information made pursuant to subdivision (f)(7) may be made in letter format. A narrative report and a letter format response to a request for information must contain the same declaration under penalty of perjury that is set forth in the Form PR-2: "I declare under penalty of perjury that this report is true and correct to the best of my knowledge and that I have not violated Labor Code §139.3."

By mutual agreement between the physician and the claims administrator, the physician may make reports in any manner and form.

(g) When the primary treating physician determines that the employee's condition is permanent and stationary, the physician shall, unless good cause is shown, report within 20 days from the date of examination any findings concerning the existence and extent of permanent impairment and limitations and any need for continuing and/or future medical care resulting from the injury. The information may be submitted on the "Primary Treating Physician's Permanent and Stationary Report" form (DWC Form PR-3 or DWC Form PR-4) contained in section 9785.3 or section 9785.4, or in such other manner which provides all the information required by Title 8, California Code of Regulations, section 10606. For permanent disability evaluation performed pursuant to the permanent disability evaluation schedule adopted on or after January 1, 2005, the primary treating physician's reports concerning the existence and extent of permanent impairment shall describe the impairment in accordance with the AMA Guides to the Evaluation on Permanent Impairment, 5th Edition (DWC Form PR-4). Qualified Medical Evaluators and Agreed Medical Evaluators may not use DWC Form PR-3 or DWC Form PR-4 to report medical-legal evaluations.

(h) Any controversies concerning this section shall be resolved pursuant to Labor Code Section 4603 or 4604, whichever is appropriate.

(i) Claims administrators shall reimburse primary treating physicians for their reports submitted pursuant to this section as required by the Official Medical Fee Schedule.

Note: Authority cited: Sections 133, 4603.5 and 5307.3, Labor Code. Reference: Sections 4061, 4061.5, 4062, 4600, 4600.3, 4603.2, 4636, 4660, 4662, 4663 and 4664, Labor Code.

History: 1. Amendment filed 11-9-77; effective thirtieth day thereafter (Register 77, No. 46).

2. Amendment of subsection (b) filed 11-11-78; effective thirtieth day thereafter (Register 78, No. 45).

3. Amendment of subsections (c) and (d) and new subsection (e) filed 7-11-89; operative 10-1-89 (Register 89, No. 28).

4. Amendment of section and Note filed 8-31-93; operative 8-31-93. Submitted to OAL for printing only pursuant to Government Code section 11351 (Register 93, No. 36).

5. New subsection (e) and subsection relettering filed 3-27-95; operative 3-27-95. Submitted to OAL for printing only pursuant to Government Code section 11351 (Register 95, No. 13).

6. Repealer and new section filed 11-9-98; operative 1-1-99 (Register 98, No. 46).

7. Amendment of subsections (e)(1), (f)(8) and (g) filed 12-22-2000; operative 1-1-2001 pursuant to Government Code section 11343.4(d) (Register 2000, No. 51).

8. Amendment of section and Note filed 5-20-2003; operative 6-19-2003 (Register 2003, No. 21).

9. Amendment of subsections (a)(1), (a)(8), (b)(3)-(4) and (g) and amendment of Note filed 12-31-2004 as an emergency; operative 1-1-2005 (Register 2004, No. 53). A Certificate of Compliance must be transmitted to OAL by 5-2-2005 or emergency language will be repealed by operation of law on the following day.

10. Certificate of Compliance as to 12-31-2004 order, including further amendment of subsections (a)(1) and (g), transmitted to OAL 4-29-2005 and filed 6-10-2005 (Register 2005, No. 23).

Ref.: Hanna §§ 5.05[6][b], [7][b], 22.02[4]–[5], 22.03[2], 22.08[3][b], 22.10; Herlick Handbook §§ 1.6, 4.1, 4.2(a), 4.19; Lawyer's Guide to AMA *Guides* and Calif. Workers' Comp. § 3.03.

§9785.2. Form PR-2 "Primary Treating Physician's Progress Report."

State of California
Division of Workers' Compensation

Additional pages attached

PRIMARY TREATING PHYSICIAN'S PROGRESS REPORT (PR-2)

Check the box (es) which indicate why you are submitting a report at this time. If the patient is "Permanent and Stationary" (i.e., has reached maximum medical improvement), do not use this form. You may use DWC Forms PR-3 or PR-4.

☐ Periodic Report (required 45 days after last report) ☐ Change in treatment plan ☐ Released from care
☐ Change in work status ☐ Need for referral or consultation ☐ Response to request for information
☐ Change in patient's condition ☐ Need for surgery or hospitalization ☐ Request for authorization ☐
Other:

Patient:
Last ______ First ______ M.I. ______ Sex ______
Address ______ City ______ State ______ Zip ______
Date of Injury ______ Date of Birth ______
Occupation ______ SS # ___-___-___ Phone ( )______
Claims Administrator:
Name ______ Claim Number ______
Address ______ City ______ State ______ Zip ______
Phone ( ) ______ FAX ( ) ______
Employer name: Employer Phone ( )

The information below must be provided. You may use this form or you may substitute or append a narrative report.

Subjective complaints:

Objective findings: (Include significant physical examination, laboratory, imaging, or other diagnostic findings.)

Diagnoses:
1. ______ ICD-9 ______
2. ______ ICD-9 ______
3. ______ ICD-9 ______

Treatment Plan: (Include treatment rendered to date. List methods, frequency and duration of planned treatment(s). Specify consultation/referral, surgery, and hospitalization. Identify each physician and non-physician provider. Specify type, frequency and duration of physical medicine services (e.g., physical therapy, manipulation, acupuncture). Use of CPT codes is encouraged. Have there been any **changes** in treatment plan? If so, why?

DWC Form PR-2
(Rev. 06-05)

Regulations

State of California
Division of Workers' Compensation

Additional pages attached

PRIMARY TREATING PHYSICIAN'S PROGRESS REPORT (PR-2)

Work Status: This patient has been instructed to:

☐ Remain off-work until__________.

☐ Return to *modified* work on________________________ with the following limitations or restrictions

(List all specific restrictions re: standing, sitting, bending, use of hands, etc.):

☐ Return to full duty on __________________with no limitations or restrictions.

Primary Treating Physician: (original signature, do not stamp) Date of exam:

____

I declare under penalty of perjury that this report is true and correct to the best of my knowledge and that I have not violated Labor Code § 139.3.

Signature: ________________________ Cal. Lic. # ________________________
Executed at: ________________________ Date: ________________________
Name: ________________________ Specialty: ________________________
Address: ________________________ Phone: ________________________

DWC Form PR-2
(Rev. 06-05)

Note: Authority cited: Sections 133, 4603.5 and 5307.3, Labor Code. Reference: Sections 4061.5, 4600, 4603.2, 4610, 4636, 4660, 4662, 4663 and 4664, Labor Code.

History: 1. New section filed 11-9-98; operative 1-1-99 (Register 98, No. 46).

2. Repealer and new form filed 12-22-2000; operative 1-1-2001 pursuant to Government Code section 11343.4(d) (Register 2000, No. 51).

3. Amendment of form filed 5-20-2003; operative 6-19-2003 (Register 2003, No. 21).

4. Amendment of section and Note filed 12-31-2004 as an emergency; operative 1-1-2005 (Register 2004, No. 53). A Certificate of Compliance must be transmitted to OAL by 5-2-2005 or emergency language will be repealed by operation of law on the following day.

5. Certificate of Compliance as to 12-31-2004 order, including further amendment of section, transmitted to OAL 4-29-2005 and filed 6-10-2005 (Register 2005, No. 23).

Ref.: Hanna §§ 5.05[6][b], 22.02[5]; Herlick Handbook § 4.2(a).

Regulations

§9785.3. Form PR-3 "Primary Treating Physician's Permanent and Stationary Report."

STATE OF CALIFORNIA

Division of Workers' Compensation

PRIMARY TREATING PHYSICIAN'S PERMANENT AND STATIONARY REPORT (PR-3)

This form is required to be used for ratings prepared pursuant to the 1997 Permanent Disability Rating Schedule. It is designed to be used by the primary treating physician to report the initial evaluation of permanent disability to the claims administrator. It should be completed if the patient has residual effects from the injury or may require future medical care. In such cases, it should be completed once the patient's condition becomes permanent and stationary.

This form should not be used by a Qualified Medical Evaluator (QME) or Agreed Medical Evaluator (AME) to report a medical-legal evaluation.

Patient:

Last Name ____________ Middle Initial ____ First Name ____________ Sex ___ Date of Birth ________

Address ____________________________ City ________________ State _____ Zip _______

Occupation ____________________ Social Security No. ________________ Phone No. ________

Claims Administrator/Insurer:

Name ____________________________ Claim No. ________________ Phone No. __________

Address ____________________________ City ____________________ State _____ Zip ________

Employer:

Name ____ Phone No. ______________

Address ______________________________ City _____________ State __________ Zip _____

You must address each of the issues below. You may substitute or append a narrative report if you require additional space to adequately report on these issues.

Date of Injury__________ Last date __________ Date of current __________ Permanent & __________

Date worked Date examination Date Stationary date Date

Description of how injury/illness occurred (e.g. Hand caught in punch press; fell from height onto back; exposed 25 years ago to asbestos):

Patient's Complaints:

DWC Form PR-3
(Rev. 06-05)

STATE OF CALIFORNIA

Division of Workers' Compensation

PRIMARY TREATING PHYSICIAN'S PERMANENT AND STATIONARY REPORT (PR-3)

Relevant Medical History:

Objective Findings:

Physical Examination: (Describe all relevant findings; include any specific measurements indicating atrophy, range of motion, strength, etc.; include bilateral measurements - injured/uninjured - for upper and lower extremity injuries.)

Diagnostic tests results (X-ray/Imaging/Laboratory/etc.)

Diagnoses (List each diagnosis; ICD-9 code must be included) ICD-9

1. ______________________ ______________
2. ______________________ ______________
3. ______________________ ______________
4. ______________________ ______________

	Yes	No	Cannot determine
Can this patient now return to his/her usual occupation?	☐	☐	☐
If not, can the patient perform another line of work?	☐	☐	☐

DWC Form PR-3
(Rev. 06-05)

STATE OF CALIFORNIA

Division of Workers' Compensation

PRIMARY TREATING PHYSICIAN'S PERMANENT AND STATIONARY REPORT (PR-3)

Subjective Findings: Provide your professional assessment of the subjective factors of disability, based on your evaluation of the patient's complaints, your examination, and other findings. List specific symptoms (e.g. pain right wrist) and their frequency, severity, and/or precipitating activity using the following definitions:

Severity: Minimal pain - an annoyance, causes no handicap in performance.
Slight pain - tolerable, causes some handicap in performance of the activity precipitating pain.
Moderate pain - tolerable, causes marked handicap in the performance of the activity precipitating pain.
Severe pain - precludes performance of the activity precipitating pain.

Frequency: Occasional - occurs roughly one fourth of the time.
Intermittent - occurs roughly one half of the time.
Frequent - occurs roughly three fourths of the time.
Constant - occurs roughly 90 to 100% of time.

Precipitating activity: Description of precipitating activity gives a sense of how often a pain is felt and thus may be used with or without a frequency modifier. If pain is constant during precipitating activity, then no frequency modifier should be used. For example, a finding of "moderate pain on heavy lifting" connotes that moderate pain is felt whenever heavy lifting occurs. In contrast, "intermittent moderate pain on heavy lifting" implies that moderate pain is only felt half the time when engaged in heavy lifting.

		Yes	No	Cannot determine
Pre-Injury Capacity	Are there any activities at home or at work that the patient cannot do as well now as could be done prior to this injury or illness?	☐	☐	☐

If yes, please describe pre-injury capacity and current capacity (e.g. used to regularly lift a 30 lb. child, now can only lift 10 lbs.; could sit for 2 hours, now can only sit for 15 mins.)

1.

2.

3.

4.

DWC Form PR-3
(Rev. 06-05)

STATE OF CALIFORNIA

Division of Workers' Compensation

PRIMARY TREATING PHYSICIAN'S PERMANENT AND STATIONARY REPORT (PR-3)

Preclusions/Work Restrictions

	Yes	No	Cannot determine
Are there any activities the patient cannot do?	☐	☐	☐

If yes, please describe all preclusions or restrictions related to work activities (e.g. no lifting more than 10 lbs. above shoulders; must use splint; keyboard only 45 mins. per hour; must have sit/stand workstation; no repeated bending). Include restrictions which may not be relevant to current job but may affect future efforts to find work on the open labor market (e.g. include lifting restriction even if current job requires no lifting; include limits on repetitive hand movements even if current job requires none).

1.

2.

3.

4.

5.

6.

Medical Treatment: Describe any continuing medical treatment related to this injury that you believe must be provided to the patient. ("Continuing medical treatment" is defined as occurring or presently planned treatment.) Also, describe any medical treatment the patient may require in the future. ("Future medical treatment" is defined as treatment which is anticipated at some time in the future to cure or relieve the employee from the effects of the injury.) Include medications, surgery, physical medicine services, durable equipment, etc.

Comments:

DWC Form PR-3
(Rev. 06-05)

STATE OF CALIFORNIA
Division of Workers' Compensation
PRIMARY TREATING PHYSICIAN'S PERMANENT AND STATIONARY REPORT (PR-3)

Apportionment:

Effective April 19, 2004, apportionment of permanent disability shall be based on causation. Furthermore, any physician who prepares a report addressing permanent disability due to a claimed industrial injury is required to address the issue of causation of the permanent disability, and in order for a permanent disability report to be complete, the report must include an apportionment determination. This determination shall be made pursuant to Labor Code Sections 4663 and 4664 set forth below:

Labor Code section 4663. Apportionment of permanent disability; Causation as basis; Physician's report; Apportionment determination; Disclosure by employee

(a) Apportionment of permanent disability shall be based on causation.

(b) Any physician who prepares a report addressing the issue of permanent disability due to a claimed industrial injury shall in that report address the issue of causation of the permanent disability.

(c) In order for a physician's report to be considered complete on the issue of permanent disability, it must include an apportionment determination. A physician shall make an apportionment determination by finding what approximate percentage of the permanent disability was caused by the direct result of injury arising out of and occurring in the course of employment and what approximate percentage of the permanent disability was caused by other factors both before and subsequent to the industrial injury, including prior industrial injuries. If the physician is unable to include an apportionment determination in his or her report, the physician shall state the specific reasons why the physician could not make a determination of the effect of that prior condition on the permanent disability arising from the injury. The physician shall then consult with other physicians or refer the employee to another physician from whom the employee is authorized to seek treatment or evaluation in accordance with this division in order to make the final determination.

(d) An employee who claims an industrial injury shall, upon request, disclose all previous permanent disabilities or physical impairments.

Labor Code section 4664. Liability of employer for percentage of permanent disability directly caused by injury; Conclusive presumption from prior award of permanent disability; Accumulation of permanent disability awards

(a) The employer shall only be liable for the percentage of permanent disability directly caused by the injury arising out of and occurring in the course of employment.

(b) If the applicant has received a prior award of permanent disability, it shall be conclusively presumed that the prior permanent disability exists at the time of any subsequent industrial injury. This presumption is a presumption affecting the burden of proof.

(c)(1) The accumulation of all permanent disability awards issued with respect to any one region of the body in favor of one individual employee shall not exceed 100 percent over the employee's lifetime unless the employee's injury or illness is conclusively presumed to be total in character pursuant to Section 4662. As used in this section, the regions of the body are the following:

STATE OF CALIFORNIA
Division of Workers' Compensation
PRIMARY TREATING PHYSICIAN'S PERMANENT AND STATIONARY REPORT (PR-3)

(A) Hearing.

(B) Vision.

(C) Mental and behavioral disorders.

(D) The spine.

(E) The upper extremities, including the shoulders.

(F) The lower extremities, including the hip joints.

(G) The head, face, cardiovascular system, respiratory system, and all other systems or regions of the body not listed in subparagraphs (A) to (F), inclusive.

(2) Nothing in this section shall be construed to permit the permanent disability rating for each individual injury sustained by an employee arising from the same industrial accident, when added together, from exceeding 100 percent.

	Yes	No
Is the permanent disability directly caused, by an injury or illness arising out of and in the course of employment?	☐	☐
Is the permanent disability caused, in whole or in part, by other factors besides this industrial injury or illness, including any prior industrial injury or illness?	☐	☐

If the answer to the second question is "yes," provide below: (1) the approximate percentage of the permanent disability that is due to factors other than the injury or illness arising out of and in the course of employment; and (2) a complete narrative description of the basis for your apportionment finding. If you are unable to include an apportionment determination in your report, state the specific reasons why you could not make this determination. You may attach your findings and explanation on a separate sheet.

DWC Form PR-3
(Rev. 06-05)

STATE OF CALIFORNIA
Division of Workers' Compensation
PRIMARY TREATING PHYSICIAN'S PERMANENT AND STATIONARY REPORT (PR-3)

List information you reviewed in preparing this report, or relied upon for the formulation of your medical opinions:

Medical Records:

Written Job Description:

Other:

DWC Form PR-3
(Rev. 06-05)

STATE OF CALIFORNIA

Division of Workers' Compensation

PRIMARY TREATING PHYSICIAN'S PERMANENT AND STATIONARY REPORT (PR-3)

Primary Treating Physician (original signature, do not stamp)

I declare under penalty of perjury that this report is true and correct to the best of my knowledge, and that I have not violated Labor Code §139.3.

Signature: ______________________ Cal. Lic. # : ______________

Executed at: ______________________ Date: ______________
(County and State)

Name (Printed): ______________________ Specialty: ______________

Address: ______________ City: __________ State: ______ Zip: ______

Telephone: ______________________

DWC Form PR-3
(Rev. 06-05)

Note: Authority cited: Sections 133, 4603.5 and 5307.3, Labor Code. Reference: Sections 4061.5, 4600, 4603.2, 4636, 4660, 4662, 4663 and 4664, Labor Code.

History: 1. New section filed 11-9-98; operative 1-1-99 (Register 98, No. 46).

2. Change without regulatory effect amending DWC Form PR-3, page 3, last sentence in the "Precipitating activity" narrative under the "Subjective Findings" section filed 12-30-98 pursuant to section 100, title 1, California Code of Regulations (Register 99, No. 1).

3. Repealer and new form filed 12-22-2000; operative 1-1-2001 pursuant to Government Code section 11343.4(d) (Register 2000, No. 51).

4. Amendment of form filed 5-20-2003; operative 6-19-2003 (Register 2003, No. 21).

5. Amendment of section and Note filed 12-31-2004 as an emergency; operative 1-1-2005 (Register 2004, No. 53). A Certificate of Compliance must be transmitted to OAL by 5-2-2005 or emergency language will be repealed by operation of law on the following day.

6. Certificate of Compliance as to 12-31-2004 order, including further amendment of section, transmitted to OAL 4-29-2005 and filed 6-10-2005 (Register 2005, No. 23).

Ref.: Hanna §§ 5.05[6][b], 22.02[5].

§9785.4. Form PR-4 "Primary Treating Physician's Permanent and Stationary Report."

STATE OF CALIFORNIA
Division of Workers' Compensation
PRIMARY TREATING PHYSICIAN'S PERMANENT AND STATIONARY REPORT (PR-4)

This form is required to be used for ratings prepared pursuant to the 2005 Permanent Disability Rating Schedule and the AMA Guides to the Evaluation of Permanent Impairment (5th Ed.). It is designed to be used by the primary treating physician to report the initial evaluation of permanent impairment to the claims administrator. It should be completed if the patient has residual effects from the injury or may require future medical care. In such cases, it should be completed once the patient's condition becomes permanent and stationary.

This form should not be used by a Qualified Medical Evaluator (QME) or Agreed Medical Evaluator (AME) to report a medical-legal evaluation.

Patient:

Last Name__________ Middle Initial ___ First Name __________ Sex ___ Date of Birth ______

Address __________ City __________ State ____ Zip _____

Occupation __________ Social Security Number __________ Phone No. ______

Claims Administrator/Insurer:

Name __________ Phone Number __________

Address __________ City __________ State ____ Zip _____

Employer:

Name __________ Phone Number __________

Address __________ City __________ State ____ Zip _____

Treating Physician:

Name __________ Phone Number __________

Address __________ City __________ State ____ Zip _____

You must address each of the issues below. You may substitute or append a narrative report if you require additional space to adequately report on these issues.

Date of Injury________ *Date* Last date worked ________ *Date* Permanent & Stationary date ________ *Date* Date of current examination ________ *Date*

Description of how injury/illness occurred (e.g. Hand caught in punch press; fell from height onto back; exposed 25 years ago to asbestos):

Patient's Complaints:

DWC Form PR-4
(Rev. 06-05)

STATE OF CALIFORNIA

Division of Workers' Compensation

PRIMARY TREATING PHYSICIAN'S PERMANENT AND STATIONARY REPORT (PR-4)

Relevant Medical History:

Objective Findings:

Physical Examination: Describe all relevant findings as required by the AMA Guides, 5th Edition. Include any specific measurements indicating atrophy, range of motion, strength, etc. Include bilateral measurements - injured/uninjured - for injuries of the extremities.

Diagnostic tests results (X-ray/Imaging/Laboratory/etc.)

Diagnoses (List each diagnosis; ICD-9 code must be included) ICD-9

1. ______________________ ______________
2. ______________________ ______________
3. ______________________ ______________
4. ______________________ ______________

Impairment Rating:

Report the whole person impairment (WPI) rating for each impairment using the AMA Guides, 5th Edition, and explain how the rating was derived. List tables used and page numbers.

Impairment WPI% Table #(s). Page #(s)

Explanation

Impairment WPI% Table #(s). Page #(s)

Explanation

Impairment WPI% Table #(s). Page #(s)

Explanation

Impairment WPI% Table #(s). Page #(s)

Explanation

DWC Form PR-4
(Rev. 06-05)

STATE OF CALIFORNIA

Division of Workers' Compensation

PRIMARY TREATING PHYSICIAN'S PERMANENT AND STATIONARY REPORT (PR-4)

Pain assessment:

If the burden of the worker's condition has been increased by pain-related impairment in excess of the pain component already incorporated in the WPI rating under Chapters 3-17 of the AMA Guides, 5th Edition, specify the additional whole person impairment rating (0% up to 3% WPI) attributable to such pain. For excess pain involving multiple impairments, attribute the pain in whole number increments to the appropriate impairments. The sum of all pain impairment ratings may not exceed 3% for a single injury.

Apportionment:

Effective April 19, 2004, apportionment of permanent disability shall be based on causation. Furthermore, any physician who prepares a report addressing permanent disability due to a claimed industrial injury is required to address the issue of causation of the permanent disability, and in order for a permanent disability report to be complete, the report must include an apportionment determination. This determination shall be made pursuant to Labor Code Sections 4663 and 4664 set forth below:

Labor Code section 4663. Apportionment of permanent disability; Causation as basis; Physician's report; Apportionment determination; Disclosure by employee

(a) Apportionment of permanent disability shall be based on causation.

(b) Any physician who prepares a report addressing the issue of permanent disability due to a claimed industrial injury shall in that report address the issue of causation of the permanent disability.

(c) In order for a physician's report to be considered complete on the issue of permanent disability, it must include an apportionment determination. A physician shall make an apportionment determination by finding what approximate percentage of the permanent disability was caused by the direct result of injury arising out of and occurring in the course of employment and what approximate percentage of the permanent disability was caused by other factors both before and subsequent to the industrial injury, including prior industrial injuries. If the physician is unable to include an apportionment determination in his or her report, the physician shall state the specific reasons why the physician could not make a determination of the effect of that prior condition on the permanent disability arising from the injury. The physician shall then consult with other physicians or refer the employee to another physician from whom the employee is authorized to seek treatment or evaluation in accordance with this division in order to make the final determination.

(d) An employee who claims an industrial injury shall, upon request, disclose all previous permanent disabilities or physical impairments.

Labor Code section 4664. Liability of employer for percentage of permanent disability directly caused by injury; Conclusive presumption from prior award of permanent disability; Accumulation of permanent disability awards

(a) The employer shall only be liable for the percentage of permanent disability directly caused by the injury arising out of and occurring in the course of employment.

(b) If the applicant has received a prior award of permanent disability, it shall be conclusively presumed that the prior permanent disability exists at the time of any subsequent industrial injury. This presumption is a presumption affecting the burden of proof.

(c)(1) The accumulation of all permanent disability awards issued with respect to any one region of the body in favor of one individual employee shall not exceed 100 percent over the employee's lifetime unless the employee's injury or illness is conclusively presumed to be total in character pursuant to Section 4662. As used in this section, the regions of the body are the following:

A) Hearing.

(B) Vision.

STATE OF CALIFORNIA
Division of Workers' Compensation
PRIMARY TREATING PHYSICIAN'S PERMANENT AND STATIONARY REPORT (PR-4)

(C) Mental and behavioral disorders.

(D) The spine.

(E) The upper extremities, including the shoulders.

(F) The lower extremities, including the hip joints.

(G) The head, face, cardiovascular system, respiratory system, and all other systems or regions of the body not listed in subparagraphs (A) to (F), inclusive.

(2) Nothing in this section shall be construed to permit the permanent disability rating for each individual injury sustained by an employee arising from the same industrial accident, when added together, from exceeding 100 percent.

	Yes	No
Is the permanent disability directly caused, by an injury or illness arising out of and in the course of employment?	☐	☐
Is the permanent disability caused, in whole or in part, by other factors besides this industrial injury or illness, including any prior industrial injury or illness?	☐	☐

If the answer to the second question is "yes," provide below: (1) the approximate percentage of the permanent disability that is due to factors other than the injury or illness arising out of and in the course of employment; and (2) a complete narrative description of the basis for your apportionment finding. If you are unable to include an apportionment determination in your report, state the specific reasons why you could not make this determination. You may attach your findings and explanation on a separate sheet.

DWC Form PR-4
(Rev. 06-05)

STATE OF CALIFORNIA
Division of Workers' Compensation
PRIMARY TREATING PHYSICIAN'S PERMANENT AND STATIONARY REPORT (PR-4)

Future Medical Treatment: Describe any continuing medical treatment related to this injury that you believe must be provided to the patient. ("Continuing medical treatment" is defined as occurring or presently planned treatment.) And describe any medical treatment the patient may require in the future. ("Future medical treatment" is defined as treatment which is anticipated at some time in the future to cure or relieve the employee from the effects of the injury.) Include medications, surgery, physical medicine services, durable equipment, etc.

Comments:

Functional Capacity Assessment:

Note: The following assessment of functional capacity is to be prepared by the treating physician, solely for the purpose of determining a claimant's ability to return to his or her usual and customary occupation, and will not to be considered in the permanent impairment rating.

Limited, but retains MAXIMUM capacities to LIFT (including upward pulling) and/or CARRY:

[ ] 10 lbs. [ ] 20 lbs. [ ] 30 lbs. [ ] 40 lbs. [ ] 50 or more lbs.

FREQUENTLY LIFT and/or CARRY:

[ ] 10 lbs. [ ] 20 lbs. [ ] 30 lbs. [ ] 40 lbs. [ ] 50 or more lbs.

OCCASIONALLY LIFT and/or CARRY:

[ ] 10 lbs. [ ] 20 lbs. [ ] 30 lbs. [ ] 40 lbs. [ ] 50 or more lbs.

STAND and/or WALK a total of:

[ ] Less than 2 HOURS per 8 hour day
[ ] Less than 4 HOURS per 8 hour day
[ ] Less than 6 HOURS per 8 hour day
[ ] Less than 8 HOURS per 8 hour day

SIT a total of:

[ ] Less than 2 HOURS per 8 hour day
[ ] Less than 4 HOURS per 8 hour day
[ ] Less than 6 HOURS per 8 hour day
[ ] Less than 8 HOURS per 8 hour day

PUSH and/or PULL (including hand or foot controls):

[ ] UNLIMITED

[ ] LIMITED (Describe degree of limitation)

DWC Form PR-4
(Rev. 06-05)

STATE OF CALIFORNIA
Division of Workers' Compensation
PRIMARY TREATING PHYSICIAN'S PERMANENT AND STATIONARY REPORT (PR-4)

ACTIVITIES ALLOWED:

	Frequently	Occasionally	Never
Climbing	[ ]	[ ]	[ ]
Balancing	[ ]	[ ]	[ ]
Stooping	[ ]	[ ]	[ ]
Kneeling	[ ]	[ ]	[ ]
Crouching	[ ]	[ ]	[ ]
Crawling	[ ]	[ ]	[ ]
Twisting	[ ]	[ ]	[ ]
Reaching	[ ]	[ ]	[ ]
Handling	[ ]	[ ]	[ ]
Fingering	[ ]	[ ]	[ ]
Feeling	[ ]	[ ]	[ ]
Seeing	[ ]	[ ]	[ ]
Hearing	[ ]	[ ]	[ ]
Speaking	[ ]	[ ]	[ ]

Describe in what ways the impaired activities are limited:

Environmental restrictions (e.g. heights, machinery, temperature extremes, dust, fumes, humidity, vibration etc.)

	Yes	No
Can this patient now return to his/her usual occupation?	☐	☐

List information you reviewed in preparing this report, or relied upon for the formulation of your medical opinions:

Medical Records:

Written Job Description:

DWC Form PR-4
(Rev. 06-05)

STATE OF CALIFORNIA
Division of Workers' Compensation
PRIMARY TREATING PHYSICIAN'S PERMANENT AND STATIONARY REPORT (PR-4)

Other:

Primary Treating Physician (original signature, do not stamp)

I declare under penalty of perjury that this report is true and correct to the best of my knowledge, and that I have not violated Labor Code §139.3.

Signature: ____________________ Cal. Lic. # : ____________________

Executed at: ____________________ Date: ____________________
(County and State)

Name (Printed): ____________________ Specialty: ____________________

DWC Form PR-4
(Rev. 06-05)

Note: Authority cited: Sections 133 and 5307.3, Labor Code. Reference: Sections 4600, 4061.5, 4603.2, 4636, 4660, 4662, 4663 and 4664, Labor Code.

History: 1. New section filed 12-31-2004 as an emergency; operative 1-1-2005 (Register 2004, No. 53). A Certificate of Compliance must be transmitted to OAL by 5-2-2005 or emergency language will be repealed by operation of law on the following day.

2. Certificate of Compliance as to 12-31-2004 order, including amendment of section, transmitted to OAL 4-29-2005 and filed 6-10-2005 (Register 2005, No. 23).

Ref.: Hanna § 22.02[5]; Herlick Handbook § 4.2(a).

§9785.5. Primary Treating Physician. [Repealed]

Note: Authority cited: Sections 133, 4061.5, 4603.5 and 5307.3, Labor Code. Reference: Sections 139 and 4061.5, Labor Code.

History: 1. New section filed 12-31-93; operative 1-1-94. Submitted to OAL for printing only pursuant to Government Code section 11351 (Register 93, No. 53).

2. Amendment of subsection (d) filed 3-27-95; operative 3-27-95. Submitted to OAL for printing only pursuant to Government Code section 11351 (Register 95, No. 13).

3. Repealer filed 11-9-98; operative 1-1-99 (Register 98, No. 46).

Ref.: Hanna § 22.08[3][b]; Herlick Handbook §§ 1.6, 4.1.

§9786. Petition for Change of Primary Treating Physician.

(a) A claims administrator desiring a change of primary treating physician pursuant to Labor Code Section 4603 shall file with the Administrative Director a petition, verified under penalty of perjury, on the "Petition for Change of Primary Treating Physician" form (DWC-Form 280 (Part A)) contained in Section 9786.1.

The petition shall be accompanied by supportive documentary evidence relevant to the specific allegations raised. A proof of service by mail declaration shall be attached to the petition indicating that (1) the completed petition (Part A), (2) the supportive documentary evidence and (3) a blank copy of the "Response to Petition for Change of Primary Treating Physician", (DWC-Form 280 (Part B)), were served on the employee or, the employee's attorney, and the employee's current primary treating physician.

(b) Good cause to grant the petition shall be clearly shown by verified statement of facts, and, where appropriate, supportive documentary evidence. Good cause includes, but is not limited to any of the following:

(1) The primary treating physician has failed to comply with Section 9785, subdivisions (e), (f)(1-7), or (g) by not timely submitting a required report or submitting a report which is inadequate due to material omissions or deficiencies;

(2) The primary treating physician has failed to comply with subdivision (f)(8) of Section 9785 by failing to submit timely or complete progress reports on two or more occasions within the 12-month period immediately preceding the filing of the petition;

(3) A clear showing that the current treatment is not consistent with the treatment plan submitted pursuant to Section 9785, subdivisions (e) or (f);

(4) A clear showing that the primary treating physician or facility is not within a reasonable geographic area as determined by Section 9780(e).

(5) A clear showing that the primary treating physician has a possible conflict of interest, including but not limited to a familial, financial or employment relationship with the employee, which has a significant potential for interfering with the physician's ability to engage in objective and impartial medical decision making.

(c)(1) Where good cause is based on inadequate reporting under subdivisions (b)(1) or (b)(2), the petition must show, by documentation and verified statement, that the claims administrator notified the primary treating physician or facility in writing of the complete requirements of Section 9785 prior to the physician's failure to properly report.

(2) Good cause shall not include a showing that current treatment is inappropriate or that there is no present need for medical treatment to cure or relieve from the effects of the injury or illness. The claims administrator's contention that current treatment is inappropriate, or that the employee is no longer in need of medical treatment to cure or relieve from the effects of the injury or illness should be directed to the Workers' Compensation Appeals Board, not the Administrative Director, in support of a Petition for Change of Primary Treating Physician.

(3) Where an allegation of good cause is based upon failure to timely issue the "Doctor's

First Report of Occupational Injury or Illness," Form DLSR 5021, within 5 working days of the initial examination pursuant to Section 9785(e)(1) or (e)(2), the petition setting forth such allegation shall be filed within 90 days of the initial examination.

(4) The failure to verify a letter response to a request for information made pursuant to Section 9785(f)(7), failure to verify a narrative report submitted pursuant to Section 9785(f)(8), or failure of the narrative report to conform to the format requirements of Section 9785(f)(8) shall not constitute good cause to grant the petition unless the claims administrator submits documentation showing that the physician was notified of the deficiency in the verification or reporting format and allowed a reasonable time to correct the deficiency.

(d) The employee, his or her attorney, and/or the primary treating physician may file with the Administrative Director a response to said petition, provided the response is verified under penalty of perjury and is filed and served on the claims administrator and all other parties no later than 20 days after service of the petition. The response may be accompanied by supportive documentary evidence relevant to the specific allegations raised in the petition. The response may be filed using the "Response to Petition for Change of Primary Treating Physician" form (DWC-Form 280 (Part B)) contained in Section 9786.1. Where the petition was served by mail, the time for filing a response shall be extended pursuant to the provisions of Code of Civil Procedure Section 1013. Unless good cause is shown, no other document will be considered by the Administrative Director except for the petition, the response, and supportive documentary evidence.

(e) The Administrative Director shall, within 45 days of the receipt of the petition, either:

(1) Dismiss the petition, without prejudice, for failure to meet the procedural requirements of this Section;

(2) Deny the petition pursuant to a finding that there is no good cause to require the employee to select a primary treating physician from the panel of physicians provided in the petition;

(3) Grant the petition and issue an order requiring the employee to select a physician from the panel of physicians provided in the petition, pursuant to a finding that good cause exists therefor;

(4) Refer the matter to the Workers' Compensation Appeals Board for hearing and determination by a Workers' Compensation Administrative Law Judge of such factual determinations as may be requested by the Administrative Director; or

(5) Issue a Notice of Intention to Grant the petition and an order requiring the submission of additional documents or information.

(f) The claims administrator's liability to pay for medical treatment by the primary treating physician shall continue until an order of the Administrative Director issues granting the petition.

(g) The Administrative Director may extend the time specified in Subsection (e) within which to act upon the claims administrator's petition for a period of 30 days and may order a party to submit additional documents or information.

Note: Authority cited: Sections 133, 139.5, 4603, 4603.2, 4603.5 and 5307.3, Labor Code. Reference: Sections 4600, 4603 and 4603.2, Labor Code.

History: 1. Repealer and new section filed 11-9-77; effective thirtieth day thereafter (Register 77, No. 46).

2. Amendment of subsections (a), (c), (d)(4), (e), and (f) filed 11-11-78; effective thirtieth day thereafter (Register 78, No. 45).

3. Amendment of subsection (a) filed 8-9-84; effective thirtieth day thereafter (Register 84, No. 35).

4. Change without regulatory effect of subsection (c) filed 7-11-86; effective upon filing (Register 86, No. 28).

5. Amendment of section and Note filed 8-31-93; operative 8-31-93. Submitted to OAL for printing only pursuant to Government Code section 11351 (Register 93, No. 36).

6. Amendment of subsections (b)(5), (d), and (g) filed 3-27-95; operative 3-27-95. Submitted to OAL for printing only pursuant to Government Code section 11351 (Register 95, No. 13).

7. Editorial correction of subsection (h) (Register 95, No. 29).

8. Editorial correction of inadvertently omitted subsection (d)(2) (Register 96, No. 52).

9. Amendment of subsection (f) and repealer and new subsection (g) filed 12-27-96; operative 12-27-96. Submitted to OAL for printing only pursuant to Government Code section 11351 (Register 96, No. 52).

10. Amendment of section heading and section filed 12-22-2000; operative 1-1-2001 pursuant to Government Code section 11343.4(d) (Register 2000, No. 51).

11. Amendment filed 5-20-2003; operative 6-19-2003 (Register 2003, No. 21).

Ref.: Hanna §§ 5.05[6][b], 5.05[7][b], 22.03[2]; Herlick Handbook §§ 1.6, 4.1.

§9786.1. Petition for Change of Primary Treating Physician; Response to Petition for Change of Primary Treating Physician (DWC Form 280 (Parts A and B)).

STATE OF CALIFORNIA
DEPARTMENT OF INDUSTRIAL RELATIONS
DIVISION OF WORKERS' COMPENSATION
ADMINISTRATIVE DIRECTOR
Post Office Box 420603
San Francisco, CA 94142

PETITION FOR CHANGE OF PRIMARY TREATING PHYSICIAN
(LABOR CODE § 4603 & TITLE 8, CALIFORNIA CODE OF REGULATIONS, § 9786)

(Print or Type Names and Addresses)

WCAB Case Nos. (If any):____________________

EMPLOYEE: ____________________

EMPLOYEE'S ADDRESS:____________________

EMPLOYEE'S ATTORNEY: ____________________

EMPLOYEE'S ATTORNEY'S ADDRESS____________________

EMPLOYER:____________________

EMPLOYER'S ADDRESS:____________________

CLAIMS ADMINISTRATOR:____________________

CLAIMS ADMINISTRATOR'S ADDRESS:____________________

CLAIMS ADMINISTRATOR'S CLAIM NUMBER(S):____________________

NAME OF PRIMARY TREATING PHYSICIAN ____________________

PRIMARY TREATING PHYSICIAN'S ADDRESS:____________________

PHYSICIAN PANEL: List below the **NAMES, ADDRESSES and MEDICAL SPECIALTIES** (e.g.-orthopedics, cardiology, etc.) of a panel of FIVE (5) physicians (to include one chiropractor if the employee is being treated by a chiropractor) available to provide treatment of the employee's injury in the event this petition is granted.

1.____________________

2.____________________

3.____________________

4.____________________

5.____________________

Petitioner states that the following constitutes good cause for issuance of an *Order Granting Petition For Change Of Primary Treating Physician:* (Additional sheets may be attached if necessary)

NOTE: Attach to this Petition any supportive evidence (medical reports, declarations, etc.) that establishes good cause for the Petition to be granted. (See Title 8, California Code of Regulations, Section 9786)

VERIFICATION

I declare under penalty of perjury under the laws of the State of California that the foregoing is true and correct.

EXECUTED AT ______________________, CALIFORNIA ON ______________
(City) (Date)

BY: ______________________ // ______________________
Original Signature of Petitioner's Representative Preparing the Petition // Name of Petitioner's Representative Preparing the Petition (Print or type)

____
(Address of Petitioner)

____

YOU MUST ATTACH A PROOF OF SERVICE BY MAIL DECLARATION INDICATING THAT: (1) PART A (PETITION FOR CHANGE OF PRIMARY TREATING PHYSICIAN) *AND* PART B (RESPONSE TO PETITION FOR CHANGE OF PRIMARY TREATING PHYSICIAN) OF THIS FORM AND (2) ALL SUPPORTIVE EVIDENCE WERE MAILED TO THE EMPLOYEE OR THE EMPLOYEE'S ATTORNEY, AND THE PRIMARY TREATING PHYSICIAN.

Notice to Employee/Employee's Attorney and Primary Treating Physician:

Pursuant to Title 8, California Code of Regulations, Section 9786(d), you may file with the Administrative Director a RESPONSE to this petition within 20 days from the date the petition was served on you. Your Response must be submitted using the *Response to Petition for Change of Treating Physician* form which is contained in Part B on Pages 3 and 4 of this form. You may attach additional sheets as needed to the Response form.

STATE OF CALIFORNIA
DEPARTMENT OF INDUSTRIAL RELATIONS
DIVISION OF WORKERS' COMPENSATION
ADMINISTRATIVE DIRECTOR
Post Office Box 420603
San Francisco, CA 94142

RESPONSE TO PETITION FOR CHANGE OF PRIMARY TREATING PHYSICIAN

(LABOR CODE § 4603 & TITLE 8, CALIFORNIA CODE OF REGULATIONS, § 9786(d))

(Print or type names and addresses)

WCAB Case Nos. (If any):______________________________

EMPLOYEE:______________________________

EMPLOYEE'S ATTORNEY______________________________

EMPLOYER:______________________________

CLAIMS ADMINISTRATOR:______________________________

CLAIMS ADMINISTRATOR'S CLAIM NUMBER:______________________________

NAME OF PRIMARY TREATING PHYSICIAN______________________________

The petition filed by or on behalf of the Claims Administrator does not establish good cause for the issuance of an *Order Granting Petition For Change Of Primary Treating Physician based on the following:* (additional sheets may be attached if necessary)

IMPORTANT: Attach to this Response any supportive documentary evidence (medical reports, affidavit and declaration, etc.) which establishes that there is not good cause for the Administrative Director to grant the Petition for Change of Primary Treating Physician. (See *Title 8, California Code of Regulations, § 9786)*

VERIFICATION

I declare under penalty of perjury under the laws of the State of California that the foregoing is true and correct.

EXECUTED AT ______________________________, CALIFORNIA ON ________________
(City) (Date)

BY: ______________________________ // ______________________________
Original Signature of Person Preparing the Response // Name of Person Preparing the Response (Print or type)

Address:
____

***NOTICE TO EMPLOYEE/EMPLOYEE'S ATTORNEY*: THE PROOF OF SERVICE BY MAIL DECLARATION BELOW MUST BE COMPLETED INDICATING A COPY OF THIS RESPONSE HAS BEEN MAILED TO THE CLAIMS ADMINISTRATOR OR ITS ATTORNEY, AND THE PRIMARY TREATING PHYSICIAN.**

***NOTICE TO PRIMARY TREATING PHYSICIAN*: THE PROOF OF SERVICE BY MAIL DECLARATION BELOW MUST BE COMPLETED INDICATING A COPY OF THIS RESPONSE HAS BEEN MAILED TO THE CLAIMS ADMINISTRATOR OR ITS ATTORNEY, AND THE EMPLOYEE OR THE EMPLOYEE'S ATTORNEY.**

PROOF OF SERVICE BY MAIL

On ______________ I served a copy of this Response to Petition for Change of Treating Physician on
(date)

______________________________ at ______________________________ and
(Claims Administrator or its Attorney) *(address)*

______________________________ at ______________________________ by
(Primary Treating Physician or Employee/ Employee's Attorney) *(address)*

placing a true copy enclosed in a sealed envelope, addressed as indicated above and with postage fully prepaid, in the U.S. Mail at______________________, California. I declare under penalty of perjury under the laws of the State of California that the foregoing is true and correct.

______________________________ // ______________________________
Original Signature of Declarant // Name of Declarant (Print or Type)

Note: Authority cited: Sections 133, 139.5, 4603, 4603.2, 4603.5, and 5307.3, Labor Code. Reference: Sections 4600, 4603 and 4603.2, Labor Code.

History: 1. New section (DWC form 280) filed 12-22-2000; operative 1-1-2001 pursuant to Government Code section 11343.4(d) (Register 2000, No. 51).

§9787. Appeal From Administrative Director's Order Granting or Denying Petition for Change of Primary Treating Physician.

Any order denying or granting the claims administrator's petition whether issued with or without hearing, shall be final and binding upon the parties unless within 20 days from service thereof the aggrieved party petitions the Workers' Compensation Appeals Board for relief in the manner prescribed by Section 10950 of the Board's Rules of Practice and Procedure.

Note: Authority cited: Sections 133, 139.5, 4603.2, 4603.5 and 5307.3, Labor Code. Reference: Sections 4600, 4603 and 4603.2, Labor Code.

History: 1. Repealer and new section filed 11-9-77; effective thirtieth day thereafter (Register 77, No. 46).

2. Amendment of section heading and section filed 12-22-2000; operative 1-1-2001 pursuant to Government Code section 11343.4(d) (Register 2000, No. 51).

3. Amendment of section and new Note filed 5-20-2003; operative 6-19-2003 (Register 2003, No. 21).

Ref.: Hanna § 22.03[2]; Herlick Handbook §§ 1.6, 4.1, 15.2.

ARTICLE 5.1
Spinal Surgery Second Opinion Procedure

§9788.01. Definitions.

As used in this Article:

(a) "Agreed second opinion physician" is a physician agreed upon by an employer and represented employee pursuant to Labor Code Section 4062 subdivision (b).

(b) "Completion of the second opinion process" occurs on the forty-fifth day after the receipt of the treating physician's report by the employer, unless the time has been extended by mutual written consent of the parties as provided in these regulations, or unless the time has been extended as provided in these regulations because the employee failed to attend an examination with the second opinion physician or agreed second opinion physician.

(c) "CPT®" means the procedure codes set forth in the American Medical Association's *Physicians' Current Procedural Terminology (CPT) 1997*, copyright 1996, American Medical Association.

(d) "Income" of a person includes the income of that person's business partner, physician member of the office of a group practice as defined in Labor Code section 139.3, spouse, cohabitant, and immediate family. Income of a second opinion physician does not include income from employment which had terminated prior to the time the physician was selected as a second opinion physician where there is no reasonable prospect of future employment.

(e) "Material familial affiliation" means a relationship in which one of the persons or entities listed in subdivision (c) of Labor Code section 4062 is the parent, child, grandparent, grandchild, sibling, uncle, aunt, nephew, niece, spouse, or cohabitant of the second opinion physician. For entities of the employer, insurer, physician, medical group, independent practice association, administrator, utilization review entity, facility, or institution mentioned in subdivision (c) of Labor Code section 4062, which are not persons, the familial affiliation shall be determined by considering the relationship of all of the officers, directors, owners and management employees, and individual claims administrators and supervisors to the second opinion physician.

(f) "Material financial affiliation" includes all of the following financial relationships between the second opinion physician and another person or entity listed in subdivision (c) of Labor Code section 4062, or parent or subsidiary or otherwise related business entity of a person or entity:

(1) One has a direct or indirect investment worth two thousand dollars or more in the other;

(2) One is a director, officer, partner, trustee, employee, or holds any position of management in the other;

(3) One has a direct or indirect interest worth two thousand dollars or more in fair market value in an interest in real estate owned or controlled by the other;

(4) One has received income of any kind, including gifts, from the other, aggregating three hundred dollars or more within the twelve months prior to the time of selection as a second opinion

physician, except that the following income shall not be counted for this purpose:

A. income for services as a second opinion physician;

B. income for services as a treating physician;

C. income for services as an agreed medical examiner;

D. income for services as a panel Qualified Medical Evaluator selected for unrepresented employees;

E. income from services as a Qualified Medical Evaluator for represented employees.

F. income for services as a Qualified Medical Evaluator for an employer from the first five cases in any twelve month period for the same employer, carrier, or administrator.

(5) One has an employment or promise of employment relationship with the other.

(g) "Material professional affiliation" is any relationship in which the second opinion physician shares office space with, or works in the same office of, any of the other persons or entities listed in subdivision (c) of Labor Code section 4062.

(h) "Parent, subsidiary, and otherwise related business entity" have the same meanings as in Section 18703.1, Title 2, Division 6 of the California Code of Regulations.

(i) "Receipt of the treating physician's report" is the day it was first received by the employer, insurance carrier, or administrator.

(j) "Retired spinal surgeon" is a physician currently licensed in the State of California who once had, but no longer has, hospital privileges to perform spinal surgery described in Section 9788.2(c)(2). "Retired spinal surgeon" does not include a physician whose hospital privileges to perform spinal surgery were either surrendered by the physician or were terminated or not renewed by the hospital, after disciplinary charges were filed or after a disciplinary investigation was commenced.

(k) "Second opinion physician" is the physician who is randomly selected pursuant to subdivision (b) of Labor Code section 4062 to render the second opinion on a treating physician's recommendation of spinal surgery.

(*l*) "Spinal surgery" includes:

(1) any of the procedures listed in the Official Medical Fee Schedule denominated by the following CPT® procedure code numbers: 22100, 22101, 22102, 22103, 22110, 22112, 22114, 22116, 22210, 22212, 22214, 22216, 22220, 22222, 22224, 22226, 22548, 22554, 22556, 22558, 22585, 22590, 22595, 22600, 22610, 22612, 22614, 22630, 22632, 22800, 22802, 22804, 22808, 22810, 22812, 22830, 22840, 22841, 22842, 22843, 22844, 22845, 22846, 22847, 22848, 22849, 22850, 22851, 22852, 22855; 22899; 62287, 62292, 63001 through 63615; and,

(2) any other procedure, which is not listed in subdivision (*l*)(1), which is a non-diagnostic invasive procedure to the spine or associated anatomical structures to perform an operative or curative procedure which is not primarily an analgesic procedure; and,

(3) any procedure which involves the introduction of energy, a foreign substance, or a device that destroys tissue in the spine and/or associated structures, including nerves and disks, or involves the implantation of devices into the spine and associated structures, including nerves and disks, and which is not primarily an analgesic procedure;

(4) Notwithstanding subdivisions (1) through (3), "spinal surgery" does not include penetration of the body by needles in the performance of acupuncture by a practitioner whose license permits the performance of acupuncture, nor does "spinal surgery" include surgery which is required because of a bona fide medical emergency.

Note: Authority cited: Sections 133, 5307.1 and 5307.3, Labor Code. Reference: Sections 4062(b) and 4600, Labor Code.

History: 1. New article 5.1 (sections 9788.01-9788.91) and section filed 7-2-2004 as an emergency; operative 7-2-2004 (Register 2004, No. 27). A Certificate of Compliance must be transmitted to OAL by 11-1-2004 or emergency language will be repealed by operation of law on the following day.

2. Certificate of Compliance as to 7-2-2004 order, including amendment of subsection (*l*)(1), transmitted to OAL 11-1-2004 and filed 12-15-2004 (Register 2004, No. 51).

Ref.: Hanna § 22.06[2][b]; Herlick Handbook § 14.4.

§9788.1. Employer's Objection To Report Of Treating Physician Recommending Spinal Surgery.

(a) An objection to the treating physician's recommendation for spinal surgery shall be written on the form prescribed by the Administrative Director in Section 9788.11. The employer shall include with the objection a copy of the treating physician's report containing the recommendation to which the employer objects. The objection shall include the employer's reasons, specific to the employee, for the objection to the recommended procedure. The form must be executed by a principal or employee of the employer, insurance carrier, or administrator.

(b) Declarations.

(1) Declaration as to receipt of treating physician's recommendation.

The employer's objection shall include one of two versions of a declaration made under penalty of perjury regarding the date the report containing the treating physician's recommendation was first received by the employer, employer's insurance carrier, or administrator, in the format of the form prescribed by Section 9788.11.

Version A of the declaration shall be used if the declarant has personal knowledge of all the facts. Version B of the declaration may be used if the recipient employer, insurance carrier or administrator has a written policy of date-stamping every piece of mail on the date it was delivered to its office, this policy is consistently followed, the declarant is knowledgeable about the policy, and the report bears a legible date stamp showing when it was received in the office.

The declaration must be executed by a principal or employee of the employer, insurance carrier, or administrator.

(2) Declaration as to service of objection.

The employer's objection shall include a declaration made under penalty of perjury, in the format of the form prescribed by Section 9788.11 as to the date and time the objection was served, and the manner in which the objection was served.

The declaration must be executed by a principal or employee of the employer, insurance carrier, or administrator.

(c) Service of Objection.

(1) The employer shall serve the objection and the report containing the treating physician's recommendation on the Administrative Director, the employee, the employee's attorney, if any, and on the treating physician within 10 days of receipt of the treating physician's report containing the recommendation. An objection which is mailed to the Administrative Director and is received more than ten days after the date of receipt of the treating physician's report is untimely unless it bears a postmark date no later than the tenth day after the date of receipt of the treating physician's report. The employer shall serve the original of the objection on the Administrative Director.

(2) Service on the Administrative Director shall be by mail or physical delivery. Service on the employee, employee's attorney, and treating physician shall be by mail or physical delivery or, if prior consent has been obtained from the recipient to be served by fax, may be by fax.

(d) If after an employer has served the objection on the Administrative Director, either the employer and a represented employee agree to an agreed second opinion physician or the employer withdraws its objection to the treating physician's recommendation for spinal surgery, the employer shall notify the Administrative Director within one working day of the agreement or withdrawal of objection. This notification may be by fax.

Note: Authority cited: Sections 133 and 5307.3, Labor Code. Reference: Sections 4062(b) and 4600, Labor Code.

History: 1. New section filed 7-2-2004 as an emergency; operative 7-2-2004 (Register 2004, No. 27). A Certificate of Compliance must be transmitted to OAL by 11-1-2004 or emergency language will be repealed by operation of law on the following day.

2. Certificate of Compliance as to 7-2-2004 order, including amendment of section, transmitted to OAL 11-1-2004 and filed 12-15-2004 (Register 2004, No. 51).

Ref.: Hanna § 22.06[2][b]; Herlick Handbook § 14.4.

§9788.11. Form for Employer's Objection To Report Of Treating Physician Recommending Spinal Surgery.

State of California
Department of Industrial Relations
Division of Workers' Compensation

OBJECTION TO TREATING PHYSICIAN'S RECOMMENDATION FOR SPINAL SURGERY

EMPLOYEE

Last Name	First Name	Other names/initials	Social Security Number	Date of Injury

W.C.A.B. Case No.	Claim No. (If Available)	Telephone (If Available)	Fax No. (If Available)

RESIDENCE ADDRESS: Street	City	State	Zip Code

EMPLOYER

Name

MAILING ADDRESS: Street	City	State	Zip Code

Insurance Carrier:

Claims Administrator:

Company providing utilization review:

Employer health care provider:

EMPLOYEE'S ATTORNEY

Name

MAILING ADDRESS: Street	City	State	Zip Code

Telephone:	Fax Number:

TREATING PHYSICIAN

Last Name:	First Name:	Other names/initials:

MAILING ADDRESS: Street	City	State	Zip Code

Telephone:	Fax Number:	E-mail:

Physician's Medical Group:

Independent Practice Association:

Exact procedure which is being objected to:

Name of facility or institution at which the proposed procedure is to be performed:

Name of facility or institution at which an alternative procedure (if any) recommended by the employer, employer health care provider, carrier, or administrator is proposed to be performed:

DWC Form 233
May 2007

Date that the treating physician's recommendation for this procedure was first received by any of employer, insurance carrier, administrator:

Name of entity which received it on that date:

Type of entity (employer, insurance carrier, or administrator):

NAME OF PERSON SIGNING THIS OBJECTION:

Name:	Company:		
MAILING ADDRESS: Street	City	State	Zip Code
Telephone:	Fax Number:	E-mail:	

Reason(s) for this objection, specific to this employee:

Declaration Regarding Receipt of Report – SEE INSTRUCTIONS

Version A

I declare under penalty of perjury of the laws of the State of California that:

1. I am employed by ________________________.
2. The enclosed physician's report was first received by the employer, insurance carrier or administrator, the name of which firm is ________________________, on ____________ (date).
3. I have personal knowledge of the above facts.

______________________ (Signature of Declarant) ____________ (date)

Version B

I declare under penalty of perjury of the laws of the State of California that:

1. I am employed by ________________________.
2. The enclosed physician's report was first received by the employer, insurance carrier or administrator, the name of which firm is ________________________, on ____________ (date).
3. The firm stated in (2), above, has a written policy of date-stamping every piece of mail on the date it is delivered to its office; this policy is consistently followed; I am knowledgeable about this policy, and the report bears a date stamp showing that it was received in the firm's office on ____________ (date).

I have personal knowledge of the facts in (1) and (3), above, and as to the facts in (2), above, I am informed and believe them to be true.

______________________ (Signature of Declarant) ____________ (date)

______________________ **(Signature of Person Executing Form)** ____________ **(Title)** ____________ **(date)**

DWC Form 233
May 2007

Declaration Regarding Service of Objection

I declare under penalty of perjury of the laws of the State of California that:

1. I am employed by ____.

2. On ______________________, I served the enclosed objection on the persons/firms served,
(date)

and on the Administrative Director, and by the means of service, indicated in the box below. If service is by mail, I further declare that I am readily familiar with the practice of the office stated in (1), above, of collection and processing of correspondence for mailing. Under that practice it would be deposited with the U.S. Postal Service on that same day with postage fully prepaid at ______________________________ California, in the ordinary course of business. I further declare that if served by mail, I either deposited the objection personally in the U.S. Mails, or that I placed it for normal collection with the office stated in (1), in time for collection and processing that same day. If service is by fax, I further declare that I transmitted a true copy to the fax numbers stated in the box below pursuant to oral and/or written agreement by the recipient to receive by fax. If service is by delivery, I further declare that I am familiar with the practice of the office stated in (1), above for messenger delivery, and I caused the objection in a sealed envelope to be delivered to a courier employed by ____ who was to personally deliver each such envelope within two working days to the office of the address at the place and on the date indicated in the box below:

Person/Firm served and Address	Means of service: e.g. mail/certified mail/fax/FedEx Fax number, if by fax	(time, if by fax)
ADMINISTRATIVE DIRECTOR		Cannot fax to Administrative Director

______________________________ ______________

(Signature of Declarant) (date)

DWC Form 233
May 2007

INSTRUCTIONS

Signing and Serving

The declarations and this form must be signed by Principals or Employees of the employer, insurance carrier, or administrator.
This form, together with the report of the treating physician containing the recommendation for treatment which is objected to, is to be mailed to the Administrative Director, Medical Unit, P.O. Box 71010, Oakland, CA 94612, and copies served by mail or physical delivery or fax on the employee, employee's attorney, and treating physician. The objection form and report may be served on the employee, employee's attorney, and treating physician by fax, but only if prior consent has been obtained from the recipient to be served by fax. This form may not be served on the Administrative Director by fax. This Objection must be sent within ten (10) days of the first receipt by any of the employer, insurance carrier, or administrator, of the treating physician's report containing the recommendation.

Declarations

The form contains two declarations to be signed under penalty of perjury. The first is a declaration specifying the date that the report containing the treating physician's recommendation was first received by the employer, insurance carrier, or administrator. The second declaration specifies the date and manner of serving of the objection.

The form includes two versions of the declaration specifying the date of receipt of the report. Only one version needs to be completed. Version A shall be completed by an employee having personal knowledge of the facts of when the report was received, such as the person who opened the mail. Version B shall be completed by an employee who knows from the date stamp when the report was received, if all mail to the firm is date-stamped on the date it is received, the signer is readily knowledgeable about the policy, the policy is consistently followed, and the report bears a legible date stamp.

The declaration regarding service of the objection must be signed by the person having knowledge of how the report was served.

DWC Form 233
May 2007

Note: Authority cited: Sections 133 and 5307.3, Labor Code. Reference: Sections 4062(b) and 4600, Labor Code.

History: 1. New section filed 7-2-2004 as an emergency; operative 7-2-2004 (Register 2004, No. 27). A Certificate of Compliance must be transmitted to OAL by 11-1-2004 or emergency language will be repealed by operation of law on the following day.

2. Certificate of Compliance as to 7-2-2004 order, including repealer and new form, transmitted to OAL 11-1-2004 and filed 12-15-2004 (Register 2004, No. 51).

3. Change without regulatory effect amending form filed 10-18-2006 pursuant to section 100, title 1, California Code of Regulations (Register 2006, No. 42).

4. Change without regulatory effect amending section filed 5-23-2007 pursuant to section 100, title 1, California Code of Regulations (Register 2007, No. 21).

Ref.: Hanna § 22.06[2][b]; Herlick Handbook § 14.4.

§9788.2. Qualifications of Spinal Surgery Second Opinion Physicians.

(a) An agreed second opinion physician may be any California licensed board-certified or board-eligible orthopaedic surgeon or neurosurgeon.

(b) The Administrative Director shall maintain a list of qualified surgeons who have applied, and whom the Administrative Director has found to be eligible to give second opinions under Labor Code §4062 (b) after random selection by the Administrative Director.

(c) To apply to be on the Administrative Director's list, a physician shall demonstrate to the satisfaction of the Administrative Director that the physician:

(1) Is currently board certified either as a neurosurgeon by the American Board of Neurological Surgery or the American Osteopathic Board of Surgery, or as an orthopaedic surgeon by either the American Board of Orthopaedic Surgery or the American Osteopathic Board of Orthopedic Surgery;

(2) Has current hospital privileges in good standing at an accredited hospital in California to perform spinal surgery without proctoring;

(3) Has an unrestricted license as a physician and surgeon in California;

(4) Has no record of previous discipline by any governmental physician licensing agency, and is not then under accusation by any governmental physician licensing agency;

(5) Has not been terminated or had discipline imposed by the Industrial Medical Council or Administrative Director in relation to the physician's role as a Qualified Medical Evaluator; is not then under accusation by the Industrial Medical Council or Administrative Director; has not been denied renewal of Qualified Medical Evaluator status, except for non-completion of continuing education or for non-payment of fees; has neither resigned nor failed to renew Qualified Medical Evaluator status while under accusation or probation by the Industrial Medical Council or Administrative Director or after notification that reappointment as a Qualified Medical Evaluator may or would be denied for reasons other than non-completion of continuing education or non-payment of fees; and has not filed any applications or forms with the Industrial Medical Council or Administrative Director which contained any untrue material statements; and

(6) Has not been convicted of any crime involving dishonesty or any crime of moral turpitude.

(d) The Administrative Director may also accept to be on the list a retired spinal surgeon who does not meet the qualifications of subdivision (c)(2), but who does meet the qualifications of subdivisions (c)(1), (c)(3), (c)(5), (c)(6), and either (c)(4) or (e), if the retired spinal surgeon met the qualifications of subdivision (c)(2) within three years of application. The qualification of such physician shall not extend longer than three years from the last time the physician met the requirements of subdivision (c)(2).

(e) The Administrative Director may also accept to be on the list a physician who does not meet the qualifications of subdivision (c)(4), but who does meet the qualifications of subdivisions (c)(1), (c)(2), (c)(5), (c)(6), and either (c)(3) or (d), if at least five years have elapsed since discipline was imposed, the physician is not currently the subject of a discipline accusation, and the Administrative Director finds that the physician has been rehabilitated.

Note: Authority: Sections 133 and 5307.3, Labor Code. Reference: Sections 4062(b) and 4600, Labor Code.

History: 1. New section filed 7-2-2004 as an emergency; operative 7-2-2004 (Register 2004, No. 27). A Certificate of Compliance must be transmitted to OAL by 11-1-2004 or emergency language will be repealed by operation of law on the following day.

2. Certificate of Compliance as to 7-2-2004 order transmitted to OAL 11-1-2004 and filed 12-15-2004 (Register 2004, No. 51).

Ref.: Hanna § 22.06[2][b]; Herlick Handbook § 14.4.

§9788.3. Application Procedures.

Physicians seeking to serve as a second opinion physician shall:

(a) Make application to the Administrative Director on the form prescribed by the Administrative Director in Section 9788.31.

(b) Furnish certified copies of their board certification and hospital privileges, and shall submit other documentation of their qualifications as the Administrative Director may require.

(c) Both after making application, and after being notified by the Administrative Director that the application has been accepted, the physician shall keep the Administrative Director informed of any change of address, telephone, or fax number.

(d) The physician shall also notify the Administrative Director within 10 days, if the California Medical Board, or any other state medical board from whom the physician is licensed, files any accusation or charges against the physician, or imposes any discipline.

Note: Authority cited: Sections 133 and 5307.3, Labor Code. Reference: Sections 4062(b) and 4600, Labor Code.

History: 1. New section filed 7-2-2004 as an emergency; operative 7-2-2004 (Register 2004, No. 27). A Certificate of Compliance must be transmitted to OAL by 11-1-2004 or emergency language will be repealed by operation of law on the following day.

2. Certificate of Compliance as to 7-2-2004 order, including new subsection (d), transmitted to OAL 11-1-2004 and filed 12-15-2004 (Register 2004, No. 51).

Ref.: Hanna § 22.06[2][b]; Herlick Handbook § 14.4.

§9788.31. Application Form.

APPLICATION FOR SPINAL SURGERY 2ND OPINION PHYSICIAN LIST
For the Department of Industrial Relations
Division of Workers' Compensation
P.O. Box 71010
Oakland, CA 94612

FOR OFFICE USE ONLY
NO.:
INPUT DATE:
INPUT BY:

BLOCK 1 (FOR BOTH NEUROSURGEONS & ORTHOPAEDISTS) PLEASE TYPE OR PRINT LEGIBLY

Please list your primary location. DO NOT USE P.O. BOX. You may provide additional office addresses at which you may schedule appointments on a separate sheet.

LAST NAME	FIRST NAME	MI	JR/SR

BUSINESS ADDRESS	CITY	ZIP + 4

MAILING ADDRESS, if different from above	CITY	ZIP + 4

(AREA CODE) PHONE NO.	(AREA CODE) FAX NO.	CAL. PROFESSIONAL LICENSE NUMBER	EXPIRATION (MM/YY)

BLOCK 2 ALL APPLICANTS

MEDICAL SCHOOL

CITY	STATE	DEGREE	YEAR COMPLETED

ALL APPLICANTS are to furnish their board certification and current hospital privileges.

PLEASE LIST:

Hospital/Facility	Location (City/State)	Type	From	To

Hospital/Facility	Location (City/State)	Type	From	To

DWC Form 232
Title 8, CCR § 9788.31
May 2007

BLOCK 3 APPLICANT MUST MEET ONE OF THE FOLLOWING REQUIREMENTS YES NO

1) I am board certified in neurosurgery by the American Board of Neurological Surgery. ☐ ☐

2) I am board certified in orthopaedics by the American Board of Orthopaedic Surgery. ☐ ☐

3) I am board certified in orthopaedics by the American Osteopathic Board of Orthopaedic Surgery. ☐ ☐

4) I am certified in neurosurgery by the American Osteopathic Board of Orthopaedic of Surgery. ☐ ☐

Date of expiration of board certification:______________________

BLOCK 4 ALL APPLICANTS YES NO

1) Have you ever been formally disciplined by a State Medical Licensing Board?
* If the answer is "Yes", please furnish full particulars on a separate sheet. ☐ ☐

2) Is any accusation by any State medical licensing board currently pending against you?
* If the answer is "Yes", please furnish full particulars on a separate sheet. ☐ ☐

3) Do you currently have hospital privileges in spinal surgery? ☐ ☐

3a) If the answer is NO, have you had privileges in spinal surgery in the past? ☐ ☐

4) Have you ever been convicted of a crime?
* If the answer is YES, please furnish all particulars on a separate sheet. ☐ ☐

5) Have you ever applied to the Industrial Medical Council or Administrative Director to be a Qualified Medical Evaluator?
* If the answer is NO, please skip to Questions in BLOCK 5. ☐ ☐

6) If the Answer to Question 5 is YES: Has the Industrial Medical Council or the Administrative Director ever denied appointment for a reason other than for failing to pass the Qualified Medical Evaluator examination, informed you that it would deny appointment for a reason other than for failing to pass the Qualified Medical Evaluator examination, or filed a statement of issues in regard to your application for appointment?
* If the answer is YES, please furnish all particulars on a separate sheet. ☐ ☐

7) If the Answer to Question 5 is YES: Have you ever filed an application or official form with the Industrial Medical Council or Administrative Director which contained an untrue material statement? ☐ ☐

8) If the Answer to Question 5 is YES: Have you ever been appointed as a Qualified Medical Evaluator? ☐ ☐

9) If the Answer to Question 8 is YES: Has the Industrial Medical Council or the Administrative Director ever suspended or terminated your appointment as a Qualified Medical Evaluator, placed you on probation, filed an accusation against you, denied reappointment, informed you that it would deny reappointment, or filed a statement of issues in regard to your appointment or reappointment?
* If the answer is YES, please furnish all particulars on a separate sheet. ☐ ☐

BLOCK 5 (FOR ALL APPLICANTS)
Most recent hospital privileges in spinal surgery.

Hospital/Facility	Date

DWC Form 232
Title 8, CCR § 9788.31
May 2007

BLOCK 6 ALL APPLICANTS

Physicians may not serve in cases in which they have a material professional, familial or financial affiliation with any of the parties or companies involved. YOU are responsible for determining whether you have one of these affiliations in any particular case, and for recusing yourself, although the Administrative Director will attempt to screen out any cases in which a conflict of interest is apparent from the names of the parties involved. So that the Administrative Director can do this screening, please list the names of all companies with which you have a material professional, familial or financial affiliation, as defined in the Regulations.

Workers' Compensation Insurance Companies

1.	3.
2.	4.

Workers' Compensation Third Party Administrators

1.	3.
2.	4.

Utilization Review Companies

1.	3.
2.	4.

Group Health Plans

1.	3.
2.	4.

Medical Group(s). (Please include the address(es) of the group)

1.	3.
2.	4.

Independent Practice Association(s). (Please include the address(es) of the association)

1.	3.
2.	4.

Hospital or Ambulatory Surgery Centers. (Please include the address(es) of the facility)

1.	3.
2.	4.

Spinal Surgery Related Drugs, Devices, Procedures or Therapies.

1.	3.
2.	4.

PROVIDE ADDITIONAL SHEETS WHEN NECESSARY

DWC Form 232
Title 8, CCR § 9788.31
May 2007

BLOCK 7 ALL APPLICANTS - PLEASE CHECK:

1) That your application is fully completed, dated and signed with an original signature. We will not accept faxed applications.

2) That all necessary documentation is attached:
- ❖ A copy of your current California Professional License.
- ❖ A copy of your board certification(s).
- ❖ Certification of your current hospital privileges.

IMPORTANT: Your application for appointment as a Second Opinion Surgeon shall be returned if it is incomplete, and it must be submitted prior to obtaining your appointment.

BLOCK 8 ALL APPLICANTS
License Status

A. My license to practice medicine is active and is neither restricted nor encumbered by suspension, interim suspension or probation.

B. I agree to notify the Administrative Director if my license to practice medicine is placed on suspension, interim suspension, probation or is restricted by my licensing agency, or if any State Medical Licensing Board files an accusation against me.

Verification

I have used all reasonable diligence in preparing and completing this application. I have reviewed this completed application and to the best of my knowledge the information contained herein and in the attached supporting documentation is true, correct and complete. I declare under penalty of perjury under the laws of the State of California that the foregoing is true and correct.

Executed on ______________ **at** ________________, **CA** ______________________
(MM/DD/YY) **County** **Applicant's Signature**

A PUBLIC DOCUMENT

PRIVACY NOTICE - The Information Practices Act of 1977 and the Federal Privacy Act require the Administrative Director to provide the following notice to individuals who are asked by a governmental entity to supply information for appointment as a Qualified Medical Evaluator (QME).

The principal purpose for requesting information from QMEs is to administer the QME program within the California workers' compensation system. Additional information may be requested if your application is denied and/or a disciplinary action is taken.

The California Labor Code requires every QME physician to meet certain statutory requirements. Physicians are required by the Labor Code to provide: name; business address/addresses; professional education; training; license number; year entered practice and other requirements deemed necessary by the Administrative Director. It is mandatory to furnish all the appropriate information requested by the Administrative Director. Failure to provide all of the requested information may result in the denial of the application.

As authorized by law, information furnished on this form may be given to: you, upon request; the public, pursuant to the Public Records Act; a governmental entity, when required by state or federal law; to any person, pursuant to a subpoena or court order or pursuant to any other exception in Civil Code § 1798.24.

An individual has a right of access to records containing his/her personal information that are maintained by the Administrative Director. An individual may also amend, correct, or dispute information in such personal records (Civil Code § 1798.34-1798.37).

Requests should be sent to:

Division of Workers' Compensation-Medical Unit
P.O. Box 71010
Oakland, CA 94612
(510) 286-3700 or (800) 794-6900
Fax: (510) 622-3467

You may request a copy of the Division of Workers' Compensation policy and procedures for inspection of records at the above address. Copies of the procedures and all records are ten cents ($0.10) per page, payable in advance. (Civil Code § 1798.33).

DWC Form 232
Title 8, CCR § 9788.31
May 2007

Note: Authority cited: Sections 133 and 5307.3, Labor Code. Reference: Sections 4062(b) and 4600, Labor Code.

History: 1. New section filed 7-2-2004 as an emergency; operative 7-2-2004 (Register 2004, No. 27). A Certificate of Compliance must be transmitted to OAL by 11-1-2004 or emergency language will be repealed by operation of law on the following day.

2. Certificate of Compliance as to 7-2-2004 order transmitted to OAL 11-1-2004 and filed 12-15-2004 (Register 2004, No. 51).

3. Change without regulatory effect amending form filed 10-18-2006 pursuant to section 100, title 1, California Code of Regulations (Register 2006, No. 42).

4. Change without regulatory effect amending form

filed 5-21-2007 pursuant to section 100, title 1, California Code of Regulations (Register 2007, No. 21).

Ref.: Hanna § 22.06[2][b]; Herlick Handbook § 14.4.

§9788.32. Administrative Director's Action on Application.

(a) After reviewing a completed application, if the Administrative Director finds that the applicant meets the qualifications, he/she shall notify the applicant by mail, and add the applicant's name to the list of second opinion physicians.

(b) If a physician applicant does not qualify only because the physician has a record of previous discipline by a governmental physician licensing agency and if at least five years have elapsed since discipline was imposed, the Administrative Director shall notify the physician that the physician may within ninety days submit written evidence of the physician's rehabilitation from the offenses or inadequacies for which discipline was imposed. If no evidence is submitted within that time period, the Administrative Director shall reject the application. If the physician submits evidence, the Administrative Director shall consider any written evidence submitted by the physician along with any other evidence the Administrative Director may obtain through investigation. The Administrative Director shall make a finding as to whether the physician has been rehabilitated from the offenses or inadequacies for which discipline was imposed. If the Administrative Director does not find that the physician has been rehabilitated, the Administrative Director shall reject the application.

(c) If the Administrative Director finally determines that an applicant does not meet the qualifications, he/she shall notify the applicant by mail that the application is rejected.

(d) An applicant whose application has been rejected may, within 30 days of the mailing of the notice of rejection, request a hearing by filing a written request for hearing with the Administrative Director. If a written request for hearing is not received by the Administrative Director within 30 days of the mailing of the notice of rejection, the applicant shall be deemed to have waived any appeal or request for hearing.

(e) Upon receipt of a written request for hearing, the Administrative Director shall serve a statement of issues, as provided in Government Code section 11504.

(f) Hearings shall be held under the procedures of Chapter 5 of Part 1 of Division 3 of Title 2 of the Government Code (commencing with section 11500) and the regulations of the Office of Administrative Hearings (California Code of Regulations, Title 1, Division 2).

(g) Failure to file timely a mailed notice of defense or failure to appear at a noticed hearing or conference shall constitute a waiver of a right to a hearing.

(h) An applicant whose application has been rejected may reapply after:

1. one year has elapsed from the date his application was rejected; or

2. the time when the deficiencies which were the reasons for rejection have been corrected; whichever occurs first.

Note: Authority cited: Sections 133 and 5307.3, Labor Code; and Sections 11400.20 and 11415.10, Government Code. Reference: Sections 4062(b) and 4600, Labor Code.

History: 1. New section filed 7-2-2004 as an emergency; operative 7-2-2004 (Register 2004, No. 27). A Certificate of Compliance must be transmitted to OAL by 11-1-2004 or emergency language will be repealed by operation of law on the following day.

2. Certificate of Compliance as to 7-2-2004 order transmitted to OAL 11-1-2004 and filed 12-15-2004 (Register 2004, No. 51).

Ref.: Hanna § 22.06[2][b]; Herlick Handbook § 14.4.

§9788.4. Removal of Physicians from the Spinal Surgery Second Opinion Physician List.

(a) The Administrative Director may remove from the list any physician whenever the Administrative Director learns:

(1) That the physician no longer meets the qualifications to be on the list; or

(2) That the California Medical Board, or any other state medical board from whom the physician is licensed, has filed any accusation against the physician; or

(3) That the physician, having been notified by the Administrative Director of the physician's selection to render a second opinion in any case, has not served the second opinion report in that case within forty-five days after the receipt of the treating physician's report by the employer, unless the employee failed to attend an examination; or

(4) That the physician's application to be on the list contained statements which were not true; or

(5) That the physician has at any time failed to disclose to the Administrative Director that the physician had a material professional, familial, or financial affiliation with any of the persons or entities listed in subdivision (c) of Labor Code section 4062 in any case in which the physician had been selected as a second opinion physician.

(6) That the physician has declined to accept assignment as a second opinion physician at any time except during a period for which the physician had notified the Administrative Director of unavailability per Section 9788.45.

(7) That the physician has filed notifications of unavailability for more than 120 days of any one year period. The first one year period shall commence with the date the physician was added to the list of spinal surgery second opinion physicians by the Administrative Director.

(b) Upon removal of a physician from the list, the Administrative Director shall advise the physician by mail of the removal, the Administrative Director's reasons for removal, and the right to request a hearing on the removal.

(c) A physician who has been mailed a notice of removal from the list may, within 30 days of the mailing of the notice of removal, request a hearing by filing a written request for hearing with the Administrative Director. If a written request for hearing is not received by the Administrative Director within 30 days of the mailing of the notice of removal, the physician shall be deemed to have waived any appeal or request for hearing.

(d) Upon receipt of a written request for hearing, the Administrative Director shall serve an accusation, as provided in Government Code section 11503.

(e) Hearings shall be held under the procedures of Chapter 5 of Part 1 of Division 3 of Title 2 of the Government Code (commencing with section 11500) and the regulations of the Office of Administrative Hearings (California Code of Regulations, Title 1, Division 2).

(f) Failure to file timely a mailed notice of defense or failure to appear at a noticed hearing or conference shall constitute a waiver of a right to a hearing.

(g) A physician who has been removed from the list may petition for reinstatement after one year has elapsed since the effective date of the decision on the physician's removal. The provisions of Government Code section 11522 shall apply to such petition.

Note: Authority cited: Sections 133 and 5307.3, Labor Code; and Sections 11400.20, 11415.10 and 11522, Government Code. Reference: Sections 4062(b) and 4600, Labor Code.

History: 1. New section filed 7-2-2004 as an emergency; operative 7-2-2004 (Register 2004, No. 27). A Certificate of Compliance must be transmitted to OAL by 11-1-2004 or emergency language will be repealed by operation of law on the following day.

2. Certificate of Compliance as to 7-2-2004 order, including amendment of section, transmitted to OAL 11-1-2004 and filed 12-15-2004 (Register 2004, No. 51).

Ref.: Hanna § 22.06[2][b]; Herlick Handbook § 14.4.

§9788.45. Unavailability of Second Opinion Physician.

A physician who will be unavailable to accept assignments for a period of 30 days or more for any reason, shall, at least 30 days prior to a period of unavailability, notify the Administrative Director in writing of the dates of the physician's unavailability.

Note: Authority cited: Sections 133 and 5307.3, Labor Code. Reference: Sections 4062(b) and 4600, Labor Code.

History: 1. New section filed 12-15-2004; operative 12-15-2004 (Register 2004, No. 51).

Ref.: Hanna § 22.06[2][b][ii].

§9788.5. Random Selection of Second Opinion Physician.

(a) Within five (5) working days of the Administrative Director's receipt of an objection to a recommendation for spinal surgery, the Administrative Director shall randomly select a physician from those listed physicians located within a thirty (30) mile radius of the employee's address, provided that six physicians are located within that radius; and if six are not located within that radius, using ever increasing radii, until at least six (6) physicians are located from which a random selection may be made. The Administrative Director shall not include among the six physicians any physician that the Administrative Director has determined, from the information submitted to the Administrative Director by the physician and by the employer objecting to the treating physician's recommendation, has a material affiliation prohibited by subdivision (c) of Labor Code section 4062. The selected second opinion physician shall notify the Administrative Director if he/she has a material professional, familial, or financial affiliation with any of the persons or entities listed in subdivision (c) of Labor Code section 4062, within five working days of the physician's receipt of notification of selection. Upon such notification, the Administrative Director shall immediately select a replacement second opinion physician.

(b) Until the Administrative Director shall have a computerized system for random selection of physicians, the Administrative Director shall manually make random selections as in subdivision (a), except that instead of using an initial thirty mile radius, the Administrative Director shall select from those physicians located within the same zipcode as the employee's address, or if there are not at least six physicians located within that zipcode, then additional adjacent zipcodes shall be used until there are at least six physicians found within the geographic area of selection.

(c) Upon selection by the Administrative Director, the second opinion physician shall, unless the physician notifies the Administrative Director of a material professional, familial, or financial affiliation, notify the parties within five working days of the physician's receipt of notification of selection of the date and time of any appointment for examination of the employee. If the physician arranges an appointment with the employee by telephone, the physician shall thereafter send the employee a written notice containing the details of the appointment.

(d) Within ten days of the selection of a second opinion physician, either the employer or the employee may object to the selection on the basis that the second opinion physician has a material professional, familial, or financial affiliation with any of the persons or entities listed in subdivision (c) of Labor Code section 4062, by filing a written objection with the Administrative Director and serving the other parties. The Administrative Director may either sustain the objection, in which case a new selection shall be made, or deny the objection.

(e) The Administrative Director shall exclude from the selection process any physician who has notified the Administrative Director of unavailability pursuant to Section 9788.45.

Note: Authority cited: Sections 133 and 5307.3, Labor Code. Reference: Sections 4062(b) and 4600, Labor Code.

History: 1. New section filed 7-2-2004 as an emergency; operative 7-2-2004 (Register 2004, No. 27). A Certificate of Compliance must be transmitted to OAL by 11-1-2004 or emergency language will be repealed by operation of law on the following day.

2. Certificate of Compliance as to 7-2-2004 order, including amendment of subsection (c) and new subsection (e), transmitted to OAL 11-1-2004 and filed 12-15-2004 (Register 2004, No. 51).

Ref.: Hanna § 22.06[2][b]; Herlick Handbook § 14.4.

§9788.6. Examination by Second Opinion Physician or Agreed Second Opinion Physician.

(a) The second opinion physician or agreed second opinion physician may physically examine the patient-employee, if the second opinion physician or agreed second opinion physician determines in his or her sole discretion that an examination of the patient-employee is required, but nevertheless must physically examine the patient-employee before finally rendering a second opinion in all cases in which the second opinion physician or agreed second opinion physician disagrees with the recommendation of the treating physician. If there is to be a physical examination of the patient-employee, the second opinion physician or agreed second opinion physician shall schedule the examination, and shall, at least ten days in advance of the scheduled examination, send written notice of the date, time, and place of the examination to the employee, the employee's attorney, if any, and the party who objected to the recommended surgery.

(b) The employer shall, and the employee may, furnish all relevant medical records to the second opinion physician or agreed second opinion physician, including x-ray, MRI, CT, and other diagnostic films, and any medical reports which describe the employee's current spinal condition or contain a recommendation for treatment of the employee's spinal diagnoses. The employer shall serve all reports and records on the employee, except for x-ray, MRI, CT and other diagnostic films and for other records which have been previously served on the employee. If a special form of transportation is required because of the employee's medical condition, it is the obligation of the employer to arrange for it. The employer shall furnish transportation expense in advance of the examination. Except for during the examination, a second opinion physician or agreed second opinion physician shall have no ex parte contact with any party.

(1) In the case of a represented employee, except for matters dealing with the scheduling of appointments, missed appointments, the furnishing of records and reports, and the availability of the report, all communications between a second opinion physician or agreed second opinion physician and any party shall be in writing, with copies served on the other parties.

(2) In the case of an unrepresented employee, except for during the examination and for matters dealing with the scheduling of appointments, missed appointments, the furnishing of records and reports, and the availability of the report, there shall be no communications between any party and a second opinion physician until after the report has been served.

(c) If the employee fails to attend an examination with a second opinion physician or agreed second opinion physician, and the physician is unable to reschedule the employee's appointment before the 35th day after receipt of the treating physician's report, the time to complete the second opinion process shall be extended for an additional 30 days. If a second opinion physician is unable to schedule another examination within the 30 additional days, the Administrative Director, upon request, will select another second opinion physician.

Note: Authority cited: Sections 133 and 5307.3, Labor Code. Reference: Sections 4062(b) and 4600, Labor Code.

History: 1. New section filed 7-2-2004 as an emergency; operative 7-2-2004 (Register 2004, No. 27). A Certificate of Compliance must be transmitted to OAL by 11-1-2004 or emergency language will be repealed by operation of law on the following day.

2. Certificate of Compliance as to 7-2-2004 order, including amendment of section, transmitted to OAL 11-1-2004 and filed 12-15-2004 (Register 2004, No. 51).

Ref.: Hanna § 22.06[2][b]; Herlick Handbook § 14.4.

§9788.7. Contents of Second Opinion and Agreed Second Opinion Physician Reports.

(a) If the second opinion physician or agreed second opinion physician disagrees with the recommendation of the treating physician, the second opinion physician's or agreed second opinion physician's report may include a recommendation for a different treatment or therapy.

(b) Reports of second opinion physicians and agreed second opinion physicians shall include, where applicable:

(1) The date of the examination;

(2) The patient's complaints;

(3) A listing of all information received from the parties reviewed in preparation of the report or relied upon for the formulation of the physician's opinion;

(4) The patient's medical history relevant to the treatment determination;

(5) Findings on record review or examination;

(6) The relevant diagnosis;

(7) The physician's opinion whether or not the proposed spinal surgery is appropriate or indicated, and any alternate treatment recommendations;

(8) The reasons for the opinion, including a reference to any treatment guidelines referred to or relied upon in assessing the proposed medical care;

(9) The signature of the physician.

(c) Second opinion physicians and agreed second opinion physicians shall serve with each report the following executed declaration made under penalty of perjury:

"In connection with the preparation and submission of the attached report of second opinion on recommended spinal surgery, I declare, on the date next written, under penalty of perjury of the laws of the State of California, that I have no material familial affiliation, material financial affiliation, or material professional affiliation prohibited by Labor Code Section 4062, subdivision (c).

____________ ____________

date signature"

Note: Authority cited: Sections 133 and 5307.3, Labor Code. Reference: Sections 4062(b) and 4600, Labor Code.

History: 1. New section filed 7-2-2004 as an emergency; operative 7-2-2004 (Register 2004, No. 27). A Certificate of Compliance must be transmitted to OAL by 11-1-2004 or emergency language will be repealed by operation of law on the following day.

2. Certificate of Compliance as to 7-2-2004 order transmitted to OAL 11-1-2004 and filed 12-15-2004 (Register 2004, No. 51).

Ref.: Hanna § 22.06[2][b]; Herlick Handbook § 14.4.

§9788.8. Time Limits For Providing Reports.

Second opinion physicians and agreed second opinion physicians shall simultaneously serve the report on the Administrative Director, the employer, the employee, and the employee's attorney, if any, as soon as possible, but in any event within forty-five days of receipt of the treating physician's report (as defined herein), unless the parties have agreed in writing to extend the time to a later date.

Note: Authority cited: Sections 133 and 5307.3, Labor Code. Reference: Sections 4062(b) and 4600, Labor Code

History: 1. New section filed 7-2-2004 as an emergency; operative 7-2-2004 (Register 2004, No. 27). A Certificate of Compliance must be transmitted to OAL by 11-1-2004 or emergency language will be repealed by operation of law on the following day.

2. Certificate of Compliance as to 7-2-2004 order, including amendment of section, transmitted to OAL 11-1-2004 and filed 12-15-2004 (Register 2004, No. 51).

Ref.: Hanna § 22.06[2][b]; Herlick Handbook § 14.4.

§9788.9. Charges for Services of Second Opinion Physician and Agreed Second Opinion Physician.

Payment for the services of the second opinion physician shall be made by the employer. The fee shall be:

(a) if the physician examines the injured worker, the same as the fee allowed under Section 9795 for a Basic Comprehensive Medical-Legal Evaluation, without modifiers which might otherwise be allowed under Section 9795(d); or,

(b) if the physician does not examine the injured worker, one half of the fee allowed under Section 9795 for a Basic Comprehensive Medical-Legal Evaluation, without modifiers which might otherwise be allowed under Section 9795(d).

Note: Authority cited: Sections 133 and 5307.3, Labor Code. Reference: Sections 4062(b) and 4600, Labor Code.

History: 1. New section filed 7-2-2004 as an emergency; operative 7-2-2004 (Register 2004, No. 27). A Certificate of Compliance must be transmitted to OAL by 11-1-2004 or emergency language will be repealed by operation of law on the following day.

2. Certificate of Compliance as to 7-2-2004 order transmitted to OAL 11-1-2004 and filed 12-15-2004 (Register 2004, No. 51).

Ref.: Hanna § 22.06[2][b]; Herlick Handbook § 14.4.

§9788.91. Filing of a Declaration of Readiness to Proceed.

(a) If the report of the second opinion physician or agreed second opinion physician concurs with the treating physician's recommendation for surgery, the employer shall authorize the surgery and communicate that authorization to the treating physician within three working days of receipt of the second opinion physician's report.

(b) If the report of the second opinion physician or agreed second opinion physician does not concur with the treating physician's recommendation for surgery, the employer shall file a declaration of readiness to proceed within 14 days of receipt of the second opinion physician's report, unless the parties agree with the determination of the second opinion physician or agreed second opinion physician, or unless the employer has authorized the surgery.

Note: Authority cited: Sections 133 and 5307.3, Labor Code. Reference: Sections 4062(b) and 4600, Labor Code.

History: 1. New section filed 7-2-2004 as an emergency; operative 7-2-2004 (Register 2004, No. 27). A Certificate of Compliance must be transmitted to OAL by 11-1-2004 or emergency language will be repealed by operation of law on the following day.

2. Certificate of Compliance as to 7-2-2004 order, including amendment of section, transmitted to OAL 11-1-2004 and filed 12-15-2004 (Register 2004, No. 51).

Ref.: Hanna § 22.06[2][b]; Herlick Handbook § 14.4.

ARTICLE 5.3
Official Medical Fee Schedule

Physician Services Rendered on or after July 1, 2004.

Inpatient Hospital Services for Services Rendered for an Admission with Date of Discharge on or after July 1, 2004.

Outpatient Services Rendered on or after July 1, 2004.

Pharmacy Services Rendered after January 1, 2004

Pathology and Laboratory Services Rendered after January 1, 2004

Durable Medical Equipment, Prosthetics, Orthotics, Supplies Services after January 1, 2004

Ambulance Services Rendered after January 1, 2004

§9789.10. Physician Services — Definitions.

(a) "Basic value" means the unit value for an anesthesia procedure that is set forth in the Official Medical Fee Schedule 2003.

(b) "CMS" means the Centers for Medicare & Medicaid Services of the United States Department of Health and Human Services.

(c) "Conversion factor" or "CF" means the factor set forth below for the applicable OMFS section:

Evaluation and Management	$8.50
Medicine	$6.15
Surgery	$153.00
Radiology	$12.50
Pathology	$1.50
Anesthesia	$34.50

(d) "CPT®" means the procedure codes set forth in the American Medical Association's *Physicians' Current Procedural Terminology (CPT) 1997*, copyright 1996, American Medical Association, or the *Physicians' Current Procedural Terminology (CPT) 1994*, copyright 1993, American Medical Association.

(e) "Medicare rate" means the physician fee schedule rate derived from the Resource Based Relative Value Scale and related data, adopted for the Calendar Year 2004, published in the Federal Register on January 7, 2004, Volume 69, No. 4, pages 1117 through 1242 (CMS-1372-IFC), as amended by CMS Manual System, Pub. 100-04 Medicare Claims Processing, Transmittal 105 (February 20, 2004). The Medicare rate for each procedure is derived by the Administrative Director utilizing the non-facility rate (or facility rate if no non-facility rate exists), and a weighted average geographic adjustment factor of 1.063.

(f) "Modifying units" means the anesthesia modifiers and qualifying circumstances as set forth in the Official Medical Fee Schedule 2003.

(g) "Official Medical Fee Schedule" or "OMFS" means Article 5.3 of Subchapter 1 of Chapter 4.5 of Title 8, California Code of Regulations (Sections 9789.10 – 9789.111), adopted pursuant to Section 5307.1 of the Labor Code for all medical services, goods, and treatment provided pursuant to Labor Code Section 4600.

(h) "Official Medical Fee Schedule 2003" or "OMFS 2003" means the Official Medical Fee Schedule incorporated into Section 9791.1 in effect on December 31, 2003, which consists of the OMFS book revised April 1, 1999 and as amended for dates of service on or after July 12, 2002.

(i) "Percentage reduction calculation" means the factor set forth in Table A for each procedure code which will result in a reduction of the OMFS 2003 rate by 5%, or a lesser percent so that the reduction results in a rate that is no lower than the Medicare rate.

(j) "Physician service" means professional medical service that can be provided by a physician, as defined in Section 3209.3 of the Labor Code, and is subject to reimbursement under the Official Medical Fee Schedule. For purposes of the OMFS, "physician service" includes service rendered by a physician or by a non-physician who is acting under the supervision, instruction, referral or prescription of a physician, including but not limited to a physician assistant, nurse practitioner, clinical nurse specialist, and physical therapist.

(k) "RVU" means the relative value unit for a particular procedure that is set forth in the Official Medical Fee Schedule 2003.

(*l*) "Time value" means the unit of time indicating the duration of an anesthesia procedure that is set forth in the Official Medical Fee Schedule 2003.

Note: Authority cited: Sections 133, 4603.5, 5307.1 and 5307.3, Labor Code. Reference: Sections 4600, 4603.2 and 5307.1, Labor Code.

History: 1. New article 5.3 (sections 9789.10-9789.110) and section filed 1-2-2004 as an emergency; operative 1-2-2004 (Register 2004, No. 2). A Certificate of Compliance must be transmitted to OAL by 5-3-2004 or emergency language will be repealed by operation of law on the following day.

2. Certificate of Compliance as to 1-2-2004 order, including amendment of article heading, new introductory paragraph and amendment of subsections (d), (e) and (g), transmitted to OAL 4-30-2004 and filed 6-15-2004 (Register 2004, No. 25).

Ref.: Hanna § 22.05[2]; Herlick Handbook § 4.19.

§9789.11. Physician Services Rendered on or After July 1, 2004.

(a) Except as specified below, or otherwise provided in this Article, the ground rule materials set forth in each individual section of the OMFS 2003 are applicable to physician services rendered on or after July 1, 2004.

(1) The OMFS 2003's "General Information and Instructions" section is not applicable.

The "General Information and Instructions, Effective for Dates of Service on or after July 1, 2004," are incorporated by reference and will be made available on the Division of Workers' Compensation Internet site http://www.dir.ca.gov/DWC/OMFS9904.htm or upon request to the Administrative Director at:

DIVISION OF WORKERS' COMPENSATION
(ATTENTION: OMFS – PHYSICIAN SERVICES)
P.O. BOX 420603
SAN FRANCISCO, CA 94142

(b) For physician services rendered on or after July 1, 2004 the maximum allowable reimbursement amount set forth in the OMFS 2003 for each procedure code is reduced by five (5) percent, except that those procedures that are reimbursed under OMFS 2003 at a rate between 100% and 105% of the Medicare rate will be reduced between zero and 5% so that the OMFS reimbursement will not fall below the Medicare rate. The reduction rate for each procedure is set forth as the adjustment factor in Table A. Reimbursement for procedures that are reimbursed under OMFS 2003 at a rate below the Medicare rate will not be reduced.

(c)(1) Table A, "OMFS Physician Services Fees for Services Rendered on or after July 1, 2004," which sets forth each individual procedure code with its corresponding relative value, conversion factor, percentage reduction calculation (between 0 and 5.0%), and maximum reimbursable fee, is incorporated by reference.

(2) Table A, "OMFS Physician Services Fees for Services Rendered on or after January 14, 2005," which sets forth each individual procedure code with its corresponding relative value, conversion factor, percentage reduction calculation (between 0 and 5.0%), and maximum reimbursable fee, is incorporated by reference.

(3) Table A, "OMFS Physician Services Fees for Services Rendered on or after May 14, 2005," which sets forth each individual procedure code with its corresponding relative value, conversion factor, percentage reduction calculation (between 0 and 5.0%), and maximum reimbursable fee, is incorporated by reference.

(4) Table A and its addenda may be obtained from the Division of Workers' Compensation Internet site http://www.dir.ca.gov/DWC/OMFS9904.htm or upon request to the Administrative Director at:

DIVISION OF WORKERS' COMPENSATION
(ATTENTION: OMFS – PHYSICIAN SERVICES)
P.O. BOX 420603
SAN FRANCISCO, CA 94142

(d)(1) Except for anesthesia services, to determine the maximum allowable reimbursement for a physician service rendered on or after July 1, 2004 the following formula is utilized: RVU × conversion factor × percentage reduction calculation = maximum reasonable fee before application of ground rules. Applicable ground rules set forth in the OMFS 2003 and the "General Information and Instructions, Effective for Dates of Service on or after July 1, 2004," are then applied to calculate the maximum reasonable fee.

(2) To determine the maximum allowable reimbursement for anesthesia services (CPT Codes 00100 through 01999) rendered after January 1, 2004, the following formula is utilized: (basic value + modifying units (if any) + time value) × (conversion factor × .95) = maximum reasonable fee.

(e) The following procedures in the Pathology and Laboratory section (both professional and technical component) will be reimbursed under this section: CPT Codes 80500, 80502; 85060 through 85102; 86077 through 86079; 87164; and 88000 through 88399. All other pathology and laboratory services will be reimbursed pursuant to Section 9789.50, including but not limited to: CPT Codes 80002 through 80440; 81000 through 85048; 85130 through 86063; 86140 through 87163; 87166 through 87999; and 89050 through 89399.

(f) For physician services rendered on or after February 15, 2007, the maximum allowable reimbursement amounts for procedure codes 99201 through 99205 and 99211 through 99215 are set forth in the February, 2007 Addendum to Table A, "OMFS Physician Services Fees for Services Rendered on or after February 15, 2007." The February, 2007 Addendum to Table A, "OMFS Physician Services Fees for Services Rendered on or after February 15, 2007", which sets forth individual procedure codes with the corresponding maximum reimbursable fees, is incorporated by reference.

Note: Authority cited: Sections 133, 4603.5, 5307.1 and 5307.3, Labor Code. Reference: Sections 4600, 4603.2 and 5307.1, Labor Code.

History: 1. New section filed 1-2-2004 as an emergency; operative 1-2-2004 (Register 2004, No. 2). A

Certificate of Compliance must be transmitted to OAL by 5-3-2004 or emergency language will be repealed by operation of law on the following day.

2. Certificate of Compliance as to 1-2-2004 order, including amendment of section heading and section, transmitted to OAL 4-30-2004 and filed 6-15-2004 (Register 2004, No. 25).

3. Amendment of subsection (a)(1), redesignation and amendment of former subsection (c) as new subsections (c)(1) and (c)(3), new subsection (c)(2) and adoption of new revision of Table A (incorporated by reference) filed 12-15-2004 as an emergency; operative 1-14-2005 (Register 2004, No. 51). A Certificate of Compliance must be transmitted to OAL by 5-16-2005 or emergency language will be repealed by operation of law on the following day.

4. Readoption of 12-15-2004 order, with additional amendments, filed 5-12-2005 as an emergency; operative 5-14-2005 (Register 2005, No. 19). A Certificate of Compliance must be transmitted to OAL by 9-12-2005 or emergency language will be repealed by operation of law on the following day.

5. Certificate of Compliance as to 5-12-2005 order transmitted to OAL 8-22-2005 and filed 9-29-2005 (Register 2005, No. 39).

6. Amendment of subsection (c)(4) and new subsection (f) submitted to the Office of Administrative Law for printing only as exempt from the Administrative Procedure Act and review by the Office of Administrative Law pursuant to section 11340(g) of the Government Code (Register 2007, No. 7).

Ref.: Hanna § 22.05[2]; Herlick Handbook § 4.19.

§9789.20. General Information for Inpatient Hospital Fee Schedule — Discharge on or after July 1, 2004.

(a) This Inpatient Hospital Fee Schedule section of the Official Medical Fee Schedule covers charges made by a hospital for inpatient services provided by the hospital.

(b) Charges by a hospital for the professional component of medical services for physician services shall be paid according to Sections 9789.10 through 9789.11.

(c) Sections 9789.20 through 9789.24 shall apply to all bills for inpatient services with a date of discharge on or after July 1, 2004. Services for discharges after January 1, 2004, but before July 1, 2004 are governed by the "emergency" regulations that were effective on January 2, 2004. Bills for services with date of admission on or before December 31, 2003 will be reimbursed in accordance with Section 9792.1.

(d) The Inpatient Hospital Fee schedule shall be adjusted to conform to any relevant changes in the Medicare payment schedule, including mid-year changes no later than 60 days after the effective date of those changes. Updates shall be posted on the Division of Workers' Compensation webpage at http://www.dir.ca.gov/DWC/dwc_home_page.htm. The annual updates to the Inpatient Hospital Fee schedule shall be effective every year on October 1.

(e) Any document incorporated by reference in Sections 9789.20 through 9789.24 is available from the Division of Workers' Compensation Internet site (http://www.dir.ca.gov/DWC/dwc_home_page.htm) or upon request to the Administrative Director at:

Division of Workers' Compensation
(Attention: OMFS)
P.O. Box 420603
San Francisco, CA 94142

Note: Authority cited: Sections 133, 4603.5, 5307.1 and 5307.3, Labor Code. Reference: Sections 4600, 4603.2, 5307.1, and 5318 Labor Code.

History: 1. New section filed 1-2-2004 as an emergency; operative 1-2-2004 (Register 2004, No. 2). A Certificate of Compliance must be transmitted to OAL by 5-3-2004 or emergency language will be repealed by operation of law on the following day.

2. Certificate of Compliance as to 1-2-2004 order, including amendment of section heading and subsections (c) and (d), transmitted to OAL 4-30-2004 and filed 6-15-2004 (Register 2004, No. 25).

Ref.: Hanna § 22.05[2]; Herlick Handbook § 4.19.

§9789.21. Definitions for Inpatient Hospital Fee Schedule.

(a) "Average length of stay" means the geometric mean length of stay for a diagnosis-related group assigned by CMS.

(b) "Capital outlier factor" means fixed loss cost outlier threshold × capital wage index × large urban add-on × (capital cost-to-charge ratio/total cost-to-charge ratio).

(1) The capital wage index, also referred to as the capital geographic factor (GAF), is specified in the Federal Register of October 6, 2003 (correcting the rule published on August 1, 2003) at Vol. 68, page 57736, Table 4A for urban areas, Table 4B on page 57743 for rural areas, and Table 4C on page 57744 for reclassified hospitals, which document is hereby incorporated by reference and will be made available upon request to the Administrative Director.

(2) The "large urban add-on" is indicated by the post-reclassification urban/rural location published in the Payment Impact File at positions

229–235. As stated in Title 42, Code of Federal Regulations, Section 412.316(b), as it is in effect on November 11, 2003, the "large urban add-on" is an additional 3% of what would otherwise be payable to the health facility.

(3) "Fixed loss cost outlier threshold" means the Medicare fixed loss cost outlier threshold for inpatient admissions. The fixed loss cost outlier threshold for FY 2004 is $31,000 as published in the Federal Register of August 1, 2003 at volume 68, number 148 at page 45477.

(c) "CMS" means the Centers for Medicare & Medicaid Services of the United States Department of Health and Human Services.

(d) "Composite factor" means the factor calculated by the administrative director for a health facility by adding the prospective operating costs and the prospective capital costs for the health facility, excluding the DRG weight and any applicable outlier and new technology payment, as determined by the federal Centers for Medicare & Medicaid Services (CMS) for the purpose of determining payment under Medicare.

(1) Prospective capital costs are determined by the following formula:

(A) Capital standard federal payment rate × capital geographic adjustment factor × large urban add-on × [1 + capital disproportionate share adjustment factor + capital indirect medical education adjustment factor]

(B) The "capital standard federal payment rate" is $414.18 as published by CMS in the Federal Register of October 6, 2003 (correcting the publication of August 1, 2003), at Vol. 68, page 57735, Table 1D, which document is hereby incorporated by reference and will be made available upon request to the Administrative Director.

(C) The "capital geographic adjustment factor" is published in the Payment Impact File at positions 243–252.

(D) The "large urban add-on" is indicated by the post-reclassification urban/rural location published in the Payment Impact File at positions 229–235. As stated in Title 42, Code of Federal Regulations, Section 412.316(b), effective November 11, 2003, the "large urban add-on" is an additional 3% of what would otherwise be payable to the health facility.

(E) The "capital disproportionate share adjustment factor" is published in the Payment Impact File at positions 117–126.

(F) The "capital indirect medical education adjustment factor" (capital IME adjustment) is published in Payment Impact File at positions 202–211.

(2) Prospective operating costs are determined by the following formula:

(A) [(Labor-related national standardized amount × operating wage index) + nonlabor-related national standardized amount] × [1 + operating disproportionate share adjustment factor + operating indirect medical education adjustment]

(B) The "labor-related national standardized amount" is $3,136.39, as published by the federal Centers for Medicare & Medicaid Services in the Federal Register of October 6, 2003 (correcting the publication of August 1, 2003), at Vol. 68 page 57735, Table 1A, which document is hereby incorporated by reference and will be made available upon request to the Administrative Director and as modified by Medicare Prescription Drug, Improvement, and Modernization Act of 2003, Public Law 108-173, §401, which document is hereby incorporated by reference and will be made available upon request to the Administrative Director.

(C) The "operating wage index" is published in the Payment Impact File at positions 253–262.

(D) The "nonlabor-related national standardized amount" is $1,274.85, as published by CMS in the Federal Register of October 6, 2003 (correcting the publication of August 1, 2003), at Vol. 68, page 57735, Table 1A, which document is hereby incorporated by reference and will be made available upon request to the Administrative Director and as modified by Medicare Prescription Drug, Improvement, and Modernization Act of 2003, Public Law 108-173, §401, which document is hereby incorporated by reference and will be made available upon request to the Administrative Director.

(E) The "operating disproportionate share adjustment factor" is published in the Payment Impact File at positions 127–136 and as modified by Medicare Prescription Drug, Improvement, and Modernization Act of 2003, Public Law 108-173, §402, which document is hereby incorporated by reference and will be made available upon request to the Administrative Director.

(F) The "operating indirect medical education adjustment" is published in the Payment Impact File at positions 212–221 and as modified by Medicare Prescription Drug, Improvement, and Modernization Act of 2003, Public Law 108-173, §502, which document is hereby incorporated by reference and will be made available upon request to the Administrative Director.

(G) For sole community hospitals, the operating component of the composite rate shall be the higher of the prospective operating costs determined using the formula in (2) or the hospital-specific rate published in the Payment Impact File at positions 137–145.

(3) A table of composite factors for each health facility in California is contained in Section 9789.23. The sole community hospital composite factors that incorporate the operating component specified in subdivision (d)(2)(G) are listed in italics in the column headed "Composite" set forth in Section 9789.23.

(e) "Costs" means the total billed charges for an admission, excluding non-medical charges such as television and telephone charges, charges for Durable Medical Equipment for in home use, charges for implantable medical devices, hardware, and/or instrumentation reimbursed under subdivision (f) of Section 9789.223, multiplied by the hospital's total cost-to-charge ratio.

(f) "Cost-to-charge ratio" means the sum of the hospital specific operating cost-to-charge ratio and the hospital specific capital cost-to-charge ratio. The operating cost-to-charge ratio for each hospital is published in the Payment Impact File at positions 161–168. The capital cost-to-charge ratio for each hospital is published in the Payment Impact File at positions 99–106.

(g) "Cost outlier case" means a hospitalization for which the hospital's costs, as defined in subdivision (e) above, exceeds the cost outlier threshold.

(h) "Cost outlier threshold" means the sum of the Inpatient Hospital Fee Schedule payment amount, the payment for new medical services and technologies reimbursed under subdivision (g) of Section 9789.22, and the hospital specific outlier factor.

(i) "Diagnosis Related Group (DRG)" means the inpatient classification scheme used by CMS for hospital inpatient reimbursement. The DRG system classifies patients based on principal diagnosis, surgical procedure, age, presence of comorbidities and complications and other pertinent data.

(j) "DRG weight" means the weighting factor for a diagnosis-related group assigned by CMS for the purpose of determining payment under Medicare. Section 9789.24 lists the DRG weights and geometric mean lengths of stay as assigned by CMS.

(k) "FY" means the CMS fiscal year October 1 through September 30.

(*l*) "Health facility" means any facility as defined in Section 1250 of the Health and Safety Code.

(m) "Inpatient" means a person who has been admitted to a health facility for the purpose of receiving inpatient services. A person is considered an inpatient when he or she is formally admitted as an inpatient with the expectation that he or she will remain at least overnight and occupy a bed, even if it later develops that such person can be discharged or is transferred to another facility and does not actually remain overnight.

(n) "Inpatient Hospital Fee Schedule maximum payment amount" is that amount determined by multiplying the DRG weight × hospital composite factor × 1.20.

(o) "Labor-related portion" is that portion of operating costs attributable to labor costs, as specified in the Federal Register of October 6, 2003 (correcting the publication of August 1, 2003), at Vol. 68, page 57735, Table 1A, which document is hereby incorporated by reference and will be made available upon request to the Administrative Director.

(p) "Medical services" means those goods and services provided pursuant to Article 2 (commencing with Section 4600) of Chapter 2 of Part 2 of Division 4 of the Labor Code.

(q) "Operating outlier factor" means ((fixed loss cost outlier threshold × ((labor-related portion × wage index) + nonlabor-related portion)) × (operating cost-to-charge ratio/ total cost-to-charge ratio)).

(1) The wage index, also referred to as operating wage index in the Payment Impact File at positions 253–262, is specified as the wage index at Federal Register of October 6, 2003 (correcting rule published on August 1, 2003) at Vol. 68, page 57736, Table 4A for urban areas; Table 4B on page 57743 for rural areas, and Table 4C on page 57744 for reclassified hospitals, which document is hereby incorporated by reference and will be made available upon request to the Administrative Director.

(2) The nonlabor-related portion is that portion of operating costs attributable to nonlabor

costs as defined in the Federal Register of October 6, 2003 (correcting the publication of August 1, 2003), at Vol. 68, page 57735, Table 1A, which document is hereby incorporated by reference and will be made available upon request to the Administrative Director.

(r) "Outlier factor" means the sum of the capital outlier factor and the operating outlier factor. A table of hospital specific outlier factors for each health facility in California is contained in Section 9789.23.

(s) "Payment Impact File" means the FY 2004 Prospective Payment System Payment Impact File (October 2003 Update) (IMPFILE04) published by the federal Centers for Medicare & Medicaid Services (CMS), which document is hereby incorporated by reference. The description of the file is found at http://cms.hhs.gov/providers/hipps/impact_rcd_lay.pdf. The file is accessible through http://cms.hhs.gov/providers/hipps/ippspufs.asp. A paper copy of the Payment Impact File, with explanatory material, is available from the Administrative Director upon request. An electronic copy is available from the Administrative Director at http://www.dir.ca.gov/DWC/dwc_home_page.htm.

(t) "Professional Component" means the charges associated with a professional service provided to a patient by a hospital based physician. This component is billed separately from the inpatient charges.

Note: Authority cited: Sections 133, 4603.5, 5307.1 and 5307.3, Labor Code. Reference: Sections 4600, 4603.2, 5307.1 and 5318, Labor Code.

History: 1. New section filed 1-2-2004 as an emergency; operative 1-2-2004 (Register 2004, No. 2). A Certificate of Compliance must be transmitted to OAL by 5-3-2004 or emergency language will be repealed by operation of law on the following day.

2. Certificate of Compliance as to 1-2-2004 order, including amendment of section, transmitted to OAL 4-30-2004 and filed 6-15-2004 (Register 2004, No. 25).

Ref.: Hanna § 22.05[2]; Herlick Handbook § 4.19.

§9789.22. Payment of Inpatient Hospital Services.

(a) Maximum payment for inpatient medical services shall be determined by multiplying 1.20 by the product of the health facility's composite factor and the applicable DRG weight. The fee determined under this subdivision shall be a global fee, constituting the maximum reimbursement to a health facility for inpatient medical services not exempted under this section. However, preadmission services rendered by a health facility more than 24 hours before admission are separately reimbursable.

(b) The maximum payment for inpatient medical services includes reimbursement for all of the inpatient operating costs specified in Title 42, Code of Federal Regulations, Section 412.2(c), effective date October 1, 2002 and revised as of October 1, 2003, which is incorporated by reference and will be made available upon request to the Administrative Director, and the inpatient capital-related costs specified in Title 42, Code of Federal Regulations, Section 412.2(d), effective date October 1, 2002 and revised as of October 1, 2003, which is incorporated by reference and will be made available upon request to the Administrative Director.

(c) The maximum payment shall include the cost items specified in Title 42, Code of Federal Regulations, Section 412.2(e)(1), (2), (3), and (5), revised as of October 1, 2003, which in incorporated by reference and will be made available upon request to the Administrative Director. The maximum allowable fees for cost item set forth at 42 C.F.R. §412.2(e)(4), "the acquisition costs of hearts, kidneys, livers, lungs, pancreas, and intestines (or multivisceral organ) incurred by approved transplantation centers," shall be based on the documented paid cost of procuring the organ or tissue.

(d) Health facilities billing for fees under this section shall present with their bill the name and address of the facility, the facility's Medicare ID number, and the applicable DRG codes. The billings shall include the principal and secondary diagnoses and surgical procedures. They shall also set forth the patient characteristics, including the DRG weight, the charges, the costs for new technology, and the length of stay.

(e) Cost Outlier cases. Inpatient services for cost outlier cases, shall be reimbursed as follows:

(1) Step 1: Determine the Inpatient Hospital Fee Schedule maximum payment amount (DRG weight × 1.2 × hospital specific composite factor).

(2) Step 2: Determine costs. Costs = (total billed charges × total cost-to-charge ratio).

(3) Step 3: Determine outlier threshold. Outlier threshold = (Inpatient Hospital Fee Schedule payment amount + hospital specific outlier factor + any new technology pass-through payment determined under Section 9789.22(g)).

(4) If costs exceed the outlier threshold, the case is a cost outlier case and the admission is reimbursed at the Inpatient Hospital Fee Schedule payment amount + new technology pass-through payment determined under Section 9789.22(g) + (0.8 × (costs − cost outlier threshold)).

(5) For purposes of determining whether a case qualifies as a cost outlier case under this subdivision, charges for implantable hardware and/or instrumentation reimbursed under subsection (f) is excluded from the calculation of costs. If an admission for DRGs 496, 497, 498, 519, 520, 531 and 532 qualifies as a cost outlier case, any implantable hardware and/or instrumentation shall be separately reimbursed under subsection (f).

(f) Implantable medical devices, hardware, and instrumentation for DRGs 496, 497, 498, 519, 520, 531 and 532 shall be separately reimbursed at the provider's documented paid cost, plus an additional 10% of the provider's documented paid cost, net of discounts and rebates, not to exceed a maximum of $250.00, plus any sales tax and/or shipping and handling charges actually paid. For purposes of this subdivision, a device is an instrument, apparatus, implement, machine, contrivance, implant, in vitro reagent, or other similar related article, including a component part, or accessory which is: (1) recognized in the official National Formulary, or the United States Pharmacopoeia, or any supplement to them; (2) intended for use in the cure, mitigation, treatment, or prevention of disease; or (3) intended to affect the structure or any function of the body, and which does not achieve any of its primary intended purposes through chemical action within or on the body and which is not dependent upon being metabolized for the achievement of any of its primary intended purposes.

(g) "New technology pass-through": Additional payments will be allowed for new medical services and technologies as provided by CMS and set forth in Title 42, Code of Federal Regulations Sections 412.87 (effective September 7, 2001 and revised as of October 1, 2003), Section 412.88 (effective September 7, 2001 and amended August 1, 2002 and August 1, 2003 and revised as of October 1, 2003), which document is hereby incorporated by reference and will be made available upon request to the Administrative Director.

(h) Sole Community Hospitals: If a hospital meets the criteria for sole community hospitals, under Title 42, Code of Federal Regulations §412.92(a), effective October 1, 2002 and revised as of October 1, 2003, and has been classified by CMS as a sole community hospital, its payment rates are determined under Title 42, Code of Federal Regulations § 412.92(d), effective October 1, 2002 and as revised as of October 1, 2003, which document is hereby incorporated by reference and will be made available upon request to the Administrative Director.

(i) Transfers

(1) Inpatient services provided by a health facility transferring an inpatient to another hospital are exempt from the maximum reimbursement formula set forth in subdivision (a). Maximum reimbursement for inpatient medical services of a health facility transferring an inpatient to another hospital shall be a per diem rate for each day of the patient's stay in that hospital, not to exceed the amount that would have been paid under Title 8, California Code of Regulations §9789.22(a). However, the first day of the stay in the transferring hospital shall be reimbursed at twice the per diem amount. The per diem rate is determined by dividing the maximum reimbursement as determined under Title 8, California Code of Regulations §9789.22(a) by the average length of stay for that specific DRG. However, if an admission to a health facility transferring a patient is exempt from the maximum reimbursement formula set forth in subdivision (a) because it satisfies one or more of the requirements of Title 8, California Code of Regulations §9789.22(j), this subdivision shall not apply. Inpatient services provided by the hospital receiving the patient shall be reimbursed under the provisions of Title 8, California Code of Regulations §9789.22(a).

(2) Post-acute care transfers exempt from the maximum reimbursement set forth in subdivision (a).

(A) When an acute care patient is discharged to a post-acute care provider which is a rehabilitation hospital or distinct part rehabilitation unit of an acute care hospital or a long-term hospital, and the patient's discharge is assigned to one of the following qualifying DRGs: 12, 14, 24, 25, 89, 90, 113, 121, 122, 130, 131, 236, 239, 243, 263, 264, 277, 278, 296, 297, 320, 321, 429, 462, 483, or 468; payment to the transferring hospital shall be made as set forth in subdivision (i)(1) of this section.

(B) When an acute care patient is discharged to a post-acute care provider and the patient's discharge is assigned to one of the following qualifying DRGs 209, 210 or 211, the payment to the transferring hospital is 50% of the amount paid under subdivision (a) of this section, plus 50% of the per diem, set forth in subdivision (i)(1) for each day, up to the full DRG amount.

(j) The following are exempt from the maximum reimbursement formula set forth in subdivision (a) and are paid on a reasonable cost basis.

(1) Critical access hospitals;

(2) Children's hospitals that are engaged in furnishing services to inpatients who are predominantly individuals under the age of 18.

(3) Cancer hospitals as defined by Title 42, Code of Federal Regulations, Section 412.23(f), effective date October 1, 2002 and as revised as of October 1, 2003, which document is hereby incorporated by reference and will be made available upon request to the Administrative Director.

(4) Veterans Administration hospitals.

(5) Long term care hospitals as defined by Title 42, Code of Federal Regulations, Section 412.23(e), effective date October 1, 2002 and as revised as of October 1, 2003, which document is hereby incorporated by reference and will be made available upon request to the Administrative Director.

(6) Rehabilitation hospital or distinct part rehabilitation units of an acute care hospital or a psychiatric hospital or distinct part psychiatric unit of an acute care hospital.

(7) The cost of durable medical equipment provided for use at home is exempt from this Inpatient Hospital Fee Schedule. The cost of durable medical equipment shall be paid pursuant to Section 9789.60.

(8) Out of state hospitals.

(k) A health facility that is not listed on the Medicare Cost Report should notify the Administrative Director and provide in writing the following information: OSHPD Licensure number, Medicare provider number, physical location, number of beds, and, if applicable, avearage FTE residents in approved training programs. If a hospital has been in operation for more than one year, information should also be provided on the precentage of inpatient days attributable to Medicaid patients.

(*l*) Any health care facility that believes its composite factor or hospital specific outlier factor was erroneously determined because of an error in tabulating data may request the Administrative Director for a re-determination of its composite factor or hospital specific outlier factor. Such requests shall be in writing, shall state the alleged error, and shall be supported by written documentation. Within 30 days after receiving a complete written request, the Administrative Director shall make a redetermination of the composite factor or hospital specific outlier factor or reaffirm the published factor.

Note: Authority cited: Sections 133, 4603.5, 5307.1, 5307.3 and 5318, Labor Code. Reference: Sections 4600, 4603.2, 5307.1 and 5318, Labor Code.

History: 1. New section filed 1-2-2004 as an emergency; operative 1-2-2004 (Register 2004, No. 2). A Certificate of Compliance must be transmitted to OAL by 5-3-2004 or emergency language will be repealed by operation of law on the following day.

2. Certificate of Compliance as to 1-2-2004 order, including amendment of section, transmitted to OAL 4-30-2004 and filed 6-15-2004 (Register 2004, No. 25).

Ref.: Hanna § 22.05[2]; Herlick Handbook § 4.19.

§9789.23. Hospital Cost to Charge Rations, Hospital Specific Outliers, and Hospital Composite Factors.

PROV	NAME	COMPOSITE	HOSP SPEC OUTLIER	COST-TO CHARGE RATIO	OPERATING CCR	CAPITAL CCR
050002	ST. ROSE HOSPITAL	8518.90	42288.50	0.4650	0.43700	0.02800
050006	ST JOSEPH - EUREKA	5163.71	30927.39	0.3791	0.36100	0.01810
050007	MILLS PENINSULA MEDICAL CENTER	6385.51	40970.00	0.2847	0.26200	0.02270
050008	CPMC - DAVIES CAMPUS	6920.34	40963.69	0.2689	0.25400	0.01490
050009	QUEEN OF THE VALLEY HOSPITAL	6278.87	38494.09	0.3324	0.30300	0.02940
050013	ST HELENA HOSPITAL	6453.06	38501.60	0.3562	0.32900	0.02720
050014	SUTTER AMADOR HOSPITAL	4976.59	30927.63	0.4007	0.34600	0.05470
050015	*NORTHERN INYO HOSPITAL*	*7728.46*	*30927.43*	*0.7577*	*0.70900*	*0.04870*
050016	ARROYO GRANDE COMMUNITY					

	HOSPITAL	5313.28	34128.70	0.2772	0.24500	0.03220
050017	MERCY GENERAL HOSPITAL	6442.48	35103.21	0.2045	0.19500	0.00950
050018	PACIFIC ALLIANCE MEDICAL CNTR	9827.02	35057.47	0.4973	0.48500	0.01230
050022	RIVERSIDE COMMUNITY	6225.81	34014.95	0.1856	0.17600	0.00960
050024	PARADISE VALLEY HOSPITAL	7744.84	33596.70	0.3942	0.36300	0.03120
050025	UCSD MEDICAL CENTER	8285.37	33596.47	0.4158	0.38300	0.03280
050026	GROSSMONT HOSPITAL	5974.07	33609.23	0.2692	0.24400	0.02520
050028	MAD RIVER COMMUNITY HOSPITAL	5247.91	30927.41	0.4440	0.42000	0.02400
050029	ST.LUKE MEDICAL CENTER	7770.34	35124.56	0.1168	0.10400	0.01280
050030	OROVILLE HOSPITAL	5893.90	31423.97	0.3975	0.36400	0.03350
050036	MEMORIAL HOSPITAL	5377.83	30927.44	0.3412	0.31800	0.02320
050038	SANTA CLARA VALLEY MEDICAL CENTER	11316.88	41220.79	0.4020	0.35900	0.04300
050039	ENLOE MEDICAL CENTER	5204.44	31424.13	0.3199	0.29600	0.02390
050040	LAC OLIVE VIEW/UCLA MEDICAL CENTER	10318.51	35130.75	0.2674	0.23600	0.03140
050042	*ST ELIZABETH COMMUNITY HOSPITAL*	*5875.16*	*33966.90*	*0.3817*	*0.35200*	*0.02970*
050043	SUMMIT MEDICAL CENTER	8652.27	42286.36	0.3003	0.28900	0.01130
050045	EL CENTRO REGIONAL MED. CTR.	6421.08	30976.17	0.4148	0.39300	0.02180
050046	OJAI VALLEY COMMUNITY HOSPITAL	5188.83	33332.87	0.6713	0.60400	0.06730
050047	CALIFORNIA PACIFIC MEDICAL CENTER	7760.92	40965.57	0.2219	0.20800	0.01390
050054	SAN GORGONIO MEMORIAL HOSPITAL	5879.30	34037.33	0.3634	0.33500	0.02840
050055	ST. LUKES HOSPITAL	9537.43	40963.50	0.3639	0.34400	0.01990
050056	ANTELOPE VALLEY HOSPITAL	7120.39	35126.94	0.2682	0.23800	0.03020
050057	KAWEAH DELTA HEALTH CARE DISTRICT	5752.68	30927.48	0.2689	0.24700	0.02190
050058	GLENDALE MEMORIAL HOSPITAL & HLTH CT	8172.54	35093.73	0.2238	0.20800	0.01580
050060	COMMUNITY MEDICAL CENTER - FRESNO	7713.28	31312.18	0.3339	0.31200	0.02190
050061	ST. FRANCIS MEDICAL CENTER	4976.16	31967.18	0.3196	0.28300	0.03660
050063	QUEEN OF ANGELS - HLLYWD PRES MC	9069.81	35108.53	0.1142	0.10400	0.01020
050065	WMC SANTA ANA	7227.14	34368.80	0.1295	0.11700	0.01250
050067	OAK VALLEY DISTRICT HOSPITAL	5838.12	33807.81	0.3332	0.32800	0.00520
050069	ST. JOSEPH HOSPITAL	5728.32	34317.09	0.2765	0.26700	0.00950
050070	KFH - SOUTH SAN FRANCISCO	6377.58	40956.94	0.8737	0.84800	0.02570
050071	KFH - SANTA CLARA	7312.45	42285.97	0.8371	0.80900	0.02810
050072	KFH - WALNUT CREEK	6728.66	42287.25	0.9025	0.86000	0.04250
050073	KFH - VALLEJO	6649.91	42255.31	0.8792	0.85800	0.02120
050075	KFH - OAKLAND	7411.05	42285.81	0.9410	0.91100	0.03000
050076	KFH - SAN FRANCISCO	7523.88	40959.71	1.0230	0.98200	0.04100
050077	SCRIPPS MERCY HOSPITAL	6765.31	33582.07	0.2634	0.24700	0.01640
050078	SAN PEDRO PENINSULA HOSPITAL	6365.22	35108.08	0.2941	0.26800	0.02610
050079	DOCTORS MEDICAL CENTER-SAN PABLO	8292.63	42285.75	0.1218	0.11800	0 00380
050082	ST. JOHN'S REGIONAL MEDICAL CENTER	6058.97	33342.53	0.3076	0.30100	0.00660
050084	ST. JOSEPH'S MEDICAL CENTER	5805.68	31887.75	0.2239	0.20800	0.01590
050088	SAN LUIS OBISPO GEN HOSPITAL	5896.41	34146.37	0.6916	0.67900	0.01260
050089	COMMUNITY HOSPITAL OF SAN BERNARDINO	8199.69	34049.24	0.2104	0.19100	0.01940
050090	SONOMA VALLEY HEALTH CARE DIST.	6030.01	37294.75	0.4118	0.37200	0.03980
050091	ST. MARY MEDICAL CENTER	10067.78	35124.11	0.2660	0.23700	0.02900
050093	SAINT AGNES MEDICAL CENTER	5262.34	31312.10	0.3450	0.32000	0.02500
050095	WASHINTON HOSPITAL DISTRICT	6582.95	42291.26	0.3580	0.32600	0.03200

050096	DOCTOR'S HOSP. OF WEST COVINA	6202.52	35126.89	0.3741	0.33200	0.04210
050099	SAN ANTONIO COMMUNITY HOSPITAL	5695.85	34032.43	0.0539	0.05000	0.00390
050100	SHARP MEMORIAL HOSPITAL	5856.29	33598.92	0.2766	0.25400	0.02260
050101	SUTTER SOLANO MEDICAL CENTER	8568.74	42213.63	0.2587	0.24300	0.01570
050102	PARKVIEW COMMUNITY HOSPITAL	6752.32	34028.07	0.4642	0.43300	0.03120
050103	WHITE MEMORIAL MEDICAL CENTER	8931.73	35112.69	0.2474	0.22400	0.02340
050104	ST. FRANCIS MEDICAL CENTER	8685.22	35106.28	0.2463	0.22500	0.02130
050107	MARIAN MEDICAL CENTER	5726.44	31967.98	0.2023	0.18300	0.01930
050108	SUTTER MEDICAL CENTER-SACRAMENTO	6618.77	35160.54	0.2191	0.19300	0.02610
050110	LOMPOC DISTRICT HOSPITAL	4976.16	31969.62	0.4431	0.41800	0.02510
050111	TEMPLE COMMUNITY HOSPITAL	8287.13	35091.83	0.3402	0.31700	0.02320
050112	SANTA MONICA HOSPITAL	6027.22	35075.65	0.4022	0.38300	0.01920
050113	SAN MATEO COUNTY GENERAL HOSPITAL	7503.91	40971.27	0.7964	0.72900	0.06740
050114	SHERMAN OAKS HOSP AND HLTH CENTER	5745.28	35110.48	0.2070	0.18800	0.01900
050115	PALOMAR MEDICAL CENTER	5967.55	33597.58	0.3131	0.28800	0.02510
050116	NORTHRIDGE HOSPITAL - ROSCO	7131.09	35110.55	0.1872	0.17000	0.01720
050117	MERCY HOSPITAL & HEALTH SYSTEM	5489.31	30927.41	0.3237	0.30600	0.01770
050118	DOCTORS HOSPITAL OF MANTECA	5146.76	31889.21	0.0734	0.07100	0.00240
050121	HANFORD COMM. MEDICAL CENTER	5344.81	30927.47	0.2635	0.24300	0.02050
050122	DAMERON HOSPITAL	5794.86	31888.60	0.2260	0.21500	0.01100
050124	VERDUGO HILLS HOSPITAL	5464.52	35135.76	0.2933	0.25700	0.03630
050125	REGIONAL MEDICAL CENTER OF SAN JOSE	8965.85	41211.15	0.3134	0.29300	0.02040
050126	VALLEY PRESBYTERIAN HOSPITAL	7697.23	35111.41	0.3098	0.28100	0.02880
050127	WOODLAND MEMORIAL HOSPITAL	5352.47	30927.49	0.3372	0.30800	0.02920
050128	TRI-CITY MEDICAL CENTER	5621.92	33615.49	0.3759	0.33800	0.03790
050129	ST. BERNARDINE MEDICAL CENTER	6836.53	34069.24	0.2409	0.21300	0.02790
050131	NOVATO COMMUNITY HOSPITAL	6377.58	40975.97	0.4536	0.40700	0.04660
050132	SAN GABRIEL VALLEY MEDICAL CENTER	7967.12	35110.09	0.2344	0.21300	0.02140
050133	RIDEOUT MEMORIAL HOSPITAL	5356.05	31430.45	0.5751	0.52300	0.05210
050135	HOLLYWOOD COMM HOSP OF HOLLYWOOD	6932.92	35124.92	0.3562	0.31700	0.03920
050136	PETALUMA VALLEY HOSPITAL	6098.02	37308.23	0.3382	0.31500	0.02320
050137	KAISER FOUND. HOSP - PANORAMA	5502.50	35105.99	0.2648	0.24200	0.02280
050138	KAISER FOUNDATION HOSPITALS - SUNSET	6413.12	35120.05	0.2522	0.22600	0.02620
050139	KAISER FOUND. HOSPITALS - BELLFLOWER	5532.29	35078.81	0.3596	0.34100	0.01860
050140	KAISER FOUND. HOSPITALS - FONTANA	5728.48	34063.73	0.5041	0.44900	0.05510
050144	BROTMAN MEDICAL CENTER	6598.12	35122.62	0.2240	0.20000	0.02400
050145	COMMUNITY HOSP. MONTEREY PENINSULA	6317.44	40466.37	0.5021	0.44700	0.05510
050148	*PLUMAS DISTRICT HOSPITAL MCARE RPT*	*5834.79*	*30927.40*	*0.5771*	*0.54700*	*0.03010*
050149	CALIFORNIA HOSPITAL MEDICAL CENTER	9679.52	35118.26	0.2460	0.22100	0.02500
050150	SIERRA NEVADA MEMORIAL HOSPITAL	5455.00	35034.36	0.4211	0.36800	0.05310
050152	SAINT FRANCIS MEMORIAL HOSPITAL	7886.23	40977.75	0.2482	0.22100	0.02720
050153	O'CONNOR HOSPITAL	6831.37	41215.30	0.2334	0.21400	0.01940
050155	MONROVIA COMMUNITY HOSPITAL	6226.61	35111.57	0.4036	0.36600	0.03760

050158	ENCINO TARZANA MEDICAL CENTER	6079.13	35101.53	0.1131	0.10400	0.00910
050159	VENTURA COUNTY MEDICAL CENTER	8764.60	33340.09	0.4350	0.41700	0.01800
050167	SAN JOAQUIN GENERAL HOSPITAL	8364.07	31886.92	0.4023	0.36500	0.03730
050168	ST. JUDE MEDICAL CENTER	5671.65	34349.58	0.2806	0.26000	0.02060
050169	PRESBYTERIAN INTERCOMMUNITY HOSP	6380.77	35111.96	0.2317	0.21000	0.02170
050172	REDWOOD MEMORIAL HOSPITAL	5193.23	30927.34	0.4090	0.39800	0.01100
050173	ANAHEIM GENERAL HOSPITAL	7468.39	34363.87	0.2870	0.26100	0.02600
050174	SANTA ROSA MEMORIAL HOSPITAL	6255.45	38491.74	0.2049	0.18600	0.01890
050175	WHITTIER HOSPITAL MEDICAL CENTER	6877.59	35099.14	0.1485	0.13700	0.01150
050177	SANTA PAULA MEMORIAL HOSPITAL	5758.22	33341.61	0.5355	0.52000	0.01550
050179	EMANUEL MEDICAL CENTER	6100.50	33806.16	0.2290	0.22300	0.00600
050180	JOHN MUIR MEDICAL CENTER	6596.80	42290.19	0.2343	0.21600	0.01830
050188	COMM HOSP.& REHAB- LOS GATOS	6426.72	41224.59	0.1369	0.12000	0.01690
050189	*MEE MEMORIAL HOSPITAL*	*6994.89*	*40519.57*	*0.4609*	*0.43800*	*0.02290*
050191	ST. MARY MEDICAL CENTER	8164.30	35094.19	0.2627	0.24400	0.01870
050192	SIERRA KINGS DISTRICT HOSPITAL	7302.47	30927.50	0.5488	0.49900	0.04980
050193	SOUTH COAST MEDICAL CENTER	5352.49	34376.71	0.3065	0.27400	0.03250
050194	WATSONVILLE COMMUNITY	7948.33	37468.81	0.2189	0.21200	0.00690
050195	WASHINGTON HOSPITAL DISTRICT	7646.53	42290.06	0.3260	0.30100	0.02500
050196	CENTRAL VALLEY GEN. HOSPITAL	5342.24	30927.42	0.2855	0.26900	0.01650
050197	SEQUOIA HEALTH SERVICES	6390.81	40966.74	0.2605	0.24300	0.01750
050204	LANCASTER COMMUNITY HOSPITAL	5633.69	35104.77	0.2720	0.24900	0.02300
050205	HUNTINGTON EAST VALLEY HOSPITAL	7563.47	35097.49	0.3623	0.33500	0.02730
050207	FREMONT MEDICAL CENTER	5648.97	31430.96	0.5495	0.51600	0.03350
050211	ALAMEDA HOSPITAL	6600.41	42288.82	0.2264	0.21200	0.01440
050214	GRANADA HILLS HOSPITAL	6941.57	35079.52	0.3610	0.34200	0.01900
050215	SAN JOSE MEDICAL CENTER	8340.87	41215.43	0.3514	0.32200	0.02940
050217	*FAIRCHILD MEDICAL CENTER*	*5286.97*	*30927.53*	*0.5556*	*0.50000*	*0.05560*
050219	COAST PLAZA DOCTORS HOSPITAL	7573.18	35091.68	0.2779	0.25900	0.01890
050222	SHARP CHULA VISTA MEDICAL CTR	6690.72	33594.22	0.2425	0.22400	0.01850
050224	HOAG MEMORIAL HOSPITAL PRESBYTERIAN	5354.71	34346.88	0.4076	0.37900	0.02860
050225	FEATHER RIVER HOSPITAL	5109.82	31424.12	0.4140	0.38300	0.03100
050226	ANAHEIM MEMORIAL MEDICAL CENTER	5935.24	34353.19	0.2765	0.25500	0.02150
050228	SAN FRANCISCO GENERAL HOSPITAL	11994.78	42286.03	0.5146	0.49700	0.01760
050230	GARDEN GROVE MEDICAL CENTER	8953.46	35124.56	0.1022	0.09100	0.01120
050231	POMONA VALLEY HOSPITAL MED CTR	7623.45	35098.03	0.2262	0.20900	0.01720
050232	FRENCH HOSPITAL MEDICAL CENTER	5320.20	34131.37	0.2515	0.22600	0.02550
050234	SHARP CORONADO HOSPITAL	5803.04	33583.04	0.2808	0.26300	0.01780
050235	PROVIDENCE SAINT JOSEPH MED. CENTER	6067.45	35102.02	0.2960	0.27200	0.02400
050236	SIMI VALLEY HOSPITAL	5708.67	35066.52	0.3289	0.31700	0.01190
050238	METHODIST HOSPITAL OF SO. CALIF.	5824.03	35134.01	0.2789	0.24500	0.03390
050239	GLENDALE ADVENTIST MEDICAL CENTER	7786.41	35095.68	0.3107	0.28800	0.02270
050240	CENTINELA HOSPITAL MEDICAL CENTER	7402.95	35130.04	0.3690	0.32600	0.04300
050242	DOMINICAN SANTA CRUZ HOSPITAL	6432.74	37438.20	0.3198	0.29000	0.02980
050243	DESERT HOSPITAL	6319.96	34085.73	0.1168	0.10100	0.01580
050245	ARROWHEAD REGIONAL MEDICAL CENTER	8536.83	34218.75	0.4889	0.34600	0.14290
050248	NATIVIDAD MEDICAL CENTER	10296.87	40444.33	0.2912	0.25200	0.03920

050251	*LASSEN COMMUNITY HOSPITAL*	*5716.37*	*32499.51*	*0.5571*	*0.52800*	*0.02910*
050253	BELLWOOD GENERAL HOSPITAL	7167.12	34357.09	0.4294	0.39400	0.03540
050254	MARSHALL HOSPITAL	5688.25	35159.08	0.3931	0.34700	0.04610
050256	ORTHOPAEDIC HOSPITAL	8255.59	35090.32	0.3877	0.36200	0.02570
050257	GOOD SAMARITAN HOSPITAL	5342.24	30927.53	0.3670	0.33000	0.03700
050261	SIERRA VIEW DISTRICT HOSPITAL	5886.24	30927.69	0.3591	0.30200	0.05710
050262	UCLA MEDICAL CENTER	8543.27	35102.65	0.4030	0.37000	0.03300
050264	SAN LEANDRO HOSPITAL	6873.42	42290.13	0.2298	0.21200	0.01780
050267	DANIEL FREEMAN MEMORIAL HOSPITAL	7407.98	35158.52	0.1357	0.11500	0.02070
050270	SMH - CHULA VISTA	7423.07	33612.36	0.2880	0.26000	0.02800
050272	REDLANDS COMMUNITY HOSPITAL	5557.04	34041.84	0.3175	0.29100	0.02650
050276	CONTRA COSTA REGIONAL MEDICAL CNTR	10372.55	42293.09	0.6541	0.58300	0.07110
050277	PACIFIC HOSPITAL OF LONG BEACH	8407.69	35120.34	0.1976	0.17700	0.02060
050278	PROVIDENCE HOLY CROSS MED. CENTER	6404.19	35084.60	0.2540	0.23900	0.01500
050279	*HI - DESERT MEDICAL CENTER*	*6375.54*	*34060.32*	*0.5186*	*0.46400*	*0.05460*
050280	MERCY MEDICAL CENTER REDDING	6161.72	33966.81	0.2756	0.25400	0.02160
050281	ALHAMBRA HOSPITAL	9105.23	35076.23	0.3363	0.32000	0.01630
050283	VALLEY MEMORIAL HOSPITAL	6595.45	42292.76	0.2358	0.21100	0.02480
050289	SETON MEDICAL CENTER	7701.79	40972.30	0.2326	0.21200	0.02060
050290	SAINT JOHN'S HOSPITAL	5471.17	35094.20	0.2121	0.19700	0.01510
050291	SUTTER MEDICAL CENTER OF SANTA ROSA	8301.24	37320.99	0.4280	0.41000	0.01800
050292	RIVERSIDE COUNTY REGIONAL MED CENTER	7715.67	34091.62	0.4570	0.39200	0.06500
050295	MERCY HOSPITAL	5239.89	30927.54	0.3786	0.33900	0.03960
050296	HAZEL HAWKINS MEM. HOSPITAL	6966.12	40499.95	0.4622	0.42900	0.03320
050298	BARSTOW COMMUNITY HOSPITAL	5879.30	34066.24	0.2681	0.23800	0.03010
050299	NORTHRIDGE HOSPITAL MEDICAL CENTERS	8717.55	35082.94	0.2704	0.25500	0.01540
050300	ST MARY REGIONAL MEDICAL CENTER	6492.36	34035.96	0.3097	0.28600	0.02370
050301	UKIAH VALLEY MEDICAL CENTER	5342.24	30927.35	0.2985	0.28900	0.00950
050305	ALTA BATES MEDICAL CENTER	7641.45	42290.32	0.2379	0.21900	0.01890
050308	EL CAMINO HOSPITAL	6429.45	41210.45	0.3369	0.31600	0.02090
050309	SUTTER ROSEVILLE MEDICAL CENTER	5679.83	35161.16	0.1568	0.13800	0.01880
050312	REDDING MEDICAL CENTER	5440.30	33974.79	0.0846	0.08200	0.00260
050313	SUTTER TRACY COMMUNITY HOSPITAL	5203.45	31886.53	0.2541	0.22800	0.02610
050315	KERN MEDICAL CENTER	8445.81	30927.42	0.3957	0.37200	0.02370
050320	ALAMEDA COUNTY MEDICAL CENTER	11104.70	42285.57	0.5491	0.53300	0.01610
050324	SCRIPPS MEM HOSPITAL-LA JOLLA	5242.66	33594.58	0.2751	0.25400	0.02110
050325	TUOLUMNE GENERAL HOSPITAL	5790.03	33525.06	0.4536	0.43600	0.01760
050327	LOMA LINDA UNIVERSITY MEDICAL CTR.	8304.85	34044.74	0.3395	0.31000	0.02950
050329	CORONA REGIONAL MEDICAL CENTER	6168.85	34040.75	0.2397	0.22000	0.01970
050331	HEALSDBURG GENERAL HOSPITAL	5806.06	37331.20	0.6056	0.59300	0.01260
050333	*SENECA DISTRICT HOSPITAL*	*6589.36*	*30927.41*	*0.5842*	*0.55100*	*0.03320*
050334	SALINAS VALLEY MEMORIAL HOSPITAL	6699.99	40515.18	0.5490	0.51900	0.03000
050335	SONORA COMMUNITY HOSPITAL	5217.48	33523.30	0.3512	0.33300	0.01820
050336	LODI MEMORIAL HOSPITAL	5371.11	31887.99	0.1796	0.16800	0.01160
050342	PIONEERS MEM. HOSPITAL	5342.24	30927.65	0.4822	0.41200	0.07020
050348	UCI MEDICAL CENTER	9516.61	34348.58	0.2479	0.23000	0.01790
050349	CORCORAN DISTRICT HOSPITAL	5342.24	30927.38	0.5201	0.49700	0.02310

050350	BEVERLY COMMUNITY HOSPITAL	7447.59	35084.42	0.3570	0.33600	0.02100
050351	TORRANCE MEMORIAL MEDICAL CENTER	5610.31	35109.50	0.2540	0.23100	0.02300
050352	*BARTON MEMORIAL HOSP*	*6006.40*	*35136.65*	*0.4390*	*0.40000*	*0.03900*
050353	LITTLE COMPANY OF MARY HOSPITAL	5816.36	35102.60	0.3202	0.29400	0.02620
050355	*SIERRA VALLEY DISTRICT HOSPITAL*	*5414.54*	*30927.45*	*0.4420*	*0.41100*	*0.03100*
050357	GOLETA VALLEY COTTAGE HOSPITAL	4976.16	31969.93	0.2798	0.26600	0.01380
050359	TULARE DISTRICT HOSPITAL	5778.91	30927.48	0.5066	0.46500	0.04160
050360	MARIN GENERAL HOSPITAL	6551.67	40969.80	0.3724	0.34300	0.02940
050366	*MARK TWAIN ST. JOSEPHS HOPITAL*	*6492.49*	*30927.45*	*0.3930*	*0.36600*	*0.02700*
050367	NORTHBAY MEDICAL CENTER	7025.81	38487.91	0.2429	0.21900	0.02390
050369	CVMC - QUEEN OF THE VALLEY	7816.48	35093.32	0.3011	0.28000	0.02110
050373	LAC+USC MEDICAL CENTER	10218.83	35085.24	0.2489	0.23400	0.01490
050376	HARBOR-UCLA MEDICAL CENTER	10538.45	35052.73	0.1814	0.17800	0.00340
050378	PACIFICA OF THE VALLEY	8920.71	35111.81	0.4611	0.41800	0.04310
050379	*MERCY WESTSIDE HOSPITAL*	*6174.48*	*30927.44*	*0.8853*	*0.82700*	*0.05830*
050380	GOOD SAMARITAN HOSPITAL	6427.47	41214.90	0.3331	0.30600	0.02710
050382	CVMC - INTERCOMMUNITY	6787.42	35095.07	0.3126	0.29000	0.02260
050385	PALM DRIVE HOSPITAL	5806.06	37306.38	0.5660	0.52500	0.04100
050390	HEMET VALLEY MEDICAL CENTER	5989.00	34044.48	0.3361	0.30700	0.02910
050391	SANTA TERESITA HOSPITAL	6062.82	35093.61	0.4131	0.38400	0.02910
050392	*TRINITY HOSPITAL*	*8130.07*	*30927.29*	*0.5827*	*0.57800*	*0.00470*
050393	DOWNEY REGIONAL MED CTR	6939.85	35114.44	0.2779	0.25100	0.02690
050394	COMM MEM HOSP OF SAN BUENAVENTURA	5200.51	33338.72	0.2343	0.22200	0.01230
050396	SANTA BARBARA COTTAGE HOSPITAL	5554.58	31968.71	0.2354	0.21700	0.01840
050397	*COALINGA REGIONAL MEDICAL CENTER*	*9883.78*	*31311.21*	*0.6421*	*0.54900*	*0.09310*
050407	CHINESE HOSPITAL	7076.82	40962.50	0.4741	0.45000	0.02410
050410	SANGER GENERAL HOSPITAL	5408.67	31312.48	0.6051	0.58000	0.02510
050411	KAISER FOUNDATION HOSPITALS -HARBOR	5519.41	35131.44	0.3153	0.27800	0.03730
050414	MERCY HOSPITAL OF FOLSOM	5468.96	35138.83	0.2653	0.24100	0.02430
050417	*SUTTER COAST HOSPITAL*	*6158.64*	*30927.60*	*0.5541*	*0.48300*	*0.07110*
050419	*MERCY MEDICAL CENTER MT. SHASTA*	*5655.40*	*33966.34*	*0.3820*	*0.35100*	*0.03100*
050420	ROBERT F. KENNEDY	7871.62	35113.22	0.3559	0.32200	0.03390
050423	*PALO VERDE HOSPITAL*	*5879.30*	*34034.55*	*0.3740*	*0.34600*	*0.02800*
050424	SCRIPPS GREEN HOSPITAL	5873.96	33597.65	0.3153	0.29000	0.02530
050425	KFH - SACRAMENTO	5729.90	35103.40	0.9724	0.92700	0.04540
050426	WEST ANAHEIM MED CTR	6458.87	34357.55	0.1952	0.17900	0.01620
050430	MODOC MEDICAL CENTER	6829.63	30927.39	0.6405	0.61000	0.03050
050432	GARFIELD MEDICAL CTR.	9813.97	35047.95	0.0709	0.07000	0.00090
050433	INDIAN VALLEY HOSPITAL	6794.19	30927.38	0.6526	0.62400	0.02860
050434	COLUSA COMMUNITY HOSPITAL	7871.23	30927.42	0.5631	0.53100	0.03210
050435	FALLBROOK DISTRICT HOSPITAL	6046.57	33571.20	0.2715	0.25800	0.01350
050438	HUNTINGTON MEMORIAL HOSPITAL	6348.94	35112.83	0.3303	0.29900	0.03130
050441	STANFORD HOSPITAL AND CLINICS	9270.96	41218.32	0.4083	0.36900	0.03930
050444	SUTTER MERCED MEDICAL CENTER	6658.33	30927.54	0.2374	0.21300	0.02440
050447	VILLA VIEW COMMUNITY HOSPITAL	7980.34	33593.92	0.6255	0.57800	0.04750
050448	RIDGECREST REGIONAL HOSPITAL	5222.60	30927.46	0.4417	0.40900	0.03270
050454	UC SAN FRANCISCO MEDICAL CENTER	11563.78	40969.80	0.2964	0.27300	0.02340
050455	SAN JOAQUIN COMMUNITY HOSPITAL	5914.82	30927.40	0.3184	0.30200	0.01640
050456	GARDENA PHYSICIAN'S HOSP INC	5571.10	35120.72	0.5060	0.45300	0.05300
050457	ST. MARY MEDICAL CENTER	7812.98	42291.55	0.2446	0.22200	0.02260
050464	DOCTORS MEDICAL CENTER OF					

	MODESTO	6839.89	33805.13	0.0548	0.05300	0.00180
050468	MEMORIAL HOSPITAL OF GARDENA	7288.15	35087.01	0.3124	0.29300	0.01940
050469	COLORADO RIVER MEDICAL CENTER	6586.06	30927.51	0.3067	0.27800	0.02870
050470	SELMA COMMUNITY HOSPITAL	5354.91	31312.17	0.2099	0.19600	0.01390
050471	GOOD SAMARITAN HOSPITAL	7382.30	35108.75	0.3460	0.31500	0.03100
050476	SUTTER LAKESIDE HOSPITAL	6505.72	30927.47	0.4729	0.43600	0.03690
050477	MIDWAY HOSPITAL MEDICAL CENTER	6482.73	35150.17	0.0979	0.08400	0.01390
050478	SANTA YNEZ VALLEY COTTAGE HOSPITAL	6596.12	31968.49	0.5204	0.47700	0.04340
050481	WEST HILLS REG MEDICAL CENTER	5471.63	35116.84	0.2444	0.22000	0.02440
050485	LONG BEACH MEMORIAL MEDICAL CENTER	6557.28	35089.74	0.4409	0.41200	0.02890
050488	EDEN MEDICAL CENTER	6866.84	42287.37	0.2837	0.27000	0.01370
050491	SANTA ANA HOSPITAL MEDICAL CENTER	5933.92	34414.54	0.2145	0.18200	0.03250
050492	CLOVIS COMMUNITY HOSPITAL	5398.86	31311.53	0.3587	0.31600	0.04270
050494	TAHOE FOREST HOSPITAL	7954.15	35047.31	0.5148	0.47600	0.03880
050496	MT. DIABLO MEDICAL CENTER	6863.33	42289.50	0.2034	0.18900	0.01440
050497	DOS PALOS MEMORIAL HOSPITAL	5342.24	30927.66	0.4365	0.37100	0.06550
050498	SUTTER AUBURN FAITH HOSPITAL	5642.87	35139.60	0.2722	0.24700	0.02520
050502	ST. VINCENT MEDICAL CENTER	7658.32	35106.84	0.2443	0.22300	0.02130
050503	SCRIPPS MEM HOSP - ENCINITAS	5244.16	33592.88	0.3037	0.28100	0.02270
050506	SIERRA VISTA REGINAL MED CTR	5606.84	34134.11	0.0963	0.08800	0.00830
050510	KFH - SAN RAFAEL	6585.05	42287.19	0.6649	0.63400	0.03090
050512	KFH - HAYWARD	6662.49	42285.39	0.8925	0.86800	0.02450
050515	KAISER FOUND. HOSPITALS - SAN DIEGO	5327.59	33603.08	0.3098	0.28300	0.02680
050516	MERCY SAN JUAN HOSPITAL	6431.84	35148.09	0.2342	0.21000	0.02420
050517	VICTOR VALLEY COMMUNITY HOSP.	7531.44	34039.12	0.3327	0.30600	0.02670
050523	SUTTER DELTA MEDICAL CENTER	7053.61	42289.23	0.2693	0.25100	0.01830
050526	HUNTINGTON BEACH MEDICAL CENTER	6480.96	34384.77	0.2601	0.23000	0.03010
050528	MEMORIAL HOSPITAL - LOS BANOS	6750.48	30927.42	0.2286	0.21500	0.01360
050531	BELLFLOWER MEDICAL CENTER	8184.24	35075.56	0.2520	0.24000	0.01200
050534	JOHN.F. KENNEDY MEMORIAL HOSP.	7621.77	34010.74	0.1668	0.15900	0.00780
050535	COASTAL COMMUNITIES HOSPITAL	8350.15	34382.31	0.1747	0.15500	0.01970
050537	SUTTER DAVIS HOSPITAL	5291.46	30927.72	0.2895	0.24000	0.04950
050539	REDBUD COMMUNITY HOSPITAL	5681.73	30927.46	0.3671	0.34000	0.02710
050541	KFH - REDWOOD CITY	6894.25	42286.77	0.8747	0.83800	0.03670
050542	KERN VALLEY HOSPITAL DISTRICT	4935.24	30927.74	0.3565	0.29200	0.06450
050543	COLLEGE HOSPITAL COSTA MESA	8000.88	34308.89	0.2286	0.22300	0.00560
050545	LANTERMAN DEVELOPMENTAL CENTER	6062.82	35047.90	1.0523	1.03900	0.01330
050546	PORTERVILLE DEVELOPMENTAL CENTER	5342.24	30927.29	0.8043	0.79800	0.00630
050547	SONOMA DEVELOPMENTAL CENTER	6443.69	37316.42	0.3395	0.32200	0.01750
050548	FAIRVIEW DEVELOPMENTAL CENTER	5933.92	34362.45	0.3600	0.32800	0.03200
050549	LOS ROBLES REGIONAL MEDICAL CENTER	5458.39	35022.24	0.2889	0.27100	0.01790
050550	CHAPMAN MEDICAL CENTER	5542.26	34418.92	0.2360	0.19900	0.03700
050551	LOS ALAMITOS MEDICAL CTR.	5606.93	34349.41	0.1079	0.10000	0.00790
050552	MOTION PICTURE AND TELEVISION FUND	5464.52	35094.17	1.0400	0.96600	0.07400
050557	MEMORIAL HOSPITAL MODESTO	5787.39	33796.21	0.1605	0.14600	0.01450
050559	DANIEL FREEMAN MARINA HOSPITAL	5627.38	35142.96	0.2860	0.24800	0.03800
050561	KAISER FOUND. HOSPITAL - WEST LA	5498.53	35117.86	0.2403	0.21600	0.02430

050567	MISSION HOSPITAL REGIONAL MED CENTER	5586.89	34351.80	0.3128	0.28900	0.02380
050568	MADERA COMMUNITY HOSPITAL	6182.58	31312.52	0.4322	0.41600	0.01620
050569	MENDOCINO COAST DISTRICT HOSPITAL	6356.15	37295.52	0.7260	0.65700	0.06900
050570	FOUNTAIN VALLEY REG MEDICAL CENTER	7633.39	34378.36	0.1435	0.12800	0.01550
050571	SUBURBAN MEDICAL CENTER	8674.18	35128.29	0.1942	0.17200	0.02220
050573	EISENHOWER MEMORIAL HOSPITAL	5310.61	34065.50	0.3106	0.27600	0.03460
050575	TRI-CITY REGIONAL MEDICAL CENTERS	7067.63	35105.78	0.3588	0.32800	0.03080
050577	SANTA MARTA HOSPITAL	8426.38	35081.24	0.4179	0.39500	0.02290
050578	MARTIN LUTHER KING, JR./DREW MEDICAL	9938.53	35118.66	0.2673	0.24000	0.02730
050579	CENTURY CITY HOSP	6326.98	35055.89	0.1627	0.15900	0.00370
050580	LAPALMA INTERCOMMUNITY HOSPITAL	6943.14	34361.56	0.3530	0.32200	0.03100
050581	LAKEWOOD REGIONAL MED. CTR.	6481.58	35101.61	0.2110	0.19400	0.01700
050583	ALVARADO COMMUNITY HOSPITAL	5943.89	33563.36	0.1303	0.12500	0.00530
050584	KPC GLOBAL MEDICAL	6778.93	34017.41	0.2581	0.24400	0.01410
050585	SAN CLEMENTE HOSPITAL	5671.70	34357.32	0.3663	0.33600	0.03030
050586	CHINO VALLEY MEDICAL CENTER	6698.22	34043.17	0.3410	0.31200	0.02900
050588	SAN DIMAS COMMUNITY HOSPITAL	6062.82	35141.82	0.1750	0.15200	0.02300
050589	PLACENTIA LINDA COMMUNITY HOSPITAL	5492.13	34315.96	0.2182	0.21100	0.00720
050590	METHODIST HOSPITAL OF SACRAMENTO	7758.10	35113.91	0.2766	0.26000	0.01660
050591	MONTEREY PARK HOSPITAL	8962.76	35083.74	0.1380	0.13000	0.00800
050592	BREA COMMUNITY HOSPITAL	5633.22	34368.71	0.4958	0.44800	0.04780
050594	WESTERN MEDICAL CENTER ANAHEIM	8264.25	35124.89	0.1618	0.14400	0.01780
050597	FOOTHILL PRESBYTERIAN HOSPITAL	5770.89	35073.75	0.4169	0.39800	0.01890
050599	UC DAVIS MEDICAL CENTER	9320.03	35144.70	0.1676	0.15100	0.01660
050601	TARZANA ENCINO REGIONAL MED CTR	6222.93	35071.46	0.0919	0.08800	0.00390
050603	SADDLEBACK MEMORIAL MEDICAL CENTER	5358.24	34343.87	0.3471	0.32400	0.02310
050604	KFH - SANTA TERESA	6425.21	41206.12	0.7839	0.75000	0.03390
050608	DELANO REGIONAL MEDICAL CNT.	7238.21	30927.68	0.2981	0.25100	0.04710
050609	KAISER FOUNDATION HOSPITALS - ANAHEIM	5927.61	35110.30	0.2785	0.25300	0.02550
050613	SETON MEDICAL CENTER	6377.58	40972.10	0.3530	0.32200	0.03100
050615	GREATER EL MONTE COMMUNITY HOSPITAL	9251.45	35103.91	0.1713	0.15700	0.01430
050616	ST. JOHN'S PLEASANT VALLEY HOSPITAL	5188.83	33335.47	0.2986	0.27500	0.02360
050618	BEAR VALLEY COMMUNITY HOSPITAL	8109.48	30927.43	0.6937	0.65100	0.04270
050623	HIGH DESERT HOSPITAL	6062.82	35073.59	0.2105	0.20100	0.00950
050624	HENRY MAYO NEWHALL MEMORIAL HOSPITAL	5609.71	35166.00	0.2148	0.18000	0.03480
050625	CEDARS-SINAI MEDICAL CENTER	7314.78	35118.00	0.2626	0.23600	0.02660
050630	INLAND VALLEY REGIONAL MEDICAL CTR	5528.51	33992.62	0.1734	0.16900	0.00440
050633	TWIN CITIES COMMUNITY HOSPITAL	5465.06	34144.33	0.0948	0.09200	0.00280
050636	POMERADO HOSPITAL	5230.52	33593.82	0.3073	0.28400	0.02330
050641	EAST L.A. DOCTOR'S HOSPITAL	8724.30	35104.74	0.3419	0.31300	0.02890
050643	PHS INDIAN HEALTH SERVICES HOSPITAL	6910.52	40759.26	0.6369	0.60600	0.03086
050644	L.A. METROPOLITAN MED. CENTER	8741.52	35137.52	0.2540	0.22200	0.03200

050662	AGNEWS DEVELOPMENTAL CENTER	7119.07	41197.62	0.6964	0.69200	0.00440
050663	LOS ANGELES COMMUNITY HOSPITAL	8807.46	35114.28	0.2878	0.26000	0.02780
050667	NELSON M. HOLDERMAN	5992.19	38402.16	0.4217	0.32200	0.09970
050668	LAGUNA HONDA HOSPITAL	7304.96	42284.90	0.6720	0.65700	0.01500
050674	KFH SOUTH SACRAMENTO	5858.56	35089.10	0.9069	0.88100	0.02590
050677	KAISER FOUND HOSP. - WOODLAND HILLS	5804.51	35101.59	0.2719	0.25000	0.02190
050678	ORANGE COAST MEMORIAL MEDICAL CENTER	6927.94	34334.74	0.3473	0.32800	0.01930
050680	VACAVALLEY HOSPITAL	6585.59	38497.36	0.2236	0.20500	0.01860
050682	KINGSBURG DISTRICT HOSPITAL	5408.67	31312.73	0.4534	0.44400	0.00940
050684	MENIFEE VALLEY MEDICAL CENTER	5299.22	34107.99	0.3423	0.28700	0.05530
050686	KAISER FOUND. HOSPITALS - RIVERSIDE	5646.28	34364.40	0.2795	0.25400	0.02550
050688	ST. LOUISE REGIONAL HOSPITAL	7119.07	41220.19	0.2836	0.25400	0.02960
050689	SAN RAMON REG. MEDICAL CENTER	6587.73	42287.56	0.1390	0.13200	0.00700
050690	KFH - SANTA ROSA	5810.35	37326.14	0.8331	0.80700	0.02610
050693	IRVINE MEDICAL CENTER	5362.06	34539.86	0.3210	0.22400	0.09700
050694	MORENO VALLEY COMMUNITY HOSPITAL	7017.97	34100.36	0.3186	0.27000	0.04860
050695	ST. DOMINIC'S HOSPITAL	5508.07	31887.90	0.2851	0.26600	0.01910
050696	USC UNIVERSITY HOSPITAL	7154.83	35145.21	0.1319	0.11400	0.01790
050697	PATIENTS' HOSPITAL OF REDDING	5409.17	33973.09	0.5307	0.50900	0.02170
050701	RANCHO SPRINGS MEDICAL CENTER	5815.09	34035.86	0.3324	0.30700	0.02540
050704	MISSION COMMUNITY HOSPITAL	8515.18	35082.87	0.4273	0.40300	0.02430
050707	RECOVERY INN OF MENLO PARK	6377.58	41003.62	0.4072	0.32200	0.08520
050708	FRESNO SURGERY CENTER	4873.98	31310.28	0.4470	0.34800	0.09900
050709	DESERT VALLEY HOSPITAL	5595.35	34022.49	0.3002	0.28200	0.01820
050710	KFH - FRESNO	4877.45	31312.36	1.0612	1.00700	0.05420
050713	LINCOLN HOSPITAL	6062.82	35067.59	1.1668	1.12300	0.04380
050714	SANTA CRUZ MATERINTY & SURGERY HOSP	5828.15	37404.83	0.5562	0.46700	0.08920
050717	RANCHO LOS AMIGOS NATL.REHAB.CTR.	7701.55	35132.30	0.2873	0.25300	0.03430
050718	VALLEY PLAZA DOCTORS HOSPITAL	5879.30	34012.62	0.4921	0.46800	0.02410
050720	TUSTIN HOSPIAL AND MEDICAL CENTER	5631.51	34358.54	0.5820	0.53300	0.04900
050722	SHARP MARY BIRCH HOSPITAL FOR WOMEN	5446.07	33603.36	0.3570	0.32600	0.03100
050723	KAISER FOUND HOSPITAL - BALDWIN	6135.46	35190.30	0.2589	0.20900	0.04990
050724	BAKERSFIELD HEART HOSPITAL	5125.48	30927.50	0.3580	0.32600	0.03200
050725	CITY OF ANGELS MEDICAL CENTER	8758.45	35276.78	0.4614	0.32200	0.13940
050726	STANISLAUS SURGICAL HOSPITAL	5260.78	33771.94	0.4169	0.31400	0.10290
050727	COMMUNITY HOSPITAL OF LONG BEACH	5475.04	35108.58	0.3580	0.32600	0.03200
050728	SUTTER WARRACK HOSPITAL	5806.06	37326.66	0.4001	0.38800	0.01210
050729	DANIEL FREEMAN HOSPITAL	7274.90	35110.94	0.2490	0.22600	0.02300
050730	DANIEL FREEMAN MARINA HOSPITAL	5689.52	35127.36	0.2740	0.24300	0.03100

Full Payment Impact File (impfile04zip) at http://www.cms.gov/providers/hipps/ippsputs.asp (Section 9789.23 reflects the modifications of the Medicare Prescription Drug, Improvement, and Modernization Act of 2003, Public Law 108-173, §§402, 402 and 502, which document is hereby incorporated by reference and will be made available upon request to the Administrative Director.

Record Layout at http://cms.hhs.gov/providers/hipps/impact_rcd_lay.pdf.

Composite Rate (in italics) reflects Sole Community Hospital adjustment

Note: Authority cited: Sections 133, 4603.5, 5307.1,

5307.3 and 5318, Labor Code. Reference: Sections 4600, 4603.2, 5307.1 and 5318, Labor Code.

History: 1. New section filed 1-2-2004 as an emergency; operative 1-2-2004 (Register 2004, No. 2). A Certificate of Compliance must be transmitted to OAL by 5-3-2004 or emergency language will be repealed by operation of law on the following day.

2. Certificate of Compliance as to 1-2-2004 order, including amendment of section heading and repealer and new section, transmitted to OAL 4-30-2004 and filed 6-15-2004 (Register 2004, No. 25).

2004 Note: It appears section 402 is cited twice in reference to Public Law 108-173 being incorporated into the revision of this section.

Ref.: Hanna § 22.05[2]; Herlick Handbook § 4.19.

§9789.24. Diagnostic Related Groups, Relative Weights, Geometric Mean Length of Stay.

DRGV21	MDC	TYPE	DRG TITLE	RELATIVE WEIGHTS	GEOMETRIC MEAN LOS
1	01	SURG	CRANIOTOMY AGE >17 W CC	3.6186	8.0
2	01	SURG	CRANIOTOMY AGE >17 W/O CC	2.0850	4.1
3	01	SURG*	CRANIOTOMY AGE 0-17	1.9753	12.7
4	01	SURG	NO LONGER VALID	0.0000	0.0
5	01	SURG	NO LONGER VALID	0.0000	0.0
6	01	SURG	CARPAL TUNNEL RELEASE	0.8092	2.2
7	01	SURG	PERIPH & CRANIAL NERVE & OTHER NERV SYST PROC W CC	2.6519	6.6
8	01	SURG	PERIPH & CRANIAL NERVE & OTHER NERV SYST PROC W/O CC	1.5453	1.9
9	01	MED	SPINAL DISORDERS & INJURIES	1.4214	4.7
10	01	MED	NERVOUS SYSTEM NEOPLASMS W CC	1.2448	4.8
11	01	MED	NERVOUS SYSTEM NEOPLASMS W/O CC	0.8571	3.0
12	01	MED	DEGENERATIVE NERVOUS SYSTEM DISORDERS	0.9259	4.5
13	01	MED	MULTIPLE SCLEROSIS & CEREBELLAR ATAXIA	0.8176	4.0
14	01	MED	INTRACRANIAL HEMORRHAGE & STROKE W INFARCT	1.2682	4.7
15	01	MED	NONSPECIFIC CVA & PRECEREBRAL OCCLUSION W/O INFARCT	0.9677	3.9
16	01	MED	NONSPECIFIC CEREBROVASCULAR DISORDERS W CC	1.2618	4.8
17	01	MED	NONSPECIFIC CEREBROVASCULAR DISORDERS W/O CC	0.6991	2.5
18	01	MED	CRANIAL & PERIPHERAL NERVE DISORDERS W CC	1.0026	4.2
19	01	MED	CRANIAL & PERIPHERAL NERVE DISORDERS W/O CC	0.7041	2.8
20	01	MED	NERVOUS SYSTEM INFECTION EXCEPT VIRAL MENINGITIS	2.7394	8.0
21	01	MED	VIRAL MENINGITIS	1.5138	5.0
22	01	MED	HYPERTENSIVE ENCEPHALOPATHY	1.0737	3.9
23	01	MED	NONTRAUMATIC STUPOR & COMA	0.8239	3.2
24	01	MED	SEIZURE & HEADACHE AGE >17 W CC	1.0121	3.7
25	01	MED	SEIZURE & HEADACHE AGE >17 W/O CC	0.6109	2.5
26	01	MED	SEIZURE & HEADACHE AGE 0-17	1.3730	2.2
27	01	MED	TRAUMATIC STUPOR & COMA, COMA >1 HR	1.3370	3.2
28	01	MED	TRAUMATIC STUPOR & COMA, COMA <1 HR AGE >17 W CC	1.3386	4.4
29	01	MED	TRAUMATIC STUPOR & COMA, COMA <1 HR AGE >17 W/O CC	0.7087	2.7
30	01	MED*	TRAUMATIC STUPOR & COMA, COMA		

			<1 HR AGE 0-17	0.3341	2.0
31	01	MED	CONCUSSION AGE >17 W CC	0.9117	3.1
32	01	MED	CONCUSSION AGE >17 W/O CC	0.5684	2.0
33	01	MED*	CONCUSSION AGE 0-17	0.2098	1.6
34	01	MED	OTHER DISORDERS OF NERVOUS SYSTEM W CC	0.9931	3.7
35	01	MED	OTHER DISORDERS OF NERVOUS SYSTEM W/O CC	0.6355	2.5
36	02	SURG	RETINAL PROCEDURES	0.6298	1.2
37	02	SURG	ORBITAL PROCEDURES	1.0575	2.5
38	02	SURG	PRIMARY IRIS PROCEDURES	0.4669	1.9
39	02	SURG	LENS PROCEDURES WITH OR WITHOUT VITRECTOMY	0.6285	1.5
40	02	SURG	EXTRAOCULAR PROCEDURES EXCEPT ORBIT AGE >17	0.8937	2.7
41	02	SURG*	EXTRAOCULAR PROCEDURES EXCEPT ORBIT AGE 0-17	0.3401	1.6
42	02	SURG	INTRAOCULAR PROCEDURES EXCEPT RETINA, IRIS & LENS	0.7064	1.9
43	02	MED	HYPHEMA	0.5382	2.4
44	02	MED	ACUTE MAJOR EYE INFECTIONS	0.6597	4.0
45	02	MED	NEUROLOGICAL EYE DISORDERS	0.7250	2.5
46	02	MED	OTHER DISORDERS OF THE EYE AGE >17 W CC	0.7936	3.4
47	02	MED	OTHER DISORDERS OF THE EYE AGE >17 W/O CC	0.5317	2.4
48	02	MED*	OTHER DISORDERS OF THE EYE AGE 0-17	0.2996	2.9
49	03	SURG	MAJOR HEAD & NECK PROCEDURES	1.7277	3.2
50	03	SURG	SIALOADENECTOMY	0.8317	1.5
51	03	SURG	SALIVARY GLAND PROCEDURES EXCEPT SIALOADENECTOMY	0.8410	1.9
52	03	SURG	CLEFT LIP & PALATE REPAIR	0.8018	1.4
53	03	SURG	SINUS & MASTOID PROCEDURES AGE >17	1.2520	2.2
54	03	SURG*	SINUS & MASTOID PROCEDURES AGE 0-17	0.4856	3.2
55	03	SURG	MISCELLANEOUS EAR, NOSE, MOUTH & THROAT PROCEDURES	0.9247	2.0
56	03	SURG	RHINOPLASTY	0.9233	1.9
57	03	SURG	T&A PROC, EXCEPT TONSILLECTOMY &/OR ADENOIDECTOMY ONLY, AGE >17	1.1029	2.4
58	03	SURG*	T&A PROC, EXCEPT TONSILLECTOMY &/OR ADENOIDECTOMY ONLY, AGE 0-17	0.2757	1.5
59	03	SURG	TONSILLECTOMY &/OR ADENOIDECTOMY ONLY, AGE >17	0.9557	1.9
60	03	SURG*	TONSILLECTOMY &/OR ADENOIDECTOMY ONLY, AGE 0-17	0.2099	1.5
61	03	SURG	MYRINGOTOMY W TUBE INSERTION AGE >17	1.2334	3.1
62	03	SURG*	MYRINGOTOMY W TUBE INSERTION AGE 0-17	0.2973	1.3
63	03	SURG	OTHER EAR, NOSE, MOUTH & THROAT O.R. PROCEDURES	1.3759	3.0
64	03	MED	EAR, NOSE, MOUTH & THROAT MALIGNANCY	1.3089	4.3
65	03	MED	DYSEQUILIBRIUM	0.5748	2.3
66	03	MED	EPISTAXIS	0.5811	2.4

67	03	MED	EPIGLOTTITIS	0.7780	2.9
68	03	MED	OTITIS MEDIA & URI AGE >17 W CC	0.6531	3.1
69	03	MED	OTITIS MEDIA & URI AGE >17 W/O CC	0.4987	2.5
70	03	MED	OTITIS MEDIA & URI AGE 0-17	0.3188	2.0
71	03	MED	LARYNGOTRACHEITIS	0.7065	2.5
72	03	MED	NASAL TRAUMA & DEFORMITY	0.6954	2.6
73	03	MED	OTHER EAR, NOSE, MOUTH & THROAT DIAGNOSES AGE >17	0.8184	3.3
74	03	MED*	OTHER EAR, NOSE, MOUTH & THROAT DIAGNOSES AGE 0-17	0.3380	2.1
75	04	SURG	MAJOR CHEST PROCEDURES	3.0437	7.7
76	04	SURG	OTHER RESP SYSTEM O.R. PROCEDURES W CC	2.8184	8.4
77	04	SURG	OTHER RESP SYSTEM O.R. PROCEDURES W/O CC	1.2378	3.5
78	04	MED	PULMONARY EMBOLISM	1.2731	5.6
79	04	MED	RESPIRATORY INFECTIONS & INFLAMMATIONS AGE >17 W CC	1.5974	6.7
80	04	MED	RESPIRATORY INFECTIONS & INFLAMMATIONS AGE >17 W/O CC	0.8400	4.3
81	04	MED*	RESPIRATORY INFECTIONS & INFLAMMATIONS AGE 0-17	1.5300	6.1
82	04	MED	RESPIRATORY NEOPLASMS	1.3724	5.1
83	04	MED	MAJOR CHEST TRAUMA W CC	0.9620	4.3
84	04	MED	MAJOR CHEST TRAUMA W/O CC	0.5371	2.6
85	04	MED	PLEURAL EFFUSION W CC	1.1927	4.8
86	04	MED	PLEURAL EFFUSION W/O CC	0.6864	2.8
87	04	MED	PULMONARY EDEMA & RESPIRATORY FAILURE	1.3430	4.8
88	04	MED	CHRONIC OBSTRUCTIVE PULMONARY DISEASE	0.9031	4.1
89	04	MED	SIMPLE PNEUMONIA & PLEURISY AGE >17 W CC	1.0463	4.9
90	04	MED	SIMPLE PNEUMONIA & PLEURISY AGE >17 W/O CC	0.6147	3.4
91	04	MED	SIMPLE PNEUMONIA & PLEURISY AGE 0-17	0.7408	3.1
92	04	MED	INTERSTITIAL LUNG DISEASE W CC	1.2024	5.0
93	04	MED	INTERSTITIAL LUNG DISEASE W/O CC	0.7176	3.3
94	04	MED	PNEUMOTHORAX W CC	1.1340	4.7
95	04	MED	PNEUMOTHORAX W/O CC	0.6166	3.0
96	04	MED	BRONCHITIS & ASTHMA AGE >17 W CC	0.7464	3.7
97	04	MED	BRONCHITIS & ASTHMA AGE >17 W/O CC	0.5505	2.9
98	04	MED*	BRONCHITIS & ASTHMA AGE 0-17	0.9662	3.7
99	04	MED	RESPIRATORY SIGNS & SYMPTOMS W CC	0.7032	2.4
100	04	MED	RESPIRATORY SIGNS & SYMPTOMS W/O CC	0.5222	1.8
101	04	MED	OTHER RESPIRATORY SYSTEM DIAGNOSES W CC	0.8654	3.3
102	04	MED	OTHER RESPIRATORY SYSTEM DIAGNOSES W/O CC	0.5437	2.1
103	PRE	SURG	HEART TRANSPLANT	18.6081	26.1
104	05	SURG	CARDIAC VALVE & OTH MAJOR CARDIOTHORACIC PROC W CARD CATH	7.9389	12.2
105	05	SURG	CATH CARDIAC VALVE & OTH MAJOR CARDIOTHORACIC PROC W/O CARD		

176	06	MED	COMPLICATED PEPTIC ULCER	1.0998	4.1
177	06	MED	UNCOMPLICATED PEPTIC ULCER W CC	0.9259	3.7
178	06	MED	UNCOMPLICATED PEPTIC ULCER W/O CC	0.6940	2.6
179	06	MED	INFLAMMATORY BOWEL DISEASE	1.0885	4.6
180	06	MED	G.I. OBSTRUCTION W CC	0.9642	4.2
181	06	MED	G.I. OBSTRUCTION W/O CC	0.5376	2.8
182	06	MED	ESOPHAGITIS, GASTROENT & MISC DIGEST DISORDERS AGE >17 W CC	0.8223	3.4
183	06	MED	ESOPHAGITIS, GASTROENT & MISC DIGEST DISORDERS AGE >17 W/O CC	0.5759	2.3
184	06	MED	ESOPHAGITIS, GASTROENT & MISC DIGEST DISORDERS AGE 0-17	0.4813	2.4
185	03	MED	DENTAL & ORAL DIS EXCEPT EXTRACTIONS & RESTORATIONS, AGE >17	0.8685	3.3
186	03	MED*	DENTAL & ORAL DIS EXCEPT EXTRACTIONS & RESTORATIONS, AGE 0-17	0.3236	2.9
187	03	MED	DENTAL EXTRACTIONS & RESTORATIONS	0.7778	3.0
188	06	MED	OTHER DIGESTIVE SYSTEM DIAGNOSES AGE >17 W CC	1.1088	4.1
189	06	MED	OTHER DIGESTIVE SYSTEM DIAGNOSES AGE >17 W/O CC	0.5987	2.4
190	06	MED	OTHER DIGESTIVE SYSTEM DIAGNOSES AGE 0-17	0.8104	3.7
191	07	SURG	PANCREAS, LIVER & SHUNT PROCEDURES W CC	4.2787	9.8
192	07	SURG	PANCREAS, LIVER & SHUNT PROCEDURES W/O CC	1.8025	4.7
193	07	SURG	BILIARY TRACT PROC EXCEPT ONLY CHOLECYST W OR W/O C.D.E. W CC	3.4211	10.4
194	07	SURG	BILIARY TRACT PROC EXCEPT ONLY CHOLECYST W OR W/O C.D.E. W/O CC	1.6030	5.7
195	07	SURG	CHOLECYSTECTOMY W C.D.E. W CC	3.0613	8.7
196	07	SURG	CHOLECYSTECTOMY W C.D.E. W/O CC	1.6117	4.8
197	07	SURG	CHOLECYSTECTOMY EXCEPT BY LAPAROSCOPE W/O C.D.E. W CC	2.5547	7.5
198	07	SURG	CHOLECYSTECTOMY EXCEPT BY LAPAROSCOPE W/O C.D.E. W/O CC	1.1831	3.8
199	07	SURG	HEPATOBILIARY DIAGNOSTIC PROCEDURE FOR MALIGNANCY	2.3953	7.0
200	07	SURG	HEPATOBILIARY DIAGNOSTIC PROCEDURE FOR NON-MALIGNANCY	3.0415	6.7
201	07	SURG	OTHER HEPATOBILIARY OR PANCREAS O.R. PROCEDURES	3.6841	10.2
202	07	MED	CIRRHOSIS & ALCOHOLIC HEPATITIS	1.3120	4.8
203	07	MED	MALIGNANCY OF HEPATOBILIARY SYSTEM OR PANCREAS	1.3482	5.0
204	07	MED	DISORDERS OF PANCREAS EXCEPT MALIGNANCY	1.1675	4.4
205	07	MED	DISORDERS OF LIVER EXCEPT MALIG, CIRR, ALC HEPA W CC	1.2095	4.6
206	07	MED	DISORDERS OF LIVER EXCEPT MALIG, CIRR, ALC HEPA W/O CC	0.7071	2.9
207	07	MED	DISORDERS OF THE BILIARY TRACT W CC	1.1539	4.0
208	07	MED	DISORDERS OF THE BILIARY TRACT		

			W/O CC	0.6601	2.3
209	08	SURG	MAJOR JOINT & LIMB REATTACHMENT PROCEDURES OF LOWER EXTREMITY	2.0327	4.4
210	08	SURG	HIP & FEMUR PROCEDURES EXCEPT MAJOR JOINT AGE >17 W CC	1.8477	6.1
211	08	SURG	HIP & FEMUR PROCEDURES EXCEPT MAJOR JOINT AGE >17 W/O CC	1.2544	4.5
212	08	SURG	HIP & FEMUR PROCEDURES EXCEPT MAJOR JOINT AGE 0-17	1.4152	3.2
213	08	SURG	AMPUTATION FOR MUSCULOSKELETAL SYSTEM & CONN TISSUE DISORDERS	1.8904	6.7
214	08	SURG	NO LONGER VALID	0.0000	0.0
215	08	SURG	NO LONGER VALID	0.0000	0.0
216	08	SURG	BIOPSIES OF MUSCULOSKELETAL SYSTEM & CONNECTIVE TISSUE	2.1107	5.0
217	08	SURG	WND DEBRID & SKN GRFT EXCEPT HAND, FOR MUSCSKELET & COMM TISS DIS	3.0020	9.0
218	08	SURG	LOWER EXTREM & HUMER PROC EXCEPT HIP, FOOT, FEMUR AGE >17 W CC	1.5750	4.3
219	08	SURG	LOWER EXTREM & HUMER PROC EXCEPT HIP, FOOT, FEMUR AGE >17 W/O CC	1.0258	2.7
220	08	SURG*	LOWER EXTREM & HUMER PROC EXCEPT HIP, FOOT, FEMUR AGE 0-17	0.5881	5.3
221	08	SURG	NO LONGER VALID	0.0000	0.0
222	08	SURG	NO LONGER VALID	0.0000	0.0
223	08	SURG	MAJOR SHOULDER, ELBOW PROC, OR OTHER UPPER EXTREMITY PROC W CC	1.0573	2.2
224	08	SURG	SHOULDER, ELBOW OR FOREARM PROC, EXC MAJOR JOINT PROC, W/O CC	0.7898	1.6
225	08	SURG	FOOT PROCEDURES	1.1704	3.6
226	08	SURG	SOFT TISSUE PROCEDURES W CC	1.5529	4.5
227	08	SURG	SOFT TISSUE PROCEDURES W/O CC	0.8190	2.1
228	08	SURG	MAJOR THUMB OR JOINT PROC, OR OTH HAND OR WRIST PROC W CC	1.1639	2.7
229	08	SURG	HAND OR WRIST PROC, EXCEPT MAJOR JOINT PROC, W/O CC	0.7064	1.8
230	08	SURG	LOCAL EXCISION & REMOVAL OF INT FIX DEVICES OF HIP & FEMUR	1.3147	3.6
231	08	SURG	NO LONGER VALID	0.0000	0.0
232	08	SURG	ARTHROSCOPY	0.9674	1.8
233	08	SURG	OTHER MUSCULOSKELET SYS & CONN TISS O.R. PROC W CC	2.0024	5.0
234	08	SURG	OTHER MUSCULOSKELET SYS & CONN. TISS O.R. PROC W/O CC	1.1977	2.2
235	08	MED	FRACTURES OF FEMUR	0.7580	3.8
236	08	MED	FRACTURES OF HIP & PELVIS	0.7358	3.9
237	08	MED	SPRAINS, STRAINS, & DISLOCATIONS OF HIP, PELVIS & THIGH	0.5983	2.9
238	08	MED	OSTEOMYELITIS	1.3564	6.5
239	08	MED	PATHOLOGICAL FRACTURES & MUSCULOSKELETAL & CONN TISS MALIGNANCY	1.0614	5.1
240	08	MED	CONNECTIVE TISSUE DISORDERS W CC	1.3153	4.9

241	08	MED	CONNECTIVE TISSUE DISORDERS W/O CC	0.6358	3.0
242	08	MED	SEPTIC ARTHRITIS	1.1695	5.3
243	08	MED	MEDICAL BACK PROBLEMS	0.7525	3.7
244	08	MED	BONE DISEASES & SPECIFIC ARTHROPATHIES W CC	0.7155	3.7
245	08	MED	BONE DISEASES & SPECIFIC ARTHROPATHIES W/O CC	0.4786	2.6
246	08	MED	NON-SPECIFIC ARTHROPATHIES	0.6063	3.0
247	08	MED	SIGNS & SYMPTOMS OF MUSCULOSKELETAL SYSTEM & CONN TISSUE	0.5724	2.6
248	08	MED	TENDONITIS, MYOSITIS & BURSITIS	0.8585	3.8
249	08	MED	AFTERCARE, MUSCULOSKELETAL SYSTEM & CONNECTIVE TISSUE	0.6744	2.5
250	08	MED	FX, SPRN, STRN & DISL OF FOREARM, HAND, FOOT AGE >17 W CC	0.7091	3.2
251	08	MED	FX, SPRN, STRN & DISL OF FOREARM, HAND, FOOT AGE >17 W/O CC	0.4578	2.3
252	08	MED*	FX, SPRN, STRN & DISL OF FOREARM, HAND, FOOT AGE 0-17	0.2553	1.8
253	08	MED	FX, SPRN, STRN & DISL OF UPARM, LOWLEG EX FOOT AGE >17 W CC	0.7581	3.7
254	08	MED	FX, SPRN, STRN & DISL OF UPARM, LOWLEG EX FOOT AGE >17 W/O CC	0.4464	2.6
255	08	MED*	FX, SPRN, STRN & DISL OF UPARM, LOWLEG EX FOOT AGE 0-17	0.2974	2.9
256	08	MED	OTHER MUSCULOSKELETAL SYSTEM & CONNECTIVE TISSUE DIAGNOSES	0.8190	3.8
257	09	SURG	TOTAL MASTECTOMY FOR MALIGNANCY W CC	0.8913	2.1
258	09	SURG	TOTAL MASTECTOMY FOR MALIGNANCY W/O CC	0.7018	1.6
259	09	SURG	SUBTOTAL MASTECTOMY FOR MALIGNANCY W CC	0.9420	1.8
260	09	SURG	SUBTOTAL MASTECTOMY FOR MALIGNANCY W/O CC	0.6854	1.2
261	09	SURG	BREAST PROC FOR NON-MALIGNANCY EXCEPT BIOPSY & LOCAL EXCISION	0.8944	1.6
262	09	SURG	BREAST BIOPSY & LOCAL EXCISION FOR NON-MALIGNANCY	0.9533	2.9
263	09	SURG	SKIN GRAFT &/OR DEBRID FOR SKN ULCER OR CELLULITIS W CC	2.0556	8.3
264	09	SURG	SKIN GRAFT &/OR DEBRID FOR SKN ULCER OR CELLULITIS W/O CC	1.0605	5.0
265	09	SURG	SKIN GRAFT &/OR DEBRID EXCEPT FOR SKIN ULCER OR CELLULITIS W CC	1.5984	4.2
266	09	SURG	SKIN GRAFT &/OR DEBRID EXCEPT FOR SKIN ULCER OR CELLULITIS W/O CC	0.8791	2.3
267	09	SURG	PERIANAL & PILONIDAL PROCEDURES	0.9574	2.9
268	09	SURG	SKIN, SUBCUTANEOUS TISSUE & BREAST PLASTIC PROCEDURES	1.1513	2.4
269	09	SURG	OTHER SKIN, SUBCUT TISS & BREAST PROC W CC	1.7747	6.0
270	09	SURG	OTHER SKIN, SUBCUT TISS & BREAST PROC W/O CC	0.8129	2.5
271	09	MED	SKIN ULCERS	1.0280	5.6
272	09	MED	MAJOR SKIN DISORDERS W CC	1.0185	4.6

273	09	MED	MAJOR SKIN DISORDERS W/O CC	0.6192	3.0
274	09	MED	MALIGNANT BREAST DISORDERS W CC	1.1574	4.7
275	09	MED	MALIGNANT BREAST DISORDERS W/O CC	0.5729	2.4
276	09	MED	NON-MALIGANT BREAST DISORDERS	0.6471	3.5
277	09	MED	CELLULITIS AGE >17 W CC	0.8805	4.7
278	09	MED	CELLULITIS AGE >17 W/O CC	0.5432	3.5
279	09	MED	CELLULITIS AGE 0-17	0.7779	4.0
280	09	MED	TRAUMA TO THE SKIN, SUBCUT TISS & BREAST AGE >17 W CC	0.7109	3.2
281	09	MED	TRAUMA TO THE SKIN, SUBCUT TISS & BREAST AGE >17 W/O CC	0.4866	2.3
282	09	MED*	TRAUMA TO THE SKIN, SUBCUT TISS & BREAST AGE 0-17	0.2586	2.2
283	09	MED	MINOR SKIN DISORDERS W CC	0.7322	3.5
284	09	MED	MINOR SKIN DISORDERS W/O CC	0.4215	2.3
285	10	SURG	AMPUTAT OF LOWER LIMB FOR ENDOCRINE, NUTRIT, & METABOL DISORDERS	2.0825	7.9
286	10	SURG	ADRENAL & PITUITARY PROCEDURES	2.0342	4.4
287	10	SURG	SKIN GRAFTS & WOUND DEBRID FOR ENDOC, NUTRIT & METAB DISORDERS	1.8899	7.7
288	10	SURG	O.R. PROCEDURES FOR OBESITY	2.1498	3.9
289	10	SURG	PARATHYROID PROCEDURES	0.9441	1.8
290	10	SURG	THYROID PROCEDURES	0.8938	1.7
291	10	SURG	THYROGLOSSAL PROCEDURES	0.6468	1.4
292	10	SURG	OTHER ENDOCRINE, NUTRIT & METAB O.R. PROC W CC	2.7336	7.3
293	10	SURG	OTHER ENDOCRINE, NUTRIT & METAB O.R. PROC W/O CC	1.3896	3.2
294	10	MED	DIABETES AGE >35	0.7800	3.5
295	10	MED	DIABETES AGE 0-35	0.7975	3.0
296	10	MED	NUTRITIONAL & MISC METABOLIC DISORDERS AGE >17 W CC	0.8639	4.0
297	10	MED	NUTRITIONAL & MISC METABOLIC DISORDERS AGE >17 W/O CC	0.5085	2.7
298	10	MED	NUTRITIONAL & MISC METABOLIC DISORDERS AGE 0-17	0.4537	2.4
299	10	MED	INBORN ERRORS OF METABOLISM	0.9466	3.8
300	10	MED	ENDOCRINE DISORDERS W CC	1.1001	4.7
301	10	MED	ENDOCRINE DISORDERS W/O CC	0.6158	2.8
302	11	SURG	KIDNEY TRANSPLANT	3.2343	7.2
303	11	SURG	KIDNEY, URETER & MAJOR BLADDER PROCEDURES FOR NEOPLASM	2.3659	6.4
304	11	SURG	KIDNEY, URETER & MAJOR BLADDER PROC FOR NON-NEOPL W CC	2.3856	6.2
305	11	SURG	KIDNEY, URETER & MAJOR BLADDER PROC FOR NON-NEOPL W/O CC	1.1854	2.8
306	11	SURG	PROSTATECTOMY W CC	1.2257	3.5
307	11	SURG	PROSTATECTOMY W/O CC	0.6145	1.7
308	11	SURG	MINOR BLADDER PROCEDURES W CC	1.5993	4.0
309	11	SURG	MINOR BLADDER PROCEDURES W/O CC	0.8991	1.7
310	11	SURG	TRANSURETHRAL PROCEDURES W CC	1.1502	2.9
311	11	SURG	TRANSURETHRAL PROCEDURES W/O CC	0.6258	1.5
312	11	SURG	URETHRAL PROCEDURES, AGE >17 W CC	1.0841	3.0

313	11	SURG	URETHRAL PROCEDURES, AGE >17 W/O CC	0.6814	1.7
314	11	SURG*	URETHRAL PROCEDURES, AGE 0-17	0.4984	2.3
315	11	SURG	OTHER KIDNEY & URINARY TRACT O.R. PROCEDURES	2.0796	3.7
316	11	MED	RENAL FAILURE	1.2987	4.9
317	11	MED	ADMIT FOR RENAL DIALYSIS	0.8503	2.4
318	11	MED	KIDNEY & URINARY TRACT NEOPLASMS W CC	1.1871	4.4
319	11	MED	KIDNEY & URINARY TRACT NEOPLASMS W/O CC	0.6771	2.2
320	11	MED	KIDNEY & URINARY TRACT INFECTIONS AGE >17 W CC	0.8853	4.3
321	11	MED	KIDNEY & URINARY TRACT INFECTIONS AGE >17 W/O CC	0.5685	3.1
322	11	MED	KIDNEY & URINARY TRACT INFECTIONS AGE 0-17	0.4625	2.8
323	11	MED	URINARY STONES W CC, &/OR ESW LITHOTRIPSY	0.8088	2.4
324	11	MED	URINARY STONES W/O CC	0.4797	1.6
325	11	MED	KIDNEY & URINARY TRACT SIGNS & SYMPTOMS AGE >17 W CC	0.6553	2.9
326	11	MED	KIDNEY & URINARY TRACT SIGNS & SYMPTOMS AGE >17 W/O CC	0.4206	2.1
327	11	MED*	KIDNEY & URINARY TRACT SIGNS & SYMPTOMS AGE 0-17	0.3727	3.1
328	11	MED	URETHRAL STRICTURE AGE >17 W CC	0.7613	2.7
329	11	MED	URETHRAL STRICTURE AGE >17 W/O CC	0.5296	1.7
330	11	MED*	URETHRAL STRICTURE AGE 0-17	0.3210	1.6
331	11	MED	OTHER KIDNEY & URINARY TRACT DIAGNOSES AGE >17 W CC	1.0618	4.2
332	11	MED	OTHER KIDNEY & URINARY TRACT DIAGNOSES AGE >17 W/O CC	0.5982	2.4
333	11	MED	OTHER KIDNEY & URINARY TRACT DIAGNOSES AGE 0-17	0.9483	3.7
334	12	SURG	MAJOR MALE PELVIC PROCEDURES W CC	1.4810	3.9
335	12	SURG	MAJOR MALE PELVIC PROCEDURES W/O CC	1.0835	2.8
336	12	SURG	TRANSURETHRAL PROSTATECTOMY W CC	0.8595	2.6
337	12	SURG	TRANSURETHRAL PROSTATECTOMY W/O CC	0.5869	1.8
338	12	SURG	TESTES PROCEDURES, FOR MALIGNANCY	1.2316	3.5
339	12	SURG	TESTES PROCEDURES, NON-MALIGNANCY AGE >17	1.1345	2.9
340	12	SURG*	TESTES PROCEDURES, NON-MALIGNANCY AGE 0-17	0.2853	2.4
341	12	SURG	PENIS PROCEDURES	1.2739	1.9
342	12	SURG	CIRCUMCISION AGE >17	0.7800	2.4
343	12	SURG*	CIRCUMCISION AGE 0-17	0.1551	1.7
344	12	SURG	OTHER MALE REPRODUCTIVE SYSTEM O.R. PROCEDURES FOR MALIGNANCY	1.3306	1.6
345	12	SURG	OTHER MALE REPRODUCTIVE SYSTEM O.R. PROC EXCEPT FOR MALIGNANCY	1.1671	3.0
346	12	MED	MALIGNANCY, MALE REPRODUCTIVE		

			SYSTEM, W CC	1.0213	4.5
347	12	MED	MALIGNANCY, MALE REPRODUCTIVE SYSTEM, W/O CC	0.5417	2.2
348	12	MED	BENIGN PROSTATIC HYPERTROPHY W CC	0.7472	3.3
349	12	MED	BENIGN PROSTATIC HYPERTROPHY W/O CC	0.4608	2.0
350	12	MED	INFLAMMATION OF THE MALE REPRODUCTIVE SYSTEM	0.7370	3.6
351	12	MED*	STERILIZATION, MALE	0.2379	1.3
352	12	MED	OTHER MALE REPRODUCTIVE SYSTEM DIAGNOSES	0.7097	2.9
353	13	SURG	PELVIC EVISCERATION, RADICAL HYSTERECTOMY & RADICAL VULVECTOMY	1.8390	4.9
354	13	SURG	UTERINE, ADNEXA PROC FOR NON-OVARIAN/ADNEXAL MALIG W CC	1.4808	4.7
355	13	SURG	UTERINE, ADNEXA PROC FOR NON-OVARIAN/ADNEXAL MALIG W/O CC	0.8912	3.0
356	13	SURG	FEMALE REPRODUCTIVE SYSTEM RECONSTRUCTIVE PROCEDURES	0.7556	1.8
357	13	SURG	UTERINE & ADNEXA PROC FOR OVARIAN OR ADNEXAL MALIGNANCY	2.2737	6.7
358	13	SURG	UTERINE & ADNEXA PROC FOR NON-MALIGNANCY W CC	1.1807	3.4
359	13	SURG	UTERINE & ADNEXA PROC FOR NON-MALIGNANCY W/O CC	0.8099	2.3
360	13	SURG	VAGINA, CERVIX & VULVA PROCEDURES	0.8661	2.2
361	13	SURG	LAPAROSCOPY & INCISIONAL TUBAL INTERRUPTION	1.0793	2.2
362	13	SURG*	ENDOSCOPIC TUBAL INTERRUPTION	0.3041	1.4
363	13	SURG	D&C, CONIZATION & RADIO-IMPLANT, FOR MALIGNANCY	0.9374	2.6
364	13	SURG	D&C, CONIZATION EXCEPT FOR MALIGNANCY	0.9098	2.9
365	13	SURG	OTHER FEMALE REPRODUCTIVE SYSTEM O.R. PROCEDURES	2.1284	5.3
366	13	MED	MALIGNANCY, FEMALE REPRODUCTIVE SYSTEM W CC	1.2826	4.8
367	13	MED	MALIGNANCY, FEMALE REPRODUCTIVE SYSTEM W/O CC	0.5588	2.3
368	13	MED	INFECTIONS, FEMALE REPRODUCTIVE SYSTEM	1.1657	5.1
369	13	MED	MENSTRUAL & OTHER FEMALE REPRODUCTIVE SYSTEM DISORDERS	0.6065	2.4
370	14	SURG	CESAREAN SECTION W CC	1.0119	4.2
371	14	SURG	CESAREAN SECTION W/O CC	0.6317	3.2
372	14	MED	VAGINAL DELIVERY W COMPLICATING DIAGNOSES	0.5520	2.7
373	14	MED	VAGINAL DELIVERY W/O COMPLICATING DIAGNOSES	0.3856	2.0
374	14	SURG	VAGINAL DELIVERY W STERILIZATION &/OR D&C	0.7402	2.5
375	14	SURG*	VAGINAL DELIVERY W O.R. PROC EXCEPT STERIL &/OR D&C	0.5806	4.4
376	14	MED	POSTPARTUM & POST ABORTION		

			DIAGNOSES W/O O.R. PROCEDURE	0.5693	2.5
377	14	SURG	POSTPARTUM & POST ABORTION DIAGNOSES W O.R. PROCEDURE	1.0321	3.1
378	14	MED	ECTOPIC PREGNANCY	0.7950	2.0
379	14	MED	THREATENED ABORTION	0.3626	2.0
380	14	MED	ABORTION W/O D&C	0.4323	1.6
381	14	SURG	ABORTION W D&C, ASPIRATION CURETTAGE OR HYSTEROTOMY	0.5257	1.5
382	14	MED	FALSE LABOR	0.2190	1.3
383	14	MED	OTHER ANTEPARTUM DIAGNOSES W MEDICAL COMPLICATIONS	0.5123	2.7
384	14	MED	OTHER ANTEPARTUM DIAGNOSES W/O MEDICAL COMPLICATIONS	0.3485	1.9
385	15	MED*	NEONATES, DIED OR TRANSFERRED TO ANOTHER ACUTE CARE FACILITY	1.3855	1.8
386	15	MED*	EXTREME IMMATURITY OR RESPIRATORY DISTRESS SYNDROME, NEONATE	4.5687	17.9
387	15	MED*	PREMATURITY W MAJOR PROBLEMS	3.1203	13.3
388	15	MED*	PREMATURITY W/O MAJOR PROBLEMS	1.8827	8.6
389	15	MED*	FULL TERM NEONATE W MAJOR PROBLEMS	3.2052	4.7
390	15	MED*	NEONATE W OTHER SIGNIFICANT PROBLEMS	1.1344	3.4
391	15	MED*	NORMAL NEWBORN	0.1536	3.1
392	16	SURG	SPLENECTOMY AGE >17	3.3164	7.1
393	16	SURG*	SPLENECTOMY AGE 0-17	1.3571	9.1
394	16	SURG	OTHER O.R. PROCEDURES OF THE BLOOD AND BLOOD FORMING ORGANS	1.9338	4.7
395	16	MED	RED BLOOD CELL DISORDERS AGE >17	0.8307	3.2
396	16	MED	RED BLOOD CELL DISORDERS AGE 0-17	0.6986	2.9
397	16	MED	COAGULATION DISORDERS	1.2648	3.7
398	16	MED	RETICULOENDOTHELIAL & IMMUNITY DISORDERS W CC	1.2360	4.5
399	16	MED	RETICULOENDOTHELIAL & IMMUNITY DISORDERS W/O CC	0.6651	2.7
400	17	SURG	NO LONGER VALID	0.0000	0.0
401	17	SURG	LYMPHOMA & NON-ACUTE LEUKEMIA W OTHER O.R. PROC W CC	2.8946	8.1
402	17	SURG	LYMPHOMA & NON-ACUTE LEUKEMIA W OTHER O.R. PROC W/O CC	1.1430	2.7
403	17	MED	LYMPHOMA & NON-ACUTE LEUKEMIA W CC	1.8197	5.8
404	17	MED	LYMPHOMA & NON-ACUTE LEUKEMIA W/O CC	0.8658	3.0
405	17	MED*	ACUTE LEUKEMIA W/O MAJOR O.R. PROCEDURE AGE 0-17	1.9241	4.9
406	17	SURG	MYELOPROLIF DISORD OR POORLY DIFF NEOPL W MAJ O.R. PROC W CC	2.7055	6.9
407	17	SURG	MYELOPROLIF DISORD OR POORLY DIFF NEOPL W MAJ O.R. PROC W/O CC	1.2410	3.2
408	17	SURG	MYELOPROLIF DISORD OR POORLY DIFF NEOPL W OTHER O.R. PROC	2.1984	4.8
409	17	MED	RADIOTHERAPY	1.2439	4.6
410	17	MED	CHEMOTHERAPY W/O ACUTE LEUKEMIA AS SECONDARY		

			DIAGNOSIS	1.0833	3.2
411	17	MED*	HISTORY OF MALIGNANCY W/O ENDOSCOPY	0.3948	4.7
412	17	MED	HISTORY OF MALIGNANCY W ENDOSCOPY	0.5679	2.5
413	17	MED	OTHER MYELOPROLIF DIS OR POORLY DIFF NEOPL DIAG W CC	1.3224	5.2
414	17	MED	OTHER MYELOPROLIF DIS OR POORLY DIFF NEOPL DIAG W/O CC	0.7370	3.2
415	18	SURG	O.R. PROCEDURE FOR INFECTIOUS & PARASITIC DISEASES	3.6276	10.4
416	18	MED	SEPTICEMIA AGE >17	1.5918	5.6
417	18	MED	SEPTICEMIA AGE 0-17	0.9612	4.4
418	18	MED	POSTOPERATIVE & POST-TRAUMATIC INFECTIONS	1.0672	4.8
419	18	MED	FEVER OF UNKNOWN ORIGIN AGE >17 W CC	0.8476	3.6
420	18	MED	FEVER OF UNKNOWN ORIGIN AGE >17 W/O CC	0.6107	2.8
421	18	MED	VIRAL ILLNESS AGE >17	0.7464	3.1
422	18	MED	VIRAL ILLNESS & FEVER OF UNKNOWN ORIGIN AGE 0-17	0.7248	2.5
423	18	MED	OTHER INFECTIOUS & PARASITIC DISEASES DIAGNOSES	1.8155	5.9
424	19	SURG	O.R. PROCEDURE W PRINCIPAL DIAGNOSES OF MENTAL ILLNESS	2.4074	8.0
425	19	MED	ACUTE ADJUSTMENT REACTION & PSYCHOSOCIAL DYSFUNCTION	0.6781	2.8
426	19	MED	DEPRESSIVE NEUROSES	0.5087	3.2
427	19	MED	NEUROSES EXCEPT DEPRESSIVE	0.5012	3.1
428	19	MED	DISORDERS OF PERSONALITY & IMPULSE CONTROL	0.7291	4.5
429	19	MED	ORGANIC DISTURBANCES & MENTAL RETARDATION	0.8291	4.5
430	19	MED	PSYCHOSES	0.6801	5.6
431	19	MED	CHILDHOOD MENTAL DISORDERS	0.6620	4.4
432	19	MED	OTHER MENTAL DISORDER DIAGNOSES	0.6513	2.9
433	20	MED	ALCOHOL/DRUG ABUSE OR DEPENDENCE, LEFT AMA	0.2904	2.2
434	20	MED	NO LONGER VALID	0.0000	0.0
435	20	MED	NO LONGER VALID	0.0000	0.0
436	20	MED	NO LONGER VALID	0.0000	0.0
437	20	MED	NO LONGER VALID	0.0000	0.0
438	20		NO LONGER VALID	0.0000	0.0
439	21	SURG	SKIN GRAFTS FOR INJURIES	1.7547	5.2
440	21	SURG	WOUND DEBRIDEMENTS FOR INJURIES	1.8878	5.8
441	21	SURG	HAND PROCEDURES FOR INJURIES	0.9662	2.1
442	21	SURG	OTHER O.R. PROCEDURES FOR INJURIES W CC	2.4200	5.6
443	21	SURG	OTHER O.R. PROCEDURES FOR INJURIES W/O CC	0.9787	2.5
444	21	MED	TRAUMATIC INJURY AGE >17 W CC	0.7475	3.2
445	21	MED	TRAUMATIC INJURY AGE >17 W/O CC	0.5015	2.3
446	21	MED*	TRAUMATIC INJURY AGE 0-17	0.2983	2.4
447	21	MED	ALLERGIC REACTIONS AGE >17	0.5238	1.9
448	21	MED*	ALLERGIC REACTIONS AGE 0-17	0.0981	2.9
449	21	MED	POISONING & TOXIC EFFECTS OF DRUGS AGE >17 W CC	0.8352	2.6
450	21	MED	POISONING & TOXIC EFFECTS OF		

			DRUGS AGE >17 W/O CC	0.4246	1.6
451	21	MED*	POISONING & TOXIC EFFECTS OF DRUGS AGE 0-17	0.2648	2.1
452	21	MED	COMPLICATIONS OF TREATMENT W CC	1.0455	3.5
453	21	MED	COMPLICATIONS OF TREATMENT W/O CC	0.5113	2.1
454	21	MED	OTHER INJURY, POISONING & TOXIC EFFECT DIAG W CC	0.8153	3.0
455	21	MED	OTHER INJURY, POISONING & TOXIC EFFECT DIAG W/O CC	0.4773	1.8
456	22		NO LONGER VALID	0.0000	0.0
457	22	MED	NO LONGER VALID	0.0000	0.0
458	22	SURG	NO LONGER VALID	0.0000	0.0
459	22	SURG	NO LONGER VALID	0.0000	0.0
460	22	MED	NO LONGER VALID	0.0000	0.0
461	23	SURG	O.R. PROC W DIAGNOSES OF OTHER CONTACT W HEALTH SERVICES	1.1692	2.2
462	23	MED	REHABILITATION	0.9747	9.0
463	23	MED	SIGNS & SYMPTOMS W CC	0.6856	3.1
464	23	MED	SIGNS & SYMPTOMS W/O CC	0.4982	2.4
465	23	MED	AFTERCARE W HISTORY OF MALIGNANCY AS SECONDARY DIAGNOSIS	0.8881	2.0
466	23	MED	AFTERCARE W/O HISTORY OF MALIGNANCY AS SECONDARY DIAGNOSIS	0.8088	2.2
467	23	MED	OTHER FACTORS INFLUENCING HEALTH STATUS	0.5274	1.9
468			EXTENSIVE O.R. PROCEDURE UNRELATED TO PRINCIPAL DIAGNOSIS	3.8454	9.4
469		**	PRINCIPAL DIAGNOSIS INVALID AS DISCHARGE DIAGNOSIS	0.0000	0.0
470		**	UNGROUPABLE	0.0000	0.0
471	08	SURG	BILATERAL OR MULTIPLE MAJOR JOINT PROCS OF LOWER EXTREMITY	3.0576	4.7
472	22	SURG	NO LONGER VALID	0.0000	0.0
473	17	MED	ACUTE LEUKEMIA W/O MAJOR O.R. PROCEDURE AGE >17	3.4885	7.4
474	04	SURG	NO LONGER VALID	0.0000	0.0
475	04	MED	RESPIRATORY SYSTEM DIAGNOSIS WITH VENTILATOR SUPPORT	3.6000	8.0
476		SURG	PROSTATIC O.R. PROCEDURE UNRELATED TO PRINCIPAL DIAGNOSIS	2.2477	8.0
477		SURG	NON-EXTENSIVE O.R. PROCEDURE UNRELATED TO PRINCIPAL DIAGNOSIS	1.8873	5.4
478	05	SURG	OTHER VASCULAR PROCEDURES W CC	2.3743	4.9
479	05	SURG	OTHER VASCULAR PROCEDURES W/O CC	1.4300	2.4
480	PRE	SURG	LIVER TRANSPLANT	9.7823	14.0
481	PRE	SURG	BONE MARROW TRANSPLANT	6.1074	19.2
482	PRE	SURG	TRACHEOSTOMY FOR FACE, MOUTH & NECK DIAGNOSES	3.4803	9.6
483	PRE	SURG	TRAC W MECH VENT 96+HRS OR PDX EXCEPT FACE, MOUTH & NECK DX OSES	16.7762	34.2

484	24	SURG	CRANIOTOMY FOR MULTIPLE SIGNIFICANT TRAUMA	5.4179	9.7
485	24	SURG	LIMB REATTACHMENT, HIP AND FEMUR PROC FOR MULTIPLE SIGNIFICANT TRA	3.2121	7.9
486	24	SURG	OTHER O.R. PROCEDURES FOR MULTIPLE SIGNIFICANT TRAUMA	4.8793	8.7
487	24	MED	OTHER MULTIPLE SIGNIFICANT TRAUMA	2.0057	5.3
488	25	SURG	HIV W EXTENSIVE O.R. PROCEDURE	4.8118	11.7
489	25	MED	HIV W MAJOR RELATED CONDITION	1.8603	6.0
490	25	MED	HIV W OR W/O OTHER RELATED CONDITION	1.0512	3.9
491	08	SURG	MAJOR JOINT & LIMB REATTACHMENT PROCEDURES OF UPPER EXTREMITY	1.7139	2.8
492	17	MED	CHEMOTHERAPY W ACUTE LEUKEMIA OR W USE OF HI DOSE CHEMOAGENT	3.8371	9.3
493	07	SURG	LAPAROSCOPIC CHOLECYSTECTOMY W/O C.D.E. W CC	1.8302	4.4
494	07	SURG	LAPAROSCOPIC CHOLECYSTECTOMY W/O C.D.E. W/O CC	1.0034	2.0
495	PRE	SURG	LUNG TRANSPLANT	8.5551	13.4
496	08	SURG	COMBINED ANTERIOR/POSTERIOR SPINAL FUSION	5.6839	6.8
497	08	SURG	SPINAL FUSION EXCEPT CERVICAL W CC	3.4056	5.2
498	08	SURG	SPINAL FUSION EXCEPT CERVICAL W/O CC	2.5319	3.6
499	08	SURG	BACK & NECK PROCEDURES EXCEPT SPINAL FUSION W CC	1.4244	3.3
500	08	SURG	BACK & NECK PROCEDURES EXCEPT SPINAL FUSION W/O CC	0.9369	2.0
501	08	SURG	KNEE PROCEDURES W PDX OF INFECTION W CC	2.6393	8.3
502	08	SURG	KNEE PROCEDURES W PDX OF INFECTION W/O CC	1.4192	5.1
503	08	SURG	KNEE PROCEDURES W/O PDX OF INFECTION	1.2233	3.0
504	22	SURG	EXTENSIVE 3RD DEGREE BURNS W SKIN GRAFT	11.6215	20.3
505	22	MED	EXTENSIVE 3RD DEGREE BURNS W/O SKIN GRAFT	2.0006	2.3
506	22	SURG	FULL THICKNESS BURN W SKIN GRAFT OR INHAL INJ W CC OR SIG TRAUMA	4.1070	12.1
507	22	SURG	FULL THICKNESS BURN W SKIN GRFT OR INHAL INJ W/O CC OR SIG TRAUMA	1.8154	6.5
508	22	MED	FULL THICKNESS BURN W/O SKIN GRFT OR INHAL INJ W CC OR SIG TRAUMA	1.3775	5.6
509	22	MED	FULL THICKNESS BURN W/O SKIN GRFT OR INH INJ W/O CC OR SIG TRAUMA	0.6426	3.1
510	22	MED	NON-EXTENSIVE BURNS W CC OR SIGNIFICANT TRAUMA	1.1812	4.6
511	22	MED	NON-EXTENSIVE BURNS W/O CC OR SIGNIFICANT TRAUMA	0.6753	3.2
512	PRE	SURG	SIMULTANEOUS PANCREAS/KIDNEY		

			TRANSPLANT	5.3405	11.1
513	PRE	SURG	PANCREAS TRANSPLANT	6.1594	8.7
514	05	SURG	NO LONGER VALID	0.0000	0.0
515	05	SURG	CARDIAC DEFIBRILLATOR IMPLANT W/O CARDIAC CATH	5.3366	3.0
516	05	SURG	PERCUTANEOUS CARDIOVASC PROC W AMI	2.6911	3.8
517	05	SURG	PERC CARDIO PROC W NON-DRUG ELUTING STENT W/O AMI	2.1598	1.8
518	05	SURG	PERC CARDIO PROC W/O CORONARY ARTERY STENT OR AMI	1.7494	2.3
519	08	SURG	CERVICAL SPINAL FUSION W CC	2.4266	3.2
520	08	SURG	CERVICAL SPINAL FUSION W/O CC	1.5780	1.7
521	20	MED	ALCOHOL/DRUG ABUSE OR DEPENDENCE W CC	0.7115	4.3
522	20	MED	ALC/DRUG ABUSE OR DEPEND W REHABILITATION THERAPY W/O CC	0.5226	7.7
523	20	MED	ALC/DRUG ABUSE OR DEPEND W/O REHABILITATION THERAPY W/O CC	0.3956	3.3
524	01	MED	TRANSIENT ISCHEMIA	0.7320	2.7
525	05	SURG	HEART ASSIST SYSTEM IMPLANT	14.1896	10.2
526	05	SURG	PERCUTNEOUS CARDIOVASULAR PROC W DRUG ELUTING STENT W AMI	2.9891	3.6
527	05	SURG	PERCUTNEOUS CARDIOVASULAR PROC W DRUG ELUTING STENT W/O AMI	2.4483	1.8
528	01	SURG	INTRACRANIAL VASCULAR PROC W PDX HEMORRHAGE	7.2205	14.2
529	01	SURG	VENTRICULAR SHUNT PROCEDURES W CC	2.2529	5.3
530	01	SURG	VENTRICULAR SHUNT PROCEDURES W/O CC	1.2017	2.8
531	01	SURG	SPINAL PROCEDURES W CC	3.0552	6.8
532	01	SURG	SPINAL PROCEDURES W/O CC	1.4482	2.9
533	01	SURG	EXTRACRANIAL PROCEDURES W CC	1.6678	2.7
534	01	SURG	EXTRACRANIAL PROCEDURES W/O CC	1.0748	1.6
535	05	SURG	CARDIAC DEFIB IMPLANT W CARDIAC CATH W AMI/HF/SHOCK	8.1560	8.1
536	05	SURG	CARDIAC DEFIB IMPLANT W CARDIAC CATH W/O AMI/HF/SHOCK	6.2775	3.9
537	08	SURG	LOCAL EXCIS & REMOV OF INT FIX DEV EXCEPT HIP & FEMUR W CC	1.8185	4.7
538	08	SURG	LOCAL EXCIS & REMOV OF INT FIX DEV EXCEPT HIP & FEMUR W/O CC	0.9919	2.1
539	17	SURG	LYMPHOMA & LEUKEMIA W MAJOR OR PROCEDURE W CC	3.3846	7.4
540	17	SURG	LYMPHOMA & LEUKEMIA W MAJOR OR PROCEDURE W/O CC	1.2891	2.9

History: 1. New section filed 1-2-2004 as an emergency; operative 1-2-2004 (Register 2004, No. 2). A Certificate of Compliance must be transmitted to OAL by 5-3-2004 or emergency language will be repealed by operation of law on the following day.

2. Certificate of Compliance as to 1-2-2004 order transmitted to OAL 4-30-2004 and filed 6-15-2004 (Register 2004, No. 25).

Ref.: Hanna § 22.05[2]; Herlick Handbook § 4.19.

§9789.30. Hospital Outpatient Departments and Ambulatory Surgical Centers — Definitions.

(a) "Adjusted Conversion Factor" means the CMS' conversion factor for 2003 of 52.151 × the market basket inflation factor of 1.034 × (0.4 + (0.6 × wage index)).

(b) "Ambulatory Payment Classifications (APC)" means the Centers for Medicare &

Medicaid Services' (CMS) list of ambulatory payment classifications of hospital outpatient services.

(c) "Ambulatory Surgical Center (ASC)" means any surgical clinic as defined in the California Health and Safety Code Section 1204, subdivision (b)(1), any ambulatory surgical center that is certified to participate in the Medicare program under Title XVIII (42 U.S.C. SEC. 1395 et seq.) of the federal Social Security Act, or any surgical clinic accredited by an accrediting agency as approved by the Licensing Division of the Medical Board of California pursuant to Health and Safety Code Sections 1248.15 and 1248.4.

(d) "Annual Utilization Report of Specialty Clinics" means the Annual Utilization Report of Clinics that is filed by February 15 of each year with the Office of Statewide Health Planning and Development by the ASCs as required by Section 127285 and Section 1216 of the Health and Safety Code.

(e) "APC Payment Rate" means CMS' hospital outpatient prospective payment system rate for Calendar Year 2004 as set forth in the Federal Register on November 7, 2003, Volume 68, No. 216, Addendum B, pages 63488 through 63655 conformed to comply with CMS-1471-CN, Federal Register, Volume 68, No. 250 (December 31, 2003), pages 75442 through 75445, and CMS-1371-IFC, Federal Register, Volume 69, No. 3 (January 6, 2004), pages 820 through 844.

(f) "APC Relative Weight" means CMS' APC relative weight as set forth in CMS' hospital outpatient prospective payment system for the Calendar Year 2004 as set forth in the Federal Register on November 7, 2003, Volume 68, No. 216, Addendum B, pages 63488 through 63655 conformed to comply with CMS-1471-CN, Federal Register, Volume 68, No. 250 (December 31, 2003), pages 75442 through 75445, and CMS-1371-IFC, Federal Register, Volume 69, No. 3 (January 6, 2004), pages 820 through 844.

(g) "CMS" means the Centers for Medicare & Medicaid Services of the United States Department of Health and Human Services.

(h) "Cost to Charge Ratio for ASC" means the ratio of the facility's total operating costs to total gross charges during the preceding calendar year.

(i) "Cost to Charge Ratio for Hospital Outpatient Department" means the hospital cost-to-charge used by the Medicare fiscal intermediary to determine high cost outlier payments.

(j) "HCPCS" means CMS' Healthcare Common Procedure Coding System, which describes products, supplies, procedures and health professional services and includes, the American Medical Associations (AMA's) Physician "Current Procedural Terminology", Fourth Edition (CPT-4) codes, alphanumeric codes, and related modifiers.

(k) "HCPCS Level I Codes" are the AMA's CPT-4 codes and modifiers for professional services and procedures.

(*l*) "HCPCS Level II Codes" are national alphanumeric codes and modifiers maintained by CMS for health care products and supplies, as well as some codes for professional services not included in the AMA's CPT-4.

(m) "Health facility" means any facility as defined in Section 1250 of the Health and Safety Code.

(n) "Hospital Outpatient Department" means any hospital outpatient department of a health facility as defined in the California Health and Safety Code Section 1250 and any hospital outpatient department that is certified to participate in the Medicare program under Title XVIII (42 U.S.C. SEC. 1395 et seq.) of the federal Social Security Act.

(o) "Hospital Outpatient Department Services" means services furnished by any health facility as defined in the California Health and Safety Code Section 1250 and any hospital that is certified to participate in the Medicare program under Title XVIII (42 U.S.C. SEC. 1395 et seq.) of the federal Social Security Act to a patient who has not been admitted as an inpatient but who is registered as an outpatient in the records of the hospital.

(p) "Market Basket Inflation Factor" means 3.4%, the market basket percentage increase determined by CMS for FY 2004, as set forth in the Federal Register on August 1, 2003, Volume 68, at page 45346.

(q) "Outpatient Prospective Payment System (OPPS)" means Medicare's payment system for outpatient services at hospitals. These outpatient services are classified according to a list of ambulatory payment classifications (APCs).

(r) "Total Gross Charges" means the facility's total usual and customary charges to patients and third-party payers before reductions for contractual allowances, bad debts, courtesy allowances and charity care.

(s) "Total Operating Costs" means the direct cost incurred in providing care to patients. Included in operating cost are: salaries and wages, rent or mortgage, employee benefits, supplies, equipment purchase and maintenance, professional fees, advertising, overhead, etc. It does not include start up costs.

(t) "Wage Index" means CMS' wage index for urban, rural and hospitals that are reclassified as described in CMS' 2004 Hospital Outpatient Prospective Payment System (HOPPS), adopted for the Calendar Year 2004, published in the Federal Register on November 7, 2003, Volume 68, No. 216, Addenda H through J, pages 63682 through 63690.

(u) "Workers' Compensation Multiplier" means the 120% Medicare multiplier required by Labor Code Section 5307.1, or the 122% multiplier that includes an extra 2% reimbursement for high cost outlier cases.

Note: Authority cited: Sections 133, 4603.5, 5307.1 and 5307.3, Labor Code. Reference: Sections 4600, 4603.2 and 5307.1, Labor Code.

History: 1. New section filed 1-2-2004 as an emergency; operative 1-2-2004 (Register 2004, No. 2). A Certificate of Compliance must be transmitted to OAL by 5-3-2004 or emergency language will be repealed by operation of law on the following day.

2. Certificate of Compliance as to 1-2-2004 order, including amendment of subsections (d)-(f), transmitted to OAL 4-30-2004 and filed 6-15-2004 (Register 2004, No. 25).

Ref.: Hanna § 22.05[2]; Herlick Handbook § 4.19.

§9789.31. Hospital Outpatient Departments and Ambulatory Surgical Centers — Adoption of Standards.

(a) The Administrative Director incorporates by reference, the Centers for Medicare and Medicaid Services' (CMS) 2004 Hospital Outpatient Prospective Payment System (HOPPS), adopted for the Calendar Year 2004, published in the Federal Register on November 7, 2003, Volume 68, No. 216, Addenda A through J, pages 63478 through 63690 (CMS-1471-FC), as changed by CMS-1471-CN, Federal Register, Volume 68, No. 250 (December 31, 2003), pages 75442 through 75445, and CMS-1371-IFC, Federal Register, Volume 69, No. 3 (January 6, 2004), pages 820 through 844. See http://www.cms.hhs.gov/regulations/hopps/. The payment system includes:

(1) Addendum A "List of Ambulatory Payment Classifications (APCs) with Status Indicators, Relative Weights, Payment Rates, and Copayment Amounts Calendar Year 2004."

(2) Addendum B "Payment Status by HCPCS Code and Related Information Calendar Year 2004."

(3) Addendum D1 "Payment Status Indicators for Hospital Outpatient Prospective Payment System."

(4) Addendum D2 "Code Conditions."

(5) Addendum E "CPT Codes Which Would Be Paid Only As Inpatient Procedures."

(6) Addendum H "Wage Index For Urban Areas"

(7) Addendum I "Wage Index For Rural Areas"

(8) Addendum J "Wage Index For Hospitals That Are Reclassified."

(b) The Administrative Director incorporates by reference the American Medical Associations' Physician "Current Procedural Terminology," 2004 Edition.

(c) The Administrative Director incorporates by reference CMS' 2004 Alphanumeric "Healthcare Common Procedure Coding System (HCPCS)."

Note: Authority cited: Sections 133, 4603.5, 5307.1 and 5307.3, Labor Code. Reference: Sections 4600, 4603.2 and 5307.1, Labor Code.

History: 1. New section filed 1-2-2004 as an emergency; operative 1-2-2004 (Register 2004, No. 2). A Certificate of Compliance must be transmitted to OAL by 5-3-2004 or emergency language will be repealed by operation of law on the following day.

2. Certificate of Compliance as to 1-2-2004 order, including amendment of subsection (a), transmitted to OAL 4-30-2004 and filed 6-15-2004 (Register 2004, No. 25).

Ref.: Hanna § 22.05[2]; Herlick Handbook § 4.19.

§9789.32. Outpatient Hospital Department and Ambulatory Surgical Center Fee Schedule — Applicability.

(a) Sections 9789.30 through 9789.38 shall be applicable to the maximum allowable fees for emergency room visits and surgical procedures rendered on or after July 1, 2004. For purposes of this section, emergency room visits shall be defined by CPT codes 99281–99285 and surgical procedures shall be defined by CPT codes 10040–69990. A facility fee is payable only for the specified emergency room and surgical codes and for supplies, drugs, devices, blood products and biologicals that are an integral part of the emergency room visit or surgical procedure. A supply, drug, device, blood product and biological is considered an integral part of an emergency room visit or surgical procedure if:

(1) the item has a status code N and is packaged into the APC payment for the emergency room visit or surgical procedure (in which case no additional fee is allowable) or,

(2) the item is furnished in conjunction with an emergency room visit or surgical procedure and has been assigned Status Code G, H or K. Payment for other services furnished in conjunction with a surgical procedure or emergency room visit shall be in accordance with subdivision (c) of this Section.

(b) Sections 9789.30 through 9789.38 apply to any hospital outpatient department as defined in Section 9789.30(n) and any hospital outpatient department that is certified to participate in the Medicare program under Title XVIII (42 U.S.C. SEC. 1395 et seq.) of the federal Social Security Act and any ASC as defined in the California Health and Safety Code Section 1204, subdivision (b)(1), any ambulatory surgical center that is certified to participate in the Medicare program under Title XVIII (42 U.S.C. SEC. 1395 et seq.) of the federal Social Security Act, and any surgical clinic accredited by an accrediting agency as approved by the Licensing Division of the Medical Board of California pursuant to Health and Safety Code Sections 1248.15 and 1248.4, performing procedures and services on an outpatient basis.

(c) The maximum allowable fees for services, drugs and supplies furnished by hospitals and ambulatory surgical centers that do not meet the requirements in (a) for a facility fee payment and are not bundled in the APC payment rate for a surgical service or emergency room visit will be determined as follows:

(1) The maximum allowable fees for professional medical services which are performed by physicians and other licensed health care providers shall be paid according to Section 9789.10 and Section 9789.11.

(2) The maximum allowable fees for organ acquisition costs and corneal tissue acquisition costs shall be based on the documented paid cost of procuring the organ or tissue.

(3) The maximum allowable fee for drugs not otherwise covered by a Medicare fee schedule payment for facility services shall be 100% of the fee prescribed by Medi-Cal pursuant to Labor Code Section 5307.1 subdivision (a), or, where applicable, Section 9789.40.

(4) The maximum allowable fee for clinical diagnostic tests shall be determined according to Section 9789.50.

(5) The maximum allowable fees for non-surgical ancillary services with a status code indicator "X" shall be determined according to Section 9789.10 and Section 9789.11.

(6) The maximum allowable fee for durable medical equipment, prosthetics and orthotics shall be determined according to Section 9789.60.

(7) The maximum allowable fee for ambulance service shall be determined according to Section 9789.70.

(d) Only hospitals may charge or collect a facility fee for emergency room visits. Only hospital outpatient departments and ambulatory surgical centers as defined in Section 9789.30(n) and Section 9789.30(c) may charge or collect a facility fee for surgical services provided on an outpatient basis.

(e) Hospital outpatient departments and ambulatory surgical centers shall not be reimbursed for procedures on the inpatient only list, Section 9789.31(a)(5), Addendum E, except that pre-authorized services rendered are payable at the pre-negotiated fee arrangement. The pre-authorization must be provided by an authorized agent of the claims administrator to the provider. The fee agreement and pre-authorization must be memorialized in writing prior to performing the medical services.

(f) Critical access hospitals and hospitals that are excluded from acute PPS are exempt from this fee schedule.

(g) Out of state hospital outpatient departments and ambulatory surgical centers are exempt from this fee schedule.

(h) Hospital outpatient departments and ambulatory surgical centers billing for facility fees and other services under this Section shall present with their bill the name and physical address of the facility, the facility's Medicare Provider Number or UPIN (or, in the absence of the Medicare number, the OSHPD Facility Number). The bill shall include the dates of service, the diagnosis and current HCPCS codes and charges for each billed service, including HCPCS codes for any items and services that are packaged into the APC payment for a significant procedure.

Note: Authority cited: Sections 133, 4603.5, 5307.1 and 5307.3, Labor Code. Reference: Sections 4600, 4603.2 and 5307.1, Labor Code.

History: 1. New section filed 1-2-2004 as an emergency; operative 1-2-2004 (Register 2004, No. 2). A Certificate of Compliance must be transmitted to OAL by 5-3-2004 or emergency language will be repealed by operation of law on the following day.

2. Certificate of Compliance as to 1-2-2004 order, including amendment of section, transmitted to OAL 4-30-2004 and filed 6-15-2004 (Register 2004, No. 25).

Ref.: Hanna § 22.05[2]; Herlick Handbook § 4.19.

§9789.33. Hospital Outpatient Departments and Ambulatory Surgical Facilities Fee Schedule — Determination of Maximum Reasonable Fee.

(a) For Services rendered on or after July 1, 2004, the maximum allowable payment for outpatient facility fees for hospital emergency room services or for surgical services performed at a hospital outpatient department or at an ambulatory surgical center shall be determined based on the following. The 1.22 factor shall be used in lieu of an additional payment for high cost outlier cases.

(1) CTP codes 99281-99285 and CPT codes 10040-69990 with status code indicators "S", "T", "X" or "V":

(APC relative weight × $52.151) × (.40 + .60 × applicable wage index) × inflation factor of 1.034 × 1.22

(A) Table A in Section 9789.34 contains an "adjusted conversion factor" which incorporates the standard conversion factor, wage index and inflation factor. The maximum payment rate for ASCs and non-listed hospitals can be determined as follows:

APC relative weight × adjusted conversion factor × 1.22

(B) Table B in Section 9789.35 contains an "adjusted conversion factor" which incorporates the standard conversion factor, wage index and inflation factor. The maximum payment rate for the listed hospitals can be determined as follows:

APC relative weight × adjusted conversion factor × 1.22

(2) Procedure codes for drugs and biologicals with status code indicator "G":

APC payment rate × 1.22

(3) Procedure codes for devices with status code indicator "H":

Documented paid costs, net of discounts and rebates, plus 10% not to exceed $250.00, plus any sales tax and/or shipping and handling charges actually paid.

(4) Procedure codes for drugs and biologicals with status code indicator "K":

APC payment rate × 1.22

(b) Alternative payment methodology. In lieu of the maximum allowable fees set forth under (a), the maximum allowable fees for a facility meeting the requirements in subdivisions (c)(1) through (c)(5) will be determined as follows:

(1) Standard payment:

(A) CTP codes 99281-99285 and CPT codes 10040-69990 with status code indicators "S", "T", "X" or "V":

(APC relative weight × $52.151) × (.40 + .60 × applicable wage index) × inflation factor of 1.034 × 1.20

(B) Procedure codes for drugs and biologicals with status code indicator "G":

APC payment rate × 1.20

(C) Procedure codes for devices with status code indicator "H":

Documented paid costs, net of discounts and rebates, plus 10% not to exceed $250.00, plus any sales tax and/or shipping and handling charges actually paid.

(D) Procedure codes for drugs and biologicals with status code indicator "K"

APC payment rate × 1.20

(2) Additional payment for high cost outlier case:

[(Facility charges × cost-to-charge ratio) – (standard payment × 2.6)] × .50

(3) In determining the additional payment, the facility's charges and payment for devices with status code indicator "H" shall be excluded from the computation.

(c) The following requirements shall be met for election of the alternative payment methodology:

(1) A facility seeking to be paid for high cost outlier cases under subdivision 9789.33(b) must file a written election using DWC Form 15 "Election for High Cost Outlier," contained in Section 9789.37 with the Division of Workers' Compensation, Medical Unit (Attention: OMFS-Outpatient). P.O. Box 420603, San Francisco, CA 94142-0603. The form must be post-marked

by March 1 of each year and shall be effective for one year commencing with services furnished on or after April 1 of the year in which the election is made.

(2) The maximum allowable fees applicable to a facility that does not file a timely election satisfying the requirements set forth in this subdivision and Section 9789.37 shall be determined under subdivision (a).

(3) The maximum allowable fees applicable to a hospital that does not participate under the Medicare program shall be determined under subdivision (a).

(4) The cost-to-charge ratio applicable to a hospital participating in the Medicare program shall be the hospital's cost-to-charge ratio used by the Medicare fiscal intermediary to determine high cost outlier payments under 42 C.F.R. § 419.43(d), which is incorporated by reference, as contained in Section 9789.38 Appendix X. The cost-to-charge ratio being used by the intermediary for services furnished on February 15 of the year the election is filed shall be included on the hospital's election form.

(5) The cost-to-charge ratio applicable to an ambulatory surgery center shall be the ratio of the facility's total operating costs to total gross charges during the preceding calendar year. Total Operating Costs are the direct costs incurred in providing care to patients. Included in operating cost are: salaries and wages, rent or mortgage, employee benefits, supplies, equipment purchase and maintenance, professional fees, advertising, overhead, etc. It does not include start up costs. Total gross charges are defined as the facility's total usual and customary charges to all patients and third-party party payers before reductions for contractual allowances, bad debts, courtesy allowances and charity care. The facility's election form, as contained in Section 9789.37 shall include a completed Annual Utilization Report of Specialty Clinics filed with Office of Statewide Health Planning and Development (OSHPD) for the preceding calendar year, which is incorporated by reference. The facility's election form shall further include the facility's total operating costs during the preceding calendar year, the facility's total gross charges during the preceding calendar year, and a certification under penalty of perjury signed by the Chief Executive Officer and a Certified Public Accountant, as to the accuracy of the information. Upon request from the Administrative Director, an independent audit may be conducted at the expense of the ASC. (Note: While ASCs may not typically file Annual Utilization Report of Specialty Clinics with OSHPD, any ASC applying for the alternative payment methodology must file the equivalent, subject to the Division of Workers' Compensation's audit.) A copy of the Annual Utilization Report of Specialty Clinics may be obtained at OSHPD's website at http://www.oshpd.ca.gov/HID/HID/clinic/util/index.htm#Forms or upon request to the Division of Workers' Compensation, Medical Unit (Attention: OMFS-Outpatient), P.O. Box 420603, San Francisco, CA 94142-0603.

(6) Before April 1 of each year the AD shall post a list of those facilities that have elected to be paid under this paragraph and the facility-specific cost-to-charge ratio that shall be used to determine additional fees allowable for high cost outlier cases. The list shall be posted on the Division of Workers' Compensation website: http://www.dir.ca.gov/DWC/dwc_home_page.htm or is available upon request to the Division of Workers' Compensation, Medical Unit (Attention: OMFS-Outpatient), P.O. Box 420603, San Francisco, CA 94142-0603.

(d) Any ambulatory surgical center that believes its cost-to-charge ratio in connection with its election to participate in the alternative payment methodology for high cost outlier cases under Section 9789.33(b) was erroneously determined because of error in tabulating data may request the Administrative Director for a redetermination of its cost-to-charge ratio. Such requests shall be in writing, shall state the alleged error, and shall be supported by written documentation. Within 30 days after receiving a complete written request, the Administrative Director shall make a redetermination of the cost-to-charge ratio or reaffirm the published cost-to-charge ratio.

(e) The OPPS rules in 42 C.F.R § 419.44 regarding reimbursement for multiple procedures are incorporated by reference as contained in Section 9789.38 Appendix X.

(f) The OPPS rules in 42 C.F.R. §§ 419.62, 419.64, and 419.66 regarding transitional pass-through payments for innovative medical devices, drugs and biologicals shall be incorporated by reference, as contained in Section 9789.38 Appendix X, except that payment for these items shall be in accordance with subdivisions (a) or (b) as applicable.

(g) The payment determined under subdivisions (a) and (b) include reimbursement for all of the included cost items specified in 42 CFR §419.2(b)(1)-(12), which is incorporated by reference, as contained in Section 9789.38 Appendix X.

(h) The maximum allowable fee shall be determined without regard to the cost items specified in 42 C.F.R. § 419.2(c)(1), (2), (3), (4), and (6), as contained in Section 9789.38 Appendix X. Cost item set forth at 42 C.F.R. § 419.2(c)(5), as contained in Section 9789.38 Appendix X, is payable pursuant to Section 9789.32(c)(1). Cost items set forth at 42 C.F.R. § 419.2(c)(7) and (8), as contained in Section 9789.38 Appendix X, are payable pursuant to Section 9789.32(c)(2).

(i) The maximum allowable fees shall be determined without regard to the provisions in 42 C.F.R. § 419.70.

Note: Authority cited: Sections 133, 4603.5, 5307.1, and 5307.3, Labor Code. Reference: Sections 4600, 4603.2, and 5307.1, Labor Code.

History: 1. New section filed 1-2-2004 as an emergency; operative 1-2-2004 (Register 2004, No. 2). A Certificate of Compliance must be transmitted to OAL by 5-3-2004 or emergency language will be repealed by operation of law on the following day.

2. Certificate of Compliance as to 1-2-2004 order, including amendment of section, transmitted to OAL 4-30-2004 and filed 6-15-2004 (Register 2004, No. 25).

3. Change without regulatory effect amending subsections (c)(1), (c)(5) and (c)(6) filed 10-18-2006 pursuant to section 100, title 1, California Code of Regulations (Register 2006, No. 42).

Ref.: Hanna § 22.05[2]; Herlick Handbook § 4.19.

§9789.34. Table A.

(See Addenda H and I set forth in Section 9789.31)

MSA Code	*Urban/Rural Area*	*Constituent Counties*	*Wage Index*	*Adjusted Conversion Factor**
680	Bakersfield, CA	Kern	0.9967	53.82
1620	Chico-Paradise, CA	Butte	1.0193	54.55
2840	Fresno, CA	Fresno Madera	1.0142	54.38
4480	Los Angeles–Long Beach, CA	Los Angeles	1.1832	59.85
4940	Merced, CA	Merced	0.9967	53.82
51700	Modesto, CA	Stanislaus	1.1275	58.05
5775	Oakland, CA	Alameda Contra Costa	1.5119	70.49
5945	Orange County, CA	Orange	1.1492	58.75
6690	Redding, CA	Shasta	1.1352	58.30
6780	Riverside–San Bernardino, CA	Riverside San Bernardino	1.1348	58.29
6920	Sacramento, CA	El Dorado Placer Sacramento	1.1845	59.89
7120	Salinas, CA	Monterey	1.4339	67.96
7320	San Diego, CA	San Diego	1.1147	57.64
7360	San Francisco, CA	Marin San Francisco San Mateo	1.4514	68.53
7400	San Jose, CA	Santa Clara	1.4626	68.89
7460	San Luis Obispo–Atascadero–Paso Robles, CA	San Luis Obispo	1.1429	58.55
7480	Santa Barbara–Santa Maria–Lompoc, CA	Santa Barbara	1.0441	55.35
7485	Santa Cruz–Watsonville, CA	Santa Cruz	1.2942	63.44
7500	Santa Rosa, CA	Sonoma	1.2877	63.23
8120	Stockton-Lodi, CA	San Joaquin	1.0404	55.23
8720	Vallejo–Fairfield–Napa, CA	Napa Solano	1.3425	65.01
8735	Ventura, CA	Ventura	1.1064	57.37
8780	Visalia–Tulare–Porterville, CA	Tulare	0.9967	53.82

9270	Yolo, CA	Yolo	0.9967	53.82
9340	Yuba City, CA	Sutter Yuba	1.0196	54.56
Non-MSA Areas of State			0.9967	53.82

* $52.151 × (.40 + .60 × applicable wage index) × inflation factor of 1.034

Note: Authority cited: Sections 133, 4603.5, 5307.1 and 5307.3, Labor Code. Reference: Sections 4600, 4603.2 and 5307.1, Labor Code.

History: 1. New section filed 1-2-2004 as an emergency; operative 1-2-2004 (Register 2004, No. 2). A Certificate of Compliance must be transmitted to OAL by 5-3-2004 or emergency language will be repealed by operation of law on the following day.

2. Certificate of Compliance as to 1-2-2004 order, including amendment of section, transmitted to OAL 4-30-2004 and filed 6-15-2004 (Register 2004, No. 25).

Ref.: Hanna § 22.05[2]; Herlick Handbook § 4.19.

§9789.35. Table B.

(See Addenda H, I and J set forth in Section 9789.31)

PROVIDER #	NAME	WIGRN - MSA WAGE INDEX	Adjusted Conversion Factor
050002	ST. ROSE HOSPITAL	1.5119	70.49
050006	ST JOSEPH - EUREKA	0.9967	53.82
050007	MILLS PENINSULA MEDICAL CENTER	1.4514	68.53
050008	CPMC - DAVIES CAMPUS	1.4514	68.53
050009	QUEEN OF THE VALLEY HOSPITAL	1.3425	65.01
050013	ST HELENA HOSPITAL	1.3425	65.01
050014	SUTTER AMADOR HOSPITAL	0.9967	53.82
050015	NORTHERN INYO HOSPITAL	0.9967	53.82
050016	ARROYO GRANDE COMMUNITY HOSPITAL	1.1429	58.55
050017	MERCY GENERAL HOSPITAL	1.1845	59.89
050018	PACIFIC ALLIANCE MEDICAL CNTR	1.1832	59.85
050022	RIVERSIDE COMMUNITY	1.1348	58.29
050024	PARADISE VALLEY HOSPITAL	1.1147	57.64
050025	UCSD MEDICAL CENTER	1.1147	57.64
050026	GROSSMONT HOSPITAL	1.1147	57.64
050028	MAD RIVER COMMUNITY HOSPITAL	0.9967	53.82
050029	ST. LUKE MEDICAL CENTER	1.1832	59.85
050030	OROVILLE HOSPITAL	1.0193	54.55
050036	MEMORIAL HOSPITAL	0.9967	53.82
050038	SANTA CLARA VALLEY MEDICAL CENTER	1.4626	68.89
050039	ENLOE MEDICAL CENTER	1.0193	54.55
050040	LAC OLIVE VIEW/UCLA MEDICAL CENTER	1.1832	59.85
050042	ST ELIZABETH COMMUNITY HOSPITAL	1.1352	58.30
050043	SUMMIT MEDICAL CENTER	1.5119	70.49
050045	EL CENTRO REGIONAL MED. CTR.	0.9967	53.82
050046	OJAI VALLEY COMMUNITY HOSPITAL	1.1064	57.37
050047	CALIFORNIA PACIFIC MEDICAL CENTER	1.4514	68.53
050054	SAN GORGONIO MEMORIAL HOSPITAL	1.1348	58.29
050055	ST. LUKES HOSPITAL	1.4514	68.53
050056	ANTELOPE VALLEY HOSPITAL	1.1832	59.85
050057	KAWEAH DELTA HEALTH CARE DISTRICT	0.9967	53.82
050058	GLENDALE MEMORIAL HOSPITAL & HLTH CT	1.1832	59.85
050060	COMMUNITY MEDICAL CENTER - FRESNO	1.0142	54.38
050061	ST. FRANCIS MEDICAL CENTER	1.0441	55.35
050063	QUEEN OF ANGELS - HLLYWD PRES MC	1.1832	59.85
050065	WMC SANTA ANA	1.1492	58.75

050067	OAK VALLEY DISTRICT HOSPITAL	1.1275	58.05
050069	ST. JOSEPH HOSPITAL	1.1492	58.75
050070	KFH - SOUTH SAN FRANCISCO	1.4514	68.53
050071	KFH - SANTA CLARA	1.5119	70.49
050072	KFH - WALNUT CREEK	1.5119	70.49
050073	KFH - VALLEJO	1.5119	70.49
050075	KFH - OAKLAND	1.5119	70.49
050076	KFH - SAN FRANCISCO	1.4514	68.53
050077	SCRIPPS MERCY HOSPITAL	1.1147	57.64
050078	SAN PEDRO PENINSULA HOSPITAL	1.1832	59.85
050079	DOCTORS MEDICAL CENTER-SAN PABLO	1.5119	70.49
050082	ST. JOHN'S REGIONAL MEDICAL CENTER	1.1064	57.37
050084	ST. JOSEPH'S MEDICAL CENTER	1.0404	55.23
050088	SAN LUIS OBISPO GEN HOSPITAL	1.1429	58.55
050089	COMMUNITY HOSPITAL OF SAN BERNARDINO	1.1348	58.29
050090	SONOMA VALLEY HEALTH CARE DIST.	1.2877	63.23
050091	HUNTINGTON PARK	1.1832	59.85
050093	SAINT AGNES MEDICAL CENTER	1.0142	54.38
050095	LAURAL GROVE HOSPITAL	1.5119	70.49
050096	DOCTOR'S HOSP. OF WEST COVINA	1.1832	59.85
050099	SAN ANTONIO COMMUNITY HOSPITAL	1.1348	58.29
050100	SHARP MEMORIAL HOSPITAL	1.1147	57.64
050101	SUTTER SOLANO MEDICAL CENTER	1.5119	70.49
050102	PARKVIEW COMMUNITY HOSPITAL	1.1348	58.29
050103	WHITE MEMORIAL MEDICAL CENTER	1.1832	59.85
050104	ST. FRANCIS MEDICAL CENTER	1.1832	59.85
050107	MARIAN MEDICAL CENTER	1.0441	55.35
050108	SUTTER MEDICAL CENTER-SACRAMENTO	1.1845	59.89
050110	LOMPOC DISTRICT HOSPITAL	1.0441	55.35
050111	TEMPLE COMMUNITY HOSPITAL	1.1832	59.85
050112	SANTA MONICA HOSPITAL	1.1832	59.85
050113	SAN MATEO COUNTY GENERAL HOSPITAL	1.4514	68.53
050114	SHERMAN OAKS HOSP AND HLTH CENTER	1.1832	59.85
050115	PALOMAR MEDICAL CENTER	1.1147	57.64
050116	NORTHRIDGE HOSPITAL - ROSCO	1.1832	59.85
050117	MERCY HOSPITAL & HEALTH SYSTEM	0.9967	53.82
050118	DOCTORS HOSPITAL OF MANTECA	1.0404	55.23
050121	HANFORD COMM. MEDICAL CENTER	0.9967	53.82
050122	DAMERON HOSPITAL	1.0404	55.23
050124	VERDUGO HILLS HOSPITAL	1.1832	59.85
050125	REGIONAL MEDICAL CENTER OF SAN JOSE	1.4626	68.89
050126	VALLEY PRESBYTERIAN HOSPITAL	1.1832	59.85
050127	WOODLAND MEMORIAL HOSPITAL	0.9967	53.82
050128	TRI-CITY MEDICAL CENTER	1.1147	57.64
050129	ST. BERNARDINE MEDICAL CENTER	1.1348	58.29
050131	NOVATO COMMUNITY HOSPITAL	1.4514	68.53
050132	SAN GABRIEL VALLEY MEDICAL CENTER	1.1832	59.85
050133	RIDEOUT MEMORIAL HOSPITAL	1.0196	54.56
050135	HOLLYWOOD COMM HOSP OF HOLLYWOOD	1.1832	59.85
050136	PETALUMA VALLEY HOSPITAL	1.2877	63.23
050137	KAISER FOUND. HOSP - PANORAMA	1.1832	59.85
050138	KAISER FOUNDATION HOSPITALS - SUNSET	1.1832	59.85
050139	KAISER FOUND. HOSPITALS - BELLFLOWER	1.1832	59.85
050140	KAISER FOUND. HOSPITALS - FONTANA	1.1348	58.29
050144	BROTMAN MEDICAL CENTER	1.1832	59.85
050145	COMMUNITY HOSP. MONTEREY PENINSULA	1.4339	67.96
050148	PLUMAS DISTRICT HOSPITAL MCARE RPT	0.9967	53.82
050149	CALIFORNIA HOSPITAL MEDICAL CENTER	1.1832	59.85
050150	SIERRA NEVADA MEMORIAL HOSPITAL	1.1845	59.89
050152	SAINT FRANCIS MEMORIAL HOSPITAL	1.4514	68.53

050153	O'CONNOR HOSPITAL	1.4626	68.89
050155	MONROVIA COMMUNITY HOSPITAL	1.1832	59.85
050158	ENCINO TARZANA MEDICAL CENTER	1.1832	59.85
050159	VENTURA COUNTY MEDICAL CENTER	1.1064	57.37
050167	SAN JOAQUIN GENERAL HOSPITAL	1.0404	55.23
050168	ST. JUDE MEDICAL CENTER	1.1492	58.75
050169	PRESBYTERIAN INTERCOMMUNITY HOSP	1.1832	59.85
050172	REDWOOD MEMORIAL HOSPITAL	0.9967	53.82
050173	ANAHEIM GENERAL HOSPITAL	1.1492	58.75
050174	SANTA ROSA MEMORIAL HOSPITAL	1.3425	65.01
050175	WHITTIER HOSPITAL MEDICAL CENTER	1.1832	59.85
050177	SANTA PAULA MEMORIAL HOSPITAL	1.1064	57.37
050179	EMANUEL MEDICAL CENTER	1.1275	58.05
050180	JOHN MUIR MEDICAL CENTER	1.5119	70.49
050188	COMM HOSP. & REHAB- LOS GATOS	1.4626	68.89
050189	MEE MEMORIAL HOSPITAL	1.4339	67.96
050191	ST. MARY MEDICAL CENTER	1.1832	59.85
050192	SIERRA KINGS DISTRICT HOSPITAL	0.9967	53.82
050193	SOUTH COAST MEDICAL CENTER	1.1492	58.75
050194	WATSONVILLE COMMUNITY	1.2942	63.44
050195	WASHINGTON HOSPITAL DISTRICT	1.5119	70.49
050196	CENTRAL VALLEY GEN. HOSPITAL	0.9967	53.82
050197	SEQUOIA HEALTH SERVICES	1.4514	68.53
050204	LANCASTER COMMUNITY HOSPITAL	1.1832	59.85
050205	HUNTINGTON EAST VALLEY HOSPITAL	1.1832	59.85
050207	FREMONT MEDICAL CENTER	1.0196	54.56
050211	ALAMEDA HOSPITAL	1.5119	70.49
050214	GRANADA HILLS HOSPITAL	1.1832	59.85
050215	SAN JOSE MEDICAL CENTER	1.4626	68.89
050217	FAIRCHILD MEDICAL CENTER	0.9967	53.82
050219	COAST PLAZA DOCTORS HOSPITAL	1.1832	59.85
050222	SHARP CHULA VISTA MEDICAL CTR	1.1147	57.64
050224	HOAG MEMORIAL HOSPITAL PRESBYTERIAN	1.1492	58.75
050225	FEATHER RIVER HOSPITAL	1.0193	54.55
050226	ANAHEIM MEMORIAL MEDICAL CENTER	1.1492	58.75
050228	SAN FRANCISCO GENERAL HOSPITAL	1.5119	70.49
050230	GARDEN GROVE MEDICAL CENTER	1.1832	59.85
050231	POMONA VALLEY HOSPITAL MED CTR	1.1832	59.85
050232	FRENCH HOSPITAL MEDICAL CENTER	1.1429	58.55
050234	SHARP CORONADO HOSPITAL	1.1147	57.64
050235	PROVIDENCE SAINT JOSEPH MED. CENTER	1.1832	59.85
050236	SIMI VALLEY HOSPITAL	1.1832	59.85
050238	METHODIST HOSPITAL OF SO. CALIF.	1.1832	59.85
050239	GLENDALE ADVENTIST MEDICAL CENTER	1.1832	59.85
050240	CENTINELA HOSPITAL MEDICAL CENTER	1.1832	59.85
050242	DOMINICAN SANTA CRUZ HOSPITAL	1.2942	63.44
050243	DESERT HOSPITAL	1.1348	58.29
050245	ARROWHEAD REGIONAL MEDICAL CENTER	1.1348	58.29
050248	NATIVIDAD MEDICAL CENTER	1.4339	67.96
050251	LASSEN COMMUNITY HOSPITAL	1.0682	56.13
050253	BELLWOOD GENERAL HOSPITAL	1.1492	58.75
050254	MARSHALL HOSPITAL	1.1845	59.89
050256	ORTHOPAEDIC HOSPITAL	1.1832	59.85
050257	GOOD SAMARITAN HOSPITAL	0.9967	53.82
050261	SIERRA VIEW DISTRICT HOSPITAL	0.9967	53.82
050262	UCLA MEDICAL CENTER	1.1832	59.85
050264	SAN LEANDRO HOSPITAL	1.5119	70.49
050267	DANIEL FREEMAN MEMORIAL HOSPITAL	1.1832	59.85
050270	SMH - CHULA VISTA	1.1147	57.64
050272	REDLANDS COMMUNITY HOSPITAL	1.1348	58.29

050276	CONTRA COSTA REGIONAL MEDICAL CNTR	1.5119	70.49
050277	PACIFIC HOSPITAL OF LONG BEACH	1.1832	59.85
050278	PROVIDENCE HOLY CROSS MED. CENTER	1.1832	59.85
050279	HI - DESERT MEDICAL CENTER	1.1348	58.29
050280	MERCY MEDICAL CENTER REDDING	1.1352	58.30
050281	ALHAMBRA HOSPITAL	1.1832	59.85
050283	VALLEY MEMORIAL HOSPITAL	1.5119	70.49
050289	SETON MEDICAL CENTER	1.4514	68.53
050290	SAINT JOHN'S HOSPITAL	1.1832	59.85
050291	SUTTER MEDICAL CENTER OF SANTA ROSA	1.2877	63.23
050292	RIVERSIDE COUNTY REGIONAL MED CENTER	1.1348	58.29
050295	MERCY HOSPITAL	0.9967	53.82
050296	HAZEL HAWKINS MEM. HOSPITAL	1.4339	67.96
050298	BARSTOW COMMUNITY HOSPITAL	1.1348	58.29
050299	NORTHRIDGE HOSPITAL MEDICAL CENTER-S	1.1832	59.85
050300	ST MARY REGIONAL MEDICAL CENTER	1.1348	58.29
050301	UKIAH VALLEY MEDICAL CENTER	0.9967	53.82
050305	ALTA BATES MEDICAL CENTER	1.5119	70.49
050308	EL CAMINO HOSPITAL	1.4626	68.89
050309	SUTTER ROSEVILLE MEDICAL CENTER	1.1845	59.89
050312	REDDING MEDICAL CENTER	1.1352	58.30
050313	SUTTER TRACY COMMUNITY HOSPITAL	1.0404	55.23
050315	KERN MEDICAL CENTER	0.9967	53.82
050320	ALAMEDA COUNTY MEDICAL CENTER	1.5119	70.49
050324	SCRIPPS MEM HOSPITAL-LA JOLLA	1.1147	57.64
050325	TUOLUMNE GENERAL HOSPITAL	1.1148	57.64
050327	LOMA LINDA UNIVERSITY MEDICAL CTR.	1.1348	58.29
050329	CORONA REGIONAL MEDICAL CENTER	1.1348	58.29
050331	HEALSDBURG GENERAL HOSPITAL	1.2877	63.23
050333	SENECA DISTRICT HOSPITAL	0.9967	53.82
050334	SALINAS VALLEY MEMORIAL HOSPITAL	1.4339	67.96
050335	SONORA COMMUNITY HOSPITAL	1.1148	57.64
050336	LODI MEMORIAL HOSPITAL	1.0404	55.23
050342	PIONEERS MEM. HOSPITAL	0.9967	53.82
050348	UCI MEDICAL CENTER	1.1492	58.75
050349	CORCORAN DISTRICT HOSPITAL	0.9967	53.82
050350	BEVERLY COMMUNITY HOSPITAL	1.1832	59.85
050351	TORRANCE MEMORIAL MEDICAL CENTER	1.1832	59.85
050352	BARTON MEMORIAL HOSP	1.1845	59.89
050353	LITTLE COMPANY OF MARY HOSPITAL	1.1832	59.85
050355	SIERRA VALLEY DISTRICT HOSPITAL	0.9967	53.82
050357	GOLETA VALLEY COTTAGE HOSPITAL	1.0441	55.35
050359	TULARE DISTRICT HOSPITAL	0.9967	53.82
050360	MARIN GENERAL HOSPITAL	1.4514	68.53
050366	MARK TWAIN ST. JOSEPHS HOPITAL	0.9967	53.82
050367	NORTHBAY MEDICAL CENTER	1.3425	65.01
050369	CVMC - QUEEN OF THE VALLEY	1.1832	59.85
050373	LAC+USC MEDICAL CENTER	1.1832	59.85
050376	HARBOR-UCLA MEDICAL CENTER	1.1832	59.85
050378	PACIFICA OF THE VALLEY	1.1832	59.85
050379	MERCY WESTSIDE HOSPITAL	0.9967	53.82
050380	GOOD SAMARITAN HOSPITAL	1.4626	68.89
050382	CVMC - INTERCOMMUNITY	1.1832	59.85
050385	PALM DRIVE HOSPITAL	1.2877	63.23
050390	HEMET VALLEY MEDICAL CENTER	1.1348	58.29
050391	SANTA TERESITA HOSPITAL	1.1832	59.85
050392	TRINITY HOSPITAL	0.9967	53.82
050393	DOWNEY REGIONAL MED CTR	1.1832	59.85
050394	COMM MEM HOSP OF SAN BUENAVENTURA	1.1064	57.37
050396	SANTA BARBARA COTTAGE HOSPITAL	1.0441	55.35

050397	COALINGA REGIONAL MEDICAL CENTER	1.0142	54.38
050407	CHINESE HOSPITAL	1.4514	68.53
050410	SANGER GENERAL HOSPITAL	1.0142	54.38
050411	KAISER FOUNDATION HOSPITALS -HARBOR	1.1832	59.85
050414	MERCY HOSPITAL OF FOLSOM	1.1845	59.89
050417	SUTTER COAST HOSPITAL	0.9967	53.82
050419	MERCY MEDICAL CENTER MT. SHASTA	1.1352	58.30
050420	ROBERT F. KENNEDY	1.1832	59.85
050423	PALO VERDE HOSPITAL	1.1348	58.29
050424	SCRIPPS GREEN HOSPITAL	1.1147	57.64
050425	KFH - SACRAMENTO	1.1845	59.89
050426	WEST ANAHEIM MED CTR	1.1492	58.75
050430	MODOC MEDICAL CENTER	0.9967	53.82
050432	GARFIELD MEDICAL CTR.	1.1832	59.85
050433	INDIAN VALLEY HOSPITAL	0.9967	53.82
050434	COLUSA COMMUNITY HOSPITAL	0.9967	53.82
050435	FALLBROOK DISTRICT HOSPITAL	1.1147	57.64
050438	HUNTINGTON MEMORIAL HOSPITAL	1.1832	59.85
050441	STANFORD HOSPITAL AND CLINICS	1.4626	68.89
050444	SUTTER MERCED MEDICAL CENTER	0.9967	53.82
050447	VILLA VIEW COMMUNITY HOSPITAL	1.1147	57.64
050448	RIDGECREST REGIONAL HOSPITAL	0.9967	53.82
050454	UC SAN FRANCISCO MEDICAL CENTER	1.4514	68.53
050455	SAN JOAQUIN COMMUNITY HOSPITAL	0.9967	53.82
050456	GARDENA PHYSICIAN'S HOSP INC	1.1832	59.85
050457	ST. MARY MEDICAL CENTER	1.5119	70.49
050464	DOCTORS MEDICAL CENTER OF MODESTO	1.1275	58.05
050468	MEMORIAL HOSPITAL OF GARDENA	1.1832	59.85
050469	COLORADO RIVER MEDICAL CENTER	0.9967	53.82
050470	SELMA COMMUNITY HOSPITAL	1.0142	54.38
050471	GOOD SAMARITAN HOSPITAL	1.1832	59.85
050476	SUTTER LAKESIDE HOSPITAL	0.9967	53.82
050477	MIDWAY HOSPITAL MEDICAL CENTER	1.1832	59.85
050478	SANTA YNEZ VALLEY COTTAGE HOSPITAL	1.0441	55.35
050481	WEST HILLS REG MEDICAL CENTER	1.1832	59.85
050485	LONG BEACH MEMORIAL MEDICAL CENTER	1.1832	59.85
050488	EDEN MEDICAL CENTER	1.5119	70.49
050491	SANTA ANA HOSPITAL MEDICAL CENTER	1.1492	58.75
050492	CLOVIS COMMUNITY HOSPITAL	1.0142	54.38
050494	TAHOE FOREST HOSPITAL	1.1845	59.89
050496	MT. DIABLO MEDICAL CENTER	1.5119	70.49
050497	DOS PALOS MEMORIAL HOSPITAL	0.9967	53.82
050498	SUTTER AUBURN FAITH HOSPITAL	1.1845	59.89
050502	ST. VINCENT MEDICAL CENTER	1.1832	59.85
050503	SCRIPPS MEM HOSP - ENCINITAS	1.1147	57.64
050506	SIERRA VISTA REGINAL MED CTR	1.1429	58.55
050510	KFH - SAN RAFAEL	1.5119	70.49
050512	KFH - HAYWARD	1.5119	70.49
050515	KAISER FOUND. HOSPITALS -SAN DIEGO	1.1147	57.64
050516	MERCY SAN JUAN HOSPITAL	1.1845	59.89
050517	VICTOR VALLEY COMMUNITY HOSP.	1.1348	58.29
050523	SUTTER DELTA MEDICAL CENTER	1.5119	70.49
050526	HUNTINGTON BEACH MEDICAL CENTER	1.1492	58.75
050528	MEMORIAL HOSPITAL - LOS BANOS	0.9967	53.82
050531	BELLFLOWER MEDICAL CENTER	1.1832	59.85
050534	JOHN.F. KENNEDY MEMORIAL HOSP.	1.1348	58.29
050535	COASTAL COMMUNITIES HOSPITAL	1.1492	58.75
050537	SUTTER DAVIS HOSPITAL	0.9967	53.82
050539	REDBUD COMMUNITY HOSPITAL.	0.9967	53.82
050541	KFH - REDWOOD CITY	1.5119	70.49

050542	KERN VALLEY HOSPITAL DISTRICT	0.9967	53.82
050543	COLLEGE HOSPITAL COSTA MESA	1.1492	58.75
050545	LANTERMAN DEVELOPMENTAL CENTER	1.1832	59.85
050546	PORTERVILLE DEVELOPMENTAL CENTER	0.9967	53.82
050547	SONOMA DEVELOPMENTAL CENTER	1.2877	63.23
050548	FAIRVIEW DEVELOPMENTAL CENTER	1.1492	58.75
050549	LOS ROBLES REGIONAL MEDICAL CENTER	1.1832	59.85
050550	CHAPMAN MEDICAL CENTER	1.1492	58.75
050551	LOS ALAMITOS MEDICAL CTR.	1.1492	58.75
050552	MOTION PICTURE AND TELEVISION FUND	1.1832	59.85
050557	MEMORIAL HOSPITAL MODESTO	1.1275	58.05
050559	DANIEL FREEMAN MARINA HOSPITAL	1.1832	59.85
050561	KAISER FOUND. HOSPITAL - WEST LA	1.1832	59.85
050567	MISSION HOSPITAL REGIONAL MED CENTER	1.1492	58.75
050568	MADERA COMMUNITY HOSPITAL	1.0142	54.38
050569	MENDOCINO COAST DISTRICT HOSPITAL	1.2877	63.23
050570	FOUNTAIN VALLEY REG MEDICAL CENTER	1.1492	58.75
050571	SUBURBAN MEDICAL CENTER	1.1832	59.85
050573	EISENHOWER MEMORIAL HOSPITAL	1.1348	58.29
050575	TRI-CITY REGIONAL MEDICAL CENTERS	1.1832	59.85
050577	SANTA MARTA HOSPITAL	1.1832	59.85
050578	MARTIN LUTHER KING, JR./DREW MEDICAL	1.1832	59.85
050579	CENTURY CITY HOSP	1.1832	59.85
050580	LAPALMA INTERCOMMUNITY HOSPITAL	1.1492	58.75
050581	LAKEWOOD REGIONAL MED. CTR.	1.1832	59.85
050583	ALVARADO COMMUNITY HOSPITAL	1.1147	57.64
050584	KPC GLOBAL MEDICAL	1.1348	58.29
050585	SAN CLEMENTE HOSPITAL	1.1492	58.75
050586	CHINO VALLEY MEDICAL CENTER	1.1348	58.29
050588	SAN DIMAS COMMUNITY HOSPITAL	1.1832	59.85
050589	PLACENTIA LINDA COMMUNITY HOSPITAL	1.1492	58.75
050590	METHODIST HOSPITAL OF SACRAMENTO	1.1845	59.89
050591	MONTEREY PARK HOSPITAL	1.1832	59.85
050592	BREA COMMUNITY HOSPITAL	1.1492	58.75
050594	WESTERN MEDICAL CENTER ANAHEIM	1.1832	59.85
050597	FOOTHILL PRESBYTERIAN HOSPITAL	1.1832	59.85
050599	UC DAVIS MEDICAL CENTER	1.1845	59.89
050601	TARZANA ENCINO REGIONAL MED CTR	1.1832	59.85
050603	SADDLEBACK MEMORIAL MEDICAL CENTER	1.1492	58.75
050604	KFH - SANTA TERESA	1.4626	68.89
050608	DELANO REGIONAL MEDICAL CNT.	0.9967	53.82
050609	KAISER FOUNDATION HOSPITALS -ANAHEIM	1.1832	59.85
050613	SETON MEDICAL CENTER	1.4514	68.53
050615	GREATER EL MONTE COMMUNITY HOSPITAL	1.1832	59.85
050616	ST. JOHN'S PLEASANT VALLEY HOSPITAL	1.1064	57.37
050618	BEAR VALLEY COMMUNITY HOSPITAL	0.9967	53.82
050623	HIGH DESERT HOSPITAL	1.1832	59.85
050624	HENRY MAYO NEWHALL MEMORIAL HOSPITAL	1.1832	59.85
050625	CEDARS-SINAI MEDICAL CENTER	1.1832	59.85
050630	INLAND VALLEY REGIONAL MEDICAL CTR	1.1348	58.29
050633	TWIN CITIES COMMUNITY HOSPITAL	1.1429	58.55
050636	POMERADO HOSPITAL	1.1147	57.64
050641	EAST L.A. DOCTOR'S HOSPITAL	1.1832	59.85
050643	PHS INDIAN HEALTH SERVICES HOSPITAL	1.4448	68.32
050644	LOS ANGELES METROPOLITAN MEDICAL CENTER	1.1832	59.85
050662	AGNEWS DEVELOPMENTAL CENTER	1.4626	68.89
050663	LOS ANGELES COMMUNITY HOSPITAL	1.1832	59.85
050667	NELSON M. HOLDERMAN	1.3425	65.01
050668	LAGUNA HONDA HOSPITAL	1.5119	70.49
050674	KFH SOUTH SACRAMENTO	1.1845	59.89

050677	KAISER FOUND. HOSP. - WOODLAND HILLS	1.1832	59.85
050678	ORANGE COAST MEMORIAL MEDICAL CENTER	1.1492	58.75
050680	VACAVALLEY HOSPITAL	1.3425	65.01
050682	KINGSBURG DISTRICT HOSPITAL	1.0142	54.38
050684	MENIFEE VALLEY MEDICAL CENTER	1.1348	58.29
050686	KAISER FOUND. HOSPITALS - RIVERSIDE	1.1492	58.75
050688	ST. LOUISE REGIONAL HOSPITAL	1.4626	68.89
050689	SAN RAMON REG. MEDICAL CENTER	1.5119	70.49
050690	KFH - SANTA ROSA	1.2877	63.23
050693	IRVINE MEDICAL CENTER	1.1492	58.75
050694	MORENO VALLEY COMMUNITY HOSPITAL	1.1348	58.29
050695	ST. DOMINIC'S HOSPITAL	1.0404	55.23
050696	USC UNIVERSITY HOSPITAL	1.1832	59.85
050697	PATIENTS' HOSPITAL OF REDDING	1.1352	58.30
050701	RANCHO SPRINGS MEDICAL CENTER	1.1348	58.29
050704	MISSION COMMUNITY HOSPITAL	1.1832	59.85
050707	RECOVERY INN OF MENLO PARK	1.4514	68.53
050708	FRESNO SURGERY CENTER	1.0142	54.38
050709	DESERT VALLEY HOSPITAL	1.1348	58.29
050710	KFH - FRESNO	1.0142	54.38
050713	LINCOLN HOSPITAL	1.1832	59.85
050714	SANTA CRUZ MATERINTY & SURGERY HOSP	1.2942	63.44
050717	RANCHO LOS AMIGOS NATL.REHAB.CTR.	1.1832	59.85
050718	VALLEY PLAZA DOCTORS HOSPITAL	1.1348	58.29
050720	TUSTIN HOSPITAL AND MEDICAL CENTER	1.1492	58.75
050722	SHARP MARY BIRCH HOSPITAL FOR WOMEN	1.1147	57.64
050723	KAISER FOUND HOSPITAL - BALDWIN	1.1832	59.85
050724	BAKERSFIELD HEART HOSPITAL	0.9967	53.82
050725	CITY OF ANGELS MEDICAL CENTER	1.1832	59.85
050726	STANISLAUS SURGICAL HOSPITAL	1.1275	58.05
050727	COMMUNTIY HOSPITAL OF LONG BEACH	1.1832	59.85
050728	SUTTER WARRACK HOSPITAL	1.2877	63.23
050729	DANIEL FREEMAN HOSPITAL	1.1832	59.85
050730	DANIEL FREEMAN MARIAN HOSPITAL	1.1832	59.85

* $52.151 × (.40 + .60 × applicable wage Index) × inflation factor of 1.034

Note: Authority cited: Sections 133, 4603.5, 5307.1 and 5307.3, Labor Code. Reference: Sections 4600, 4603.2 and 5307.1, Labor Code.

History: 1. New section filed 1-2-2004 as an emergency; operative 1-2-2004 (Register 2004, No. 2). A Certificate of Compliance must be transmitted to OAL by 5-3-2004 or emergency language will be repealed by operation of law on the following day.

2. Certificate of Compliance as to 1-2-2004 order, including amendment, transmitted to OAL 4-30-2004 and filed 6-15-2004 (Register 2004, No. 25).

Ref.: Hanna § 22.05[2]; Herlick Handbook § 4.19.

§9789.36. Update of Rules to Reflect Changes in the Medicare Payment System.

Sections 9789.30 through 9789.38 shall be adjusted to conform to any relevant changes in the Medicare payment schedule, including mid-year changes, no later than 60 days after the effective date of those changes. Updates shall be posted on the Division of Workers' Compensation webpage at http://www.dir.ca.gov/DWC/dwc_home_page.htm. The annual updates to the Hospital Outpatient Departments and Ambulatory Surgical Centers Fee Schedule shall be effective every year on January 1.

Note: Authority cited: Sections 133, 4603.5, 5307.1 and 5307.3, Labor Code. Reference: Sections 4600, 4603.2 and 5307.1, Labor Code.

History: 1. New section filed 1-2-2004 as an emergency; operative 1-2-2004 (Register 2004, No. 2). A Certificate of Compliance must be transmitted to OAL by 5-3-2004 or emergency language will be repealed by operation of law on the following day.

2. Certificate of Compliance as to 1-2-2004 order, including amendment of section, transmitted to OAL 4-30-2004 and filed 6-15-2004 (Register 2004, No. 25).

Ref.: Hanna § 22.05[2]; Herlick Handbook § 4.19.

§9789.37. DWC Form 15 Election for High Cost Outlier.

State of California
Department of Industrial Relations
DIVISION OF WORKERS' COMPENSATION

ELECTION FOR HIGH COST OUTLIER

Labor Code § 5307.1; Title 8, California Code of Regulations § 9789.37
For the 12 month period commencing on April 1, 20____.

This Election is filed with the Administrative Director pursuant to Labor Code Section 5307.1, and Title 8, California Code of Regulations Section 9789.33. A provider who elects to participate in the alternative payment methodology for high cost outlier cases under Section 9789.33, subdivision (b) in lieu of the maximum allowable fees set forth under Section 9789.33 subdivision (a), shall file this form by March 1 of each year providing the requested information to the Administrative Director. The maximum allowable fees applicable to a facility that does not file a timely election satisfying the requirements set forth in Section 9789.33, subdivision (b), shall be determined under subdivision (a).

1. PROVIDER'S NAME: ____________________
2. OSHPD FACILITY NUMBER: ____________________
3. MEDICARE PROVIDER NUMBER: ____________________
4. CONTACT PERSON AND PHONE NUMBER: ____________________

Hospital Outpatient Department Cost-to-Charge Ratio

Pursuant to Section 9789.33(c)(4), the cost-to-charge ratio applicable to a hospital outpatient department participating in the Medicare program shall be the hospital's cost-to-charge ratio used by the Medicare fiscal intermediary to determine high cost outlier payments under 42 CFR 419.43(d). List below the cost-to-charge ratio being used by the intermediary for services furnished on February 15 of the year this election is filed:

5. Cost-to-charge ratio ____________________

____________________ Signature and Title ____________________ Date

Ambulatory Surgical Center (ASC) Cost-to-Charge Ratio

Pursuant to Section 9789.33(c)(5), the cost-to-charge ratio applicable to an ambulatory surgery center shall be the ratio of the facility's total operating costs to total gross charges during the preceding calendar year. Total gross charges is defined as the facility's total usual and customary charges to patients and third-party payers before reductions for contractual allowances, bad debts, courtesy allowances and charity care.

6. Provide:
   (a) The facility's total operating costs during the preceding calendar year ____________________
   (b) The facility's total gross charges during the preceding calendar year ____________________
   (c) Provide county where facility is located ____________________

7. Attach completed Annual Utilization Report of Specialty Clinics (OSHPD) which is incorporated by reference, and may be obtained at OSHPD's website at http://www.oshpd.ca.gov/HID/HID/clinic/util/index.htm#Forms or is available upon request to the Administrative Director at: Division of Workers' Compensation (Attention: OMFS-Outpatient), P.O. Box 420603, San Francisco, CA 94142.

Upon request from the Administrative Director, an independent audit may be conducted at the expense of the ASC.

8. We, the undersigned, declare under penalty of perjury under the laws of the State of California that the foregoing, and attachment(s), are true and correct.

____________________ Signature, Chief Executive Officer ____________________ Date

____________________ Signature, Certified Public Accountant ____________________ Date

DWC Form 15 (1/1/04)

Note: Authority cited: Sections 133, 4603.5, 5307.1

and 5307.3, Labor Code. Reference: Sections 4600, 4603.2 and 5307.1, Labor Code.

History: 1. New section filed 1-2-2004 as an emergency; operative 1-2-2004 (Register 2004, No. 2). A Certificate of Compliance must be transmitted to OAL by 5-3-2004 or emergency language will be repealed by operation of law on the following day.

2. Certificate of Compliance as to 1-2-2004 order transmitted to OAL 4-30-2004 and filed 6-15-2004 (Register 2004, No. 25).

Ref.: Hanna § 22.05[2]; Herlick Handbook § 4.19.

§9789.38. Appendix X.

The federal regulations as incorporated by reference and/or referred to in Sections 9789.30 through 9789.36 are set forth below in numerical order.

42 C.F.R. § 419.2

Basis of payment.

(a) Unit of payment. Under the hospital outpatient prospective payment system, predetermined amounts are paid for designated services furnished to Medicare beneficiaries. These services are identified by codes established under the Centers for Medicare & Medicaid Services Common Procedure Coding System (HCPCS). The prospective payment rate for each service or procedure for which payment is allowed under the hospital outpatient prospective payment system is determined according to the methodology described in subpart C of this part. The manner in which the Medicare payment amount and the beneficiary copayment amount for each service or procedure are determined is described in subpart D of this part.

(b) Determination of hospital outpatient prospective payment rates: Included costs. The prospective payment system establishes a national payment rate, standardized for geographic wage differences, that includes operating and capital-related costs that are directly related and integral to performing a procedure or furnishing a service on an outpatient basis. In general, these costs include, but are not limited to

(1) Use of an operating suite, procedure room, or treatment room;

(2) Use of recovery room;

(3) Use of an observation bed;

(4) Anesthesia, certain drugs, biologicals, and other pharmaceuticals; medical and surgical supplies and equipment; surgical dressings; and devices used for external reduction of fractures and dislocations;

(5) Supplies and equipment for administering and monitoring anesthesia or sedation;

(6) Intraocular lenses (IOLs);

(7) Incidental services such a venipuncture;

(8) Capital-related costs;

(9) Implantable items used in connection with diagnostic x-ray tests, diagnostic laboratory tests, and other diagnostic tests;

(10) Durable medical equipment that is implantable;

(11) Implantable prosthetic devices (other than dental) which replace all or part of an internal body organ (including colostomy bags and supplies directly related to colostomy care), including replacement of these devices; and;

(12) Costs incurred to procure donor tissue other than corneal tissue.

(c) Determination of hospital outpatient prospective payment rates: Excluded costs. The following costs are excluded from the hospital outpatient prospective payment system.

(1) The costs of direct graduate medical education activities as described in §413.86 of this chapter.

(2) The costs of nursing and allied health programs as described in §413.86 of this chapter.

(3) The costs associated with interns and residents not in approved teaching programs as described in §415.202 of this chapter.

(4) The costs of teaching physicians attributable to Part B services for hospitals that elect cost-based reimbursement for teaching physicians under §415.160.

(5) The reasonable costs of anesthesia services furnished to hospital outpatients by qualified nonphysician anesthetists (certified registered nurse anesthetists and anesthesiologists' assistants) employed by the hospital or obtained under arrangements, for hospitals that meet the requirements under §412.113(c) of this chapter.

(6) Bad debts for uncollectible deductibles and coinsurances as described in §413.80(b) of this chapter.

(7) Organ acquisition costs paid under Part B.

(8) Corneal tissue acquisition costs.

42 C.F.R. § 419.32

Calculation of prospective payment rates for hospital outpatient services.

(a) Conversion factor for 1999. CMS calculates a conversion factor in such a manner that payment for hospital outpatient services furnished in 1999 would have equaled the base expenditure target calculated in § 419.30, taking into account APC group weights and estimated service frequencies and reduced by the amounts that would be payable in 1999 as outlier payments under § 419.43(d) and transitional pass-through payments under § 419.43(e).

(b) Conversion factor for calendar year 2000 and subsequent years.

(1) Subject to paragraph (b)(2) of this section, the conversion factor for a calendar year is equal to the conversion factor calculated for the previous year adjusted as follows:

(i) For calendar year 2000, by the hospital inpatient market basket percentage increase applicable under section 1886(b)(3)(B)(iii) of the Act reduced by one percentage point.

(ii) For calendar year 2001 —

(A) For services furnished on or after January 1, 2001 and before April 1, 2001, by the hospital inpatient market basket percentage increase applicable under section 1886(b)(3)(B)(iii) of the Act reduced by one percentage point; and

(B) For services furnished on or after April 1, 2001 and before January 1, 2002, by the hospital inpatient market basket percentage increase applicable under section 1886(b)(3)(B)(iii) of the Act, and increased by a transitional percentage allowance equal to 0.32 percent.

(iii) For the portion of calendar year 2002 that is affected by these rules, by the hospital inpatient market basket percentage increase applicable under section 1886(b)(3)(B)(iii) of the Act reduced by one percentage point, without taking into account the transitional percentage allowance referenced in § 419.32(b)(ii)(B).

(iv) For calendar year 2003 and subsequent years, by the hospital inpatient market basket percentage increase applicable under section 1886(b)(3)(B)(iii) of the Act.

(2) Beginning in calendar year 2000, CMS may substitute for the hospital inpatient market basket percentage in paragraph (b) of this section a market basket percentage increase that is determined and applied to hospital outpatient services in the same manner that the hospital inpatient market basket percentage increase is determined and applied to inpatient hospital services.

(c) Payment rates. The payment rate for services and procedures for which payment is made under the hospital outpatient prospective payment system is the product of the conversion factor calculated under paragraph (a) or paragraph (b) of this section and the relative weight determined under § 419.31(b).

(d) Budget neutrality.

(1) CMS adjusts the conversion factor as needed to ensure that updates and adjustments under § 419.50(a) are budget neutral.

(2) In determining adjustments for 2004 and 2005, CMS will not take into account any additional expenditures per section 1833(t)(14) of the Act that would not have been made but for enactment of section 621 of the Medicare Prescription Drug, Improvement, and Mordernization Act of 2003.

42 C.F.R. § 419.43

Adjustments to national program payment and beneficiary copayment amounts.

(a) General rule. CMS determines national prospective payment rates for hospital outpatient department services and determines a wage adjustment factor to adjust the portion of the APC payment and national beneficiary copayment amount attributable to labor-related costs for relative differences in labor and labor-related costs across geographic regions in a budget neutral manner.

(b) Labor-related portion of payment and copayment rates for hospital outpatient services. CMS determines the portion of hospital outpatient costs attributable to labor and labor-related costs (known as the "labor-related portion" of hospital outpatient costs) in accordance with § 419.31(c)(1).

(c) Wage index factor. CMS uses the hospital inpatient prospective payment system wage index established in accordance with part 412 of this chapter to make the adjustment referred to in paragraph (a) of this section.

(d) Outlier adjustment —

(1) General rule. Subject to paragraph (d)(4) of this section, CMS provides for an additional payment for a hospital outpatient service (or group of services) not excluded under paragraph (f) of this section for which a hospital's charges, adjusted to cost, exceed the following:

(i) A fixed multiple of the sum of —

(A) The applicable Medicare hospital outpatient payment amount determined under § 419.32(c), as adjusted under § 419.43 (other than for adjustments under this paragraph (d) or paragraph (e) of this section); and

(B) Any transitional pass-through payment under paragraph (e) of this section.

(ii) At the option of CMS, a fixed dollar amount.

(2) Amount of adjustment. The amount of the additional payment under paragraph (d)(1) of this section is determined by CMS and approximates the marginal cost of care beyond the applicable cutoff point under paragraph (d)(1) of this section.

(3) Limit on aggregate outlier adjustments —

(i) In general. The total of the additional payments made under this paragraph (d) for covered hospital outpatient department services furnished in a year (as estimated by CMS before the beginning of the year) may not exceed the applicable percentage specified in paragraph (d)(3)(ii) of this section of the total program payments (sum of both the Medicare and beneficiary payments to the hospital) estimated to be made under this part for all hospital outpatient services furnished in that year. If this paragraph is first applied to less than a full year, the limit applies only to the portion of the year.

(ii) Applicable percentage. For purposes of paragraph (d)(3)(i) of this section, the term "applicable percentage" means a percentage specified by CMS up to (but not to exceed) —

(A) For a year (or portion of a year) before 2004, 2.5 percent; and

(B) For 2004 and thereafter, 3.0 percent.

(4) Transitional authority. In applying paragraph (d)(1) of this section for hospital outpatient services furnished before January 1, 2002, CMS may —

(i) Apply paragraph (d)(1) of this section to a bill for these services related to an outpatient encounter (rather than for a specific service or group of services) using hospital outpatient payment amounts and transitional pass-through payments covered under the bill; and

(ii) Use an appropriate cost-to-charge ratio for the hospital or CMHC (as determined by CMS), rather than for specific departments within the hospital.

(e) Budget neutrality. CMS establishes payment under paragraph (d) of this section in a budget-neutral manner excluding services and groups specified in paragraph (f) of this section.

(f) Excluded services and groups. Drugs and biologicals that are paid under a separate APC and devices of branchytherapy, consisting of a seed or seeds (including radioactive source) are excluded from qualification for outlier payments.

42 C.F.R. § 419.44

(a) Multiple surgical procedures. When more than one surgical procedure for which payment is made under the hospital outpatient prospective payment system is performed during a single surgical encounter, the Medicare program payment amount and the beneficiary copayment amount are based on —

(1) The full amounts for the procedure with the highest APC payment rate; and

(2) One-half of the full program and the beneficiary payment amounts for all other covered procedures.

(b) Terminated procedures. When a surgical procedure is terminated prior to completion due to extenuating circumstances or circumstances that threaten the well-being of the patient, the Medicare program payment amount and the beneficiary copayment amount are based on —

(1) The full amounts if the procedure is discontinued after the induction of anesthesia or after the procedure is started; or

(2) One-half of the full program and the beneficiary coinsurance amounts if the procedure is discontinued after the patient is prepared for surgery and taken to the room where the procedure is to be performed but before anesthesia is induced.]

42 C.F.R. § 419.62

Transitional pass-through payments: General rules.

(a) General. CMS provides for additional payments under §§ 419.64 and 419.66 for certain innovative medical devices, drugs, and biologicals.

(b) Budget neutrality. CMS establishes the additional payments under §§ 419.64 and 419.66 in a budget neutral manner.

(c) Uniform prospective reduction of pass-through payments. (1) If CMS estimates before the beginning of a calendar year that the total amount of pass-through payments under §§ 419.64 and 419.66 for the year would exceed the applicable percentage (as described in paragraph (c)(2) of this section) of the total amount of Medicare payments under the outpatient prospective payment system. CMS will reduce, pro rata, the amount of each of the additional payments under §§ 419.64 and 419.66 for that year to ensure that the applicable percentage is not exceeded.

(2) The applicable percentages are as follows:

(i) For a year before CY 2004, the applicable percentage is 2.5 percent.

(ii) For 2004 and subsequent years, the applicable percentage is a percentage specified by CMS up to (but not to exceed) 2.0 percent.

(d) CY 2002 incorporated amount. For the portion of CY 2002 affected by these rules, CMS incorporated 75 percent of the estimated pass-through costs (before the incorporation and any pro rata reduction) for devices into the procedure APCs associated with these devices.

42 C.F.R. § 419.64

Transitional pass-through payments: drugs and biologicals.

(a) Eligibility for pass-through payment. CMS makes a transitional pass-through payment for the following drugs and biologicals that are furnished as part of an outpatient hospital service:

(1) Orphan drugs. A drug or biological that is used for a rare disease or condition and has been designated as an orphan drug under section 526 of the Federal Food, Drug and Cosmetic Act if payment for the drug or biological as an outpatient hospital service was being made on August 1, 2000.

(2) Cancer therapy drugs and biologicals. A drug or biological that is used in cancer therapy, including, but not limited to, a chemotherapeutic agent, an antiemetic, a hematopoietic growth factor, a colony stimulating factor, a biological response modifier, and a bisphosphonate if payment for the drug or biological as an outpatient hospital service was being made on August 1, 2000.

(3) Radiopharmaceutical drugs and biological products. A radiopharmaceutical drug or biological product used in diagnostic, monitoring, and therapeutic nuclear medicine services if payment for the drug or biological as an outpatient hospital service was being made on August 1, 2000.

(4) Other drugs and biologicals. A drug or biological that meets the following conditions:

(i) It was first payable as an outpatient hospital service after December 31, 1996.

(ii) CMS has determined the cost of the drug or biological is not insignificant in relation to the amount payable for the applicable APC (as calculated under § 419.32(c)) as defined in paragraph (b) of this section.

(b) Cost. CMS determines the cost of a drug or biological to be not insignificant if it meets the following requirements:

(1) Services furnished before January 1, 2003. The expected reasonable cost of a drug or biological must exceed 10 percent of the applicable APC payment amount for the service related to the drug or biological.

(2) Services furnished after December 31, 2002. CMS considers the average cost of a new drug or biological to be not insignificant if it meets the following conditions:

(i) The estimated average reasonable cost of the drug or biological in the category exceeds 10 percent of the applicable APC payment amount for the service related to the drug or biological.

(ii) The estimated average reasonable cost of the drug or biological exceeds the cost of the drug or biological portion of the APC payment amount for the related service by at least 25 percent.

(iii) The difference between the estimated reasonable cost of the drug or biological and the estimated portion of the APC payment amount for the drug or biological exceeds 10 percent of the APC payment amount for the related service.

(c) Limited period of payment. CMS limits the eligibility for a pass-through payment under this section to a period of at least 2 years, but not more than 3 years, that begins as follows:

(1) For a drug or biological described in paragraphs (a)(1) through (a)(3) of this section — August 1, 2000.

(2) For a drug or biological described in paragraph (a)(4) of this section — the date that CMS makes its first pass-through payment for the drug or biological.

(d) Amount of pass-through payment. (1) Subject to any reduction determined under 419.62(b), the pass-through payment for a drug or biological as specified in section 1842(o)(1)(A) and (o)(1)(D)(i) of the Act is 95 percent of the average wholesale price of the drug or biological minus the portion of the APC payment CMS determines is associated with the drug or biological.

(2) Subject to any reduction determined under 419.62(b), the pass-through payment for a drug or biological as specified in section 1842(o)(1)(B) and (o)(1)(E)(i) of the act is 85 percent of the average wholesale price, determined as of April 1, 2003, of the drug or biological minus the portion of the APC payment CMS determines is associated with the drug or biological.

42 C.F.R. § 419.66

Transitional pass-through payments: medical devices.

(a) General rule. CMS makes a pass-through payment for a medical device that meets the requirements in paragraph (b) of this section and that is described by a category of devices established by CMS under the criteria in paragraph (c) of this section.

(b) Eligibility. A medical device must meet the following requirements:

(1) If required by the FDA, the device must have received FDA approval or clearance (except for a device that has received an FDA investigational device exemption (IDE) and has been classified as a Category B device by the FDA in accordance with §§ 405.207 and 405.211 of this chapter) or another appropriate FDA exemption.

(2) The device is determined to be reasonable and necessary for the diagnosis or treatment of an illness or injury or to improve the functioning of a malformed body part (as required by section 1862(a)(1)(A) of the Act).

(3) The device is an integral and subordinate part of the service furnished, is used for one patient only, comes in contact with human tissue, and is surgically implanted or inserted whether or not it remains with the patient when the patient is released from the hospital.

(4) The device is not any of the following:

(i) Equipment, an instrument, apparatus, implement, or item of this type for which depreciation and financing expenses are recovered as depreciable assets as defined in Chapter 1 of the Medicare Provider Reimbursement Manual (CMS Pub. 15-1).

(ii) A material or supply furnished incident to a service (for example, a suture, customized surgical kit, or clip, other than radiological site marker).

(iii) A material that may be used to replace human skin (for example, a biological or synthetic material).

(c) Criteria for establishing device categories. CMS uses the following criteria to establish a category of devices under this section:

(1) CMS determines that a device to be included in the category is not described by any of the existing categories or by any category previously in effect, and was not being paid for as an outpatient service as of December 31, 1996.

(2) CMS determines that a device to be included in the category has demonstrated that it will substantially improve the diagnosis or treatment of an illness or injury or improve the functioning of a malformed body part compared to the benefits of a device or devices in a previously established category or other available treatment.

(3) Except for medical devices identified in paragraph (e) of this section, CMS determines the cost of the device is not insignificant as described in paragraph (d) of this section.

(d) Cost criteria. CMS considers the average cost of a category of devices to be not insignificant if it meets the following conditions:

(1) The estimated average reasonable cost of devices in the category exceeds 25 percent of the applicable APC payment amount for the service related to the category of devices.

(2) The estimated average reasonable cost of the devices in the category exceeds the cost of the device-related portion of the APC payment amount for the related service by at least 25 percent.

(3) The difference between the estimated average reasonable cost of the devices in the category and the portion of the APC payment amount for the device exceeds 10 percent of the APC payment amount for the related service.

(e) Devices exempt from cost criteria. The following medical devices are not subject to the cost requirements described in paragraph (d) of this section, if payment for the device was being made as an outpatient service on August 1, 2000:

(1) A device of brachytherapy.

(2) A device of temperature-monitored cryoablation.

(f) Identifying a category for a device. A device is described by a category, if it meets the following conditions:

(1) Matches the long descriptor of the category code established by CMS.

(2) Conforms to guidance issued by CMS relating to the definition of terms and other information in conjunction with the category descriptors and codes.

(g) Limited period of payment for devices. CMS limits the eligibility for a pass-through payment established under this section to a period of at least 2 years, but not more than 3 years beginning on the date that CMS establishes a category of devices.

(h) Amount of pass-through payment. Subject to any reduction determined under § 419.62(b), the pass-through payment for a device is the hospital's charge for the device, adjusted to the actual cost for the device, minus the amount included in the APC payment amount for the device.

Note: Authority cited: Sections 133, 4603.5, 5307.1 and 5307.3, Labor Code. Reference: Sections 4600, 4603.2 and 5307.1, Labor Code.

History: 1. New section filed 1-2-2004 as an emergency; operative 1-2-2004 (Register 2004, No. 2). A Certificate of Compliance must be transmitted to OAL by 5-3-2004 or emergency language will be repealed by operation of law on the following day.

2. Certificate of Compliance as to 1-2-2004 order, including amendment of section, transmitted to OAL 4-30-2004 and filed 6-15-2004 (Register 2004, No. 25).

Ref.: Hanna § 22.05[2]; Herlick Handbook § 4.19.

§9789.40. Pharmacy.

(a) The maximum reasonable fee for pharmaceuticals and pharmacy services rendered after January 1, 2004 is 100% of the reimbursement prescribed in the relevant Medi-Cal payment system, including the Medi-Cal professional fee for dispensing. Medi-Cal rates will be made available on the Division of Workers' Compensation's Internet Website (http://www.dir.ca.gov/DWC/dwc_home_page.htm) or upon request to the Administrative Director at:
DIVISION OF WORKERS' COMPENSATION
(ATTENTION: OMFS – PHARMACY)
P.O. BOX 420603
SAN FRANCISCO, CA 94142.

(b) For a pharmacy service or drug that is not covered by a Medi-Cal payment system, the maximum reasonable fee paid shall not exceed the drug cost portion of the fee determined in accordance with this subdivision, plus $7.25 professional fee for dispensing or $8.00 if the patient is in a skilled nursing facility or in an intermediate care facility. The maximum fee shall include only a single professional dispensing fee for dispensing for each dispensing of a drug.

(1) If the National Drug Code for the drug product as dispensed is not in the Medi-Cal database, and the National Drug Code for the underlying drug product from the original labeler appears in the Medi-Cal database, then the maximum fee shall be the drug cost portion of the reimbursement allowed pursuant to section 14105.45 of the Welfare and Institutions Code using the National Drug Code for the underlying drug product from the original labeler as it appears in the Medi-Cal database, calculated on a per unit basis, plus the professional fee allowed by subdivision (b) of this section.

(2) If the National Drug Code for the drug product as dispensed is not in the Medi-Cal database and the National Drug Code for the underlying drug product from the original labeler is not in the Medi-Cal database, then the maximum fee shall be 83 percent of the average wholesale price of the lowest priced therapeutically equivalent drug, calculated on a per unit basis, plus the professional fee allowed by subdivision (b) of this section.

(c) For purposes of this section:

(1) "therapeutically equivalent drugs" means drugs that have been assigned the same Therapeutic Equivalent Code starting with the letter "A" in the Food and Drug Administration's publication "Approved Drug Products with Therapeutic Equivalence Evaluations" ("Orange Book".) The Orange Book any be accessed through the Food and Drug Administration's website: http://www.fda.gov/cder/orange/default.htm.;

(2) "National Drug Code for the underlying drug product from the original labeler" means the National Drug Code of the drug product actually utilized by the repackager in producing the repackaged product.

(d) The changes made to this Section in February, 2007, shall be applicable to all pharmaceuticals dispensed or provided on or after March 1, 2007.

Note: Authority cited: Sections 133, 4603.5, 5307.1 and 5307.3, Labor Code. Reference: Sections 4600, 4603.2 and 5307.1, Labor Code.

History: 1. New section filed 1-2-2004 as an emergency; operative 1-2-2004 (Register 2004, No. 2). A Certificate of Compliance must be transmitted to OAL by 5-3-2004 or emergency language will be repealed by operation of law on the following day.

2. Certificate of Compliance as to 1-2-2004 order, including redesignation of existing section as subsection (a) and new subsection (b), transmitted to OAL 4-30-2004 and filed 6-15-2004 (Register 2004, No. 25).

3. Amendment of subsections (a) and (b) and new subsections (b)(1)-(d) filed 2-28-2007; operative 2-28-2007. Submitted to OAL for printing purposes only pursuant to Government Code section 11343.8, as exempt from the APA and OAL review pursuant to Government Code section 11340.9(g) (Register 2007, No. 9).

Ref.: Hanna § 22.05[2]; Herlick Handbook § 4.19.

§9789.50. Pathology and Laboratory.

(a) Effective for services after January 1, 2004, the maximum reasonable fees for pathology and laboratory services shall not exceed one hundred twenty (120) percent of the rate for the same procedure code in the CMS' Clinical Diagnostic Laboratory Fee Schedule, as established by Sections 1833 and 1834 of the Social Security Act (42 U.S.C. §§ 1395l and 1395m) and applicable to California. The Clinical Diagnostic Laboratory Fee Schedule, which can be found on the CMS Internet Website (http://www.cms.hhs.gov/paymentsystems) is incorporated by reference and will be made available on the Division of Workers' Compensation's Internet Website (http://www.dir.ca.gov/DWC/dwc_home_page.htm) or upon request to the Administrative Director at:

Division of Workers' Compensation (Attention: OMFS)
P.O. Box 420603
San Francisco, CA 94142

(b) The following procedures in the Special Services and Reports section of the OMFS 2003 will not be valid for services rendered after January 1, 2004: CPT Codes 99000, 99001, 99017, 99019, 99020, 99021, 99026, and 99027.

(c) For any pathology and laboratory service not covered by a Medicare payment system, the maximum reasonable fee paid shall not exceed the fee specified in the OMFS 2003.

Note: Authority cited: Sections 133, 4603.5, 5307.1 and 5307.3, Labor Code. Reference: Sections 4600, 4603.2 and 5307.1, Labor Code.

History: 1. New section filed 1-2-2004 as an emergency; operative 1-2-2004 (Register 2004, No. 2). A Certificate of Compliance must be transmitted to OAL by 5-3-2004 or emergency language will be repealed by operation of law on the following day.

2. Certificate of Compliance as to 1-2-2004 order, including new subsection (c), transmitted to OAL 4-30-2004 and filed 6-15-2004 (Register 2004, No. 25).

Ref.: Hanna § 22.05[2]; Herlick Handbook § 4.19.

§9789.60. Durable Medical Equipment, Prosthetics, Orthotics, Supplies.

(a) For services, equipment, or goods provided after January 1, 2004, the maximum reasonable reimbursement for durable medical equipment, supplies and materials, orthotics, prosthetics, and miscellaneous supplies and services shall not exceed one hundred twenty (120) percent of the rate set forth in the CMS' Durable Medical Equipment, Prosthetics/Orthotics, and Supplies (DMEPOS) Fee Schedule, as established by Section 1834 of the Social Security Act (42 U.S.C. § 1395m) and applicable to California. The DMEPOS Fee Schedule, which can be found on the CMS Internet Website (http://www.cms.hhs.gov/paymentsystems) is incorporated by reference and will be made available on the Division of Workers' Compensation's Internet Website (http://www.dir.ca.gov/DWC/dwc_home_page.htm) or upon request to the Administrative Director at:

Division of Workers' Compensation (Attention: OMFS)
P.O. Box 420603
San Francisco, CA 94142

(b) The following procedures in the Special Services and Reports section of the OMFS 2003 will not be valid for services rendered after January 1, 2004: CPT Code 99002.

(c) For durable medical equipment, supplies and materials, orthotics, prosthetics, and miscellaneous supplies and services not covered by a Medicare payment system, the maximum reasonable fee paid shall not exceed the fee specified in the OMFS 2003.

Note: Authority cited: Sections 133, 4603.5, 5307.1 and 5307.3, Labor Code. Reference: Sections 4600, 4603.2 and 5307.1, Labor Code.

History: 1. New section filed 1-2-2004 as an emergency; operative 1-2-2004 (Register 2004, No. 2). A Certificate of Compliance must be transmitted to OAL by 5-3-2004 or emergency language will be repealed by operation of law on the following day.

2. Certificate of Compliance as to 1-2-2004 order, including amendment of subsection (b) and new subsection (c), transmitted to OAL 4-30-2004 and filed 6-15-2004 (Register 2004, No. 25).

Ref.: Hanna § 22.05[2]; Herlick Handbook § 4.19.

§9789.70. Ambulance Services.

(a) The maximum reasonable fee for ambulance services rendered after January 1, 2004 shall not exceed 120% of the applicable fee for the Calendar Year 2006 set forth in CMS's Ambulance Fee Schedule, which is established pursuant to Section 1834 of the Social Security Act (42 U.S.C. §1395m) and applicable to California. The Ambulance Fee Schedule, which can be found at the CMS Internet Website http://www.cms.hhs.gov/suppliers/ambulance is incorporated by reference and will be made available on the Division of Workers' Compensation's Internet Website (http://www.dir.ca.gov/DWC/dwc_home_page.htm) or upon request to the Administrative Director at:

Division of Workers' Compensation (Attention: OMFS)
P.O. Box 420603
San Francisco, CA 94142

(b) For any ambulance service not covered by a Medicare payment system, the maximum reasonable fee paid shall not exceed the fee specified in the OMFS 2003.

Note: Authority cited: Sections 133, 4603.5, 5307.1 and 5307.3, Labor Code. Reference: Sections 4600, 4603.2 and 5307.1, Labor Code.

History: 1. New section filed 1-2-2004 as an emergency; operative 1-2-2004 (Register 2004, No. 2). A Certificate of Compliance must be transmitted to OAL by 5-3-2004 or emergency language will be repealed by operation of law on the following day.

2. Certificate of Compliance as to 1-2-2004 order, including designation and amendment of first paragraph as subsection (a) and new subsection (b), transmitted to OAL 4-30-2004 and filed 6-15-2004 (Register 2004, No. 25).

Ref.: Hanna § 22.05[2]; Herlick Handbook § 4.19.

§9789.80. Skilled Nursing Facility. [Reserved]

§9789.90. Home Health Care. [Reserved]

§9789.100. Outpatient Renal Dialysis. [Reserved]

§9789.110. Update of Rules to Reflect Changes in the Medicare Payment System.

The OMFS shall be adjusted within 60 days to conform to any relevant changes in the Medicare and Medi-Cal payment systems as required by law. The Administrative Director shall determine the effective date of the change and issue an order informing the public of the change and the effective date. Such order shall be posted on the Division's Internet Website: http://www.dir.ca.gov/DWC/dwc_home_page.htm.

Note: Authority cited: Sections 133, 4603.5, 5307.1 and 5307.3, Labor Code. Reference: Sections 4600, 4603.2 and 5307.1, Labor Code.

History: 1. New section filed 1-2-2004 as an emergency; operative 1-2-2004 (Register 2004, No. 2). A Certificate of Compliance must be transmitted to OAL by 5-3-2004 or emergency language will be repealed by operation of law on the following day.

2. Certificate of Compliance as to 1-2-2004 order, including amendment of section, transmitted to OAL 4-30-2004 and filed 6-15-2004 (Register 2004, No. 25).

Ref.: Hanna § 22.05[2]; Herlick Handbook § 4.19.

§9789.111. Effective Date of Fee Schedule Provisions.

(a) The OMFS regulations for Physician Services (Sections 9789.10–9789.11) are effective for services rendered on or after July 1, 2004. Services rendered after January 1, 2004, but before July 1, 2004 are governed by the "emergency" regulations that were effective on January 2, 2004.

(b) The OMFS regulations for Inpatient Services (Sections 9789.20–9789.24) are effective for inpatient hospital admissions with dates of discharge on or after July 1, 2004. Services for discharges after January 1, 2004, but before July 1, 2004 are governed by the "emergency" regulations that were effective on January 2, 2004. Bills for services with date of admission on or before December 31, 2003 will be reimbursed in accordance with Section 9792.1.

(c) The OMFS regulations for Outpatient Services (Sections 9789.30–9789.38) are effective for services rendered on or after July 1, 2004. Services rendered after January 1, 2004, but before July 1, 2004 are governed by the "emergency" regulations that were effective on January 2, 2004.

(d) The OMFS regulation for pharmacy (Section 9789.40) is effective for services rendered after January 1, 2004.

(e) The OMFS regulation for Pathology and Laboratory (Section 9789.50) is effective for services rendered after January 1, 2004.

(f) The OMFS regulation for Durable Medical Equipment, Prosthetics, Orthotics, Supplies (Section 9789.60) is effective for services rendered after January 1, 2004.

(g) The OMFS regulation for Ambulance Services is effective for services rendered after January 1, 2004.

Note: Authority cited: Sections 133, 4603.5, 5307.1 and 5307.3, Labor Code. Reference: Sections 4600, 4603.2 and 5307.1, Labor Code.

History: 1. New section filed 6-15-2004; operative 7-1-2004 (Register 2004, No. 25).

Ref.: Hanna § 22.05[2]; Herlick Handbook § 4.19.

ARTICLE 5.5
Application of the Official Medical Fee Schedule (Treatment)

§9790. Authority.

The rules and regulations contained in this Article are adopted pursuant to the authority contained in Sections 133, 4603.5, 5307.1 and 5307.3 of the California Labor Code.

Note: Authority cited: Sections 133, 4603.5, 5307.1 and 5307.3, Labor Code. Reference: Sections 4600, 4603.2 and 5307.1, Labor Code.

History: 1. New Article 5.5 (Sections 9790–9792) filed 11-9-77; effective thirtieth day thereafter (Register 77, No. 46).

2. Amendment of section and Note filed 10-7-93; operative 1-1-94 (Register 93, No. 41). This filing is exempt from much of the APA (including OAL review) pursuant to Government Code section 11351.

Ref.: Herlick Handbook § 1.6.

§9790.1. Definitions.

(a) "Capital outlier factor" means (California fixed loss cost outlier threshold × geographic adjustment factor × large urban add-on × (capital cost-to-charge ratio to total cost-to-charge ratio)). The geographic adjustment factor is specified in the *Federal Register* of August 1, 2000 at Vol. 65, page 47126, Table 1a, which document is hereby incorporated by reference and will be made available upon request to the Administrative Director. The "large urban add-on" is indicated by the post-reclassification urban/rural location published in the Payment Impact File at positions 229-235. As stated in Title 42, Code of Federal Regulations, Section 412.316(b), as it is in effect on September 29, 2000, the "large urban add-on" is an additional 3% of what would otherwise be payable to the health facility.

(b) "California fixed loss cost outlier threshold" means the factor calculated by adjusting the Medicare fixed loss cost outlier threshold for California workers' compensation inpatient admissions. The California fixed loss cost outlier threshold is $14,500.

(c) "Composite factor" means the factor calculated by the administrative director for a health facility by adding the prospective operating costs and the prospective capital costs for the health facility, excluding the DRG weight and any applicable outlier payment, as determined by the federal Health Care Financing Administration for the purpose of determining reimbursement under Medicare.

(1) Prospective capital costs are determined by the following formula:

Capital standard federal payment rate × capital wage index × large urban add-on × [1 + capital disproportionate share adjustment factor + capital indirect medical education adjustment factor]

The "capital standard federal payment rate" is $382.03 as published by HCFA in the *Federal Register* of August 1, 2000, at Vol. 65, page 47127, Table 1d, which document is hereby incorporated by reference and will be made available upon request to the Administrative Director.

The "capital wage index" was published in the Payment Impact File at positions 243-252.

The "large urban add-on" is indicated by the post-reclassification urban/rural location published in the Payment Impact File at positions 229-235. As stated in Title 42, Code of Federal Regulations, Section 412.316(b), as it is in effect on September 29, 2000, the "large urban add-on" is an additional 3% of what would otherwise be payable to the health facility.

The "capital disproportionate share adjustment factor" was published in the Payment Impact File at positions 117-126.

The "capital indirect medical education adjustment factor" (capital IME adjustment) was published in Payment Impact File at positions 202-211.

(2) Prospective operating costs are determined by the following formula:

[(Labor-related national standardized amount × operating wage index) + nonlabor-related national standardized amount] × [1 + operating disproportionate share adjustment factor + operating indirect medical education adjustment]

The "labor-related national standardized amount" is $2,864.19 for large urban areas and $2,818.85 for other areas, as published by the federal Health Care Financing Administration [HCFA] in the *Federal Register* of August 1, 2000, at Vol. 65, page 47126, Table 1a, which document is hereby incorporated by reference and will be made available upon request to the Administrative Director. The "labor-related national standardized amount" is $2,894.99 for large urban area sole community hospitals and $2,849.16 for other areas sole community hospitals, as published by the federal Health Care Financing Administration [HCFA] in the *Fed-*

eral Register of August 1, 2000, at Vol. 65, page 47127, Table 1e, which document is hereby incorporated by reference and will be made available upon request to the Administrative Director.

The "operating wage index" was published in the Payment Impact File at positions 253-262.

The "nonlabor-related national standardized amount" is $1,164.21 for large urban areas and $1,145.78 for other areas, as published by HCFA in the *Federal Register* of August 1, 2000, at Vol. 65, page 47126, Table 1a, which document is hereby incorporated by reference and will be made available upon request to the Administrative Director. The "nonlabor-related national standardized amount" is $1,176.73 for large urban area sole community hospitals and $1,158.10 for other areas sole community hospitals as published by the federal Health Care Financing Administration [HCFA] in the *Federal Register* of August 1, 2000, at Vol. 65, page 47127, Table 1e, which document is hereby incorporated by reference and will be made available upon request to the administrative director.

The "operating disproportionate share adjustment factor" was published in the Payment Impact File at positions 127-136.

The "operating indirect medical education adjustment" was published in the Payment Impact File at positions 212-221.

(3) A table of composite factors for each health facility in California is contained in Appendix A to Section 9792.1.

(d) "Costs" means the total billed charges for an admission, excluding non-medical charges such as television and telephone charges, multiplied by the hospital's total cost-to-charge ratio. For DRGs 496 through 500, for purposes of determining whether an admission is a cost outlier, "costs" exclude implantable hardware and/or instrumentation reimbursed under subsection (7) of Section 9792.1.

(e) "Cost-to-charge ratio" means the sum of the hospital specific operating cost-to-charge ratio and the hospital specific capital cost-to-charge ratio. The operating cost-to-charge ratio for each hospital was published in the Payment Impact File at positions 161-168. The capital cost-to-charge ratio for each hospital was published in the Payment Impact File at positions 99-106. A table of hospital specific capital cost-to-charge, operating cost-to-charge and total cost-to-charge ratios for each health facility in California is contained in Appendix A to Section 9792.1.

(f) "Cost outlier case" means a hospitalization for which the hospital's costs, as defined in subdivision (d) above, exceed the Inpatient Hospital Fee Schedule payment amount by the hospital's outlier factor. If costs exceed the cost outlier threshold, the case is a cost outlier case.

(g) "Cost outlier threshold" means the sum of the Inpatient Hospital Fee Schedule payment amount plus the hospital specific outlier factor.

(h) "DRG weight" means the weighting factor for a diagnosis-related group assigned by the Health Care Financing Administration for the purpose of determining reimbursement under Medicare. A table is contained in Appendix B to Section 9792.1. Appendix B shows DRG weights as assigned by HCFA and, where applicable, "Revised DRG weights" in italics.

(i)(1) "Revised DRG weight" means the product of the DRG weight multiplied by the ratio set forth in subsection (i)(2) for 48 specified DRGs to reflect the different resource usage between the workers' compensation population and the Medicare population.

(2) The ratios that were applied to the DRG weights are contained in the column identified as "DWC Revised Ratio" in Appendix B of Section 9792.1.

(j) "Health facility" means any facility as defined in Section 1250 of the Health and Safety Code.

(k) "Inpatient" means a person who has been admitted to a health facility for the purpose of receiving inpatient services. A person is considered an inpatient when he or she is formally admitted as an inpatient with the expectation that he or she will remain at least overnight and occupy a bed, even if it later develops that such person can be discharged or is transferred to another facility and does not actually remain overnight.

(*l*) "Inpatient Hospital Fee Schedule payment amount" is that amount determined by multiplying the DRG weight × hospital composite factor × 1.2.

(m) "Labor-related portion" is that portion of operating costs attributable to labor costs, as specified in the *Federal Register* of August 1, 2000 at Vol. 65, page 47126, Table 1a, which document is hereby incorporated by reference and will be made available upon request to the Administrative Director.

(n) "Medical services" means those goods and services provided pursuant to Article 2 (commencing with Section 4600) of Chapter 2 of Part 2 of Division 4 of the Labor Code.

(o) "Average length of stay" means the geometric mean length of stay for a diagnosis-related group assigned by the Health Care Financing Administration.

(p) "Operating outlier factor" means ((California fixed loss cost outlier threshold × ((labor-related portion × MSA wage index) + nonlabor-related portion)) × (operating cost-to-charge ratio to total cost-to-charge ratio)). The MSA wage index is specified at *Federal Register* of August 1, 2000 at Vol. 65, page 47149, Table 4a, which document is hereby incorporated by reference and will be made available upon request to the Administrative Director. The nonlabor-related portion is that portion of operating costs as defined in the *Federal Register* of August 1, 2000 at Vol. 65, page 47126, Table 1a, which document is hereby incorporated by reference and will be made available upon request to the Administrative Director.

(q) "Outlier factor" means the sum of the capital outlier factor and the operating outlier factor. A table of hospital specific outlier factors for each health facility in California is contained in Appendix A to Section 9792.1.

(r) "Payment Impact File" means the FY 2001 Prospective Payment System Payment Impact File (August 2000 Update) (IMPCTF01.EXE) published by the federal Health Care Financing Administration, which document is hereby incorporated by reference. The description of the file is found at http://www.hcfa.gov/stats/impctf01.doc. The file is accessible through http://www.hcfa.gov/stats/pufiles.htm#ppfexmtp. A paper copy of the Payment Impact File, with explanatory material, is available from the Administrative Director upon request. An electronic copy is available from the Administrative Director at http://www.dir.ca.gov.

Note: Authority cited: Sections 133, 4603.5, 5307.1 and 5307.3, Labor Code. Reference: Sections 4600, 4603.2 and 5307.1, Labor Code.

History: 1. New section filed 10-7-93; operative 1-1-94 (Register 93, No. 41). This filing is exempt from much of the APA (including OAL review) pursuant to Government Code section 11351.

2. New subsections (a)-(c)(2), subsection relettering, and new subsection (g) filed 12-31-96; operative 12-31-96 pursuant to Government Code section 11343.4(d). Submitted to OAL for printing only pursuant to Government Code section 11351 (Register 97, No. 1).

3. New subsections (a)(1)-(3), amendment of subsections (b) and (c)(2) and new subsection (h) filed 2-23-99; operative 4-1-99 (Register 99, No. 9).

4. Amendment filed 5-30-2001; operative 6-29-2001. Submitted to OAL for printing only pursuant to Government Code section 11340.9(g) (Register 2001, No. 23).

Ref.: Hanna § 22.05[2]; Herlick Handbook § 1.6.

§9791. Services Covered.

Except as provided in this article, the Official Medical Fee Schedule applies to all covered medical services provided, referred or prescribed by physicians (as defined in Section 3209.3 of the Labor Code), regardless of the type of facility in which the medical services are performed, including clinic and hospital-based physicians working on a contract basis. The Schedule shall not apply to inpatient medical services provided by employees of a health facility, medical-legal expenses authorized under Section 4621 of the Labor Code, and medical expenses payable pursuant to Section 9795. Nothing contained in this schedule shall preclude any hospital as defined in subdivisions (a), (b), or (f) of Section 1250 of the Health and Safety Code, or any surgical facility which is licensed under subdivision (b) of Section 1204 of the Health and Safety Code, or any ambulatory surgical center that is certified to participate in the Medicare program under Title XVIII (42 U.S.C. Sec. 1395 et seq.) of the federal Social Security Act, or any surgical clinic accredited by the Accreditation Association for Ambulatory Health Care (AAAHC), from charging and collecting a facility fee for the use of the emergency room or operating room of the facility.

Note: Authority cited: Sections 133, 4603.5, 5307.1 and 5307.3, Labor Code. Reference: Sections 4600, 4603.2 and 5307.1, Labor Code.

History: 1. Amendment of section and new Note filed 10-7-93; operative 1-1-94 (Register 93, No. 41). This filing is exempt from much of the APA (including OAL review) pursuant to Government Code section 11351.

2. Amendment filed 10-11-95; operative 10-11-95. Submitted to OAL for printing only pursuant to Government Code section 11351 (Register 95, No. 41).

Ref.: Hanna § 22.05[2]; Herlick Handbook §§ 1.6, 4.19.

§9791.1. Medical Fee Schedule.

The Official Medical Fee Schedule shall include the procedures, procedure numbers, descriptions, instructions, and unit values adopted by the Administrative Director, effective January 1, 1994; as revised for services on or after January 1, 1996; and as thereafter revised and adopted. The Official California Workers' Compensation Medical Fee Schedule (Revised April 1, 1999, and as amended for dates of service on or after 7/12/02) is hereby incorporated by reference. An order form for purchasing a copy of the Schedule can be obtained by contacting the Division of Workers' Compensation at the following address:

DIVISION OF WORKERS' COMPENSATION
(ATTENTION: OMFS ORDER)
P.O. BOX 420603
SAN FRANCISCO, CALIFORNIA 94142

The amendments of the OMFS for dates of service on or after 7/12/02 may be obtained either by purchasing them from the Division or they may be downloaded at no charge from the Division's website at (http://www.dir.ca.gov/workers'_comp.html).

Note: Authority cited: Sections 133, 4603.5, 5307.1 and 5307.3, Labor Code. Reference: Sections 4600, 4603.2 and 5307.1, Labor Code.

History: 1. New section filed 8-14-81; effective thirtieth day thereafter (Register 81, No. 33).

2. Amendment filed 8-29-84; effective thirtieth day thereafter (Register 84, No. 35).

3. Change without regulatory effect filed 7-11-86; effective upon filing (Register 86, No. 28).

4. Amendment filed 5-18-87; operative 5-18-87 (Register 87, No. 21).

5. Amendment of section and Note filed 10-7-93; operative 1-1-94 (Register 93, No. 41). This filing is exempt from much of the APA (including OAL review) pursuant to Government Code section 11351.

6. Amendment filed 10-11-95; operative 10-11-95. Submitted to OAL for printing only pursuant to Government Code section 11351 (Register 95, No. 41).

7. Amendment of section incorporating by reference "The Official California Workers' Compensation Medical Fee Schedule" (revised April 1, 1999) filed 2-19-99; operative 4-1-99 (Register 99, No. 8).

8. Change without regulatory effect amending section filed 6-12-2002 pursuant to section 100, title 1, California Code of Regulations (Register 2002, No. 24).

Ref.: Hanna § 22.05[2]; Herlick Handbook §§ 1.6, 4.19.

§9792. Determination of the Fee.

(a) The fee is determined by the use of the Official Medical Fee Schedule as defined in Section 9791.1 of these rules. For services provided on and after January 1, 1994, the conversion factors to be applied to unit values in the schedule are as follows:

Determination of the Fee

Evaluation and Management Services Section	$7.15
Medicine Section	$6.15
Surgery Section	$153.00
Radiology Section	$12.50
Pathology Section	$1.50
Anesthesia Section	$34.50

(b) For services in the Evaluation and Management Services Section provided on and after April 1, 1999, the conversion factor to be applied to unit values in the schedule is $8.50.

(c) The conversion factor shall be multiplied by the listed unit value (also known as relative value) of the procedure as set forth in the Official Medical Fee Schedule to establish the reasonable maximum fee. A medical provider or a licensed health care facility may be paid a fee in excess of the reasonable maximum fees if the fee is reasonable, accompanied by itemization, and justified by an explanation of extraordinary circumstances related to the unusual nature of the services rendered; however, in no event shall a physician charge in excess of his or her usual fee.

Note: Authority cited: Sections 133, 4603.5, 5307.1 and 5307.3, Labor Code. Reference: Sections 4600, 4603.2 and 5307.1, Labor Code.

History: 1. Amendment filed 4-11-79; designated effective 7-1-79 (Register 79, No. 15).

2. Amendment filed 8-14-81; effective thirtieth day thereafter (Register 81, No. 33).

3. Amendment filed 11-5-82; designated effective 1-1-83 (Register 82, No. 45).

4. Amendment filed 11-23-83; effective thirtieth day thereafter (Register 83, No. 48).

5. Amendment filed 8-29-84; effective thirtieth day thereafter (Register 84, No. 35).

6. Editorial correction (Register 84, No. 48).

7. Amendment filed 1-10-85; effective upon filing pursuant to Government Code section 11346.2(d) (Register 85, No. 2).

8. Amendment filed 7-1-87; operative 7-1-87 (Register 87, No. 28).

9. Amendment of section and Note filed 10-7-93; operative 1-1-94 (Register 93, No. 41). This filing is exempt from much of the APA (including OAL review) pursuant to Government Code section 11351.

10. New subsection (a) designator, new subsection (b), and amendment of newly designated subsection (c) filed 2-19-99; operative 4-1-99 (Register 99, No. 8).

Ref.: Hanna §§ 5.05[10][d], 22.05[2]; Herlick Handbook § 1.6.

§9792.1. Payment of Inpatient Services of Health Facilities.

(a) Maximum reimbursement for inpatient medical services shall be determined by multiplying 1.20 by the product of the health facility's composite factor and the applicable DRG weight or revised DRG weight if a revised weight has been adopted by the administrative director. The fee determined under this subdivision shall be a global fee, constituting the maximum reimbursement to a health facility for inpatient medical services not exempted under this section. However, preadmission services rendered by a health facility more than 24 hours before admission are separately reimbursable.

(b) Health facilities billing for fees under this section shall present with their bill the name and address of the facility, the facility's Medicare ID number, and the applicable DRG codes.

(c) The following are exempt from the maximum reimbursement formula set forth in subdivision (a):

(1) Inpatient services for the following diagnoses: Psychiatry (DRGs 424-432), Substance Abuse (DRGs 433-437), Organ Transplants (DRGs 103, 302, 480, 481, 495), Rehabilitation (DRG 462 and inpatient rehabilitation services provided in any rehabilitation center that is authorized by the Department of Health Services in accordance with Title 22, §§70301, 70595 70603 of the California Code of Regulations to provide rehabilitation services), Tracheostomies (DRGs 482, 483), and Burns (DRGs 475 and 504-511).

(2) Inpatient services provided by a Level I or Level II trauma center, as defined in Title 22, California Code of Regulations sections 100260, 100261, to a patient with an immediately life threatening or urgent injury.

(3) Inpatient services provided by a health facility for which there is no composite factor.

(4) Inpatient services provided by a health facility located outside the State of California.

(5) The cost of durable medical equipment provided for use at home.

(6) Inpatient services provided by a health facility transferring an inpatient to another hospital. Maximum reimbursement for inpatient medical services of a health facility transferring an inpatient to another hospital shall be a per diem rate for each day of the patient's stay in that hospital, not to exceed the amount that would have been paid under Title 8, California Code of Regulations §9792.1(a). However, the first day of the stay in the transferring hospital shall be reimbursed at twice the per diem amount. The per diem rate is determined by dividing the maximum reimbursement as determined under Title 8, California Code of Regulations §9792.1(a) by the average length of stay for that specific DRG. However, if an admission to a health facility transferring a patient is exempt from the maximum reimbursement formula set forth in subdivision (a) because it satisfies one or more of the requirements of Title 8, California Code of Regulations §9792.1(c)(1) through (c)(4), subdivision (c)(6) shall not apply. Inpatient services provided by the hospital receiving the patient shall be reimbursed under the provisions of Title 8, California Code of Regulations §9792.1(a).

(7) Implantable hardware and/or instrumentation for DRGs 496 through 500, where the admission occurs on or after April 13, 2001. Implantable hardware and/or instrumentation for DRGs 496 through 500, where the admission occurs on or after April 13, 2001, shall be separately reimbursed at the provider's documented paid cost, plus an additional 10% of the provider's documented paid cost not to exceed a maximum of $250.00, plus any sales tax and/or shipping and handling charges actually paid.

(8) Cost Outlier cases. Inpatient services for cost outlier cases where the admission occurs on or after June 29, 2001, shall be reimbursed as follows:

Step 1: Determine the Inpatient Hospital Fee Schedule payment amount (DRG relative weight × 1.2 × hospital specific composite factor).

Step 2: Determine costs. Costs = (total billed charges × total cost-to-charge ratio).

Step 3: Determine outlier threshold. Outlier threshold = (Inpatient Hospital Fee Schedule payment amount + hospital specific outlier factor).

If costs exceed the outlier threshold, the case is a cost outlier case and the admission is reimbursed at the Inpatient Hospital Fee Schedule payment amount + (0.8 × (costs - cost outlier threshold)).

NOTE: For purposes of determining whether a case qualifies as a cost outlier case under this subsection, implantable hardware and/or instrumentation reimbursed under subsection (8) below is excluded from the calculation of costs. Once an admission for DRGs 496 through 500 qualifies as a cost outlier case, any implantable hardware and/or instrumentation shall be separately reimbursed under subsection (8) below.

(d) Any health care facility that believes its composite factor or hospital specific outlier factor was erroneously determined because of an error in tabulating data may request the Administrative Director for a re-determination of its composite factor or hospital specific outlier factor. Such requests shall be in writing, shall state the alleged error, and shall be supported by written documentation. Within 30 days after receiving a complete written request, the Administrative Director shall make a redetermination of the composite factor or hospital specific outlier factor or reaffirm the published factor.

(e) This section, except as provided in subsections (c)(7) and (c)(8), shall apply to covered inpatient hospital stays for which the day of admittance is on or after April 1, 1999.

(f) Subsections (c)(7) and (c)(8) shall remain in effect only through December 31, 2001, and shall not apply to admissions occurring on or after January 1, 2002.

AN IMPORTANT NOTE CONCERNING SUBSECTIONS (c)(7) AND (c)(8):

Labor Code Section 5318, (as added by Statutes of 2001, chapter 252, effective January 1, 2002,) provides that: "Notwithstanding any other provision of law, the termination date of December 31, 2001, provided in Section 9792.1(f) of Title 8 of the California Code of Regulations shall be extended until the effective date of new regulations adopted by the administrative director, as required by Section 5307.1, providing for the biennial review of the fee schedule for health care facilities." Sections 9792.1(c)(7) and (c)(8) will therefore remain in effect for admissions on or after January 1, 2002, and will not sunset.

Note: Authority cited: Sections 133, 4603.5, 5307.1, 5307.3 and 5318, Labor Code. Reference: Sections 4600, 4603.2, 5307.1 and 5318, Labor Code.

History: 1. New section filed 12-31-96; operative 12-31-96 pursuant to Government Code section 11343.4(d). Submitted to OAL for printing only pursuant to Government Code section 11351 (Register 97, No. 1).

2. Amendment of section and new appendices A-C filed 2-23-99; operative 4-1-99 (Register 99, No. 9).

3. New subsection (c)(8), amendment of subsection (e) and new subsection (f) filed 3-14-2001; operative 4-13-2001. Submitted to OAL for printing only pursuant to Government Code section 11343(a)(1) (Register 2001, No. 22).

4. Amendment of section and repealer and new Appendices A and B filed 5-30-2001; operative 6-29-2001. Submitted to OAL for printing only pursuant to Government Code section 11340.9(g) (Register 2001, No. 23).

5. Change without regulatory effect adding final two paragraphs and amending Note filed 12-31-2001 pursuant to section 100, title 1, California Code of Regulations (Register 2002, No. 1).

Ref.: Hanna § 22.05[2]; Herlick Handbook §§ 1.6, 4.19.

Appendix A. Hospital Composite Factors and Cost to Charge Rations [Appendix Not Reproduced]

Appendix B. DRG Weights and Revised DRG Weights 2001 Rates (California revisions shown in italics incorporate the DWC Revised Ratios) [Appendix Not Reproduced]

Editor's Note: For text of Appendix A and/or Appendix B, please see Barclays *Official California Code of Regulations.*

Ref.: Hanna § 22.05[2].

§9792.5. Payment for Medical Treatment.

(a) As used in this section:

(1) "Claims Administrator" has the same meaning specified in Section 9785(a)(3).

(2) "Medical treatment" means the treatment to which an employee is entitled under Labor Code Section 4600.

(3) "Physician" has the same meaning specified in Labor Code Section 3209.3.

(4) "Required report" means a report which must be submitted pursuant to Section 9785.

(5) "Treating physician" means the "primary treating physician" as that term is defined by Section 9785(a)(1).

(b) Any properly documented bill for medical treatment within the planned course, scope and duration of treatment reported under Section 9785 which is provided or authorized by the treating physician shall be paid by the claims administrator within sixty days from receipt of each separate itemized bill and any required reports, unless the bill is contested, as specified in subdivisions (d), and (e), within thirty working days of receipt of the bill. Any amount not contested within the thirty working days or not paid within the sixty day period shall be increased 10%, and shall carry interest at the same rate as judgments in civil actions retroactive to the date of receipt of the bill.

For purposes of this Section, treatment which is provided or authorized by the treating physician includes but is not limited to treatment provided by a "secondary physician" as that term is defined by Section 9785(a)(2).

(c) To be properly documented, a bill for medical treatment which exceeds the amount presumed reasonable in the Official Medical Fee Schedule adopted pursuant to Labor Code Section 5307.1, must be accompanied by an itemization and explanation for the excess charge.

(d) A claims administrator who objects to all or any part of a bill for medical treatment shall notify the physician or other authorized provider of the objection within thirty working days after receipt of the bill and any required report and shall pay any uncontested amount within sixty days after receipt of the bill. If a required report is not received with the bill, the periods to object or pay shall commence on the date of receipt of the bill or report, whichever is received later. If the claims administrator receives a bill and believes that it has not received a required report to support the bill, the claims administrator shall so inform the medical provider within thirty working days of receipt of the bill. An objection will be deemed timely if sent by first class mail and postmarked on or before the thirtieth working day after receipt, or if personally delivered or sent by electronic facsimile on or before the thirtieth working day after receipt. Any notice of objection shall include or be accompanied by all of the following:

(1) An explanation of the basis for the objection to each contested procedure and charge. The original procedure codes used by the physician or authorized provider shall not be altered. If the objection is based on appropriate coding of a procedure, the explanation shall include both the code reported by the provider and the code believed reasonable by the claims administrator.

(2) If additional information is necessary as a prerequisite to payment of the contested bill or portions thereof, a clear description of the information required.

(3) The name, address, and telephone number of the person or office to contact for additional information concerning the objection.

(4) A statement that the treating physician or authorized provider may adjudicate the issue of the contested charges before the Workers' Compensation Appeals Board.

(e) An objection to charges from a hospital, outpatient surgery center, or independent diagnostic facility shall be deemed sufficient if the provider is advised, within the thirty working day period specified in subdivision (d), that a request has been made for an audit of the billing, when the results of the audit are expected, and contains the name, address, and telephone number of the person or office to contact for additional information concerning the audit.

(f) Any contested charge for medical treatment provided or authorized by the treating physician which is determined by the appeals board to be payable shall carry interest at the same rate as judgments in civil actions from the date the amount was due until it is paid.

Note: Authority cited: Sections 133, 4603.5 and 5307.3, Labor Code. Reference: Sections 4603.2 and 5307.1, Labor Code.

History: 1. New section filed 4-13-93; operative 4-13-93. Submitted to OAL for printing only pursuant to Government Code section 11351 (Register 93, No. 16).

2. Amendment of subsections (b), (d), (d)(1), (f) and (g) filed 9-25-95; operative 9-25-95. Submitted to OAL for printing only pursuant to Government Code section 11351 (Register 95, No. 39).

3. Change without regulatory effect amending section and Note filed 6-12-2002 pursuant to section 100, title 1, California Code of Regulations (Register 2002, No. 24).

Ref.: Hanna §§ 5.05[6][b], 22.05[1], 22.05[3]; Herlick Handbook § 1.6.

ARTICLE 5.5.1
Utilization Review Standards

§9792.6. Utilization Review Standards—Definitions.

As used in this Article:

(a) "ACOEM Practice Guidelines" means the American College of Occupational and Environmental Medicine's Occupational Medicine Practice Guidelines, Second Edition.

(b) "Authorization" means assurance that appropriate reimbursement will be made for an approved specific course of proposed medical treatment to cure or relieve the effects of the industrial injury pursuant to section 4600 of the Labor Code, subject to the provisions of section 5402 of the Labor Code, based on the Doctor's First Report of Occupational Injury or Illness," Form DLSR 5021, or on the "Primary Treating Physician's Progress Report," DWC Form PR-2, as contained in section 9785.2, or in narrative form containing the same information required in the DWC Form PR-2.

(c) "Claims Administrator" is a self-administered workers' compensation insurer, an insured employer, a self-administered self-insured employer, a self-administered legally uninsured employer, a self-administered joint powers authority, a third-party claims administrator or other entity subject to Labor Code section 4610. The claims administrator may utilize an entity contracted to conduct its utilization review responsibilities.

(d) "Concurrent review" means utilization review conducted during an inpatient stay.

(e) "Course of treatment" means the course of medical treatment set forth in the treatment plan contained on the "Doctor's First Report of Occupational Injury or Illness," Form DLSR 5021, or on the "Primary Treating Physician's Progress Report," DWC Form PR-2, as contained in section 9785.2 or in narrative form containing the same information required in the DWC Form PR-2.

(f) "Emergency health care services" means health care services for a medical condition manifesting itself by acute symptoms of sufficient severity such that the absence of immediate medical attention could reasonably be expected to place the patient's health in serious jeopardy.

(g) "Expedited review" means utilization review conducted when the injured worker's condition is such that the injured worker faces an imminent and serious threat to his or her health, including, but not limited to, the potential loss of life, limb, or other major bodily function, or the normal timeframe for the decision-making process would be detrimental to the injured worker's life or health or could jeopardize the injured worker's permanent ability to regain maximum function.

(h) "Expert reviewer" means a medical doctor, doctor of osteopathy, psychologist, acupuncturist, optometrist, dentist, podiatrist, or chiropractic practitioner licensed by any state or the District of Columbia, competent to evaluate the specific clinical issues involved in the medical treatment services and where these services are within the individual's scope of practice, who has been consulted by the reviewer or the utilization review medical director to provide specialized review of medical information.

(i) "Health care provider" means a provider of medical services, as well as related services or goods, including but not limited to an individual provider or facility, a health care service plan, a health care organization, a member of a preferred provider organization or medical provider network as provided in Labor Code section 4616.

(j) "Immediately" means within 24 hours after learning the circumstances that would require an extension of the timeframe for decisions specified in subdivisions (b)(1), (b)(2) or (c) and (g)(1) of section 9792.9.

(k) "Material modification" is when the claims administrator changes utilization review vendor or makes a change to the utilization review standards as specified in section 9792.7.

(*l*) "Medical Director" is the physician and surgeon licensed by the Medical Board of California or the Osteopathic Board of California who holds an unrestricted license to practice medicine in the State of California. The Medical Director is responsible for all decisions made in the utilization review process.

(m) "Medical services" means those goods and services provided pursuant to Article 2 (commencing with Labor Code section 4600) of Chapter 2 of Part 2 of Division 4 of the Labor Code.

(n) "Prospective review" means any utilization review conducted, except for utilization review conducted during an inpatient stay, prior to the delivery of the requested medical services.

(o) "Request for authorization" means a written confirmation of an oral request for a specific course of proposed medical treatment pursuant to Labor Code section 4610(h) or a written request for a specific course of proposed medical treatment. An oral request for authorization must be followed by a written confirmation of the request within seventy-two (72) hours. Both the written confirmation of an oral request and the written request must be set forth on the "Doctor's First Report of Occupational Injury or Illness," Form DLSR 5021, section 14006, or on the Primary Treating Physician Progress Report, DWC Form PR-2, as contained in section 9785.2, or in narrative form containing the same information required in the PR-2 form. If a narrative format is used, the document shall be clearly marked at the top that it is a request for authorization.

(p) "Retrospective review" means utilization review conducted after medical services have been provided and for which approval has not already been given.

(q) "Reviewer" means a medical doctor, doctor of osteopathy, psychologist, acupuncturist, optometrist, dentist, podiatrist, or chiropractic practitioner licensed by any state or the District of Columbia, competent to evaluate the specific clinical issues involved in medical treatment services, where these services are within the scope of the reviewer's practice.

(r) "Utilization review plan" means the written plan filed with the Administrative Director pursuant to Labor Code section 4610, setting forth the policies and procedures, and a description of the utilization review process.

(s) "Utilization review process" means utilization management functions that prospectively, retrospectively, or concurrently review and approve, modify, delay, or deny, based in whole or in part on medical necessity to cure or relieve, treatment recommendations by physicians, as defined in Labor Code section 3209.3, prior to, retrospectively, or concurrent with the provision of medical treatment services pursuant to Labor Code section 4600. Utilization review does not include determinations of the work-relatedness of injury or disease, or bill review for the purpose of determining whether the medical services were accurately billed.

(t) "Written" includes a facsimile as well as communications in paper form.

Note: Authority cited: Sections 133, 4603.5 and 5307.3, Labor Code. Reference: Sections 3209.3, 4062, 4600, 4600.4, 4604.5 and 4610, Labor Code.

History: 1. New section filed 7-20-95; operative 7-20-95. Submitted to OAL for printing only pursuant to Government Code section 11351 (Register 95, No. 29).

2. Amendment of subsections (a)(4), (c)(1), (c)(3)(iii)-(iv) and (c)(4)(i)-(iii) filed 11-9-98; operative 1-1-99 (Register 98, No. 46).

3. New article 5.5.1 (sections 9792.6-9792.11) and repealer and new section filed 12-9-2004 as an emergency; operative 12-13-2004 (Register 2004, No. 50). A Certificate of Compliance must be transmitted to OAL by 4-12-2005 or emergency language will be repealed by operation of law on the following day.

4. New article 5.5.1 (sections 9792.6-9792.11) and repealer and new section refiled 4-6-2005 as an emergency; operative 4-12-2005 (Register 2005, No. 14). A Certificate of Compliance must be transmitted to OAL by 8-10-2005 or emergency language will be repealed by operation of law on the following day.

5. Certificate of Compliance as to 4-6-2005 order, including amendment of section and Note, transmitted to OAL 8-10-2005 and filed 9-22-2005 (Register 2005, No. 38).

§9792.7. Utilization Review Standards—Applicability.

(a) Effective January 1, 2004, every claims administrator shall establish and maintain a utilization review process for treatment rendered on or after January 1, 2004, regardless of date of injury, in compliance with Labor Code section 4610. Each utilization review process shall be set forth in a utilization review plan which shall contain:

(1) The name, address, phone number, and medical license number of the employed or designated medical director, who holds an unrestricted license to practice medicine in the state of California issued pursuant to section 2050 or section 2450 of the Business and Professions Code.

(2) A description of the process whereby requests for authorization are reviewed, and decisions on such requests are made, and a description of the process for handling expedited reviews.

(3) A description of the specific criteria utilized routinely in the review and throughout the decision-making process, including treatment protocols or standards used in the process. A description of the personnel and other sources used in the development and review of the criteria, and methods for updating the criteria. Prior to and until the Administrative Director adopts a medical treatment utilization schedule pursuant to Labor Code section 5307.27, the written policies and procedures governing the utilization review process shall be consistent with the recommended standards set forth in the American College of Occupational and Environmental Medicine's Occupational Medicine Practice Guidelines, Second Edition. The Adminis-

trative Director incorporates by reference the American College of Occupational and Environmental Medicine's Occupational Medicine Practice Guidelines (ACOEM), Second Edition (2004), published by OEM Press. A copy may be obtained from OEM Press, 8 West Street, Beverly Farms, Massachusetts 01915 (www.oempress.com). After the Administrative Director adopts a medical treatment utilization schedule pursuant to Labor Code section 5307.27, the written policies and procedures governing the utilization review process shall be consistent with the recommended standards set forth in that schedule.

(4) A description of the qualifications and functions of the personnel involved in decision-making and implementation of the utilization review plan.

(5) A description of the claims administrator's practice, if applicable, of any prior authorization process, including but not limited to, where authorization is provided without the submission of the request for authorization.

(b)(1) The medical director shall ensure that the process by which the claims administrator reviews and approves, modifies, delays, or denies requests by physicians prior to, retrospectively, or concurrent with the provision of medical services, complies with Labor Code section 4610 and these implementing regulations.

(2) A reviewer who is competent to evaluate the specific clinical issues involved in the medical treatment services, and where these services are within the reviewer's scope of practice, may, except as indicated below, delay, modify or deny, requests for authorization of medical treatment for reasons of medical necessity to cure or relieve the effects of the industrial injury.

(3) A non-physician reviewer may be used to initially apply specified criteria to requests for authorization for medical services. A non-physician reviewer may approve requests for authorization of medical services. A non-physician reviewer may discuss applicable criteria with the requesting physician, should the treatment for which authorization is sought appear to be inconsistent with the criteria. In such instances, the requesting physician may voluntarily withdraw a portion or all of the treatment in question and submit an amended request for treatment authorization, and the non-physician reviewer may approve the amended request for treatment authorization. Additionally, a non-physician reviewer may reasonably request appropriate additional information that is necessary to render a decision but in no event shall this exceed the time limitations imposed in section 9792.9 subdivisions (b)(1), (b)(2) or (c). Any time beyond the time specified in these paragraphs is subject to the provisions of subdivision (g)(1)(A) through (g)(1)(C) of section 9792.9.

(c) The complete utilization review plan, consisting of the policies and procedures, and a description of the utilization review process, shall be filed by the claims administrator, or by the external utilization review organization contracted by the claims administrator to perform the utilization review, with the Administrative Director. In lieu of filing the utilization review plan, the claims administrator may submit a letter identifying the external utilization review organization which has been contracted to perform the utilization review functions, provided that the utilization review organization has filed a complete utilization review plan with the Administrative Director. A modified utilization review plan shall be filed with the Administrative Director within 30 calendar days after the claims administrator makes a material modification to the plan.

(d) Upon request by the public, the claims administrator shall make available the complete utilization review plan, consisting of the policies and procedures, and a description of the utilization review process.

(1) The claims administrator may make available the complete utilization review plan, consisting of the policies and procedures and a description of the utilization review process, through electronic means. If a member of the public requests a hard copy of the utilization review plan, the claims administrator may charge reasonable copying and postage expenses related to disclosing the complete utilization review plan. Such charge shall not exceed $0.25 per page plus actual postage costs.

Note: Authority cited: Sections 133, 4603.5 and 5307.3, Labor Code. Reference: Sections 4062, 4600, 4600.4, 4604.5 and 4610, Labor Code.

History: 1. New section filed 12-9-2004 as an emergency; operative 12-13-2004 (Register 2004, No. 50). A Certificate of Compliance must be transmitted to OAL by 4-12-2005 or emergency language will be repealed by operation of law on the following day.

2. New section refiled 4-6-2005 as an emergency; operative 4-12-2005 (Register 2005, No. 14). A Certificate of Compliance must be transmitted to OAL by

8-10-2005 or emergency language will be repealed by operation of law on the following day.

3. Certificate of Compliance as to 4-6-2005 order, including amendment of section, transmitted to OAL 8-10-2005 and filed 9-22-2005 (Register 2005, No. 38).

Ref.: Hanna § 22.05[6][c]; Herlick Handbook §§ 1.6, 4.19.

§9792.8. Utilization Review Standards—Medically-Based Criteria.

(a)(1) The criteria shall be consistent with the schedule for medical treatment utilization adopted pursuant to Labor Code section 5307.27. Prior to adoption of the schedule, the criteria or guidelines used in the utilization review process shall be consistent with the American College of Occupational and Environmental Medicine's (ACOEM) Practice Guidelines, Second Edition. The guidelines set forth in the ACOEM Practice Guidelines shall be presumptively correct on the issue of extent and scope of medical treatment until the effective date of the utilization schedule adopted pursuant to Labor Code section 5307.27. The presumption is rebuttable and may be controverted by a preponderance of the scientific medical evidence establishing that a variance from the guidelines is reasonably required to cure or relieve the injured worker from the effects of his or her injury.

(2) For all conditions or injuries not addressed by the ACOEM Practice Guidelines or by the official utilization schedule after adoption pursuant to Labor Code section 5307.27, authorized treatment shall be in accordance with other evidence-based medical treatment guidelines that are generally recognized by the national medical community and are scientifically based. Treatment may not be denied on the sole basis that the treatment is not addressed by the ACOEM Practice Guidelines until adoption of the medical treatment utilization schedule pursuant to Labor Code section 5307.27. After the Administrative Director adopts a medical treatment utilization schedule pursuant to Labor Code section 5307.27, treatment may not be denied on the sole basis that the treatment is not addressed by that schedule.

(3) The relevant portion of the criteria or guidelines used shall be disclosed in written form to the requesting physician, the injured worker, and if the injured worker is represented by counsel, the injured worker's attorney, if used as the basis of a decision to modify, delay, or deny services in a specific case under review. The claims administrator may not charge an injured worker, the injured worker's attorney or the requesting physician for a copy of the relevant portion of the criteria or guidelines used to modify, delay or deny the treatment request.

(4) Nothing in this section precludes authorization of medical treatment not included in the specific criteria under section 9792.8(a)(3).

Note: Authority cited: Sections 133, 4603.5 and 5307.3, Labor Code. Reference: Sections 4062, 4600, 4600.4, 4604.5 and 4610, Labor Code.

History: 1. New section filed 12-9-2004 as an emergency; operative 12-13-2004 (Register 2004, No. 50). A Certificate of Compliance must be transmitted to OAL by 4-12-2005 or emergency language will be repealed by operation of law on the following day.

2. New section refiled 4-6-2005 as an emergency; operative 4-12-2005 (Register 2005, No. 14). A Certificate of Compliance must be transmitted to OAL by 8-10-2005 or emergency language will be repealed by operation of law on the following day.

3. Certificate of Compliance as to 4-6-2005 order, including amendment of section, transmitted to OAL 8-10-2005 and filed 9-22-2005 (Register 2005, No. 38).

Ref.: Hanna § 22.05[6][c]; Herlick Handbook §§ 1.6, 4.19.

§9792.9. Utilization Review Standards—Timeframe, Procedures and Notice Content.

(a) The request for authorization for a course of treatment as defined in section 9792.6(e) must be in written form.

(1) For purposes of this section, the written request for authorization shall be deemed to have been received by the claims administrator by facsimile on the date the request was received if the receiving facsimile electronically date stamps the transmission. If there is no electronically stamped date recorded, then the date the request was transmitted. A request for authorization transmitted by facsimile after 5:30 PM Pacific Time shall be deemed to have been received by the claims administrator on the following business day as defined in Labor Code section 4600.4 and in section 9 of the Civil Code. The copy of the request for authorization received by a facsimile transmission shall bear a notation of the date, time and place of transmission and the facsimile telephone number to which the request was transmitted or be accompanied by an unsigned copy of the affidavit or

certificate of transmission which shall contain the facsimile telephone number to which the request was transmitted. The requesting physician must indicate the need for an expedited review upon submission of the request.

(2) Where the request for authorization is made by mail, and a proof of service by mail exists, the request shall be deemed to have been received by the claims administrator five (5) days after the deposit in the mail at a facility regularly maintained by the United States Postal Service. Where the request for authorization is delivered via certified mail, return receipt mail, the request shall be deemed to have been received by the claims administrator on the receipt date entered on the return receipt. In the absence of a proof of service by mail or a dated return receipt, the request shall be deemed to have been received by the claims administrator on the date stamped as received on the document.

(b) The utilization review process shall meet the following timeframe requirements:

(1) Prospective or concurrent decisions shall be made in a timely fashion that is appropriate for the nature of the injured worker's condition, not to exceed five (5) working days from the date of receipt of the written request for authorization.

(2) If appropriate information which is necessary to render a decision is not provided with the original request for authorization, such information may be requested by a reviewer or non-physician reviewer within five (5) working days from the date of receipt of the written request for authorization to make the proper determination. In no event shall the determination be made more than 14 days from the date of receipt of the original request for authorization by the health care provider.

(A) If the reasonable information requested by the claims administrator is not received within 14 days of the date of the original written request by the requesting physician, a reviewer may deny the request with the stated condition that the request will be reconsidered upon receipt of the information requested.

(3) Decisions to approve a physician's request for authorization prior to, or concurrent with, the provision of medical services to the injured worker shall be communicated to the requesting physician within 24 hours of the decision. Any decision to approve a request shall be communicated to the requesting physician initially by telephone or facsimile. The communication by telephone shall be followed by written notice to the requesting physician within 24 hours of the decision for concurrent review and within two business days for prospective review.

(4) Decisions to modify, delay or deny a physician's request for authorization prior to, or concurrent with the provision of medical services to the injured worker shall be communicated to the requesting physician initially by telephone or facsimile. The communication by telephone shall be followed by written notice to the requesting physician, the injured worker, and if the injured worker is represented by counsel, the injured worker's attorney within 24 hours of the decision for concurrent review and within two business days of the decision for prospective review. In addition, the non-physician provider of goods or services identified in the request for authorization, and for whom contact information has been included, shall be notified in writing of the decision modifying, delaying, or denying a request for authorization that shall not include the rationale, criteria or guidelines used for the decision.

(5) For purposes of this section "normal business day" means a business day as defined in Labor Code section 4600.4 and Civil Code section 9.

(c) When review is retrospective, decisions shall be communicated to the requesting physician who provided the medical services and to the individual who received the medical services, and his or her attorney/designee, if applicable, within 30 days of receipt of the medical information that is reasonably necessary to make this determination. In addition, the non-physician provider of goods or services identified in the request for authorization, and for whom contact information has been included, shall be notified in writing of the decision modifying, delaying, or denying a request for authorization that shall not include the rationale, criteria or guidelines used for the decision.

(d) Failure to obtain prior authorization for emergency health care services shall not be an acceptable basis for refusal to cover medical services provided to treat and stabilize an injured worker presenting for emergency health care services. Emergency health care services, however, may be subjected to retrospective review. Documentation for emergency health care services shall be made available to the claims administrator upon request.

(e) Prospective or concurrent decisions related to an expedited review shall be made in a timely fashion appropriate to the injured worker's condition, not to exceed 72 hours after the receipt of the written information reasonably necessary to make the determination. The requesting physician must indicate the need for an expedited review upon submission of the request. Decisions related to expedited review refer to the following situations:

(1) When the injured worker's condition is such that the injured worker faces an imminent and serious threat to his or her health, including, but not limited to, the potential loss of life, limb, or other major bodily function, or

(2) The normal timeframe for the decision-making process, as described in subdivision (b), would be detrimental to the injured worker's life or health or could jeopardize the injured worker's permanent ability to regain maximum function.

(f) The review and decision to deny, delay or modify a request for medical treatment must be conducted by a reviewer, who is competent to evaluate the specific clinical issues involved in the medical treatment services, and where these services are within the scope of the individual's practice.

(g)(1) The timeframe for decisions specified in subdivisions (b)(1), (b)(2) or (c) may only be extended by the claims administrator under the following circumstances:

(A) The claims administrator is not in receipt of all of the necessary medical information reasonably requested.

(B) The reviewer has asked that an additional examination or test be performed upon the injured worker that is reasonable and consistent with professionally recognized standards of medical practice.

(C) The claims administrator needs a specialized consultation and review of medical information by an expert reviewer.

(2) If subdivisions (A), (B) or (C) above apply, the claims administrator shall immediately notify the requesting physician, the injured worker, and if the injured worker is represented by counsel, the injured worker's attorney in writing, that the claims administrator cannot make a decision within the required timeframe, and specify the information requested but not received, the additional examinations or tests required, or the specialty of the expert reviewer to be consulted. The claims administrator shall also notify the requesting physician, the injured worker, and if the injured worker is represented by counsel, the injured worker's attorney of the anticipated date on which a decision will be rendered. This notice shall include a statement that if the injured worker believes that a bona fide dispute exists relating to his or her entitlement to medical treatment, the injured worker or the injured worker's attorney may file an Application for Adjudication of Claim and Request for Expedited Hearing, DWC Form 4, in accordance with sections 10136(b)(1), 10400, and 10408. In addition, the non-physician provider of goods or services identified in the request for authorization, and for whom contact information has been included, shall be notified in writing of the decision to extend the timeframe and the anticipated date on which the decision will be rendered in accordance with this subdivision. The written notification shall not include the rationale, criteria or guidelines used for the decision.

(3) Upon receipt of information pursuant to subdivisions (A), (B), or (C) above, and (b)(2)(A), the claims administrator shall make the decision to approve, and the reviewer shall make a decision to modify or deny the request for authorization within five (5) working days of receipt of the information for prospective or concurrent review. The decision shall be communicated pursuant to subdivisions (b)(3) or (b)(4).

(4) Upon receipt of information pursuant to subdivisions (A), (B), or (C) above, the claims administrator shall make the decision to approve, and the reviewer shall make a decision to modify or deny the request for authorization within thirty (30) days of receipt of the information for retrospective review.

(h) Every claims administrator shall maintain telephone access from 9:00 AM to 5:30 PM Pacific Time, on normal business days, for health care providers to request authorization for medical services. Every claims administrator shall have a facsimile number available for physicians to request authorization for medical services. Every claims administrator shall maintain a process to receive communications from health care providers requesting authorization for medical services after business hours. For purposes of this section "normal business day" means a business day as defined in Labor Code section 4600.4 and Civil Code section 9. In addition, for purposes of this section the requirement that the claims administrator maintain a process to receive communications from requesting physicians after business hours shall be satisfied by maintaining a voice mail system or a facsimile number for after business hours requests.

(i) A written decision approving a request for treatment authorization under this section shall specify the specific medical treatment service approved.

(j) A written decision modifying, delaying or denying treatment authorization under this section shall be provided to the requesting physician, the injured worker, and if the injured worker is represented by counsel, the injured worker's attorney and shall contain the following information:

(1) The date on which the decision is made.

(2) A description of the specific course of proposed medical treatment for which authorization was requested.

(3) A specific description of the medical treatment service approved, if any.

(4) A clear and concise explanation of the reasons for the claims administrator's decision.

(5) A description of the medical criteria or guidelines used pursuant to section 9792.8, subdivision (a)(3).

(6) The clinical reasons regarding medical necessity.

(7) A clear statement that any dispute shall be resolved in accordance with the provisions of Labor Code section 4062, and that an objection to the utilization review decision must be communicated by the injured worker or the injured worker's attorney on behalf of the injured worker to the claims administrator in writing within 20 days of receipt of the decision. It shall further state that the 20-day time limit may be extended for good cause or by mutual agreement of the parties. The letter shall further state that the injured worker may file an Application for Adjudication of Claim and Request for Expedited Hearing, DWC Form 4, showing a bona fide dispute as to entitlement to medical treatment in accordance with sections 10136(b)(1), 10400, and 10408.

(8) Include the following mandatory language:

Either

"If you want further information, you may contact the local state Information and Assistance office by calling [enter district I & A office telephone number closest to the injured worker] or you may receive recorded information by calling 1-800-736-7401.

or

"If you want further information, you may contact the local state Information and Assistance office closest to you. Please see attached listing (attach a listing of I&A offices and telephone numbers) or you may receive recorded information by calling 1-800-736-7401."

and

"You may also consult an attorney of your choice. Should you decide to be represented by an attorney, you may or may not receive a larger award, but, unless you are determined to be ineligible for an award, the attorney's fee will be deducted from any award you might receive for disability benefits. The decision to be represented by an attorney is yours to make, but it is voluntary and may not be necessary for you to receive your benefits."

In addition, the non-physician provider of goods or services identified in the request for authorization, and for whom contact information has been included, shall be notified in writing of the decision modifying, delaying, or denying a request for authorization that shall not include the rationale, criteria or guidelines used for the decision.

(9) Details about the claims administrator's internal utilization review appeals process, if any, and a clear statement that the appeals process is on a voluntary basis, including the following mandatory statement:

"If you disagree with the utilization review decision and wish to dispute it, you must send written notice of your objection to the claims administrator within 20 days of receipt of the utilization review decision in accordance with Labor Code section 4062. You must meet this deadline even if you are participating in the claims administrator's internal utilization review appeals process."

(k) The written decision modifying, delaying or denying treatment authorization provided to the requesting physician shall also contain the name and specialty of the reviewer or expert reviewer, and the telephone number in the United States of the reviewer or expert reviewer. The written decision shall also disclose the hours of availability of either the review, the expert reviewer or the medical director for the treating physician to discuss the decision which shall be, at a minimum, four (4) hours per week during normal business hours, 9:00 AM to 5:30 PM.,

Pacific Time or an agreed upon scheduled time to discuss the decision with the requesting physician. In the vent the reviewer is unavailable, the requesting physician may discuss the written decision with another reviewer who is competent to evaluate the specific clinical issues involved in the medical treatment services.

(*l*) Authorization may not be denied on the basis of lack of information without documentation reflecting an attempt to obtain the necessary information from the physician or from the provider of goods or services identified in the request for authorization either by facsimile or mail.

Note: Authority cited: Sections 133, 4603.5 and 5307.3, Labor Code. Reference: Sections 4062, 4600, 4600.4, 4604.5 and 4610, Labor Code.

History: 1. New section filed 12-9-2004 as an emergency; operative 12-13-2004 (Register 2004, No. 50). A Certificate of Compliance must be transmitted to OAL by 4-12-2005 or emergency language will be repealed by operation of law on the following day.

2. New section refiled 4-6-2005 as an emergency; operative 4-12-2005 (Register 2005, No. 14). A Certificate of Compliance must be transmitted to OAL by 8-10-2005 or emergency language will be repealed by operation of law on the following day.

3. Certificate of Compliance as to 4-6-2005 order, including amendment of section, transmitted to OAL 8-10-2005 and filed 9-22-2005 (Register 2005, No. 38).

Ref.: Hanna § 22.05[6][c][iii]–[iv]; Herlick Handbook §§ 1.6, 4.19.

§9792.10. Utilization Review Standards—Dispute Resolution.

(a)(1) If the request for authorization of medical treatment is not approved, or if the request for authorization for medical treatment is approved in part, any dispute shall be resolved in accordance with Labor Code section 4062.

(2) An objection to a decision disapproving in whole or in part a request for authorization of medical treatment, must be communicated to the claims administrator by the injured worker or the injured worker's attorney in writing within 20 days of receipt of the utilization review decision. The 20-day time limit may be extended for good cause or by mutual agreement of the parties.

(3) Nothing in this paragraph precludes the parties from participating in an internal utilization review appeal process on a voluntary basis provided the injured worker and if the injured worker is represented by counsel, the injured worker's attorney have been notified of the 20-day time limit to file an objection to the utilization review decision in accordance with Labor Code section 4062.

(4) Additionally, the injured worker or the injured worker's attorney may file an Application for Adjudication of Claim, and a Request for Expedited Hearing, DWC Form 4, in accordance with sections 10136(b)(1), 10400, and 10408, and request an expedited hearing and decision on his or her entitlement to medical treatment if the request for medical treatment is not authorized within the time limitations set forth in section 9792.9, or when there exists a bona fide dispute as to entitlement to medical treatment.

(b) The following requirements shall be met prior to a concurrent review decision to deny authorization for medical treatment and to resolve disputes:

(1) In the case of concurrent review, medical care shall not be discontinued until the requesting physician has been notified of the decision and a care plan has been agreed upon by the requesting physician that is appropriate for the medical needs of the injured worker. In addition, the non-physician provider of goods or services identified in the request for authorization, and for whom contact information has been included, shall be notified in writing of the decision modifying, delaying, or denying a request for authorization that shall not include the rationale, criteria or guidelines used for the decision.

(2) Medical care provided during a concurrent review shall be medical treatment that is reasonably required to cure or relieve from the effects of the industrial injury.

Note: Authority cited: Sections 133, 4603.5 and 5307.3, Labor Code. Reference: Sections 4062, 4600, 4600.4, 4604.5 and 4610, Labor Code.

History: 1. New section filed 12-9-2004 as an emergency; operative 12-13-2004 (Register 2004, No. 50). A Certificate of Compliance must be transmitted to OAL by 4-12-2005 or emergency language will be repealed by operation of law on the following day.

2. New section refiled 4-6-2005 as an emergency; operative 4-12-2005 (Register 2005, No. 14). A Certificate of Compliance must be transmitted to OAL by 8-10-2005 or emergency language will be repealed by operation of law on the following day.

3. Certificate of Compliance as to 4-6-2005 order, including amendment of subsection (b)(1), transmitted

to OAL 8-10-2005 and filed 9-22-2005 (Register 2005, No. 38).

Ref.: Hanna § 22.05[6][c]; Herlick Handbook §§ 1.6, 4.19.

§9792.11. Investigation Procedures: Labor Code §4610 Utilization Review Violations.

(a) To carry out the responsibilities mandated by Labor Code Section 4610(i), the Administrative Director, or his or her designee, shall investigate the utilization review process of any employer, insurer or other entity subject to the provisions of section 4610. The investigation shall include, but not be limited to, review of the practices, files, documents and other records, whether electronic or paper, of the claims administrator, and any other person responsible for utilization review processes for an employer. As used in sections 9792.11 through 9792.15, the phrase 'utilization review organization' includes any person or entity with which the employer, or an insurer, or third party administrator, contracts to fulfill part or all of the employer's utilization review responsibilities under Labor Code section 4610 and Title 8 of the California Code of Regulations, sections 9792.6 through 9792.15.

(b) Notwithstanding Labor Code section 129(a) through (d) and section 129.5 subdivisions (a) through (d), the Administrative Director, or his or her designee, may conduct a utilization review investigation pursuant to Labor Code section 4610, which may include, but is not limited to, an audit of files and other records.

(c) The Administrative Director, or his or her designee, may conduct a utilization review investigation at any location where Labor Code Section 4610 utilization review processes occur, as follows:

(1) For utilization review organizations:

(A) A Routine Investigation shall be initiated at each known utilization review organization at least once every three (3) years. The investigation shall include a review of a random sample of requests for authorization, as defined by section 9792.6(o), received by the utilization review organization during the three most recent full calendar months preceding the date of the issuance of the Notice of Utilization Review Investigation. The investigation may also include a review of any credible complaints received by the Administrative Director since the time of the previous investigation. If there has not been a previous investigation, the investigation may include a review of any credible complaints received by the Administrative Director since the effective date of sections 9792.11 through 9792.15.

(B) Target Investigations:

1. A Return Target Investigation of the same investigation subject shall be conducted within 18 months of the date of the previous investigation if the performance rating was less than eighty-five percent.

2. A Special Target Investigation may be conducted at any time based on credible information indicating the possible existence of a violation of Labor Code section 4610 or sections 9792.6 through 9792.12.

3. The Return Target Investigation and the Special Target Investigation may include: (i) a review of the requests for authorization previously investigated which contained violations; (ii) a review of the file or files pertaining to the complaint or possible violation; (iii) a random sample of requests for authorization received by the utilization review organization during the three most recent full calendar months preceding the date of the issuance of the Notice of Utilization Review Investigation; (iv) a sample of a specific type of request for authorization; and (v) any credible complaints received by the Administrative Director since the time of any prior investigation. If there has not been a previous investigation, the investigation may include a review of any credible complaints received by the Administrative Director since the effective date of sections 9792.11 through 9792.15.

(2) For a claims administrator:

(A) A Routine Investigation shall be initiated at each claims adjusting location at least once every five (5) years concurrent with the profile audit review done pursuant to Labor Code sections 129 and 129.5. The investigation shall include a review of a random sample of requests for authorization, as defined by section 9792.6(o), received by the claims administrator during the three most recent full calendar months preceding the date of the issuance of the Notice of Utilization Review Investigation. The investigation may also include a review of any credible complaints received by the Administrative Director since the time of the previous investigation. If there has not been a previous investigation, the investigation may include a review of any credible complaints received by the Administrative Director since the effective date of sections 9792.11 through 9792.15.

(B) Target Investigations:

1. A Return Target Investigation of the same investigation subject shall be conducted within 18 months of the date of any previous investigation if the performance rating was less than eighty-five percent.

2. A Special Target Investigation may be conducted at any time based on credible information indicating the possible existence of a violation of Labor Code section 4610 or sections 9792.6 through 9792.12.

3. The Return Target Investigation and the Special Target Investigation may include: (i) a review of the requests for authorization previously investigated which contained violations; (ii) a review of the file or files pertaining to the complaint or possible violation; (iii) a random sample of requests for authorization received by the claims administrator during the three most recent full calendar months preceding the date of the issuance of the Notice of Utilization Review Investigation; (iv) a sample of a specific type of request for authorization; and (v) any credible complaints received by the Administrative Director since the time of any prior investigation. If there has not been a previous investigation, the investigation may include a review of any credible complaints received by the Administrative Director since the effective date of sections 9792.11 through 9792.15.

(d) The number of requests for authorization randomly selected for investigation shall be determined based on the following table:

Population of requests for authorization received during a three month calendar period	*Sample Size*
5 or less	all
6-10	1 less than total
11-13	2 less than total
14-16	3 less than total
17-18	4 less than total
19-20	5 less than total
21-23	6 less than total
24	17
25-26	18
27-29	19
30-31	20
32-33	21
34-36	22
37-39	23
40-41	24
42-44	25
45-48	26
49-51	27
52-55	28
56-58	29
59-62	30
63-67	31
68-72	32
73-77	33
78-82	34
83-88	35
89-95	36
96-102	37
103-110	38
111-119	39
120-128	40
129-139	41
140-151	42
152-164	43
165-179	44
180-197	45
198-217	46
218-241	47
242-269	48
270-304	49
305-346	50
347-399	51
400-468	52
469-562	53
563-696	54
697-905	55
906-1,272	56
1,273-2,091	57
2,092-5,530	58
5,531 +	59

(e) Complaints concerning utilization review procedures may be submitted with any supporting documentation to the Division of Workers' Compensation using the sample complaint form that is posted on the Division's website at:

http://www.dir.ca.gov/dwc/FORMS/UtilizationReviewcomplaintform.pdf

Complaints should be mailed to DWC Medical Unit-UR, P.O. Box 71010, Oakland, CA 94612, attention UR Complaints or emailed to DWCManagedCare@dir.ca.gov. Complaints received by the Division of Workers' Compensation will be reviewed and investigated, if necessary, to determine if the complaints are credible and indicate the possible existence of a violation of Labor Code section 4610 or sections 9792.6 through 9792.12.

(f) Administrative penalties may be assessed for any failure to comply with Labor Code section 4610, or sections 9792.6 through 9792.12 of Title 8, California Code of Regulations, except that the penalties listed in section 9792.12(a)(6) through (14) and (b) shall only be imposed if the request was subject to the Labor Code section 4610 utilization review process.

(g) In the event an investigation of utilization review processes is done at the claims administrator's adjusting location, concurrent with a profile audit review done pursuant to Labor Code section 129 or 129.5, the administrative penalty amounts for each violation of Labor Code section 4610 or sections 9792.6 through 9792.12 of Title 8, California Code of Regulations, shall be governed by sections 9792.11 through 9792.15. Any such administrative penalty for utilization review process violations shall apply in lieu of the administrative penalty amount allowed under the audit regulations at section 10111.2(b)(8)[vi] of Title 8, California Code of Regulations. In addition, any report of findings from the investigation and any Order to Show Cause re: Assessment of Administrative Penalties prepared by the Administrative Director, or his or her designee, based on violations of Labor Code section 4610 or sections 9792.6 through 9792.12 of Title 8, California Code of Regulations, shall be prepared separately from any audit report or assessment of administrative penalties made pursuant to Labor Code section 129 and 129.5. The Order to Show Cause re: Assessment of Administrative Penalties for violations of sections 9792.6 et seq of Title 8 of the California Code of Regulations shall be governed by sections 9792.11 through 9792.15.

(h) The Administrative Director, or his or her designee, may also utilize the provisions of Government Code sections 11180 through 11191 to determine whether any violations of the requirements in Labor Code section 4610 or sections 9792.6 through 9792.12 of Title 8, California Code of Regulations, have occurred.

(i) Sections 9792.11 through 9792.15 of Title 8 of the California Code of Regulations shall apply to any Labor Code section 4610 utilization review investigation conducted on or after the effective date of sections 9792.11 through 9792.15 and for conduct which occurred on or after the effective date of sections 9792.11 through 9792.15.

(j) Unless the Administrative Director in his or her discretion determines that advance notice will render a Special Target or Return Target Investigation less useful, the claims administrator or utilization review organization shall be notified of its selection for an Investigation. Claims administrators and utilization review organizations shall be sent a Notice of Utilization Review Investigation. The Notice of Utilization Review Investigation shall require the investigation subject to provide the following:

(1) A description of the system used to identify each request for authorization (if applicable). To the extent the system identifies any of the following information in an electronic format, the claims administrator or utilization review organization shall provide in an electronic format a list of each and every request for authorization received at the investigation site during a three month calendar period specified by the Administrative Director, or his or her designee, and the following data elements: i) a unique identifying number for each request for authorization if one has been assigned; ii) the name of the injured worker; iii) the claim number used by the claims adjuster; iv) the initial date of receipt of the request for authorization; v) the type of review (expedited prospective, prospective, expedited concurrent, concurrent, retrospective, appeal); vi) the disposition (approve, deny, delay, modify, withdrawal); and, vii) if applicable, the type of person who withdrew the request (requesting physician, claims adjuster, injured employee or his or her attorney, or other person). In the event the claims administrator or utilization review organization is not able to provide the list in an electronic format, the list shall be provided in such a form that the listed requests for authorization are sorted in the following order: by type of utilization review, type of disposition, and date of receipt of the initial request;

(2) A description of all media used to transmit, share, record or store information received and transmitted in reference to each request, whether printed copy, electronic, fax, diskette, computer drive or other media;

(3) A legend of any and all numbers, letters and other symbols used to identify the disposition (e.g. approve, deny, modify, delay or withdraw), type of review (expedited prospective, prospective, expedited concurrent, concurrent,

retrospective, appeal), and other abbreviations used to document individual requests for authorization and a data dictionary for all data elements provided;

(4) A description of the methods by which the medical director for utilization review ensures that the process by which requests for authorization are reviewed and approved, modified, delayed, or denied is in compliance with Labor Code section 4610 and sections 9792.6 through 9792.10, as required by sections 9792.6(*l*) and 9792.7(b) of Title 8 of the California Code of Regulations; and

(5) The following additional information, may be requested by the Administrative Director or his or her designee, as applicable to the type of entity investigated: i) whether utilization review services are provided externally; ii) the name(s) of the utilization review organization(s); iii) the name and address of the employer; and iv) the name and address of the insurer.

(k) The utilization review organization or claims administrator shall provide the requested information listed in subdivision (j) within fourteen (14) calendar days of receipt of the Notice of Utilization Review Investigation. Based on the information provided, the Administrative Director, or his or her designee, shall provide the claims administrator or utilization review organization with a Notice of Investigation Commencement, which shall include a list of randomly selected requests for authorization from a three month calendar period designated by the Administrative Director and complaint files (if applicable) for investigation.

(*l*) For utilization review organizations: Within fourteen (14) calendar days of receipt from the Administrative Director, or his or her designee, of the Notice of Investigation Commencement, the utilization review organization shall deliver to the Administrative Director, or his or her designee, a true and complete copy of all records, whether electronic or paper, for each request for authorization listed. Copies of the records shall be delivered with a statement signed under penalty of perjury by the custodian of records for the location at which the records are held, attesting that all of the records produced are true, correct and complete copies of the originals, in his or her possession. After reviewing the records, the Administrative Director, or his or her designee, shall determine if an onsite investigation is required. If an onsite investigation is required, fourteen (14) calendar days notice shall be provided to the utilization review organization.

(m) For claims administrators: The Notice of Investigation Commencement shall be provided to the claims administrator at least fourteen (14) calendar days prior to the commencement of the onsite investigation. The claims administrator shall produce for the Administrative Director, or his or her designee, on the first day of commencement of the onsite investigation, the true, correct and complete copies, whether electronic or paper, whether located onsite or offsite, of each request for authorization identified by the Administrative Director or his or her designee, together with a statement signed under penalty of perjury by the custodian of records for the location at which the records are held, attesting that all of the records produced are true, correct and complete copies of the originals.

(n) In the event the Administrative Director, or his or her designee, determines additional records or files are needed for review during the course of an onsite investigation, the claims administrator or utilization review organization shall produce the requested records in the manner described by subdivision 9792.11(k), within one (1) working day when the records are located at the site of investigation, and within five (5) working days when the records are located at any other site. Any such request by the Administrative Director or his or her designee also may include records or files pertaining to any complaint alleging violations of Labor Code sections 4610 or sections 9792.6 through 9792.12 of Title 8 of the California Code of Regulations. The Administrative Director or his or her designee may extend the time for production of the requested records for good cause.

(o) If the date or deadline in sections 9792.9(b) and 9792.9(c) of Title 8 of the California Code of Regulations to perform any act related to utilization review practices falls on a weekend or holiday, for the purposes of assessing penalties, the act may be performed on the next normal business day, as defined by Labor Code section 4600.4 and Civil Code section 9. This subdivision shall not apply in cases involving concurrent or expedited review. The timelines in sections 9792.9(b) of Title 8 of the California Code of Regulations shall only be extended as provided under section 9792.9(g) of that title.

(p) If the claims administrator or utilization review organization does not record the date a document is received, it shall be deemed received by using the method set out in section 9792.9(a)(2), except that:

(1) where the request for authorization is made by mail through the U.S. postal service and no proof of service by mail exists, the request shall be deemed to have been received by the claims administrator, or utilization review organization on whichever date is earlier, either the receipt date stamped by the addressee or within five (5) calendar days of the date stated in the request for authorization or where the addressee can show a delay in mailing by the postmark date on the mailing envelope then: (A) within five (5) calendar days of the postmark date, if the place of mailing and place of address are both within California; (B) within ten (10) calendar days if the place of address is within the United States but outside of California; or (C) within twenty (20) calendar days if the place of address is outside of the United States; and

(2) where the request for authorization is made by express mail, overnight mail or courier without any proof of service, the request shall be deemed received by the addressee on the date specified in any written confirmation of delivery.

(q) Upon initiating a Special Target Investigation, the Administrative Director, or his or her designee, shall provide to the claims administrator or the utilization review organization a written description of the factual information or of the complaint containing factual information or a copy of the complaint that triggered the utilization review investigation, unless the Administrative Director or his or her designee determines that providing the information would make the investigation less useful. The claims administrator or utilization review organization shall have ten (10) business days upon receipt of the written description or copy of the complaint to provide a written response to the Administrative Director or his or her designee. After reviewing the written response, the Administrative Director, or his or her designee, shall either close the investigation without' the assessment of administrative penalties or conduct further investigation to determine whether a violation exists and whether to impose penalty assessments.

(r) For utilization review organizations: The files and other records, whether electronic or paper, that pertain to the utilization review process shall be retained for at least three (3) years following either: (1) the most recent utilization review decision for each injured employee, or (2) the date on which any appeal from the assessment of penalties for violations of Labor Code section 4610 or sections 9792.6 through 9792.12 is final, whichever date is later. Claims administrators shall retain their claim files as set forth in section 10102 of Title 8 of the California Code of Regulations.

(s) Upon receipt of a notice of Routine or Target Investigation or any other request from the Administrative Director, or his or her designee, to review all files and other records pertaining to the employer's utilization review process, whether electronic or paper, that are created or held outside of California, the claims administrator or utilization review organization shall either deliver all such requested files and other records to an address in California specified by the Administrative Director, or his or her designee, or reimburse the Administrative Director for the actual expenses of each investigator who travels outside of California to the place where the records are held, including the per diem expenses, travel expenses and compensated overtime of the investigators.

(t) A preliminary investigation report will be provided to the claims administrator or utilization review organization. The preliminary investigation report shall consist of the preliminary notice of utilization review penalty assessments, the performance rating, and may include one or more requests for additional documentation or compliance. A conference to discuss the preliminary investigation report shall be scheduled, if necessary, within twenty-one calendar days from the issuance of the preliminary findings. Following the conference, the Administrative Director or his or her designee shall issue an Order to Show Cause Re: Assessment of Administrative Penalty (which shall include the final investigation report), as set forth in section 9792.15.

(u) The claims administrator or utilization review organization may stipulate to the allegations and final report set forth in the Order to Show Cause.

(v) Within forty-five (45) calendar days of the service of the Order to Show Cause Re: Assessment of Administrative Penalties, if no answer has been filed, or within 15 calendar days after any and all appeals have become final, the claims administrator or utilization review organization shall provide the following:

(1) A notice, which shall include a copy of the final investigation report, the measures actually implemented to abate such conditions, and the website address for the Division where the performance rating and summary of violations is posted. If a hearing was conducted under section 9792.15, the notice shall include the Final Determination in lieu of the final investigation report.

(2) For utilization review organizations: the notice must be served on any employer or third party claims administrator that contracted with the utilization review organization and whose utilization review process was assessed with a penalty pursuant to section 9792.12, and any insurer whose utilization review process was assessed with a penalty pursuant to section 9792.12.

(3) For claims administrators: the notice must be served on any self-insured employer and any insurer whose utilization review process was assessed with a penalty pursuant to section 9792.12.

(4) The notice shall be served by certified mail.

(5) Documentation of compliance with this section shall be served on the Administrative Director within thirty calendar days from the date the notice was served.

Note: Authority cited: Sections 11180-11191, Government Code; and Sections 133, 4610 and 5307.3, Labor Code. Reference: Sections 129, 129.5, 4062, 4600, 4600.4, 4604.5, 4610 and 4614, Labor Code.

History: 1. New section filed 6-7-2007; operative 6-7-2007 pursuant to Government Code section 11343.4 (Register 2007, No. 23). For prior history, see Register 2005, No. 38.

Ref.: Hanna § 22.05[6][c]; Herlick Handbook §§ 1.6, 4.19.

§9792.12. Administrative Penalty Schedule for Labor Code §4610 Utilization Review Violations.

(a) Mandatory Administrative Penalties. Notwithstanding Labor Code section 129.5(c)(1) through (c)(3), the penalty amount that shall be assessed for each failure to comply with the utilization review process required by Labor Code section 4610 and sections 9792.6 through 9792.12 of Title 8 of the California Code of Regulations, is:

(1) For failure to establish a Labor Code section 4610 utilization review plan: $50,000;

(2) For failure to include all of the requirements of section 9792.7(a) in the utilization review plan: $5,000;

(3) For failure to file the utilization review plan or a letter in lieu of a utilization review plan with the Administrative Director as required by section 9792.7(c): $10,000;

(4) For failure to file a modified utilization review plan with the Administrative Director within 30 calendar days after the claims administrator makes a material modification to the plan as required by section 9792.7(c): $5,000;

(5) For failure to employ or designate a physician as a medical director, as defined in section 9792.6(*l*), of the utilization review process, as required by section 9792.7(b): $50,000;

(6) For issuance of a decision to modify or deny a request for authorization regarding a medical treatment, procedure, service or product where the requested treatment, procedure or service is not within the reviewer's scope of practice (as set forth by the reviewer's licensing board): $25,000;

(7) For failure to comply with the requirement that only a licensed physician may modify, delay, or deny requests for authorization of medical treatment for reasons of medical necessity to cure or relieve, except as provided for in Labor Code section 4604.5(d) and section 9792.9(b)(2) and (3): $25,000;

(8) For failure of a non-physician reviewer (person other than a reviewer, expert reviewer or medical director as defined in section 9792.6 of Title 8 of the California Code of Regulations), who approves an amended request to possess an amended written request for treatment authorization as provided under section 9792.7(b)(3) when a physician has voluntarily withdrawn a request in order to submit an amended request: $1,000;

(9) For failure to communicate the decision in response to a request for an expedited review, as defined in section 9792.6(g), in a timely fashion, as required by section 9792.9: $15,000;

(10) For failure to approve the request for authorization solely on the basis that the condition for which treatment was requested is not addressed by the medical treatment utilization schedule adopted pursuant to section 5307.27 of the Labor Code: $5,000;

(11) For failure to discuss or document attempts to discuss reasonable options for a care

plan with the requesting physician as required by Labor Code section 4610(g)(3)(B), prior to denying authorization of or discontinuing medical care, in the case of concurrent review: $10,000;

(12) For failure to respond to the request for authorization by the injured employee's requesting treating physician, in the case of a non-expedited concurrent review: $2,000;

(13) For failure to respond to the request for authorization by the injured employee's requesting treating physician, in the case of a non-expedited prospective review: $1,000;

(14) For failure to respond to the request for authorization by the injured employee's requesting treating physician, in the case of a retrospective review: $500;

(15) For failure to disclose or otherwise to make available, if requested, the Utilization Review criteria or guidelines to the public, as required by Labor Code section 4610, subdivision (f)(5) and section 9792.7(d) of Title 8 of the California Code of Regulations: $100.

(16) For failure to timely serve the Administrative Director with documentation of compliance pursuant to section 9792.11(v)(5): $500.

(17) For failure to timely comply with any compliance requirement listed in the Final Report if no timely answer was filed or any compliance requirement listed in the Determination and Order after any and all appeals have become final: $500.

(b) Additional Penalties and Remediation.

(1) After conducting a Routine or Return Target Investigation, the Administrative Director, or his or her designee, shall calculate the investigation subject's performance rating based on its review of the randomly selected requests. The investigation subject's performance rating may also be calculated after conducting a Special Target Investigation. The performance rating will be calculated as follows:

(A) The factor for failure to make and/or provide a timely response to a request for authorization shall be determined by dividing the number of randomly selected requests with violations involving failure to make or provide a timely response to a request for authorization by the total number of randomly selected requests.

(B) The factor for notice(s) with faulty content shall be determined by dividing the number of requests involving notice(s) with faulty content by the total number of randomly selected requests.

(C) The factor for failure to issue notice(s) to all appropriate parties shall be determined by the number of requests involving the failure to issue notice(s) to all appropriate parties by the total number of randomly selected requests.

(D) The investigation subject's investigation performance rating will be determined by adding the factors calculated pursuant to subsections (b)(1)(A) through (b)(1)(C), dividing the total by three, subtracting from one, and multiplying by one-hundred.

(E) If the investigation subject's performance rating meets or exceeds eighty-five percent, the Administrative Director, or his or her designee, shall assess no penalties for the violations listed in this subdivision. If the performance rating is less than eighty-five percent, the violations shall be assessed as set forth below in (b)(2) through (b)(5):

(2) For the types of violations listed below in (b)(4) and (b)(5), each violation shall have a penalty amount, as specified of $100 in (b)(4) or $50 in (b)(5). The penalty amount specified in (b)(4) and (b)(5) shall be waived if the investigation subject's performance rating meets or exceeds eighty-five percent, or if following a Routine Investigation the claims administrator or utilization review organization agrees in writing to:

(A) Deliver to the Administrative Director, or his or her designee, within no more than thirty (30) calendar days from the date of the agreement or the number of days otherwise specified, written evidence, tendered with a declaration made under penalty of perjury, that explains or demonstrates how the violation has been abated in compliance with the applicable statute or regulations and the terms of abatement specified by the Administrative Director; and

(B) Grant the Administrative Director, or his or her designee, entry, upon request and within the time frame specified in the agreement, to the site at which the violation was found for a Return Target Investigation for the purpose of verifying compliance with the abatement measures reported in subdivision 9792.12(b)(1)(A) above and agree to a review of randomly selected requests for authorization; and

(C) Reinstatement of the penalty amount previously waived for each such instance, in the event the violative condition is not abated within the time period specified by the Administrative Director, or his or her designee, or in the event that such abatement measures are not consistent with abatement terms specified by the Administrative Director, or his or her designee.

(3) In the event the Administrative Director, or his or her designee, returns for a Return Target Investigation, after the initial violation has become final, and the subject fails to meet the performance standard of 85%, the amount of penalty shall be calculated as described below and in no event shall the penalty amount be waived:

(A) The penalty amount for each violation shall be multiplied by two for a second investigation, but in no event shall the total penalties for the violations exceed $100,000;

(B) The penalty amount for each violation shall be multiplied by five for a third investigation, but in no event shall the total penalties for the violations exceed $200,000;

(C) The penalty amount for each violation shall be multiplied by ten for a fourth investigation, but in no event shall the total penalties for the violations exceed $400,000.

(4) For each of the violations listed below, the penalty amount shall be $100.00 for each instance found by the Administrative Director, or his or her designee:

(A) For failure to immediately notify all parties in the manner described in section 9792.9(g)(2) of the basis for extending the decision date for a request for medical treatment;

(B) For failure to document efforts to obtain information from the requesting party prior to issuing a denial of a request for authorization on the basis of lack of reasonable and necessary information;

(C) For failure to make a decision to approve or modify or deny the request for authorization, within five (5) working days of receipt of the requested information for prospective or concurrent review, and to communicate the decision as required by section 9792.9(g)(3);

(D) For failure to make and communicate a retrospective decision to approve, modify, or deny the request, within thirty (30) working days of receipt of the information, as required by section 9792.9(g)(4);

(E) For failure to include in the written decision that modifies, delays or denies authorization, all of the items required by section 9792.9(j);

(F) For failure to disclose or otherwise to make available, if requested, the Utilization Review criteria or guidelines, to the injured employee whose case is under review, as required by Labor Code section 4610(f)(5) and section 9792.8(a)(3) Title 8 of the California Code of Regulations.

(5) For each of the violations listed below, the penalty amount shall be $50.00 for each instance found by the Administrative Director, or his or her designee:

(A) For failure by a non-physician or physician reviewer to timely notify the requesting physician, as required by section 9792.9(b)(2), that additional information is needed in order to make a decision in compliance with the timeframes contained in section 9792.9(b);

(B) For failure to communicate the decision to approve to the requesting physician in the case of prospective or concurrent review, by phone or fax within 24 hours of the decision, as required by Labor Code section 4610(g)(3)(A) and in accordance with section 9792.9(b)(3) of Title 8 of the California Code of Regulations;

(C) For failure to send a written notice of the decision to modify, delay or deny to the requesting party, and to the injured employee and to his or her attorney if any, within twenty four (24) hours of making the decision for concurrent review, or within two business days for prospective review, as required by Labor Code section 4610(g)(3)(A) and section 9792.9(b)(4) of Title 8 of the California Code of Regulations;

(D) For failure to communicate a decision in the case of retrospective review as required by section 9792.9(c) within thirty (30) days of receipt of the medical information that was reasonably necessary to make the determination;

(E) For failure to provide immediately a written notice to the requesting party that a decision on the request for authorization cannot be made within fourteen (14) days for prospective and concurrent reviews, or within thirty (30) days for retrospective in accordance with section 9792.9(g)(2);

(F) For failure to document that one of the following events occurred prior to the claims administrator providing written notice for delay under Labor Code section 4610(g)(5):

(1) the claims administrator had not received all of the information reasonably necessary and requested;

(2) the employer or claims administrator has requested a consultation by an expert reviewer;

(3) the physician reviewer has requested an additional examination or test be performed;

(G) For failure to explain in writing the reason for delay as required by section 9792.9(g)(2) of Title 8 of the California Code of Regulations when the decision to delay was made under one of the circumstances listed in section 9792.9(g)(1).

(6) After the time to file an answer to the Order to Show Cause Re: Assessment of Administrative Penalties has elapsed and no answer has been filed or after any and all appeals have become final, the Administrative Director, or his or her designee, shall post on the website for the Division of Workers' Compensation the performance rating and summary of violations for each utilization review investigation.

(c) The penalty amounts specified for violations under subsection 9792.12(a) and (b) above may, in the discretion of the Administrative Director, be reduced after consideration of the factors set out in section 9792.13 of Title 8 of the California Code of Regulations. Failure to abate a violation found under section 9792.12(b)(4) and (b)(5), in the time period or in a manner consistent with that specified by the Administrative Director, or his or her designee, shall result in the assessment of the full original penalty amount proposed by the Administrative Director for that violation.

Note: Authority cited: Sections 133, 4610 and 5307.3, Labor Code. Reference: Sections 129, 129.5, 4062, 4600, 4600.4, 4604.5, 4610 and 4614, Labor Code.

History: 1. New section filed 6-7-2007; operative 6-7-2007 pursuant to Government Code section 11343.4 (Register 2007, No. 23).

§9792.13. Assessment of Administrative Penalties — Penalty Adjustment Factors.

(a) In any investigation that the Administrative Director deems appropriate, the Administrative Director, or his or her designee, may mitigate a penalty amount imposed under section 9792.12 after considering each of these factors:

(1) The medical consequences or gravity of the violation(s);

(2) The good faith of the claims administrator or utilization review organization. Mitigation for good faith shall be determined based on documentation of attempts to comply with the Labor Code and regulations and shall result in a reduction of 20% for each applicable penalty;

(3) The history of previous penalties;

(4) The frequency of violations found during the investigation giving rise to a penalty;

(5) Penalties may be mitigated outside the above mitigation guidelines in extraordinary circumstances, when strict application of the mitigation guidelines would be clearly inequitable; and

(6) In the event an objection or appeal is filed pursuant to subsection 9792.15 of these regulations, whether the claims administrator or utilization review organization abated the alleged violation within the time period specified by the Administrative Director or his or her designee.

(b) The Administrative Director, or his or her designee, may assess both an administrative penalty under Labor Code section 4610 and a civil penalty under subdivision (e) of Labor Code section 129.5 based on the same violation(s).

(c) The Administrative Director, or his or her designee, shall not collect payment for an administrative penalty under Labor Code section 4610 from both the utilization review organization and the claims administrator for an assessment based on the same violation(s).

(d) Where an injured worker's or a requesting provider's refusal to cooperate in the utilization review process has prevented the claims administrator or utilization review organization from determining whether there is a legal obligation to perform an act, the Administrative Director, or his or her designee, may forego a penalty assessment for any related act or omission. The claims administrator or utilization review organization shall have the burden of proof in establishing both the refusal to cooperate and that such refusal prevented compliance with the relevant applicable statute or regulation.

Note: Authority cited: Sections 133, 4610 and 5307.3, Labor Code. Reference: Sections 129, 129.5, 4062, 4600, 4600.4, 4604.5, 4610 and 4614, Labor Code.

History: 1. New section filed 6-7-2007; operative 6-7-2007 pursuant to Government Code section 11343.4 (Register 2007, No. 23).

§9792.14. Liability for Penalty Assessments.

(a) If more than one claims administrator or utilization review organization has been responsible for a claim file, utilization review file or other file that is being investigated, penalties may be assessed against each such entity for the violation(s) that occurred during the time each such entity had responsibility for the file or for the utilization review process.

(b) The claims administrator or utilization review organization is liable for all penalty assessments made against it, except that if the subject of the investigation is acting as an agent, the agent and the principal are jointly and severally liable for all penalty assessments resulting from a given investigation. This paragraph does not prohibit an agent and its principal from allocating the administrative penalty liability between them. Liability for civil penalties assessed pursuant to Labor Code section 129.5(e) for violations under Labor Code section 4610 or sections 9792.6 through 9792.10 of Title 8 of the California Code of Regulations shall not be allocated.

(c) Successor liability may be imposed on a claims administrator or utilization review organization that has merged with, consolidated, or otherwise continued the business of a corporation, other business entity or other person that was cited by the Administrative Director for violations of Labor Code section 4610 or sections 9792.6 through 9792.12. The surviving entity or person responsible for administering the utilization review process for an employer, shall assume and be liable for all the liabilities, obligations and penalties of the prior corporation or business entity. Successor liability will be imposed if there has been a substantial continuity of business operations and/or the new business uses the same or substantially the same work force.

Note: Authority cited: Sections 133, 4610 and 5307.3, Labor Code. Reference: Sections 129, 129.5, 4062, 4600, 4600.4, 4604.5, 4610 and 4614, Labor Code.

History: 1. New section filed 6-7-2007; operative 6-7-2007 pursuant to Government Code section 11343.4 (Register 2007, No. 23).

§9792.15. Administrative Penalties Pursuant to Labor Code §4610 — Order to Show Cause, Notice of Hearing, Determination and Order, and Review Procedure.

(a) Pursuant to Labor Code section 4610(i), the Administrative Director shall issue an Order to Show Cause Re: Assessment of Administrative Penalty when the Administrative Director, or his or her designee (the investigating unit of the Division of Workers' Compensation), has reason to believe that an employer, insurer or other entity subject to Labor Code section 4610 has failed to meet any of the requirements of this section or of any regulation adopted by the Administrative Director pursuant to the authority of section 4610.

(b) The order shall be in writing and shall include all of the following:

(1) Notice that an administrative penalty may be assessed;

(2) The final investigation report, which shall consist of the notice of utilization review penalty assessment, the performance rating, and may include one or more requests for documentation or compliance;

(c) The order shall be served personally or by registered or certified mail.

(d) Within thirty (30) calendar days after the date of service of the Order to Show Cause Re: Assessment of Administrative Penalties, the claims administrator or utilization review organization may pay the assessed administrative penalties or file an answer as the respondent with the Administrative Director, in which the respondent may:

(1) Admit or deny in whole or in part any of the allegations set forth in the Order to Show Cause;

(2) Contest the amount of any or all proposed administrative penalties;

(3) Contest the existence of any or all of the violations;

(4) Set forth any affirmative and other defenses;

(5) Set forth the legal and factual bases for each defense.

(e) Any allegation and proposed penalty stated in the Order to Show Cause that is not contested shall be paid within thirty (30) calendar days after the date of service of the Order to Show Cause.

(f) Failure to timely file an answer shall constitute a waiver of the respondent's right to an evidentiary hearing. Unless set forth in the answer, all defenses to the Order to Show Cause shall be deemed waived. If the answer is not timely filed, within ten (10) days of the date for filing the answer, the respondent may file a written request for leave to file an answer. The respondent may also file a written request for leave to assert additional defenses, which the

Administrative Director may grant upon a showing of good cause.

(g) The answer shall be in writing and signed by, or on behalf of, the claims administrator or utilization review organization and shall state the respondent's mailing address. It need not be verified or follow any particular form.

(1) The respondent must file the original and one copy of the answer on the Administrative Director and concurrently serve one copy of the answer on the investigating unit of the Division of Workers' Compensation (designated by the Administrative Director). The original and all copies of any filings required by this section shall have a proof of service attached.

(h) Within sixty (60) calendar days of the issuance of the Order to Show Cause Re: Assessment of Administrative Penalty, the Administrative Director shall issue the Notice of the date, time and place of a hearing. The date of the hearing shall be at least ninety calendar days from the date of service of the Notice. The Notice shall be served personally or by registered or certified mail. Continuances will not be allowed without a showing of good cause.

(i) At any time before the hearing, the Administrative Director may file or permit the filing of an amended complaint or supplemental Order to Show Cause. All parties shall be notified thereof. If the amended complaint or supplemental Order to Show Cause presents new charges, the Administrative Director shall afford the respondent a reasonable opportunity to prepare its defense, and the respondent shall be entitled to file an amended answer.

(j) At the Administrative Director's discretion, the Administrative Director may proceed with an informal pre-hearing conference with the respondent in an effort to resolve the contested matters. If any or all of the violations or proposed penalties in the Order to Show Cause, the amended Order or the supplemental Order remain contested, those contested matters shall proceed to an evidentiary hearing.

(k) Whenever the Administrative Director's Order to Show Cause has been contested, the Administrative Director may designate a hearing officer to preside over the hearing. The authority of the Administrative Director or the designated hearing officer shall include, but is not limited to: conducting a pre-hearing settlement conference; setting the date for an evidentiary hearing and any continuances; issuing subpoenas for the attendance of any person residing anywhere within the state as a witness or party at any pre-hearing conference and hearing; issuing subpoenas duces tecum for the production of documents and things at the hearing; presiding at the hearings; administering oaths or affirmations and certifying official acts; ruling on objections and motions; issuing pre-hearing orders; and preparing a Recommended Determination and Opinion based on the hearing.

(*l*) The Administrative Director or the designated hearing officer shall set the time and place for any pre-hearing conference on the contested matters in the Order to Show Cause, and shall give sixty (60) calendar days written notice to all parties.

(m) The pre-hearing conference may address one or more of the following matters:

(1) Exploration of settlement possibilities;

(2) Preparation of stipulations;

(3) Clarification of issues;

(4) Rulings on the identity of witnesses and limitation of the number of witnesses;

(5) Objections to proffers of evidence;

(6) Order of presentation of evidence and cross-examination;

(7) Rulings regarding issuance of subpoenas and protective orders;

(8) Schedules for the submission of written briefs and schedules for the commencement and conduct of the hearing;

(9) Any other matters as shall promote the orderly and prompt conduct of the hearing.

(n) The Administrative Director or the designated hearing officer shall issue a pre-hearing order incorporating the matters determined at the pre-hearing conference. The Administrative Director or the designated hearing officer may direct one or more of the parties to prepare the pre-hearing order.

(o) Not less than thirty (30) calendar days prior to the date of the evidentiary hearing, the respondent shall file and serve the original and one copy of a written statement with the Administrative Director or the designated hearing officer specifying the legal and factual bases for its answer and each defense, listing all witnesses the respondent intends to call to testify at the hearing, and appending copies of all documents and other evidence the respondent intends to introduce into evidence at the hearing. A copy of the written statement and its attachments shall also concurrently be served on the investigating unit of the Division of Workers' Compensation. If the written statement and supporting evidence are not timely filed and served, the Administrative Director or the designated hearing officer shall dismiss the answer and issue a written Determination based on the evidence provided by the investigating unit of the Division of Workers' Compensation. Within ten (10) calendar days of the date for filing the written statement and supporting evidence, the respondent may file a written request for leave to file a written statement and supporting evidence. The Administrative Director or the designated hearing officer may grant the request, upon a showing of good cause. If leave is granted, the written statement and supporting evidence must be filed and served no later than ten (10) calendar days prior to the date of the hearing.

(p) Oral testimony shall be taken only on oath or affirmation.

(q)(1) Each party shall have these rights: to call and examine witnesses, to introduce exhibits; to cross-examine opposing witnesses on any matter relevant to the issues even though that matter was not covered in the direct examination; to impeach any witness regardless of which party first called him or her to testify; and to rebut the evidence.

(2) In the absence of a contrary order by the Administrative Director or the designated hearing officer, the investigating unit of the Division of Workers' Compensation shall present evidence first.

(3) The hearing need not be conducted according to the technical rules relating to evidence and witnesses, except as hereinafter provided. Any relevant evidence shall be admitted if it is the sort of evidence on which responsible persons are accustomed to rely in the conduct of serious affairs, regardless of the existence of any common law or statutory rule which might make the admission of the evidence improper over objection in civil actions.

(4) Hearsay evidence may be used for the purpose of supplementing or explaining other evidence but upon timely objection shall not be sufficient in itself to support a finding unless it would be admissible over objection in civil actions. An objection is timely if made before submission of the case to the Administrative Director or to the designated hearing officer.

(r) The written affidavit or declaration of any witness may be offered and shall be received into evidence provided that (i) the witness was listed in the written statement pursuant to section 9792.15(n); (ii) the statement is made by affidavit or by declaration under penalty of perjury; (iii) copies of the statement have been delivered to all opposing parties at least twenty (20) days prior to the hearing; and (iv) no opposing party has, at least ten (10) days before the hearing, delivered to the proponent of the evidence a written demand that the witness be produced in person to testify at the hearing. The Administrative Director or the designated hearing officer shall disregard any portion of the statement received pursuant to this regulation that would be inadmissible if the witness were testifying in person, but the inclusion of inadmissible matter does not render the entire statement inadmissible. Upon timely demand for production of a witness in lieu of admission of an affidavit or declaration, the proponent of that witness shall ensure the witness appears at the scheduled hearing and the proffered declaration or affidavit from that witness shall not be admitted. If the Administrative Director or the designated hearing officer determines that good cause exists that prevents the witness from appearing at the hearing, the declaration may be introduced in evidence, but it shall be given only the same effect as other hearsay evidence.

(s) The Administrative Director or the designated hearing officer shall issue a written Determination and Order Assessing Penalty, if any, including a statement of the basis for the Determination and each penalty assessed, within sixty (60) days of the date the case was submitted for decision, which shall be served on all parties. This requirement is directory and not jurisdictional.

(t) The Administrative Director shall have sixty (60) calendar days to adopt or modify the Determination and Order Assessing Penalty issued by the Administrative Director or the designated hearing officer. In the event the recommended Determination and Order of the designated hearing officer is modified, the Administrative Director shall include a statement of the basis for the Determination and Order Assessing Penalty signed and served by the Administrative Director, or his or her designee. If the Administrative Director does not act within sixty (60) calendar days, then the recommended Determination and Order shall become the Determination and Order on the sixty-first calendar day.

(u) The Determination and Order Assessing Penalty shall be served on all parties personally or by registered or certified mail by the Administrative Director.

(v) The Determination and Order Assessing Penalty, if any, shall become final on the day it is served, unless the aggrieved party files a timely Petition Appealing the Determination of the Administrative Director. All findings and assessments in the Determination and Order Assessing Penalty not contested in the Petition Appealing the Determination of the Administrative Director shall become final as though no petition were filed.

(w) At any time prior to the date the Determination and Order Assessing Penalty becomes final, the Administrative Director or designated hearing officer may correct the Determination and Order Assessing Penalty for clerical, mathematical or procedural error(s).

(x) Penalties assessed in a Determination and Order Assessing Penalty shall be paid within thirty (30) calendar days of the date the Determination and Order became final. A timely filed Petition Appealing the Determination of the Administrative Director shall toll the period for paying the penalty assessed for the item appealed.

(y) All appeals from any part or the entire Determination and Order Assessing Penalty shall be made in the form of a Petition Appealing the Determination of the Administrative Director, in conformance with the requirements of chapter 7, part 4 of Division 4 of the Labor Code. Any such Petition Appealing the Determination of the Administrative Director shall be filed at the Appeals Board in San Francisco (and not with any district office of the Workers' Compensation Appeals Board), in the same manner specified for petitions for reconsideration.

Note: Authority cited: Sections 133, 4610 and 5307.3, Labor Code. Reference: Sections 129, 129.5, 4062, 4600, 4600.4, 4604.5, 4610, 4614 and 5300, Labor Code.

History: 1. New section filed 6-7-2007; operative 6-7-2007 pursuant to Government Code section 11343.4 (Register 2007, No. 23).

ARTICLE 5.5.2
Medical Treatment Utilization Schedule

§9792.20. Medical Treatment Utilization Schedule — Definitions.

As used in this Article:

(a) "American College of Occupational and Environmental Medicine (ACOEM)" is a medical society of physicians and other health care professionals specializing in the field of occupational and environmental medicine, dedicated to promoting the health of workers through preventive medicine, clinical care, research, and education.

(b) "ACOEM Practice Guidelines" means the American College of Occupational and Environmental Medicine's Occupational Medicine Practice Guidelines, 2nd Edition (2004). The Administrative Director incorporates the ACOEM Practice Guidelines by reference. A copy may be obtained from the American College of Occupational and Environmental Medicine, 25 Northwest Point Blvd., Suite 700, Elk Grove Village, Illinois, 60007-1030 (www.acoem.org).

(c) "Claims administrator" is a self-administered workers' compensation insurer, a self-administered self-insured employer, a self-administered legally uninsured employer, a self-administered joint powers authority, a third-party claims administrator, or the California Insurance Guarantee Association.

(d) "Evidence-based" means based, at a minimum, on a systematic review of literature published in medical journals included in MEDLINE.

(e) "Functional improvement" means either a clinically significant improvement in activities of daily living or a reduction in work restrictions as measured during the history and physical exam, performed and documented as part of the evaluation and management visit billed under the Official Medical Fee Schedule (OMFS) pursuant to Sections 9789.10-9789.111; and a reduction in the dependency on continued medical treatment.

(f) "Medical treatment" is care which is reasonably required to cure or relieve the employee from the effects of the industrial injury consistent with the requirements of sections 9792.20-9792.23.

(g) "Medical treatment guidelines" means the most current version of written recommendations revised within the last five years which are systematically developed by a multidisciplinary process through a comprehensive literature search to assist in decision-making about the appropriate medical treatment for specific clinical circumstances.

(h) "MEDLINE" is the largest component of PubMed, the U.S. National Library of Medicine's database of biomedical citations and abstracts that is searchable on the Web. Its website address is www.pubmed.gov.

(i) "Nationally recognized" means published in a peer-reviewed medical journal; or developed, endorsed and disseminated by a national organization with affiliates based in two or more U.S. states; or currently adopted for use by one or more U.S. state governments or by the U.S. federal government; and is the most current version.

(j) "Peer reviewed" means that a medical study's content, methodology and results have been evaluated and approved prior to publication by an editorial board of qualified experts.

(k) "Scientifically based" means based on scientific literature, wherein the body of literature is identified through performance of a literature search in MEDLINE, the identified literature is evaluated, and then used as the basis for the guideline.

(*l*) "Strength of Evidence" establishes the relative weight that shall be given to scientifically based evidence.

Note: Authority cited: Sections 133, 4603.5, 5307.3 and 5307.27, Labor Code. Reference: Sections 77.5, 4600, 4604.5 and 5307.27, Labor Code.

History: 1. New article 5.5.2 (sections 9792.20-9792.23) and section filed 6-15-2007; operative 6-15-2007 pursuant to Government Code section 11343.4 (Register 2007, No. 24).

Ref.: Hanna § 22.05[6][b].

§9792.21. Medical Treatment Utilization Schedule.

(a) The Administrative Director adopts the Medical Treatment Utilization Schedule consisting of Sections 9792.20 through Section 9792.23. The Administrative Director adopts and incorporates by reference the following medical treatment guidelines into the Medical Treatment Utilization Schedule:

(1) The American College of Occupational and Environmental Medicine's Occupational Medicine Practice Guidelines (ACOEM Practice Guidelines), Second Edition (2004). A copy may be obtained from the American College of Occupational and Environmental Medicine, 25 Northwest Point Blvd., Suite 700, Elk Grove Village, Illinois, 60007-1030 (www.acoem.org).

(2) Acupuncture Medical Treatment Guidelines

The Acupuncture Medical Treatment Guidelines set forth in this subdivision shall supersede the text in the ACOEM Practice Guidelines, Second Edition, relating to acupuncture, except for shoulder complaints, and shall address acupuncture treatment where not discussed in the ACOEM Practice Guidelines.

(A) Definitions:

(i) "Acupuncture" is used as an option when pain medication is reduced or not tolerated, it may be used as an adjunct to physical rehabilitation and/or surgical intervention to hasten functional recovery. It is the insertion and removal of filiform needles to stimulate acupoints (acupuncture points). Needles may be inserted, manipulated, and retained for a period of time. Acupuncture can be used to reduce pain, reduce inflammation, increase blood flow, increase range of motion, decrease the side effect of medication-induced nausea, promote relaxation in an anxious patient, and reduce muscle spasm.

(ii) "Acupuncture with electrical stimulation" is the use of electrical current (microamperage or milli-amperage) on the needles at the acupuncture site. It is used to increase effectiveness of the needles by continuous stimulation of the acupoint. Physiological effects (depending on location and settings) can include endorphin release for pain relief, reduction of inflammation, increased blood circulation, analgesia through interruption of pain stimulus, and muscle relaxation. It is indicated to treat chronic pain conditions, radiating pain along a nerve pathway, muscle spasm, inflammation, scar tissue pain, and pain located in multiple sites.

(iii) "Chronic pain for purposes of acupuncture" means pain that persists for at least 30 days beyond the usual course of an acute disease or a reasonable time for an injury to heal or that is associated with a chronic pathological process that causes continuous pain (e.g., reflex sympathetic dystrophy). The very definition of chronic pain describes a delay or outright failure to relieve pain associated with some specific illness or accident.

(B) Indications for acupuncture or acupuncture with electrical stimulation include the following presenting complaints in reference to the following ACOEM Practice Guidelines Chapter Headings:

(i) Neck and Upper Back Complaints

(ii) Elbow Complaints

(iii) Forearm, Wrist, and Hand Complaints

(iv) Low Back Complaints

(v) Knee Complaints

(vi) Ankle and Foot Complaints

(vii) Pain, Suffering, and the Restoration of Function

(C) Frequency and duration of acupuncture or acupuncture with electrical stimulation may be performed as follows:

(i) Time to produce functional improvement: 3 to 6 treatments.

(ii) Frequency: 1 to 3 times per week

(iii) Optimum duration: 1 to 2 months

(D) Acupuncture treatments may be extended if functional improvement is documented as defined in Section 9792.20(e).

(E) It is beyond the scope of the Acupuncture Medical Treatment Guidelines to state the precautions, limitations, contraindications or adverse events resulting from acupuncture or acupuncture with electrical stimulations. These decisions are left up to the acupuncturist.

(b) The Medical Treatment Utilization Schedule is intended to assist in the provision of medical treatment by offering an analytical framework for the evaluation and treatment of injured workers and to help those who make decisions regarding the medical treatment of injured workers understand what treatment has been proven effective in providing the best medical outcomes to those workers, in accordance with section 4600 of the Labor Code.

(c) Treatment shall not be denied on the sole basis that the condition or injury is not addressed by the Medical Treatment Utilization Schedule. In this situation, the claims administrator shall authorize treatment if such treatment is in accordance with other scientifically and evidence-based, peer-reviewed, medical treatment guidelines that are nationally recognized by the medical community, in accordance with subdivisions (b) and (c) of section 9792.22, and pursuant to the Utilization Review Standards found in Section 9792.6 through Section 9792.10.

Note: Authority cited: Sections 133, 4603.5, 5307.3 and 5307.27, Labor Code. Reference: Sections 77.5, 4600, 4604.5 and 5307.27, Labor Code.

History: 1. New section filed 6-15-2007; operative 6-15-2007 pursuant to Government Code section 11343.4 (Register 2007, No. 24).

Ref.: Hanna § 22.05[6][b], [c][i].

§9792.22. Presumption of Correctness, Burden of Proof and Strength of Evidence.

(a) The Medical Treatment Utilization Schedule is presumptively correct on the issue of extent and scope of medical treatment and diagnostic services addressed in the Medical Treatment Utilization Schedule for the duration of the medical condition. The presumption is rebuttable and may be controverted by a preponderance of scientific medical evidence establishing that a variance from the schedule is reasonably required to cure or relieve the injured worker from the effects of his or her injury. The presumption created is one affecting the burden of proof.

(b) For all conditions or injuries not addressed by the Medical Treatment Utilization Schedule, authorized treatment and diagnostic services shall be in accordance with other scientifically and evidence-based medical treatment guidelines that are nationally recognized by the medical community.

(c)(1) For conditions or injuries not addressed by either subdivisions (a) or (b) above; for medical treatment and diagnostic services at variance with both subdivisions (a) or (b) above; or where a recommended medical treatment or diagnostic service covered under subdivision (b) is at variance with another treatment guideline also covered under subdivision (b), the following ACOEM's strength of evidence rating methodology is adopted and incorporated as set forth below, and shall be used to evaluate scientifically based evidence published in peer-reviewed, nationally recognized journals to recommend specific medical treatment or diagnostic services:

(A) Table A — Criteria Used to Rate Randomized Controlled Trials

Studies shall be rated using the following 11 criteria. Each criterion shall be rated 0, 0.5, or 1.0, thus the overall ratings range from 0-11. A study is considered low quality if the composite rating was 3.5 or less, intermediate quality if rated 4-7.5, and high quality if rated 8-11.

Criteria	*Rating Explanation*
Randomization: Assessment of the degree that randomization was both reported to have been performed and successfully* achieved through analyses of comparisons of variables between the two groups. *Simply allocating individuals to groups does not constitute sufficient grounds to assess the success of randomization. The groups must be comparable; otherwise, the randomization was unsuccessful.	Rating is "0" if the study is not randomized or reports that it was and subsequent analyses of the data/tables suggest it either was not randomized or was unsuccessful. Rating is "0.5" if there is mention of randomization and it appears as if it was performed, however there are no data on the success of randomization, it appears incomplete, or other questions about randomization cannot be adequately addressed. Rating is "1.0" if randomization is specifically stated and data reported on subgroups suggests that the study did achieve successful randomization.
Treatment Allocation Concealed: Concealment of the allocation scheme from all involved, not just the patient.	Rating is "0" if there is no description of how members of the research team or subjects would have not been able to know how they were going to receive a particular treatment, or the process used would not be concealed. Rating is "0.5" if the article mentions how allocation was concealed, but the concealment was either partial involving only some of those involved or other questions about it are unable to be completely addressed. Rating is "1.0" if there is a concealment process described that would conceal the treatment allocation to all those involved.
Baseline Comparability: Measures how well the baseline groups are comparable (e.g., age, gender, prior treatment).	Rating is "0" if analyses show that the groups were dissimilar at baseline or it cannot be assessed. Rating is "0.5" if there is general comparability, though one variable may not be comparable. Rating is "1.0" if there is good comparability for all variables between the groups at baseline.
Patient Blinded	Rating is "0" if there is no mention of blinding of the patient. Rating is "0.5" if it mentions blinding, but the methods are unclear. Rating is "1.0" if the study reports blinding, describes how that was carried out, and would plausibly blind the patient.
Provider Blinded	Rating is "0" if there is no mention of blinding of the provider. Rating is "0.5" if it mentions blinding, but the methods are unclear. Rating is "1.0" if the study reports blinding, describes how that was carried out and would plausibly blind the provider.
Assessor Blinded	Rating is "0" if there is no mention of blinding of the assessor.

Criteria	*Rating Explanation*
	Rating is "0.5" if it mentions blinding, but the methods are unclear. Rating is "1.0" if the study reports blinding, describes how that was carried out and would plausibly blind the assessor.
Controlled for Co-interventions: The degree to which the study design controlled for multiple interventions (e.g., a combination of stretching exercises and anti-inflammatory medication or mention of not using other treatments during the study).	Rating is "0" if there are multiple interventions or no description of how this was avoided. Rating is "0.5" if there is brief mention of this potential problem. Rating is "1.0" if there is a detailed description of how co-interventions were avoided.
Compliance Acceptable: Measures the degree of non-compliance.	Rating is "0" if there is no mention of non-compliance. Rating is "0.5" if non-compliance is briefly addressed and the description suggests that there was compliance, but a complete assessment is not possible. Rating is "1.0" if there are specific data and the non-compliance rate is less than 20%.
Dropout Rate: Measures the drop-out rate.	Rating is "0" if there is no mention of drop-outs or it cannot be inferred from the data presented. Rating is "0.5" if the drop-out issue is briefly addressed and the description suggests that there were few drop-outs, but a complete assessment is not possible. Rating is "1.0" if there are specific data and the drop-out rate is under 20%.
Timing of Assessments: Timing rates the timeframe for the assessments between the study groups.	Rating is "0" if the timing of the evaluations is different between the groups. Rating is "0.5" if the timing is nearly identical (e.g., one day apart). Rating is "1.0" if the timing of the assessments between the groups is identical.
Analyzed by Intention to Treat: This rating is for whether the study was analyzed with an intent to treat analysis.	Rating is "0" if it was not analyzed by intent to treat. Rating is "0.5" if there is not mention of intent to treat analysis, but the results would not have been different (e.g., there was nearly 100% compliance and no drop-outs). Rating is "1.0" if the study specifies analyses by intention to treat.

Criteria	*Rating Explanation*
Lack of Bias: This rating does not enter into the overall rating of an article. This is an overall indication of the degree to which biases are felt to be present in the study.	Rating is "0" if there are felt to be significant biases that are uncontrolled in the study and may have influenced the study's results.
	Rating is "0.5" if there are felt to be some biases present, but the results are less likely to have been influenced by those biases.
	Rating is "1.0" if there are few biases, or those are well controlled and unlikely to have influenced the study's results.

(B) Table B — Strength of Evidence Ratings

Levels of evidence shall be used to rate the quality of the body of evidence. The body of evidence shall consist of all studies on a given topic that are used to develop evidence-based recommendations. Levels of evidence shall be applied when studies are relevant to the topic and study working populations. Study outcomes shall be consistent and study data shall be homogeneous.

A	**Strong evidence-base:** One or more well-conducted systematic reviews or meta-analyses, or two or more high-quality studies.
B	**Moderate evidence-base:** At least one high-quality study, a well-conducted systematic review or meta-analysis of lower quality studies or multiple lower-quality studies relevant to the topic and the working population.
C	**Limited evidence-base:** At least one study of intermediate quality.
I	**Insufficient Evidence:** Evidence is insufficient or irreconcilable.

(2) Evidence shall be given the highest weight in the order of the strength of evidence.

Note: Authority cited: Sections 133, 4603.5, 5307.3 and 5307.27, Labor Code. Reference: Sections 77.5, 4600, 4604.5 and 5307.27, Labor Code.

History: 1. New section filed 6-15-2007; operative 6-15-2007 pursuant to Government Code section 11343.4 (Register 2007, No. 24).

Ref.: Hanna § 22.05[6][b], [c][i].

§9792.23. Medical Evidence Evaluation Advisory Committee.

(a)(1) The Medical Director shall create a medical evidence evaluation advisory committee to provide recommendations to the Medical Director on matters concerning the medical treatment utilization schedule. The recommendations are advisory only and shall not constitute scientifically based evidence.

(A) If the Medical Director position becomes vacant, the Administrative Director shall appoint a competent person to temporarily assume the authority and duties of the Medical Director as set forth in this section, until such time that the Medical Director position is filled.

(2) The members of the medical evidence evaluation advisory committee shall be appointed by the Medical Director, or his or her designee, and shall consist of 17 members of the medical community holding the following licenses: Medical Doctor (M.D.) board certified by an American Board of Medical Specialties (ABMS) approved specialty board; Doctor of Osteopathy (D.O.) board certified by an ABMS or American Osteopathic Association (AOA) approved specialty board; M.D. board certified by a Medical Board of California (MBC) approved specialty board; Doctor of Chiropractic (D.C.); Physical Therapy (P.T.); Occupational Therapy (O.T.); Acupuncture (L.Ac.); Psychology (PhD.); or Doctor of Podiatric Medicine (DPM), and representing the following specialty fields:

(A) One member shall be from the orthopedic field;

(B) One member shall be from the chiropractic field;

(C) One member shall be from the occupational medicine field;

(D) One member shall be from the acupuncture medicine field;

(E) One member shall be from the physical therapy field;

(F) One member shall be from the psychology field;

(G) One member shall be from the pain specialty field;

(H) One member shall be from the occupational therapy field;

(I) One member shall be from the psychiatry field;

(J) One member shall be from the neurosurgery field;

(K) One member shall be from the family physician field;

(L) One member shall be from the neurology field;

(M) One member shall be from the internal medicine field;

(N) One member shall be from the physical medicine and rehabilitation field;

(O) One member shall be from the podiatrist field;

(P) Two additional members shall be appointed at the discretion of the Medical Director or his or her designee.

(3) In addition to the seventeen members of the medical evidence evaluation advisory committee appointed under subdivision (a)(2) above, the Medical Director, or his or her designee, may appoint an additional three members to the medical evidence evaluation advisory committee as subject matter experts for any given topic.

(b) The Medical Director, or his or her designee, shall serve as the chairperson of the medical evidence evaluation advisory committee.

(c) To evaluate evidence when making recommendations to revise, update or supplement the medical treatment utilization schedule, the members of the medical evidence evaluation advisory committee shall:

(1) Apply the requirements of subdivision (b) of Section 9792.22 in reviewing medical treatment guidelines to insure that the guidelines are scientifically and evidence-based, and nationally recognized by the medical community;

(2) Apply the ACOEM's strength of evidence rating methodology to the scientific evidence as set forth in subdivision (c) of Section 9792.22 after identifying areas in the guidelines which do not meet the requirements set forth in subdivision (b) of Section 9792.22;

(3) Apply in reviewing the scientific evidence, the ACOEM's strength of evidence rating methodology for treatments where there are no medical treatment guidelines or where a guideline is developed by the Administrative Director, as set forth in subdivision (c) of Section 9792.22.

(d) The members of the medical evidence evaluation advisory committee, except for the three subject matter experts, shall serve a term of two year period, but shall remain in that position until a successor is selected. The subject matter experts shall serve as members of the medical evidence evaluation advisory committee until the evaluation of the subject matter guideline is completed. The members of the committee shall meet as necessary, but no less than four (4) times a year.

(f) The Administrative Director, in consultation with the Medical Director, may revise, update, and supplement the medical treatment utilization schedule as necessary.

Note: Authority cited: Sections 133, 4603.5, 5307.3 and 5307.27, Labor Code. Reference: Sections 77.5, 4600, 4604.5 and 5307.27, Labor Code.

History: 1. New section filed 6-15-2007; operative 6-15-2007 pursuant to Government Code section 11343.4 (Register 2007, No. 24).

2007 Note: No subsection (e) was promulgated.

Ref.: Hanna § 22.05[6][b].

ARTICLE 5.6
Medical-Legal Expenses and Comprehensive Medical-Legal Evaluations

§9793. Definitions.

As used in this article:

(a) "Claim" means a claim for compensation as evidenced by either the filing of a claim form pursuant to Section 5401 of the Labor Code or notice or knowledge of an injury under Section 5400 or 5402 of the Labor Code.

(b) "Contested claim" means any of the following:

(1) Where the claims administrator has rejected liability for a claimed benefit.

(2) Where the claims administrator has failed to accept liability for a claim and the claim has become presumptively compensable under Section 5402 of the Labor Code.

(3) Where the claims administrator has failed to respond to a demand for the payment of compensation after the expiration of any time period fixed by statute for the payment of indemnity benefits, including where the claims administrator has failed to either commence the

payment of temporary disability indemnity or issue a notice of delay within 14 days after knowledge of an employee's injury and disability as provided in Section 4650 of the Labor Code.

(4) Where the claims administrator has accepted liability for a claim and a disputed medical fact exists.

(c) "Comprehensive medical-legal evaluation" means an evaluation of an employee which (A) results in the preparation of a narrative medical report prepared and attested to in accordance with Section 4628 of the Labor Code, any applicable procedures promulgated under Section 139.2 of the Labor Code, and the requirements of Section 10606 and (B) is either:

(1) performed by a Qualified Medical Evaluator pursuant to subdivision (h) of Section 139.2 of the Labor Code, or

(2) performed by a Qualified Medical Evaluator, Agreed Medical Evaluator, or the primary treating physician for the purpose of proving or disproving a contested claim, and which meets the requirements of paragraphs (1) through (5), inclusive, of subdivision (g).

(d) "Claims Administrator" means a self-administered insurer providing security for the payment of compensation required by Divisions 4 and 4.5 of the Labor Code, a self-administered self-insured employer, a group self-insurer, or a third-party claims administrator for a self-insured employer, insurer, legally uninsured employer, group self-insurer, or joint powers authority.

(e) "Disputed medical fact" means an issue in dispute, including an objection to a medical determination made by a treating physician under Section 4062 of the Labor Code, concerning (1) the employee's medical condition, (2) the cause of the employee's medical condition, (3) treatment for the employee's medical condition, (4) the existence, nature, duration or extent of temporary or permanent disability caused by the employee's medical condition, or (5) the employee's medical eligibility for rehabilitation services.

(f) "Follow-up medical-legal evaluation" means an evaluation which includes an examination of an employee which (A) results in the preparation of a narrative medical report prepared and attested to in accordance with Section 4628 of the Labor Code, any applicable procedures promulgated under Section 139.2 of the Labor Code, and the requirements of Section 10606, (B) is performed by a qualified medical evaluator, agreed medical evaluator, or primary treating physician within nine months following the evaluator's examination of the employee in a comprehensive medical-legal evaluation and (C) involves an evaluation of the same injury or injuries evaluated in the comprehensive medical-legal evaluation.

(g) "Medical-legal expense" means any costs or expenses incurred by or on behalf of any party or parties, the administrative director, or the appeals board for X-rays, laboratory fees, other diagnostic tests, medical reports, medical records, medical testimony, and as needed, interpreter's fees, for the purpose of proving or disproving a contested claim. The cost of medical evaluations, diagnostic tests, and interpreters is not a medical-legal expense unless it is incidental to the production of a comprehensive medical-legal evaluation report, follow-up medical-legal evaluation report, or a supplemental medical-legal evaluation report and all of the following conditions exist:

(1) The report is prepared by a physician, as defined in Section 3209.3 of the Labor Code.

(2) The report is obtained at the request of a party or parties, the administrative director, or the appeals board for the purpose of proving or disproving a contested claim and addresses the disputed medical fact or facts specified by the party, or parties or other person who requested the comprehensive medical-legal evaluation report. Nothing in this paragraph shall be construed to prohibit a physician from addressing additional related medical issues.

(3) The report is capable of proving or disproving a disputed medical fact essential to the resolution of a contested claim, considering the substance as well as the form of the report, as required by applicable statutes, regulations, and case law.

(4) The medical-legal examination is performed prior to receipt of notice by the physician, the employee, or the employee's attorney, that the disputed medical fact or facts for which the report was requested have been resolved.

(5) In the event the comprehensive medical-legal evaluation is served on the claims administrator after the disputed medical fact or facts for which the report was requested have been resolved, the report is served within the time frame specified in Section 139.2(j)(1) of the Labor Code.

(h) "Medical-legal testimony" means expert testimony provided by a physician at a deposition or workers' compensation appeals board hearing, regarding the medical opinion submitted by the physician.

(i) "Medical research" is the investigation of medical issues. It includes investigating and reading medical and scientific journals and texts. "Medical research" does not include reading or reading about the *Guides for the Evaluation of Permanent Impairment* (any edition), treatment guidelines (including guidelines of the American College of Occupational and Environmental Medicine), the Labor Code, regulations or publications of the Division of Workers' Compensation (including the *Physicians' Guide*), or other legal materials.

(j) "Primary treating physician" is the treating physician primarily responsible for managing the care of the injured worker in accordance with subdivision (a) of Section 9785.

(k) "Reports and documents required by the administrative director" means an itemized billing, a copy of the medical-legal evaluation report, and any verification required under Section 9795(c).

(*l*) "Supplemental medical-legal evaluation" means an evaluation which (A) does not involve an examination of the patient, (B) is based on the physician's review of records, test results or other medically relevant information which was not available to the physician at the time of the initial examination, (C) results in the preparation of a narrative medical report prepared and attested to in accordance with Section 4628 of the Labor Code, any applicable procedures promulgated under Section 139.2 of the Labor Code, and the requirements of Section 10606 and (D) is performed by a qualified medical evaluator, agreed medical evaluator, or primary treating physician following the evaluator's completion of a comprehensive medical-legal evaluation.

Note: Authority cited: Sections 133, 4627, 5307.3 and 5307.6, Labor Code. Reference: Sections 4061, 4061.5, 4062, 4620, 4621, 4622, 4625, 4628, 4650, 5307.6 and 5402, Labor Code.

History: 1. New article 5.6 (sections 9793-9795) filed 1-10-85; designated effective 3-1-85 (Register 85, No. 2).

2. Change without regulatory effect filed 7-11-86; effective upon filing (Register 86, No. 28).

3. Repealer and new section filed 8-3-93; operative 8-3-93. Submitted to OAL for printing only pursuant to Government Code section 11351 (Register 93, No. 32).

4. Amendment of article heading, section and Note filed 12-31-93; operative 1-1-94. Submitted to OAL for printing only pursuant to Government Code section 11351 (Register 93, No. 53).

5. Change without regulatory effect amending subsections (f) and (i) filed 6-12-2002 pursuant to section 100, title 1, California Code of Regulations (Register 2002, No. 24).

6. Amendment of subsections (a) and (b)(3), new subsection (i), subsection relettering and amendment of newly designated subsection (j) filed 6-30-2006; operative 7-1-2006. Submitted to OAL for filing with the Secretary of State and printing only pursuant to Government Code section 11340.9(g) (Register 2006, No. 26).

Ref.: Hanna §§ 5.04[2][a], 22.09[1], 22.09[3], 23.13[2][b], 23.13[3]; Herlick Handbook §§ 1.6, 4.21, 10.3; W. Cal. Sum., 2 "Workers' Compensation" §273.

§9794. Reimbursement of Medical-Legal Expenses.

(a) The cost of comprehensive, follow-up and supplemental medical-legal evaluation reports, diagnostic tests, and medical-legal testimony, regardless of whether incurred on behalf of the employee or claims administrator, shall be billed and reimbursed as follows:

(1) X-rays, laboratory services and other diagnostic tests shall be billed and reimbursed in accordance with the official medical fee schedule adopted pursuant to Labor Code Section 5307.1. In no event shall the claims administrator be liable for the cost of any diagnostic test provided in connection with a comprehensive medical-legal evaluation report unless the subjective complaints and physical findings that warrant the necessity for the test are included in the medical-legal evaluation report. Additionally, the claims administrator shall not be liable for the cost of diagnostic tests, absent prior authorization by the claims administrator, if adequate medical information is already in the medical record provided to the physician.

(2) The cost of comprehensive, follow-up and supplemental medical-legal evaluations, and medical-legal testimony shall be billed and reimbursed in accordance with the schedule set forth in Section 9795.

(b) All medical-legal expenses shall be paid within 60 days after receipt by the employer of the reports and documents required by the administrative director unless the claims administrator, within this period, contests its liability for such payment.

(c) A claims administrator who contests all or any part of a bill for medical-legal expense, or who contests a bill on the basis that the expense does not constitute a medical-legal expense, shall pay any uncontested amount and notify the physician or other provider of the objection within sixty days after receipt of the reports and documents required by the administrative director. Any notice of objection shall include or be accompanied by all of the following:

(1) An explanation of the basis for the objection to each contested procedure and charge. The original procedure codes used by the physician or other provider shall not be altered. If the objection is based on appropriate coding of a procedure, the explanation shall include both the code reported by the provider and the code believed reasonable by the claims administrator, and shall include the claim's administrator's rationale as to why its code more accurately reflects the service provided. If the claims administrator denies liability for the entire medical-legal expense, the objection shall set forth the legal, medical or factual basis for the denial.

(2) If additional information is necessary as a prerequisite to payment of the contested bill or portions thereof, a clear description of the information required.

(3) The name, address, and telephone number of the person or office to contact for additional information concerning the objection.

(4) A statement that the physician or other provider may adjudicate the issue of the contested charges before the Workers' Compensation Appeals Board.

A form objection which does not identify the specific deficiencies of the report in question shall not satisfy the requirements of this subdivision.

(d) All reports and documents required by the administrative director shall be included in or attached to the medical-legal report when it is filed and served on the parties pursuant to Section 10608 or served on the parties pursuant to Section 4061 or 4062 of the Labor Code.

(e) Physicians shall keep and maintain for three years, and shall make available to the administrative director by date of examination upon request, copies of all billings for medical-legal expense.

(f) A physician may not charge, nor be paid, any fees for services in violation of Section 139.3 of the Labor Code or subdivision (d) of Section 5307.6 of the Labor Code;

(g) Claims administrator shall retain, for three years, the following information for each comprehensive medical evaluation for which the claims administrator is billed:

(1) name and specialty of medical evaluator;

(2) name of the employee evaluated;

(3) date of examination;

(4) the amount billed for the evaluation;

(5) the date of the bill;

(6) the amount paid for the evaluation, including any penalties and interest;

(7) the date payment was made.

This information may be stored in paper or electronic form and shall be made available to the administrative director upon request. This information shall also be made available, upon request, to any party to a case, where the requested information pertains to an evaluation obtained in the case.

Note: Authority cited: Sections 133, 4627, 5307.3 and 5307.6, Labor Code. Reference: Sections 4620, 4621, 4622, 4625, 4626, 4628 and 5307.6, Labor Code.

History: 1. Repealer and new section filed 8-3-93; operative 8-3-93. Submitted to OAL for printing only pursuant to Government Code section 11351 (Register 93, No. 32).

2. Amendment of subsections (a)-(c)(1) and (e), and new subsections (f)-(h) filed 12-31-93; operative 1-1-94. Submitted to OAL for printing only pursuant to Government Code section 11351 (Register 93, No. 53).

3. Repealer of subsection (h) filed 2-14-96; operative 2-14-96. Submitted to OAL for printing only pursuant to Government Code section 11351 (Register 96, No. 7).

4. Editorial correction of subsection (a) (Register 2001, No. 22).

Ref.: Hanna §§ 10.50[2][a], 22.09[2]–[4], 27.01[8][b][ii]; Herlick Handbook §§ 1.6, 4.21, 10.3.

§9795. Reasonable Level of Fees for Medical-Legal Expenses, Follow-up, Supplemental and Comprehensive Medical-Legal Evaluations and Medical-Legal Testimony.

(a) The schedule of fees set forth in this section shall be prima facie evidence of the reasonableness of fees charged for medical-legal evaluation reports, and fees for medical-legal testimony.

Reports by treating or consulting physicians, other than comprehensive, follow-up or supplemental medical-legal evaluations, regardless of whether liability for the injury has been accepted at the time the treatment was provided or the report was prepared, shall be subject to the Official Medical Fee Schedule adopted pursuant to Labor Code Section 5307.1 rather than to the fee schedule set forth in this section.

(b) The fee for each evaluation is calculated by multiplying the relative value by $12.50, and adding any amount applicable because of the modifiers permitted under subdivision (d). The fee for each medical-legal evaluation procedure includes reimbursement for the history and physical examination, review of records, preparation of a medical-legal report, including typing and transcription services, and overhead expenses. The complexity of the evaluation is the dominant factor determining the appropriate level of service under this section; the times to perform procedures is expected to vary due to clinical circumstances, and is therefore not the controlling factor in determining the appropriate level of service.

(c) Medical-legal evaluation reports and medical-legal testimony shall be reimbursed as follows:

CODE	*B.R.*	*PROCEDURE DESCRIPTION*
ML100		*Missed Appointment for a Comprehensive or Follow-Up Medical-Legal Evaluation.* This code is designed for communication purposes only. It does not imply that compensation is necessarily owed.

CODE	*RV*	*PROCEDURE DESCRIPTION*
ML101	5	*Follow-up Medical-Legal Evaluation.* Limited to a follow-up medical-legal evaluation by a physician which occurs within nine months of the date on which the prior medical-legal evaluation was performed. The physician shall include in his or her report verification, under penalty of perjury, of time spent in each of the following activities: review of records, face-to-face time with the injured worker, and preparation of the report. Time spent shall be tabulated in increments of 15 minutes or portions thereof, rounded to the nearest quarter hour. The physician shall be reimbursed at the rate of RV 5, or his or her usual and customary fee, whichever is less, for each quarter hour.

CODE	*RV*	*PROCEDURE DESCRIPTION*
ML102	50	*Basic Comprehensive Medical-Legal Evaluation.* Includes all comprehensive medical-legal evaluations other than those included under ML 103 or ML 104.

CODE	*RV*	*PROCEDURE DESCRIPTION*
ML103	75	*Complex Comprehensive Medical-Legal Evaluation.* Includes evaluations which require three of the complexity factors set forth below.

In a separate section at the beginning of the report, the physician shall clearly and concisely specify which of the following complexity factors were required for the evaluation, and the circumstances which made these complexity factors applicable to the evaluation. An evaluator who specifies complexity factor (3) must also provide a list of citations to the sources reviewed, and excerpt or include copies of medical evidence relied upon:

(1) Two or more hours of face-to-face time by the physician with the injured worker;

(2) Two or more hours of record review by the physician;

(3) Two or more hours of medical research by the physician;

(4) Four or more hours spent on any combination of two of the complexity factors (1)-(3), which shall count as two complexity factors. Any complexity factor in (1), (2), or (3) used to make this combination shall not also be used as the third required complexity factor;

(5) Six or more hours spent on any combination of three complexity factors (1)-(3), which shall count as three complexity factors;

(6) Addressing the issue of medical causation, upon written request of the party or parties requesting the report, or if a bona fide issue of medical causation is discovered in the evaluation;

(7) Addressing the issue of apportionment, when determination of this issue requires the physician to evaluate the claimant's employment by three or more employers, three or more injuries to the same body system or body region as delineated in the Table of Contents of *Guides to the Evaluation of Permanent Impairment* (Fifth Edition), or two or more or more injuries involving two or more body systems or body regions as delineated in that Table of Contents. The Table of Contents of *Guides to the Evaluation of Permanent Impairment* (Fifth Edition), published by the American Medical Association, 2000, is incorporated by reference.

(8) Addressing the issue of medical monitoring of an employee following a toxic exposure to chemical, mineral or biologic substances;

(9) A psychiatric or psychological evaluation which is the primary focus of the medical-legal evaluation.

(10) Addressing the issue of denial or modification of treatment by the claims administrator following utilization review under Labor Code section 4610.

CODE RV PROCEDURE DESCRIPTION

Regulations

ML104 5 *Comprehensive Medical-legal Evaluation Involving Extraordinary Circumstances.* The physician shall be reimbursed at the rate of RV 5, or his or her usual and customary hourly fee, whichever is less, for each quarter hour or portion thereof, rounded to the nearest quarter hour, spent by the physician for any of the following:

(1) An evaluation which requires four or more of the complexity factors listed under ML 103; In a separate section at the beginning of the report, the physician shall clearly and concisely specify which four or more of the complexity factors were required for the evaluation, and the circumstances which made these complexity factors applicable to the evaluation. An evaluator who specifies complexity factor (3) must also provide a list of citations to the sources reviewed, and excerpt or include copies of medical evidence relied upon.

(2) An evaluation involving prior multiple injuries to the same body part or parts being evaluated, and which requires three or more of the complexity factors listed under ML 103, including three or more hours of record review by the physician;

(3) A comprehensive medical-legal evaluation for which the physician and the parties agree, prior to the evaluation, that the evaluation involves extraordinary circumstances. When billing under this code for extraordinary circumstances, the physician shall include in his or her report (i) a clear, concise explanation of the extraordinary circumstances related to the medical condition being evaluated which justifies the use of this procedure code, and (ii) verification under penalty of perjury of the total time spent by the physician in each of these activities: reviewing the records, face-to-face time with the injured worker, preparing the report and, if applicable, any other activities.

CODE RV PROCEDURE DESCRIPTION

ML105	5	Fees for medical-legal testimony. The physician shall be reimbursed at the rate of RV 5, or his or her usual and customary fee, whichever is less, for each quarter hour or portion thereof, rounded to the nearest quarter hour, spent by the physician. The physician shall be entitled to fees for all itemized reasonable and necessary time spent related to the testimony, including reasonable preparation and travel time. The physician shall be paid a minimum of one hour for a scheduled deposition.
CODE	*RV*	*PROCEDURE DESCRIPTION*
ML106	5	Fees for supplemental medical-legal evaluations. The physician shall be reimbursed at the rate of RV 5, or his or her usual and customary fee, whichever is less, for each quarter hour or portion thereof, rounded to the nearest quarter hour, spent by the physician. Fees will not be allowed under this section for supplemental reports following the physician's review of (A) information which was available in the physician's office for review or was included in the medical record provided to the physician prior to preparing the initial report or (B) the results of laboratory or diagnostic tests which were ordered by the physician as part of the initial evaluation.

(d) The services described by Procedure Codes ML101 through ML106 may be modified under the circumstances described in this subdivision. The modifying circumstances shall be identified by the addition of the appropriate modifier code, which is reported by a two-digit number placed after the usual procedure number separated by a hyphen. The modifiers available are the following:

–92 Performed by a primary treating physician. This modifier is added solely for identification purposes, and does not change the normal value of the service.

–93 Interpreter needed at time of examination, or other circumstances which impair communication between the physician and the injured worker and significantly increase the time needed to conduct the examination. Requires a description of the circumstance and the increased time required for the examination as a result. Where this modifier is applicable, the value for the procedure is modified by multiplying the normal value by 1.1. This modifier shall only be applicable to ML 102 and ML 103.

–94 Evaluation and medical-legal testimony performed by an Agreed Medical Evaluator. Where this modifier is applicable, the value of the procedure is modified by multiplying the normal value by 1.25. If modifier -93 is also applicable for an ML-102 or ML-103, then the value of the procedure is modified by multiplying the normal value by 1.35.

–95 Evaluation performed by a panel selected Qualified Medical Evaluator. This modifier is added solely for identification purposes, and does not change the normal value of any procedure.

(e) Requests for duplicate reports shall be in writing. Duplicate reports shall be separately reimbursable and shall be reimbursed in the same manner as set forth in the Official Medical Fee Schedule adopted pursuant to Labor Code Section 5307.1.

(f) This section shall apply to medical-legal evaluation reports where the examination occurs on or after the effective date of this section. The 2006 amendments to this section shall apply to: (1) medical-legal evaluation reports where the medical examination to which the report refers occurs on or after the effective date of the 2006 amendments; (2) medical-legal testimony provided on or after the effective date of the 2006 amendments; and (3) supplemental medical legal reports that are requested on or after the effective date of the 2006 amendments regardless of the date of the original examination.

Note: Authority cited: Sections 133, 4627, 5307.3 and 5307.6, Labor Code. Reference: Sections 139.2, 4061, 4061.5, 4062, 4620, 4621, 4622, 4625, 4626, 4628, 5307.6 and 5402, Labor Code.

History: 1. Repealer and new section filed 8-3-93; operative 8-3-93. Submitted to OAL for printing only pursuant to Government Code section 11351 (Register 93, No. 32).

2. Change without regulatory effect amending subsection (a) and subsection (c) medical-legal evaluation procedure code ML104 filed 8-27-93 pursuant to section 100, title 1, California Code of Regulations (Register 93, No. 35).

3. Amendment of section heading, section and Note filed 12-31-93; operative 1-1-94. Submitted to OAL for printing only pursuant to Government Code section 11351 (Register 93, No. 53).

4. Amendment filed 2-24-99; operative 4-1-99 (Register 99, No. 9).

5. Change without regulatory effect amending subsections (b) and (d) filed 6-12-2002 pursuant to section 100, title 1, California Code of Regulations (Register 2002, No. 24).

6. Amendment of section and Note filed 6-30-2006; operative 7-1-2006. Submitted to OAL for filing with the Secretary of State and printing only pursuant to Government Code section 11340.9(g) (Register 2006, No. 26).

Ref.: Hanna §§ 5.04[2][b], 22.09[3], 23.13[2][b], 27.01[8][b][ii], 30.05; Herlick Handbook §§ 1.6, 4.21, 10.3.

ARTICLE 5.7
Fees for Interpreter Services

§9795.1. Definitions.

As used in this article:

(a) "Certified" means an interpreter who is certified in accordance with subdivision (e) of Section 11513 of the Government Code or Section 68562 of the Government Code.

(b) "Claims Administrator" means a self-administered insurer providing security for the payment of compensation required by Divisions 4 and 4.5 of the Labor Code, a self-administered self-insured employer, or a third-party claims administrator for a self-insured employer, insurer, legally uninsured employer, or joint powers authority.

(c) "Full day" means services performed which exceed one-half day, up to 8 hours.

(d) "One-half day" means:

(1) When appearing at any Workers' Compensation Appeals Board hearing, daytime arbitration or formal rehabilitation conference, all or any part of a morning or afternoon session.

(2) When appearing at a deposition, all or any part of 3.5 hours.

(3) When appearing at an evening arbitration, all or any part of 3 hours.

(e) "Provisionally certified" means an interpreter who is deemed to be qualified to perform services under this article, when a certified interpreter cannot be present, by (A) the residing officer at an appeals board hearing, arbitration, or formal rehabilitation conference, at the request of a party or parties, or (B) agreement of the parties for any services provided under this article other than at an appeals board hearing, arbitration, or formal rehabilitation conference.

(f) "Qualified interpreter" means an interpreter who is certified or provisionally certified.

(g) "Travel time" means the time an interpreter actually travels to and from the place where service is to be rendered and his or her place of business.

(h) "Market rate" means that amount an interpreter has actually been paid for recent interpreter services provided in connection with the preparation and resolution of an employee's claim.

Note: Authority cited: Sections 133, 5307.3, 5710 and 5811, Labor Code. Reference: Sections 4600, 4620, 4621, 5710 and 5811, Labor Code; and Sections 11513 and 68562, Government Code.

History: 1. New article 5.7 (sections 9795.1-9795.4) and section filed 1-28-94; operative 1-28-94. Submitted to OAL for printing only pursuant to Government Code section 11351 (Register 94, No. 4).

2. Repealer of subsection (g), subsection relettering, and new Note filed 12-30-96; operative 12-30-96 pursuant to Government Code section 11343.4(d). Submitted to OAL for printing only pursuant to Government Code section 11351 (Register 97, No. 1).

Ref.: Herlick Handbook §§ 1.6, 14.33.

§9795.2. Notice of Right to Interpreter.

The notice of hearing, deposition, or other setting shall include a statement explaining the right to have an interpreter present if they do not proficiently speak or understand the English language. Where a party is designated to serve a notice, it shall be the responsibility of that party to include this statement in the notice.

Note: Authority cited: Sections 133, 5307.3, 5710 and 5811, Labor Code. Reference: Sections 4600, 4620, 4621, 5710 and 5811, Labor Code; and Sections 11513 and 68562, Government Code.

History: 1. New section filed 1-28-94; operative 1-28-94. Submitted to OAL for printing only pursuant to Government Code section 11351 (Register 94, No. 4).

2. New Note filed 12-30-96; operative 12-30-96 pursuant to Government Code section 11343.4(d). Submitted to OAL for printing only pursuant to Government Code section 11351 (Register 97, No. 1).

Ref.: Hanna §§ 23.13[3], 23.14[1][c], 26.04[1], 33.01[4], 35.53[3]; Herlick Handbook §§ 1.6, 14.33.

§9795.3. Fees for Interpreter Services.

(a) Fees for services performed by a qualified interpreter, where the employee does not proficiently speak or understand the English language, shall be paid by the claims administrator for any of the following events:

(1) An examination by a physician to which an injured employee submits at the requests of the claims administrator, the administrative director, or the appeals board;

(2) A comprehensive medical-legal evaluation as defined in subdivision (c) of Section 9793, a follow-up medical-legal evaluation as defined in subdivision (f) of Section 9793, or a supplemental medical-legal evaluation as defined in subdivision (k) of Section 9793; provided, however, that payment for interpreter's fees by the claims administrator shall not be required under this paragraph unless the medical report to which the services apply is compensable in accordance with Article 5.6. Nothing in this paragraph, however, shall be construed to relieve the party who retains an interpreter from liability to pay the interpreter's fees in the event the claims administrator is not liable.

(3) A deposition of an injured employee or any person claiming benefits as a dependent of an injured employee, at the request of the claims administrator, including the following related events:

(i) Preparation of the deponent immediately prior to the deposition,

(ii) Reading of a deposition to a deponent prior to signing, and,

(iii) Reading of prior volumes to a deponent in preparation for continuation of a deposition.

(4) An appeals board hearing, arbitration, or formal rehabilitation conference.

(5) An informal rehabilitation conference.

(6) A conference held by an information and assistance officer pursuant to Chapter 2.5 (commencing with Section 5450) of Part 4 of Division 4 of the Labor Code to assist in resolving a dispute between an injured employee and a claims administrator.

(7) Other similar settings determined by the Workers' Compensation Appeals Board to be reasonable and necessary to determine the validity and extent of injury to an employee.

(b) The following fees for interpreter services provided by a certified interpreter shall be presumed to be reasonable:

(1) For an appeal board hearing, arbitration, deposition, or formal rehabilitation conference: interpreter fees shall be billed and paid at the greater of the following (i) at the rate for one-half day or one full day as set forth in the Superior Court fee schedule for interpreters in the county where the service was provided, or (ii) at the market rate. The interpreter shall establish the market rate for the interpreter's services by submitting documentation to the claims administrator, including a list of recent similar services performed and the amounts paid for those services. Services over 8 hours shall be paid at the rate of one-eighth the full day rate for each hour of service over 8 hours.

(2) For all other events listed under subdivision (a), interpreter fees shall be billed and paid at the rate of $11.25 per quarter hour or portion thereof, with a minimum payment of two hours, or the market rate, whichever is greater. The interpreter shall establish the market rate for the interpreter's services by submitting documentation to the claims administrator, including a list of recent similar services performed and the amounts paid for those services.

(3) The fee in paragraph (1) or (2) shall include, when requested and adequately documented by the interpreter, payment for mileage and travel time where reasonable and necessary to provide the service, and where the distance between the interpreter's place of business and the place where the service was rendered is over 25 miles. Travel time is not deemed reasonable and necessary where a qualified interpreter listed in the master listing for the county where the service is to be provided can be present to provide the service without the necessity of excessive travel.

(i) Mileage shall be paid at the minimum rate adopted by the Director of the Department of Personnel Administration pursuant to Section 19820 of the Government Code for non-represented (excluded) employees at Title 2, CCR § 599.631(a).

(ii) Travel time shall be paid at the rate of $5.00 per quarter hour or portion thereof.

(c) Unless notified of a cancellation at least 24 hours prior to the time the service is to be provided, the interpreter shall be paid no less than the minimum fee.

(d) Nothing in this section shall preclude payment to an interpreter or agency for interpreting services based on an agreement made in advance of services between the interpreter or agency and the claims administrator, regardless of whether or not such payment is less than, or exceeds, the fees set forth in this section.

(e) The fees set forth in subdivision (b) shall be presumed reasonable for services provided by provisionally certified interpreters only if efforts to obtain a certified interpreter are documented and submitted to the claims administrator with the bill for services. Efforts to obtain a certified interpreter shall also be disclosed in any document based in whole or in part on information obtained through a provisionally certified interpreter.

Note: Authority cited: Sections 133, 5307.3, 5710 and 5811, Labor Code. Reference: Sections 4600, 4620, 4621, 5710 and 5811, Labor Code; and Sections 11513 and 68562, Government Code.

History: 1. New section filed 1-28-94; operative 1-28-94. Submitted to OAL for printing only pursuant to Government Code section 11351 (Register 94, No. 4).

2. Amendment of subsections (b)(1) and (b)(2), repealer of subsection (b)(3), subsection renumbering, amendment of newly designated subsection (b)(4) and subsection (d), and new Note filed 12-30-96; operative 12-30-96 pursuant to Government Code section 11343.4(d). Submitted to OAL for printing only pursuant to Government Code section 11351 (Register 97, No. 1).

Ref.: Hanna §§ 22.07[2][a], 23.03[2], 23.13[3], 25.41[2], 27.01[8][a]; Herlick Handbook §§ 1.6, 14.33.

§9795.4. Time for Payment; Effective Date.

(a) All expenses for interpreter services shall be paid within 60 days after receipt by the claims administrator of the bill for services unless the claims administrator, within this period, contests its liability for such payment, or the reasonableness or the necessity of incurring such expenses. A claims administrator who contests all or any part of a bill for interpreter services shall pay the uncontested amount and notify the interpreter of the objection within 60 days after receipt of the bill. Any notice of objection shall include all of the following:

(1) An explanation of the basis of the objection.

(2) If additional information is needed as a prerequisite to payment of a contested bill or portions thereof, a clear description of the information required.

(3) The name, address and telephone number of the person or office to contact for additional information concerning the objection.

(4) A statement that the interpreter may adjudicate the issue of the contested charge before the Workers' Compensation Appeals Board.

(b) Any bill for interpreter's services which constitutes a medical-legal expense as defined in subdivision (g) of Section 9793 and which is neither paid nor contested within the time limits set forth herein shall be subject to the penalties and interest set forth in Section 4622 of the Labor Code.

(c) This article shall be effective for services provided on and after the effective date of this article which pertain to injuries occurring on or after January 1, 1994. Amendments to this article which became effective in 1996 shall apply to interpreting services provided on or after April 1, 1997.

Note: Authority cited: Sections 133, 5307.3, 5710 and 5811, Labor Code. Reference: Sections 4600, 4620, 4621, 5710 and 5811, Labor Code; and Sections 68562 and 11513, Government Code.

History: 1. New section filed 1-28-94; operative 1-28-94. Submitted to OAL for printing only pursuant to Government Code section 11351 (Register 94, No. 4).

2. Amendment of subsection (c) and Note filed 12-30-96; operative 12-30-96 pursuant to Government Code section 11343.4(d). Submitted to OAL for printing only pursuant to Government Code section 11351 (Register 97, No. 1).

Ref.: Hanna §§ 23.03[2][e], 22.13[3], 33.01[5], 33.53[3][b]; Herlick Handbook §§ 1.6, 14.33.

ARTICLE 6
Consulting Physician, Certification of

§9796. Certification of Consulting Physician, How Initiated.

When an injured employee requests an employer to secure certification of a consulting physician under Labor Code Section 4602, the employer shall direct a letter in triplicate to the Division of Industrial Accidents, attention Medical Director, 525 Golden Gate Avenue, Room 201, San Francisco, California 94102, containing the following information:

(a) The name and address of the injured employee;

(b) The name and address of the consulting physician chosen;

(c) The field of practice of the consulting physician.

Note: Authority cited: Sections 124, 127, 133, 138.2, 138.3, 138.4, 139, 139.5, 139.6, 4600, 4601, 4602, 4603, 4603.2, 4603.5, 5307.3, 5450, 5451, 5452, 5453, 5454 and 5455, Labor Code. Reference: Chapters 442, 709 and 1172, Statutes of 1977; and Chapter 1017, Statutes of 1976.

History: 1. Amendment filed 11-7-78; effective thirtieth day thereafter (Register 78, No. 45).

2. Change without regulatory effect filed 7-11-86; effective upon filing (Register 86, No. 28).

Ref.: Hanna §§ 5.05[8], 22.04; Herlick Handbook §§ 1.6, 4.2(b).

§9799. Criterion for Certifying Competence.

The criterion to be followed by the Administrative Director in certifying the competence of the consulting physician chosen by the injured employee is that the field of practice is related to the injury or the problem for which consultation was requested.

Ref.: Hanna § 22.04; Herlick Handbook §§ 1.6, 4.2(b).

§9802. Notification by Administrative Director.

The Administration Director will notify the employer and employee as to the competence of a consulting physician within twelve (12) days of the date of the receipt of the request for such certification.

Ref.: Hanna §§ 5.05[8], 22.04; Herlick Handbook §§ 1.6, 4.2(b).

ARTICLE 7
Schedule for Rating Permanent Disabilities

§9805. Schedule for Rating Permanent Disabilities, Adoption, Amendment.

The method for the determination of percentages of permanent disability is set forth in the Schedule for Rating Permanent Disabilities, which has been adopted by the Administrative Director effective January 1, 2005, and which is hereby incorporated by reference in its entirety as though it were set forth below. The schedule adopts and incorporates the American Medical Association (AMA) *Guides to the Evaluation of Permanent Impairment 5th Edition*. The schedule shall be effective for dates of injury on or after January 1, 2005 and for dates of injury prior to January 1, 2005, in accordance with subdivision (d) of Labor Code section 4660, and it shall be amended at least once every five years.

The schedule may be downloaded from the Division of Workers' Compensation website at http://www.dir.ca.gov/dwc/dwcrep.htm.

Note: Authority cited: Sections 133 and 5307.3, Labor Code. Reference: Sections 4660, 4662, 4663 and 4664, Labor Code.

History: 1. Amendment filed 12-8-69; designated effective 1-1-70 (Register 69, No. 50).

2. Amendment filed 12-14-72; designated effective 1-1-73 (Register 72, No. 51).

3. Editorial correction (Register 81, No. 31).

4. Amendment filed 7-15-83; effective thirtieth day thereafter (Register 83, No. 30).

5. Editorial correction of 7-15-83 order redesignating effective date to 8-1-83 pursuant to Government Code Section 11346.2(d) filed 7-19-83 (Register 83, No. 30).

6. Amendment of section and Note filed 12-31-2004 as an emergency; operative 1-1-2005 (Register 2004, No. 53). A Certificate of Compliance must be transmitted to OAL by 5-2-2005 or emergency language will be repealed by operation of law on the following day.

7. Certificate of Compliance as to 12-31-2004 order, including further amendment of section, transmitted to OAL 4-29-2005 and filed 6-10-2005 (Register 2005, No. 23).

Ref.: Hanna §§ 1.12[6], 8.02[3], 8.02[4][a], 32.01[3][a][i], 32.03[1]; Herlick Handbook § 1.6; Lawyer's Guide to AMA *Guides* and Calif. Workers' Comp. §§ 2.02, 2.03, 3.02, 3.03, 6.03.

§9805.1. Data Collection, Evaluation, and Revision of Schedule.

The Administrative Director shall: (1) collect for 18 months permanent disability ratings under the 2005 Permanent Disability Rating Schedule (PDRS) effective for injuries occurring on or after 1/1/05 and effective for injuries occurring on or after 4/19/04 and before 1/1/05 where there has been either no comprehensive medical-legal report or no report by a treating physician indicating the existence of permanent disability, or when the employer is not required to provide the notice required by Labor Code Section 4601 to the injured employee; (2) evaluate the data to determine the aggregate effect of the diminished future earning capacity adjustment on the permanent partial disability ratings under the 2005 PDRS; and (3) revise, if necessary, the diminished future earning capacity adjustment to reflect consideration of an employee's diminished future earning capacity for injuries based on the data collected. If the Administrative Director determines that there is not a sufficient amount of data to perform a statistically valid evaluation, the Administrative Director shall continue to collect data until a valid statistical sample is obtained. If there is a statistically valid sample of data that the Administrative Director determines supports a revision to the diminished future earning capacity adjustment, the Administrative Director shall revise the PDRS before the mandatory five year statutory revision contained in Labor Code section 4660(c).

Note: Authority cited: Sections 133 and 5307.3, Labor Code. Reference: Sections 4660, 4662, 4663 and 4664, Labor Code.

History: 1. New section filed 6-10-2005; operative 6-10-2005 (Register 2005, No. 23).

Ref.: Hanna § 8.02[4][a]; Herlick Handbook § 6.1; Lawyer's Guide to AMA *Guides* and Calif. Workers' Comp. §§ 2.02, 2.03, 3.02, 3.03, 6.03.

ARTICLE 8
Benefit Notices; Claims Administrator's Duties and Responsibilities; Claim Form and Notice of Potential Eligibility for Benefits; Regulatory Authority of the Administrative Director

§9810. General Provisions.

(a) This Article applies to benefit notices prepared on or after its effective date. Amendments to this Article filed with the Secretary of State on December 11, 2007 shall become effective for notices required to be sent on or after April 9, 2008.

(b) The Administrative Director may issue and revise from time to time a Benefit Notice Instruction Manual as a guide for completing and serving the notices required by this Article.

(c) Benefit notice letters, excepting those notices whose language or format are set forth in statute or where a specific notice form has been adopted as a regulation, may be produced on the claims administrator's letterhead. Unless sent on the claims administrator's letterhead, all notice letters shall identify the claims administrator's name, mailing address and telephone number, the employee's name, employer's name, the claim number, the date the notice was sent to the employee, and the date of injury. All notices shall clearly identify the name and telephone number and mailing address of the individual claims examiner responsible for the payment and adjusting of the claim, and shall include a notation if one or more attachments are being sent with the notice and shall clearly state that additional information may be obtained from an Information and Assistance officer with the Division of Workers' Compensation. If the employer offers additional disability benefits in addition to those provided by law under workers' compensation, the claims administrator may incorporate the information within the notices required by these regulations. A single benefit notice may encompass multiple events.

(d) Benefit notices, excepting those notices whose language or format are set forth in statute or specific notice forms adopted by regulation, may be produced in any format developed by the claims administrator. Each such benefit notice shall contain all relevant notice elements required by either statute or regulation. The Administrative Director shall make sample notices that comply with these requirements available on the DWC website.

(e) The claims administrator shall provide copies to the employee, upon request, of all medical reports, relevant to any benefit notice issued, or which are not required to be provided along with a notice and have not yet been provided to the employee other than psychiatric reports which the physician has recommended not be provided to the employee.

(f) The claims administrator shall send a copy of each benefit notice, and any enclosures not previously served on the attorney, concurrently to the attorney of any represented employee.

(g) Any deadline for reply which is measured from the date a notice is sent, and all rights protected within the deadline, are extended if the notice is sent by mail, as follows: by 5 days if the place of mailing and the place of address are in the same state of the United States; by 10 days if the place of mailing and the place of address are in different states of the United States; by 20 days if the place of mailing is in and the place of address is outside the United States. All notices shall be mailed from the United States.

(h) Copies of all benefit notices sent to injured workers shall be maintained by the claims administrator in the claims file. In lieu of retaining a copy of any attachments to the notice, the claims administrator may identify the attachments by name and revision date on the notice. These copies may be maintained in paper or electronic form.

(i) All benefit notices shall be made available in English and Spanish, as appropriate.

Note: Authority cited: Sections 59, 124, 133, 138.3, 138.4, 139.5(a)(2), 4061(a), (b), (d) and 5307.3, Labor Code. Reference: Sections 138.4, 139.5(a)(3), 4061 and 4650(a)–(d), Labor Code.

History: 1. Repealer of article 8 (sections 9810–9878, not consecutive) and new article 8 (sections 9810–9817) filed 7-15-83; effective thirtieth day thereafter (Register 83, No. 30). For prior history, see Registers 81, No. 42; 79, No. 30; 78, No. 45; 73, Nos. 51 and 38; 72, No. 51; and 66, No. 20.

2. Editorial correction of 7-15-83 order redesignating effective date to 8-1-83 pursuant to Government Code section 11346.2(d) filed 7-19-83 (Register 83, No. 30).

3. Editorial correction of 7-15-83 order filed 8-11-83 (Register 83, No. 33).

4. Amendment of article heading, section and Note filed 1-7-94; operative 1-7-94. Submitted to OAL for printing only pursuant to Government Code section 11351 (Register 94, No. 1).

5. Repealer of subsection (d) and subsection relettering filed 7-7-2004; operative 8-1-2004 pursuant to Government Code section 11343.4 (Register 2004, No. 28).

6. Repealer and new article heading and amendment of section and Note filed 12-11-2007; operative 4-9-2008 (Register 2007, No. 50).

Ref.: Hanna §§ 1.12[6], 7.03[1], 9.06; Herlick Handbook §§ 1.6, 9.3, 14.3.

§9811. Definitions.

As used in this Article:

(a) "Claims Administrator" means a self-administered insurer providing security for the payment of compensation required by Divisions 4 and 4.5 of the Labor Code, a self-administered self-insured employer, a self-administered joint powers authority, a self-administered legally uninsured, a third-party claims administrator for a self-insured employer, insurer, legally uninsured employer, or joint powers authority, or an administrator for an alternative dispute resolution (ADR) program established under Labor Code section 3201.5 or 3201.7.

(b) "Date of knowledge of injury" means the date the employer had knowledge of a worker's injury or claim of injury.

(c) "Date of knowledge of injury and disability" means the date the employer had knowledge of (1) a worker's injury or claim of injury, and (2) the worker's inability or claimed inability to work because of the injury.

(d) "Duration" means any known period of time for which benefits are to be paid, or, where benefits will continue for an unknown period of time the event that will occur which will determine when benefits will terminate.

(e) "Employee" includes dependent(s) in the event of any injury which results in death.

(f) "Employee's (or claimant's) remedies", means a statement of the employee's rights of which an employee or claimant shall be informed in benefit notices when specified in these regulations.

Every benefit notice, excepting those mandatory notices set forth in statute or where a specific notice form has been adopted as a regulation, shall include a mandatory statement of employee's (or claimant's) remedies:

For claims not falling under an alternative dispute resolution program (ADR) program under Labor Code sections 3201.5 or 3201.7, the following language shall be used:

You have a right to disagree with decisions affecting your claim. If you have any questions regarding the information provided to you in this notice, please call: (*insert adjuster's name and telephone number*). However, if you are represented by an attorney, you should call your attorney, not the claims adjuster. If you want further information on your rights to benefits or disagree with our decision, you may contact your local state Information & Assistance Office of the Division of Workers' Compensation by calling (*insert local I&A number*).

For recorded information and a list of offices, call (800)736-7401. You may also visit the DWC website at:

http://www.dir.ca.gov/DWC/dwc_home_page.htm

You also have a right to consult with an attorney of your choice. Should you decide to be represented by an attorney, you may or may not receive a larger award, but, unless you are determined to be ineligible for an award, the attorney's fee will be deducted from any award you might receive for disability benefits. The decision to be represented by an attorney is yours to make, but it is voluntary and may not be necessary for you to receive your benefits.

To resolve a dispute, you may apply to [**choose appropriate option(s)**] the Workers'

Compensation Appeals Board, the Vocational Rehabilitation Unit, or the Administrative Director.

For employees subject to an ADR program under Labor Code sections 3201.5 or 3201.7, the claims administrator may substitute the following language where appropriate:

You have a right to disagree with decisions affecting your claim. If you have any questions regarding the information provided to you in this notice, please call: (*insert adjuster's name and telephone number*) or, (*insert name of ombudsperson or mediator if employee is subject to an ADR agreement*). However, if you are represented by an attorney, you should call your attorney, not the claims adjuster, ombudsperson or mediator. If you want further information on your rights to benefits or disagree with our decision, you may also contact your local state Information & Assistance Office of the Division of Workers' Compensation by calling (*insert local I&A number*). Please be sure to inform the Information and Assistance Officer that you are subject to an alternative dispute resolution program.

For recorded information and a list of offices, call (800)736-7401. You may also visit the DWC website at:

http://www.dir.ca.gov/DWC/dwc_home_page.htm

NOTE: For employees subject to an ADR program under Labor Code section 3201.5, the claims administrator may include the following language if appropriate under the provisions of the ADR program:

In accordance with the (*insert union name*) agreement, active participation by an attorney is not allowed in the Ombudsman and Mediation stages of the ADR workers' compensation process. Your right to obtain legal advice is not limited and you may obtain such at your own expense at anytime. If the Ombudsman and Mediation stages of dispute resolution are unsuccessful and a written request for Arbitration has been timely filed, attorney participation is allowed.

(g) "Employer" means any person or entity defined as an employer by Labor Code Section 3300.

(h) "Injury" means any injury as defined in Labor Code Section 3208 which results in medical treatment beyond first aid, lost time beyond the date of injury, or death.

(i) "Permanent and stationary status," means the point when the employee has reached maximal medical improvement his or her condition is well stabilized and unlikely to change substantially in the next year with or without medical treatment.

Note: Authority cited: Sections 59, 133, 138.3, 138.4 and 5307.3, Labor Code. Reference: Sections 138.4, 139.5(c), (d), 3201.5, 3201.7, 3208, 3300, 3351, 3351.5, 3700, 3753, 4635(a), 4650(a)–(d), 4653, 4654, 4700 and 4701, Labor Code; Sections 11651 and 11652, Insurance Code; Sections 2330 and 2332, Civil Code.

History: 1. Amendment of section and Note filed 1-7-94; operative 1-7-94. Submitted to OAL for printing only pursuant to Government Code section 11351 (Register 94, No. 1).

2. Amendment of section and Note filed 12-11-2007; operative 4-9-2008 (Register 2007, No. 50).

Ref.: Hanna §§ 7.03[1], 9.06, 32.07[1], 32.07[4], 35.11[3]; Herlick Handbook §§ 1.6, 9.3, 14.3.

§9812. Benefit Payment and Notice.

(a) Temporary Disability Notices. When an injury causes or is claimed to cause temporary disability:

(1) Notice of First Temporary Disability Indemnity Payment. The first time the claims administrator pays temporary disability indemnity, the claims administrator shall advise the employee of the amount of temporary disability indemnity due, how it was calculated, and the duration and schedule of indemnity payments. The notice shall be sent no later than the 14th day after the employer's date of knowledge of injury and disability. A copy of the most recent version of the DWC informative pamphlet "Temporary Disability Fact Sheet" shall be provided with the notice.

(2) Notice of Delay in Any Temporary Disability Indemnity Payment. If the employee's entitlement to any period of temporary disability indemnity cannot be determined within 14 days of the date of knowledge of injury and disability, the claims administrator shall advise the employee within the 14-day period of the delay, the reasons for it, the need, if any, for additional information required to make a determination, and when a determination is likely to be made. If the claims administrator cannot make a determination by the date specified in a notice to the injured worker, the claims administrator shall send a subsequent delay notice to the injured worker, not later than the determination date specified in the previous delay notice, notifying the injured worker of the revised date by which

the claims administrator now expects the determination to be made.

(A) Where the delay is related to a medical issue, the notice shall advise an unrepresented employee of one of the following options:

1. If the injured worker has already received a comprehensive medical evaluation and either party disputes the results of that evaluation, the injured worker may be asked to return to that physician for a new evaluation.

2. If no comprehensive medical evaluation has taken place, the injured worker may obtain an evaluation by a Qualified Medical Evaluator obtained from a panel issued by the DWC Medical Unit pursuant to Labor Code section 4062.1. The notice shall include the claims administrator's decision on whether the claims administrator accepts or refutes the treating physician's evaluation of the employee's temporary disability status and shall be accompanied by the form prescribed by the DWC Medical Unit with which to request assignment of a panel of Qualified Medical Evaluators. The notice shall advise the injured worker of the 10 day time limit in which a panel may be requested and in which an appointment must be made following receipt of the panel.

The notice shall contain the following warning in not less than 12 point font at the top of the first page: You may lose important rights if you do not take certain actions within 10 days. Read this letter and any enclosed fact sheets very carefully.

(B) Where the delay is related to a medical issue, the notice shall advise a represented employee of one of the following options:

1. For dates of injury from January 1, 1994 through December 31, 2004, if the injured worker has already received a comprehensive medical evaluation, he or she may be asked to return to that physician for a new evaluation. If no comprehensive medical evaluation has taken place, an evaluation may be obtained from an Agreed Medical Evaluator if the parties agree or, if no agreement on an Agreed Medical Evaluator can be reached, the injured worker may be evaluated by a Qualified Medical Evaluator and that arrangements for obtaining this evaluation should be discussed with the injured worker's attorney.

2. For dates of injury on or after January 1, 2005, if the injured worker has already received a comprehensive medical evaluation, he or she may be asked to return to that physician for a new evaluation. If no comprehensive medical evaluation has taken place, an evaluation may be obtained from an Agreed Medical Evaluator if the parties agree or, if no agreement on an Agreed Medical Evaluator can be reached, the injured worker may be evaluated by a Qualified Medical Evaluator obtained from a panel issued by the DWC Medical Unit pursuant to Labor Code section 4062.2 and that arrangements for obtaining this evaluation should be discussed with the injured worker's attorney.

A copy of the most recent version of the DWC informative pamphlet "QME/AME Fact Sheet" shall be provided with the notice.

The additional delay notices shall comply with all requirements for an original delay notice, except that no copy of the DWC informative pamphlet "QME/AME Fact Sheet" need be provided with the notice unless it has been revised since it was last provided.

(3) Notice of Denial of Any Temporary Disability Indemnity Payment. If the claims administrator denies liability for the payment of any period for which an employee claims temporary disability indemnity, the notice shall advise the employee of the denial and the reasons for it. The notice shall be sent within 14 days after the determination to deny was made.

(A) Where the denial is related to a medical issue, the notice shall advise an unrepresented employee of one of the following options:

1. If the denial is based on a comprehensive medical evaluation, the injured worker may file an Application for Adjudication of Claim with the WCAB.

2. If the injured worker has already received a comprehensive medical evaluation, and either party disputes the results of that evaluation, the injured worker may be asked to return to that physician for a new evaluation.

3. If no comprehensive medical evaluation has taken place, the injured worker may obtain an evaluation by a Qualified Medical Evaluator obtained from a panel issued by the DWC Medical Unit pursuant to Labor Code section 4062.1. The notice shall include the claims administrator's decision on whether the claims administrator accepts or refutes the treating physician's evaluation of the employee's temporary disability status and shall be accompanied by the form prescribed by the DWC Medical Unit with which to request assignment of a panel of Qualified Medical Evaluators. The notice shall advise the injured worker of the 10

day time limit in which a panel may be requested and in which an appointment must be made following receipt of the panel.

The notice shall contain the following warning in not less than 12 point font at the top of the first page: You may lose important rights if you do not take certain actions within 10 days. Read this letter and any enclosed fact sheets very carefully.

(B) Where the denial is related to a medical issue, the notice shall advise a represented employee of one of the following options:

1. If the denial is based on a comprehensive medical evaluation, the injured worker may file an Application for Adjudication of Claim with the WCAB.

2. For dates of injury from January 1, 1994 through December 31, 2004, if the injured worker has already received a comprehensive medical evaluation, he or she may be asked to return to that physician for a new evaluation. If no comprehensive medical evaluation has taken place, an evaluation may be obtained from an Agreed Medical Evaluator if the parties agree or, if no agreement on an Agreed Medical Evaluator can be reached, the injured worker may be evaluated by a Qualified Medical Evaluator and that arrangements for obtaining this evaluation should be discussed with the injured worker's attorney.

3. For dates of injury on or after January 1, 2005 if the injured worker has already received a comprehensive medical evaluation, he or she may be asked to return to that physician for a new evaluation. If no comprehensive medical evaluation has taken place, an evaluation may be obtained from an Agreed Medical Evaluator if the parties agree or, if no agreement on an Agreed Medical Evaluator can be reached, the injured worker may be evaluated by a Qualified Medical Evaluator obtained from a panel issued by the DWC Medical Unit pursuant to Labor Code section 4062.2 and that arrangements for obtaining this evaluation should be discussed with the injured worker's attorney.

A copy of the relevant DWC informative pamphlet(s) "TD Fact Sheet," "QME/AME Fact Sheet" and/or "Permanent Disability Fact Sheet" shall be provided at this time.

(b) Notice of Resumed Benefit Payments (TD, SC, PD, VRTD/VRMA). If the payment of temporary disability indemnity, salary continuation, permanent disability indemnity, or vocational rehabilitation temporary disability indemnity or maintenance allowance is resumed after terminating any of these benefits, the claims administrator shall advise the employee of the amount of indemnity due and the duration and schedule of payments. Notice shall be sent within 14 days after the employer's date of knowledge of the entitlement to additional benefits.

(c) Notice of Changed Benefit Rate, Payment Amount or Schedule (TD, SC, PD, VRTD/VRMA). When the claims administrator changes the benefit rate, payment amount or benefit payment schedule for temporary disability indemnity, salary continuation, permanent disability indemnity, or vocational rehabilitation temporary disability indemnity or maintenance allowance, the claims administrator shall advise the employee, as applicable, of the amount of the new benefit rate and the reason the rate is being changed, or of the new benefit payment schedule. Notice shall be given before or with the new payment.

(d) Notice that Benefits Are Ending (TD, SC, PD, VRTD/VRMA). With the last payment of temporary disability indemnity, permanent disability indemnity, salary continuation, or vocational rehabilitation temporary disability indemnity or maintenance allowance, the claims administrator shall advise the employee of the ending of indemnity payments and the reason, and shall make an accounting of all compensation paid to or on behalf of the employee in the species of benefit to which the notice refers, including the dates and amounts paid and any related penalties. If the decision to end payment of indemnity was made after the last payment, the claims administrator shall send the notice and accounting within 14 days of the last payment.

(1) The notice, except a notice that VRMA is ending, shall advise an unrepresented employee one of the following options:

(A) If the injured worker has already received a comprehensive medical evaluation, and either party disputes the results of that evaluation, the injured worker may be asked to return to that physician for a new evaluation.

(B) If no comprehensive medical evaluation has taken place, the injured worker may obtain an evaluation by a Qualified Medical Evaluator obtained from a panel issued by the DWC Medical Unit pursuant to Labor Code section 4062.1. The notice shall include the claims administrator's decision on whether the claims administrator accepts or refutes the treating physician's evaluation of the employee's temporary disability status or permanent impairment and shall be accompanied by the form prescribed by the DWC Medical Unit with which to request assignment of a panel of Qualified Medical Evaluators. The notice shall advise the injured worker of the 10 day time limit in which a panel may be requested and in which an appointment must be made following receipt of the panel.

The notice shall contain the following warning in not less than 12 point font at the top of the first page: You may lose important rights if you do not take certain actions within 10 days. Read this letter and any enclosed fact sheets very carefully.

(2) The notice, except a notice that VRMA is ending, shall advise a represented employee:

(A) If the injured worker has already received a comprehensive medical evaluation, he or she may be asked to return to that physician for a new evaluation.

(B) If no comprehensive medical evaluation has taken place, an evaluation may be obtained from an Agreed Medical Evaluator if the parties agree or, if no agreement on an Agreed Medical Evaluator can be reached, the injured worker may be evaluated by a Qualified Medical Evaluator obtained from a panel issued by the DWC Medical Unit pursuant to Labor Code section 4062.2 and that arrangements for obtaining this evaluation should be discussed with the injured worker's attorney.

A copy of the relevant DWC informative fact sheet pamphlet(s) "TD Fact Sheet," "QME/AME Fact Sheet" and/or "Permanent Disability Fact Sheet" shall be provided at this time.

(e) Permanent Disability Notices For Injuries That Occurred Prior To 1991:

(1) Existence and Extent of Permanent Disability is Known. Within 14 days after the claims administrator knows that the injury has caused permanent disability and knows the extent of that disability, the claims administrator shall advise the employee of the amount of the weekly permanent disability indemnity payment, how it was calculated, the duration and frequency of payments, the date payments can be expected to begin and the total amount to be paid.

(2) Existence of Permanent Disability is Known, Extent is Uncertain. If the claims administrator knows that the injury has caused permanent disability but cannot determine its extent within the 14 days after the last payment of temporary disability indemnity, or within 14 days after knowledge that the employee's injury has resulted in permanent disability if there was no compensable temporary disability, the claims administrator nevertheless shall make timely payment of permanent disability indemnity and shall advise the employee of the amount of the weekly permanent disability indemnity payment, how it was calculated, the duration and schedule of payments, and the claims administrator's reasonable estimate of the amount of permanent disability indemnity to be paid.

The claims administrator shall notify the employee that his or her medical condition will be monitored until the extent of permanent disability can be determined and that the disability payments will be revised at that time if appropriate. Within 14 days after the claims administrator determines the extent of permanent disability indemnity benefits, the claims administrator shall notify the employee as provided by paragraph (1).

(3) Existence of Permanent Disability is Uncertain. If the existence of permanent disability is uncertain, the claims administrator shall advise the employee within 14 days after the last payment of temporary disability indemnity, or within 14 days of receiving a claim or medical report alleging the existence of permanent disability if the claims administrator paid no temporary disability, that the claims administrator cannot yet determine whether the injury will cause permanent disability. The notice shall specify the reasons for the delay in determination, the need, if any, for additional information required to make a determination, and when the determination is likely to be made. If the claims administrator cannot make a determination by the date it specified in a notice to the injured worker, the claims administrator shall send a subsequent notice to the injured worker, not later than the determination date specified in the previous notice, notifying the injured worker of the date by which the claims administrator now expects the determination to be made. The additional delay notices shall comply with all requirements for an original delay notice. If the reason for the delay is that the employee's medical condition is not permanent and stationary, the claims administrator shall advise the employee that his or her medical condition will be monitored until it is permanent and stationary, at which time an evaluation will be per-

formed to determine the amount of permanent disability indemnity, if any, due the employee. Within 14 days after the claims administrator determines that permanent disability exists, the claims administrator shall notify the employee of the commencement of permanent disability indemnity payments as provided by paragraph (1) or (2).

(4) Notice That No Permanent Disability Exists. If the claims administrator alleges that the injury has caused no permanent disability, the claims administrator shall advise the employee within 14 days after the claims administrator determines that the injury has caused no permanent disability.

(f) Permanent Disability Notices for Injuries Occurring in 1991, 1992, 1993.

(1) Condition Not Permanent and Stationary (P & S), May Cause Permanent Disability—Notice of Monitoring Until P&S Date. If the injury has resulted or may result in permanent disability but the employee's medical condition is not permanent and stationary, the claims administrator shall advise the employee, together with the last payment of temporary disability indemnity, that permanent disability indemnity is or may be payable but that the amount cannot be determined because the employee's medical condition has not yet reached a stationary status. The notice shall advise the employee that his or her medical condition will be monitored until it is permanent and stationary, at which time a medical evaluation will be performed to determine the existence and extent of permanent impairment or limitations and the need for continuing medical care. The notice shall advise the employee of the estimated date when a determination is likely to be made, and the claimant's remedies. If the claims administrator cannot make a determination of A) permanent and stationary status, B) the existence and extent of permanent impairment or limitations, and C) the need for continuing medical care by the date it specified in a monitoring notice to the injured worker, the claims administrator shall send a subsequent notice to the injured worker, not later than the determination date specified in the previous notice, notifying the injured worker of the date by which the claims administrator now expects the determination to be made. The additional notice shall comply with all requirements of the original delay notice.

(2) Condition Becomes Permanent and Stationary, May Cause Permanent Disability—Notice of Qualified Medical Evaluator (QME) Procedures. Within 5 working days after receiving information indicating that the employee's condition is permanent and stationary and has caused or may have caused permanent disability, the claims administrator shall advise the employee that his or her medical condition is permanent and stationary and of the procedures for evaluating permanent disability and need for continuing medical care.

(A) The notice shall advise an unrepresented employee of one of the following options:

1. If the injured worker has already received a comprehensive medical evaluation, and either party disputes the results of that evaluation, the injured worker may be asked to return to that physician for a new evaluation.

2. If no comprehensive medical evaluation has taken place, the injured worker may obtain an evaluation by a Qualified Medical Evaluator obtained from a panel issued by the DWC Medical Unit pursuant to Labor Code section 4062.1. The notice shall include the claims administrator's decision on whether the claims administrator accepts or refutes the treating physician's evaluation of the employee's permanent and stationary status and/or need for future medical care and shall be accompanied by the form prescribed by the DWC Medical Unit with which to request assignment of a panel of Qualified Medical Evaluators. The notice shall advise the injured worker of the 10 day time limit in which a panel may be requested and in which an appointment must be made following receipt of the panel.

The notice shall contain the following warning in not less than 12 point font at the top of the first page: You may lose important rights if you do not take certain actions within 10 days. Read this letter and any enclosed fact sheets very carefully.

(B) The notice shall advise a represented employee:

If the injured worker has already received a comprehensive medical evaluation, he or she may be asked to return to that physician for a new evaluation. If no comprehensive medical evaluation has taken place, an evaluation may be obtained from an Agreed Medical Evaluator if the parties agree or, if no agreement on an Agreed Medical Evaluator can be reached, the injured worker may be evaluated by a Qualified Medical Evaluator and that arrangements for obtaining this evaluation should be discussed with the injured worker's attorney.

A copy of the most recent version of the DWC informative pamphlet "QME/AME Fact Sheet" shall be provided with the notice.

(3) Notice of Permanent Disability Indemnity Payment When Injury Causes Permanent Disability. If the claims administrator knows that the employee has sustained permanent disability, whether or not its extent is known and whether or not the employee's medical condition is permanent and stationary, the claims administrator shall advise the employee of the weekly permanent disability indemnity payment, how it was calculated, the duration and schedule of payments, and the claims administrator's reasonable estimate of permanent disability indemnity to be paid, within 14 days after knowledge that the employee's injury has resulted in permanent disability, whichever is later.

(A) The notice shall advise an unrepresented employee of one of the following options:

1. If the estimate is based on a comprehensive medical evaluation, the injured worker may file an Application for Adjudication of Claim with the WCAB.

2. If the injured worker has already received a comprehensive medical evaluation, and either party disputes the results of that evaluation, the injured worker may be asked to return to that physician for a new evaluation.

3. If no comprehensive medical evaluation has taken place, the injured worker may obtain an evaluation by a Qualified Medical Evaluator obtained from a panel issued by the DWC Medical Unit pursuant to Labor Code section 4062.1. The notice shall include the claims administrator's decision on whether the claims administrator accepts or refutes the treating physician's evaluation of the employee's permanent impairment and shall be accompanied by the form prescribed by the DWC Medical Unit with which to request assignment of a panel of Qualified Medical Evaluators. The notice shall advise the injured worker of the 10 day time limit in which a panel may be requested and in which an appointment must be made following receipt of the panel.

The notice shall contain the following warning in not less than 12 point font at the top of the first page: You may lose important rights if you do not take certain actions within 10 days. Read this letter and any enclosed fact sheets very carefully.

(B) The notice shall advise a represented employee of one of the following options:

1. If the determination is based on a comprehensive medical evaluation, the injured worker may file an Application for Adjudication of Claim with the WCAB.

2. If the injured worker has already received a comprehensive medical evaluation, he or she may be asked to return to that physician for a new evaluation.

3. If no comprehensive medical evaluation has taken place, an evaluation may be obtained from an Agreed Medical Evaluator if the parties agree or, if no agreement on an Agreed Medical Evaluator can be reached, the injured worker may be evaluated by a Qualified Medical Evaluator and that arrangements for obtaining this evaluation should be discussed with the injured worker's attorney.

(4) Notice That No Permanent Disability Exists. If the claims administrator alleges that the injury has caused no permanent disability, the claims administrator shall advise the employee that no permanent disability indemnity is payable. This notice shall be sent within 14 days after the claims administrator determines that the injury has caused no permanent disability. The notice shall advise the employee of the process to obtain a formal medical evaluation to contest the determination that the employee has no permanent disability. If the basis for the claims administrator's determination is a medical report, a copy of the most recent version of the DWC informative pamphlet "QME/AME Fact Sheet," shall be provided with the notice.

(A) The notice shall advise an unrepresented employee of one of the following options:

1. If the determination is based on a comprehensive medical evaluation, the injured worker may file an Application for Adjudication of Claim with the WCAB.

2. If the injured worker has already received a comprehensive medical evaluation, and either party disputes the results of that evaluation, the injured worker may be asked to return to that physician for a new evaluation.

3. If no comprehensive medical evaluation has taken place, the injured worker may obtain an evaluation by a Qualified Medical Evaluator

obtained from a panel issued by the DWC Medical Unit pursuant to Labor Code section 4062.1. The notice shall include the claims administrator's decision on whether the claims administrator accepts or refutes the treating physician's evaluation of the employee's permanent impairment and shall be accompanied by the form prescribed by the DWC Medical Unit with which to request assignment of a panel of Qualified Medical Evaluators. The notice shall advise the injured worker of the 10 day time limit in which a panel may be requested and in which an appointment must be made following receipt of the panel.

The notice shall contain the following warning in not less than 12 point font at the top of the first page: You may lose important rights if you do not take certain actions within 10 days. Read this letter and any enclosed fact sheets very carefully.

(B) The notice shall advise a represented employee of one of the following options:

1. If the determination is based on a comprehensive medical evaluation, the injured worker may file an Application for Adjudication of Claim with the WCAB.

2. If the injured worker has already received a comprehensive medical evaluation, he or she may be asked to return to that physician for a new evaluation. If no comprehensive medical evaluation has taken place, an evaluation may be obtained from an Agreed Medical Evaluator if the parties agree or, if no agreement on an Agreed Medical Evaluator can be reached, the injured worker may be evaluated by a Qualified Medical Evaluator and that arrangements for obtaining this evaluation should be discussed with the injured worker's attorney.

(g) Permanent Disability Notices For Injuries Occurring on or after 1/1/94. For injuries occurring on or after January 1, 1994:

(1) Condition Not Permanent and Stationary, May Cause Permanent Disability—Notice of Monitoring Until P&S Date. If the injury has resulted or may result in permanent disability but the employee's medical condition is not permanent and stationary, the claims administrator shall advise the employee together with the last payment of temporary disability indemnity, that permanent disability indemnity is or may be payable but that the amount cannot be determined because the employee's medical condition has not yet reached a stationary status. The notice shall advise the employee that his or her medical condition will be monitored until it is permanent and stationary, at which time a medical evaluation will be performed to determine the existence and extent of permanent impairment or limitations and the need for continuing medical care. The notice shall advise the employee of the estimated date when a determination is likely to be made. If the claims administrator cannot make a determination of A) permanent and stationary status, B) the existence and extent of permanent impairment or limitations, and C) the need for continuing medical care by the date it specified in a monitoring notice to the injured worker, the claims administrator shall send a subsequent notice to the injured worker, not later than the determination date specified in the previous notice, notifying the injured worker of the date by which the claims administrator now expects the determination to be made. The additional notice shall comply with all requirements of the original notice.

(2) Condition Becomes Permanent and Stationary, Causes Permanent Disability—Notice of QME/AME Procedures. Together with the last payment of temporary disability or within 14 days of knowledge that the injury is permanent and stationary or has caused permanent disability, the claims administrator shall provide notice of the procedures available to obtain a QME or AME evaluation. The claims administrator shall advise the employee of the claims administrator's estimate of the amount of permanent disability indemnity payable, the basis for the estimate, and whether there is need for continuing medical care. A copy of the medical report on which the estimate of permanent disability was based, and a copy of the most recent version of the DWC informative pamphlets, QME/AME Fact Sheet and/or Temporary Disability Fact Sheet, shall be provided with the notice.

(A) The notice shall advise an unrepresented employee of one of the following options:

1. If the injured worker has already received a comprehensive medical evaluation, and either party disputes the results of that evaluation, the injured worker may be asked to return to that physician for a new evaluation.

2. If no comprehensive medical evaluation has taken place, the injured worker may obtain an evaluation by a Qualified Medical Evaluator obtained from a panel issued by the DWC

Medical Unit pursuant to Labor Code section 4062.1.

The notice shall include the claims administrator's decision on whether the claims administrator accepts or refutes the treating physician's evaluation of the employee's permanent impairment and shall be accompanied by the form prescribed by the DWC Medical Unit with which to request assignment of a panel of Qualified Medical Evaluators. The notice shall advise the injured worker of the 10 day time limit in which a panel may be requested and in which an appointment must be made following receipt of the panel.

The notice shall contain the following warning in not less than 12 point font at the top of the first page: You may lose important rights if you do not take certain actions within 10 days. Read this letter and any enclosed fact sheets very carefully.

(B) If the claims administrator is not requesting a rating from the Disability Evaluation Unit, the notice shall also advise the worker that he or she may contact an Information and Assistance Officer to have the treating physician's evaluation reviewed and rated by the Disability Evaluation Unit.

(C) If the claims administrator has or will be requesting a rating from the Disability Evaluation Unit on the treating physician's evaluation, the notice shall advise the employee that he or she will be receiving a rating based on the treating physician's evaluation from the Disability Evaluation Unit.

(D) The notice shall advise a represented employee of one of the following options:

1. For dates of injury from January 1, 1994 through December 31, 2004, if the injured worker has already received a comprehensive medical evaluation, he or she may be asked to return to that physician for a new evaluation. If no comprehensive medical evaluation has taken place, an evaluation may be obtained from an Agreed Medical Evaluator if the parties agree or, if no agreement on an Agreed Medical Evaluator can be reached, the injured worker may be evaluated by a Qualified Medical Evaluator and that arrangements for obtaining this evaluation should be discussed with the injured worker's attorney.

2. For dates of injury on or after January 1, 2005 if the injured worker has already received a comprehensive medical evaluation, he or she may be asked to return to that physician for a new evaluation. If no comprehensive medical evaluation has taken place, an evaluation may be obtained from an Agreed Medical Evaluator if the parties agree or, if no agreement on an Agreed Medical Evaluator can be reached, the injured worker may be evaluated by a Qualified Medical Evaluator obtained from a panel issued by the DWC Medical Unit pursuant to Labor Code section 4062.2 and that arrangements for obtaining this evaluation should be discussed with the injured worker's attorney.

(3) Notice That No Permanent Disability Exists. If the claims administrator alleges that the injury has caused no permanent disability, the claims administrator shall advise the employee that no permanent disability indemnity is payable. This notice shall be sent together with the last payment of temporary disability indemnity or within 14 days after the claims administrator determines that the injury has caused no permanent disability. A copy of the medical report on which the determination of no permanent disability was based, and a copy of the most recent version of the DWC informative pamphlets, QME/AME Fact Sheet and Permanent Disability Fact Sheet shall be provided with the notice. A copy of the DWC form prescribed by the Administrative Director for requesting assignment of a panel of Qualified Medical Evaluators shall be provided with the notice unless the employee is represented by an attorney.

(A) The notice shall advise an unrepresented employee of one of the following options:

1. If the determination is based on a comprehensive medical evaluation, the injured worker may file an Application for Adjudication of Claim with the WCAB.

2. If the injured worker has already received a comprehensive medical evaluation, and either party disputes the results of that evaluation, the injured worker may be asked to return to that physician for a new evaluation.

3. If no comprehensive medical evaluation has taken place, the injured worker may obtain an evaluation by a Qualified Medical Evaluator obtained from a panel issued by the DWC Medical Unit pursuant to Labor Code section 4062.1. The notice shall also advise of the procedure for requesting the panel and shall be accompanied by the form prescribed by the DWC Medical Unit with which to request assignment of a panel of Qualified Medical Evaluators. The notice shall advise the injured worker

of the 10 day time limit in which a panel may be requested and in which an appointment must be made following receipt of the panel.

The notice shall contain the following warning in not less than 12 point font: You may lose important rights if you do not take certain actions within 10 days. Read this letter and any enclosed fact sheets very carefully.

(B) If the denial is based upon the treating physician's report, the notice shall also advise the worker that he or she may contact an Information and Assistance office to have the treating physician's evaluation review and rated by the Disability Evaluation Unit.

(C) If the claims administrator requests a rating from the Disability Evaluation Unit on the treating physician's report, the notice shall advise the employee that he or she will be receiving a rating based on the treating physician's evaluation from the Disability Evaluation Unit.

(D) The notice shall advise a represented employee of one of the following options:

1. If the determination is based on a comprehensive medical evaluation, the injured worker may file an Application for Adjudication of Claim with the WCAB.

2. For dates of injury from January 1, 1994 through December 31, 2004, if the injured worker has already received a comprehensive medical evaluation, he or she may be asked to return to that physician for a new evaluation. If no comprehensive medical evaluation has taken place, an evaluation may be obtained from an Agreed Medical Evaluator if the parties agree or, if no agreement on an Agreed Medical Evaluator can be reached, the injured worker may be evaluated by a Qualified Medical Evaluator and that arrangements for obtaining this evaluation should be discussed with the injured worker's attorney.

3. For dates of injury on or after January 1, 2005 if the injured worker has already received a comprehensive medical evaluation, he or she may be asked to return to that physician for a new evaluation. If no comprehensive medical evaluation has taken place, an evaluation may be obtained from an Agreed Medical Evaluator if the parties agree or, if no agreement on an Agreed Medical Evaluator can be reached, the injured worker may be evaluated by a Qualified Medical Evaluator obtained from a panel issued by the DWC Medical Unit pursuant to Labor Code section 4062.2 and that arrangements for obtaining this evaluation should be discussed with the injured worker's attorney.

(4) Notice of Permanent Disability Indemnity Payment When Injury Causes Permanent Disability. If the claims administrator knows that the employee has sustained permanent disability, whether or not its extent is known and whether or not the employee's medical condition is permanent and stationary, the claims administrator shall advise the employee of the weekly permanent disability indemnity payment, how it was calculated, the duration and schedule of payments, and the claims administrator's reasonable estimate of permanent disability indemnity to be paid, within 14 days after the last payment of temporary disability indemnity, or within 14 days after knowledge that the employee's injury has resulted in permanent disability, whichever is later. A copy of the most recent version of the DWC informative pamphlet "Permanent Disability Fact Sheet," shall be provided with the notice.

For injuries occurring on or after January 1, 2005, the claims administrator shall, concurrently with any increased or decreased payment, notify the injured worker of any increase or decrease in the amount of the injured worker's permanent disability payments, pursuant to Labor Code section 4658, subdivision (d) resulting from the employer's offer of regular, modified or alternative work or resulting from the employer's failure to offer, or the employer's early termination of, regular, modified or alternative work. The information required by this subdivision shall be given in the appropriate PD payment start notice, PD payment resumption notice or notice of change in rate, payment amount or payment schedule.

(h) Notices to Dependents in Death Cases. In a case of fatal injury which is or is claimed to be compensable under the workers' compensation laws of this state, or involving accrued compensation which was not paid to an injured employee before the employee's death, the claims administrator shall advise the dependent(s) of the status of any benefits to which they may be entitled or which they have claimed as a result of the employee's death. As used in this subsection, "dependent" includes any person who may be or has claimed to be entitled to workers' compensation benefits as the result of an employee's death (including compensation which was accrued and unpaid to an injured worker before his or her death), and also includes the parent or legal guardian of minor dependent children. The claims administrator shall send each dependent a copy of all notices concerning benefits claimed by, or which may be payable to, that dependent, including notices sent to a different dependent if the benefits paid to the different dependent affect the amount payable to the other claimant. If the claims administrator discovers a new dependent after having sent a notice, the claims administrator shall send copies of each prior notice which concerned benefits to which the newly-discovered dependent might be entitled, to that dependent.

(1) Benefit Payment Schedule. If the claims administrator pays death benefits (including compensation which was accrued and unpaid to an injured worker before his or her death), the claims administrator shall advise each affected dependent of the amount of the death benefit payable to the dependent, how it was calculated, the duration and schedule of payments and other pertinent information. Notice is required within 14 days after the claims administrator's date of knowledge both of the death and of the identity and address of the dependent.

(2) Notice of Changed Benefit Rate, Amount or Schedule or that Benefits are Ending. If the claims administrator changes the benefit rate, amount or payment schedule, or ends payment, of a death benefit to a dependent, the claims administrator shall advise the affected dependent of the change and the reason for it, or of the new payment schedule. A notice that benefits are ending shall include an accounting of all compensation paid to the claimant. A notice that payment is ending shall be sent with the last payment unless the decision to end payment was made after that payment; in that case it shall be sent within 14 days of the last payment. Other notices concerning changed payments shall be sent before or with the changed payment, but not later than 14 days after the last payment which was made before the change.

(3) Delay in Determining Benefits. If the claims administrator cannot determine entitlement to some or all death benefits, the claims administrator shall advise each affected dependent of the delay, the reasons for it, the need, if any, for additional information required to make a determination, and when a determination is likely to be made. Notice is required within 14 days after the claims administrator's date of knowledge of the death, the identity and address of the affected dependent, and the nature of the benefit claimed or which might be due. If the claims administrator cannot make a determination by the date it specified in a notice to the affected dependent(s), the claims administrator shall send a subsequent notice to the affected dependent(s), not later than the determination date specified in the previous notice, notifying the affected dependent(s) of the date by which the claims administrator now expects the determination to be made. The additional delay notices shall include the employee's remedies and shall comply with all requirements for an original delay notice.

(4) Notices Denying Death Benefits. If the claims administrator denies liability for the payment of any or all death benefits, the claims administrator shall advise the affected dependent(s) of the denial and the reasons for it. The notice shall be sent within 14 days after the determination to deny was made.

(i) Notice Denying Liability for All Compensation Benefits. If the claims administrator denies liability for the payment of all workers' compensation benefits for any claim except a claim for death benefits, including medical-only claims, the claims administrator shall advise the employee of the denial and the reasons for it. The notice shall be sent no later than 14 days after the determination to deny was made. A copy of the most recent version of the DWC informative pamphlet "QME/AME Fact Sheet" shall be provided with the notice.

For claims reported on or after April 19, 2004, if an injured worker has filed a completed claim form with the employer, the claims administrator shall advise the injured worker to send for consideration of payment, all bills for medical services provided between the date the completed claim form was given to the employer and the date that liability for the claim is rejected, unless he or she has done so already. The claims administrator shall also advise the employee that the maximum payment for medical services that were provided consistent with the applicable treatment guidelines is $10,000.

A copy of the Notice Denying Liability for All Compensation Benefits shall be served on all lien claimants or all persons or entities who can reasonably be identified by the claims administrator from information in the claims file to be potential lien claimants on account of their having furnished benefits, goods or services for which a lien may be filed under Labor Code sections 4903 through 4906, inclusive.

(j) Notice of Delay in Determining All Liability. If the claims administrator cannot determine whether the employer has any liability for an injury, other than an injury causing death, within 14 days of the date of knowledge of injury, the claims administrator shall advise the employee within the 14-day period of the delay, the reasons for it, the need, if any, for additional information required to make a determination, and when a determination is likely to be made. If the claims administrator cannot make a determination by the date it specified in a notice to the injured worker, the claims administrator shall send a subsequent notice to the injured worker, not later than the determination date specified in the previous notice, notifying the injured worker of the date by which the claims administrator now expects the determination to be made. The additional delay notices shall comply with all requirements for an original delay notice. Where the delay is related to a medical issue, a copy of the most recent version of the DWC informative pamphlet "QME/AME Fact Sheet" shall be provided with the notice.

(1) For injuries on or after January 1, 1990, if the claims administrator sends a notice of a delay in its decision whether to accept or deny liability for the claim, the notice shall include an explanation that the claim is presumed to be compensable if not denied within 90 days from the filing of the claim form, and that this presumption can be rebutted only with evidence discovered after the 90-day period.

(2) For claims reported on or after April 19, 2004, regardless of the date of injury, if the claims administrator sends a notice of delay in its decision whether to accept or deny liability for the claim, the notice shall include an explanation that Labor Code section 5402(c), provides that within one working day after an employee files a claim form, the employer shall authorize the provision of all treatment, consistent with the applicable treatment guidelines, for the alleged injury; and shall continue to provide treatment until the date that liability is rejected. The notice shall advise the injured worker that the employer's liability for medical treatment under this Labor Code section is limited to ten thousand dollars ($10,000).

Note: Authority cited: Sections 59, 133, 138.3, 138.4, 139.5(a)(2), 4636(d), 4637 and 5307.3, Labor Code. Reference: Sections 138.4, 139.5, 4061(a), (b), 4061(d), 4061(e), 4061(f), 4062.1, 4650(a)–(d), 4658(d), 4661.5, 4700, 4701, 4702, 4703, 4703.5, 4903–4906 and 5402, Labor Code.

History: 1. Repealer and new section filed 7-11-89; operative 10-1-89 (Register 89 No. 28).

2. Amendment of section and Note filed 1-7-94; operative 1-7-94. Submitted to OAL for printing only pursuant to Government Code section 11351 (Register 94, No. 1).

3. Amendment of section and Note filed 12-11-2007; operative 4-9-2008 (Register 2007, No. 50).

Ref.: Hanna §§ 7.03[1], 9.06, 22.06[2][a], 25.20[4], 35.11[3], 35.12; Herlick Handbook §§ 1.6, 6.6, 9.3, 14.3, 16.3.

§9813. Vocational Rehabilitation Notices.

(a) The following notices are applicable to dates of injury through December 31, 2003. This section shall not apply to dates of injury on or after January 1, 2004.

(1) Notice of First Payment. The first time the claims administrator pays vocational rehabilitation temporary disability or maintenance allowance, the claims administrator shall advise the employee of the amount of indemnity due, how it was calculated, and the duration and schedule of indemnity payments. The notice is due by the 14th day after the employee requested vocational rehabilitation services. The notice shall include, if applicable, the employee's option to add an amount from permanent disability benefits to increase the maintenance allowance payments to the temporary disability rate.

(2) Delay in Providing Vocational Rehabilitation. If upon receipt of a medical report which indicates that an employee is likely to be precluded from his or her usual and customary occupation, or upon receipt of a request for vocational rehabilitation services the claims administrator cannot determine the employee's entitlement to vocational rehabilitation services, a notice of delay shall be sent. The notice shall be sent no later than 10 days from the date of receipt of the medical report or no later than 10 days from receipt of the employee's request for services.

The delay notice shall explain the reason for delay, the need, if any, for additional information required to make a determination and the date by which a determination is likely to be made. If the claims administrator cannot make a determination by the date it specified in a notice to the injured worker, the claims administrator shall send a subsequent notice to the injured worker, not later than the determination date specified in the previous notice, notifying the injured worker of the date by which the claims administrator now expects the determination to be made. The additional delay notices shall include the employee's remedies and shall comply with all requirements for an original delay notice.

(3) Denial of Vocational Rehabilitation Benefits. The claims administrator shall advise the employee of its determination that an employee is not a qualified injured worker, the reasons for it, enclosed a copy of the document in which the determination is based and the employee's remedies. The notice shall include a DWC Form RU 103 Request for Dispute Resolution. The notice is due within 10 days of either:

(A) A request for vocational rehabilitation services; or

(B) Receipt of a treating physician's final report determining medical eligibility subsequent to 90 days of aggregate total temporary disability; or

(C) Receipt of the document upon which the claims administrator relied for its determination.

If the claims administrator denies liability for rehabilitation services but remains liable for paying VRTD or VRMA benefits, the notice shall explain the distinction between the terminated and continuing rehabilitation benefits.

If the denial is on the basis that the employee is not medically eligible, a copy of the most recent version of the DWC informative pamphlet "QME/AME Fact Sheet" shall be provided to the employee.

(4) Interruption or Deferral of Vocational Rehabilitation Services. Within 10 days after agreeing to interrupt or defer vocational rehabilitation services, the claims administrator shall advise the employee of the interruption and the dates it will be in effect. The claims administrator shall send a like notice within 10 days after agreeing to a new or extended period of interruption. The notice shall include an explanation of the specific steps he or she must take to notify the claims administrator that he or she is ready to resume participation (e.g., written or telephonic communication to the claims administrator, the agreed Qualified Rehabilitation Representative or the employee's representative), and information regarding the likely termination of the employee's rights to vocational rehabilitation should the employee fail to request services within 5 years from the date of injury.

If the parties agree to an interruption or deferral which extends beyond the statutory period, the notice shall advise the employee that failure to request services within the agreed upon time frame is likely to terminate the employee's rights to rehabilitation services.

For injuries occurring on or after 1/1/94 where an interruption occurs during a vocational rehabilitation plan, the notice shall explain that the plan must by law be completed within 18 months of approval.

(b) Vocational Rehabilitation Notices for Injuries Occurring Prior to 1990.

(1) Potential Eligibility for Rehabilitation. Within 10 days of receipt of a physician's report or knowledge of a physician's opinion indicating that an employee may be permanently precluded from his or her usual and customary occupation or the position in which he or she was engaged at the time of injury, or if the employee has been totally temporarily disabled for an aggregate of 180 days, the claims administrator shall notify the employee within 10 days of the 180th day of his or her potential eligibility for vocational rehabilitation services. The notice shall include all of the following information:

(A) An explanation of the vocational rehabilitation services and rehabilitation temporary disability benefits available to the employee;

(B) Instructions how the employee may apply for vocational rehabilitation (e.g., by written or telephonic communication to the claims administrator, the agreed Qualified Rehabilitation Representative or the employee's representative);

(C) Notice of the employee's right to participate in selecting an agreed rehabilitation counselor;

(D) Notice that vocational rehabilitation benefits may not be settled or otherwise converted to cash payments;

(E) Either an offer of vocational rehabilitation services, or notice of delay or denial notice in accordance with Section 9813(a)(2) or (3).

(c) Vocational Rehabilitation Notices for Injuries Occurring in 1990, 1991, 1992 or 1993.

(1) At 90 days of Aggregate Temporary Disability Benefits. The claims administrator shall notify the worker no later than 10 days after an employee has accrued 90 days of aggregate temporary total disability benefits of the assignment of the Qualified Rehabilitation Representative (QRR) for the purpose of explaining the employee's potential entitlement to vo-

cational rehabilitation services. The notice shall include a statement that the QRR will be assisting the employee in the development of a job description to submit to the treating physician for an opinion regarding whether the employee may be released to his or her usual and customary occupation. The notice shall further state that the employee will be notified of the physician's opinion when available.

(2) Potential Eligibility for Rehabilitation. Within 10 days of receipt of a physician's report or knowledge of a physician's opinion indicating that an employee is medically eligible for vocational rehabilitation, or if prior notice has not been sent, within 10 days after the employee has been totally temporarily disabled for an aggregate of more than 365 days, the claims administrator shall notify the employee of his or her potential eligibility for vocational rehabilitation services. The notice shall include the following information:

(A) The "*Help in Returning to Work*" pamphlet published by the Division of Workers' Compensation;

(B) If the notice contains an offer of services, the notice shall include instructions on how to apply for vocational rehabilitation services (e.g., by written or telephonic communication to the claims administrator, the agreed Qualified Rehabilitation Representative or the employee's representative);

(C) If the notice contains an offer of services, the notice shall state that failure to apply within 90 days of receipt of this notice may terminate the employee's entitlement to vocational rehabilitation services;

(D) If the notice contains an offer of services, information on the employee's right to assist in the selection of an agreed upon Qualified Rehabilitation Representative;

(E) If the notice contains an offer of services, advice that the employee may request an evaluation of his or her ability to benefit from the provision of services prior to accepting or rejecting vocational rehabilitation services;

(F) The notice may include a statement from the claims administrator that every effort will be made to identify a modified or alternate job with the same employer to speed the employee's return to the labor market.

(G) Either an offer of vocational rehabilitation services, or a delay or denial notice in accordance with Section 9813(a)(2) or (3) of these regulations.

(3) Reminder of Potential Eligibility. If the employee has not requested vocational rehabilitation services after notification of medical eligibility, the claims administrator shall remind the employee of his or her right to vocational rehabilitation services. The notice shall be made not earlier than 45 nor later than 70 days after the employee's receipt of the Notice of Potential Eligibility.

(4) Intention to Withhold Maintenance Allowance for Failure to Cooperate. If the employee unreasonably fails to cooperate in the provision of vocational rehabilitation services, the claims administrator shall give the employee written notice of any intention to withhold payment of vocational rehabilitation maintenance allowance, the reasons, and the employee's right to object within 10 days of receiving the notice. The notice shall be made at least 15 days before ending payment of vocational rehabilitation maintenance allowance. The notice shall include a DWC Form RU 103 "Request for Dispute Resolution".

(d) Vocational Rehabilitation Notices for Injuries Occurring on or after January 1, 1994 and before January 1, 2004.

(1) At 90 days of Aggregate Temporary Disability Benefits. The claims administrator shall notify the employee no later than 10 days after the employee accrues 90 days of aggregate temporary total disability benefits of the employee's potential rights to vocational rehabilitation. The notice shall include the "*Help in Returning to Work*" pamphlet as set forth in section 10133.2 of these regulations;

(2) Potential Eligibility for Rehabilitation. Within 10 days of receipt of a physician's report or knowledge of a physician's opinion indicating that an employee is medically eligible for vocational rehabilitation, or if prior notice has not been sent within 10 days after the employee has been totally temporarily disabled for an aggregate of 365 days, the claims administrator shall notify the employee of his or her potential eligibility for vocational rehabilitation services. The notice shall indicate the following information:

(A) The "*Help in Returning to Work*" pamphlet as set forth in section 10133.2 of these regulations;

(B) If the notice contains an offer of services, the notice shall include instructions on how to apply for vocational rehabilitation services (e.g., by written or telephonic communication to the claims administrator, the agreed Qualified Rehabilitation Representative or the employee's representative);

(C) If the notice contains an offer of services, the notice shall state that failure to apply within 90 days of receipt of this notice may terminate the employee's entitlement to vocational rehabilitation services;

(D) If the notice contains an offer of services, information on the employee's right to assist in the selection of an agreed upon Qualified Rehabilitation Representative;

(E) If the notice contains an offer of services, advice that the employee may request an evaluation of their ability to benefit from the provision of services prior to accepting or rejecting vocational rehabilitation services. The employee must further be advised that fees for such an evaluation are included within the forty-five hundred dollars ($4,500) maximum fees available for counseling services.

(F) The notice shall include a statement from the claims administrator whether a modified or alternate job with the employer is available. In the event that additional investigation into the availability of alternate or modified work is required, a final notice regarding the availability of modified or alternate work shall be sent within 30 days. This time limit may be extended by agreement of the parties.

(G) Either an offer of vocational rehabilitation services, or delay or denial notice in accordance with paragraph (2) or (3) of subdivision (a).

(3) Reminder of Potential Eligibility. If the employee has not requested vocational rehabilitation services after notification of medical eligibility, the claims administrator shall remind the employee of his or her right to vocational rehabilitation services. The notice shall be made not earlier than 45 nor later than 70 days after the employee's receipt of the Notice of Potential Eligibility.

(4) Intention to Withhold Maintenance Allowance for Failure to Cooperate. If the employee unreasonably fails to cooperate in the provision of vocational rehabilitation services, the claims administrator shall give the employee written notice of any intention to withhold payment of vocational rehabilitation maintenance allowance, the reasons, and the employee's right to object within 10 days of receiving the notice. The notice shall be made at least 15 days before ending payment of vocational rehabilitation maintenance allowance. The Notice shall include a DWC Form RU 103 "Request for Dispute Resolution".

Note: Authority cited: Sections 59, 133, 138.3, 138.4, 139.5(a)(2), 4636(d), 4637 and 5307.3, Labor Code. Reference: Sections 138.4, 139.5, 4061(a), (b), (d), 4636, 4637, 4641, 4643, 4644, 4650(a)–(d), 4661.5, 4700, 4701, 4702, 4703, 4703.5, 4903(a) and 5402, Labor Code.

History: 1. Repealer filed 7-11-89; operative 10-1-89 (Register 89, No. 28).

2. New section filed 1-7-94; operative 1-7-94. Submitted to OAL for printing only pursuant to Government Code section 11351 (Register 94, No. 1). For prior history, see Register 89, No. 28.

3. Amendment of subsections (a)(2)-(a)(3)(C), (c)(2), (c)(2)(B)-(E), (d)(2) and (d)(2)(B)-(E) filed 2-21-95; operative 2-21-95. Submitted to OAL for printing only pursuant to Government Code section 11351 (Register 95, No. 8).

4. Amendment of subsections (a), (a)(2)-(3), (a)(3)(C), (c)(4)-(d)(1), (d)(2)(A) and (d)(4) filed 12-11-2007; operative 4-9-2008 (Register 2007, No. 50).

Ref.: Hanna §§ 35.31[1][a]–[b], 35.81; Herlick Handbook §§ 1.6, 6.6, 9.3, 14.3, 16.3.

§9813.1. Notice of Supplemental Job Displacement Benefit, Notice of Offer of Modified or Alternative Work. For Injuries Occurring on or After January 1, 2004.

(a) Notice of Potential Right to Supplemental Job Displacement Benefit (SJDB). Within 10 days of the last payment of temporary disability indemnity, if such notice has not previously been provided, the claims administrator shall advise the employee of his or her potential right to the supplemental job displacement benefit. The claims administrator shall use the mandatory form "Notice of Potential Right to Supplemental Job Displacement Benefit" that is set forth in section 10133.52 of these regulations. The notice shall be sent to the employee by certified mail.

(b) Notice of Offer of Modified or Alternative Work. Within 30 days of the termination of temporary disability indemnity payments, the employer may offer, in the form and manner prescribed by section 10133.53 of these regulations, modified or alternative work accommodating the employee's work restrictions, lasting at least 12 months.

Note: Authority cited: Sections 59, 133, 138.3, 138.4, 4658.5 and 5307.3, Labor Code. Reference: Sections 124, 4658.1, 4658.5 and 4658.6, Labor Code.

History: 1. New section filed 12-11-2007; operative 4-9-2008 (Register 2007, No. 50).

Ref.: Hanna §§ 7.02[3][d][vi], 35.110[1].

§9813.2. Return to Work Notices. For Injuries Occurring on or After January 1, 2005.

Notice of Offer of Regular Work, Notice of Offer of Modified or Alternative Work. Within 60 calendar days from the date that the condition of an injured employee with permanent partial disability becomes permanent and stationary:

(a) If an employer does not serve the employee with a notice of offer of regular work, modified work or alternative work as set forth in section 10002, each payment of permanent partial disability remaining to be paid to the employee from the date of the end of the 60 day period shall be paid in accordance with Labor Code section 4658(d)(1) and increased by 15 percent.

(b) If an employer serves the employee with a notice of offer of regular work, modified work or alternative work as set forth in section 10002(b)(3) and (4), each payment of permanent partial disability remaining to be paid from the date the offer was served on the employee shall be paid in accordance with Labor Code section 4658(d)(1) and decreased by 15 percent, regardless of whether the employee accepts or rejects the offer.

(c) The employer shall use Form DWC-AD 10133.53 (Section 10133.53) to offer modified or alternative work, or Form DWC-AD 10003 (Section 10003) to offer regular work. The claims administrator may serve the offer of work on behalf of the employer.

Note: Authority cited: Sections 59, 133, 138.3, 138.4, 4658 and 5307.3, Labor Code. Reference: Sections 124, 4658 and 4658.1, Labor Code.

History: 1. New section filed 12-11-2007; operative 4-9-2008 (Register 2007, No. 50).

Ref.: Hanna §§ 7.02[3][d][vi], 35.110[1].

§9814. Salary Continuation.

In relation to periods of temporary disability, where an employer provides salary or other payments in lieu of or in excess of temporary disability indemnity, the claims administrator or employer shall comply with the notice requirements of this article which apply to temporary disability. In addition, the claims administrator or employer shall include a full explanation of the salary continuation plan with the initial notice.

Note: Authority cited: Sections 59, 133, 138.4, 139.5(a)(2), 4637 and 5307.3, Labor Code. Reference: Sections 4650(a), (c), (d), (g), 4800, 4804.1, 4806 and 4850-4850.7, Labor Code.

History: 1. Amendment filed 7-11-89; operative 10-1-89 (Register 89, No. 28).

2. Amendment of section and Note filed 1-7-94; operative 1-7-94. Submitted to OAL for printing only pursuant to Government Code section 11351 (Register 94, No. 1).

Ref.: Hanna § 7.03[1]; Herlick Handbook §§ 1.6, 6.6, 9.3, 14.3.

§9815. Corrected Notice.

If information in any notice, or the action taken as reflected in the notice, was incorrect or incomplete, the claims administrator shall provide the employee with a corrected notice within 14 days of knowledge of the error or omission. The notice shall be identified as a "Corrected Notice" and explain the nature and reason for the correction. Any additional benefits due as a result of the error or omission shall be paid or provided with the notice, if not previously provided.

Note: Authority cited: Sections 59, 133, 138.4, 139.5(a)(2), 4637 and 5307.3, Labor Code. Reference: Sections 138.4, 139.5, 4061(a), (b), (d), 4636, 4637, 4641, 4643, 4644, 4650(a) through (d), 4661.5, 4700, 4701, 4702, 4703, 4703.5, 4903(a) and 5402, Labor Code.

History: 1. Amendment of section and Note filed 1-7-94; operative 1-7-94. Submitted to OAL for printing only pursuant to Government Code section 11351 (Register 94, No. 1).

Ref.: Hanna §§ 7.03[1], 32.07[4]; Herlick Handbook §§ 1.6, 6.6, 9.3, 14.3, 16.3.

§9816. Repealed.

Note: Authority cited: Sections 138.3 and 138.4, Labor Code. Reference: Sections 138.3, 138.4 and 5453, Labor Code.

History: 1. Repealer filed 1-7-94; operative 1-7-94. Submitted to OAL for printing only pursuant to Government Code section 11351 (Register 94, No. 1).

§9817. Repealed.

Note: Authority cited: Sections 138.3 and 138.4, Labor Code. Reference: Sections 138.4, 4650, 4651, 4700–4703 and 5402, Labor Code.

History: 1. Repealer filed 1-7-94; operative 1-7-94. Submitted to OAL for printing only pursuant to Government Code section 11351 (Register 94, No. 1).

ARTICLE 8.1
Workers' Compensation Advertising By Non-Attorneys and Non-Physicians; Prohibition of False or Misleading Advertising

§9820. Definitions.

As used in this article:

(a) Administrative Director. The Administrative Director of the Division of Workers' Compensation or the Director's duly authorized representative designee, or delegee.

(b) Advertisement. Any form of communication, in writing, photograph or picture, electronic broadcasting or transmission, that solicits any person to:

(1) file a workers' compensation claim, or,

(2) use any workers' compensation services as defined in subsection (k), or,

(3) engage or consult counsel or a medical care provider or clinic to consider a workers' compensation claim.

The form of advertisement may include, but is not limited to, advertising by newspaper, magazine, circular, form letter, publication, billboard, card, label, placard, transit advertisement, business card, envelope, book, list, directory, radio, motion picture, video, television, or electronic mail.

(c) Advertiser. Any person who sends, publishes, broadcasts, transmits or communicates an advertisement as defined in subsection (b); or who causes or pays in whole or in part for the sending, publishing, broadcasting, transmission or communication of such an advertisement either for himself or on behalf of another person. However, advertiser does not include the following persons if the person's principal business is other than providing workers' compensation services:

(1) a publisher, printer, distributor or circulator of a newspaper, magazine, book, or other writing;

(2) an operator of a broadcasting station, movie or video production company;

(3) an operator of premises where advertisements are displayed;

(4) a person while working as an employee of any persons exempted in paragraphs 1 through 3 of this subsection.

(d) Attorney. A person who holds a valid, active license to practice law in California at the time the advertisement governed by these regulations is published.

(e) False or misleading advertisement. An advertisement that:

(1) Is false or misleading pursuant to Labor Code Section 139.43(a) or 139.45(b).

(2) Violates any provision of Labor Code Section 5433.

(3) Offers or implies that the advertiser can or will dissuade, delay or impede a claimant from pursuing a legitimate work injury claim; or can or will provide false or inaccurate evidence or opinion in support of or in opposition to a work injury claim.

(4) Fails to include the notice as specified in Labor Code Section 5432 or Title 8 CCR Section 9823(b).

(5) Fails to comply with any requirement of this article.

(6) Is placed in furtherance of business operations conducted in violation of law, or when the advertiser has not complied with any requirement of this article.

(f) Him, Himself or His. These terms include "her", "herself" or "hers" when the person is female, and "it", "itself" or "its" when referring to an artificial person.

(g) Owner. A person who has a direct or indirect ownership interest in a business which provides workers' compensation services, or a person who has a direct or indirect claim to all or a portion of the income of a business which provides workers' compensation services.

(h) Person. Any natural or artificial person or combination of persons, including without limitation a corporation, partnership, trust, or unincorporated association.

(i) Physician. A person who holds a valid, active license to practice in California at the time the advertisement governed by these regulations is published, as any of the following medical practitioners: a medical or osteopathic physician and surgeon; a psychologist; a chiropractor; a podiatrist; a dentist; or an optometrist.

(j) Referral panelist. A person who will receive or has agreed to receive referrals of clients from a workers' compensation referral service.

(k) Workers' compensation services means services provided by any of the following:

(1) A workers' compensation medical or medical-legal provider, which means any person who provides medical treatment or evaluation of injuries or alleged injuries, including work injuries.

(2) A workers' compensation non-attorney advisor or representative, which means any person who is not an attorney who advises or represents persons in connection with injuries or alleged injuries, including work injuries.

(3) A workers' compensation referral service, which means any person who refers persons to medical or medical-legal providers, non-attorney advisors or representatives, or attorneys who advise or represent persons in connection with injuries or alleged injuries, including work injuries.

(4) A workers' compensation advertiser, which means any person who advertises or solicits for any or all of the preceding three categories of persons.

This definition includes persons who provide services for several types of injuries, as long as work injuries are included.

Note: Authority cited: Sections 59, 133, 139.43(b) and 5307.3, Labor Code. Reference: Sections 7, 139.43(a), (b), (d), 139.45 and 5430-5434, Labor Code.

History: 1. New article 8.1 and section filed 12-31-93; operative 1-1-94. Submitted to OAL for printing only pursuant to Government Code section 11351 (Register 93, No. 53).

2. Amendment of article 8.1 heading filed 8-7-95; operative 8-7-95. Submitted to OAL for printing only pursuant to Government Code section 11351 (Register 95, No. 32).

Ref.: Hanna § 1.23; Herlick Handbook §§ 1.6, 9.3, 9.18.

§9821. Coverage and Exclusions.

(a) This article does not apply to attorneys, as defined in Section 9820(d), or physicians, as defined in Section 9820(i). Nothing in this article shall be construed to obviate or lessen the obligations of attorneys or physicians under Labor Code Sections 5430 through 5434, or under other provisions of law. A person who was not licensed to practice in California at the time of the act or omission is not considered an attorney or physician under this article, and these regulations apply to such a person.

(b) This article does not apply to government agencies, labor organizations as defined in Labor Code Section 1117, charitable organizations, or non-profit tax-exempt bar associations whose primary business or purpose is other than providing workers' compensation services as defined in Section 9820(k), or to agents or employees of any of these exempt entities while acting for them.

(c) This article does apply to all other advertisers, as defined in Section 9820(c), even though an advertiser who is subject to this article may also be subject to attorney or physician workers' compensation advertising laws because the person advertises with or for an attorney or physician.

(d) The provisions of this article are not exclusive. The Administrative Director may use the remedies in this article and any other remedies provided by law.

(e) Any waiver of this article is void as against public policy.

(f) This article shall not be construed to authorize the unlawful practice of law or medicine by any person.

Note: Authority cited: Sections 59, 133, 139.43(b) and 5307.3, Labor Code. Reference: Sections 7, 139.43(a), (b), (d), 139.45 and 5430-5434, Labor Code.

History: 1. New section filed 12-31-93; operative 1-1-94. Submitted to OAL for printing only pursuant to Government Code section 11351 (Register 93, No. 53).

2. Amendment of subsection (a) filed 8-7-95; operative 8-7-95. Submitted to OAL for printing only pursuant to Government Code section 11351 (Register 95, No. 32).

Ref.: Hanna § 1.23; Herlick Handbook §§ 1.6, 9.3, 9.18.

§9822. Severability.

If any portion of this article, or the application of any part of it to any person or circumstance, is held to be invalid, the rest of the article and its application to any other person or circumstance remain valid.

Note: Authority cited: Sections 59, 133, 139.43(b) and 5307.3, Labor Code. Reference: Sections 7, 139.43(a), (b), (d), 139.45 and 5430-5434, Labor Code.

History: 1. New section filed 12-31-93; operative 1-1-94. Submitted to OAL for printing only pursuant to Government Code section 11351 (Register 93, No. 53).

Ref.: Herlick Handbook §§ 1.6, 9.3, 9.18.

§9823. General Workers' Compensation Advertising Rules.

All advertisements shall comply with the following rules:

(a) No advertisement shall be false or misleading.

(b) All advertisements shall include the written or spoken fraud notices, in the manner set forth in Labor Code Section 5432(a), (b).

(c) If an advertisement includes a testimonial, it must not overstate or distort the facts or results of the person's case, and must qualify the testimonial by stating immediately before or after it: (1) that each person's case is different and that the reader's or viewer's results will not necessarily be the same as the example; (2) in the case of a spoken or pictorial testimonial when the speaker is not relating his or her own experience, that the reader, model or performer is an actor and not the actual person involved in the case. The advertisement must give the qualifying information in a similar manner and with similar emphasis as the testimonial.

(d) The advertiser must identify himself either by his true legal name or by a fictitious business name that was duly filed under Division 7, Part 3, Chapter 5 of the Business & Professions Code before using the fictitious name in an advertisement, and which fictitious name filing had not expired at the time of the advertisement. However, no such advertised name shall violate subsection (e). Notwithstanding the general provisions of the fictitious business name law, an advertiser must file its fictitious business statement before using it in an advertisement.

(e) An advertisement for a person who is not a physician (as defined in Section 9820(i)) may not use the terms "medical", "physician", or "doctor"; nor a term describing a specific area of medical practice such as "surgeon", "osteopath", "psychologist", "chiropractor", "podiatrist", "dentist", "optometrist", etc.; nor their linguistic variants; nor any similar designation implying that the person is a physician; in the advertiser's name or to describe the advertiser's services. In addition, an advertisement for a person who is not licensed as a physician in the specific area of medical practice named in the advertisement may not include a term describing a specific area of medical practice. However, an advertisement for a medical referral service may use the terms as provided in Section 9828(a).

(f) An advertisement for a person who is not an attorney (as defined in Section 9820(d)) may not use the terms "legal", "attorney", "law firm", "law office", "law center", "counselor at law", "specialist in workers' compensation law"; nor their linguistic variants; nor any similar designation implying that the person is an attorney; in the advertiser's name nor to describe the advertiser's services. However, an advertisement for a legal referral service may use the terms as provided in Section 9828(b).

Note: Authority cited: Sections 59, 133, 139.43(b) and 5307.3, Labor Code. Reference: Sections 7, 139.43(a), (b), (d), 139.45 and 5430-5434, Labor Code.

History: 1. New section filed 12-31-93; operative 1-1-94. Submitted to OAL for printing only pursuant to Government Code section 11351 (Register 93, No. 53).

Ref.: Hanna § 1.23; Herlick Handbook §§ 1.6, 9.3, 9.18.

§9824. Identification as Representative.

An advertisement for a workers' compensation non-attorney advisor or representative shall identify the advertiser as a non-attorney as follows: *"The advertiser is a representative [or an advisor] who is not an attorney."* This notice shall be advertised in the same manner (size, typeface, display, etc.) required for the notice specified in Section 9823(b).

Note: Authority cited: Sections 59, 133, 139.43(b) and 5307.3, Labor Code. Reference: Sections 7, 139.43(a), (b), (d), 139.45 and 5430-5434, Labor Code.

History: 1. New section filed 12-31-93; operative 1-1-94. Submitted to OAL for printing only pursuant to Government Code section 11351 (Register 93, No. 53).

Ref.: Hanna § 1.23; Herlick Handbook §§ 1.6, 9.3, 9.18.

§9825. Representative's WCAB Qualification.

No person shall advertise as or on behalf of a non-attorney advisor or representative whose right to practice before the Workers' Compensation Appeals Board is suspended or revoked when the advertisement is published.

Note: Authority cited: Sections 59, 133, 139.43(b) and 5307.3, Labor Code. Reference: Sections 7, 139.43(a), (b), (d), 139.45 and 5430-5434, Labor Code.

History: 1. New section filed 12-31-93; operative 1-1-94. Submitted to OAL for printing only pursuant to Government Code section 11351 (Register 93, No. 53).

Ref.: Herlick Handbook §§ 1.6, 9.3, 9.18.

§9826. Advertisement by Unlicensed Attorney.

No person shall advertise as or on behalf of a non-attorney advisor or representative whose California license to practice law is suspended or revoked when the advertisement is published, without stating in the advertisement: *"The advertiser is a representative [*or *an advisor] whose license to practice law has been suspended [*or *revoked]."* This notice shall be advertised in the same manner (size, typeface, display, etc.) required for the notice specified in Section 9823(b). This section does not permit advertising by a person whose right to practice before the WCAB, as well as his license to practice law, is suspended or revoked.

Note: Authority cited: Sections 59, 13, 139.43(b) and 5307.3, Labor Code. Reference: Sections 7, 139.43(a), (b), (d), 139.45 and 5430-5434, Labor Code.

History: 1. New section filed 12-31-93; operative 1-1-94. Submitted to OAL for printing only pursuant to Government Code section 11351 (Register 93, No. 53).

Ref.: Hanna § 1.23; Herlick Handbook §§ 1.6, 9.3, 9.18.

§9827. Advertisement by Unlicensed Medical Provider.

No person shall advertise medical goods or services whose provision requires a license, by or on behalf of a person who does not hold a valid, active license to provide the goods or services when the advertisement is published.

Note: Authority cited: Sections 59, 133, 139.43(b) and 5307.3, Labor Code. Reference: Sections 7, 139.43(a), (b), (d), 139.45 and 5430-5434, Labor Code.

History: 1. New section filed 12-31-93; operative 1-1-94. Submitted to OAL for printing only pursuant to Government Code section 11351 (Register 93, No. 53).

Ref.: Herlick Handbook §§ 1.6, 9.3, 9.18.

§9828. Use of Terms "Medical", "Legal", or Comparable Terms.

An advertisement for workers' compensation referral services shall not use any of the following terms or their linguistic variants, nor any similar designation, in its name or to describe its services: (1) "medical", "physician", or "doctor"; (2) a term describing a specific area of medical practice such as "surgeon", "osteopath", "psychologist", "chiropractor", "podiatrist", "dentist", "surgeon", "optometrist", or the like; (3) "legal", "attorney", "law firm", "law office", "law center", "counselor at law", "specialist in workers' compensation law", except:

(a) An advertisement for a medical referral service may use the terms "medical referral" or "physician referral" if the service refers persons who respond to the advertisement only to physicians (as defined in Subsection 9820(i)). It may also use the term "medical referral" if it refers for goods or services by medical providers outside the fields of practice listed in subsection 9820(i), only to persons licensed to provide those other goods or services. It may use the term "referral" preceded by the name of a specific type of physician, such as "chiropractic referral", "podiatric referral", etc., if it restricts its referrals to physicians of the type named.

(b) An advertisement for a legal referral service may use the terms "legal referral" or "attorney referral" if the service refers persons who respond to the advertisement only to attorneys (as defined in Subsection 9820(d)).

Note: Authority cited: Sections 59, 133, 139.43(b) and 5307.3, Labor Code. Reference: Sections 7, 139.43(a), (b), (d), 139.45 and 5430-5434, Labor Code.

History: 1. New section filed 12-31-93; operative 1-1-94. Submitted to OAL for printing only pursuant to Government Code section 11351 (Register 93, No. 53).

Ref.: Herlick Handbook §§ 1.6, 9.3, 9.18.

§9829. Information Required from Referral Panelists.

Each advertiser of workers' compensation referral services shall require each medical, legal or non-attorney advisor or representative who will receive referrals from the referral service to supply the following information in writing, before receiving any referrals:

(a) In the case of all referral panelists, the information required by Section 9831.

(b) In the case of all referral panelists, an agreement that the panelist will inform the referral service in writing of any change in the information supplied, within 10 days of the change.

(c) In the case of an attorney, physician or other medical care referral panelist, the date the panelist was licensed to practice in California (if a license is required for that field of practice); that the license is then active and in good standing; and the panelist's specialty area of practice, if any, including the name of any specialty board or certification and date of that certification which the panelist holds.

(d) In the case of a non-attorney advisor or representative, a statement that the panelist is then entitled to appear before the Workers' Compensation Appeals Board.

Note: Authority cited: Sections 59, 133, 139.43(b) and 5307.3, Labor Code. Reference: Sections 7, 139.43(a), (b), (d), 139.45 and 5430-5434, Labor Code.

History: 1. New section filed 12-31-93; operative 1-1-94. Submitted to OAL for printing only pursuant to Government Code section 11351 (Register 93, No. 53).

Ref.: Herlick Handbook §§ 1.6, 9.3, 9.18.

§9830. Information Supplied to Referral Panelists.

Each advertiser of workers' compensation referral services shall give each referral panelist a copy of each advertisement it will use to refer clients to the panelist, on or before the date the advertisement is published. The advertiser shall notify the panelist in writing, with the copy of the advertisement, that the panelist may object to the advertiser's using that advertisement to attract or refer clients to the panelist. If a panelist notifies the service that (s)he objects to the advertisement, the service shall not refer any clients who respond to that advertisement to a panelist who objected to it.

The advertiser shall maintain written records of each objection to an advertisement, containing a copy of the advertisement, the identity of the panelist who objected to it, and the date of the objection. During the period any objection is in force to an advertisement then being published, the advertiser shall ask each respondent to identify the advertisement to which the person is responding, and shall not refer the respondent to any panelist who objected to that advertisement.

Note: Authority cited: Sections 59, 133, 139.43(b) and 5307.3, Labor Code. Reference: Sections 7, 139.43(a), (b), (d), 139.45 and 5430-5434, Labor Code.

History: 1. New section filed 12-31-93; operative 1-1-94. Submitted to OAL for printing only pursuant to Government Code section 11351 (Register 93, No. 53).

Ref.: Herlick Handbook §§ 1.6, 9.3, 9.18.

§9831. Registration Statement.

Every advertiser shall prepare, retain, and make available to the administrative director upon request a written registration statement. The information in the statement shall be verified by a declaration under penalty of perjury signed by the advertiser (if an individual), or by each owner of the advertiser (if a business entity). Whenever a material change occurs in the information in the statement, the advertiser shall within 10 days of the change revise the statement.

The statement shall contain the following information:

(a) The full legal name of the advertiser, and any other name(s) under which the person will advertise or do business.

(b) The advertiser's business form and place of organization; if the advertiser is a corporation, a copy of its articles of incorporation and bylaws and any amendments to them; if the advertiser is a partnership, a copy of the partnership agreement and any amendments to it; if the advertiser is an unincorporated organization a copy of its written organizational documents and any amendments to them; if the advertiser has filed or uses a fictitious business name, a copy of each fictitious business name statement showing the place(s) of filing.

(c) The complete street address or addresses of all locations at which the advertiser does or proposes to do business, and a designation of one such location in California as its principal place of business in the state.

(d) A listing of all telephone numbers to be used by the advertiser and the address where each telephone using each of these telephone numbers is located.

(e) The name of, and the office held by, the advertiser's officers, directors, trustees, general and limited partners, sole proprietor, and owners, as the case may be, and the names of those persons who have management responsibilities in connection with the advertiser's business activities.

(f) For each person whose name is disclosed under subdivision (e): the complete address of his principal residence; his driver's license number and state of issuance; and the number, licensing agency, and status of each professional license (s)he holds.

(g) A statement identifying any person disclosed under subdivision (e) who:

(1) has been convicted of or has pleaded guilty or no contest to a felony or misdemeanor violation of any offense related to workers' compensation, or of fraud, theft, embezzlement, fraudulent conversion, or misappropriation of property; or

(2) is or has been the subject of any civil or administrative action alleging acts in violation of any workers' compensation law, or of fraud, theft, embezzlement, fraudulent conversion, or misappropriation of property, or of the use of unfair, unlawful, or deceptive business practices.

The statement shall identify the person, court or administrative agency in which the case was filed, the case number, title of the case, and the result of the case.

Note: Authority cited: Sections 59, 133, 139.43(b) and 5307.3, Labor Code. Reference: Sections 7, 139.43(a), (b), (d), 139.45 and 5430-5434, Labor Code.

History: 1. New section filed 12-31-93; operative 1-1-94. Submitted to OAL for printing only pursuant to Government Code section 11351 (Register 93, No. 53).

Ref.: Hanna § 1.23; Herlick Handbook §§ 1.6, 9.3, 9.18.

§9832. Maintenance of and Access to Records.

Every advertiser shall maintain the following records, at its principal place of business in California, of its business of providing workers' compensation services:

(a) Complete financial records using generally accepted accounting principles, as defined by the American Institute of Certified Public Accountants and the Financial Standards Board.

(b) A copy of all of its workers' compensation advertisements (whether in print, video or audio media) published within the preceding two years. The records shall include a copy of the advertisement and the dates and places of each publication, including as applicable the name and city of publication of a periodical, or the station call letters and city location of any radio or television station.

(c) Its registration statement required by Section 9831.

(d) For workers' compensation referral services, a record of all objections to advertisements as required by Section 9830.

(e) For workers' compensation referral services, a single record listing all referral panelists, including each panelist's: (1) name; (2) address(es) at which (s)he will consult with clients; (3) profession, professional license number and state of issuance; (4) if the panelist works for a business, the name of the business and his status with it (owner, employee or independent contractor); (5) date (s)he became a panelist; and (6) the date (s)he ended the status as a panelist if applicable.

The service shall update the record to show any change in a panelist's status within 10 days of knowledge of the change. The record shall continue to list each panelist who ends his status as such, for two years after the person's status as a panelist ended.

(f) The advertiser shall maintain all records required by this section for at least two years after: (1) for advertisements, the date of its last publication; (2) for financial records, the end of the calendar year to which the records refer in whole or in part; (3) for registration statements or statement changes, the end of the calendar year to which the statement or change relates; (4) for objections to advertisements, the later of the date of the objection or the date the advertisement was last published; (5) for the combined listing of referral panelists required by Subsection (e) (in its current updated form), the date the service publishes its last advertisement.

(g) The advertiser shall make all records required by this section available for inspection and copying by any representative of the Department of Industrial Relations, the Department of Justice, or district or city attorney, during the advertiser's normal business hours but at least between 9:00 a.m. and 5:00 p.m. Monday through Friday (excepting holidays). In addition, if necessary in the judgment of the inspector to protect the integrity of an investigation, the advertiser shall allow, and an inspector may conduct or continue inspection and copying during other hours or days.

Note: Authority cited: Sections 59, 133, 139.43(b) and 5307.3, Labor Code. Reference: Sections 7, 139.43(a), (b), (d), 139.45 and 5430-5434, Labor Code; Sections 11180-11191, Government Code.

History: 1. New section filed 12-31-93; operative 1-1-94. Submitted to OAL for printing only pursuant to Government Code section 11351 (Register 93, No. 53).

Ref.: Hanna § 1.23; Herlick Handbook §§ 1.6, 9.3, 9.18.

§9833. Right to Conduct Investigation.

The Administrative Director may investigate any violation of this article, of the Workers' Compensation Truth in Advertising Act of 1992 (Labor Code §§5430 et seq.), of Section 139.43 of the Labor Code, or of any other provision of law now or hereafter enacted concerning workers' compensation advertising by persons other than attorneys or physicians. For this purpose (s)he may employ all rights and remedies possessed or delegated under Government Code §§11180 et seq.

Note: Authority cited: Sections 59, 133, 139.43(b) and 5307.3, Labor Code. Reference: Sections 7, 139.43(a), (b), (d), 139.45 and 5430-5434, Labor Code; and Sections 11180-11191, Government Code.

History: 1. New section filed 12-31-93; operative 1-1-94. Submitted to OAL for printing only pursuant to Government Code section 11351 (Register 93, No. 53).

Ref.: Herlick Handbook §§ 1.6, 9.3, 9.18.

§9834. Order to Produce Documents or Provide Information.

The Administrative Director may issue and serve on any advertiser, or the advertiser's employees or agents, an order requiring the advertiser, employee or agent to provide information, copies and access to any information related to workers' compensation advertising subject to regulation under this article. The advertiser, employee or agent shall comply with the order within the time specified in it. The Administrative Director may serve the order by any method reasonably calculated to give notice to the person served.

Note: Authority cited: Sections 59, 133, 139.43(b) and 5307.3, Labor Code. Reference: Sections 7, 133.49(a), (b), (d), 139.45 and 5430-5434, Labor Code; Sections 11180-11191, Government Code.

History: 1. New section filed 12-31-93; operative 1-1-94. Submitted to OAL for printing only pursuant to Government Code section 11351 (Register 93, No. 53).

2. Editorial correction of Note (Register 98, No. 46).

Ref.: Herlick Handbook §§ 1.6, 9.3, 9.18.

§9835. Compliance Orders.

(a) The Administrative Director may issue and serve on any advertiser, or the advertiser's employees or agents, a compliance order requiring the advertiser, employee or agent to cease and desist from committing any violation, or to comply with any requirement, of this article. The Administrative Director may serve the order by any method reasonably calculated to give notice to the person served.

(b) The Administrative Director's order may include, but is not limited to, the following provisions: (1) an order to stop using an advertisement or to use it only with specified modifications; (2) an order to advertise or otherwise disseminate corrective information, either by the advertiser at its expense, or by the Administrative Director at the advertiser's expense; (3) an order to pay the Administrative Director's investigation and enforcement costs.

(c) The advertiser, employee or agent shall comply with the order within the time specified in it.

Note: Authority cited: Sections 59, 133, 139.43(b) and 5307.3, Labor Code. Reference: Sections 7, 139.43(a), (b), (d), 139.45 and 5430-5434, Labor Code.

History: 1. New section filed 12-31-93; operative 1-1-94. Submitted to OAL for printing only pursuant to Government Code section 11351 (Register 93, No. 53).

Ref.: Herlick Handbook §§ 1.6, 9.3, 9.18.

§9836. Other Remedies; Cumulative Remedies.

The Administrative Director may institute civil proceedings against any person for violation of this article or of the statutes which may be investigated under this article, or may refer any violation for civil, criminal or professional disciplinary proceedings to the Attorney General, a district or city attorney, or other authorities having jurisdiction of the matter.

The Administrative Director's remedies in this article are cumulative and not exclusive, and the exercise of any or all of them is discretionary.

Note: Authority cited: Sections 59, 133, 139.43(b) and 5307.3, Labor Code. Reference: Sections 7, 139.43(a), (b), (d), 139.45 and 5430-5434, Labor Code.

History: 1. New section filed 12-31-93; operative 1-1-94. Submitted to OAL for printing only pursuant to Government Code section 11351 (Register 93, No. 53).

Ref.: Herlick Handbook §§ 1.6, 9.3, 9.18.

§9837. Hearing.

(a) Any person aggrieved by an order issued under Sections 9834 or 9835 may request a hearing before the administrative director or an administrative law judge which shall be shall be held in accordance with the Administrative Procedure Act [Chapter 5, (commencing with Section 11500), of Part 1 of Division 3 of Title 2 of the Government Code], and the administrative director shall have all of the powers granted under that act.

Note: Authority cited: Sections 59, 133, 139.43(b) and 5307.3, Labor Code. Reference: Sections 7, 139.43(a), (b), (d), 139.45 and 5430-5434, Labor Code.

History: 1. New section filed 12-31-93; operative 1-1-94. Submitted to OAL for printing only pursuant to Government Code section 11351 (Register 93, No. 53).

Ref.: Herlick Handbook §§ 1.6, 9.3, 9.18.

ARTICLE 8.5
Employee Information

§9880. Written Notice to New Employees.

(a) Every employer shall provide to every new employee, either at the time of hire or by the end of the first pay period, the Written Notice to New Employees concerning the rights, benefits and obligations under worker's compensation law. The content of the notice must be approved by the Administrative Director.

(b) The notice shall be easily understandable. It shall be available in both English and Spanish where there are Spanish-speaking employees.

(c) The notice provided shall be in writing, in non-technical terms and shall include the following information:

(1) The name of the current compensation insurance carrier of the employer at the time of distribution, or when such is the fact, that the employer is self-insured, and who is responsible for claims adjustment;

(2) How to get emergency medical treatment, if needed;

(3) The kind of events, injuries and illnesses covered by workers' compensation;

(4) The injured employee's right to receive medical care;

(5) How to obtain appropriate medical care for a job injury;

(6) The role and function of the primary treating physician;

(7) The rights of the employee to select and change the treating physician pursuant to the provisions of Labor Code Sections 4600 to 4601;

(8) A form that the employee may use as an optional method for notifying the employer of the name of the employee's "personal physician," as defined by Labor Code Section 4600, or "personal chiropractor," as defined by Labor Code Section 4601;

(9) The rights of the employee to receive temporary disability indemnity, permanent disability indemnity, vocational rehabilitation services, supplemental job displacement benefits, and death benefits, as appropriate;

(10) To whom the injuries should be reported;

(11) The existence of time limits for the employer to be notified of an occupational injury;

(12) The protections against discrimination provided pursuant to Section 132a; and

(13) The location and telephone number of the nearest information and assistance officer, including an explanation of services available.

Note: Authority cited: Sections 133, 138.3, 138.4, 3550, 3551 and 5307.3, Labor Code. Reference: Sections 139.5, 139.6, 3550, 3551, 3600, 4600, 4601, 4603, 4650, 4651, 4658.5, 4658.6, 4700, 4702 and 4703, Labor Code.

History: 1. New Article 8.5 (Sections 9880-9882) filed 1-28-76 as an emergency; effective upon filing (Register 76, No. 5).

2. Certificate of Compliance filed 1-29-76 (Register 76, No. 5).

3. Repealer and new section filed 11-9-77; effective thirtieth day thereafter (Register 77, No. 46).

4. Amendment filed 10-16-81; effective thirtieth day thereafter (Register 81, No. 42).

5. Editorial correction restoring Article 8.5 (Sections 9880-9883), which was inadvertently repealed by a 7-15-83 order (Register 83, No. 33).

6. Repealer and new section filed 7-11-89; operative 10-1-89 (Register 89, No. 28).

7. Amendment of section and Note filed 7-7-2004; operative 8-1-2004 pursuant to Government Code section 11343.4 (Register 2004, No. 28).

Ref.: Hanna § 22.01[3]; Herlick Handbook §§ 1.6, 9.3; W. Cal. Sum., 2 "Workers' Compensation" §225.

§9881. Posting of Notice to Employees.

(a) Every employer shall post and keep

posted in a conspicuous location frequented by employees during the hours of the workday a Notice to Employees.

(b) The Notice to Employees poster shall be easily understandable. It shall be posted in both English and Spanish where there are Spanish-speaking employees.

(c) The Notice to Employees poster shall include the following information:

(1) The name of the current compensation insurance carrier of the employer, or when such is the fact, that the employer is self-insured, and who is responsible for claims adjustment.

(2) How to get emergency medical treatment, if needed.

(3) Emergency telephone numbers for physician, hospital, ambulance, police and firefighting services.

(4) The kinds of events, injuries and illnesses covered by workers' compensation.

(5) Advice that the employer may not be responsible for compensation because of an injury due to the employee's voluntary participation in any off-duty recreational, social, or athletic activity that is not a part of the employee's work-related duties.

(6) The injured employee's right to receive medical care.

(7) The rights of the employee to select and change the treating physician pursuant to the provisions of Labor Code Section 4600.

(8) The rights of the employee to receive temporary disability indemnity, permanent disability indemnity, vocational rehabilitation services, supplemental job displacement benefits, and death benefits, as appropriate.

(9) To whom the injuries should be reported.

(10) The existence of time limits for the employer to be notified of an occupational injury.

(11) The protections against discrimination provided pursuant to Labor Code Section 132a.

(12) The location and telephone number of the nearest information and assistance officer.

(c) The employer may post the Administrative Director's approved Notice to Employee Poster provided in Section 9881.1. If the employer chooses not to use the Notice to Employee Poster provided in Section 9881.1, the employer may use a poster which meets the posting requirements of Labor Code Section 3550, includes the information required by this regulation, and has been approved by the Administrative Director.

Note: Authority cited: Sections 133, 138.3, 139.6, 3550 and 5307.3, Labor Code. Reference: Sections 139.5, 3550, 3600, 4600, 4601, 4603, 4658.5 and 4658.6, Labor Code.

History: 1. Repealer and new section filed 7-11-89; operative 10-1-89 (Register 89, No. 28).

2. Amendment of section heading, section and Note filed 7-7-2004; operative 8-1-2004 pursuant to Government Code section 11343.4 (Register 2004, No. 28).

Ref.: Hanna §§ 4.25[5], 22.01[3]; Herlick Handbook §§ 1.6, 8.7, 9.3.

§9881.1. Notice to Employees Poster.

STATE OF CALIFORNIA - DEPARTMENT OF INDUSTRIAL RELATIONS
Division of Workers' Compensation

Notice to Employees—Injuries Caused By Work

You may be entitled to workers' compensation benefits if you are injured or become ill because of your job. Workers' compensation covers most work-related physical or mental injuries and illnesses. An injury or illness can be caused by one event (such as hurting your back in a fall) or by repeated exposures (such as hurting your wrist from doing the same motion over and over).

Benefits. Workers' compensation benefits include:

- **Medical Care:** Doctor visits, hospital services, physical therapy, lab tests, x-rays, and medicines that are reasonably necessary to treat your injury. You should never see a bill. For injuries occurring on or after 1/1/04, there is a limit on some medical services.
- **Temporary Disability (TD) Benefits:** Payments if you lose wages while recovering.
- **Permanent Disability (PD) Benefits:** Payments if your injury causes a permanent disability.
- **Vocational Rehabilitation:** Services and payments if your injury prevents you from returning to your usual job or occupation. This benefit applies to injuries that occurred prior to 1/1/04.
- **Supplemental Job Displacement Benefit:** A nontransferable voucher payable to a state approved school if you are injured on or after 1/1/04, the injury results in a permanent disability, you don't return to work within 60 days after TD ends, and your employer does not offer modified or alternative work.
- **Death Benefits:** Paid to dependents of a worker who dies from a work-related injury or illness.

Naming Your Own Physician Before Injury. You may be able to choose the doctor who will treat you for a job injury or illness during the first 30 days after the injury. If eligible, you must tell your employer, in writing, the name and address of your personal physician *before* you are injured. For instructions, see the written information about workers' compensation that your employer is now required to give to new employees.

If You Get Hurt:

1. **Get Medical Care.** If you need first aid, contact your employer. If you need emergency care, call for help immediately. Emergency phone numbers:

   Ambulance ____________ Fire Dept. ____________ Police ____________

   Doctor ____________ Hospital ____________

2. **Report Your Injury.** Report the injury immediately to your supervisor or to.
   Employer representative ____________ phone number ____________.
   Don't delay. There are time limits. If you wait too long, you may lose your right to benefits. Your employer is required to provide you a claim form within one working day after learning about your injury. Within one working day after an employee files a claim form, the employer shall authorize the provision of all treatment, consistent with the applicable treating guidelines, for the alleged injury and shall continue to provide treatment until the date that liability for the claim is accepted or rejected. Until the date the claim is accepted or rejected, liability for medical treatment shall be limited to ten thousand dollars ($10,000).

3. **See Your Primary Treating Physician (PTP).** This is the doctor with overall responsibility for treating your injury or illness. If you named your personal physician before injury (see above), you may see him or her for treatment in certain circumstances. Otherwise, your employer has the right to select the physician who will treat you for the first 30 days. You may be able to switch to a doctor of your choice after 30 days. Special rules apply if your employer offers a Health Care Organization (HCO) or after 1/1/05, has a medical provider network. Contact your employer for more information.

Discrimination: It is illegal for your employer to punish or fire you for having a work injury or illness, for filing a claim, or testifying in another person's workers' compensation case. If proven, you may receive lost wages, job reinstatement, increased benefits, and costs and expenses up to limits set by the state.

Questions? Learn more about workers' compensation by reading the information that your employer is required to give you at time of hire. If you have questions, see your employer or the claims administrator (who handles workers' compensation claims for your employer):

Claims Administrator ____________

Address ____________ City ____________ State ____ Zip ____

Phone ____________ Policy Expiration Date ____________

The employer is insured for workers' compensation by ____________
(Enter "self-insured" if appropriate)

If the workers' compensation policy has expired, contact a Labor Commissioner at the Division of Labor Standards Enforcement - their number can be found in your local White Pages under California State Government, Department of Industrial Relations.

You can get free information from a State Division of Workers' Compensation Information & Assistance Officer. The nearest Information & Assistance Officer is at:

Address ____________ City ____________ Phone ____________

Hear recorded information and a list of local offices by calling toll-free (800) 736-7401. Learn more online: www.dir.ca.gov.

False claims and false denials. Any person who makes or causes to be made any knowingly false or fraudulent material statement or material representation for the purpose of obtaining or denying workers' compensation benefits or payments is guilty of a felony and may be fined and imprisoned.

Your employer may not be liable for the payment of workers' compensation benefits for any injury that arises from your voluntary participation in any **off-duty, recreational, social, or athletic activity** that is not part of your work-related duties.

DWC 7 (8/1/04)

ESTADO DE CALIFORNIA - DEPARTAMENTO DE RELACIONES INDUSTRIALES
Division De Compensación Al Trabajador

Aviso a los Empleados—Lesiones Causadas por el Trabajo

Es posible que usted tenga derecho a beneficios de compensación para trabajadores, si usted se lesiona o se enferma a causa de su trabajo. La compensación para trabajadores cubre la mayoría de las lesiones y enfermedades físicas o mentales relacionadas con el trabajo. Una lesión o enfermedad puede ser causada por un evento (como por ejemplo el lastimarse la espalda en una caida) o por acciones repetidas (como por ejemplo lastimarse la muñeca por hacer el mismo movimiento una y otra vez).

Beneficios. Los beneficios de compensación para trabajadores incluyen:

- **Atención Médica:** Consultas con el médico, servicios de hospital, terapia física, análisis de laboratorio, radiografías y medicinas que son razonablemente necesarias para tratar su lesión. Usted nunca deberá ver un cobro. Para lesiones que ocurren en o después de 1/1/04, hay un límite de visitas para ciertos servicios médicos.
- **Beneficios por Incapacidad Temporal** (TD): Pagos, si usted pierde sueldos, mientras se recupera.
- **Beneficios por Incapacidad Permanente (PD):** Pagos, si su lesión le ocasiona una incapacidad permanente.
- **Rehabilitación Vocacional:** Servicios y pagos, si su lesión no le permite regresar a su empleo u ocupación normal. Este beneficio para lesiones que ocurrieron antes de 1/1/04.
- **Beneficio Suplementario por Desplazamiento de Trabajo:** Unc vale no-transferible pagadero a una escuela aprobada por el estado si se lesiona en o después de 1/1/04, la lesión le ocasiona una incapacidad permanente, no regresa al trabajo en un plazo de 60 días después que los pagos por incapacidad temporal terminan, y su empleador no le ofrece un trabajo modificado o alterno.
- **Beneficios por Muerte:** Pagados a los dependientes de un(a) trabajador(a) que muera a causa de una lesión o enfermedad relacionada con el trabajo.

Designación de su Propio Médico Antes de una Lesión. Es posible que usted pueda elegir al médico que le atenderá a causa de una lesión o enfermedad relacionada con el trabajo durante los primeros 30 días después de la lesión. Si elegible, usted tiene que decirle al empleador, por escrito, el nombre y la dirección de su médico personal, *antes* de que usted se lesione. Para instrucciones, vea la información escrita sobre la compensación para trabajadores, que ahora se le exige a su empleador darle a los empleados nuevos.

Si Usted se Lastima:

1. **Obtenga Atención Médica.** Si usted necesita primeros auxilios, comuníquese con su empleador. Si usted necesita atención de emergencia, pida ayuda inmediatamente. Los números de teléfono de emergencia son:

   Ambulancia ______ Dept. de Bomberos ______ Policía ______

   Doctor ______ Hospital ______

2. **Reporte su Lesión.** Reporte la lesión inmediatamente a su supervisor(a) o a:
   El/la representante del empleador ______ Número de teléfono ______.
   No se demore. Hay límites de tiempo. Si usted espera demasiado, es posible que usted pierda su derecho a beneficios. A su empleador se le exige proporcionarle un formulario de reclamo, en un plazo de un dia laboral, a partir de que sepa lo referente a su lesión. El empleador autorizará todo tratamiento médico consistente con las directivas de tratamiento applicables a la lesión o enfermedad, durante el primer día laboral después que el empleado efectúa un reclamo para beneficios de compensación, y continuará proveyendo este tratamiento hasta la fecha en que el reclamo sea aceptado o rechazado. Hasta la fecha en que el reclamo sea aceptado o rechazado, el tratamiento médico será limitado a diez mil dólares ($10,000).

3. **Consulte al Médico Primario que le Atienda (PTP).** Este es el médico con toda la responsabilidad para dar el tratamiento para su lesión o enfermedad. Si usted designó a su médico personal antes de la lesión (vea uno de los párrafos anteriores), usted puede consultarlo para el tratamiento en ciertas circunstancias. De otra forma, su empleador tiene derecho a seleccionar al médico que le atenderá durante los primeros 30 días. Es posible que usted pueda cambiar al médico de su preferencia después de 30 días. Hay reglas especiales que son aplicables cuando su empleador ofrece una Organización del Cuidado Médico (HCO) o depués de 1/1/05 tiene un Sistema de Proveedores de Atención Médica. Hable con su empleador para más información.

Discriminación: Es ilegal que su empleador le castigue o despida por sufrir una lesión o enfermedad en el trabajo, por presentar un reclamo o por atestiguar en el caso de compensación para trabajadores de otra persona. Si es probado, puede ser que usted reciba pagos por pérdida de sueldos, reposición del trabajo, aumento de beneficios, y gastos hasta un límite establecido por el estado.

¿Preguntas? Obtenga más información sobre la compensación para trabajadores, leyendo la información que ahora se le exige a su empleador darle a los empleados nuevos. Si usted tiene preguntas, vea a su empleador o al/a la administrador(a) de reclamos (que maneja los reclamos de compensación para trabajadores por su empleador):

Administrador(a) de Reclamos ______

Dirección ______ Ciudad ______ Estado ____ Código postal ______

Teléfono ______ Fecha de Vencimiento de la Póliza ______

El empleador está asegurado para compensación para trabajadores con ______
(Anote "autoasegurado" si es pertinente)

Si la póliza de compensación para trabajadores se ha vencido, comuníquese con el Comisionado del Trabajo, en la Division of Labor Standards Enforcement. Su número puede encontrarse en las Páginas Blancas de su guía telefónica local, bajo el encabezado en inglés de *California State Government, Department of Industrial Relations*.

Usted puede obtener información gratuita de un Oficial de Asistencia e Información, de la División de Compensación al Trabajador. El Oficial de Asistencia e Información más cercano se localiza en:

Dirección ______ Ciudad ______ Teléfono ______

Usted puede escuchar información grabada, y una lista de las oficinas locales, llamando al número gratuito **(800) 736-7401.** Usted puede obtener más información en el Internet en: **www.dir.ca.gov.** Enlácese a la sección de Compensación para Trabajadores.

Los reclamos falsos y rechazos falsos del reclamo. Cualquier persona que haga o que ocasione que se haga una declaración o una representación relevante intencionalmente falsa o fraudulenta, con el fin de obtener, o negar beneficios o pagos de compensación para trabajadores, es culpable de un delito grave y puede resultar en una multa y encarcelación.

Es posible que su empleador o asegurador no sea responsible por el pago de beneficios de compensación laboral debido a una lesión causada por la participación voluntaria del empleado en cualquier **actividad recreativa, social, o atlética** fuera del trabajo que no sea parte de los deberes laborales del empleado.

DWC 7 (8/1/04)

Note: Authority cited: Sections 133, 138.3, 139.6, 3550 and 5307.3, Labor Code. Reference: Sections 3550, 4600, 4601, 4603, 4604.5, 4616, 4658.5 and 4658.6, Labor Code.

History: 1. New section filed 7-7-2004; operative 8-1-2004 pursuant to Government Code section 11343.4 (Register 2004, No. 28).

Ref.: Hanna § 22.01[3].

§9882. Repealed.

Note: Authority cited: Sections 133, 138.3, 138.4, 139.6, and 5402, Labor Code. Reference: Sections 132(a), 139.5, 3600, 4600, 4601, 4650, 4658, 4700, 4701, 4702, 4703, 4401–4411 and 5400–5412, Labor Code.

History: 1. Repealer and new section filed 7-11-89; operative 10-1-89 (Register 89, No. 28).

2. Repealer filed 7-7-2004; operative 8-1-2004 pursuant to Government Code section 11343.4 (Register 2004, No. 28).

§9883. Publication of Information, Approval, Spanish Translation.

(a) Insurers, employers or private enterprises may prepare and publish for their use or sale the Notice to Employees poster and/or the Written Notice to New Employees required by this Article upon prior approval of the form and content by the Administrative Director. The Notice to Employees poster and/or Written Notice to New Employees may include a logotype. The addition only of a logotype to a previously approved Notice to Employees poster or Written Notice to New Employees does not require additional approval.

(1) Any published Written Notice to New Employees shall be available in English and Spanish and shall include the information specified in Section 9880.

(2) Any published Notice to Employees poster shall be available in English and Spanish, where there are Spanish-speaking employees, and shall include the information specified in Section 9881.

(b) All matter published subsequent to the effective date of this regulation shall indicate that the written informational material has been approved by the Administrative Director.

(c) Publications other than those of the Administrative Director or the Workers' Compensation Appeals Board may reflect the employer, private publisher or insurance carrier identifier or logotype.

Note: Authority cited: Sections 133, 139.6, 3550, 3551 and 5307, Labor Code. Reference: Sections 139.6, 3550 and 3551, Labor Code.

History: 1. New section filed 7-27-79; effective thirtieth day thereafter (Register 79, No. 30).

2. Change without regulatory effect of NOTE filed 7-11-86; effective upon filing (Register 86, No. 28).

3. Repealer and new section filed 7-11-89; operative 10-1-89 (Register 89, No. 28).

4. Amendment of section and Note filed 7-7-2004; operative 8-1-2004 pursuant to Government Code section 11343.4 (Register 2004, No. 28).

Ref.: Hanna § 22.01[3]; Herlick Handbook § 1.6.

§9884. Exceptions.

The requirements of this article shall not apply to injuries where the employee files an application for adjudication of claim with the appeals board.

Note: Authority cited: Sections 138.4, Labor Code. Reference: Section 5402, Labor Code.

History: 1. New section filed 7-11-89; operative 10-1-89 (Register 89, No. 28).

2. Editorial correction to History 1 (Register 96, No. 52).

Ref.: Hanna § 24.01[2]; Herlick Handbook § 1.6.

ARTICLE 9
Computation of Life Pensions, Tables For

§9885. U. S. Life Tables. [Repealed]

Note: Authority cited: Sections 127, 133, 138.2, 138.3, 139.5, 139.6, 4603.2, 4603.5, 5307.1, 5307.3 and 5450–5455, Labor Code.

History: 1. New section filed 11-9-70; designated effective 1-1-71 (Register 70, No. 46).

2. Amendment filed 11-9-77; effective thirtieth day thereafter (Register 77, No. 46).

3. Amendment filed 8-29-84; effective thirtieth day thereafter (Register 84, No. 35).

4. Repealer of article 9 (section 9885) and section filed 1-17-2001; operative 1-17-2001 pursuant to Government Code section 11343.4(c) (Register 2001, No. 3).

Ref.: Herlick Handbook § 1.6.

ARTICLE 10
Employee Death, Notice of

§9900. Employer.

(a) Each employer shall notify the Administrative Director of the death of every employee, regardless of the cause of death, except where the employer has actual knowledge or notice that the deceased employee left a surviving minor child.

(b) Notification shall be made on the Division of Industrial Accidents Form 510, "Notice of Employee Death" (See Section 9910).

(c) The Notice of Employee Death shall be filed within 60 days of the employer's notice or knowledge of the employee death.

(d) The employer may forward the "Notice of Employee Death" to his workmens' compensation insurer for subsequent submission to the Administrative Director.

Note: Authority cited: Sections 133, 138.2, 138.3, 139.5, 139.6, 4603.2, 4603.5, 5307.1, 5307.3 and 5450–5455, Labor Code.

History: 1. Amendment of subsection (a) filed 11-9-77; effective thirtieth day thereafter (Register 77, No. 46) For prior history, see Register 73, No. 28.

Ref.: Hanna §§ 23.14[2][e], 25.20[6]; Herlick Handbook §§ 1.6, 7.18.

§9905. Notice.

If the Notice required in Section 9900 is incomplete or otherwise deficient, the Administrative Director may require a further explanation or additional information from the employer, or his insurance carrier.

Ref.: Hanna § 25.20[6]; Herlick Handbook § 1.6.

§9910. DIA Form 510: Notice of Employee Death.

STATE OF CALIFORNIA
DEPARTMENT OF INDUSTRIAL RELATIONS
DIVISION OF INDUSTRIAL ACCIDENTS

FORWARD TO
P.O. BOX 4,400
SAN FRANCISCO, CA 9414

NOTICE OF EMPLOYEE DEATH

EACH EMPLOYER SHALL NOTIFY THE ADMINISTRATIVE DIRECTOR OF THE DEATH OF EVERY EMPLOYEE, **REGARDLESS OF THE CAUSE OF DEATH**, EXCEPT WHERE THE EMPLOYER HAS ACTUAL KNOWLEDGE OR NOTICE THAT THE DECEASED EMPLOYEE LEFT A SURVIVING **MINOR CHILD** (TITLE 8, CHAPTER 4.5, SECTION 9900).

DECEASED EMPLOYEE:

NAME: ______________________ AGE: ______ SOCIAL SECURITY NUMBER: ______________

LAST KNOWN ADDRESS: ______________________

NAME, RELATIONSHIP AND LAST KNOWN ADDRESS OF NEXT OF KIN: ______________________

____

JOB TITLE AND NATURE OF DUTIES: ______________________

____

DATE, TIME AND PLACE OF ACCIDENT: ______________________

DATE, TIME AND PLACE OF DEATH: ______________________

CIRCUMSTANCES OF DEATH (DESCRIBE FULLY THE EVENTS WHICH RESULTED IN DEATH. TELL WHAT HAPPENED. USE ADDITIONAL SHEET IF NECESSARY):

____

CAUSE OF DEATH (ATTACH COPY OF DEATH CERTIFICATE OR CORONER'S REPORT):

____

HAVE ANY WORKERS' COMPENSATION DEATH BENEFITS BEEN PROVIDED IN CONNECTION WITH THIS DEATH? ____ YES ____ NO

(IF YES, TO WHOM: ______________________)

ATTACH A COPY OF THE FORM 5020, "EMPLOYER'S REPORT OF OCCUPATIONAL INJURY OR ILLNESS," IF ONE WAS FILED.

PLEASE NOTE:

IF THE DEATH IS WORK-CONNECTED, THE EMPLOYER ALSO IS REQUIRED TO REPORT THE DEATH:

TO HIS OR HER WORKERS' COMPENSATION INSURANCE CARRIER AND TO THE NEAREST OFFICE OF THE DIVISION OF INDUSTRIAL SAFETY IMMEDIATELY BY TELEPHONE OR TELEGRAPH. AN EMPLOYER'S REPORT OF OCCUPATIONAL INJURY OR ILLNESS SHOULD ALSO BE FILED WITH THE WORKERS' COMPENSATION INSURANCE CARRIER.

( ) INSURED ( ) SELF-INSURED ( ) LEGALLY UNINSURED

EMPLOYER: ______________________

STREET: ______________________

CITY/STATE: ______________ ZIP: ________

TELEPHONE: ______________________
(INCLUDE AREA CODE)

INSURANCE CARRIER OR ADJUSTING AGENT: ______________________

STREET: ______________________

CITY/STATE: ______________ ZIP: ________

TELEPHONE: ______________________
(INCLUDE AREA CODE)

BY: ______________________

TITLE: ______________________ DATE: ____________

DIA 510 (Rev. 9/84)

History: 1. Amendment filed 7-11-73 as an emergency; effective upon filing. Certificate of Compliance included (Register 73, No. 28).

2. Amendment filed 11-9-77; effective thirtieth day thereafter (Register 77, No. 46).

3. Repealer and new section filed 8-29-84; effective thirtieth day thereafter (Register 84, No. 35).

Ref.: Herlick Handbook § 1.6.

§9914. Reproduction of Form 510, Notice of Employee Death.

(a) Employers and insurers may reproduce DIA Form 510, in which the heading may be rearranged to permit printing of:

(1) The insurance carrier's or employer's name, address and telephone number.

(2) Instructions for forwarding the form and number of copies required.

(b) The spacing, arrangement, sequence or language shall not otherwise be altered.

History: 1. Amendment filed 7-11-73 as an emergency; effective upon filing. Certificate of Compliance included (Register 73, No. 28).

Ref.: Hanna § 25.20[6]; Herlick Handbook § 1.6.

§9918. Service on Administrative Director.

The Notice of Employee Death, DIA Form 510, shall be mailed to the Administrative Director, Division of Industrial Accidents, P.O. Box 422400, San Francisco, California 94142.

This P.O. Box is to be used only for the notices required in Section 9900 and not for any other functions of the Administrative Director or Division of Industrial Accidents.

Ref.: Hanna § 25.20[6]; Herlick Handbook § 1.6.

ARTICLE 10.5
Operation of the Information and Assistance Program of the Division of Workers' Compensation

§9921. Operative Date.

The provisions of this Article are effective immediately upon adoption.

Ref.: Herlick Handbook § 1.6.

§9922. Purpose.

This Article is being adopted to implement Section 139.6 and Article 2.5 of Part 4 of Division 4 of the Labor Code by providing that the State, through the Division of Workers' Compensation, establish an affirmative impartial service to employees, employers, claims administrators, labor unions, medical providers, and all others subject to or interested in the workers' compensation laws of the State of California. This service shall be provided so that all such parties are informed of the provisions of the workers' compensation laws, that benefits due are paid promptly, that disputes and misunderstandings are resolved informally insofar as possible, and that premature and unnecessary litigation be minimized.

Note: Authority cited: Sections 133, 139.6, 5307.3 and 5450, Labor Code. Reference: Sections 5450-5455, Labor Code.

History: 1. Amendment filed 2-16-95; operative 2-16-95. Submitted to OAL for printing only pursuant to Government Code section 11351 (Register 95, No. 7).

Ref.: Hanna §§ 1.12[11], 1.12[14], 23.03[1]; Herlick Handbook §§ 1.6, 1.9.

§9923. Designation.

(a) Pursuant to Labor Code Section 139.6, the Administrative Director shall appoint a person or persons thoroughly familiar with the Workers' Compensation Program in California to be responsible for informing the general public, labor unions, employees, employers, claims administrators, medical providers and all other interested parties of the rights, benefits and obligations of the workers' compensation law, including the creation and existence of the Information and Assistance Program.

(b) In each district office of the Division of Workers' Compensation (Workers' Compensation Appeals Board) and at the Division headquarters the Administrative Director shall appoint an Information and Assistance Officer, and such Deputy Information and Assistance Officers as the work of the district office and headquarters may require. The Administrative Director shall provide office facilities and clerical support appropriate to the functions of such Information and Assistance Officer.

Note: Authority cited: Sections 133, 139.6, 5307.3 and 5450, Labor Code. Reference: Sections 5450-5455, Labor Code.

History: 1. Amendment filed 2-16-95; operative 2-16-95. Submitted to OAL for printing only pursuant to Government Code section 11351 (Register 95, No. 7).

Ref.: Hanna §§ 1.12[11], 23.03[1]; Herlick Handbook §§ 1.6, 1.9.

§9924. Scope of Duties.

Each Information and Assistance Officer shall be responsible for the performance of the following duties:

(a) Provide continuing information concerning the rights, benefits and obligations under the workers' compensation laws of the State of California to employees, employers, medical providers, claims administrators and other interested parties.

(b) Assist in the prompt resolution of misunderstandings, disputes, and controversies arising out of claims for compensation, without formal proceedings, to the end that full and timely compensation benefits are furnished.

(c) Distribute such information pamphlets in English, Spanish and other languages as needed that have been prepared and approved by the Administrative Director to all inquiring employees and to such other parties that may request copies of the same.

(d) Establish and maintain liaison with the persons located in the geographic area served by the district office, with other affected State agencies, with organizations representing employees, employers, claims administrators and the medical community.

(e) Discharge such other duties consistent with the purposes of this Article as from time to time may be delegated by the Administrative Director.

Note: Authority cited: Sections 133, 139.6, 5307.3 and 5451, Labor Code. Reference: Sections 5450-5455, Labor Code.

History: 1. Amendment of subsections (a), (c) and (d) filed 2-16-95; operative 2-16-95. Submitted to OAL for printing only pursuant to Government Code section 11351 (Register 95, No. 7).

Ref.: Hanna §§ 1.12[11], 1.12[14], 23.03[1]; Herlick Handbook §§ 1.6, 1.9.

§9925. Use of Other Division Facilities.

In undertaking his or her duties, the Information and Assistance Officer may use the services of the Industrial Medical Council, the Disability Evaluation Unit, the Rehabilitation Unit, the Audit Unit and any other unit or units of the Division of Workers' Compensation available to aid in the resolution of disputes.

Copies of medical reports, permanent disability rating evaluations, earnings data and other pertinent information obtained by the Information and Assistance Officer shall be furnished to all parties involved in a dispute.

Note: Authority cited: Sections 133, 136.6, 5307.3 and 5451, Labor Code. Reference: Sections 5450-5455, Labor Code.

History: 1. Amendment filed 2-16-95; operative 2-16-95. Submitted to OAL for printing only pursuant to Government Code section 11351 (Register 95, No. 7).

Ref.: Hanna § 23.03[2][c]; Herlick Handbook §§ 1.6, 1.9.

§9926. Referrals to a Qualified Medical Evaluator.

Upon the submission of a matter to an Information and Assistance Officer, the Officer, with the agreement of a party to pay the cost and with the consent of an unrepresented employee, may request that the Administrative Director direct the injured employee to be examined by a Qualified Medical Evaluator selected by the Medical Director, within the scope of the qualified medical evaluator's professional training, for the purpose of addressing any pertinent clinical question other than those issues specified in Labor Code Section 4061.

Note: Authority cited: Sections 133, 139.6, 5307.3, 5451 and 5703.5(b), Labor Code. Reference: Sections 5450-5455, Labor Code.

History: 1. Amendment of section heading and section filed 2-16-95; operative 2-16-95. Submitted to OAL for printing only pursuant to Government Code section 11351 (Register 95, No. 7).

Ref.: Hanna §§ 1.12[2][a], 22.07[4], 23.03[2][c]; Herlick Handbook §§ 1.6, 1.9.

§9927. Jurisdiction.

(a) Any party to a claim may consult with an Information and Assistance Officer at any time to seek advice and assistance in the resolution of any misunderstanding, dispute, or controversy. The request for assistance need not be in writing, or be in any particular form, but it shall apprise the Information and Assistance Officer of the nature of the dispute and any other pertinent information to facilitate an appropriate inquiry by the Information and Assistance Officer. The Information and Assistance Officer shall communicate with the parties and provide information and assistance in resolving disputes.

(b) If an Application for Adjudication of Claim has been filed with the Workers' Compensation Appeals Board, any party may consult with an Information and Assistance Officer to seek assistance in resolving controverted issues or misunderstandings at any time prior to the filing of a Declaration of Readiness to Proceed. If the employee is not represented or by consent of the parties, the Information and Assistance Officer may continue to provide assistance after a filing of a Declaration of Readiness to Proceed.

(c) The Information and Assistance Officer shall provide assistance to asbestos workers in obtaining benefits from the Asbestos Workers' Account and/or the responsible employer pursuant to Section 4410 of the Labor Code.

(d) When the injured worker is not represented by an attorney or other representative, and either a Compromise and Release agreement or Stipulations with Request for Award, other than those presented at or subsequent to a regularly scheduled hearing, has been filed with the Workers' Compensation Appeals Board, the information and assistance officer shall: review the documents; contact the parties when indicated; coordinate with other units within the Division of Workers' Compensation; seek to determine that the employee is aware of the significance of the agreement; and make recommendations to the parties and the workers' compensation judge. The Manager of the Information and Assistance Unit shall notify the Presiding Workers' Compensation Judge when this service cannot be provided timely.

Note: Authority cited: Sections 133, 139.6 and 5307.3, Labor Code. Reference: Sections 5450–5455, Labor Code.

History: 1. Amendment filed 10-16-81; effective thirtieth day thereafter (Register 81, No. 42).

2. Amendment filed 7-15-83; effective thirtieth day thereafter (Register 83, No. 30).

3. Editorial correction of 7-15-83 order redesignating effective date to 8-1-83 pursuant to Government Code Section 11346.2(d) filed 7-19-83 (Register 83, No. 30).

4. Repealer of subsection (d), subsection relettering and amendment of newly designated subsection (d) filed 2-16-95; operative 2-16-95. Submitted to OAL for printing only pursuant to Government Code section 11351 (Register 95, No. 7).

Ref.: Hanna §§ 1.12[11], 1.12[12][b], 1.12[13], 23.03[2][b], 23.03[3]; Herlick Handbook §§ 1.6, 1.9.

§9928. Procedures for Mediation and Recommendations.

(a) The Information and Assistance Officer is not bound by technical or formal rules of procedure but may make inquiries into any matter referred to him or her in a manner best suited to protect the rights of all parties and to achieve substantial justice.

(b) When there is a dispute regarding the provision of workers' compensation benefits, the employee, claims administrator or any party may request the Information and Assistance Officer to mediate the dispute. The Information and Assistance Officer will attempt to resolve the dispute by mediation, which may include a conference. The officer shall make appropriate inquiries to determine the contentions of the parties, identify the matters which may prevent amicable resolution, and afford all parties an opportunity to present their positions.

(c) In the event a dispute is not resolved through mediation, the Information and Assistance Officer shall issue a recommendation as soon as possible.

(d) In order to toll the statutes of limitations pursuant to Section 5454 of the Labor Code, the Information and Assistance Officer must notify in writing all parties to any misunderstanding, dispute or controversy of the fact that said Information and Assistance Officer has taken under consideration the misunderstanding, dispute or controversy submitted to him or her for a recommendation.

(e) Upon issuing a recommendation, the Officer shall advise the parties of his or her recommendation in a written communication which describes in non-technical terms the nature of the differences, the proposed resolution and the rationale used in arriving at that resolution. The communication shall also advise the parties that the tolling of any applicable statute of limitations will cease 60 days after the issuance of the recommendation, and shall further advise the parties of their right to obtain a decision from the appeals board if the recommendation is not accepted by the parties. In the event a party does not accept the recommendation of the Information and Assistance Officer, the party must notify all other parties in writing within 30 days of receipt of the recommendation. Where the Information and Assistance Officer feels that further mediation may resolve the dispute, he or she will notify the parties of the availability of the Information and Assistance Officer to provide such further mediation.

Note: Authority cited: Sections 133, 139.6, 5307.3, 5451 and 5453, Labor Code. Reference: Sections 5450-5455, Labor Code.

History: 1. Amendment of section heading and subsections (b), (c) and (e) filed 2-16-95; operative 2-16-95. Submitted to OAL for printing only pursuant to Government Code section 11351 (Register 95, No. 7).

Ref.: Hanna §§ 1.12[12][a], 1.12[12][c], 23.03[2][d]; Herlick Handbook §§ 1.6, 1.9.

§9928.1. Procedures for Asbestos Workers.

When consulted by an asbestos worker or his/her representative, the Information and Assistance Officer shall aid the worker in procuring those records, reports and other information which are necessary for the identification of responsible employers and insurance carriers, and in obtaining information required by the Asbestos Workers' Account before payments may be made pursuant to Section 4406.

Note: Authority cited: Sections 5307.3 and 5451, Labor Code. Reference: Sections 139.6, 4410 and 5451, Labor Code.

History: 1. New section filed 10-16-81; effective thirtieth day thereafter (Register 81, No. 42).

Ref.: Hanna §§ 1.12[13], 23.03[3]; Herlick Handbook §§ 1.6, 1.9.

§9929. Costs.

(a) Except as otherwise provided by this Section or by Section 5452 of the Labor Code, no fees or costs shall be charged to any party for services provided by the Division of Industrial Accidents under this Article.

(b) If the employee is represented, such representative may request that the Information and Assistance Officer refer the matter to a Workers' Compensation Judge for the determination of the value of the services of such representative. The Information and Assistance Officer shall, thereafter, refer such request to the Presiding Judge of the office which has jurisdiction over the claim.

Ref.: Hanna §§ 1.12[11], 20.02[2][d], 23.03[2][e]; Herlick Handbook §§ 1.6, 1.9, 10.2.

ARTICLE 11
Document Copy and Electronic Transaction Fees

§9990. Fees for Transcripts; Copies of Documents; Certifications; Case File Inspection; Electronic Transactions.

The Division will charge and collect fees for copies of records or documents. For the purposes of this section, "records" includes any writing containing information relating to the conduct of the public's business which is prepared, owned, or used by the Division, regardless of the physical form or characteristics. "Writing" means handwriting, typewriting, printing, photostatting, photographing and every other means of recording any form of communication thereof, and all papers, maps, magnetic tapes, photographic films and prints, electronic facsimiles, any form of stored computer data, magnetic cards or disks, drums, and other documents.

Fees will be charged and collected by the Division as follows:

(a) For copies of papers, records or documents, not certified or otherwise authenticated, one dollar ($1.00) for the first copy and twenty cents ($0.20) for each additional copy of the same page, except to the injured worker to whom the fee will be ten cents ($.10) per page.

(1) State sales tax and postage will be added to this fee.

(b) For certification of copies of official records or documents and orders of evidence taken or proceedings had, ten dollars ($10.00) for each certification.

(1) Where the Division is requested to both copy and certify a document, the fee is the sum of the fees prescribed in (a) and (b) above.

(c) For paper transcripts of any testimony, three dollars ($3.00) for each page of the first copy of transcripts; thereafter, one dollar and fifty cents ($1.50) for each page of additional copies of the transcript.

(1) Sales tax and postage will be added to this fee.

(2) Transcripts delivered on a medium other than paper shall be compensated at the same rate set for paper transcripts, except an additional fee shall be charged to cover the cost of the medium and any copies thereof.

(d) For inspection of a case file not stored in the place where the inspection is requested, ten dollars ($10.00) plus any postage or other delivery costs, except when requested by an injured employee or his or her attorney or his or her representative of record.

(e) For electronic records maintained by the Division:

(1) Listing of WCAB new case filings:

(A) $305.00 per transmission for WCAB new case opening records transmitted to the requester on tape.

(B) $85.00 per download for WCAB new case opening records transmitted to the requester by direct electronic download.

Paper copies of the WCAB new case opening records provided in addition to the electronic data will be subject to a separate charge of $0.10 per page, plus postage.

(2) Electronic response to an electronic inquiry concerning a case's status, a lien's status, or other case specific information available in electronic form, through EDEX (the Division's Electronic Data Exchange program), twenty cents ($0.20) per transaction.

(3) The Division will provide electronic copies of WCAB new case opening records or EDEX access only pursuant to a written agreement with the administrative director.

(4) Copies of existing electronic records, other than those electronic records set forth in subsections (e)(1) or (e)(2), that constitute disclosable public records, will be provided as required by law, for the Division's actual costs of retrieving and transmitting the data, including programming and processing time, storage media, postage or shipping costs and sales tax. All programming and processing time required to create new data sorts of existing electronically maintained records will be charged at the Division's standard rate of $40.00 per hour, billed in fifteen (15) minute increments.

(f) Copies of Division records containing information that is privileged or otherwise nondisclosable will be redacted before release.

Note: Authority cited: Sections 127, 133, 138.7 and 5307.3, Labor Code. Reference: Sections 127 and 138.7, Labor Code.

History: 1. Amendment of subsection (a) filed 11-7-78; effective thirtieth day thereafter (Register 78, No. 45). For former history, see Registers 77, No. 46; 75, No. 32; and 73, No. 51.

2. Amendment filed 8-29-84; effective thirtieth day thereafter (Register 84, No. 35).

3. Amendment of article and section headings and text filed 1-28-94; operative 1-28-94 (Register 94, No. 4). Submitted to OAL for printing only pursuant to Government Code section 11351.

4. Amendment of section and Note filed 8-22-2000; operative 9-21-2000 (Register 2000, No. 34).

Ref.: Hanna §§ 23.13[1], 34.21[2]; Herlick Handbook § 1.6.

§9992. Payment of Fees in Advance.

Payment of fees in Section 9990 must accompany the request, either in cash or by check or money order made payable to the Division of Workers' Compensation, except as otherwise provided in the establishment of payment accounts.

Note: Authority cited: Sections 127, 133 and 5307.3, Labor Code. Reference: Section 127, Labor Code.

History: 1. Amendment filed 1-28-94; operative 1-28-94 (Register 94, No. 4). Submitted to OAL for printing only pursuant to Government Code section 11351.

Ref.: Hanna §§ 1.12[5][b], 23.13[1]; Herlick Handbook § 1.6.

§9994. Payment for Transcripts.

For transcripts of testimony or other proceeding of record, a deposit fee based on the number of paper pages, as estimated by the division, shall be paid by the requesting party in advance. If the actual fee exceeds the deposit, the purchaser will be notified of the balance to be paid prior to release of the transcripts or any copies. Any excess deposit will be returned to the purchaser.

Note: Authority cited: Sections 127, 133 and 5307.3, Labor Code. Reference: Section 127, Labor Code.

History: 1. Amendment of section heading and text filed 1-28-94; operative 1-28-94 (Register 94, No. 4). Submitted to OAL for printing only pursuant to Government Code section 11351.

Ref.: Hanna § 23.13[1]; Herlick Handbook § 1.6.

ARTICLE 12
Return to Work

§10001. Definitions.

As used in this Article:

(a) "Alternative work" means work (1) offered either by the employer who employed the injured worker at the time of injury, or by another employer where the previous employment was seasonal work, (2) that the employee has the ability to perform, (3) that offers wages and compensation that are at least 85 percent of those paid to the employee at the time of injury, and (4) that is located within a reasonable commuting distance of the employee's residence at the time of injury.

(b) "Claims Administrator" means a self-administered insurer providing security for the payment of compensation required by Divisions 4 and 4.5 of the Labor Code, a self-administered self-insured employer, a self-administered joint powers authority, a self-administered legally uninsured, or a third-party claims administrator for a self-insured employer, insurer, legally uninsured employer, or joint powers authority.

(c) "Modified Work" means regular work modified so that the employee has the ability to perform all the functions of the job and that offers wages and compensation that are at least 85 percent of those paid to the employee at the time of injury, and located within a reasonable commuting distance of the employee's residence at the time of injury.

(d) "Permanent and stationary" means the point in time when the employee has reached maximal medical improvement, meaning his or her condition is well stabilized, and unlikely to change substantially in the next year with or without medical treatment, based on (1) an opinion from a treating physician, AME, or QME; (2) a judicial finding by a Workers' Compensation Administrative Law Judge, the Workers' Compensation Appeals Board, or a court; or (3) a stipulation that is approved by a Workers' Compensation Administrative Law Judge or the Workers' Compensation Appeals Board.

(e) "Regular Work" means the employee's usual occupation or the position in which the employee was engaged at the time of injury and that offers wages and compensation equivalent to those paid to the employee at the time of injury, and located within a reasonable commuting distance of the employee's residence at the time of injury.

(f) "Seasonal Work" means employment as a daily hire, a project hire, or an annual season hire.

Note: Authority cited: Sections 133, 139.48 and 5307.3, Labor Code. Reference: Sections 139.48 and 4658.1, Labor Code; *Henry v. WCAB* (1998) 68 Cal.App.4th 981.

History: 1. New section filed 6-30-2006; operative 7-1-2006. Submitted to OAL for filing with the Secretary of State and printing only pursuant to Government Code section 11340.9(g) (Register 2006, No. 38). For prior history, see Register 96, No. 52.

Ref.: Hanna § 7.02[3][d][i]–[iv]; Herlick Handbook § 5.20.

§10002. Offer of Work; Adjustment of Permanent Disability Payments.

(a) This section shall apply to all injuries occurring on or after January 1, 2005, and to the following employers:

(1) Insured employers who employed 50 or more employees at the time of the most recent policy inception or renewal date for the insurance policy that was in effect at the time of the employee's injury;

(2) Self-insured employers who employed 50 or more employees at the time of the most recent filing by the employer of the Self-Insurer's Annual Report that was in effect at the time of the employee's injury; and

(3) Legally uninsured employers who employed 50 or more employees at the time of injury.

(b) Within 60 calendar days from the date that the condition of an injured employee with permanent partial disability becomes permanent and stationary:

(1) If an employer does not serve the employee with a notice of offer of regular work, modified work or alternative work for a period of at least 12 months, each payment of permanent partial disability remaining to be paid to the employee from the date of the end of the 60 day period shall be paid in accordance with Labor Code section 4658(d)(1) and increased by 15 percent.

(2) If an employer serves the employee with a notice of offer of regular work, modified work or alternative work for a period of at least 12 months, and in accordance with the requirements set forth in paragraphs (3) and (4), each payment of permanent partial disability remaining to be paid from the date the offer was served on the employee shall be paid in accordance with Labor Code section 4658(d)(1) and decreased by 15 percent, regardless of whether the employee accepts or rejects the offer.

(3) The employer shall use Form DWC-AD 10133.53 (Section 10133.53) to offer modified or alternative work, or Form DWC-AD 10003 (Section 10003) to offer regular work. The claims administrator may serve the offer of work on behalf of the employer.

(4) The regular, alternative, or modified work that is offered by the employer pursuant to paragraph (2) shall be located within a reasonable commuting distance of the employee's residence at the time of the injury, unless the employee waives this condition. This condition shall be deemed to be waived if the employee accepts the regular, modified, or alternative work, and does not object to the location within 20 calendar days of being informed of the right to object. The condition shall be conclusively deemed to be satisfied if the offered work is at the same location and the same shift as the employment at the time of injury.

(c) If the claims administrator relies upon a permanent and stationary date contained in a medical report prepared by the employee's treating physician, QME, or AME, but there is subsequently a dispute as to an employee's permanent and stationary status, and there has been a notice of offer of work served on the employee in accordance with subdivision (b), the claims administrator may withhold 15% from each payment of permanent partial disability remaining to be paid from the date the notice of offer was served on the employee until there has been a final judicial determination of the date that the employee is permanent and stationary pursuant to Labor Code section 4062.

(1) Where there is a final judicial determination that the employee is permanent and stationary on a date later than the date relied on by the employer in making its offer of work, the employee shall be reimbursed any amount withheld up to the date a new notice of offer of work is served on the employee pursuant to subdivision (b).

(2) Where there is a final judicial determination that the employee is not permanent and stationary, the employee shall be reimbursed any amount withheld up to the date of the determination.

(3) The claims administrator is not required to reimburse permanent partial disability benefit payments that have been withheld pursuant to this subdivision during any period for which the employee is entitled to temporary disability benefit payments.

(d) If the employee's regular work, modified work, or alternative work that has been offered by the employer pursuant to paragraph (1) of subdivision (b) and has been accepted by the employee, is terminated prior to the end of the period for which permanent partial disability benefits are due, the amount of each remaining permanent partial disability payment from the date of the termination shall be paid in accordance with Labor Code section 4658 (d) (1), as though no decrease in payments had been imposed, and increased by 15 percent. An employee who voluntarily terminates his or her regular work, modified work, or alternative work shall not be eligible for the 15 percent increase in permanent partial disability payments pursuant to this subdivision.

(e) Nothing in this section shall prevent the parties from settling or agreeing to commute the permanent disability benefits to which an employee may be entitled. However, if the permanent disability benefits are commuted by a Workers' Compensation Administrative Law Judge or the Workers' Compensation Appeals Board pursuant to Labor Code section 5100, the commuted sum shall account for any adjustment that would have been required by this section if payment had been made pursuant to Labor Code section 4658.

(f) When the employer offers regular, modified or alternative work to the employee that meets the conditions of this section and subsequently learns that the employee cannot lawfully perform regular, modified or alternative work, the employer is not required to provide the regular, modified or alternative work.

(g) If the employer offers regular, modified, or alternative seasonal work to the employee, the offer shall meet the following requirements:

(1) the employee was hired for seasonal work prior to injury;

(2) the offer of regular, modified or alternative seasonal work is of reasonably similar hours and working conditions to the employee's previous employment, and the one year requirement may be satisfied by cumulative periods of seasonal work;

(3) the work must commence within 12 months of the date of the offer; and

(4) The offer meets the conditions set forth in this section.

Note: Authority cited: Sections 133, 139.48 and 5307.3, Labor Code. Reference: Sections 139.48 and 4658, Labor Code; *Del Taco v. WCAB* (2000) 79 Cal.App.4th 1437; *Anzelde v. WCAB* (1996) 61 Cal. Comp. Cases 1458 (Writ denied); and *Henry v. WCAB* (1998) 68 Cal.App.4th 981.

History: 1. New section filed 6-30-2006; operative 7-1-2006. Submitted to OAL for filing with the Secretary of State and printing only pursuant to

Government Code section 11340.9(g) (Register 2006, No. 38). For prior history, see Register 96, No. 52.

Ref.: Hanna § 7.02[3][d][i]–[iv]; Herlick Handbook § 5.20.

§10003. Form [DWC AD 10003 Notice of Offer of Work].

DWC-AD 10003 NOTICE OF OFFER OF REGULAR WORK
For injuries occurring on or after 1/1/05

THIS SECTION TO BE COMPLETED BY EMPLOYER OR CLAIMS ADMINISTRATOR:

Claims Administrator:____________________ Claim Number:____________
(Name of Claims Administrator)

Based on the opinion of__treating physician QME AME____________, you are able to return to
(Name of Physician)

your usual occupation or the position you held at the time of your injury on____________.
(Date)

Date you are eligible to return to job:____________(as stated in the above physician's report)

Employer:____________________
(Name of Firm)

Job Title:____________________

Starting Date:____________________

__ This position is at the same location and shift as your pre-injury position.

__ This position is at a different location than your pre-injury position, as follows:____________

____

__ This position is for a different shift than your pre-injury position, as follows:____________
(start time) (end time)

You may contact ____________________concerning this position. Phone No.:____________
(Name of Contact Person)

You must return the completed form to the employer or claims administrator listed here:

____
(Name of Employer or Claims Administrator) (Mailing address)

This position is expected to last for a total of at least 12 months of work. If this position does not last for a total of at least 12 months of work, you may be entitled to an increase in your permanent disability benefit payments.

This position provides wages and compensation of $____________, that are equivalent to or more than the wages and compensation paid to you at the time of your injury.

I,____________________, have obtained the above job offer information from your employer.
(Name of Claims Administrator)

If the job offered is at a different location than the job you held at the time of your injury, and you believe the commuting distance to this job from the residence where you lived at the time of your injury is not reasonable, you may object to the job offer as not being within a reasonable commuting distance. You may also waive this commuting distance requirement. You will be considered to have waived this requirement if you accept the above offer of work or do not reject the offer within twenty calendar days of receipt of this notice.

MANDATORY FORMAT
STATE OF CALIFORNIA
September 2006
8 CCR 10003

Page1 of 3

THIS SECTION TO BE COMPLETED BY EMPLOYEE: **Claim Number**____________________

The employee must accept, reject, or object to this offer for regular work and return this form to the employer or claims administrator listed on page one within 20 calendar days of receipt of the offer or it will be deemed that the employee has waived the right to object to the location or shift. The employee should keep a copy of this form for his or her records.

Name of employee:________________________ Date offer received:____________________

I understand that if my disability is permanent and stationary and the employer has fulfilled its legal obligations related to this offer, my remaining permanent disability payments will be decreased by 15% whether I accept or reject this offer.

Offer of Regular Work at Same Location and/or Shift

__ I accept this offer of regular work.

__ I reject this offer of work. Reason:____

Note: If either party has a dispute or objection regarding the offer of regular work, or if the employee rejects the offer of regular work, that party may file a Declaration of Readiness with the local district office of the Workers' Compensation Appeals Board (WCAB).

Offer of Regular Work at a Different Location and/or Shift

I understand that I have the right to object to a work offer when the location or shift is different than what I had at the time of my injury.

__ I accept the offer and waive my right to object to the job location or shift as not being within a reasonable commuting distance from the residence where I lived at the time of my injury.

__ I reject this offer of work. Reason: ____

__ I object to this offer because the job location that has been offered is different than the job location I held at the time of my injury, and I do not believe this job allows a reasonable commute from my residence. I understand if the claims administrator does not agree with this objection, my remaining permanent disability weekly benefit payment may be decreased by 15%.

__ I object to this offer because the job shift that has been offered is different than the job shift I held at the time of my injury. I understand if the claims administrator does not agree with this objection, my remaining permanent disability weekly benefit payment may be decreased by 15%.

Note: If either party has a dispute or objection regarding the offer of regular work, or if the employee rejects the offer of regular work, that party may file a Declaration of Readiness with the local district office of the Workers' Compensation Appeals Board (WCAB).

________________________________ Date: ____________________
Signature

Page 2 of 3

Proof of Service By Mail or Hand Delivery

I am a resident of the County of ______________________. I am over the age of eighteen years and not a party to the within matter. My business address is:

____.

On ________________________, I served the **Notice of Offer of Regular Work** on the party/parties listed below by either method of service described below:

A. Placing a true copy of the **Notice of Offer of Regular Work** in a sealed envelope with postage fully prepaid addressed to each person whose name and address is given below by depositing the envelope in the United States mail.

Or

B. Personally serving a true copy of the **Notice of Offer of Regular Work** on each person whose name and address is given below.

Enter the name of the party and indicate the type of service in the box (either A or B as described above.)

Name of Party:	Type of Service
______________________________	☐
______________________________	☐
______________________________	☐
______________________________	☐

I declare under penalty of perjury under the laws of the State of California that the foregoing is true and correct.

Executed at

______________________________ on ______________________.

Signature: ______________________________

MANDATORY FORMAT
STATE OF CALIFORNIA
September 2006
8 CCR 10003

Page 3 of 3

Note: Authority cited: Sections 133, 139.48 and 5307.3, Labor Code. Reference: Sections 139.48 and 4658, Labor Code.

History: 1. New section filed 6-30-2006; operative 7-1-2006. Submitted to OAL for filing with the Secretary of State and printing only pursuant to Government Code section 11340.9(g) (Register 2006, No. 38). For prior history, see Register 96, No. 52.

Ref.: Hanna § 7.02[3][d][i]–[iv]; Herlick § 5.20.

§10004. Return to Work Program.

(a) This section shall apply to injuries occurring on or after July 1, 2004;

(b) An "Eligible Employer" means any employer, except the state or an employer eligible to secure the payment of compensation pursuant to subdivision (c) of Section 3700, who, based on the employer's payroll records or other equivalent documentation or evidence, employed 50 or fewer full-time employees on the date of injury.

(c) "Full-time employee" means an employee who, during the period of his or her employment within the year preceding the injury, worked an average of 32 or more hours per week.

(d) The Return to Work Program is administered by the Administrative Director for the purpose of promoting the employee's early and sustained return to work following a work-related injury or illness.

(e) This program shall be funded by the Return to Work Fund, which shall consist of all penalties collected pursuant to Labor Code section 5814.6 and transfers made to this fund by the Administrative Director from the Workers' Compensation Administrative Revolving Fund established pursuant to Labor Code section 62.5. The reimbursement offered to eligible employees as set forth in this section shall be available only to the extent funds are available.

(f) An eligible employer shall be entitled to reimbursement through this program for expenses incurred to make workplace modifications to accommodate an employee's return to modified or alternative work, up to the following maximum amounts:

(1) $1,250 to accommodate each temporarily disabled employee, for expenses incurred in allowing such employee to perform modified or alternative work within physician-imposed temporary work restrictions; and

(2) $2,500 to accommodate each permanently disabled employee, for expenses incurred in returning such employee to sustained modified or alternative work within physician-imposed permanent work restrictions; however, if an employer who has received reimbursement for a temporarily disabled employee under paragraph (1) is also requesting reimbursement for the same employee for accommodation of permanent disability, the maximum available reimbursement is $2,500. For the purpose of this subdivision, "sustained modified or alternative work" is work anticipated to last at least 12 months.

(g) Reimbursement shall be provided for any of the following expenses, provided they are specifically prescribed by a physician or are reasonably required by restrictions set forth in a medical report:

(1) modification to worksite;

(2) equipment;

(3) furniture;

(4) tools; or

(5) any other necessary costs reasonably required to accommodate the employee's restrictions.

(h) An eligible employer seeking reimbursement pursuant to subdivision (d) shall submit a "Request for Reimbursement of Accommodation Expenses" (Form DWC AD 10005, section 10005) to the Division of Workers' Compensation Return to Work Program within ninety (90) calendar days from the date of the expenditure for which the employer is seeking reimbursement. As a condition to reimbursement, the expenditure shall not have been paid or covered by the employer's insurer or any source of funding other than the employer. The filing date may be extended upon a showing of good cause for such extension. The employer shall attach to its request copies of all pertinent medical reports that contain the work restrictions being accommodated, any other documentation supporting the request, and all receipts for accommodation expenses. Requests should be sent to the mailing address for the Division of Workers' Compensation Return to Work Program that is listed in the web site of the Division of Workers' Compensation, at:

http://www.dir.ca.gov/dwc/dwc_home_page.htm

(i) The Administrative Director or his or her designee shall review each "Request for Reimbursement of Accommodation Expenses," and within sixty (60) business days of receipt shall provide the employer with notice of one of the following:

(1) that the request has been approved, together with a check for the reimbursement allowed, and an explanation of the allowance, if less than the maximum amounts set forth in subdivision (d); or

(2) that the request has been denied, with an explanation of the basis for denial; or

(3) that the request is deficient or incomplete and indicating what clarification or additional information is necessary.

(j) In the event there are insufficient funds in the Return to Work Fund to fully reimburse an employer or employers for workplace modification expenses as required by this section, the Administrative Director shall utilize the following priority list in establishing the amount of reimbursement or whether reimbursement is allowed, in order of decreasing priority as follows:

(1) Employers who have not previously received any reimbursement under this program;

(2) Employers who have not previously received any reimbursement under this program for the employee who is the subject of the request;

(3) Employers who are seeking reimbursement for accommodation required in returning a permanently disabled employee to sustained modified or alternative work; and,

(4) Employers who are requesting reimbursement for accommodation required by a temporarily disabled employee.

(k) An eligible employer may appeal the Administrative Director's notice under subdivision (i) by filing a Declaration of Readiness to Proceed with the local district office of the Workers' Compensation Appeals Board within twenty calendar days of the issuance of the notice, together with a petition entitled "Appeal of Administrative Director's Reimbursement Allowance," setting forth the basis of the appeal. A copy of the Declaration of Readiness to Proceed and the petition shall be concurrently served on the Administrative Director.

Note: Authority cited: Sections 133, 139.48 and 5307.3, Labor Code. Reference: Sections 62.5, 139.48 and 5814.6, Labor Code.

History: 1. New article 12 (sections 10004-10005) and section filed 7-19-2006; operative 8-18-2006 (Register 2006, No. 29). For prior history of article 12 (sections 10001-10021), see Register 88, No. 21; Register 95, No. 7 and Register 96, No. 52.

Ref.: Hanna § 7.02[3][d][i]–[iv]; Herlick § 5.20.

§10005. Form [DWC AD 10005 Request for Reimbursement of Accommodation Expenses].

Request for Reimbursement of Accommodation Expenses
For injuries on or after July 1, 2004
Form DWC AD 10005

Name of Employer: ______________ Address of Employer: ______________

Phone Number: ______________ Name of Injured Employee: ______________

WCAB number (if applicable): ______________ Claim Number ______________

Job Title (at time of injury): ______________

Job Duties (attach job description if available): ______________

Date of Injury: ______________

Reimbursement is requested for expenses to accommodate a:

_____ temporarily disabled employee ($1250 maximum)

_____ permanently disabled employee ($2500 maximum)

Employee's work restrictions and accommodation required (attach treating physician's, QME or AME report):

Itemized list of costs for which reimbursement is requested (attach all receipts):

1. Modification to worksite (list all work done and total cost) Cost

2. Equipment, furniture and/or tools (list each item and cost) Cost

3. Any other accommodation expenses: Cost

(Attach additional sheets if necessary)

Total Costs: ______________

The above costs have not been paid for and are not covered by the insurance carrier or any other source.

I declare that the information I have provided on this form is true and correct under penalty of perjury.

Signature of employer or employer's representative ______________ Date ______________

Form DWC AD 10005 (August 18, 2006)

MANDATORY FORMAT
STATE OF CALIFORNIA
8 CCR Section 10005

Note: Authority cited: Sections 133, 139.48 and 5307.3, Labor Code. Reference: Sections 62.5, 139.48 and 5814.6, Labor Code.

History: 1. New section filed 7-19-2006; operative 8-18-2006 (Register 2006, No. 29). For prior history, see Register 96, No. 52.

Ref.: Hanna § 7.02[3][d][i]–[iv]; Herlick Handbook § 5.20.

§10006. Notice to Employee. [Repealed]

Note: Authority cited: Sections 133, 138.4, 139.5 and 5307.3, Labor Code. Reference: Chapter 1435, 1974 Stats.

History: 1. Repealer and new section filed 5-17-88; operative 7-1-88 (Register 88, No. 21). For prior history, see Register 83, No. 30.

2. Repealer of section filed 12-27-96; operative 12-27-96. Submitted to OAL for printing only pursuant to Government Code section 11351 (Register 96, No. 52).

§10007. Reports to Bureau. [Repealed]

Note: Authority cited: Sections 133, 138.4, 139.5 and 5307.3, Labor Code. Reference: Chapter 1435, 1974 Stats.

History: 1. Repealer and new section filed 5-17-88; operative 7-1-88 (Register 88, No. 21). For prior history, see Register 83, No. 30.

2. Repealer of section filed 12-27-96; operative 12-27-96. Submitted to OAL for printing only pursuant to Government Code section 11351 (Register 96, No. 52).

§10007.1. Entitlement Issues. [Repealed]

Note: Authority cited: Section 139.5, Labor Code. Reference: Section 133, Labor Code.

History: 1. New section filed 6-15-81; effective thirtieth day thereafter (Register 81, No. 25).

2. Repealer filed 5-17-88; operative 7-1-88 (Register 88, No. 21).

§10008. Identification of Need for Vocational Rehabilitation Services. [Repealed]

Note: Authority cited: Sections 133, 138.4, 139.5 and 5307.3, Labor Code. Reference: Chapter 1435, 1974 Stats.

History: 1. Repealer and new section filed 5-17-88; operative 7-1-88 (Register 88, No. 21). For prior history, see Register 83, No. 30.

2. Repealer of section filed 12-27-96; operative 12-27-96. Submitted to OAL for printing only pursuant to Government Code section 11351 (Register 96, No. 52).

§10009. Initiation of Vocational Rehabilitation Services. [Repealed]

Note: Authority cited: Sections 133, 138.4, 139.5 and 5307.3, Labor Code. Reference: Chapter 1435, 1974 Stats.

History: 1. Repealer and new section filed 5-17-88; operative 7-1-88 (Register 88, No. 21). For prior history, see Register 79, No. 30.

2. Repealer of section filed 12-27-96; operative 12-27-96. Submitted to OAL for printing only pursuant to Government Code section 11351 (Register 96, No. 52).

§10010. Independent Vocational Evaluators. [Repealed]

Note: Authority cited: Sections 133, 138.4, 139.5 and 5307.3, Labor Code. Reference: Chapter 1435, 1974 Stats.

History: 1. Repealer and new section filed 5-17-88; operative 7-1-88 (Register 88, No. 21). For prior history, see Register 75, No. 1.

2. Repealer of section filed 12-27-96; operative 12-27-96. Submitted to OAL for printing only pursuant to Government Code section 11351 (Register 96, No. 52).

§10011. Vocational Rehabilitation Plans. [Repealed]

Note: Authority cited: Sections 133, 138.4, 139.5 and 5307.3, Labor Code. Reference: Chapter 1435, 1974 Stats.

History: 1. Repealer and new section filed 5-17-88; operative 7-1-88 (Register 88, No. 21). For prior history, see Register 83, No. 30.

2. Repealer of section filed 12-27-96; operative 12-27-96. Submitted to OAL for printing only pursuant to Government Code section 11351 (Register 96, No. 52).

§10012. Plan Approval. [Repealed]

Note: Authority cited: Sections 133, 138.4, 139.5 and 5307.3, Labor Code. Reference: Chapter 1435, 1974 Stats.

History: 1. Repealer and new section filed 5-17-88; operative 7-1-88 (Register 88, No. 21). For prior history, see Register 79, No. 30.

2. Repealer of section filed 12-27-96; operative 12-27-96. Submitted to OAL for printing only pursuant to Government Code section 11351 (Register 96, No. 52).

§10013. Entitlement Issues. [Repealed]

Note: Authority cited: Sections 133, 138.4, 139.5 and 5307.3, Labor Code. Reference: Chapter 1435, 1974 Stats.

History: 1. Repealer and new section filed 5-17-88; operative 7-1-88 (Register 88, No. 21). For prior history, see Register 83, No. 30.

2. Repealer of section filed 12-27-96; operative 12-27-96. Submitted to OAL for printing only pursuant to Government Code section 11351 (Register 96, No. 52).

§10014. Bureau Resolution of Disputes. [Repealed]

Note: Authority cited: Sections 133, 138.4, 139.5 and 5307.3, Labor Code. Reference: Chapter 1435, 1974 Stats.

History: 1. Repealer and new section filed 5-17-88; operative 7-1-88 (Register 88, No. 21). For prior history, see Register 79, No. 30. (c)

2. Repealer of section filed 12-27-96; operative 12-27-96. Submitted to OAL for printing only pursuant to Government Code section 11351 (Register 96, No. 52).

§10015. Interruption of Services. [Repealed]

Note: Authority cited: Sections 133, 138.4, 139.5 and 5307.3, Labor Code. Reference: Chapter 1435, 1974 Stats.

History: 1. Repealer and new section filed 5-17-88; operative 7-1-88 (Register 88, No. 21). For prior history, see Register 83, No. 30.

2. Repealer of section filed 12-27-96; operative 12-27-96. Submitted to OAL for printing only pursuant to Government Code section 11351 (Register 96, No. 52).

§10016. Conclusion of Vocational Rehabilitation Services. [Repealed]

Note: Authority cited: Sections 133, 138.4, 139.5 and 5307.3, Labor Code. Reference: Chapter 1435, 1974 Stats.

History: 1. Repealer and new section filed 5-17-88; operative 7-1-88 (Register 88, No. 21). For prior history, see Register 83, No. 30.

2. Repealer of section filed 12-27-96; operative 12-27-96. Submitted to OAL for printing only pursuant to Government Code section 11351 (Register 96, No. 52).

§10017. Reinstatement of Vocational Rehabilitation Benefits. [Repealed]

Note: Authority cited: Sections 133, 138.4, 139.5 and 5307.3, Labor Code. Reference: Chapter 1435, 1974 Stats.

History: 1. Repealer and new section filed 5-17-88; operative 7-1-88 (Register 88, No. 21). For prior history, see Register 83, No. 30.

2. Repealer of section filed 12-27-96; operative 12-27-96. Submitted to OAL for printing only pursuant to Government Code section 11351 (Register 96, No. 52).

§10018. Vocational Rehabilitation Temporary Disability Indemnity. [Repealed]

Note: Authority cited Sections 133, 138.4, 139.5 and 5307.3, Labor Code. Reference: Chapter 1435, 1974 Stats.

History: 1. New section filed 5-17-88; operative 7-1-88 (Register 88, No. 21).

2. Repealer of section filed 12-27-96; operative 12-27-96. Submitted to OAL for printing only pursuant to Government Code section 11351 (Register 96, No. 52).

§10019. Bureau File Retention.

Note: Authority cited: Sections 133, 138.4, 139.5 and 5307.3, Labor Code. Reference: Chapter 1435, 1974 Stats.

History: 1. New section filed 5-17-88; operative 7-1-88 (Register 88, No. 21).

2. Renumbering and amendment of former section 10019 to section 10134 filed 2-16-95; operative 2-16-95. Submitted to OAL for printing only pursuant to Government Code §11351 (Register 95, No. 7).

§10020. Enforcement of Notice and Reporting Requirements. [Repealed]

Note: Authority cited: Sections 133, 138.4, 139.5 and 5307.3, Labor Code. Reference: Chapter 1435, 1974 Stats.

History: 1. New section filed 5-17-88; operative 7-1-88 (Register 88, No. 21).

2. Repealer of section filed 12-27-96; operative 12-27-96. Submitted to OAL for printing only pursuant to Government Code section 11351 (Register 96, No. 52).

§10021. Rehabilitation of Industrially Injured Inmates.

Note: Authority cited: Sections 133, 138.4, 139.5 and 5307.3, Labor Code. Reference: Chapter 1435, 1974 Stats.

History: 1. New section filed 5-17-88; operative 7-1-88 (Register 88, No. 21).

2. Renumbering of former section 10021 to new section 10133.4 filed 12-27-96; operative 12-27-96. Submitted to OAL for printing only pursuant to Government Code section 11351 (Register 96, No. 52).

SUBCHAPTER 1.5 INJURIES ON OR AFTER JANUARY 1, 1990

ARTICLE 1 Audit, General Definitions

§10100. Definitions—Prior to January 1, 1994.

The following definitions apply in Articles 1 through 7 of this Subchapter for injuries occurring on or after January 1, 1990 and before January 1, 1994.

(a) Adjusting Location. The office where claims are administered.

(b) Administrative Director. The Administrative Director of the Division of Workers' Compensation or his/her duly authorized representative.

(c) Audit. Any audit performed by the Audit Unit of the Division of Workers' Compensation pursuant to Labor Code Sections 129 and 129.5.

(d) Claims Administrator. A self-administered insurer providing security for the payment of compensation required by Divisions 4 and 4.5 of the Labor Code, a self-administered self-insured employer, or a third-party claims administrator for a self-insured employer, insurer, legally uninsured employer, or joint powers authority.

(e) Claim File. A record, either in legible paper or electronic form which can be produced into legible paper, containing all of the information specified in Section 10101 and related documents pertaining to a given work-injury claim.

(f) Claim Log. A handwritten or printed ledger maintained by the claims administrator listing each work injury case by the date the injury was reported to the claims administrator and listing the date of injury. The claim log contents are specified in Section 10103.

(g) Compensation. Compensation as defined in Labor Code Section 3207.

(h) Duly Authorized Representative. A designated employee or unit of the Department of Industrial Relations.

(i) DWC. The Division of Workers' Compensation of the Department of Industrial Relations.

(j) Employee. An employee, his or her dependents or his agent.

(k) Indemnity Case. A work-injury claim which has or may result in any of the following benefits:

(1) Temporary Disability

(2) Permanent Disability

(3) Life Pension

(4) Death Benefits

(5) Vocational Rehabilitation

(*l*) Insurer. Any company, group or entity in, or which has been in, the business of transacting workers' compensation insurance for employers subject to the workers' compensation laws of this state. The term insurer includes the State Compensation Insurance Fund.

(m) Investigation. The process of examining and evaluating a claim to determine the nature and extent of all legally required benefits, if any, which are due under the claim. Investigation may include formal or informal methods of gathering information relevant to evaluating the claim such as: obtaining employment records, obtaining earnings records, informal or formal interviews of the employee, employer, or witnesses, deposition of parties or witnesses, obtaining expert opinion where an issue requires an expert opinion for its resolution, such as obtaining a medical-legal evaluation.

(n) Issue Date. The date upon which a notice of penalty assessment or an order of the Administrative Director is served.

(o) Joint Powers Authority. Any county, city, city and county, municipal corporation, public district, public agency, or political subdivision of the state, but not the state itself, including in a pooling arrangement under a joint exercise of powers agreement for the purpose of securing a certificate of consent to self-insure workers' compensation claims under Labor Code Section 3700(c).

(p) Medical-Only Claim. A work-injury case which requires compensation only for medical treatment by a physician.

(q) Medical Fee Schedule. Official schedule promulgated by the Administrative Director pursuant to Labor Code Section 5307.1. Refer to

Title 8 of existing CCR Section 9791.1 through Section 9792.

(r) Non-Random. Any method of selecting an audit subject which is specific to that audit subject, based on any or all of the factors provided in Labor Code Section 129(b).

(s) Notice of Compensation Due. The Notice of Assessment issued pursuant to Labor Code Section 129(c).

(t) Open Claim. A work-injury claim in which future payment of compensation may be due or for which reserves for the future payment of compensation are maintained.

(u) Payment Schedule. The two-week cycle of indemnity payments due on the day designated with the first payment as required by Labor Code Section 4650(c) or 4702(b).

(v) Random. Any method of selecting an audit subject which is not based on factors specific to that audit subject, but instead which chooses subjects from a broad cross-section of possible subjects. Random selection methods may stratify by general groups and need not be statistically precise.

(w) Self-insured Employer. An employer that has been issued a certificate of consent to self-insure as provided by Labor Code Section 3700(b) or (c), including a joint powers authority or the State of California as a legally uninsured employer.

(x) Third-Party Administrator. An agent under contract to administer the workers' compensation claims of an insurer, self-insured employer, or joint powers authority.

(y) VRMA. Vocational rehabilitation maintenance allowance.

(z) Work-Injury Claim. A claim for an injury that is reported or reportable to the Division of Labor Statistics and Research pursuant to Sections 6409, 6409.1 and 6413 of the Labor Code.

Note: Authority cited: Sections 59, 133, 129.5, 138.4 and 5307.3, Labor Code. Reference: Sections 7, 124, 129, 129.5, 3700, 3702.1, 4636, 4650(c), 5307.1 and 5402, Labor Code.

History: 1. New section filed 1-18-90; operative 1-18-90 (Register 90, No. 4). New section is exempt from review by OAL pursuant to Government Code Section 11351.

2. Amendment of section heading, text and Note filed 1-28-94; operative 1-28-94. Submitted to OAL for printing only pursuant to Government Code section 11351 (Register 94, No. 4).

Ref.: Hanna § 10.50[2][b]; Herlick Handbook §§ 1.6, 9.5.

§10100.1. Definitions—On or After January 1, 1994.

The following definitions apply in Articles 1 through 7 of this Subchapter for injuries occurring on or after January 1, 1994.

(a) Adjusting Location. The office where claims are administered.

(b) Administrative Director. The Administrative Director of the Division of Workers' Compensation or the Director's duly authorized representative, designee, or delegee.

(c) Audit. An audit performed under Labor Code Sections 129 and 129.5.

(d) Audit Subject. A single adjusting location of a claims administrator which has been selected for audit. If a claims administrator has more than one adjusting location, other locations may be selected as separate audit subjects. In its discretion, the Audit Unit may combine more than one adjusting location of a claims administrator as a single non-random audit subject.

(e) Audit Unit. The organizational unit within the Division of Workers' Compensation which audits insurers, self-insured employers and third-party administrators pursuant to Labor Code Sections 129 and 129.5.

(f) Claim. A request for compensation for an injury arising out of and in the course of employment, whether disputed or not, or notice or knowledge that such an injury has occurred or is alleged to have occurred.

(g) Claim File. A record in paper or electronic form, or a combination, containing all of the information specified in Section 10101.1 of these Regulations and all documents or entries related to the provision or denial of benefits.

(h) Claim Log. A handwritten or printed ledger maintained by the claims administrator listing each work-injury claim as specified in Section 10103.1 of these Regulations.

(i) Claims Administrator or Administrator. A self-administered workers' compensation insurer, a self-administered self-insured employer, a self-administered legally uninsured employer, a self-administered joint powers authority, or a third-party claims administrator for an insurer, a self-insured employer, a legally-uninsured employer or a joint powers authority.

(j) Closed Claim. A work-injury claim in which future payment of compensation cannot be reasonably expected to be due.

(k) Compensation. Every benefit or payment, including vocational rehabilitation, medical, and medical-legal expenses, conferred by Divisions 1 and 4 of the Labor Code on an injured employee or the employee's dependents.

(*l*) Date of Knowledge of Injury and Disability. The date the employer had knowledge or reasonably can be expected to have had knowledge of (1) a worker's injury or claim for injury, and (2) the worker's inability or claimed inability to work because of the injury.

(m) Denied Claim. A claim for which all liability has been denied at any time, even if the claim was accepted before or after the denial. A claim which otherwise meets this definition is a denied claim even if medical-legal expenses were paid.

(n) Employee. An employee, or in the case of the employee's death, his or her dependent, as each is defined in Division 4 of the Labor Code, or the employee's or dependent's agent.

(o) First Payment of Temporary Disability Indemnity. (1) The first payment of temporary disability indemnity made to an injured worker for a work injury; or (2) the first resumed payment of temporary disability indemnity following any period of one or more days for which no temporary disability indemnity was payable for that work injury; or (3) the first resumed payment of temporary disability indemnity following issuance of a lawful notice that temporary disability benefits were ending.

(p) Indemnity Claim. A work-injury claim which has resulted or may result in entitlement to any of the following benefits: temporary disability indemnity or salary continuation in lieu of temporary disability indemnity, permanent disability indemnity, death benefits, or vocational rehabilitation.

(q) Insurer. Any company, group, or entity in, or which has been in, the business of transacting workers' compensation insurance for employers subject to the workers' compensation laws of this state. The term insurer includes the State Compensation Insurance Fund.

(r) Investigation. The process of examining and evaluating a claim to determine the nature and extent of all legally required benefits, if any, which are due under the claim. Investigation may include formal or informal methods of gathering information relevant to evaluating the claim such as: obtaining employment records; obtaining earnings records; informal or formal interviews of the employee, employer, or witnesses; deposition of parties or witnesses; obtaining expert opinion where an issue requires an expert opinion for its resolution, such as obtaining a medical-legal evaluation.

(s) Joint Powers Authority. Any county, city, city and county, municipal corporation, public district, public agency, or political subdivision of the state, but not the state itself, included in a pooling arrangement under a joint exercise of powers agreement for the purpose of securing a certificate of consent to self-insure workers' compensation claims under Labor Code Section 3700(c).

(t) Medical-Only Claim. A work-injury claim in which no indemnity benefits are payable.

(u) Non-Random. Any method of selecting an audit subject which is specific to that audit subject, based on any or all of the factors provided in Labor Code Section 129(b).

(v) Notice of Compensation Due. The Notice of Assessment issued pursuant to Labor Code Section 129(c).

(w) Open Claim. A work-injury claim in which future payment of compensation may be due or for which reserves for the future payment of compensation are maintained.

(x) Payment Schedule. Either:

(1) The two-week cycle of indemnity payments due on the day designated with the first payment as required by Labor Code Section 4650(c) or 4702(b), including any lawfully changed payment schedule; or

(2) The two-week cycle of payments of vocational rehabilitation maintenance allowance (VRMA) required by Title 8, California Code of Regulations, Division 1, Chapter 4.5, Subchapter 1.5, Article 7, Section 10125.1.

(y) Random. Any method of selecting an audit subject which is not based on factors specific to that audit subject, but instead which chooses subjects from a broad cross-section of possible subjects. Random selection methods may stratify by general groups and need not be statistically precise.

(z) Record of Payment. An accurate written or electronic record of all compensation payments in a claim file, including but not limited to:

(1) The check number, date the check was issued, name of the payee, amount, and for

indemnity payments the time period(s) covered by the payment;

(2) All dates for which salary continuation as defined by Labor Code Section 4650(g) was provided instead of direct indemnity payments; the dates for which salary continuation was authorized; and documentation when applicable that sick leave or other leave credits were restored for any periods for which salary continuation was payable;

(3) A copy of each bill received which included a medical progress or work status report; and either a copy of each other bill received or documentation of the contents of that bill showing the date and description of the service provided, provider's name, amount billed, date the claims administrator received the bill, and date and amount paid.

(aa) Self-insured Employer. An employer, either as an individual employer or as a group of employers, that has been issued a certificate of consent to self-insure as provided by Labor Code Section 3700(b) or (c), including a joint powers authority or the State of California as a legally uninsured employer.

(bb) Third-Party Administrator. An agent under contract to administer the workers' compensation claims of an insurer, self-insured employer, or joint powers authority.

(cc) VRMA. Vocational rehabilitation maintenance allowance.

Note: Authority cited: Sections 59, 133, 129.5, 138.4, 5307.3, Labor Code. Reference: Sections 7, 124(a), 129(a), (b), (c), 129.5(a), (b), 3700, 3702.1, 4636, 4650(c), 5307.1, 5402, Labor Code.

History: 1. New section filed 1-28-94; operative 1-28-94. Submitted to OAL for printing only pursuant to Government Code section 11351 (Register 94, No. 4).

2. Amendment of subsection (i) filed 2-14-96; operative 2-14-96. Submitted to OAL for printing only pursuant to Government Code section 11351 (Register 96, No. 7).

3. Editorial correction of subsection (d) (Register 2000, No. 45).

Ref.: Hanna § 10.50[2][a]; Herlick Handbook §§ 1.6, 9.5.

§10100.2. Definitions.

The following definitions apply in Articles 1 through 7 of this Subchapter for audits conducted on or after January 1, 2003.

(a) Adjusting Location. The office where claims are administered. Separate underwriting companies, self-administered, self-insured employers, and/or third-party administrators operating at one location shall be combined as one audit subject for the purposes of audits conducted pursuant to Labor Code Section 129(b) only if claims are administered under the same management at that location.

Where claims are administered from an office that includes a satellite office at another location, claims administered at the satellite office(s) will be considered as part of the single adjusting location for auditing purposes when demonstrated that the claims are under the same immediate management.

(b) Administrative Director. The Administrative Director of the Division of Workers' Compensation or the Director's duly authorized representative, designee, or delegee.

(c) Audit. An audit performed under Labor Code Sections 129 and 129.5.

(d) Audit Subject. A single adjusting location of a claims administrator which has been selected for audit. If a claims administrator has more than one adjusting location, other locations shall be considered as separate audit subjects for the purposes of implementing Labor Code Sections 129(a) and 129(b). However, the Audit Unit at its discretion may combine more than one adjusting location of a claims administrator as a single targeted audit subject, or may designate one insurer, insurer group, or self-insured employer at one or more third-party administrator adjusting locations as a single targeted audit subject.

(e) Audit Unit. The organizational unit within the Division of Workers' Compensation which audits and/or investigates insurers, self-insured employers and third-party administrators pursuant to Labor Code Sections 129 and 129.5.

(f) Claim. A request for compensation, or record of an occurrence in which compensation reasonably would be expected to be payable for an injury arising out of and in the course of employment.

(g) Claim File. A record in paper or electronic form, or a combination, containing all of the information specified in Section 10101.1 of these Regulations and all documents or entries related to the provision, delay, or denial of benefits.

(h) Claim Log. A handwritten, printed, or electronically maintained listing maintained by the claims administrator listing each work-injury claim as specified in Section 10103.2 of these Regulations.

(i) Claims Administrator or Administrator. A self-administered workers' compensation insurer, a self-administered self-insured employer, a self-administered legally uninsured employer, a self-administered joint powers authority, or a third-party claims administrator for an insurer, a self-insured employer, a legally-uninsured employer or a joint powers authority.

(j) Closed Claim. A work-injury claim in which future payment of compensation cannot be reasonably expected to be due.

(k) Compensation. Every benefit or payment, including vocational rehabilitation, medical, and medical-legal expenses, conferred by Divisions 1 and 4 of the Labor Code on an injured employee or the employee's dependents.

(*l*) Date of Knowledge of Injury and Disability. The date the employer had knowledge or reasonably can be expected to have had knowledge, pursuant to Labor Code Section 5402, of (1) a worker's injury or claim for injury, and (2) the worker's inability or claimed inability to work because of the injury.

(m) Denied Claim. A claim for which all liability has been denied at any time, even if the claim was accepted before or after the denial. A claim which otherwise meets this definition is a denied claim even if medical-legal expenses were paid.

(n) Employee. An employee, or in the case of the employee's death, his or her dependent, as each is defined in Division 4 of the Labor Code, or the employee's or dependent's agent.

(o) First Payment of Temporary Disability Indemnity. (1) The first payment of temporary disability indemnity made to an injured worker for a work injury; or (2) the first resumed payment of temporary disability indemnity following any period of one or more days for which no temporary disability indemnity was payable for that work injury; or (3) the first resumed payment of temporary disability indemnity following issuance of a lawful notice that temporary disability benefits were ending.

(p) General Business Practice. Conduct that can be distinguished by a reasonable person from an isolated event. The conduct can include a single practice and/or separate, discrete acts or omissions in the handling of several claims.

(q) Indemnity Claim. A work-injury claim that has resulted in the payment of any of the following benefits: temporary disability indemnity or salary continuation in lieu of temporary disability indemnity, permanent disability indemnity, death benefits, or vocational rehabilitation.

(r) Insurer. Any company, group, or entity in, or which has been in, the business of transacting workers' compensation insurance for employers subject to the workers' compensation laws of this state. The term insurer includes the State Compensation Insurance Fund.

(s) Investigation.

(1) As conducted by a claims administrator, an investigation is the process of examining and evaluating a claim to determine the nature and extent of all legally required benefits, if any, which are due under the claim. Investigation may include formal or informal methods of gathering information relevant to evaluating the claim such as: obtaining employment records; obtaining earnings records; informal or formal interviews of the employee, employer, or witnesses; deposition of parties or witnesses; and, obtaining expert opinion where an issue requires an expert opinion for its resolution, such as obtaining a medical-legal evaluation.

(2) As conducted by the Audit Unit, an investigation is the process of reviewing and evaluating, pursuant to Section 10106.5 of these regulations and/or Government Code Sections 11180 through 11191, the extent to which a claims administrator meets its compensation obligations under the California Labor Code or Administrative Director's regulations. An investigation may be conducted concurrently as part of an on-going audit without separate notice issued by the Audit Unit, or may be conducted independently from a specific audit in order to determine if an audit will be conducted, or to determine the nature and extent of business practices for which one or more civil penalties may be assessed pursuant to Labor Code Section 129.5(e).

(t) Joint Powers Authority. Any county, city, city and county, municipal corporation, public district, public agency, or political subdivision of the state, but not the state itself, included in a pooling arrangement under a joint exercise of powers agreement for the purpose of securing a certificate of consent to self-insure workers' compensation claims under Labor Code Section 3700(c).

(u) Knowingly committed. Acting with knowledge of the facts of the conduct. A corporation is presumed to have knowledge of facts any employee receives while acting within the scope of his or her authority. A corporation is presumed to have knowledge of information contained in its records.

(v) Medical-Only Claim. A work-injury claim in which no indemnity benefits have been paid.

(w) Notice of Compensation Due. The Notice of Assessment issued pursuant to Labor Code Section 129(c).

(x) Open Claim. A work-injury claim in which future payment of compensation may be due or for which reserves for the future payment of compensation are maintained.

(y) Payment Schedule. Either:

(1) The two-week cycle of indemnity payments due on the day designated with the first payment as required by Labor Code Section 4650(c) or 4702(b), including any lawfully changed payment schedule; or

(2) The two-week cycle of payments of vocational rehabilitation maintenance allowance (VRMA) required by Title 8, California Code of Regulations, Division 1, Chapter 4.5, Subchapter 1.5, Article 7, Section 10125.1.

(z) Record of Payment. An accurate written or electronic record of all compensation payments in a claim file, including but not limited to:

(1) The check number, date the check was issued, name of the payee, amount, and for indemnity payments, including self-imposed increases, penalties, and/or interest, the time period(s) covered by the payment;

(2) All dates for which salary continuation as defined by Labor Code Section 4650(g) was provided instead of direct indemnity payments; the dates for which salary continuation was authorized; and documentation when applicable that sick leave or other leave credits were restored for any periods for which salary continuation was payable;

(3) A copy of each bill received which included as part of the bill a medical progress or work status report; and either a copy of each other bill received or documentation of the contents of that bill showing the date and description of the service provided, provider's name, amount billed, date the claims administrator received the bill, and date and amount paid.

(aa) Self-insured Employer. An employer, either as an individual employer or as a group of employers, that has been issued a certificate of consent to self-insure as provided by Labor Code Section 3700(b) or (c), including a joint powers authority or the State of California as a legally uninsured employer.

(bb) Third-Party Administrator. An agent under contract to administer the workers' compensation claims of an insurer, a self-insured employer, a legally uninsured employer. or a self-insured joint powers authority. The term third-party administrator includes the State Compensation Insurance Fund for locations that administer claims for legally uninsured and self-insured employers, and also includes Managing General Agents.

(cc) VRMA. Vocational rehabilitation maintenance allowance.

Note: Authority cited: Sections 59, 129.5, 133, 138.4 and 5307.3, Labor Code. Reference: Sections 7, 124(a), 129(a), (b), (c), 129.5(a), (b), 3700, 3702.1, 4636, 4650(c), 5307.1 and 5402, Labor Code.

History: 1. New section filed 12-30-2002; operative 1-1-2003 pursuant to Government Code section 11343.4 (Register 2003, No. 1).

ARTICLE 2
Claims Administration and Recordkeeping

§10101. Claim File—Contents.

This section applies to maintenance of claims files for injuries occurring before January 1, 1994.

Every claims administrator shall maintain a claim file of each work-injury claim including claims which were denied. All open claim files shall be kept at the adjusting location for the file. The file shall contain but not be limited to:

(a) An employer date stamped copy of the Employee's Claim for Workers' Compensation Benefits, DWC Form 1, or documentation of reasonable attempts to obtain the form.

(b) Employers Report of Occupational Injury or Illness, DLSR Form 5020, or documentation of reasonable attempts to obtain it.

(c) Every notice or report sent to the Division of Workers' Compensation.

(d) A copy of every Doctor's First Report of Occupational Injury or Illness, DLSR Form 5021, or documentation of reasonable attempts to obtain them.

(e) The original or a copy of every medical report pertaining to the claim, or documentation of reasonable attempts to obtain them.

(f) All orders or awards of the Workers' Compensation Appeals Board pertaining to the claim.

(g) A record of payment of compensation.

(h) A copy of the application(s) for adjudication of claim filed with the Workers' Compensation Appeals Board, if any.

(i) Copies of all notices sent to the employee pursuant to the requirements of the Benefit Notice Program established by Labor Code Section 138.4 and the notices required by Article 2.6 of Chapter 2 of Part 2 of the Labor Code, commencing with Section 4635.

Note: Authority cited: Sections 59, 129.5, 133, 138.4, 4603.5 and 5307.3, Labor Code. Reference: Sections 124, 129, 129.5, 138.3, 138.4, 139.5, 4061, 4453, 4454, 4600, 4603.2, 4621, 4622, 4636, 4637, 4641, 4643, 4644, 4650, 4701 through 4703.5, 5401, 6409 and 6409.1, Labor Code.

History: 1. New section filed 1-18-90; operative 1-18-90 (Register 90, No. 4). New section is exempt from review by OAL pursuant to Government Code Section 11351.

2. Amendment of article heading, section heading, text and Note filed 1-28-94; operative 1-28-94. Submitted to OAL for printing only pursuant to Government Code section 11351 (Register 94, No. 4).

Ref.: Herlick Handbook §§ 1.6, 9.5.

§10101.1. Claim File—Contents.

This section applies to maintenance of claim files for injuries occurring on or after January 1, 1994.

Every claims administrator shall maintain a claim file of each work-injury claim including claims which were denied. All open claim files shall be kept at the adjusting location for the file. The file shall contain but not be limited to:

(a) Either (1) a copy of the Employee's Claim for Workers' Compensation Benefits, DWC Form 1, showing the employer's date of knowledge of injury, the date the employer provided the form to the employee and the date the employer received the completed form from the employee; or (2) if the employee did not return the claim form, documentation of the date the employer provided a claim form to the employee. If the administrator cannot obtain the form or determine that the form was provided to the employee by the employer, the file shall contain documentation that the administrator has provided the claim form to the employee as required by Title 8, California Code of Regulations Section 10119.

(b) A copy of the Employer's Report of Occupational Injury or Illness, DLSR Form 5020, or documentation of reasonable attempts to obtain it;

(c) A copy of every notice or report sent to the Division of Workers' Compensation.

(d) A copy of every Doctor's First Report of Occupational Injury or Illness, DLSR Form 5021, or documentation of reasonable attempts to obtain them.

(e) The original or a copy of every medical report pertaining to the claim, or documentation of reasonable attempts to obtain them.

(f) All orders or awards of the Workers' Compensation Appeals Board or the Rehabilitation Unit pertaining to the claim.

(g) A record of payment of compensation.

(h) A copy of the application(s) for adjudication of claim filed with the Workers' Compensation Appeals Board, if any.

(i) Copies of the following notices sent to the employee:

(1) Benefit notices, including vocational rehabilitation notices, required by Title 8, California Code of Regulations, Division 1, Chapter 4.5, Subchapter 1, Article 8, beginning with Section 9810, or by Title 8, California Code of Regulations, Division 1, Chapter 4.5, Subchapter 1.5, Article 7, beginning with Section 10122;

(2) Notices related to the Qualified Medical Evaluation process required by Labor Code Section 4061;

(j) Documentation sufficient to determine the injured worker's average weekly earnings in accordance with Labor Code Sections 4453 through 4459. Unless the claims administrator accepts liability to pay the maximum temporary disability rate, including any increased maximum due under Labor Code §4661.5, the information shall include:

(1) Documentation whether the employee received the following earnings, and if so, the amount or fair market value of each: tips, commissions, bonuses, overtime, and the market value of board, lodging, fuel, or other advantages as part of the worker's remuneration, which can be estimated in money, said documentation to include the period of time, not exceeding one year, as may conveniently be taken to determine an average weekly rate of pay;

(2) Documentation of concurrent earnings from employment other than that in which the injury occurred, or that there were no concurrent

earnings, or of reasonable attempts to determine this information;

(3) If earnings at the time of injury were irregular, documentation of earnings from all sources of employment for one year prior to the injury, or of reasonable attempts to determine this information.

(4) If the foregoing information results in less than maximum earnings, documentation of the worker's earning capacity, including documentation of any increase in earnings likely to have occurred but for the injury (such as periodic salary increases or increased earnings upon completion of training status), or of reasonable attempts to determine this information.

(k) Notes and documentation related to the provision, delay, or denial of benefits, including any electronically stored documentation.

(*l*) Notes and documentation evidencing the legal, factual, or medical basis for non-payment or delay in payment of compensation benefits or expenses.

(m) Notes describing telephone conversations relating to the claim which are of significance to claims handling, including the dates of calls, substance of calls, and identification of parties to the calls.

Note: Authority cited: Sections 59, 129.5, 133, 138.4, 4603.5 and 5307.3, Labor Code. Reference: Sections 124, 129, 129.5, 138.3, 138.4, 139.5, 4061, 4453, 4454, 4600, 4603.2, 4621, 4622, 4636, 4637, 4641, 4643, 4644, 4650, 4701 through 4703.5, 5401, 6409 and 6409.1, Labor Code.

History: 1. New section filed 1-28-94; operative 1-28-94. Submitted to OAL for printing only pursuant to Government Code section 11351 (Register 94, No. 4).

Ref.: Herlick Handbook §§ 1.6, 9.5.

§10102. Retention of Claim Files.

(a) All claim files shall be maintained at least until the latest of the following dates:

(1) five years from the date of injury;

(2) one year from the date compensation was last provided;

(3) all compensation due or which may be due has been paid;

(4) if an audit has been conducted within the time specified in (a)(1), until the findings of an audit of the file have become final.

(b) Open and closed claim files may be maintained in whole or in part in an electronic or other non-paper storage medium.

Note: Authority cited: Sections 59, 129.5(b), 133, 138.4, 4603.5 and 5307.3, Labor Code. Reference: Sections 124(a), 129(a) through (c), 129.5(a), (b), (d), 138.3, 4061, 4453, 4454, 4600, 4603.2(b), 4621, 4622, 4636, 4637, 4641, 4643, 4644, 4650, 4701 through 4703.5, 5401(a), 5401.6, 5405 and 5804, Labor Code.

History: 1. New section filed 1-18-90; operative 1-18-90 (Register 90, No. 4). New section is exempt from review by OAL pursuant to Government Code section 11351.

2. Renumbering of former section 10103 to section 10102, and renumbering and amendment of former section 10102 to section 10103 filed 1-28-94; operative 1-28-94. Submitted to OAL for printing only pursuant to Government Code section 11351 (Register 94, No. 4).

Ref.: Herlick Handbook §§ 1.6, 9.5.

§10103. Claim Log—Contents and Maintenance.

This section shall govern claim log maintenance prior to January 1, 1994.

(a) Every claims administrator shall produce a claim log of all work-injury claims maintained at each adjusting location, prepared chronologically in alphanumeric or numeric ascending order, or in a combination thereof.

(b) The claim log shall contain at least the following information:

(1) Name of injured.

(2) The claims administrator's claim number.

(3) Date of injury.

(4) An indication as to whether the work-injury claim is an indemnity or medical-only case.

(5) An entry if all liability for a claim has been denied.

(6) For self-insurer, when a Certificate of Consent to Self-Insure has been issued, an entry identifying the corporation employing the injured.

(c) The claim log of a former self-insurer shall be maintained and made available to the audit unit within 5 days of request.

(d) A claims administrator shall provide a copy of a claim log within 14 days of receiving a written request from the Administrative Director.

Note: Authority cited: Sections 59, 129.5, 133 and 5307.3, Labor Code. Reference: Sections 124, 129, 129.5, 138.4, 3702.8 and 5401, Labor Code.

History: 1. New section filed 1-18-90; operative 1-18-90 (Register 90, No. 4). New section is exempt from review by OAL pursuant to Government Code Section 11351.

2. Renumbering of former section 10102 to section 10103, and renumbering and amendment of former section 10103 to section 10102 filed 1-28-94; operative 1-28-94. Submitted to OAL for printing only pursuant to Government Code section 11351 (Register 94, No. 4).

3. Amendment of subsection (b)(6) filed 2-14-96; operative 2-14-96. Submitted to OAL for printing only pursuant to Government Code section 11351 (Register 96, No. 7).

Ref.: Herlick Handbook §§ 1.6, 9.5.

§10103.1. Claim Log—Contents and Maintenance.

This section shall govern claim log maintenance on or after January 1, 1994.

(a) The claims administrator shall maintain annual claim logs listing all work-injury claims, open and closed. Each year's log shall be maintained for at least five years from the end of the year covered. Separate claim logs shall be maintained for each self-insured employer and each insurer for each adjusting location.

(b) Each entry in the claim log shall contain at least the following information:

(1) Name of injured worker.

(2) Claims administrator's claim number.

(3) Date of injury.

(4) An indication whether the claim is an indemnity or medical-only claim.

(5) An entry if all liability for a claim has been denied at any time. All liability is considered to have been denied even if the administrator accepted liability for medical-legal expense.

(6) If the claim log is for a self-insured employer and a Certificate of Consent to Self-Insure has been issued, the name of the corporation employing the injured worker. If the claim log consists of claims for two or more members of an insurer group, each entry on the log shall identify the insurer.

(c) The entries on a log provided to the Administrative Director shall reflect current information, to show at least any changes in status of a claim which occurred 45 days or more before the claim log was provided. However, once all liability for a claim has been denied the log shall designate the claim as a denial, even if the claim was later accepted.

(d) The claim log of each former self-insured employer and each self-insured employer which changes or terminates the use of a third-party administrator shall be maintained by that self-insured employer as required by subsection (a).

(e) A claims administrator shall provide a copy of a claim log within 14 days of receiving a written request from the Administrative Director.

Note: Authority cited: Sections 59, 129.5, 133 and 5307.3, Labor Code. Reference: Sections 124, 129, 129.5, 138.4, 3702.8 and 5401, Labor Code.

History: 1. New section filed 1-28-94; operative 1-28-94. Submitted to OAL for printing only pursuant to Government Code section 11351 (Register 94, No. 4).

2. Amendment of subsection (b)(6) filed 2-14-96; operative 2-14-96. Submitted to OAL for printing only pursuant to Government Code section 11351 (Register 96, No. 7).

Ref.: Hanna § 10.50[2][a]; Herlick Handbook §§ 1.6, 9.5.

§10103.2. Claim Log—Contents and Maintenance.

This section shall govern claim log maintenance on or after January 1, 2003.

(a) The claims administrator shall maintain annual claim logs listing all work-injury claims, open and closed. Each year's log shall be maintained for at least five years from the end of the year covered. Separate claim logs shall be maintained for each self-insured employer and each insurer for each adjusting location.

(b) Each entry in the claim log shall contain at least the following information:

(1) Name of injured worker.

(2) Claims administrator's claim number.

(3) Date of injury.

(4) An indication whether the claim is an indemnity or medical-only claim.

(5) An entry if all liability for a claim has been denied at any time. All liability is considered to have been denied even if the administrator accepted liability for medical-legal expense.

(6) If the claim log is for a self-insured employer and a Certificate of Consent to Self-Insure has been issued, the name of the corporation employing the injured worker. If the claim log consists of claims for two or more members of an insurer group, the log shall identify the insurer for each claim.

(7) If the claim has been transferred from one adjusting location to another, the address of the new location shall be identified on the initial adjusting location's log. Claims that are transferred from one adjusting location to another shall be listed on the claim log of the new adjusting location for the year in which the claim was initially reported, not for the year in which the claim was transferred.

(c) The entries on a log provided to the Administrative Director shall reflect current information, to show at least any changes in status of a claim which occurred 45 days or more before the claim log was provided. However, once all liability for a claim has been denied the log shall designate the claim as a denial, even if the claim was later accepted.

(d) The claim log of each former self-insured employer and each self-insured employer that changes or terminates the use of a third-party administrator shall be maintained by that self-insured employer as required by subsection (a).

(e) A claims administrator shall provide a copy of a claim log within 14 days of receiving a written request from the Administrative Director.

Note: Authority cited: Sections 59, 129.5, 133 and 5307.3, Labor Code. Reference: Sections 124, 129, 129.5, 138.4, 3702.8 and 5401, Labor Code.

History: 1. New section filed 12-30-2002; operative 1-1-2003 pursuant to Government Code section 11343.4 (Register 2003, No. 1).

§10104. Annual Report of Inventory.

Each claims administrator shall maintain, and shall file with the Administrative Director, an Annual Report of Inventory for each of its adjusting locations. The report shall be filed annually by April 1. It shall include the name, address, and telephone number of the adjusting location and the name and title of the person responsible for audit coordination. Reports due on or after April 1, 2003 shall report, as of the preceding January 1, the numbers of indemnity, denied, and medical-only claims reported to the claims administrator during the preceding calendar year for insurers and private self-insured employers, or fiscal year for public self-insured employers. If the administrator adjusts for more than one entity at that location, the report shall give the total numbers of claims at that location and shall also identify the numbers of claims for each self-insured employer or insurer liable for the payment of compensation.

Note: Authority cited: Sections 59, 129.5(b), 133 and 5307.3, Labor Code. Reference: Sections 129(a), (b) and 129.5(a), (b), (d), Labor Code.

History: 1. Renumbering of former section 10104 to section 10105 and new section filed 1-28-94; operative 1-28-94. Submitted to OAL for printing only pursuant to Government Code section 11351 (Register 94, No. 4).

2. Amendment filed 12-30-2002; operative 1-1-2003 pursuant to Government Code section 11343.4 (Register 2003, No. 1).

3. Amendment filed 10-6-2003; operative 12-1-2003 (Register 2003, No. 41).

Ref.: Hanna § 10.50[2][a]; Herlick Handbook §§ 1.6, 9.5.

ARTICLE 3
Auditing

§10105. Auditing, Discretion of the Administrative Director.

To carry out the responsibility pursuant to Labor Code Section 129(a) and Section 129(b), the Administrative Director or his/her representative shall audit claims administrators' claim files and claim logs at such reasonable times as he/she deems necessary. The Administrative Director or his/her representative may also utilize the provisions of Government Code Sections 11180 through 11191.

Note: Authority cited: Sections 59, 129.5, 133 and 5307.3, Labor Code. Reference: Sections 129 and 129.5, Labor Code.

History: 1. New article 3 heading, repealer of former section 10105 and renumbering and amendment of former section 10104 to section 10105 filed 1-28-94; operative 1-28-94. Submitted to OAL for printing only pursuant to Government Code section 11351 (Register 94, No. 4). For prior history, see Register 90, No. 4.

2. Amendment filed 12-30-2002; operative 1-1-2003 pursuant to Government Code section 11343.4 (Register 2003, No. 1).

Ref.: Hanna § 1.12[8]; Herlick Handbook §§ 1.6, 9.5.

§10106. Random and Non-Random Audit Subject Selection; Complaint/Information Investigation.

(a) In its discretion, the Audit Unit may treat an affiliated group of insurers at a single adjusting location as individual insurers, or may combine all or any of them as a single insurer audit subject. In its discretion, the Audit Unit may treat parent and subsidiary self-insured employers at a single adjusting location as individual self-insureds, or may combine all or any of them as a single self-insured audit subject.

(b) The final selection of audit subjects shall be within the discretion of the Audit Unit. The Audit Unit may investigate information or complaints instead of, or in addition to, conducting an audit. Investigations and/or audits may be conducted if complaints or information indicate the possible existence of claims handling practices which would be assessed as a civil penalty under Labor Code Section 129.5(d).

(c) The Audit Unit shall select at least half of its audit subjects at random from any available listing of adjusting locations of workers' compensation insurers, self-insured employers, self-insured joint powers authorities, legally uninsured employers, and third-party administrators. If, after the results of an audit become final, none of the criteria qualifying an audit subject for a return non-random audit pursuant to subsection (f) of this section exist, the audit subject shall be removed from the pool of potential random audit subject selection for three years. However, eligibility under this subsection for removal from the pool for random audit subject selection shall not bar the non-random selection of the audit subject pursuant to this section or Labor Code Section 129(b).

(d) In order to establish priorities for audits pursuant to Labor Code §129(b), the Audit Unit shall review and compile complaints and information that indicate a claims administrator is failing to meet its obligations under Divisions 1 or 4 of the Labor Code or regulations of the administrative director.

(1) The information and complaints shall be tracked and compiled into a list of Claims Administrators Identified for Potential Non-Random Investigation as follows:

(i) Complaints or information available to the Audit Unit which indicate possible violations of the kind which, if found on audit, would be subject to the assessment of administrative penalties or issuance of notices of compensation due shall be retained in potential audit subject files by claims adjusting locations. Factual information and complaints shall be weighted on the basis of apparent severity of the alleged violation, using the assessment categories set forth in the subsections (a) through (d) of §10111 and §10111.1 to set a point value.

An alleged violation that would fall within subsection (a) is given one point, an alleged violation that would fall within subsection (b) is given five points, an alleged violation that would fall within subsection (c) is given ten points, and an alleged violation that would fall within subsec tion (d) is given fifty points. When multiple violations are alleged in one complaint, each potential violation is given the appropriate point(s).

Points assigned for violations which are evidenced by decisions or findings rendered by the WCAB or Rehabilitation Unit shall be multiplied by ten.

(ii) Periodically, the audit unit shall review and analyze the complaint and information data in order to establish a list of Claims Administrators Identified for Potential Non-Random Investigation. The total number of points assigned to a claims administrator at an adjusting location shall be compared to the total number of claims reported at that claims adjusting location as indicated on the Annual Report of Inventory or the Self Insurer's Annual Report. The claims administrators shall be ranked on the list of Claims Administrators Identified for Potential Non-Random Investigation on the basis of the ratio of weighted complaints to case load size at each adjusting location. It is within the discretion of the Audit Unit to determine when new lists shall be established.

(2) The audit unit shall select any number of the highest ranking claims adjusting locations for investigation from the list of Claims Administrators Identified for Potential Non-Random Investigation.

(i) The Audit Unit shall notify the claims administrator that it will conduct an investigation, and shall specify the files it will review by providing the names of the injured workers. The Audit Unit shall give the claims administrator a minimum of three working days notice of the date of commencement of the investigation. Notice may be given by telephone. The claim files shall be made available to the Audit Unit at the time of the commencement of the investigation. The Audit Unit may examine claim files and require a claims administrator to provide documents and information.

(ii) The Audit Unit shall examine the selected files and shall assign points for each violation found in the files in accordance with the point system set forth in subsection (d)(1)(i), except that there shall be no multiplier for violations evidenced by decisions or findings of the WCAB or Rehabilitation Unit. Points shall be assigned for every violation found in the file, both violations that were alleged in the complaints and additional violations found by the audit unit.

(iii) The Audit Unit shall send a notice to the claims administrator which outlines the violations found in the files investigated. The claims administrator may request copies of the complaints relating to the files investigated. The complaints may be kept confidential by the audit unit if confidentiality is requested by the complainant.

(iv) The claims administrator may present documentation and/or argument to the Audit Unit to disprove any or all of the violations found by the audit unit in the investigated files. The documentation and argument must be postmarked or personally delivered to the Audit Unit within fourteen days of receipt of the letter outlining the violations.

(v) The Audit Unit shall consider documents and argument submitted by the claims administrator to disprove the violations found in the investigated files and determine whether there is a basis to alter any of the points previously assigned.

(vi) The adjusting locations shall then be ranked on a list of Claims Administrators Identified for Potential Non-Random Audit on the basis of the ratio of violation points to the number of claims investigated at each adjusting location.

(e) The Audit Unit shall select non-random audit subjects from the list of Claims Administrators Identified for Potential Non-Random Audit, and shall endeavor to give priority in scheduling audits to those administrators that have been assigned the most points. However, the audit unit may also consider the results and recency of prior audits at the adjusting location, the resources of the audit unit, and the need to conduct random audits, in scheduling investigations and audits. The Audit Unit is not required to investigate or audit every claims administrator on the list, nor is it required to investigate or audit in the order in which claims administrators appear on the list.

If the Audit Unit is able to conduct more non-random audits than the number appearing on the list of Claims Administrators Identified for Potential Non-Random Audit, it may select any number of the next highest ranking adjusting locations appearing on the list of Claims Administrators Identified for Potential Non-Random Investigation. The adjusting locations shall then be investigated and ranked according to subsection (d)(2).

(f) Prior audit results shall be used independently as factual information to support selection of a claims administrator for non-random audit.

(1) The Audit Unit shall return for a repeat non-random audit of denied files of the audit subject within one to three years of the results of an audit becoming final if there is more than one unsupported denial and the number of unsupported denials exceeds 5% of the audited denied claims.

(2) The Audit Unit shall return for a repeat non-random audit of indemnity files of the audit subject within one to three years of the results of an audit becoming final if:

(i) The number of randomly selected audited files with violations involving the failure to pay indemnity exceeds 20% of the audited files in which indemnity is accrued and payable and the average amount of unpaid indemnity exceeds $200.00 per file in which indemnity is accrued and payable, or

(ii) The numbers of randomly selected files with violations involving the late first payments of temporary disability indemnity, permanent disability indemnity, vocational rehabilitation maintenance allowance, late subsequent indemnity payments, and late payments of death benefits, as mitigated for frequency under Section 10111.1(e)(3)(i) through (v), exceeds 30% of the audited files in which those indemnity payments have been made, and the number of audited files with violations involving the failure to issue benefit notices, as assessed under Section 10111.1(a)(7)(ii) of these regulations, exceeds 30% of the files in which there is a requirement to issue those notices.

(g) The Audit Unit shall send a claims administrator selected for non-random audit a Notice of Audit in accordance with §10107. The Notice of Audit for a non-random audit may be appealed as follows:

(i) Within 7 days after receiving a Notice of Audit the claims administrator may appeal its selection for audit by filing and serving a request for an appeals conference or a request for a written decision by the Administrative Director without a conference.

(ii) Within 21 days after the request for a written decision or an appeals conference is filed, the appellant shall file with the Administrative Director and serve a written statement setting forth the legal and factual basis of the appeal, and including documentation or other evidence which supports the appellant's position.

(iii) If a request for an appeals conference or a request for a written decision without conference or if the written statement and documentation are not timely filed and served under Subsections (g)(i) and (g)(ii), the claims administrator shall be deemed to have finally waived the issue of the propriety of its selection for audit. The claims administrator will be precluded from raising the issue at any subsequent appeals of Notices of Penalty Assessment or Notices of Compensation Due.

(iv) Service and filing are timely if the documents are placed in the United States mail, first class postage prepaid, or personally delivered between the hours of 8:00 a.m. and 5:00 p.m., within the periods specified in Subsections (g)(i) and (g)(ii). The original and all copies of any filing shall attach proof of service as provided in Section 10514.

(v) The appeal process shall be governed by Section 10115.2.

Note: Authority cited: Sections 59, 129.5, 133 and 5307.3, Labor Code. Reference: Sections 7, 53, 111, 124, 129 and 129.5, Labor Code; and Sections 11180, 11180.5, 11181 and 11182, Government Code.

History: 1. Relocation of article 3 heading to article 5 and repealer and new section filed 1-28-94; operative 1-28-94. Submitted to OAL for printing only pursuant to Government Code section 11351 (Register 94, No. 4). For prior history, see Register 90, No. 4.

2. Amendment of subsection (b), (d)(2), and (e) filed 2-14-96; operative 2-14-96. Submitted to OAL for printing only pursuant to Government Code section 11351 (Register 96, No. 7).

3. Amendment of section and Note filed 10-26-98; operative 11-25-98 (Register 98, No. 44).

Ref.: Herlick Handbook § 9.5.

§10106.1. Routine and Targeted Audit Subject Selection; Complaint Tracking; Appeal of Targeted Audit Selection.

For audits conducted on or after January 1, 2003:

(a) The Division of Workers' Compensation shall maintain and update annually a list of known adjusting locations of California workers' compensation claims. The list will be based on information provided to the Division in Annual Reports of Inventory submitted pursuant to Section 10104, data submitted to the Division's Workers' Compensation Information System pursuant to Labor Code Section 138.6, and any other sources of information available. The list shall include all known adjusting locations, located in or out of California, of insurers, self-administered self-insured employers, and third-party administrators that administer California workers' compensation claims.

(b) The Audit Unit shall select each adjusting location from the list of adjusting locations for routine profile audit review pursuant to Labor Code Section 129(b)(1) at least once every five years. Audit subjects may be selected in any order, and routine audits may be scheduled by the Audit Unit in a manner to best minimize travel expenses and utilize audit personnel efficiently.

(1) For routine audit subject selection pursuant to Labor Code Section 129(b)(1), if the adjusting location includes claims of more than one insurance underwriting company, self-insured employer, or third-party administrator at the location and all claims at that location share the same local management, the location will be considered as one audit subject.

(2) Eligibility under this subsection for removal from the pool for routine audit subject selection shall not bar the targeted selection of the audit subject pursuant to subsections (c)(2), (c)(3), (c)(4), Labor Code Section 129(b)(3), or for investigation and/or audit pursuant to Section 10106.5 of these regulations.

(c) The Audit Unit shall target audit subjects based on prior audit results pursuant to Labor Code Section 129(b)(2) and subsection (c)(1) of this regulation. Pursuant to Labor Code Section 129(b)(3), the Audit Unit may also target audit subjects based on subsections (c)(2) through (c)(5) of this regulation.

(1) Audit results shall be used independently as factual information to support selection of a claims administrator for a return, targeted audit as follows:

(A) When a final audit report is issued, the report will include a final performance rating. The final performance rating will be calculated in the same manner as the performance audit review performance rating as set forth in Section 10107.1(c)(3), except that the rating shall be determined based on audit findings from all randomly selected claims, including additional claims selected pursuant to Sections 10107.1(d)(1) and (e)(1).

(B) If the audit subject's performance rating calculated pursuant to Section 10107.1(c)(3) or (d)(3) fails to meet or exceed the worst 10% of performance ratings for all audits conducted in the three calendar years before the year preceding the current audit, the Audit Unit will return for a targeted audit of the audit subject within two years of the date the audit findings become final.

(C) In the final audit report, the Audit Unit shall notify the audit subject that a return, targeted audit will be conducted based upon its performance rating. The return target audit shall be conducted in addition to any penalties assessed as a result of the qualifying audit.

(D) Any appeal of the audit subject's selection for a targeted audit based upon the audit findings must be made in the same manner as an appeal of the Notice of Penalty Assessment as set forth in Section 10115.1, and must be made within seven days of receipt of the audit findings upon which the selection for targeted audit is based.

(2) Audit subjects may be selected for targeted audit based on final decisions or findings of the WCAB issued pursuant to Labor Code Section 5814 as follows:

(A) The Division of Workers' Compensation will regularly submit copies of WCAB decisions, findings, and/or awards issued pursuant to Labor Code Section 5814 to the Audit Unit.

(B) Approximately once per year the audit unit will establish a list of claims administrators identified for potential targeted audit based on the documentation provided pursuant to subsection (c)(2)(A). For each adjusting location, the total number of decisions, findings, and/or awards issued pursuant to Labor Code Section 5814 shall be compared to the total number of claims reported at that claims adjusting location for the last year for that potential audit subject, as indicated on the Annual Report of Inventory or the Self Insurer's Annual Report, or as indicated in the data reported by the claims administrator to the Division of Workers' Compensation as part of the Workers' Compensation Information System pursuant to Labor Code Section 138.6. The Audit Unit may obtain data runs or claim logs from the claims administrator to verify the accuracy of the claims reported.

(C) The Audit Unit may select for target audit the highest-ranking subjects, based on the ratios of decisions, findings, and/or awards issued pursuant to Labor Code Section 5814 compared to the number of claims reported at the adjusting location, from the list. The Audit Unit may consider the results and recency of prior audits at the adjusting location, the resources of the Audit Unit, and the need to conduct routine audits in scheduling targeted audits. The Audit Unit is not required to audit every claims administrator on the list, nor is it required to audit in the order in which claims administrators appear on the list.

(D) The Audit Unit shall send the audit subject selected for targeted audit a Notice of Audit in accordance with §10107.1(a).

(3) The Audit Unit may also target audit subjects based on credible complaints and/or information received by the Division of Workers' Compensation that indicate possible claims handling violations, except that the Audit Unit will not target audit subjects based only on anonymous complaints unless the complaint(s) is supported by credible documentation. Complaints received by the Division of Workers' Compensation may be kept confidential if confidentiality is requested by the complaining party. In order to establish priorities for audits pursuant to this subsection, the Audit Unit shall review and compile complaints and information that indicate claims administrator adjusting locations are failing to meet their obligations under Divisions 1 or 4 of the Labor Code or regulations of the administrative director. Approximately once per year, complaints and information alleging improper claims handling shall be tracked and compiled into a list of claims administrators identified for potential target audits in two manners:

(A) On the basis of overall gravity and frequency of potential violations as measured by assigned points:

(i) Complaints or information indicating possible violations of the kind which, if found on audit, would be subject to the assessment of administrative penalties or issuance of notices of compensation due shall be weighted on the basis of apparent severity of the alleged violation. One point shall be assigned for each $100.00 in penalties assessable under the corresponding violations in Sections 10111 through 10111.2 of these regulations.

(ii) The Audit Unit may select for target audit the highest-ranking subjects, based on points assigned compared to the number of claims reported at the adjusting location. The Audit Unit may consider the results and recency of prior audits at the adjusting location, the resources of the Audit Unit, and the need to conduct routine audits in scheduling targeted audits. The Audit Unit is not required to audit every claims administrator on the list, nor is it required to audit in the order in which claims administrators appear on the list.

(iii) The Audit Unit shall send the audit subject selected for targeted audit a Notice of Audit in accordance with § 10107.1(a).

(B) On the basis of credible complaints or information indicating claims handling for which a civil penalty may be assessed pursuant to Labor Code Section 129.5(e):

(i) The Audit Unit may select for target audit the highest-ranking subjects based on the ratios of complaints or information regarding specific claims practices compared to the number of claims. In considering the potential for specific poor claims practices, the Audit Unit may consider the results and recency of prior audits at the adjusting location, the resources of the Audit Unit, and the need to conduct routine audits in scheduling targeted audits. The Audit Unit is not required to audit every claims administrator on the list, nor is it required to audit in the order in which claims administrators appear on the list.

(ii) The Audit Unit shall send the audit subject selected for targeted audit a Notice of Audit in accordance with §10107.1(a).

(4) The Audit Unit may also select targeted audit subjects based on data from the Workers' Compensation Information System which indicates the claims administrator is failing to meet its obligations, including, but not limited to, high percentages of possible violations compared to other claims administrators. Possible violations include high percentages of apparent late first and/or subsequent indemnity payments, either overall or by class of indemnity, and/or high ratios of denied claims to indemnity claims

(5) The Audit Unit may also target an audit subject for any of the following:

(A) Failure to produce a claim for the Audit Unit within 30 days of receipt of a written request in a profile audit review conducted pursuant to Labor Code Section 129(b).

(B) Failure to pay or appeal pursuant to Section 10115 any Notice of Compensation Due issued by the Audit Unit.

(6) For target audits, the Audit Unit may randomly select claims pursuant to Section 10107.1 of these regulations and/or target claims based on information indicating the possible existence of specific claims handling practices.

(7) For target audits and/or for targeted claims in any audit, the Audit Unit is not required to audit an entire claim file, but may audit only those parts of the claim file that pertain to the complaint or to a specific type of possible violation(s).

(8) The Notice of Audit for a targeted audit selected pursuant to subsections (c)(2) through (c)(5) may be appealed as follows:

(A) Within 7 days after receiving a Notice of Audit the claims administrator may appeal its selection for audit by filing with the Administrative Director and serving on the Audit Unit a request for an appeals conference or a request for a written decision without a conference.

(B) Within 21 days after the request for a written decision or an appeals conference is filed, the appellant shall file with the Administrative Director and serve the Audit Unit with a written statement setting forth the legal and factual basis of the appeal, and including documentation or other evidence which supports the appellant's position.

(C) If a request for an appeals conference or a request for a written decision without conference or if the written statement and documentation are not timely filed and served under Section 10115.1(g)(1) and (g)(2), the claims administrator shall be deemed to have waived any issue concerning its selection for audit. The claims administrator will be precluded from raising the issue at any subsequent appeals of Notices of Penalty Assessment or Notices of Compensation Due.

(D) Service and filing are timely if the documents are placed in the United States mail, first class postage prepaid, or personally delivered between the hours of 8:00 a.m. and 5:00 p.m., within the periods specified in Section 10115.1(g). The original and all copies of any filing shall attach proof of service as provided in Section 10975.

(E) The appeal process shall be governed by Section 10115.2.

Note: Authority cited: Sections 59, 129, 129.5, 133, 138.6 and 5307.3, Labor Code. Reference: Sections 7, 53, 111, 124, 129 and 129.5, Labor Code; and Sections 11180, 11181 and 11182, Government Code.

History: 1. New section filed 12-30-2002; operative 1-1-2003 pursuant to Government Code section 11343.4 (Register 2003, No. 1).

2. Change without regulatory effect redesignating and amending former subsections (c)(8)(i)-(v) to subsections (c)(8)(A)-(E) filed 5-1-2003 pursuant to section 100, title 1, California Code of Regulations (Register 2003, No. 18).

Ref.: Hanna § 1.12[8].

§10106.5. Civil Penalty Investigation.

Notwithstanding Sections 10106 and 10107 of these regulations, if the Audit Unit has information indicating the possible existence of claims handling practices which would be assessable as a civil penalty under Labor Code Section 129.5(e), it may conduct an investigation and/or audit pursuant to Labor Code Sections 129 and 129.5. The Audit Unit may also utilize the provisions of Government Code Sections 11180 through 11191 as the delagee of the Administrative Director's powers as a department head.

The Audit Unit shall report any suspected fraudulent activity uncovered during an audit and/or investigation to the appropriate law enforcement agencies, including but not limited to the Department of Insurance Fraud Bureau and the appropriate District Attorney having jurisdiction over the audit subject.

Note: Authority cited: Sections 129.5, 133 and 5307.3, Labor Code. Reference: Sections 11180 through 11191, Government Code; and Sections 59, 60, 111, 124, 129 and 129.5, Labor Code.

History: 1. New section filed 10-26-98; operative 11-25-98 (Register 98, No. 44).

2. Amendment filed 12-30-2002; operative 1-1-2003 pursuant to Government Code section 11343.4 (Register 2003, No. 1).

Ref.: Hanna § 1.12[8]; Herlick Handbook §§ 1.6, 9.5.

§10107. Notice of Audit; Claim File Selection; Production of Claim Files; Auditing Procedure.

(a) Once a subject has been selected for an audit, the Audit Unit shall serve a Notice of Audit on the claims administrator. The Notice shall inform the administrator of its selection for audit, and shall include a request to provide the Audit Unit with a claim log or logs. The audit subject shall provide two copies of the specified claim log(s) within fourteen days of the date of the receipt of the Notice. The Audit Unit may select any or all claim files for audit.

(b) The Audit Unit shall send the audit subject a Notice of Audit Commencement identifying the files to be audited, except that no notice need be given to audit claim files which are the subject of inquiries or complaints. The audit shall commence no less than fourteen days from the date the Notice was sent, unless the audit subject agrees to earlier commencement.

(c) The Audit Unit shall randomly select separate samples of indemnity, denied, and medical-only files from two years' of the audit subject's claim logs, except that if the earliest of the last two completed years has already been the subject of an audit, claims will be randomly selected from only the last completed year.

(1) The total number of indemnity files randomly selected for audit will be determined based on the following table:

Population	*Sample Size*
8 or less	all
9-15	1 less than total
16-19	2 less than total
20-23	3 less than total
24-27	4 less than total
28-30	5 less than total
31-33	6 less than total
34-36	7 less than total
37-38	8 less than total
39-41	9 less than total
42	32
43-44	33
45	34
46-47	35
48-49	36
50-51	37
52-53	38
54-55	39
56-57	40
58-59	41
60-61	42
62-63	43
64-65	44
66-67	45
68-70	46
71-72	47
73-74	48
75-77	49
78-79	50
80-82	51
83-84	52
85-87	53
88-89	54
90-92	55

Population	*Sample Size*
93-95	56
96-98	57
99-101	58
102-104	59
105-107	60
108-110	61
111-114	62
115-117	63
118-120	64
121-124	65
125-128	66
129-131	67
132-135	68
136-139	69
140-143	70
144-148	71
149-152	72
153-156	73
157-161	74
162-166	75
167-171	76
172-176	77
177-181	78
182-187	79
188-192	80
193-198	81
199-204	82
205-210	83
211-217	84
218-223	85
224-230	86
231-238	87
239-245	88
246-253	89
254-261	90
262-270	91
271-279	92
280-288	93
289-298	94
299-308	95
309-319	96
320-330	97
331-342	98
343-354	99
355-367	100
368-381	101
382-396	102
397-411	103
412-427	104
428-444	105
445-463	106
464-482	107
483-503	108
504-525	109
526-549	110
550-575	111
576-603	112
604-633	113
634-665	114
666-700	115
701-739	116
740-781	117
782-827	118
828-879	119
880-936	120
937-1,000	121
1,001-1,072	122
1,073-1,154	123
1,155-1,248	124
1,249-1,356	125
1,357-1,483	126
1,484-1,633	127
1,634-1,814	128
1,815-2,036	129
2,037-2,315	130
2,316-2,677	131
2,678-3,163	132
3,164-3,852	133
3,853-4,904	134
4,905-6,710	135
6,711-10,530	136
10,531-23,993	137
23,994 +	138

(2) In conducting the audit, the Audit Unit shall calculate the frequency of files with violations as percentages of the files with exposure for violations after the following number of randomly selected indemnity files are audited:

Population	*Sample Size*
5 or less	all
6-10	1 less than total
11-13	2 less than total
14-16	3 less than total
17-18	4 less than total
19-20	5 less than total
21-23	6 less than total
24	17
25-26	18
27-29	19
30-31	20
32-33	21
34-36	22
37-39	23

Population	*Sample Size*
40-41	24
42-44	25
45-48	26
49-51	27
52-55	28
56-58	29
59-62	30
63-67	31
68-72	32
73-77	33
78-82	34
83-88	35
89-95	36
96-102	37
103-110	38
111-119	39
120-128	40
129-139	41
140-151	42
152-164	43
165-179	44
180-197	45
198-217	46
218-241	47
242-269	48
270-304	49
305-346	50
347-399	51
400-468	52
469-562	53
563-696	54
697-905	55
906-1,272	56
1,273-2,091	57
2.092-5,530	58
5,531 +	59

If any of the following criteria are met after auditing the sample size as set forth in this subsection (c)(2), the Audit Unit will proceed to audit the remaining number of randomly selected indemnity files selected for audit pursuant to subsection (c)(1):

(i) The number of randomly selected audited files with violations involving the failure to pay indemnity exceeds 20% of those files in which indemnity is accrued and payable and the average amount of unpaid indemnity exceeds $200.00 per file in which indemnity is accrued and payable;

(ii) The numbers of randomly selected files with violations involving the late first payments of temporary disability indemnity, permanent disability indemnity, vocational rehabilitation maintenance allowance, late subsequent indemnity payments, and late payments of death benefits, as mitigated for frequency under Section 10111.1(e)(3)(i) through (v), exceeds 30% of the files in which those indemnity payments have been made;

(iii) The number of randomly selected audited files with violations involving the failure to issue benefit notices, as assessed under Section 10111.1(a)(7)(ii) of these regulations, exceeds 30% of those files in which there is a requirement to issue those notices.

The determination of whether or not to audit the number of files selected pursuant to subsection (c)(1) of this section shall not be the subject of appeal, and no preliminary report of findings will be issued to the audit subject before the determination is made.

(d) The total numbers of denied files and medical-only files randomly selected for audit will be determined based on the following table:

Population	*Sample Size*
6 or less	all
7-10	1 less than total
11-14	2 less than total
15-17	3 less than total
18	14
19-20	15
21	16
22-23	17
24-25	18
26-27	19
28-29	20
30-31	21
32-33	22
34-36	23
37-38	24
39-41	25
42-43	26
44-46	27
47-49	28
50-52	29
53-55	30
56-59	31
60-63	32
64-67	33
68-71	34
72-75	35
76-80	36
81-85	37
86-90	38

Population	*Sample Size*
91-96	39
97-102	40
103-109	41
110-116	42
117-124	43
125-132	44
133-141	45
142-151	46
152-163	47
164-175	48
176-189	49
190-205	50
206-222	51
223-242	52
243-265	53
266-292	54
293-323	55
324-360	56
361-405	57
406-461	58
462-531	59
532-623	60
624-749	61
750-931	62
932-1,217	63
1,218-1,731	64
1,732-2,934	65
2,935-8,990	66
8,991 +	67

(e) In addition to randomly selected indemnity, denied, and medical-only files, the Audit Unit may also select for audit any or all files for which the Division of Workers' Compensation has received complaints within the past three years.

(f) The audit subject shall pay all expenses of an audit of an adjusting location outside the State of California, including per diem, travel expense, and compensated overtime of audit personnel.

(g) The audit subject shall make each of the claim files selected for audit available at the audit site at the time of audit commencement. If claim files are maintained in an electronic or other non-paper storage medium, the claims administrator shall, upon request, provide to the Audit Unit direct computer access to electronic claim files and/or legible printed paper copies of the claim files, including all records of compensation payments.

(h) The Audit Unit shall have discretion to audit files in addition to those identified with the Notice of Audit Commencement. The audit subject shall make each of the additional files selected for audit available at the audit site within 14 days of receipt of written notice identifying the additional files.

(i) The audit subject shall provide the auditor(s) an adequate, safe, and healthful work space during the audit, which allows the auditors a reasonable degree of privacy. If this work space is not provided, the Audit Unit may require the audit subject to deliver the files to the nearest Audit Unit office for completion of the audit.

(j) The Audit Unit may obtain and retain copies of documentation or information from claim files to support the assessment of penalties.

(k) The audit subject shall have the opportunity to discuss preliminary findings and provide additional information at a post-audit conference.

(*l*) The Audit Unit may at any time request additional information or documentation in order to complete its audit. Such information may include documentation that, as specified by Labor Code Sections 3751(a) and 3752, compensation has not been reduced or affected by any insurance, contribution, or other benefit due to or received by or from the employee. The audit subject shall provide any requested documentation or other information within thirty days from the Audit Unit's request, unless the Audit Unit extends the time for good cause.

(m) The Audit Unit shall issue a report of audit findings which may include, but is not limited to, the following: one or more requests for additional documentation or compliance, Notices of Intention to Issue Notice of Compensation Due, Preliminary Notices of Penalty Assessments, Notices of Compensation Due, or Notices of Penalty Assessments. If any additional requested documentation is not provided within thirty days of receipt of the report, additional audit penalties may be assessed under Section 10111.1(d)(2) of these Regulations.

Note: Authority cited: Sections 59, 129.5, 133 and 5307.3, Labor Code. Reference: Sections 11180, 11180.5, 11181 and 11182, Government Code; and Sections 111, 124, 129, 129.5, 3751 and 3752, Labor Code.

History: 1. Repealer and new section filed 1-28-94; operative 1-28-94. Submitted to OAL for printing only pursuant to Government Code section 11351 (Register 94, No. 4). For prior history, see Register 90, No. 4.

2. New subsections (c)-(e), subsection relettering, amendment of newly designated subsection (g) and amendment of Note filed 10-26-98; operative 11-25-98 (Register 98, No. 44).

Ref.: Hanna § 10.50[2][a]; Herlick Handbook §§ 1.6, 9.5.

§10107.1. Notice of Audit; Claim File Selection; Production of Claim Files; Auditing Procedure.

For audits conducted on or after January 1, 2003:

(a) Once a subject has been selected for an audit, the Audit Unit shall serve a Notice of Audit on the claims administrator. The Notice shall inform the administrator of its selection for audit, and may include a request to provide the Audit Unit with a claim log or logs. If the Audit Unit has requested claim logs, the audit subject shall provide two copies of the specified claim log(s) within fourteen days of the date of the receipt of the Notice.

(b) At least 14 days before the audit is scheduled, the Audit Unit shall send the audit subject a Notice of Audit Commencement identifying the claims to be audited. The audit shall commence no less than fourteen days from the date the Notice was sent, unless the audit subject and Audit Unit agrees to earlier commencement.

(c) For profile audit reviews conducted pursuant to Labor Code Section 129(b)(1), the Audit Unit shall randomly select samples of indemnity claims from the most recent three years of the audit subject's claim logs or from the list of claims for those years as reported to the Division of Workers' Compensation pursuant to Labor Code Section 138.6 as part of the Workers' Compensation Information System. If any of the years have been the subject of a previous audit, claims will be randomly selected from the most recent unaudited year(s).

(1) The initial number of indemnity claims randomly selected for audit will be determined based on the following table:

Population	*Sample Size*
5 or less	all
6-10	1 less than total
11-13	2 less than total
14-16	3 less than total
17-18	4 less than total
19-20	5 less than total
21-23	6 less than total
24	17
25-26	18
27-29	19
30-31	20
32-33	21
34-36	22
37-39	23
40-41	24
42-44	25
45-48	26
49-51	27
52-55	28
56-58	29
59-62	30
63-67	31
68-72	32
73-77	33
78-82	34
83-88	35
89-95	36
96-102	37
103-110	38
111-119	39
120-128	40
129-139	41
140-151	42
152-164	43
165-179	44
180-197	45
198-217	46
218-241	47
242-269	48
270-304	49
305-346	50
347-399	51
400-468	52
469-562	53
563-696	54
697-905	55
906-1,272	56
1,273-2,091	57
2,092-5,530	58
5,531 +	59

(2) In addition to the randomly selected indemnity claims, the Audit Unit may audit any claims for which it has received a complaint or information indicating a failure to pay indemnity, including any companion claim needed to ascertain the extent to which benefits have been provided.

(3) After reviewing the claims selected pursuant to subsection (1), the Audit Unit shall

calculate the audit subject's profile audit review performance rating based on its review of the randomly selected claims. The profile audit review performance rating will be calculated as follows:

(A) The factor for the failure to pay accrued and undisputed indemnity shall be determined by

(i-a) Dividing the number of randomly selected claims with violations involving the failure to pay indemnity by the number of randomly selected claims with accrued and payable indemnity, whether paid or not, to produce a frequency rate.

(i-b) Dividing the total amount of unpaid indemnity in randomly selected claims by the number of randomly selected claims with accrued and payable indemnity, whether paid or not, to produce an average amount of unpaid indemnity per file with the obligation to pay indemnity.

(i-c) Dividing the average amount of unpaid indemnity per randomly selected audited claim with the obligation to pay indemnity for the audit subject by the average amount of unpaid indemnity per randomly selected audited claim for all audit subjects for the three calendar years before the year preceding the year in which the current audit is being conducted, to produce a severity rate.

(i-d) Multiplying the frequency rate by the severity rate by a modifier of 2 to determine the factor for the failure to pay accrued and undisputed indemnity.

(ii) The factor for the late first payment of temporary disability indemnity and issuance of first temporary disability notices shall be determined by dividing the number of randomly selected claims with violations involving the late first payment of temporary disability indemnity, or in claims that involve salary continuation in lieu of first temporary disability payments, the late issuance of the first temporary disability notice by the number of randomly selected claims in which temporary disability payments or first temporary disability notices were issued.

(iii) The factor for the late first payment of permanent disability indemnity, vocational rehabilitation maintenance allowance, and death benefits shall be determined by dividing the numbers of randomly selected claims with violations involving late first payments of those benefits by the numbers of randomly selected claims with payments for those benefits. In calculation of this factor, claims shall be counted for each type of exposure and late first payment.

(iv) The factor for late subsequent indemnity payments shall be determined by dividing the number of randomly selected claims with violations involving late indemnity payments subsequent to first payment by the number of randomly selected claims with subsequent indemnity payments.

(v) The factor for failure to comply with requirements for notices advising injured employees of the process for selecting Agreed Medical Examiners and/or Qualified Medical Examiners, and for failure to comply with the requirements for notices advising injured workers of potential eligibility for vocational rehabilitation pursuant to Labor Code Section 4637 shall be determined by dividing the numbers of randomly selected claims with violations involving the failure to issue the notices by the numbers of randomly selected claims with the requirement to issue the notices. In calculation of this factor, claims shall be counted for each type of exposure and violation.

(vi) The audit subject's profile audit review performance rating will be determined by adding the factors calculated pursuant to subsections (c)(3)(A)(i) through (c)(3)(A)(v).

(B) If the audit subject's profile audit review performance rating meets or exceeds the worst 20% of performance ratings for all final audit reports issued over the three calendar years before the year preceding the current audit, the Audit Unit will issue Notices of Compensation Due pursuant to Section 10110 but will assess no administrative penalties for violations found in the profile audit review.

(C) If the audit subject's profile audit review performance rating fails to meet or exceed the rating of the worst 20% of performance ratings as calculated based on all final audit findings as published in the Annual DWC Audit Reports over the three calendar years before the year preceding the current audit, the Audit Unit will conduct a Full Compliance Audit by randomly selecting and auditing an additional sample of indemnity claims pursuant to subsection (d). Written notification of the Audit Unit's intent to proceed to a Full Compliance Audit, showing the calculation of the profile audit review performance rating, will be provided to the audit subject in time for the timely filing of an objection. The audit subject may dispute whether or not a Full Compliance Audit is merited under this subsection at a post-profile audit review conference. Following the post-profile audit review conference, the Audit Unit may continue with the Full Compliance Audit. The audit subject may appeal the issues pursuant to Section 10115.1 following the issuance of the final audit report. Failure of the audit subject to raise issues related to failing to meet or exceed the profile audit review performance standard during the post-profile audit review conference shall constitute a waiver of appeal on those issues.

(d) If the audit subjects fails to meet or exceed the profile audit review performance standard, the Audit Unit shall conduct a Full Compliance Audit by selecting and auditing an additional sample of indemnity claims.

(1) The total number of indemnity claims randomly selected for audit, including the number audited pursuant to subsection (c)(1), will be determined based on the following table:

Population	*Sample Size*
8 or less	all
9-15	1 less than total
16-19	2 less than total
20-23	3 less than total
24-27	4 less than total
28-30	5 less than total
31-33	6 less than total
34-36	7 less than total
37-38	8 less than total
39-41	9 less than total
42	32
43-44	33
45	34
46-47	35
48-49	36
50-51	37
52-53	38
54-55	39
56-57	40
58-59	41
60-61	42
62-63	43
64-65	44
66-67	45
68-70	46
71-72	47
73-74	48
75-77	49
78-79	50
80-82	51

Population	*Sample Size*
83-84	52
85-87	53
88-89	54
90-92	55
93-95	56
96-98	57
99-101	58
102-104	59
105-107	60
108-110	61
111-114	62
115-117	63
118-120	64
121-124	65
125-128	66
129-131	67
132-135	68
136-139	69
140-143	70
144-148	71
149-152	72
153-156	73
157-161	74
162-166	75
167-171	76
172-176	77
177-181	78
182-187	79
188-192	80
193-198	81
199-204	82
205-210	83
211-217	84
218-223	85
224-230	86
231-238	87
239-245	88
246-253	89
254-261	90
262-270	91
271-279	92
280-288	93
289-298	94
299-308	95
309-319	96
320-330	97
331-342	98
343-354	99
355-367	100
368-381	101
382-396	102
397-411	103
412-427	104

Population	*Sample Size*
428-444	105
445-463	106
464-482	107
483-503	108
504-525	109
526-549	110
550-575	111
576-603	112
604-633	113
634-665	114
666-700	115
701-739	116
740-781	117
782-827	118
828-879	119
880-936	120
937-1,000	121
1,001-1,072	122
1,073-1,154	123
1,155-1,248	124
1,249-1,356	125
1,357-1,483	126
1,484-1,633	127
1,634-1,814	128
1,815-2,036	129
2,037-2,315	130
2,316-2,677	131
2,678-3,163	132
3,164-3,852	133
3,853-4,904	134
4,905-6,710	135
6,711-10,530	136
10,531-23,993	137
23,994 +	138

(2) In addition to the randomly selected indemnity claims, the Audit Unit may audit any claims for which it has received a complaint or information indicating a failure to pay indemnity or late-paid indemnity, including any companion claim needed to ascertain the extent to which benefits have been provided.

(3) After reviewing the claims selected pursuant to subsection (1), the Audit Unit shall calculate the audit subject's full compliance audit performance rating.

(A) The audit subject's full compliance audit performance rating will be calculated pursuant to subsection (c)(3)(A), except that it shall be based on the review of all claims selected pursuant to subsection (d)(1).

(B) If the audit subject's full compliance audit performance rating meets or exceeds the worst 10% of performance ratings for all final audit reports issued over the three calendar years before the year preceding the current audit, the Audit Unit will issue Notices of Compensation Due pursuant to Section 10110 and will assess administrative penalties only for violations involving unpaid and late paid compensation, pursuant to Labor Code Section 129.5(c)(2).

(e) If the audit subject's full compliance audit performance rating fails to meet or exceed the rating of the worst 10% of performance ratings for all final audit reports issued over the three calendar years before the year preceding the current audit, the Audit Unit will audit all claims selected for audit for all violations, and also randomly select a sample of denied claims. Notification of the Audit Unit's intent to audit a sample of denied claims and assess penalties pursuant to Labor Code Section 129.5(c)(3) will be provided to the audit subject based on findings at a meet and confer audit review conference. At that time the audit subject may dispute whether or not it met or exceeded the Full Compliance Audit performance standard. Following the meet and confer audit review conference, the Audit Unit may continue with the Full Compliance Audit. The audit subject may appeal pursuant to Section 10115.1 following the issuance of the final audit report. Failure of the audit subject to raise issues related to failing to meet or exceed the full compliance audit performance standard during the meet and confer audit review conference shall constitute a waiver of appeal on those issues.

(1) The number of denied claims randomly selected for audit will be based on the following table:

Population	*Sample Size*
6 or less	all
7-10	1 less than total
11-14	2 less than total
15-17	3 less than total
18	14
19-20	15
21	16
22-23	17
24-25	18
26-27	19
28-29	20
30-31	21
32-33	22
34-36	23
37-38	24

Population	*Sample Size*
39-41	25
42-43	26
44-46	27
47-49	28
50-52	29
53-55	30
56-59	31
60-63	32
64-67	33
68-71	34
72-75	35
76-80	36
81-85	37
86-90	38
91-96	39
97-102	40
103-109	41
110-116	42
117-124	43
125-132	44
133-141	45
142-151	46
152-163	47
164-175	48
176-189	49
190-205	50
206-222	51
223-242	52
243-265	53
266-292	54
293-323	55
324-360	56
361-405	57
406-461	58
462-531	59
532-623	60
624-749	61
750-931	62
932-1,217	63
1,218-1,731	64
1,732-2,934	65
2,935-8,990	66
8,991 +	67

(2) In addition to the random samples of indemnity and denied claims and claims for which the Division received complaints or information indicating unpaid or late-paid compensation, the Audit Unit may select for audit any claims for which it received complaints or information over the past three years that indicate the possible existence of any claims handling violations.

(f) Following the conclusion of the audit, the Audit Unit shall issue a report of audit findings which may include, but is not limited to, the following: one or more requests for additional documentation or compliance, Notices of Intention to Issue Notice of Compensation Due, Preliminary Notices of Penalty Assessments, Notices of Compensation Due, or Notices of Penalty Assessments. If any additional requested documentation is not provided within thirty days of receipt of the report, additional audit penalties may be assessed under Section 10111.1(d)(2) of these Regulations.

(g) The audit subject shall pay all expenses of an audit of an adjusting location outside the State of California, including per diem, travel expense, and compensated overtime of audit personnel.

(h) The audit subject shall make each of the claim files selected for audit available at the audit site at the time of audit commencement. If claim files are maintained in an electronic or other non-paper storage medium, the claims administrator shall, upon request, provide to the Audit Unit direct computer access to electronic claim files and/or legible printed paper copies of the claim files, including all records of compensation payments. If a randomly selected indemnity, medical-only, or denied claim has been incorrectly classified as to type by the audit subject, the Audit Unit may randomly select an additional correctly designated claim file for audit, and may also assess penalties as appropriate in the misdesignated claim initially selected. If the audit subject fails to produce a claim selected for audit, the Audit Unit may assess a penalty for failure to produce the claim pursuant to Section 10111.2(b)(3) and may also select for audit another claim of the same type to complete the random sample. If the audit subject has transferred a claim selected for audit to a different adjusting location of the company being audited, the audit subject shall nonetheless produce the claim for audit within five working days of request, unless additional time is agreed upon by both the Audit Unit and the audit subject.

(i) The Audit Unit shall have discretion to audit claims in addition to those identified with the Notice of Audit Commencement. The audit subject shall make each of the additional claims selected for audit available at the audit site as follows:

(1) Open claims and closed claims stored on site within one working day of request;

(2) Closed claims stored off site within five working days of request, unless additional time is agreed upon by both the Audit Unit and the audit subject.

(j) The audit subject shall provide the auditor(s) an adequate, safe, and healthful workspace during the audit, which allows the auditors a reasonable degree of privacy. If this workspace is not provided, the Audit Unit may require the audit subject to deliver the files to the nearest Audit Unit office for completion of the audit.

(k) The Audit Unit may obtain and retain copies of documentation or information from claim files to support the assessment of penalties.

(*l*) The audit subject shall have the opportunity to discuss preliminary findings and provide additional information at a post-audit conference.

(m) The Audit Unit may at any time request additional information or documentation related to the claims being audited in order to complete its audit. Such information may include documentation that, as specified by Labor Code Sections 3751(a) and 3752, compensation has not been reduced or affected by any insurance, contribution, or other benefit due to or received by or from the employee. The audit subject shall provide any requested documentation or other information within thirty days from the Audit Unit's request, unless the Audit Unit extends the time for good cause.

Note: Authority cited: Sections 59, 129.5, 133 and 5307.3, Labor Code. Reference: Sections 11180, 11180.5, 11181 and 11182, Government Code; and Sections 111, 124, 129, 129.5, 3751 and 3752, Labor Code.

History: 1. New section filed 12-30-2002; operative 1-1-2003 pursuant to Government Code section 11343.4 (Register 2003, No. 1).

2. Change without regulatory effect amending subsections (c)(3)(A)(i-a) and (c)(3)(A)(i-c) filed 5-1-2003 pursuant to section 100, title 1, California Code of Regulations (Register 2003, No. 18).

3. Amendment of subsection (c)(3)(A)(v) filed 10-6-2003; operative 12-1-2003 (Register 2003, No. 41).

Ref.: Hanna § 1.12[8]; Herlick Handbook § 9.5.

§10108. Audit Violations—General Rules.

The following general rules apply to audits and audit processes under Labor Code §§129, 129.5:

(a) If the date or deadline (including any applicable extension) to perform any act falls on a weekend or holiday, the act may be performed on the last business day before or the first business day after the weekend or holiday. A payment date which is changed under this provision shall not change the normal dates for later payments in an existing two-week payment schedule.

(b) For the purpose of imposing audit penalties, if the claims administrator does not record the date it received a document, it shall be deemed received five days after the latest date the sender wrote on the document.

(c) Audit penalties will be based on each claim's status when the claim is audited. If, at the time of the audit, the claims administrator has failed to perform a required act, but remedies the failure prior to the issuance of the audit report, the claims administrator will nonetheless be accountable for the violation as a failure to act and audit findings related to the violation will be based on the failure to perform the act. Unless these regulations specifically provide otherwise, the penalty for an unlawful delay of more than 30 days in performing an act is the same as the penalty for not performing the act. However, the penalty will be mitigated for good faith because the act, though late, was eventually performed. There will be no mitigation for good faith, however, if the act was performed after notification to the audit subject that the claim was selected for audit. In such cases where there is an unlawful delay of more than 30 days in performing an act and the act was performed only after the audit subject was notified that the claim was selected for audit, violations will be calculated as though there was a failure to perform the act rather than late performance of the act. A lawful delay is a delay permitted by law or regulation, and for which the claims administrator has given a proper and timely notice of delay when such a notice is required. Any other delay is an unlawful delay.

(d) Penalties will not be assessed during the period a claims administrator is actively investigating its liability for provision of benefits or payment of compensation, provided that a Notice of Delay has been timely and properly issued in accordance with §9812 or §9813. However, penalties shall still be issued for violations during the period of delay for: failure to object to medical treatment bills in accordance with §9792.5, or failure to object to or pay bills for medical legal expense in accordance with §9794.

(e) Penalties will not be assessed for an act or omission where an injured worker's unreasonable refusal to cooperate in the investigation has prevented the claims administrator from determining its legal obligation to perform the act.

(f) Where a penalty is provided for failure to pay mileage fees related to medical treatment or evaluation, a penalty will be imposed if payment is not made at a rate that is at least the greater of the following: (i) thirty-four cents per mile, or (ii) the minimum rate adopted by the Director of the Department of Personnel Administration pursuant to Section 19820 of the Government Code for non-represented (excluded) employees at Title 2, CCR §599.631(a).

(g) Failure, delay, or refusal to pay compensation benefits or expenses shall be subject to the applicable penalties under §10111 or §10111.1 unless the legal, factual, or medical basis for the failure, refusal, or delay is documented in the claim file.

(h) The Audit Unit will not assess penalties for violations of failure to make payment of indemnity due if the total indemnity is less than ten dollars ($10.00) aggregate per claim.

(i) Nothing in these regulations will bar the assessment of a civil penalty under Labor Code Section 129.5(e), whether or not the audit subject meets or exceeds performance rating standards calculated pursuant to Section 10107.1(c)(3) or (d)(3).

(j) Claims that are randomly selected for audit pursuant to Sections 10107.1(c)(1) and (d)(1) will be considered as randomly selected claims for purposes of determining whether or not an audit subject meets or exceeds performance standards pursuant to Sections 10107.1(c)(3) or (d)(3), whether or not complaints or information indicating claims handling violations in those claims have been received by the Audit Unit. If the Audit Unit cannot ascertain the extent to which benefits have been paid on a claim randomly selected for audit without auditing a companion or master claim to that claim, the Audit Unit may add the companion or master claim to the sample. The companion or master claims will be considered as randomly selected claims for purposes of determining whether or not the audit subject meets or exceeds performance standards pursuant to Sections Section 10107.1(c)(3) and/or (d)(3).

(k) Notwithstanding Section 10111.2(a) and (b), penalties may be assessed for failure to timely submit an accurate Annual Report of Inventory regardless of whether or not an audit has been conducted, or, if an audit was conducted, whether or not the audit subject's performance rating in the key performance areas calculated pursuant to Section 10107(c) warrants the audit of a full sample of indemnity claims pursuant to Section 10107(c)(4), or a return, targeted audit based on performance in those areas pursuant to Section 10106(c)(2).

(*l*) Notwithstanding penalty amounts established pursuant to Section 10111.2, penalties for late performance of an act may not exceed penalty amounts for the failure to perform an act.

(m) If more than one claims administrator has adjusted a claim file that is being audited or investigated, penalties will be assessed against the audit subject only for violations that occurred subsequent to the date the audit subject began adjusting the claim file, except that the audit subject will be assessed penalties for the failure to pay compensation due if the claim was open when transferred to the audit subject or re-opened subsequent to its transfer and the compensation remained unpaid. The claims administrator is required to correct any failures to issue notices which are still pertinent, to recalculate and correct any improperly calculated payments due to the worker, and to pay any interest and increase due for late paid medical payments.

(n) Successor liability may be imposed on a claims administrator or insurer that has merged with, consolidated, or otherwise continued the business of a corporation or other business entity that is a responsible party and failed to meet its obligations under Divisions 1 and 4 of the Labor Code or regulations of the administrative director. The surviving claims administrator shall assume and be liable for all the liabilities, obligations and penalties of the prior corporation or business entity. Successor liability will be imposed if there has been a substantial continuity of business operations; and/or the new business uses the same or substantially the same work force. In such circumstances, due consideration of the appropriateness of penalties with respect to the history of previous violations pursuant to Labor Code Section 129.5(b)(3) will encompass findings related to the last audit of the predecessor claims administrator applied in conjunction with audit results of the successor claims administrator pursuant to Section 10111.2(c)(4) of these regulations.

Note: Authority cited: Sections 59, 129.5, 133, 138.3, 138.4 and 5307.3, Labor Code. Reference: Sections 124, 129, 129.5, 4600 and 4621, Labor Code; and Sections 7, 9, 10 and 11, Civil Code.

History: 1. Renumbering of former section 10108 to section 10111 and new section filed 1-28-94; operative 1-28-94. Submitted to OAL for printing only pursuant to Government Code section 11351 (Register 94, No. 4).

2. Amendment of subsection (e) filed 2-14-96; operative 2-14-96. Submitted to OAL for printing only pursuant to Government Code section 11351 (Register 96, No. 7).

3. Amendment of subsection (c) filed 10-26-98; operative 11-25-98 (Register 98, No. 44).

4. Amendment of subsections (c) and (f) and new subsections (h)-(n) filed 12-30-2002; operative 1-1-2003 pursuant to Government Code section 11343.4 (Register 2003, No. 1).

Ref.: Hanna § 1.12[8]; Herlick Handbook §§ 1.6, 9.5.

§10109. Duty to Conduct Investigation; Duty of Good Faith.

(a) To comply with the time requirements of the Labor Code and the Administrative Director's regulations, a claims administrator must conduct a reasonable and timely investigation upon receiving notice or knowledge of an injury or claim for a workers' compensation benefit.

(b) A reasonable investigation must attempt to obtain the information needed to determine and timely provide each benefit, if any, which may be due the employee.

(1) The administrator may not restrict its investigation to preparing objections or defenses to a claim, but must fully and fairly gather the pertinent information, whether that information requires or excuses benefit payment. The investigation must supply the information needed to provide timely benefits and to document for audit the administrator's basis for its claims decisions. The claimant's burden of proof before the Appeal Board does not excuse the administrator's duty to investigate the claim.

(2) The claims administrator may not restrict its investigation to the specific benefit claimed if the nature of the claim suggests that other benefits might also be due.

(c) The duty to investigate requires further investigation if the claims administrator receives later information, not covered in an earlier investigation, which might affect benefits due.

(d) The claims administrator must document in its claim file the investigatory acts undertaken and the information obtained as a result of the investigation.

(e) Insurers, self-insured employers and third-party administrators shall deal fairly and in good faith with all claimants, including lien claimants.

Note: Authority cited: Sections 59, 129.5, 133 and 5307.3, Labor Code. Reference: Article 14, Section 4, California Constitution; Sections 124, 129, 133, 4061, 4550, 4600, 4636 through 4638, 4650, 4701 through 4703.5, 5402 and 5814, Labor Code; *Ramirez v. WCAB*, 10 Cal.App.3d 227, 88 CR 865, 35 CCC 383 (1970); and Section 790.03(h)(3), (5), (13), Insurance Code.

History: 1. Relocation of article 4 heading to article 6, renumbering of former section 10109 to section 10113 and new section filed 1-28-94; operative 1-28-94. Submitted to OAL for printing only pursuant to Government Code section 11351 (Register 94, No. 4).

Ref.: Hanna § 10.50[2][a]; Herlick Handbook §§ 1.6, 9.5.

ARTICLE 4
Notices of Compensation Due

§10110. Notice of Intention to Issue a Notice of Compensation Due; Notice of Compensation Due; Review by Workers' Compensation Appeals Board.

(a) If as the result of an audit, the Administrative Director determines that compensation is due and unpaid to an employee, (s)he shall serve on the audit subject, personally or by first class mail, a Notice of Intention to Issue a Notice of Compensation Due specifying the amount, reason and period for which compensation is due. If liability for compensation is clear but the amount cannot be determined from information in the claim file, the Administrative Director may direct the claims administrator to gather the necessary additional information.

(b) The audit subject may file an Objection to the Notice of Intention within 14 days of receipt. The Objection shall state in detail the reasons the compensation found due is disputed and may include supporting documentation and legal argument.

(c) The Administrative Director will review any Objection, and may set the matter for an administrative meeting, which may be included as part of a post audit conference. The administrative meeting or the post audit conference may be set on the Administrative Director's own initiative or at the request of the audit subject. After review, the Administrative Director shall either dismiss the Notice of Intention to Issue a Notice of Compensation Due or issue a Notice of Compensation Due.

(d) If no timely Objection is submitted, the Administration Director may issue a Notice of Compensation Due. A Notice of Compensation Due which was issued without a timely Objection shall be final without right of further review unless the Workers' Compensation Appeals Board agrees to hear an appeal after a late Objection.

(e) A Notice of Compensation Due shall specify the amount, reason and period for which compensation is due and shall order payment of the compensation to the employee or dependent. The Notice of Compensation Due shall be served on the insurer, self-insured employer or third-party administrator personally or by certified or registered mail, and a copy shall be sent by first class mail to the affected employee or dependent. The compensation due must be paid within 15 days of receipt of the Notice of Compensation Due unless appealed to the Workers Compensation Appeals Board in accordance with Section 10115 of these Rules and the applicable rules of the Workers' Compensation Appeals Board.

Note: Authority cited: Sections 59, 129.5, 133, 4603.5 and 5307.3, Labor Code. Reference: Sections 129, 139.5, 3207, 4453, 4550, 4600, 4621, 4636 through 4638, 4639, 4653, 4658, 4659, 4660, 4661.5, 4701-4703.5, 4900 and 4902, Labor Code; and Section 10952, Title 8, California Code of Regulations.

History: 1. New article 4 heading, renumbering of former section 10110 to section 10114 and new section filed 1-28-94; operative 1-28-94. Submitted to OAL for printing only pursuant to Government Code section 11351 (Register 94, No. 4).

Ref.: Hanna §§ 1.12[9][a]–[b], 10.50[2][a]; Herlick Handbook §§ 1.6, 9.5.

ARTICLE 5
Administrative Penalties

§10111. Schedule of Administrative Penalties for injuries on or after January 1, 1990, but Before January 1, 1994.

The administrative penalties set forth in subsections (a) through (d) of this section will be imposed for injuries occurring on or after January 1, 1990, but before January 1, 1994, subject to any applicable mitigation or exacerbation under subsection (e) of this section.

(a) A penalty of up to $100 for each violation shall be assessed when there is:

(1) Failure to make full payment of 10% self-imposed increase when temporary disability indemnity or permanent disability indemnity is overdue. The penalty for this violation is:

If the self-imposed increase was not paid or was only partially paid, the audit penalty is based on the amount of the underlying indemnity and is as follows:

$25 if the late-paid indemnity totals not more than 3 days;

$50 if the late-paid indemnity totals more than 3 but not more than 7 days;

$75 if the late-paid indemnity totals more than 7 but not more than 14 days;

$100 if the late paid indemnity totals more than 14 days.

(2) Failure to provide first permanent disability payment when due and/or within 14 days after temporary disability payments are terminated. The penalty for this violation is:

$25 if the first payment was made 1 to 2 days late;

$50 if the first payment was made 3 to 7 days late;

$75 if the first payment was made 8 to 14 days late;

$100 if the first payment was made more than 14 days late.

(3) Failure to respond to a written request for medical treatment of injured worker within 20 days of the date of request. The penalty for this violation is:

$25 for a response made from 1 to 7 days late;

$50 for a response made from 8 to 15 days late;

$75 for a response made from 16 to 34 days late;

$100 for failure to respond for more than 35 days.

(4) Failure to provide, upon request, any transportation costs when due to injured worker for medical care. The penalty for this violation is:

$25 for $10 or less in expense;

$50 for more than $10, to $20, in expense;

$75 for more than $20, to $40, in expense;

$100 for more than $40 in expense.

(5) Failure to document average weekly earnings if temporary disability indemnity is being paid at less than the maximum rate. The penalty for this violation is $100.

(6) Failure to make the first payment of temporary disability indemnity not later than 14 days after the date of the employer's knowledge of injury and disability pursuant to Labor Code Section 4650(a). The penalty for this violation is:

$25 if the first payment was made 1 to 2 days late;

$50 if the first payment was made 3 to 7 days late;

$75 if the first payment was made 8 to 14 days late, and/or if all indemnity then due was not paid but was paid with a subsequent payment;

$100 if the first payment was made more than 14 days late, and/or if all indemnity then due was not paid with the first payment and remains unpaid at the time of audit.

(7) Failure to follow the Rules and Regulations established by the Administrative Director for the purpose of carrying out the workers' compensation provisions in Labor Code Section 3200 through Section 6002. The penalty for this violation is:

[i] For each failure to include in a claim file a copy of the Employee's Claim for Worker's Compensation Benefits, DWC Form 1, showing the date the form was provided to and received from the employee, or documentation of the date the claim form was provided to the employee if the employee did not return the form, the penalty is:

$100 if there were any late indemnity payments, or if notice of acceptance of the claim was not issued within 90 days after the employer's date of knowledge of injury and disability, or if the claim was denied.

[ii] For each failure to issue a notice of benefits as required by Title 8, California Code of Regulations, Division 1, Chapter 4.5, Subchapter 1, Article 8, beginning with Section 9810, or by Title 8, California Code of Regulations, Division 1, Chapter 4.5, Subchapter 1.5, Article 7, beginning with Section 10122, unless penalties apply and are assessed under Section 10111(b)(2) of these regulations, the penalty is $100.

[iii] For each notice of benefits which was not issued timely as provided in Title 8, California Code of Regulations, Division 1, Chapter 4.5, Subchapter 1, Article 8, beginning with Section 9810, or as provided in Title 8, California Code of Regulations, Division 1, Chapter 4.5, Subchapter 1.5, Article 7, beginning with Section 10122, the penalty is:

$25 for each notice of first, resumed, changed or final payment of temporary disability indemnity, wage continuation, death benefits, permanent disability indemnity, or VRMA which was issued from 1 to 7 days late;

$50 for each notice of first, resumed, changed or final payment of temporary disability indemnity, wage continuation, death benefits, permanent disability indemnity, or VRMA which was issued more than 7 days late, and for each delay in decision notice or denial notice which was issued from 1 to 7 days late;

$75 for each delay in decision notice or denial notice which was issued more than 7 days late.

[iv] For each Notice of Benefits required by Title 8, California Code of Regulations, Division 1, Chapter 4.5, Subchapter 1, Article 8, beginning with Section 9810, or by Title 8, California Code of Regulations, Division 1, Chapter 4.5, Subchapter 1.5, Article 7, beginning with Section 10122, which was materially inaccurate or incomplete, except an inaccurate or incomplete denial notice, the penalty is $25. For a materially inaccurate or incomplete denial notice the penalty is $100.

[v] For each failure to include in a claim file, or document attempts to obtain, any of the required contents specified in Section 10101, the penalty is $100.

[vi] For each failure to comply with any regulation of the Administrative Director, not otherwise assessed in these Regulations, the penalty is $100.

(8) Failure to pay or object to all documented Medical-Legal expenses within 60 days of receipt of billing and any required reports as provided for in Labor Code 4622. The penalty for this violation is:

$50 for each bill which was paid more than 60 days from receipt with interest and a 10% increase;

$75 for each bill which was paid more than 60 days from receipt where either interest or a 10% increase was not included;

$100 for each bill which was paid more than 60 days from receipt where neither interest nor a 10% increase was paid;

$100 for each bill which was not paid where no timely objection was sent.

(9) Failure to pay or object to expenses for medical treatment within 60 days of receipt of the bill and any required reports. The penalty for this violation is:

$25 for each bill of $100 or less, excluding interest and penalty;

$50 for each bill of more than $100, but no more than $200, excluding interest and penalty;

$75 for each bill of more than $200, but no more than $300, excluding interest and penalty;

$100 for each bill of more than $300, excluding interest and penalty.

(10) Failure to pay within ten days any indemnity due, which is not specified in subsections (a)(1) through (a)(9). The penalty for this violation is:

$25 for late payment of 3 days of indemnity or less;

$50 for late payment of more than 3 but no more than 7 days of indemnity;

$75 for late payment of more than 7 days of indemnity, or failure to pay 3 days of indemnity or less;

$100 for failure to pay more than 3 days of indemnity.

(b) A penalty of up to $500 for each violation shall be assessed when there is:

(1) Failure to maintain and provide a written claim log as defined in Section 10100(g) to the audit unit commencing July 1, 1990, and thereafter. The claim log shall contain all claims received, whether liability has been accepted, and distinguish between Indemnity and Medical-only claims. The penalty for this violation is:

$25 for each failure to list on a claim log one or more of the following: employee's name; claim number; date of injury;

$25 for each misdesignation of an indemnity file as a medical-only file on the claim log;

$100 for each failure to identify subsidiary self-insured employers on the log;

$100 for each failure to identify the underwriting insurance company of an insurance group;

$100 for each failure to designate a denied claim on the log;

$100 for each claim not listed on the log;

$250 for each failure to provide the claim log to the Audit Unit within 14 days of receipt of a written request if the claim log was provided more than 14 but no more than 30 days from receipt of the request;

$500 for each failure for more than 30 days from receipt of a written request, to provide the claim log to the Audit Unit.

(2) Failure to comply with Labor Code Sections 4636, 4637 and 4644. The penalty for this violation is:

[i] The penalty for each failure to assign a qualified rehabilitation representative immediately after 90 days of aggregate temporary disability indemnity is $100 if the assignment was made or the employee returned to his or her usual and customary occupation more than 10 but not more than 20 days after 90 days of aggregate total disability, and an additional $100 for each additional delay of not more than 10 days, to a maximum penalty of $500.

[ii] The penalty for each failure to issue notice of medical eligibility for vocational rehabilitation services (if not previously issued) within 10 days after knowledge of a physician's opinion that the employee is medically eligible, or for failure to issue notice within 10 days after 366 days of aggregate total temporary disability, is $100 if the notice was issued not more than 10 days late, and an additional $100 for each additional delay of not more than 10 days, to a maximum penalty of $500.

[iii] The penalty for each failure to notify an injured employee of the reasons he or she is not entitled to any, or to any further, vocational rehabilitation services, and the procedure for contesting the determination of non-eligibility, is $100 if notification was issued more than 10 but not more than 20 days after the determination, and an additional $100 for each additional delay of not more than 10 days, to a maximum penalty of $500.

(c) A penalty of up to $1,000 for each violation shall be assessed when there is:

(1) Failure to pay or appeal penalties provided for in the Notice of Compensation Due within 15 days of the date of receipt of the Notice. The penalty for this violation is:

$250 for each assessment paid more than 15 but not more than 30 days after receipt;

$500 for each assessment paid more than 30 but not more than 45 days after receipt;

$1,000 for each assessment not paid within 45 days after receipt.

(2) Failure to comply with or appeal any final order of the Workers' Compensation Appeals Board within 30 days of service. The penalty for this violation is:

$250 for full compliance in more than 30 but not more than 45 days from the date of service, or for any late payment or failure to pay interest due;

$500 for full compliance (other than a late interest payment) in more than 45 but not more than 60 days from the date of service;

$750 for full compliance (other than a late interest payment) in more than 60 but not more than 75 days from the date of service;

$1,000 if there was not full compliance (other than failure to pay interest) within 75 days of the date of service.

(d) A penalty of up to $5,000 for each violation shall be assessed when there is:

(1) Failure to produce, on a second request, a legible paper copy of a claim files within 5 days of written notice by the Administrative Director or his representatives. The penalty for this violation is:

$100 if the file was produced not more than 3 days late;

$250 if the file was produced more than 3 but not more than 14 days late;

$500 if the file was produced more than 14 but not more than 29 days late;

$1,000 if the file was produced more than 29 but not more than 40 days late;

$2500 if the file was produced more than 40 days late but not more than 90 days late.

$5000 if the was produced more than 90 days late or was not produced.

(2) Denial of liability for a claim without supporting documentation.

The total penalty shall be determined by applying the penalty assessment amount listed in [i] for gravity, subtracting the amount listed in [ii] for good faith if applicable, and increasing or decreasing the penalty as applicable for history and frequency as set forth in [iii] and [iv]:

[i] For a claim involving potential for medical treatment only the penalty is $3,500;

For a claim involving potential for medical treatment and either temporary or permanent disability the penalty is $4,000;

For a claim involving potential for medical treatment and both temporary and permanent disability the penalty is $4,500;

For a claim involving potential for medical treatment, temporary disability, permanent disability and vocational rehabilitation the penalty is $5,000;

For a claim involving potential for death benefits the penalty is $5,000.

[ii] The penalty will be reduced by $1,000 for good faith if there was a reasonable attempt to investigate the claim.

[iii] Reduction or increase of the penalty for history shall be based on the following:

An audit subject having no prior Audit Unit history will receive a $500 reduction;

An audit subject having a prior Audit Unit history of no more than one audited unsupported denial will receive a $500 reduction;

An audit subject having a prior Audit Unit history of more than one audited unsupported denial but no more than 5% of audited denials as unsupported will receive no reduction or increase for history;

An audit subject having a prior Audit Unit history of more than one audited unsupported denial and more than 5% of audited denials as unsupported will receive a $500 increase.

[iv] Reduction or increase of the penalty for frequency shall be based on the following:

An audit subject having no more than one audited unsupported denial will receive a $500 reduction;

An audit subject having more than one audited unsupported denial but no more than 5% of audited denials which are unsupported will receive no reduction or increase for frequency;

An audit subject having more than one audited unsupported denial and more than 5% of audited denials which are unsupported will receive an increase of $500.

[v] The total amount assessed for a denial shall be reduced by 50% if the claim was accepted after the denial without evidence that the acceptance was the result of litigation or of the claim's selection for audit.

(3) Except as provided in subsection (d)(1) of this section, failure to comply with or appeal any lawful written request or order of the Administrative Director regarding a claim filed within 30 days. The penalty for this violation is:

$500 if there was compliance in more than 30 but not more than 40 days from receipt or order;

$1,000 if there was compliance in more than 40 but not more than 60 days from receipt of the request or order;

$2,500 if there was compliance in more than 60 but not more than 90 days of receipt fo the request or order;

$5,000 for failure to comply within 90 days of receipt of the request or order.

(4) Failure by a claims administrator to provide a claim form within 24 hours upon request of an injured worker or his/her agent. The penalty for this violation is:

$500 if the claim form was provided in more than 1 but not more than 5 working days from receipt of the request, if benefits were being provided to the employee at the time of the request;

$1,000 if the claim form was not provided within 5 working days of receipt of the request, if benefits were being provided to the employee at the time of the request;

$3,000 if the claim form was provided in more than 1 but not more than 5 working days from receipt of the request, if benefits were not being provided to the employee at the time of the request;

$5,000 if the claim form was not provided within 5 working days of receipt of the request, if benefits were not being provided to the employee at the time of the request.

(e) The penalties otherwise applicable under subsections (a) through (d) of this section shall be modified, if warranted, for good faith, history, and frequency in the same manner as penalties are modified for acts or omissions occurring on or after January 1, 1994 by Section 10111.1(e) of this Article.

Note: Authority cited: Sections 59, 129.5, 133, 138.3, 138.4, 139.5, 4603.5, 4627 and 5307.3, Labor Code. Reference: Sections 124, 129, 129.5, 4061, 4453, 4454, 4550, 4600, 4603.2, 4621, 4622, 4625, 4636 through 4638, 4639, 4641, 4642, 4650, 4651, 4701 through 4703.5, 4706, 4706.5, 5401, 5401.6, 5402, 5800 and 5814, Labor Code; and Section 2629.1(e), (f), Unemployment Insurance Code.

History: 1. New section filed 1-18-90; operative 1-18-90 (Register 90, No. 4). New section is exempt from review by OAL pursuant to Government Code Section 11351.

2. Relocation and amendment of article heading, renumbering of former section 10111 to section 10114 subsections (g)-(h) and renumbering and amendment of former section 10108 to section 10111 filed 1-28-94; operative 1-28-94. Submitted to OAL for printing only pursuant to Government Code section 11351 (Register 94, No. 4).

3. Editorial correction by official state publisher of subsection (a)(2) (Register 95, No. 32).

4. Amendment of subsections (a), (a)(6), (a)(7)[ii], (a)(7)[iv] and (b)(1) filed 2-14-96; operative 2-14-96. Submitted to OAL for printing only pursuant to Government Code section 11351 (Register 96, No. 7).

5. Amendment of subsection (b)(1) filed 7-30-96; operative 7-30-96 pursuant to Government Code section 11343.4(d) (Register 96, No. 31).

Ref.: Hanna § 10.50[2][b]; Herlick Handbook §§ 1.6, 9.5.

§10111.1. Schedule of Administrative Penalties for Injuries On or After January 1, 1994.

The administrative penalties set forth in subsections (a) through (d) of this section will be imposed for injuries occurring on or after January 1, 1994, subject to any applicable mitigation or exacerbation under subsection (e) of this section. Penalties will not be assessed for violations occurring during the period January 1, 1994 through March 31, 1994 for acts or omissions for which there previously existed no audit penalties.

(a) The following Group A violations carry penalties of up to $100:

(1) The penalty for each failure to pay the 10% self-imposed increase with a late indemnity payment in accordance with Labor Code Section 4650(d) is:

$25 if the self-imposed increase was paid after the late indemnity payment;

If the self-imposed increase was not paid or was only partially paid, the audit penalty is based on the amount of the underlying indemnity and is as follows:

$25 if the late-paid indemnity totals not more than 3 days;

$50 if the late-paid indemnity totals more than 3 but not more than 7 days;

$75 if the late-paid indemnity totals more than 7 but not more than 14 days;

$100 if the late paid indemnity totals more than 14 days.

(2) The penalty for each failure to make the first payment of permanent disability indemnity within 14 days after the last payment of temporary disability indemnity, or within 14 days of knowledge of the existence of permanent disability when there is no temporary disability, is:

$25 if the first payment was made 1 to 2 days late;

$50 if the first payment was made 3 to 7 days late;

$75 if the first payment was made 8 to 14 days late;

$100 if the first payment was made more than 14 days late;

(3) The penalty for each failure to object or pay to the injured worker, within 60 days of receiving a request, reimbursement for the reasonable expense incurred for self-procured medical treatment in accordance with Labor Code Section 4600, is:

$25 for $100 or less in expense;

$50 for more than $100, to $200, in expense;

$75 for more than $200, to $400, in expense;

$100 for more than $400 in expense.

(4) The penalty for each failure to pay mileage fees and bridge tolls when notifying the employee of a medical evaluation scheduled by the claims administrator, in accordance with Labor Code Sections 4600 through 4621; or to pay mileage fees and bridge tolls within 14 days of receiving notice of a medical evaluation scheduled by the administrative director or the appeals board; or to object or pay the injured worker for any other transportation, temporary disability, meal or lodging expense incurred to obtain medical treatment or evaluation, within 60 days of receiving a request, is:

$25 for $10 or less in expense;

$50 for more than $10, to $50, in expense;

$75 for more than $50, to $100, in expense;

$100 for more than $100 in expense.

(5) The penalty for each failure to document a factual basis for paying less than the maximum indemnity rate is $100.

(6) The penalty for each failure to make temporary disability, permanent disability, death benefits or VRMA payments according to the payment schedule defined by Section 10100.1(x) of these regulations is:

$25 for each payment made 1 to 2 days late;

$50 for each payment made 3 to 7 days late;

$75 for each payment made 8 to 14 days late;

$100 for each payment made more than 14 days late.

(7) The penalty for each failure to comply with any regulation of the Administrative Director specified in this subsection is:

[i] For each failure to include in a claim file a copy of the Employee's Claim for Worker's Compensation Benefits, DWC Form 1, showing the date the form was provided to and received from the employee, or documentation of the date the claim form was provided to the employee if the employee did not return the form, the penalty is:

$100 if there was any late indemnity payments, or if notice of acceptance of the claim was not issued within 90 days after the employer's date of knowledge of injury and disability, or if the claim was denied.

[ii] For each failure to issue a notice of benefits as required by Title 8, California Code of Regulations, Division 4.5, Chapter 1, Article 8, beginning with Section 9810, or by Title 8, California Code of Regulations, Division 4.5, Chapter 1.5, Article 7, beginning with Section 10122, unless penalties apply and are assessed under Section 10111.1(b)(2), (b)(3), (b)(4), (b)(5), (b)(6), (b)(7) or (b)(8) of these Rules, the penalty is $100.

[iii] For each Notice of Benefits which was not issued timely as provided in Title 8, California Code of Regulations, Division 1, Chapter 4.5, Subchapter 1, Article 8, beginning with Section 9810, or as provided in Title 8, California Code of Regulations, Division 1, Chapter 4.5, Subchapter 1.5, Article 7, beginning with Section 10122, unless penalties apply and are assessed under Section 10111.1(b)(2), (b)(3), (b)(4), (b)(5), (b)(6), (b)(7) or (b)(8) of these regulations, the penalty is:

$25 for each notice of first, resumed, changed or final payment of temporary disability indemnity, wage continuation, death benefits, permanent disability indemnity, or VRMA which was issued from 1 to 7 days late;

$50 for each notice of first, resumed, changed or final payment of temporary disability indemnity, wage continuation, death benefits, permanent disability indemnity, or VRMA which was issued more than 7 days late, and for each delay in decision notice which was issued from 1 to 7 days late;

$75 for each delay in decision notice which was issued more than 7 days late.

[iv] For each notice of benefits required by Title 8, California Code of Regulations, Division 1, Chapter 4.5, Subchapter 1, Article 8, beginning with Section 9810, (except a materially misleading denial notice assessed under Section 10111.1(b)(9)), or by Title 8, California Code of Regulations, Division 1, Chapter 4.5, Subchapter 1.5, Article 7, beginning with Section 10122, which is materially inaccurate or incomplete, the penalty is $25.

[v] For each failure to include in a claim file, or document attempts to obtain, any of the required contents specified in Section 10101.1(b), (c), (d), (e), (f), (g), (h), (i), (j) of these Regulations, the penalty is $100.

[vi] For each failure to comply with any regulation of the Administrative Director, not otherwise assessed in this Subchapter, the penalty is $100.

(8) The penalty for each failure to pay or object to a billing for a medical-legal expense, in the manner required by Section 9794, within 60

days of receiving the bill and all reports and documents required by the Administrative Director incident to the services, is:

$25 for each bill which was paid more than 60 days from receipt with interest and a 10% increase;

$50 for each bill which was paid more than 60 days from receipt where either interest or a 10% increase was not included;

$75 for each bill which was paid more than 60 days from receipt where neither interest nor a 10% increase was paid.

$100 for each bill which was not paid at the time the audit subject was notified the claim was selected for audit where no timely objection was sent.

(9) The penalty for each failure to pay or object to, within 60 days of receipt, in the manner required by law or regulation, a bill for medical treatment provided or authorized by the treating physician, is as follows when the bill remains unpaid at the time the audit subject is notified that the claim was selected for audit. For the purpose of this penalty the treating physician will be presumed chosen by the employee unless the claims administrator demonstrates otherwise:

$25 for each bill of $100 or less, excluding interest and penalty;

$50 for each bill of more than $100, but no more than $200 excluding interest and penalty;

$75 for each bill of more than $200, but no more than $300, excluding interest and penalty;

$100 for each bill of more than $300, excluding interest and penalty.

(10) The penalty for each failure to pay or object to, within 60 days of receipt, in the manner required by law or regulation, a bill for medical treatment provided or authorized by the treating physician, is as follows when the bill was paid before the audit subject was notified that the claim was selected for audit:

$25 for each bill which included a 10% increase and interest with the late payment of any uncontested amount of the bill, in accordance with Labor Code Section 4603.2;

$50 for each bill which included either a 10% increase or interest with the late payment of any uncontested amount of the bill, in accordance with Labor Code Section 4603.2;

$75 for any bill which included neither a 10% increase nor interest with the late payment of any uncontested amount of the bill, in accordance with Labor Code Section 4603.2.

(11) The penalty for each failure to pay or object to a vocational rehabilitation bill within 60 days of receipt, as required by Title 8, California Code of Regulations, Sections 10132 and 10132.1, is:

$25 for each bill of $100 or less;

$50 for each bill of more than $100, but no more than $200;

$75 for each bill of more than $200, but no more than $300;

$100 for each bill of more than $300.

(12) The penalty for each failure to make a required first payment of temporary disability indemnity within 14 days after the employer's date of knowledge of injury and disability is:

$25 if the first payment was made 1 to 7 days late;

$50 if the first payment was made 8 to 14 days late;

$75 if the first payment was made 15 to 21 days late;

$100 if the first payment was made more than 21 days late.

(13) The penalty for each underpayment of an indemnity payment (including death benefits and VRMA), when the balance of the indemnity was paid late, is:

$25 for late payment of the equivalent of 3 days of indemnity or less;

$50 for late payment of the equivalent of more than 3 but no more than 7 days of indemnity;

$75 for late payment of the equivalent of more than 7 but no more than 14 days of indemnity;

$100 for the late payment of the equivalent of more than 14 days of indemnity.

(14) The penalty for each failure to make a first payment of VRMA or death benefit when due is:

$25 if the first payment was made 1 to 7 days late;

$50 if the first payment was made 8 to 14 days late;

$75 if the first payment was made 15 to 21 days late;

$100 if the first payment was made more than 21 days late.

(b) The following Group B violations carry penalties of up to $500:

(1) The penalty for each failure to maintain or provide to the Audit Unit a claim log which complies with these Regulations is:

$25 for each failure to list on a claim log one or more of the following: employee's name; claim number; date of injury;

$25 for each misdesignation of an indemnity file as a medical-only file on the claim log;

$100 for each failure to identify self-insured employers on the log as required by Section 10103.1(b)(6) of these Regulations;

$100 for each failure to identify the underwriting insurance company of an insurance group;

$100 for each failure to designate a denied claim on the log;

$100 for each claim not listed on the log;

$250 for each failure to provide the claim log to the Audit Unit within 14 days of receipt of a written request if the claim log was provided more than 14 but no more than 30 days from receipt of the request;

$500 for each failure for more than 30 days from receipt of a written request, to provide the claim log to the Audit Unit.

(2) The penalty for each failure to provide information regarding the Americans with Disabilities Act, the Fair Employment and Housing Act, and workers' compensation vocational rehabilitation as required by Labor Code Section 4636(a) immediately after 90 days of aggregate temporary disability indemnity is $100 if the information was provided or the employee returned to his or her usual and customary occupation more than 10 but not more than 20 days after 90 days of aggregate total disability, and an additional $100 for each additional delay of not more than 10 days, to a maximum penalty of $400 if the notice was issued more than 30 days late, and $500 if the notice was overdue more than 40 days and was not issued at the time the audit subject was notified that the claim was selected for audit.

(3) The penalty for each failure to issue notice of medical eligibility for vocational rehabilitation services (if not previously issued) within 10 days after knowledge of a physician's opinion that the employee is medically eligible, or for failure to issue notice within 10 days after 366 days of aggregate total temporary disability, is $100 if the notice was issued not more than 10 days late, and an additional $100 for each additional delay of not more than 10 days, to a maximum penalty of $400 if the notice was issued more than 30 days late, and $500 if the notice was overdue more than 40 days and was not issued at the time the audit subject was notified that the claim was selected for audit. Where the injured worker is represented by an attorney and documentation in the claim file indicates that the injured worker's attorney has received a copy of the physician's report indicating the employee is medically eligible for vocational rehabilitation, and if the knowledge is of a physician's opinion other than the injured worker's treating physician, a physician selected from a panel provided by the Industrial Medical Council, or an agreed medical examiner, the penalty shall be assessed at 20% of the amount otherwise assessed under this subsection and shall not exceed $100.

(4) The penalty for each failure to provide the employee with a copy of the treating physician's final report together with notice of the procedure to contest the treating physician's determination, in accordance with Labor Code Section 4636(d), immediately upon receipt of that report, is $100 for compliance more than 10 but not more than 20 days after receipt of the treating physician's final report, and an additional $100 for each additional delay of not more than 10 days, to a maximum penalty of $400 if the notice was issued more than 30 days late, and $500 if the notice was overdue more than 40 days and was not issued at the time the audit subject was notified that the claim was selected for audit.

(5) The penalty for each failure to notify an injured employee of the reasons he or she is not entitled to any, or to any further, vocational rehabilitation services, and the procedure for contesting the determination of non-eligibility, as required by Sections 9813(a)(3) and 10131, is $100 if notification was issued more than 10 but not more than 20 days after the determination, and an additional $100 for each additional delay of not more than 10 days, to a maximum penalty of $400 if the notice was issued more than 30 days late, and $500 if the notice was overdue more than 40 days and was not issued at the time the audit subject was notified that the claim was selected for audit.

(6) The penalty for each failure to notify an injured employee that his or her injury may have caused permanent disability and the procedures for evaluating the permanent disability, or of the employer's position that the injury has caused no permanent disability and the employee's remedies, in the manner provided by Title 8,

California Code of Regulations, Division 1, Chapter 4.5, Subchapter 1, Article 8, beginning with Section 9810; is $100 if the notice was issued up to 10 days late, and an additional $100 for each additional delay of not more than 10 days, to a maximum penalty of $400 if the notice was issued more than 30 days late, and $500 if the notice was overdue more than 40 days and was not issued at the time the audit subject was notified that the claim was selected for audit.

(7) The penalty for each failure to notify a claimant of the denial of all death benefits claimed by that person (except a denial limited to all or any of: burial expense, benefits which were due to the injured worker before his or her death, or medical-legal expense), in the manner provided by Title 8, California Code of Regulations, Division 1, Chapter 4.5, Subchapter 1, Article 8, beginning with Section 9810, is $100 if the notice was issued up to 10 days late, and an additional $100 for each additional delay of not more than 10 days, to a maximum penalty of $400 if the notice was issued more than 30 days late, and $500 if the notice was overdue more than 40 days and was not issued at the time the audit subject was notified that the claim was selected for audit.

(8) The penalty for each failure to send a notice denying liability for all workers' compensation benefits, in accordance with Title 8, California Code of Regulations, Division 4.5, Chapter 1, Article 8, beginning with Section 9810, is $100 if the notice was issued up to 10 days late, and an additional $100 for each additional delay of not more than 10 days, to a maximum penalty of $400 if the notice was issued more than 30 days late, and $500 if the notice was overdue more than 40 days and was not issued at the time the audit subject was notified that the claim was selected for audit.

(9) The penalty for each notice denying lability for all workers' compensation benefits, which was materially misleading, is $500. The penalty for each materially incomplete denial notice is $100.

(10) The penalty for each failure to pay any uncontested penalty assessment in a Notice of Penalty Assessments within 15 days of receipt of the Notice of Penalty Assessments is:

$100 for each assessment paid more than 15 but not more than 30 days after receipt;

$300 for each assessment paid more than 30 but not more than 45 days after receipt;

$500 for each assessment not paid within 45 days after receipt.

(11) The penalty for each failure to comply with Section 10104 of this Subchapter is:

$100 for each period of 1 to 14 days' delay in filing the Annual Report of Inventory, to a maximum penalty of $500 for each Annual Report of Inventory;

$500 for each Annual Report of Inventory that overstates or understates the number of claims by 10% or more.

(c) The following Group C violations carry penalties of up to $1,000:

(1) The penalty for each failure to pay compensation as ordered in a Notice of Compensation Due within 15 days of receipt, if no timely Request for Review of Notice of Compensation Due was filed, is:

$250 if the compensation was paid more than 15 but not more than 30 days from receipt of notice;

$500 if the compensation was paid more than 30 but not more than 45 days from receipt of notice;

$1,000 for failure to pay the compensation within 45 days of receipt of notice.

(2) The penalty for each termination, interruption or deferral of vocational rehabilitation services other than as provided by Labor Code Sections 4637(b), 4644(b) is $1,000.

(3) The penalty for each failure to pay or denial of rehabilitation maintenance allowance, temporary disability indemnity, or salary continuation in lieu of temporary disability indemnity, without a factual, medical or legal basis for the failure or denial, is:

$100 for the equivalent of 3 days or less of unpaid indemnity;

$200 for the equivalent of more than 3 but not more than 7 days of unpaid indemnity;

$300 for the equivalent of more than 7 but not more than 14 days of unpaid indemnity;

$500 for the equivalent of more than 14 but not more than 21 days of unpaid indemnity;

$750 for the equivalent of more than 21 but not more than 28 days of unpaid indemnity;

$1,000 for the equivalent of more than 28 days of unpaid indemnity.

(4) The penalty for each failure to pay permanent disability indemnity based on a reasonable estimate of permanent disability, or denial of permanent disability indemnity, without a factual, medical or legal basis, is:

$200 for up to 6 weeks of unpaid indemnity;

$400 for more than 6 but not more than 15 weeks of unpaid indemnity;

$750 for more than 15 but not more than 30 weeks of unpaid indemnity;

$1,000 for more than 30 weeks of unpaid indemnity.

(5) The penalty for each failure to pay or denial of death benefits to any claimant without a factual, medical or legal basis for the failure or denial, is:

$100 for the equivalent of 3 days or less of unpaid indemnity under Labor Code §4701(b), or for up to $300 of unpaid burial expenses;

$200 for the equivalent of more than 3 but not more than 7 days of unpaid indemnity under Labor Code §4701(b), or for more than $300, up to $600, of unpaid burial expenses;

$300 for the equivalent of more than 7 but not more than 14 days of unpaid indemnity under Labor Code §4701(b), or for more than $600, up to $900, of unpaid burial expenses;

$500 for the equivalent of more than 14 but not more than 21 days of unpaid indemnity under Labor Code §4701(b), or for more than $900, up to $1,500, of unpaid burial expenses;

$750 for the equivalent of more than 21 but not more than 28 days of unpaid indemnity under Labor Code §4701(b), or for more than $1,500, up to $2,250, of unpaid burial expenses;

$1,000 for the equivalent of more than 28 days of unpaid indemnity under Labor Code §4701(b), or for more than $2,250 of unpaid burial expenses.

The penalty for each failure to pay or denial of payment to any claimant of compensation which was accrued and unpaid to the injured worker at the time of the worker's death is the same penalty which would apply for failure to pay or denial of payment of that compensation to the injured worker.

The penalty under this subsection does not supersede the penalty under subsection 10111.1(d)(1).

(6) The penalty for each failure to investigate a claim as provided by Section 10109 of these Regulations is:

$250 if the failure to investigate involved a claim for medical treatment only, with no reasonable expectation of liability for indemnity payments;

$500 if the failure to investigate involved a claim or reasonable expectation of liability for temporary or permanent disability indemnity or vocational rehabilitation benefits;

$1,000 if the failure to investigate involved a claim or reasonable expectation of liability for death benefits, or a combination of two or more of the following classes of benefits temporary or permanent disability indemnity or vocational rehabilitation.

This penalty does not supersede a penalty for denial of claim without an investigation and documentation supporting a factual, medical, or legal basis for denial as set forth in Section 10111.1(d)(1) of this subchapter.

(d) The following Group D violations carry penalties of up to $5,000:

(1) The penalty for each denial of all liability for a claim without documentation supporting a factual, medical, or legal basis for the denial is specified in this subsection.

In order to avoid a penalty, the denial must state a legal, factual or medical basis recognized by applicable law and documented by information in the claim file. An employee's purported waiver of benefits in a compensable case is not a ground to deny liability.

The gravity portion of the penalty is based on the class or classes of benefits potentially payable if benefits were provided. The total penalty shall be determined by the applying the penalty assessment amount listed in [i] for gravity, subtracting the amount listed in [ii] for good faith if applicable, and increasing or decreasing the penalty as applicable for history and frequency as set forth in [iii] and [iv]:

[i] For a claim involving potential for medical treatment only the penalty is $3,500;

For a claim involving potential for medical treatment and either temporary or permanent disability the penalty is $4,000;

For a claim involving potential for medical treatment and both temporary and permanent disability the penalty is $4,500;

For a claim involving potential for medical treatment, temporary disability, permanent disability and vocational rehabilitation the penalty is $5,000;

For a claim involving potential for death benefits the penalty is $5,000.

[ii] The penalty will be reduced by $1,000 for good faith if there was a reasonable attempt to investigate the claim.

[iii] Reduction or increase of the penalty for history shall be based on the following:

An audit subject having no prior Audit Unit history will receive a $500 reduction;

An audit subject having a prior Audit Unit history of no more than one audited unsupported denial will receive a $500 reduction;

An audit subject having a prior Audit Unit history of more than one audited unsupported denial but no more than 5% of audited denials as unsupported will receive no reduction or increase for history;

An audit subject having a prior Audit Unit history of more than one audited unsupported denial and more than 5% of audited denials as unsupported will receive a $500 increase.

[iv] Reduction of the penalty for frequency shall be based on the following:

An audit subject having no more than one audited unsupported denial will receive a $500 reduction;

An audit subject having more than one audited unsupported denial but no more than 5% of audited denials which are unsupported will receive no reduction or increase for frequency;

An audit subject having more than one audited denial and more than 5% of audited denials which are unsupported will receive an increase of $500.

[v] The total amount assessed for a denial shall be reduced by 50% if the claim was accepted after the denial without evidence that the acceptance was the result of litigation or of the claim's selection for audit.

(2) The penalty for each failure to comply with, show good cause for non-compliance with, or contest, within 30 days of receipt, any written request or order of the Administrative Director or Audit Unit which is not specified in subsections (b)(1), (c)(1), or (d)(5) of this section is:

$500 if there was compliance in more than 30 but not more than 40 days from receipt of the request or order;

$1,000 if there was compliance in more than 40 but not more than 60 days from receipt of the request or order;

$2,500 if there was compliance in more than 60 but not more than 90 days of receipt of the request or order;

$5,000 for failure to comply within 90 days of receipt of the request or order.

(3) The penalty for each failure by a claims administrator to provide a claim form within one working day of receipt of a request from an injured worker or the worker's agent is:

$500 if the claim form was provided in more than 1 but not more than 5 working days from receipt of the request, if benefits were being provided to the employee at the time of the request;

$1,000 if the claim form was not provided within 5 working days of receipt of the request, if benefits were being provided to the employee at the time of the request;

$3,000 if the claim form was provided in more than 1 but not more than 5 working days from receipt of the request, if benefits were not being provided to the employee at the time of the request;

$5,000 if the claim form was not provided within 5 working days of receipt of the request, if benefits were not being provided to the employee at the time of the request.

(4) The penalty for each failure to comply in full with any final award or order of the Workers' Compensation Appeals Board or the Rehabilitation Unit within 20 days of service, allowing an additional five days for service by mail, is:

For any failure to pay all amounts payable as awarded or ordered, including interest, when partial nonpayment is due to a miscalculation or oversight and all other amounts have been paid, the penalty amount shall be determined based on the equivalent amount of unpaid indemnity as assessed under subsection (c)(3) of this section.

For late payment of an award or order, the penalty is:

$500 for compliance in more than 20 but not more than 35 days from the date of service;

$1,000 for compliance (other than a late interest payment) in more than 35 but not more than 60 days from the date of service;

$2,500 for compliance (other than a late interest payment) in more than 60 but not more than 90 days from the date of service;

$5,000 if there was not compliance (other than failure to pay interest) within 90 days of the date of service.

Penalties will be assessed separately for both late payment and the failure to pay a portion of an award or order.

(5) The penalty for each failure to produce a legible paper copy of a claim file as required by Section 10107 or at the time specified by the Administrative Director is:

$100 if the file was produced not more than 3 days late;

$250 if the file was produced more than 3 but not more than 14 days late;

$500 if the file was produced more than 14 but not more than 29 days late;

$1,000 if the file was produced more than 29 days late but not more than 40 days late;

$2,500 if the file was produced more than 40 days late but not more than 90 days late;

$5000 if the was produced more than 90 days late or was not produced.

(6) The penalty for providing a backdated or otherwise altered or fraudulent document to the Audit Unit, or intentionally withholding a document from the Audit Unit, which would have the effect of avoiding liability for the payment of compensation or an audit penalty is:

$5,000 for each backdated, altered, or withheld document. The amount of the penalty is not subject to reduction based on frequency, history, or good faith as set forth in subsection (e) of this section.

The claims administrator shall not be subjected to penalty under this subsection if it demonstrates by clear and convincing evidence that the backdating, alteration, or withholding of the document was due solely to unintentional clerical error.

(e) The penalties otherwise applicable under subsections (a) through (d) of this section shall be modified by any applicable provision of this subsection (e). However, the method of modifying penalties for unsupported denials is set forth in Section 10111(d)(2) and Section 10111.1(d)(1) and is not governed by this subsection (e).

(1) Modification for the gravity of each violation is included within the penalty assessment amounts listed in subsections (a) through (d);

(2) Modification for the good faith of the audit subject shall be determined based on documentation of attempts to comply with requirements of the Labor Code and the Administrative Director's regulations, and may result in a reduction of 20% for each applicable violation.

(3) Modification for frequency shall be considered for each type of violation. Frequency shall be determined by comparing the number of audited files which were randomly selected pursuant to Section 10107(c) and (d) of these regulations in which there is an assessment for a specific type of violation to the total number of those randomly selected audited files in which the possibility of that type of violation exists. The frequency of violations in the complaint files selected for audit pursuant to Section 10107(e) shall not be used to determine penalty amounts for these categories, except the mitigation or exacerbation of penalty amounts based on frequency of violations in the randomly selected files shall be applied to the audited complaint files.

[i] If there are assessments for late first payments of temporary disability indemnity in 10% or less of the audited files in which payments of temporary disability indemnity are made, the penalty amounts of these assessments will be reduced by 20%. If there are assessments for late first payments of temporary disability indemnity in more than 30% of the audited files in which payments of temporary disability indemnity are made, the penalty amounts of these assessments will be increased by 20%,

[ii] If there are assessments for late first payments of permanent disability indemnity in 10% or less of the audited files in which payments of permanent disability indemnity are made, the penalty amounts of these assessments will be reduced by 20%. If there are assessments for late first payments of permanent disability indemnity in more than 30% of the audited files in which payments of permanent disability indemnity are made, the penalty amounts of these assessments will be increased by 20%.

[iii] If there are assessments for late first payments of vocational rehabilitation maintenance allowance in 10% or less of the audited files in which payments of maintenance allowance in 10% or less of the audited files in which payments of maintenance allowance are made, the penalty amounts of these assessments will be reduced by 20%. If there are assessments for late first payments of vocational rehabilitation maintenance allowance in more than 30% of the audited files in which payments of maintenance allowance are made, the penalty amounts of these assessments will be increased by 20%.

[iv] If there are assessments involving late subsequent payments, including any payment in which all indemnity then due is not paid with that payment but is paid with a subsequent payment as assessed under subsection (a)(13) of this section, of temporary disability indemnity, permanent disability indemnity, or vocational rehabilitation maintenance allowance in 10% or less of the audited files in which these subsequent payments were made, the penalty amounts

of these assessments will be reduced by 20%. If the number of audited files with assessments for late subsequent payments of temporary disability indemnity, permanent disability indemnity, or vocational rehabilitation maintenance allowance exceeds 30% of the total number of audited files with subsequent payments of these benefits, the penalty amounts of these assessments will be increased by 20%.

[v] If there are assessments involving late payments of death benefits in 10% or less of the audited files in which these payments were made, the penalty amounts of these assessments will be reduced by 20%. If the number of audited files with assessments for late payments of death benefits exceeds 30% of the total number of audited files with payments of death benefits, the penalty amounts of these assessments will be increased by 20%.

[vi] If there are assessments involving failure to issue benefit notices (other than notices specifically mentioned elsewhere in this subsection (3)) in 10% or less of the audited files in which these benefit notices are required, no penalties will be assessed for those violations. If the number of audited files with assessments for failure to issue these notices exceeds 10%, but does not exceed 20%, the penalty amounts of these assessments will be reduced by 20%. If the number of audited files with assessments for failure to issue these notices exceeds 30% of the total number of audited files in which these notices are required, the penalty amounts of these assessments will be increased by 20%.

[vii] If there are assessments involving late provision of benefit notices (other than notices specifically mentioned elsewhere in this subsection (3)) in 10% or less of the audited files in which these benefit notices are required, no penalties will be assessed for those violations. If the number of audited files with assessments for late issuance of these notices exceeds 10%, but does not exceed 20%, the penalty amounts of these assessments will be reduced by 20%. If the number of audited files with assessments for late issuance of these notices exceeds 30% of the total number of audited files in which these notices were required and issued, the penalty amounts of these assessments will be increased by 20%.

[viii] If there are assessments involving the failure to pay or object to medical expenses within 60 days of receipt of the billing in 10% or less of the audited files with a requirement to pay or object to medical bills within 60 days of receipt of billing, the penalty amounts of these assessments will be reduced by 20%. if the number of audited files with assessments for failure to pay or object to medical expenses within 60 days of receipt of the billing exceeds 30% of the total number of audited files in which there was a requirement to pay or object to medical bills within 60 days of receipt of billing, the penalty amounts of these assessments will be increased by 20%.

[ix] If there are assessments involving the failure to pay or object to medical-legal expenses within 60 days of receipt of the billing in 10% or less of the audited files containing medical-legal expenses, the penalty amounts of these assessments will be reduced by 20%. If the number of audited files with assessments for failure to pay or object to medical-legal expenses within 60 days of receipt of the billing exceeds 30% of the total number of audited files in which there was a requirement to pay or object to medical-legal expenses within 60 days of receipt of billing, the penalty amounts of these assessments will be increased by 20%.

[x] If there are assessments involving the failure to pay or object to vocational rehabilitation expenses within 60 days of receipt of the billing in 10% or less of the audited files containing vocational rehabilitation expenses, the penalty amounts of these assessments will be reduced by 20%. If the number of audited files with assessments for failure to pay or object to vocational rehabilitation expenses within 60 days of receipt of the billing exceeds 30% of the total number of audited files in which there was a requirement to pay or object to vocational rehabilitation expenses within 60 days of receipt of billing, the penalty amounts of these assessments will be increased by 20%.

[xi] For injuries before January 1, 1994, if there are assessments involving the failure to assign a qualified rehabilitation representative within 10 days after 90 days of aggregate total disability in 10% or less of the audited files with 90 or more days of aggregate total disability, the penalty amounts of these assessments will be reduced by 20%. If the number of audited files with assessments involving the failure to assign a qualified rehabilitation representative within 10 days after 90 days of aggregate total disability exceeds 30% of the total number of audited files in which there was a requirement to assign a qualified rehabilitation representative within

10 days after 90 days of aggregate total disability, the penalty amounts of these assessments will be increased by 20%.

[xii] For injuries on or after January 1, 1994, if there are assessments involving the failure to provide information to the employee required by Labor Code Section 4636(a) within 10 days after 90 days of aggregate total disability in 10% or less of the audited files with 90 or more days of aggregate total disability, the penalty amounts of these assessments will be reduced by 20%. If the number of audited files with assessments involving the failure to provide the information specified in Section 4636(a) within 10 days after 90 days of aggregate total disability exceeds 30% of the total number of audited files in which there was a requirement to provide the information specified in Section 4636(a) within 10 days after 90 days of aggregate total disability, the penalty amounts of these assessments will be increased by 20%.

[xiii] If there are assessments involving the failure to notify an employee in a timely manner of potential eligibility for vocational rehabilitation in 10% or less of the audited files in which these notices are required, the penalty amounts of these assessments will be reduced by 20%. If the number of audited files with assessments involving the failure to notify an employee in a timely manner of potential eligibility for vocational rehabilitation exceeds 30% of the total number of audited files in which these notices are required, the penalty amounts of these assessments will be increased by 20%.

[xiv] If there are assessments involving the failure to notify an employee in a timely manner of non-eligibility for vocational rehabilitation in 10% or less of the audited files in which these notices are required, the penalty amounts of these assessments will be reduced 20%. If the number of audited files with assessments involving the failure to notify an employee in a timely manner of non-eligibility for vocational rehabilitation exceeds 30% of the total number of audited files in which these notices are required, the penalty amounts of these assessments will be increased by 20%.

[xv] If there are assessments involving the failure to notify an employee in a timely manner of the procedure for evaluating the employee's permanent disability, as required by Title 8, California Code of Regulations, Sections 9812(f)(2), 9812(f)(4), (g)(2), or (g)(3), in 10% or less of the audited files in which these notices are required, the penalty amounts of these assessments will be reduced by 20%. If the number of audited audited files with assessments for failure to issue these notices exceeds 30% of the total number of audited files in which these notices are required, the penalty amounts of these assessments will be increased by 20%.

[xvi] If there are assessments involving the failure to notify an employee or claimant in a timely manner of the denial of all liability for a claim, or of all liability for death benefits, in 10% or less of the audited files in which these notices are required, the penalty amounts of these assessments will be reduced by 20%. If the number of audited files with assessments for failure to issue these notices exceeds 30% of the total number of audited files in which these notices are required, the penalty amounts of these assessments will be increased by 20%.

[xvii] If there is an assessment for the failure to timely respond to a request to provide or authorize medical treatment in no more than one audited file, the penalty amount of that assessment will be reduced by 20%. If the number of audited files with assessments for the failure to timely respond to a request to provide or authorize medical treatment, the penalty amounts for these assessments will be increased by 20%.

[xviii] If there are assessments involving the failure to pay temporary disability indemnity, permanent disability indemnity, death benefits, vocational rehabilitation maintenance allowance, self-imposed increase for late indemnity payment, interest, or penalty in 5% or less of the audited files in which any of these forms of compensation are accrued and payable, the penalty amounts of these assessments will be reduced by 20%. If the number of audited files with assessments for the failure to pay any of these forms of compensation is more than 20% of the audited files in which any of these forms of compensation is accrued and payable, the penalty amounts of these assessments will be increased by 20%.

[xix] If there are assessments for failure to include items or properly designate entries on a claim log, and if no more than ten, or no more than 1%, of the entries on the log are affected, whichever is smaller, the penalty amounts of these assessments will be reduced by 20%. If more than fifty, or more than 5% of the entries on the log are affected, whichever is smaller, the penalty amounts of these assessments will be increased by 20%.

[xx] If there are other violations assessed which are not specified in [i] through [xix] above in 5% or less of the audited files, the penalty amounts of these assessments will be reduced by 20%. If the number of audited files with assessments exceeds 20% of the audited files, the penalty amounts of these assessments will be increased by 20%.

(4) Modification of the history of previous violations, if any, shall be based on prior audits of the audit subject at the current adjusting location. However, no modification for history shall apply if a valid comparison cannot be made between the current and prior audit(s). The penalty shall be modified for history as follows:

[i] There will be a reduction of 20% of any penalty for which there was no increase in the penalty amount based on frequency as described in subsections (e)(3)[i] through (3)[xx] above in the previous audit, and for which there was a reduction in the penalty amount based on frequency in the present audit at the audited adjusting location.

[ii] There will be an increase of 20% of any penalty for which there was an increase in the penalty amount based on frequency as described in subsections (3)[i] through (3)[xx] above in the previous audit, and for which there was no decrease in the penalty amount based on frequency of violations in the present audit at the audited adjusting location, provided that any increased penalty is limited to the maximum provided by statute and regulation for the violation.

(5) No administrative penalties shall be assessed if the only violations found in an audit are violations which do not involve the denial of a claim without supporting documentation, or failure to pay or late payment of compensation, and the violations are found in 20% or less of the indemnity files audited.

(6) Penalties may be mitigated outside the above mitigation guidelines in extraordinary circumstances, when strict application of the mitigation guidelines would be clearly inequitable.

Note: Authority cited: Sections 59, 129.5, 133, 138.3, 138.4, 139.5, 4603.5, 4627 and 5307.3, Labor Code. Reference: Sections 124, 129, 129.5, 4061, 4453, 4454, 4550, 4600, 4603.2, 4621, 4622, 4625, 4636 through 4638, 4639, 4641, 4642, 4650, 4651, 4701 through 4703.5, 4706, 4706.5, 5401, 5401.6, 5402, 5800 and 5814, Labor Code; and Section 2629.1(e), (f), Unemployment Insurance Code.

History: 1. New section filed 1-28-94; operative 1-28-94. Submitted to OAL for printing only pursuant to Government Code section 11351 (Register 94, No. 4).

2. Editorial correction inserting omitted text in subsection (e)(3)[xviii] (Register 95, No. 32).

3. Amendment of subsections (a)(7)[ii]-(a)(7)[iv], (b)(1), (b)(9), (d)(1) and (e)(3)[xv] filed 2-14-96; operative 2-14-96. Submitted to OAL for printing only pursuant to Government Code section 11351 (Register 96, No. 7).

4. Amendment filed 10-26-98; operative 11-25-98 (Register 98, No. 44).

Ref.: Hanna §§ 10.50[2][a], 10.50[2][c].

§10111.2. Full Compliance Audit Penalty Schedules; Target Audit Penalty Schedule.

(a) For full compliance audits conducted on or after January 1, 2003, administrative penalties will be assessed pursuant to this subsection (a) for audit subjects that fail to meet or exceed the profile audit review performance standards calculated pursuant to Section 10107.1(c)(3) but meet or exceed the full compliance audit performance standards calculated pursuant to Section 10107.1(d)(3). However, for violations in claims with dates of injury from January 1, 1990 through December 31, 1993, penalty amounts may not exceed the amounts that would be assessed pursuant to Section 10111, and for violations in claims with dates of injury from January 1, 1994 through December 31, 2002, penalty amounts may not exceed the amounts that would be assessed pursuant to Section 10111.1:

(1) The penalty for each failure to pay the 10% self-imposed increase due because of a late indemnity payment is:

If the self-imposed increase was not paid or was only partially paid, the audit penalty is based on the amount of the underlying indemnity and is as follows:

$50 if the late-paid indemnity totals not more than 3 days;

$100 if the late-paid indemnity totals more than 3 but not more than 7 days;

$150 if the late-paid indemnity totals more than 7 but not more than 14 days;

$200 if the late paid indemnity totals more than 14 but not more than 21 days;

$300 if the late paid indemnity totals more than 21 but not more than 28 days;

$500 if the late paid indemnity totals more than 28 days.

(2) The penalty for each failure to pay or denial of rehabilitation maintenance allowance, temporary disability indemnity, or salary continuation in lieu of temporary disability indemnity, without a factual, medical or legal basis for the failure or denial, is:

$200 for the equivalent of 3 days or less of unpaid indemnity;

$400 for the equivalent of more than 3 but not more than 7 days of unpaid indemnity;

$600 for the equivalent of more than 7 but not more than 14 days of unpaid indemnity;

$1,000 for the equivalent of more than 14 but not more than 21 days of unpaid indemnity;

$1,500 for the equivalent of more than 21 but not more than 28 days of unpaid indemnity;

$2,000 for the equivalent of more than 28 but not more than 35 days of unpaid indemnity;

$3,000 for the equivalent of more than 35 but not more than 42 days of unpaid indemnity;

$5,000 for the equivalent of more than 42 days of unpaid indemnity.

(3) The penalty for each failure to pay permanent disability indemnity based on a reasonable estimate of permanent disability, or denial of permanent disability indemnity, without a factual, medical or legal basis, is:

$400 for up to 6 weeks of unpaid indemnity;

$800 for more than 6 but not more than 15 weeks of unpaid indemnity;

$1,500 for more than 15 but not more than 30 weeks of unpaid indemnity;

$2,000 for more than 30 but not more than 50 weeks of unpaid indemnity;

$3,000 for more than 50 but not more than 95 weeks of unpaid indemnity;

$5,000 for more than 95 weeks of unpaid indemnity.

(4) The penalty for each failure to pay death benefits pursuant to Labor Code Section 4701 to any claimant without a factual, medical or legal basis for the failure, is:

$200 for the equivalent of 3 days or less of unpaid indemnity or for no more than $300 of unpaid burial expenses;

$400 for the equivalent of more than 3 but not more than 7 days of unpaid indemnity or for more than $300, but not more than $600, of unpaid burial expenses;

$600 for the equivalent of more than 7 but not more than 14 days of unpaid indemnity or for more than $600, but no more than $900, of unpaid burial expenses;

$1,000 for the equivalent of more than 14 but not more than 21 days of unpaid indemnity or for more than $900, but no more than $1,500, of unpaid burial expenses;

$1,500 for the equivalent of more than 21 but not more than 28 days of unpaid indemnity or for more than $1,500, but no more than $2,000, of unpaid burial expenses;

$3,000 for the equivalent of more than 28 but not more than 42 days of unpaid indemnity or for more than $2,250 of unpaid burial expenses;

$5,000 for the equivalent of more than 42 days of unpaid indemnity.

The penalty for each failure to pay to any claimant compensation which was accrued and unpaid to the injured worker at the time of the worker's death is the same penalty which would apply for failure to pay that compensation to the injured worker.

(5) The penalty for each late first payment of temporary disability indemnity is:

$100 if the first payment was made 1 to 3 days late;

$200 if the first payment was made 4 to 7 days late;

$250 if the first payment was made 8 to 14 days late;

$300 if the first payment was made 15 to 21 days late;

$400 if the first payment was made 22 to 30 days late.

Penalty amounts for payments made over 30 days late are assessed pursuant to Sections 10108(c) and subsection (a)(2) of this section.

(6) The penalty for each late first payment of permanent disability is:

$100 if the first payment was made 1 to 3 days late;

$200 if the first payment was made 4 to 7 days late;

$250 if the first payment was made 8 to 14 days late;

$300 if the first payment was made 15 to 21 days late;

$400 if the first payment was made 22 to 30 days late.

Penalty amounts for payments made over 30 days late are assessed pursuant to Sections 10108(c) and subsection (a)(3) of this section.

For purposes of this subsection, the first payment of permanent disability indemnity shall be considered late if not made within 14 days after the last payment of temporary disability indemnity, or within 14 days of knowledge of the existence of permanent disability, whichever last occurs.

(7) The penalty for each late first payment of VRMA or death benefit is:

$100 if the first payment was made 1 to 3 days late;

$200 if the first payment was made 4 to 7 days late;

$250 if the first payment was made 8 to 14 days late;

$300 if the first payment was made 15 to 21 days late;

$400 if the first payment was made 22 to 30 days late.

Penalty amounts for payments made over 30 days late are assessed pursuant to Sections 10108(c) and subsection (a)(2) of this section.

(8) The penalty for each underpayment of temporary disability, permanent disability, death benefits, or VRMA, when the balance of the indemnity was paid late, or late paid self-imposed increases, not paid together with the late indemnity payment is:

$100 for late payment of the equivalent of 3 days of indemnity or less, except it is $25 for late paid self-imposed increases;

$200 for late payment of the equivalent of more than 3 but no more than 7 days of indemnity, except it is $50 for late paid self-imposed increases;

$250 for late payment of the equivalent of more than 7 but no more than 14 days of indemnity, except it is $75 for late paid self-imposed increases;

$300 for late payment of the equivalent of more than 14 but no more than 21 days of indemnity, except it is $100 for late paid self-imposed increases;

$400 for the late payment of the equivalent of more than 21 days of indemnity, except it is $125 for late paid self-imposed increases.

Penalty amounts for underpayments made more than 30 days late are governed by Section 10108(c).

(9) The penalty for each failure to make temporary disability, permanent disability, death benefits or VRMA payments according to the payment schedule defined by Section 10100.2(y) is:

$100 for each payment made 1 to 3 days late;

$200 for each payment made 4 to 7 days late;

$250 for each payment made 8 to 14 days late;

$300 for each payment made 15 to 21 days late;

$400 for each payment made 22 to 30 days late.

Penalty amounts for payments made more than 30 days late are governed by Section 10108(c).

(10) Penalty amounts assessed pursuant to subsections (a)(1) through (a)(9) will be increased by 100% if the failure to pay or late payment was in violation of an award or order of the Workers' Compensation Appeals Board or an order of the Rehabilitation Unit.

(11) Notwithstanding Labor Code Section 129.5(c)(1) and whether or not the audit subject has met or exceeded performance standards calculated pursuant to Section 10107.1(c)(3), penalties will be assessed for failure to pay, or late or partial payment of, a Notice of Compensation Due issued as a result of an audit. Penalties will be assessed as follows:

A penalty in the same amount as the total of the penalties applicable under subsections (a)(1) through (a)(4) and (a)(10) will be assessed for any compensation paid more than 15 but not more than 30 days after receipt of the Notice of Compensation Due;

A penalty in the amount of 200% of the total of the penalties applicable under subsections (a)(1) through (a)(4) and (a)(10) will be assessed for any compensation paid more than 30 but not more than 60 days late;

A penalty in the amount of 300% of the total of the penalties applicable under subsections (a)(1) through (a)(4) and (a)(10) will be assessed for any compensation not paid within 60 days.

(12) Notwithstanding Labor Code Section 129.5(c)(2) and whether or not the audit subject has met or exceeded performance standards calculated pursuant to Section 10107.1(d)(3), additional penalties will be assessed for late payment or failure of the audit subject to pay any administrative penalties assessed pursuant to this section that are not timely appealed pursuant to Section 10115.1. Penalties will be assessed as follows:

An additional penalty of 50% of the amount of each late paid penalty will be assessed for each penalty paid more than 30 but not more than 60 days from receipt of the Notice of Penalty Assessments;

An additional penalty of 100% of the amount of each applicable penalty will be assessed for each penalty not paid within 60 days of receipt of the Notice of Penalty Assessments.

(b) For full compliance audits conducted on or after January 1, 2003, administrative penalties will be assessed pursuant to subsection (a) and this subsection (b) for audit subjects that fail to meet or exceed the full compliance audit performance standards calculated pursuant to Section 10107.1(d)(3). However, for violations in claims with dates of injury from January 1, 1990 through December 31, 1993, penalty amounts may not exceed the amounts that would be assessed pursuant to Section 10111, and for violations in claims with dates of injury from January 1, 1994 through December 31, 2002, penalty amounts may not exceed the amounts that would be assessed pursuant to Section 10111.1:

(1) The penalty for each failure to investigate a claim as provided by Section 10109 of these Regulations is:

$500 if the failure to investigate involved a claim for medical treatment only, with no reasonable expectation of liability for indemnity payments, or if the failure to investigate involved the need for medical treatment or testing, but did not involve uncompensated lost time or permanent disability;

$1,000 if the failure to investigate involved a claim for or reasonable expectation of liability for only one of the following classes of benefits: temporary disability; permanent disability indemnity; or, vocational rehabilitation;

$2,500 if the failure to investigate involved a claim or reasonable expectation of liability for any combination two of the following classes of benefits: temporary disability; permanent disability indemnity; or, vocational rehabilitation;

$5,000 if the failure to investigate involved a claim or reasonable expectation of liability for death benefits, or for all of the following classes of benefits: temporary disability; permanent disability indemnity; and, vocational rehabilitation.

(2) The penalty for each denial of all liability for a claim without documentation supporting a factual, medical, or legal basis for the denial is specified in this subsection.

In order to avoid a penalty, the denial must state a legal, factual or medical basis recognized by applicable law and documented by information in the claim file. An employee's waiver of benefits in an otherwise clearly compensable case is not a ground to deny liability.

The penalty is $2,500 for a claim involving the potential for medical treatment only, with no potential for liability for indemnity payments;

The penalty is $4,000 for a claim involving the potential liability for medical treatment and for only one of the following classes of benefits: temporary disability; permanent disability indemnity; or, vocational rehabilitation;

The penalty is $4,500 for a claim involving the potential liability for medical treatment and for any combination of two of the following classes of benefits: temporary disability; permanent disability indemnity; or, vocational rehabilitation;

The penalty is $5,000 for a claim involving the potential liability for death benefits, or for all of the following classes of benefits: medical treatment, temporary disability; permanent disability indemnity; and, vocational rehabilitation.

The penalty will be reduced by 20% for good faith if there was an incomplete investigation of the claim.

The total amount assessed for a denial shall be reduced by 50% if the claim was accepted after the denial without evidence that the acceptance was the result of litigation or of the claim's selection for audit.

(3) The penalty for each failure to produce a legible paper copy of a claim file as required by Section 10107 or at the time specified by the Administrative Director is:

$100 if the file was produced not more than 3 days late;

$250 if the file was produced more than 3 but not more than 14 days late;

$500 if the file was produced more than 14 but not more than 29 days late;

$1,000 if the file was produced more than 29 days late but not more than 40 days late;

$2,500 if the file was produced more than 40 days late but not more than 90 days late;

$5000 if the was produced more than 90 days late or was not produced.

(4) The penalty for providing a backdated or otherwise altered or fraudulent document to the Audit Unit, or intentionally withholding a document from the Audit Unit, which would have the effect of avoiding liability for the payment of compensation or an audit penalty is: $5,000 for each backdated, altered, or withheld document.

(5) The penalty for each failure to object or pay to the injured worker, within 60 days of receiving a request, reimbursement for the reasonable expense incurred for self-procured medical treatment in accordance with Labor Code Section 4600, is:

$100 for $100 or less in expense;

$200 for more than $100, to $500, in expense;

$300 for more than $500, to $1,000, in expense;

$500 for more than $1,000 in expense.

(6) The penalty for each failure to pay reasonable expenses of transportation, meals, and lodging incident to reporting to an examination, together with one day of temporary disability indemnity for each day of wages lost when submitting to the examination, when notifying the employee of a medical evaluation scheduled by the claims administrator in accordance with Labor Code Sections 4600 through 4621; or to pay these expenses within 14 days of receiving notice of a medical evaluation scheduled by the Administrative Director or the appeals board; or to object or pay the injured worker for any reasonable transportation expenses incurred to obtain medical treatment or evaluation, within 60 days of receiving a request, is:

$100 for more than $10, to $100, in expense;

$200 for more than $100, to $300, in expense;

$300 for more than $300, to $500, in expense.

$500 for more than $500 in expense.

(7) The penalty for each failure to document a factual basis for paying less than the maximum indemnity rate is:

$50 if the total indemnity, paid and unpaid, totals not more than 3 days;

$100 if the total indemnity totals more than 3 but not more than 7 days;

$150 if the total indemnity totals more than 7 but not more than 14 days;

$200 if the total indemnity totals more than 14 but not more than 21 days;

$300 if the total indemnity totals more than 21 but not more than 28 days;

$500 if the total indemnity totals more than 28 days.

(8) The penalty for each failure to comply with any regulation of the Administrative Director specified in this subsection is:

[i] For each failure to include in a claim file a copy of the Employee's Claim for Worker's Compensation Benefits, DWC Form 1, showing the date the form was provided to and received from the employee, or documentation of the date the claim form was provided to the employee if the employee did not return the form, the penalty is:

$100 if there was any late indemnity payments, or if notice of acceptance of the claim was not issued within 90 days after the employer's date of knowledge of injury and disability, or if the claim was denied.

[ii] For each failure to issue a notice of benefits as required by Title 8, California Code of Regulations, Division 4.5, Chapter 1, Article 8, beginning with Section 9810, or by Title 8, California Code of Regulations, Division 4.5, Chapter 1.5, Article 7, beginning with Section 10122, unless penalties are assessed pursuant to subsections (b)(14) through (b)(20), the penalty is $100.

[iii] For each Notice of Benefits that was not issued timely as provided in Title 8, California Code of Regulations, Division 1, Chapter 4.5, Subchapter 1, Article 8, beginning with Section 9810, or as provided in Title 8, California Code of Regulations, Division 1, Chapter 4.5, Subchapter 1.5, Article 7, beginning with Section 10122, unless penalties are assessed pursuant to subsections (b)(14) through (b)(20), the penalty is:

$25 for each notice of first, resumed, changed or final payment of temporary disability indemnity, wage continuation, death benefits, permanent disability indemnity, or VRMA that was issued from 1 to 7 days late;

$50 for each notice of first, resumed, changed or final payment of temporary disability indemnity, wage continuation, death benefits, permanent disability indemnity, or VRMA that was issued more than 7 days late, and for each delay in decision notice which was issued from 1 to 7 days late;

$75 for each delay in decision notice, that was, issued more than 7 days late.

[iv] For each notice of benefits required by Title 8, California Code of Regulations, Division 1, Chapter 4.5, Subchapter 1, Article 8, beginning with Section 9810, (except a materially misleading denial notice assessed under subsection (b)(21) or by Title 8, California Code of Regulations, Division 1, Chapter 4.5, Subchapter 1.5, Article 7, beginning with Section 10122, that is materially inaccurate or incomplete, the penalty is $25.

[v] For each failure to include in a claim file, or document attempts to obtain, any of the required contents specified in Section 10101.1(b), (c), (d), (e), (f), (g), (h), (i), (j) of these Regulations, the penalty is $100.

[vi] For each failure to comply with any regulation of the Administrative Director, not otherwise assessed in this Subchapter, the penalty is $100.

(9) The penalty for each failure to pay or object to a billing for a medical-legal expense, in the manner required by Section 9794, within 60 days of receiving the bill and all reports and documents required by the Administrative Director incident to the services, is:

$100 for each bill that was paid more than 60 days from receipt with interest and a 10% increase;

$200 for each bill that was paid more than 60 days from receipt where either interest or a 10% increase was not included;

$300 for each bill that was paid more than 60 days from receipt where neither interest nor a 10% increase was paid.

$500 for each bill that was not paid at the time the audit subject was notified the claim was selected for audit where no timely objection was sent.

(10) The penalty for each failure to pay or object, in the manner required by law or regulation, to a bill for medical treatment provided or authorized by the treating physician, is as follows when the bill remains unpaid at the time the audit subject is notified that the claim was selected for audit:

$100 for each bill of $100 or less, excluding interest and penalty;

$200 for each bill of more than $100, but no more than $500 excluding interest and penalty;

$300 for each bill of more than $500, but no more than $1,000, excluding interest and penalty;

$500 for each bill of more than $1,000, excluding interest and penalty.

(11) The penalty for each failure to pay or object, in the manner required by law or regulation, to a bill for medical treatment provided or authorized by the treating physician, is as follows when the bill was paid before the audit subject was notified that the claim was selected for audit:

$100 for each bill that included a 10% increase and interest with the late payment of any uncontested amount of the bill, in accordance with Labor Code Section 4603.2; $200 for each bill that included either a 10% increase or interest with the late payment of any uncontested amount of the bill, in accordance with Labor Code Section 4603.2; $300 for each bill that included neither a 10% increase nor interest with the late payment of any uncontested amount of the bill, in accordance with Labor Code Section 4603.2.

(12) The penalty for each failure to pay or object to a vocational rehabilitation bill within 60 days of receipt, as required by Title 8, California Code of Regulations, Sections 10132 and 10132.1, is:

$25 for each bill of $100 or less;

$50 for each bill of more than $100, but no more than $200;

$75 for each bill of more than $200, but no more than $300;

$100 for each bill of more than $300.

(13) The penalty for each failure to maintain or provide to the Audit Unit a claim log that complies with these Regulations is:

$25 for each failure to list on a claim log one or more of the following: employee's name; claim number; date of injury;

$25 for each misdesignation of an indemnity claim as a medical-only claim on the claim log;

$100 for each failure to identify self-insured employers on the log as required by Section 10103.1(b)(6) of these Regulations;

$100 for each failure to identify the underwriting insurance company of an insurance group;

$100 for each failure to designate a denied claim on the log;

$100 for each claim not listed on the log;

$250 for each failure to provide the claim log to the Audit Unit within 14 days of receipt of a written request if the claim log was provided more than 14 but no more than 30 days from receipt of the request;

$500 for each failure for more than 30 days from receipt of a written request, to provide the claim log to the Audit Unit.

(14) The penalty for each failure to provide information regarding the Americans with Disabilities Act, the Fair Employment and Housing Act, and workers' compensation vocational rehabilitation as required by Labor Code Section 4636(a) immediately after 90 days of aggregate temporary disability indemnity is $100 if the information was provided or the employee re-

turned to his or her usual and customary occupation more than 10 but not more than 20 days after 90 days of aggregate total disability, and an additional $100 for each additional delay of not more than 10 days, to a maximum penalty of $400 if the notice was issued more than 30 days late, and $500 if the notice was overdue more than 40 days and was not issued at the time the audit subject was notified that the claim was selected for audit.

(15) The penalty for each failure to issue notice of medical eligibility for vocational rehabilitation services (if not previously issued) within 10 days after knowledge of a physician's opinion that the employee is medically eligible, or for failure to issue notice within 10 days after 366 days of aggregate total temporary disability, is $100 if the notice was issued not more than 10 days late, and an additional $100 for each additional delay of not more than 10 days, to a maximum penalty of $400 if the notice was issued more than 30 days late, and $500 if the notice was overdue more than 40 days and was not issued at the time the audit subject was notified that the claim was selected for audit. Where the injured worker is represented by an attorney and documentation in the claim file indicates that the injured worker's attorney has received a copy of the physician's report indicating the employee is medically eligible for vocational rehabilitation, and if the knowledge is of a physician's opinion other than the injured worker's treating physician, a physician selected from a panel provided by the Industrial Medical Council, or an agreed medical examiner, the penalty shall be assessed at 20% of the amount otherwise assessed under this subsection and shall not exceed $100.

(16) The penalty for each failure to provide the employee with a copy of the treating physician's final report together with notice of the procedure to contest the treating physician's determination, in accordance with Labor Code Section 4636(d), immediately upon receipt of that report, is $100 for compliance more than 10 but not more than 20 days after receipt of the treating physician's final report, and an additional $100 for each additional delay of not more than 10 days, to a maximum penalty of $400 if the notice was issued more than 30 days late, and $500 if the notice was overdue more than 40 days and was not issued at the time the audit subject was notified that the claim was selected for audit. However, if a separate penalty is assessed under subsection (b)(17) for the violation, no penalty will be assessed under this subsection. If the injured worker was notified of the procedure to contest the treating physician's determination, but no copy of the treating physician's final report was provided with the notice, the maximum penalty shall be $100 under this subsection.

(17) The penalty for each failure to notify an injured employee of the reasons he or she is not entitled to any, or to any further, vocational rehabilitation services, and the procedure for contesting the determination of non-eligibility, as required by Sections 9813(a)(3) and 10131, is $100 if notification was issued more than 10 but not more than 20 days after the determination, and an additional $100 for each additional delay of not more than 10 days, to a maximum penalty of $400 if the notice was issued more than 30 days late, and $500 if the notice was overdue more than 40 days and was not issued at the time the audit subject was notified that the claim was selected for audit.

(18) The penalty for each failure to notify an injured employee that his or her injury may have caused permanent disability and the procedures for evaluating the permanent disability, or of the employer's position that the injury has caused no permanent disability and the employee's remedies, in the manner provided by Title 8, California Code of Regulations, Division 1, Chapter 4.5, Subchapter 1, Article 8, beginning with Section 9810; is $100 if the notice was issued up to 10 days late, and an additional $100 for each additional delay of not more than 10 days, to a maximum penalty of $400 if the notice was issued more than 30 days late, and $500 if the notice was overdue more than 40 days and was not issued at the time the audit subject was notified that the claim was selected for audit.

(19) The penalty for each failure to notify a claimant of the denial of all death benefits claimed by that person (except a denial limited to all or any of: burial expense, benefits which were due to the injured worker before his or her death, or medical-legal expense), in the manner provided by Title 8, California Code of Regulations, Division 1, Chapter 4.5, Subchapter 1, Article 8, beginning with Section 9810, is $100 if the notice was issued up to 10 days late, and an additional $100 for each additional delay of not more than 10 days, to a maximum penalty of $400 if the notice was issued more than 30 days late, and $500 if the notice was overdue more

than 40 days and was not issued at the time the audit subject was notified that the claim was selected for audit.

(20) The penalty for each failure to send a notice denying liability for all workers' compensation benefits, in accordance with Title 8, California Code of Regulations, Division 4.5, Chapter 1, Article 8, beginning with Section 9810, is $100 if the notice was issued up to 10 days late, and an additional $100 for each additional delay of not more than 10 days, to a maximum penalty of $400 if the notice was issued more than 30 days late, and $500 if the notice was overdue more than 40 days and was not issued at the time the audit subject was notified that the claim was selected for audit.

(21) The penalty for each notice denying liability for all workers' compensation benefits, which was materially misleading, is $500.

The penalty for each materially incomplete denial notice is $100.

(22) The penalty for each termination, interruption or deferral of vocational rehabilitation services other than as provided by Labor Code Sections 4637(b), 4644(b) is $1,000.

(23) The penalty for each failure to comply with, show good cause for non-compliance with, or contest, within 30 days of receipt, any written request or order of the Administrative Director or Audit Unit which is not specified in subsections (a)(10) or (b)(14) of this section is:

$500 if there was compliance in more than 30 but not more than 40 days from receipt of the request or order;

$1,000 if there was compliance in more than 40 but not more than 60 days from receipt of the request or order;

$2,500 if there was compliance in more than 60 but not more than 90 days of receipt of the request or order;

$5,000 for failure to comply within 90 days of receipt of the request or order.

(24) The penalty for each failure to comply with any final award or order of the Workers' Compensation Appeals Board or the Rehabilitation Unit which is not assessed pursuant to subdivision (a)(10), is:

For late compliance with an award or order compliance with an award must be within 20 days of service, plus an additional five days for service by mail), the penalty is:

$500 for compliance in more than 20 but not more than 35 days from the date of service

$1,000 for compliance (other than a late interest payment) in more than 35 but not more than 60 days from the date of service;

$2,500 for compliance (other than a late interest payment) in more than 60 but not more than 90 days from the date of service;

$5,000 if there was not compliance (other than failure to pay interest) within 90 days of the date of service.

Penalties will be assessed separately for both late compliance and the failure to pay a portion of an award or order.

(25) The penalty for each failure by a claims administrator to provide a claim form within one working day of receipt of a request from an injured worker or the worker's agent is:

$500 if the claim form was provided in more than 1 but not more than 5 working days from receipt of the request, if benefits were being provided to the employee at the time of the request;

$1,000 if the claim form was not provided within 5 working days of receipt of the request, if benefits were being provided to the employee at the time of the request;

$3,000 if the claim form was provided in more than 1 but not more than 5 working days from receipt of the request, if benefits were not being provided to the employee at the time of the request;

$5,000 if the claim form was not provided within 5 working days of receipt of the request, if benefits were not being provided to the employee at the time of the request.

(26) The penalty for each failure to comply with Section 10104 of this Subchapter is:

$100 for each period of 1 to 14 days' delay in filing the Annual Report of Inventory, to a maximum penalty of $500 for each Annual Report of Inventory;

$500 for each Annual Report of Inventory that overstates or understates the number of claims by 10% or more.

(c) Mitigation of penalty amounts pursuant to Labor Code Section 129.5(b)(1) through (b)(7) will be applied as follows:

(1) Mitigation for gravity of the violation is included within the penalty amounts set forth in subsections (a) and (b).

(2) Mitigation for good faith of the insurer, self-insured employer, or third-party administrator will be determined based on documentation of attempts to comply with requirements of the

Labor Code and the Administrative Director's regulations, and will result in a reduction of 20% for each applicable violation.

(3) Mitigation for frequency is considered as included within the numbers of penalties and their amounts established by this section and in conjunction with the frequency of violations that determines whether or not the audit subject meets or exceeds the profile audit review performance standards and/or full compliance audit performance standards pursuant to Sections 10107.1(c)(3) and (d)(3).

(4) Mitigation for history shall be determined as follows:

(A) For audits that meet or exceed the full compliance audit performance standard, penalty amounts will be reduced by 20%, after modification for good faith, if any, in instances in which the audit subject met or exceeded the profile audit review performance standards in the audit preceding the current audit. No reduction shall apply if the preceding audit occurred before January 1, 2003.

(B) For audits that fail to meet or exceed the full compliance audit performance standards, mitigation for history shall be determined pursuant to Labor Code Section 129.5(e).

(5) Mitigation based on whether or not the audit subject has met or exceeded the profile audit review performance standard is determined pursuant to Labor Code Section 129.5(c)(1) and (c)(2).

(6) Mitigation based on whether or not the audit subject has met or exceeded the full compliance audit performance standard is determined pursuant to Labor Code Section 129.5(c)(3).

(7) Consideration of penalty amounts based on the size of the audit subject location pursuant to Labor Code Section 129.5(c)(3) shall be based on the number of indemnity claims reported at the audit subject's location for the last audited year. For audit subjects that fail to meet or exceed the full compliance audit performance standards calculated pursuant to Section 10107.1(d)(3), after penalty amounts are calculated pursuant to subsections (a)(1) through (c)(6) of this section, penalty amounts will be modified based on the size of the adjusting location as follows:

Number of indemnity claims reported at the audit subject location in last audited year:	Multiply the penalty amount calculated pursuant to subsections (a)(1) through (c)(6) of this section by the following factor:
Less than 65:	1.0
65-99	1.2
100-249	1.4
250-499	1.6
500-749	1.8
750-999	2.0
1,000-1,499	2.4
1,500-1,999	2.8
2,000-3,499	3.6
3,500 or more	7.2

(8) The Audit Unit may assess penalties pursuant to subsections (a), (b), and (c) in target audits in which the claims were audited to evaluate specific practices but in which full compliance audit samples of claims were not randomly selected pursuant to Section 10107.1(c) through (e).

Note: Authority cited: Sections 59, 129, 129.5, 133, 138.3, 138.4, 139.5, 4603.5, 4627 and 5307.3, Labor Code. Reference: Sections 124, 129, 129.5, 4061, 4453, 4454, 4550, 4600, 4603.2, 4621, 4622, 4625, 4636-4638, 4639, 4641, 4642, 4650, 4951, 4701-4703.5, 4706, 4706.5, 5401, 5401.6, 5402, 5800 and 5814, Labor Code; and Section 2629.1(e) and (f), Unemployment Insurance Code.

History: 1. New section filed 12-30-2002; operative 1-1-2003 pursuant to Government Code section 11343.4 (Register 2003, No. 1).

2. Change without regulatory effect amending subsection (b)(8)[iv] filed 5-1-2003 pursuant to section 100, title 1, California Code of Regulations (Register 2003, No. 18).

3. Amendment of subsections (a)(1) and (a)(8), new subsection (a)(9), subsection renumbering, amendment of newly designated subsections (a)(10)-(11) and subsection (b)(23), new subsection (b)(24) and subsection renumbering filed 10-6-2003; operative 12-1-2003 (Register 2003, No. 41).

Ref.: Hanna § 10.50[2][b].

§10112. Liability for Penalty Assessments.

The audit subject is liable for all penalty assessments, except that if the audit subject is acting as a third-party administrator, the client of that third-party administrator which secures the payment of compensation is jointly and severally liable with the administrator for all penalty assessments except civil penalties imposed under Labor Code Section 129.5(d). Without affecting DWC's rights, a third-party administrator and its client may agree how to allocate the audit penalty expense between them.

Note: Authority cited: Sections 59, 129.5, 133 and 5307.3, Labor Code. Reference: Sections 129, 129.5 and 3200-6002, Labor Code.

History: 1. Renumbering of former section 10112 to section 10115 and new section filed 1-28-94; operative 1-28-94. Submitted to OAL for printing only pursuant to Government Code section 11351 (Register 94, No. 4).

Ref.: See Labor Code §4651; Hanna §§ 1.12[10], 10.50[1]; Herlick Handbook §§ 1.6, 9.5, 15.2.

ARTICLE 5.5
Administrative Penalties Pursuant to Labor Code Section 5814.6

§10112.1. Definitions.

As used in this article:

(a) "Adjusting location" means the office where claims are administered. Separate underwriting companies, employers that are both self-administered and self-insured, and/or third-party administrators operating at one location shall be combined as one adjusting location only if claims are administered under the same management at that location. Where claims are administered from an office that includes a satellite office at another location, claims administered at the satellite office(s) will be considered as part of the single adjusting location for investigation and auditing purposes under this article when it is demonstrated that the claims are under the same immediate management.

(b) "Administrative Director" means the Administrative Director of the Division of Workers Compensation, including his or her designee.

(c) "Claim" means a request for compensation, or record of an occurrence in which compensation reasonably would be expected to be payable for an injury arising out of and in the course of employment.

(d) "Claim file" means a record in paper or electronic form, or any combination, containing all of the information specified in section 10101.1 of Title 8 of the California Code of Regulations and all documents or entries related to the provision, payment, delay, or denial of benefits or compensation under Divisions 1, 4 or 4.5 of the Labor Code.

(e) "Claims administrator" means a self-administered workers' compensation insurer; a self-administered self-insured employer; a self-administered legally uninsured employer; a self-administered joint powers authority; or a third-party claims administrator for an insurer, a self-insured employer, a legally uninsured employer or a joint powers authority.

(f) "Compensation" means every benefit or payment, including vocational rehabilitation, supplemental job displacement benefits, medical treatment, medical and medical-legal expenses, conferred by Divisions 1 and 4 of the Labor Code on an injured employee or the employee's dependents.

(g) "Compensation order" means any award, order or decision issued by the Workers' Compensation Appeals Board or the Division of Workers' Compensation vocational rehabilitation unit by which a party is entitled to payment of compensation.

(h) "Concurrent medical treatment authorization" means authorization requested or provided during an inpatient stay.

(i) "Determination and Order" means Determination and Order in re Labor Code § 5814.6 Administrative Penalties.

(j) "Employee" means every person in the service of another, as defined under Article 2 of Chapter 2 of Part 1 of Division 4 of the Labor Code (Sections 3350 et seq.), or in the case of the employee's death, his or her dependent, as each is defined in Division 4 of the Labor Code, or the employee's or dependent's agent or attorney.

(k) "Employer" shall have the same meaning as the word 'employer' as defined in Division 4 of the Labor Code (sections 3300 et seq.).

(*l*) "General business practice" means a pattern of violations of Labor Code section 5814 at a single adjusting location that can be distinguished by a reasonable person from an isolated event. The pattern of violations must occur in the handling of more than one claim. The pattern of violations may consist of one type of act or omission, or separate, discrete acts or omissions in the handling of more than one claim. However, where a claim file with a violation of Labor Code section 5814 has been adjusted at multiple adjusting locations, that claim file may be considered when determining the general business practice of any of the adjusting locations where the conduct that caused the violation occurred even if the file has been transferred to a different adjusting location.

(m) "Indemnity" means payments made directly to an eligible person as a result of a work injury and as required under Division 4 of the Labor Code, including but not limited to temporary disability indemnity, salary continuation in lieu of temporary disability indemnity, permanent disability indemnity, vocational rehabilitation temporary disability indemnity, vocational rehabilitation maintenance allowance, life pension and death benefits.

(n) "Insurer" means any company, group, or entity in, or which has been in, the business of transacting workers' compensation insurance for one or more employers subject to the workers' compensation laws of this state. The term insurer includes the State Compensation Insurance Fund.

(o) "Investigation" means the process used by the Administrative Director, or his or her designee, pursuant to Section 10112.2 and/or Government Code sections 11180 through 11191, to determine whether a violation of Labor Code section 5814.6 has occurred, including but not limited to reviewing, evaluating, copying and preserving electronic and paper records, files, accounts and other things, and interviewing potential witnesses.

(p) "Joint powers authority" means any county, city, city and county, municipal corporation, public district, public agency, or political subdivision of the state, but not the state itself, included in a pooling arrangement under a joint exercise of powers agreement for the purpose of securing a certificate of consent to self-insure workers' compensation claims under Labor Code Section 3700(c).

(q) "Knowingly" means acting with knowledge of the facts of the conduct at issue. For the purposes of this article, a corporation has knowledge of the facts an employee receives while acting within the scope of his or her authority. A corporation has knowledge of information contained in its records and of the actions of its employees performed in the scope and course of employment. An employer or insurer has knowledge of information contained in the records of its third-party administrator and of the actions of the employees of the third-party administrator performed in the scope and course of employment.

(r) "Notice of Assessment" means Notice of Labor Code § 5814.6 Administrative Penalty Assessment.

(s) "Penalty award" means a final order or final award by the Workers' Compensation Appeals Board to pay penalties due to a violation of section 5814 of the Labor Code.

(t) "Petition Appealing Determination and Order" means Petition Appealing Determination and Order of the Administrative Director in re Labor Code § 5814.6 Administrative Penalties.

(u) "Proof of service" means an affidavit or declaration made under penalty of perjury and filed with one or more documents required to be filed, setting out a description of the document(s) being served, the names and addresses of all persons served, whether service was made personally or by mail, the date of service, and the place of service or the address to which mailing was made.

(v) "Prospective medical treatment authorization" means authorization requested or provided prior to the delivery of the medical services.

(w) "Recommended Determination and Order" means Recommended Determination and Order in re Labor Code § 5814.6 Administrative Penalties.

(x) "Retrospective medical treatment authorization" means authorization requested or provided after medical services have been provided and for which services approval has not already been given.

(y) "Salary continuation" means payment made to an injured employee as provided under Division 4 of the Labor Code.

(z) "Serve" means to file or deliver a document or to cause it to be delivered to the Administrative Director or his or her designee, or to such other person as is required under this article.

(aa) "Stipulated Order" means a Notice of Assessment that was timely paid.

(bb) "Supplemental job displacement benefits" means benefits as described under Labor Code section 4658.5 and sections 10133.50–10133.59 of Title 8 of the California Code of Regulations.

(cc) "Third-party administrator" means an agent under contract to administer the workers' compensation claims of an insurer, a self-insured employer, a legally uninsured employer, a self-insured joint powers authority or on behalf of the California Insurance Guarantee Association. The term third-party administrator includes the State Compensation Insurance Fund for locations that administer claims for legally uninsured and self-insured employers, and also includes managing general agents.

(dd) "Utilization review files" means those files, documents or records, whether paper or electronic, containing information that documents an employer or insurer utilization review process required under Division 4 of the Labor Code.

(ee) "Workers' Compensation Appeals Board" means the Appeals Board, commissioners, deputy commissioners, presiding workers' compensation judges and workers' compensation administrative law judges.

Note: Authority cited: Sections 133, 5307.3 and 5814.6, Labor Code. Reference: Sections 129.5, 139.48, 5814 and 5814.6, Labor Code.

History: 1. Change without regulatory effect renumbering former subchapter 1.8, article 1 (sections 10225–10225.2) to subchapter 1.5, article 5.5 (sections 10112.1–10112.3) and renumbering former section 10225 to section 10112.1 filed 4-7-2008 pursuant to section 100, title 1, California Code of Regulations (Register 2008, No. 15).

§10112.2. Schedule of Administrative Penalties Pursuant to Labor Code §5814.6.

(a) Administrative penalties shall only be imposed under this section based on violations of Labor Code section 5814, after more than one penalty award has been issued by the Workers' Compensation Appeals Board on or after June 1, 2004 based on conduct occurring on or after April 19, 2004 for unreasonable delay or refusal to pay compensation within a five year time period. The five year period of time shall begin on the date of issuance of any penalty award not previously subject to an administrative penalty assessment pursuant to Labor Code section 5814.6.

(b) The Division of Workers' Compensation shall at least monthly submit copies of WCAB decisions, findings, and/or awards issued pursuant to Labor Code section 5814 to the Audit Unit.

(c) The Audit Unit shall obtain monthly Labor Code section 5814 activity reports and shall determine if the decisions, findings, and/or awards are final. If more than one final penalty award has been issued on or after June 1, 2004 against a claims administrator at a single adjusting location, the Audit Unit may proceed with an investigation.

(d) To determine whether a violation described in Labor Code section 5814.6 has occurred, and notwithstanding Labor Code section 129(a) through (d) and section 129.5 subdivisions (a) through (c) and sections 10106, 10106.1, 10107 and 10107.1 of Title 8 of the California Code of Regulations, the Administrative Director, or his or her designee, may conduct an investigation, which may include but is not limited to an audit of claims and/or utilization review files. The investigation may be independent of, or may be conducted concurrently with, an audit conducted pursuant to Labor Code section 129 and 129.5.

(e) The Administrative Director, or his or her designee, may also utilize the provisions of Government Code sections 11180 through 11191 to carry out the responsibilities mandated by Labor Code section 5814.6.

(f) The Administrative Director may issue a Notice of Assessment under this article in conjunction with an order to show cause pursuant to section 10113 of Title 8 of the California Code of Regulations, charging both an administrative penalty under this section and a civil penalty under subdivision (e) of Labor Code section 129.5 in the same pleading, however only one penalty may be imposed by the Administrative Director following the hearing on such charges.

(g) Pursuant to Labor Code section 5814.6, the Administrative Director, or his or her designee, shall issue a Notice of Assessment for administrative penalties against an employer and/or insurer as follows:

(1) $100,000 for when the Administrative Director, or his or her designee, has evidence to support a finding that an employer or insurer knowingly violated Labor Code section 5814 with a frequency that indicates a general business practice, and additionally for each applicable penalty award, the following;

(2) $30,000 for each penalty award by the Workers' Compensation Appeals Board for a violation of Labor Code section 5814 for an unreasonable delay or refusal to comply with an existing compensation order;

(3) For each penalty award by the Workers' Compensation Appeals Board for a violation of Labor Code section 5814 for an unreasonable delay or refusal to make a payment of temporary disability benefits or salary continuation payments in lieu of temporary disability; vocational

rehabilitation maintenance allowance, life pension, or death benefits:

(A) $5,000 for 14 days or less of indemnity benefits;

(B) $10,000 for 15 days through 42 days of indemnity benefits;

(C) $15,000 for more than 42 days of indemnity benefits.

(4) For each penalty award by the Workers' Compensation Appeals Board for a violation of Labor Code section 5814 for an unreasonable delay or refusal to provide authorization for medical treatment:

(A) $1,000 for retrospective medical treatment authorization;

(B) $5,000 for prospective or concurrent medical treatment authorization;

(C) $15,000 for prospective or concurrent medical treatment authorization when the employee's condition is such that the employee faces an imminent and serious threat to his or her health.

(5) For each penalty award by the Workers' Compensation Appeals Board for a violation of Labor Code section 5814 for an unreasonable delay or refusal to reimburse an employee for self-procured medical treatment costs:

(A) $1,000 for medical treatment costs of $100 or less, excluding interest and penalty;

(B) $2,000 for medical treatment costs of more than $100 to $300, excluding interest and penalty;

(C) $3,000 for medical treatment costs of more than $300 to $500, excluding interest and penalty;

(D) $5,000 for medical treatment costs of more than $500, excluding interest and penalty.

(6) $2,500 for each penalty award by the Workers' Compensation Appeals Board for a violation of Labor Code section 5814 for an unreasonable delay or refusal to provide the the supplemental job displacement benefit, as required by section 10133.51(b) and section 10133.56(c), respectively, of Title 8 of the California Code of Regulations.

(7) $2,500 for each penalty award by the Workers' Compensation Appeals Board for a violation of Labor Code section 5814 for an unreasonable delay or refusal to make payment to an injured worker as reimbursement for payment for services provided for a supplemental job displacement benefit voucher, or where the unreasonable delay or refusal to pay the training provider causes an interruption in the employee's retraining.

(8) For each penalty award by the Workers' Compensation Appeals Board for a violation of Labor Code section 5814 for an unreasonable delay or refusal to make a payment of permanent disability indemnity benefits:

(A) $1,000 for 15 weeks or less of indemnity benefits;

(B) $5,000 for more than 15 but not more than 50 weeks of indemnity benefits;

(C) $7,500 for more than 50 but not more than 95 weeks of indemnity benefits;

(D) $15,000 for more than 95 weeks of indemnity benefits.

(9) $2,500 for any other penalty award by the Workers' Compensation Appeals Board pursuant to Labor Code section 5814 not otherwise specified in this section.

(h) In cases that the Administrative Director deems appropriate, the Administrative Director, or his or her designee, may mitigate a penalty imposed under this section after considering each of these factors:

(1) The consequences and gravity of the violation(s).

(2) The good faith of the claims administrator.

(3) The history of previous penalty awards under Labor Code section 5814.

(4) The number and type of the violations.

(5) The time period in which the violations occurred.

(6) The size of the claims adjusting location.

(i) Each administrative penalty assessed under this section shall be doubled upon a second Order (which may be a Stipulated Order or a final Determination and Order) by the Administrative Director under Labor Code § 5814.6 against the same employer or insurer within a five (5) year period. Each administrative penalty under this section shall be tripled upon a third Order (which may be a Stipulated Order or a final Determination and Order) by the Administrative Director under Labor Code § 5814.6 against the same employer or insurer within the same five (5) year period.

(j) In no event shall the administrative penalties assessed against a single employer or insurer in a single Stipulated Order or final Determination and Order after doubling or tripling exceed $400,000.

Note: Authority cited: Sections 133, 5307.3 and 5814.6, Labor Code. Reference: Sections 129.5, 139.48, 5814 and 5814.6, Labor Code; and Sections 11180–11191, Government Code.

History: 1. Change without regulatory effect renumbering former section 10225.1 to section 10112.2 filed 4-7-2008 pursuant to section 100, title 1, California Code of Regulations (Register 2008, No. 15).

§10112.3. Notice of Administrative Penalty Assessment, Appeal Hearing Procedures and Review.

(a) Pursuant to Labor Code section 5814.6, the Administrative Director shall issue a Notice of Assessment when the Administrative Director, or his or her designee (the investigating unit of the Division of Workers Compensation), has evidence to support a finding that an employer or insurer has knowingly violated section 5814 with a frequency that indicates a general business practice.

(b) Successor liability may be imposed on a corporation or other business entity that has merged with, consolidated with, or otherwise continued the business of an employer or insurer that is subject to penalties under Labor Code section 5814.6. The surviving entity shall assume and be liable for all the liabilities, obligations and penalties of the prior employer or insurer. Successor liability will be imposed if there has been a substantial continuity of business operations and/or the new business uses the same or substantially the same work force.

(c) The Notice of Assessment shall be in writing and shall contain all of the following:

(1) The basis for the penalty assessment, including a statement of the alleged violations and the amount of each proposed penalty;

(2) A description of the methods for paying or appealing the penalty assessment.

(d) The Notice of Assessment shall be served personally or by registered or certified mail.

(e) Within thirty (30) calendar days after the date of service of the Notice of Assessment, the employer or insurer may pay the penalties as assessed or file an appeal with the Administrative Director.

(f) If the employer or insurer pays the penalties within thirty (30) calendar days, the Notice of Assessment shall be deemed a Stipulated Order.

(g) If the employer or insurer files an appeal of the Notice of Assessment with the Administrative Director, the appeal shall:

(1) Admit or deny, in whole or in part any of the allegations set forth in the Notice;

(2) Appeal the existence of any or all of the alleged violations;

(3) Appeal the amount of any or all the penalties assessed;

(4) Set forth any affirmative and other defenses;

(5) Set forth the legal and factual bases for each defense and each ground for appeal. Any item listed in the Notice of Assessment but not appealed shall be paid within thirty (30) calendar days after the date of service of the Notice of Assessment.

(h) Failure to timely file an appeal shall constitute a waiver of the appellant's right to an evidentiary hearing. Unless set forth in the appeal, all defenses to the Notice of Assessment shall be deemed waived. The appellant may also file a written request for leave to assert additional defenses which the Administrative Director may grant upon a showing of good cause.

(i) The appeal shall be in writing signed by, or on behalf of, the employer or insurer, and shall state the appellant's mailing address. The appeal shall be verified, under penalty of perjury, by the employer or insurer. If the appellant is a corporation, the verification may be signed by an officer of the corporation. In the event the appellant is not the employer, the employer's address shall be provided and the employer shall be included on the proof of service.

(1) The appellant shall file the original and one copy of the appeal on the Administrative Director and concurrently serve one copy of the appeal on the investigating unit of the Division of Workers Compensation designated by the Administrative Director. The original and all copies of any filings required by this section shall have a proof of service attached.

(j) At any time before the hearing, the Administrative Director may file or permit the filing of an amended Notice of Assessment. All parties shall be notified thereof. If the amended Notice of Assessment presents new allegations or new penalties, the Administrative Director shall afford the Appellant a reasonable opportunity to prepare its defense, and the Appellant shall be entitled to file an amended appeal.

(k) At the Administrative Director's discretion, the Administrative Director may proceed with an informal pre-hearing conference with the appellant in an effort to resolve the contested matters. If any or all of the proposed penalties in

Notice of Assessment or the amended Notice of Assessment remain contested, those contested matters shall proceed to an evidentiary hearing.

(*l*) Whenever the Administrative Director's Notice of Assessment has been contested, the Administrative Director may designate a hearing officer to preside over the hearing. The authority of the Administrative Director or any designated hearing officer includes, but is not limited to: conducting a prehearing settlement conference; setting the date for an evidentiary hearing and any continuances; issuing subpoenas for the attendance of any person residing anywhere within the state as a witness or party at any pre-hearing conference and hearing; issuing subpoenas duces tecum for the production of documents and things at the hearing; presiding at hearings; administering oaths or affirmations and certifying official acts; ruling on objections and motions; issuing prehearing orders; and preparing a Recommended Determination and Order based on the hearing.

(m) The Administrative Director, or the designated hearing officer, shall set the time and place for any prehearing conference on the contested matters in a Notice of Hearing and shall give sixty (60) calendar days written notice to all parties.

(n) The prehearing conference may address one or more of the following matters:

(1) Exploration of settlement possibilities.

(2) Preparation of stipulations.

(3) Clarification of issues.

(4) Rulings on identity and limitation of the number of witnesses.

(5) Objections to proffers of evidence.

(6) Order of presentation of evidence and cross-examination.

(7) Rulings regarding issuance of subpoenas and protective orders.

(8) Schedules for the submission of written briefs and schedules for the commencement and conduct of the hearing.

(9) Any other matters as shall promote the orderly and prompt conduct of the hearing.

(o) The Administrative Director, or the designated hearing officer, shall issue a prehearing conference order incorporating the matters determined at the prehearing conference. The Administrative Director, or the designated hearing officer, may direct one or more of the parties to prepare the prehearing conference order.

(p) Not less than 30 calendar days prior to the date of the pre-hearing conference, or if no pre-hearing conference is set, not less than 30 calendar days prior to the date of the evidentiary hearing, the Appellant shall file and serve the original and one copy of a written statement with the Administrative Director, or the designated hearing officer, specifying the legal and factual bases for its appeal and each defense, listing all witnesses the Appellant intends to call to testify at the hearing, and appending copies of all documents and other evidence the Appellant intends to introduce into evidence at the hearing. A copy of the written statement and its attachments shall also concurrently be served on the investigating unit of the Division of Workers' Compensation. If the Appellant's written statement and supporting evidence are not timely filed and served, the Administrative Director, or the designated hearing officer, shall dismiss the appeal and the violations and penalties as stated in the Notice of Assessment shall be final, due and payable. Within ten (10) calendar days of the date for filing the written statement and supporting evidence, the Appellant may file a written request for leave to file a written statement and supporting evidence. The Administrative Director, or the designated hearing officer, may grant the request, upon a showing of good cause. If leave is granted, the written statement and supporting evidence must be filed and served no later than ten (10) calendar days prior to the date of the hearing.

(q) Oral testimony shall be taken only on oath or affirmation.

(r)(1) Each party shall have these rights: to call and examine witnesses, to introduce exhibits; to cross-examine opposing witnesses on any matter relevant to the issues even though that matter was not covered in the direct examination; to impeach any witness regardless of which party first called him or her to testify; and to rebut the evidence.

(2) In the absence of a contrary order by the Administrative Director, or the designated hearing officer, the investigating unit of the Division of Worker's Compensation shall present evidence first.

(3) The hearing need not be conducted according to the technical rules relating to evidence and witnesses, except as hereinafter provided. Any relevant evidence shall be admitted if it is the sort of evidence on which responsible persons are accustomed to rely in the conduct of

serious affairs, regardless of the existence of any common law or statutory rule which might make improper the admission of the evidence over objection in civil actions.

(4) Hearsay evidence may be used for the purpose of supplementing or explaining other evidence but over timely objection shall not be sufficient in itself to support a finding unless it would be admissible over objection in civil actions. An objection is timely if made before submission of the case to the Administrative Director, or to the designated hearing officer.

(s) The written affidavit or declaration of any witness may be offered and shall be received into evidence provided that (i) the witness was listed in the written statement pursuant to section 10112.3(p), (ii) the statement is made by affidavit or by declaration under penalty of perjury, (iii) copies of the statement have been delivered to all opposing parties at least 20 calendar days prior to the hearing, and (iv) no opposing party has, at least 10 calendar days before the hearing, delivered to the proponent of the evidence a written demand that the witness be produced in person to testify at the hearing. The Administrative Director, or the designated hearing officer, shall disregard any portion of the statement received pursuant to this regulation that would be inadmissible if the witness were testifying in person, but the inclusion of inadmissible matter does not render the entire statement inadmissible. Upon timely demand for production of a witness in lieu of admission of an affidavit or declaration, the proponent of that witness shall ensure the witness appears at the scheduled hearing and the proffered declaration or affidavit from that witness shall not be admitted. If the Administrative Director, or the designated hearing officer, determines that good cause exists that prevents the witness from appearing at the hearing, the declaration may be introduced in evidence, but it shall be given only the same effect as other hearsay evidence.

(t) The Administrative Director, or the designated hearing officer, shall issue a written Recommended Determination and Order, granting or denying the appeal, in whole or part, and affirming or amending the penalty assessment(s). The Recommended Determination and Order shall include a statement of the basis for the decision and each penalty assessed. It shall be served on all parties within sixty (60) calendar days of the date the case was submitted for determination. This requirement is directory and not jurisdictional.

(u) The Administrative Director shall have up to sixty (60) calendar days to adopt or modify the Recommended Determination and Order issued by the Administrative Director or the designated hearing officer. In the event the Recommended Determination and Order is modified, the Administrative Director shall include a statement of the basis for the Determination and Order. If the Administrative Director does not act within sixty (60) calendar days, then the Recommended Determination and Order shall become the Determination and Order on the sixty-first calendar day.

(v) The Determination and Order shall be served on all parties personally or by registered or certified mail by the Administrative Director.

(w) The Determination and Order, if any, shall become final on the date it was served, unless the aggrieved party files a timely Petition Appealing Determination and Order within twenty (20) days. A timely filed Petition Appealing the Determination and Order tolls the period for paying any disputed penalty. All findings and assessments in the Determination and Order that are not contested in the Petition Appealing Determination and Order shall become final as though no such petition was filed.

(x) At any time prior to the date the Determination and Order becomes final, the Administrative Director may correct the Determination and Order for clerical, mathematical or procedural error.

(y) Penalties assessed in a Determination and Order shall be paid within thirty (30) calendar days of the date the Determination and Order has been served, if no Petition Appealing Determination and Order has been filed. The penalties shall be deposited into the Return-to-Work-Fund.

(z) All appeals from any part or the entire Determination and Order shall be made in the form of a Petition Appealing the Determination and Order, in conformance with the requirements of chapter 7, part 4 of Division 4 of the Labor Code. Any such Petition Appealing the Determination and Order shall be filed at the Workers' Compensation Appeals Board in San Francisco (and not with any district office of the Workers' Compensation Appeals Board), in the same manner specified for petitions for reconsideration.

Note: Authority cited: Sections 133, 5307.3 and 5814.6, Labor Code. Reference: Sections 129.5, 139.48, 5300, 5814, 5814.6 and 5900 et seq., Labor Code.

History: 1. Change without regulatory effect renumbering former section 10225.2 to section 10112.3, including amendment of subsection (s), filed 4-7-2008 pursuant to section 100, title 1, California Code of Regulations (Register 2008, No. 15).

ARTICLE 6
Civil Penalty

§10113. Order to Show Cause Re: Assessment of Civil Penalty and Notice of Hearing.

(a) If an audit subject fails to meet the full compliance audit performance standards in two consecutive full compliance audits, the Audit Unit shall refer the audit subject to the Administrative Director for the possible assessment of a civil penalty pursuant to Labor Code Section 129.5(e). Nothing in these regulations shall prohibit the Audit Unit from referring any audit subject to the Administrative Director for the possible assessment of a civil penalty under Labor Code Section 129.5(e) for any other reason. If the Administrative Director has reason to believe that an employer, insurer, or third-party administrator has knowingly committed or performed any of the practices set forth in Labor Code Section 129.5(e), (s)he shall issue an Order to Show Cause Re: Assessment of Civil Penalty and Notice of Hearing.

(b) The order shall be in writing and shall contain all of the following:

(1) Notice that a civil penalty not to exceed $100,000 per audit subject named in the order may be assessed;

(2) The basis for the assessment, including a statement of the alleged violations;

(3) Notice of the date, time and place of hearing. Continuances will not be allowed without a showing of good cause.

(c) The order shall be served personally or by registered or certified mail.

Note: Authority cited: Sections 59, 129, 129.5, 133 and 5307.3, Labor Code. Reference: Sections 7, 124, 129 and 129.5, Labor Code.

History: 1. New section filed 1-18-90; operative 1-18-90 (Register 90, No. 4). New section is exempt from review by OAL pursuant to Government Code Section 11351.

2. Relocation and amendment of article heading, renumbering of former section 10113 to section 10115.1 and renumbering and amendment of former section 10109 to section 10113 filed 1-28-94; operative 1-28-94. Submitted to OAL for printing only pursuant to Government Code section 11351 (Register 94, No. 4).

3. Amendment of subsections (a), (b)(2) and Note filed 10-26-98; operative 11-25-98 (Register 98, No. 44).

4. Amendment of section and Note filed 12-30-2002; operative 1-1-2003 pursuant to Government Code section 11343.4 (Register 2003, No. 1).

Ref.: Hanna §§ 1.12[2], [7], 10.51[2][a], [b]; Herlick Handbook §§ 1.6, 9.5, 15.2.

§10113.1. Answer to Order to Show Cause.

(a) Within 30 days after service of the Order to Show Cause Re Assessment of Civil Penalties the claims administrator may file with the Administrative Director an Answer to the Order to Show Cause in which the claims administrator may:

(1) Admit or deny in whole or in part any of the allegations of set forth in the Order to Show Cause;

(2) Set forth any affirmative defenses.

(b) Failure to timely file an Answer shall constitute a waiver of the claims administrator's right to a hearing. Unless set forth in the Answer, all defenses to the Order to Show cause shall be deemed waived. If the Answer is not timely filed, the claims administrator may file a written request for leave to file an Answer. The claims administrator may also file a written request for leave to assert additional defenses. The Administrative Director may grant relief upon a showing of good cause.

(c) The Answer shall be in writing signed by or on behalf of the claims administrator and shall state the claims administrator's mailing address. It need not be verified or follow any particular form.

(d) The claims administrator must file the original and one copy of the Answer on the Administrative Director and concurrently serve one copy of the Answer on the Audit Unit. The original and all copies of any filings shall have a proof of service.

Note: Authority cited: Sections 59, 129, 129.5, 133 and 5307.3, Labor Code Reference: Sections 129 and 129.5, Labor Code.

History: 1. New section filed 12-30-2002; operative 1-1-2003 pursuant to Government Code section 11343.4 (Register 2003, No. 1).

Ref.: Hanna § 10.51[2][a.1].

§10113.2. Amended Complaint or Supplemental Order to Show Cause Before Submission of Case.

At any time before the hearing, the Administrative Director may file or permit the filing of an amended complaint or supplemental Order to Show Cause. All parties shall be notified thereof. If the amended or supplemental Order to Show Cause presents new charges, the Administrative Director shall afford the claims administrator a reasonable opportunity to prepare its defense thereto, and it shall be entitled to file an amended Answer.

Note: Authority cited: Sections 59, 129, 129.5, 133 and 5307.3, Labor Code. Reference: Sections 129 and 129.5, Labor Code.

History: 1. New section filed 12-30-2002; operative 1-1-2003 pursuant to Government Code section 11343.4 (Register 2003, No. 1).

Ref.: Hanna § 10.51[2][a.2]; Herlick Handbook §§ 1.6, 9.5.

§10113.3. Administrative Director's Designation of Hearing Officer.

The Administrative Director may delegate authority to a Workers' Compensation Administrative Law Judge to act as the Hearing Officer. The delegation may include the following authority: to conduct a prehearing conference; to conduct the civil penalty hearing; to issue subpoenas for the attendance of witnesses at the conference; to issue subpoena duces tecum for the production of documents; and to prepare a Recommended Determination.

Note: Authority cited: Sections 59, 129, 129.5, 133 and 5307.3, Labor Code. Reference: Sections 129 and 129.5, Labor Code.

History: 1. New section filed 12-30-2002; operative 1-1-2003 pursuant to Government Code section 11343.4 (Register 2003, No. 1).

Ref.: Hanna § 10.51[2][a.3].

§10113.4. Written Statement and Supporting Evidence.

(a) Not less than 30 calendar days prior to the date of hearing, the claims administrator shall file and serve a written statement with the Administrative Director specifying its legal and factual bases for its Answer. The written statement shall also list all witnesses the claims administrator intends to call to testify at the hearing, and copies of all documents and all other evidence the claims administrator intends on introducing into evidence must be served with the written statement. If the written statement and supporting evidence are not timely filed and served, the Administrative Director shall dismiss the Answer and issue a written Determination. If the written statement and supporting evidence are not timely filed and served, the claims administrator may file a written request for leave to file a written statement and supporting evidence. The written request for leave must be filed and served no later than the date of the hearing. The Administrative Director may grant the request for leave to file the written statement and supporting evidence and continue the hearing, upon a showing of good cause.

(b) The claims administrator must file the original and one copy of the written statement and all supporting evidence on the Administrative Director and concurrently serve one copy of the written statement and all supporting evidence on the Audit Unit. The original and all copies of any filings shall have a proof of service.

Note: Authority cited: Sections 59, 129, 129.5, 133 and 5307.3, Labor Code. Reference: Sections 129 and 129.5, Labor Code.

History: 1. New section filed 12-30-2002; operative 1-1-2003 pursuant to Government Code section 11343.4 (Register 2003, No. 1).

Ref.: Hanna § 10.51[2][b].

§10113.5. Prehearing Conference; Subject Matter; Prehearing Order.

(a) The Administrative Director or designee shall set the time and place for the prehearing conference, and shall give reasonable written notice to all parties.

(b) The prehearing conference may deal with one or more of the following matters:

(1) Exploration of settlement possibilities.

(2) Preparation of stipulations.

(3) Clarification of issues.

(4) Rulings on identity and limitation of the number of witnesses.

(5) Objections to proffers of evidence.

(6) Order of presentation of evidence and cross-examination.

(7) Rulings regarding issuance of subpoenas and protective orders.

(8) Schedules for the submission of written briefs and schedules for the commencement and conduct of the hearing.

(9) Any other matters as shall promote the orderly and prompt conduct of the hearing.

(c) The Administrative Director or designee shall issue a prehearing order incorporating the matters determined at the prehearing conference. The Administrative Director or designee may direct one or more of the parties to prepare a prehearing order.

Note: Authority cited: Sections 59, 129, 129.5, 133 and 5307.3, Labor Code. Reference: Sections 129 and 129.5, Labor Code.

History: 1. New section filed 12-30-2002; operative 1-1-2003 pursuant to Government Code section 11343.4 (Register 2003, No. 1).

Ref.: Hanna § 10.51[2][a.5].

§10113.6. Subpoenas.

The Administrative Director or designee may issue subpoenas for the attendance of persons and the production of documents or other things, to compel the attendance of persons residing anywhere within the State.

Note: Authority cited: Sections 59, 129, 129.5, 133 and 5307.3, Labor Code. Reference: Sections 129 and 129.5, Labor Code.

History: 1. New section filed 12-30-2002; operative 1-1-2003 pursuant to Government Code section 11343.4 (Register 2003, No. 1).

Ref.: Hanna § 10.51[2][a.3].

§10114. Hearing.

(a) The hearing shall be held at the place, time and date noticed, unless a continuance has been granted for good cause.

(b) A record of the hearing shall be made.

(c) Any claims administrator that fails to meet the full compliance audit performance standards in two consecutive full compliance audits shall be rebuttably presumed to have engaged in a general business practice of discharging and administering its compensation obligations in a manner causing injury to those dealing with it. With regard to any other bases for the assessment of a civil penalty, the Audit Unit will have the burden to prove a prima facie case that a violation of 129.5(e) occurred. The claims administrator may cross-examine the witnesses. The claims administrator may then present any testimony to rebut the Audit Unit's testimony, and the Audit Unit may cross-examine. The Designated Hearing Officer may choose to ask questions for clarification of the record.

Note: Authority cited: Sections 59, 129.5, 133 and 5307.3, Labor Code. Reference: Sections 7, 124 and 129.5, Labor Code.

History: 1. New section filed 1-18-90; operative 1-18-90 (Register 90, No. 4). New section is exempt from review by OAL pursuant to Government Code Section 11351.

2. Renumbering of former section 10114 to section 10115.2 and renumbering and amendment of former sections 10110 and 10111 to section 10114 filed 1-28-94; operative 1-28-94. Submitted to OAL for printing only pursuant to Government Code section 11351 (Register 94, No. 4).

3. Amendment of section heading, repealer of subsections (a), (b), (d), (e), (g) and (h), subsection relettering and new subsection (c) filed 12-30-2002; operative 1-1-2003 pursuant to Government Code section 11343.4 (Register 2003, No. 1).

Ref.: Hanna §§ 10.51[2][b]–[c]; Herlick Handbook §§ 1.6, 9.5, 15.2.

§10114.1. Evidence; Examination of Witnesses.

(a) Oral evidence shall be taken only on oath or affirmation.

(b) Each party shall have these rights: to call and examine witnesses, to introduce exhibits; to cross-examine opposing witnesses on any matter relevant to the issues even though that matter was not covered in the direct examination; to impeach any witness regardless of which party first called him or her to testify; and to rebut the evidence.

(c) In the absence of a contrary order by the Hearing Officer, the Audit Unit shall present its evidence first.

(d) The hearing need not be conducted according to technical rules relating to evidence and witnesses, except as hereinafter provided. Any relevant evidence shall be admitted if it is the sort of evidence on which responsible persons are accustomed to rely in the conduct of serious affairs, regardless of the existence of any common law or statutory rule which might make improper the admission of the evidence over objection in civil actions.

(e) Hearsay evidence may be used for the purpose of supplementing or explaining other evidence but over timely objection shall not be sufficient in itself to support a finding unless it would be admissible over objection in civil actions. An objection is timely if made before submission of the case or on reconsideration.

(f) The rules of privilege shall be effective to the extent that they are otherwise required by statute to be recognized at the hearing.

Note: Authority cited: Sections 59, 129, 129.5, 133 and 5307.3, Labor Code. Reference: Sections 7, 124 and 129.5, Labor Code.

History: 1. New section filed 12-30-2002; operative 1-1-2003 pursuant to Government Code section 11343.4 (Register 2003, No. 1).

Ref.: Hanna § 10.51[2][b].

§10114.2. Affidavits.

The written affidavit or declaration of any witness may be offered and shall be received into evidence provided that (i) the witness was listed in the written statement pursuant to section 10113.4, (ii) the statement is made by affidavit or by declaration under penalty of perjury, (iii) copies of the statement have been delivered to all opposing parties at least 20 days prior to the hearing, and (iv) no opposing party has, at least 10 days before the hearing, delivered to the proponent of the evidence a written demand that the witness be produced in person to testify at the hearing. The Hearing Officer shall disregard any portion of the statement received pursuant to this regulation that would be inadmissible if the witness were testifying in person, but the inclusion of inadmissible matter does not render the entire statement inadmissible.

Note: Authority cited: Sections 59, 129, 129.5, 133 and 5307.3, Labor Code. Reference: Sections 7, 124 and 129.5, Labor Code.

History: 1. New section filed 12-30-2002; operative 1-1-2003 pursuant to Government Code section 11343.4 (Register 2003, No. 1).

Ref.: Hanna § 10.51[2][b].

§10114.3. Oaths.

In any proceedings under this chapter the Administrative Director or his designated hearing officer, has power to administer oaths and affirmations and to certify to official acts.

Note: Authority cited: Sections 59, 129, 129.5, 133 and 5307.3, Labor Code. Reference: Sections 7, 124 and 129.5, Labor Code.

History: 1. New section filed 12-30-2002; operative 1-1-2003 pursuant to Government Code section 11343.4 (Register 2003, No. 1).

Ref.: Hanna § 10.51[2][b].

§10114.4. Determination.

(a) The Administrative Director shall issue a written Determination, including a statement of the basis for the Determination, within 60 days of the date the case was submitted for decision. This requirement is directory and not jurisdictional.

(b) The Determination shall be served on the audit subject personally or by registered or certified mail. If the Determination assesses a civil penalty, the Determination shall become final 7 days after the audit subject receives it, and the audit subject shall pay the amount assessed within 30 days after receiving the Determination, but the 30-day period shall be tolled if the audit subject files a timely appeal pursuant to Section 10953.

Note: Authority cited: Sections 59, 129, 129.5, 133 and 5307.3, Labor Code. Reference: Sections 7, 124 and 129.5, Labor Code.

History: 1. New section filed 12-30-2002; operative 1-1-2003 pursuant to Government Code section 11343.4 (Register 2003, No. 1).

Ref.: Hanna § 10.51[2][c].

ARTICLE 7
Appeals

§10115. Appeal of Notice of Compensation Due.

An audit subject which has filed a timely Objection under Section 10110 of these Rules may seek further review of a Notice of Compensation Due by filing an appeal with the Workers Compensation Appeals Board, and serving copies of the appeal on the injured worker, any other person to whom the payment is due as specified in the Notice of Compensation Due, and the Administrative Director, within 15 days of receiving the Notice.

Note: Authority cited: Sections 59, 129.5, 133, 4603.5 and 5307.3, Labor Code. Reference: Sections 129, 129.5, 3207, 4550, 4600, 4621, 4636 through 4638, 4639, 4701 through 4703.5, 4900 and 4902, Labor Code; and Section 10952, Title 8, California Code of Regulations.

History: 1. New section filed 1-18-90; operative 1-18-90 (Register 90, No. 4). New section is exempt from review by OAL pursuant to Government Code Section 11351.

2. Relocation and amendment of article heading, renumbering of former section 10115 to 10115.2 subsections (i)-(*l*) and new section filed 1-28-94; operative 1-28-94. Submitted to OAL for printing only pursuant to Government Code section 11351 (Register 94, No. 4). For prior history, see Register 90, No. 4.

Ref.: Hanna § 1.12[9][b]; Herlick Handbook §§ 1.6, 9.5.

§10115.1. Appeal of Notice of Penalty Assessment—Filing and Contents.

(a) Within 7 days after receiving a Notice of Penalty Assessment issued under Labor Code Section 129.5(a) and (c), the claims administrator may appeal all or a portion of the penalty assessments in the Notice by filing with the Administrative Director and serving the Audit Unit with a request for an appeals conference or a request for a written decision without a conference.

(b) If a request for a written decision or request for appeals conference is not timely filed and served, the Notice of Penalty Assessment will become final 7 days after the claims administrator received it, and must be paid in accordance with Labor Code §129.5(c) within 15 days of receipt.

(c) The request shall be in writing in a form specified by the Administrative Director and shall include at least the following information:

(1) The name and address of the person filing the request;

(2) A copy of the Notice of Penalty Assessment which is disputed.

(d) Within 21 days after the request for a written decision or appeals conference is filed, the appellant shall file with the Administrative Director and serve the Audit Unit with a written statement listing the assessments appealed, specifying the legal or factual basis of the appeal, and including documentation or other evidence, if any, which supports the appellant's position. If the written statement and supporting documentation are not timely filed and served, the the Administrative Director shall dismiss the request for written decision or appeals conference. The Notice of Penalty Assessment becomes final on the date of the Administrative Director's notice of dismissal. Penalties shall be paid within 15 days of receipt of the notice of dismissal.

(e) The appellant is deemed to have finally waived any legal or factual basis for appeal which is not stated in a timely filed appeal or timely filed supporting statement. However, the appellant may move the Administrative Director, upon a written showing of good cause filed and served not later than thirty days after its written statement was timely filed, for leave to amend its appeal or statement to add a legal or factual basis for appeal not previously stated. The motion shall attach a copy of the proposed amendment. The motion may include a request to file additional supporting documentation, which shall also be attached. If leave to amend is granted, the proposed amendment shall be deemed filed on the date the Administrative Director's order is served.

(f) Documentation which the appellant did not file with its appeal or supporting statement (including an amended appeal and statement allowed under subsection (e)) will not be admitted into evidence in support of the appeal without a showing of good cause. Good cause requires the appellant to show that the additional documentation was not reasonably available to accompany its appeal statement, and also requires that the appellant serve a copy of the proposed additional documentation on the Audit Unit before the hearing, as soon as the document becomes available.

(g) The appellant shall mail or deliver an original and one copy of its request under subsection (a) and its statement, documentation and any motion under subsections (d) or (e) to the office of the Administrative Director at the address shown in the report of audit findings. Requests, statements, documentation and motions are timely if they were:

(1) Placed in the United States mail in a fully prepaid, sealed envelope postmarked within the times specified in subsections (a), (d) and (e); or,

(2) Delivered to the office of the Administrative Director between the hours of 8:00 a.m. and 5:00 p.m. within the periods specified in subsections (a), (d) and (e).

If a date to submit a request under subsection (a) or to submit a filing under subsections (d) or (e) falls on a weekend or holiday, that date is extended to the next business day.

(h) The appellant shall serve two copies of any request, statement, document or motion filed with the Administrative Director concurrently on the Audit Unit, by the same means of delivery as the original which was filed with the Administrative Director. The original and all copies of any filing shall attach proof of service, which may be made as provided in Title 8, California Code of Regulations, Section 10975.

(i) If a request for a written decision or an appeals conference, or a written statement in support of the appeal, contests only a portion of a Notice of Penalty Assessment, the portions of which are not appealed (or not included in the supporting statement(s)) shall become final on the same date an entire Notice of Penalty Assessment would become final if not timely appealed or supported, and appellant shall pay the uncontested assessments by the date payment would be due under subsection (b) if an entire Notice of Penalty Assessment were involved.

Note: Authority cited: Sections 59, 129.5, 133 and 5307.3, Labor Code. Reference: Sections 129 and 129.5, Labor Code.

History: 1. Renumbering and amendment of former section 10113 to section 10115.1 filed 1-28-94; operative 1-28-94. Submitted to OAL for printing only pursuant to Government Code section 11351 (Register 94, No. 4).

2. Amendment of subsection (i) filed 2-14-96; operative 2-14-96. Submitted to OAL for printing only pursuant to Government Code section 11351 (Register 96, No. 7).

3. Amendment of subsections (a) and (d) filed 12-30-2002; operative 1-1-2003 pursuant to Government Code section 11343.4 (Register 2003, No. 1).

Ref.: Hanna §§ 10.50[3][a], 10.50[3][b][i]–[iii]; Herlick Handbook §§ 1.6, 9.5.

§10115.2. Appeal of Notice of Penalty Assessment; Conference Process and Delegation of Authority; Notice of Findings, Service.

(a) The Administrative Director may appoint a designee to conduct the appeal conference.

(b) The conference shall be held at the place, time, and date scheduled unless, upon a showing of good cause, a continuance has been granted. Notice of the conference date will be provided to the parties no later than thirty days before the conference.

(c) The appeals conference is an informal hearing in which the parties are given an opportunity to explain their positions and to present evidence in support of their positions. The conference need not be conducted in accordance with the formal rules of evidence, and legal representation is not required.

(d) The conference will be tape recorded, unless a party chooses to have it recorded by a court reporter. The Administrative Director and the opposing party shall be notified no later than five days before the conference that a party will supply a court reporter. The party choosing to use a court reporter is responsible for making the arrangements and for paying the costs of the reporter and transcription, including the cost of a copy of the transcript for the Administrative Director.

(e) Either party may present live testimony or documentary evidence at the conference. The Administrative Director may issue subpoenas for the attendance of witnesses at the conference, or subpoenas duces tecum for the production of documents, if requested by a party in writing within a reasonable time before the conference. Any person who is subpoenaed to appear may, instead of appearing at the time specified in the subpoena, agree with the party at whose request the subpoena was issued to appear at another time or upon agreed notice. Any failure to appear according to that agreement may be treated in all respects as a failure to appear in response to the original subpoena. The facts establishing or disproving the agreement and failure to appear may be proved by an affidavit of any person having personal knowledge of the facts.

(f) All testimony shall be made on oath or affirmation administered by the Administrative Director or designee.

(g) The Administrative Director or the Director's designee shall preside over the conference and shall have authority to admit any testimony or documentary evidence into the record which (s)he deems relevant and to decide any issues which arise during the conference including objections to evidence, privileges, claims and defenses.

(h) If the appellant fails to appear at the conference, the Administrative Director shall dismiss the request for conference and issue an order affirming the notice of penalty assessment.

(i) Within 15 days of the date the appeal is submitted for decision, the Administrative Director shall issue a Notice of Findings. When a written decision without a conference was requested, the date of submission is the date the Administrative Director receives the Audit Unit's written response to the appeal unless that date is extended by the Administrative Director for good cause. The time limits for action by the Administrative Director are directory and not jurisdictional.

(j) The Notice of Findings shall be served on the appellant by registered or certified mail, and is final for purposes of judicial review upon receipt.

(k) The appellant must pay any amount found due by the Administrative Director within 30 days after receiving the Notice of Findings, but the 30-day period shall be tolled if the appellant files a timely petition for writ of mandate, as to any assessment included for review in the petition proceeding, until that proceeding has become final.

(*l*) The appellant may file a petition for a writ of mandate from the Administrative Director's Notice of Findings in accordance with Labor Code Section 129.5(e). The deadline for filing the petition for writ is 30 days after receipt of the Notice of Findings.

Note: Authority cited: Sections 59, 129.5, 133 and 5307.3, Labor Code. Reference: Sections 7, 129 and 129.5, Labor Code.

History: 1. Renumbering and amendment of former sections 10114 and 10115 to section 10115.2 filed 1-28-94; operative 1-28-94. Submitted to OAL for printing only pursuant to Government Code section 11351 (Register 94, No. 4).

Ref.: Hanna §§ 1.12[8], 10.50[3][b][iv]–[v]; Herlick Handbook §§ 1.6, 9.5.

§10115.3. Appeal of Civil Penalty. [Repealed]

Note: Authority cited: Sections 59, 129.5, 133 and 5307.3, Labor Code. Reference: Sections 7, 124 and 129.5, Labor Code.

History: 1. Renumbering and amendment of former section 10112 to section 10115.3 filed 1-28-94; operative 1-28-94. Submitted to OAL for printing only pursuant to Government Code section 11351 (Register 94, No. 4).

2. Repealer filed 12-30-2002; operative 1-1-2003 pursuant to Government Code section 11343.4 (Register 2003, No. 1).

ARTICLE 6
Claim Form: Availability, Filing, Acknowledgement of Receipt, Dismissal [Renumbered]

§10116. General: Definitions. [Renumbered]

Note: Authority cited: Sections 133 and 5307.3, Labor Code. Reference: Sections 5401, 5401.7, 5402 and 5404.5, Labor Code.

History: 1. New section filed 1-18-90; operative 1-18-90 (Register 90, No. 4). New section is exempt from review by OAL pursuant to Government Code Section 11351.

2. Amendment of subsection (a) filed 4-13-93; operative 4-13-93. Submitted to OAL for printing only pursuant to Government Code section 11351 (Register 93, No. 16).

3. New subsection (a), subsection relettering, and amendment of article heading, newly designated subsections (b) and (c) and Note filed 12-31-93; operative 1-1-94. Submitted to OAL for printing only pursuant to Government Code section 11351 (Register 93, No. 53).

4. Change without regulatory effect renumbering former article 6 (sections 10116–10121) to article 9 (sections 10136–10142) and renumbering former section 10116 to section 10136 filed 4-7-2008 pursuant to section 100, title 1, California Code of Regulations (Register 2008, No. 15).

§10116.1. General: Employer Obligation. [Renumbered]

Note: Authority cited: Sections 133 and 5307.3, Labor Code. Reference: Sections 5401 and 3200-6208, Labor Code.

History: 1. New section filed 1-18-90; operative 1-18-90 (Register 90, No. 4). New section is exempt from review by OAL pursuant to Government Code section 11351.

2. Amendment of Note filed 12-31-93; operative 1-1-94. Submitted to OAL for printing only pursuant to Government Code section 11351 (Register 93, No. 53).

3. Change without regulatory effect renumbering former section 10116.1 to section 10137 filed 4-7-2008 pursuant to section 100, title 1, California Code of Regulations (Register 2008, No. 15).

§10117.1. Claim Form and Notice of Potential Eligibility for Benefits. [Renumbered]

Note: Authority cited: Sections 133 and 5307.3, Labor Code. Reference: Sections 5401, 5401.7 and 5402, Labor Code.

History: 1. New section filed 7-7-2004; operative 8-1-2004 pursuant to Government Code section 11343.4 (Register 2004, No. 28).

2. Change without regulatory effect renumbering former section 10117.1 to section 10138 filed 4-7-2008 pursuant to section 100, title 1, California Code of Regulations (Register 2008, No. 15).

§10118.1. Workers' Compensation Claim Form (DWC 1) and Notice of Potential Eligibility. [Renumbered]

Note: Authority cited: Sections 133 and 5307.3, Labor Code. Reference: Sections 139.5, 4600, 4604.5, 4616, 4658.5, 4658.6, 5401, 5401.7 and 5402, Labor Code.

History: 1. New section filed 7-7-2004; operative 8-1-2004 pursuant to Government Code section 11343.4 (Register 2004, No. 28).

2. Change without regulatory effect renumbering former section 10118.1 to section 10139 filed 4-7-2008 pursuant to section 100, title 1, California Code of Regulations (Register 2008, No. 15).

§10119. Employer's Responsibility to Process Claim Form, Claims Administrator's Duty to Provide Claim Form. [Renumbered]

Note: Authority cited: Sections 133 and 5307.3, Labor Code. Reference: Sections 5401 and 5402, Labor Code.

History: 1. New section filed 1-18-90; operative 1-18-90 (Register 90, No. 4). New section is exempt from review by OAL pursuant to Government Code section 11351.

2. Repealer of section 10119 and renumbering of former section 10121 to section 10119 filed 4-13-93; operative 4-13-93. Submitted to OAL for printing only pursuant to Government Code section 11351 (Register 93, No. 16).

3. Amendment of section heading, section and Note filed 12-31-93; operative 1-1-94. Submitted to OAL for printing only pursuant to Government Code section 11351 (Register 93, No. 53).

4. Change without regulatory effect renumbering former section 10119 to section 10140 filed 4-7-2008 pursuant to section 100, title 1, California Code of Regulations (Register 2008, No. 15).

§10120. Dismissal of Inactive Claim by Operation of Law After Notice. [Renumbered]

Note: Authority cited: Sections 133, 5307.3 and 5404.5, Labor Code. Reference: Sections 5401, 5402 and 5404.5, Labor Code.

History: 1. New section filed 12-31-93; operative 1-1-94. Submitted to OAL for printing only pursuant to Government Code section 11351 (Register 93, No. 53).

2. Change without regulatory effect renumbering former section 10120 to section 10141 filed 4-7-2008 pursuant to section 100, title 1, California Code of Regulations (Register 2008, No. 15).

§10121. Date of Denial for Purposes of End of Tolling of Limitations Period. [Renumbered]

Note: Authority cited: Sections 133 and 5307.3, Labor Code. Reference: Section 5401, Labor Code.

History: 1. New section filed 12-31-93; operative 1-1-94. Submitted to OAL for printing only pursuant to Government Code section 11351 (Register 93, No. 53).

2. Change without regulatory effect renumbering former section 10121 to section 10142 filed 4-7-2008 pursuant to section 100, title 1, California Code of Regulations (Register 2008, No. 15).

ARTICLE 7
Vocational Rehabilitation

§10122. Definitions.

The following definitions apply to this article and are in addition to those as set forth in Labor Code section 4635:

(a) Alternative Work: A job or occupation, other than modified work, with the same employer which is compatible with the injured employee's work restrictions. Alternative work for injuries occurring on or after 1/1/94 shall also meet the criteria of Labor Code Section 4644(a)(6).

(b) Claims Administrator. The person or entity responsible for the payment of compensation for a self-administered insurer providing security for the payment of compensation required by Divisions 4 and 4.5 of the Labor Code, a self-administered self-insured employer, or a third-party claims administrator for a self-insured employer, insurer, legally uninsured employer, or joint powers authority.

(c) Correct Rehabilitation Unit District Office. The district office venue assigned by the Rehabilitation Unit.

(d) Employer. The person or entity that employed the injured employee at the time of injury.

(e) In-House Qualified Rehabilitation Representative. An employee of the claims administrator who is capable of developing and implementing a vocational rehabilitation plan and whose experience and regular duties involve the evaluation, counseling or placement of disabled persons, and who is familiar with this article and Article 2.6 (commencing with Section 4635) of Chapter 2 of Part 2 of Division 4 of the Labor Code.

(f) Insurer. Has the same meaning as in Labor Code Section 3211.

(g) Modified Work: An injured employee's usual and customary job or occupation with the same employer after modification to accommodate required work restrictions. Modification includes, but is not limited to, changing or excluding certain tasks, reducing the time devoted to certain tasks, modifying the work station, changing the work location, and providing helpful equipment or tools. Modified work for injuries occurring on or after 1/1/94, shall meet the criteria of Labor Code Section 4644(a)(5). An Employer's provision of ergonomic or safety equipment or devices for injury prevention purposes shall not give rise to liability for vocational rehabilitation services.

(h) Notices. Required notices letters generated by the claims administrator and directed to the injured employee.

(i) Parties. The employee, claims administrator and their designated representatives, if any.

(j) Rehabilitation Provider. A person or entity providing vocational rehabilitation services for a fee.

(k) Rehabilitation Unit. The unit established within the Division of Workers' Compensation.

(*l*) Regular Position: A position arising from the ongoing business needs of the employer which consists of defined activities that can be reasonably viewed as required or prudent in view of the company's business objectives and is expected to last at least 12 months.

(m) Represented Employee: An injured employee who has retained an attorney-at-law who is a member in good standing of the State Bar of California.

Note: Authority cited: Sections 133, 139.5 and 5307.3, Labor Code. Reference: Sections 124, 139.5, 4635 and 4644, Labor Code.

History: 1. New section filed 1-18-90; operative 1-18-90 (Register 90, No. 4). New section is exempt from review by OAL pursuant to Government Code section 11351.

2. Change without regulatory effect amending section filed 1-22-91 pursuant to section 100, title 1, California Code of Regulations (Register 91, No. 10).

3. Amendment filed 12-31-93; operative 1-1-94. Submitted to OAL for printing only pursuant to Government Code section 11351 (Register 93, No. 53).

4. Amendment of subsections (d), (e), (g) and (*l*), new subsections (m) and (n), and amendment of Note filed 8-26-98; operative 9-25-98 (Register 98, No. 35).

5. Amendment alphabetizing definitions and relettering subsections filed 1-29-2003; operative 1-29-2003 pursuant to Government Code section 11343.4 (Register 2003, No. 5).

6. Change without regulatory effect repealing subsection (b) and relettering subsections filed 5-1-2003 pursuant to section 100, title 1, California Code of Regulations (Register 2003, No. 18).

Ref.: Hanna §§ 35.40[1], 35.41[3]; Herlick Handbook §§ 16.1, 16.7, 16.16.

§10122.1. Weekend or Holiday Deadlines.

If the date or deadline (including any applicable extension) to perform any act falls on a weekend or state holiday (as defined by Government Code §6700 and §6701), the act may be performed on the first business day after the weekend or holiday.

Note: Authority cited: Sections 133, 138.4, 139.5 and 5307.3, Labor Code. Reference: Sections 133, 139.5 and 4637, Labor Code.

History: 1. New section filed 1-29-2003; operative 1-29-2003 pursuant to Government Code section 11343.4 (Register 2003, No. 5).

Ref.: Hanna §§ 25.20[5], 35.31[1][b], 35.40[3][a], 35.50[2][e]; Herlick Handbook § 16.3.

§10123. Reporting Requirements.

(a) Except for notices required by this article to be sent to an employee, all forms or correspondence submitted to the Rehabilitation Unit shall include:

(1) Rehabilitation Unit file number, or

(2) Case Initiation Document or promulgated form requesting actionwhich includes the Rehabilitation Unit file number as the cover sheet for the information being submitted.

Documents which have neither a Rehabilitation Unit file number or a Case Initiation Document will be returned to the sender with instructions for proper filing.

(b) All forms, notices, reports and other communications subject to Labor Code section 139.5 and article 2.6 commencing with Labor Code section 4635 are to be served simultaneously on all parties.

(c) All forms and reports as required by this article shall be submitted to the correct Rehabilitation Unit District Office in the manner prescribed by the Administrative Director.

(1) Incomplete forms or forms with incomplete information attached may be returned to the sender. Each form has instructions as to the reports/information which must be attached.

(2) A form filed without the attachments and a specific listing of all enclosures as required by the instruction section of the form is deemed incomplete and shall be denied or returned to sender for proper submission. All incomplete requests will be date stamped.

(3) The Rehabilitation Unit shall serve a copy of the transmittal information upon the other parties when a form is returned.

(d) Filing instructions and venue lists shall be provided upon request by the Rehabilitation Unit. Requests shall be submitted to:

Rehabilitation Unit Headquarters
P. O. Box 420603
San Francisco, CA 94142

(e) All forms submitted to the Rehabilitation Unit shall bear original signatures and shall be on forms as issued by the Administrative Director or forms approved by the Administrative Director.

(1) No forms, notices or reports shall be forwarded to the Rehabilitation Unit when the claims administrator has raised a good faith issue of injury arising out of and occurring in the course of employment, until the claims administrator has accepted liability for the injury or there has been a finding of injury by the Workers' Compensation Appeals Board.

(2) Any requests for provision of rehabilitation services and for intervention/dispute resolution require confirmation by the employee or his/her representative that liability for the injury has been accepted.

Forms sent to the Rehabilitation Unit when a good faith issue of injury exists or where there has been no confirmation of acceptance of injury, shall be returned to the sender.

(f) All required notices shall be sent to the employee and his or her attorney, if any, on a timely basis by the claims administrator in the form and manner prescribed by the Administrative Director. Failure to provide notices timely shall subject the insurer, third party administrator or self-insured employer to administrative or civil penalties. The notices are timely when sent according to the requirements of Section 9813.

(g) The insurer shall advise the employer of a potential refund as described in Labor Code section 4638 no later than the required date of the initial notice of potential eligibility.

(h) The claims administrator shall retain a true copy of all notices sent to the employee and shall provide the unit with a copy upon request.

(i) When an employer, claims administrator or an employee chooses to be represented in matters pending before the Rehabilitation Unit, the represented party or representative shall notify the Rehabilitation Unit by completing and filing DWC Form RU-101, "Case Initiation Document." Notice of representation to the Appeals Board shall not be considered notice to the Rehabilitation Unit.

Note: Authority cited: Sections 133, 139.5 and 5307.3, Labor Code. Reference: Sections 139.5, 4636, 4637, 4638 and 4645, Labor Code.

History: 1. New section filed 1-18-90; operative 1-18-90 (Register 90, No. 4). New section is exempt from review by OAL pursuant to Government Code Section 11351.

2. Change without regulatory effect amending section filed 1-22-91 pursuant to section 100, title 1, California Code of Regulations (Register 91, No. 10).

3. Amendment of subsections (a)(2), (c)(2), (d), (e), (e)(1) and (f), repealer of subsections (f)(1)-(g)(2) and subsection relettering, and amendment of newly designated subsections (g)-(i) filed 12-31-93; operative 1-1-94. Submitted to OAL for printing only pursuant to Government Code section 11351 (Register 93, No. 53).

4. Change without regulatory effect amending subsection (f) and Note filed 3-14-94 pursuant to section 100, title 1, California Code of Regulations (Register 94, No. 11).

5. Amendment of subsection (g) filed 2-21-95; operative 2-21-95. Submitted to OAL for printing only pursuant to Government Code section 11351 (Register 95, No. 8).

Ref.: Hanna §§ 35.05[4][a]–[c], 35.31[1][b], 35.41[1][a], 35.50[1]; Herlick Handbook §§ 16.1, 16.3, 16.5, 16.12, 16.16.

§10123.1. Reproduction of Forms, Notices.

Any person or entity may reproduce all the forms required by this article and Article 2.6 of Chapter 2, Part 2 of Division 4 of the Labor Code (commencing with section 4635), including the pamphlet entitled "Help In Returning To Work-94" (Section 10133.2), and may only modify the heading to permit imprinting the name, address, telephone number and logo-type or other identifier of an employer, insurer or third party administrator.

The forms may be reproduced on white paper and must otherwise be comparable in type size, typestyle and format, to that promulgated by the Administrative Director in this section.

Note: Authority cited: Sections 133, 139.5 and 5307.3, Labor Code. Reference: Sections 139.5, 4636, 4637, 4638 and 4645, Labor Code.

History: 1. Change without regulatory effect adding new section filed 1-22-91 pursuant to section 100, title 1, California Code of Regulations (Register 91, No. 10).

2. Editorial correction of printing error restoring section 10123.2 (Register 91, No. 31).

3. Renumbering and amendment of former section 10123.2 to section 10123.1 filed 12-31-93; operative 1-1-94. Submitted to OAL for printing only pursuant to Government Code section 11351 (Register 93, No. 53).

4. Amendment filed 2-21-95; operative 2-21-95. Submitted to OAL for printing only pursuant to Government Code section 11351 (Register 95, No. 8).

5. Amendment of first paragraph filed 8-7-95; operative 8-7-95. Submitted to OAL for printing only pursuant to Government Code section 11351 (Register 95, No. 32).

6. Amendment of first paragraph filed 9-11-95; operative 9-11-95. Submitted to OAL for printing only pursuant to Government Code section 11351 (Register 95, No. 37).

Ref.: Hanna § 35.05[4][a]; Herlick Handbook § 16.1.

§10123.2. Unrepresented Employees.

The Rehabilitation Unit shall assist an unrepresented worker in complying with section 10123 of these regulations. Such assistance may include directing the worker to the correct Rehabilitation Unit district office, obtaining all reports and/or obtaining information necessary to make a determination on disputed issues.

Note: Authority cited: Sections 133, 139.5, 139.6 and 5307.3, Labor Code. Reference: Sections 139.5, 4636, 4637, 4638 and 4645, Labor Code.

History: 1. Change without regulatory effect adding new section filed 1-22-91 pursuant to section 100, title 1, California Code of Regulations (Register 91, No. 10).

2. Editorial correction of printing error restoring section 10123.1 (Register 91, No. 31).

3. Renumbering of former section 10123.1 to section 10123.2 filed 12-31-93; operative 1-1-94. Submitted to OAL for printing only pursuant to Government Code section 11351 (Register 93, No. 53).

Ref.: Hanna §§ 35.05[3], 35.05[4][a]; Herlick Handbook § 16.1.

§10123.3. Referral to Rehabilitation Providers; Facilities.

(a) An insurer may not refer an injured worker to a rehabilitation provider or facility in which the insurer has a proprietary interest. Nothing in this subdivision shall be construed to restrict or prohibit return-to-work services provided by a health care organization certified under Section 4600.5 of the Labor Code.

(b) A rehabilitation provider may not refer an injured worker to a work evaluation facility or education or training program in which the rehabilitation provider has a proprietary interest or contractual relationship, express or implied. This extends to the provider's spouse, employer, co-employee or any party with whom he or she has entered into a contract, express or implied.

(c) An in-house qualified rehabilitation representative may provide vocational rehabilitation services only if the expenses charged to a claim for such services are disclosed to the insured and agreed to in advance.

(d) This section applies only to injuries which occur or or after January 1, 1994.

Note: Authority cited: Sections 133, 139.5, 139.6 and 5307.3, Labor Code. Reference: Section 139.5(h), Labor Code.

History: 1. New section filed 12-31-93; operative 1-1-94. Submitted to OAL for printing only pursuant to Government Code section 11351 (Register 93, No. 53).

Ref.: Hanna § 35.57; Herlick Handbook § 16.1.

§10124. Identification of Medical Eligibility.

(a) For Injuries Occurring on or after 1/1/90 through 12/31/93 at 90 days of Aggregate Total Temporary Disability.

Within 25 days of receipt of the assignment required by subdivision (a) of Labor Code section 4636, the qualified rehabilitation representative shall:

(1) Meet with the employee to explain the services available to assist the employee in returning to work. If the employee's medical eligibility for vocational rehabilitation services has not yet been determined, the qualified rehabilitation representative shall assist the employee and confer with the employer in the joint development of a job description, using either DWC Form RU-91, "Description of Employee's Job Duties" or a narrative description, which may include a video tape of the tasks, worksite and equipment.

(2) Submit DWC Form RU-90, "Treating Physician's Report of Disability Status," and the job description to the employee's treating physician and request the physician to determine the employee's medical eligibility for vocational rehabilitation services.

(3) Provide the injured worker with the "Help In Returning to Work" pamphlet published by the Department of Industrial Relations, Division of Workers' Compensation.

(b) For Injuries Occurring on or after 1/1/94.

When 90 days of aggregate total disability occurs, the claims administrator shall, within 10 days, provide the employee "Help In Returning to Work-94" along with information on how to contact an Information and Assistance officer. (Reference 9813(d)(1).

(1) If the employee's medical eligibility for vocational rehabilitation services has not yet been determined, the claims administrator shall assist the employee in the joint development of a job description, using DWC Form RU-91, Description of Employee's Job Duties or a narrative description which may include a video tape of the tasks, worksite and equipment. If the employee unreasonably refuses to participate in the development of a joint job description, the employer's description shall be presumed to be the joint description.

(2) In the event that a dispute regarding the job duties cannot be resolved by the parties, the claims administrator shall submit this dispute to the Rehabilitation Unit. The Rehabilitation Unit will resolve the dispute on an expedited basis.

(3) The claims administrator must submit the DWC Form RU 90 "Treating Physician's Report of Disability Status", and the job description to the employee's treating physician and request the physician to determine the employee's medical eligibility for vocational rehabilitation services. In the event the treating physician is unable to determine if the employee is medically eligible for services, the claims administrator shall continue to contact the physician at no less than 60 day intervals until the physician can make a determination.

Note: Authority cited: Sections 133, 139.5 and 5307.3, Labor Code. Reference: Sections 139.5 and 4636, Labor Code.

History: 1. Change without regulatory effect renumbering and amending former section 10124 to section 10127.1 and former section 10124.1 to section 10124 filed 1-22-91 pursuant to section 100, title 1, California Code of Regulations (Register 91, No. 10). For prior history, see Register 90, No. 4.

2. Editorial correction of printing error restoring section 10124 (Register 91, No. 31).

3. Amendment of section heading and section filed 12-31-93; operative 1-1-94. Submitted to OAL for printing only pursuant to Government Code section 11351 (Register 93, No. 53).

4. Change without regulatory effect amending subsection (b) filed 3-14-94 pursuant to section 100, title 1, California Code of Regulations (Register 94, No. 11).

5. Amendment of subsections (b)-(b)(1) filed 2-21-95; operative 2-21-95. Submitted to OAL for printing only pursuant to Government Code section 11351 (Register 95, No. 8).

Ref.: Hanna §§ 35.31[1][a], 35.40[4]; Herlick Handbook §§ 16.1, 16.4, 16.6.

§10124.1. Identification of Vocational Feasibility.

(a) The Qualified Rehabilitation Representative (QRR) selected pursuant to Labor Code section 4637(a)(5) shall determine the employee's "vocational feasibility" as defined in Labor Code section 4635(a)(2). The QRR's determination of vocational feasibility may include the following steps:

(1) an initial evaluation meeting;

(2) an assessment of existing employment skills;

(3) consideration of the current physical limitations and work restrictions contained in the medical record;

(4) an assessment of the injured employee's perception of his or her physical capacities;

(5) an identification of vocational strengths;

(6) an identification of factors that may prevent or enhance participation in vocational rehabilitation services; and

(7) the use of vocational testing and/or work evaluation services when appropriate.

(b) The QRR shall prepare an initial report using DWC Form RU-120 addressing the employee's vocational feasibility prior to completing the "Vocational Rehabilitation Plan", DWC Form RU 102. The QRR shall thereafter continue to address the employee's vocational feasibility using DWC Form RU-121. For employees injured on or after 1/1/94, where all of the events contained in Section 10125 have occurred, the fees for reports required by this section shall be attributable to the maximum aggregate fees provided for in Section 10132.

(c) The QRR's report of vocational nonfeasibility shall identify the specific factor(s) preventing the employee from benefiting from the provision of vocational rehabilitation services. The report shall further identify any recommended action the employee should pursue in order to attain vocational feasibility.

(d) Where the QRR determines an employee lacks vocational feasibility, the claims administrator may, after notice to the employee pursuant to Sections 9812(d) or 9813(a)(3), discontinue vocational rehabilitation services and vocational rehabilitation temporary disability or maintenance allowance payments.

(e) The employee may dispute the claims administrator's discontinuance of benefits under subdivision (d) by filing a "Request for Dispute Resolution", DWC Form RU-103, pursuant to Section 10127(c) or (d). Notwithstanding Section 10127(e), the Rehabilitation Unit shall consider the dispute on an expedited basis, and shall issue a determination within ten (10) days of receipt of the RU-103.

Note: Authority cited: Sections 133, 138.4, 139.5 and 5307.3, Labor Code. Reference: Sections 4635 and 4637, Labor Code.

History: 1. New section filed 5-30-2001; operative 6-29-2001 (Register 2001, No. 22). For prior history, see Register 91, No. 46.

§10125. Maximum Vocational Rehabilitation Expenditures for Injuries Occurring On or After 1/1/94.

The maximum expenditure for counseling fees, training, maintenance allowance, and costs associated with and arising out of vocational rehabilitation services shall begin when all of the following events have occurred:

(a) The claims administrator has identified the employee as medically eligible for vocational rehabilitation services and has sent a notice of potential eligibility to the employee;

(b) The employee has received notice in writing that confirms the lack of alternate or modified work with the employer;

(c) The employee has made a request for vocational rehabilitation services.

Nothing in this article shall be construed to limit or discourage the use of additional public or private resources in addition to the maximum expenditure payable by the insurer as a part of a vocational rehabilitation plan.

Note: Authority cited: Sections 133, 139.5 and 5307.3, Labor Code. Reference: Sections 139.5, 4636, 4638 and 4642, Labor Code.

History: 1. Renumbering of former section 10125 to section 10127.2 and new section filed 12-31-93; operative 1-1-94. Submitted to OAL for printing only pursuant to Government Code section 11351 (Register 93, No. 53).

Ref.: Hanna §§ 35.05[1], 35.31[1][b], 35.40[3][a]; Herlick Handbook §§ 16.1, 16.5, 16.6.

§10125.1. Vocational Rehabilitation Maintenance Allowance.

(a) Vocational Rehabilitation Maintenance Allowance (VRMA) payments shall be made every 14 days on the day designated with the first payment.

(b) If the employee fails to reasonably cooperate with the provisions of vocational rehabilitation services subsequent to a request, the claims administrator may notify the worker of the claims administrator's intent to withhold the employee's maintenance allowance in accordance with Section 9813 (c)(4) and (d)(4). Failure to cooperate includes unreasonable failure to attend scheduled meetings and unreasonable failure to follow-up on tasks assigned in the development or implementation of a vocational rehabilitation plan.

(c) When the injured worker is receiving or should be receiving VRMA, the maintenance allowance payable during any delay caused by the employer or claims administrator shall be paid to the injured worker at the temporary disability rate. "Delay" includes any delay in the employer's provision of notice to the employee in accordance with subdivision (d) of Section 4636 of the Labor Code. For injuries occurring on or after 1/1/94, such payments will not be counted against the maximum allowable expenditure for vocational rehabilitation services or against the 52 week limitation on maintenance allowance payments.

Note: Authority cited: Sections 133, 139.5 and 5307.3, Labor Code. Reference: Sections 139.5, 4636, 4638 and 4642, Labor Code.

History: 1. New section filed 12-31-93; operative 1-1-94. Submitted to OAL for printing only pursuant to Government Code section 11351 (Register 93, No. 53).

2. Change without regulatory effect amending subsection (a) filed 3-14-94 pursuant to section 100, title 1, California Code of Regulations (Register 94, No. 11).

3. Amendment of subsection (c) filed 2-21-95; operative 2-21-95. Submitted to OAL for printing only pursuant to Government Code section 11351 (Register 95, No. 8).

Ref.: Hanna § 35.11[3]; Herlick Handbook §§ 16.1, 16.5, 16.7.

§10125.2. Vocational Rehabilitation Additional Living Expenses.

Additional living expenses to an employee that are necessitated by the provision of vocational rehabilitation services may include, but are not limited to, reasonable costs for food, lodging, transportation, clothing, and dependent care. The employee may elect to waive provision of additional living expenses provided such waiver is documented in the "Vocational Rehabilitation Plan", DWC Form RU-102.

Note: Authority cited: Sections 133, 139.5 and 5307.3, Labor Code. Reference: Sections 139.5 and 4641, Labor Code.

History: 1. New section filed 8-26-98; operative 9-25-98 (Register 98, No. 35).

Ref.: Hanna § 35.14[1]; Herlick Handbook §§ 16.1, 16.5.

§10125.3. Entitlement to Vocational Rehabilitation Temporary Disability or Vocational Rehabilitation Maintenance Allowance.

An employee shall be entitled to continuous payments of vocational rehabilitation temporary disability (VRTD), or for injury dates on or after 1/1/90 where the employee is permanent and stationary, vocational rehabilitation maintenance allowance (VRMA), during any period of entitlement to vocational rehabilitation services, including periods while participating in eligibility evaluation, plan development and during pendency of plan approval and implementation. However, entitlement to VRTD or VRMA payments, in addition to any other requirements, shall be contingent upon the employee's cooperation in and availability to receive vocational rehabilitation services. VRTD shall be payable in the same manner and at the same rate as temporary disability indemnity. For dates of injury on or after 1/1/94, VRMA payments shall not exceed 52 weeks in the aggregate unless the overall cap on vocational rehabilitation services may be exceeded pursuant to Labor Code Sections 139.5, 4642 or 4644.

Note: Authority cited: Sections 133, 138.4, 139.5 and 5307.3, Labor Code. Reference: Sections 139.5, 4642 and 4644, Labor Code.

History: 1. New section filed 8-26-98; operative 9-25-98 (Register 98, No. 35).

Ref.: Hanna §§ 35.11[2], 35.11[3], 35.12; Herlick Handbook §§ 16.1, 16.5.

§10126. Vocational Rehabilitation; Plans and Offers of Modified or Alternative Work.

(a) For Injuries occurring prior to 1/1/94,

(1) Within ninety (90) days after determination of the employee's vocational feasibility, the claims administrator shall either:

(a)(a) Submit Vocational Rehabilitation Plan, DWC Form RU-102, agreed to by the parties with appropriate attachments or;

(b)(b) Advise the Rehabilitation Unit of any dispute by filing a "Request For Dispute Resolution", DWC Form RU-103, to the Rehabilitation Unit, attaching a summary of the informal conference and the results thereof, including identification of the issues, issues resolved, issues pending, position of the parties and the rationale/supporting information for the position(s).

(2) A vocational rehabilitation plan that provides for modified or alternative work with the same employer and has been agreed to by the employer and employee shall not be subject to Rehabilitation Unit approval prior to implementation.

(3) Where a question arises concerning the duration of alternate plans of equal merit, the unit shall approve the plan that expedites the employee's return to suitable gainful employment.

(b) For Injuries Occurring On Or After 1/1/94.

(1) Offers to provide alternative or modified employment with the employer which meet the criteria of Labor Code Section 4644(a)(5), (6), or (7) do not require a written plan nor approval from the Rehabilitation Unit. The offer shall be made on DWC Form RU-94. The injured employee shall accept or reject a bona fide offer within 30 calendar days of receipt of the offer. In the event that the offer is not accepted or rejected within 30 days, the offer is deemed rejected unless the time period for reply is extended by the employer or by the terms and conditions of a collective bargaining agreement. The claims administrator shall submit a copy of the acceptance or rejection of the re-employment offer to the Rehabilitation Unit within 30 days of the acceptance or rejection.

(2) Plans developed for unrepresented employees or plan developed without the service of a Qualified Rehabilitation Representative require the approval of the Rehabilitation Unit. The plan must be submitted, on DWC Form RU 102, to the Rehabilitation Unit within 15 days of the agreement to the provisions of the plan.

(3) Agreed plans developed by a Qualified Rehabilitation Representative for represented

employees do not require Rehabilitation Unit approval. The claims administrator shall submit a copy of the plan to the Rehabilitation Unit upon submission of the Notice of Termination of Vocational Rehabilitation Services at the time of completion.

(4) Plans which provide the employee with discretionary monies to be used on a non-specific and/or self-directed basis must be reviewed by the Rehabilitation Unit to determine whether the plan is in conflict with Labor Code Section 4646. Any plan found to be in conflict with Labor Code Section 4646 shall not terminate an insurer's liability to provide vocational rehabilitation services and any money expended on such a plan shall not be counted against the maximum expenditure for vocational rehabilitation services.

(5) An employee may be granted a waiver of the services of a Qualified Rehabilitation Representative if the employee has made substantial progress towards the completion of a certificate or degree program from a community college, California State University, or the University of California. Substantial progress includes but is not limited to situations where the employee can demonstrate all of the following:

(a)(a) The employee is, was, or will be enrolled as a full-time student taking 12 units or more;

(b)(b) The employee has completed 35% or more of the units necessary to complete the degree or certificate program and has attained at least a "C" grade in those courses necessary to complete the degree or certificate program;

(c)(c) The employee has produced a letter of recommendation from the school in which the employee is enrolled supporting the employee's course of study from one of the following: the Dean of Admissions, the school department head or the school counselor. Accompanying the letter shall be an outline of the courses to be taken and the estimated time frames for completion of each course.

(d)(d) The employee has identified the vocational goal to be achieved, the resources and time frames required to achieve the goal and, if the goal extends beyond the maximum expenditures and time frames allowed, the alternative resources available to the employee to complete the program.

The Rehabilitation Unit will assist the employee in completing the DWC Form RU 102.

(c) All plans must contain a description of the level of participation expected of the employee in order to continue to receive maintenance allowance. If the employee fails to adhere to the agreement, the claims administrator may petition to withhold the employee's maintenance allowance as described in Section 9813.

(d) Nothing shall preclude the claims administrator or employee from requesting the Rehabilitation Unit to approve a modification of the plan because of an unforeseen circumstance arising subsequent to the initial plan agreement.

(e) Within 15 days after the employee and claims administrator have agreed to the terms and conditions of a vocational rehabilitation plan, the plan shall be submitted to the Rehabilitation Unit for review and approval where approval is required. Within thirty (30) days of receipt of a properly submitted, documented and signed plan, the Rehabilitation Unit shall approve or disapprove the plan. If disapproval is not made within thirty (30) days of receipt of a properly submitted plan, the plan shall be deemed approved.

Notice of approval shall issue only in instances where the plan has been previously disapproved. Plan commencement shall not be deemed approval.

(f) Plans that are in conflict with Labor Code Section 139.5(h) or Section 10123.3 of these regulations shall not terminate the insurer's liability to provide vocational rehabilitation services and, for injuries occurring on or after 1/1/94, shall not be counted against the maximum expenditure for vocational rehabilitation services.

(g) A vocational rehabilitation plan is complete when the claims administrator and employee have fulfilled their respective obligations specified in the plan or when applicable maximum expenditures for vocational rehabilitation services have been reached, whichever occurs first.

(h) For injuries occurring on or after 1/1/94, a rehabilitation plan must be completed within 18 consecutive months from the date of plan approval, or, if approval is not required, from the date of plan commencement. Except as provided in Subdivision (i), the job placement period in a plan shall not exceed 60 days.

(i) For employees injured on or after 1/1/94 who initiate rehabilitation benefits or services pursuant to Section 10125 on or after 1/1/98, the period of job placement in a rehabilitation plan may be up to 90 days where the plan exclusively utilizes transferable skills and experience for direct placement.

(j) A second vocational rehabilitation plan will not be provided where the claims administrator has fulfilled its obligations under the plan and the employee has completed, or with reasonable diligence could have completed the vocational rehabilitation plan, unless the employee can demonstrate a deterioration of his or her disability to the point where the employee is unable to meet the physical demands of the first plan.

(k) Private providers of vocational training selected to provide training as part of a vocational rehabilitation plan shall have either approval from the Bureau for Private Postsecondary and Vocational Education, approval from a California state agency that has an agreement with the Bureau for the regulation and oversight of non-degree-granting private postsecondary institutions, accreditation from the Western Association of Schools and Colleges, or certification from the Federal Aviation Administration.

(*l*) Vocational rehabilitation plans for employees who lack English language proficiency may include English language training when necessary to return the employee to suitable gainful employment.

Note: Authority cited: Sections 133, 139.5 and 5307.3, Labor Code. Reference: Sections 139.5, 4638 and 4644, Labor Code.

History: 1. New section filed 1-18-90; operative 1-18-90 (Register 90, No. 4). New section is exempt from review by OAL pursuant to Government Code section 11351.

2. Change without regulatory effect amending section filed 1-22-91 pursuant to section 100, title 1, California Code of Regulations (Register 91, No. 10).

3. Amendment of section heading and section filed 12-31-93; operative 1-1-94. Submitted to OAL for printing only pursuant to Government Code section 11351 (Register 93, No. 53).

4. Change without regulatory effect amending subsections (c)(c) and (c) filed 3-14-94 pursuant to title 1, section 100, California Code of Regulations (Register 94, No. 11).

5. Amendment of section heading, amendment of subsections (a)(2), (b)(1) and (h), new subsection (i), subsection relettering, amendment of newly designated subsections (j) and (k) and new subsection (*l*) filed 8-26-98; operative 9-25-98 (Register 98, No. 35).

Ref.: Hanna §§ 35.18, 35.30[2], 35.40[2A], 35.41[1][b], 35.41[3]; Herlick Handbook §§ 16.1, 16.6, 16.7, 16.8.

§10127. Dispute Resolution.

When there is a dispute regarding the provision of vocational rehabilitation services, either the employee or claims administrator may request the Rehabilitation Unit to resolve the dispute. All requests for dispute resolution shall be submitted as follows:

(a) If the request for dispute resolution results from an employee's objection to the claims administrator's intention to withhold maintenance payment pursuant to section 4643:

(1) The employee shall forward to the Rehabilitation Unit request for Dispute Resolution DWC Form RU 103 to the correct Rehabilitation Unit district office with copy to all parties;

(2) The employee shall state his/her position with full explanation of his/her objection, and attach the same to the request for Rehabilitation Unit dispute resolution; copies shall be served on all parties;

(3) The Rehabilitation Unit shall schedule and hold a conference and issue a determination within ten (10) days of the date of receipt of the employee's objection.

(b) If a dispute exists regarding identification of a vocational goal for injuries occurring on or after 1/1/94, the parties may contact the Rehabilitation Unit for a telephone conference discussion. The Rehabilitation Unit Consultant will provide direction, issue a determination or schedule a conference to be held on an expedited basis within 10 days.

(c) Excluding (a) above, all other requests for Rehabilitation Unit dispute resolution shall be submitted by completing a Request For Dispute Resolution, DWC Form RU-103, and attaching all medical and vocational reports not previously submitted to the Rehabilitation Unit, along with a format summary of the Informal Conference. The format summary identifies the disputed issues and the positions of the parties, including supporting information which shall be attached. The request for dispute resolution and all attached documentation shall be served on the parties.

(d) Excluding (a) above, and in instances where an informal conference is either impossible or impractical:

(1) The requesting party shall:

(aa) Complete the request form;

(bb) Attach all pertinent medical and vocational reports not previously submitted to the Rehabilitation Unit;

(cc) Clearly identify why an informal conference is inappropriate.

(dd) Clearly state the issue(s) and identify supporting information for each issue and position;

(ee) Serve copies on all parties.

(2) Upon receipt of the request above, the opposing party shall have twenty (20) days to forward their position with supporting information to the Rehabilitation Unit with copies to all parties.

(3) Upon receipt of all information, the Rehabilitation Unit shall either issue its determination based on the record, will ask for additional information, set the matter for formal conference, or direct the parties to meet informally.

(e) Pursuant to (b), (c) and (d) above, the Rehabilitation Unit shall issue a determination within fifty (50) days of the receipt of the original request. Where a determination denying a request issues, any further requests for dispute resolution must be accompanied with a new or updated DWC Form RU-103.

(f) When a dispute arises concerning the cost-effectiveness of providing vocational rehabilitation services outside of California, the Rehabilitation Unit may assign an Independent Vocational Evaluator (IVE) or Qualified Rehabilitation Representative (QRR), at the expense of the employer and subject to the maximum vocational rehabilitation expenditure contained in Labor Code Section 139.5, to assist the Unit in issuing a determination pursuant to Labor Code Section 4644(g).

Note: Authority cited: Sections 133, 139.5 and 5307.3, Labor Code. Reference: Sections 139.5, 4639, 4644 and 4645, Labor Code.

History: 1. New section filed 1-18-90; operative 1-18-90 (Register 90, No. 4). New section is exempt from review by OAL pursuant to Government Code Section 11351.

2. Change without regulatory effect amending section filed 1-22-91 pursuant to section 100, title 1, California Code of Regulations (Register 91, No. 10).

3. Amendment of first paragraph and subsection (a), new subsection (b) and subsection relettering, and amendment of newly designated subsection (c), (d) and (e) filed 12-31-93; operative 1-1-94. Submitted to OAL for printing only pursuant to Government Code section 11351 (Register 93, No. 53).

4. Amendment of subsections (d)(2)-(e), new subsection (f) and amendment of Note filed 8-26-98; operative 9-25-98 (Register 98, No. 35).

Ref.: Hanna §§ 35.42, 35.53[1]–[2], 35.70; Herlick Handbook §§ 16.1, 16.8, 16.12.

§10127.1. Conferences.

(a) Upon receipt of "Request for Dispute Resolution," DWC Form RU-103, the Rehabilitation Unit shall determine if a formal conference is necessary. Notices shall be served by the Rehabilitation Unit on all parties, identifying the time, date, and location of any conference. Where the request is initiated by an unrepresented employee, the Rehabilitation Unit or an Information & Assistance Officer may assist the employee in completing and serving the form.

(b) Rehabilitation Unit Conferences shall be held on the date and time scheduled. Any party unable to attend the conference, may submit his/her position, on the issue(s) in writing, to the Rehabilitation Unit district office holding the conference. Following the conference, the Rehabilitation Unit shall issue a determination based on its file, information provided during the conference, and any written positions submitted prior to or at the time of the conference.

(c) If the dispute is resolved by the parties before the conference has been held, the party who requested the conference shall contact the Rehabilitation Unit for permission to cancel the conference. If permission to cancel is given, the requesting party shall notify all parties of the cancellation, and forward, in writing to the Rehabilitation Unit, with copies to all parties, notification that the conference has been cancelled. The requesting party shall include in the notification the issue(s) in dispute and the resolution reached by the parties.

(d) Except where the conference is held pursuant to Labor Code Section 4643, a determination shall be issued within thirty (30) days of the date of conference unless additional information is requested by the Rehabilitation Unit, in which case, determination shall be issued thirty (30) days from the date of receipt of all further requested information.

Note: Authority cited: Sections 133, 139.5 and 5307.3, Labor Code. Reference: Sections 139.5, 4638 and 4639, Labor Code.

History: 1. Change without regulatory effect renumbering and amending former section 10127.1 filed 1-22-91 pursuant to section 100, title 1, California Code of Regulations (Register 91, No. 10).

Ref.: Hanna §§ 35.53[1], 35.53[3]; Herlick Handbook §§ 16.1, 16.12.

§10127.2. Independent Vocational Evaluator.

(a) The Rehabilitation Unit Headquarters shall maintain a list of Qualified Rehabilitation Representatives (QRR) who meet the requirements of an Independent Vocational Evaluator (IVE) pursuant to Labor Code section 4635(c). A QRR who meets the qualifications specified in Labor Code Section 4635(c) may apply to be included on the IVE list throughout the year. The IVE list shall be reviewed and revised on a yearly basis, and shall be made available upon request.

(b) The parties are encouraged to select a QRR whenever a dispute is raised regarding the assignment of a QRR. If the parties cannot agree on the selection of a QRR within fifteen (15) days, either party may request the Rehabilitation Unit to appoint an IVE. To request an IVE either party must file a Request for Dispute Resolution, DWC Form RU-103, with the correct Rehabilitation Unit district office.

(c) Within fifteen (15) days of receipt of the request, the Rehabilitation Unit shall appoint an IVE with notice served simultaneously on the IVE and all parties. The assignment shall be made in rotation from a panel of all independent vocational evaluators in the geographic area included within the venue of the correct rehabilitation unit district office and who meet the language and specialty requirements, if any, of the employee.

(d) Upon receipt of notification of the IVE appointment, the claims administrator shall forward all medical and vocational reports to the IVE within ten (10) days. If the IVE is unable to meet with the employee within ten (10) days of receipt of the medical and vocational reports, upon notification from either party, the Rehabilitation Unit shall appoint another IVE.

(e) The IVE shall communicate with the injured worker throughout the provision of rehabilitation services. Except as specified in Administrative Rule 10127.2(d) above, no party shall communicate with the IVE regarding the evaluation unless otherwise directed by the Rehabilitation Unit except for communications initiated by the IVE. All such communications shall be confirmed in writing by the IVE.

(f) The Rehabilitation Unit may order that vocational rehabilitation services be provided by an Independent Vocational Evaluator at the expense of the employer, subject to the maximum expenditure for counseling fees set forth in Labor Code Section 139.5 for injuries occurring on or after 1/1/94, upon a finding of any of the following:

(1) The claims administrator failed to provide vocational rehabilitation services in a timely manner subsequent to the employee requesting vocational rehabilitation services;

(2) An independent vocational evaluation is necessary for the rehabilitation unit to determine if an employee is vocationally feasible;

(3) An independent vocational evaluation is necessary for the Rehabilitation Unit to determine if a vocational rehabilitation plan meets the requirements of this article; or

(4) The employee and qualified rehabilitation representative cannot agree on a vocational goal.

Note: Authority cited: Sections 133, 139.5 and 5307.3, Labor Code. Reference: Sections 4635 and 4639, Labor Code.

History: 1. New section filed 1-18-90; operative 1-18-90 (Register 90, No. 4). New section is exempt from review by OAL pursuant to Government Code section 11351.

2. Change without regulatory effect amending section filed 1-22-91 pursuant to section 100, title 1, California Code of Regulations (Register 91, No. 10).

3. Renumbering of former section 10125 to section 10127.2 and amendment of subsections (d)-(f)(1) filed 12-31-93; operative 1-1-94. Submitted to OAL for printing only pursuant to Government Code section 11351 (Register 93, No. 53).

Ref.: Hanna § 35.40[3][a]–[c]; Herlick Handbook §§ 16.1, 16.6.

§10127.3. Qualified Rehabilitation Representative (QRR).

(a) The provision of vocational rehabilitation services shall be provided by individuals who meet the definition of a QRR as defined in Labor Code Section 4635(b), except where a QRR Waiver has been granted.

(b) When an employee is determined to be medically eligible and chooses to participate in a vocational rehabilitation program he/she is to be referred immediately to a QRR selected in agreement between the employee and claims administrator, pursuant to Labor Code Section 4637.

(c) If the agreement on a QRR cannot be reached within 15 days either party may request the Unit appoint an Independent Vocational Evaluator (IVE).

(d) The referral to the QRR shall include all pertinent and narrative medical and vocational reports to assist the QRR in the evaluation process.

Note: Authority cited: Sections 133, 138.4, 139.5 and 5307.3, Labor Code. Reference: Sections 4635, 4637 and 4640, Labor Code.

History: 1. New section filed 1-29-2003; operative 1-29-2003 pursuant to Government Code section 11343.4 (Register 2003, No. 5).

Ref.: Hanna § 35.40[1]; Herlick Handbook § 16.6.

§10128. Request for Order of Rehabilitation Services.

If the claims administrator fails to voluntarily provide services, subsequent to the employee's written demand with substantiation of eligibility for services upon the claims administrator, the employee may, on DWC Form RU-103 "Request for Dispute Resolution", request the Rehabilitation Unit to order the provisions of vocational rehabilitation services at the expense of the employer. A copy of the demand and copies of all medical and vocational reports including a listing of documents shall be attached with a completed Case Initiation Document, DWC form RU-101. Medical reports filed by the parties will be returned upon request.

Note: Authority cited: Sections 133, 139.5 and 5307.3, Labor Code. Reference: Sections 139.5 and 4639, Labor Code.

History: 1. Change without regulatory effect renumbering and amending former section 10128 to section 10131.1 and former section 10130 to section 10128 filed 1-22-91; operative 1-22-91 (Register 91, No. 10). For prior history, see Register 90, No. 4.

2. Amendment filed 12-31-93; operative 1-1-94. Submitted to OAL for printing only pursuant to Government Code section 11351 (Register 93, No. 53).

Ref.: Hanna § 35.50[1]; Herlick Handbook §§ 16.1, 16.4, 16.8, 16.9.

§10129. Interruption/Deferral of Services For Injuries Occurring Prior to 1/1/94.

(a) The provision of vocational rehabilitation services may be interrupted or deferred upon the request of the employee and agreement by the claims administrator, or if the agreement cannot be reached, upon a finding of good cause by the Rehabilitation Unit.

The claims administrator shall within 10 days of the agreement, confirm the deferral or interruption in writing to the employee including advice concerning procedures to be followed by the employee to commence or continue vocational rehabilitation services.

(b) The period of deferral or interruption may be extended upon agreement of the employee and claims administrator. If the employee and claims administrator are unable to agree to an extension of the deferral or interruption period, the Rehabilitation Unit may order an extension of the deferral or interruption period upon a finding that the extension is in the best interests of the employee.

(c) If the claims administrator fails to commence or continue vocational rehabilitation services after receipt of a timely request from the employee, the employee may request the Rehabilitation Unit to order the provision of vocational rehabilitation services pursuant to section 10128.

(d) If the employer offers the employee modified or alternate employment, the claims administrator may request the Rehabilitation Unit to determine whether the employer's offer provides the employee with suitable gainful employment. If the Rehabilitation Unit finds the employer's offer reasonable and appropriate, the employee shall not be entitled to the development or implementation of an additional plan.

Note: Authority cited: Sections 133, 139.5 and 5307.3, Labor Code. Reference: Sections 139.5 and 4644, Labor Code.

History: 1. Change without regulatory effect renumbering and amending former section 10129 to section 10132 and former section 10131 to section 10129 filed 1-22-91; operative 1-22-91 (Register 91, No. 10). For prior history, see Register 90, No. 4.

2. Amendment of section heading, subsections (a)-(c), new subsection (d) filed 12-31-93; operative 1-1-94. Submitted to OAL for printing only pursuant to Government Code section 11351 (Register 93, No. 53).

Ref.: Hanna §§ 35.41[3], 35.70, 35.80; Herlick Handbook §§ 16.1, 16.9.

§10129.1. Interruption/Deferral of Services for Injuries Occurring on or After 1/1/94.

(a) An employee may defer rehabilitation services subsequent to being advised of medical eligibility for services, but prior to accepting services, only if the employer has not offered to provide alternative or modified work not exceeding the medical restrictions.

(b) An employee may interrupt rehabilitation services subsequent to accepting services. The interruption shall be for an agreed upon period of time. If the employee had previously agreed to a plan at the time of interruption, the claims administrator shall provide the notice specified in Section 9813(a)(4).

(c) If a dispute arises concerning an employee's request to defer or interrupt rehabilitation services, the employee may be granted a deferral or interruption upon a finding of good cause by the Rehabilitation Unit.

Note: Authority cited: Sections 133, 139.5 and 5307.3, Labor Code. Reference: Sections 139.5 and 4644, Labor Code.

History: 1. New section filed 12-31-93; operative 1-1-94. Submitted to OAL for printing only pursuant to Government Code section 11351 (Register 93, No. 53).

2. New subsection (c) filed 2-25-99; operative 2-25-99 pursuant to Government Code section 11343.3(d) (Register 99, No. 9).

Ref.: Hanna § 35.80; Herlick Handbook §§ 16.1, 16.9.

§10130. Request for Reinstatement of Vocational Rehabilitation Services.

Request for reinstatement of vocational rehabilitation services following an interruption or deferral shall be made in accordance with Labor Code section 4644(b).

All other requests for reinstatement of services shall initially be submitted to the claims administrator. If the claims administrator fails to reinstate services and the employee wishes a determination of entitlement to further rehabilitation services, all such requests shall be directed to the correct Rehabilitation Unit district office on DWC Form RU-103, "Request for Dispute Resolution".

Note: Authority cited: Sections 133, 139.5 and 5307.3, Labor Code. Reference: Section 4644, Labor Code.

History: 1. Change without regulatory effect renumbering and amending former section 10130 to section 10128 and former section 10132 to section 10130 filed 1-22-91; operative 1-22-91 (Register 91, No. 10). For prior history, see Register 90, No. 4.

2. Amendment filed 12-31-93; operative 1-1-94. Submitted to OAL for printing only pursuant to Government Code section 11351 (Register 93, No. 53).

Ref.: Hanna §§ 25.20[5], 35.70, 35.83; Herlick Handbook §§ 16.1, 16.11, 16.14.

§10131. Termination of Vocational Rehabilitation Services.

(a) When the employer/claims administrator elects to terminate rehabilitation services of an employee injured before 1/1/90, prior to such termination, the claims administrator shall provide the employee with a "Request for Conclusion of Rehabilitation Benefits", DWC Form RB-105. For employees injured on or after 1/1/90, the claims administrator shall provide the employee with a "Notice of Termination of Rehabilitation Services," DWC RU-105. The notice must be sent within 10 days of the circumstances set forth in Labor Code section 4644(a) with copies sent to all parties, including the Rehabilitation Unit, with proof of service. The copy forwarded to the Rehabilitation Unit shall include the Rehabilitation Unit file number or a RU 101 attached.

(b) If the employee wishes to object to the "Request for Conclusion of Rehabilitation Benefits", DWC Form RB-105 or the "Notice of Termination of Vocational Rehabilitation Services", DWC Form RU-105, the objection must be filed with the Rehabilitation Unit within twenty days using the "Request for Dispute Resolution", DWC Form RU-103. The claims administrator shall provide the employee with a RU-103 with the "Request for Conclusion of Rehabilitation Benefits", DWC Form RB-105, or "Notice of Termination of Vocational Rehabilitation Services" DWC Form RU-105. Absent timely objection by the employee, the employer's liability for vocational rehabilitation services will be presumed terminated.

(c) When the employee objects to the claims administrator's "Request for Conclusion of Rehabilitation Benefits", DWC Form RB-105 or "Notice of Termination of Vocational Rehabilitation Services", DWC Form RU-105, the Rehabilitation Unit shall, within thirty (30) days of the employee's objection, hold a conference or otherwise obtain the employee's reasons for objection together with substantiating evidence and issue its decision.

(d) For injuries occurring on or after 1/1/94. When the employer offers modified or alternative work to the employee on the DWC Form RU-94 that meets the conditions of Labor Code Section 4644(a)(5), (6), or (7) and subsequently learns that the employee cannot lawfully perform modified or alternative work due to the employee's immigration status, the employer is not required to provide vocational rehabilitation services.

(e) An employer's obligation to provide modified or alternative work to a seasonal employee is terminated after 12 months if the following conditions apply:

(1) The employee was hired on a seasonal basis prior to injury;

(2) The offer or modified or alternative work is on a similar seasonal basis to the employee's previous employment; and

(3) The offer is made on the DWC Form RU-94 that meets the conditions of Labor Code Section 4644(a)(5), (6), or (7).

(f) For dates of injuries on or after 1/1/03, where the employee and employer have agreed to settle the employee's right to prospective vocational rehabilitation services for an amount not to exceed $10,000 for the employee's use in self-directed rehabilitation, the employer/claims administrator's liability for vocational rehabilitation services is terminated.

Note: Authority cited: Sections 133, 139.5 and 5307.3, Labor Code. Reference: Sections 139.5, 4644 and 4646, Labor Code.

History: 1. Change without regulatory effect renumbering and amending former section 10131 to section 10129 and former section 10133 to section 10131 filed 1-22-91; operative 1-22-91 (Register 91, No. 10). For prior history, see Register 90, No. 4.

2. Amendment of section heading and section filed 12-31-93; operative 1-1-94. Submitted to OAL for printing only pursuant to Government Code section 11351 (Register 93, No. 53).

3. Amendment filed 12-27-96; operative 12-27-96. Submitted to OAL for printing only pursuant to Government Code section 11351 (Register 96, No. 52).

4. Amendment of subsection (a), new subsections (d)-(f) and amendment of Note filed 3-25-2003; operative 3-25-2003 pursuant to Government Code section 11343.4 (Register 2003, No. 13).

Ref.: Hanna §§ 10.50[2][a], 35.70, 35.80, 35.81; Herlick Handbook §§ 2.3, 16.1, 16.4, 16.7, 16.10.

§10131.1. Declination of Rehabilitation.

(a) A request for conclusion of rehabilitation benefits, or a notice of termination of vocational rehabilitation services on the basis that the employee has declined rehabilitation services must be made in the form and manner set forth by the Administrative Director in section 10131 of these rules by using DWC Form RB-105 or DWC Form RU-105.

(b) Absent timely objection by the employee to the "Request for Conclusion of Rehabilitation Benefits", DWC Form RB-105 or the "Notice of Termination of Vocational Rehabilitation Services", DWC Form RU-105, the employer's liability for vocational rehabilitation services will be presumed terminated when:

(1)(A) The employee, with a date of injury prior to 1/1/90, received a notice of potential entitlement to rehabilitation services, immediately following the claims administrator's knowledge of potential medical eligibility or immediately following 180 days of aggregate total disability, or

(B) The employee with a date of injury on or after 1/1/90 has received a notice of potential eligibility pursuant to Labor Code section 4637(a); and,

(2) If the injury occurred between 1/1/90 and 12/31/93, the employee has received a full explanation by a Qualified Rehabilitation Representative of his/her rights and obligations pertaining to vocational services pursuant to Labor Code section 4636(a); or

(3) If the injury occurred on or after 1/1/94, the employee has received a notice of his/her rights and obligations as required in Section 9813(d)(2).

(c) The employee and his/her representative, if any, must sign a declination of rehabilitation on the form prescribed by the Administrative Director.

(d) The claims administrator shall submit a "Request for Conclusion of Rehabilitation Benefits", DWC Form RB-105 for employees with a date of injury prior to 1/1/90, to the correct Rehabilitation Unit district office with copies to all parties. A "Notice of Termination of Vocational Rehabilitation Services", DWC Form RU-105, shall be submitted for employees with dates of injury on or after 1/1/90 to the correct Rehabilitation Unit district office with copies to all parties. The request shall be accompanied with the notice of potential eligibility and either (i) the signed "Statement of Decline of Rehabilitation Benefits", DWC Form RB-107, for employees with dates of injury prior to 1/1/90 or (ii) an "Employee Statement of Declination of Vocational Rehabilitation Services," DWC Form RU-107, for employees with dates of injury between 1/1/90 and 12/31/93 or (iii) an "Employee Statement of Declination of Vocational

Rehabilitation Services", DWC Form RU-107A, for employees with dates of injury on or after 1/1/94.

Note: Authority cited: Sections 133, 139.5 and 5307.3, Labor Code. Reference: Section 4641 and 4644, Labor Code.

History: 1. Change without regulatory effect renumbering and amending former section 10128 to section 10131.1 filed 1-22-91 pursuant to section 100, title 1, California Code of Regulations (Register 91, No. 10).

2. Amendment filed 12-31-93; operative 1-1-94. Submitted to OAL for printing only pursuant to Government Code section 11351 (Register 93, No. 53).

3. Change without regulatory effect amending subsection (b)(2) filed 3-14-94 pursuant to title 1, section 100, California Code of Regulations (Register 94, No. 11).

4. Amendment filed 12-27-96; operative 12-27-96. Submitted to OAL for printing only pursuant to Government Code section 11351 (Register 96, No. 52).

5. Amendment of subsection (d) filed 8-26-98; operative 9-25-98 (Register 98, No. 35).

Ref.: Hanna § 35.32; Herlick Handbook §§ 16.1, 16.4, 16.10.

§10131.2. Settlement of Prospective Vocational Rehabilitation.

(a) A represented employee who was injured on or after January 1, 2003 can settle prospective vocational rehabilitation services for an amount not to exceed $10,000 in self directed vocational rehabilitation when the following conditions have been met;

(1) The settlement of the employee's rights to prospective vocational rehabilitation services shall be set forth on the DWC Form RU-122;

(2) Prior to entering into any settlement agreement, the attorney for the represented employee shall fully disclose and explain to the employee the nature and quality of the rights and privileges being waived; and

(3) The "Settlement of Prospective Vocational Rehabilitation Services" shall be submitted on the DWC Form RU-122 for employees with a date of injury on or after January 1, 2003 to the correct Rehabilitation Unit office with copies to all parties.

(b) The Rehabilitation Unit may only disapprove a settlement agreement upon a finding that receipt of rehabilitation services is necessary to return the employee to suitable gainful employment. If disapproval is not made within ten (10) days of the Rehabilitation Unit's receipt of a fully executed agreement, the agreement shall be deemed approved.

Note: Authority cited: Sections 133, 139.5 and 5307.3, Labor Code. Reference: Sections 139.5, 4644 and 4646, Labor Code.

History: 1. New section filed 1-29-2003; operative 1-29-2003 pursuant to Government Code section 11343.4 (Register 2003, No. 5). For prior history, see Register 96, No. 13.

Ref.: Hanna §§ 29.03[3], 35.41[3], 35.54; Herlick Handbook § 16.5.

§10132. Fee Schedule.

(a) The Fee Schedule promulgated by the Administrative Director shall be deemed reasonable for providers of vocational rehabilitation services pursuant to Labor Code section 139.5. For services provided to employees injured on or after 1/1/94, the maximum aggregate permissible fees paid for evaluation, plan development and job placement may not exceed $4500, nor may the maximum aggregate permissible fees in each phase of the fee schedule be exceeded.

(b) For injuries occurring prior to 1/1/94, the fee schedule promulgated by the Administrative Director effective 1/1/94 shall be presumed reasonable for services to employees who are determined medically eligible on or after 1/1/94.

(c) For employees who were determined medically eligible prior to 1/1/94, the fee schedule promulgated by the Administrative Director effective 1/23/91 shall apply.

(d) For employees injured on or after 1/1/94 who initiate rehabilitation benefits or services pursuant to Section 10125 on or after 1/1/98, the fee schedule promulgated by the Administrative Director effective 1/1/98 shall apply.

(e) Rehabilitation providers and claims administrators may enter into agreements with any party to provide services at rates less than those provided by the Fee Schedule. Any agreements, however, shall be made in writing prior to the provision of such rehabilitation services. Fees that are charged back to a file by an in-house QRR who is providing rehabilitation services shall not exceed this fee schedule and are subject to the maximum permissible fees for counseling for injuries occurring on or after 1/1/94.

(f) Charges by a claims administrator for the activities of an employee supervising outside rehabilitation providers shall not exceed this fee schedule and shall not be attributed to the maximum permissible fees for counseling. These charges shall be attributed as expenses and not losses for the purposes of insurance rating pursuant to Labor Code Section 139.5(i) for injuries occurring on or after 1/1/94.

(g) Disputes pertaining to the application of the Fee Schedule shall be initially determined by the Rehabilitation Unit.

(h) Service provided by persons other than the firm in which the Qualified Rehabilitation Representative is employed must be clearly identified and billed separately.

(i) Qualified Rehabilitation Representatives appointed by the Rehabilitation Unit to act in the capacity of an independent Vocational Evaluator shall strictly adhere to the fee schedule.

(j) All billings from vocational rehabilitation service providers are due and payable within sixty (60) days of receipt by the claims administrator unless within the sixty (60) day period an objections filed contesting the billing or any portion thereof. Any portion of the billing not contested shall be paid within the sixty day period. Absent objection as described, billings not paid within sixty days from the date of receipt are subject to penalty under Labor Code sections 129 and 129.5. A copy of each billing shall be sent to the employee, and his or her representative, if any, at the time the bill is sent to the claims administrator.

Note: Authority cited: Sections 129, 129.5, 133, 139.5 and 5307.3, Labor Code. Reference: Sections 4635, 4636, 4638 and 4639, Labor Code.

History: 1. Change without regulatory effect renumbering and amending former section 10132 to section 10130 and new section 10132 filed 1-22-91; operative 1-22-91 (Register 91, No. 10). For prior history, see Register 90, No. 4.

2. Amendment filed 12-31-93; operative 1-1-94. Submitted to OAL for printing only pursuant to Government Code section 11351 (Register 93, No. 53).

3. New subsection (c) and subsection relettering filed 2-21-95; operative 2-21-95. Submitted to OAL for printing only pursuant to Government Code section 11351 (Register 95, No. 8).

4. Amendment of subsections (a)-(c), new subsection (d), subsection relettering and amendment of newly designated subsection (f) filed 8-26-98; operative 9-25-98 (Register 98, No. 35).

Ref.: Hanna § 35.05[1]; Herlick Handbook § 16.1.

§10132.1. Reasonable Fee Schedule.

VOCATIONAL REHABILITATION FEE SCHEDULE

All billings for casework provided are to be itemized in tenths of an hour, unless alternative agreements are made under Section 10132(c).

Non-billable costs include: postage, clerical services, photocopies, in-house waiting time, attempts telephone contacts, and in-house staffing. If detailed documentation of these activities is required, the activity is billable at the normal hourly rate of actual time spent.

Adjustments to the Fee Schedule will be reviewed by the Administrative Director of the Division of Worker's Compensation on an annual basis. Recommendations regarding adjustments to the Fee Schedule shall be reviewed by the Rehabilitation Advisory Committee prior to public hearings.

Professional Hourly Rate $65.00

Vocational Evaluation Modules:

Work Sample Testing, Vocational Testing, Situational Assessment, or related activities in a group setting shall be subject to the following fee schedule. Includes report.

Service Code #	*Item Description*	*Schedule*
60	One Day	$175
61	Three Day	$375
62	Five Day	$500
63	Eight Day	$800
30	90 Day QRR Benefit Call	Actual time at professional hourly rate, not to exceed 5 Hours
	Includes all contacts to schedule appointments, preparation of RU90/91, visit verification, employer contact, first physician contact. Subsequent contacts to be billed at professional hourly rate.	
31	Job Analysis of Position at Time of Injury	Actual time at professional hourly rate, not to exceed 5 Hours

Includes contacts to schedule appointment, site visit, document completion, document review with employee/attorney, securing signatures and completed report.

PHASE A: EVALUATION OF VOCATIONAL FEASIBILITY AND PLAN DEVELOPMENT MAXIMUM AGGREGATE PERMISSIBLE FEES NOT TO EXCEED $3000

32 Initial Evaluation — Actual time, not to exceed 5 Hours

Includes initial file review, scheduling contact with employee, contact with employee and representative, if any, interview, assessment of vocational feasibility and completed Initial Evaluation Summary, Form RU-120. Billing for the RU-120 shall not exceed 1.2 hours. The QRR must review with the employee the report and his or her initial recommendations regarding the employee's likely ability to benefit from the provision of rehabilitation services and regarding the nature, extent and cost of any additional services.

60,61, 62,63 Vocational/Work Evaluation Services — Appropriate module

To be used at most appropriate module if required to assist in the evaluation of vocational feasibility.

34 Vocational Testing & Report. — Actual time at Professional Hourly Rate, not to exceed 5 Hours or most appropriate module (and related service code) if testing is done at a vocational/work evaluation facility.

Includes administration and scoring of a standard battery of vocational tests.

35 Counseling & Research Service — Actual Time at Professional Hourly Rate

Includes professional time meeting with employee, assessment of transferrable skills, guidance through vocational exploration, test interpretation with employee, labor market assessment and resource research, determination of physical appropriateness of a proposed vocational goal.

43 DWC Form RU-102 — Actual time at professional hourly rate, not to exceed 1 Hour

All required documents and cover latter completion for plans involving modified or alternative work.

44 DWC Form RU-102 — Actual time, at professional hourly rate, not to exceed 2 Hours

All required documents and cover letter completion for plans involving Direct placement, OJT, Training, Self-Employment.

45 Plan Monitoring — Actual time, by report

Includes activities necessary to oversee the employee's successful completion of the plan. May entail contacts with employee, training facility or OJT employer.

PHASE B: PLAN MONITORING AND JOB PLACEMENT MAXIMUM AGGREGATE PERMISSIBLE FEES NOT TO EXCEED $3500.

46 Plan Monitoring Report — Actual time, not to exceed .5 hours

41	Job Seeking Skills All activity directed to providing the employee with skills, resume preparation, and personal presentation necessary to obtain employment.	Actual time, not to exceed 4 hours at $65 hour
42	Job Placement Job placement services, placement follow-up and placement counseling.	Actual time at $65/hour

INTERPHASE SERVICES (pertains to all phases, to be charged during the phase in which the activity occurs and included within the maximum aggregate expenditure for each phase)

21	Travel Rate	Not to exceed $32.50/hour plus $0.24 per mile
51	Telephone Calls	Actual time
52	File Review/New Document Review After an initial review, file review is billable activity only for re-opening or re-activation of a file, or for conference preparation purposes. Review of new medical/legal reports, or work evaluation reports, upon receipt, is billable activity.	Actual Time at $65.00
35	Counseling & Research Services	Actual Time at Professional Hourly Rate
53	Reporting For narrative reports at the request of a party unless otherwise specified, three-tenths of an hour per page, up to one and one half hour maximum.	The fee for completion of the Vocational Rehabilitation Progress Report, Form RU-121, is .5 hours at Professional Hourly Rate.
54	Rehabilitation Unit Conference, Informal Conference & Professional Appearance Preparation time up to one hour.	Actual time at professional rate.

Education & Training:
As between schools of equal merit, preference will be given to those schools who have reduced their tuition rates by 10% from published 1989 tuition rates, in accordance with the reduction required by Labor Code section 139.5(a)(4). Documentation reflecting the tuition reduction shall be available upon request. Private Vocational schools may not charge a tuition rate for rehabilitation students which is greater than the lowest rate than that given to the general public.

90	Extraordinary Services/Expenses For Dates of Injury prior to 1/1/94: It is recognized that there can occasionally be exceptional circumstances which may require services and fees beyond those listed. Billings above the recommended fee schedule shall require additional documentation prior authorization for excess billings should be obtained before service delivery.	

Note: Authority cited: Sections 133, 139.5 and 5307.3, Labor Code. Reference: Sections 4635, 4636, 4638 and 4639, Labor Code.

History: 1. Change without regulatory effect adding new section filed 1-22-91; operative 1-22-91 (Register 91, No. 10). For prior history, see Register 90, No. 4.

2. Amendment filed 12-31-93; operative 1-1-94. Submitted to OAL for printing only pursuant to Government Code section 11351 (Register 93, No. 53).

3. Amendment filed 2-21-95; operative 2-21-95. Submitted to OAL for printing only pursuant to Government Code section 11351 (Register 95, No. 8).

4. Amendment of fee schedule filed 3-26-96; operative 3-26-96. Submitted to OAL for printing only pursuant to Government Code section 11351 (Register 96, No. 13).

5. Amendment of fee schedule filed 8-26-98; operative 9-25-98 (Register 98, No. 35).

Ref.: Hanna § 35.05[1]; Herlick Handbook §§ 16.1, 16.6.

§10133. Forms, Form Filing Instructions & Notices.

The forms and form filing instructions govern the procedures for the use and completion of the forms required by the Rehabilitation Unit. Unless otherwise specified each form may be used for all dates of injuries.

Form RU-90 "Treating Physician's Report of Disability Status"

Form Filing Instructions

Form RU-91 "Description of Employee's Job Duties"

Form Filing Instructions

Form RU-94 "Notice of Offer of Modified or Alternative Work"

Form Filing Instructions

Form RU-102 "Vocational Rehabilitation Plan"

Form Filing Instructions

Form RU-103 "Request for Dispute Resolution"

Form Filing Instructions

Form RB-105 "Request for Conclusion of Rehabilitation Benefits"

Form Filing Instructions

Form RU-105 "Notice of Termination of Vocational Rehabilitation Services"

Form Filing Instructions

Form RB-107 "Statement of Decline of Vocational Rehabilitation Benefits"

Form Filing Instructions

Form RU-107 "Employee Statement of Declination of Vocational Rehabilitation Services"

Form Filing Instructions

Form RU-107A "Statement of Declination of Vocational Rehabilitation Services"

Form Filing Instructions

Form RU-120 "Initial Evaluation Summary"

Form Filing Instructions

Form RU-121 "Vocational Rehabilitation Progress Report"

Form Filing Instructions

Form RU-122 "Settlement of Prospective Vocational Rehabilitation Services"

Form Filing Instructions

Note: Authority cited: Sections 133, 138.4, 139.5 and 5307.3, Labor Code. Reference: Sections 139.5, 4635, 4636, 4637, 4638, 4641, 4644 and 4646, Labor Code.

History: 1. Change without regulatory effect renumbering and amending former section 10133 to section 10131 and new section 10133 filed 1-22-91; operative 1-22-91 (Register 91, No. 10). For prior history, see Register 90, No. 4.

2. New Form RU-94, repealer and new Forms RU-102, RU-105 and RU-107, and repealer of Forms RU-104, RU-105-W, RU-500-W.1, RU-500-X, RU-500-Y and RU-500-Z filed 12-31-93; operative 1-1-94. Submitted to OAL for printing only pursuant to Government Code section 11351 (Register 93, No. 53).

3. Amendment of forms RU-91 and RU-103 filed 2-21-95; operative 2-21-95. Submitted to OAL for printing only pursuant to Government Code section 11351 (Register 95, No. 8).

4. Amendment of Forms RU-102 and RU-105 filed 8-26-98; operative 9-25-98 (Register 98, No. 35).

5. Repealer and new forms RU-94 and RU-103 filed 2-25-99; operative 2-25-99 pursuant to Government Code section 11343.3(d) (Register 99, No. 9).

6. Relocation of Forms RU-90, RU-91, RU-94, RU-102, RU-103, RU-105 and RU-107A to sections 10133.10, 10133.11, 10133.12, 10133.13, 10133.14, 10133.16 and 10133.19 filed 1-29-2003; operative 1-29-2003 pursuant to Government Code section 11343.4 (Register 2003, No. 5).

7. Amendment of section heading, new section text, and amendment of Note filed 1-29-2003; operative 1-29-2003 pursuant to Government Code section 11343.4 (Register 2003, No. 13.)

Ref.: Hanna §§ 35.05[4][a], 35.30[5], 35.31[1][a], 35.51[1], 35.81; Herlick Handbook §§ 16.1, 16.12.

§10133.1. Standardized Report Forms. [Repealed]

Note: Authority cited: Sections 133, 138.4, 139.5 and 5307.3, Labor Code. Reference: Section 139.5, Labor Code.

History: 1. New section filed 2-16-95; operative 2-16-95. Submitted to OAL for printing only pursuant to Government Code §11351 (Register 95, No. 7).

2. Amendment of subsections (a) and (b) and relocation and amendment of forms RU-120 and RU-121 from section 10133.3 to section 10133.1 filed 8-26-98; operative 9-25-98 (Register 98, No. 35).

3. Relocation of Form RU-120 to section 10133.20 and repealer of section filed 1-29-2003; operative 1-29-2003 pursuant to Government Code section 11343.4 (Register 2003, No. 5).

§10133.2. Pamphlets.

(a) "Help in Returning to Work"

Help In Returning To Work

Vocational Rehabilitation Benefits for Workers Injured after January 1, 1994

What is vocational rehabilitation?

Vocational rehabilitation is a workers' compensation benefit that helps injured workers return to work.

You generally qualify for vocational rehabilitation if you can no longer do your old job, and your employer does not offer you another.

If you qualify, a plan to return you to work will usually be developed by a vocational counselor - - with assistance from you and your claims administrator, the person who is handling your claim for your employer or your employer's insurance company.

California law limits the amount of money for rehabilitation services.

How do I find out if I'm eligible for vocational rehabilitation services?

When you are off work for 90 days, your claims administrator will give the doctor who is treating you a job description that lists the exact duties you performed at work.

Your claims administrator will ask for your help in preparing this job description. This is to make sure that your doctor has an accurate picture of your job duties

Your participation is very important, because if you do not assist, the claims administrator may send your doctor the employer's description of your job.

If you need help filling out the job description form, you may contact the Division of Workers' Compensation (DWC) Information and Assistance office.

Once your doctor reports whether you can return to your job, you will receive a letter from the claims administrator and a copy of the doctor's report regarding medical eligibility.

If you are unable to return to your old job, your employer will decide whether you can return to other work with your disability. You should receive a notice in about a month from the date you receive the notice of potential eligibility from the claims administrator.

If your employer offers you work within your medical restrictions, and you reject or fail to accept the job within 30 days of the offer, you will not qualify for rehabilitation services.

What if the job my employer offered does not work out?

You may still be entitled to rehabilitation services if the job doesn't last for 12 months or your disability prevents you from performing the tasks.

If you have concerns, talk to your employer, claims administrator, or Information and Assistance officer.

What if my employer does not offer me a job?

You will receive an offer of vocational rehabilitation services. You have 90 days to accept. You may ask for an evaluation to help you decide.

If you want services but can't start immediately, you should let your claims administrator know and ask about the possibility of delaying services.

If you do not wish rehabilitation at all, you may decline these services by signing a form. This ends your employer's obligation to provide rehabilitation services at a later date.

Can I settle my vocational rehabilitation services?

No, for injuries which occurred prior to January 1, 2003. California law does not permit prospective vocational rehabilitation services to be settled.

Yes, for injuries which occur on or after January 1, 2003. An employer and represented employee may agree to settle rights to prospective vocational rehabilitation services with a one-time payment not to exceed $10,000 for use in self directed vocational rehabilitation.

If I accept vocational rehabilitation, what should I expect?

You and your claims administrator can choose an agreed upon counselor who will develop a rehabilitation plan for your. This can include job modification, job placement assistance, short-term training, and self-employment possibilities - - whatever is the best way to return to work

You also have the right to request a change of counselor.

What income do I receive if I accept vocational rehabilitation?

If you are receiving temporary disability payments when you start vocational rehabilitation, you may continue receiving them until your doctor reports your condition is "permanent and stationary." When this occurs, you will then receive a maintenance allowance of up to $246 per week. There is a 52-week limit to the maintenance allowance that counts against the $16,000 cap. It is better for you to start your rehabilitation as soon as possible. You may also receive advance payments of permanent disability benefits to supplement the maintenance allowance.

What are the limits of vocational rehabilitation?

The California Legislature has placed very strict limits on rehabilitation plans:

* The plan must be completed within 18 months.
* Vocational rehabilitation maintenance allowance payments are limited to a total of 52 weeks.
* Once you agree to a plan, changes are limited.
* Total cost, including maintenance allowance, counseling fees, services and expenses, are generally limited to $16,000.

What if I'm already enrolled in a college or university?

If you are already enrolled and have made substantial progress toward a degree or certificate at a community college, California State University, or the University of California, you may be able to waive the services of a rehabilitation counselor. Funds normally paid for counseling may then be used to help pay for the college or university program in which you are enrolled. Contact the DWC Rehabilitation Unit for details.

What other services or benefits could I receive as part of the vocational rehabilitation benefit?

* Transportation allowance at a rate specified by the State of California.
* Specific costs required for your rehabilitation plan, such as the cost of re-training, supplies, tools and equipment, tuition and student fees.
* Reasonable additional living expenses, such as temporary relocation costs during evaluation or training. This consists of the costs of your food and lodging when you are required to be away from home.
* Reasonable relocation expenses if permanent relocation is required.
* Remember, total costs cannot be more than $16,000 except in very limited circumstances.

What are my responsibilities?

You are expected to:

* Take an active role in your rehabilitation.
* Complete assignments.
* Be on time for all appointments, classes, interviews and scheduled meetings.
* Notify your rehabilitation counselor immediately if you are unable to keep appointments.
* Maintain an accurate, complete travel expense log.
* Stay in contact with and immediately notify your counselor of any problems.
* Keep your counselor and claims administrator advised of any change of your address or phone number.
* Be available for rehabilitation services Monday through Friday, during reasonable business hours.

You should be aware that if you do not participate fully, your maintenance allowance may be stopped.

What are the claims administrator responsibilities?

The claims administrator in a timely manner:

* assists you in returning to work with your employer.
* pays your benefits that are due.
* pays for rehabilitation services and expenses that are agreed upon.

* notifies you of changes in benefits
* submits required paperwork to DWC
* responds to your questions.

If your claims administrator causes a delay in the provision of services, you may be entitled to additional benefits that could extend beyond the $16,000 limitation. You must file a Request for Dispute Resolution (DWC Form RU-103) if you wish a written determination as to whether there was a delay.

How do I request assistance from the DWC Rehabilitation Unit?

We hope that you can resolve problems informally with your claims administrator. However, the DWC Rehabilitation Unit is the agency responsible for resolving disputes in vocational rehabilitation.

You can contact the Rehabilitation Unit by phone, or you may request assistance by completing a Request for Dispute Resolution (DWC RU-103).

There is also a toll-free information number you may call for a recorded message - - 1-800-736-7401. You may also request any forms or printed information that you may need by calling the toll free number.

Should I have an attorney represent me? How much will it cost?

Both the DWC rehabilitation consultant and the information and assistance officer are available to help at no cost to you.

If you decide you want the services of any attorney, you will be represented on matters involving your workers' compensation claim(s). Your attorney will represent you before the Workers' Compensation Appeals Board and Rehabilitation Unit. Your attorney will also represent you in proceedings before any appellate court, or any proceedings designed to execute on an award.

You should be aware that your weekly vocational rehabilitation maintenance allowance payment (VRMA) may be reduced to pay the attorney. Generally 12% of your weekly VRMA is set aside for payment of attorney fees. For example, if you are entitled to the maximum rate of $246 per week, a 12% reduction means that you would receive $216.48 per week. For this reason, you should discuss fees with the attorney.

You may or may not be entitled to other rights.

The federal Americans with Disabilities Act (ADA) prohibits discrimination against qualified individuals. Qualified individuals include persons who have a physical or mental impairment that substantially limits one or more life activities and who can perform essential job functions. The employer is required to provide a reasonable accommodation if it would not impose an "undue hardship" on the employer.

For information on the Americans with Disabilities Act, call the Equal Opportunity Commission at 1-800-USA-EEOC.

The state Department of Fair Employment and Housing (FEHA) administers California laws that prohibit harassment or discrimination in employment, housing and public accommodations. If you feel an employer has discriminated against you and you want information, the phone number is 1-800-884-1684.

Here is how to get helpful information:

This publication is intended to answer the most frequently asked questions. It may not necessarily provide a solution for your particular problem, because the specific facts of your situation may call for a different approach. The information contained here is general in nature, and not intended as a substitute for legal advice.

If you have more questions after reading this publication, contact one of the DWC Information and Assistance offices or Rehabilitation offices listed in the white pages of your telephone directory under "State Government Offices, Department of Industrial Relations" or contact the web site at: www.dir.ca.gov

ANYONE WHO KNOWINGLY FILES OR ASSISTS IN THE FILING OF A FALSE WORKERS' COMPENSATION CLAIM MAY BE FINED UP TO $50,000 AND SENT TO PRISON FOR UP TO FIVE YEARS.

[Insurance Code Section 1871.4]

State of California
Department of Industrial Relations
Division of Workers Compensation
Rehabilitation Unit

Note: Authority cited: Sections 133, 139.5, 139.6 and 5307.3, Labor Code. Reference: Sections 139.5, 4636 and 4646, Labor Code.

History: 1. New section filed 2-21-95; operative 2-21-95. Submitted to OAL for printing only pursuant to Government Code section 11351 (Register 95, No. 8).

2. Amendment of section and Note filed 1-29-2003; operative 1-29-2003 pursuant to Government Code section 11343.4 (Register 2003, No. 5).

Ref.: Herlick Handbook §§ 16.1, 16.16.

§10133.3. Rehabilitation Unit File Retention.

(a) The unit shall retain its files until 90 days from the date of the filing of the "Notice of Termination of Rehabilitation Services", DWC RU 105, unless a timely objection to the notice is filed by the employee. File retention shall be extended to 90 days beyond a final decision of the appeals board on a petition which appeals a unit finding, decision or determination. If no activity on a file is reported to the Rehabilitation Unit for more than 18 months, the Unit shall not retain its file.

(b) When the parties, subsequent to the time limits in subsection (a), request a determination by the unit, the unit may require the parties to provide copies of pertinent notices, reports and documents which are necessary for the unit to make its determination.

Note: Authority cited: Sections 133, 138.4, 139.5 and 5307.3, Labor Code. Reference: Section 139.5, Labor Code.

History: 1. Renumbering and amendment of former section 10019 to section 10134 filed 2-16-95; operative 2-16-95. Submitted to OAL for printing only pursuant to Government Code §11351 (Register 95, No. 7).

2. Amendment of section number filed 8-8-95; operative 8-8-95. Submitted to OAL for printing only pursuant to Government Code section 11351 (Register 95, No. 32).

3. Amendment of subsection (a) and relocation of forms RU-120 and RU-121 from section 10133.3 to section 10133.1 filed 8-26-98; operative 9-25-98 (Register 98, No. 35).

Ref.: Hanna § 35.81; Herlick Handbook § 16.1.

§10133.4. Rehabilitation of Industrially Injured Inmates.

(a) Inmates of a state penal or correctional institution may be eligible for workers' compensation benefits, including the provision of vocational rehabilitation services, for injuries which occur during their incarceration and while engaged in assigned work or employment. As used in this section:

(1) "Assigned work or employment" means work performed in any pay or non-pay position in a work program under the direction and with the approval of a duly authorized inmate leadman or supervisory leadman or Department of Corrections employee. The term does not include skill centers, vocational training or academic education programs (except for physical fitness training and forestry training which are authorized by Labor Code Section 3365 as prerequisites to fire suppression duties) or activities which are clearly not encompassed within the duties and responsibilities of the position to which assigned.

(2) "Inmate of a state penal or correctional institution" means a person committed to the custody of the Department of Corrections; and who is in a facility, camp, hospital, or institution of the Department of Corrections for the purpose of confinement, treatment, employment, training, or discipline; or who has been temporarily removed by the Department of Corrections from a facility under its jurisdiction with or without custody, for the performance of assigned work. The term does not include a prisoner who has escaped or who has been released on parole.

(3) "Director," as cited in subdivision (b) of Section 5069 of the Penal Code, means the Director of Corrections. In addition to the requirements of Sections 10123, 10124 and 10126, the Director of Corrections shall provide notice of the availability of vocational rehabilitation services to inmates disabled for 28 calendar days or more, on a form prescribed by the director. A copy of such form shall be sent to the Department of Rehabilitation.

(b) Notwithstanding Section 10125.1, an injured inmate who otherwise qualifies for vocational rehabilitation services shall not be entitled to vocational rehabilitation maintenance allowance payments while serving in a state penal or correctional institution.

(c) Vocational rehabilitation services to determine an inmate's eligibility as a qualified injured worker, and to develop any required vocational rehabilitation plan, shall be provided by a rehabilitation representative chosen by the Department of Corrections. Such services shall be provided the inmate as soon as it is feasible and prior to the inmate's release from custody, if possible, with the intent of preparing the inmate for suitable gainful employment upon release. Nothing shall bar the development and implementation of a plan, however, prior to the inmate's release, using modified work or an otherwise suitable work position meeting the definition of assigned work or employment under subsection (a) of this section.

Note: Authority cited: Sections 133, 138.4, 139.5 and 5307.3, Labor Code. Reference: Sections 3351 and 3370, Labor Code; and Section 5069, Penal Code.

History: 1. Renumbering of former section 10021 to new section 10133.4 and amendment of section and Note filed 12-27-96; operative 12-27-96. Submitted to OAL for printing only pursuant to Government Code section 11351 (Register 96, No. 52).

Ref.: Hanna § 35.30[5]; Herlick Handbook §§ 16.1, 16.17.

§10133.10. Form RU-90 "Treating Physician's Report of Disability Status" and Form Filing Instructions.

TREATING PHYSICIAN'S REPORT OF DISABILITY STATUS

INSTRUCTIONS: Pursuant to requirements of the California Labor Code, please complete this form and return it to the claims administrator listed below within 15 days of receipt with a copy to the Qualified Rehabilitation Representative.

EMPLOYEE NAME: (LAST) (FIRST) (M.I.)	SS#	DATE OF INJURY

EMPLOYER NAME:

Attached is a description of the employee's job duties. Based on your examination, including the history provided by the patient and the enclosed job description, choose one of the following:

_______ I expect to release the employee to return to the pre-injury occupation on or about ______________________.

_______ The employee's permanent disability as a result of the injury whether or not combined with the effects of a prior injury or disability, if any is likely to preclude the employee from returning to work at the pre-injury occupation.

Is the employee currently physically able to participate in vocational rehabilitation services? ________ Yes ______No

If yes, please describe any physical limitations: ______________________________

____

If employee is not physically able to participate in vocational services, please estimate when participation may be possible.

____

_______ At this time, I am unable to give an opinion concerning the employee's ability to return to the pre-injury occupation.

I expect to be able to provide an opinion on or about: ______________________________

Please advise also if the employee is currently physically able to perform light duties if modified or alternative work is available:

_______ Yes, with the following limitations: ______________________________

_______ No

Physician's Name: ______________________________ Date:______________

Physician's Signature: ______________________________

Please return to: Employer/Insurer/Adjusting Agent

____

Address: (Street) (City) (State) (Zip)

____

Send a copy to Qualified Rehabilitation Representative:

____

Address: (Street) (City) (State) (Zip)

State of California
DWC Form RU-90 (12/90)

Rehabilitation Unit
California Division of Workers' Compensation

Form RU-90

TREATING PHYSICIAN'S REPORT OF DISABILITY STATUS

Purpose:
To allow early identification of employee's potential need for vocational rehabilitation services, the claims administrator or Qualified Rehabilitation Representative must solicit the treating physician's opinion concerning the employee's ability to return to previous employment.

Submitted by:
Qualified Rehabilitation Representative assigned by claims administrator, if the injury is before 1/1/94 or claims administrator if the injury is on or after 1/1/94.

When submitted:
At 90 days of aggregate temporary disability and thereafter at 60 day intervals, or less, until medical eligibility has been determined.

Where submitted:
To the treating physician. **Do not file the RU-90 or RU-91 with the Rehabilitation Unit unless specifically requested or when submitting information as part of a dispute.**

Form completion:
The Qualified Rehabilitation Representative or claims administrator completes the identification data on the form and the treating physician is responsible for the completion of the remainder of the form, including signature. **Be sure to fill in the claims administrator name and address or the doctor may become confused and return the form to the Rehabilitation Unit.** Upon completion, the treating physician returns the form to the claims administrator with a copy to the Qualified Rehabilitation Representative, if applicable, and injured worker.

Accompanying document:
Description of Employee's Job Duties (RU-91) must be included when the RU-90 is initially sent to the treating physician.

Response to RU-90:
The claims administrator within 10 days of receipt of the final Treating Physician's Report Of Disability Status (RU-90), shall notify the employee of his/her status using the prescribed Notice of Potential Eligibility or Denial of Vocational Rehabilitation Services, whichever is applicable.

The completed RU-90 is a medical report and is to be served on all parties by the claims administrator with the previously completed RU-91.

Rehabilitation Unit action:
None.

Note: Authority cited: Sections 133, 139.5 and 5307.3, Labor Code. Reference: Sections 4636 and 4637, Labor Code.

History: 1. New section, relocation of Form RU-90 from section 10133 to section 10133.10, and new form filing instructions filed 1-29-2003; operative 1-29-

2003 pursuant to Government Code section 11343.4 (Register 2003, No. 5).

Ref.: Hanna §§ 35.05[4][a], 35.31[1][a]; Herlick Handbook §§ 16.3, 16.4, 16.8, 16.9, 16.12, 16.16.

§10133.11. Form RU-91 "Description of Employee's Job Duties" and Form Filing Instructions.

State of California
Division of Workers' Compensation

DESCRIPTION OF EMPLOYEE'S JOB DUTIES

INSTRUCTIONS: This form shall be developed jointly by the employer and employee and is intended to describe the employee's job duties. The completed form will be reviewed by the treating doctor to determine whether the employee is able to return to his/her job. This is an important document and should accurately show the requirements of the employee's job. If the employee needs help in completing this form, the employee may contact the Information and Assistance Officer at the Division of Workers' Compensation. The phone number can be found in the State Government section of the phone book.

EMPLOYEE NAME:	(LAST)	(FIRST)	(M.I.)	CLAIM #:
EMPLOYER NAME:		JOB ADDRESS:		
JOB TITLE:		HRS. WORKED PER DAY:		HRS. WORKED PER WEEK:

DESCRIPTION OF JOB RESPONSIBILITIES: (DESCRIBE ALL JOB DUTIES)

1. Check the frequency of activity required of the employee to perform the job.

ACTIVITY (Hours per day)	NEVER 0 hours	OCCASIONALLY up to 3 hours	FREQUENTLY 3–6 hours	CONSTANTLY 6–8+ hours
Sitting				
Walking				
Standing				
Bending (neck)				
Bending (waist)				
Squatting				
Climbing				
Kneeling				
Crawling				
Twisting (neck)				
Twisting (waist)				
Hand Use: Dominant hand Right___ Left___				
Is repetitive use of hand required?				
Simple Grasping (right hand)				
Simple Grasping (left hand)				
Power Grasping (right hand)				
Power Grasping (left hand)				
Fine Manipulation (right hand)				
Fine Manipulation (left hand)				
Pushing & Pulling (right hand)				
Pushing & Pulling (left hand)				
Reaching (above shoulder level)				
Reaching (below shoulder level)				

DWC Form RU-91 (1/95)

2. Please indicate the daily Lifting and Carrying requirements of the job:
Indicate the height the object is lifted from floor, table or overhead location and the distance the object is carried.

	LIFTING					CARRYING				
	Never 0 hours	Occasionally up to 3 hours	Frequently 3–6 hours	Constantly 6–8+ hours	Height	Never 0 hours	Occasionally up to 3 hours	Frequently 3–6 hours	Constantly 6–8+ hours	Distance
0–10 lbs.										
11–25 lbs.										
26–50 lbs.										
51–75 lbs.										
76–100 lbs.										
100+ lbs.										

Describe the heaviest item required to carry and the distance to be carried: ____________________

3. Please indicate if your job requires:

	YES	NO	(IF YES, PLEASE BRIEFLY DESCRIBE)
a. Driving cars, trucks, forklifts and other equipment?	☐	☐	
b. Working around equipment and machinery?	☐	☐	
c. Walking on uneven ground?	☐	☐	
d. Exposure to excessive noise?	☐	☐	
e. Exposure to extremes in temperature, humidity or wetness?	☐	☐	
f. Exposure to dust, gas, fumes, or chemicals?	☐	☐	
g. Working at heights?	☐	☐	
h. Operation of foot controls or repetitive foot movement?	☐	☐	
i. Use of special visual or auditory protective equipment?	☐	☐	
j. Working with bio-hazards such as: bloodborne pathogens, sewage, hospital waste, etc.	☐	☐	

Employee Comments:

Employer Comments:

EMPLOYER CONTACT NAME:	EMPLOYER CONTACT TITLE:
EMPLOYER REPRESENTATIVE SIGNATURE:	DATE:
EMPLOYEE'S SIGNATURE:	DATE:
QUALIFIED REHAB. REPRESENTATIVE SIGNATURE: (IF APPLICABLE)	DATE:

DWC Form RU-91 (1/95)

Rehabilitation Unit
California Division of Workers' Compensation

Form RU-91

DESCRIPTION OF EMPLOYEE'S JOB DUTIES

Purpose:
To obtain a job description which is to be forwarded to the employee's treating physician when an injury or illness results in disability exceeding 90 days.

Submitted by:

1. Qualified Rehabilitation Representative, if the injury is before 1/1/94, or
2. Claims Administrator if the injury is on or after 1/1/94.

When prepared:
If the injury is before 1/1/94, the QRR meets with the employee to jointly complete this form and provides a copy of the form in conjunction with the RU-90 to the employee's treating physician. If the injury is on or after 1/1/94, the claims administrator consults with the injured worker in completing the RU-91 and then submits it to the treating physician.

When submitted:
To the treating physician. **Do not file the RU-90 or RU-91 with the Rehabilitation Unit unless specifically requested or when submitting information as part of a dispute.**

Form completion:
Qualified Rehabilitation Representative or claim administrator, in consultation with the employee and employer, completes the entire form.

Accompanying document:
The RU-91 is to be attached to the RU-90 and submitted to the treating doctor.

Rehabilitation Unit action:
None.

Note: Authority cited: Sections 133, 139.5 and 5307.3, Labor Code. Reference: Sections 4636 and 4637, Labor Code.

History: 1. New section, relocation and amendment of Form RU-91 from section 10133 to section 10133.11, and new form filing instructions filed 1-29-2003; operative 1-29-2003 pursuant to Government Code section 11343.4 (Register 2003, No. 5).

Ref.: Hanna § 35.05[4][a]; Herlick Handbook §§ 16.3, 16.4, 16.8, 16.9, 16.12, 16.16.

§10133.12. Form RU-94 "Notice of Offer of Modified or Alternative Work" and Form Filing Instructions.

NOTICE OF OFFER OF MODIFIED OR ALTERNATIVE WORK

THIS SECTION COMPLETED BY EMPLOYER OR CLAIMS ADMINISTRATOR:

Employer (name of firm)______________________________ is offering you the position of a (name of job) ______________________________.

Attach a list of the duties required of the position.

You may contact ________________________ concerning this offer. Phone No.: ____________

Date of offer: ____________________. Date job starts: ____________________.

Claims Administrator:______________________________Claim Number:______________

NOTICE TO EMPLOYEE Name of employee: ______________________

Date offer received: ______________________

You have 30 calendar days from receipt to accept or reject this offer of modified or alternative work. If you reject this job offer, you will not be entitled to rehabilitation services unless:

Modified Work

A. The proposed modification(s) to accommodate required work restrictions are inadequate.
B. The modified job will not last 12 months.

Alternative Work

A. You cannot perform the essential functions of the job; or
B. The job is not a regular position lasting at least 12 months; or
C. Wages and compensation offered were less than 85% paid at the time of injury; or
D. The job is beyond a reasonable commuting distance from residence at time of injury.

THIS SECTION TO BE COMPLETED BY EMPLOYEE

__ I accept this offer of Modified or Alternative work.

__ I reject this offer of Modified or Alternative work and understand that I am not entitled to vocational rehabilitation services.

______________________________ Date ______________
Signature

I feel I cannot accept this offer because:

NOTICE TO THE PARTIES

If the offer is not accepted or rejected within 30 days of the offer, the offer is deemed to be rejected by the employee.

The employer or claims administrator must forward a completed copy of this agreement to the Rehabilitation Unit with a Notice of Termination (DWC Form RU-105) within 30 days of acceptance or rejection.
If a dispute occurs regarding the above offer or agreement, either party may request the Rehabilitation Unit to resolve the dispute by filing a Request for Dispute Resolution (DWC Form RU-103) at the applicable Rehabilitation Unit. The Rehabilitation Unit venue is the same as the Workers' Compensation Appeals Board. If no WCAB case exists, file with a Rehabilitation Unit at the appropriate district office.

MANDATORY FORMAT
STATE OF CALIFORNIA
DWC-RU-94 (01/03) §10133.12

Rehabilitation Unit
California Division of Workers' Compensation

Form RU-94

NOTICE OF OFFER OF MODIFIED OR ALTERNATIVE WORK

Purpose:
To document an offer of modified or alternative work by the employer at the time of injury. The form also documents the acceptance or rejection of modified or alternate work by the injured employee. The RU-94 is to be used only for injuries which occur on or after 1-1-94.

Submitted by:
The claims administrator obtains the response of the injured worker and submits the form to the Rehabilitation Unit.

When prepared:
The form is prepared at the time of the offer of modified or alternative work by the employer or claims administrator. This form is not to be used to document a plan for modified or alternate work offered subsequent to advising the worker that modified or alternative work was **not** available.

Where submitted:
Initially to the injured worker within 30 days of the acceptance or rejection of the offer, then it is submitted to the Rehabilitation Unit, together with a RU-105.

Form completion:
The employer or claims administrator completes the information in the top box. The employee completes the section so marked.

Accompanying document:
The RU-94 is submitted with a RU-105 Notice of Termination. The submitted RU-94 must also include a list of duties required of the position and wages offered.

Rehabilitation Unit action:
The Rehabilitation Unit will not take action unless the employee objects by filing a RU-103, Request for Dispute Resolution, to the Notice of Termination.

Note: -If the offer is not accepted or rejected within 30 days of the offer, the offer is deemed to be rejected by the employee. The employer has the option to file a RU-105, Notice of Termination, or extend the 30-day period by mutual agreement.

Note: Authority cited: Sections 133, 139.5 and 5307.3, Labor Code. Reference: Sections 4636 and 4637, Labor Code.

History: 1. New section, relocation and amendment of Form RU-94 from section 10133 to section 10133.12, and new form filing instructions filed 1-29-2003; operative 1-29-2003 pursuant to Government Code section 11343.4 (Register 2003, No. 5).

Ref.: Hanna § 35.05[4][a]; Herlick Handbook §§ 16.3, 16.4, 16.8, 16.9, 16.12, 16.16.

§10133.13. Form RU-102 "Vocational Rehabilitation Plan" and Form Filing Instructions.

VOCATIONAL REHABILITATION PLAN	REHABILITATION USE ONLY

Social Security Number	**WCAB Number**	**Rehab Unit Number**
Employee Name (Last) (First)	(MI)	Date of Birth
Address (Street) (City)	(State)	(Zip)

Employer Name	**Insurance Company Name; Or, If Self-Insured, Certificate Name**
Address	Adjusting Agency Name (if adjusted)
City, State, Zip	Claims Mailing Address
Date of Injury / **Claim Number**	City, State, Zip Phone No.
Employee Representative	**Employer Representative**
Firm Name	Firm Name
Address	Address
City, State, Zip Phone No.	City, State, Zip Phone No.

Qualified Rehabilitation Representative	
Firm Name	Representative Name
Address (Street, City, State, Zip)	Phone No.

SECTION A

OCCUPATION AT INJURY	EARNINGS AT INJURY
DESCRIBE TYPE OF INJURY AND MEDICAL RESTRICTIONS (both industrial and non-industrial. Also identify medical report relied upon):	
SUMMARY OF EMPLOYEE'S EDUCATIONAL AND VOCATIONAL BACKGROUND AND EXPLANATION OF HOW TRANSFERRABLE SKILLS HAVE BEEN USED IN SELECTION OF THE PLAN OBJECTIVE:	
REHAB UNIT APPROVAL IS REQUIRED DUE TO: Check one: ____ Unrepresented Injured Worker ____ QRR Waiver ____ Pre '94 Dates of Injury ____ Discretionary Monies	Initials

(Voc. Rehab.) §10133.13

Mandatory Format
State of California
DWC Form RU-102 (1/03)

SECTION B

VOCATIONAL OBJECTIVE	ESTIMATED WEEKLY EARNINGS UPON COMPLETION

Type of Plan

With Same Employer

- ☐ **1. Modified Job**
- ☐ **2. Alternative Work**

With New Employer

- ☐ **3. Direct Placement**
- ☐ **4. On-The-Job Training**
- ☐ **5. Educational Training**
- ☐ **6. Self-Employment**

DESCRIBE NATURE AND EXTENT OF REHABILITATION PLAN:

DATE VOCATIONAL FEASIBILITY DETERMINED:______________________

PLAN COMMENCEMENT DATE:______________________

EXPECTED COMPLETION DATE (Including placement assistance):______________________

#WEEKS OF TRAINING______________________#DAYS OF PLACEMENT ASSISTANCE

INITIALS

(Voc. Rehab.) §10133.13

Mandatory Format
State of California
DWC Form RU-102 (1/03)

BUDGET FOR VOCATIONAL REHABILITATION PLAN EXPENDITURES

Identify incurred and estimated costs for this rehabilitation plan. For injuries on or after 1/1/94, the maximum expenditure for vocational rehabilitation expenses shall not exceed $16,000.

RESOURCES TO EMPLOYEE

$__________Weekly VRMA Rate $__________withheld for attorney fees; $__________Payment to employee

VRMA/VRTD paid prior to plan (including attorney fees) Total: $ __________

Dates: From __________to__________

VRMA/VRTD to be paid during plan (including attorney fees) Total: $ __________

Dates: From __________to__________

Transportation Expenses to be paid as follows: $__________per__________ Total: $ __________

PLAN EXPENDITURES

Training/Tuition fees, if any (specify recipient): $__________ Total: $ __________

Other Costs (specific type, recipient and method of payment)

__________ $__________ / __________ Total: $ __________

__________ $__________ / __________ Total: $ __________

__________ $__________ / __________ Total: $__________

__________ $__________ / __________ Total: $__________

FEES FOR EVALUATION, PLAN DEVELOPMENT & PLACEMENT

(List Evaluation and Plan Development fees to date and estimated fees for Plan Monitoring and Placement)

Phase I: Evaluation $__________ DOIs on /after 1/1/94 where VR was initiated on/after 1/1/98

Phase II Plan Development $__________ Phase A: $__________

Plan Monitoring $__________ Phase B $__________

Phase III Placement $__________ Total: $__________

TOTAL ESTIMATE OF PLAN EXPENDITURES: $__________

ADDITIONAL RESOURCES TO EMPLOYEE

Permanent Disability Supplement paid to date: $__________ / Week Total: $__________

Permanent Disability Supplement to be paid: $__________ / Week Total: $__________

Other resources to be provided to employee (identify source and amount):

__________ $__________ / __________ Total: $__________

__________ $__________ / __________ Total: $__________

SECTION C

1. List results of vocational testing, if any, and how they support the vocational objective:

2. Describe why this employee will be employable in the vocational objective of this plan. Include assessment of labor market.

INITIALS

(Voc. Rehab.) §10133.13

Mandatory Format
State of California
DWC Form RU-102 (1/03)

SECTION D

RESPONSIBILITIES OF THE CLAIMS ADMINISTRATOR:

The claims administrator shall provide in a timely manner all vocational services and benefits necessitated by the agreed upon vocational rehabilitation plan and as required by the Labor Code. I verify that the insurer does not have a proprietary interest in the rehabilitation provider or facilities used in the development or implementation of this plan.

Other:

Signature

RESPONSIBILITIES OF THE EMPLOYEE:

The employee shall be available and reasonably cooperate in the provision of vocational rehabilitation services. The employee shall arrive on time and participate in all scheduled activities; if for any reason the employee does not, he or she must immediately provide an explanation to the Qualified Rehabilitation Representative.

The employee shall follow the requirements of all facilities and persons providing vocational rehabilitation services. The employee shall notify the Qualified Rehabilitation Representative about anything that may interfere with scheduled completion of this plan.

Other

SECTION E

VERIFICATION OF THE QUALIFIED REHABILITATION REPRESENTATIVE

1. This plan was developed by me as the Qualified Rehabilitation Representative or as an Independent Vocational Evaluator. It is my opinion that the services contained in this plan will provide the employee with the opportunity to return to suitable gainful employment.
2. The employee was not referred for services for evaluation, education or training to a facility in which I, my spouse, my employer or co-employee has a proprietary interest or which I, my spouse, my employer or co-employee has a contractual relationship.

Signature	Date
Firm Name & Address	

SECTION F

PLAN AGREEMENT

Signature of the claims administrator and employee on this plan shall be deemed to be an agreement that claims administrator and employee intend to comply with all the plan's provisions.

Failure of the claims administrator to provide in a timely manner all services required by the plan may result in the employee being entitled to additional services.

Failure of the employee to comply with the provisions and schedules developed for this plan may result in termination of the employer's liability for rehabilitation services.

I have read and understand all four pages of this plan and agree with all of the plan's provisions.

NAME OF EMPLOYEE	SIGNATURE	DATE
NAME OF EMPLOYEE REPRESENTATIVE (if any):	SIGNATURE	DATE
PERSON AUTHORIZING THE PROVISION OF THIS PLAN ON BEHALF OF THE EMPLOYER/CLAIMS ADMINISTRATOR NAME		
SIGNATURE	DATE	

PERSONS SIGNING THIS SECTION SHALL ALSO INITIAL THE OTHER THREE PAGES IN THE INITIAL BOX

(Voc. Rehab.) §10133.13

Mandatory Format
State of California
DWC Form RU-102 (1/03)

Rehabilitation Unit
California Division of Workers' Compensation

Form RU-102

VOCATIONAL REHABILITATION PLAN*

PLANS FOR REPRESENTED EMPLOYEES INJURED ON OR AFTER 1/1/94

Purpose:
To document objectives and methods to be used to implement a proposed rehabilitation plan.

Submitted by:
Claims Administrator

When submitted:
The Claims Administrator submits the form with a RU-105 at the completion of the plan.

Where submitted:
With the applicable Rehabilitation Unit district office. The Rehabilitation Unit's venue is the same as the WCAB. If no WCAB case exists, file with a Rehabilitation Unit within the county where the injured employee resides.

Form completion:
See the following page for information on properly completing the form. **Please note:** This form must be completed using type no smaller than 10 point. All information must be contained within the section provided.

Accompanying documents:
Within 10 days of plan completion, submit the RU-102 along with a RU-105 Notice of Termination. **Medical and vocational reports should not be attached.**

Rehabilitation Unit action:
Statistical recording.

Copy:
All parties

PLANS FOR UNREPRESENTED EMPLOYEE OR WITH A QRR WAIVER AND ALL PLANS FOR EMPLOYEES INJURED BEFORE 1/1/94

Purpose:
To document objectives and methods to be used to implement a proposed rehabilitation plan.

Submitted by:
Claims Administrator

When submitted:
Immediately upon development of a rehabilitation plan which has been agreed to by the parties. If a waiver of Qualified Rehabilitation Representative is requested, **whether represented or not**, the plan must be submitted for approval.

Where submitted:

With the applicable Rehabilitation Unit district office. The Rehabilitation Unit's venue is the same as the WCAB's. If no WCAB case exists, file with a Rehabilitation Unit within the county where the injured employee resides.

Form completion:
See the following page for information on properly completing the form. **Please note:** This form must be completed using type no smaller than 10 point. All information must be contained within the section provided.

Accompanying documents:
Include all supporting medical and vocational reports not previously submitted.

Rehabilitation Unit action:
If disapproval is not made within 30 days of a properly documented plan, the plan is deemed approved. A notice of approval will issue in instances where disapproval previously issued.

Copy:
All parties.

INFORMATION ON HOW TO PROPERLY COMPLETE THE FORM RU-102

Form completion:
Submit only if the employee is a Qualified Injured Worker. The RU-102 is prepared by a Qualified Rehabilitation Representative (QRR). In filing out the form, avoid continuation of information to additional sheets. An extension of the information requested on the RU-102 to additional sheets should be limited to only the situation where there is an OJT agreement which describes the responsibilities of the parties and details of training.

Page 1:
The QRR completes the required information. The box in the lower left hand corner are for the parties to initial to show their agreement with the plan. Employee level of participation must be described.

Page 2:
The QRR completes the information and the parties initial the page. The RU-102 is used for modified or alternative work plans when the offer of modified or alternate work is made subsequent to the initiation of rehab services. The box in the lower left hand corner is for the parties to initial to show agreement. If training, education, or tutoring is

a part of the plan, the counselor must select a facility or program approved by the council for Private Post Secondary and Vocational Education.

Page 3:

For injuries before 1/1/94--This page describes expected costs of the plan. There is not a legislatively required limit of $16,000 on total costs.

For injuries on or after 1/1/94--The purpose of the budget is to plan the estimated expenditures. The total budget for rehabilitation services may not exceed $16,000 including QRR fees. For QRR's fees, please refer to the fee schedule in the administrative rules.

This page may be helpful as a counseling tool to show the injured worker that greater expenditures in one area must be balanced with savings in others areas or the development of additional monetary resources.

Description of specific items on Page 3

VRMA/VRTD to date - refers to the rate and sum of VRMA payments made since the claims administrator sent the notice of potential eligibility and the injured worker requested rehabilitation services.

VRMA/VRTD to be paid - refers to the rate and sum of VRMA payments during the plan.

If the claims administrator is withholding for attorney fees, the should be calculated along with the actual weekly benefit payment so the worker will know how much he or she actually receives.

Any allocation for **TRANSPORTATION EXPENSES** such as gas money or public transit tickets must be calculated.

Any **TRAINING/TUITION FEES** and the training provider must be listed.

OTHER COSTS - such as clothing, tools, books, babysitting, relocation costs, or any other plan costs not itemized above on the form should be listed.

FEES FOR EVALUATION, PLAN DEVELOPMENT AND PLACEMENT and other expenditures from the fee schedule must be listed.

To insure that total plan costs do not exceed $16,000 add the following:

1) VRMA/VRTD paid to date -- total
2) VRMA/VRTD to be paid -- total
3) Transportation expenses -- total
4) Total of plan expenditures
5) Total of fees for evaluation, plan development, and placement

The injured worker must insure that he can meet his living expenses during the plan by adding the total weekly benefit payment to employee to the permanent disability supplement to be paid and any other confirmed financial resources which are listed. In addition, the injured worker can calculate expenditures for legal and rehabilitation fees by adding the total of amount withheld for attorney fees and the total of fees for evaluation, plan development and placement.

Regarding section C-2, labor market surveys are not required. Labor market assessment should include information from the California Occupational Information System if it is available.

The box in the lower left hand corner is for the parties to initial to show agreements.

Page 4:

This is the signature page. Please note: The claims administrator is expected to sign space in Section D as well as Section F.

Please note: Any plan, whether the employee is represented or not, which provides funds to the employee to be disbursed at the employee's discretion or on a non-specific basis must be submitted for review to the Rehabilitation Unit to determine whether the plan is in conflict with Labor Code Section 4646 as required by AD 10126(b)(4).

Note: Authority cited: Sections 133, 139.5 and 5307.3, Labor Code. Reference: Sections 4635, 4636 and 4638, Labor Code.

History: 1. New section, relocation and amendment of Form RU-102 from section 10133 to section 10133.13, and new form filing instructions filed 1-29-2003; operative 1-29-2003 pursuant to Government Code section 11343.4 (Register 2003, No. 5).

Ref.: Hanna §§ 35.05[4][a], 35.14[1]; Herlick Handbook §§ 16.3, 16.4, 16.8, 16.9, 16.12, 16.16.

§10133.14. Form RU-103 "Request for Dispute Resolution" and Form Filing Instructions.

Request for Dispute Resolution

___Original ___Response

Has employer accepted this claim? ___ Yes ___ No
Has liability for injury been found by the WCAB? ___ Yes ___ No
Has more than 90 days of TTD been paid? ___ Yes ___ No

Rehabilitation Use Only

Social Security Number | **WCAB Number** | **Rehab Unit Number**

Employee Name (Last) (First) (MI) Date of Birth

Address (Street) (City) (State) (Zip)

Employer Name | **Insurance Company Name; Or, if Self-Insured, Certificate Name**

Address | Adjusting Agency Name (if adjusted)

City, State, Zip | Claims Mailing Address

Date of Injury **Claim Number** | City, State, Zip Phone No.

Employee Representative | **Employer Representative**

Firm Name | Firm Name

Address | Address

City, State, Zip Phone No. | City, State, Zip Phone No.

Qualified Rehabilitation Representative

Firm Name Representative Name

Address (Street, City, State, Zip) Phone No.

The Rehabilitation Unit is requested to resolve the following dispute on an expedited basis because the parties disagree on : (Check the single issue which applies)

___ The identification of a vocational goal (for injuries after 1/1/94)
___ The selection of a Independent Vocational Evaluator
___The description of the employee's job duties at the time of injury (for injuries after 1/1/94)
___The employee objects to the attached Notice of Intent to Withhold Maintenance Allowance

Non-Expedited Issues: (Check the issue(s) that apply)

___ The employee objects to a Notice of Termination
___ The employee's medical eligibility for vocational rehabilitation services. Medical report relied upon by requester:___________
___ The employer has failed to provide vocational rehabilitation services and benefits. My QRR preference is: (if any)___________
On what date should the employer have provided vocational rehabilitation services? ______/______/______ (Attach explanation)
Date last worked_____/______/______ Date of last temporary disability ______/______/______
___ The employee requested reinstatement and the employer failed to respond. On what date was request made to claims administrator? _____/______/______
How does the employee substantiate this request? [Attach supporting document(s)]
___ This is in response to a previously submitted RU-103 dated ______/______/______
___ Other disputed issues (please describe the nature):

Summary of Parties' Informal Efforts to Resolve this Dispute

An informal conference was held on ______________________. A summary of the conference, including a list of attendees, issues addressed, agreements reached and other unresolved issues is attached. If an informal conference was not held, attach explanation.

Copies of this request with copies of medical and vocational reports have been served on:

Name of Requester **Date** | **Signature**

(Voc. Rehab.) §10133.14

Mandatory Format
State of California
DWC Form RU-103 (01/03)

Rehabilitation Unit
California Division of Workers' Compensation

Form RU-103

REQUEST FOR DISPUTE RESOLUTION

Purpose:
To request the Rehabilitation Unit to resolve a disputed rehabilitation issue.

Submitted by:
Any party of interest.

When submitted:
The form should only be submitted after all informal methods to resolve the rehabilitation dispute have been exhausted or in response to a RU-103 filed by the other party, or in response to a RU-105 Notice with which the employee disagrees.

Where submitted:
With the applicable Rehabilitation Unit district office. The Rehabilitation Unit's venue is the same as the WCAB's. If no WCAB case exists, file with a Rehabilitation Unit within the county where the injured employee resides.

Form completion:
This form will be returned or the request denied if:

- Liability for injury is in dispute.
- The form is incomplete.
- The requester has not attempted to resolve the dispute or such attempts have not been thoroughly documented on the form.
- Copies of all medical and vocational reports not previously filed are not attached.

Accompanying document:
Attach all medical and vocational reports not previously filed.

Response to RU-103:
The other parties shall have fifteen (15) days to respond by forwarding their position via a RU-103, with supporting information, to the correct Rehabilitation Unit District office with copies to all parties.

Rehabilitation Unit action:
The Rehabilitation Unit shall either issue a determination based on the record, request additional information, or set the matter for formal conference.

Copy:
All parties.
Please note: An expedited dispute resolution conference is to resolve a single issue as identified on the RU-103. If other issues are raised, a subsequent conference will be scheduled or a determination will be issued on the record.

Note: Authority cited: Sections 133, 139.5 and 5307.3, Labor Code. Reference: Section 4638, Labor Code.

History: 1. New section, relocation and amendment of Form RU-103 from section 10133 to section 10133.14, and new form filing instructions filed 1-29-2003; operative 1-29-2003 pursuant to Government Code section 11343.4 (Register 2003, No. 5).

Ref.: Hanna §§ 35.05[4][a], 35.11[3]; Herlick Handbook §§ 16.3, 16.4, 16.8, 16.9, 16.12, 16.16.

§10133.15. Form RB-105 "Request for Conclusion of Rehabilitation Benefits" and Form Filing Instructions.

REQUEST FOR CONCLUSION OF REHABILITATION BENEFITS			Rehabilitation Use Only
Social Security Number	**WCAB Number**		**Rehab Unit Number**
Employee Name (Last) (First)	(MI)		Date of Birth
Address (Street)	(City)	(State)	(Zip)
Employer Name		**Insurance Company Name; Or, if Self-Insured, Certificate Name**	
Address		Adjusting Agency Name (if adjusted)	
City, State, Zip		Claims Mailing Address	
Date of Injury	**Claim Number**	City, State, Zip	Phone No.
Employee Representative		**Employer Representative**	
Firm Name		Firm Name	
Address		Address	
City, State, Zip	Phone No.	City, State, Zip	Phone No.
Qualified Rehabilitation Representative			
Firm Name		Representative Name	
Address (Street, City, State, Zip)			Phone No.

The Employer/Insurer requests Rehabilitation Unit approval of conclusion of vocational rehabilitation services because:

- ❑ The qualified injured worker completed a vocational rehabilitation plan.
- ❑ The employee is not a qualified injured worker or the employee failed to cooperate in the provision of vocational rehabilitation services to determine the employee's eligibility as a qualified injured worker.
- ❑ The qualified injured worker unreasonably failed to complete an approved vocational rehabilitation plan.
- ❑ The employee declined, on the prescribed form, to accept the provision of vocational rehabilitation services.
- ❑ The employee failed to request timely reinstatement of vocational rehabilitation services.
- ❑ None of the above reasons apply and all necessary and reasonable vocational rehabilitation services have been provided.

The basis for this request is substantiated in the attached reports and is summarized as follows:

NOTICE TO EMPLOYEE

If you object to this request, you (or your attorney, if you are represented) must submit your written objections and the reasons for them to the Rehabilitation Unit within 20 days of the date of this request. The objection should be made on the Request for Dispute Resolution Form RU-103 and a copy must be sent to the employer/insurer.

Within specified time limits and subject to certain criteria, you may request reinstatement of vocational rehabilitation benefits. Requests must be in writing, accompanied by supporting facts and submitted to the Rehabilitation Unit within one year of either a finding of permanent disability or approval of a Compromise and Release by the Workers' Compensation Appeals Board, or within 5 years from the date of your injury. The Rehabilitation Unit will determine if the vocational rehabilitation services previously provided were sufficient or if you are entitled to additional services.

(Voc. Rehab.) §10133.15

State of California
DWC Form RB-105 (01/03)

SUMMARY OF VOCATIONAL REHABILITATION BENEFITS PROVIDED

Date Rehab Services Commenced:____________ Rehab Plan Type: ____________

Rehab Plan Goal____________

Date Rehab Services Completed: ____________ Return To Work: Yes ❑ Date:____________ No ❑

Employee's New Job Title: ____________ Wages $________per________

1. The employee has been paid $____________in temporary disability indemnity benefits at the rate of $____________per week, beginning____________ and ending____________ for the injury occurring on____________.

2. Vocational rehabilitation services provided to the employee include: (check where applicable)

❑ Job Analysis ❑ Vocational Evaluation ❑ Vocational Testing

❑ Situational Assessments

❑ Labor Market Survey ❑ Financial Analysis ❑ Training: Number of weeks: ________

❑ Placement Services: Number of Weeks:________ ❑ Other (Specify)____________

COPIES OF THIS NOTICE HAVE BEEN SENT TO:	SUBMITTED BY:
	COMPANY
	SIGNATURE
	DATE

(Voc. Rehab.) §10133.15

State of California
DWC Form RB-105 (01/03)

Rehabilitation Unit
California Division of Workers' Compensation

Form RB–105

REQUEST FOR CONCLUSION OF REHABILITATION BENEFITS

Purpose:
To request the Rehabilitation Unit's approval of conclusion of rehabilitation services for injuries before 1–1–90. For injuries on or after 1–1–90, use the Notice of Termination of Rehabilitation Services (RU–105).

Submitted by:
Claims Administrator.

When submitted:
Within ten (10) days of the circumstances as described on the form.

Where submitted:
To the applicable Rehabilitation Unit district office. The Rehabilitation Unit's venue is the same as the WCAB's. If no WCAB case exists, file with a Rehabilitation Unit within the county where the injured employee resides.

Form completion:
Please note this form will be returned or the request denied if:

- The box was not checked for the reason of the request.
- The request lacks substantiation as required.
- Copies have not been sent to the employee and his/her representative, if represented.
- The copy of service section is incomplete.

Accompanying documents:
Relevant medical and vocational reports.

Rehabilitation Unit action:
When the employee objects to the RB–105, the rehabilitation unit will hold a conference or otherwise obtain the reason for objection and issue its decision. If the employee objects, a RU–103 (Request For Dispute Resolution) must be filed. Check the box *"the requesting party objects to the request for termination or conclusion of vocational rehabilitation benefits"* and provide the reasons for the objection.

Copy:
All parties.

Note: Authority cited: Sections 133, 139.5 and 5307.3, Labor Code. Reference: Sections 4637, 4643 and 4644, Labor Code.

History: 1. New section and new Form RB-105 and form filing instructions filed 1-29-2003; operative 1-29-2003 pursuant to Government Code section 11343.4 (Register 2003, No. 5).

2. Change without regulatory effect repealing Form RB-105 and adopting new Form RB-105 filed 5-1-2003 pursuant to section 100, title 1, California Code of Regulations (Register 2003, No. 18).

§10133.16. Form RU-105 "Notice of Termination of Vocational Rehabilitation Services" and Form Filing Instructions.

NOTICE OF TERMINATION OF VOCATIONAL REHABILITATION SERVICES			Rehabilitation Use Only
Social Security Number	**WCAB Number**		**Rehab Unit Number**
Employee Name (Last)	(First)	(MI)	Date of Birth
Address (Street)	(City)	(State)	(Zip)
Employer Name		**Insurance Company Name; Or, if Self-Insured, Certificate Name**	
Address		Adjusting Agency Name (if adjusted)	
City, State, Zip		Claims Mailing Address	
Date of Injury	**Claim Number**	City, State, Zip	Phone No.
Employee Representative		**Employer Representative**	
Firm Name		Firm Name	
Address		Address	Phone No.
City, State, Zip	Phone No.	City, State, Zip	
Qualified Rehabilitation Representative Firm Name		Representative Name	
Address (Street, City, State, Zip)			Phone No.

CLOSURE REASONS (Check one box which applies)

- ☐ 1. The employee declines and has signed the RU-107 or RU-107A.
- ☐ 2. The qualified employee completes a vocational rehabilitation plan.
- ☐ 3. The qualified employee unreasonably fails to complete a vocational rehabilitation plan.
- ☐ 4. The employee has not requested vocational rehabilitation within 90 days.
- ☐ 5. The employer offers and the employee accepts/rejects modified work lasting 12 months, even if the employee voluntarily quits prior to the end of the 12 month period. *(Attach RU-94)*
- ☐ 6. The employer offers and the employee accepts/rejects alternative work meeting all of the conditions listed in Labor Code §4644(a)(6). Attach RU-94.
- ☐ 7. The employer offers and the employee accepts a job not meeting criteria of #5 or #6. *(Attach RU-94)*

NOTICE TO EMPLOYEE

If you agree with the above, no further action is required on your part, and we will not be providing vocational rehabilitation services in the future.

If you disagree with our determination that we have no further liability to provide vocational rehabilitation services, you or your representative must submit your written objections and the reasons for them to the Rehabilitation Unit within twenty (20) days of receipt of this Notice. The form to use to make your objection is enclosed. Be sure to send a copy to me. The Rehabilitation Unit will then determine if you are to be given further services. Please send a copy of this Notice, with your objection, to the Rehabilitation Unit located at: *(insert Rehabilitation Unit address)*

If you have any questions about this notice, you may contact me at: ______________________________

(Voc. Rehab.) §10133.16

Mandatory Format
State of California

DWC Form RU–105 (5/03)

SUMMARY OF SERVICES PROVIDED

		RU-94 Offer		
Number of weeks of VRMA: (Within the cap)	_____	☐ Modified Job (L.C 4644 (a)(5))	☐ Alternate Job (L.C. 4644 (a)(6))	☐ "Other Job" (L.C. 4644 (a)(7))
Total Amount of paid VRMA: (Within the cap)	$_____	Did employee RTW? Yes_____ No_____		
Total Amount of PD supplement:	$_____	If Yes, employee's new job title:_____		
Amount Paid for QRR:	$_____	Wages: $_____ per _____ (Hour/Week/Month)		

	DOIs on/after 1/1/94	Plan Completion		
		Plan Type		
VR initiated before 1/1/98	VR initiated on/after 1/1/98			
Phase I: $_____ Phase II: $_____ Phase III: $_____	Phase A: $_____ Phase B $_____	☐ Direct Placement	☐ OJT	☐ Training
		☐ Self Employment	☐ Modified Job	☐ Alternate Job
Total Cost of QRR Services:	$_____	Employed in Plan Objective: Yes_____ No_____		
QRR Name:_____		If Yes, employee's new job title:_____		
Total Cost of Other VR Services:	$_____	Wages: $_____ per _____ (Hour/Week/Month)		
Amt. Withheld for Employee's Attorney (if any)	$_____			

PROOF OF SERVICE BY MAIL

I am a citizen of the United States and a resident of the County of: _____. I am over the age of eighteen years and not a party to the within matter. My business address is:_____.

On _____, I served the Notice of Termination of Vocational Rehabilitation Services on the parties listed below by placing a true copy thereof enclosed in a sealed envelope with postage fully prepaid, and thereafter deposited in the U.S. Mail at the place so addressed.

I declare under penalty of perjury under the laws of the State of California that the foregoing is true and correct. Executed at_____on_____20_____.

Signature

Copies Served On:

(Voc. Rehab.) §10133.16

Mandatory Format
State of California

DWC Form RU–105 (5/03)

Rehabilitation Unit
California Division of Workers' Compensation

RU–105

NOTICE OF TERMINATION OF REHABILITATION SERVICES

Purpose:
To notify the employee of the employer's termination of liability to provide rehabilitation services. It is not to be used for non–feasibility. This notice is not to be used for injuries prior to 1990.

Submitted by:
Claims Administrator to the injured employee and representative.

When submitted:
Within 10 days of the circumstances set forth in LC §4644(a).

Where submitted:
Original of the notice is sent to the employee and a copy to the applicable Rehabilitation Unit district office. The Rehabilitation Unit's venue is the same as the WCAB. If no WCAB case exists, file with a Rehabilitation Unit within the county where the injured employee resides.

Accompanying documents:

- RU–94 for DOI's on or after 1/1/94 where an offer of modified or alternate work has been accepted or rejected.
- Agreed upon plans for represented injured workers whose date of injury is on or after 1/1/94. (See 1994–1999 rules – AR 10126b(3))
- All declination forms and *Notice of Potential Eligibility*.
- A copy of proof of service.

Rehabilitation Unit action:
When the employee objects to the notice of termination, the Rehabilitation Unit will hold a conference or otherwise obtain the employee's reason for objection and issue its decision.

Notes: Copies of medical or vocational reports are not required to be submitted to the Rehabilitation Unit when filing a copy of the RU–105 on injuries subsequent to 1/1/90.

All RU–105 Notices must have a "Proof of Service" as required by AR 10131(a). For further information of "Proof of Service" see 8 Cal 10514.

Note: Authority cited: Sections 133, 139.5 and 5307.3, Labor Code. Reference: Sections 4637 and 4644, Labor Code.

History: 1. New section, relocation and amendment of Form RU-105 from section 10133 to section 10133.16, and new form filing instructions filed 1-29-2003; operative 1-29-2003 pursuant to Government Code section 11343.4 (Register 2003, No. 5).

2. Change without regulatory effect repealing Form RU-105 and adopting new Form RU-105 filed 5-1-2003 pursuant to section 100, title 1, California Code of Regulations (Register 2003, No. 18).

Ref.: Hanna § 35.05[4]; Herlick Handbook §§ 16.3, 16.4, 16.8, 16.9, 16.12, 16.16.

§10133.17. Form RB-107 "Statement of Decline of Vocational Rehabilitation Benefits" and Form Filing Instructions.

State of California
Division of Workers' Compensation

STATEMENT OF DECLINE OF VOCATIONAL REHABILITATION BENEFITS

INSTRUCTIONS: This form shall be signed and dated by the employee and the employee's representative (if any) when the employee declines the provision of vocational rehabilitation services and sent to the employer/insurer. When the choice to decline services occurs subsequent to the commencement of vocational rehabilitation services, this form shall be submitted by the employer/insurer to the Rehabilitation Unit with the Request for Conclusion of Rehabilitation Benefits Form RB-105.	REHABILITATION UNIT USE ONLY

EMPLOYEE NAME: (FIRST) (MIDDLE) (LAST)	RU CASE # if any:

NOTICE TO EMPLOYEE

Employees who have had industrial injuries may be entitled to receive vocational rehabilitation benefits if they are likely to be precluded from returning to their employment and would benefit from the provision of vocational rehabilitation services.

This benefit, known as vocational rehabilitation, varies with the employee's needs and abilities. This may include an evaluation to identify the type of vocational rehabilitation services which can help the employee to return to suitable employment. These services may involve changing the demands of the employee's usual job; assisting the employee to obtain new employment compatible with his/her abilities; or training the employee for a new occupation.

When the employee is a qualified injured worker, all vocational rehabilitation costs are paid by the employer or its insurer. The employee continues to receive temporary disability indemnity payments during the period of entitlement to vocational rehabilitation services.

The employee has the right to choose whether he/she will accept the provision of vocational rehabilitation services. Regardless of the employee's choice, other workers' compensation benefits will not be affected.

If the employee declines rehabilitation benefits now, he/she may be able to request future consideration of these benefits within statutory time limits. The request must be in writing and submitted to the Rehabilitation0 Unit within one year of either a finding of permanent disability or approval of a compromise and release by the Workers' Compensation Appeals Board, or within 5 years from the date of injury. The Rehabilitation Unit will determine entitlement to services.

STATEMENT OF EMPLOYEE

I have read and understand this notice and I choose to decline the provision of vocational rehabilitation benefits.

EMPLOYEE'S SIGNATURE:
EMPLOYEE REPRESENTATIVE'S SIGNATURE (if represented):
DATE:

State of California
DWC Form RB-107 (pre 1/1/90)

Rehabilitation Unit
California Division of Workers' Compensation

Form RB-107

STATEMENT OF DECLINE OF VOCATIONAL REHABILITATION BENEFITS

Purpose:
To record the employee's declination of rehabilitation services for injuries before 1/1/90.

Submitted by:
Claims Administrator

When submitted:
When the employee chooses to decline Vocational Rehabilitation Services.

Where submitted:
With the RB-105 to the applicable office of the Rehabilitation Unit

Form completion:
Identifying data completed by Claims Administrator.
Statement of employee completed by injured worker with signature of injured worker and attorney, if represented.

Accompanying documents:
Request for Conclusion Form RB-105

Response to RU-103:
The other parties shall have twenty (20) days to respond by forwarding their position, with supporting information, to the applicable Rehabilitation Unit district office with copies to all parties.

Rehabilitation Unit action:
If the employee objects to the Request for Conclusion, the Rehabilitation Unit shall, within 30 days, schedule a conference or otherwise obtain the employee's reason for objection with substantiating evidence and issue its determination.

Copy:
All parties.

Note: Authority cited: Sections 133, 139.5 and 5307.3, Labor Code. Reference: Sections 4641 and 4644, Labor Code.

History: 1. New section and new Form RB-107 and form filing instructions filed 1-29-2003; operative 1-29-2003 pursuant to Government Code section 11343.4 (Register 2003, No. 5).

Ref.: Herlick Handbook §§ 16.3, 16.4, 16.8, 16.9, 16.12, 16.16.

§10133.18. Form RU-107 "Employee Statement of Declination of Vocational Rehabilitation Services" and Form Filing Instructions.

State of California
Division of Workers' Compensation

EMPLOYEE STATEMENT OF DECLINATION OF VOCATIONAL REHABILITATION SERVICES

INSTRUCTIONS: This form is to be used when the employee declines rehabilitation following notification of medical eligibility. It must be signed by the employee and his/her representative, if any, and submitted by the employer to the Rehabilitation Unit along with a properly completed Notice of Termination of Vocational Rehabilitation Services (DWC Form RU-105). If a Rehabilitation Unit case does not exist, it must be accompanied by a Case Initiation Document (DWC Form RU-101).

Employee Name: Last	First	M.I.	RU Case #:

NOTICE TO EMPLOYEE

The purpose of this form is to formally record your desire to end your right to rehabilitation benefits. If you decline rehabilitation services, your right for rehabilitation services will end upon the approval of the Rehabilitation Unit. This means your employer will not be required to provide rehabilitation services to you at a later date, unless otherwise determined pursuant to the Rules and Regulations of the Workers' Compensation Appeals Board in accordance with Labor Code Section 5410.

DESCRIPTION OF VOCATIONAL REHABILIATION SERVICES

If you had a work-related injury which prevents you from doing your former job, you are entitled to receive rehabilitation services. The amount of services you receive will depend on your needs and abilities.

Some rehabilitation plans call for your former job to be modified, or for a different job with your same employer or a new employer. Other plans involve training for a new type of work. All of the rehabilitation costs are paid by your employer. During rehabilitation, you will receive a maintenance allowance. You have a right to an evaluation to determine the vocational options available to you prior to making a decision. Your right to rehabilitation is separate from your other workers' compensation benefits and cannot under the Labor Code be terminated by a cash payment to you. If you are not ready to participate now in rehabilitation, but might be later, it is possible to delay your participation in rehabilitation for a period of time.

If you want more information, you may contact the Rehabilitation Unit or the Office of Benefit Determination, at no charge, or contact an attorney.

STATEMENT OF DECLINATION

This form must be signed by the injured employee.

The injured employee states:
I have read this Statement of Declination of Vocational Rehabilitation Services.
I have received the pamphlet *Help in Returning to Work.*
I decline rehabilitation.
I have met with a QRR.
I understand by signing this form I am giving up a service to which I may be entitled.

EMPLOYEE SIGNATURE:____________________ **Date:**__________

Representative's signature, if any.

The representative states:
I have reviewed this form with my client and
I have explained the effects of declining vocational rehabilitation benefits.

EMPLOYEE REPRESENTATIVE'S SIGNATURE:____________________ **Date:**__________

REHABILITATION UNIT USE ONLY

State of California
DWC Form RU-107 (12/90)

Estado de California
División de Compensación al Trabajador

DECLARACIÓN DEL EMPLEADO DE RENUNCIA A LOS SERVICIOS DE REHABILITACIÓN VOCACIONAL

INSTRUCCIONES: Se debe utilizar este formulario cuando un empleado renuncia a la rehabilitación después de habérsele infonnado que por motivos médicos tiene derecho a ella. Debe ser firmado por el empleado y su representante, si lo tuviere, y presentado a la Unidad de Rehabilitación por el patrón junto con un formulario de Solicitud para Terminar los Servicios de Rehabilitación (Fomulario DWC RU- 105) debidamente llenado. Si el caso no tuviera un número de la Unidad de Rehabilitación, este fonmlario debe ir acompañado del formulario Documento de Iniciación de Casos (Formulario DWC RU- 101).

Nombre del empleado: Apellido	Primer nombre	Inicial	**# de caso UR:**

AVISO AL EMPLEADO

El propósito de este formulario es registrar oficialmente el hecho que usted desea terminar su derecho a recibir beneficios de rehabilitación. Si usted renuncia a los servicios de rehabilitación, el derecho que usted tiene a ellos finalizará una vez que la Unidad de Rehabilitación haya aprobado su decisión. Esto significa que su patrón ya no estará obligado a proporcionarle servicios de rehabilitación en una fecha posterior, a menos que las reglas y reglamentos de la Junta de Apelaciones de Compensación al Trabajador estipulen lo contrario de acuerdo con la Sección 5410 del Código Laboral.

DESCRIPCION DE LOS SERVICIOS DE REHABILITACIÓN VOCACIONAL

Si usted ha sufrido una lesion que se relaciona con su trabajo y que le impide seguir desempeñando su trabajo anterior, usted tiene derecho a recibir servicios de rehabilitación. La cantidad de servicios qu reciba de sus necesidades y de las destrezas que usted tenga.

Algunos planes de rehabilitación contemplan que su trabajo anterior se modifique, o que se le proporcione otro trabajo con el mismo patrón o un patrón nuevo. Otros planes incluyen capacitación para un nuevo tipo de trabajo. Su patrón paga todos los costos de su rehabilitación. Durante su rehabilitación, usted recibrá un subsidio de mantenimiento. Usted tiene derecho a que se le evalúe antes de que tenga que tomar una decisión para determinar que alternativas de rehabilitación tiene. El derecho que usted tiene a la rehabilitación es un derecho adicional a los demás derechos que tiene de recibir beneficios de Compensación al Trabajador y no se pueden cancelar con un pago en efectivo. Si usted no está listo para participar en este momento en la rehabilitación, pero podria estario en una fecha posterior, es posible postergar su participación en la rehabilitación durante un tiempo.

Si desea mayor información al respecto, puede ponerse en contacto con la Unidad de Rehabilitación de la Oficina de Determinación de Beneficios, sin costo alguno, o puede habits con un abogado.

DECLARACIÓN DE RENUNCIA

Este formulario debe ser firmado por el empleado lastimado.

El empleado lastimado declara:

He leído esta declaración de Renuncia de los Servicios de Rehabilitación Vocacional.
He recibido el folleto *Ayuda para Regresar a Trabajar.*
Renuncio a recibir rehabilitación.
He conversado con un Representante Calificado de Rehabilitación (QRR).
Comprendo que al firmar este formulario estoy renunciando un servicio al que tengo derecho.

FIRMA DEL EMPLEADO: ______________________ **Fecha:** ______________

Firma del representante, si lo hubiere.

El representante declara:

He revisado este formulario con mi cliente y
Le he explicado las consecuencias de renunciar a los beneficios de rehabilitación vocacional.

FIRMA DEL REPRESENTANTE DEL EMPLEADO: ______________________ **Fecha:** ______________

Estado de California
Formulario DWC RU-107 (12/90)

Rehabilitation Unit
California Division of Workers' Compensation

Form RU-107

EMPLOYEE STATEMENT OF DECLINATION OF VOCATIONAL REHABILITATION SERVICES

Purpose:
To record the employee's declination of rehabilitation services for injuries between 1/1/90 and 12/31/93, inclusive.

Submitted by:
Claims Administrator.

When submitted:
When the employee chooses to decline vocational rehabilitation services.

Where submitted:
With the RU-105 to the applicable Rehabilitation Unit district office

Form completion:
Identifying data completed by Claims Administrator
Signature of employee and attorney, if represented.

Accompanying documents:
Notice of Termination of Rehabilitation Services RU-105;
A copy of the *Notice of Potential Eligibility;*
Verification of the 90 day explanation of rights by a QRR;

Response to the RU-103:
The other parties shall have twenty (20) days to respond by forwarding their position, with supporting information, to the applicable Rehabilitation Unit district office with copies to all parties.

Rehabilitation Unit action:
If the employee objects to the employer's Notice of Termination, the Rehabilitation Unit shall, within 30 days, schedule a conference or otherwise obtain the employee's reason for objection together with substantiating evidence and issue its decision.

Copy:
All parties.

Note: Authority cited: Sections 133, 139.5 and 5307.3, Labor Code. Reference: Sections 4641 and 4644, Labor Code.

History: 1. New section and new Form RU-107 and form filing instructions filed 1-29-2003; operative 1-29-2003 pursuant to Government Code section 11343.4 (Register 2003, No. 5).

Ref.: Hanna § 35.05[4][a]; Herlick Handbook §§ 16.3, 16.4, 16.8, 16.9, 16.12, 16.16.

§10133.19. Form RU-107A "Statement of Declination of Vocational Rehabilitation Services" and Form Filing Instructions.

State of California
Division of Workers' Compensation

STATEMENT OF DECLINE OF VOCATIONAL REHABILITATION SERVICES

INSTRUCTIONS: This form is to be used for injuries occurring on or after 1/1/94, when the employee declines rehabilitation following notification of medical eligibility. It must be signed by the employee and his/her representative, if any, and submitted by the claims administrator to the Rehabilitation Unit along with a properly completed Notice of Termination of Vocational Rehabilitation Services (DWC Form RU-105). If a Rehabilitation Unit case does not exist, it must be accompanied by a Case Initiation Document (DWC Form RU-101).

Employee Name: Last	First	M.I.	**RU Case #:**

NOTICE TO EMPLOYEE

The purpose of this form is to formally record your desire to end your right to rehabilitation benefits. If you decline rehabilitation services, your right to rehabilitation services will end. This means your employer will not be required to provide rehabilitation services to you at a later date, unless otherwise determined pursuant to the Rules and Regulations of the Workers' Compensation Appeals Board in accordance with Labor Code Section 5410.

DESCRIPTION OF VOCATIONAL REHABILITATION SERVICES

If you had a work-related injury or illness which prevents you from doing your former job and your employer cannot take you back, you are entitled to receive rehabilitation services. The amount of services you receive will depend on your needs and abilities.

Vocational rehabilitation services help you to get another job, through job placement or training, whichever is best for you. The rehabilitation costs, including counselor fees and maintenance allowance, are paid by your employer subject to the statutory limits. You have a right to an evaluation to determine the vocational options available to you prior to making this decision. Your right to rehabilitation is separate from your other workers' compensation benefits and cannot under the Labor Code be terminated by a cash payment to you. If you are not ready to participate now in rehabilitation, but might be later, it may be possible to delay your participation in rehabilitation for a period of time.

If you want more information, you may contact an Information and Assistance officer with the Division of Workers' Compensation, at no charge, or you may contact an attorney.

STATEMENT OF DECLINATION

This form must be signed by the injured employee.

The injured employee states:

I have read this Statement of Decline of Vocational Rehabilitation Services.
I have received the pamphlet *Help in Returning to Work-94.*
I decline rehabilitation.
I understand by signing this form I am giving up a service to which I am entitled.

EMPLOYEE'S SIGNATURE: ______________________ **Date:** ____________

Representative's signature, if any.

The representative states:

I have reviewed this form with my client and
I have explained the effects of declining vocational rehabilitation benefits.

EMPLOYEE'S REPRESENTATIVE SIGNATURE: ______________ **Date:** ________

REHABILITATION UNIT USE ONLY

State of California
DWC Form RU-107A (1/94)

Estado de California
División de Compensación al Trabajador

DECLARACIÓN DEL EMPLEADO DE RECHAZO DE SERVICIOS VOCACIONALES DE REHABILITACIÓN

INSTRUCCIONES: Se usa este formulario para lesiones que ocurrieron el o después del 1/1/94, cuando el empleado decide no aceptar participar en rehabilitación después que se le notifica que reúne los requisitos por razones médicas. El empleado o su representante, si lo tiene, tiene que firmarlo, y el administrador de reclamos tiene que presentarlo a la Unidad de Rehabilitación junto con una Notificación de Terminación de los Servicios de Rehabilitación Vocacional debidamente lleno (Formulario DWC RU-105). Si no existe un caso de la Unidad de Rehabilitación, tiene que ir acompañado de un Documento de Iniciación de Caso (Formulario DWC RU-101).

Nombre del empleado: Apellido	Primer nombre	Inicial	**# de caso UR:**

NOTIFICACIÓN AL EMPLEADO

El propósito de este formulario es el de formalmente registrar sus deseos de terminar su derecho a beneficios de rehabilitación. Si usted rechaza los servicios de rehabilitación, terminará su derecho a recibir servicios de rehabilitación. Esto significa que no se le exigirá a su patrón que le proporcione a usted servicios de rehabilitación en una fecha posterior, a menos que se decida de otra manera en conformidad con la Reglas y Ordenamientos de la Directiva de Apelaciones de Compensación para Trabajadores según lo estipulado por la Sección 5410 del Código Laboral.

DESCRIPCION DE LOS SERVICIOS VOCIONALES DE REHABILITACIÓN

Si usted sufrió una lesión o enfermedad relacionada al trabajo que le impide desempeñar su trabajo anterior y su patrón no puede emplearle de nuevo, usted tiene derecho a recibir servicios de rehabilitación. La cantidad de servicios que usted reciba dependerá de sus necesidades y habilidades.

Los servicios vocacionales de rehabilitación le ayudan a obtener otro empleo, por medio de una colocación en un empleo o entrenamiento-lo que sea mejor para usted. Su patrón paga el costo de la rehabilitación, así como los honorarios del consejero y la asignación de mantenimiento, los cuales están sujetos a límites estatutorios. Usted tiene el derecho a una evaluación para que se determinen las opciones vocacionales que hay a su disposición, antes que tome esta decisión. Su derecho a rehabilitación es algo separado de sus otros beneficios de compensación para trabajadores, y no puede ser terminado en conformidad con el Código Laboral con un pago en efectivo que se la haga a usted. Si usted no está preparado para participar ahora en la rehabilitación pero Io puede estar después, es posible posponer durante un período de tiempo su participación en rehabilitación.

Si desea más información, puede comunicarse con un oficial de Asistencia e Información de la División de Compensación para Trabajadores, sin cargo alguno, o usted puede comunicarse con un abogado.

DECLARACIÓN DE RECHAZO

Este formulario tiene que ser firmado por el empleado lesionado.

El empleado lesionado declara:

He leído esta declaración de Rechazo de Servicios Vocacionales de Rehabilitación.
He recibido el folleto *Ayuda para Regresar a Trabajar-94 (Help in Returning to Work-94).*
Rechazo participar en rehabilitación.
Entiendo que al firmar este formulario estoy renunciando a recibir un servicio al que tengo derecho.

FIRMA DEL EMPLEADO: ______________________________ **Fecha:** ______________

Firma del representante, si lo hay.

El representante declara:

He revisado este formulario juntamente con mi cliente y
Le he explicado los efectos de este rechazo de los beneficios de rehabilitación vocacional.

FIRMA DEL REPRESENTANTE DEL EMPLEADO: ______________________ **Fecha:** ______________

SOLO PARA USO DE LA UNIDAD DE REHABILITACIÓN

Estado de California
Formulario DWC RU-107A (1/94)

Rehabilitation Unit
California Division of Workers' Compensation

Form RU-107A

EMPLOYEE STATEMENT OF DECLINATION OF VOCATIONAL REHABILITATION SERVICES

Purpose:
To record the employee's declination of rehabilitation services for injuries on or after 1/1/94.

Submitted by:
Claims Administrator

When submitted:
When the employee chooses to decline vocational rehabilitation services.

Where submitted:
With the RU-105 to the applicable Rehabilitation Unit district office

Form completion:
Identifying data completed by Claims Administrator; signature of employee and attorney, if represented.

Accompanying documents:
Notice of Termination of Rehabilitation Services (RU-105)
A copy of the *Notice of Potential Eligibility*.

Rehabilitation Unit action:
If the employee objects to the Notice of Termination, the Rehabilitation Unit shall, within 30 days, schedule a conference or otherwise obtain the employee's reason for objection together with substantiating evidence and issue its decision.

Copy:
All parties.

Note: Authority cited: Sections 133, 139.5 and 5307.3, Labor Code. Reference: Sections 4641 and 4644, Labor Code.

History: 1. New section, relocation and amendment of Form RU-107-A from section 10133 to section 10133.19, and new form filing instructions filed 1-29-2003; operative 1-29-2003 pursuant to Government Code section 11343.4 (Register 2003, No. 5).

Ref.: Hanna § 35.05[4][a]; Herlick Handbook §§ 16.3, 16.4, 16.8, 16.9, 16.12, 16.16.

§10133.20. Form RU-120 "Initial Evaluation Summary" and Form Filing Instructions.

INITIAL EVALUATION SUMMARY

Claims Administrator:	Employee:	
Address:	Claim #:	DOI:
City/State/Zip:	Employer:	
Contact Name:	Date of Initial Evaluation:	

Reason for Referral:

_____Full Service _____Evaluation Only

Initial Meeting and Impressions: Vocationally Feasible? ____Yes ____No _____Deferred (Explain)

Summary:

Recommendations:

Plan of Action:

Next Reporting Date:

QRR (Print Name): Telephone:	Signature:	Date:

Attachments: a) Data Sheet b) ____________ c) ____________ d) ____________	Copies Sent To: a) ____________ b) ____________ c) ____________ d) ____________

DWC Form RU-120 (Page 1 of 4) (Rev. 1/03)

INITIAL EVALUATION DATA SHEET

PERSONAL INFORMATION: Name:

Male: Female: | Social Security No.: | DOB:

Phone No.: | CA Driver's License No.: | Exp. Date:

License Restrictions (Explain):

Distance willing to travel to work (one way): | Areas willing to drive:

Reliable vehicle available for transportation (full-time): ____________Yes ____________No
If no, what method of transportation will be used?:

Willing to relocate? Yes No | Work Shifts: All Days All Shifts M-F Only 8-5 Only

Describe issues which may interfere with employee's participation in services:

SOCIO-FAMILY FINANCIAL HISTORY

Marital status: Married Single Divorced Widowed Separated

Number of Dependents Living at Home: | Ages: | Child Support Payments? ___Yes___No
Amount: $

Child care required: Yes No | Estimated amount per week: $

Able to financially support self throughout duration of services: ___Yes ___No (Explain):

Receiving VRMA? Yes No | Amount per week: $

Receiving PD Supplement? Yes No | Amount per week: $

Other sources of income (explain):

EDUCATIONAL BACKGROUND

High School Graduate? ____Yes ____ No
Year: | Name & Location of High School:

If not HS graduate, GED? ____Yes Year: ____
If No GED - Last grade completed: | Post-HS Studies: ___Certificate ___AA/AS ___BA/BS
Area of Study: Year:

English Language
Speak ___Yes___No
Read ___Yes___No Level ____________
Write ___Yes___No Level ____________

Other Language: ____________
Speak ____Yes____ No
Read ____Yes____ No
Write ____Yes____ No

Employee's List of Perceived Work Skills:

MILITARY SERVICE: Dates of Service: Branch:

Special Skills:

VOCATIONAL HISTORY

Company, Location	Dates Employed From	To	Job Title	Salary	Reason for Leaving

MEDICAL FILE REVIEW

Treating Physician: Phone:

Address:

Medical Restrictions:

Permanent & Stationary	Yes	No	Date:

Medical Restrictions/Limitations (specify medical report and date relied upon):

Current Medications (specify medical report and date relied upon):

Currently in Physical Therapy: ____________Yes _______No Days/Times:

Non-Industrially Related Medical Conditions (explain):

PRESENT PHYSICAL TOLERANCES (Subjective)

Sitting _______minutes	Lifting _______ # of Pounds: _______	Reaching
Standing _______minutes	Climb Steps: Can _______Cannot_______	Below shoulder _______Yes_____No
Driving _______minutes	Bending: Can _______ Cannot _______	At shoulder _______Yes_____No
Walking _______minutes	Dominant Hand: Rt. _______ Lft. _______	Handling/Feeling _______Yes_____No
		Pushing/Pulling _______Yes_____No

Vision Restriction _____Yes _____No Ready to Return to Work _______Yes_____No

Supplemental Medical/Physical Information:

VOCATIONAL CONSIDERATIONS

Preliminary Assessment of Transferable Skills:

Client's Expressed Interest/Expectations of Vocational Rehabilitation:

Observations (Comments on Appearance, Rapport, Cooperation, Attitude):

VOCATIONAL FEASIBILITY FACTORS

Can the employee reasonably benefit from the provision of vocational rehabilitation services?

INVESTIGATION OF MODIFIED/ALTERNATIVE EMPLOYMENT

	Available	Contact:
	Not Available	Title:
	Unknown/Not Requested	Date of Conduct:

EXPLANATION OF VOCATONAL REHABILITATION PROCESS
(Check Box For All Issues Covered With Employee)

	EE Role		Caps/Limits on VR		Termination Process
	QRR Role		VRMA		Reinstatement Process
	Carrier/ER Role		Dispute Resolution Process		Interruption Process
	Rehab Unit Role		Effect of Delays		Allowable Costs
	Help RTW Brochure		Plan Definition		Nature, Extent Added Costs
	Plan Hierarchy		Plan Parameters		Other (Explain)

Rehabilitation Unit
California Division of Workers' Compensation

Form RU-120

INITIAL EVALUATION SUMMARY

Purpose:
To document the findings and recommendations of the Qualified Rehabilitation Representative who conducts the initial evaluation. Per AR §10132.1, such assessment is to include an initial assessment of the worker's ability to benefit from VR services.

Submitted by:
Qualified Rehabilitation Representative (QRR).

When submitted:
The Rehabilitation Unit encourages an expeditious assessment of employee skills and vocational feasibility. The RU-120 should be submitted not later than 30 days from completion of the initial interview unless otherwise agreed to.

Where submitted:
To the claims administrator with copies to all parties. If the QRR is functioning as an Independent Vocational Evaluator (IVE), the RU-120 would be filed directly with the Rehabilitation Unit with copies to all parties.

Form completion:
This form is to be completed by the QRR. The purpose of the form is to obtain comprehensive, yet concise, information which is critical for assessing vocational feasibility and developing an appropriate plan per the California Standards Governing Timeliness and Quality of Vocational Rehabilitation Services. Information gathered for each section must fit within the section designated for that category and the typeface must be no smaller than 10 point. The cost of additional or more detailed reports shall be borne by the party requesting them.

Accompanying documents:
None

Rehabilitation Unit action:
None.

Copy:
All parties.

Note: Authority cited: Sections 133, 138.4, 139.5 and 5307.3, Labor Code. Reference: Section 139.5, Labor Code.

History: 1. New section, relocation and amendment of Form RU-120 from section 10133 to section 10133.20, and new form filing instructions filed 1-29-2003; operative 1-29-2003 pursuant to Government Code section 11343.4 (Register 2003, No. 5).

Ref.: Hanna §§ 35.05[4], 35.40[4]; Herlick Handbook §§ 16.3, 16.4, 16.8, 16.9, 16.12, 16.16.

Regulations

§10133.21. Form RU-121 "Vocational Rehabilitation Progress Report" and Form Filing Instructions.

VOCATIONAL REHABILITATION PROGRESS REPORT

Claims Administrator:	Employee:	
Address:	Claim #:	DOI:
City/State/Zip:	Employer:	
Contact Name:	Report Date:	Period Covered:
Anticipated Plan Submission Date:	Date Vocational Feasibility:	
Plan Goal:	Plan Start Date:	Plan Completion Date:
Dates of Meetings/Appointments/Classes Attended:	Dates of Missed Meetings/Appointments/Classes:	

Services Provided:

Summary of Activities and Comments:

Recommendations/Plan of Action:

Next Reporting Date:

QRR (Print Name):	Signature:	Date:
Telephone Number:		

Attachments:	Copies Sent To:	VR Initiated Pre 1998	VR Initiated Post 12/31/97
		Phase I: $	Phase A: $
		Phase II: $	
		Phase III: $	Phase B: $
Report Prep Time: mins		Cum. Total: $	Cum. Total: $

DWC Form RU-121 (Rev. 9/98)

Rehabilitation Unit
California Division of Workers' Compensation

Form RU-121

VOCATIONAL REHABILITATION PROGRESS REPORT

Purpose:
To report on the progress of the employee who is receiving vocational rehabilitation services.

Submitted by:
Qualified Rehabilitation Representative (QRR)

When submitted:
Reports are done no less often than once per month unless otherwise agreed to, due to cap considerations. The QRR shall report to all parties within 10 days of the completion of services.

Where submitted:
To the claims administrator with copies to all parties. If the QRR is functioning as an Independent Vocational Evaluator, the RU-121 would be filed directly with the Rehabilitation Unit with copies to all parties.

Form completion:
This form is to be completed by the QRR. The purpose of the form is to obtain comprehensive, yet concise, information on the progress of vocational services. The information gathered for each section must fit within the section designated for that category and the typeface must be no smaller than 10 point. The cost of additional or more detailed reports shall be borne by the party requesting them.

Accompanying documents:
None

Rehabilitation Unit action:
None.

Copy:
All parties.

Note: Authority cited: Sections 133, 138.4, 139.5 and 5307.3, Labor Code. Reference: Section 139.5, Labor Code.

History: 1. New section and new Form RU-121 and form filing instructions filed 1-29-2003; operative 1-29-2003 pursuant to Government Code section 11343.4 (Register 2003, No. 5).

Ref.: Hanna §§ 35.05[4], 35.41[3]; Herlick Handbook §§ 16.3, 16.4, 16.8, 16.9, 16.12, 16.16.

§10133.22. Form RU-122 "Settlement of Prospective Vocational Rehabilitation Services" and Form Filing Instructions.

SETTLEMENT OF PROSPECTIVE VOCATIONAL REHABILITATION SERVICES [LC § 4646 (b)]	REHABILITATION USE ONLY

Social Security No:	Claim Number:	WCAB Case No. (if any):	RU Case No. (if any):
Employee Name (Last) (First) (MI)			Date of Birth
Address (Street) (City) (State) (Zip Code)			

Date of Injury	If Self Insured, Certificate Name or Insurer Name
Employer Name	Adjusting Agency Name (if adjusted)
Employer Address	Claims Mailing Address
City, State, Zip Code	City, State, Zip Code
Employee's Attorney	Employer's Representative
Firm Name	Firm Name
Address	Address
City, State, Zip Code Phone No.	City, State, Zip Code Phone No.
Qualified Rehabilitation Representative *(if any)*	
Firm Name	
Address	
City, State, Zip Code Phone No.	

In accordance with Labor Code 4646:

1. The parties to this agreement are the employee __________________ and the employer or claims administrator______________________.

2. All parties agree that any vocational rehabilitation benefits paid and accrued prior to the date this agreement has been signed are separate and distinct funds from the amount settled in this agreement.

3. The parties hereby agree to settle the employee's right to prospective Vocational Rehabilitation services with a one-time payment to the employee for the sum of $ ______________, less the sum of $ ______________, as reasonable attorney's fee. The requested attorney's fee will be held in trust by the employer subject to approval and subsequent order by the Workers' Compensation Appeals Board.

4. The employee's attorney has fully disclosed and explained to the employee the nature and quality of the rights and privileges being waived and settled by the parties. The employee has knowingly and voluntarily agreed to relinquish his or her rehabilitation rights.

Employee's signature ______________________________ Date ______________

Employee's Attorney's signature ______________________ Date ______________

Qualified Interpreter's signature ______________________ Date ______________
(if needed)

5. The employee understands and agrees that the settlement is to be applied to his/her self-directed vocational rehabilitation, such as direct placement, training, self-employment.

Signatures

Employee____ Date______________

Employee's Attorney________________________________ Date______________

Employer's Representative___________________________ Date______________

Determination of the Rehabilitation Unit

The Rehabilitation Unit has reviewed this Settlement Agreement pursuant to Labor Code § 4646 (b) and (c). The Rehabilitation Unit, hereby, **approves** this Settlement Agreement.

Rehabilitation Unit Consultant____________________________ **Date**______________

OR

The Rehabilitation Unit has reviewed the Settlement Agreement pursuant to Labor Code § 4646 (b) and it is, hereby, **disapproved**. Reason for Disapproval:______________________________
____

Rehabilitation Unit Consultant____________________________ **Date**______________

The Rehabilitation Unit shall approve or disapprove the settlement agreement of vocational rehabilitation. If disapproval is not made within ten (10) days of receipt of a fully executed agreement, the agreement shall be deemed approved.

This Agreement is Final. Any aggrieved party must file an appeal with the Workers' Compensation Appeals Board within twenty (20) days from the date this Agreement is approved, deemed approved or disapproved.

If Vocational Rehabilitation Services were commenced:

Summary of Services Provided

Number of weeks of VRMA: ______________________________

Total Amount VRMA Paid: $______________________________

Total Amount of PD Supplement: $______________________________

Amount Paid QRR for:

DOI's on or after 1/1/03

Phase A: $________________

Phase B: $________________

Total costs of QRR services $______________________________

QRR Name ______________________________

Total other costs of rehabilitation services: $______________________________

Amount withheld for Employee's Representative, if any: $______________________________

If plan developed, plan type: ______________________________

Completed by: ______________________________ Date: ______________

Rehabilitation Unit
California Division of Workers' Compensation

Form RU-122

SETTLEMENT OF PROSPECTIVE VOCATIONAL REHABILITATION SERVICES

Purpose:
To record the agreement between the employee and the employer to settle prospective vocational rehabilitation services for injuries on or after 1/1/03.

Submitted by:
Any party.

When Submitted:
When the parties have agreed to settle prospective vocational rehabilitation services.

Where Submitted:
To the applicable Rehabilitation Unit district office. The Rehabilitation Unit's venue is the same as the WCAB. If no WCAB case exists, file with a Rehabilitation Unit within the county where the injured employee resides.

Form Completion:
Identifying data completed by claims administrator
Signature of employee, employee's representative and claims administrator

Accompanying documents:
None.

Rehabilitation Unit Action:
The Rehabilitation Unit shall either issue a determination based on the record, request additional information , or set the matter for formal conference.

Copy:
All parties

Note: Authority cited: Sections 133, 138.4, 139.5 and 5307.3, Labor Code. Reference: Sections 139.5 and 4646, Labor Code.

History: 1. New section and new Form RU-122 and form filing instructions filed 1-29-2003; operative 1-29-2003 pursuant to Government Code section 11343.4 (Register 2003, No. 5).

Ref.: Hanna § 35.05[4]; Herlick Handbook §§ 16.3, 16.4, 16.8, 16.9, 16.12, 16.16.

ARTICLE 7.5
Supplemental Job Displacement Benefit

§10133.50. Definitions.

(a) The following definitions apply for injuries occurring on or after January 1, 2004:

(1) Alternative Work. Work that the employee has the ability to perform, that offers wages and compensation that are at least 85 percent of those paid to the employee at the time of injury, and that is located within reasonable commuting distance of the employee's residence at the time of injury.

(2) Approved Training Facility. A training or skills enhancement facility or institution that meets the requirements of section 10133.58.

(3) Claims Administrator. The person or entity responsible for the payment of compensation for a self-administered insurer providing security for the payment of compensation required by Divisions 4 and 4.5 of the Labor Code, a self-administered self-insured employer, or a third-party claims administrator for a self-insured employer, insurer, legally uninsured employer, or joint powers authority.

(4) Employer. The person or entity that employed the injured employee at the time of injury.

(5) Essential Functions. Job duties considered crucial to the employment position held or desired by the employee. Functions may be considered essential because the position exists to perform the function, the function requires specialized expertise, serious results may occur if the function is not performed, other employees are not available to perform the function or the function occurs at peak periods and the employer cannot reorganize the work flow.

(6) Insurer. Has the same meaning as in Labor Code section 3211.

(7) Modified Work. Regular work modified so that the employee has the ability to perform all the functions of the job and that offers wages and compensation that are at least 85 percent of those paid to the employee at the time of injury, and located within a reasonable commuting distance of the employee's residence at the time of injury.

(8) Nontransferable Training Voucher. A document provided to an employee that allows the employee to enroll in education-related training or skills enhancement. The document shall include identifying information for the employee and claims administrator, specific information regarding the value of the voucher pursuant to Labor Code section 4658.5.

(9) Notice. A required letter or form generated by the claims administrator and directed to the injured employee.

(10) Offer of Modified or Alternative Work. An offer to the injured employee of medically appropriate employment with the date-of-injury employer in a form and manner prescribed by the Administrative Director.

(11) Parties. The employee, the claims administrator and their designated representatives, if any.

(12) Permanent Partial Disability Award. A final award of permanent partial disability determined by a Workers' Compensation Administrative Law Judge or the Workers' Compensation Appeals Board.

(13) Regular Work. The employee's usual occupation or the position in which the employee was engaged at the time of injury and that offers wages and compensation equivalent to those paid to the employee at the time of injury, and located within a reasonable commuting distance of the employee's residence at the time of injury.

(14) Supplemental Job Displacement Benefit. An educational retraining or skills enhancement allowance for injured employees whose employers are unable to provide work consistent with the requirements of Labor Code section 4658.6.

(15) Vocational & Return to Work Counselor (VRTWC). A person or entity capable of assisting a person with a disability with development of a return to work strategy and whose regular duties involve the evaluation, counseling and placement of disabled persons. A VRTWC must have at least an undergraduate degree in any field and three or more years full time experience in conducting vocational evalua-

tions, counseling and placement of disabled adults.

(16) Work Restrictions. Permanent medical limitations on employment activity established by the treating physician, Qualified Medical Examiner or Agreed Medical Examiner.

Note: Authority cited: Sections 133, 4658.5 and 5307.3, Labor Code. Reference: Sections 124, 4658.1, 4658.5 and 4658.6, Labor Code.

History: 1. New article 7.5 (sections 10133.50-10133.60) and section filed 6-6-2005; operative 8-1-2005 (Register 2005, No. 23).

Ref.: Hanna § 35.110[1]; Herlick Handbook § 16.22.

§10133.51. Notice of Potential Right to Supplemental Job Displacement Benefit.

(a) This section and section 10133.52 shall only apply to injuries occurring on or after January 1, 2004.

(b) Within 10 days of the last payment of temporary disability, if not previously provided, the claims administrator shall send the employee, by certified mail, the mandatory form "Notice of Potential Right to Supplemental Job Displacement Benefit Form" that is set forth in Section 10133.52.

Note: Authority cited: Sections 133, 4658.5 and 5307.3, Labor Code. Reference: Section 4658.5, Labor Code.

History: 1. New section filed 6-6-2005; operative 8-1-2005 (Register 2005, No. 23).

Ref.: Hanna § 35.110[1]; Herlick Handbook § 16.22.

§10133.52. "Notice of Potential Right to Supplemental Job Displacement Benefit Form."

Notice of Potential Right to Supplemental Job Displacement Benefit Form

(Mandatory Form)

If your injury causes permanent partial disability, which prevented you from returning to work within 60 days of the last payment of temporary disability, and the claims administrator has not provided you with a Form DWC-AD 10133.53 "Notice of Offer of Modified or Alternative Work," you may be eligible for a supplemental job displacement benefit in the form of a nontransferable voucher for education-related retraining or skill enhancement, or both, at state approved or accredited schools.

The amount of the voucher for the supplemental job displacement benefit will be as follows:

Up to four thousand dollars ($4,000) for a permanent partial disability award of less than 15%.

Up to six thousand dollars ($6,000) for a permanent partial disability award between 15 and 25%.

Up to eight thousand dollars ($8,000) for a permanent partial disability award between 26 and 49%.

Up to ten thousand dollars ($10,000) for a permanent partial disability award between 50 and 99%.

A permanent partial disability award is issued by a Workers' Compensation Administrative Law Judge or the Workers' Compensation Appeals Board. You may also settle your potential eligibility for a voucher as part of a compromise and release settlement for a lump sum payment. Any settlement must be reviewed and approved by a Workers' Compensation Administrative Law Judge.

The voucher may be used for payment of tuition, fees, books, and other expenses required by the school for retraining or skill enhancement. Not more than 10 percent of the voucher moneys may be used for vocational or return to work counseling. A list of vocational return to work counselors is available on the Division of Workers' Compensation's website www.dir.ca.gov or upon request.

If you are eligible, and you have not already settled the benefit, you will receive the voucher from the claims administrator within 25 calendar days from the date the permanent partial disability award is issued by the Workers' Compensation Administrative Law Judge or the Workers' Compensation Appeals Board.

If modified or alternative work is available, you will receive a Form DWC-AD 10133.53 "Notice of Offer of Modified or Alternative Work" from the claims administrator within 30 days of the termination of temporary disability indemnity payments. The claims administrator will not be required to pay for supplemental job displacement benefits if the offer for modified or alternative work meets the following conditions:

(1) You have the ability to perform the essential functions of the job provided;

(2) the job provided is in a regular position lasting at least 12 months;

(3) the job provided offers wages and compensation that are at least 85 percent of those paid to you at the time of the injury; and

(4) the job is located within reasonable commuting distance of your residence at the time of injury.

If there is a dispute regarding the Supplemental Job Displacement Benefit, the employee or claims administrator may file Form DWC-AD 10133.55 "Request for Dispute Resolution before the Administrative Director."

If you have a question or need more information, you can contact your employer or the claims administrator listed below. You can also contact a State Division of Workers' Compensation Information and Assistance Officer.

Date: ____________

Name of Claims Administrator: ____________

Phone No.: ________

Address of Claims Administrator: ____________

Email (optional): ____________

Note: Authority cited: Sections 133, 4658.5 and 5307.3, Labor Code. Reference: Section 4658.5, Labor Code.

History: 1. New section filed 6-6-2005; operative 8-1-2005 (Register 2005, No. 23).

Ref.: Hanna § 35.110[1]; Herlick Handbook § 16.22.

§10133.53. Form DWC-AD 10133.53 "Notice of Offer of Modified or Alternative Work."

DWC-AD 10133.53 NOTICE OF OFFER OF MODIFIED OR ALTERNATIVE WORK
For injuries occurring on or after 1/1/04

THIS SECTION COMPLETED BY CLAIMS ADMINISTRATOR:

Employer (name of firm) ________________ is offering you the position of a (name of job) ________________.
You may contact ________________ concerning this offer. Phone No.: ________
Date of offer: ________ Date job starts: ________
Claims Administrator: ________________ Claim Number: ________

NOTICE TO EMPLOYEE Name of employee: ________________
Date of injury: ________________ Date offer received: ________

You have 30 calendar days from receipt to accept or reject the attached offer of modified or alternative work. Regardless of whether you accept or reject this offer, the remainder of your permanent disability payments may be decreased by 15%. However, if you fail to respond in 30 days or reject this job offer, you will not be entitled to the supplemental job displacement benefit unless:

Modified Work ☐ **or Alternative Work** ☐

A. You cannot perform the essential functions of the job; or
B. The job is not a regular position lasting at least 12 months; or
C. Wages and compensation offered are less than 85% paid at the time of injury; or
D. The job is beyond a reasonable commuting distance from residence at time of injury.

THIS SECTION TO BE COMPLETED BY EMPLOYEE

___ I accept this offer of Modified or Alternative work.
___ I reject this offer of Modified or Alternative work and understand that I am not entitled to the Supplemental Job Displacement Benefit.

I under stand that if I voluntarily quit prior to working in this position for 12 months, I may not be entitled to the Supplemental Job Displacement Benefit.

________________ Date ________
Signature

I feel I cannot accept this offer because:

NOTICE TO THE PARTIES

If the offer is <u>not</u> accepted or rejected within 30 days of the offer, the offer is deemed to be rejected by the employee.

The employer or claims administrator must forward a completed copy of this agreement to the Administrative Director within 30 days of acceptance or rejection. (A.D., "SJDB." Division of Workers' Compensation, P.O. Box 420603, S.F., CA 94142–0603) If a dispute occurs regarding the above offer or agreement, either party may request the Administrative Director to resolve the dispute by filing a Request for Dispute Resolution (Form DWC-AD 10133.55) with the Administrative Director.

MANDATORY FORM (Page 1 of 3)
STATE OF CALIFORNIA
(08/06)

DWC–AD 10133.53 NOTICE OF OFFER OF MODIFIED OR ALTERNATIVE WORK
For injuries occurring on or after 1/1/04

POSITION REQUIREMENTS

Actual job title:

Wages: $ per Hour___ Week___ Month___

Is salary of modified/alternative work the same as pre-injury job? Yes ___ No ___

Is salary of modified/alternative work at least 85% of pre-injury job? Yes ___ No ___

Will job last at least 12 months? Yes ___ No ___

Is the job a regular position required by the employer's business? Yes ___ No ___

Work location: ________________________________

Duties required of the position:

Description of activities to be performed (if not stated in job description):

Physical requirements for performing work activities (include modifications to usual and customary job):

Name of doctor who approved job restrictions (optional):____________________ Date of report::____________

Date of last payment of Temporary Total Disability:

Preparer's Name:

Preparer's Signature: Date

DWC-AD 10133.53 NOTICE OF OFFER OF MODIFIED OR ALTERNATIVE WORK
For injuries occurring on or after 1/1/04

Proof of Service By Mail

I am a citizen of the United States and a resident of the County of ____________________, I am over the age of eighteen years and not a party to the within matter.

My business address is:

____

On ____________________, I served the **Notice of Offer of Modified or Alternative Work** on the parties listed below by placing a true copy thereof enclosed in a sealed envelope with postage fully prepaid, and thereafter deposited in the U. S. Mail at the place so addressed.

I declare under penalty of perjury under the laws of the State of California that the foregoing is true and correct.

Executed at ____________________ on ____________________.

Signature: ____________________

Copies Served On:

MANDATORY FORM (Page 3 of 3)
STATE OF CALIFORNIA
(08/06)

Note: Authority cited: Sections 133, 4658 and 5307.3, Labor Code. Reference: Sections 4658, 4658.1, 4658.5 and 4658.6, Labor Code.

History: 1. New section filed 6-6-2005; operative 8-1-2005 (Register 2005, No. 23).

2. Amendment filed 7-19-2006; operative 8-18-2006 (Register 2006, No. 29). For prior history, see Register 96, No. 52.

Ref.: Hanna § 35.110[1]; Herlick Handbook § 16.22.

§10133.54. Dispute Resolution.

(a) This section and section 10133.55 shall only apply to injuries occurring on or after January 1, 2004.

(b) When there is a dispute regarding the Supplemental Job Displacement Benefit, the employee, or claims administrator may request the Administrative Director to resolve the dispute.

(c) The party requesting the Administrative Director to resolve the dispute shall:

(1) Complete Form DWC-AD 10133.55 "Request for Dispute Resolution before the Administrative Director;"

(2) Clearly state the issue(s) and identify supporting information for each issue and position;

(3) Attach all pertinent documents;

(4) Submit the original request and all attached documents to the Administrative Director and serve a copy of the request and all attached documents on all parties; and

(5) Sign and date the proof of service section of Form DWC-AD 10133.55 "Request for Dispute Resolution before the Administrative Director."

(d) The opposing party shall have twenty (20) calendar days from the date of the proof of service of the Request to submit the original response and all attached documents to the Administrative Director and serve a copy of the response and all attached documents on all parties.

(e) The Administrative Director or his or her designee may request additional information from the parties.

(f) The Administrative Director or his or her designee shall issue a written determination and order based solely on the request, response, and any attached documents within thirty (30) calendar days of the date the opposing party's response and supporting information is due. If the Administrative Director or his or her designee requests additional information, the written determination shall be issued within thirty (30) calendar days from the receipt of the additional information. In the event no decision is issued within sixty (60) calendar days of the date the opposing party's response is due or within sixty (60) calendar days of the Administrative Director's receipt of the requested additional information, whichever is later, the request shall be deemed to be denied.

(g) Either party may appeal the determination and order of the Administrative Director by filing a written petition together with a Declaration of Readiness to Proceed pursuant to section 10414 with the local district office of the Workers' Compensation Appeals Board within twenty calendar days of the issuance of the decision or within twenty days after a request is deemed denied pursuant to subdivision (f). The petition shall set forth the specific factual and/or legal reason(s) for the appeal. A copy of the petition and a copy of the Declaration of Readiness to Proceed shall be concurrently served on the Administrative Director.

Note: Authority cited: Sections 133, 4658.5 and 5307.3, Labor Code. Reference: Sections 4658.5 and 4658.6, Labor Code.

History: 1. New section filed 6-6-2005; operative 8-1-2005 (Register 2005, No. 23).

Ref.: Hanna § 35.110[2]; Herlick Handbook § 16.22.

§10133.55. Form DWC-AD 10133.55 "Request for Dispute Resolution Before the Administrative Director."

DWC-AD 10133.55 **Request for Dispute Resolution Before the Administrative Director** **(For injuries occurring on or after 1/1/04)** ___Original ___Response	Has employer accepted this claim? ___Yes ___No Has liability for injury been found by the WCAB? ___Yes ___No Has it been more than 60 days since TTD ended? ___Yes ___No Has PPD award been stipulated, issued/approved? ___Yes ___No	**DWC Use Only**
Social Security Number	**WCAB Number**	**DWC Unit Number**

Employee Name (Last)	(First)	(MI)	Phone	Date of Birth	
Address (Street)	(City)	(State)	(Zip)		

Employer Name Phone	**Insurance Company Name; Or, if Self-Insured, Certificate Name**
Address	Adjusting Agency Name (if adjusted)
City, State, Zip	Claims Mailing Address
Date of Injury / **Claim Number**	City, State, Zip Phone No.
Employee Representative (if any)	**Employer Representative**
Firm Name	Firm Name
Address	Address
City, State, Zip Phone No.	City, State, Zip Phone No.

Vocational & Return to Work Counselor (if applicable)	
Firm Name	Representative Name
Address (Street, City, State, Zip	Phone No.

The Administrative Director is requested to resolve the following dispute because the parties disagree on: (Please describe and attach all pertinent documents)

Summary of Parties' Informal Efforts to Resolve this Dispute	**Proof of Service: I declare under penalty of perjury under the laws of the State of California that on the date written below, I mailed a copy of this request with a copy of any documents included with this request to the following parties at the following addresses:** **Administrative Director, (SJDB), Division of Workers' Compensation, P.O. Box 420603, San Francisco, CA 94142–0603**
Name of Requester **Date**	**Signature** **Date**

(Mandatory Form DWC–AD 10133.55 (08/06))

Note: Authority cited: Sections 133, 4658.5 and 5307.3, Labor Code. Reference: Section 4658.5, Labor Code.

History: 1. New section filed 6-6-2005; operative 8-1-2005 (Register 2005, No. 23).

2. Amendment filed 7-19-2006; operative 8-18-2006 (Register 2006, No. 29). For prior history, see Register 96, No. 52.

Ref.: Herlick Handbook § 16.22.

§10133.56. Requirement to Issue Supplemental Job Displacement Nontransferable Training Voucher.

(a) This section and section 10133.57 shall only apply to injuries occurring on or after January 1, 2004.

(b) The employee shall be eligible for the Supplemental Job Displacement Benefit when:

(1) the injury causes permanent partial disability; and

(2) within 30 days of the termination of temporary disability indemnity payments, the claims administrator does not offer modified or alternative work in accordance with Labor Code section 4658.6; and

(3) either the injured employee does not return to work for the employer within 60 days of the termination of temporary disability benefits; or

(4) in the case of a seasonal employee, where the employee is unable to return to work within 60 days of the termination of temporary disability benefits because the work season has ended, the injured employee does not return to work on the next available work date of the next work season.

(c) When the requirements under subdivision (b) have been met, the claims administrator shall provide a nontransferable voucher for education-related retraining or skill enhancement or both to the employee within 25 calendar days from the issuance of the permanent partial disability award by the Workers' Compensation Administrative Law Judge or the Workers' Compensation Appeals Board.

(d) The voucher shall be issued to the employee allowing direct reimbursement to the employee upon the employee's presentation to the claims administrator of documentation and receipts or as a direct payment to the provider of the education related training or skill enhancement and/or to the VRTWC.

(e) The voucher must indicate the appropriate level of money available to the employee in compliance with Labor Code section 4658.5.

(f) The mandatory voucher form is set forth in Section 10133.57.

(g) The voucher shall certify that the school is approved and if outside of California, approval is required similarly to the Bureau for Private Postsecondary (BPPVE).

(h) The claims administrator shall issue the reimbursement payments to the employee or direct payments to the VRTWC and the training providers within 45 calendar days from receipt of the completed voucher, receipts and documentation.

Note: Authority cited: Sections 133, 4658.5, 4658.6 and 5307.3, Labor Code. Reference: Sections 4658.5 and 4658.6, Labor Code.

History: 1. New section filed 6-6-2005; operative 8-1-2005 (Register 2005, No. 23).

Ref.: Hanna § 35.110[3]; Herlick Handbook § 16.22.

§10133.57. Form DWC-AD 10133.57 "Supplemental Job Displacement Nontransferable Training Voucher Form."

Supplemental Job Displacement Nontransferable Training Voucher Form

(Form DWC-AD 10133.57 — Mandatory Form)

For injuries occurring on or after 1/1/04

You have been determined eligible for this nontransferable, Supplemental Job Displacement Voucher. This voucher may be used for the payment of tuition, fees, books, and other expenses required by a state approved or accredited school that you enroll in for the purpose of education related retraining or skill enhancement, or both.

The state approved or accredited school will be reimbursed upon receipt of a documented invoice for tuition, fees, books and other required expenses required by the school for retraining or skill enhancement. If you pay for the eligible expenses, you may be reimbursed for these expenses upon submission of documented receipts. No more than 10 percent of the value of this voucher may be used for vocational or return to work counseling. If you decide to voluntarily withdraw from a program, you may not be entitled to a full refund of the voucher amount utilized.

Please present this original letter to the state approved or accredited school and/or the Vocational & Return to Work Counselor of your choice, chosen from the list developed by the Division of Workers' Compensation's Administrative Director, in order to initiate your training and return to work counseling. A list of Vocational & Return to Work Counselors is available on the Division of Workers' Compensation's website www.dir.ca.gov or upon request. The school and/or counselor should contact me regarding direct payment from your supplemental job displacement benefit.

Injured Employee Information: Upon completing the voucher form the injured employee must return the form with receipts and documentation to the claims administrator immediately for reimbursement. (The claims administrator must complete Nos. 1-8 of this voucher form prior to sending it to the injured employee.)

1. Injured Employee Name ___________
2. Address ___________
City ________ State ______ Zip Code ______
3. Claim Number ___________
Phone Number ___________

Claims Administrator

4. Name ___________
5. Claims Mailing Address ___________
6. City ________ State ______ Zip Code ______
7. Claims Representative ___________
Phone Number ________
8. $______ is available to the injured employee based on ______% of Permanent Partial Disability Award

The injured employee must complete Nos. 9-19 and sign and date this voucher form.

(VRTWC) Vocational Return to Work Counselor (if any)

9. Name ___________
Phone Number ___________
10. Address ___________
11. City ________ State ______ Zip Code ______
12. Funds used for vocational and return to work counseling $________ (10% maximum of voucher value)

Training Provider Details (Attach additional pages for each provider if necessary.)

13. Provider Name ___________
14. Provider Address ___________
Phone Number ___________
15. City ________ State ______ Zip Code ______
16. Provider approval number ___________
17. Expiration Date ___________
18. Provider Contact Name ___________
19. Training Cost ________

Injured Employee Signature ___________ Date ______

Note to Claims Administrator: Upon receipt of voucher, receipts and documentation from the employee, reimbursement payments to the employee or direct payments to VRTWC and training providers must be made within 45 calendar days.

Note: Authority cited: Sections 133, 4658.5 and 5307.3, Labor Code. Reference: Section 4658.5, Labor Code.

History: 1. New section filed 6-6-2005; operative 8-1-2005 (Register 2005, No. 23).

Ref.: Hanna § 35.110[3]; Herlick Handbook § 16.22.

§10133.58. State Approved or Accredited Schools.

(a) This section shall only apply to injuries occurring on or after January 1, 2004.

(b) Private providers of education-related retraining or skill enhancement selected to provide training as part of a supplemental job displacement benefit shall be:

(1) approved by the Bureau for Private Postsecondary and Vocational Education (www.bppve.ca.gov), or a California state agency that has an agreement with the Bureau for the regulation and oversight of non-degree-granting private postsecondary institutions;

(2) accredited by one of the Regional Associations of Schools and Colleges authorized by the United States Department of Education; or

(3) certified by the Federal Aviation Administration.

(c) Any training outside of California must be approved by an agency in that state similar to the Bureau for Private Postsecondary and Vocational Education.

Note: Authority cited: Sections 133, 4658.5 and 5307.3, Labor Code. Reference: Section 4658.5, Labor Code.

History: 1. New section filed 6-6-2005; operative 8-1-2005 (Register 2005, No. 23).

Ref.: Hanna § 35.110[4]; Herlick Handbook § 16.22.

§10133.59. The Administrative Director's List of Vocational Return to Work Counselors.

(a) This section shall only apply to injuries occurring on or after January 1, 2004.

(b) The Administrative Director shall maintain a list of Vocational & Return to Work Counselors (VRTWC) who perform the work of assisting injured employees. A VRTWC who meets the qualifications specified in Section 10133.50(a)(15) must apply to the Administrative Director to be included on the list throughout the year. The list shall be reviewed and revised on a yearly basis, and shall be made available on the website www.dir.ca.gov or upon request.

(c) The injured employee may select a Vocational & Return to Work Counselor whenever the assistance of a Vocational & Return to Work Counselor is needed to facilitate an employee's vocational training or return to work in connection with the Supplemental Job Displacement Benefit set forth in this Article.

(d) The injured employee shall be responsible for providing the VRTWC with any necessary medical reports. However, a claims administrator shall provide a VRTWC with any medical reports, including permanent and stationary medical reports, upon an employee's written request and a signed release waiver.

(e) The VRTWC shall communicate with the injured employee regarding the evaluation.

Note: Authority cited: Sections 133, 4658.5 and 5307.3, Labor Code. Reference: Section 4658.5, Labor Code.

History: 1. New section filed 6-6-2005; operative 8-1-2005 (Register 2005, No. 23).

Ref.: Hanna § 35.110[5]; Herlick Handbook § 16.22.

§10133.60. Termination of Claims Administrator's Liability for the Supplemental Job Displacement Benefit.

(a) For injuries occurring on or after January 1, 2004, the claims administrator's liability to provide a supplemental job displacement voucher shall end if either (a)(1) or (a)(2) occur:

(1) the claims administrator offers modified or alternative work to the employee, meeting the requirements of Labor Code §4658.6, on DWC-AD Form 10133.53 "Notice of Offer of Modified or Alternative Work";

(A) If the claims administrator offers modified or alternative work to the employee for 12 months of seasonal work, the offer shall meet the following requirements:

1. the employee was hired on a seasonal basis prior to injury; and

2. the offer of modified or alternative work is on a similar seasonal basis to the employee's previous employment;

(2) the maximum funds of the voucher have been exhausted.

Note: Authority cited: Sections 133 and 5307.3, Labor Code. Reference: Sections 4658.1, 4658.5, 4658.6 and 5410, Labor Code; and Henry v. WCAB (1998) 68 Cal.App.4th 981.

History: 1. New section filed 6-6-2005; operative 8-1-2005 (Register 2005, No. 23).

Ref.: Hanna § 35.110[6]; Herlick Handbook § 16.22.

ARTICLE 8
Attorney Fee Disclosure Statement

§10134. Attorney Fee Disclosure Statement Form.

State of California
Department of Industrial Relations
Division of Workers' Compensation

FEE DISCLOSURE STATEMENT

If you choose to be represented by an attorney, your attorney's fees will be deducted from your benefits. The fee will be approved by the Workers' Compensation Appeals Board, with consideration given to the: (1) responsibility assumed by the attorney; (2) care exercised in representing you; (3) time involved; and, (4) results obtained.

Attorney's fees normally range from 9% to 12% of the benefits awarded. If your attorney has also represented you before the Rehabilitation Unit, there may also be a fee allowed for this representation.

There are certain circumstances where your employer (or his/her insurer) may be liable to pay your attorney's fees. For example, if employer disputes a permanent disability evaluation obtained when you were not represented by an attorney, your employer may be liable for any attorney fees you incur because of the dispute.

If at any time you no longer wish to be represented by the attorney, you may withdraw from representation by notifying the attorney. If you withdraw from representation, the fee amount found by a workers' compensation judge to be the fair value of any work the attorney did in your case will be deducted from your award.

An Information and Assistance Officer may be able to answer your questions concerning your workers' compensation benefits at no charge to you. He/She may be able to resolve your problems without the need for litigation.

Call this toll-free number: 1-800-736-7401.

Employee's Signature ______________________ Date __________

Employee's Name ______________________

Attorney's Signature ______________________ Date __________

Attorney's Name ______________________

Address ______________________

____

____

Phone No. (____)______________________

Any person who makes or causes to be made any knowingly false or fraudulent material statement or material representation for the purpose of obtaining or denying workers' compensation benefits or payments is guilty of felony.

DWC Form 3 (Rev. 3/93)

Estado de California
Departamento de Relaciones Indu .ales
División de Compensaciones al Trabajador

DECLARACION DE REVELACION DE HONORARIOS

Si Ud. escoge ser representado por un abogado, los honorarios de su abogado serán deducidos de sus beneficios. Los honorarios serán aprobados por el Directorio de Apelaciones de Compensaciones al Trabajador, se le dará consideración a lo siguiente: (1) responsabilidad asumida por el abogado; (2) el cuidado ejercido en representarlo a Ud.; (3) tiempo dedicado; y (4) resultados obtenidos.

Los honorarios del abogado normalmente fluctúan entre un 9% a un 12% de los beneficios otorgados. Si su abogado también lo ha representado a Ud. ante la Unidad de Rehabilitación, también puede ser que se permitan honorarios por esta representación.

Hay ciertas circunstancias en que su empleador (o la compañía de seguros de correspondiente) pueda ser responsable u obligado a pagar sus honorarios de abogado. Por ejemplo, si su empleador disputa una evaluación de incapacidad permanente obtenida cuando Ud. no ha sido representado por un abogado, su empleador puede ser responsable u obligado a pagar cualquier honorario de abogado incurrido por la disputa.

Si en cualquier momento Ud. no desea continuar siendo representado por un abogado, Ud. puede retirar la representación con una notificación a su abogado. Si retira Ud. su representación, la cantidad de honorarios será determinada por el juez por cualquier trabajo que el abogado haya efectuado en su caso y esta será deducida de su beneficio otorgado.

Un Oficial de Información y Asistencia podrá responder a sus preguntas en relación a sus beneficios de compensación sin costo alguno para Ud. El podrá resolver sus problemas sin necesidad de litigación. Llame a éste número de teléfono gratis: 1-800-736-7401.

Firma del Empleado ______________________ Fecha ______________

Nombre del Empleado ______________________

Firma del Abogado ______________________ Fecha ______________

Nombre del Abogado ______________________

Dirección: ______________________

____

____

Número de Teléfono (____) ______________

Toda aquella persona que con conocimiento haga o cause que se produzca cualquier declaración o representación material falsa o fraudulenta con el fin de obtener o negar beneficios o pagos de compensación a trabajadores lesionados es culpable de un crimen mayor "felonía".

Note: Authority cited: Sections 133 and 5307.3, Labor Code. Reference: Section 4906(e), Labor Code.

History: 1. New section filed 1-18-90; operative 1-18-90 (Register 90, No. 4). New section is exempt from from review by OAL pursuant to Government Code Section 11351.

2. Repealer and new section filed 4-13-93; operative 4-13-93. Submitted to OAL for printing only pursuant to Government Code section 11351 (Register 93, No. 16).

Ref.: Hanna § 25.01[4]; Herlick Handbook §§ 10.2, 16.16; W. Cal. Sum., 2 "Workers' Compensation" §354.

§10135. Required Use of Form.

Every attorney or his/her agent who consults with an injured worker or dependent is required to furnish the attorney fee disclosure statement form set forth in Section 10134 of this Article to the injured worker or dependent at the initial consultation.

Note: Authority cited: Sections 133 and 5307.3, Labor Code. Reference: Section 4906(e), Labor Code.

History: 1. New section filed 1-18-90; operative 1-18-90 (Register 90, No. 4). New section is exempt from review by OAL pursuant to Government Code Section 11351.

2. Amendment filed 4-13-93; operative 4-13-93. Submitted to OAL for printing only pursuant to Government Code section 11351 (Register 93, No. 16).

Ref.: Hanna §§ 20.01[4], 25.01[4]; Herlick Handbook § 10.2.

§10135.1. Service of Form.

Within 15 days of the employee's and attorney's execution of the disclosure form, a copy of the disclosure form shall be mailed to the employer or, if known, to the employer's insurer or third-party administrator.

Note: Authority cited: Sections 133 and 5307.3, Labor Code. Reference: Section 4906(e), Labor Code.

History: 1. New section filed 4-13-93; operative 4-13-93. Submitted to OAL for printing only pursuant to Government Code section 11351 (Register 93, No. 16).

Ref.: Hanna §§ 20.01[4], 25.01[4]; Herlick Handbook § 10.2.

ARTICLE 9
Claim Form: Availability, Filing, Acknowledgement of Receipt, Dismissal

§10136. General: Definitions.

As used in this Article, the following definitions apply:

(a) Claims Administrator. A self-administered workers' compensation insurer, a self-administered self-insured employer, a self-administered joint powers authority, or a third-party claims administrator for an insurer, a self-insured employer, a legally-uninsured employer or a joint powers authority; or an attorney or agent of any of those entities.

(b) Claim Form. The official Division of Workers' Compensation DWC Form 1 Employee's Claim for Workers' Compensation Benefits, as set forth in Section 10139 of this Article.

(c) Employee. An employee, a person claiming to be an employee, his or her dependents, or agent.

Note: Authority cited: Sections 133 and 5307.3, Labor Code. Reference: Sections 5401, 5401.7, 5402 and 5404.5, Labor Code.

History: 1. New section filed 1-18-90; operative 1-18-90 (Register 90, No. 4). New section is exempt from review by OAL pursuant to Government Code Section 11351.

2. Amendment of subsections (b), (b)(3), (b)(4) and (c), repealer of subsections (b)(5), (d), (e) and (f), and new subsection (d) filed 4-13-93; operative 4-13-93. Submitted to OAL for printing only pursuant to Government Code section 11351 (Register 93, No. 16)

3. Change without regulatory effect repealing article 9 heading, renumbering former article 6 to new article 9, renumbering former section 10136 to section 10252 and renumbering former section 10116 to section 10136, including amendment of subsection (b), filed 4-7-2008 pursuant to section 100, title 1, California Code of Regulations (Register 2008, No. 15).

§10137. General: Employer Obligation.

Nothing in this article shall abrogate the duty of an employer to provide timely compensation to an injured worker, even if the employee has not completed and filed the form required by Labor Code Section 5401 and this article.

Note: Authority cited: Sections 133 and 5307.3, Labor Code. Reference: Sections 5401 and 3200–6208, Labor Code.

History: 1. New section filed 1-18-90; operative 1-18-90 (Register 90, No. 4). New section is exempt from review by OAL pursuant to Government Code Section 11351.

2. Repealer and new section filed 4-13-93; operative 4-13-93. Submitted to OAL for printing only pursuant to Government Code section 11351 (Register 93, No. 16)

3. Change without regulatory effect renumbering former section 10137 to section 10252.1 and renumber-

ing former section 10116.1 to section 10137 filed 4-7-2008 pursuant to section 100, title 1, California Code of Regulations (Register 2008, No. 15).

§10138. Claim Form and Notice of Potential Eligibility for Benefits.

The employee's form for filing a workers' compensation claim (DWC 1) and the Notice of Potential Eligibility for Benefits is a mandatory form set forth in Section 10139 of this Article. The employer portion of the form may also include other information pertinent to the claim, including a logo or other employer-identifying information, but such information shall in no way impose additional duties or prohibitions on the employee or delay the processing of the claim. The claim form consists of an original and three (3) copies.

Note: Authority cited: Sections 133 and 5307.3, Labor Code. Reference: Sections 5401, 5401.7 and 5402, Labor Code.

History: 1. Change without regulatory effect renumbering former section 10117.1 to section 10138, including amendment of section, filed 4-7-2008 pursuant to section 100, title 1, California Code of Regulations (Register 2008, No. 15).

§10139. Workers' Compensation Claim Form (DWC 1) and Notice of Potential Eligibility.

Workers' Compensation Claim Form (DWC 1) & Notice of Potential Eligibility
Formulario de Reclamo de Compensación para Trabajadores (DWC 1) y Notificación de Posible Elegibilidad

If you are injured or become ill, either physically or mentally, because of your job, including injuries resulting from a workplace crime, you may be entitled to workers' compensation benefits. Attached is the form for filing a workers' compensation claim with your employer. **You should read all of the information below.** Keep this sheet and all other papers for your records. You may be eligible for some or all of the benefits listed depending on the nature of your claim. If required you will be notified by the claims administrator, who is responsible for handling your claim, about your eligibility for benefits.

To file a claim, complete the "Employee" section of the form, keep one copy and give the rest to your employer. Your employer will then complete the "Employer" section, give you a dated copy, keep one copy and send one to the claims administrator. Benefits can't start until the claims administrator knows of the injury, so complete the form as soon as possible.

Medical Care: Your claims administrator will pay all reasonable and necessary medical care for your work injury or illness. Medical benefits may include treatment by a doctor, hospital services, physical therapy, lab tests, x-rays, and medicines. Your claims administrator will pay the costs directly so you should never see a bill. For injuries occurring on or after 1/1/04, there is a limit on some medical services.

The Primary Treating Physician (PTP) is the doctor with the overall responsibility for treatment of your injury or illness. Generally your employer selects the PTP you will see for the first 30 days, however, in specified conditions, you may be treated by your predesignated doctor. If a doctor says you still need treatment after 30 days, you may be able to switch to the doctor of your choice. Special rules apply if your employer offers a Health Care Organization (HCO) or after 1/1/05, has a medical provider network. Contact your employer for more information. If your employer has not put up a poster describing your rights to workers' compensation, you may choose your own doctor immediately.

Within one working day after an employee files a claim form, the employer shall authorize the provision of all treatment, consistent with the applicable treating guidelines, for the alleged injury and shall continue to provide treatment until the date that liability for the claim is accepted or rejected. Until the date the claim is accepted or rejected, liability for medical treatment shall be limited to ten thousand dollars ($10,000).

Disclosure of Medical Records: After you make a claim for workers' compensation benefits, your medical records will not have the same privacy that you usually expect. If you don't agree to voluntarily release medical records, a workers' compensation judge may decide what records will be released. If you request privacy, the judge may "seal" (keep private) certain medical records.

Payment for Temporary Disability (Lost Wages): If you can't work while you are recovering from a job injury or illness, you will receive temporary disability payments. These payments may change or stop when your doctor says you are able to return to work. These benefits are tax-free. Temporary disability payments are two-thirds of your average weekly pay, within minimums and maximums set by state law. Payments are not made for the first three days you are off the job unless you are hospitalized overnight or cannot work for more than 14 days.

Si Ud. se lesiona o se enferma, ya sea física o mentalmente, debido a su trabajo, incluyendo lesiones que resulten de un crimen en el lugar de trabajo, es posible que Ud. tenga derecho a beneficios de compensación para trabajadores. Se adjunta el formulario para presentar un reclamo de compensación para trabajadores con su empleador. **Ud. debe leer toda la información a continuación.** Guarde esta hoja y todos los demás documentos para sus archivos. Es posible que usted reúna los requisitos para todos los beneficios, o parte de éstos, que se enumeran, dependiendo de la índole de su reclamo. Si se requiere, el/la administrador(a) de reclamos, quien es responsable del manejo de su reclamo, le notificará a usted, lo referente a su elegibilidad para beneficios.

Para presentar un reclamo, complete la sección del formulario designada para el "Empleado", guarde una copia, y déle el resto a su empleador. Entonces, su empleador completará la sección designada para el "Empleador", le dará a Ud. una copia fechada, guardará una copia, y enviará una al/a la administrador(a) de reclamos. Los beneficios no pueden comenzar hasta, que el/la administrador(a) de reclamos se entere de la lesión, así que complete el formulario lo antes posible.

Atención Médica: Su administrador(a) de reclamos pagará toda la atención médica razonable y necesaria, para su lesión o enfermedad relacionada con el trabajo. Es posible que los beneficios médicos incluyan el tratamiento por parte de un médico, los servicios de hospital, la terapia física, los análisis de laboratorio y las medicinas. Su administrador(a) de reclamos pagará directamente los costos, de manera que usted nunca verá un cobro. Para lesiones que ocurren en o después de 1/1/04, hay un límite de visitas para ciertos servicios médicos.

El Médico Primario que le Atiende-*Primary Treating Physician PTP* es el médico con toda la responsabilidad para dar el tratamiento para su lesión o enfermedad. Generalmente, su empleador selecciona al *PTP* que Ud. verá durante los primeros 30 días. Sin embargo, en condiciones específicas, es posible que usted pueda ser tratado por su médico pre-designado. Si el doctor dice que usted aún necesita tratamiento después de 30 días, es posible que Ud. pueda cambiar al médico de su preferencia. Hay reglas especiales que son aplicables cuando su empleador ofrece una Organización del Cuidado Médico (HCO) o depués de 1/1/05 tiene un Sistema de Proveedores de Atención Médica. Hable con su empleador para más información. Si su empleador no ha colocado un poster describiendo sus derechos para la compensación para trabajadores, Ud. puede seleccionar a su propio médico inmediatamente.

El empleador autorizará todo tratamiento médico consistente con las directivas de tratamiento applicables a la lesión o enfermedad, durante el primer día laboral después que el empleado efectúa un reclamo para beneficios de compensación, y continuará proveyendo este tratamiento hasta la fecha en que el reclamo sea aceptado o rechazado. Hasta la fecha en que el reclamo sea aceptado o rechazado, el tratamiento médico será limitado a diez mil dólares ($10,000).

Divulgación de Expedientes Médicos: Después de que Ud. presente un reclamo para beneficios de compensación para los trabajadores, sus expedientes médicos no tendrán la misma privacidad que usted normalmente espera. Si Ud. no está de acuerdo en divulgar voluntariamente los expedientes médicos, un(a) juez de compensación para trabajadores posiblemente decida qué expedientes se revelarán. Si Ud. solicita privacidad, es posible que el/la juez "selle" (mantenga privados) ciertos expedientes médicos.

Pago por Incapacidad Temporal (Sueldos Perdidos): Si Ud. no puede trabajar, mientras se está recuperando de una lesión o enfermedad relacionada con el trabajo, Ud. recibirá pagos por incapacidad temporal. Es posible que estos pagos cambien o paren, cuando su médico diga que Ud. está en condiciones de regresar a trabajar. Estos beneficios son libres de

Workers' Compensation Claim Form (DWC 1) & Notice of Potential Eligibility
Formulario de Reclamo de Compensación para Trabajadores (DWC 1) y Notificación de Posible Elegibilidad

Return to Work: To help you to return to work as soon as possible, you should actively communicate with your treating doctor, claims administrator, and employer about the kinds of work you can do while recovering. They may coordinate efforts to return you to modified duty or other work that is medically appropriate. This modified or other duty may be temporary or may be extended depending on the nature of your injury or illness.

Payment for Permanent Disability: If a doctor says your injury or illness results in a permanent disability, you may receive additional payments. The amount will depend on the type of injury, your age, occupation, and date of injury.

Vocational Rehabilitation (VR): If a doctor says your injury or illness prevents you from returning to the same type of job and your employer doesn't offer modified or alternative work, you may qualify for VR. If you qualify, your claims administrator will pay the costs, up to a maximum set by state law. VR is a benefit for injuries that occurred prior to 2004.

Supplemental Job Displacement Benefit (SJDB): If you do not return to work within 60 days after your temporary disability ends, and your employer does not offer modified or alternative work, you may qualify for a nontransferable voucher payable to a school for retraining and/or skill enhancement. If you qualify, the claims administrator will pay the costs up to the maximum set by state law based on your percentage of permanent disability. SJDB is a benefit for injuries occurring on or after 1/1/04.

Death Benefits: If the injury or illness causes death, payments may be made to relatives or household members who were financially dependent on the deceased worker.

It is illegal for your employer to punish or fire you for having a job injury or illness, for filing a claim, or testifying in another person's workers' compensation case (Labor Code 132a). If proven, you may receive lost wages, job reinstatement, increased benefits, and costs and expenses up to limits set by the state.

You have the right to disagree with decisions affecting your claim. If you have a disagreement, contact your claims administrator first to see if you can resolve it. If you are not receiving benefits, you may be able to get State Disability Insurance (SDI) benefits. Call State Employment Development Department at (800) 480-3287.

You can obtain free information from an information and assistance officer of the State Division of Workers' Compensation, or you can hear recorded information and a list of local offices by calling **(800) 736-7401**. You may also go to the DWC web site at **www.dir.ca.gov**. Link to Workers' Compensation.

You can consult with an attorney. Most attorneys offer one free consultation. If you decide to hire an attorney, his or her fee will be taken out of some of your benefits. For names of workers' compensation attorneys, call the State Bar of California at (415) 538-2120 or go to their web site at **www.californiaspecialist.org**.

impuestos. Los pagos por incapacidad temporal son dos tercios de su pago semanal promedio, con cantidades mínimas y máximas establecidas por las leyes estatales. Los pagos no se hacen durante los primeros tres días en que Ud. no trabaje, a menos que Ud. sea hospitalizado(a) de noche, o no pueda trabajar durante más de 14 días.

Regreso al Trabajo: Para ayudarle a regresar a trabajar lo antes posible, Ud. debe comunicarse de manera activa con el médico que le atienda, el/la administrador(a) de reclamos y el empleador, con respecto a las clases de trabajo que Ud. puede hacer mientras se recupera. Es posible que ellos coordinen esfuerzos para regresarle a un trabajo modificado, o a otro trabajo, que sea apropiado desde el punto de vista médico. Este trabajo modificado, u otro trabajo, podría extenderse o no temporalmente, dependiendo de la índole de su lesión o enfermedad.

Pago por Incapacidad Permanente: Si el doctor dice que su lesión o enfermedad resulta en una incapacidad permanente, es posible que Ud. reciba pagos adicionales. La cantidad dependerá de la clase de lesión, su edad, su ocupación y la fecha de la lesión.

Rehabilitación Vocacional: Si el doctor dice que su lesión o enfermedad no le permite regresar a la misma clase de trabajo, y su empleador no le ofrece trabajo modificado o alterno, es posible que usted reúna los requisitos para rehabilitación vocacional. Si Ud. reúne los requisitos, su administrador(a) de reclamos pagará los costos, hasta un máximo establecido por las leyes estatales. Este es un beneficio para lesiones que ocurrieron antes de 2004.

Beneficio Suplementario por Desplazamiento de Trabajo: Si Ud. no vuelve al trabajo en un plazo de 60 días después que los pagos por incapcidad temporal terminan, y su empleador no ofrece un trabajo modificado o alterno, es posible que usted reúne los requisitos para recibir un vale no-transferible pagadero a una escuela para recibir un nuevo entrenamiento y/o mejorar su habilidad. Si Ud. reúne los requisitios, el administrador(a) de reclamos pagará los costos hasta un máximo establecido por las leyes estatales basado en su porcentaje del incapicidad permanente. Este es un beneficio para lesiones que ocurren en o después de 1/1/04.

Beneficios por Muerte: Si la lesión o enfermedad causa la muerte, es posible que los pagos se hagan a los parientes o a las personas que vivan en el hogar, que dependían económicamente del/de la trabajador(a) difunto(a).

Es ilegal que su empleador le castigue o despida, por sufrir una lesión o enfermedad en el trabajo, por presentar un reclamo o por atestiguar en el caso de compensación para trabajadores de otra persona. (El Codigo Laboral sección 132a). Si es probado, puede ser que usted reciba pagos por perdida de sueldos, reposición del trabajo, aumento de beneficios, y gastos hasta un límite establecido por el estado.

Ud. tiene derecho a estar en desacuerdo con las decisiones que afecten su reclamo. Si Ud. tiene un desacuerdo, primero comuníquese con su administrador(a) de reclamos, para ver si usted puede resolverlo. Si usted no está recibiendo beneficios, es posible que Ud. pueda obtener beneficios de Seguro Estatal de Incapacidad (SDI). Llame al Departamento Estatal del Desarrollo del Empleo (EDD) al (800) 480-3287.

Ud. puede obtener información gratis, de un oficial de información y asistencia, de la División estatal de Compensación al Trabajador *(Division of Workers' Compensation – DWC)*, o puede escuchar información grabada, así como una lista de oficinas locales, llamando al **(800) 736-7401**. Ud. también puede ir al sitio electrónico en el Internet de la DWC en **www.dir.ca.gov**. Enlácese a la sección de Compensación para Trabajadores.

Ud. puede consultar con un(a) abogado(a). La mayoría de los abogados ofrecen una consulta gratis. Si Ud. decide contratar a un(a) abogado(a), sus honorarios se tomarán de sus beneficios. Para obtener nombres de abogados de compensación para trabajadores, llame a la Asociación Estatal de Abogados de California *(State Bar)* al (415) 538-2120, ó vaya a su sitio electrónico en el Internet en **www.californiaspecialist.org**.

State of California
Department of Industrial Relations
DIVISION OF WORKERS' COMPENSATION

Estado de California
Departamento de Relaciones Industriales
DIVISION DE COMPENSACIÓN AL TRABAJADOR

WORKERS' COMPENSATION CLAIM FORM (DWC 1)

PETITION DEL EMPLEADO PARA DE COMPENSACIÓN DEL TRABAJADOR (DWC 1)

Employee: Complete the **"Employee"** section and give the form to your employer. Keep a copy and mark it **"Employee's Temporary Receipt"** until you receive the signed and dated copy from your employer. You may call the Division of Workers' Compensation and hear recorded information at **(800) 736-7401**. An explanation of workers' compensation benefits is included as the cover sheet of this form.

You should also have received a pamphlet from your employer describing workers' compensation benefits and the procedures to obtain them.

Any person who makes or causes to be made any knowingly false or fraudulent material statement or material representation for the purpose of obtaining or denying workers' compensation benefits or payments is guilty of a felony.

Empleado: *Complete la sección **"Empleado"** y entregue la forma a su empleador. Quédese con la copia designada **"Recibo Temporal del Empleado"** hasta que Ud. reciba la copia firmada y fechada de su empleador. Ud. puede llamar a la Division de Compensación al Trabajador al **(800) 736-7401** para oir información gravada. En la hoja cubierta de esta forma esta la explicatión de los beneficios de compensación al trabjador.*

Ud. también debería haber recibido de su empleador un folleto describiendo los benficios de compensación al trabajador lesionado y los procedimientos para obtenerlos.

Toda aquella persona que a propósito haga o cause que se produzca cualquier declaración o representación material falsa o fraudulenta con el fin de obtener o negar beneficios o pagos de compensación a trabajadores lesionados es culpable de un crimen mayor "felonía".

Employee—complete this section and see note above ***Empleado—complete esta sección y note la notación arriba.***

1. Name. *Nombre.* ____________ Today's Date. *Fecha de Hoy.* ____________
2. Home Address. *Dirección Residencial.* ____________
3. City. *Ciudad.* ____________ State. *Estado.* ____________ Zip. *Código Postal.* ____________
4. Date of Injury. *Fecha de la lesión (accidente).* ____________ Time of Injury. *Hora en que ocurrió.* ______ a.m. ______ p.m.
5. Address and description of where injury happened. *Dirección/lugar dónde occurió el accidente.* ____________
6. Describe injury and part of body affected. *Describa la lesión y parte del cuerpo afectada.* ____________
7. Social Security Number. *Número de Seguro Social del Empleado.* ____________
8. Signature of employee. *Firma del empleado.* ____________

Employer—complete this section and see note below. ***Empleador—complete esta sección y note la notación abajo.***

9. Name of employer. *Nombre del empleador.* ____________
10. Address. *Dirección.* ____________
11. Date employer first knew of injury. *Fecha en que el empleador supo por primera vez de la lesión o accidente.* ____________
12. Date claim form was provided to employee. *Fecha en que se le entregó al empleado la petición.* ____________
13. Date employer received claim form. *Fecha en que el empleado devolvió la petición al empleador.* ____________
14. Name and address of insurance carrier or adjusting agency. *Nombre y dirección de la compañía de seguros o agencia adminstradora de seguros.* ____________
15. Insurance Policy Number. *El número de la póliza de Seguro.* ____________
16. Signature of employer representative. *Firma del representante del empleador.* ____________
17. Title. *Título.* ____________ 18. Telephone. *Teléfono.* ____________

Employer: You are required to date this form and provide copies to your insurer or claims administrator and to the employee, dependent or representative who filed the claim within **one working day** of receipt of the form from the employee.

SIGNING THIS FORM IS NOT AN ADMISSION OF LIABILITY

Empleador: *Se requiere que Ud. feche esta forma y que provéa copias a su compañía de seguros, administrador de reclamos, o dependiente/representante de reclamos y al empleado que hayan presentado esta petición dentro del plazo de **un día hábil** desde el momento de haber sido recibida la forma del empleado.*

EL FIRMAR ESTA FORMA NO SIGNIFICA ADMISION DE RESPONSABILIDAD

☐ Employer copy/*Copia del Empleador* ☐ Employee copy/ *Copia del Empleado* ☐ Claims Administrator/*Administrador de Reclamos* ☐ Temporary Receipt/*Recibo del Empleado*

7/1/04 Rev.

Note: Authority cited: Sections 133 and 5307.3, Labor Code. Reference: Sections 139.5, 4600, 4604.5, 4616, 4658.5, 4658.6, 5401, 5401.7 and 5402, Labor Code.

History: 1. Change without regulatory effect renumbering former section 10118.1 to section 10139 filed 4-7-2008 pursuant to section 100, title 1, California Code of Regulations (Register 2008, No. 15).

§10140. Employer's Responsibility to Process Claim Form, Claims Administrator's Duty to Provide Claim Form.

(a) Within one working day of receipt of a claim form, the employer shall date the claim form and provide a dated copy of the form to the employee and the employer's claims administrator.

(b) If the claims administrator obtains knowledge that the employer has not provided a claim form, it shall provide one to the employee within three working days of its knowledge that the form was not provided.

(c) If the claims administrator cannot determine if the employer has provided a claim form to the employee, the claims administrator shall provide one to the employee within 30 days of the administrator's date of knowledge of the claim.

Note: Authority cited: Sections 133 and 5307.3, Labor Code. Reference: Sections 5401 and 5402, Labor Code.

History: 1. Change without regulatory effect renumbering former section 10119 to section 10140 filed 4-7-2008 pursuant to section 100, title 1, California Code of Regulations (Register 2008, No. 15).

§10141. Dismissal of Inactive Claim by Operation of Law After Notice.

(a) Where a claim form has been filed for an injury that occurred prior to January 1, 1994, the claim has been denied, and there has been no activity for 180 days, the claims administrator may issue a notice of dismissal of the claim as follows:

(1) The notice shall include the following:

NOTICE REGARDING WORKERS' COMPENSATION CLAIM

You applied for workers' compensation benefits. A copy of your claim form is attached. We have not heard from you since we sent you a letter denying your claim on ___________ [Date]. Your case has been inactive for at least 180 days. If you are still claiming benefits, you must file an Application for Adjudication of Claim with the Workers' Compensation Appeal Board within 180 days of the date this notice is served on you. The date of service is listed at the bottom of this form. IF YOU DO NOT FILE THE APPLICATION BY THE DEADLINE, THE CLAIM WILL AUTOMATICALLY BE DISMISSED "BY OPERATION OF LAW". This means you will not be able to claim benefits for the injury or illness listed on the claim form unless you file the Application for Adjudication of Claim by the deadline. Please call me at ___________ [phone number] if you want more information or help figuring out the deadline for filing an Application.

You can get the Application form, help figuring out the deadline for filing an Application, and information about your claim by calling the State of California Division of Workers' Compensation Information and Assistance Office. [Enter telephone number of district Information and Assistance Office closest to injured workers' residence.] You may hear recorded information by calling 1-800-736-7401. You may also consult an attorney.

____

[Claims Administrator Representative]

Date Notice Is Served:__________

(2) The blank(s) in the prescribed notice language shall be completed by the claims administrator to specify the information described in brackets. The date of service of the Notice shall be inserted on the Notice by the claims administrator or process server to accurately reflect the date service is effected in accordance with the Code of Civil Procedure as specified in subsection (d).

(b) Where a claim form has been filed for an injury that occurred prior to January 1, 1994, benefits have been furnished, and there has been no activity for 180 days, the claims administrator may issue a notice of dismissal of the claim as follows:

(1) The notice shall include the following:

NOTICE REGARDING WORKERS' COMPENSATION CLAIM

You applied for workers' compensation benefits. A copy of your claim form is attached. Your case has been inactive for at least 180 days.

Your right to workers' compensation benefits will end on ___________ [Insert date – either five years from the date of injury or one year from the last furnishing of benefits, whichever is later], unless you file an Application for Adjudication of Claim by that date. That date is ___________ [insert either "five years from the date of your injury", or "one year from the date of the last benefit provided to you."]

IF YOU DO NOT FILE THE APPLICATION BY THE DEADLINE, THE CLAIM WILL AUTOMATICALLY BE DISMISSED "BY OPERATION OF LAW". This means you will not be able to claim further benefits for the injury or illness listed on the claim form unless you file the Application for Adjudication of Claim by the deadline. Please call me at ___________ [phone number] if you want more information.

You can get the application form and information about your claim by calling the State of California Division of Workers' Compensation Information and Assistance Office at ___________ [Enter telephone number of district Information and Assistance Office closest to injured worker's residence.] You may hear recorded information by calling 1-800-736-7401. You may also consult an attorney.

____

[Claims Administrator Representative]

(2) The date of last furnishing of benefits shall be the latter of: the latest date of receipt by the employee of medical or rehabilitation services, or the latest date that payment of any compensation benefit was mailed or personally delivered to the employee or any service provider.

(3) The blanks in the prescribed notice language shall be completed by the claims administrator to specify the information described in brackets.

(c) The Notice under (a)(2) and (b)(2) shall further contain the date(s) of injury, name of the employee, the name of the employer, identification of the claims administrator, including address and telephone number, and claim number, if any. A copy of the claim form(s) shall be attached to the notice prior to service.

(d) The claims administrator shall serve notice on the employee in the manner prescribed for a summons in a civil action in accordance with Article 3 (commencing with Section 415.10) of Chapter 4 of Title 5 of the Code of Civil Procedure.

If the employee is represented by an attorney, the claims administrator shall in addition serve a copy of the notice on the attorney by personal delivery or first class mail. Where no Application for Adjudication of Claim has been filed, but the Workers' Compensation Appeals Board has assigned a case number to the matter because of a pre-Application filing, the claims administrator shall also serve a copy of the notice on the appeals board. Proof of service shall be made in accordance with Title 8, CCR section 10975.

(e) The occurrence of any of the following during the 180 days prior to service of the notice is evidence that the claim is not inactive and there can be no dismissal under (a)(1) or (a)(2): the employee has made demand for payment or provision of benefits (whether indemnity, medical, or other), the claims administrator has knowledge that there are benefits due and unpaid, there has been treatment rendered for the industrial injury, there has been a medical-legal evaluation of the employee, there has been a deposition in regard to the claim, the claims administrator has other knowledge that the employee is actively pursuing his or her claim.

Note: Authority cited: Sections 133, 5307.3 and 5404.5, Labor Code. Reference: Sections 5401, 5402 and 5404.5, Labor Code.

History: 1. Change without regulatory effect renumbering former section 10120 to section 10141 filed 4-7-2008 pursuant to section 100, title 1, California Code of Regulations (Register 2008, No. 15).

§10142. Date of Denial for Purposes of End of Tolling of Limitations Period.

For purposes of Labor Code Section 5401(c), the date "the claim is denied" for determining when the claim form ceases to toll the specified limitations periods is:

(a) the date the written denial notice is personally served, or

(b) five days after the written denial notice is placed in the mail if the address is within the State of California, ten days if the address is outside the State of California, but within the United States and twenty days if the address is outside of the United States.

The written denial notice must be issued in accordance with the notice regulations in Title 8, CCR, Subchapter 1, Article 8, Sections 9810 et seq. in order to cease the claim form's tolling of the limitations periods.

Note: Authority cited: Sections 133 and 5307.3, Labor Code. Reference: Section 5401, Labor Code.

History: 1. Change without regulatory effect renumbering former section 10121 to section 10142 filed 4-7-2008 pursuant to section 100, title 1, California Code of Regulations (Register 2008, No. 15).

SUBCHAPTER 1.6 PERMANENT DISABILITY RATING DETERMINATION

§10150. Disability Evaluation Unit.

The Disability Evaluation Unit, under the direction and authority of the Administrative Director, will issue permanent disability ratings as required under this subchapter utilizing the Schedule for Rating Permanent Disabilities adopted by the Administrative Director. The Disability Evaluation Unit will prepare the following kinds of rating determinations:

(a) Formal rating determinations
(b) Summary rating determinations
(c) Consultative rating determinations
(d) Informal rating determinations.

Note: Authority cited: Sections 133 and 5307.3, Labor Code. Reference: Sections 124, 4061, 4660, 4662, 4663 and 4664, Labor Code.

History: 1. New section filed 4-25-91; operative 4-25-91 (Register 91, No. 26). New section is exempt from review by OAL pursuant to Government Code section 11351.

2. Amendment of subchapter 1.6 heading filed 12-27-96; operative 12-27-96. Submitted to OAL for printing only pursuant to Government Code section 11351 (Register 96, No. 52).

3. Amendment of section heading, section and Note filed 12-31-2004 as an emergency; operative 1-1-2005 (Register 2004, No. 53). A Certificate of Compliance must be transmitted to OAL by 5-2-2005 or emergency language will be repealed by operation of law on the following day.

4. Certificate of Compliance as to 12-31-2004 order transmitted to OAL 4-29-2005 and filed 6-10-2005 (Register 2005, No. 23).

Ref.: Hanna §§ 1.12[15], 32.05[1]; Herlick Handbook §§ 6.19, 6.20, 14.4; Lawyer's Guide to AMA *Guides* and Calif. Workers' Comp. §§ 2.02, 2.06[4].

§10151. Schedule for Rating Permanent Disabilities. [Repealed]

Note: Authority cited: Sections 4660, 133, 4061, 5307.3 and 5307.4, Labor Code. Reference: Sections 124 and 4061, Labor Code.

History: 1. New section filed 12-30-96; operative 12-30-96 pursuant to Government Code section 11343.4(d). Submitted to OAL for printing only pursuant to Government Code section 11351 (Register 97, No. 1).

2. Repealer filed 12-31-2004 as an emergency; operative 1-1-2005 (Register 2004, No. 53). A Certificate of Compliance must be transmitted to OAL by 5-2-2005 or emergency language will be repealed by operation of law on the following day.

3. Certificate of Compliance as to 12-31-2004 order transmitted to OAL 4-29-2005 and filed 6-10-2005 (Register 2005, No. 23).

§10152. Disability, When Considered Permanent.

A disability is considered permanent when the employee has reached maximal medical improvement, meaning his or her condition is well stabilized, and unlikely to change substantially in the next year with or without medical treatment.

Note: Authority cited: Sections 133 and 5307.3, Labor Code. Reference: Sections 124, 4061, 4062, 4062.01, 4062.1, 4660, 4662, 4663 and 4664, Labor Code.

History: 1. New section filed 4-25-91; operative 4-25-91 (Register 91, No. 26). New section is exempt from review by OAL pursuant to Government Code section 11351.

2. Amendment of section and Note filed 12-31-2004 as an emergency; operative 1-1-2005 (Register 2004, No. 53). A Certificate of Compliance must be transmitted to OAL by 5-2-2005 or emergency language will be repealed by operation of law on the following day.

3. Certificate of Compliance as to 12-31-2004 order transmitted to OAL 4-29-2005 and filed 6-10-2005 (Register 2005, No. 23).

Ref.: Hanna §§ 8.01, 8.03, 32.02[1]; Herlick Handbook §§ 6.19, 6.20, 14.4; Lawyer's Guide to AMA *Guides* and Calif. Workers' Comp. § 3.03.

§10154. Permanent Disability Rating Determinations, Kinds. [Repealed]

Note: Authority cited: Sections 133, 5307.3 and 5307.4, Labor Code. Reference: Sections 124. 4061, 5452, 5701 and 5703.5, Labor Code.

History: 1. New section filed 4-25-91; operative 4-25-91 (Register 91, No. 26). New section is exempt from review by OAL pursuant to Government Code section 11351.

2. New subsection (d) filed 12-27-96; operative 12-27-96. Submitted to OAL for printing only pursuant to Government Code section 11351 (Register 96, No. 52).

3. Repealer filed 12-31-2004 as an emergency; operative 1-1-2005 (Register 2004, No. 53). A Certificate

of Compliance must be transmitted to OAL by 5-2-2005 or emergency language will be repealed by operation of law on the following day.

4. Certificate of Compliance as to 12-31-2004 order transmitted to OAL 4-29-2005 and filed 6-10-2005 (Register 2005, No. 23).

§10156. Formal Rating Determinations.

A formal rating determination will be prepared by the Disability Evaluation Unit when requested by the Appeals Board or a Workers' Compensation Judge on a form specified for that purpose by the Administrative Director. The form will provide for a description of the disability to be rated, the occupation of the injured employee, the employee's age at the time of injury, the date of injury, the formula used, and a notice of submission in accordance with Appeals Board Rules of Practice and Procedure.

Note: Authority cited: Sections 133 and 5307.3, Labor Code. Reference: Sections 124, 4061, 4660, 4662, 4663, 4664 and 5701, Labor Code.

History: 1. New section filed 4-25-91; operative 4-25-91 (Register 91, No. 26). New section is exempt from review by OAL pursuant to Government Code section 11351.

2. Amendment of section and Note filed 12-31-2004 as an emergency; operative 1-1-2005 (Register 2004, No. 53). A Certificate of Compliance must be transmitted to OAL by 5-2-2005 or emergency language will be repealed by operation of law on the following day.

3. Certificate of Compliance as to 12-31-2004 order transmitted to OAL 4-29-2005 and filed 6-10-2005 (Register 2005, No. 23).

Ref.: Hanna § 32.05[6][a]; Herlick Handbook §§ 6.19, 6.20, 14.4; Lawyer's Guide to AMA *Guides* and Calif. Workers' Comp. §§ 2.02, 2.06[4].

§10158. Formal Rating Determinations As Evidence.

Formal rating determinations prepared by disability evaluators shall be deemed to constitute evidence only as to the relation between the disability or impairment standard(s) described and the percentage of permanent disability.

Note: Authority cited: Sections 133 and 5307.3, Labor Code. Reference: Sections 124, 4061, 4660, 4662, 4663 and 4664, Labor Code.

History: 1. New section filed 4-25-91; operative 4-25-91 (Register 91, No. 26). New section is exempt from review by OAL pursuant to Government Code section 11351.

2. Amendment of section and Note filed 12-31-2004 as an emergency; operative 1-1-2005 (Register 2004, No. 53). A Certificate of Compliance must be transmitted to OAL by 5-2-2005 or emergency language will be repealed by operation of law on the following day.

3. Certificate of Compliance as to 12-31-2004 order transmitted to OAL 4-29-2005 and filed 6-10-2005 (Register 2005, No. 23).

Ref.: Hanna § 32.05[2]; Herlick Handbook §§ 6.19, 6.20, 14.4; Lawyer's Guide to AMA *Guides* and Calif. Workers' Comp. §§ 2.02, 2.06[4].

§10160. Summary Rating Determinations, Comprehensive Medical Evaluation of Unrepresented Employee.

(a) The Disability Evaluation Unit will prepare a summary rating determination upon receipt of a properly prepared request. A properly prepared request shall consist of:

(1) A completed Request for Summary Rating Determination, DEU Form 101;

(2) A completed Employee's Disability Questionnaire, DEU Form 100;

(3) A comprehensive medical evaluation of an unrepresented employee from a Qualified Medical Evaluator.

(b) The insurance carrier or self-insured employer shall provide the employee with an Employee's Disability Questionnaire (DEU Form 100) prior to the appointment scheduled with the Qualified Medical Evaluator. The employee will be instructed in the form and manner prescribed by the Administrative Director to complete the questionnaire and provide it to the Qualified Evaluator at the time of the examination.

(c) The insurance carrier, self-insured employer or injured worker shall complete a Request for Summary Rating Determination (DEU Form 101), a copy of which shall be served on the opposing party. The requesting party shall send the request, including proof of service of the request on the opposing party, to the Qualified Medical Evaluator together with all medical reports and medical records relating to the case prior to the scheduled examination with the Qualified Medical Evaluator. The request shall include the appropriate address of the Disability Evaluation Unit. A listing of all of the offices of the Disability Evaluation Unit, with each office's area of jurisdiction, will be provided, upon request, by any office of the Disability Evaluation Unit or any Information and Assistance Office.

(d) When a summary rating determination has been requested, the Qualified Medical Evaluator shall submit all of the following documents to the Disability Evaluation Unit at the location indicated on the DEU Form 101 and shall concurrently serve copies on the employee and claims administrator:

1. Request for Summary Rating Determination of Qualified Medical Evaluator's Report (DEU Form 101) as a cover sheet to the evaluation report;

2. Employee's Disability Questionnaire (DEU Form 100);

3. Comprehensive medical evaluation by the Qualified Medical Evaluator, including the Qualified Medical Evaluator's Findings Summary Form (IMC Form 1002).

(e) No request for a summary rating determination will be considered to be received until the DEU Form 100, the DEU Form 101, and the comprehensive medical evaluation have been received by the office of the Disability Evaluation Unit having jurisdiction over the employee's area of residence. In the event an employee does not have a completed Employee's Disability Questionnaire (DEU Form 100) at the time of his or her appointment with a Qualified Medical Evaluator, the medical evaluator shall provide this form to the employee for completion prior to the evaluation. Any requests received on or after April 1, 1994 without all the required documents will be returned to the sender.

(f) Any request for the rating of a supplemental comprehensive medical evaluation report shall be made no later than twenty days from the receipt of the report and shall be accompanied by a copy of the correspondence to the evaluator soliciting the supplemental evaluation, together with proof of service of the correspondence on the opposing party.

Note: Authority cited: Sections 133 and 5307.3, Labor Code. Reference: Sections 124, 4061, 4062, 4062.01, 4062.1, 4062.2, 4062.5, 4064, 4067, 4660, 4662, 4663 and 4664, Labor Code.

History: 1. New section filed 4-25-91; operative 4-25-91 (Register 91, No. 26). New section is exempt from review by OAL pursuant to Government Code section 11351.

2. Amendment of section filed 1-28-94; operative 1-28-94. Submitted to OAL for printing only pursuant to Government Code section 11351 (Register 94, No. 4).

3. Amendment of section heading and text filed 2-21-95; operative 2-21-95. Submitted to OAL for printing only pursuant to Government Code section 11351 (Register 95, No. 8).

4. Amendment of subsections (c)-(d) and (f) and amendment of Note filed 12-31-2004 as an emergency; operative 1-1-2005 (Register 2004, No. 53). A Certificate of Compliance must be transmitted to OAL by 5-2-2005 or emergency language will be repealed by operation of law on the following day.

5. Certificate of Compliance as to 12-31-2004 order, including amendment of subsections (a)(2), (b), (d) and (e), transmitted to OAL 4-29-2005 and filed 6-10-2005 (Register 2005, No. 23).

Ref.: Hanna §§ 22.06[1][b], 32.05[3][b][ii]; Herlick Handbook §§ 6.19, 6.20, 14.4.

§10160.1. Summary Rating Determinations, Report of Primary Treating Physician for Unrepresented Employee.

For injuries on or after January 1, 1994, the insurance carrier, self-insured employer or the employee may request a summary rating of the primary treating physician's report prepared in accordance with Section 9785.5. The request may be made by completing a Request for Summary Rating Determination of Primary Treating Physician's Report (DEU Form 102) and sending the request to the Disability Evaluation Unit together with a copy of the primary treating physician's report. A copy of the request form and a copy of the primary treating physician's report must be served concurrently on the non-requesting party, including a proof of service on the non-requesting party.

Note: Authority cited: Sections 133, 5307.3 and 5307.4, Labor Code. Reference: Sections 124, 4061, 4061.5, 4062, 4062.1, 4062.2, 4062.5, 4064 and 4067, Labor Code.

History: 1. New section filed 2-21-95; operative 2-21-95. Submitted to OAL for printing only pursuant to Government Code section 11351 (Register 95, No. 8).

Ref.: Hanna § 32.05[3][b][ii]; Herlick Handbook §§ 6.19, 6.20, 14.4.

§10160.5. Summary Rating Determinations, Represented Employees.

(a) For injuries on or after January 1, 1991 and before January 1, 1994, the Disability Evaluation Unit will prepare a summary rating determination in cases where the injured worker is represented only if requested by a party. A summary rating determination will be prepared only upon receipt of a properly prepared request. A properly prepared request shall consist of:

(1) A completed Request for Summary Rating Determination (DEU Form 101);

(2) An evaluation by a Qualified Medical Evaluator or Agreed Medical Evaluator.

(b) The requesting party shall complete a Request for Summary Rating Determination (DEU Form 101) and submit it together with all medical reports and medical records concerning the case to the medical evaluator. The medical evaluator shall send the completed medical evaluation report together with the Request for Summary Rating Determination to the office of the Disability Evaluation Unit designated by the Administrative Director and specific on the Request for Summary Rating Determination (DEU Form 101) and shall simultaneously serve the party or parties requesting the evaluation.

(c) Notwithstanding the provisions of subdivision (b), a party may request a summary rating determination following receipt of a medical report prepared by a Qualified Medical Evaluator or Agreed Medical Evaluator on a represented case. The party shall send the Request for Summary Rating Determination (DEU Form 101) and the medical report to the DEU office designated by the Administrative Director and shall simultaneously serve the other party.

(d) If a case is settled prior to receipt of a summary rating which has been requested, the requesting party shall notify the DEU office to which the request was directed.

Note: Authority cited: Sections 133, 5307.3 and 5307.4, Labor Code. Reference: Sections 124, 4061, 4062, 4062.1, 4062.2, 4062.5, 4064 and 4067, Labor Code.

History: 1. New section filed 4-25-91; operative 4-25-91 (Register 91, No. 26). New section is exempt from review by OAL pursuant to Government Code section 11351.

2. Amendment of section filed 1-28-94; operative 1-28-94. Submitted to OAL for printing only pursuant to Government Code section 11351 (Register 94, No. 4).

3. Amendment of section heading and subsections (a)-(c), repealer of subsection (d), subsection relettering, and amendment of redesignated subsection (d) filed 2-21-95; operative 2-21-95. Submitted to OAL for printing only pursuant to Government Code section 11351 (Register 95, No. 8).

Ref.: Hanna § 32.05[3][b][i]; Herlick Handbook §§ 6.19, 6.20, 14.4.

§10161. Forms.

(a) Employee's Disability Questionnaire (DEU Form 100) (revised 4/05).

(b) Request for Summary Determination of Qualified Medical Evaluator's Report (DEU Form 101) (revised 4/05).

(c) Request for Summary Determination of Primary Treating Physician's Report (DEU Form 102)

STATE OF CALIFORNIA
Division of Workers' Compensation
Disability Evaluation Unit

EMPLOYEE'S DISABILITY QUESTIONNAIRE

This form will aid the doctor in determining your permanent impairment or disability. Please complete this form and give it to the physician who will be performing the evaluation. The doctor will include this form with his or her report and submit it to the Disability Evaluation Unit, with a copy to you and your claims administrator.

Employee	Employer
Social Security No.	Nature of employer's business
Street and Number	
City, State, Zip Code	Claim number
Date of Injury	Date of Birth

PLEASE ANSWER THE FOLLOWING QUESTIONS FULLY, using reverse side if needed:

How was your evaluating doctor selected? (check one)

☐ From a list of doctors provided by the State of California, Division of Workers' Compensation.

☐ Other (explain)____________________

What is the name of the doctor who will be doing the evaluation?____________________

When is your examination scheduled?____________________

What were your job duties at the time of your injury?

What is the disability resulting from your injury?

How does this injury affect you in your work?

Have you ever had a disability as a result of another injury or illness? If so, when?____________________

Please describe the disability?____________________

Sign here ____________________ Date: ____________________

DEU Form 100
(Rev. 06-05)

REQUEST FOR SUMMARY RATING DETERMINATION
of Qualified Medical Evaluator's Report
State of California
Division of Workers' Compensation
Disability Evaluation Unit

DEU Use Only

INSTRUCTIONS TO THE CLAIMS ADMINISTRATOR:

1. Use this form if employee is unrepresented and has not filed an application for adjudication.
2. Complete this form and forward it along with a complete copy of all medical reports and medical records concerning this case to the physician scheduled to evaluate the existence and extent of permanent impairment or disability.
3. Send the EMPLOYEE'S DISABILITY QUESTIONNAIRE, DEU FORM 100 to the employee in time for the medical evaluation.
4. **This form must be served on the employee prior to the evaluation. Be sure to complete the proof of service.**

INSTRUCTIONS TO THE PHYSICIAN:

1. If the employee is unrepresented, review and comment upon the Employee's Disability Questionnaire, (DEU Form 100), in your report. (If the employee does not have a completed Form 100 at the time of the appointment, please provide the form to the employee.)
2. Submit your completed medical evaluation and, if the employee is unrepresented, the DEU Form 100, to the Disability Evaluation Unit district office listed below. **PLEASE USE THIS FORM AS A COVER SHEET FOR SUBMISSION TO THE DISABILITY EVALUATION UNIT.**
3. Serve a copy of your report and the Form 100 upon the claims administrator and the employee.

Date of first medical report indicating the existence of permanent impairment or disability: ____________
Last date for which temporary disability indemnity was paid: ____________

SUBMIT TO: DISABILITY EVALUATION UNIT
Mailing Address:
City, State, Zip:

CLAIMS ADMINISTRATOR
Company:
Mailing Address:
City, State, Zip:
Claim No:
Phone No:
Adjustor:
EMPLOYER:

PHYSICIAN:
EXAM DATE:

EMPLOYEE
Name:
Mailing Address:
City, State, Zip:
Date of Injury:
Date of Birth:
Social Security #:
WCAB Case No. (if any):

OCCUPATION: ____________________________
(Please attach job description or job analysis, if available)

WEEKLY GROSS EARNINGS: ____________________ (Attach a wage statement/DLSR 5020 if earnings are less than maximum. Include the value of additional advantages provided such as meals, lodging, etc. If earnings are irregular or for less than 30 hours per week, include a detailed description of all earnings of the employee from all sources, including other employers, for one year prior to the date of injury. Benefits will be calculated at MAXIMUM RATE unless a complete and detailed statement of earnings is attached.)

DEU Form 101
(Rev. 06-05)

PROOF OF SERVICE BY MAIL

On ______________________, I served a copy of this Request for Summary Rating Determination on
(date)

______________________________ at ______________________________
(name of employee) *(address)*

by placing a true copy enclosed in a sealed envelope with postage fully prepaid, and deposited in the U.S. Mail. I declare under penalty of perjury under the laws of the State of California that the foregoing is true and correct.

Signature______________________________

DEU Form 101
(Rev. 06-05)

REQUEST FOR SUMMARY RATING DETERMINATION
of Primary Treating Physician's Report

State of California
Division of Workers' Compensation
Disability Evaluation Unit

DEU Use Only

To be used for injuries which occur on or after January 1, 1994.

INSTRUCTIONS :
1. Complete this form and send it to the Disability Evaluation Unit along with a copy of the primary treating physician's report.
2. This form and any attachments including a copy of the primary treating physician's report must be served on the other party .
3. If you receive the completed form from the other party and you disagree with the description of the occupation or earnings, please attach the correct information to a copy of this form and send it to the Disability Evaluation Unit. You must also send a copy of your objection to the other party.

REQUEST IS MADE BY:
____ Employee
____ Claims Administrator

PHYSICIAN:
EXAM DATE:

CLAIMS ADMINISTRATOR
Company:
Mailing Address:
City, State, Zip:
Claim No:
Phone No.:
Adjustor:

EMPLOYEE
Name:
Mailing Address:
City, State, Zip:
Date of Injury:
Date of Birth:
Social Security #:
WCAB Case No. (if any):

EMPLOYER:______________________________

NATURE OF EMPLOYER'S BUSINESS:______________________________________

JOB TITLE:____________________________

DESCRIBE THE GENERAL DUTIES OF THE JOB (Attach job description or job analysis, if available):
____
____

WEEKLY GROSS EARNINGS: $______________________ Attach a wage statement/DLSR 5020 if earnings are less than maximum. Include the value of additional advantages provided such as meals, lodging, etc. If earnings are irregular or for less than 30 hours per week, include a detailed description of all earnings of the employee from all sources, including other employers, for one year prior to the date of injury. Benefits will be calculated at MAXIMUM RATE unless a complete and detailed statement of earnings is received.

PROOF OF SERVICE BY MAIL

On ______________ I served a copy of this Request for Summary Rating Determination on
(date)
____ at ______________________________ by placing
(name of employee or claims administrator) *(address)*
a true copy enclosed in a sealed envelope with postage fully prepaid, and deposited in the U.S. Mail. I declare under penalty of perjury under the laws of the State of California that the foregoing is true and correct.

Signature________________________________

DEU FORM 102 (2/95)

Note: Authority cited: Sections 133 and 5307.3, Labor Code. Reference: Sections 124, 4061, 4062, 4062.01, 4062.1, 4062.2, 4062.5, 4064, 4067, 4660, 4662, 4663 and 4664, Labor Code.

History: 1. New section filed 4-25-91; operative 4-25-91 (Register 91, No. 26). New section is exempt from review by OAL pursuant to Government Code section 11351.

2. Repealer and new DEU Form 100 filed 1-28-94; operative 1-28-94. Submitted to OAL for printing only pursuant to Government Code section 11351 (Register 94, No. 4).

3. Editorial correction restoring inadvertently omitted subsection (b) (Register 95, No. 8).

4. Amendment of subsections (a), (b) and forms 100 and 101; and new subsection (c) and form 102 filed 2-21-95; operative 2-21-95. Submitted to OAL for printing only pursuant to Government Code section 11351 (Register 95, No. 8).

5. Certificate of Compliance as to 12-31-2004 order, including further amendment of section and forms and amendment of Note, transmitted to OAL 4-29-2005 and filed 6-10-2005 (Register 2005, No. 23).

Ref.: Hanna § 32.05[3][b][i]–[ii]; Herlick Handbook §§ 6.19, 6.20, 14.4.

§10161.1. Reproduction of Forms.

The Request for Summary Rating Determination (DEU Form 101), the Employee's Permanent Disability Questionnaire (DEU Form 100), and the Request for Summary Rating Determination of the primary treating physician (DEU Form 102) may be reproduced by automated office equipment or other means as long as the content is identical to the specified form.

History: 1. New section filed 2-21-95; operative 2-21-95. Submitted to OAL for printing only pursuant to Government Code section 11351 (Register 95, No. 8).

2. Amendment of section number filed 8-8-95; operative 8-8-95. Submitted to OAL for printing only pursuant to Government Code section 11351 (Register 95, No. 32).

Ref.: Hanna §§F11.01[2], F11.02[2], F11.03[2]; Herlick Handbook §§ 6.19, 6.20, 14.4.

§10162. Summary Rating Determination, Apportionment.

In cases where the injured worker is not represented and a Qualified Medical Evaluator's formal medical evaluation indicates apportionment of the permanent disablility, a summary rating determination will not be made until a Workers' Compensation Judge has reviewed the medical evaluation to determine if the apportionment is inconsistent with the law. The determination of the Workers' Compensation Judge will not be admissible in any judicial proceeding.

Upon receipt of a formal medical evaluation which apportions the disability, the Disability Evaluation Unit will transmit the medical evaluation to the Presiding Workers' Judge of the office of the Appeals Board designated by the Disability Evaluation Unit, with a request to review the apportionment to determine whether it is inconsistent with the law. The Workers' Compensation Judge will make the determination and respond to the Disability Evaluation within 45 days.

If the Workers' Compensation Judge refers the medical report back to the Qualified Medical Evaluator for correction or clarification, the Qualified Medical Evaluator shall provide a response to the Workers' Compensation Judge within 30 days of the referral. If no response is received, the Workers' Compensation Judge will make a determination whether the apportionment is inconsistent with the law, and a summary rating determination will be made.

In cases where the injured worker is represented and an Agreed Medical Evaluator or Qualified Medical Evaluator apportions the permanent disability, the Disability Evaluation Unit will issue a summary rating determination "Before Apportionment."

Note: Authority cited: Sections 133, 5307.3 and 5307.4, Labor Code. Reference: Sections 124 and 4061, Labor Code.

History: 1. New section filed 4-25-91; effective 4-25-91 (Register 91, No. 26).

Ref.: Hanna § 32.05[3][d]; Herlick Handbook §§ 6.19, 6.20, 14.4.

§10163. Apportionment Referral.

STATE OF CALIFORNIA
Department of Industrial Relations
Division of Workers' Compensation
DISABILITY EVALUATION UNIT

APPORTIONMENT REFERRAL

Date: ____________________

TO: Presiding Workers' Comp. Judge, ____________________
(Office)

FROM: Disability Evaluation Unit, ____________________
(Office)

SUBJECT: DEU File:
Employee:
QME:
Date of Report:

The attached formal medical evaluation report indicates that part or all of the permanent disability may be subject to apportionment pursuant to Labor Code Section 4663 and/or Labor Code Section 4664. Please determine whether the apportionment is inconsistent with the law.

If you believe the apportionment is inconsistent with the law, you may refer the report back to the medical evaluator for correction or clarification. If you receive no response from the medical evaluator within 30 days from your request, please make your determination based on the original report.

After checking the appropriate space, sign and date the bottom of this form and return it with the medical report to the DEU office listed above.

Thank you.

The apportionment: IS CONSISTENT _______ or
IS NOT CONSISTENT _______ with the law.

____________________, **Workers' Compensation Judge**
(Signature)

____
(Date)

NOTE: This memorandum is an administrative document and is not admissible in any judicial proceeding.

DEU Form 105
(Rev. 06-05)

Note: Authority cited: Sections 133 and 5307.3, Labor Code. Reference: Sections 124, 4061, 4062, 4062.01, 4062.1, 4062.2, 4062.5, 4064, 4067, 4660, 4662, 4663 and 4664, Labor Code.

History: 1. New section filed 4-25-91; operative 4-25-91 (Register 91, No. 26). New section is exempt from review by OAL pursuant to Government Code section 11351.

2. Amendment of section and Note filed 12-31-2004 as an emergency; operative 1-1-2005 (Register 2004, No. 53). A Certificate of Compliance must be transmitted to OAL by 5-2-2005 or emergency language will be repealed by operation of law on the following day.

3. Certificate of Compliance as to 12-31-2004 order, including further amendment of Note, transmitted to OAL 4-29-2005 and filed 6-10-2005 (Register 2005, No. 23).

Ref.: Hanna § F11.06[2]; Herlick Handbook §§ 6.19, 6.20, 14.4.

§10164. Summary Rating Determinations, Reconsideration If Employee Is Unrepresented.

(a) Requests for reconsideration of the summary rating determination must be filed with the Administrative Director in writing within 30 days of receipt of the summary rating determination. The request shall clearly specify the reasons the summary rating determination should be reconsidered and shall be accompanied by a copy of the summary rating, a copy of the comprehensive medical evaluation, proof of service on the other party and any other information necessary to support the request. Reconsideration of a summary rating may be granted by the administrative director for one or more of the following reasons:

(1) the summary rating was incorrectly calculated,

(2) the comprehensive medical evaluation failed to address one or more issues;

(3) the comprehensive medical evaluation failed to completely address one or more issues;

(4) the comprehensive medical evaluation was not prepared in accordance with required procedures, including the procedures of the Industrial Medical Council promulgated under paragraph (2) or (3) of subdivision (j) of Section 139.2.

Requests for reconsideration which are not based on one of the above reasons will be denied.

(b) The Administrative Director shall not accept or consider, as a basis for a request for reconsideration, a supplemental or follow-up evaluation which was requested by a party after a summary rating determination has already been issued to the parties.

(c) If the Administrative Director determines that an additional evaluation from another Qualified Medical Evaluator is necessary, the matter shall be referred to the Executive Medical Director of the Industrial Medical Council for the provision of another Qualified Medical Evaluator.

Note: Authority cited: Sections 133, 5307.3 and 5307.4, Labor Code. Reference: Sections 124 and 4061, Labor Code.

History: 1. New section filed 4-25-91; operative 4-25-91 (Register 91, No. 26). New section is exempt from review by OAL pursuant to Government Code section 11351.

2. Amendment of section filed 1-28-94; operative 1-28-94. Submitted to OAL for printing only pursuant to Government Code section 11351 (Register 94, No. 4).

3. Amendment of section heading, repealer of subsection (a), subsection relettering, amendment of redesignated subsection (a), new subsections (a)(1)-(4) and (b) and amendment of subsection (c) filed 2-21-95; operative 2-21-95. Submitted to OAL for printing only pursuant to Government Code section 11351 (Register 95, No. 8).

Ref.: Hanna § 32.05[3][c]; Herlick Handbook §§ 6.19, 6.20, 14.4.

§10165. Service of Summary Rating Determination and Notice of Options Following Permanent Disability Rating.

Within the time specified in Labor Code Section 4061(h), the Office of Benefit Determination shall serve the permanent disability rating determination on the employee and employer by first class mail. At the same time, the employee shall also be served with the Notice of Options Following Permanent Disability Rating.

Note: Authority cited: Sections 133, 5307.3 and 5307.4, Labor Code. Reference: Sections 124 and 4061, Labor Code.

History: 1. New section filed 4-25-91; effective 4-25-91 (Register 91, No. 26).

Ref.: Hanna § 32.05[3][c]; Herlick Handbook §§ 6.19, 6.20, 14.4.

§10165.5. Notice of Options Following Disability Rating (DEU Form 110).

STATE OF CALIFORNIA
Department of Industrial Relations
Division of Workers' Compensation
DISABILITY EVALUATION UNIT

NOTICE OF OPTIONS FOLLOWING DISABILITY RATING

This is a disability rating determination (Rating) prepared by the State of California Disability Evaluation Unit within the Division of Workers' Compensation. It describes your percentage of disability. This percentage is based on your limitations as reported by the doctor, your potential loss of future earning capacity, your age, and the type of work you were doing at the time of your injury. If the rating indicates that you have some permanent disability, you should automatically begin to receive permanent disability payments. Payments are made in installments, every two weeks, for the number of weeks shown on the rating, less any permanent disability payments made to you prior to the rating.

If the rating is not disputed by you or your employer, you do not have to take any action to receive your benefits. We do want you to know that you may have two options you may want to consider. They are:

1) STIPULATED FINDINGS AND AWARD;
2) COMPROMISE AND RELEASE;

1) STIPULATED FINDINGS AND AWARD

If you and the employer, carrier or agent, accept the rating, written agreements may be submitted to the Workers' Compensation Appeals Board (WCAB) requesting that an Award be made without the need for a hearing. We recommend this option when the rating is not disputed, and you have a need for future medical care. A Workers' Compensation Judge will review the stipulations and issue an award.

ADVANTAGES

- A stipulated award is a quick, easy way to settle your case while protecting your rights;
- There is no need to take time off work to go to a hearing;
- The Division of Workers' Compensation will review the settlement to protect your rights at no cost to you; there is no need to hire a lawyer;
- If your condition worsens, you can apply for additional payments anytime within five years from the date of your injury;
- If you need additional medical care or you are to receive a life pension (rating of 70% or more), your rights to future benefits can be fully protected and a judge can enforce the award if there later becomes a problem.
- You may request a lump sum payment of all or part of your permanent disability if you can show a financial need or hardship. However, a Workers' Compensation Judge must first be convinced that it would be in your best interest.

DISADVANTAGES

- You normally will not receive a lump sum payment, but will receive your benefits in payments every two weeks.

2) COMPROMISE AND RELEASE

A Compromise and Release Agreement is a settlement which usually permanently closes all aspects of a workers' compensation claim except for vocational rehabilitation benefits, including any provision for future medical care.

The Compromise and Release is paid in one lump sum to you. It must be reviewed and approved by a Workers' Compensation Judge.

ADVANTAGES

- You may receive more money than you would receive under a Stipulated Findings and Award because you are giving up your future rights in exchange for money.
- If the employer or insurance company disputes the rating, a Compromise and Release will assure you receive an agreed amount of money now rather than risk getting nothing or a lesser amount later.
- You will receive your benefits in one lump sum.

DISADVANTAGES

- A Compromise and Release usually permanently releases the employer from all future responsibilities. After your case has been resolved by a Compromise and Release Agreement, you cannot ask for more medical treatment at your employer's expense, nor can you claim additional benefits if your disability or condition becomes worse. Also, if you later die as a result of the injury, your dependents would not be entitled to death benefits.
- Once a Workers' Compensation Judge has approved your Compromise and Release, the settlement is final and it cannot be set aside except in very rare circumstances.

If you would like more information, you can receive recorded information free of charge, by calling 1-800-736-7401 or you may contact your local Information and Assistance officer (listed in the state government section of your telephone book under Department of Industrial Relations, Division of Workers' Compensation). You may also consult an attorney of your choice.

SPECIAL NOTICE TO UNREPRESENTED INJURED WORKERS

If you disagree with the rating because you believe that the rating was improperly calculated or that the doctor failed to address any or all issues or failed to properly rate your impairment, you may request administrative review of the rating within 30 days of receipt of the rating, from the Administrative Director of the Division of Workers' Compensation. In some cases, you may be entitled to an additional medical evaluation or a different medical specialist. Your request should include a copy of the rating and a copy of the report from the doctor. A copy of the request must be sent to your claims adjustor.

If you have questions about whether to request administrative review of your rating or whether another medical evaluation is appropriate, you should contact the local Information and Assistance Officer listed in the state government section of your telephone book under Department of Industrial Relations, Division of Workers' Compensation. They can tell you how to file the request if you decide to do so.

DEU Form 110
(Rev. 06-05)

3

Note: Authority cited: Sections 133 and 5307.3, Labor Code. Reference: Sections 124, 4061, 4062, 4062.01, 4062.1, 4062.2, 4062.5, 4064, 4067, 4660, 4662, 4663 and 4664, Labor Code.

History: 1. New section filed 4-25-91; operative 4-25-91 (Register 91, No. 26). New section is exempt from review by OAL pursuant to Government Code section 11351.

2. Amendment of section filed 1-28-94; operative 1-28-94. Submitted to OAL for printing only pursuant to Government Code section 11351 (Register 94, No. 4).

3. Amendment of section and Note filed 12-31-2004 as an emergency; operative 1-1-2005 (Register 2004, No. 53). A Certificate of Compliance must be transmitted to OAL by 5-2-2005 or emergency language will be repealed by operation of law on the following day.

4. Certificate of Compliance as to 12-31-2004 order, including further amendment of section and Note,

transmitted to OAL 4-29-2005 and filed 6-10-2005 (Register 2005, No. 23).

Ref.: Hanna § 32.05[3][c]; Herlick Handbook §§ 6.19, 6.20, 14.4.

§10166. Consultative Rating Determinations.

(a) The Disability Evaluation Unit will prepare consultative rating determinations upon request of the Workers' Compensation Appeals Board, Workers' Compensation Judges, Settlement Conference Referees, Arbitrators, Workers' Compensation Judges Pro-Tempore and Information & Assistance Officers.

(b) Consultative rating determinations may be requested for the purpose of determining the ratable significance of factors, reviewing proposed Compromise and Release Agreements for adequacy, determining commuted values, resolving occupational questions or any other matters within the expertise of the disability evaluators. These rating determinations are the "informal ratings" referred to in subsection (k) of section 10301 of the Workers' Compensation Appeals Board Rules of Practice and Procedure. Consultative Rating Determinations will not be admissible in judicial proceedings.

(c) The Disability Evaluation Unit may also prepare consultative rating determinations upon receipt of reasonable requests from employers, injured workers or their respective representatives. A request is not considered reasonable where an insurance carrier or self-insurer seeks a consultative rating determination for the purpose of terminating its self-insurer seeks a consultative rating determination for the purpose of terminating its liability or for negotiating a Compromise and Release settlement where the injured worker has no representative. Consultative rating determinations shall not to be used as a substitute for summary rating determinations.

(d) In all cases the person making a request for a consultative rating determination will provide the Disability Evaluation Unit with the occupation and age of the injured worker at the time of injury.

(e) No consultative rating determination will be provided on cases in which an application for adjudication of claim has been filed with the Appeals Board without prior written authorization of the Appeals Board, a Workers' Compensation Judge, Settlement Conference Referee, Arbitrator, Workers' Compensation Judge Pro-Tempore, or Information & Assistance Officer. In cases where an application has been filed, the disability evaluator may require that any request for consultative rating determination be accompanied by the Appeals Board file.

Note: Authority cited: Sections 133, 5307.3 and 5307.4, Labor Code. Reference: Sections 123.6, 123.7, 124, 5275, 5451, 5502, 5701 and 5703.5, Labor Code.

History: 1. New section filed 4-25-91; operative 4-25-91 (Register 91, No. 26). New section is exempt from review by OAL pursuant to Government Code section 11351.

2. Amendment of section filed 1-28-94; operative 1-28-94. Submitted to OAL for printing only pursuant to Government Code section 11351 (Register 94, No. 4).

Ref.: Hanna § 32.05[5]; Herlick Handbook §§ 6.19, 6.20, 14.4.

§10167. Informal Ratings.

An informal rating will be prepared by the Disability Evaluation Unit upon the request of both the employee and/or his/her representative and the employer, or at the request of an Information and Assistance Officer providing the necessary information. Such requests shall be submitted on forms and in a manner prescribed by the Administrative Director. Informal ratings shall be issued only in those instances where an Application for Adjudication of Claim has not been filed with the Appeals Board. All medical reports pertaining to the case must be submitted with the request.

The Disability Evaluation Unit may request the employee to submit to a medical examination as provided for under Labor Code Sections 4050, 4600, and 5703.5.

The Disability Evaluation Unit will issue the informal rating on a form prescribed for that purpose by the Administrative Director, which will contain a statement that the informal rating is not: a) a finding, award, order or decision of the Appeals Board, and b) evidence as to the existence of the factors of disability.

Where the informal rating indicates a life pension, or provision for future medical treatment appears indicated, the Disability Evaluation Unit will forward a copy of the rating to an Information and Assistance Officer for the purpose of obtaining a stipulated award, or other action as may be appropriate.

Self-ratings prepared by the employer are not acceptable substitutes for informal ratings prepared by the Disability Evaluation Unit.

Note: Authority cited: Sections 133 and 5307.3, Labor Code. Reference: Section 4061, Labor Code.

History: 1. New section filed 12-27-96; operative 12-27-96. Submitted to OAL for printing only pursuant to Government Code section 11351 (Register 96, No. 52).

Ref.: Hanna §§ 23.04, 31.10[2], 32.05[4]; Herlick Handbook §§ 6.19, 6.20, 10.2, 14.4.

§10168. Records, Destruction of.

(a) The Disability Evaluation Unit's copies of requests for, and instructions on formal rating determinations, together with the disability evaluator's work notes shall be destroyed by the unit two years after the date of issuance of the formal rating determination by the disability evaluator.

(b) Requests for summary rating determinations and informal ratings, the documents and reports pertaining thereto, the rating and work notes of the disability evaluators, shall be destroyed by the unit two years after issuance of the summary or informal rating, unless there is evidence of on-going activity.

The approval of the Department of Finance, as required by the provisions of Government Code section 14755, is recognized.

Note: Authority cited: Sections 133, 135 and 5307.3, Labor Code. Reference: Sections 135 and 4061, Labor Code; and Section 14755, Government Code.

History: 1. New section filed 4-25-91; operative 4-25-91 (Register 91, No. 26). New section is exempt from review by OAL pursuant to Government Code section 11351.

2. Amendment filed 3-27-95; operative 3-27-95. Submitted to OAL for printing only pursuant to Government Code section 11351 (Register 95, No. 13).

3. Amendment of section and Note filed 12-27-96; operative 12-27-96. Submitted to OAL for printing only pursuant to Government Code section 11351 (Register 96, No. 52).

Ref.: See Labor Code §124; Herlick Handbook §§ 6.19, 6.20, 14.4.

§10169. Commutation Tables and Instructions.

Table 1 ("Present Value of Permanent Disability at 3% Interest") as issued in January 2001, Table 2 ("Present Value of Life Pension at 3% Interest for a Male") as issued in July 2001, Table 3 ("Present Value of Life Pension at 3% Interest for a Female") as issued in July 2001, and "Commutation Instructions" as issued in January 2001, are hereby incorporated by reference in their entirety as though they were set forth below. The tables and instructions are available from any office of the Division of Workers' Compensation and may be accessed and printed from the Division's homepage at www.dir.ca.gov.

Note: Authority cited: Sections 133, 5100, 5101, 5307.3 and 5307.4, Labor Code. Reference: Sections 5100 and 5101, Labor Code.

History: 1. New section filed 1-17-2001; operative 1-17-2001 pursuant to Government Code section 11343.4(c) (Register 2001, No. 3).

2. Change without regulatory effect amending section filed 7-18-2001 pursuant to section 100, title 1, California Code of Regulations (Register 2001, No. 29).

Ref.: Hanna §§ 9.03[4], 27.02[6]; Herlick Handbook § 6.7.

§10169.1. Commutation of Life Pension and Permanent Disability Benefits.

(a) Determinations of the present value of a life pension under Labor Code Section 5101(b) shall be made in accordance with the Commutation Instructions contained in Section 10169, and shall be based on the actuarial data contained in Section 10169, Table 2 ("Present Value of Life Pension at 3% Interest for a Male") or Table 3 ("Present Value of Life Pension at 3% Interest for a Female").

(b) Determinations of the present value of permanent disability indemnity under Labor Code Section 5101(b) shall be made in accordance with the Commutation Instructions contained in Section 10169, and shall be based on the actuarial data contained in Section 10169, Table 1 ("Present Value of Permanent Disability at 3% Interest").

(c) The Administrative Director shall periodically revise Tables 2 and 3 of Section 10169 to incorporate revisions to the "U. S. Life Tables" and "Actuarial Tables Based On The U.S. Life Tables" issued by the United States government following each decennial census.

Note: Authority cited: Sections 133, 5100, 5101, and 5307.3, and 5307.4, Labor Code. Reference: Sections 5100, 5100.5, 5100.6, 5101, Labor Code.

History: 1. New section filed 1-17-2001; operative 1-17-2001 pursuant to Government Code section 11343.4(c) (Register 2001, No. 3).

Ref.: Hanna §§ 9.03[4], 27.02[6]; Herlick Handbook § 6.7.

SUBCHAPTER 1.7

§10175. Definitions.

As used in this subchapter:

(a) "Employer" means any person defined as an employer in Section 3300 of the Labor Code who has secured the payment of workers' compensation benefits as required by Section 3700 of the Labor Code.

(b) "Exclusive provider of care option" means an option chosen by an employee under Section 10180 under which medical, surgical, and hospital treatment for both occupational and non-occupational injuries and illness are provided to the employee through one health care service plan.

(c) "Health care service plan" means any of the following which offer a managed care product:

(1) A health care service plan licensed under Section 1353 of the Health and Safety Code (Knox-Keene Health Care Service Plan Act);

(2) A disability insurer authorized to transact health insurance or disability income insurance pursuant to Part 2 of Division 2 of the Insurance Code.

(3) An insurer authorized to transact workers' compensation insurance in California, including the State Compensation Insurance Fund.

(4) The state or an employer who has secured a certificate of consent to self-insure from the Director of Industrial Relations pursuant to Labor Code Section 3700.

(5) Multi-employer collectively bargained employee welfare benefit plans or an employee welfare benefit plan sponsored by a recognized exclusive bargaining agent for State employees.

(d) "Managed care product" means a system of medical care which provides for all of the following:

(1) All medical and health care services required under Section 4600 of the Labor Code in a manner that is timely, effective, and accessible to the employee. This shall include making available to an employee, within 5 days of a request, the services of any type of physician, as defined in Section 3209.3 of the Labor Code, including a chiropractor, following an initial visit with the employee's primary care physician, when treatment for an occupational injury or illness falls within the scope of practice of the requested type of physician.

(2) Appropriate case management, including direction of injured employees to appropriate medical service providers within a network for all non-emergency services.

(3) Appropriate financial incentives to reduce service costs and utilization without sacrificing the quality of service, and mechanisms to identify and correct quality deficiencies.

(4) Adequate methods of quality assurance, peer review and service utilization review to prevent inappropriate or excessive treatment, and exclusion from participation those providers who violate treatment standards.

(5) Expertise in providing medical reports necessary for the prompt, proper administration of compensation, including those required under Sections 9785 and 10978.

(6) A procedure for resolving disputes concerning the provision of health care services under the plan, which shall be equivalent to that specified in Section 1368 of the Health and Safety Code.

(7) A program involving cooperative efforts by the employees, the employer, physicians, and other participants to promote employee wellness, workplace health and safety, and early return to work.

(8) Adequate mechanisms to assure coordinated case management goals and incentives among all providers of workers' compensation for employees with occupational injuries and diseases.

(e) "Principal place of business" means the location at which the majority of the employer's employees are employed.

(f) "Small employer" means an employer who on at least 50 percent of its working days during the calendar quarter preceding submission of the proposal under which the employer participates in the pilot project employed not more than fifty (50) employees.

(g) "Traditional health benefit plan" means a plan of medical coverage for non-occupational injuries and illness provided by the employer, through a contract between the employer and a health care provider, or through a purchasing cooperative specifically authorized by state law.

(h) "Traditional workers' compensation provider" means a health care provider chosen pursuant to Labor Code Section 4600 or 4601.

Note: Authority cited: Sections 133, 4612 and 5307.3, Labor Code. Reference: Section 4612, Labor Code.

History: 1. New subchapter 1.7 and section filed 8-31-93; operative 8-31-93. Submitted to OAL for printing only pursuant to Government Code section 11351 (Register 93, No. 36).

§10176. Eligible Employers and Employees.

(a) Employers whose principal place of business is in any of the following counties may participate in the pilot project:

(1) Los Angeles;

(2) San Diego;

(3) Santa Clara;

(4) Sacramento.

(b) Employees of employers eligible to participate in the pilot project who are employed in counties other than those enumerated in subdivision (a) are not precluded from participation in the project.

(c) Nothing in this section shall be construed to prohibit participation by employers whose principal place of business is not within one of the four counties listed in subdivision (a) above if the employer is specifically authorized to do so by statute.

Note: Authority cited: Sections 133, 4612 and 5307.3, Labor Code. Reference: Section 4612, Labor Code.

History: 1. New section filed 8-31-93; operative 8-31-93. Submitted to OAL for printing only pursuant to Government Code section 11351 (Register 93, No. 36).

§10177. Eligible Applicants.

(a) Pilot project plan proposals may be submitted to the administrative director by any one or combination of the following entities or authorized agents thereof:

(1) Employers

(2) Health care service plans

(3) Health insurance purchasing cooperatives specifically authorized under state law.

Note: Authority cited: Sections 133, 4612 and 5307.3, Labor Code. Reference: Section 4612, Labor Code.

History: 1. New section filed 8-31-93; operative 8-31-93. Submitted to OAL for printing only pursuant to Government Code section 11351 (Register 93, No. 36).

§10178. Pilot Project Proposal Requirements.

(a) Proposals submitted to the administrative director for final approval shall include all of the following:

(1) A description of the manner in which health care services are to be provided, including the administrative and organizational structure, how each component of the managed care product will be provided, and the standards and procedures under which an employee who selects the exclusive provider of care option will be permitted to change health care service plans.

(2) The business name and tax identification number of the employer or employee, the approximate number and occupations of participating employees, the health care service plan or provider of health care services, and any other parties required in the operation of the proposal. The proposal shall include signed authorization from all necessary parties, other than the employees, confirming their commitment to the plan. In the case of a proposal under which only small employers will participate, the proposal may specify the method by which employers will be selected to participate in lieu of identifying and obtaining commitments from participating employers and identifying the approximate number and occupations of participating employees.

(3) The method whereby employees will be informed of their rights and options under the proposal, including the right to obtain a decision from the Workers' Compensation Appeals Board in the case of disputes over compensation for injuries compensable under Division 4 (commencing with Section 3200) of the Labor Code. Materials to be used for this purpose shall be submitted with the proposal. Materials shall include a description of the dispute resolution process, a description of dependent coverage, a description of the method and frequency of employee choice of health care provider, and a description of any other incentives offered to employees by employers to participate in the plan.

(4) The dispute resolution process under the exclusive provider of care option, including the process made available to employees to voluntarily resolve issues subject to the jurisdiction of the appeals board, as well as the process for resolving disputes which are not subject to the jurisdiction of the appeals board.

(5) A description of how dependents will be covered under the proposal, and if co-payments, premium shares, deductibles, or other charges are to be assessed against employees or dependents for non-occupational injuries and illness, the amount of such charges and how these

charges will be determined and segregated in a manner to assure compliance with subdivision (a) of Section 3751 of the Labor Code.

(6) The method and frequency of employee choice as to whether the employee will receive medical care under an exclusive provider of care option.

(7) A description of any incentives offered by an employer to employees to encourage participation in the exclusive provider of care option.

(8) Verification of agreement to participate executed by an authorized representative of each exclusive or certified bargaining agent which represents employees of the employer.

(9) The method by which any workers' compensation liability of the employer incurred during the pilot project will be paid after an employee's or employer's participation in the pilot project terminates.

(10) An agreement to provide the administrative director, in the form and manner prescribed by the Administrative Director, with information necessary to evaluate the plan and compliance with this subchapter.

(11) An agreement by the participating employers, or by another participating entity on the behalf of these employers, to pay a proportionate share of the cost of the evaluation of the pilot projects approved under this subchapter, based on the number of participating employees. Nothing in this paragraph shall be construed to require participating employers to pay a share of the evaluation cost if other funding sources are authorized by statute and alternative funding is obtained for this purpose.

Note: Authority cited: Sections 133, 4612 and 5307.3, Labor Code. Reference: Section 4612, Labor Code.

History: 1. New section filed 8-31-93; operative 8-31-93. Submitted to OAL for printing only pursuant to Government Code section 11351 (Register 93, No. 36).

§10179. Selection of Proposals; Priorities; Pilot Termination.

(a) Initial applications will be accepted from the date the Request for Applications is issued until March 31, 1994.

(b) The following will be given priority in selecting participants in the pilot project:

(1) Joint labor-management proposals.

(2) Proposals targeting employers who have previously not offered health benefits for non-occupational injuries and illness to their employees.

(3) Proposals which include appropriate control groups to assist the evaluation process.

(4) Proposals which provide for coordinated administration of indemnity benefits, as well as medical benefits, including workers' compensation temporary disability benefits, state disability insurance benefits, and private disability benefits, while retaining separate administration of the compensation required under Division 4 (commencing with Section 3200) of the Labor Code.

(5) Proposals which will operate in more than one pilot project county.

(6) Proposals which provide parity in coverage between occupational and non-occupational injuries and illness.

(7) Proposals which will commence on January 1, 1994.

(c) Proposals approved for participation in the pilot project shall commence no earlier than January 1, 1994 and shall terminate no later than December 31, 1997.

Note: Authority cited: Sections 133, 4612 and 5307.3, Labor Code. Reference: Section 4612, Labor Code.

History: 1. New section filed 8-31-93; operative 8-31-93. Submitted to OAL for printing only pursuant to Government Code section 11351 (Register 93, No. 36).

2. Amendment of section and section heading filed 10-11-94; operative 10-11-94 (Register 94, No. 41).

§10180. Employee Choice of Plans.

(a) An employee participating in a proposal approved by the administrative director must be offered a choice between the following:

(1) Receiving medical benefits under an exclusive provider of care option for both occupational and non-occupational injuries and illness;

(2) Receiving medical benefits for non-occupational injuries and illness from a traditional health benefit plan and receiving medical treatment for occupational injuries and illness from a traditional workers' compensation provider.

(b) Employees may be permitted to choose between the two options specified in subdivision (a) in the following ways:

(1) The employee selects an option only once, either (i) before the plan begins in the case

of current employees, or (ii) at the time of employment in the case of persons employed after the initial selection period for current employees.

(2) After the initial election, the employee is permitted to change options annually, during an open enrollment period made available to all participating employees.

(c) Nothing in this section shall be construed to preclude an employee from changing plans at any time for good cause, as specified in the approved pilot project proposal or in the rules of the health care service plan.

Note: Authority cited: Sections 133, 4612 and 5307.3, Labor Code. Reference: Section 4612, Labor Code.

History: 1. New section filed 8-31-93; operative 8-31-93. Submitted to OAL for printing only pursuant to Government Code section 11351 (Register 93, No. 36).

§10181. Records, Claims Administration, Auditing, and Termination.

(a) Nothing in this subchapter shall relieve any employer, health care provider or their agents from any of the requirements or obligations contained in Division 1 (commencing with Section 1) of this Title, except for the requirements of Sections 9780.1, 9781, and 9782 to the extent an approved pilot project proposal conflicts with the requirements of these sections.

(b) Administration and accounting of the payment of workers' compensation benefits under this pilot project shall be solely for the purpose of complying with the workers' compensation laws of the State of California and shall be separate from the administration of other employee welfare benefits within the meaning of 29 U.S.C. Section 1002(1). However, any benefit provided by a government plan, church plan, or benefits plan maintained solely for the purpose of compliance with unemployment compensation or disability insurance laws, within the meaning of 29 U.S.C. 1003, may be combined with the administration of workers' compensation under an exclusive provider of care option.

(c) Nothing in this subchapter or a pilot project plan shall be construed to relieve any person, including an employer or physician, from any reporting requirements concerning occupational injuries or illness, or to preclude or in any way inhibit the adjudication of issues involving occupational injuries, including whether an injury or illness is compensable under Division 4 (commencing with Section 3200) of the Labor Code, before the Workers' Compensation Appeals Board.

(d) An employer's participation in this pilot project shall terminate automatically, without any action by the administrative director, when an employer fails to secure the payment of workers' compensation in the manner prescribed by Section 3700 of the Labor Code.

Note: Authority cited: Sections 133, 4612 and 5307.3, Labor Code. Reference: Sections 3700, 4612, 5300, 6409 and 6409.1, Labor Code.

History: 1. New section filed 8-31-93; operative 8-31-93. Submitted to OAL for printing only pursuant to Government Code section 11351 (Register 93, No. 36).

SUBCHAPTER 1.8 ADMINISTRATIVE DIRECTOR – ADMINISTRATIVE RULES COLLECTIVE BARGAINING AGREEMENTS UNDER LABOR CODE SECTIONS 3201.5 AND 3201.7

§10200. Definitions.

As used in this subchapter:

(a) "Employee" means an employee covered under either:

(1) A provision of a collective bargaining agreement recognized by the Administrative Director pursuant to Labor Code section 3201.5; or

(2) A labor-management agreement recognized by the Administrative Director pursuant to Labor Code section 3201.7.

(b) "Employer" means either:

(1) For the purpose of Labor Code section 3201.5, a private employer or group of employers actually engaged in construction, construction maintenance, or activities limited to rock, sand, gravel, cement and asphalt operations, heavy-duty mechanics, surveying, and construction inspection in California. A public entity may be a member of a group of employers.

(2) For the purpose of Labor Code section 3201.7, a private employer, group of employers, or a city or county that is self-insured in compliance with Labor Code section 3700.

(c) "Labor-management agreement" under Labor Code section 3201.7 (or 3201.7 provision) means a provision, clause, addendum, or other section of a collective bargaining agreement that establishes or would establish any program permitted under Labor Code section 3201.7(a). Such a program shall be maintained solely for the purpose of complying with the requirements of Division 4 the Labor Code and shall be administered separately from any other employee benefit plan.

(d) "Provision of a collective bargaining agreement" under Labor Code section 3201.5 (or "3201.5 provision") means a provision, clause, addendum, or other section of a collective bargaining agreement that establishes or would establish any program permitted under Labor Code section 3201.5(a). Such a program shall be maintained solely for the purpose of complying with the requirements of Division 4 the Labor Code and shall be administered separately from any other employee benefit plan.

(e) "Union" means a bona fide labor organization that is the recognized or certified exclusive bargaining representative of the employees of an employer. A labor organization is bona fide under this regulation if:

(1) it actually represents employees in California as to wages, hours and working conditions,

(2) its officers have been elected by secret ballot or otherwise in a manner consistent with federal law, and

(3) it is free of domination or interference by any employer and has received no improper assistance or support from any employer.

Note: Authority cited: Sections 133, 3201.5 and 5307.3, Labor Code. Reference: Sections 3201.5 and 3201.7, Labor Code.

History: 1. New subchapter 1.8 and section filed 8-8-95; operative 8-8-95. Submitted to OAL for printing only pursuant to Government Code section 11351 (Register 95, No. 32).

2. Amendment of section and Note filed 4-22-2004 as an emergency; operative 4-22-2004 (Register 2004, No. 17). A Certificate of Compliance must be transmitted to OAL by 8-20-2004 or emergency language will be repealed by operation of law on the following day.

3. Certificate of Compliance as to 4-22-2004 order, including further amendment of section, transmitted to OAL 8-20-2004 and filed 10-4-2004 (Register 2004, No. 41).

Ref.: Herlick Handbook § 3.4.

§10201. Procedure for Determining Eligibility Under Labor Code Section 3201.5.

(a) Every employer and union proposing to establish any program permitted by Labor Code section 3201.5 shall jointly request the Administrative Director to determine eligibility, as follows:

(1) Employers shall submit the following documents:

(A) Upon its original application and whenever it is renegotiated thereafter, a copy of the underlying collective bargaining agreement and the approximate number of employees who will be covered thereby. The collective bargaining agreement shall be complete, including side letters and all appendices and other documents referred to in the agreement that relate to the program permitted by Labor Code section 3201.5, including but not limited to trust agreements and agreements concerning providers. If the application is on behalf of a group of employers, the application shall clearly define the group and shall state whether all the members of the group are bound by the 3201.5 provision, or whether each member must individually agree to be bound.

(B) Upon its original application and annually thereafter, evidence of a valid and active license where that license is required by law as a condition of doing business in the state within the industries set forth in subdivision (a) of Section 3201.5.

(C) Upon its original application and annually thereafter, a statement signed under penalty of perjury, that no action has been taken by any administrative agency or court of the United States to invalidate the collective bargaining agreement.

(D) Upon its original application and annually thereafter, the name, address, and telephone number of the contact person of the employer.

(E) Upon its original application and annually thereafter, evidence that the employer is actually engaged in construction, construction maintenance, or activities limited to rock, sand, gravel, cement and asphalt operations, heavy-duty mechanics, surveying, or construction inspection in California, or has a plan for immediate engagement in one of those businesses.

(F) Upon its original application and annually thereafter, evidence that the employer:

(i) is developing or projecting an annual workers' compensation insurance premium, in

California, of two hundred fifty thousand dollars ($250,000) or more, or has paid an annual workers' compensation insurance premium, in California, of two hundred fifty thousand dollars ($250,000) in at least one of the previous three years; or

(ii) is a group of employers engaged in a workers' compensation safety group complying with Sections 11656.6 and 11656.7 of the Insurance Code, and established pursuant to a joint labor management safety committee or committees, which develops or projects annual workers' compensation insurance premiums of two million dollars ($2,000,000) or more; or

(iii) is an employer or group of employers that is self-insured in compliance with Section 3700 that has projected annual workers' compensation costs that meet the requirements of, and that meet the other requirements of, paragraph (i) in the case of employers, or paragraph (ii) in the case of groups of employers; or

(iv) is an employer, who is properly signatory to a project agreement, and is covered by an owner or general contractor provided wrap-up insurance policy applicable to a single construction site that develops workers' compensation insurance premiums of two million dollars ($2,000,000) or more with respect to those employees covered by that wrap-up insurance policy.

Every member of a group of employers must maintain separately administered workers' compensation insurance or a self-insurance program distinct from all other types of insurance. Every member must maintain this insurance or self-insurance in one of the ways enumerated in Labor Code section 3700; but it is not necessary that all members maintain insurance or a self-insurance program in the same way. Every member must meet one of the minimum premium or cost requirements listed in paragraphs (i) through (iv) above.

(G) Upon its original application and annually thereafter a statement that it is able and willing to supply the data required by Labor Code section 3201.5(i).

(H) If the application is on behalf of a group of employers, evidence that:

(i) membership in the group is limited to employers that meet all the criteria of Labor Code section 3201.5 and these regulations;

(ii) the group shall, on behalf of its individual members, provide the data required by Labor Code section 3201.5(i);

(iii) the group shall maintain records of its membership satisfactory to the Administrative Director for the purpose of readily ascertaining the facts required by Section 10201(e)(3). Membership records shall include evidence of security for the payment of compensation for each member, including the insurance policy number, or a copy of the certificate of self-insurance issued pursuant to Labor Code section 3700. Membership records shall also include the approximate number of employees for each individual member of the group who is bound by the collective bargaining agreement. Copies of membership records shall be delivered to the Administrative Director on request.

(2) Unions shall submit the following documents:

(A) Upon its original application and annually thereafter, a copy of its most recent LM-2 or LM-3 filing with the United States Department of Labor, along with a statement, signed under penalty of perjury, that the document is a true and correct copy.

(B) Upon its original application and annually thereafter, the name, address, and telephone number of the contact person or persons of the collective bargaining representative or representatives.

(C) Upon its original application and annually thereafter evidence that the union is a bona fide labor organization in that:

(i) it actually represents employees engaged in construction, construction maintenance, or activities limited to rock, sand, gravel, cement and asphalt operations, heavy-duty mechanics, surveying, and construction inspection in California as to wages, hours and working conditions,

(ii) its officers have been elected by secret ballot or otherwise in a manner consistent with federal law, and

(iii) it is free of domination or interference of any employer and has received no improper assistance or support from any employer.

It will be presumed that a union is bona fide if for a period of five years it has actually entered into collective bargaining agreements with employers in California and has filed all appropriate reports with the United States Department of Labor in that period. If a union is not presumed to be bona fide, it shall present evidence satisfactory to the Administrative Director that it meets the criteria of a bona fide labor organization.

(3) Any person may submit documents to the Administrative Director that bear on the eligibility of an applicant. Copies of all such documents received shall be sent to the applicants for comment.

(b) [Reserved for regulation relating to confidentiality]

(c) Issuance of a Letter of Eligibility

Within 30 days after receiving an application, the Administrative Director shall notify the applicants that the application is complete or shall specify what further information is needed to complete the application. Within 30 days after the time an application is completed, the Administrative Director shall either (1) issue a letter of eligibility, or (2) deny eligibility. If eligibility is denied, the Administrative Director shall inform the parties of the reasons therefor. For good cause and upon written notice to the applicants, the Administrative Director may extend the periods of notification for an additional 30 days.

(d) Period of Eligibility

The letter of eligibility shall state the beginning date of eligibility, which shall be no earlier than 15 days before the parties submitted their request to the Administrative Director under this section. A letter of eligibility shall remain valid for the same period as the 3201.5 provision of the collective bargaining agreement, but no longer then three years from the date of issuance of the letter. Upon the effective date of this regulation, the Administrative Director shall re-issue letters of eligibility to parties which have already received them.

(e) Effect of a Letter of Eligibility

(1) A letter of eligibility is a determination by the Administrative Director that the parties meet the eligibility requirements of Labor Code section 3201.5. A letter of eligibility is not a determination by the Administrative Director that the collective bargaining agreement or any part of it is in compliance with Labor Code section 3201.5.

(2) A 3201.5 provision is valid and binding only if there was a letter of eligibility in effect at the time of injury.

(3) A letter of eligibility issued to a group of employers shall be valid as to an individual member of the group if all the following facts are established as of the time the provision is alleged to be in effect and at the time of injury:

(A) the group of employers possessed a current letter of eligibility;

(B) the individual employer was a member of the group;

(C) the individual employer had signed the 3201.5 provision;

(D) the individual employer was actually engaged in construction, construction maintenance, or activities limited to rock, sand, gravel, cement and asphalt operations, heavy-duty mechanics, surveying, or construction inspection in California and possesses a valid and active license as required by Labor Code section 3201.5(a); and

(E) the individual employer was is compliance with Labor Code section 3201.5(c).

(f) Renewal of Eligibility

(1) At least 30 days prior to the expiration of the letter of eligibility, the parties shall submit to the Administrative Director updated copies of the documents and other evidence required by subdivision (a) of this Section. However, if certain documents and other evidence are completely unchanged since the submission of the previous annual report required by Section 10204, the party responsible for submitting the updates may instead submit a statement under penalty of perjury that there has been no change in the document or evidence since the previous annual report. The Administrative Director may nonetheless require any party to submit the actual documents or evidence.

(2) Within 30 days after receiving the information required under subdivision (f)(1), the Administrative Director shall either: (1) renew the letter of eligibility for the same period of time set forth in subdivision (d); or (2) deny eligibility. If eligibility is denied, the Administrative Director shall inform the parties of the reasons therefor.

(g) All insurers, self-insured employers, and third party administrators who adjust claims subject to a Section 3201.5 provision shall comply with the applicable provisions of Section 138.4 of the Labor Code and shall comply with the administrative regulations contained in Title 8, Cal. Code Regs., Division 1, Chapter 4.5:

(1) Subchapter 1: Article 1.1, commencing with Section 9700; Article 5, commencing with Section 9780; Article 6, commencing with Section 9796; Article 8, commencing with Section 9810; Article 8.5, commencing with Section 9880; Article 10, commencing with Section 9900;

(2) Subchapter 1.5: Article 1, commencing with Section 10100; Article 2, commencing with

Section 10101; Article 3, commencing with Section 10105; Article 4, commencing with Section 10110; Article 5, commencing with Section 10111; Article 6, commencing with Section 10113; Article 7, commencing with Section 10115; Article 6, commencing with Section 10116; Article 7, commencing with Section 10122; and,

(3) Subchapter 1.6, commencing with Section 10150.

Note: Authority cited: Sections 133, 3201.5 and 5307.3, Labor Code. Reference: Section 3201.5, Labor Code.

History: 1. New section filed 8-8-95; operative 8-8-95. Submitted to OAL for printing only pursuant to Government Code section 11351 (Register 95, No. 32).

2. Amendment filed 4-22-2004 as an emergency; operative 4-22-2004 (Register 2004, No. 17). A Certificate of Compliance must be transmitted to OAL by 8-20-2004 or emergency language will be repealed by operation of law on the following day.

3. Certificate of Compliance as to 4-22-2004 order, including further amendment of section, transmitted to OAL 8-20-2004 and filed 10-4-2004 (Register 2004, No. 41).

Ref.: Hanna § 1.04[4]; Herlick Handbook § 3.4.

§10202. Procedure for Recognizing Labor-Management Agreements Under Labor Code Section 3201.7.

(a) Any union in an industry not covered by Labor Code section 3201.5 who seeks to negotiate a 3201.7 provision with an employer shall file a petition with the Administrative Director, verified under penalty of perjury, on the "Petition for Permission to Negotiate a Section 3201.7 Labor-Management Agreement" form (DWC Form RGS-1), contained in Section 10202.1. A proof of service by mail declaration shall be attached to the petition indicating that the complete petition, including all attachments, was served on the employer, or group of employers.

(b) Within 10 days after receiving a petition, the Administrative Director shall notify the union that the petition is complete or shall specify what further information is needed to complete the petition. Within 30 days after the time the petition is completed, the Administrative Director shall either (1) issue to the union and employer, or group of employers, a letter of eligibility to negotiate a 3201.7 provision, or (2) deny the petition. If the petition is denied, the Administrative Director shall inform the union of the reasons therefor. For good cause and upon written notice to the union, the Administrative Director may extend the periods of notification for an additional 30 days.

(c) The letter of eligibility to negotiate shall remain valid for a period not to exceed one year from the date of issuance. Upon joint request by the union and the employer, or group of employers, an additional one year period to negotiate a 3201.7 agreement shall be granted.

(d) Upon receipt of the letter of eligibility to negotiate, the union and employer, or group of employers, may negotiate a 3201.7 provision. A negotiated and signed 3201.7 provision between a union and employer, or group of employers, will be recognized by the Department of Industrial Relations as valid and binding upon application by the parties to the Administrative Director.

(1) The employer, or group of employers, shall submit the following documents with the application:

(A) Upon its original application and whenever it is renegotiated thereafter, a copy of the 3201.7 provision, and the approximate number of employees who will be covered thereby. If the application is on behalf of a group of employers, the application shall clearly define the group and shall state whether all the members of the group are bound by the 3201.7 provision, or whether each member must individually agree to be bound.

(B) Upon its original application and annually thereafter, a statement signed under penalty of perjury, that no action has been taken by any administrative agency or court of the United States to invalidate the collective bargaining agreement.

(C) Upon its original application and annually thereafter, the name, address, and telephone number of the contact person of the employer, or group of employers.

(D) Upon its original application and annually thereafter, evidence of a valid and active license where that license is required by law as a condition of doing business in the state.

(E) Upon its original application and annually thereafter, evidence that the employer:

(i) is developing or projecting an annual workers' compensation insurance premium, in California, of fifty thousand dollars ($50,000) or more, and employing at least fifty (50) employees, or has paid an annual workers' compensation insurance premium, in California, of fifty thousand dollars ($50,000), and employing at least fifty (50) employees in at least one of the previous three years; or

(ii) is a group of employers engaged in a workers' compensation safety group complying with Sections 11656.6 and 11656.7 of the Insurance Code, and established pursuant to a joint labor management safety committee or committees, that develops or projects annual workers' compensation insurance premiums of five hundred thousand dollars ($500,000) or more; or

(iii) is an employer or group of employers, including cities and counties, that is self-insured in compliance with Labor Code section 3700 that has projected annual workers' compensation costs that meet the requirements of, and that meet the other requirements of, paragraph (i) in the case of employers, or paragraph (ii) in the case of groups of employers.

(F) Upon its original application and annually thereafter a statement that it is able and willing to supply the data required by Labor Code section 3201.7(h).

(G) If the application is on behalf of a group of employers, evidence that:

(i) membership in the group is limited to employers that meet all the criteria of Labor Code section 3201.7 and these regulations;

(ii) the group shall, on behalf of its individual members, provide the data required by Labor Code section 3201.7(h);

(iii) the group shall maintain records of its membership satisfactory to the Administrative Director for the purpose of readily ascertaining the facts required by subdivision (h) of the section. Membership records shall include evidence of security for the payment of compensation for each member, including the insurance policy number, or a copy of the certificate of self-insurance issued pursuant to Labor Code section 3700. Membership records shall also include the approximate number of employees for each individual member of the group who is bound by the collective bargaining agreement. Copies of membership records shall be delivered to the Administrative Director on request.

(2) Unions shall submit the following documents with the application:

(A) Upon its original application and annually thereafter, a copy of its most recent LM-2 or LM-3 filing with the United States Department of Labor, along with a statement, signed under penalty of perjury, that the document is a true and correct copy.

(B) Upon its original application and annually thereafter, the name, address, and telephone number of the contact person or persons of the collective bargaining representative or representatives.

(C) Upon its original application and annually thereafter evidence that the union is a bona fide labor organization in that:

(i) its officers have been elected by secret ballot or otherwise in a manner consistent with federal law, and

(ii) it is free of domination or interference of any employer and has received no improper assistance or support from any employer.

It will be presumed that a union is bona fide if for a period of five years it has actually entered into collective bargaining agreements with employers in California and has filed all appropriate reports with the United States Department of Labor in that period. If a union is not presumed to be bona fide, it shall present evidence satisfactory to the Administrative Director that it meets the criteria of a bona fide labor organization.

(e) Every member of a group of employers must maintain separately administered workers' compensation insurance or a self-insurance program distinct from all other types of insurance. Every member must maintain this insurance or self-insurance in one of the ways enumerated in Labor Code section 3700; but it is not necessary that all members maintain insurance or a self-insurance program in the same way. Every member must meet one of the minimum premium or cost requirements listed above in subdivision (d)(1)(E), paragraphs (i) through (iii).

(f) Any person may submit documents to the Administrative Director that bear on the application of the union and employer, or group of employers. Copies of all such documents received shall be sent to the union and employer, or group of employers, for comment.

(g) Within 30 days after receiving the application, the Administrative Director shall notify the union and employer, or group of employers, that the application is complete or shall specify what further information is needed to complete the application. Within 30 days after the time the application is completed, the Administrative Director shall either (1) issue to the union and employer, or group of employers, a letter recognizing the 3201.7 provision, or (2) deny the application. If the application is denied, the Administrative Director shall inform the union and employer, or group of employers, of the reasons therefor. For good cause and upon written notice to the union and employer, or group of employers, the Administrative Director may extend the periods of notification for an additional 30 days.

(h) The recognition of the Section 3201.7 provision is a determination by the Administrative Director that the parties meet the eligibility requirements of Labor Code section 3201.7. Recognition is not a determination by the Administrative Director that the 3201.7 agreement, or any part of it, is in compliance with Labor Code section 3201.7.

(1) A 3201.7 provision is valid and binding only if there was a complete application filed with the Administrative Director at the time of injury.

(2) A 3201.7 provision negotiated and signed by a group of employers shall be valid as to an individual member of the group if all the following facts are established as of the time the provision is alleged to be in effect and at the time of injury:

(A) the group of employers has a complete application filed with the Administrative Director;

(B) the individual employer was a member of the group;

(C) the individual employer had signed the 3201.7 provision;

(D) the individual employer was is compliance with Labor Code section 3201.7(c).

(i) All insurers, self-insured employers, and third party administrators who adjust claims subject to a Section 3201.7 provision shall comply with the applicable provisions of Section 138.4 of the Labor Code and the administrative regulations contained in Title 8, Cal. Code Regs., Division 1, Chapter 4.5:

(1) Subchapter 1: Article 1.1, commencing with Section 9700; Article 5, commencing with Section 9780; Article 6, commencing with Section 9796; Article 8, commencing with Section 9810; Article 8.5, commencing with Section 9880; Article 10, commencing with Section 9900;

(2) Subchapter 1.5: Article 1, commencing with Section 10100; Article 2, commencing with Section 10101; Article 3, commencing with Section 10105; Article 4, commencing with Section 10110; Article 5, commencing with Section 10111; Article 6, commencing with Section 10113; Article 7, commencing with Section 10115; Article 6, commencing with Section 10116; Article 7, commencing with Section 10122; and,

(3) Subchapter 1.6, commencing with Section 10150.

Note: Authority cited: Sections 133 and 5307.3, Labor Code. Reference: Section 3201.7, Labor Code.

History: 1. New section filed 8-8-95; operative 8-8-95. Submitted to OAL for printing only pursuant to Government Code section 11351 (Register 95, No. 32).

2. Amendment of section heading, repealer and new section and amendment of Note filed 4-22-2004 as an emergency; operative 4-22-2004 (Register 2004, No. 17). A Certificate of Compliance must be transmitted to OAL by 8-20-2004 or emergency language will be repealed by operation of law on the following day.

3. Certificate of Compliance as to 4-22-2004 order, including further amendment of section, transmitted to OAL 8-20-2004 and filed 10-4-2004 (Register 2004, No. 41).

Ref.: Hanna §§ 1.04[4], 1.04A[1]; Herlick Handbook § 3.4.

§10202.1. Petition for Permission to Negotiate a Section 3201.7 Labor-Management Agreement (DWC Form RGS-1).

STATE OF CALIFORNIA
Department of Industrial Relations
Division of Workers' Compensation
Administrative Director
Post Office Box 420603
San Francisco, CA 94142-0603
Telephone: (415) 703-4600

Petition for Permission to Negotiate a Section 3201.7
Labor-Management Agreement

Labor Code § 3201.7; Title 8, California Code of Regulations § 10202

Please submit the following information to the Administrative Director of the Division of Workers' Compensation to obtain a letter advising the below-named union and employer, or group of employers, of their eligibility to enter into negotiations for the purpose of reaching agreement on a labor-management agreement authorized by Section 3201.7 of the California Labor Code.

(Print or Type Name and Addresses)

1. Union Information
Name of Union:
Contact Person and Title:
Principal Address:

2. Employer Information (For group of employers, please use separate pages to list all individual employers.)
Name of Employer:
Contact Person and Title:
Federal Employers Identification Number (FEIN):
Principal Business of Employer:
Principal Address:

3. Please describe the bargaining unit or units to be covered by the Section 3201.7 labor-management agreement, and provide the approximate number of employees in the unit(s).

4. Please attach proof of the union's status as the exclusive bargaining representative of the employees in the above-described bargaining unit(s).

5. Please attach a copy of the current collective bargaining agreement or agreements in effect between the union and the employer.

I declare under penalty of perjury under the laws of the State of California that the foregoing is true and correct.

EXECUTED AT ___________ (City), CALIFORNIA ON ___________ (Date)

BY: ____, TITLE: __________

(Original Signature of Union Representative)

You must attach a proof of service by mail declaration indicating that the petition and all supporting evidence was mailed to the employer, or for a group of employers, all individual employers.

DWC Form RGS-1 (012004)

Note: Authority cited: Sections 133 and 5307.3, Labor Code. Reference: Section 3201.7, Labor Code.

History: 1. New section filed 4-22-2004 as an emergency; operative 4-22-2004 (Register 2004, No.

17). A Certificate of Compliance must be transmitted to OAL by 8-20-2004 or emergency language will be repealed by operation of law on the following day.

2. Certificate of Compliance as to 4-22-2004 order, including further amendment of section, transmitted to OAL 8-20-2004 and filed 10-4-2004 (Register 2004, No. 41).

Ref.: See Labor Code §3201.5; Hanna § 1.04A[1]; Herlick Handbook § 14.4.

§10203. Reporting Data.

(a)(1) On or before March 31 of every year, every employer subject to either a 3201.5 or 3201.7 provision shall provide the information specified in subdivision (b) for the previous calendar year. For each claim with a date of injury on or after January 1, 2004, the information reported under subdivision (b)(8) through (16) in the first mandatory reporting year under subdivision (b)(8), shall also be updated annually thereafter for the following three calendar years.

(2) To provide the information required in subdivision (b), the employer shall either:

(A) Provide the information on a form prescribed by the administrative director, either DWC Form GV-1, as set forth in Section 10203.1, or DWC Form GV-2, as set forth in Section 10203.2; or

(B) Provide the administrative director with written authorization to collect the information from the appropriate claims administrator. If the administrative director is unable to obtain the information with the written authorization, the employer shall remain responsible for obtaining and submitting the information.

(3) Groups of employers shall report the information required by this section on behalf of its members. The information shall be reported as to every individual employer covered by the 3201.5 or 3201.7 provision. Groups shall also report aggregated figures for all employers in the group covered by the 3201.5 or 3201.7 provision.

(b) The report shall contain the following information:

(1) The name of the individual employer and the union.

(2) The principal business of the employer.

(3) The dates the 3201.5 or 3201.7 provision were in effect during the previous calendar year.

(4) The name of the insurer, if any, and the insurance policy number. If self-insured, the name and certificate number of the self-insured employer.

(5) The name, address and telephone number of any administrator, ombudsperson, mediator or arbitrator employed in an alternative dispute resolution system.

(6) Hours worked by covered employees, reported by trade or craft.

(7) Payroll in accordance with the rules of the Workers' Compensation Insurance Rating Bureau [WCIRB]. Payroll shall be reported by class code as set by the WCIRB.

(8) The number of claims filed in the previous calendar year pursuant to Labor Code section 5401. The claims shall be reported in the following categories:

A. The number of claims that were medical only. As to those claims, there shall also be a report on the total amount of paid costs and the total amount of incurred costs.

B. The number of claims that included a claim for indemnity. As to those claims, there shall also be a report on total amount of paid costs and total amount of incurred costs in each of the following categories: temporary disability, permanent disability, life pensions, death benefits, vocational rehabilitation, medical services, and medical-legal expenses.

(9) The number of claims filed pursuant to Labor Code section 5401 in the previous calendar year that were resolved and the number that remained unresolved on December 31 of the previous calendar year. These numbers together should equal the total number reported in subdivision (b)(8). For the purpose of this section, "resolved" means one in which ultimate liability has been determined, even though payments may be made beyond the reporting period.

(10) Of the claims that were filed and/or resolved in the previous calendar year, the number that were resolved with a denial of compensability.

(11) Of the claims that were filed and/or resolved in the previous calendar year, the number that were resolved at each of the following stages: before mediation, at or after mediation, at or after arbitration, at or after the appeals board, or at or after the court of appeals. If the 3201.5 or 3201.7 provision contains another dispute resolution procedure, whether instead of or in addition to arbitration or mediation, the report must identify the type of procedure, its stage in the overall alternate dispute

resolution process, and the same respective information regarding the resolution of claims.

(12) The title and case number of every application filed with the appeals board in the previous calendar year concerning a claim alleged by any party to fall within the 3201.5 or 3201.7 provision, regardless of whether the employee had the right to file such an application.

(13) The title and court number of every civil action, including petitions for writs and injunctions in any court, state or federal, filed in the previous calendar year, that concerned a claim alleged by any party to fall within the 3201.5 or 3201.7 provision.

(14) The number of injuries and illnesses reported on the United States Department of Labor OSHA Form No. 300 for those employees covered by the 3201.5 or 3201.7 provision. The same number multiplied by 200,000 and divided by hours worked (as reported in subdivision (b)(6)).

(15) The number of employees covered by the 3201.5 or 3201.7 provision who participated in vocational rehabilitation.

(16) If the 3201.5 or 3201.7 provision established a light-duty or return to work program, the number of employees who participated in that program.

(17) For employers covered by a 3201.7 provision, an employee survey that measures worker satisfaction with the 3201.7 alternative dispute resolution procedures. The survey shall be designed and administered by agreement between the employer and the union.

(c) In addition to the data above, the employer may include in its report any explanatory material, narrative account, or comment that the employer believes is necessary to understand the data.

(d) Notwithstanding this section, all employers shall be subject to the reporting requirements of the Workers' Compensation Information System, Title 8, Cal. Code Regs., Section 9700 et seq.

(e) The data obtained by the Administrative Director pursuant to Section 10203 shall be confidential and not subject to public disclosure under any law of this state. However, the Division of Workers' Compensation may create derivative works based on the collective bargaining agreements and data. Those derivative works shall not be confidential, but shall be public.

Note: Authority: Sections 133, 3201.5 and 5307.3, Labor Code. Reference: Sections 3201.5, 3201.7 and 3201.9, Labor Code.

History: 1. New section filed 2-14-96; operative 2-14-96. Submitted to OAL for printing only pursuant to Government Code section 11351 (Register 96, No. 7).

2. Amendment of subsections (a)(1), (b)3., (b)8., (b)9.-11. and (b)13.-15. filed 12-27-96; operative 12-27-96. Submitted to OAL for printing only pursuant to Government Code section 11351 (Register 96, No. 52).

3. Amendment of section and Note filed 4-22-2004 as an emergency; operative 4-22-2004 (Register 2004, No. 17). A Certificate of Compliance must be transmitted to OAL by 8-20-2004 or emergency language will be repealed by operation of law on the following day.

4. Certificate of Compliance as to 4-22-2004 order, including further amendment of section, transmitted to OAL 8-20-2004 and filed 10-4-2004 (Register 2004, No. 41).

Ref.: Hanna § 1.04[4]; Herlick Handbook § 3.4.

11. Telephone number of ombudsperson: ( )
(Note: If there is more than one ombudsperson, attach additional sheets with the required information).
12. Name of mediator employed in an ADR system (if any):
13. Address of mediator:
14. Telephone number of mediator: ( )
(Note: If there is more than one mediator, attach additional sheets with the required information).
15. Name of arbitrator employed in an ADR system (if any):
16. Address of arbitrator:
17. Telephone number of arbitrator: ( )
(Note: If there is more than one arbitrator, attach additional sheets with the required information).
18. Total person hours worked by covered employees, indicate by trade or craft:

Trade:	Person Hours:
Trade:	Person Hours:
Trade:	Person Hours:
Trade:	Person Hours:
Trade:	Person Hours:
Trade:	Person Hours:
Trade:	Person Hours:
Trade:	Person Hours:
Trade:	Person Hours:
Trade:	Person Hours:

(Note: If there are more trades represented, attach additional sheets with the required information on person hours worked.)
19. Attach payroll for the employer(s) in accordance with the rules of the Workers' Compensation Insurance Rating Bureau (WCIRB). Payroll shall be reported by class code as set by the WCIRB and provided in table format.

Questions 20 through 45 apply to claims filed in the previous calendar year pursuant to Labor Code §§ 5401 or 5402. For claims with a date of injury on or after January 1, 2003, the information reported shall be for the year in which the claim was filed, and the subsequent calendar years until the claim is resolved. However, information from no more than four calendar years (including the year the claim was filed) shall be reported on each claim.

20. Number of claims that were medical only:
21. Total amount of paid costs for medical only claims:
22. Total amount of incurred costs for medical only claims:
23. Number of claims that included a claim for indemnity:
24. Total amount of paid temporary disability for indemnity claims:
25. Total amount of incurred temporary disability for indemnity claims:
26. Total amount of paid permanent disability for indemnity claims:
27. Total amount of incurred permanent disability for indemnity claims:
28. Total amount of paid life pensions for indemnity claims:
29. Total amount of incurred life pensions for indemnity claims:
30. Total amount of paid death benefits for indemnity claims:
31. Total amount of incurred death benefits for indemnity claims:
32. Total amount of paid vocational rehabilitation for indemnity claims:
33. Total amount of incurred vocational rehabilitation for indemnity claims:
34. Total amount of paid medical services for indemnity claims:
35. Total amount of incurred medical services for indemnity claims:
36. Total amount of paid medical legal expenses for indemnity claims:

37. Total amount of incurred medical legal expenses for indemnity claims:

38. Number of claims that were resolved (resolved means one in which ultimate liability has been determined, even though payments may be made beyond the reporting period):

39. Number of claims that remained unresolved:

Note: The numbers in questions 38 and 39 added together should equal the summation of the number of medical only claims (question 20) and indemnity claims (question 23).

40. The number of claims that were resolved with a denial of compensability:

41. The number of claims that were resolved before mediation:

42. The number of claims that were resolved at or after mediation:

43. The number of claims that were resolved at or after arbitration.

Note: For employers, or group of employers, who utilize an alternative dispute resolution system that includes resolution procedures in addition to or in place of mediation and/or arbitration, please identify on an attachment each resolution procedure used and the number of claims that were resolved using that procedure.

44. The number of claims that were resolved at or after the Workers' Compensation Appeals Board (WCAB):

45. The number of claims that were resolved at or after the court of appeals:

46. Provide the title and number of every application filed with the WCAB during the previous calendar year concerning the claim alleged by any party to fall within the Section 3201.5 or 3201.7 provision, regardless of whether the employee had the right to file such a application (example in italics):

Title:	*Jane Doe vs. ABC Co*	Number:	*SFO 0123456*
Title:		Number:	
Title:		Number:	
Title:		Number:	
Title:		Number:	
Title:		Number:	
Title:		Number:	

Note: If there are more applications, attach additional sheets with the required information.

47. Provide the title and court number of every civil action, including petitions for writs and injunctions in any court, state or federal, filed in the previous calendar year, that concerned a claim alleged by any party to fall within the Section 3201.5 or 3201.7 provision (example in italics):

Title:	*Jane Doe vs. ABC Co*	Number:	*Alameda County No 3 76052*
Title:		Number:	
Title:		Number:	
Title:		Number:	
Title:		Number:	
Title:		Number:	
Title:		Number:	
Title:		Number:	
Title:		Number:	
Title:		Number:	

Note: If there are more civil actions, attach additional sheets with the required information.

48. The number of injuries and illnesses reported in the previous calendar year on the United States Department of Labor OSHA Form No. 300 for those employees covered by the Section 3201.5 or 3201.7 provision:

49. The number of employees covered by the Section 3201.5 or 3201.7 provision who participated in vocational rehabilitation:

50. The number of employees covered by the Section 3201.5 or 3201.7 provision who participated in a light duty program or modified return to work programs established under Section 3201.5 or 3201.7:

51. For an employer, or group of employers, who is covered by a 3201.7 provision, please provide an employee survey that measures worker satisfaction with the applicable 3201.7 alternative dispute resolution procedures. The survey shall be designed and administered by agreement between the employer and the union.

52. Please attach any explanatory material, narrative account or comment that you believe would enable the Division to understand your response(s).

Programs are encouraged to submit updated information covering prior calendar year claims reported to Division of Workers' Compensation.

DWC Form GV-1 (012004)

Note: Authority cited: Sections 133, and 5307.3, Labor Code. Reference: Sections 3201.5, 3201.7, and 3201.9, Labor Code.

History: 1. New section filed 4-22-2004 as an emergency; operative 4-22-2004 (Register 2004, No. 17). A Certificate of Compliance must be transmitted to OAL by 8-20-2004 or emergency language will be repealed by operation of law on the following day.

2. Certificate of Compliance as to 4-22-2004 order, including further amendment of section, transmitted to OAL 8-20-2004 and filed 10-4-2004 (Register 2004, No. 41).

Ref.: Hanna § 1.04[4]; Herlick Handbook § 14.4.

§10203.2. Individual Employer Annual Report (DWC Form GV-2).

STATE OF CALIFORNIA
Department of Industrial Relations
Division of Workers' Compensation
Administrative Director
Post Office Box 420603
San Francisco, CA 94142
Telephone: (415) 703-4600

Individual Employer Annual Report

Labor Code §§ 3201.5 and 3201.7; Title 8, California Code of Regulations § 10203

For the 12 month period ending December 31, 20______.

The following information is being obtained by the Administrative Director pursuant to Labor Code §§ 3201.5 and 3201.7, and Title 8, California Code of Regulations Section 10203. An individual employer who is participating in a Section 3201.5 or 3201.7 program with a group of employers shall provide the information requested in this form to the administrator of the Section 3201.5 or 3201.7 program, or the contact person or persons identified in Title 8, California Code of Regulations § 10201(a)(1)(D) and (2)(B) or §10202(d)(1)(C) or (2)(B). The information provided to the program shall be confidential and not subject to public disclosure under any law of this state. However, the Division of Workers' Compensation may create derivative works based on collective bargaining agreements and data. Those derivative works shall not be confidential, but shall be public. The information provided by the employer shall be maintained by the administrator of the program and is available for inspection by the Administrative Director upon reasonable written request.

Name of Program:
Statute Authorizing Program (circle one): 3201.5 – Construction 3201.7 – Other

1. Employer Information.
Name:
FEIN:
Principal business of employer (please circle one or more):

3201.5: construction construction maintenance rock, sand, gravel, cement and asphalt operations heavy-duty mechanics surveying construction inspection
3201.7: education and health services financial activities government information leisure and hospitality manufacturing natural resources and mining professional and business services transportation and utilities wholesale and retail trade other (specify)

2. Name of union participating in the Section 3201.5 or 3201.7 agreement:

3. Dates that the Section 3201.5 or 3201.7 provision was in effect during the previous calendar year:
Beginning date: Ending date:

4. Name of insurer:

5. Insurance policy number:

5a. If an employer is legally self-insured under authority of the Department of Industrial Relations' Office of Self-Insurance Plans, list certificate number and name:

6. Attach payroll in accordance with the rules of the Workers' Compensation Insurance Rating Bureau (WCIRB). Payroll shall be reported by class code as set by the WCIRB and provided in table format.

7. Total person hours worked by covered employees, indicate by trade or craft:

Trade: Person Hours:

Trade: Person Hours:

Trade: Person Hours:

(Note: If there are more trades represented, attach additional sheets with the required information on person hours worked.)

Questions 8 through 27 apply to claims filed in the previous calendar year pursuant to Labor Code §§ 5401 or 5402. For claims with a date of injury on or after January 1, 2003, the information reported shall be for the year in which the claim was filed, and the subsequent calendar years until the claim is resolved. However, information from no more than four calendar years (including the year the claim was filed) shall be reported on each claim.

8. Number of claims that were medical only:

9. Total amount of paid costs for medical only claims:

10. Total amount of incurred costs for medical only claims:

11. Number of claims that included a claim for indemnity:

12. Total amount of paid temporary disability for indemnity claims:

13. Total amount of incurred temporary disability for indemnity claims:

14. Total amount of paid permanent disability for indemnity claims:

15. Total amount of incurred permanent disability for indemnity claims:

16. Total amount of paid life pensions for indemnity claims:

17. Total amount of incurred life pensions for indemnity claims:

18. Total amount of paid death benefits for indemnity claims:

19. Total amount of incurred death benefits for indemnity claims:

20. Total amount of paid vocational rehabilitation for indemnity claims:

21. Total amount of incurred vocational rehabilitation for indemnity claims:

22. Total amount of paid medical services for indemnity claims:

23. Total amount of incurred medical services for indemnity claims:

24. Total amount of paid medical legal expenses for indemnity claims:

25. Total amount of incurred medical legal expenses for indemnity claims:

26. Number of claims that were resolved (resolved means one in which ultimate liability has been determined, even though payments may be made beyond the reporting period):

27. Number of claims that remained unresolved:

Note: The numbers in questions 26 and 27 added together should equal the summation of the number of medical only claims (question 8) and indemnity claims (question 11).

28. The number of claims that were resolved with a denial of compensability:

29. The number of claims that were resolved before mediation:

30. The number of claims that were resolved at or after mediation:

31. The number of claims that were resolved at or after arbitration.

Note: For employers who utilize a alternative dispute resolution system that includes resolution procedures in addition to or in place of mediation and/or arbitration, please identify on an attachment each resolution procedure used and the number of claims that were resolved using that procedure.

32. The number of claims that were resolved at or after the Workers' Compensation Appeals Board (WCAB):

33. The number of claims that were resolved at or after the court of appeals:

34. Provide the title and number of every application filed with the WCAB during the previous calendar year concerning the claim alleged by any party to fall within the Section 3201.5 or 3201.7 provision, regardless of whether the employee had the right to file such a application (example in italics):

Title: *Jane Doe vs. ABC Co* Number: *SFO 0123456*
Title: Number:

Note: If there are more applications, attach additional sheets with the required information.

35. Provide the title and court number of every civil action, including petitions for writs and injunctions in any court, state or federal, filed in the previous calendar year, that concerned a claim alleged by any party to fall within the Section 3201.5 or 3201.7 provision (example in italics):

Title: *Jane Doe vs. ABC Co* Number: *Alameda County No 3 76052*
Title: Number:

Note: If there are more civil actions, attach additional sheets with the required information.

36. The number of injuries and illnesses reported in the previous calendar year on the United States Department of Labor OSHA Form No. 300 for those employees covered by the Section 3201.5 or 3201.7 provision:

37. The number of employees covered by the Section 3201.5 or 3201.7 provision who participated in vocational rehabilitation:

38. The number of employees covered by the Section 3201.5 or 3201.7 provision who participated in a light duty program or modified return to work programs established under Section 3201.5 or 3201.7:

39. For an employer who is covered by a 3201.7 provision, please provide an employee survey that measures worker satisfaction with the applicable 3201.7 alternative dispute resolution procedures. The survey shall be designed and administered by agreement between the employer and the union.

40. Please attach any explanatory material, narrative account or comment that you believe would enable the Division to understand your response(s).

Programs are encouraged to submit updated information covering prior calendar year claims reported to Division of Workers' Compensation.

DWC Form GV-2 (012004)

Note: Authority cited: Sections 133 and 5307.3, Labor Code. Reference: Sections 3201.5, 3201.7 and 3201.9, Labor Code.

History: 1. New section filed 4-22-2004 as an emergency; operative 4-22-2004 (Register 2004, No. 17). A Certificate of Compliance must be transmitted to OAL by 8-20-2004 or emergency language will be repealed by operation of law on the following day.

2. Certificate of Compliance as to 4-22-2004 order, including further amendment of section, transmitted to OAL 8-20-2004 and filed 10-4-2004 (Register 2004, No. 41).

Ref.: Hanna § 1.04[4]; Herlick Handbook § 14.4.

§10204. Annual Reports.

(a) On or before March 31 of every year, the parties covered by the 3201.5 or 3201.7 provision shall submit updated copies of the documents and other evidence required by Section 10201 or Section 10202. However, if certain documents and other evidence are completely unchanged since the previous submission, the party responsible for submitting the annual update may instead submit a statement under penalty of perjury that there has been no change in the document or evidence since the previous submission. The Administrative Director may nonetheless require any party to submit the actual documents or evidence.

(b) If the parties have not submitted the updated documents required by this section, or if the employer has not timely submitted the data required by Section 10203 the Administrative Director may, after notice and an opportunity to respond, either: (1) revoke a letter of eligibility issued pursuant to Labor Code section 3201.5; (2) revoke the recognition given to the labor-management agreement negotiated pursuant to Labor Code section 3201.7; or (3) take such other steps as he or she deems necessary to secure the parties' compliance with reporting requirements.

Note: Authority cited: Sections 133, 3201.5 and 5307.3, Labor Code. Reference: Sections 3201.5, 3201.7 and 3201.9, Labor Code.

History: 1. New section filed 8-8-95; operative 8-8-95. Submitted to OAL for printing only pursuant to Government Code section 11351 (Register 95, No. 32).

2. Amendment of subsection (a) filed 2-14-96; operative 2-14-96. Submitted to OAL for printing only

pursuant to Government Code section 11351 (Register 96, No. 7).

3. Amendment of section and Note filed 4-22-2004 as an emergency; operative 4-22-2004 (Register 2004, No. 17). A Certificate of Compliance must be transmitted to OAL by 8-20-2004 or emergency language will be repealed by operation of law on the following day.

4. Certificate of Compliance as to 4-22-2004 order transmitted to OAL 8-20-2004 and filed 10-4-2004 (Register 2004, No. 41).

Ref.: Hanna § 1.04[4]; Herlick Handbook § 3.4.

SUBCHAPTER 1.8.1 ADMINISTRATIVE DIRECTOR — OTHER ADMINISTRATIVE PENALTIES

ARTICLE 1 Administrative Penalties Pursuant to Labor Code Section 5814.6 [Renumbered]

§10225. Definitions. [Renumbered]

Note: Authority cited: Sections 133, 5307.3 and 5814.6, Labor Code. Reference: Sections 129.5, 139.48, 5814 and 5814.6, Labor Code.

History: 1. New subchapter 1.8.1 (sections 10225–10225.2) and section filed 4-26-2007; operative 5-26-2007 (Register 2007, No. 17).

2. Change without regulatory effect renumbering former subchapter 1.8, article 1 (sections 10225–10225.2) to subchapter 1.5, article 5.5 (sections 10112.1–10112.3) and renumbering former section 10225 to section 10112.1 filed 4-7-2008 pursuant to section 100, title 1, California Code of Regulations (Register 2008, No. 15).

§10225.1. Schedule of Administrative Penalties Pursuant to Labor Code §5814.6. [Renumbered]

Note: Authority cited: Sections 133, 5307.3 and 5814.6, Labor Code. Reference: Sections 129.5, 139.48, 5814 and 5814.6, Labor Code; and Sections 11180–11191, Government Code.

History: 1. New section filed 4-26-2007; operative 5-26-2007 (Register 2007, No. 17).

2. Change without regulatory effect renumbering former section 10225.1 to section 10112.2 filed 4-7-2008 pursuant to section 100, title 1, California Code of Regulations (Register 2008, No. 15).

§10225.2. Notice of Administrative Penalty Assessment, Appeal Hearing Procedures and Review. [Renumbered]

Note: Authority cited: Sections 133, 5307.3 and 5814.6, Labor Code. Reference: Sections 129.5, 139.48, 5300, 5814, 5814.6 and 5900 et seq., Labor Code.

History: 1. New section filed 4-26-2007; operative 5-26-2007 (Register 2007, No. 17).

2. Change without regulatory effect renumbering former section 10225.2 to section 10112.3 filed 4-7-2008 pursuant to section 100, title 1, California Code of Regulations (Register 2008, No. 15).

SUBCHAPTER 1.9 RULES OF THE COURT ADMINISTRATOR

§10250. Payment of Medical Provider and Medical-Legal Lien Claimant Initial Lien Filing Fees.

(a) At the time of filing of the initial lien in each case, every medical provider or medical-legal lien claimant, except the Veterans Administration, the Medi-Cal program, or a public hospital, shall be responsible for payment of the initial lien filing fee required of providers by Labor Code Section 4903.05. For purposes of this section, the term "initial lien" means any lien filed in a case on or after January 1, 2004 by a lien claimant who has not previously filed a lien in the same or in any related case. When the medical provider or medical-legal lien claimant files a single initial lien in more than one related case involving the same employee or dependent, only a single filing fee shall be required. For purposes of this section, a case shall be deemed related if the case alleges injury to the same or substantially same body parts.

(b) When filing the initial lien in writing, the medical provider or medical-legal lien claimant shall submit a check or money order in the amount of one hundred dollars ($100), made payable to "DWC Revolving Fund." The check or money order for the filing fee shall be attached to the front of the lien form and shall contain the words "lien filing fee" and the Workers' Compensation Appeals Board case number, if available, in the memo section of the check or money order.

(c) If no application exists for the employee at the time of the initial lien filing, the lien claimant must file any necessary application(s) together with the lien. When the medical provider or medical-legal lien claimant files the application, the filing fee required by Labor Code Section 4903.05 shall be submitted together with the application. In such cases, the WCAB case number shall be filled in by the WCAB on the check or money order at such time as the case number is assigned. If the lien claimant wishes to receive a conformed copy of the application, the lien claimant shall submit a postage paid, pre-addressed return envelope together with the application(s).

(d) When the medical provider or medical-legal lien claimant files liens in written form in more than one case at the same time, the filing fees for each lien may be paid with a single check or money order by attaching a list of the available WCAB case numbers for the cases in which the filing fees are paid to the check covering those cases. If the list includes cases in which the lien claimant is filing an application together with the lien, the lien claimant shall provide the name of the employee, the employee's social security number, and the date(s) of injury on the list instead of a WCAB case number. A single list may include existing cases and cases where the lien claimant is filing the application.

(e) No initial lien, filed in writing, shall be accepted for filing on or after January 1, 2004 unless accompanied by full payment for the filing fee required by Labor Code Section 4903.05. Any initial lien delivered for filing on or after January 1, 2004 without payment of the initial lien filing fee shall be discarded without notice to the party submitting it, unless a postage paid, pre-addressed return envelope is submitted with the lien. Until receipt of proper payment, the lien shall not be deemed to have been received or filed for any purpose.

(f) A medical provider or medical-legal lien claimant shall be billed on a monthly basis for all liens filed electronically through the EDEX system, or as otherwise designated by DWC, in the preceding month. Within 30 calendar days of receipt of the billing, the medical provider or medical-legal lien claimant shall submit a check or money order for the total filing fee billed. The check or money order, made payable to "DWC Revolving Fund," shall be submitted to:

LIEN FILING FEE PAYMENT UNIT
DIVISION OF WORKERS' COMPENSATION
P.O. BOX 420603
SAN FRANCISCO, CA 94142-0603

(g) The WCAB will not order or enforce payment of any medical treatment or medical-legal lien filed on or after January 1, 2004 without prior payment of the filing fee required by Labor Code Section 4903.05.

(h) When the attorney for the employee or dependent or any assignee of the lien claimant files the initial medical or medical-legal lien, that filing shall be deemed to have been made by an agent for the medical provider or medical-legal lien claimant and payment of the filing fee required by Labor Code Section 4903.05 shall be required of the filing party as if the lien had been filed directly by the medical provider or medical-legal lien claimant.

Note: Authority cited: Section 4903.05, Labor Code. Reference: Sections 4903.05 and 5307, Labor Code.

History: 1. New subchapter 1.9 (section 10250) and section filed 12-31-2003 as an emergency; operative 1-1-2004 (Register 2004, No. 1). A Certificate of Compliance must be transmitted to OAL by 4-30-2004 or emergency language will be repealed by operation of law on the following day.

2. Certificate of Compliance as to 1-1-2004 order transmitted to OAL 4-30-2004; disapproved by OAL and order of repeal filed 6-15-2004 (Register 2004, No. 27).

3. New subchapter 1.9 (section 10250) and section filed 6-30-2004; operative 6-30-2004 pursuant to Government Code section 11343.4 (Register 2004, No. 27).

Ref.: Hanna § 30.04.

§10252. Filing the Request.

(a) The Administrative Director shall establish a uniform expedited hearing calendar in all offices of the Division of Workers' Compensation.

(b) An applicant is entitled to an expedited priority hearing and decision upon the filing of an Application for Adjudication of Claim and Request for Expedited Hearing, DWC Form 4, showing a bona fide dispute as to:

(1) entitlement to medical treatment;

(2) entitlement to temporary disability payments or amount;

(3) appeal from a decision and order of the rehabilitation unit, enforcement thereof, or termination; or

(4) liability for benefits among employers;

(c) The request for expedited hearing must be on the form set forth in Section 10252.1, DWC Form 4, and must be filed with an Application for Adjudication of Claim.

(d) Within two (2) days of receipt of the Request for Expedited Hearing, the Request shall be reviewed for compliance with Subdivision (b).

Note: Authority cited: Sections 133 and 5307.3, Labor Code. Reference: Section 5502(b), Labor Code.

History: 1. Change without regulatory effect renumbering former section 10136 to section 10252, including amendment of subsection (c), filed 4-7-2008 pursuant to section 100, title 1, California Code of Regulations (Register 2008, No. 15).

§10252.1. Form.

WORKERS COMPENSATION APPEALS BOARD
STATE OF CALIFORNIA

CASE NO.:

REQUEST FOR EXPEDITED
HEARING AND DECISION
[LABOR CODE SECTION 5502(b)]

____
Applicant

vs.

____
Defendants

The applicant herein, having filed an Application for Adjudication of Claim this date, requests that this case be set for expedited hering and decision at

______________________________ on the following issues:
Workers' Compensation Appeals Board

_______ Entitlement to Medical Treatment per L.C. 4600
_______ Entitlement to Temporary Disability, or Disagreement on Amount of Temporary Disability
_______ Appeal from Decision and Order of Rehabilitation Bureau
_______ Entitlement to Compensation in Dispute Because of Disagreement between Employers and/or Carriers

Explanation: ______________________________

____

APPLICANT STATES UNDER PENALTY OF PERJURY THAT THERE IS A BONA FIDE DISPUTE; THAT HE/SHE IS PRESENTLY READY TO PROCEED TO HEARING; THAT HIS/HER DISCOVERY IS COMPLETE ON SAID ISSUES; THAT THE TIME REQUIRED FOR HEARING WILL BE ______________________________

Name (Print or Type) ______________________________

Signature of applicant ______________________________

Signature of attorney (if represented) ______________________________

Date: ______________________________

INSTRUCTION FOR FILING

This request must be filed with an Application for Adjudication of Claim at the appropriate district office of the Appeals Board.

SERVICE

Type or print names and addresses of parties, including attorneys and representatives served with a copy of this request.

______________________________ ______________________________

DWC Form 4 (02/93)

WORKERS' COMPENSATION APPEALS BOARD
STATE OF CALIFORNIA

CASE NO.:

SOLICTITUD PARA EXPEDIR
LA AUDICION Y DECISION
[CODIGO DEL TRABAJO SECCION 5502(b)]

____
Demandante

Contra

____
Demandado

Eldemandante en esta, ha presentado una aplicacion para beneficios en esta fecha, el requiere que este caso sea dirigido para espedir la audicion y decision a ______________________________
Oficina de La Compensacion de Trabajadores de la Junta de Apelacion
en los siguientes asuntos:

________ Tener Derecho a Tratamiento Medico segun L.C. 4600
________ Tener Derecho de Incapacitado Temporal, o estar de desacuerdo con la cantidad de la Incapacidad
________ Temporal
________ Apelacion de la Decision y Orden del Bureau de Rehabilitacion
________ Tener Derecho a recibir compensacion en Litigio por desacuerdo entre el Empresario y/o Compania de
________ Seguros

Explicacion: ______________________________

____

____

EL DEMANDANTE DECLARA BAJO MULTO DE PERJURIO QUE AQUI EXISTE UN LITIGIO DE BONA FIDE; QUE EL/ELLA ESTA AHORA PREPARADA PARA PROCEDER CON LA AUDICION; QUE SU DESCUBRIMIENTO ESTA COMPLETO CON LAS CUESTIONES DICHAS; QUE LA REQUERIDA HORA SERA ______________

Nombre (Escribe en letra de imprenta o maquina) ______________

Firma del Demandante______________

Firma del Abogado (si es representado) ______________

Fecha ______________

INSTRUCCIONES PARA SER PRESENTADO

Esta solicitud debe ser presentada con la Demanda de Adjuicio en una Oficina de Compensacion de Trabajadores.

SERVICIO

Escriba a maquina o en letra de imprenta los nombres y direcciones de las personas que hayan recibidos una copia de esta demanda, inluyendo los abogados y los representantes

______________ ______________

DWC Form 4 (02/93)

Note: Authority cited: Sections 133 and 5307.3, Labor Code. Reference: Section 5502(b), Labor Code.

History: 1. Change without regulatory effect renumbering former section 10137 to section 10252.1 filed 4-7-2008 pursuant to section 100, title 1, California Code of Regulations (Register 2008, No. 15).

SUBCHAPTER 2 WORKERS' COMPENSATION APPEALS BOARD—RULES OF PRACTICE AND PROCEDURE

ARTICLE 1 General

§10300. Adoption, Amendment or Rescission of Rules.

Notices required by Labor Code Sections 5307 and 5307.4 shall be served by the Appeals Board by regular mail, fax, electronic mail or any similar technology, not less than thirty (30) days prior to the date of hearing on those who have on file with the Secretary of the Workers' Compensation Appeals Board in San Francisco a written request for notification. Notice of action taken shall be served on the same persons by regular mail within thirty (30) days following the filing of any order pertaining to the rules with the Secretary of State.

Note: Authority cited: Section 5307, Labor Code. Reference: Section 5307.4, Labor Code.

History: 1. Repeal of chap. 4.5 (Industrial Accident Commission—Rules of Practice and Procedure) and new chap. 4.5 filed by Industrial Accident Commission 12-27-65; effective thirtieth day thereafter (Register 65, No. 25). For former chap. 4.5, see Registers 58, No. 14; 59, No. 21; 61, No. 9; 61, No. 12; 62, No. 7; 62, No. 21; 63, No. 2; 65, Nos. 5, 13 and 22.

2. Ratification and adoption by Workmen's Compensation Appeals Board, of regulations filed by Industrial Accident Commission on 12-27-65, filed 1-26-66 (Register 66, No. 3).

3. Repealer of subchapter 2 (articles 1-19, sections 10300-10957, not consecutive and Appendix) and new subchapter 2 (articles 1-20, sections 10300-10958, not consecutive) filed 6- 1-81; designated effective 7-1-81 (Register 81, No. 23). For prior history, see Registers 79, No. 1; 78, No. 3; 77, No. 49; 76, No. 3; 75, No. 35; 75, No. 15; 75, No. 11; 74, No. 6; 73, No. 51; 73, No. 36; 73, No. 6; 68, No. 29; 66, No. 8; 66, No. 7; and 65, No. 25.

4. Amendment filed 12-23-93; operative 1-1-94. Submitted to OAL for printing only pursuant to Government Code section 11351 (Register 93, No. 52).

Ref.: Hanna §§ 1.11[4], 23.10[3]; Herlick Handbook § 1.6; W. Cal. Sum., 2 "Workers' Compensation" §§13, 345.

§10301. Definitions.

As used in this chapter:

(a) "Administrative Director" means the Administrative Director of the Division of Workers' Compensation.

(b) "Appeals Board" means the commissioners and deputy commissioners of the Workers' Compensation Appeals Board acting en banc or in panels.

(c) "Applicant" means any person asserting a right to relief under the provisions of Labor Code Section 5300.

(d) "Application for Adjudication" or "application" means the initial pleading that asserts a right to relief under the provisions of Labor Code Section 5300.

(e) "Declaration of Readiness to Proceed" or "Declaration of Readiness" means a request for a proceeding before the Workers' Compensation Appeals Board.

(f) "Declaration of Readiness to Proceed to Expedited Hearing" means a request for a proceeding before the Workers' Compensation Appeals Board pursuant to Labor Code section 5502(b).

(g) "Defendant" means any person against whom a right to relief is claimed.

(h) To "file" a document means to deliver the document or cause it to be delivered to the Workers' Compensation Appeals Board district office with venue or to the Appeals Board for the purpose of having it included in the Workers' Compensation Appeals Board case file.

(i) "Hearing" means any trial, mandatory settlement conference, rating mandatory settlement conference, status conference, or priority conference.

(j) "Lien claimant" means any person claiming payment under the provisions of Labor Code section 4903 or 4903.1.

(k) "Mandatory settlement conference" means a proceeding before the Workers' Compensation Appeals Board to assist the parties in resolving their dispute or, if the dispute cannot be resolved, to frame the issues and stipulations in preparation for a trial.

(*l*) "Party" means an Applicant or Defendant, or a lien claimant where the applicant's case has been settled by way of a compromise and release, or where the applicant chooses not to proceed with his or her case.

(m) "Petition" means any request for action by the Workers' Compensation Appeals Board other than an Application for Adjudication, an Answer or a Declaration of Readiness to Proceed.

(n) "Priority conference" means a proceeding before the Workers' Compensation Appeals Board in which the applicant is represented by an attorney and the issues in dispute at the time of the proceeding include employment and/or injury arising out of and in the course of employment.

(o) "Rating mandatory settlement conference" means a mandatory settlement conference conducted to facilitate determination of the existence and extent of permanent disability through the use of informal ratings issued by the Disability Evaluation Unit, where the only unresolved issues are permanent disability and the need for future medical treatment.

(p) "Record of proceedings" means the pleadings, Declaration of Readiness to Proceed, minutes of hearings and summary of evidence, transcripts, if prepared and filed, proof of service, evidence received in the course of a proceeding, exhibits marked but not received into evidence, notices, petitions, briefs, findings, orders, decisions and awards, and arbitrator's file, if any.

(q) "Regular hearing" means a trial.

(r) To "serve" a document means to personally deliver a copy of the document, or send it in a manner permitted by these rules, to a party, lien claimant, or attorney who is entitled to a copy of the document.

(s) "Status conference" means a proceeding set for the purpose of ascertaining if there are genuine disputes requiring resolution by the Workers' Compensation Appeals Board, of providing assistance to the parties in resolving disputes, of narrowing the issues, and of facilitating preparation and trial if a trial is necessary. A status conference includes a lien conference.

(t) "Submission" means the closing of the record to the receipt of further evidence or argument.

(u) "Trial" means a proceeding set for the purpose of receiving evidence.

(v) "Workers' Compensation Appeals Board" means the Appeals Board, commissioners, deputy commissioners, presiding workers' compensation judges and workers' compensation judges.

Note: Authority cited: Sections 133 and 5307, Labor Code.

History: 1. Amendment of section and Note filed 12-19-2002; operative 1-1-2003. Submitted to OAL for printing only pursuant to Government Code section 11351 (Register 2002, No. 51).

Ref.: See Labor Code §5307; Hanna §§ 26.01[1], 26.03[1], 32.05[5]; Herlick Handbook §§ 1.6, 14.29; W. Cal. Sum., 2 "Workers' Compensation" §13.

§10302. Working Title of Referees and Referees in Charge.

The Appeals Board hereby declares its intent that the working or organizational titles of "referee" and "referee in charge" shall be respectively "workers' compensation judge" and "presiding workers' compensation judge."

Note: Authority cited: Section 5307, Labor Code. Reference: Sections 123.5, 5309, 5310 and 5312, Labor Code.

Ref.: Herlick Handbook §§ 1.2, 1.6; W. Cal. Sum., 2 "Workers' Compensation" §395.

§10304. Article and Section Headings.

Article and section headings shall not be deemed to limit or modify the meaning or intent of the provisions of any section hereof.

Note: Authority cited: Sections 133 and 5307, Labor Code. Reference: Sections 133 and 5307, Labor Code.

Ref.: Herlick Handbook § 1.6.

§10306. Case Names.

Each case shall be filed in the database of the Division of Workers' Compensation under the name of the person claimed to have been injured, whether or not that person is an applicant. Reference to the case shall be by the name of the injured person and the Workers' Compensation Appeals Board case number.

Note: Authority cited: Sections 133 and 5307, Labor Code. Reference: Section 126, Labor Code.

History: 1. Amendment of section heading and section filed 12-19-2002; operative 1-1-2003. Submitted to OAL for printing only pursuant to Government Code section 11351 (Register 2002, No. 51).

Ref.: Hanna §§ 1.11[5][b], 23.12[3], 25.06[1]; Herlick Handbook § 1.6; W. Cal. Sum., 2 "Workers' Compensation" §349.

§10308. Official Address Record.

The Workers' Compensation Appeals Board shall maintain in each case file an official address record, which shall contain the names and addresses of all parties and lien claimants, and their attorneys or agents of record.

Note: Authority cited: Sections 133 and 5307, Labor Code. Reference: Section 126, Labor Code.

History: 1. Amendment filed 12-19-2002; operative 1-1-2003. Submitted to OAL for printing only pursuant to Government Code section 11351 (Register 2002, No. 51).

Ref.: Herlick Handbook §§ 1.6, 14.5.

§10322. Workers' Compensation Appeals Board Records Not Subject to Subpoena.

The records, files and proceedings of the Workers' Compensation Appeals Board shall not be taken from its offices either on informal request or in response to a subpoena duces tecum or any order issued out of any other court or tribunal. Except as precluded by Civil Code Section 1798.24, or Government Code Section 6254, certified copies of portions of the records desired by litigants shall be delivered upon payment of fees as provided in the Rules of the Administrative Director.

Note: Authority cited: Sections 133 and 5307, Labor Code. Reference: Sections 127, 5811, Labor Code.

History: 1. Amendment filed 12-19-2002; operative 1-1-2003. Submitted to OAL for printing only pursuant to Government Code section 11351 (Register 2002, No. 51).

Ref.: Hanna § 1.11[5][b]; Herlick Handbook § 1.6.

§10324. Ex Parte Communications.

No document, including letters or other writings, shall be filed by a party or lien claimant with the Workers' Compensation Appeals Board unless service of a copy thereof is made on all parties together with the filing of proof of service as provided for in Rule 10514. No party or lien claimant shall discuss with the Appeals Board or a workers' compensation judge the merits of any case pending before the Appeals Board or that judge without the presence of all necessary parties to the proceeding, except as provided by these rules.

Note: Authority cited: Sections 133 and 5307, Labor Code. Reference: Section 5708, Labor Code.

History: 1. Amendment filed 12-19-2002; operative 1-1-2003. Submitted to OAL for printing only pursuant to Government Code section 11351 (Register 2002, No. 51).

Ref.: Hanna §§ 23.01, 23.14[2][a]; Herlick Handbook § 14.5.

ARTICLE 2
Powers, Duties and Responsibilities

§10340. Appeals Board Decisions and Orders.

In accordance with Labor Code Section 115, the following orders, decisions and awards shall be issued only by the Appeals Board:

(a) All orders dismissing, denying and granting petitions for reconsideration and decisions thereon.

(b) All decisions that terminate proceedings on reconsideration, including, but not limited to, findings, orders, awards, orders approving or disapproving compromise and release, orders allowing or disallowing liens, and orders for dismissal.

(c) All orders, including interim and interlocutory orders, made after reconsideration has been granted and while proceedings are pending on reconsideration, including but not limited to, orders taking off calendar, orders joining or dismissing parties, and orders allowing or disallowing liens. Unless otherwise instructed by the Appeals Board, the authority of the workers' compensation judge to whom a case has been referred for proceedings on reconsideration is as set out in Section 10862 of these Rules.

(d) Except for sanctions and contempt, orders in disciplinary proceedings against attorneys or other agents.

(e) Decisions on remittitur.

(f) Orders disqualifying a workers' compensation judge under Labor Code Section 5311.

Note: Authority cited: Sections 133 and 5307, Labor Code. Reference: Sections 115, 5311, Labor Code.

History: 1. Amendment of subsections (b) and (d) filed 12-19-2002; operative 1-1-2003. Submitted to OAL for printing only pursuant to Government Code section 11351 (Register 2002, No. 51).

Ref.: Hanna §§ 1.11[6][b], 26.10[1]; Herlick Handbook §§ 1.6, 14.5; W. Cal. Sum., 2 "Workers' Compensation" §395.

§10341. En Banc Decisions.

En banc decisions of the Appeals Board are binding on panels of the Appeals Board and workers' compensation judges as legal precedent under the principle of *stare decisis*.

Note: Authority cited: Sections 133 and 5307, Labor Code. Reference: Section 115, Labor Code.

History: 1. New section filed 12-19-2002; operative 1-1-2003. Submitted to OAL for printing only pursuant to Government Code section 11351 (Register 2002, No. 51).

Ref.: Hanna § 28.35[1]; Herlick Handbook §§ 1.2, 14.34; W. Cal. Sum., 2 "Workers' Compensation" §13.

§10342. Appeals Board, Member Orders.

The following orders may be issued only by the Appeals Board or a member thereof:

(a) approving undertakings on stays of proceedings on reconsideration and petitions for writ of review; and

(b) directing exhumation or autopsy.

Note: Authority cited: Sections 133 and 5307, Labor Code. Reference: Sections 115, 5706, 5707 and 6002, Labor Code.

History: 1. Amendment filed 12-23-93; operative 1-1-94. Submitted to OAL for printing only pursuant to Government Code section 11351 (Register 93, No. 52).

Ref.: See Labor Code §§6000, 6001; Hanna §§ 1.11[6][b], 26.10[1], 27.11[3]; Herlick Handbook §§ 1.6, 14.5.

§10344. Appeals Board, Commissioner, Deputy Commissioner and Presiding Workers' Compensation Judge Orders.

The following may be issued only by the Appeals Board, a commissioner, a deputy commissioner or a presiding workers' compensation judge:

(a) orders issuing certified copies of orders, decisions or awards except that a certified copy may be issued by a presiding workers' compensation judge only if the time for seeking reconsideration and judicial review has expired, and no proceedings are pending on reconsideration or judicial review;

(b) orders staying, quashing and recalling writs of execution and fixing and approving undertakings thereon;

(c) orders directing entry of satisfaction of judgment; and

(d) orders issuing, recalling, quashing, discharging and staying writs of attachment and fixing and approving undertakings thereon.

Note: Authority cited: Sections 133 and 5307, Labor Code. Reference: Sections 6000, 6001 and 6002, Labor Code.

Ref.: Hanna §§ 1.11[3][d], 26.10[1], 27.11[4][a]; Herlick Handbook §§ 1.6, 14.5.

§10346. Assignment or Transfer of Cases.

(a) The presiding workers' compensation judge has full responsibility for the assignment of cases to the workers' compensation judges of each office. The presiding workers' compensation judge shall transfer to another workers' compensation judge the proceedings on any case in the event of the death, extended absence, unavailability, or disqualification of the workers' compensation judge to whom it has been assigned, and may otherwise reassign those cases if no oral testimony has been received therein, or if the requirements of Labor Code Section 5700 have been waived. To the extent practicable and fair, supplemental proceedings shall be assigned to the workers' compensation judge who heard the original proceedings.

Any conflict that may arise between presiding workers' compensation judges of different offices respecting assignment of a case, venue, or priority of hearing where there is conflict in calendar settings will be resolved by a deputy commissioner of the Appeals Board.

(b) If a compromise and release or stipulations with request for award have not been approved, disapproved, or noticed for trial on the issue of adequacy and other disputed issues within 45 days after filing, the file shall be transferred to the presiding judge for review.

Note: Authority cited: Sections 133 and 5307, Labor Code. Reference: Sections 5309 and 5310, Labor Code.

History: 1. Amendment of section and Note filed 12-19-2002; operative 1-1-2003. Submitted to OAL for printing only pursuant to Government Code section 11351 (Register 2002, No. 51).

Ref.: See Labor Code §6002; Hanna §§ 1.11[3][d], 26.03[1]; Herlick Handbook §§ 1.6, 14.5, 14.31.

§10347. Assignment of Judges.

Where practicable, different judges shall be assigned to conduct the mandatory settlement conference or conference(s) pursuant to Labor Code section 5502(c) and the trial.

Note: Authority cited: Sections 133 and 5307, Labor Code. Reference: Sections 5309 and 5310, Labor Code.

History: 1. New section filed 12-19-2002; operative 1-1-2003. Submitted to OAL for printing only pursuant to Government Code section 11351 (Register 2002, No. 51). For prior history, see Register 96, No. 43.

Ref.: See Labor Code §5311; Hanna § 26.04[1][d]; Herlick Handbook §§ 14.30, 14.34.

§10348. Authority of Workers' Compensation Judges.

In any case that has been regularly assigned to a workers' compensation judge, the judge shall have full power, jurisdiction and authority to hear and determine all issues of fact and law presented and to issue any interim, interlocutory and final orders, findings, decisions and awards as may be necessary to the full adjudication of the case, including the fixing of the amount of the bond required in Labor Code section 3715. Orders, findings, decisions and awards issued by a workers' compensation judge shall be the orders, findings, decisions and awards of the Workers' Compensation Appeals Board unless reconsideration is granted.

A workers' compensation judge or a deputy commissioner may issue writs or summons, warrants of attachment, warrants of commitment and all necessary process in proceedings for direct and hybrid contempt in a like manner and to the same extent as courts of record.

Note: Authority cited: Sections 133 and 5307, Labor Code. Reference: Sections 121, 134, 5309 and 5310, Labor Code.

History: 1. Amendment exempt from OAL review pursuant to Government Code section 11351 filed 12-19-90; operative 1-1-91 (Register 91, No. 7).

2. Amendment of first paragraph filed 12-19-2002; operative 1-1-2003. Submitted to OAL for printing only pursuant to Government Code section 11351 (Register 2002, No. 51).

Ref.: Hanna §§ 1.11[3][b]–[c], 21.09[1], 26.03[1], 26.10[1]; Herlick Handbook §§ 1.6, 13.4, 14.4; W. Cal. Sum., 2 "Workers' Compensation" §14.

§10349. Orders Equivalent to Notices of Intention.

An order with a clause rendering the order null and void if an objection showing good cause is filed within ten (10) days shall be deemed equivalent to a ten (10) day notice of intention.

Note: Authority cited: Sections 133 and 5307, Labor Code. Reference: Section !, Labor Code.

History: 1. New section filed 12-19-2002; operative 1-1-2003. Submitted to OAL for printing only pursuant to Government Code section 11351 (Register 2002, No. 51). For prior history, see Register 96, No. 43.

Ref.: See Labor Code §§121, 123.7, 134, 5309, 5310; Hanna § 23.14[1][c]; Herlick Handbook § 14.43.

§10350. Trials: Appointment and Authority of Pro Tempore Workers' Compensation Judges.

A presiding workers' compensation judge may appoint and assign a pro tempore workers' compensation judge to conduct a trial on any issue in any proceeding before the Workers' Compensation Appeals Board and to make and file a finding, opinion, order, decision or award based thereon. Before assignment of a particular pro tempore workers' compensation judge, the parties or their representatives shall submit a request and written stipulation to the presiding workers' compensation judge. The request and written stipulation shall set out in full the name and the office address of the attorney agreed upon to conduct the trial as a pro tempore workers' compensation judge.

If a case is off calendar or has not before been set on the trial calendar, the request and written stipulation must be filed with a Declaration of Readiness to Proceed pursuant to Section 10414. The presiding workers' compensation judge, upon approval of the request for trial by a pro tempore workers' compensation judge, will assign the case to the trial calendar making appropriate arrangements to provide the pro tempore workers' compensation judge with facilities and staff at a time and place convenient to the Workers' Compensation Appeals Board and the pro tempore workers' compensation judge.

At the time of any conference hearing, the parties or their representatives may file the same request and written stipulation which will be submitted to the presiding workers' compensation judge who will assign the case to the trial calendar in the same manner as set forth above.

Pro tempore workers' compensation judges will have all the authority and powers of workers' compensation judges as set forth in the Labor Code and Rules of Practice and Procedure of the Workers' Compensation Appeals Board including inquiry into adequacy of and approval of compromise and release agreements and stipulated findings including the authority to issue appropriate findings, awards and orders. Pro tempore workers' compensation judges shall be bound by the Rules of Practice and Procedure of the Workers' Compensation Appeals Board (including Articles 6, 7 and 8).

Note: Authority cited: Sections 133 and 5307, Labor Code. Reference: Sections 123.7, 5309 and 5310, Labor Code.

History: 1. New section filed 5-25-82; designated effective 7-1-82 (Register 82, No. 22).

2. Amendment of section heading, section and Note filed 12-19-2002; operative 1-1-2003. Submitted to OAL for printing only pursuant to Government Code section 11351 (Register 2002, No. 51).

Ref.: See Labor Code §121; Hanna § 1.11[3][e]; Herlick Handbook §§ 1.6, 14.5.

§10351. Conference Hearings: Appointment and Authority of Pro Tempore Workers' Compensation Judges.

A pro tempore workers' compensation judge shall in any case filed have the same power as a workers' compensation judge to conduct conference hearings, including mandatory settlement conferences, rating mandatory settlement conferences and status conferences; to inquire into the adequacy of and to approve compromise and release agreements; to approve stipulated findings and to issue appropriate awards based on the stipulations; to frame stipulations and issues and make interim and interlocutory orders at the conference hearing.

The presiding workers' compensation judge may assign a pro tempore workers' compensation judge to any conference hearing calendar including rating mandatory settlement conferences or status conferences. The name of the pro tempore workers' compensation judge shall appear on the notice of hearing. Failure to object to the assignment within five days of service of notice of conference hearing shall constitute a waiver of any objection to proceeding before the pro tempore workers' compensation judge assigned to the mandatory settlement conference hearing, rating mandatory settlement conference or status conference.

Note: Authority cited: Sections 133 and 5307, Labor Code. Reference: Sections 123.7, 5309 and 5310, Labor Code.

History: 1. New section filed 5-25-82; designated effective 7-1-82 (Register 82, No. 22).

2. Amendment of section and Note filed 12-19-2002; operative 1-1-2003. Submitted to OAL for printing only pursuant to Government Code section 11351 (Register 2002, No. 51).

Ref.: See Labor Code §121; Hanna § 1.11[3][e]; Herlick Handbook §§ 1.6, 14.5.

§10352. Reconsideration of Pro Tempore Workers' Compensation Judge's Orders, Decisions or Awards.

Any final order, decision or award filed by a pro tempore workers' compensation judge shall be subject to the reconsideration process as set forth in Labor Code Sections 5900 through 5911.

Note: Authority cited: Sections 133 and 5307, Labor Code. Reference: Sections 121, 123.7, 5309, 5310 and 5900–5911, Labor Code.

History: 1. New section filed 5-25-82; designated effective 7-1-82 (Register 82, No. 22).

2. Editorial correction of NOTE filed 2-2-83 (Register 83, No. 6).

Ref.: Hanna § 1.11[3][e]; Herlick Handbook §§ 1.6, 14.4.

§10353. Settlement Conference Authority.

(a) In accordance with Labor Code section 5502, subdivision (e)(2), the workers' compensation judge shall have authority to inquire into the adequacy and completeness, including provision for lien claims, of compromise and release agreements or stipulations with request for award or orders, and to issue orders approving compromise and release agreements or awards or orders based upon approved stipulations. The workers' compensation judge may make orders and rulings regarding admission of evidence and discovery matters, including admission of offers of proof and stipulations of testimony where appropriate and necessary for resolution of the dispute(s) by the workers' compensation judge, and may submit and decide the dispute(s) on the record pursuant to the agreement of the parties. The workers' compensation judge shall not hear sworn testimony at any conference.

(b) The workers' compensation judge may temporarily adjourn a conference to a time certain to facilitate a specific resolution of the dispute(s) subject to Labor Code section 5502, subdivision (e)(1).

Subject to the provisions of Labor Code Section 5502.5 and Rule 10416, upon a showing of good cause, the workers' compensation judge may continue a mandatory settlement conference to a date certain, may continue it to a status conference on a date certain, or may take the case off calendar. In such a case, the workers' compensation judge shall note the reasons for the continuance or order taking off calendar in the minutes. The minutes shall be served on all parties and lien claimants, and their representatives.

(c) Absent resolution of the dispute(s), the parties shall file at the mandatory settlement conference a joint pre-trial statement setting forth the issues and stipulations for trial, witnesses, exhibits, and the proposed permanent disability rating as provided by Labor Code Section 4065. The parties may modify their proposed ratings only when evidence, relevant to the proposed ratings, and disclosed or obtained after the mandatory settlement conference, becomes admissible pursuant to Labor Code Section 5502, subdivision (e)(3).

A summary of conference proceedings including the joint pre-trial conference statement and the disposition shall be filed by the workers' compensation judge in the record of the proceedings on a form prescribed and approved by the Appeals Board and shall be served on the parties.

Note: Authority cited: Sections 133, 5307 and 5502, Labor Code. Reference: Sections 5502 and 5502.5, Labor Code.

History: 1. New section exempt from OAL review pursuant to Government Code section 11351, filed 12-19-90; operative 1-1-91 (Register 91, No. 7).

2. Amendment of section heading and text filed 12-23-93; operative 1-1-94. Submitted to OAL for printing only pursuant to Government Code section 11351 (Register 93, No. 52).

3. Amendment of section and Note filed 12-19-2002; operative 1-1-2003. Submitted to OAL for printing only pursuant to Government Code section 11351 (Register 2002, No. 51).

Ref.: See Labor Code §5500; Hanna §§ 26.04[2], 30.22[1a]; Herlick Handbook §§ 1.6, 14.32.

ARTICLE 3
Parties and Joinder

§10360. Necessary Parties.

Any applicant other than the injured employee shall join the injured employee as a party. In such instances the Application for Adjudication shall include the injured employee's address if known or, if not known, a statement of that fact.

Note: Authority cited: Sections 133 and 5307, Labor Code. Reference: Sections 126, 5307.5 and 5503, Labor Code.

History: 1. Amendment of section and Note filed 12-19-2002; operative 1-1-2003. Submitted to OAL for printing only pursuant to Government Code section 11351 (Register 2002, No. 51).

Ref.: Hanna § 26.01[2][a]; Herlick Handbook §§ 1.6, 14.11; W. Cal. Sum., 2 "Workers' Compensation" §352.

§10364. Parties Applicant.

(a) Any person in whom any right to relief is alleged to exist may appear, or be joined, as an applicant in any case or controversy before the Workers' Compensation Appeals Board. A lien claimant may become a party where the applicant's case has been settled by way of a compromise and release, or where the applicant chooses not to proceed with his or her case.

(b) Any person against whom any right to relief is alleged to exist may be joined as a defendant.

(c) In death cases, all persons who may be dependents shall either join or be joined as applicants so that the entire liability of the employer or the insurer may be determined in one proceeding.

Note: Authority cited: Sections 133 and 5307, Labor Code. Reference: Sections 5300, 5303, 5307.5, 5500 and 5503, Labor Code.

History: 1. New subsection (a) designator and new subsections (b) and (c) filed 10-21-96; operative 11-1-96. Submitted to OAL for printing only pursuant to Government Code section 11351 (Register 96, No. 43).

2. Amendment of subsection (a) filed 12-19-2002; operative 1-1-2003. Submitted to OAL for printing only pursuant to Government Code section 11351 (Register 2002, No. 51).

Ref.: Hanna §§ 22.10, 25.05[3], 25.10[7], 26.01[2][a]; Herlick Handbook §§ 1.6, 14.11; W. Cal. Sum., 2 "Workers' Compensation" §352.

§10368. Repealed.

Note: Authority cited: Sections 133 and 5307, Labor Code. Reference: Sections 5300, 5303, 5307.5, 5500 and 5503, Labor Code.

History: 1. Repealer filed 10-21-96; operative 11-1-96. Submitted to OAL for printing only pursuant to Government Code section 11351 (Register 96, No. 43).

§10372. Repealed.

Note: Authority cited: Sections 133 and 5307, Labor Code. Reference: Sections 5300, 5303, 5307.5, 5500 and 5503, Labor Code.

History: 1. Repealer filed 10-21-96; operative 11-1-96. Submitted to OAL for printing only pursuant to Government Code section 11351 (Register 96, No. 43).

§10380. Joinder of Parties.

After filing of an Application for Adjudication, the Appeals Board, a workers' compensation judge may order the joinder of additional parties necessary for the full adjudication of the case. A party not present or represented at the time of joinder shall be served with copies of the order of joinder, the application, minutes of hearing and summary of evidence, medical reports and other documents, as directed in the order of joinder. The Workers' Compensation Appeals Board may designate the party or parties who are to make service.

Note: Authority cited: Sections 133 and 5307, Labor Code. Reference: Sections 5307.5 and 5316, Labor Code.

History: 1. Amendment exempt from OAL review pursuant to Government Code section 11351, filed 12-19-90; operative 1-1-91 (Register 91, No. 7).

2. Amendment filed 12-19-2002; operative 1-1-2003. Submitted to OAL for printing only pursuant to Government Code section 11351 (Register 2002, No. 51).

Ref.: Hanna §§ 1.11[3][c], 1.11[6][c], 23.14[2][f], 26.01[2][a], 26.03[1]; Herlick Handbook §§ 1.6, 14.11; W. Cal. Sum., 2 "Workers' Compensation" §352.

ARTICLE 4
Filing of Documents

§10390. Place and Time of Filing Documents.

After the filing and processing of the application for adjudication, all papers and documents required to be filed by the Rules of Practice and Procedure of the Workers' Compensation Appeals Board or which request action by the Workers' Compensation Appeals Board shall be filed with the office of the Workers' Compensation Appeals Board district office where the case has been assigned for hearing except where the case is pending before the Appeals Board in San Francisco for action on a petition for reconsideration or removal.

After a petition for reconsideration or petition for removal has been properly filed pursuant to Rule 10840 or 10843 and after the 15 days for amendment or correction allowed by Rule 10859 or 10843 and until the Appeals Board issues its decision on a petition for reconsideration or removal, all requests for action relating to the reconsideration process, requests for withdrawal of the petitions for reconsideration or petitions to remove or notifications of change of address from the parties or lien claimants shall be filed with the Appeals Board in San Francisco. All other mail unnecessary to the reconsideration or removal process shall be filed with the district office where the case was heard and from which the decision issued.

Documents received in any other district office or the office of the Appeals Board in San Francisco, except as provided in this rule, shall not be accepted for filing or deemed filed and shall not be acknowledged or returned to the filing party and may be discarded. Such document, however, may be returned where the filing party includes a self addressed envelope with sufficient return postage. The Workers' Compensation Appeals Board, in any proceeding, may excuse a failure to comply with this rule resulting from mistake inadvertence, surprise, or excusable neglect.

Except where the document is filed at the mandatory settlement conference or hearing, the person who received the document for filing shall affix on it an appropriate endorsement as evidence of the fact and date of receipt, which endorsement may be made by handwriting, by hand stamp, by electrical mail received time and date stamp, or by any other appropriate means. Documents filed by mail are deemed filed on the date they are received by the Workers' Compensation Appeals Board, not on the date of posting.

Note: Authority cited: Sections 133 and 5307, Labor Code. Reference: Section 126, Labor Code.

History: 1. Repealer and new section filed 12-23-93; operative 1-1-94. Submitted to OAL for printing only pursuant to Government Code section 11351 (Register 93, No. 52).

2. Amendment filed 12-19-2002; operative 1-1-2003. Submitted to OAL for printing only pursuant to Government Code section 11351 (Register 2002, No. 51).

Ref.: Hanna § 23.12[2]; Herlick Handbook §§ 1.6, 14.5, 14.15, 15.3, 15.4.

§10391. Filing of Copies of Documents.

A document that has been sent directly to the Workers' Compensation Appeals Board by fax or e-mail will not be accepted for filing.

The Workers' Compensation Appeals Board will accept for filing a fax copy, photocopy, or other reproduction of a properly executed Application for Adjudication, Answer to an Application for Adjudication, Petition, Declaration of Readiness, Compromise and Release, or Stipulations with Request for Award.

Any reproduction of a document filed under this section is presumed to be an accurate representation of the original document. If a party alleges that a reproduction filed under this section is inaccurate or unreliable, the party filing the reproduction has the burden of proving by a preponderance of the evidence, that the reproduction is an accurate representation of the original document.

Note: Authority cited: Sections 133 and 5307, Labor Code. Reference: Section 126, Labor Code.

History: 1. New section filed 12-19-2002; operative 1-1-2003. Submitted to OAL for printing only pursuant to Government Code section 11351 (Register 2002, No. 51).

Ref.: Hanna § 23.12[2]; Herlick Handbook §§ 14.11, 14.15.

§10392. Form and Size Requirements for Filed Documents.

All pleadings, letters, petitions, briefs and notices filed with the Workers' Compensation Appeals Board by any party or lien claimant shall be on 8½ × 11 inch paper with two holes punched at the top and centered to fit the Workers' Compensation Appeals Board file. All documents shall include in the heading the name of the injured employee and the Workers' Compensation Appeals Board case number. All pleadings, petitions and briefs shall be double spaced, except that quotations may be single spaced.

Where, on the same day, a party files two or more medical reports in the same case, the party shall attach them to a transmittal letter that shall list each report by name of physician and date of report. The transmittal letter shall include the name of the injured employee and the Workers' Compensation Appeals Board case number.

Note: Authority cited: Sections 133 and 5307, Labor Code. Reference: Section 126, Labor Code.

History: 1. Amendment filed 12-23-93; operative 1-1-94. Submitted to OAL for printing only pursuant to Government Code section 11351 (Register 93, No. 52).

2. Amendment filed 12-19-2002; operative 1-1-2003. Submitted to OAL for printing only pursuant to Government Code section 11351 (Register 2002, No. 51).

Ref.: Hanna §§ 22.08[4][d], 23.12[2], 25.07[3], 26.06[12][b][iii], 28.21[1]; Herlick Handbook §§ 1.6, 14.5.

§10395. Improper Filing of Documents.

The following documents shall not be filed with or sent to the Workers' Compensation Appeals Board:

(a) Letters to opposing parties or counsel;

(b) Subpoenas;

(c) Notices of taking deposition;

(d) Medical appointment letters;

(e) Proofs of service ordered pursuant to Rule 10500;

(f) Medical reports, except as required by Rules 10608 and 10615;

(g) Any other document which is not required to be filed by the Rules of Practice and Procedure of the Workers' Compensation Appeals Board or which does not request action by the Workers' Compensation Appeals Board.

This rule shall not prevent admission into evidence of any document relevant to an issue pending before the Workers' Compensation Appeals Board.

Documents improperly filed pursuant to this rule and received in any district office or the office of the Appeals Board in San Francisco shall neither be accepted for filing nor deemed filed for any purpose and shall not be acknowledged or returned to the filing party, and may be discarded.

Note: Authority cited: Sections 133 and 5307, Labor Code. Reference: Section 126, Labor Code.

History: 1. New section filed 5-25-82; designated effective 7-1-82 (Register 82, No. 22).

2. Amendment filed 12-23-93; operative 1-1-94. Submitted to OAL for printing only pursuant to Government Code section 11351 (Register 93, No. 52).

3. New subsections (e)-(f), subsection relettering and amendment of last paragraph filed 12-19-2002; operative 1-1-2003. Submitted to OAL for printing only pursuant to Government Code section 11351 (Register 2002, No. 51).

Ref.: Hanna §§ 23.12[2], 25.41[2], 25.43; Herlick Handbook §§ 1.6, 14.5.

§10396. Duty to Furnish Correct Address.

(a) Every party and lien claimant having an interest in an active case pending before the Workers' Compensation Appeals Board shall advise the Workers' Compensation Appeals Board and all other known interested parties of any change of address by promptly furnishing the correct and current mailing address.

Every lien claimant having an interest in an active case pending before the Workers' Compensation Appeals Board shall advise all known interested parties of any change in the identity or telephone number of the person with authority to resolve the lien by promptly furnishing the correct name and daytime telephone number of that person to the interested parties, and shall advise the Workers' Compensation Appeals Board of any such change after a Declaration of Readiness is filed.

(b) Every party and lien claimant having an interest in an inactive case shall advise all other known interested parties and known interested lien claimants of any change of address by promptly furnishing the correct and current mailing address.

Note: Authority cited: Sections 133 and 5307, Labor Code. Reference: Section 126, Labor Code.

History: 1. Amendment filed 12-19-2002; operative 1-1-2003. Submitted to OAL for printing only pursuant to Government Code section 11351 (Register 2002, No. 51).

Ref.: Hanna § 23.14A; Herlick Handbook §§ 1.6, 10.1, 14.2, 14.5.

ARTICLE 5
Pleadings

§10400. Applications.

Proceedings for adjudication of rights and liabilities before the Workers' Compensation Appeals Board shall be initiated by the filing of an Application for Adjudication, Compromise and Release Agreement or Stipulations with Request for Award.

Applications for Adjudication shall be filed with the Workers' Compensation Appeals Board office with the proper venue. Upon filing, the application shall be assigned a case number and placed in the case file. The person filing the application shall be notified that the application has been filed and shall be given a case number that he or she shall serve on all other parties and lien claimants.

Note: Authority cited: Sections 133 and 5307, Labor Code. Reference: Sections 126, 5316 and 5500, Labor Code.

History: 1. Repealer and new section exempt from OAL review pursuant to Government Code section 11351 filed 12-19-90; operative 1-1-91 (Register 91, No. 7).

2. Amendment of section filed 6-11-92 with Secretary of State by Workers' Compensation Appeals Board; operative 6-11-92. Submitted to OAL for printing only pursuant to Government Code section 11351 (Register 92, No. 24).

3. Amendment filed 12-23-93; operative 1-1-94. Submitted to OAL for printing only pursuant to Government Code section 11351 (Register 93, No. 52).

4. Editorial correction of article heading (Register 93, No. 53).

5. Amendment of section and Note filed 12-19-2002; operative 1-1-2003. Submitted to OAL for printing only pursuant to Government Code section 11351 (Register 2002, No. 51).

Ref.: Hanna §§ 25.05[1], 25.06[1], 29.03[8]; Herlick Handbook §§ 1.6, 14.5, 14.11, 14.13, 14.15; W. Cal. Sum., 2 "Workers' Compensation" §387.

§10401. Separate Application for Each Injury.

A separate Application for Adjudication shall be filed for each separate injury for which benefits are claimed even though the employer is the same in each case. Separate pleadings shall be filed in each case.

All claims of all persons arising out of the same injury to the same employee shall be filed in the same proceeding.

Note: Authority cited: Sections 133 and 5307, Labor Code. Reference: Sections 3208.2 and 5500, Labor Code.

Ref.: Hanna §§ 25.05[2], 31.01; Herlick Handbook §§ 1.6, 14.5, 14.14.

§10402. Minors, Incompetents as Applicants.

If the Applicant is a minor or incompetent, the Application for Adjudication shall be accompanied by a Petition for Appointment of a Guardian ad Litem and Trustee. In those instances where the minor has the right of nomination, the nomination shall be included in the petition.

Note: Authority cited: Sections 133 and 5307, Labor Code. Reference: Sections 5307.5 and 5500, Labor Code.

History: 1. Amendment exempt from OAL review pursuant to Government Code section 11351 filed 12-19-90; operative 1-1-91 (Register 91, No. 7).

2. Repealer of second paragraph filed 12-19-2002; operative 1-1-2003. Submitted to OAL for printing only pursuant to Government Code section 11351 (Register 2002, No. 51).

Ref.: Hanna §§ 24.05[1], 25.05[1], 31.21[3]; Herlick Handbook §§ 1.6, 14.5.

§10403. Repealed.

History: 1. Amendment filed 5-25-82; designated effective 7-1-82 (Register 82, No. 22).

2. Repealer and new section exempt from OAL review pursuant to Government Code section 11351 filed 12-19-90; operative 1-1-91 (Register 91, No. 7).

3. Repealer of section filed 6-11-92 with Secretary of State by Workers' Compensation Appeals Board; operative 6-11-92. Submitted to OAL for printing only pursuant to Government Code section 11351 (Register 92, No. 24).

§10404. Labor Code Section 4906(g) Statement.

The employee, insurer, employer and the attorneys for each party shall comply with Labor Code Section 4906(g) by filing a statement under penalty of perjury wherein it is declared that the party on whose behalf the declaration is made has not violated Labor Code Section 139.3, has not offered, delivered, received, or accepted any unlawful rebate, refund, commission, preference, patronage dividend, discount or other consideration, whether in the form of money or otherwise, as compensation or inducement for any referred examination or evaluation by a physician. Except as otherwise provided herein, failure to comply with this rule shall result in refusal to file or process that party's application for adjudication or answer. If any of the above parties are not available, cannot be located or are unwilling to sign a declaration under penalty of perjury setting forth in specific detail the reasons that the party is not available, cannot be located or is unwilling to sign as well as good faith efforts to locate the party may be filed with the application or answer. If the presiding workers' compensation judge or designee determines from the facts set forth in the declaration that good cause has been established, he or she may accept the application or answer for filing. For the purpose of this rule, a compromise and release agreement or stipulations with request for award shall not be treated as an application for adjudication.

Note: Authority cited: Sections 133 and 5307, Labor Code. Reference: Sections 4906(g), Labor Code.

History: 1. New section filed 12-23-93; operative 1-1-94. Submitted to OAL for printing only pursuant to Government Code section 11351 (Register 93, No. 52). For prior history, see Register 91, No. 7.

2. Amendment filed 12-19-2002; operative 1-1-2003. Submitted to OAL for printing only pursuant to Government Code section 11351 (Register 2002, No. 51).

Ref.: Hanna §§ 25.06[3], 25.23, 25.27; Herlick Handbook §§ 1.6, 14.5, 14.15.

§10405. Request for Findings of Fact.

A request for findings of fact under Government Code Sections 21164, 21166, 21537, 21538, 21540, or 21540.5 or under Labor Code Sections 4800.5(d), 4801, 4804.2, 4807 or 4851 is a proceeding separate from a claim for workers' compensation benefits even though it arises out of the same incident, injury or exposure. The request for findings of fact shall be filed separately and a separate file folder and record of the proceeding will be maintained, but the request for findings of fact may be consolidated for hearing with a claim for workers' compensation benefits under the provisions of Section 10590 of these Rules.

Note: Authority cited: Sections 133 and 5307, Labor Code. Reference: Sections 21164, 21166, 21537, 21538, 21540 and 21540.5, Government Code; Sections 4800.5(d), 4801, 4804.2, 4807 and 4851, Labor Code.

History: 1. Amendment of section and Note filed 12-19-2002; operative 1-1-2003. Submitted to OAL for printing only pursuant to Government Code section 11351 (Register 2002, No. 51).

Ref.: Hanna §§ 33.02[2], 33.02[3][c], 33.02[4][c], 33.02[5][d]; Herlick Handbook §§ 1.6, 14.5, 14.17.

§10406. Pre-Application and Miscellaneous Proceedings. [Repealed]

Note: Authority cited: Sections 133 and 5307, Labor Code. Reference: Sections 132a, 4553, 4751 and 5401, Labor Code.

History: 1. New section exempt from OAL review pursuant to Government Code section 11351 filed 12-19-90; operative 1-1-91 (Register 91, No. 7).

2. Amendment filed 12-23-93; operative 1-1-94. Submitted to OAL for printing only pursuant to Government Code section 11351 (Register 93, No. 52).

3. Repealer filed 12-19-2002; operative 1-1-2003. Submitted to OAL for printing only pursuant to Government Code section 11351 (Register 2002, No. 51).

§10407. Dismissal of Claim Form—Labor Code Section 5404.5. [Renumbered]

Note: Authority cited: Sections 133 and 5307, Labor Code. Reference: Section 5404.5, Labor Code.

History: 1. New section filed 12-23-93; operative 1-1-94. Submitted to OAL for printing only pursuant to Government Code section 11351 (Register 93, No. 52).

2. Renumbering of former section 10407 to new section 10583 filed 12-19-2002; operative 1-1-2003. Submitted to OAL for printing only pursuant to Government Code section 11351 (Register 2002, No. 51).

§10408. Forms of Application.

The Application for Adjudication for compensation benefits and death benefits shall be on forms prescribed and approved by the Appeals Board.

Venue shall be at the district office where the Application for Adjudication is filed pursuant to Labor Code Section 5501.5.

Note: Authority cited: Sections 133 and 5307, Labor Code. Reference: Sections 5500 and 5501.5, Labor Code.

History: 1. Amendment filed 12-23-93; operative 1-1-94. Submitted to OAL for printing only pursuant to Government Code section 11351 (Register 93, No. 52).

2. Amendment filed 12-19-2002; operative 1-1-2003. Submitted to OAL for printing only pursuant to Government Code section 11351 (Register 2002, No. 51).

Ref.: Hanna §§ 22.05[6][c][iii]–[iv], 23.12[1], 31.20[2]; Herlick Handbook §§ 1.6, 14.5, 14.15; W. Cal. Sum., 2 "Workers' Compensation" §387.

§10410. Objection to Venue.

Any employer or carrier listed on the initial Application for Adjudication may file an objection to venue selected under Labor Code section 5501.5(a)(3) within 30 days after notice of the case number is served on the party.

Note: Authority cited: Sections 133 and 5307, Labor Code. Reference: Section 5501.5, Labor Code.

History: 1. New section filed 12-19-2002; operative 1-1-2003. Submitted to OAL for printing only pursuant to Government Code section 11351 (Register 2002, No. 51).

Ref.: Hanna § 25.27; Herlick Handbook § 14.15.

§10411. Petition for Change of Venue.

A petition for change of venue shall be filed at the district office with venue. Any objection to a petition for a change of venue shall be filed within 10 days of the filing of the petition. The presiding judge or his or her designee shall grant or deny a petition for change of venue, or serve notice of a status conference concerning the petition, within 30 days of the filing of the petition.

Note: Authority cited: Sections 133 and 5307, Labor Code. Reference: Section 5501.6, Labor Code.

History: 1. New section filed 12-19-2002; operative 1-1-2003. Submitted to OAL for printing only pursuant to Government Code section 11351 (Register 2002, No. 51).

Ref.: Hanna § 25.27; Herlick Handbook § 14.15.

§10412. Location of File After Venue Change.

When an order changing venue is issued, the Workers' Compensation Appeals Board file shall be sent forthwith to the district office to which venue was changed and that district office shall retain the file until 1) another order changing venue is issued, or 2) the case is inactive and the file is ready to be sent to the state records center or destroyed.

Note: Authority cited: Sections 133 and 5307, Labor Code. Reference: Sections 126 and 5501.6, Labor Code.

History: 1. New section filed 12-19-2002; operative 1-1-2003. Submitted to OAL for printing only pursuant to Government Code section 11351 (Register 2002, No. 51). For prior history, see Register 93, No. 52.

Ref.: Hanna § 25.27; Herlick Handbook § 14.15.

§10414. Declaration of Readiness to Proceed.

Applications or petitions shall not be placed on calendar for mandatory settlement conferences, status conferences, priority conferences, or any other hearing unless one of the parties has filed and served a Declaration of Readiness to Proceed in the form prescribed by the Appeals Board. The Declaration of Readiness shall be served on all other parties and lien claimants. The declarant shall state under penalty of perjury the specific efforts made to resolve the issues stated and, unless a status conference or priority conference is requested, that he or she is presently ready to proceed on those issues.

A simple statement in the declaration setting forth efforts to resolve the dispute or noting the opposing party's failure to respond within fifteen (15) days to an effort to resolve the dispute shall constitute an adequate description for the purposes of this rule.

A false declaration or certification by an attorney or representative may give rise to proceedings under Labor Code Section 134 for contempt or Labor Code Section 5813 for sanctions.

If a party is represented by an attorney or representative any Declaration of Readiness filed on behalf of the party shall be executed by the attorney or representative.

These rules shall not prohibit the Workers' Compensation Appeals Board from requiring proceedings on its own motion.

Note: Authority cited: Sections 133 and 5307, Labor Code. Reference: Sections 134, 5502 and 5813, Labor Code.

History: 1. Amendment exempt from OAL review pursuant to Government Code section 11351 filed 12-19-90; operative 1-1-91 (Register 91, No. 7).

2. Amendment of section filed 6-11-92 with Secretary of State by Workers' Compensation Appeals Board; operative 6-11-92. Submitted to OAL for printing only pursuant to Government Code section 11351 (Register 92, No. 24).

3. Amendment of first paragraph filed 12-23-93; operative 1-1-94. Submitted to OAL for printing only pursuant to Government Code section 11351 (Register 93, No. 52).

4. Amendment of section and Note filed 12-19-2002; operative 1-1-2003. Submitted to OAL for printing only pursuant to Government Code section 11351 (Register 2002, No. 51).

Ref.: Hanna §§ 23.14[2][d], 25.08[1]; Herlick Handbook §§ 1.6, 14.5, 14.7, 14.8, 14.18, 14.30.

§10415. Declaration of Readiness to Proceed to Expedited Hearing.

An expedited hearing shall not be placed on calendar unless a party has filed a Declaration of Readiness to Proceed to Expedited Hearing. However, the Workers' Compensation Appeals Board may schedule an expedited hearing on its own motion.

Note: Authority cited: Sections 133 and 5307, Labor Code. Reference: Section 5502(b), Labor Code.

History: 1. New section filed 12-19-2002; operative 1-1-2003. Submitted to OAL for printing only pursuant to Government Code section 11351 (Register 2002, No. 51).

Ref.: Hanna §§ 23.14[2][c], 24.11[1][c], 25.09[2], 25.23, 26.02[1]; Herlick Handbook §§ 14.8, 14.18.

§10416. Objection to Declaration of Readiness to Proceed.

Any objection to a Declaration of Readiness to Proceed shall be filed and served within ten (10) days after service of the Declaration. The objection shall set forth, under penalty of perjury, specific reason(s) why the case should not be set or why the requested proceedings are inappropriate.

A false declaration or certification filed under this section by an attorney or representative may give rise to proceedings under Labor Code section 134 for contempt or Labor Code section 5813 for sanctions.

If a party is represented, the attorney or representative shall execute any objection to the Declaration of Readiness to Proceed on behalf of the party.

If a party has received a copy of the Declaration of Readiness to Proceed and has not filed an objection under this section, that party shall be deemed to have waived any and all objections to proceeding on the issues specified in the declaration, absent extraordinary circumstances.

Note: Authority cited: Sections 133 and 5307, Labor Code. Reference: Sections 134 and 5813, Labor Code.

History: 1. Amendment exempt from OAL review pursuant to Government Code section 11351 filed 12-19-90; operative 1-1-91 (Register 91, No. 7).

2. Amendment of first paragraph filed 12-23-93; operative 1-1-94. Submitted to OAL for printing only pursuant to Government Code section 11351 (Register 93, No. 52).

3. Amendment of section and Note filed 12-19-2002; operative 1-1-2003. Submitted to OAL for printing only pursuant to Government Code section 11351 (Register 2002, No. 51).

Ref.: Hanna § 25.08[2]; Herlick Handbook §§ 1.6, 14.5, 14.8.

§10417. Walk-Through Calendar Setting.

Each district office shall establish a procedure allowing a party or law firm representing a party or parties to file up to five (5) Declarations of Readiness per day in person and immediately be notified of the date that the cases are scheduled for conference. Each Declaration of Readiness shall be served at least 10 days prior to filing and, when filed, shall be accompanied by any objection to the Declaration of Readiness. Within five (5) days of filing, the person filing the Declaration of Readiness shall notify in writing all other parties and lien claimants of the date, time, and location of the conference and the identity of the assigned judge. At the conference, the judge shall consider the issues in the Declaration of Readiness and the issues raised by any objection to it.

Note: Authority cited: Sections 133 and 5307, Labor Code. Reference: Section 5316 and 5502, Labor Code.

History: 1. Amendment exempt from OAL review pursuant to Government Code section 11351 filed 12-19-90; operative 1-1-91 (Register 91, No. 7).

2. Amendment filed 12-23-93; operative 1-1-94. Submitted to OAL for printing only pursuant to Government Code section 11351 (Register 93, No. 52).

3. Renumbering of former section 10417 to section 10420 and new section 10417 filed 12-19-2002; operative 1-1-2003. Submitted to OAL for printing only pursuant to Government Code section 11351 (Register 2002, No. 51).

Ref.: See Labor Code §§5310, 5311; Hanna §§ 24.11[1][b], [c], 25.08[4]; Herlick Handbook § 14.8.

§10418. Letters of Appointment for Medical Examinations. [Renumbered]

Note: Authority cited: Sections 133 and 5307, Labor Code. Reference: Sections 5401 and 5703, Labor Code.

History: 1. Amendment exempt from OAL review pursuant to Government Code section 11351 filed 12-19-90; operative 1-1-91 (Register 91, No. 7).

2. Amendment filed 12-23-93; operative 1-1-94. Submitted to OAL for printing only pursuant to Government Code section 11351 (Register 93, No. 52).

3. Renumbering of former section 10418 to section 10430 filed 12-19-2002; operative 1-1-2003. Submitted to OAL for printing only pursuant to Government Code section 11351 (Register 2002, No. 51).

§10420. Setting the Case.

The Workers' Compensation Appeals Board, upon the receipt of a Declaration of Readiness to Proceed, may, in its discretion, set the case for a type of proceeding other than that requested. The Workers' Compensation Appeals Board may on its own motion set any case for conference or trial.

Note: Authority cited: Sections 133 and 5307, Labor Code. Reference: Section 5310, Labor Code.

History: 1. Renumbering and amendment of former section 10417 to new section 10420 filed 12-19-2002; operative 1-1-2003. Submitted to OAL for printing only pursuant to Government Code section 11351 (Register 2002, No. 51).

Ref.: Hanna § 25.08[1]; Herlick Handbook §§ 1.6, 14.5.

§10430. Letters of Appointment for Medical Examinations.

After the filing of an Application for Adjudication, each party will notify all other parties, and their attorneys or representatives, of any medical appointment scheduled for the purposes of medical-legal evaluation. That notice shall be given at the same time the injured worker is advised of the appointment.

Note: Authority cited: Sections 133 and 5307, Labor Code. Reference: Sections 5401 and 5703, Labor Code.

History: 1. Renumbering and amendment of former section 10418 to new section 10430 filed 12-19-2002; operative 1-1-2003. Submitted to OAL for printing only pursuant to Government Code section 11351 (Register 2002, No. 51).

Ref.: Hanna §§ 21.09[2][b], 22.07[1][b]; Herlick Handbook §§ 1.6, 14.5.

§10440. Pleadings—Serious and Willful Misconduct.

All allegations that an injury was caused by either the serious and willful misconduct of the employee or of the employer must be separately pleaded and must set out in sufficient detail the specific basis upon which the charge is founded so that the adverse parties and the Workers' Compensation Appeals Board may be fully advised.

Note: Authority cited: Sections 133 and 5307, Labor Code. Reference: Sections 4550, 4551, 4552, 4553, 4553.1, Labor Code.

History: 1. Amendment of section heading filed 12-19-2002; operative 1-1-2003. Submitted to OAL for printing only pursuant to Government Code section 11351 (Register 2002, No. 51).

Ref.: Hanna §§ 10.03, 25.05[4], 25.25, 31.20[3]; Herlick Handbook §§ 1.6, 9.8, 10.2, 14.5, 14.16, 14.36; W. Cal. Sum., 2 "Workers' Compensation" §§316, 387.

§10445. Allegations.

All allegations that an injury was caused by serious and willful misconduct shall:

(a) When the charge of serious and willful misconduct is based on more than one theory, set forth each theory separately.

(b) Whenever the charge of serious and willful misconduct is predicated upon the violation of a particular safety order, set forth the correct citation or reference and all of the particulars required by Labor Code Section 4553.1.

Note: Authority cited: Sections 133 and 5307, Labor Code. Reference: Sections 4550, 4551, 4552, 4553, 4553.1, Labor Code.

History: 1. Repealer of last paragraph filed 12-19-2002; operative 1-1-2003. Submitted to OAL for printing only pursuant to Government Code section 11351 (Register 2002, No. 51).

Ref.: Hanna §§ 10.03, 25.05[4], 31.20[3]; Herlick Handbook §§ 1.6, 9.8, 14.5, 14.16, 14.36; W. Cal. Sum., 2 "Workers' Compensation" §387.

§10447. Pleadings—Discrimination.

Any person seeking to initiate proceedings under Labor Code Section 132a other than prosecution for misdemeanor must file a petition therefor setting forth specifically and in detail the nature of each violation alleged and facts relied on to show the same, and the relief sought. Each alleged violation must be separately pleaded so that the adverse party or parties and the Workers' Compensation Appeals Board may be fully advised of the specific basis upon which the charge is founded.

The Workers' Compensation Appeals Board may refer, or any worker may complain of, suspected violations of the criminal misdemeanor provisions of Labor Code Section 132a to the Division of Labor Standards Enforcement or directly to the Office of the Public Prosecutor.

Note: Authority cited: Sections 133 and 5307, Labor Code. Reference: Section 132a, Labor Code.

History: 1. Editorial correction filed 2-2-83 (Register 83, No. 6).

2. Amendment of section heading and repealer of second paragraph filed 12-19-2002; operative 1-1-2003. Submitted to OAL for printing only pursuant to Government Code section 11351 (Register 2002, No. 51).

Ref.: Hanna §§ 10.11[4], 25.05[5]; Herlick Handbook §§ 1.6, 9.12, 14.5, 14.16, 14.37.

§10450. Petitions.

A request for action by the Workers' Compensation Appeals Board, other than an Application for Adjudication, an Answer or Declaration of Readiness, shall be made by petition filed at the district office of the Workers' Compensation Appeals Board with venue. The caption of each petition shall contain the title and number of the case and shall indicate the type of relief sought.

Any document previously filed with the Workers' Compensation Appeals Board should not be attached to a petition; any such document that is attached to a petition may be discarded.

Note: Authority cited: Sections 133 and 5307, Labor Code. Reference: Section 126, Labor Code.

History: 1. Amendment of section and Note filed 12-19-2002; operative 1-1-2003. Submitted to OAL for printing only pursuant to Government Code section 11351 (Register 2002, No. 51).

Ref.: See Labor Code §§133, 5307; Hanna §§ 11.42[5][f], 25.05[4], 25.26, 27.02[5][a], 31.10[2]–[3]; Herlick Handbook §§ 1.6, 10.2, 14.5, 14.19; W. Cal. Sum., 2 "Workers' Compensation" §390.

§10452. Petition for Disqualification of Judge.

Proceedings to disqualify a workers' compensation judge under Labor Code Section 5311 shall be initiated by the filing of a petition for disqualification supported by an affidavit or declaration under penalty of perjury stating in detail facts establishing grounds for disqualification of the workers' compensation judge to whom a case or proceeding has been assigned.

If the workers' compensation judge assigned to hear the matter and the grounds for disqualification are known, the petition for disqualification shall be filed not more than 10 days after service of notice of hearing. In no event shall any such petition be allowed after the swearing of the first witness.

A petition for disqualification shall be referred to and determined by a panel of three commissioners of the Appeals Board in the same manner as a petition for reconsideration.

Note: Authority cited: Section 5307, Labor Code. Reference: Sections 5310 and 5311, Labor Code.

Ref.: Hanna § 26.03[2]; Herlick Handbook §§ 1.6, 14.5, 14.19.

§10453. Petition for Automatic Reassignment of Trial or Expedited Hearing to Another Workers' Compensation Judge.

A party shall be entitled to automatic reassignment of a trial or expedited hearing to another workers' compensation judge in accordance with the provisions of this section. An injured worker shall be entitled to one reassignment of a judge for trial or expedited hearing. If the injured worker has not exercised the right to automatic reassignment and one or more lien claimants have become parties and no testimony has been taken, the lien claimants shall be entitled to one reassignment of judge for a trial, which may be exercised by any of them. The defendants shall be entitled to one reassignment of judge for a trial or expedited hearing, which may be exercised by any of them.

If the parties are first notified of the identity of the workers' compensation judge assigned for trial or expedited hearing by a notice of trial served by mail, to exercise the right to automatic reassignment a party must file a petition requesting reassignment not more than five (5) days after the service of the notice of trial or expedited hearing. The presiding judge or a person designated by the presiding judge shall rule on any petition for automatic reassignment. If a petition for automatic reassignment is granted, a new notice of trial or expedited hearing shall be served.

If the parties are first notified of the identity of the workers' compensation judge assigned for trial at a mandatory settlement conference, at a status conference, at a lien conference, at a priority conference, or upon reassignment at the time of trial, to exercise the right to automatic reassignment a party must make an oral motion immediately upon learning the name of the judge to whom the case has been assigned for trial. The motion shall be acted upon immediately by the presiding workers' compensation judge or a person designated by the presiding judge.

In no event shall any motion or petition for reassignment be entertained after the swearing of the first witness at a trial or expedited hearing.

If a party files a petition or makes a motion for automatic reassignment and no other workers' compensation judge is available in the office, the assignment shall be made by a deputy commissioner of the Appeals Board.

Unless required for the convenience of the Workers' Compensation Appeals Board, no continuance shall be granted by reason of a petition or motion under this section. If a continuance is granted, another trial or expedited hearing shall be scheduled as early as possible.

Consolidated cases are to be considered as one case within the meaning of this section. This section is not applicable to conference hearings.

Note: Authority cited: Section 5307, Labor Code. Reference: Section 5310, Labor Code.

History: 1. Editorial correction filed 2-2-83 (Register 83, No. 6).

2. Amendment of section heading, section and Note filed 12-19-2002; operative 1-1-2003. Submitted to OAL for printing only pursuant to Government Code section 11351 (Register 2002, No. 51).

Ref.: See Labor Code §5311; Hanna § 26.03[1A]; Herlick Handbook § 14.19.

§10454. Automatic Reassignment After Reversal.

Notwithstanding Rule 10453, where the Appeals Board reverses a decision of a workers' compensation judge on an issue of the statute of limitations, jurisdiction, employment, or injury arising out of and in the course of employment, and remands the case for further proceedings, the party who filed the petition for reconsideration that resulted in the reversal shall be entitled to automatic reassignment of the case to another workers' compensation judge upon a motion or petition requesting reassignment filed at the district office within 30 days after the decision of the Appeals Board becomes final.

Note: Authority cited: Sections 133 and 5307, Labor Code. Reference: Section 5310, Labor Code.

History: 1. Renumbering of former section 10454 to new section 10455 and new section 10454 filed 12-19-2002; operative 1-1-2003. Submitted to OAL for printing only pursuant to Government Code section 11351 (Register 2002, No. 51).

Ref.: See Labor Code §5803; Hanna §§ 26.03[1A], 28.36[4]; Herlick Handbook § 14.5; W. Cal. Sum., 2 "Workers' Compensation" §§427, 432.

§10455. Petition to Reopen.

Petitions invoking the continuing jurisdiction of the Workers' Compensation Appeals Board under Labor Code Section 5803 shall set forth specifically and in detail the facts relied upon to establish good cause for reopening.

Note: Authority cited: Sections 133 and 5307, Labor Code. Reference: Section 5803, Labor Code.

History: 1. Renumbering of former section 10454 to new section 10455 filed 12-19-2002; operative 1-1-2003. Submitted to OAL for printing only pursuant to Government Code section 11351 (Register 2002, No. 51).

Ref.: Hanna §§ 28.03[1][a], 31.04[4][a]; Herlick Handbook §§ 1.6, 14.5, 14.9.

§10458. Petition for New and Further Disability.

The jurisdiction of the Workers' Compensation Appeals Board under Labor Code Section 5410 shall be invoked by a petition setting forth specifically and in detail the facts relied upon to establish new and further disability.

If no prior Application for Adjudication has been filed, jurisdiction shall be invoked by the filing of an original Application for Adjudication.

Note: Authority cited: Sections 133 and 5307, Labor Code. Reference: Section 5803, Labor Code.

Ref.: Hanna §§ 25.05[2], 31.05[5]; Herlick Handbook §§ 1.6, 14.5, 14.9, 14.19.

§10462. Petition to Terminate Liability; Filing.

A petition to terminate liability for continuing temporary disability indemnity under a findings and award, decision or order of the Appeals Board or a workers' compensation judge shall be filed within 10 days of the termination of the payments or other compensation. Failure to file such a petition within 10 days may affect the right to credit for an overpayment of temporary disability indemnity.

Note: Authority cited: Sections 133 and 5307, Labor Code. Reference: Sections 4650, 4651.1, Labor Code.

History: 1. Amendment filed 12-19-2002; operative 1-1-2003. Submitted to OAL for printing only pursuant to Government Code section 11351 (Register 2002, No. 51).

Ref.: Hanna §§ 7.02[1], 31.10[1][a]; Herlick Handbook §§ 1.6, 14.5, 14.19; W. Cal. Sum., 2 "Workers' Compensation" §433.

§10464. Contents of Petition to Terminate Liability.

A petition to terminate liability for temporary total disability indemnity shall conform substantially to the form provided by the Appeals Board and shall include:

(a) the correct title and date of filing of the prior order or decision, liability under which is sought to be terminated;

(b) the date upon which it is claimed that liability terminated;

(c) the grounds upon which it is claimed liability should be terminated;

(d) whether permanent disability is being advanced and, if so, the approximate date to which such indemnity will be paid;

(e) whether the employee is presently working, according to information available to the petitioner;

(f) a computer printout showing the dates and the amounts of disability indemnity that have been paid, and the periods covered shall be attached; and

(g) proof of service upon the opposing parties.

All medical reports in the possession of the petitioner that have not previously been served and filed shall accompany the petition. The petition also shall contain a statement, in underlined capital letters, that an order terminating liability for temporary total disability indemnity may issue unless objection thereto is made on behalf of the employee within 14 days after service of the petition.

Note: Authority cited: Sections 133 and 5307, Labor Code. Reference: Sections 4650, 4651.1, Labor Code.

History: 1. Amendment filed 12-19-2002; operative 1-1-2003. Submitted to OAL for printing only pursuant to Government Code section 11351 (Register 2002, No. 51).

Ref.: Hanna §§ 23.14[2][i], 31.10[1][a]; Herlick Handbook §§ 1.6, 14.5, 14.19.

§10466. Objections to Petition, Hearing, Interim Order.

If written objection to the petition to terminate is not received within fourteen (14) days of its proper filing and service, the Workers' Compensation Appeals Board may order temporary disability compensation terminated, in accordance with the facts as stated in the petition or in such other manner as may appear appropriate on the record. If the petition to terminate is not properly completed or executed in accordance with Section 10464, the Workers' Compensation Appeals Board may summarily deny or dismiss the petition.

Objection to the petition by the employee shall be filed in writing within fourteen (14) days of service of the petition, and shall state the facts in support of the employee's contention that the petition should be denied, and shall be accompanied by a Declaration of Readiness to Proceed to Expedited Hearing. All supporting medical reports shall be attached to the objection. The objection shall also show that service of the objection and the reports attached thereto has been made upon petitioner or counsel.

Upon the filing of a timely objection, where it appears that the employee is not or may not be working and is not or may not be receiving disability indemnity, the petition to terminate shall be set for expedited hearing not less than ten (10) nor more than thirty (30) days from the date of the receipt of the objection.

If complete disposition of the petition to terminate cannot be made at the hearing, the workers' compensation judge assigned thereto, based on the record, including the allegations of the petition, the objection thereto, and the evidence (if any) at said hearing, shall forthwith issue an interim order directing whether temporary disability indemnity shall or shall not continue during the pendency of proceedings on the petition to terminate. Said interim order shall not be considered a final order, and will not preclude a complete adjudication of the petition to terminate or the issue of temporary disability or any other issue after full hearing of the issues.

Note: Authority cited: Sections 133 and 5307, Labor Code. Reference: Sections 4650 and 4651.1, Labor Code.

History: 1. Amendment of section and Note filed 12-19-2002; operative 1-1-2003. Submitted to OAL for printing only pursuant to Government Code section 11351 (Register 2002, No. 51).

Ref.: Hanna §§ 23.14[2][i], 31.10[1][a]–[c]; Herlick Handbook §§ 1.6, 14.5.

§10470. Medical Reports. [Repealed]

Note: Authority cited: Sections 133 and 5307, Labor Code. Reference: Sections 5703, 5401, 5270 and 5277, Labor Code.

History: 1. Amendment exempt from OAL review pursuant to Government Code section 11351 filed 12-19-90; operative 1-1-91 (Register 91, No. 7).

2. Repealer filed 12-19-2002; operative 1-1-2003. Submitted to OAL for printing only pursuant to Government Code section 11351 (Register 2002, No. 51).

§10480. Answers.

An Answer to each Application for Adjudication shall be filed and served ten (10) days after service of the Declaration of Readiness to Proceed required by rule 10414 or 10415.

Note: Authority cited: Sections 133 and 5307, Labor Code. Reference: Section 5500, Labor Code.

History: 1. Amendment exempt from OAL review pursuant to Government Code section 11351 filed 12-19-90; operative 1-1-91 (Register 91, No. 7).

2. Amendment filed 12-23-93; operative 1-1-94. Submitted to OAL for printing only pursuant to Government Code section 11351 (Register 93, No. 52).

3. Amendment filed 12-19-2002; operative 1-1-2003. Submitted to OAL for printing only pursuant to Government Code section 11351 (Register 2002, No. 51).

Ref.: Hanna §§ 23.14[2][c], 25.23; Herlick Handbook §§ 1.6, 14.5, 14.18.

§10484. Procedural Requirement.

The Answer used by the parties shall conform to a form prescribed and approved by the Appeals Board. Additional matters may be pleaded as deemed necessary by the answering party.

A general denial is not an answer within this rule. The Answer shall be accompanied by a proof of service upon the opposing parties.

Evidence upon matters and affirmative defenses not pleaded by Answer will be allowed only upon such terms and conditions as the Appeals Board or workers' compensation judge may impose in the exercise of sound discretion.

Note: Authority cited: Sections 133 and 5307, Labor Code. Reference: Sections 5500, 5505, Labor Code.

History: 1. Amendment filed 12-23-93; operative 1-1-94. Submitted to OAL for printing only pursuant to Government Code section 11351 (Register 93, No. 52).

2. Amendment of second paragraph filed 12-19-2002; operative 1-1-2003. Submitted to OAL for printing only pursuant to Government Code section 11351 (Register 2002, No. 51).

Ref.: Hanna §§ 23.12[1], 25.22[1], 25.23, 26.06[3]; Herlick Handbook §§ 1.6, 14.5, 14.18; W. Cal. Sum., 2 "Workers' Compensation" §389.

§10488. Repealed.

Note: Authority cited: Sections 133 and 5307, Labor Code. Reference: Sections 5500 and 5505, Labor Code.

History: 1. Repealer filed 12-23-93; operative 1-1-94. Submitted to OAL for printing only pursuant to Government Code section 11351 (Register 93, No. 52).

§10490. Demurrer, Judgment on the Pleadings, and Summary Judgment Not Permitted; Unintelligible Pleadings.

Demurrers, petitions for judgment on the pleadings, and petitions for summary judgment are not permitted. A continuance may be granted upon timely request and upon such terms as may be reasonable under the circumstances or may be ordered by the Workers' Compensation Appeals Board on its own motion if:

(a) a pleading is so uncertain, unintelligible or ambiguous as to render it impossible for the Workers' Compensation Appeals Board to understand or act upon it; or

(b) any party is prejudiced by omission or ambiguity of necessary allegations sufficient to prevent that party from adequately presenting a cause of action or defense.

Note: Authority cited: Sections 133 and 5307, Labor Code. Reference: Sections 5500 and 5708, Labor Code.

History: 1. Amendment of section heading and section filed 12-19-2002; operative 1-1-2003. Submitted to OAL for printing only pursuant to Government Code section 11351 (Register 2002, No. 51).

Ref.: Hanna § 25.25; Herlick Handbook §§ 1.6, 14.5, 14.43; W. Cal. Sum., 2 "Workers' Compensation" §389.

§10492. When Pleadings Deemed Amended.

The pleadings shall be deemed amended to conform to the stipulations and statement of issues agreed to by the parties on the record. Pleadings may be amended by the Workers' Compensation Appeals Board to conform to proof.

Note: Authority cited: Sections 133 and 5307, Labor Code. Reference: Section 5702, Labor Code.

Ref.: Herlick Handbook §§ 1.6, 14.5, 14.18; W. Cal. Sum., 2 "Workers' Compensation" §390.

§10496. Awards and Orders Without Hearing.

Awards and orders may be based upon stipulations of parties in open court or upon written stipulations signed by the parties.

Note: Authority cited: Sections 133 and 5307, Labor Code. Reference: Section 5702, Labor Code.

Ref.: Hanna §§ 23.11[3], 26.06[2], 27.02[5][a]; Herlick Handbook §§ 1.6, 14.5, 14.44; W. Cal. Sum., 2 "Workers' Compensation" §391.

§10497. Rejection of Stipulations.

No finding shall be made contrary to a stipulation of the parties on an issue without giving the parties notice and an opportunity to present evidence thereon.

Note: Authority cited: Sections 133 and 5307, Labor Code. Reference: Section 5702, Labor Code.

Ref.: Hanna § 23.11[3]; Herlick Handbook §§ 1.6, 14.5, 14.44.

ARTICLE 6
Service

§10500. Service.

Upon filing an Application for Adjudication, the filing party shall serve a copy of the application on all other parties. If the applicant is the injured worker or dependent and is unrepresented, the injured worker's or dependent's application and accompanying documents shall be served by the Workers' Compensation Appeals Board on the parties listed on the application or on the address record in the case file. If a case number has been previously assigned by the Workers' Compensation Appeals Board, that number must be affixed to the application, and service thereof is deemed service of a conformed copy for the purposes of Labor Code Section 5501. If a case number has not been assigned either before or at the time of filing of the application, notification of the case number assigned to the application by the Workers' Compensation Appeals Board shall constitute service of a conformed copy for the purpose of Labor Code section 5501.

Except as provided below, the Workers' Compensation Appeals Board may, in its discretion, designate a party or lien claimant, or their representative, to make service of notices of the time and place of hearing, orders approving compromise and release, awards based upon stipulations with request for award and any interim or procedural orders. The party, lien claimant, or representative designated to make service shall retain the proof of service and shall not file it unless ordered to do so by the Workers' Compensation Appeals Board.

The Workers' Compensation Appeals Board shall serve all parties and lien claimants of record notice of any final order, decision, or award issued by a workers' compensation judge on a disputed issue after submission.

Note: Authority cited: Sections 133 and 5307, Labor Code. Reference: Sections 5316 and 5504, Labor Code.

History: 1. Repealer and new section exempt from OAL review pursuant to Government Code section 11351 filed 12-19-90; operative 1-1-91 (Register 91, No. 7).

2. Amendment filed 12-16-92; operative 2-1-93 and exempt from OAL review pursuant to Government Code section 11351 (Register 92, No. 51).

3. Amendment of section and Note filed 12-23-93; operative 1-1-94. Submitted to OAL for printing only pursuant to Government Code section 11351 (Register 93, No. 52).

4. Amendment filed 12-19-2002; operative 1-1-2003. Submitted to OAL for printing only pursuant to Government Code section 11351 (Register 2002, No. 51).

Ref.: Hanna §§ 23.14[1][b]–[c], 23.14[2][a]–[b], 25.06[1], 30.22[1]; Herlick Handbook §§ 1.6, 14.5, 14.11, 14.12, 14.30; W. Cal. Sum., 2 "Workers' Compensation" §§388, 394, 408.

§10501. Service in Death Cases.

When an Application for Adjudication, stipulations with request for award or compromise and release is filed in a death case in which there is a bona fide issue as to partial or total dependency, the filing party shall serve copies of the documents on the Department of Industrial Relations, Death Without Dependents Unit.

Note: Authority cited: Sections 133 and 5307, Labor Code. Reference: Section 4706.5, Labor Code.

History: 1. Amendment of section heading and section filed 12-19-2002; operative 1-1-2003. Submitted to OAL for printing only pursuant to Government Code section 11351 (Register 2002, No. 51).

Ref.: Hanna §§ 23.14[1][b], 25.06[1]; Herlick Handbook §§ 1.6, 14.5, 14.30.

§10505. Service by the Parties.

Service of any document may be made by mail or personal service. Service of any document may be made by facsimile transmission by agreement of the parties of lien claimants, or where authorized or requested by the receiving party or lien claimant.

Service of all documents other than those specified in Sections 10500 and 10501 shall be made by the parties and lien claimants.

Note: Authority cited: Sections 133, 5307 and 5316, Labor Code. Reference: Section 5316, Labor Code.

History: 1. Amendment of section heading and text filed 12-23-93; operative 1-1-94. Submitted to OAL for printing pursuant to Government Code section 11351 (Register 93, No. 52).

2. Amendment filed 12-19-2002; operative 1-1-2003. Submitted to OAL for printing only pursuant to Government Code section 11351 (Register 2002, No. 51).

Ref.: Hanna §§ 23.14[2][a], 23.14[3], 27.01[4]; Herlick Handbook §§ 1.6, 10.1, 14.4, 14.11, 14.12, 14.30; W. Cal. Sum., 2 "Workers' Compensation" §388.

§10506. Service: Mailbox.

Where a district office of the Workers' Compensation Appeals Board maintains mailboxes for outgoing documents and allows consenting parties, lien claimants, and attorneys to obtain their documents from their mailboxes, documents so obtained shall be deemed to have been served on the party, lien claimant, or attorney by mail on the date of service specified on the document.

Note: Authority cited: Sections 133 and 5307, Labor Code. Reference: Section 5316, Labor Code.

History: 1. New section filed 12-19-2002; operative 1-1-2003. Submitted to OAL for printing only pursuant to Government Code section 11351 (Register 2002, No. 51).

Ref.: Hanna §§ 23.14[3], 27.01[4]; Herlick Handbook § 14.12.

§10507. Mail and Fax Service.

The time requirements of Code of Civil Procedure Section 1013(a) shall govern all service by mail and fax.

Note: Authority cited: Sections 133 and 5307, Labor Code. Reference: Section 5316, Labor Code.

History: 1. Amendment of section heading and section filed 12-19-2002; operative 1-1-2003. Submitted to OAL for printing only pursuant to Government Code section 11351 (Register 2002, No. 51).

Ref.: Hanna §§ 23.14[3], 27.01[4], 28.20, 28.24; Herlick Handbook §§ 1.6, 14.5, 14.12, 14.30, 15.4; W. Cal. Sum., 2 "Workers' Compensation" §388.

§10510. Service on Attorney or Agent.

Except as otherwise provided by Rule 10500, service shall be made on all attorneys or agents of record unless the party or lien claimant is unrepresented, in which event service shall be made on the party or lien claimant.

Note: Authority cited: Sections 133 and 5307, Labor Code. Reference: Section 5316, Labor Code.

History: 1. Amendment filed 12-23-93; operative 1-1-94. Submitted to OAL for printing only pursuant to Government Code section 11351 (Register 93, No. 52).

Ref.: Hanna §§ 23.14[2][a], 23.14[3]; Herlick Handbook §§ 1.6, 10.1, 14.4, 14.30; W. Cal. Sum., 2 "Workers' Compensation" §388.

§10514. Proof of Service by Parties and Lien Claimants.

Proof of service by parties or lien claimants may be made by:

(a) affidavit or declaration of service;

(b) written statement endorsed upon the document served and signed by the party making the statement;

(c) letter of transmittal.

The proof of service shall set forth the names and addresses of persons served, whether service was made personally or by mail, the date of service, the place of personal service or the address to which mailing was made.

The proof of service shall be filed with the documents to which the proof of service pertains. A proof of service filed at any other time may be discarded by the Workers' Compensation Appeals Board.

Note: Authority cited: Sections 133 and 5307, Labor Code. Reference: Section 5316, Labor Code.

History: 1. Amendment of section heading and text filed 12-23-93; operative 1-1-94. Submitted to OAL for printing only pursuant to Government Code section 11351 (Register 93, No. 52).

2. Amendment filed 12-19-2002; operative 1-1-2003. Submitted to OAL for printing only pursuant to Government Code section 11351 (Register 2002, No. 51).

Ref.: Hanna §§ 23.14[2][q], 25.06[1]; Herlick Handbook §§ 1.6, 14.5, 14.11, 14.12, 14.30, 14.43.

§10520. Proof of Service by Workers' Compensation Appeals Board.

Proof of service by the Workers' Compensation Appeals Board may be made by endorsement on the document served, setting forth the fact of service on the persons listed on the official address record on the date of service. The endorsement shall state whether service was made personally or by mail, the date of service and the signature of the person making the service.

Note: Authority cited: Sections 133 and 5307, Labor Code. Reference: Section 5316, Labor Code.

History: 1. Amendment filed 12-19-2002; operative 1-1-2003. Submitted to OAL for printing only pursuant to Government Code section 11351 (Register 2002, No. 51).

Ref.: Hanna § 23.14[1][e]; Herlick Handbook §§ 1.6, 14.5, 14.11, 14.30.

ARTICLE 7
Subpoenas

§10530. Subpoenas.

The Workers' Compensation Appeals Board shall issue subpoenas and subpoenas duces tecum upon request in accordance with the provisions of Code of Civil Procedure Sections 1985 and 1987.5 and Government Code Section 68097.1. Subpoenas and subpoenas duces tecum shall be on forms prescribed and approved by the Appeals Board and for injuries occurring on or after January 1, 1990, shall contain, in addition to the requirements of Code of Civil Procedure Section 1985, an affidavit that a claim form has been duly filed pursuant to Labor Code Section 5401, subdivision (c).

Note: Authority cited: Sections 133 and 5307, Labor Code. Reference: Sections 130 and 5401, Labor Code; 1985 and 1987.5, Code of Civil Procedure; and Section 68097.1, Government Code.

History: 1. Amendment exempt from OAL review pursuant to Government Code section 11351 filed 12-19-90; operative 1-1-91 (Register 91, No. 7).

Ref.: Hanna §§ 25.10[2][a], 25.29[3][a], 25.43; Herlick Handbook §§ 1.6, 14.5.

§10532. Notice to Appear or Produce.

A notice to appear or produce in accordance with Code of Civil Procedure Section 1987 is permissible in proceedings before the Workers' Compensation Appeals Board.

Note: Authority cited: Sections 133 and 5307, Labor Code. Reference: Section 132, Labor Code.

Ref.: Hanna §§ 25.43, 26.05[3]; Herlick Handbook §§ 1.6, 14.20, 14.43.

§10534. Microfilm.

Where records or other documentary evidence have been recorded or reproduced using the methods described in Section 1551 of the Evidence Code and the original records destroyed, the film, legible print thereof or electronic recording shall be produced in response to a subpoena duces tecum. A party offering a film or electronic recording in evidence may be required to provide legible prints thereof or reproductions from the electronic recording.

The expense of:

(a) inspecting reproductions shall be paid by the party making the inspection; and

(b) obtaining microfilm prints shall be borne by the party requiring the same.

Note: Authority cited: Sections 133 and 5307, Labor Code. Reference: Section 130, Labor Code.

History: 1. Amendment of section and Note filed 12-19-2002; operative 1-1-2003. Submitted to OAL for printing only pursuant to Government Code section 11351 (Register 2002, No. 51).

Ref.: See Labor Code §132.

§10536. Witness Fees and Subpoenas.

Medical examiners appointed by the Workers' Compensation Appeals Board or agreed to by the parties when subpoenaed for cross-examination at the Workers' Compensation Appeals Board or deposition shall be paid by the party requiring the attendance of the witness in accordance with the Rules of the Administrative Director.

Failure to serve the subpoena and tender the fee in advance based on the estimated time of the trial or deposition may be treated by the Workers' Compensation Appeals Board as a waiver of the right to examine the witness. Service and payment of the fee may be made by mail if the witness so agrees.

Note: Authority cited: Sections 133 and 5307, Labor Code. Reference: Sections 130, 131, 4621 and 5710, Labor Code; and Section 2034(i)(2), Code of Civil Procedure.

History: 1. Repealer and new section exempt from OAL review pursuant to Government Code section 11351 filed 12-19-90; operative 1-1-91 (Register 91, No. 7).

2. Amendment of section and Note filed 12-19-2002; operative 1-1-2003. Submitted to OAL for printing only pursuant to Government Code section 11351 (Register 2002, No. 51).

Ref.: See Labor Code §§132, 134; Hanna §§ 22.08[6][c], 23.13[2][b], 26.05[3]; Herlick Handbook § 1.6.

§10537. Subpoena for Medical Witness.

A subpoena requiring the appearance of a medical witness before the Workers' Compensation Appeals Board must be served not less than ten (10) days before the time the witness is required to appear and testify.

Note: Authority cited: Sections 133 and 5307, Labor Code. Reference: Section 132, Labor Code.

Ref.: Hanna § 26.05[3]; Herlick Handbook §§ 1.6, 14.43.

ARTICLE 8
Hearings

§10541. Submission at Conference.

A workers' compensation judge may receive evidence and submit an issue or issues for decision at a conference hearing if the parties so agree.

Note: Authority cited: Sections 133 and 5307, Labor Code. Reference: Sections 5708 and 5709, Labor Code.

History: 1. Amendment filed 12-23-93; operative 1-1-94. Submitted to OAL for printing only pursuant to Government Code section 11351 (Register 93, No. 52).

2. Amendment of section heading, section and Note filed 12-19-2002; operative 1-1-2003. Submitted to OAL for printing only pursuant to Government Code section 11351 (Register 2002, No. 51).

Ref.: Hanna § 26.04[1][d]; Herlick Handbook §§ 1.6, 14.30; W. Cal. Sum., 2 "Workers' Compensation" §394.

§10544. Notice of Hearing.

The Workers' Compensation Appeals Board shall serve or cause to be served notice of the time and place of hearings on all parties and lien claimants, and their attorneys or other agents of record, as provided in Rule 10500.

Notice of hearing shall be given at least ten (10) days before the date of hearing, except where:

(a) notice is waived;

(b) a different time is expressly agreed to by all parties and concurred in by the Workers' Compensation Appeals Board; or

(c) the proceedings are governed by Article 19 pertaining to claims against the Subsequent Injuries Fund.

Note: Authority cited: Sections 133 and 5307, Labor Code. Reference: Section 5504, Labor Code.

History: 1. Amendment filed 12-23-93; operative 1-1-94. Submitted to OAL for printing only pursuant to Government Code section 11351 (Register 93, No. 52).

2. Amendment of section and Note filed 12-19-2002; operative 1-1-2003. Submitted to OAL for printing only pursuant to Government Code section 11351 (Register 2002, No. 51).

Ref.: See Labor Code §5505; Hanna §§ 23.14[1][c], 24.11[1][b], 26.03[1], 26.04[1][b]; Herlick Handbook §§ 1.6, 14.30; W. Cal. Sum., 2 "Workers' Compensation" §§388, 394, 396.

§10548. Continuances; Appearances in Settled Cases.

(a) Continuances are not favored. Requests for continuances are inconsistent with the requirement that workers' compensation proceedings be expeditious. Continuances will be granted only upon a clear showing of good cause. Where possible, reassignment pursuant to Rule 10346 shall be used to avoid continuances.

(b) When the parties represent to the Workers' Compensation Appeals Board that a case has been settled, the case shall be taken off calendar and no appearances shall be required.

Note: Authority cited: Sections 133 and 5307, Labor Code. Reference: Article XIV, Section 4, California Constitution; and Section 5502.5, Labor Code.

History: 1. Amendment of section heading, section and Note filed 12-19-2002; operative 1-1-2003. Submitted to OAL for printing only pursuant to Government Code section 11351 (Register 2002, No. 51).

Ref.: Hanna §§ 25.09[1], 26.02[3]; Herlick Handbook §§ 1.6, 14.31; W. Cal. Sum., 2 "Workers' Compensation" §396.

§10555. Priority Conference Calendar.

A priority conference will be set upon the filing of a Declaration of Readiness requesting a priority conference that shows that the applicant is represented by an attorney and that the issues in dispute include employment and/or injury arising out of and in the course of employment. Upon a showing of good cause, the workers' compensation judge may continue the matter to a status conference. At each priority or status conference, the parties shall be prepared to set the matter for trial or to provide a plan to complete discovery. To the extent possible, all priority and status conferences in a case shall be conducted by the same workers' compensation judge. When discovery is complete, or when the workers' compensation judge determines that the parties have had sufficient time to complete reasonable discovery, the case shall be set for trial as expeditiously as possible.

Note: Authority cited: Sections 133 and 5307, Labor Code. Reference: Section 5502(c), Labor Code.

History: 1. New section filed 12-19-2002; operative 1-1-2003. Submitted to OAL for printing only pursuant to Government Code section 11351 (Register 2002, No. 51).

Ref.: Hanna §§ 24.11[1][c], 25.09[2], 26.02[1]; Herlick Handbook § 14.30.

§10560. Submission at Single Trial.

The parties are expected to submit for decision all matters properly in issue at a single trial and to produce at the trial all necessary evidence, including witnesses, documents, medical reports, payroll statements and all other matters considered essential in the proof of a party's claim or defense. However, a workers' compensation judge may order that the issues in a case be bifurcated and tried separately upon a showing of good cause.

Note: Authority cited: Sections 133 and 5307, Labor Code. Reference: Article XIV, Section 4, California Constitution; and Section 5708, Labor Code.

History: 1. Repealer and new section heading and section and amendment of Note filed 12-19-2002; operative 1-1-2003. Submitted to OAL for printing only pursuant to Government Code section 11351 (Register 2002, No. 51).

Ref.: Hanna § 26.02[3]; W. Cal. Sum., 2 "Workers' Compensation" §396.

§10561. Sanctions.

On its own motion or upon the filing of a petition pursuant to Rule 10450, the Workers' Compensation Appeals Board may order payment of reasonable expenses, including attorney's fees and costs and, in addition, sanctions as provided in Labor Code section 5813. Before issuing such an order, the alleged offending party or attorney must be given notice and an opportunity to be heard. In no event shall the Workers' Compensation Appeals Board impose a monetary sanction pursuant to Labor Code section 5813 where the one subject to the sanction acted with reasonable justification or other circumstances make imposition of the sanction unjust.

A bad faith action or tactic is one that results from a willful failure to comply with a statutory or regulatory obligation or from a willful intent to disrupt or delay the proceedings of the Workers' Compensation Appeals Board.

A frivolous bad faith action or tactic is one that is done for an improper motive or is indisputably without merit.

Violations subject to the provisions of Labor Code Section 5813 shall include but are not limited to the following:

Failure to appear or appearing late at a conference or trial shall be deemed a bad faith action or tactic solely intended to cause unnecessary delay where a reasonable excuse is not offered or the offending party has demonstrated a pattern of such conduct.

Filing a pleading, petition or legal document shall be deemed a bad faith action or tactic that is frivolous or solely intended to cause unnecessary delay unless there is some reasonable justification for filing the document.

Failure to timely serve evidentiary documents, including but not limited to medical reports pursuant to rule 10608, shall be deemed a bad faith action or tactic that is frivolous or solely intended to cause unnecessary delay unless that failure resulted from mistake, inadvertence, or excusable neglect.

Failing to comply with the Workers' Compensation Appeals Board's Rules of Practice and Procedure or an order of the Workers' Compensation Appeals Board, including an order of discovery, shall be deemed a bad faith action or tactic that is frivolous or solely intended to cause unnecessary delay unless that failure results from mistake, inadvertence, surprise, or excusable neglect.

This rule shall apply only to applications filed on or after January 1, 1994.

Note: Authority cited: Sections 133 and 5307, Labor Code. Reference: Section 5813, Labor Code.

History: 1. New section filed 12-23-93; operative 1-1-94. Submitted to OAL for printing only pursuant to Government Code section 11351 (Register 93, No. 52).

2. Amendment filed 12-19-2002; operative 1-1-2003. Submitted to OAL for printing only pursuant to Government Code section 11351 (Register 2002, No. 51).

Ref.: Hanna §§ 23.15, 27.01[8][a]; Herlick Handbook §§ 1.6, 13.4, 14.42.

§10562. Failure to Appear.

(a) Where a party served with notice of trial fails to appear either in person or by attorney or representative, the workers' compensation judge may

(1) dismiss the application after issuing a ten (10) day notice of intention to dismiss, or

(2) hear the evidence and, after service of the minutes of hearing and summary of evidence that shall include a ten (10) day notice of intention to submit, make such decision as is just and proper.

(b) Where a party served with notice of a mandatory settlement conference fails to appear at the conference, the workers' compensation judge may

(1) dismiss the application after issuing a ten (10) day notice of intention to dismiss, or

(2) close discovery and forward the case to the presiding workers' compensation judge to set for trial.

(c) Where a party, after notice, fails to appear at either a trial or a conference and good cause is shown for failure to appear, the workers' compensation judge may take the case off calendar or may continue the case to a date certain.

(d) Where a lien claimant served with notice of a conference fails to appear at the conference either in person or by attorney or representative, and fails to have a person with settlement authority available by telephone, the workers' compensation judge may

(1) dismiss the lien claim after issuing a ten (10) day notice of intention to dismiss with or without prejudice, or

(2) close discovery and forward the case to the presiding workers' compensation judge to set for trial.

(e) Where a lien claimant served with notice of a trial fails to appear, the workers' compensation judge may

(1) dismiss the lien claim after issuing a ten (10) day notice of intention to dismiss with or without prejudice, or

(2) hear the evidence and, after service of the minutes of hearing and summary of evidence that shall include a ten (10) day notice of intention to submit, make such decision as is just and proper, or

(3) defer the issue to the lien and submit the case on the remaining issues.

(f) If the workers' compensation judge defers a lien issue, upon the issuance of his or her decision on the remaining issues, the workers' compensation judge shall

(1) issue a ten (10) day notice of intention to order payment of the lien in full or in part, or

(2) issue a ten (10) day notice of intention to disallow the lien, or

(3) continue the lien issue to a lien conference.

Note: Authority cited: Sections 133 and 5307, Labor Code. Reference: Article XIV, Section 4, California Constitution; and Sections 5502(e) and 5708, Labor Code.

History: 1. Repealer and new section filed 12-23-93; operative 1-1-94. Submitted to OAL for printing only pursuant to Government Code section 11351 (Register 93, No. 52). For prior history, see Register 91, No. 7.

2. Amendment of section and Note filed 12-19-2002; operative 1-1-2003. Submitted to OAL for printing only pursuant to Government Code section 11351 (Register 2002, No. 51).

Ref.: See Labor Code §5404.5; Hanna §§ 21.09[2][c], 26.01[3], 26.04[2], 30.22[1]; Herlick Handbook §§ 1.6, 10.1, 13.4, 14.43; W. Cal. Sum., 2 "Workers' Compensation" §396.

§10563. Appearances Required.

Unless the notice otherwise provides, the applicant shall be present at a mandatory settlement conference as provided in Labor Code section 5502, subdivision (e) and the defendant and lien claimants whose liens have not been resolved or withdrawn shall have a person available with settlement authority. The person designated by the defendant to be available with settlement authority need not be present if an attorney or representative who is present can obtain immediate authority by telephone. The representative of the lien claimant with settlement authority must be present or available by telephone. Government entities shall have a person available with settlement authority to the fullest extent allowed by law.

At the time of trial, all parties shall be present and the defendants shall have a person available with settlement authority in the same manner as set forth above. If a lien claimant whose lien has not been resolved or withdrawn is not present at the time of trial, the lien claimant shall have a person available with settlement authority in the same manner as set forth above.

Note: Authority cited: Sections 133 and 5307, Labor Code. Reference: Sections 5502(e) and 5708, Labor Code.

History: 1. Amendment filed 5-25-82; designated effective 7-1-82 (Register 82, No. 22).

2. Amendment exempt from OAL review pursuant to Government Code section 11351 filed 12-19-90; operative 1-1-91 (Register 91, No. 7).

3. Editorial correction of History 1 (Register 96, No. 52).

4. Amendment of section and Note filed 12-19-2002; operative 1-1-2003. Submitted to OAL for printing only pursuant to Government Code section 11351 (Register 2002, No. 51).

Ref.: See Labor Code §§111, 130; Hanna § 26.04[1][c]; Herlick Handbook §§ 1.6, 14.31, 14.34, 14.43.

§10564. Interpreters.

Subject to the Rules of the Administrative Director, the Workers' Compensation Appeals Board may in any case appoint an interpreter and fix the interpreter's compensation. It shall be the responsibility of any party producing a witness requiring an interpreter to arrange for the presence of a qualified interpreter.

For injuries before January 1, 1994, interpreter's fees that are reasonably, actually and necessarily incurred and that are not allowed under Labor Code Section 4600 shall be allowed as costs under Labor Code Section 5811. Recovery shall be allowed in the amount charged by the interpreter unless:

(1) proof of unreasonableness is entered by the party contesting the reasonableness of the charge, or

(2) the charge is manifestly unreasonable.

For injuries on or after January 1, 1994, interpreter's fees that are reasonably, actually and necessarily incurred shall be allowed as provided by Labor Code Sections 4600, 5710 and 5811 as amended July 16, 1993. Interpreter's fees as defined in Labor Code section 4620, that are reasonably, actually and necessarily incurred as provided in Labor Code section 4621, shall be allowed in accordance with the fee schedule set by the Administrative Director.

Note: Authority cited: Sections 133 and 5307, Labor Code. Reference: Sections 4600, 4621, 5710 and 5811, Labor Code.

History: 1. Amendment of section and Note filed 12-23-93; operative 1-1-94. Submitted to OAL for printing only pursuant to Government Code section 11351 (Register 93, No. 52).

2. Amendment of section and Note filed 12-19-2002; operative 1-1-2003. Submitted to OAL for printing

only pursuant to Government Code section 11351 (Register 2002, No. 51).

Ref.: See Labor Code §4620; Hanna §§ 23.13[3], 26.05[3], 27.01[8][a]; Herlick Handbook §§ 1.6, 14.33.

§10566. Minutes of Hearing and Summary of Evidence.

Minutes of hearing and summary of evidence shall be prepared at the conclusion of each hearing and filed in the record of proceedings. They shall include:

(a) The names of the commissioners, deputy commissioner or workers' compensation judge, reporter, the parties present, attorneys or other agents appearing therefor and witnesses sworn;

(b) The place and date of said hearing;

(c) All interlocutory orders, admissions and stipulations, the issues and matters in controversy, a descriptive listing of all exhibits received for identification or in evidence (with the identity of the party offering the same) and the disposition, which shall include the time and action, if any, required for submission;

(d) A summary of the evidence required by Labor Code Section 5313 that shall include a fair and unbiased summary of the testimony given by each witness;

(e) If motion pictures are shown, a brief summary of their contents;

(f) A fair statement of any offers of proof.

If the disposition is an order taking off calendar or a continuance, the reason therefor shall be given.

Note: Authority cited: Sections 133 and 5307, Labor Code. Reference: Section 5313, Labor Code.

History: 1. Amendment of subsection (d) filed 12-19-2002; operative 1-1-2003. Submitted to OAL for printing only pursuant to Government Code section 11351 (Register 2002, No. 51).

Ref.: Hanna §§ 26.04[1][d], 26.08; Herlick Handbook § 1.6.

§10570. Minute Orders.

Interlocutory or interim orders, including dismissal of improper or unnecessary parties, may be entered upon the minutes of hearing and will become the order of the Workers' Compensation Appeals Board upon the filing thereof.

Note: Authority cited: Sections 133 and 5307, Labor Code. Reference: Section 5307.5, Labor Code.

Ref.: Herlick Handbook §§ 1.6, 14.43.

§10578. Waiver of Summary of Evidence.

The summary of evidence need not be filed upon waiver by the parties or upon issuance of a stipulated order, decision or award.

Note: Authority cited: Sections 133 and 5307, Labor Code. Reference: Section 5702, Labor Code.

History: 1. Amendment filed 12-19-2002; operative 1-1-2003. Submitted to OAL for printing only pursuant to Government Code section 11351 (Register 2002, No. 51).

Ref.: Hanna § 23.11[3]; Herlick Handbook § 1.6.

§10580. Evidence Taken Without Notice.

Transcripts or summaries of testimony taken without notice and copies of all reports and other matters added to the record, otherwise than during the course of an open hearing, shall be served upon the parties to the proceeding. Unless it is otherwise expressly provided, the parties shall be allowed 10 days after service of the testimony and reports within which to produce evidence in explanation or rebuttal or to request further proceedings before the case shall be deemed submitted for decision.

Note: Authority cited: Sections 133 and 5307, Labor Code. Reference: Section 5704, Labor Code.

History: 1. Amendment filed 12-19-2002; operative 1-1-2003. Submitted to OAL for printing only pursuant to Government Code section 11351 (Register 2002, No. 51).

Ref.: Hanna §§ 23.14[1][d], 26.06[11]; Herlick Handbook § 1.6; W. Cal. Sum., 2 "Workers' Compensation" §399.

§10582. Inactive Cases, Procedure, Subsequent Action.

This rule applies to injuries occurring before January 1, 1990 and on or after January 1, 1994.

An Application for Adjudication filed without an accompanying Declaration of Readiness to Proceed will be placed in inactive status.

Cases set for hearing may be removed from the active calendar by an order taking off calendar.

Cases in off calendar status may be restored to the active calendar upon the filing and serving of a properly executed Declaration of Readiness to Proceed.

Unless a case is activated for hearing within one year after the filing of the Application for Adjudication or the entry of an order taking off calendar, the case may be dismissed after notice and opportunity to be heard. Such dismissals may be entered at the request of an interested party or upon the Workers' Compensation Appeals Board's own motion for lack of prosecution. A case may be dismissed after issuance of a ten (10) day notice of intention to dismiss and an opportunity to be heard, but not by an order with a clause rendering the order null and void if an objection showing good cause is filed.

A petition by a defendant to dismiss the case must be accompanied by a copy of a letter mailed to the applicant and, if represented, to the applicant's attorney or representative, more than thirty (30) days before the filing of the petition to dismiss. This letter must state that it is the intention of the persons signing the letter to file a petition for dismissal thirty (30) days after the date of that letter unless the applicant or his attorney or representative shows in writing some good reason for not dismissing the case. A copy of the reply, if any, must be attached to the petition to dismiss. A copy of the petition must be served on all parties and all lien claimants.

Note: Authority cited: Sections 133 and 5307, Labor Code. Reference: Section 5405 and 5406, Labor Code.

History: 1. Amendment exempt from OAL review pursuant to Government Code section 11351 filed 12-19-90; operative 1-1-91 (Register 91, No. 7).

2. Amendment of first paragraph filed 12-23-93; operative 1-1-94. Submitted to OAL for printing only pursuant to Government Code section 11351 (Register 93, No. 52).

3. Amendment of second and third paragraphs and amendment of Note filed 12-19-2002; operative 1-1-2003. Submitted to OAL for printing only pursuant to Government Code section 11351 (Register 2002, No. 51).

Ref.: See Labor Code §111; Hanna §§ 23.11[5][c], 23.14[2][j], 25.05[1], 31.14[5]; Herlick Handbook §§ 1.6, 14.8, 14.43; W. Cal. Sum., 2 "Workers' Compensation" §367.

§10583. Dismissal of Claim Form—Labor Code Section 5404.5.

Where an application for adjudication for an injury on or after January 1, 1990 and before January 1, 1994, has not been filed by any of the parties, an employer or insurer seeking dismissal of a claim form for lack of prosecution shall solely utilize the procedures set forth in Labor Code Section 5404.5 and shall not seek an order of dismissal from the Appeals Board by the filing of an application for adjudication, a request for pre-application determination or any other petition or request.

Note: Authority cited: Sections 133 and 5307, Labor Code. Reference: Section 5404.5, Labor Code.

History: 1. Renumbering of former section 10407 to new section 10583 filed 12-19-2002; operative 1-1-2003. Submitted to OAL for printing only pursuant to Government Code section 11351 (Register 2002, No. 51).

Ref.: Hanna § 25.20[2]; Herlick Handbook §§ 1.6, 14.43.

§10589. Consolidated Cases.

Consolidation of two or more related cases may be ordered for the purpose of receiving evidence. Whether consolidation is ordered or a master file is designated to accommodate exhibits rests in the sound discretion of the Workers' Compensation Appeals Board. In exercising that discretion, the Workers' Compensation Appeals Board shall take into consideration the complexity of the issues involved and the potential prejudice of any party. Under consolidation, all documentary evidence previously received in an individual case shall be reintroduced in the consolidated proceedings under a master file, if so designated. When so adduced, the evidence shall be deemed part of the record of each of the several consolidated cases. Evidence received subsequent to the order of consolidation shall be similarly received with like force and effect.

Any request or petition to consolidate cases assigned to different workers' compensation judges in the same office of the Workers' Compensation Appeals Board shall be referred to the presiding workers' compensation judge of that office.

Note: Authority cited: Sections 133 and 5307, Labor Code. Reference: Sections 5303 and 5708, Labor Code.

History: 1. Renumbering of former section 10590 to new section 10589, including amendment of section and Note, filed 12-19-2002; operative 1-1-2003. Submitted to OAL for printing only pursuant to Government Code section 11351 (Register 2002, No. 51).

Ref.: Hanna § 26.03[1]; Herlick Handbook §§ 1.6, 14.5, 14.17.

§10590. Consolidated Cases—Same Injured Worker.

For cases involving the same injured worker, any request or petition to consolidate cases assigned to different offices for hearing in one office shall be first referred to the presiding workers' compensation judges of the offices to which the cases are assigned; if the presiding workers' compensation judges cannot agree, the conflict shall be resolved by the court administrator upon referral by a presiding judge.

Note: Authority cited: Sections 133 and 5307, Labor Code. Reference: Section 5303, Labor Code.

History: 1. Amendment exempt from OAL review pursuant to Government Code section 11351 filed 12-19-90; operative 1-1-91 (Register 91, No. 7).

2. Renumbering of former section 10590 to new section 10589 and new section 10590 filed 12-19-2002; operative 1-1-2003. Submitted to OAL for printing only pursuant to Government Code section 11351 (Register 2002, No. 51).

Ref.: See Labor Code §§5316, 5502; Hanna § 23.16; Herlick Handbook § 14.5; W. Cal. Sum., 2 "Workers' Compensation" §352.

§10591. Consolidating Cases—Multiple Injured Workers.

For cases involving two or more injured workers, any request or petition to consolidate cases assigned to different offices for hearing in one office of the Workers' Compensation Appeals Board shall be first referred to the court administrator. The court administrator shall set the request for conference to obtain agreement of all the parties to the place of hearing. If the parties do not agree to the place of hearing, the court administrator shall make a determination of the request for consolidation, giving due consideration to whether there are common issues of fact and law as well as whether judicial economy and expediency warrant and justify the request. Any party aggrieved by the determination of the court administrator may request proceedings pursuant to Labor Code section 5310.

Note: Authority cited: Sections 133 and 5307, Labor Code. Reference: Sections 5303, 5310 and 5708, Labor Code.

History: 1. New section filed 12-23-93; operative 1-1-94. Submitted to OAL for printing only pursuant to Government Code section 11351 (Register 93, No. 52).

2. Amendment of section heading, section and Note filed 12-19-2002; operative 1-1-2003. Submitted to OAL for printing only pursuant to Government Code section 11351 (Register 2002, No. 51).

Ref.: See Labor Code §§5316, 5502; Hanna § 23.16; Herlick Handbook §§ 1.6, 14.5.

§10592. Pleadings in Consolidated Cases.

Where cases are consolidated, joint minutes of hearing, summaries of evidence and opinions may be used.

Note: Authority cited: Sections 133 and 5307, Labor Code. Reference: Sections 5303 and 5313, Labor Code.

History: 1. Amendment of section and Note filed 12-19-2002; operative 1-1-2003. Submitted to OAL for printing only pursuant to Government Code section 11351 (Register 2002, No. 51).

Ref.: See Labor Code §5316; Hanna § 23.14[2][k]; Herlick Handbook §§ 1.6, 14.5.

ARTICLE 9
Evidence and Reports

§10600. Evidence and Reports.

The filing of a document does not signify its receipt in evidence, and, except for the documents listed in section 10750 of these Rules, only those documents that have been received in evidence shall be included in the record of proceedings on the case.

Note: Authority cited: Sections 133 and 5307, Labor Code. Reference: Section 5708, Labor Code.

History: 1. Amendment of section and Note filed 12-19-2002; operative 1-1-2003. Submitted to OAL for printing only pursuant to Government Code section 11351 (Register 2002, No. 51).

Ref.: See Labor Code §§5703, 5709; Hanna § 26.06[4]; Herlick Handbook §§ 1.6, 14.5, 14.27; W. Cal. Sum., 2 "Workers' Compensation" §399.

§10601. Copies of Reports and Records.

Where documents, including videotapes, are to be offered into evidence, copies shall be served on all adverse parties no later than the mandatory settlement conference, unless a satisfactory showing is made that the documents were not available for service by that time.

Note: Authority cited: Sections 133 and 5307, Labor Code. Reference: Section 5502(e), Labor Code.

History: 1. Amendment of section heading, section and Note filed 12-19-2002; operative 1-1-2003. Submitted to OAL for printing only pursuant to Government Code section 11351 (Register 2002, No. 51).

Ref.: See Labor Code §§5703, 5708, 5709; Hanna §§ 23.14[2][h], 26.06[12][e]; Herlick Handbook §§ 1.6, 14.5, 14.27.

§10602. Formal Permanent Disability Rating Determinations.

The Workers' Compensation Appeals Board may request the Disability Evaluation Unit to prepare a formal rating determination on a form prescribed for that purpose by the Administrative Director. The request may refer to an accompanying medical report or chart for the sole purpose of describing measurable physical elements of the condition that are clearly and exactly identifiable. In every instance the request shall describe the factors of disability in full.

The report of the Disability Evaluation Unit in response to the request shall constitute evidence only as to the percentage of the permanent disability based on the factors described, and the report shall not constitute evidence as to the existence of the permanent disability described.

The report of the Disability Evaluation Unit shall be filed and served on the parties and shall include or be accompanied by a notice that the case shall be submitted for decision seven (7) days after service unless written objection is made within that time.

Note: Authority cited: Sections 133 and 5307, Labor Code. Reference: Sections 4660 and 5708, Labor Code.

History: 1. Amendment of section heading, section and Note filed 12-19-2002; operative 1-1-2003. Submitted to OAL for printing only pursuant to Government Code section 11351 (Register 2002, No. 51).

Ref.: Hanna §§ 23.14[1][a], 26.06[12][d], 32.02[7], 32.05[6][a]–[c][i]; Herlick Handbook §§ 1.6, 6.8, 14.5, 14.28, 14.29; Lawyer's Guide to AMA *Guides* and Calif. Workers' Comp. § 2.06[4].

§10604. Certified Copies.

Certified copies of the reports or records of any governmental agency, division or bureau shall be admissible in evidence in lieu of the original reports or records.

Note: Authority cited: Sections 133 and 5307, Labor Code. Reference: Sections 5703 and 5708, Labor Code.

History: 1. Amendment of section and Note filed 12-19-2002; operative 1-1-2003. Submitted to OAL for printing only pursuant to Government Code section 11351 (Register 2002, No. 51).

Ref.: See Labor Code §5709; Hanna § 26.06[12][e]; Herlick Handbook §§ 1.6, 14.5.

§10605. Reproductions of Documents.

A nonerasable optical image reproduction provided that additions, deletions, or changes to the original document are not permitted by the technology, a photostatic, microfilm, microcard, miniature photographic, or other photographic copy or reproduction, or an enlargement thereof, of a writing is admissible as the writing itself if the copy or reproduction was made and preserved as a part of the records of a business (as defined by Evidence Code Section 1270) in the regular course of that business. The introduction of the copy, reproduction, or enlargement does not preclude admission of the original writing if it is still in existence. The Workers' Compensation Appeals Board may require the introduction of a hard copy printout of the document.

A printed representation of images stored on a video or digital medium is presumed to be an accurate representation of the images it purports to represent. This presumption is a presumption affecting the burden of producing evidence. If a party to an action introduces evidence that a printed representation of images stored on a video or digital medium is inaccurate or unreliable, the party introducing the printed representation into evidence has the burden of proving by a preponderance of the evidence, that the printed representation is an accurate representation of the existence and content of the images that it purports to represent.

Note: Authority cited: Sections 133 and 5307, Labor Code. Reference: Section 5708, Labor Code.

History: 1. New section filed 12-19-2002; operative 1-1-2003. Submitted to OAL for printing only pursuant to Government Code section 11351 (Register 2002, No. 51).

Ref.: Hanna § 26.06[12][e]; Herlick Handbook §§ 14.27, 14.40.

§10606. Physicians' Reports as Evidence.

The Workers' Compensation Appeals Board favors the production of medical evidence in the form of written reports. Direct examination of a medical witness will not be received at a trial except upon a showing of good cause. A continuance may be granted for rebuttal testimony subject to Labor Code Section 5502.5.

These reports should include where applicable:

(a) the date of the examination;

(b) the history of the injury;

(c) the patient's complaints;

(d) a listing of all information received from the parties reviewed in preparation of the report or relied upon for the formulation of the physician's opinion;

(e) the patient's medical history, including injuries and conditions, and residuals thereof, if any;

(f) findings on examination;

(g) a diagnosis;

(h) opinion as to the nature, extent, and duration of disability and work limitations, if any;

(i) cause of the disability;

(j) treatment indicated;

(k) opinion as to whether or not permanent disability has resulted from the injury and whether or not it is stationary. If stationary, a description of the disability with a complete evaluation;

(*l*) apportionment of disability, if any;

(m) a determination of the percent of the total causation resulting from actual events of employment, if the injury is alleged to be a psychiatric injury;

(n) the reasons for the opinion; and,

(o) the signature of the physician.

Failure to comply with (a) through (o) will be considered in weighing the evidence.

In death cases, the reports of non-examining physicians may be admitted into evidence in lieu of oral testimony.

All medical-legal reports shall comply with the provisions of Labor Code Section 4628. Except as otherwise provided by the Labor Code, including Labor Code Sections 4628 and 5703, and the rules of practice and procedure of the Appeals Board, failure to comply with the requirements of this section will not make the report inadmissible but will be considered in weighing the evidence.

Note: Authority cited: Sections 133 and 5307, Labor Code. Reference: Sections 4603.2, 4628, 5703, 5708 and 5709, Labor Code.

History: 1. New subsections (i), (j) and (k) filed 5-25-82; designated effective 7-1-82 (Register 82, No. 22).

2. Editorial correction of subsection (h) filed 2-2-83 (Register 83, No. 6).

3. Amendment filed 12-23-93; operative 1-1-94. Submitted to OAL for printing only pursuant to Government Code section 11351 (Register 93, No. 52).

4. Amendment of section and Note filed 12-19-2002; operative 1-1-2003. Submitted to OAL for printing only pursuant to Government Code section 11351 (Register 2002, No. 51).

Ref.: See Labor Code §4600; Hanna §§ 22.08[3][a]–[3][b], 22.08[3][d], 22.08[5][a], 23.14[2][g], 25.10[2][b]; Herlick Handbook §§ 1.6, 13.4, 14.5, 14.21, 14.23, 14.38; Lawyer's Guide to AMA *Guides* and Calif. Workers' Comp. § 3.03.

§10607. Computer Printouts of Benefits Paid.

If a party requests that a defendant provide a computer printout of benefits paid, within twenty (20) days the defendant shall provide the requesting party with a current computer printout of benefits paid. The printout shall include the date and amount of each payment of temporary disability indemnity, permanent disability indemnity, and vocational rehabilitation maintenance allowance, and the period covered by each payment, and the date, payee, and amount of each payment for medical treatment. This request may not be made more frequently than once in a one-hundred-twenty (120) day period unless there is a change in indemnity payments.

A defendant that has paid benefits shall have a current computer printout of benefits paid available for inspection at every mandatory settlement conference.

Note: Authority cited: Sections 133 and 5307, Labor Code. Reference: Sections 5502(e) and 5708, Labor Code.

History: 1. New section filed 12-19-2002; operative 1-1-2003. Submitted to OAL for printing only pursuant to Government Code section 11351 (Register 2002, No. 51).

Ref.: Herlick Handbook §§ 14.20, 14.32.

§10608. Filing and Service of Physicians' Reports.

(a) After the filing of an Application for Adjudication, if a party is requested by another party or lien claimant to serve copies of physicians' reports relating to the claim, the party receiving the request shall serve copies of the reports on the requesting party or lien claimant within six (6) days of the request; the party receiving the request shall serve a copy of any subsequently-received physician's report within six (6) days of receipt of the report.

(b) A Declaration of Readiness to Proceed, a Declaration of Readiness to Proceed to Expedited Hearing, or an objection to either shall be accompanied by the physicians' reports that are in the possession or under control of the declarant. At the time of filing, it shall be the duty of the declarant to serve copies of physicians' reports that have not been previously served and that are in the possession or under the control of the declarant on all other parties and all lien claimants requesting service.

(c) Within six (6) days after service of the Declaration of Readiness to Proceed or Declaration of Readiness to Proceed to Expedited Hearing, all other parties and lien claimants shall serve upon the opposing parties copies of all reports of physicians that are in their possession or under their control, and that have not been previously served. All reports that have not been previously filed, and whose filing is not required by subsection (b), shall be filed at the next hearing.

(d) All physicians' reports that have not been previously filed shall be filed upon the filing of a compromise and release or stipulations with request for award.

(e) Any report filed in violation of this section may be discarded by the Workers' Compensation Appeals Board.

(f) X-rays shall not be transmitted to the Workers' Compensation Appeals Board except under a specific order directing their production.

Note: Authority cited: Sections 133 and 5307, Labor Code. Reference: Sections 5001, 5502, 5703 and 5708, Labor Code.

History: 1. Repealer and new section filed 12-23-93; operative 1-1-94. Submitted to OAL for printing only pursuant to Government Code section 11351 (Register 93, No. 52).

2. Amendment of section heading, section and Note filed 12-19-2002; operative 1-1-2003. Submitted to OAL for printing only pursuant to Government Code section 11351 (Register 2002, No. 51).

Ref.: See Labor Code §§4600, 4621, 5709; Hanna §§ 22.08[4][a], 23.14[2][g], 25.08[3], 26.06[12][b][iii], 30.25[3]; Herlick Handbook §§ 1.6, 10.3, 13.4, 14.5, 14.21, 14.25.

§10609. Service on Lien Claimants. [Repealed]

Note: Authority cited: Sections 133 and 5307, Labor Code. Reference: Sections 4903.1, 5708 and 5709, Labor Code.

History: 1. Repealer filed 12-19-2002; operative 1-1-2003. Submitted to OAL for printing only pursuant to Government Code section 11351 (Register 2002, No. 51).

§10610. Cross-Examination of Physicians. [Repealed]

Note: Authority cited: Sections 133 and 5307, Labor Code. Reference: Article XIV, Section 4, California Constitution; Sections 4621 and 5709, Labor Code.

History: 1. Amendment of Note filed 12-23-93; operative 1-1-94. Submitted to OAL for printing only pursuant to Government Code section 11351 (Register 93, No. 52).

2. Repealer filed 12-19-2002; operative 1-1-2003. Submitted to OAL for printing only pursuant to Government Code section 11351 (Register 2002, No. 51).

§10615. Continuing Duty to Serve.

During the continuing jurisdiction of the Workers' Compensation Appeals Board, the parties have a continuing duty to serve on each other and any lien claimant requesting service any physicians' reports received.

Note: Authority cited: Sections 133 and 5307, Labor Code.

History: 1. Repealer and new section filed 12-23-93; operative 1-1-94. Submitted to OAL for printing only pursuant to Government Code section 11351 (Register 93, No. 52).

2. Editorial correction of first sentence (Register 96, No. 5).

3. Amendment of section heading, repealer and new section and new Note filed 12-19-2002; operative 1-1-2003. Submitted to OAL for printing only pursuant to Government Code section 11351 (Register 2002, No. 51).

Ref.: Hanna §§ 21.09[2][b], 22.08[4][a], 23.12[2], 23.14[2][g], 25.07[1], 26.06[12][a]; Herlick Handbook § 9.16.

§10616. Employer-Maintained Records.

A written communication from a physician containing any information listed in Section 10606 that is contained in any record maintained by the employer in the employer's capacity as employer will be deemed to be a physician's report and shall be filed and served as required in Sections 10608 and 10615. Records from an employee assistance program are not required to be filed or served unless ordered by the Workers' Compensation Appeals Board.

Note: Authority cited: Sections 133 and 5307, Labor Code. Reference: Sections 4600, 5703 and 5708, Labor Code.

History: 1. Amendment of section and Note filed 12-19-2002; operative 1-1-2003. Submitted to OAL for printing only pursuant to Government Code section 11351 (Register 2002, No. 51).

Ref.: See Labor Code §5709; Hanna §§ 22.08[4][a], 23.14[2][g], 25.07[4]; Herlick Handbook §§ 1.6, 14.5, 14.21.

§10618. X-Rays.

On order of the Appeals Board or workers' compensation judge, a party shall forthwith transmit all X-rays to the person designated in the order.

X-rays shall be subpoenaed only when they are relevant to pending issues and there is a present and bona fide intent to offer them in evidence. X-rays produced in violation of this rule will be ordered returned to their original custodian at the expense of the party causing them to be produced.

Upon reasonable request of a party, X-rays in the possession of, or subject to the control of, an adverse party or lien claimant shall be made available for examination by the requesting party or persons designated by that party at a time or place convenient to the persons to make the examination.

Note: Authority cited: Sections 133 and 5307, Labor Code. Reference: Sections 4600 and 5708, Labor Code.

History: 1. Amendment of section heading, section and Note filed 12-19-2002; operative 1-1-2003. Submitted to OAL for printing only pursuant to Government Code section 11351 (Register 2002, No. 51).

Ref.: See Labor Code §5709; Hanna §§ 22.08[4][c], 26.06[12][f]; Herlick Handbook §§ 1.6, 14.5, 14.21.

§10619. Subpoena of X-Rays. [Repealed]

Note: Authority cited: Sections 133, 5307, 5708 and 5709, Labor Code. Reference: Sections 4600, 5708 and 5709, Labor Code.

History: 1. Repealer filed 12-19-2002; operative 1-1-2003. Submitted to OAL for printing only pursuant to Government Code section 11351 (Register 2002, No. 51).

§10620. Examination of X-Rays. [Repealed]

Note: Authority cited: Sections 133 and 5307, Labor Code. Reference: Sections 4600, 5708 and 5709, Labor Code.

History: 1. Repealer filed 12-19-2002; operative 1-1-2003. Submitted to OAL for printing only pursuant to Government Code section 11351 (Register 2002, No. 51).

§10622. Failure to Comply.

Disclosure, service and filing of all medical reports in the possession and control of every party to a proceeding, except as otherwise expressly provided, is essential to and required in the expeditious determination of controversies.

The Workers' Compensation Appeals Board may decline to receive in evidence, either at or subsequent to hearing, any report offered under the provisions of Labor Code Section 5703 by a party who has failed to comply with the provisions of Rules 10600, 10608, 10615, 10616 or 10618. A medical report shall not be refused admission into evidence at a hearing, solely upon the ground of a late filing, where examination was diligently sought and said report came into possession or control of the party offering it within the preceding seven (7) days.

Where a willful suppression of a medical report is shown to exist in violation of these rules, it shall be presumed that the findings, conclusions and opinions therein contained would be adverse, if produced.

The remedies in this section are cumulative to all others authorized by law.

Note: Authority cited: Sections 133 and 5307, Labor Code. Reference: Section 5708, Labor Code.

History: 1. Amendment of section and Note filed 12-19-2002; operative 1-1-2003. Submitted to OAL for printing only pursuant to Government Code section 11351 (Register 2002, No. 51).

Ref.: See Labor Code §§111, 5709; Hanna §§ 22.08[4][e], 23.14[2][g], 25.07[5], 26.03[1], 26.06[12][b][iii]–[iv]; Herlick Handbook §§ 1.6, 9.16, 14.5, 14.21, 14.24; W. Cal. Sum., 2 "Workers' Compensation" §399.

§10626. Hospital and Physicians' Records.

Subject to Labor Code section 3762, all parties, their attorneys, agents and physicians shall be entitled to examine and make copies of all or any part of physician, hospital, or dispensary records that are relevant to the claims made and the issues pending in a proceeding before the Workers' Compensation Appeals Board.

A party offering such records shall designate the particular portion or portions thereof believed to be relevant, specifically stating where in the records it may be found. The Workers' Compensation Appeals Board prefers that the designation be in writing and before the hearing.

Note: Authority cited: Sections 133 and 5307, Labor Code. Reference: Section 4600, Labor Code.

History: 1. Amendment filed 12-19-2002; operative 1-1-2003. Submitted to OAL for printing only pursuant to Government Code section 11351 (Register 2002, No. 51).

Ref.: Hanna §§ 22.08[4][c], 25.07[6], 26.06[12][c]; Herlick Handbook §§ 1.6, 14.5, 14.21.

§10630. Return of Exhibits.

No exhibits filed or received in evidence will be released into the custody of a party, his attorney or other agent, except upon stipulation of the parties or by order of the Appeals Board or a workers' compensation judge.

Sixty (60) days after decision is final in any proceeding, or after a case has been ordered off calendar, the Workers' Compensation Appeals Board may, on its own motion, with or without notice, return:

(a) to the owners or persons producing the same, all exhibits of a physical, mechanical or demonstrative evidentiary character, unless some other disposition is expressly provided for; and

(b) to the respective owners or custodians, all permanent office records, X-rays, laboratory, clinical and hospital records and charts.

Upon expiration of five (5) years after filing the application, there being no proceedings pending, the Workers' Compensation Appeals Board may, with or without notice, make such order disposing of exhibits as deemed proper. Where proper written requests covering disposition of the exhibits are on file, they will be returned or disposed of in accordance therewith.

Note: Authority cited: Sections 133 and 5307, Labor Code. Reference: Section 126, Labor Code.

History: 1. Amendment of last paragraph filed 12-19-2002; operative 1-1-2003. Submitted to OAL for printing only pursuant to Government Code section 11351 (Register 2002, No. 51).

Ref.: Hanna §§ 1.11[5][c], 26.06[12][f], 26.09; Herlick Handbook §§ 1.6, 14.5, 14.21.

§10631. Specific Finding of Fact—Labor Code Section 139.2(d)(2).

Where a qualified medical evaluator's report has been considered and rejected pursuant to Labor Code section 139.2, subdivision (d)(2), the workers' compensation judge or Appeals Board shall make and serve a specific finding on the qualified medical evaluator and the Industrial Medical Council at the time of decision on the regular workers' compensation issues. The specific finding may be included in the decision.

If the Appeals Board, on reconsideration, affirms or sets aside the specific finding of fact filed by a workers' compensation judge, it shall advise the qualified medical evaluator and the Industrial Medical Council at the time of service of its decision on the petition for reconsideration. If the workers' compensation judge does not make a specific finding and the Appeals Board, on reconsideration, makes a specific finding of rejection pursuant to Labor Code Section 139.2, subdivision (d)(2), it shall serve its specific finding on the qualified medical evaluator and the Industrial Medical Council at the time it serves its decision after reconsideration.

Rejection of a qualified medical evaluator's report pursuant to Labor Code section 139.2, subdivision (d)(2) shall occur where the qualified medical evaluator's report does not meet the minimum standards prescribed by the provisions of Rule 10606 and the regulations of the Industrial Medical Council.

This rule shall apply to injuries on or after January 1, 1994.

Note: Authority cited: Sections 133 and 5307, Labor Code. Reference: Section 139.2(d)(2), Labor Code.

History: 1. New section filed 12-23-93; operative 1-1-94. Submitted to OAL for printing only pursuant to Government Code section 11351 (Register 93, No. 52).

2. Amendment of first paragraph filed 12-19-2002; operative 1-1-2003. Submitted to OAL for printing only pursuant to Government Code section 11351 (Register 2002, No. 51).

Ref.: Hanna § 1.12[2A]; Herlick Handbook §§ 1.6, 14.5, 14.21.

§10632. Labor Code Section 4065—Evidence.

Where the provisions of Labor Code Section 4065 apply, the workers' compensation judge shall receive into evidence the "proposed ratings" submitted by the parties.

Note: Authority cited: Sections 133 and 5307, Labor Code. Reference: Section 4065, Labor Code.

History: 1. New section filed 12-23-93; operative 1-1-94. Submitted to OAL for printing only pursuant to Government Code section 11351 (Register 93, No. 52).

2. Amendment filed 12-19-2002; operative 1-1-2003. Submitted to OAL for printing only pursuant to Government Code section 11351 (Register 2002, No. 51).

Ref.: Hanna § 22.06[9]; Herlick Handbook §§ 1.6, 14.5, 14.21, 14.28.

§10633. Proposed Rating—Labor Code Section 4065.

A "proposed rating" pursuant to Labor Code Section 4065 shall include the appropriate disability numbers for each part of the body resulting in permanent disability and a standard rating of the factors of disability.

Where the provisions of Labor Code Section 4065 have been used to determine permanent disability, the workers' compensation judge shall comply with Labor Code Section 5313 and state the evidence relied upon and the reasons or grounds on which selection of the proposed rating is based.

Note: Authority cited: Sections 133 and 5307, Labor Code. Reference: Section 4065, Labor Code.

History: 1. New section filed 12-23-93; operative 1-1-94. Submitted to OAL for printing only pursuant to Government Code section 11351 (Register 93, No. 52).

2. Amendment of first paragraph filed 12-19-2002; operative 1-1-2003. Submitted to OAL for printing only pursuant to Government Code section 11351 (Register 2002, No. 51).

Ref.: Hanna § 22.06[9]; Herlick Handbook §§ 1.6, 14.5, 14.21, 14.28.

§10634. Labor Code Section 4628(k) Requests.

Failure to comply with Labor Code Section 4628, subdivision (k) shall not make the medical report inadmissible as evidence and eliminate liability for medical-legal costs where good cause has been shown for the failure to comply and, after notice of non-compliance, compliance takes place within a reasonable period of time or within a time prescribed by the workers' compensation judge.

Note: Authority cited: Sections 133 and 5307, Labor Code. Reference: Section 4628(k), Labor Code.

History: 1. New section filed 12-23-93; operative 1-1-94. Submitted to OAL for printing only pursuant to Government Code section 11351 (Register 93, No. 52).

Ref.: Hanna § 22.09[5]; Herlick Handbook §§ 1.6, 14.5, 14.21.

§10635. Repealed.

Note: Authority cited: Sections 133 and 5307, Labor Code. Reference: Sections 4600, 4624 and 4625, Labor Code.

History: Repealer exempt from OAL review pursuant to Government Code section 11351 filed 12-19-90; operative 1-1-91 (Register 91, No. 7).

ARTICLE 10
Medical Examiners

§10700. Impartial Medical Examiners. [Repealed]

Note: Authority cited: Sections 133 and 5703, Labor Code. Reference: Sections 139.1 and 5703.5, Labor Code.

History: 1. Repealer and new section exempt from OAL review pursuant to Government Code section 11351 filed 12-19-90; operative 1-1-91 (Register 91, No. 7).

2. Repealer filed 12-19-2002; operative 1-1-2003. Submitted to OAL for printing only pursuant to Government Code section 11351 (Register 2002, No. 51).

§10705. Repealed.

Note: Authority cited: Sections 133 and 5307, Labor Code. Reference: Article XIV, Section 4, California Constitution.

History: 1. Repealer filed 10-21-96; operative 11-1-96. Submitted to OAL for printing only pursuant to Government Code section 11351 (Register 96, No. 43).

§10715. Orders Directing Applicants to Report for Medical Examination. [Repealed]

Note: Authority cited: Sections 133 and 5307, Labor Code. Reference: Section 139, Labor Code.

History: 1. Editorial correction filed 2-2-83 (Register 83, No. 6).

2. Repealer filed 12-19-2002; operative 1-1-2003. Submitted to OAL for printing only pursuant to Government Code section 11351 (Register 2002, No. 51).

§10718. Prohibited Communication.

All correspondence concerning the examination and reports of a physician appointed pursuant to Labor Code Section 5701 or 5703.5 shall be made through the Workers' Compensation Appeals Board, and no party, attorney or representative shall communicate with that physician with respect to the merits of the case unless ordered to do so by the Workers' Compensation Appeals Board.

Note: Authority cited: Sections 133 and 5307, Labor Code. Reference: Sections 5701 and 5703.5, Labor Code.

History: 1. Amendment of section and Note filed 12-19-2002; operative 1-1-2003. Submitted to OAL for printing only pursuant to Government Code section 11351 (Register 2002, No. 51).

Ref.: Hanna § 22.07[3]; Herlick Handbook §§ 1.6, 14.22.

§10722. Filing and Service of Medical Reports. [Repealed]

Note: Authority cited: Sections 133 and 5307, Labor Code. Reference: Sections 139, 5703.5, 5708, Labor Code.

History: 1. Repealer filed 12-19-2002; operative 1-1-2003. Submitted to OAL for printing only pursuant to Government Code section 11351 (Register 2002, No. 51).

§10727. Cross-Examination by Deposition.

The Workers' Compensation Appeals Board favors cross-examination of medical witnesses by way of deposition. Reasonable costs in connection with such deposition shall be allowed under Labor Code Section 4621.

Note: Authority cited: Sections 133 and 5307, Labor Code. Reference: Article XIV, Section 4, California Constitution; and Section 5708, Labor Code.

History: 1. Amendment of section and Note filed 12-19-2002; operative 1-1-2003. Submitted to OAL for printing only pursuant to Government Code section 11351 (Register 2002, No. 51).

Ref.: See Labor Code §4600; Hanna §§ 22.08[6][c], 25.41[2]; Herlick Handbook §§ 1.6, 14.5, 14.26, 14.38.

ARTICLE 11
Transcript of Testimony

§10740. Transcripts.

Unless otherwise ordered by a commissioner, a deputy commissioner, or a presiding workers' compensation judge, testimony taken at hearings in compensation proceedings will not be transcribed except upon the request of a party accompanied by the fee prescribed in the Rules of the Administrative Director.

Requests for transcription of testimony shall be in writing, served on all other parties, directed to the transcript clerk and accompanied by a deposit fee based on the transcript clerk's estimate of the number of pages to be transcribed. If the actual fee exceeds the deposit, the purchaser shall pay the balance of the fee before the transcript is released. Any excess deposit will be returned to the purchaser.

No person shall make a photographic copy of a transcript from the Board file except upon payment prescribed by law for a copy of the transcript.

Note: Authority cited: Sections 133 and 5307, Labor Code. Reference: Sections 127 and 5708, Labor Code.

History: 1. Amendment of first paragraph filed 12-19-2002; operative 1-1-2003. Submitted to OAL for printing only pursuant to Government Code section 11351 (Register 2002, No. 51).

Ref.: Hanna § 23.12[4]; Herlick Handbook § 1.6.

ARTICLE 12
Record of Proceedings

§10750. Record of Proceedings.

The record of proceedings consists of: the pleadings, declarations of readiness to proceed, minutes of hearing and summary of evidence, transcripts, if prepared and filed, proofs of service, evidence received in the course of a hearing, exhibits marked but not received in evidence, notices, petitions, briefs, findings, orders, decisions and awards. Documents that are in the Workers' Compensation Appeals Board file but have not been received in evidence are not part of the evidentiary record.

Note: Authority cited: Sections 133 and 5307, Labor Code. Reference: Sections 126 and 5708, Labor Code.

History: 1. Amendment of section and Note filed 12-19-2002; operative 1-1-2003. Submitted to OAL for printing only pursuant to Government Code section 11351 (Register 2002, No. 51).

Ref.: Hanna §§ 1.11[5][a], 23.12[3]; Herlick Handbook § 1.6.

§10751. Legal File.

The Workers' Compensation Appeals Board's legal file includes the record of proceedings. Upon approval of compromise and release or stipulations with request for award, all medical reports that have been filed shall be transferred to the legal file.

Note: Authority cited: Sections 133 and 5307, Labor Code. Reference: Section 126, Labor Code.

History: 1. New section filed 12-19-2002; operative 1-1-2003. Submitted to OAL for printing only

pursuant to Government Code section 11351 (Register 2002, No. 51).

Ref.: Hanna §§ 1.11[5][b], 23.12[3].

§10753. Inspection of Files.

Except as provided in Section 10754 of these Rules or otherwise, any person legally may inspect the contents of any Workers' Compensation Appeals Board file at the district office where the file is located at a time convenient to the Workers' Compensation Appeals Board and during regular office hours. The file and the records and documents contained therein may not be removed from the district office for copying or for any other purpose. Copying operators must operate their equipment in the room assigned to them and any person copying a file must put papers back in the file in their original order and any person viewing or copying a file must return the file in the same order and condition in which it was received.

A file will not be sent from one office to another for inspection except for good cause by order of a workers' compensation judge and upon the payment of a fee required by the Administrative Director. At the request of a party to the case, or his or her attorney, a file that has been transferred to a record storage center for storage will be made available for inspection through the office from which the file was transferred. Files that have been transferred to a record storage center will be made available for inspection by any other person upon payment of the fee required by the Administrative Director.

Although the following documents may be retained in a Workers' Compensation Appeals Board file folder for the sake of convenience, they are not a part of the file and may be removed from the file before it is made available for inspection by any person:

(a) Decisions, reports, opinions, orders, recommendations and other documents that are in the process of preparation, or, although fully prepared, have not yet been signed and filed.

(b) Agreed Medical Examiner or Qualified Medical Examiner reports and ratings that have been received but have not yet been served.

(c) The working papers, personal notes, deliberation records, and other private notations made by a workers' compensation judge, commissioner, deputy commissioner or Appeals Board attorney in the course of hearing or deliberation relating to the case.

(d) Any legal memorandum or analysis prepared by a workers' compensation judge, commissioner, deputy commissioner, Appeals Board attorney or legal assistant to assist a workers' compensation judge, deputy commissioner or commissioner in his deliberations concerning a case.

Except as provided in Rule 10754, a party, or his or her attorney or representative, may inspect the legal file and any medical reports that have been filed; any other person may inspect only the legal file.

Note: Authority cited: Sections 133 and 5307, Labor Code. Reference: Section 126, Labor Code.

History: 1. Amendment of section and Note filed 12-19-2002; operative 1-1-2003. Submitted to OAL for printing only pursuant to Government Code section 11351 (Register 2002, No. 51).

Ref.: See Labor Code §111; Hanna §§ 1.11[5][b], 23.12[3]; Herlick Handbook § 1.6.

§10754. Sealed Documents.

Where a medical report, medical record or other document filed in a case contains references to or discusses the mental or emotional health of any person, sexual habits or practice, use of or addiction to alcohol or other drugs, or other matter of similar character such that the workers' compensation judge to whom the case is assigned determines that public inspection of the document should not be permitted, the workers' compensation judge may order the document to be sealed. If an order is made that a document or documents be sealed, the order shall be filed in the record of the proceedings and the sealed document or documents shall be placed in a sealed envelope, which shall be removed from the file before the file is made available for public inspection.

Sealed documents in a case shall be made available for inspection by any party to the case or by his representative on order of a workers' compensation judge and subject to any reasonable conditions and limitations as the workers' compensation judge may impose. Sealed documents shall not otherwise be made available for public inspection except by order of a workers' compensation judge which shall be made only on a showing that good cause exists to permit the inspection.

Note: Authority cited: Sections 133 and 5307, Labor Code. Reference: Section 5708, Labor Code.

History: 1. Amendment filed 12-19-2002; operative 1-1-2003. Submitted to OAL for printing only

pursuant to Government Code section 11351 (Register 2002, No. 51).

Ref.: Hanna §1.11[5][b]; Herlick Handbook § 1.6.

§10755. Destruction of Records.

Following a period of:

(a) two years after date of last entry thereon, the Workers' Compensation Appeals Board may destroy any miscellaneous record, not otherwise expressly covered by these Rules, which is kept and maintained in the proceeding of cases, case files and decisions; and

(b) five years after the date of filing of the Application for Adjudication or upon transfer to archive storage, whichever date first occurs, the Workers' Compensation Appeals Board may eliminate from the case file and destroy:

(1) extra copies of pleadings, notices, findings, orders, decisions, awards and other documents; and

(2) correspondence and other miscellaneous material not part of the legal record in the case, excepting originals of all medical reports found in the correspondence section of the file.

The approval of the Department of Finance, as required by the provisions of Government Code Section 14755, will be obtained before action under this section.

Note: Authority cited: Sections 133 and 5307, Labor Code. Reference: Section 135, Labor Code.

Ref.: Hanna §§ 1.11[5][c], 26.09; Herlick Handbook § 1.6.

§10758. Destruction of Case Files.

Following a period of five (5) years after the filing of the Application or other opening document, the Workers' Compensation Appeals Board may destroy, without microphotographic or other reproduction, the file in each case.

A case file may be destroyed by the Workers' Compensation Appeals Board after its contents, as stripped in accordance with Section 10755, have been reproduced in a manner permitted by law. The reproduction may be destroyed after a period of five (5) years from the date of filing of the Application or other opening document.

The approval of the Department of Finance, as required by the provisions of Labor Code Section 135, will be obtained before action under this rule.

Note: Authority cited: Sections 133 and 5307, Labor Code. Reference: Section 135, Labor Code.

History: 1. Amendment filed 10-21-96; operative 11-1-96. Submitted to OAL for printing only pursuant to Government Code section 11351 (Register 96, No. 43).

2. Amendment filed 12-19-2002; operative 1-1-2003. Submitted to OAL for printing only pursuant to Government Code section 11351 (Register 2002, No. 51).

Ref.: Hanna § 1.11[5][c]; Herlick Handbook § 1.6.

§10762. Reporters' Notes.

Stenographic reporters' notes shall be retained for a period of six (6) years after the taking of them and thereafter may be destroyed or otherwise disposed of.

The approval of the Department of Finance, as required by the provisions of Government Code Section 14755, will be obtained before action under this rule.

Note: Authority cited: Sections 133 and 5307, Labor Code. Reference: Section 14755, Government Code; and Section 5708, Labor Code.

History: 1. Amendment of first paragraph and Note filed 12-19-2002; operative 1-1-2003. Submitted to OAL for printing only pursuant to Government Code section 11351 (Register 2002, No. 51).

Ref.: Hanna § 1.11[5][c]; Herlick Handbook § 1.6.

ARTICLE 13
Liens

§10770. Lien Procedure.

(a) Any lien claimant under Labor Code sections 4903 or 4903.1 shall file its lien in writing upon a form approved by the Appeals Board or electronically as approved by the Administrative Director. Lien claims filed in writing shall be accompanied by a full statement or itemized voucher supporting the lien and justifying the right to reimbursement and proof of service. All liens, along with a full statement or itemized voucher supporting the lien, shall be served upon the applicant, the injured worker (or, if deceased, upon worker's dependents), the employer, the insurance carrier and the respective attorneys or other representatives of record. Service of a lien on a party shall constitute notice to it of the existence of the lien.

(b) The Workers' Compensation Appeals Board shall not accept for filing a lien that does not bear a case number previously assigned by the Workers' Compensation Appeals Board for the injury.

(c) The lien claimant shall provide the name, mailing address, and daytime telephone number of a person who will be available at the time of all conferences and trials, and will have authority to resolve the lien on behalf of the lien claimant.

(d) After a lien has been filed, the lien claimant shall continue to serve amendments to the lien on the parties. After a lien has been filed, amendments to the lien shall be filed only upon the filing of a Declaration of Readiness, compromise and release, or stipulations with request for award or order, or upon receipt of a notice of hearing. An amendment to a lien filed at any other time, and any attachments thereto, will not be filed and may be discarded by the Workers' Compensation Appeals Board. If a lien has been filed electronically, upon the filing of a Declaration of Readiness, compromise and release, or stipulations with request for award or order, or upon receipt of a notice of hearing, the lien claimant shall file a full statement or itemized voucher supporting the lien unless the lien claimant advises in writing, or electronically, that the lien has been resolved or withdrawn.

(e) The lien claimant shall be notified by the Workers' Compensation Appeals Board when a hearing is scheduled.

Note: Authority cited: Sections 133 and 5307, Labor Code. Reference: Sections 4903 and 4903.1, Labor Code.

History: 1. Amendment exempt from OAL review pursuant to Government Code section 11351 filed 12-19-90; operative 1-1-91 (Register 91, No. 7).

2. Amendment filed 12-23-93; operative 1-1-94. Submitted to OAL for printing only pursuant to Government Code section 11351 (Register 93, No. 52).

3. Amendment filed 12-19-2002; operative 1-1-2003. Submitted to OAL for printing only pursuant to Government Code section 11351 (Register 2002, No. 51).

Ref.: Hanna §§ 20.04[1], 23.14[2][*l*], 30.20[1]–[2], 30.22[1]; Herlick Handbook §§ 1.6, 10.1, 10.7; W. Cal. Sum., 2 "Workers' Compensation" §§394, 408.

§10771. Medical-Legal Expense.

Lien claims for the expenses set forth in Labor Code section 4622 shall not be filed with the Workers' Compensation Appeals Board until the 60-day period for voluntary payment has elapsed, unless the lien claimant certifies the fee request has been rejected in writing.

Note: Authority cited: Sections 133 and 5307, Labor Code. Reference: Sections 4903 and 4903.1, Labor Code.

History: 1. Amendment exempt from OAL review pursuant to Government Code section 11351 filed 12-19-90; operative 1-1-91 (Register 91, No. 7).

2. Amendment of section and Note filed 12-19-2002; operative 1-1-2003. Submitted to OAL for printing only pursuant to Government Code section 11351 (Register 2002, No. 51).

Ref.: See Labor Code §§4620, 4621; Hanna §§ 22.09[2], 30.20[3], 30.21[2][a]; Herlick Handbook §§ 1.6, 10.1, 10.3.

§10772. Unemployment Compensation Disability Liens.

When an unemployment compensation disability lien is filed by the Employment Development Department, there shall be a rebuttable presumption that the amounts stated therein have been paid to the injured worker by the Employment Development Department.

In any case involving a lien claim for unemployment compensation disability benefits or unemployment compensation benefits and extended duration benefits where it appears that further benefits may have been paid subsequent to the filing of the claim of lien, the workers' compensation judge shall notify the lien claimant when the case is ready for decision or for order approving compromise and release and the lien claimant shall have five (5) days thereafter in which to file and serve an amended lien reflecting all payments made to and including the date of filing of the amended lien.

In cases where a compromise and release is filed and continuing unemployment compensation disability benefits or unemployment compensation benefits and extended duration benefits are being paid, the workers' compensation judge will ascertain the full amount of the lien claim as of the time of the approval of the compromise and release so that the allocation made under the authority of Labor Code Section 4904 may be changed to reflect unemployment compensation disability or unemployment compensation and extended duration payments to the date of decision.

Note: Authority cited: Sections 133 and 5307, Labor Code. Reference: Sections 4903 and 4904, Labor Code.

Ref.: Hanna §§ 29.04[3][b], 30.24[3], 30.25[3]; Herlick Handbook §§ 1.6, 10.6, 10.7, 10.8, 10.9, 10.10.

§10773. Law Firm Employees.

(a) Law firm employees not holding current active membership in the State Bar may appear on behalf of the law firm if:

(1) the client has been fully informed of the involvement of the law firm employee and that the person is not a current active member of the State Bar of California;

(2) in all proceedings where the law firm employee appears and in all documents the person has prepared, the person appearing or preparing the documents is identified and it is fully disclosed that the person is not licensed to practice law in the State of California; and

(3) the attorney directly responsible for supervising the law firm employee appearing in any proceedings is identified.

(b) A workers' compensation judge shall not approve any compromise and release agreement or stipulations with request for award signed by a law firm employee who is not currently an active member of the State Bar of California without the specific written authorization of the attorney directly responsible for supervising the law firm employee.

Note: Authority cited: Sections 133 and 5307, Labor Code. Reference: Section 4907, Labor Code.

History: 1. New section filed 12-19-2002; operative 1-1-2003. Submitted to OAL for printing only pursuant to Government Code section 11351 (Register 2002, No. 51). For prior history, see Register 96, No. 43.

Ref.: See Labor Code §4903.4; Hanna § 20.01[1][a]; Herlick Handbook § 10.2.

ARTICLE 14
Attorneys and Representatives

§10774. Substitution or Dismissal of Attorneys.

Substitution or dismissal of attorneys must be made in the manner provided by Code of Civil Procedure Sections 284, 285 and 286. Dismissal of agents may be made by serving and filing a statement of dismissal.

Note: Authority cited: Sections 133 and 5307, Labor Code. Reference: Sections 4903 and 4906, Labor Code.

Ref.: Hanna §§ 20.01[3], 21.09[2][b], 26.01[1]; Herlick Handbook §§ 1.6, 10.2; W. Cal. Sum., 2 "Workers' Compensation" §§353, 432.

§10775. Reasonable Attorney's Fee.

In establishing a reasonable attorney's fee, the workers' compensation judge or arbitrator shall consider the

(a) responsibility assumed by the attorney,

(b) care exercised in representing the applicant,

(c) time involved,

(d) results obtained.

Reference will be made to guidelines contained in the Policy and Procedural Manual and workers' compensation judges and arbitrators shall at all times comply with Labor Code section 5313 by setting forth the reasons or grounds for applying the guidelines in any fee determination.

Through its power to grant reconsideration on its own motion, the Appeals Board shall exercise authority to ascertain the extent to which these guidelines are followed.

Note: Authority cited: Sections 133 and 5307, Labor Code. Reference: Sections 4903 and 4906, Labor Code.

History: 1. Amendment exempt from OAL review pursuant to Government Code section 11351 filed 12-19-90; operative 1-1-91 (Register 91, No. 7).

2. Amendment of first and penultimate paragraphs filed 12-19-2002; operative 1-1-2003. Submitted to OAL for printing only pursuant to Government Code section 11351 (Register 2002, No. 51).

Ref.: Hanna §§ 20.02[1][b], 20.03[1]–[2], 21.03[7], 28.36[2][c], 29.04[3][e]; Herlick Handbook §§ 1.6, 10.2; W. Cal. Sum., 2 "Workers' Compensation" §§354, 355, 356.

§10776. Approval of Attorney's Fee.

(a) No request for payment or demand for payment of a fee shall be made by any attorney for, or agent of, a worker or dependent of a worker until the fee has been approved or set by the Workers' Compensation Appeals Board.

(b) No attorney or agent shall accept any money from a worker or dependent of a worker for the purpose of representing the worker or dependent of a worker before the Workers' Compensation Appeals Board or in any appellate procedure related thereto until the fee has been approved or set by the Workers' Compensation Appeals Board or an appellate court.

(c) Any agreement between any attorney or agent and a worker or dependent of a worker for payment of a fee shall be submitted to the Workers' Compensation Appeals Board for approval within ten (10) days after the agreement is made.

Note: Authority cited: Sections 133 and 5307, Labor Code. Reference: Sections 4903 and 4906, Labor Code.

History: 1. Amendment of subsections (a)-(b) filed 12-19-2002; operative 1-1-2003. Submitted to OAL for printing only pursuant to Government Code section 11351 (Register 2002, No. 51).

Ref.: Hanna §§ 20.02[1][a]–[b], 21.09[2][b], 25.01[4], 30.03[2], 35.51[2]; Herlick Handbook §§ 1.6, 10.2.

§10778. Request for Increase of Attorney's Fee.

All requests for an increase in attorney's fee shall be accompanied by proof of service on the applicant of written notice of the attorney's adverse interest and of the applicant's right to seek independent counsel. Failure to so notify the applicant may constitute grounds for dismissal of the request for increase in fee.

Note: Authority cited: Sections 133 and 5307, Labor Code. Reference: Sections 4903 and 4906, Labor Code.

Ref.: Hanna §§ 20.05, 23.14[2][n], 30.03[3]; Herlick Handbook §§ 1.6, 10.2.

§10779. Disbarred and Suspended Attorneys.

An attorney who has been disbarred or suspended by the Supreme Court for reasons other than nonpayment of State Bar fees, or who has been placed on involuntary inactive enrollment status by the State Bar, or who has resigned while disciplinary action is pending shall be deemed unfit to appear as a representative of any party before the Workers' Compensation Appeals Board during the time that the attorney is precluded from practicing law in this state. Any attorney claiming to be qualified to appear as a representative before the Workers' Compensation Appeals Board despite disbarment, suspension or resignation may file a petition for permission to appear. The petition shall set forth in detail:

(1) the facts leading to the disbarment, suspension or resignation; and

(2) the facts and circumstances alleged by the attorney to establish competency, qualification and moral character to appear as a representative before the Workers' Compensation Appeals Board. The petition shall be verified, shall be filed in the San Francisco office of the Appeals Board and a copy thereof served on the State Bar of California.

Note: Authority cited: Sections 133 and 5307, Labor Code. Reference: Section 4907, Labor Code.

History: 1. Amendment of first paragraph filed 12-19-2002; operative 1-1-2003. Submitted to OAL for printing only pursuant to Government Code section 11351 (Register 2002, No. 51).

Ref.: Hanna § 20.01[1][b]; Herlick Handbook §§ 1.6, 10.2.

ARTICLE 15
Findings, Awards and Orders

§10780. Dismissal Orders.

Except as provided in Rule 10562 and 10582 and unless good cause to the contrary appears, orders of dismissal of claim forms for injuries on or after January 1, 1990 and before January 1, 1994, and orders of dismissal of applications for adjudication for injuries before January 1, 1990 and on or after January 1, 1994, shall issue forthwith when requested by the employee. All other orders of dismissal of claim forms for injuries occurring on or after January 1, 1990 and before January 1, 1994, or orders of dismissal of applications for adjudication for injuries occurring before January 1, 1990 and on or after January 1, 1994, shall issue only after service of a notice of intention allowing at least fifteen (15) days for the adverse parties to show good cause to the contrary, and not by an order with a clause rendering the order null and void if an objection showing good cause is filed.

Note: Authority cited: Sections 133 and 5307, Labor Code.

History: 1. Repealer and new section filed 12-23-93; operative 1-1-94. Submitted to OAL for printing only pursuant to Government Code section 11351 (Register 93, No. 52).

2. Amendment of section and Note filed 12-19-2002; operative 1-1-2003. Submitted to OAL for printing only pursuant to Government Code section 11351 (Register 2002, No. 51).

Ref.: Hanna §§ 23.11[5][b], 23.14[1][c], 25.26, 31.04[4][b]; Herlick Handbook §§ 1.6, 14.43; W. Cal. Sum., 2 "Workers' Compensation" §390.

§10782. Repealed.

Note: Authority cited: Section 5307, Labor Code. Reference: Section 5313, Labor Code.

History: 1. Repealer filed 10-21-96; operative 11-1-96. Submitted to OAL for printing only pursuant to

Government Code section 11351 (Register 96, No. 43).

ARTICLE 16
Executions and Certified Copies

§10820. When Certified Copies Will Issue.

Certified copies of findings and awards or other final orders for the purpose of having judgment entered and execution issued by the clerk of a superior court shall be issued only upon written request of a person entitled to benefits thereunder or by the attorney or authorized representative, and upon payment of the fees prescribed by the Rules of the Administrative Director.

Certified copies of such orders and awards against authorized insurance carriers, authorized self-insured employers, the State of California and all political subdivisions thereof shall be issued only upon receipt of a written request showing good cause therefor.

Every request for a certified copy of any final order must state whether proceedings are pending on reconsideration or judicial review, whether a petition for reconsideration or a writ of review has been filed, and whether the decision, a certified copy of which is requested has become final.

Nothing in these rules, however, shall limit the power of the Workers' Compensation Appeals Board to issue a certified copy at any time upon its own motion without charge.

Note: Authority cited: Sections 133 and 5307, Labor Code. Reference: Sections 5806, 5807 and 5808, Labor Code.

History: 1. Amendment of section and Note filed 12-19-2002; operative 1-1-2003. Submitted to OAL for printing only pursuant to Government Code section 11351 (Register 2002, No. 51).

Ref.: See Labor Code §§130, 134, 5105, 5809, 6000, 6001, 6002; Hanna §§ 27.10[3][a], 27.10[4], 27.11[2][a]; Herlick Handbook § 1.6; W. Cal. Sum., 2 "Workers' Compensation" §410.

§10825. Withholding Certified Copies.

As an alternative to the issuance of an order staying execution, the Workers' Compensation Appeals Board may direct by order that no certified copy be issued. Such an order shall have the same effect as an order staying execution issued under similar circumstances.

(a) Before staying execution or issuing order withholding issuance of a certified copy of an order, decision or award, the Workers' Compensation Appeals Board in its discretion may require the filing of a bond from an approved surety equivalent to twice the probable amount of liability in the case.

(b) The bond shall be filed in the record of the case.

Note: Authority cited: Sections 133 and 5307, Labor Code. Reference: Sections 130, 134, 5105, 5806, 5807, 5808, 5809, 6000, 6001 and 6002, Labor Code.

Ref.: Hanna §§ 27.10[2][d], 27.10[3][b], 27.11[2][a], 27.11[3][b]; Herlick Handbook § 1.6.

§10828. Necessity for Bond.

Where a party intending to file for writ of review requests a stay of execution or withholding issuance of a certified copy of the order, decision or award that is the subject of the party's complaint, the request will ordinarily be granted, conditioned upon the filing of a bond from an approved surety equivalent to twice the probable amount of liability in the case.

Note: Authority cited: Sections 133 and 5307, Labor Code. Reference: Sections 5808, 5956, 6000, 6001 and 6002, Labor Code.

History: 1. Amendment of section and Note filed 12-19-2002; operative 1-1-2003. Submitted to OAL for printing only pursuant to Government Code section 11351 (Register 2002, No. 51).

Ref.: See Labor Code §§134, 5105, 5806, 5807, 5809; Hanna §§ 27.10[2][e], 27.10[3][b], 27.11[2][a]; Herlick Handbook § 1.6.

§10832. Repealed.

Note: Authority cited: Sections 133 and 5307, Labor Code. Reference: Sections 134 and 5300, Labor Code.

History: 1. Repealer filed 10-21-96; operative 11-1-96. Submitted to OAL for printing only pursuant to Government Code section 11351 (Register 96, No. 43).

ARTICLE 17
Reconsideration

§10840. Filing Petitions for Reconsideration and Answers.

Petitions for reconsideration from final orders, decisions or awards and answers thereto shall be filed at the district office of the Workers'

Compensation Appeals Board from which the order, decision or award issued. Petitions for reconsideration from final orders, decisions or awards issued by the Appeals Board in San Francisco and answers thereto shall be filed at the office of the Appeals Board in San Francisco. Petitions for reconsideration received in any district office or the office of the Appeals Board in San Francisco, except as provided by this rule, shall neither be accepted for filing nor deemed filed for any purpose.

Note: Authority cited: Sections 133 and 5307, Labor Code. Reference: Section 5900 and 5905, Labor Code.

History: 1. Repealer and new section filed 12-16-92; operative 2-1-93 and exempt from OAL review pursuant to Government Code section 11351 (Register 92, No. 51).

2. Amendment of section heading and text filed 12-23-93; operative 1-1-94. Submitted to OAL for printing only pursuant to Government Code section 11351 (Register 93, No. 52).

Ref.: Hanna §§ 23.12[2], 28.23, 28.24; Herlick Handbook §§ 1.6, 15.1, 15.3, 15.4; W. Cal. Sum., 2 "Workers' Compensation" §418.

§10842. Contents of Petition for Reconsideration and Answer.

All petitions for reconsideration shall conform to the requirements of Section 10392 of these Rules.

Every petition for reconsideration shall fairly state all the material evidence relative to the point or points at issue. Each contention contained in a petition for reconsideration shall be separately stated and clearly set forth.

Copies of documents that have already been received in evidence or that have already been made part of the legal file shall not be attached as exhibits to petitions for reconsideration or answers to petitions for reconsideration. Documents attached in violation of this rule may be detached from the petition for reconsideration or answer and discarded.

Note: Authority cited: Sections 133 and 5307, Labor Code. Reference: Sections 126, 5900 and 5902, Labor Code.

History: 1. New section filed 5-25-82; designated effective 7-1-82 (Register 82, No. 22).

2. Amendment of section heading and text filed 12-23-93; operative 1-1-94. Submitted to OAL for printing only pursuant to Government Code section 11351 (Register 93, No. 52).

3. Amendment of last paragraph filed 12-19-2002; operative 1-1-2003. Submitted to OAL for printing only pursuant to Government Code section 11351 (Register 2002, No. 51).

Ref.: Hanna §§ 28.21[1], 28.24; Herlick Handbook §§ 1.6, 15.1, 15.3; W. Cal. Sum., 2 "Workers' Compensation" §419.

§10843. Petitions to Remove.

(a) Petitions to remove and responses or answers thereto shall be filed with the district office of the Workers' Compensation Appeals Board from which relief is sought or from which an order subject to the removal process issued. Petitions to remove received in any district office except as provided by this rule shall neither be accepted for filing nor deemed filed for any purpose and may be discarded.

(b) At any time within twenty (20) days after the service of the order or decision, or of the occurrence of the action in issue, any party may petition for removal based upon one or more of the following grounds:

(1) The order, decision or action will result in significant prejudice.

(2) The order, decision or action will result in irreparable harm.

The petitioner must also demonstrate that reconsideration will not be an adequate remedy after the issuance of a final order, decision or award. Failure to file the petition to remove timely shall constitute valid ground for dismissing the petition to remove.

(c) A copy of the petition to remove shall be served forthwith upon all parties by the petitioner. Any adverse party may file an answer within ten (10) days after service. No supplemental petitions, pleadings or responses shall be considered unless requested or approved by the Appeals Board.

(d) The workers' compensation judge may, within fifteen (15) days of the filing of the petition to remove, rescind the order or decision in issue, or take action to resolve the issue raised in the petition to remove. If the judge so acts, or if the petitioner withdraws the petition at any time, the petition to remove will be deemed automatically dismissed, requiring no further action by the Appeals Board. The issuance of a new order or decision, or the occurrence of a new action, will recommence the time period for filing a petition to remove as described above.

(e) The filing of a petition to remove does not terminate the judge's authority to proceed in a case or require the judge to continue or cancel a previously scheduled hearing absent direction from the Appeals Board. After a petition to remove has been filed, the workers' compensation judge shall consult with the presiding workers' compensation judge prior to proceeding in the case or continuing or canceling a scheduled hearing.

Note: Authority cited: Sections 133 and 5307, Labor Code. Reference: Section 5310, Labor Code.

History: 1. New section filed 12-23-93; operative 1-1-94. Submitted to OAL for printing only pursuant to Government Code section 11351 (Register 93, No. 52).

2. Amendment filed 12-12-2000; operative 1-1-2001. Submitted to OAL for printing only pursuant to Government Code section 11351 (Register 2000, No. 50).

3. Amendment filed 12-19-2002; operative 1-1-2003. Submitted to OAL for printing only pursuant to Government Code section 11351 (Register 2002, No. 51).

Ref.: Hanna §§ 1.11[3][f], 26.03[4]; Herlick Handbook §§ 1.6, 15.1, 15.3.

§10846. Skeletal Petitions.

A petition for reconsideration may be denied if it contains no more than allegations of the statutory grounds for reconsideration unsupported by specific references to the record and principles of law involved.

Note: Authority cited: Sections 133 and 5307, Labor Code. Reference: Section 5902, Labor Code.

Ref.: Hanna § 28.21[1]; Herlick Handbook §§ 1.6, 15.1, 15.3, 15.4.

§10848. Supplemental Petitions.

When a petition for reconsideration has been timely filed, supplemental petitions or pleadings or responses other than the answer shall be considered only when specifically requested or approved by the Appeals Board. Supplemental petitions or pleadings or responses other than the answer, except as provided by this rule, shall neither be accepted nor deemed filed for any purpose and shall not be acknowledged or returned to the filing party.

Note: Authority cited: Sections 133 and 5307, Labor Code. Reference: Section 5900, Labor Code.

History: 1. Repealer and new section filed 12-23-93; operative 1-1-94. Submitted to OAL for printing only pursuant to Government Code section 11351 (Register 93, No. 52).

Ref.: Hanna § 28.21[3]; Herlick Handbook §§ 1.6, 15.1, 15.3, 15.4.

§10850. Proof of Service.

Service of copies of a petition for reconsideration, removal, or disqualification shall be made on all parties to the case and on any lien claimant, the validity of whose lien is specifically questioned by the petition, and to any case that has been consolidated therewith pursuant to Section 10590. Failure to file proof of service shall constitute valid ground for dismissing the petition.

Note: Authority cited: Sections 133 and 5307, Labor Code. Reference: Sections 5310, 5311, 5902 and 5903, Labor Code.

History: 1. Amendment of section and Note filed 12-19-2002; operative 1-1-2003. Submitted to OAL for printing only pursuant to Government Code section 11351 (Register 2002, No. 51).

Ref.: Hanna §§ 23.14[2][o], 28.23; Herlick Handbook §§ 1.6, 15.1, 15.3, 15.4.

§10852. Insufficiency of Evidence.

Where reconsideration is sought on the ground that findings are not justified by the evidence, the petition shall set out specifically and in detail how the evidence fails to justify the findings.

Note: Authority cited: Sections 133 and 5307, Labor Code. Reference: Sections 5902 and 5903, Labor Code.

History: 1. Amendment filed 12-19-2002; operative 1-1-2003. Submitted to OAL for printing only pursuant to Government Code section 11351 (Register 2002, No. 51).

Ref.: Hanna § 28.22[1]; Herlick Handbook §§ 1.6, 15.1, 15.3, 15.4.

§10856. Allegations of Newly Discovered Evidence and Fraud.

Where reconsideration is sought on the ground of newly discovered evidence that could not with reasonable diligence have been produced before submission of the case or on the ground that the decision had been procured by fraud, the petition must contain an offer of proof, specific and detailed, providing:

(a) the names of witnesses to be produced;

(b) a summary of the testimony to be elicited from the witnesses;

(c) a description of any documentary evidence to be offered;

(d) the effect that the evidence will have on the record and on the prior decision; and

(e) as to newly discovered evidence, a full and accurate statement of the reasons why the testimony or exhibits could not reasonably have been discovered or produced before submission of the case.

A petition for reconsideration sought upon these grounds may be denied if it fails to meet the requirements of this rule, or if it is based upon cumulative evidence.

Note: Authority cited: Sections 133 and 5307, Labor Code. Reference: Sections 5902 and 5903, Labor Code.

History: 1. Amendment filed 12-19-2002; operative 1-1-2003. Submitted to OAL for printing only pursuant to Government Code section 11351 (Register 2002, No. 51).

Ref.: Hanna §§ 28.22[2], 28.32; Herlick Handbook §§ 1.6, 15.1, 15.3, 15.4; W. Cal. Sum., 2 "Workers' Compensation" §419.

§10858. Correction of Errors.

Before a petition for reconsideration is filed, a workers' compensation judge may correct the decision for clerical, mathematical or procedural error or amend the decision for good cause under the authority and subject to the limitations set out in Sections 5803 and 5804 of the Labor Code.

Note: Authority cited: Sections 133 and 5307, Labor Code. Reference: Section 5309, Labor Code.

Ref.: Hanna §§ 28.03[1][c], 28.03[2]; Herlick Handbook §§ 1.6, 14.34, 15.1, 15.3.

§10859. Orders After Filing of Petition for Reconsideration.

After a petition for reconsideration has been timely filed, a workers' compensation judge may, within the period of fifteen (15) days following the date of filing of that petition for reconsideration, amend or modify the order, decision or award or rescind the order, decision or award and conduct further proceedings. Further proceedings shall be initiated within 30 days from the order of recession. The time for filing a petition for reconsideration pursuant to Labor Code section 5903 will run from the filing date of the new, amended or modified decision. After this period of fifteen (15) days has elapsed, a workers' compensation judge shall not make any order in the case nor correct any error until the Appeals Board has denied or dismissed the petition for reconsideration or issued a decision after reconsideration.

Note: Authority cited: Section 5307, Labor Code. Reference: Sections 5906, 5907 and 5908.5, Labor Code.

History: 1. Repealer and new section filed 12-16-92; operative 2-1-93 and exempt from OAL review pursuant to Government Code section 11351 (Register 92, No. 51).

2. Amendment filed 12-19-2002; operative 1-1-2003. Submitted to OAL for printing only pursuant to Government Code section 11351 (Register 2002, No. 51).

Ref.: Hanna §§ 23.12[2], 26.10[1], 28.03[2], 28.25; Herlick Handbook §§ 1.6, 15.1, 15.3.

§10860. Report of Workers' Compensation Judge.

Petitions for reconsideration, petitions for removal and petitions for disqualification shall be referred to the workers' compensation judge from whose decisions or actions relief is sought. The workers' compensation judge shall prepare a report that shall contain:

(a) a statement of the contentions raised by the petition;

(b) a discussion of the support in the record for the findings of fact and the conclusions of law that serve as a basis for the decision or order as to each contention raised by the petition, or, in the case of a petition for disqualification, a specific response to the allegations and, if appropriate, a discussion of any failure by the petitioner to comply with the procedures set forth in Rule 10452, and

(c) the action recommended on the petition.

The workers' compensation judge shall send the report and the Workers' Compensation Appeals Board's file to the Appeals Board within 15 days after the petition is filed unless the Appeals Board grants an extension of time. The workers' compensation judge shall serve a copy of the report on the parties and any lien claimant, the validity of whose lien is specifically questioned by the petition, at the time it is sent to the Appeals Board.

Note: Authority cited: Sections 133 and 5307, Labor Code. Reference: Sections 5900 and 5906, Labor Code.

History: 1. Amendment filed 12-23-93; operative 1-1-94. Submitted to OAL for printing only pursuant to Government Code section 11351 (Register 93, No. 52).

2. Amendment filed 12-19-2002; operative 1-1-2003. Submitted to OAL for printing only pursuant to Government Code section 11351 (Register 2002, No. 51).

Ref.: Hanna §§ 26.03[2], 26.03[4], 28.35[2]; Herlick Handbook §§ 1.6, 15.1, 15.3; W. Cal. Sum., 2 "Workers' Compensation" §424.

§10862. Hearing After Reconsideration Granted.

Where reconsideration has been granted and the case referred to a workers' compensation judge for proceedings on reconsideration, the workers' compensation judge shall, upon the conclusion thereof, prepare and serve upon the parties a summary of evidence received in the proceedings after reconsideration granted.

Unless otherwise instructed by the panel before which a case is pending, the workers' compensation judge to whom the case has been assigned for further proceedings may rule on requests for postponement, continuance of further hearing, join additional parties, dismiss unnecessary parties where such dismissal is not opposed by any other party to the case, make all interlocutory or procedural orders that are agreed to by all parties, issue subpoenas, rule on motions for discovery, rule on all evidentiary motions and objections, and make all other rulings necessary to expedite and facilitate the trial and disposition of the case. The workers' compensation judge shall not order a medical examination, obtain a recommended disability evaluation, make an order taking the case off calendar, nor make an order approving or disapproving compromise and release.

Note: Authority cited: Sections 133 and 5307, Labor Code. Reference: Sections 5309 and 5313, Labor Code.

History: 1. Amendment of section and Note filed 12-19-2002; operative 1-1-2003. Submitted to OAL for printing only pursuant to Government Code section 11351 (Register 2002, No. 51).

Ref.: Hanna §§ 26.10[1], 28.36[1], 28.36[2][a]; Herlick Handbook §§ 1.6, 15.1, 15.3; W. Cal. Sum., 2 "Workers' Compensation" §422.

§10864. Authority of Workers' Compensation Judge After Decision After Reconsideration.

After a decision after reconsideration has become final, subsequent orders and decisions in a case may be made by any workers' compensation judge to whom the case is assigned pursuant to Section 10348, including orders approving or disapproving compromise and release, orders allowing or disallowing liens, orders for enforcement of the decision of the Appeals Board, orders granting or denying petitions to reopen, orders rescinding, altering or amending the decision of the Appeals Board for good cause under Labor Code Section 5803, orders for increased compensation under Labor Code Section 5814, orders terminating liability, orders for commutation and orders resolving issues that the Board in its decision has left for determination by a workers' compensation judge.

A workers' compensation judge may not make an order correcting a decision after reconsideration for clerical, mathematical, or procedural error. Requests for such correction shall be acted on by the panel that made the decision or if the composition of the Board has changed, by the successor panel.

Note: Authority cited: Sections 133 and 5307, Labor Code. Reference: Sections 5900, 5910 and 5911, Labor Code.

History: 1. Amendment filed 5-25-82; designated effective 7-1-82 (Register 82, No. 22).

2. Amendment filed 12-19-2002; operative 1-1-2003. Submitted to OAL for printing only pursuant to Government Code section 11351 (Register 2002, No. 51).

Ref.: Hanna §§ 28.03[2], 28.36[3]; Herlick Handbook §§ 1.6, 14.34, 15.1, 15.3.

§10865. Reconsideration—Labor Code Sections 3201.5 and 3201.7.

A petition for reconsideration from an arbitration decision made pursuant to Labor Code Section 3201.5(a)(1) or Section 3201.7(a)(1) shall be filed directly with the office of the Appeals Board in San Francisco within twenty (20) days of the service of the final order, decision, or award made and filed by the arbitrator or board of arbitrators. A copy of the petition for reconsideration shall be served on the arbitrator or arbitration board.

The petition for reconsideration shall be captioned so as to identify it as a Petition for Reconsideration from Arbitrator's Decision Under Labor Code section 3201.5 or 3201.7, and shall set forth the injured worker's name, date of birth, social security number, and the date on which the arbitrator or board of arbitrators served the arbitration decision. Proof of service of the arbitration decision on the parties shall be either by a verified statement of the arbitrator indicating the date of service and listing the names and addresses of the persons served or by written acknowledgment of receipt by the parties at the time of the arbitration proceedings. In addition, a copy of that portion of the collective bargaining agreement relating to the arbitration and reconsideration processes shall be submitted by the petitioner.

Upon receiving the petition for reconsideration, the arbitrator or board of arbitrators shall forward to the Appeals Board in San Francisco the record of proceedings, including the transcript of proceedings, if any, a summary of testimony if the proceedings were not transcribed, the documentary evidence submitted by each of the parties, and an opinion that sets forth the rationale for the decision as to each contention raised by the petition.

After the arbitration decision has been made, the arbitrator or board of arbitrators shall maintain possession of the record of proceedings until the time for filing a petition for reconsideration has passed. Thereafter one of the parties may be designated custodian of the arbitration record as provided for in the collective bargaining agreement.

Note: Authority cited: Sections 133 and 5307, Labor Code. Reference: Sections 3201.5 and 3201.7, Labor Code.

History: 1. New section filed 12-23-93; operative 1-1-94. Submitted to OAL for printing only pursuant to Government Code section 11351 (Register 93, No. 52).

2. Amendment of section heading, section and Note filed 12-19-2002; operative 1-1-2003. Submitted to OAL for printing only pursuant to Government Code section 11351 (Register 2002, No. 51).

Ref.: Hanna §§ 28.27, 33.01[6]; Herlick Handbook §§ 1.6, 15.1, 15.3.

§10866. Reconsideration of Arbitrator's Decisions or Awards.

Any final order, decision or award filed by an arbitrator under Labor Code Sections 5270 through 5275 shall be subject to the reconsideration process as set forth in Labor Code Sections 5900 through 5911 and Rules 10840 and 10842.

The parties, respectively, shall serve the arbitrator with the petition for reconsideration and the answer.

Note: Authority cited: Sections 133 and 5307, Labor Code. Reference: Sections 5275, 5277(c) and 5900–5911, Labor Code.

History: 1. New section filed 12-23-93; operative 1-1-94. Submitted to OAL for printing only pursuant to Government Code section 11351 (Register 93, No. 52).

2. Amendment of section and Note filed 12-19-2002; operative 1-1-2003. Submitted to OAL for printing only pursuant to Government Code section 11351 (Register 2002, No. 51).

Ref.: Hanna § 28.26; Herlick Handbook §§ 1.6, 15.1, 15.3.

§10867. Report of Arbitrator.

When a petition for reconsideration is filed from any final order, decision or award made by an arbitrator under Labor Code Sections 5270 through 5275, the arbitrator shall prepare and serve a report on reconsideration as provided in Rule 10860 and shall concurrently forward the arbitrator's file and the original report to the presiding workers' compensation judge, who shall promptly forward the Workers' Compensation Appeals Board's file and the arbitrator's file and report to the Appeals Board.

Note: Authority cited: Sections 133 and 5307, Labor Code. Reference: Sections 5275, 5277(c) and 5900–5911, Labor Code.

History: 1. New section filed 12-23-93; operative 1-1-94. Submitted to OAL for printing only pursuant to Government Code section 11351 (Register 93, No. 52).

2. Amendment of section and Note filed 12-19-2002; operative 1-1-2003. Submitted to OAL for printing only pursuant to Government Code section 11351 (Register 2002, No. 51).

Ref.: Hanna § 28.26; Herlick Handbook §§ 1.6, 15.3.

§10868. Reconsideration of Settlement Conference Referees' Decisions or Awards. [Repealed]

Note: Authority cited: Sections 133 and 5307, Labor Code. Reference: Sections 111, 5502 and 5900, Labor Code.

History: 1. New section filed 12-23-93; operative 1-1-94. Submitted to OAL for printing only pursuant to Government Code section 11351 (Register 93, No. 52).

2. Repealer filed 12-19-2002; operative 1-1-2003. Submitted to OAL for printing only pursuant to Government Code section 11351 (Register 2002, No. 51).

§10869. Report of Settlement Conference Referee. [Repealed]

Note: Authority cited: Sections 133 and 5307, Labor Code. Reference: Sections 111, 5502 and 5307, Labor Code.

History: 1. New section filed 12-23-93; operative 1-1-94. Submitted to OAL for printing only pursuant to Government Code section 11351 (Register 93, No. 52).

2. Repealer filed 12-19-2002; operative 1-1-2003. Submitted to OAL for printing only pursuant to Government Code section 11351 (Register 2002, No. 51).

ARTICLE 18
Settlements

§10870. Approval of Compromise and Release.

Agreements that provide for the payment of less than the full amount of compensation due or to become due and undertake to release the employer from all future liability will be approved only where it appears that a reasonable doubt exists as to the rights of the parties or that approval is in the best interest of the parties. No agreement shall relieve an employer of liability for vocational rehabilitation benefits unless the Workers' Compensation Appeals Board makes a finding that there is a good faith issue which, if resolved against the injured employee, would defeat the employee's right to all workers' compensation benefits.

Note: Authority cited: Sections 133 and 5307, Labor Code. Reference: Sections 4646, 5001, 5002 and 5100.6, Labor Code.

History: 1. Amendment of article 18 heading and amendment of section and Note filed 12-19-2002; operative 1-1-2003. Submitted to OAL for printing only pursuant to Government Code section 11351 (Register 2002, No. 51).

Ref.: Hanna §§ 29.01[5], 29.02[3][b], 29.03[3], 29.04[2][a], 35.54; Herlick Handbook §§ 1.6, 11.1, 11.4, 11.5, 16.5, 16.15; W. Cal. Sum., 2 "Workers' Compensation" §363.

§10874. Form.

Every compromise and release agreement shall comply with the provisions of Labor Code Sections 5003–5004 and conform to a form provided by the Appeals Board.

Note: Authority cited: Sections 133 and 5307, Labor Code. Reference: Sections 5001, 5002, 5003 and 5004, Labor Code.

Ref.: Hanna §§ 23.12[1], 29.01[5], 29.03[1], 29.07[1]; Herlick Handbook §§ 1.6, 11.1, 11.2; W. Cal. Sum., 2 "Workers' Compensation" §363.

§10875. Procedures—Labor Code Section 3761.

Where the insurer has attached a declaration to the compromise and release agreement or stipulations with request for award that it has complied with the provisions of Labor Code Sections 3761, subdivision (a), and 3761, subdivision (b), the Workers' Compensation Appeals Board may approve the compromise and release or stipulations with request for award without hearing or further proceedings.

Where a workers' compensation judge or the Appeals Board has approved a compromise and release or stipulations with request for award and the insurer has failed to show proof of service pursuant to Labor Code Section 3761, subdivision (b), the workers' compensation judge or the Appeals Board, after giving notice and an opportunity to be heard to the insurer, shall award expenses as provided in Labor Code Section 5813 upon request by the employer.

Any request for relief under Labor Code Section 3761, subdivision (b), or Labor Code Section 3761, subdivision (d), shall be made by the filing of a petition pursuant to Rule 10450, together with a Declaration of Readiness to Proceed.

This rule shall apply to injuries on or after January 1, 1994.

Note: Authority cited: Sections 133 and 5307, Labor Code. Reference: Section 3761, Labor Code.

History: 1. New section filed 12-23-93; operative 1-1-94. Submitted to OAL for printing only pursuant to Government Code section 11351 (Register 93, No. 52).

2. Amendment of penultimate paragraph filed 12-19-2002; operative 1-1-2003. Submitted to OAL for printing only pursuant to Government Code section 11351 (Register 2002, No. 51).

Ref.: Hanna §§ 2.34, 29.01[5], 29.04[7]; Herlick Handbook §§ 1.6, 11.1, 14.32.

§10878. Settlement Document as an Application.

The filing of a compromise and release agreement or stipulations with request for award shall constitute the filing of an application which may, in the Workers' Compensation Appeals Board's discretion, be set for hearing, reserving to the parties the right to put in issue facts that might otherwise have been admitted in the compromise and release agreement or stipulations with request for award. If a hearing is held with this document used as an application, the defendants shall have available to them all defenses that were available as of the date of filing of this document. The Workers' Compensation Appeals Board may thereafter either approve the settlement agreement or disapprove it and issue findings and award after hearing has been held and the matter submitted for decision.

Note: Authority cited: Sections 133 and 5307, Labor Code. Reference: Sections 5001, 5002, 5500 and 5702, Labor Code.

History: 1. Amendment of section heading, section and Note filed 12-19-2002; operative 1-1-2003. Submitted to OAL for printing only pursuant to Government Code section 11351 (Register 2002, No. 51).

Ref.: See Labor Code §§5003, 5004, 5005; Hanna §§ 29.01[4]–[5]; Herlick Handbook §§ 1.6, 11.1, 11.2, 11.3, 14.44; W. Cal. Sum., 2 "Workers' Compensation" §363.

§10882. Action on Settlement Agreement.

The Workers' Compensation Appeals Board shall inquire into the adequacy of all compromise and release agreements and stipulations with request for award, and may set the matter for hearing to take evidence when necessary to determine whether the agreement should be approved or disapproved, or issue findings and awards.

Note: Authority cited: Sections 133 and 5307, Labor Code. Reference: Sections 5001, 5002 and 5702, Labor Code.

History: 1. Amendment of section heading, section and Note filed 12-19-2002; operative 1-1-2003. Submitted to OAL for printing only pursuant to Government Code section 11351 (Register 2002, No. 51).

Ref.: See Labor Code §§5003, 5004, 5005; Hanna §§ 29.01[5], 29.04[2][a]; Herlick Handbook §§ 1.6, 11.1; W. Cal. Sum., 2 "Workers' Compensation" §363.

§10886. Service on Lien Claimants.

Where a lien claim is on file with the Workers' Compensation Appeals Board or where a party has been served with a lien, and a compromise and release agreement or stipulations with request for award or order is filed, a copy of the compromise and release agreement or stipulations shall be served on the lien claimant.

No lien claim shall be disallowed or reduced unless the lien claimant has been given notice and an opportunity to be heard.

Note: Authority cited: Sections 133 and 5307, Labor Code. Reference: Sections 4903, 4903.1, 4903.4, 4904, 4904.1, 4905 and 4906, Labor Code.

History: 1. Amendment exempt from OAL review pursuant to Government Code section 11351 filed 12-19-90; operative 1-1-91 (Register 91, No. 7).

2. Amendment filed 12-19-2002; operative 1-1-2003. Submitted to OAL for printing only pursuant to Government Code section 11351 (Register 2002, No. 51).

Ref.: Hanna §§ 23.14[2][m], 29.01[5], 29.03[8], 29.04[3][b]–[c], 30.24[2][a]; Herlick Handbook §§ 1.6, 11.1, 11.2, 10.1.

§10888. Resolution of Liens.

Before issuance of an order approving compromise and release that resolves a case or an award that resolves a case based upon the stipulations of the parties, if there remain any liens that have not been resolved or withdrawn, the parties shall make a good-faith attempt to contact the lien claimants and resolve their liens. A good-faith attempt requires at least one contact of each lien claimant by telephone or letter.

After issuing an order approving compromise and release that resolves a case or an award that resolves a case based upon the stipulations of the parties, if there remain any liens that have not been resolved or withdrawn, the workers' compensation judge shall

(1) set the case for a lien conference, or

(2) issue a ten (10) day notice of intention to order payment of any such lien in full or in part, or

(3) issue a ten (10) day notice of intention to disallow any such lien. Upon a showing of good cause, the workers' compensation judge may once continue a lien conference to another lien conference. If a lien cannot be resolved at a lien conference, the workers' compensation judge shall set the case for trial.

An agreement to "pay, adjust or litigate" a lien, or its equivalent, or an award leaving a lien to be adjusted, is not a resolution of the lien.

Note: Authority cited: Sections 133 and 5307, Labor Code. Reference: Sections 4903, 4903.1, 4904, 5001, 5002 and 5702, Labor Code.

History: 1. New section filed 12-19-2002; operative 1-1-2003. Submitted to OAL for printing only pursuant to Government Code section 11351 (Register 2002, No. 51).

Ref.: Hanna §§ 23.14[2][m], 29.03[8], 30.24[1], [2][a]; Herlick Handbook §§ 10.1, 11.1, 14.44.

§10890. Walk-Through Documents.

(a) A "walk-through" document is a document that is presented to a workers' compensation judge for immediate action.

(b) A party may present the following walk-through documents to a workers' compensation judge during conference calendars and mandatory settlement conference calendars:

(1) Compromise and releases;

(2) Stipulations with request for award;

(3) Petitions for attorney's fees for representation of the applicant in vocational rehabilitation;

(4) Petitions for attorney's fees for representation of the applicant at a deposition; and

(5) Petitions to compel attendance at a medical examination or deposition.

(c) At any time, a party may present to the presiding judge a petition to stay an action by an opposing party pending a hearing. The presiding judge may act on the petition or assign it to another judge for action. A party who walks through a petition to stay an action shall provide notice to the opposing party or parties in accordance with subsections (b) and (c) of Rule 379 of the California Rules of Court.

(d) Each walk-through settlement document (a compromise and release or stipulations with request for award) shall be accompanied by a proof of service showing that the document was served on all lien claimants whose liens have not been resolved and any other defendant who may be liable for payment of additional compensation.

Each petition for attorney's fees for representation of the applicant in vocational rehabilitation shall be accompanied by a proof of service showing that the petition was served on the injured worker and the defendant alleged to be liable for paying the fees.

Each petition for attorney's fees for representation of the applicant at a deposition shall be accompanied by a proof service showing that the petition was served upon the defendant alleged to be liable for paying the fees.

Each petition to compel attendance at a medical examination or deposition shall be accompanied by a proof of service showing that the petition was served upon the injured worker, the injured worker's attorney, and any other defendant who may be liable for payment of additional compensation.

(e) A workers' compensation judge who is presented with a walk-through settlement document shall approve it, disapprove it, suspend action on it, or accept it for later review and action. If a workers' compensation judge is presented with so many walk-through documents that review of them will interfere with cases scheduled for conference, the judge may refer to the presiding judge as many walk-through cases as are necessary to allow timely consideration of the cases scheduled for conference.

(f) A walk-through document may be presented only to a workers' compensation judge at the district office that has venue. If an injured worker has existing cases at two or more district offices that have venue, a walk-through settlement may be presented to a judge at any office having venue over an existing case that is settled by the walk-through document. An existing case is a case that has been filed and assigned a case number prior to the filing of the walk-through document.

(g) A walk-through document may be presented to any workers' compensation judge during a conference calendar or mandatory settlement conference calendar except as follows:

(1) If a judge has taken testimony, any walk-through document in that case must be presented to the judge who took testimony if that judge works at the district office to which the case is assigned, unless the presiding judge allows it to be presented to another judge.

(2) If a judge has reviewed a settlement document and declined to approve it, a walk-through settlement document in that case must be presented to the same judge, if that judge works at the district office to which the case is assigned, unless the presiding judge allows it to be presented to another judge.

(h) If an injured worker is not represented by an attorney, the worker must be present when a walk-through settlement document is presented to the judge unless the settlement has previously been reviewed with the injured worker by an Information and Assistance officer.

(i) Each district office will have clerical staff available to obtain files and create new files for walk-through cases from 8:00 a.m. to 11:00 a.m. and 1:00 p.m. to 4:00 p.m. when conferences are scheduled except that, with the approval of the Administrative Director, in order to meet operational needs, a district office may require up to one day's notice of a party's intention to walk through a document and may require that documents requiring the creation of a new case file be filed up to one day prior to walking them through.

Note: Authority cited: Sections 133 and 5307, Labor Code. Reference: Sections 4053, 4054, 5001, 5002, 5702 and 5710, Labor Code.

History: 1. New section filed 12-19-2002; operative 1-1-2003. Submitted to OAL for printing only pursuant to Government Code section 11351 (Register 2002, No. 51).

Ref.: Hanna § 23.11[2]; Herlick Handbook §§ 14.20, 14.21, 14.30A, 14.44, 16.16.

ARTICLE 19
Subsequent Injuries Fund

§10940. Application.

All claims against the Subsequent Injuries Fund shall be by an application in writing setting forth the date and nature of the industrial injury, together with all factors of disability alleged to have pre-existed said injury. Allegations of additional factors must be by amended application.

All applications against the Subsequent Injuries Fund shall be filed with the Appeals Board and a copy shall be served by mail on the Division of Workers' Compensation, Subsequent Injuries Fund, in accordance with Sections 10505 and 10507. Where joinder of the Subsequent Injuries Fund has been ordered by the workers' compensation judge or the Appeals Board, the applicant shall forthwith file and serve an application as provided herein.

Note: Authority cited: Sections 133 and 5307, Labor Code. Reference: Sections 4750, 4751, 4753, 4753.5 and 4754.5, Labor Code.

History: 1. Amendment filed 6-28-83; designated effective 7-1-83 pursuant to Government Code Section 11346.2(d) (Register 83, No. 27).

2. Amendment of last paragraph filed 12-19-2002; operative 1-1-2003. Submitted to OAL for printing only pursuant to Government Code section 11351 (Register 2002, No. 51).

Ref.: Hanna §§ 23.14[2][p], 25.05[7], 31.20[4][b], 32.05[6][b]; Herlick Handbook §§ 1.6, 6.21, 14.17; W. Cal. Sum., 2 "Workers' Compensation" §§301, 396.

§10942. Service.

Service of all documents directed to the Subsequent Injuries Fund shall be made on the Division of Workers' Compensation, Subsequent Injuries Fund.

Note: Authority cited: Sections 133 and 5307, Labor Code. Reference: Sections 4750, 4751, 4753, 4753.5 and 4754.5, Labor Code.

History: 1. Amendment filed 6-28-83; designated effective 7-1-83 pursuant to Government Code Section 11346.2(d) (Register 83, No. 27).

2. Amendment filed 12-19-2002; operative 1-1-2003. Submitted to OAL for printing only pursuant to Government Code section 11351 (Register 2002, No. 51).

Ref.: Hanna §§ 23.14[2][p], 31.20[4][b]; Herlick Handbook §§ 1.6, 6.21, 14.17, 14.43.

§10944. Notice of Hearing. [Repealed]

Note: Authority cited: Sections 133 and 5307, Labor Code. Reference: Section 5502, Labor Code.

History: 1. Repealer filed 12-19-2002; operative 1-1-2003. Submitted to OAL for printing only pursuant to Government Code section 11351 (Register 2002, No. 51).

Ref.: Herlick Handbook §§ 1.6, 6.21, 14.17.

§10946. Medical Reports.

When an application is filed against the Subsequent Injuries Fund, any party who has previously filed medical reports shall forthwith serve copies on the Division of Workers' Compensation, Subsequent Injuries Fund, and in no case later than the mandatory settlement conference, unless service is waived by the Division of Workers' Compensation, Subsequent Injuries Fund.

Note: Authority cited: Sections 133 and 5307, Labor Code.

History: 1. Amendment filed 6-28-83; designated effective 7-1-83 pursuant to Government Code Section 11346.2(d) (Register 83, No. 27).

2. Amendment of section and Note filed 12-19-2002; operative 1-1-2003. Submitted to OAL for printing only pursuant to Government Code section 11351 (Register 2002, No. 51).

Ref.: Hanna §§ 23.14[2][p], 31.20[4][b]; Herlick Handbook §§ 1.6, 6.21, 14.17.

ARTICLE 20
Review of Administrative Orders

§10950. Appeal from Order Granting or Denying Petition for Order Requiring Employee to Select Employer-Designated Physician.

(a) Where either party petitions the Workers' Compensation Appeals Board within twenty

(20) days pursuant to Section 9787 as the result of a grant or denial pursuant to Section 9786(e)(2) or Section 9786(e)(3) of the Rules of the Administrative Director, the matter shall be referred to a workers' compensation judge for hearing and determination of the issues raised. A party aggrieved by the determination of the workers' compensation judge may seek relief therefrom within the same time and in the same manner specified for petitions for reconsideration. The petition for reconsideration shall be filed in the district office having venue.

(b) Any party aggrieved by an order issued pursuant to Section 9786(e)(4) of the rules of the Administrative Director may petition the Appeals Board for relief therefrom within twenty (20) days from the date of the issuance of the order in the same manner specified for petitions for reconsideration, including the filing of the petition for reconsideration and answers thereto at the district office of the Workers' Compensation Appeals Board from which the decision issued.

Note: Authority cited: Sections 133 and 5307, Labor Code. Reference: Sections 4603, 4604 and 5302, Labor Code.

History: 1. Amendment of section and Note filed 12-19-2002; operative 1-1-2003. Submitted to OAL for printing only pursuant to Government Code section 11351 (Register 2002, No. 51).

Ref.: See Labor Code §4600; Hanna § 22.03[2]; Herlick Handbook §§ 1.6, 4.3, 15.1, 15.2.

§10952. Appeal of Notice of Compensation Due.

A notice of compensation due, issued pursuant to Labor Code Section 129, may be appealed by the filing of an Appeal of Notice of Compensation Due with the Workers' Compensation Appeals Board and service of the Appeal of Notice of Compensation Due on the injured worker or dependent and the audit unit within fifteen (15) days of receipt of the notice of compensation due. The Appeal of Notice of Compensation Due shall be filed at or referred to the district office where venue has already been determined by previous filing or application or, if venue has not been determined, a district office in accordance with Labor Code Section 5501.5.

The filing of an objection to a notice of intention to issue notice of compensation due shall be a prerequisite for the filing of an Appeal of Notice of Compensation Due. Failure to timely file an objection to notice of intention to issue notice of compensation due may result in dismissal of the Appeal of Notice of Compensation Due.

The Appeal of Notice of Compensation Due shall set out the factual and legal basis for contesting the notice of compensation due and shall include the audit unit's file number. The Appeal of Notice of Compensation Due shall be accompanied by a copy of the notice of compensation due, a Declaration of Readiness, an Application for Adjudication if one has not been previously filed, and any other documents deemed relevant. The copy of the Appeal of Notice of Compensation Due sent to the injured worker shall inform the injured worker of the right to consult an attorney.

The case number assigned to the Application for Adjudication shall be assigned to the Appeal of Notice of Compensation Due.

An Appeal of Notice of Compensation Due shall be set for a hearing before a workers' compensation judge within forty-five (45) days of filing with the Workers' Compensation Appeals Board unless the employee's claim is before the Workers' Compensation Appeals Board on other substantive issues in which case the appeal may be considered with these other issues. The audit unit, insurer, self-insured employer or third party administrator and the injured worker shall receive notice of the date and time of hearing as well as copies of any other notices or orders issued by the Workers' Compensation Appeals Board. Following the hearing, the workers' compensation judge shall issue findings of fact and an order affirming, modifying or rescinding the notice of compensation due, which complies with Labor Code section 5313.

If the injured worker is represented by an attorney, the workers' compensation judge may determine the amount of attorney fees reasonably incurred in resisting the Appeal of Notice of Compensation Due and may assess reasonable attorney fees as a cost upon the employer filing the Appeal of Notice of Compensation Due in accordance with Labor Code section 129(c).

Note: Authority cited: Sections 133 and 5307, Labor Code. Reference: Sections 129, 5300 and 5301, Labor Code.

History: 1. New section filed 6-11-92 with Secretary of State by Workers' Compensation Appeals Board; operative 6-11-92. Submitted to OAL for printing only pursuant to Government Code section 11351 (Register 92, No. 24).

2. Amendment filed 12-19-2002; operative 1-1-2003. Submitted to OAL for printing only pursuant to Government Code section 11351 (Register 2002, No. 51).

Ref.: Hanna §§ 1.12[9][b], 2.02[1][d]; Herlick Handbook §§ 1.6, 9.5, 15.1, 15.2.

§10953. Petition Appealing Audit Penalty Assessment—Labor Code Section 129.5(g).

An insurer, self-insured employer, or third-party administrator may file a petition appealing from a civil penalty assessment issued pursuant to subdivision (e) of Labor Code section 129.5, together with a Declaration of Readiness requesting a mandatory settlement conference, at the district office of the Workers' Compensation Appeals Board closest to petitioner within seven days after receipt of the notice. If petitioner is domiciled out of state, the petition shall be filed at the San Francisco district office. Petitioner shall attach a copy of the notice of penalty assessment and any other evidence it wishes to submit. Petitioner shall serve upon the Administrative Director copies of all documents filed. Upon stipulation of petitioner and the Administrative Director, the matter may be submitted for decision at the mandatory settlement conference. Otherwise, it shall be set for trial.

Note: Authority cited: Sections 133 and 5307, Labor Code. Reference: Section 129.5(g), Labor Code.

History: 1. New section filed 12-19-2002; operative 1-1-2003. Submitted to OAL for printing only pursuant to Government Code section 11351 (Register 2002, No. 51).

Ref.: Hanna § 10.51[2][c], [d]; Herlick Handbook § 9.5.

§10955. Rehabilitation Appeals.

(a) Appeals from decisions of the Division of Workers' Compensation Rehabilitation Unit or an arbitrator appointed pursuant to Labor Code Sections 4645, subdivisions (b) and (c), shall be commenced as follows:

(1) if an Application for Adjudication is already on file, by filing a Declaration of Readiness and a petition setting forth the reason for the appeal;

(2) if no Application for Adjudication is on file, by filing an application, a Declaration of Readiness, and a petition setting forth the reason for the appeal.

(b) The party appealing from a decision of the Rehabilitation Unit shall file and serve copies of the decision and other documents that the appealing party deems relevant. The opposing party may file and serve copies of whatever additional documents the opposing party deems relevant.

A copy of all pleadings, notices and orders shall be served on the Division of Workers' Compensation, Rehabilitation Unit.

Note: Authority cited: Sections 133 and 5307, Labor Code. Reference: Sections 139.5, 4645 and 5500, Labor Code.

History: 1. Repealer and new section filed 12-23-93; operative 1-1-94. Submitted to OAL for printing only pursuant to Government Code section 11351 (Register 93, No. 52).

2. Amendment filed 12-19-2002; operative 1-1-2003. Submitted to OAL for printing only pursuant to Government Code section 11351 (Register 2002, No. 51).

Ref.: Hanna § 35.72[3]; Herlick Handbook §§ 1.6, 15.1, 16.1, 16.12, 16.13, 15.2.

§10956. Rehabilitation Records. [Repealed]

Note: Authority cited: Sections 133 and 5307, Labor Code. Reference: Sections 139.5, 5708 and 5709, Labor Code.

History: 1. Repealer filed 12-19-2002; operative 1-1-2003. Submitted to OAL for printing only pursuant to Government Code section 11351 (Register 2002, No. 51).

Ref.: Herlick Handbook §§ 1.6, 15.1, 15.2, 16.13.

§10957. Deposition of Rehabilitation Consultants.

Depositions of Rehabilitation Unit consultants will not be taken except on terms and conditions as ordered by a workers' compensation judge.

Note: Authority cited: Sections 133 and 5307, Labor Code. Reference: Section 5708, Labor Code.

History: 1. Amendment of section and Note filed 12-19-2002; operative 1-1-2003. Submitted to OAL for printing only pursuant to Government Code section 11351 (Register 2002, No. 51).

Ref.: Hanna § 35.72[5]; Herlick Handbook §§ 1.6, 14.5, 15.1, 15.2, 16.13.

§10958. Hearing and Burden of Proof.

Proceedings instituted under Section 10955 shall be assigned, heard and determined in the same manner as proceedings instituted for the collection of other compensation except that the burden of proof shall be on the person disputing the finding or determination of the Rehabilitation Unit.

Note: Authority cited: Sections 133 and 5307, Labor Code. Reference: Section 5708, Labor Code.

History: 1. Amendment of section and Note filed 12-19-2002; operative 1-1-2003. Submitted to OAL for printing only pursuant to Government Code section 11351 (Register 2002, No. 51).

Ref.: See Labor Code §5709; Hanna § 35.72[5]; Herlick Handbook §§ 1.6, 15.1, 15.2, 16.1, 16.13.

ARTICLE 21 General [Repealed]

§10960. Operative Effect of Rules 10300 through 10958. [Repealed]

Note: Authority cited: Sections 133 and 5307, Labor Code. Reference: Statutes of 1989, Chapters 892 and 893; and Statutes of 1993, Chapter 121.

History: 1. Repealer and new section filed 12-23-93; operative 1-1-94. Submitted to OAL for printing only pursuant to Government Code section 11351 (Register 93, No. 52). For prior history, see Register 90, No. 5.

2. Repealer of article 21 (sections 10960-10964) and section filed 12-19-2002; operative 1-1-2003. Submitted to OAL for printing only pursuant to Government Code section 11351 (Register 2002, No. 51).

§10961. Operative Effect of Rules 10960 through 10999. [Repealed]

Note: Authority cited: Sections 133 and 5307, Labor Code. Reference: Statutes of 1989, Chapters 892 and 893; and Statutes of 1993, Chapter 121.

History: 1. New section filed 1-12-90; operative 1-12-90 (Register 90, No. 5). This section is exempt from review by OAL pursuant to Government Code Section 11351.

2. Change without regulatory effect filed 1-26-90 (Register 90, No. 5).

3. Amendment filed 12-23-93; operative 1-1-94. Submitted to OAL for printing only pursuant to Government Code section 11351 (Register 93, No. 52).

4. Repealer filed 12-19-2002; operative 1-1-2003. Submitted to OAL for printing only pursuant to Government Code section 11351 (Register 2002, No. 51).

§10962. Repealed.

Note: Authority cited: Sections 133 and 5307, Labor Code. Reference: Section 5502, subdivision (d), Labor Code.

History: 1. New section filed 1-12-90; operative 1-12-90 (Register 90, No. 5). This section is exempt from review by OAL pursuant to Government Code section 11351.

2. Change without regulatory effect filed 1-26-90 (Register 90, No. 5).

3. Repealer filed 10-21-96; operative 11-1-96. Submitted to OAL for printing only pursuant to Government Code section 11351 (Register 96, No. 43).

§10963. Administrative Director of the Division of Workers' Compensation. [Repealed]

Note: Authority cited: Sections 133 and 5307, Labor Code. Reference: Sections 110 and 111, Labor Code.

History: 1. New section filed 1-12-90; operative 1-12-90 (Register 90, No. 5). This section is exempt from review by OAL pursuant to Government Code Section 11351.

2. Change without regulatory effect filed 1-26-90 (Register 90, No. 5).

3. Repealer filed 12-19-2002; operative 1-1-2003. Submitted to OAL for printing only pursuant to Government Code section 11351 (Register 2002, No. 51).

§10964. Office of Benefit Determination. [Repealed]

Note: Authority cited: Sections 133 and 5309, Labor Code. Reference: Section 124, Labor Code.

History: 1. New section filed 1-12-90; operative 1-12-90 (Register 90, No. 5). This section is exempt from review by OAL pursuant to Government Code Section 11351.

2. Change without regulatory effect filed 1-26-90 (Register 90, No. 5).

3. Repealer filed 12-19-2002; operative 1-1-2003. Submitted to OAL for printing only pursuant to Government Code section 11351 (Register 2002, No. 51).

ARTICLE 22 Pleadings [Repealed]

§10965. Repealed.

Note: Authority cited: Sections 133 and 5307, Labor Code. Reference: Section 5500, Labor Code.

History: 1. New section filed 1-12-90; operative 1-12-90 (Register 90, No. 5). This section is exempt from review by OAL pursuant to Government Code section 11351.

2. Change without regulatory effect filed 1-26-90 (Register 90, No. 5).

3. Repealer filed 12-23-93; operative 1-1-94. Submitted to OAL for printing only pursuant to Government Code section 11351 (Register 93, No. 52).

§10966. Declaration of Readiness to Proceed. [Repealed]

Note: Authority cited: Sections 133 and 5307, Labor Code. Reference: Sections 134, 5500 and 5502, Labor Code.

History: 1. New section filed 1-12-90; operative 1-12-90 (Register 90, No. 5). This section is exempt from review by OAL pursuant to Government Code section 11351.

2. Change without regulatory effect filed 1-26-90 (Register 90, No. 5).

3. Amendment exempt from OAL review pursuant to Government Code section 11351 filed 12-19-90; operative 1-1-91 (Register 91, No. 7).

4. Amendment of section filed 6-11-92 with Secretary of State by Workers' Compensation Appeals Board; operative 6-11-92. Submitted to OAL for printing only pursuant to Government Code section 11351 (Register 92, No. 24).

5. Amendment filed 12-23-93; operative 1-1-94. Submitted to OAL for printing only pursuant to Government Code section 11351 (Register 93, No. 52).

6. Repealer of article 22 (sections 10966-10967) and section filed 12-19-2002; operative 1-1-2003. Submitted to OAL for printing only pursuant to Government Code section 11351 (Register 2002, No. 51).

§10967. Objection to Declaration of Readiness to Proceed. [Repealed]

Note: Authority cited: Sections 133 and 5307, Labor Code. Reference: Sections 134, 5500 and 5502, Labor Code.

History: 1. New section filed 1-12-90; operative 1-12-90 (Register 90, No. 5). This section is exempt from review by OAL pursuant to Government Code section 11351.

2. Change without regulatory effect filed 1-26-90 (Register 90, No. 5).

3. Amendment exempt from OAL review pursuant to Government Code section 11351 filed 12-19-90; operative 1-1-91 (Register 91, No. 7).

4. Amendment filed 12-23-93; operative 1-1-94. Submitted to OAL for printing only pursuant to Government Code section 11351 (Register 93, No. 52).

5. Repealer filed 12-19-2002; operative 1-1-2003. Submitted to OAL for printing only pursuant to Government Code section 11351 (Register 2002, No. 51).

§10968. Repealed.

Note: Authority cited: Sections 133 and 5307, Labor Code. Reference: Section 5500, Labor Code.

History: 1. New section filed 1-12-90; operative 1-12-90 (Register 90, No. 5). This section is exempt from review by OAL pursuant to Government Code Section 11351.

2. Change without regulatory effect filed 1-26-90 (Register 90, No. 5).

3. Repealer filed 12-23-93; operative 1-1-94. Submitted to OAL for printing only pursuant to Government Code section 11351 (Register 93, No. 52).

§10969. Repealed.

Note: Authority cited: Sections 133 and 5307, Labor Code. Reference: Section 5500, Labor Code.

History: 1. New section filed 1-12-90; operative 1-12-90 (Register 90, No. 5). This section is exempt from review by OAL pursuant to Government Code Section 11351.

2. Change without regulatory effect filed 1-26-90 (Register 90, No. 5).

3. Repealer filed 12-23-93; operative 1-1-94. Submitted to OAL for printing only pursuant to Government Code section 11351 (Register 93, No. 52).

§10973. Repealed.

Note: Authority cited: Sections 133 and 5307, Labor Code. Reference: Section 5316, Labor Code.

History: 1. New section filed 1-12-90; operative 1-12-90 (Register 90, No. 5). This section is exempt from review by OAL pursuant to Government Code Section 11351.

2. Change without regulatory effect filed 1-26-90 (Register 90, No. 5).

3. Repealer of article heading and section filed 12-23-93; operative 1-1-94. Submitted to OAL for printing only pursuant to Government Code section 11351 (Register 93, No. 52).

§10974. Repealed.

Note: Authority cited: Sections 133 and 5307, Labor Code. Reference: Section 5316, Labor Code.

History: 1. New section filed 1-12-90; operative 1-12-90 (Register 90, No. 5). This section is exempt from review by OAL pursuant to Government Code Section 11351.

2. Change without regulatory effect filed 1-26-90 (Register 90, No. 5).

3. Repealer filed 12-23-93; operative 1-1-94. Submitted to OAL for printing only pursuant to Government Code section 11351 (Register 93, No. 52).

§10975. Repealed.

Note: Authority cited: Sections 133 and 5307, Labor Code. Reference: Section 5316, Labor Code.

History: 1. Repealer filed 12-23-93; operative 1-1-94. Submitted to OAL for printing only pursuant to Government Code section 11351 (Register 93, No. 52).

§10976. Repealed.

Note: Authority cited: Sections 133 and 5307, Labor Code. Reference: Sections 5502 and 5709, Labor Code.

History: 1. New section filed 1-12-90; operative 1-12-90 (Register 90, No. 5). This section is exempt from review by OAL pursuant to Government Code section 11351.

2. Change without regulatory effect filed 1-26-90 (Register 90, No. 5).

3. Repealer of article heading and section filed 12-23-93; operative 1-1-94. Submitted to OAL for printing only pursuant to Government Code section 11351 (Register 93, No. 52).

§10977. Repealed.

Note: Authority cited: Sections 133 and 5307, Labor Code. Reference: Section 5504, Labor Code.

History: 1. New section filed 1-12-90; operative 1-12-90 (Register 90, No. 5). This section is exempt from review by OAL pursuant to Government Code section 11351.

2. Change without regulatory effect filed 1-26-90 (Register 90, No. 5).

3. Repealer filed 12-23-93; operative 1-1-94. Submitted to OAL for printing only pursuant to Government Code section 11351 (Register 93, No. 52).

§10978. Repealed.

Note: Authority cited: Sections 133 and 5307, Labor Code. Reference: Sections 4620, 4628, 5703, 5708 and 5709, Labor Code.

History: 1. New section filed 1-12-90; operative 1-12-90 (Register 90, No. 5). This section is exempt from review by OAL pursuant to Government Code section 11351.

2. Change without regulatory effect filed 1-26-90 (Register 90, No. 5).

3. Amendment exempt from OAL review pursuant to Government Code section 11351 filed 12-19-90; operative 1-1-91 (Register 91, No. 7).

4. Repealer of article heading and section filed 12-23-93; operative 1-1-94. Submitted to OAL for printing only pursuant to Government Code section 11351 (Register 93, No. 52).

§10979. Repealed.

Note: Authority cited: Sections 133 and 5307, Labor Code. Reference: Sections 4620, 5500, 5703, 5708 and 5709, Labor Code.

History: 1. New section filed 1-12-90; operative 1-12-90 (Register 90, No. 5). This section is exempt from review by OAL pursuant to Government Code section 11351.

2. Change without regulatory effect filed 1-26-90 (Register 90, No. 5).

3. Amendment exempt from OAL review pursuant to Government Code section 11351 filed 12-19-90; operative 1-1-91 (Register 91, No. 7).

4. Repealer filed 12-23-93; operative 1-1-94. Submitted to OAL for printing only pursuant to Government Code section 11351 (Register 93, No. 52).

§10980. Repealed.

Note: Authority cited: Sections 133 and 5307, Labor Code. Reference: Article XIV, Section 4, California Constitution; and Sections 4600 through 5709, Labor Code.

History: 1. New section filed 1-12-90; operative 1-12-90 (Register 90, No. 5). This section is exempt from review by OAL pursuant to Government Code section 11351.

2. Change without regulatory effect filed 1-26-90 (Register 90, No. 5).

3. Repealer filed 12-23-93; operative 1-1-94. Submitted to OAL for printing only pursuant to Government Code section 11351 (Register 93, No. 52).

ARTICLE 23
Medical Examiners
[Repealed]

§10984. Impartial Medical Examiners. [Repealed]

Note: Authority cited: Sections 133 and 5307, Labor Code. Reference: Sections 122 and 139, Labor Code.

History: 1. New section filed 1-12-90; operative 1-12-90 (Register 90, No. 5). This section is exempt from review by OAL pursuant to Government Code Section 11351.

2. Change without regulatory effect filed 1-26-90 (Register 90, No. 5).

3. Amendment of article heading filed 12-23-93; operative 1-1-94. Submitted to OAL for printing only

pursuant to Government Code section 11351 (Register 93, No. 52).

4. Repealer of article 23 (section 10984) filed 12-19-2002; operative 1-1-2003. Submitted to OAL for printing only pursuant to Government Code section 11351 (Register 2002, No. 51).

§10985. Repealed.

Note: Authority, Sections 133 and 5307, Labor Code. Reference: Section 4903.4, Labor Code.

History: 1. New section filed 1-12-90; operative 1-12-90 (Register 90, No. 5). This section is exempt from review by OAL pursuant to Government Code section 11351.

2. Change without regulatory effect filed 1-26-90 (Register 90, No. 5).

3. Repealer of article heading and section filed 12-23-93; operative 1-1-94. Submitted to OAL for printing only pursuant to Government Code section 11351 (Register 93, No. 52).

§10986. Repealed.

Note: Authority cited: Sections 133 and 5307, Labor Code. Reference: Section 4903.4, Labor Code.

History: 1. New section filed 1-12-90; operative 1-12-90 (Register 90, No. 5). This section is exempt from review by OAL pursuant to Government Code section 11351.

2. Change without regulatory effect filed 1-26-90 (Register 90, No. 5).

3. Repealer filed 12-23-93; operative 1-1-94. Submitted to OAL for printing only pursuant to Government Code section 11351 (Register 93, No. 52).

ARTICLE 24
Attorneys and Representatives [Repealed]

§10987. Pre-Application Attorney Fees. [Repealed]

Note: Authority cited: Sections 133 and 5307, Labor Code. Reference: Sections 4903 and 4906, Labor Code.

History: 1. New section filed 1-12-90; operative 1-12-90 (Register 90, No. 5). This section is exempt from review by OAL pursuant to Government Code Section 11351.

2. Change without regulatory effect filed 1-26-90 (Register 90, No. 5).

3. Amendment of article heading and section filed 12-23-93; operative 1-1-94. Submitted to OAL for printing only pursuant to Government Code section 11351 (Register 93, No. 52).

4. Repealer of article 24 (sections 10987-10987.3) and section filed 12-19-2002; operative 1-1-2003. Submitted to OAL for printing only pursuant to Government Code section 11351 (Register 2002, No. 51).

§10987.1. Information Request Form. [Repealed]

Note: Authority cited: Sections 133, 5307, 5407 and 5401.7, Labor Code. Reference: Section 5401.5, Labor Code.

History: 1. New section exempt from OAL review pursuant to Government Code section 11351, filed 12-19-90; operative 1-1-91 (Register 91, No. 7).

2. Amendment of section filed 6-11-92 with Secretary of State by Workers' Compensation Appeals Board; operative 6-11-92. Submitted to OAL for printing only pursuant to Government Code section 11351 (Register 92, No. 24).

3. Repealer filed 12-19-2002; operative 1-1-2003. Submitted to OAL for printing only pursuant to Government Code section 11351 (Register 2002, No. 51).

§10987.2. Information Response Form. [Repealed]

Note: Authority cited: Sections 133, 5307 and 5401.6, Labor Code. Reference: Section 5401.6, Labor Code.

History: 1. New section exempt from OAL review pursuant to Government Code section 11351, filed 12-19-90; operative 1-1-91 (Register 91, No. 7).

2. Amendment of section filed 6-11-92 with Secretary of State by Workers' Compensation Appeals Board; operative 6-11-92. Submitted to OAL for printing only pursuant to Government Code section 11351 (Register 92, No. 24).

3. Repealer filed 12-19-2002; operative 1-1-2003. Submitted to OAL for printing only pursuant to Government Code section 11351 (Register 2002, No. 51).

§10987.3. Operative Effect of Rules 10987.1 and 10987.2. [Repealed]

Note: Authority cited: Sections 133 and 5307, Labor Code. Reference: Section 4903 and 4906, Labor Code; and Statutes of 1993, Chapter 121.

History: 1. New section filed 12-23-93; operative 1-1-94. Submitted to OAL for printing only pursuant to Government Code section 11351 (Register 93, No. 52).

2. Repealer filed 12-19-2002; operative 1-1-2003. Submitted to OAL for printing only pursuant to Government Code section 11351 (Register 2002, No. 51).

§10988. Repealed.

Note: Authority cited: Sections 133 and 5307, Labor Code. Reference: Sections 5277(c), 5275(d), and 5900 through 5911, Labor Code.

History: 1. New section filed 1-12-90; operative 1-12-90 (Register 90, No. 5). This section is exempt from review by OAL pursuant to Government Code section 11351.

2. Change without regulatory effect filed 1-26-90 (Register 90, No. 5).

3. Amendment exempt from OAL review pursuant to Government Code section 11351 filed 12-19-90; operative 1-1-91 (Register 91, No. 7).

4. Repealer of article heading and section filed 12-23-93; operative 1-1-94. Submitted to OAL printing only pursuant to Government Code section 11351 (Register 93, No. 52).

§10989. Repealed.

Note: Authority cited: Sections 133 and 5307, Labor Code. Reference: Sections 5275(c), 5275(d), and 5900 through 5911, Labor Code.

History: 1. New section filed 1-12-90; operative 1-12-90 (Register 90, No. 5). This section is exempt from review by OAL pursuant to Government Code section 11351.

2. Change without regulatory effect filed 1-26-90 (Register 90, No. 5).

3. Amendment exempt from OAL review pursuant to Government Code section 11351 filed 12-19-90; operative 1-1-91 (Register 91, No. 7).

4. Repealer filed 12-23-93; operative 1-1-94. Submitted to OAL for printing only pursuant to Government Code section 11351 (Register 93, No. 52).

§10990. Repealed.

Note: Authority cited: Sections 133 and 5307, Labor Code. Reference: Sections 111 and 5502, Labor Code.

History: 1. New section filed 1-12-90; operative 1-12-90 (Register 90, No. 5). This section is exempt from review by OAL pursuant to Government Code section 11351.

2. Change without regulatory effect filed 1-26-90 (Register 90, No. 5).

3. Amendment exempt from OAL review pursuant to Government Code section 11351 filed 12-19-90; operative 1-1-91 (Register 91, No. 7).

4. Repealer filed 12-23-93; operative 1-1-94. Submitted to OAL for printing only pursuant to Government Code section 11351 (Register 93, No. 52).

§10991. Repealed.

Note: Authority cited: Sections 133 and 5307, Labor Code. Reference: Sections 111 and 5502, Labor Code.

History: 1. New section filed 1-12-90; operative 1-12-90 (Register 90, No. 5). This section is exempt from review by OAL pursuant to Government Code section 11351.

2. Change without regulatory effect filed 1-26-90 (Register 90, No. 5).

3. Amendment exempt from OAL review pursuant to Government Code section 11351 filed 12-19-90; operative 1-1-91 (Register 91, No. 7).

4. Repealer filed 12-23-93; operative 1-1-94. Submitted to OAL for printing only pursuant to Government Code section 11351 (Register 93, No. 52).

§10992. Repealed.

Note: Authority cited: Sections 133 and 5307, Labor Code. Reference: Sections 139.5, 4645(d) and 5500, Labor Code.

History: 1. New section filed 1-12-90; operative 1-12-90 (Register 90, No. 5). This section is exempt from review by OAL pursuant to Government Code section 11351.

2. Change without regulatory effect filed 1-26-90 (Register 90, No. 5).

3. Repealer of article heading and section filed 12-23-93; operative 1-1-94. Submitted to OAL for printing only pursuant to Government Code section 11351 (Register 93, No. 52).

ARTICLE 22
Arbitration

§10995. Mandatory Arbitration.

This rule applies to injuries occurring on or after January 1, 1990.

Any Application for Adjudication that lists one or more disputes involving an issue set forth in Labor Code section 5275, subdivision (a), shall be accompanied by an arbitration submittal form prescribed and approved by the Appeals Board. The arbitration submittal form shall indicate that either:

(1) an arbitrator has been selected pursuant to Labor Code section 5271, subdivision (a), or

(2) an unsuccessful attempt has been made to select an arbitrator and the presiding workers' compensation judge is requested pursuant to Labor Code section 5271, subdivision (b), to assign a panel of five arbitrators.

If the parties have agreed to an arbitrator pursuant to Labor Code section 5271, subdivision (c), the presiding workers' compensation judge shall, within six (6) days of receipt of the arbitration submittal form, order the issue or issues in dispute submitted for arbitration pursuant to Labor Code sections 5272, 5273, 5276 and 5277.

If the arbitration submittal form requests a panel pursuant to Labor Code section 5271, subdivision (b), the presiding workers' compensation judge shall, within six (6) days of receipt of the arbitration submittal form, serve on each of the parties an identical list of five arbitrators selected at random pursuant to Labor Code 5271(b). For each party in excess of one party in the capacity of employer and one party in the capacity of injured employee or lien claimant, the presiding workers' compensation judge shall randomly select two additional arbitrators to add to the panel in accordance with the selection process set forth in Labor Code section 5721, subdivision (c). Each of the parties shall strike two arbitrators from the list and return it to the presiding workers' compensation judge within six (6) days after service. Failure to timely return the list shall constitute a waiver of a party's right to participate in the selection process. If one arbitrator remains, the presiding workers' compensation judge shall, within six (6) days of return of the lists from the parties, order the issue or issues submitted for arbitration before the selected arbitrator pursuant to Labor Code sections 5272, 5273, 5276 and 5277. If more than one arbitrator remains on the panel, the presiding workers' compensation judge shall randomly select an arbitrator from the remaining panelists.

If the parties to the dispute have stricken all the arbitrators from the panel, the presiding workers' compensation judge shall, within six (6) days of receipt of the last of the returned lists, serve on each of the parties to the dispute a new list of five arbitrators and any additional arbitrators required by Labor Code section 5271 subdivision (c) selected at random but excluding the names of the arbitrators on the prior list. Each of the parties to the dispute shall again strike two arbitrators from the list and return it to the presiding workers' compensation judge within six (6) days after service. This procedure shall continue until one or more arbitrators remain on the lists returned to the presiding workers' compensation judge.

The parties shall provide all necessary materials to the arbitrator. The Workers' Compensation Appeals Board file shall remain in the custody of the district office.

Note: Authority cited: Sections 133 and 5307, Labor Code. Reference: Sections 5270 through 5277, Labor Code.

History: 1. New section filed 1-12-90; operative 1-12-90 (Register 90, No. 5). This section is exempt from review by OAL pursuant to Government Code section 11351.

2. Change without regulatory effect filed 1-26-90 (Register 90, No. 5).

3. Amendment exempt from OAL review pursuant to Government Code section 11351 filed 12-19-90; operative 1-1-91 (Register 91, No. 7).

4. Amendment of article heading filed 12-23-93; operative 1-1-94. Submitted to OAL for printing only pursuant to Government Code section 11351 (Register 93, No. 52).

5. Renumbering of former article 25 to article 22 and amendment of section filed 12-19-2002; operative 1-1-2003. Submitted to OAL for printing only pursuant to Government Code section 11351 (Register 2002, No. 51).

Ref.: Hanna §§ 33.01[1][b], 33.01[3][b]–[c], [d]; Herlick Handbook §§ 1.6, 14.32; W. Cal. Sum., 2 "Workers' Compensation" §392.

§10996. Voluntary Arbitration.

At any time, the parties may agree to submit any issue for arbitration pursuant to Labor Code section 5275, subdivision (b), by submitting an arbitration submittal form prescribed and approved by the Appeals Board that indicates that the parties have selected an arbitrator from the list prepared by the presiding workers' compensation judge pursuant to Labor Code section 5271, subdivision (a) and by filing an Application for Adjudication if one has not been previously filed.

Within six (6) days of receipt of the arbitration submittal form, the presiding workers' compensation judge shall order the issues in dispute submitted for arbitration pursuant to Labor Code sections 5272, 5273, 5276 and 5277.

Any final decision, order or award from the arbitrator, together with the notice of claim form and the record developed as set forth in Labor Code sections 5276 and 5277, shall be filed with the presiding workers' compensation judge.

If the parties are unable to agree to an arbitrator under Labor Code section 5271, subdivision (a), the parties may agree to follow the procedures for selecting an arbitrator under Labor Code section 5271, subdivision (b) and (c), as set forth in rule 10995.

The parties shall provide all necessary materials to the arbitrator. The Workers' Compensation Appeals Board file shall remain in the custody of the district office.

Note: Authority cited: Sections 133 and 5307, Labor Code. Reference: Sections 5270 through 5277, Labor Code.

History: 1. New section filed 1-12-90; operative 1-12-90 (Register 90, No. 5). This section is exempt from review by OAL pursuant to Government Code section 11351.

2. Change without regulatory effect filed 1-26-90 (Register 90, No. 5).

3. Amendment exempt from OAL review pursuant to Government Code section 11351 filed 12-19-90; operative 1-1-91 (Register 91, No. 7).

4. Amendment filed 12-19-2002; operative 1-1-2003. Submitted to OAL for printing only pursuant to Government Code section 11351 (Register 2002, No. 51).

Ref.: Hanna §§ 33.01[2][a]–[b], 33.01[3[b], 33.01[4]; Herlick Handbook §§ 1.6, 14.32; W. Cal. Sum., 2 "Workers' Compensation" §392.

§10997. Request for Arbitration.

In no event will arbitration be permitted after the taking of testimony in any proceeding.

Note: Authority cited: Sections 133 and 5307, Labor Code. Reference: Sections 5270 through 5277, Labor Code.

History: 1. New section filed 1-12-90; operative 1-12-90 (Register 90, No. 5). This section is exempt from review by OAL pursuant to Government Code section 11351.

2. Change without regulatory effect filed 1-26-90 (Register 90, No. 5).

3. Amendment exempt from OAL review pursuant to Government Code section 11351 filed 12-19-90; operative 1-1-91 (Register 91, No. 7).

4. Amendment filed 12-19-2002; operative 1-1-2003. Submitted to OAL for printing only pursuant to Government Code section 11351 (Register 2002, No. 51).

Ref.: Hanna § 33.01[2][a]; Herlick Handbook §§ 1.6, 14.32.

§10998. Disqualification of Arbitrator.

This rule applies to injuries occurring on or after January 1, 1990, except that this rule applies regardless of the date of injury for voluntary arbitration pursuant to Labor Code section 5275, subdivision (b).

After service of a list of panel members pursuant to rule 10995, any party may, within six (6) days, petition the workers' compensation judge to remove any member from the panel pursuant to section 170.1 of the Code of Civil Procedure. In event the presiding workers' compensation judge finds cause under section 170.1 of the Code of Civil Procedure, the presiding workers' compensation judge shall remove the member or members of the panel challenged and add to the original list the appropriate number of arbitrators at random to make a full panel and, within six (6) days, serve the list on the parties.

In event the presiding workers' compensation judge selects an arbitrator pursuant to rule 10995, the parties will have six (6) days after service of the name of the arbitrator to petition to disqualify that arbitrator pursuant to section 170.1 of the Code of Civil Procedure. If the presiding workers' compensation judge finds cause, the presiding workers' compensation judge shall assign another arbitrator pursuant to Labor Code section 5271, subdivision (d) and order the issue or issues in dispute submitted to that arbitrator.

Note: Authority cited: Sections 133 and 5307, Labor Code. Reference: Section 5271(d), Labor Code.

History: 1. New section filed 1-12-90; operative 1-12-90 (Register 90, No. 5). This section is exempt from review by OAL pursuant to Government Code section 11351.

2. Change without regulatory effect filed 1-26-90 (Register 90, No. 5).

3. Amendment exempt from OAL review pursuant to Government Code section 11351 filed 12-19-90; operative 1-1-91 (Register 91, No. 7).

4. Amendment of first paragraph and Note filed 12-19-2002; operative 1-1-2003. Submitted to OAL for printing only pursuant to Government Code section 11351 (Register 2002, No. 51).

Ref.: Hanna § 33.01[3][d]; Herlick Handbook §§ 1.6, 14.32.

§10999. Arbitrator Fee and Cost Disputes.

Any dispute involving an arbitrator's fee or cost shall be resolved by the presiding workers' compensation judge of the appropriate local office or, in his or her absence, the acting presiding workers' compensation judge.

Any request to resolve a dispute about arbitrator fees or costs must be accompanied by any written agreement pertaining to arbitrator fees or costs and a statement that shall include the nature of the dispute and an itemization of the hours spent in actual arbitration hearing, in preparation for arbitration, and in preparation of the decision. The statement shall also include an itemization of the verifiable costs including use of facility, reporters and transcript preparation.

An arbitrator fee shall not exceed a reasonable amount. In establishing a reasonable fee, the Presiding Workers' Compensation Judge shall consider:

(a) responsibility assumed by the arbitrator;

(b) experience of the arbitrator;

(c) number and complexity of the issues being arbitrated;

(d) time involved; and

(e) expeditiousness and completeness of issue resolution.

The presiding workers' compensation judge of each local office shall maintain statistics on all arbitration fees awarded pursuant to Labor Code section 5273(c) including the amount thereof and rationale or basis for the award pursuant to (a) through (e) herein above.

Arbitration costs will be allowed in a reasonable amount pursuant to Labor Code section 5273, subdivision (a).

Note: Authority cited: Sections 133 and 5307, Labor Code. Reference: Section 5273(c), Labor Code.

History: 1. New section filed 1-12-90; operative 1-12-90 (Register 90, No. 5). This section is exempt from review by OAL pursuant to Government Code section 11351.

2. Change without regulatory effect filed 1-26-90 (Register 90, No. 5).

3. Amendment exempt from OAL review pursuant to Government Code section 11351 filed 12-19-90; operative 1-1-91 (Register 91, No. 7).

4. Amendment of section and Note filed 12-19-2002; operative 1-1-2003. Submitted to OAL for printing only pursuant to Government Code section 11351 (Register 2002, No. 51).

Ref.: Hanna § 33.01[5]; Herlick Handbook §§ 1.6, 14.32.

CHAPTER 7
DIVISION OF LABOR STATISTICS AND RESEARCH

SUBCHAPTER 1
OCCUPATIONAL INJURY OR ILLNESS REPORTS AND RECORDS

ARTICLE 1
Reporting of Occupational Injury or Illness

§14000. Definitions.

As used in this Article:

Computer input media. Techniques and means by which information or data can be entered into a computer system. Examples include magnetic tape, diskette, and telecommunications.

Division. The Division of Labor Statistics and Research of the Department of Industrial Relations.

Occupational illness. Any abnormal condition or disorder caused by exposure to environmental factors associated with employment, including acute and chronic illnesses or diseases which may be caused by inhalation, absorption, ingestion, or direct contact.

Self-insured employer. An employer who has secured from the Director of Industrial Relations a certificate of consent to self-insure against workers' compensation claims pursuant to Labor Code Section 3700.

Note: Authority cited: Section 6410, Labor Code. Reference: Sections 3700, 6409(b), 6410, Labor Code.

History: 1. New §§14000 to 14504, inclusive, filed 3-3-47; effective thirtieth day thereafter (Register 7).

2. Amendment filed 5-16-73; designated effective 7-1-73 (Register 73, No. 20).

3. Amendment filed 4-15-74; designated effective 6-1-74 (Register 74, No. 16).

4. Repealer and new section filed 2-8-80; designated effective 5-1-80 (Register 80, No. 6).

5. Amendment filed 3-18-87; effective thirtieth day thereafter (Register 87, No. 12).

6. Amendment 6-14-89; operative 7-14-89 (Register 89, No. 25).

7. Amendment of section and Note filed 1-14-93; operative 2-16-93 (Register 93, No. 3).

Ref.: Hanna §§ 22.08[2], 25.20[3].

§14001. Employer.

(a) Every employer shall file a complete report of every occupational injury or occupational illness to each employee which results in lost time beyond the date of such injury or illness or which requires medical treatment beyond first aid, as defined in Labor Code Section 5401(a). As used in this subdivision, "lost time" means absence from work for a full day or shift beyond the date of the injury or illness.

(b) In the event an employer has filed a report of injury or illness pursuant to subdivision 14001(a), and the employee subsequently dies as a result of the reported injury or illness, the employer shall file an amended report indicating such death, within five days after the employer is notified or learns of the death.

(c) The report(s) required by subdivisions 14001(a) and (b) shall be made on Form 5020, Rev. 6, Employer's Report of Occupational Injury or Illness, reproduced in accordance with Section 14005, or by use of computer input media, prescribed by the Division and compatible with the Division's computer equipment. However, reports may be submitted on Form 5020, Rev. 5 until June 30, 1993.

(d) In the case of a self-insured employer, the reports required by subdivision 14001(a) and (b) shall be filed directly with the Division within five days after the employer obtains knowledge of the injury, illness or death. In addition, the self-insured employer shall transmit the doctor's report filed in accordance with Section 14003 to the Division within five days of receipt.

(e) In the case of an insured employer, the report required by subdivisions 14001(a) and (b) shall be filed with the insurer within five days after such insured employer obtains knowledge of the injury, illness or death.

(f) To assure timely filing of the doctor's first report, the employer, upon request by the physician, shall immediately disclose the name and address of the employer's workers' compensation insurance provider.

Note: Authority cited: Section 6410, Labor Code. Reference: Sections 5401(a), 6409(a), 6409.1(a), Labor Code.

History: 1. New section filed 3-3-47; effective thirtieth day thereafter (Register 7).

2. Amendment filed 11-26-51; effective thirtieth day thereafter (Register 26, No. 5).

3. Repealer filed 5-16-73; designated effective 7-1-73 (Register 73, No. 20).

4. New section filed 2-8-80; designated effective 5-1-80 (Register 80, No. 6).

5. Amendment of subsection (b) filed 1-13-83; effective thirtieth day thereafter (Register 83, No. 3).

6. Amendment of subsections (b)–(d) filed 3-18-87; effective thirtieth day thereafter (Register 87, No. 12).

7. Amendment filed 6-14-89; operative 7-14-89 (Register 89, No. 25).

8. Editorial correction of printing error in subsections (a) and (b) (Register 90, No. 6).

9. Amendment of subsection (a), new subsection (b), subsection relettering, amendments of newly designated subsections (c)-(e), new subsection (f), and amendments of Note filed 1-14-93; operative 2-16-93 (Register 93, No. 3).

Ref.: Hanna §§ 22.08[2], 25.20[3].

§14002. Insurer.

(a) Immediately upon receipt, the insurer shall transmit to the Division the reports filed by the insured employer, as required by subdivisions 14001(a) and (b). The report(s) filed shall be on either Form 5020, Rev. 6, or the computer input media prescribed by the Division.

(b) In addition, the insurer shall transmit the doctor's report filed in accordance with Section 14003 to the Division within five days of receipt.

Note: Authority cited: Section 6410, Labor Code. Reference: Sections 6409(a), 6409.1(a), Labor Code.

History: 1. New section filed 5-16-73; designated effective 7-1-73 (Register 73, No. 20).

2. Amendment filed 4-15-74; designated effective 6-1-74 (Register 74, No. 16).

3. Repealer and new section filed 2-8-80; designated effective 5-1-80 (Register 80, No. 6).

4. Amendment of subsection (a) filed 3-18-87; effective thirtieth day thereafter (Register 87, No. 12).

5. Amendment filed 6-14-89; operative 7-14-89 (Register 89, No. 25).

6. Editorial correction of printing error in subsection (b) (Register 90, No. 6).

7. Amendment of subsection (a) filed 1-14-93; operative 2-16-93 (Register 93, No. 3).

Ref.: Hanna §§ 22.08[2], 25.20[3].

§14003. Physician.

(a) Every physician, as defined in Labor Code Section 3209.3, who attends an injured employee shall file, within five days after initial examination, a complete report of every occupational injury or occupational illness to such employee, with the employer's insurer, or with the employer, if self-insured. The injured or ill employee, if able to do so, shall complete a portion of such report describing how the injury or illness occurred. Unless the report is transmitted on computer input media, the physician shall file the original signed report with the insurer or self-insured employer.

(b) If treatment is for pesticide poisoning or for a condition suspected to be pesticide poisoning, the physician shall also file a complete report directly with the Division within five days after initial treatment. In no case shall treatment administered for pesticide poisoning or suspected pesticide poisoning be deemed to be first aid treatment.

(c) The reports required by this Section shall be made on Form 5021, Rev. 4, Doctor's First Report of Occupational Injury or Illness (sample forms may be secured from the Division), upon a form reproduced in accordance with Section 14007, or by use of computer input media prescribed by the Division and compatible with the Division's computer equipment. However, reports may be submitted on Revision 3 of Form 5021 until June 30, 1993.

(d) Physicians who use computerized data collection and reporting systems shall keep the injured worker's statement with the patient's medical records.

Note: Authority cited: Section 6410, Labor Code. Reference: Sections 6409(a), 6409.3, 6410, Labor Code.

History: 1. New section filed 2-8-80; designated effective 5-1-80 (Register 80, No. 6).

2. Amendment of subsection (c) filed 1-13-83; effective thirtieth day thereafter (Register 83, No. 3).

3. Amendment filed 6-14-89; operative 7-14-89 (Register 89, No. 25).

4. Editorial correction of printing error in subsection (a) (Register 90, No. 6).

5. Amendment of subsections (a) and (c) filed 1-14-93; operative 2-16-93 (Register 93, No. 3).

6. Editorial correction of printing error in subsection (c) (Register 93, No. 44).

Ref.: Hanna § 22.08[2].

§14004. Employer's Report of Occupational Injury or Illness, Form 5020, Rev. 7.

State of California
EMPLOYER'S REPORT OF OCCUPATIONAL INJURY OR ILLNESS

Please complete in triplicate (type if possible) Mail two copies to:

OSHA CASE NO.

FATALITY ☐

Any person who makes or causes to be made any knowingly false or fraudulent material statement or material representation for the purpose of obtaining or denying workers compensation benefits or payments is guilty of a felony.

California law requires employers to report within **five days** of knowledge every occupational injury or illness which results in lost time beyond the date of the incident **OR** requires medical treatment beyond first aid. If an employee subsequently dies as a result of a previously reported injury or illness, the employer must file within **five days** of knowledge an amended report indicating death. In addition, every serious injury, illness, or death must be **reported immediately** by telephone or telegraph to the nearest office of the California Division of Occupational Safety and Health.

EMPLOYER

1. FIRM NAME — 1a. Policy Number
2. MAILING ADDRESS: (Number, Street, City, Zip) — 2a. Phone Number
3. LOCATION if different from Mailing Address (Number, Street, City and Zip) — 3a. Location Code
4. NATURE OF BUSINESS; e.g.. Painting contractor, wholesale grocer, sawmill, hotel, etc. — 5. State unemployment insurance acct.no
6. TYPE OF EMPLOYER: ☐ Private ☐ State ☐ County ☐ City ☐ School District ☐ Other Gov't, Specify: ____________

INJURY OR ILLNESS

7. DATE OF INJURY / ONSET OF ILLNESS (mm/dd/yy)
8. TIME INJURY/ILLNESS OCCURRED ________ AM ________ PM
9. TIME EMPLOYEE BEGAN WORK ________ AM ________ PM
10. IF EMPLOYEE DIED, DATE OF DEATH (mm/dd/yy)
11. UNABLE TO WORK FOR AT LEAST ONE FULL DAY AFTER DATE OF INJURY? ☐ Yes ☐ No
12. DATE LAST WORKED (mm/dd/yy)
13. DATE RETURNED TO WORK (mm/dd/yy)
14. IF STILL OFF WORK, CHECK THIS BOX: ☐
15. PAID FULL DAYS WAGES FOR DATE OF INJURY OR LAST DAY WORKED? ☐ Yes ☐ No
16. SALARY BEING CONTINUED? ☐ Yes ☐ No
17. DATE OF EMPLOYER'S KNOWLEDGE /NOTICE OF INJURY/ILLNESS (mm/dd/yy)
18. DATE EMPLOYEE WAS PROVIDED CLAIM FORM FORM (mm/dd/yy)
19. SPECIFIC INJURY/ILLNESS AND PART OF BODY AFFECTED, MEDICAL DIAGNOSIS if available, e.g.. Second degree burns on right arm, tendonitis on left elbow, lead poisoning
20. LOCATION WHERE EVENT OR EXPOSURE OCCURRED (Number, Street, City, Zip) — 20a. COUNTY
21. ON EMPLOYER'S PREMISES? ☐ Yes ☐ No
22. DEPARTMENT WHERE EVENT OR EXPOSURE OCCURRED, e.g.. Shipping department, machine shop.
23. Other Workers injured or ill in this event? ☐ Yes ☐ No
24. EQUIPMENT, MATERIALS AND CHEMICALS THE EMPLOYEE WAS USING WHEN EVENT OR EXPOSURE OCCURRED, e.g.. Acetylene, welding torch, farm tractor, scaffold
25. SPECIFIC ACTIVITY THE EMPLOYEE WAS PERFORMING WHEN EVENT OR EXPOSURE OCCURRED, e.g.. Welding seams of metal forms, loading boxes onto truck.
26. HOW INJURY/ILLNESS OCCURRED. DESCRIBE SEQUENCE OF EVENTS. SPECIFY OBJECT OR EXPOSURE WHICH DIRECTLY PRODUCED THE INJURYIILLNESS, e.g.. Worker stepped back to inspect work and slipped on scrap material. As he fell, he brushed against fresh weld, and burned right hand. USE SEPARATE SHEET IF NECESSARY
27. Name and address of physician (number, street, city, zip) — 27a. Phone Number
28. Hospitalized as an inpatient overnight? ☐ No ☐ Yes If yes then, name and address of hospital (number, street, city, zip) — 28a. Phone Number
29. Employee treated in emergency room? ☐ Yes ☐ No

ATTENTION This form contains information relating to employee health and must be used in a manner that protects the confidentiality of employees to the extent possible while the information is being used for occupational safety and health purposes. See CCR Title 8 14300.29 (b)(6)-(10) & 14300.35(b)(2)(E)2.
Note: Shaded boxes indicate confidential employee information as listed in CCR Title 8 14300.35(b)(2)(E)2*.

EMPLOYEE

30. EMPLOYEE NAME — 31. SOCIAL SECURITY NUMBER — 32. DATE OF BIRTH (mm/dd/yy)
33. HOME ADDRESS (Number, Street, City,Zip) — 33a. PHONE NUMBER
34. SEX ☐ Male ☐ Female
35. OCCUPATION (Regular job title, NO initials, abbreviations or numbers)
36. DATE OF HIRE (mm/dd/yy)
37. EMPLOYEE USUALLY WORKS ______ hours per day, ______ days per week, ______ total weekly hours
37a. EMPLOYMENT STATUS ☐ regular, full-time ☐ part-time ☐ temporary ☐ seasonal
37b. UNDER WHAT CLASS CODE OF YOUR POLICY WHERE WAGES ASSIGNED
38. GROSS WAGES/SALARY $ __________ per __________
39. OTHER PAYMENTS NOT REPORTED AS WAGESISALARY (e.g. tips, meals, overtime, bonuses, etc.)? ☐ Yes ☐ No

Please do not use this column: CASE NUMBER; OWNERSHIP; INDUSTRY; OCCUPATION; SEX; AGE; DAILY HOURS; DAYS PER WEEK; WEEKLY HOURS; WEEKLY WAGE; COUNTY; NATURE OF INJURY; PART OF BODY; SOURCE; EVENT; SECONDARY SOURCE; EXTENT OF INJURY

Completed By (type or print) — Signature & Title — Date (mm/dd/yy)

• Confidential information may be disclosed only to the employee, former employee, or their personal representative (CCR Title 8 14300.35), to others for the purpose of processing a workers' compensation or other insurance claim; and under certain circumstances to a public health or law enforcement agency or to a consultant hired by the employer (CCR Title 8 14300.30). CCR Title 8 14300.40 requires provision upon request to certain state and federal workplace safety agencies.

FORM 5020 (Rev7) June 2002

FILING OF THIS FORM IS NOT AN ADMISSION OF LIABILITY

Note: Authority cited: Sections 6409.1(a), 6410, and 6410.5, Labor Code. Reference: Sections 6409.1(a) and 6410, Labor Code.

History: 1. New section filed 2-8-80; designated effective 5-1-80 (Register 80, No. 6).

2. Amendment filed 1-13-83; effective thirtieth day thereafter (Register 83, No. 3).

3. Repealer and new section filed 3-18-7; effective thirtieth day thereafter (Register 87, No. 12).

4. Repealer and new section filed 1-14-93; operative 2-16-93 (Register 93, No. 3).

5. Amendment of section heading and new revision of Form 5020 filed 9-19-2002; operative 10-19-2002 (Register 2002, No. 38).

Ref.: Hanna § 25.20[3].

§14005. Reproduction of the Employer's Report.

(a) Insurers and self-insured employers shall reproduce Form 5020, Rev. 7, Employer's Report of Occupational Injury or Illness. In reproducing the form, all of the following conditions shall be met:

(1) The title of the reproduced form shall read: State of California Employer's Report of Occupational Injury or Illness. The size of type may be reduced to meet space requirements, but the words "Employer's Report of Occupational Injury or Illness" shall be in bold face type.

(2) The form shall prominently contain filing instructions and the following statements:

(A) "Any person who makes or causes to be made any knowingly false or fraudulent material statement or material representation for the purpose of obtaining or denying workers' compensation benefits or payments is guilty of a felony."

(B) "ATTENTION: This form contains information relating to employee health and must be used in a manner that protects the confidentiality of employees to the extent possible while the information is being used for occupational safety and health purposes." Reference: Section 14300.29(b)(6)-(10)

(C) Shaded boxes indicate confidential employee information as listed in CCR Title 8 14300.35(b)(2)(E)2.

(D) Confidential information may be disclosed to the employee, former employee, or their personal representative (8 CCR 14300.35), to others for the purpose of processing a workers' compensation or other insurance claim; and under certain circumstances to a public health or law enforcement agency or to a consultant hired by the employer (8 CCR 14300.30). 8 CCR 14300.40 requires provision upon request to certain state and federal workplace safety agencies.

(3) The notice block, coding column in the right hand margin, subheadings, spacing, numbering, arrangement, sequence and text of Questions 1 through 39 shall not be altered. However, self-insured employers may eliminate Questions 1A, 2A, 3A, and 37b from reproduced forms and utilize the space to collect other information.

Except as otherwise specified in this Section, any other modification to the content or layout of Form 5020, Rev. 7 may be made only with prior approval of a written request to:

DEPARTMENT OF INDUSTRIAL RELATIONS
CHIEF, DIVISION OF LABOR STATISTICS AND RESEARCH
P. O. BOX 420603
SAN FRANCISCO, CA 94142-0603

(4) Reproduced forms shall be printed on 81/2, by 11, paper stock.

(b) Insurers, self-insured employers or other persons reproducing Form 5020, Rev. 7 may rearrange the header block to permit imprinting the following:

(1) Name and address of the insurer, self-insured employer or claims administrator;

(2) Instructions for completing and filing the form;

(3) Coding lines or boxes for special use by the insurer, self-insured employer or claims administrator.

(c) The size of the header block may be altered to gain space for additional questions, which may be included at the bottom of the form, following Question 39, provided the proposed form has been reviewed and approved by the Division. The reverse of the form may be used for additional information or questions.

Note: Authority cited: Sections 6410 and 6410.5, Labor Code. Reference: Sections 5401.7, 6409.1(a) and 6410, Labor Code.

History: 1. New section filed 2-8-80; designated effective 5-1-80 (Register 80, No. 6).

2. Amendment of subsections (a) and (c) filed 1-13-83; effective thirtieth day thereafter (Register 83, No. 3).

3. Amendment filed 3-18-87; effective thirtieth day thereafter (Register 87, No. 12).

4. Amendment of subsection (a) filed 6-14-89; operative 7-14-89 (Register 89, No. 25).

5. Amendment of section and Note filed 1-14-93; operative 2-16-93 (Register 93, No. 3).

6. Amendment filed 9-19-2002; operative 10-19-2002 (Register 2002, No. 38).

Ref.: Hanna § 25.20[3].

Regulations

§14006. Form 5021, Rev. 4, Doctor's First Report of Occupational Injury or Illness.

STATE OF CALIFORNIA

DOCTOR'S FIRST REPORT OF OCCUPATIONAL INJURY OR ILLNESS

Within 5 days of your initial examination, for every occupational injury or illness, send two copies of this report to the **employer's workers' compensation insurance carrier** or the **self-insured employer.** Failure to file a timely doctor's report may result in assessment of a civil penalty. **In the case of diagnosed or suspected pesticide poisoning,** send a copy of this report to Division of Labor Statistics and Research, P.O. Box 420603, San Francisco, CA 94142-0603, and notify your local health officer by telephone within 24 hours.

1. **INSURER NAME AND ADDRESS**
2. **EMPLOYER NAME**
3. Address No. and Street City Zip
4. Nature of business (e.g., food manufacturing, building construction, retailer of women's clothes)
5. **PATIENT NAME** (first name, middle initial, last name) 6. Sex ☐ Male ☐ Female 7. Date of Birth Mo. Day Yr.
8. Address: No. and Street City Zip 9. Telephone number ( )
10. Occupation (Specific job title) 11. Social Security Number
12. Injured at: No. and Street City County
13. Date and hour of injury or onset of illness Mo. Day Yr. Hour ______ a.m. ______ p.m. 14. Date last worked Mo. Day Yr.
15. Date and hour of first examination or treatment Mo. Day Yr. Hour ______ a.m. ______ p.m. 16. Have you (or your office) previously treated patient? ☐ Yes ☐ No

PLEASE DO NOT USE THIS COLUMN: Case No. / Industry / County / Age / Hazard / Disease / Hospitalization / Occupation / Return Date/Code

Patient please complete this portion, if able to do so. Otherwise, doctor please complete immediately. Inability or failure of a patient to complete this portion shall not affect his/her rights to workers' compensation under the California Labor Code.

17. **DESCRIBE HOW THE ACCIDENT OR EXPOSURE HAPPENED** (Give specific object, machinery or chemical. Use reverse side if more space is required.)

18. **SUBJECTIVE COMPLAINTS** (Describe fully. Use reverse side if more space is required.)

19. **OBJECTIVE FINDINGS** (Use reverse side if more space is required.)
    A. Physical examination
    B. X-ray and laboratory results (State if none or pending.)

20. **DIAGNOSIS** (if occupational illness specify etiologic agent and duration of exposure.) Chemical or toxic compounds involved? ☐ Yes ☐ No
    ICD-9 Code ___ ___ ___ . ___ ___

21. Are your findings and diagnosis consistent with patient's account of injury or onset of illness? ☐ Yes ☐ No If "no", please explain.

22. Is there any other current condition that will impede or delay patient's recovery? ☐ Yes ☐ No If "yes", please explain.

23. **TREATMENT RENDERED** (Use reverse side if more space is required.)

24. If further treatment required, specify treatment plan/estimated duration.

25. If hospitalized as inpatient, give hospital name and location Date admitted Mo. Day Yr. Estimated stay

26. **WORK STATUS**—Is patient able to perform usual work? ☐ Yes ☐ No
    If "no", date when patient can return to: Regular work ___/___/___
    Modified work ___/___/___ Specify restrictions ______

Doctor's Signature ______ CA License Number ______
Doctor Name and Degree (please type) ______ IRS Number ______
Address ______ Telephone Number ( )

FORM 5021 (REV. 4) 1992

Any person who makes or causes to be made any knowingly false or fraudulent material statement or material representation for the purpose of obtaining or denying workers' compensation benefits or payments is guilty of a felony

Note: Authority cited: Sections 6409(a), 6410, 6410.5, 6413.5, Labor Code; and Section 2950, Health and Safety Code. Reference: Sections 5401.7, 6410, Labor Code.

History: 1. New section filed 2-8-80; designated effective 5-1-80 (Register 80, No. 6).

2. Repealer and new section filed 6-14-89; operative 7-14-89 (Register 89, No. 25).

3. Repealer and new section filed 1-14-93; operative 2-16-93 (Register 93, No. 3).

Ref.: Hanna § 22.08[2].

§14007. Reproduction of the Doctor's Report.

(a) Insurers, self-insured employers, doctors, clinics, hospitals and other persons may reproduce Form 5021, Rev. 4, Doctor's First Report of Occupational Injury or Illness, if all of the following conditions are met:

(1) The title of the reproduced form shall read: Doctor's First Report of Occupational Injury or Illness State of California. The size of type may be reduced to meet space requirements, but the words "Doctor's First Report of Occupational Injury or Illness" shall be in bold face type.

(2) Filing instructions in the heading shall include the requirement for the physician to file a copy of the report directly with the Division of Labor Statistics and Research in the case of pesticide poisoning or suspected pesticide poisoning, and the statement "Failure to file a timely doctor's report may result in assessment of a civil penalty."

(3) The form shall prominently contain the following statement: "Any person who makes or causes to be made any knowingly false or fraudulent material statement or material representation for the purpose of obtaining or denying workers' compensation benefits or payments is guilty of a felony."

(4) Reproduced forms shall be printed on 8½″ x 11″ paper stock.

(5) The subheadings, arrangement, sequence and text of Questions 1 through 25, the coding column and the signature section shall not be altered, except that Question 1 may be eliminated on forms printed with the insurer's or self-insured employer's name at the top.

(b) Insurers, self-insured employers, doctors, clinics, hospitals and other persons reproducing Form 5021, Rev. 4, may rearrange the heading to permit imprinting:

(1) The name and address of such insurer, self-insured employer, doctor, clinic, hospital or other persons;

(2) Coding lines or boxes for special use by the person reproducing the form;

(3) Instructions for forwarding the form and the number of copies required.

(c) Insurers, self-insured employers and other persons reproducing Form 5021, Rev. 4, may use the back of the form for additional information, questions, or skeleton diagrams.

(d) Except as otherwise specified in subdivision 14007(b), any other modification to the content or layout of Form 5021, Rev. 4 may be made only with prior approval of a written request to the Division at the address shown in subdivision 14005(a)(3).

Note: Authority cited: Sections 6410, 6410.5, Labor Code. Reference: Sections 5401.7, 6410, Labor Code.

History: 1. New section filed 2-8-80; designated effective 5-1-80 (Register 80, No. 6).

2. Amendment of subsection (a) filed 1-13-83; effective thirtieth day thereafter (Register 83, No. 3).

3. Amendment filed 6-14-89; operative 7-14-89 (Register 89, No. 25).

4. Editorial correction of printing error in subsection (a)(2) (Register 90, No. 6).

5. Amendment of section and Note filed 1-14-93; operative 2-16-93 (Register 93, No. 3).

Ref.: Hanna § 22.08[2].

ARTICLE 2
Employer Records of Occupational Injury or Illness

§14300. Purpose.

The purpose of this rule (Article 2) is to require employers to record work-related fatalities, injuries and illnesses.

Note 1: Recording a work-related injury, illness, or fatality does not mean that the employer or employee was at fault, that a Cal/OSHA regulation has been violated, or that the employee is eligible for workers' compensation or other benefits.

Note 2: All employers covered by the California Occupational Safety and Health Act are covered by the provisions of Article 2. However, because of the partial exemptions provided by Sections 14300.1 and 14300.2, most employers do not have to keep OSHA injury and illness records unless they are asked in writing to do so by OSHA, the Bureau of Labor Statistics (BLS), or a state agency operating under the authority of OSHA or the BLS. For example, employers with 10 or fewer employees and establishments in certain industry classifications listed in Section 14300.2, Appendix A, are partially exempt from keeping Cal/OSHA injury and illness records.

Note: Authority cited: Section 6410, Labor Code. Reference: Section 6410, Labor Code.

History: 1. Repealer of former article 2 (sections 14300-14400), and new article 2 (sections 14300-14300.48) and section filed 1-15-2002; operative 1-15-2002 pursuant to Government Code section 11343.4 (Register 2002, No. 3). For prior history of article 2, see Register 83, No. 3.

§14300.1. Partial Exemption for Employers with 10 or Fewer Employees.

(a) Basic requirement.

(1) If your company had ten (10) or fewer employees at all times during the last calendar year, you do not need to keep Cal/OSHA injury and illness records unless OSHA or the BLS informs you in writing that you must keep records under the provisions of Section 14300.41 or Section 14300.42. However, all employers must continue to file reports of occupational injuries and illnesses with the Division of Labor Statistics and Research as required by Article 1 of this subchapter, and to immediately report to the Division of Occupational Safety and Health any workplace incident that results in serious injury or illness, or death, as required by Title 8 Section 342.

(2) If your company had more than ten (10) employees at any time during the last calendar year, you must keep Cal/OSHA injury and illness records unless your establishment is classified as a partially exempt industry under Section 14300.2.

(b) Implementation.

(1) Is the partial exemption for size based on the size of my entire company or on the size of an individual establishment?

The partial exemption for size is based on the number of employees in the entire company.

(2) How do I determine the size of my company to find out if I qualify for the partial exemption for size?

To determine if you are exempt because of size, you need to determine your company's peak employment during the last calendar year. If you had 10 or fewer employees at all times in the last calendar year, your company qualifies for the partial exemption for size.

Note: Authority cited: Section 6410, Labor Code. Reference: Section 6410, Labor Code.

History: 1. New section filed 1-15-2002; operative 1-15-2002 pursuant to Government Code section 11343.4 (Register 2002, No. 3).

§14300.2. Partial Exemption for Establishments in Certain Industries.

(a) Basic requirement.

(1) If you are a public or private sector employer and all of your establishments are classified in the retail, service, finance, insurance or real estate industries listed in Table 1 in Appendix A of this section, you do not need to keep Cal/OSHA injury and illness records required by Article 2 unless the government asks you to keep the records under Section 14300.41 or Section 14300.42. However, all employers must report to the Division of Occupational Safety and Health any workplace incident that results in a serious injury or illness, or death, as required at Title 8 Section 342.

(2) If one or more of your establishments are classified in a non-exempt industry, you must keep Cal/OSHA injury and illness records required by Article 2 for all such establishments except those partially exempted because of size under Section 14300.1.

(b) Implementation.

(1) Does the partial industry classification exemption apply only to the types of establishments in the retail, service, finance, insurance or real estate industries listed in Table 1?

Yes. Establishments classified in agriculture; mining; construction; manufacturing; transportation; communication, electric, gas and sanitary services; or wholesale trade, and those establishments in the retail, service, finance, insurance and real estate industries not specifically listed in Table 1 in Appendix A are not eligible for the partial industry classification exemption.

(2) Is the partial industry classification exemption based on the industry classification of my entire company or on the classification of individual establishments operated by my company?

The partial industry classification exemption applies to individual establishments. If a company has several establishments engaged in different classes of activities, some of the company's establishments may be required to keep records, while others may be exempt.

(3) How do I determine the Standard Industrial Classification code for my company or for individual establishments?

You determine your Standard Industrial Classification (SIC) code by using the Standard Industrial Classification Manual, Executive Office of the President, Office of Management and Budget. You may contact the nearest office of the Division of Occupational Safety and Health for help in determining your SIC code. The SIC Manual can also be viewed at the Internet site for OSHA, www.osha.gov.

Appendix A to Section 14300.2

Public and private sector employers are not required to keep Cal/OSHA injury and illness records for any establishment classified in the following Standard Industrial Classification (SIC) codes, unless they are asked in writing to do so by OSHA, the Bureau of Labor Statistics (BLS), or a state agency operating under the authority of OSHA or the BLS. All employers, including those partially exempted by reason of size or industry classification, must report to the Division of Occupational Safety and Health any workplace incident that results in a serious injury or illness, or death, as required at Title 8 Section 342.

Table 1
Partially Exempt Industries in California

SIC Code	*Industry Description*
525	Hardware Stores
542	Meat and Fish Markets
544	Candy, Nut, and Confectionery Stores
545	Dairy Products Stores
546	Retail Bakeries
549	Miscellaneous Food stores
551	New and Used Car Dealers
552	Used Car Dealers
554	Gasoline Service Stations
557	Motorcycle Dealers
56	Apparel and Accessory Stores
573	Radio, Television, and Computer Stores
58	Eating and Drinking Places
591	Drug Stores and Proprietary Stores
592	Liquor Stores
594	Miscellaneous Shopping Goods Stores
599	Retail Stores, Not Elsewhere Classified
60	Depository Institutions (banks and savings institutions)
61	Nondepository
62	Security and Commodity Brokers
63	Insurance Carriers
64	Insurance Agents, Brokers and Services
653	Real Estate Agents and Managers
654	Title Abstract Offices
67	Holding and Other Investment Offices
722	Photographic Studios, Portrait
723	Beauty Shops
731	Advertising Services
732	Credit Reporting and Collection Services
733	Mailing, Reproduction and Stenographic Services
737	Computer and Data Processing Services
738	Miscellaneous Business Services
764	Reupholstery and Furniture Repair
782	Motion Picture Distribution and Allied Services
783	Motion Picture Theaters
784	Video Tape Rental
791	Dance Studios, Schools, and Halls
792	Producers, Orchestras, Entertainers
793	Bowling Centers
801	Offices and Clinics of Medical Doctors
802	Offices and Clinics of Dentists
803	Offices of Osteopathic
804	Offices of Other Health Practitioners
807	Medical and Dental Laboratories
809	Health and Allied Services, Not Elsewhere Classified
81	Legal Services
82	Educational Services (schools, colleges, universities and libraries)
832	Individual and Family Services
835	Child Day Care Services
839	Social Services, Not Elsewhere Classified
841	Museums and Art Galleries

724	Barber Shops	86	Membership Organizations
725	Shoe Repair and Shoeshine Parlors	87	Engineering, Accounting, Research, Management, and Related Services
726	Funeral Service and Crematories		
729	Miscellaneous Personal Services	899	Services, Not Elsewhere Classified

NOTE: In California, establishments in SIC Code 781 (Motion Picture Production and Allied Services) are required to record. Federal law does not require these establishments to record. This is the only difference between the list of establishments shown in Table 1 above and the list shown in the equivalent federal rule at 29 CFR 1904.2.

Note: Authority cited: Section 6410, Labor Code. Reference: Section 6410, Labor Code.

History: 1. New section and Appendix A filed 1-15-2002; operative 1-15-2002 pursuant to Government Code section 11343.4 (Register 2002, No. 3).

§14300.3. Keeping Records for More than One Agency.

If you create records to comply with another government agency's injury and illness recordkeeping requirements, OSHA will consider those records as meeting OSHA's recordkeeping requirements if OSHA accepts the other agency's records under a memorandum of understanding with that agency, or if the other agency's records contain the same information as this article requires you to record. You may contact the nearest office of the Division of Occupational Safety and Health for help in determining whether your records meet the requirements of this article.

Note: Authority cited: Section 6410, Labor Code. Reference: Section 6410, Labor Code.

History: 1. New section filed 1-15-2002; operative 1-15-2002 pursuant to Government Code section 11343.4 (Register 2002, No. 3).

§14300.4. Recording Criteria.

(a) Basic requirement. Each employer required by this article to keep records of fatalities, injuries, and illnesses must record each fatality, injury and illness that:

(1) Is work-related; and

(2) Is a new case; and

(3) Meets one or more of the general recording criteria of Section 14300.7 or the application to specific cases of Section 14300.8 through Section 14300.12.

(b) Implementation.

What sections of this rule describe recording criteria for recording work-related injuries and illnesses?

The list below indicates which sections of the rule address each topic

(1) Determination of work-relatedness. See Section 14300.5;

(2) Determination of a new case. See Section 14300.6;

(3) General recording criteria. See Section 14300.7; and

(4) Additional criteria. (Needlestick and sharps injury cases, medical removal cases, hearing loss cases, tuberculosis cases, and musculoskeletal disorder cases.) See Section 14300.8 though Section 14300.12.

Note: Authority cited: Section 6410, Labor Code. Reference: Section 6410, Labor Code.

History: 1. New section filed 1-15-2002; operative 1-15-2002 pursuant to Government Code section 11343.4 (Register 2002, No. 3).

§14300.5. Determination of Work-Relatedness.

(a) Basic requirement. You must consider an injury or illness to be work-related if an event or exposure in the work environment either caused or contributed to the resulting condition or significantly aggravated a pre-existing injury or illness. Work-relatedness is presumed for injuries and illnesses resulting from events or exposures occurring in the work environment, unless an exception in Section 14300.5(b)(2) specifically applies.

(b) Implementation.

(1) What is the "work environment"?

Work environment is defined as "the establishment and other locations where one or more employees are working or are present as a condition of their employment. The work environment includes not only physical locations, but also the equipment or materials used by the employee during the course of his or her work."

(2) Are there situations where an injury or illness occurs in the work environment and is not considered work-related?

Yes. An injury or illness occurring in the work environment that falls under one of the following exceptions is not work-related, and therefore is not recordable:

(A) At the time of the injury or illness, the employee was present in the work environment as a member of the general public rather than as an employee.

(B) The injury or illness involves signs or symptoms that surface at work but result solely from a non-work-related event or exposure that occurs outside the work environment.

(C) The injury or illness results solely from voluntary participation in a wellness program or in a medical, fitness, or recreational activity such as blood donation, physical examination, flu shot, exercise class, racquetball, or baseball.

(D) The injury or illness is solely the result of an employee eating, drinking, or preparing food or drink for personal consumption (whether bought on the employer's premises or brought in). For example, if the employee is injured by choking on a sandwich while in the employer's establishment, the case would not be considered work-related.

Note: If the employee is made ill by ingesting food contaminated by workplace contaminants (such as lead), or gets food poisoning from food supplied by the employer, the case would be considered work-related.

(E) The injury or illness is solely the result of an employee doing personal tasks (unrelated to their employment) at the establishment outside of the employee's assigned working hours.

(F) The injury or illness is solely the result of personal grooming, self-medication for a non-work-related condition, or is intentionally self-inflicted.

(G) The injury or illness is caused by a motor vehicle accident and occurs on a company parking lot or company access road while the employee is commuting to or from work.

(H) The illness is the common cold or flu (Note: contagious diseases such as tuberculosis, brucellosis, hepatitis A, or plague are considered work-related if the employee is infected at work).

(I) The illness is a mental illness. Mental illness will not be considered work-related unless the employee voluntarily provides the employer with an opinion from a physician or other licensed health care professional with appropriate training and experience (psychiatrist, psychologist, psychiatric nurse practitioner, etc.) stating that the employee has a mental illness that is work-related.

(3) How do I handle a case if it is not obvious whether the precipitating event or exposure occurred in the work environment or occurred away from work?

In these situations, you must evaluate the employee's work duties and environment to decide whether or not one or more events or exposures in the work environment either caused or contributed to the resulting condition or significantly aggravated a pre-existing condition.

(4) How do I know if an event or exposure in the work environment "significantly aggravated" a pre-existing injury or illness?

A pre-existing injury or illness has been significantly aggravated, for purposes of Cal/OSHA injury and illness recordkeeping required by this Article, when an event or exposure in the work environment results in any of the following:

(A) Death, provided that the pre-existing injury or illness would likely not have resulted in death but for the occupational event or exposure.

(B) Loss of consciousness, provided that the pre-existing injury or illness would likely not have resulted in loss of consciousness but for the occupational event or exposure.

(C) One or more days away from work, or days of restricted work, or days of job transfer that otherwise would not have occurred but for the occupational event or exposure.

(D) Medical treatment in a case where no medical treatment was needed for the injury or illness before the workplace event or exposure, or a change in medical treatment was necessitated by the workplace event or exposure.

(5) Which injuries and illnesses are considered pre-existing conditions?

An injury or illness is a pre-existing condition if it resulted solely from a non-work-related event or exposure that occurred outside the work environment.

(6) How do I decide whether an injury or illness is work-related if the employee is on travel status at the time the injury or illness occurs?

Injuries and illnesses that occur while an employee is on travel status are work-related if, at the time of the injury or illness, the employee was engaged in work activities "in the interest of the employer." Examples of such activities include travel to and from customer contacts, conducting job tasks, and entertaining or being entertained to transact, discuss, or promote business (work-related entertainment includes only entertainment activities being engaged in at the direction of the employer).

Injuries or illnesses that occur when the employee is on travel status do not have to be recorded if they meet one of the following exceptions:

EXCEPTION 1: When a traveling employee checks into a hotel, motel, or other temporary residence, he or she establishes a "home away from home." You must evaluate the employee's activities after he or she checks into the hotel, motel, or other temporary residence for their work-relatedness in the same manner as you evaluate the activities of a non-traveling employee. When the employee checks into the temporary residence, he or she is considered to have left the work environment. When the employee begins work each day, he or she re-enters the work environment. If the employee has established a "home away from home" and is reporting to a fixed worksite each day, you also do not consider injuries or illnesses work-related if they occur while the employee is commuting between the temporary residence and the job location.

EXCEPTION 2: Injuries or illnesses are not considered work-related if they occur while the employee is on a personal detour from a reasonably direct route of travel (e.g., has taken a side trip for personal reasons).

(7) How do I decide if a case is work-related when the employee is working at home?

Injuries and illnesses that occur while an employee is working at home, including work in a home office, will be considered work-related if the injury or illness occurs while the employee is performing work for pay or compensation in the home, and the injury or illness is directly related to the performance of work rather than to the general home environment or setting. For example, if an employee drops a box of work documents and injures his or her foot, the case is considered work-related. If an employee's fingernail is punctured by a needle from a sewing machine used to perform garment work at home, becomes infected and requires medical treatment, the injury is considered work-related. If an employee is injured because he or she trips on the family dog while rushing to answer a work phone call, the case is not considered work-related. If an employee working at home is electrocuted because of faulty home wiring, the injury is not considered work-related.

Note: Authority cited: Section 6410, Labor Code. Reference: Section 6410, Labor Code.

History: 1. New section filed 1-15-2002; operative 1-15-2002 pursuant to Government Code section 11343.4 (Register 2002, No. 3).

§14300.6. Determination of New Cases.

(a) Basic requirement. You must consider an injury or illness to be a "new case" if:

(1) The employee has not previously experienced a recorded injury or illness of the same type that affects the same part of the body, or

(2) The employee previously experienced a recorded injury or illness of the same type that affected the same part of the body but had recovered completely (all signs and symptoms had disappeared) from the previous injury or illness and an event or exposure in the work environment caused the signs or symptoms to reappear.

(b) Implementation.

(1) When an employee experiences the signs or symptoms of a chronic work-related illness, do I need to consider each recurrence of signs or symptoms to be a new case?

No. For occupational illnesses where the signs or symptoms may recur or continue in the absence of an exposure in the workplace, the case must only be recorded once. Examples may include occupational cancer, asbestosis, byssinosis and silicosis.

(2) When an employee experiences the signs or symptoms of an injury or illness as a result of an event or exposure in the workplace, such as an episode of occupational asthma, must I treat the episode as a new case?

Yes. Because the episode or recurrence was caused by an event or exposure in the workplace, the incident must be treated as a new case.

(3) May I rely on a physician or other licensed health care professional to determine whether a case is a new case or a recurrence of an old case?

You are not required to seek the advice of a physician or other licensed health care professional. However, if you do seek such advice, you must follow the physician or other licensed health care professional's recommendation about whether the case is a new case or a recurrence. If you receive recommendations from two or more physicians or other licensed health care professionals, you must make a decision as to which recommendation is the most authoritative (best documented, best reasoned, or most authoritative), and record the case based upon that recommendation.

Note: Authority cited: Section 6410, Labor Code. Reference: Section 6410, Labor Code.

History: 1. New section filed 1-15-2002; operative 1-15-2002 pursuant to Government Code section 11343.4 (Register 2002, No. 3).

§14300.7. General Recording Criteria.

(a) Basic requirement. You must consider an injury or illness to meet the general recording criteria, and therefore to be recordable, if it results in any of the following as detailed in subsections (b)(2) through (b)(6) of this section: death, days away from work, restricted work or transfer to another job, medical treatment beyond first aid, or loss of consciousness. You must also consider a case to meet the general recording criteria if it involves a significant injury or illness diagnosed by a physician or other licensed health care professional as detailed in subsection (b)(7) of this section, even if it does not result in death, days away from work, restricted work or job transfer, medical treatment beyond first aid, or loss of consciousness.

(b) Implementation.

(1) How do I decide if a case meets one or more of the general recording criteria?

A work-related injury or illness must be recorded if it results in one or more of the following:

(A) Death, See Section 14300.7(b)(2)

(B) Days away from work, See Section 14300.7(b)(3)

(C) Restricted work or transfer to another job, See Section 14300.7(b)(4)

(D) Medical treatment beyond first aid, See Section 14300.7(b)(5)

(E) Loss of consciousness, See Section 14300.7(b)(6)

(F) A significant injury or illness diagnosed by a physician or other licensed health care professional. See Section 14300.7(b)(7)

(2) How do I record a work-related injury or illness that results in a fatality?

You must record an injury or illness that results in a fatality, as defined in Section 14300.46 of this Article, by entering a mark on the Cal/OSHA Form 300 in the column labeled for cases resulting in death. You must also report any work-related fatality or serious injury or illness to the Division of Occupational Safety and Health within eight (8) hours, as required by Title 8 Section 342.

(3) How do I record a work-related injury or illness that results in days away from work?

When an injury or illness involves one or more days away from work, you must record the injury or illness on the Cal/OSHA Form 300 with a mark in the space for cases involving days away and an entry of the number of calendar days away from work in the number of days column. If the employee is out for an extended period of time, you must enter an estimate of the days that the employee will be away, and update the day count when the actual number of days is known.

(A) Do I count the day on which the injury occurred or the illness began?

No. You begin counting days away on the day after the injury occurred or the illness began.

(B) How do I record an injury or illness when a physician or other licensed health care professional recommends that the worker stay at home but the employee comes to work anyway?

You must record these injuries and illnesses on the Cal/OSHA Form 300 using the check box for cases with days away from work and enter the number of calendar days away recommended by the physician or other licensed health care professional. If a physician or other licensed health care professional recommends days away, you should encourage your employee to follow that recommendation. However, the days away must be recorded whether the injured or ill employee follows the physician or licensed health care professional's recommendation or not. If you receive recommendations from two or more physicians or other licensed health care professionals, you may make a decision as to which recommendation is the most authoritative, and record the case based upon that recommendation.

(C) How do I handle a case when a physician or other licensed health care professional recommends that the worker return to work but the employee stays at home anyway?

In this situation, you must end the count of days away from work on the date the physician or other licensed health care professional recommends that the employee return to work.

(D) How do I count weekends, holidays, or other days the employee would not have worked anyway?

You must count the number of calendar days the employee was unable to work as a result of the injury or illness, regardless of whether or not the employee was scheduled to work on those day(s). Weekend days, holidays, vacation days or other days off are included in the total number of days recorded if the employee would not have been able to work on those days because of a work-related injury or illness.

(E) How do I record a case in which a worker is injured or becomes ill on a Friday and reports to work on a Monday, and was not scheduled to work on the weekend?

You need to record this case only if you receive information from a physician or other licensed health care professional indicating that the employee should not have worked, or should have performed only restricted work, during the weekend. If so, you must record the injury or illness as a case with days away from work or restricted work, and enter the day counts, as appropriate.

(F) How do I record a case in which a worker is injured or becomes ill on the day before scheduled time off such as a holiday, a planned vacation, or a temporary plant closing?

You need to record a case of this type only if you receive information from a physician or other licensed health care professional indicating that the employee should not have worked, or should have performed only restricted work, during the scheduled time off. If so, you must record the injury or illness as a case with days away from work or restricted work, and enter the day counts, as appropriate.

(G) Is there a limit to the number of days away from work I must count?

Yes. You may "cap" the total days away at 180 calendar days. You are not required to keep track of the number of calendar days away from work if the injury or illness resulted in more than 180 calendar days away from work and/or days of job transfer or restriction. In such a case, entering 180 in the total days away column will be considered adequate.

(H) May I stop counting days if an employee who is away from work because of an injury or illness retires or leaves my company?

Yes. If the employee leaves your company for some reason unrelated to the injury or illness, such as retirement, a plant closing, or to take another job, you may stop counting days away from work or days of restriction/job transfer. If the employee leaves your company because of the injury or illness, you must estimate the total number of days away or days of restriction/job transfer and enter the day count on the Cal/OSHA Form 300.

(I) If a case occurs in one year but results in days away during the next calendar year, do I record the case in both years?

No. You only record the injury or illness once. You must enter the number of calendar days away for the injury or illness on the Cal/OSHA Form 300 for the year in which the injury or illness occurred. If the employee is still away from work because of the injury or illness when you prepare the annual summary, estimate the total number of calendar days you expect the employee to be away from work, use this number to calculate the total for the annual summary, and then update the initial log entry later when the day count is known or reaches the 180-day cap.

(4) How do I record a work-related injury or illness that results in restricted work or job transfer?

When an injury or illness involves restricted work or job transfer but does not involve death or days away from work, you must record the injury or illness on the Cal/OSHA Form 300 by placing a mark in the space for job transfer or restriction and an entry of the number of restricted or transferred days in the restricted workdays column.

(A) How do I decide if the injury or illness resulted in restricted work?

Restricted work occurs when, as the result of a work-related injury or illness:

1. You keep the employee from performing one or more of the routine functions of his or her job, or from working the full workday that he or she would otherwise have been scheduled to work; or

2. A physician or other licensed health care professional recommends that the employee not perform one or more of the routine functions of his or her job, or not work the full workday that he or she would otherwise have been scheduled to work.

(B) What is meant by "routine functions"?

For recordkeeping purposes, an employee's routine functions are those work activities the employee regularly performs at least once per week.

(C) Do I have to record restricted work or job transfer if it applies only to the day on which the injury occurred or the illness began?

No. You do not have to record restricted work or job transfers if you, or the physician or other licensed health care professional, impose the restriction or transfer only for the day on which the injury occurred or the illness began.

(D) If you or a physician or other licensed health care professional recommends a work restriction, is the injury or illness automatically recordable as a "restricted work" case?

No. A recommended work restriction is recordable only if it affects one or more of the employee's routine job functions. To determine whether this is the case, you must evaluate the restriction in light of the routine functions of the injured or ill employee's job. If the restriction from you or the physician or other licensed health care professional keeps the employee from performing one or more of his or her routine job functions, or from working the full workday the injured or ill employee would otherwise have worked, the employee's work has been restricted and you must record the case.

(E) How do I record a case where the worker works only for a partial work shift because of a work-related injury or illness?

A partial day of work is recorded as a day of job transfer or restriction for recordkeeping purposes, except for the day on which the injury occurred or the illness began.

(F) If the injured or ill worker produces fewer goods or services than he or she would have produced prior to the injury or illness but otherwise performs all of the routine functions of his or her work, is the case considered a restricted work case?

No. The case is considered restricted work only if the worker does not perform all of the routine functions of his or her job or does not work the full shift that he or she would otherwise have worked.

(G) How do I handle vague restrictions from a physician or other licensed health care professional, such as that the employee engage only in "light duty" or "take it easy for a week"?

If you are not clear about the physician or other licensed health care professional's recommendation, you may ask that person whether the employee can do all of his or her routine job functions and work all of his or her normally assigned work shift. If the answer to both of these questions is "Yes," then the case does not involve a work restriction and does not have to be recorded as such. If the answer to one or both of these questions is "No," the case involves restricted work and must be recorded as a restricted work case. If you are unable to obtain this additional information from the physician or other licensed health care professional who recommended the restriction, record the injury or illness as a case involving restricted work.

(H) What do I do if a physician or other licensed health care professional recommends a job restriction meeting the definition in Section 14300.7(b)(4)(A), but the employee does all of his or her routine job functions anyway?

You must record the injury or illness on the Cal/OSHA Form 300 as a restricted work case. If a physician or other licensed health care professional recommends a job restriction, you should ensure that the employee complies with that restriction. If you receive recommendations from two or more physicians or other licensed health care professionals, you may make a decision as to which recommendation is the most authoritative, and record the case based upon that recommendation.

(I) How do I decide if an injury or illness involved a transfer to another job?

If you assign an injured or ill employee to a job other than his or her regular job for part of the day, the case involves transfer to another job.

Note: This does not include the day on which the injury or illness occurred.

(J) Are transfers to another job recorded in the same way as restricted work cases?

Yes. Both job transfer and restricted work cases are recorded in the same box on the Cal/OSHA Form 300. For example, if you assign, or a physician or other licensed health care professional recommends that you assign, an injured or ill worker to his or her routine job duties for part of the day and to another job for the rest of the day, the injury or illness involves a job transfer. You must record an injury or illness that involves a job transfer by placing a check in the box for job transfer.

(K) How do I count days of job transfer or restriction?

You count days of job transfer or restriction in the same way you count days away from work, using Sections 14300.7(b)(3)(A) to (H), above. The only difference is that, if you permanently assign the injured or ill employee to a job that has been modified or permanently changed in a manner that eliminates the routine functions the employee was restricted from performing, you may stop the day count when the modification or change is made permanent. You must count at least one day of restricted work or job transfer for such cases.

(5) How do I record an injury or illness that involves medical treatment beyond first aid?

If a work-related injury or illness results in medical treatment beyond first aid, you must record it on the Cal/OSHA Form 300. If the injury or illness did not involve death, one or more days away from work, one or more days of restricted work, or one or more days of job transfer, you enter a mark in the box for cases where the employee received medical treatment but remained at work and was not transferred or restricted.

(A) What is the definition of medical treatment?

"Medical treatment" means the management and care of a patient to combat disease or disorder. For the purposes of Article 2, medical treatment does not include:

1. Visits to a physician or other licensed health care professional solely for observation or counseling;

2. The conduct of diagnostic procedures, such as x-rays and blood tests, including the administration of prescription medications used solely for diagnostic purposes (e.g., eye drops to dilate pupils); or

3. "First aid" as defined in subsection (b)(5)(B) of this section.

(B) What is "first aid"?

For the purposes of Article 2, "first aid" means the following:

1. Using a nonprescription medication at nonprescription strength (for medications available in both prescription and non-prescription form, a recommendation by a physician or other licensed health care professional to use a nonprescription medication at prescription strength is considered medical treatment for recordkeeping purposes);

2. Administering tetanus immunizations (other immunizations, such as Hepatitis B vaccine or rabies vaccine, are considered medical treatment);

3. Cleaning, flushing or soaking wounds on the surface of the skin;

4. Using wound coverings such as bandages, Band-AidsE, gauze pads, etc.; or using butterfly bandages or Steri-StripsE (other wound closing devices such as sutures, staples, etc. are considered medical treatment);

5. Using hot or cold therapy;

6. Using any non-rigid means of support, such as elastic bandages, wraps, non-rigid back belts, etc. (devices with rigid stays or other systems designed to immobilize parts of the body are considered medical treatment for recordkeeping purposes);

7. Using temporary immobilization devices while transporting an accident victim (e.g., splints, slings, neck collars, backboards, etc.);

8. Drilling of a fingernail or toenail to relieve pressure, or draining fluid from a blister;

9. Using eye patches;

10. Removing foreign bodies from the eye using only irrigation or a cotton swab;

11. Removing splinters or foreign material from areas other than the eye by irrigation, tweezers, cotton swabs or other simple means;

12. Using finger guards;

13. Using massages (physical therapy or chiropractic treatment are considered medical treatment for recordkeeping purposes); or

14. Drinking fluids for relief of heat stress.

(C) Are any other procedures included in first aid?

No. This is a complete list of all treatments considered first aid for purposes of Article 2.

(D) Does the professional status of the person providing the treatment have any effect on what is considered first aid or medical treatment?

No. The treatments listed in Section 14300.7(b)(5)(B) of this Article are considered to be first aid regardless of the professional status of the person providing the treatment. Even when these treatments are provided by a physician or other licensed health care professional, they are considered first aid for the purposes of Article 2. Similarly, treatment beyond first aid is considered to be medical treatment even when it is provided by someone other than a physician or other licensed health care professional.

(E) What if a physician or other licensed health care professional recommends medical treatment but the employee does not follow the recommendation?

If a physician or other licensed health care professional recommends medical treatment, you should encourage the injured or ill employee to follow that recommendation. However, you must record the case even if the injured or ill employee does not follow the physician or other licensed health care professional's recommendation.

(6) Is every work-related injury or illness case involving a loss of consciousness recordable?

Yes. You must record a work-related injury or illness if the worker becomes unconscious, regardless of the length of time the employee remains unconscious.

(7) What is a "significant" diagnosed injury or illness that is recordable under the general criteria even if it does not result in death, days away from work, restricted work or job transfer, medical treatment beyond first aid, or loss of consciousness?

Work-related cases involving cancer, chronic irreversible disease, a fractured or cracked bone, or a punctured eardrum must always be recorded under the general criteria at the time of diagnosis by a physician or other licensed health care professional.

Note to Section 14300.7: Most significant injuries and illnesses will result in one of the criteria listed in Section 14300.7(a): death, days away from work, restricted work or job transfer, medical treatment beyond first aid, or loss of consciousness. However, there are some significant injuries, such as a punctured eardrum or a fractured toe or rib, for which neither medical treatment nor work restrictions may be recommended. In addition, there are some significant progressive diseases, such as byssinosis, silicosis, and some types of cancer, for which medical treatment or work restrictions may not be recommended at the time of diagnosis but are likely to be recommended as the disease progresses. Cancer, chronic irreversible diseases, fractured or cracked bones, and punctured eardrums are generally considered significant injuries and illnesses, and must be recorded at the initial diagnosis even if medical treatment or work restrictions are not recommended, or are postponed, in a particular case.

Note: Authority cited: Section 6410, Labor Code. Reference: Section 6410, Labor Code.

History: 1. New section filed 1-15-2002; operative 1-15-2002 pursuant to Government Code section 11343.4 (Register 2002, No. 3).

§14300.8. Recording Criteria for Needlestick and Sharps Injuries.

(a) Basic requirement. You must record all work-related needlestick injuries and cuts from sharp objects that are contaminated with another person's blood or other potentially infectious material (as defined by Title 8, Section 5193). You must enter the case on the Cal/OSHA Form 300 as an injury. To protect the employee's privacy, you may not enter the employee's name on the Cal/OSHA Form 300 (see the requirements for privacy cases in Subsections 14300.29(b)(6) through 14300.29(b)(9)).

Note: The requirements of this section are not limited to health care and related establishments.

(b) Implementation.

(1) What does "other potentially infectious material" mean?

The term "other potentially infectious materials" is defined in the standard for Bloodborne Pathogens at Title 8 Section 5193(b) and includes the following materials:

(A) Human bodily fluids, tissues and organs, and

(B) Other materials infected with the HIV, hepatitis B virus (HBV) or hepatitis C virus (HCV) such as laboratory cultures or tissues from experimental animals.

(2) Does this mean that I must record all cuts, lacerations, punctures, and scratches?

No. You need to record cuts, lacerations, punctures, and scratches only if they are work-related and involve contamination with another person's blood or other potentially infectious material. If the cut, laceration, or scratch involves a clean object, or a contaminant other than blood or other potentially infectious material, you need to record the case only if it meets one or more of the recording criteria in Section 14300.7.

(3) If I record an injury and the employee is later diagnosed with an infectious bloodborne disease, do I need to update the Cal/OSHA Form 300?

Yes. You must update the classification of the case on the Cal/OSHA Form 300 if the case results in death, days away from work, restricted work, or job transfer. You must also update the description to identify the infectious disease and change the classification of the case from an injury to an illness.

(4) What if one of my employees is splashed or exposed to blood or other potentially infectious material without being cut or scratched? Do I need to record this incident?

You need to record such an incident on the Cal/OSHA Form 300 as an illness if:

(A) It results in the diagnosis of a bloodborne illness, such as HIV, hepatitis B, or hepatitis C; or

(B) It meets one or more of the recording criteria in Section 14300.7.

Note: Authority cited: Section 6410, Labor Code. Reference: Section 6410, Labor Code.

History: 1. New section filed 1-15-2002; operative 1-15-2002 pursuant to Government Code section 11343.4 (Register 2002, No. 3).

§14300.9. Recording Criteria for Cases Involving Medical Removal Under Cal/OSHA Standards.

(a) Basic requirement. If an employee is medically removed under the medical surveillance requirements of a Title 8 standard, you must record the case on the Cal/OSHA Form 300.

(b) Implementation.

(1) How do I classify medical removal cases on the Cal/OSHA Form 300?

You must enter each medical removal case on the Cal/OSHA Form 300 as either a case involving days away from work or a case involving restricted work activity, depending on how you decide to comply with the medical removal requirement. If the medical removal is the result of a chemical exposure, you must enter the case on the Cal/OSHA Form 300 by checking the "poisoning" column.

(2) Do all of Cal/OSHA's standards have medical removal provisions?

No. Some Title 8 standards, such as the standards covering bloodborne pathogens and noise, do not have medical removal provisions. Many Title 8 standards that cover specific chemical substances have medical removal provisions. These standards include, but are not limited to, lead, cadmium, methylene chloride, formaldehyde, and benzene.

(3) Do I have to record a case where I voluntarily removed the employee from exposure before the medical removal criteria in a Cal/OSHA standard are met?

No. If the case involves voluntary medical removal before the medical removal levels required by a Cal/OSHA standard, you do not need to record the case on the Cal/OSHA Form 300.

Note: Authority cited: Section 6410, Labor Code. Reference: Section 6410, Labor Code.

History: 1. New section filed 1-15-2002; operative 1-15-2002 pursuant to Government Code section 11343.4 (Register 2002, No. 3).

§14300.10. Recording Criteria for Cases Involving Occupational Hearing Loss.

(a) Basic requirement. If an employee's hearing test (audiogram) reveals that the employee has experienced a work-related Standard Threshold Shift (STS) in hearing in one or both ears, and the employee's total hearing level is 25 decibels (dB) or more above audiometric zero (averaged at 2000, 3000, and 4000 Hz) in the same ear(s) as the STS, you must record the case on the Cal/OSHA Form 300.

(b) Implementation.

(1) What is a Standard Threshold Shift? A Standard Threshold Shift, or STS, is defined in the occupational noise exposure standard at section 5097(d)(8) as a change in hearing threshold, relative to the baseline audiogram for that employee, of an average of 10 decibels (dB) or more at 2000, 3000, and 4000 hertz (Hz) in one or both ears.

(2) How do I evaluate the current audiogram to determine whether an employee has an STS and a 25-dB hearing level?

(i) STS. If the employee has never previously experienced a recordable hearing loss, you must compare the employee's current audiogram with that employee's baseline audiogram. If the employee has previously experienced a recordable hearing loss, you must compare the employee's current audiogram with the employee's revised baseline audiogram (the audiogram reflecting the employee's previous recordable hearing loss case).

(ii) 25-dB loss. Audiometric test results reflect the employee's overall hearing ability in comparison to audiometric zero. Therefore, using the employee's current audiogram, you must use the average hearing level at 2000, 3000, and 4000 Hz to determine whether or not the employee's total hearing level is 25 dB or more.

(3) May I adjust the current audiogram to reflect the effects of aging on hearing?

Yes. When you are determining whether an STS has occurred, you may age adjust the employee's current audiogram results by using Tables F as appropriate, in Appendix F of Title 8 General Industry Safety Orders, Article 105, section 5095 to 5100. You may not use an age adjustment when determining whether the employee's total hearing level is 25 dB or more above audiometric zero.

(4) Do I have to record the hearing loss if I am going to retest the employee's hearing?

No, if you retest the employee's hearing within 30 days of the first test, and the retest does not confirm the recordable STS, you are not required to record the hearing loss case on the Cal/OSHA 300 Log. If the retest confirms the recordable STS, you must record the hearing loss illness within seven (7) calendar days of the retest. If subsequent audiometric testing performed under the testing requirements of the noise standard at section 5097 indicates that an STS is not persistent, you may erase or line-out the recorded entry.

(5) Are there any special rules for determining whether a hearing loss case is work-related?

No. You must use the rules in section 14300.5 to determine if the hearing loss is work-related. If an event or exposure in the work environment either caused or contributed to the hearing loss, or significantly aggravated a pre-existing hearing loss, you must consider the case to be work related.

(6) If a physician or other licensed health care professional determines the hearing loss is not work-related, do I still need to record the case?

If a physician or other licensed health care professional determines that the hearing loss is not work-related or has not been significantly aggravated by occupational noise exposure, you are not required to consider the case work-related or to record the case on the Cal/OSHA Form 300.

(7) How do I complete the Form 300 for a hearing loss case?

When you enter a recordable hearing loss case on the Cal/OSHA Form 300, you must check the 300 Log column for hearing loss.

Note: Authority cited: Section 6410, Labor Code. Reference: Section 6410, Labor Code; and 29 Code of Federal Regulations Section 1904.10.

History: 1. New section filed 1-15-2002; operative 1-15-2002 pursuant to Government Code section 11343.4 (Register 2002, No. 3).

2. Repealer and new section filed 12-30-2002; operative 1-1-2003 pursuant to Government Code section 11343.4 (Register 2003, No. 1).

3. Amendment of subsections (a) and (a)(7) and amendment of Note filed 4-23-2004; operative 4-23-2004 pursuant to Government Code section 11343.4 (Register 2004, No. 17).

4. Change without regulatory effect amending subsections (a) and (b)(7) filed 8-22-2007 pursuant to section 100, title 1, California Code of Regulations (Register 2007, No. 34).

§14300.11. Recording Criteria for Work-Related Tuberculosis Cases.

(a) Basic requirement. If any of your employees has been occupationally exposed to anyone with a known case of active tuberculosis (TB), and that employee subsequently develops a tuberculosis infection, as evidenced by a positive skin test or diagnosis by a physician or other licensed health care professional, you must record the case on the Cal/OSHA Form 300 by checking the "respiratory condition" column.

(b) Implementation.

(1) Do I have to record, on the Cal/OSHA Form 300, a positive TB skin test result obtained at a pre-employment physical?

No. You do not have to record it because the employee was not occupationally exposed to a known case of active tuberculosis in your workplace.

(2) May I line-out or erase a recorded TB case if I obtain evidence that the case was not caused by occupational exposure?

Yes. You may line-out or erase the case from the Cal/OSHA Form 300 under the following circumstances:

(A) The worker is living in a household with a person who has been diagnosed with active TB;

(B) The Public Health Department has identified the worker as a contact of an individual with a case of active TB unrelated to the workplace; or

(C) A medical investigation shows that the employee's infection was caused by exposure to TB away from work, or proves that the case was not related to the workplace TB exposure.

Note: Authority cited: Section 6410, Labor Code. Reference: Section 6410, Labor Code.

History: 1. New section filed 1-15-2002; operative 1-15-2002 pursuant to Government Code section 11343.4 (Register 2002, No. 3).

§14300.12. Recording Criteria for Cases Involving Work-Related Musculoskeletal Disorders.

Record work-related injuries and illnesses involving muscles, nerves, tendons, ligaments, joints, cartilage and spinal discs in accordance with the requirements applicable to any injury or illness under Sections 14300.5, 14300.6, 14300.7, and 14300.29. For entry (M) on the Cal/OSHA

Form 300, you must check either the entry for "injury" or for "all other illnesses."

Note: Authority cited: Section 6410, Labor Code. Reference: Section 6410, Labor Code; and 29 Code of Federal Regulations Section 1904.12.

History: 1. New section filed 1-15-2002; operative 1-15-2002 pursuant to Government Code section 11343.4 (Register 2002, No. 3).

2. Amendment of section and new Note filed 12-30-2002; operative 1-1-2003 pursuant to Government Code section 11343.4 (Register 2003, No. 1).

3. Amendment of section and Note filed 4-23-2004; operative 4-23-2004 pursuant to Government Code section 11343.4 (Register 2004, No. 17).

4. Change without regulatory effect amending section filed 8-22-2007 pursuant to section 100, title 1, California Code of Regulations (Register 2007, No. 34).

§14300.29. Forms.

(a) Basic requirement. You must use Cal/OSHA 300, 300A, and 301 forms, or equivalent forms, for recordable injuries and illnesses. The Cal/OSHA Form 300 is called the Log of Work-Related Injuries and Illnesses, the Cal/OSHA Form 300A is called the Summary of Work-Related Injuries and Illnesses, and the Cal/OSHA Form 301 is called the Injury and Illness Incident Report. Appendices A through C give samples of the Cal/OSHA forms. Appendices D through F provide elements for development of equivalent forms consistent with Section 14300.29(b)(4) requirements. Appendix G is a worksheet to assist in completing the Cal/OSHA Form 300A.

(b) Implementation.

(1) What do I need to do to complete the Cal/OSHA Form 300?

You must enter information about your establishment at the top of the Cal/OSHA Form 300 by entering a one or two line description for each recordable injury or illness, and summarizing this information on the Cal/OSHA Form 300A at the end of the year.

(2) What do I need to do to complete the Cal/OSHA Form 301 Incident Report?

You must complete a Cal/OSHA 301 Incident Report form, or an equivalent form, for each injury or illness required to be entered on the Cal/OSHA Form 300.

(3) How quickly must each injury or illness be recorded?

You must enter each recordable injury or illness on the Cal/OSHA Form 300 and Cal/OSHA Form 301 Incident Report within seven (7) calendar days of receiving information that a recordable injury or illness has occurred.

(4) What is an equivalent form?

An equivalent form is one that has the same information, is as readable and understandable to a person not familiar with it, and is completed using the same instructions as the Cal/OSHA form it replaces.

(5) May I keep my records on a computer?

Yes. If the computer can produce equivalent forms when they are needed, as described under Sections 14300.35 and 14300.40, you may keep your records using a computer system.

(6) Are there situations where I do not put the employee's name on the forms for privacy reasons?

Yes. If you have a "privacy concern case," as described in subsection (b)(7) of this section, you may not enter the employee's name on the Cal/OSHA Form 300. Instead, enter "privacy case" in the space normally used for the employee's name. This will protect the privacy of the injured or ill employee when another employee, a former employee, or an authorized employee representative is provided access to the Cal/OSHA Form 300 under Section 14300.35(b)(2). You must keep a separate, confidential list of the case numbers and employee names for your privacy concern cases so you can update the cases and provide the information to the government if asked to do so.

(7) How do I determine if an injury or illness is a privacy concern case?

You must consider the following injuries or illnesses to be privacy concern cases:

(A) An injury or illness to an intimate body part or the reproductive system;

(B) An injury or illness resulting from a sexual assault;

(C) Mental illnesses;

(D) HIV infection, hepatitis, or tuberculosis;

(E) Needlestick injuries and cuts from sharp objects that are contaminated with another person's blood or other potentially infectious material (see Section 14300.8 for definitions); and

(F) Other illnesses, if the employee independently and voluntarily requests that his or her name not be entered on the log.

(8) May I classify any other types of injuries and illnesses as privacy concern cases?

No. This is a complete list of all injuries and illnesses considered privacy concern cases for purposes of Article 2.

(9) If I have removed the employee's name, but still believe that the employee may be identified from the information on the forms, is there anything else that I can do to further protect the employee's privacy?

Yes. If you have a reasonable basis to believe that information describing the privacy concern case may be personally identifiable even though the employee's name has been omitted, you may use discretion in describing the injury or illness on both the Cal/OSHA forms 300 and 301. You must enter enough information to identify the cause of the incident and the general severity of the injury or illness, but you do not need to include details of an intimate or private nature. For example, a sexual assault case could be described as "injury from assault," or an injury to a reproductive organ could be described as "lower abdominal injury."

(10) What must I do to protect employee privacy if I wish to provide access to the Cal/OSHA forms 300 and 301 to persons other than government representatives, employees, former employees or authorized representatives?

If you decide to voluntarily disclose the forms to persons other than government representatives, employees, former employees or authorized representatives (as required by Sections 14300.35 and 14300.40), you must remove or hide the employees' names and other personally identifying information, except for the following cases. You may disclose the forms with personally identifying information only:

(A) to an auditor or consultant hired by the employer to evaluate the safety and health program;

(B) to the extent necessary for processing a claim for workers' compensation or other insurance benefits; or

(C) to a public health authority or law enforcement agency for uses and disclosures for which consent, an authorization, or opportunity to agree or object is not required under Department of Health and Human Services Standards for Privacy of Individually Identifiable Health Information, 45 CFR.164.512.

Note: Authority cited: Section 6410, Labor Code. Reference: Section 6410, Labor Code; and 29 Code of Federal Regulations Section 1904.29.

History: 1. New section filed 1-15-2002; operative 1-15-2002 pursuant to Government Code section 11343.4 (Register 2002, No. 3).

2. Amendment of subsection (b)(7)(F) filed 12-30-2002; operative 1-1-2003 pursuant to Government Code section 11343.4 (Register 2003, No. 1).

3. Amendment of subsections (a), (b)(1)-(3), (b)(6) and (b)(7)(F) and amendment of Note filed 4-23-2004; operative 4-23-2004 pursuant to Government Code section 11343.4 (Register 2004, No. 17).

4. Change without regulatory effect amending subsections (a), (b)(1)-(3) and (b)(6) filed 8-22-2007 pursuant to section 100, title 1, California Code of Regulations (Register 2007, No. 34).

§14300.30. Multiple Establishments.

(a) Basic requirement. You must keep a separate Cal/OSHA Form 300 for each establishment that is expected to be in operation for one year or longer.

(b) Implementation.

(1) Do I need to keep injury and illness records for short-term establishments (i.e., establishments that will exist for less than a year)?

Yes. However, you do not have to keep a separate Cal/OSHA Form 300 for each such establishment. You may keep one Cal/OSHA Form 300 that covers all of your short-term establishments. You may also include the short-term establishments' recordable injuries and illnesses on a Cal/OSHA Form 300 that covers short-term establishments for individual company divisions or geographic regions.

(2) May I keep the records for all of my establishments at my headquarters location or at some other central location?

Yes. You may keep the records for an establishment at your headquarters or other central location if you:

(A) Transmit information about the injuries and illnesses from the establishment to the central location within seven (7) calendar days of receiving information that a recordable injury or illness has occurred.

Exception: If you have an establishment in SIC Code 781 and it is operated at a location that is remote from your central location, you must transmit the information to the central location within the lesser of 30 calendar days of learning of the injury or illness, or 7 calendar days of termination of operations at the remote location;

(B) Produce and send the records from the central location to the establishment within the time frames required by Section 14300.35 and Section 14300.40 when you are required to provide records to a government representative, employee, former employee or employee representative;

(C) Have the address and telephone number of the central location or headquarters where records are kept available at each worksite; and

(D) Have personnel available at the central location or headquarters where records are kept during normal business hours to transmit information from the records maintained there as required by Section 14300.35 and Section 14300.40.

(3) Some of my employees work at several different locations or do not work at any of my establishments at all. How do I record cases for these employees?

You must link each of your employees with one of your establishments, for recordkeeping purposes. You must record each injury and illness on the Cal/OSHA Form 300 of the injured or ill employee's establishment, or on a Cal/OSHA Form 300 that covers that employee's short-term establishment.

(4) How do I record an injury or illness when an employee of one of my establishments is injured or becomes ill while visiting or working at another of my establishments, or while working away from any of my establishments?

If the injury or illness occurs at one of your establishments, you must record the injury or illness on the Cal/OSHA Form 300 of the establishment at which the injury or illness occurred. If the employee is injured or becomes ill and is not at one of your establishments, you must record the case on the Cal/OSHA Form 300 for the establishment at which the employee normally works.

Note: Authority cited: Section 6410, Labor Code. Reference: Section 6410, Labor Code.

History: 1. New section filed 1-15-2002; operative 1-15-2002 pursuant to Government Code section 11343.4 (Register 2002, No. 3).

§14300.31. Covered Employees.

(a) Basic requirement. You must record on the Cal/OSHA Form 300 the recordable injuries and illnesses of all employees on your payroll, whether they are labor, executive, hourly, salary, part-time, seasonal, or migrant workers. You also must record the recordable injuries and illnesses that occur to employees who are not on your payroll if you supervise these employees on a day-to-day basis. If your establishment is organized as a sole proprietorship or partnership, the owner or partners are not considered employees for recordkeeping purposes.

(b) Implementation.

(1) If a self-employed person is injured or becomes ill while doing work at my establishment, do I need to record the injury or illness?

No. Self-employed individuals are not covered by the Cal/OSHA Act or this regulation.

(2) If I obtain employees from a temporary help service, employee leasing service, or personnel supply service, do I have to record an injury or illness occurring to one of those employees?

You must record these injuries and illnesses if you supervise these employees on a day-to-day basis.

(3) If an employee in my establishment is a contractor's employee, must I record an injury or illness occurring to that employee?

If the contractor's employee is under the day-to-day supervision of the contractor, the contractor is responsible for recording the injury or illness. If you supervise the contractor employee's work on a day-to-day basis, you must record the injury or illness.

(4) Must the personnel supply service, temporary help service, employee leasing service, or contractor also record the injuries or illnesses occurring to temporary, leased or contract employees that I supervise on a day-to-day basis?

No. You and the temporary help service, employee leasing service, personnel supply service, or contractor should coordinate your efforts to make sure that each injury and illness is recorded only once: either on your Cal/OSHA Form 300 (if you provide day-to-day supervision) or on the other employer's Cal/OSHA Form 300 (if that company provides day-to-day supervision).

Note: Authority cited: Section 6410, Labor Code. Reference: Section 6410, Labor Code.

History: 1. New section filed 1-15-2002; operative 1-15-2002 pursuant to Government Code section 11343.4 (Register 2002, No. 3).

§14300.32. Annual Summary.

(a) Basic requirement. At the end of each calendar year, you must:

(1) Review the Cal/OSHA Form 300 to verify that the entries are complete and accurate, and correct any deficiencies identified;

(2) Create an annual summary of injuries and illnesses recorded on the Cal/OSHA Form 300 using the Cal/OSHA Form 300A Annual Summary of Work-related Injuries and Illnesses;

(3) Certify the annual summary; and

(4) Post the annual summary.

(b) Implementation.

(1) How extensively do I have to review the Cal/OSHA Form 300 entries at the end of the year?

You must review the entries as extensively as necessary to make sure that they are complete and correct.

(2) How do I complete the annual summary?

You must:

(A) Total the columns on the Cal/OSHA Form 300 (if you had no recordable cases, enter zeros for each column total); and

(B) Enter the calendar year covered, the company's name, establishment name, establishment address, annual average number of employees covered by the Cal/OSHA Form 300, and the total hours worked by all employees covered by the Cal/OSHA Form 300.

(C) If you are using an equivalent form other than the Cal/OSHA 300A, as permitted under Section 14300.29(b)(4), the annual summary you use must also include the employee access and employer penalty statements found on the Cal/OSHA Form 300A.

(3) How do I certify the annual summary?

A company executive must certify that he or she has examined the Cal/OSHA Form 300 and that he or she reasonably believes, based on his or her knowledge of the process by which the information was recorded, that the annual summary is correct and complete.

(4) Who is considered a company executive?

The company executive who certifies the log must be one of the following persons:

(A) An owner of the company (this is required only if the company is a sole proprietorship or partnership);

(B) An officer of the corporation;

(C) The highest ranking company official working at the establishment; or

(D) The immediate supervisor of the highest ranking company official working at the establishment.

(5) How do I post the annual summary?

You must post a copy of the annual summary in each establishment in a conspicuous place or places where notices to employees are customarily posted. You must ensure that the posted annual summary is not altered, defaced or covered by other material.

(6) When do I have to post the annual summary?

You must post the annual summary no later than February 1 of the year following the year covered by the records and keep the posting in place until April 30.

(7) What must be done for employees who do not normally report at least weekly to a location where the annual summary is posted for the establishment at which they work? Employers are required to present or mail the annual summary to each employee who receives pay during the February through April posting period who does not normally report at least weekly to a location where the annual summary is posted for the establishment to which they are linked for recordkeeping purposes as described at Section 14300.30(b)(3).

(8) Do I have to post the annual summary at locations where I no longer have operations or employees?

For multi-establishment employers where operations have closed down in some establishments during the calendar year, it will not be necessary to post summaries for those establishments.

Note: Authority cited: Section 6410, Labor Code. Reference: Section 6410, Labor Code.

History: 1. New section filed 1-15-2002; operative 1-15-2002 pursuant to Government Code section 11343.4 (Register 2002, No. 3).

§14300.33. Retention and Updating.

(a) Basic requirement. You must save the Cal/OSHA Form 300, the privacy case list (if one exists), the Cal/OSHA Form 300A, and the Cal/OSHA Form 301 Incident Reports for five (5) years following the end of the calendar year that these records cover.

(b) Implementation.

(1) Do I have to update the Cal/OSHA 300 Form during the five-year storage period?

Yes. During the storage period, you must update your stored Cal/OSHA 300 forms to include newly discovered recordable injuries or illnesses and to show any changes that have occurred in the classification of previously recorded injuries and illnesses. If the description or outcome of a case changes, you must remove or line out the original entry and enter the new information.

(2) Do I have to update the Cal/OSHA 300A Annual Summary of Work-related Injuries and Illnesses?

No. You are not required to update the annual summary, but you may do so if you wish.

(3) Do I have to update the Cal/OSHA 301 Incident Reports?

No. You are not required to update the Cal/OSHA 301 Incident Reports, but you may do so if you wish.

Note: Authority cited: Section 6410, Labor Code. Reference: Section 6410, Labor Code.

History: 1. New section filed 1-15-2002; operative 1-15-2002 pursuant to Government Code section 11343.4 (Register 2002, No. 3).

§14300.34. Change in Establishment Ownership.

If your establishment changes ownership, you are responsible for recording and reporting work-related injuries and illnesses only for that period of the year during which you owned the establishment. You must transfer the records required by this article to the new owner. The new owner must save all records of the establishment kept by the prior owner, as required by Section 14300.33 of this Article, but need not update or correct the records of the prior owner.

Note: Authority cited: Section 6410, Labor Code. Reference: Section 6410, Labor Code.

History: 1. New section filed 1-15-2002; operative 1-15-2002 pursuant to Government Code section 11343.4 (Register 2002, No. 3).

§14300.35. Employee Involvement.

(a) Basic requirement. Your employees and their representatives must be involved in the recordkeeping system in several ways.

(1) You must inform each employee of how he or she is to report an injury or illness to you.

(2) You must provide limited access to your injury and illness records for your employees and their representatives.

(b) Implementation.

(1) What must I do to make sure that employees report work-related injuries and illnesses to me?

(A) You must set up a way for employees to report work-related injuries and illnesses promptly; and

(B) You must tell each employee how to report work-related injuries and illnesses to you.

(2) Do I have to give my employees and their representatives access to the injury and illness records required by this article?

Yes. Your employees, former employees, their personal representatives, and their authorized employee representatives have the right to access the injury and illness records required by this article, with some limitations, as discussed below.

(A) Who is an authorized employee representative?

An authorized employee representative is an authorized collective bargaining agent of employees.

(B) Who is a "personal representative" of an employee or former employee?

A personal representative is:

1. Any person that the employee or former employee designates as such, in writing; or

2. The legal representative of a deceased or legally incapacitated employee or former employee.

(C) If an employee or his or her representative asks for access to the Cal/OSHA Form 300 and annual summary when do I have to provide it?

When an employee, former employee, personal representative, or authorized employee representative asks for copies of your current or stored Cal/OSHA 300 forms or a current or stored annual summary for an establishment the employee or former employee has worked in, you must give the requester a copy of the relevant Cal/OSHA 300 forms and annual summaries by the end of the next business day.

Exception: If your establishment is in SIC Code 781, you must give the requester the information within 7 calendar days.

(D) May I remove the names of the employees or any other information from the Cal/OSHA Form 300 before I give copies to an employee, former employee, or employee representative?

No. You must leave the names on the Cal/OSHA Form 300. However, to protect the privacy of injured and ill employees, you may not record the employee's name on the Cal/OSHA Form 300 for certain "privacy concern cases," as specified in Sections 14300.29(b)(6) through 14300.29(b)(9).

(E) If an employee or representative asks for access to the Cal/OSHA 301 Incident Report, when do I have to provide it?

1. When an employee, former employee, or personal representative asks for a copy of the Cal/OSHA Form 301 Incident Report describing an injury or illness to that employee or former employee, you must give the requester a copy of the Cal/OSHA 301 Incident Report containing that information by the end of the next business day.

Exception: If your establishment is in SIC Code 781, you must give the requester the information within 7 calendar days.

2. When an authorized employee representative asks for copies of the Cal/OSHA 301 Incident Reports or equivalent forms for an establishment where the agent represents employees under a collective bargaining agreement, you must give copies of those forms to the authorized employee representative within seven (7) calendar days but with the following personally identifying information deleted:

1. Name;
2. Address;
3. Date of birth;
4. Date of hire;
5. Gender;
6. Name of physician;
7. Location where treatment was provided;
8. Whether the employee was treated in an emergency room; and
9. Whether the employee was hospitalized overnight as an in-patient.

(F) May I charge for the copies?

No. You may not charge for these copies the first time they are provided. However, if one of the designated persons asks for additional copies, you may assess a reasonable charge for retrieving and copying the records.

(c) With the exception of provisions to protect the privacy of employees in subsections (b)(2)(D) and (b)(2)(E) of this section and in subsections (b)(6) through (b)(10) in Section 14300.29, nothing in this section shall be deemed to preclude employees and employee representatives from collectively bargaining to obtain access to information relating to occupational injuries and illnesses in addition to the information made available under this section.

Note: Authority cited: Section 6410, Labor Code. Reference: Section 6410, Labor Code.

History: 1. New section filed 1-15-2002; operative 1-15-2002 pursuant to Government Code section 11343.4 (Register 2002, No. 3).

§14300.36. Prohibition Against Discrimination.

Section 11(c) of the Act and Sections 6310 and 6311 of the Labor Code prohibit you from discriminating against an employee for reporting a work-related fatality, injury, or illness. These provisions of the Labor Code also protect the employee who files a safety and health complaint, asks for access to records required by this article, or otherwise exercises any rights afforded by the Act or Sections 6310 and 6311 of the Labor Code.

Note: Authority cited: Sections 50.7 and 6410, Labor Code. Reference: Sections 50.7, 98.7, 6310, 6311 and 6410, Labor Code.

History: 1. New section filed 1-15-2002; operative 1-15-2002 pursuant to Government Code section 11343.4 (Register 2002, No. 3).

§14300.38. Variances from the Recordkeeping Rule.

(a) Basic requirement for private employers. If you are a private employer and wish to keep records in a different manner from the manner prescribed by the provisions of this article, you may submit a variance petition to the Assistant Secretary of Labor for Occupational Safety and Health (Assistant Secretary), U. S. Department of Labor, Washington, DC 20210. You can obtain a variance only if you can show that your alternative recordkeeping system:

(1) Collects the same information as this article requires;

(2) Meets the purposes of the Act; and

(3) Does not interfere with the administration of the Act.

(b) Implementation of the basic requirement for private employers.

(1) What do I need to include in my variance petition?

You must include the following items in your petition:

(A) Your name and address;

(B) A list of the State(s) where the variance would be used;

(C) The address(es) of the establishment(s) involved;

(D) A description of why you are seeking a variance;

(E) A description of the different recordkeeping procedures you propose to use;

(F) A description of how your proposed procedures will collect the same information as would be collected by the provisions of this article and achieve the purpose of the Act; and

(G) A statement that you have informed your employees of the petition by giving them or their authorized representative a copy of the petition and by posting a statement summarizing the petition in the same way as notices are posted under Title 8 Section 340.

(2) How will the Assistant Secretary handle my variance petition?

The Assistant Secretary will take the following steps to process your variance petition.

(A) The Assistant Secretary will offer your employees and their authorized representatives an opportunity to submit written data, views, and arguments about your variance petition.

(B) The Assistant Secretary may allow the public to comment on your variance petition by publishing the petition in the Federal Register. If the petition is published, the notice will establish a public comment period and may include a schedule for a public meeting on the petition.

(C) After reviewing your variance petition and any comments from your employees and the public, the Assistant Secretary will decide whether or not your proposed recordkeeping procedures will meet the purposes of the Act, will not otherwise interfere with the Act, and will provide the same information as required by the provisions of this article provide. If your procedures meet these criteria, the Assistant Secretary may grant the variance subject to such conditions as he or she finds appropriate.

(D) If the Assistant Secretary grants your variance petition, OSHA will publish a notice in the Federal Register to announce the variance. The notice will include the practices the variance allows you to use, any conditions that apply, and the reasons for allowing the variance.

(3) If I apply for a variance, may I use my proposed recordkeeping procedures while the Assistant Secretary is processing the variance petition?

No. Alternative recordkeeping practices are only allowed after the variance is approved. You must comply with the provisions of this article while the Assistant Secretary is reviewing your variance petition.

(4) If I have already been cited by the Division of Occupational Safety and Health for not following the provisions of this article, will my variance petition have any effect on the citation and penalty?

No. In addition, the Assistant Secretary may elect not to review your variance petition if it includes an element for which you have been cited and the citation is still under review by a court, an Administrative Law Judge (ALJ), or the California Occupational Safety and Health Appeals Board.

(5) If I receive a variance, may the Assistant Secretary revoke the variance at a later date?

Yes. The Assistant Secretary may revoke your variance if he or she has good cause. The procedures revoking a variance will follow the same process as are used for reviewing variance petitions, as outlined in Section 14300.38(b)(2). Except in cases of willfulness or where necessary for public safety, the Assistant Secretary will:

(A) Notify you in writing of the facts or conduct that may warrant revocation of your variance; and

(B) Provide you, your employees, and authorized employee representatives with an opportunity to participate in the revocation procedures.

(c) Variances from the recordkeeping rule for public employers. A public agency employer wishing to keep records in a different manner from the manner prescribed in this article may write a letter to the Chief of the Division of Labor Statistics and Research stating his or her request. Such requests should include the information described in subsection (b)(1) of this section for private employer requests for variances from requirements of this article. The provisions of subsections (b)(2) through (b)(5) of this section will also apply to variance requests from public agency employers except that the determining authority will be the Chief of the Division of Labor Statistics and Research.

Note: Authority cited: Section 6410, Labor Code. Reference: Section 6410, Labor Code.

History: 1. New section filed 1-15-2002; operative 1-15-2002 pursuant to Government Code section 11343.4 (Register 2002, No. 3).

§14300.40. Providing Records to Government Representatives.

(a) Basic requirement. When an authorized government representative asks for the records you keep under the provisions of this article, you must provide within four (4) business hours, access to the original recordkeeping documents requested as well as, if requested, one set of copies free of charge.

Exception: If your establishment is in SIC Code 781, you must make a reasonable effort to comply as required by this section within 4 business hours of receiving the request. If it is not possible to comply with that deadline with reasonable effort, you must comply no later than by the end of the next business day.

(b) Implementation.

(1) What government representatives have the right to get copies of the records I keep as required by Article 2?

The government representatives authorized to receive the records are:

(A) A representative of the Chief of the Division of Occupational Safety and Health, or of the Director of the Department of Health Services;

(B) A representative of the Secretary of the U.S. Department of Labor conducting an inspection or investigation under the Act; and

(C) A representative of the Secretary of the U.S. Department of Health and Human Services (including the National Institute for Occupational Safety and Health—NIOSH) conducting an investigation under Section 20(b) of the Act;

(2) Do I have to produce the records within four (4) hours if my records are kept at a location in a different time zone?

Your response will be considered to be timely if you give the records to the government representative within four (4) business hours of the request. If you maintain the records at a location in a different time zone, you may use the business hours of the establishment at which the records are located when calculating the deadline.

Note: Authority cited: Section 6410, Labor Code. Reference: Section 6410, Labor Code.

History: 1. New section filed 1-15-2002; operative 1-15-2002 pursuant to Government Code section 11343.4 (Register 2002, No. 3).

§14300.41. Annual OSHA Injury and Illness Survey.

(a) Basic requirement. If you receive OSHA's annual survey form, you must fill it out and send it to OSHA or OSHA's designee, as stated on the survey form. You must report the following information for the year described on the form:

(1) the number of workers you employed;

(2) the number of hours worked by your employees; and

(3) the requested information from the records that you keep under the provisions of this article.

(b) Implementation.

(1) Does every employer have to send data to OSHA or its designee?

No. Each year, OSHA or its designee sends injury and illness survey forms to employers in certain industries. In any year, some employers will receive an OSHA survey form and others will not. You do not have to send injury and illness data to OSHA or its designee unless you receive a survey form.

(2) How quickly do I need to respond to an OSHA survey form?

You must send the survey reports to OSHA or its designee by mail or other means described in the survey form, within 30 calendar days, or by the date stated in the survey form, whichever is later.

(3) Do I have to respond to an OSHA survey form if I am normally exempt from keeping OSHA injury and illness records?

Yes. Even if you are exempt from keeping injury and illness records under Section 14300.1 to Section 14300.3, OSHA or its designee may inform you in writing that it will be collecting injury and illness information from you in the following year. If you receive such a letter, you must keep the injury and illness records required by this article and make a survey report for the year covered by the survey.

(4) Do I have to answer the OSHA survey form if I am located in a State-Plan State?

Yes. All employers who receive survey forms must respond to the survey, even those in State-Plan States.

(5) Does this section affect the Division of Occupational Safety and Health's authority to inspect my workplace?

No. Nothing in this section affects the Division of Occupational Safety and Health's statutory authority to investigate conditions related to occupational safety and health.

Note: Authority cited: Section 6410, Labor Code. Reference: Section 6410, Labor Code.

History: 1. New section filed 1-15-2002; operative 1-15-2002 pursuant to Government Code section 11343.4 (Register 2002, No. 3).

§14300.42. Requests from the Bureau of Labor Statistics for Data.

(a) Basic requirement. If you receive a Survey of Occupational Injuries and Illnesses Form from the Bureau of Labor Statistics (BLS), or a BLS designee, you must promptly complete the form and return it following the instructions contained on the survey form.

(b) Implementation.

(1) Does every employer have to send data to the BLS?

No. Each year, the BLS sends injury and illness survey forms to randomly selected employers and uses the information to create the Nation's occupational injury and illness statistics. In any year, some employers will receive a BLS survey form and others will not. You do not have to send injury and illness data to the BLS unless you receive a survey form.

(2) If I get a survey form from the BLS, what do I have to do?

If you receive a Survey of Occupational Injuries and Illnesses Form from the Bureau of Labor Statistics (BLS), or a BLS designee, you must promptly complete the form and return it, following the instructions contained on the survey form.

(3) Do I have to respond to a BLS survey form if I am normally exempt from keeping injury and illness records as required by this article?

Yes. Even if you are exempt from keeping injury and illness records under one or more of the provisions of Section 14300.1 to Section 14300.3, the BLS may inform you in writing that it will be collecting injury and illness information from you in the coming year. If you receive such a letter, you must keep the injury and illness records required by this article and make a survey report for the year covered by the survey.

(4) Do I have to answer the BLS survey form if I am located in a State-Plan State?

Yes. All employers who receive a survey form must respond to the survey, even those in State-Plan States.

Note: Authority cited: Section 6410, Labor Code. Reference: Section 6410, Labor Code.

History: 1. New section filed 1-15-2002; operative 1-15-2002 pursuant to Government Code section 11343.4 (Register 2002, No. 3).

§14300.43. Annual Summary and Posting of the 2001 Data.

(a) Basic requirement. If you were required to keep Cal/OSHA Form 200 in 2001, you must post a 2001 annual summary from the Cal/OSHA Form 200 of occupational injuries and illnesses for each establishment.

(b) Implementation.

(1) What do I have to include in the annual summary?

(A) You must include a copy of the totals from the 2001 Cal/OSHA Form 200 Log and Summary and the following information from that form:

1. The calendar year covered;
2. Your company name;
3. The name and address of the establishment; and
4. The certification signature, title and date.

(B) If no injuries or illnesses occurred at your establishment in 2001, you must enter zeros on the totals line and post the 2001 annual summary.

(2) When am I required to summarize and post the 2001 information?

(A) You must complete the annual summary by February 1, 2002; and

(B) You must post a copy of the annual summary in each establishment in a conspicuous place or places where notices to employees are customarily posted. You must ensure that the annual summary is not altered, defaced or covered by other material.

(3) You must post the 2001 annual summary from February 1, 2002 to March 1, 2002.

Note: Authority cited: Section 6410, Labor Code. Reference: Section 6410, Labor Code.

History: 1. New section filed 1-15-2002; operative 1-15-2002 pursuant to Government Code section 11343.4 (Register 2002, No. 3).

§14300.44. Retention and Updating of Old Forms.

You must save your copies of the Cal/OSHA 200 forms and supplementary records for each occupational injury or illness for five years following the year to which they relate and continue to provide access to the data as though these forms were the Cal/OSHA 300 and 301 forms, as provided for in Section 14300.35 and Section 14300.40. You are not required to update your old Cal/OSHA 200 forms and supplementary records.

Note: Authority cited: Section 6410, Labor Code. Reference: Section 6410, Labor Code.

History: 1. New section filed 1-15-2002; operative 1-15-2002 pursuant to Government Code section 11343.4 (Register 2002, No. 3).

§14300.46. Definitions.

The Act. The Act means the federal Occupational Safety and Health Act of 1970 (29 U.S.C. 651 et seq.). The definitions contained in Section 3 of the Act (29 U.S.C. 652) and related interpretations apply to such terms when used in this article.

Authorized representative. See subsection 14300.35(b)(2)(A).

BLS. The Bureau of Labor Statistics in the U. S. Department of Labor.

Cal/OSHA. The California Occupational Safety and Health Program within the California Department of Industrial Relations.

Cal/OSHA Form 300 means the Cal/OSHA Form 300 Log of Work-Related Injuries and Illnesses (Rev. 7/2007)

Cal/OSHA Form 300A means the Cal/OSHA Form 300A Annual Summary of Work-Related Injuries and Illnesses (Rev. 7/2007)

Company. A public or private employer.

Covered employees. See Section 14300.31.

Equivalent form. See subsection 14300.29(b)(4).

Establishment. An establishment is a single physical location where business is conducted or where services or industrial operations are performed. For activities where employees do not work at a single physical location, such as construction; transportation; communications, electric, gas and sanitary services; and similar operations, the establishment is represented by main or branch offices, terminals, stations, etc. that either supervise such activities or are the base from which personnel carry out these activities.

(A) Can one business location include two or more establishments?

Normally, one business location has only one establishment. Under limited conditions, the employer may consider two or more separate establishments that share a single location to be separate establishments. An employer may divide one location into two or more establishments only when:

1. Each of the establishments represents a distinctly separate business;

2. Each establishment is engaged in a different economic activity;

3. No one industry description in the Standard Industrial Classification Manual (1987) applies to the joint activities of the establishments; and

4. Separate reports are routinely prepared for each establishment on the number of employees, their wages and salaries, sales or receipts, and other business information. For example, if an employer operates a construction company at the same location as a lumberyard, the employer may consider each business to be a separate establishment.

(B) Can an establishment include more than one physical location?

Yes, but only under certain conditions. An employer may combine two or more physical locations into a single establishment only when:

1. The employer operates the locations as a single business operation under common management;

2. The locations are all located in close proximity to each other; and

3. The employer keeps one set of business records for the locations, such as records on the number of employees, their wages and salaries, sales or receipts, and other kinds of business information. For example, one manufacturing establishment might include the main plant, a warehouse a few blocks away, and an administrative services building across the street.

(C) If an employee telecommutes from home, is his or her home considered a separate establishment?

No. For employees who telecommute from home, the employee's home is not an establishment and a separate Cal/OSHA Form 300 is not required. Employees who telecommute must be linked to one of your establishments under Section 14300.30(b)(3).

Fatality. Any occupational injury or illness which results in death, regardless of the time between injury and death, or the length of the illness.

First aid. See subsection 14300.7(b)(5)(B).

General recording criteria. See Section 14300.7.

Injury or illness. An injury or illness is an abnormal condition or disorder. Injuries include cases such as, but not limited to, a cut, fracture, sprain, or amputation. Illnesses include both acute and chronic illnesses, such as, but not limited to, a skin disease, respiratory disorder, or poisoning. (Note: Injuries and illnesses are recordable only if they are new, work-related cases that meet one or more of recording criteria provisions in this article.)

Job transfer. See subsection 14300.7(b)(4).

Medical treatment. See subsection 14300.7(b)(5)(A).

New case. See Section 14300.6.

OSHA. The Occupational Safety and Health Administration in the U.S. Department of Labor.

Personal representative. See subsection 14300.35(b)(2)(B).

Physician or other licensed health care professional. A physician or other licensed health care professional is an individual whose legally permitted scope of practice (i.e., license, registration, or certification) allows him or her to independently perform, or be delegated the responsibility to perform, the activities described by this regulation.

Pre-existing condition. See subsection 14300.5(b)(5).

Privacy concern case. See subsection 14300.29(b)(6).

Recordable. An injury or illness is "recordable" for the purposes of this article if it satisfies the conditions requiring recording found in subsection (a) of Section 14300.4.

Routine functions. See subsection 14300.7(b)(4)(B).

Restricted work. See subsection 14300.7(b)(4)(A).

Significant injury or illness. See subsection 14300.7(b)(7).

Work environment. See subsection 14300.5(b)(1).

You. "You" means an employer as defined by Sections 3300 and 3301 of the Labor Code.

Note: Authority cited: Section 6410, Labor Code. Reference: Section 6410, Labor Code.

History: 1. New section filed 1-15-2002; operative 1-15-2002 pursuant to Government Code section 11343.4 (Register 2002, No. 3).

2. Change without regulatory effect adding definitions of "Cal/OSHA Form 300" and "Cal/OSHA Form 300A," filed 8-22-2007 pursuant to section 100, title 1, California Code of Regulations (Register 2007, No. 34).

§14300.47. Recordkeeping Requirements for Employers Covered by the Federal Mine Safety and Health Act.

Employers whose employees' occupational injuries and illnesses are required to be recorded under the Federal Mine Safety and Health Act of 1977 are not required to comply with the recordkeeping requirements of this article to the extent that so complying would result in duplicating information, provided access to the records required by Code of Federal Regulations, Title 30, Chapter 1, Subchapter I, commencing with Section 50.20 is granted to authorized representatives of the official mine safety agency of the State.

Note: Authority cited: Section 6410, Labor Code. Reference: Section 6410, Labor Code.

History: 1. New section filed 1-15-2002; operative 1-15-2002 pursuant to Government Code section 11343.4 (Register 2002, No. 3).

§14300.48. Effective Date.

The provisions of this article take effect on January 1, 2002 or on the effective date of the regulation, whichever is later.

Note: Authority cited: Section 6410, Labor Code. Reference: Section 6410, Labor Code.

History: 1. New section and Appendices A-G filed 1-15-2002; operative 1-15-2002 pursuant to Government Code section 11343.4 (Register 2002, No. 3).

2. Amendment of appendices A, B, D and E and amendment of Notes for appendices D and E filed 4-23-2004; operative 4-23-2004 pursuant to Government Code section 11343.4 (Register 2004, No. 17).

3. Change without regulatory effect amending appendices A, B, D and E filed 8-22-2007 pursuant to section 100, title 1, California Code of Regulations (Register 2007, No. 34).

Appendix A. Log of Work-Related Injuries and Illnesses

Editor's Note: For the text of Appendix A, please see Barclays *Official California Code of Regulations*.

Appendix B. Annual Summary of Work-Related Injuries and Illnesses

Editor's Note: For the text of Appendix B, please see Barclays *Official California Code of Regulations.*

Appendix C. Injury and Illness Incident Report

Editor's Note: For the text of Appendix C, please see Barclays *Official California Code of Regulations.*

Appendix D. Required Elements for the Cal/OSHA 300 Equivalent Form

I. California employers who are required to record work-related injuries and illnesses on the Cal/OSHA Form 300 may use an equivalent form that includes all of the following instructions and information.

Log of Work-Related Injuries and Illnesses

Instruction: You must record information about every work-related death and about every work-related injury or illness that involves loss of consciousness, restricted work activity or job transfer, days away from work, or medical treatment beyond first aid. You must also record significant work-related injuries and illnesses that are diagnosed by a physician or licensed health care professional. You must also record work-related injuries and illnesses that meet any of the specific recording criteria listed in 8 CCR 14300.8 through 14300.12. Feel free to use two lines for a single case if you need to. You must complete an Injury and Illness Incident Report (Cal/OSHA Form 301) or equivalent form for each injury or illness recorded on this form. If you're not sure whether a case is recordable, contact the nearest office of the Division of Occupational Safety and Health for assistance.

Establishment Name & Address

Identify the Person (A)-(C)

A. Case Number

B. Employee's Name

C. Job Title

Describe the Case (D)-(F):

D. Date of Injury or illness

E. Where the event occurred

F. Describe the injury or illness, part(s) of the body affected, and object/substance that directly injured or made the person ill

Classify the Case (G)-(M)

Using these four categories (G)-(J), indicate only the most serious result for each case:

G. "Death"

H. "Days away from work"

I. Remained at work as "Other recordable cases"

J. Remained at work with "Job transfer or restriction"

Enter the number of days the injured or ill worker was:

K. Number of days the injured or ill worker was "Away from work"

L. Number of days the injured or ill worker was "On job transfer or restrictions"

M. Indicate an injury or, one type of illness:

(1) Injury column

(2) Skin disorder column

(3) Respiratory condition column

(4) Poisoning column

(5) Occupational hearing loss

(6) All other illnesses column

Page Totals (for columns (G)-(M))

Instruction: Transfer these totals to the Summary page (Cal/OSHA Form 300A) before you post it.

Instructions for privacy concerns:

"ATTENTION: This form contains information relating to employee health and must be used in a manner that protects the confidentiality of employees to the extent possible while the information is being used for occupational safety and health purposes."

Note: Privacy Concern Cases: employers using forms equivalent to the Cal/OSHA 300 are required to follow the privacy concern disclosure restrictions specified in Section 14300.29(b)(6)-(10).

Note: Additional Criteria. Beginning January 1, 2002, employers are required to record the following as specific injury and illness conditions. These are:

1. Injury from a needle or other sharp object that is contaminated with blood or OPIM (Reference: Section 14300.8)

2. Cases of medical removal under the requirements of a Cal/OSHA standard. (Reference: Section 14300.9)

3. Tuberculosis infection as evidenced by a positive skin test or diagnosis by a physician. (Reference: Section 14300.11)

Note: Authority cited: Section 6410, Labor Code. Reference: Section 6410, Labor Code; and 29 Code of Federal Regulations Section 1904.10.

Appendix E. Required Elements for the Cal/OSHA Form 300A, Annual Summary of Work-Related Injuries and Illnesses Equivalent Form.

A. Employers who are required to complete the Cal/OSHA Form 300A may use an equivalent form that provides all of the following information:

1. The number of cases:

(G) The total number of deaths

(H) The total number of cases with days away from work

(I) The total number of cases with job transfers or restriction

(J) The total number of other recordable cases

2. The number of days:

(K) The total number of days away from work

(L) The total number of days of job transfer or restriction

(M) Injury and Illness Types, the total numbers of:

1. Injuries
2. Skin disorders
3. Respiratory conditions
4. Poisonings
5. Hearing loss
6. All other illnesses

3. Posting requirement statement: "Post this Annual Summary from February 1 to April 30 of the year following the year covered by the form."

4. Establishment information:

- The establishment name
- Street address
- City, State, Zip
- Industry description
- The Standard Industry Classification Code, if known.

5. Employment information

- The annual average number of employees.
- The total hours worked by all employees last year.

(For assistance in calculating the annual average number of employees, and total hours worked, refer to Appendix G.)

6. Sign Here:

- Admonition: "Knowingly falsifying this statement may result in a fine."
- Certification statement: "I certify that I have examined this document and that to the best of my knowledge the entries are true, accurate, and complete."
- Space for the signature of the company executive, and title.
- Phone number of signatory.
- Date of the certification.

Note: Authority cited: Section 6410, Labor Code. Reference: Section 6410, Labor Code; and 29 Code of Federal Regulations Section 1904.29.

Appendix F. Required Elements for the Cal/OSHA 301 Injury and Illness Incident Report Equivalent Form

I. An employer that is required to fill out a Cal/OSHA Form 301 may use an equivalent form that provides the following items of information:

A. Information about the employee:

1. Full name

2. Home street address, city, state and Zip code

3. Date of birth

4. Date hired

5. Employee gender

B. Information about the physician or other health care professional:

6. Name of the physician or other health care professional who treated the employee

7. Name and complete address of the facility where the employee received treatment (if applicable)

8. If the employee was treated in an emergency room (yes or no)

9. If the employee was hospitalized overnight as an in-patient (yes or no)

C. Information about the case:

10. The case number matching the Cal/OSHA Log 300 (or equivalent) entry

11. The date of the injury or illness

12. Time of employee began work AM/PM

13. Time of the event AM/PM; or indication that the time cannot be determined

14. Description of what the employee was doing just before the incident occurred

15. Description of what happened; how the injury/illness occurred

16. The specific injury/illness, part(s) of the body affected, and medical diagnosis if available

17. Identify the object or substance that directly harmed the employee

18. If the employee died, the date of death

D. The name of the person the form was completed by

E. The title of the person who completed the form

F. The phone number of the person who completed the form

Appendix G. Worksheet to Help You Fill Out the Annual Summary

Editor's Note: For the text of Appendix G, please see Barclays *Official California Code of Regulations*

§14301. Log and Summary of Occupational Injuries and Illnesses. [Repealed]

Note: Authority cited: Section 6410, Labor Code. Reference: Section 6410, Labor Code.

History: 1. New sections (14301-14315) filed 5-22-75; designated effective 7-1-75 (Register 75, No. 21).

2. Amendment of subsection (b) filed 11-29-77; effective thirtieth day thereafter (Register 77, No. 49).

3. Amendment of subsections (a) and (b) filed 1-13-83; effective thirtieth day thereafter (Register 83, No. 3).

4. Repealer filed 1-15-2002; operative 1-15-2002 pursuant to Government Code section 11343.4 (Register 2002, No. 3).

§14303. Period Covered. [Repealed]

Note: Authority cited: Section 6410, Labor Code. Reference: Section 6410, Labor Code.

History: 1. Amendment filed 1-13-83; effective thirtieth day thereafter (Register 83, No. 3). For prior history, see Register 75, No. 21.

2. Repealer filed 1-15-2002; operative 1-15-2002 pursuant to Government Code section 11343.4 (Register 2002, No. 3).

§14304. Supplementary Record. [Repealed]

Note: Authority cited: Section 6410, Labor Code. Reference: Section 6410, Labor Code.

History: 1. Amendment filed 2-8-80; designated effective 5-1-80 (Register 80, No. 6). For prior history, see Register 75, No. 21.

2. Amendment of subsection (b)(1) filed 1-13-83; effective thirtieth day thereafter (Register 83, No. 3).

3. Amendment of subsection (b)(1) filed 3-18-87; effective thirtieth day thereafter (Register 87, No. 12).

4. Amendment of subsection (b)(1) filed 1-14-93; operative 2-16-93 (Register 93, No. 3).

5. Repealer filed 1-15-2002; operative 1-15-2002 pursuant to Government Code section 11343.4 (Register 2002, No. 3).

§14305. Annual Summary. [Repealed]

Note: Authority cited: Section 6410, Labor Code. Reference: Section 6410, Labor Code.

History: 1. Amendment of subsection (c) filed 5-6-76 as procedural and organizational; effective upon filing (Register 76, No. 19).

2. Amendment of subsection (a) and (c) filed 11-29-77; effective thirtieth day thereafter (Register 77, No. 49).

3. Amendment filed 1-13-83; effective thirtieth day thereafter (Register 83, No. 3).

4. Repealer filed 1-15-2002; operative 1-15-2002 pursuant to Government Code section 11343.4 (Register 2002, No. 3).

§14307. Retention of Records. [Repealed]

Note: Authority cited: Section 6410, Labor Code. Reference: Section 6410, Labor Code.

History: 1. Amendment filed 1-3-79; effective thirtieth day thereafter (Register 79, No. 1).

2. Amendment filed 1-13-83; effective thirtieth day thereafter (Register 83, No. 3).

3. Repealer filed 1-15-2002; operative 1-15-2002 pursuant to Government Code section 11343.4 (Register 2002, No. 3).

§14308. Access to Records. [Repealed]

Note: Authority cited: Section 6410, Labor Code. Reference: Section 6410, Labor Code.

History: 1. Amendment filed 10-5-78; effective thirtieth day thereafter (Register 78, No. 40).

2. Amendment filed 1-13-83; effective thirtieth day thereafter (Register 83, No. 3).

3. Repealer filed 1-15-2002; operative 1-15-2002 pursuant to Government Code section 11343.4 (Register 2002, No. 3).

§14309. Falsification, or Failure to Keep Records. [Repealed]

Note: Authority cited: Section 6410, Labor Code. Reference: Sections 6410, 6426 and 6431, Labor Code.

History: 1. Amendment of subsection (b) filed 1-13-83; effective thirtieth day thereafter (Register 83, No. 3).

2. Repealer filed 1-15-2002; operative 1-15-2002 pursuant to Government Code section 11343.4 (Register 2002, No. 3).

§14310. Change of Ownership. [Repealed]

Note: Authority cited: Section 6410, Labor Code. Reference: Section 6410, Labor Code.

History: 1. New Note filed 1-13-83; effective thirtieth day thereafter (Register 83, No. 3).

2. Repealer filed 1-15-2002; operative 1-15-2002 pursuant to Government Code section 11343.4 (Register 2002, No. 3).

§14311. Definitions. [Repealed]

Note: Authority cited: Section 6410, Labor Code. Reference: Section 6410, Labor Code.

History: 1. Amendment of subsection (e) filed 1-13-83; effective thirtieth day thereafter (Register 83, No. 3).

2. New subsection (f) filed 7-19-84; designated effective 8-1-84 pursuant to Government Code Section 11346.2(d) (Register 84, No. 29).

3. Repealer filed 1-15-2002; operative 1-15-2002 pursuant to Government Code section 11343.4 (Register 2002, No. 3).

§14312. Petitions for Recordkeeping Exceptions. [Repealed]

Note: Authority cited: Section 6410, Labor Code. Reference: Section 6410, Labor Code.

History: 1. Amendment filed 1-13-83; effective thirtieth day thereafter (Register 83, No. 3).

2. Repealer filed 1-15-2002; operative 1-15-2002 pursuant to Government Code section 11343.4 (Register 2002, No. 3).

§14313. Employees Not in Fixed Establishments. [Repealed]

Note: Authority cited: Section 6410, Labor Code. Reference: Section 6410, Labor Code.

History: 1. New Note filed 1-13-83; effective thirtieth day thereafter (Register 83, No. 3).

2. Repealer filed 1-15-2002; operative 1-15-2002 pursuant to Government Code section 11343.4 (Register 2002, No. 3).

§14314. Small Employers. [Repealed]

Note: Authority cited: Section 6410, Labor Code. Reference: Section 6410, Labor Code.

History: 1. Amendment filed 11-29-77; effective thirtieth day thereafter (Register 77, No. 49).

2. Amendment filed 2-8-80; designated effective 5-1-80 (Register 80, No. 6).

3. Amendment filed 1-13-83; effective thirtieth day thereafter (Register 83, No. 3).

4. Repealer filed 1-15-2002; operative 1-15-2002 pursuant to Government Code section 11343.4 (Register 2002, No. 3).

§14315. Employers Covered by the Federal Mine Safety and Health Act. [Repealed]

Note: Authority cited: Section 6410, Labor Code. Reference: Section 6410, Labor Code.

History: 1. Amendment filed 1-13-83; effective thirtieth day thereafter (Register 83, No. 3).

2. Repealer filed 1-15-2002; operative 1-15-2002 pursuant to Government Code section 11343.4 (Register 2002, No. 3).

§14316. Private Sector Establishments Classified in Standard Industrial Classification Codes (SIC) 52-89, (except 52-55, 57, 70, 75, 76, 781, 79 and 80), in Accordance with the 1972 Edition of the "Standard Industrial Classification Manual," Incorporating the 1977 Supplement, Published by the Office of Management and Budget, Executive Office of the President. [Repealed]

Note: Authority cited: Section 6410, Labor Code. Reference: Section 6410, Labor Code.

History: 1. New section filed 7-19-84; designated effective 8-1-84 pursuant to Government Code Section 11346.2(d) (Register 84, No. 29).

2. Repealer filed 1-15-2002; operative 1-15-2002 pursuant to Government Code section 11343.4 (Register 2002, No. 3).

§14400. Statistical Surveys. [Repealed]

Note: Authority cited: Sections 6410 and 6411, Labor Code. Reference: Section 6411, Labor Code.

History: 1. New section filed 5-22-75; designated effective 7-1-75 (Register 75, No. 21).

2. Amendment filed 11-29-77; effective thirtieth day thereafter (Register 77, No. 49).

3. New Note filed 1-13-83; effective thirtieth day thereafter (Register 83, No. 3).

4. Repealer filed 1-15-2002; operative 1-15-2002 pursuant to Government Code section 11343.4 (Register 2002, No. 3).

SUBCHAPTER 2
REPORTS OF INJURY TO BE FILED BY THE CALIFORNIA DEPARTMENT OF CORRECTIONS

ARTICLE 1
Prison Labor

§14900. Prison Labor.

Section 6413(a) of the Labor requires that, except for the injuries specifically exempted by the section itself, injury reports shall be filed for every injury to any state prisoner (inmate) resulting from any labor performed by the prisoner (inmate). No reports need be filed if "disability resulting from such injury does not last through the day or does not require medical service other than ordinary first aid treatment."

Note: Authority cited: Section 6413, Labor Code.

History: 1. New Group 2 (Sections 14900-14920, not consecutive) filed 9-23-74; designated effective 11-1-74 (Register 74, No. 39).

ARTICLE 2
Reports to Be Filed by the Department of Corrections

§14901. Department of Corrections' Report of Injury (Form 5030).

The report shall be submitted in duplicate (Form 5030), to the Division of Labor Statistics and Research on a standard form (Form 5030) approved by the Department of Conections and the Division of Labor Statistics and Research, Department of Industrial Relations. The following information shall be included on the standard form:

Name, address and phone number of correctional institution;

Name, inmate number, sex, and date of birth of injured inmate;

Date of incarceration;

Type of labor (work) when injured and extent of total experience at that type of labor, and extent of prison training and safety training in that type of labor;

Extent of supervision over work methods used:

Where did the injury occur;

What was the object or substance that directly injured inmate:

Nature of injury and part of body affected;

What was the primary correctable cause of this accident;

What arrangements could be made to eliminate hazard;

Name of physician;

Date of injury;

Was injured unable to work on any day after injury;

Actual or estimated date of injured's recovery;

Date of death if injured died.

§14902. Agreement Between Parties.

By agreement between the parties concerned Form 5030 may be modified as needs for pertinent information arise.

§14903. Color of Form 5030.

The copy of the form to be used for transmission to the Division of Labor Statistics and Research must be printed on light blue stock.

§14904. Time of Filing.

The report shall be filed within five days after the injury.

§14910. Physician or Surgeon (Report Form 5031).

(a) Every physician or surgeon who attends, within a Department of Corrections institution, any injured inmate shall file with the Division of

Labor Statistics and Research a complete report of such injury unless disability resulting from such ingury does not last through the day or does not require medical service other than ordinary first aid treatment.

(b) The report shall be submitted in duplicate to the Division of Labor statistics and Research on a standard form (Form 5031) approved by the Department of Corrections and the Division of Labor Statistics and Research, Department of Industrial Relations. Pertinent data requried will include a statement as to the cause of the injury and the nature and extent of injury.

§14911. Agreement Between Parties.

By agreement between the parties concerned Form 5031 may be modified as needs for pertinent information arise.

§14912. Color of Form 5031.

The copy of the form to be used for transmission to the Division of Labor Statistics and Research must be printed on light blue stock.

§14913. Time of Filing Form 5031.

The report shall be filed within five days after first treatment.

§14920. Effective Date.

The California Department of Corrections shall commence submitting said reports on all injuries occurring January 1, 1975, and thereafter.

CHAPTER 8
OFFICE OF THE DIRECTOR

SUBCHAPTER 2
ADMINISTRATION OF SELF-INSURANCE PLANS

ARTICLE 1
Definitions

§15200. Repealed.

Note: Authority cited for Group 2: Sections 54, 55, 3702.10, Labor Code. Reference: Sections 54, 55, 3702.10, Labor Code.

History: 1. New Group 2 (§§15200-15203, 15210-15213, 15220-15221, 15230, 15250-15253, 15300-15303, 15350-15352, 15360-15363, 15400-15403 and 15420-15423) filed 4-23-56; effective thirtieth day thereafter (Register 56, No. 8).

2. Repealer of Group 2, and new Group 2 (§§15200-15203, 15210-15213, 15220, 15221, 15230, 15250-15252, 15300-15303, 15350-15352, 15360-15362, 15400-15405, 15420-15423) filed 6-17-66; effective thirtieth day thereafter (Register 66, No. 18). For prior amendments, see Registers 56, No. 19; 58, No. 7; 61, No. 7; 61, No. 10

3. Amendment filed 6-1-72; effective thirtieth day thereafter (Register 72, No. 23).

4. Amendment of article heading, repealer of section, and amendment of Note filed 12-22-92; operative 1-21-93 (Register 93, No. 2).

§15201. Definitions.

The following definitions apply in Articles 1 through 13 of these regulations:

(a) Adjusting Location. The office address designated in accordance with Section 15402 of these regulations where:

(1) The named administrator of the self insurer fulfills his/her function; and

(2) The original records called for in Article 9 of these regulations are maintained.

In the event that claims are administered at the home of a telecommuting adjuster, the location shall be considered as a separate adjusting location for reporting and audit purposes unless the telecommuting adjuster reports to a California location of the administrator no less than weekly.

(b) Administrative Director. The Administrative Director of the Division of Workers' Compensation within the Department of Industrial Relations.

(c) Administrative Agency. The person or firm that performs the day-to-day claims administration functions of a workers' compensation self insurance program. The administrative agency may be:

(1) An independent contractor possessing a certificate to administer and designated by a self-insurer to be the administrative agency for all or a portion of its claims; or

(2) A partnership or corporation possessing a master certificate to self insure, which administers its own claims and the claims of other affiliate or subsidiary self insurers issued affiliate or subsidiary certificates to self insure under the same master certificate number;

(3) A joint powers authority possessing a master certificate to self insure, which self

administers in whole or part the claims of its affiliate public self insurers issued affiliate certificates to self insure under the same master certificate number of the joint powers authority; or

(4) The claims department of an insurance carrier admitted to transact workers' compensation insurance in California, which is exempt from the requirement to possess a certificate to administer under Labor Code Section 3702.1(a).

(d) Administrator. A competent person pursuant to Section 15452 of these regulations, at an adjusting location, who is responsible for day-to-day management of an employer's self-insurance workers' compensation program. The responsibility includes but is not limited to, the making and reviewing of decisions relating to the furnishing of all workers' compensation benefits in accordance with law and the maintenance of the self insurer's claim records.

(e) Affiliate Certificate.

(1) A type of certificate to self insure issued to a private self insurer that has common ownership to another private self insurer holding a master certificate to self insure, but the affiliated certificate holder is not a subsidiary to the master certificate holder; or

(2) A type of certificate to self insure issued to a public self insurer that is a member of a joint powers authority for pooling of workers' compensation liabilities with the master certificate number issued to the joint powers authority.

(3) A type of certificate to self insure issued to a private self insurer that is a member of a group self-insurance plan for pooling of workers' compensation liabilities with the master certificate number issued to the group self insurer.

(f) Alternative Composite Deposit. A security deposit system pursuant to Labor Code Section 3701.8 whereby all eligible private self insurers collectively secure, in whole or in part, aggregate self insured worker's compensation liabilities through the Self Insurer's Security Fund.

(g) Audit. Any examination of self insured workers' compensation claim files performed by or at the request of the Office of Self Insurance Plans pursuant to Labor Code Section 3702.6.

(h) Board of Trustees. In group self insurance, it is the representative body selected by the group member to be responsible for managing the assets and directing the affairs of the group self insurer corporation and assuring the group self insurer, through the group members, is financially sound and able to meet the workers' compensation liabilities under the statutes and regulations applicable in California.

(i) Cancellation of Surety Bond. An act whereby the surety gives written notice to the Manager, as beneficiary of the workers' compensation self insurance surety bond, that the surety is terminating its contractual obligations under the named bond pursuant to Sections 996.320 and 996.330 of the Code of Civil Procedure and the liability of the surety bond after the effective date of the cancellation is set forth in Section 996.360 of the Code of Civil Procedure.

(j) Certificate to Self Insure. A Certificate of Consent to Self-Insure issued to an employer pursuant to Section 3700(b) of the Labor Code.

(k) Certificate to Administer. A Certificate of Consent to Administer self insured workers' compensation claims issued to an administrative agency, except exempt insurance carriers, pursuant to Labor Code Section 3702.1.

(*l*) Claim File. A separate case file containing all pertinent documents and matters relating to a specific or companion work-injury claim. The claim file contents are specified in Section 15400 of these regulations.

(m) Claim Log. A manual or electronic listing of workers' compensation claims maintained by the self insurer or administrative agency for the self insurer. The claim log for private self insurers shall list each work injury claim by the calendar year in which the claim was reported to the employer or the claims administrator, whichever first occurred, and the claim log for public self insurers shall list each work injury claim by the fiscal year in which the claim was reported. The claim log contents are specified in Section 15400.1 of these regulations.

(n) Compensation. Compensation as defined in Labor Code Section 3207.

(o) Contribution. The amount of payments required of each group member in order to fund the compensation and deposit obligations of the group self insurer.

(p) Director. The Director of the Department of Industrial Relations.

(q) Exoneration of Surety Bond. The discharge of a surety from all past, present and future liability under its workers' compensation self insurance surety bond by the execution of a

"Release of Surety", Form A4-24 (Rev. 11/92) by the Manager.

(r) First Aid. First Aid as defined in Labor Code Section 5401(a).

(s) Group Self Insurer. A private, non-profit, mutual benefit corporation pursuant to Part 3 (commencing with Section 7110) of Division 2 of Title 1 of the Corporation Code established for the sole purpose of operating a group workers' compensation self-insurance fund. Said self-insurance fund to pool California workers' compensation liabilities for two or more private employers in the same industry under the California workers' compensation statutes and regulations.

(t) Group Member. A private employer issued an Affiliate Certificate as a member in a group self-insurance program that has, in turn, been issued a Certificate to Self Insure as a group self insurer.

(u) Group Administrator. The individual authorized to serve as the representative of a group self insurer and its group members in carrying out the policies of the Board of Trustees of the Group Self Insurer and managing the activities of the group self insurer corporation.

(v) Indemnity Agreement and Power of Attorney. The written agreement executed by each group member or proposed group member of a group self insurer pursuant to Section 15479 of these regulations.

(w) Indemnity Claim. A work-injury case which has or may result in any of the following benefits:

(1) Temporary Disability or salary in lieu thereof

(2) Permanent Disability

(3) Life Pension

(4) Death Benefits

(5) Vocational Rehabilitation

(x) Industry. Employer classification as determined using the first two digits of the Standard Industrial Classification Code (SIC Code), provided by the Department of Commerce, Bureau of Management and Budget.

(y) Joint Powers Authority. A public entity created by agreement of two or more public agencies pursuant to Division 7, Chapter 5, Article 1, Sections 6500 et seq. of the Government Code. These regulations apply only to Joint Powers Authorities who have among their purposes for existence, the forming of workers' compensation liability pooling arrangements.

(z) Labor Code. The Labor Code of the State of California.

(aa) Manager. The Manager, Office of Self-Insurance Plans, in the Department of Industrial Relations.

(bb) Medical-Only Claim. A work-injury case which does not result in compensable lost time but results in medical treatment beyond first aid.

NOTE: Payment of medical examinations pursuant to Labor Code Section 4600 will be considered a medical payment.

(cc) Open Claim. A work-injury case in which it appears that one or more future payments of workers' compensation benefits may be due.

(dd) Release of Surety Bond. Action of Manager of Self Insurance Plans by which a surety is exonerated. A released surety bond does not constitute part of the security deposit of a self insured entity.

(ee) Security Fund. The Self Insurer's Security Fund as established by Labor Code section 3742.

(ff) Self-Insurer. An individual public or private sector employer or joint powers authority or private group of employers that has been issued and lawfully holds a valid Certificate to Self-Insure its workers' compensation liabilities pursuant to:

(1) The provisions of Section 29(a), Chapter 586, Laws of 1917 and amendments thereto; and/or

(2) Labor Code, Section 3700(b) and 3700(c).

(gg) Special Audit. Any audit performed other than that in accordance with Labor Code Section 3702.6.

(hh) Subsidiary Certificate. A type of certificate to self insure issued to a subsidiary of a self-insurer, where the self insurer holds the master certificate to self insure.

(ii) Termination of Surety Bond. See definition of "Cancellation of Surety Bond".

(jj) Work-Injury Claim. An injury that is reported or reportable to the Division of Labor Statistics and Research pursuant to Labor Code Sections 6409, 6409.1 and 6413.

Note: Authority cited: Sections 54, 55, 3701.8 and 3702.10, Labor Code. Reference: Sections 59, 129, 3700, 3701, 3701.5, 3701.8, 3702, 3702.3, 3702.5, 3702.6, 3702.10, 3703, 3705, 3740-3747 and 3850, Labor Code; Section 6500, Government Code; and Sections 995.430, 996.320 and 996.330, Code of Civil Procedure.

History: 1. Repealer and new section filed 12-3-69; effective thirtieth day thereafter (Register 69, No. 49).

2. Repealer and new section filed 6-1-72; effective thirtieth day thereafter (Register 72, No. 23).

3. Repealer and new section filed 11-19-75; effective thirtieth day thereafter (Register 75, No. 47).

4. Amendment placing the defined terms in alphabetical order, removal of letter designators, amendment of existing terms, addition of terms "Administrative Director," "Affiliate Certificate," "Certificate to Administer," and "Joint Powers Authority" and addition of Note filed 12-22-92; operative 1-21-93 (Register 93, No. 2).

5. New definitions "Cancellation of Surety Bond," "Exoneration of Surety Bond," "Release of Surety Bond," and "Termination of Surety Bond" and amendment of Note filed 8-12-93; operative 9-13-93 (Register 93, No. 33).

6. Amendment filed 6-30-94; operative 6-30-94 (Register 94, No. 26).

7. Amendment of section and Note filed 5-30-2003 as an emergency; operative 5-30-2003 (Register 2003, No. 22). A Certificate of Compliance must be transmitted to OAL by 9-29-2003 or emergency language will be repealed by operation of law on the following day.

8. Certificate of Compliance as to 5-30-2003 order transmitted to OAL 9-29-2003 and filed 11-12-2003 (Register 2003, No. 46).

9. Amendment of subsections (a)(2) and (m) filed 2-9-2006; operative 3-11-2006 (Register 2006, No. 6).

Ref.: Hanna § 1.19.

§15202. Advisory Committee.

The Manager shall appoint an ad hoc committee to advise the Manager on proposed regulations relating to self-insurance.

Note: Authority cited: Sections 54, 55, 3702.10, Labor Code. Reference: Sections 54, 55, 59, 3702.10, 6160, Labor Code.

History: 1. Repealer and new section filed 6-1-72; effective thirtieth day thereafter (Register 72, No. 23).

2. Amendment of section and addition of Note filed 12-22-92; operative 1-21-93 (Register 93, No. 2).

ARTICLE 2
Certificate to Self Insure

§15203. Application.

(a) Every employer desiring to procure an initial certificate to self-insure its workers' compensation liabilities shall make application on;

(1) Form A4-1 (Rev. 2/92) for private individual employer applicants seeking an individual Certificate to Self Insure;

(2) Form A4-2 (Rev. 2/92) for public employer applicants;

(3) Form A4-3 (Rev. 1/94) for a private group employer and their members seeking an group Certificate to Self Insure.

(4) Form A4-3M (Rev 1/94) for each member of a group seeking an affiliate certificate.

(5) Form A4-5 (Rev. 11/97) for an interim self insurer seeking a permanent Certificate to Self Insure.

NOTE 1: The current application forms for private and public employers are contained in Plates A-1, A-2, A-3 and A-4 of the Appendix following the last article in these Group 2 regulations.

NOTE 2: A new application may be required when an existing self insurer reincorporates, merges, changes ownership, or adds a new or separate subsidiary or affiliate to its existing workers' compensation self insurance program. In some cases, it may be possible to amend and transfer an existing certificate without a new application.

(b) A complete application to self insure by a private employer (Form A4-1 (Rev. 2/92) shall include all attachments requested on the application form itself, and, as applicable, the following:

(1) A current, certified, independently audited financial statement complete with all schedules and notes for the past three years;

NOTE: The application of a private sector subsidiary or affiliate may include the consolidated financial statement of its parent in lieu of the subsidiary's financial statement.

(2) An unaudited financial statement or published quarterly report, or a consolidated financial statement for the current year or portion thereof;

(3) An Agreement of Assumption and Guarantee of Liabilities for each self insurer and subsidiary or affiliate applicant executed by the parent employer or majority owner, or partners;

(4) A Resolution authorizing the application to self insure and empowering employees or officers of the applicant employer to sign the application form and any other necessary documents on behalf of the applicant employer;

(5) A Resolution by the general partners, or parent corporation authorizing the execution of the Agreement of Assumption and Guarantee of Liabilities on behalf of a subsidiary or affiliate applicant employer;

(6) Original Certificates of Status or other appropriate registration documents showing that the applicant employer is licensed or registered to do business in California;

(7) An evaluation of the applicant's injury and illness prevention program or proof of a DOSH inspection pursuant to Section 15353 of these regulations; and

(8) Payment of any required application filing fee.

(c) A complete application to self insure by a public employer (Form A4-2 (Rev. 2/92) shall include all attachments requested on the public sector application form and, as applicable, the following:

(1) An Agreement of Assumption and Guarantee of Liabilities for the predecessor agency due to a unification, merger, realignment of the boundaries of an existing self insured public agency, or name change by the successor or surviving public agency;

(2) A Resolution authorizing the application to self insure and empowering employees or officers of the applicant employer or joint powers authority to sign the application form and any other necessary documents on behalf of the applicant.

(3) All public applicants shall indicate the proposed start up date of its self insurance program as part of its application.

(d) A complete application to self insure on a Form A4-3 (Rev. 1/94) by a private group of employers shall include all the attachments requested in the application form itself, and, as applicable, the following:

(1) A proforma financial statement prepared by an independent, certified public accountant with all schedules and notes for the group applicant;

(2) A current, certified, independently audited financial statement with all schedules and notes for each proposed group member for the past two years;

NOTE: The application of a private sector subsidiary or affiliate of any group member may include the consolidated financial statement of its parent in lieu of the subsidiary or affiliate financial statement;

(3) An unaudited financial statement or published quarterly report, or consolidated financial statement for the current year or portion thereof;

(4) An Agreement of Assumption and Guarantee of Liabilities of Workers' Compensation Liabilities For Group Members [Form A4-3G (Rev 1/94)] for each or listing each proposed group member and any subsidiary or affiliate of each proposed group member executed by the group administrator of the group applicant, as required in Section 15203.1 of these regulations;

(5) A Resolution by the Board of Trustees [Form GR-1 (Rev. 1/94)] of the group applicant authorizing the application to become a group self insurer and empowering the group administrator and other employees or officers or Trustees of the group applicant to sign the application form and any other necessary documents on behalf of the group applicant, and, if granted a Certificate to Self Insure, the group self insurer as required in Section 15203.3(d) of these regulations.

(6) A Resolution by the Board of Trustees of the group applicant authorizing the execution of an Agreement of Assumption and Guarantee For Workers' Compensation Liabilities on behalf of the proposed group members and any future members of the group self insurer granted an Affiliate Certificate;

(7) An original Certificate of Status or other appropriate registration documents showing the group applicant and each group member is licensed or registered to do business in California;

(8) An evaluation of the group applicant and group members injury and illness prevention program or proof of a DOSH inspection pursuant to Section 15353 of these regulations;

(9) An original, executed Indemnity Agreement and Power of Attorney of Joint and Several Liability between the group applicant and each proposed member pursuant to Section 15479 of these regulations.

(10) Payment of the required application fee as required by Section 15204 of these regulations.

(11) A copy of the Initial Feasibility Study as required in Section 15471 of these regulations.

(12) Agreement and Undertaking for Security Deposit.

(13) Completed application forms from proposed members.

(e) A complete application to self insure on a Form A4-4 (Rev. 1/94) by each member of a group shall include all the attachments requested in the application form itself, and, as applicable, the following:

(1) A current copy of the applicant's certified, independently audited, financial statement complete with all schedules and notes; or

(2) A current copy of the applicant's reviewed financial statement prepared by a certified public accountant, complete with all schedules and notes, provided the private group self insurer can demonstrate and maintain a consolidated minimum net worth twice that required in Section 15203.2(f).

NOTE: If the report of the financial condition is dated more than 12 months prior to the date of this application, the Director may require interim financial statement certified by the appropriate finance officer and dated not less than 3 months from the date of this application.

(3) Resolution to be Self Insured as a Member of the Group Self Insurer.

(4) Indemnity Agreement and Power of Attorney, as required in section 15479.

(f) To any joint powers authority which pools the workers' compensation liabilities of its public agency members, the Manager shall issue a Certificate to Self Insure to the joint powers authority and the master certificate number to the joint powers authority. All members of the joint powers authority shall be issued an affiliate certificate numbers under the certificate number issued to the joint powers authority.

(g) An applicant for self insurance filing a private individual employer application, an interim self insurer application or a public employer application will be notified in writing within 14 days, that an application is complete or deficient. An applicant for self insurance filing a private group employer application, will be notified in writing within 30 days, that an application is complete or deficient. A notice indicating that the application is deficient will include a list of items required to be included or completed.

(h) Upon receipt of a complete private individual employer application or an interim self insurer application, the applicant will be notified within 45 days of the Director's decision to allow self insurance. The maximum processing time for a private individual employer application is 45 days, the minimum time is 21 days and the median time is 30 days.

(i) Upon receipt of a complete public entity application, the applicant will be notified within 30 days of approval of application. The maximum processing time for a public employer application is 30 days, the minimum time is 7 days and the median time is 14 days.

(j) Upon receipt of a complete private group employer application, the applicant will be notified within 90 days of the approval of the application. The maximum processing time for a private group employer application is 90 days, the minimum time is 30 days and the median time is 60 days.

Note: Authority cited: Sections 54, 55, 59 and 3702.10, Labor Code. Reference: Sections 3700, 3700(b), 3701, 3702, 3702.5 and 6401.7(a), Labor Code; and Sections 15374-15378, Government Code.

History: 1. Repealer and new section filed 6-1-72; effective thirtieth day thereafter (Register 72, No. 23).

2. Amendment filed 11-19-75; effective thirtieth day thereafter (Register 75, No. 47).

3. Amendment filed 11-21-78; effective thirtieth day thereafter (Register 78, No. 47).

4. New article 2 heading, newly designated subsections (a) and (b)-(b)(1), new subsections (b)(2)-(g)(1), amendment of Note, and repealer of form filed 12-22-92; operative 1-21-93 (Register 93, No. 2).

5. Amendment filed 6-30-94; operative 6-30-94 (Register 94, No. 26).

6. Amendment of subsection (a)(4), new subsection (a)(5), amendment of Note 1 and amendment of subsections (g) and (h) filed 6-4-98; operative 7-4-98 (Register 98, No. 23).

Ref.: Hanna §§ 1.19, 2.11[1].

§15203.1. Agreement of Assumption and Guarantee of Subsidiary's or Affiliate's Liabilities.

(a) Each private subsidiary or affiliate applicant for a Certificate to Self Insure shall provide an Agreement of Assumption and Guarantee of Liabilities executed by the parent company, general partners, or owners having controlling ownership in accordance with Section 15211.2 of these regulations.

If the parent entity, general partner(s), or owners having controlling ownership will not execute the Assumption and Guarantee agreement, the Director may:

(1) Require a deposit level of 200% of the master certificate holder's, subsidiary's or affiliate's estimated future liabilities for the payment of compensation, or higher, in lieu of the Agreement of Assumption and Guarantee of Liabilities; or

(2) Deny the application to self insure by the private applicant.

(b) Private group self insurers shall provide an individual Agreement of Assumption and Guarantee of Liabilities of Workers' Compensation Liabilities For Group Members for each group member or a single agreement listing all group members and all subsidiary or affiliates of each group member executed by the group administrator of the group applicant. If the group self insurer or group applicant will not execute the Agreement of Assumption and Guarantee of Liabilities of Workers' Compensation Liabilities For Group Members for each group member, the Director:

(1) may require a deposit level of 200% of the group self insurer's estimated future liabilities for the payment of compensation, or higher, in lieu of the Agreement of Assumption and Guarantee of Liabilities; or

(2) may deny the application to self insure by the private group applicant or group member.

Note: Authority cited: Sections 54, 55 and 3702.10, Labor Code. Reference: Sections 59, 3550, 3700, 3701, 3701.5, 3702, 3702.10 and 3705, Labor Code.

History: 1. New section filed 11-21-78; effective thirtieth day thereafter (Register 78, No. 47).

2. Amendment of section heading and text filed 12-22-92; operative 1-21-93 (Register 93, No. 2).

3. Amendment filed 6-30-94; operative 6-30-94 (Register 94, No. 26).

§15203.2. Continuing Financial Capacity.

(a) All private self insurers and all private group self insurers, shall submit annually a current, certified, independently audited financial statement complete with all notes and schedules. If the private self insurer did not prepare a current, certified, independently audited financial statement, the self insurer shall advise the Manager of that fact in writing and submit a consolidated financial statement prepared by an independent certified public accountant (CPA).

(b) Any joint powers authority which is solely responsible for the self insurance claims of its public members shall submit annually to the Manager a consolidated report of its financial condition, and/or if available, a current, certified, independently audited financial statement complete with all notes and schedules.

(c) All private group members of a private group self insurer shall annually submit a current, certified, independently audited financial statement complete with all notes and schedules to the Board of Trustees of the group self insurer. The group administrator shall make any of the financial statements available to the Manager upon request and shall advise the Manager of any group member not having a certified, independently audited financial statement.

Exception: A private group member authorized to self insure pursuant to Section 15203(e)(2), shall annually submit a current, reviewed financial statement to the Board of Trustees of the group self insurer.

(d) Impairment of solvency indicated by a marked reduction in financial strength or the lack of an independently prepared, audited financial statement, or the lack of the minimum net worth requirement set forth in subsection (e) of this section is good cause for increased security deposit or involuntary revocation of any Certificate to Self Insure, Affiliate Certificate or Subsidiary Certificate by the Director.

(e) After July 1, 1994, all private individual employer applicants for a master Certificate to Self Insure shall demonstrate and maintain a current net worth of at least $5,000,000 and average net income for the past 5 years of at least $500,000.

Exception: Any existing private self insurer granted a Certificate to Self Insure prior to the July 1, 1994 shall only need to maintain a net worth of at least $2,200,000 and an average net income for the past 5 years of at least $300,000.

(f) All private group self insurers shall demonstrate and maintain a consolidated net worth of the group members of at least $5,000,000 and a consolidated annual net income of the group members of $500,000, and sufficient income to fund:

(1) the group self insurer's actuarially projected claim liabilities at the 80% confidence level;

(2) to pay the expected administrative expenses to operate the group self insurer's business operations; and

(3) to post the security deposit required.

Note: Consolidated net worth and consolidated net income of group members shall be determined only from members with current certified, independently audited financial statement.

Note: Authority cited: Sections 54, 55 and 3702.10, Labor Code. Reference: Sections 59, 3700, 3701, 3702 and 3702.10, Labor Code.

History: 1. New section filed 12-22-92; operative 1-21-93 (Register 93, No. 2).

2. Amendment of section and Note filed 6-30-94; operative 6-30-94 (Register 94, No. 26).

§15203.3. Resolution To Authorize Self Insurance for a Private Sector Applicant or Group Applicant.

(a) The resolution to authorize self insurance of workers' compensation required as part of the application for a certificate to self insure by any private sector applicant or private group self insurer shall be adopted by the Board of Directors of each corporation, or the general partners of an applicant partnership or joint venture, or owner of an applicant sole proprietorship, or Board of Trustees of an applicant group self insurer. The resolution to authorize self insurance shall include the following:

(1) A statement identifying the applicant by corporate or other legal name, the state of registration, and the date that the resolution was adopted;

(2) Identify by title of appointed officers or other company employees who have the authority to sign the application, execute any and all documents required for the application and do subsequent acts as required to maintain self insurance approval.

(b) If a private self insurer or group self insurer reincorporates, merges, or changes its identity, a new resolution shall be submitted to the Manager within 30 days to ratify the maintenance of the self insured's responsibility under the successor's identity. The Manager may extend the period of time for good cause.

(c) A model corporate resolution shall be included as part of the application form and the Manager shall provide separate model resolutions to self insurers which are partnerships or other non-corporate structures upon request.

(d) A group self insurer resolution Form GR-1 (Rev. 1/94) shall be attached as part of the private group employer application and executed by the group applicant Board of Trustees.

Note: The current group self insurer resolution, Form GR-1 (Rev. 1/94), is contained in Plate B of the Appendix following the last article of these Group 2 regulations.

Note: Authority cited: Sections 54, 55 and 3702.10, Labor Code. Reference: Sections 59, 3700, 3701, 3702 and 3702.10, Labor Code.

History: 1. New section filed 11-21-78; effective thirtieth day thereafter (Register 78, No. 47).

2. Amendment filed 1-19-79; effective thirtieth day thereafter (Register 79, No. 3).

3. Amendment of section heading and text filed 12-22-92; operative 1-21-93 (Register 93, No. 2).

4. Amendment of section heading and text filed 6-30-94; operative 6-30-94 (Register 94, No. 26).

§15203.4. Resolution to Self Insure for Public Entities.

(a) The resolution of the governing body of a public entity or joint powers authority seeking approval for a certificate to self insure shall be executed by the governing board and attached to the application form. The resolution shall be sealed with the seal of the adopting agency or the resolution's signatures shall be notarized.

Note: The officers of the joint powers authority which is the holder of the master Certificate to Self Insure may sign documents on behalf of the affiliated members of the JPA for self insurance purposes, including the Self Insurer's Annual Report.

Note: Authority cited: Sections 54, 55, and 3702.10, Labor Code. Reference: Sections 59, 3700, 3702 and 3702.10, Labor Code.

History: 1. New section filed 12-22-92; operative 1-21-93 (Register 93, No. 2).

§15203.5. Agreement and Undertaking for Security Deposit.

(a) All private employer applicants for self insurance shall execute an Agreement and Undertaking For Security Deposit as part of the application process.

(b) All security deposits shall be posted in accordance with the provisions of the Agreement and Undertaking.

(c) The form of such agreement and undertaking shall be supplied by the Manager as part of the application (Form A4-1 (Rev. 2/92) for a private individual employer and Form A4-GAU (1/94) for a private group self insurer).

Note: The current agreement and undertaking form is contained in Plate H of the Appendix following the last Article of these Group 2 regulations. This agreement is contained in the application form for applicants to be self-insured after January 1, 1993. The Agreement and Undertaking for Security Deposit Form for a Group Self Insurer (Form A4-GAU (1/94) is in the Appendix following the Application for a Certificate of Consent to Self Insure By A Group of Employers.

Note: Authority cited: Sections 54, 55 and 3702.10, Labor Code. Reference: Sections 59, 3701, 3701.5 and 3702.10, Labor Code.

History: 1. New section filed 11-21-78; effective thirtieth day thereafter (Register 78, No. 47).

2. Renumbering and amendment of former section 15203.5 to section 15203.6 and renumbering and amendment of former section 15213 to section 15203.5 filed 12-22-92; operative 1-21-93 (Register 93, No. 2).

3. Amendment of subsection (c) and following Note filed 6-30-94; operative 6-30-94 (Register 94, No. 26).

§15203.6. Delayed Start-up of a Self Insurance Program.

(a) The certificate to self insure for public and private employers shall be initially valid for six months after the date of approval by the Director. If the self insurer has not initiated its self insurance program within the initial six month period, the approval of the certificate to self insure shall be void and a new application shall be filed for approval. Once the self insurance program has been initiated in the initial 6 month period, the certificate to self insure shall be valid until revoked by order of the Director.

Note: A private employer applicant which fails to initiate a self insurance program within three months of notification of approval by the Director may be required to establish current good standing with the Secretary of State and to provide current financial information before issuance of a certificate to self insure.

Note: Authority cited: Sections 54, 55 and 3702.10, Labor Code. Reference: Sections 59, 3700, 3702.10, Labor Code.

History: 1. Renumbering and amendment of former section 15203.5 to section 15203.6 filed 12-22-92; operative 1-21-93 (Register 93, No. 2).

§15203.7. Issuance of the Certificate to Self Insure and Notice to Employees of Self Insured Status.

(a) Upon the Director's approval of an employer's application and, if required, the posting of an assumption agreement and adequate security deposit with the Department, within seven days the self insurer shall receive confirmation of its self insured status by receipt of a Certificate to Self Insure issued and signed by the Manager.

(b) The original Certificate to Self Insure or a copy of the original certificate to self insure shall be prominently displayed at the self insurer's principal place of business in California.

(c) Notice to employees of workers' compensation coverage as required by Labor Code Section 3550 shall be accomplished by display of a copy of the self insurer's certificate to self insure accompanied by a notice stating the name of the person(s) or administrative agency responsible for claims adjustment.

(d) If a self insurer is required to provide evidence of its approved self insured status to prove compliance with Labor Code Section 3700, the Manager shall provide a Certification of Self Insurance upon request from the certificate holder.

Note: A sample Certificate of Self Insurance is contained in Plate C of the Appendix following the last article in these Group 2 regulations.

Note: Authority cited: Sections 54, 55 and 3702.10, Labor Code. Reference: Sections 59, 3550, 3700, 3701, 3702, 3702.10, Labor Code.

History: 1. Renumbering and amendment of former section 15203.7 to section 15203.8 and new section filed 12-22-92; operative 1-21-93 (Register 93, No. 2).

§15203.8. Change in Status.

(a) The self insurer, public or private shall notify the Manager in writing within 30 days of the following actions:

(1) Any amendment to the self insurer's articles, charter, or agreement of incorporation, association, or co-partnership which changes its identity or business structure or ownership in a material manner from the status as it existed at the time of issuance of its certificate to self insure; or

(2) The self insurer proposes to cease doing business entirely, proposes to cease doing business in California, or proposes to dispose of, by sale or otherwise, the controlling interest of the business for which the certificate to self insure was issued.

(b) If any self insurer desires to retain its self insured status following any amendment to the articles, charter, or agreement of incorporation, association, or copartnership which changes its identity or business structure or ownership, the self insurer shall provide to the Manager the following information:

(1) A written description of the date the event(s) occurred;

(2) Copies of Certificates of Status or other appropriate registration documents filed with the Secretary of State in which the self insurer is incorporated concerning the change of the self insurer's status; and

(3) Written notice indicating that the certificate holder will continue to provide an annual financial statement or that a financial statement will be issued by a parent corporation.

(c) If a self insured corporation reincorporates, merges, or changes its identity, a new resolution shall be submitted to the Manager in accordance with Section 15203.3 of these regulations.

Note: Authority cited: Sections 54, 55 and 3702.10, Labor Code. Reference: Sections 59, 3700, 3701, 3701.5, 3702, 3702.3, 3702.10 and 3703, Labor Code.

History: 1. New section filed 11-21-78; effective thirtieth day thereafter (Register 78, No. 47).

2. Renumbering and amendment of former section 15203.7 to section 15203.8 filed 12-22-92; operative 1-21-93 (Register 93, No. 2).

3. Amendment of subsection (a) filed 6-30-94; operative 6-30-94 (Register 94, No. 26).

§15203.9. Validity of Certificate to Self Insure.

(a) A certificate to self insure shall be valid only to the private corporation, partnership, company, subsidiary, affiliate public entity, joint powers authority, group self insurer, or private group member to which the certificate to self insure, affiliate certificate or subsidiary certificate was issued. Each subsidiary or affiliate shall be issued its own certificate to self insure.

(b) Except as provided in Labor Code Section 3701.7, the Manager shall issue a new certificate to self insure with an effective date no earlier than the date the application and all other documents or information required by these regulations were submitted and deemed a complete application.

Note: Authority cited: Sections 54, 55 and 3702.10, Labor Code. Reference: Sections 59, 3701, 3701.5 and 3702.10, Labor Code.

History: 1. New section filed 12-22-92; operative 1-21-93 (Register 93, No. 2).

2. Amendment of subsection (a) filed 6-30-94; operative 6-30-94 (Register 94, No. 26).

§15203.10. Reinstatement of a Certificate to Self Insure.

(a) A self insurer, who because of a legal change in business or corporate structure or in its legal name, has had its self insurance privilege terminated may have its certificate to self insure reinstated without lapse, providing the employer can requalify for self insurance.

(b) To request reinstatement of a certificate to self insure, the applicant shall submit to the Manager a complete application and a statement that the applicant assumes and guarantees all workers' compensation liabilities incurred during its prior period of self insurance, and will be responsible for any additional self insured liabilities incurred after termination of its certificate to self insure. The Manager shall accept the statement of the employer's assumption of all past liabilities if signed by a corporate officer, attested to by the corporate secretary and sealed with the corporate seal. This must be confirmed within 90 days by execution of the standard Agreement of Assumption and Guarantee of Liabilities and an Assumption Resolution as part of the application before the certificate to self insure can be reinstated.

Note: Authority cited: Sections 54, 55 and 3702.10, Labor Code. Reference: Sections 59, 3700, 3701, 3702, 3702.10, Labor Code.

History: 1. New section filed 12-22-92; operative 1-21-93 (Register 93, No. 2).

§15204. Application Filing Fee.

(a) Each private employer making application for a certificate to self insure shall at the time of filing the application, pay a non-refundable filing fee on the following basis:

(1) A filing fee to accompany a single application or the first of more than one application submitted together shall be $500;

(2) For each additional application submitted with the first application, the filing fee shall be an additional $100;

(3) Any subsequent applications, determined by the Manager to be necessary but not submitted with the original filing of an application, shall be considered a new application and the filing fee will be $500;

(b) Any subsequent filing of an application by an existing private self insurer to add a new subsidiary or affiliate, or required due to merger, acquisition, or reincorporation shall be considered a new application and shall be subject to the payment of the fees set forth in subsection (a).

(c) No application filing fee shall be required from a public entity making application for a certificate to self insure.

(d) Each private group self insurer making an application to obtain a certificate to self insure for the group shall at the time of filing of the group application, pay a non-refundable filing fee on the following basis:

(1) A filing fee for the group applicant as set forth in subsection (a)(1) of this section;

(2) An additional filing fee for each proposed group member submitted at the same time as the group application as set forth in subsection (a)(2) of this section;

(3) Any subsequent group member filings determined by the Manager to be necessary but not submitted with the original group application will pay a non-refundable application fee as set forth in subsection (a)(3) of this section; and

(4) Any subsequent filing of an application by an existing group self insurer to add new group members, or required due to merger, acquisition, or reincorporation shall be considered a new application and shall be subject to the payment of fees as set forth in subsection (a) of this section.

Note: Authority cited: Sections 54, 55 and 3702.10, Labor Code. Reference: Sections 59, 3700, 3702.5 and 3702.10, Labor Code.

History: 1. New section filed 11-19-75; effective thirtieth day thereafter (Register 75, No. 47).

2. Amendment of section heading and text and adoption of Plates A-1 through C and Plate H filed 12-22-92; operative 1-21-93 (Register 93, No. 2).

3. Change without regulatory effect relocating Appendix Plates to section 15463 filed 9-14-93 pursuant to title 1, section 100, California Code of Regulations (Register 93, No. 38).

4. Designation of subsection (a) and new subsections (d)-(d)(4) filed 6-30-94; operative 6-30-94 (Register 94, No. 26).

§15205. Interim Certificates.

(a) The Manager may issue an Interim Certificate of Consent to Self Insure to a subsidiary or affiliate of an existing private self insurer. The Interim Certificate of Consent to Self Insure will be issued for a period not to exceed 180-days. An application for a permanent Certificate to Self Insure as set forth in Section 15203 and the application filing fees as set forth in Section 15204 just be submitted within 90 days of issuance of an interim certificate.

(b) To qualify for an Interim Certificate, the existing private self insurer must demonstrate the following:

(1) Net worth on the last financial report filed with the Manager of Self Insurance Plans, pursuant to Section 15203.2, that shows at least $10 million in net worth,

(2) The private self insurer holding the Master Certificate of Consent to Self Insure has furnished proof satisfactory to the Manager of financial responsibility and ability to guarantee the payment of any compensation due.

(3) The subsidiary or affiliate being added to the self insurance program does not represent more than 50% of the annual payroll of the existing self insurer as reported on the most recent Self Insurers' Annual Report.

(c) A request for an Interim Certificate shall be made by the existing private self insurer in writing to the Manager and provide the following information on each subsidiary or affiliate new to the self insurance program:

(1) The full legal name, state of incorporation, and Federal Tax Identification Number;

(2) The requested effective date of the Interim Certificate;

(3) The annual payroll of the subsidiary or affiliate during the last 12 months; or, the latest 12-month period for which payroll figures are available and what 12 month period is being reported.

(4) A statement that the Master Certificate holder shall be financially responsible to pay all workers' compensation claims arising out of the period of time its subsidiary or affiliate is granted an Interim Certificate;

NOTE: The Manager shall prepare a model letter that will contain all the necessary information to permit the private self insurer to request issuance of an Interim Certificate. The Manager shall provide this model letter to the self insurer upon request.

(d) Upon receipt of a written request for an Interim Certificate from a private self insurer meeting the requirements set forth in Section 15205(b) and (c), the Manager shall issue the Interim Certificate within 14 days.

(1) An applicant for an interim certificate will be notified in writing within 14 days if the application is incomplete and what specific information is required.

(e) To qualify for a permanent Certificate of Consent to Self Insure, the Interim Self Insurer will be required to comply with subsections 15203(b)(3)-(b) and (b)(8) and to submit Application Form A4-5 (Rev. 11/97).

Note: Sections 54, 55 and 3702.10, Labor Code. Reference: Sections 59, 3700, 3702.5 and 3702.10, Labor Code.

History: 1. New section filed 2-26-97; operative 3-28-97 (Register 97, No. 9).

2. Amendment of subsection (e) filed 6-4-98; operative 7-4-98 (Register 98, No. 23).

Ref.: Hanna § 2.11[1].

ARTICLE 3
Security Deposit Requirements

§15210. Security Deposit.

(a) Public self insurers are not required to post or maintain a security deposit with the Director for workers' compensation liabilities.

(b) Private self insurers shall post and maintain a security deposit, in accordance with the provisions of Labor Code Section 3701 and the requirements of Article 3 of this subchapter 2 and/or in accordance with Labor Code Section 3701.8 and Article 3.1 of this subchapter 2.

(c) The minimum required security deposit pursuant to Labor Code Section 3701 for existing, private self insurer's shall be equal to:

(1) 135 percent of the private self insurer's estimated future liabilities for the payment of compensation for known claims, adjusted by any previously documented reductions to known claim liability for specific excess insurance coverage pursuant to Section 15300(e) of these regulations; and

(2) a deposit, consisting of the average annual estimated future liability for the past five (5) years reported on the Self Insurer's Annual Report, posted in advance for liabilities of the current year; and

(3) an adjustment to reduce the liability to be reported on individual claims due to any new documentation of specific excess insurance coverage not previously reported pursuant to Section 15300(e) of these regulations.

The required deposit may be increased at the Director's discretion as set forth in Article 3 of these regulations. Said future liability may be ascertained from any relevant source.

(d) New private self insurers shall initially post a security deposit pursuant to Labor Code Section 3701 in an amount equal to the greater of the following:

(1) The prior three (3) years' incurred liability; or

(2) The statutory minimum required by Labor Code Section 3701(b); or

(3) A higher amount approved by the Director.

(e) The addition of a new subsidiary or affiliate private self insurer to the holder of an existing Certificate to Self Insure shall initially post a security deposit pursuant to Labor Code Section 3701 in an amount equal to the greater of the following:

(1) The average one year incurred liability for the new subsidiary or affiliate self insurer based upon the prior three years' incurred liability; or

(2) A higher amount approved by the Director.

(f) Security deposit shall be posted in the form of:

(1) A surety bond executed on State issued bond and rider forms pursuant to Section 15212 of these regulations;

(2) An irrevocable letter of credit issued by a bank or savings institution or other financial institution pursuant to Section 15215 of these regulations;

(3) Approved securities in the form of government issued or corporate issued securities, meeting the requirements of Section 15213 of these regulations;

(4) Cash in trust deposited pursuant to requirements of Section 15214 of these regulations; or

(5) Any combination of one or more of the above four types of security deposit.

(g) Failure to maintain the required amount of deposit or to post an acceptable form of deposit as set forth in this Article shall be good cause for assessment of civil penalties pursuant to Labor Code Section 3702.9(a) by the Manager and/or, in the Director's discretion, revocation of the Certificate to Self Insure.

(h) Failure to post and maintain the required amount of security deposit for a period of 60 days shall be good cause for the Manager to summarily revoke a Certificate of Consent to Self-Insure. The summary revocation of the Self Insurer's Certificate of Consent will provide for a 15-day notice of termination, without a hearing.

(1) Notwithstanding subsection (h) above, the employer may still request a hearing on the Manager's Revocation Order before the Director as provided in Article 11 of this subchapter 2.

(2) A self insurer requesting a hearing pursuant to subsection (h)(1) shall be required to provide proof of workers' compensation coverage under a policy from an admitted carrier for the period of time without security deposit or proof of compliance with the Manager's request to post security.

Note: Authority cited: Sections 54, 55, 3701.8 and 3702.10, Labor Code. Reference: Sections 59, 3700, 3701, 3701.5, 3701.8, 3702, 3702.3, 3702.6, 3702.10 and 3740-3745, Labor Code.

History: 1. Amendment of article heading, section heading and text and adoption of Note filed 12-22-92; operative 1-21-93 (Register 93, No. 2).

2. Change without regulatory effect amending subsection (f)(3) filed 8-27-98 pursuant to section 100, title 1, California Code of Regulations (Register 98, No. 35).

3. Change without regulatory effect amending subsections (c)(1) and (c)(3) filed 4-9-2003 pursuant to

section 100, title 1, California Code of Regulations (Register 2003, No. 15).

4. Amendment of section and Note filed 5-30-2003 as an emergency; operative 5-30-2003 (Register 2003, No. 22). A Certificate of Compliance must be transmitted to OAL by 9-29-2003 or emergency language will be repealed by operation of law on the following day.

5. Certificate of Compliance as to 5-30-2003 order, including amendment of subsection (h)(1), transmitted to OAL 9-29-2003 and filed 11-12-2003 (Register 2003, No. 46).

Ref.: Hanna § 1.19.

§15210.1. Adjustments in the Amount of Security Deposit.

(a) Any amount of the security deposit required pursuant to Labor Code Section 3701 shall be reviewed by the Manager at least annually following receipt of the private Self-Insurer's Annual Report.

(b) The private self insurer shall post any annual increase in security deposit required pursuant to Labor Code Section 3701 indicated in the deposit calculations contained in the Self-Insurer's Annual Report or as determined by the Manager due to an audit, change in the self-insured employer's program or change in deposit rate. The deposit shall cover both prior known liabilities; plus an advance deposit for the current year liabilities based on an average estimated future liability of claims for the past 5 years; minus credit for liabilities above the retention level of specific excess workers' compensation insurance policies as reported on the current year annual report. This deposit posting is due no later than May 1 each year.

(c) At the request of any private self insurer for a reduction or where a decrease in security deposit is indicated in the deposit calculations on the annual report, no reduction of security deposit already posted shall be made without prior written authorization of the Manager. Self Insurance Plans shall review each certificate holder's annual report and the certificate holder's file to determine the extent to which a decrease in deposit, if any, may be authorized.

(d) For good cause, the Manager shall require the private self insurer to post and maintain additional security deposit or adjust the deposit rate for a specific private self insurer above the statutory minimum deposit set forth in Labor Code Sections 3701, 3701.7, and 3701.8. Good cause includes, but is not limited to, understated future liability of claims on the Self-Insurer's Annual Report; a pattern of understated liabilities in claim files audited in an audit; failure to report all claims; poor administration of claims or payment of benefits due injured workers found in the audit results of the Office of Benefits Audits and Enforcement in the Division of Workers' Compensation or audits by Self Insurance Plans; lack of an effective safety and health program as indicated by final citations issued by the Division of Occupational Safety and Health showing repeat or willful violation of safety and health regulations; impairment of financial condition of the self insurer; the result of evaluation of an application to self-insure; or to cover a period of unlawful self insurance; or being required to post security deposit in whole or part pursuant to Section 3701.8 of the Labor Code and Article 3.1 (commencing with Section 15220) of this subchapter 2.

(e) Whenever the Manager determines that a deposit increase is required to be posted by a self insurer, the Manager shall send written notice to the self insurer pursuant to Labor Code Section 3701(b) and (j) of the amount of deposit due in order to create a perfected security interest for the Self Insurer's Security Fund.

(f) Any increase in a required self insurer's security deposit due to understated liabilities on the private employer's Self Insurer's Annual Report, shall be reported to the Security Fund. The Security Fund shall be authorized to adjust the deposit assessment for the alternative composite deposit.

Note: Authority cited: Sections 54, 55, 3701.8 and 3702.10, Labor Code. Reference: Sections 59, 3700, 3701, 3701.5, 3701.7, 3701.8, 3702, 3702.3, 3702.6, 3702.10, 3740, 3741, 3742, 6319(f), 6401.7, Labor Code.

History: 1. New section filed 12-22-92; operative 1-21-93 (Register 93, No. 2).

2. Change without regulatory effect amending subsection (e) filed 8-27-98 pursuant to section 100, title 1, California Code of Regulations (Register 98, No. 35).

3. Amendment of section and Note filed 5-30-2003 as an emergency; operative 5-30-2003 (Register 2003, No. 22). A Certificate of Compliance must be transmitted to OAL by 9-29-2003 or emergency language will be repealed by operation of law on the following day.

4. Certificate of Compliance as to 5-30-2003 order transmitted to OAL 9-29-2003 and filed 11-12-2003 (Register 2003, No. 46).

§15210.2. Deposit Adjustment Upon Revocation of Certificate to Self Insure.

(a) As part of the revocation of a Certificate to Self Insure pursuant to Sections 15422 and 15423 of these regulations, the Manager shall determine the need for a special revocation audit of the claims of any private self insurer and the need for a deposit adjustment to secure future liabilities of the revoked private self insurer pursuant to Labor Code Section 3701 and/or Section 3701.8.

(b) The amount of deposit or deposit rate required by the Manager on a revocation of a private self insurer's certificate to self insure may be at an amount or rate above the minimum required by Labor Code Section 3701 and/or Section 3701.8. The Manager in his/her discretion shall adjust the rate of deposit or the amount of deposit down to the statutory minimum required to secure the remaining workers' compensation liabilities for a revoked self insurer as necessary over time as the liabilities of the remaining claims inventory are run off by the administrator.

Note: Authority cited: Sections 54, 55, 3701.8 and 3702.10, Labor Code. Reference: Sections 59, 129, 3700, 3701, 3701.5, 3701.8, 3702, 3702.3, 3702.6, 3702.8, 3740-3745, Labor Code.

History: 1. New section filed 12-22-92; operative 1-21-93 (Register 93, No. 2).

2. Amendment of section heading, section and Note filed 5-30-2003 as an emergency; operative 5-30-2003 (Register 2003, No. 22). A Certificate of Compliance must be transmitted to OAL by 9-29-2003 or emergency language will be repealed by operation of law on the following day.

3. Certificate of Compliance as to 5-30-2003 order transmitted to OAL 9-29-2003 and filed 11-12-2003 (Register 2003, No. 46).

§15210.3. Insurance Coverage.

(a) Any self insurer shall be permitted to insure any part of its liability to secure the payment of compensation pursuant to Labor Code Section 3700 with a standard workers' compensation insurance policy issued by a carrier. Full coverage of a self insurer's workers' compensation liability under a standard workers' compensation insurance policy shall be good cause for revocation of the certificate to self insure.

(b) All self insurers shall provide the Manager with information on any standard workers' compensation insurance policies, specific excess workers' compensation insurance coverage, and any aggregate excess (stop loss) workers' compensation insurance coverage carried, as part of the Self Insurer's Annual Report or upon the request of the Manager. Evidence of any of these three types of insurance coverage shall also be provided to the Manager in the form of a Certificate of Insurance from the carrier, along with any changes, cancellations, revisions, or new policies.

(c) Upon the request of the Manager, the self insurer shall provide a Certificate of Insurance or a copy of the workers' compensation insurance policy or policies maintained by the self insurer.

(d) Specific workers' compensation insurance policies are not required to be purchased or maintained by any self insurer. A self insurer who elects to purchase an aggregate excess policy shall not be given any credit toward the security deposit to be posted due to aggregate excess insurance coverage.

Exception: Every Private group self insurer shall purchase and maintain specific excess workers' compensation insurance policy coverage as set forth in Section 15478 of these regulations.

(e) Any self insurer who elects to purchase an aggregate workers' compensation excess policy shall not be given any credit by the Manager toward the security deposit to be posted due to aggregate excess insurance coverage.

Note: Authority cited: Sections 54, 55 and 3702.10, Labor Code. Reference: Sections 59, 129, 3700, 3701, 3701.5, 3702, 3740, 3743 and 3744, Labor Code.

History: 1. New section filed 12-22-92; operative 1-21-93 (Register 93, No. 2).

2. Amendment of subsections (c)-(e) filed 6-30-94; operative 6-30-94 (Register 94, No. 26).

§15211. Deposits for Subsidiary and Affiliate Self-Insurers.

(a) With the approval of the Manager, any subsidiary or affiliate private self insurer may post a separate deposit for its workers' compensation liabilities as part of the total security deposit posted to secure the liabilities under any Certificate to Self Insure issued to any self insured program. When approved, each subsidiary or affiliate self insurer posting its own deposit shall report its workers' compensation liabilities on the self insurer's annual report as a separate reporting location.

(b) Subsidiary and affiliated self insurers may be included in the security deposit of a holding corporation that has a certificate to self insure.

(1) For purposes of these regulations, Section 189 of the California Corporations Code shall be used to define "subsidiary corporation" and "holding corporation."

(2) For purposes of these regulations, legal entities with common ownership are sufficient to qualify for a common security deposit and may be included as co-principals on the same surety bond, or as named entities on a letter of credit, or as co-trustors on securities or a cash deposit.

(c) The Manager may require certification or other proof of stock ownership of the self-insured subsidiary corporation or corporations before allowing a self insurer to be included in the deposit of another self insurer.

(d) If the private holding corporation loses its power to elect a majority of the directors of a subsidiary self-insured corporation or corporations, the holding corporation and subsidiary corporation or corporations shall notify the Manager within 30 days of the event.

(e) Each type of security deposit posted by a private group self insurer shall be applicable to the liabilities of all members of the group self insurer and shall be amended, if necessary, to include all new members added to the group self insurer.

Note: Authority cited: Sections 54, 55 and 3702.10, Labor Code. Reference: Sections 129, 3700, 3700(b), 3701, 3702, 3702.5, 3702.6, 3703, 3704, 3705 and 3740-3745, Labor Code; and Section 189, Corporations Code.

History: 1. Amendment filed 6-1-72; effective thirtieth day thereafter (Register 72, No. 23).

2. Amendment filed 11-19-75; effective thirtieth day thereafter (Register 75, No. 47).

3. Amendment filed 11-21-78; effective thirtieth day thereafter (Register 78, No. 47).

4. Editorial correction to remove duplicate history note (Register 78, No. 50).

5. Amendment filed 12-22-92; operative 1-21-93 (Register 93, No. 2).

6. Amendment of subsection (a) and new subsection (e) filed 6-30-94; operative 6-30-94 (Register 94, No. 26).

7. Editorial correction of History 6 (Register 96, No. 52).

§15211.1. Appeals to Increase in Security Deposit Due to Impaired Financial Condition of Self-Insurer.

(a) Where the Manager has required an increase in security deposit due to the impaired financial status of the self insurer and the self insurer wishes to appeal the Manager's decision, upon receipt of the written appeal, the Manager shall order a detailed, third-party financial evaluation of the private self insurer in order to determine the employer's financial strength. Such a third party financial evaluation shall include, but not be limited to, a Dun & Bradstreet Risk Assessment Report. The cost of the third party financial evaluation report shall be paid by the self insurer. Upon receipt of the evaluation report, the appeal will be considered by the Manager.

Note: Authority cited: Sections 54, 55 and 3702.10, Labor Code. Reference: Section 3701, Labor Code.

History: 1. New section filed 6-1-72; effective thirtieth day thereafter (Register 72, No. 23).

2. Repealer and new section filed 11-19-75; effective thirtieth day thereafter (Register 75, No. 47).

3. Repealer and new section filed 12-22-92; operative 1-21-93 (Register 93, No. 2).

§15211.2. Agreement of Assumption and Guarantee of Liabilities.

(a) At the discretion of the Manager, the workers' compensation liabilities of a self-insurer may be assumed and guaranteed in whole or part by any other legal entity or person.

(b) The agreement of assumption and guarantee of liabilities shall be written upon a form provided by the Manager (Form A4-6 (Rev. 11/97)).

NOTE: The current Agreement forms are contained in Plate D of the Appendix following the last Article of these Subchapter 2 regulations.

(c) Regardless of whether a private affiliate or subsidiary or the self insurer's parent company's financial condition is relied upon to qualify a subsidiary, affiliate or master self insurer for self insurance, the private subsidiary, affiliate or master self insurer shall provide an agreement of assumption and guarantee of liabilities executed by the owner, or controlling partners, or holding corporation or other entity acceptable to the Manager.

EXCEPTION: At the discretion of the Director, the parental assumption agreement may be waived, but if waived, the Manager shall require the self insurer to post and maintain a minimum of a 200% deposit rate, in lieu of the assumption agreement.

(d) A corporate guarantor shall provide a Board of Directors resolution which authorizes the assumption and guarantee of the liabilities of the affiliated or subsidiary company or public agency and the board resolution shall grant signature authority to the person or position title of the person signing the agreement.

NOTE 1: The assumption resolution may be worded in such a manner as to be applicable to only the specific applicants to self insure or the assumption resolution may list all present subsidiaries or affiliates and authorize the addition of future, unnamed additions to the assumption resolution as an attachment without execution of a new resolution.

NOTE 2: The Manager shall provide an acceptable model resolution to any party upon request. The current model assumption resolutions are contained in Plate E of the Appendix following the last Article of these Subchapter 2 regulations.

(e) When a self insurer reincorporates, merges, or changes its identity, the surviving entity shall execute a new Agreement of Assumption and Guarantee of Liabilities and a new assumption resolution to cover the liabilities of the prior self insurer as part of the reapplication process to continue self insurance of workers' compensation liabilities.

(f) A foreign entity (i.e. outside the United States) may execute a parental Agreement of Assumption and Guarantee of Liabilities for a subsidiary or affiliate self insurer provided such foreign entity:

(1) executes in the English language the Agreement of Assumption and Guarantee of Liabilities and the assumption resolution; and

(2) includes a statement in the Agreement of Assumption and Guarantee of Liabilities that, in the event of the Director's need to enforce the Agreement of Assumption executed by the foreign entity on behalf of a self-insured subsidiary or subsidiaries, the foreign entity will:

(A) become subject to the jurisdiction of California courts and administrative agencies; and

(B) become controlled by California law in the resolution of any dispute under the assumption and guarantee agreement.

(g) Execution of an agreement of assumption and guarantee of liabilities shall not reduce the amount of security deposit required to be posted by any self insurer as set forth in Section 15210 and 15210.1.

(h) An Assumption and Guarantee Agreement may be terminated upon receipt of a written notice of such termination and take effect 30 days after receipt of the written termination notice.

NOTE: The Director may approve an earlier termination date without 30 days' advance notice where a self-insurer is sold to a new owner and workers' compensation liabilities are either covered by an insurance policy or the new owner executes an Assumption and Guarantee Agreement effective on or before the date of the sale.

Note: Authority cited: Sections 54, 55 and 3702.10, Labor Code. Reference: Sections 59, 129, 3700, 3701, 3701.5, 3702, 3702.5, 3702.6, 3702.10, 3703, 3705 and 3740-3744, Labor Code.

History: 1. New section filed 11-19-75; effective thirtieth day thereafter (Register 75, No. 47).

2. Amendment filed 11-21-78; effective thirtieth day thereafter (Register 78, No. 47).

3. Amendment filed 12-22-92; operative 1-21-93 (Register 93, No. 2).

4. Editorial correction of subsection (f)(2)(A) (Register 98, No. 8).

5. Change without regulatory effect amending subsection (b) filed 2-17-98 pursuant to section 100, title 1, California Code of Regulations (Register 98, No. 8).

6. Amendment of subsection (c) filed 6-25-98; operative 7-25-98 (Register 98, No. 26).

§15211.3. Agreement and Undertaking for Security Deposit.

(a) All security deposits shall be posted in accordance with the provisions of the Agreement and Undertaking, as required in Section 15203.5 of these regulations.

Note: Authority cited: Sections 54, 55 and 3702.10, Labor Code. Reference: Sections 59, 3701, 3701.5, 3702, 3702.6, 3702.10, 3703, 3705, 3740-3745, Labor Code.

History: 1. New section filed 12-22-92; operative 1-21-93 (Register 93, No. 2).

§15212. Surety Bonds.

(a) Surety bonds shall be accepted by the Manager only if written by an "admitted surety insurer" as defined by California Code of Civil Procedure, Chapter 2, Bonds and Undertaking, Section 995.120(a).

(b) A surety bond underwritten by an organization owned and/or controlled by the self insurer, who is also the principal on the surety bond, shall be rejected by the Manager unless the surety company is financially independent of its parent.

(c) The Manager shall make available, upon request of any self insurer, an appropriate quantity of surety bond forms (Form A4-20 (Rev. 11/92)), increase riders (Form A4-21b (Rev. 4/92)) decrease riders (Form A4-21a (Rev. 4/92)), name change riders (Form A4-22 (Rev. 4/92)), and special form change riders (Form A4-23 (Rev. 4/92)), and Release of Surety (Form A4-24 (11/92)), California Code of Regulations, Title 11, Chapter 2, Section 25, which are hereby incorporated by reference.

Note: The current surety bond forms and rider forms are contained in Plates F-1 through F-6 of the Appendix immediately following the last Article in these Subchapter 2 regulations.

(d) A surety bond accepted by the Manager as security deposit shall be continuous in form. Surety bonds shall be exonerated only by their terms and cancelled only according to the specific language in the bond form. Exoneration of a surety bond by the Manager shall only be done when the bond language includes a release provision and the self insurer has substituted another acceptable security deposit or combination of acceptable deposits that totals to the amount determined by the Director to be required as a security deposit.

Note: Bond forms previously accepted as security deposit have differing terms and conditions from the current surety bond forms and some of the prior bond forms may not include a release provision in the bond language. Such bonds cannot be exonerated by the Manager unless the prior bond form is changed to the current terms and conditions by means of reinstatement of the surety bond, if cancelled, and execution of a Special Form Change Rider.

(e) The surety company shall submit a Notice of Cancellation in writing to the Manager on any surety bond according to the terms of the bond. The surety shall give the Manager written notice at least (thirty) 30 days in advance of the effective date of cancellation of an existing surety bond. After receipt of the written cancellation notice and receipt of a replacement security deposit, as set forth in subsection (d) and (g), in the amount required by the Director, the Manager may issue a Release of Surety to the surety company for the cancelled bond.

(f) Surety bonds and all riders to the surety bonds shall be executed by the surety company's Attorney-In-Fact and the Attorney-In-Fact's appointment or power of attorney must accompany all copies of the bond or rider being submitted.

Note: The Attorney-In-Fact does not need to be a California Attorney-In-Fact.

(g) The self insurer shall substitute the deposit represented by the penal sum of the cancelled surety bond with another acceptable form of security deposit, in the full amount required by the Director, within thirty (30) days of the receipt of bond cancellation notice to the Manager.

Exceptions:

(1) A surety bond issued prior to the effective date of these regulations where the bond secures liabilities of a former self insurer.

(2) An active self insurer in the process of revocation on the effective date of this regulation of its self insurance authority and which has fully insured its workers' compensation liabilities with a standard workers' compensation policy from an admitted carrier prior to the effective date of this regulation.

(h) The surety company or its parent company shall have and maintain an acceptable credit rating as set forth below:

(1) Standard and Poors Insurer Financial Strength Rating of A or better rating, or

(2) A.M. Best Company, Financial Strength Rating of B+ or better rating.

(i) A surety bond shall be replaced by the self insurer in the event the surety is placed in conservatorship, or is seized, or declares insolvency, or the current credit rating is below the ratings required in subsection (h).

Note: Authority cited: Sections 54, 55 and 3702.10, Labor Code. Reference: Sections 3700, 3700(b), 3701, 3701.5, 3702.10, 3703, 3705 and 3740-3744, Labor Code; and Sections 995.120(a) and 995.430, Code of Civil Procedure.

History: 1. Repealer and new section filed 12-22-92; operative 1-21-93 (Register 93, No. 2).

2. Amendment filed 8-12-93; operative 9-13-93 (Register 93, No. 33).

3. New subsections (h)-(i) and amendment of Note filed 11-2-2001; operative 12-2-2001 (Register 2001, No. 44).

Ref.: See Labor Code §§59, 129, 3702, 3702.5, 3702.6.

§15213. Approved Securities.

(a) Approved securities shall be only those securities which meet the following:

(1) Securities are corporate or Federal, State or municipal government bonds or notes in book entry form, having a rating of AA or better by Standard and Poor's Rating Service or a rating of Aa or better by Moody's Investors Service Guide or a rating of AA or better by Fitch Investors Service Guide;

Exception 1. Securities issued by the State of California shall have a rating of B or better.

Exception 2. Securities in registered, physical form that meet all requirements of this section are acceptable until January 1, 1997 for posting by a self insurer. After that date, all securities shall be in book entry form.

(2) Securities shall be delivered in the name of the "Treasurer, State of California in trust for (insert the legal name of the self insurer)" or similar legible abbreviation to a custodian account designated by the State Treasurer.*

(3) Securities previously accepted and registered in the name of "Treasurer State of California" or "Treasurer of State of California in trust for [legal name of self insurer(s)] liabilities pursuant to Labor Code Sections 3700 and 3701" shall not have to be reregistered, but will be held until maturity or released by order of the Manager or Director.

(4) Mortgage backed securities shall not be acceptable and zero-coupon securities shall not be accepted.

(5) Securities issued by the self insurer or its subsidiaries, or its affiliated companies or parent companies, shall not be accepted for that particular self insurer's security deposit.

(b) Any private self insurer desiring to post or have released approved securities shall provide the Manager with a complete description of the security or securities, including the following:

(1) Whether the security is registered or book entry type;

(2) Complete name of security;

(3) Interest rate of security;

(4) Original issue date of security;

(5) Date of maturity of security;

(6) Par value of security;

(7) Current market value of security;

(8) Name of delivery agent and the telephone number of delivery agent who will actually deliver the security to the State on behalf of the self insured employer.
[Note: This is usually a bank or brokerage firm.]; and

(9) The name and address where interest checks are to be sent for registered securities or a bank name and bank account number for wire transfer of interest payments for book entry securities.

(10) The self insurer's Federal Taxpayer Identification Number for interest payments on the securities.

(c) Approval by the Manager or Director, or other person authorized in writing by the Director, to the State Treasurer shall be required on all securities to be posted or released and the Manager shall transmit the approval order to the State Treasurer.

Note: The current model letter to request approval of securities is contained in Plate G of the Appendix following the last Article in these Subchapter 2 regulations.

(d) The Manager shall value approved securities at par value or market value, whichever is less, when computing the security deposit represented by the securities for any private self insurer. Each self insurer posting securities shall provide a statement of the current market value of the security or securities annually to the Manager on their Self Insurer's Annual Report as required by Section 15251(b)(6).

(e) No approved security shall be accepted for deposit at above its par value. Additional deposits of approved securities shall be required at any time when the market value of an approved security falls below its par value.

(f) The Manager may order called or matured securities to be redeemed by the State Treasurer and the resulting cash returned to or deposited in trust on behalf of the self-insured.

(g) Any self insurer with securities on deposit may request the release of the securities upon the posting of replacement security or upon the determination of the Manager that the securities represent surplus deposit above that required by Labor Code Section 3701 and these regulations.

*Note: The usual practice of the State Treasurer is to contact the delivery agent for the specific wire instructions for processing the securities transaction into or out of the State Treasurer's custodian account.

Note: Authority cited: Sections 54, 55 and 3702.10, Labor Code. Reference: Sections 59, 3700, 3701,

3701.5, 3702, 3702.6, 3702.10, 3703, 3705 and 3740-3745, Labor Code.

History: 1. Editorial correction to Form Nos. A4-30 and A4-31 (Register 74, No. 47).

2. Repealer and new section filed 12-22-92; operative 1-21-93 (Register 93, No. 2).

3. Amendment of subsections (a)(1) and (a)(2), repealer and new subsection (a)(3), and addition of footnote to subsection (a)(2) filed 12-23-96; operative 1-1-97 pursuant to Government Code section 11343.4(d) (Register 96, No. 52).

§15214. Cash in Trust.

(a) Cash shall be presented to the Manager in the form of a corporate check, cashier's check, certified check or money order and shall be made payable to "The Department of Industrial Relations In Trust For [the legal name of the self insurer]." A wire transfer of funds to a bank or savings institution if approved in advance by the Manager may be used.

Note 1: Cash deposits shall be deposited by the Office of Self-Insurance Plans on the same day received or on the following business day with a bank or savings institution meeting the credit standards contained in Section 15215(e) into an interest bearing passbook savings account or into a certificate of deposit not exceeding one year in duration with an automatic rollover upon maturity. The passbook account or certificate shall be set up in such a manner to show the cash deposit is held in trust for the private self insurer by the Department of Industrial Relations, as the depositor, and the private self insurer has no ability to control any part of the account or certificate. The passbook or original certificate shall be held by the bank pending written instruction from Self-Insurance Plans signed by the Manager to deliver the passbook or certificate to the State Treasurer, who shall be the custodian of the deposit.

Note 2: A private self insurer desiring to deposit cash to be held in trust as part of its security deposit should contact the Manager in advance of sending a cash deposit to the Office of Self-Insurance Plans. The private self insurer may advise the Manager in writing of any preference for a bank or savings institution into which the cash is to be deposited by the Department and length of the deposit term. However, the selection of the bank or savings institution and length of term of the deposit is at the discretion of the Manager.

(b) Negotiable certificates of deposit in book entry format, bearer form or registered form may be deposited with prior arrangements made with the manager and subject to approval of the Manager as with any other registered securities pursuant to Section 15212.1 of these regulations.

(c) By order of the Manager, physical possession of the passbook or certificate of deposit shall be transferred from the financial institution to the State Treasurer. The passbook or certificate shall be released only upon written order of the Director and the Manager or other person designated by the Director.

(d) The Manager shall provide the private self insurer depositing cash with a written receipt for the deposit.

(e) The private self insurer may request and the Manager shall authorize the payment of any interest on the cash deposit to be sent to the self insurer from the bank or savings institution.

Note: Authority cited: Sections 54, 55 and 3702.10, Labor Code. Reference: Sections 59, 3700, 3701, 3701.5, 3702, 3702.6, 3702.10, 3703, 3705, 3740-3745, Labor Code.

History: 1. New section filed 12-22-92; operative 1-21-93 (Register 93, No. 2).

§15215. Letters of Credit.

(a) An irrevocable standby letter of credit may be accepted by the Manager as all or part of the security deposit for a private self insurer. The Manager shall determine whether the letter of credit submitted is acceptable and if its language and format meets the requirements of this Section.

(b) Irrevocable letters of credit shall be issued by and payable at a branch in the continental United States, Alaska or Hawaii. The issuing bank or savings institution may be:

(1) A State of California chartered bank or savings institution; or

(2) A federally chartered bank or savings institution; or

(3) Any other foreign or domestic bank or savings institution; or

(4) A group (syndication) of domestic or foreign banks or savings institutions.

(c) The Manager shall provide a model letter of credit format and language that will meet the requirements for acceptance. The letter of credit shall include, but not be limited to, the following provisions:

(1) The letter of credit will be automatically extended without amendment for an additional 1 year from the expiry date or any subsequent expiry date unless, at least 45 days before the expiry date, the Manager is notified in writing by the bank or savings institution that the letter of credit will not be renewed;

(2) The letter of credit can be called if the self insurer fails to pay its workers' compensation liabilities; or the self insurer files bankruptcy; or the self insurer fails to renew or substitute acceptable security by ten days prior to the expiry date of the letter of credit; or any combination of these events;

(3) The letter of credit is not subject to any qualification or condition by the issuing or confirming bank or savings institution and is the bank or savings institution's individual obligation which is in no way contingent upon reimbursement;

(4) Payment of any amount under the letter of credit shall be made only by wire transfer in the name of "The Department of Industrial Relations In Trust For [the legal name of the self insurer]" to an account of the State Controller, State of California, at a designated bank;

(5) All letters of credit shall include a statement that if legal proceedings are initiated by any party with respect to the payment of any letter of credit, it is agreed that such proceedings shall be subject to the jurisdiction of California courts and administrative agencies and subject to California law; and

(6) Letters of credit shall be subject to the Uniform Customs and Practices for Documentary Credits, 1993 Revision, ICC Publication No. 500, which is hereby incorporated by reference, and a reference to this publication shall be included within the text of the letter of credit.

(7) Discrepancy fees, if any, shall be payable by the self insurer.

Note: A model single bank letter of credit (Revised 7/94) is contained in Plate I of the Appendix following the last Article in these Subchapter 2 regulations.

(d) A syndicated letter of credit shall include all the language of the single bank issued letter of credit and in addition:

(1) Authorize all demands for payment to be presented at a designated branch ("agent bank") of one of the participating banks or savings institutions;

(2) Include a draft to be presented for payment of all or part of the credit available under the letter of credit;

(3) Permit any participating bank's portion of the total credit available to be drawn upon if the participating bank's credit rating falls below the acceptable credit rating level specified in subsection (e) of this Section; and

(4) State that the obligations of the banks or savings institutions issuing a syndicated letter of credit are several and not joint, and neither the agent bank or savings institution or any other participating bank or savings institution shall be responsible for or otherwise liable for the failure of any other participating bank or savings institution to perform its obligations under the syndicated letter of credit. The failure of any participating bank or savings institution to perform its obligations under the syndicated letter of credit shall also not relieve any other participating bank or savings institution of its obligations under the syndicated letter of credit.

(e) The issuing bank(s) or savings institution(s) or the parent holding corporation of an unrated bank or savings institution issuing a letter of credit shall have at the time of issuance of the letter of credit an acceptable credit rating as set forth below:

(1) An "Aaa", "Aa", "A" long term certificate of deposit (CD) rating for the bank or savings institution in the current monthly edition of "Moody's Statistical Handbook" prepared by Moody's Investors Service, Inc., New York; or

(2) An "AAA", "AA" or "A" long term certificate of deposit (CD) rating for the bank or savings institution in the current quarterly edition or monthly supplement of "Financial Institutions Ratings" prepared by Standard & Poor's Corporation, New York; or

(3) An "AAA", "AA+" or "AA" credit quality rating for the issuing financial institution along with a CD/Debt Credit Limit Code above the dollar amount of the letter of credit as well as a Credit Limit Maturity Code of "a, b, c or d" in the current annual edition of "GFI Credit Ratings", or the latest monthly "GFI Bank Letter" supplement thereto; or

(4) Federally chartered instrumentalities of the United States operating under authority of the Farm Credit Act of 1971, as amended.

(f) A letter of credit issued by a bank or savings institution or syndication of banks or savings institutions that does not meet the credit rating set forth in subsection (e) at the time of issuance shall be accepted by the Manager with a confirming letter of credit issued by a bank or savings institution meeting the criteria of subsection (e). The confirming letter of credit shall state that the confirming bank or savings institution is primarily obligated to pay on demand the full amount of the letter of credit regardless of reimbursement from the bank or savings institution whose letter of credit is being confirmed.

Note: Advising letters of credit shall not be accepted in lieu of the confirmation requirement for the letter of credit bank with an unacceptable credit rating.

(g) If a bank or savings institution's rating subsequent to the issuance of the letter of credit falls below the acceptable rating level as set forth in subsection (e), the Manager shall, within 60 days of the publication of the lower credit rating, require the self insurer to:

(1) Replace the letter of credit with a new letter of credit issued by a bank or savings institution with an acceptable credit rating; or

(2) Confirm the letter of credit by a bank or savings institution with an acceptable rating.

Note: Authority cited: Sections 54, 55 and 3702.10, Labor Code. Reference: Sections 59, 3700, 3701, 3701.5, 3702, 3702.3, 3702.6, 3702.10, 3740, 3741 and 3742, Labor Code.

History: 1. New section filed 12-22-92; operative 1-21-93 (Register 93, No. 2).

2. New subsection (e)(3) and subsection redesignation, and amendment of subsections (e)(1) and (2) filed 3-24-94; operative 4-25-94 (Register 94, No. 12).

3. Amendment of subsection (c)(6) and (c)(7) Note filed 12-1-94; operative 1-2-95 (Register 94, No. 48).

§15216. Administration of Defaulted Self-Insurer's Claims.

(a) In the event the self insurer fails to pay workers' compensation benefits due, the cost of administration and legal expenses of existing and new claims shall be made from the security deposit set aside for this purpose pursuant to Labor Code Section 3701.5.

(b) If claims have been administered from out of state, the Director may order all remaining and future claims to be administered from California or may turn them over to the Self-Insurer's Security Fund.

(c) The Manager shall determine the adequacy of the existing security deposit to pay the defaulting self insurer's workers' compensation liabilities within 90 days of the Manager's determination that the self-insured has defaulted, and shall report his/her findings to the Director and the Self Insurer's Security Fund.

(d) If it is necessary for the Director to call or cash any security deposit, a trust shall be established by the Manager to receive the funds from the deposit, except in the following situations:

(1) Where the surety company elects, and the Director approves, handling of the claims directly by the provider of the surety bond; or

(2) Where the funds and responsibility for the claims are turned over to the Self-Insurer's Security Fund pursuant to Labor Code Section 3701.5.

(e) In the event of a default, all security deposits, regardless of form that is posted by the self insured employer, shall be the first in order to be called upon to pay benefits due. If any portion of the defaulting self insurer's liabilities are secured in whole or part by an alternative composite deposit posted by the Security Fund, the alternative composite deposit shall be next in order to be called upon to pay benefits due. The Director may at his/her discretion call any portion of the entire security deposit posted at any time without waiting for the exhaustion of all funds in the prior level or call order contained in this subsection.

(f) The Manager shall advise the Self-Insurers' Security Fund of the receipt of any verified information indicating a self-insurer's failure to pay benefits due, the filing of bankruptcy, or inability to post and maintain required security deposit.

(g) The Director, at his/her discretion, may order the Security Fund to assume full liability for any self insurer's insolvency or failure to pay benefits regardless of whether or not there is a shortfall in the deposit to pay benefits due.

Note: Authority cited: Sections 54, 55, 3701.8 and 3702.10, Labor Code. Reference: Sections 59, 129, 3701, 3701.5, 3701.8, 3702, 3702.3, 3702.6, 3703, 3705 and 3740-3745, Labor Code.

History: 1. New section filed 12-22-92; operative 1-21-93 (Register 93, No. 2).

2. Amendment of section and Note filed 5-30-2003 as an emergency; operative 5-30-2003 (Register 2003, No. 22). A Certificate of Compliance must be transmitted to OAL by 9-29-2003 or emergency language will be repealed by operation of law on the following day.

3. Certificate of Compliance as to 5-30-2003 order transmitted to OAL 9-29-2003 and filed 11-12-2003 (Register 2003, No. 46).

Ref.: Herlick Handbook § 3.20.

ARTICLE 3.1
Alternative Composite Deposits

§15220. Participation in Alternative Composite Deposits.

(a) All private self insured employers, active or revoked, shall be annually determined by the Manager to be either eligible or non-eligible for participation in the alternative composite deposit program. Participation shall be as a fully participating self insured employer or as a partially participating self insured employer as provided in subsection (c)(1).

(b) All non-eligible self insurers shall be deemed "excluded". The following self insured employers shall be excluded from the alternative composite deposit program:

(1) Any new private sector self insured employer during their first three full years of self insurance. An employer shall be considered a new self insured employer if, when it applied to become self insured, it did not possess an active Certificate of Consent to Self Insure issued pursuant to Labor Code Section 3700(b) for itself or for its parent, a subsidiary, or an affiliate employer.

(2) Any former private self insured employer that possesses a revoked Certificate of Consent to Self-Insure and is no longer required to submit a Self-Insurer's Annual Report pursuant to Section 15251 of this subchapter 2 because all known claims costs have been reported and all known claims are closed.

(3) Any former private self insured employer that possesses a revoked Certificate of Consent to Self Insure and is required to post no more than the minimum security deposit amount pursuant to Labor Code Section 3701(b).

(4) Any current or former private self insured employer to the extent it has sold off all or any portion of its workers' compensation liabilities under a special excess workers compensation insurance policy to an admitted carrier and has continued to post security deposit to secure such sold off liabilities for 3 years from the policy issuance date.

(5) All private group self insurers of workers' compensation liabilities as provided for in Article 13 of this subchapter 2.

(6) Any private self insured employer to the extent that it transfers any or all of its existing self insured workers' compensation liabilities to either: (A) a fully insured employer, such as in the merger, reorganization, sale or spin off of a division or subsidiary; or, (B) a carrier through a contractual sell off that is not a special excess workers' compensation insurance policy pursuant to Labor Code Section 3702.8(c) and (d).

(7) Any current or former private self insured employer that has defaulted on the payment of its self insured workers' compensation liabilities and whose liabilities have been turned over to the Security Fund by the Director.

(8) Any current or former private self insured employer that has failed to post the full amount of security deposit required by Section 15210 for more than 60 consecutive days.

(9) Any former private self insured employer that has posted a surety bond that contains no provision to release the carrier's liabilities under the surety bond.

(10) Any private self insured employer that does not meet the minimum credit rating criteria for participation in the alternative composite deposit contained in subsection (d)(3).

(11) Any current or former private legally self insured employer that is a member of a public sector healthcare joint powers authority pursuant to Government Code Section 6527.

(12) Any self insured employer that has been specifically excluded by written request of the Security Fund. Notwithstanding other requirements of this section, the Security Fund may submit a written request to the Manager that any private self-insured employer otherwise excluded from participation in the alternative composite deposit program be included, and the Manager, upon such written request, may grant the request; the written request shall identify the private self-insured employer and shall state the reasons that such private self-insured employer should be included in the alternative composite deposit.

(c) All private self insured employers determined by the Manager to be eligible shall be required to participate in the alternative composite deposit program.

(1) The Manager shall identify each eligible participant as one of the following:

(A) Fully participating employer, or

(B) Partially participating employer.

(d) To qualify as a fully participating private self insured employer, the employer shall meet all the following requirements:

(1) The employer is not excluded by subsection (b) of this regulation;

(2) The self insured employer meets the minimum financial requirements in its last published annual financial report as provided in Section 15203.2;

(3) The employer possesses an acceptable credit rating on the date of the Security Fund's written alternative composite deposit proposal. An acceptable credit rating shall be any "A" or

any "B" rating or equivalent as determined by section 15220.1, in either of the following publications:

(A) Moody's Investor Service Corporate Finance monthly subscription rating guide entitled "Moody's Global Rating Guide", or

(B) Standard & Poor's Credit Market Services monthly subscription rating guide entitled "Global Ratings Handbook".

In the event that ratings have been determined pursuant to both subsection (d)(3)(A) and (B), and the ratings differ, the most recently published rating shall be utilized.

(e) The following self insured employers shall qualify as partially participating members of the alternative composite deposit program:

(1) The employer is not excluded by subsection (b) of this regulation;

(2) The employer meets the qualifications of subsection (d) but has been identified as a partially participating self insured employer by action of the Manager for cause. Cause may include, but is not limited to, failure to provide a parental agreement of assumption and guarantee; failure to file a complete and timely Self Insurer's Annual Report; failure to post the required security deposit by the required date; failure to report all claim liabilities or to estimate claims liabilities pursuant to Section 15300 of these regulations as determined in a routine audit or special audit; and/or, failure to post alternate deposit for new subsidiaries or affiliates of the self insurer after the end of the cycle for the previous year's alternate composite deposit.

(f) Excluded self insured employers shall not be eligible for any portion of their security deposit to be covered by the alternative composite deposit. The excluded private self insurer shall continue to secure its workers' compensation liabilities as required in Article 3 and to pay assessments as provided in Article 4 of this subchapter 2.

(g) Any private self insured employer that is eligible only as a partially participating member or is excluded to participate in the alternative composite deposit shall post the balance of the amount of required security deposit with the Director pursuant to Labor Code Section 3701 and Article 3 of this subchapter 2.

(h) For cause, the Manager may downgrade an eligible private self insured employer from:

(1) fully participating employer to partially participating employer as provided in subsection (e)(2); or

(2) from partially participating employer to excluded.

Cause may include, but is not limited to, failure to submit the Self Insurers' Annual Report and/or failure to estimate future claim liabilities on the Self Insurers' Annual Report fully pursuant to Section 15300 as determined in an audit; inclusion of claim liabilities of subsidiaries or affiliates in their self insurance program that have not been granted a Certificate to Self Insure by the Director; failure to post a security deposit pursuant to Labor Code Section 3701 and these regulations; failure to meet the financial requirements for self insurance pursuant to Section 15203.1; failure to submit an Assumption and Guarantee Agreement pursuant to Section 15203.1; and/or, failure to pay any assessments, fees, and/or penalties pursuant to Labor Code Section 3702.9, this article, and/or Articles 4 or 9 of this subchapter 2.

Note: Authority cited: Sections 3701, 3701.8 and 3702.10, Labor Code. Reference: Sections 3701 and 3701.8, Labor Code; and Section 6527, Government Code.

History: 1. New article 3.1 (sections 15220-15220.8) and section filed 5-30-2003 as an emergency; operative 5-30-2003 (Register 2003, No. 22). A Certificate of Compliance must be transmitted to OAL by 9-29-2003 or emergency language will be repealed by operation of law on the following day. For prior history of sections 15220-15221, see Register 93, No. 2.

2. Certificate of Compliance as to 5-30-2003 order transmitted to OAL 9-29-2003 and filed 11-12-2003 (Register 2003, No. 46).

3. Amendment of subsections (b)(12) and (d)(3)(B) and amendment of Note filed 7-6-2004 as an emergency; operative 7-6-2004 (Register 2004, No. 28). A Certificate of Compliance must be transmitted to OAL by 11-3-2004 or emergency language will be repealed by operation of law on the following day.

4. Amendment of subsections (b)(12) and (d)(3)(B) and amendment of Note refiled 11-3-2004 as an emergency; operative 11-3-2004 (Register 2004, No. 45). A Certificate of Compliance must be transmitted to OAL by 3-3-2005 or emergency language will be repealed by operation of law on the following day.

5. Certificate of Compliance as to 11-3-2004 order transmitted to OAL 1-26-2005 and filed 3-8-2005 (Register 2005, No. 10).

§15220.1. Financial Information.

(a) In addition to the existing requirements to provide the current financial statement to the

Manager contained in Section 15203.2 of these regulations, the Manager shall require financial information that includes designated general information and key financial items from such financial statement required by Section 15203.2, in a format approved by the Director pursuant to subsection (c)(3), from any private self insured employer that:

(1) does not have public financial statements (such as closely held or privately held employers) or has no published credit rating; and

(2) has a required security deposit equal to or greater than $2,000,000 or fails to meet the financial requirements to be self insured as contained in Section 15203.2.

(b) Financial information shall include the following designated general information and key financial items:

(1) General Information Items:

(A) Name of Employer

(B) Date of Last Annual Financial Statement

(2) Key Financial Information:

(A) Cash and Marketable Securities

(B) Inventory

(C) Total Current Assets

(D) Total Intangible Assets

(E) Total Assets

(F) Total Short Term Debt

(G) Total Current Liabilities

(H) Total Long Term Debt

(I) Long Term Pension Obligations

(J) Total Liabilities

(K) Total Shareholders' Equity

(L) Total Preferred Stock

(M) Retained Earnings

(N) Net Sales

(O) Cost of Goods Sold

(P) Selling, General & Administrative Expenses

(Q) Operating Profit/ (Loss)

(R) Earnings before Interest and Taxes

(S) Total Interest Expenses

(T) Rental Expense

(U) Net Income

(V) Depreciation & Amortization

(W) Extraordinary Items

(c) A private self insured employer that fails to file the financial information as determined by this section shall be ineligible to participate as a fully participating member in the current alternative composite deposit.

(1) The Manager shall utilize available financial information to assign a non-investment grade rating to any self insured employer that fails to submit financial information for eligibility as a partial participating member.

(2) The Manager shall be authorized to determine that a private self insurer that fails to submit financial information be ineligible for partial participation in the current alternative composite deposit program.

(3) After December 31, 2004, the financial information required by subsection (b) shall be submitted to the Manager electronically in a format provided by the Manager.

(d) Pursuant to Labor Code Section 3701.8(b)(5), the Manager may provide to the Security Fund any financial information needed to set the deposit assessments for self-insured employers participating in the alternative composite deposit program and to secure the composite deposit.

Note: Authority cited: Sections 3701.8 and 3702.10, Labor Code. Reference: Sections 3701.8 and 3702.10, Labor Code.

History: 1. New section filed 5-30-2003 as an emergency; operative 5-30-2003 (Register 2003, No. 22). A Certificate of Compliance must be transmitted to OAL by 9-29-2003 or emergency language will be repealed by operation of law on the following day.

2. Certificate of Compliance as to 5-30-2003 order, including amendment of subsection (a), subsection relettering and new subsection (d) — form A4-7, transmitted to OAL 9-29-2003 and filed 11-12-2003 (Register 2003, No. 46).

3. Amendment of section heading and subsections (a), (b) and (c)-(c)(2), new subsection (c)(3) and repealer and new subsection (d) filed 7-6-2004 as an emergency; operative 7-6-2004 (Register 2004, No. 28). A Certificate of Compliance must be transmitted to OAL by 11-3-2004 or emergency language will be repealed by operation of law on the following day.

4. Amendment of section heading and subsections (a), (a)(2) and (c)-(c)(2), new subsection (c)(3) and repealer and new subsection (d) refiled 11-3-2004 as an emergency; operative 11-3-2004 (Register 2004, No. 45). A Certificate of Compliance must be transmitted to OAL by 3-3-2005 or emergency language will be repealed by operation of law on the following day.

5. Certificate of Compliance as to 11-3-2004 order transmitted to OAL 1-26-2005 and filed 3-8-2005 (Register 2005, No. 10).

§15220.2. Listing of Security Deposit Amount Required.

(a) The Manager shall annually prepare a listing of the security deposit amount required to secure workers' compensation liabilities for each private self insured employer pursuant to Labor Code Section 3701 and Article 3 of this subchapter 2. This listing of required security deposits shall be calculated by using the total amount of liability reported on the private self insured employer's year-end Self Insurer's Annual Report, and shall reflect deposit adjustments from audit results, additions of subsidiaries or affiliates, each applicable rate of deposit, and/or other deposit adjustments as determined by the Manager for all private self insured employers. This list shall be submitted to the Director annually.

(b) Any private self insured employer that fails to file its Self Insurer's Annual Report as required by Section 15251 of this subchapter 2 by April 1 of each year shall be deemed by the Manager to have twice the liabilities indicated on the prior year's Annual Report for the purpose of determining and recording the required security deposit in the above listing.

(c) The Manager shall provide the listing of required security deposits to the Security Fund. The Manager may submit the listing in a series of partially complete lists as the Self Insurers' Annual Reports are processed each year.

Note: Authority cited: Section 3701.8 and 3701.10, Labor Code. Reference: Sections 3701.8 and 3702.10, Labor Code.

History: 1. New section filed 5-30-2003 as an emergency; operative 5-30-2003 (Register 2003, No. 22). A Certificate of Compliance must be transmitted to OAL by 9-29-2003 or emergency language will be repealed by operation of law on the following day.

2. Certificate of Compliance as to 5-30-2003 order transmitted to OAL 9-29-2003 and filed 11-12-2003 (Register 2003, No. 46).

§15220.3. Alternative Composite Deposits.

(a) The Security Fund shall secure the aggregate security deposit amount required, in whole or part, for all eligible private self insured employers in the alternative composite deposit program, utilizing any one or combination of security instruments listed in Labor Code Section 3701 and/or Section 3701.8 and as provided for in subsection (b) of this section.

(b) These security instruments may include, but not be limited to, letters of credit, surety bonds, approved securities, and cash subject to the regulatory requirements for each contained in Article 3 (commencing with Section 15210) of this subchapter 2. It may also include, but not be limited to, insurance coverage, such as specific or aggregate excess policies, or special excess workers' compensation policies; or other financial instruments, such as commercial paper or reinsurance contracts; or the Security Fund's own secured or unsecured indebtedness; or financial guarantees, including the Security Fund's own guarantee backed by cash or securities.

(c) The Security Fund shall submit a written proposal as required in subsection (d) each year that the Security Fund proposes to replace individual security deposits with an aggregate composite deposit.

(d) Each formal written proposal for an alternative composite deposit to the Manager shall include:

(1) A complete description of the proposed composite deposit including what portions are cash and non-cash; any retentions, deductibles, or co-payments that are contemplated in each layer, if any; and any insurance or reinsurance being utilized as part of the proposal;

(2) A list of all proposed self insured employers to be covered; their amount of coverage; their applicable credit rating or equivalent credit rating as determined by Section 15220.1 of this subchapter 2; and the credit rating agency utilized to determine the credit rating;

(3) Specification of the call order, if any, of the instruments proposed to be posted as part of the alternative composite deposit.

(4) A proposed starting date for the proposed alternative composite deposit that is at least 30 days after the date of the official written proposal to the Manager.

(e) The Manager shall advise the Director of all written proposals submitted by the Security Fund for an alternative composite deposit and the details of the proposal.

(f) The Manager shall review and approve or reject the alternative composite deposit proposal in whole or part and shall advise the Security Fund of the decision within 30 days. If approved, the Security Fund shall have 30 days to post the alternative composite deposit instruments(s) with the Director, unless the Security Fund's approved proposal sets forth some other acceptable timetable for delivery of the instrument(s).

(g) The Manager shall not release security deposits posted by individual self insured employers pursuant to Labor Code Section 3701 until after the alternative composite deposit permitted by Labor Code Section 3701.8 is fully posted.

(h) The Security Fund may subsequently propose additions, extensions, replacements, substitutions, or other changes to the initial alternative composite deposit posted with the Manager, in whole or part, in the same manner as set forth in this section. Approval and posting of any changes in the alternative composite deposit shall comply with the provisions of this section.

(i) The Security Fund may provide its own guarantee for any portion of the alternative composite deposit in the form of a retention, a deductible, or its own guarantee, provided the guaranteed amount is secured by segregated cash or securities posted with the Director as set forth in Section 15220.8.

(j) At the time the Security Fund submits the written proposal each year as required by subsection (d), it shall list the self-insurers that it proposes to include in whole or in part in the composite deposit. Notwithstanding Section 15210.1(b) of these regulations, each self-insurer listed for inclusion shall have 60 days from the date of notification of the increase or until July 1 of that year, whichever is sooner, to post any indicated increase in security deposit, and that increase shall be either included in the composite deposit proposed by the Security Fund or separately posted, as required.

Note: Authority cited: Sections 3701.8 and 3702.10, Labor Code. Reference: Section 3701.8, Labor Code.

History: 1. New section filed 5-30-2003 as an emergency; operative 5-30-2003 (Register 2003, No. 22). A Certificate of Compliance must be transmitted to OAL by 9-29-2003 or emergency language will be repealed by operation of law on the following day.

2. Certificate of Compliance as to 5-30-2003 order transmitted to OAL 9-29-2003 and filed 11-12-2003 (Register 2003, No. 46).

3. Amendment of subsection (b) and new subsection (j) filed 7-6-2004 as an emergency; operative 7-6-2004 (Register 2004, No. 28). A Certificate of Compliance must be transmitted to OAL by 11-3-2004 or emergency language will be repealed by operation of law on the following day.

4. Amendment of subsection (b) and new subsection (j) refiled 11-3-2004 as an emergency; operative 11-3-2004 (Register 2004, No. 45). A Certificate of Compliance must be transmitted to OAL by 3-3-2005 or emergency language will be repealed by operation of law on the following day.

5. Certificate of Compliance as to 11-3-2004 order transmitted to OAL 1-26-2005 and filed 3-8-2005 (Register 2005, No. 10).

§15220.4. Deposit Assessments by the Security Fund for Participants of the Alternative Composite Deposit.

(a) The Security Fund shall collect an annual deposit assessment from all private self insurers participating in the alternative composite deposit as follows:

(1) A pro-rata cash contribution to build the net worth of the Security Fund to pay existing or future defaults on covered workers' compensation liabilities of eligible private self insured employers under an alternative composite deposit. This portion of the deposit assessment shall be called the Default Loss Fund Fee.

(2) A pro-rata cash contribution to pay the cost of any aggregate loss protection in excess of the level of liability provided through the Default Loss Fund. This portion of the deposit assessment shall be called the Excess Liability Protection Fee.

(3) A pro-rata cash contribution to fund security deposit shortfalls from existing private self insurer insolvencies and defaults formerly funded exclusively by the Security Fund's Insolvency Assessment pursuant to Labor Code Section 3745. This portion of the deposit assessment shall be called the Pre-Existing Deposit Shortfall Fee.

Exception: Private self insurers whose Certificate of Consent to Self Insure was revoked before January 1, 2003, shall remain subject to the assessments as provided by Labor Code Section 3745.

(b) Each private self insured employer participating in an alternative composite deposit with the Security Fund shall be required to annually pay the Security Fund deposit assessment.

(c) The Security Fund shall determine the pro-rata amount of the deposit assessment for each fully participating and partially participating private self insured employer based on all the following:

(1) Labor Code Section 3701.8(b) requirements;

(2) the cost of the security instruments permitted in Section 15220.2 including any cash holdings that will make up the Default Loss Fund and/or the Excess Liability Protection Fee

portions of any alternative composite deposit proposed to the Director;

(3) the amount of the security deposit required by the Manager for each participating private self insured employer to secure its self insured workers' compensation liabilities;

(4) the participating private self insured employer's credit ratings or equivalent credit ratings as determined by Sections 15220, 15220.1, or Section 15220.3;

(5) an amount, if needed, for the pro-rata share of incurred but not fully reported liabilities aggregated across all private self insurers;

(6) an amount for the pro-rata share of pre-existing, unfunded defaulted liabilities of the Self Insurers' Security Fund to be collected for funding cash flow needs by the Pre-Existing Deposit Shortfall Fee;

(7) other measures of each private self insured employer's contribution to the cost of the alternative composite deposit proposed to the Director; and

(8) the amount, if any, of the security deposit required to be separately posted with the Director pursuant to Labor Code Section 3701 to secure that portion of the employer's self insured workers' compensation liabilities that is not secured in the alternative composite deposit.

(d) Where the participating self insurer has more than one credit rating from the credit rating agencies and the ratings are not in agreement, the most recently published credit rating shall be used to calculate the deposit assessment.

(e) Excluded private self insured employers shall be required to participate in the assessments. The Manager shall determine the amount of each deposit assessment due from private self insured employers excluded from participation in any alternative composite deposit and submit it to the Security Fund. The Security Fund shall collect the deposit assessments from excluded employers.

(f) The Security Fund may repay any indebtedness incurred as contemplated by Section 15220.3 from the annual deposit assessment. At the time the annual deposit assessment is determined, it may not be known whether any such indebtedness will be incurred, or the amount or repayment terms thereof. Accordingly, a portion of the annual deposit assessment may be contingent upon the actual incurrence of such indebtedness and delayed until the amount and repayment terms are known.

(g) If the Manager increases the security deposit requirement of a participating self-insured employer after the Security Fund has issued the annual assessment for the alternative composite deposit, the amount of the increase may be addressed through a supplemental assessment or by the posting of additional deposit separately as a partially participating self-insurer.

Note: Authority cited: Sections 3701, 3701.8, 3702.10 and 3745, Labor Code. Reference: Sections 3701, 3701.8, 3701.8(b), 3702.10 and 3745, Labor Code.

History: 1. New section filed 5-30-2003 as an emergency; operative 5-30-2003 (Register 2003, No. 22). A Certificate of Compliance must be transmitted to OAL by 9-29-2003 or emergency language will be repealed by operation of law on the following day.

2. Certificate of Compliance as to 5-30-2003 order, including amendment of Note, transmitted to OAL 9-29-2003 and filed 11-12-2003 (Register 2003, No. 46).

3. Amendment of subsection (c)(4), new subsections (d), (f) and (g) and subsection relettering filed 7-6-2004 as an emergency; operative 7-6-2004 (Register 2004, No. 28). A Certificate of Compliance must be transmitted to OAL by 11-3-2004 or emergency language will be repealed by operation of law on the following day.

4. Amendment of subsection (c)(4), new subsections (d), (f) and (g) and subsection relettering refiled 11-3-2004 as an emergency; operative 11-3-2004 (Register 2004, No. 45). A Certificate of Compliance must be transmitted to OAL by 3-3-2005 or emergency language will be repealed by operation of law on the following day.

5. Certificate of Compliance as to 11-3-2004 order transmitted to OAL 1-26-2005 and filed 3-8-2005 (Register 2005, No. 10).

§15220.5. Deposit Assessments; Failure to Pay; Assessment Liability.

(a) Each alternative composite deposit posted with the Director by the Security Fund shall be a binding agreement for all private self insured employers, fully participating and non-fully participating.

(b) Individual deposit assessment determinations, billings, and collection of these individual deposit assessments from participating private self insured employers shall be the responsibility of the Security Fund. The Security Fund shall advise the Manager in writing of any employer that fails to pay the assessment within the time period allocated by the Security Fund.

(c) The Manager shall assess a civil penalty pursuant to Labor Code Section 3701.8(d) against each private self insured employer who fails to pay the deposit assessment in the time allocated by the Security Fund. In addition to the civil penalty, the private self insured employer shall post a separate security deposit pursuant to Labor Code Section 3701 within 30 days of notice by the Manager.

(d) Failure by any participating private self insured employer to pay the deposit assessment in the time specified by the Security Fund, and/or failure to post and maintain the full amount of required security deposit pursuant to Labor Code Section 3701 for 60 days shall be good cause for the Manager to summarily revoke the private self insured employer's Certificate to Self Insure without a hearing as set forth in Section 15210.1.

(e) Any civil penalty assessed by the Manager pursuant to Labor Code Section 3701.8 shall not be discharged by the employer subsequently posting a security deposit. Any civil penalty or unpaid portion of the deposit assessment shall not be discharged by revocation of the employers' Certificate of Consent to Self Insure.

Note: Authority cited: Sections 3701.8 and 3702.10, Labor Code. Reference: Section 3701.8, Labor Code.

History: 1. New section filed 5-30-2003 as an emergency; operative 5-30-2003 (Register 2003, No. 22). A Certificate of Compliance must be transmitted to OAL by 9-29-2003 or emergency language will be repealed by operation of law on the following day.

2. Certificate of Compliance as to 5-30-2003 order transmitted to OAL 9-29-2003 and filed 11-12-2003 (Register 2003, No. 46).

§15220.6. New Self Insurers Fair Share Contribution Surcharge Fee.

(a) The Security Fund shall develop and track an annual historical schedule of cash contributions covering the initial ten years of the alternative security deposit program to build the net worth of the Default Loss Fund. A private self insured employer issued a Certificate to Self Insure after January 1, 2004, shall be surcharged a fair share contribution for the portion of the initial ten years that they did not contribute to the Default Loss Fund. This initial ten-year contribution for new self insurers shall be called the "New Self Insurer Fair Share Contribution Surcharge Fee" and shall be assessed and collected as a surcharge in addition to any other payment required of that new private self insurer into the Default Loss Fund. The Self Insurers Fair Share Contribution may be calculated as an average over a period of up to ten years.

(b) All funds collected from the New Self Insurer Fair Share Contribution Surcharge Fee shall be subject to the requirements of Section 15220.8.

Note: Authority cited: Sections 3701.8 and 3702.10, Labor Code. Reference: Section 3701.8, Labor Code.

History: 1. New section filed 5-30-2003 as an emergency; operative 5-30-2003 (Register 2003, No. 22). A Certificate of Compliance must be transmitted to OAL by 9-29-2003 or emergency language will be repealed by operation of law on the following day.

2. Certificate of Compliance as to 5-30-2003 order transmitted to OAL 9-29-2003 and filed 11-12-2003 (Register 2003, No. 46).

§15220.7. Appeals of Deposit Assessments and Appeals of Deposit Assessment Penalties.

(a) Any private self insured employer assessed a deposit assessment by the Security Fund may object or appeal the calculation or any other aspect of its deposit assessment to the Director as set forth in Article 11 (commencing with Section 15430). However, it shall be a condition precedent of such appeal that the full amount of the deposit assessment must first be paid to the Security Fund.

(b) Any private self insured employer assessed a civil penalty by the Manager for non-payment of the deposit assessment may appeal any civil penalties resulting from non-payment of the deposit assessment to the Director as set forth in Article 11 (commencing with Section 15430).

Note: Authority cited: Sections 3701.8 and 3702.10, Labor Code. Reference: Section 3701.8, Labor Code.

History: 1. New section filed 5-30-2003 as an emergency; operative 5-30-2003 (Register 2003, No. 22). A Certificate of Compliance must be transmitted to OAL by 9-29-2003 or emergency language will be repealed by operation of law on the following day.

2. Certificate of Compliance as to 5-30-2003 order transmitted to OAL 9-29-2003 and filed 11-12-2003 (Register 2003, No. 46).

§15220.8. Requirements for Use and Investment of Cash Generated from Deposit Assessments.

(a) The Security Fund shall provide the Director with a detailed accounting report of the monies collected for each deposit assessment within 90 days of the payment due date of the assessment.

(b) The accounting report shall include a summary of all funds collected, costs of each instrument posted as alternative composite deposit, all commissions and costs due or paid related to the alternative deposit system for that cycle, and any remaining excess funds.

(c) Following the purchase of any non-cash financial instruments to secure the liabilities of the alternative composite deposit, excess funds collected by the Security Fund in any deposit assessment and any additional funds subsequently collected shall be posted with the Director.

(d) All remaining cash collected from the assessments shall be deposited with the Director or as provided in subsection (f).

(e) All Security Fund cash deposits posted with the Director shall be held in the name of "Director of Industrial Relations in Trust for Self Insurers' Security Fund".

(f) The Director shall deposit and invest the Security Fund's cash in the Surplus Money Investment Fund pursuant to Labor Code Section 3702.5(b) and subject to the restrictions of use contained in Labor Code Section 3701.8, or the Director may permit the Security Fund to hire its own funds manager and invest the deposited cash on behalf of the Security Fund outside of the State Treasury subject to the following:

(1) As a condition precedent to the Security Fund managing such funds, the Security Fund shall adopt a cash investment policy outlining the types of investments in which such cash may be invested to preserve and protect the principal.

(2) The Security Fund shall insure that the Investment Fund manager submit a quarterly report to the Manager covering any of the Director's cash managed by the Security Fund.

(3) None of the Director's cash may be commingled with Security Fund cash, nor may any specific investments made with the Director's cash be commingled in the same instrument with Security Fund cash.

(4) Regardless of whether the Director or the Security Fund manages the cash posted, the funds shall remain in the name of the Director as set forth in subsection (e) of this section until such time as the Director may order any or all of the funds released to the Security Fund or refunded to the private self insured employers.

(g) Whenever the Director initially turns over the compensation liabilities of a private self insured employer to the Security Fund pursuant to Labor Code Section 3701.5 and such liabilities are covered in whole or part by the cash portion of an alternative composite deposit, the Director shall order the Manager to release enough cash to fund the payment of expected workers' compensation benefits for the remainder of the calendar year. If the amount released is inadequate, the Manager in consultation with the Security Fund shall advise the Director and request the Director to authorize the release of an additional amount to fund the payment of benefits and expenses for the period.

(h) The Security Fund shall annually notify the Manager and the Director in writing of the amount of funds that it will need to operate for the next calendar year for payment of benefits due, legal and administrative expenses, and other expenses of the Security Fund that will be funded from alternative composite deposits. The Manager shall be authorized to release the cash portion of the funds to the Self Insurers' Security Fund's possession.

Note: Authority cited: Sections 3701.8 and 3702.10, Labor Code. Reference: Section 3701.8, Labor Code.

History: 1. New section filed 5-30-2003 as an emergency; operative 5-30-2003 (Register 2003, No. 22). A Certificate of Compliance must be transmitted to OAL by 9-29-2003 or emergency language will be repealed by operation of law on the following day.

2. Certificate of Compliance as to 5-30-2003 order transmitted to OAL 9-29-2003 and filed 11-12-2003 (Register 2003, No. 46).

ARTICLE 4
Assessments

§15230. Private Sector License Fee Assessment.

(a) After July 1, 2001, an annual license fee shall be assessed by the Manager against each private self-insurer and paid by each private self-insurer on the following basis:

Number of Employees	Single Adjusting Location *
0 – 2999	$4000
3000 – 6999	$6000
7000 and Over	$8000

*An additional $300 per adjusting location for every location over 1.

Note: The above table shall apply against the last full year Self-Insurer's Annual Report submitted. If two or more annual reports are prepared from separate records at the same address, they shall be counted as separate adjusting locations.

(b) If the above table fails to produce sufficient funds to meet the total anticipated costs for the administration of the self-insurance program by the Director, an additional charge per employee covered by each self-insurance plan shall be made to cover these costs.

(c) The Manager shall invoice each private self-insurer on or before October 1 of each year, an assessment for the total cost of administration of the private Self-Insurance Plans program for the current fiscal year. The assessment is due 30 days after invoice mailing.

(d) Each new private sector self-insurer granted a certificate shall pay a pro-rata share of the annual license fee as determined by the Manager based on the information provided on the application. The fee shall be adjusted and pro-rated for the portion of the fiscal year remaining. The payment of the fee shall be made within thirty (30) days from the date of billing.

(e) Each private self insured certificate holder whose certificate is revoked after June 30, 2001, shall pay the full license fee' assessment for the next five full calendar years after the date of revocation order or until their security deposit reaches the statutory minimum.

Note: Authority cited: Sections 54, 55, 3702.5 and 3702.10, Labor Code. Reference: Sections 59, 3700, 3702.5 and 3702.10, Labor Code.

History: 1. Repealer of article 4 (section 15230) and new article 4 (sections 15230-15233) filed 6-1-72; effective thirtieth day thereafter (Register 72, No. 23).

2. Amendment filed 1-21-92; operative 2-20-92 (Register 92, No. 13).

3. New subsection (e) filed 7-27-93; operative 8-26-93 (Register 93, No. 31).

4. Amendment of article heading filed 6-30-94; operative 6-30-94 (Register 94, No. 26).

5. Amendment of subsections (a), (c) and (e) filed 4-19-2001; operative 5-19-2001 (Register 2001, No. 16).

§15231. Public Sector License Fee.

A public sector self-insurer shall not be subject to the payment of the annual license fee assessment.

Note: Authority cited: Sections 54, 55 and 3702.10, Labor Code. Reference: Sections 59, 3700, 3702.5 and 3702.10, Labor Code.

History: 1. Amendment filed 11-19-75; effective thirtieth day thereafter (Register 75, No. 47).

2. Amendment filed 11-21-78; effective thirtieth day thereafter (Register 78, No. 47).

3. Amendment filed 1-21-92; operative 2-20-92 (Register 92, No. 13).

§15232. User Funding Assessment.

The Manager shall collect the user funding assessment from all self-insurers and the State of California as set forth in Sections 15600–15610 of these regulations.

Note: Authority cited: Sections 54, 55, 62.5 and 3702.10, Labor Code. Reference: Sections 59, 62.5, 3700, 3702.9 and 3702.10, Labor Code.

History: 1. Amendment filed 11-21-78; effective thirtieth day thereafter (Register 78, No. 47).

2. Amendment filed 1-21-92; operative 2-20-92 (Register 92, No. 13).

3. Editorial correction by official state publisher of section heading (Register 96, No. 36).

§15233. Fraud Investigation and Prosecution Assessment.

The Manager shall collect the state fraud investigation and prosecution surcharge from all self insurers and the State of California as set forth in Sections 15600-15610 of these regulations.

Note: Authority cited: Sections 54, 55, 62.5, 62.6 and 3702.10, Labor Code. Reference: Sections 59, 3700, 3702.5 and 3702.10, Labor Code.

History: 1. New section filed 6-30-94; operative 6-30-94 (Register 94, No. 26).

§15234. Cal/OSHA Targeted Inspection and Consultation Assessment.

The Manager shall collect the Cal/OSHA Targeted Inspection and Consultation Assessment from all affected self insurers as set forth in Sections 15600 and 15601.7 of these regulations.

Note: Authority cited: Sections 54, 55, 62.7, 62.9 and 3702.10, Labor Code. Reference: Sections 59, 62.7, 62.9, 3700, 3702.5 and 3702.10, Labor Code.

History: 1. New section filed 9-6-96; operative 10-6-96 (Register 96, No. 36).

ARTICLE 5
Self Insurer's Annual Report

§15250. Repealed.

Note: Authority cited: Sections 54, 55 and 3702.10, Labor Code. Reference: Sections 55 and 3702.10, Labor Code.

History: 1. Repealer and new section filed 6-1-72; effective thirtieth day thereafter (Register 72, No. 23).

2. Amendment filed 11-19-75; effective thirtieth day thereafter (Register 75, No. 47).

3. Amendment filed 11-21-78; effective thirtieth day thereafter (Register 78, No. 47).

4. Amendment of article heading filed 10-16-92; operative 11-16-92 (Register 92, No. 42).

5. Repealer of section and amendment of Note filed 12-22-92; operative 1-21-93 (Register 93, No. 2).

§15250.1. Repealed.

Note: Authority cited: Sections 54, 55 and 3702.10, Labor Code. Reference: Sections 54, 55 and 3702.10, Labor Code.

History: 1. New section filed 6-1-72; effective thirtieth day thereafter (Register 72, No. 23).

2. Repealer of text and new Note filed 10-16-92; operative 11-16-92 (Register 92, No. 42).

§15251. Self Insurer's Annual Report.

(a) Every self-insurer shall file a Self-Insurer's Annual Report on forms supplied by the Manager as follows:

(1) Form A4-40a (Rev. 6/2001) for individual private self insurers;

(2) Form A4-40b (Rev. 4/92) for public self insurers without a Joint Power Authority;

(3) Form A4-40c (Rev. 4/92) for public sector self insurers that belong to a Joint Powers Authority;

(4) Form A4-40d (Rev. 1/94) for private group self insurers. The filing of the annual report by each self insurer and each former self insurer shall continue until all the self-insured workers' compensation claims are resolved and all benefit payments have been made.

Note 1: Sample generic Annual Report forms are contained in Plates J-1, and J-2 and J-3 of the Appendix following the last Article of these Group 2 regulations. When the forms are distributed by the Manager, the forms shall contain appropriate reporting year and prior year designations and shall be color-coded for ease of identification.

(b) For private self insurers, individual or with a group, the report shall be filed on or before March 1 of each year and shall include the following information:

(1) General Information.

(A) Certificate to Self Insure number, status of certificate, and period of report.

(B) Name and address of master certificate holder, state of incorporation, federal tax identification number, and first four digits of North American Industry Classification System (NAICS).

(C) List of all subsidiaries or affiliate companies that are covered by the master certificate to self insure, their state of incorporation, and their subsidiary/affiliate certificate number.

(D) Notification of any reincorporation, merger, change in name or identity or any additions to the self insurance program by the master certificate holder or any subsidiary/affiliate company during the reporting period.

(E) Name and address of person to whom all correspondence related to self insurance should be addressed.

(F) Employment and wages paid in that calendar year as reported to Employment Development Department on the employer's Form DE-6 Quarterly Report.

Exception: A Certificate to Self Insure that is revoked for three full years is not required to submit this employment and wage information.

(2) Claims Liability and Administrator Information.

(A) A Liabilities by Reporting Location report shall be submitted by each claims administrator administering claims for the said self insurer and shall include:

(1.) All claims reported on or before December 31 of each of the five prior calendar years (January 1 through December 31), showing indemnity and medical payments grouped as incurred liability, paid to date and future liability.

(2.) All open claims reported prior to the 5 years shall also be reported as in subsection (b)(2)(A)(1.) above in a single line entry;

(3.) For the reporting year of the annual report the total of indemnity and medical future liability, the total estimated future liability of claims, the total benefits paid, number of medical only cases reported, number of indemnity cases reported; number of fatality cases, number of claims for which the employer or administrator was notified of representation by an attorney or legal representative in the reporting year, and number of new applications for adjudication received for any claims that year.

(4.) Total number of open indemnity cases in all years.

(5.) Name, address and Certificate to Administer number of the self insurer's claims administrator.

(6.) Notification of any change in administrator during the period covered by the report and, if applicable, the name and address of the prior administrator.

(7.) A certification by the qualified claims administrator that the report is true, correct and complete with respect to the workers' compensation liabilities incurred and paid, signed and dated with the name and address of the said administrator completing the Liabilities by Reporting Location page.

(B) An additional separate Liabilities by Reporting Location report shall be submitted if any of the following occur:

(1.) Separate security deposits are posted by a single self insured certificate holder.

(2.) A self insured certificate is merged into an other self insured certificate by Self Insurance Plans. The administrator shall run-off the liabilities of the non-surviving certificate for a five year period. At the end of the five year period, all remaining open claims will be merged into the 'new companies' liability report.

Note: When certifcate files are merged together, all new claims after the file certificate date shall be reported as claims of the surviving certificate holder.

(3) Location of Claims Records Information. The name and address of any location other than the current administrator where self insurance claims records are stored.

(4) Insurance Information. Name and policy number of any standard workers' compensation insurance policy, specific excess workers' compensation insurance policy, or aggregate worker's compensation insurance policy held by the self insurer along with policy issue date and retention levels of liability of the policies.

(5) Open Indemnity Claims Information. List of all open indemnity claims by reporting location by year, and alphabetically within each year.

(A) Show name of claimant, date of injury, description of injury, amount of benefits paid-to-date in indemnity and medical payments and estimated future liability of claim for indemnity and medical benefits.

Note: Computer Loss Runs showing the information requested and organized as set forth in this subsection will be acceptable in lieu of the open indemnity claim page in Appendix J-1 and J-2.

(B) Show any open claim reported to the carrier of a specific excess insurance policy, and for which the carrier has not denied in writing the claim liability in whole or part above the retention level of the policy. The listing to include the name of the claimant, claim number, date of injury, description of injury, carrier name and policy number, policy coverage period, retention level of policy and paid to date in indemnity or medical benefits, and the estimated future liability of the claim minus the total unpaid employer retention, which equals the total unpaid carrier liability. The listing must also state if the claim has been reported to a carrier, if the claim has been accepted by the carrier, if the carrier has denied any part of the liability of the claim.

1. Specific Excess Coverage Calculation. A calculation which includes a total of all unpaid carrier liability times the applicable deposit rate for the self insurer. This number will be included in the deposit calculation as provided for in Section 15251(b)(7).

(6) Deposit Calculation Information. A Deposit Calculation which includes the estimated future liability from the Liabilities Report times the deposit rate factor to determine a minimum deposit required for known liabilities; plus a deposit in advance for the current new year based on the average estimated future liability of claims for the past 5 years to secure average unpaid liability in the current year's new claims; less any credit for claims exceeding the retention level of any specific excess insurance policy for which the carrier has accepted liability in writing to arrive at the deposit required calculation. The total of the current security deposit is then subtracted from the minimum deposit required to determine if a deposit increase is due or a deposit decrease is indicated.

(7) Company Officer Certification Information. The name, title, address, phone number and original signature of the authorized company officer by Board Resolution to the certification that the report is true, correct and complete and acknowledging the company's responsibility to

post and maintain the required security deposit that is due as a result of this report.

(c) For public self insurers, with or without a joint powers authority, the report shall be filed by October 1 of each year to cover liabilities during the July 1-June 30 fiscal year and shall include:

(1) General Information.

(A) Name and address of master certificate holder (individual agency or joint powers authority as applicable), federal tax identification number, and type of public agency.

(B) Agency name of affiliates and certificate numbers of all joint power's members.

(C) A certification by the individual public agency or joint powers authority official that the report is true, correct and complete.

(D) Notification of any reincorporation, merger, change in name or identity or any additions to the self insurance program by the master certificate holder or any subsidiary/affiliate company during the reporting period, and identification of any employees not included in the self insurance program.

(E) Name and address of person to whom all correspondence related to self insurance should be addressed.

(F) Employment and wages paid in that fiscal year as reported to Employment Development Department on the employer's Form DE-6 Quarterly Report.

Exception: A Certificate to Self Insure that is revoked is not required to submit this information.

(2) Liability Report and Administrator Information.

(A) A Liabilities Report which shall include:

(1.) All claims reported shall be on a fiscal year basis (starting July 1 and ending June 30 of the reporting years), with all claims reported on or before June 30 of each of the five prior fiscal years, showing indemnity and medical payments grouped as incurred liability, paid to date and future liability.

(2.) All open claims reported prior to the 5 years shall also be reported as required in (b)(2)(a)(1.), but in a single line entry.

(3.) Joint Powers Authorities (JPA) shall report the consolidated liabilities of all members of the JPA on one Liabilities Report.

(B) A Liabilities by Reporting Location Report is also required to be completed in full for each claims adjusting location.

Note 1: A reporting location report is required to be submitted in addition to the consolidated report, if one certificate is merged into the file of a second certificate (i.e. merger of school districts).

(3) Claims Information for reporting year shall meet the requirements in subsection (b)(2)(A)(3.)-(4).

(A) List of all open indemnity claims for a Joint Powers Authority may be consolidated into a single listing for the entire JPA.

(4) Claims Administrator Information shall meet the requirements in subsection (b)(2)(A)(5.)-(7.).

(5) Location of Claims Records Information. The public self insurer shall comply with Section 15251(b)(3).

(6) Insurance Information. The public self insurer shall comply with Section 15251(b)(4).

(7) Open Indemnity Claims Information. The public self insurer shall comply with Section 15251(b)(5)(A)-(B).

(8) Funding of Liabilities Information.

(A) A Funding of Liabilities report for a self insured public entity without joint power authority membership shall include:

(1.) Method agency uses to fund the outstanding worker's compensation liabilities.

(2.) A statement indicating if the agency funds for incurred but not reported claims and if yes, the amount.

(3.) A statement indicating if the funding is set aside solely to pay the agency's workers' compensation liabilities, and if yes, the amount.

(4.) A statement indicating if the agency has an outside independent claims auditor review the case reserve practices and general claims management.

(5.) A statement indicating if the agency has an outside independent actuary to review future liability funding and the date of any such review.

(B) A Funding of Liabilities Report for each self-insured entity with joint power authority membership shall include:

(1.) Method joint power authority uses to fund the outstanding worker's compensation liabilities.

(2.) A statement indicating if the joint power authority sets aside aggregate funding for incurred but not reported claims.

(3.) A statement indicating if the joint power authority had an outside independent claims auditor review the claims.

(4.) A statement indicating if the joint power authority had an actuary study of the joint power authority's funding of worker's compensation liabilities by an outside, independent actuary.

(5.) A statement indicating if the joint power authority had an annual financial audit conducted by a certified public accountant.

(6.) A statement indicating who establishes the level of funding for the joint power authority worker's compensation claims.

(7.) A statement indicating if a member of the joint power authority can leave and take their claims liability and claims with them when they withdraw their membership.

(8.) A statement indicating if the joint power authority had authority under it governing document to assess joint power authority members for additional funding, if necessary.

(d) The Manager may, for good cause, require any self insurer to submit a Self Insurer's Annual Report covering a six-month interim period, in addition to the annual report specified in subsection (b) and (c) of this section.

(1) For private self insurers, such interim reports, when required, shall cover the period starting January 1 and ending June 30 of each year and shall be due on September 1 of each year.

(2) Public self insurer's interim reports shall cover July 1 through December 31 and shall be due on March 1 of each year.

(e) The Manager shall assess the civil penalty set forth in Labor Code Section 3702.9(a) against any self insurer for failure to file a complete and timely Self Insurer's Annual Report. Continued failure to file an Annual Report sixty days after assessment of civil penalties pursuant to Section 3702.9(a) shall be good cause for revocation of a certificate to self insure.

(f) For good cause shown by the self insurer or its administrative agency, the Manager may grant additional time to a self insurer to file the report without penalty.

(g) Unless otherwise approved by the Manager, the consolidated liabilities report (page 2 of the annual report) and reporting location reports (page 3 of the annual report) shall be signed by a competent person pursuant to Section 15452 of these regulations, in the employment of the self insurer or administrative agency for the self-insurance plan.

(1) The employer's certification on the Self Insurer's report shall be signed by:

(A) an officer or employee of the self insurer authorized by the Board of Director's Resolution to sign documents for self insurance matters; or

(B) an authorized public self insurer officer or employee; or

(C) an authorized officer or employee of the joint powers authority to which the public agency is a member; or

(D) an authorized officer or employee of the Self Insurer's Security Fund where the Director has turned over responsibility for an insolvent private self insurer's claim liability to the Fund pursuant to Labor Code Section 3701.5(c).

Note: Authority cited: Sections 54, 55 and 3702.10, Labor Code. Reference: Sections 59, 129, 3700, 3701.5, 3702.2, 3702.3, 3702.9 and 3702.10, Labor Code.

History: 1. Amendment filed 6-1-72; effective thirtieth day thereafter (Register 72, No. 23).

2. Amendment of section heading and text filed 10-16-92; operative 11-16-92 (Register 92, No. 42).

3. Amendment of subsections (a) and (b)(5)(B) and new subsection (b)(5)(B)1 filed 8-10-93; operative 8-10-93 (Register 93, No. 33).

4. Amendment of subsections (a)-(b), (b)(1)(F) Exception and (b)(5)(B) filed 6-30-94; operative 6-30-94 (Register 94, No. 26).

5. Change without regulatory effect amending subsections (b)(1)(F) and (c)(1)(F) filed 10-18-95 pursuant to section 100, title 1, California Code of Regulations (Register 95, No. 42).

6. Amendment filed 5-7-2001; operative 6-6-2001 (Register 2001, No. 19).

7. Change without regulatory effect amending subsection (a)(1) and form A4-40a (incorporated by reference) filed 8-1-2001 pursuant to section 100, title 1, California Code of Regulations (Register 2001, No. 31).

8. Change without regulatory effect amending subsection (b)(2)(A)(7.) filed 4-7-2003 pursuant to section 100, title 1, California Code of Regulations (Register 2003, No. 15).

Ref.: Hanna §§ 1.19, 2.11[2], 2.11[3].

§15252. Repealed.

Note: Authority cited: Sections 54, 55 and 59, Labor Code. Reference: Sections 129, 3700, 3700(b), 3701, 3702, 3702.5, 3702.6, 3703, 3704, 3705, Labor Code.

History: 1. Amendment filed 12-3-69; effective thirtieth day thereafter (Register 69, No. 49).

2. Repealer and new section filed 6-1-72; effective thirtieth day thereafter (Register 72, No. 23).

3. Amendment filed 11-19-75; effective thirtieth day thereafter (Register 75, No. 47).

4. Amendment filed 11-21-78; effective thirtieth day thereafter (Register 78, No. 47).

5. Repealer filed 10-16-92; operative 11-16-92 (Register 92, No. 42).

Ref.: Hanna §§ 1.19, 2.11[2].

§15253. Repealed.

Note: Authority cited: Sections 54, 55 and 3702.10, Labor Code.

History: 1. New section filed 6-1-72; effective thirtieth day thereafter (Register 72, No. 23).

2. Amendment filed 11-21-78; effective thirtieth day thereafter (Register 78, No. 47).

3. Repealer of text and amendment of Note filed 10-16-92; operative 11-16-92 (Register 92, No. 42).

ARTICLE 6
Estimating Work Injury Claims and Medical Reports

§15300. Estimating and Reporting Work Injury Claims.

(a) A list of open indemnity claims shall be submitted with each self insurer's annual report as required by Section 15251(b)(5)(A)-(B) and (c)(7).

(b) The administrator shall set a realistic estimate of future liability for each indemnity claim listed on the self insurer's annual report based on computations which reflect the probable total future cost of compensation and medical benefits due or that can reasonably expected to be due over the life of the claim. Each estimate listed on the self insurer's annual report shall be based on information in possession of the administrator at the-ending date of the period of time covered by the annual report. Estimated future liabilities listed on the annual report must represent the probable total future cost of compensation for the injury or disease based on information documented as in possession of the administrator at the ending date of the period of time covered by the annual report. In setting estimates of future liability, the administrator shall adhere to the following principles:

(1) Each estimate of future liability shall separately reflect an indemnity component and a medical component. The indemnity component shall include the estimated future cost of all temporary disability, permanent disability, death benefits including burial costs, and vocational rehabilitation including vendor costs. The medical component shall include the estimated future cost of all medical treatment, including costs of medical cost containment programs if those costs are allocated to the particular claim, and the estimated future cost of medical evaluations. Estimates of future liability shall include any increases in compensation in either component reasonably expected to be payable pursuant to Labor Code Sections 132a, 4553, and/or 5814.

(2) In estimating future permanent disability costs, where there are conflicting permanent disability ratings, the estimate shall be based on the higher rating unless there is sufficient evidence in the claim file to support a lower estimate.

(3) In estimating future medical costs where the injured worker's injury has not reached maximum medical improvement or permanent and stationary status, the estimate shall be based on projected costs for the total anticipated period of treatment throughout the life of the claim.

(4) In estimating future medical costs where the injured worker's injury has reached maximum medical improvement or permanent and stationary status, the estimate shall be based on average annual costs over the past three years since the injury reached maximum medical improvement or permanent and stationary status, or a lesser period if three years have not passed since the injury reached maximum medical improvement or permanent and stationary status, projected over the life expectancy of the injured worker. Estimates shall include any additional costs such as medical procedures or surgeries that can reasonably be expected over the life of the claim.

(5) Estimates based on average past costs shall be increased to include any costs that can reasonably be expected to occur that are not included within the averages. Estimates based on average past costs may be reduced to account for any treatment not reasonably expected to occur in the future based on medical documentation in possession of the administrator.

(6) Estimates of future medical costs based on average past costs shall not be reduced based

on undocumented anticipated reductions in frequency of treatment or to reflect the substitution of treatments with a lower cost than utilized by the injured worker that may be available but that the injured worker is not utilizing. Estimates based on average past costs may be reduced based on reductions in the approved medical fee schedule and based on utilization review, except that reductions in estimates based on utilization review may not be reduced if the reductions are reasonably disputed. Estimates of future liability may be reduced based on the expectation of a third party recovery only in instances where an Order allowing credit has been issued pursuant to Labor Code Section 3861.

(7) Estimates of lifetime medical care and life pension benefits shall be determined based on the injured worker's life expectancy according to the most recent U.S. Life Expectancy Tables as reported by the U.S. Department of Health and Human Services, Centers for Disease Control and Prevention. Note: the most recent life expectancy tables can be found at http://www.cdc.gov/nchs/datawh/nchsdefs/lifeexpectancy.htm.

(8) Estimates of permanent disability shall not be reduced based on apportionment unless the claim file includes documentation supporting apportionment.

(9) Estimates shall not be reduced to reflect present value of future benefits.

(c) All medical-only claims reported on the self insurer's annual report shall be estimated on the basis of computations which will develop the total future cost of medical benefits due or that can reasonably expected to be due based on information documented as in possession of the administrator at the ending date of the period of time covered by the annual report.

(d) Estimates of future liability shall not be decreased based on projected third party recoveries or projected reimbursements from aggregate excess insurance, nor shall reported paid costs be decreased based on third party recoveries or aggregate excess insurance reimbursements.

(e) The incurred liability estimate on known claims may be capped at the retention level of any specific excess workers' compensation insurance policy to the extent that each claim has not been denied in writing by the carrier. The self insurer's claims administrator shall list each claim covered by a specific excess insurance policy on Part VI-B of the Self Insurer's Annual Report. An adjustment to the total deposit required to be posted shall be made for claims covered by specific excess insurance policy on the annual report to the extent that they meet the requirements in Section 15251(b)(5)(B) of these regulations.

(f) Estimates of incurred liability, payments-made-to-date and estimated future liability of all compensation benefits shall be made immediately available at the time of audit if not already documented in the claim file, or when requested by the Manager.

(g) The administrator shall adjust the estimate immediately upon receipt of medical reports, orders of the Appeals Board, or other relevant information that affects the valuation of the claim. Each estimate shall be reviewed no less than annually. Estimates set by a prior administrator shall be reviewed by the current administrator before filing the Self Insurer's Annual Report.

Note: Authority cited: Sections 54, 55 and 3702.10, Labor Code. Reference: Sections 54, 55, 59, 129, 132a, 3700, 3702.3, 3702.6, 3702.10, 3703, 3740-3745, 3861, 4553 and 5814, Labor Code.

History: 1. Amendment filed 12-3-69; effective thirtieth day thereafter (Register 69, No. 49).

2. Amendment of article heading, section heading, section and new Note filed 8-10-93; operative 9-9-93 (Register 93, No. 33).

3. Repealer and new subsection (b), new subsections (b)(1)-(4), amendment of subsection (c), repealer and new subsection (d), new subsection (g) and amendment of Note filed 2-9-2006; operative 3-11-2006 (Register 2006, No. 6).

§15301. Revision of Estimates.

The Manager shall have authority to revise private sector self insurer's estimates when information from any relevant source in the Manager's possession indicates the estimates are inaccurate or inadequate. Deposit recalculations shall be made at the same time or after the self-insurer has been notified of the Manager's revisions and given an opportunity to object to the increases in deposit or revision to liability estimates.

Note: Authority cited: Sections 54, 55 and 3702.10, Labor Code. Reference: Sections 54, 55, 59, 129, 3700, 3701.5, 3702.3, 3702.6, 3702.10 and 3740-3745, Labor Code.

History: 1. Amendment of section and new Note filed 8-10-93; operative 9-9-93 (Register 93, No. 33).

§15302. Medical Reports.

The Manager, when deemed necessary for proper administration of self-insurance, may require a self-insurer to provide a true copy of any relevant medical report in the possession of the self-insurer, its agent, or representative.

Note: Authority cited: Sections 54, 55 and 3702.10, Labor Code. Reference: Sections 54, 55, 59, 129, 3700, 3701, 3701.5, 3702, 3702.3, 3702.6, 3702.10 and 3740-3745, Labor Code.

History: 1. Amendment filed 11-19-75; effective thirtieth day thereafter (Register 75, No. 47).

2. Amendment of section and new Note filed 8-10-93; operative 9-9-93 (Register 93, No. 33).

§15303. Medical, Surgical, Hospital Contract.

No contract for medical, surgical, or hospital services shall relieve the self-insurer from reporting the total future determined and estimated cost of said services in accordance with Section 15300 of these regulations. For purposes of this section, a valid and effective policy of workers' compensation insurance providing for full payment of medical, surgical, or hospital services shall not be construed as a contract for medical, surgical, or hospital services.

Note: Authority cited: Sections 54, 55 and 3702.10, Labor Code. Reference: Sections 54, 55, 59, 129, 3700, 3701, 3701.5, 3702.3, 3702.6, 3703 and 3740-3745, Labor Code.

History: 1. Amendment filed 11-19-75; effective thirtieth day thereafter (Register 75, No. 47).

2. Amendment of section and new Note filed 8-10-93; operative 9-9-93 (Register 93, No. 33).

ARTICLE 7
Injury and Illness Prevention Program

§15350. Repealed.

Note: Authority cited: Sections 54 and 55, Labor Code. Reference: Sections 3700, 3701, 3702, 3702.5, 3702.6, 3703, 3704, 3705, Labor Code.

History: 1. Amendment filed 12-3-69; effective thirtieth day thereafter (Register 69, No. 49).

2. Amendment filed 11-19-75; effective thirtieth day thereafter (Register 75, No. 47).

3. Amendment of article heading, repealer of section, and adoption of Note filed 12-18-92; operative 1-19-93 (Register 92, No. 51).

§15350.1. Repealed.

Note: Authority cited: Sections 54 and 55, Labor Code. Reference: Sections 3700, 3700(b), 3701, 3702, 3702.5, 3702.6, 3703, 3704 and 3705, Labor Code.

History: 1. Amendment filed 11-21-78; effective thirtieth day thereafter (Register 78, No. 47).

2. Repealer of section and amendment of Note filed 12-18-92; operative 1-19-93 (Register 92, No. 51).

§15350.2. Repealed.

Note: Authority cited: Sections 54 and 55, Labor Code. Reference: Sections 3700, 3700(b), 3701, 3702, 3702.5, 3702.6, 3703, 3704 and 3705, Labor Code.

History: 1. Amendment filed 11-21-78; effective thirtieth day thereafter (Register 78, No. 47).

2. Repealer of section and amendment of Note filed 12-18-92; operative 1-19-93 (Register 92, No. 51).

§15350.5. Repealed.

Note: Authority cited: Sections 54 and 55, Labor Code. Reference: Sections 3700, 3700(b), 3701, 3702, 3702.5, 3702.6, 3703, 3704, 3705, Labor Code.

History: 1. Amendment filed 11-21-78; effective thirtieth day thereafter (Register 78, No. 47).

2. Repealer of section and amendment of Note filed 12-18-92; operative 1-19-93 (Register 92, No. 51).

§15351. Repealed.

Note: Authority cited: Sections 54 and 55, Labor Code. Reference: Sections 3700, 3700(b), 3701, 3702, 3702.5, 3702.6, 3703, 3704, 3705, Labor Code.

History: 1. Repealer and new section filed 6-1-72; effective thirtieth day thereafter (Register 72, No. 23).

2. Amendment filed 11-19-75; effective thirtieth day thereafter (Register 75, No. 47).

3. Repealer of section and adoption of Note filed 12-18-92; operative 1-19-93 (Register 92, No. 51).

§15352. Repealed.

Note: Authority cited: Sections 54 and 55, Labor Code. Reference: Sections 3700, 3700(b), 3701, 3702, 3702.5, 3702.6, 3703, 3704, 3705, Labor Code.

History: 1. Repealer and new section filed 6-1-72; effective thirtieth day thereafter (Register 72, No. 23).

2. Amendment filed 11-19-75; effective thirtieth day thereafter (Register 75, No. 47).

3. Repealer of section and adoption of Note filed 12-18-92; operative 1-19-93 (Register 92, No. 51).

§15353. Injury and Illness Prevention Program.

(a) As part of the application process, a private sector applicant for a Certificate to Self-Insure shall provide one of the following:

(1) an independent evaluation of the applicant employer's injury and illness prevention program as set forth in Labor Code Section 6314.5 and 6401.7 and Section 3203 of Title 8, California Code of Regulations prepared by an independent, licensed, California professional engineer, or a Certified Safety Professional, and/or a Certified Industrial Hygienist.

(A) The evaluation preparer shall be considered independent if: (i) the preparer or the preparer's firm has had no business dealings with the applicant employer or its owner for the prior two years; (ii) the preparer is not or has not been employed by the applicant employer's present or prior insurance carrier or insurance broker during the past 5 years; and (iii) the preparer or preparer's firm has not been employed by the applicant employer or its parent in a safety and health or accident prevention capacity during the past 5 years.

(B) The evaluation report preparer shall disclose any such business relationships noted in subsection (a)(1)(A) of this Section in the evaluation report. The Manager shall reject a submitted evaluation report where a conflict of interest may exist between the evaluation preparer and the applicant employer as set forth in Subsection (a)(1)(A); or

(2) Written report or citation of a Division of Occupational Safety and Health (DOSH) inspection of the applicant employer's injury and illness prevention program pursuant to Labor Code Section 6314.5 and 6401.7 and Section 3203 of Title 8, California Code of Regulations. The Division of Occupational Safety and Health (DOSH) inspection shall have been conducted within 120 days of the date of application to become self insured.

(b) An evaluation report pursuant to subsection (a) that shows the applicant for a Certificate to Self Insure to be without an effective injury prevention program shall be good cause for denial of the application for self insurance by the Director without prejudice to reapplication at a later date.

(c) The applicant employer must abate all serious violations found in the safety and health evaluation report. Written verification of abatement must be sent from the evaluation preparer to Self Insurance Plans.

Note: The pamphlet "A sample of an Injury and Illness Prevention Program" can be obtained from the Cal/OSHA Consultation Services.

Note: Authority cited: Sections 54, 55 and 3702.10, Labor Code. Reference: Sections 59, 3700, 3702, 3702.10, 6314.5, 6319 and 6401.7, Labor Code.

History: 1. New section filed 11-21-78; effective thirtieth day thereafter (Register 78, No. 47).

2. Amendment of section heading, section and Note filed 12-18-92; operative 1-19-93 (Register 92, No. 51).

§15354. Willful or Repeat Violation of Injury Prevention Program by a Self Insurer.

Any private employer self insurer identified to the Director by the Division of Occupational Safety and Health pursuant to Labor Code Section 6319(f) shall provide proof of abatement of the repeat or willful violation of Section 3203 of Title 8, California Code of Regulations to the Manager. Failure to abate shall be good cause to revoke the Certificate to Self Insure issued to that self insurer after the opportunity for a hearing before the Director.

Note: Authority cited: Sections 54, 55 and 3702.10, Labor Code. Reference: Sections 54, 55, 59, 3700, 3702, 3702.10, 6314.5, 6319, 6401.7, Labor Code.

History: 1. New section filed 12-18-92; operative 1-19-93 (Register 92, No. 51).

ARTICLE 8
Transfer of Liabilities

§15360. Transfer of Claim Liabilities.

A current or former self insurer may transfer claim liabilities to a third party as set forth in subsections (a) through (e) of this section.

(a) Self-insured workers' compensation claim liabilities cannot be transferred to another entity without first applying for and receiving permission from the Director. Except as provided in Labor Code Section 3702.8(c), the claim liabilities being transferred shall be assumed and guaranteed with the standard Agreement of Assumption and Guarantee of Liabilities as provided for in Section 15211.2 of these regulations, with an assumption resolution executed by the Board of Directors if a corporation, by the general partners if a partnership, or by the owners if a sole proprietorship of the entity taking over the liabilities.

(1) The new holder of claim liabilities shall post the security deposit determined necessary by the Manager pursuant to Article 3 of these regulations.

(2) The Manager shall be provided with copies of the necessary documents involved in a

sale or transfer of claim liabilities from a self-insurer to another party.

(3) All other duties of a self insured employer in Labor Code Section 3702.8(a) shall be complied with by the self insured employer.

(b) The Manager may authorize the contractual transfer of claim liabilities, other than through a special excess worker's compensation insurance policy, from a self-insurer to an admitted worker's compensation insurance carrier provided:

(1) A copy of the signed contract between the self-insurer and carrier is provided to the Manager;

(2) The self-insurer continues to post the amount of deposit required by the Manager pursuant to Article 3 of these regulations;

(3) The claims contractually transferred to the carrier are administered in California by an admitted carrier or by a administrative agency holding a Certificate to Administer;

(4) Self Insurer's Annual Reports are submitted by the self-insurer as required by these regulations until all claims are resolved; and

(5) All other duties of a self insurer in Labor Code Section 3702.8(a) are complied with by the self insured employer.

(c) Where a former self-insurer transfers liabilities to a carrier via a special excess workers' compensation insurance policy as provided in Labor Code Section 3702.8(c), but no carrier performance bond is posted, the self-insurer's security deposit shall be held for three years before release.

(d) Claim liabilities of a member public agency of a pooling workers' compensation joint powers authority may be transferred if:

(1) The joint powers authority agreement permits a member public agency to take their claim liabilities out of the joint powers authority pool if the public agency elects to do so;

(2) The public agency member elects to transfer its claim liability; and

(3) The claims are transferred to another workers' compensation joint authority, or to a self administered or administrative agency administered or carrier administered self insurance program.

(e) Private group self insurers and their group members claim liabilities shall not be transferred and shall remain the liability of the group self insurer.

Exception: Claim liabilities of a former group member may be transferred pursuant to Labor Code Section 3702.8(c).

Note: Authority cited: Sections 54, 55 and 3702.10, Labor Code. Reference: Sections 129, 3700, 3700(b), 3701, 3702, 3702.5, 3702.6, 3702.8, 3703, 3705 and 3740-3745, Labor Code.

History: 1. Amendment of article heading, repealer of section 15360, and renumbering and amendment of former section 15361.5 to section 15360 filed 10-27-93; operative 11-26-93 (Register 93, No. 44).

2. Amendment filed 6-30-94; operative 6-30-94 (Register 94, No. 26).

§15361. Repealed.

Note: Authority cited: Sections 54, 55 and 3702.10, Labor Code. Reference: Sections 54, 55 and 3702.10, Labor Code.

History: 1. Amendment filed 6-1-72; effective thirtieth day thereafter (Register 72, No. 23).

2. Repealer filed 10-27-93; operative 11-26-93 (Register 93, No. 44).

§15361.5. Renumbered.

Note: Authority cited: Sections 54, 55 and 59, Labor Code. Reference: Sections 129, 3700, 3700(b), 3701, 3702, 3702.5, 3702.6, 3703, 3704 and 3705, Labor Code.

History: 1. New section filed 11-21-78; effective thirtieth day thereafter (Register 78, No. 47).

2. Renumbering and amendment of former section 15361.5 to section 15360 filed 10-27-93; operative 11-26-93 (Register 93, No. 44).

§15362. Repealed.

Note: Authority cited: Sections 54, 55 and 59, Labor Code. Reference: Sections 129, 3700, 3700(b), 3701, 3702, 3702.5, 3702.6, 3703, 3704 and 3705, Labor Code.

History: 1. Amendment filed 11-21-78; effective thirtieth day thereafter (Register 78, No. 47).

2. Repealer filed 10-27-93; operative 11-26-93 (Register 93, No. 44).

ARTICLE 9
Recordkeeping and Audits

§15400. Claim File.

(a) Every self-insurer or its administrative agency shall keep a claim file of each indemnity and medical-only work-injury occurring on or after January 1, 1990, in accordance with Title 8, Section 10101 and Section 10101.1.

(b) For work injuries occurring prior to January 1, 1990, every self insurer shall keep a claim file including those claims which were denied. Said claim file shall contain, but not be limited to, a copy of:

(1) Employers Report of Occupational Injury or Illness, Form No. 5020;

(2) Every report made to the Administrative Director of the Division of Industrial Accidents; including but not limited to the letter of denial to the employee;

(3) Doctor's First Report of Occupational Injury or Illness, Form No. 5021;

(4) Every subsequent relevant medical report;

(5) All applicable orders of the Workers' Compensation Appeals Board and reports relating thereto;

(6) A record of payment of compensation benefits as compensation is defined in Section 3207 of the Labor Code, together with a record of the periods covered by disability payments, including a copy of DIA Form 500, Notice of Termination of Benefits;

(c) For injuries reported on or after January 1, 2006, each self administering self insurer and claims administrative agency shall maintain a claim file for each indemnity and medical-only claim, including denied claims, and shall ensure that each file is complete and current for each claim. Contents of claim files may be in hard copy, in electronic form, or some combination of hard copy and electronic form. Files maintained in hard copy shall be in chronological order with the most recently dated documents on top, or subdivided into sections such as medical reports, benefit notices, correspondence, claim notes, and vocational rehabilitation. In addition to the contents specified in Title 8, California Code of Regulations, Section 10101.1, each indemnity file shall contain itemized written documentation showing the basis for the calculation of estimated future liability and for each change in estimated future liability for the claim. Files or portions of files maintained in electronic form shall be easily retrievable.

Note: Authority cited: Sections 54, 55, 59 and 3702.10, Labor Code. Reference: Sections 59, 129, 3700, 3700(b), 3701, 3702, 3702.1, 3702.5, 3702.6, 3703, 3704 and 3705, Labor Code.

History: 1. Amendment filed 12-3-69; effective thirtieth day thereafter (Register 69, No. 49).

2. Amendment filed 11-19-75; effective thirtieth day thereafter (Register 75, No. 47).

3. New subsection (g) filed 11-21-78; effective thirtieth day thereafter (Register 78, No. 47).

4. Amendment filed 2-19-92; operative 3-20-92 (Register 92, No. 13).

5. Change without regulatory effect amending subsection (a) filed 11-3-96 pursuant to section 100, title 1, California Code of Regulations (Register 96, No. 46).

6. Repealer and new subsection (c) filed 2-9-2006; operative 3-11-2006 (Register 2006, No. 6).

1992 Note: The use of a "Reserve Worksheet" developed by the administrator to document initial estimates of incurred liability and subsequent adjustments to the estimate is recommended.

Ref.: Hanna § 2.11[2].

§15400.1. Claim Log.

(a) After January 1, 1993, every self-insurer or its administrative agency shall maintain:

(1) a manually prepared log of all work injury claims for each self-insurer at each adjusting location in accordance with Title 8, Section 10103 and 10103.1; or

(2) a computerized log of claims for each self-insurer at each adjusting location in accordance with Title 8, Section 10103 and 10103.1.

(b) The claim log shall be maintained at each of the self-insurer's or its administrative agency's claims adjusting locations. The claim log at each location shall be kept current and shall include all claims reported to the adjusting location.

(c) A claim log shall be found to be materially deficient if it fails to contain the elements of Title 8, Section 10103 and 10103.1; or fails to include all reported claims; or is not provided to the Manager or any subsequent administrator in readable form.

Note: Authority cited: Sections 54, 55 and 3702.10, Labor Code. Reference: Sections 59, 129, 3700, 3702.1 and 3702.10, Labor Code.

History: 1. New sections 15400.1, 15400.2, and 15400.3 filed 12-3-69; effective thirtieth day thereafter (Register 69, No. 49).

2. Amendment filed 2-19-92; operative 3-20-92 (Register 92, No. 13).

3. Change without regulatory effect amending subsections (a)(1)-(2) and (c) filed 10-18-95 pursuant to section 100, title 1, California Code of Regulations (Register 95, No. 42).

4. Change without regulatory effect amending subsections (a)(1)-(2) and (c) filed 1-9-98 pursuant to section 100, title 1, California Code of Regulations (Register 98, No. 2).

§15400.2. Maintenance of Records.

(a) All claim files shall be kept and maintained for a period of five years from the date of injury or from the date on which the last provision of compensation benefits occurred as defined in Labor Code Section 3207, whichever is later. Claim files with awards for future benefits shall not be destroyed, but two years after the date of the last provision of workers' compensation benefits as defined in Labor Code Section 3207, they may be converted to an inactive or closed status by the administrator, but only if there is no reasonable expectation that future benefits will be claimed or provided.

(b) Inactive and closed claim files may be microfilmed for storage, however, the original paper files shall be maintained for at least two years after the claim has been closed or become inactive. Such microfilmed files must be readily reproducible into legible paper form if requested by the Manager for audit.

(c) All claim files and the claim logs shall be kept and maintained in California unless the Manager has given written approval to a self insurer or former self insurer to administer its workers' compensation self-insurance plan from a location outside of California.

(d) All claim files and claim logs, together with records of all compensation benefit payments, shall be readily available for inspection by the Manager or his representative.

Note: Authority cited: Sections 54, 55 and 3702.10, Labor Code. Reference: Sections 59, 129, 3700, 3702.1 and 3702.10, Labor Code.

History: 1. Amendment filed 2-19-92; operative 3-20-92 (Register 92, No. 13).

2. Amendment of subsection (a) filed 2-9-2006; operative 3-11-2006 (Register 2006, No. 6).

Ref.: Hanna § 2.11[2].

§15400.3. Repealed.

Note: Authority cited: Sections 54, 55 and 3702.10, Labor Code. Reference: Sections 55 and 3702.10, Labor Code.

History: 1. New section 15400.3 filed 12-3-69; effective thirtieth day thereafter (Register 69, No. 49).

2. Repealer filed 2-19-92; operative 3-20-92 (Register 92, No. 13).

§15401. Repealed.

Note: Authority cited: Sections 54, 55 and 3702.10, Labor Code. Reference: Sections 55 and 3702.10, Labor Code.

History: 1. New section 15401 filed 12-3-69; effective thirtieth day thereafter (Register 69, No. 49).

2. Repealer filed 2-19-92; operative 3-20-92 (Register 92, No. 13).

§15401.1. Repealed.

Note: Authority cited: Sections 54, 55 and 3702.10, Labor Code. Reference: Sections 55 and 3702.10, Labor Code.

History: 1. New section filed 6-1-72; effective thirtieth day thereafter (Register 72, No. 23).

2. Amendment filed 11-19-75; effective thirtieth day thereafter (Register 75, No. 47).

3. Repealer filed 2-19-92; operative 3-20-92 (Register 92, No. 13).

§15401.2. Repealed.

Note: Authority cited: Sections 54, 55 and 3702.10, Labor Code. Reference: Sections 59 and 3702.10, Labor Code.

History: 1. New section filed 11-19-75; effective thirtieth day thereafter (Register 75, No. 47).

2. Repealer filed 2-19-92; operative 3-20-92 (Register 92, No. 13).

§15402. Notice of Change of Administrator and Location of Records.

(a) Each self-insurer or administrative agency shall annually report on the Self Insurer's Annual Report form to the Manager the name, title, and office address of the person or persons appointed to administer the employer's self-insurance plan and of the location or locations of records required to be kept and maintained pursuant to Section 15400 of these regulations.

(b) The new administrator shall report any changes of the administrative agency administering the employer's self-insurance plan, or any change of location or locations of records in writing to the Manager no later than the date of such change.

Note: Authority cited: Sections 54, 55 and 3702.10, Labor Code. Reference: Sections 59, 129, 3700, 3702.1 and 3702.10, Labor Code.

History: 1. Amendment filed 6-1-72; effective thirtieth day thereafter (Register 72, No. 23).

2. Amendment filed 11-19-75; effective thirtieth day thereafter (Register 75, No. 47).

3. Amendment filed 2-19-92; operative 3-20-92 (Register 92, No. 13).

1992 Note: Reporting required by subsection (b) may be done by submitting a "Report of Changes" on the appropriate Division of Workers' Compensation AE Form 101 or AE Form 102 (see Plate L-1 and L-2 of the Appendix).

§15402.1. Self Insurer's Interim Report.

(a) A self-insurer and its administrative agency shall jointly submit to the Manager a self-insurer's annual report, covering any interim period between regularly scheduled reporting periods whenever any of the following changes occur in the administration of the employer's self insurance plan:

(1) A change from an agency-administered plan to another agency-administered plan, (i.e. from one third party administrator to another third party administrator);

(2) A change from an agency-administered plan to a self-administered plan;

(3) A change from a self-administered plan to an agency-administered plan; or

(b) The interim Self Insurers Annual Report shall be made by the former administrator on the applicable form as required by Section 15251 of these regulations, showing the self-insurer's claims experience as of the date of the change of administrative agencies.

(c) The interim self insurer's annual report shall be due within thirty (30) days of the change of administrators. The self insurer shall provide a copy to the new administrator and three (3) copies to the Manager. The Manager may supply the new administrator with a copy of the interim report.

(d) The new administrator shall submit the year end self insurer's annual report for the self insurer which includes the total loss experience of all open and closed claims from all administrative agencies handling the self insurer's claims during the reporting period.

Note: Authority cited: Sections 54, 55 and 3702.10, Labor Code. Reference: Sections 59, 129, 3700, 3702.1, 3702.2 and 3702.10, Labor Code.

History: 1. New section filed 6-1-72; effective thirtieth day thereafter (Register 72, No. 23).

2. Amendment filed 11-19-75; effective thirtieth day thereafter (Register 75, No. 47).

3. Amendment filed 2-19-92; operative 3-20-92 (Register 92, No. 13).

4. Change without regulatory effect amending subsection (b) filed 12-24-96 pursuant to Government Code section 11343.4(d) (Register 96, No. 52).

5. Repealer of subsection (a)(4) filed 5-10-2001; operative 6-9-2001 (Register 2001, No. 19).

§15402.2. Report of Transfer of Records.

(a) After July 1, 1992, at the time of a change of administration of a self insurance plan, as set forth in Section 15402.1(a) of these regulations, the former administrative agency or previously self administering self insurer shall submit to the Manager and to the new administrative agency a written report containing the following:

(1) A list of all open and closed claims for the self insurer in the possession of the former administrative agency as of the date of the transfer; and

(2) A written description of the physical location of all claimed files, the required claim logs, and any computer data files of the self insurer's plan. Physical location shall include claim files sent to storage and where stored; files sent to the self insurer; and files sent to the new administrator.

(b) Except where specified in a contractual agreement between the self insurer and the former administrative agency, all claim files, claim logs and computerized data files shall be the property of the self insurer and shall be returned to the self insurer or delivered to the new administrator or administrative agency designated by the self insurer.

(c) Failure of an administrative agency or self insurer to provide a Report of Transfer of Records as set forth in this section may be good cause for revocation of a certificate to administer.

Note: Authority cited: Sections 54, 55 and 3702.10, Labor Code. Reference: Sections 59, 129, 3700, 3702, 3702.1, 3702.2, 3702.7 and 3702.10, Labor Code.

History: 1. New section filed 11-19-75; effective thirtieth day thereafter (Register 75, No. 47).

2. Amendment filed 2-19-92; operative 3-20-92 (Register 92, No. 13).

§15402.3. Notice of Change of Membership in a Joint Powers Authority or in a Private Group Self Insurer.

(a) The joint powers authority shall notify the Manager when a Public entity with an affiliate certificate to self insure changes its membership from the existing joint powers authority to

(1) another joint powers authority;

(2) a carrier insured plan or;

(3) an independent self insured plan.

(b) The group administrator of each private group self insurer shall notify the Manager when any group member holding an Affiliate Certificate changes its membership from the existing group self insurer to:

(1) another private group self insurer;

(2) a carrier insured plan; or

(3) an independent self insured plan.

(c) The Manager shall be notified no later than the date of such change.

Note: Authority cited: Sections 54, 55 and 3702.10, Labor Code. Reference: Sections 59, 3700, 3702.5 and 3702.10, Labor Code.

History: 1. New section filed 2-19-92; operative 3-20-92 (Register 92, No. 13).

2. Amendment of section heading, new subsections (b)-(b)(3) and subsection redesignation filed 6-30-94; operative 6-30-94 (Register 94, No. 26).

§15402.4. Transfer of Claim Files and Computerized Claim File Data Information.

(a) Upon change of an administrative agency, all open claims shall be transferred immediately to the new administrative agency, unless otherwise provided by agreement between the self insurer, former administrator and new administrator.

(b) All closed claim files in the possession of the former administrator shall be transferred to the new administrator within 30 days, unless otherwise provided by agreement between the self insurer, former administrator and new administrator.

(c) All computerized claim file data showing all historical claim information, including payments and reserve data as of the date of the transfer of the open claim files shall be provided by the former administrator on the date that all open claim files are transferred, unless otherwise provided for by written agreement between the self insurer, former administrator and the new administrator. In the event that an agreement precludes the transfer of electronic claim contents of claims being transferred to the new administrator, the former administrator will provide hard copies of any required contents to the new administrator at its own expense. The closing date of the transactions on the computerized data shall coincide with the date of the physical transfer of the claim files to the new administrator. In the event that computerized data pertaining to the specific administration is changed by the former administrator after the physical claims have been transferred and the data provided to the new administrator, the former administrator shall provide reported computerized information to the new administrator within 14 days of any such changes.

Note: Authority cited: Sections 54, 55 and 3702.10, Labor Code. Reference: Sections 59, 129, 3700, 3702.1 and 3702.10, Labor Code.

History: 1. New section filed 2-19-92; operative 3-20-92 (Register 92, No. 13).

2. Amendment of subsection (c) filed 2-9-2006; operative 3-11-2006 (Register 2006, No. 6).

§15403. Audits.

(a) Pursuant to Labor Code Sections 129 and 3702.6, the Manager may order an audit of any self insurer or individual claim file at such reasonable times as is deemed necessary. Such audits shall include, but not be limited to, an audit of the files and records required by Section 15400 of these regulations. Such files and records shall be made readily available by the self insured employer or its administrative agency.

(b) In the event of an audit, the Manager may require that claims administered at the home of a telecommuting adjuster be presented for audit at a California office location of the administrator, or at a California location of the self insured employer.

Note: Authority cited: Sections 54, 55 and 3702.10, Labor Code. Reference: Sections 59, 129, 3700, 3702 and 3702.6, Labor Code.

History: 1. Amendment filed 6-1-72; effective thirtieth day thereafter (Register 72, No. 23).

2. Amendment filed 2-19-92; operative 3-20-92 (Register 92, No. 13).

3. Amendment designating first paragraph as subsection (a) and new subsection (b) filed 2-9-2006; operative 3-11-2006 (Register 2006, No. 6).

Ref.: Hanna § 1.19.

§15403.1. Notice of Special Audit.

When in the discretion of the Manager, a special audit as defined in Section 15201 of these regulations is necessary, the Manager shall notify the self-insurer of the requirement in writing fourteen (14) calendar days prior to the special audit and give the reasons therefor.

Note: Authority cited: Sections 54, 55 and 3702.10, Labor Code. Reference: Sections 59, 129, 3702.6 and 3702.10, Labor Code.

History: 1. New section filed 6-1-72; effective thirtieth day thereafter (Register 72, No. 23).

2. Repealer and new section filed 11-19-75; effective thirtieth day thereafter (Register 75, No. 47).

3. Amendment filed 2-19-92; operative 3-20-92 (Register 92, No. 13).

§15403.2. Repealed.

Note: Authority cited: Sections 54, 55 and 3702.10, Labor Code. Reference: Sections 59, 129, 3700, 3701 and 3702.10, Labor Code.

History: 1. New section filed 11-19-75; effective thirtieth day thereafter (Register 75, No. 47).

2. Amendment filed 11-21-78; effective thirtieth day thereafter (Register 78, No. 47).

3. Repealer filed 2-19-92; operative 3-20-92 (Register 92, No. 13).

§15404. Expenses of Out-of-State Audit.

The audit of any self insurer, pursuant to Section 15403 of these regulations, at locations outside of the State of California, shall be at the expense of the self-insurer. The Manager shall bill the self insurer for the expense incurred in making such out-of-state audit.

Note: Authority cited: Sections 54, 55 and 3702.10, Labor Code. Reference: Sections 59, 129, 3702.6 and 3702.10, Labor Code.

History: 1. Amendment filed 2-19-92; operative 3-20-92 (Register 92, No. 13).

§15404.1. Expense of Revoked Certificate Audit.

A self-insurer whose certificate to self insure has been revoked shall pay any expenses incurred by the Director or his representative in conducting an audit pursuant to Section 15425 of these regulations. The Manager shall bill the self insurer for expenses incurred.

Note: Authority cited: Sections 54, 55 and 3702.10, Labor Code. Reference: Sections 59, 129, 3702.6 and 3702.10, Labor Code.

History: 1. New section filed 6-1-72; effective thirtieth day thereafter (Register 72, No. 23).

2. Amendment filed 2-19-92; operative 3-20-92 (Register 92, No. 13).

§15404.2. Expense of Special Audit.

A self-insurer shall pay the expenses incurred whenever a special audit as defined in Section 15201, of these regulations, is ordered by the Manager pursuant to Sections 15403, 15404 and 15404.1 of these regulations. The Manager shall bill the self insurer for expenses incurred.

Note: Authority cited: Sections 54, 55 and 3702.10, Labor Code. Reference: Sections 59, 129, 3702.6 and 3702.10, Labor Code.

History: 1. New section filed 11-19-75; effective thirtieth day thereafter (Register 75, No. 47).

2. Amendment filed 2-19-92; operative 3-20-92 (Register 92, No. 13).

3. Change without regulatory effect amending section filed 10-18-95 pursuant to section 100, title 1, California Code of Regulations (Register 95, No. 42).

§15405. Confidentiality.

(a) Financial information submitted to the Director or Manager to establish the solvency and worth of any self insurer, applicant to be self insured, third party administrator, or of a guarantor of a self insurer or applicant to be self insured shall be considered confidential in accordance with Government Code Sections 6254 and 6255.

(b) Information obtained from any audit regarding the nature, extent or financial liability of any specific self insurer's workers' compensation claims, together with any and all like information regarding a specific self insurer's claims or financial condition, shall be confidential and shall be used solely for the purpose of applying the provisions of these regulations.

(c) The list of open claims and list of claims reported to excess insurance carriers in the Self Insurers Annual Report and any claims logs submitted to the Manager shall be confidential.

(d) The Manager shall disclose any financial or claims information to the Self Insurers' Security Fund on any private self insurer whose liabilities have been turned over to the Fund pursuant to Labor Code Section 3742 et seq. The Manager shall also disclose any financial information to the Self Insurers' Security Fund on any private self insurer who has filed bankruptcy, been unable to pay their liabilities, or failed to post an increase in deposit due that would potentially put the Fund in jeopardy for the self insurer's liabilities.

(e) At the written request of the Chief of the Division of Workers' Compensation, Office of Benefits and Enforcement, the Manager shall provide a copy of any audit report to the Division of Workers' Compensation. The self insured employer and/or administrator shall be notified of the release of the audit report to the Division of Workers' Compensation.

(f) Subject to the described conditions, the financial and audit information shall not be disclosed to any other department, entity or person without an order from an appropriate court or administrative subpoena from an agency of the State. The self-insured entity shall be promptly advised of the court order or subpoena by the Manager.

Note: Authority cited: Sections 54, 55 and 3702.10, Labor Code. Reference: Sections 59, 129, 3700, 3702.6 and 3702.10, Labor Code; and Sections 6254 and 6255, Government Code.

History: 1. Amendment filed 2-19-92; operative 3-20-92 (Register 92, No. 13).

§15406. Repealed.

Note: Authority cited: Sections 54, 55 and 3702.10, Labor Code. Reference: Sections 59, 3700, 3702.5 and 3702.10, Labor Code.

History: 1. New section filed 11-21-78; effective thirtieth day thereafter (Register 78, No. 47).

2. Repealer filed 2-19-92; operative 3-20-92 (Register 92, No. 13).

ARTICLE 10
Revocation of a Certificate to Self Insure or Certificate to Administer and Continuing Jurisdiction

§15420. Compliance With Statutes and Regulatory Requirements.

Self-insured employers and their administrative agencies shall comply with applicable regulations governing the administration of self-insurance pursuant to Labor Code Sections 129, and 3700-3709.5, which are adopted in accordance with the provisions of the California Administrative Procedure Act (Government Code, Title 2, Division 3, Part 1, Chapters 3.5 [commencing with Section 11340]). Failure to comply with these statutes governing administration of self insurance or with these regulations may be good cause for revocation of a Certificate to Self Insure or Certificate to Administer or other action by the Director.

Note: Authority cited: Sections 54, 55 and 3702.10, Labor Code. Reference: Sections 54, 55, 59, 129, 3700, 3701, 3701.5, 3702, 3702.3, 3702.5, 3702.6, 3702.10, 3703, 3705, 3740-3745, Labor Code.

History: 1. Repealer of Article 10 (§§15420-15423) and new Article 10 (§§15420-15427) filed 6-1-72; effective thirtieth day thereafter (Register 72, No. 23). For prior history, see Register 69, No. 49.

2. Amendment of article heading, section heading and section and new Note filed 11-24-93; operative 12-24-93 (Register 93, No. 48).

§15421. Repealed.

Note: Authority cited: Sections 55 and 3702.10, Labor Code. Reference: Sections 54, 55 and 3702.10, Labor Code.

History: 1. Repealer filed 11-24-93; operative 12-24-93 (Register 93, No. 48).

§15422. Voluntary Revocation.

Any self-insurer or administrative agency may voluntarily request that its Certificate to Self Insure or Certificate to Administer be revoked at any time by informing the Manager in writing. The Director shall revoke the Certificate to Self Insure or Certificate to Administer after the self-insurer or administrative agency has:

(a) Shown to the satisfaction of the Director that the self-insurer or administrative agency has established a program to discharge all liabilities and all responsibilities incurred by the self-insurer or administrator during the period the Certificate to Self Insure or Certificate to Administer was in force; and

(b) Surrendered the Certificate to Self Insure or Certificate to Administer.

Note: Authority cited: Sections 54, 55 and 3702.10, Labor Code. Reference: Sections 54, 55, 59, 129, 3700, 3701, 3701.5, 3702, 3702.3, 3702.5, 3702.6, 3703, 3705 and 3740-3745, Labor Code.

History: 1. Amendment of section and new Note filed 11-24-93; operative 12-24-93 (Register 93, No. 48).

Ref.: Hanna § 2.11[3].

§15423. Revocation.

Revocation for Cause. Proceedings to revoke a Certificate to Self Insure or Certificate to Administer for good cause as defined in Labor Code Section 3702 and in these regulations shall be after Notice of Intent and opportunity for a hearing in accordance with Article 11 of these Regulations. The Notice of Intention to Revoke a Certificate to Self Insure or Certificate to Administer shall include a clear description of cause for revocation.

Note: Authority cited: Sections 54, 55, 59, 129, 3700, 3700(b), 3701, 3701.5, 3702, 3702.5, 3702.6, 3703, 3705 and 3740-3745, Labor Code. Reference: Sections 129, 3700, 3700(b), 3701, 3702, 3702.5, 3702.6, 3703, 3705, Labor Code.

History: 1. Repealer and new section filed 11-21-78; effective thirtieth day thereafter (Register 78, No. 47).

2. Amendment of section heading and section and Note filed 11-24-93; operative 12-24-93 (Register 93, No. 48).

Ref.: Hanna § 2.11[3].

§15424. Revoked Certificate Report.

The Director shall require a former self-insurer whose certificate to self insure has been revoked to continue to submit self-insurer's annual reports pursuant to Section 15251 of these regulations, setting forth the status of all open work-injury claims until all claims are resolved.

Note: Authority cited: Sections 54, 55 and 3702.10, Labor Code. Reference: Sections 54, 55, 59, 129, 3700, 3701, 3701.5, 3702, 3702.3, 3702.6, 3702.10, 3703, 3705, 3740-3745, Labor Code.

History: 1. Amendment of section and new Note filed 11-24-93; operative 12-24-93 (Register 93, No. 48).

Ref.: Hanna § 2.11[3].

§15425. Revoked Certificate Audit.

Pursuant to Sections 15403 and 15427 of these regulations, the Manager shall continue to audit the work-injury cases of any former self-insurer whose certificate to self insure has been revoked.

Note: Authority cited: Sections 54, 55 and 3702.10, Labor Code. Reference: Sections 54, 55, 59, 129, 3700, 3701, 3701.5, 3702, 3702.3, 3702.6, 3702.10, 3703, 3705, 3740-3745, Labor Code.

History: 1. Amendment of section and new Note filed 11-24-93; operative 12-24-93 (Register 93, No. 48).

§15426. Release of Security Deposit.

(a) Upon any revocation of a private employer's certificate to self-insure, a new deposit level shall be determined by the Manager to be sufficient to secure all actual and potential liabilities. The former self insurer shall continue to be responsible to increase the deposit at the written request of the Manager as required in Section 15210 of these regulations.

(b) Except as provided in Labor Code Section 3702.8(c), the deposit shall not be reduced below the statutory minimum pursuant to Labor Code Section 3701.

Note: Authority cited: Sections 54, 55 and 3702.10, Labor Code. Reference: Sections 54, 55, 59, 129, 3700, 3701, 3701.5, 3702, 3702.3, 3702.6, 3702.10, 3703, 3705, 3740-3745, Labor Code.

History: 1. Amendment of section heading and newly designated subsection (a), and new subsection (b) and Note filed 11-24-93; operative 12-24-93 (Register 93, No. 48).

§15427. Continuing Jurisdiction.

After revocation of a certificate to self insure, the Director's jurisdiction over work injuries sustained during the period of self-insurance shall continue until all liabilities and all responsibilities have been terminated in accordance with law.

Note: Authority cited: Sections 54, 55 and 3702.10, Labor Code. Reference: Sections 54, 55, 59, 129, 3700, 3701, 3701.5, 3702, 3702.3, 3702.6, 3702.10, 3703, 3705, 3740-3745, Labor Code.

History: 1. Amendment of section and new Note filed 11-24-93; operative 12-24-93 (Register 93, No. 48).

Ref.: Hanna § 2.11[3].

§15428. Administration of Claims After Revocation.

(a) A private sector self insurer whose certificate to self insure has been revoked shall continue to provide competent administration of workers' compensation claims incurred during the period of self insurance in accordance with Sections 15450-15463 of these regulations, and the claims shall be administered from within the State of California.

(b) If it is determined by the Manager that the claims are not being competently administered, the Manager shall arrange for the claims administration. The cost of administration shall be borne by the former self insurer.

Note: Authority cited: Sections 54, 55 and 3702.10, Labor Code. Reference: Sections 54, 55, 59, 129, 3700, 3701, 3701.5, 3702, 3702.3, 3702.6, 3702.10, 3703, 3705, 3740-3745, Labor Code.

History: 1. New section filed 11-24-93; operative 12-24-93 (Register 93, No. 48).

Ref.: Hanna § 2.11[3].

ARTICLE 11
Hearing and Appeal Procedures

§15430. Hearing.

The Director may initiate an investigation or hold a hearing to implement the law and regulations with respect to the following self insurance matters:

(a) Disputes specified in Labor Code section 3701.5(g) arising between or among a surety, the issuer of an agreement of assumption and guarantee of workers' compensation liabilities, the issuer of a letter of credit, any custodian of the security deposit, a self-insured employer, or the Self-Insurers' Security Fund;

(b) Disputes between any self-insurer and the Manager involving action by the Manager to involuntarily revoke an existing certificate for cause pursuant to Labor Code section 3702;

(c) Disputes involving action by the Manager to revoke or deny issuance of a certificate to administer pursuant to Labor Code sections 3702.1 and 3702.7;

(d) An appeal by a private sector self-insurer concerning the amount of the security deposit to be posted pursuant to Labor Code section 3701(b) or section 15210 of these regulations;

(e) An appeal by any self-insurer concerning any civil penalty assessment made pursuant to Labor Code section 3702.9;

(f) The appeal of an employer alleging its application for a certificate or by an administrator that its application for a certificate to administer has not been processed in a timely manner;

(g) To determine whether good cause exists to revoke any self-insurers' certificate for willful or repeat serious violations of occupational safety and health regulations as noted in Cal/OSHA citations issued by the Division of Occupational Safety and Health;

(h) An appeal by a private self insurer concerning the calculation, posting, or any other aspect of its deposit assessment after payment of the deposit assessment in the time provided to the Security Fund, and;

(i) An appeal by a private self insurer of any civil penalty assessed for failure to pay a deposit assessment to the Security Fund.

Note: Authority cited: Sections 54, 55, 3701.8 and 3702.10, Labor Code. Reference: Sections 59, 3700, 3701, 3701.5, 3701.8, 3702, 3702.1, 3702.5, 3702.6, 3702.7, 3702.9, 3705, and 3740-3747, Labor Code. Sections 11181-11188, 15378, Government Code.

History: 1. New article 11 (sections 15430-15437) filed 11-21-78; effective thirtieth day thereafter (Register 78, No. 47).

2. Amendment filed 12-17-90; operative 1-16-91 (Register 91, No. 6).

3. Change without regulatory effect amending subsection (d) filed 6-13-2000 pursuant to section 100, title 1, California Code of Regulations (Register 2000, No. 24).

4. Amendment of subsections (c) and (g), new subsections (h)-(i) and amendment of Note filed 5-30-2003 as an emergency; operative 5-30-2003 (Register 2003, No. 22). A Certificate of Compliance must be transmitted to OAL by 9-29-2003 or emergency language will be repealed by operation of law on the following day.

5. Certificate of Compliance as to 5-30-2003 order transmitted to OAL 9-29-2003 and filed 11-12-2003 (Register 2003, No. 46).

§15430.1. Definitions.

As used in Article 11, the following definitions shall apply:

Aggrieved Party. Any person aggrieved as a result of the failure to pass a Self Insurance Administrator examination pursuant to Labor Code Section 3702.1(b) or the revocation of a certificate to administer pursuant to Labor Code Sections 3702.1(a) or 3702.7 and as prescribed in Article 12 of these regulations.

Appeals Board. The California Workers' Compensation Appeals Board.

Certificate. See Section 15201 for definition.

Certificate to Administer. A Certificate of Consent to Administer issued to an administrative agency, except exempt insurance carriers, pursuant to Section 3702.1 of the Labor Code.

Custodian of a Security Deposit. The Office of the State Treasurer for Cash Deposits and Approved Securities; the Manager of Self Insurance Plans for surety bonds and letters of credit.

Employer. Any private corporation or other private business entity or public agency as defined in Labor Code Section 3300 that has or did have a Certificate of Consent to Self Insure or any such private entity or public agency seeking a Certificate of Consent to Self-Insure pursuant to Labor Code Sections 3700 and 3701.

Letter of Credit, Maker of. Any financial institution providing an irrevocable letter of credit to a self-insured employer pursuant to Labor Code Section 3701.

SISF. Self-Insurers' Security Fund (SISF), a non-profit entity created pursuant to Labor Code Section 3740 et seq.

Surety. Any corporation authorized to provide surety bonds in the State of California and providing a surety bond to a self-insured employer pursuant to Labor Code Section 3701.

Note: Authority cited: Sections 54, 55, 3702.10, Labor Code. Reference: Sections 3300, 3700, 3701, 3701.5, 3702.1, 3702.7, 3740–3747, Labor Code; and Sections 11181–11188, Government Code.

History: 1. New section filed 12-17-90; operative 1-16-91 (Register 91, No. 6).

§15431. Delegation of Authority.

(a) The Manager of Self-Insurance Plans is the authorized representative of the Director. The Manager is authorized to:

(1) Issue notice of intention to revoke a certificate and to deny a request for a certificate or a certificate to administer;

(2) Receive requests for a hearing by parties enumerated in Section 15430 of these regulations;

(3) Schedule hearings;

(4) Perform all administrative duties as required to conduct a hearing, including granting of extensions of time requested in writing upon a showing of good cause;

(5) Hear and determine an appeal by any party aggrieved by the result of the self-insurance administrator examination; and

(6) Hear and determine an appeal regarding the revocation of a certificate to administer prescribed in Article 12 of these regulations.

(b) In all other hearings and appeals the Director or hearing officer shall perform all functions necessary to conduct a hearing.

Note: Authority cited: Sections 54, 55, 3702.10, Labor Code. Reference: Sections 59, 3700, 3701, 3701.5, 3702, 3702.1, 3702.7, 3740–3747, Labor Code; and Sections 11181–11188, 15378, Government Code.

History: 1. Amendment filed 12-17-90; operative 1-16-91 (Register 91, No. 6).

Ref.: Hanna § 1.19.

§15431.1. Appeals and/or Requests for Hearings.

(a) Appeals and/or requests for hearing under this article by an employer or aggrieved party shall be in writing and shall include the following information:

(1) Name and address of the person making the appeal or requesting the hearing (i.e. the requesting party);

(2) The specific nature of the request (For example, "This request is to review action denying or revoking a certificate to administer"; or "This request is to appeal the failure to pass the self-insurance administrator's examination");

(3) A statement of the requesting party's rationale, basis, evidence, facts, reasoning, arguments, documentation, or other supporting material which establishes and supports the position of the requesting party;

(4) A statement of whether the requesting party wishes a formal hearing or a written decision only on the matter; and

(5) When a formal hearing is requested, an additional statement estimating the number of witnesses, if any, to be called by the requesting party at the hearing and the amount of time the requesting party will require to present its case at the hearing.

(b) Requests for a hearing or appeal pursuant to Section 15430 of these regulations shall be; mailed or delivered to: Manager, Self-Insurance Plans, 2265 Watt Avenue, Suite 1, Sacramento, CA 95825.

(c) An appeal or request for a hearing from an employer or aggrieved party must be served upon the director in writing within twenty-one (21) calendar days after receipt of:

(1) Notice of intention to revoke or deny a certificate to self-insure;

(2) Notice of the default of a self-insured employer or surety;

(3) Notice of a failing score on the self-insurance administrator's examination;

(4) Notice of intent to revoke a certificate to administer; or

(5) The decision by the Manager not to renew or grant a certificate to administer.

(d) A hearing on a claim that Self-Insurance Plans has not timely processed an application as required by Government Code Section 15378 may be requested at any time.

(e) An appeal or request for hearing shall be deemed timely received if the request is postmarked or delivered to the Director or the Manager by the end of business on the twenty second (22nd) calendar day after receipt of the notice or decision being appealed, as set forth in subsection (c) of this section.

(f) The written appeal or hearing request shall be:

(1) Placed in the United States mail in a fully prepaid, postmarked and sealed envelope; or

(2) Delivered to an overnight mail delivery service for delivery the following day; or

(3) Delivered by messenger or in person to the Office of Self-Insurance Plans.

Note: Authority cited: Sections 54, 55, 3702.10, Labor Code. Reference: Sections 59, 3700, 3701, 3701.5, 3702, 3702.1, 3702.7, 3702.9, 3702.10, 3740–3747, Labor Code; and Sections 11181–11188, 15378, Government Code.

History: 1. New section filed 12-17-90; operative 1-16-91 (Register 91, No. 6).

2. Change without regulatory effect amending subsection (b) filed 10-18-95 pursuant to section 100, title 1, California Code of Regulations (Register 95, No. 42).

§15431.2. Complaints.

(a) Any self-insured employer, administrator, the Self-Insurers' Security Fund, or injured employee of a self-insured employer may file a complaint to the Manager in writing concerning the failure of any self-insured employer or administrator to provide timely payment of benefits due or to fund the payment of such benefits.

(b) The Manager shall review any complaints received and may investigate the complaint, determine what benefits may be due and order payment thereof, audit the claim records of the self-insurer or administrator, and take action to revoke the certificate or certificate to administer for cause.

(c) The Manager shall not seek to substitute his/her judgement for that of the Workers' Compensation Appeals Board on any adjudicated claim and may refuse to consider the complaint of any injured worker's entitlement to benefits or self-insurer where the matter involved in the complaint is awaiting the decision of the Appeals Board.

(d) Any written complaint shall include the following information:

(1) The basis of jurisdiction of the Director;

(2) The relief or action requested;

(3) The grounds for the requested relief or action;

(4) The facts involved in the complaint;

(5) A statement of whether or not the specific claim or claims is being adjudicated before the Workers' Compensation Appeals Board and the Appeal number of the claim before the Appeals Board; and

(6) The name of the parties known to the complainant against which any relief is sought or who have an interest in the proceeding. The complaint shall be served on these other persons who may have an interest in the proceedings by the person submitting the complaint.

Note: Authority cited: Sections 54, 55, 3702.10, Labor Code. Reference: Sections 59, 3700, 3701, 3701.5, 3702, 3702.1, 3702.7, 3702.9, 3702.10, 3740–3747, Labor Code; and Sections 11181–11188, 15378, Government Code.

History: 1. New section filed 12-17-90; operative 1-16-91 (Register 91, No. 6).

§15432. Hearings; Special Requirements: Failure to Appear.

(a) Before seeking reconsideration by the Director an appeal shall be first made to the Manager in matters of:

(1) A failing score on any self-insurance administrator's examination; or

(2) The revocation of a certificate to administer or denial of a renewal of a certificate to administer.

(b) A written waiver of review by the Manager shall constitute satisfaction of section 15432(a) and allow immediate reconsideration by the Director in the matter.

(c) The SISF shall have thirty (30) days to contest a decision by the Director to require it to assume administration on behalf of a defaulting self-insured employer. The SISF shall not be required to bring a complaint action under section 15431.2 of these regulations within any specific time against a defaulting self-insurer, surety, custodian of securities or maker of a letter of credit after assuming the liabilities of responsible parties under Labor Code Sections 3743-3744. Nothing in this subsection shall be construed as to allow SISF to withhold or delay payments in any event.

(d) Failure to Appear.

(1) If after service of notice of hearing or continuance, a party fails to appear at the hearing either in person or by representative, the Director or the designated hearing officer may:

(A) Continue the proceeding; or

(B) After notice, dismiss the proceeding as a default and uphold the action appealed from, if the non-appearing party is the party requesting the hearing; or

(C) Receive evidence, including admissions, affidavit or declarations of the party, establish a prima facie case and render a decision.

(2) A party who has defaulted, and against whom a decision or determination is upheld,

nevertheless has the right to make a showing by way of mitigation as to any remedy. The Director may consider documentary evidence or hold a hearing, and may decide to alter the remedy, both in the discretion of the Director.

Note: Authority cited: Sections 54, 55, 3702.10, Labor Code. Reference: Sections 59, 3700, 3701, 3701.5, 3702, 3702.1, 3702.5, 3702.6, 3702.7, 3702.9, 3702.10, 3705, 3740–3747, Labor Code; and Sections 11181–11188, 15378, Government Code.

History: 1. Amendment filed 12-17-90; operative 1-16-91 (Register 91, No. 6).

§15433. Hearing Officer: Appointment and Delegation of Authority.

(a) The appointed hearing officer shall have full power, jurisdiction and authority to:

(1) Hold a hearing and ascertain facts for the information of the Director;

(2) Hold a pre-hearing conference and/or to certify official acts;

(3) Regulate the course of the hearing;

(4) Join and dismiss parties in a complaint proceeding pursuant to Section 15431.2 of these regulations;

(5) Grant a withdrawal, disposition or amendment;

(6) Order a continuance or to extend the submittal date of the proceeding;

(7) Approve a stipulation voluntarily entered into by the parties;

(8) Administer oaths and affirmations;

(9) Rule on objections, privileges, defenses, and the receipt of relevant and material evidence;

(10) Request a party at any time to state his theory concerning any fact or issue in the proceeding;

(11) Hear and determine all issues of fact and law presented; and

(12) Issue interlocutory and final orders, findings and decisions as may be necessary for full adjudication of the matter.

(b) The hearing officer may issue subpoenas and subpoenas duces tecum in the name of the Director for the attendance of persons and the production of testimony, books, documents, or other things, to compel attendance of persons residing anywhere within the state, subject to the provisions of Government Code section 11185.

(c) For purposes of an appeal or hearing to be heard by the Manager, the Manager shall exercise the power of a designated hearing officer.

Note: Authority cited: Sections 54, 55, 3702.10, Labor Code. Reference: Sections 59, 3700, 3701, 3701.5, 3702, 3702.1, 3702.5, 3702.6, 3702.7, 3702.9, 3702.10, 3705, 3740–3747, Labor Code; Sections 11181–11188, 15378, Government Code; and Sections 1985–2031, 2033–2036, Code of Civil Procedure.

History: 1. Amendment filed 12-17-90; operative 1-16-91 (Register 91, No. 6).

§15434. Hearing Procedures.

(a) The affected employer, surety, any custodian of a surety deposit, maker of a letter of credit, the SISF, an aggrieved party, and any other affected parties or persons shall be notified of the time and place of the hearing by a notice issued by the Director, designated hearing officer or the Manager and such notice to be served on all parties.

(b) Notification shall be placed in the U.S. mail in a fully prepaid, postmarked and sealed envelope at least twenty-one (21) calendar days in advance of the hearing. Without good cause being shown and a written request for extended time to respond, the time to respond shall not be extended beyond the twenty-one (21) days by California Code of Civil Procedure Section 1013.

(c) The employer, surety, custodian of a security deposit, maker of a letter of credit, the SISF, an aggrieved party, and any other party, shall be given an opportunity to present evidence and/or written or oral arguments in support of its position.

(d) The hearing need not be conducted according to the technical rules of evidence. In the interest of expeditious and inexpensive adjudication, evidence by way of affidavit or declaration shall be allowed under the following conditions:

(1) At any time fifteen (15) days or more prior to the hearing date or continued hearing date, a party may mail or deliver to the opposing party or parties a copy of any affidavit or declaration which is proposed to be introduced in evidence, together with a notice as provided in subsection (2). Unless an opposing party, within ten (10) days after such mailing or deliver, mails or delivers to the proponent a request to cross-examine the affiant or declarant, his right to cross-examine such affiant or declarant is waived and the affidavit or declaration, if introduced into evidence, shall be given the

same effect as if the affiant or declarant had testified orally. If an opportunity to cross-examine an affiant or declarant is not afforded after request therefor is made as herein provided, the affidavit or declaration may be introduced into evidence, but shall be given only the same effect as other hearsay evidence.

(2) The notice referred to in subsection (1) shall be substantially in the following form:

"The accompanying affidavit or declaration of (here insert name of affiant or declarant) will be introduced as evidence at the hearing in (here insert title and docket number of proceeding). (Here insert name) will not be called to testify orally and you will not be entitled to question him unless you notify (name of the proponent, representative, agent or attorney) at (here insert address) that you wish to cross-examine him. To be effective, your request must be mailed or delivered to (here insert name of proponent, representative, agent or attorney) on or before (here insert date ten (10) days after the date of mailing or delivering the affidavit or declaration to the opposing party)."

(e) All witnesses testifying before the hearing officer shall testify under oath, affirmation or penalty of perjury.

(f) Upon written request to the Director and for good cause shown, an aggrieved party may request the production of his or her own test and application records from Self-Insurance Plans. At the time of hearing or, upon written request to the Director and for good cause, an aggrieved party may request inspection of his/her own test records prior to the time of hearing.

(g) Discovery. The parties shall have the right to take depositions and to obtain discovery and to that end may exercise all of the same rights, remedies, and procedures, and shall be subject to all of the same duties, liabilities and obligations as provided in Part 4, Title 3, Chapter 3, of the Code of Civil Procedure, except that applications to the court or requests for relief from the court shall be considered as applications or requests of the hearing officer. All discovery shall be completed not less than fifteen (15) days prior to the date set for hearing, unless the Director, upon a showing of good cause, makes an order granting an extension of the time within which discovery must be completed. The hearing officer shall not have authority to impose monetary sanctions.

(h) Subpoena of Witnesses; Subpoena Duces Tecum. Subject to the provisions of Title 2, Division 3, Part 1, Chapter 2, of the Government Code and before the hearing has commenced, the Director shall issue a subpoena and subpoena duces tecum at the request of a party for attendance of a person or production of a document, object or thing determined to be reasonably relevant to the issues to be decided at the hearing.

After the hearing has commenced, the Director may issue a subpoena and subpoena duces tecum as follows:

(1) The subpoenaing party shall prepare the affidavit of good cause required by Section 1985 of the Code of Civil Procedure before a subpoena duces tecum will be issued.

(2) A subpoenaing party shall comply with Section 1985.3 of the Code of Civil Procedure. A person not a party to the matter, is not obliged to attend as a witness in any matter under this article at a place out of the county in which he resides, unless the distance is less than fifty (50) miles from his place of residence. A party or party-identified witness may be obliged to attend a deposition in like manner as in Code of Civil Procedure Section 2025.

(i) The hearing shall be recorded by audio recorder. Parties wishing a written transcript shall pay the cost of a transcription or may provide a certified reporter at the time of hearing. A copy of the recorded proceedings shall be provided to the Director if reconsideration is requested.

(j) The Director may appoint an interpreter and fix the interpreter's compensation in any matter where an interpreter is requested by the parties or determined to be needed by the Director or his/her designee. It shall be the responsibility of any party producing a witness requiring an interpreter to arrange for the presence of a qualified interpreter. Interpreter fees are to be paid by the party requesting the use of the interpreter. It shall be the responsibility of the party seeking to use an interpreter to show that the interpreter is proficient in the appropriate language and has sufficient knowledge relating to the terminology and procedures generally used in hearings before the Director to function satisfactorily. The Director may disqualify an interpreter due to conflict of interest, bias, prejudice, partiality or for disclosure of confidential or privileged information.

(k) A request for intervention may be allowed by the Director or designated hearing officer in like manner as in California Code of Civil Procedure Section 387.

(*l*) In the interests of the expeditious resolution of all disputes, the Director may allow time for settlement of disputes. The Director shall approve settlement of any dispute regarding a third-party administrator examination, a revocation of a third-party certificate or certificate of consent to self-insure. The Director, in his discretion, may approve resolution of disputes involving the Self-Insurers' Security Fund. Approval by the Director of disputes involving SISF is necessary only after a formal hearing on the merits has begun.

(m) An official address record shall be maintained by the Director or the designated hearing officer. Each party shall furnish one address and one telephone number, for itself or its representative, to which all communications by the Director and other parties shall be directed. If the address is a Post Office Box, a physical address shall also be provided for use when physical delivery other than by mail is intended. All communications by the Director or hearing officer, including all notices and decisions and determinations, shall be made to the addresses on the official address record. Service of anything required to be served shall be acceptable if mailed by registered or certified mail, with return receipt, if mailed to the official address. Legal service may also be made by personal delivery to the official address.

(n) No party or representative of a party shall communicate with a hearing officer on the merits of a matter except in the presence of the other parties or their representatives. No written communication shall be directed to a hearing officer or the Director unless it shows on the face of it or on an attached proof of service that the communication has been simultaneously served on other parties. No written communications in violation of this rule shall be received by the hearing officer or Director. The Director, after a hearing officer has been designated and while the hearing officer is continuing to act on the case, shall not communicate with the hearing officer about the merits of the matter before the hearing officer.

(o) Foundation Evidence. Evidence of the genuineness of any document, and of the authenticity of records, shall be by affidavit or declaration only, unless good cause is shown by a party for the necessity for testimony in the presence of the hearing officer. At the discretion of the hearing officer, any other evidence of a foundational nature shall also be by declaration or affidavit, except where good cause is shown why it should be otherwise.

Note: Authority cited: Sections 54, 55, 3702.10, Labor Code. Reference: Sections 59, 3700, 3701, 3701.5, 3702, 3702.1, 3702.5, 3702.6, 3702.7, 3702.9, 3702.10, 3705, 3740–3747, Labor Code; Sections 11181–11188, 15378, Government Code; and Sections 1985–2031, 2033–2036, Code of Civil Procedure.

History: 1. Amendment filed 12-17-90; operative 1-16-91 (Register 91, No. 6).

§15435. Decision.

(a) The hearing officer shall conduct the hearing and provide a written recommendation to the Director and make available the entire record of the hearing. A matter is deemed submitted to the Director either at the close of the hearing, or, at the discretion of the hearing officer, upon the submission of any post-hearing briefs or arguments requested or allowed by the hearing officer.

(b) The decision of the Director shall reflect a summary of evidence, findings of fact and conclusions of law, together with citations to the controlling statutes applied in rendering the decision, and any determinations made by the Director.

(c) The decision shall be mailed within ninety (90) days of the date of submission, with copies to all parties of record. Issuance of a decision may be delayed to allow settlement, or as the interests of justice may require, in which case the Director shall give all parties of record written notice of such delay.

(d) The Director shall make determinations, as required, as to whether there was at the time of the notice of intention or at the time of the decision, good cause to revoke or deny a certificate or certificate to administer.

(e) If the Director determines that an appellant's application was not processed within the time limits which the Director has adopted in these regulations pursuant to Government Code section 15378, the decision shall include a refund of the fees paid by that appellant for that application.

(f) The decision of the Director shall be final, unless reconsideration pursuant to Section 15436 of these regulations is requested.

Note: Authority cited: Sections 54, 55, 3702.10, Labor Code. Reference: Sections 59, 3700, 3701, 3701.5, 3702, 3702.1, 3702.5, 3702.6, 3702.7, 3702.9,

3702.10, 3705, 3740–3747, Labor Code; Sections 11181–11188, 15378, Government Code; and Sections 1985–2031, 2033–2036, Code of Civil Procedure.

History: 1. Amendment filed 12-17-90; operative 1-16-91 (Register 91, No. 6).

§15436. Reconsideration.

(a) The Director has the discretion to reconsider and to take whatever action is appropriate and necessary to support and facilitate a decision or determination. The Director, in his/her discretion, may grant a stay of enforcement in any proceeding where reconsideration or appeal is initiated.

(b) The employer, surety, custodian of a security deposit, the SISF, or an aggrieved party, upon receipt of the decision, shall have ten (10) calendar days to request reconsideration of the decision by the Director. The request must be in writing and shall be limited to the grounds specified in Labor Code Section 5903.

(c) Upon receipt of a request for reconsideration, the Director may:

(1) Decline reconsideration;

(2) Grant reconsideration and issue an amended decision or determination after reconsideration based only upon the record and additional argument and evidence offered in the request for reconsideration and any response thereto; or,

(3) If the Director deems that, based upon the request for reconsideration and any response, further hearing is merited, grant reconsideration and hold further hearing pursuant to these regulations, and issue a decision or determination after reconsideration.

(d) A decision or determination of the Director, where reconsideration by the Director has been requested but not granted, becomes final upon service of the notice that reconsideration is declined. A decision or determination of the Director where reconsideration by the Director has been granted, becomes final upon service of the decision or determination after reconsideration.

(e) All requests for reconsideration by the Director shall be served on all other parties of record by the requesting party at the time of service on the Director. The Director shall not accept requests for reconsideration without a declaration of service attached indicating that all other parties to the matter, as reflected on the official address record, have been served with the request for reconsideration.

(f) If a party to a proceeding is adversely affected for the first time by the decision or determination after reconsideration, that party may then request further reconsideration of the original decision or determination after reconsideration.

Note: Authority cited: Sections 54, 55, 3702.10, Labor Code. Reference: Sections 59, 3700, 3701, 3701.5, 3702, 3702.1, 3702.5, 3702.6, 3702.7, 3702.9, 3702.10, 3705, 3740–3747, Labor Code; Sections 11181–11188, 15378, Government Code; and Sections 1985–2031, 2033–2036, Code of Civil Procedure.

History: 1. Amendment filed 12-17-90; operative 1-16-91 (Register 91, No. 6).

§15437. Appellate Review.

(a) Appeal from an adverse decision of the Director with regard to failure to pass the Self-Insurance Administrator examination or revocation of a Certificate to Administer, or with regard to the Office of Self Insurance Plans' timeliness of processing an application, shall be made to the Superior Court of California by writ as provided in the Code of Civil Procedure. A condition precedent to such appeal shall be exhaustion of all appeal requirements specified in this Article.

(b) Appeal from a decision or determination of the Director after hearing arising from a dispute between or among a surety, the issuer of an agreement of assumption and guarantee of workers' compensation liabilities, the issuer of a letter of credit, a custodian of a security deposit, an employer, or the SISF, concerning the posting, renewal, termination, exoneration, or return of all or any portion of the security deposit, or any liability arising out of the posting or failure to post security, or adequacy of the security or reasonableness of administrative costs, including legal fees, may be taken to the Superior Court, as provided in Labor Code Section 3701.5(g).

(c) Appeal from a determination of the Director after hearing in a proceeding under Labor Code Section 3702.8 involving private employers who have ceased to be self-insured employers may be taken to the Appeals Board. After January 1, 1991 such appeals shall be taken to the appropriate Superior Court by petition for writ of mandate.

(d) Appeal from a decision or determination of the Director after hearing which denies an application for a certificate or which revokes a certificate pursuant to Labor Code Section

3702(b), may be taken to the Appeals Board. It shall be a condition precedent to the filing of such an appeal that the appealing employer shall have first obtained workers' compensation insurance. A Certificate of Insurance showing the current existence of such insurance, issued by the insurer, shall be filed as part of the appeal.

(e) Appeal of any other determination of the Director may be taken to the Appeals Board.

(f) All appeals to the Appeals Board under this section shall be governed by Article 1 of Chapter 7 of Part 4 of Division 4 of the Labor Code, Reconsideration. Appeals shall be filed with the Appeals Board within twenty (20) days after service of the final decision or determination of the Director. Where service is by mail, the time to file shall be extended as provided in Code of Civil Procedure Section 1013.

Note: Authority cited: Sections 54, 55, 3702.10, Labor Code. Reference: Sections 59, 3700, 3701, 3701.5, 3702, 3702.1, 3702.5, 3702.6, 3702.7, 3702.8, 3702.9, 3702.10, 3705, 3740–3747, Labor Code; Sections 11181–11188, 15378, Government Code; and Sections 1985–2031, 2033–2036, Code of Civil Procedure.

History: 1. Renumbering and amendment of former section 15437 to section 15438 and new section 15437 filed 12-17-90; operative 1-16-91 (Register 91, No. 6).

§15438. Severability.

If any provision of these regulations or the application thereof to any party or circumstances is held invalid, such invalidity shall not affect other provisions or applications of these regulations which can be given effect without the invalid provision or applications and to this end the provisions of the regulations are severable.

Note: Authority cited: Sections 54, 55, 3702.10, Labor Code. Reference: Sections 59, 3700, 3701, 3701.5, 3702, 3702.1, 3702.5, 3702.6, 3702.7, 3702.9, 3702.10, 3705, 3740–3747, Labor Code; Sections 11181–11188, 15378, Government Code; and Sections 1985–2031, 2033–2036, Code of Civil Procedure.

History: 1. Renumbering and amendment of former Section 15437 to Section 15438 filed 12-17-90; operative 1-16-91 (Register 91, No. 6).

ARTICLE 12
Claims Administration

§15450. Certificate to Administer.

(a) A valid Certificate to Administer issued by the Manager shall be in the possession of each claims administrator, whether a person, firm, corporation, joint powers authority or self insured employer, to administer or adjust workers' compensation self insurance claims.

EXCEPTION 1: An insurer admitted to transact workers' compensation insurance in California is exempt from this requirement pursuant to Labor Code Section 3702.1(a);

NOTE: An insurance company subsidiary not admitted to transact workers' compensation insurance in California and engaged in the administration or adjustment of claims for a self insured employer is not exempt.

EXCEPTION 2: A private self insurer that administers its own claims and/or the claims of other private self insurers with common ownership or which are in the same Master Certificate file is exempt from this requirement.

EXCEPTION 3: A joint powers authority that holds a Master Certificate of Consent to Self Insure and administers its own claims; and/or the claims of other public self insurers which have an affiliate Certificate under the same Master Certificate file number held by the joint powers authority; and/or the claims of a former member of the joint powers authority is exempt from this requirement.

EXCEPTION 4: A public self insurer that administers its own agency's claims is exempt from this requirement.

(b) Application for a Certificate to Administer shall be made on forms provided by Self-Insurance Plans (Form A4-50 (Rev. 4/91)). A complete application shall include the application form, and fees in accordance with Section 15454.

NOTE: The current application form is contained in Plate L of the Appendix following the last Article of these Group 2 regulations.

(1) The applicant will be notified in writing within 14 days of receipt if the application is deficient.

(2) A certificate to administer will be issued within 30 days of receipt of a complete application.

(c) The Certificate to Administer expires June 30 and reapplication must be made prior to June 1 for the subsequent renewal period. The applicant may request the Certificate to Administer to be issued for a period of 1, 2 or 3 years.

(d) Failure to comply with Articles 6 and 9 of these regulations or engaging in improper practices as described in Labor Code Section

3702(a) is good cause for revocation or non-renewal of the Certificate to Administer.

Note: Authority cited: Sections 54, 55, 59, and 3702.10, Labor Code. Reference: Sections 59, 3702 and 3702.1, Labor Code. Government Code Sections 15375, 15376.

History: 1. New article 12 (sections 15450-15463, not consecutive) filed 1-27-86; effective thirtieth day thereafter (Register 86, No. 5).

2. Amendment of article and section headings filed 2-19-92; operative 3-20-92 (Register 92, No. 13).

3. Amendment of subsections (a), (b)(2) and (d) filed 2-9-2006; operative 3-11-2006 (Register 2006, No. 6).

Ref.: Hanna § 2.11[3].

§15450.1. Third Party Claims Administration for New Private Self Insurers.

(a) Each private self insurer granted an initial, individual Certificate to Self Insure workers' compensation liabilities that has not been self insured or previously self insured for a total of three full years shall contract with a third party claims administrator for the first three (3) full calendar years of self insurance. The self insured employer's third party claims administrator shall hold a Certificate to Administer pursuant to Section 15450 of these regulations.

(b) Each private group self insurer granted its initial Certificate to Self Insure workers' compensation liabilities shall contract with a third party administrator for the first five (5) full calendar years of self insurance. The group self insurer's third party claims administrator shall hold a Certificate to Administer pursuant to Section 15450 of these regulations.

Note: Authority cited: Sections 54, 55, 59 and 3702.10, Labor Code. Reference: Sections 3700, 3701, 3701.5, 3702, 3702.1, 3702.2 and 3702.3, Labor Code.

History: 1. New section filed 6-30-94; operative 6-30-94 (Register 94, No. 26). For prior history, see Register 92, No. 13.

2. Amendment of subsections (a) and (b) and repealer of subsection (c) filed 2-9-2006; operative 3-11-2006 (Register 2006, No. 6).

Ref.: Hanna § 2.11[3].

§15452. Administrator Competence.

(a) Each self insurer or third party administrative agency shall conduct the administration of each self insurance program through the services of a competent person or persons located in California.

Exception 1: Upon a showing of good cause, the Manager may authorize administration from locations outside California by an administrator with staff who has demonstrated individual competence. The desire to consolidate claims from other states in one location or the desire to reduce expenses related to utilizing a third party administer are not good cause for out-of-state administration. The demonstration of individual competence of an out-of-state administrator is not in itself good cause for out-of-state administration.

Exception 2: The Manager shall not authorize claims administration outside of the State of California for any private group self insurer.

(b) Any person may demonstrate individual competence as an administrator for a self-administered self insurer or an agency administered self insurance program by successfully passing the written examination designed to test technical knowledge of workers' compensation law and claims administration. The Manager shall ensure that the test shall be administered at least twice a fiscal year (July 1 to June 30).

(c) Application for the administrator's examination shall be made on forms provided by the Manager (Form A4-100, Rev. 9/91). A complete application shall include the application form and fees in accordance with subsection (d) of this section. The applicant will be notified in writing within 14 days if the application is deficient. Confirmation of the test date will be sent two weeks before the scheduled test date.

(d) The fee to take the Self Insurance Administrator's examination shall be $150. The fee shall not be refundable after confirmation of entrance to the exam has been issued by the Office of Self Insurance Plans.

Exception 1: Upon a written showing of good cause, the Manager may authorize a refund of the application fee.

(e) Upon passing the written examination a Certificate of Achievement will be issued within eight weeks of the test date.

(f) Each adjusting location of a third party administrative agency or a self-administered self insurer shall have at least one person who has passed the self insurance administrator's examination. All workers' compensation self insurance claims at such reporting locations shall be administered and adjusted under the direct supervision of a person who has passed the self insurance administrator's examination. Supervision of claims decisions, setting of estimates of future liability of claims, and proper payment of benefits to injured workers shall be made or reviewed by a person who has passed the self insurance administrator's examination.

(g) Lack of competent administrators at any adjusting location shall be good cause for revocation of the certificate to administer for that location and may be grounds to revoke the certificate to self insure.

Note: Authority cited: Sections 54, 55, 59, and 3702.10, Labor Code. Reference: Sections 59, 3702, 3702.1 and 3702.10, Labor Code; and Sections 15375 and 15376, Government Code.

History: 1. Amendment filed 2-19-92; operative 3-20-92 (Register 92, No. 13).

2. New (a) Exception 2 and amendment of Note filed 6-30-94; operative 6-30-94 (Register 94, No. 26).

3. Amendment of subsections (a)-(f) filed 2-9-2006; operative 3-11-2006 (Register 2006, No. 6).

Ref.: Hanna § 2.11[3].

§15454. Certificate to Administer: Fees.

(a) The certificate fee shall be paid no later than June 1 in the year of application and shall be sufficient to cover the 1 to 3 year period of the application submitted, and shall accompany the application form. The fee is not prorated in the initial year of each application cycle and is not refundable for any portion of the current fiscal year.

(b) The minimum fee for each private certificate to administer the first adjusting location is $1,000 per year. There is an additional charge of $200 per year for each additional claims adjusting location.

(c) Public applicants are exempt from the payment of a fee for the Certificate to Administer provided all claims administered are for public self insurers. A public administrator for private sector self insurers shall pay the certificate fees due for a private Certificate to Administer.

Note: Authority cited: Sections 54, 55, 59, and 3702.10, Labor Code. Reference: Sections 59, 3702.1, 3702.5 and 3702.10, Labor Code.

History: 1. Amendment filed 2-19-92; operative 3-20-92 (Register 92, No. 13).

2. Amendment of subsection (b) filed 2-9-2006; operative 3-11-2006 (Register 2006, No. 6).

Ref.: Hanna § 2.11[3].

§15456. Repealed.

Note: Authority cited: Sections 54, 55 and 3702.10, Labor Code. Reference: Sections 59, 3702.1 and 3702.10, Labor Code.

History: 1. New section filed 1-27-86; effective thirtieth day thereafter (Register 86, No. 5).

2. Repealer filed 2-19-92; operative 3-20-92 (Register 92, No. 13).

Ref.: Hanna § 2.11[3].

§15458. Claims Administration and Recordkeeping.

Workers' compensation claims and claim files shall be administered and maintained in accordance with the provisions of Articles 6 and 9 of these regulations.

Note: Authority cited: Sections 54, 55 and 3702.10, Labor Code. Reference: Sections 59, 129, 3700, 3701, 3702.1 and 3702.10, Labor Code.

History: 1. New section filed 1-27-86; effective thirtieth day thereafter (Register 86, No. 5).

2. Amendment filed 2-19-92; operative 3-20-92 (Register 92, No. 13).

Ref.: Hanna § 2.11[3].

§15459. Notification of Willful Failure to Pay Benefits.

The claims administrator shall notify the Manager in writing within three days of a self insured employer's willful failure to provide adequate funding for the timely payment of worker's compensation benefits in accordance with provision of the Labor Code.

Note: Authority cited: Sections 54, 55 and 3702.10, Labor Code. Reference: Sections 59, 129, 3700, 3701, 3702.1 and 3702.10, Labor Code.

History: 1. New section filed 1-27-86; effective thirtieth day thereafter (Register 86, No. 5).

2. Amendment filed 2-19-92; operative 3-20-92 (Register 92, No. 13).

Ref.: Hanna § 2.11[3].

§15461. Repealed.

Note: Authority cited: Sections 54, 55 and 3702.10, Labor Code. Reference: Sections 59, 3702, 3702.1 and 3702.10, Labor Code.

History: 1. New section filed 1-27-86; effective thirtieth day thereafter (Register 86, No. 5).

2. Repealer filed 2-19-92; operative 3-20-92 (Register 92, No. 13).

Ref.: Hanna § 2.11[3].

§15463. Revocation of Certificate.

(a) The Manager may issue a Notice of Intent to Revoke to any holder of a Certificate to Administer. The notice shall indicate the cause for the revocation action and advise the holder of the Certificate of the right to a hearing.

(b) The procedure for revocation of a Certificate of Consent to Administer shall be in accordance with Article 11 of these regulations.

Note: Authority cited: Sections 54, 55, 59 and 3702.10, Labor Code. Reference: Sections 59, 3702.1, 3702.7 and 3702.10, Labor Code.

History: 1. Amendment and new forms filed 2-19-92; operative 3-20-92 (Register 92, No. 13).

2. New Appendix plates D, E, F1-F6, G and I filed 12-22-92; operative 1-21-93 (Register 93, No. 2).

3. Amendment of Plate F-6 filed 8-12-93; operative 9-13-93 (Register 93, No. 33).

4. Change without regulatory effect relocating Appendix Plates A-1, A-2, B, C, and H from section 15204 to section 15463 filed 9-14-93 pursuant to title 1, section 100, California Code of Regulations (Register 93, No. 38).

5. Amendment of forms filed 6-30-94; operative 6-30-94 (Register 94, No. 26).

6. Amendment of Appendix Plate I filed 12-1-94; operative 1-2-95 (Register 94, No. 48).

7. Change without regulatory effect renumbering a portion of Form A4-3 (Agreement of Assumption and Guarantee of Workers' Compensation Liabilities) to new Form A4-6, including amendments, filed 2-17-98 pursuant to section 100, title 1, California Code of Regulations (Register 98, No. 8).

8. Amendment adding new form A4-5 filed 6-4-98; operative 7-4-98 (Register 98, No. 23).

9. Amendment filed 2-9-2006; operative 3-11-2006 (Register 2006, No. 6).

Editor's Note: The following forms are available from:

STATE OF CALIFORNIA
DEPARTMENT OF INDUSTRIAL RELATIONS
OFFICE OF SELF-INSURANCE PLANS
2848 Arden Way, Suite 105
Sacramento, Ca. 95825
(916) 483-3392

Application for a Certificate to Self-Insure
—Form No. A4-1 (2/92)

Application for a Public Entity Certificate to Self-Insure
—Form A4-2 (REV. 2-92)

Model Corporate Resolution Authorizing Application to the Director of Industrial Relations, State of California for a Certificate to Self-Insure Workers' Compensation Liabilities
—(3/92)

Model Partnership Agreement Authorizing Application for a Certificate to Self-Insure Workers' Compensation Liabilities
—(3/92)

Certificate of Self-Insurance of Workers' Compensation

Agreement of Assumption and Guarantee of Workers' Compensation Liabilities
—Form A4-3 (Revised 8/90)

Application for a Certificate of Consent to Self-Insure by a Group of Employers
—Form A4-3 (1-94)

Personal Agreement of Assumption & Guarantee of Workers' Compensation Liabilities
—Form A4-3A (2/91)

Model Resolution for Agreements of Parental Assumption and Guarantee

Model Partnership Agreement and Guarantee Resolution

Agreement of Assumption and Guarantee of Workers' Compensation Liabilities for Group Members
—Form A4-3G (Rev. 1/94)

Application for an Affiliate to Self-Insure as a Member of a Group Self-Insurer
—Form A4-3M (1/94)

Application for a Permanent Certificate to Self-Insure by an Interim Self Insurer
—Form A4-5 (Rev. 11/97)

Agreement of Assumption and Guarantee of Workers' Compensation Liabilities
—Form A4-6 (Rev. 11/97)

Indemnity Agreement and Power of Attorney
—Form A4-8 (Rev. 1/94)

Surety Bond
—Form No. A4-20 (4/92)

Surety Bond—Decrease Rider
—Form A4-21a (4/92)

Surety Bond—Increase Rider
—Form A4-21b (4/92)

Surety Bond—Name Change Rider
—Form A4-22 (4/92)

Surety Bond—Special Form Change Rider
—Form A4-23 (4/92)

Surety Bond—Release of Surety
—Form A4-24 (11/92)

Model Letter to Request Approval of Securities

Informational Bulletin—Letter of Credit
—Revised (1/95)

Syndicated Letter of Credit

Certificate of Drawing

Amendment to Irrevocable Standby Letter of Credit
—(7/92)

Agreement and Undertaking for Security Deposit
—Form A4-32 (12/92)

Private Group Self-Insurer's Annual Report
—Form A4-40d (1/94)

Application for a Certificate of Consent to Administer Workers' Compensation Self-Insurance Claims
—Form No. A4-50 (4/91)

Application for Self-Insurance Administrator's Examination
—Form No. A4-100 (9/91)

Workers' Compensation Self-Insured/Self-Administered Employer Report of Changes
—AE Form 101 (10/90)

Workers' Compensation Adjusting Agency/Third-Party Administrator Report of Changes
—AE Form 102 (10/90)

Agreement and Undertaking for Security Deposit
—Form A4-GAU (1/94)

Group Resolution Authorizing Application to the Director of Industrial Relations, State of California for a Certificate of Self-Insure Workers' Compensation Liabilities
—Form GR-1 (Rev. 1/94)

Resolution of Agreement of Assumption and Guarantee of Workers' Compensation Liabilities for a Group Self-Insurer
—Form GR-2 (Rev. 1/94)

Ref.: Hanna § 2.11[3].

ARTICLE 13
Group Self Insurance

§15470. General.

(a) A California non-profit, mutual benefit corporation for the sole purpose of operating a group workers' compensation self insurance fund to pool compensation liabilities of two or more private employers shall be established by the organizers or members of any applicant group self insurer pursuant to Part 3 (commencing with Section 7110) of Division 2 of Title 1 of the Corporations Code. This non-profit, mutual benefit corporation shall be the "group self insurer".

(b) The group self insurer will make application for a Certificate to Self Insure to the Manager as provided in Article 2 of these regulations and, if granted approval by the Director, shall be the holder of the Certificate to Self Insure.

(c) Each proposed group member shall also make application for an Affiliate Certificate to Self Insure to the Manager, as provided in Article 2 of these regulations, and if granted by the Director, shall be the holder of an Affiliate Certificate to Self Insure under the Certificate to Self Insure granted to the group self insurer.

(d) The group self insurer shall post and maintain a security deposit with the Manager as set forth in Article 3 of these regulations to secure the expected workers' compensation liabilities of the group self insurer, based on the prior history of liabilities of all its members.

(e) The group self insurer shall file a Self Insurer's Annual Report as set forth in Article 5 of these regulations and shall estimate compensation liabilities as set forth in Article 6 of these regulations.

(f) The group self insurer shall comply with the transfer of liability requirements of Article 8.

(g) The group self insurer shall fall under the continuing jurisdiction of the Director and any Certificates to Self Insure or Affiliate Certificates issued to a group self insurer or a group member may be revoked as set forth in Article 10 of these regulations.

(h) Hearing and appeal procedures set forth in Article 11 shall be applicable to self insurance matters set forth in Section 15430 involving group self insurers or group members.

(i) The group self insurer shall comply with recordkeeping and audit requirements in Article 9 and the claims administration requirements of Article 12 of these regulations.

Note: Authority cited: Sections 54, 55 and 3702.10, Labor Code. Reference: Sections 59, 3700, 3701, 3701.5, 3702, 3702.2, 3702.5 and 3702.10, Labor Code.

History: 1. New article 13 and section filed 6-30-94; operative 6-30-94 (Register 94, No. 26).

§15471. Initial Feasibility Study.

(a) Accompanying each group self insurer's initial application for a Certificate To Self Insure required by Section 15203 of these regulations, shall also be an feasibility study prepared by an independent risk management individual or firm addressing all of the following:

(1) The advantages and disadvantages of group self insurance for the proposed group members as compared to the options of individual self insurance, or coverage under a policy issued by a carrier(s);

(2) Identification of all proposed group members and the combined total payroll for the proposed group self insurer;

(3) A consolidated summary of the historical workers' compensation claims loss experience and the allocated loss expenses of the proposed group members for the three most recent, completed, full policy years, as well as, the current partially completed policy year to the most current quarter under the current policy;

(4) An evaluation of the historical workers' compensation claims costs for the group members and actuarial projection of the expected claims costs for the first five years of the group operation. The actuarial projection to be prepared by (A) an independent person with a designation of Fellow of the Casualty Actuarial Society (FCAS); or (B) by a member of the American Academy of Actuaries (MAAA) with current experience in making California workers' compensation actuarial projections.

(5) A five year proforma financial statement including, as a minimum, an income statement, balance sheet, projected cash flows, and claims payout projections. The proforma financial statement must include a detailed separation of assets, liabilities, retained earnings, taxes, and dividends. If any claims costs are discounted, the interest rate assumptions and payout patterns must be described and based on reasonable assumptions. The claims payout schedule shall be calculated using the 80th percent confidence level figures from the actuarial study.

(6) A summary of the specific details of the group self insurer's operating plan including, but not limited to:

(A) The legal and organizational structure;

(B) Method of governance;

(C) General management of the pool, including underwriting policies, insurance coverage, billing, etc.

(D) Rating plans or premiums or other means by which group funding during the first five years of operation will generated and the amounts to be generated by the methods proposed for each of the first 5 years of operation;

(7) The first 12 month budget of the group self insurer;

(8) Excess Insurance Coverage including estimated cost, attachment point of specific excess coverage policy and aggregate excess policy (if any), and maximum liability of each excess policy;

(9) Summary of the third party claims administration agency chosen to handle the group self insurer's claims;

(10) Safety and loss control services that will be available from the group self insurer to group members;

(11) Underwriting requirements for initial and subsequent member selection into the group self insurer, including particular emphasis as to whether any underwriting requirement would be excluded from coverage by the specific excess or aggregate excess insurance coverage;

(12) Name of certified public accountant that will prepare annual financial reports for the group self insurer;

(13) Name of actuary and their professional actuarial designation who will prepare actuarial reports for the group self insurer and the frequency of such evaluation reports;

(14) Means by which the group self insurer will post the required security deposit and how that cost or deposit will be allocated to the group members;

(15) Any fidelity coverage and errors and omissions coverage that will be maintained by the group;

Note: Authority cited: Sections 54, 55 and 3702.10, Labor Code. Reference: Sections 3700, 3701 and 3702.1, Labor Code.

History: 1. New section filed 6-30-94; operative 6-30-94 (Register 94, No. 26).

§15472. Minimum Net Worth of a Group Self Insurer.

(a) Each applicant group and each group self insurer granted a Certificate to Self Insure shall have and maintain a minimum net worth as provided in Section 15203.2(f).

(b) The group administrator shall maintain a copy of the current and immediate past year's independently audited financial statement of each group member in the files of the group self insurer.

(c) The group administrator shall immediately advise the Manager in writing if at any time the consolidated net worth of the group members of the self insurer fall below the minimum amount set forth in subsection (a) of this section.

Note: Authority cited: Sections 54, 55 and 3702.10, Labor Code. Reference: Sections 3700, 3701, 3701.5, 3702, 3702.2 and 3702.10, Labor Code.

History: 1. New section filed 6-30-94; operative 6-30-94 (Register 94, No. 26).

§15473. Homogeneity of Group Members.

(a) Each group self insurer shall maintain homogeneity of its group members by one of the following methods:

(1) All group members shall have the same, predominant, two digit Standard Industrial Classification Code (SIC Code) as found in the Standard Industrial Classification Code Manual published by the United States Department of Commerce; or

(2) All group members are required in the by-laws of the group self insurer or by laws of the group applicant to be members in good standing in a specific industry trade association, and each trade association sponsored group self insurer is limited to one, designated three digit Standard Industrial Classification Code industry grouping.

Note: A trade association may sponsor more than one group self insurer, but each would be limited to a single 3 digit SIC Code industry grouping.

(b) The Manager shall also consider any other information available on the nature of the business of each group member and may require the group applicant or group self insurer to present additional information to verify that all group member applicants meet the requirements of subsection (a) of this section.

Note: Authority cited: Sections 54, 55 and 3702.10, Labor Code. Reference: Sections 3700 and 3702.10, Labor Code.

History: 1. New section filed 6-30-94; operative 6-30-94 (Register 94, No. 26).

§15474. Reporting Periods.

All group self insurers shall administer their self insurance program on a calendar year basis. Regardless of initial start-up date of any group self insurer, the self insurer shall file an annual report as required by Section 15251, for the remaining months of that calendar year.

Note: Authority cited: Sections 54, 55 and 3702.10, Labor Code. Reference: Sections 3700, 3702.1, 3702.2 and 3702.10, Labor Code.

History: 1. New section filed 6-30-94; operative 6-30-94 (Register 94, No. 26).

§15475. Board of Trustees.

(a) Each group self insurer shall have a Board of Trustees that is responsible for all operations of the group self insurer.

(b) Each trustee on the Board of Trustees shall be elected by the group members or, if each group member has a seat on the Board of Trustees, the trustee may be appointed by the group member. At least two-thirds of the trustees shall be employees or officers of the group members.

(c) The duties of the Board of Trustees shall include the responsibility to approve the request of any proposed member to join the group self insurer, subject to subsequent application and approval of the group member by the Director of Industrial Relations.

(d) The Board of Trustees shall take all necessary precautions to protect assets of the group self insurer, including all of the following:

(1) Designate a "Group Administrator" to administer the financial affairs and normal day-to-day operations of the group self insurer. The group administrator shall not be an owner, operator or employee of the third party administrator handling the claims of the group self insurer;

(2) Furnish a fidelity bond in an amount determined by the Board of Trustees to be an amount sufficient to assure the integrity of member or group funds handled by the Trustees, the Group Administrator, and employees of the group self insurer. Evidence of such bond shall be provided to the Manager upon request.

(3) Require the third party administrator handling the workers' compensation claims of the group self insurer to carry sufficient fidelity bond for the funds handled and errors and omissions coverage for the claims handled to protect the integrity of the group self insurer's funds;

(4) Restrict disbursements to the payment and expenses of handling claims, administrative expenses, posting of security deposit, and other expenses necessary for operating the group self insurer;

(5) Establish necessary bank accounts and accounting procedures for control of funds and accurate financial reporting;

(6) Audit the financial accounts and records of the group self insurer annually immediately after the December 31 close of the reporting year by an independent, certified public accountant;

(7) Hire an actuary to conduct an actuarial review of the group self insurer's claims to establish a level of cash needed to fund anticipated claims;

(8) Insure that all group members pay their share of group expenses, that none of the funds collected are extended as credit to any group member for the payment of premiums, and collect delinquent accounts from any group member;

(9) The Board of Trustees, the group administrator, or fiscal agent shall not utilize any of the funds collected from group members for any purpose not directly related to the payment of compensation liabilities of the group self insurer, posting of security deposit, payment of assessments and penalties as a group self insurer or the reasonable costs of operation of the group self insurer. Excess moneys not needed for current operation of the group self insurer shall be invested by the Board of Trustees, at its discretion, into California government bonds and notes, U.S. Treasury Notes and bonds, U.S. Government Agency issues, investment share accounts in savings and loans or credit unions whose deposits are insured by a federal agency, and savings accounts or certificates of deposit issued by a duly chartered commercial bank. Deposits in banks, savings and loans, or credit unions shall be limited to institutions in the State of California and shall not exceed the federally insured amount in any one account.

(e) The Board of Trustees may delegate specific functions to the group administrator of the group self insurer, including, but not limited to:

(1) contracting with the third party claims administrator for the handling of claims;

(2) determining the premium or other means of cost sharing to be charged each group member;

(3) investing surplus moneys subject to the restrictions of subsection (d) of this section and any others adopted by the Board of Trustees in addition to those contained in subsection (d);

(4) reviewing and accepting applications from prospective members to the group self insurer; and

(5) executing the Agreement of Assumption and Guarantee For Group Members or the Indemnity Agreement on behalf of the group self insurer.

All delegated functions shall be specifically defined in the group self insurer's by-laws.

Note: Authority cited: Sections 54, 55 and 3702.10, Labor Code. Reference: Sections 3700, 3700.1, 3701, 3701.5, 3702.1, 3702.2 and 3702.10, Labor Code.

History: 1. New section filed 6-30-94; operative 6-30-94 (Register 94, No. 26).

§15476. Advance Premium Discounts.

The Board of Trustees of a group self insurer using a premium plan may not authorize advance premium discounts to any member.

Note: Authority cited: Sections 54, 55 and 3702.10, Labor Code. Reference: Sections 3700, 3701 and 3702.10, Labor Code.

History: 1. New section filed 6-30-94; operative 6-30-94 (Register 94, No. 26).

§15477. Surplus or Insufficient Funding.

(a) Any surplus moneys for a calendar year in excess of the amount necessary to fulfill all compensation obligations for that calendar year, including a provision for incurred but not reported claims, may be declared to be refundable by the Board of Trustees of the group self insurer at any time.

(1) The amount of such declaration shall be a fixed liability of the group self insurer at the time of the declaration and any surplus in the compensation loss fund shall be held for a minimum period of 12 months from the date of the Board of Trustees' declaration.

(2) The date of payment of such refund shall be as agreed to by the Board of Trustees, except that the moneys not needed to satisfy the compensation loss fund requirements as established by the aggregate excess contract, may be refunded immediately after the end of the calendar year.

Note: It is the intent of this regulation to assure that total assets of the group self insurer are greater than the total liabilities of the group self insurer in each calendar year.

(b) In the event that member funds collected and investment income associated with any calendar year are insufficient to completely fund all reported claims and expenses for that year, unfunded amounts by calendar year shall be immediately reported to the Manager with a proposed plan to achieve full funding. The plan to achieve full funding for all claims is subject to approval by the Manager. The plan to achieve full funding may include, but is not limited to, all of the following:

(1) Use of group self insurer funds collected in other calendar years, but that are unnecessary for the payment of claims or expenses for the calendar year collected;

(2) Use of investment earnings associated with other calendar years, but not necessary for

the payment of claims or expenses in the calendar year in which the earnings are associated;

(3) Special assessment of all group self insurer members by the Board of Trustees to make up the funding insufficiency.

(d) If the plan to achieve full funding for all claims is not approved by the Manager, the Manager may order the Board of Trustees of the group self insurer to immediately assess the group members for the full amount of the deficiency and/or order that any surplus funds or dividends distributed to group members during the previous 12 calendar months from the date of the discovery of the funding deficiency by the group self insurer by immediately returned.

(e) If the Manager determines that actions specified in subsection (d) of this section will not achieve full funding of all claim liability for the group self insurer, the Manager may request the Director to order an outside Conservator be appointed at the expense of the group self insurer to manage the financial affairs of the group self insurer and to take whatever steps may be necessary in order to return a financially troubled group self insurer to full financial solvency.

Note: Authority cited: Sections 54, 55 and 3702.10, Labor Code. Reference: Sections 3700, 3701, 3701.5 and 3702.10, Labor Code.

History: 1. New section filed 6-30-94; operative 6-30-94 (Register 94, No. 26).

Editor's Note: There is no subsection (c).

§15478. Excess Insurance.

(a) All group self insurers shall have and maintain in full force a specific excess workers' compensation insurance policy issued by a admitted casualty insurance carrier authorized to transact such business in the State by the Department of Insurance. The specific excess policy shall not have a minimum retention level above $500,000 and the policy may not be canceled or renewed without prior written notice to the Manager and the group self insurer at least 30 days prior to the date of cancellation or non-renewal by the carrier.

(b) Any group self insurer may have and maintain in full force an aggregate excess workers' compensation insurance policy issued by an admitted casualty insurance carrier authorized to conduct such business in the State of California. The aggregate policy may not be canceled or renewed without prior written notice to the Manager and the group self insurer at least 30 days prior to the date of cancellation or nonrenewal by the carrier.

Note: No credit toward security deposit will be given for aggregate excess coverage as set forth in Section 15210.3.

(c) If a group self insurer for any reason is unable to pay compensation due or to post security deposit required or both, and the Director orders the Self Insurer's Security Fund to assume the liabilities of the group self insurer pursuant to Labor Code Section 3701.5, the specific excess carrier or aggregate excess carrier shall make all payments due directly to the Security Fund as would have been made by the excess carrier to the group self insurer after the retention level of the policy had been reached.

(d) The group self insurer may not own its own specific excess or aggregate excess carrier that issues the policy for the group self insurer.

Note: Authority cited: Sections 54, 55 and 3702.10, Labor Code. Reference: Sections 3700, 3701, 3701.5, 3702.10 and 3740-3747, Labor Code.

History: 1. New section filed 6-30-94; operative 6-30-94 (Register 94, No. 26).

§15479. Indemnity Agreement and Power of Attorney.

(a) Each group member of a group self insurer shall execute an indemnity agreement and power of attorney that shall be on either a Form A4-8 (Rev 1/94), Indemnity Agreement and Power of Attorney or another form of an Indemnity Agreement and Power of Attorney which shall be subject to the approval of the Manager.

(b) The indemnity agreement and power of attorney shall contain, in substance, the following provisions:

(1) An agreement under which each member of a group self insurer agrees to assume and discharge, jointly and severally, any compensation liability under Labor Code Section 3700-3705 of any and all other employers that are parties to the group self insurer indemnity agreement; and,

(2) The agreement provides that, in addition to the rights of the group self insurer to enforce the indemnity agreement, in the event of a failure of the group self insurer to enforce such rights after reasonable notice to the group self insurer, the Director of Industrial Relations shall have the right independently to enforce the indemnity agreement on behalf of the group self insurer including the joint and several liability

of group members for payment of all compensation liabilities under the indemnity agreement and the liability of group members for any unpaid contributions and assessments; and

(3) Provisions requiring that the Board of Trustees of the group self insurer designate and appoint a group administrator empowered to accept the service of process on behalf of the group members and authorized to act for and bind the group self insurer and all group members in all transactions relating to or arising out of the operation of the group self insurer; and

(4) Provisions for the right of the Director of Industrial Relations to substitute an outside Conservator for the group administrator; and

(5) A provision granting full power of attorney and signature authority to the group administrator of the group self insurer to execute documents, enter contracts, accept service of process on behalf of the group self insurer, and conduct the general business of the group self insurer, and, that said signature of the group administrator shall bind each and every group member jointly and severally.

Note: A copy of Form A4-8 (Rev 1/94), Indemnity Agreement and Power of Attorney, is contained in the Appendix following the last Article of these Group 2 regulations.

Note: Authority cited: Sections 54, 55 and 3702.10, Labor Code. Reference: Sections 3700, 3701, 3701.5, 3702, 3702.1, 3702.2, 3702.3, 3702.5, 3702.7 and 3702.10, Labor Code.

History: 1. New section filed 6-30-94; operative 6-30-94 (Register 94, No. 26).

§15480. Termination of Membership in a Group.

(a) No group member in a group self insurer may be canceled or terminated from membership in a group self insurer unless at least 60 days advance written notice has been given to the group member and to the Manager.

(b) The group self insurer shall remain liable for all compensation liabilities of any group member resulting from any claim with a date of injury during the period of membership in the group self insurer, including the 60 day period required for termination of membership.

Exception 1: The group self insurer's liability for claims shall terminate on the date of issuance of a standard workers' compensation insurance policy issued by a admitted carrier.

Exception 2: A former self insurer's claims may be transferred to a carrier as set forth in Labor Code Section 3702.8(c) under a special excess workers' compensation policy.

(c) Notice to the Manager of termination of a group member from a group self insurer as set forth in subsection (a) of this section shall be good cause for revocation of the Affiliate Certificate issued to the group member on the termination date or the policy issue date as set forth in subsection (b) of this section.

Note: Authority cited: Sections 54, 55 and 3702.10, Labor Code. Reference: Sections 3700, 3701, 3701.5, 3702 and 3702.10, Labor Code.

History: 1. New section filed 6-30-94; operative 6-30-94 (Register 94, No. 26).

§15481. Actuarial Certification of Losses.

(a) At least every other year, each group self insurer shall have an actuarial analysis done of its historical loss development and a projection of anticipated loss development. The actuary performing this study shall be either:

(1) Associate or Fellow of the Casualty Actuary Society; or

(2) Member of the American Academy of Actuaries.

(b) The analysis and results of the study shall be presented to the group self insurers' Board of Trustees and made available in written form to the Board of Trustees and to any group member requesting a copy. The study shall be commenced immediately following the close of the ninth month of each calendar year and the written report presented to the Board of Trustees by January 1 of the new calendar year.

(c) The written actuarial report shall be provided to the Manager by March 1 of each required year it is prepared by the group administrator.

(d) The Board of Trustees shall ensure that funding of claims losses for the group shall be based on the actuarial projection at the 80% confidence level.

Note: Sample By Laws. A sample of bylaws for a Group Self Insurer to assist groups in developing a set of by-laws is in the appendix following these regulations.

Note: Authority cited: Sections 54, 55 and 3702.10, Labor Code. Reference: Sections 3700, 3701, 3701.5 and 3702.10, Labor Code.

History: 1. New section filed 6-30-94; operative 6-30-94 (Register 94, No. 26).

SUBCHAPTER 2.05 ENFORCEMENT OF WORKERS' COMPENSATION COVERAGE, PENALTY ASSESSMENT ORDERS, STOP ORDERS AND POSTING AND NOTICE REQUIREMENTS

ARTICLE 1 Delegation of Enforcement Authority

§15550. Delegation of Enforcement Authority.

The Director of Industrial Relations delegates concurrent authority to enforce Labor Code Sections 3700, 3710, 3710.1, 3710.2, 3711, 3712, 3713, 3714, 3718, 3722, 3723, 3725, 3726 and 3727 to the Division of Labor Standards Enforcement.

Note: Authority cited: Sections 55 and 3710, Labor Code. Reference: Sections 3700, 3710, 3710.1, 3710.2, 3711, 3712, 3713, 3714, 3718, 3722, 3723, 3725, 3726 and 3727, Labor Code.

History: 1. New Group 2.05 (Articles 1-15, Sections 15550-15596) filed 6-27-79; effective thirtieth day thereafter (Register 79, No. 26).

ARTICLE 2 Definitions

§15551. Direction to File Verified Statement.

"Direction to File Verified Statement" means the notice sent pursuant to Labor Code Section 3722 to employers found by the Workers' Compensation Appeals Board not to have secured the payment of compensation.

Note: Authority cited: Sections 55 and 3710, Labor Code. Reference: Sections 3700, 3710, 3710.1, 3710.2, 3711, 3712, 3713, 3714, 3718, 3722, 3723, 3725, 3726 and 3727, Labor Code.

§15552. Director.

"Director" means the Director of Industrial Relations or his designated agents or delegees.

Note: Authority cited: Sections 55 and 3710, Labor Code. Reference: Sections 3700, 3710, 3710.1, 3710.2, 3711, 3712, 3713, 3714, 3718, 3722, 3723, 3725, 3726 and 3727, Labor Code.

§15553. Division.

"Division" means Division of Labor Standards Enforcement unless otherwise specified.

Note: Authority cited: Sections 55 and 3710, Labor Code. Reference: Sections 3700, 3710, 3710.1, 3710.2, 3711, 3712, 3713, 3714, 3718, 3722, 3723, 3725, 3726 and 3727, Labor Code.

§15554. Findings.

"Findings" means Findings issued by the Division after a hearing on the objection to a Penalty Assessment Order or a Stop Order.

Note: Authority cited: Sections 55 and 3710, Labor Code. Reference: Sections 3700, 3710, 3710.1, 3710.2, 3711, 3712, 3713, 3714, 3718, 3722, 3723, 3725, 3726 and 3727, Labor Code.

§15555. Issue.

"Issue" means to issue and serve a Stop Order, a Penalty Assessment Order or a Notice on the employer.

Note: Authority cited: Sections 55 and 3710, Labor Code. Reference: Sections 3700, 3710, 3710.1, 3710.2, 3711, 3712, 3713, 3714, 3718, 3722, 3723, 3725, 3726 and 3727, Labor Code.

§15556. Notice of Findings on Penalty Assessment Order or Stop Order.

"Notice of Findings on Penalty Assessment Order or Stop Order" means the notice issued by the Division to an employer after a hearing on the objection to a Penalty Assessment Order or a Stop Order.

Note: Authority cited: Sections 55 and 3710, Labor Code. Reference: Sections 3700, 3710, 3710.1, 3710.2, 3711, 3712, 3713, 3714, 3718, 3722, 3723, 3725, 3726 and 3727, Labor Code.

§15557. Penalty Assessment Order.

"Penalty Assessment Order" means an order issued by the Division to an employer requiring the payment of penalties as set forth in Labor Code Sections 3710.1, 3711 or 3722.

Note: Authority cited: Sections 55 and 3710, Labor Code. Reference: Sections 3700, 3710, 3710.1, 3710.2, 3711, 3712, 3713, 3714, 3718, 3722, 3723, 3725, 3726 and 3727, Labor Code.

§15558. Special Judgment.

"Special Judgment" means the judgment entered by the clerk of the Superior Court pursuant to Labor Code Section 3726.

Note: Authority cited: Sections 55 and 3710, Labor Code. Reference: Sections 3700, 3710, 3710.1, 3710.2, 3711, 3712, 3713, 3714, 3718, 3722, 3723, 3725, 3726 and 3727, Labor Code.

§15559. Stop Order.

"Stop Order" means an order issued by the Director pursuant to Labor Code Section 3710.1 to an employer prohibiting the use of employees' labor until the employer secures the payment of compensation as required by Labor Code Section 3700.

Note: Authority cited: Sections 55 and 3710, Labor Code. Reference: Sections 3700, 3710, 3710.1, 3710.2, 3711, 3712, 3713, 3714, 3718, 3722, 3723, 3725, 3726 and 3727, Labor Code.

§15560. Uninsured Employer.

"Uninsured Employer" means any employer who has failed to secure the payment of compensation as required by Labor Code Section 3700.

Note: Authority cited: Sections 55 and 3710, Labor Code. Reference: Sections 3700, 3710, 3710.1, 3710.2, 3711, 3712, 3713, 3714, 3718, 3722, 3723, 3725, 3726 and 3727, Labor Code.

§15561. Verified Statement.

"Verified Statement" means a written form sent by the Workers' Compensation Appeals Board to an employer upon which such employer is directed to indicate (under penalty of perjury) the number of employees in his employ on the date of injury and submit this statement to the Division.

Note: Authority cited: Sections 55 and 3710, Labor Code. Reference: Sections 3700, 3710, 3710.1, 3710.2, 3711, 3712, 3713, 3714, 3718, 3722, 3723, 3725, 3726 and 3727, Labor Code.

§15562. Verified Petition.

"Verified Petition" means a written statement made and signed by an employer either (1) under oath taken before a notary public or other officer authorized to take affidavits and to administer oaths or (2) under a declaration stating in substance "I declare under penalty of perjury that the foregoing is true and correct" and further stating the date and place of execution. This petition is to be used by an employer who wishes to object to a Penalty Assessment Order and thereby request an administrative appeals.

Note: Authority cited: Sections 55 and 3710, Labor Code. Reference: Sections 3700, 3710, 3710.1, 3710.2, 3711, 3712, 3713, 3714, 3718, 3722, 3723, 3725, 3726 and 3727, Labor Code.

ARTICLE 3
Investigation of Employer's Workers' Compensation Status

§15563. Access to Places of Labor.

The Division, its deputies and agents shall have free access to information about workers' compensation coverage in all places of labor. The Division shall investigate any employer to determine whether he has secured the payment of workers' compensation as required by law.

Note: Authority cited: Sections 55 and 3710, Labor Code. Reference: Sections 3700, 3710, 3710.1, 3710.2, 3711, 3712, 3713, 3714, 3718, 3722, 3723, 3725, 3726 and 3727, Labor Code.

Ref.: Hanna § 10.20.

§15564. Inquiry Into Workers' Compensation Status.

The Division shall inquire of any employer the status of such employer's workers' compensation coverage pursuant to Section 3711 of the Labor Code.

Note: Authority cited: Sections 55 and 3710, Labor Code. Reference: Sections 3700, 3710, 3710.1, 3710.2, 3711, 3712, 3713, 3714, 3718, 3722, 3723, 3725, 3726 and 3727, Labor Code.

Ref.: Hanna § 10.20.

§15565. Posting Notice of Workers' Compensation Carrier.

Each employer is required to post a notice of his workers' compensation carrier at his headquarters or branch office together with the date of the expiration of his policy and the telephone number of the nearest office of the Labor Commissioner so that employees may call to report expiration of such coverage (as required by Labor Code Section 3713). Failure to post such notice is a misdemeanor.

Note: Authority cited: Sections 55 and 3710, Labor Code. Reference: Sections 3700, 3710, 3710.1, 3710.2, 3711, 3712, 3713, 3714, 3718, 3722, 3723, 3725, 3726 and 3727, Labor Code.

Ref.: Hanna § 10.26.

ARTICLE 4
Penalties

§15566. Assessment of Penalty.

Insured employers shall be assessed penalties for the failure or refusal to furnish information concerning the status of their workers' compensation coverage. Uninsured employers shall be assessed penalties for the failure to secure the payment of workers' compensation coverage for their employees.

Note: Authority cited: Sections 55 and 3710, Labor Code. Reference: Sections 3700, 3710, 3710.1, 3710.2, 3711, 3712, 3713, 3714, 3718, 3722, 3723, 3725, 3726 and 3727, Labor Code.

Ref.: Hanna § 10.22[1].

§15567. Penalty Assessment Orders.

Penalties shall be assessed by the issuance of Penalty Assessment Orders and shall be served as prescribed in these regulations.

Note: Authority cited: Sections 55 and 3710, Labor Code. Reference: Sections 3700, 3710, 3710.1, 3710.2, 3711, 3712, 3713, 3714, 3718, 3722, 3723, 3725, 3726 and 3727, Labor Code.

Ref.: Hanna § 10.22[1].

§15568. Types of Penalty Assessment Orders.

(a) Penalties in non-injury cases.

(1) A fifty ($50) dollar penalty shall be assessed against an insured employer who fails or refuses to make a written response as to the status of his workers' compensation insurance when directed to do so by the Division.

(2) A one hundred ($100) dollar penalty shall be assessed an uninsured employer for each employee in his employ and not necessarily actually working at the time, a Stop Order is served upon him for failing to carry workers' compensation coverage on his employees.

(b) Penalties in Injury Cases.

(1) A one hundred ($100) dollar penalty per employee employed on the date of a claimed injury shall be assessed the employer where the Workers' Compensation Appeals Board finds (a) the employer was uninsured and (b) the injury was not compensable.

(2) A five hundred ($500) dollar penalty per employee employed on the date of injury shall be assessed an employer where the Workers' Compensation Appeals Board finds (a) the employer was uninsured and (b) the injury was compensable.

Note: Authority cited: Sections 55 and 3710, Labor Code. Reference: Sections 3700, 3710, 3710.1, 3710.2, 3711, 3712, 3713, 3714, 3718, 3722, 3723, 3725, 3726 and 3727, Labor Code.

Ref.: Hanna § 10.22[2].

§15569. Maximum Penalties.

The maximum penalties that may be assessed under Section 15568(a)(2) and Section 15568(b)(1) and (b)(2) shall not exceed ten thousand ($10,000) dollars.

Note: Authority cited: Sections 55 and 3710, Labor Code. Reference: Sections 3700, 3710, 3710.1, 3710.2, 3711, 3712, 3713, 3714, 3718, 3722, 3723, 3725, 3726 and 3727, Labor Code.

§15570. Number of Employees.

(a) Uninsured Employers in Non-Injury Cases. When issuing a one hundred ($100) dollar Penalty Assessment Order against an uninsured employer, the number of employees employed by such employer, and not necessarily those actually working at the time, in non-injury cases shall be ascertained by the Division at the time the Stop Order is served.

(b) Uninsured Employers in Injury Cases.

(1) After the issuance of a final decision of the Workers' Compensation Appeals Board, the Appeals Board shall mail to the uninsured employer and the Division a copy of the final decision and notice of the provisions of Labor Code Sections 3710.1 and 3722 which require such employer to pay penalties of one hundred ($100) dollars per employee and five hundred ($500) dollars per employee in non-compensable and compensable cases, respectively.

(2) In order to establish the number of employees, such employer shall submit to the Division within ten (10) days after service of the aforementioned documents by the Workers' Compensation Appeals Board, a verified statement of the number of employees in his employ on the date of injury.

(3) If such employer fails to submit to the Division a verified statement indicating the number of employees employed or if the Division disputes the accuracy of such verified statement, on the date of injury the Division shall issue a Penalty Assessment Order using such information regarding the number of such employees as the Division may have or otherwise obtain.

(4) Notice of the Penalty Assessment Order shall be mailed to the employer at his residence or usual place of business by registered or certified mail.

(5) The employer to whom the assessment is directed may file within twenty (20) days after receipt thereof a verified petition in writing, objecting to the assessment and setting forth the grounds for his objection.

(6) If such employer does not file a a petition with the Division within said twenty (20) days, such assessment shall become conclusive and the amount thereof shall be due and payable from the employer so assessed to the Division for deposit in the State Treasury to the credit of the Uninsured Employers Fund.

Note: Authority cited: Sections 55 and 3710, Labor Code. Reference: Sections 3700, 3710, 3710.1, 3710.2, 3711, 3712, 3713, 3714, 3718, 3722, 3723, 3725, 3726 and 3727, Labor Code.

ARTICLE 5
Stop Order

§15571. When Issued.

Where an employer is found to be without workers' compensation insurance as required by law, the Division shall issue and serve a Stop Order on such employer (1) prohibiting his use of employee labor until he acquires coverage and (2) requiring him to pay lost wages to his employees affected by the work stoppage, not exceeding ten (10) days' pay, pending compliance by such employer.

Note: Authority cited: Sections 55 and 3710, Labor Code. Reference: Sections 3700, 3710, 3710.1, 3710.2, 3711, 3712, 3713, 3714, 3718, 3722, 3723, 3725, 3726 and 3727, Labor Code.

Ref.: Hanna § 10.21[1].

§15571.5. When Effective.

A Stop Order shall be effective immediately upon service and shall remain in effect during any appeal proceedings, unless and until the employer acquires workers' compensation coverage.

Note: Authority cited: Sections 55 and 3710, Labor Code. Reference: Sections 3700, 3710, 3710.1, 3710.2, 3711, 3712, 3713, 3714, 3718, 3722, 3723, 3725, 3726 and 3727, Labor Code.

Ref.: Hanna § 10.21[1].

§15572. Failure to Observe Stop Order Constitutes Misdemeanor.

Such Stop Order shall inform the employer that failure to observe same constitutes a misdemeanor, and if the employer if convicted thereof, the court is required to impose a mandatory jail sentence in the county jail of not less than ten (10) days and a fine of not less than three hundred ($300) dollars.

Note: Authority cited: Sections 55 and 3710, Labor Code. Reference: Sections 3700, 3710, 3710.1, 3710.2, 3711, 3712, 3713, 3714, 3718, 3722, 3723, 3725, 3726 and 3727, Labor Code.

Ref.: Hanna § 10.21[3].

§15573. Injunctive Relief.

Where an uninsured employer fails to comply with a Stop Order, the Division may seek injunctive relief from the courts.

Note: Authority cited: Sections 55 and 3710, Labor Code. Reference: Sections 3700, 3710, 3710.1, 3710.2, 3711, 3712, 3713, 3714, 3718, 3722, 3723, 3725, 3726 and 3727, Labor Code.

Ref.: Hanna § 10.21[3].

ARTICLE 6
Contents of Orders, of Direction to File Verified Statement and of Verified Statement

§15574. Stop Order.

The Stop Order issued and served on the uninsured employer pursuant to Labor Code Section 3710.1 shall contain the following information:

(a) The uninsured employer shall cease and desist the use of employee labor until he obtains the required workers' compensation coverage.

(b) Such employer shall be assessed a penalty of one hundred ($100) dollars per employee employed at the time the Stop Order is issued and served for failure to have obtained workers' compensation.

(c) The correct name and legal entity of the employer, the employer's address, the date, the time, the place of issuance, the signature and the name of the official who issues the Stop Order.

(d) The appeal procedure for objecting to a Stop Order.

Note: Authority cited: Sections 55 and 3710, Labor Code. Reference: Sections 3700, 3710, 3710.1, 3710.2, 3711, 3712, 3713, 3714, 3718, 3722, 3723, 3725, 3726 and 3727, Labor Code.

Ref.: Hanna § 10.21[1].

§15575. Penalty Assessment Orders.

(a) $50 Penalty Assessment Order. This order, issued pursuant to Labor Code Section 3711 shall contain the following information:

(1) The employer has failed to furnish a written statement to the Division stating the

name of his workers' compensation insurance carrier.

(2) Failure to furnish such statement within ten (10) days constitutes prima facie evidence of the employer's neglect or failure to comply with the coverage requirements of the law.

(3) The employer, by virtue of the Order, is assessed a penalty of fifty ($50) dollars for such failure.

(4) The correct name and legal entity of the employer, the employer's address, the date, the place of issuance, the signature and the name of the official who issues the order.

(5) The appeal procedure for objecting to this penalty assessment order.

(6) The procedure used by the Division to obtain a judgment against the employer, should he fail to pay the assessment.

(b) $100 Non-Injury Penalty Assessment Order. The order, issued pursuant to Labor Code Section 3710.1 shall contain the following information:

(1) The employer has been found to be without the required workers' compensation insurance.

(2) The employer, by virtue of the Order, is assessed a penalty of one hundred ($100) dollars per employee employed at the time the Order is issued for failure to have workers' compensation coverage.

(3) The correct name and legal entity of the employer, the employer's address, the date, the time, the place of issuance, the signature and the name of the official who issued the Order.

(4) The appeal procedure for objecting to the Penalty Assessment Order.

(5) The procedure used by the Division to obtain a judgment against the employer, should he fail to pay the assessment.

(c) $100 Injury-related Penalty Assessment Order. The order, issued pursuant to Labor Code Section 3710.1 shall contain the following information:

(1) The Workers' Compensation Appeals Board has found the employer to be uninsured in a claimed injury and that such injury is noncompensable.

(2) The employer, by virtue of the Order, is assessed a penalty of one hundred ($100) dollars employee employed on the date of such claimed injury.

(3) The correct name and legal entity of the employer, the employer's address, the date, the place of issuance, the signature and the name of the official who issued the Order.

(4) The appeal procedure for objecting to the Order.

(5) The procedure used by the Division to obtain a judgment against the employer, should he fail to pay the assessment.

(d) $500 Injury-related Penalty Assessment Order. The Order issued pursuant to Labor Code Section 3722 shall contain the following information:

(1) The Workers' Compensation Appeals Board has found the employer to be uninsured and the claimed injury compensable.

(2) The employer, by virtue of the Order, is assessed a penalty of five hundred ($500) dollars per employee employed on the date of injury.

(3) The correct name and legal entity of the employer, the employer's address, the date, the place of issuance, the signature and the name of the official who issued the Order.

(4) The appeal procedure for objecting to the Order.

(5) The procedure used by the Division to obtain a judgment against the employer, should he fail to pay the assessment.

Note: Authority cited: Sections 55 and 3710, Labor Code. Reference: Sections 3700, 3710, 3710.1, 3710.2, 3711, 3712, 3713, 3714, 3718, 3722, 3723, 3725, 3726 and 3727, Labor Code.

Ref.: Hanna § 10.22[3].

§15576. Direction to File Verified Statement.

The statement, which shall be mailed to the employer by the Workers' Compensation Appeals Board simultaneously with the issuance and service of Findings of Fact, Findings and Order or Findings and Award, shall contain the following information:

(a) The Workers' Compensation Appeals Board has found the employer to be without the required workers' compensation coverage.

(b) The Division shall assess the employer a penalty of one hundred ($100) dollars or five hundred ($500) dollars per employee at the time of the injury pursuant to Labor Code Sections 3710.1 and 3722, respectively.

(c) The employer is requested to complete and submit to the Division within ten (10) days the verified statement on the reverse side of the Direction to File Verified Statement indicating the number of employees employed on the date of injury.

(d) The Division may dispute the accuracy of such verified statement.

(e) The Appeal procedure for objecting to the one hundred ($100) dollar injury-related Penalty Assessment Order (Labor Code Section 3710.1) and to the five hundred ($500) dollar injury-related Penalty Assessment Order (Labor Code Section 3722).

Note: Authority cited: Sections 55 and 3710, Labor Code. Reference: Sections 3700, 3710, 3710.1, 3710.2, 3711, 3712, 3713, 3714, 3718, 3722, 3723, 3725, 3726 and 3727, Labor Code.

§15577. Verified Statement.

The verified statement, which shall be mailed to the employer by the Workers' Compensation Appeals Board simultaneously with the issuance of Findings of Fact, Findings and Order or Findings and Award, shall be found on the reverse side of the Direction to File Verified Statement and shall contain the following information:

(a) That the employer must complete the verified statement and submit the requested information to the Division.

(b) The number of employees in the employer's employ on the date of injury.

(c) A certification under penalty of perjury by the employer that such number is true and correct.

(d) The employer's signature, address and the date and place of execution thereof.

ARTICLE 7
Service of Stop Order and Penalty Assessment Order

§15578. Service.

Any Stop Order or Penalty Assessment Order under the law and pursuant to these regulations issued to and served upon an employer may be served as follows:

(a) By delivering a copy of same to the employer if the employers is an individual;

(b) By delivering a copy of same to any general partner of the employer if the employer is a partnership;

(c) By delivering a copy of same to any person specified in Section 416.10 of the Code of Civil Procedure (specified corporate officers or designated agent) if the employer is a corporation;

(d) By any other manner authorized under the Code of Civil Procedure for the service of process in a civil action.

Note: Authority cited: Sections 55 and 3710, Labor Code. Reference: Sections 3700, 3710, 3710.1, 3710.2, 3711, 3712, 3713, 3714, 3718, 3722, 3723, 3725, 3726 and 3727, Labor Code.

ARTICLE 8
Review of Proceedings and Withdrawal Proceedings

§15579. Review of Proceedings to Correct Designation of Legal Entity or Clerical Error.

(a) During an appeal hearing, a hearing officer may establish the correct legal entity of the employer and may amend any necessary documents to reflect said true legal entity.

(b) The Division may correct a clerical error where such error has been made in an order, or decision until it becomes final to conform with the facts and the intended wording.

Note: Authority cited: Sections 55 and 3710, Labor Code. Reference: Sections 3700, 3710, 3710.1, 3710.2, 3711, 3712, 3713, 3714, 3718, 3722, 3723, 3725, 3726 and 3727, Labor Code.

§15580. Withdrawal of Orders.

The Division may withdraw a Stop Order or a Penalty Assessment Order:

(a) Where investigation indicates the employer had secured the payment of compensation as required by Section 3700 of the Labor Code at the time of service of such Orders; or

(b) Where an insured employer responded in writing within the prescribed time to a request to furnish the status of his workers' compensation coverage; or

(c) Where investigation indicates the employer had no employees.

Note: Authority cited: Sections 55 and 3710, Labor Code. Reference: Sections 3700, 3710, 3710.1, 3710.2, 3711, 3712, 3713, 3714, 3718, 3722, 3723, 3725, 3726 and 3727, Labor Code.

Ref.: Hanna §§ 10.21[4], 10.22[6].

ARTICLE 9
Appeal Procedures

§15581. Stop Order.

Where an employer objects to a Stop Order and desires a hearing thereon, such employer may make an oral or written request for a hearing. Upon receipt of such request, the Division shall set the matter for a hearing with five (5) days from the date of receipt thereof.

Note: Authority cited: Sections 55 and 3710, Labor Code. Reference: Sections 3700, 3710, 3710.1, 3710.2, 3711, 3712, 3713, 3714, 3718, 3722, 3723, 3725, 3726 and 3727, Labor Code.

§15582. Penalty Assessment Orders.

An employer may object to a Penalty Assessment Order within twenty (20) days after the service of the Order by filing a verified petition objecting to said Penalty Assessment Order and setting forth the ground(s) for such objections which are as set forth in Section 15584 of this Article. Upon the filing of such petition within the time prescribed, the Division shall set the matter for hearing within thirty (30) days thereafter.

Note: Authority cited: Sections 55 and 3710, Labor Code. Reference: Sections 3700, 3710, 3710.1, 3710.2, 3711, 3712, 3713, 3714, 3718, 3722, 3723, 3725, 3726 and 3727, Labor Code.

§15583. Grounds of Objection.

The grounds of objection are as follows:

(a) The Division acted without or in excess of its jurisdiction;

(b) The Stop Order, Penalty Assessment Orders, or Notice were not properly served;

(c) The correct legal entity is not set forth in the Order or Notice;

(d) The employer was legally insured for workers' compensation;

(e) No employment relationship exists between the workers and the person assessed or enjoined;

(f) The Division committed mistake, error or omission; or

(g) The Division acted arbitrarily, capriciously and in abuse of its discretion.

Note: Authority cited: Sections 55 and 3710, Labor Code. Reference: Sections 3700, 3710, 3710.1, 3710.2, 3711, 3712, 3713, 3714, 3718, 3722, 3723, 3725, 3726 and 3727, Labor Code.

§15584. Matters Not Grounds for Objection.

The following reasons which may be asserted are not sufficient or valid grounds for objection:

(a) Ignorance of the law;

(b) The employer's assertion that the workers' compensation insurance premiums are excessive; or

(c) The employer's mistaken belief that he had such insurance.

Note: Authority cited: Sections 55 and 3710, Labor Code. Reference: Sections 3700, 3710, 3710.1, 3710.2, 3711, 3712, 3713, 3714, 3718, 3722, 3723, 3725, 3726 and 3727, Labor Code.

ARTICLE 10
Hearing

§15585. Proceedings Under Oath.

All testimony adduced at the hearing shall taken under oath. The hearing officer shall administer such oath.

Note: Authority cited: Sections 55 and 3710, Labor Code. Reference: Sections 3700, 3710, 3710.1, 3710.2, 3711, 3712, 3713, 3714, 3718, 3722, 3723, 3725, 3726 and 3727, Labor Code.

§15586. Proceedings Shall Be Recorded.

Any proceedings heard before the Division shall be recorded.

Note: Authority cited: Sections 55 and 3710, Labor Code. Reference: Sections 3700, 3710, 3710.1, 3710.2, 3711, 3712, 3713, 3714, 3718, 3722, 3723, 3725, 3726 and 3727, Labor Code.

§15587. Conduct of Hearing.

Any Party to the hearing is entitled to be heard, to present evidence and to cross examine witnesses appearing at the hearing, but the Division is not bound by common law or statutory rules of evidence or procedure.

Note: Authority cited: Sections 55 and 3710, Labor Code. Reference: Sections 3700, 3710, 3710.1, 3710.2, 3711, 3712, 3713, 3714, 3718, 3722, 3723, 3725, 3726 and 3727, Labor Code.

§15588. Right to Subpoenas and Subpoenas Duces Tecum.

(a) Subpoenas.

Upon request of any party to a hearing on a Penalty Assessment Order or Stop Order, the Division may issue subpoenas for the attendance of witnesses before the Division at the time and place of hearing. Said subpoenas shall be served in the manner provided for serving subpoenas in civil actions. The Division shall not issue subpoenas in blank.

(b) Subpoenas Duces Tecum.

Upon the request of any party to a hearing on a Penalty Assessment Order or Stop Order, accompanied by a declaration of materiality thereof in the manner provided for in Section 1985 of the Code of Civil Procedure, the Division may issue subpoenas duces tecum requiring witnesses or parties to produce any books, documents or other materials under their control which they are bound by law to produce at the time and place of hearing. Subpoenas duces tecum served hereunder shall be served as provided therefor in civil actions.

Note: Authority cited: Sections 55 and 3710, Labor Code. Reference: Sections 3700, 3710, 3710.1, 3710.2, 3711, 3712, 3713, 3714, 3718, 3722, 3723, 3725, 3726 and 3727, Labor Code.

§15589. Custody of Papers Filed With the Division.

Books, documents and other material admitted into evidence may be withdrawn only on condition that an exact copy of any such books, documents or other materials sought to be removed, be offered in evidence in lieu thereof. In such event, there shall be made on the face of any such copy so admitted, a notation that the same is identical to the original withdrawn, and such notation shall be dated and signed by both the employer and the hearing officer.

Note: Authority cited: Sections 55 and 3710, Labor Code. Reference: Sections 3700, 3710, 3710.1, 3710.2, 3711, 3712, 3713, 3714, 3718, 3722, 3723, 3725, 3726 and 3727, Labor Code.

§15590. Decision of the Division.

(a) Stop Order. At the conclusion of a hearing on a Stop Order, the Division shall immediately affirm or dismiss said Stop Order. In addition, the Division shall issue and serve on any party to the hearing by registered or certified mail a written Notice of Findings and Findings within twenty-four (24) hours after the conclusion of such hearing.

(b) Penalty Assessment Order. The decision of the Division on any Penalty Assessment Order shall consist of Notice of Findings and written Findings which shall be served on any party to the hearing by registered or certified mail within fifteen (15) days after said hearing.

Note: Authority cited: Sections 55 and 3710, Labor Code. Reference: Sections 3700, 3710, 3710.1, 3710.2, 3711, 3712, 3713, 3714, 3718, 3722, 3723, 3725, 3726 and 3727, Labor Code.

Ref.: Hanna §§ 10.21[2], 10.22[4].

ARTICLE 11
Writ of Review

§15591. Employer's Right to Writ of Review.

An employer, upon receipt of Findings affirming or modifying any Penalty Assessment Order may file a Writ of Review from any such Findings to the appropriate superior court upon the execution by such employer of a bond to the State in double the amount so found due and ordered paid by such employer conditioned that such employer will pay any judgment and costs rendered against him for such assessment.

Note: Authority cited: Sections 55 and 3710, Labor Code. Reference: Sections 3700, 3710, 3710.1, 3710.2, 3711, 3712, 3713, 3714, 3718, 3722, 3723, 3725, 3726 and 3727, Labor Code.

Ref.: Hanna § 10.22[4].

ARTICLE 12
Special Judgment Procedure as to Penalty Assessment Orders

§15592. Procedures After Hearing or in the Absence of a Hearing.

(a) Where a hearing has been held and Notice of Findings and Findings have been issued and served on the uninsured employer, and after ten (10) days have expired since the issuance and service thereof, certified copies of the Penalty Assessment Order and the Findings shall be filed with the Judgment (Special) for the Uninsured Employers Fund with the clerk of the superior court who shall enter a judgment in favor of the Director of Industrial Relations as Administrator of the Uninsured Employers Fund, and against the uninsured employer in the amount shown on the Findings unless a Writ of Review has been filed within the said ten (10)-day period.

(b) Where a petition objecting to a Penalty Assessment Order has not been filed, a hearing has not been held and twenty (20) days have expired since the issuance and service of the Penalty Assessment Order, a certified copy of the Penalty Assessment Order may be filed with the Judgment (Special) for the Uninsured Employers Fund with the clerk of the superior court who shall enter a judgment in favor of the Director of Industrial Relations, as Administrator of the Uninsured Employers Fund, and against the uninsured employer in the amount shown on the assessment order.

(c) Upon the entry of a Special Judgment by the clerk of the superior court under Section 15592 (a) and (b) a Notice of Entry of Judgment (Special) for the Uninsured Employers Fund shall be filed and served upon the employer by regular first-class mail.

(d) After full payment has been made of a Judgment (Special) for the Uninsured Employers Fund, an Acknowledgment of Full Satisfaction of Judgment may be filed with the clerk of the superior court.

Note: Authority cited: Sections 55 and 3710, Labor Code. Reference: Sections 3700, 3710, 3710.1, 3710.2, 3711, 3712, 3713, 3714, 3718, 3722, 3723, 3725, 3726 and 3727, Labor Code.

§15593. Procedures Subsequent to Entry of Judgment.

After a Judgment (Special) has been entered and Notice of Entry of such Judgment has been mailed to the employer and he has failed or refused to pay such judgment, the Division may obtain a writ of execution thereon.

Note: Authority cited: Sections 55 and 3710, Labor Code. Reference: Sections 3700, 3710, 3710.1, 3710.2, 3711, 3712, 3713, 3714, 3718, 3722, 3723, 3725, 3726 and 3727, Labor Code.

ARTICLE 14
Penalty Liens

§15594. Recording of Penalty Lien.

Where the employer has failed to secure the payment of compensation, the Division shall file with the county recorder of any county in which such employer's property may be located, a certificate of the amount of penalty due from such employer and such amount shall be a lien in favor of the Division from the date of such filing against the real property and personal property of the employer within the county in which such certificate is filed in accordance with Labor Code Secton 3727.

Note: Authority cited: Sections 55 and 3710, Labor Code. Reference: Sections 3700, 3710, 3710.1, 3710.2, 3711, 3712, 3713, 3714, 3718, 3722, 3723, 3725, 3726 and 3727, Labor Code.

Ref.: Hanna § 10.22[7].

§15595. Cancellation of Penalty Lien.

Upon Payment of the penalty assessment and upon the employer's request, the Division shall issue a certificate of cancellation of penalty assessment which may be recorded by the employer at his expense.

Note: Authority cited: Sections 55 and 3710, Labor Code. Reference: Sections 3700, 3710, 3710.1, 3710.2, 3711, 3712, 3713, 3714, 3718, 3722, 3723, 3725, 3726 and 3727, Labor Code.

Ref.: Hanna § 10.22[7].

ARTICLE 15
Notice of Right to Benefits

§15596. Notice of Employee's Right to Workers' Compensation Benefits.

(a) Employers shall notify, orally or in writing, every new employee, either at the time the employee is hired or by the end of his first pay period, of the employee's right to receive workers' compensation benefits should he be injured on the job at any time while in such employer's employ.

(b) Employers who need not give such notice are owners or occupants of residential dwellings whose employees perform duties which are incidental to the ownership, maintenance or use of the dwelling, including the care and supervision of children or whose duties are personal and not in the course of the trade, business, profession or occupation of such owner or occupant if such employees are employed for less than fifty-two (52) hours during a ninety (90)-day period and earn less than one hundred ($100) dollars.

Note: Authority cited: Sections 55 and 3710, Labor Code. Reference: Sections 3700, 3710, 3710.1, 3710.2, 3711, 3712, 3713, 3714, 3718, 3722, 3723, 3725, 3726 and 3727, Labor Code.

SUBCHAPTER 2.06 WORKERS' COMPENSATION—ADMINISTRATION REVOLVING FUND ASSESSMENT, UNINSURED EMPLOYERS BENEFITS TRUST FUND ASSESSMENT, SUBSEQUENT INJURIES BENEFITS TRUST FUND ASSESSMENTS, FRAUD SURCHARGE AND CAL–OSHA TARGETED INSPECTION ASSESSMENT

ARTICLE 1 Definitions

§15600. Definitions.

(a) Assessable Premium. The premium to which the assessment and/or surcharge is to be applied is the premium the insured is charged after all rating adjustments (experience rating, schedule rating, premium discounts, expense constants, retrospective rating, etc.) except for adjustments resulting from the application of deductible plans or the return of policyholder dividends.

(b) Assessment. Includes those assessments levied upon insured and self-insured employers to establish and maintain the Workers' Compensation Administration Revolving Fund, the Uninsured Employers Benefits Trust Fund, and the Subsequent Injuries Benefits Employers Trust Fund.

(c) Base Year. For purposes of calculating the self-insured employer assessment factors, that time period as provided by the Office of Self-Insurance Plans pursuant to section 15602. For public self-insured employers, the base year is a fiscal year basis. For private self-insured employers, the base year is a calendar year basis.

(d) Director. The Director of the Department of Industrial Relations.

(e) Expected total current year premium. Total direct workers' compensation premium of all insurers as reported to the Department of Insurance's designated licensed rating organization for the period of January 1 through June 30 of the year immediately preceding the assessment, and adjusted by the Department of Insurance's designated licensed rating organization, to a full year basis.

(f) Indemnity. The payments made by a self-insured employer directly to injured employees or their dependents as compensation pursuant to Labor Code divisions 4 and 4.5 including vocational rehabilitation maintenance and salary continuation payments pursuant to Labor Code sections 4800 and 4850.

(g) Inception date. The inception date of a workers' compensation insurance policy is the normal anniversary rating date of a workers' compensation insurance policy as defined in the California Workers' Compensation Insurance Manual published by the Workers' Compensation Insurance Rating Bureau.

(h) Insured employer. Any employer, including any agency or division of the State of California, who secures workers' compensation insurance coverage under provisions of subdivision (a) of Labor Code section 3700.

(i) Insurer. Any person, including the State Compensation Insurance Fund, authorized to transact workers' compensation insurance in California.

(j) Payroll. Remuneration subject to workers' compensation insurance premium for insured employers and that remuneration to employees of a self-insured employer which would be subject to premium charges if the employer were an insured employer.

(k) Revolving Fund. The Workers' Compensation Administration Revolving Fund established pursuant to the provisions of Labor Code section 62.5.

(*l*) Revolving Fund Assessment. The user fee assessment levied upon insured and self-insured employers to establish and maintain the Workers' Compensation Administration Revolving Fund.

(m) Self-insured employer. Any employer who is authorized by the Director to self-insure its workers' compensation liability under subdivisions (b) or (c) of Labor Code section 3700. A self-insured employer shall include the State of California. For the limited purposes of the Targeted Inspection Assessment, the term "self-insured employer" shall not include the State of California or a public agency employer.

(n) Subsequent Injuries Fund. The Subsequent Injuries Benefits Trust Fund established pursuant to the provisions of Labor Code section 62.5.

(o) Subsequent Injuries Fund Assessment. The user fee assessment levied upon insured and self-insured employers to establish and maintain the Subsequent Injuries Benefits Trust Fund.

(p) Surcharge. Surcharge means the "State Fraud Investigation and Prosecution Surcharge" assessed under authority of Labor Code Section 62.6.

(q) Targeted Inspection Assessment. The user fee assessment levied upon self-insured employers to establish and maintain the Cal-OSHA Targeted Inspection and Consultation Fund established pursuant to the provisions of Labor Code section 62.7.

(r) Uninsured Employers Fund. The Uninsured Employers Benefits Trust Fund established pursuant to the provisions of Labor Code section 62.5.

(s) Uninsured Employers Fund Assessment. The user fee assessment levied upon insured and self-insured employers to establish and maintain the Uninsured Employers Benefits Trust Fund.

Note: Authority cited: Sections 54, 55 and 62.5, Labor Code; and Section 1872.83, Insurance Code. Reference: Sections 51, 62.5, 62.6, 3700 and 3701, Labor Code; Section 1872.83, Insurance Code.

History: 1. New section filed 4-18-90 as an emergency; operative 4-18-90 (Register 90, No. 18). A Certificate of Compliance must be transmitted to OAL within 120 days or emergency language will be repealed by operation of law on 8-16-90.

2. Certificate of Compliance as to 4-18-90 order including amendment adding subsections (c) and (k) and renumbering existing subsections transmitted to OAL 8-14-90 and filed 9-13-90 (Register 90, No. 43).

3. Amendment of article heading, amendment of subsections (a), (b) and (g), new subsection (*l*), and amendment of Note filed 1-15-93 as an emergency; operative 1-15-93 (Register 93, No. 3). A Certificate of Compliance must be transmitted to OAL 5-17-93 or emergency language will be repealed by operation of law on the following day.

4. Certificate of Compliance as to 1-15-93 order including repealer of subsection (b), subsection relettering, and amendment of newly designated subsection (f) transmitted to OAL 5-10-93 and filed 6-16-93 (Register 93, No. 25).

5. Amendment of subchapter heading and subsection (b), new subsection (e) and subsection redesignation, amendment of subsections (f) and (l), new subsection (m) and amendment of Note filed 9-6-94 as an emergency; operative 9-6-94 (Register 94, No. 36). A Certificate of Compliance must be transmitted to OAL by 1-4-95 or emergency language will be repealed by operation of law on the following day.

6. Certificate of Compliance as to 9-6-94 order including amendment of subsection (a), new subsection (j), subsection relettering and amendment of subsection (k) transmitted to OAL 12-30-94 and filed 2-15-95 (Register 95, No. 7).

7. Amendment of subsection (a), new subsection (d), repealer of subsection (n), subsection relettering and amendment of Note filed 11-14-95 as an emergency; operative 12-1-95 (Register 95, No. 46). A Certificate of Compliance must be transmitted to OAL by 3-30-96 or emergency language will be repealed by operation of law on the following day.

8. Certificate of Compliance as to 11-14-95 order transmitted to OAL 3-29-96 and filed 5-8-96 (Register 96, No. 19).

9. New subsection (a), repealer of subsection (m), and subsection relettering filed 11-10-97; operative 11-10-97 pursuant to Government Code section 11343.4(d) (Register 97, No. 46).

10. Change without regulatory effect amending subchapter heading and subsections (a) and (b), repealing subsections (k) and (*l*), relettering subsections and amending Note filed 12-15-99 pursuant to section 100, title 1, California Code of Regulations (Register 99, No. 51).

11. Amendment of subchapter heading, amendment of subsections (a) and (b), new subsections (k) and (*l*), subsection relettering, and amendment of Note filed 1-14-2000 as an emergency; operative 1-14-2000 (Register 2000, No. 2). A Certificate of Compliance must be transmitted to OAL by 5-15-2000 or emergency language will be repealed by operation of law on the following day.

12. Certificate of Compliance as to 1-14-2000 order transmitted to OAL 5-9-2000 and filed 6-15-2000 (Register 2000, No. 24).

13. Amendment of subchapter heading and subsections (b), (c) and (k), new subsections (n), (o) and (q)-(s) and subsection relettering filed 12-18-2003; operative 12-18-2003. Submitted to OAL for printing only (Register 2003, No. 51).

ARTICLE 2
Determination of Assessments and/or Surcharge

§15601. Determination of Revolving Fund, Subsequent Injuries Fund, and Uninsured Employers Fund Total Assessment.

On or before November 1 of each year, the Director shall, in accordance with Labor Code Section 62.5:

(a) Determine the total amount of funds appropriated for the Division of Workers' Compensation;

(b) Determine the aggregate amount of the assessment for the Subsequent Injuries Fund; and

(c) Determine the aggregate amount of the assessment for the Uninsured Employers Fund.

Note: Authority cited: Sections 54, 55 and 62.5, Labor Code. Reference: Section 62.5, Labor Code.

History: 1. New section filed 4-18-90 as an emergency; operative 4-18-90 (Register 90, No. 18). A Certificate of Compliance must be transmitted to OAL within 120 days or emergency language will be repealed by operation of law on 8-16-90.

2. Certificate of Compliance as to 4-18-90 order transmitted to OAL 8-14-90 and filed 9-13-90 (Register 90, No. 43).

3. New article 2 heading, amendment of section heading, amendment of subsection (a) and repealer of subsection (b) filed 1-15-93 as an emergency; operative 1-15-93 (Register 93, No. 3). A Certificate of Compliance must be transmitted to OAL 5-17-93 or emergency language will be repealed by operation of law on the following day.

4. Certificate of Compliance as to 1-15-93 order transmitted to OAL 5-10-93 and filed 6-16-93 (Register 93, No. 25).

5. Amendment of article heading, section and Note filed 9-6-94 as an emergency; operative 9-6-94 (Register 94, No. 36). A Certificate of Compliance must be transmitted to OAL by 1-4-95 or emergency language will be repealed by operation of law on the following day.

6. Certificate of Compliance as to 9-6-94 order including amendment of Note transmitted to OAL 12-30-94 and filed 2-15-95 (Register 95, No. 7).

7. Change without regulatory effect repealing section filed 12-15-99 pursuant to section 100, title 1, California Code of Regulations (Register 99, No. 51).

8. New section filed 1-14-2000 as an emergency; operative 1-14-2000 (Register 2000, No. 2). A Certificate of Compliance must be transmitted to OAL by 5-15-2000 or emergency language will be repealed by operation of law on the following day.

9. Certificate of Compliance as to 1-14-2000 order transmitted to OAL 5-9-2000 and filed 6-15-2000 (Register 2000, No. 24).

10. Amendment of section heading and section filed 12-18-2003; operative 12-18-2003. Submitted to OAL for printing only (Register 2003, No. 51).

§15601.5. Ascertainment of State Fraud Investigation and Prosecution Surcharge.

On or before September 1 of each year, the Director shall ascertain from the Fraud Assessment Commission the aggregate amount of the surcharge to be assessed.

The aggregate amount of the surcharge shall be allocated between insured and self-insured employers by applying the same proportional allocation and collection methodology as used to collect the Workers' Compensation Administration Revolving Fund Assessment.

Note: Authority cited: Sections 54 and 55, Labor Code. Reference: Section 62.6, Labor Code.

History: 1. New section filed 1-15-93 as an emergency; operative 1-15-93 (Register 93, No. 3). A Certificate of Compliance must be transmitted to OAL 5-17-93 or emergency language will be repealed by operation of law on the following day.

2. Certificate of Compliance as to 1-15-93 order transmitted to OAL 5-10-93 and filed 6-16-93 (Register 93, No. 25).

3. Amendment of Note filed 9-6-94 as an emergency; operative 9-6-94 (Register 94, No. 36). A Certificate of Compliance must be transmitted to OAL by 1-4-95 or emergency language will be repealed by operation of law on the following day.

4. Certificate of Compliance as to 9-6-94 order including amendment of Note transmitted to OAL 12-30-94 and filed 2-15-95 (Register 95, No. 7).

§15601.6. Repealed.

Note: Authority cited: Sections 54, 55, 62.5, 62.6 and 62.7, Labor Code. Reference: Section 62.7, Labor Code.

History: 1. New section filed 9-6-94 as an emergency; operative 9-6-94 (Register 94, No. 36). A Certificate of Compliance must be transmitted to OAL by 1-4-95 or emergency language will be; repealed by operation of law on the following day.

2. Certificate of Compliance as to 9-6-94 order including amendment of subsections (b)-(c) and repealer of subsection (d) transmitted to OAL 12-30-94 and filed 2-15-95 (Register 95, No. 7).

3. Repealer filed 11-14-95 as an emergency; operative 12-1-95 (Register 95, No. 46). A Certificate of Compliance must be transmitted to OAL by 3-30-96 or emergency language will be repealed by operation of law on the following day.

4. Certificate of Compliance as to 11-14-95 order transmitted to OAL 3-29-96 and filed 5-8-96 (Register 96, No. 19).

§15601.7. Determination of Self Insured Employers Subject to the Targeted Inspection Assessment.

On or before September 1 of each year, the Manager of Self-Insurance Plans shall identify for the Director each Private Self Insurer subject to the Targeted Inspection Assessment as determined below.

(a) The Targeted Inspection Assessment shall apply to each Self Insurer in each grouping set forth in subsection (b) that has a current 1-year average number of indemnity claims per 100 employees as calculated in subsection (e) below, that is equal to or in excess of 125 percent of the 3 year base figure determined for each grouping in subsection (d) of this section.

(b) The Manager shall categorize all private self insurers into groups for the purpose of calculating the Targeted Inspection Assessment. All private self insurers shall be categorized into groups by the first digit of their Standard Industrial Classification Code (SIC Code) as reported on Page 1 of the Self Insurer's Annual Report for the reporting period immediately prior to the current budget year. For purposes of such categorization, each private group self insurer shall be considered as a single entity. The Manager may correct the SIC Code reported for cause or where the Manager believes an error was made by the self insurer in designating their SIC Code on the Annual Report.

(c) For each SIC Code grouping set forth in subsection (a), the Manager shall calculate the historical average number of indemnity claims per 100 employees from the Consolidated Liabilities page of the full year Self Insurer's Annual Reports submitted by the members in each SIC Code group for the 3 year reporting period immediately prior to the current 1-year period used to calculate the individual self insurer's indemnity claims per 100 employees.

(d) The Manager shall calculate a figure that will be 125 percent of each SIC Code grouping's 3 year historical average number of indemnity claims per 100 employees.

(e) For each private self insurer, the Manager shall calculate an individual 1-year number of indemnity claims per 100 employees, using information reported by each self insurer on its last full year Self Insurer's Annual Report submitted for the reporting period immediately prior to the current budget year. In this calculation, the manager shall divide the total number of indemnity claims reported in the most recent claim year by the total number of California employees reported, with the result multiplied by 100. Any self insurer with less than 100 total employees shall be considered to have 100 employees for purposes of this calculation.

Note: Authority cited: Sections 54, 55, 62.7 and 62.9, Labor Code. Reference: Section 62.7 and 62.9, Labor Code.

History: 1. New section filed 9-6-94 as an emergency; operative 9-6-94 (Register 94, No. 36). A Certificate of Compliance must be transmitted to OAL by 1-4-95 or emergency language will be repealed by operation of law on the following day.

2. Certificate of Compliance as to 9-6-94 order including amendment of first paragraph and subsections (a), (d), and (e), repealer of subsections (b)-(b)(3), and new subsection (b) transmitted to OAL 12-30-94 and filed 2-15-95 (Register 95, No. 7).

3. Amendment of section and Note filed 11-10-97; operative 11-10-97 pursuant to Government Code section 11343.4(d) (Register 97, No. 46).

4. Amendment of subsection (b) filed 12-18-2003; operative 12-18-2003. Submitted to OAL for printing only (Register 2003, No. 51).

§15601.8. Determination of Insured Employers' Payroll and Premium Data.

On or before September 1 of each year, the Director shall request that the Department of Insurance direct the designated licensed rating organization to provide the Director with a statement for each insurer authorized to transact workers' compensation insurance in the state of California showing the total payroll and premium generated by that insurer on policies subject to an experience modification of 1.25 or more for the most recent policy year available.

Note: Authority cited: Sections 54, 55 and 62.7, Labor Code. Reference: Section 62.7, Labor Code.

History: 1. New section filed 9-6-94 as an emergency; operative 9-6-94 (Register 94, No. 36). A Certificate of Compliance must be transmitted to OAL by 1-4-95 or emergency language will be repealed by operation of law on the following day.

2. Certificate of Compliance as to 9-6-94 order including amendment of section transmitted to OAL 12-30-94 and filed 2-15-95 (Register 95, No. 7).

§15602. Allocation of Revolving Fund Assessment, Subsequent Injuries Fund Assessment, Uninsured Employers Fund Assessment, and/or Fraud Surcharge Among Insured and Self-Insured Employers.

(a) Not later than November 1 of each year, the Director shall determine the proportional payroll allocation factors to use to determine the total insured employer Revolving Fund Assessment, Subsequent Injuries Fund Assessment, Uninsured Employers Fund Assessment, and Fraud Surcharge, and the total self-insured employer Revolving Fund Assessment, Subsequent

Injuries Fund Assessment, Uninsured Employers Fund Assessment, and Fraud Surcharge as follows:

(1) The aggregate payroll of all insured employers shall be determined from payroll information provided by the Department of Insurance's designated licensed rating organization for the most recent period available.

(2) The aggregate payroll of all self-insured employers shall be determined from payroll information provided by the Office of Self-Insurance Plans of the Department of Industrial Relations excluding payroll of insured employees of the State of California for the most recent base year available.

(3) The total payroll information shall then be determined by combining the most recent insured employer payroll with the most recent self-insured employer payroll.

(4) The insured employer proportional payroll allocation factor shall be determined by dividing the insured employer payroll by the total combined payroll.

(5) The self-insured employer proportional payroll allocation factor shall be determined by dividing the self-insured employer payroll by the total combined payroll. The self-insured employer payroll shall not include that portion of the State of California's payroll which was covered by a policy of insurance.

(b) The total insured employer Revolving Fund Assessment, Subsequent Injuries Fund Assessment, Uninsured Employers Fund Assessment, and/or Fraud Surcharge shall be determined by multiplying each respective assessment and/or surcharge by the insured employer proportional payroll allocation factor.

(c) The total self-insured employer Revolving Fund Assessment, Subsequent Injuries Fund Assessment, Uninsured Employers Fund Assessment, and/or Fraud Surcharge shall be determined by multiplying each respective assessment and/or surcharge by the self-insured employer proportional payroll allocation factor.

Note: Authority cited: Sections 54, 55, 62.5 and 62.6, Labor Code. Reference: Sections 62.5 and 62.6, Labor Code.

History: 1. New section filed 4-18-90 as an emergency; operative 4-18-90 (Register 90, No. 18). A Certificate of Compliance must be transmitted to OAL within 120 days or emergency language will be repealed by operation of law on 8-16-90.

2. Certificate of Compliance as to 4-18-90 order including amendment to subsection (a) transmitted to OAL 8-14-90 and filed 9-13-90 (Register 90, No. 43).

3. Amendment of section heading, section and Note filed 1-15-93 as an emergency; operative 1-15-93 (Register 93, No. 3). A Certificate of Compliance must be transmitted to OAL 5-17-93 or emergency language will be repealed by operation of law on the following day.

4. Certificate of Compliance as to 1-15-93 order including amendment of subsection (a)(2) transmitted to OAL 5-10-93 and filed 6-16-93 (Register 93, No. 25).

5. Amendment of subsections (a)(1) and (3) and Note filed 9-6-94 as an emergency; operative 9-6-94 (Register 94, No. 36). A Certificate of Compliance must be transmitted to OAL by 1-4-95 or emergency language will be repealed by operation of law on the following day.

6. Certificate of Compliance as to 9-6-94 order including amendment of section heading, subsections (a)-(a)(2), (b), (c) and Note transmitted to OAL 12-30-94 and filed 2-15-95 (Register 95, No. 7).

7. Change without regulatory effect amending section heading, section and Note filed 12-15-99 pursuant to section 100, title 1, California Code of Regulations (Register 99, No. 51).

8. Amendment of section heading, section and Note filed 1-14-2000 as an emergency; operative 1-14-2000 (Register 2000, No. 2). A Certificate of Compliance must be transmitted to OAL by 5-15-2000 or emergency language will be repealed by operation of law on the following day.

9. Certificate of Compliance as to 1-14-2000 order transmitted to OAL 5-9-2000 and filed 6-15-2000 (Register 2000, No. 24).

10. Amendment of section heading and section filed 12-18-2003; operative 12-18-2003. Submitted to OAL for printing only (Register 2003, No. 51).

§15603. Determination of Insured and Self-Insured Employer Revolving Fund Assessment, Subsequent Injuries Fund Assessment, Uninsured Employers Fund Assessment, and Fraud Surcharge Factors.

(a) The insured employer Revolving Fund Assessment, Subsequent Injuries Fund Assessment, Uninsured Employers Fund Assessment, and Fraud Surcharge factors shall be determined by dividing the total amount of each respective insured employer assessment and the total amount of the insured employer surcharge, as the case may be, by the expected total current year premium, as determined by the Department of

Insurance's designated licensed rating organization.

(b) The self-insured employer Revolving Fund Assessment, Subsequent Injuries Fund Assessment, Uninsured Employers Fund Assessment, and/or Fraud Surcharge factors shall be determined by dividing the total amount of each respective self-insured employer assessment or surcharge, as the case may be, by the total amount of workers' compensation indemnity paid under California law by all self-insured employers during the most recent base year available, as determined by the Office of Self-Insurance Plans.

Note: Authority cited: Sections 54, 55 and 62.5, Labor Code. Reference: Sections 62.5 and 62.6, Labor Code.

History: 1. New section filed 4-18-90 as an emergency; operative 4-18-90 (Register 90, No. 18). A Certificate of Compliance must be transmitted to OAL within 120 days or emergency language will be repealed by operation of law on 8-16-90.

2. Certificate of Compliance as to 4-18-90 order including amendment to subsection (b) transmitted to OAL 8-14-90 and filed 9-13-90 (Register 90, No. 43).

3. Amendment of section and Note filed 1-15-93 as an emergency; operative 1-15-93 (Register 93, No. 3). A Certificate of Compliance must be transmitted to OAL 5-17-93 or emergency language will be repealed by operation of law on the following day.

4. Certificate of Compliance as to 1-15-93 order including amendment of section (a)(2) transmitted to OAL 5-10-93 and filed 6-16-93 (Register 93, No. 25).

5. Amendment of section heading and text filed 9-6-94 as an emergency; operative 9-6-94 (Register 94, No. 36). A Certificate of Compliance must be transmitted to OAL by 1-4-95 or emergency language will be repealed by operation of law on the following day.

6. Certificate of Compliance as to 9-6-94 order transmitted to OAL 12-30-94 and filed 2-15-95 (Register 95, No. 7).

7. Amendment of subsection (a) filed 11-14-95 as an emergency; operative 12-1-95 (Register 95, No. 46). A Certificate of Compliance must be transmitted to OAL by 3-30-96 or emergency language will be repealed by operation of law on the following day.

8. Certificate of Compliance as to 11-14-95 order transmitted to OAL 3-29-96 and filed 5-8-96 (Register 96, No. 19).

9. Change without regulatory effect amending section heading, section and Note filed 12-15-99 pursuant to section 100, title 1, California Code of Regulations (Register 99, No. 51).

10. Amendment of section heading, section and Note filed 1-14-2000 as an emergency; operative 1-14-2000 (Register 2000, No. 2). A Certificate of Compliance must be transmitted to OAL by 5-15-2000 or emergency language will be repealed by operation of law on the following day.

11. Certificate of Compliance as to 1-14-2000 order transmitted to OAL 5-9-2000 and filed 6-15-2000 (Register 2000, No. 24).

12. Amendment of section heading and section filed 12-18-2003; operative 12-18-2003. Submitted to OAL for printing only (Register 2003, No. 51).

§15603.5. Repealed.

Note: Authority cited: Sections 54, 55 and 62.7, Labor Code. Reference: Section 62.7, Labor Code.

History: 1. New section filed 9-6-94 as an emergency; operative 9-6-94 (Register 94, No. 36). A Certificate of Compliance must be transmitted to OAL by 1-4-95 or emergency language will be repealed by operation of law on the following day.

2. Certificate of Compliance as to 9-6-94 order including amendment of section and Note transmitted to OAL 12-30-94 and filed 2-15-95 (Register 95, No. 7).

3. Repealer filed 11-14-95 as an emergency; operative 12-1-95 (Register 95, No. 46). A Certificate of Compliance must be transmitted to OAL by 3-30-96 or emergency language will be repealed by operation of law on the following day.

4. Certificate of Compliance as to 11-14-95 order transmitted to OAL 3-29-96 and filed 5-8-96 (Register 96, No. 19).

§15604. Surplus in Funding.

(a) In the event of an unexpended surplus in the Workers' Compensation Administration Revolving Fund balance for a fiscal year, the balance shall be carried forward and credited to the subsequent year's Revolving Fund assessment.

(b) In the event of an unexpended surplus in the Subsequent Injuries Fund balance for a fiscal year, the balance shall be carried forward and credited to the subsequent year's Subsequent Injuries Fund Assessment.

(c) In the event of an unexpended surplus in the Uninsured Employers Fund balance for a fiscal year, the balance shall be carried forward and credited to the subsequent year's Uninsured Employers Fund Assessment.

Note: Authority cited: Sections 54, 55 and 62.5, Labor Code. Reference: Section 62.5, Labor Code.

History: 1. Renumbering of former section 15604 to section 15605 and new section 15604 filed 1-15-93 as an emergency; operative 1-15-93 (Register 93, No. 3). A Certificate of Compliance must be transmitted to

OAL 5-17-93 or emergency language will be repealed by operation of law on the following day.

2. Certificate of Compliance as to 1-15-93 order transmitted to OAL 5-10-93 and filed 6-16-93 (Register 93, No. 25).

3. Change without regulatory effect repealing section filed 12-15-99 pursuant to section 100, title 1, California Code of Regulations (Register 99, No. 51).

4. New section filed 1-14-2000 as an emergency; operative 1-14-2000 (Register 2000, No. 2). A Certificate of Compliance must be transmitted to OAL by 5-15-2000 or emergency language will be repealed by operation of law on the following day.

5. Certificate of Compliance as to 1-14-2000 order transmitted to OAL 5-9-2000 and filed 6-15-2000 (Register 2000, No. 24).

6. Amendment filed 12-18-2003; operative 12-18-2003. Submitted to OAL for printing only (Register 2003, No. 51).

ARTICLE 3
Collection of Assessments and/or Surcharges

§15605. Collection of the Revolving Fund Assessment, Subsequent Injuries Fund Assessment, Uninsured Employers Fund Assessment, and Fraud Surcharge from Self-Insured Employers.

(a) The Director designates the Manager of Self-Insurance Plans to collect the Revolving Fund Assessment, Subsequent Injuries Fund Assessment, Uninsured Employers Fund Assessment, and/or Fraud Surcharge from self-insured employers on the Director's behalf.

(b) No later than December 1 of each year, the Manager of Self-Insurance Plans shall bill each self-insured employer for the amount of the individual self-insured employer's Revolving Fund Assessment, Subsequent Injuries Fund Assessment, Uninsured Employers Fund Assessment, and/or Fraud Surcharge. The billing shall identify each assessment and/or surcharge separately and shall include the calculations utilized to determine each assessment factor. Each individual assessment and/or surcharge shall be determined by multiplying the self-insured employer assessment factor by the total amount of worker's compensation indemnity paid and reported by each self-insured employer on its Self-Insurer's Annual Report during the base year, as determined by the Office of Self-Insurance Plans. The Self-Insurer's Annual Report shall include all indemnity payments as defined in section 15600 (e).

(c) The amount of any assessment and/or surcharge shall be paid to the Office of Self-Insurance Plans within 30 days of the billing. Upon the request of any Joint Powers Authority, the Manager may agree to bill the Joint Powers Authority directly for the total amount of each assessment and/or surcharge owed by its public agency members.

(d) In the event the Manager collects funds in excess of the total self-insured employer assessment in the (1) Revolving Fund Assessment; (2) Subsequent Injuries Fund Assessment: (3) Uninsured Employers Fund Assessment; and/or (4) Fraud Surcharge, such excess funds shall be paid over to the Director to be held in a trust account and credited to the next year's respective assessments and/or surcharge on self-insured employers.

(e) Should the Manager determine that any self-insured employer has understated or overstated its total payroll or indemnity paid on the self-insured employer's annual report, the Manager may issue a corrected billing.

(f) If an employer has paid the assessments and/or surcharge as an insured employer, and during the year of such assessments and/or surcharge is granted a certificate of consent to self-insure, the newly self-insured employer is not required to pay an additional assessments and/or surcharge as a self-insured employer for the current assessments and/or surcharge year. Such an employer shall submit to the Manager a copy of the assessments and/or surcharge billing paid as insured employer in lieu of payment as a self-insured employer.

(g) A self-insured employer that does not have a self-insurers' annual report on file with the Office of Self-Insurance Plans which covers the base year of the assessments and/or surcharge, and that did not pay the assessments and/or surcharge for the base year as an insured employer, shall pay the assessments and/or surcharge through the Office of Self-Insurance Plans.

(1) To enable the Manager to determine such self-insured employer's liability for the assessments and/or surcharge, each such self-insured employer shall file a report prescribed by the Manager, setting forth such self-insured employer's total annual payroll for the base year, and the total workers' compensation pre-

mium paid for each calendar quarter of the preceding year.

(2) The Manager shall bill the self-insured employer by applying the self-insured employer assessment factors to the last annual premium paid by the self-insured employer until the self-insured employer's experience as a self-insured employer exceeds two complete calendar years for private self-insured employers or two complete fiscal years for public self-insured employers.

(h) A self-insured employer that ceases to be self-insured and ceases to operate as a functioning employer with no legal requirement to secure the payment of compensation, but continues to have open workers' compensation claims arising from the period of self-insurance, shall continue to be liable for assessments and/or surcharge for a period of 3 calendar years following the termination, revocation, or surrender of the employer's certificate of consent to self-insure. The Manager shall bill the former self-insured employer in accordance with this Section.

Note: Authority cited: Sections 54, 55 and 62.5, Labor Code; and Section 1872.83, Insurance Code. Reference: Sections 62.5 and 62.6, Labor Code; and Section 1872.83, Insurance Code.

History: 1. New section filed 4-18-90 as an emergency; operative 4-18-90 (Register 90, No. 18). A Certificate of Compliance must be transmitted to OAL within 120 days or emergency language will be repealed by operation of law on 8-16-90.

2. Certificate of Compliance as to 4-18-90 order including amendment to subsections (b), (c) and (e) and adding subsection (f), (g) and (h) transmitted to OAL 8-14-90 and filed 9-13-90 (Register 90, No. 43).

3. Renumbering of former section 15605 to section 15606 and renumbering of former section 15604 to section 15605 and amendment of section heading, section, and Note filed 1-15-93 as an emergency; operative 1-15-93 (Register 93, No. 3). A Certificate of Compliance must be transmitted to OAL 5-17-93 or emergency language will be repealed by operation of law on the following day.

4. Editorial correction restoring inadvertently omitted article heading (Register 93, No. 25).

5. Certificate of Compliance as to 1-15-93 order including amendment of subsection (F) transmitted to OAL 5-10-93 and filed 6-16-93 (Register 93, No. 25).

6. Amendment of article heading, section heading, subsections (a), (e), (f) and (h) and Note filed 9-6-94 as an emergency; operative 9-6-94 (Register 94, No. 36). A Certificate of Compliance must be transmitted to OAL by 1-4-95 or emergency language will be repealed by operation of law on the following day.

7. Certificate of Compliance as to 9-6-94 order including amendment of subsections (a)-(c) transmitted to OAL 12-30-94 and filed 2-15-95 (Register 95, No. 7).

8. Amendment of subsection (f) filed 11-14-95 as an emergency; operative 12-1-95 (Register 95, No. 46). A Certificate of Compliance must be transmitted to OAL by 3-30-96 or emergency language will be repealed by operation of law on the following day.

9. Certificate of Compliance as to 11-14-95 order transmitted to OAL 3-29-96 and filed 5-8-96 (Register 96, No. 19).

10. Change without regulatory effect amending section heading, section and Note filed 12-15-99 pursuant to section 100, title 1, California Code of Regulations (Register 99, No. 51).

11. Amendment of section heading, section and Note filed 1-14-2000 as an emergency; operative 1-14-2000 (Register 2000, No. 2). A Certificate of Compliance must be transmitted to OAL by 5-15-2000 or emergency language will be repealed by operation of law on the following day.

12. Certificate of Compliance as to 1-14-2000 order transmitted to OAL 5-9-2000 and filed 6-15-2000 (Register 2000, No. 24).

13. Amendment of section heading and section filed 12-18-2003; operative 12-18-2003. Submitted to OAL for printing only (Register 2003, No. 51).

§15605.5. Repealed.

Note: Authority cited: Sections 54, 55 and 62.7, Labor Code. Reference: Section 62.7, Labor Code.

History: 1. New section filed 9-6-94 as an emergency; operative 9-6-94 (Register 94, No. 36). A Certificate of Compliance must be transmitted to OAL by 1-4-95 or emergency language will be repealed by operation of law on the following day.

2. Certificate of Compliance as to 9-6-94 order including amendment of section transmitted to OAL 12-30-94 and filed 2-15-95 (Register 95, No. 7).

3. Repealer filed 11-14-95 as an emergency; operative 12-1-95 (Register 95, No. 46). A Certificate of Compliance must be transmitted to OAL by 3-30-96 or emergency language will be repealed by operation of law on the following day.

4. Certificate of Compliance as to 11-14-95 order transmitted to OAL 3-29-96 and filed 5-8-96 (Register 96, No. 19).

§15606. Collection of Advances Against Insured Employers.

(a) Not later than December 1 of each year, the Director shall notify each workers' compensation insurer, of the amounts due from the insurer on behalf of its policyholders for, respectively, the Revolving Fund Assessment, Subsequent Injuries Fund Assessment, Uninsured Employers Fund Assessment, and the Fraud Surcharge levied pursuant to the authority of Labor Code Sections 62.5 and 62.6 and these regulations. The notice shall include a bill that sets forth separately the total amounts of the assessments and the surcharge.

(b) The Insurer advances against the Revolving Fund Assessment, Subsequent Injuries Fund Assessment, Uninsured Employers Fund Assessment, and Fraud Surcharge amounts shall be calculated by multiplying the insurer's California direct written workers' compensation premium as reported in the most recent year's financial statement on file with the Insurance Commissioner, multiplied by the ratio of the expected total current year premium to the total direct written workers' compensation premium of all insurers as reported in the latest year's annual financial statements on file with the Insurance Commissioner by the respective factors determined pursuant to subsection (a) of Section 15603 of these regulations.

(c) Where the amount of the assessments or surcharge owed is less than $5.00 the Director may elect not to bill the insurer therefor.

(d) Each insurer shall pay to the Director one half of the amounts billed under subsection (a) on behalf of its insured employers on or before the following January 1. Each insurer shall pay the balance of the assessments and surcharge to the Director on the following April 1.

(e) Upon agreement of the affected insurers, the Director may elect to consolidate in one billing the assessments and surcharge of all insured employers that are insured by insurers under the same management, direction and control.

(f) In the event the Director collects advances from insurers in excess of the total assessments and surcharge due from insured employers in the (1) Revolving Fund Assessment; (2) Subsequent Injuries Fund Assessment: (3) Uninsured Employers Fund Assessment; and/or (4) Fraud Surcharge, the excess funds shall be held by the Director in a trust account and credited to the subsequent year's total respective assessments and surcharge on insured employers.

(g) Commencing with the assessment payment due April 1, 1993, the insurer shall submit a summary report on a form provided by the Director, which includes the following information: (1) the total amount of assessments and surcharges billed insured employers by the insurer; (2) the respective factors used by the insurer in assessing and surcharging insured employers.

(h) The summary report due April 1, 1993 shall include the information specified in this subsection for all workers' compensation insurance policies with an inception date between August 1, 1990 and December 31, 1991. Commencing April 1, 1994, the summary report shall include the information specified in this subsection for all workers' compensation insurance policies with an inception date in the next preceding calendar years.

Note: Authority cited: Sections 54, 55 and 62.5, Labor Code; and Section 1872.83, Insurance Code. Reference: Sections 62.5 and 62.6, Labor Code; and Section 1872.83, Insurance Code.

History: 1. New section filed 4-18-90 as an emergency; operative 4-18-90 (Register 90, No. 18). A Certificate of Compliance must be transmitted to OAL within 120 days or emergency language will be repealed by operation of law on 8-16-90.

2. Certificate of Compliance as to 4-18-90 order including amendment to subsection (a), (d) and (e) transmitted to OAL 8-14-90 and filed 9-13-90 (Register 90, No. 43).

3. Renumbering of former section 15606 to 15607 and renumbering of former section 15605 to section 15606 and amendment of section and Note filed 1-15-93 as an emergency; operative 1-15-93 (Register 93, No. 3). A Certificate of Compliance must be transmitted to OAL 5-17-93 or emergency language will be repealed by operation of law on the following day.

4. Certificate of Compliance as to 1-15-93 order including amendment of subsection (a) and repealer of subsection (e)(3) transmitted to OAL 5-10-93 and filed 6-16-93 (Register 93, No. 25).

5. Amendment of subsections (a)-(d) and Note filed 9-6-94 as an emergency; operative 9-6-94 (Register 94, No. 36). A Certificate of Compliance must be transmitted to OAL by 1-4-95 or emergency language will be repealed by operation of law on the following day.

6. Certificate of Compliance as to 9-6-94 order including amendment of section heading, repealer of subsections (a)-(e) and new subsections (a)-(i) transmitted to OAL 12-30-94 and filed 2-15-95 (Register 95, No. 7).

7. Amendment of subsections (a)-(b), repealer of subsection (c), subsection relettering and amendment of Note filed 11-14-95 as an emergency; operative 12-1-95 (Register 95, No. 46). A Certificate of Com-

pliance must be transmitted to OAL by 3-30-96 or emergency language will be repealed by operation of law on the following day.

8. Certificate of Compliance as to 11-14-95 order transmitted to OAL 3-29-96 and filed 5-8-96 (Register 96, No. 19).

9. Change without regulatory effect amending section and Note filed 12-15-99 pursuant to section 100, title 1, California Code of Regulations (Register 99, No. 51).

10. Amendment of section and Note filed 1-14-2000 as an emergency; operative 1-14-2000 (Register 2000, No. 2). A Certificate of Compliance must be transmitted to OAL by 5-15-2000 or emergency language will be repealed by operation of law on the following day.

11. Certificate of Compliance as to 1-14-2000 order transmitted to OAL 5-9-2000 and filed 6-15-2000 (Register 2000, No. 24).

12. Amendment of subsections (a), (b) and (f) filed 12-18-2003; operative 12-18-2003. Submitted to OAL for printing only (Register 2003, No. 51).

§15607. Collection of Revolving Fund Assessment, Subsequent Injuries Fund Assessment, Uninsured Employers Fund Assessment, and Fraud Surcharge from Insured Employers.

(a) Every insurer shall collect the Revolving Fund Assessment, Subsequent Injuries Fund Assessment, Uninsured Employers Fund Assessment, and Fraud Surcharge required by this article and Labor Code Sections 62.5 and 62.6, respectively, from each employer insured by it by applying a separate charge to all workers' compensation insurance policies issued by such insurer with an inception date in the year beginning January 1 after the determinations required by Sections 15601 and 15601.5 of these regulations. The amount of the assessment and surcharge shall be determined by multiplying the insured employer's estimated annual assessable premium by the assessment factors determined by the Director pursuant to subsection (a) of section 15603. The assessment factors in effect on the inception date of the policy shall be used to calculate the separate charges relative to that policy, including any additional or return premium.

(b) The respective amounts of the Revolving Fund Assessment, Subsequent Injuries Fund Assessment, Uninsured Employers Fund Assessment, and Fraud surcharge shall each be rounded to the nearest whole dollar, and be respectively shown in the policy as "Workers' Compensation Administration Revolving Fund Assessment (amount)," "Subsequent Injuries Benefits Trust Fund Assessment (amount)," "Uninsured Employers Benefits Trust Fund Assessment (amount)," and "State Fraud Surcharge (amount)".

(c) Commencing with policies effective on and after January 1, 1993, the insured employer's separate charges calculated under subsection (a) above shall be collected in full with the initial payment of assessable premium. If additional premium becomes due under the policy, the final amount of the separate charges shall be adjusted with the final premium bill for the policy. In the case of a retrospective rated policy, the respective assessment and/or surcharge should be applied to the policy premium at issuance, with recalculation at audit, and application of the factors to any retrospective adjustment premium.

(d) Notwithstanding the requirements of this Section, an insurer may elect not to bill an insured employer for the assessments and surcharge for the additional premium due under the policy if the amount of the additional assessments or surcharge does not exceed $10.00. In the event a return premium is due the employer, the insurer shall return a pro rata share of assessments and surcharge previously paid by the employer unless the assessments and surcharge overpayment does not exceed $10.00.

(e) A self-insurer whose certificate has been revoked during the base year or during the calendar year prior to the current assessments and/or surcharge billing by the Manager shall be exempt from payment of the assessments and/or surcharge as a self-insurer.

(f) If an employer has paid the assessments and/or surcharge as a self-insured employer, and during the year of such assessment and/or surcharge obtains a policy of workers' compensation insurance, the newly insured employer is not required to make assessments and/or surcharge payments as an insured employer for that year's assessments and/or surcharge. Such an employer shall submit to the insurer a copy of the assessments and/or surcharge billing paid as a self-insured employer, in lieu of payment as an insured employer.

Note: Authority cited: Sections 54, 55 and 62.5, Labor Code; and Section 1872.83, Insurance Code. Reference: Sections 62.5 and 62.6, Labor Code; and Section 1872.83, Insurance Code.

History: 1. New section filed 4-18-90 as an emergency; operative 4-18-90 (Register 90, No. 18). A Certificate of Compliance must be transmitted to OAL within 120 days or emergency language will be repealed by operation of law on 8-16-90.

2. Certificate of Compliance as to 4-18-90 order including amendment to subsections (a), (b), and (c) and adding subsection (d) transmitted to OAL 8-14-90 and filed 9-13-90 (Register 90, No. 43).

3. Renumbering of former section 15607 to 15608 and renumbering of former section 15606 to section 15607 and amendment of section heading, section, and Note filed 1-15-93 as an emergency; operative 1-15-93 (Register 93, No. 3). A Certificate of Compliance must be transmitted to OAL 5-17-93 or emergency language will be repealed by operation of law on the following day.

4. Certificate of Compliance as to 1-15-93 order including amendment of subsections (b) and (d) transmitted to OAL 5-10-93 and filed 6-16-93 (Register 93, No. 25).

5. Amendment of subsections (a), (b), (d) and Note filed 9-6-94 as an emergency; operative 9-6-94 (Register 94, No. 36). A Certificate of Compliance must be transmitted to OAL by 1-4-95 or emergency language will be repealed by operation of law on the following day.

6. Certificate of Compliance as to 9-6-94 order including amendment of section heading, subsections (a), (b), and (d), and Note transmitted to OAL 12-30-94 and filed 2-15-95 (Register 95, No. 7).

7. Amendment of subsections (a) and (d), and new subsections (e)-(f) filed 11-14-95 as an emergency; operative 12-1-95 (Register 95, No. 46). A Certificate of Compliance must be transmitted to OAL by 3-30-96 or emergency language will be repealed by operation of law on the following day.

8. Certificate of Compliance as to 11-14-95 order transmitted to OAL 3-29-96 and filed 5-8-96 (Register 96, No. 19).

9. Amendment of subsections (a), (c) and (d) filed 11-10-97; operative 11-10-97 pursuant to Government Code section 11343.4(d) (Register 97, No. 46).

10. Change without regulatory effect amending section heading, section and Note filed 12-15-99 pursuant to section 100, title 1, California Code of Regulations (Register 99, No. 51).

11. Amendment of section heading, section and Note filed 1-14-2000 as an emergency; operative 1-14-2000 (Register 2000, No. 2). A Certificate of Compliance must be transmitted to OAL by 5-15-2000 or emergency language will be repealed by operation of law on the following day.

12. Certificate of Compliance as to 1-14-2000 order transmitted to OAL 5-9-2000 and filed 6-15-2000 (Register 2000, No. 24).

13. Amendment of section heading and section filed 12-18-2003; operative 12-18-2003. Submitted to OAL for printing only (Register 2003, No. 51).

§15607.5. Repealed.

Note: Authority cited: Sections 54, 55 and 62.7, Labor Code. Reference: Section 62.7, Labor Code.

History: 1. New section filed 9-6-94 as an emergency; operative 9-6-94 (Register 94, No. 36). A Certificate of Compliance must be transmitted to OAL by 1-4-95 or emergency language will be repealed by operation of law on the following day.

2. Certificate of Compliance as to 9-6-94 order including designation of subsections (a)-(e), amendment of subsections (b) and (d), and new subsections (f)-(g) transmitted to OAL 12-30-94 and filed 2-15-95 (Register 95, No. 7).

3. Repealer filed 11-14-95 as an emergency; operative 12-1-95 (Register 95, No. 46). A Certificate of Compliance must be transmitted to OAL by 3-30-96 or emergency language will be repealed by operation of law on the following day.

4. Certificate of Compliance as to 11-14-95 order transmitted to OAL 3-29-96 and filed 5-8-96 (Register 96, No. 19).

§15608. Assessment and/or Surcharge Collection in Excess of Insured Employer Assessment Advance.

If the summary report required by subsections (g) and (h) of Section 15606 of these regulations shows that the insurer has collected assessments and surcharges from employers in excess of the advances paid to the Director for policies incepting in the calendar year covered by the summary report, the insurer shall pay the excess amount to the Director upon submission of the summary report. The Director shall hold any excess amounts in a trust account and either credit the respective amounts to any deficiency in the current assessments and surcharge, or, if there is no deficiency, to the subsequent year's respective assessments and/or surcharges on insured employers.

Note: Authority cited: Sections 54, 55 and 62.5, Labor Code; and Section 1872.83, Insurance Code. Reference: Sections 62.5 and 62.6, Labor Code; and Section 1872.83, Insurance Code.

History: 1. New section filed 4-18-90 as an emergency; operative 4-18-90 (Register 90, No. 18). A Certificate of Compliance must be transmitted to OAL within 120 days or emergency language will be repealed by operation of law on 8-16-90.

2. Certificate of Compliance as to 4-18-90 order including amendment transmitted to OAL 8-14-90 and filed 9-13-90 (Register 90, No. 43).

3. Renumbering of former section 15608 to 15609 and renumbering of former section 15607 to section 15608 and amendment of section heading, section, and Note filed 1-15-93 as an emergency; operative

1-15-93 (Register 93, No. 3). A Certificate of Compliance must be transmitted to OAL 5-17-93 or emergency language will be repealed by operation of law on the following day.

4. Certificate of Compliance as to 1-15-93 order transmitted to OAL 5-10-93 and filed 6-16-93 (Register 93, No. 25).

5. Amendment of Note filed 9-6-94 as an emergency; operative 9-6-94 (Register 94, No. 36). A Certificate of Compliance must be transmitted to OAL by 1-4-95 or emergency language will be repealed by operation of law on the following day.

6. Certificate of Compliance as to 9-6-94 order including amendment of section transmitted to OAL 12-30-94 and filed 2-15-95 (Register 95, No. 7).

7. Amendment of section and Note filed 11-14-95 as an emergency; operative 12-1-95 (Register 95, No. 46). A Certificate of Compliance must be transmitted to OAL by 3-30-96 or emergency language will be repealed by operation of law on the following day.

8. Certificate of Compliance as to 11-14-95 order transmitted to OAL 3-29-96 and filed 5-8-96 (Register 96, No. 19).

9. Change without regulatory effect amending section heading, section and Note filed 12-15-99 pursuant to section 100, title 1, California Code of Regulations (Register 99, No. 51).

10. Amendment of section heading, section and Note filed 1-14-2000 as an emergency; operative 1-14-2000 (Register 2000, No. 2). A Certificate of Compliance must be transmitted to OAL by 5-15-2000 or emergency language will be repealed by operation of law on the following day.

11. Certificate of Compliance as to 1-14-2000 order transmitted to OAL 5-9-2000 and filed 6-15-2000 (Register 2000, No. 24).

12. Amendment filed 12-18-2003; operative 12-18-2003. Submitted to OAL for printing only (Register 2003, No. 51).

§15609. Credit for Undercollection.

(a) When an insurer demonstrates to the Director, within one year of the final audit conducted for premium adjustments for the policies with inception dates in the year subject to assessment, that the total assessments and/or surcharges, respectively, collected from its insured employers is less than the respective assessment and surcharge amounts advanced by the insurer under Section 15606 for that assessment year, the Director shall credit the amount of the difference against the subsequent year's respective advances due from the insurer on behalf of its insured employers.

(b) No insurer shall receive any credit for any portion of an undercollection against advances paid by that insurer that is due to the insurer's failure to properly bill a policyholder for the appropriate assessments and/or surcharges applicable to the premium for that policyholder's policy.

Note: Authority cited: Sections 54, 55 and 62.5, Labor Code; and Section 1872.83, Insurance Code. Reference: Sections 62.5 and 62.6, Labor Code; and Section 1872.83, Insurance Code.

History: 1. New section filed 4-18-90 as an emergency; operative 4-18-90 (Register 90, No. 18). A Certificate of Compliance must be transmitted to OAL within 120 days or emergency language will be repealed by operation of law on 8-16-90.

2. Certificate of Compliance as to 4-18-90 order including amendment transmitted to OAL 8-14-90 and filed 9-13-90 (Register 90, No. 43).

3. Repealer of former section 15609 and renumbering and amendment of former section 15608 to section 15609 filed 1-15-93 as an emergency; operative 1-15-93 (Register 93, No. 3). A Certificate of Compliance must be transmitted to OAL 5-17-93 or emergency language will be repealed by operation of law on the following day.

4. Certificate of Compliance as to 1-15-93 order transmitted to OAL 5-10-93 and filed 6-16-93 (Register 93, No. 25).

5. Amendment of section and Note filed 9-6-94 as an emergency; operative 9-6-94 (Register 94, No. 36). A Certificate of Compliance must be transmitted to OAL by 1-4-95 or emergency language will be repealed by operation of law on the following day.

6. Certificate of Compliance as to 9-6-94 order including amendment of section transmitted to OAL 12-30-94 and filed 2-15-95 (Register 95, No. 7).

7. Amendment filed 5-8-96; operative 5-8-96 pursuant to Government Code section 11343.4(d) (Register 96, No. 19).

8. New subsection (a) designator and new subsection (b) filed 11-10-97; operative 11-10-97 pursuant to Government Code section 11343.4(d) (Register 97, No. 46).

9. Change without regulatory effect amending section and Note filed 12-15-99 pursuant to section 100, title 1, California Code of Regulations (Register 99, No. 51).

10. Amendment of section and Note filed 1-14-2000 as an emergency; operative 1-14-2000 (Register 2000, No. 2). A Certificate of Compliance must be transmitted to OAL by 5-15-2000 or emergency language will be repealed by operation of law on the following day.

11. Certificate of Compliance as to 1-14-2000 order transmitted to OAL 5-9-2000 and filed 6-15-2000 (Register 2000, No. 24).

§15610. Collections of 1995 Interim Targeted Inspection Assessment. [Repealed]

History: 1. New section filed 4-18-90 as an emergency; operative 4-18-90 (Register 90, No. 18). A Certificate of Compliance must be transmitted to OAL within 120 days or emergency language will be repealed by operation of law on 8-16-90.

2. Certificate of Compliance as to 4-18-90 order transmitted to OAL 8-14-90 and filed 9-13-90 (Register 90, No. 43).

3. Repealer filed 1-15-93 as an emergency; operative 1-15-93 (Register 93, No. 3). A Certificate of Compliance must be transmitted to OAL 5-17-93 or emergency language will be repealed by operation of law on the following day.

4. Certificate of Compliance as to 1-15-93 order transmitted to OAL 5-10-93 and filed 6-16-93 (Register 93, No. 25).

5. New section filed 2-15-95; operative 3-17-95 (Register 95, No. 7).

6. Repealer filed 12-18-2003; operative 12-18-2003. Submitted to OAL for printing only (Register 2003, No. 51).

§15611. Collection of Interim Assessments.

(a) Notwithstanding the provisions of this subchapter, if the Director determines that there are insufficient funds to support the Workers' Compensation Administration Revolving Fund, the Subsequent Injuries Fund or the Uninsured Employers Fund for fiscal year 2003-2004, or any fiscal year thereafter, the Director may collect a single interim assessment for these respective funds, in an amount determined by the Director, to provide sufficient funding for these funds.

(b) Any assessment collected under this Section shall not reduce the amount to be collected in the subsequent year's assessments, except as provided by Section 15608 of these regulations.

(c) Any assessment collected under this Section shall be included on the next annual report required under Section 15606(g) of these regulations.

Note: Authority cited: Sections 54, 55 and 62.5, Labor Code. Reference: Section 62.5, Labor Code.

History: 1. New section filed 12-18-2003; operative 12-18-2003. Submitted to OAL for printing only (Register 2003, No. 51).

SUBCHAPTER 2.1 ILLEGALLY UNINSURED EMPLOYERS. DETERMINATIONS BY THE DIRECTOR: PRIMA FACIE ILLEGALLY UNINSURED, CORPORATE PARENT AND SUBSTANTIAL SHAREHOLDER; NOTICE; HEARINGS; APPEALS

ARTICLE 1 General

§15710. Definitions.

The following definitions are applicable to this group. Terms not defined here but used in the Labor Code shall have their meaning as so used. All references to the code or to code sections refer to the California Labor Code unless otherwise stated.

(a) Prima facie illegally uninsured. In addition to examples provided in the code, an employer against which there is any evidence from which, after considering any contradicting evidence except any testimony or statements by the employer or related persons, a reasonable person could conclude that the employer, as of the time of the injury, had not secured the payment of compensation as provided by code Section 3700.

(b) Prima facie a parent. A corporation against which there is any evidence from which, after considering any contradictory evidence except testimony or statements of shareholders, officers or beneficial owners of the parent or its subsidiary, a reasonable person could conclude that the corporation had been at the time of the injury or has been, at any subsequent time the parent of a corporation which, as of the time of the injury, had not secured the payment of compensation as provided by code Section 3700.

(c) Prima facie a substantial shareholder. A person against which there is any evidence from which, after considering any contradictory evidence except testimony or statements of that person or of related persons or other shareholders, a reasonable person could conclude that the person had been at the time of the injury or has been at any subsequent time a substantial shareholder in a corporation or the parent of a corporation, which corporation, as of the time of the injury, had not secured the payment of compensation as provided by code Section 3700.

(d) Prima facie case. A case for which there is any evidence from which, after considering any contradictory evidence, a reasonable person could conclude that the case were established as likely to be true.

(e) Director. The Director of Industrial Relations or his designated agents or delegates.

(f) Illegally uninsured. The status of having employees, one of whom was injured arising out of and in the course of the employee's employment at a time when the employer had not secured the payment of compensation as required by code Section 3800.

(g) Appeals board. The California Workers Compensation Appeals Board.

Note: Authority cited: Sections 54, 55, 59, 3702.10, 3710 and 3715, Labor Code. Reference: Sections 3715, 3717.2, 3720, 3720.1 and 3721, Labor Code.

History: 1. New section filed 6-19-89; operative 7-19-89 (Register 89, No. 27). For history of former Group 2.1 (Sections 15600-15670 and Sections 15700-15780, not consecutive), see Register 83, No. 31.

Ref.: Hanna §§ 10.24[2], 10.24[8][a].

§15711. Delegation of Authority.

The director delegates authority to the Chief of the Claims Bureau of the Uninsured Employers Fund to make the determinations under Labor Code Sections 3715(c), 3720(c), and 3720.1(a), to reconsider determinations made pursuant to code Sections 3715(c) and 3720.1(a), to file liens, to remove liens erroneously filed, to remove liens pursuant to code Section 3720(c), to collect funds on liens, refund funds erroneously collected, issue the notices pursuant to code Section 3715(d), and otherwise to administer the program relating to liens issued prior to the issuance of findings and awards of the appeals board, in appeals board cases involving illegally uninsured employers. The Chief of the Claims Bureau may, as he or she deems necessary, delegate all or any part of the authority granted herein to the area supervisors within the Claims Bureau.

History: 1. New section filed 6-19-89; operative 7-19-89 (Register 89, No. 27). For history of former Group 2.1 (Sections 15600-15670 and Sections 15700-15780, not consecutive), see Register 83, No. 31.

Ref.: Hanna §§ 10.24[2], 10.24[8][a].

ARTICLE 2
Determinations by Director

§15720. Determinations.

The director shall make all determinations under code Section 3715(c) of whether a person involved in a claim before the Appeals Board is prima facie illegally uninsured. The director may make determinations pursuant to code Section 3715(c) in any case in which the director, as administrator of the Uninsured Employers Fund, has been joined or otherwise made a party. In all cases where the employer or alleged employer is a corporation and where the director has not petitioned the appeals board to make a determination under code Section 3717.2 or, pending a determination in such cases, the director may make determinations pursuant to code Section 3720.1 of status of prima facie a parent or prima facie a substantial shareholder. The director shall record written reasons for his determinations. These reasons shall be included with the notice of determination.

Note: Authority cited: Sections 54, 55, 59, 3702.10, 3710 and 3715, Labor Code. Reference: Sections 3715, 3717.2, 3720, 3720.1 and 3721, Labor Code.

Ref.: Hanna § 10.24[2].

§15721. Negative Inferences.

If information or documentary proof has been requested by the director from the alleged uninsured employer, and the alleged uninsured employer has not supplied such information or documents, and if the information, documents or copies thereof can reasonably be assumed to be in the possession or control of the alleged uninsured employer, the director shall infer from the failure to comply with the request that the documents do not exist, or that the information or the contents of the documents establish that the alleged uninsured employer was illegally uninsured, or that there was substantial shareholder or parent status, whichever is applicable.

Note: Authority cited: Sections 54, 55, 59, 3702.10, 3710 and 3715, Labor Code. Reference: Sections 3715, 3717.2, 3720, 3720.1 and 3721, Labor Code.

History: 1. New section filed 6-19-89; operative 7-19-89 (Register 89, No. 27). For history of former Group 2.1 (Sections 15600-15670, not consecutive), see Register 83, No. 31.

Ref.: Hanna §§ 10.24[2], 10.24[8][a].

§15722. Reconsideration of Section 3715(c) Determinations; Finality.

Upon receipt of written protest or application for reconsideration from an aggrieved person, of a determination that an employer was prima facie illegally uninsured, the Chief of the Claims Bureau, Uninsured Employers Fund, on the director's behalf, shall informally reconsider the determination. The aggrieved person shall furnish a statement of reasons why the determination was in error, and any evidence in support of the position of the aggrieved person. The Chief of the Claims Bureau may uphold, rescind, or alter the original determination. The decision after reconsideration shall be mailed to the aggrieved person and to other persons to whom the original notice was sent, within five working days after receipt of the protest or application for reconsideration. A request for reconsideration under this section shall be a prerequisite to a filing of a petition with the appeals board pursuant to code Section 3715(d). For purposes of the time within which the petition must be filed with appeals board, the determination shall not be considered to be final until after the decision after reconsideration is mailed.

Note: Authority cited: Sections 54, 55, 59, 3702.10, 3710 and 3715, Labor Code. Reference: Sections 3715, 3717.2, 3720, 3720.1 and 3721, Labor Code.

History: 1. New section filed 6-19-89; operative 7-19-89 (Register 89, No. 27). For history of former Group 2.1 (Sections 15600-15670 and Sections 15700-15780, not consecutive), see Register 83, No. 31.

Ref.: Hanna § 10.24[3].

§15723. Reconsideration of Section 3720.1(a) Determinations; Finality.

Upon receipt of written protest or application for reconsideration from an aggrieved person of a determination that a person was prima facie a parent or a substantial shareholder, the Chief of the Claims Bureau, Uninsured Employers Fund, on the director's behalf, shall informally reconsider the determination. The aggrieved person shall furnish a statement of reasons why the determination was in error, and any evidence in support of the position of the aggrieved person. The Chief of the Claims Bureau may uphold, rescind, or alter the original determination. The decision after reconsideration shall be mailed to the aggrieved person, and to other persons to whom the original notice was sent, within five working days after receipt of the protest or application for reconsideration. A request for reconsideration under this section shall be a prerequisite to a filing of a request for a hearing pursuant to code Section 3720.1(b). A request for hearing filed prior to a protest or application for reconsideration shall be deemed a request for reconsideration. The time for filing a request for formal hearing shall not begin to run until the notice of decision after reconsideration is issued.

Note: Authority cited: Sections 54, 55, 59, 3702.10, 3710 and 3715, Labor Code. Reference: Sections 3715, 3717.2, 3720, 3720.1 and 3721, Labor Code.

History: 1. New section filed 6-19-89; operative 7-19-89 (Register 89, No. 27). For history of former Group 2.1 (Sections 15600-15670, not consecutive), see Register 83, No. 31.

Ref.: Hanna § 10.24[8][b].

ARTICLE 3
Hearings Under Code Section 3720.1

§15730. Administrative Hearing.

Upon the petition of an aggrieved person, if the petition is not treated as a request for informal reconsideration pursuant to Section 15723, the director shall hold a hearing to review prima facie substantial shareholder or parent status.

Note: Authority cited: Sections 54, 55, 59, 3702.10, 3710 and 3715, Labor Code. Reference: Sections 3715, 3717.2, 3720, 3720.1 and 3721, Labor Code.

History: 1. New section filed 6-19-89; operative 7-19-89 (Register 89, No. 27). For history of former Group 2.1 (Sections 15600-15670, not consecutive), see Register 83, No. 31.

Ref.: Hanna § 10.24[8][b].

§15731. Delegation of Authority.

The director delegates authority to the Chief Counsel of the Department of Industrial Relations to appoint hearing officers and to issue the notices for hearings held pursuant to code section 3720.1(b). The hearing officer appointed shall not have been involved in the representation of the director before the appeals board in that particular case.

Note: Authority cited: Sections 54, 55, 59, 3702.10, 3710 and 3715, Labor Code. Reference: Sections 3715, 3717.2, 3720, 3720.1 and 3721, Labor Code.

Ref.: Hanna § 10.24[8][b].

§15732. Conduct of Hearing.

(a) Hearing Officer. The hearing officer shall have full authority as the director would to make all decisions necessary for the proper conduct of the hearing and for the making of a decision thereon. Not limiting the foregoing, the hearing officer may administer oaths, take testimony, admit or exclude evidence, schedule the hearing, continue or adjourn the hearing, require a statement of contentions, issue a subpoena and subpoena duces tecum for the attendance of a person and the production of testimony, books, or documents, and to decide when the case is submitted for decision.

(b) Admissible Evidence. The California Evidence Code and the common law rules of evidence shall not apply in the hearing, and the hearing officer may admit, consider, and rely upon evidence which would not be admissible if such rules of evidence governed.

(c) Testimony under Oath. All witnesses testifying before the hearing officer shall testify under oath, affirmation or penalty of perjury.

(d) Transcripts. The hearing shall be recorded by audio tape recording. A party desiring a transcript must pay for the transcription or provide and pay for a court reporter. In either case, a copy of the transcript must be provided to the director.

(e) Witness fees. Costs of subpoenaing witnesses are to be borne by the party requesting the subpoena.

(f) Documents. If a person seeking to establish that the person is not a parent or substantial shareholder does not produce corporate documents which relate the ownership of the applicable corporation, and there is evidence that the person was a shareholder or owner of a beneficial interest in the corporation, the hearing officer may presume that the corporate documents not produced would contain evidence establishing the opposite of the contention asserted by the person not offering them.

History: 1. New section filed 6-19-89; operative 7-19-89 (Register 89, No. 27). For history of former Group 2.1 (Sections 15600–15670, not consecutive), see Register 83, No. 31.

Ref.: Hanna § 10.24[8][b].

SUBCHAPTER 2.1.1 UNINSURED EMPLOYERS FUND AND SUBSEQUENT INJURIES FUND BENEFITS TO ALIENS

ARTICLE 1 Limitations on Benefits

§15740. Limitations on Uninsured Employers Fund and Subsequent Injuries Fund Benefits for Aliens.

(a) All eligibility requirements contained herein shall be applied without regard to the race, creed, color, gender, religion, or national origin of the individual applying for the public benefit.

(b) Pursuant to Section 411 of the Personal Responsibility and Work Opportunity Reconciliation Act of 1996, (Pub. L. No. 104-193 (PRWORA)), (8 U.S.C. §1621), and notwithstanding any other provision of this division, aliens who are not qualified aliens, nonimmigrant aliens under the Immigration and Nationality Act (INA) (8 U.S.C. §1101 et seq.), or aliens paroled into the United States under Section 212(d)(5) of the INA (8 U.S.C. §1182(d)(5)), for less than one year, are not eligible to receive benefits, including death benefits as the dependent of a deceased employee, from the UEF or SIF as set forth in Labor Code Sections 3716, 3716.2 and 4750-4755.

(c) A qualified alien is an alien who, at the time he or she applies for, receives, or attempts to receive benefits from the UEF or SIF, including death benefits as the dependent of a deceased employee, is, under Section 431(b) of the PRWORA (8 U.S.C. §1641(b) and (c)), any of the following:

(1) An alien lawfully admitted for permanent residence under the INA (8 U.S.C. §1101 et seq.).

(2) An alien who is granted asylum under Section 208 of the INA (8 U.S.C. §1158).

(3) A refugee who is admitted to the United States under Section 207 of the INA (8 U.S.C. §1157).

(4) An alien who is paroled into the United States under Section 212(d)(5) of the INA (8 U.S.C. §1182(d)(5)) for a period of at least one year.

(5) An alien whose deportation is being withheld under Section 243(h) of the INA (8 U.S.C. §1253(h)) (as in effect immediately before the effective date of Section 307 of division C of Public Law 104-208) or Section 241(b)(2) of such Act (8 U.S.C. §1251(b)(3)) (as amended by Section 305(a) of division C of Public Law 104-208).

(6) An alien who is granted conditional entry pursuant to Section 203(a)(7) of the INA as in effect prior to April 1, 1980 (8 U.S.C. §1153(a)(7)) (See editorial note under 8 U.S.C. §1101, "Effective Date of 1980 Amendment").

(7) An alien who is a Cuban or Haitian entrant (as defined in Section 501(e) of the Refugee Education Assistance Act of 1980 (8 U.S.C. §1522 note)).

(8) An alien who, under Section 431(c)(1) of the PRWORA (8 U.S.C. §1641(c)(1), meets all of the conditions of subparagraphs (A), (B), (C), and (D) below:

(A) The alien has been battered or subjected to extreme cruelty in the United States by a spouse or a parent, or by a member of the spouse's or parent's family residing in the same household as the alien, and the spouse or parent of the alien consented to, or acquiesced in, such battery or cruelty. For purposes of this subsection, the term "battered or subjected to extreme cruelty" includes, but is not limited to being the victim of any act or threatened act of violence including any forceful detention, which results or threatens to result in physical or mental injury. Rape, molestation, incest (if the victim is a minor), or forced prostitution shall be considered acts of violence.

(B) There is a substantial connection between such battery or cruelty and the need for the benefits to be provided in the opinion of the UEF or SIF. For purposes of this subsection, the following circumstances demonstrate a substantial connection between the battery or cruelty and the need for the benefits to be provided:

(i) The benefits are needed to enable the alien to become self-sufficient following separation from the abuser.

(ii) The benefits are needed to enable the alien to escape the abuser and/or the community in which the abuser lives, or to ensure the safety of the alien from the abuser.

(iii) The benefits are needed due to a loss of financial support resulting from the alien's separation from the abuser.

(iv) The benefits are needed because the battery or cruelty, separation from the abuser, or work absences or lower job performance resulting from the battery or extreme cruelty or from legal proceedings relating thereto (including resulting child support, child custody, and divorce actions) cause the alien to lose his or her job or to earn less or to require the alien to leave his or her job for safety reasons.

(v) The benefits are needed because the alien requires medical attention or mental health counseling, or has become disabled, as a result of the battery or extreme cruelty.

(vi) The benefits are needed because the loss of a dwelling or source of income or fear of the abuser following separation from the abuser jeopardizes the alien's ability to care for his or her children (e.g., inability to house, feed, or clothe children or to put children into a day care for fear of being found by the abuser).

(vii) The benefits are needed to alleviate nutritional risk or need resulting from the abuse or following separation from the abuser.

(viii) The benefits are needed to provide medical care during a pregnancy resulting from the abuser's sexual assault or abuse of, or relationship with, the alien and/or to care for any resulting children.

(ix) Where medical coverage and/or health care services are needed to replace medical coverage or health care services the alien had when living with the abuser.

(C) The alien has been approved or has a petition pending which sets forth a prima facie case for:

(i) status as a spouse or child of a United States citizen pursuant to clause (ii), (iii), or (iv) of Section 204(a)(1)(A) of the INA (8 U.S.C. §1154(a)(1)(A)(ii), (iii) or (iv)),

(ii) classification pursuant to clause (ii) or (iii) of Section 204(a)(1)(B) of the INA (8 U.S.C. §1254(a)(1)(B)(ii) or (iii)),

(iii) cancellation of removal under 8 U.S.C. §1229b as in effect prior to April 1, 1997,

(iv) status as a spouse or child of a United States citizen pursuant to clause (i) of Section 204(a)(1)(A) of the INA (8 U.S.C. §1154(a)(1)(A)) or classification pursuant to clause (i) of Section 204(a)(1)(B) of the INA (8 U.S.C. §1154(a)(1)(B)(i)).

(v) cancellation of removal pursuant to Section 204A(b)(2) of the INA (8 U.S.C. §1229b(b)(2)).

(D) For the period for which benefits are sought, the individual responsible for the battery or cruelty does not reside in the same household or family eligibility unit as the individual subjected to the battery or cruelty.

(9) An alien who meets all of the conditions of subparagraphs (A), (B), (C), (D) and (E) below:

(A) The alien has a child who has been battered or subjected to extreme cruelty in the United States by a spouse or a parent of the alien (without the active participation of the alien in the battery or cruelty), or by a member of the spouse's or parent's family residing in the same household as the alien, and the spouse or parent consented or acquiesced to such battery or cruelty. For purposes of this subsection, the term "battered or subjected to extreme cruelty" includes, but is not limited to being the victim of any act or threatened act of violence including any forceful detention, which results or threatens to result in physical or mental injury. Rape, molestation, incest (if the victim is a minor), or forced prostitution shall be considered as acts of violence.

(B) The alien did not actively participate in such battery or cruelty.

(C) There is a substantial connection between such battery or cruelty and the need for the benefits to be provided-in the opinion of the UEF or SIF. For purposes of this subsection, the following circumstances demonstrate a substantial connection between the battery or cruelty and the need for the benefits to be provided:

(i) The benefits are needed to enable the alien's child to become self-sufficient following separation from the abuser.

(ii) The benefits are needed to enable the alien's child to escape the abuser and/or the community in which the abuser lives, or to ensure the safety of the alien's child from the abuser.

(iii) The benefits are needed due to a loss of financial support resulting from the alien's child's separation from the abuser.

(iv) The benefits are needed because the battery or cruelty, separation from the abuser, or work absences or lower job performance resulting from the battery or extreme cruelty or from legal proceedings relating thereto (including resulting child support, child custody, and divorce actions) cause the alien's child to lose his or her job or to earn less or to require the alien's child to leave his or her job for safety reasons.

(v) The benefits are needed because the alien's child requires medical attention or mental health counseling, or has become disabled, as a result of the battery or extreme cruelty.

(vi) The benefits are needed because the loss of a dwelling or source of income or fear of the abuser following separation from the abuser jeopardizes the alien's child's ability to care for his or her children (e.g., inability to house, feed, or clothe children or to put children into a day care for fear of being found by the abuser).

(vii) The benefits are needed to alleviate nutritional risk or need resulting from the abuse or following separation from the abuser.

(viii) The benefits are needed to provide medical care during a pregnancy resulting from the abuser's sexual assault or abuse of, or relationship with, the alien's child and/or to care for any resulting children.

(ix) Where medical coverage and/or health care services are needed to replace medical coverage or health care services the alien's child had when living with the abuser.

(D) The alien meets the requirements of subsection (c)(8)(C) above.

(E) For the period for which benefits are sought, the individual responsible for the battery or cruelty does not reside in the same household or family eligibility unit as the individual subjected to the battery or cruelty.

(10) An alien child who meets all of the conditions of subparagraphs (A), (B), and (C) below:

(A) The alien child resides in the same household as a parent who has been battered or subjected to extreme cruelty in the United States by that parent's spouse or by a member of the spouse's family residing in the same household as the parent and the spouse consented or acquiesced to such battery or cruelty. For purposes of this subsection, the term "battered or subjected to extreme cruelty" includes, but is not limited to being the victim of any act or threatened act of violence including any forceful detention, which results or threatens to result in physical or mental injury. Rape, molestation, incest (if the victim is a minor), or forced prostitution shall be considered acts of violence.

(B) There is a substantial connection between such battery or cruelty and the need for the benefits to be provided in the opinion of the UEF or SIF. For purposes of this subsection, the following circumstances demonstrate a substantial connection between the battery or cruelty and the need for the benefits to be provided:

(i) The benefits are needed to enable the alien child's parent to become self-sufficient following separation from the abuser.

(ii) The benefits are needed to enable the alien child's parent to escape the abuser and/or the community in which the abuser lives, or to ensure the safety of the alien child's parent from the abuser.

(iii) The benefits are needed due to a loss of financial support resulting from the alien child's parent's separation from the abuser.

(iv) The benefits are needed because the battery or cruelty, separation from the abuser, or work absences or lower job performance resulting from the battery or extreme cruelty or from legal proceedings relating thereto (including resulting child support, child custody, and divorce actions) cause the alien child's parent to lose his or her job or to earn less or to require the alien child's parent to leave his or her job for safety reasons.

(v) The benefits are needed because the alien child's parent requires medical attention or mental health counseling, or has become disabled, as a result of the battery or extreme cruelty.

(vi) The benefits are needed because the loss of a dwelling or source of income or fear of the abuser following separation from the abuser jeopardizes the alien child's parent's ability to care for his or her children (e.g., inability to house, feed, or clothe children or to put children into a day care for fear of being found by the abuser).

(vii) The benefits are needed to alleviate nutritional risk or need resulting from the abuse or following separation from the abuser.

(viii) The benefits are needed to provide medical care during a pregnancy resulting from the abuser's sexual assault or abuse of, or relationship with, the alien child's parent and/or to care for any resulting children.

(ix) Where medical coverage and/or health care services are needed to replace medical coverage or health care services the alien child's parent had when living with the abuser.

(c) The alien child meets the requirements of subsection (c)(8)(C) above.

(d) For purposes of this section, "nonimmigrant" is defined the same as in Section 101(a)(15) of the INA (8 U.S.C. §1101(a)(15)).

(e) For purposes of establishing eligibility for Uninsured Employers Fund (UEF) and Subsequent Injuries Fund (SIF) benefits, all of the following must be met:

(1) The applicant must declare himself or herself to be a citizen of the United States or a qualified alien under subsection (c), a nonimmigrant alien under subsection (d), or an alien paroled into the United States for less than one year under Section 212(d)(5) of the INA (8 U.S.C. §1182(d)(5)). The applicant shall declare that status through use of the "Statement of Citizenship, Alienage, and Immigration Status for State Public Benefits," Form UEF-1.

(2) The applicant must present documents of a type acceptable to the Immigration and Naturalization Services (INS) which serve as reasonable evidence of the applicant's declared status.

(3) The applicant must complete and sign Form UEF-1.

(4) Where authorized by the INS, the documentation presented by an alien as reasonable evidence of the alien's declared immigration status must be submitted to the INS for verification through the Systematic Alien Verification for Entitlements (SAVE) system procedures as follows:

(A) Unless the primary SAVE system is unavailable for use, the primary SAVE system verification must be used to access the biographical/immigration status computer record contained in the Alien Status Verification Index maintained by the INS. Subject to subparagraph (B), this procedure must be used to verify the status of all aliens who claim to be qualified aliens and who present an INS-issued document that contains an alien registration or alien admission number.

(B) In any of the following cases, the secondary SAVE system verification procedure must be used to forward copies of original INS documents evidencing an alien's status as a qualified alien, as a nonimmigrant alien under the INA, or as an alien paroled into the United States under Section 212(d)(5) of the INA (8 U.S.C. §1182(d)(5)), for less than one year:

(i) The primary SAVE system is unavailable for verification.

(ii) A primary check of the Alien Status Verification Index instructs the Uninsured Employers Fund or Subsequent Injuries Fund to "institute secondary verification."

(iii) The document presented indicates immigration status but does not include an alien registration or alien admission number.

(iv) The Alien Status Verification Index record includes the alien registration or admission number on the document presented by the alien but does not match other information contained in the document.

(v) The document is suspected to be counterfeit or to have been altered.

(vi) The document includes an alien registration number in the A60 000 000 (not yet issued) or A80 000 000 (illegal border crossing) series.

(vii) The document is a fee receipt from INS for replacement of a lost, stolen, or unreadable INS document.

(viii) The document is one of the following: an INS Form I-181b notification letter issued in connection with an INS Form I-181 Memorandum of Creation of Record of Permanent Residence, an Arrival-Departure Record (INS Form

I-94) or a foreign passport stamped "PROCESSED FOR I-551, TEMPORARY EVIDENCE OF LAWFUL PERMANENT RESIDENCE" that INS issued more than one year before the date of application for benefits from the UEF or SIF.

(5) Where verification through the SAVE system is not available, if the documents presented do not on their face reasonably appear to be genuine or to relate to the individual presenting them, the government entity that originally issued the document should be contacted for verification. With regard to naturalized citizens and derivative citizens presenting certificates of citizenship and aliens, the INS is the appropriate government entity to contact for verification. The UEF or SIF should request verification by the INS by filing INS Form G-845 with copies of the pertinent documents provided by the applicant with the local INS office. If the applicant has lost his her original documents, or presents expired documents or is unable to present any documentation evidencing his or her immigration status, the applicant should be referred to the local INS office to obtain documentation.

(6) If the INS advises that the applicant has citizenship status or immigration status which makes him or her a qualified alien under the PRWORA, the INS verification should be accepted. If the INS advises that it cannot verify that the applicant has citizenship status or an immigration status that makes him or her a qualified alien, benefits shall be denied and the applicant notified of his or her rights to appeal the denial of benefits.

(7) Provided that the alien has completed and signed Form UEF-1 under penalty of perjury, eligibility for UEF or SIF benefits shall not be delayed, denied, reduced or terminated while the status of the alien is verified.

(f) Pursuant to Section 432(d) of the PRWORA (8 U.S.C. §1642(d)), the UEF or SIF shall assure that a nonprofit charitable organization that provides federal, state, or local public benefits shall not be required to determine, verify, or otherwise require proof of eligibility of any applicant or beneficiary with respect to his or her immigration status or alienage.

(g) Pursuant to Section 434 of the PRWORA (8 U.S.C. §1644), where the UEF or SIF reasonably believes that an alien is unlawfully in the State based on the failure of the alien to provide reasonable evidence of the alien's declared status, after an opportunity to do so, said alien shall be reported to the Immigration and Naturalization Service.

(h) Nothing in this section shall be construed to withdraw eligibility for medical treatment required for an emergency medical condition under Section 411(b) of the PRWORA (8 U.S.C. §1621(b(1)).

(i) Any applicant who is denied benefits, or whose benefits are terminated, pursuant to subsections (b) and (e), may file a Request for Administrative Review of benefit determination with the UEF Manager within 20 days of service of the notice of denial or termination of benefits from the UEF or SIF. The Request for Administrative Review shall be verified under penalty of perjury with proof of service on all parties, and shall provide a statement of reasons, as well as any relevant evidence, explaining why the determination of the UEF or SIF was in error.

(j) Upon receipt of the Request for Administrative Review, the UEF Manager shall informally reconsider the determination and shall issue a decision granting or denying the request within 45 days. A Request for Administrative Review as provided in subsection (i) shall be a prerequisite to the filing of a petition before the Workers' Compensation Appeals Board pursuant to subsection (k).

(k) Any applicant aggrieved by a decision of the UEF Manager on a Request for Administrative Review of benefit determination may file, within 20 days of service of the decision, a petition for relief before the Workers' Compensation Appeals Board. The petition shall be filed at the appeals board office that is designated for applications for adjudication of claim pursuant to Labor Code Section 5501.5., and shall be assigned to a workers' compensation judge for hearing and determination of the issues raised. A party aggrieved by the determination of the workers' compensation judge may seek relief from the determination in the same manner as specified for petitions for reconsideration pursuant to Labor Code Section 5900.

Note: Authority cited: Sections 54, 55, 59, 3702.10, 3716, 3716.1, 3716.2 and 4751, Labor Code. Reference: Sections 1621, 1641 and 1642, Title 8, United States Code; and Sections 3716, 3716.1, 3716.2, 4750-4755 and 5501.5, Labor Code.

History: 1. New subchapter 2.1.1, article 1 (sections 15740-15741) and section filed 10-28-98; operative 11-27-98 (Register 98, No. 44).

Ref.: See Labor Code §§4751–4755; Hanna §§ 1.21, 2.13, 31.20[4][a]; Herlick Handbook §§ 2.3, 3.19, 6.21.

§15741. Statement of Citizenship, Alienage, and Immigration Status for State Public Benefits, Form UEF-1.

STATE OF CALIFORNIA
DEPARTMENT OF INDUSTRIAL RELATIONS
UNINSURED EMPLOYERS FUND-SUBSEQUENT INJURIES FUND

STATEMENT OF CITIZENSHIP, ALIENAGE, AND IMMIGRATION STATUS FOR STATE PUBLIC BENEFITS

Name of Applicant (the person seeking Uninsured Employers Fund or Subsequent Injuries Fund benefits)
Date

Name of Person Acting for Applicant, if any
Relationship to Applicant

STATE PUBLIC BENEFITS TO CITIZENS AND ALIENS

Citizens and nationals of the United States who meet all eligibility requirements may receive Uninsured Employers Fund or Subsequent Injuries Fund benefits and must fill out Sections A and D.

Aliens who meet all eligibility requirements may also receive Uninsured Employers Fund or Subsequent Injuries Fund benefits and must complete SECTIONS A, B, C and D of this form.

SECTION A: CITIZENSHIP/IMMIGRATION STATUS DECLARATION

1. Is the applicant a citizen or national of the United States?

Yes ☐ No ☐

If the answer to the above question is "Yes", where was he/she born?
___________ (State or Country)

2. To establish citizenship or nationality, please submit one of the documents on List A (attached to this form) which is legible and unaltered to establish proof.

IF YOU ARE A CITIZEN OR NATIONAL OF THE UNITED STATES, GO DIRECTLY TO SECTION D. IF YOU ARE AN ALIEN, PLEASE COMPLETE SECTION B, AND, IF NECESSARY, SECTION C.

SECTION B: ALIEN STATUS DECLARATION

IMPORTANT: Please indicate the applicant's alien status below, and submit documents evidencing such status. The alien status documents listed for each category are the most commonly used documents that the United States Immigration and Naturalization Service (INS) provides to aliens in those categories. You can provide other acceptable evidence of your alien status even if not listed below. Where authorized by the INS, the documents you provide will be submitted to the INS for verification through the Systematic Alien Verification for Entitlements ("SAVE") system. Should verification through the "SAVE" system be unavailable, the validity of the documents you provide may be verified directly with the issuing government agency.

1. An alien lawfully admitted for permanent residence under the Immigration and Naturalization Act (INA). (Evidence includes: ☐

- INS Form I-551 (Alien Registration Receipt Card, commonly known as a "green card"); or
- Unexpired Temporary I-551 stamp in foreign passport or on INS Form I-94.

2. An alien who is granted asylum under section 208 of the INA. (Evidence includes: ☐
   - INS Form I-94 annotated with stamp showing grant of asylum under section 208 of the INA;
   - INS Form I-688B (Employment Authorization Card) annotated "274a.12(a)(5)";
   - INS Form I-766 (Employment Authorization Document) annotated "A5";
   - Grant letter from the Asylum Office of INS; or
   - Order of an immigration judge granting asylum.)
3. A refugee admitted to the United States under section 207 of the INA. (Evidence includes: ☐
   - INS Form I-94 annotated with stamp showing admission under section 207 of the INA;
   - INS Form I-688B (Employment Authorization Card) annotated "274a.12(a)(3)";
   - INS Form I-766 (Employment Authorization Document) annotated "A3"; or
   - INS Form I-571 (Refugee Travel Document).
4. An alien paroled into the United States for at least one year under section 212(d)(5) of the INA. (Evidence includes: ☐
   - INS Form I-94 with stamp showing admission for at least one year under section 212(d)(5) of the INA. (Applicant cannot aggregate periods of admission for less than one year to meet the one-year requirement.)
5. An alien whose deportation is being withheld under section 243(h) of the INA (as in effect immediately prior to September 30, 1996) or Section 241(b)(3) of such Act (as amended by section 305(a) of division C of Public Law 104-208). (Evidence includes: ☐
   - INS Form I-688B (Employment Authorization Card) annotated "274a.12(a)(10)";
   - INS Form I-766 (Employment Authorization Document) annotated "A10"; or
   - Order from an immigration judge showing deportation withheld under section 243(h) of the INA as in effect prior to April 1, 1997, or removal withheld under section 241(b)(3) of the INA.)
6. An alien who is granted conditional entry under section 203(a)(7) of the INA as in effect prior to April 1, 1980. (Evidence includes: ☐
   - INS Form I-94 with stamp showing admission under Section 203(a)(7) of the INA;
   - INS Form I-688B (Employment Authorization Card) annotated "274a.12(a)(3)"; or
   - INS Form I-766 (Employment Authorization Document) annotated "A3").
7. An alien who is a Cuban or Haitian entrant (as defined in section 501(e) of the Refugee Education Assistance Act of 1980). (Evidence includes: ☐
   - INS Form I-551 (Alien Registration Receipt Card, commonly known as a "green card") with the code CU6, CU7, or CH6;
   - Unexpired temporary I-551 stamp in foreign passport or on INS Form I-94 with the code CU6 or CU7; or
   - INS Form I-94 with stamp showing parole as "Cuban/Haitian Entrant" under Section 212(d)(5) of the INA.)
8. An alien paroled into the United States for less than one year under section 212(d)(5) of the INA. (Evidence includes INS Form I-94 showing this status.) ☐
9. An alien not in categories 1 through 8 who has been admitted to ☐

the United States for a limited period of time (a non-immigrant). Non-immigrants are persons who have temporary status for a specific purpose. (Evidence includes INS Form I-94 showing this status.)

SECTION C: DECLARATION FOR BATTERED ALIENS

IMPORTANT: Complete this section if the applicant, the applicant's child or the applicant child's parent has been battered or subjected to extreme cruelty in the United States.

1. Has the INS or the EOIR granted a petition or application filed by or on behalf of the applicant, the applicant's child, or the applicant's child's parent under the INA or found that a pending petition sets forth a prima facie case? Evidence includes one of the documents on List B (attached hereto) ☐
2. Has the applicant, the applicant's child, or the applicant child's parent been battered or subjected to extreme cruelty in the United States by a spouse or parent, or by a spouse's or parent's family member living in the same house (where the spouse or parent consented to, or acquiesced in the battery or cruelty)? ☐

SECTION D:

I DECLARE UNDER PENALTY OF PERJURY UNDER THE LAWS OF THE STATE OF CALIFORNIA THAT THE ANSWERS I HAVE GIVEN ARE TRUE AND CORRECT TO THE BEST OF MY KNOWLEDGE.

Applicant's Signature: ____________________ Date: ____________
Signature of Person
Acting for Applicant: ____________________ Date: ____________

LIST "A"

(For Applicants for Uninsured Employers Fund or Subsequent Injuries Fund benefits who are citizens or nationals of the United States.)

A. Primary Evidence

- A birth certificate showing birth in one of the 50 States, the District of Columbia, Puerto Rico (on or after January 13, 1941), Guam, the U.S. Virgin Islands (on or after January 17, 1917), American Samoa, Swain's Island or the Northern Mariana Islands, unless the person was born to foreign diplomats residing in the U.S.

Note: If the document shows that the individual was born in Puerto Rico, the U.S. Virgin Islands or the Northern Mariana Islands before these areas became part of the U.S., the individual may be a collectively naturalized citizen—(see Paragraph C below).

- United States passport (except limited passports, which are issued for periods of less than five years);
- Report of birth abroad of a U.S. citizen (FS-240) (issued by the Department of State to U.S. citizens);
- Certificate of birth (FS-545) (issued by a foreign service post) or Certification of Report of Birth (DS-1350) (issued by the Department of State), copies of which are available from the Department of State;
- Certificate of Naturalization (N-550 or N-570) (issued by INS through a Federal or State court, or through administrative naturalization after December 1990 to individuals who are individually naturalized; the N-570 is a replacement certificate issued when the N-550 has been lost or mutilated or the individual's name has been changed);
- Certificate of Citizenship (N-560 or N-561) (issued by the INS to individuals who derive U.S. citizenship through a parent; the N-561 is a replacement certificate issued when the N-560 has been lost or mutilated or the individual's name has been changed);

- United States Citizen Identification Card (I-197) (issued by the INS until April 7, 1983 to U.S. citizens living near the Canadian or Mexican border who needed it for frequent border crossings) (formerly Form I-179, last issued in February 1974);
- Northern Mariana Identification Card (issued by the INS to a collectively naturalized citizen of the U.S. who was born in the Northern Mariana Islands before November 3, 1986);
- Statement provided by a U.S. consular officer certifying that the individual is a U.S. citizen (this is given to an individual born outside the U.S. who derives citizenship through a parent but does not have an FS-240, FS-545 or DS-1350); or
- American Indian Card with a classification code "KIC" and a statement on the back (identifying U.S. citizen members of the Texas Band of Kickapoos living near the U.S./Mexican border).

B. Secondary Evidence

If the applicant cannot present one of the documents listed in A above, the following may be relied upon to establish U.S. citizenship or nationality:

- Religious record recorded in one of the 50 States, the District of Columbia, Puerto Rico (on or after January 13, 1941), Guam, the U.S. Virgin Islands (on or after January 17, 1917), American Samoa, Swain's Island or the Northern Mariana Islands (unless the person was born to foreign diplomats residing in such a jurisdiction) within three months after birth showing that the birth occurred in such jurisdiction and the date of birth or the individual's age at the time the record was made;
- Evidence of civil service employment by the U.S. government before June 1, 1976;
- Early school records (preferably from the first school) showing the date of admission to the school, the child's date and place of birth, and the name(s) and place(s) of birth of the parent(s);
- Census record showing name, U.S. citizenship or a U.S. place of birth, and date of birth or age of applicant;
- Adoption Finalization Papers showing the child's name and place of birth in one of the 50 States, the District of Columbia, Puerto Rico (on or after January 13, 1941), Guam, the U.S. Virgin Islands (on or after January 17, 1917), American Samoa, Swain's Island or the Northern Mariana Islands (unless the person was born to foreign diplomats residing in such a jurisdiction) or, where or adoption is not finalized and the State or other jurisdiction listed above in which the child was born will not release a birth certificate prior to final adoption, a statement from a state-approved adoption agency showing the child's name and place of birth in one of such jurisdictions (NOTE: the source of the information must be an original birth certificate and must be indicated in the statement); or
- Any other document that establishes a U.S. place of birth or in some way indicates U.S. citizenship (e.g., a contemporaneous hospital record of birth in that hospital in one of the 50 States, the District of Columbia, Puerto Rico (on or after January 13, 1941), Guam, the U.S. Virgin Islands (on or after January 17, 1917), American Samoa, Swain's Island or the Northern Mariana Islands (unless the person was born to foreign diplomats residing in such a jurisdiction).

C. Collective Naturalization

If the applicant cannot present one of the documents listed in A or B above, the following may be relied upon to establish U.S. citizenship for collectively naturalized individuals:

Puerto Rico:

- Evidence of birth in Puerto Rico on or after April 11, 1899 and the applicant's statement that he or she was residing in the U.S., a U.S. possession or Puerto Rico on January 13, 1941; or
- Evidence that the applicant was a Puerto Rican citizen and the applicant's statement that he or she was residing in Puerto Rico on March 1, 1917 and that he or she did not take an oath of allegiance to Spain.

U.S. Virgin Islands:

- Evidence of birth in the U.S. Virgin Islands, and the applicant's statement of residence in the U.S., a U.S. possession or the U.S. Virgin Islands on February 25, 1927;

- The applicant's statement indicating residence in the U.S. Virgin Islands as a Danish citizen on January 17, 1917 and residence in the U.S., a U.S. possession or the U.S. Virgin Islands on February 25, 1927, and that he or she did not make a declaration to maintain Danish citizenship; or
- Evidence of birth in the U.S. Virgin Islands and the applicant's statement indicating residence in the U.S., a U.S. possession or territory or the Canal Zone on June 28, 1932.

Northern Mariana Islands (NMI) (formerly part of the Trust Territory of the Pacific Islands (TTPI));

- Evidence of birth in the NMI, TTPI citizenship and residence in the NMI, the U.S., or a U.S. territory or possession on November 3, 1986 (NMI local time) and the applicant's statement that he or she did not owe allegiance to a foreign state on November 4, 1986 (NMI local time);
- Evidence of TTPI citizenship, continuous residence in the NMI since before November 3, 1981 (NMI local time), voter registration prior to January 1, 1975 and the applicant's statement that he or she did not owe allegiance to a foreign state on November 4, 1986 (NMI local time); or
- Evidence of continuous domicile in the NMI since before January 1, 1974 and the applicant's statement that he or she did not owe allegiance to a foreign state on November 4, 1986 (NMI local time). Note: If a person entered the NMI as a nonimmigrant and lived in the NMI since January 1, 1974, this does not constitute continuous domicile and the individual is not a U.S. citizen.

D. Derivative Citizenship

If the applicant cannot present one of the documents listed in A or B above, you should make a determination of derivative U.S. citizenship in the following situations:

Applicant born abroad to two U.S. citizen parents:

- Evidence of the U.S. citizenship of the parents and the relationship of the applicant to the parents, and evidence that at least one parent resided in the U.S. or an outlying possession prior to the applicant's birth.

Applicant born abroad to a U.S. citizen parent and a U.S. non-citizen national parent:

- Evidence that one parent is a U.S. citizen and that the other is a U.S. non-citizen national, evidence of the relationship of the applicant to the U.S. citizen parent, and evidence that the U.S. citizen parent resided in the U.S., a U.S. possession, American Samoa or Swain's Island for a period of at least one year prior to the applicant's birth.

Applicant born out of wedlock abroad to a U.S. citizen mother:

- Evidence of the U.S. citizenship of the mother, evidence of the relationship to the applicant and, for births on or before December 24, 1952, evidence that the mother resided in the U.S. prior to the applicant's birth or, for births after December 24, 1952, evidence that the mother had resided, prior to the child's birth, in the U.S. or a U.S. possession for a period of one year.

Applicant born in the Canal Zone or the Republic of Panama:

- A birth certificate showing birth in the Canal Zone on or after February 26, 1904 and before October 1, 1979 and evidence that one parent was a U.S. citizen at the time of the applicant's birth; or
- A birth certificate showing birth in the Republic of Panama on or after February 26, 1904 and before October 1, 1979 and evidence that at least one parent was a U.S. citizen and employed by the U.S. government or the Panama Railroad Company or its successor in title.

All other situations where an applicant claims to have a U.S. citizen parent and an alien parent, or claims to fall within one of the above categories but is unable to present the listed documentation:

- If the applicant is in the U.S., refer him or her to the local INS office for determination of U.S. citizenship;
- If the applicant is outside the U.S., refer him or her to the State Department for a U.S. citizenship determination.

E. Adoption of Foreign-Born Child by U.S. Citizen

- If the birth certificate shows a foreign place of birth and the applicant cannot be determined to be a naturalized citizen under any of the above criteria, obtain other evidence of U.S. citizenship;
- Since foreign-born adopted children do not automatically acquire U.S. citizenship by virtue of adoption by U.S. citizens, refer the applicant to the local INS district office for a determination of U.S. citizenship if the applicant provides no evidence of U.S. citizenship.

F. U.S. Citizenship by Marriage

A women acquired U.S. citizenship through marriage to a U.S. citizen before September 22, 1922. Ask for: Evidence of U.S. citizenship of the husband, and evidence showing the marriage occurred before September 22, 1922.

Note: If the husband was an alien at the time of the marriage, and became naturalized before September 22, 1922, the wife also acquired naturalized citizenship. If the marriage terminated, the wife maintained her U.S. citizenship if she was residing in the U.S. at that time and continued to reside in the U.S.

LIST "B"

(For Applicants for Uninsured Employers Fund or Subsequent Injuries Fund benefits who are citizens or nationals of the United States.)

A. Documentation Evidencing an Approved Petition or Application

- INS Form I-551 ("Resident Alien Card" or "Alien Registration Receipt Card" commonly known as a "green card") with one of the following INS class of admission ("COA") codes printed on the front of a white card or the back of a pink card; AR1, AR6, C20 through C29, CF1, CF2, CR1, CR2, CR6, CR7, CX1 through CX3, CX6 through CX8, F20 through F29, FX1 through FX3, FX6 through FX8, IF1, IF2, IR1 through IR4, IR6 through IR9, IW1, IW2, IW6, IW7, MR6, MR7, P21 through P23, or P26 through P28.

If an alien claiming approved status presents a code different than those enumerated, or if you cannot determine the class of admission from the I-551 stamp, you should file INS Form G-845, and the G-845 Supplement (mark item six on the Supplement) (attached hereto) along with a copy of the document(s) presented, with the local INS office in order to determine whether the applicant gained his or her status because he or she was the spouse, widow, or child of a U.S. citizen or the spouse, child, or unmarried son or daughter of an LPR (lawful permanent resident).

- INS Form I-551 with one of the following COA codes stamped on the lower left side of the back of a pink card: IB1 through IB3, IB6 through IB8, B11, B12, B16, B17, B20 through B29, B31 through B33, B36 through B38, BX1 through BX3, or BX6 through BX8.
- INS Form I-551 with COA code Z13.
- Unexpired Temporary I-551 stamp in foreign passport or on INS Form I-94 with one of the COA codes specified in the Subsections (1)-(3), above.
- INS Form I-797 indicating approval of an INS I-130 petition (only I-130 petitions describing the following relationships may be accepted: husbands or wives of U.S. citizens or LPRs, unmarried children under 21 years old of U.S. citizens or LPRs, or unmarried children 21 or older of LPRs), or approval of an I-360 petition (only I-360 approvals based on status as a widow/widower of a U.S. citizen or as a self-petitioning spouse or child of an abusive U.S. citizen or LPR may be accepted).
- A final order of an Immigration Judge or the Board of Immigration Appeals granting suspension of deportation under section 244(a)(3) of the INA as in effect prior to April 1, 1997, or cancellation of removal under section 240A(b)(2) of the INA.

B. Documentation Demonstrating that the Applicant has Established a Prima Facie Case

- INS Form I-797 indicating that the applicant has established a prima facie case; or
- An immigration court or Board of Immigration Appeals order indicating that the applicant has established a prima facie case for suspension of deportation under INA section 244(a)(3) as in effect prior to April 1, 1997, or cancellation of removal under section 240A(b)(2) of the INA.

C. Documentation Indicating that the Applicant has Filed a Petition or that a Petition has been Filed on the Applicant's Behalf, as Applicable, but with no Evidence of Approval of the Petition or Establishment of a Prima Facie Case

The benefit provider shall determine from the documentation when the petition was filed and take the actions set forth below:

- Applicants with petitions filed before June 7, 1997 should have an INS Form I-797 indicating filing of the I-360 petition by "self-petitioning spouse [or child] of abusive U.S.C. or LPR," a file-stamped copy of the petition, or another document demonstrating filing (including a cash register or computer-generated receipt indicating filing of Form I-360).
- Applicants with petitions filed after June 7, 1997 should have an INS Form I-797 indicating filing of the I-360 petition.

D. Documentation Indicating that the Applicant has filed a Petition or that a Petition was filed on His or Her Behalf, as Applicable

The following must indicate that the applicant is the widow/widower of a U.S. citizen, the husband or wife of a U.S. Citizen or LPR, the unmarried child under age 21 of a U.S. citizen or LPR, or the unmarried child age 21 or older of an LPR):

- For aliens on whose behalf a petition has been filed: INS Form I-797 indicating filing of an INS I-130 petition, a file-stamped copy of the petition, or another document demonstrating filing (including a cash register or computer-generated receipt indicating filing of Form I-130) (a sample copy of Form I-130 is attached to this Exhibit).
- For self-petitioning widows or widowers: a file-stamped copy of the INS I-360 petition, or another document demonstrating filing (including a cash register or computer-generated receipt indicating filing of Form I-360).

E. Documentation Indicating that the INS has Initiated Deportation or Removal Proceedings in which Relief may be Available

- an "Order to Show Cause";
- a "Notice to Appear"; or
- a "Notice of Hearing in Deportation Proceedings."

F. Minimal or no Documentation Regarding the Claimed Filing

If the applicant has some documentation, but it is insufficient to demonstrate filing, establishment of prima facie case or approval of a petition, you should fax the INS Request Form on your agency letterhead, as well as a copy of any document(s) provided by the applicant, to the INS Vermont Service Center in order to determine the applicant's status. If the applicant has no documentation, but is certain that a petition has been filed by his or her spouse or parent, you should fax the INS Request Form to the INS Vermont Service Center.

Note: Authority cited: Sections 54, 55, 59, 3702.10, 3716, 3716.1, 3716.2 and 4751, Labor Code. Reference: Sections 1621, 1641 and 1642, Title 8, United States Code; and Sections 3716, 3716.1, 3716.2 and 4750-4755, Labor Code.

History: 1. New section filed 10-28-98; operative 11-27-98 (Register 98, No. 44).

Ref.: See Labor Code §§4751–4755.

TITLE 10
INVESTMENTS

CHAPTER 5
INSURANCE COMMISSIONER

SUBCHAPTER 3
INSURERS

ARTICLE 20
Standards Applicable to Workers' Compensation Claims Adjusters and Medical Billing Entities and Certification of Those Standards by Insurers

§2592. Authority and Purpose.

These regulations are promulgated pursuant to authority granted to the Insurance Commissioner under the provisions of Section 11761 of the California Insurance Code. The purpose of these regulations is to set forth the minimum standards of training, experience, and skill that workers' compensation claims adjusters, including adjusters working for medical billing entities, must possess to perform their duties with regard to workers' compensation claims and to specify how insurers must meet and certify those standards to the Insurance Commissioner.

Note: Authority cited: Section 11761, Insurance Code. Reference: Section 11761, Insurance Code.

History: 1. New article 20 (sections 2592-2592.14) and section filed 1-23-2006; operative 2-22-2006 (Register 2006, No. 4).

Ref.: Hanna §§ 2.11[4], 2.37[1]-[7]; Herlick Handbook § 3.15.

§2592.01. Definitions.

As used in this article:

(a) "Certify" means a written statement made under penalty of perjury.

(b) "Claims adjuster" means a person who, on behalf of an insurer, including an employee or agent of an entity that is not an insurer, is responsible for determining the validity of a workers' compensation claim. The claims adjuster may also establish a case reserve, approve and process all workers' compensation benefits, may hire investigators, attorneys or other professionals and may negotiate settlements of claims. "Claims adjuster" also means a person who is responsible for the immediate supervision of a claims adjuster but does not mean an attorney representing the insurer or a person whose primary function is clerical. "Claims adjuster" also includes an experienced claims adjuster. "Claims adjuster" does not include the medical director or physicians utilized by an insurer for the utilization review process pursuant to Labor Code section 4610.

(c) "Classroom" means any space sufficiently designed so that the instructor and students can communicate with a high degree of privacy and relative freedom from outside interference. The instructor or the person or persons assisting the instructor may be physically present or may communicate with students by means of an electronic medium, including, but not limited to, audio, video, computer, or Internet.

(d) "Course" means any program of instruction taken or given to satisfy the requirements of Insurance Code Section 11761.

(e) "Curriculum" means a course of study that satisfies the requirements of Insurance Code Section 11761. The curriculum must provide sufficient content, including time allocated to each subject area, to enable claims adjusters, medical-only claims adjusters, and medical bill reviewers to meet minimum standards of training, experience, and skill to perform their duties with regard to workers' compensation claims.

(f) "Experienced claims adjuster" means a person who has had at least five (5) years within the past eight (8) years of on-the-job experience adjusting California workers' compensation claims or supervising claims adjusters handling California workers' compensation claims and is designated as an experienced claims adjuster by an insurer. A person who has successfully completed the written examination specified by Title 8, Section 15452 of the California Code of Regulations is also considered an experienced claims adjuster, provided that he or she has either (1) worked as a workers' compensation claims adjuster or supervised workers' compensation claims adjusters continuously since passing the examination and is designated as an experienced claims adjuster by an insurer or (2) passed the examination within the previous five (5) years and is designated as an experienced claims adjuster by an insurer. "Experienced claims adjuster" also includes a person who has already been trained and designated a claims adjuster and now meets the requirements of experience or examination completion noted above and is designated an experienced claims adjuster by an insurer.

(g) "Experienced medical-only claims adjuster" means a person who has had at least three (3) years within the past five (5) years of on-the-job experience adjusting California workers' compensation medical-only claims and is designated as an experienced medical-only claims adjuster by an insurer.

(h) "Experienced medical bill reviewer" means a person who has had at least three (3) years within the past five (5) years of on-the-job experience reviewing California workers' compensation medical bills and is designated as an experienced medical bill reviewer by a medical billing entity or by an insurer.

(i) "Instructor" means a person who conveys curriculum content to students on behalf of an insurer, a training entity, or a medical billing entity. An instructor shall have had at least five (5) years within the past eight (8) years of on-the-job experience adjusting California workers' compensation claims and have been designated as a claims adjuster by an insurer or be an individual who has had at least eight (8) years of experience in California workers' compensation within the past twelve (12) years. Persons knowledgeable about specific workers' compensation issues who are not instructors may train students under the direction of an instructor.

(j) "Insurer" means an insurance company admitted to transact workers' compensation insurance in California, the State Compensation Insurance Fund, an employer that has secured a certificate of consent to self-insure from the Department of Industrial Relations pursuant to Labor Code Section 3700(b) or (c), or a third party administrator that has secured a certificate of consent pursuant to Labor Code Section 3702.1.

(k) "Medical bill reviewer" means a person who is not a claims adjuster or medical-only claims adjuster and who only reviews or adjusts workers' compensation medical bills on behalf of an insurer, including employees or agents of the insurer or employees or agents of a medical billing entity. "Medical bill reviewer" also includes an experienced medical bill reviewer.

(*l*) "Medical billing entity" means a third party that reviews or adjusts workers' compensation medical bills for insurers.

(m) "Medical-only claims adjuster" means a person who, on behalf of an insurer, including an employee or agent of an entity that is not an insurer, is responsible for determining the validity of workers' compensation claims only involving medical workers' compensation benefits, as defined under Article 2 (commencing with Labor Code section 4600) of Chapter 2 of Part 2 of Division 4 of the Labor Code. The medical-only claims adjuster may also establish medical treatment reserves, approve and process medical benefits, and negotiate settlement of medical benefit claims. "Medical-only claims adjuster" also means a person who is responsible for the immediate supervision of a medical-only claims adjuster but does not mean an attorney representing the insurer or a person whose primary function is clerical. "Medical-only claims adjuster" also includes an experienced medical-only claims adjuster. "Medical-only claims adjuster" does not include the medical director or physicians utilized by an insurer for the utilization review process pursuant to Labor Code section 4610.

(n) "Post-designation training" means a course of study provided to trained or experienced workers' compensation claims adjusters and medical-only claims adjusters who have been designated by an insurer or provided to trained or experienced medical bill reviewers who have been designated by an insurer or medical billing entity. Post-designation training also includes seminars, workshops, or other informational meetings pertaining to California workers' compensation.

(o) "Student" or "trainee" means an individual taking a course that is required for that person in order to be a workers' compensation claims adjuster, medical-only claims adjuster, or medical bill reviewer.

(p) "Training" means to provide a course of instruction that includes the topics specified in Sections 2592.03 and 2592.04.

(q) "Training entity" means any person or organization that provides instructors or curriculum to an insurer or medical billing entity.

Note: Authority cited: Section 11761, Insurance Code. Reference: Section 11761, Insurance Code.

History: 1. New section filed 1-23-2006; operative 2-22-2006 (Register 2006, No. 4).

Ref.: Hanna §§ 2.11[4], 2.37[1]-[5]; Herlick Handbook § 3.15.

§2592.02. Training Required for Claims Adjusters and Medical-Only Claims Adjusters.

(a) Every insurer shall require all claims adjusters and medical-only claims adjusters who handle workers' compensation claims on the insurer's behalf, other than those who are defined in subdivisions (f) and (g) of Section 2592.01, to be trained pursuant to these subparagraphs:

(1) The insurer shall require at least 160 hours of training for claims adjusters, at least 120 hours of which shall be conducted in a classroom with an instructor. The insurer shall require at least 80 hours of training for medical-only claims adjusters, at least 50 hours of which shall be conducted in a classroom with an instructor. Any training not conducted in a classroom with an instructor may be done on the job under the supervision of an instructor or an experienced claims adjuster.

(2) A medical-only claims adjuster who has completed 80 hours of training pursuant to this section may be designated as a claims adjuster upon completion of 80 additional hours of workers' compensation claims training, 70 hours of which shall be in a classroom with an instructor, provided that such training is completed within six months of the claims adjuster beginning to adjust claims that include more than medical benefits.

(b) The training required by this section shall be completed within a twelve (12) consecutive month period, during which time a claims adjuster or medical-only claims adjuster trainee may adjust claims under the supervision of an instructor or experienced claims adjuster. No individual may adjust claims on behalf of one or more insurers for a combined total of more than twelve (12) months unless such individual has been trained pursuant to this article. However, if a claims adjuster or medical-only claims adjuster trainee requires leave from his or her employment because of illness, disability, military service, or leave required or permitted by state or federal law, and the leave has begun after the training has started, the training shall be completed within a period not to exceed 24 months after the commencement of the training.

(c) Any classes or courses taken within three (3) years before the effective date of these regulations that satisfy the curriculum requirement may be used to meet the hourly requirements upon verification by the student to the insurer of the type of course taken, the course of study, the date or dates taken, the person or organization providing the class or course, and the number of hours taken.

(d) Upon the effective date of these regulations, every insurer shall require a minimum of 30 hours of post-designation training every two (2) years for all claims adjusters and 20 hours of training every two (2) years for all medical-only claims adjusters.

(e) Post-designation training may include seminars, workshops, or other informational meetings pertaining to California workers' compensation and need not be in a classroom with an instructor. Such training shall be verified by the insurer with the type of course taken, the subject matter, the date or dates taken, the location of the training, the person or organization providing the training, and the number of hours taken.

(f) Failure of a claims adjuster or medical-only claims adjuster who has received a designation pursuant to subdivisions (a) or (b) of section 2592.05 to fulfill the requirements for post-designation training every two years pursuant to subdivisions (d) and (e) above shall result in that person being no longer considered a designated claims adjuster or medical-only claims adjuster. That person shall not be authorized to adjust claims until the requisite number of hours of post-designation training is completed.

(g) The insurer may provide the designation training directly or by sending its employees or its agents to be trained by a training entity for the entire designation curriculum. An insurer shall certify to the Insurance Commissioner that the course of instruction provided for training meets all the requirements set forth in this article and that all of the claims adjusters and medical-only claims adjusters who adjust claims on behalf of the insurer have actually attended the training for the required number of hours, in the manner provided for in sections 2592.07 and 2592.08.

(h) A claims adjuster or medical-only claims adjuster who has completed the training required by this section shall not be required to be re-trained and re-designated in order to adjust claims for a different insurer.

(i) An insurer may not authorize an individual to act in the capacity of claims adjuster or medical-only claims adjuster who has not been trained and designated pursuant to this article or who is not an experienced claims adjuster or an experienced medical-only claims adjuster and designated pursuant to this article, except that an individual who is undergoing training may adjust claims under the direct supervision of an instructor or experienced claims adjuster.

Note: Authority cited: Section 11761, Insurance Code. Reference: Section 11761, Insurance Code.

History: 1. New section filed 1-23-2006; operative 2-22-2006 (Register 2006, No. 4).

Ref.: Hanna § 2.37[2], [5]; Herlick Handbook § 3.15.

§2592.03. Curriculum.

(a) The course of study required by Section 2592.02 for claims adjusters shall include, but not be limited to, the following topics:

(1) Historical overview of the workers' compensation system.

(2) Organizational structure of the system.

(3) The workers' compensation insurance policy, its forms and endorsements, insurance principles of compensation.

(4) Concepts and terminology.

(5) Benefit provisions.

(6) Compensability.

(7) Notice requirements.

(8) Temporary disability.

(9) Permanent disability, including evaluation and rating.

(10) Death benefits.

(11) Return to work and vocational rehabilitation.

(12) Cumulative trauma.

(13) Serious and willful misconduct.

(14) Workers' Compensation Appeals Board procedures, forms, hearings, and penalties.

(15) Investigation.

(16) Fraud.

(17) Medical terminology.

(18) Knowledge and use of utilization guidelines (American College of Occupational and Environmental Medicine or other guidelines approved by the Administrative Director of the Division of Workers' Compensation.)

(19) Medical evidence.

(20) Medical dispute resolution (Qualified Medical Examiners, spinal surgery second opinions, pre-designation of physicians, independent medical reviewers, utilization review.)

(21) Fee schedules.

(22) Liens.

(23) Apportionment.

(24) Subrogation.

(25) Reserving.

(26) Ethical issues.

(b) The course of study required for the training of medical-only claims adjusters shall include, at a minimum, all the topics specified in subdivision (a) above, with the exception of (8), (9), (10), (11), (13), and (23).

(c) The course of study required by Section 2592.02(d) for post-designation training shall include changes in the law that affect workers' compensation claims and any other topics relevant to the work of a claims adjuster or medical-only claims adjuster as specified in subdivision (a) above.

Note: Authority cited: Section 11761, Insurance Code. Reference: Section 11761, Insurance Code.

History: 1. New section filed 1-23-2006; operative 2-22-2006 (Register 2006, No. 4).

Ref.: Hanna § 2.37[2], [5]; Herlick Handbook § 3.15.

§2592.04. Training Required for Medical Bill Reviewers.

(a) Every insurer shall require all medical bill reviewers, other than those defined in section 2592.01(h), including employees and agents of medical billing entities used by the insurer, to be trained. The insurer shall require at least 40 hours of training for medical bill reviewers, at least 30 hours of which shall be conducted in a classroom by an instructor. No more than ten (10) hours of training may be done on the job.

(b) The training required by this section shall be completed within a twelve (12) month period, during which time a medical bill review trainee may review bills under the supervision of an instructor, experienced medical bill reviewer, or experienced claims adjuster. No individual may review medical bills on behalf of one or more insurers for a combined total of more than twelve (12) months unless the individual has been trained pursuant to this article.

(c) Any classes or courses taken within one (1) year before the effective date of these regulations that satisfy the curriculum requirement of subdivision (h) below may be used to meet the hourly requirements upon verification by the student to the insurer or medical billing entity of the type of course taken, the course of study, the date or dates taken, the person or organization providing the class or course, and the number of hours taken.

(d) Upon the effective date of these regulations, every insurer shall require a minimum of 16 hours every two (2) years of post-designation training for all medical bill reviewers and shall include in the post-designation training changes in the law affecting medical bill reviewers and topics as specified in subdivision (h) below.

(e) Failure of a medical bill reviewer designated pursuant to subdivisions (a) or (c) of section 2592.05 to fulfill the requirements for post-designation training every two years pursuant to subdivision (d) above shall result in that person being no longer considered a designated medical bill reviewer. That person shall not be authorized to review medical bills until the requisite number of hours of post-designation training is completed.

(f) The insurer may provide the designation training directly or by sending its employees or agents to be trained by a training entity for the entire designation curriculum. The insurer shall require all medical billing entities that review or adjust medical billings on its behalf to have the medical billing entities' employees or agents trained directly by the medical billing entity, the insurer, or by a training entity for the entire designation curriculum. The insurer shall certify, in the manner provided for in sections 2592.07 and 2592.09, that the course of instruction provided or that is provided by its medical billing entities meets all the requirements set forth in this article and that all medical bill reviewers of the insurer and its medical billing entities have actually attended the training for the required number of hours.

(g) A medical bill reviewer who has received a Designation as having completed the training required by this article shall not be required to be re-trained and re-designated in order to review medical bills for a different insurer.

(h) The curriculum for the training of medical bill reviewers shall include, but not be limited to, the following topics:

(1) The correct use of billing codes and detection of improper use of billing codes.

(2) All fee schedules applicable in California to workers' compensation medical care, including statutes and regulations authorizing the fee schedules.

(3) Workers' compensation benefit provisions.

(4) Fraud.

(5) Medical terminology.

(6) Utilization guidelines (American College of Occupational and Environmental Medicine or other guidelines approved by the Administrative Director of the Division of Workers' Compensation.)

(7) Medical evidence.

(8) Liens.

(9) Ethical issues.

(i) An insurer may not authorize an individual to act in the capacity of a medical bill reviewer who has not been trained pursuant to this article or who is not an experienced medical bill reviewer, except that an individual who is undergoing training may review medical bills under the direct supervision of an instructor, experienced medical bill reviewer or experienced claims adjuster.

Note: Authority cited: Section 11761, Insurance Code. Reference: Section 11761, Insurance Code.

History: 1. New section filed 1-23-2006; operative 2-22-2006 (Register 2006, No. 4).

Ref.: Hanna § 2.37[3], [5]; Herlick Handbook § 3.15.

§2592.05. Designation.

(a) A Designation shall be provided by the insurer to any person who successfully completes the claims adjuster, medical-only claims adjuster, or medical bill reviewer training required by sections 2592.02 and 2592.03 or section 2592.04, respectively. The Designation for a claims adjuster, medical-only claims adjuster or a medical bill reviewer shall be in the form specified in Section 2592.10 or 2592.11, respectively.

(b) An Experienced Claims Adjuster or Experienced Medical-Only Claims Adjuster Designation shall be provided by the insurer to a person as defined in Section 2592.01(f) or (g), respectively. The Experienced Claims Adjuster or Experienced Medical-Only Claims Adjuster Designation shall be in the form specified in Section 2592.12.

(c) An Experienced Medical Bill Reviewer Designation shall be provided by the insurer to a person as defined in Section 2592.01(h). The Experienced Medical Bill Reviewer Designation shall be in the form specified in Section 2592.13.

(d) An insurer shall provide to the claims adjuster, medical-only claims adjuster or medical bill reviewer a Post-Designation Training Form that states the course and hours taken for the post-designation training following the completion of the required training. The Post-Designation Training Form shall be on the form specified in Section 2592.14.

(e) A medical billing entity may provide medical bill reviewer and experienced medical bill reviewer Designations and Post-Designation Training Forms to its employees or agents that meet the requirements of this article so long as the insurer using the medical billing entity confirms that the medical billing entity has met all requirements of this article and obtains copies of all records required by this article.

Note: Authority cited: Section 11761, Insurance Code. Reference: Section 11761, Insurance Code.

History: 1. New section filed 1-23-2006; operative 2-22-2006 (Register 2006, No. 4).

Ref.: Hanna § 2.37[5], [24]; Herlick Handbook § 3.15.

§2592.06. Maintenance of Records.

(a) An insurer shall maintain copies of the Designation forms pertaining to trained and experienced claims adjusters, medical-only claims adjusters and medical bill reviewers in its employ or acting on its behalf, notwithstanding whether or not that person was designated by it or was employed or trained by or on behalf of another insurer or a medical billing entity, as long as the claims adjuster, medical-only claims adjuster, or medical bill reviewer is in its employ or acting on its behalf and thereafter for five (5) years.

(b) An insurer shall maintain copies of the Post-Designation Training Forms as long as the claims adjuster, medical-only claims adjuster, or medical bill reviewer is in its employ or acting on its behalf, notwithstanding whether or not that person received post-designation training by that insurer or was employed or trained by or on behalf of another insurer or medical billing entity, and thereafter for five (5) years.

(c) If a trained or experienced claims adjuster, medical-only claims adjuster, or medical bill reviewer is employed by or works on behalf of an insurer that did not designate him or her, the insurer that did designate the claims adjuster, medical-only claims adjuster, or medical bill reviewer shall send copies of the Designation Forms to the current insurer within 20 working days after a request for the Designation Forms has been received.

(d) All insurers shall maintain a record of all courses given or taken by claims adjusters, medical-only claims adjusters, or medical bill reviewers to comply with this article. The record shall include:

(1) The name and business address of all students, along with the beginning and ending date of the training of the student and a statement of whether or not the student has completed the training in all topic areas required to be covered.

(2) A complete description of the curriculum, including all topics covered with a detailed statement of how much time was spent training students in each topic, the name of the entity providing the instruction, and the name of the instructor or instructors and any persons who instructed under the direction of the instructor.

(e) All insurers shall maintain a record of all post-designation courses, seminars, workshops, or other training taken by claims adjusters, medical-only claims adjusters, and medical bill reviewers employed by or acting on their behalf. The record shall also include the dates of such training, the time spent in the training, and the topics covered.

(f) All records maintained pursuant to this article shall be made available to the Insurance Commissioner and to the Administrative Director of the Division of Workers' Compensation. Copies of all Designation Forms maintained pursuant to the article and issued to a claims adjuster, medical-only claims adjuster, or medical bill reviewer shall be provided by the insurer that issued the forms to that person within 20 working days of a request for copies of the forms from the claims adjuster, medical-only claims adjuster, or medical bill reviewer.

(g) Upon the request of a policyholder or an injured worker whose claim is being adjusted, the insurer shall provide to the requesting policyholder or injured worker a copy of the Designation Form of the claims adjuster, medical-only claims adjuster, or medical bill reviewer handling the claim demonstrating that person's qualifications in adjusting that claim.

Note: Authority cited: Section 11761, Insurance Code. Reference: Section 11761, Insurance Code.

History: 1. New section filed 1-23-2006; operative 2-22-2006 (Register 2006, No. 4).

Ref.: Hanna § 2.37[6]; Herlick Handbook § 3.15.

§2592.07. Certification and Submission of Documents.

(a) Each insurer shall submit to the commissioner annually by July 1 of each year a document certifying the following:

(1) the total number of persons adjusting claims on its behalf;

(2) the total number of claims adjusters and medical-only claims adjusters who are trained or experienced;

(3) the percentage of the claims adjusters and medical-only claims adjusters who are trained or experienced;

(4) all persons adjusting claims on behalf of the insurer are designated to do so or are in training; and

(5) the course of instruction provided for training of all claims adjusters and medical-only claims adjusters meets all requirements of this article and that all claims adjusters and medical-only claims adjusters have attended training for the required number of hours to be qualified to adjust workers' compensation claims.

The document, which shall be on the form specified in Section 2592.08, shall be signed under penalty of perjury by the person or executive officer responsible for the insurer's claims operations. The commissioner shall publish the information contained in this document on the Department of Insurance public website.

(b) Each insurer shall submit to the commissioner annually by July 1 of each year a document certifying the following:

(1) the total number of medical bill reviewers reviewing medical bills on its behalf;

(2) the total number of medical bill reviewers who are trained or experienced;

(3) the percentage of the medical bill reviewers who are trained or experienced medical bill reviewers;

(4) all persons reviewing medical bills on its behalf are designated to do so or are in training; and

(5) the course of instruction provided for training of all medical bill reviewers of the insurer and of medical billing entities used by the insurer meets all requirements set forth in this article and that all medical bill reviewers of the insurer and of medical billing entities used by the insurer have attended training for the required number of hours to be qualified to perform medical bill review.

The document, which shall be on the form specified in Section 2592.09, shall be signed under penalty of perjury by the person or executive officer responsible for the insurer's claims operations. The commissioner shall publish the information contained in this document on the Department of Insurance public website.

Note: Authority cited: Section 11761, Insurance Code. Reference: Section 11761, Insurance Code.

History: 1. New section filed 1-23-2006; operative 2-22-2006 (Register 2006, No. 4).

Ref.: Hanna § 2.37[2], [3], [7]; Herlick Handbook § 3.15.

§2592.08. Insurer Annual Certification Form—Claims Adjusters and Medical-Only Claims Adjusters.

ANNUAL CERTIFICATION OF CLAIMS ADJUSTERS AND MEDICAL-ONLY CLAIMS ADJUSTERS

To the Insurance Commissioner of the State of California Pursuant to California Insurance Code Section 11761 and California Code of Regulations, Title 10, Sections 2592.02 and 2592.07

As the person or officer responsible for the claims operation of:

____

(Name of Insurer)

☐ Insurance Company ☐ Self-Insured Employer
☐ Third-Party Administrator
(Check One)

I hereby certify the following regarding California workers' compensation claims:

1. The total number of persons adjusting claims on this insurer's behalf is: __________.

2. The total number of experienced or trained claims adjusters and medical-only claims adjust-

ers adjusting claims on the insurer's behalf is: ____________.

3. The percentage of experienced or trained claims adjusters and medical-only claims adjusters adjusting claims on the insurer's behalf is: ________%

4. All persons adjusting claims on behalf of this insurer are designated to do so or are in training.

5. The course of instruction provided for training of all claims adjusters and medical-only claims adjusters meets all requirements set forth in Article 20 (commencing with section 2592) of Subchapter 3, Chapter 5, Title 10, California Code of Regulations, and that all claims adjusters and medical-only claims adjusters have attended training for the required number of hours to be qualified to adjust workers' compensation claims.

I certify under the penalty of perjury under the laws of the State of California that the foregoing is true and correct:

________________ ________________

(Date and Place) (Signature)

Name of person certifying (print or type):

Title of person certifying:

Business address:

Note: Authority cited: Section 11761, Insurance Code. Reference: Section 11761, Insurance Code.

History: 1. New section filed 1-23-2006; operative 2-22-2006 (Register 2006, No. 4).

Ref.: Hanna § 2.37[2], [7]; Herlick Handbook § 3.15.

§2592.09. Insurer Annual Certification Form—Medical Bill Reviewers.

ANNUAL CERTIFICATION OF MEDICAL BILL REVIEWERS

To the Insurance Commissioner of the State of California Pursuant to California Insurance Code Section 11761 and California Code of Regulations, Title 10, Sections 2592.04 and 2592.07

As the person or officer responsible for the claims operation of:

____

(Name of Insurer)

☐ Insurance Company ☐ Self-Insured Employer

☐ Third-Party Administrator

(Check One)

I hereby certify the following regarding California workers' compensation claims:

1. The total number of medical bill reviewers reviewing medical bills on this insurer's behalf is: ____________.

2. The total number of experienced or trained medical bill reviewers reviewing medical bills on this insurer's behalf is: ____________.

3. The percentage of experienced or trained medical bill reviewers reviewing medical bills on this insurer's behalf is: ________%

4. All persons reviewing medical bills on behalf of this insurer are designated to do so or are in training.

5. The course of instruction provided for training of all medical bill reviewers of this insurer and of medical billing entities used by this insurer meets all requirements set forth in Article 20 (commencing with section 2592) of Subchapter 3, Chapter 5, Title 10, California Code of Regulations, and that all medical bill reviewers of this insurer and of medical billing entities used by this insurer have attended training for the required number of hours to be qualified to perform medical bill review.

I certify under the penalty of perjury under the laws of the State of California that the foregoing is true and correct:

________________ ________________

(Date and Place) (Signature)

Name of person certifying (print or type):

Title of person certifying:

Business address:

Note: Authority cited: Section 11761, Insurance Code. Reference: Section 11761, Insurance Code.

History: 1. New section filed 1-23-2006; operative 2-22-2006 (Register 2006, No. 4).

Ref.: Hanna § 2.37[3], [7]; Herlick Handbook § 3.15.

§2592.10. Designation—Claims Adjuster and Medical-Only Claims Adjuster.

CLAIMS ADJUSTER or MEDICAL-ONLY CLAIMS ADJUSTER DESIGNATION

This Designation is awarded to

____

(Adjuster's Name)

for: ☐ **Claims Adjuster** ☐ **Medical-Only Claims Adjuster**

(Check Only One)

as a result of successfully completing the required hours for workers' compensation training pursuant to California Insurance Code Section 11761 and California Code of Regulations, Title 10, Sections 2592.02 and 2592.03

Total Hours of Training Completed:

____

Designation Given By:

____

(Name of Insurance Company, Self-Insured Employer, or Third-Party Administrator)

________________ ________________

(Date) (Signature)

Name of person awarding designation (print or type):

Title of person awarding designation:

Business address:

Note: Authority cited: Section 11761, Insurance Code. Reference: Section 11761, Insurance Code.

History: 1. New section filed 1-23-2006; operative 2-22-2006 (Register 2006, No. 4).

Ref.: Hanna § 2.37[4]; Herlick Handbook § 3.15.

§2592.11. Designation—Medical Bill Reviewer.

MEDICAL BILL REVIEWER DESIGNATION

This Designation is awarded to

____

(Medical Bill Reviewer's Name)

for Medical Bill Reviewer Training

as a result of successfully completing the required hours for workers' compensation training pursuant to California Insurance Code Section 11761 and California Code of Regulations, Title 10, Section 2592.04

Total Hours of Training Completed:

____

Designation Given By:

____

(Name of Insurer or Medical Billing Entity)

________________ ________________

(Date) (Signature)

Name of person awarding designation (print or type):

Title of person awarding designation:

Business address:

Note: Authority cited: Section 11761, Insurance Code. Reference: Section 11761, Insurance Code.

History: 1. New section filed 1-23-2006; operative 2-22-2006 (Register 2006, No. 4).

Ref.: Hanna § 2.37[4]; Herlick Handbook § 3.15.

§2592.12. Designation—Experienced Claims Adjuster and Medical-Only Claims Adjuster.

EXPERIENCED CLAIMS ADJUSTER OR EXPERIENCED MEDICAL-ONLY CLAIMS ADJUSTER DESIGNATION

This Designation is awarded to

____

(Adjuster's Name)

for: ☐ Experienced Claims Adjuster

☐ Experienced Medical-Only Claims Adjuster

(Check Only One)

as a result of meeting the experience requirements for workers' compensation claims experience pursuant to California Insurance Code Section 11761 and California Code of Regulations, Title 10, Sections 2592.01 and 2592.05

Total Years of California Experience At Time of Designation: ________

and/or

Date Completed Examination Pursuant to Title 8, CCR Section 15452: _______

Designation Given By:

____

(Name of Insurance Company, Self-Insured Employer, or Third-Party Administrator)

______________ ______________

(Date) (Signature)

Name of person awarding designation (print or type):

Title of person awarding designation:

Business address:

Note: Authority cited: Section 11761, Insurance Code. Reference: Section 11761, Insurance Code.

History: 1. New section filed 1-23-2006; operative 2-22-2006 (Register 2006, No. 4).

Ref.: Hanna § 2.37[4]; Herlick Handbook § 3.15.

§2592.13. Designation—Experienced Medical Bill Reviewer.

EXPERIENCED MEDICAL BILL REVIEWER DESIGNATION

This Designation is awarded to

____

(Medical Bill Reviewer's Name)

for Experienced Medical Bill Reviewer

as a result of meeting the requirements for workers' compensation medical bill reviewing experience pursuant to California Insurance Code Section 11761 and California Code of Regulations, Title 10, Sections 2592.01 and 2592.05

Total Years of California Experience At Time of Designation: ________

Designation Given By:

____

(Name of Insurer or Medical Billing Entity)

______________ ______________

(Date) (Signature)

Name of person awarding designation (print or type):

Title of person awarding designation:

Business address:

Note: Authority cited: Section 11761, Insurance Code. Reference: Section 11761, Insurance Code.

History: 1. New section filed 1-23-2006; operative 2-22-2006 (Register 2006, No. 4).

Ref.: Hanna § 2.37[4]; Herlick Handbook § 3.15.

§2592.14. Post-Designation Training Form.

POST-DESIGNATION TRAINING FORM

____

(Adjuster's or Medical Bill Reviewer's Name)

☐ **Claims Adjuster**
☐ **Medical-Only Claims Adjuster**
☐ **Medical Bill Reviewer**
(Check Only One)

has successfully completed the post-designation workers' compensation training and hours noted below pursuant to California Insurance Code Section 11761 and California Code of Regulations, Title 10, Sections 2592.02, 2592.03, 2592.04, and 2592.05

Name and Topic of Post-Designation Training Taken:

____

Total Hours of Post-Designation Training Completed: ________

Date of Post-Designation Training:

____

Post-Designation Training Verified By:

____

(Name of Insurer or Medical Billing Entity)

__________________ __________________

(Date) (Signature)

Name of person awarding designation (print or type):

Title of person awarding designation:

Business address:

Note: Authority cited: Section 11761, Insurance Code. Reference: Section 11761, Insurance Code.

History: 1. New section filed 1-23-2006; operative 2-22-2006 (Register 2006, No. 4).

Ref.: Hanna § 2.37[5]; Herlick Handbook § 3.15.

TABLES AND SCHEDULES

Revisions by James T. Stewart*

SYNOPSIS

---

*James T. Stewart is a graduate of the University of California at Berkeley with over 30 years' experience from both the applicant and the defense perspective of California workers' compensation. He is a Legal Assistant or Paralegal with Cole, Fisher, Bosquez-Flores, Cole & O'Keefe in Fresno. He has revised these Tables and Schedules annually since asked to do so for the 1992 edition.

He is the author of the *Work Comp Index*, the *Rehab Index*, and the *SB 899 Index*. Table 14 is adapted from his 1993 *Work Comp Index*. Table 18 is adapted from his *Work Comp Index* and *Rehab Index*. The newest edition of the *Work Comp Index* is the 7th. The 8th is not expected until mid-2010 at the earliest.

If you have questions concerning these tables, or if you would like more information regarding his books, on work days, 8:00 A.M. to 3:00 P.M., call (559) 485-0700, ext 237, or fax (559) 485-3804. On workday evenings, 5:00 P.M. to 8:00 P.M., call or fax (559) 291-3238. The same number may be used on weekends or holidays, but calls may not be returned until the next business day.

e-mail: stewshe@comcast.net

James T. Stewart
c/o Cole, Fisher, Bosquez-Flores, Cole & O'Keefe
P.O. Box 391
Fresno, CA 93708-0391

PART 1. Commutation

TABLE 1

Commutation: Present Value of Permanent Disability

TABLE 1 - PRESENT VALUE OF PERMANENT DISABILITY

Use this table to commute, i.e. determine the present value of permanent disability benefits. The "Wks" column refers to the number of weeks of PD being commuted. The "PV" column contains the present value (PV) at $1 per week of the corresponding number of weeks of PD. A fractional number of weeks of PD may be commuted using interpolation. See Examples A, B and C under Commutation Procedures for an illustration of various types of commutations.

Wks	PV	Wks	PV	Wks	PV	Wks	PV
1	0.9989	45	44.4058	89	86.7442	133	128.0402
2	1.9977	46	45.3801	90	87.6945	134	128.9671
3	2.9955	47	46.3533	91	88.6437	135	129.8930
4	3.9932	48	47.3264	92	89.5929	136	130.8188
5	4.9898	49	48.2985	93	90.5410	137	131.7436
6	5.9864	50	49.2706	94	91.4892	138	132.6684
7	6.9819	51	50.2416	95	92.4362	139	133.5922
8	7.9774	52	51.2125	96	93.3833	140	134.5159
9	8.9717	53	52.1824	97	94.3293	141	135.4386
10	9.9661	54	53.1523	98	95.2753	142	136.3613
11	10.9593	55	54.1210	99	96.2202	143	137.2830
12	11.9525	56	55.0898	100	97.1651	144	138.2047
13	12.9446	57	56.0575	101	98.1090	145	139.1253
14	13.9367	58	57.0252	102	99.0529	146	140.0459
15	14.9277	59	57.9918	103	99.9956	147	140.9655
16	15.9187	60	58.9583	104	100.9384	148	141.8851
17	16.9085	61	59.9238	105	101.8801	149	142.8036
18	17.8984	62	60.8893	106	102.8219	150	143.7221
19	18.8871	63	61.8537	107	103.7625	151	144.6396
20	19.8759	64	62.8181	108	104.7032	152	145.5571
21	20.8635	65	63.7814	109	105.6428	153	146.4736
22	21.8511	66	64.7447	110	106.5823	154	147.3900
23	22.8376	67	65.7069	111	107.5209	155	148.3054
24	23.8241	68	66.6691	112	108.4594	156	149.2209
25	24.8095	69	67.6302	113	109.3968	157	150.1352
26	25.7948	70	68.5914	114	110.3343	158	151.0496
27	26.7791	71	69.5514	115	111.2707	159	151.9630
28	27.7634	72	70.5114	116	112.2071	160	152.8763
29	28.7465	73	71.4704	117	113.1424	161	153.7886
30	29.7297	74	72.4293	118	114.0778	162	154.7009
31	30.7117	75	73.3872	119	115.0121	163	155.6122
32	31.6937	76	74.3450	120	115.9463	164	156.5235
33	32.6747	77	75.3018	121	116.8796	165	157.4337
34	33.6556	78	76.2586	122	117.8128	166	158.3440
35	34.6354	79	77.2143	123	118.7449	167	159.2532
36	35.6152	80	78.1700	124	119.6771	168	160.1624
37	36.5939	81	79.1246	125	120.6082	169	161.0706
38	37.5726	82	80.0792	126	121.5393	170	161.9788
39	38.5502	83	81.0327	127	122.4694	171	162.8859
40	39.5278	84	81.9862	128	123.3994	172	163.7931
41	40.5043	85	82.9387	129	124.3284	173	164.6992
42	41.4808	86	83.8911	130	125.2574	174	165.6054
43	42.4562	87	84.8425	131	126.1854	175	166.5105
44	43.4315	88	85.7939	132	127.1133	176	167.4156

Tables & Schedules

Wks	PV	Wks	PV	Wks	PV	Wks	PV
177	168.3197	231	216.4008	285	263.0333	339	308.2609
178	169.2237	232	217.2776	286	263.8837	340	309.0857
179	170.1268	233	218.1535	287	264.7332	341	309.9096
180	171.0298	234	219.0293	288	265.5827	342	310.7334
181	171.9319	235	219.9042	289	266.4312	343	311.5564
182	172.8339	236	220.7790	290	267.2797	344	312.3793
183	173.7349	237	221.6529	291	268.1272	345	313.2013
184	174.6359	238	222.5268	292	268.9747	346	314.0233
185	175.5359	239	223.3996	293	269.8213	347	314.8444
186	176.4359	240	224.2725	294	270.6679	348	315.6655
187	177.3349	241	225.1444	295	271.5135	349	316.4856
188	178.2339	242	226.0163	296	272.3591	350	317.3057
189	179.1318	243	226.8872	297	273.2038	351	318.1250
190	180.0298	244	227.7581	298	274.0485	352	318.9442
191	180.9267	245	228.6280	299	274.8922	353	319.7625
192	181.8236	246	229.4979	300	275.7359	354	320.5807
193	182.7196	247	230.3669	301	276.5786	355	321.3981
194	183.6155	248	231.2358	302	277.4214	356	322.2155
195	184.5104	249	232.1037	303	278.2632	357	323.0319
196	185.4053	250	232.9717	304	279.1050	358	323.8483
197	186.2992	251	233.8386	305	279.9458	359	324.6638
198	187.1931	252	234.7056	306	280.7866	360	325.4794
199	188.0860	253	235.5716	307	281.6265	361	326.2939
200	188.9789	254	236.4376	308	282.4664	362	327.1085
201	189.8707	255	237.3026	309	283.3054	363	327.9222
202	190.7626	256	238.1676	310	284.1443	364	328.7359
203	191.6535	257	239.0316	311	284.9823	365	329.5486
204	192.5443	258	239.8956	312	285.8203	366	330.3613
205	193.4342	259	240.7586	313	286.6573	367	331.1732
206	194.3240	260	241.6217	314	287.4944	368	331.9850
207	195.2129	261	242.4838	315	288.3305	369	332.7959
208	196.1017	262	243.3458	316	289.1665	370	333.6068
209	196.9896	263	244.2069	317	290.0017	371	334.4168
210	197.8774	264	245.0680	318	290.8368	372	335.2268
211	198.7642	265	245.9281	319	291.6710	373	336.0358
212	199.6511	266	246.7882	320	292.5052	374	336.8449
213	200.5369	267	247.6474	321	293.3385	375	337.6530
214	201.4227	268	248.5065	322	294.1718	376	338.4612
215	202.3075	269	249.3647	323	295.0041	377	339.2684
216	203.1924	270	250.2228	324	295.8364	378	340.0757
217	204.0762	271	251.0800	325	296.6677	379	340.8820
218	204.9600	272	251.9372	326	297.4991	380	341.6883
219	205.8428	273	252.7935	327	298.3295	381	342.4937
220	206.7257	274	253.6497	328	299.1600	382	343.2991
221	207.6075	275	254.5049	329	299.9895	383	344.1036
222	208.4893	276	255.3602	330	300.8190	384	344.9081
223	209.3701	277	256.2145	331	301.6475	385	345.7117
224	210.2510	278	257.0688	332	302.4760	386	346.5153
225	211.1308	279	257.9221	333	303.3037	387	347.3180
226	212.0106	280	258.7754	334	304.1313	388	348.1207
227	212.8894	281	259.6278	335	304.9579	389	348.9224
228	213.7683	282	260.4801	336	305.7846	390	349.7242
229	214.6461	283	261.3315	337	306.6104	391	350.5250
230	215.5239	284	262.1829	338	307.4361	392	351.3259

Wks	PV	Wks	PV	Wks	PV	Wks	PV
393	352.1259	447	394.6693	501	435.9309	555	475.9494
394	352.9258	448	395.4451	502	436.6834	556	476.6792
395	353.7249	449	396.2201	503	437.4350	557	477.4082
396	354.5239	450	396.9951	504	438.1866	558	478.1372
397	355.3220	451	397.7691	505	438.9374	559	478.8653
398	356.1202	452	398.5432	506	439.6882	560	479.5935
399	356.9174	453	399.3165	507	440.4381	561	480.3208
400	357.7147	454	400.0897	508	441.1880	562	481.0481
401	358.5110	455	400.8620	509	441.9371	563	481.7746
402	359.3073	456	401.6344	510	442.6862	564	482.5012
403	360.1028	457	402.4058	511	443.4344	565	483.2268
404	360.8982	458	403.1773	512	444.1826	566	483.9525
405	361.6927	459	403.9479	513	444.9300	567	484.6774
406	362.4873	460	404.7185	514	445.6774	568	485.4022
407	363.2809	461	405.4882	515	446.4239	569	486.1263
408	364.0745	462	406.2579	516	447.1704	570	486.8503
409	364.8673	463	407.0268	517	447.9161	571	487.5735
410	365.6600	464	407.7956	518	448.6618	572	488.2968
411	366.4518	465	408.5636	519	449.4067	573	489.0192
412	367.2437	466	409.3316	520	450.1515	574	489.7416
413	368.0346	467	410.0987	521	450.8955	575	490.4632
414	368.8256	468	410.8658	522	451.6395	576	491.1847
415	369.6156	469	411.6321	523	452.3827	577	491.9055
416	370.4056	470	412.3983	524	453.1258	578	492.6263
417	371.1948	471	413.1637	525	453.8681	579	493.3462
418	371.9839	472	413.9291	526	454.6104	580	494.0662
419	372.7722	473	414.6936	527	455.3519	581	494.7853
420	373.5605	474	415.4581	528	456.0934	582	495.5044
421	374.3478	475	416.2217	529	456.8340	583	496.2228
422	375.1352	476	416.9854	530	457.5747	584	496.9411
423	375.9217	477	417.7481	531	458.3145	585	497.6586
424	376.7081	478	418.5109	532	459.0543	586	498.3761
425	377.4937	479	419.2728	533	459.7932	587	499.0928
426	378.2793	480	420.0347	534	460.5322	588	499.8095
427	379.0640	481	420.7958	535	461.2703	589	500.5254
428	379.8487	482	421.5568	536	462.0084	590	501.2413
429	380.6325	483	422.3170	537	462.7457	591	501.9563
430	381.4163	484	423.0772	538	463.4830	592	502.6714
431	382.1992	485	423.8365	539	464.2194	593	503.3857
432	382.9821	486	424.5959	540	464.9559	594	504.0999
433	383.7641	487	425.3543	541	465.6915	595	504.8134
434	384.5462	488	426.1128	542	466.4271	596	505.5268
435	385.3273	489	426.8704	543	467.1619	597	506.2395
436	386.1085	490	427.6280	544	467.8967	598	506.9521
437	386.8887	491	428.3848	545	468.6306	599	507.6640
438	387.6690	492	429.1415	546	469.3646	600	508.3758
439	388.4484	493	429.8974	547	470.0977	601	509.0868
440	389.2277	494	430.6533	548	470.8308	602	509.7979
441	390.0062	495	431.4084	549	471.5631	603	510.5081
442	390.7847	496	432.1634	550	472.2954	604	511.2183
443	391.5623	497	432.9176	551	473.0269	605	511.9278
444	392.3399	498	433.6718	552	473.7583	606	512.6372
445	393.1167	499	434.4251	553	474.4890	607	513.3458
446	393.8934	500	435.1784	554	475.2196	608	514.0544

Wks	PV	Wks	PV	Wks	PV	Wks	PV
609	514.7622	663	552.4057	717	588.9151	771	624.3245
610	515.4701	664	553.0922	718	589.5809	772	624.9702
611	516.1771	665	553.7779	719	590.2459	773	625.6152
612	516.8841	666	554.4636	720	590.9110	774	626.2602
613	517.5903	667	555.1486	721	591.5753	775	626.9045
614	518.2965	668	555.8335	722	592.2396	776	627.5488
615	519.0019	669	556.5177	723	592.9031	777	628.1924
616	519.7074	670	557.2018	724	593.5667	778	628.8359
617	520.4120	671	557.8852	725	594.2295	779	629.4788
618	521.1166	672	558.5686	726	594.8923	780	630.1216
619	521.8204	673	559.2512	727	595.5543	781	630.7637
620	522.5242	674	559.9339	728	596.2164	782	631.4058
621	523.2273	675	560.6157	729	596.8777	783	632.0472
622	523.9303	676	561.2975	730	597.5390	784	632.6886
623	524.6325	677	561.9786	731	598.1995	785	633.3292
624	525.3347	678	562.6597	732	598.8601	786	633.9699
625	526.0362	679	563.3400	733	599.5199	787	634.6098
626	526.7376	680	564.0203	734	600.1797	788	635.2497
627	527.4382	681	564.6998	735	600.8388	789	635.8889
628	528.1389	682	565.3793	736	601.4978	790	636.5281
629	528.8387	683	566.0581	737	602.1561	791	637.1666
630	529.5386	684	566.7368	738	602.8144	792	637.8051
631	530.2376	685	567.4148	739	603.4720	793	638.4428
632	530.9367	686	568.0928	740	604.1296	794	639.0806
633	531.6349	687	568.7701	741	604.7864	795	639.7176
634	532.3332	688	569.4473	742	605.4432	796	640.3546
635	533.0306	689	570.1237	743	606.0993	797	640.9909
636	533.7281	690	570.8002	744	606.7553	798	641.6272
637	534.4248	691	571.4759	745	607.4107	799	642.2628
638	535.1215	692	572.1516	746	608.0660	800	642.8984
639	535.8174	693	572.8265	747	608.7206	801	643.5333
640	536.5133	694	573.5014	748	609.3752	802	644.1682
641	537.2084	695	574.1756	749	610.0290	803	644.8023
642	537.9035	696	574.8497	750	610.6829	804	645.4365
643	538.5978	697	575.5231	751	611.3360	805	646.0699
644	539.2921	698	576.1965	752	611.9891	806	646.7033
645	539.9856	699	576.8692	753	612.6415	807	647.3360
646	540.6792	700	577.5418	754	613.2938	808	647.9688
647	541.3719	701	578.2137	755	613.9455	809	648.6007
648	542.0646	702	578.8855	756	614.5971	810	649.2327
649	542.7566	703	579.5567	757	615.2480	811	649.8640
650	543.4486	704	580.2278	758	615.8989	812	650.4953
651	544.1397	705	580.8981	759	616.5490	813	651.1259
652	544.8309	706	581.5685	760	617.1992	814	651.7564
653	545.5213	707	582.2381	761	617.8486	815	652.3863
654	546.2117	708	582.9077	762	618.4980	816	653.0162
655	546.9013	709	583.5765	763	619.1467	817	653.6453
656	547.5909	710	584.2453	764	619.7954	818	654.2744
657	548.2797	711	584.9134	765	620.4434	819	654.9029
658	548.9686	712	585.5815	766	621.0913	820	655.5313
659	549.6566	713	586.2488	767	621.7385	821	656.1590
660	550.3447	714	586.9161	768	622.3857	822	656.7867
661	551.0320	715	587.5827	769	623.0322	823	657.4137
662	551.7192	716	588.2493	770	623.6787	824	658.0407

Wks	PV	Wks	PV	Wks	PV	Wks	PV
825	658.6670	879	691.9749	933	724.2793		
826	659.2933	880	692.5824	934	724.8685		
827	659.9189	881	693.1891	935	725.4569		
828	660.5445	882	693.7958	936	726.0454		
829	661.1694	883	694.4019	937	726.6332		
830	661.7943	884	695.0079	938	727.2210		
831	662.4184	885	695.6133	939	727.8081		
832	663.0426	886	696.2187	940	728.3952		
833	663.6661	887	696.8233	941	728.9817		
834	664.2895	888	697.4280	942	729.5681		
835	664.9123	889	698.0320	943	730.1539		
836	665.5350	890	698.6360	944	730.7397		
837	666.1571	891	699.2393	945	731.3249		
838	666.7791	892	699.8426	946	731.9100		
839	667.4005	893	700.4453	947	732.4945		
840	668.0218	894	701.0479	948	733.0789		
841	668.6425	895	701.6498	949	733.6628		
842	669.2631	896	702.2518	950	734.2466		
843	669.8831	897	702.8531				
844	670.5030	898	703.4543				
845	671.1222	899	704.0549				
846	671.7415	900	704.6555				
847	672.3600	901	705.2554				
848	672.9786	902	705.8553				
849	673.5964	903	706.4545				
850	674.2142	904	707.0537				
851	674.8314	905	707.6523				
852	675.4485	906	708.2508				
853	676.0650	907	708.8487				
854	676.6814	908	709.4466				
855	677.2971	909	710.0437				
856	677.9129	910	710.6409				
857	678.5279	911	711.2375				
858	679.1430	912	711.8340				
859	679.7573	913	712.4298				
860	680.3717	914	713.0256				
861	680.9853	915	713.6208				
862	681.5990	916	714.2160				
863	682.2119	917	714.8105				
864	682.8249	918	715.4050				
865	683.4371	919	715.9988				
866	684.0494	920	716.5926				
867	684.6610	921	717.1857				
868	685.2725	922	717.7789				
869	685.8834	923	718.3713				
870	686.4943	924	718.9638				
871	687.1045	925	719.5556				
872	687.7147	926	720.1474				
873	688.3242	927	720.7386				
874	688.9337	928	721.3297				
875	689.5425	929	721.9202				
876	690.1513	930	722.5106				
877	690.7594	931	723.1004				
878	691.3675	932	723.6902				

Tables & Schedules

TABLE 2
Commutation: Present Value of Life Pension for a Male

TABLE 2 - PRESENT VALUE OF LIFE PENSION FOR A MALE

Use this table to commute, i.e. determine the present value (PV) of life pension benefits for a male. The "Age on DOC" column refers to the age of the injured employee as of the date of the commutation. The columns labeled "0, 1, 2, 3. . ." refer to the period of years between the DOC and the commencement of life pension, commonly referred to as the "deferral period". The number at the intersection of the row (representing age) and column (representing deferral period) contains the present value at $1 per week for that combination of age and deferral period. Fractional ages and commencement delays can be accommodated using interpolation. See Examples D, E, and F under Commutation Procedures. This table is based on the U.S. Decennial Life Tables for 1989-91.

Age on DOC	Number of years between date of commutation (DOC) and commencement of life pension														
	0	1	2	3	4	5	6	7	8	9	10	11	12	13	14
15	1401.79	1350.43	1300.62	1252.31	1205.48	1160.07	1116.06	1073.39	1032.04	991.95	953.10	915.45	878.96	843.60	809.32
16	1392.18	1340.83	1291.03	1242.75	1195.94	1150.56	1106.58	1063.94	1022.62	982.57	943.76	906.14	869.68	834.35	800.11
17	1382.60	1331.25	1281.46	1233.20	1186.41	1141.05	1097.09	1054.48	1013.18	973.16	934.37	896.77	860.34	825.04	790.83
18	1372.97	1321.63	1271.85	1223.59	1176.81	1131.47	1087.53	1044.94	1003.66	963.65	924.88	887.30	850.89	815.62	781.44
19	1363.21	1311.87	1262.09	1213.84	1167.08	1121.75	1077.82	1035.24	993.97	953.98	915.22	877.67	841.28	806.02	771.87
20	1353.22	1301.88	1252.11	1203.87	1157.11	1111.80	1067.88	1025.31	984.06	944.08	905.34	867.80	831.44	796.21	762.08
21	1343.02	1291.68	1241.91	1193.68	1146.93	1101.62	1057.71	1015.15	973.91	933.95	895.22	857.71	821.37	786.16	752.07
22	1332.57	1281.23	1231.47	1183.24	1136.50	1091.20	1047.29	1004.74	963.52	923.57	884.86	847.37	811.05	775.88	741.81
23	1321.88	1270.54	1220.78	1172.55	1125.81	1080.52	1036.62	994.08	952.87	912.94	874.25	836.78	800.49	765.35	731.31
24	1310.88	1259.54	1209.78	1161.56	1114.83	1069.53	1025.65	983.12	941.92	902.01	863.35	825.91	789.65	754.54	720.54
25	1299.58	1248.24	1198.48	1150.26	1103.53	1058.25	1014.37	971.86	930.68	890.80	852.16	814.75	778.52	743.44	709.49
26	1287.93	1236.59	1186.83	1138.62	1091.89	1046.62	1002.76	960.28	919.12	879.26	840.65	803.27	767.08	732.04	698.13
27	1275.93	1224.59	1174.84	1126.63	1079.92	1034.67	990.83	948.36	907.23	867.40	828.83	791.49	755.33	720.34	686.47
28	1263.61	1212.27	1162.53	1114.33	1067.63	1022.39	978.57	936.13	895.03	855.23	816.70	779.40	743.29	708.34	674.52
29	1250.98	1199.64	1149.91	1101.72	1055.04	1009.82	966.02	923.61	882.54	842.78	804.28	767.02	730.96	696.06	662.29
30	1238.06	1186.73	1137.00	1088.82	1042.16	996.96	953.19	910.80	869.77	830.04	791.58	754.37	718.35	683.50	649.78
31	1224.84	1173.51	1123.79	1075.63	1028.98	983.80	940.05	897.70	856.70	817.01	778.59	741.42	705.45	670.65	636.99
32	1211.32	1160.00	1110.28	1062.13	1015.50	970.34	926.62	884.30	843.33	803.68	765.31	728.18	692.25	657.51	623.92
33	1197.48	1146.16	1096.45	1048.31	1001.70	956.56	912.87	870.58	829.65	790.03	751.70	714.62	678.76	644.08	610.56
34	1183.31	1131.99	1082.29	1034.17	987.57	942.46	898.80	856.54	815.64	776.07	737.79	700.76	664.96	630.35	596.91
35	1168.82	1117.50	1067.81	1019.70	973.12	928.04	884.40	842.18	801.32	761.79	723.56	686.59	650.85	616.32	582.97
36	1153.99	1102.68	1052.99	1004.90	958.34	913.28	869.68	827.48	786.66	747.18	709.01	672.10	636.45	602.01	568.76
37	1138.83	1087.52	1037.85	989.77	943.23	898.19	854.62	812.46	771.68	732.25	694.14	657.32	621.75	587.41	554.28
38	1123.31	1072.01	1022.34	974.27	927.75	882.74	839.20	797.08	756.35	716.99	678.95	642.21	606.75	572.52	539.51
39	1107.41	1056.11	1006.45	958.40	911.90	866.91	823.40	781.33	740.67	701.38	663.42	626.78	591.43	557.33	524.46
40	1091.11	1039.80	990.16	942.12	895.64	850.69	807.23	765.21	724.62	685.41	647.56	611.03	575.80	541.84	509.13
41	1074.38	1023.09	973.45	925.43	878.98	834.07	790.66	748.72	708.20	669.09	631.35	594.94	559.86	526.06	493.53
42	1057.25	1005.95	956.33	908.33	861.92	817.06	773.72	731.85	691.43	652.43	614.81	578.55	543.63	510.01	477.69
43	1039.71	988.42	938.81	890.84	844.48	799.68	756.41	714.63	674.32	635.44	597.96	561.87	527.13	493.72	461.63
44	1021.80	970.52	920.93	873.00	826.69	781.95	738.77	697.09	656.90	618.16	580.84	544.93	510.40	477.22	445.37
45	1003.55	952.27	902.71	854.82	808.57	763.91	720.82	679.26	639.20	600.61	563.48	527.77	493.46	460.53	428.96
46	984.99	933.72	884.19	836.34	790.15	745.58	702.59	661.16	621.24	582.83	545.90	510.41	476.35	443.70	412.44
47	966.15	914.89	865.39	817.60	771.47	726.99	684.12	642.82	603.07	564.86	528.14	492.89	459.11	426.76	395.84
48	947.04	895.79	846.32	798.58	752.53	708.15	665.41	624.26	584.70	546.69	510.21	475.24	441.76	409.74	379.18
49	927.65	876.42	826.98	779.29	733.33	689.07	646.46	605.49	566.13	528.35	492.14	457.47	424.32	392.67	362.49
50	907.98	856.76	807.36	759.74	713.88	669.74	627.30	586.52	547.38	509.86	473.94	439.60	406.81	375.55	345.79

(Present Value of Life Pension for a Male - con't)

Age on DOC	Number of years between date of commutation (DOC) and commencement of life pension														
	0	1	2	3	4	5	6	7	8	9	10	11	12	13	14
51	888.05	836.85	787.49	739.96	694.21	650.21	607.94	567.37	528.48	491.25	455.65	421.67	389.27	358.43	329.12
52	867.93	816.75	767.44	719.99	674.36	630.53	588.45	548.12	509.50	472.58	437.33	403.73	371.74	341.35	312.52
53	847.65	796.48	747.24	699.88	654.38	610.71	568.85	528.78	490.46	453.88	419.00	385.80	354.26	324.34	296.02
54	827.23	776.08	726.89	679.64	634.29	590.81	549.19	509.39	471.40	435.17	400.70	367.93	336.86	307.45	279.65
55	806.69	755.57	706.45	659.31	614.12	570.85	529.49	489.99	452.34	416.50	382.45	350.15	319.57	290.69	263.46
56	786.06	734.96	685.91	638.90	593.89	550.85	509.76	470.59	433.31	397.88	364.28	332.47	302.42	274.09	247.46
57	765.34	714.27	665.31	618.44	573.62	530.84	490.05	451.22	414.33	379.34	346.21	314.92	285.42	257.69	231.69
58	744.61	693.57	644.71	597.99	553.39	510.86	470.39	431.93	395.45	360.92	328.30	297.54	268.63	241.53	216.22
59	723.94	672.93	624.17	577.61	533.23	490.98	450.84	412.76	376.72	342.67	310.57	280.39	252.11	225.68	201.09
60	703.35	652.39	603.73	557.34	513.18	471.22	431.42	393.75	358.16	324.61	293.07	263.50	235.89	210.18	186.35
61	682.82	631.89	583.34	537.12	493.20	451.55	412.12	374.87	339.75	306.74	275.80	246.89	219.98	195.04	172.00
62	662.31	611.41	562.97	516.94	473.29	431.96	392.91	356.11	321.50	289.07	258.77	230.57	204.43	180.28	158.08
63	641.80	590.95	542.64	496.81	453.43	412.44	373.81	337.48	303.44	271.64	242.03	214.59	189.24	165.94	144.61
64	621.35	570.55	522.37	476.75	433.66	393.03	354.84	319.05	285.61	254.48	225.63	198.98	174.48	152.05	131.62
65	600.97	550.22	502.17	456.78	413.99	373.76	336.06	300.84	268.05	237.66	209.59	183.78	160.15	138.64	119.15
66	580.64	529.94	482.04	436.88	394.43	354.64	317.47	282.87	250.80	221.18	193.94	169.01	146.30	125.73	107.22
67	560.33	509.68	461.93	417.05	374.98	335.68	299.10	265.18	233.86	205.06	178.70	154.69	132.94	113.36	95.86
68	540.05	489.46	441.90	397.33	355.68	316.92	280.98	247.80	217.28	189.35	163.91	140.87	120.12	101.58	85.14
69	519.90	469.38	422.03	377.80	336.63	298.46	263.21	230.79	201.13	174.10	149.63	127.59	107.89	90.43	75.09
70	499.97	449.53	402.42	358.56	317.90	280.36	245.83	214.23	185.45	159.38	135.90	114.92	96.32	79.98	65.75
71	480.35	430.00	383.14	339.69	299.57	262.68	228.91	198.16	170.30	145.22	122.80	102.92	85.46	70.26	57.13
72	461.09	410.84	364.25	321.23	281.68	245.47	212.49	182.61	155.72	131.68	110.37	91.64	75.34	61.27	49.23
73	442.23	392.08	345.77	303.19	264.22	228.72	196.56	167.61	141.74	118.80	98.64	81.09	65.95	53.00	42.05
74	423.71	373.67	327.66	285.54	247.17	212.42	181.14	153.17	128.38	106.60	87.63	71.27	57.27	45.44	35.56
75	405.48	355.54	309.84	268.21	230.50	196.56	166.21	139.31	115.67	95.09	77.33	62.15	49.30	38.58	29.75
76	387.49	337.68	292.31	251.22	214.22	181.15	151.83	126.07	103.64	84.28	67.73	53.73	42.05	32.42	24.61
77	369.79	320.10	275.10	234.59	198.37	166.26	138.05	113.49	92.29	74.17	58.84	46.05	35.51	26.95	20.12
78	352.36	302.83	258.23	218.36	183.02	151.97	124.93	101.60	81.65	64.77	50.69	39.08	29.67	22.15	16.25
79	335.28	285.90	241.76	202.63	168.25	138.32	112.48	80.39	71.72	56.12	43.27	32.85	24.52	17.99	12.97
80	318.61	269.42	225.82	187.50	154.14	125.35	100.74	79.92	62.54	48.22	36.60	27.33	20.05	14.46	10.24
81	302.57	253.60	210.57	173.11	140.78	113.13	89.75	70.23	54.16	41.11	30.69	22.52	16.23	11.50	8.00
82	287.28	238.54	196.10	159.48	128.16	101.68	79.56	61.35	46.57	34.76	25.51	18.39	13.03	9.06	6.19
83	272.73	224.21	182.33	146.53	116.25	90.97	70.14	53.24	39.75	29.16	21.03	14.89	10.36	7.07	4.74
84	258.66	210.35	169.04	134.11	104.94	80.92	61.42	45.85	33.64	24.26	17.18	11.95	8.16	5.47	3.59
85	244.80	196.73	156.08	122.13	94.17	71.48	53.36	39.16	28.23	20.00	13.91	9.50	6.36	4.17	2.68
86	231.26	183.47	143.57	110.70	84.03	62.73	46.03	33.18	23.50	16.35	11.16	7.48	4.91	3.15	1.98
87	218.27	170.80	131.70	99.97	74.63	54.76	39.48	27.96	19.45	13.28	8.89	5.84	3.75	2.35	1.44
88	205.91	158.77	120.52	89.97	66.01	47.59	33.71	23.45	16.01	10.72	7.04	4.52	2.84	1.73	1.03
89	194.15	147.37	110.02	80.72	58.20	41.22	28.68	19.58	13.11	8.60	5.53	3.47	2.12	1.26	0.73
90	183.01	136.62	100.24	72.27	51.19	35.61	24.32	16.28	10.69	6.86	4.31	2.63	1.57	0.91	0.51
91	172.58	126.63	91.29	64.67	44.99	30.72	20.57	13.50	8.67	5.44	3.33	1.98	1.15	0.64	0.35
92	163.03	117.54	83.25	57.92	39.55	26.48	17.38	11.16	7.00	4.28	2.55	1.47	0.83	0.44	0.23
93	154.41	109.37	76.09	51.95	34.79	22.83	14.66	9.20	5.63	3.35	1.94	1.08	0.58	0.30	0.15
94	146.60	101.99	69.64	46.63	30.60	19.65	12.33	7.54	4.49	2.60	1.45	0.78	0.40	0.20	0.09
95	139.36	95.15	63.72	41.81	26.85	16.85	10.31	6.14	3.55	1.99	1.07	0.55	0.27	0.12	0.05

TABLE 3
Commutation: Present Value of Life Pension for a Female

TABLE 3 - PRESENT VALUE OF LIFE PENSION FOR A FEMALE

Use this table to commute, i.e. determine the present value (PV) of life pension benefits for a female. The "Age on DOC" column refers to the age of the injured employee as of the date of the commutation. The columns labeled "0, 1, 2. . . " refer to the period of years between the DOC and the commencement of life pension, commonly referred to as the "deferral period". The number at the intersection of the row (representing age) and column (representing deferral period) contains the present value at $1 per week for that combination of age and deferral period. Fractional ages and commencement delays can be accommodated using interpolation. See Examples D, E, and F under Commutation Procedures. This table is based on the U.S. Decennial Life Tables for 1989-91.

Age on DOC	Number of years between date of commutation (DOC) and commencement of life pension														
	0	1	2	3	4	5	6	7	8	9	10	11	12	13	14
15	1475.06	1423.69	1373.83	1325.44	1278.48	1232.92	1188.70	1145.80	1104.17	1063.77	1024.57	986.54	949.64	913.83	879.09
16	1466.91	1415.54	1365.68	1317.30	1270.35	1224.79	1180.59	1137.69	1096.07	1055.68	1016.49	978.47	941.57	905.78	871.05
17	1458.60	1407.23	1357.38	1309.00	1262.06	1216.50	1172.30	1129.41	1087.80	1047.42	1008.23	970.22	933.33	897.55	862.83
18	1450.11	1398.74	1348.89	1300.52	1253.57	1208.03	1163.83	1120.95	1079.33	1038.96	999.78	961.77	924.90	889.12	854.41
19	1441.41	1390.04	1340.19	1291.81	1244.88	1199.33	1155.14	1112.26	1070.65	1030.28	991.11	953.11	916.24	880.47	845.78
20	1432.45	1381.08	1331.24	1282.87	1235.93	1190.39	1146.20	1103.32	1061.72	1021.36	982.20	944.20	907.34	871.59	836.90
21	1423.26	1371.89	1322.04	1273.67	1226.74	1181.20	1137.02	1094.14	1052.55	1012.19	973.03	935.05	898.20	862.46	827.79
22	1413.81	1362.44	1312.59	1264.22	1217.29	1171.76	1127.58	1084.71	1043.12	1002.77	963.62	925.65	888.81	853.08	818.43
23	1404.09	1352.73	1302.88	1254.52	1207.59	1162.05	1117.88	1075.01	1033.43	993.09	953.95	915.99	879.17	843.45	808.82
24	1394.10	1342.73	1292.89	1244.52	1197.60	1152.07	1107.89	1065.04	1023.46	983.13	944.01	906.06	869.25	833.56	798.94
25	1383.82	1332.45	1282.60	1234.24	1187.32	1141.79	1097.63	1054.78	1013.21	972.89	933.78	895.85	859.06	823.38	788.78
26	1373.23	1321.86	1272.02	1223.66	1176.74	1131.22	1087.06	1044.22	1002.67	962.36	923.27	885.35	848.58	812.93	778.35
27	1362.34	1310.97	1261.13	1212.77	1165.86	1120.35	1076.20	1033.37	991.83	951.54	912.46	874.57	837.82	802.19	767.64
28	1351.13	1299.77	1249.93	1201.58	1154.67	1109.17	1065.03	1022.22	980.69	940.42	901.36	863.49	826.76	791.16	756.64
29	1339.64	1288.28	1238.44	1190.10	1143.20	1097.71	1053.58	1010.78	969.27	929.02	889.98	852.13	815.43	779.85	745.37
30	1327.86	1276.49	1226.66	1178.32	1131.43	1085.95	1041.83	999.05	957.56	917.32	878.31	840.48	803.81	768.27	733.82
31	1315.77	1264.41	1214.58	1166.25	1119.37	1073.90	1029.79	987.02	945.55	905.34	866.35	828.55	791.91	756.40	721.99
32	1303.38	1252.02	1202.20	1153.87	1107.00	1061.54	1017.45	974.70	933.24	893.05	854.09	816.32	779.71	744.24	709.88
33	1290.68	1239.32	1189.50	1141.18	1094.31	1048.86	1004.79	962.06	920.62	880.46	841.52	803.79	767.22	731.79	697.48
34	1277.65	1226.29	1176.47	1128.16	1081.30	1035.87	991.81	949.10	907.69	867.55	828.65	790.95	754.43	719.05	684.79
35	1264.28	1212.92	1163.11	1114.80	1067.96	1022.54	978.50	935.81	894.43	854.32	815.45	777.80	741.32	706.00	671.81
36	1250.57	1199.21	1149.41	1101.11	1054.28	1008.87	964.86	922.19	880.84	840.77	801.94	764.34	727.92	692.66	658.54
37	1236.51	1185.16	1135.36	1087.07	1040.25	994.87	950.87	908.24	866.92	826.89	788.11	750.56	714.21	679.02	644.97
38	1222.12	1170.76	1120.97	1072.69	1025.89	980.53	936.56	893.95	852.67	812.69	773.97	736.48	700.20	665.09	631.13
39	1207.37	1156.02	1106.24	1057.97	1011.19	965.84	921.90	879.33	838.10	798.17	759.51	722.09	685.88	650.87	617.01
40	1192.28	1140.93	1091.15	1042.90	996.13	950.82	906.91	864.38	823.20	783.33	744.73	707.40	671.28	636.36	602.61
41	1176.83	1125.48	1075.71	1027.48	980.73	935.45	891.58	849.10	807.97	768.17	729.65	692.40	656.38	621.57	587.95
42	1161.02	1109.68	1059.92	1011.70	964.99	919.74	875.91	833.49	792.43	752.69	714.27	677.11	641.20	606.51	573.02
43	1144.87	1093.54	1043.79	995.59	948.90	903.69	859.92	817.56	776.56	736.92	698.58	661.54	625.75	591.19	557.84
44	1128.37	1077.04	1027.31	979.13	932.48	887.31	843.60	801.30	760.39	720.84	682.61	645.68	610.02	575.61	542.41
45	1111.55	1060.22	1010.51	962.36	915.75	870.63	826.98	784.76	743.94	704.48	666.37	629.57	594.05	559.79	526.77
46	1094.42	1043.10	993.40	945.28	898.71	853.65	810.07	767.93	727.20	687.86	649.88	613.21	577.85	543.76	510.92
47	1076.99	1025.68	976.00	927.92	881.39	836.39	792.89	750.84	710.22	671.00	633.14	596.63	561.43	527.52	494.89
48	1059.29	1007.98	958.32	910.27	863.80	818.87	775.44	733.49	692.98	653.89	616.18	579.83	544.81	511.10	478.69
49	1041.29	989.99	940.36	892.35	845.93	801.07	757.73	715.88	675.50	636.54	598.99	562.81	527.99	494.51	462.32
50	1023.01	971.72	922.10	874.14	827.78	783.00	739.76	698.02	657.77	618.96	581.58	545.60	511.00	477.74	445.81

(Present Value of Life Pension for a Female - con't)

Age on DOC	Number of years between date of commutation (DOC) and commencement of life pension														
	0	1	2	3	4	5	6	7	8	9	10	11	12	13	14
51	1004.44	953.16	903.58	855.66	809.37	764.67	721.53	679.92	639.81	601.17	563.98	528.21	493.83	460.82	429.16
52	985.64	934.37	884.82	836.95	790.73	746.12	703.09	661.61	621.65	583.20	546.21	510.66	476.52	443.78	412.41
53	966.59	915.33	865.81	818.00	771.85	727.34	684.43	643.09	603.31	565.04	528.27	492.96	459.09	426.63	395.56
54	947.30	896.05	846.57	798.81	752.74	708.33	665.56	624.38	584.78	546.72	510.18	475.12	441.53	409.37	378.63
55	927.76	876.52	827.07	779.38	733.40	689.11	646.47	605.47	566.07	528.23	491.93	457.15	423.86	392.03	361.63
56	907.96	856.74	807.33	759.70	713.82	669.66	627.18	586.37	547.17	509.58	473.55	439.06	406.08	374.59	344.57
57	887.93	836.72	787.36	739.81	694.04	650.02	607.71	567.09	528.13	490.79	455.04	420.87	388.23	357.11	327.49
58	867.69	816.50	767.19	719.73	674.08	630.21	588.09	547.68	508.96	471.89	436.45	402.60	370.33	339.61	310.43
59	847.31	796.14	746.89	699.52	653.99	610.28	568.34	528.16	489.70	452.92	417.80	384.31	352.43	322.14	293.43
60	826.80	775.65	726.45	679.17	633.77	590.23	548.50	508.55	470.36	433.88	399.10	366.00	334.55	304.73	276.52
61	806.13	755.00	705.86	658.68	613.42	570.05	528.54	488.84	450.93	414.79	380.38	347.69	316.70	287.39	259.73
62	785.28	734.18	685.10	638.03	592.92	549.74	508.45	469.02	431.43	395.64	361.64	329.41	298.92	270.15	243.07
63	764.26	713.18	664.18	617.22	572.27	529.29	488.24	449.11	411.85	376.46	342.91	311.17	281.22	253.03	226.57
64	743.09	692.03	643.11	596.27	551.49	508.72	467.94	429.13	392.25	357.29	324.22	293.01	263.64	236.08	210.28
65	721.77	670.74	621.89	575.19	530.58	488.05	447.57	409.11	372.64	338.15	305.61	274.97	246.22	219.32	194.23
66	700.30	649.30	600.54	553.97	509.56	467.30	427.14	389.07	353.05	319.07	287.09	257.07	228.98	202.79	178.47
67	678.66	627.69	579.02	532.61	488.43	446.45	406.66	369.02	333.50	300.08	268.70	239.34	211.96	186.54	163.06
68	656.86	605.92	557.36	511.12	467.20	425.56	386.17	349.00	314.02	281.19	250.46	221.81	195.21	170.64	148.07
69	634.95	584.06	535.61	489.58	445.94	404.67	365.72	329.06	294.66	262.46	232.44	204.56	178.82	155.17	133.57
70	613.01	562.16	513.85	468.05	424.73	383.85	345.38	309.26	275.47	243.96	214.70	187.68	162.86	140.20	119.64
71	591.10	540.30	492.14	446.59	403.61	363.15	325.18	289.65	256.52	225.76	197.34	171.24	147.41	125.80	106.35
72	569.26	518.52	470.52	425.24	382.62	342.61	305.17	270.26	237.85	207.92	180.42	155.31	132.54	112.05	93.75
73	547.52	496.85	449.03	404.02	361.78	322.24	285.38	251.16	219.55	190.51	164.00	139.96	118.32	98.99	81.91
74	525.89	475.27	427.64	382.92	341.08	302.06	265.84	232.38	201.65	173.59	148.14	125.23	104.78	86.69	70.87
75	504.31	453.76	406.32	361.92	320.52	282.08	246.58	213.97	184.19	157.19	132.88	111.18	91.99	75.20	60.67
76	482.73	432.25	385.02	340.98	300.09	262.32	227.63	195.95	167.23	141.37	118.28	97.86	80.00	64.55	51.35
77	461.16	410.77	363.78	320.16	279.86	242.85	209.05	178.41	150.82	126.19	104.41	85.35	68.86	54.78	42.92
78	439.67	389.38	342.69	299.56	259.94	223.77	190.96	161.43	135.07	111.75	91.35	73.71	58.64	45.94	35.43
79	418.43	368.26	321.91	279.33	240.46	205.21	173.48	145.15	120.09	98.17	79.21	63.01	49.37	38.07	28.87
80	397.59	347.55	301.58	259.61	221.56	187.30	156.71	129.66	105.99	85.52	68.03	53.30	41.10	31.17	23.24
81	377.23	327.34	281.79	240.48	203.30	170.09	140.73	115.04	92.82	73.84	57.86	44.61	33.84	25.23	18.47
82	357.39	307.65	262.55	221.95	185.71	153.65	125.60	101.34	80.62	63.17	48.71	36.94	27.54	20.16	14.48
83	338.06	288.51	243.89	204.06	168.84	138.02	111.36	88.59	69.41	53.52	40.59	30.26	22.16	15.92	11.21
84	319.25	269.88	225.81	186.83	152.72	123.23	98.03	76.81	59.22	44.92	33.49	24.52	17.61	12.40	8.56
85	300.95	251.80	208.33	170.30	137.41	109.31	85.65	66.04	50.09	37.34	27.34	19.64	13.83	9.54	6.44
86	283.27	234.38	191.59	154.59	122.98	96.35	74.30	56.35	42.01	30.76	22.09	15.56	10.73	7.25	4.78
87	266.38	217.76	175.70	139.77	109.51	84.44	64.05	47.75	34.96	25.11	17.68	12.20	8.24	5.43	3.49
88	250.27	201.93	160.64	125.86	97.05	73.61	54.88	40.18	28.86	20.32	14.02	9.46	6.24	4.02	2.51
89	234.86	186.83	146.39	112.88	85.61	63.82	46.73	33.57	23.64	16.31	11.01	7.26	4.67	2.92	1.77
90	220.16	172.49	133.01	100.88	75.21	55.06	39.55	27.85	19.21	12.97	8.56	5.50	3.44	2.09	1.23
91	206.39	159.15	120.71	89.99	65.89	47.33	33.33	22.99	15.52	10.24	6.58	4.12	2.50	1.47	0.83
92	193.80	146.99	109.58	80.23	57.63	40.58	28.00	18.90	12.47	8.02	5.02	3.04	1.79	1.01	0.54
93	182.30	135.91	99.51	71.48	50.33	34.72	23.44	15.46	9.95	6.22	3.78	2.21	1.25	0.67	0.34
94	171.64	125.66	90.26	63.56	43.85	29.60	19.53	12.56	7.86	4.77	2.80	1.58	0.85	0.43	0.20
95	161.63	116.10	81.76	56.40	38.08	25.12	16.15	10.11	6.13	3.60	2.03	1.09	0.55	0.26	0.10

TABLE 4
Commutation: Instructions with Examples

COMMUTATION INSTRUCTIONS

The following examples illustrate various methods of commuting permanent disability and life pension benefits. Examples A, B and C apply to permanent disability and utilize Table 1, "Present Value of Fixed Annuity at 3% Interest". Examples D, E and F apply to life pension and utilize Tables 2 and 3 (for males and females respectively), "Present Value of Lifetime Annuity at 3% Interest..."

EXAMPLE A: COMMUTATION OF ALL REMAINING PD

In this example, all PD due for the period after the date of commutation is commuted.

Assumed facts for Example A:

Date of injury: 4/10/96
PD commencement date: 2/20/98
Date of commutation (DOC): 5/14/99

PD rating: 65%
Weekly PD rate: $164
Number of weeks of indemnity corresponding to 65% PD: 386.25

1) Determine weeks of PD remaining after date of commutation (DOC).

a)	#days from PD commencement through DOC inclusive..........	449
b)	Divide by 7 days/week..........	÷ 7
c)	#weeks from PD commencement through DOC..........	64.1429
d)	Total weeks of PD	386.2500
e)	Subtract weeks elapsed through DOC (from 1c)..........	– 64.1429
f)	Weeks of PD remaining after date of commutation..........	322.1071

2) Determine PV of weeks of PD remaining after DOC (1f).

a)	PV of #weeks just above 1f* (PV of 323 wks)..........	295.0041
b)	Subtract next lower PV from table* (PV of 322 wks)..........	–294.1718
c)	Difference of 2a and 2b..........	.8323
d)	Multiply by fractional portion of 1f..........	× .1071
e)	PV of fractional week..........	.0891
f)	Add 2b	+ 294.1718
g)	PV of weeks remaining after DOC..........	294.2609

* Values for 2a and 2b taken from PV column of Table 1.

(continued on next page)

(Example A continued)

3) Determine commuted value of all PD due for period after DOC.

a)	PV of weeks remaining after DOC (from 2g)...........................	294.2609
b)	Multiply by PD rate..	× 164
c)	Commuted value of all PD due for period after DOC................	$48,258.79

Summary of Example A:

- On date of commutation (DOC), $48,258.79 would be due and payable. This is the commuted value of all remaining PD. If payment is made at a later date, interest at 10% per annum is due for the period from DOC to date of actual payment. For example, if the payment in this instance is made on 5/26/99, i.e. twelve days after the date of commutation, interest of $158.66 would be due calculated as follows: 48,258.79 X 12 X .1 ÷ 365*.

  * The formula for calculation of interest is:
  (Commuted value) X (#Days between DOC and payment date) X .1 ÷ 365

EXAMPLE B: COMMUTATION OF PD "OFF THE FAR END" TO PRODUCE A SPECIFIC LUMP SUM

In this example, sufficient monies are to be commuted off the far end of the PD award to produce a payment on the date of commutation of $11,500. All facts are identical to those used in Example A. The calculation of the number of weeks of PD remaining after DOC used in this example is illustrated in step 1 of Example A. The calculation of the PV of weeks remaining after DOC used in this example is illustrated in step 2 of Example A.

Assumed facts:

Date of injury: 4/10/96
PD commencement date: 2/20/98
Date of commutation (DOC): 5/14/99

PD rating: 65%
Weekly PD rate: $164
Number of weeks of indemnity corresponding to 65% PD: 386.25

Weeks of PD remaining after DOC (1f from Example A): 322.1071
PV of weeks remaining after DOC (2g from Example A): 294.2609

1) Determine PV (at $1/week) of amount to be commuted.

a)	Amount to be commuted..	11,500
b)	Divide by weekly PD rate..	÷ 164
c)	PV of amount to be commuted...	70.1220

(continued on next page)

Tables & Schedules

(Example B continued)

2) Determine PV of weeks remaining after commutation off far end.

a)	PV of weeks remaining after DOC (2g from Ex. A)...............	294.2609
b)	Subtract PV of amount to be commuted (1c from above).........	– 70.1220
c)	PV of weeks remaining after commutation off far end..............	224.1389

3) Determine number of weeks of PD remaining after commutation off far end.

a)	PV just above 2c* (corresponding to 240 wks PD)................	224.2725
b)	Subtract PV just below 2c* (corresp. to 239 wks PD).............	– 223.3996
c)	Difference of 3a and 3b (PV of 240th week)..........................	.8729

*Values for 3a and 3b taken from PV column of Table 1.

d)	PV of weeks remaining after commut. off far end (2c).............	224.1389
e)	Subtract 3b (PV of 239 weeks)..	– 223.3996
f)	Difference of 3d and 3e..	.7393
g)	Divide by 3c (PV of 240th week)...	÷ .8729
h)	Proportional amount of 240th week..	.8469
i)	Add to 239 weeks..	+ 239.0000
j)	#weeks PD remaining after commutation off far end...............	239.8469

4) Determine amount of PD due after commutation off far end.

a)	#weeks PD remaining after commutation off far end (3j)..........	239.8469
b)	Multiply by PD rate..	× 164
c)	PD still owed for period after DOC...	$39,334.89

5) Determine number of weeks of PD eliminated from the far end.

a)	# weeks PD before commut. off far end (1f from Ex. A)..........	322.1071
b)	Subtract #weeks PD remaining after commut. (3j).................	– 239.8469
c)	#weeks PD eliminated from far end...	82.2602

Summary of Example B:

- On date of commutation (DOC), $11,500 would be due and payable. If payment is made after the DOC, interest is due at 10% per annum. See Summary of Example A for interest calculation.
- Following the payment of $11,500, the claims administrator would still owe 239.8469 weeks of PD (3j) payable on a biweekly basis in the total amount of $39,334.89 (4c).
- The number of weeks of PD eliminated from the far end as a result of the commutation would be 82.2602 (5c).

(Continued on next page)

EXAMPLE C: COMMUTATION OF PD BY UNIFORM REDUCTION OF PAYMENTS

In this example, sufficient monies are commuted by uniform reduction of all future payments of PD to produce a payment on the date of commutation of $11,500. All facts from Example A apply here. The calculation of number of weeks of PD remaining after DOC used in this example is illustrated in step 1 of Example A. The calculation of PV of remaining weeks used in this example is illustrated in step 2 of Example A.

Assumed facts:

Date of injury: 4/10/96
PD commencement date: 2/20/98
Date of commutation (DOC): 5/14/99

PD rating: 65%
Weekly PD rate: $164
Number of weeks of indemnity corresponding to 65% PD: 386.25

Lump sum to be paid on DOC: $11,500
Number of weeks of PD remaining after DOC (1f from Example A): 322.1071
PV of weeks of PD remaining after DOC (2g from Ex. A): 294.2609

1) Determine amount of reduction required to produce lump sum

a)	Amount desired to be commuted..	$11,500
b)	Divide by PV of remaining weeks (2g from Ex. A)...............	÷ 294.2609
c)	Amount of reduction after rounding to nearest whole cent..........	$39.08

2) Determine new PD rate after reduction

a)	Weekly PD rate	164.00
b)	Subtract amount of reduction (1c)..	− 39.08
c)	New PD rate after reduction..	$124.92

3) Determine amount of PD still owed for period after DOC

a)	#weeks of PD remaining after DOC (1f from Example A).......	322.1071
b)	Multiply by new PD rate after reduction (2c).........................	× 124.92
c)	Amount of PD still owed for period after DOC.......................	$40,237.62

Summary of Example C:

- On date of commutation (DOC), $11,500 would be due and payable. If payment is made after DOC, interest is due at 10% per annum. See Summary of Example A for interest calculation.
- As a result of the commutation, payments for the period following the DOC would be due at the reduced weekly rate of $124.92 (2c).
- Following the payment of $11,500, the balance of PD benefits owed would be 322.1071 weeks payable on a biweekly basis in the total amount of $40,237.62 (3c).

(Continued on next page)

Tables & Schedules

EXAMPLE D - COMMUTATION OF ALL REMAINING LIFE PENSION AFTER LIFE PENSION HAS COMMENCED

In this example, the commutation occurs after the commencement of life pension. On the date of commutation, all life pension indemnity owed for the period thereafter is commuted.

Assumed facts for Example D:

Date of birth (DOB): 8/25/45
Date of injury: 4/10/87
Life pension commencement date: 3/21/98
Date of commutation: 5/14/99

Life pension rate: $33.92
Gender: male

1) Determine exact age on date of commutation.

a)	Number of days from DOB through DOC*............................	19620
b)	Divide by number of days per year......................................	÷ 365.24
c)	Exact age on date of commutation..	53.718

* Note that in determining exact age, the actual date of birth is not counted as the first day of the period. That is, an individual does not become one day old until the day after the DOB. This differs from the determination of the number of days for a period of benefits when the commencement date is counted as the first day of the period. See, for example, step 1a of Example A.

2) Determine PV of life pension as of exact age on DOC

a)	PV for age in table below 1c* (age 53)..................................	847.65
b)	PV for age in table above 1c (age 54)*..................................	– 827.23
c)	Difference of 2a and 2b..	20.42
d)	Multiply by fractional portion of age from 1c..........................	× .718
e)	Interpolation adjustment for 2d..	14.66
f)	PV for age in table below 1c* (from 2a above)........................	847.65
g)	Subtract 2e	– 14.66
h)	PV of life pension as of exact age on DOC..............................	832.99

* Value taken from column titled "Immed." in Table 2. [A note to our readers from LexisNexis Matthew Bender: "Immed." means the column in Table 2 labeled "0" years between DOC and the start of the life pension.]

3) Determine commuted value of all life pension indemnity due after DOC

a)	PV of life pension as of exact age on DOC (from 2h)..............	832.99
b)	Multiply by life pension rate..	× 33.92
c)	Commuted value of all life pension due after DOC	$28.255.02

(Continued on next page)

(Example D continued)

Summary of Example D:

- On date of commutation, $28,255.02, the commuted value of all life pension indemnity for the period after DOC, would be due and payable(3c). No further life pension indemnity would be due. If payment was made after DOC, interest would be due at 10% per annum. See Summary of Example A for interest calculation.

EXAMPLE E - COMMUTATION OF ALL LIFE PENSION INDEMNITY PRIOR TO COMMENCEMENT OF LIFE PENSION

In this example, the commutation of all life pension is done prior to commencement of life pension while the injured worker is still receiving PD. Calculation of exact age at DOC used in this example is illustrated in step 1 of Example†D.

Assumed facts for Example E:

Date of birth: 8/25/45
Date of injury: 4/10/96
PD commencement: 11/15/97
Date of commutation (DOC): 5/14/99

Total weeks of PD: 525.50 (based on 81% PD rating)
Life pension rate: $65.42
Gender: female
Exact age on DOC (from 1c of Example D): 53.718

1) Determine number of years between date of commutation (DOC) and commencement of life pension.

a)	Total weeks of PD		525.5
b)	Multiply by 7 days per week		× 7
c)	Total days of PD	3678.5	
d)	Subtract #days from PD commence through DOC inclusive		– 546.0
e)	Number of days from DOC to LP commencement		3132.5
f)	Divide by 365.24 days/year		÷ 365.24
g)	Period in years from DOC to start of LP*		8.577

* This is the period for which the commencement of LP is "deferred". It determines which columns are used in Tables 2 (for males) or 3 (for females). In this example, you would use columns entitled "Year 8" and "Year 9" in Table 3.

Tables & Schedules

(Continued on next page)

(Example E continued)

2) Determine PV of life pension for exact age at date of commutation (53.718 years from 1c of Example D) and for exact deferral period (8.577 years from†2g above).

a)	PV for age 53 deferred 8 years (from Table 3)......................	603.31
b)	Subtract PV for age 54 deferred 8 years (from Table 3)..........	584.78
c)	Difference of 2a and 2b..	18.53
d)	Multiply by fractional portion of age at DOC..........................	× .718
e)	Interpolation adjustment for age..	13.30
f)	PV for age 53 deferred 8 years (from Table 3)......................	603.31
g)	Subtract PV for age 53 deferred 9 years (from Table 3)..........	– 565.04
h)	Difference of 2f and 2g..	38.27
i)	Multiply by fractional portion of deferral period (from 1g)..........	× .577
j)	Interpolation adjustment for deferral period............................	22.08
k)	PV for age 53 deferred 8 years (from 2a).............................	603.31
l)	Subtract sum of 2e and 2j..	– 35.38
m)	PV of life pension (for age 53.718 deferred 8.577 years)..........	567.93

3) Determine commuted value of all LP as of DOC

a)	PV of life pension (from 2m)..	567.93
b)	Multiply by LP rate..	× 65.42
c)	Commuted value of all life pension......................................	$37,153.98

Summary of Example E:

- On date of commutation (DOC), $37,153.98, the commuted value of all life pension indemnity (3c), would be due and payable. No life pension would be due thereafter. (This amount would not include the commuted value of any future PD indemnity. If payment were made after DOC, interest would be due at 10% per annum. See Summary of Example A for interest calculation. To commute future PD, use the method illustrated in Example A.)

(Continued on next page)

EXAMPLE F - COMMUTATION OF PORTION OF REMAINING LIFE PENSION (LP) AFTER LP COMMENCEMENT BY UNIFORM REDUCTION OF LIFE PENSION PAYMENTS

In this example, the commutation of a portion of life pension is done after LP commencement. Sufficient monies are commuted through uniform reduction of payments from remaining life pension to produce an amount payable on the date of commutation of $11,500.

Assumed facts for Example F:

Date of birth (DOB): 8/25/45
Date of injury: 4/10/87
Life pension commencement date: 3/21/98
Date of commutation (DOC): 5/14/99

Life pension rate: $33.92
Gender: female
Lump sum to be paid on DOC: $11,500

1) Determine exact age on date of commutation.

a)	Number of days from DOB through DOC*..........................	19620
b)	Divide by number of days per year..................................	÷ 365.24
c)	Exact age on date of commutation.....................................	53.718

* Note that in determining exact age, the actual date of birth is not counted as the first day of the period. That is, an individual does not become one day old until the day after the DOB. This differs from the determination of the number of days for a period of benefits when the commencement date is counted as the first day of the period. See, for example, step 1a of Example A.

2) Determine PV of life pension as of exact age on DOC

a)	PV for age in table below 1c* (age 53)................................	966.59
b)	PV for age in table above 1c (age 54)*...............................	– 947.30
c)	Difference of 2a and 2b..	19.29
d)	Multiply by fractional portion of age from 1c.........................	× .718
e)	Interpolation adjustment for 2d..	13.85
f)	PV for age in table below 1c* (from 2a above)......................	966.59
g)	Subtract 2e	– 13.85
h)	PV of life pension as of exact age on DOC..........................	952.74

* Value taken from column titled "Immed." in Table 3.

(Example F continued on next page)

Tables & Schedules

(Example F continued)

3) Calculate amount of reduction in LP rate necessary to produce desired lump sum.

a)	Amount to be commuted..	$11,500
b)	Divide by PV of LP (2h from above)...................................	÷ 952.74
c)	Amount of weekly reduction in LP (after rounding).................	$12.07

4) Calculate LP rate after commutation.

a)	LP rate before commutation...	$33.92
b)	Subtract weekly reduction in LP (from 3c above)...................	– $12.07
c)	LP rate after commutation..	$21.85

Summary of Example F:

- On date of commutation, $11,500 would be due and payable. If payment were made after DOC, interest would be due at 10% per annum. See Summary of Example A for interest calculation.
- The life pension, when due, would be paid at the reduced rate of $21.85.

[Editor's Note: Several persons have asked for a method to commute a given percentage of remaining life pension. The following is a method contributed by James T. Stewart using the "Assumed facts for Example F," supra, however, instead of commuting $11,500 from the LP, assume instead 12% has been ordered commuted from the life pension for, e.g., attorney's fees. The example is the same through step 2). This method may be employed for any ongoing life pension or 100% PD award.

3) Calculate amount of reduction in LP rate assuming 12% is commuted.

a)	PV of LP from 2) h), supra, ...	952.74
b)	Multiply by $33.92 LP rate before commutation	× $33.92
c)	Present value of all remaining LP (~, supra D) ...	$32,316.94
d)	Multiply by 12%, reduced to a decimal, 0.12	× 0.12
e)	Commuted amount to paid to attorney	$3,878.03

4) Recalculation of LP rate after commutation of 12% $33.92

a)	Multiply LP by 12%	× 0.12
b)	Amount each future LP payment is reduced	$4.07
c)	Future payments of LP will be made at $33.92 - 4.07 = $29.85 [An alternate way would be to multiply $33.92 by 0.88 = $29.85]	

PART 2. Interest

TABLE 5
Interest: Ten Percent Annually (One Lump Sum Due)

Labor Code §5800; Code of Civil Procedure §685.010

Days	Interest	Days	Interest	Days	Interest
1	0.000274	61	0.016712	121	0.033151
2	0.000548	62	0.016986	122	0.033425
3	0.000822	63	0.017260	123	0.033699
4	0.001096	64	0.017534	124	0.033973
5	0.001370	65	0.017808	125	0.034247
6	0.001644	66	0.018082	126	0.034521
7	0.001918	67	0.018356	127	0.034795
8	0.002192	68	0.018630	128	0.035068
9	0.002466	69	0.018904	129	0.035342
10	0.002740	**70**	0.019178	**130**	0.035616
11	0.003014	71	0.019452	131	0.035890
12	0.003288	72	0.019726	132	0.036164
13	0.003562	73	0.020000	133	0.036438
14	0.003836	74	0.020274	134	0.036712
15	0.004110	75	0.020548	135	0.036986
16	0.004384	76	0.020822	136	0.037260
17	0.004658	77	0.021096	137	0.037534
18	0.004932	78	0.021370	138	0.037808
19	0.005205	79	0.021644	139	0.038082
20	0.005479	**80**	0.021918	**140**	0.038356
21	0.005753	81	0.022192	141	0.038630
22	0.006027	82	0.022466	142	0.038904
23	0.006301	83	0.022740	143	0.039178
24	0.006575	84	0.023014	144	0.039452
25	0.006849	85	0.023288	145	0.039726
26	0.007123	86	0.023562	146	0.040000
27	0.007397	87	0.023836	147	0.040274
28	0.007671	88	0.024110	148	0.040548
29	0.007945	89	0.024384	149	0.040822
30	0.008219	**90**	0.024658	**150**	0.041096
31	0.008493	91	0.024932	151	0.041370
32	0.008767	92	0.025205	152	0.041644
33	0.009041	93	0.025479	153	0.041918
34	0.009315	94	0.025753	154	0.042192
35	0.009589	95	0.026027	155	0.042466
36	0.009863	96	0.026301	156	0.042740
37	0.010137	97	0.026575	157	0.043014
38	0.010411	98	0.026849	158	0.043288
39	0.010685	99	0.027123	159	0.043562
40	0.010959	**100**	0.027397	**160**	0.043836
41	0.011233	101	0.027671	161	0.044110
42	0.011507	102	0.027945	162	0.044384
43	0.011781	103	0.028219	163	0.044658
44	0.012055	104	0.028493	164	0.044932
45	0.012329	105	0.028767	165	0.045205
46	0.012603	106	0.029041	166	0.045479
47	0.012877	107	0.029315	167	0.045753
48	0.013151	108	0.029589	168	0.046027
49	0.013425	109	0.029863	169	0.046301
50	0.013699	**110**	0.030137	**170**	0.046575
51	0.013973	111	0.030411	171	0.046849
52	0.014247	112	0.030685	172	0.047123
53	0.014521	113	0.030959	173	0.047397
54	0.014795	114	0.031233	174	0.047671
55	0.015068	115	0.031507	175	0.047945
56	0.015342	116	0.031781	176	0.048219
57	0.015616	117	0.032055	177	0.048493
58	0.015890	118	0.032329	178	0.048767
59	0.016164	119	0.032603	179	0.049041
60	0.016438	**120**	0.032877	**180**	0.049315

Days	Interest	Days	Interest	Days	Interest
181	0.049589	243	0.066575	305	0.083562
182	0.049863	244	0.066849	306	0.083836
183	0.050137	245	0.067123	307	0.084110
184	0.050411	246	0.067397	308	0.084384
185	0.050685	247	0.067671	309	0.084658
186	0.050959	248	0.067945	**310**	0.084932
187	0.051233	249	0.068219	311	0.085205
188	0.051507	**250**	0.068493	312	0.085479
189	0.051781	251	0.068767	313	0.085753
190	0.052055	252	0.069041	314	0.086027
191	0.052329	253	0.069315	315	0.086301
192	0.052603	254	0.069589	316	0.086575
193	0.052877	255	0.069863	317	0.086849
194	0.053151	256	0.070137	318	0.087123
195	0.053425	257	0.070411	319	0.087397
196	0.053699	258	0.070685	**320**	0.087671
197	0.053973	259	0.070959	321	0.087945
198	0.054247	**260**	0.071233	322	0.088219
199	0.054521	261	0.071507	323	0.088493
200	0.054795	262	0.071781	324	0.088767
201	0.055068	263	0.072055	325	0.089041
202	0.055342	264	0.072329	326	0.089315
203	0.055616	265	0.072603	327	0.089589
204	0.055890	266	0.072877	328	0.089863
205	0.056164	267	0.073151	329	0.090137
206	0.056438	268	0.073425	**330**	0.090411
207	0.056712	269	0.073699	331	0.090685
208	0.056986	**270**	0.073973	332	0.090959
209	0.057260	271	0.074247	333	0.091233
210	0.057534	272	0.074521	334	0.091507
211	0.057808	273	0.074795	335	0.091781
212	0.058082	274	0.075068	336	0.092055
213	0.058356	275	0.075342	337	0.092329
214	0.058630	276	0.075616	338	0.092603
215	0.058904	277	0.075890	339	0.092877
216	0.059178	278	0.076164	**340**	0.093151
217	0.059452	279	0.076438	341	0.093425
218	0.059726	**280**	0.076712	342	0.093699
219	0.060000	281	0.076986	343	0.093973
220	0.060274	282	0.077260	344	0.094247
221	0.060548	283	0.077534	345	0.094521
222	0.060822	284	0.077808	346	0.094795
223	0.061096	285	0.078082	347	0.095068
224	0.061370	286	0.078356	348	0.095342
225	0.061644	287	0.078630	349	0.095616
226	0.061918	288	0.078904	**350**	0.095890
227	0.062192	289	0.079178	351	0.096164
228	0.062466	**290**	0.079452	352	0.096438
229	0.062740	291	0.079726	353	0.096712
230	0.063014	292	0.080000	354	0.096986
231	0.063288	293	0.080274	355	0.097260
232	0.063562	294	0.080548	356	0.097534
233	0.063836	295	0.080822	357	0.097808
234	0.064110	296	0.081096	358	0.098082
235	0.064384	297	0.081370	359	0.098356
236	0.064658	298	0.081644	**360**	0.098630
237	0.064932	299	0.081918	361	0.098904
238	0.065205	**300**	0.082192	362	0.099178
239	0.065479	301	0.082466	363	0.099452
240	0.065753	302	0.082740	364	0.099726
241	0.066027	303	0.083014	365	0.100000
242	0.066301	304	0.083288		

Example using Table 5:

Note: Per "Summary of Example A" in Table 4, Commutation Instructions, the formula for calculating annual interest on a lump sum due, the function of Table 5, is $\frac{(\text{Lump Sum Due} \times \text{\# of Days of Interest}) \times 0.1}{365}$

Assume an award issued 23 days ago and the amount accrued, or due as of the date of the award is 64 weeks @ $140.00/week = $8,960.00. That amount will be owed, plus interest on the total amount due for 23 days, plus interest due on $140.00/week for 3 weeks 2 days. (Table 6 calculates this last period.)

Interest due on Accrued PD using the formula above is:
[$8,960.00 × 23 days × 0.1] ÷ 365 = **$56.46** [same as second step below]

Per Table 5, 23 days = 0.006301 which × $8,960.00 = interest due: **$56.46**

Summary of Accrued PD plus interest to date Award is paid:

1. Accrued PD indemnity, 64 wks @ $140.00 = ... $8,960.00
2. Plus Interest due on Accrued, 0.006301 × $8,960.00 = **+ 56.46**
3. Total, Accrued PD plus Interest on Accrued PD = . . . $9,016.46

SUMMARY: TABLES 5 AND 6

Payments due on PD award in example, issued 23 days prior to payment:

Steps:

1. Accrued PD, 64 weeks @ $140/week = ... $8,960.00
2. Interest due on Accrued PD (See above, this page) = ... 56.46
3. 23 days of PD due after Award, calculated as follows:
   23 days ÷ 7 days/wk = 3.28571 which × $140/wk = . . 460.00
4. Interest on 3 wks 2 days @ $140/wk (from Table 6) = . . + 1.70
5. **Total amount due on the 23rd day after the award = . $9,478.16**

The decimal value in the third step above (3.28571) which calculates 23 days (3 weeks 2 days) of PD owed after the award, may also be obtained by adding to "3 weeks" the value for "2 days" from Table 19, 0.28571, for the total, 3.28571. (I prefer to divide 23 days by 7 days/week to get the decimal.)

To calculate interest owed on a lump sum beyond the one year shown in Table 5, e.g., 1 year and 56 days, use the following method:

1 year = 365 days . 0.100000
Plus 56 days +0.015342
1 year and 56 days . 0.115342 (Multiply this times the lump sum due.)

Try the formula at top of this page: 365 + 56 = 421 days. It's much easier!

TABLE 6
Interest: Ten Percent Weekly (Successive Payments of $1/Week)

Labor Code §5800; Code of Civil Procedure §685.020

Weeks	Interest Due	Weeks	Interest Due
1	0.0019	27	0.7250
2	0.0057	28	0.7786
3	0.0116	29	0.8343
4	0.0191	30	0.8917
5	0.0287	31	0.9513
6	0.0403	32	1.0125
7	0.0537	33	1.0759
8	0.0690	34	1.1411
9	0.0863	35	1.2083
10	0.1054	36	1.2773
11	0.1266	37	1.3483
12	0.1496	38	1.4211
13	0.1746	39	1.4958
14	0.2014	40	1.5726
15	0.2301	41	1.6513
16	0.2609	42	1.7317
17	0.2934	43	1.8143
18	0.3280	44	1.8986
19	0.3644	45	1.9850
20	0.4027	46	2.0731
21	0.4430	47	2.1633
22	0.4851	48	2.2553
23	0.5293	49	2.3493
24	0.5753	50	2.4451
25	0.6233	51	2.5430
26	0.6731	52	2.6427

Days	Interest Due	Days	Interest Due
1	0.0002739	4	0.001096
2	0.0005479	5	0.001370
3	0.0008218	6	0.001644

Add Interest Due for whole weeks and days together. Multiply the result by the weekly comp rate to determine the total interest due, e.g., following the example in Table 5:

23 days equals 3 weeks plus 2 days: Interest from Table 6, above:

	3 weeks	=	0.0116
	+ 2 days	=	+ 0.0005479
(Used in Table 5, step 4.)	Interest	=	0.0121479 × $140.00/week = **$1.70**

The amount shown seems trivial, however when payments are made many weeks after an award, e.g., after an appeal, several hundred dollars may be involved.

For instance, assume 60 weeks of Successive Payments at $140 are due since the award issued. PD due, 60 wks × $140 = $8,400, but how much interest is owed? Calculate the first 52 weeks of Successive Payments using Table 6, above. Then add interest owing on that lump sum *for the remaining time* (8 weeks in this example) from Table 5. Then add interest on the final 8 weeks for successive weekly payments due per Table 6 as follows:

1. Per Table 6, 52 successive weeks = 2.6427 and × $140 = .. **$369.98**
2. At the end of 1 year, 52 wks × $140 = **$7,280** is due. Interest on this amount is due for 8 wks × 7 days/wk = 56 days, and per, Table 5, interest on 56 days = 0.015342 and × **$7,280** =...... 111.69
3. 8 wks of payments from Table 6 above is 0.0690 and × $140 = + 9.66
   Interest Due on 60 Successive Payments of $140/week = .. $491.33

Tables & Schedules

TABLE 7
Interest: Seven Percent Annually (One Lump Sum Due)
Labor Code §4622

Days	Interest	Days	Interest	Days	Interest
1	0.000192	61	0.011699	121	0.023205
2	0.000384	62	0.011890	122	0.023397
3	0.000575	63	0.012082	123	0.023589
4	0.000767	64	0.012274	124	0.023781
5	0.000959	65	0.012466	125	0.023973
6	0.001151	66	0.012658	126	0.024164
7	0.001342	67	0.012849	127	0.024356
8	0.001534	68	0.013041	128	0.024548
9	0.001726	69	0.013233	129	0.024740
10	0.001918	70	0.013425	130	0.024932
11	0.002110	71	0.013616	131	0.025123
12	0.002301	72	0.013808	132	0.025315
13	0.002493	73	0.014000	133	0.025507
14	0.002685	74	0.014192	134	0.025699
15	0.002877	75	0.014384	135	0.025890
16	0.003068	76	0.014575	136	0.026082
17	0.003260	77	0.014767	137	0.026274
18	0.003452	78	0.014959	138	0.026466
19	0.003644	79	0.015151	139	0.026658
20	0.003836	80	0.015342	140	0.026849
21	0.004027	81	0.015534	141	0.027041
22	0.004219	82	0.015726	142	0.027233
23	0.004411	83	0.015918	143	0.027425
24	0.004603	84	0.016110	144	0.027616
25	0.004795	85	0.016301	145	0.027808
26	0.004986	86	0.016493	146	0.028000
27	0.005178	87	0.016685	147	0.028192
28	0.005370	88	0.016877	148	0.028384
29	0.005562	89	0.017068	149	0.028575
30	0.005753	90	0.017260	150	0.028767
31	0.005945	91	0.017452	151	0.028959
32	0.006137	92	0.017644	152	0.029151
33	0.006329	93	0.017836	153	0.029342
34	0.006521	94	0.018027	154	0.029534
35	0.006712	95	0.018219	155	0.029726
36	0.006904	96	0.018411	156	0.029918
37	0.007096	97	0.018603	157	0.030110
38	0.007288	98	0.018795	158	0.030301
39	0.007479	99	0.018986	159	0.030493
40	0.007671	100	0.019178	160	0.030685
41	0.007863	101	0.019370	161	0.030877
42	0.008055	102	0.019562	162	0.031068
43	0.008247	103	0.019753	163	0.031260
44	0.008438	104	0.019945	164	0.031452
45	0.008630	105	0.020137	165	0.031644
46	0.008822	106	0.020329	166	0.031836
47	0.009014	107	0.020521	167	0.032027
48	0.009205	108	0.020712	168	0.032219
49	0.009397	109	0.020904	169	0.032411
50	0.009589	110	0.021096	170	0.032603
51	0.009781	111	0.021288	171	0.032795
52	0.009973	112	0.021479	172	0.032986
53	0.010164	113	0.021671	173	0.033178
54	0.010356	114	0.021863	174	0.033370
55	0.010548	115	0.022055	175	0.033562
56	0.010740	116	0.022247	176	0.033753
57	0.010932	117	0.022438	177	0.033945
58	0.011123	118	0.022630	178	0.034137
59	0.011315	119	0.022822	179	0.034329
60	0.011507	120	0.023014	180	0.034521

Days	Interest	Days	Interest	Days	Interest
181	0.034712	243	0.046603	305	0.058493
182	0.034904	244	0.046795	306	0.058685
183	0.035096	245	0.046986	307	0.058877
184	0.035288	246	0.047178	308	0.059068
185	0.035479	247	0.047370	309	0.059260
186	0.035671	248	0.047562	310	0.059452
187	0.035863	249	0.047753	311	0.059644
188	0.036055	250	0.047945	312	0.059836
189	0.036247	251	0.048137	313	0.060027
190	0.036438	252	0.048329	314	0.060219
191	0.036630	253	0.048521	315	0.060411
192	0.036822	254	0.048712	316	0.060603
193	0.037014	255	0.048904	317	0.060795
194	0.037205	256	0.049096	318	0.060986
195	0.037397	257	0.049288	319	0.061178
196	0.037589	258	0.049479	320	0.061370
197	0.037781	259	0.049671	321	0.061562
198	0.037973	260	0.049863	322	0.061753
199	0.038164	261	0.050055	323	0.061945
200	0.038356	262	0.050247	324	0.062137
201	0.038548	263	0.050438	325	0.062329
202	0.038740	264	0.050630	326	0.062521
203	0.038932	265	0.050822	327	0.062712
204	0.039123	266	0.051014	328	0.062904
205	0.039315	267	0.051205	329	0.063096
206	0.039507	268	0.051397	330	0.063288
207	0.039699	269	0.051589	331	0.063479
208	0.039890	270	0.051781	332	0.063671
209	0.040082	271	0.051973	333	0.063863
210	0.040274	272	0.052164	334	0.064055
211	0.040466	273	0.052356	335	0.064247
212	0.040658	274	0.052548	336	0.064438
213	0.040849	275	0.052740	337	0.064630
214	0.041041	276	0.052932	338	0.064822
215	0.041233	277	0.053123	339	0.065014
216	0.041425	278	0.053315	340	0.065205
217	0.041616	279	0.053507	341	0.065397
218	0.041808	280	0.053699	342	0.065589
219	0.042000	281	0.053890	343	0.065781
220	0.042192	282	0.054082	344	0.065973
221	0.042384	283	0.054274	345	0.066164
222	0.042575	284	0.054466	346	0.066356
223	0.042767	285	0.054658	347	0.066548
224	0.042959	286	0.054849	348	0.066740
225	0.043151	287	0.055041	349	0.066932
226	0.043342	288	0.055233	350	0.067123
227	0.043534	289	0.055425	351	0.067315
228	0.043726	290	0.055616	352	0.067507
229	0.043918	291	0.055808	353	0.067699
230	0.044110	292	0.056000	354	0.067890
231	0.044301	293	0.056192	355	0.068082
232	0.044493	294	0.056384	356	0.068274
233	0.044685	295	0.056575	357	0.068466
234	0.044877	296	0.056767	358	0.068658
235	0.045068	297	0.056959	359	0.068849
236	0.045260	298	0.057151	360	0.069041
237	0.045452	299	0.057342	361	0.069233
238	0.045644	300	0.057534	362	0.069425
239	0.045836	301	0.057726	363	0.069616
240	0.046027	302	0.057918	364	0.069808
241	0.046219	303	0.058110	365	0.070000
242	0.046411	304	0.058301		

PART 3. Legislation

TABLE 8

SB 899: Rationale for Revisions to PD Tables 17A and 17B

The 2005 Schedule for Rating Permanent Disabilities (PDRS) applies prospectively and only to injuries on and after the effective date of the Schedule adopted on 1/1/05, per 4/04 L.C. §4660(d).

Per 4/04 L.C. §4660(d), the 2005 PDRS Schedule also applies to injuries where there has been either no medical-legal report or a report by a treating physician indicating the existence of PD or when no L.C. §4061 notice has been required for claims arising prior to 1/1/05.

Per 4/04 L.C. §4658(d)(1), the weeks of PD changed by SB 899 (Table 17A), "... shall apply to injuries on or after the effective date of the revised permanent disability schedule adopted by the administrative director pursuant to Section 4660." This was done 1/1/05.

Thus, I believe the 2005 PDRS and the 2004 PD Table 17B, or for earlier injuries, 17C, apply for injuries before 1/1/05 where there has been either no medical-legal report or a report by a treating physician indicating the existence of PD, or no notice under L.C. §4061 is not required.

Some persons believe the medical-legal report before 1/1/05 need not comment on the existence of PD and only reports by a treating physician must find the existence of PD to qualify. These persons believe the fact of a medical-legal report prior to 1/1/05 is sufficient.

Others believe there is no limit to the application of the 2005 PDRS if there has been no medical-legal report, etc., as discussed above. They believe the 2005 PDRS should apply to all injuries before 1/1/05 if the criteria are met in 4/04 L.C. §4660(d). Others claim payment of TD in 2004 implies the requirement, eventually, of a L.C. §4061 notice, so the 1997 PDRS applies.

I have done my best to understand these statutes and when and why they apply. Neither I nor Matthew Bender/LexisNexis™ *can offer guarantees.* Case law will eventually sort out how these statutes are to be applied. In the meantime, "Let the reader beware!"

Readers are cautioned to obtain legal advice prior to relying on this or any table or other commentary on legal matters. Go to original sources, e.g., 2005 regulations in T8CCR dealing with the use of the Post-SB 899 changes in PD evaluation per 4/04 L.C. §4660(e).

Other places to check include reliable sources such as magazines/bulletins by CWCI, CWCR, and CWCE as well as DWC Newslines at:

http://www.dir.ca.gov/dwc/dwc_newsline.html
Subscribers may also log on to **http://www.lexis.com**

+/− 15% for employers of 50 or more employees, L.C. §4658(d)(2), (3): PD is increased if no mod/alt work is offered within 60 days of becoming P&S per (d)(2). PD is decreased if mod/alt work is offered, (d)(3)(B). Tables to do this are not provided since the *increase or decrease depends on how many unpaid weeks of PD remain at the time the offer is made* and may change if the employee is later terminated for cause or quits within 1 year. 10/21/06 T8CCR §§10001–10003:
If RTW offered, PD = (Wks before offer × \$/wk rate) + (Remaining wks × \$/wk rate × 0.85)
If no RTW offer, PD = (e.g., 60 days/7 × \$/wk rate) + (Remaining wks × \$/wk rate × 1.15)

James T. Stewart; Clovis, CA 10/02/06

PART 4. Calendar Information

TABLE 9
Number of Days Between Two Dates

Date	Jan	Feb	Mar	Apr	May	Jun	Jul	Aug	Sep	Oct	Nov	Dec	Date
1	1	32	60	91	121	152	182	213	244	274	305	335	**1**
2	2	33	61	92	122	153	183	214	245	275	306	336	**2**
3	3	34	62	93	123	154	184	215	246	276	307	337	**3**
4	4	35	63	94	124	155	185	216	247	277	308	338	**4**
5	5	36	64	95	125	156	186	217	248	278	309	339	**5**
6	6	37	65	96	126	157	187	218	249	279	310	340	**6**
7	7	38	66	97	127	158	188	219	250	280	311	341	**7**
8	8	39	67	98	128	159	189	220	251	281	312	342	**8**
9	9	40	68	99	129	160	190	221	252	282	313	343	**9**
10	10	41	69	100	130	161	191	222	253	283	314	344	**10**
11	11	42	70	101	131	162	192	223	254	284	315	345	**11**
12	12	43	71	102	132	163	193	224	255	285	316	346	**12**
13	13	44	72	103	133	164	194	225	256	286	317	347	**13**
14	14	45	73	104	134	165	195	226	257	287	318	348	**14**
15	15	46	74	105	135	166	196	227	258	288	319	349	**15**
16	16	47	75	106	136	167	197	228	259	289	320	350	**16**
17	17	48	76	107	137	168	198	229	260	290	321	351	**17**
18	18	49	77	108	138	169	199	230	261	291	322	352	**18**
19	19	50	78	109	139	170	200	231	262	292	323	353	**19**
20	20	51	79	110	140	171	201	232	263	293	324	354	**20**
21	21	52	80	111	141	172	202	233	264	294	325	355	**21**
22	22	53	81	112	142	173	203	234	265	295	326	356	**22**
23	23	54	82	113	143	174	204	235	266	296	327	357	**23**
24	24	55	83	114	144	175	205	236	267	297	328	358	**24**
25	25	56	84	115	145	176	206	237	268	298	329	359	**25**
26	26	57	85	116	146	177	207	238	269	299	330	360	**26**
27	27	58	86	117	147	178	208	239	270	300	331	361	**27**
28	28	59	87	118	148	179	209	240	271	301	332	362	**28**
29	29	*	88	119	149	180	210	241	272	302	333	363	**29**
30	30		89	120	150	181	211	242	273	303	334	364	**30**
31	31		90		151		212	243		304		365	**31**

* On leap years, February has 29 days and the year, 366 days. Add 1 to every number after February 29th. The following are leap years. To determine leap years other than as listed, divide date by 4:

1924	1944	1964	1984	2004	2024	2044	2064
1928	1948	1968	1988	2008	2028	2048	2068
1932	1952	1972	1992	2012	2032	2052	2072
1936	1956	1976	1996	2016	2036	2056	2076
1940	1960	1980	2000	2020	2040	2060	2080

Date	Jan	Feb	Mar	Apr	May	Jun	Jul	Aug	Sep	Oct	Nov	Dec	Date
1	366	397	425	456	486	517	547	578	609	639	670	700	**1**
2	367	398	426	457	487	518	548	579	610	640	671	701	**2**
3	368	399	427	458	488	519	549	580	611	641	672	702	**3**
4	369	400	428	459	489	520	550	581	612	642	673	703	**4**
5	370	401	429	460	490	521	551	582	613	643	674	704	**5**
6	371	402	430	461	491	522	552	583	614	644	675	705	**6**
7	372	403	431	462	492	523	553	584	615	645	676	706	**7**
8	373	404	432	463	493	524	554	585	616	646	677	707	**8**
9	374	405	433	464	494	525	555	586	617	647	678	708	**9**
10	375	406	434	465	495	526	556	587	618	648	679	709	**10**
11	376	407	435	466	496	527	557	588	619	649	680	710	**11**
12	377	408	436	467	497	528	558	589	620	650	681	711	**12**
13	378	409	437	468	498	529	559	590	621	651	682	712	**13**
14	379	410	438	469	499	530	560	591	622	652	683	713	**14**
15	380	411	439	470	500	531	561	592	623	653	684	714	**15**
16	381	412	440	471	501	532	562	593	624	654	685	715	**16**
17	382	413	441	472	502	533	563	594	625	655	686	716	**17**
18	383	414	442	473	503	534	564	595	626	656	687	717	**18**
19	384	415	443	474	504	535	565	596	627	657	688	718	**19**
20	385	416	444	475	505	536	566	597	628	658	689	719	**20**
21	386	417	445	476	506	537	567	598	629	659	690	720	**21**
22	387	418	446	477	507	538	568	599	630	660	691	721	**22**
23	388	419	447	478	508	539	569	600	631	661	692	722	**23**
24	389	420	448	479	509	540	570	601	632	662	693	723	**24**
25	390	421	449	480	510	541	571	602	633	663	694	724	**25**
26	391	422	450	481	511	542	572	603	634	664	695	725	**26**
27	392	423	451	482	512	543	573	604	635	665	696	726	**27**
28	393	424	452	483	513	544	574	605	636	666	697	727	**28**
29	394	*	453	484	514	545	575	606	637	667	698	728	**29**
30	395		454	485	515	546	576	607	638	668	699	729	**30**
31	396		455		516		577	608		669		730	**31**

Example: Subtract first or earliest date from last date

Last day disabled: Oct.22. 1996 (see below. 1)* 660 + 1 = ... 661

First day disabled: Feb. 8. 1995 .... – <u>39</u>

Number of days between two dates. <u>***not inclusive***</u> (see below. 2 & 3) 622

Since we are subtracting dates. add one to answer to make inclusive. 622 +1 = . <u>**623**</u>

* 1996 was a leap year: See prior page for other dates.

Additional notes:

1. Whenever leap year is involved. add one extra day to any period that includes February 29th.
2. The number of days given "between" two dates in this table is <u>***not inclusive***</u>. Thus. you will always need to add one day if you are subtracting dates. For example. from January 1 to January 3 is three days. but if you subtract the two numbers you need to add one to make the result inclusive.
3. If you add three days to January 1. you need to subtract one day to make the result inclusive.
4. The two pages above apply for up to two years. If more years are involved. add 365 days/year.

PART 5. The Schedules for Rating Permanent Disabilities

TABLE 10

Schedule for Rating Permanent Disabilities—General Introduction

Schedule for Rating Permanent Disabilities (See Table 8, supra): Regulations for Title 8 of the California Code of Regulations were adopted by the A. D. on January 1, 2005 per 4/19/04 L.C. § 4660(e). This PD Schedule is often called the "Post-SB 899 Schedule," [1] or the "1/05 Schedule." The previous schedule is the "4/97 Schedule" which was effective 4/1/97 to 12/31/04, with exceptions as noted in Table 8. Injuries prior to 4/1/97 are rated per the "Pre-4/97 Schedule."

Earlier editions of the *Workers' Compensation Laws of California*, e.g., the 2003 or 2004 edition, reprints in Table 10 the "Introduction and Instructions" to the 4/1/97 Schedule, pages 1–1 to 1–14, as well as "Combining Multiple Disabilities," pages 7–12 to 7–14.

When reading medical reports, pay particular attention to combining of disabilities by physicians. The method for combining disabilities in California in the Post-SB 899 Schedule is different from the method used in the AMA Guides, 5th ed. See the chart in the back of the schedule, pages 8-1 to 8-4 and the "Formula for Combining Impairments and Disabilities," page 1-10 as well as "Adjusting AMA Impairments and Combining Ratings," page 1-11.

The following instructions from page 1-11 in the Post-SB 899 Schedule discusses different methods from those in the AMA Guides, 5th ed. for combining disabilities:

> Impairments with disability numbers in the 16.01 and 17.01 series are converted to whole person impairment and adjusted before being combined with any other impairment of the same extremity.
>
> Impairments of an individual extremity are adjusted and combined at the whole person level with other impairments of the same extremity before being combined with impairments of other body parts. For example, an impairment of the left knee and ankle would be combined before further combination with an impairment of the opposing leg or the back.

Physicians should describe impairments in extremities and NOT combine them per the AMA Guides 5th ed. The answer obtained per the Guides will almost certainly be "wrong" per California's 1/1/05 *Schedule for Rating Permanent Disabilities.*

---

[1] The new Post-SB 899 Schedule is reprinted in Table 11 A

Tables & Schedules

TABLE 11

Guidelines for Work Capacity and Excerpts From the Schedule for Rating Permanent Disabilities, 4/1/97 to 12/31/04

Page numbers refer to the *Schedule* (See Table 8 for exceptions)

These apply to pulmonary, heart disease, abdominal weakness and spinal disabilities. Guidelines g) and h) may apply to lower extremity disabilities. (*)

a) **Disability Precluding Very Heavy Lifting 10%**

contemplates the individual has lost approximately one-quarter of his pre-injury capacity for lifting.

[A statement "inability to lift 50 pounds" is not meaningful. The total lifting effort, including weight, distance, endurance, frequency, body position and similar factors should be considered with reference to the particular individual.]

b) **Disability Precluding Very Heavy Work 15%**

contemplates the individual has lost approximately one-quarter of his pre-injury capacity for performing such activities as bending, stooping, lifting, pushing, pulling and climbing or other activities involving comparable physical effort.

c) **Disability Precluding Heavy Lifting 20%**

contemplates the individual has lost approximately one-half of his pre-injury capacity for lifting.

[see statement regarding lifting under a) above.]

d) **Disability Precluding Heavy Lifting, Repeated Bending and Stooping 25%**

contemplates the individual has lost approximately half of his pre-injury capacity for lifting, bending and stooping.

e) **Disability Precluding Heavy Work 30%**

contemplates the individual has lost approximately half of his pre-injury capacity for performing such activities as bending, stooping, lifting, pushing, pulling, and climbing or other activities involving comparable physical effort.

f) **Disability Resulting in Limitation to Light Work 50%**

contemplates the individual can do work in a standing or walking position, with a minimum of demands for physical effort.

g) **Disability Resulting in Limitation to Semi-Sedentary Work 60%**

contemplates the individual can do work approximately one-half the time in a sitting position, and approximately one-half the time in a standing or walking position, with a minimum of demands for physical effort whether standing, walking or sitting.

h) **Disability Resulting in Limitation to Sedentary Work 70%**

contemplates the individual can do work predominantly in a sitting position at a bench, desk or table with a minimum of demands for physical effort and with some degree of walking and standing being permitted.

(*) This amendment applies to injuries occurring on or after 1/1/73 to 12/31/04 (See Table 8).
This amendment applies to injuries occurring on or after 1/1/70 to 12/31/04 (See Table 8).

LOWER EXTREMITY GUIDELINES FOR INJURIES 4/1/97 TO 12/31/04 [1,2] (SEE TABLE 8)

WORK CAPACITY AS INDEX	STANDARD RATING
Disability Precluding Squatting and/or Kneeling .... contemplates loss of approximately 90–100% of worker's pre-injury capacity for squatting and/or kneeling.	**5%**
Disability Precluding Climbing .... contemplates loss of approximately 90–100% of worker's pre-injury capacity for climbing.	**10%**
Disability Precluding Walking Over Uneven Ground .... contemplates loss of approximately 90–100% of worker's pre-injury capacity for walking over rough terrain.	**10%**
Disability Precluding Very Heavy Lifting .... contemplates loss of approximately 90–100% of worker's pre-injury capacity for lifting.	**10%**
Disability Precluding Climbing, Walking Over Uneven Ground, Squatting, Kneeling, Crouching, Crawling, and Pivoting, or other activities involving comparable physical effort.	**20%**
Disability Precluding Prolonged Weight-Bearing .... contemplates ability to do work approximately 75% of time in standing and walking position, and requires sitting approximately 25% of time.	**20%**
Disability Precluding Heavy Lifting .... contemplates loss of approximately 50% of worker's pre-injury capacity for lifting.	**20%**
Disability Precluding Heavy Lifting, and Precluding Climbing, Walking Over Uneven Ground, Squatting, Kneeling, Crouching, Crawling, and Pivoting, or other activities involving comparable physical effort.	**30%**
Disability Precluding Heavy Lifting, Prolonged Weight-Bearing, and Precluding Climbing, Walking Over Uneven Ground, Squatting, Kneeling, Crouching, Crawling, and Pivoting, or other activities involving comparable physical effort.	**40%**
Disability Resulting in Limitation of Weight-bearing to Half Time .... contemplates ability to do work approximately 50% of time in standing and walking position, and requires sitting approximately 50% of time.	**40%**
Disability Resulting in Limitation to Semi-Sedentary Work .... contemplates ability to do work approximately 50% of the time in a sitting position, and approximately 50% the time in a standing or walking position, with a minimum of demands for physical effort whether standing, walking or sitting.	**60%**
Disability Resulting in Limitation to Sedentary Work .... contemplates ability to do work predominantly in a sitting position at a bench, desk or table with a minimum of demands for physical effort and with some degree of walking and standing being permitted.	**70%**

---

1. Need for orthopedic appliances may be considered in conjunction with other elements comprising the disability.
2. When warranted by facts and evidence, additional factors may be considered resulting in a change in the disability rating.

SPINE AND TORSO GUIDELINES FOR INJURIES 4/1/97 TO 12/31/04 [1,2] (SEE TABLE 8)

WORK CAPACITY OR SUBJECTIVE FACTOR AS INDEX [3,4,5] **STANDARD RATING**

{Editorial Comment: Disability factors in these guidelines essentially duplicate the **Guidelines for Work Capacity** quoted on the first page of Table 11, except for additional entries as noted below.}

Disability Resulting from Constant Slight Pain **10%**
contemplates an individual with pain which can be tolerated, but causes some handicap in performance of activity. {Previously noted on page 13-B of Schedule}

Disability Precluding Repetitive Motions of Neck or Back **15%**
contemplates the individual has lost approximately 50% of pre-injury capacity for flexing, extending, bending, and rotating neck or back.

Disability Resulting from Constant Slight to Moderate Pain **30%**
{Previously noted on page 13-B of Schedule}

Disability Precluding Substantial Work **40%**
contemplates the individual has lost approximately 75% of pre-injury capacity for performing such activities as bending, stooping, lifting, pushing, pulling, and climbing or other activities involving comparable physical effort.

Disability Resulting from Constant Moderate Pain **50%**
contemplates an individual with pain which can be tolerated, but causes marked handicap in performance of activity. {Previously noted on page 13-B of Schedule}

---

1. Either or both indexes of disability may be used to describe a particular condition. The final rating is to be based on the index yielding the higher rating.
2. When warranted by facts and evidence, additional factors may be considered resulting in a change in the disability rating.
3. Guidelines using work capacity as an index apply to neck, back, pelvis, heart, pulmonary and abdominal disabilities.
4. Guidelines using subjective factors as index apply to neck, back, pelvis and abdominal disabilities. Subjective disability should be identified as prescribed in 8 CCR § 9727.
5. Objective factors of disability may be considered in conjunction with spine or torso pain.

Comparison of Disability Numbers for 4/1/97 vs. Prior Schedule[1]

Note: See Table 8 for possible application of Post-SB 899 PD Schedule

4/1/97 Schedule (D/A 4/1/97-12/31/04)		**Pre-4/1/97 Schedule** (D/A before 4/1/97)	
1.1	Paralysis	1.1	Paralysis
1.3	Epilepsy	1.3	Epilepsy
1.4	Psychiatric	1.4	Neurosis: Psychiatric Disability
1.5	Post-traumatic Head Synd.	1.5	Post-traumatic Head Syndrome
1.6	Vertigo	1.6	Vertigo
1.7	Headaches	1.7	Headaches
1.8	Cognitive Disability	1.8	Mental Deterioration
2.1	Sight-Cosmetic	2.141	Loss of Sight w. Marked Blemish
2.2 - 2.6	Vision	2.1- 2.8	Impairment of Visual Acuity
2.7	Lacrimation	2.61	Chronic Lacrimation (Tears)
3.1	Hearing Loss	3.1	Loss of Hearing
4.1	Cosmetic	4.1	Cosmetic Disfigurement
4.3 - 4.4	Skull	4.3 - 4.4	Skull Apertures
4.5	Jaw	4.5	Tooth, Mouth, & Jaw Injuries
4.7	Nose	4.7	Nose Injuries Affecting Function
5.2	Speech	5.2	Disabilities Affecting Speech
5.31	Smell	5.31	Loss of Sense of Smell
5.32	Taste	5.32	Loss of Sense of Taste
5.33	Smell, Taste	5.33	Loss of Sense of Taste & Smell
6.1	Skin - Preclude Outside Work		(Unscheduled)[2]
6.2	Skin - Preclude Wet Work		(Unscheduled)
7.1	Arm Amputation	7.1	Loss of Arm
7.3	Shoulder	7.3	Impairment, Function, Shoulder
7.5	Elbow	7.52	Impair, Elbow 70°- 100° Flexion
7.6	Forearm	7.54	Loss of Rotation of Forearm
7.7	Wrist	7.7	Impairment of Function, Wrist

Finger Amputations: T = Thumb; I = Index; M = Middle; R = Ring; & L = Little

8.11	Thumb Amputation	8.1	Thumb
8.12	Index Amputation	8.2	Index Finger
8.13	Middle Amputation	8.3	Middle Finger
8.14	Ring Amputation	8.4	Ring Finger
8.15	Little Amputation	8.5	Little Finger
8.2	Thumb + Index	9.1	Thumb & any one finger
	(Combine Disabilities)[3]	9.2	Index & any one finger
	(Combine Disabilities)	9.3	Middle & Ring or Little Finger
	(Combine Disabilities)	9.4	Ring and Little Fingers
8.3	T+I+M Amp	10.1	Thumb, Index, and Middle
	(Combine Disabilities)	10.2	Index, Middle, & Ring Fingers
	(Combine Disabilities)	10.3	Middle, Ring and Little Fingers
	(Combine Disabilities)	11.1	Thumb, Index, Middle & Ring
8.4	I+M+R+L Amp	11.2	Index, Middle, Ring & Little
8.5	All Fingers Amputation	12.1	Thumb and All Fingers

Tables & Schedules

4/1/97 Schedule (D/A 4/1/97-12/31/04) **Pre-4/1/97 Schedule** (D/A < 4/1/97), contd.

Note: See Table 8 for possible application of Post-SB 899 PD Schedule

Finger Immobility: T = Thumb; I = Index; M = Middle; R = Ring; & L = Little

9.11	Thumb Immobility	13.1	Thumb
9.12	Index Immobility	13.2	Index Finger
9.13	Middle Immobility	13.3	Middle Finger
9.14	Ring Immobility	13.4	Ring Finger
9.15	Little Immobility	13.5	Little Finger
9.2	T+I Immobility	14.1	Thumb & Index Finger
9.3	T+I+M Immobility	15.1	Thumb, Index & Middle
9.4	I+M+R+L Immobility	16.2	Index, Middle, Ring & Little
9.5	Immobility Thumb/Fingers	17.1	Thumb & All Fingers
10.5	Grip	16.8	Loss of Grasping Power
11.1	Pulmonary	6.1	Chronic . . . Pulmonary Tissues
11.3	Heart	6.3	Heart Disease
11.5	Rib Cage	6.5	Injuries to the Rib Cage
12.1	Spine	18.1	Neck, Spine or Pelvis
12.3	Spine - Paralysis	18.3	Spinal Cord . . . Paralysis
13.1	Abdomen - Hernia	19.1	Inoperable Hernia
13.2	Abdomen Organs	19.3	Loss/Impair Abdominal Organs
14.1	Leg Amputation	20.1	Amputations, Legs (or foot)
14.2	Toe Amputation	20.7	Amputations, toes
14.3	Leg Short	20.811	Shortening Lower Extremities
14.4	Hip	21.1-21.2	Motion, Hip/Other Dis., Hip
14.5	Knee, Thigh	21.3-21.4	Motion, Knee/Other Dis., Knee
14.531	Atrophy of Thigh Muscles	21.441	Thigh Atrophy
14.6	Ankle, Calf	21.5-21.6	Motion, Ankle/Other Dis., Ankle
14.631	Atrophy of Calf Muscles	21.641	Calf Atrophy
14.7	Toe Immobility	21.7	Impairment of Function, Toes
14.8	Post-thrombosis	21.8	Post Thrombophlebitic Disability

---

1. Entries for disability numbers such as "1.1" assume "1.1–" referring to the entire category beginning 1.1 et seq. An attempt has been made to keep the original wording of the disabilities, but some definitions have been shortened for the sake of brevity.

2. *Unscheduled* ratings are those which by definition are not contained within the Schedule. They rely on the judgment, experience and expertise of the disability evaluator.

3. *Combine Disabilities* refers to the calculation of a disability by combining data one has, such as the loss of an index finger with the loss of another finger, to reach a disability which represents the loss of the two fingers, even though the schedule does not specifically list the loss of those two fingers. Consult a rating manual for instructions. To combine disabilities generally, see the *4/1/97 Schedule*, pages 7-12 to 7-14.

TABLE 11A
Permanent Disability Revised Schedule (2005 PDRS)

ARNOLD SCHWARZENEGGER
GOVERNOR OF CALIFORNIA

SCHEDULE FOR RATING PERMANENT DISABILITIES

UNDER THE PROVISIONS OF THE

LABOR CODE OF THE STATE OF CALIFORNIA

Compiled and Published by
STATE OF CALIFORNIA

LABOR AND WORKFORCE DEVELOPMENT AGENCY
DEPARTMENT OF INDUSTRIAL RELATIONS
DIVISION OF WORKERS' COMPENSATION

ANDREA LYNN HOCH
Administrative Director

January 2005

AUTHORITY

Labor Code section 4660, amended effective April 19, 2004, provides:

4660(a) In determining the percentages of permanent disability, account shall be taken of the nature of the physical injury or disfigurement, the occupation of the injured employee, and his or her age at the time of the injury, consideration being given to an employee's diminished future earning capacity.

(b)(1) For purposes of this section, the "nature of the physical injury or disfigurement" shall incorporate the descriptions and measurements of physical impairments and the corresponding percentages of impairments published in the American Medical Association (AMA) Guides to the Evaluation of Permanent Impairment (5th Edition).

(2) For purposes of this section, an employee's diminished future earning capacity shall be a numeric formula based on empirical data and findings that aggregate the average percentage of long-term loss of income resulting from each type of injury for similarly situated employees. The administrative director shall formulate the adjusted rating schedule based on empirical data and findings from the Evaluation of California's Permanent Disability Rating Schedule, Interim Report (December 2003), prepared by the RAND Institute for Civil Justice, and upon data from additional empirical studies.

(c) The Administrative Director shall amend the schedule for the determination of the percentage of permanent disability in accordance with this section at least once every five years. This schedule shall be available for public inspection and, without formal introduction in evidence, shall be prima facie evidence of the percentage of permanent disability to be attributed to each injury covered by the schedule.

(d) The schedule shall promote consistency, uniformity, and objectivity. The schedule and any amendment thereto or revision thereof shall apply prospectively and shall apply to and govern only those permanent disabilities that result from compensable injuries received or occurring on and after the effective date of the adoption of the schedule, amendment or revision, as the fact may be. For compensable claims arising before January 1, 2005, the schedule as revised pursuant to changes made in legislation enacted during the 2003-04 Regular and Extraordinary Sessions shall apply to the determination of permanent disabilities when there has been either no comprehensive medical-legal report or no report by a treating physician indicating the existence of permanent disability, or when the employer is not required to provide the notice required by Section 4061 to the injured worker.

(e) On or before January 1, 2005, the administrative director shall adopt regulations to implement the changes made to this section by the act that added this subdivision.

Pursuant to this authority, the Administrative Director has adopted this revised Schedule for Rating Permanent Disabilities.

TABLE OF CONTENTS

SECTION 1 - INTRODUCTION AND INSTRUCTIONS

SECTION 1 – INTRODUCTION AND INSTRUCTIONS

I. INTRODUCTION

This Schedule for Rating Permanent Disabilities (hereinafter referred to as the "Schedule") has been adopted by the Administrative Director pursuant to Labor Code section 4660. In accordance with this section, the schedule shall be amended at least once every five years.

The extent of permanent disability that results from an industrial injury can be assessed once an employee's condition becomes permanent and stationary. Permanent and stationary is defined as the point in time when the employee has reached maximal medical improvement (MMI), meaning his or her condition is well stabilized and unlikely to change substantially in the next year with or without medical treatment. (AMA Guides, p. 2.)

The calculation of a permanent disability rating is initially based on a evaluating physician's impairment rating, in accordance with the medical evaluation protocols and rating procedures set forth in the American Medical Association (AMA) *Guides to the Evaluation of Permanent Impairment, 5th Edition* (hereinafter referred to as the "AMA Guides"), which is hereby incorporated by reference.

Initial impairment ratings are consolidated by body part (see *Adjusting AMA Impairments and Combining Ratings* on page 1-11) and converted to a whole person impairment rating (hereinafter referred to as "impairment standard"). The impairment standard is then adjusted to account for diminished future earning capacity, occupation and age at the time of injury to obtain a final permanent disability rating.

A permanent disability rating can range from 0% to 100%. Zero percent signifies no reduction of earning capacity, while 100% represents permanent total disability. A rating between 0% and 100% represents permanent partial disability. Permanent total disability represents a level of disability at which an employee has sustained a total loss of earning capacity. Some impairments are conclusively presumed to be totally disabling. (Lab. Code, §4662.)

Each rating corresponds to a fixed number of weeks of compensation. Compensation is paid based on the number of weeks and the weekly compensation rate, in accordance with Labor Code section 4658.

II RATING PROCEDURES

A. Use of the AMA Guides

The AMA Guides are used by evaluating physicians to determine the extent of an individual's impairment. The AMA Guides use different scales to describe impairment for different parts and regions of the body. For example, finger impairment is measured using a finger scale that can range from 0% to 100%. Other commonly used scales in the AMA Guides are the hand, upper extremity, foot, lower extremity and whole person scales.

The scales that correspond to different body regions are equivalent to a percentage of the whole person scale; therefore these scales are converted to the whole person scale to determine the appropriate impairment rating. For example, an upper extremity impairment in the range of 0% to 100% is equivalent to a whole person impairment in the range of 0% to 60%. The upper extremity impairment is converted to a whole person impairment by multiplying by .6.

When combining two or more ratings to create a composite rating, the ratings must be expressed in the same scale. (See *Formula for combining impairments and disabilities* on page 1-10.)

The whole person impairment scale is referred to as WPI (whole person impairment). The upper and lower extremity scales are referred to as UE (upper extremity) and LE (lower extremity), respectively.

A final permanent disability rating is obtained only after the impairment rating obtained from an evaluating physician is adjusted for diminished future earning capacity, occupation and age at the time of injury.

B. Calculation of Rating

This schedule utilizes an impairment number and an impairment standard. The impairment standard is then modified to reflect diminished future earning capacity, the occupation and the age at the time of injury.

1. *Impairment Number*

The impairment number identifies the body part, organ system and/or nature of the injury and takes the form of "xx.xx.xx.xx". The first two digits correspond to the chapter number in the AMA Guides which address the body part/organ system. Subsequent pairs of digits further refine the identification of the impairment.

For example, soft tissue lesion of the neck rated under the range of motion (ROM) method would be represented as follows:

15.	01.	02.	02
Spine	Neck	ROM method	Soft tissue lesion

Under Section 2 of the Permanent Disability Rating Schedule, an appropriate impairment number can be found for most impairments.

2. *Impairment Standard*

After identification of the appropriate disability number(s), the next step is to calculate all relevant impairment standard(s) for the impairments being evaluated. An impairment standard is a whole person impairment rating under the AMA Guides, provided by the evaluating physician.

If an impairment based on an objective medical condition is not addressed by the AMA Guides, physicians should use clinical judgment, comparing measurable impairment resulting from the unlisted objective medical condition to measurable impairment resulting from similar objective medical conditions with similar impairment of function in performing activities of daily living. (AMA Guides, p. 11.)

A single injury can result in multiple impairments of several parts of the body. For example, an injury to the arm could result in limited elbow range of motion and shoulder instability. Multiple impairments must be combined in a prescribed manner to produce a final overall rating. (See, *Adjusting AMA Impairments and Combining Ratings* on page 1-11.)

It is not always appropriate to combine all impairment standards resulting from a single injury, since two or more impairments may have a duplicative effect on the function of the injured body part. The AMA Guides provide some direction on what impairments can be used in combination. Lacking such guidance, it is necessary for the evaluating physician to exercise his or her judgment in avoiding duplication.

The impairment standard is assumed to represent the degree of impairment for a theoretical average worker, i.e., a worker with average occupational demands on all parts of the body and at the average age of 39.

3. *Adjustment for Diminished Future Earning Capacity*

The adjustment for diminished future earning capacity (FEC) is applied to the impairment standard in accordance with procedures outlined in section 2 of the Schedule. An impairment must be expressed using the whole person impairment scale before applying the FEC adjustment.

The methodology and FEC Adjustment table is premised on a numerical formula based on empirical data and findings that aggregate the average percentage of long-term loss of income resulting from each type of injury for similarly situated employees. The empirical data was obtained from the interim report, "Evaluation of California's Permanent Disability Rating Schedule (December 2003), prepared by the RAND Institute for Justice. The result is that the injury categories are placed into different ranges (based on the ratio of standard ratings to proportional wage losses). Each of these ranges will generate a FEC adjustment between 10% and 40% for each injury category.

(a) Summary of Methodology:

1. RAND data was used to establish the ratio of average California standard ratings to proportional wage losses for each of 22 injury categories. (*Data for Adjusting Disability Ratings to Reflect Diminished Future Earnings and Capacity in Compliance with SB 899*, December 2004, RAND Institute for Civil Justice, Seabury, Reville, Neuhauser.) These ratios are listed in Table B.

2. The range of the ratios for all injury categories is .45 to 1.81. This numeric range was divided into eight evenly spaced ranges. (See the Range of Ratios columns in Table A.) Each injury category will fall within one of these eight ranges, based on its rating/wage loss ratio.

3. A series of FEC adjustment factors were established to correspond to the eight ranges described above. (See column 4 of Table A.) The smallest adjustment factor is 1.1000 which will result in a 10% increase when applied to the AMA whole person impairment rating. The largest is 1.4000 which will result in a 40% increase. The six intermediate adjustment factors are determined by dividing the difference between 1.1 and 1.4 into seven equal amounts.

4. The formula for calculating the maximum and minimum adjustment factors is **([1.81/a] x .1) +1** where a equals the minimum or maximum rating/loss ratio from Table B. AMA whole person impairment ratings for injury categories that correspond to a greater relative loss of earning capacity will receive a higher FEC adjustment. For example, a psychiatric impairment receives a higher FEC adjustment because RAND data shows that a relatively high wage loss corresponds to the average psychiatric standard permanent disability rating. A hand impairment would receive a lower FEC adjustment because RAND data shows a relatively low wage loss relative to the average psychiatric standard permanent disability rating.

The FEC rank and adjustment factors that correspond to relative earnings for the eight evenly-divided ranges are listed in Table A. The ratio of earnings to losses and the corresponding rank for each injury category are listed in Table B. To adjust an impairment standard for earning capacity, multiply it by the appropriate adjustment factor from Table A and round to the nearest whole number percentage. Alternatively, a table is provided at the end of Section 2 of the Schedule which provides the earning capacity adjustment for all impairment standards and FEC ranks.

Table A

Range of Ratios			
Low	High	FEC Rank	Adjustment Factor
1.647	1.810	One	1.100000
1.476	1.646	Two	1.142857
1.305	1.475	Three	1.185714
1.134	1.304	Four	1.228571
0.963	1.133	Five	1.271429
0.792	0.962	Six	1.314286
0.621	0.791	Seven	1.357143
0.450	0.620	Eight	1.400000

Table B

Part of the Body	Ratio of Rating over Losses	FEC Rank
Hand/fingers	1.810	One
Vision	1.810	One
Knee	1.570	Two
Other	1.530	Two
Ankle	1.520	Two
Elbow	1.510	Two
Loss of grasping power	1.280	Four
Wrist	1.210	Four
Toe(s)	1.110	Five
Spine Thoracic	1.100	Five
General lower extremity	1.100	Five
Spine Lumbar	1.080	Five
Spine Cervical	1.060	Five
Hip	1.030	Five
General upper extremity	1.000	Five
Heart disease	0.970	Five
General Abdominal	0.950	Six
PT head syndrome	0.930	Six
Lung disease	0.790	Seven
Shoulder	0.740	Seven
Hearing	0.610	Eight
Psychiatric	0.450	Eight

The FEC Rank for the "Other" category is based on average ratings and proportional earning losses for the following impairments:

Impaired rib cage
Cosmetic disfigurement
General chest impairment
Facial disfigurement or impairment
Impaired mouth or jaw
Speech impairment
Impaired nose
Impaired nervous system
Vertigo
Impaired smell
Paralysis
Mental Deterioration
Epilepsy
Skull aperture

4. Occupational Grouping

After the rating is adjusted for diminished future earning capacity, it is then modified to take into account the requirements of the specific occupation that the employee was engaged in when injured.

The Schedule divides the labor market into 45 numbered occupational groups. Each group is assigned a three-digit code called an occupational group number. The first digit of the code refers to the arduousness of the duties, ranking jobs from 1 to 5 in ascending order of physical arduousness; the second digit separates occupations into broad categories sharing common characteristics; the third digit differentiates between occupations within these groups. (See Occupational Group Chart in Section 3B of the Schedule for a breakdown of all occupational groups.)

To identify the appropriate occupational group number, look up the occupation in the list contained in Section 3A of the Schedule. Each job title is listed along with its corresponding group number. The appropriate occupation can generally be found listed under a scheduled or alternative job title. If the occupation cannot be found, an appropriate occupational group is determined by analogy to a listed occupation(s) based on a comparison of duties. (The table Occupational Group Characteristics in Section 3C of the Schedule provides a description of each occupational group to facilitate the determination of a group number.)

5. *Occupational Variant*

Section 4 of the Schedule contains tables that cross-reference impairment numbers and occupational group numbers to produce an "occupational variant," which is expressed as a letter. These tables are designed so that variant "F" represents average demands on the injured body part for the particular impairment being rated, with letters "E", "D" and "C" representing progressively lesser demands, and letters "G" through "J" reflecting progressively higher demands.

6. *Occupational Adjustment*

After the rating has been adjusted for diminished future earning capacity, the rating is adjusted next for occupation by reference to tables found in Section 5 of the Schedule. To use this section, find the earning capacity-adjusted rating in the column entitled "Rating" and then read across the table to the column headed with the appropriate occupational variant. The intersection of the row and column contains the occupation-adjusted rating.

7. *Age Adjustment*

Finally, the rating is adjusted to account for the worker's age on the date of injury. Section 6 of the Schedule contains tables for determining the age adjustment. To use this section, find the occupation-adjusted rating in the column entitled "Rating" and read across the table to the column with the injured worker's age on the date of injury.

8. *Final Permanent Disability Rating*

The number identified on the age adjustment table represents the final overall permanent disability rating percentage for a single impairment. (See Subdivisions C.1. and C.2. on pages 10 and 11 to combine multiple impairments and disabilities.)

9. *Rating Formula*

The final rating is generally expressed as a rating formula, as in the following example:

15.01.02.02 – 8 - [5]10 - 470H – 13 – 11%

Each component is described below:

15.01.02.02 – Impairment number for cervical spine, soft tissue lesion

8% – Impairment standard

10% – Rating after adjustment for earning capacity based on FEC rank 5

470 – Occupational group number for Furniture assembler, heavy

H – Occupational variant

13% – Rating after occupational adjustment

11% – Rating after adjustment for age of 30

C. Additional Rating Procedures

1. Formula for Combining Impairments and Disabilities

Impairments and disabilities are generally combined using the following formula where "a" and "b" are the decimal equivalents of the impairment or disability percentages:

$$a + b(1-a)$$

For example, the result of combining 15% and 25% would be calculated as follows:

$$.25 + .15(1-.25)$$
$$.25 + .15(.75)$$
$$.25 + .1125 = .3625 = 36\%$$

Impairment ratings must be expressed in the same scale to be combined. For example, it would be inappropriate to combine 15% UE with 20% WPI. Likewise, one cannot combine an impairment rating with a disability rating.

Except as specified in the section below, when combining three or more ratings on the same scale into a single rating, combine the two largest ratings first, rounding the result to the nearest whole percent. Then combine that result with the next larger rating, and so on, until all ratings are combined. Each successive calculation result must be rounded before performing the next.

2. ***Adjusting AMA Impairments and Combining Ratings***

As used here, the term "adjusting" refers to adjusting an AMA impairment rating for diminished future earning capacity, occupation and age.

Except as specified below, all impairments are converted to the whole person scale, adjusted, and then combined to determine a final overall disability rating.

Multiple impairments involving the hand or foot are combined using standard AMA Guides protocols. The resulting impairment is converted to whole person impairment and adjusted before being combined with other impairments of the same extremity.

Multiple impairments such as those involving a single part of an extremity, e.g. two impairments involving a shoulder such as shoulder instability and limited range of motion, are combined at the upper extremity level, then converted to whole person impairment and adjusted before being combined with other parts of the same extremity. Note that some impairments of the same body part may not be combined because of duplication.

Impairments with disability numbers in the 16.01 and 17.01 series are converted to whole person impairment and adjusted before being combined with any other impairment of the same extremity.

Impairments of an individual extremity are adjusted and combined at the whole person level with other impairments of the same extremity before being combined with impairments of other body parts. For example, an impairment of the left knee and ankle would be combined before further combination with an impairment of the opposing leg or the back.

The composite rating for an extremity (after adjustments) may not exceed the amputation value of the extremity adjusted for earning capacity, occupation and age. The occupational variant used to rate an entire extremity shall be the highest variant of the involved individual impairments.

3. *Rating Impairment Based on Pain*

Pursuant to Chapter 18 of the AMA Guides, a whole person impairment rating based on the body or organ rating system of the AMA Guides (Chapters 3 through 17) may be increased by 0% up to 3% WPI if the burden of the worker's condition has been increased by pain-related impairment in excess of the pain component already incorporated in the WPI rating in Chapters 3-17. (AMA Guides, p. 573.)

A physician may perform a formal pain-related impairment assessment if deemed necessary to justify the increase of an impairment rating based on the body or organ rating system. (See Section 18.3f of the AMA Guides starting on page 575.)

The maximum allowance for pain resulting from a single injury is 3% WPI regardless of the number of impairments resulting from that injury.

The addition of up to 3% for pain is to be made at the whole person level. For example, if an elbow impairment were to be increased by 3% for pain, the rating for the elbow would first be converted to the whole person scale, and then increased. The resultant rating would then be adjusted for diminished future earning capacity, occupation and age.

In the case of multiple impairments, the evaluating physician shall, when medically justifiable, attribute the pain in whole number increments to the appropriate impairments. The additional percentage added for pain will be applied to the respective impairments as described in the preceding paragraph.

4. *Rating Psychiatric Impairment*

Psychiatric impairment shall be evaluated by the physician using the Global Assessment of Function (GAF) scale shown below. The resultant GAF score shall then be converted to a whole person impairment rating using the GAF conversion table below.

(a) Instructions for Determining a GAF score:

STEP 1: Starting at the top level of the GAF scale, evaluate each range by asking "is either the individual's symptom severity OR level of functioning worse than what is indicated in the range description?"

STEP 2: Keep moving down the scale until the range that best matches the individual's symptom severity OR the level of functioning is reached, whichever is worse.

STEP 3: Look at the next lower range as a double-check against having stopped prematurely. This range should be too severe on both symptom severity and level of functioning. If it is, the appropriate range has been reached (continue with step 4). If not, go back to step 2 and continue moving down the scale.

STEP 4: To determine the specific GAF rating within the selected 10 point range, consider whether the individual is functioning at the higher or lower end of the 10 point range. For example, consider an individual who hears voices that do not influence his behavior (e.g., someone with long-standing Schizophrenia who accepts his hallucinations as part of his illness). If the voices occur relatively infrequently (once a week or less) a rating of 39 or 40 might be most appropriate. In contrast, if the individual hears voices almost continuously, a rating of 31 or 32 would be more appropriate.

(b) Global Assessment of Functioning (GAF) Scale

Consider psychological, social, and occupational functioning on a hypothetical continuum of mental health-illness. Do not include impairment in functioning due to physical (or environmental) limitations.

Code	
91 – 100	Superior functioning in a wide range of activities, life's problems never seem to get out of hand, is sought out by others because of his or her many positive qualities. No symptoms.
81 – 90	Absent or minimal symptoms (e.g., mild anxiety before an exam), good functioning in all areas, interested and involved in a wide range of activities, socially effective, generally satisfied with life, no more than everyday problems or concerns (e.g., an occasional argument with family members).
71 – 80	If symptoms are present, they are transient and expectable reactions to psychosocial stressors (e.g., difficulty concentrating after family argument); no more than slight impairment in social, occupational, or school functioning (e.g., temporarily falling behind in schoolwork).
61 – 70	Some mild symptoms (e.g., depressed mood and mild insomnia) OR some difficulty in social, occupational, or school functioning (e.g., occasional truancy, or theft within the household), but generally functioning pretty well, has some meaningful interpersonal relationships.
51 – 60	Moderate symptoms (e.g., flat affect and circumstantial speech, occasional panic attacks) OR moderate difficulty in social, occupational, or school functioning (e.g. few friends, conflicts with peers or co-workers).
41 – 50	Serious symptoms (e.g., suicidal ideation, severe obsessional rituals, frequent shoplifting) OR any serious impairment in social, occupational, or school functioning (e.g., no friends, unable to keep a job).

31 – 40	Some impairment in reality testing or communication (e.g., speech is at times illogical, obscure, or irrelevant) OR major impairment in several areas, such as work or school, family relations, judgment thinking, or mood (e.g.. depressed man avoids friends, neglects family, and is unable to work; child frequently beats up younger children, is defiant at home and is failing at school).
21 – 30	Behavior is considerably influenced by delusions or hallucinations OR serious impairment in communication or judgment (e.g., sometimes incoherent, acts grossly inappropriately, suicidal preoccupation) OR inability to function in almost all areas (e.g., stays in bed all day; no job, home or friends).
11 – 20	Some danger of hurting self or others (e.g., suicide attempts without clear expectation of death; frequently violent; manic excitement) OR occasionally fails to maintain minimal personal hygiene (e.g., smears feces) OR gross impairment in communication (e.g., largely incoherent or mute).
1 – 10	Persistent danger of severely hurting self or others (e.g., recurrent violence) OR persistent inability to maintain minimal personal hygiene OR serious suicidal act with clear expectation of death.
0	Inadequate information.

(c) Converting the GAF Score to a Whole Person Impairment

Locate the GAF score in the table below and read across to determine the corresponding whole person impairment (WPI) rating.

GAF	WPI	GAF	WPI	GAF	WPI	GAF	WPI
1	90	34	63	67	5	100	0
2	89	35	61	68	3		
3	89	36	59	69	2		
4	88	37	57	70	0		
5	87	38	55	71	0		
6	87	39	53	72	0		
7	86	40	51	73	0		
8	85	41	48	74	0		
9	84	42	46	75	0		
10	84	43	44	76	0		
11	83	44	42	77	0		
12	82	45	40	78	0		
13	82	46	38	79	0		
14	81	47	36	80	0		
15	80	48	34	81	0		
16	80	49	32	82	0		
17	79	50	30	83	0		
18	78	51	29	84	0		
19	78	52	27	85	0		
20	77	53	26	86	0		
21	76	54	24	87	0		
22	76	55	23	88	0		
23	75	56	21	89	0		
24	74	57	20	90	0		
25	73	58	18	91	0		
26	73	59	17	92	0		
27	72	60	15	93	0		
28	71	61	14	94	0		
29	71	62	12	95	0		
30	70	63	11	96	0		
31	69	64	9	97	0		
32	67	65	8	98	0		
33	65	66	6	99	0		

SECTION 2 – IMPAIRMENT NUMBER/EARNING CAPACITY ADJUSTMENT

Use this section to determine an impairment number and a future earning capacity (FEC) rank for each body part being evaluated. Then use the table at the end of this section to adjust the impairment standard for earning capacity. If the impairment is not addressed by the AMA Guides, choose the closest applicable impairment number, and replace the last pair of digits with the number 99. For example, a condition that was analogized to a spinal cord disorder affecting the respiratory system (impairment no. 13.10.01.00) would take the impairment number 13.10.01.99.

# Impairment	FEC Rank	Impairment
03 – CARDIOVASCULAR SYSTEM – HEART & AORTA		
03.01.00.00	5	Valvular Heart Disease
03.02.00.00	5	Coronary Heart Disease
03.03.00.00	5	Congenital Heart Disease
03.04.00.00	5	Cardiomyopathies
03.05.00.00	5	Pericardial Heart Disease
03.06.00.00	5	Arrhythmia
04 – CARDIOVASCULAR SYSTEM – SYSTEMIC & PULMONARY ARTERIES		
04.01.00.00	5	Hypertensive Cardiovascular Disease
04.02.00.00	5	Aortic Disease
04.03.01.00	5	Peripheral Vascular Disease, Upper Extremities
04.03.02.00	5	Peripheral Vascular Disease, Lower Extremities
04.04.00.00	7	Pulmonary Circulation Disease
05 – RESPIRATORY SYSTEM		
05.01.00.00	7	Asthma
05.02.00.00	7	Respiratory Disorders
05.03.00.00	7	Cancer
06 – DIGESTIVE SYSTEM		
06.01.00.00	6	Upper Digestive Tract
06.02.00.00	6	Colon, Rectum, Anus
06.03.00.00	6	Enterocutaneous Fistulas
06.04.00.00	6	Liver/Biliary Tract
06.05.00.00	6	Hernias
07 – URINARY & REPRODUCTIVE SYSTEMS		
07.01.00.00	2	Upper Urinary Tract
07.02.00.00	2	Urinary Diversion
07.03.00.00	2	Bladder
07.04.00.00	2	Urethra
07.05.00.00	2	Reproductive System

Impairment#	FEC Rank	Impairment
08 – SKIN		
08.01.00.00	2	Disfigurement
08.02.00.00	2	Scars & Skin Grafts
08.03.00.00	2	Contact Dermatitis
08.04.00.00	2	Latex Allergy
08.05.00.00	2	Skin Cancer
09 – HEMATOPOIETIC SYSTEM		
09.01.00.00	2	Hematopoietic Impairment
10 – ENDOCRINE SYSTEM		
10.01.00.00	2	Diabetes Mellitus
11 – EAR, NOSE & THROAT		
11.01.01.00	8	Ear – Hearing Impairment
11.01.02.00	8	Ear – Vestibular Disorder
11.02.01.00	2	Face/cosmetic
11.02.02.00	2	Face/eye/cosmetic
11.03.01.00	2	Nose/Throat/Related Structures – Respiration
11.03.02.00	2	Nose/Throat/Related Structures – Mastication & Deglutition
11.03.03.00	2	Nose/Throat/Related Structures – Olfaction & Taste
11.03.04.00	2	Nose/Throat/Related Structures – Voice & Speech
12 – VISUAL SYSTEM		
12.01.00.00	1	Visual Acuity
12.02.00.00	1	Visual Field
12.03.00.00	1	Visual System
13 – CENTRAL & PERIPHERAL NERVOUS SYSTEM		
13.01.00.00	6	Consciousness Disorder
13.02.00.00	2	Episodic Neurologic Disorder
13.03.00.00	6	Arousal Disorder
13.04.00.00	2	Cognitive Impairment

# Impairment	FEC Rank	Impairment
13.05.00.00	2	Language Disorder
13.06.00.00	8	Behavioral/Emotional Disorder
13.07.01.00	2	Cranial Nerve – Olfactory
13.07.02.00	1	Cranial Nerve – Optic
13.07.03.00	2	Cranial Nerve – Oculomotor, Trochlear & Abducens
13.07.04.00	2	Cranial Nerve – Trigeminal
13.07.05.00	2	Cranial Nerve – Facial
13.07.06.01	8	Cranial Nerve – Vestibulocochlear – Vertigo
13.07.06.02	8	Cranial Nerve – Vestibulocochlear – Tinnitus
13.07.07.00	2	Cranial Nerve – Glossopharyngeal & Valgus
13.07.08.00	2	Cranial Nerve – Spinal Accessory
13.07.09.00	2	Cranial Nerve – Hypoglossal
13.08.00.00	5	Station, Gait, Movement
13.09.00.00	5	Upper Extremities
13.10.01.00	7	Spinal Cord Disorder – Respiratory
13.10.02.00	2	Spinal Cord Disorder – Urinary
13.10.03.00	2	Spinal Cord Disorder – Anorectal
13.10.04.00	2	Spinal Cord Disorder – Sexual
13.11.01.01	5	Chronic Pain – Upper Extremities – Causalgia
13.11.01.02	5	Chronic Pain – Upper Extremities – Post-traumatic Neuralgia
13.11.01.03	5	Chronic Pain – Upper Extremities – Reflex Sympathetic Dystrophy
13.11.02.01	5	Chronic Pain – Lower Extremities – Causalgia
13.11.02.02	5	Chronic Pain – Lower Extremities – Post-traumatic Neuralgia
13.11.02.03	5	Chronic Pain – Lower Extremities – Reflex Sympathetic Dystrophy
13.12.01.01	5	Peripheral Nerve System – Spine – Sensory
13.12.01.02	5	Peripheral Nerve System – Spine – Motor
13.12.02.01	5	Peripheral Nerve System – Upper Extremity – Sensory
13.12.02.02	5	Peripheral Nerve System – Upper Extremity – Motor
13.12.03.01	5	Peripheral Nerve System – Lower Extremity – Sensory
13.12.03.02	5	Peripheral Nerve System – Lower Extremity – Motor

Impairment#	FEC Rank	Impairment
14 – MENTAL & BEHAVIORIAL DISORDERS		
14.01.00.00	8	Psychiatric – Mental and Behavioral
15 – SPINE		
15.01.01.00	5	Cervical – Diagnosis-related Estimate (DRE)
15.01.02.01	5	Cervical – Range of Motion (ROM) – Fracture
15.01.02.02	5	Cervical – Range of Motion – Soft Tissue Lesion
15.01.02.03	5	Cervical – Range of Motion – Spondylolysis, no operation
15.01.02.04	5	Cervical – Range of Motion – Stenosis, with operation
15.01.02.05	5	Cervical – Range of Motion – Nerve Root/Spinal Cord-Sensory
15.01.02.06	5	Cervical – Range of Motion – Nerve Root/Spinal Cord – Motor
15.02.01.00	5	Thoracic – Diagnosis-related Estimate
15.02.02.01	5	Thoracic – Range of Motion – Fracture
15.02.02.02	5	Thoracic – Range of Motion – Soft Tissue Lesion
15.02.02.03	5	Thoracic – Range of Motion – Spondylolysis, no operation
15.02.02.04	5	Thoracic – Range of Motion – Stenosis, with operation
15.02.02.05	5	Thoracic – Range of Motion – Nerve Root/Spinal Cord – Sensory
15.02.02.06	5	Thoracic – Range of Motion – Nerve Root/Spinal Cord – Motor
15.03.01.00	5	Lumbar – Diagnosis-related Estimate
15.03.02.01	5	Lumbar – Range of Motion – Fracture
15.03.02.02	5	Lumbar – Range of Motion – Soft Tissue Lesion
15.03.02.03	5	Lumbar – Range of Motion – Spondylolysis, no operation
15.03.02.04	5	Lumbar – Range of Motion – Stenosis, with operation
15.03.02.05	5	Lumbar – Range of Motion – Nerve Root/Spinal Cord – Sensory
15.03.02.06	5	Lumbar – Range of Motion – Nerve Root/Spinal Cord – Motor
15.04.01.00	5	Corticospinal Tract – One Upper Extremity
15.04.02.00	5	Corticospinal Tract – Two Upper Extremities
15.04.03.00	5	Corticospinal Tract – Station/Gait Disorder

# Impairment	FEC Rank	Impairment
15.04.04.00	2	Corticospinal Tract – Bladder Impairment
15.04.05.00	2	Corticospinal Tract – Anorectal Impairment
15.04.06.00	2	Corticospinal Tract – Sexual Impairment
15.04.07.00	7	Corticospinal Tract – Respiratory Impairment
15.05.01.00	5	Pelvic – Healed Fracture
15.05.02.00	5	Pelvic – Healed Fracture with Displacement
15.05.03.00	5	Pelvic – Healed Fracture with Deformity
16 – UPPER EXTREMITIES		
16.01.01.01	5	Arm – Amputation/Deltoid insertion proximally
16.01.01.02	5	Arm – Amputation/Bicipital insertion proximally
16.01.01.03	5	Arm – Amputation/Wrist proximally
16.01.01.04	5	Arm – Amputation/All fingers at MP joint proximally
16.01.02.01	5	Arm – Peripheral neuropathy – Brachial plexus
16.01.02.02	4	Arm – Peripheral neuropathy – Entrapment/compression – Carpal tunnel
16.01.02.03	5	Arm – Peripheral neuropathy – Entrapment/compression – Other
16.01.02.04	5	Arm – Peripheral neuropathy – CRPS I
16.01.02.05	5	Arm – Peripheral neuropathy – CRPS II
16.01.03.00	5	Arm – Peripheral vascular
16.01.04.00	4	Arm – Grip/pinch strength
16.01.05.00	5	Arm – Other
16.02.01.00	7	Shoulder – Range of motion
16.02.02.00	7	Shoulder – Other
16.03.01.00	2	Elbow/forearm – Range of motion
16.03.02.00	2	Elbow/forearm – Other
16.04.01.00	4	Wrist – Range of motion
16.04.02.00	4	Wrist – Other
16.05.01.00	1	Hand/multiple fingers – Range of motion
16.05.02.00	1	Hand/multiple fingers – Amputation
16.05.03.00	1	Hand/multiple fingers – Sensory
16.05.04.00	1	Hand/multiple fingers – Other
16.06.01.01	1	Thumb – Range of motion
16.06.01.02	1	Thumb – Amputation

Impairment#	FEC Rank	Impairment
16.06.01.03	1	Thumb – Sensory
16.06.01.04	1	Thumb – Other
16.06.02.01	1	Index – Range of motion
16.06.02.02	1	Index – Amputation
16.06.02.03	1	Index – Sensory
16.06.02.04	1	Index – Other
16.06.03.01	1	Middle – Range of motion
16.06.03.02	1	Middle – Amputation
16.06.03.03	1	Middle – Sensory
16.06.03.04	1	Middle – Other
16.06.04.01	1	Ring – Range of motion
16.06.04.02	1	Ring – Amputation
16.06.04.03	1	Ring – Sensory
16.06.04.04	1	Ring – Other
16.06.05.01	1	Little – Range of motion
16.06.05.02	1	Little – Amputation
16.06.05.03	1	Little – Sensory
16.06.05.04	1	Little – Other
17 – LOWER EXTREMITIES		
17.01.01.00	5	Leg – Limb Length
17.01.02.01	5	Leg – Amputation/Knee proximally
17.01.02.02	5	Leg – Amputation/MTP joint proximally
17.01.03.00	5	Leg – Skin Loss
17.01.04.00	5	Leg – Peripheral Nerve
17.01.05.00	5	Leg – Vascular
17.01.06.00	5	Leg – Causalgia/RSD
17.01.07.00	5	Leg – Gait Derangement
17.01.08.00	5	Leg – Other
17.02.10.00	5	Pelvis – Diagnosis-based estimate (DBE) – Fracture
17.03.01.00	5	Hip – Muscle Atrophy
17.03.02.00	5	Hip – Ankylosis
17.03.03.00	5	Hip – Arthritis
17.03.04.00	5	Hip – Range of Motion

# Impairment	FEC Rank	Impairment
17.03.05.00	5	Hip – Muscle Strength
17.03.06.00	5	Hip – Other
17.03.10.01	5	Hip – Diagnosis-based Estimate – Hip/Replacement
17.03.10.02	5	Hip – Diagnosis-based Estimate – Hip/Femoral Neck Fracture
17.03.10.03	5	Hip – Diagnosis-based Estimate – Hip/Arthroplasty
17.03.10.04	5	Hip – Diagnosis-based Estimate – Trochanteric bursitis
17.04.10.00	5	Femur – Diagnosis-based Estimate – Fracture
17.05.01.00	2	Knee – Muscle Atrophy
17.05.02.00	2	Knee – Ankylosis
17.05.03.00	2	Knee – Arthritis
17.05.04.00	2	Knee – Range of Motion
17.05.05.00	2	Knee – Muscle Strength
17.05.06.00	2	Knee – Other
17.05.10.01	2	Knee – Diagnosis-based Estimate – Subluxation/dislocation
17.05.10.02	2	Knee – Diagnosis-based Estimate – Fracture
17.05.10.03	2	Knee – Diagnosis-based Estimate – Patellectomy
17.05.10.04	2	Knee – Diagnosis-based Estimate – Menisectomy
17.05.10.05	2	Knee – Diagnosis-based Estimate – Cruciate/collateral Ligament
17.05.10.06	2	Knee – Diagnosis-based Estimate – Plateau Fracture
17.05.10.07	2	Knee – Diagnosis-based Estimate – Supra/Intercondylar Fracture
17.05.10.08	2	Knee – Diagnosis-based Estimate – Total Replacement
17.05.10.09	2	Knee – Diagnosis-based Estimate – Proximal Tibial osteotomy
17.06.10.00	5	Tibia/fibula – Diagnosis-based Estimate – fracture
17.07.01.00	2	Ankle – Muscle Atrophy
17.07.02.00	2	Ankle – Ankylosis
17.07.03.00	2	Ankle – Arthritis

Impairment#	FEC Rank	Impairment
17.07.04.00	2	Ankle – Range of Motion
17.07.05.00	2	Ankle – Muscle Strength
17.07.06.00	2	Ankle – Other
17.07.10.01	2	Ankle – Diagnosis-based Estimate – Ligament Instability
17.07.10.02	2	Ankle – Diagnosis-based Estimate – Fracture
17.08.01.00	2	Foot – Muscle Atrophy
17.08.02.00	2	Foot – Ankylosis
17.08.03.00	2	Foot – Arthritis
17.08.04.00	2	Foot – Range of Motion
17.08.05.00	2	Foot – Muscle Strength
17.08.06.00	2	Foot – Other
17.08.10.01	2	Foot – Diagnosis-based Estimate – Hind Foot Fracture
17.08.10.02	2	Foot – Diagnosis-based Estimate – Loss of Tibia
17.08.10.03	2	Foot – Diagnosis-based Estimate – Intra-articular Fracture
17.08.10.04	2	Foot – Diagnosis-based Estimate – Calvus
17.08.10.05	2	Foot – Diagnosis-based Estimate – Rocker Bottom
17.08.10.06	2	Foot – Diagnosis-based Estimate – Avascular Necrosis
17.08.10.07	2	Foot – Diagnosis-based Estimate – Metatarsal fracture
17.09.01.00	5	Toes – Muscle Atrophy
17.09.02.00	5	Toes – Ankylosis
17.09.03.00	5	Toes – Arthritis
17.09.04.00	5	Toes – Range of Motion
17.09.05.00	5	Toes – Muscle Strength
17.09.06.00	5	Toes – Amputation
17.09.07.00	5	Toes – Other
18 – PAIN		
18.00.00.00	Variable	Pain – use FEC rank for involved body part.

FUTURE EARNING CAPACITY (FEC) ADJUSTMENT TABLE

Directions: To adjust for earning capacity, look up the impairment standard in the top row (bolded numbers), and read down to the entry corresponding to the applicable future earning capacity rank

FEC	AMA Whole Person Impairment Standard																			
Rank	**1**	**2**	**3**	**4**	**5**	**6**	**7**	**8**	**9**	**10**	**11**	**12**	**13**	**14**	**15**	**16**	**17**	**18**	**19**	**20**
One	1	2	3	4	6	7	8	9	10	11	12	13	14	15	17	18	19	20	21	22
Two	1	2	3	5	6	7	8	9	10	11	13	14	15	16	17	18	19	21	22	23
Three	1	2	4	5	6	7	8	9	11	12	13	14	15	17	18	19	20	21	23	24
Four	1	2	4	5	6	7	9	10	11	12	14	15	16	17	18	20	21	22	23	25
Five	1	3	4	5	6	8	9	10	11	13	14	15	17	18	19	20	22	23	24	25
Six	1	3	4	5	7	8	9	11	12	13	14	16	17	18	20	21	22	24	25	26
Seven	1	3	4	5	7	8	10	11	12	14	15	16	18	19	20	22	23	24	26	27
Eight	1	3	4	6	7	8	10	11	13	14	15	17	18	20	21	22	24	25	27	28

FEC	AMA Whole Person Impairment Standard																			
Rank	**21**	**22**	**23**	**24**	**25**	**26**	**27**	**28**	**29**	**30**	**31**	**32**	**33**	**34**	**35**	**36**	**37**	**38**	**39**	**40**
One	23	24	25	26	28	29	30	31	32	33	34	35	36	37	39	40	41	42	43	44
Two	24	25	26	27	29	30	31	32	33	34	35	37	38	39	40	41	42	43	45	46
Three	25	26	27	28	30	31	32	33	34	36	37	38	39	40	42	43	44	45	46	47
Four	26	27	28	29	31	32	33	34	36	37	38	39	41	42	43	44	45	47	48	49
Five	27	28	29	31	32	33	34	36	37	38	39	41	42	43	45	46	47	48	50	51
Six	28	29	30	32	33	34	35	37	38	39	41	42	43	45	46	47	49	50	51	53
Seven	29	30	31	33	34	35	37	38	39	41	42	43	45	46	48	49	50	52	53	54
Eight	29	31	32	34	35	36	38	39	41	42	43	45	46	48	49	50	52	53	55	56

FEC Rank	AMA Whole Person Impairment Standard 41	42	43	44	45	46	47	48	49	50	51	52	53	54	55	56	57	58	59	60
One	45	46	47	48	50	51	52	53	54	55	56	57	58	59	61	62	63	64	65	66
Two	47	48	49	50	51	53	54	55	56	57	58	59	61	62	63	64	65	66	67	69
Three	49	50	51	52	53	55	56	57	58	59	60	62	63	64	65	66	68	69	70	71
Four	50	52	53	54	55	57	58	59	60	61	63	64	65	66	68	69	70	71	72	74
Five	52	53	55	56	57	58	60	61	62	64	65	66	67	69	70	71	72	74	75	76
Six	54	55	57	58	59	60	62	63	64	66	67	68	70	71	72	74	75	76	78	79
Seven	56	57	58	60	61	62	64	65	67	68	69	71	72	73	75	76	77	79	80	81
Eight	57	59	60	62	63	64	66	67	69	70	71	73	74	76	77	78	80	81	83	84

FEC Rank	AMA Whole Person Impairment Standard 61	62	63	64	65	66	67	68	69	70	71	72	73	74	75	76	77	78	79	80
One	67	68	69	70	72	73	74	75	76	77	78	79	80	81	83	84	85	86	87	88
Two	70	71	72	73	74	75	77	78	79	80	81	82	83	85	86	87	88	89	90	91
Three	72	74	75	76	77	78	79	81	82	83	84	85	87	88	89	90	91	92	94	95
Four	75	76	77	79	80	81	82	84	85	86	87	88	90	91	92	93	95	96	97	98
Five	78	79	80	81	83	84	85	86	88	89	90	92	93	94	95	97	98	99	100	100
Six	80	81	83	84	85	87	88	89	91	92	93	95	96	97	99	100	100	100	100	100
Seven	83	84	86	87	88	90	91	92	94	95	96	98	99	100	100	100	100	100	100	100
Eight	85	87	88	90	91	92	94	95	97	98	99	100	100	100	100	100	100	100	100	100

FEC Rank	AMA Whole Person Impairment Standard 81	82	83	84	85	86	87	88	89	90	91	92	93	94	95	96	97	98	99	100
One	89	90	91	92	94	95	96	97	98	99	100	100	100	100	100	100	100	100	100	100
Two	93	94	95	96	97	98	99	100	100	100	100	100	100	100	100	100	100	100	100	100
Three	96	97	98	100	100	100	100	100	100	100	100	100	100	100	100	100	100	100	100	100
Four	100	100	100	100	100	100	100	100	100	100	100	100	100	100	100	100	100	100	100	100
Five	100	100	100	100	100	100	100	100	100	100	100	100	100	100	100	100	100	100	100	100
Six	100	100	100	100	100	100	100	100	100	100	100	100	100	100	100	100	100	100	100	100
Seven	100	100	100	100	100	100	100	100	100	100	100	100	100	100	100	100	100	100	100	100
Eight	100	100	100	100	100	100	100	100	100	100	100	100	100	100	100	100	100	100	100	100

SECTION 3 - OCCUPATIONS AND GROUP NUMBERS

Section 3 contains two parts. Part A contains an alphabetized list of occupations with their scheduled occupational group numbers. Find the occupation in the alphabetical list and record the associated group number. Note that some occupations may have more than one title and that all variations may not be listed. Also note that some titles may appear more than once, but pertain to different industries. Care should be taken to ensure that the industry designated also matches the occupation under consideration.

Part B contains an occupational group chart which illustrates the overall system for classifying occupations into groups. Part C contains a description and sample occupations of each group. This information may be useful if the occupation cannot be located in Part A. Simply determine the basic functions and activities of the occupation under consideration and relate it to a comparable scheduled occupation to determine the appropriate group number.

After establishing the occupation and group number, turn to Section 4 to determine the occupational variant.

PART A – LIST OF OCCUPATIONS AND GROUP NUMBERS

Group No.	Occupation	Industry
111	ABSTRACTOR	profess. & kin.
110	ACADEMIC DEAN	education
110	ACCOUNT EXECUTIVE	business ser.
111	ACCOUNT INFORMATION CLERK	utilities
111	ACCOUNTANT	profess. & kin.
111	ACCOUNTANT, PROPERTY	profess. & kin.
111	ACCOUNTING CLERK	clerical
590	ACROBAT	amuse. & rec.
210	ACTOR	amuse. & rec.
310	ACUPRESSURIST	medical ser.
211	ADDRESSING MACHINE OPERATOR	clerical
111	ADMINISTRATIVE ANALYST	any industry
211	ADMINISTRATIVE CLERK	clerical
212	ADMINISTRATOR, HEALTH CARE FACILITY	medical ser.
111	ADMISSIONS EVALUATOR	education
212	AIR ANALYST	profess. & kin.
481	AIR CONDITIONING INSTALLER SERV., WINDOW UNIT	construction
480	AIR HAMMER OPERATOR	construction
212	AIR TRAFFIC CONTROL SPECIALIST, TOWER	government ser.
380	AIRCRAFT BODY REPAIRER	air trans.
380	AIRCRAFT BONDED STRUCTURES REPAIRER	aircraft mfg.
460	AIRCRAFT SERVICE WORKER	air trans.
341	AIRCRAFT SERVICE ATTENDANT	air trans.
380	AIRFRAME AND POWER PLANT MECHANIC	aircraft mfg.
213	AIRLINE TRANSPORTATION AGENT	air trans.
213	AIRPLANE INSPECTOR	air trans.
250	AIRPLANE PILOT, COMMERCIAL	air trans.
322	AIRPLANE FLIGHT ATTENDANT	air trans.
380	ALARM SERVICE TECHNICIAN	business ser.
111	ALARM SIGNAL OPERATOR	any industry
560	AMBULANCE ATTENDANT	medical ser.
560	AMBULANCE DRIVER	medical ser.
340	AMUSEMENT PARK ATTENDANT	amuse. & rec.
210	AMUSEMENT PARK ENTERTAINER	amuse. & rec.
220	ANESTHESIOLOGIST	medical ser.
310	ANGIOGRAM TECHNOLOGIST	medical ser.
491	ANIMAL KEEPER	amuse. & rec.
390	ANIMAL TRAINER	amuse. & rec.
491	ANIMAL RIDE ATTENDANT	amuse. & rec.
210	ANNOUNCER	radio-tv broad.
460	ANODIZER	any industry
380	ANTENNA INSTALLER	any industry
380	ANTENNA INSTALLER, SATELLITE COMMUNICATIONS	any industry
110	APPEALS REFEREE	government ser.
111	APPOINTMENT CLERK	clerical
212	APPRAISER, ART	any industry
212	APPRAISER, BUSINESS EQPT.	any industry
213	APPRAISER, REAL ESTATE	real estate
330	ARBOR PRESS OPERATOR	any industry
370	ARC CUTTER	welding
212	ARCHITECT	profess. & kin.
111	ARCHIVIST	profess. & kin.
320	ARMATURE BANDER	any industry
350	ARMORED CAR DRIVER	business ser.
390	ARMORED CAR GUARD	business ser.
111	ART DIRECTOR	motion picture
221	ARTIFICIAL FLOWER MAKER	button & notion
220	ARTIFICIAL PLASTIC EYE MAKER	optical goods
480	ASPHALT RAKER	construction
351	ASPHALT SURFACE HEATER OPERATOR	construction
351	ASPHALT DISTRIBUTOR TENDER	construction
351	ASPHALT PAVING MACHINE OPERATOR	construction
120	ASSEMBLER	jewelry-silver.
221	ASSEMBLER	house. appl.
221	ASSEMBLER, ELECTRIC MOTOR	elec. equip.
370	ASSEMBLER, INTERNAL COMBUSTION ENGINE	engine-turbine
370	ASSEMBLER, MOTOR VEHICLE	auto. mfg.
221	ASSEMBLER, MUSICAL INSTRUMENTS	musical inst.

Group No.	Occupation	Industry
320	ASSEMBLER, OFFICE MACHINES	office machines
221	ASSEMBLER, PRODUCTION	any industry
120	ASSEMBLER, SEMICONDUCTOR	electron. comp.
221	ASSEMBLER, SMALL PRODUCTS	any industry
380	ASSEMBLER, SUBASSEMBLY	aircraft mfg.
380	ASSEMBLER-INSTALLER, GENERAL	aircraft mfg.
590	ATHLETE, PROFESSIONAL	amuse. & rec.
390	ATHLETIC TRAINER	amuse. & rec.
111	ATTENDANCE CLERK	education
111	AUCTION CLERK	retail trade
210	AUCTIONEER	retail trade
212	AUDIO OPERATOR	radio-tv broad.
221	AUDIO VIDEO REPAIRER	any industry
251	AUDIOVISUAL PRODUCTION SPECIALIST	profess. & kin.
111	AUDIT CLERK	clerical
111	AUDITOR	profess. & kin.
251	AUDITOR, FIELD	profess. & kin.
330	AUTOCLAVE OPERATOR	aircraft mfg.
370	AUTOMATED EQUIPMENT INSTALLER	machinery mfg.
370	AUTOMOBILE ASSEMBLER	auto. mfg.
340	AUTOMOBILE DETAILER	automotive ser.
111	AUTOMOBILE LOCATOR	retail trade
321	AUTOMOBILE UPHOLSTERER	automotive ser.
340	AUTOMOBILE WASHER & POLISHER	automotive ser.
460	AUTOMOBILE WRECKER	wholesale tr.
370	AUTOMOBILE ACCESSORIES INSTALLER	automotive ser.
370	AUTOMOBILE BODY REPAIRER	automotive ser.
214	AUTOMOBILE REPAIR SERVICE ESTIMATOR	automotive ser.
370	AUTOMOBILE SERVICE STATION MECHANIC	automotive ser.
321	AUTO PAINTER	any industry
380	AWNING MAKER	tex. prod., nec.
240	BABYSITTER	domestic ser.
460	BAGGAGE HANDLER	r.r. trans.
212	BAGGAGE SCREENER, AIRPO	air transport.
214	BAGGER	retail trade; groceries
490	BAILIFF	government ser.

Group No.	Occupation	Industry
322	BAKER	hotel & rest.
460	BAKER HELPER	bakery products
420	BAKER	bakery products
322	BAKERY SUPERVISOR	bakery products
330	BAND-SAWING MACHINE OPERATOR	fabrication, nec
230	BAND SAWMILL OPERATOR	saw. & plan.
211	BANK CLERK	financial
290	BARBER	personal ser.
330	BARREL ASSEMBLER	wood. container
460	BARREL FILLER	beverage
322	BARTENDER	hotel & rest.
221	BASKET MAKER	wood. container
230	BATCH STILL OPERATOR	chemical
321	BATTERY ASSEMBLER, DRY CELL	elec. equip.
321	BATTERY REPAIRER	any industry
290	BEAUTICIAN	personal ser.
230	BED LASTER	boot & shoe
491	BEEKEEPER	agriculture
360	BELLHOP	hotel & rest.
221	BENCH WORKER	optical goods
330	BENDING MACHINE OPERATOR	any industry
493	BICYCLE MESSENGER	business ser.
320	BICYCLE REPAIRER	any industry
480	BILLBOARD & SIGN ERECTOR	fabrication, nec
480	BILLBOARD ERECTOR HELPER	construction
112	BILLING CLERK	clerical
213	BILLPOSTER	business ser.
230	BINDERY WORKER	print. & pub.
212	BIOCHEMIST	profess. & kin.
110	BIOLOGY SPECIMEN TECHNICIAN	profess. & kin.
320	BIOMEDICAL EQUIPMENT TECHNICIAN	profess. & kin.
430	BLACKSMITH	forging
460	BLACKSMITH HELPER	forging
480	BLASTER	mining; construction
332	BLENDER	petrol. refin.
240	BLIND AIDE	personal ser.
330	BLISTER MACHINE OPERATOR	any industry
220	BLOCKER AND CUTTER, CONTACT LENS	optical goods

Group No.	Occupation	Industry
221	BLOCKER, HAND	hat & cap
230	BLUEPRINTING MACHINE OPERATOR	any industry
380	BOAT REPAIRER	ship-boat mfg.
380	BOAT RIGGER	retail trade
380	BOATBUILDER, WOOD	ship-boat mfg.
390	BODYGUARD	personal ser.
332	BOILER OPERATOR	any industry
332	BOILER TENDER	any industry
430	BOILERMAKER	struct. metal
460	BOILERMAKER HELPER	struct. metal
111	BONDING AGENT	business ser.
322	BONER, MEAT	meat products
221	BOOK REPAIRER	any industry
320	BOOKBINDER	print. & pub.
112	BOOKKEEPER	clerical
112	BOOKKEEPER, GENERAL LEDGER	clerical
351	BOOM CONVEYOR OPERATOR	any industry
330	BORING MACHINE OPERATOR	woodworking
230	BOTTLE PACKER	beverage
390	BOUNCER	amuse. & rec.
390	BOUNTY HUNTER	business ser.
221	BOW MAKER	any industry
493	BOWLER, PROFESSIONAL	amuse. and rec.
331	BOWLING BALL MOLDER	toy-sport equip.
321	BOX MAKER, PAPERBOARD	any industry
321	BOX MAKER, WOOD	wood. container
230	BOX PRINTING MACHINE OPERATOR	any industry
230	BOX BLANK MACHINE OPERATOR	wood. container
460	BOX FOLDING MACHINE OPERATOR	paper goods
321	BOX SPRING MAKER	furniture
211	BRAILLE OPERATOR	print. & pub.
111	BRAILLE PROOFREADER	nonprofit org.
370	BRAKE REPAIRER	automotive ser.
330	BRAKE PRESS OPERATOR	any industry
330	BRAZING MACHINE OPERATOR	welding
330	BREAD WRAPPING MACHINE OPERATOR	any industry
332	BREWERY CELLAR WORKER	beverage
331	BRICK AND TILE MAKING MACHINE OPERATOR	brick & tile
481	BRICKLAYER	construction
481	BRICKLAYER APPRENTICE	construction
480	BRICKLAYER HELPER	construction
482	BRIDGE MAINTENANCE WORKER	construction
482	BRIDGE WORKER	construction
331	BRIQUETTE MACHINE OPERATOR	fabrication, nec
330	BROACHING MACHINE OPERATOR, PRODUCTION	machine shop
321	BROOM STITCHER	fabrication, nec
492	BUCKER	logging
111	BUDGET ANALYST	government ser.
321	BUFFER	any industry
230	BUFFING MACHINE TENDER, AUTOMATIC	any industry
480	BUILDING CLEANER, OUTSIDE	any industry
213	BUILDING INSPECTOR	government ser.
213	BUILDING INSPECTOR	insurance
380	BUILDING MAINTENANCE REPAIRER	any industry
351	BULLDOZER OPERATOR	any industry
380	BURGLAR ALARM INSTALLER/REPAIRER	business ser.
330	BURNING MACHINE OPERATOR	welding
250	BUS DRIVER	motor trans.
322	BUS PERSON	hotel & rest.
110	BUSINESS MANAGER	amuse. & rec.
111	BUSINESS REPRESENTATIVE, LABOR UNION	profess. & kin.
420	BUTCHER, ALL-ROUND	meat products
322	BUTCHER, MEAT	hotel & rest.
240	BUTLER	domestic ser.
460	BUTTERMAKER	dairy products
230	BUTTONHOLE AND BUTTON SEWING MACHINE OPERATOR	garment
320	CABINETMAKER	woodworking
320	CABLE ASSEMBLER AND SWAGER	aircraft mfg.
350	CABLE CAR OPERATOR	r.r. transportation
380	CABLE INSTALLER-REPAIRER	utilities
380	CABLE MAINTAINER	utilities
480	CABLE PULLER	construction
380	CABLE SPLICER	construction
481	CABLE TELEVISION INSTALLER	radio-tv broad.
380	CABLE TESTER	tel. & tel.
120	CAD DESIGNER	profess. & kindred

Group No.	Occupation	Industry
360	CADDIE	amuse. & rec.
322	CAFETERIA ATTENDANT	hotel & rest.
480	CAGER	mine & quarry
221	CAKE DECORATOR	bakery products
120	CALLIGRAPHER	profess. & kin.
360	CAMERA OPERATOR	motion picture
220	CAMERA REPAIRER	photo. appar.
390	CAMP COUNSELOR	amuse. & rec.
340	CAMPGROUND ATTENDANT	amuse. & rec.
230	CAN-FILLING AND CLOSING MACHINE TENDER	can. & preserv.
221	CANDLEMAKER	fabrication, nec
331	CANDY MAKER	sugar & conf.
221	CANER	furniture
230	CANNERY WORKER, HAND OR MACHINE	can. & preserv.
420	CANVAS REPAIRER	any industry
230	CAP-LINING MACHINE OPERATOR	any industry
320	CAPACITOR ASSEMBLER	elec. equip.
211	CARD DEALER	amusement and rec.
322	CAR HOP	hotel & rest.
460	CARBIDE POWDER PROCESSOR	machine shop
110	CARDIAC MONITOR TECHNICIAN	medical ser.
212	CARDIOPULMONARY TECHNOLOGIST	medical ser.
240	CARDROOM ATTENDANT	amuse. & rec.
360	CARGO AGENT	air trans.
380	CARPENTER	construction
380	CARPENTER APPRENTICE	construction
480	CARPENTER HELPER	construction
380	CARPENTER, ACOUSTICAL	construction
380	CARPENTER, MAINTENANCE	any industry
380	CARPENTER, RAILCAR	railroad equip.
481	CARPENTER, ROUGH	construction
380	CARPENTER, SHIP	ship-boat mfg.
480	CARPET CUTTER	retail trade
481	CARPET LAYER	retail trade
321	CARPET SEWER	carpet & rug
230	CARPET WEAVER	carpet & rug
480	CARPET LAYER HELPER	retail trade
120	CARTOGRAPHER	prof. & kindred
330	CARTON-FORMING MACHINE OPERATOR	any industry
460	CARTON-FORMING MACHINE TENDER	paper goods
120	CARTOONIST, MOTION PICTURES	motion picture
111	CASEWORKER	social ser.
320	CASH REGISTER SERVICER	any industry
111	CASHIER	clerical
214	CASHIER-CHECKER	retail trade
230	CASING MACHINE OPERATOR	meat products
330	CASTER	smelt. & refin.
331	CASTER	jewelry-silver.
320	CASTING REPAIRER	any industry
322	CATERER	personal ser.
491	CATTLE HERDER	agriculture
480	CAULKER	construction
330	CELLOPHANE BAG MACHINE OPERATOR	paper goods
481	CEMENT MASON	construction
480	CEMENT SPRAYER, NOZZLE	construction
480	CEMENT MASON HELPER	construction
480	CEMENTER, OILWELL	petrol. & gas
331	CENTER MACHINE OPERATOR	sugar & conf.
380	CENTRAL OFFICE REPAIRER	tel. & tel.
331	CENTRIFUGAL EXTRACTOR OPERATOR	any industry
230	CENTRIFUGE OPERATOR, PLASMA PROCESSING	medical ser.
230	CENTRIFUGE SEPARATOR OPERATOR	chemical
110	CEPHALOMETRIC ANALYST	medical ser.
331	CERAMIC COATER, MACHINE	any industry
460	CHAIN OFFBEARER	saw. & plan.
492	CHAIN SAW OPERATOR	logging
331	CHAR CONVEYOR TENDER	sugar & conf.
230	CHARGE PREPARATION TECHNICIAN	electron. comp.
492	CHASER	logging
250	CHAUFFEUR	any industry
111	CHECK CASHIER	business ser.
360	CHECKER	laundry & rel.
214	CHECKER, GROCERY	retail trade

Group No.	Occupation	Industry
360	CHECKER, UNLOADER	clerical
360	CHECKER, WAREHOUSE	retail trade
240	CHECKROOM ATTENDANT	any industry
322	CHEESE CUTTER	dairy products
322	CHEESEMAKER	dairy products
322	CHEF DE FROID	hotel & rest.
212	CHEMICAL ENGINEER	profess. & kin.
212	CHEMICAL LABORATORY TECHNICIAN	profess. & kin.
230	CHEMICAL PREPARER	chemical
212	CHEMIST	profess. & kin.
240	CHILD MONITOR	domestic ser.
111	CHILD SUPPORT OFFICER	government ser.
340	CHILD-CARE ATTENDANT, HANDICAPPED	education
340	CHILDREN'S INSTITUTION ATTENDANT	any industry
341	CHIMNEY SWEEP	any industry
460	CHIPPER, ROUGH	any industry
311	CHIROPRACTOR	medical ser.
311	CHIROPRACTOR ASSISTANT	medical ser.
460	CHOCOLATE PRODUCTION MACHINE OPERATOR	sugar & conf.
560	CHOKE SETTER	logging
492	CHOPPER	logging
491	CHRISTMAS TREE FARM WORKER	forestry
320	CHUCKING LATHE OPERATOR	machine shop
330	CIRCULAR SAWYER, STONE	stonework
212	CIVIL ENGINEER	profess. & kin.
251	CLAIM ADJUSTER, FIELD	insurance; business ser.
111	CLAIM ADJUSTER, INSIDE	insurance
111	CLAIMS CLERK	insurance
221	CLAY MODELER	any industry
340	CLEANER, COMMERCIAL OR INSTITUTIONAL	any industry
340	CLEANER, EQUIPMENT	any industry
340	CLEANER, HOSPITAL	medical ser.
340	CLEANER, LABORATORY EQUIPMENT	any industry
341	CLEANER, WINDOW	any industry
210	CLERGY MEMBER	profess. & kin.
111	CLERK, ADVERTISING SPACE	print. & pub.
111	CLERK, ANIMAL HOSPITAL	medical ser.
112	CLERK, BILLING	clerical
111	CLERK, COLLECTION	clerical
111	CLERK, CONTRACT, AUTOMOBILE	retail trade
111	CLERK, COURT	government ser.
111	CLERK, CREDIT	clerical
111	CLERK, ELECTION	government ser.
214	CLERK, FILE	clerical
211	CLERK, GENERAL	clerical
211	CLERK, INVENTORY CONTROL	clerical
214	CLERK, SALES	retail trade
360	CLERK, SHIPPING	clerical
112	CLERK, STATISTICAL	clerical
111	CLERK, WIRE TRANSFER	financial
112	CLERK-TYPIST	clerical
110	CLINICAL PSYCHOLOGIST	profess. & kin.
330	CLOTH PRINTER	any industry
221	CLOTH TESTER, QUALITY	textile
390	COACH, PROFESSIONAL ATHLETES	amuse. & rec.
331	COATER OPERATOR	any industry
331	COATING MACHINE OPERATOR	paper & pulp
320	COBBLER	boot & shoe
322	COFFEEMAKER	hotel & rest.
230	COFFEE ROASTER	food prep., nec
230	COIL WINDER	elec. equip.
221	COIL WINDER, REPAIR	any industry
214	COIN COUNTER AND WRAPPER	clerical
251	COIN MACHINE COLLECTOR	business ser.
370	COIN MACHINE SERVICE REPAIRER	svc. ind. mach.
111	COLLECTION CLERK	clerical
251	COLLECTOR, OUTSIDE	clerical
230	COLOR PRINTER OPERATOR	photofinishing
111	COLUMNIST/COMMENTATOR	print. & pub.
111	COMMUNITY ORGANIZATION WORKER	social serv.
250	COMMUNITY SERVICE OFFICER, PATROL	social serv.
240	COMPANION	domestic ser.
221	COMPOSITOR, TYPESETTER	print. & pub.
230	COMPOUNDER	petrol. refin.
360	COMPRESSED GAS PLANT WORKER	chemical

Group No.	Occupation	Industry
332	COMPRESSOR OPERATOR	any industry
112	COMPUTER KEYBOARD OPERATOR	clerical
230	COMPUTER OPERATOR, MAINFRAME	clerical
111	COMPUTER PROCESSING SCHEDULER	clerical
112	COMPUTER PROGRAMMER	profess. & kin.
320	COMPUTER REPAIRER	office machines
111	COMPUTER SECURITY SPECIALIST	profess. & kin.
320	COMPUTER SET-UP PERSON	business serv.
111	COMPUTER SUPPORT ANALYST	profess. & kin.
351	CONCRETE PAVING MACHINE OPERATOR	construction
480	CONCRETE STONE FINISHER	concrete prod.
480	CONCRETE VIBRATOR OPERATOR	construction
340	CONDUCTOR, ALL RAILS	r.r. trans.
213	CONDUCTOR, PASSENGER CAR	r.r. trans.
370	CONSTRUCTION EQUIPMENT MECHANIC	construction
110	CONSULTANT, EDUCATION	education
230	CONTACT LENS MOLDER	optical goods
330	CONTOUR BAND SAW OPERATOR, VERTICAL	machine shop
213	CONTRACTOR	construction
120	CONTROLS DESIGNER	profess. & kin.
360	CONVEYOR FEEDER-OFFBEARER	any industry
360	CONVEYOR TENDER	any industry
370	CONVEYOR MAINTENANCE MECHANIC	any industry
360	CONVEYOR SYSTEM OPERATOR	any industry
322	COOK	domestic ser.
322	COOK	any industry
322	COOK ASSISTANT	hotel & rest.
322	COOK, CHIEF	hotel & rest.
322	COOK, FAST FOOD	hotel & rest.
322	COOK, PASTRY	hotel & rest.
322	COOK, SPECIALTY	hotel & rest.
110	COORDINATOR, SKILL-TRAINING PROGRAM	government ser.
111	COPY READER	print. & pub.
111	COPY WRITER	profess. & kin.
112	COPYIST	any industry
480	CORE DRILL OPERATOR	any industry

Group No.	Occupation	Industry
330	COREMAKER	paper goods
331	COREMAKER, FLOOR	foundry
490	CORRECTION OFFICER	government ser.
290	COSMETOLOGIST	personal ser.
110	COUNSELOR	profess. & kin.
390	COUNSELOR, CAMP	amuse. & rec.
322	COUNTER ATTENDANT, CAFETERIA	hotel & rest.
250	COURIER	any industry
111	COURT CLERK	government ser.
112	COURT REPORTER	clerical
491	COWPUNCHER	agriculture
360	CRANE FOLLOWER	any industry
360	CRANE HOOKER	any industry
351	CRANE OPERATOR	any industry
360	CRATE MAKER	any industry
111	CREDIT AUTHORIZER	clerical
111	CREDIT CLERK	clerical
111	CREDIT COUNSELOR	profess. & kin.
460	CREMATOR	personal ser.
111	CREW SCHEDULER	air trans.
230	CRIMPING MACHINE OPERATOR	any industry
330	CROSSBAND LAYER	millwork-plywood
460	CRUSHER OPERATOR	concrete prod.
112	CRYPTOGRAPHIC MACHINE OPERATOR	clerical
330	CRYSTAL GROWER	comm. equip.
330	CRYSTAL SLICER	electron. comp.
212	CURATOR	museums
211	CURRENCY COUNTER	financial
340	CUSTODIAN	any industry
360	CUSTODIAN, ATHLETIC EQUIPMENT	amuse. & rec.
211	CUSTODIAN, PROPERTY	government ser.
211	CUSTOMER SERVICE CLERK	retail trade
213	CUSTOMER SERVICE REPRESENTATIVE	utilities
112	CUSTOMER SERVICE REPRESENTATIVE – INSIDE	utilities
212	CUSTOMS BROKER	financial
330	CUT-OFF SAW OPERATOR	woodworking
330	CUT-OFF SAW OPERATOR, METAL	machine shop
230	CUTTER	photofinishing
330	CUTTER OPERATOR	any industry

Group No.	Occupation	Industry
230	CUTTER, MACHINE	any industry
230	CUTTING MACHINE OPERATOR, AUTOMATED	aircraft mfg.
460	CUTTING MACHINE OPERATOR	textile
330	CUTTING MACHINE TENDER	any industry
460	CYLINDER FILLER	chemical
460	CYLINDER PRESS FEEDER	print. & pub.
120	CYTOTECHNOLOGIST	medical ser.
460	DAIRY PROCESSING EQUIPMENT OPERATOR	dairy products
590	DANCER	amuse. & rec.
111	DATA BASE ADMINISTRATOR	profess. & kin.
380	DATA COMMUNICATIONS INSTALLER	any industry
112	DATA ENTRY CLERK	clerical
221	DECAL APPLIER	any industry
491	DECKHAND	water trans., fishing & hunt.
331	DECONTAMINATOR, RADIOACTIVE MATERIAL	any industry
221	DECORATOR	bakery products
380	DECORATOR, SPECIAL EVENT	any industry
480	DECORATOR, STREET AND BUILDING	any industry
322	DELI CUTTER-SLICER	retail trade
250	DELIVERER, CAR RENTAL	automotive ser.
250	DELIVERER, FLORAL ARRANGEMENTS	retail trade
213	DELIVERER, NON-DRIVING	clerical
250	DELIVERER, PIZZA	retail trade
212	DEMONSTRATOR	retail trade
212	DENTAL ASSISTANT	medical ser.
220	DENTAL HYGIENIST	medical ser.
220	DENTAL LABORATORY TECHNICIAN	protective dev.
220	DENTIST	medical ser.
490	DEPUTY, COURT	government ser.
480	DERRICK WORKER, WELL SERVICE	petrol. & gas
230	DESIGN PRINTER, BALLOON	rubber goods
490	DETECTIVE	government ser.
390	DETECTIVE, STORE	retail trade
212	DIALYSIS TECHNICIAN	medical ser.
330	DIE CASTING MACHINE OPERATOR	foundry
330	DIE CUTTER	any industry
120	DIE DESIGNER	machine shop
320	DIE MAKER	machine shop
320	DIE SINKER	machine shop
322	DIETARY AIDE, HOSPITAL SERVICES	medical ser.
212	DIETITIAN, CLINICAL	profess. & kin.
322	DINING ROOM ATTENDANT	hotel & rest.
351	DINKEY OPERATOR	any industry
221	DIPPER	jewelry-silver.
331	DIPPER	any industry
110	DIRECTOR, FUNDRAISING	nonprofit org.
110	DIRECTOR, MOTION PICTURE	motion picture
212	DIRECTOR, RECREATION CENTER	social ser.
110	DIRECTOR, REGULATORY AGENCY	government ser.
110	DIRECTOR, RESEARCH AND DEVELOPMENT	any industry
110	DIRECTOR, SERVICE	retail trade
210	DIRECTOR, SOCIAL	hotel & rest.
112	DIRECTORY ASSISTANCE OPERATOR	tel. & tel.
322	DISHWASHER, HAND OR MACHINE	hotel & rest.
111	DISPATCHER, MOTOR VEHICLE	clerical
380	DISPLAY MAKER	fabrication, nec
330	DISPLAY SCREEN FABRICATOR	electron. comp.
360	DISPLAYER, MERCHANDISE	retail trade
460	DISTILLERY WORKER, GENERAL	beverage
221	DISTRESSER	furniture
480	DITCH DIGGER	construction
492	DIVER	any industry
230	DIVIDING MACHINE OPERATOR	bakery products
111	DOCUMENT PREPARER, MICROFILMING	business ser.
491	DOG CATCHER	government ser.
491	DOG GROOMER	personal ser.
251	DOG LICENSER	nonprofit org.
560	DOLLY PUSHER	radio-tv broad.
390	DOUBLE	motion picture
460	DOUGH BRAKE MACHINE OPERATOR	bakery products
322	DOUGH MOLDER, HAND	bakery products
322	DOUGHNUT MAKER	bakery products
330	DOWEL MACHINE OPERATOR	woodworking
120	DRAFTER, ARCHITECTURAL	profess. & kin.

Group No.	Occupation	Industry
120	DRAFTER, ASSISTANT	profess. & kin.
120	DRAFTER, CIVIL	profess. & kin.
120	DRAFTER, ELECTRICAL	profess. & kin.
120	DRAFTER, ELECTROMECHANISMS DESIGN	profess. & kin.
120	DRAFTER, LANDSCAPE	profess. & kin.
120	DRAFTER, MECHANICAL	profess. & kin.
351	DRAGLINE OPERATOR	any industry
380	DRAPERY HANGER	retail trade
110	DRAWINGS CHECKER, ENGINEERING	profess. & kin.
221	DRESSMAKER	any industry
230	DRIER OPERATOR	food prep., nec
331	DRIER OPERATOR	chemical
330	DRILL PRESS OPERATOR	machine shop
330	DRILL PRESS OPERATOR, NUMERICAL CONTROL	machine shop
321	DRILLER, HAND	any industry
240	DRIVE-IN THEATER ATTENDANT	amuse. & rec.
251	DRIVER'S LICENSE EXAMINER	government ser.
350	DRIVER, NEWSPAPER DELIVERY	wholesale tr.
430	DROPHAMMER OPERATOR	aircraft mfg.
430	DRUM STRAIGHTENER	any industry
340	DRY CLEANER	laundry & rel.
331	DRY-PRESS OPERATOR	brick & tile
380	DRY WALL APPLICATOR	construction
481	DUCT INSTALLER	construction
330	DYNAMITE PACKING MACHINE OPERATOR	chemical
212	ECHOCARDIOGRAPH TECHNICIAN	medical ser.
110	EDITOR, MANAGING, NEWSPAPER	print. & pub.
111	EDITOR, NEWSPAPER	print. & pub.
111	EDITOR, PUBLICATIONS	print. & pub.
112	EDITORIAL WRITER	print. & pub.
221	EGG CANDLER	any industry
380	ELECTRIC METER INSTALLER	utilities
221	ELECTRIC MOTOR ASSEMBLER	elec. equip.
320	ELECTRIC MOTOR CONTROL UNIT ASSEMBLER	elec. equip.
320	ELECTRIC SIGN ASSEMBLER	fabrication, nec
212	ELECTRICAL ENGINEER	profess. & kin.
212	ELECTRICAL TECHNICIAN	profess. & kin.

Group No.	Occupation	Industry
221	ELECTRICAL APPLIANCE REPAIRER, SMALL	any industry
370	ELECTRICAL APPLIANCE SERVICER	any industry
460	ELECTRICAL APPLIANCE UNCRATER	any industry
221	ELECTRICAL INSTRUMENT REPAIRER	any industry
380	ELECTRICIAN	construction
380	ELECTRICIAN	ship-boat mfg.
380	ELECTRICIAN APPRENTICE	construction
380	ELECTRICIAN HELPER	any industry
370	ELECTRICIAN, AUTOMOTIVE	automotive ser.
380	ELECTRICIAN, MAINTENANCE	any industry
380	ELECTRICIAN, POWERHOUSE	utilities
460	ELECTROLESS PLATER, PRINTED CIRCUIT BOARD PANELS	electron. comp.
290	ELECTROLOGIST	personal ser.
220	ELECTROMECHANICAL TECHNICIAN	inst. & app.
320	ELECTROMEDICAL EQUIPMENT REPAIRER	any industry
212	ELECTROMYOGRAPHIC TECHNICIAN	medical ser.
221	ELECTRONIC COMPONENT PROCESSOR	electron. comp.
221	ELECTRONICS ASSEMBLER	comm. equip.
212	ELECTRONICS TECHNICIAN	profess. & kin.
221	ELECTRONICS TESTER	comm. equip.
212	ELECTRONICS DESIGN ENGINEER	profess. & kin.
351	ELEVATING GRADER OPERATOR	construction
482	ELEVATOR CONSTRUCTOR	construction
380	ELEVATOR EXAMINER AND ADJUSTER	any industry
460	ELEVATOR OPERATOR, FREIGHT	any industry
380	ELEVATOR REPAIRER	any industry
111	ELIGIBILITY WORKER	government ser.
420	EMBALMER	personal ser.
331	EMBOSSER	any industry
230	EMBOSSING PRESS OPERATOR	print. & pub.
460	EMERGENCY MEDICAL TECHNICIAN	medical ser.
111	EMPLOYEE RELATIONS SPECIALIST	profess. & kin.
111	EMPLOYMENT INTERVIEWER	profess. & kin.
320	ENGINE LATHE OPERATOR	machine shop
213	ENGINEER, AERONAUTICAL TEST	aircraft mfg.
111	ENGINEER, AERONAUTICAL DESIGN	aircraft mfg.

Group No.	Occupation	Industry
212	ENGINEER, AGRICULTURAL	profess. & kin.
212	ENGINEER, AUTOMOTIVE	auto. mfg.
111	ENGINEER, BIOMEDICAL	profess. & kin.
212	ENGINEER, CHEMICAL	profess. & kin.
212	ENGINEER, CIVIL	profess. & kin.
111	ENGINEER, ELECTRO-OPTICAL	profess. & kin.
212	ENGINEER, ELECTRONICS DESIGN	profess. & kin.
212	ENGINEER, FACTORY LAY-OUT	profess. & kin.
213	ENGINEER, FIELD SERVICE	profess. & kin.
212	ENGINEER, MECHANICAL	profess. & kin.
111	ENGINEER, NUCLEAR	profess. & kin.
111	ENGINEER, PACKAGING	profess. & kin.
111	ENGINEER, POWER DISTRIBUTION	utilities
111	ENGINEER, PRODUCT SAFETY	profess. & kin.
212	ENGINEER, RAILROAD	profess. & kin.
213	ENGINEER, SOILS	profess. & kin.
320	ENGRAVER, HAND, HARD METALS	engraving
120	ENGRAVER, HAND, SOFT METALS	engraving; jewelry
230	ENGRAVER, MACHINE	engraving
213	ENVIRONMENTAL ANALYST	profess. & kin.
111	EQUAL OPPORTUNITY REPRESENTATIVE	government ser.
340	EQUIPMENT CLEANER	any industry
370	EQUIPMENT INSTALLER, VEHICLES	any industry
111	ESCROW OFFICER	profess. & kin.
111	ESTATE PLANNER	insurance
213	ESTIMATOR/CRUISER	forestry
221	ETCHED CIRCUIT PROCESSOR	electron. comp.
221	ETCHER	engraving
320	ETCHER, HAND	print. & pub.
370	EVAPORATIVE COOLER INSTALLER	any industry
111	EXAMINER	government ser.
390	EXERCISE PHYSIOLOGIST	medical ser.
491	EXERCISER, HORSE	amuse. & rec.
380	EXHIBIT BUILDER	museums
111	EXPEDITER	clerical
360	EXPEDITER, MATERIAL	clerical
380	EXPERIMENTAL AIRCRAFT MECHANIC	aircraft mfg.
213	EXTERMINATOR	business ser.
480	EXTERMINATOR, TERMITE	business ser.
213	EXTRA, ACTOR	amuse. & rec.; motion picture
330	EXTRUDER OPERATOR	rubber goods
220	EYEGLASS LENS CUTTER	optical goods
230	FABRIC STRETCHER	furniture
320	FABRICATING MACHINE OPERATOR, METAL	any industry
221	FABRICATOR, FOAM RUBBER	any industry
330	FABRICATOR/ASSEMBLER, METAL PRODUCTS	any industry
210	FACULTY MEMBER, COLLEGE OR UNIVERSITY	education
492	FALLER	logging
492	FALLER, TIMBER	logging
491	FARM LABORER, GENERAL	agriculture
351	FARM MACHINE OPERATOR	agriculture
491	FARMER, GENERAL	agriculture
491	FARMWORKER, FRUIT	agriculture
491	FARMWORKER, VEGETABLE	agriculture
120	FASHION ARTIST	retail trade
251	FASHION COORDINATOR	retail trade
212	FASHION DESIGNER	profess. & kin.
322	FAST FOODS WORKER	hotel & rest.
460	FEEDER	print. & pub.
331	FELTING MACHINE OPERATOR	tex. prod., nec
481	FENCE ERECTOR	construction
330	FIBERGLASS LAMINATOR	ship-boat mfg.;vehicles nec.
330	FIBERGLASS MACHINE OPERATOR	glass products
213	FIELD ENGINEER	radio-tv broad.
214	FILE CLERK	clerical
221	FILLER	tex. prod., nec
230	FILM DEVELOPER	motion picture
230	FILM OR VIDEOTAPE EDITOR	motion picture
230	FILM PRINTER	motion picture
214	FILM OR TAPE LIBRARIAN	clerical
331	FILTER OPERATOR	any industry
460	FILTER PRESS OPERATOR	any industry
320	FINAL ASSEMBLER	office machines
110	FINANCIAL PLANNER	profess. & kin.
110	FINANCIAL AIDS OFFICER	education
120	FINGERNAIL FORMER	personal ser.

Group No.	Occupation	Industry
490	FIRE FIGHTER	any industry
490	FIRE LOOKOUT	forestry
490	FIRE RANGER	forestry
320	FIRE EXTINGUISHER REPAIRER	any industry
490	FIRE INSPECTOR	government serv.
332	FIRER, HIGH PRESSURE	any industry
320	FIRESETTER	elec. equip.
360	FIREWORKS DISPLAY SPECIALIST	any industry
490	FISH AND GAME WARDEN	government ser.
322	FISH CLEANER	can. & preserv.
491	FISH FARMER	fishing & hunt.
491	FISH HATCHERY LABORER	fishing & hunt.
492	FISHER, DIVING	fishing & hunt.
491	FISHER, LINE	fishing & hunt.
491	FISHER, NET	fishing & hunt.
481	FITTER	construction, pipe lines
430	FITTER, METAL	any industry
320	FIXTURE REPAIRER-FABRICATOR	any industry
213	FLAGGER, TRAFFIC CONTROL	construction
230	FLATWORK FINISHER	laundry & rel.
322	FLIGHT ATTENDANT	air trans.
212	FLIGHT ENGINEER	air trans.
211	FLIGHT INFORMATION EXPEDITER	air trans.
380	FLOOR LAYER	construction
480	FLOOR FINISHER HELPER	construction
221	FLORIST	retail trade
460	FLOUR BLENDER	grain-feed mills
230	FOLDER SEAMER, AUTOMATIC	any industry
230	FOLDING MACHINE OPERATOR	print. & pub.
330	FOLDING MACHINE OPERATOR	paper goods
330	FOLDING MACHINE OPERATOR	textile
322	FOOD ASSEMBLER, KITCHEN	hotel & rest.
492	FOREST WORKER	forestry
490	FOREST FIRE FIGHTER	forestry
213	FORESTER	profess. & kin.
491	FORESTER AIDE	forestry
460	FORGE HELPER	forging
430	FORGING PRESS OPERATOR	forging
351	FORKLIFT OPERATOR	any industry
481	FORM BUILDER	construction
480	FORM STRIPPER	construction
480	FORM TAMPER	construction
480	FORM TAMPER OPERATOR	construction
320	FORMER, HAND	any industry
331	FORMING MACHINE OPERATOR	glass mfg.
111	FORMS ANALYST	profess. & kin.
331	FOURDRINIER MACHINE OPERATOR	paper & pulp
470	FRAME REPAIRER	furniture
370	FRAME STRAIGHTENER	motor-bicycles
230	FREEZER OPERATOR	dairy products
491	FRUIT PICKER	agriculture
360	FRUIT BUYING INSPECTOR	can. & preserv.
331	FRUIT GRADER OPERATOR	agriculture
332	FUEL ATTENDANT, PLANT	any industry
480	FUMIGATOR	business ser.
212	FUND RAISER	nonprofit org.
340	FUNERAL ATTENDANT	personal ser.
560	FUNERAL CAR CHAUFFEUR	personal ser.
212	FUNERAL DIRECTOR	personal ser.
341	FURNACE CLEANER	any industry
380	FURNACE INSTALLER AND REPAIRER, HOT AIR	any industry; utilities
321	FURNITURE ASSEMBLER	furniture
470	FURNITURE ASSEMBLER/HEAVY	woodworking
360	FURNITURE CRATER	any industry
221	FURNITURE FINISHER	woodworking
560	FURNITURE MOVER	motor trans.
321	FURNITURE UPHOLSTERER	any industry
221	FURRIER	fur goods
370	GARAGE SERVICER, TRANSPORTATION EQUIPMENT	any industry
560	GARBAGE COLLECTOR, MANUAL	motor trans.
491	GARDENER	domestic ser.
221	GARMENT CUTTER, HAND	any industry
321	GARMENT CUTTER, MACHINE	any industry
332	GAS COMPRESSOR OPERATOR	any industry
332	GAS ENGINE OPERATOR	any industry
320	GAS METER ADJUSTER	utilities
212	GATE AGENT	air trans.
213	GEOLOGIST	profess. & kin.
221	GIFT WRAPPER	retail trade
221	GILDER, METAL LEAF	any industry
230	GINNER	agriculture

Group No.	Occupation	Industry
221	GLASS BLOWER, HAND	glass mfg
420	GLASS CUTTER	any industry
221	GLASS FINISHER	glass products
370	GLASS INSTALLER	automotive ser.
370	GLASS INSTALLER	woodworking
321	GLASS POLISHER	glass mfg.
380	GLAZIER	construction
330	GLUER	woodworking
251	GOLF COURSE RANGER	amuse. & rec.
390	GOLF INSTRUCTOR	amuse. & rec.
493	GOLFER, PROFESSIONAL	amuse. & rec.
340	GOLF RANGE ATTENDANT	amuse. & rec.
360	GRAINER, MACHINE	any industry
110	GRANT COORDINATOR	profess. & kin.
230	GRANULATOR OPERATOR	sugar & conf.
120	GRAPHIC DESIGNER	profess. & kin.
480	GRAVE DIGGER	real estate
340	GREASER	any industry
460	GREEN CHAIN OFFBEARER	millwork-plywood
331	GRINDER OPERATOR	grain-feed mills
320	GRINDER OPERATOR, PRECISION	machine shop
330	GRINDER SET-UP OPERATOR, CENTERLESS	machine shop
330	GRINDER, BENCH	any industry
321	GRINDER, DISK, BELT OR WHEEL	any industry
330	GRINDER, TOOL	any industry
460	GRINDER-CHIPPER, ROUGH	any industry
330	GRINDING MACHINE TENDER	machine shop
482	GRIP	amuse. & rec.
482	GRIP, PROPERTY HANDLER	motion picture
482	GRIP, STAGE CONSTRUCTION	motion picture
214	GROCERY CHECKER	retail trade
230	GROMMET MACHINE OPERATOR	any industry
491	GROOM	any industry
491	GROUNDSKEEPER	any industry
490	GROUP SUPERVISOR	government ser.
490	GUARD, CORRECTIONAL FACILITY	government ser.
240	GUARD, SCHOOL-CROSSING	government ser.
590	GUIDE, ALPINE	personal ser.
213	GUIDE, ESTABLISHMENT	any industry
491	GUIDE, HUNTING AND FISHING	amuse. & rec.
220	GUNSMITH	any industry

Group No.	Occupation	Industry
290	HAIR STYLIST	personal ser.
211	HAND LABELER	any industry
380	HANDYPERSON	any industry
110	HARBOR MASTER	government ser.
380	HARDWOOD FLOOR LAYER	construction
320	HARNESS MAKER	leather prod.
230	HAT AND CAP SEWER	hat & cap
110	HAZARDOUS WASTE MANAGEMENT SPECIALIST	government ser.
110	HEARING OFFICER	government ser.
112	HEARING REPORTER	clerical
330	HEAT TREATER	heat treating
430	HEATER	forging
380	HEATING AND AIR CONDITIONING INSTALLER-SERVICER	construction
230	HEMMER, AUTOMATIC	tex. prod., nec
420	HIDE PULLER	meat products
480	HOD CARRIER	construction
351	HOISTING ENGINEER	any industry
111	HOLTER SCANNING TECHNICIAN	medical ser.
340	HOME ATTENDANT	personal ser.
491	HORSESHOER	agriculture
213	HORTICULTURIST	profess. & kin.
111	HOSPITAL ADMITTING CLERK	medical ser.
240	HOST/HOSTESS	any industry
211	HOTEL CLERK	hotel & rest.
470	HOUSEHOLD APPLIANCE INSTALLER	any industry
340	HOUSEKEEPER, DOMESTIC	domestic ser.; hotel & rest.
332	HYDROELECTRIC STATION OPERATOR	utilities
331	ICE CREAM MAKER	dairy products
460	ICE CUTTER	food prep., nec
120	ILLUSTRATOR	profess. & kin.
110	IMPORT-EXPORT AGENT	any industry
111	INDUSTRIAL ENGINEER	profess. & kin.
213	INDUSTRIAL HYGIENIST	profess. & kin.
111	INFORMATION CLERK	clerical
111	INFORMATION AND REFERRAL AIDE	government ser.
230	INJECTION WAX MOLDER	foundry; jewelry-silver.

Group No.	Occupation	Industry
230	INJECTION MOLDING MACHINE TENDER	plastic prod.
330	INKER	print. & pub.
460	INMATE, LABORER	any industry
120	INSPECTOR	jewelry-silver.
221	INSPECTOR	plastic prod.
221	INSPECTOR	pharmaceut.
213	INSPECTOR, AGRICULTURAL COMMODITIES	government ser.
213	INSPECTOR, AIR CARRIER	government ser.
213	INSPECTOR, AIRPLANE	air trans.
221	INSPECTOR, CANNED FOOD RECONDITIONING	can. & preserv.
320	INSPECTOR, EDDY CURRENT	steel & rel.
221	INSPECTOR, ELECTRONICS	comm. equip.
221	INSPECTOR, FABRIC	any industry
251	INSPECTOR, FOOD AND DRUG	government ser.
321	INSPECTOR, FURNITURE	furniture
221	INSPECTOR, GARMENT	any industry
221	INSPECTOR, GLASS	any industry
251	INSPECTOR, HEALTH CARE FACILITIES	government ser.
120	INSPECTOR, JEWEL	clock & watch
213	INSPECTOR, METAL FABRICATING	any industry
221	INSPECTOR, METAL FINISH	any industry
221	INSPECTOR, PRINTED CIRCUIT BOARDS	electron. comp.
251	INSPECTOR, QUALITY ASSURANCE	government ser.
251	INSPECTOR, TRANSPORTATION	motor trans.
213	INSPECTOR, WEIGH STATION	government ser.
493	INSTRUCTOR, AEROBICS	amuse. & rec.
251	INSTRUCTOR, DRIVING	education
390	INSTRUCTOR, PHYSICAL EDUCATION	education
390	INSTRUCTOR, SPORTS	amuse. & rec.
214	INSTRUCTOR, VOCATIONAL TRAINING	education
320	INSTRUMENT REPAIRER	any industry
220	INSTRUMENT MAKER AND REPAIRER	any industry
380	INSULATION WORKER	construction
221	INTEGRATED CIRCUIT FABRICATOR	electron. comp.
120	INTEGRATED CIRCUIT LAYOUT DESIGNER	profess. & kin.
214	INTERIOR DESIGNER	profess. & kin.
220	INTERNIST	medical ser.
210	INTERPRETER	profess. & kin.
212	INTERPRETER, DEAF	profess. & kin.
111	INTERVIEWER, EMPLOYMENT	profess. & kin.
212	INTERVIEWER/SURVEY WORKER	clerical
360	INVENTORY CLERK	clerical
251	INVESTIGATOR	government ser.
111	INVESTIGATOR, CREDIT FRAUD	retail trade
251	INVESTIGATOR, INSIDE/OUTSIDE	business ser.
490	INVESTIGATOR, VICE	government ser.
110	INVESTMENT ANALYST	financial
111	INVOICE CONTROL CLERK	clerical
491	IRRIGATOR, GRAVITY FLOW	agriculture
491	IRRIGATOR, SPRINKLING SYSTEM	agriculture
480	JACKHAMMER OPERATOR	mine & quarry
490	JAILER	government ser.
340	JANITOR	any industry
120	JEWELER	jewelry-silver.
320	JIG MAKER	machine shop
330	JIG-BORING MACHINE OPERATOR, NUMERICAL CONTROL	machine shop
330	JIGSAW OPERATOR	woodworking
212	JOB ANALYST	profess. & kin.
110	JOB DEVELOPMENT SPECIALIST	profess. & kin.
320	JOB SETTER, HONING	machine shop
590	JOCKEY	amuse. & rec.
380	JOINER	ship-boat mfg.
330	JOINTER OPERATOR	woodworking
110	JUDGE	government ser.
221	KEY CUTTER	any industry
230	KICK PRESS OPERATOR	any industry
230	KILN OPERATOR	woodworking
360	KILN WORKER	pottery & porc.
322	KITCHEN HELPER	hotel & rest.
230	KNITTING MACHINE OPERATOR, HOSIERY	knitting
330	KNITTING MACHINE OPERATOR	knitting
492	KNOT BUMPER	logging

Group No.	Occupation	Industry
212	LABORATORY ASSISTANT, BLOOD AND PLASMA	medical ser.
340	LABORATORY EQUIPMENT CLEANER	any industry
220	LABORATORY TESTER	any industry
460	LABORER	meat products
460	LABORER	pharmaceut.
460	LABORER, CHEMICAL PROCESSING	chemical
480	LABORER, CONCRETE PAVING	construction
480	LABORER, CONCRETE MIXING PLANT	construction
480	LABORER, CONSTRUCTION	construction
491	LABORER, FARM	agriculture
360	LABORER, GENERAL	plastic prod.
460	LABORER, GENERAL	machine shop
460	LABORER, GENERAL	nonfer. metal
460	LABORER, GENERAL	steel & rel.
460	LABORER, MILL	woodworking
460	LABORER, PETROLEUM REFINERY	petrol. refin.
480	LABORER, ROAD	construction
460	LABORER, SHIPYARD	ship-boat mfg.
480	LABORER, WRECKING & SALVAGING	construction
460	LABORER, YARD	paper & pulp
331	LACQUERER	plastic prod.
330	LAMINATING MACHINE FEEDER	wood prod., nec.
330	LAMINATING MACHINE OPERATOR	furniture
430	LAMINATING PRESS OPERATOR	plastic prod.
330	LAMINATOR	ship-boat mfg.;vehicles nec.
213	LAND SURVEYOR	profess. & kin.
491	LANDSCAPE GARDENER	agriculture
370	LASER TECHNICIAN/REPAIRER	electron. comp.
230	LASER BEAM MACHINE OPERATOR	welding
230	LASER BEAM TRIM OPERATOR	electron. comp.
330	LATHE OPERATOR, NUMERICAL CONTROL	machine shop
330	LATHE OPERATOR, SWING-TYPE	woodworking
330	LATHE OPERATOR, WOOD-TURNING	woodworking
460	LATHE SPOTTER	millwork-plywood
330	LATHE TENDER	machine shop
380	LATHER, METAL OR WOOD	construction

Group No.	Occupation	Industry
340	LAUNDERER, HAND	laundry & rel.
491	LAWN SERVICE WORKER	agriculture
110	LAWYER	profess. & kin.
320	LAY-OUT MAKER	sheet metal; any industry
120	LAY-OUT TECHNICIAN	optical goods
491	LEAD PONY RIDER, RACETRACK	amuse. & rec.
221	LEATHER CUTTER	leather prod.
230	LEATHER GARMENT PRESSER	laundry & rel.
320	LEATHER WORKER	leather prod.
110	LEGISLATIVE ASSISTANT	government ser.
220	LENS EXAMINER	optical goods
230	LENS HARDENER	optical goods
320	LENS MOUNTER, OPTICAL	optical goods
220	LENS POLISHER, HAND	optical goods
220	LENS FABRICATING MACHINE TENDER	optical goods
214	LIBRARIAN	library
212	LIBRARIAN, CATALOG	library
214	LIBRARY ASSISTANT	library
211	LICENSE CLERK	government ser.
590	LIFEGUARD	amuse. & rec.
250	LIGHT RAIL CAR OPERATOR	r.r. trans.
341	LIGHT FIXTURE SERVICER	any industry
482	LINE INSTALLER-REPAIRER	tel. & tel.; utilities
341	LINE SERVICE ATTENDANT	air trans.
213	LINE WALKER	petrol. & gas
360	LINEN ROOM CLERK	hotel & rest.
110	LITERARY AGENT	business ser.
491	LIVESTOCK YARD ATTENDANT	any industry
460	LOADER/UNLOADER	any industry
110	LOAN OFFICER	financial
212	LOCATION MANAGER	motion picture
120	LOCK ASSEMBLER	cutlery-hrdwr.
221	LOCKSMITH	any industry
250	LOCOMOTIVE ENGINEER	r.r. trans.
213	LOG SCALER	logging
491	LOG SORTER	logging
492	LOGGER, ALL-ROUND	logging
351	LOGGING TRACTOR OPERATOR	forestry
370	LOOM FIXER	narrow fabrics
340	LUBRICATION SERVICER	automotive ser.

Group No.	Occupation	Industry
320	LUGGAGE REPAIRER	any industry
221	LUMBER GRADER	woodworking
460	LUMBER HANDLER/STACKER	woodworking
360	LUMBER SORTER	woodworking
350	LUNCH TRUCK DRIVER	hotel & rest.
370	MACHINE ASSEMBLER/BUILDER	machinery mfg.
360	MACHINE FEEDER	any industry
460	MACHINE FEEDER, RAW STOCK	tex. prod., nec
330	MACHINE MOLDER	foundry
230	MACHINE OPERATOR, ROOFING MATERIALS	build. mat., nec
320	MACHINE SET-UP OPERATOR	machine shop
221	MACHINE TESTER	office machines
320	MACHINIST	machine shop
320	MACHINIST, AUTOMOTIVE	automotive ser.
370	MACHINIST, BENCH	machinery mfg.
112	MAGNETIC TAPE COMPOSER OPERATOR	print. & pub.
211	MAIL CLERK	clerical
230	MAILING MACHINE OPERATOR	print. & pub.
370	MAINTENANCE MACHINIST	machine shop
470	MAINTENANCE MECHANIC	any industry
380	MAINTENANCE REPAIRER, BUILDING	any industry
470	MAINTENANCE REPAIRER, INDUS. MACHINES & PLANTS	any industry
480	MAINTENANCE WORKER, MUNICIPAL	government ser.
311	MAKE-UP ARTIST, BODY	amuse. & rec.
110	MANAGEMENT ANALYST	profess. & kin.
212	MANAGEMENT TRAINEE	any industry
212	MANAGER, ADVERTISING AGENCY	business ser.
212	MANAGER, APARTMENT HOUSE	real estate
213	MANAGER, AUTOMOBILE SERVICE STATION	retail trade
110	MANAGER, BENEFITS	profess. & kin.
110	MANAGER, BUS TRANSPORTATION	motor trans.
212	MANAGER, CONVENTION	hotel & rest.
212	MANAGER, CUSTOMER SERVICES	business ser.
213	MANAGER, DAIRY FARM	agriculture
110	MANAGER, DATA PROCESSING	profess. & kin.
110	MANAGER, DEPARTMENT	any industry
212	MANAGER, FAST FOOD SERVICES	retail trade
110	MANAGER, HOTEL OR MOTEL	hotel & rest.
212	MANAGER, HOTEL RECREATIONAL FACILITIES	amuse. & rec.
212	MANAGER, LABOR RELATIONS	profess. & kin.
212	MANAGER, MOBILE HOME PARK	real estate
213	MANAGER, NURSERY	agriculture
111	MANAGER, OFFICE	any industry
212	MANAGER, PARTS	retail trade
111	MANAGER, PERSONNEL	profess. & kin.
213	MANAGER, PROPERTY	real estate
212	MANAGER, QUALITY CONTROL	profess. & kin.
212	MANAGER, RETAIL STORE	retail trade
212	MANAGER, STAGE	amuse. & rec.
212	MANAGER, THEATER	amuse. & rec.
110	MANAGER, TRAFFIC	air trans.; any industry
212	MANAGER, VEHICLE LEASING AND RENTAL	automotive ser.
212	MANAGER, WAREHOUSE	any industry
120	MANICURIST	personal ser.
330	MARBLE POLISHER, MACHINE	stonework
481	MARBLE SETTER	construction
480	MARBLE SETTER HELPER	construction
211	MARKER	retail trade
111	MARKET RESEARCH ANALYST	profess. & kin.
221	MASKER, PARTS	any industry
311	MASSEUR/MASSEUSE	personal ser.
212	MASTER CONTROL OPERATOR	radio-tv broad.
221	MAT CUTTER, PICTURE FRAMES	wood prod., nec
360	MATERIAL EXPEDITER	clerical
460	MATERIAL STACKER	any industry
321	MATTRESS MAKER	furniture
322	MEAT CARVER, DISPLAY	hotel & rest.
322	MEAT CLERK	retail trade
322	MEAT CUTTER	retail trade
331	MEAT GRINDER	meat products
380	MECHANIC, AIRCRAFT	aircraft mfg.
370	MECHANIC, AUTOMOBILE	automotive ser.
470	MECHANIC, DIESEL	any industry
370	MECHANIC, FRONT-END	automotive ser.
481	MECHANIC, POWERHOUSE	utilities

Group No.	Occupation	Industry
380	MECHANIC, RADAR	any industry
370	MECHANIC, RADIATOR	automotive ser.
481	MECHANIC, REFRIGERATION	svc. ind. mach.
370	MECHANIC, ROCKET ENGINE COMPONENT	aircraft mfg.
470	MECHANIC, SAFE AND VAULT	business ser.
370	MECHANIC, SMALL ENGINE	any industry
370	MECHANIC, TRACTOR	automotive ser.
370	MECHANIC, TRANSMISSION	automotive ser.
370	MECHANIC, TUNE-UP	automotive ser.
214	MEDIA SPECIALIST, SCHOOL LIBRARY	library
212	MEDICAL ASSISTANT, OFFICE	medical ser.
220	MEDICAL LABORATORY TECHNOLOGIST	medical ser.
470	MEDICAL EQUIPMENT REPAIRER	protective dev.
212	MEDICAL LABORATORY TECHNICIAN	medical ser.
211	MEDICAL RECORD CLERK	medical ser.
321	MELTER	jewelry-silver.
340	MENTAL RETARDATION AIDE, INSTITUTION	medical ser.
213	MESSENGER, NON-DRIVING	clerical
430	METAL FABRICATOR	any industry
321	METAL GRINDER AND FINISHER	any industry
321	METAL SPRAYER, PRODUCTION	any industry
331	METAL CLEANER, IMMERSION	any industry
230	METALLIZATION EQUIPMENT TENDER, SEMICONDUCTORS	comm. equip.
212	METALLURGICAL TESTER	profess. & kin.
213	METER READER	utilities
320	METER REPAIRER	any industry
220	MICROELECTRONICS TECHNICIAN	electron. comp.
230	MICROFILM PROCESSOR	business ser.
212	MICROPHONE BOOM OPERATOR	motion picture
491	MILKER, MACHINE	agriculture
331	MILL OPERATOR	any industry
320	MILLING MACHINE OPERATOR, NUMERICAL CONTROL	machine shop
481	MILLWRIGHT	any industry
480	MILLWRIGHT HELPER	any industry
213	MINE INSPECTOR	mine & quarry
560	MINER	mine & quarry
560	MINER HELPER	mine & quarry
221	MINIATURE SET CONSTRUCTOR	motion picture
460	MIXER	paint & varnish
460	MIXER, CLAY	brick & tile
480	MIXER, CONCRETE	construction
460	MIXER, DOUGH	bakery products
460	MIXER, FLOUR	bakery products
480	MIXER, MORTAR	construction
221	MIXER, PAINT (HAND)	any industry
460	MIXER, PAINT (MACHINE)	any industry
331	MIXER, SAND (MACHINE)	foundry
331	MIXING MACHINE OPERATOR	food prep., nec
460	MIXING MACHINE OPERATOR	any industry
380	MOBILE HOME ASSEMBLER	mfd. bldgs.
212	MOBILE HOME PARK MANAGER	real estate
240	MODEL	garment
221	MODEL MAKER	any industry
240	MODEL, ARTISTS'	any industry
213	MODEL, PHOTOGRAPHERS'	any industry
321	MOLD REPAIRER	any industry
221	MOLD AND MODEL MAKER, PLASTER	concrete prod.
330	MOLDER	aircraft mfg.
420	MOLDER, HAND	brick & tile
320	MOLDER, PATTERN	foundry
230	MOLDING MACHINE TENDER, COMPRESSION	plastic prod.
340	MORGUE ATTENDANT	medical ser.
230	MOTION PICTURE PROJECTIONIST	amuse. & rec.
351	MOTOR-GRADER OPERATOR	construction
351	MOTORBOAT OPERATOR	any industry
370	MOTORCYCLE ASSEMBLER	motor-bicycles
250	MOTORCYCLE DRIVER, DELIVERY	retail trade
490	MOTORCYCLE POLICE OFFICER	government ser.
370	MOTORCYCLE REPAIRER	automotive ser.
120	MOUNTER, HAND	photofinishing
310	MRI TECHNOLOGIST	medical ser.
370	MUFFLER INSTALLER	automotive ser.
460	MUNITIONS HANDLER	ordnance
212	MUSEUM ATTENDANT & GUIDE	museums
380	MUSEUM PREPARATOR	museums

Group No.	Occupation	Industry
220	MUSICIAN, INSTRUMENTAL	amuse. & rec.
330	NAILING MACHINE OPERATOR	any industry
111	NAVIGATOR	air trans.
360	NEWS GATHERING TECHNICIAN	radio-tv broad.
210	NEWSCASTER	radio-tv broad.
330	NIBBLER OPERATOR	any industry
111	NIGHT AUDITOR	hotel & rest.
460	NITROGLYCERIN DISTRIBUTOR	chemical
310	NUCLEAR MEDICINE TECHNOLOGIST	medical ser.
330	NUMERICAL CONTROL MACHINE OPERATOR	machine shop
340	NURSE AIDE	medical ser.
220	NURSE ANESTHETIST	medical ser.
212	NURSE CASE MANAGER	medical ser.
311	NURSE, GENERAL DUTY	medical ser.
311	NURSE, LICENSED VOCATIONAL	medical ser.
311	NURSE, PRIVATE DUTY	medical ser.
212	NURSE, SCHOOL	medical ser.
311	NURSE-MIDWIFE	medical ser.
460	NUT ROASTER	can. & preserv.
212	OCCUPATIONAL ANALYST	profess. & kin.
311	OCCUPATIONAL THERAPIST	medical ser.
340	OCCUPATIONAL THERAPY AIDE	medical ser.
213	OCCUPATIONAL SAFETY AND HEALTH INSPECTOR	government ser.
211	OFFICE CLERK, GENERAL	clerical
320	OFFICE MACHINE SERVICER	any industry
330	OFFSET PRESS HELPER	print. & pub.
230	OFFSET DUPLICATING MACHINE OPERATOR	clerical
230	OFFSET PRESS OPERATOR	print. & pub.
480	OIL WELL DRILLER	petrol. & gas
340	OILER	any industry
332	OPERATING ENGINEER	any industry
332	OPERATING ENGINEER, REFRIGERATION	any industry
111	OPTICAL ENGINEER	profess. & kin.
220	OPTICIAN, DISPENSING	optical goods
220	OPTICIAN, LENS GRINDER	optical goods
220	OPTOMETRIST	medical ser.
491	ORCHARD SPRAYER, HAND	agriculture
360	ORDER CHECKER	clerical
111	ORDER CLERK	clerical
214	ORDER CLERK	clerical
214	ORDER FILLER, CATALOG SALES	retail trade
460	ORDERLY	medical ser.
481	ORNAMENTAL IRON WORKER	construction
120	ORTHODONTIC TECHNICIAN	protective dev.
320	ORTHOTICS TECHNICIAN	protective dev.
310	ORTHOTIST	medical ser.
331	OVEN TENDER	bakery products
351	OVERHEAD CRANE OPERATOR	any industry
331	OXIDIZED FINISH PLATER	any industry
221	OXIDIZER	jewelry-silver.
330	PACKAGE SEALER, MACHINE	any industry
330	PACKAGER, MACHINE	any industry
360	PACKER, AGRICULTURAL PRODUCE	agriculture
360	PACKER, HAND	any industry
380	PAINTER	construction
480	PAINTER HELPER	construction
221	PAINTER, AIRBRUSH	any industry
482	PAINTER, BRIDGE, STRUCTURAL STEEL	construction
321	PAINTER, BRUSH	any industry
120	PAINTER, HAND, DECORATIVE	any industry
380	PAINTER, SIGN	any industry
321	PAINTER, SPRAY GUN	any industry
321	PAINTER, TOUCH-UP	any industry
350	PAINTER, TRAFFIC LINE	construction
380	PAINTER, TRANSPORTATION EQUIPMENT	aircraft mfg.
230	PALLETIZER OPERATOR, AUTOMATIC	any industry
230	PAPER CUTTER, MACHINE	beverage
460	PAPER-BALING MACHINE TENDER	any industry
331	PAPER-MAKING MACHINE OPERATOR	paper & pulp
460	PAPERCUTTING MACHINE OPERATOR	print. & pub.
380	PAPERHANGER	construction
321	PARACHUTE RIGGER	air trans.
211	PARALEGAL	profess. & kin.
490	PARAMEDIC	medical ser.

Group No.	Occupation	Industry
211	PARIMUTUEL TICKET SELLER	amuse. & rec.
490	PARK RANGER	government ser.
250	PARKING ENFORCEMENT OFFICER	government ser.
240	PARKING LOT ATTENDANT, BOOTH	automotive serv.
214	PARKING LOT ATTENDANT	automotive ser.
490	PAROLE OFFICER	profess. & kin.
214	PARTS CLERK	clerical
214	PARTS ORDER AND STOCK CLERK	clerical
460	PASTEURIZER	dairy products
250	PATROL OFFICER, VOLUNTEER	government serv.
230	PATTERN-PUNCHING MACHINE OPERATOR	tex. prod., nec
320	PATTERNMAKER, ALL-AROUND	foundry
320	PATTERNMAKER, METAL	foundry
320	PATTERNMAKER, WOOD	foundry
221	PEELER, HAND	can. & preserv.
230	PEELER, MACHINE	can. & preserv.
320	PERCUSSION INSTRUMENT REPAIRER	any industry
310	PERFUSIONIST	medical ser.
390	PERSONAL TRAINER	amuse. & rec.
111	PERSONNEL RECORDS CLERK	clerical
111	PERSONNEL RECRUITER	profess. & kin.
220	PHARMACIST	medical ser.
220	PHLEBOTOMIST	medical ser.
211	PHOTOCOPYING MACHINE OPERATOR	clerical
221	PHOTOENGRAVER	print. & pub.
221	PHOTOFINISHING LABORATORY WORKER	photofinishing
213	PHOTOGRAPHER	amuse. & rec.
212	PHOTOGRAPHER, STILL	profess. & kin.
221	PHOTOGRAPHIC PLATE MAKER	electron. comp.
213	PHOTOJOURNALIST	print. & pub.
230	PHOTOTYPESETTER OPERATOR	print. & pub.
310	PHYSIATRIST	medical ser.
311	PHYSICAL THERAPIST	medical ser.
340	PHYSICAL THERAPY AIDE	medical ser.
212	PHYSICIAN ASSISTANT	medical ser.
220	PHYSICIAN, GENERAL PRACTITIONER	medical ser.
320	PIANO TECHNICIAN	any industry
221	PIANO TUNER	any industry
491	PICKER, FRUIT	agriculture
330	PICKING MACHINE OPERATOR	any industry
221	PICTURE FRAMER	retail trade
351	PILE-DRIVER OPERATOR	construction
370	PINSETTER ADJUSTER, AUTOMATIC	toy-sport equip.
380	PINSETTER MECHANIC, AUTOMATIC	any industry
380	PIPE COVERER AND INSULATOR	ship-boat mfg.
481	PIPE FITTER	construction
480	PIPE LAYER	construction
481	PIPE FITTER HELPER	construction
480	PIPE LAYER HELPER	construction
380	PIPE ORGAN TUNER AND REPAIRER	any industry
480	PIPELINER	pipe lines
214	PIT BOSS/FLOOR PERSON	amusement & rec.
330	PLANER OPERATOR	woodworking
430	PLANER OPERATOR, METAL CASTINGS	machine shop
212	PLANT ENGINEER	profess. & kin.
321	PLASTER MAKER	nonmet. min.
320	PLASTER MOLDER	foundry
420	PLASTER DIE MAKER	pottery & porc.
380	PLASTERER	construction
480	PLASTERER HELPER	construction
230	PLATEN PRESS FEEDER	print. & pub.
230	PLATEN PRESS OPERATOR	print. & pub.
330	PLATER	electroplating
460	PLATER, ELECTROLESS, PRINTED CIRCUIT BOARDS	electron. comp.
460	PLATER, HOT DIP	galvanizing
460	PLATER, PRINTED CIRCUIT BOARD PANELS	electron. comp.
221	PLATER, SEMICONDUCTOR WAFERS & COMPONENTS	electron. comp.
230	PLEATING MACHINE OPERATOR	any industry
481	PLUMBER	construction
481	PLUMBER APPRENTICE	construction
481	PLUMBER HELPER	construction
370	PNEUMATIC TOOL REPAIRER	any industry
380	PNEUMATIC TUBE REPAIRER	any industry
220	PODIATRIST	medical ser.
251	POLICE ARTIST	government ser.

Group No.	Occupation	Industry
490	POLICE CAPTAIN	government ser.
111	POLICE CLERK	government ser.
490	POLICE OFFICER	government ser.
490	POLICE OFFICER, STATE HIGHWAY	government ser.
120	POLISHER, EYEGLASS FRAMES	optical goods
321	POLISHER/BUFFER	any industry
330	POLISHING MACHINE OPERATOR	any industry
212	POLYGRAPH EXAMINER	profess. & kin.
360	PORTER	air trans.
360	PORTER, BAGGAGE	hotel & rest.
330	POTTERY MACHINE OPERATOR	pottery & porc.
322	POULTRY DRESSER	agriculture
430	POWER BRAKE OPERATOR	any industry
230	POWER BARKER OPERATOR	paper & pulp
332	POWER PLANT OPERATOR	utilities
330	POWER PRESS TENDER	any industry
332	POWER REACTOR OPERATOR	utilities
351	POWER SHOVEL OPERATOR	any industry
481	POWERHOUSE MECHANIC	utilities
370	PRECISION ASSEMBLER & REPAIRER	aircraft mfg.
320	PRECISION ASSEMBLER, BENCH	aircraft mfg.
110	PRESIDENT	any industry
230	PRESS OPERATOR	laundry & rel.
330	PRESS OPERATOR, CYLINDER	print. and pub.
430	PRESS OPERATOR, HEAVY DUTY	any industry
331	PRESS OPERATOR, MEAT	meat products
230	PRESS OPERATOR, OFFSET	print. & pub.
330	PRESS OPERATOR, ROTOGRAVURE	print. & pub.
321	PRESSER, ALL-AROUND	laundry & rel.
221	PRESSER, HAND	any industry
321	PRESSER, MACHINE	any industry
230	PRINT DEVELOPER, AUTOMATIC	photofinishing
221	PRINTED CIRCUIT BOARD ASSEMBLER, HAND	comm. equip.
120	PRINTED CIRCUIT DESIGNER	profess. & kin.
320	PRINTER, JOB	print. & pub.
390	PROBATION OFFICER	profess. & kin.
251	PROCESS SERVER	business ser.
360	PRODUCE CLERK, RETAIL	retail trade
212	PRODUCER	radio-tv broad.
212	PROMPTER	amuse. & rec.
211	PROOFREADER	print. & pub.

Group No.	Occupation	Industry
111	PROOFREADER, PRODUCTION	print. & pub.
380	PROP MAKER	amuse. & rec.
320	PROSTHETICS TECHNICIAN	protective dev.
310	PROSTHETIST	medical ser.
311	PSYCHIATRIC TECHNICIAN	medical ser.
340	PSYCHIATRIC WARD ATTENDANT	medical ser.
110	PSYCHOLOGIST, CLINICAL	profess. & kin.
110	PSYCHOLOGIST, COUNSELING	profess. & kin.
110	PUBLIC HEALTH SERVICE OFFICER	government ser.
380	PUBLIC ADDRESS SETTER-UP & SERVICER	any industry
111	PUBLIC RELATIONS REPRESENTATIVE	profess. & kin.
212	PULMONARY FUNCTION TECHNICIAN	medical ser.
470	PUMP INSTALLER	any industry
370	PUMP SERVICER	any industry
330	PUMP MACHINE OPERATOR	any industry
332	PUMP STATION OPERATOR, WATERWORKS	waterworks
330	PUNCH PRESS OPERATOR	any industry
430	PUNCH PRESS OPERATOR, AUTOMATIC	any industry
251	PURCHASING AGENT	profess. & kin.
111	PURSER	water trans.
321	PUTTY GLAZER, POTTERY	any industry
221	QUALITY ASSURANCE MONITOR	auto. mfg.
212	QUALITY CONTROL TECHNICIAN	profess. & kin.
480	QUARRY WORKER	mine & quarry
120	QUICK SKETCH ARTIST	amuse. & rec.
221	RACKET STRINGER	toy-sport equip.
330	RADIAL ARM SAW OPERATOR	woodworking
320	RADIAL DRILL PRESS SETUP	machine shop
310	RADIATION THERAPY TECHNOLOGIST	medical ser.
212	RADIOGRAPHER, INDUSTRIAL	any industry
310	RADIOLOGIC TECHNOLOGIST	medical ser.
380	RADIOLOGICAL EQUIPMENT SPECIALIST	inst. & app.
212	RADIOTELEPHONE OPERATOR	any industry
481	RAILROAD CAR BUILDER	railroad equip.
481	RAILWAY CAR REPAIRER	railroad equip.

Group No.	Occupation	Industry
460	RAMP ATTENDANT	air trans.
111	RATER	insurance
251	REAL ESTATE AGENT	profess. & kin.
321	REAMER, HAND	machine shop
330	REAMING MACHINE TENDER	nonfer. metal
111	RECEPTIONIST	clerical
212	RECORDING ENGINEER	radio-tv broad.
360	RECORDING STUDIO SET-UP WORKER	recording
230	RECORDIST	motion picture
214	RECREATION AIDE	social ser.
310	RECREATIONAL THERAPIST	medical ser.
111	RECRUITER, PERSONNEL	profess. & kin.
111	REGISTRATION CLERK	government ser.
212	REHABILITATION CENTER MANAGER	government ser.
481	REINFORCING IRON WORKER	construction
221	REPAIRER	furniture
220	REPAIRER, ART OBJECTS	any industry
320	REPAIRER, OFFICE MACHINES	any industry
320	REPAIRER, SALVAGED PARTS	any industry
320	REPAIRER, SMALL APPLIANCE	house. appl.
320	REPAIRER, WIND INSTRUMENT	any industry
220	REPAIRER/ADJUSTER	office machines
251	REPORTER	print. & pub.
110	REPORTS ANALYST	profess. & kin.
213	REPOSSESSOR	clerical
460	RESAW OPERATOR	woodworking
111	RESEARCHER	profess. & kin.
111	RESERVATION CLERK	clerical
111	RESERVATIONS AGENT	air trans.
311	RESPIRATORY THERAPIST	medical ser.
340	RESPIRATORY THERAPY AIDE	medical ser.
240	REST ROOM ATTENDANT	any industry
380	RESTORATION TECHNICIAN	museums
214	RETAIL CLERK	retail trade
111	REVIEWER, FINAL APPLICATION	insurance
330	REWINDER OPERATOR	paper goods
230	RICE GRADER	grain-feed mills
240	RIDE OPERATOR	amuse. & rec.
482	RIGGER	ship-boat mfg.
482	RIGGER, HIGH	amuse. & rec.
481	RIGGER/SLINGER	any industry
330	RIPSAW OPERATOR	woodworking
230	RIVET AND BOLT MAKER	any industry
330	RIVETER, HYDRAULIC	any industry
481	RIVETER, PNEUMATIC	any industry
330	RIVETING MACHINE OPERATOR, AUTOMATIC	aircraft mfg.
330	RIVETING MACHINE OPERATOR	any industry
351	ROAD ROLLER OPERATOR	construction
330	ROBOTIC MACHINE OPERATOR	aircraft mfg.
470	ROBOTICS SERVICE TECHNICIAN	machinery mfg.
351	ROCK DRILL OPERATOR	construction
560	ROLL TENDER/SETTER	print. & pub.
330	ROLLER MACHINE OPERATOR	metal prod., nec
230	ROLLING MILL ATTENDANT	steel & rel.
380	ROOFER	construction
480	ROOFER HELPER	construction
322	ROOM SERVICE CLERK	hotel & rest.
480	ROTARY DRILLER	petrol. & gas
480	ROTARY DRILLER HELPER	petrol. & gas
230	ROUGHER, BAR MILL	steel & rel.
480	ROUGHNECK	petrol. & gas
480	ROUSTABOUT	petrol. & gas
211	ROUTER	clerical
330	ROUTER OPERATOR	any industry
330	ROUTER OPERATOR	woodworking
460	RUBBER CUTTER	rubber goods
230	RUBBER MILL OPERATOR	plastic-synth.
340	RUG CLEANER, HAND OR MACHINE	laundry & rel.
321	RUG REPAIRER	laundry & rel.
420	SADDLE MAKER	leather prod.
212	SAFETY ENGINEER	profess. & kin.
212	SAFETY MANAGER	profess. & kin.
380	SAIL MAKER	ship-boat mfg.
322	SALAD MAKER	water trans.
212	SALES AGENT, INSURANCE	insurance
214	SALES CLERK	retail trade
251	SALES REP, FARM, GARDEN EQPT. & SUPPLIES	wholesale tr.
212	SALES REP, ADVERTISING	print. & pub.
251	SALES REP, COMPUTERS AND EDP SYSTEMS	wholesale tr.

Group No.	Occupation	Industry
212	SALES REP, DATA PROCESSING SERVICES	business ser.
251	SALES REP, DOOR-TO-DOOR	retail trade
212	SALES REP, FINANCIAL SERVICES	financial
251	SALES REP, LIVESTOCK	wholesale tr.
251	SALES REP, OFFICE MACHINES	retail trade
251	SALES REP, RECREATION, SPORTING GOODS	wholesale tr.
251	SALES REP, SECURITY SYSTEMS	business ser.
212	SALES REP, UPHOLSTERY, FURNITURE REPAIR	retail trade
251	SALES REP, WOMEN'S AND GIRLS' APPAREL	wholesale tr.
251	SALESPERSON, AUTOMOBILES	retail trade
214	SALESPERSON, GENERAL MERCHANDISE	retail trade
214	SALESPERSON, PARTS	retail trade
214	SALESPERSON, SHOES	retail trade
430	SALVAGE CUTTER	welding
480	SANDBLASTER	any industry
330	SANDER, MACHINE	woodworking
322	SANDWICH MAKER	hotel & rest.
331	SAUSAGE MAKER	meat products
331	SAUSAGE STUFFER	meat products
321	SAW BLADE FILER	any industry
360	SAWMILL WORKER	saw. & plan.
330	SAWYER	plastic prod.; plastic-synth.
230	SAWYER, CIRCULAR HEAD	saw. & plan.
230	SAWYER, CORK SLABS	wood prod., nec
330	SAWYER, TRIMMER	saw. & plan.
111	SCHEDULER	clerical
212	SCHOOL PRINCIPAL	education
111	SCOREBOARD OPERATOR	amuse. & rec.
251	SCOUT, PROFESSIONAL SPORTS	amuse. & rec.
460	SCRAP HANDLER	any industry
320	SCREEN MAKER, PHOTOGRAPHIC PROCESS	any industry
221	SCREEN MAKER, WALLPAPER	paper goods
330	SCREW MACHINE OPERATOR, MULTIPLE SPINDLE	machine shop
330	SCROLL MACHINE OPERATOR	struct. metal

Group No.	Occupation	Industry
321	SCULPTOR	stonework
112	SECRETARY	clerical
112	SECRETARY, LEGAL	clerical
112	SECRETARY, MEDICAL	medical ser.
112	SECRETARY, SOCIAL	clerical
212	SECURITY GUARD, GATE	any industry
213	SECURITY GUARD, PLANT	any industry
390	SECURITY OFFICER	any industry
230	SEED PELLETER	agriculture
212	SEISMOLOGIST	profess. & kin.
330	SEMICONDUCTOR PROCESSOR	electron. comp.
380	SEPTIC TANK INSTALLER	construction
480	SEPTIC TANK SERVICER	construction
214	SERVICE MANAGER	automotive ser.
213	SERVICE REPRESENTATIVE	utilities
340	SERVICE STATION ATTENDANT	automotive ser.
213	SET DESIGNER	motion picture
320	SETTER, AUTOMATIC SPINNING LATHE	any industry
360	SET-UP PERSON, TRADE SHOW	retail trade
480	SEWAGE DISPOSAL WORKER	sanitary ser.
221	SEWER, HAND	any industry
480	SEWER LINE REPAIRER	sanitary ser.
341	SEWER PIPE CLEANER	business ser.
230	SEWING MACHINE OPERATOR	tex. prod., nec
370	SEWING MACHINE REPAIRER	any industry
330	SHAPER OPERATOR	woodworking
330	SHAPING MACHINE OPERATOR	machine shop
430	SHEAR OPERATOR	any industry
370	SHEETMETAL MECHANIC	any industry
320	SHEETMETAL FABRICATING MACHINE OPERATOR	any industry
491	SHELLFISH GROWER	fishing & hunt.
490	SHERIFF, DEPUTY	government ser.
481	SHIPFITTER	ship-boat mfg.
480	SHIPFITTER HELPER	ship-boat mfg.
360	SHIPPING AND RECEIVING CLERK	clerical
214	SHIPPING CHECKER	clerical
380	SHIPWRIGHT	ship-boat mfg.
221	SHOE REPAIRER	personal ser.
214	SHOP ESTIMATOR	automotive ser.
210	SHOW HOST/HOSTESS	radio-tv broad.

Group No.	Occupation	Industry
250	SHUTTLE BUS DRIVER	any industry
380	SIDER	construction
341	SIGN POSTER	any industry
120	SIGN WRITER, HAND	any industry
221	SILK SCREEN ETCHER	engraving
221	SILK SCREEN PRINTER	any industry
221	SILK SCREEN FRAME ASSEMBLER	any industry
220	SILVERSMITH	jewelry-silver.
210	SINGER	amuse. & rec.
493	SKI INSTRUCTOR	amuse. & rec.
240	SKI LIFT OPERATOR	amuse. & rec.
590	SKI PATROLLER	amuse. & rec.
221	SKI REPAIRER, PRODUCTION	toy-sport equip.
420	SKINNER	meat products
480	SKIP TENDER	mine & quarry
111	SKIP TRACER	clerical
460	SLASHER TENDER	textile
230	SLICING MACHINE OPERATOR	bakery products
460	SLITTING MACHINE OPERATOR HELPER	any industry
331	SLURRY BLENDER	cement
370	SMOG TECHNICIAN	automotive ser.
590	SMOKE JUMPER	forestry
351	SNOWPLOW OPERATOR	government ser.
230	SOAP MAKER	soap & rel.
111	SOCIAL WORKER	social ser.
111	SOFTWARE ENGINEER	profess. & kin.
213	SOIL CONSERVATIONIST	profess. & kin.
481	SOLAR ENERGY SYSTEM INSTALLER	any industry
470	SOLAR FABRICATION TECHNICIAN	machine shop
120	SOLDERER	jewelry-silver.
111	SORTER	clerical
221	SORTER, AGRICULTURAL PRODUCE	agriculture
221	SORTER, REMNANT	textile
214	SORTER-PRICER	nonprofit org.
212	SOUND MIXER	motion picture
212	SOUND EFFECTS TECHNICIAN	radio-tv broad.
322	SOUS CHEF	hotel & rest.
490	SPECIAL AGENT	government ser.
390	SPECIAL POLICEMAN	any industry
212	SPEECH PATHOLOGIST	profess. & kin.
331	SPINNER	sugar & conf.

Group No.	Occupation	Industry
430	SPINNER, HYDRAULIC	any industry
330	SPINNING LATHE OPERATOR	any industry
221	SPORTS EQUIPMENT REPAIRER	any industry
221	SPOT CLEANER	laundry & rel.
111	SPOTTER, PHOTOGRAPHIC	photofinishing
330	SPRAY PAINTING MACHINE OPERATOR	any industry
460	SPREADER MACHINE, CLOTH	textile
491	STABLE ATTENDANT	any industry
230	STAMPING PRESS OPERATOR	any industry
390	STAND-IN	motion picture
330	STAPLING MACHINE OPERATOR	any industry
380	STATION INSTALLER AND REPAIRER	tel. & tel.
332	STATIONARY ENGINEER	any industry
111	STATISTICIAN, APPLIED	profess. & kin.
340	STEAM CLEANER	automotive ser.
482	STEEL ERECTOR	construction
380	STEEL PLATE CAULKER	any industry
482	STEEPLE JACK	construction
112	STENOCAPTIONER	radio-tv broad.
112	STENOGRAPHER	clerical
112	STENOTYPE OPERATOR	clerical
330	STEREOTYPE CASTER & MOLDER	print. & pub.
230	STERILIZER	medical ser.
351	STEVEDORE	water trans.
230	STILL TENDER	any industry
230	STITCHER, STANDARD MACHINE	boot & shoe
230	STITCHER, WIRE, SADDLE AND SIDE	print. & pub.
214	STOCK CLERK	clerical
360	STOCK CLERK	clerical
360	STOCK CLERK	retail trade
214	STOCK CLERK, AUTOMOTIVE EQPT.	clerical
321	STONE CARVER	stonework
480	STONE DRILLER	stonework
220	STONE SETTER	jewelry-silver.
480	STONE SPLITTER OPERATOR	stonework
321	STONECUTTER, HAND	stonework
330	STONECUTTER, MACHINE	stonework
380	STONEMASON	construction
120	STONER	jewelry-silver.
470	STOVE REFINISHER	any industry
321	STRAIGHTENER, HAND	any industry

Group No.	Occupation	Industry
330	STRAIGHTENING PRESS OPERATOR	any industry
330	STRANDING MACHINE OPERATOR	elec. equip.
460	STRAPPING MACHINE OPERATOR	wood. container
340	STREET CLEANER/SWEEPER, MANUAL	government ser.
380	STREET LIGHT SERVICER	utilities
351	STREET SWEEPER OPERATOR	government ser.
111	STRESS ANALYST	aircraft mfg.
212	STRESS TEST TECHNICIAN	medical ser.
230	STRETCHING MACHINE TENDER, FRAME	leather mfg.
221	STRIPER & LETTERER, HAND, MOTORCYCLES	any industry
331	STRIPPER-ETCHER, PRINTED CIRCUIT BOARDS	electron. comp.
482	STRUCTURAL STEEL WORKER	construction
482	STRUCTURAL STEEL WORKER HELPER	construction
380	STUCCO MASON	construction
590	STUNT PERFORMER	amuse. & rec.
320	SUBASSEMBLER	machinery mfg.
332	SUBSTATION OPERATOR	utilities
250	SUBWAY CAR OPERATOR	r.r. trans.
332	SUPERCALENDER OPERATOR	paper & pulp
212	SUPERINTENDENT, BUILDING	any industry
213	SUPERINTENDENT, CONSTRUCTION	construction
212	SUPERINTENDENT, PLANT PROTECTION	any industry
360	SUPPLY CLERK	clerical
220	SURGEON	medical ser.
230	SURGICAL DRESSING MAKER, MACHINE	protective dev.
212	SURGICAL TECHNICIAN	medical ser.
213	SURVEYOR	surveying/carto-graphic
360	SURVEYOR HELPER	any industry
340	SWIMMING POOL SERVICER	any industry
111	SWITCHBOARD OPERATOR, POLICE DISTRICT	government ser.
331	SYRUP MAKER	beverage
111	SYSTEMS ANALYST	profess. & kin.
111	SYSTEMS PROGRAMMER	profess. & kin.
230	TACKING MACHINE OPERATOR	any industry
221	TAILOR, ALTERATION	garment
221	TAILOR, CUSTOM	garment
460	TANK CLEANER	any industry
380	TAPER	construction
120	TAPER, PRINTED CIRCUIT LAYOUT	electron. comp.
330	TAPPING MACHINE TENDER	nut & bolt
111	TAX CLERK	clerical
111	TAX PREPARER	business ser.
250	TAXI DRIVER	motor trans.
311	TAXIDERMIST	profess. & kin.
214	TEACHER AIDE	education
212	TEACHER, ADULT EDUCATION	education
214	TEACHER, ELEMENTARY SCHOOL	education
214	TEACHER, INDUSTRIAL ARTS	education
214	TEACHER, LEARNING DISABLED	education
214	TEACHER, MUSIC	education
390	TEACHER, PHYSICAL EDUCATION	education
214	TEACHER, PHYSICALLY IMPAIRED	education
214	TEACHER, PRESCHOOL/KINDERGARTEN	education
212	TEACHER, SECONDARY SCHOOL	education
214	TEACHER, VOCATIONAL TRAINING	education
120	TECHNICAL ILLUSTRATOR	profess. & kin.
112	TELEGRAPH OPERATOR	clerical
112	TELEPHONE OPERATOR	clerical
112	TELEPHONE ANSWERING SERVICE OPERATOR	business ser.
350	TELEPHONE DIRECTORY DELIVERER	business ser.
111	TELEVISION CONSOLE MONITOR	radio-tv broad.
380	TELEVISION RECEIVER/ANTENNA INSTALLER	any industry
470	TELEVISION TECHNICIAN	radio-tv broad.
320	TELEVISION AND RADIO REPAIRER	any industry
211	TELLER	financial
214	TELLER, VAULT	financial
320	TEMPLATE MAKER	any industry
380	TERRAZZO INSTALLER	construction
480	TERRAZZO INSTALLER HELPER	construction
220	TEST TECH, SEMICONDUCTOR PROCESSING EQUIPMENT	electron. comp.
320	TESTER, NONDESTRUCTIVE	profess. & kin.

Group No.	Occupation	Industry
212	TESTING MACHINE OPERATOR, METAL	profess. & kin.
370	THERMAL CUTTER, HAND	welding
330	THERMAL CUTTING-MACHINE OPERATOR	welding
320	THERMOSTAT REPAIRER	inst. & app.
221	THREAD CUTTER, HAND OR MACHINE	any industry
330	THREADING MACHINE OPERATOR	machine shop
321	THROWER	pottery & porc.
212	TICKET AGENT	any industry
213	TICKET INSPECTOR, TRANSPORTATION	r.r. transportation
230	TICKET PRINTER	any industry
240	TICKET TAKER	amuse. & rec.
330	TILE MAKER	brick & tile
380	TILE SETTER	construction
480	TILE SETTER HELPER	construction
330	TIMBER-SIZER OPERATOR	saw. & plan.
212	TIME AND MOTION STUDY ANALYST	profess. & kin.
321	TIRE BUILDER, AUTOMOBILE	rubber tire
460	TIRE CHANGER	automotive ser.
460	TIRE MOLDER	rubber tire
321	TIRE RECAPPER	automotive ser.
460	TIRE REPAIRER	automotive ser.
420	TIRE TRIMMER, HAND	rubber tire
211	TITLE SEARCHER	real estate
211	TOLL COLLECTOR	government ser.
220	TOOL DESIGNER	profess. & kin.
330	TOOL DRESSER	any industry
320	TOOL MAKER	machine shop
320	TOOL MAKER, BENCH	machine shop
120	TOOL PROGRAMMER, NUMERICAL CONTROL	electron. comp.
360	TOOL AND EQUIPMENT RENTAL CLERK	business ser.
360	TOOL CRIB ATTENDANT	clerical
430	TORCH STRAIGHTENER AND HEATER	any industry
221	TOUCH-UP PAINTER, HAND	any industry
482	TOWER ERECTOR	construction
212	TOXICOLOGIST	pharmaceut.
221	TOY ASSEMBLER	toy-sport equip.
351	TRACTOR OPERATOR	any industry
351	TRACTOR CRANE OPERATOR	any industry
111	TRAFFIC CLERK	business ser.
212	TRAFFIC ENGINEER	government ser.
490	TRAFFIC OFFICER	government ser.
111	TRAIN DISPATCHER	r.r. trans.
112	TRANSCRIBING MACHINE OPERATOR	clerical
370	TRANSFORMER ASSEMBLER	elec. equip.
111	TRANSLATOR, DOCUMENTS	profess. & kin.
492	TREE CUTTER	agriculture
491	TREE PRUNER, LOW LEVEL/BUCKET	agriculture
482	TREE SURGEON	agriculture
482	TREE TRIMMER	tel. & tel.
230	TRIMMER, MACHINE	garment
322	TRIMMER, MEAT	meat products
221	TROPHY ASSEMBLER	jewelry-silver.
350	TRUCK DRIVER	any industry
350	TRUCK DRIVER, CONCRETE MIXING	construction
350	TRUCK DRIVER, DUMP TRUCK	any industry
350	TRUCK DRIVER, GARBAGE	motor trans.
350	TRUCK DRIVER, LOGS	logging
351	TRUCK DRIVER, ROAD OILING	construction
350	TRUCK DRIVER, SALES ROUTE	retail trade
350	TRUCK DRIVER, TANK TRUCK	petrol. refin.
350	TRUCK DRIVER, TOW TRUCK	automotive ser.
350	TRUCK DRIVER, TRACTOR-TRAILER	any industry
460	TRUCK LOADER	any industry
460	TRUCK DRIVER HELPER	any industry
380	TRUSS BUILDER, CONSTRUCTION	construction
320	TUBE ASSEMBLER, CATHODE RAY	electron. comp.
221	TUBE BENDER, HAND	any industry
341	TUBE CLEANER	any industry
330	TUBULAR FURNITURE MAKER	any industry
111	TUMOR REGISTRAR	medical ser.
332	TURBINE ATTENDANT	utilities
332	TURBINE OPERATOR	utilities
330	TURRET LATHE OPERATOR	machine shop
212	TUTOR	education
221	TYPESETTER/COMPOSITOR	print. & pub.

Group No.	Occupation	Industry
230	TYPESETTING MACHINE TENDER	print. & pub.
112	TYPIST	clerical
212	ULTRASOUND TECHNOLOGIST	medical ser.
214	UMPIRE	amuse. & rec.
110	UNDERWRITER, MORTGAGE LOAN	financial
321	UPHOLSTERY REPAIRER	furniture
110	URBAN PLANNER	profess. & kin.
370	USED CAR RENOVATOR	retail trade
240	USHER	amuse. & rec.
330	UTILITY OPERATOR	saw. & plan.
320	VACUUM CLEANER REPAIRER	any industry
351	VACUUM CLEANER OPERATOR, INDUSTRIAL	any industry
250	VALET, PARKING	automotive serv.
330	VARIETY SAW OPERATOR	woodworking
112	VARITYPE OPERATOR	clerical
214	VAULT CASHIER	business ser.
213	VENDOR	amuse. & rec.
340	VENETIAN BLIND CLEANER AND REPAIRER	any industry
311	VETERINARIAN	medical ser.
311	VETERINARIAN, LABORATORY ANIMAL CARE	medical ser.
311	VETERINARY TECHNICIAN	medical ser.
212	VIDEOTAPE OPERATOR, STUDIO	radio-tv broad.
110	VOCATIONAL REHABILITATION CONSULTANT	government ser.
212	VOICE PATHOLOGIST	profess. & kin.
221	WAFER FAB OPERATOR	electron. comp.
322	WAITER/WAITRESS	hotel & rest.
480	WALLPAPER REMOVER, STEAM	construction
360	WAREHOUSE WORKER	any industry
331	WASHER, MACHINE	any industry
340	WASHER, MACHINE	laundry & rel.
460	WASHING MACHINE LOADER AND PULLER	laundry & rel.
460	WASTE DISPOSAL ATTENDANT, RADIOACTIVE	any industry
332	WASTE TREATMENT OPERATOR	chemical
332	WASTEWATER TREATMENT PLANT OPERATOR	sanitary ser.
220	WATCH REPAIRER	clock & watch

Group No.	Occupation	Industry
380	WATER METER INSTALLER	waterworks
332	WATER PUMP TENDER	any industry
460	WATER SOFTENER SERVICER AND INSTALLER	business ser.
332	WATER TREATMENT PLANT OPERATOR	waterworks
481	WAYSMAN	ship-boat mfg.
230	WEAVER, TEXTILE	nonmet. min.
330	WEB PRESS OPERATOR HELPER, OFFSET	print. & pub.
330	WEB PRESS OPERATOR	print. & pub.
360	WEIGHER, PRODUCTION	any industry
214	WEIGHER, SHIPPING AND RECEIVING	clerical
240	WEIGHT REDUCTION SPECIALIST	personal services
460	WELDER HELPER	welding
430	WELDER, ARC	welding
370	WELDER, COMBINATION	welding
370	WELDER, GAS	welding
370	WELDER, GUN	welding
370	WELDER, PRODUCTION LINE	welding
430	WELDER, TACK	welding
380	WELDER-FITTER	welding
330	WELDING MACHINE OPERATOR, ARC	welding
480	WELL DIGGER	construction
480	WELL PULLER	petrol. & gas
480	WELL DRILL OPERATOR	construction
480	WELL DRILL OPERATOR HELPER	construction
320	WHEEL LACER AND TRUER	motor-bicycles
482	WIND GENERATING ELECTRIC POWER INSTALLER	construction
482	WIND TURBINE TECHNICIAN	construction; utilities
330	WINDER	paper goods
460	WINDER OPERATOR, FLOOR COVERINGS	fabrication
230	WINDER, MAGNETIC TAPE	recording
330	WINDER, YARN	tex. prod., nec
330	WINDING-MACHINE OPERATOR, CLOTH	textile
341	WINDOW CLEANER	any industry

Group No.	Occupation	Industry	Group No.	Occupation	Industry
380	WINDOW REPAIRER	any industry			
213	WINE MAKER	beverage			
240	WINE STEWARD/STEWARDESS	hotel & rest.			
332	WINERY WORKER	beverage			
221	WIRE HARNESS ASSEMBLER	elec. equip.			
330	WIRE DRAWING MACHINE TENDER	nonfer. metal			
230	WIRE WRAPPING MACHINE OPERATOR	electron. comp.			
330	WOOD-CARVING MACHINE OPERATOR	woodworking			
321	WOOL AND PELT GRADER	meat products			
112	WORD PROCESSING MACHINE OPERATOR	clerical			
330	WRAPPING MACHINE OPERATOR	any industry			
480	WRECKER, CONSTRUCTION	construction			
112	WRITER, PROSE, FICTION AND NONFICTION	profess. & kin.			
112	WRITER, TECHNICAL PUBLICATIONS	profess. & kin.			
212	XRAY OPERATOR, INDUSTRIAL	any industry			
310	XRAY TECHNOLOGIST	medical ser.			
460	YARD ATTENDANT, BUILDING MATERIALS	retail trade			
351	YARDER OPERATOR, FIXED/PORTABLE	logging			

PART B - OCCUPATIONAL GROUP CHART

	OCCUPATION DESIGNATOR	STRENGTH DESIGNATOR				
		1 Very Light	2 Light	3 Medium	4 Heavy	5 Very Heavy
1	Professional, Technical, Clerical	110, 111, 112 Case worker Auditor Editor	210, 211, 212, 213, 214 Adm. clerk Bank clerk Clerk, general	310, 311 Physical therapist Chiropractor Psych. tech.		
2	Hand Intensive	120 Drafter, civil Cartoonist Assemb/semi-cond.	220, 221 Dentist Microelect. tech. Surgeon	320, 321, 322 Die maker Meter repair Precision assem.	420 Butcher Saddle maker Hide puller	
3	Machine Operators, Tenders		230 Coil winder Cutter, machine Palletizer oper.	330, 331, 332 Bend. mach. Oper. Cut-off sawyer Laminating mach.	430 Boiler maker Metal fabricator Welder-arc	
4	Cleaners, Attendants		240 Child monitor Restroom attend. Ticket taker	340, 341 Auto washer Janitor Nurse's aide		
5	Drivers		250, 251 Coin-mach. collector Bus driver	350, 351 Truckdriver/ Tractor-trailer Truckdriver/ dump		
6	Laborers, Material Handlers			360 Warehouse worker Crate maker Material expediter	460 Baker's helper Material stacker Ramp attendant	560 Ambul. Attendant Furniture mover Miner
7	Mechanics, Installers, Repairers, Servicers			370 Mechanic-tractor Precision assemb. Welder, gas	470 Mechanic-diesel Furn. assemb/heavy TV tech.	

OCCUPATION DESIGNATOR		1 Very Light	2 Light	3 Medium	4 Heavy	5 Very Heavy
8	Construction Workers			380 Electrician Carpenter-Const Handy person	480, 481, 482 Bricklayer Carpenter/ Rough Millwright	
9	Miscellaneous		290 Beautician Barber Cosmetologist	390 Security officer Counselor, camp	490, 491, 492, 493 Farm laborer Gardener Log sorter	590 Athlete Jockey Dancer

PART C – OCCUPATIONAL GROUP CHARACTERISTICS

Group 110

Professional Occupations

Some use of keyboards but less than 112 or 112; greater standing and walking demands than 112 and 120.

Typical occupations: Lawyer, Loan Officer, Urban Planner

Spine	C
Shoulder	C
Elbow	D
Wrist	D
Finger motion.	F
Grip	D
Leg	D
Psych	J

Group 111

Professional and Clerical Occupations

Substantial use of keyboards; greater demands for standing and walking than 112 and 120.

Typical occupations: Accountant, Claims Clerk, Reservations Agent

Spine	C
Shoulder	D
Elbow	F
Wrist	G
Finger motion	G
Grip	E
Leg	D
Psych	I

Group 112

Mostly Clerical Occupations

Highest demand for use of keyboard; prolonged sitting.

Typical occupations: Billing Clerk, Computer Keyboard Operator, Secretary

Spine	D
Shoulder	D
Elbow	G
Wrist	H
Finger motion	I
Grip	E
Leg	C
Psych	I

Group 120

Most Technical Occupations

Precision work requiring skill and dexterity; use of hand tools; more sitting than 110 and 111.

Typical occupations: Electrical drafter, Illustrator, Jeweler

Spine	D
Shoulder	E
Elbow	G
Wrist	H
Finger motion	H
Grip	F
Leg	C
Psych	I

Group 210

Mostly Professional Occupations

Extensive speech and hearing; standing and sitting; may require driving to business locations; other physical demands at the lower end of the light category.

Typical occupations: Actor, Announcer. Clergy member

Spine	D
Shoulder	C
Elbow	D
Wrist	D
Finger motion	E
Grip	C
Leg	E
Psych	I

Group 211

Mostly Clerical Occupations

Emphasis on frequent fingering, handling, and possibly some keyboard work; spine and leg demands similar to 210.

Typical occupations: Bank clerk, Inventory clerk, License clerk

Spine	D
Shoulder	D
Elbow	F
Wrist	G
Finger motion	G
Grip	E
Leg	E
Psych	H

Group 212

Mostly Professional and Medical Occupations

Work predominantly performed indoors, but may require driving to locations of business; less use of hands than 211; slightly higher demands on spine than 210 & 211.

Typical occupations: Chemist, Dialysis Technician, Secondary School Teacher

Spine	E
Shoulder	E
Elbow	E
Wrist	F
Finger motion	F
Grip	E
Leg	E
Psych	J

Group 213

Mostly Professional Occupations

Work performed indoors and outdoors; occasional climbing and uneven ground required, therefore spine and legs have slightly higher variants for this strength level.

Typical occupations: Airplane Inspector, Meter Reader, Property Manager

Spine	F
Shoulder	E
Elbow	E
Wrist	E
Finger motion	F
Grip	E
Leg	F
Psych	I

Group 214

Clerical (physically active) Occupations; Educators, & Retail Sales Occupations

Very high demand for speech, hearing and vision; high demand for fingering and handling; spine and leg demands at highest level for 200 series.

Typical occupations: Auto Shop Estimator, Elementary School Teacher, Retail Sales Clerk

Spine	F
Shoulder	F
Elbow	F
Wrist	G
Finger motion	G
Grip	F
Leg	F
Psych	I

Group 220

Fine precision Occupations in medical, electronic and optical industries

Very high demands for vision; high demands for hand activity – use of hand tools; highest variants in this strength category for fingering and arm Disabilities.

Typical occupations: Dental Hygienist, Instrument Maker & Repairer, Surgeon

Spine	E
Shoulder	F
Elbow	G
Wrist	H
Finger motion	H
Grip	F
Leg	E
Psych	J

Group 221

Light Assembly Occupations, Food Preparation Occupations

Vision important; repetitive fingering and use of hand tools; similar to 220 for all parts of body except for wrist and finger motion which is one variant lower.

Spine	E
Shoulder	F
Elbow	G
Wrist	G
Finger motion	G
Grip	F
Leg	E
Psych	F

Typical occupations: Assembler, small products Inspector, electronics Produce Sorter

Group 230

Machine Operator and Tenders

Average demands for this strength level on spine and legs; hand activities are most significant.

Spine	E
Shoulder	F
Elbow	F
Wrist	F
Finger motion	G
Grip	G
Leg	E
Psych	F

Typical occupations: Bottle Packer, Circular Saw Operator' Offset Press Operator

Group 240

Mostly Attendants (providing services)

Minimal hand activities; low on arm activities; average for 200 series on spine and legs.

Spine	E
Shoulder	D
Elbow	E
Wrist	E
Finger motion	E
Grip	D
Leg	E
Psych	G

Typical occupations: Host/Hostess, Parking Lot Attendant, booth,Weight Reduction Specialist

Group 250

Public Transportation Drivers & Light Delivery Drivers

Operates light automotive equipment over public thoroughfares; vision, hearing and other head disabilities important; highest variants for spine and leg activities in 200 series (along with 213 & 214); grip demands similar to 251.

Spine	F
Shoulder	F
Elbow	G
Wrist	F
Finger motion	F
Grip	F
Leg	F
Psych	H

Typical occupations: Parking Enforcement Officer, Subway Car Operator, Taxi Driver

Group 251

Outside Sales, Inspectors, & Business Agents (performing extensive driving to reach business locations)

Work requires extensive driving of light automotive equipment over public thoroughfares to reach business locations; vision, hearing and other head disabilities important; average demand for spine and leg activities for this strength level; arms are one variant lower that 250.

Spine	E
Shoulder	D
Elbow	F
Wrist	E
Finger motion	F
Grip	F
Leg	E
Psych	I

Typical occupations: Food & Drug Inspector, Real Estate Agent. Sales, Rep. sporting goods

Group 290

Personal Attendants	Spine	E
	Shoulder	G
Vision important; cosmetic appearance important; arms variants at high end for 200 series.	Elbow	G
	Wrist	H
	Finger motion	G
	Grip	F
Typical occupations: Hair Stylist	Leg	E
	Psych	H

Group 310

Medical Occupations	Spine	F
	Shoulder	F
Low end of 300 series for most parts of body; head disabilities, including speech, hearing, PTHS are highest in 300 series.	Elbow	F
	Wrist	F
	Finger motion	F
	Grip	F
	Leg	F
Typical occupations: Acupressurist, MRI Technologist, X-ray Technologist	Psych	I

Group 311

Mostly Medical Occupations	Spine	G
	Shoulder	F
Medical treatments performed result in higher spine demands; head disabilities are at the highest levels.	Elbow	G
	Wrist	G
	Finger motion	G
	Grip	F
Typical occupations: Masseur/Masseuse Nurse – LVN, Psychiatric Technician	Leg	F
	Psych	J

Group 320

Assemblers	Spine	F
	Shoulder	F
Precision work requiring use of hand tools; highest arm variants for the 320 series; lower end variants for 300 series for spine & leg (same as 321 & 322); highest head variants in 320 series.	Elbow	H
	Wrist	I
	Finger motion	H
	Grip	H
	Leg	F
	Psych	H
Typical occupations: Machinist, Office Machine Servicer, Television & Radio Repairer		

Group 321

Assemblers	Spine	F
	Shoulder	F
Use of hand tools required; precision requirements less than 320 – arm variants slightly lower; same demand on spine and legs as 320 & 322.	Elbow	G
	Wrist	H
	Finger motion	G
	Grip	G
	Leg	F
Typical occupations: Furniture	Psych	F

Assembler, Garment Cutter, machine Painter, spray gun

Group 322

Description	Body part	Rating
Food Preparation and Service Occupations	Spine	F
	Shoulder	F
	Elbow	G
Least precise work in 320 series – arm variants the lowest; spine & legs same as 320 & 321	Wrist	G
	Finger motion	G
	Grip	G
	Leg	F
Typical occupations: Airline Flight Attendant, Cook, Waiter/Waitress	Psych	G

Group 330

Description	Body part	Rating
Press Operators, Sawyers, etc.	Spine	F
	Shoulder	F
Most demanding on arms of machine operations series (330s); spine and legs at lower end for 300 series, & same as 331 & 322.	Elbow	G
	Wrist	F
	Finger motion	G
	Grip	G
	Leg	F
Typical occupations: Blister Machine Operator, Power Press Tender, Tubular Furniture Maker	Psych	F

Group 331

Description	Body part	Rating
Machine Tending & Processing	Spine	F
	Shoulder	F
Observation and control of machinery; occasional stooping required; mechanical adjustments performed; variants similar to 332.	Elbow	F
	Wrist	F
	Finger motion	F
	Grip	F
	Leg	F
Typical occupations: Coating Machine Op, Mixing Machine Op, food prep; Washer, machine	Psych	F

Group 332

Description	Body part	Rating
Observation of Large Stationary Equipment	Spine	F
	Shoulder	F
	Elbow	F
Work performed in a plant or other large facility, some mechanical adjustments of machinery performed lowest variants for 300 series for most parts of body.	Wrist	E
	Finger motion	F
	Grip	F
	Leg	F
	Psych	G
Typical occupations: Brewery Cellar Worker, Power Reactor Operator, Stationary Engineer		

Group 340

Description	Body part	Rating
Mostly Cleaners	Spine	G
	Shoulder	F
Work involves cleaning equipment and/or buildings; operation of cleaning devices, some lifting , some climbing, lowest variants for head disabilities of 300 series; lower end of 300 series for arms; highest demands are for spine & leg activities	Elbow	G
	Wrist	F
	Finger motion	F
	Grip	F
	Leg	G
	Psych	D
Typical occupations: Auto Washer & Polisher, Janitor, Nurse Aide		

Group 341

Cleaners (working at high levels)	Spine	G
	Shoulder	G
Work generally performed at high levels – higher end of 300 series for spine & legs; average demands on arms.	Elbow	G
	Wrist	F
	Finger motion	F
	Grip	F
	Leg	G
Typical occupations: Aircraft Service Attendant, Sign Poster, Window Cleaner	Psych	D

Group 350

Truck Drivers	Spine	G
	Shoulder	F
Operate heavy vehicle over public thoroughfares; may do some loading of materials, may tie down loads, may hook up hoses, etc., and performs related duties; head disabilities highest in 300 series.	Elbow	H
	Wrist	F
	Finger motion	G
	Grip	G
	Leg	G
	Psych	H
Typical occupations: Armored Car Driver, Lunch Truck Driver, Truck Driver		

Group 351

Heavy Equipment Operators	Spine	G
	Shoulder	G
Operates heavy construction equipment at work sites; arm demands at lower end of 300 series; spine & leg demands at higher end of 300 series.	Elbow	H
	Wrist	G
	Finger motion	G
	Grip	G
	Leg	G
	Psych	G
Typical occupations: Crane Operator, Forklift Operator, Snowplow Operator		

Group 360

Porters, Packers	Spine	G
	Shoulder	G
Significant lifting and carrying required; significant walking required; may occasionally climb at low levels; variants are "G" for most parts of body; head disabilities are mostly "F"or lower.	Elbow	G
	Wrist	F
	Finger motion	F
	Grip	G
	Leg	G
	Psych	E
Typical occupations: Clerk, Shipping; Conveyor Tender; Warehouse worker		

Group 370

Mechanical Assembly, Installation, Repairers	Spine	G
	Shoulder	G
	Elbow	I
Mechanical work on automobiles, machinery and other equipment, requiring a combination of some skill and significant physical effort; highest variants in 300 series for arm	Wrist	J
	Finger motion	H
	Grip	H
	Leg	G
	Psych	H

and head disabilities

Typical occupations: Automobile Accessories Installer; Mechanic, automobile; Welder, Combination

Group 380

Skilled Construction Work

Work requires construction of buildings or large structure; strenuous demands on arms, legs & spine result in highest variants in 300 series; significant climbing required.

Typical occupations: Burglar Alarm, Carpenter Electrician

Spine	H
Shoulder	H
Elbow	I
Wrist	J
Finger motion	H
Grip	H
Leg	I
Psych	H

Group 390

Security Officers, Coaches

Inside and outside work requiring significant walking, some uneven ground, and climbing –leg demands are most significant aspect of duties; work may be high risk but not necessarily highly physical; demands for arms & spine are at middle of 300 series.

Typical occupations: Bodyguard, Instructor, Physical education, Security Officer

Spine	G
Shoulder	G
Elbow	G
Wrist	G
Finger motion	G
Grip	G
Leg	H
Psych	H

Group 420

Meat Processing +

Heavy demands placed on arms; spine demand similar to most in 400 series; leg demands lowest in 400 series.

Typical occupations: Baker, Butcher, Glass Cutter

Spine	H
Shoulder	G
Elbow	H
Wrist	I
Finger motion	G
Grip	H
Leg	G
Psych	F

Group 430

Machine-assisted Metal Shaping

Heavy demands on spine & legs in lifting & carrying; work performed at ground level; requires use of heavy hand tools or force with arms.

Typical occupations: Boilermaker, Power Brake Operator, Shear Operator

Spine	H
Shoulder	H
Elbow	I
Wrist	H
Finger motion	H
Grip	H
Leg	H
Psych	G

Group 460

Material Handlers & Machine Loaders & Unloaders

Strenuous demands on spine & legs for lifting and carrying heavy objects; lowest demand for specialized arm activities in 400 series.

Typical occupations: Baggage Handler, Chain Offbearer, Laborer,

Spine	H
Shoulder	G
Elbow	G
Wrist	G
Finger motion	F
Grip	G
Leg	H
Psych	E

Group 470

Description	Body part	Rating
Installers & Repairers	Spine	H
	Shoulder	H
Strenuous demands on all parts of body – variants are at the higher end of the 400 series.	Elbow	I
	Wrist	J
	Finger motion	H
	Grip	H
Typical occupations: Household Appliance Installer, Maintenance Mechanic, Television Technician	Leg	H
	Psych	H

Group 480

Description	Body part	Rating
Construction Helpers, Oil Field Workers & Some Skilled Construction Workers	Spine	I
	Shoulder	H
	Elbow	H
	Wrist	G
Heavy laboring work at construction sites or other work sites; very strenuous use of spine for lifting and exerting force; heavy demands on arms (similar to 492); leg requirements lower than for 481 & 492.	Finger motion	G
	Grip	G
	Leg	H
	Psych	E
Typical occupations: Carpenter Helper; Laborer, construction; Roughneck		

Group 481

Description	Body part	Rating
Skilled Construction Workers	Spine	I
	Shoulder	H
Work requires construction of buildings or large structures; skilled work performed at various levels, with significant demands for climbing, but lower demands on legs than 482; strenuous use of arms (same as 470).	Elbow	I
	Wrist	J
	Finger motion	H
	Grip	H
	Leg	I
	Psych	H
Typical occupations: Cable Television Installer, Millwright, Pipe Fitter		

Group 482

Description	Body part	Rating
Skilled Construction Workers	Spine	J
	Shoulder	I
Construction and maintenance work performed at high and dangerous levels – balance required; demands on spine & legs similar to 590; very strenuous use of arms.	Elbow	J
	Wrist	J
	Finger motion	I
	Grip	J
	Leg	J
	Psych	I
Typical occupations: Bridge Maintenance Worker, Grip (movie industry), Tree Trimmer		

Group 490

Description	Body part	Rating
Mostly Sworn Officers – Police & Fire (legal presumptions apply)	Spine	I
	Shoulder	I
	Elbow	I
Workers called upon to perform demanding activities in unpredictable and dangerous circumstances;	Wrist	H
	Finger motion	H
	Grip	I

significant demands on all parts of body.	Leg	I
	Psych	J
Typical occupations: Fire Fighter, Paramedic.Police Officer		

Group 491

Agricultural & Livestock Workers	Spine	H
	Shoulder	G
Work requires tending the land and/or caring for animals; physical demands & variants similar to 460 but slightly lower in mental demands.	Elbow	G
	Wrist	G
	Finger motion	F
	Grip	G
	Leg	H
	Psych	D
Typical occupations: Dog Catcher; Farmer, General; Gardener		

Group 492

Logging & Fishing Occupations	Spine	I
	Shoulder	H
Very physical work performed outside; high demand on spine & legs for balancing, working on rugged terrain, and climbing; arm and other variants similar to 560.	Elbow	H
	Wrist	H
	Finger motion	G
	Grip	H
	Leg	I
	Psych	E
Typical occupations: Bucker, Logger, all-round		

Group 493

Mostly Professional Athletes	Spine	H
	Shoulder	H
Substantial athletic performance required but less arduous than Group 590	Elbow	H
	Wrist	H
	Finger motion	G
	Grip	H
Typical occupations: Bowler, professional, Ski instructor, Aerobic instructor	Leg	I
	Psych	H

Group 560

Mostly Material Handlers	Spine	J
	Shoulder	H
Requires lifting of large and/or very heavy objects or exerting very significant force – very strenuous demands placed on spine & legs.	Elbow	H
	Wrist	H
	Finger motion	G
	Grip	H
	Leg	I
Typical occupations: Ambulance Attendant; Furniture Mover; Garbage Collector, manual	Psych	D

Group 590

Mostly Professional Athletes	Spine	J
	Shoulder	J
Peak athletic performance requiring whole body strength with specialized training and skills; highest variants for all parts of the body.	Elbow	J
	Wrist	J
	Finger motion	I
	Grip	J
	Leg	J
Typical occupations: Athlete, professional; Stunt Performer	Psych	I

SECTION 4 - OCCUPATIONAL VARIANTS

Use this section to determine the occupational variant for the particular impairment and occupation under consideration.

Locate the row on which the impairment number appears*, and the column headed by the group number. Record the letter appearing at the intersection of the row and column. This letter is the "Occupational Variant" which is represented by a letter between "C" and "J" inclusive.

After establishing the occupational variant, turn to Section 5, page 5-1 to adjust the rating for occupation.

*All impairment numbers contain eight numbers in the form XX.XX.XX.XX. Ranges of impairment numbers with the same variants are represented in two ways. As an example, numbers beginning with 03.01-, 03.02- and 03.03- are represented as 03.01--03.03. And all impairment numbers beginning with 13.11.01- are shown as 13.11.01.XX.

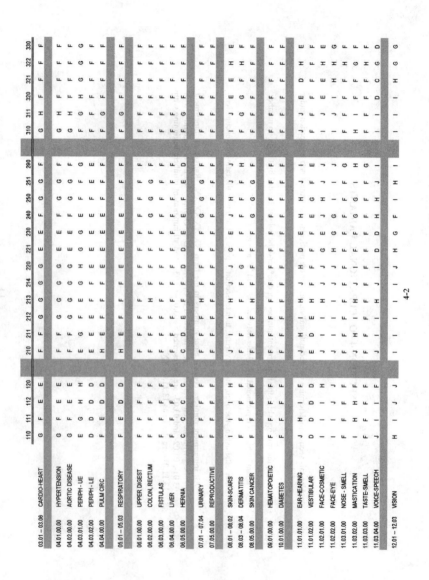

		110	111	112	120	210	211	212	213	214	220	221	230	240	250	251	290	310	311	320	321	322	330
03.01 – 03.06	CARDIO-HEART	G	F	E	E	F	F	G	G	G	G	E	E	F	G	G	F	G	H	F	F	F	F
04.01.00.00	HYPERTENSION	G	F	E	E	F	F	G	G	G	G	E	E	F	G	G	F	G	H	F	F	F	F
04.02.00.00	AORTIC DISEASE	G	F	E	E	F	F	G	G	G	G	E	E	F	G	G	F	G	H	F	F	F	F
04.03.01.00	PERIPH - UE	E	G	H	H	E	G	F	E	G	H	G	G	E	F	F	G	F	G	H	G	G	G
04.03.02.00	PERIPH - LE	D	D	D	D	E	E	E	F	F	E	E	E	E	F	E	E	F	F	F	F	F	F
04.04.00.00	PULM CIRC	F	E	D	D	H	E	F	F	F	E	E	E	E	F	F	F	F	G	F	F	F	F
05.01 – 05.03	RESPIRATORY	F	E	D	D	H	E	F	F	F	E	E	E	E	F	F	F	F	G	F	F	F	F
06.01.00.00	UPPER DIGEST	F	F	F	F	F	F	F	F	F	F	F	F	F	F	F	F	F	F	F	F	F	F
06.02.00.00	COLON, RECTUM	F	F	F	F	F	F	F	H	F	F	F	F	G	G	G	F	F	F	F	F	F	F
06.03.00.00	FISTULAS	F	F	F	F	F	F	F	F	F	F	F	F	F	F	F	F	F	F	F	F	F	F
06.04.00.00	LIVER	F	F	F	F	F	F	F	F	F	F	F	F	F	F	F	F	F	F	F	F	F	F
06.05.00.00	HERNIA	C	C	C	C	C	D	E	F	F	D	D	E	E	F	E	D	F	G	F	F	F	F
07.01 – 07.04	URINARY	F	F	F	F	F	F	F	H	F	F	F	F	G	G	G	F	F	F	F	F	F	F
07.05.00.00	REPRODUCTIVE	F	F	F	F	F	F	F	F	F	F	F	F	F	F	F	F	F	F	F	F	F	F
08.01 – 08.02	SKIN-SCARS	I	I	I	H	J	I	I	H	J	J	G	E	J	H	J	J	I	J	E	E	H	E
08.03 – 08.04	DERMATITIS	F	F	F	F	F	F	F	F	F	G	F	F	F	F	F	H	F	G	G	F	H	F
08.05.00.00	SKIN CANCER	F	F	F	F	F	F	F	H	F	F	F	F	G	G	G	F	F	F	F	F	F	F
09.01.00.00	HEMATOPOIETIC	F	F	F	F	F	F	F	F	F	F	F	F	F	F	F	F	F	F	F	F	F	F
10.01.00.00	DIABETES	F	F	F	F	F	F	F	F	F	F	F	F	F	F	F	F	F	F	F	F	F	F
11.01.01.00	EAR-HEARING	J	H	I	F	J	H	I	H	J	H	D	E	H	H	J	I	J	J	E	D	H	E
11.01.02.00	VESTIBULAR	D	D	D	D	E	D	E	H	F	F	F	F	E	G	F	E	F	F	F	F	F	F
11.02.01.00	FACE-COSMETIC	I	I	I	H	J	I	I	H	J	J	G	E	J	H	J	J	I	J	E	E	H	E
11.02.02.00	FACE-EYE	I	I	J	J	J	I	I	I	J	J	H	G	G	I	I	J	I	J	I	H	H	G
11.03.01.00	NOSE - SMELL	F	F	F	F	F	F	F	F	F	F	F	F	F	F	F	G	F	F	F	F	H	F
11.03.02.00	MASTICATION	I	H	H	F	J	H	I	H	J	I	F	F	G	G	I	H	H	I	F	F	G	F
11.03.03.00	TASTE-SMELL	F	F	F	F	F	F	F	F	F	F	F	F	F	F	F	G	F	F	F	F	H	F
11.03.04.00	VOICE-SPEECH	J	I	I	F	J	I	I	H	J	I	D	D	H	H	J	I	I	I	D	C	G	D
12.01 – 12.03	VISION	H	I	J	J	I	I	I	I	I	J	H	G	F	I	H	I	I	I	I	H	G	G

		331	332	340	341	350	351	360	370	380	390	420	430	460	470	480	481	482	490	491	492	493	560	590
03.01 -- 03.06	CARDIO-HEART	F	F	G	G	H	G	G	G	H	H	H	H	H	H	H	H	I	I	H	H	I	H	J
04.01.00.00	HYPERTENSION	F	F	G	G	H	G	G	G	H	H	H	H	H	H	H	H	I	I	H	H	I	H	J
04.02.00.00	AORTIC DISEASE	F	F	G	G	H	G	G	G	H	H	H	H	H	H	H	H	I	I	H	H	I	H	J
04.03.01.00	PERIPH - UE	F	F	F	F	G	G	G	H	H	G	H	H	G	H	G	H	J	I	G	H	I	H	J
04.03.02.00	PERIPH - LE	F	F	G	G	G	G	G	G	I	H	G	H	H	H	H	I	J	I	H	I	I	I	J
04.04.00.00	PULM CIRC	F	F	G	G	G	G	G	G	H	H	G	H	G	H	H	H	I	I	G	H	I	H	J
05.01 -- 05.03	RESPIRATORY	F	F	G	G	G	G	G	G	H	H	G	H	G	H	H	H	I	I	G	H	I	H	J
06.01.00.00	UPPER DIGEST	F	F	F	F	F	F	F	F	F	F	F	F	F	F	F	F	F	F	F	F	F	F	F
06.02.00.00	COLON, RECTUM	F	F	F	H	G	G	F	F	H	G	F	F	F	F	H	H	H	H	H	H	H	G	H
06.03.00.00	FISTULAS	F	F	F	F	F	F	F	F	F	F	F	F	F	F	F	F	F	F	F	F	F	F	F
06.04.00.00	LIVER	F	F	F	F	F	F	F	F	F	F	F	F	F	F	F	F	F	F	F	F	F	F	F
06.05.00.00	HERNIA	F	F	G	G	G	F	G	G	H	G	H	H	H	H	H	H	J	H	H	H	H	I	J
07.01 -- 07.04	URINARY	F	F	F	H	G	G	F	F	H	G	F	F	F	F	H	H	H	H	H	H	H	G	H
07.05.00.00	REPRODUCTIVE	F	F	F	F	F	F	F	F	F	F	F	F	F	F	F	F	F	F	F	F	F	F	F
08.01 -- 08.02	SKIN-SCARS	E	E	G	E	G	E	F	F	F	H	E	E	F	F	E	F	E	J	E	E	I	E	I
08.03 -- 08.04	DERMATITIS	G	F	G	G	F	F	F	G	G	F	H	F	F	G	F	G	F	F	F	F	F	F	F
08.05.00.00	SKIN CANCER	F	F	F	H	G	G	F	F	H	G	F	F	F	F	H	H	H	H	H	H	H	G	H
09.01.00.00	HEMATOPOIETIC	F	F	F	F	F	F	F	F	F	F	F	F	F	F	F	F	F	F	F	F	F	F	F
10.01.00.00	DIABETES	F	F	F	F	F	F	F	F	F	F	F	F	F	F	F	F	F	F	F	F	F	F	F
11.01.01.00	EAR-HEARING	E	G	F	E	H	G	G	G	G	H	D	F	F	G	F	G	H	I	F	F	I	F	I
11.01.02.00	VESTIBULAR	F	F	F	I	G	G	F	H	J	G	F	G	F	H	G	J	J	I	F	H	I	H	J
11.02.01.00	FACE-COSMETIC	E	E	G	E	G	E	F	F	F	H	E	E	F	F	E	F	E	J	E	E	I	E	I
11.02.02.00	FACE - EYE	F	G	F	F	I	H	F	H	H	H	G	G	F	H	F	H	I	J	F	G	I	F	I
11.03.01.00	NOSE - SMELL	F	F	F	F	H	F	F	F	G	H	F	G	F	F	F	G	I	J	F	G	F	F	J
11.03.02.00	MASTICATION	F	F	F	F	G	F	F	F	F	G	F	F	F	F	F	F	G	H	F	G	F	F	G
11.03.03.00	TASTE-SMELL	F	F	F	F	F	F	F	F	F	G	F	F	F	F	F	F	F	G	F	F	F	F	F
11.03.04.00	VOICE-SPEECH	D	F	G	F	H	F	G	F	G	H	C	D	F	F	F	G	G	I	F	G	H	F	H
12.01 -- 12.03	VISION	F	G	F	F	I	H	F	H	H	G	G	G	F	H	F	H	I	I	F	G	I	F	I

		110	111	112	120	210	211	212	213	214	220	221	230	240	250	251	290	310	311	320	321	322	330
13.01.00.00	CONSCIOUSNESS	I	H	H	H	H	H	H	I	H	H	G	F	G	H	H	G	H	H	H	F	G	F
13.02.00.00	EPISODIC NEURO	H	G	I	I	H	G	H	I	H	I	H	F	F	J	I	H	I	I	I	G	H	H
13.03.00.00	AROUSAL	I	H	H	H	H	H	H	I	H	H	G	F	G	H	H	G	H	H	H	F	G	F
13.04.00.00	COGNITIVE IMP	I	H	H	H	H	H	H	I	H	H	G	F	G	H	H	G	H	H	H	F	G	F
13.05.00.00	LANGUAGE DISOR	J	I	I	F	J	I	I	H	J	I	D	D	H	H	J	I	I	I	D	C	G	D
13.06.00.00	BEHAV-EMOT	J	I	I	H	I	H	J	I	I	J	F	F	G	H	I	H	I	J	H	F	G	F
13.07.01.00	CRANIAL-OLFACTORY	F	F	F	F	F	F	F	F	F	F	F	F	F	F	F	G	F	F	F	F	H	F
13.07.02.00	CRANIAL-OPTIC	H	I	J	J	I	I	I	I	I	J	H	G	F	I	H	I	I	I	I	H	G	G
13.07.03.00	CRANIAL-OCULO	H	I	J	J	I	I	I	I	I	J	H	G	F	I	H	I	I	I	I	H	G	G
13.07.04.00	CRANIAL-TRIGEM	I	H	H	F	J	H	I	H	J	I	F	F	G	G	I	H	H	I	F	F	G	F
13.07.05.00	CRANIAL-FACIAL	I	I	I	H	J	I	I	H	J	J	G	E	J	H	J	J	I	J	E	E	H	E
13.07.06.01	CRANIAL-VERTIGO	D	D	D	D	E	D	E	H	F	F	F	F	E	G	F	E	F	F	F	F	F	F
13.07.06.02	CRANIAL-TINNITUS	J	H	I	F	J	H	I	H	J	H	D	E	H	H	J	I	J	J	E	D	H	E
13.07.07.00	CRANIAL-GLOSSO	F	F	F	F	F	F	F	F	F	F	F	F	F	F	F	F	F	F	F	F	F	F
13.07.08.00	CRANIAL-SPINAL ACC	This impairment can affect swallowing and speech, head turning and shoulder motion. Use variant from 11.03.04.00, 15.01.XX.XX, or 16.02.01.00 as appropriate.																					
13.07.09.00	CRANIAL-HYPOGLOS	J	I	I	F	J	I	I	H	J	I	D	D	H	H	J	I	I	I	D	C	G	D
13.08.00.00	STATION GAIT	D	D	C	C	E	E	E	F	F	E	E	E	E	F	E	E	F	F	F	F	F	F
13.09.00.00	UPPER EXTREM	E	G	H	H	E	G	F	E	G	H	G	G	E	F	F	G	F	G	H	G	G	G
13.10.01.00	SPINAL-RESPIR	F	E	D	D	H	E	F	F	F	E	E	E	E	F	F	F	F	G	F	F	F	F
13.10.02.00	SPINAL-URINARY	F	F	F	F	F	F	F	H	F	F	F	F	G	G	G	F	F	F	F	F	F	F
13.10.03.00	SPINAL-ANORECT	F	F	F	F	F	F	F	H	F	F	F	F	G	G	G	F	F	F	F	F	F	F
13.10.04.00	SPINAL-SEXUAL	F	F	F	F	F	F	F	F	F	F	F	F	F	F	F	F	F	F	F	F	F	F
13.11.01.XX	PAIN-UE	E	G	H	H	E	G	F	E	G	H	G	G	E	F	F	G	F	G	H	G	G	G
13.11.02.XX	PAIN-LE	D	D	C	C	E	E	E	F	F	E	E	E	E	F	E	E	F	F	F	F	F	F
13.12.01.XX	PERIPH-SPINE	C	C	D	D	D	D	E	F	F	E	E	E	E	F	E	E	F	G	F	F	F	F
13.12.02.XX	PERIPH-UE	E	G	H	H	E	G	F	E	G	H	G	G	E	F	F	G	F	G	H	G	G	G
13.12.03.XX	PERIPH-LE	D	D	C	C	E	E	E	F	F	E	E	E	E	F	E	E	F	F	F	F	F	F
14.01.00.00	PSYCHIACTRIC	J	I	I	H	I	H	J	I	I	J	F	F	G	H	I	H	I	J	H	F	G	F

		331	332	340	341	350	351	360	370	380	390	420	430	460	470	480	481	482	490	491	492	493	560	590
13.01.00.00	CONSCIOUSNESS	F	F	D	H	H	G	E	H	I	G	F	H	E	H	F	I	J	I	D	G	G	E	J
13.02.00.00	EPISODIC NEURO	G	G	F	I	J	J	F	I	J	G	G	I	G	I	H	J	J	J	G	H	G	H	J
13.03.00.00	AROUSAL	F	F	D	H	H	G	E	H	I	G	F	H	E	H	F	I	J	I	D	G	G	E	J
13.04.00.00	COGNITIVE IMP	F	F	D	H	H	G	E	H	I	G	F	H	E	H	F	I	J	I	D	G	G	E	J
13.05.00.00	LANGUAGE DISOR	D	F	G	F	H	F	G	F	G	H	C	D	F	F	F	G	G	I	F	G	H	F	H
13.06.00.00	BEHAV-EMOT	F	G	D	D	H	G	E	H	H	H	F	G	E	H	E	H	I	J	D	E	H	D	I
13.07.01.00	CRANIAL-OLFACTORY	F	F	F	F	F	F	F	F	F	G	F	F	F	F	F	F	F	G	F	F	F	F	F
13.07.02.00	CRANIAL-OPTIC	F	G	F	F	I	H	F	H	H	G	G	G	F	H	F	H	I	I	F	G	I	F	I
13.07.03.00	CRANIAL-OCULO	F	G	F	F	I	H	F	H	H	G	G	G	F	H	F	H	I	I	F	G	I	F	I
13.07.04.00	CRANIAL-TRIGEM	F	F	F	F	G	F	F	F	F	G	F	F	F	F	F	F	G	H	F	G	G	F	G
13.07.05.00	CRANIAL-FACIAL	E	E	G	E	G	E	F	F	F	H	E	E	F	F	E	F	E	J	E	E	H	E	I
13.07.06.01	CRANIAL-VERTIGO	F	F	F	I	G	G	F	H	J	G	F	G	F	H	G	J	J	I	F	H	I	H	J
13.07.06.02	CRANIAL-TINNITUS	E	G	F	E	H	G	G	G	G	H	D	F	F	G	F	G	H	I	F	F	I	F	I
13.07.07.00	CRANIAL-GLOSSO	F	F	F	F	F	F	F	F	F	F	F	F	F	F	F	F	F	F	F	F	F	F	F
13.07.08.00	CRANIAL-SPINAL ACC	This impairment can affect swallowing and speech, head turning and shoulder motion. Use variant from 11.03.04.00, 15.01.XX.XX, or 16.02.01.00 as appropriate.																						
13.07.09.00	CRANIAL-HYPOGLOS	D	F	G	F	H	F	G	F	G	H	C	D	F	F	F	G	G	I	F	G	H	F	H
13.08.00.00	STATION GAIT	F	F	G	G	G	G	G	G	I	H	G	H	H	H	H	I	J	I	H	I	I	I	J
13.09.00.00	UPPER EXTREM	F	F	F	F	G	G	G	H	H	G	H	H	G	H	G	H	J	I	G	H	H	H	J
13.10.01.00	SPINAL-RESPIR	F	F	G	G	G	G	G	G	H	H	G	H	G	H	H	H	I	I	G	H	I	H	J
13.10.02.00	SPINAL-URINARY	F	F	F	H	G	G	F	F	H	G	F	F	F	F	H	H	H	H	H	H	H	G	H
13.10.03.00	SPINAL-ANORECT	F	F	F	H	G	G	F	F	H	G	F	F	F	F	H	H	H	H	H	H	H	G	H
13.10.04.00	SPINAL-SEXUAL	F	F	F	F	F	F	F	F	F	F	F	F	F	F	F	F	F	F	F	F	F	F	F
13.11.01.XX	PAIN-UE	F	F	F	F	G	G	G	H	H	G	H	H	G	H	G	H	J	I	G	H	H	H	J
13.11.02.XX	PAIN-LE	F	F	G	G	G	G	G	G	I	H	G	H	H	H	H	I	J	I	H	I	I	I	J
13.12.01.XX	PERIPH-SPINE	F	F	G	G	G	G	G	G	H	G	H	H	H	H	I	I	J	I	H	I	H	J	J
13.12.02.XX	PERIPH-UE	F	F	F	F	G	G	G	H	H	G	H	H	G	H	G	H	J	I	G	H	H	H	J
13.12.03.XX	PERIPH-LE	F	F	G	G	G	G	G	G	I	H	G	H	H	H	H	I	J	I	H	I	I	I	J
14.01.00.00	PSYCHIACTRIC	F	G	D	D	H	G	E	H	H	H	F	G	E	H	E	H	I	J	D	E	H	D	I

		110	111	112	120	210	211	212	213	214	220	221	230	240	250	251	290	310	311	320	321	322	330
15.01 – 15.03	SPINE-DRE-ROM	C	C	D	D	D	D	E	F	F	E	E	E	E	F	E	E	F	G	F	F	F	F
15.04.01.00	CORTIC-ONE UE	E	G	H	H	E	G	F	E	G	H	G	G	E	F	F	G	F	G	H	G	G	G
15.04.02.00	CORTIC-TWO UE	E	G	H	H	E	G	F	E	G	H	G	G	E	F	F	G	F	G	H	G	G	G
15.04.03.00	CORTIC-GAIT	D	D	C	C	E	E	E	F	F	E	E	E	E	F	E	E	F	F	F	F	F	F
15.04.04.00	CORTIC-BLADDER	F	F	F	F	F	F	F	H	F	F	F	F	G	G	G	F	F	F	F	F	F	F
15.04.05.00	CORTIC-ANOREC	F	F	F	F	F	F	F	H	F	F	F	F	G	G	G	F	F	F	F	F	F	F
15.04.06.00	CORTIC-SEXUAL	F	F	F	F	F	F	F	F	F	F	F	F	F	F	F	F	F	F	F	F	F	F
15.04.07.00	CORTIC-RESPIR	F	E	D	D	H	E	F	F	F	E	E	E	E	F	F	F	F	G	F	F	F	F
15.05.XX.XX	PELVIC	C	C	D	D	D	D	E	F	F	E	E	E	E	F	E	E	F	G	F	F	F	F
16.01.01.XX	ARM-AMPUT	E	G	H	H	E	G	F	E	G	H	G	G	E	F	F	G	F	G	H	G	G	G
16.01.02.01	BRACHIAL PLEX	E	G	H	H	E	G	F	E	G	H	G	G	E	F	F	G	F	G	H	G	G	G
16.01.02.02	CARPAL TUNNEL	D	G	H	H	D	G	F	E	G	H	G	F	E	F	E	H	F	G	I	H	G	F
16.01.02.03	ENTRAP-OTHER	E	G	H	H	E	G	F	E	G	H	G	G	E	F	F	G	F	G	H	G	G	G
16.01.02.04	CRPS I	E	G	H	H	E	G	F	E	G	H	G	G	E	F	F	G	F	G	H	G	G	G
16.01.02.05	CRPS II	E	G	H	H	E	G	F	E	G	H	G	G	E	F	F	G	F	G	H	G	G	G
16.01.03.00	PERIPH VASC	E	G	H	H	E	G	F	E	G	H	G	G	E	F	F	G	F	G	H	G	G	G
16.01.04.00	ARM-GRIP/PINCH	D	E	E	F	C	E	E	E	F	F	F	G	D	F	F	F	F	F	H	G	G	G
16.01.05.00	ARM-OTHER	E	G	H	H	E	G	F	E	G	H	G	G	E	F	F	G	F	G	H	G	G	G
16.02.01.00	SHOULER-ROM	C	D	D	E	C	D	E	E	F	F	F	F	D	F	D	G	F	F	F	F	F	F
16.02.02.00	SHOULDER-OTHER	E	G	H	H	E	G	F	E	G	H	G	G	E	F	F	G	F	G	H	G	G	G
16.03.01.00	ELBOW-ROM	D	F	G	G	D	F	E	E	F	G	G	F	E	G	F	G	F	G	H	G	G	G
16.03.02.00	ELBOW-OTHER	E	G	H	H	E	G	F	E	G	H	G	G	E	F	F	G	F	G	H	G	G	G
16.04.01.00	WRIST-ROM	D	G	H	H	D	G	F	E	G	H	G	F	E	F	E	H	F	G	I	H	G	F
16.04.02.00	WRIST-OTHER	E	G	H	H	E	G	F	E	G	H	G	G	E	F	F	G	F	G	H	G	G	G
16.05.XX.XX	HAND	F	G	I	H	E	G	F	F	G	H	G	G	E	F	F	G	F	G	H	G	G	G
16.06.01.XX	THUMB	F	G	G	H	E	G	F	F	G	H	H	G	E	F	F	H	F	G	H	G	G	G
16.06.02.XX	INDEX	F	H	I	I	E	H	G	F	H	I	H	G	E	F	F	H	G	H	I	H	H	G
16.06.03.XX	MIDDLE	F	H	I	I	E	H	G	F	H	I	H	G	E	F	F	H	G	H	I	H	H	G
16.06.04.XX	RING	F	G	I	G	E	G	F	F	G	G	G	F	E	F	F	F	F	G	H	G	G	F
16.06.05.XX	LITTLE	F	G	I	G	E	G	F	F	G	G	G	F	E	F	F	F	F	G	H	G	G	F

		331	332	340	341	350	351	360	370	380	390	420	430	460	470	480	481	482	490	491	492	493	560	590
15.01 – 15.03	SPINE-DRE-ROM	F	F	G	G	G	G	G	G	H	G	H	H	H	H	I	I	J	I	H	I	H	J	J
15.04.01.00	CORTIC-ONE UE	F	F	F	F	G	G	G	H	H	G	H	H	G	H	G	H	J	I	G	H	H	H	J
15.04.02.00	CORTIC-TWO UE	F	F	F	F	G	G	G	H	H	G	H	H	G	H	G	H	J	I	G	H	H	H	J
15.04.03.00	CORTIC-GAIT	F	F	G	G	G	G	G	G	I	H	G	H	H	H	H	I	J	I	H	I	I	I	J
15.04.04.00	CORTIC-BLADDER	F	F	F	H	G	G	F	F	H	G	F	F	F	F	H	H	H	H	H	H	H	G	H
15.04.05.00	CORTIC-ANOREC	F	F	F	H	G	G	F	F	H	G	F	F	F	F	H	H	H	H	H	H	H	G	H
15.04.06.00	CORTIC-SEXUAL	F	F	F	F	F	F	F	F	F	F	F	F	F	F	F	F	F	F	F	F	F	F	F
15.04.07.00	CORTIC-RESPIR	F	F	G	G	G	G	G	G	H	H	G	H	G	H	H	H	I	I	G	H	I	H	J
15.05.XX.XX	PELVIC	F	F	G	G	G	G	G	G	H	G	H	H	H	H	I	I	J	I	H	I	H	J	J
16.01.01.XX	ARM-AMPUT	F	F	F	F	G	G	G	H	H	G	H	H	G	H	G	H	J	I	G	H	H	H	J
16.01.02.01	BRACHIAL PLEX	F	F	F	F	G	G	G	H	H	G	H	H	G	H	G	H	J	I	G	H	H	H	J
16.01.02.02	CARPAL TUNNEL	F	E	F	F	F	G	F	J	J	G	I	H	G	J	G	J	J	H	G	H	H	H	J
16.01.02.03	ENTRAP-OTHER	F	F	F	F	G	G	G	H	H	G	H	H	G	H	G	H	J	I	G	H	H	H	J
16.01.02.04	CRPS I	F	F	F	F	G	G	G	H	H	G	H	H	G	H	G	H	J	I	G	H	H	H	J
16.01.02.05	CRPS II	F	F	F	F	G	G	G	H	H	G	H	H	G	H	G	H	J	I	G	H	H	H	J
16.01.03.00	PERIPH VASC	F	F	F	F	G	G	G	H	H	G	H	H	G	H	G	H	J	I	G	H	H	H	J
16.01.04.00	ARM-GRIP/PINCH	F	F	F	F	G	G	G	H	H	G	H	H	G	H	G	H	J	I	G	H	H	H	J
16.01.05.00	ARM-OTHER	F	F	F	F	G	G	G	H	H	G	H	H	G	H	G	H	J	I	G	H	H	H	J
16.02.01.00	SHOULER-ROM	F	F	F	G	F	G	G	G	H	G	G	H	G	H	H	H	I	I	G	H	H	H	J
16.02.02.00	SHOULDER-OTHER	F	F	F	F	G	G	G	H	H	G	H	H	G	H	G	H	J	I	G	H	H	H	J
16.03.01.00	ELBOW-ROM	F	F	G	G	H	H	G	I	I	G	H	I	G	I	H	I	J	I	G	H	H	H	J
16.03.02.00	ELBOW-OTHER	F	F	F	F	G	G	G	H	H	G	H	H	G	H	G	H	J	I	G	H	H	H	J
16.04.01.00	WRIST-ROM	F	E	F	F	F	G	F	J	J	G	I	H	G	J	G	J	J	H	G	H	H	H	J
16.04.02.00	WRIST-OTHER	F	F	F	F	G	G	G	H	H	G	H	H	G	H	G	H	J	I	G	H	H	H	J
16.05.XX.XX	HAND	F	F	F	F	G	G	F	H	H	G	G	H	F	H	G	H	I	H	F	G	G	G	I
16.06.01.XX	THUMB	F	F	F	F	G	G	F	H	H	G	H	H	G	H	G	H	I	H	G	H	G	H	I
16.06.02.XX	INDEX	F	F	F	F	G	G	F	I	I	G	G	H	F	I	G	I	I	H	F	G	G	G	I
16.06.03.XX	MIDDLE	F	F	F	F	G	G	F	I	I	G	G	H	F	I	G	I	I	H	F	G	G	G	I
16.06.04.XX	RING	F	F	F	F	F	F	F	H	H	G	G	H	F	H	G	H	H	H	F	G	G	G	I
16.06.05.XX	LITTLE	F	F	F	F	F	F	F	H	H	G	G	H	F	H	G	H	H	H	F	G	G	G	I

		110	111	112	120	210	211	212	213	214	220	221	230	240	250	251	290	310	311	320	321	322	330
17.01.01.00	LEG-LENGTH	C	C	C	C	D	D	D	E	D	D	D	D	D	D	D	D	D	E	E	E	E	E
17.01.02.XX	LEG-AMPUT	D	D	C	C	E	E	E	F	F	E	E	E	E	F	E	E	F	F	F	F	F	F
17.01.03.00	LEG-SKIN LOSS	D	D	D	D	E	E	E	F	F	E	E	E	E	F	E	E	F	F	F	F	F	F
17.01.04.00	LEG-PERIPH NRV	D	D	C	C	E	E	E	F	F	E	E	E	E	F	E	E	F	F	F	F	F	F
17.01.05.00	LEG-VASCULAR	D	D	D	D	E	E	E	F	F	E	E	E	E	F	E	E	F	F	F	F	F	F
17.01.06.00	LEG-CAUSALGIA	D	D	C	C	E	E	E	F	F	E	E	E	E	F	E	E	F	F	F	F	F	F
17.01.07.00	LEG-GAIT	D	D	C	C	E	E	E	F	F	E	E	E	E	F	E	E	F	F	F	F	F	F
17.01.08.00	LEG-OTHER	D	D	C	C	E	E	E	F	F	E	E	E	E	F	E	E	F	F	F	F	F	F
17.02.10.00	PELVIS-FX	D	D	C	C	E	E	E	F	F	E	E	E	E	F	E	E	F	F	F	F	F	F
17.03.XX.XX	HIP	D	D	C	C	E	E	E	F	F	E	E	E	E	F	E	E	F	F	F	F	F	F
17.04.10.00	FEMUR-FX	D	D	C	C	E	E	E	F	F	E	E	E	E	F	E	E	F	F	F	F	F	F
17.05.XX.XX	KNEE	D	D	C	C	E	E	E	F	F	E	E	E	E	F	E	E	F	F	F	F	F	F
17.06.10.00	TIBIA-FX	D	D	C	C	E	E	E	F	F	E	E	E	E	F	E	E	F	F	F	F	F	F
17.07.XX.XX	ANKLE	D	D	C	C	E	E	E	F	F	E	E	E	E	F	E	E	F	F	F	F	F	F
17.08.01.00	FOOT-ATROPHY	D	D	C	C	E	E	E	F	F	E	E	E	E	F	E	E	F	F	F	F	F	F
17.08.02.00	FOOT-ANKYLOSIS	C	C	C	C	D	D	D	E	D	D	D	D	D	D	D	D	D	E	E	E	E	E
17.08.03.00	FOOT-ARTHRITIS	D	D	C	C	E	E	E	F	F	E	E	E	E	F	E	E	F	F	F	F	F	F
17.08.04.00	FOOT-ROM	C	C	C	C	D	D	D	E	D	D	D	D	D	D	D	D	D	E	E	E	E	E
17.08.05.00	FOOT-STRENGTH	D	D	C	C	E	E	E	F	F	E	E	E	E	F	E	E	F	F	F	F	F	F
17.08.06.00	FOOT-OTHER	D	D	C	C	E	E	E	F	F	E	E	E	E	F	E	E	F	F	F	F	F	F
17.08.10.XX	FOOT-DBE	D	D	C	C	E	E	E	F	F	E	E	E	E	F	E	E	F	F	F	F	F	F
17.09.01.00	TOE-ATROPHY	C	C	C	C	D	D	D	E	D	D	D	D	D	D	D	D	D	E	E	E	E	E
17.09.02.00	TOE-ANKYLOSIS	C	C	C	C	D	D	D	E	D	D	D	D	D	D	D	D	D	E	E	E	E	E
17.09.03.00	TOE-ARTHRITIS	C	C	C	C	D	D	D	E	D	D	D	D	D	D	D	D	D	E	E	E	E	E
17.09.04.00	TOE-ROM	C	C	C	C	D	D	D	E	D	D	D	D	D	D	D	D	D	E	E	E	E	E
17.09.05.00	TOE-STRENGTH	D	D	C	C	E	E	E	F	F	E	E	E	E	F	E	E	F	F	F	F	F	F
17.09.06.00	TOE-AMPUTATION	D	D	C	C	E	E	E	F	F	E	E	E	E	F	E	E	F	F	F	F	F	F
17.09.07.00	TOE-OTHER	D	D	C	C	E	E	E	F	F	E	E	E	E	F	E	E	F	F	F	F	F	F

		331	332	340	341	350	351	360	370	380	390	420	430	460	470	480	481	482	490	491	492	493	560	590
17.01.01.00	LEG-LENGTH	E	F	E	G	E	E	E	F	G	F	F	F	F	F	G	G	H	G	F	G	I	G	H
17.01.02.00	LEG-AMPUT	F	F	G	G	G	G	G	G	I	H	G	H	H	H	H	I	J	I	H	I	I	I	J
17.01.03.00	LEG-SKIN LOSS	F	F	G	G	G	G	G	G	I	H	G	H	H	H	H	I	J	I	H	I	I	I	J
17.01.04.00	LEG-PERIPH NRV	F	F	G	G	G	G	G	G	I	H	G	H	H	H	H	I	J	I	H	I	I	I	J
17.01.05.00	LEG-VASCULAR	F	F	G	G	G	G	G	G	I	H	G	H	H	H	H	I	J	I	H	I	I	I	J
17.01.06.00	LEG-CAUSALGIA	F	F	G	G	G	G	G	G	I	H	G	H	H	H	H	I	J	I	H	I	I	I	J
17.01.07.00	LEG-GAIT	F	F	G	G	G	G	G	G	I	H	G	H	H	H	H	I	J	I	H	I	I	I	J
17.01.08.00	LEG-OTHER	F	F	G	G	G	G	G	G	I	H	G	H	H	H	H	I	J	I	H	I	I	I	J
17.02.10.00	PELVIS-FX.	F	F	G	G	G	G	G	G	I	H	G	H	H	H	H	I	J	I	H	I	I	I	J
17.03.XX.XX	HIP	F	F	G	G	G	G	G	G	I	H	G	H	H	H	H	I	J	I	H	I	I	I	J
17.04.10.00	FEMUR-FX	F	F	G	G	G	G	G	G	I	H	G	H	H	H	H	I	J	I	H	I	I	I	J
17.05.XX.XX	KNEE	F	F	G	G	G	G	G	G	I	H	G	H	H	H	H	I	J	I	H	I	I	I	J
17.06.10.00	TIBIA-FX	F	F	G	G	G	G	G	G	I	H	G	H	H	H	H	I	J	I	H	I	I	I	J
17.07.XX.XX	ANKLE	F	F	G	G	G	G	G	G	I	H	G	H	H	H	H	I	J	I	H	I	I	I	J
17.08.01.00	FOOT-ATROPHY	F	F	G	G	G	G	G	G	I	H	G	H	H	H	H	I	J	I	H	I	I	I	J
17.08.02.00	FOOT-ANKYLOSIS	E	F	E	G	E	E	E	F	G	F	F	F	F	F	G	G	H	G	F	G	I	G	H
17.08.03.00	FOOT-ARTHRITIS	F	F	G	G	G	G	G	G	I	H	G	H	H	H	H	I	J	I	H	I	I	I	J
17.08.04.00	FOOT-ROM	E	F	E	G	E	E	E	F	G	F	F	F	F	F	G	G	H	G	F	G	I	G	H
17.08.05.00	FOOT-STRENGTH	F	F	G	G	G	G	G	G	I	H	G	H	H	H	H	I	J	I	H	I	I	I	J
17.08.06.00	FOOT-OTHER	F	F	G	G	G	G	G	G	I	H	G	H	H	H	H	I	J	I	H	I	I	I	J
17.08.10.XX	FOOT-DBE	F	F	G	G	G	G	G	G	I	H	G	H	H	H	H	I	J	I	H	I	I	I	J
17.09.01.00	TOE-ATROPHY	E	F	E	G	E	E	E	F	G	F	F	F	F	F	G	G	H	G	F	G	H	G	H
17.09.02.00	TOE-ANKYLOSIS	E	F	E	G	E	E	E	F	G	F	F	F	F	F	G	G	H	G	F	G	H	G	H
17.09.03.00	TOE-ARTHRITIS	E	F	E	G	E	E	E	F	G	F	F	F	F	F	G	G	H	G	F	G	H	G	H
17.09.04.00	TOE-ROM	E	F	E	G	E	E	E	F	G	F	F	F	F	F	G	G	H	G	F	G	H	G	H
17.09.05.00	TOE-STRENGTH	F	F	G	G	G	G	G	G	I	H	G	H	H	H	H	I	J	I	H	I	H	I	J
17.09.06.00	TOE-AMPUTATION	F	F	G	G	G	G	G	G	I	H	G	H	H	H	H	I	J	I	H	I	H	I	J
17.09.07.00	TOE-OTHER	F	F	G	G	G	G	G	G	I	H	G	H	H	H	H	I	J	I	H	I	H	I	J

SECTION 5 - OCCUPATIONAL ADJUSTMENT

Use this table to adjust the rating for occupation.

Locate the row on which the rating (after adjustment for diminished future earning capacity) appears and the column headed by the occupation variant (obtained from the Occupational Variant Table in Section 4). Record the number appearing at the intersection of this row and column. This is the rating after adjustment for occupation.

After adjusting the rating for occupation, turn to Section 6, page 6-1 to adjust for age.

OCCUPATIONAL ADJUSTMENT TABLE

Standard Rating Percent	C	D	E	F	G	H	I	J	Standard Rating Percent	C	D	E	F	G	H	I	J
0	0	0	0	0	0	0	0	0									
1	1	1	1	1	2	2	2	2	**26**	19	22	24	26	29	31	34	37
2	1	2	2	2	3	3	4	4	**27**	20	23	25	27	30	33	35	38
3	2	2	3	3	4	5	5	6	**28**	21	24	26	28	31	34	36	39
4	3	3	4	4	5	6	7	8	**29**	22	24	27	29	32	35	37	40
5	3	4	4	5	6	7	8	9	**30**	23	25	28	30	33	36	38	41
6	4	5	5	6	7	8	9	11	**31**	24	26	29	31	34	37	40	43
7	5	5	6	7	8	10	11	12	**32**	25	27	30	32	35	38	41	44
8	6	6	7	8	9	11	12	14	**33**	25	28	30	33	36	39	42	45
9	6	7	8	9	11	12	14	15	**34**	26	29	31	34	37	40	43	46
10	7	8	9	10	12	13	15	16	**35**	27	30	32	35	38	41	44	47
11	7	9	10	11	13	14	16	18	**36**	28	31	33	36	39	42	45	48
12	8	10	11	12	14	16	17	19	**37**	29	32	34	37	40	43	46	49
13	9	10	12	13	15	17	18	20	**38**	30	32	35	38	41	44	47	50
14	10	11	13	14	16	18	20	22	**39**	31	33	36	39	42	45	48	51
15	11	12	14	15	17	19	21	23	**40**	32	34	37	40	43	46	49	52
16	11	13	14	16	18	20	22	24	**41**	33	35	38	41	44	47	50	54
17	12	14	15	17	19	21	23	26	**42**	34	36	39	42	45	48	51	55
18	13	15	16	18	20	22	24	27	**43**	35	37	40	43	46	49	52	56
19	14	15	17	19	21	24	26	28	**44**	36	38	41	44	47	50	53	57
20	15	16	18	20	22	25	27	29	**45**	36	39	42	45	48	51	54	58
21	16	17	19	21	23	26	28	31	**46**	37	40	43	46	49	52	55	59
22	16	18	20	22	24	27	29	32	**47**	38	41	44	47	50	53	56	60
23	17	19	21	23	26	28	31	33	**48**	39	42	45	48	51	54	57	61
24	18	20	22	24	27	29	32	34	**49**	40	43	46	49	52	55	58	62
25	18	21	23	25	28	30	33	36	**50**	41	44	47	50	53	56	59	62

OCCUPATIONAL ADJUSTMENT TABLE

Standard Rating Percent	C	D	E	F	G	H	I	J	Standard Rating Percent	C	D	E	F	G	H	I	J
51	42	45	48	51	54	57	60	64	**76**	68	70	73	76	78	80	82	84
52	43	46	49	52	55	58	61	65	**77**	69	71	74	77	79	81	83	85
53	44	47	50	53	56	59	62	65	**78**	70	72	75	78	80	82	84	86
54	45	48	51	54	57	60	63	66	**79**	71	74	76	79	81	83	84	86
55	46	49	52	55	58	61	64	67	**80**	72	75	77	80	82	83	85	87
56	47	50	53	56	59	62	65	68	**81**	73	76	78	81	83	84	86	88
57	48	51	54	57	60	63	66	69	**82**	74	77	79	82	84	85	87	88
58	49	52	55	58	61	64	67	70	**83**	76	78	81	83	84	86	87	89
59	50	53	56	59	62	65	68	71	**84**	77	79	82	84	85	87	88	90
60	51	54	57	60	63	66	69	72	**85**	78	81	83	85	86	88	89	90
61	52	55	58	61	64	67	69	72	**86**	79	82	84	86	87	89	90	91
62	53	56	59	62	65	68	70	73	**87**	81	83	85	87	88	89	90	92
63	54	57	60	63	66	69	71	74	**88**	82	84	86	88	89	90	91	92
64	55	58	61	64	67	69	72	75	**89**	84	85	87	89	90	91	92	93
65	56	59	62	65	68	70	73	76	**90**	85	87	88	90	91	92	93	94
66	57	60	63	66	69	71	74	77	**91**	86	88	89	91	92	93	93	94
67	58	61	64	67	70	72	75	77	**92**	88	89	91	92	93	93	94	95
68	59	62	65	68	71	73	76	78	**93**	89	91	92	93	94	94	95	96
69	60	63	66	69	71	74	76	79	**94**	91	92	93	94	95	95	96	96
70	61	64	67	70	72	75	77	80	**95**	93	93	94	95	96	96	97	97
71	62	65	68	71	73	76	78	80	**96**	94	94	95	96	96	97	98	98
72	63	66	69	72	74	77	79	81	**97**	95	96	96	97	97	98	98	98
73	65	67	70	73	75	77	79	82	**98**	97	97	98	98	98	98	98	99
74	66	68	71	74	76	78	80	83	**99**	98	99	99	99	99	99	100	100
75	67	69	72	75	77	79	81	83	**100**	100	100	100	100	100	100	100	100

SECTION 6 - AGE ADJUSTMENT

Use this table to modify the rating for age.

Locate the row on which the rating (already adjusted for earning capacity and occupation) appears, and the column headed by the age at time of injury. Record the number appearing at the intersection of the row and column. This is the rating adjusted for earning capacity, occupation and age.

Rating	AGE AT TIME OF INJURY									
	21 and under	22 - 26	27 - 31	32 - 36	37 - 41	42 - 46	47 - 51	52 - 56	57 - 61	62 and over
1	1	1	1	1	1	1	1	1	1	1
2	2	2	2	2	2	2	2	3	3	3
3	2	2	3	3	3	3	3	4	4	4
4	3	3	3	4	4	4	5	5	5	6
5	4	4	4	5	5	5	6	6	6	7
6	5	5	5	6	6	6	7	7	8	8
7	5	6	6	7	7	8	8	9	9	10
8	6	6	7	7	8	9	9	10	10	11
9	7	7	8	8	9	10	10	11	12	12
10	8	8	9	9	10	11	11	12	13	13
11	8	9	10	10	11	12	13	13	14	15
12	9	10	10	11	12	13	14	15	15	16
13	10	11	11	12	13	14	15	16	16	17
14	11	11	12	13	14	15	16	17	18	19
15	12	12	13	14	15	16	17	18	19	20
16	12	13	14	15	16	17	18	19	20	21
17	13	14	15	16	17	18	19	20	21	22
18	14	15	16	17	18	19	20	21	23	24
19	15	16	17	18	19	20	22	23	24	25
20	16	17	18	19	20	21	23	24	25	26
21	17	18	19	20	21	22	24	25	26	27
22	17	18	20	21	22	23	25	26	28	29
23	18	19	20	22	23	24	26	27	29	30
24	19	20	21	23	24	25	27	28	30	31
25	20	21	22	24	25	27	28	29	31	32

	AGE AT TIME OF INJURY									
Rating	**21 and under**	**22 - 26**	**27 - 31**	**32 - 36**	**37 - 41**	**42 - 46**	**47 - 51**	**52 - 56**	**57 - 61**	**62 and over**
26	21	22	23	25	26	28	29	31	32	33
27	22	23	24	26	27	29	30	32	33	35
28	23	24	25	27	28	30	31	33	34	36
29	24	25	26	28	29	31	32	34	36	37
30	24	25	27	28	30	32	33	35	37	38
31	25	26	28	30	31	33	35	36	38	39
32	26	27	29	31	32	34	36	37	39	40
33	27	28	30	32	33	35	37	38	40	42
34	28	29	31	33	34	36	38	39	41	43
35	29	30	32	34	35	37	39	41	42	44
36	30	31	33	35	36	38	40	42	43	45
37	31	32	34	36	37	39	41	43	44	46
38	32	33	35	37	38	40	42	44	46	47
39	33	34	36	38	39	41	43	45	47	48
40	34	35	37	39	40	42	44	46	48	50
41	35	36	38	40	41	43	45	47	49	51
42	36	37	39	41	42	44	46	48	50	52
43	36	37	39	41	43	45	47	49	51	53
44	37	38	40	42	44	46	48	50	52	54
45	38	39	41	43	45	47	49	51	53	55
46	39	40	42	44	46	48	50	52	54	56
47	40	41	43	45	47	49	51	53	55	57
48	41	42	44	46	48	50	52	54	56	58
49	42	43	45	47	49	51	53	55	57	59
50	43	44	46	48	50	52	54	56	58	60

	AGE AT TIME OF INJURY									
Rating	21 and under	22 - 26	27 - 31	32 - 36	37 - 41	42 - 46	47 - 51	52 - 56	57 - 61	62 and over
51	44	45	47	49	51	53	55	57	59	61
52	45	46	48	50	52	54	56	58	60	62
53	46	47	49	51	53	55	57	59	61	63
54	47	48	50	52	54	56	58	60	62	64
55	48	49	51	53	55	57	59	61	63	65
56	49	50	52	54	56	58	60	62	64	66
57	50	51	53	55	57	59	61	63	65	67
58	51	53	55	57	58	60	62	64	66	68
59	52	54	56	58	59	61	63	65	67	69
60	53	55	57	59	60	62	64	66	68	70
61	54	56	58	60	61	63	65	67	69	71
62	55	57	59	61	62	64	66	68	69	71
63	57	58	60	62	63	65	67	69	70	72
64	58	59	61	63	64	66	68	70	71	73
65	59	60	62	64	65	67	69	71	72	74
66	60	61	63	65	66	68	70	72	73	75
67	61	62	64	66	67	69	70	72	74	76
68	62	63	65	67	68	70	71	73	75	77
69	63	64	66	68	69	71	72	74	76	78
70	64	65	67	69	70	72	73	75	76	78
71	65	66	68	70	71	73	74	76	77	79
72	66	67	69	71	72	74	75	77	78	80
73	68	69	70	72	73	75	76	78	79	81
74	69	70	71	73	74	76	77	79	80	82
75	70	71	72	74	75	77	78	80	81	83

Rating	AGE AT TIME OF INJURY									
	21 and under	22 - 26	27 - 31	32 - 36	37 - 41	42 - 46	47 - 51	52 - 56	57 - 61	62 and over
76	71	72	73	75	76	78	79	80	82	83
77	72	73	74	76	77	79	80	81	82	84
78	73	74	75	77	78	80	81	82	83	85
79	74	75	76	78	79	81	82	83	84	86
80	76	77	78	79	80	81	82	84	85	86
81	77	78	79	80	81	82	83	85	86	87
82	78	79	80	81	82	83	84	86	87	88
83	79	80	81	82	83	84	85	86	87	89
84	80	81	82	83	84	85	86	87	88	89
85	81	82	83	84	85	86	87	88	89	90
86	83	83	84	85	86	87	88	89	90	91
87	84	85	85	86	87	88	89	90	91	92
88	85	86	86	87	88	89	90	91	91	92
89	86	87	87	88	89	90	91	91	92	93
90	88	88	89	89	90	91	91	92	93	93
91	89	89	90	90	91	92	92	93	94	94
92	90	90	91	92	92	93	93	94	94	95
93	91	92	92	93	93	94	94	95	95	96
94	92	93	93	94	94	95	95	95	96	96
95	94	94	94	95	95	96	96	96	97	97
96	95	95	95	96	96	96	97	97	97	98
97	96	96	97	97	97	97	97	98	98	98
98	97	98	98	98	98	98	98	98	99	99
99	99	99	99	99	99	99	99	99	99	99
100	100	100	100	100	100	100	100	100	100	100

SECTION 7 – EXAMPLES

The examples in this section illustrate all the basic components of disability rating including converting AMA scales, adjusting for diminished future earning capacity, occupation and age.

Example A – Multiple impairments within a single extremity

A 30-year-old stevedore injures his right arm resulting in the following impairment ratings:

Limited motion of index finger = 50% Digit impairment
Limited motion of ring finger = 80% Digit impairment
Limited motion of shoulder = 20% Upper extremity (UE)
Shoulder instability = 12% UE

1. Follow AMA protocols[1] for combining individual finger impairments into one overall hand impairment. The hand impairment for this example is 18%.

2. Convert hand impairment[2] to whole person scale.

   18% Hand impairment × .9 = 16% UE

   16 % UE × .6 = 10% Whole person impairment (WPI)

3. Combine[3] shoulder impairments.

   20% UE C 12% UE = 30% UE

4. Convert overall shoulder impairment to whole person scale

   30% UE × .6 = 18% WPI

5. Apply earning capacity, occupation and age adjustments[4] to hand and shoulder ratings:

   Hand: 16.05.01.00 – 10 – [1]11 – 351G – 13 – 11 PD

   Shoulder: 16.02.02.00 – 18 – [7]24 – 351G – 27 – 24 PD

6. Combine adjusted ratings for hand and shoulder to obtain final disability.

   24% PD C 11% PD = 32% PD

   The final overall PD rating for this example is 32%.

Example B – Applying the single extremity maximum

A 30-year-old stevedore sustains an injury to his left leg resulting in the following impairment ratings:

Amputation of left leg below knee = 80% LE
Limited motion of left knee = 35% LE
Pain in stump is substantially aggravated by performing ADL's = 3% add-on[5]

---

[1] See Chapter 16 of the AMA Guides, 5th edition for protocols.
[2] See AMA Guides, 5th edition, pages 438-439, for upper extremity conversion factors.
[3] The symbol used to represent the operation of combining is "C". Use the Combined Values Chart on page 8-2 of the Schedule to combine ratings.
[4] Rating adjustments and formulas are explained in Section 1 of this Schedule.
[5] See Section 1 of PDRS for information regarding add-on's for pain.

1. Convert individual impairments[6] to the whole person scale.

   Left leg amputation: 80% LE × .4 = 32% WPI
   Left knee motion: 35% LE × .4 = 14% WPI

2. Apply 3% add-on for pain.

   32% WPI + 3% WPI = 35% WPI

3. Apply earning capacity, occupation and age adjustments[7] to each whole person impairment.

   L leg amp.: 17.01.02.02 – 35 – [5]45 – 351G – 48 – 44 PD
   L knee motion: 17.05.04.00 – 14 – [2]16 – 351G–18 – 16 PD

4. Combine[8] the adjusted impairments for the left leg.

   44% PD C 16% PD = 53% PD

5. Calculate the maximum value for a single leg adjusted for earning capacity, age and occupation. The maximum rating for a leg before adjustments is 40%.

   17.01.02.01 – 40 – [5]51 – 351G – 54 – 50 PD

6. Compare the results of step 4 and 5 above. Choose the lower as the final value. The correct disability rating for the left leg is 50% PD.

Example C – Multiple impairments to different regions of body

A 30-year-old stevedore sustains injuries to his right arm, low back and legs resulting in the following impairment ratings.

Herniated lumbar disk (DRE Category 3) = 10% WPI

Limited motion of right index finger = 50% Digit impairment
Limited motion of right ring finger = 80% Digit impairment
Limited motion of right shoulder = 20% Upper extremity (UE)
Right shoulder instability = 12% UE

Amputation of left leg two inches below knee = 80% LE
Limited motion of left knee = 35% LE
Pain in stump is substantially aggravated by performing ADL's = 3% add-on[9]

Limited motion of right knee = 8% LE

1. Calculate disability rating for the back by adjusting the back impairment rating for earning capacity, occupation and age.

   15.03.01.00 – 10 – [5]13 – 351G – 15 – 13 PD

[6] See AMA Guides, 5th edition, page 527, for lower extremity conversion factors.
[7] Rating adjustments and formulas are explained in Section 1 of this Schedule.
[8] The symbol used to represent the operation of combining is "C". Use the Combined Values Chart on page 8-2 of the Schedule to combine ratings.
[9] See Section 1 of PDRS for information regarding add-on's for pain.

2. Calculate disability rating for right arm in accordance with Example A above. The overall disability rating for the arm is 39% PD after adjustment for earning capacity, occupation and age.

3. Calculate the disability rating for the left leg in accordance with Example B above. The overall disability rating for the left leg is 61% PD after adjustment for earning capacity, occupation and age.

4. Calculate disability rating for the right leg as follows:

   a. Convert the lower extremity impairment rating for the right knee to whole person impairment.

      8% LE × .4 = 3% WPI

   b. Adjust the right knee impairment rating for earning capacity, occupation and age.

      17.05.04.00 – 3 – [2]4 – 351G – 5 – 4 PD

5. Combine the ratings for the right arm, back, and each leg in the order from the largest to the smallest. The final overall PD rating for this example is 71%.

   50% PD (left leg) C 32% PD (right arm) = 66% PD
   66% PD C 13% PD (back) = 70% PD
   70% PD C 4% PD (right leg) = 71% PD

SECTION 8 - COMBINED VALUES CHART

Use this chart to combine two or more impairments, or two or more disabilities. When combining groups of three or more values, always combine the larger two first, and then successively combine the result with the next smaller until all values are combined.

COMBINED VALUES CHART

DIRECTIONS: To combine any two values, locate the larger value on the left side of the chart, and the smaller value at the bottom of the chart. The intersection of that row and column contains the combined value.

1	2																																																	
2	3	4																																																
3	4	5	6																																															
4	5	6	7	8																																														
5	6	7	8	9	10																																													
6	7	8	9	10	11	12																																												
7	8	9	10	11	12	13	14																																											
8	9	10	11	12	13	14	14	15																																										
9	10	11	12	13	14	14	15	16	17																																									
10	11	12	13	14	15	15	16	17	18	19																																								
11	12	13	14	15	15	16	17	18	19	20	21																																							
12	13	14	15	16	16	17	18	19	20	21	22	23																																						
13	14	15	16	16	17	18	19	20	21	22	23	23	24																																					
14	15	16	17	17	18	19	20	21	22	23	23	24	25	26																																				
15	16	17	18	18	19	20	21	22	23	24	24	25	26	27	28																																			
16	17	18	19	19	20	21	22	23	24	24	25	26	27	28	29	29																																		
17	18	19	19	20	21	22	23	24	24	25	26	27	28	29	29	30	31																																	
18	19	20	20	21	22	23	24	25	25	26	27	28	29	29	30	31	32	33																																
19	20	21	21	22	23	24	25	25	26	27	28	29	30	30	31	32	33	34	34																															
20	21	22	22	23	24	25	26	26	27	28	29	30	30	31	32	33	34	34	35	36																														
21	22	23	23	24	25	26	27	27	28	29	30	30	31	32	33	34	34	35	36	37	38																													
22	23	24	24	25	26	27	27	28	29	30	31	31	32	33	34	34	35	36	37	38	38	39																												
23	24	25	25	26	27	28	28	29	30	31	31	32	33	34	35	35	36	37	38	38	39	40	41																											
24	25	26	26	27	28	29	29	30	31	32	32	33	34	35	35	36	37	38	38	39	40	41	41	42																										
25	26	27	27	28	29	30	30	31	32	33	33	34	35	36	36	37	38	39	39	40	41	42	42	43	44																									
26	27	27	28	29	30	30	31	32	33	33	34	35	36	36	37	38	39	39	40	41	42	42	43	44	45	45																								
27	28	28	29	30	31	31	32	33	34	34	35	36	36	37	38	39	39	40	41	42	42	43	44	45	45	46	47																							
28	29	29	30	31	32	32	33	34	34	35	36	37	37	38	39	40	40	41	42	42	43	44	45	45	46	47	47	48																						
29	30	30	31	32	33	33	34	35	35	36	37	38	38	39	40	40	41	42	42	43	44	45	45	46	47	47	48	49	50																					
30	31	31	32	33	34	34	35	36	36	37	38	38	39	40	41	41	42	43	43	44	45	45	46	47	48	48	49	50	50	51																				
31	32	32	33	34	34	35	36	37	37	38	39	39	40	41	41	42	43	43	44	45	45	46	47	48	48	49	50	50	51	52	52																			
32	33	33	34	35	35	36	37	37	38	39	39	40	41	42	42	43	44	44	45	46	46	47	48	48	49	50	50	51	52	52	53	54																		
33	34	34	35	36	36	37	38	38	39	40	40	41	42	42	43	44	44	45	46	46	47	48	48	49	50	50	51	52	52	53	54	54	55																	
34	35	35	36	37	37	38	39	39	40	41	41	42	43	43	44	45	45	46	47	47	48	49	49	50	51	51	52	52	53	54	54	55	56	56																
35	36	36	37	38	38	39	40	40	41	42	42	43	43	44	45	45	46	47	47	48	49	49	50	51	51	52	53	53	54	55	55	56	56	57	58															
36	37	37	38	39	39	40	40	41	42	42	43	44	44	45	46	46	47	48	48	49	49	50	51	51	52	53	53	54	55	55	56	56	57	58	58	59														
37	38	38	39	40	40	41	41	42	43	43	44	45	45	46	46	47	48	48	49	50	50	51	51	52	53	53	54	55	55	56	57	57	58	58	59	60	60													
38	39	39	40	40	41	42	42	43	44	44	45	45	46	47	47	48	49	49	50	50	51	52	52	53	54	54	55	55	56	57	57	58	58	59	60	60	61	62												
39	40	40	41	41	42	43	43	44	44	45	46	46	47	48	48	49	49	50	51	51	52	52	53	54	54	55	55	56	57	57	58	59	59	60	60	61	62	62	63											
40	41	41	42	42	43	44	44	45	45	46	47	47	48	48	49	50	50	51	51	52	53	53	54	54	55	56	56	57	57	58	59	59	60	60	61	62	62	63	63	64										
41	42	42	43	43	44	45	45	46	46	47	47	48	49	49	50	50	51	52	52	53	53	54	55	55	56	56	57	58	58	59	59	60	60	61	62	62	63	63	64	65	65									
42	43	43	44	44	45	45	46	47	47	48	48	49	50	50	51	51	52	52	53	54	54	55	55	56	57	57	58	58	59	59	60	61	61	62	62	63	63	64	65	65	66	66								
43	44	44	45	45	46	46	47	48	48	49	49	50	50	51	52	52	53	53	54	54	55	56	56	57	57	58	58	59	60	60	61	61	62	62	63	64	64	65	65	66	66	67	68							
44	45	45	46	46	47	47	48	48	49	50	50	51	51	52	52	53	54	54	55	55	56	56	57	57	58	59	59	60	60	61	61	62	62	63	64	64	65	65	66	66	67	68	68	69						
45	46	46	47	47	48	48	49	49	50	51	51	52	52	53	53	54	54	55	55	56	57	57	58	58	59	59	60	60	61	62	62	63	63	64	64	65	65	66	66	67	68	68	69	69	70					
46	47	47	48	48	49	49	50	50	51	51	52	52	53	54	54	55	55	56	56	57	57	58	58	59	60	60	61	61	62	62	63	63	64	64	65	65	66	67	67	68	68	69	69	70	70	71				
47	48	48	49	49	50	50	51	51	52	52	53	53	54	54	55	55	56	57	57	58	58	59	59	60	60	61	61	62	62	63	63	64	64	65	66	66	67	67	68	68	69	69	70	70	71	71	72			
48	49	49	50	50	51	51	52	52	53	53	54	54	55	55	56	56	57	57	58	58	59	59	60	60	61	62	62	63	63	64	64	65	65	66	66	67	67	68	68	69	69	70	70	71	71	72	72	73		
49	50	50	51	51	52	52	53	53	54	54	55	55	56	56	57	57	58	58	59	59	60	60	61	61	62	62	63	63	64	64	65	65	66	66	67	67	68	68	69	69	70	70	71	71	72	72	73	73	74	
50	51	51	52	52	53	53	54	54	55	55	56	56	57	57	58	58	59	59	60	60	61	61	62	62	63	63	64	64	65	65	66	66	67	67	68	68	69	69	70	70	71	71	72	72	73	73	74	74	75	75
	1	**2**	**3**	**4**	**5**	**6**	**7**	**8**	**9**	**10**	**11**	**12**	**13**	**14**	**15**	**16**	**17**	**18**	**19**	**20**	**21**	**22**	**23**	**24**	**25**	**26**	**27**	**28**	**29**	**30**	**31**	**32**	**33**	**34**	**35**	**36**	**37**	**38**	**39**	**40**	**41**	**42**	**43**	**44**	**45**	**46**	**47**	**48**	**49**	**50**

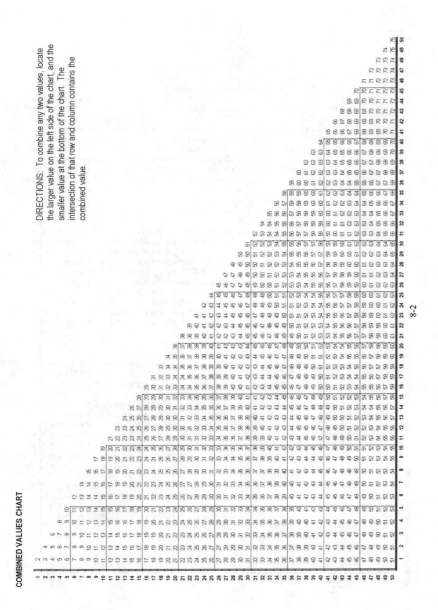

COMBINED VALUES CHART (CON'T)

	1	2	3	4	5	6	7	8	9	10	11	12	13	14	15	16	17	18	19	20	21	22	23	24	25	26	27	28	29	30	31	32	33	34	35	36	37	38	39	40	41	42	43	44	45	46	47	48	49	50
51	51	52	52	53	53	54	54	55	55	56	56	57	57	58	58	59	59	60	60	61	61	62	62	63	63	64	64	65	65	66	66	67	67	68	68	69	69	70	70	71	71	72	72	73	73	74	74	75	75	76
52	52	53	53	54	54	55	55	56	56	57	57	58	58	59	59	60	60	61	61	62	62	63	63	64	64	64	65	65	66	66	67	67	68	68	69	69	70	70	71	71	72	72	73	73	74	74	75	75	76	76
53	53	54	54	55	55	56	56	57	57	58	58	59	59	60	60	61	61	61	62	62	63	63	64	64	65	65	66	66	67	67	68	68	69	69	69	70	70	71	71	72	72	73	73	74	74	75	75	76	76	77
54	54	55	55	56	56	57	57	58	58	59	59	60	60	60	61	61	62	62	63	63	64	64	65	65	66	66	66	67	67	68	68	69	69	70	70	71	71	71	72	72	73	73	74	74	75	75	76	76	77	77
55	55	56	56	57	57	58	58	59	59	60	60	60	61	61	62	62	63	63	64	64	64	65	65	66	66	67	67	68	68	69	69	69	70	70	71	71	72	72	73	73	73	74	74	75	75	76	76	77	77	78
56	56	57	57	58	58	59	59	60	60	60	61	61	62	62	63	63	63	64	64	65	65	66	66	67	67	67	68	68	69	69	70	70	71	71	71	72	72	73	73	74	74	74	75	75	76	76	77	77	78	78
57	57	58	58	59	59	60	60	60	61	61	62	62	63	63	63	64	64	65	65	66	66	66	67	67	68	68	69	69	69	70	70	71	71	72	72	72	73	73	74	74	75	75	75	76	76	77	77	78	78	79
58	58	59	59	60	60	61	61	61	62	62	63	63	63	64	64	65	65	66	66	66	67	67	68	68	69	69	69	70	70	71	71	71	72	72	73	73	74	74	74	75	75	76	76	76	77	77	78	78	79	79
59	59	60	60	61	61	61	62	62	63	63	64	64	64	65	65	66	66	66	67	67	68	68	68	69	69	70	70	70	71	71	72	72	73	73	73	74	74	75	75	75	76	76	77	77	77	78	78	79	79	80
60	60	61	61	62	62	62	63	63	64	64	64	65	65	66	66	66	67	67	68	68	68	69	69	70	70	70	71	71	72	72	72	73	73	74	74	74	75	75	76	76	76	77	77	78	78	78	79	79	80	80
61	61	62	62	63	63	63	64	64	65	65	65	66	66	66	67	67	68	68	68	69	69	70	70	70	71	71	72	72	72	73	73	73	74	74	75	75	75	76	76	77	77	77	78	78	79	79	79	80	80	81
62	62	63	63	64	64	64	65	65	65	66	66	67	67	67	68	68	68	69	69	70	70	70	71	71	72	72	72	73	73	73	74	74	75	75	75	76	76	76	77	77	78	78	78	79	79	79	80	80	81	81
63	63	64	64	64	65	65	66	66	66	67	67	67	68	68	69	69	69	70	70	70	71	71	72	72	72	73	73	73	74	74	74	75	75	76	76	76	77	77	77	78	78	79	79	79	80	80	80	81	81	82
64	64	65	65	65	66	66	67	67	67	68	68	68	69	69	69	70	70	70	71	71	72	72	72	73	73	73	74	74	74	75	75	76	76	76	77	77	77	78	78	78	79	79	79	80	80	81	81	81	82	82
65	65	66	66	66	67	67	67	68	68	69	69	69	70	70	70	71	71	71	72	72	72	73	73	73	74	74	74	75	75	76	76	76	77	77	77	78	78	78	79	79	79	80	80	80	81	81	81	82	82	83
66	66	67	67	67	68	68	68	69	69	69	70	70	70	71	71	71	72	72	72	73	73	73	74	74	75	75	75	76	76	76	77	77	77	78	78	78	79	79	79	80	80	80	81	81	81	82	82	82	83	83
67	67	68	68	68	69	69	69	70	70	70	71	71	71	72	72	72	73	73	73	74	74	74	75	75	75	76	76	76	77	77	77	78	78	78	79	79	79	80	80	80	81	81	81	82	82	82	83	83	83	84
68	68	69	69	69	70	70	70	71	71	71	72	72	72	72	73	73	73	74	74	74	75	75	75	76	76	76	77	77	77	78	78	78	79	79	79	80	80	80	80	81	81	81	82	82	82	83	83	83	84	84
69	69	70	70	70	71	71	71	71	72	72	72	73	73	73	74	74	74	75	75	75	76	76	76	76	77	77	77	78	78	78	79	79	79	80	80	80	80	81	81	81	82	82	82	83	83	83	84	84	84	85
70	70	71	71	71	72	72	72	72	73	73	73	74	74	74	75	75	75	75	76	76	76	77	77	77	78	78	78	78	79	79	79	80	80	80	81	81	81	81	82	82	82	83	83	83	84	84	84	84	85	85
71	71	72	72	72	72	73	73	73	74	74	74	74	75	75	75	76	76	76	77	77	77	77	78	78	78	79	79	79	79	80	80	80	81	81	81	81	82	82	82	83	83	83	83	84	84	84	85	85	85	86
72	72	73	73	73	73	74	74	74	75	75	75	75	76	76	76	76	77	77	77	78	78	78	78	79	79	79	80	80	80	80	81	81	81	82	82	82	82	83	83	83	83	84	84	84	85	85	85	85	86	86
73	73	74	74	74	74	75	75	75	75	76	76	76	77	77	77	77	78	78	78	78	79	79	79	79	80	80	80	81	81	81	81	82	82	82	82	83	83	83	84	84	84	84	85	85	85	85	86	86	86	87
74	74	75	75	75	75	76	76	76	76	77	77	77	77	78	78	78	78	79	79	79	79	80	80	80	81	81	81	81	82	82	82	82	83	83	83	83	84	84	84	84	85	85	85	85	86	86	86	86	87	87
75	75	76	76	76	76	77	77	77	77	78	78	78	78	79	79	79	79	80	80	80	80	81	81	81	81	82	82	82	82	83	83	83	83	84	84	84	84	85	85	85	85	86	86	86	86	87	87	87	87	88
76	76	76	77	77	77	77	78	78	78	78	79	79	79	79	80	80	80	80	81	81	81	81	82	82	82	82	82	83	83	83	83	84	84	84	84	85	85	85	85	86	86	86	86	87	87	87	87	88	88	88
77	77	77	78	78	78	78	79	79	79	79	80	80	80	80	80	81	81	81	81	82	82	82	82	83	83	83	83	83	84	84	84	84	85	85	85	85	86	86	86	86	86	87	87	87	87	88	88	88	88	89
78	78	78	79	79	79	79	80	80	80	80	80	81	81	81	81	82	82	82	82	82	83	83	83	83	84	84	84	84	84	85	85	85	85	85	86	86	86	86	87	87	87	87	87	88	88	88	88	89	89	89
79	79	79	80	80	80	80	80	81	81	81	81	82	82	82	82	82	83	83	83	83	83	84	84	84	84	84	85	85	85	85	86	86	86	86	86	87	87	87	87	87	88	88	88	88	88	89	89	89	89	90
80	80	80	81	81	81	81	81	82	82	82	82	82	83	83	83	83	83	84	84	84	84	84	85	85	85	85	85	86	86	86	86	86	87	87	87	87	87	88	88	88	88	88	89	89	89	89	89	90	90	90
81	81	81	82	82	82	82	82	83	83	83	83	83	83	84	84	84	84	84	85	85	85	85	85	86	86	86	86	86	87	87	87	87	87	87	88	88	88	88	88	89	89	89	89	89	90	90	90	90	90	91
82	82	82	83	83	83	83	83	83	84	84	84	84	84	85	85	85	85	85	85	86	86	86	86	86	87	87	87	87	87	87	88	88	88	88	88	88	89	89	89	89	89	90	90	90	90	90	90	91	91	91
83	83	83	84	84	84	84	84	84	85	85	85	85	85	85	86	86	86	86	86	86	87	87	87	87	87	87	88	88	88	88	88	88	89	89	89	89	89	89	90	90	90	90	90	90	91	91	91	91	91	92
84	84	84	84	85	85	85	85	85	85	86	86	86	86	86	86	87	87	87	87	87	87	88	88	88	88	88	88	88	89	89	89	89	89	89	90	90	90	90	90	90	91	91	91	91	91	91	92	92	92	92
85	85	85	85	86	86	86	86	86	86	87	87	87	87	87	87	87	88	88	88	88	88	88	88	89	89	89	89	89	89	90	90	90	90	90	90	90	91	91	91	91	91	91	91	92	92	92	92	92	92	93
86	86	86	86	87	87	87	87	87	87	87	88	88	88	88	88	88	88	89	89	89	89	89	89	89	90	90	90	90	90	90	90	90	91	91	91	91	91	91	91	92	92	92	92	92	92	92	93	93	93	93
87	87	87	87	88	88	88	88	88	88	88	88	89	89	89	89	89	89	89	89	90	90	90	90	90	90	90	91	91	91	91	91	91	91	91	92	92	92	92	92	92	92	92	93	93	93	93	93	93	93	94
88	88	88	88	88	89	89	89	89	89	89	89	89	90	90	90	90	90	90	90	90	91	91	91	91	91	91	91	91	91	92	92	92	92	92	92	92	92	93	93	93	93	93	93	93	93	94	94	94	94	94
89	89	89	89	89	90	90	90	90	90	90	90	90	90	91	91	91	91	91	91	91	91	91	92	92	92	92	92	92	92	92	92	93	93	93	93	93	93	93	93	93	94	94	94	94	94	94	94	94	94	95
90	90	90	90	90	91	91	91	91	91	91	91	91	91	91	92	92	92	92	92	92	92	92	92	92	93	93	93	93	93	93	93	93	93	93	94	94	94	94	94	94	94	94	94	94	95	95	95	95	95	95
91	91	91	91	91	91	92	92	92	92	92	92	92	92	92	92	92	93	93	93	93	93	93	93	93	93	93	93	94	94	94	94	94	94	94	94	94	94	94	95	95	95	95	95	95	95	95	95	95	95	96
92	92	92	92	92	92	92	93	93	93	93	93	93	93	93	93	93	93	93	94	94	94	94	94	94	94	94	94	94	94	94	94	95	95	95	95	95	95	95	95	95	95	95	95	96	96	96	96	96	96	96
93	93	93	93	93	93	93	93	94	94	94	94	94	94	94	94	94	94	94	94	94	94	95	95	95	95	95	95	95	95	95	95	95	95	95	95	96	96	96	96	96	96	96	96	96	96	96	96	96	96	97
94	94	94	94	94	94	94	94	94	95	95	95	95	95	95	95	95	95	95	95	95	95	95	95	95	96	96	96	96	96	96	96	96	96	96	96	96	96	96	96	96	96	97	97	97	97	97	97	97	97	97
95	95	95	95	95	95	95	95	95	95	96	96	96	96	96	96	96	96	96	96	96	96	96	96	96	96	96	96	96	96	97	97	97	97	97	97	97	97	97	97	97	97	97	97	97	97	97	97	97	97	98
96	96	96	96	96	96	96	96	96	96	96	96	96	97	97	97	97	97	97	97	97	97	97	97	97	97	97	97	97	97	97	97	97	97	97	97	97	97	98	98	98	98	98	98	98	98	98	98	98	98	98
97	97	97	97	97	97	97	97	97	97	97	97	97	97	97	97	97	98	98	98	98	98	98	98	98	98	98	98	98	98	98	98	98	98	98	98	98	98	98	98	98	98	98	98	98	98	98	98	98	98	99
98	98	98	98	98	98	98	98	98	98	98	98	98	98	98	98	98	98	98	98	98	98	98	98	98	99	99	99	99	99	99	99	99	99	99	99	99	99	99	99	99	99	99	99	99	99	99	99	99	99	99
99	99	99	99	99	99	99	99	99	99	99	99	99	99	99	99	99	99	99	99	99	99	99	99	99	99	99	99	99	99	99	99	99	99	99	99	99	99	99	99	99	99	99	99	99	99	99	99	99	99	100

COMBINED VALUES CHART (CON'T)

	51	52	53	54	55	56	57	58	59	60	61	62	63	64	65	66	67	68	69	70	71	72	73	74	75	76	77	78	79	80	81	82	83	84	85	86	87	88	89	90	91	92	93	94	95	96	97	98	99	
51	76																																																	
52	76	77																																																
53	77	77	78																																															
54	77	78	78	79																																														
55	78	78	79	79	80																																													
56	78	79	79	80	80	81																																												
57	79	79	80	80	81	81	82																																											
58	79	80	80	81	81	82	82	82																																										
59	80	80	81	81	82	82	82	83	83																																									
60	80	81	81	82	82	82	83	83	84	84																																								
61	81	81	82	82	82	83	83	84	84	84	85																																							
62	81	82	82	83	83	83	84	84	84	85	85	86																																						
63	82	82	83	83	83	84	84	84	85	85	86	86	86																																					
64	82	83	83	83	84	84	85	85	85	86	86	86	87	87																																				
65	83	83	84	84	84	85	85	85	86	86	86	87	87	87	88																																			
66	83	84	84	84	85	85	85	86	86	86	87	87	87	88	88	88																																		
67	84	84	84	85	85	85	86	86	86	87	87	87	88	88	88	89	89																																	
68	84	85	85	85	86	86	86	87	87	87	88	88	88	88	89	89	89	90																																
69	85	85	85	86	86	86	87	87	87	88	88	88	89	89	89	89	90	90	90																															
70	85	86	86	86	87	87	87	87	88	88	88	89	89	89	90	90	90	90	91	91																														
71	86	86	86	87	87	87	88	88	88	88	89	89	89	90	90	90	90	91	91	91	92																													
72	86	87	87	87	87	88	88	88	89	89	89	89	90	90	90	90	91	91	91	92	92	92																												
73	87	87	87	88	88	88	88	89	89	89	89	90	90	90	91	91	91	91	92	92	92	92	93																											
74	87	88	88	88	88	89	89	89	89	90	90	90	90	91	91	91	91	92	92	92	92	93	93	93																										
75	88	88	88	89	89	89	89	90	90	90	90	91	91	91	91	92	92	92	92	93	93	93	93	94	94																									
76	88	88	89	89	89	89	90	90	90	90	91	91	91	91	92	92	92	92	93	93	93	93	94	94	94	94																								
77	89	89	89	89	90	90	90	90	91	91	91	91	91	92	92	92	92	93	93	93	93	94	94	94	94	94	95																							
78	89	89	90	90	90	90	91	91	91	91	91	92	92	92	92	93	93	93	93	93	94	94	94	94	95	95	95	95																						
79	90	90	90	90	91	91	91	91	91	92	92	92	92	92	93	93	93	93	93	94	94	94	94	95	95	95	95	95	96																					
80	90	90	91	91	91	91	91	92	92	92	92	92	93	93	93	93	93	94	94	94	94	94	95	95	95	95	95	96	96	96																				
81	91	91	91	91	91	92	92	92	92	92	93	93	93	93	93	94	94	94	94	94	94	95	95	95	95	95	96	96	96	96	96																			
82	91	91	92	92	92	92	92	92	93	93	93	93	93	94	94	94	94	94	94	95	95	95	95	95	96	96	96	96	96	96	97	97																		
83	92	92	92	92	92	93	93	93	93	93	93	94	94	94	94	94	94	95	95	95	95	95	95	96	96	96	96	96	96	97	97	97	97																	
84	92	92	92	93	93	93	93	93	93	94	94	94	94	94	94	95	95	95	95	95	95	96	96	96	96	96	96	96	97	97	97	97	97	97																
85	93	93	93	93	93	93	94	94	94	94	94	94	94	95	95	95	95	95	95	96	96	96	96	96	96	96	97	97	97	97	97	97	97	98	98															
86	93	93	93	94	94	94	94	94	94	94	95	95	95	95	95	95	95	96	96	96	96	96	96	96	97	97	97	97	97	97	97	97	98	98	98	98														
87	94	94	94	94	94	94	94	95	95	95	95	95	95	95	95	96	96	96	96	96	96	96	96	97	97	97	97	97	97	97	98	98	98	98	98	98	98													
88	94	94	94	94	95	95	95	95	95	95	95	95	96	96	96	96	96	96	96	96	97	97	97	97	97	97	97	97	97	98	98	98	98	98	98	98	98	99												
89	95	95	95	95	95	95	95	95	95	96	96	96	96	96	96	96	96	96	97	97	97	97	97	97	97	97	97	98	98	98	98	98	98	98	98	98	99	99	99											
90	95	95	95	95	96	96	96	96	96	96	96	96	96	96	97	97	97	97	97	97	97	97	97	97	98	98	98	98	98	98	98	98	98	98	99	99	99	99	99	99										
91	96	96	96	96	96	96	96	96	96	96	96	97	97	97	97	97	97	97	97	97	97	97	98	98	98	98	98	98	98	98	98	98	98	99	99	99	99	99	99	99	99									
92	96	96	96	96	96	96	97	97	97	97	97	97	97	97	97	97	97	97	98	98	98	98	98	98	98	98	98	98	98	98	98	99	99	99	99	99	99	99	99	99	99	99								
93	97	97	97	97	97	97	97	97	97	97	97	97	97	97	98	98	98	98	98	98	98	98	98	98	98	98	98	98	99	99	99	99	99	99	99	99	99	99	99	99	99	99	100							
94	97	97	97	97	97	97	97	97	98	98	98	98	98	98	98	98	98	98	98	98	98	98	98	98	99	99	99	99	99	99	99	99	99	99	99	99	99	99	99	99	99	100	100	100						
95	98	98	98	98	98	98	98	98	98	98	98	98	98	98	98	98	98	98	98	99	99	99	99	99	99	99	99	99	99	99	99	99	99	99	99	99	99	99	99	100	100	100	100	100	100					
96	98	98	98	98	98	98	98	98	98	98	98	98	99	99	99	99	99	99	99	99	99	99	99	99	99	99	99	99	99	99	99	99	99	99	99	99	99	99	100	100	100	100	100	100	100	100				
97	99	99	99	99	99	99	99	99	99	99	99	99	99	99	99	99	99	99	99	99	99	99	99	99	99	99	99	99	99	99	99	99	99	100	100	100	100	100	100	100	100	100	100	100	100	100	100			
98	99	99	99	99	99	99	99	99	99	99	99	99	99	99	99	99	99	99	99	99	99	99	99	100	100	100	100	100	100	100	100	100	100	100	100	100	100	100	100	100	100	100	100	100	100	100	100	100		
99	100	100	100	100	100	100	100	100	100	100	100	100	100	100	100	100	100	100	100	100	100	100	100	100	100	100	100	100	100	100	100	100	100	100	100	100	100	100	100	100	100	100	100	100	100	100	100	100	100

PART 6. Medical-Legal Fee Schedule: Excerpts

TABLE 12
Medical-Legal Fee Schedule, adopted 8/3/93:

[8 Cal. Code Reg. §9795]

Evaluation Type and Code:	Description:	Amount Presumed Reasonable
FOLLOW-UP EVAL **ML101**: RV 5	Within 9 mos. paid @ lesser of U&C or $62.50/¼ hr =	**$250.00/hr**
BASIC EVAL **ML102**: RV 50	All evaluations, other than Supplemental, Complex or Extraordinary	**$625.00**
COMPLEX EVAL **ML103**: RV 75	<u>INCLUDES THREE OR MORE OF THE FOLLOWING:</u> 1) 2 or more hours physician face-to-face with patient; 2) 2 or more hours of record review by the physician; 3) 2 or more hours of medical research by physician; 4) 4 or more hours on 2 of 3 above complexity factors; 5) 6 or more hours on any combination of 3 factors; 6) Addressing the issue of medical causation; 7) Addressing the issue of apportionment, old or new Schedule; 8) Monitoring after toxic chemical, mineral or biologic exposure; 9) Psychiatric/Psychological evaluation is primary focus of eval; 10) Denial/Mod of treatment after UR, L.C. §4610	**$937.50**
Extraordinary [1, 4] **Eval ML104**: RV 5	Eval requires: 4 or more ML-103 factors; prior injuries to same body part; complex medical issues + 3 of 6 factors & 3 hrs spent; & AME after QMEs; verification of time spent; contents of report true per L.C. § 4628(j): Lesser of U&C or $62.50/¼hr or	**$250/hr**
Med-Legal Testimony [1, 4] **ML105**: RV 5	1 hour minimum for depo & including reasonable preparation & travel time: Lesser of U&C or $62.50/¼hr or	**$250/hr**
Supplemental Med-Legal Eval [1, 4] **ML106**, RV 5	Not for review of information previously available or for tests ordered at initial eval: Lesser of U&C or $62.50/¼hr or .	**$250/hr**

Circumstances Allowing Modification: Per Exam or Per Hour[2]

Evaluation Type:	Modifier -93	Modifier -94	Modifier -93 & -94
With →	**Interpreter** [3]	**AME** [4]	**Interpreter & AME** [4]
Multiplier →	**× 1.1**	**× 1.25**	**× 1.35**
Follow-up	(Not applicable)[4]	$312.50/hr	($312.50/hr) [4]
Basic ($625.00) [4]	$687.50	$781.25	$843.75
Complex (937.50) [4]	$1,031.25	$1,171.88	$1,265.63
Extraordinary	(Not applicable)[4]	$312.50/hr	($312.50/hr) [4]

[1] Comprehensive Medical-Legal Evaluation Involving Extraordinary Circumstances; Medical-Legal Testimony, or Supplemental Medical-Legal Evaluations, 8 Cal. Code Reg. §9795, ML104/105/106.

[2] Modifier -92: Evaluation by Primary Treating Physician, before 7/1/06; after 7/1/06 for info only; Follow-up = $160.00/hr before 7/1/06, and after, $250.00/hr; Basic = $500.00; Complex = $750.00; Modifiers -95, -96 and -97 are to identify only & do not affect values.

[3] Or other circumstances which significantly increase the time necessary to conduct the examination.

[4] Modifier -93 is **only applicable to ML 102 or ML 103** while -94 applies to an evaluation or testimony by an AME at $250.00/hr × 1.25 = $312.50/hr. (Use of an interpreter's may take longer, i.e., more hours, but there is no additional fee, just more hours at $312.50/hour.)

PART 7. Death Benefits

TABLE 13

Death Benefits Payable for Total and Partial Dependency

Injuries Occurring On or After January 1, 1983
Labor Code §4702

Status of Dependency	Death From Injury On Or After					
	1/1/83	1/1/84	1/1/91	7/1/94	7/1/96	1/1/06
A. 1 total and no partial dependents	60,000	70,000	95,000	115,000	125,000	250,000
B. 2 or more total dependents regardless of the number of partial dependents	85,000	95,000	115,000	135,000	145,000	290,000
C. 3 or more total dependents, regardless of the number of partial dependents	85,000	95,000	115,000	150,000	160,000	320,000
D. 1 total and one or more partial dependents	60,000*	70,000*	95,000*	115,000*	125,000*	250,000*
* Plus 4 times the amount annually devoted to the support of any partial dependents, with the *total paid*, not to exceed:	85,000	95,000	115,000	125,000	145,000	290,000
E. No total and one or more partial dependents	4 times [*8 times o/a 1/1/06*] the amount annually devoted to the support of partial dependents, not to exceed:					
	60,000	70,000	95,000	115,000	125,000	250,000
F. No total and no partial dependents, L.C. § 4702(a)(6)(B)	Injury on or after 1/1/04: $250,000 to be paid to the estate of the deceased employee. Unconstitutional per decision in Six Flags, Inc. vs. WCAB (Rackchamroon) 71 CCC 1759					

Death Benefits are payable in installments in the same manner and amounts as temporary disability indemnity per Labor Code §4702(b).

Maximum Burial Expense Benefit: Labor Code §4701(a)

Date of Injury	Maximum Benefit	
1/1/79 to 12/31/85	1,500	All employees
1/1/86 to 12/31/88	1,500	Public employees
1/1/89 to 12/31/90	2,000	Public employees
1/1/86 to 12/31/90	2,000	All other employees
1/1/91 to present	5,000	All employees

Tables & Schedules

PART 8. Indemnity and Earnings

TABLE 14
Maximum/Minimum Indemnity and Earnings

(Adapted from *Work Comp Index* 1993)

Temporary Total Disability

Date of Injury	Earnings, Average Weekly	Rate Paid/Week
7-1-94	$ 0.00 – $ 126.00	Actual earnings
to	126.01 – 189.00	$126.00
6-30-95	189.01 – 609.00 × 2/3 = up to	406.00
	Labor Code §4453(a)(5)	
7-1-95	$ 0.00 – $ 126.00	Actual earnings
to	126.01 – 189.00	$126.00
6-30-96	189.01 – 672.00 × 2/3 = up to	448.00
	Labor Code §4453(a)(6)	
7-1-96	$ 0.00 – $ 126.00	Actual earnings
to	126.01 – 189.00	$126.00
12-31-02	189.01 – 735.00 × 2/3 = up to	490.00
	Labor Code §4453(a)(7)	
2003	$ 0.00 – $ 189.00	$126.00
	189.01 – $ 903.00 × 2/3 = up to	$602.00
	Labor Code §4453(a)(8)	
2004	$ 0.00 – $ 189.00	$126.00
	189.01 – $1,092.00 × 2/3 = up to	$728.00
	Labor Code §4453(a)(9)	
2005	$ 0.00 – $ 189.00	$126.00
	189.01 – $1,260.00 × 2/3 = up to	$840.00
	Labor Code §4453(a)(10)	
2006	$ 0.00 – $ 189.00 + COLA per SAWW	$126.00 *
	189.01 – $1,260.00 + COLA per SAWW × 2/3	$840.00 *
	Labor Code §4453(a)(10)	
2007	$ 0.00 – $ 189.00 + 4.95932% = $ **198.37** & × 2/3 =	$132.25 *
	198.38 – $1,260.00 + 4.95932% = **$1,322.49** & × 2/3 =	$881.66 *
	Labor Code §4453(a)(10) + SAWW	
2008	$ 0.00 – $ 198.37 + 3.93181% = $ **206.17** & × 2/3 =	$137.45 *
	206.18 – $1,322.49 + 3.93181% = **$1,374.49** & × 2/3 =	$916.33 *
	Labor Code §4453(a)(10) + SAWW	
2009	$ 0.00 – $ 215.55 + 4.54843% = $ **215.55** & × 2/3 =	$143.70 *
	215.56 – $1,374.49 + 4.54843% = **$1,437.01** & × 2/3 =	$958.01 *
	Labor Code §4453(a)(10) + SAWW	

*** TD SAWW increases apply to the maximum/minimum *rates*, not to the amount paid.**

TTD paid 2 or more yrs after injury: Check for a possible rate increase or 104 wks under L.C. §§ 4661.5, 4656(c)(1), (2). Supplemental job displacement vouchers may apply for injuries o/a 1/1/04, L.C. §§ 4658.5, 4658.6 and generally T8CCR §§10133.50 – 10133.60. For employers of 50 or more employees, 2005+, see Table 8 re calculating PD +/– 15%.

Permanent Partial Disability (PD): Minimum and Maximum Rates

Date of Injury		Min – Max PD Rate and Labor Code Section	
1-1-91 to 6-30-94			
	1:0 to 24:3	$70 – $140	L.C. §4453(b)(2)
	25:0 to 99:3	$70 – $148	L.C. §4453(b)(4)
7-1-94 to 6-30-95			
	1:0 to 14:3	$70 – $140	L.C. §4453(b)(2)
	15:0 to 24:3	$70 – $148	L.C. §4453(b)(3)
	25:0 to 69:3	$70 – $158	L.C. §4453(b)(5)
	70:0 to 99:3	$70 – $168	L.C. §4453(b)(6)
7-1-95 to 6-30-96			
	1:0 to 14:3	$70 – $140	L.C. §4453(b)(2)
	15:0 to 24:3	$70 – $154	L.C. §4453(b)(3)
	25:0 to 69:3	$70 – $164	L.C. §4453(b)(5)
	70:0 to 99:3	$70 – $198	L.C. §4453(b)(6)
7-1-96 to 12-31-02			
	1:0 to 14:3	$70 – $140	L.C. §4453(b)(2)
	15:0 to 24:3	$70 – $160	L.C. §4453(b)(3)
	25:0 to 69:3	$70 – $170	L.C. §4453(b)(5)
	70:0 to 99:3	$70 – $230	L.C. §4453(b)(6)
2003:	1:0 to 69:3	$100–$185	L.C. §4453(b)(6)
	70:0 to 99:3	$100–$230	L.C. §4453(b)(7)
2004:	1:0 to 69:3	$105–$200	L.C. §4453(b)(6)
	70:0 to 99:3	$105–$250	L.C. §4453(b)(7)
2005:	1:0 to 69:3	$105–$220	L.C. §4453(b)(6)
	70:0 to 99:3	$105–$270	L.C. §4453(b)(7)
2006:	1:0 to 69:3	$130–$230	L.C. §4453(b)(6)
to?	70:0 to 99:3	$130–$270	L.C. §4453(b)(7)

Life Pension **(LP), PD ≥ 70:0**
Maximum weekly earnings, *Labor Code* §4659
(Minimum wage for PD/LP, per L.C. §4453 above, e.g. $105 × ⅔ = $70.00/wk P.D.)

Formula: (PD – 60) × 0.015 × Earnings, e.g., for 77% PD, 12/20/02 injury @ max
(77 – 60) × 0.015 × $257.69 = $65.71/week

Effective Dates	**AWW**: Minimum/Max	PD 70:0 to 99:3 **Paid**: Min/wk	Max/wk
07-01-94 to 06-30-95	$105.00 to $157.69	$15.75 to	$94.02
07-01-95 to 06-30-96	$105.00 to $207.69	$15.75 to	$123.84
07-01-96 to 12-31-02	$105.00 to $257.69	$15.75 to	$153.65
01-01-03 to 12-31-03*	$150.00 to $257.69	$22.50 to	$153.65
01-01-04 to 12-31-04*	$157.50 to $257.69	$23.55 to	$153.65
01-01-05 to 12-31-05*	$157.50 to $257.69	$23.55 to	$153.65
01-01-06 + COLA*	$195.00 to $515.38	$29.25 to	$307.30

* For injuries o/a 1/1/03, beginning on 1/1/04, a Cost of Living Adjustment (COLA) is to be made to the ***Life Pension*** or ***Permanent Total Disability*** ***rate paid each year*** based on an *increase*, if any, in the state average weekly wage (SAWW) compared to the prior year, L.C. § 4659(c).

Increases in SAWW effective 1/1/09 calculate to 1.0454843%. Calculations on following page list annual increases through 2009 and give annual multiplication factors.

Questions remain as to ***exactly*** how these annual COLA increases are going to be calculated, and paid. Commutations raise additional questions. Hopefully legislative or regulatory clarification will be provided.

Tables & Schedules

Additional Information to Aid in Using Table 14

The 1st page of Table 14 gives maximum and minimum wages and TD rates paid. Increases in SAWW here apply only to the **maximum and minimum wages**, not to rates paid.

The 2nd page of Table 14 covers first Permanent Partial Disability & max/min rates paid. The 2nd part of this page covers **Life Pension & 100%** Permanent Total Disability **paid.** This latter part has a Cost of Living Adjustment (COLA) based on the annual change in State Average Weekly Wage (SAWW). These increases ***apply to payments made***, as noted.

SAWW data is based on the year ending March 31 per the U.S. Dept of Labor. Readers may call (202) 693-3039 or write Div. of Fiscal & Actuarial Services, Room C-4514; 200 Constitution Ave., NW; Washington, DC 20210. Data used for 2009 is from their web site:

http://ows.doleta.gov/unemploy/content/data.asp

Calculations of Change in State Average Weekly Wage by Year

Year	DWCNewsline	SAWW	Current ÷ Prior = Increase (Except for 2004)
2003	18-03 (12/22/03) ...	$794.95 ...	(Not relevant, this table)
2004	18-03 (12/22/03) ...	$790.50 ...	790.50 ÷ 794.95 = 0.9944021 **(No Increase)**
2005	64-04 (12/15/04) ...	$806.11 ...	806.11 ÷ 790.50 = **1.0191668**
2006	80-05 (12/20/05) ...	$838.42 ...	838.42 ÷ 806.11 = **1.0400813**
2007	54-06 (10/10/06) ...	$880.00 ...	880.00 ÷ 838.42 = **1.0495932**
2008	66-07 (10/03/07) ...	$914.60 ...	914.60 ÷ 880.00 = **1.0393181**
2009	66-08 (10/31/08) ...	$956.20 ...	956.20 ÷ 914.60 = **1.0454843**

Example: Assume a 100% PD award on an injury in 2006 with an average weekly wage of $900.00/week. The TD rate is 2/3rds of that or $600.00/wk. The PD rate is the same until 1/1/07. Then, per L.C. §4659(c), the rate paid will increase annually as follows:

The initial rate paid, $600.00/wk × **1.0495932** = $629.76/wk., the rate paid for **2007**
On 1/1/08 the 2007 rate, $629.76/wk × **1.0393181** = $654.52/wk., the rate paid for **2008**
On 1/1/09 the 2008 rate, $654.52/wk × **1.0454843** = $684.29/wk., the rate paid for **2009**

As noted above, questions remain as to ***exactly*** how these annual COLA increases are going to be calculated, and paid. For instance, for injuries o/a 1/1/03, will increases be applied retroactively to Life Pension Payments which do not begin until many years in the future when the PD is paid out and the Life Pension begins? Commutations raise additional questions. Hopefully, legislative or regulatory clarification will be provided.

TABLE 15
Percentage of Permanent Disability to Weeks of Indemnity

The permanent disability rating schedule which became effective for **injuries occurring April 1, 1972 to December 31, 1991** provided for an increase in indemnity as the percent of disability increased as follows:

Percentage Range of Permanent Disability Rating	Number of Weeks For Each 1% Within the Range
Under 10	3
10 - 19.75	4
20 - 29.75	5
30 - 49.75	6
50 - 69.75	7
70 - 99.75	8

The cumulative effect of the formula precludes the use of a straight-line method of calculating the number of weeks of benefits. Therefore, to determine the number of weeks of indemnity for a permanent disability rating, we must either refer to a chart or use one of the following equations. ("R" is the permanent disability rating.)

If "R" is Between	Then total Number of Weeks is
1% - 9.75%	3 R
10% - 19.75%	4(R - 9.75) + 29.25
20% - 29.75%	5(R - 19.75) + 69.25
30% - 49.75%	6(R - 29.75) + 119.25
50% - 69.75%	7(R - 49.75) + 239.25
70% - 99.75%	8(R - 69.75) + 379.25

% of PD	Injuries 1/1/92 to 12/31/02
1% - 9.75%	3 R
10% - 19.75%	4(R - 9.75) + 29.25
20% - 24.75%	5(R - 19.75) + 69.25
25% - 29.75%	6(R - 24.75) + 94.25
30% - 49.75%	7(R - 29.75) + 124.25
50% - 69.75%	8(R - 49.75) + 264.25
70% - 99.75%	9(R - 69.75) + 424.25

% of PD	1/1/03 to 12/31/03	1/1/04 to 12/31/04	%PD 01/01/05 to ? See Table 8	
1 - 9.75	3R (3 × Rating)	4R (4 × Rating)	0.25-9.75	3R (3 × Rating)
10 - 19.75	4(R - 9.75) + 29.25	5(R - 9.75) + 39	10-14.75	4(R- 9.75)+ 29.25
20 - 24.75	5(R - 19.75) + 69.25	5(R - 19.75) + 89	15-24.75	5(R- 19.75)+ 74.25
25 - 29.75	6(R - 24.74) + 94.25	6(R - 24.75) + 114	25-29.75	6(R- 24.75)+ 99.25
30 - 49.75	7(R - 29.75) + 124.25	7(R - 29.75) + 144	30-49.75	7(R- 29.75)+129.25
50 - 69.75	8(R - 49.75) + 264.25	8(R - 49.75) + 284	50-69.75	8(R- 49.75)+269.25
70 - 99.75	9(R - 69.75) + 424.25	9(R - 69.75) + 444	70-99.75	16(R-69.75)+429.25

Example: Injury of 12-20-03. Calculate the number of weeks of P.D. for **37%**:
7(**37** - 29.75) + 124.25 = 7(7.25) + 124.25 = 50.75 + 124.25 = 175.00 weeks

Tables & Schedules

TABLE 16
Instructions for Applying New and Old Permanent Partial Disability Benefit Rates to Table 17

1. Match the date of injury to the appropriate column in Table 17. Weeks of indemnity paid do not increase for injuries on or after 1992. However, the maximum permanent partial disability rates vary as the percentage of disability increases. The minimum paid is $70/week for all injuries on or after 1/1/84.

2. If the injury occurred in 1983, the maximum is $130/week and the minimum is $50/week. To calculate the amount owed for a given percent of permanent disability, multiply the number of weeks in the second column from the left (next to the % of P.D.) by the applicable weekly P.D. rate.

3. If the date of injury is from 1/1/77 to 12/31/82, the maximum is $70/week and the minimum, $30/week. From 4/1/72 to 12/31/76 the maximum was also $70/week, but the minimum was $20/week. To calculate the amount owed for a given percent of permanent disability, multiply the number of weeks in the second column from the left (next to the percent of P.D.) by the weekly P.D. rate. The minimum P.D. rate is $70/week for injuries on or after 1/1/84.

4. Note: Whenever the P.D. rate is less than $70 (1983 and prior) and the percent of disability is 29½ or less, compare with pre–1972 rates which were 4 weeks for each percent of P.D., but with a maximum of $52.50. The higher benefit applies.

5. Permanent disability rates are subject to the maximum/minimum values in effect on the date of injury. The following are three different methods for calculating the permanent partial disability rate from an average weekly wage, e.g. of $125 per week:
 (1) Multiply by 2 & divide by 3: Earnings of $125.00 × 2 ÷ 3 = **$83.33**;
 (2) Multiply by 0.66667: Earnings of $125.00 × 0.66667 = **$83.33**; or
 (3) Divide by 1.5: Earnings of $125.00 ÷ 1.5 = **$83.33** (The first method is most common.)

Summary: Permanent Partial Disability (PD) and Minimum / Maximum Rates

Date of Injury:	**Min**	**Max** Weekly Rates	
04/01/72 to 12/31/76	$20	$ 70	(Table 17 is for injuries on or after 1984.
01/01/77 to 12/31/82	$30	$ 70	Steps 2, 3 & 4 above calculate PD for
01/01/83 to 12/31/83	$50	$130	dates of injury back to 04/01/72 from the
01/01/84 to 12/31/90	$70	$140	1st # of weeks column in Table 17.)

Subsequent Minimum / Maximum weekly values depending on the Percent of PD:

Date of Injury:	**Min**	**Max** 1:0–14:3	**Max** 15:0–24:3	**Max** 25:0–69:3	**Max** 70:0–99:3
01/01/91 to 06/30/94	**$70**	$140	$140	$148	$148
07/01/94 to 06/30/95	**$70**	$140	$148	$158	$168
07/01/95 to 06/30/96	**$70**	$140	$154	$164	$198
07/01/96 to 12/31/02	**$70**	$140	$160	$170	$230

Date of Injury	**Min**	**Max** 1:0–69:3	**Max** 70:0–99:3	
01/01/03 to 12/31/03	**$100**	$185	$230	Plus Life Pension
01/01/04 to 12/31/04	**$105**	$200	$250	See Table 14, page 2
01/01/05 to 12/31/05	**$105**	$220	$270	"
01/01/06 to 12/31/06	**$130**	$230	$270	"

PART 9. Permanent Disability: Weeks/Percents

Table 17 A, Permanent Disability Indemnity: For injuries o/a the adoption of the 2005 Permanent Disability Rating Schedule (PDRS) on 1/1/05, per L.C. §§4658(d), 4660(d)

See Table 8 and Issues regarding the 2005 PDRS

This table applies to injuries o/a the 1/01/05 adoption of the Permanent Disability Rating Schedule (PDRS).

Use Table 17B for injuries from 1/01/03 to 12/31/04 and Table 17C for injuries from 1984 to 12/31/02.

These Tables are believed to be correct, but can not be "guaranteed."

% of PD	SB 899 Weeks of PD	2004 PD: See Table 17 B	(+/– 15%?) 2005 PD: @ Minimum $105/wk	2005 PD: Maximum 1 – 69 % @ $220/wk; 70 – 99 % @ $270/wk	(+/– 15%?) 2006 PD: @ Minimum $130/wk	2006 PD: Maximum 1 – 69 % @ $230/wk; 70 – 99 % @ $270/wk
1	3.00		$315.00	$660.00	$390.00	$690.00
2	6.00		$630.00	$1,320.00	$780.00	$1,380.00
3	9.00		$945.00	$1,980.00	$1,170.00	$2,070.00
4	12.00		$1,260.00	$2,640.00	$1,560.00	$2,760.00
5	**15.00**		**$1,575.00**	**$3,300.00**	**$1,950.00**	**$3,450.00**
6	18.00		$1,890.00	$3,960.00	$2,340.00	$4,140.00
7	21.00		$2,205.00	$4,620.00	$2,730.00	$4,830.00
8	24.00		$2,520.00	$5,280.00	$3,120.00	$5,520.00
9	27.00		$2,835.00	$5,940.00	$3,510.00	$6,210.00
10	**30.25**		**$3,176.25**	**$6,655.00**	**$3,932.50**	**$6,957.50**
11	34.25		$3,596.25	$7,535.00	$4,452.50	$7,877.50
12	38.25		$4,016.25	$8,415.00	$4,972.50	$8,797.50
13	42.25		$4,436.25	$9,295.00	$5,492.50	$9,717.50
14	46.25		$4,856.25	$10,175.00	$6,012.50	$10,637.50
15	**50.50**		**$5,302.50**	**$11,110.00**	**$6,565.00**	**$11,615.00**
16	55.50		$5,827.50	$12,210.00	$7,215.00	$12,765.00
17	60.50		$6,352.50	$13,310.00	$7,865.00	$13,915.00
18	65.50		$6,877.50	$14,410.00	$8,515.00	$15,065.00
19	70.50		$7,402.50	$15,510.00	$9,165.00	$16,215.00
20	**75.50**		**$7,927.50**	**$16,610.00**	**$9,815.00**	**$17,365.00**
21	80.50		$8,452.50	$17,710.00	$10,465.00	$18,515.00
22	85.50		$8,977.50	$18,810.00	$11,115.00	$19,665.00
23	90.50		$9,502.50	$19,910.00	$11,765.00	$20,815.00
24	95.50		$10,027.50	$21,010.00	$12,415.00	$21,965.00
25	**100.75**		**$10,578.75**	**$22,165.00**	**$13,097.50**	**$23,172.50**

If date of injury is 1/1/03 to 12/31/04, use Table 17B. If date of injury is 1/1/84 to 12/31/02, usc Table 17C

Table 17 A, Permanent Disability Indemnity: For injuries o/a the adoption of the 2005 Permanent Disability Rating Schedule (PDRS) on 1/1/05, per L.C. §§4658(d), 4660(d)

See Table 8 and Issues regarding the 2005 PDRS

This table applies to injuries o/a the 1/01/05 adoption of the Permanent Disability Rating Schedule (PDRS).

Use Table 17B for injuries from 1/01/03 to 12/31/04 and Table 17C for injuries from 1984 to 12/31/02.

These Tables are believed to be correct, but can not be "guaranteed."

% of PD	SB 899 Weeks of PD	2004 PD: See Table 17 B	(+/– 15%?) 2005 PD: @ Minimum $105/wk	2005 PD: Maximum 1 - 69 % @ $220/wk; 70 – 99 % @ $270/wk	(+/– 15%?) 2006 PD: @ Minimum $130/wk	2006 PD: Maximum 1 - 69 % @ $230/wk; 70 – 99 % @ $270/wk
26	106.75		$11,208.75	$23,485.00	$13,877.50	$24,552.50
27	112.75		$11,838.75	$24,805.00	$14,657.50	$25,932.50
28	118.75		$12,468.75	$26,125.00	$15,437.50	$27,312.50
29	124.75		$13,098.75	$27,445.00	$16,217.50	$28,692.50
30	**131.00**		**$13,755.00**	**$28,820.00**	**$17,030.00**	**$30,130.00**
31	138.00		$14,490.00	$30,360.00	$17,940.00	$31,740.00
32	145.00		$15,225.00	$31,900.00	$18,850.00	$33,350.00
33	152.00		$15,960.00	$33,440.00	$19,760.00	$34,960.00
34	159.00		$16,695.00	$34,980.00	$20,670.00	$36,570.00
35	**166.00**		**$17,430.00**	**$36,520.00**	**$21,580.00**	**$38,180.00**
36	173.00		$18,165.00	$38,060.00	$22,490.00	$39,790.00
37	180.00		$18,900.00	$39,600.00	$23,400.00	$41,400.00
38	187.00		$19,635.00	$41,140.00	$24,310.00	$43,010.00
39	194.00		$20,370.00	$42,680.00	$25,220.00	$44,620.00
40	**201.00**		**$21,105.00**	**$44,220.00**	**$26,130.00**	**$46,230.00**
41	208.00		$21,840.00	$45,760.00	$27,040.00	$47,840.00
42	215.00		$22,575.00	$47,300.00	$27,950.00	$49,450.00
43	222.00		$23,310.00	$48,840.00	$28,860.00	$51,060.00
44	229.00		$24,045.00	$50,380.00	$29,770.00	$52,670.00
45	**236.00**		**$24,780.00**	**$51,920.00**	**$30,680.00**	**$54,280.00**
46	243.00		$25,515.00	$53,460.00	$31,590.00	$55,890.00
47	250.00		$26,250.00	$55,000.00	$32,500.00	$57,500.00
48	257.00		$26,985.00	$56,540.00	$33,410.00	$59,110.00
49	264.00		$27,720.00	$58,080.00	$34,320.00	$60,720.00
50	**271.25**		**$28,481.25**	**$59,675.00**	**$35,262.50**	**$62,387.50**

If date of injury is 1/1/03 to 12/31/04, use Table 17B. If date of injury is 1/1/84 to 12/31/02, use Table 17C

Table 17 A, Permanent Disability Indemnity: For injuries o/a the adoption of the 2005 Permanent Disability Rating Schedule (PDRS) on 1/1/05, per L.C. §§4658(d), 4660(d)

See Table 8 and Issues regarding the 2005 PDRS

This table applies to injuries o/a the 1/01/05 adoption of the Permanent Disability Rating Schedule (PDRS).

Use Table 17B for injuries from 1/01/03 to 12/31/04 and Table 17C for injuries from 1984 to 12/31/02.

These Tables are believed to be correct, but can not be "guaranteed."

% of PD	SB 899 Weeks of PD	2004 PD: See Table 17 B	(+/– 15%?) 2005 PD: @ Minimum $105/wk	2005 PD: Maximum 1 – 69 % @ $220/wk; 70 – 99 % @ $270/wk	(+/– 15%?) 2006 PD: @ Minimum $130/wk	2006 PD: Maximum 1 – 69 % @ $230/wk; 70 – 99 % @ $270/wk
51	279.25		$29,321.25	$61,435.00	$36,302.50	$64,227.50
52	287.25		$30,161.25	$63,195.00	$37,342.50	$66,067.50
53	295.25		$31,001.25	$64,955.00	$38,382.50	$67,907.50
54	303.25		$31,841.25	$66,715.00	$39,422.50	$69,747.50
55	**311.25**		**$32,681.25**	**$68,475.00**	**$40,462.50**	**$71,587.50**
56	319.25		$33,521.25	$70,235.00	$41,502.50	$73,427.50
57	327.25		$34,361.25	$71,995.00	$42,542.50	$75,267.50
58	335.25		$35,201.25	$73,755.00	$43,582.50	$77,107.50
59	343.25		$36,041.25	$75,515.00	$44,622.50	$78,947.50
60	**351.25**		**$36,881.25**	**$77,275.00**	**$45,662.50**	**$80,787.50**
61	359.25		$37,721.25	$79,035.00	$46,702.50	$82,627.50
62	367.25		$38,561.25	$80,795.00	$47,742.50	$84,467.50
63	375.25		$39,401.25	$82,555.00	$48,782.50	$86,307.50
64	383.25		$40,241.25	$84,315.00	$49,822.50	$88,147.50
65	**391.25**		**$41,081.25**	**$86,075.00**	**$50,862.50**	**$89,987.50**
66	399.25		$41,921.25	$87,835.00	$51,902.50	$91,827.50
67	407.25		$42,761.25	$89,595.00	$52,942.50	$93,667.50
68	415.25		$43,601.25	$91,355.00	$53,982.50	$95,507.50
69	423.25		$44,441.25	$93,115.00	$55,022.50	$97,347.50
70	**433.25**		**$45,491.25**	**$116,977.50**	**$56,322.50**	**$116,977.50**
71	449.25		$47,171.25	$121,297.50	$58,402.50	$121,297.50
72	465.25		$48,851.25	$125,617.50	$60,482.50	$125,617.50
73	481.25		$50,531.25	$129,937.50	$62,562.50	$129,937.50
74	497.25		$52,211.25	$134,257.50	$64,642.50	$134,257.50
75	**513.25**		**$53,891.25**	**$138,577.50**	**$66,722.50**	**$138,577.50**

If date of injury is 1/1/03 to 12/31/04, use Table 17B. If date of injury is 1/1/84 to 12/31/02, use Table 17C

Table 17 A, Permanent Disability Indemnity: For Injuries o/a the adoption of the 2005 Permanent Disability Rating Schedule (PDRS) on 1/1/05, per L.C. §§4658(d), 4660(d)

See Table 8 and Issues regarding the 2005 PDRS	**% of PD**	**SB 899** Weeks of PD	**2004 PD:** See Table 17 B	(+/- 15%?) 2005 PD: @ Minimum $105/wk	2005 PD: Maximum 1 - 69 % @ $220/wk; 70 - 99 % @ $270/wk	(+/- 15%?) 2006 PD: @ Minimum $130/wk	2006 PD: Maximum 1 - 69 % @ $230/wk; 70 - 99 % @ $270/wk
	76	529.25		$55,571.25	$142,897.50	$68,802.50	$142,897.50
	77	545.25		$57,251.25	$147,217.50	$70,882.50	$147,217.50
	78	561.25		$58,931.25	$151,537.50	$72,962.50	$151,537.50
	79	577.25		$60,611.25	$155,857.50	$75,042.50	$155,857.50
This table applies to injuries o/a the 1/01/05 adoption of the Permanent Disability Rating Schedule (PDRS).	**80**	**593.25**		**$62,291.25**	**$160,177.50**	**$77,122.50**	**$160,177.50**
	81	609.25		$63,971.25	$164,497.50	$79,202.50	$164,497.50
	82	625.25		$65,651.25	$168,817.50	$81,282.50	$168,817.50
	83	641.25		$67,331.25	$173,137.50	$83,362.50	$173,137.50
	84	657.25		$69,011.25	$177,457.50	$85,442.50	$177,457.50
Use Table 17B for injuries from 1/01/03 to 12/31/04 and Table 17C for injuries from 1984 to 12/31/02.	**85**	**673.25**		**$70,691.25**	**$181,777.50**	**$87,522.50**	**$181,777.50**
	86	689.25		$72,371.25	$186,097.50	$89,602.50	$186,097.50
	87	705.25		$74,051.25	$190,417.50	$91,682.50	$190,417.50
	88	721.25		$75,731.25	$194,737.50	$93,762.50	$194,737.50
	89	737.25		$77,411.25	$199,057.50	$95,842.50	$199,057.50
These Tables are believed to be correct, but can not be "guaranteed."	**90**	**753.25**		**$79,091.25**	**$203,377.50**	**$97,922.50**	**$203,377.50**
	91	769.25		$80,771.25	$207,697.50	$100,002.50	$207,697.50
	92	785.25		$82,451.25	$212,017.50	$102,082.50	$212,017.50
	93	801.25		$84,131.25	$216,337.50	$104,162.50	$216,337.50
	94	817.25		$85,811.25	$220,657.50	$106,242.50	$220,657.50
	95	**833.25**		**$87,491.25**	**$224,977.50**	**$108,322.50**	**$224,977.50**
	96	849.25		$89,171.25	$229,297.50	$110,402.50	$229,297.50
	97	865.25		$90,851.25	$233,617.50	$112,482.50	$233,617.50
	98	881.25		$92,531.25	$237,937.50	$114,562.50	$237,937.50
	99	897.25		$94,211.25	$242,257.50	$116,642.50	$242,257.50

100 % Permanent Total Disability is paid at the Temporary Total Disability rate for life per Labor Code § 4659(b)

Table 17 B, Permanent Disability Indemnity, Injuries 2003 through 12-31-04, but **see warnings** in Table 8

% of PD Injuries on/after 1/1/03	2003 Weeks of PD	2003 PD: @ Minimum $100/wk	Max 1 - 69:3 @ $185/wk 70 to 99:3 @ $230/wk	2004 Weeks of PD	2004 PD: @ Minimum $105/wk	Max 1 - 69:3 @ $200/wk 70 to 99:3 @ $250/wk
1	**3.00**	**300.00**	**555.00**	**4.00**	**420.00**	**800.00**
2	6.00	600.00	1,110.00	8.00	840.00	1,600.00
3	9.00	900.00	1,665.00	12.00	1,260.00	2,400.00
4	12.00	1,200.00	2,220.00	16.00	1,680.00	3,200.00
5	**15.00**	**1,500.00**	**2,775.00**	**20.00**	**2,100.00**	**4,000.00**
6	18.00	1,800.00	3,330.00	24.00	2,520.00	4,800.00
7	21.00	2,100.00	3,885.00	28.00	2,940.00	5,600.00
8	24.00	2,400.00	4,440.00	32.00	3,360.00	6,400.00
9	27.00	2,700.00	4,995.00	36.00	3,780.00	7,200.00
10	**30.25**	**3,025.00**	**5,596.25**	**40.25**	**4,226.25**	**8,050.00**
11	34.25	3,425.00	6,336.25	45.25	4,751.25	9,050.00
12	38.25	3,825.00	7,076.25	50.25	5,276.25	10,050.00
13	42.25	4,225.00	7,816.25	55.25	5,801.25	11,050.00
14	46.25	4,625.00	8,556.25	60.25	6,326.25	12,050.00
15	**50.25**	**5,025.00**	**9,296.25**	**65.25**	**6,851.25**	**13,050.00**
16	54.25	5,425.00	10,036.25	70.25	7,376.25	14,050.00
17	58.25	5,825.00	10,776.25	75.25	7,901.25	15,050.00
18	62.25	6,225.00	11,516.25	80.25	8,426.25	16,050.00
19	66.25	6,625.00	12,256.25	85.25	8,951.25	17,050.00
20	**70.50**	**7,050.00**	**13,042.50**	**90.25**	**9,476.25**	**18,050.00**
21	75.50	7,550.00	13,967.50	95.25	10,001.25	19,050.00
22	80.50	8,050.00	14,892.50	100.25	10,526.25	20,050.00
23	85.50	8,550.00	15,817.50	105.25	11,051.25	21,050.00
24	90.50	9,050.00	16,742.50	110.25	11,576.25	22,050.00
25	**95.75**	**9,575.00**	**17,713.75**	**115.50**	**12,127.50**	**23,100.00**

Injuries 1/1/03 to 12/31/04. If no PD per AME/QME/Treater until o/a 1/1/05, or if no L.C. § 4061 notice due, see Table 8

This table is for injuries 1/1/03 to 12/31/04. From 4/19/04 to 12/31/04 if there was NO medical-legal report or a treating physician's report stating there is permanent disability or NO notice was due per L.C. §4061, this table is to be used together with the Post-SB 899 PD Schedule which was adopted by the A.D. on 1/1/05.

For injuries o/a approval of the Post-SB 899 Schedule on 1/1/05, use Table 17 A and the Post-SB 899 Schedule.

Table 8 cites statutes involved and gives the rationale supporting when to use Table 17 A and 17 B. Case law hopefully will provide clarification soon. Meanwhile, if you are in doubt, seek legal advice.

These tables are not "guaranteed" to be correct, either as to content or when they do and do not apply.

For a more detailed explanation and for additional places to seek clarification, **SEE TABLE 8**.

Use this table if date of injury is 1/1/03 to 12/31/04 and if PD **has been found** or notice due, L.C. §4061. If D/A is 1/1/84 to 12/31/02, use Table 17 C

Table 17 B, Permanent Disability Indemnity, Injuries 2003 through 12-31-04, but **see warnings** in Table 8

% of PD Injuries on/after 1/1/03	2003 Weeks of PD	2003 PD: @ Minimum $100/wk	Max 1 - 69:3 @ $185/wk 70 to 99:3 @ $230/wk	2004 Weeks of PD	2004 PD: @ Minimum $105/wk	Max 1 - 69:3 @ $200/wk 70 to 99:3 @ $250/wk
26	101.75	10,175.00	18,823.75	121.50	12,757.50	24,300.00
27	107.75	10,775.00	19,933.75	127.50	13,387.50	25,500.00
28	113.75	11,375.00	21,043.75	133.50	14,017.50	26,700.00
29	119.75	11,975.00	22,153.75	139.50	14,647.50	27,900.00
30	**126.00**	**12,600.00**	**23,310.00**	**145.75**	**15,303.75**	**29,150.00**
31	133.00	13,300.00	24,605.00	152.75	16,038.75	30,550.00
32	140.00	14,000.00	25,900.00	159.75	16,773.75	31,950.00
33	147.00	14,700.00	27,195.00	166.75	17,508.75	33,350.00
34	154.00	15,400.00	28,490.00	173.75	18,243.75	34,750.00
35	**161.00**	**16,100.00**	**29,785.00**	**180.75**	**18,978.75**	**36,150.00**
36	168.00	16,800.00	31,080.00	187.75	19,713.75	37,550.00
37	175.00	17,500.00	32,375.00	194.75	20,448.75	38,950.00
38	182.00	18,200.00	33,670.00	201.75	21,183.75	40,350.00
39	189.00	18,900.00	34,965.00	208.75	21,918.75	41,750.00
40	**196.00**	**19,600.00**	**36,260.00**	**215.75**	**22,653.75**	**43,150.00**
41	203.00	20,300.00	37,555.00	222.75	23,388.75	44,550.00
42	210.00	21,000.00	38,850.00	229.75	24,123.75	45,950.00
43	217.00	21,700.00	40,145.00	236.75	24,858.75	47,350.00
44	224.00	22,400.00	41,440.00	243.75	25,593.75	48,750.00
45	**231.00**	**23,100.00**	**42,735.00**	**250.75**	**26,328.75**	**50,150.00**
46	238.00	23,800.00	44,030.00	257.75	27,063.75	51,550.00
47	245.00	24,500.00	45,325.00	264.75	27,798.75	52,950.00
48	252.00	25,200.00	46,620.00	271.75	28,533.75	54,350.00
49	259.00	25,900.00	47,915.00	278.75	29,268.75	55,750.00
50	**266.25**	**26,625.00**	**49,256.25**	**286.00**	**30,030.00**	**57,200.00**

Injuries 1/1/03 to 12/31/04. If no PD per AME/QME/Treater until o/a 1/1/05, or if no L.C. § 4061 notice due, see Table 8

This table is for injuries 1/1/03 to 12/31/04. From 4/19/04 to 12/31/04 if there was NO medical-legal report or a treating physician's report stating there is permanent disability or NO notice was due per L.C. §4061, this table is to be used together with the Post-SB 899 PD Schedule which was adopted by the A.D. on 1/1/05.

For injuries o/a approval of the Post-SB 899 Schedule on 1/1/05, use Table 17 A and the Post-SB 899 Schedule.

Table 8 cites statutes involved and gives the rationale supporting when to use Table 17 A and 17 B. Case law hopefully will provide clarification soon. Meanwhile, if you are in doubt, seek legal advice.

These tables are not "guaranteed" to be correct, either as to content or when they do and do not apply.

For a more detailed explanation and for additional places to seek clarification, **SEE TABLE 8.**

Use this table if date of injury is 1/1/03 to 12/31/04 and if PD **has been found** or notice due, L.C. §4061. If D/A is 1/1/84 to 12/31/02, use Table 17 C

Table 17 B, Permanent Disability Indemnity, Injuries 2003 through 12-31-04, but **see warnings** in Table 8

% of PD Injuries on/after 1/1/03	2003 Weeks of PD	2003 PD: @ Minimum $100/wk	Max 1 - 69:3 @ $185/wk 70 to 99:3 @ $230/wk	2004 Weeks of PD	2004 PD: @ Minimum $105/wk	Max 1 - 69:3 @ $200/wk 70 to 99:3 @ $250/wk
51	274.25	27,425.00	50,736.25	294.00	30,870.00	58,800.00
52	282.25	28,225.00	52,216.25	302.00	31,710.00	60,400.00
53	290.25	29,025.00	53,696.25	310.00	32,550.00	62,000.00
54	298.25	29,825.00	55,176.25	318.00	33,390.00	63,600.00
55	**306.25**	**30,625.00**	**56,656.25**	**326.00**	**34,230.00**	**65,200.00**
56	314.25	31,425.00	58,136.25	334.00	35,070.00	66,800.00
57	322.25	32,225.00	59,616.25	342.00	35,910.00	68,400.00
58	330.25	33,025.00	61,096.25	350.00	36,750.00	70,000.00
59	338.25	33,825.00	62,576.25	358.00	37,590.00	71,600.00
60	**346.25**	**34,625.00**	**64,056.25**	**366.00**	**38,430.00**	**73,200.00**
61	354.25	35,425.00	65,536.25	374.00	39,270.00	74,800.00
62	362.25	36,225.00	67,016.25	382.00	40,110.00	76,400.00
63	370.25	37,025.00	68,496.25	390.00	40,950.00	78,000.00
64	378.25	37,825.00	69,976.25	398.00	41,790.00	79,600.00
65	**386.25**	**38,625.00**	**71,456.25**	**406.00**	**42,630.00**	**81,200.00**
66	394.25	39,425.00	72,936.25	414.00	43,470.00	82,800.00
67	402.25	40,225.00	74,416.25	422.00	44,310.00	84,400.00
68	410.25	41,025.00	75,896.25	430.00	45,150.00	86,000.00
69	418.25	41,825.00	77,376.25	438.00	45,990.00	87,600.00
70	***426.50***	***42,650.00***	***98,095.00***	***446.25***	***46,856.25***	***111,562.50***
71	435.50	43,550.00	100,165.00	455.25	47,801.25	113,812.50
72	444.50	44,450.00	102,235.00	464.25	48,746.25	116,062.50
73	453.50	45,350.00	104,305.00	473.25	49,691.25	118,312.50
74	462.50	46,250.00	106,375.00	482.25	50,636.25	120,562.50
75	**471.50**	**47,150.00**	**108,445.00**	**491.25**	**51,581.25**	**122,812.50**

Injuries 1/1/03 to 12/31/04. If no PD per AME/QME/Treater until o/a 1/1/05, or if no L.C. § 4061 notice due, see Table 8

This table is for injuries 1/1/03 to 12/31/04. From 4/19/04 to 12/31/04 if there was NO medical-legal report or a treating physician's report stating there is permanent disability or NO notice was due per L.C. §4061, this table is to be used together with the Post-SB 899 PD Schedule which was adopted by the A.D. on 1/1/05.

For injuries o/a approval of the Post-SB 899 Schedule on 1/1/05, use Table 17 A and the Post-SB 899 Schedule.

Table 8 cites statutes involved and gives the rationale supporting when to use Table 17 A and 17 B. Case law hopefully will provide clarification soon. Meanwhile, if you are in doubt, seek legal advice.

These tables are not "guaranteed" to be correct, either as to content or when they do and do not apply.

For a more detailed explanation and for additional places to seek clarification, **SEE TABLE 8.**

Use this table if date of injury is 1/1/03 to 12/31/04 and if PD **has been found** or notice due, L.C. §4061. If D/A is 1/1/84 to 12/31/02, use Table 17 C

Table 17 B, Permanent Disability Indemnity, Injuries 2003 through 12/31/04, but see warnings in Table 8

% of PD Injuries on/after 1/1/03	2003 Weeks of PD	2003 PD: @ Minimum $100/wk	Max 1 - 69:3 @ $185/wk 70 to 99:3 @ $230/wk	2004 Weeks of PD	2004 PD: @ Minimum $105/wk	Max 1 - 69:3 @ $200/wk 70 to 99:3 @ $250/wk
76	480.50	48,050.00	110,515.00	500.25	52,526.25	125,062.50
77	489.50	48,950.00	112,585.00	509.25	53,471.25	127,312.50
78	498.50	49,850.00	114,655.00	518.25	54,416.25	129,562.50
79	507.50	50,750.00	116,725.00	527.25	55,361.25	131,812.50
80	**516.50**	**51,650.00**	**118,795.00**	**536.25**	**56,306.25**	**134,062.50**
81	525.50	52,550.00	120,865.00	545.25	57,251.25	136,312.50
82	534.50	53,450.00	122,935.00	554.25	58,196.25	138,562.50
83	543.50	54,350.00	125,005.00	563.25	59,141.25	140,812.50
84	552.50	55,250.00	127,075.00	572.25	60,086.25	143,062.50
85	**561.50**	**56,150.00**	**129,145.00**	**581.25**	**61,031.25**	**145,312.50**
86	570.50	57,050.00	131,215.00	590.25	61,976.25	147,562.50
87	579.50	57,950.00	133,285.00	599.25	62,921.25	149,812.50
88	588.50	58,850.00	135,355.00	608.25	63,866.25	152,062.50
89	597.50	59,750.00	137,425.00	617.25	64,811.25	154,312.50
90	**606.50**	**60,650.00**	**139,495.00**	**626.25**	**65,756.25**	**156,562.50**
91	615.50	61,550.00	141,565.00	635.25	66,701.25	158,812.50
92	624.50	62,450.00	143,635.00	644.25	67,646.25	161,062.50
93	633.50	63,350.00	145,705.00	653.25	68,591.25	163,312.50
94	642.50	64,250.00	147,775.00	662.25	69,536.25	165,562.50
95	**651.50**	**65,150.00**	**149,845.00**	**671.25**	**70,481.25**	**167,812.50**
96	660.50	66,050.00	151,915.00	680.25	71,426.25	170,062.50
97	669.50	66,950.00	153,985.00	689.25	72,371.25	172,312.50
98	678.50	67,850.00	156,055.00	698.25	73,316.25	174,562.50
99	687.50	68,750.00	158,125.00	707.25	74,261.25	176,812.50

Injuries 1/1/03 to 12/31/04. If no PD per AME/QME/Treater until o/a 1/1/05, or if no L.C. § 4061 notice due, see Table 8

This table is for injuries 1/1/03 to 12/31/04. From 4/19/04 to 12/31/04 if there was NO medical-legal report or a treating physician's report stating there is permanent disability or NO notice was due per L.C. §4061, this table is to be used together with the Post-SB 899 PD Schedule which was adopted by the A.D. on 1/1/05.

For injuries o/a approval of the Post-SB 899 Schedule on 1/1/05, use Table 17 A and the Post-SB 899 Schedule.

Table 8 cites statutes involved and gives the rationale supporting when to use Table 17 A and 17 B. Case law hopefully will provide clarification soon. Meanwhile, if you are in doubt, seek legal advice.

These tables are not "guaranteed" to be correct, either as to content or when they do and do not apply.

For a more detailed explanation and for additional places to seek clarification, **SEE TABLE 8.**

100 % Permanent Total Disability is paid at the Temporary Total Disability rate for life per Labor Code § 4659(b)

Table 17 C, Permanent Disability Indemnity, Injuries 1984 through 2002

% of P.D.	1984-'91 # of WEEKS	Minimum @ $70/wk ≥ 1984	Maximum 1984 to 12-31-90	1991 @ $148/wk, ≥ 25%	1-1-92+ # of WEEKS	to 6-30-94 @ $148 ≥ 25% Total $	7-1-94 to 6-30-95 Max / Week	7-1-94 to 6-30-95 Total $	7-1-95 to 6-30-96 Max / Week	7-1-95 to 6-30-96 Total $	7-1-96 to 12-31-02 Max / Week	7-1-96 to 12-31-02 Total $
1.00	3.00	210.00	420.00	420.00	**3.00**	420.00	140	420.00	140	420.00	140	420.00
1.25	3.75	262.50	525.00	525.00	3.75	525.00	140	525.00	140	525.00	140	525.00
1.50	4.50	315.00	630.00	630.00	4.50	630.00	140	630.00	140	630.00	140	630.00
1.75	5.25	367.50	735.00	735.00	5.25	735.00	140	735.00	140	735.00	140	735.00
2.00	6.00	420.00	840.00	840.00	**6.00**	840.00	140	840.00	140	840.00	140	840.00
2.25	6.75	472.50	945.00	945.00	6.75	945.00	140	945.00	140	945.00	140	945.00
2.50	7.50	525.00	1,050.00	1,050.00	7.50	1,050.00	140	1,050.00	140	1,050.00	140	1,050.00
2.75	8.25	577.50	1,155.00	1,155.00	8.25	1,155.00	140	1,155.00	140	1,155.00	140	1,155.00
3.00	9.00	630.00	1,260.00	1,260.00	**9.00**	1,260.00	140	1,260.00	140	1,260.00	140	1,260.00
3.25	9.75	682.50	1,365.00	1,365.00	9.75	1,365.00	140	1,365.00	140	1,365.00	140	1,365.00
3.50	10.50	735.00	1,470.00	1,470.00	10.50	1,470.00	140	1,470.00	140	1,470.00	140	1,470.00
3.75	11.25	787.50	1,575.00	1,575.00	11.25	1,575.00	140	1,575.00	140	1,575.00	140	1,575.00
4.00	12.00	840.00	1,680.00	1,680.00	**12.00**	1,680.00	140	1,680.00	140	1,680.00	140	1,680.00
4.25	12.75	892.50	1,785.00	1,785.00	12.75	1,785.00	140	1,785.00	140	1,785.00	140	1,785.00
4.50	13.50	945.00	1,890.00	1,890.00	13.50	1,890.00	140	1,890.00	140	1,890.00	140	1,890.00
4.75	14.25	997.50	1,995.00	1,995.00	14.25	1,995.00	140	1,995.00	140	1,995.00	140	1,995.00
5.00	15.00	1,050.00	2,100.00	2,100.00	**15.00**	2,100.00	140	2,100.00	140	2,100.00	140	2,100.00
5.25	15.75	1,102.50	2,205.00	2,205.00	15.75	2,205.00	140	2,205.00	140	2,205.00	140	2,205.00
5.50	16.50	1,155.00	2,310.00	2,310.00	16.50	2,310.00	140	2,310.00	140	2,310.00	140	2,310.00
5.75	17.25	1,207.50	2,415.00	2,415.00	17.25	2,415.00	140	2,415.00	140	2,415.00	140	2,415.00
6.00	18.00	1,260.00	2,520.00	2,520.00	**18.00**	2,520.00	140	2,520.00	140	2,520.00	140	2,520.00
6.25	18.75	1,312.50	2,625.00	2,625.00	18.75	2,625.00	140	2,625.00	140	2,625.00	140	2,625.00
6.50	19.50	1,365.00	2,730.00	2,730.00	19.50	2,730.00	140	2,730.00	140	2,730.00	140	2,730.00
6.75	20.25	1,417.50	2,835.00	2,835.00	20.25	2,835.00	140	2,835.00	140	2,835.00	140	2,835.00
7.00	21.00	1,470.00	2,940.00	2,940.00	**21.00**	2,940.00	140	2,940.00	140	2,940.00	140	2,940.00
7.25	21.75	1,522.50	3,045.00	3,045.00	21.75	3,045.00	140	3,045.00	140	3,045.00	140	3,045.00
7.50	22.50	1,575.00	3,150.00	3,150.00	22.50	3,150.00	140	3,150.00	140	3,150.00	140	3,150.00
7.75	23.25	1,627.50	3,255.00	3,255.00	23.25	3,255.00	140	3,255.00	140	3,255.00	140	3,255.00
8.00	24.00	1,680.00	3,360.00	3,360.00	**24.00**	3,360.00	140	3,360.00	140	3,360.00	140	3,360.00
8.25	24.75	1,732.50	3,465.00	3,465.00	24.75	3,465.00	140	3,465.00	140	3,465.00	140	3,465.00
8.50	25.50	1,785.00	3,570.00	3,570.00	25.50	3,570.00	140	3,570.00	140	3,570.00	140	3,570.00
8.75	26.25	1,837.50	3,675.00	3,675.00	26.25	3,675.00	140	3,675.00	140	3,675.00	140	3,675.00
9.00	27.00	1,890.00	3,780.00	3,780.00	**27.00**	3,780.00	140	3,780.00	140	3,780.00	140	3,780.00
9.25	27.75	1,942.50	3,885.00	3,885.00	27.75	3,885.00	140	3,885.00	140	3,885.00	140	3,885.00
9.50	28.50	1,995.00	3,990.00	3,990.00	28.50	3,990.00	140	3,990.00	140	3,990.00	140	3,990.00
9.75	29.25	2,047.50	4,095.00	4,095.00	29.25	4,095.00	140	4,095.00	140	4,095.00	140	4,095.00
10.00	30.25	2,117.50	4,235.00	4,235.00	**30.25**	4,235.00	140	4,235.00	140	4,235.00	140	4,235.00
10.25	31.25	2,187.50	4,375.00	4,375.00	31.25	4,375.00	140	4,375.00	140	4,375.00	140	4,375.00
10.50	32.25	2,257.50	4,515.00	4,515.00	32.25	4,515.00	140	4,515.00	140	4,515.00	140	4,515.00
10.75	33.25	2,327.50	4,655.00	4,655.00	33.25	4,655.00	140	4,655.00	140	4,655.00	140	4,655.00

Table 17 C, Permanent Disability Indemnity, Injuries 1984 through 2002

% of P.D.	1984-'91 # of Weeks	Minimum @ $70/wk ≥ 1984	Maximum 1984 to 12-31-90	1991 @ $148/wk, ≥ 25%	1-1-92+ # of Weeks	to 6-30-94 @ $148 ≥ 25% Total $	7-1-94 to 6-30-95 Max / Week	7-1-94 to 6-30-95 Total $	7-1-95 to 6-30-96 Max / Week	7-1-95 to 6-30-96 Total $	7-1-96 to 12-31-02 Max / Week	7-1-96 to 12-31-02 Total $
11.00	34.25	2,397.50	4,795.00	4,795.00	**34.25**	4,795.00	140	4,795.00	140	4,795.00	140	4,795.00
11.25	35.25	2,467.50	4,935.00	4,935.00	35.25	4,935.00	140	4,935.00	140	4,935.00	140	4,935.00
11.50	36.25	2,537.50	5,075.00	5,075.00	36.25	5,075.00	140	5,075.00	140	5,075.00	140	5,075.00
11.75	37.25	2,607.50	5,215.00	5,215.00	37.25	5,215.00	140	5,215.00	140	5,215.00	140	5,215.00
12.00	38.25	2,677.50	5,355.00	5,355.00	**38.25**	5,355.00	140	5,355.00	140	5,355.00	140	5,355.00
12.25	39.25	2,747.50	5,495.00	5,495.00	39.25	5,495.00	140	5,495.00	140	5,495.00	140	5,495.00
12.50	40.25	2,817.50	5,635.00	5,635.00	40.25	5,635.00	140	5,635.00	140	5,635.00	140	5,635.00
12.75	41.25	2,887.50	5,775.00	5,775.00	41.25	5,775.00	140	5,775.00	140	5,775.00	140	5,775.00
13.00	42.25	2,957.50	5,915.00	5,915.00	**42.25**	5,915.00	140	5,915.00	140	5,915.00	140	5,915.00
13.25	43.25	3,027.50	6,055.00	6,055.00	43.25	6,055.00	140	6,055.00	140	6,055.00	140	6,055.00
13.50	44.25	3,097.50	6,195.00	6,195.00	44.25	6,195.00	140	6,195.00	140	6,195.00	140	6,195.00
13.75	45.25	3,167.50	6,335.00	6,335.00	45.25	6,335.00	140	6,335.00	140	6,335.00	140	6,335.00
14.00	46.25	3,237.50	6,475.00	6,475.00	**46.25**	6,475.00	140	6,475.00	140	6,475.00	140	6,475.00
14.25	47.25	3,307.50	6,615.00	6,615.00	47.25	6,615.00	140	6,615.00	140	6,615.00	140	6,615.00
14.50	48.25	3,377.50	6,755.00	6,755.00	48.25	6,755.00	140	6,755.00	140	6,755.00	140	6,755.00
14.75	49.25	3,447.50	6,895.00	6,895.00	49.25	6,895.00	140	6,895.00	140	6,895.00	140	6,895.00
15.00	50.25	3,517.50	7,035.00	7,035.00	**50.25**	7,035.00	**148**	**7,437.00**	**154**	**7,738.50**	**160**	**8,040.00**
15.25	51.25	3,587.50	7,175.00	7,175.00	51.25	7,175.00	148	7,585.00	154	7,892.50	160	8,200.00
15.50	52.25	3,657.50	7,315.00	7,315.00	52.25	7,315.00	148	7,733.00	154	8,046.50	160	8,360.00
15.75	53.25	3,727.50	7,455.00	7,455.00	53.25	7,455.00	148	7,881.00	154	8,200.50	160	8,520.00
16.00	54.25	3,797.50	7,595.00	7,595.00	**54.25**	7,595.00	148	8,029.00	154	8,354.50	160	8,680.00
16.25	55.25	3,867.50	7,735.00	7,735.00	55.25	7,735.00	148	8,177.00	154	8,508.50	160	8,840.00
16.50	56.25	3,937.50	7,875.00	7,875.00	56.25	7,875.00	148	8,325.00	154	8,662.50	160	9,000.00
16.75	57.25	4,007.50	8,015.00	8,015.00	57.25	8,015.00	148	8,473.00	154	8,816.50	160	9,160.00
17.00	58.25	4,077.50	8,155.00	8,155.00	**58.25**	8,155.00	148	8,621.00	154	8,970.50	160	9,320.00
17.25	59.25	4,147.50	8,295.00	8,295.00	59.25	8,295.00	148	8,769.00	154	9,124.50	160	9,480.00
17.50	60.25	4,217.50	8,435.00	8,435.00	60.25	8,435.00	148	8,917.00	154	9,278.50	160	9,640.00
17.75	61.25	4,287.50	8,575.00	8,575.00	61.25	8,575.00	148	9,065.00	154	9,432.50	160	9,800.00
18.00	62.25	4,357.50	8,715.00	8,715.00	**62.25**	8,715.00	148	9,213.00	154	9,586.50	160	9,960.00
18.25	63.25	4,427.50	8,855.00	8,855.00	63.25	8,855.00	148	9,361.00	154	9,740.50	160	10,120.00
18.50	64.25	4,497.50	8,995.00	8,995.00	64.25	8,995.00	148	9,509.00	154	9,894.50	160	10,280.00
18.75	65.25	4,567.50	9,135.00	9,135.00	65.25	9,135.00	148	9,657.00	154	10,048.50	160	10,440.00
19.00	66.25	4,637.50	9,275.00	9,275.00	**66.25**	9,275.00	148	9,805.00	154	10,202.50	160	10,600.00
19.25	67.25	4,707.50	9,415.00	9,415.00	67.25	9,415.00	148	9,953.00	154	10,356.50	160	10,760.00
19.50	68.25	4,777.50	9,555.00	9,555.00	68.25	9,555.00	148	10,101.00	154	10,510.50	160	10,920.00
19.75	69.25	4,847.50	9,695.00	9,695.00	69.25	9,695.00	148	10,249.00	154	10,664.50	160	11,080.00
20.00	70.50	4,935.00	9,870.00	9,870.00	**70.50**	9,870.00	148	10,434.00	154	10,857.00	160	11,280.00
20.25	71.75	5,022.50	10,045.00	10,045.00	71.75	10,045.00	148	10,619.00	154	11,049.50	160	11,480.00
20.50	73.00	5,110.00	10,220.00	10,220.00	73.00	10,220.00	148	10,804.00	154	11,242.00	160	11,680.00
20.75	74.25	5,197.50	10,395.00	10,395.00	74.25	10,395.00	148	10,989.00	154	11,434.50	160	11,880.00

Table 17 C, Permanent Disability Indemnity, Injuries 1984 through 2002

% of P.D.	1984-'91 # of WEEKS	Minimum @ $70/wk ≥ 1984	Maximum 1984 to 12-31-90	1991 @ $148/wk, ≥ 25%	1-1-92+ # of WEEKS	to 6-30-94 @ $148 ≥ 25% Total $	7-1-94 to 6-30-95 Max / Week	7-1-94 to 6-30-95 Total $	7-1-95 to 6-30-96 Max / Week	7-1-95 to 6-30-96 Total $	7-1-96 to 12-31-02 Max / Week	7-1-96 to 12-31-02 Total $
21.00	75.50	5,285.00	10,570.00	10,570.00	**75.50**	10,570.00	148	11,174.00	154	11,627.00	160	12,080.00
21.25	76.75	5,372.50	10,745.00	10,745.00	76.75	10,745.00	148	11,359.00	154	11,819.50	160	12,280.00
21.50	78.00	5,460.00	10,920.00	10,920.00	78.00	10,920.00	148	11,544.00	154	12,012.00	160	12,480.00
21.75	79.25	5,547.50	11,095.00	11,095.00	79.25	11,095.00	148	11,729.00	154	12,204.50	160	12,680.00
22.00	80.50	5,635.00	11,270.00	11,270.00	**80.50**	11,270.00	148	11,914.00	154	12,397.00	160	12,880.00
22.25	81.75	5,722.50	11,445.00	11,445.00	81.75	11,445.00	148	12,099.00	154	12,589.50	160	13,080.00
22.50	83.00	5,810.00	11,620.00	11,620.00	83.00	11,620.00	148	12,284.00	154	12,782.00	160	13,280.00
22.75	84.25	5,897.50	11,795.00	11,795.00	84.25	11,795.00	148	12,469.00	154	12,974.50	160	13,480.00
23.00	85.50	5,985.00	11,970.00	11,970.00	**85.50**	11,970.00	148	12,654.00	154	13,167.00	160	13,680.00
23.25	86.75	6,072.50	12,145.00	12,145.00	86.75	12,145.00	148	12,839.00	154	13,359.50	160	13,880.00
23.50	88.00	6,160.00	12,320.00	12,320.00	88.00	12,320.00	148	13,024.00	154	13,552.00	160	14,080.00
23.75	89.25	6,247.50	12,495.00	12,495.00	89.25	12,495.00	148	13,209.00	154	13,744.50	160	14,280.00
24.00	90.50	6,335.00	12,670.00	12,670.00	**90.50**	12,670.00	148	13,394.00	154	13,937.00	160	14,480.00
24.25	91.75	6,422.50	12,845.00	12,845.00	91.75	12,845.00	148	13,579.00	154	14,129.50	160	14,680.00
24.50	93.00	6,510.00	13,020.00	13,020.00	93.00	13,020.00	148	13,764.00	154	14,322.00	160	14,880.00
24.75	94.25	6,597.50	13,195.00	13,195.00	94.25	13,195.00	148	13,949.00	154	14,514.50	160	15,080.00
25.00	95.50	6,685.00	**13,370.00**	**14,134.00**	**95.75**	**14,171.00**	**158**	**15,128.50**	**164**	**15,703.00**	**170**	**16,277.50**
25.25	96.75	6,772.50	13,545.00	14,319.00	97.25	14,393.00	158	15,365.50	164	15,949.00	170	16,532.50
25.50	98.00	6,860.00	13,720.00	14,504.00	98.75	14,615.00	158	15,602.50	164	16,195.00	170	16,787.50
25.75	99.25	6,947.50	13,895.00	14,689.00	100.25	14,837.00	158	15,839.50	164	16,441.00	170	17,042.50
26.00	100.50	7,035.00	14,070.00	14,874.00	**101.75**	15,059.00	158	16,076.50	164	16,687.00	170	17,297.50
26.25	101.75	7,122.50	14,245.00	15,059.00	103.25	15,281.00	158	16,313.50	164	16,933.00	170	17,552.50
26.50	103.00	7,210.00	14,420.00	15,244.00	104.75	15,503.00	158	16,550.50	164	17,179.00	170	17,807.50
26.75	104.25	7,297.50	14,595.00	15,429.00	106.25	15,725.00	158	16,787.50	164	17,425.00	170	18,062.50
27.00	105.50	7,385.00	14,770.00	15,614.00	**107.75**	15,947.00	158	17,024.50	164	17,671.00	170	18,317.50
27.25	106.75	7,472.50	14,945.00	15,799.00	109.25	16,169.00	158	17,261.50	164	17,917.00	170	18,572.50
27.50	108.00	7,560.00	15,120.00	15,984.00	110.75	16,391.00	158	17,498.50	164	18,163.00	170	18,827.50
27.75	109.25	7,647.50	15,295.00	16,169.00	112.25	16,613.00	158	17,735.50	164	18,409.00	170	19,082.50
28.00	110.50	7,735.00	15,470.00	16,354.00	**113.75**	16,835.00	158	17,972.50	164	18,655.00	170	19,337.50
28.25	111.75	7,822.50	15,645.00	16,539.00	115.25	17,057.00	158	18,209.50	164	18,901.00	170	19,592.50
28.50	113.00	7,910.00	15,820.00	16,724.00	116.75	17,279.00	158	18,446.50	164	19,147.00	170	19,847.50
28.75	114.25	7,997.50	15,995.00	16,909.00	118.25	17,501.00	158	18,683.50	164	19,393.00	170	20,102.50
29.00	115.50	8,085.00	16,170.00	17,094.00	**119.75**	17,723.00	158	18,920.50	164	19,639.00	170	20,357.50
29.25	116.75	8,172.50	16,345.00	17,279.00	121.25	17,945.00	158	19,157.50	164	19,885.00	170	20,612.50
29.50	118.00	8,260.00	16,520.00	17,464.00	122.75	18,167.00	158	19,394.50	164	20,131.00	170	20,867.50
29.75	119.25	8,347.50	16,695.00	17,649.00	124.25	18,389.00	158	19,631.50	164	20,377.00	170	21,122.50
30.00	120.75	8,452.50	16,905.00	17,871.00	**126.00**	18,648.00	158	19,908.00	164	20,664.00	170	21,420.00
30.25	122.25	8,557.50	17,115.00	18,093.00	127.75	18,907.00	158	20,184.50	164	20,951.00	170	21,717.50
30.50	123.75	8,662.50	17,325.00	18,315.00	129.50	19,166.00	158	20,461.00	164	21,238.00	170	22,015.00
30.75	125.25	8,767.50	17,535.00	18,537.00	131.25	19,425.00	158	20,737.50	164	21,525.00	170	22,312.50

Table 17 C, Permanent Disability Indemnity, Injuries 1984 through 2002

% of P.D.	1984-'91 # of Weeks	Minimum @ $70/wk ≥ 1984	Maximum 1984 to 12-31-90	1991 @ $148/wk, ≥ 25%	1-1-92+ # of Weeks	to 6-30-94 @ $148 ≥ 25% Total $	7-1-94 to 6-30-95 Max / Week	7-1-94 to 6-30-95 Total $	7-1-95 to 6-30-96 Max / Week	7-1-95 to 6-30-96 Total $	7-1-96 to 12-31-02 Max / Week	7-1-96 to 12-31-02 Total $
31.00	126.75	8,872.50	17,745.00	18,759.00	**133.00**	19,684.00	158	21,014.00	164	21,812.00	170	22,610.00
31.25	128.25	8,977.50	17,955.00	18,981.00	134.75	19,943.00	158	21,290.50	164	22,099.00	170	22,907.50
31.50	129.75	9,082.50	18,165.00	19,203.00	136.50	20,202.00	158	21,567.00	164	22,386.00	170	23,205.00
31.75	131.25	9,187.50	18,375.00	19,425.00	138.25	20,461.00	158	21,843.50	164	22,673.00	170	23,502.50
32.00	132.75	9,292.50	18,585.00	19,647.00	**140.00**	20,720.00	158	22,120.00	164	22,960.00	170	23,800.00
32.25	134.25	9,397.50	18,795.00	19,869.00	141.75	20,979.00	158	22,396.50	164	23,247.00	170	24,097.50
32.50	135.75	9,502.50	19,005.00	20,091.00	143.50	21,238.00	158	22,673.00	164	23,534.00	170	24,395.00
32.75	137.25	9,607.50	19,215.00	20,313.00	145.25	21,497.00	158	22,949.50	164	23,821.00	170	24,692.50
33.00	138.75	9,712.50	19,425.00	20,535.00	**147.00**	21,756.00	158	23,226.00	164	24,108.00	170	24,990.00
33.25	140.25	9,817.50	19,635.00	20,757.00	148.75	22,015.00	158	23,502.50	164	24,395.00	170	25,287.50
33.50	141.75	9,922.50	19,845.00	20,979.00	150.50	22,274.00	158	23,779.00	164	24,682.00	170	25,585.00
33.75	143.25	10,027.50	20,055.00	21,201.00	152.25	22,533.00	158	24,055.50	164	24,969.00	170	25,882.50
34.00	144.75	10,132.50	20,265.00	21,423.00	**154.00**	22,792.00	158	24,332.00	164	25,256.00	170	26,180.00
34.25	146.25	10,237.50	20,475.00	21,645.00	155.75	23,051.00	158	24,608.50	164	25,543.00	170	26,477.50
34.50	147.75	10,342.50	20,685.00	21,867.00	157.50	23,310.00	158	24,885.00	164	25,830.00	170	26,775.00
34.75	149.25	10,447.50	20,895.00	22,089.00	159.25	23,569.00	158	25,161.50	164	26,117.00	170	27,072.50
35.00	150.75	10,552.50	21,105.00	22,311.00	**161.00**	23,828.00	158	25,438.00	164	26,404.00	170	27,370.00
35.25	152.25	10,657.50	21,315.00	22,533.00	162.75	24,087.00	158	25,714.50	164	26,691.00	170	27,667.50
35.50	153.75	10,762.50	21,525.00	22,755.00	164.50	24,346.00	158	25,991.00	164	26,978.00	170	27,965.00
35.75	155.25	10,867.50	21,735.00	22,977.00	166.25	24,605.00	158	26,267.50	164	27,265.00	170	28,262.50
36.00	156.75	10,972.50	21,945.00	23,199.00	**168.00**	24,864.00	158	26,544.00	164	27,552.00	170	28,560.00
36.25	158.25	11,077.50	22,155.00	23,421.00	169.75	25,123.00	158	26,820.50	164	27,839.00	170	28,857.50
36.50	159.75	11,182.50	22,365.00	23,643.00	171.50	25,382.00	158	27,097.00	164	28,126.00	170	29,155.00
36.75	161.25	11,287.50	22,575.00	23,865.00	173.25	25,641.00	158	27,373.50	164	28,413.00	170	29,452.50
37.00	162.75	11,392.50	22,785.00	24,087.00	**175.00**	25,900.00	158	27,650.00	164	28,700.00	170	29,750.00
37.25	164.25	11,497.50	22,995.00	24,309.00	176.75	26,159.00	158	27,926.50	164	28,987.00	170	30,047.50
37.50	165.75	11,602.50	23,205.00	24,531.00	178.50	26,418.00	158	28,203.00	164	29,274.00	170	30,345.00
37.75	167.25	11,707.50	23,415.00	24,753.00	180.25	26,677.00	158	28,479.50	164	29,561.00	170	30,642.50
38.00	168.75	11,812.50	23,625.00	24,975.00	**182.00**	26,936.00	158	28,756.00	164	29,848.00	170	30,940.00
38.25	170.25	11,917.50	23,835.00	25,197.00	183.75	27,195.00	158	29,032.50	164	30,135.00	170	31,237.50
38.50	171.75	12,022.50	24,045.00	25,419.00	185.50	27,454.00	158	29,309.00	164	30,422.00	170	31,535.00
38.75	173.25	12,127.50	24,255.00	25,641.00	187.25	27,713.00	158	29,585.50	164	30,709.00	170	31,832.50
39.00	174.75	12,232.50	24,465.00	25,863.00	**189.00**	27,972.00	158	29,862.00	164	30,996.00	170	32,130.00
39.25	176.25	12,337.50	24,675.00	26,085.00	190.75	28,231.00	158	30,138.50	164	31,283.00	170	32,427.50
39.50	177.75	12,442.50	24,885.00	26,307.00	192.50	28,490.00	158	30,415.00	164	31,570.00	170	32,725.00
39.75	179.25	12,547.50	25,095.00	26,529.00	194.25	28,749.00	158	30,691.50	164	31,857.00	170	33,022.50
40.00	180.75	12,652.50	25,305.00	26,751.00	**196.00**	29,008.00	158	30,968.00	164	32,144.00	170	33,320.00
40.25	182.25	12,757.50	25,515.00	26,973.00	197.75	29,267.00	158	31,244.50	164	32,431.00	170	33,617.50
40.50	183.75	12,862.50	25,725.00	27,195.00	199.50	29,526.00	158	31,521.00	164	32,718.00	170	33,915.00
40.75	185.25	12,967.50	25,935.00	27,417.00	201.25	29,785.00	158	31,797.50	164	33,005.00	170	34,212.50

Table 17 C, Permanent Disability Indemnity, Injuries 1984 through 2002

% of P.D.	1984-'91 # of WEEKS	Minimum @ $70/wk ≥ 1984	Maximum 1984 to 12-31-90	1991 @ $148/wk, ≥ 25%	1-1-92+ # of WEEKS	to 6-30-94 @ $148 ≥ 25% Total $	7-1-94 to 6-30-95 Max / Week	7-1-94 to 6-30-95 Total $	7-1-95 to 6-30-96 Max / Week	7-1-95 to 6-30-96 Total $	7-1-96 to 12-31-02 Max / Week	7-1-96 to 12-31-02 Total $
41.00	186.75	13,072.50	26,145.00	27,639.00	**203.00**	30,044.00	158	32,074.00	164	33,292.00	170	34,510.00
41.25	188.25	13,177.50	26,355.00	27,861.00	204.75	30,303.00	158	32,350.50	164	33,579.00	170	34,807.50
41.50	189.75	13,282.50	26,565.00	28,083.00	206.50	30,562.00	158	32,627.00	164	33,866.00	170	35,105.00
41.75	191.25	13,387.50	26,775.00	28,305.00	208.25	30,821.00	158	32,903.50	164	34,153.00	170	35,402.50
42.00	192.75	13,492.50	26,985.00	28,527.00	**210.00**	31,080.00	158	33,180.00	164	34,440.00	170	35,700.00
42.25	194.25	13,597.50	27,195.00	28,749.00	211.75	31,339.00	158	33,456.50	164	34,727.00	170	35,997.50
42.50	195.75	13,702.50	27,405.00	28,971.00	213.50	31,598.00	158	33,733.00	164	35,014.00	170	36,295.00
42.75	197.25	13,807.50	27,615.00	29,193.00	215.25	31,857.00	158	34,009.50	164	35,301.00	170	36,592.50
43.00	198.75	13,912.50	27,825.00	29,415.00	**217.00**	32,116.00	158	34,286.00	164	35,588.00	170	36,890.00
43.25	200.25	14,017.50	28,035.00	29,637.00	218.75	32,375.00	158	34,562.50	164	35,875.00	170	37,187.50
43.50	201.75	14,122.50	28,245.00	29,859.00	220.50	32,634.00	158	34,839.00	164	36,162.00	170	37,485.00
43.75	203.25	14,227.50	28,455.00	30,081.00	222.25	32,893.00	158	35,115.50	164	36,449.00	170	37,782.50
44.00	204.75	14,332.50	28,665.00	30,303.00	**224.00**	33,152.00	158	35,392.00	164	36,736.00	170	38,080.00
44.25	206.25	14,437.50	28,875.00	30,525.00	225.75	33,411.00	158	35,668.50	164	37,023.00	170	38,377.50
44.50	207.75	14,542.50	29,085.00	30,747.00	227.50	33,670.00	158	35,945.00	164	37,310.00	170	38,675.00
44.75	209.25	14,647.50	29,295.00	30,969.00	229.25	33,929.00	158	36,221.50	164	37,597.00	170	38,972.50
45.00	210.75	14,752.50	29,505.00	31,191.00	**231.00**	34,188.00	158	36,498.00	164	37,884.00	170	39,270.00
45.25	212.25	14,857.50	29,715.00	31,413.00	232.75	34,447.00	158	36,774.50	164	38,171.00	170	39,567.50
45.50	213.75	14,962.50	29,925.00	31,635.00	234.50	34,706.00	158	37,051.00	164	38,458.00	170	39,865.00
45.75	215.25	15,067.50	30,135.00	31,857.00	236.25	34,965.00	158	37,327.50	164	38,745.00	170	40,162.50
46.00	216.75	15,172.50	30,345.00	32,079.00	**238.00**	35,224.00	158	37,604.00	164	39,032.00	170	40,460.00
46.25	218.25	15,277.50	30,555.00	32,301.00	239.75	35,483.00	158	37,880.50	164	39,319.00	170	40,757.50
46.50	219.75	15,382.50	30,765.00	32,523.00	241.50	35,742.00	158	38,157.00	164	39,606.00	170	41,055.00
46.75	221.25	15,487.50	30,975.00	32,745.00	243.25	36,001.00	158	38,433.50	164	39,893.00	170	41,352.50
47.00	222.75	15,592.50	31,185.00	32,967.00	**245.00**	36,260.00	158	38,710.00	164	40,180.00	170	41,650.00
47.25	224.25	15,697.50	31,395.00	33,189.00	246.75	36,519.00	158	38,986.50	164	40,467.00	170	41,947.50
47.50	225.75	15,802.50	31,605.00	33,411.00	248.50	36,778.00	158	39,263.00	164	40,754.00	170	42,245.00
47.75	227.25	15,907.50	31,815.00	33,633.00	250.25	37,037.00	158	39,539.50	164	41,041.00	170	42,542.50
48.00	228.75	16,012.50	32,025.00	33,855.00	**252.00**	37,296.00	158	39,816.00	164	41,328.00	170	42,840.00
48.25	230.25	16,117.50	32,235.00	34,077.00	253.75	37,555.00	158	40,092.50	164	41,615.00	170	43,137.50
48.50	231.75	16,222.50	32,445.00	34,299.00	255.50	37,814.00	158	40,369.00	164	41,902.00	170	43,435.00
48.75	233.25	16,327.50	32,655.00	34,521.00	257.25	38,073.00	158	40,645.50	164	42,189.00	170	43,732.50
49.00	234.75	16,432.50	32,865.00	34,743.00	**259.00**	38,332.00	158	40,922.00	164	42,476.00	170	44,030.00
49.25	236.25	16,537.50	33,075.00	34,965.00	260.75	38,591.00	158	41,198.50	164	42,763.00	170	44,327.50
49.50	237.75	16,642.50	33,285.00	35,187.00	262.50	38,850.00	158	41,475.00	164	43,050.00	170	44,625.00
49.75	239.25	16,747.50	33,495.00	35,409.00	264.25	39,109.00	158	41,751.50	164	43,337.00	170	44,922.50
50.00	241.00	16,870.00	33,740.00	35,668.00	**266.25**	39,405.00	158	42,067.50	164	43,665.00	170	45,262.50
50.25	242.75	16,992.50	33,985.00	35,927.00	268.25	39,701.00	158	42,383.50	164	43,993.00	170	45,602.50
50.50	244.50	17,115.00	34,230.00	36,186.00	270.25	39,997.00	158	42,699.50	164	44,321.00	170	45,942.50
50.75	246.25	17,237.50	34,475.00	36,445.00	272.25	40,293.00	158	43,015.50	164	44,649.00	170	46,282.50

Table 17 C, Permanent Disability Indemnity, Injuries 1984 through 2002

% of P.D.	1984-'91 # of WEEKS	Minimum @ $70/wk ≥ 1984	Maximum 1984 to 12-31-90	1991 @ $148/wk, ≥ 25%	1-1-92+ # of WEEKS	to 6-30-94 @ $148 ≥ 25% Total $	7-1-94 to 6-30-95 Max / Week	Total $	7-1-95 to 6-30-96 Max / Week	Total $	7-1-96 to 12-31-02 Max / Week	Total $
51.00	248.00	17,360.00	34,720.00	36,704.00	**274.25**	40,589.00	158	43,331.50	164	44,977.00	170	46,622.50
51.25	249.75	17,482.50	34,965.00	36,963.00	276.25	40,885.00	158	43,647.50	164	45,305.00	170	46,962.50
51.50	251.50	17,605.00	35,210.00	37,222.00	278.25	41,181.00	158	43,963.50	164	45,633.00	170	47,302.50
51.75	253.25	17,727.50	35,455.00	37,481.00	280.25	41,477.00	158	44,279.50	164	45,961.00	170	47,642.50
52.00	255.00	17,850.00	35,700.00	37,740.00	**282.25**	41,773.00	158	44,595.50	164	46,289.00	170	47,982.50
52.25	256.75	17,972.50	35,945.00	37,999.00	284.25	42,069.00	158	44,911.50	164	46,617.00	170	48,322.50
52.50	258.50	18,095.00	36,190.00	38,258.00	286.25	42,365.00	158	45,227.50	164	46,945.00	170	48,662.50
52.75	260.25	18,217.50	36,435.00	38,517.00	288.25	42,661.00	158	45,543.50	164	47,273.00	170	49,002.50
53.00	262.00	18,340.00	36,680.00	38,776.00	**290.25**	42,957.00	158	45,859.50	164	47,601.00	170	49,342.50
53.25	263.75	18,462.50	36,925.00	39,035.00	292.25	43,253.00	158	46,175.50	164	47,929.00	170	49,682.50
53.50	265.50	18,585.00	37,170.00	39,294.00	294.25	43,549.00	158	46,491.50	164	48,257.00	170	50,022.50
53.75	267.25	18,707.50	37,415.00	39,553.00	296.25	43,845.00	158	46,807.50	164	48,585.00	170	50,362.50
54.00	269.00	18,830.00	37,660.00	39,812.00	**298.25**	44,141.00	158	47,123.50	164	48,913.00	170	50,702.50
54.25	270.75	18,952.50	37,905.00	40,071.00	300.25	44,437.00	158	47,439.50	164	49,241.00	170	51,042.50
54.50	272.50	19,075.00	38,150.00	40,330.00	302.25	44,733.00	158	47,755.50	164	49,569.00	170	51,382.50
54.75	274.25	19,197.50	38,395.00	40,589.00	304.25	45,029.00	158	48,071.50	164	49,897.00	170	51,722.50
55.00	276.00	19,320.00	38,640.00	40,848.00	**306.25**	45,325.00	158	48,387.50	164	50,225.00	170	52,062.50
55.25	277.75	19,442.50	38,885.00	41,107.00	308.25	45,621.00	158	48,703.50	164	50,553.00	170	52,402.50
55.50	279.50	19,565.00	39,130.00	41,366.00	310.25	45,917.00	158	49,019.50	164	50,881.00	170	52,742.50
55.75	281.25	19,687.50	39,375.00	41,625.00	312.25	46,213.00	158	49,335.50	164	51,209.00	170	53,082.50
56.00	283.00	19,810.00	39,620.00	41,884.00	**314.25**	46,509.00	158	49,651.50	164	51,537.00	170	53,422.50
56.25	284.75	19,932.50	39,865.00	42,143.00	316.25	46,805.00	158	49,967.50	164	51,865.00	170	53,762.50
56.50	286.50	20,055.00	40,110.00	42,402.00	318.25	47,101.00	158	50,283.50	164	52,193.00	170	54,102.50
56.75	288.25	20,177.50	40,355.00	42,661.00	320.25	47,397.00	158	50,599.50	164	52,521.00	170	54,442.50
57.00	290.00	20,300.00	40,600.00	42,920.00	**322.25**	47,693.00	158	50,915.50	164	52,849.00	170	54,782.50
57.25	291.75	20,422.50	40,845.00	43,179.00	324.25	47,989.00	158	51,231.50	164	53,177.00	170	55,122.50
57.50	293.50	20,545.00	41,090.00	43,438.00	326.25	48,285.00	158	51,547.50	164	53,505.00	170	55,462.50
57.75	295.25	20,667.50	41,335.00	43,697.00	328.25	48,581.00	158	51,863.50	164	53,833.00	170	55,802.50
58.00	297.00	20,790.00	41,580.00	43,956.00	**330.25**	48,877.00	158	52,179.50	164	54,161.00	170	56,142.50
58.25	298.75	20,912.50	41,825.00	44,215.00	332.25	49,173.00	158	52,495.50	164	54,489.00	170	56,482.50
58.50	300.50	21,035.00	42,070.00	44,474.00	334.25	49,469.00	158	52,811.50	164	54,817.00	170	56,822.50
58.75	302.25	21,157.50	42,315.00	44,733.00	336.25	49,765.00	158	53,127.50	164	55,145.00	170	57,162.50
59.00	304.00	21,280.00	42,560.00	44,992.00	**338.25**	50,061.00	158	53,443.50	164	55,473.00	170	57,502.50
59.25	305.75	21,402.50	42,805.00	45,251.00	340.25	50,357.00	158	53,759.50	164	55,801.00	170	57,842.50
59.50	307.50	21,525.00	43,050.00	45,510.00	342.25	50,653.00	158	54,075.50	164	56,129.00	170	58,182.50
59.75	309.25	21,647.50	43,295.00	45,769.00	344.25	50,949.00	158	54,391.50	164	56,457.00	170	58,522.50
60.00	311.00	21,770.00	43,540.00	46,028.00	**346.25**	51,245.00	158	54,707.50	164	56,785.00	170	58,862.50
60.25	312.75	21,892.50	43,785.00	46,287.00	348.25	51,541.00	158	55,023.50	164	57,113.00	170	59,202.50
60.50	314.50	22,015.00	44,030.00	46,546.00	350.25	51,837.00	158	55,339.50	164	57,441.00	170	59,542.50
60.75	316.25	22,137.50	44,275.00	46,805.00	352.25	52,133.00	158	55,655.50	164	57,769.00	170	59,882.50

Table 17 C, Permanent Disability Indemnity, Injuries 1984 through 2002

% of P.D.	1984-'91 # of Weeks	Minimum @ $70/wk ≥ 1984	Maximum 1984 to 12-31-90	1991 @ $148/wk, ≥ 25%	1-1-92+ # of Weeks	to 6-30-94 @ $148 ≥ 25% Total $	7-1-94 to 6-30-95 Max / Week	7-1-94 to 6-30-95 Total $	7-1-95 to 6-30-96 Max / Week	7-1-95 to 6-30-96 Total $	7-1-96 to 12-31-02 Max / Week	7-1-96 to 12-31-02 Total $
61.00	318.00	22,260.00	44,520.00	47,064.00	354.25	52,429.00	158	55,971.50	164	58,097.00	170	60,222.50
61.25	319.75	22,382.50	44,765.00	47,323.00	356.25	52,725.00	158	56,287.50	164	58,425.00	170	60,562.50
61.50	321.50	22,505.00	45,010.00	47,582.00	358.25	53,021.00	158	56,603.50	164	58,753.00	170	60,902.50
61.75	323.25	22,627.50	45,255.00	47,841.00	360.25	53,317.00	158	56,919.50	164	59,081.00	170	61,242.50
62.00	325.00	22,750.00	45,500.00	48,100.00	362.25	53,613.00	158	57,235.50	164	59,409.00	170	61,582.50
62.25	326.75	22,872.50	45,745.00	48,359.00	364.25	53,909.00	158	57,551.50	164	59,737.00	170	61,922.50
62.50	328.50	22,995.00	45,990.00	48,618.00	366.25	54,205.00	158	57,867.50	164	60,065.00	170	62,262.50
62.75	330.25	23,117.50	46,235.00	48,877.00	368.25	54,501.00	158	58,183.50	164	60,393.00	170	62,602.50
63.00	332.00	23,240.00	46,480.00	49,136.00	370.25	54,797.00	158	58,499.50	164	60,721.00	170	62,942.50
63.25	333.75	23,362.50	46,725.00	49,395.00	372.25	55,093.00	158	58,815.50	164	61,049.00	170	63,282.50
63.50	335.50	23,485.00	46,970.00	49,654.00	374.25	55,389.00	158	59,131.50	164	61,377.00	170	63,622.50
63.75	337.25	23,607.50	47,215.00	49,913.00	376.25	55,685.00	158	59,447.50	164	61,705.00	170	63,962.50
64.00	339.00	23,730.00	47,460.00	50,172.00	378.25	55,981.00	158	59,763.50	164	62,033.00	170	64,302.50
64.25	340.75	23,852.50	47,705.00	50,431.00	380.25	56,277.00	158	60,079.50	164	62,361.00	170	64,642.50
64.50	342.50	23,975.00	47,950.00	50,690.00	382.25	56,573.00	158	60,395.50	164	62,689.00	170	64,982.50
64.75	344.25	24,097.50	48,195.00	50,949.00	384.25	56,869.00	158	60,711.50	164	63,017.00	170	65,322.50
65.00	346.00	24,220.00	48,440.00	51,208.00	386.25	57,165.00	158	61,027.50	164	63,345.00	170	65,662.50
65.25	347.75	24,342.50	48,685.00	51,467.00	388.25	57,461.00	158	61,343.50	164	63,673.00	170	66,002.50
65.50	349.50	24,465.00	48,930.00	51,726.00	390.25	57,757.00	158	61,659.50	164	64,001.00	170	66,342.50
65.75	351.25	24,587.50	49,175.00	51,985.00	392.25	58,053.00	158	61,975.50	164	64,329.00	170	66,682.50
66.00	353.00	24,710.00	49,420.00	52,244.00	394.25	58,349.00	158	62,291.50	164	64,657.00	170	67,022.50
66.25	354.75	24,832.50	49,665.00	52,503.00	396.25	58,645.00	158	62,607.50	164	64,985.00	170	67,362.50
66.50	356.50	24,955.00	49,910.00	52,762.00	398.25	58,941.00	158	62,923.50	164	65,313.00	170	67,702.50
66.75	358.25	25,077.50	50,155.00	53,021.00	400.25	59,237.00	158	63,239.50	164	65,641.00	170	68,042.50
67.00	360.00	25,200.00	50,400.00	53,280.00	402.25	59,533.00	158	63,555.50	164	65,969.00	170	68,382.50
67.25	361.75	25,322.50	50,645.00	53,539.00	404.25	59,829.00	158	63,871.50	164	66,297.00	170	68,722.50
67.50	363.50	25,445.00	50,890.00	53,798.00	406.25	60,125.00	158	64,187.50	164	66,625.00	170	69,062.50
67.75	365.25	25,567.50	51,135.00	54,057.00	408.25	60,421.00	158	64,503.50	164	66,953.00	170	69,402.50
68.00	367.00	25,690.00	51,380.00	54,316.00	410.25	60,717.00	158	64,819.50	164	67,281.00	170	69,742.50
68.25	368.75	25,812.50	51,625.00	54,575.00	412.25	61,013.00	158	65,135.50	164	67,609.00	170	70,082.50
68.50	370.50	25,935.00	51,870.00	54,834.00	414.25	61,309.00	158	65,451.50	164	67,937.00	170	70,422.50
68.75	372.25	26,057.50	52,115.00	55,093.00	416.25	61,605.00	158	65,767.50	164	68,265.00	170	70,762.50
69.00	374.00	26,180.00	52,360.00	55,352.00	418.25	61,901.00	158	66,083.50	164	68,593.00	170	71,102.50
69.25	375.75	26,302.50	52,605.00	55,611.00	420.25	62,197.00	158	66,399.50	164	68,921.00	170	71,442.50
69.50	377.50	26,425.00	52,850.00	55,870.00	422.25	62,493.00	158	66,715.50	164	69,249.00	170	71,782.50
69.75	379.25	26,547.50	53,095.00	56,129.00	424.25	62,789.00	158	67,031.50	164	69,577.00	170	72,122.50
70.00	381.25	26,687.50	53,375.00	56,425.00	426.50	63,122.00	**168**	**71,652.00**	**198**	**84,447.00**	**230**	**98,095.00**
70.25	383.25	26,827.50	53,655.00	56,721.00	428.75	63,455.00	168	72,030.00	198	84,892.50	230	98,612.50
70.50	385.25	26,967.50	53,935.00	57,017.00	431.00	63,788.00	168	72,408.00	198	85,338.00	230	99,130.00
70.75	387.25	27,107.50	54,215.00	57,313.00	433.25	64,121.00	168	72,786.00	198	85,783.50	230	99,647.50

Tables & Schedules

Table 17 C, Permanent Disability Indemnity, Injuries 1984 through 2002

% of P.D.	1984-'91 # of WEEKS	Minimum @ $70/wk ≥ 1984	Maximum 1984 to 12-31-90	1991 @ $148/wk, ≥ 25%	1-1-92+ # of WEEKS	to 6-30-94 @ $148 ≥ 25% Total $	7-1-94 to 6-30-95 Max / Week	Total $	7-1-95 to 6-30-96 Max / Week	Total $	7-1-96 to 12-31-02 Max / Week	Total $
71.00	389.25	27,247.50	54,495.00	57,609.00	**435.50**	64,454.00	168	73,164.00	198	86,229.00	230	100,165.00
71.25	391.25	27,387.50	54,775.00	57,905.00	437.75	64,787.00	168	73,542.00	198	86,674.50	230	100,682.50
71.50	393.25	27,527.50	55,055.00	58,201.00	440.00	65,120.00	168	73,920.00	198	87,120.00	230	101,200.00
71.75	395.25	27,667.50	55,335.00	58,497.00	442.25	65,453.00	168	74,298.00	198	87,565.50	230	101,717.50
72.00	397.25	27,807.50	55,615.00	58,793.00	**444.50**	65,786.00	168	74,676.00	198	88,011.00	230	102,235.00
72.25	399.25	27,947.50	55,895.00	59,089.00	446.75	66,119.00	168	75,054.00	198	88,456.50	230	102,752.50
72.50	401.25	28,087.50	56,175.00	59,385.00	449.00	66,452.00	168	75,432.00	198	88,902.00	230	103,270.00
72.75	403.25	28,227.50	56,455.00	59,681.00	451.25	66,785.00	168	75,810.00	198	89,347.50	230	103,787.50
73.00	405.25	28,367.50	56,735.00	59,977.00	**453.50**	67,118.00	168	76,188.00	198	89,793.00	230	104,305.00
73.25	407.25	28,507.50	57,015.00	60,273.00	455.75	67,451.00	168	76,566.00	198	90,238.50	230	104,822.50
73.50	409.25	28,647.50	57,295.00	60,569.00	458.00	67,784.00	168	76,944.00	198	90,684.00	230	105,340.00
73.75	411.25	28,787.50	57,575.00	60,865.00	460.25	68,117.00	168	77,322.00	198	91,129.50	230	105,857.50
74.00	413.25	28,927.50	57,855.00	61,161.00	**462.50**	68,450.00	168	77,700.00	198	91,575.00	230	106,375.00
74.25	415.25	29,067.50	58,135.00	61,457.00	464.75	68,783.00	168	78,078.00	198	92,020.50	230	106,892.50
74.50	417.25	29,207.50	58,415.00	61,753.00	467.00	69,116.00	168	78,456.00	198	92,466.00	230	107,410.00
74.75	419.25	29,347.50	58,695.00	62,049.00	469.25	69,449.00	168	78,834.00	198	92,911.50	230	107,927.50
75.00	421.25	29,487.50	58,975.00	62,345.00	**471.50**	69,782.00	168	79,212.00	198	93,357.00	230	108,445.00
75.25	423.25	29,627.50	59,255.00	62,641.00	473.75	70,115.00	168	79,590.00	198	93,802.50	230	108,962.50
75.50	425.25	29,767.50	59,535.00	62,937.00	476.00	70,448.00	168	79,968.00	198	94,248.00	230	109,480.00
75.75	427.25	29,907.50	59,815.00	63,233.00	478.25	70,781.00	168	80,346.00	198	94,693.50	230	109,997.50
76.00	429.25	30,047.50	60,095.00	63,529.00	**480.50**	71,114.00	168	80,724.00	198	95,139.00	230	110,515.00
76.25	431.25	30,187.50	60,375.00	63,825.00	482.75	71,447.00	168	81,102.00	198	95,584.50	230	111,032.50
76.50	433.25	30,327.50	60,655.00	64,121.00	485.00	71,780.00	168	81,480.00	198	96,030.00	230	111,550.00
76.75	435.25	30,467.50	60,935.00	64,417.00	487.25	72,113.00	168	81,858.00	198	96,475.50	230	112,067.50
77.00	437.25	30,607.50	61,215.00	64,713.00	**489.50**	72,446.00	168	82,236.00	198	96,921.00	230	112,585.00
77.25	439.25	30,747.50	61,495.00	65,009.00	491.75	72,779.00	168	82,614.00	198	97,366.50	230	113,102.50
77.50	441.25	30,887.50	61,775.00	65,305.00	494.00	73,112.00	168	82,992.00	198	97,812.00	230	113,620.00
77.75	443.25	31,027.50	62,055.00	65,601.00	496.25	73,445.00	168	83,370.00	198	98,257.50	230	114,137.50
78.00	445.25	31,167.50	62,335.00	65,897.00	**498.50**	73,778.00	168	83,748.00	198	98,703.00	230	114,655.00
78.25	447.25	31,307.50	62,615.00	66,193.00	500.75	74,111.00	168	84,126.00	198	99,148.50	230	115,172.50
78.50	449.25	31,447.50	62,895.00	66,489.00	503.00	74,444.00	168	84,504.00	198	99,594.00	230	115,690.00
78.75	451.25	31,587.50	63,175.00	66,785.00	505.25	74,777.00	168	84,882.00	198	100,039.50	230	116,207.50
79.00	453.25	31,727.50	63,455.00	67,081.00	**507.50**	75,110.00	168	85,260.00	198	100,485.00	230	116,725.00
79.25	455.25	31,867.50	63,735.00	67,377.00	509.75	75,443.00	168	85,638.00	198	100,930.50	230	117,242.50
79.50	457.25	32,007.50	64,015.00	67,673.00	512.00	75,776.00	168	86,016.00	198	101,376.00	230	117,760.00
79.75	459.25	32,147.50	64,295.00	67,969.00	514.25	76,109.00	168	86,394.00	198	101,821.50	230	118,277.50
80.00	461.25	32,287.50	64,575.00	68,265.00	**516.50**	76,442.00	168	86,772.00	198	102,267.00	230	118,795.00
80.25	463.25	32,427.50	64,855.00	68,561.00	518.75	76,775.00	168	87,150.00	198	102,712.50	230	119,312.50
80.50	465.25	32,567.50	65,135.00	68,857.00	521.00	77,108.00	168	87,528.00	198	103,158.00	230	119,830.00
80.75	467.25	32,707.50	65,415.00	69,153.00	523.25	77,441.00	168	87,906.00	198	103,603.50	230	120,347.50

Table 17 C, Permanent Disability Indemnity, Injuries 1984 through 2002

% of P.D.	1984-'91 # of WEEKS	Minimum @ $70/wk ≥ 1984	Maximum 1984 to 12-31-90	1991 @ $148/wk, ≥ 25%	1-1-92+ # of WEEKS	to 6-30-94 @ $148 ≥ 25% Total $	7-1-94 to 6-30-95 Max / Week	7-1-94 to 6-30-95 Total $	7-1-95 to 6-30-96 Max / Week	7-1-95 to 6-30-96 Total $	7-1-96 to 12-31-02 Max / Week	7-1-96 to 12-31-02 Total $
81.00	469.25	32,847.50	65,695.00	69,449.00	**525.50**	77,774.00	168	88,284.00	198	104,049.00	230	120,865.00
81.25	471.25	32,987.50	65,975.00	69,745.00	527.75	78,107.00	168	88,662.00	198	104,494.50	230	121,382.50
81.50	473.25	33,127.50	66,255.00	70,041.00	530.00	78,440.00	168	89,040.00	198	104,940.00	230	121,900.00
81.75	475.25	33,267.50	66,535.00	70,337.00	532.25	78,773.00	168	89,418.00	198	105,385.50	230	122,417.50
82.00	477.25	33,407.50	66,815.00	70,633.00	**534.50**	79,106.00	168	89,796.00	198	105,831.00	230	122,935.00
82.25	479.25	33,547.50	67,095.00	70,929.00	536.75	79,439.00	168	90,174.00	198	106,276.50	230	123,452.50
82.50	481.25	33,687.50	67,375.00	71,225.00	539.00	79,772.00	168	90,552.00	198	106,722.00	230	123,970.00
82.75	483.25	33,827.50	67,655.00	71,521.00	541.25	80,105.00	168	90,930.00	198	107,167.50	230	124,487.50
83.00	485.25	33,967.50	67,935.00	71,817.00	**543.50**	80,438.00	168	91,308.00	198	107,613.00	230	125,005.00
83.25	487.25	34,107.50	68,215.00	72,113.00	545.75	80,771.00	168	91,686.00	198	108,058.50	230	125,522.50
83.50	489.25	34,247.50	68,495.00	72,409.00	548.00	81,104.00	168	92,064.00	198	108,504.00	230	126,040.00
83.75	491.25	34,387.50	68,775.00	72,705.00	550.25	81,437.00	168	92,442.00	198	108,949.50	230	126,557.50
84.00	493.25	34,527.50	69,055.00	73,001.00	**552.50**	81,770.00	168	92,820.00	198	109,395.00	230	127,075.00
84.25	495.25	34,667.50	69,335.00	73,297.00	554.75	82,103.00	168	93,198.00	198	109,840.50	230	127,592.50
84.50	497.25	34,807.50	69,615.00	73,593.00	557.00	82,436.00	168	93,576.00	198	110,286.00	230	128,110.00
84.75	499.25	34,947.50	69,895.00	73,889.00	559.25	82,769.00	168	93,954.00	198	110,731.50	230	128,627.50
85.00	501.25	35,087.50	70,175.00	74,185.00	**561.50**	83,102.00	168	94,332.00	198	111,177.00	230	129,145.00
85.25	503.25	35,227.50	70,455.00	74,481.00	563.75	83,435.00	168	94,710.00	198	111,622.50	230	129,662.50
85.50	505.25	35,367.50	70,735.00	74,777.00	566.00	83,768.00	168	95,088.00	198	112,068.00	230	130,180.00
85.75	507.25	35,507.50	71,015.00	75,073.00	568.25	84,101.00	168	95,466.00	198	112,513.50	230	130,697.50
86.00	509.25	35,647.50	71,295.00	75,369.00	**570.50**	84,434.00	168	95,844.00	198	112,959.00	230	131,215.00
86.25	511.25	35,787.50	71,575.00	75,665.00	572.75	84,767.00	168	96,222.00	198	113,404.50	230	131,732.50
86.50	513.25	35,927.50	71,855.00	75,961.00	575.00	85,100.00	168	96,600.00	198	113,850.00	230	132,250.00
86.75	515.25	36,067.50	72,135.00	76,257.00	577.25	85,433.00	168	96,978.00	198	114,295.50	230	132,767.50
87.00	517.25	36,207.50	72,415.00	76,553.00	**579.50**	85,766.00	168	97,356.00	198	114,741.00	230	133,285.00
87.25	519.25	36,347.50	72,695.00	76,849.00	581.75	86,099.00	168	97,734.00	198	115,186.50	230	133,802.50
87.50	521.25	36,487.50	72,975.00	77,145.00	584.00	86,432.00	168	98,112.00	198	115,632.00	230	134,320.00
87.75	523.25	36,627.50	73,255.00	77,441.00	586.25	86,765.00	168	98,490.00	198	116,077.50	230	134,837.50
88.00	525.25	36,767.50	73,535.00	77,737.00	**588.50**	87,098.00	168	98,868.00	198	116,523.00	230	135,355.00
88.25	527.25	36,907.50	73,815.00	78,033.00	590.75	87,431.00	168	99,246.00	198	116,968.50	230	135,872.50
88.50	529.25	37,047.50	74,095.00	78,329.00	593.00	87,764.00	168	99,624.00	198	117,414.00	230	136,390.00
88.75	531.25	37,187.50	74,375.00	78,625.00	595.25	88,097.00	168	100,002.00	198	117,859.50	230	136,907.50
89.00	533.25	37,327.50	74,655.00	78,921.00	**597.50**	88,430.00	168	100,380.00	198	118,305.00	230	137,425.00
89.25	535.25	37,467.50	74,935.00	79,217.00	599.75	88,763.00	168	100,758.00	198	118,750.50	230	137,942.50
89.50	537.25	37,607.50	75,215.00	79,513.00	602.00	89,096.00	168	101,136.00	198	119,196.00	230	138,460.00
89.75	539.25	37,747.50	75,495.00	79,809.00	604.25	89,429.00	168	101,514.00	198	119,641.50	230	138,977.50
90.00	541.25	37,887.50	75,775.00	80,105.00	**606.50**	89,762.00	168	101,892.00	198	120,087.00	230	139,495.00
90.25	543.25	38,027.50	76,055.00	80,401.00	608.75	90,095.00	168	102,270.00	198	120,532.50	230	140,012.50
90.50	545.25	38,167.50	76,335.00	80,697.00	611.00	90,428.00	168	102,648.00	198	120,978.00	230	140,530.00
90.75	547.25	38,307.50	76,615.00	80,993.00	613.25	90,761.00	168	103,026.00	198	121,423.50	230	141,047.50

Table 17 C, Permanent Disability Indemnity, Injuries 1984 through 2002

% of P.D.	1984-'91 # of WEEKS	Minimum @ $70/wk ≥ 1984	Maximum 1984 to 12-31-90	1991 @ $148/wk, ≥ 25%	1-1-92+ # of WEEKS	to 6-30-94 @ $148 ≥ 25% Total $	7-1-94 to 6-30-95 Max / Week	7-1-94 to 6-30-95 Total $	7-1-95 to 6-30-96 Max / Week	7-1-95 to 6-30-96 Total $	7-1-96 to 12-31-02 Max / Week	7-1-96 to 12-31-02 Total $
91.00	549.25	38,447.50	76,895.00	81,289.00	**615.50**	91,094.00	168	103,404.00	198	121,869.00	230	141,565.00
91.25	551.25	38,587.50	77,175.00	81,585.00	617.75	91,427.00	168	103,782.00	198	122,314.50	230	142,082.50
91.50	553.25	38,727.50	77,455.00	81,881.00	620.00	91,760.00	168	104,160.00	198	122,760.00	230	142,600.00
91.75	555.25	38,867.50	77,735.00	82,177.00	622.25	92,093.00	168	104,538.00	198	123,205.50	230	143,117.50
92.00	557.25	39,007.50	78,015.00	82,473.00	**624.50**	92,426.00	168	104,916.00	198	123,651.00	230	143,635.00
92.25	559.25	39,147.50	78,295.00	82,769.00	626.75	92,759.00	168	105,294.00	198	124,096.50	230	144,152.50
92.50	561.25	39,287.50	78,575.00	83,065.00	629.00	93,092.00	168	105,672.00	198	124,542.00	230	144,670.00
92.75	563.25	39,427.50	78,855.00	83,361.00	631.25	93,425.00	168	106,050.00	198	124,987.50	230	145,187.50
93.00	565.25	39,567.50	79,135.00	83,657.00	**633.50**	93,758.00	168	106,428.00	198	125,433.00	230	145,705.00
93.25	567.25	39,707.50	79,415.00	83,953.00	635.75	94,091.00	168	106,806.00	198	125,878.50	230	146,222.50
93.50	569.25	39,847.50	79,695.00	84,249.00	638.00	94,424.00	168	107,184.00	198	126,324.00	230	146,740.00
93.75	571.25	39,987.50	79,975.00	84,545.00	640.25	94,757.00	168	107,562.00	198	126,769.50	230	147,257.50
94.00	573.25	40,127.50	80,255.00	84,841.00	**642.50**	95,090.00	168	107,940.00	198	127,215.00	230	147,775.00
94.25	575.25	40,267.50	80,535.00	85,137.00	644.75	95,423.00	168	108,318.00	198	127,660.50	230	148,292.50
94.50	577.25	40,407.50	80,815.00	85,433.00	647.00	95,756.00	168	108,696.00	198	128,106.00	230	148,810.00
94.75	579.25	40,547.50	81,095.00	85,729.00	649.25	96,089.00	168	109,074.00	198	128,551.50	230	149,327.50
95.00	581.25	40,687.50	81,375.00	86,025.00	**651.50**	96,422.00	168	109,452.00	198	128,997.00	230	149,845.00
95.25	583.25	40,827.50	81,655.00	86,321.00	653.75	96,755.00	168	109,830.00	198	129,442.50	230	150,362.50
95.50	585.25	40,967.50	81,935.00	86,617.00	656.00	97,088.00	168	110,208.00	198	129,888.00	230	150,880.00
95.75	587.25	41,107.50	82,215.00	86,913.00	658.25	97,421.00	168	110,586.00	198	130,333.50	230	151,397.50
96.00	589.25	41,247.50	82,495.00	87,209.00	**660.50**	97,754.00	168	110,964.00	198	130,779.00	230	151,915.00
96.25	591.25	41,387.50	82,775.00	87,505.00	662.75	98,087.00	168	111,342.00	198	131,224.50	230	152,432.50
96.50	593.25	41,527.50	83,055.00	87,801.00	665.00	98,420.00	168	111,720.00	198	131,670.00	230	152,950.00
96.75	595.25	41,667.50	83,335.00	88,097.00	667.25	98,753.00	168	112,098.00	198	132,115.50	230	153,467.50
97.00	597.25	41,807.50	83,615.00	88,393.00	**669.50**	99,086.00	168	112,476.00	198	132,561.00	230	153,985.00
97.25	599.25	41,947.50	83,895.00	88,689.00	671.75	99,419.00	168	112,854.00	198	133,006.50	230	154,502.50
97.50	601.25	42,087.50	84,175.00	88,985.00	674.00	99,752.00	168	113,232.00	198	133,452.00	230	155,020.00
97.75	603.25	42,227.50	84,455.00	89,281.00	676.25	100,085.00	168	113,610.00	198	133,897.50	230	155,537.50
98.00	605.25	42,367.50	84,735.00	89,577.00	**678.50**	100,418.00	168	113,988.00	198	134,343.00	230	156,055.00
98.25	607.25	42,507.50	85,015.00	89,873.00	680.75	100,751.00	168	114,366.00	198	134,788.50	230	156,572.50
98.50	609.25	42,647.50	85,295.00	90,169.00	683.00	101,084.00	168	114,744.00	198	135,234.00	230	157,090.00
98.75	611.25	42,787.50	85,575.00	90,465.00	685.25	101,417.00	168	115,122.00	198	135,679.50	230	157,607.50
99.00	613.25	42,927.50	85,855.00	90,761.00	**687.50**	101,750.00	168	115,500.00	198	136,125.00	230	158,125.00
99.25	615.25	43,067.50	86,135.00	91,057.00	689.75	102,083.00	168	115,878.00	198	136,570.50	230	158,642.50
99.50	617.25	43,207.50	86,415.00	91,353.00	692.00	102,416.00	168	116,256.00	198	137,016.00	230	159,160.00
99.75	619.25	43,347.50	86,695.00	91,649.00	694.25	102,749.00	168	116,634.00	198	137,461.50	230	159,677.50

100% P. D. = Temporary Total Disability Rate for Life, Labor Code § 4659(b)

PART 10. Glossary

TABLE 18
Glossary of Terms and Abbreviations Commonly Used in Workers' Compensation

(Adapted from the *Work Comp Index* and the *Rehab Index*, by James T. Stewart)

AA, A/A or EEA	Applicant's Attorney or "Employee's Attorney"
AC	Appeals Council (SSA)
ACOEM	American College of Occupational and Environmental Medicine
A.D.	Administrative Director, acting, Ms. Carrie Nevans
ADA	Americans with Disabilities Act (Federal)
ADJ (EAMS)	"A district office adjudication case."
ADJ PJ (EAMS)	"The presiding judge (PJ) in the district office."
Adjourn (heading) (EAMS)	When a hearing is ended and another must be scheduled later
Adjudicate	The deciding of case by a WCALJ (aka, "WCJ" or "judge") who issues an "Opinion" or "Findings and Award" (F&A)
ADL	Activities of Daily Living, from AMA Guides, infra
Ad Litem	Usually as in "guardian ad litem," a person appointed as a guardian of a minor or adult person incompetent to manage their own affairs for the purpose of the litigation of a claim
ADR	Alternative Dispute Resolution, L.C. §3201.7, "carve out"
ALJ	Administrative Law Judge, now usually "WCALJ" is a Workers' Compensation Administrative Law Judge or WCJ
AMA Findings	Findings of a physician regarding, e.g., limitation of ADL's
AMA Guides	*American Medical Association Guides to the Evaluation of Permanent Impairment* © (5th Ed.), per L.C. §4660(b)(1)
AME	Agreed Medical Examiner, Examination, or Evaluator
AME Dance	Requirement parties must attempt to agree to an AME when employee is represented, L.C. §§4061(c), 4062.2 o/a 1/1/05
Answer	A formal response by the party, usually the employer or employer's representative, opposing the party who filed an Application for Adjudication of Claim
AOE/COE	Arising Out Of Employment and occurring in the Course Of Employment
Ap, AP or App	Application for Adjudication of Claim, usually filed by the employee or his or her representative; usually spoken, with the full word, "application" used in written form
Appeal (EAMS)	"A request by a case participant to change a case decision."
Appeals Board	Workers' Compensation Appeals Board, including local offices and "The WCAB" in San Francisco
Applicant	A party, usually the employee, who files an Application

Tables & Schedules

Apportionment	The process of removing from a PD award portions not owed by a defendant because the disability or impairment either pre-existed or would have existed regardless of injury; L.C. §§4663, 4664; the Sup. Ct. of Calif. has resolved some questions, **Brodie, Welcher, et al. vs. WCAB 72 CCC 565**
A.R. §, or Rules §	"Administrative Rules §," referring to Title 8 of the Code of Regulations, usually, "CCR §" or "T8CCR §," see "Rules," infra
Authority™	CD-ROM published by Matthew Bender (Lexis) containing the CCCs, Hanna, L.C., Title 8 of the Code of Regulations (see "L.C." below); also, a published opinion by a District Court of Appeal or the Supreme Court of California
Authority	A published opinion by a District Court of Appeal or the Supreme Court of California or WCAB en banc opinion
Award	Award by WCAB, as in "Findings and Award," or F & A
AWW or AWE	Average Weekly Wage or Earnings
Baseball Arbitration	Ratings proposed by each party contesting other's QME, Prior L.C. §§4065, 5502(d)(3), repealed 2002
Board	Workers' Compensation Appeals Board
BRBS	Benefits Review Board Service–Longshore Reporter; Matthew Bender; 1275 Broadway; Albany, NY 12204 (800) 223-1940
Brigham	Christopher Brigham; one of the authors of the "AMA Guides," supra and a frequent lecturer regarding them
BUE or BUEX	Bilateral Upper Extremities; UE or UEX, Upper Extremities
Bureau	Rehabilitation Bureau, now Rehabilitation Unit
C and R or C&R	Compromise and Release, a final settlement in "Comp"
CA or C/A	Claims Administrator, L.C. §138.4; CCR §§9793(d)
CAAA	California Applicants' Attorneys Association
Cal. Rptr.	*West's California Reporter*
Cancel (hearing) (EAMS)	Cancellation of a scheduled hearing; previously called "OTOC"
Carve Out	Collective bargaining agreement in certain industries, e.g., construction, L.C. §3201.5, using alternative dispute resolution with WCAB having appellate jurisdiction
CCC	*California Compensation Cases* [Add 35 to the number preceding CCC for the year of the case]; by Matthew Bender® (one of the Lexis™ Publishing Companies) 201 Mission St.; San Francisco, CA 94105-1831 (800) 223-1940
CCR § or T8CCR §	Title 8 of the Code of Regulations Section…
CEB	Continuing Education of the Bar's book, *California Workers' Compensation Practice*, a.k.a., "The CEB Book"
CE or C/E	Claims Examiner (same as "CA," supra)
CHSWC	Commission on Health and Safety and Workers' Compensation; acronym pronounced, "Cheese-Wiz"
CIGA	California Insurance Guarantee Association

Client (EAMS)	Used to identify the primary client in the case; essentially the EE
CME	Comprehensive Medical Examiner/Examination
CMS	Centers for Medicare and Medicaid Services of the U.S. Dept. of Health and Human Services; T8CCR §9789.10(b)
COBRA	Group health coverage offered some employees under Federal law after employment terminates
COE	Course Of Employment, see "AOE/COE," above
COLA	Cost of Living Adjustment (See Table 14)
Commutation	Reducing a sum of money due at a certain rate, for a period Commutation of time, to its present value
Comp	Workers' Compensation, Government Code §24
Companion case (EAMS)	Cases sharing a common factor, e.g., the EE, D/A where there are multiple EEs hurt the same way, same ER, CC or lien claimant
Complete (hearing) (EAMS)	Recording details of a hearing, e.g., attendees, date/time of hearing, notes about disposition and orders relating to the case(s)
Consolidate	Thc process of bringing together for a hearing separate claims to avoid delay and duplication of effort; in EAMS, a "Consolidated case," where all evidence is filed in one case number for all cases
Continue (hearing) (EAMS)	A hearing is postponed prior to the date of the hearing and then is rescheduled for another date
Contribution	A process where defendant #1 seeks to recover from #2 for payments made by #1 which are allegedly owed by #2; e.g., L.C. §5500.5(e)
CPT	Current Procedural Terminology; a 5 digit code for billing medical procedures; T8CCR §9789.10(d)
CSIMS	California Society of Industrial Medicine and Surgery
CT	Cumulative Trauma, L.C. §5500.5
CT Scan or CAT Scan	Computerized Axial Tomography; combines separate X-Rays to produce detailed pictures, especially of bones {See "MRI"}
CWCR	*California Workers' Compensation Reporter* [Add 72 to the number preceding *CWCR* for the year of the issue]
Cytokine testing	Testing of DNA for cytokines released when exposed to toxic substances each with their own "signature," including chronic pain http://www.cytokineinstitute.com/
DA, D/A or DOI	Depending on context, Defense Attorney or Date of Accident or Injury (D.A. is District Attorney)
DC, DefAtty, INSA	Defense Counsel, Defense Attorney, or "Insurance Attorney" (D.C. = Dr. of Chiropractic)
DCA	District Court of Appeal
Δ or Def	Greek letter "Delta," not spoken, meaning "Defendant," i.e., either an employer, adjusting agent or representative

Demand	A proposal to settle made by employee or attorney; a counter proposal by the defendant is called an "Offer"
Depo	Deposition; a statement under oath recorded by Ct. reporter
DEU	Disability Evaluation Unit
DI, D/I or DOI	Date of Injury (D/A = Date of Accident)
Dicta	Comments made by a court in a decision concerning something not then being decided
DIR	Division of Industrial Relations
DME	Durable Medical Equipment; CCR §9789.60
Doctor shopping	Seeking a "favorable" medical opinion from another doctor
DR, DRP or DOR	Declaration of Readiness to Proceed
DRE	Diagnosis-Related Estimate from "AMA Guides" for e.g., describing spine impairment as opposed to "ROM" which utilizes Range Of Motion
DWC	Division of Workers' Compensation
DWC-1	Claim Form, an official report of injury by employee to employer
DWCNewsline	http://www.dir.ca.gov/dwc/dwc_newsline.html
E and O or E&O	Errors and Omissions insurance coverage, e.g., by an insurance agent, claims person or attorney
EAMS	Electronic Adjudication Management System (paperless) which the DWC "launched" 8/25/08 at all WCAB offices, statewide; pronunciation of acronym rhymes with "Screams"; terms used in EAMS here shown as "(EAMS)"; see generally, http://www.dir.ca.gov/dwc/EAMS/EAMS.htm
EBM	Evidence Based Medicine, L.C. §5307.27
EDD	Employment Development Dept. pays State Disability SDI or UI (Unemployment)
EDEX	DWC's Electronic Data Exchange system, replaced by EAMS, supra, which will ultimately do much more; see generally, http://www.dir.ca.gov/dwc/edex.html
EE, ee	Employee or attorney, written only
EEOC	Equal Employment Opportunity Commission (Federal)
e-forms (EAMS)	Forms submitted to the WCAB electronically as opposed to hard copy which has to be scanned
Employer, ER or Def	Employer, insurance carrier, self-insured or their attorneys
Employer (EAMS)	Per EAMS glossary, "Used to describe any group that needs to be registered in EAMS that is an entity of more than one person."
en banc or in bank	A decision made by all of the members of a court or, e.g., the WCAB Commissioners (binding on WCJs, CCR §10341)
EOP or EOB	Explanation Of Payment or Benefit
ER, ERA	Employer, Employer's Attorney
ERISA	Federal law governing retirement plans

Esq. . . . . Esquire (English title) now indicating a person is an attorney

Estoppel . . . . A legal "stopping" of a party from making an argument, e.g., that an employee took too long to report an injury, but since the employer and/or CA failed to provide notice to the employee of their rights and duties after knowledge of the injury; see Reynolds vs. WCAB 39 CCC 768

et al. . . . . Latin for "et allia" meaning "and others"

et seq. . . . . Latin for "et sequens" meaning "and the following"

ex parte . . . . Latin "for one party"; all "parties" are supposed to appear at the same time before a judge with no private conversations with the judge regarding an issue remaining to be decided; also, a letter sent to an AME with no copy to other "parties" at the same time; CCR §10334; L.C. §4062.2(f), (g)

F and A, F&A . . . . . . Findings and Award, a decision by the WCAB

FA&O . . . . Findings Award and Order

Far End . . . . Commutation off the far end of the Award, i.e., calculated from the end of a series of payments back towards present

FCE . . . . Functional Capacity Evaluation

FEHA & FEHC . . . . . Fair Employment Housing Act (State anti-discrimination) & Fair Employment Housing Commission

FME . . . . Formal Medical Evaluation

GAF . . . . Global Assessment of Function, from *AMA Guides*

Going and Coming . . . General rule that injuries during a normal commute are not industrial, with many exceptions

Guardian ad litem . . . . Guardian appointed only for the case being litigated

Guides . . . . See, "AMA Guides," infra

Hanna . . . . *California Law of Employee Injuries and Workers' Compensation,* Revised 2nd Edition; Matthew Bender; 1275 Broadway; Albany, NY 12204 (800) 223-1940

HCO . . . . Health Care Organization, e.g., as in L.C. §4600.5

Hearing (EAMS) . . . . "This is a meeting before a hearing official."

Hearing official (EAMS) . . . . "A judge or rehabilitation consultant."

Herlick . . . . Herlick, California Workers' Compensation Law (6th Ed. a treatise; there is also a handbook, e.g. the 27th ed., for 2008)

HIPAA . . . . Health Insurance Portability and Accountability Act of 1996 (HIPAA, Title II); deals with privacy of medical records

Home (EAMS) . . . . . "A link in EAMS that will take you back to the home page."

I and A Officer . . . . . Information and Assistance Officer

IC . . . . Insurance Carrier

ICD-9 . . . . International Classification of Diseases, 9th Ed. for coding of a medical diagnosis

IDL . . . . Industrial Disability Leave (State employees)

Tables & Schedules

IEA	Insurance Educational Association; 100 California St., #100; San Francisco, CA 94111
IJ or IW	Injured person or worker, also "EE" or "applicant"
IMC	Industrial Medical Council, since eliminated; see "Medical Unit" which has many of the same functions
IME	Independent or Impartial Medical Examiner, not a doctor chosen by one of the parties; called "QME" for Qualified Medical Examiner for injuries on or after 1-1-90
IMR	Independent Medical Review, L.C. §4616.4, T8CCR §§9768.1–9768.4
Impairment	Loss of use or damage to a body part or function as measured against activities of daily living; results in disability
In Pro Per	An individual acting as his or her own attorney
INS, INSA	Insurance Co. or "Defendant" + A = their attorney
Insider (EAMS)	A DWC newsletter about EAMS: http://www.dir.ca.gov/dwc/EAMS/EAMS_Insider/EAMS_Insider.htm
Jones Act	46 U.S.C §688 providing protection for merchant seaman (the act is near the end of the section which follows these Tables and Schedules)
Joinder	Adding parties after filing an AP, CCR §§10360–10380
Judge	Since 1993, L.C. §27, has changed Workers' Compensation "Judge," (WCJ) to "Referee," (WCR), then to "Workers' Compensation Administrative Law Judge," (WCALJ), but they are usually called a "Judge" or "WCJ"
L.C.	Labor Code of California, as cited in *Workers' Compensation Laws of California* which contains the Labor Code and most other laws relating to Workers' Comp in Calif. It is often called, "The Labor Code Book," but it contains much more. Matthew Bender; 1275 Broadway; Albany, NY 12204. Ph. (800) 223-1940
Larson	Larson's Workers' Compensation Law; Matthew Bender; 1275 Broadway; Albany, NY 12204. Ph. (800) 223-1940
Lawyer's Guide	*The Lawyer's Guide to the AMA Guides and California Workers' Compensation* by Robert G. Rassp, published by LexisNexis™
LDW	Last Day Worked
Legacy system (EAMS)	"The current system of record, like DEU's system or the WCAB online system."
LEX	Lower Extremity (UEX, upper extremity)
Lexis or LexisNexis™	The largest publisher of "Law Books" in the world
LHWCA or L & H . . .	Longshore and Harbor Workers' Compensation Act
Linked case (EAMS) . . .	Cases with some relationship with each other are "linked." These cases need to be designated as "master" or "non-master" cases
LTD	Long Term Disability

Master case (EAMS) . . .	"... Actions taken on cases linked to the master case are noted on the master case rather than the linked case."
MDT	Multiple Disability Table, noted at the end of the various PD Schedules. See the one at the end of Table 11A, infra
Med – Legal	Medical – Legal examination or expense, at request of a party; employee's is owed by def. L.C. §§4620–4622
Mediator	A person hired by parties to assist in reaching agreements; differs from an "Arbitrator" who is more similar to a judge
Medical Unit	http://www.dir.ca.gov/imc/imchp.html DWC – Medical Unit P.O. Box 71010 Oakland, CA 94612 **Street Address:** 1515 Clay Street, 18th floor Oakland CA 94612 Phone: 510-286-3700 or 800-794-6900 **NOTE: ALL PACKAGES, CERTIFIED MAIL AND PRIORITY MAIL MUST BE SENT TO THE STREET ADDRESS ONLY**
MMI	Maximum Medical Improvement, CCR §10152
MPN	Medical Provider Network, 4/04 L.C. §4616
MRI	Magnetic Resonance Imaging, especially useful in showing soft tissue structures better than X-Ray or CAT Scans
MSA	Medicare Set Aside (also "Set-Aside" or Setaside) Trust
MSC	Mandatory Settlement Conference, L.C. §5502(d)
MTUS	Medical Treatment Utilization Schedule
Navigation (EAMS) . . .	"Navigation supplies related links to other screens as found on the current EAMS screen. EAMS offers both top level and left-handed navigation."
New and Further	Petition to Reopen for New and Further Disability
New PD Schedule	The Permanent Disability Evaluation Schedule effective 1/1/05 & sometimes earlier, with exceptions, L.C. §4660(d)
NOPE	Notice of Potential Eligibility for rehab, T8CCR §9813
Noteworthy Panel Decisions	LexisNexis™ editorial consultants deem a panel decision noteworthy because it does one or more of the following: (1) Establishes a new rule of law, applies an existing rule to a set of facts significantly different from those stated in other decisions, or modifies, or criticizes with reasons given, an existing rule; (2) Resolves or creates an apparent conflict in the law; (3) Involves a legal issue of continuing public interest; (4) Makes a significant contribution to legal literature by reviewing either the development of workers' compensation law or the legislative, regulatory, or judicial history of a constitution, statute, regulation, or other written law; and/or (5) Makes a contribution to the body of law available to attorneys, claims personnel, judges, the Board, and others seeking to understand the workers' compensation law of California. WCAB panel decisions are citeable authority, particularly on issues of contemporaneous administrative construction of statutory language

[see Griffin v. WCAB (1989) 209 Cal. App. 3d 1260, 1264, fn 2, 54 Cal. Comp. Cases 145]. However, WCAB panel decisions are not binding precedent, as are en banc decisions, on all other Appeals Board panels and workers' compensation judges [see Gee v. Workers' Comp. Appeals Bd. (2002) 96 Cal. App. 4th 1418, 1425 fn. 6, 67 Cal. Comp. Cases 236].

Notice comments (EAMS) . . . . Comments on notices sent out to participants by EAMS

Numbers . . . .
- 132a . . . . . L.C. §132a, Discrimination {"a" not in "( )"}
- 139.5 . . . . L.C. §139.5 Vocational Rehabilitation
- 1013 . . . . . Civ. Pro. §1013 Time for service by mail
- 1877.3 . . . . Ins. Code §1877.3 Duty to report fraud
- 3202 . . . . L.C. §3202 Liberal construction by courts
- 3600 . . . . . L.C. §3600(a) 10 Reasons to deny a claim
- 4060 . . . . . L.C. §4060 Comprehensive med-legal exam
- 4061 . . . . . L.C. §4061 Notice of PD; Formal med exam
- 4062 . . . . . L.C. §4062 EE/ER objection to med. finding
- 4600 . . . . . L.C. §4600 Medical treatment
- 4601 . . . . . L.C. §4601 Employee requests new doctor
- 4650(d) . . . L.C. §4650(d) Self imposed 10% penalty
- 4660(d) . . . L.C. §4660(d) Old or New PD Schedule?
- 4663 . . . . 4/04 L.C. §4663 Apportionment to causation
- 4800/4850 L.C. §4800 or 4850 1 year leave with pay
- 4906(g) . . . L.C. §4906(g) "Use a fork, go to jail!"
- 5020 . . . . . L.C. §5020 Employer's Report of Injury
- 5021 . . . . . L.C. §5021 Dr.'s 1st Report of Occ. Injury
- 5500.5 . . . . L.C. §5500.5 Cumulative Trauma
- 5813 . . . . . L.C. §5813 Sanctions for bad-faith actions
- 5814 . . . . . L.C. §5814 10% penalty, unreasonable delay
- 9785 . . . . . CCR §9785 Dr.'s duty to report to adjuster
- 9813 . . . . . CCR §9813 Rehab notices
- 10125.1 . . . CCR §10125.1 Delay VRMA not, $16k cap

NCM . . . . Nurse Case Manager

OACR . . . . Order Approving C&R

Occupational Group . . . Numbered groups of occupations from the *Schedule for Evaluation of Permanent Disability*, two digit numbers for injuries up to 3/31/97 and three digit #s on or after 4/1/97

OCDJR . . . . Other Cases Denied Judicial Review as reported in the CCC

OCR (EAMS) . . . . . . Optical Character Recognition; paper forms more easily scanned

Old PD Schedule . . . . The 4/1/97 Schedule for evaluating Permanent Disability effective 4/1/97 to 12/31/04, with exceptions, L.C. §4660(d); there were earlier schedules

OMFS . . . . Official Medical Fee Schedule; T8CCR §9789.10 et seq.

OSHA . . . . Occupational Safety and Health Act

OTOC . . . . Order Taking Off Calendar

π . . . . Greek letter, pi, sometimes written as "TT." It is used for "plaintiff" in tort claims. In "comp" it = applicant or "EE"

P&A . . . . Points and Authorities; legal brief supporting a position

P&S	Permanent and Stationary, CCR §9785(a)(8); maximum medical improvement, CCR §10152
PA	Physician's Assistant
Panel QME	Panel of 3 QMEs assigned by Medical Unit at the request of a party; Represented EE, D/A o/a 1/1/05, L.C. §4062.2; Unrepresented EE, injury o/a 4/19/04, L.C. §4062.1
Participant (EAMS)	A person or employer, registered in EAMS, which may be linked to a case becoming a "case participant"
PD or PPD	Permanent Disability or Permanent Partial Disability
PDA	Permanent Disability Advance
PDR	Permanent Disability Rating
PDRS	Permanent Disability Rating Schedule; see "Schedule," infra
Peer Review	Treating Dr. and U.R. Dr. review of treatment proposed
PERS	Public Employees' Retirement System
Person (EAMS)	Per EAMS glossary, "The term used for any single person that needs to be listed in EAMS in order to act as a party in a case. Single-owner businesses will be listed as 'employers'."
Petition	A pleading or prayer for relief, e.g., a Petition for a Writ of Review or for the enforcement of an Award
PPET	Policy, Program Evaluation and Training Unit
PPM	WCAB's Policy and Procedure Manual
PPO	Preferred Provider Organization (Medical)
PQME or 3PQME	Panel QME or 3 Panel QME; see "Panel QME," supra
PR-2	PTP Progress Report, CCR §9785.2
PR-3	PTP P&S Report, 4/97 PD Schedule, CCR §9785.3
PR-4	PTP P&S Report, 1/05 PD Schedule, CCR §9785.4
Pre-Designation	Selection of a physician before injury; L.C. §4600(d)
Prima Facie	The bare minimum elements of a claim, which, if not refuted, will allow a party to prevail
Primary (EAMS)	Usage depends on context, e.g., "Primary client" refers to the injured worker in EAMS
PRN	A doctor's release of patient to return "as needed"
Pro Bono	Usually legal services rendered free of charge to the indigent
Pro Per or "in pro per"	A person is "in pro per," when acting as their own attorney
PSI	Permissibly Self-Insured
PTP	Primary Treating Physician, 8 Cal. Code Reg. §9785
QIW	Qualified Injured Worker (for vocational rehabilitation)
QME	Qualified Medical Evaluator, Examiner or Examination
QRR	Qualified Rehabilitation Representative
Quash	To nullify or set aside, e.g., a subpoena or notice to produce

Tables & Schedules

Rand Study . . . . Evaluation of California's Permanent Disability Rating Schedule, Interim Report (12/03), prepared by the RAND Institute for Civil Justice, 4/04 L.C. §4660(b)(2)

Rassp, Robert G. . . . . Author of *The Lawyer's Guide to the AMA Guides and California Workers' Compensation* by LexisNexis™

Rating . . . . A calculation of the percentage of permanent disability

RB . . . . Rehabilitation Bureau, now called the Rehabilitation Unit

Recon . . . . Petition for Reconsideration, 1st level of appeal in "comp"; see also "Writ," infra for more information

Referee or WCR . . . . Workers' Comp Referee, see "Judge," or "WCJ," L.C. §27

Rehab or Voc Rehab . . . Vocational rehabilitation, not "medical rehab" or treatment following an injury, 4/04 L.C. §139.5; includes all services reasonably necessary to return an injured employee to work for injuries from 1975 to 12/31/03. {Thereafter, replaced by the Supplemental Job Displacement Voucher, **1/04** L.C. §4658.5}

Removal . . . . Petition requesting Ap be "removed" to main WCAB in S.F., CCR §10843

Reschedule (hearing)
EAMS . . . . "Setting a new date for a hearing before the original has occurred. (See: continue)"

Retro . . . . Retroactive benefits claimed, e.g., "retro VRMA"

ROM . . . . Range Of Motion; method of calculation of impairment

RRTW . . . . Release to Return to Work; RTW, Return to Work

RU . . . . Rehabilitation Unit, formerly the Rehabilitation Bureau

Rules or A.R. . . . . . . Rules and Regulations of the Administrative Director, Title 8 California Code of Regulations, or more commonly T8CCR

RX, Rx or R_x . . . . . . Prescription; R_x is used more by doctors

§ or §§ . . . . Section or sections, e.g., L.C. §§4600–4601

S & W . . . . Serious and Willful misconduct of employee or employer

SAWE . . . . Statutory Average Weekly Earnings

SAWW . . . . State Average Weekly Wage in, e.g., L.C. §4659(c)

SB 899 . . . . Senate Bill 899, approved 4/19/04; massive w/c reform

Schedule . . . . *Schedule for Rating Permanent Disabilities*: The "Pre-4/1/97 Schedule" applies to injuries before 4/1/97. The "4/97 Schedule" (or "1997 PDRS") is for injuries 4/1/97 to 12/31/04, with exceptions. The "1/05 Schedule" (or "2005 PDRS") is for injuries o/a 1/1/05, though it sometimes applies earlier, per L.C. §4660(d), and is reprinted in Table 11 A. For use, see Tables 8 & 10, infra.)

Schedule (hearing)
(EAMS) . . . . "The first time a hearing is scheduled."

SCIF . . . . State Compensation Insurance Fund, pronounced "skiff"

SDT . . . . Subpoena Duces Tecum; request for, e.g., medical records

Self-Procured . . . . . . Medical treatment of employee not authorized by employer

SGE . . . . Suitable Gainful Employment

SIF	Subsequent Injuries Fund, L.C. §§4751 to 4755
SII, or SIP	Self Imposed Increase or Penalty, L.C. §4650(d)
Silberman	*California Vocational Rehabilitation*, by Leonard J. Silberman & Susan Wulz Silberman, 6th Ed, revised by Joseph Capurro & James Westman; James Publishing; P.O. Box 25202; Santa Ana, CA 92799-5202; Ph (800) 440-4780
SIU	Special Investigation Unit, insurance carriers writing "comp" required to maintain a fraud unit, 9/04 Ins. Code 1875.24
SJDV, or SJDB	Supplemental Job Displacement Voucher (or "Benefit"), L.C. §4658.5; applies to injuries o/a 1/1/04
SOL or S.O.L.	Statute of Limitations
Split	Difference between 2 PD ratings; not always "split" 50-50
SSA	Social Security Administration
SSD	Social Security Disability (payments)
SSDI	Social Security Disability Indemnity
SSI	Supplemental Security Income (Social Security welfare benefit payable to disabled and poor persons)
SSN	Social Security Number
SSPG	Social Security Practice Guide by NOSSCR (National Organization of Social Security Claimant's Representatives); Matthew Bender; 1275 Broadway; Albany, NY 12204 (800) 223-1940
SSSO	Spinal Surgery Second Opinion
Standard Rating	A level of PD before adjusting for age and occupation
State Disability	Disability insurance provided by the Employment Development Department (EDD)
Status (employer) (EAMS)	"Shows whether the employer has cases that are active in EAMS."
Status (person) (EAMS)	"Shows whether the person has a case or cases that are active in EAMS. A person's status stays active until death. After that the status is closed."
Statute	Statute of Limitations
Stip or Stips	Stipulations with Request for Award and Award; an agreement signed by the parties and approved by a WCJ having the same effect as a Findings and Award
Stips & Issues	Pretrial Conference Statement noting agreements as well as issues in dispute, proposed ratings, listing exhibits & disclosing witnesses, L.C. §5502(e)(3)
STP	Secondary Treating Physician
Strikes	Represented EE, injury o/a 1/1/05, L.C. §4062.2(c), each "side" strikes 1 of 3 doctors & Dr. left is the "Panel QME"
Subrogation	Def's claim for payment from 3rd party which is alleged to have caused injury; L.C. §§3850–3864; Ins. Code §11662
Sub Rosa	Private investigation, usually a video of employee

Tables & Schedules

Summary Rating	CCR §§10160–10165; one of several ratings done by DEU
SWAG	Scientific Wild-Assed Guess, see, e.g., L.C. §4663 & EBM
SX	Surgery or Symptoms, depending on context; medical abbr.
T8CCR § or CCR §	Title 8 of the Calif. Code of Regulations Section
Tables, e.g., Table 14 . . .	These Tables and Schedules
Take Nothing	"... used to indicate a finding of no entitlement to any benefits at all ..." Editorial in Title Records, Inc. vs WCAB (Shahbazian) 25 CWCR 205 @ p206
TD, TTD or TDI	Temporary Total Disability Indemnity
Tort	A civil claim, e.g., for negligence causing a personal injury
TPA	Third Party Administrator (of a self-insured employer)
TPD	Temporary Partial Disability Indemnity
TX	Treatment, i.e., Medical Treatment
U and C	Usual and Customary employment
UEF	Uninsured Employers Fund
UEX	Upper Extremities; BUE, bilateral upper extremities
UI	Unemployment Insurance
UIAB	Unemployment Insurance Appeals Board
UR	Utilization Review, L.C. §5307.27, CCR §§9792.6–9791.11
USL&H	U.S. Longshore and Harbor Workers' Compensation Act
VA	Veteran's Administration
Voucher	Supplemental Job Displacement Voucher, L.C. §4658.5
VR or Voc Rehab	Vocational Rehabilitation or "Rehab"; L.C. §139.5 sunsets 1/1/09
VRMA	Vocational Rehabilitation Maintenance Allowance, injuries o/a 1/1/90; L.C. §139.5(c), (d)
VRTD	Vocational Rehabilitation Temporary Total Disability, injuries 1975 to 12/31/89
W-2 Form	Earnings statement for tax purposes showing annual wages
W/C, w/c or W.C.	Workers' Compensation, "Work Comp" or "Comp"
WCAB	Workers' Compensation Appeals Board
WCC	WorkCompCentral.com
WCCP	Workers' Comp Claims Professional
WCIRB	Workers' Compensation Insurance Rating Bureau
WCALJ or WCJ	Workers' Compensation Administrative Law Judge, (L.C. §27), but "WCJ" or "Judge" is often used
WCI	*Work Comp Index*, 7th Ed., 5/08, by James T. Stewart; see infra
WCR	Workers' Compensation Referee; see WCALJ, supra
Work Comp Index	An alphabetical by subject Index to Workers' Comp in Calif.; 7th Ed. by James T. Stewart; 1937 Santa Ana; Clovis, CA 93611-4126; Ph/Fax (559) 291–3238; e-mail: stewshe@comcast.net
WP or WPI	Whole Person; WPI, "Whole Person Impairment"

Window period	Injuries occurring from 1990 to 1993
Writ	Petition for Writ of Review, the 2nd level of appeal to a Dist. Court of Appeal following a lost petition for Recon to "The" WCAB in San Francisco, not the local WCAB district office

PART 11. Indemnity Calculations

TABLE 19
Miscellaneous

To obtain a TD, PD or VRMA rate: Earnings × 2 ÷ 3 = or,

Earnings ÷ 1.5 = (subject to earnings maximum/minimums)

If you have the rate and want to calculate the earnings it was derived from, reverse the process:

Earnings × 3 ÷ 2 = or, Earnings × 1.5 =

If your calculator has a date key, remember to make answers *inclusive*, or running from one date, to ***& including*** another date:

When *subtracting* dates, ***add 1 to*** answer
When *adding* dates, ***1 from*** answer

Rounding %'s of PD

Rounding for injuries on/after 4/1/97 is to the nearest whole percent, per the *Schedule for Rating Permanent Disabilities*, April 1997. Quarter %'s are given in Table 17 C through 12-31-02 due to requests for continuity in the tables & for compromises.

Days as a part of a week

1	0.14286
2	0.28571
3	0.42857
4	0.57143
5	0.71429
6	0.85714

Temporary Partial Disability (TPD) or "Wage Loss," L.C. §§4654, 4657

Assume D/A 8-15-04, payment to be made 8-30-04 & earnings of $1,500.00/wk. The employee was returned to work for ½ days only from 8/17/04 to 8/30/04 and is paid $750.00/week. How is "TPD" calculated? (Were payment > 2 yrs, see L.C. §4661.5)

$1,092.00	Maximum allowable earnings for TD, injuries 1-1-04 to 12-31-04
– 750.00	Less wages earned upon return to work
$ 342.00	= "Wage Loss"/week and × 2/3 = $228.00/wk TPD due

Concurrent employment: L.C. §4453(c)(2), "Where the employee is working for two or more employers at or about the time of the injury …" average weekly wage (AWW) is total earnings from both, but not greater than at the hourly rate where injured. Thus, if employer #1 pays $10/hr, but employer #2 pays $12/hr and injury occurs with employer #2, total earnings are used. However, if injury occurs with employer #1, hours worked at employer #2 are multiplied by the rate at employer #1. Assume 20 hrs/wk worked at each employer: $10/hr × 20 hrs = $200 (#1) and $12/hr × 20 hrs/wk = $240/wk (#2). Thus, an injury at employer #2 produces an AWW of $440/wk, but only $400/wk if injury is at employer #1.

SB 899: To decrease or increase PD by 15%, multiply PD **RATE** by 0.85 or 1.15.

PART 12. Longshore and Harbor Workers' Compensation Act

TABLE 20
Maximum and Minimum Compensation Rates Under Longshore and Harbor Workers' Compensation Act

(Reprinted with Permission of Laughlin, Falbo, Levy & Moresi)

EFFECTIVE DATE	MINIMUM	MAXIMUM	INCREASE
Pre – 11/26/72	$ 18.00	$ 70.00	
11/26/72	$ 65.90	$167.00	
10/01/73	$ 70.18	$210.54	6.49%
10/01/74	$ 74.57	$261.00	6.26%
10/01/75	$ 79.60	$318.38	6.74%
10/01/76	$ 85.64	$342.54	7.59%
10/01/77	$ 91.81	$367.22	7.21%
10/01/78	$ 99.20	$396.78	8.05%
10/01/79	$106.57	$426.26	7.43%
10/01/80	$114.06	$456.24	7.03%
10/01/81	$124.18	$496.70	8.87%
10/01/82	$131.18	$524.70	5.64%
10/01/83	$137.09	$548.34	4.51%
10/01/84	$144.92	$579.66	5.00%
10/01/85	$148.81	$595.24	2.69%
10/01/86	$151.33	$605.32	1.69%
10/01/87	$154.24	$616.96	1.92%
10/01/88	$159.06	$636.24	3.13%
10/01/89	$165.16	$660.62	3.83%
10/01/90	$170.54	$682.14	3.26%
10/01/91	$174.99	$699.96	2.61%
10/01/92	$180.29	$721.14	3.03%
10/01/93	$184.58	$738.30	2.38%
10/01/94	$190.23	$760.92	3.06%
10/01/95	$195.61	$782.44	2.83%
10/01/96	$200.27	$801.06	2.38%
10/01/97	$208.94	$835.74	4.33%
10/01/98	$217.94	$871.76	4.31%
10/01/99	$225.32	$901.28	3.39%
10/01/00	$233.46	$933.82	3.61%
10/01/01	$241.52	$966.08	3.45%
10/01/02	$249.14	$996.54	3.15%
10/01/03	$257.70	$1,030.78	3.44%
10/01/04	$261.79	$1,047.16	1.59%
10/01/05	$268.41	$1,073.64	2.53%
10/01/06	$278.61	$1,114.44	3.80%
10/01/07	$290.09	$1,160.36	4.12%
10/01/08	$300.16	$1,200.62	3.47%

Note: Between 11/26/72 and 9/28/84, the max/min comp rates for employees covered under the Non-appropriated Funds Instrumentality Act were based on pay schedules set for Federal employees under 5 U.S.C. §5332, and are not included here. Effective 9/28/84, the same max/min rates apply to all employees covered under the LHWCA and its extensions, except the Defense Base Act which has no minimum comp rate, 42 U.S.C. §1652(a).

TABLE 21
Weeks of Compensation Awarded for Permanent Impairment Under Longshore and Harbor Workers' Compensation Act

Member Involved	Weeks
Arm	312
Leg	288
Hand	244
Foot	205
One Eye	160
Hearing Loss (Both Ears)	200
Hearing Loss (One Ear)	52
Thumb	75
1st Finger	46
2nd Finger	30
3rd Finger	25
Great Toe	38
Other Toes	16

NOTE: Loss of sight in both eyes, or of the use of two limbs, represents permanent total disability. For rating percentages other than those above, computation should be in proportion to figures in the above table.

UNITED STATES CODE

SYNOPSIS

TITLE 5
GOVERNMENT ORGANIZATION AND EMPLOYEES

PART III
EMPLOYEES

SUBPART A
GENERAL PROVISIONS

CHAPTER 21
DEFINITIONS

§2105. Employee.

SUBPART G
INSURANCE AND ANNUITIES

CHAPTER 81
COMPENSATION FOR WORK INJURIES

SUBCHAPTER II
EMPLOYEES OF NONAPPROPRIATED FUND INSTRUMENTALITIES

§8171. Compensation for work injuries; generally.

§8172. Employees not citizens or residents of the United States.

§8173. Liability under this subchapter exclusive.

TITLE 26
INTERNAL REVENUE CODE

SUBTITLE A
INCOME TAXES

CHAPTER 1
NORMAL TAXES AND SURTAXES

SUBCHAPTER B
COMPUTATION OF TAXABLE INCOME

PART III
ITEMS SPECIFICALLY EXCLUDED FROM GROSS INCOME

§101. Certain death benefits.

§104. Compensation for injuries or sickness.

SUBTITLE F
PROCEDURE AND ADMINISTRATION

CHAPTER 64
COLLECTION

SUBCHAPTER C
LIEN FOR TAXES

PART II
LIENS

§6323. Validity and priority against certain persons.

U.S.C.

SUBCHAPTER D
SEIZURE OF PROPERTY FOR COLLECTION OF TAXES

PART II
LEVY

§6334. Property exempt from levy.

TITLE 28
JUDICIARY AND JUDICIAL PROCEDURE

PART IV
JURISDICTION AND VENUE

CHAPTER 83
COURTS OF APPEALS

§1291. Final decisions of district courts.

CHAPTER 85
DISTRICT COURTS; JURISDICTION

§1333. Admiralty, maritime and prize cases.
§1346. United States as defendant.

CHAPTER 87
DISTRICT COURTS; VENUE

§1402. United States as defendant.

PART VI
PARTICULAR PROCEEDINGS

CHAPTER 161
UNITED STATES AS PARTY GENERALLY

§2401. Time for commencing action against United States.
§2402. Jury trial in actions against United States.
§2412. Costs and fees.

CHAPTER 171
TORT CLAIMS PROCEDURE

§2671. Definitions.
§2672. Administrative adjustment of claims.
§2674. Liability of United States.
§2675. Disposition by federal agency as prerequisite.
§2676. Judgment as bar.
§2677. Compromise.
§2678. Attorney fees; penalty.
§2679. Exclusiveness of remedy.
§2680. Exceptions.

TITLE 33
NAVIGATION AND NAVIGABLE WATERS

CHAPTER 18
LONGSHORE AND HARBOR WORKERS' COMPENSATION

§901. Short title.
§902. Definitions.
§903. Coverage.
§904. Liability for compensation.
§905. Exclusiveness of liability.
§906. Compensation.
§907. Medical services and supplies.
§908. Compensation for disability.
§909. Compensation for death.
§910. Determination of pay.
§911. Guardian for minor or incompetent.
§912. Notice of injury or death.
§913. Filing of claims.
§914. Payment of compensation.
§915. Invalid agreements.
§916. Assignment and exemption from claims of creditors.
§917. Lien against compensation.
§918. Collection of defaulted payments; special fund.
§919. Procedure in respect of claims.
§920. Presumptions.
§921. Review of compensation orders.
§921a. Appearance of attorneys for Secretary, deputy commissioner, or Board.
§922. Modification of awards.
§923. Procedure before the deputy commissioner or Board.
§924. Witnesses.
§925. Witness fees.
§926. Costs in proceedings brought without reasonable grounds.
§927. Powers of deputy commissioners or Board.
§928. Fees for services.
§929. Record of injury or death.
§930. Reports to Secretary.
§931. Penalty for misrepresentation.
§932. Security for compensation.
§933. Compensation for injuries where third persons are liable.
§934. Compensation notice.
§935. Substitution of carrier for employer.
§936. Insurance policies.
§937. Certificate of compliance with chapter.

TITLE 40
PUBLIC BUILDINGS, PROPERTY, AND WORKS

SUBTITLE II
PUBLIC BUILDINGS AND WORKS

PART A
GENERAL

CHAPTER 31
GENERAL

SUBCHAPTER VI
MISCELLANEOUS

TITLE 42
THE PUBLIC HEALTH AND WELFARE

CHAPTER 11
COMPENSATION FOR DISABILITY OR DEATH TO PERSONS EMPLOYED AT MILITARY, AIR, AND NAVAL BASES OUTSIDE THE UNITED STATES

CHAPTER 12
COMPENSATION FOR INJURY, DEATH, OR DETENTION OF EMPLOYEES OF CONTRACTORS WITH THE UNITED STATES OUTSIDE THE UNITED STATES

SUBCHAPTER I
COMPENSATION, REIMBURSEMENT, ETC., BY SECRETARY OF LABOR

SUBCHAPTER II
MISCELLANEOUS PROVISIONS

TITLE 43
PUBLIC LANDS

CHAPTER 29
SUBMERGED LANDS

SUBCHAPTER III
OUTER CONTINENTAL SHELF LANDS

TITLE 45
RAILROADS

CHAPTER 2
LIABILITY FOR INJURIES TO EMPLOYEES

§51. Liability of common carriers by railroad, in interstate or foreign commerce, for injuries to employees from negligence; employee defined.
§52. Carriers in territories or other possessions of United States.
§53. Contributory negligence; diminution of damages.
§54. Assumption of risks of employment.
§54a. Regulation, standard, or requirement under chapter 201 of title 49, United States Code, deemed to be statute under sections 3 and 4.
§55. Contract, rule, regulation, or device exempting from liability; set-off.
§56. Actions; limitation; concurrent jurisdiction of courts.
§57. Who included in term "common carrier."
§58. Duty or liability of common carriers and rights of employees under other acts not impaired.
§59. Survival of right of action of person injured.
§60. Penalty for suppression of voluntary information incident to accidents; separability.

TITLE 46
SHIPPING

SUBTITLE III
MARITIME LIABILITY

CHAPTER 301
GENERAL LIABILITY PROVISIONS

§30101. Extension of jurisdiction to cases of damage or injury on land.
§30104. Personal injury to or death of seamen.
§30105. Restriction on recovery by non-citizens and non-resident aliens for incidents in waters of other countries.
§30106. Time limit on bringing maritime action for personal injury or death.

CHAPTER 303
DEATH ON THE HIGH SEAS

§30301. Short title.
§30302. Cause of action.
§30303. Amount and apportionment of recovery.
§30304. Contributory negligence.
§30305. Death of plaintiff in pending action.
§30306. Foreign cause of action.
§30307. Commercial aviation accidents.
§30308. Nonapplication.

CHAPTER 309
SUITS IN ADMIRALTY AGAINST THE UNITED STATES

§30901. Short title.
§30902. Definition.
§30903. Waiver of immunity.
§30904. Exclusive remedy.
§30905. Period for bringing action.
§30906. Venue.
§30907. Procedure for hearing and determination.
§30908. Exemption from arrest or seizure.
§30909. Security.
§30910. Exoneration and limitation.
§30911. Costs and interest.
§30912. Arbitration, compromise, or settlement.
§30913. Payment of judgment or settlement.

CHAPTER 311
SUITS INVOLVING PUBLIC VESSELS

§31101. Short title.
§31102. Waiver of immunity.
§31103. Applicable procedure.
§31104. Venue.
§31105. Security when counterclaim filed.
§31106. Exoneration and limitation.
§31107. Interest.
§31108. Arbitration, compromise, or settlement.
§31109. Payment of judgment or settlement.
§31110. Subpoenas to officers or members of crew.
§31111. Claims by nationals of foreign countries.
§31112. Lien not recognized or created.

PROVISIONS Of The UNITED STATES CODE

TITLE 5
GOVERNMENT ORGANIZATION AND EMPLOYEES

PART III
EMPLOYEES

SUBPART A
GENERAL PROVISIONS

CHAPTER 21
DEFINITIONS

§2105. Employee.

[Subsections (a) and (b) Not Reproduced]

(c) An employee paid from nonappropriated funds of the Army and Air Force Exchange Service, Army and Air Force Motion Picture Service, Navy Ship's Stores Ashore, Navy exchanges, Marine Corps exchanges, Coast Guard exchanges, and other instrumentalities of the United States under the jurisdiction of the armed forces conducted for the comfort, pleasure, contentment, and mental and physical improvement of personnel of the armed forces is deemed not an employee for the purpose of—

(1) laws administered by the Office of Personnel Management, except—

(A) section 7204;

(B) as otherwise specifically provided in this title;

(C) the Fair Labor Standards Act of 1938;

(D) for the purpose of entering into an interchange agreement to provide for the noncompetitive movement of employees between such instrumentalities and the competitive service; or

(E) subchapter V of chapter 63, which shall be applied so as to construe references to benefit programs to refer to applicable programs for employees paid from nonappropriated funds; or

(2) subchapter I of chapter 81, chapter 84 (except to the extent specifically provided therein), and section 7902 of this title.

This subsection does not affect the status of these nonappropriated fund activities as Federal instrumentalities.

[Subsections (d)–(f) Not Reproduced]

(November 5, 1990, Pub. L. 101-508, Title VII, §7202(b), 104 Stat. 1388-855; February 5, 1993, Pub. L. 103-3, §201(b)(1), (2), 107 Stat. 23; October 29, 1994, Pub. L. 103-424, §7, 108 Stat. 4364; Sept. 23, 1996, Pub. L. 104-201, Div. A, Title III, §370(b), 110 Stat. 2499; Nov. 18, 1997, Pub. L. 105-85, Div. B, Title XXVIII, §2871(c)(2), 111 Stat. 2015.)

SUBPART G
INSURANCE AND ANNUITIES

CHAPTER 81
COMPENSATION FOR WORK INJURIES

SUBCHAPTER II
EMPLOYEES OF NONAPPROPRIATED FUND INSTRUMENTALITIES

§8171. Compensation for work injuries; generally.

(a) The Longshore and Harbor Workers' Compensation Act (33 U.S.C. 901 et seq.) applies with respect to disability or death resulting from injury, as defined by section 2(2) of such Act (33 U.S.C. 902(2)), occurring to an employee of a nonappropriated fund instrumentality described by section 2105(c) of this title, or to a volunteer providing such an instrumentality with services accepted under section 1588 of title 10, who is—

(1) a United States citizen or a permanent resident of the United States or a territory or possession of the United States employed outside the continental United States; or

(2) employed inside the continental United States.

However, that part of section 3(a) of such Act (33 U.S.C. 903(a)) which follows the second comma does not apply to such an employee.

(b) For the purpose of this subchapter, the term "employer" in section 2(4) of the Longshore and Harbor Workers' Compensation Act (33 U.S.C. 902(4)) includes the nonappropriated fund instrumentalities described by section 2105(c) of this title.

(c) The Secretary of Labor may—

(1) extend compensation districts established under section 39(b) of the Longshore and Harbor Workers' Compensation Act (33 U.S.C. 939(b)), or establish new districts to include the areas outside the continental United States; and

(2) assign to each district one or more deputy commissioners as the Secretary considers advisable.

(d) Judicial proceedings under sections 18 and 21 of the Longshore and Harbor Workers' Compensation Act (33 U.S.C. 918 and 921) with respect to an injury or death occurring outside the continental United States shall be instituted in the district court within the territorial jurisdiction of which is located the office of the deputy commissioner having jurisdiction with respect to the injury or death. (October 5, 1994, Pub. L. 103-337, Div. A, Title X, §§1061(c), 1070(d)(8)(A), 108 Stat. 2847, 2858, 2859; February 10, 1996, Pub. L. 104-106 §1505(b)(1), 110 Stat. 514.)

§8172. Employees not citizens or residents of the United States.

In case of disability or death resulting from injury, as defined by section 2(2) of the Longshore and Harbor Workers' Compensation Act (33 U.S.C. 902(2)), occurring to an employee of a nonappropriated fund instrumentality described by section 2105(c) of this title who is—

(1) not a citizen or permanent resident of the United States or a territory or possession of the United States; and

(2) employed outside the continental United States;

compensation shall be provided in accordance with regulations prescribed by the Secretary of the military department concerned and approved by the Secretary of Defense or regulations prescribed by the Secretary of Transportation, as the case may be. (July 5, 1994, Pub. L. 103-272, §4(b)(3), 108 Stat. 1361; October 5, 1994, Pub. L. 103-337, Div. A, Title X, §1070(d)(8)(B), 108 Stat. 2859; February 10, 1996, Pub. L. 104-106 §1505(b)(2), 110 Stat. 514.)

§8173. Liability under this subchapter exclusive.

The liability of the United States or of a nonappropriated fund instrumentality described by section 2105(c) of this title, with respect to the disability or death resulting from injury, as defined by section 2(2) of the Longshore and Harbor Workers' Compensation Act (33 U.S.C. 902(2)), of an employee referred to by sections 8171 and 8172 of this title, shall be determined as provided by this subchapter. This liability is exclusive and instead of all other liability of the United States or the instrumentality to the employee, his legal representative, spouse, dependents, next of kin, and any other person otherwise entitled to recover damages from the United States or the instrumentality because of the disability or death in a direct judicial proceeding, in a civil action, or in admiralty, or by an administrative or judicial proceeding under a workmen's compensation statute or under a Federal tort liability statute. (October 5, 1994, Pub. L. 103-337, Div. A, Title X, §1070(d)(8)(B), 108 Stat. 2859; February 10, 1996, Pub. L. 104-106 §1505(b)(2), 110 Stat. 514.)

TITLE 26
INTERNAL REVENUE CODE

SUBTITLE A
INCOME TAXES

CHAPTER 1
NORMAL TAXES AND SURTAXES

SUBCHAPTER B
COMPUTATION OF TAXABLE INCOME

PART III
ITEMS SPECIFICALLY EXCLUDED FROM GROSS INCOME

§101. Certain death benefits.

[Subsection (a) Not Reproduced]

(b) **[Repealed August 20, 1996]** Employees' death benefits.—

(1) General rule. Gross income does not include amounts received (whether in a single sum or otherwise) by the beneficiaries or the estate of an employee, if such amounts are paid by or on behalf of an employer and are paid by reason of the death of an employee.

(2) Special rules for paragraph (1)—

A. $5,000 limitation. The aggregate amounts excludable under paragraph (1) with respect to the death of any employee shall not exceed $5,000.

[Subsections (b)(2)B.–(h) Not Reproduced]

(i) Certain employee death benefits payable by reason of death of certain terrorist victims or astronauts.

(1) In general. Gross income does not include amounts (whether in a single sum or otherwise) paid by an employer by reason of the death of an employee who is a specified terrorist victim (as defined in section 692(d)(4)).

(2) Limitation.

(A) In general. Subject to such rules as the Secretary may prescribe, paragraph (1) shall not apply to amounts which would have been payable after death if the individual had died other than as a specified terrorist victim (as so defined).

(B) Exception. Subparagraph (A) shall not apply to incidental death benefits paid from a plan described in section 401(a) and exempt from tax under section 501(a).

(3) Treatment of self-employed individuals. For purposes of paragraph (1), the term "employee" includes a self-employed individual (as defined in section 401(c)(1)).

(4) Relief with respect to astronauts. The provisions of this subsection shall apply to any astronaut whose death occurs in the line of duty.

(j) Treatment of certain employer-owned life insurance contracts.

(1) General rule. In the case of an employer-owned life insurance contract, the amount excluded from gross income of an applicable policyholder by reason of paragraph (1) of subsection (a) shall not exceed an amount equal to the sum of the premiums and other amounts paid by the policyholder for the contract.

(2) Exceptions. In the case of an employer-owned life insurance contract with respect to which the notice and consent requirements of paragraph (4) are met, paragraph (1) shall not apply to any of the following:

(A) Exceptions based on insured's status. Any amount received by reason of the death of an insured who, with respect to an applicable policyholder—

(i) was an employee at any time during the 12-month period before the insured's death, or

U.S.C.

(ii) is, at the time the contract is issued—

(I) a director,

(II) a highly compensated employee within the meaning of section 414(q) [26 USCS § 414(q)] (without regard to paragraph (1)(B)(ii) thereof), or

(III) a highly compensated individual within the meaning of section 105(h)(5) [26 USCS § 105(h)(5)], except that "35 percent" shall be substituted for "25 percent" in subparagraph (C) thereof.

(B) Exception for amounts paid to insured's heirs. Any amount received by reason of the death of an insured to the extent—

(i) the amount is paid to a member of the family (within the meaning of section 267(c)(4) [26 USCS § 267(c)(4)]) of the insured, any individual who is the designated beneficiary of the insured under the contract (other than the applicable policyholder), a trust established for the benefit of any such member of the family or designated beneficiary, or the estate of the insured, or

(ii) the amount is used to purchase an equity (or capital or profits) interest in the applicable policyholder from any person described in clause (i).

(3) Employer-owned life insurance contract.

(A) In general. For purposes of this subsection, the term "employer-owned life insurance contract" means a life insurance contract which—

(i) is owned by a person engaged in a trade or business and under which such person (or a related person described in subparagraph (B)(ii)) is directly or indirectly a beneficiary under the contract, and

(ii) covers the life of an insured who is an employee with respect to the trade or business of the applicable policyholder on the date the contract is issued.

For purposes of the preceding sentence, if coverage for each insured under a master contract is treated as a separate contract for purposes of sections 817(h), 7702, and 7702A [26 USCS § § 817(h), 7702, and 7702A], coverage for each such insured shall be treated as a separate contract.

(B) Applicable policyholder. For purposes of this subsection—

(i) In general. The term "applicable policyholder" means, with respect to any employer-owned life insurance contract, the person described in subparagraph (A)(i) which owns the contract.

(ii) Related persons. The term "applicable policyholder" includes any person which—

(I) bears a relationship to the person described in clause (i) which is specified in section 267(b) or 707(b)(1) [26 USCS § 267(b) or 707(b)(1)], or

(II) is engaged in trades or businesses with such person which are under common control (within the meaning of subsection (a) or (b) of section 52 [26 USCS § 52]).

(4) Notice and consent requirements. The notice and consent requirements of this paragraph are met if, before the issuance of the contract, the employee—

(A) is notified in writing that the applicable policyholder intends to insure the employee's life and the maximum face amount for which the employee could be insured at the time the contract was issued,

(B) provides written consent to being insured under the contract and that such coverage may continue after the insured terminates employment, and

(C) is informed in writing that an applicable policyholder will be a beneficiary of any proceeds payable upon the death of the employee.

(5) Definitions. For purposes of this subsection—

(A) Employee. The term "employee" includes an officer, director, and highly compensated employee (within the meaning of section 414(q) [26 USCS § 414(q)]).

(B) Insured. The term "insured" means, with respect to an employer-owned life insurance contract, an individual covered by the contract who is a United States citizen or resident. In the case of a contract covering the joint lives of 2 individuals, references to an insured include both of the individuals. (August 20, 1996, Pub. L. 104-188 §1402(a), 110 Stat. 1789; Jan. 23, 2002, Pub. L. 107-134 §102(a), 115 Stat. 2429; Nov. 11, 2003, Pub. L. 108-121, Title I, § 110(b)(1), (2), 117 Stat. 1342; Pub. L. 109-280, Title VIII, Subtitle F, §863(a), (c)(1), 120 Stat. 1021, 1024.)

2006 Note: Act Aug. 17, 2006, P.L. 109-280, Title VIII, Subtitle F, § 863(d), 120 Stat. 1024, provides: "The amendments made by this section [adding 26 USCS § 101(j)] shall apply to life insurance contracts issued after the date of the enactment of this Act, except for a contract issued after such date pursuant to an exchange described in section 1035 of the Internal

Revenue Code of 1986 [26 USCS § 1035] for a contract issued on or prior to that date. For purposes of the preceding sentence, any material increase in the death benefit or other material change shall cause the contract to be treated as a new contract except that, in the case of a master contract (within the meaning of section 264(f)(4)(E) of such Code [26 USCS § 264(f)(4)(E)]), the addition of covered lives shall be treated as a new contract only with respect to such additional covered lives.".

2003 Note: The amendments made by Pub. L. 108–121 shall apply to amounts paid after December 31, 2002, with respect to deaths occurring after such date. Pub. L. 108–121, Title I, §110(b)(3), 117 Stat. 1342.

2002 Note: Application of Jan. 23, 2001 amendment; waiver of limitations. Act Jan. 23, 2002, P.L. 107-134, Title I, Subtitle A, §102(b), 115 Stat. 2429, provides:

(1) Effective date. The amendment made by this section [adding subsec. (i) of this section] shall apply to taxable years ending before, on, or after September 11, 2001.

(2) Waiver of limitations. If refund or credit of any overpayment of tax resulting from the amendments made by this section [adding subsec. (i) of this section] is prevented at any time before the close of the 1-year period beginning on the date of the enactment of this Act by the operation of any law or rule of law (including res judicata), such refund or credit may nevertheless be made or allowed if claim therefor is filed before the close of such period.

1996 Note: The repeal of subsection (b) made by §1402(a) of Pub. L. 104-188 applies with respect to decedents dying after August 20, 1996. Pub. L. 104-188 §1402(c).

The Publisher has retained the language of repealed subsection (b), above, for use in cases in which the decedent died prior to August 20, 1996.

§104. Compensation for injuries or sickness.

(a) In general.—Except in the case of amounts attributable to (and not in excess of) deductions allowed under section 213 (relating to medical, etc., expenses) for any prior taxable year, gross income does not include—

(1) amounts received under workmen's compensation acts as compensation for personal injuries or sickness;

(2) the amount of any damages (other than punitive damages) received (whether by suit or agreement and whether as lump sums or as periodic payments) on account of personal physical injuries or physical sickness;

(3) amounts received through accident or health insurance (or through an arrangement having the effect of accident or health insurance) for personal injuries or sickness (other than amounts received by an employee, to the extent such amounts (A) are attributable to contributions by the employer which were not includible in the gross income of the employee, or (B) are paid by the employer);

(4) amounts received as a pension, annuity, or similar allowance for personal injuries or sickness resulting from active service in the armed forces of any country or in the Coast and Geodetic Survey or the Public Health Service, or as a disability annuity payable under the provisions of section 808 of the Foreign Service Act of 1980; and

(5) amounts received by an individual as disability income attributable to injuries incurred as a direct result of a terroristic or military action (as defined in section 692(c)(2)). For purposes of paragraph (3), in the case of an individual who is, or has been, an employee within the meaning of section 401(c)(1) (relating to self-employed individuals), contributions made on behalf of such individual while he was such an employee to a trust described in section 401(a) which is exempt from tax under section 501(a), or under a plan described in section 403(a), shall, to the extent allowed as deductions under section 404, be treated as contributions by the employer which were not includible in the gross income of the employee. For purposes of paragraph (2), emotional distress shall not be treated as a physical injury or physical sickness. The preceding sentence shall not apply to an amount of damages not in excess of the amount paid for medical care (described in subparagraph (A) or (B) of section 213(d)(1)) attributable to emotional distress.

(b) Termination of application of subsection (a)(4) in certain cases.—

(1) In general.—Subsection (a)(4) shall not apply in the case of any individual who is not described in paragraph (2).

(2) Individuals to whom subsection (a)(4) continues to apply.—An individual is described in this paragraph if—

(A) on or before September 24, 1975, he was entitled to receive any amount described in subsection (a)(4),

(B) on September 24, 1975, he was a member of any organization (or reserve component thereof) referred to in subsection (a)(4) or under a binding written commitment to become such a member,

(C) he receives an amount described in subsection (a)(4) by reason of a combat-related injury, or

(D) on application therefor, he would be entitled to receive disability compensation from the Veterans' Administration.

(3) Special rules for combat-related injuries.—For purposes of this subsection, the term "combat-related injury" means personal injury or sickness—

(A) which is incurred—

(i) as a direct result of armed conflict,

(ii) while engaged in extrahazardous service, or

(iii) under conditions simulating war; or

(B) which is caused by an instrumentality of war.

In the case of an individual who is not described in subparagraph (A) or (B) of paragraph (2), except as provided in paragraph (4), the only amounts taken into account under subsection (a)(4) shall be the amounts which he receives by reason of a combat-related injury.

(4) Amount excluded to be not less than veterans' disability compensation.—In the case of any individual described in paragraph (2), the amounts excludable under subsection (a)(4) for any period with respect to any individual shall not be less than the maximum amount which such individual, on application therefor, would be entitled to receive as disability compensation from the Veterans' Administration.

(c) Application of prior law in certain cases.—The phrase "(other than punitive damages)" shall not apply to punitive damages awarded in a civil action—

(1) which is a wrongful death action, and

(2) with respect to which applicable State law (as in effect on September 13, 1995 and without regard to any modification after such date) provides, or has been construed to provide by a court of competent jurisdiction pursuant to a decision issued on or before September 13, 1995, that only punitive damages may be awarded in such an action.

This subsection shall cease to apply to any civil action filed on or after the first date on which the applicable State law ceases to provide (or is no longer construed to provide) the treatment described in paragraph (2).

(d) Cross references.—

(1) For exclusion from employee's gross income of employer contributions to accident and health plans, see section 106.

(2) For exclusion of part of disability retirement pay from the application of subsection (a)(4) of this section, see section 1403 of Title 10, United States Code (relating to career compensation laws). (December 19, 1989, Pub. L. 101-239, Title VII, §7641(a), 103 Stat. 2379; August 20, 1996, Pub. L. 104-188 §1605, 110 Stat. 1838, 1839; August 21, 1996, Pub. L. 104-191 §311(b), 110 Stat. 2053; January 23, 2002, Pub. L. 107-134 §113(a), 115 Stat. 2435).

2002 Note: The amendments made by this section shall apply to taxable years ending on or after September 11, 2001. Pub. L. 107-134 §113(c).

1996 Notes: The amendments to subsections (a) [closing paragraph], (a)(2), (c), and (d) made by Pub. L. 104-188 §1605 apply to amounts received after August 20, 1996, in taxable years ending after this date; except, the amendments made by Pub. L. 104-188 §1605 shall not apply to any amount received under a written binding agreement, court decree, or mediation award in effect on (or issued on or before) September 13, 1995. Pub. L. 104-188 §1605(d).

The amendment to subsection (a)(3) by Pub. L. 104-191 §311(b) applies to taxable years beginning after December 31, 1996. Pub. L. 104-191 §311(c).

Ref.: W. Cal. Sum., 4 "Secured Transactions in Personal Property" §§164, 166, 6 "Torts" §§1557, 1558, 8 "Constitutional Law" §873.

SUBTITLE F
PROCEDURE AND ADMINISTRATION

CHAPTER 64
COLLECTION

SUBCHAPTER C
LIEN FOR TAXES

PART II
LIENS

§6323. Validity and priority against certain persons.

[Subsection (a) Not Reproduced]

(b) Protection for certain interests even though notice filed.—Even though notice of a lien imposed by section 6321 has been filed, such lien shall not be valid—

[Subsections (b)(1)–(7) Not Reproduced]

(8) Attorneys' liens.—With respect to a judgment or other amount in settlement of a claim or of a cause of action, as against an attorney who, under local law, holds a lien upon or a contract enforceable against such judgment or amount, to the extent of his reasonable compensation for obtaining such judgment or procuring such settlement, except that this paragraph shall not apply to any judgment or amount in settlement of a claim or of a cause of action against the United States to the extent that the United States offsets such judgment or amount against any liability of the taxpayer to the United States.

[Subsections (b)(9)–(i) Not Reproduced]

(Aug. 16, 1954, ch 736, 68A Stat. 779; Feb. 26, 1964, P.L. 88-272, Title II, §236(a), (c)(1), 78 Stat. 127, 128; July 5, 1966, P.L. 89-493, §17(a), 80 Stat. 266; Nov. 2, 1966, P.L. 89-719, Title I, §101(a), 80 Stat. 1125; Oct. 4, 1976, P.L. 94-455, Title XII, §1202(h)(2), Title XIX, §1906(b)(13)(A), Title XX, §2008(c), 90 Stat. 1688, 1834, 1892; Nov. 6, 1978, P.L. 95-600, Title VII, §702(q)(1), (2), 92 Stat. 2937, 2938; Oct. 22, 1986, P.L. 99-514, Title XV, §1569(a), 100 Stat. 2764; Nov. 10, 1988, P.L. 100-647, Title I, §1015(s)(1), 102 Stat. 3573; Nov. 5, 1990, P.L. 101-508, Title XI, §§11317(b), 11704(a)(26), 104 Stat. 1388-458, 1388-519; July 30, 1996, P.L. 104-168, Title V, §501(a), 110 Stat. 1460; July 22, 1998, P.L. 105-206, Title I, §1102(d)(1)(A), Title III, §3435(a), (b), 112 Stat. 704, 760, 761.)

SUBCHAPTER D
SEIZURE OF PROPERTY FOR COLLECTION OF TAXES

PART II
LEVY

§6334. Property exempt from levy.

(a) Enumeration.—There shall be exempt from levy—

[Subsections (1)–(6) Not Reproduced]

(7) Workmen's Compensation.—Any amount payable to an individual as workmen's compensation (including any portion thereof payable with respect to dependents) under a workmen's compensation law of the United States, any State, the District of Columbia, or the Commonwealth of Puerto Rico.

[Subsections (a)(8)–(g) Not Reproduced]

(Aug. 16, 1954, ch 736, 68A Stat. 784; Aug. 28, 1958, P.L. 85-840, Title IV, §406, 72 Stat. 1047; June 21, 1965, P.L. 89-44, Title VIII, §812(a), 79 Stat. 170; Nov. 2, 1966, P.L. 89-719, Title I, §104(c), 80 Stat. 1137; Dec. 30, 1969, P.L. 91-172, Title IX, §945(a), 83 Stat. 729; Oct. 4, 1976, P.L. 94-455, Title XII, §1209(a)-(c), Title XIX, §1906(b)(13)(A), 90 Stat. 1709, 1710, 1834; Sept. 3, 1982, P.L. 97-248, Title III, §347(a), 96 Stat. 638; July 18, 1984, P.L. 98-369, Div B, Title VI, §2661(o)(5), 98 Stat. 1159; Oct. 22, 1986, P.L. 99-514, Title XV, §1565(a), 100 Stat. 2763; Nov. 10, 1988, P.L. 100-647, Title I, §1015(o), Title VI, §6236(c), 102 Stat. 3572, 3738; Aug. 6, 1991, P.L. 102-83, §5(c)(2), 105 Stat. 406; July 30, 1996, P.L. 104-168, Title V, §502(a)-(c), 110 Stat. 1461; Aug. 22, 1996, P.L. 104-193, Title I, §110(l)(3) [110(l)(6)], 110 Stat. 2173; Aug. 5, 1997, P.L. 105-33, Title V,

§5514(a)(2), (3), 111 Stat. 620; Aug. 5, 1997, P.L. 105-34, Title III, §312(d)(1), Title X, §1025(a), 111 Stat. 839, 924; July 22, 1998, P.L. 105-206, Title III, §§3431(a)-(c), 3445(a), (b), 112 Stat. 758, 762, 763.)

TITLE 28
JUDICIARY AND JUDICIAL PROCEDURE

PART IV
JURISDICTION AND VENUE

CHAPTER 83
COURTS OF APPEALS

§1291. Final decisions of district courts.

The courts of appeals (other than the United States Court of Appeals for the Federal Circuit) shall have jurisdiction of appeals from all final decisions of the district courts of the United States, the United States District Court for the District of the Canal Zone, the District Court of Guam, and the District Court of the Virgin Islands, except where a direct review may be had in the Supreme Court. The jurisdiction of the United States Court of Appeals for the Federal Circuit shall be limited to the jurisdiction described in sections 1292(c) and (d) and 1295 of this title. (June 25, 1948, c. 646, 62 Stat. 929; October 31, 1951, c. 655, §48, 65 Stat. 726; July 7, 1958, Pub. L. 85–508 §12(e), 72 Stat. 348; April 2, 1982, Pub. L. 97–164 §124, 96 Stat. 36.)

CHAPTER 85
DISTRICT COURTS; JURISDICTION

§1333. Admiralty, maritime and prize cases.

The district courts shall have original jurisdiction, exclusive of the courts of the States, of:

(1) Any civil case of admiralty or maritime jurisdiction, saving to suitors in all cases all other remedies to which they are otherwise entitled.

(2) Any prize brought into the United States and all proceedings for the condemnation of property taken as prize. (June 25, 1948, c. 646, 62 Stat. 931; May 24, 1949, c. 139, §79, 63 Stat. 101.)

Ref.: W. Cal. Sum., 2 "Workers' Compensation" §126.

§1346. United States as defendant.

[Subsection (a) Not Reproduced]

(b)(1) Subject to the provisions of chapter 171 of this title, the district courts, together with the United States District Court for the District of the Canal Zone and the District Court of the Virgin Islands, shall have exclusive jurisdiction of civil actions on claims against the United States, for money damages, accruing on and after January 1, 1945, for injury or loss of property, or personal injury or death caused by the negligent or wrongful act or omission of any employee of the Government while acting within the scope of his office or employment, under circumstances where the United States, if a private person, would be liable to the claimant in accordance with the law of the place where the act or omission occurred.

(2) No person convicted of a felony who is incarcerated while awaiting sentencing or while serving a sentence may bring a civil action against the United States or an agency, officer, or employee of the Government, for mental or emotional injury suffered while in custody without a prior showing of physical injury.

(c) The jurisdiction conferred by this section includes jurisdiction of any set-off, counterclaim, or other claim or demand whatever on the part of the United States against any plaintiff commencing an action under this section.

[Subsections (d)–(g) Not Reproduced]

(June 25, 1948, ch 646, 62 Stat. 933; April 25, 1949, ch 92, §2(a), 63 Stat. 62; May 24, 1949, ch 139, §80(a), (b), 63 Stat. 101; Oct. 31, 1951, ch 655, §50(b), 65 Stat. 727; July 30, 1954, ch 648, §1, 68 Stat. 589; July 7, 1958, P.L. 85-508, §12(e), 72 Stat. 348; Aug. 30, 1964, P.L. 88-519, 78 Stat. 699; Nov. 2, 1966, P.L. 89-719, Title II, §202(a), 80 Stat. 1148; July 23, 1970, P.L. 91-350, §1(a), 84 Stat. 449; Oct. 25, 1972, P.L. 92-562, §1, 86 Stat. 1176; Oct. 4, 1976, P.L. 94-455, Title XII, §1204(c)(1), Title XIII, 1306(b)(7), 90 Stat. 1697, 1719; Nov. 1, 1978, P.L. 95-563, §14(a), 92 Stat. 2389; April 2, 1982, P.L. 97-164, Title I, Part A, §129, 96 Stat. 39; Sept. 3, 1982, P.L. 97-248, Title IV, §402(c)(17), 96 Stat. 669; April 26, 1996, P.L. 104-134, Title I [Title VIII, §806], 110 Stat. 1321-75; May 2, 1996, P.L. 104-140, §1(a), 110 Stat. 1327; Oct. 26, 1996, P.L. 104-331, §3(b)(1), 110 Stat. 4069.)

Ref.: W. Cal. Sum., 5 "Torts" §§205–207, 209, 6 "Torts" §1538.

CHAPTER 87
DISTRICT COURTS; VENUE

§1402. United States as defendant.

[Subsection (a) Not Reproduced]

(b) Any civil action on a tort claim against the United States under subsection (b) of section 1346 of this title may be prosecuted only in the judicial district where the plaintiff resides or wherein the act or omission complained of occurred.

[Subsections (c) and (d) Not Reproduced]

(June 25, 1948, ch 646, 62 Stat. 937; Sept. 2, 1958, P.L. 85-920, 72 Stat. 1770; Nov. 2, 1966, P.L. 89-719, Title II, §202(b), 80 Stat. 1149; Oct. 25, 1972, P.L. 92-562, §2, 86 Stat. 1176; April 2, 1982, P.L. 97-164, Title I, Part A, §131, 96 Stat. 39.)

Ref.: W. Cal. Sum., 5 "Torts" §209.

PART VI
PARTICULAR PROCEEDINGS

CHAPTER 161
UNITED STATES AS PARTY GENERALLY

§2401. Time for commencing action against United States.

[Subsection (a) Not Reproduced]

(b) A tort claim against the United States shall be forever barred unless it is presented in writing to the appropriate Federal agency within two years after such claim accrues or unless action is begun within six months after the date of mailing, by certified or registered mail, of notice of final denial of the claim by the agency to which it was presented. (June 25, 1948, c. 646, 62 Stat. 971, as amended April 25, 1949, c. 92, §1, 63 Stat. 62; Pub. L. 86–238 §1(3), 73 Stat. 472; July 18, 1966, Pub. L. 89–506 §7, 80 Stat. 306.)

Ref.: W. Cal. Sum., 5 "Torts" §209.

§2402. Jury trial in actions against United States.

Subject to chapter 179 of this title [28 USCS §§ 3901 et seq.], any action against the United States under section 1346 [28 USCS § 1346] shall be tried by the court without a jury, except that any action against the United States under section 1346(a)(1) [28 USCS § 1346(a)(1)] shall, at the request of either party to such action, be tried by the court with a jury. (June 25, 1948, ch 646, 62 Stat. 971; July 30, 1954, ch. 648, §2(a), 68 Stat. 589; Oct. 26, 1996, P.L. 104-331, §3(b)(3), 110 Stat. 4069.)

Ref.: W. Cal. Sum., 5 "Torts" §209.

§2412. Costs and fees.

(a)(1) Except as otherwise specifically provided by statute, a judgment for costs, as enumerated in section 1920 of this title, but not including the fees and expenses of attorneys, may be awarded to the prevailing party in any civil action brought by or against the United States or any agency or any official of the United States acting in his or her official capacity in any court having jurisdiction of such action. A judgment for costs when taxed against the United States shall, in an amount established by statute, court rule, or order, be limited to reimbursing in whole or in part the prevailing party for the costs incurred by such party in the litigation.

(2) A judgment for costs, when awarded in favor of the United States in an action brought by the United States, may include an amount equal to the filing fee prescribed under section 1914(a) of this title. The preceding sentence shall not be construed as requiring the United States to pay any filing fee.

(b) Unless expressly prohibited by statute, a court may award reasonable fees and expenses of attorneys, in addition to the costs which may be awarded pursuant to subsection (a), to the prevailing party in any civil action brought by or against the United States or any agency or any official of the United States acting in his or her official capacity in any court having jurisdiction of such action. The United States shall be liable for such fees and expenses to the same extent that any other party would be liable under the common law or under the terms of any statute which specifically provides for such an award.

(c)(1) Any judgment against the United States or any agency and any official of the United States acting in his or her official capacity for costs pursuant to subsection (a) shall be paid as provided in sections 2414 and 2517 of this title and shall be in addition to any relief provided in the judgment.

(2) Any judgment against the United States or any agency and any official of the United States acting in his or her official capacity for fees and expenses of attorneys pursuant to subsection (b) shall be paid as provided in sections 2414 and 2517 of this title, except that if the basis for the award is a finding that the United States acted in bad faith, then the award shall be paid by any agency found to have acted in bad faith and shall be in addition to any relief provided in the judgment.

(d)(1)(A) Except as otherwise specifically provided by statute, a court shall award to a prevailing party other than the United States fees and other expenses, in addition to any costs awarded pursuant to subsection (a), incurred by that party in any civil action (other than cases sounding in tort), including proceedings for judicial review of agency action, brought by or against the United States in any court having jurisdiction of that action, unless the court finds that the position of the United States was substantially justified or that special circumstances make an award unjust.

(B) A party seeking an award of fees and other expenses shall, within thirty days of final judgment in the action, submit to the court an application for fees and other expenses which shows that the party is a prevailing party and is eligible to receive an award under this subsection, and the amount sought, including an itemized statement from any attorney or expert witness representing or appearing in behalf of the party stating the actual time expended and the rate at which fees and other expenses were computed. The party shall also allege that the position of the United States was not substantially justified. Whether or not the position of the United States was substantially justified shall be determined on the basis of the record (including the record with respect to the action or failure to act by the agency upon which the civil action is based) which is made in the civil action for which fees and other expenses are sought.

(C) The court, in its discretion, may reduce the amount to be awarded pursuant to this subsection, or deny an award, to the extent that the prevailing party during the course of the proceedings engaged in conduct which unduly and unreasonably protracted the final resolution of the matter in controversy.

(D) If, in a civil action brought by the United States or a proceeding for judicial review of an adversary adjudication described in section 504(a)(4) of title 5, the demand by the United States is substantially in excess of the judgment finally obtained by the United States and is unreasonable when compared with such judgment, under the facts and circumstances of the case, the court shall award to the party the fees and other expenses related to defending against the excessive demand, unless the party has committed a willful violation of law or otherwise acted in bad faith, or special circumstances make an award unjust. Fees and expenses awarded under this subparagraph shall be paid only as a consequence of appropriations provided in advance.

(2) For the purposes of this subsection—

(A) "fees and other expenses" includes the reasonable expenses of expert witnesses, the reasonable cost of any study, analysis, engineering report, test, or project which is found by the court to be necessary for the preparation of the party's case, and reasonable attorney fees (The amount of fees awarded under this subsection shall be based upon prevailing market rates for the kind and quality of the services furnished, except that (i) no expert witness shall be compensated at a rate in excess of the highest rate of compensation for expert witnesses paid by the United States; and (ii) attorney fees shall not be awarded in excess of $125 per hour unless the court determines that an increase in the cost of living or a special factor, such as the limited availability of qualified attorneys for the proceedings involved, justifies a higher fee.);

(B) "party" means (i) an individual whose net worth did not exceed $2,000,000 at the time the civil action was filed, or (ii) any owner of an unincorporated business, or any partnership, corporation, association, unit of local government, or organization, the net worth of which did not exceed $7,000,000 at the time the civil action was filed, and which had not more than 500 employees at the time the civil action was filed; except that an organization described in section 501(c)(3) of the Internal Revenue Code of 1954 (26 U.S.C. 501(c)(3)) exempt from taxation under section 501(a) of such Code, or a cooperative association as defined in section 15(a) of the Agricultural Marketing Act (12 U.S.C. 1141j(a)), may be a party regardless of the net worth of such organization or cooperative association or for purposes of subsection (d)(1)(D), a small entity as defined in section 601 of title 5;

(C) "United States" includes any agency and any official of the United States acting in his or her official capacity;

(D) "position of the United States" means, in addition to the position taken by the United States in the civil action, the action or failure to act by the agency upon which the civil action is based; except that fees and expenses may not be awarded to a party for any portion of the litigation in which the party has unreasonably protracted the proceedings;

(E) "civil action brought by or against the United States" includes an appeal by a party, other than the United States, from a decision of a contracting officer rendered pursuant to a disputes clause in a contract with the Government or pursuant to the Contract Disputes Act of 1978;

(F) "court" includes the United States Claims Court [United States Court of Federal Claims] and the United States Court of Appeals for Veterans Claims;

(G) "final judgment" means a judgment that is final and not appealable, and includes an order of settlement;

(H) "prevailing party", in the case of eminent domain proceedings, means a party who obtains a final judgment (other than by settlement), exclusive of interest, the amount of which is at least as close to the highest valuation of the property involved that is attested to at trial on behalf of the property owner as it is to the highest valuation of the property involved that is attested to at trial on behalf of the Government; and

(I) "demand" means the express demand of the United States which led to the adversary adjudication, but shall not include a recitation of the maximum statutory penalty (i) in the complaint, or (ii) elsewhere when accompanied by an express demand for a lesser amount.

(3) In awarding fees and other expenses under this subsection to a prevailing party in any action for judicial review of an adversary adjudication, as defined in subsection (b)(1)(C) of section 504 of title 5, United States Code, or an adversary adjudication subject to the Contract Disputes Act of 1978, the court shall include in that award fees and other expenses to the same extent authorized in subsection (a) of such section, unless the court finds that during such adversary adjudication the position of the United States was substantially justified, or that special circumstances make an award unjust.

(4) Fees and other expenses awarded under this subsection to a party shall be paid by any agency over which the party prevails from any funds made available to the agency by appropriation or otherwise.

(5) [Repealed]

(e) The provisions of this section shall not apply to any costs, fees, and other expenses in connection with any proceeding to which section 7430 of the Internal Revenue Code of 1954 applies (determined without regard to subsections (b) and (f) of such section). Nothing in the preceding sentence shall prevent the awarding under subsection (a) of section 2412 of title 28, United States Code, of costs enumerated in section 1920 of such title (as in effect on October 1, 1981).

(f) If the United States appeals an award of costs or fees and other expenses made against the United States under this section and the award is affirmed in whole or in part, interest shall be paid on the amount of the award as affirmed. Such interest shall be computed at the rate determined under section 1961(a) of this title, and shall run from the date of the award through the day before the date of the mandate of affirmance. (June 25, 1948, c. 646, §1, 62 Stat. 973; July 18, 1966, Pub.L. 89-507, §1, 80 Stat. 308; Oct. 21, 1980, Pub.L. 96-481, Title II, §204(a), (c), 94 Stat. 2327, 2329; Sept. 3, 1982, Pub.L. 97-248, Title II, Subtitle G, §292(c), 96 Stat. 574; Aug. 5, 1985, Pub.L. 99-80, §§2, 6, 99 Stat. 184, 186; Oct. 29, 1992, Pub.L. 102-572, Title III, §301(a), Title V, §§502(b), 506(a), 106 Stat. 4511, 4512, 4513; Dec. 21, 1995, Pub.L. 104-66, Title I, Subtitle I, §1091(b), 109 Stat. 722; March 29, 1996, Pub.L. 104-121, Title II, Subtitle C, §232, 110 Stat. 863; Nov. 11, 1998, Pub.L. 105-368, Title V, Subtitle B, §512(b)(1)(B), 112 Stat. 3342.)

2002 Note: Act Dec. 6, 2002, Pub. L. 107-330, §403, 116 Stat. 2833, provides: "The authority of the United States Court of Appeals for Veterans Claims to award reasonable fees and expenses of attorneys under section 2412(d) of title 28, United States Code, shall include authority to award fees and expenses, in an amount determined appropriate by the United States Court of Appeals for Veterans Claims, of individuals admitted to practice before the Court as non-attorney practitioners under subsection (b) or (c) of Rule 46 of the Rules of Practice and Procedure of the United States Court of Appeals for Veterans Claims."

CHAPTER 171
TORT CLAIMS PROCEDURE

§2671. Definitions.

As used in this chapter and sections 1346(b) and 2401(b) of this title, the term "Federal agency" includes the executive departments, the judicial and legislative branches, the military departments, independent establishments of the United States, and corporations primarily acting as instrumentalities or agencies of the United States, but does not include any contractor with the United States.

"Employee of the government" includes (1) officers or employees of any federal agency, members of the military or naval forces of the United States, members of the National Guard while engaged in training or duty under section 115, 316, 502, 503, 504, or 505 of title 32, and persons acting on behalf of a federal agency in an official capacity, temporarily or permanently in the service of the United States, whether with or without compensation, and (2) any officer or employee of a Federal public defender organization, except when such officer or employee performs professional services in the course of providing representation under section 3006A of title 18.

"Acting within the scope of his office or employment", in the case of a member of the military or naval forces of the United States or a member of the National Guard as defined in section 101(3) of title 32, means acting in line of duty. (June 25, 1948, c. 646, 62 Stat. 982, amended May 24, 1949, c. 139 §124, 63 Stat. 106; July 18, 1966, Pub. L. 89–506 §8, 80 Stat. 306; Dec. 29, 1981, Pub. L. 97-124, §1, 95 Stat. 1666; Nov. 18, 1988, Pub. L. 100-694 §3, 102 Stat. 4564; Oct. 30, 2000, P.L. 106-398, §1, 114 Stat. 1654; Nov. 13, 2000, P.L. 106-518, Title IV, §401, 114 Stat. 2421.)

Ref.: W. Cal. Sum., 5 "Torts" §§205, 206.

§2672. Administrative adjustment of claims.

The head of each Federal agency or his designee, in accordance with regulations prescribed by the Attorney General, may consider, ascertain, adjust, determine, compromise, and settle any claim for money damages against the United States for injury or loss of property or personal injury or death caused by the negligent or wrongful act or omission of any employee of the agency while acting within the scope of his office or employment, under circumstances where the United States, if a private person, would be liable to the claimant in accordance with the law of the place where the act or omission occurred: Provided, That any award, compromise, or settlement in excess of $25,000 shall be effected only with the prior written approval of the Attorney General or his designee. Notwithstanding the proviso contained in the preceding sentence, any award, compromise, or settlement may be effected without the prior written approval of the Attorney General or his or her designee, to the extent that the Attorney General delegates to the head of the agency the authority to make such award, compromise, or settlement. Such delegations may not exceed the authority delegated by the Attorney General to the United States attorneys to settle claims for money damages against the United States. Each Federal agency may use arbitration, or other alternative means of dispute resolution under the provisions of subchapter IV of chapter 5 of title 5, to settle any tort claim against the United States, to the extent of the agency's authority to award, compromise, or settle such claim without the prior written approval of the Attorney General or his or her designee.

Subject to the provisions of this title relating to civil actions on tort claims against the United States, any such award, compromise, settlement, or determination shall be final and conclusive on all officers of the Government, except when procured by means of fraud.

Any award, compromise, or settlement in an amount of $2,500 or less made pursuant to this section shall be paid by the head of the Federal agency concerned out of appropriations available to that agency. Payment of any award, compromise, or settlement in an amount in excess of $2,500 made pursuant to this section or made by the Attorney General in any amount pursuant to section 2677 of this title shall be paid in a manner similar to judgments and compromises in like causes and appropriations or funds available for the payment of such judgments and compromises are hereby made available for the payment of awards, compromises, or settlements under this chapter.

The acceptance by the claimant of any such award, compromise, or settlement shall be final and conclusive on the claimant, and shall constitute a complete release of any claim against the United States and against the employee of the government whose act or omission gave rise to the claim, by reason of the same subject matter. (June 25, 1948, c. 646, 62 Stat. 983, amended April 25, 1949, c. 92, §2(b), 63 Stat. 62; May 24, 1949, c. 139, §125, 63 Stat. 106; September 23, 1950, c. 1010, §9, 64 Stat. 987; September 8, 1959, Pub. L. 86–238, 73 Stat. 471; July 18, 1966, Pub. L. 89–506 §§1, 9(a), 80 Stat. 306; November 15, 1990, Pub. L. 101-552, §8(a), 104 Stat. 2746.)

Ref.: W. Cal. Sum., 5 "Torts" §§205–207, 209.

§2674. Liability of United States.

The United States shall be liable, respecting the provisions of this title relating to tort claims, in the same manner and to the same extent as a private individual under like circumstances, but shall not be liable for interest prior to judgment or for punitive damages.

If, however, in any case wherein death was caused, the law of the place where the act or omission complained of occurred provides, or has been construed to provide, for damages only punitive in nature, the United States shall be liable for actual or compensatory damages, measured by the pecuniary injuries resulting from such death to the persons respectively, for whose benefit the action was brought, in lieu thereof.

With respect to any claim under this chapter, the United States shall be entitled to assert any defense based upon judicial or legislative immunity which otherwise would have been available to the employee of the United States whose act or omission gave rise to the claim, as well as any other defenses to which the United States is entitled.

With respect to any claim to which this section applies, the Tennessee Valley Authority shall be entitled to assert any defense which otherwise would have been available to the employee based upon judicial or legislative immunity, which otherwise would have been available to the employee of the Tennessee Valley Authority whose act or omission gave rise to the claim as well as any other defenses to which the Tennessee Valley Authority is entitled under this chapter. (June 25, 1948, c. 646, 62 Stat. 983; November 18, 1988, Pub. L. 100-694, §§4, 9(c), 102 Stat. 4564, 4567.)

Ref.: W. Cal. Sum., 5 "Torts" §§205, 207.

§2675. Disposition by federal agency as prerequisite.

(a) An action shall not be instituted upon a claim against the United States for money damages for injury or loss of property or personal injury or death caused by the negligent or wrongful act or omission of any employee of the Government while acting within the scope of his office or employment, unless the claimant shall have first presented the claim to the appropriate Federal agency and his claim shall have been finally denied by the agency in writing and sent by certified or registered mail. The failure of an agency to make final disposition of a claim within six months after it is filed shall, at the option of the claimant any time thereafter, be deemed a final denial of the claim for purposes of this section. The provisions of this subsection shall not apply to such claims as may be asserted under the Federal Rules of Civil Procedure by third party complaint, cross-claim, or counterclaim.

(b) Action under this section shall not be instituted for any sum in excess of the amount of the claim presented to the federal agency, except where the increased amount is based upon newly discovered evidence not reasonably discoverable at the time of presenting the claim to the federal agency, or upon allegation and proof of intervening facts, relating to the amount of the claim.

(c) Disposition of any claim by the Attorney General or other head of a federal agency shall not be competent evidence of liability or amount of damages. (June 25, 1948, c. 646, §1, 62 Stat. 983, amended May 24, 1949, c. 139, §126, 63 Stat. 107; July 18, 1966, Pub. L. 89–506, §2, 80 Stat. 306.)

Ref.: W. Cal. Sum., 5 "Torts" §209.

§2676. Judgment as bar.

The judgment in an action under section 1346(b) of this title shall constitute a complete bar to any action by the claimant, by reason of the same subject matter, against the employee of the government whose act or omission gave rise to the claim. (June 25, 1948, c. 646, 62 Stat. 984.)

Ref.: W. Cal. Sum., 5 "Torts" §209.

§2677. Compromise.

The Attorney General or his designee may arbitrate, compromise, or settle any claim cognizable under section 1346(b) of this title, after the commencement of an action thereon. (June 25, 1948, c. 646, 62 Stat. 984; July 18, 1966, Pub. L. 506 §3, 80 Stat. 307.)

Ref.: W. Cal. Sum., 5 "Torts" §209.

§2678. Attorney fees; penalty.

No attorney shall charge, demand, receive, or collect for services rendered, fees in excess of 25 per centum of any judgment rendered pursuant to section 1346(b) of this title or any settlement made pursuant to section 2677 of this title, or in excess of 20 per centum of any award, compromise, or settlement made pursuant to section 2672 of this title.

Any attorney who charges, demands, receives, or collects for services rendered in connection with such claim any amount in excess of that allowed under this section, if recovery be had, shall be fined not more than $2,000 or imprisoned not more than one year, or both. (June 25, 1948, c. 646, 62 Stat. 984; July 18, 1966, Pub. L. 89–506 §4, 80 Stat. 307.)

Ref.: W. Cal. Sum., 5 "Torts" §205.

§2679. Exclusiveness of remedy.

(a) The authority of any federal agency to sue and be sued in its own name shall not be construed to authorize suits against such federal agency on claims which are cognizable under section 1346(b) of this title, and the remedies provided by this title in such cases shall be exclusive.

(b)(1) The remedy against the United States provided by sections 1346(b) and 2672 of this title for injury or loss of property, or personal injury or death, arising or resulting from the negligent or wrongful act or omission of any employee of the Government while acting within the scope of his office or employment is exclusive of any other civil action or proceeding for money damages by reason of the same subject matter against the employee whose act or omission gave rise to the claim or against the estate of such employee. Any other civil action or proceeding for money damages arising out of or relating to the same subject matter against the employee or the employee's estate is precluded without regard to when the act or omission occurred.

(2) Paragraph (1) does not extend or apply to a civil action against an employee of the Government—

(A) which is brought for a violation of the Constitution of the United States, or

(B) which is brought for a violation of a statute of the United States under which such action against an individual is otherwise authorized.

(c) The Attorney General shall defend any civil action on proceeding brought in any court against any employee of the Government or his estate for any such damage or injury. The employee against whom such civil action or proceeding is brought shall deliver within such time after date of service or knowledge of service as determined by the Attorney General, all process served upon him or an attested true copy thereof to his immediate superior or to whomever was designated by the head of his department to receive such papers and such person shall promptly furnish copies of the pleadings and process therein to the United States attorney for the district embracing the place wherein the proceeding is brought, to the Attorney General, and to the head of his employing Federal agency.

(d)(1) Upon certification by the Attorney General that the defendant employee was acting within the scope of his office or employment at the time of the incident out of which the claim arose, any civil action or proceeding commenced upon such claim in a United States district court shall be deemed an action against the United States under the provisions of this title and all references thereto, and the United States shall be substituted as the party defendant.

(2) Upon certification by the Attorney General that the defendant employee was acting within the scope of his office or employment at the time of the incident out of which the claim arose, any civil action or proceeding commenced upon such claim in a State court shall be removed without bond at any time before trial by the Attorney General to the district court of the United States for the district and division embracing the place in which the action or proceeding is pending. Such action or proceeding shall be deemed to be an action or proceeding brought against the United States under the provisions of this title and all references thereto, and the United States shall be substituted as the party defendant. This certification of the Attorney General shall conclusively establish scope of office or employment for purposes of removal.

(3) In the event that the Attorney General has refused to certify scope of office or employment under this section, the employee may at any time before trial petition the court to find and certify that the employee was acting within the scope of his office or employment. Upon such certification by the court, such action or proceeding shall be deemed to be an action or proceeding brought against the United States under the provisions of this title and all references thereto, and the United States shall be substituted as the party defendant. A copy of the petition shall be served upon the United States in accordance with the provisions of Rule 4(d)(4) of the Federal Rules of Civil Procedures. In the event the petition is filed in a civil action or proceeding pending in a State court, the action or proceeding may be removed without bond by the Attorney General to the district court of the United States for the district and division embracing the place in which it is pending. If, in considering the petition, the district court determines that the employee was not acting within the scope of his office or employment, the action or proceeding shall be remanded to the State court.

TITLE 33
NAVIGATION AND NAVIGABLE WATERS

CHAPTER 18
LONGSHORE AND HARBOR WORKERS' COMPENSATION

§901. Short title.

This chapter may be cited as "Longshore and Harbor Workers' Compensation Act." (March 4, 1927, ch 509, §1, 44 Stat. 1424; Sept. 28, 1984, Pub.L. 98-426, §27(d)(1), 98 Stat. 1654.)

Ref.: W. Cal. Sum., 2 "Workers' Compensation" §§130, 135.

§902. Definitions.

When used in this Act—

(1) The term "person" means individual, partnership, corporation, or association.

(2) The term "injury" means accidental injury or death arising out of and in the course of employment, and such occupational disease or infection as arises naturally out of such employment or as naturally or unavoidably results from such accidental injury, and includes an injury caused by the willful act of a third person directed against an employee because of his employment.

(3) The term "employee" means any person engaged in maritime employment, including any longshoreman or other person engaged in longshoring operations, and any harbor-worker including a ship repairman, shipbuilder, and shipbreaker, but such term does not include—

(A) individuals employed exclusively to perform office clerical, secretarial, security, or data processing work;

(B) individuals employed by a club, camp, recreational operation, restaurant, museum, or retail outlet;

(C) individuals employed by a marina and who are not engaged in construction, replacement, or expansion of such marina (except for routine maintenance);

(D) individuals who (i) are employed by suppliers, transporters, or vendors, (ii) are temporarily doing business on the premises of an employer described in paragraph (4), and (iii) are not engaged in work normally performed by employees of that employer under this Act;

(E) aquaculture workers;

(F) individuals employed to build, repair, or dismantle any recreational vessel under sixty-five feet in length;

(G) a master or member of a crew of any vessel; or

(H) any person engaged by a master to load or unload or repair any small vessel under eighteen tons net;

if individuals described in clauses (A) through (F) are subject to coverage under a State workers' compensation law.

(4) The term "employer" means an employer any of whose employees are employed in maritime employment, in whole or in part, upon the navigable waters of the United States (including any adjoining pier, wharf, dry dock, terminal, building way, marine railway, or other adjoining area customarily used by an employer in landing, unloading, repairing, or building a vessel).

(5) The term "carrier" means any person or fund authorized under section 32 [33 U.S.C.S. §932] to insure under this Act and includes self-insurers.

(6) The term "Secretary" means the Secretary of Labor.

(7) The term "deputy commissioner" means the deputy commissioner having jurisdiction in respect of an injury or death.

(8) The term "State" includes a Territory and the District of Columbia.

(9) The term "United States" when used in a geographical sense means the several States and Territories and the District of Columbia, including the territorial waters thereof.

(10) "Disability" means incapacity because of injury to earn the wages which the employee was receiving at the time of injury in the same or any other employment; but such term shall mean permanent impairment, determined (to the extent covered thereby) under the guides to the evaluation of permanent impairment promulgated and modified from time to time by the American Medical Association, in the case of an individual whose claim is described in section 910(d)(2) [33 U.S.C.S. §910(d)(2)].

(11) "Death" as a basis for a right to compensation means only death resulting from an injury.

(12) "Compensation" means the money allowance payable to an employee or to his dependents as provided for in this Act, and includes funeral benefits provided therein.

(13) The term "wages" means the money rate at which the service rendered by an employee is compensated by an employer under the contract of hiring in force at the time of the injury, including the reasonable value of any advantage which is received from the employer and included for purposes of any withholding of tax under subtitle C of the Internal Revenue Code of 1954 [26 U.S.C.S. §§ 3101 et seq.] (relating to employment taxes). The term wages does not include fringe benefits, including (but not limited to) employer payments for or contributions to a retirement, pension, health and welfare, life insurance, training, social security or other employee or dependent benefit plan for the employee's or dependent's benefit, or any other employee's dependent entitlement.

(14) "Child" shall include a posthumous child, a child legally adopted prior to the injury of the employee, a child in relation to whom the deceased employee stood in loco parentis for at least one year prior to the time of injury, and a stepchild or acknowledged illegitimate child dependent upon the deceased, but does not include married children unless wholly dependent on him. "Grandchild" means a child as above defined of a child as above defined. "Brother" and "sister" include stepbrothers and stepsisters, half brothers and half sisters, and brothers and sisters by adoption, but does not include married brothers nor married sisters unless wholly dependent on the employee. "Child," "grandchild," "brother," and "sister" include only a person who is under eighteen years of age, or who, though eighteen years of age or over, is (1) wholly dependent upon the employee and incapable of self-support by reason of mental or physical disability, or (2) a student as defined in paragraph (19) [(18)] of this section.

(15) The term "parent" includes stepparents and parents by adoption, parents-in-law, and any person who for more than three years prior to the death of the deceased employee stood in the place of a parent to him, if dependent on the injured employee.

(16) The terms "widow or widower" includes only the decedent's wife or husband living with or dependent for support upon him or her at the time of his or her death; or living apart for justifiable cause or by reason of his or her desertion at such time.

(17) The terms "adoption" or "adopted" means legal adoption prior to the time of the injury.

(18) The term "student" means a person regularly pursuing a full-time course of study or training at an institution which is—

(A) a school or college or university operated or directly supported by the United States, or by any State or local government or political subdivision thereof,

(B) a school or college or university which has been accredited by a State or by a State recognized or nationally recognized accrediting agency or body,

(C) a school or college or university not so accredited but whose credits are accepted, on transfer, by not less than three institutions which are so accredited, for credit on the same basis as if transferred from an institution so accredited, or

(D) an additional type of educational or training institution as defined by the Secretary, but not after he reaches the age of twenty-three or has completed four years of education beyond the high school level, except that, where his twenty-third birthday occurs during a semester or other enrollment period, he shall continue to be considered a student until the end of such semester or other enrollment period. A child shall not be deemed to have ceased to be a student during any interim between school years if the interim does not exceed five months and if he shows to the satisfaction of the Secretary that he has a bona fide intention of continuing to pursue a full-time course of education or training during the semester or other enrollment period immediately following the interim or during periods of reasonable duration during which, in the judgment of the Secretary, he is prevented by factors beyond his control from pursuing his education. A child shall not be deemed to be a student under this Act during a period of service in the Armed Forces of the United States.

(19) The term "national average weekly wage" means the national average weekly earnings of production or nonsupervisory workers on private nonagricultural payrolls.

(20) The term "Board" shall mean the Benefits Review Board.

(21) Unless the context requires otherwise, the term "vessel" means any vessel upon which or in connection with which any person entitled to benefits under this Act suffers injury or death arising out of or in the course of his employment, and said vessel's owner, owner pro hac vice, agent, operator, charter or bare boat charterer, master, officer, or crew member.

(22) The singular includes the plural and the masculine includes the feminine and neuter. (March 4, 1927, c. 509, §2, 44 Stat. 1424; June 25, 1938, c. 685, §1, 52 Stat. 1164; Oct. 27, 1972, Pub.L. 92-576, §§2(a)(b) 3, 5(b), 15(c), 18(b), 20(c), 86 Stat. 1251, 1262; Sept. 28, 1984, Pub.L. 98-426, §§2, 5(a)(2), 27(a)(1), 98 Stat. 1639, 1641, 1654.)

Ref.: W. Cal. Sum., 2 "Workers' Compensation" §§136, 137.

§903. Coverage.

(a) Disability or death; injuries occurring upon navigable waters of United States. Except as otherwise provided in this section, compensation shall be payable under this Act in respect of disability or death of an employee, but only if the disability or death results from an injury occurring upon the navigable waters of the United States (including any adjoining pier, wharf, dry dock, terminal, building way, marine railway, or other adjoining area customarily used by an employer in loading, unloading, repairing, dismantling, or building a vessel).

(b) Governmental officers and employees. No compensation shall be payable in respect of the disability or death of an officer or employee of the United States, or any agency thereof, or of any State or foreign government, or any subdivision thereof.

(c) Intoxication; willful intention to kill. No compensation shall be payable if the injury was occasioned solely by the intoxication of the employee or by the willful intention of the employee to injure or kill himself or another.

(d) Small vessels.

(1) No compensation shall be payable to an employee employed at a facility of an employer if, as certified by the Secretary, the facility is engaged in the business of building, repairing, or dismantling exclusively small vessels (as defined in paragraph (3) of this subsection), unless the injury occurs while upon the navigable waters of the United States or while upon any adjoining pier, wharf, dock, facility over land for launching vessels, or facility over land for hauling, lifting, or drydocking vessels.

(2) Notwithstanding paragraph (1), compensation shall be payable to an employee—

(A) who is employed at a facility which is used in the business of building, repairing, or dismantling small vessels if such facility receives Federal maritime subsidies; or

(B) if the employee is not subject to coverage under a State workers' compensation law.

(3) For purposes of this subsection, a small vessel means—

(A) a commercial barge which is under 900 lightship displacement tons; or

(B) a commercial tugboat, towboat, crew boat, supply boat, fishing vessel, or other work vessel which is under 1,600 tons gross as measured under section 14502 of title 46, United States Code, or an alternate tonnage measured under section 14302 of that title as prescribed by the Secretary under section 14104 of that title.

(e) Credit for benefits paid under other laws. Notwithstanding any other provision of law, any amounts paid to an employee for the same injury, disability, or death for which benefits are claimed under this Act pursuant to any other workers' compensation law or section 20 of the Act of March 4, 1915 (38 Stat. 1185, chapter 153; 46 U.S.C. 688 [46 U.S.C.S. Appx §688]) (relating to recovery for injury to or death of seamen) shall be credited against any liability imposed by this Act. (March 4, 1927, c. 509. §3, 44 Stat. 1426; Oct. 27, 1972, Pub.L. 92-576, §§2(c), 21, 86 Stat. 1251, 1265; Sept. 28, 1984, Pub.L. 98-426, §3, 98 Stat. 1640, as amended October 19, 1996, Pub. L. 104–324, §703, 110 Stat. 3933.)

Ref.: W. Cal. Sum., 2 "Workers' Compensation" §136.

§904. Liability for compensation.

(a) Every employer shall be liable for and shall secure the payment to his employees of the compensation payable under sections 907, 908, and 909 of this title. In the case of an employer who is a subcontractor, only if such subcontractor fails to secure the payment of compensation shall the contractor be liable for and be required to secure the payment of compensation. A subcontractor shall not be deemed to have failed to secure the payment of compensation if the contractor has provided insurance for such compensation for the benefit of the subcontractor.

(b) Compensation shall be payable irrespective of fault as a cause for the injury. (March 4, 1927, c. 509, §4, 44 Stat. 1426; Sept. 28, 1984, Pub.L. 98-426, §4(a), 98 Stat. 1641.)

§905. Exclusiveness of liability.

(a) The liability of an employer prescribed in section 904 of this title shall be exclusive and in place of all other liability of such employer to the employee, his legal representative, husband or wife, parents, dependents, next of kin, and anyone otherwise entitled to recover damages from such employer at law or in admiralty on account of such injury or death, except that if an employer fails to secure payment of compensation as required by this chapter, an injured employee, or his legal representative in case death results from the injury, may elect to claim compensation under the chapter, or to maintain an action at law or in admiralty for damages on account of such injury or death. In such action the defendant may not plead as a defense that the injury was caused by the negligence of a fellow servant, or that the employee assumed the risk of his employment, or that the injury was due to the contributory negligence of the employee. For purposes of this subsection, a contractor shall be deemed the employer of a subcontractor's employees only if the subcontractor fails to secure the payment of compensation as required by section 904 of this title.

(b) In the event of injury to a person covered under this chapter caused by the negligence of a vessel, then such person, or anyone otherwise entitled to recover damages by reason thereof, may bring an action against such vessel as a third party in accordance with the provisions of section 933 of this title, and the employer shall not be liable to the vessel for such damages directly or indirectly and any agreements or warranties to the contrary shall be void. If such person was employed by the vessel to provide stevedoring services, no such action shall be permitted if the injury was caused by the negligence of persons engaged in providing stevedoring services to the vessel. If such person was employed to provide shipbuilding, repairing, or breaking services and such person's employer was the owner, owner pro hac vice, agent, operator, or character of the vessel, no such action shall be permitted, in whole or in part or directly or indirectly, against the injured person's employer (in any capacity, including as the vessel's owner, owner pro hac vice, agent, operator, or charterer) or against the employees of the employer. The liability of the vessel under this subsection shall not be based upon the warranty of seaworthiness or a breach thereof at the time the injury occurred. The remedy provided in this subsection shall be exclusive of all other remedies against the vessel except remedies available under this chapter.

(c) In the event that the negligence of a vessel causes injury to a person entitled to receive benefits under this chapter by virtue of section 1333 of Title 43, then such person, or anyone otherwise entitled to recover damages by reason thereof, may bring an action against such vessel in accordance with the provisions of subsection (b) of this section. Nothing contained in subsection (b) of this section shall preclude the enforcement according to its terms of any reciprocal indemnity provision whereby the employer of a person entitled to receive benefits under this chapter by virtue of section 1333 of Title 43 and the vessel agree to defend and indemnify the other for cost of defense and loss or liability for damages arising out of or resulting from death or bodily injury to their employees. (March 4, 1927, ch. 509, §5, 44 Stat. 1426; Oct. 27, 1972, Pub. L. 92-576, §18(a), 86 Stat. 1263; Sept. 28, 1984, Pub. L. 98-426, §§4(b), 5(a)(1), (b), 98 Stat. 1641.)

Ref.: W. Cal. Sum., 2 "Workers' Compensation" §§130, 135, 139, 141, 142.

§906. Compensation.

(a) No compensation shall be allowed for the first three days of the disability, except the benefits provided for in section 907 of this title: Provided, however, That in case the injury results in disability of more than fourteen days, the compensation shall be allowed from the date of the disability.

(b)(1) Compensation for disability or death (other than compensation for death required by this chapter to be paid in a lump sum) shall not exceed an amount equal to 200 per centum of the applicable national average weekly wage, as determined by the Secretary under paragraph (3).

(2) Compensation for total disability shall not be less than 50 per centum of the applicable national average weekly wage determined by the Secretary under paragraph (3), except that if the employee's average weekly wages as computed under section 10 are less that 50 per centum of such national average weekly wage, he shall receive his average weekly wages as compensation for total disability.

(3) As soon as practicable after June 30 of each year, and in any event prior to October 1 of such year, the Secretary shall determine the national average weekly wage for the three consecutive calendar quarters ending June 30. Such determination shall be the applicable national average weekly wage for the period beginning with October 1 of that year and ending with September 30 of the next year. The initial determination under this paragraph shall be made as soon as practicable after the enactment of this subsection.

(c) Determinations under subsection (b)(3) of this section with respect to a period shall apply to employees or survivors currently receiving compensation for permanent total disability or death benefits during such period, as well as those newly awarded compensation during such period. (March 4, 1927, ch 509, §6, 44 Stat. 1426; June 24, 1948, ch 623, §1, 62 Stat. 602; July 26, 1956, ch 735, §1, 70 Stat. 654; July 14, 1961, P.L. 87-87, §1, 75 Stat. 203; Oct. 27, 1972, P.L. 92-576, §§4, 5(a), 86 Stat. 1252; Sept. 28, 1984, P.L. 98-426, §6, 98 Stat. 1641.)

§907. Medical services and supplies.

(a) The employer shall furnish such medical, surgical, and other attendance or treatment, nurse and hospital service, medicine, crutches, and apparatus, for such period as the nature of the injury or the process of recovery may require.

(b) The employee shall have the right to choose an attending physician authorized by the Secretary to provide medical care under this chapter as hereinafter provided. If, due to the nature of the injury, the employee is unable to select his physician and the nature of the injury requires immediate medical treatment and care, the employer shall select a physician for him. The Secretary shall actively supervise the medical care rendered to injured employees, shall require periodic reports as to the medical care being rendered to injured employees, shall have authority to determine the necessity, character, and sufficiency of any medical aid furnished or to be furnished, and may, on his own initiative or at the request of the employer, order a change of physicians or hospitals when in his judgment such change is desirable or necessary in the interest of the employee or where the charges exceed those prevailing within the community for the same or similar services or exceed the provider's customary charges. Change of physicians at the request of employees shall be permitted in accordance with regulations of the Secretary.

(c)(1)(A) The Secretary shall annually prepare a list of physicians and health care providers in each compensation district who are not authorized to render medical care or provide medical services under this chapter. The names of physicians and health care providers contained on the list required under this subparagraph shall be made available to employees and employers in each compensation district through posting and insuch other forms as the Secretary may prescribe.

(B) Physicians and health care providers shall be included on the list of those not authorized to provide medical care and medical services pursuant to subparagraph (A) when the Secretary determines under this section, in accordance with the procedures provided in subsection (j) of this section, that such physician or health care provider—

(i) has knowingly and willfully made, or caused to be made, any false statement or misrepresentation of a material fact for use in a claim for compensation or claim for reimbursement of medical expenses under this chapter;

(ii) has knowingly and willfully submitted, or caused to be submitted, a bill or request for payment under this chapter containing a charge which the Secretary finds to be substantially in excess of the charge for the service, appliance, or supply prevailing within the community or in excess of the provider's customary charges, unless the Secretary finds there is good cause for the bill or request containing the charge;

(iii) has knowingly and willfully furnished a service, appliance, or supply which is determined by the Secretary to be substantially in excess of the need of the recipient thereof or to be of a quality which substantially fails to meet professionally recognized standards;

(iv) has been convicted under any criminal statute (without regard to pending appeal thereof) for fraudulent activities in connection with any Federal or State program for which payments are made to physicians or providers of similar services, appliances, or supplies; or

(v) has otherwise been excluded from participation in such program.

(C) Medical services provided by physicians or health care providers who are named on the list published by the Secretary pursuant to subparagraph (A) of this section shall not be reimbursable under this chapter, except that the Secretary shall direct the reimbursement of medical claims for services rendered by such physicians or health care providers in cases where the services were rendered in an emergency.

(D) A determination under subparagraph (B) shall remain in effect for a period of not less than three years and until the Secretary finds an gives notice to the public that there is a reasonably assurance that the basis for the determination will not reoccur.

(E) A provider of a service, appliance, or supply shall provide to the Secretary such information and certification as the Secretary may require to assure that this subsection is enforced.

(2) Whenever the employer or carrier acquires knowledge of the employee's injury, through written notice or otherwise as prescribed by this chapter, the employer or carrier shall forthwith authorize medical treatment and care from a physician selected by an employee pursuant to subsection (b) of this section. An employee may not select a physician who is on the list required by paragraph (1) of this subsection. An employee may not change physicians after his initial choice unless the employer, carrier, or deputy commissioner has given prior consent for such change. Such consent shall be given in cases where an employee's initial choice was ot of a specialist whose services are necessary for and appropriate to the proper care and treatment of the compensable injury or disease. In all other cases, consent may be given upon a showing of good cause for change.

(d)(1) An employee shall not be entitled to recover any amount expended by him for medical or other treatment or services unless—

(A) the employer shall have refused or neglected a request to furnish such services and the employee has complied with subsections (b) and (c) of this section and the applicable regulations; or

(B) the nature of the injury required such treatment and services and the employer or his superintendent or foreman having knowledge of such injury shall have neglected to provide or authorize same.

(2) No claim for medical or surgical treatment shall be valid and enforceable against such employer unless, within ten days following the first treatment, the physician giving such treatment furnishes to the employer and the deputy commissioner a report of such injury or treatment, on a form prescribed by the Secretary. The Secretary may excuse the failure to furnish such report within the ten-day period whenever he finds it to be in the interest of justice to do so.

(3) The Secretary may, upon application by a party in interest, make an award for the reasonable value of such medical or surgical treatment so obtained by the employee.

(4) If at any time the employee unreasonably refuses to submit to medical or surgical treatment, or to an examination by a physician selected by the employer, the Secretary or administrative law judge may, by order, suspend the payment of further compensation during such time as such refusal continues, and no compensation shall be paid at any time during the period of such suspension, unless the circumstances justified the refusal.

(e) In the event that medical questions are raised in any case, the Secretary shall have the power to cause the employee to be examined by a physician employed or selected by the Secretary and to obtain from such physician a report containing his estimate of the employee's physical impairment and such other information as may be appropriate. Any party who is dissatisfied with such report may request a review or reexamination of the employee by one or more different physicians employed or selected by the Secretary. The Secretary shall order such review or reexamination unless he finds that it is clearly unwarranted. Such review or reexamination shall be completed within two weeks from the date ordered unless the Secretary finds that because of extraordinary circumstances a longer period is required. The Secretary shall have the power in his discretion to charge the cost of examination or review under this subsection to the employer, if he is a self-insurer, or to the insurance company which is carrying the risk, in appropriate cases, or to the special fund in section 44.

(f) An employee shall submit to a physical examination under subsection (e) at such place as the Secretary may require. The place, or places, shall be designated by the Secretary and shall be reasonably convenient for the employee. No physician selected by the employer, carrier, or employee shall be present at or participate in any manner in such examination, nor shall conclusions of such physicians as to the nature or extent of impairment or the cause of impairment be available to the examining physician unless otherwise ordered, for good cause, by the Secretary. Such employer or carrier shall, upon request, be entitled to have the employee examined immediately thereafter and upon the same premises by a qualified physician or physicians in the presence of such physician as the employee may select, if any. Proceedings shall be suspended and no compensation shall be payable for any period during which the employee may refuse to submit to examination.

(g) All fees and other charges for medical examinations, treatment, or service shall be limited to such charges as prevail in the community for such treatment, and shall be subject to regulation by the Secretary. The Secretary shall issue regulations limiting the nature and extent of medical expenses chargeable against the employer without authorization by the employer or the Secretary.

(h) The liability of an employer for medical treatment as herein provided shall not be affected by the fact that his employee was injured through the fault or negligence of a third party not in the same employ, or that suit has been brought against such third party. The employer shall, however, have a cause of action against such third party to recover any amounts paid by him for such medical treatment in like manner as provided in section 933(b) of this title.

(i) Unless the parties to the claim agree, the Secretary shall not employ or select any physician for the purpose of making examinations or reviews under subsection (e) of this section who, during such employment, or during the period of two years prior to such employment, has been employed by, or accepted or participated in any fee relating to a workmen's compensation claim from any insurance carrier or any self-insurer.

(j)(1) The Secretary shall have the authority to make rules and regulations and to establish procedures, not inconsistent with the provisions of this chapter, which are necessary or appropriate to carry out the provisions of subsection (c) of this section, including the nature and extent of the proof and evidence necessary for actions under this section and the methods of taking and furnishing such proof and evidence.

(2) Any decision to take action with respect to a physician or health care provider under this section shall be based on specific findings of fact by the Secretary. The Secretary shall provide notice of these findings and an opportunity for a hearing pursuant to section 556 of Title 5 for a provider who would be affected by a decision under this section. A request for a hearing must be filed with the Secretary within thirty days after notice of the findings is received by the provider making such request. If a hearing is held, the Secretary shall, on the basis of evidence adduced at the hearing, affirm, modify, or reverse the findings of fact and proposed action under this section.

(3) For the purpose of any hearing, investigation, or other proceeding authorized or directed under this section, the provisions of section[s] 49 and 50 of Title 15 (relating to the attendance of witnesses and the production of books, papers, and documents) shall apply to the jurisdiction, powers, and duties of the Secretary or any officer designated by him.

(4) Any physician or health care provider, after any final decision of the Secretary made after a hearing to which he was a party, irrespective of the amount in controversy, may obtain a review of such decision by a civil action commenced within sixty days after the mailing to him of notice of such decision, but the pendency of such review shall not operate as a stay upon the effect of such decision. Such action shall be brought in the court of appeals of the United States for the judicial circuit in which the plaintiff resides or has his principal place of business, or the Court of Appeals for the District of Columbia. As part of his answer, the Secretary shall file a certified copy of the transcript of the record of the hearing, including all evidence submitted in connection therewith. The findings of fact of the Secretary, if based on substantial evidence in the record as a whole, shall be conclusive.

(k)(1) Nothing in this chapter prevents an employee whose injury or disability has been established under this chapter from relying in good faith on treatment by prayer or spiritual means alone, in accordance with the tenets and practice of a recognized church or religious denomination, by an accredited practitioner of such recognized church or religious denomination, and on nursing services rendered in accordance with such tenets and practice, without suffering loss or diminution of the compensation or benefits under this chapter. Nothing in this subsection shall be construed to except an employee from all physical examinations required by this chapter.

(2) If an employee refuses to submit to medical or surgical services solely because, in adherence to the tenets and practice of a recognized church or religious denomination, the employee relies upon prayer or spiritual means alone for healing, such employee shall not be considered to have unreasonably refused medical or surgical treatment under subsection (d) of this section.

§908. Compensation for disability.

Compensation for disability shall be paid to the employee as follows:

(a) Permanent total disability: In case of total disability adjudged to be permanent 66⅔ per centum of the average weekly wages shall be paid to the employee during the continuance of such total disability. Loss of both hands, or both arms, or both feet, or both legs, or both eyes, or of any two thereof shall, in the absence of conclusive proof to the contrary, constitute permanent total disability. In all other cases permanent total disability shall be determined in accordance with the facts.

(b) Temporary total disability: In case of disability total in character but temporary in quality 66⅔ per centum of the average weekly wages shall be paid to the employee during the continuance thereof.

(c) Permanent partial disability: In case of disability partial in character but permanent in quality, the compensation shall be 66⅔ per centum of the average weekly wages, which shall be in addition to compensation for temporary total disability or temporary partial disability paid in accordance with subdivision (b) or subdivision (e) of this section respectively, and shall be paid to the employee, as follows:

(1) Arm lost, three hundred and twelve weeks' compensation.

(2) Leg lost, two hundred and eighty-eight weeks' compensation.

(3) Hand lost, two hundred and forty-four weeks' compensation.

(4) Foot lost, two hundred and five weeks' compensation.

(5) Eye lost, one hundred and sixty weeks' compensation.

(6) Thumb lost, seventy-five weeks' compensation.

(7) First finger lost, forty-six weeks' compensation.

(8) Great toe lost, thirty-eight weeks' compensation.

(9) Second finger lost, thirty weeks' compensation.

(10) Third finger lost, twenty-five weeks' compensation.

(11) Toe other than great toe lost, sixteen weeks' compensation.

(12) Fourth finger lost, fifteen weeks' compensation.

(13) Loss of hearing:

(A) Compensation for loss of hearing in one ear, fifty-two weeks.

(B) Compensation for loss of hearing in both ears, two hundred weeks.

(C) An audiogram shall be presumptive evidence of the amount of hearing loss sustained as of the date thereof, only if (i) such audiogram was administered by a licensed or certified audiologist or a physician who is certified in otolaryngology, (ii) such audiogram, with the report thereon, was provided to the employee at the time it was administered, and (iii) no contrary audiogram made at that time is produced.

(D) The time for filing a notice of injury, under section 912 of this title, or a claim for compensation, under section 913 of this title, shall not begin to run in connection with any claim for loss of hearing under this section, until the employee has received an audiogram, with the accompanying report thereon, which indicates that the employee has suffered a loss of hearing.

(E) Determinations of loss of hearing shall be made in accordance with the guides for the evaluation of permanent impairment as promulgated and modified from time to time by the American Medical Association.

(14) Phalanges: Compensation for loss of more than one phalange of a digit shall be the same as for loss of the entire digit. Compensa-

tion for loss of the first phalange shall be one-half of the compensation for loss of the entire digit.

(15) Amputated arm or leg: Compensation for an arm or a leg, if amputated at or above the elbow or the knee, shall be the same as for a loss of the arm or leg; but, if amputated between the elbow and the wrist or the knee and the ankle, shall be the same as for loss of a hand or foot.

(16) Binocular vision or per centum of vision: Compensation for loss of binocular vision or for 80 per centum or more of the vision of an eye shall be the same as for loss of the eye.

(17) Two or more digits: Compensation for loss of two or more digits, or one or more phalanges of two or more digits, of a hand or foot may be proportioned to the loss of use of the hand or foot occasioned thereby, but shall not exceed the compensation for loss of a hand or foot.

(18) Total loss of use: Compensation for permanent total loss of use of a member shall be the same as for loss of the member.

(19) Partial loss or partial loss of use: Compensation for permanent partial loss or loss of use of a member may be for proportionate loss or loss of use of the member.

(20) Disfigurement: Proper and equitable compensation not to exceed $7,500 shall be awarded for serious disfigurement of the face, head, or neck or of other normally exposed areas likely to handicap the employee in securing or maintaining employment.

(21) Other Cases: In all other cases in the class of disability, the compensation shall be 66⅔ per centum of the difference between the average weekly wages of the employee and the employee's wage-earning capacity thereafter in the same employment or otherwise, payable during the continuance of partial disability.

(22) In any case in which there shall be a loss of, or loss of use of, more than one member or parts of more than one member set forth in paragraphs (1) to (19) of this subdivision, not amounting to permanent total disability, the award of compensation shall be for the loss of, or loss of use of, each such member or part thereof, which awards shall run consecutively, except that where the injury affects only two or more digits of the same hand or foot, paragraph (17) of this subdivision shall apply.

(23) Notwithstanding paragraphs (1) through (22), with respect to a claim for permanent partial disability for which the average weekly wages are determined under section 910(d)(2) of this title, the compensation shall be 66⅔ per centum of such average weekly wages multiplied by percentage of permanent impairment, as determined under the guides referred to in section 902(10) of this title, payable during the continuance of such impairment.

(d)(1) If an employee who is receiving compensation for permanent partial disability pursuant to subdivision (c)(1)–(20) of this section dies from causes other than the injury, the total amount of the award unpaid at the time of death shall be payable to or for the benefit of his survivors, as follows:

(A) if the employee is survived only by a widow or widower, such unpaid amount of the award shall be payable to such widow or widower,

(B) if the employee is survived only by a child or children, such unpaid amount of the award shall be paid to such child or children in equal shares,

(C) if the employee is survived by a widow or widower and a child or children, such unpaid amount of the award shall be payable to such survivors in equal shares,

(D) if there be no widow or widower and no surviving child or children, such unpaid amount of the award shall be paid to the survivors specified in section 909(d) of this title (other than a wife, husband, or child); and the amount to be paid each such survivor shall be determined by multiplying such unpaid amount of the award by the appropriate percentage specified in section 909(d) of this title, but if the aggregate amount to which all such survivors are entitled, as so determined, is less than such unpaid amount of the award, the excess amount shall be divided among such survivors pro rata according to the amount otherwise payable to each under this subparagraph.

(2) Notwithstanding any other limitation in section 909 of this title, the total amount of any award for permanent partial disability pursuant to subdivision (c)(1)–(20) of this section unpaid at time of death shall be payable in full in the appropriate distribution.

(3) An award for disability may be made after the death of the injured employee. Except where compensation is payable under subdivision (c)(21) of this section, if there be no survivors as prescribed in this section, then the compensation payable under this subsection shall

be paid to the special fund established under section 944(a) of this title.

(e) Temporary partial disability: In case of temporary partial disability resulting in decrease of earning capacity the compensation shall be two-thirds of the difference between the injured employee's average weekly wages before the injury and his wage-earning capacity after the injury in the same or another employment, to be paid during the continuance of such disability, but shall not be paid for a period exceeding five years.

(f) Injury increasing disability:

(1) In any case in which an employee having an existing permanent partial disability suffers injury, the employer shall provide compensation for such disability as is found to be attributable to that injury based upon the average weekly wages of the employee at the time of the injury. If following an injury falling within the provisions of subdivision (c)(1)–(20) of this section, the employee is totally and permanently disabled, and the disability is found not to be due solely to that injury, the employer shall provide compensation for the applicable prescribed period of weeks provided for in that section for the subsequent injury, or for one hundred and four weeks, whichever is the greater, except that, in the case of an injury falling within the provisions of section 908(c)(13) of this title, the employer shall provide compensation for the lesser of such periods. In all other cases of total permanent disability or of death, found not to be due solely to that injury, of an employee having an existing permanent partial disability, the employer shall provide in addition to compensation under paragraphs (b) and (e) of this section, compensation payments or death benefits for one hundred and four weeks only. If following an injury falling within the provisions of subdivision (c)(1)-(20) of this section, the employee has a permanent partial disability and the disability is found not to be due solely to that injury, and such disability is materially and substantially greater than that which would have resulted from the subsequent injury alone, the employer shall provide compensation for the applicable period of weeks provided for in that section for the subsequent injury, or for one hundred and four weeks, whichever is the greater, except that, in the case of an injury falling with the provisions of section 908(c)(13) of this title, the employer shall provide compensation for the lesser of such periods.

In all other cases in which the employee has a permanent partial disability, found not to be due solely to that injury, and such disability is materially and substantially greater than that which would have resulted from the subsequent injury alone, the employer shall provide in addition to compensation under paragraphs (b) and (e) of this section, compensation for one hundred and four weeks only.

(2)(A) After cessation of the payments for the period of weeks provided for herein, the employee or his survivor entitled to benefits shall be paid the remainder of the compensation that would be due out of the special fund established in section 944 of this title, except that the special fund shall not assume responsibility with respect to such benefits (and such payments shall not be subject to cessation) in the case of any employer who fails to comply with section 932(a) of this title.

(B) After cessation of payments for the period of weeks provided for in this subsection, the employer or carrier responsible for payment of compensation shall remain a party to the claim, retain access to all records relating to the claim, and in all other respects retain all rights granted under this chapter prior to cessation of such payments.

(3) Any request, filed after September 28, 1984, for apportionment of liability to the special fund established under section 944 of this title for the payment of compensation benefits, and a statement of the grounds therefore, shall be presented to the deputy commissioner prior to the consideration of the claim by the deputy commissioner. Failure to present such request prior to such consideration shall be an absolute defense to the special fund's liability for the payment of any benefits in connection with such claim, unless the employer could not have reasonably anticipated the liability of the special fund prior to the issuance of a compensation order.

(g) Maintenance for employees undergoing vocational rehabilitation: An employee who as a result of injury is or may be expected to be totally or partially incapacitated for a remunerative occupation and who, under the direction of the Secretary as provided by section 939(c) of this title, is being rendered fit to engage in a remunerative occupation, shall receive additional compensation necessary for his maintenance, but such additional compensation shall not exceed $25 a week. The expense shall be paid out of the special fund established in section 944 of this title.

(h) The wage-earning capacity of an injured employee in cases of partial disability under subdivision (c) (21) of this section or under subdivision (e) of this section shall be determined by his actual earnings if such actual earnings fairly and reasonably represent his wage-earning capacity: Provided, however, that if the employee has no actual earnings or his actual earnings do not fairly and reasonably represent his wage-earning capacity, the deputy commissioner may, in the interest of justice, fix such wage-earning capacity as shall be reasonable, having due regard to the nature of his injury, the degree of physical impairment, his usual employment, and any other factors or circumstances in the case which may affect his capacity to earn wages in his disabled condition, including the effect of disability as it may naturally extend into the future.

(i)(1) Whenever the parties to any claim for compensation under this chapter, including survivors benefits, agree to a settlement, the deputy commissioner or administrative law judge shall approve the settlement within thirty days unless it is found to be inadequate or procured by duress. Such settlement may include future medical benefits if the parties so agree. No liability of any employer, carrier, or both for medical disability, or death benefits shall be discharged unless the application for settlement is approved by the deputy commissioner or administrative law judge. If the parties to the settlement are represented by counsel, then agreements shall be deemed approved unless specifically disapproved within thirty days after submission for approval.

(2) If the deputy commissioner disapproves an application for settlement under paragraph (1), the deputy commissioner shall issue a written statement within thirty days containing the reasons for disapproval. Any party to the settlement may request a hearing before an administrative law judge in the manner prescribed by this chapter. Following such hearing, the administrative law judge shall enter an order approving or rejecting the settlement.

(3) A settlement approved under this section shall discharge the liability of the employer or carrier, or both. Settlements may be agreed upon at any stage of the proceeding including after entry of a final compensation order.

(4) the special fund shall not be liable for reimbursement of any sums paid or payable to an employee or any beneficiary under such settlement, or otherwise voluntarily paid prior to such settlement by the employer or carrier, or both.

(j)(1) The employer may inform a disabled employee of his obligation to report to the employer not less than semiannually any earnings from employment or self-employment, on such forms as the Secretary shall specify in regulations.

(2) An employee who—

(A) fails to report the employee's earnings under paragraph (1) when requested, or

(B) knowingly and willfully omits or understates any part of such earnings, and who is determined by the deputy commissioner to have violated clause (A) or (B) of this paragraph, forfeits his right to compensation with respect to any period during which the employee was required to file such report.

(3) Compensation forfeited under this subsection, if already paid, shall be recovered by a deduction from the compensation payable to the employee in any amount and on such schedule as determined by the deputy commissioner.

§909. Compensation for death.

If the injury causes death, the compensation therefore shall be known as a death benefit and shall be payable in the amount and to or for the benefit of the persons following:

(a) Reasonable funeral expenses not exceeding $3,000.

(b) If there be a widow or widower an no child of the deceased, to such widow or widower 50 per centum of the average wages of the deceased, during widowhood, or dependent widowerhood, with two years' compensation in one sum upon remarriage; and if there be a surviving child or children of the deceased, the additional amount of 16⅔ per centum of such wages for each such child; in case of the death or remarriage of such widow or widower, if there be one surviving child of the deceased employee, such child shall have his compensation increased to 50 per centum of such wages, and if there be more than one surviving child of the deceased employee, to such children, in equal parts, 50 per centum of such wages increased by 16⅔ per centum of such wages for each child in excess of one: Provided, That the total amount payable shall in no case exceed 66⅔ per centum of such wages. The deputy commissioner having jurisdiction over the claim may, in his discretion, require the appointment of a guardian for the purpose of receiving the compensation of a minor child. In the absence of such a requirement the appointment of a guardian for such purposes shall not be necessary.

(c) If there be one surviving child of the deceased, but no widow or widower, then for the support of such child 50 per centum of the wages of the deceased; and if there be more than one surviving child of the deceased, but no widow or dependent husband, then for the support of such children, in equal parts 50 per centum of such wages increased by 16⅔ per centum of such wages for each child in excess of one: Provided, That the total amount payable shall in no case exceed 66⅔ per centum of such wages.

(d) If there be no surviving wife or husband or child, or if the amount payable to a surviving wife or husband and to children shall be less in the aggregate than 66⅔ per centum of the average wages of the deceased; then for the support of grandchildren or brothers and sisters, if dependent upon the deceased at the time of the injury, and any other persons who satisfy the definition of the term "dependent" in section 152 of Title 26, but are not otherwise eligible under this section, 20 per centum of such wages for the support of each such person during such dependency and for the support of each parent, or grandparent, of the deceased if dependent upon him at the time of the injury, 25 per centum of such wages during such dependency. But in no case shall the aggregate amount payable under this subdivision exceed the difference between 66⅔ per centum of such wages and the amount payable as hereinbefore provided to widow or widower and for the support of surviving child or children.

(e) In computing death benefits the average weekly wages of the deceased shall be considered to have been not less than the national average weekly wage as prescribed in section 906(b) of this title, but—

(1) the total weekly benefits shall not exceed the lesser of the average weekly wages of the deceased or the benefit which the deceased employee would have been eligible to receive under section 906(b)(1) of this title; and

(2) in the case of a claim based on death due to an occupational disease for which the time of injury (as determined under section 910(i) of this title) occurs after the employee has retired, the total weekly benefits shall not exceed one fifty-second part of the employee's average annual earnings during the 52-week period preceding retirement.

(f) All questions of dependency shall be determined as of the time of the injury.

(g) Aliens: Compensation under this chapter to aliens not residents (or about to become nonresidents) of the United States or Canada shall be the same in amount as provided for residents, except that dependents in any foreign country shall be limited to surviving wife and child or children, or if there be no surviving wife or child or children, to surviving father or mother whom the employee has supported, either wholly or in part, for the period of one year prior to the date of the injury, and except that the Secretary may, at his option or upon the application of the insurance carrier shall, commute all future installments of compensation to be paid to such aliens by paying or causing to be paid to them one-half of the commuted amount of such future installments of compensation as determined by the Secretary.

§910. Determination of pay.

Except as otherwise provided in this Chapter, the average weekly wage of the injured employee at the time of the injury shall be taken as the basis upon which to compute compensation and shall be determined as follows:

(a) If the injured employee shall have worked in the employment in which he was working at the time of the injury, whether for the same or another employer, during substantially the whole of the year immediately preceding his injury, his average annual earnings shall consist of three hundred times the average daily wage or salary for a six-day worker and two hundred and sixty times the average daily wage or salary for a five-day worker, which he shall have earned in such employment during the days when so employed.

(b) If the injured employee shall not have worked in such employment during substantially the whole of such year, his average annual earnings, if a six-day worker, shall consist of three hundred times the average daily wage or salary, and, if a five-day worker, two hundred and sixty times the average daily wage or salary, which an employee of the same class working substantially the whole of such immediately preceding year in the same or in similar employment in the same or a neighboring place shall have earned in such employment during the days when so employed.

(c) If either of the foregoing methods of arriving at the average annual earnings of the injured employee cannot reasonably and fairly be applied, such average annual earnings shall be such sum as, having regard to the previous earnings of the injured employee in the employment in which he was working at the time of the injury, and of other employees of the same or most similar class working in the same or most similar employment in the same or neighboring locality, or other employment of such employee, including the reasonable value of the services of the employee if engaged in self-employment, shall reasonably represent the annual earning capacity of the injured employee.

(d)(1) The average weekly wages of an employee shall be one fifty-second part of his average annual earnings.

(2) Notwithstanding paragraph (1), with respect to any claim based on a death or disability due to an occupational disease for which the time of injury (as determined under subsection (i) of this section) occurs—

(A) within the first year after the employee has retired, the average weekly wages shall be one fifty-second part of his average annual earnings during the 52-week period preceding retirement; or

(B) more than one year after the employee has retired, the average weekly wage shall be deemed to be the national average weekly wage (as determined by the Secretary pursuant to section 906(b) of this title) applicable at the time of the injury.

(e) If it be established that the injured employee was a minor when injured, and that under normal conditions his wages should be expected to increase during the period of disability the fact may be considered in arriving at his average weekly wages.

(f) Effective October 1 of each year, the compensation or death benefits payable for permanent total disability or death arising out of injuries subject to this chapter shall be increased by the lesser of—

(1) a percentage equal to the percentage (if any) by which the applicable national weekly wage for the period beginning on such October 1, as determined under section 906(b) of this title, exceeds the applicable national average weekly wage, as so determined, for the period beginning with the preceding October 1; or

(2) five per centum.

(g) The weekly compensation after adjustment under subsection (f) shall be fixed at the nearest dollar. No adjustment of less than $1 shall be made, but in no event shall compensation or death benefits be reduced.

(h)(1) Not later than ninety days after October 27, 1972, the compensation to which an employee or his survivor is entitled due to total permanent disability or death which commenced or occurred prior to October 27, 1972 shall be adjusted. The amount of such adjustment shall be determined in accordance with regulations of the Secretary by designating as the employee's average weekly wage the applicable national average weekly wage determined under section 906(b) of this title and (A) computing the compensation to which such employee or survivor would be entitled if the disabling injury or death had occurred on the day following October 27, 1972 and (B) subtracting therefrom the compensation to which such employee or survivor was entitled on October 27, 1972; except that no such employee or survivor shall receive total compensation amounting to less than that to which he was entitled on October 27, 1972. Notwithstanding the foregoing sentence, where such an employee or his survivor was awarded compensation as the result of death or permanent total disability at less than the maximum rate that was provided in this Act at the time of the injury which resulted in the death or disability, then his average weekly wage shall be determined by increasing his average weekly wage at the time of such injury by the percentage which the applicable national average weekly wage has increased between the year in which the injury occurred and the first day of the first month following October 27, 1972. Where such injury occurred prior to 1947, the Secretary shall determine, on the basis of such economic data as he deems relevant, the amount by which the employee's average weekly wage shall be increased for the pre-1947 period.

(2) Fifty per centum of any additional compensation or death benefit paid as a result of the adjustment required by paragraphs (1) and (3) of this subsection shall be paid out of the special fund established under section 944 of this title, and 50 per centum shall be paid from appropriations.

(3) For the purposes of subsections (f) and (g) an injury which resulted in permanent total disability or death which occurred prior to October 27, 1972 shall be considered to have occurred on the day following such October 27, 1972 date.

(i) For purposes of this section with respect to a claim for compensation for death or disability due to an occupational disease which does not immediately result in death or disability, the time of injury shall be deemed to be the date on which the employee or claimant becomes aware, or in the exercise of reasonable diligence or by reason of medical advice should have been aware, of the relationship between the employment, the disease, and the death or disability.

§911. Guardian for minor or incompetent.

The deputy commissioner may require the appointment by a court of competent jurisdiction, for any person who is mentally incompetent or a minor, of a guardian or other representative to receive compensation payable to such person under this chapter and to exercise the powers granted to or to perform the duties required of such person under this chapter.

§912. Notice of injury or death.

(a) Notice of an injury or death in respect of which compensation is payable under this Act shall be given within thirty days after the date of such injury or death, or thirty days after the employee or beneficiary is aware, or in the exercise of reasonable diligence or by reason of medical advice should have been aware, of a relationship between the injury or death and the employment, except that in the case of an occupational disease which does not immediately result in a disability or death, such notice shall be given within one year after the employee or claimant becomes aware, or in the exercise of reasonable diligence or by reason of medical advice should have been aware, of the relationship between the employment, the disease, and the death or disability. Notice shall be given (1) to the deputy commissioner in the compensation district in which the injury occurred, and (2) to the employer.

(b) Such notice shall be in writing, shall contain the name and address of the employee and a statement of the time, place, nature, and cause of the injury or death, and shall be signed by the employee or by some person on his behalf, or in case of death, by any person claiming to be entitled to compensation for such death or by a person on his behalf.

(c) Notice shall be given to the deputy commissioner by delivering it to him or sending it by mail addressed to his office, and to the employer by delivering it to him or by sending it by mail addressed to him at his last known place of business. If the employer is a partnership, such notice may be given to any partner, or if a corporation, such notice may be given to any agent or officer thereof upon whom legal process may be served or who is in charge of the business in the place where the injury occurred. Each employer shall designate those agents or other responsible officials to receive such notice, except that the employer shall designate as its representatives individuals among first line supervisors, local plan management, and personnel office officials. Such designations shall be made in accordance with regulations prescribed by the Secretary and the employer shall notify his employees and the Secretary of such designation in a manner prescribed by the Secretary in regulations.

(d) Failure to give such notice shall not bar any claim under this Act (1) if the employer (or his agent or agents or other responsible official or officials designated by the employer pursuant to subsection (c)) of this section or the carrier had knowledge of the injury or death, (2) the deputy commissioner determines that the employer or carrier has not been prejudiced by failure to give such notice, or (3) if the deputy commissioner excuses such failure on the ground that (i) notice, while not given to a responsible official designated by the employer pursuant to subsection (c) of this section, was given to an official of the employer or the employer's insurance carrier, and that the employer or carrier was not prejudiced due to the failure to provide notice to a responsible official designated by by employer pursuant to subsection (c) of this section, or (ii) for some satisfactory reason such notice could not be given; nor unless objection to such failure is raised before the deputy commissioner at the first hearing of a claim for compensation in respect of such injury or death.

§913. Filing of claims.

(a) Except as otherwise provided in this section, the right to compensation for disability or death under this Act shall be barred unless a claim therefore is filed within one year after the injury or death. If payment of compensation has been made without an award on account of such injury or death, a claim may be filed within one year after the date of the last payment. Such claim shall be filed with the deputy commissioner in the compensation district in which such injury or death occurred. The time for filing a claim shall not begin to run until the employee or beneficiary is aware, or by the exercise of reasonable diligence should have been aware, of the relationship between the injury or death and the employment.

(b)(1) Notwithstanding the provisions of subdivision (a) of this section failure to file a claim within the period prescribed in such subdivision shall not be a bar to such right unless objection to such failure is made at the first hearing of such claim in which all parties in interest are given reasonable notice and opportunity to be heard.

(2) Notwithstanding the provisions of subsection (a) of this section, a claim for compensation for death or disability due to an occupational disease which does not immediately result in such death or disability shall be timely if filed within two years after the employee or claimant becomes award, or in the exercise of reasonable diligence or by reason of medical advice should have been aware, of the relationship between the employment, the disease, and the death or disability, or within one year of the date of the last payment of compensation, whichever is later.

(c) If a person who is entitled to compensation under this Act is mentally incompetent or a minor, the provisions of subdivision (a) shall not be applicable so long as such person has no guardian or other authorized representative, but shall be applicable in the case of a person who is mentally incompetent or a minor from the date of appointment of such guardian or other representative, or in the case of a minor, if no guardian is appointed before he becomes of age, from the date he becomes of age.

(d) Where recovery is denied to any person, in a suit brought at law or in admiralty to recover damages in respect of injury or death, on the ground that such person was an employee and that the defendant was an employer within the meaning of this Act and that such employer had secured compensation to such employee under this Act, the limitation of time prescribed in subdivision (a) shall begin to run only from the date of termination of such suit.

§914. Payment of compensation.

(a) Compensation under this Act shall be paid periodically, promptly, and directly to the person entitled thereto, without an award, except where liability to pay compensation is controverted by the employer.

(b) The first installment of compensation shall become due on the fourteenth day after the employer has been notified pursuant to section 912 of this title, or the employer has knowledge of the injury or death, on which date all compensation then due shall be paid. Thereafter compensation shall be paid, in installments, semi-monthly, except where the deputy commissioner determines that payment in installments should be made monthly or at some other period.

(c) Upon making the first payment, and upon suspension of payment for any cause, the employer shall immediately notify the deputy commissioner, in accordance with a form prescribed by the Secretary, that payment of compensation has begun or has been suspended, as the case may be.

(d) If the employer controverts the right to compensation he shall file with the deputy commissioner on or before the fourteenth day after he has knowledge of the alleged injury or death, a notice, in accordance with a from prescribed by the Secretary, stating that the right to compensation is controverted, the name of the claimant, the name of the employer, the date of the alleged injury or death, and the grounds upon which the right to compensation is controverted.

(e) If any installment of compensation payable without an award is not paid within fourteen days after it becomes due, as provided in subdivision (b) of this section, there shall be added to such unpaid installment an amount equal to 10 per centum thereof, which shall be paid at the same time as, but in addition to, such installment, unless notice is filed under subdivision (d) of this section, or unless such nonpayment is excused by the deputy commissioner after a showing by the employer that owing to conditions over which he had no control such installment could not be paid within the period prescribed for the payment.

(f) If any compensation, payable under the terms of an award, is not paid within ten days after it becomes due, there shall be added to such unpaid compensation an amount equal to 20 per centum thereof, which shall be paid at the same time as, but in addition to, such compensation, unless review of the compensation order making such award is had as provided in section 21 and an order staying payment has been issued by the Board or court.

(g) Within sixteen days after final payment of compensation has been made, the employer shall send to the deputy commissioner a notice, in accordance with a form prescribed by the Secretary, stating that such final payment has been made, the total amount of compensation paid, the name of the employee and of any other person to whom the compensation has been paid, the date of the injury or death, and the date to which compensation has been paid. If the employer fails to so notify the deputy commissioner within such time the Secretary shall assess against such employer a civil penalty in the amount of $100.

(h) The deputy commissioner (1) may upon his own initiative at any time in a case in which payments are being made without an award, and (2) shall in any case where right to compensation is controverted, or where payments of compensation have been stopped or suspended, upon receipt of notice from any person entitled to compensation or from the employer, that the right to compensation is controverted, or that payments of compensation have been stopped or suspended, make such investigations, cause such medical examinations to be made, or hold such hearings, and take such further action as he considers will properly protect the rights of all parties.

(i) Whenever the deputy commissioner deems it advisable he may require any employer to make a deposit with the Treasurer of the United States to secure the prompt and convenient payment of such compensation and payments therefrom upon any awards shall be made upon order of the deputy commissioner.

(j) If the employer has made advance payments of compensation, he shall be entitled to be reimbursed out of any unpaid installment or installments of compensation due.

(k) An injured employee or in case of death his dependents or personal representative, shall give receipts for payment of compensation to the employer paying the same and such employer shall produce the same for inspection by the deputy commissioner, whenever required.

§915. Invalid agreements.

(a) No agreement by an employee to pay any portion of premium paid by his employer to a carrier or to contribute to a benefit fund or department maintained by such employer for the purpose of providing compensation or medical services and supplies as required by this Act shall be valid, and any employer who makes a deduction for such purpose from the pay of any employee entitled to the benefits of this Act shall be guilty of a misdemeanor and upon conviction thereof shall be punished by a fine of not more than $1,000.

(b) No agreement by an employee to waive his right to compensation under this Act shall be valid.

§916. Assignment and exemption from claims of creditors.

No assignment, release, or commutation of compensation or benefits due or payable under this Act, except as provided by this Act, shall be valid, and such compensation and benefits shall be exempt from all claims of creditors and from levy, execution, and attachment or other remedy for recovery or collection of a debt, which exemption may not be waived.

§917. Lien against compensation.

Where a trust fund which complies with section 302(c) of the Labor-Management Relations Act of 1947 (29 U.S.C 186(c)) established pursuant to a collective-bargaining agreement in effect between an employer and an employee covered under this chapter has paid disability benefits to an employee which the employee is legally obligated to repay by reason of his entitlement to compensation under this chapter or under a settlement, the Secretary shall authorize a lien on such compensation in favor of the trust fund for the amount of such payments.

§918. Collection of defaulted payments; special fund.

(a) In case of default by the employer in the payment of compensation due under any award of compensation for a period of thirty days after the compensation is due and payable, the person to whom such compensation is payable may, within one year after such default, make application to the deputy commissioner making the compensation order or a supplementary order declaring the amount of the default. After investigation, notice, and hearing, as provided in section 919 of this title, the deputy commissioner shall make a supplementary order, declaring the amount of the default, which shall be filed in the same manner as the compensation order. In case the payment in default is in installment of the award, the deputy commissioner may, in his discretion, declare the whole of the award as the amount of default. The applicant may file a certified copy of such supplementary order with the clerk of the Federal district court for the judicial district in which the employer has his principal place of business or maintains an office, or for the judicial district in which the injury occurred. In case such principal place of business or office or place where the injury occurred is in the District of Columbia, a copy of such supplementary order may be filed with the clerk of the Supreme Court of the District of Columbia. Such supplementary order of the deputy commissioner shall be final, and the court shall upon the filing of the copy enter judgment for the amount declared in default by the supplementary order if such supplementary order is in accordance with law. Review of the judgment so entered may be had as in civil suits for damages at common law. Final proceedings to execute the judgment may be had by writ of execution in the form used by the courts in suits at common law in actions of assumpsit. No fee shall be required for filing the supplementary order nor for entry of judgment thereon, and the applicant shall not be liable for costs in a proceeding for review of the judgment unless the court shall otherwise direct. The court shall modify such judgment to conform to any later compensation order upon presentation of a certified copy thereof to the court.

(b) In cases where judgment cannot be satisfied by reason of the employer's insolvency or other circumstances precluding payment, the Secretary of Labor may, in his discretion and to the extent he shall determine advisable after consideration of current commitments, payable from the special fund established in section 944 of this title, make payment from such fund upon any award made under this chapter, and in addition provide any necessary medical, surgical, and other treatment required by section 7 of the chapter in any case of disability where there has been a default in furnishing medical treatment by reason of the insolvency of the employer. Such an employer shall be liable for payment into such fund of the amounts paid therefrom by the Secretary of Labor under this subsection; and for the purpose of enforcing this liability, the Secretary of Labor for the benefit of the fund shall be subrogated to all the rights of the person receiving such payments or benefits as against the employer and may by a proceeding in the name of the Secretary of Labor under this section or under subsection (c) of section 921 of this title, or both, by seek to recover the amount of the default or so much thereof as in the judgment of the Secretary is possible, or the Secretary may settle and compromise any such claim.

§919. Procedure in respect of claims.

(a) Subject to the provisions of section 913 of this title a claim for compensation may be filed with the deputy commissioner in accordance with regulations prescribed by the Secretary at any time after the first seven days of disability following any injury, or at any time after death, and the deputy commissioner shall have full power and authority to hear and determine all questions in respect of such claim.

(b) Within ten days after such claim is filed the deputy commissioner, in accordance with regulations prescribed by the Secretary, shall notify the employer and any other person (other than the claimant), whom the deputy commissioner considers an interested party, that a claim has been filed. Such notice may be served personally upon the employer or other person, or sent to such employer or person by registered mail.

(c) The deputy commissioner shall make or cause to be made such investigations as he considers necessary in respect of the claim, and upon application of any interested party shall order a hearing thereon. If a hearing on such claim is ordered the deputy commissioner shall give the claimant and other interested parties at least ten days' notice of such hearing, served personally upon the claimant and other interested parties or sent to such claimant and other interested parties by registered mail or by certified mail, and shall within twenty days after such hearing is had, by order, reject the claim or make an award in respect of the claim. If no hearing is ordered within twenty days after notice is given as provided in subsection (b) of this section, the deputy commissioner shall, by order reject the claim or make an award in respect to the claim.

(d) Notwithstanding any other provisions of this Act, any hearing held under this Act shall be conducted in accordance with the provisions of section 554 of title 5 of the United States Code. Any such hearing shall be conducted by an administrative law judge qualified under section 3105 of that title. All powers, duties, and responsibilities vested by this Act, on the date of enactment of the Longshoremen's and Harbor Workers' Compensation Act Amendments of 1972, in the deputy commissioners with respect to such hearings shall be vested in such administrative law judges.

(e) The order rejecting the claim or making the award (referred to in this chapter as a compensation order) shall be filed in the office of the deputy commissioner, and a copy thereof shall be sent by registered mail or by certified mail to the claimant and to the employer at the last known address of each.

(f) An award of compensation for disability may be made after the death of an injured employee.

(g) At any time after a claim has been filed with him, the deputy commissioner may, with the approval of the Secretary, transfer such case to any other deputy commissioner for the purpose of making investigation, taking testimony, making physical examinations or taking such other necessary action therein as may be directed.

(h) An injured employee claiming or entitled to compensation shall submit to such physical examination by a medical officer of the United States or by a duly qualified physician designated or approved by the Secretary as the deputy commissioner may require. The place or places shall be reasonably convenient for the employee. Such physician or physicians as the employee, employer, or carrier may select and pay for may participate in an examination if the employee, employer, or carrier so request. Proceedings shall be suspended and no compensation be payable for any period during which the employee may refuse to submit to examination. (As amended June 11, 1960, Pub. L. 86–507, §1, 74 Stat. 202; March 27, 1978, Pub. L. 95–251, §2(a)(10), 92 Stat. 183.)

§920. Presumptions.

In any proceeding for the enforcement of a claim for compensation under this chapter it shall be presumed, in the absence of substantial evidence to the contrary—

(a) That the claim comes within the provisions of this chapter.

(b) That sufficient notice of such claim has been given.

(c) That the injury was not occasioned solely by the intoxication of the injured employee.

(d) That the injury was not occasioned by the willful intention of the injured employee to injure or kill himself or another.

§921. Review of compensation orders.

(a) A compensation order shall become effective when filed in the office of the deputy commissioner as provided in section 19, and, unless proceedings for the suspension or setting aside of such order are instituted as provided in subdivision (b) of this section, shall become final at the expiration of the thirtieth day thereafter.

(b)(1) There is hereby established a Benefits Review Board which shall be composed of five members appointed by the Secretary from among individuals who are especially qualified to serve on such Board. The Secretary shall designate one of the members of the Board to serve as chairman. The Chairman shall have the authority, as delegated by the Secretary, to exercise all administrative functions necessary to operate the Board.

(2) For the purpose of carrying out its functions under this Act, three members of the Board shall constitute a quorum and official action can be taken only on the affirmative vote of at least three members.

(3) The Board shall be authorized to hear and determine appeals raising a substantial question of law or fact taken by any party in interest from decisions with respect to claims of employees under this Act and the extensions thereof. The Board's orders shall be based upon the hearing record. The findings of fact in the decision under review by the Board shall be conclusive if supported by substantial evidence in the record considered as a whole. The payment of the amounts required by an award shall not be stayed pending final decision in any such proceeding unless ordered by the Board. No stay shall be issued unless irreparable injury would otherwise ensue to the employer or carrier.

(4) The Board may, on its own motion or at the request of the Secretary, remand a case to the administrative law judge for further appropriate action. The consent of the parties in interest shall not be a prerequisite to a remand by the Board.

(5) Notwithstanding paragraphs (1) through (4), upon application of the Chairman of the

Board, the Secretary may designate up to four Department of Labor administrative law judges to serve on the Board temporarily, for not more than one year. The Board is authorized to delegate to panels of three members any or all of the powers which the Board may exercise. Each such panel shall have no more than one temporary member. Two members shall constitute a quorum of a panel. Official adjudicative action may be taken only on the affirmative vote of at least two members of a panel. Any party aggrieved by a decision of a panel of the Board may, within thirty days after the date of entry of the decision, petition the entire permanent Board for review of the panel's decision. Upon affirmative vote of the majority of the permanent members of the Board, the petition shall be granted. The Board shall amend its Rules of Practice to conform with this paragraph. Temporary members, while serving as members of the Board, shall be compensated at the same rate of compensation as regular members.

(c) Any person adversely affected or aggrieved by a final order of the Board may obtain a review of that order in the United States court of appeals for the circuit in which the injury occurred, by filing in such court within sixty days following the issuance of such Board order a written petition praying that the order be modified or set aside. A copy of such petition shall be forthwith transmitted by the clerk of the court, to the Board, and to the other parties, and thereupon the Board shall file in the court the record in the proceedings as provided in section 2112 of title 28, United States Code. Upon such filing, the court shall have jurisdiction of the proceeding and shall have the power to give a decree affirming, modifying, or setting aside, in whole or in part, the order of the Board and enforcing same to the extent that such order is affirmed or modified. The orders, writs, and processes of the court in such proceedings may run, be served, and be returnable anywhere in the United States. The payment of the amounts required by an award shall not be stayed pending final decision in any such proceeding unless ordered by the court. No stay shall be issued unless irreparable injury would otherwise ensue to the employer or carrier. The order of the court allowing any stay shall contain a specific finding, based upon evidence submitted to the court and identified by reference thereto, that irreparable damage would result to the employer, and specifying the nature of the damage.

(d) If any employer or his officers or agents fails to comply with a compensation order making an award, that has become final, any beneficiary of such award or the deputy commissioner making the order, may apply for the enforcement of the order to the Federal district court for the judicial district in which the injury occurred (or to the United States District Court for the District of Columbia if the injury occurred in the District). If the court determines that the order was made and served in accordance with law, and that such employer or his officers or agents have failed to comply therewith, the court shall enforce obedience to the order by writ of injunction or by other proper process, mandatory or otherwise, to enjoin upon such person and his officers and agents compliance with the order.

(e) Proceedings for suspending, setting aside, or enforcing a compensation order, whether rejecting a claim or making an award, shall not be instituted otherwise than as provided in this section and section 18. (March 4, 1927, c. 509, §21, 44 Stat. 1436; Oct. 27, 1972, Pub.L. 92-576, §15(a), (b), 86 Stat. 1261, 1262; March 27, 1978, Pub.L. 95-251, §2(a)(10), 92 Stat. 183; Sept. 28, 1984, Pub.L. 98-426, §15, 98 Stat. 1649.)

2004 Note: Act Dec. 8, 2004, P.L. 108-447, Div F, Title I, 118 Stat. 3121, provides: "No funds made available by this Act [Div F of Act Dec. 8, 2004, P.L. 108-447; for full classification, consult USCS Tables volumes] may be used by the Solicitor of Labor to participate in a review in any United States court of appeals of any decision made by the Benefits Review Board under section 21 of the Longshore and Harbor Workers' Compensation Act (33 U.S.C. 921) where such participation is precluded by the decision of the United States Supreme Court in Director, Office of Workers' Compensation Programs v. Newport News Shipbuilding, 115 S. Ct. 1278 [131 L. Ed. 2d 160] (1995), notwithstanding any provisions to the contrary contained in Rule 15 of the Federal Rules of Appellate Procedure: *Provided further*, That no funds made available by this Act may be used by the Secretary of Labor to review a decision under the Longshore and Harbor Workers' Compensation Act (33 U.S.C. 901 et seq.) that has been appealed and that has been pending before the Benefits Review Board for more than 12 months: *Provided further*, That any such decision pending a review by the Benefits Review Board for more than 1 year shall be considered affirmed by the Benefits Review Board on the 1-year anniversary of the filing of the appeal, and shall be considered the final order of the Board for purposes of obtaining a review in the United States courts of appeals: *Provided further*, That these provisions shall not be applicable to the review or appeal of any decision issued under the Black Lung Benefits Act (30 U.S.C. 901 et seq.)."

Similar provisions were contained in Acts April 26, 1996, P.L. 104-134, Title I, 110 Stat. 1321-218, as amended May 2, 1996, P.L. 104-140, §1(a), 110 Stat. 1327; Sept. 30, 1996, P.L. 104-208, Div A, Title I, §101(e) [Title I], 110 Stat. 3009-241; Nov. 13, 1997, P.L. 105-78, Title I, 111 Stat. 1475; Oct. 21, 1998, P.L. 105-277, Div A, §101(f) [Title I], 112 Stat. 2681-345; Nov. 29, 1999, P.L. 106-113, Div B, §1000(a)(4), 113 Stat. 1535 (enacting into law Title I of H.R. 3424 (113 Stat. 1501A-224), as introduced on Nov. 17, 1999); Dec. 21, 2000, P.L. 106-554, §1(a)(1), 114 Stat. 2763 (enacting into law Title I of H.R. 5656 (114 Stat. 2763A-10), as introduced on Dec. 14, 2000); Jan. 10, 2002, P.L. 107-116, Title I, 115 Stat. 2185; Feb. 20, 2003, P.L. 108-7, Div G, Title I, 117 Stat. 306; Jan. 23, 2004, P.L. 108-199, Div E, Title I, 118 Stat. 234.

§921a. Appearance of attorneys for Secretary, deputy commissioner, or Board.

Attorneys appointed by the Secretary shall represent the Secretary, the deputy commissioner, or the Board in any court proceedings under section 921 of this title or other provisions of this chapter except for proceedings in the Supreme Court of the United States. (October 27, 1972, Pub. L. 92-576, §16, 86 Stat. 1262.)

§922. Modification of awards.

Upon his own initiative, or upon the application of any party in interest (including an employer or carrier which has been granted reief under section 908(f) of this title), on the ground of a change in conditions or because of a mistake in a determination of fact by the deputy commissioner, the deputy commissioner may, at any time prior to one year after the date of the last payment of compensation, whether or not a compensation order has been issued, or at any time prior to one year after the rejection of a claim, review a compensation case (including a case under which payments are made pursuant to section 944(i) of this title) in accordance with the procedure prescribed in respect of claims in section 919 of this title, and in accordance with such section issue a new compensation order which may terminate, continue, reinstate, increase, or decrease such compensation, or award compensation. Such new order shall not affect any compensation previously paid, except that an award increasing the compensation rate may be made effective from the date of the injury, and if any part of the compensation due or to become due is unpaid, an award decreasing the compensation rate may be made effective from the date of the injury, and any payment made prior thereto in excess of such decreased rate shall be deducted from any unpaid compensation, in such manner and by such method as may be determined by the deputy commissioner with the approval of the Secretary. This section does not authorize the modification of settlements.

Ref.: W. Cal. Sum., 2 "Workers' Compensation" §135.

§923. Procedure before the deputy commissioner or Board.

(a) In making an investigation or inquiry or conducting a hearing the deputy commissioner or Board shall not be bound by common law or statutory rules of evidence or by technical or formal rules of procedure, except as provided by this Act; but may make such investigation or inquiry or conduct such hearing in such manner as to best ascertain the rights of the parties. Declarations of a deceased employee concerning the injury in respect of which the investigation or inquiry is being made or the hearing conducted shall be received in evidence and shall, if corroborated by other evidence, be sufficient to establish the injury.

(b) Hearings before a deputy commissioner or Board shall be open to the public and shall be stenographically reported, and the deputy commissioners or Board, subject to the approval of the Secretary are authorized to contract for the reporting of such hearings. The Secretary shall by regulation provide for the preparation of a record of the hearings and other proceedings before the deputy commissioners or Board.

§924. Witnesses.

No person shall be required to attend as a witness in any proceeding before a deputy commissioner at a place outside of the State of his residence and more than one hundred miles from his place of residence, unless his lawful mileage and fee for one day's attendance shall be first paid or tendered to him; but the testimony of any witness may be taken by deposition or interrogatories according to the rules of practice of the Federal district court for the judicial district in which the case is pending (or of the Supreme Court of the District of Columbia if the case is pending in the District).

§925. Witness fees.

Witnesses summoned in a proceeding before a deputy commissioner or whose depositions are taken shall receive the same fees and mileage as witnesses in courts of the United States.

§926. Costs in proceedings brought without reasonable grounds.

If the court having jurisdiction of proceedings in respect of any claim or compensation order determines that the proceedings in respect of such claim or order have been instituted or continued without reasonable ground, the costs of such proceedings shall be assessed against the party who has so instituted or continued such proceedings.

§927. Powers of deputy commissioners or Board.

(a) The deputy commissioner or Board shall have power to preserve and enforce order during any such proceedings; to issue subpoenas for, to administer oaths to, and to compel the attendance and testimony of witnesses, or the production of books, papers, documents, and other evidence, or the taking of depositions before any designated individual competent to administer oaths; to examine witnesses and to do all things conformable to law which may be necessary to enable him effectively to discharge the duties of his office.

(b) If any person in proceedings before a deputy commissioner or Board disobeys or resists any lawful order or process, or misbehaves during a hearing or so near the place thereof as to obstruct the same, or neglects to produce, after having been ordered to do so, any pertinent book, paper, or document, or refuses to appear after having been subpoenaed, or upon appearing refuses to take the oath as a witness, or after having taken the oath refuses to be examined according to law, the deputy commissioner or Board shall certify the facts to the district court having jurisdiction in the place in which he is sitting (or to the Supreme Court of the District of Columbia if he is sitting in such District) which shall thereupon in a summary manner hear the evidence as to the acts complained of, and, if the evidence so warrants, punish such person in the same manner and to the same extent as for a contempt committed before the court, or commit such person upon the same conditions as if the doing of the forbidden act had occurred with reference to the process of or in the presence of the court.

§928. Fees for services.

(a) If the employer or carrier declines to pay any compensation on or before the thirtieth day after receiving written notice of a claim for compensation having been filed from the deputy commissioner, on the ground that there is no liability for compensation within the provisions of this Act, and the person seeking benefits shall thereafter have utilized the services of an attorney at law in the successful prosecution of his claim, there shall be awarded, in addition to the award of compensation, in a compensation order, a reasonable attorney's fee against the employer or carrier in an amount approved by the deputy commissioner, Board, or court, as the case may be, which shall be paid directly by the employer or carrier to the attorney for the claimant in a lump sum after the compensation order becomes final.

(b) If the employer or carrier pays or tenders payment of compensation without an award pursuant to section 914(a) and (b) of this title, and thereafter a controversy develops over the amount of additional compensation, if any, to which the employee may be entitled, the deputy commissioner or Board shall set the matter for an informal conference and following such conference the deputy commissioner or Board shall recommend in writing a disposition of the controversy. If the employer or carrier refuse to accept such written recommendation, within fourteen days after its receipt by them, they shall pay or tender to the employee in writing the additional compensation, if any, to which they believe the employee is entitled. If the employee refuses to accept such payment or tender of compensation, and thereafter utilizes the services of an attorney at law, and if the compensation thereafter awarded is greater than the amount paid or tendered by the employer or carrier, a reasonable attorney's fee based solely upon the difference between the amount awarded and the amount tendered or paid shall be awarded in addition to the amount of compensation. The forgoing sentence shall not apply if the controversy relates to degree or length of disability, and if the employer or carrier offers to submit the case for evaluation by physicians employed or selected by the Secretary, as authorized in section 907(e) and offers to tender an amount of compensation based upon the degree or length of disability found by the independent medical report at such time as an evaluation of disability can be made. If the claimant is successful in review proceedings before the Board or court in any such case an award may be made in favor of the claimant and against the employer or carrier for a reasonable attorney's fee for claimant's counsel in accord with the above provisions. In all other cases any claim for legal services shall not be assessed against the employer or carrier.

(c) In all cases fees for attorneys representing the claimant shall be approved in the manner herein provided. If any proceedings are had before the Board or any court for review of any action, award, order, or decision, the Board or court may approve an attorney's fee for the work done before it by the attorney for the claimant. An approved attorney's fee, in cases in which the obligation to pay the fee is upon the claimant, may be made a lien upon the compensation due under an award; and the deputy commissioner, Board, or court shall fix in the award approving the fee, such lien and manner of payment.

(d) In cases where an attorney's fee is awarded against an employer or carrier there may be further assessed against such employer or carrier as costs, fees and mileage for necessary witnesses attending the hearing at the instance of claimant. Both the necessity for the witness and the reasonableness of the fees of expert witnesses must be approved by the hearing officer, the Board, or the court, as the case may be. The amounts awarded against an employer or carrier as attorney's fees, costs, fees and mileage for witnesses shall not in any respect affect or diminish the compensation payable under this chapter.

(e) A person who receives a fee, gratuity, or other consideration on account of services rendered as a representative of a claimant, unless the consideration is approved by the deputy commissioner, administrative law judge, Board, or court, or who makes it a business to solicit employment for a lawyer, or for himself, with respect to a claim or award for compensation under this chapter shall, upon conviction thereof, for each offense be punished by a fine of not more than $1,000 or be imprisoned for not more than one year, or both.

§929. Record of injury or death.

Every employer shall keep a record in respect of any injury to an employee. Such record shall contain such information of disease, other disability, or death in respect of such injury as the Secretary may by regulation require, and shall be available to inspection by the Secretary or by any State authority at such times and under such conditions as the Secretary may by regulation prescribe.

§930. Reports to Secretary.

(a) Within ten days from the date of any injury, which causes loss of one or more shifts of work, or death or from the date that the employer has knowledge of a disease or infection in respect of such injury, the employer shall send to the Secretary a report setting forth (1) the name, address, and business of the employer; (2) the name, address, and occupation of the employee; (3) the cause and nature of the injury or death; (4) the year, month, day, and hour when and the particular locality where the injury or death occurred; and (5) such other information as the Secretary may require. A copy of such report shall be sent at the same time to the deputy commissioner in the compensation district in which the injury occurred. Notwithstanding the requirements of this subsection, each employer shall keep a record of each and every injury regardless of whether such injury results in the loss of one or more shifts of work.

(b) Additional reports in respect of such injury and of the condition of such employee shall be sent by the employer to the Secretary and to such deputy commissioner at such times and in such manner as the Secretary may prescribe.

(c) Any report provided for in subdivision (a) or (b) shall not be evidence of any fact stated in such report in any proceeding in respect of any such injury or death on account of which the report is made.

(d) The mailing of any such report and copy in a stamped envelope, within the time prescribed in subdivisions (a) or (b), to the Secretary and deputy commissioner, respectively, shall be a compliance with this section.

(e) Any employer, insurance carrier, or self-insured employer who knowingly and willfully fails or refuses to send any report required by this section or knowingly or willfully makes a false statement or misrepresentation in any such report shall be subject to a civil penalty not to exceed $10,000 for each such failure, refusal, false statement, or misrepresentation.

(f) Where the employer or the carrier has been given notice, or the employer (or his agent in charge of the business in the place where the injury occurred) or the carrier has knowledge, of any injury or death of an employee and fails, neglects, or refuses to file report thereof as required by the provisions of subdivision (a) of this section, the limitations in subdivision (a) of section 913 of this title of this Act shall not begin to run against the claim of the injured employee or his dependents entitled to compensation, or in favor of either the employer or the carrier, until such report shall have been furnished as required by the provisions of subdivision (a) of this section.

§931. Penalty for misrepresentation.

(a)(1) Any claimant or representative of a claimant who knowingly and willfully makes a false statement or representation for the purpose of obtaining a benefit or payment under this chapter shall be guilty of a felony, and on conviction thereof shall be punished by a fine not to exceed $10,000, by imprisonment not to exceed five years, or by both.

(2) The United States attorney for the district in which the injury is alleged to have occurred shall make every reasonable effort to promptly investigate each complaint made under this subsection.

(b)(1) No representation fee of a claimant's representative shall be approved by the deputy commissioner, an administrative law judge, the Board, or a court pursuant to section 928 of this title, if the claimant's representative is on the list of individuals who are disqualified from representing claimants under this chapter maintained by the Secretary pursuant to paragraph (2) of this subsection.

(2)(A) The Secretary shall annually prepare a list of those individuals in each compensation district who have represented claimants for a fee in cases under this chapter and who are not authorized to represent claimants. The names of individuals contained on the list required under this subparagraph shall be made available to employees and employers in each compensation district through posting and in such other forms as the Secretary may prescribe.

(B) Individuals shall be included on the list of those not authorized to represent claimants under this chapter if the Secretary determines under this section, in accordance with the procedure provided in subsection (j) of section 907 of this title, that such individual—

(i) has been convicted (without regard to pending appeal) of any crime in connection with the representation of a claimant under this chapter or any workers' compensation statute;

(ii) has engaged in fraud in connection with the presentation of a claim under this or any workers' compensation statute, including, but not limited to, knowingly making false representations, concealing or attempting to conceal material facts with respect to a claim, or soliciting or otherwise procuring false testimony;

(iii) has been prohibited from representing claimants before any other workers' compensation agency for reasons of professional misconduct which are similar in nature to those which would be grounds for disqualification under this paragraph; or

(iv) has accepted fees for representing claimants under this chapter which were not approved, or which were in excess of the amount approved pursuant to section 928 of this title.

(C) Notwithstanding subparagraph (B), no individual who is on the list required to be maintained by the Secretary pursuant to this section shall be prohibited from presenting his or her own claim or from representing without fee, a claimant who is a spouse, mother, father, sister, brother, or child of such individual.

(D) A determination under subparagraph (A) shall remain in effect for a period of not less than three years and until the Secretary finds and gives notice to the public that there is reasonable assurance that the basis for the determination will not reoccur.

(3) No employee shall be liable to pay a representation fee to any representative whose fee has been disallowed by reason of the operation of this paragraph.

(4) The Secretary shall issue such rules and regulations as are necessary to carry out this section.

(c) A person including, but not limited to, an employer, his duly authorized agent, or an employee of an insurance carrier who knowingly and willfully makes a false statement or representation for the purpose of reducing, denying, or terminating benefits to an injured employee, or his dependents pursuant to section 909 of this title if the injury results in death, shall be punished by a fine not to exceed

$10,000, by imprisonment not to exceed five years, or by both.

§932. Security for compensation.

(a) Every employer shall secure the payment of compensation under this chapter—

(1) By insuring and keeping insured the payment of such compensation with any stock company or mutual company or association, or with any other person or fund, while such person or fund is authorized (A) under the laws of the United States or of any State, to insure workmen's compensation, and (B) by the Secretary, to insure payment of compensation under this chapter; or

(2) By furnishing satisfactory proof to the Secretary of his financial ability to pay such compensation and receiving an authorization from the Secretary to pay such compensation directly. The Secretary may, as condition to such authorization, require such employer to deposit in a depository designated by the Secretary either an indemnity bond or securities (at the option of the employer) of a kind and in an amount determined by the Secretary, based on the employer's financial condition, the employer's previous record of payments, and other relevant factors, and subject to such conditions as the Secretary may prescribe, which shall include authorization to the Secretary in case of default to sell any such securities sufficient to pay compensation awards or to bring suit upon such bonds, to procure, prompt payment of compensation under this chapter. Any employer securing compensation in accordance with the provisions of this paragraph shall be known as a self-insurer.

(b) In granting authorization to any carrier to insure payment of compensation under this chapter the Secretary may take into consideration the recommendation of any State authority having supervision over carriers or over workmen's compensation, and may authorize any carrier to insure the payment of compensation under this chapter in a limited territory. Any marine protection and indemnity mutual insurance corporation or association, authorized to write insurance against liability for loss or damage from personal injury and death, and for other losses and damages, incidental to or in respect of the ownership, operation, or chartering of vessels on a mutual assessment plan, shall be deemed a qualified carrier to insure compensation under this chapter. The Secretary may suspend or revoke any such authorization for good cause shown after a hearing at which the carrier shall be entitled to be heard in person or by counsel and to present evidence. No suspension or revocation shall affect the liability of any carrier already incurred.

§933. Compensation for injuries where third persons are liable.

(a) If on account of a disability or death for which compensation is payable under this chapter the person entitled to such compensation determines that some other person than the employer or a person or persons in his employ is liable in damages, he need not elect whether to receive such compensation or to recover damages against such third person.

(b) Acceptance of compensation under an award in a compensation order filed by the deputy commissioner, an administrative law judge, or the Board shall operate as an assignment to the employer of all rights of the person, entitled to compensation to recover damages against such third person unless such person shall commence an action against such third person within six months after such acceptance. If the employer fails to commence an action against such third person within ninety days after the cause of action is assigned under this section, the right to bring such action shall revert to the person entitled to compensation. For the purpose of this subsection, the term "award" with respect to a compensation order means a formal order issued by the deputy commissioner, an administrative law judge, or Board.

(c) The payment of such compensation into the fund established in section 944 of this title shall operate as an assignment to the employer of all right of the legal representative of the deceased (hereinafter referred to as "representative") to recover damages against such third person.

(d) Such employer on account of such assignment may either institute proceedings for the recovery of such damages or may compromise with such third person either without or after instituting such proceeding.

(e) Any amount recovered by such employer on account of such assignment, whether or not as the result of a compromise, shall be distributed as follows:

(1) The employer shall retain an amount equal to—

(A) the expenses incurred by him in respect to such proceedings or compromise (including a reasonable attorney's fee as determined by the deputy commissioner or Board);

(B) the cost of all benefits actually furnished by him to the employee under section 907 of this title;

(C) all amounts paid as compensation,

(D) the present value of all amounts thereafter payable as compensation, such present value to be computed in accordance with a schedule prepared by the Secretary, and the present value of the cost of all benefits thereafter to be furnished under section 907 of this title, to be estimated by the deputy commissioner, and the amounts so computed and estimated to be retained by the employer as a trust fund to pay such compensation and the cost of such benefits as they become due, and to pay any sum finally remaining in excess thereof to the person entitled to compensation or to the representative; and

(2) The employer shall pay any excess to the person entitled to compensation or to the representative.

(f) If the person entitled to compensation institutes proceedings within the period prescribed in subdivision (b) of this section the employer shall be required to pay as compensation under this chapter a sum equal to the excess of the net amount which the Secretary determines is payable on account of such injury or death over the net amount recovered against such third person. Such net amount shall be equal to the actual amount recovered less the expenses reasonably incurred by such person in respect to such proceedings (including reasonable attorneys' fees).

(g)(1) If the person entitled to compensation (or the person's representative) enters into a settlement with a third person referred to in subsection (a) of this section for an amount less than the compensation to which the person (or the person's representative) would be entitled under this chapter, the employer shall be liable for compensation as determined under subsection (f) of this section only if written approval of the settlement is obtained from the employer and the employer's carrier, before the settlement is executed, and by the person entitled to compensation (or the person's representative). The approval shall be made on a form provided by the Secretary and shall be filed in the office of the deputy commissioner within thirty days after the settlement is entered into.

(2) If no written approval of the settlement is obtained and filed as required by paragraph (1), or if the employee fails to notify the employer of any settlement obtained from or judgment rendered against a third person, all rights to compensation and medical benefits under this chapter shall be terminated, regardless of whether the employer or the employer's insurer has made payments or acknowledged entitlement to benefits under this chapter.

(3) Any payments by the special fund established under section 944 of this title shall be a lien upon the proceeds of any settlement obtained from or judgment rendered against a third person referred to under subsection (a) of this section. Notwithstanding any other provision of law, such lien shall be enforceable against such proceeds, regardless of whether the Secretary on behalf of the special fund has agreed to or has received actual notice of the settlement or judgment.

(4) Any payments by a trust fund described n section 917 of this title shall be a lien upon the proceeds of any settlement obtained from or judgment recorded against a third person referred to under subsection (a) of this section. Such lien shall have priority over a lien under paragraph (3) of this subsection.

(h) Where the employer is insured and the insurance carrier has assumed the payment of the compensation, the insurance carrier shall be subrogated to all the rights of the employer under this section.

(i) The right to compensation or benefits under this chapter shall be the exclusive remedy to an employee when he is injured, or to his eligible survivors or legal representatives if he is killed, by the negligence or wrong of any other person or persons in the same employ: Provided, That this provision shall not affect the liability of a person other than an officer or employee of the employer.

Ref.: W. Cal. Sum., 2 "Workers' Compensation" §§135, 138, 139.

§934. Compensation notice.

Every employer who has secured compensation under the provisions of this chapter shall keep posted in a conspicuous place or places in and about his place or places of business typewritten or printed notices, in accordance with a form prescribed by the Secretary, stating that such employer has secured the payment of compensation in accordance with the provisions of this chapter. Such notices shall contain the name and address of the carrier, if any, with whom the employer has secured payment of compensation and the date of the expiration of the policy.

§935. Substitution of carrier for employer.

In any case where the employer is not a self-insurer, in order that the liability for compensation imposed by this chapter may be most effectively discharged by the employer, and in order that the administration of this chapter in respect of such liability may be facilitated, the Secretary shall by regulation provide for the discharge, by the carrier for such employer, of such obligations and duties of the employer in respect of such liability, imposed by this chapter upon the employer, as it considers proper in order to effectuate the provisions of this chapter. For such purposes (1) notice to or knowledge of an employer of the occurrence of the injury shall be notice to or knowledge of the carrier, (2) jurisdiction of the employer by a deputy commissioner, the Board, or the Secretary, or any court under this chapter shall be jurisdiction of the carrier, and (3) any requirement by a deputy commissioner, the Board, or the Secretary, or any court under any compensation order, finding, or decision shall be binding upon the carrier in the same manner and to the same extent as upon the employer.

§936. Insurance policies.

(a) Every policy or contract of insurance issued under authority of this chapter shall contain (1) a provision to carry out the provisions of section 935 of this title, and (2) a provision that insolvency or bankruptcy of the employer and/or discharge therein shall not relieve the carrier from payment of compensation for disability or death sustained by an employee during the life of such policy or contract.

(b) No contract or policy of insurance issued by a carrier under this Act shall be canceled prior to the date specified in such contract or policy for its expiration until at least thirty days have elapsed after a notice of cancellation has been sent to the deputy commissioner and to the employer in accordance with the provisions of subdivision (c) of section 912 of this title.

§937. Certificate of compliance with chapter.

No stevedoring firm shall be employed in any compensation district by a vessel or by hull owners until it presents to such vessel or hull owners a certificate issued by a deputy commissioner assigned to such district that it has complied with the provisions of this Act requiring the securing of compensation to its employees. Any person violating the provisions of this section shall be punished by a fine of not more than $1,000, or by imprisonment for not more than one year, or by both such fine and imprisonment.

§938. Penalties.

(a) Any employer required to secure the payment of compensation under this Act who fails to secure such compensation shall be guilty of a misdemeanor and, upon conviction thereof, shall be punished by a fine of not more than $10,000, or by imprisonment for not more than one year, or by both such fine and imprisonment; and in any case where such employer is a corporation, the president, secretary, and treasurer thereof shall be also severally liable to such fine or imprisonment as herein provided for the failure of such corporation to secure the payment of compensation; and such president, secretary, and treasurer shall be severally personally liable, jointly with such corporation, for any compensation or other benefit which may accrue under the said Act in respect to any injury which may occur to any employee of such corporation while it shall so fail to secure the payment of compensation as required by section 932 of this title.

(b) Any employer who knowingly transfers, sells, encumbers, assigns, or in any manner disposes of, conceals, secrets, or destroys any property belonging to such employer, after one of his employees has been injured within the purview of this chapter, and with intent to avoid the payment of compensation under this chapter to such employee or his dependents, shall be guilty of a misdemeanor and, upon conviction thereof, shall be punished by a fine of not more than $10,000, or by imprisonment for not more than one year, or by both such fine and imprisonment; and in any case where such employer is a corporation, the president, secretary, and treasurer thereof shall be also severally liable to such penalty of imprisonment as well as jointly liable with such corporation for such fine.

(c) This section shall not affect any other liability of the employer under this chapter.

§939. Administration by Secretary.

(a) Except as otherwise specifically provided, the Secretary of Labor shall administer the provisions of this chapter, and for such purpose the Secretary is authorized (1) to make such rules and regulations; (2) to appoint and fix the compensation of such temporary technical assistants and medical advisers, and, subject to the provisions of the civil service laws, to appoint, and, in accordance with the Classification Act of 1949, to fix the compensation of such deputy commissioners (except deputy commissioners appointed under subdivision (a) of section 940 of this title) and other officers and employees; and (3) to make such expenditures (including expenditures for personal services and rent at the seat of government and elsewhere, for law books, books of reference, periodicals, and for printing and binding) as may be necessary in the administration of this chapter. All expenditures of the Secretary in the administration of this chapter shall be allowed and paid as provided in section 945 of this title upon the presentation of itemized vouchers therefor approved by the Secretary.

(b) The Secretary shall establish compensation districts, to include the high seas and the areas within the United States to which this chapter applies, and shall assign to each such district one or more deputy commissioners, as the Secretary deems advisable. Judicial proceedings under sections 918 and 921 of this title of this chapter in respect of any injury or death occurring on the high seas shall be instituted in the district court within whose territorial jurisdiction is located the office of the deputy commissioner having jurisdiction in respect of such injury or death (or in the Supreme Court of the District of Columbia if such office is located in such District).

(c)(1) The Secretary shall, upon request, provide persons covered by this chapter with information and assistance relating to the chapter's coverage and compensation and the procedures for obtaining such compensation and including assistance in processing a claim. The Secretary may, upon request, provide persons covered by this Act with legal assistance in processing a claim. The Secretary shall also provide employees receiving compensation information on medical, manpower, and vocational rehabilitation services and assist such employees in obtaining the best such services available.

(2) The Secretary shall direct the vocational rehabilitation of permanently disabled employees and shall arrange with the appropriate public or private agencies in States or Territories, possessions, or the District of Columbia for such rehabilitation. The Federal Board for Vocational Education shall cooperate with the Secretary in such educational work. The Secretary may in his discretion furnish such prosthetic appliances or other apparatus made necessary by an injury upon which an award has been made under this chapter to render a disabled employee fit to engage in a remunerative occupation. Where necessary rehabilitation services are not available otherwise, the Secretary of Labor may, in his discretion, use the fund provided for in section 944 in such amounts as may be necessary to procure such services, including necessary prosthetic appliances or other apparatus. This fund shall also be available in such amounts as may be authorized in annual appropriations for the Department of Labor for the costs of administering this subsection.

§940. Deputy commissioners.

(a) The Secretary may appoint as deputy commissioners any member of any board, commission, or other agency of a State to act as deputy commissioner for any compensation district or part thereof in such State, and may make arrangements with such board, commission, or other agency for the use of the personnel and facilities thereof in the administration of this chapter. The Secretary may make such arrangements as may be deemed advisable by it for the payment of expenses of such board, commission, or other agency, incurred in the administration of this chapter pursuant to this section, and for the payment of salaries to such board, commission, or other agency, or the members thereof, and may pay any amounts agreed upon to the proper officers of the State, upon vouchers approved by the Secretary.

(b) In any Territory of the United States or in the District of Columbia a person holding an office under the United States may be appointed deputy commissioner and for services rendered as deputy commissioner may be paid compensation, in addition to that he is receiving from the United States, in an amount fixed by the

Secretary in accordance with the Classification Act of 1949.

(c) Deputy commissioners (except deputy commissioners appointed under subdivision (a) of this section) may be transferred from one compensation district to another and may be temporarily detailed from one compensation district for service in another in the discretion of the Secretary.

(d) Each deputy commissioner shall maintain and keep open during reasonable business hours an office, at a place designated by the Secretary, for the transaction of business under this chapter, at which office he shall keep his official records and papers. Such office shall be furnished and equipped by the Secretary, who shall also furnish the deputy commissioner with all necessary clerical and other assistants, records, books, blanks, and supplies. Wherever practicable such office shall be located in a building owned or leased by the United States; otherwise the Secretary shall rent suitable quarters.

(e) If any deputy commissioner is removed from office, or for any reason ceases to act as such deputy commissioner, all of his official records and papers and office equipment shall be transferred to his successor in office or, if there be no successor, then to the Secretary or to a deputy commissioner designated by the Secretary.

(f) Neither a deputy commissioner or Board member nor any business associate of a deputy commissioner or Board member shall appear as attorney in any proceeding under this chapter, and no deputy commissioner or Board member shall act in any such case in which he is interested, or when he is employed by any party in interest or related to any party in interest by consanguinity or affinity within the third degree, as determined by the common law.

§941. Safety rules and regulations.

(a) Safe place of employment; installation of safety devices and safeguards. Every employer shall furnish and maintain employment and places of employment which shall be reasonably safe for his employees in all employments covered by this Act and shall install, furnish, maintain, and use such devices and safeguards with particular reference to equipment used by and working conditions established by such employers as the Secretary may determine by regulation or order to be reasonably necessary to protect the life, health, and safety of such employees, and to render safe such employment and places of employment, and to prevent injury to his employees. However, the Secretary may not make determinations by regulation or order under this section as to matters within the scope of title 52 of the Revised Statutes and Acts supplementary or amendatory thereto, the Act of June 15, 1917 (ch. 30, 40 Stat. 220), as amended or section 4(e) of the Act of August 7, 1953 (ch. 345, 67 Stat. 462), as amended [43 U.S.C.S. § 1333(e)].

(b) Studies and investigations by Secretary. The Secretary, in enforcing and administering the provisions of this section, is authorized in addition to such other powers and duties as are conferred upon him—

(1) to make studies and investigations with respect to safety provisions and the causes and prevention of injuries in employments covered by this Act, and in making such studies and investigations to cooperate with any agency of the United States or with any State agency engaged in similar work;

(2) to utilize the services of any agency of the United States or any State agency engaged in similar work (with the consent of such agency) in connection with the administration of this section;

(3) to promote uniformity in safety standards in employments covered by this Act through cooperative action with any agency of the United States or with any State agency engaged in similar work;

(4) to provide for the establishment and supervision of programs for the education and training of employers and employees in the recognition, avoidance, and prevention of unsafe working conditions in employments covered by this Act, and to consult with and advise employers as to the best means of preventing injuries;

(5) to hold such hearings, issue such orders, and make such decisions, based upon findings of fact, as are deemed to be necessary to enforce the provisions of this section, and for such purposes the Secretary and the district courts shall have the authority and jurisdiction provided by section 5 of the Act of June 30, 1936 (ch. 881, 49 Stat. 2036), as amended [41 U.S.C.S. §39], and the Secretary shall be represented in any court proceedings as provided in the Act of May 4, 1928 (ch. 502, 45 Stat. 490), as amended [33 U.S.C.S. §921a].

(c) Inspection of places and practices of employment. The Secretary or his authorized representative may inspect such places of employment, question such employees, and investigate such conditions, practices, or matters in connection with employment subject to this Act, as he may deem appropriate to determine whether any person has violated any provision of this section, or any rule or regulation issued thereunder, or which may aid in the enforcement of the provisions of this section. No employer or other person shall refuse to admit the Secretary or his authorized representatives to any such place or shall refuse to permit any such inspection.

(d) Requests for advice; variations from safety rules and regulations. Any employer may request the advice of the Secretary or his authorized representative, in complying with the requirements of any rule or regulation adopted to carry out the provisions of this section. In case of practical difficulties or unnecessary hardships, the Secretary in his discretion may grant variations from any such rule or regulation, or particular provisions thereof, and permit the use of other or different devices if he finds that the purpose of the rule or regulation will be observed by the variation and the safety of employees will be equally secured thereby. Any person affected by such rule or regulation, or his agent, may request the Secretary to grant such variation, stating in writing the grounds on which his request is based. Any authorization by the Secretary of a variation shall be in writing, shall describe the conditions under which the variation shall be permitted, and shall be published as provided in section 3 of the Administrative Procedure Act (ch. 324, 60 Stat. 237), as amended [5 U.S.C.S. §552]. A properly indexed record of all variations shall be kept in the office of the Secretary and open to public inspection.

(e) Jurisdiction to restrain violations. The United States district courts, [together with the District Court for the Territory of Alaska], shall have jurisdiction for cause shown, in any action brought by the Secretary, represented as provided in the Act of May 4, 1928 (ch. 502, 45 Stat. 490), as amended [33 U.S.C.S. §921a], to restrain violations of this section or of any rule, regulation, or order of the Secretary adopted to carry out the provisions of this section.

(f) Violations and penalties. Any employer who, willfully, violates or fails or refuses to comply with the provisions of subsection (a) of this section, or with any lawful rule, regulation, or order adopted to carry out the provisions of this section, and any employer or other person who willfully interferes with, hinders, or delays the Secretary or his authorized representative in carrying out his duties under subsection (c) of this section by refusing to admit the Secretary or his authorized representative to any place, or to permit the inspection or examination of any employment or place of employment, or who willfully hinders or delays the Secretary or his authorized representative in the performance of his duties in the enforcement of this section, shall be guilty of an offense, and, upon conviction thereof, shall be punished for each offense by a fine of not less than $ 100 nor more than $ 3,000; and in any case where such employer is a corporation, the officer who willfully permits any such violation to occur shall be guilty of an offense, and, upon conviction thereof, shall be punished also for each offense by a fine of not less than $100 nor more than $ 3,000. The liability hereunder shall not affect any other liability of the employer under this Act.

(g) Inapplicability to certain employments.

(1) The provisions of this section shall not apply in the case of any employment relating to the operations for the exploration, production, or transportation by pipeline of mineral resources upon the navigable waters of the United States, nor under the authority of the Act of August 7, 1953 (ch. 345, 67 Stat. 462) [43 U.S.C.S. §§1331 et seq.], nor in the case of any employment in connection with lands (except filled in, made or reclaimed lands) beneath the navigable waters as defined in the Act of May 22, 1953 (ch. 65, 67 Stat. 29) [43 U.S.C.S. §§1301 et seq.] nor in the case of any employment for which compensation in case of disability or death is provided for employees under the authority of the Act of May 17, 1928 (ch. 612, 45 Stat. 600), as amended, nor under the authority of the Act of August 16, 1941 (ch. 357, 55 Stat. 622), as amended [42 U.S.C.S. §§1651 et seq.].

(2) The provisions of this section, with the exception of paragraph (1) of subsection (b), shall not be applied under the authority of the Act of September 7, 1916 (ch. 458, 39 Stat. 742), as amended [5 U.S.C.S. §§8101 et seq.].

(March 4, 1927, c. 509, §41, 44 Stat. 1444; Aug. 23, 1958, Pub.L. 85-742, §1, 72 Stat. 835; Dec. 21, 1982, Pub.L. 97-375, Title I, §110(b), 96 Stat. 1820.)

§942. Annual report.

The Secretary shall make to Congress at the end of each fiscal year, a report of the administration of this chapter for the preceding fiscal year, including a detailed statement of receipts of and expenditures from the fund established in section 944 of this title, together with such recommendations as the Secretary deems advisable. Such report shall include the annual report required under section 426(b) of the Black Lung Benefits Act (30 U.S.C. 936(b)) and shall be identified as the Annual Report of the Office of Workers' Compensation Programs. (As amended December 21, 1995, Pub. L. 104-66 §1102(b)(1), 109 Stat. 722.)

§944. Special fund.

(a) There is established in the Treasury of the United States a special fund.

(b) The Treasurer is authorized to disburse moneys from such fund only upon order of the Secretary. He shall be required to give bond in an amount to be fixed and with securities to be approved by the Secretary of the Treasury and the Comptroller General of the United States conditioned upon the faithful performance of his duty as custodian of such fund.

(c) Payments into such fund shall be made as follows:

(1) Whenever the Secretary determines that there is no person entitled under this chapter to compensation for the death of an employee which would otherwise be compensable under this chapter, the appropriate employer shall pay $5,000 as compensation for the death of such an employee.

(2) At the beginning of each calendar year the Secretary shall estimate the probable expenses of the fund during that calendar year and the amount of payments required (and the schedule therefor) to maintain adequate reserves in the fund. Each carrier and self-insurer shall make payments into the fund on a prorated assessment by the Secretary determined by—

(A) computing the ratio (expressed as a percent) of (i) the carrier's or self-insured's workers' compensation payments under this chapter during the preceding calendar year, to (ii) the total of such payments by all carriers and self-insureds under this chapter during such year,

(B) computing the ratio expressed as a percent) of (i) the payments under section 908 (f) of this title during the preceding calendar year which are attributable to the carrier or self-insured, to (ii) the total of such payments during such year attributable to all carriers and self-insureds;

(C) dividing the sum of the percentages computed under subparagraphs (A) and (B) for the carrier or self-insured by two; and

(D) multiplying the percent computed under subparagraph (C) by such probable expenses of the fund (as determined under the first sentence of this paragraph).

(3) All amounts collected as fines and penalties under the provisions of this chapter shall be paid into such fund.

(d)(1) For the purpose of making rules, regulations, and determinations under this section under and for providing enforcement thereof, the Secretary may investigate and gather appropriate data from each carrier and self-insurer. For that purpose, the Secretary may enter and inspect such places and records (and make such transcriptions thereof), question such employees, and investigate such facts, conditions, practices, or matters as he may deem necessary or appropriate.

(2) Each carrier and self-insurer shall make, keep, and preserve such records, and make such reports and provide such additional information, as prescribed by regulation or order of the Secretary, as the Secretary deems necessary or appropriate to carry out his responsibilities under this section.

(3) For the purpose of any hearing or investigation related to determinations or the enforcement of the provisions of this section, the provisions of sections 49 and 50 of Title 15 (relating to the attendance of witnesses and the production of books, papers, and documents) are hereby made applicable to the jurisdiction, powers, and duties of the Secretary of Labor.

(e) The Treasurer of the United States shall deposit any moneys paid into such fund into such depository banks as the Secretary may designate and may invest any portions of the funds which, in the opinion of the Secretary, is not needed for current requirements, in bonds or notes of the United States or of any Federal land bank.

(f) Neither the United States nor the Secretary shall be liable in respect of payments authorized under section 908 of this title in an amount greater than the money or property deposited in or belonging to such fund.

(g) The Comptroller General of the United States shall audit the account for such fund, but the action of the Secretary in making payments from such fund shall be final and not subject to review, and the Comptroller General is authorized and directed to allow credit in the accounts of any disbursing officer of the Secretary for payments made from such fund authorized by the Secretary.

(h) All civil penalties provided for in this Act shall be collected by civil suit brought by the Secretary.

(i) The proceeds of this fund shall be available for payments:

(1) Pursuant to section 910 of this title with respect to certain initial and subsequent annual adjustments in compensation for total permanent disability or death.

(2) Under section 8(f) and (g), under section 18(b), and under section 39(c).

(3) To repay the sums deposited in the fund pursuant to subsection (d).

(4) To defray the expense of making examinations as provided in section 907(e).

(j) Audit to Congress. The fund shall be audited annually and the results of such audit shall be included in the annual report required by section 42 [33 USCS § 942].

(k) [Redesignated] (March 4, 1927, ch 509, §44, 44 Stat. 1444; July 26, 1956, ch 735, §8, 70 Stat. 656; Oct. 27, 1972, P.L. 92-576, §8, 86 Stat. 1256; Sept. 28, 1984, P.L. 98-426, §24, 27(a)(2) in part, 98 Stat. 1653, 1654.)

§948. Laws inapplicable.

Nothing in section 183, 184 to 186, or 189 of Title 46, shall be held to limit the amount for which recovery may be had (1) in any suit at law or in admiralty where an employer has failed to secure compensation as required by this chapter, or (2) in any proceeding for compensation any addition to compensation, or any civil penalty.

§948a. Discrimination against employees who bring proceedings; penalties; deposit of payments in special fund; civil actions; entitlement to restoration of employment and compensation, qualifications requirement; liability of employer for penalties and payments; insurance policy exemption from liability.

It shall be unlawful for any employer or his duly authorized agent to discharge or in any other manner discriminate against an employee as to his employment because such employee has claimed or attempted to claim compensation from such employer, or because he has testified or is about to testify in a proceeding under this chapter. The discharge or refusal to employ a person who has been adjudicated to have filed a fraudulent claim for compensation is not a violation of this section. Any employer who violates this section shall be liable to a penalty of not less than $100, or more than $1,000, as may be determined by the deputy commissioner. All such penalties shall be paid to the deputy commissioner for deposit in the special fund as described in section 944 of this title, and if not paid may be recovered in a civil action brought in the appropriate United States district court. Any employee so discriminated against shall be restored to his employment and shall be compensated by his employer for any loss of wages arising out of such discrimination: Provided, That if such employee shall cease to be qualified to perform the duties of his employment, he shall not be entitled to such restoration and compensation. The employer alone and not his carrier shall be liable for such penalties and payments. Any provision in an insurance policy undertaking to relieve the employer from the liability for such penalties and payments shall be void.

§949. Effect of unconstitutionality.

If any part of this chapter is adjudged unconstitutional by the courts, and such adjudication has the effect of invalidating any payment of compensation under this chapter, the period intervening between the time the injury was sustained and the time of such adjudication shall not be computed as a part of the time prescribed by law for the commencement of any action against the employer in respect of such injury; but the amount of any compensation paid under this chapter on account of such injury shall be deducted from the amount of damages awarded in such action in respect of such injury.

§950. Separability.

If any provision of this chapter is declared unconstitutional or the applicability thereof to any person or circumstances is held invalid, the validity of the remainder of the chapter and the applicability of such provision to other persons and circumstances shall not be affected thereby.

TITLE 40
PUBLIC BUILDINGS, PROPERTY, AND WORKS

SUBTITLE II
PUBLIC BUILDINGS AND WORKS

PART A
GENERAL

CHAPTER 31
GENERAL

SUBCHAPTER VI
MISCELLANEOUS

§3172. Extension of state workers' compensation laws to buildings, works, and property of the Federal Government.

(a) Authorization of extension. The state authority charged with enforcing and requiring compliance with the state workers' compensation laws and with the orders, decisions, and awards of the authority may apply the laws to all land and premises in the State which the Federal Government owns or holds by deed or act of cession, and to all projects, buildings, constructions, improvements, and property in the State and belonging to the Government, in the same way and to the same extent as if the premises were under the exclusive jurisdiction of the State in which the land, premises, projects, buildings, constructions, improvements, or property are located.

(b) Limitation on relinquishing jurisdiction. The Government under this section does not relinquish its jurisdiction for any other purpose.

(c) Nonapplication. This section does not modify or amend subchapter I of chapter 81 of title 5 [5 USCS §§ 8101 et seq.]. (Aug. 21, 2002, P.L. 107-217, § 1, 116 Stat. 1154.)

Ref.: W. Cal. Sum., 7 "Constitutional Law" §19.

TITLE 42
THE PUBLIC HEALTH AND WELFARE

CHAPTER 11
COMPENSATION FOR DISABILITY OR DEATH TO PERSONS EMPLOYED AT MILITARY, AIR, AND NAVAL BASES OUTSIDE THE UNITED STATES

§1651. Compensation authorized.

(a) Places of employment. Except as herein modified, the provisions of the Longshoremen's and Harbor Workers' Compensation Act, as amended [33 U.S. Code 901–950], shall apply in respect to the injury or death of any employee engaged in any employment—

(1) at any military, air, or naval base acquired after January 1, 1940, by the United States from any foreign government; or

(2) upon any lands occupied or used by the United States for military or naval purposes in any Territory or possession outside the continental United States (including the United States Naval Operating Base, Guantanamo Bay, Cuba; and the Canal Zone); or

(3) upon any public work in any Territory or possession outside the continental United States (including the United States Naval Operating Base, Guantanamo Bay, Cuba; and the Canal Zone), if such employee is engaged in employment at such place under the contract of a contractor (or any subcontractor or subordinate subcontractor with respect to the contract of such contractor) with the United States; but nothing in this paragraph shall be construed to apply to any employee of such a contractor or subcontractor who is engaged exclusively in furnishing materials or supplies under his contract;

(4) under a contract entered into with the United States or any executive department, independent establishment, or agency thereof (including any corporate instrumentality of the United States), or any subcontract or subordinate contract with respect to such contract, where such contract is to be performed outside the continental United States and at places not within the areas described in subparagraphs (1), (2), and (3) of this subdivision, for the purpose of engaging in public work, and every such contract shall contain provisions requiring that the contractor (and subcontractor or subordinate contractor with respect to such contract) (1) shall, before commencing performance of such contract, provide for securing to or on behalf of employees engaged in such public work under such contract the payment of compensation and other benefits under the provisions of this Act [42 U.S. Code 1651–1654], and (2) shall maintain in full force and effect during the term of such contract, subcontract or subordinate contract, or while employees are engaged in work performed thereunder, the said security for the payment of such compensation and benefits, but nothing in this paragraph shall be construed to apply to any employee of such contractor or subcontractor who is engaged exclusively in furnishing materials or supplies under his contract;

(5) under a contract approved and financed by the United States or any executive department, independent establishment, or agency thereof (including any corporate instrumentality of the United States), or any subcontract or subordinate contract with respect to such contract, where such contract is to be performed outside the continental United States, under the Mutual Security Act of 1954 [22 U.S. Code, chapter 24], as amended (other than title II of

chapter II thereof unless the Secretary of Labor, upon the recommendation of the head of any department or other agency of the United States, determines a contract financed under a successor provision of any successor Act should be covered by this section), and not otherwise within the coverage of this section, and every such contract shall contain provisions requiring that the contractor (and subcontractor or subordinate contractor with respect to such contract) (A) shall, before commencing performance of such contract, provide for securing to or on behalf of employees engaged in work under such contract the payment of compensation and other benefits under the provisions of this chapter, and (B) shall maintain in full force and effect during the term of such contract, subcontract, or subordinate contract, or while employees are engaged in work performed thereunder, the said security for the payment of such compensation and benefits, but nothing in this paragraph shall be construed to apply to any employee of such contractor or subcontractor who is engaged exclusively in furnishing materials or supplies under his contract;

(6) outside the continental United States by an American employer providing welfare or similar services for the benefit of the Armed Forces pursuant to appropriate authorization by the Secretary of Defense; irrespective of the place where the injury or death occurs, and shall include any injury or death occurring to any such employee during transportation to or from his place of employment, where the employer or the United States provides the transportation or the cost thereof.

(b) Definitions. As used in this section—

(1) the term "public work" means any fixed improvement or any project, whether or not fixed, involving construction, alteration, removal or repair for the public use of the United States or its allies, including but not limited to projects or operations under service contracts and projects in connection with the national defense or with war activities, dredging, harbor improvements, dams, roadways, and housing, as well as preparatory and ancillary work in connection therewith at the site or on the project;

(2) the term "allies" means any nation with which the United States is engaged in a common military effort or with which the United States has entered into a common defensive military alliance;

(3) the term "war activities" includes activities directly relating to military operations;

(4) the term "continental United States" means States and the District of Columbia.

(c) Liability as exclusive. The liability of an employer, contractor (or any subcontractor or subordinate contractor with respect to the contract of such contractor) under this Act [42 U.S. Code 1651–1654] shall be exclusive and in place of all other liability of such employer, contractor, subcontractor, or subordinate contractor to his employees (and their dependents) coming within the purview of this Act, under the workmen's compensation law of any State, Territory, or other jurisdiction, irrespective of the place where the contract of hire of any such employee may have been made or entered into.

(d) "Contractor" defined. As used in this section, the term "contractor" means any individual, partnership, corporation, or association, and includes any trustee, receiver, assignee, successor, or personal representative thereof, and the rights, obligations, liability, and duties of the employer under such Longshoremen's and Harbor Workers' Compensation Act [33 U.S. Code 901–950] shall be applicable to such contractor.

(e) Contracts within section; waiver of application of section. The liability under this chapter of a contractor, subcontractor, or subordinate contractor engaged in public work under subparagraphs (3) and (4), subdivision (a) of this section, and the conditions set forth therein, shall become applicable to contracts and subcontracts heretofore entered into but not completed at the time of the approval of this chapter, and the liability under this chapter of a contractor, subcontractor or subordinate contractor engaged in performance of contracts, subcontracts, or subordinate contracts specified in subparagraph (5), subdivision (a) of this section, and the conditions set forth therein, shall hereafter be applicable to the remaining terms of such contracts, subcontracts, and subordinate contracts entered into prior to but not completed on the date of enactment of any successor Act to the Mutual Security Act of 1954, as amended, and contracting officers of the United States are authorized to make such modifications and amendments of existing contracts as may be necessary to bring such contracts into conformity with the provisions of this chapter. No rights shall arise in any employee or his dependent under subparagraphs (3) and (4) of subdivision (a) of this section, prior to two months after the approval of this chapter. Upon the recommendation of the head of any department or other agency of the United States, the Secretary of Labor, in the exercise of his discretion, may waive the application of this section with respect to any contract, subcontract, or subordinate contract, work location under such contracts, or classification of employees. Upon recommendation of any employer referred to in paragraph (6) of subsection (a) of this section, the Secretary of Labor may waive the application of this section to any employee or class of employees of such employer, or to any place of employment of such an employee or class of employees.

(f) Liability to prisoners of war and protected persons. The liability under this chapter of a contractor, subcontractor, or subordinate contractor engaged in public work under paragraphs (1), (2), (3), and (4) of subsection (a) of this section or in any work under paragraph (5) of subsection (a) of this section does not apply with respect to any person who is a prisoner of war or a protected person under the Geneva Conventions of 1949 and who is detained or utilized by the United States. (As amended June 30, 1958, Pub. L. 85–477, ch. V, §502(a)(1)–(3), 72 Stat. 272; August 8, 1958, Pub. L. 85–608, Title II, §201, 72 Stat. 537; June 25, 1939, Pub. L. 86–70, §40, 73 Stat. 150; July 24, 1959, Pub. L. 86–108, ch. VII, §701(a), 73 Stat. 257; September 4, 1961, Pub. L. 87–195, Pt. IV, §701, 75 Stat. 463.)

Note: 22 U.S. Code, Chapter 24, as cited in subsection (a)(5), was repealed with certain exceptions by §640(a) of Public Law 87–195.

§1652. Computation of benefits; application to aliens and nonnationals.

(a) The minimum limit on weekly compensation for disability, established by section 6(b) [33 U.S. Code 906(b)], and the minimum limit on the average weekly wages on which death benefits are to be computed, established by section 9(e) [33 U.S. Code 909(e)], of the Longshoremen's and Harbor Workers' Compensation Act, approved March 4, 1927 (44 Stat. 1424), as amended [33 U.S. Code 901–950], shall not apply in computing compensation and death benefits under this Act [42 U.S. Code 1651–1654].

(b) Compensation for permanent total or permanent partial disability under section 8(c)(21) of the Longshoremen's and Harbor Workers' Compensation Act [33 U.S. Code 908(c)(21)], or for death under this Act [42 U.S. Code 1651–1654] to aliens and nonnationals of the United States not residents of the United States or Canada shall be in the same amount as provided for residents, except that dependents in any foreign country shall be limited to surviving wife and child or children, or if there be no surviving wife or child or children, to surviving father or mother whom the employee has supported, either wholly or in part, for the period of one year immediately prior to the date of the injury, and except that the Secretary of Labor may, at his option or upon the application of the insurance carrier shall, commute all future installments of compensation to be paid to such aliens or nonnationals of the United States by paying or causing to be paid to them one-half of the commuted amount of such future installments of compensation as determined by the Secretary. (August 16, 1941, c. 357, §2, 55 Stat. 623.)

§1653. Compensation districts; judicial proceedings.

(a) The Secretary of Labor is authorized to extend compensation districts established under the Longshoremen's and Harbor Workers' Compensation Act, approved March 4, 1927 (44 Stat. 1424) [33 U.S. Code 901–950], or to establish new compensation districts, to include any area to which this Act [42 U.S. Code 1651–1654] applies; and to assign to each such district one or more deputy commissioners, as the Secretary may deem necessary.

(b) Judicial proceedings provided under sections 18 and 21 [33 U.S. Code 918 and 921] of the Longshoremen's and Harbor Workers' Compensation Act in respect to a compensation order made pursuant to this Act [42 U.S. Code 1651–1654] shall be instituted in the United States district court of the judicial district wherein is located the office of the deputy commissioner whose compensation order is involved if his office is located in a judicial district, and if not so located, such judicial proceedings shall be instituted in the judicial district nearest the base at which the injury or death occurs. (August 16, 1941, c. 357, §3, 55 Stat. 623.)

§1654. Persons excluded from benefits.

This Act [42 U.S. Code 1651–1654] shall not apply in respect to the injury or death of (1) an employee subject to the provisions of the Federal Employees' Compensation Act [5 U.S. Code 751–793]; (2) an employee engaged in agriculture, domestic service, or any employment that is casual and not in the usual course of the trade, business, or profession of the employer; and (3) a master or member of a crew of any vessel. (August 16, 1941, c. 357, §4, 55 Stat. 623.)

§1655. Requirement for Department of Defense to adopt an acquisition strategy for Defense Base Act insurance.

(a) In General.—The Secretary of Defense shall adopt an acquisition strategy for insurance required by the Defense Base Act (42 U.S.C. 1651 et seq.) which minimizes the cost of such insurance to the Department of Defense and to defense contractors subject to such Act.

(b) Criteria.—The Secretary shall ensure that the acquisition strategy adopted pursuant to subsection (a) addresses the following criteria:

(1) Minimize overhead costs associated with obtaining such insurance, such as direct or indirect costs for contract management and contract administration.

(2) Minimize costs for coverage of such insurance consistent with realistic assumptions regarding the likelihood of incurred claims by contractors of the Department.

(3) Provide for a correlation of premiums paid in relation to claims incurred that is modeled on best practices in government and industry for similar kinds of insurance.

(4) Provide for a low level of risk to the Department.

(5) Provide for a competitive marketplace for insurance required by the Defense Base Act to the maximum extent practicable.

(c) Options.—In adopting the acquisition strategy pursuant to subsection (a), the Secretary shall consider such options (including entering into a single Defense Base Act insurance contract) as the Secretary deems to best satisfy the criteria identified under subsection (b).

(d) Report.—

(1) Not later than 270 days after the date of enactment of this Act, the Secretary shall submit to the Committees on Armed Services of the Senate and the House of Representatives, the Committee on Homeland Security and Governmental Affairs of the Senate, and the Committee on Oversight and Government Reform of the House of Representatives a report on the acquisition strategy adopted pursuant to subsection (a).

(2) The report shall include a discussion of each of the options considered pursuant to subsection (c) and the extent to which each option addresses the criteria identified under subsection (b), and shall include a plan to implement within 18 months after the date of enactment of this Act the acquisition strategy adopted by the Secretary.

(e) Review of Acquisition Strategy.—As considered appropriate by the Secretary, but not less often than once every 3 years, the Secretary shall review and, as necessary, update the acquisition strategy adopted pursuant to subsection (a) to ensure that it best addresses the criteria identified under subsection (b). (Oct. 14, 2008, Pub. L. 110-417, [Div A,] Title VIII, Subtitle E, § 843, 122 Stat. 4540.)

CHAPTER 12
COMPENSATION FOR INJURY, DEATH, OR DETENTION OF EMPLOYEES OF CONTRACTORS WITH THE UNITED STATES OUTSIDE THE UNITED STATES

SUBCHAPTER I
COMPENSATION, REIMBURSEMENT, ETC., BY SECRETARY OF LABOR

§1701. Compensation for injury or death resulting from war-risk hazard.

(a) Injury or death.—In case of injury or death resulting from injury—

(1) to any person employed by a contractor with the United States, if such person is an employee specified in the Act of August 16, 1941 (Public Law Numbered 208, Seventy-seventh Congress), as amended [42 U.S. Code 1651–1654], and no compensation is payable with respect to such injury or death under such Act; or

(2) to any person engaged by the United States under a contract for his personal services outside the continental United States; or

(3) to any person employed outside the continental United States as a civilian employee paid from non-appropriated funds administered by the Army and Air Force Exchange Service, Army and Air Force Motion Picture Service, Navy Ship's Store Ashore, Navy exchanges, Marine Corps exchanges, officers' and noncommissioned officers' open messes, enlisted men's club, service clubs, special service activities, or any other instrumentality of the United States under the jurisdiction of the Department of Defense and conducted for the mental, physical and morale improvement of personnel of the Department of Defense and their dependents; or

(4) to any person who is an employee specified in section 1(a)(5) of the Defense Base Act, as amended, if no compensation is payable with respect to such injury or death under such Act, or to any person engaged under a contract for his personal services outside the United States approved and financed by the United States under the Mutual Security Act of 1954, as amended (other than title II of chapter II thereof unless the Secretary of Labor, upon the recommendation of the head of any department or other agency of the United States Government, determines a contract financed under a successor provision of any successor Act should be covered by this section): Provided, That in cases where the United States is not a formal party to contracts approved and financed under the Mutual Security Act of 1954, as amended, the Secretary, upon the recommendation of the head of any department or agency of the United States, may, in the exercise of his discretion, waive the application of the provisions of this subparagraph with respect to any such contracts, subcontracts, or subordinate contracts, work location under such contracts, subcontracts, or subordinate contracts, or classification of employees; or

(5) to any person employed or otherwise engaged for personal services outside the continental United States by an American employer providing welfare or similar services for the benefit of the Armed Forces pursuant to appropriate authorization by the Secretary of Defense, and such injury proximately results from a war-risk hazard, whether or not such person then actually was engaged in the course of his employment, the provisions of sections 751–756, 757–781, 783–791 and 793 of Title 5, and as modified by this chapter, shall apply with respect thereto in the same manner and to the same extent as if the person so employed were a civil employee of the United States and were injured while in the performance of his duty, and any compensation found to be due shall be paid from the compensation fund established pursuant to section 785 of Title 5. This subsection shall not be construed to include any person who would otherwise come within the purview of sections 751–756, 757–781, 783–791 and 793 of Title 5.

(b)(1) Any person specified in subsection (a) of this section who—

(A) is found to be missing from his place of employment, whether or not such person then

U.S.C.

actually was engaged in the course of his employment, under circumstances supporting an inference that his absence is due to the belligerent action of a hostile force or person, or

(B) is known to have been taken by a hostile force or person as a prisoner, hostage, or otherwise, or

(C) is not returned to his home or to the place where he was employed by reason of the failure of the United States or its contractor to furnish transportation, until such time as he is returned to his home, to the place of his employment, or is able to be returned to the jurisdiction of the United States, shall, under such regulations as the Secretary may prescribe, be regarded solely for the purposes of this subsection as totally disabled, and the same benefits as are provided for such disability under this subchapter shall be credited to his account and be payable to him for the period of such absence or until his death is in fact established or can be legally presumed to have occurred: Provided, That if such person has dependents residing in the United States or its Territories or possessions (including the United States Naval Operating Base, Guantanamo Bay, Cuba, the Canal Zone, and the Philippine Islands), the Secretary during the period of such absence may disburse a part of such compensation, accruing for such total disability, to such dependents, which shall be equal to the monthly benefits otherwise payable for death under this subchapter, and the balance of such compensation for total disability shall accrue and be payable to such person upon his return from such absence. Any payment made pursuant to this subsection shall not in any case be included in computing the maximum aggregate or total compensation payable for disability or death, as provided in section 1702(a) of this title: Provided further, That no such payment to such person or his dependent, on account of such absence, shall be made during any period such person or dependent, respectively, has received, or may be entitled to receive, any other payment from the United States, either directly or indirectly, because of such absence, unless such person or dependent refunds or renounces such other benefit or payment for the period claimed.

Benefits found to be due under this subsection shall be paid from the compensation fund established pursuant to section 785 of Title 5: Provided, That the determination of dependents, dependency, and amounts of payments to dependents shall be made in the manner specified in sections 751–756, 757–781, 783–791 and 793 of Title 5: Provided further, That claim for such detention benefits shall be filed in accordance with and subject to the limitation provisions of sections 751–756, 757–781, 783–791 and 793 of Title 5, as modified by section 1706(c) of this title: And provided further, That except in cases of fraud or willful misrepresentation, the Secretary may waive recovery of money erroneously paid under this subdivision whenever he finds that such recovery would be impracticable or would cause hardship to the beneficiary affected: And provided further, That where such person is found to be missing from his place of employment, whether or not such person then actually was engaged in the course of his employment, under circumstances supporting an inference that his absence is due to the belligerent action of a hostile force or person or is known to have been taken by a hostile force or person as a prisoner, hostage, or otherwise, the amount of benefits to be credited to the account of such person under this subsection, and for the purposes of this subsection only, shall be 100 per centum of the average weekly wages of such person, except that in computing such benefits such average weekly wages (a) shall not exceed the average weekly wages paid to civilian employees of the United States in the same or most similar occupation in the area nearest to the place of employment where such person was last employed, and (b) shall not exceed the average weekly wages of such absent person at the time such absence began; and 70 per centum of such average weekly wage so determined shall be disbursed to the dependent or dependents of such person, irrespective of the limitations of section 909 of Title 33, but should there be more than one such dependent, the distribution of such 70 per centum shall be proportionate to the percentages allowed for dependents by section 909 of Title 33, and if such manner of disbursement in any case would result in injustice or excessive allowance for a dependent, the Secretary may, in his discretion, modify such percentage or apportionment to meet the requirements of the case; and in such cases benefits for detention shall accrue from January 1, 1942, unless the beginning of absence occurred upon a later date in which event benefits shall accrue from such later date, and for the period of such absence shall be 100 per centum of the average weekly wages, determined as herein provided: And provided further, That compensation for disability under this subchapter (except under allowance for scheduled losses of members of functions of the body, within the purview of section 1702(a) of this title) shall not be paid in any case in respect to any period of time during which benefits for detention may accrue under this subchapter in the same case, and should a person entitled to benefits for detention also be entitled to workmen's compensation or similar benefits under any other law, agreement, or plan (except allowances for scheduled losses of members or functions of the body), where such other benefits are paid or to be paid directly or indirectly by the United States, the amount thereof accruing as to the period of absence shall be taken into account and the benefits credited to the account of the detained person reduced accordingly: And provided further, That where through mistake of fact, absence of proof of death, or error through lack of adequate information or otherwise, payments as for detention have in any case been erroneously made or credited, any resulting overpayment of detention benefits (the recovery of which is not waived as otherwise provided for in this section) shall be recouped by the Secretary in such manner as he shall determine from any unpaid accruals to the account of the detained person, and if such accruals are insufficient for such purpose, then from any allowance of compensation for injury or death in the same case (whether under this subchapter or under any other law, agreement, or plan, if the United States pays, or is obligated to pay, such benefits, directly or indirectly), but only to the extent of the amount of such compensation benefits payable for the particular period of such overpayment, and in cases of erroneous payments of compensation for injury or death, made through mistake of fact, whether under this subchapter or under any other law, agreement, or plan (if the United States is obligated to pay such compensation, directly or indirectly), the Secretary is authorized to recoup from any unpaid benefits for detention, the amount of any overpayment thus arising; and any amounts recovered under this section shall be covered into such compensation fund, and for the foregoing purposes the Secretary shall have a right of lien, intervention, and recovery in any claim or proceeding for compensation.

(2) Upon application by such person, or someone on his behalf, the Secretary may, under such regulations as he may prescribe, furnish transportation or the cost thereof (including reimbursement) to any such person from the point where his release from custody by a hostile force or person is effected, to his home, the place of his employment, or other place within the jurisdiction of the United States; but no transportation, or the cost thereof, shall be furnished under this paragraph where such person is furnished such transportation, or the cost thereof, under any agreement with his employer or under any other provision of law.

(3) In the case of death of any such person, if his death occurred away from his home, the body of such person shall, in the discretion of the Secretary, and if so desired by his next of kin, near relative, or legal representative, be embalmed and transported in a hermetically sealed casket or other appropriate container to the home of such person or to such other place as may be designated by such next of kin, near relative, or legal representative. No expense shall be incurred under this paragraph by the Secretary in any case where death takes place after repatriation, unless such death proximately results from a war-risk hazard.

(4) Such benefits for detention, transportation expenses of repatriated persons, and expenses of embalming, providing sealed or other appropriate container, and transportation of the body, and attendants (if required), as approved by the Secretary, shall be paid out of the compensation fund established under section 785 of Title 5.

(c) Compensation for permanent total or permanent partial disability or for death payable under this section to persons who are not citizens of the United States and who are not residents of the United States or Canada, shall be in the same amount as provided for residents; except that dependents in any foreign country shall be limited to surviving wife or husband and child or children, or if there be no surviving wife or husband or child or children, to surviving father or mother whom such person has supported, either wholly or in part, for the period of one year immediately prior to the date of the injury; and except that the Secretary, at his option, may commute all future installments of compensation to be paid to such persons by paying to them one-half of the commuted amount of such future installments of compensation as determined by the Secretary.

(d) The provisions of this section shall not apply in the case of any person (1) whose residence is at or in the vicinity of the place of his employment, and (2) who is not living there solely by virtue of the exigencies of his employment, unless his injury or death resulting from injury occurs or his detention begins while in the course of his employment, or (3) who is a prisoner of war or a protected person under the Geneva Conventions of 1949 and who is detained or utilized by the United States. (As amended June 30, 1958, Pub. L. 85–477, ch. V, §502(g), 72 Stat. 273; August 8, 1958, Pub. L. 85–608, Title 1, §§101, 104, Title IV, §401, 72 Stat. 536, 537, 539; June 25, 1959, Pub. L. 86–70, §42(a), 73 Stat. 151, September 4, 1961, Pub. L. 87–195, Pt. IV, §702, 75 Stat. 463.)

§1702. Application of Longshore and Harbor Workers' Compensation Act.

(a) In the administration of the provisions of subchapter I of chapter 81 of Title 5, with respect to cases coming within the purview of section 1701 of this title, the scale of compensation benefits and the provisions for determining the amount of compensation and the payment thereof as provided in sections 908 and 909 of Title 33, so far as the provisions of said sections can be applied under the terms and conditions set forth therein, shall be payable in lieu of the benefits, except medical benefits, provided under subchapter I of chapter 81 of Title 5: Provided, That the total compensation payable under this subchapter for injury or death shall in no event exceed the limitations upon compensation as fixed in section 914(m) of Title 33 as such section may from time to time be amended except that the total compensation shall not be less than that provided for in the original enactment of this chapter.

(b) For the purpose of computing compensation with respect to cases coming within the purview of section 1701 of this title, the provisions of sections 906 and 910 of Title 33 shall be applicable: Provided, That the minimum limit on weekly compensation for disability, established by section 906(b) of Title 33, and the minimum limit on the average weekly wages on which death benefits are to be computed, established by section 909(e) of Title 33, shall not apply in computing compensation under this subchapter. (December 2, 1942, c. 668, Title I, §103, 56 Stat. 1031; as amended July 3, 1948, c. 826, §4(c), 62 Stat. 1242; August 8, 1958, Pub. L. 85–608, Title I, §102, 72 Stat. 536.)

§1703. "Contractor with the United States" defined.

As used in this subchapter [42 U.S. Code 1701–1706], the term "contractor with the United States" includes any subcontractor or subordinate subcontractor with respect to the contract of such contractor. (December 2, 1942, c. 668, Title I, §103, 56 Stat. 1031.)

§1704. Reimbursement.

(a) Payments reimbursable; filing claim for reimbursement; regulations for payment of direct benefits. Where any employer or his insurance carrier or compensation fund pays or is required to pay benefits—

(1) to any person or fund on account of injury or death of any person coming within the purview of this subchapter [42 U.S. Code 1701–1706] or the Act of August 16, 1941 (Public Law Numbered 208, Seventy-seventh Congress), as amended [42 U.S. Code 1651–1654], if such injury or death arose from a war-risk hazard, which are payable under any workmen's compensation law of the United States or of any State, Territory, or possession of the United States, or other jurisdiction; or

(2) to any person by reason of any agreement outstanding on the date of enactment of this Act (Dec. 2, 1942) made in accordance with a contract between the United States and any contractor therewith to pay benefits with respect to the death of any employee of such contractor occurring under circumstances not entitling such person to benefits under any workmen's compensation law or to pay benefits with respect to the death of any employee of such contractor occurring under circumstances not entitling such person to benefits under any workmen's compensation law or to pay benefits with respect to the failure of the United States or its contractor to furnish transportation upon the completion of the employment of any employee of such contractor to his home or to the place where he was employed; or

(3) to any person by reason of an agreement approved or authorized by the United States under which a contractor with the United States has agreed to pay workmen's compensation benefits or benefits in the nature of workmen's compensation benefits to an injured employee or his dependents on account of detention by a hostile force or person or on account of injury or death arising from a war-risk hazard; such employer, carrier, or fund shall be entitled to be

reimbursed for all benefits so paid or payable, including funeral and burial expenses, medical, hospital, or other similar costs for treatment and care; and reasonable and necessary claims expense in connection therewith. Claim for such reimbursement shall be filed with the Secretary under regulations promulgated by him, and such claims, or such part thereof as may be allowed by the Secretary, shall be paid from the compensation fund established under section 785 of Title 5. The Secretary may, under such regulations as he shall prescribe, pay such benefits, as they accrue and in lieu of reimbursement, directly to any person entitled thereto, and the insolvency of such employer, insurance carrier, or compensation fund shall not affect the right of the beneficiaries of such benefits to receive the compensation directly from the said compensation fund established under section 785 of Title 5. The Secretary may also, under such regulations as he shall prescribe, use any private facilities, or such Government facilities as may be available, for the treatment or care of any person entitled thereto. (As amended August 8, 1958, Pub. L. 85–608, Title I, §104, 72 Stat. 537.)

(b) Charging of premiums as prohibiting reimbursement. No reimbursement shall be made under this subchapter [42 U.S. Code 1701–1706] in any case in which the Secretary finds that the benefits paid or payable were on account of injury, detention, or death which arose from a war-risk hazard for which a premium (which included an additional charge or loading for such hazard) was charged. (Dec. 2, 1942, c. 668, Title I, sec. 104, 56 Stat. 1031.)

(c) Injury or death occurring within any State. The provisions of this section shall not apply with respect to benefits on account of any injury or death occurring within any State. (Added by Pub. L. 86–70, §42(b), 73 Stat. 151, effective June 25, 1959.)

§1705. Receipt of workmen's compensation benefits.

(a) No benefits shall be paid or furnished under the provisions of this title [42 U.S. Code 1701–1706] for injury or death to any person who recovers or receives workmen's compensation benefits for the same injury or death under any other law of the United States, or under the law of any State, Territory, possession, foreign country, or other jurisdiction, or benefits in the nature of workmen's compensation benefits payable under an agreement approved or authorized by the United States pursuant to which a contractor with the United States has undertaken to provide such benefits.

(b) The Secretary shall have a lien and a right of recovery, to the extent of any payments made under this subchapter [42 U.S. Code 1701–1706] on account of injury or death, against any compensation payable under any other workmen's compensation law on account of the same injury or death; and any amounts recovered under this subsection shall be covered into the fund established under section 35 of such Act of September 7, 1916, as amended [5 U.S. Code 785].

(c) Where any person specified in section 1701(a) of this title, or the dependent, beneficiary, or allottee of such person, receives or claims wages, payments in lieu of wages, insurance benefits for disability or loss of life (other than workmen's compensation benefits), and the cost of such wages, payments, or benefits is provided in whole or in part by the United States, the amount of such wages, payments, or benefits shall be credited in such manner as the Secretary shall determine, against any payments to which any such person is entitled under this subchapter.

Where any person specified in section 1701(a) of this title, or any dependent, beneficiary, or allottee of such person, or the legal representative or estate of any such entities, after having obtained benefits under this subchapter, seeks through any proceeding, claim, or otherwise, brought or maintained against the employer, the United States, or other person, to recover wages, payments in lieu of wages, or any sum claimed as for services rendered, or for failure to furnish transportation, or for liquidated or unliquidated damages under the employment contract, or any other benefit, and the right in respect thereto is alleged to have accrued during or as to any period of time in respect of which payments under this title in such case have been made, and in like cases where a recovery is made or allowed, the Secretary shall have the right of intervention and a lien and right of recovery to the extent of any payments paid and payable under this subchapter in such case, provided the cost of such wages, payments in lieu of wages, or other such right, may be directly or indirectly paid by the United States; and any amounts recovered under this subsection shall be covered into the fund established under section 785 of Title 5.

(d) Where a national of a foreign government is entitled to benefits on account of injury or death resulting from a war-risk hazard, under the laws of his native country or any other foreign country, the benefits of this subchapter [42 U.S. Code 1701–1706] shall not apply.

(e) If at the time a person sustains an injury coming within the purview of this subchapter [42 U.S. Code 1701–1706] said person is receiving workmen's compensation benefits on account of a prior accident or disease, said person shall not be entitled to any benefits under this title during the period covered by such workmen's compensation benefits unless the injury from a war-risk hazard increases his disability, and then only to the extent such disability has been so increased. (December 2, 1942, c. 668, Title I, §105, 56 Stat. 1032; as amended December 23, 1943, c. 380, Title I, 57 Stat. 511, the amendment to become effective as of December 2, 1942, 1946 Reorg. Plan No. 2, §3, effective July 16, 1946, 11 F.R. 7873, 60 Stat. 1095.)

§1706. Administration.

(a) The provisions of this subchapter [42 U.S. Code 1701–1706] shall be administered by the Secretary of Labor, and the Secretary is authorized to make rules and regulations for the administration thereof and to contract with insurance carriers for the use of the service facilities of such carriers for the purpose of facilitating administration.

(b) In administering the provisions of this title [42 U.S. Code 1701–1706] the Secretary may enter into agreements or cooperative working arrangements with other agencies of the United States or of any State (including the District of Columbia, Hawaii, Alaska, Puerto Rico, and the Virgin Islands) or political subdivisions thereof, and with other public agencies and private persons, agencies, or institutions, within and outside the United States, to utilize their services and facilities and to compensate them for such use. The Secretary may delegate to any officer or employee, or to any agency, of the United States or of any State, or of any political subdivision thereof, or Territory or possession of the United States, such of his powers and duties as he finds necessary for carrying out the purposes of this subchapter.

(c) The Secretary, in his discretion, may waive the limitation provisions of such Act of September 7, 1916, as amended [5 U.S. Code 751–793] with respect to notice of injury and filing of claims under this title, whenever the Secretary shall find that, because of circumstances beyond the control of an injured person or his beneficiary, compliance with such provisions could not have been accomplished within the time therein specified. (December 2, 1942, c. 668, Title I, §106, 56 Stat. 1033.)

SUBCHAPTER II MISCELLANEOUS PROVISIONS

§1711. Definitions.

When used in this Act [42 U.S. Code 1701–1717]—

(a) The term "Secretary" means the Secretary of Labor.

(b) The term "war-risk hazard" means any hazard arising during a war in which the United States is engaged; during an armed conflict in which the United States is engaged, whether or not war has been declared; or during a war or armed conflict between military forces of any origin, occurring within any country in which a person covered by this chapter is serving; from—

(1) the discharge of any missile (including liquids and gas) or the use of any weapon, explosive, or other noxious thing by a hostile force or person or in combating an attack or an imagined attack by a hostile force or person; or

(2) action of a hostile force or person, including rebellion or insurrection against the United States or any of its Allies; or

(3) the discharge or explosion of munitions intended for use in connection with a war or armed conflict with a hostile force or person as defined herein (except with respect to employees of a manufacturer, processor, or transporter or munitions during the manufacture, processing, or transporting thereof, or while stored on the premises of the manufacturer, processor, or transporter; or

(4) the collision of vessels in convoy or the operation of vessels or aircraft without running lights or without other customary peacetime aids to navigation; or

(5) the operation of vessels or aircraft in a zone of hostilities or engaged in war activities.

(c) The term "hostile force or person" means any nation, any subject of a foreign nation, or any other person serving a foreign nation (1) engaged in a war against the United States or any of its allies, (2) engaged in armed conflict, whether or not war has been declared, against the United States or any of its allies, or (3) engaged in a war or armed conflict between military forces of any origin in any country in which a person covered by this chapter is serving.

(d) The term "allies" means any nation with which the United States is engaged in a common military effort or with which the United States has entered into a common defensive military alliance.

(e) The term "war activities" includes activities directly relating to military operations.

(f) The term "continental United States" means the States and the District of Columbia. (As amended June 29, 1957, Pub. L. 85–70, 71 Stat. 242; August 8, 1958, Pub. L. 85–608, Title I, §§103, 104, 72 Stat. 536; Pub. L. 86–70, §42(c), 73 Stat. 151, effective June 25, 1959.)

§1712. Disqualification from benefits.

No person convicted in a court of competent jurisdiction of any subversive act against the United States or any of its Allies, committed after the declaration by the President on May 27, 1941, of the national emergency, shall be entitled to compensation or other benefits under Title 1 [42 U.S. Code 1701–1706], nor shall any compensation be payable with respect to his death or detention under such title, and upon indictment or the filing of an information charging the commission of any such subversive act, all such compensation or other benefits shall be suspended and remain suspended until acquittal or withdrawal of such charge, but upon conviction thereof or upon death occurring prior to a final disposition thereof, all such payments and all benefits under such title shall be forfeited and terminated. If the charge is withdrawn, or there is an acquittal, all such compensation withheld shall be paid to the person or persons entitled thereto. (December 2, 1942, c. 668, Title II, §202, 56 Stat. 1034.)

§1713. Fraud; penalties.

Whoever, for the purpose of causing an increase in any payment authorized to be made under this Act [42 U.S. Code 1701–1717], or for the purpose of causing any payment to be made where no payment is authorized hereunder, shall knowingly make or cause to be made, or aid or abet in the making of any false statement, representation, affidavit, or document in connection with such an application, or claim, shall be guilty of a misdemeanor and upon conviction thereof shall be fined not more than $1,000 or imprisoned for not more than one year, or both. (December 2, 1942, c. 668, Title II, §203, 56 Stat. 1034.)

§1714. Legal services.

No claim for legal services or for any other services rendered in respect of a claim or award for compensation under Title I [42 U.S. Code 1701–1706] to or on account of any person shall be valid unless approved by the Secretary; and any claim so approved shall, in the manner and to the extent fixed by the said Secretary, be paid out of the compensation payable to the claimant; and any person who receives any fee, other consideration, or any gratuity on account of services so rendered, unless such consideration or gratuity is so approved, or who solicits employment for another person or for himself in respect of any claim or award for compensation under Title I [42 U.S. Code 1701–1706] shall be guilty of a misdemeanor and upon conviction thereof shall, for each offense, be fined not more than $1,000 or imprisoned not more than one year, or both. (December 2, 1942, c. 668, Title II, §204, 56 Stat. 1034.)

§1715. Finality of Secretary's decisions.

The action of the Secretary in allowing or denying any payment under Title I [42 U.S. Code 1701–1706] shall be final and conclusive on all questions of law and fact and not subject to review by any other official of the United States or by any court by mandamus or otherwise, and the Comptroller General is authorized and directed to allow credit in the accounts of any certifying or disbursing officer for payments in accordance with such action. (December 2, 1942, c. 668, Title II, §205, 56 Stat. 1034.)

§1716. Presumption of death or detention.

A determination that an individual is dead or a determination that he has been detained by a hostile force or person may be made on the basis of evidence that he has disappeared under circumstances such as to make such death or detention appear probable. (As amended August

8, 1958, Pub. L. 85–608, Title I, §104, 72 Stat. 537.)

§1717. Assignment of benefits; execution, levy, etc., against benefits.

The right of any person to any benefit under Title I [42 U.S. Code 1701–1706] shall not be transferable or assignable at law or in equity except to the United States, and none of the moneys paid or payable (except money paid hereunder as reimbursement for funeral expenses or as reimbursement with respect to payments of workmen's compensation or in the nature of workmen's compensation benefits), or rights existing under such title, shall be subject to execution, levy, attachment, garnishment, or other legal process or to the operation of any bankruptcy or insolvency law. (December 2, 1942, c. 668, Title II, §207, 56 Stat. 1035.)

TITLE 43
PUBLIC LANDS

CHAPTER 29
SUBMERGED LANDS

SUBCHAPTER III
OUTER CONTINENTAL SHELF LANDS

§1331. Definitions.

When used in this subchapter—

(a) The term "outer Continental Shelf" means all submerged lands lying seaward and outside of the area of lands beneath navigable waters as defined in section 1301 [See note, below] of this title, and of which the subsoil and seabed appertain to the United States and are subject to its jurisdiction and control;

[Subsections (b)–(q) Not Reproduced]

Note: Section 1301 provides the following definition of the term "lands beneath navigable waters":

(1) all lands within the boundaries of each of the respective States which are covered by nontidal waters that were navigable under the laws of the United States at the time such State became a member of the Union, or acquired sovereignty over such lands and waters thereafter, up to the ordinary high water mark as heretofore or hereafter modified by accretion, erosion, and reliction;

(2) all lands permanently or periodically covered by tidal waters up to but not above the line of mean high tide and seaward to a line three geographical miles distance from the cost line of each such State and to the boundary line of each such State where in any case such boundary as it existed seaward (or into the Gulf of Mexico) beyond three geographical miles, and

(3) all filed in, made, or reclaimed lands which formerly were lands beneath navigable waters, as hereinabove defined.

Ref.: W. Cal. Sum., 2 "Workers' Compensation" §144.

§1333. Laws and regulations governing lands.

[Subsection (a) Not Reproduced]

(b) Longshore and Harbor Workers' Compensation Act applicable; definitions. With respect to disability or death of an employee resulting from any injury occurring as the result of operations conducted on the outer Continental Shelf for the purpose of exploring for, developing, removing, or transporting by pipeline the natural resources, or involving rights to the natural resources, of the subsoil and seabed of the outer Continental Shelf, compensation shall be payable under the provisions of the Longshoremen's and Harbor Workers' Compensation Act. For the purposes of the extension of the provisions of the Longshoremen's and Harbor Workers' Compensation Act under this section—

(1) the term "employee" does not include a master or member of a crew of any vessel, or an officer or employee of the United States or any agency thereof or of any State or foreign government, or of any political subdivision thereof;

(2) the term "employer" means an employer any of whose employees are employed in such operations; and

(3) the term "United States" when used in a geographical sense includes the outer Continental Shelf and artificial islands and fixed structures thereon.

[Subsections (c)–(f) Not Reproduced]

TITLE 43
PUBLIC LANDS

CHAPTER 29
SUBMERGED LANDS

Ref. by Longshore and Harbor Workers' Compensation Act

§1333. Laws and regulations governing lands

[Subsection (a) Not Reproduced]

(b) Longshore and Harbor Workers' Compensation Act applicable; definitions. With respect to disability or death of an employee resulting from any injury occurring as the result of operations conducted on the outer Continental Shelf for the purpose of exploring for, developing, removing, or transporting by pipeline the natural resources, or involving rights to the natural resources, of the subsoil and seabed of the outer Continental Shelf, compensation shall be payable under the provisions of the Longshoremen's and Harbor Workers' Compensation Act. For the purposes of the extension of the provisions of the Longshoremen's and Harbor Workers' Compensation Act under this section—

(1) the term "employee" does not include a master or member of a crew of any vessel, or an officer or employee of the United States or any agency thereof or of any State or foreign government, or of any political subdivision thereof;

(2) the term "employer" means an employer any of whose employees are employed in such operations; and

(3) the term "United States" when used in a geographical sense includes the outer Continental Shelf and artificial islands and fixed structures thereon.

[Subsections (c)-(f) Not Reproduced]

SUBCHAPTER III
OUTER CONTINENTAL SHELF LANDS

§1331. Definitions

When used in this subchapter—

(a) The term "outer Continental Shelf" means all submerged lands lying seaward and outside of the area of lands beneath navigable waters as defined in section 1301 [See note below] of this title, and of which the subsoil and seabed appertain to the United States and are subject to its jurisdiction and control;

[Subsections (b)-(q) Not Reproduced]

Note: Section 1301 provides the following definition of "lands beneath navigable waters":

(1) all lands within the boundaries of each of the respective States which are covered by nontidal waters that were navigable under the laws of the United States at the time such State became a member of the Union, or acquired sovereignty over such lands and waters thereafter, up to the ordinary high water mark as heretofore or hereafter modified by accretion, erosion, and reliction;

(2) all lands permanently or periodically covered by tidal waters up to but not above the line of mean high tide and seaward to a line three geographical miles distant from the coast line of each such State and to the boundary line of each such State where in any case such boundary as it existed seaward (or into the Gulf of Mexico) beyond three geographical miles, and

(3) all filled in, made, or reclaimed lands which formerly were lands beneath navigable waters, as hereinabove defined.

TITLE 45
RAILROADS

CHAPTER 2
LIABILITY FOR INJURIES TO EMPLOYEES

§51. Liability of common carriers by railroad, in interstate or foreign commerce, for injuries to employees from negligence; employee defined.

Every common carrier by railroad while engaging in commerce between any of the several States or Territories, or between any of the States and Territories, or between the District of Columbia or any of the States or Territories and any foreign nation or nations, shall be liable in damages to any person suffering injury while he is employed by such carrier in such commerce, or, in case of the death of such employee, to his or her personal representative for the benefit of the surviving widow or husband and children of such employee; and, if none, then of such employee's parents; and, if none, then of the next of kin dependent upon such employee, for such injury or death resulting in whole or in part from the negligence of any of the officers, agents, or employees of such carrier, or by reason of any defect or insufficiency, due to its negligence, in its cars, engines, appliances, machinery, track, roadbed, works, boats, wharves, or other equipment.

Any employee of a carrier, any part of whose duties as such employee shall be the furtherance of interstate or foreign commerce; or shall, in any way directly or closely and substantially, affect such commerce as above set forth shall, for the purpose of this Act [45 U.S. Code 51–60], be considered as being employed by such carrier in such commerce and shall be considered as entitled to the benefits of this Act and of an Act entitled "An Act relating to the liability of common carriers by railroad to their employees in certain cases" (approved April 22, 1908), as the same has been or may hereafter be amended. (April 22, 1908, c. 149, §1, 35 Stat. 65, August 11, 1939, c. 685, §1, 53 Stat. 1404.)

Ref.: CACI Nos. 2900, 2920, 2941, 2942 (Matthew Bender); W. Cal. Sum., 2 "Workers' Compensation" §§118, 120, 121, 123, 6 "Torts" §§1008, 1383, 7 "Constitutional Law" §§25, 42.

§52. Carriers in territories or other possessions of United States.

Every common carrier by railroad in the Territories, the District of Columbia, the Panama Canal Zone, or other possessions of the United States shall be liable in damages to any person suffering injury while he is employed by such carrier in any of said jurisdictions, or, in case of the death of such employee, to his or her personal representative, for the benefit of the surviving widow or husband and children of such employee; and, if none, then of such employee's parents; and, if none, then of the next of kin dependent upon such employee, for such injury or death resulting in whole or in part from the negligence of any of the officers, agents, or employees of such carrier, or by reason of any defect or insufficiency, due to its negligence, in its cars, engines, appliances, machinery, track, roadbed, works, boats, wharves, or other equipment. (April 22, 1908, c. 149, §2, 35 Stat. 65.)

§53. Contributory negligence; diminution of damages.

In all actions hereafter brought against any such common carrier by railroad under or by virtue of any of the provisions of this chapter [45 U.S. Code 51–60] to recover damages for personal injuries to an employee or where such injuries have resulted in his death, the fact that the employee may have been guilty of contributory negligence shall not bar a recovery, but the damages shall be diminished by the jury in proportion to the amount of negligence attributable to such employee: Provided, That no such employee who may be injured or killed shall be held to have been guilty of contributory negligence in any case where the violation by such common carrier of any statute enacted for the safety of employees contributed to the injury or death of such employee. (April 22, 1908, c. 149, §3, 35 Stat. 66.)

Ref.: CACI Nos. 2904, 2920 (Matthew Bender); W. Cal. Sum., 2 "Workers' Compensation" §§123, 124.

§54. Assumption of risks of employment.

In any action brought against any common carrier under or by virtue of any of the provisions of this Act [45 U.S. Code 51–60] to recover damages for injuries to, or the death of, any of its employees, such employee shall not be held to have assumed the risks of his employment in any case where such injury or death resulted in whole or in part from the negligence of any of the officers, agents, or employees of such carrier; and no employee shall be held to have assumed the risks of his employment in any case where the violation by such common carrier of any statute enacted for the safety of employees contributed to the injury or death of such employee. (April 22, 1908, c. 149, §4, 35 Stat. 66; August 11, 1939, c. 685, §1, 53 Stat. 1404.)

Ref.: CACI No. 2920 (Matthew Bender); W. Cal. Sum., 2 "Workers' Compensation" §§123, 124.

§54a. Regulation, standard, or requirement under chapter 201 of title 49, United States Code, deemed to be statute under sections 3 and 4.

A regulation, standard, or requirement in force, or prescribed by the Secretary of Transportation under chapter 201 of title 49, United States Code [49 U.S.C.S. §§20101 et seq.], or by a State agency that is participating in investigative and surveillance activities under section 20105 of title 49, is deemed to be a statute under sections 3 and 4 of this Act [45 U.S.C.S. §§53, 54]. (April 22, 1908, c. 149, §4A, as added July 5, 1994, Pub.L. 103-272, §4(i), 108 Stat. 1365.)

Ref.: CACI No. 2920 (Matthew Bender).

§55. Contract, rule, regulation, or device exempting from liability; set-off.

Any contract, rule, regulation, or device whatsoever, the purpose or intent of which shall be to enable any common carrier to exempt itself from any liability created by this chapter [45 U.S. Code 51–60], shall to that extent be void: Provided, That in any action brought against any such common carrier under or by virtue of any of the provisions of this chapter, such common carrier may set off therein any sum it has contributed or paid to any insurance, relief benefit, or indemnity that may have been paid to the injured employee or the person entitled thereto on account of the injury or death for which said action was brought. (April 22, 1908, c. 149, §5, Stat. 66.)

Ref.: CACI Nos. 2941, 2942 (Matthew Bender).

§56. Actions; limitation; concurrent jurisdiction of courts.

No action shall be maintained under this chapter [45 U.S. Code 51–60] unless commenced within three years from the day the cause of action accrued.

Under this chapter an action may be brought in a district court of the United States, in the district of the residence of the defendant, or in which the cause of action arose, or in which the defendant shall be doing business at the time of commencing such action. The jurisdiction of the courts of the United States under this chapter shall be concurrent with that of the courts of the several States. (April 22, 1908, c. 149, §6, 35 Stat. 66; April 5, 1910, c. 143, §1, 36 Stat. 291; March 3, 1911, c. 231, §291, 36 Stat. 1167; August 11, 1939, c. 685, §2, 53 Stat. 1404; June 25, 1948, c. 646, §18, 62 Stat. 989.)

Ref.: MB Prac. Guide: Cal. Contract Lit., §3.08[3]; CACI No. 2922 (Matthew Bender); W. Cal. Sum., 2 "Workers' Compensation" §119.

§57. Who included in term "common carrier."

The term "common carrier" as used in this chapter [45 U.S. Code 51–60] shall include the receiver or receivers or other persons or corporations charged with the duty of the management and operation of the business of a common carrier. (April 22, 1908, c. 149, §7, 35 Stat. 66.)

Ref.: CACI No. 2925 (Matthew Bender).

§58. Duty or liability of common carriers and rights of employees under other acts not impaired.

Nothing in this chapter shall be held to limit the duty or liability of common carriers or to impair the rights of their employees under any other Act or Acts of Congress. (April 22, 1908, c. 149, §8, 35 Stat. 66.)

§59. Survival of right of action of person injured.

Any right of action given by this chapter [45 U.S. Code 51–60] to a person suffering injury shall survive to his or her personal representative, for the benefit of the surviving widow or husband and children of such employee, and, if none, then of such employee's parents; and, if none, then of the next of kin dependent upon such employee, but in such cases there shall be only one recovery for the same injury. (April 22, 1908, c. 149, §9, 35 Stat. 66; April 5, 1910, c. 143, §2, 36 Stat. 291.)

Ref.: CACI No. 2942 (Matthew Bender).

§60. Penalty for suppression of voluntary information incident to accidents; separability.

Any contract, rule, regulation, or device whatsoever, the purpose, intent, or effect of which shall be to prevent employees of any common carrier from furnishing voluntarily information to a person in interest as to the facts incident to the injury or death of any employee, shall be void, and whoever, by threat, intimidation, order, rule, contract, regulation, or device whatsoever, shall attempt to prevent any person from furnishing voluntarily such information to a person in interest, or whoever discharges or otherwise disciplines or attempts to discipline any employee for furnishing voluntarily such information to a person in interest, shall, upon conviction thereof, be punished by a fine of not more than $1,000 or imprisoned for not more than one year, or by both such fine and imprisonment, for each offense: Provided, That nothing herein contained shall be construed to void any contract, rule or regulation with respect to any information contained in the files of the carrier, or other privileged or confidential reports.

If any provision of this Act [45 U.S. Code 51–60] is declared unconstitutional or the applicability thereof to any person or circumstances is held invalid, the validity of the remainder of the Act and the applicability of such provision to other persons and circumstances shall not be affected thereby. (Added August 11, 1939, by c. 685, §3, 53 Stat. 1404.)

TITLE 46
SHIPPING

SUBTITLE III
MARITIME LIABILITY

CHAPTER 301
GENERAL LIABILITY PROVISIONS

§30101. Extension of jurisdiction to cases of damage or injury on land.

(a) In general. The admiralty and maritime jurisdiction of the United States extends to and includes cases of injury or damage, to person or property, caused by a vessel on navigable waters, even though the injury or damage is done or consummated on land.

(b) Procedure. A civil action in a case under subsection (a) may be brought in rem or in personam according to the principles of law and the rules of practice applicable in cases where the injury or damage has been done and consummated on navigable waters.

(c) Actions against United States.

(1) Exclusive remedy. In a civil action against the United States for injury or damage done or consummated on land by a vessel on navigable waters, chapter 309 or 311 of this title [46 USCS §§30901 et seq. or 31101 et seq.], as appropriate, provides the exclusive remedy.

(2) Administrative claim. A civil action described in paragraph (1) may not be brought until the expiration of the 6-month period after the claim has been presented in writing to the agency owning or operating the vessel causing the injury or damage. (Oct. 6, 2006, P.L. 109-304, §6(c), 120 Stat. 1509.)

§30104. Personal injury to or death of seamen.

A seaman injured in the course of employment or, if the seaman dies from the injury, the personal representative of the seaman may elect to bring a civil action at law, with the right of trial by jury, against the employer. Laws of the United States regulating recovery for personal injury to, or death of, a railway employee apply to an action under this section. (Oct. 6, 2006, P.L. 109-304, §6(c), 120 Stat. 1510; Jan. 8, 2008, P.L. 110-181, §3521(a), 122 Stat. 596.)

2008 Note: Act Jan. 8, 2008, P.L. 110-181, Div C, Title XXXV, Subtitle C, §3521(b), 122 Stat. 596, provides: "The amendment made by subsection (a) [amending this section] shall be effective as if included in the enactment of Public Law 109-304 [enacted Oct. 6, 2006].".

§30105. Restriction on recovery by non-citizens and non-resident aliens for incidents in waters of other countries.

(a) Definition. In this section, the term "continental shelf" has the meaning given that term in article I of the 1958 Convention on the Continental Shelf.

(b) Restriction. Except as provided in subsection (c), a civil action for maintenance and cure or for damages for personal injury or death may not be brought under a maritime law of the United States if—

(1) the individual suffering the injury or death was not a citizen or permanent resident alien of the United States at the time of the incident giving rise to the action;

(2) the incident occurred in the territorial waters or waters overlaying the continental shelf of a country other than the United States; and

(3) the individual suffering the injury or death was employed at the time of the incident by a person engaged in the exploration, development, or production of offshore mineral or energy resources, including drilling, mapping, surveying, diving, pipelaying, maintaining, repairing, constructing, or transporting supplies, equipment, or personnel, but not including trans-

U.S.C.

porting those resources by a vessel constructed or adapted primarily to carry oil in bulk in the cargo spaces.

(c) Nonapplication. Subsection (b) does not apply if the individual bringing the action establishes that a remedy is not available under the laws of—

(1) the country asserting jurisdiction over the area in which the incident occurred; or

(2) the country in which the individual suffering the injury or death maintained citizenship or residency at the time of the incident. (Oct. 6, 2006, P.L. 109-304, §6(c), 120 Stat. 1510.)

§30106. Time limit on bringing maritime action for personal injury or death.

Except as otherwise provided by law, a civil action for damages for personal injury or death arising out of a maritime tort must be brought within 3 years after the cause of action arose. (Oct. 6, 2006, P.L. 109-304, §6(c), 120 Stat. 1511.)

CHAPTER 303
DEATH ON THE HIGH SEAS

§30301. Short title.

This chapter [46 USCS §§30301 et seq.] may be cited as the "Death on the High Seas Act". (Oct. 6, 2006, P.L. 109-304, §6(c), 120 Stat. 1511.)

§30302. Cause of action.

When the death of an individual is caused by wrongful act, neglect, or default occurring on the high seas beyond 3 nautical miles from the shore of the United States, the personal representative of the decedent may bring a civil action in admiralty against the person or vessel responsible. The action shall be for the exclusive benefit of the decedent's spouse, parent, child, or dependent relative. (Oct. 6, 2006, P.L. 109-304, §6(c), 120 Stat. 1511.)

§30303. Amount and apportionment of recovery.

The recovery in an action under this chapter [46 USCS §§30301 et seq.] shall be a fair compensation for the pecuniary loss sustained by the individuals for whose benefit the action is brought. The court shall apportion the recovery among those individuals in proportion to the loss each has sustained. (Oct. 6, 2006, P.L. 109-304, §6(c), 120 Stat. 1511.)

§30304. Contributory negligence.

In an action under this chapter [46 USCS §§30301 et seq.], contributory negligence of the decedent is not a bar to recovery. The court shall consider the degree of negligence of the decedent and reduce the recovery accordingly. (Oct. 6, 2006, P.L. 109-304, §6(c), 120 Stat. 1511.)

§30305. Death of plaintiff in pending action.

If a civil action in admiralty is pending in a court of the United States to recover for personal injury caused by wrongful act, neglect, or default described in section 30302 of this title [46 USCS §30302], and the individual dies during the action as a result of the wrongful act, neglect, or default, the personal representative of the decedent may be substituted as the plaintiff and the action may proceed under this chapter [46 USCS §§30301 et seq.] for the recovery authorized by this chapter [46 USCS §§30301 et seq.]. (Oct. 6, 2006, P.L. 109-304, §6(c), 120 Stat. 1511.)

§30306. Foreign cause of action.

When a cause of action exists under the law of a foreign country for death by wrongful act, neglect, or default on the high seas, a civil action in admiralty may be brought in a court of the United States based on the foreign cause of action, without abatement of the amount for which recovery is authorized. (Oct. 6, 2006, P.L. 109-304, §6(c), 120 Stat. 1511.)

§30307. Commercial aviation accidents.

(a) Definition. In this section, the term "nonpecuniary damages" means damages for loss of care, comfort, and companionship.

(b) Beyond 12 nautical miles. In an action under this chapter [46 USCS §§30301 et seq.], if the death resulted from a commercial aviation accident occurring on the high seas beyond 12 nautical miles from the shore of the United States, additional compensation is recoverable for nonpecuniary damages, but punitive damages are not recoverable.

(c) Within 12 nautical miles. This chapter [46 USCS §§30301 et seq.] does not apply if the death resulted from a commercial aviation accident occurring on the high seas 12 nautical miles or less from the shore of the United States. (Oct. 6, 2006, P.L. 109-304, §6(c), 120 Stat. 1512.)

§30308. Nonapplication.

(a) State law. This chapter [46 USCS §§30301 et seq.] does not affect the law of a State regulating the right to recover for death.

(b) Internal waters. This chapter [46 USCS §§30301 et seq.] does not apply to the Great Lakes or waters within the territorial limits of a State. (Oct. 6, 2006, P. L. 109-304, §6(c), 120 Stat. 1512.)

CHAPTER 309 SUITS IN ADMIRALTY AGAINST THE UNITED STATES

§30901. Short title.

This chapter [46 USCS §§30901 et seq.] may be cited as the "Suits in Admiralty Act". (Oct. 6, 2006, P.L. 109-304, §6(c), 120 Stat. 1517.)

§30902. Definition.

In this chapter [46 USCS §§30901 et seq.], the term "federally-owned corporation" means a corporation in which the United States owns all the outstanding capital stock. (Oct. 6, 2006, P.L. 109-304, §6(c), 120 Stat. 1517.)

§30903. Waiver of immunity.

(a) In general. In a case in which, if a vessel were privately owned or operated, or if cargo were privately owned or possessed, or if a private person or property were involved, a civil action in admiralty could be maintained, a civil action in admiralty in personam may be brought against the United States or a federally-owned corporation. In a civil action in admiralty brought by the United States or a federally-owned corporation, an admiralty claim in personam may be filed or a setoff claimed against the United States or corporation.

(b) Non-jury. A claim against the United States or a federally-owned corporation under this section shall be tried without a jury. (Oct. 6, 2006, P.L. 109-304, §6(c), 120 Stat. 1518.)

§30904. Exclusive remedy.

If a remedy is provided by this chapter [46 USCS §§30901 et seq.], it shall be exclusive of any other action arising out of the same subject matter against the officer, employee, or agent of the United States or the federally-owned corporation whose act or omission gave rise to the claim. (Oct. 6, 2006, P.L. 109-304, §6(c), 120 Stat. 1518.)

§30905. Period for bringing action.

A civil action under this chapter [46 USCS §§30901 et seq.] must be brought within 2 years after the cause of action arose. (Oct. 6, 2006, P.L. 109-304, §6(c), 120 Stat. 1518.)

§30906. Venue.

(a) In general. A civil action under this chapter [46 USCS §§30901 et seq.] shall be brought in the district court of the United States for the district in which—

(1) any plaintiff resides or has its principal place of business; or

(2) the vessel or cargo is found.

(b) Transfer. On a motion by a party, the court may transfer the action to any other district court of the United States. (Oct. 6, 2006, P.L. 109-304, §6(c), 120 Stat. 1518.)

§30907. Procedure for hearing and determination.

(a) In general. A civil action under this chapter [46 USCS §§30901 et seq.] shall proceed and be heard and determined according to the principles of law and the rules of practice applicable in like cases between private parties.

(b) In rem.

(1) Requirements. The action may proceed according to the principles of an action in rem if—

(A) the plaintiff elects in the complaint; and

(B) it appears that an action in rem could have been maintained had the vessel or cargo been privately owned and possessed.

(2) Effect on relief in personam. An election under paragraph (1) does not prevent the plaintiff from seeking relief in personam in the same action. (Oct. 6, 2006, P.L. 109-304, §6(c), 120 Stat. 1518.)

§30908. Exemption from arrest or seizure.

The following are not subject to arrest or seizure by judicial process in the United States:

(1) A vessel owned by, possessed by, or operated by or for the United States or a federally-owned corporation.

(2) Cargo owned or possessed by the United States or a federally-owned corporation. (Oct. 6, 2006, P.L. 109-304, §6(c), 120 Stat. 1518.)

§30909. Security.

Neither the United States nor a federally-owned corporation may be required to give a bond or admiralty stipulation in a civil action under this chapter [46 USCS §§30901 et seq.]. (Oct. 6, 2006, P.L. 109-304, §6(c), 120 Stat. 1519.)

§30910. Exoneration and limitation.

The United States is entitled to the exemptions from and limitations of liability provided by law to an owner, charterer, operator, or agent of a vessel. (Oct. 6, 2006, P.L. 109-304, §6(c), 120 Stat. 1519.)

§30911. Costs and interest.

(a) In general. A judgment against the United States or a federally-owned corporation under this chapter [46 USCS §§30901 et seq.] may include costs and interest at the rate of 4 percent per year until satisfied. Interest shall run as ordered by the court, except that interest is not allowable for the period before the action is filed.

(b) Contract providing for interest. Notwithstanding subsection (a), if the claim is based on a contract providing for interest, interest may be awarded at the rate and for the period provided in the contract. (Oct. 6, 2006, P.L. 109-304, §6(c), 120 Stat. 1519.)

§30912. Arbitration, compromise, or settlement.

The Secretary of a department of the United States Government, or the board of trustees of a federally-owned corporation, may arbitrate, compromise, or settle a claim under this chapter [46 USCS §§30901 et seq.]. (Oct. 6, 2006, P.L. 109-304, §6(c), 120 Stat. 1519.)

§30913. Payment of judgment or settlement.

(a) In general. The proper accounting officer of the United States shall pay a final judgment, arbitration award, or settlement under this chapter [46 USCS §§30901 et seq.] on presentation of an authenticated copy.

(b) Source of payment. Payment shall be made from an appropriation or fund available specifically for the purpose. If no appropriation or fund is specifically available, there is hereby appropriated, out of money in the Treasury not otherwise appropriated, an amount sufficient to pay the judgment, award, or settlement. (Oct. 6, 2006, P.L. 109-304, §6(c), 120 Stat. 1519.)

CHAPTER 311
SUITS INVOLVING PUBLIC VESSELS

§31101. Short title.

This chapter [46 USCS §§31101 et seq.] may be cited as the "Public Vessels Act". (Oct. 6, 2006, P.L. 109-304, §6(c), 120 Stat. 1521.)

§31102. Waiver of immunity.

(a) In general. A civil action in personam in admiralty may be brought, or an impleader filed, against the United States for—

(1) damages caused by a public vessel of the United States; or

(2) compensation for towage and salvage services, including contract salvage, rendered to a public vessel of the United States.

(b) Counterclaim or setoff. If the United States brings a civil action in admiralty for damages caused by a privately owned vessel, the owner of the vessel, or the successor in interest, may file a counterclaim in personam, or claim a setoff, against the United States for damages arising out of the same subject matter. (Oct. 6, 2006, P.L. 109-304, §6(c), 120 Stat. 1521.)

§31103. Applicable procedure.

A civil action under this chapter [46 USCS §§31101 et seq.] is subject to the provisions of chapter 309 of this title [46 USCS §§30901 et seq.] except to the extent inconsistent with this chapter [46 USCS §§31101 et seq.]. (Oct. 6, 2006, P.L. 109-304, §6(c), 120 Stat. 1521.)

§31104. Venue.

(a) In general. A civil action under this chapter [46 USCS §§31101 et seq.] shall be brought in the district court of the United States for the district in which the vessel or cargo is found within the United States.

(b) Vessel or cargo outside territorial waters. If the vessel or cargo is outside the territorial waters of the United States—

(1) the action shall be brought in the district court of the United States for any district in which any plaintiff resides or has an office for the transaction of business; or

(2) if no plaintiff resides or has an office for the transaction of business in the United States, the action may be brought in the district court of the United States for any district. (Oct. 6, 2006, P.L. 109-304, §6(c), 120 Stat. 1521.)

§31105. Security when counterclaim filed.

If a counterclaim is filed for a cause of action for which the original action is filed under this chapter [46 USCS §§31101 et seq.], the respondent to the counterclaim shall give security in the usual amount and form to respond to the counterclaim, unless the court for cause shown orders otherwise. The proceedings in the original action shall be stayed until the security is given. (Oct. 6, 2006, P.L. 109-304, §6(c), 120 Stat. 1522.)

§31106. Exoneration and limitation.

The United States is entitled to the exemptions from and limitations of liability provided by law to an owner, charterer, operator, or agent of a vessel. (Oct. 6, 2006, P.L. 109-304, §6(c), 120 Stat. 1522.)

§31107. Interest.

A judgment in a civil action under this chapter [46 USCS §§31101 et seq.] may not include interest for the period before the judgment is issued unless the claim is based on a contract providing for interest. (Oct. 6, 2006, P.L. 109-304, §6(c), 120 Stat. 1522.)

§31108. Arbitration, compromise, or settlement.

The Attorney General may arbitrate, compromise, or settle a claim under this chapter [46 USCS §§31101 et seq.] if a civil action based on the claim has been commenced. (Oct. 6, 2006, P.L. 109-304, §6(c), 120 Stat. 1522.)

§31109. Payment of judgment or settlement.

The proper accounting officer of the United States shall pay a final judgment, arbitration award, or settlement under this chapter [46 USCS §§31101 et seq.] on presentation of an authenticated copy. Payment shall be made from any money in the Treasury appropriated for the purpose. (Oct. 6, 2006, P.L. 109-304, §6(c), 120 Stat. 1522.)

§31110. Subpoenas to officers or members of crew.

An officer or member of the crew of a public vessel may not be subpoenaed in a civil action under this chapter [46 USCS §§31101 et seq.] without the consent of—

(1) the Secretary of the department or the head of the independent establishment having control of the vessel at the time the cause of action arose; or

(2) the master or commanding officer of the vessel at the time the subpoena is issued. (Oct. 6, 2006, P.L. 109-304, §6(c), 120 Stat. 1522.)

§31111. Claims by nationals of foreign countries.

A national of a foreign country may not maintain a civil action under this chapter [46 USCS §§31101 et seq.] unless it appears to the satisfaction of the court in which the action is brought that the government of that country, in similar circumstances, allows nationals of the United States to sue in its courts. (Oct. 6, 2006, P.L. 109-304, §6(c), 120 Stat. 1522.)

§31112. Lien not recognized or created.

This chapter [46 USCS §§31101 et seq.] shall not be construed as recognizing the existence of or as creating a lien against a public vessel of the United States. (Oct. 6, 2006, P.L. 109-304, §6(c), 120 Stat. 1522.)

INDEX

ABBREVIATIONS

NOTE: Entries previously cited to Calif. Administrative Code are now cited to Calif. Code of Regulations (CCR).

B&P	Business and Professions Code
CA Const	California Constitution
2 CCR	California Code of Regulations (Title 2)
8 CCR	California Code of Regulations (Title 8)
10 CCR	California Code of Regulations (Title 10)
CCP	California Code of Civil Procedure
CC	Civil Code
Ed	Education Code
Ev	Evidence Code
Gov	Government Code
Har&N	Harbors and Navigation Code
H&S	Health and Safety Code
Ins	Insurance Code
Lab	Labor Code
Mil&Vet	Military and Veterans Code
Pen	Penal Code
Table	Tables and Schedules
UI	Unemployment Insurance Code
USC	United States Code
Veh	Vehicle Code
W&I	Welfare and Institutions Code

How To Use This Index

This Index is arranged according to Code sections, rather than page numbers. To locate an individual Code section, first find your material in the Index. Then refer to the Table of Abbreviations, above, to identify the individual Code. Under each Code in this book, sections are arranged in numerical order.

For example, "Lab §3600" under "Suicide" means Section 3600 of the Labor Code. Find the Labor Code tab on the back cover of this book and follow it to the Labor Code. Then find Section 3600 within the Labor Code.

Some Code sections, such as the Civil Code and Government Code, do not have tabs. They can generally be found in the Miscellaneous Provisions section.

INDEX

A

Index

Index

B

Index

E

Index

F

Index

Index

I

Index

Index

K

L

Index

Index

Index

Index

Index

N

Index

Index

P

Index

Index

Index

Q

Index

R

Index

S

Index

Index

Index

T

Index

U

Index

W

Index

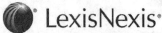